AMERICA'S
FILM LEGACY

AMERICA'S FILM LEGACY

THE AUTHORITATIVE GUIDE TO THE LANDMARK MOVIES IN THE NATIONAL FILM REGISTRY

DANIEL EAGAN

continuum

NEW YORK • LONDON

2010

The Continuum International Publishing Group Inc
80 Maiden Lane, New York, NY 10038

The Continuum International Publishing Group Ltd
The Tower Building, 11 York Road, London SE1 7NX

www.continuumbooks.com

Printed in the United States of America

Library of Congress Cataloging-in-Publication Data
A catalog record for this book is available from the Library of Congress.

ISBN 978-0826-41849-4 (hardcover)
ISBN 978-0826-42977-3 (paperback)

Contents

Acknowledgments

So many people helped with this book that it is impossible to list them individually. I apologize for any inadvertent omissions. Charles Silver at the Museum of Modern Art helped me screen many of the Registry titles, and provided access to the museum's extensive files. Josie L. Walters-Johnson and Zoran Sinobad at the Library of Congress arranged for me to use the Motion Picture & Television Reading Room. Dennis Doros at Milestone Film & Video supplied prints, photographs, and background materials for several titles, and also introduced me to film archivists and restorers. Gary Palmucci and Rodrigo Brandão at Kino International provided help with several titles, as did Brian Carmody and Brett Sharlow at Criterion. Author and editor Kevin Lally supplied titles and helped rearrange my assignments at *Film Journal International*. Bruce Goldstein, head of repertory at New York City's Film Forum, not only scheduled several Registry titles, but also helped me locate hard-to-find films. Ben Model, a piano accompanist and a producer of the Silent Clowns Film Series in New York City, tracked down critical titles. Aubrey Gaby Miller, senior publicist at the American Museum of Natural History, helped with that museum's collection. Executive director Cynthia Close and Frank Aveni at Documentary Educational Resource provided titles and photographs. Ivan Zimmerman offered legal advice. Support also came from Arlene S. Balkanksy, Bonnie Lafave, and Rick Prelinger. Rob Potter and Lorna Lentini offered valuable advice copy editing, saving me from many embarrassing mistakes.

I'd like to thank the following for help with specific titles: *Marian Anderson: The Lincoln Memorial Concert*: Blaine Bartell. *The Buffalo Creek Flood: An Act of Man*: Mimi Pickering. *Chulas Fronteras*: Les Blank, Chris Strachwitz. *The Curse of Quon Gwon*: Michael Pogorzelski, director, and Brian Meacham, public access coordinator, Academy Film Archive; Arthur Fong, DeepFocus Productions. *Czechoslovakia 1918–1968*: Robert Fresco, Terry Sanders. *Disneyland Dream*: Robbins Barstow. *Dont Look Back*: D A Pennebaker, Chris Hegedus, Frazer Pennebaker. *The Drums of Winter*: Leonard Kamerling, curator of film, Alaska Documentary Collections, University of Alaska Museum of the North. *Fox Movietone News: Jenkins Orphanage Band*: Scott Allen, University of South Carolina Newsfilm Archive. *Garlic Is As Good As Ten Mothers*: Les Blank. *Kannapolis, NC*: Karen McGlynn, visual materials archivist, Rare Book, Manuscript, and Special Collections Library, Duke University. *King . . . A Filmed Record*: Richard Kaplan. *Let's All Go to the Lobby*: Robert Mack, Filmack Studios. *Miss Lulu Bett*: Jonathan Bank, Mint Theater Company. *Motion Painting No. 1*: Cindy Keefer, Center for Visual Music. *Multiple SIDosis*: Ross Lipman. . . . *no lies*: Mitchell W. Block. *On the Bowery*: Michael Rogosin. *Our Day*: Martha Kelly, Dan Streible. *Powers of Ten*: Eames Demetrios. *Serene Velocity*: Ernie Gehr. *Sherman's March*: Ross McElwee. *Siege*: Sam Bryan. *George Stevens World War II Footage* and *The March*: George Stevens, Jr. *Think of Me First as a Person*: George Ingmire. *A Time Out of War*: Terry Sanders, American Film Foundation. *To Fly*: Greg MacGillivray, MacGillivray Freeman Films.

Finally, David Barker and his staff at Continuum displayed patience and guidance throughout the writing and editing process. My wife Melissa provided advice, encouragement, and editing skills. I will never be able to express how much she means to me.

Introduction

Developed in the late 1880s, motion pictures evolved from a sideshow novelty to the twentieth century's dominant art form. Today they still wield an overwhelming influence over both high and low culture. Identifying the most significant movies among the thousands of features, shorts, cartoons, experimental, and institutional titles was one of the reasons behind the National Film Registry. Established in 1988, the Registry singles out twenty-five movies a year; its total is now up to five hundred.

To gain an understanding of film, you could take a course in school, read histories, or consult other lists, perhaps Academy Award Best Picture winners, or any one of a number of AFI 100 Greatest compilations. But if you only paid attention to awards, you might never find out about *The House in the Middle*, or *Sky High*, or the Marx Brothers or Fred Astaire. And many lists are weighted toward recent releases from major studios. The National Film Registry acts as a corrective to commercially driven surveys. It includes independent, experimental, and animated films, the movies that helped establish the medium and then turned it into art. The Registry has no commercial ties, no angles to exploit, no axes to grind. It's compiled by filmmakers and historians, but also by the public. It is the definitive list of the American movies you need to know, whether blockbusters or flops, those made with hundred-million-dollar budgets or filmed in somebody's kitchen.

Why start another list? Because the movies that have been such an important part of our lives turned out to be a lot more fragile than anyone thought they would be.

One reason for that fragility is film itself. Film used to be made of celluloid, a synthetic material invented in 1868. When treated with camphor and nitric and sulfuric acids, the cellulose from cotton turned into a lightweight, flexible plastic that could fill in as a replacement for ivory and tortoiseshell. Celluloid became shirt collars, piano keys, Christmas ornaments, and, in 1889, chemists started to use it as a backing for photographic emulsion.

Transparent, strong even when thin, celluloid is an excellent medium for holding emulsion, a layer of silver oxide about .001 inch thick that contains the photographic record. Unfortunately, celluloid is also volatile. It's brittle when dry, moldy when wet. It burns, explosively in the case of nitrate, but dramatically enough even when safety stock. And if it doesn't catch fire, it will break down to its original elements. It mildews, rots, and given the chance reverts to a toxic pile of powdery ash or a bubbling, vinegary goo.

That's not all. Film tears. It rips. It scratches, folds, and creases. It stretches and shrinks, warps and flattens. Its sprocket holes enlarge, pull apart, and eventually shred. The emulsion flakes, chips, and peels. Then it fades away entirely.

Film is bulky and expensive to keep. It's stored on shelves, in file cabinets, under beds, in attics and garages, in bank vaults and self-storage centers and under ice-skating rinks. It's even more expensive to project than to store. And before, during, and after it's wound through projectors, film gets snipped, hole-punched, chopped, scraped, spliced, and yanked through rewinders.

Film is cut, censored, stolen, lost at sea, lost in the mail, lost off trucks, even lost in projection booths. It's bombed to oblivion during wars, burned in great smoking piles by studios, looted and hidden by collectors. It's banned from exhibition, withdrawn from circulation, used as fill by editors, melted for its silver.

The result? Half of all films made before 1950 are presumed lost. Up to 80 percent of all silent features no longer exist. Many of the films that do survive from the silent and early sound eras are in unstable condition, and could easily be considered lost as well.

Only a few years ago, many filmmakers doubted that our country's most important movies would survive the millennium. Even as markets for movies, both old and new, mushroomed in the late 1980s, it became increasingly apparent to film scholars and archivists that our film heritage was in dire condition.

In its early days, film was considered as disposable as newspapers. Producers would process prints until negatives wore out, and then simply shoot their movie over again. When sound arrived, some studios discarded their libraries of silent films. Storage reels were mislabeled or lost. Originals were mistakenly discarded as duplicates. Studios dissolved or went bankrupt, with the rights of film libraries lost in a haze of lawsuits. Copyrights were mishandled, and films fell into the public domain, with poor quality bootlegs flooding the market. Many executives simply couldn't foresee the economic windfall that video outlets and cable channels would bring, and allowed their B-movies, shorts, and newsreels to decay.

Paradoxically, advances in technologies—new film formats, computer special effects, digital sound—have made it even more difficult to preserve films. Every new technology threatens an older one. Once popular color and sound processes, widescreen formats, 3-D films, and even video formats have been made obsolete, or are becoming so.

Today, movies aren't just cans on shelves anymore. They are made up of many elements: stereo soundtracks, camera negatives, mattes, computer programs, and more. Preservationists as well as engineers trying to transfer movies to video are stymied by missing elements. Soundtracks are gone, reference negatives have faded or shrunk, and often the only prints that still exist have been cut. Right now it's almost impossible to reassemble the materials needed to reproduce the special effects in recent science fiction films. Some directors don't even know where the elements to their films are.

Preservationists have to deal with issues beyond the mere survival of films. They have to protect the actual content and structure of movies from commercial interests. In the 1980s, these included colorizing black-and-white films and cropping widescreen films. Even classics could be edited to fit television time slots, or onto videocassettes. And films that seemed to have no commercial value could disappear from simple neglect.

In the 1980s, angry filmmakers denounced studios that refused to protect their works, or else diluted their power through colorization, panning and scanning, and editing. Industry icons John Huston, Frank Capra, and James Stewart joined contemporary filmmakers like Martin Scorsese and Sydney Pollack in lobbying Congress for a film preservation bill. In hearings before legislators, they pointed out how films as important as *It's a Wonderful Life* and *Citizen Kane* were in danger of being ruined.

In an effort to stop colorization in particular, Representatives Robert J. Mrazek (D-NY) and Sidney Yates (D-Ill) introduced the National Film Preservation Act in 1988. The bill authorized the Library of Congress to select twenty-five American films each year that were "culturally, historically, or esthetically significant." The Library of Congress holds an archival print of each film selected; furthermore, the films must be labeled if they are altered from their original formats. Part publicity stunt, part a genuine effort to shape the direction of preservation, the list is updated annually, with new additions announced each December.

Anyone can nominate a film, by mail or on the Internet, but the actual selections are made by members of the National Film Preservation Board. To be nominated, a film must be at least ten years old. Details about the legislative history of the Registry can be found at *http://www.loc.gov/film/filmabou.html.* You can vote for specific titles by e-mail by checking *http://www.loc.gov/film/vote.html.*

Unlike lists compiled by magazines or organizations, the National Film Registry has no agenda other than quality. And the titles don't depend on individual fads or whims. These are the most important, and in many cases the best films ever made in this country. They cover the gamut of motion picture styles: actualities from the nineteenth century, documentaries, travelogues, propaganda films, cartoons, experimental shorts, and every type of feature film imaginable, from Oscar-winning Hollywood epics to obscure independent pieces.

Viewing these films has given me the chance to see remarkable artists like Duke Ellington and Lydia Mendoza performing in their prime. It has brought historical events like the Tacoma Narrows Bridge collapse and the Hindenburg disaster to life. The films form a record of wars, labor struggles, generational conflicts, and crime, but also of romance, humor, and inspiration. Themes and patterns emerge over the years. Farmers fare poorly, seduced by city sirens, ruined by fires, floods and drought, run off the land by financiers, attacked by Indians, crooks, and soldiers. Miners have it worse: jailed for complaining about wages, drowned in cave-ins and floods, bludgeoned to death and shot in the back by police. Strikes, marches, and demonstrations occur repeatedly, even in a musical like *Swing Time*.

The Registry films cover the extremes of human existence, from chain gangs and concentration camps to parties and honeymoons. Suicide is the driving force in a half-dozen titles. Executions are common as well, in both comedies and dramas. On the other hand, meals, kisses, and weddings are too numerous to count. Several films focus on children, and three feature childbirth. "Three" defines one of the many coincidences and convergences in the Registry. Three films have "duck" in the title. There are three "nights," three "wilds," three "littles." Three deal with the Gullah dialect, and three end with nuclear explosions.

While many titles in the National Film Registry are indisputable classics, some will be obscure to most filmgoers. Only a dozen have come out since 1990; more than twice that number were released before 1916. No other print or online movie guide contains entries for all of the National Film Registry titles. Yet they form the history of movies in the United States. *America's Film Legacy* is your opportunity to learn why these films are judged to be among our country's most important works of art.

How to Read the Entries

Individual film entries are listed in roughly chronological order, in part to avoid repeating facts about film techniques or biographical details about filmmakers. For each film I've tried to include all the pertinent information about how and when it was made. Each entry is structured as follows:

Title: In most cases, this is the title of the film as it appears on screen. Early movies did not have official titles. *Dickson Experimental Sound Film* (1894) was supplied later by historians, for example. Some films have more than one title. *The John C. Rice–May Irwin Kiss* (1896) is also known as *The Kiss*, *The May Irwin Kiss*, *The Picture of a Kiss*, and *Kiss Scene*. Where confusion may arise, I've listed alternate titles in the alphabetical index of titles.

The distributor, listed after the title, refers to the person or company responsible for getting a film into theaters. Most National Film Registry entries were distributed by the so-called major studios: Columbia, MGM, Paramount, RKO, Twentieth Century-Fox, Warner Brothers, Universal. Note that some distributors, like Edison and Thanhouser, are no longer in business. Distributors are distinct from production companies, which financed the filming process, although some shared duties. For some independent and experimental movies, especially those not released theatrically, the filmmaker is listed as the distributor.

Release date: Generally this is the earliest date a film was shown in theaters, although there are many exceptions. Some films were made in separate parts over several years, like the *Why We Fight* (1943–45) series. In these cases, the films are listed after the last portion was completed—1945, not 1943, for *Why We Fight*. Films that were not released theatrically, like *Marian Anderson: The Lincoln Memorial Concert* (1939), are usually listed by the year they were made.

Silent/Sound and **Color/B&W** are self-evident. I've noted silent films with musical scores only when the scores were recorded at the same time, such as *Sunrise* (1927).

Aspect ratio describes the shape of the frame. Early movies had widely varying aspect ratios, but by the turn of the twentieth century, 1.33 to 1 was the industry standard. This is roughly equivalent to the shape of pre-flat-panel television screens. When sound was introduced, the ratio was adjusted slightly to 1.37 to accommodate the soundtrack. With some exceptions this standard lasted until the 1950s, when widescreen processes became prevalent. Widescreen aspect ratios varied from 1.66 to 2.35, with 1.85—similar to a widescreen TV—the dominant choice in the last two decades.

Some films, like *Shane* (1953), were photographed in one format and projected in another. In these cases I've tried to list the filmmaker's preferred format.

Running time: basically how long it takes to project a film. Early films were sold by the foot, and until the 1920s running times were measured in lengths: actual feet at first, later by reels. A reel could hold 1,000 feet of film; two reels referred to a short that for convenience's sake I will estimate at about twenty minutes long.

But these films were photographed by hand-cranked cameras and exhibited by hand-cranked projectors. Both steps could either speed up or slow down a film's running time. The introduction of electric cameras and sound equipment standardized filmmaking speeds at 24 fps (frames per second). In many cases it's unclear what fps was for earlier films; estimates range from 14 to 20 fps.

Furthermore, many films exist only in battered, cut prints, minus intertitles, individual shots, and sometimes entire scenes. Determining a precise running time for some films is an impossible task, so the timings listed in this book should be treated as estimates.

MPAA ratings have been assigned by the Motion Picture Association of America (MPAA) since 1968. Originally these comprised G, M, R, and X; currently, they are G, PG, PG-13, R, and NC-17. Some films released prior to the implementation of the MPAA system were rated later; these are indicated under "Additional Credits." Explanations for ratings can be found at *http://www.filmratings.com/*.

Cast includes the performers who received screen credit, with the names of the characters they played in parentheses. Alternate names are included in brackets. Early films did not list actors; I've included those who could be verified under either "Cast" or "Additional Cast."

Credits are usually listed in this order: director, writer, producer, director of photography, production designer, music, sound, costume, make-up, casting. Credits have changed over the years: yesterday's art director is today's production designer, for example.

Additional cast: Many performers did not receive screen credit. Their names can be determined through studio payroll files or, in some cases, through visual identification. This category is by no means exhaustive.

Additional credits include personnel who contributed to a film without credit, or who were replaced during the production. It is also an opportunity to list alternate titles, production and release dates, and other pertinent information.

Awards are based on records from the Academy of Motion Picture Arts and Sciences (*http://www.oscars.org/awardsdatabase*).

Other versions include sequels, prequels, remakes, and other relevant titles. For example, *The Big T.N.T. Show* (1966) is not officially a sequel to *The T.A.M.I. Show* (1964), but is listed because it followed the same style and format and was made by many of the same filmmakers. For the most part I do not include foreign-language remakes, or films that include generic characters. It would be pointless to list every vampire movie under *Dracula* (1931), for example.

Availability: One of the goals of the National Film Registry legislation is to store an archival copy of each title at the Library of Congress. Technically, every film can be screened there. On a more practical level, a number of Registry films can be seen in libraries, museums, and archives across the country. Most are available for the home market as well. When possible, I've listed the distributor, release date, and ISBN and UPC numbers, and, if applicable, websites for these titles. I have not included older home-market formats like 8mm, or newer ones like Blu-Ray. An increasing number of films can be viewed online, through the Library of Congress American Memory site (*http://www.loc.gov/rr/mopic/ndlmps.html*), the Internet Archive (*www.archive.org*), and other sites.

The 500 Films, in Chronological Order

1973 Frank Film
American Graffiti
Enter the Dragon
Mean Streets
Badlands
The Sting
1974 Blazing Saddles
. . . no lies
The Conversation
Chinatown
Antonia: A Portrait of the Woman
A Woman Under the Influence
The Godfather Part II
Young Frankenstein
Fuji
1975 Nashville
Jaws
The Rocky Horror Picture Show
The Buffalo Creek Flood: An Act of Man
One Flew Over the Cuckoo's Nest
1960–75 Think of Me First as a Person
1976 Taxi Driver
The Outlaw Josey Wales
To Fly!
Harlan County U.S.A.
Rocky
Network
Chulas Fronteras
1977 Killer of Sheep
Annie Hall
Star Wars
Eraserhead
Close Encounters of the Third Kind
1978 National Lampoon's Animal House
Days of Heaven
Halloween
The Deer Hunter
Powers of Ten
1979 Manhattan
Alien

Apocalypse Now
The Black Stallion
All That Jazz
Free Radicals
1980 Garlic Is As Good As Ten Mothers
Return of the Secaucus Seven
Atlantic City
The Life and Times of Rosie the Riveter
Raging Bull
1981 Raiders of the Lost Ark
1982 Chan Is Missing
E.T. The Extra-Terrestrial
Blade Runner
Fast Times at Ridgemont High
Koyaanisqatsi
Tootsie
1983 El Norte
1984 This Is Spinal Tap
Stranger Than Paradise
The Terminator
1985 Back to the Future
1986 Sherman's March
Hoosiers
1988 Tin Toy
The Thin Blue Line
Uksuum Cauyai: The Drums of Winter
1989 sex, lies, and videotape
Do the Right Thing
Water and Power
1990 GoodFellas
Dances With Wolves
1991 Daughters of the Dust
Boyz n the Hood
Beauty and the Beast
1992 Unforgiven
1993 Groundhog Day
Schindler's List
1994 Hoop Dreams
1995 Toy Story
1996 Fargo

An Alphabetical List of the Films

Clash of the Wolves 1925

Close Encounters of the Third Kind 1977

Cologne: From the Diary of Ray and Esther 1939

Commandment Keeper Church, Beaufort, South Carolina, May, 1940 1940

Conversation, The 1974

Cool Hand Luke 1967

Cool World, The 1964

Cops 1922

Corner in Wheat, A 1909

Court Jester, The 1956

Crowd, The 1928

Curse of Quon Gwon, The 1916–17

Czechoslovakia 1918–1968 1969

Dance, Girl, Dance 1940

Dances With Wolves 1990

Daughter of Shanghai 1937

Daughters of the Dust 1991

David Holzman's Diary 1967

Day the Earth Stood Still, The 1951

Days of Heaven 1978

Dead Birds 1965

Deer Hunter, The 1978

Deliverance 1972

Destry Rides Again 1939

Detour 1945

Dickson Experimental Sound Film 1894

Disneyland Dream 1956

D.O.A. 1950

Docks of New York, The 1928

Dodsworth 1936

Dog Star Man 1964

Dont Look Back 1967

Do the Right Thing 1989

Double Indemnity 1944

Dr. Strangelove or: How I Learned to Stop Worrying and Love the Bomb 1964

Dracula 1931

Drums of Winter, The see Uksuum Cauyai: The Drums of Winter 1988

Duck Amuck 1953

Duck and Cover 1951

Duck Soup 1933

Early Abstractions #1–5, 7, 10 1939–56

Easy Rider 1969

Eaux d'Artifice 1953

El Norte 1983

Emperor Jones, The 1933

Empire 1964

Endless Summer, The 1966

Enter the Dragon 1973

Eraserhead 1977

E.T. The Extra-Terrestrial 1982

Evidence of the Film, The 1913

Exploits of Elaine, The 1914

Face in the Crowd, A 1957

Fall of the House of Usher, The 1928

Fantasia 1940

Fargo 1996

Fast Times at Ridgemont High 1982

Fatty's Tintype Tangle 1915

Film Portrait 1972

Five Easy Pieces 1970

Flash Gordon 1936

Flesh and the Devil 1926

Flower Drum Song 1957

Foolish Wives 1922

Footlight Parade 1933

Force of Evil 1948

Forgotten Frontier, The 1931

Four Horsemen of the Apocalypse, The 1921

42nd Street 1933

Fox Movietone News: Jenkins Orphanage Band 1928

Frankenstein 1931

Frank Film 1973

Freaks 1932

Free Radicals 1979

French Connection, The 1971

Freshman, The 1925

From Here to Eternity 1953

From Stump to Ship 1930

From the Manger to the Cross 1912

Fuji 1974

Fury 1936

Garlic Is As Good As Ten Mothers 1980

General, The 1927

George Stevens: World War II Footage 1944–46

Gerald McBoing Boing 1951

Gertie the Dinosaur 1914

Giant 1956

Gigi 1958

Glimpse of the Garden 1957

Godfather, The 1972

Godfather Part II, The 1974

Going My Way 1944

Gold Diggers of 1933 1933

Gold Rush, The 1925

Gone with the Wind 1939

GoodFellas 1990

Graduate, The 1967

Grand Hotel 1932

Grapes of Wrath, The 1940

Grass: A Nation's Battle for Life 1925

Great Dictator, The 1940

Great Train Robbery, The 1903

Greed 1924

Groundhog Day 1993

Gun Crazy 1950

Gunga Din 1939

Gus Visser and His Singing Duck *see* Theodore
    Case Sound Tests: Gus Visser and His Singing
    Duck 1924–26

Hallelujah 1929

Halloween 1978

Hands Up 1926

Harlan County U.S.A. 1976

Harold and Maude 1971

Heiress, The 1949

Hell's Hinges 1916

High Noon 1952

High School 1968

Hindenburg Disaster Newsreel Footage 1937

His Girl Friday 1940

Hitch-Hiker, The 1953

Hoop Dreams 1994

Hoosiers 1986

Hospital 1970

Hospital, The 1971

House I Live In, The 1945

House in the Middle, The 1954

House of Usher 1960

How Green Was My Valley 1941

How the West Was Won 1962

H_2O 1929

Hunters, The 1957

Hustler, The 1961

I Am a Fugitive from a Chain Gang 1932

Imitation of Life 1934

Immigrant, The 1917

In a Lonely Place 1950

In Cold Blood 1967

Inside Nazi Germany 1938

In the Heat of the Night 1967

In the Land of the Head Hunters 1914

In the Street 1948

Intolerance 1916

Invasion of the Body Snatchers 1956

Invisible Man, The 1933

It 19270

Italian, The 1915

It Happened One Night 1934

It's a Wonderful Life 1946

Jailhouse Rock 1957

Jammin' the Blues 1944

Jam Session 1942

Jaws 1975

Jazz on a Summer's Day 1960

Jazz Singer, The 1927

Jeffries-Johnson World's Championship Boxing
    Contest 1910

Jenkins Orphanage Band *see* Fox Movietone
    News: Jenkins Orphanage Band, 1928

John C. Rice–May Irwin Kiss, The 1896

Johnny Guitar 1954

Kannapolis, NC 1940–41

Killer of Sheep 1977

Killers, The 1946

King . . . A Filmed Record . . . Montgomery to
    Memphis 1970

King Kong 1933

Kiss, The *see* John C. Rice–May Irwin Kiss,
    The 1896

Kiss Me Deadly 1955

Knute Rockne All American 1940

Koyaanisqatsi 1982

Lady Eve, The 1941

Lady Helen's Escapade 1909
Lady Windermere's Fan 1925
Lambchops 1929
Land Beyond the Sunset, The 1912
Lassie Come Home 1943
Last Command, The 1928
Last of the Mohicans, The 1920
Last Picture Show, The 1971
Laura 1944
Lawrence of Arabia 1962
Learning Tree, The 1969
Let's All Go to the Lobby 1957
Letter from an Unknown Woman 1948
Life and Death of 9413 A Hollywood Extra,
    The 1928
Life and Times of Rosie the Riveter, The 1980
Life of Emile Zola, The 1937
Little Caesar 1931
Little Fugitive 1953
Little Miss Marker 1934
Living Desert, The 1953
Lost World, The 1925
Louisiana Story 1948
Love Finds Andy Hardy 1938
Love Me Tonight 1932
Magical Maestro 1952
Magnificent Ambersons, The 1942
Making of an American, The 1920
Maltese Falcon, The 1941
Manchurian Candidate, The 1962
Manhatta 1921
Manhattan 1979
Man Who Shot Liberty Valance, The 1962
March, The 1964
March of Time: Inside Nazi Germany, The
    see Inside Nazi Germany 1938
Marian Anderson: The Lincoln Memorial Concert
    1939
Marty 1955
MASH 1970
Master Hands 1936
Matrimony's Speed Limit 1913
May Irwin Kiss, The see The John C. Rice–May
    Irwin Kiss 1896

Mean Streets 1973
Medium Cool 1969
Meet Me in St. Louis 1944
Melody Ranch 1940
Memphis Belle, The 1944
Meshes of the Afternoon 1943
Midnight Cowboy 1969
Mighty Like a Moose 1926
Mildred Pierce 1945
Miracle of Morgan's Creek, The 1944
Miracle on 34th Street 1947
Miss Lulu Bett 1921
Modern Times 1936
Modesta 1956
Mom and Dad 1945
Morocco 1930
Motion Painting No. 1 1947
Movie, A 1958
Mr. Smith Goes to Washington 1939
Multiple SIDosis 1970
Music Box, The 1932
Music Man, The 1962
My Darling Clementine 1946
My Man Godfrey 1936
Naked City, The 1948
Naked Spur, The 1953
Nanook of the North 1922
Nashville 1975
National Lampoon's Animal House 1978
National Velvet 1944
Naughty Marietta 1935
Network 1976
Night at the Opera, A 1935
Night of the Hunter, The 1955
Night of the Living Dead 1968
Ninotchka 1939
. . . no lies 1974
North by Northwest 1959
Nostalgia 1971
Nothing But a Man 1964
Notorious 1946
Now, Voyager 1942
Nutty Professor, The 1963
OffOn 1968

Oklahoma! 1955

One Flew Over the Cuckoo's Nest 1975

One Froggy Evening 1956

One Week 1920

On the Bowery 1957

On the Waterfront 1954

Our Day 1938

Outlaw Josey Wales, The 1976

Out of the Past 1947

Ox-Bow Incident, The 1943

Pass the Gravy 1928

Paths of Glory 1957

Patton 1970

Pawnbroker, The 1965

Pearl, The 1948

Peege 1972

Perils of Pauline, The 1914

Peter Pan 1924

Phantom of the Opera, The 1925

Philadelphia Story, The 1940

Pinocchio 1940

Place in the Sun, A 1951

Planet of the Apes 1968

Plow That Broke the Plains, The 1936

Point of Order 1964

Poor Little Rich Girl, The 1917

Popeye the Sailor Meets Sindbad the Sailor 1936

Porky in Wackyland 1938

Power of the Press, The 1928

Powers of Ten 1978

President McKinley Inauguration Footage 1901

Primary 1960

Princess Nicotine; or, The Smoke Fairy 1909

Prisoner of Zenda, The 1937

Producers, The 1968

Psycho 1960

Public Enemy, The 1931

Pull My Daisy 1959

Punch Drunks 1934

Pups is Pups 1930

Raging Bull 1980

Raiders of the Lost Ark 1981

Raisin in the Sun, A 1961

Rear Window 1954

Rebel Without a Cause 1955

Red Dust 1932

Red River 1948

Regeneration 1915

Reminiscences of a Journey to Lithuania 1971–72

Republic Steel Strike Riots Newsreel Footage 1937

Return of the Secaucus Seven 1980

Ride the High Country 1962

Rip Van Winkle 1896

River, The 1937

Road to Morocco 1942

Rocky 1976

Rocky Horror Picture Show, The 1975

Roman Holiday 1953

Rose Hobart 1936

Sabrina 1954

Safety Last! 1923

Salesman 1969

Salomé 1922

Salt of the Earth 1954

San Francisco Earthquake and Fire, April 18, 1906

San Pietro *see* Battle of San Pietro, The 1945

Scarface 1932

Schindler's List 1993

Searchers, The 1956

Serene Velocity 1970

Sergeant York 1941

Seven Brides for Seven Brothers 1954

7th Heaven 1927

7th Voyage of Sinbad, The 1958

sex, lies, and videotape 1989

Sex Life of the Polyp, The 1928

Shadow of a Doubt 1943

Shadows 1959

Shaft 1971

Shane 1953

She Done Him Wrong 1933

Sherlock Jr. 1924

Sherman's March 1986

Shock Corridor 1963

Shop Around the Corner, The 1940

Show Boat 1936

Show People 1928

Siege 1940

Singin' in the Rain 1952

Sky High 1922

Snow-White 1933

Snow White and the Seven Dwarfs 1937

Some Like It Hot 1959

Son of the Sheik, The 1926

So's Your Old Man 1926

Sound of Music, The 1965

Stagecoach 1939

Star Is Born, A 1954

Star Theatre *see* Building Up and Demolishing the
    Star Theatre 1901

Star Wars 1977

Steamboat Willie 1928

Sting, The 1973

St. Louis Blues 1929

Stormy Weather 1943

Stranger Than Paradise 1984

Streetcar Named Desire, A 1951

Strong Man, The 1926

Sullivan's Travels 1941

Sunrise 1927

Sunset Boulevard 1950

Sweet Smell of Success 1957

Swing Time 1936

Tabu 1931

Tacoma Narrows Bridge Collapse 1940

Tall T, The 1957

T.A.M.I. Show, The 1964

Tarzan and His Mate 1934

Taxi Driver 1976

Teenage Command Performance
    see The T.A.M.I. Show 1964

Tell-Tale Heart, The 1953

Ten Commandments, The 1956

Terminator, The 1984

Tess of the Storm Country 1914

Tevye 1939

Theodore Case Sound Tests: Gus Visser and His
    Singing Duck 1924–26

There It Is 1928

Thief of Bagdad, The 1924

Thin Blue Line, The 1988

Thing from Another World, The 1951

Think of Me First as a Person 1960–75

Thin Man, The 1934

This Is Cinerama 1952

This Is Spinal Tap 1984

Three Little Pigs 1933

Through Navajo Eyes 1966

Time for Burning, A 1967

Time Out of War, A 1954

Tin Toy 1988

To Be or Not To Be 1942

To Fly! 1976

To Kill a Mockingbird 1962

Tol'able David 1921

Tom, Tom the Piper's Son 1969–71

Tootsie 1982

Topaz 1945

Top Hat 1935

Touch of Evil 1958

Toy Story 1995

Traffic in Souls 1913

Trance and Dance in Bali 1936–39

Treasure of the Sierra Madre, The 1948

Trouble in Paradise 1932

Tulips Shall Grow 1942

12 Angry Men 1957

Twelve O'Clock High 1949

2001: A Space Odyssey 1968

Uksuum Cauyai: The Drums of Winter 1988

Unforgiven 1992

Verbena Tragica 1939

Vertigo 1958

Water and Power 1989

Wedding March, The 1928

West Side Story 1961

Westinghouse Works 1904

What's Opera, Doc? 1957

Where Are My Children? 1916

White Fawn's Devotion 1910

White Heat 1949

Why Man Creates 1968

Why We Fight 1943–45

Wild and Woolly 1917

Wild Bunch, The 1969

Blacksmithing Scene

An old technology captured by the new: W.K.L. Dickson's
Blacksmithing Scene. Courtesy of Kino International

Edison Manufacturing Company, 1893. Silent, B&W, 1.33, 30 seconds.
Credits: Filmmakers: W.K.L. Dickson, William Heise. Filmed before
early May 1893. Exhibited May 9, 1893.
Available: Kino Video DVD *Edison: The Invention of the Movies* (2005).
UPC: 738329038328.

Movies would not exist the way we know them today
if it weren't for Thomas Alva Edison, the coun
try's most famous inventor. Most of the technical
aspects of film—the size, sprocket holes, vertical
orientation, etc.—can·be traced back to Edison's
factory in Menlo Park, New Jersey. Although many
inventions and devices exploited the persistence of
vision, using shutters to suggest that individual
pictures were moving together as one motion,
Edison was the prime instigator of a·machine that
utilized photographs on film.

Edison, inspired by the work of photographer
Eadweard Muybridge, embarked on his motion
picture project in 1888. In October of that year he
wrote, "I am experimenting upon an instrument
which does for the Eye what the phonograph does
for the Ear, which is the recording and reproduction of things in motion, and in such a form as
to be both Cheap practical and convenient. This
apparatus I call a Kinetoscope 'Moving View.'" As
Charles Musser notes in *Before the Nickelodeon*,
Edison took the phonograph analogy seriously.
He originally envisioned a cylinder covered with
thousands of tiny photographs arranged in spirals.

A microscope lens would pass over them as the
cylinder turned. Edison wanted the machine connected to a phonograph, so the user could hear
sound while watching what would work out to a
half-hour film.

The inventor may also have been inspired by
the stereopticon, an extremely popular parlor toy
that gave viewers three-dimensional views of almost
anything on the planet. It was the single most
widespread visual toy for decades, and even today
it's easy to find piles of stereopticon slides molder-
ing in flea markets and antique stores. (The devices
themselves have become more expensive.) Edison
originally saw film as a single-user medium, like
the stereopticon, with one person at a time looking
through a lens or "peephole" into a darkened area
where photographs were exhibited. Possibly he
thought the machine would be a consumer item,
like the stereopticon.

But the device proved impractical on so many
levels that it had to be abandoned. By this time
Edison had assigned William Kennedy Laurie
Dickson, one of the key figures in early film, to the
project. Born in France to British parents, Dickson
was fascinated by Edison's work, and paid his way
to New Jersey when he was twenty-three in order
to work for the inventor.

During a trip to Europe in 1889, Edison saw
work by Étienne-Jules Marey, a Frenchman who

had found a way to photograph images on a film strip. Edison incorporated Marey's ideas into his designs. In October 1890, Dickson and his assistant William Heise built a camera that advanced a ¾ inch strip of film through a horizontal feeder. Edison exhibited the device in May 1891. Again, it was a machine that only one person at a time could use.

Dickson and Edison built a vertical-feed motion picture camera in the summer of 1892. This one used a film strip that was 1½ inches wide. (Two apocryphal stories surround the size of film. One has Edison using his thumb and forefinger to indicate the approximate size he wanted, which came out to be close to 35mm. Another, from a Kodak historian, says that readily available 70mm strips were cut in half to supply Edison with film stock.) Surviving footage includes *A Hand-Shake* (1892), which documents Dickson and Heise demonstrating exactly that.

Musser, the preeminent historian of early film, has reconstructed two of the earliest Edison films from notebook pages covered with photographs. Musser oversaw the re-animation of the photographs, and the results are almost unbearably exciting glimpses into the past. *Monkeyshines*, as Musser has named the two films, has the inexplicable power and urgency of a nightmare. This is the first recorded motion that survives, a poignant look into vanished lives.

Edison planned to display his invention at the World's Columbian Exposition in Chicago. He needed films to show, and authorized construction of the world's first movie studio in December 1892. Finished in February 1893, the tiny, wood-frame building was covered with tarpaper and dubbed the "Black Maria." Its roof could be opened to let in sunlight, and the entire building rotated to follow the sun. *Blacksmithing Scene* was one of the first films shot there. In fact, it is one of the first extant attempts to "make" a film rather than simply record an action. While photography was still prized by many at the time for recording the "truth," nothing about *Blacksmithing Scene* is true—not even its title, which was supplied later.

The three men in the film aren't blacksmiths, they aren't in a smithy, and they aren't working on metal. (It's also doubtful that they're drinking alcohol.) They are instead performers on a set pretending to be doing something. Even in 1893, Edison's workers are confronted with the conflict between capturing and representing reality. Dickson is well aware of this split, because he plays the scene for laughs.

It's surprising how much attention to detail Dickson, Heise, and the others paid to their sets and costumes, already a crucial part of filmmaking. The anvil and sledgehammers used in the film are real, as are the leather aprons worn by the actors. No one worried about the background, which is left black. The lens Dickson used worked best for medium and medium close-up shots. The camera was probably stationed ten to twelve feet away, enabling the crew to capture the actors in full figure. (Another apocryphal early film story has cameramen shooting full-length shots of people because they were afraid audiences wouldn't understand figures whose feet were out of frame. But Dickson had composed three-quarter and close-up shots before *Blacksmithing Scene*.) Musser points out the possibly intentional contrast between Edison's state-of-the-art machine shop and the primitive smithy shown in the film, adding a level of self-awareness and irony that we don't usually attribute to early films.

On May 9, 1893, a talk at the Brooklyn Institute compared various motion picture devices, most based on "magic lanterns." Frames from *Blacksmith Scene* were projected onto a screen, and after the talk the four hundred audience members were allowed to watch the film, individually through an Edison peephole Kinetoscope. That makes *Blacksmithing Scene* the first film to be shown publicly.

The following April, a kinetoscope parlor opened in Manhattan. Each film cost five cents to see, and *Blacksmithing Scene* was one of the films on display. Dickson continued to make films for Edison, notably the *Dickson Experimental Sound Film*.

Dickson Experimental Sound Film

Edison Manufacturing Company, 1894–95. Sound, B&W, 1.33. 21 seconds at 30 fps.

Cast: W.K.L. Dickson, other unidentified workers.

Credits: Directed by W.K.L. Dickson. Photographer: William Heise.

Additional Credits: Produced between September 1894 and April 2 1895 in the Black Maria studio in West Orange, New Jersey. Note: Title supplied later.

Available: Online at the Library of Congress American Memory (*memory. loc.gov*) and Internet Archive (*www.archive.org*) websites. Image Entertainment DVD *More Treasures from American Film Archives, 1894–1931* (2004). ISBN: 0-9747099-1-3. UPC: 0-14381-2271-2-3.

Inventor Thomas Alva Edison had always envisioned combining sound and images for motion pictures, which, as he put it, would do "for the Eye what the phonograph does for the Ear." In *The Conversations*, a series of interviews between Oscar-winning editor Walter Murch and novelist Michael Ondaatje, Murch notes that "Edison's rationale was that people might be interested to see the faces of the people who sang on his records. Cinema began as a music video!"

William Kennedy Laurie Dickson, perhaps the most significant figure in the early development of movies, was also a violinist who assisted in the Edison recording department. This department prepared material for another of Edison's inventions, the wax cylinder phonograph. Dickson later testified that he completed a successful sound film in 1889 in which he greeted Edison upon the inventor's return to his lab after a European trip. This footage no longer exists.

Sometime between September 1894 and April 1895, Dickson synchronized sound to film for what later historians have called the *Dickson Experimental Sound Film*. He did this by playing a violin into a recording horn attached to a wax cylinder machine and simultaneously filming the scene with a camera. While this film was not intended for public viewing, Edison workers did complete other sound films for a new invention, the "kinetophone." This device combined the single-user kinetoscopes with phonographs. Customers could hear music for films through rubber earphones attached to the machines.

The device was not a success, possibly because of its expense (some $400). According to film historian Charles Musser, by 1900, only forty-five had been sold. By that point the industry trend had shifted from peep show viewers to movies projected onto screens, which made synchronizing sound considerably more difficult. Edison would try again in 1913 with a complicated process that ran cables from a phonograph behind the screen back to projectors, but abandoned this as well by 1915.

When Edison died in 1931, his archives became part of the Edison Historical Site, under the control of the National Park Service. In 1942, the Museum of Modern Art copied the Dickson piece from nitrate to safety film, but it wasn't until 1960 that the accompanying wax cylinder was found in a metal canister by the Edison Historical Site staff. It was labeled "Dickson—Violin by W.K.L. Dixon with Kineto." (National Park Service catalog number: EDIS 30142; E-number: E-6018-1.) Four years later they discovered that the cylinder had broken into two pieces.

In 1998, members of the Domitor society, a group devoted to the study of early cinema, were instrumental in trying to recover sound from the broken cylinder. Funded in part by the Library of Congress, curators rerecorded the sound onto tape. On June 5th, the film was seen with its music track for the first time in a hundred years. Synchronization was poor, but the viewers succeeded in identifying the music being played as the "Song of the Cabin Boy" from *Les cloches de Corneville*, an 1877 opera by Robert Planquette. It was a popular enough work to be translated in English as *The Chimes of Normandy*; according to historian Spencer Sundell, the opera had a longer run than the original production of *H.M.S. Pinafore*.

In 2000, while working on *Apocalypse Now Redux*, Walter Murch took over the task of synching sound and film. As he wrote on the online Cinema Audio Society Discussion Board, "[The] problem was the film was shot at 40fps [frames per second], not 24, and the sound was running wild on a cracked 1890's cylinder. Plus inter-government agency red tape (the film is in the hands of the Library of Congress, the sound is at the National Park Service). So they sent it to me (neutral mediator) to put in synch, which was easy enough given the time-stretching and compressing powers of the Avid [a computer editing program]." With his assistant Sean Cullen, Murch selected synchronization points—when the violinist starts playing, for example—and then adjusted the music track. "Before the film begins you hear someone say 'The rest of you fellows ready? Go ahead!' (the first 'speed' and 'action' captured on wax)," he wrote. "It was very moving, when the sound finally fell into synch: the scratchiness of the image and the sound dissolved away and you felt the immediate presence of these young men playing around with a fast-emerging technology."

Because the film showed two men dancing together, it has been categorized as a gay film (and the first gay film at that). It's impossible to say with certainty what the intentions of Dickson and his fellow workers were, but there were no female workers in his group, and thus little likelihood that a woman would have been available to join in the filming. "Song of the Cabin Boy," which describes being at sea without women, was an amusingly appropriate choice for their shooting conditions.

To Murch, another appealing aspect of the project was the chance to hear people speaking naturally for the first time. As he explained to Ondaatje, "There's a formality to all recordings of the human voice we have from that period, very much like the photographs of people sitting in their Sunday best, looking right at the camera." Since the original sound fragment was over two minutes long, Murch hopes to use modern technology to one day decipher the conversations muffled in the background.

The John C. Rice–May Irwin Kiss

Edison, 1896. Silent, B&W, 1.33. Length: 50 feet (approximately 20 seconds).
Cast: May Irwin (Widow Jones), John C. Rice [John C. Hilburg] (Billie Bike).
Credits: Directed and photographed by William Heise.
Additional Credits: Based on characters in *The Widow Jones* by John J. McNally. Filmed April 1896.
Other Versions: Edison released a remake of sorts, *The Kiss*, with different actors, in 1900.
Available: Kino Video DVD, *Edison: The Invention of the Movies* (2005). UPC: 7-38329-03832-8.

Also known as *The Kiss*, *Kiss Scene*, *The May Irwin Kiss*, and *The Picture of a Kiss*, *The John C. Rice–May Irwin Kiss* is perhaps the most familiar nineteenth-century film. Short and succinct, it shows actress May Irwin and actor John C. Rice enacting the climax to the play *The Widow Jones*. The actors are shot in medium close-up, against a black background, lit by the sun overhead.

If you don't know the play, the film may not make much sense. It has the immediacy of a home movie. Viewers are dropped into an alien setting, with no explanation of the people on the screen or what they are doing. Filmmaker William Heise doesn't try to define the performers as characters in a story—through the use of props, for example. He assumes that if you are watching *The Kiss*, you already know about the plot to *The Widow Jones*. You also already know who these people are, as well as their histories and relationships. For viewers at the end of the nineteenth century, especially those in New York, this could very well have been true.

Largely forgotten today, May Irwin was once one of the most recognizable actresses in the country. Around her name swirl most of the significant theatrical names of the late nineteenth century. She was born Ada Campbell in Ontario in 1862 and educated in a convent school with her older sister Georgia. They attracted some local attention as singers, enough so that their widowed mother brought them to the United States in search of work. Appearing in Buffalo, New York, in 1875, they were named "The Irwin Sisters" by a theater manager. (Georgia by this time was appearing as "Flo.") Two years later they were performing in New York City, for showman Tony Pastor and others.

In 1883, Irwin signed with Augustin Daly, the most influential playwright and producer in the city. His stable of actors included John Drew, Otis Skinner, and Ada Rehan. Irwin developed as a comedienne, appearing in Sir Arthur Wing Pinero's *Girls and Boys* at the end of the year, and then in a series of Daly's own plays. After touring with Daly's troupe in London, Irwin left to join a Boston theater company, giving up legitimate roles to concentrate on music hall skits. One such farce, *Home Rule*, was written by former newspaper critic John J. McNally.

In 1893 she was hired by Charles Frohman, one of the primary architects of the "star system," to appear with the highly respected Henry Miller in *His Wedding Day*. In a comic afterpiece, she introduced "After the Ball," the first song to sell a million copies of sheet music. She would later introduce "A Hot Time in the Old Town."

Starting in 1893, McNally and others began writing full-length "entertainments" for Irwin. These were essentially light comedies with music, and in a way set a template for musical comedies in the early twentieth century. One was *The Widow Jones*, in which she played Beatrice Jones, a somewhat stout woman who avoided romantic entanglements by pretending to be a widow. In it she introduced a ragtime song, "I'm Looking for de Bully," which she sang in an exaggerated African American dialect, an unfortunate contribution to the growing trend of "coon songs." (It appeared in sheet music as "Mary Irwin's Bully Song," with words and music by Charles. E. Trevathan. Trevathan, a sports writer for a Chicago newspaper, claimed that he heard "Mama Lou" sing it in a St. Louis bordello run by Babe Connors.)

Stout and matronly, Irwin resembles character actors like Marie Dressler or Marjorie Main. It was a coup for Edison and his staff to film her. The motion picture division was in financial trouble, with almost no library of titles to exploit. The idea of selling individual kinetoscope machines had been replaced with the concept of projecting movies onto a screen. Instead of one customer per film viewing, exhibitors could sell many tickets for each screening. In April 1896 this was still a new experience for everyone involved. Films had only recently been shown to the public at all, at Koster & Bial's Music Hall earlier that month.

The film was sponsored by the *New York World*, which publicized both the film and the play in the April 26, 1896, edition of its *Sunday World*. Kissing on stage had become a growing concern, or at least a viable subject for an article. In its piece, the *World* pretended to discuss the topic seriously, although it was actually exploiting kissing in general and the play and movie in particular. Along with illustrations of the kiss, the article described *The Widow Jones* and the film, and explained how to see them. This three-pronged publicity scheme benefited everyone involved, with newspaper, play, and movie all promoting themselves and each other.

While it's always risky to cite cinema firsts, this still stands as the first of countless kisses ever recorded on film. Edison's staff was not shy about advertising. Here's how the Edison catalog promoted the Irwin film: "They get ready to kiss, begin to kiss, and kiss and kiss and kiss in a way that brings down the house every time." At $7.50 a copy, *The Kiss* was the company's most popular title of the year, based on the number of copies sold. (At that time, exhibitors would purchase individual films outright, then assemble their own program of shorts.) By the fall *The Kiss* was often being used to close a film program.

According to historian Charles Musser, this was the first film that disrupted the lives of its cast. Based on his stage portrayal, Rice became a bona fide star. Irwin, thirty-four at the time, thought that he made her play "old" on stage, and had him replaced with an actor named Dickson. Rice in turn developed a vaudeville act with his wife that was based on the film. In his playlet, called *A School for Acting*, he taught her how to kiss for the movies. Meanwhile, the public clamored for a reunion between Irwin and Rice. She reluctantly acceded.

Irwin starred in a brief revival of the play in 1902, and appeared in several subsequent hits. By the early twentieth century, she had her own management company, and full control of her career. She starred in another film, *Mrs. Black Is Back*, based on a 1904 play by George V. Hobart. Plot synopses describe a dizzying whirl of mistaken identities, cross-dressing, blackface, slapstick car crashes, and broad humor, like an exercise program that causes Mrs. Black to gain ten pounds. It was filmed partially at her summer home on the St. Lawrence River in upstate New York. Her last comic stage role was in 1919's *On the Hiring Line*.

Irwin retired from show business completely in 1922. Her first husband, whom she married in 1878, died in 1886. Her second marriage, to her manager in 1907, lasted until her death. Irwin died of pneumonia following a stroke in 1938.

The Kiss was one of the last films shot at the Black Maria, which had become obsolete in less than a decade. The distance from New York to the West Orange, New Jersey, studio was a factor, as it was difficult to convince performers to travel such a long way to appear in an untested medium. One filmmaker who tried to work there found the trash-filled studio's ceiling stuck open, so that performers had to work in the cold. Filmmakers were discovering that they could assemble a "studio" almost anywhere there was sunlight—on the roof of a Manhattan office building, for example.

So much history surrounds this short film, from the rise of theater as a business to race relations, the growth of a celebrity culture, and using public relations as an advertising tool. Movies would grow vastly more complex in the coming years, but for the most part they would not stray very far from the strategies and tactics employed in *The Kiss*.

Rip Van Winkle

Joseph Jefferson in his signature role as Rip Van Winkle.

American Mutoscope, 1896. Silent, B&W, 1.33. 4 minutes.

Cast: Joseph Jefferson (Rip Van Winkle).

Credits: Directed by William K.L. Dickson. Based on the story by Washington Irving and the play by Joseph Jefferson and Dion Boucicault. Photography: G.W. Bitzer. Released September 1896.

Available: Image Entertainment DVD, *More Treasures from American Film Archives 1894–1931* (2004). ISBN: 0-9747099-1-3. UPC: 0-14381-2271-2-3.

Washington Irving wrote the short story "Rip Van Winkle" while he was living in Birmingham, England; it was featured in *The Sketch Book*, first printed in England in 1820. Irving based his story on German folk tales, although folklorists have also found antecedents in Jewish and Chinese myths. A mix of the supernatural and gentle sermonizing, it has become one of the most recognizable stories in American literature.

Born in 1828 in Philadelphia, Joseph Jefferson was the fourth generation of actors in his family, making his debut at the age of four in a blackface routine with "Jim Crow" Rice. Later a set designer and manager as well as a performer, he organized his own theater troupe before traveling to Europe in 1856. Back in the United States he starred in *Our American Cousin*, earning praise for his natural acting and comic timing. He also appeared as Caleb Plummer in a version of *The Cricket on the Hearth* written by the Irish actor Dion Boucicault.

Around this time Jefferson experimented with a version of *Rip Van Winkle* he patched together from extant plays. In mourning over the death of his wife, the actor spent the Civil War years in Australia, where he toured in *Rip Van Winkle* and *The Cricket on the Hearth*, among other plays. In 1865, Jefferson was in London, where he asked Boucicault to help him prepare a new version of *Rip Van Winkle*. Their collaboration opened at the Adelphi Theatre that September. The following year Jefferson premiered it at the Olympic Theatre in New York City.

Jefferson and Boucicault took several liberties with Irving's original story, emphasizing rural comedy, largely in the form of Rip's heavy drinking and harebrained plans to make money. According to curator and historian Scott Simmon, the play's impact was so strong that its plot essentially replaced Irving's in the American imagination.

Jefferson's performance in particular was a sensation. The actor went on to play the part for fourteen years straight, and returned to it repeatedly until shortly before his death. He became such a noted and respected actor that he succeeded Edwin Booth as president of the Players Club in New York. In 1880, he appeared as "Bob Acres" in a famous reworking of *The Rivals*, garnering new praise for his restrained, realistic performing. In 1882, he and Booth helped form the Actors Fund. Jefferson continued touring the world as Rip Van Winkle, Caleb Plummer, Bob Acres, and in other parts. By 1889, when he had built an estate on Buzzards Bay in Massachusetts, he was arguably the most famous actor in the country. That same year his *Autobiography* appeared in *Century Magazine*.

Jefferson was an early investor in the American Mutoscope Company, founded by William Kennedy Laurie Dickson, Harry Marvin, Herman Casler, and Elias Koopman in Canastota, near Syracuse, New York. Dickson was still working for Thomas Edison when he helped design the mutoscope, a stand-alone machine that displayed flip-cards through a peephole to individual viewers. The mutograph camera used 70mm film, a distinct improvement over the 35mm used in Edison's kinetograph. With the peephole industry in jeopardy, Dickson encouraged the others to design a film projector, which became known as the Biograph.

By December 1895, the company had completed a total of six films, some of them tests. Working on the roof of new headquarters in New York City, Dickson quickly doubled the studio's output, making films that closely resembled those he had shot for Edison two years earlier. Sometimes working with Dickson was Billy Bitzer, moonlighting from his job at the Magic Introduction Company.

Dickson and Bitzer brought the firm's sole camera to Buzzards Bay in August 1896, to film Jefferson performing eight scenes from *Rip Van Winkle*. These were: *Rip's Toast* (No. 45 in the Biograph catalog), *Rip Meets the Dwarf* (No. 46); *Rip and the Dwarf*; *Rip Leaving Sleepy Hollow* (No. 52); *Rip's Toast to Hudson and Crew*; *Rip's Twenty Years' Sleep* (No. 50), *Awakening of Rip*; and *Rip Passing Over Hill*. All were photographed in what would be considered today a wide or long shot, in one of two camera setups on either side of a large rock on Jefferson's estate. The actor was assisted by four costumed "dwarves" who were as tall as he was.

Simmon's notes for the films point out that Jefferson astutely chose incidents from the play that were largely pantomimed on stage, reducing the need for explanatory titles (which at the time would be affixed to individual mutoscopes or printed in programs). Customers could see all eight clips one after the other in an arcade.

At the same time, Charles B. Jefferson, the actor's son, was touring vaudeville with a show called *Sandow's Olympia*, built around the famous strongman Eugen Sandow. One of the "acts" was American Mutoscope's sole functioning projector, which the Jefferson scion used to show seven shorts, including three of his father's *Rip Van Winkle* scenes. That fall the Biograph was the sole act in a program of films, first at the Olympia Theater, then at Koster & Bial's Music Hall. Headlining the program during election week were scenes of future president William McKinley. Joseph Jefferson was represented by his "Toast Scene from *Rip Van Winkle*."

When American Mutoscope (which quickly became American Mutoscope and Biograph Company, and then simply the Biograph Company) projectors went on sale, the company offered its films as well. Exhibitors could purchase any one or all eight *Rip Van Winkle* scenes and display them in any order they liked. The films were so popular that Biograph edited them together as *Rip Van Winkle* in 1903, a year before Jefferson's final stage performance. (He died in 1905.) To copyright the material, Biograph made what were called "paper prints" and registered them with the Library of Congress. These poor quality 35mm dupes were all that survived when the library began preservation efforts in 1988.

With hit films like *The John C. Rice–May Irwin Kiss* (1896), Biograph quickly became the most popular studio in the country. When D.W. Griffith became a Biograph staff director in 1908, it also became one of the most innovative firms in the industry. By that time Jefferson's son Thomas had taken over the part of Rip Van Winkle on stage, and in two film versions. Boucicault died in 1890; his son, Dion, Jr., was also an actor, but had more impact as a theatrical producer, notably of J.M. Barrie's *Peter Pan*. (His sister Nina originated the role on stage.) So while the eight brief shots that make up *Rip Van Winkle* may seem unprepossessing today, they connect us to some of the most significant figures and trends in our cultural history.

President McKinley Inauguration Footage

Edison Manufacturing Company, 1901. Silent, B&W, 1.33. 3 minutes.
Credits (Off-Screen): Cinematography attributed to Edwin S. Porter, James H. White. The inauguration took place on March 4, 1901. Edison sold the footage under two titles: *President McKinley and Escort Going to the Capitol and President McKinley Taking the Oath of Office*.
Available: These films can be screened online or downloaded at the Library of Congress American Memory website, *http://memory.loc.gov*.

William McKinley, the twenty-fifth president of the United States, was one of the first presidential candidates to make full use of modern media. Born in Ohio in 1843, he was a Civil War veteran and governor of Ohio before running for election against

William Jennings Bryan in 1896. His campaign manager Mark Hanna blanketed the country with leaflets, posters, and pamphlets, outspending the Bryan campaign by a twelve-to-one ratio. Two Biograph shorts, *McKinley at Home, Canton, O.* and *McKinley and Hobart Parade at Canton, O.* (both 1896), were filmed with the candidate's cooperation and shown during a rally in New York City in October (Garret A. Hobart was McKinley's running mate). Press accounts described "great applause" and "pandemonium" during the screenings. The inauguration of 1897 was photographed by at least four motion picture companies.

We call these films "actualities" today, separate from the dramas, comedies, and novelties that made up fiction film of the time. They resemble broadcast news footage, and showed dignitaries, street scenes, parades and other civic events. But many were faked re-creations, especially after the outbreak of the Spanish-American War in 1898. As a result of the ten-week war, Cuba became a republic, and the United States took control of Puerto Rico and the Philippines. Once the war ended, McKinley was filmed inspecting Camp Wikoff on Long Island.

Bryan ran against McKinley again in 1900, but he was also running against what many felt was a victory in a popular war. Bryan was at the forefront of a reform movement that would eventually spread throughout American society. Names aligned to the movement would include Woodrow Wilson, Theodore Roosevelt, and many more reformers whose ideas would be adopted by the creative community. A side result was that a new realism emerged in art, something that film could depict better than any other medium. Within two decades, everything that Bryan had fought for would be enacted into legislation.

The McKinley inauguration footage is actually two separate films: *President McKinley and Escort Going to the Capitol* and *President McKinley Taking the Oath*. Edison crews shot the films on March 4, 1901, and released them less than two weeks later, on March 16. An optimistic synopsis provided by the company describes the parade to the capitol in glowing terms. Shooting at Pennsylvania Avenue and Fifteenth Street in Washington, D.C., the camera shows mounted police, the grand marshal and his staff, Troop A, the personal escort of the president, McKinley himself with congressmen riding in his carriage, followed by carriages containing various cabinet secretaries and celebrities like Admiral George Dewey. The synopsis notes that the Edison camera was "within twenty feet of the President's carriage when it passed."

Audiences of the time were presumably more familiar with the stream of celebrities who were photographed. But even in 1901, this was at best a blurry version of reality. And without that shot synopsis, it would be almost impossible to determine who is in the frame during much of the footage. What may startle viewers today is the amount and bulk of clothes that everyone seemed to wear. Bystanders who step in front of the camera, blocking the view, add another touch of authenticity.

Going to the Capitol survives in a version that is about two minutes long; *Taking the Oath* lasts about fifty seconds. They were sent as paper prints to the Library of Congress in order to secure copyrights. Consequently, the clarity of the image suffers. The bulky cameras had not yet been equipped with fluid-head tripods, making it difficult to pan or tilt while filming. Edwin S. Porter, who had recently been hired by Edison, may have been one of the cameramen. That could explain the empty sidewalk that fills almost a third of some compositions, a characteristic of many of his films.

McKinley set a more ghoulish precedent as well. He was filmed attending the 1901 Great Exposition in Buffalo, New York, on the day before he was shot by the anarchist Leon Frank Czolgosz. Edison cameramen outside the exposition's Temple of Music captured the stunned reaction of crowds to news of the attack. McKinley died of gangrene on September 14. His assassination prompted a raft of films, including one that reenacted Czolgosz's subsequent electrocution. American filmmakers at the time refrained from dramatizing the actual assassination itself, although some staged versions were filmed in France.

Building Up and Demolishing the Star Theatre

Last days of the Star Theatre.

American Mutoscope and Biograph Company, 1901. Silent, B&W, 1.33. 3 minutes.

Credits: Photographed by Frederick C. Armitage.

Additional Credits: Copyrighted April 18, 1901.

Available: The Library of Congress American Memory website (*http://memory.loc.gov/ammem*). Image Entertainment DVD *Treasures from American Film Archives* (2000). UPC: 0-14381-9706-2-3. Image Entertainment DVD *Unseen Cinema: Early American Avant-Garde Film 1894–1941*, volume 5 (2005). UPC: 0-14381-0592-2-9.

For every filmmaker impressed by how accurately cinematography captured reality, others were just as happy to learn how easily the medium could distort it. Frederick C. Armitage put one of the most fundamental camera tricks—stop-motion photography—to use in *Star Theatre*. To achieve a stop-motion effect, you only have to shut down a camera, change something within the frame, and then start the camera up again. You can shift, add or delete a person or prop, and if you don't move the camera or alter the lighting, you can achieve magical effects. People vanish or pop up with no warning. A woman can change into a man, or into a girl, or into an inanimate object. You can switch a human for a dummy, commit murder, and then switch back to the human, now playing a corpse.

You can also change nothing at all, and simply record the passing of time. This is the basis of time-lapse photography, a technique that by

illuminating patterns and progressions can help demystify our world.

In *Démolition d'un mur* (*Falling Wall*, 1895), Louis Lumière used a second effect—running film backward through the projector—to make the impossible come true: a building wall knocked over by workers springs back upright. It was a popular enough film to be copied by the American Mutoscope Company in 1897 as *Throwing Over a Wall*.

Details about the origins of American Mutoscope are covered in *Rip Van Winkle* (1896). By 1898, it was arguably the most successful film company in the world, and in the business year ending in May 1899, it produced five hundred new titles for sale. American Mutoscope made money with two machines: the Mutoscope, a flip-card peephole device that was sold to arcades; and the Biograph, a 70mm projector that was leased to traveling showmen or theaters. (The company eventually became known as Biograph.)

According to film historian Charles Musser, almost all of the early Biograph movies were made up of single shots lasting about a half minute. Many were actualities tied to sporting events and landscape views. Some were filmed in a makeshift studio built on the roof of 841 Broadway, where the company had offices. By 1897, Biograph was filming multipart movies, like a Christmas scene made up of four episodes. In 1898, its hits included faked images of the battleship *Maine* released to exploit the Spanish-American War.

The war proved a financial gold mine for the company, now run by Wallace McCutcheon. He sent cameramen Billy Bitzer and Arthur Marvin to Cuba to cover the fighting; they made up one of three production units in the company. By 1899, after the company officially changed its name to the American Mutoscope and Biograph Company, it had four main cinematographers under employment: Bitzer, Marvin, C. Fred Ackerman, and Frederick S. Armitage.

Details about Armitage's life are frustratingly vague. Film historian Paul Spehr wrote that he made an experimental sound film, *The Gay Old Boy* (1899). Musser credits him with most of Biograph's studio films from 1899 to May 1900. After going on location, he returned to studio work, splitting duties with Marvin. Musser also points out that as general manager, McCutcheon acted as a sort of producer, and may have initiated many of the actualities.

Formerly known as Wallack's Theatre, the Star Theatre was on the northeast corner of Broadway and Thirteenth Street, across from the Biograph office. According to an April 7, 1901, article in the *New York Times*, the theater was the site of the American debuts for Henry Irving, Sarah Bernhardt, and Ellen Terry. R.M. Gulick & Co. took over the lease in 1895 (the Wallack troupe had long since moved uptown), and in 1899 plans were announced to replace the building with a new structure for the Rogers, Peet & Co. clothing store. (A new Star Theatre opened at Lexington Avenue and 107th Street.)

According to the *Times* article, demolition of the Star Theatre was scheduled to begin on May 1, but the April 18 copyright on the film indicates that the work occurred earlier. Taking advantage of the Biograph office's views, Armitage set up a camera that framed the entire building. He used "a specially devised electric apparatus" to shoot every four minutes, eight hours a day, recording the process from start to finish. He also shot about thirty seconds of standard exposures at the beginning and end of the demolition, using this as a sort of narrative framework.

Star Theatre displays the capabilities of film in a manner so vivid that competing art forms must have seemed obsolete to viewers at the time. No other medium could capture the event—could answer the question, "What happens next?"—so clearly and easily. Running the film in reverse, lifting the theater back up from rubble, bordered on the miraculous. "The effect is very extraordinary," as Biograph publicists put it.

Armitage shot hundreds of subjects for Biograph, including actualities in New York and Rhode Island, and several records of stage performers, like the cakewalking Eugenie Fougère and "mirror dancer" Ameta. He also filmed Buffalo Bill's Wild West show and President Theodore Roosevelt and his staff. When Biograph moved to a new studio at 11 East Fourteenth Street, Armitage began photographing with artificial light.

Armitage was hired by the Edison company in July 1908, a few months after D.W. Griffith arrived at Biograph. (The next Biograph title on the Registry is *Lady Helen's Escapade*, 1909). At Edison, Armitage headed the camera department, coordinated editing assignments, and shot films, most of them directed by J. Searle Dawley. Stop-motion effects helped make *King Kong* (1933) so spectacular, and are used in everything from commercials to music videos today. The same is true for time-lapse photography, an important component of films like *Koyaanisqatsi* (1983). Ironically, Andy Warhol's *Empire* (1964) took the same basic approach as *Star Theatre* while discarding Armitage's effects. In a happy coincidence, the Star Theatre building site is now a Regal Union Square cineplex.

The Great Train Robbery

Edison, 1903. Silent, B&W with tints and hand coloring, 1.33. 12 minutes.

Cast: Justus D. Barnes (Chief bandit), Walter Cameron (Sheriff), George M. Anderson (Slain passenger/Man forced to dance to gunshots/Bandit), Mary Snow, Donald Gallaher.

Credits: Written, photographed, edited, and directed by Edwin S. Porter. Additional photography: J. Blair Smith. Assistant director: George M. Anderson.

Additional Credits: Possibly based in part on Scott Marble's 1896 play *The Great Train Robbery*. Production dates: November, 1903. Photographed in New York City and New Jersey. Released December, 1903.

Other Versions: Reshot (illegally) by Sigmund Lubin as *The Great Train Robbery* (1904). Remade by Porter with child actors as *The Little Train Robbery* (1905).

Available: Kino Video DVD, *Edison: The Invention of the Movies* (2005). UPC: 7-38329-03832-8.

This scene of Justus D. Barnes shooting at his viewers, sometimes hand-colored, could appear at the beginning or the end of *The Great Train Robbery*.

It can be hard to adjust to the past. In literature and music, as well as movies, the past can seem slow, obvious, and at the same time filled with odd, unexpected touches too far removed from our experiences to decipher easily—which makes *The Great Train Robbery* an even more remarkable achievement. The blockbuster of its time, it has lost none of its power to entertain over the past hundred years. Of all the silent films, it needs the fewest excuses or qualifications. From its era, only *A Trip to the Moon* (1902) has remained as firm a part of our cultural consciousness.

The Great Train Robbery is so accomplished, so modern in its outlook and technique, that you wonder why it didn't have a greater impact on contemporary filmmakers. True, within a year Sigmund Lubin shot a bootleg version, and Edison released a weak parody in 1905 in which the adult roles were acted by children. But for years, *The Great Train Robbery* remained the only twelve-minute film that succeeded on a creative as well as a commercial level.

It was directed by Edwin S. Porter, one of the medium's preeminent figures. Born in 1870, he grew up in Connellsville, Pennsylvania, about fifty miles from Pittsburgh. As a child he remembered seeing lantern shows, precursors to movies that combined projected slides and lectures into shows with titles like *Sights and Scenes in Europe*. Porter developed an early interest in electricity, sharing a patent at the age of twenty-one for a lamp regulator. After serving

in the Navy, he worked for Raff & Gammon, distributors of Edison's Vitagraph motion picture projector. He helped project the first public screening of Edison films on April 23, 1896.

Porter freelanced for the next three years, designing projectors and occasionally selling footage to Edison. In 1900 he began working at the Edison labs, first as a mechanic, then as a cameraman. Soon he was in charge of all motion picture production, directing most of the studio's releases himself. Film historian Charles Musser has outlined Porter's slow, unsteady growth as an artist; not much of his early work is very interesting apart from its historical significance. His titles can be broken down into "actualities," street scenes or depictions of tourist sites, and imitations of the trick films made by Georges Méliès.

By 1902, Porter had assimilated industry trends regarding subject matter and editing. Films had originally consisted of single shots that were sold separately. Bits of action too short to be sold individually had to be spliced together, which helped lead to "story" films like *Pie, Tramp and the Bulldog* (1901), where editing supplied the narrative. Porter also began experimenting with editing as a means of controlling time. In *Appointment by Telephone* and *Jack and the Beanstalk* (both 1902), and especially *Life of an American Fireman* (1903), Porter used editing to suggest simultaneous action—a building on fire and a fire truck racing to the rescue, for example.

Most cinematography of the period operated on the principle of delivering the equivalent of "the best seat in the house" to moviegoers; that is, straight-ahead, eye-level compositions, as if viewing the stage from a center seat in a theater. But "the best seat in the house" isn't a constant, it changes. Sometimes it's up close, so you can see the actress's tears, sometimes it's in the balcony, so you can see all of the action unfold. The ability to shift the point of view—to go closer into the story or pull back to show a wider view—is one of the fundamental differences between stage and screen.

This conceptual leap is one of the distinctive features of *The Great Train Robbery*. Porter's camera becomes a part of the story; in a way, it is a character itself. It hurtles along the top of a train, picks its way through a forest, watches a backwoods social. The camera abandons the stage proscenium, adopting oblique angles, high viewpoints, even tilting and panning—moving through space—as the story demands. Previous films may have used the same devices, but they had never been integrated as fully into a fictional story of this length. Porter's style makes the events in *The Great Train Robbery* seem like they are actually happening. Placing the camera immediately behind a crook as he throws a victim's body from a coal tender involves the viewer in the story to a far greater degree than if watching it at a distance, from a perpendicular angle.

In *The Great Train Robbery*, Porter doesn't just shift positions; he shifts time itself, another major difference between stage and screen. Not only do some actions precede others, but actions occur at the same time. The crooks escape while a station-master telegraphs for help; a posse forms while the crooks are riding through a forest. (It's not clear exactly how comfortable Porter was with these ideas. Historians like Musser and Eileen Bowser have discussed in detail Porter's "temporal overlaps" and other aberrances in time. For that matter, D.W. Griffith was doing the same thing as late as 1915's *The Birth of a Nation*).

Of course, just as important as technique was narrative. While it was not the first Western, or even the first crime film, *The Great Train Robbery* set out the elements of what would become the Western genre so clearly and cleverly that they have been imitated ever since. *The Great Train Robbery* has it all: bandits overcoming technology, senseless violence, hoedowns, horse chases, shoot-outs, the innocent in peril and the evil brought to justice. Throw in special effects like stop-motion photography, matte shots, and the occasional use of color, and you have the 1903 equivalent of a big-budget Hollywood blockbuster.

Oddly, Porter did not do much to capitalize on his success. In his subsequent films he returned to a plodding, proscenium-oriented style that looked increasingly old-fashioned. Audiences began to prefer films from the rival Biograph studio. Max Aronson, who had at least three roles in the film, later became one of the medium's earliest stars, "Broncho Billy" Anderson. Porter is also represented on the Registry by *Tess of the Storm Country* (1914), an important vehicle for Mary Pickford.

Westinghouse Works

American Mutoscope and Biograph Company, 1904. Silent, B&W, 1.33. Approximately 53 minutes.
Credits: Photography: G.W. "Billy" Bitzer.
Available: Online at the Library of Congress American Memory website (*http://memory.loc.gov/ammem/*). *Panorama View* is on the Image Entertainment DVD *Unseen Cinema: Early American Avant-Garde Film 1894–1941 (2005)*. UPC: 0-14381-0592-2-9. *Panoramic View Aisle B Westinghouse Works*, *Girls Winding Armatures*, and an untitled short are on the Image Entertainment DVD *More Treasures from American Film Archives* (2004). UPC: 0-12381-2271-2-3.

Comprised of some twenty titles, *Westinghouse Works* is a collection of short films shot in and around various Westinghouse companies near Pittsburgh, Pennsylvania, in April and May of 1904. They show the Westinghouse Air Brake Company, Westinghouse Machine Company, and Westinghouse Electric & Manufacturing Company. The latter was time considered the largest and most progressive factory in the world. More than 18,000 employees worked at the three sites; many more worked for various Westinghouse partners and subsidiaries throughout the world.

One of the earliest concerns for filmmakers was how to make money from the process. Theaters in urban areas were controlled by film exchanges, which sold titles outright. The earliest filmmakers sometimes carried their equipment with them from town to town. These entrepreneurs followed a newspaper model, filming local figures and buildings and then showing the results in theaters, often that same day. It was a risky tactic, requiring an investment of time and money with no guarantee that it would pay off.

Some filmmakers found it easier to find a patron or company to finance production before it started, basically offering themselves out for hire. Filmed commercials start appearing almost immediately after the first exhibitions, and in fact could be seen as an outgrowth of the advertising that plastered curtains and backdrops in theaters, or were projected on lantern slides in between performances. Studios routinely filmed civic groups for pay; the films were shown at benefit dinners, or at special screenings in theaters rented for the occasion.

Westinghouse Works constitutes some of the earliest extant examples of what became known as industrial films. Much like annual reports, they were intended to showcase companies for their investors and workers. They aren't strictly commercials, because they don't generally advertise individual products, and because they usually have a limited exhibition. But they can't be considered documentaries, either, because they are made according to guidelines set out by the companies paying for them. In style and technique they are more like public service announcements, only without the public service.

Many filmmakers have worked on industrials, including Robert Altman and Spike Lee. *Westinghouse Works* was shot by one of the most celebrated cinematographers in the medium, Billy Bitzer. Born in Massachusetts in 1872, G.W. Bitzer worked as a mechanic and electrician for the Magic Introduction Company, which started out marketing novelties and optical toys before evolving into the American Mutoscope and Biograph Company (AM&B). He became the company's leading cameraman, perfecting his technique by shooting street scenes, actualities, and fictionalized re-creations of news events. He would go on to photograph many of D.W. Griffith's most important films, including *The Birth of a Nation* (1915) and *Intolerance* (1916). (Both films are on the Registry.)

While the exact financial details are unclear, Westinghouse executives apparently commissioned AM&B to film at least twenty-nine shorts about their companies and workers. The films were screened for employees in Pittsburgh, and later at the Louisiana Purchase Exposition in St. Louis, where they were a notable success. (That's the same Louisiana Purchase Exposition that prompted the song, "Meet Me in St. Louis." Perhaps Judy Garland's family in the movie *Meet Me in St. Louis,* another Registry film, saw the shorts themselves when they attended the fair.)

Apart from tests, the *Westinghouse Works* films were the first to be shot with new mercury vapor lamps, lights manufactured by a Westinghouse subsidiary. They were photographed between April 13 and May 16, 1904. Some of the shorts document the gigantic Westinghouse Electric & Manufacturing plant, including an enormous aisle in the main building almost 1,200 feet long. Taken from overhead cranes that traversed the floor, they could be the first crane shots in film history.

Most of the titles document workers working, either winding armaments for use in generators, casting metal parts, or performing tasks no longer readily identifiable. One film shows nothing more than Westinghouse "girls" punching a time clock. Another is just a medium shot of a steam whistle. Others document the exterior of the Westinghouse compound from trains that circled the factory buildings.

Bitzer mostly used stationary cameras and fixed lenses and simply devoted an entire reel of film to one job or position, grinding away at the same shot until the film ran out two-and-a-half minutes later. Editing at that time was still little more than gluing one reel to another. Although we can piece together a narrative today, with establishing shots of the factory buildings followed by workers punching in and then getting to work, there is no indication of how or even if the films were cut together. Presumably they were shown as a sort of animated PowerPoint lecture, with a narrator providing information about what was being seen. A newspaper review from the time refers to a "pleasing" musical accompaniment by organist Walter E. Hall.

Apart from appreciating the sheer beauty of early film stock, lenses, and projection speeds, *Westinghouse Works* can be enjoyed as part of a cinematic style that extends to works by artists like H. Lee Waters, whose *Kannapolis* (1940–41) is also on the Registry. In addition to glimpses of life a hundred years ago, the films offer unintended suspense: Will the train make it over the bridge or around a corner before Bitzer runs out of film?

The films were restored from paper prints deposited with the Library of Congress in 1904. New prints were struck starting in 1992, and have been screened very infrequently since then. The library assigned titles to the surviving films, which themselves had no title cards. Some were copyrighted under similar names, but Biograph records could be contradictory. Number 8, which the LOC calls *Panorama Exterior, Westinghouse Works*, for example, was listed as *Railroad from Pittsburg to Stewart, Westinghouse works* in Biograph catalogs, but its shooting title in productions records was *Railroad panorama, Pittsburg to Stewart, Westinghouse works*. Here are the extant titles:

1. Assembling a Generator, Westinghouse Works
2. Assembling and Testing Turbines, Westinghouse Works
3. Casting a Guide Box, Westinghouse Works
4. Coil Winding Machines, Westinghouse Works
5. Coil Winding Section E, Westinghouse Works
6. Girls Taking Time Checks, Westinghouse Works
7. Girls Winding Armatures
8. Panorama Exterior, Westinghouse Works
9. Panorama of Machine Co. Aisle, Westinghouse Works
10. Panorama View Street Car Motor Room, Westinghouse Works
11. Panoramic View Aisle B, Westinghouse Works
12. Steam Hammer, Westinghouse Works
13. Steam Whistle, Westinghouse Works
14. Taping Coils, Westinghouse Works
15. Tapping a furnace, Westinghouse Works
16. Testing a Rotary, Westinghouse Works
17. Testing Large Turbines, Westinghouse Works
18. Welding the Big Ring, Westinghouse Works
19. Westinghouse Air Brake Co., Westinghouse Co. Works (Casting Scene)
20. Westinghouse Air Brake Co., Westinghouse Co. Works (Moulding Scene)
21. Westinghouse Air Brake Co.

San Francisco Earthquake and Fire, April 18, 1906

[Producer unknown], 1906. Silent, tinted B&W, 1.33. Approximately 13 minutes.
Credits: Unknown.
Available: The Library of Congress American Memory website (*http://memory.loc.gov/ammem*).

The San Francisco earthquake struck the city at 5:12 a.m. on the morning of April 18, 1906. (For years it was thought that the quake registered 8.2 or 8.3 on the Richter scale, but recent measurements indicate that the quake was closer to 7.9.) The quake lasted less than a minute, but destroyed large portions of the city. Water mains broke, leaving fire hydrants dry; when crumbled chimneys, shorted-out electrical wires, and ruptured gas pipes ignited, there was no way to stop the spreading fires. The disaster ultimately killed at least 3,000, and left 225,000 people—over half of the 400,000 who lived in San Francisco at the time—homeless.

Civic response was remarkable. That morning General Frederick Funston alerted the Presidio military base, and within two hours his soldiers were patrolling the city. Mayor Eugene Schmitz, his administration dogged by accusations of corruption, took a strong stand, ordering looters shot. He also authorized Army engineers to begin dynamiting unsafe building. And he sent boats to Oakland asking for help.

The Navy dispatched help immediately. The first relief train arrived that night from Los Angeles. By 4:00 a.m. the next morning, William Taft, President Theodore Roosevelt's secretary of war, sent rescue trains west. Legislation passed through Congress to pay relief bills. Rations came from Oregon and the Dakotas. The Army donated almost all of its tents, and within a month almost 10 percent of its soldiers were taking part in the relief effort. It's hard not to contrast the government's response to the impact of Hurricane Katrina on New Orleans almost one hundred years later.

The footage that makes up *San Francisco Earthquake and Fire, April 18, 1906* was shot sometime between the actual earthquake and early May. It is a stark account of what happened to the city: a combination of static shots depicting the aftermath of the quake, and solemn pans across devastated landscapes. The photographer, producer, and distributor are unknown, but the footage was seen widely throughout the country. Many other cameramen came to record the disaster, including Robert K. Bonine from Edison. But for impact this footage is hard to dismiss.

Accustomed today to structured news stories shot in color and heavy with voice-over, we may find it hard at first to piece together a "narrative" from individual shots. But you can fashion a story out of the film, a fairly far-reaching and linear account of the aftermath of the earthquake. It starts with stark, featureless landscapes, smoldering piles of rubbish, tiny humans scurrying about the wreckage. We see the first attempts to deal with the destruction as firemen tear down the tottering brick walls of St. Patrick's Church. But soon the camera records happier scenes, bearing in closely on stoic, upbeat survivors picnicking in the streets. By the end of the film crowds overflow the frame. Trolleys, cars, wagons, and ferries have returned, life and commerce have resumed. The message for viewers is that San Francisco and its people survived, and that the city, or something like it, would recover.

The reality was harsher. It took years for the city to regain its footing. Once the largest U.S. city west of the Mississippi, it was superceded by Los Angeles and Seattle. This film and the other actualities shot at the time became important fundraising tools. *San Francisco* could be the most effective of the lot, in part because of the story it tells about the quake. So it's all the more striking to note that it's impossible to determine who actually gave the film this structure. To a large extent, the shots in the film could have been taken in any order. Newspaper accounts pinpoint the razing of St. Patrick's Church to May 9, 1906. (In fact, another cameraman recording the event also captured this cameraman in his frame.) Trolley service didn't resume until May 1st. Those dates are fixed, but just about everything else in the film could have been photographed anytime after April 18th.

Did the unknown cameraman picture the story as he was shooting it, or was it assembled later, by trial and error, over the course of many screenings?

Bonine, the Edison cameraman sent to record the effects of the San Francisco earthquake, shot thirteen separate short films: panoramas, rescue scenes, even a travelogue from a car. He made no attempt to tie the films together, although they were assembled by others into a program used for fundraising. So little of Bonine's footage remains that it's unfair to compare it to the anonymous *San Francisco*. Still, many of the preceding films in the Registry came from Edison workers, *San Francisco* is also interesting as an example of a different style of filmmaking. Compared to most Edison actualities, the camerawork here seems a lot freer, looser. The pans feel smoother, less jarring, and the general quality of the cinematography—exposures, focus, composition—is more assured. Notice how the cameraman avoids backlighting, which would make it harder to see the characters in his shots. Often he's closer to the action, to the center of focus, than the Edison cameramen. At this point in film history, the cameraman not only determined the visual style of the film but was essentially the director, production designer, producer, and often the editor as well—since in most releases, shots simply began and ended and then were glued together. Within half a decade, all these jobs would be taken over by professionals devoted to specific crafts.

Intertitles are used to break up many of the shots, a decision that could have been made later by the distributor, or by anyone who purchased a print. (Toward the end of the surviving versions of *San Francisco*, a different typeface is used in a shot of passengers disembarking from an Oakland ferry. That could have meant that the film was cobbled together from different sources, and may have in fact been shot by more than one person.)

Today we see these intertitles as interrupting the action, but at the time viewers may have been more comfortable with their presence. In some venues the intertitles would have been replaced by a narrator standing behind or next to the screen. The decision of when to break a shot with intertitles would continue to be a vexing one right up to the introduction of sound. Thus, intertitles may have contributed to the development of the reaction shot, a way of cutting away from and then back to a character.

Lady Helen's Escapade

American Mutoscope and Biograph Co., 1909. Silent, B&W, 1.33. Approximately 8 minutes (765 feet).

Cast: Florence Lawrence (Lady Helen), David Miles (Violinist), Anita Henrie, Owen Moore (Boyfriend), Dorothy West (Maid), Herbert Prior (Footman; also policeman), Mack Sennett, John R. Cumpson, Arthur V. Johnson, Vivian Prescott, Dorothy Bernard (Dinner guests).

Credits: Directed by D.W. Griffith. Written by Stanner E.V. Taylor. Photographed by G.W. Bitzer.

Additional Credits: Photographed from the Library of Congress Paper Film Collection by Renovare Company. Released April 19, 1909.

Available: The Library of Congress.

Released in April 1909, this modest comedy is the first of four films in the Registry directed by D.W. Griffith. Often credited with inventing many of the elements of film grammar (claims that he repeated in a famous trade paper advertisement in 1913), Griffith is usually cited as the first important director in movies. The reality is more complicated, but there is no question that Griffith changed the medium in a way that few others did.

Born on a farm in Kentucky in 1875, David Wark Griffith was one of seven children. His father Jacob was a doctor, soldier, prospector, farmer, gambler, and politician who was emotionally distant from his children. He died when David was ten. The debt-ridden family moved to Louisville, where David clerked in a department store and started acting. He was touring by 1896, and moved to New York City when he was twenty-four. Many years of deprivation followed, including stints of physical labor. In 1906, he married Linda Arvidson in San Francisco.

Aware of his limitations as an actor, Griffith tried writing plays and poetry. He broke into movies at Biograph, the nickname for the American Mutoscope and Biograph Company, headquartered on East 14th Street in Manhattan. It was run at the time by Edwin S. Porter (*The Great Train Robbery*, 1903). Griffith acted, sold some scenarios that were filmed, then hinted that he would like to direct. For his first film as director, *The Adventures of Dollie* (1908), he screened other movies for tips on technique, went to Broadway to cast actors outside the Biograph staff, shot on locations in three different states, and combined two separate rivers into one adventure sequence. In other words, he approached the job purposefully, treating the production above all as a serious endeavor. Soon he was the chief Biograph director, turning out a one-reel film every week.

The hard work and scuffling Griffith endured earlier helped when success finally arrived. He could draw on his own life experiences, on acting friendships built over the years, and on his knowledge of stage technique and repertoire when it came time to direct. Between 1909 and 1912 he would make hundreds of films, ransacking plays, books, poems, and songs for material. He was paid by the foot, getting a small royalty—it had reached 10 percent by the time he left—of every one of his films Biograph sold to exhibitors. To make money, he had to shoot as much as possible.

Griffith paid attention to the mechanical aspects of moviemaking. He formed a creative collaboration with G.W. Bitzer, the most accomplished cinematographer in the country. Together they learned how to use close-ups, fades, cross-cutting, parallel editing. Griffith broke scenes into different camera set-ups, different angles, enabling the use of reaction shots. He developed a stock company of actors and filmmakers, helping to establish the careers of Mary Pickford, Dorothy and Lillian Gish, Mae Marsh, Blanche Sweet, Donald Crisp, Raoul Walsh, Christy Cabanne, Mack Sennett, and many others.

Florence Lawrence, on the other hand, was already a successful film performer when she was hired by Biograph. Born Florence Bridgwood in 1886 in Hamilton, Ontario, the daughter of actress Lotta Lawrence, Florence was on stage herself by the age of three. She acted in her mother's touring company until 1907, when they were hired by Edison. Lawrence's film debut was *Daniel Boone* that year. In 1908 she switched to Vitagraph, which at the time produced the most popular films in the country. There she appeared in *Richard III* with Florence Turner, another stage veteran. Turner was forming an immense following, but remained anonymous to her fans because producers refused to identify the actors in their films. Turner was simply "The Vitagraph Girl."

Perhaps at the suggestion of Biograph actor Harry Salter, Griffith saw Lawrence in Vitagraph's *The Despatch Bearer* (1907), and lured her away to his studio in September 1908. (Lawrence later married Salter.) The actress brought a freshness and youthful vitality to Biograph product, whether appearing in adaptations of classics or in knockabout comedies. As he did with all Biograph actors, Griffith cast her in supporting parts as well as leads, but Lawrence's personality was so strong that she developed an enthusiastic audience. She received fan mail addressed to "The Biograph Girl," and film reviewers speculated about her identity.

Although studio records are unreliable, some sources credit the actress with thirty-eight movies in 1908, and sixty-five in 1909. *Lady Helen's Escapade* is typical of Biograph's output at the time. The film has three sets, props and costumes recycled from other films, and a dozen or so performers playing broad, familiar stereotypes. The camera has to frame as many as nine performers at a time, ruling out close-ups. The actors compensate by gesticulating vigorously, striving to stand out from their makeup and costumes.

Lawrence, who is in almost every frame, doesn't have to try so hard. Even when playing petulant or bored, as she does here, she projects a warmth and friendliness that is entirely winning. Unlike that of many of her contemporaries, her looks translate well to the present. But more important, she has in common with most great movie stars the ability to communicate directly with viewers, to bring them in on the joke, to include them in the action. (A few years later, writers would credit Lawrence, and specifically *Lady Helen's Escapade*, with introducing the concept of costume design to movies.)

Although *Lady Helen's Escapade* has aspects of the assembly line, with its perfunctory staging and threadbare sets, it provides a window into a world of almost alien class and economic systems. Lawrence plays Helen, a woman wealthy enough to have at least three servants waiting on her, but one who is bored with life. Food, clothing, shopping mean nothing to her, but a chance notice in a newspaper spurs her into sudden action. She takes a job as a waitress in a boarding house, where she swoons over a tall, handsome violinist who accompanies a singer after a meal. To get to this point, she has to put up with relentless come-ons from dandies with slicked-back hair who have no compunction about forcing themselves on the hired help.

In tone and temperament, Lawrence is not far removed from the madcap heiress Carole Lombard played in *My Man Godfrey* (1936). She doesn't get mad at the men who try to paw her; she is indifferent to them, smarter than their best tricks, single-minded in her goal. Film curator Eileen Bowser

unearthed one review of *Lady Helen's Escapade* that cited Lawrence's "very great personal attraction" and "very fine dramatic ability." Along with John R. Cumpson, the actress was in the midst of a comedy series based on the characters "Mr. and Mrs. Jones." She was so popular that in 1910, Carl Laemmle hired her for his new IMP studio.

In a masterstroke of publicity, Laemmle planted a story that Lawrence was killed by a streetcar in St. Louis, then took out ads denouncing the "lie" perpetrated by IMP enemies. In the ads Laemmle identified Lawrence by name as "The Imp Girl" and former "Biograph Girl." According to Bowser, this was not the first time a film actress had been identified. While Lawrence went to St. Louis to "prove she was not dead," Florence Turner was introducing a song called "The Vitagraph Girl" in Brooklyn movie theaters and being profiled in the *New York Dramatic Mirror*. No matter who came first, the star system was put into irrevocable motion.

Biograph would not identify its performers until 1913. By that time Griffith had established himself as the most important director working in the United States. He was arguably the first who tried to evoke feelings, nostalgia, and memories in his movies; the first to establish emotional tones and moods. Other filmmakers were intent only on building a reality for what they were adapting—a play, a song lyric, a newspaper headline. They were trying to capture the window, the door, the harbor, the train, the baby, the battleship. Griffith went beyond that, using a field or forest to mean "rural," a homestead for "nostalgia." He would pan across a valley, a shot that did nothing to advance the story, but everything to create an atmosphere. He was among the first to suggest that film could be more than a photographic record, that it could be the equivalent to another medium, an art form in itself, rather than an imitation or duplication of something else.

According to biographer Kelly R. Brown, Lawrence was seriously injured performing a stunt in 1914. Eight years later she attempted a comeback, but her time had passed. In a gesture of charity at the start of the sound era, she was hired by MGM to appear as an occasional extra (ironically, MGM hired Florence Turner as well). Suffering from a bone marrow disease, Lawrence committed suicide in 1938. Many of her Biograph titles survive, fortunately including *Lady Helen's Escapade*.

Princess Nicotine; or, The Smoke Fairy

Some of the special effects methods from 1909's *Princess Nicotine* are still in use today.

Vitagraph, 1909. Silent, B&W, 1.33. 5 minutes.
Cast: Paul Panzer, Gladys Hulette.
Credits: Produced by J. Stuart Blackton. Photographed by Tony Gaudio.
Additional Credits: Copyrighted August 10, 1909.
Available: Image Entertainment DVD *Treasures from American Film Archives* (2000). UPC: 0-14381-9706-2-3.

Trick films constituted a large portion of movie titles in the first decades of cinema. In fact, trick films helped validate the medium, as they could only exist in cinema, and could not be transferred to stage or print. The first trick films relied on stop-motion animation, on the fact that while the camera was stopped, objects could be shifted within a frame. Once projected, they seemed to be jumping around, or could appear or disappear.

Starting in 1896, the French director Georges Méliès made hundreds of trick films (as well as dramas and "actualities"); his *A Trip to the Moon* (1902) was a worldwide sensation that inspired imitators both in Europe and the United States. By 1909, the special effects arsenal had grown to include several other cinematic tricks, all of which were put to use in *Princess Nicotine; or, The Smoke Fairy*.

Princess Nicotine was produced and most likely directed by J. Stuart Blackton, one of the most significant figures in early film. Born in England in 1875, he came to the United States with his family when he was eleven. He worked as a carpenter while taking night classes at City College in New York. When he was twenty, he was working as a reporter and illustrator for the New York *World*. On assignment to interview Thomas Alva Edison, he so impressed the inventor that he was asked to film his "lightning sketches," a skit he performed in clubs. *Blackton, The Evening World Cartoonist* (1896) prompted Blackton to buy his own motion picture camera.

With his friend and magician Albert E. Smith, Blackton formed what would become the Vitagraph Company. He starred in the studio's first two films, *The Burglar on the Roof* and *Tearing Down the Spanish Flag* (both 1898). The former is an important step forward in fictional narratives, and the latter is considered by some the first propaganda film. In succeeding years, Blackton and Smith alternated faked footage of the Spanish-American War with actualities, dramas, and comedies. *Humorous Phases of a Funny Face* (1906) was the most advanced animated film of its time. Apart from his drawing, Blackton also paid attention to editing and camera placement. He developed a studio system in which he oversaw the work of several productions at once. On top of his other achievements, Blackton helped expand the scope of movies. The same year he produced *Princess Nicotine*, his Vitagraph studio released versions of *King Lear*, *Oliver Twist*, and a biography of Napoleon.

Princess Nicotine was shot by Tony Gaudio. Born Gaetano Antonio Gaudio in Cosenza, Italy, in 1885, he worked for his father and brother, portrait photographers in Rome, before shooting films for various Italian movie companies. (His first was *Napoleon Crossing the Alps* in 1903.) By 1906 he was working in New York City, and in 1908 he was hired to run the Vitagraph film labs. According to film historian Scott Simmon, Gaudio achieved many of his effects in *Princess Nicotine* with mirrors and a camera lens that could achieve a deep depth of field.

Simmon points to *The Animated Matches* (1908, directed by Émile Cohl) as the inspiration for *Princess Nicotine*. Matches that move by themselves play a part in *Princess Nicotine*, but the film seems more concerned with the hallucinogenic haze smoker Paul Panzer (a German star of the 1914 serial *The Perils of Pauline*, and later an extra in hundreds of films) experiences. The stop-motion matches and other props, and scenes shot with mirrors that combined the human characters with tiny "sprites," were just two of the

film's special effects. Gaudio and Blackton also used double exposures, hidden wires that could lift or lower objects, mattes and an iris effect to simulate a magnifying glass, and copious amounts of smoke. Another trick was the use of oversized props such as a giant pipe bowl. Props like these became a favorite device in films as various as *Peter Pan* (1924), Laurel and Hardy's *Brats* (1930), and *The Incredible Shrinking Man* (1957).

Princess Nicotine is also notable for its understated humor, like a little cigarette who has trouble climbing into a cigar box. The film so impressed audiences at the time that it was the subject of an article in *Scientific American* and a chapter in Frederick Talbot's *Motion Pictures: How They Are Made and Worked*. While it is not as unsettling a trick film as *The Red Spectre* (1907), or as outrageous as Edison's *Dream of a Rarebit Fiend* (1905), *Princess Nicotine* is charming, well-paced, and not nearly as innocent as the filmmakers pretend.

A Corner in Wheat

Biograph, 1909. Silent, B&W, 1.33. 14 minutes.
Cast: Frank Powell (W. J. Hammond, The Wheat King), Grace Henderson (The Wheat King's Wife), James Kirkwood (Farmer), Linda Arvidson (Farmer's Wife), W. Chrystie Miller (Farmer's Father), Gladys Egan (Farmer's Daughter), Henry Walthall (Wheat King's Assistant), William J. Butler (Ruined wheat trader), Blanche Sweet (Woman in white hat/Grain elevator visitor); Frank Evans, Robert Harron, Mack Sennett, Owen Moore, George Nichols, Charles Craig (Brokers on exchange floor).
Credits: Directed by D.W. Griffith. Suggested by Frank Norris's *The Pit*. Photographed by G.W. Bitzer.
Additional Credits: Screenplay by Frank Woods. Also based on *The Octopus* and "A Deal in Wheat" by Frank Norris. Produced November 1909. Released December 13, 1909.
Available: Kino Video DVD *Griffith Masterworks Biograph Shorts* (2002). UPC: 7-38329-02682-0.

Made a few months after *Lady Helen's Escapade*, *A Corner in Wheat* was one of scores of films D.W. Griffith directed in 1909. While he showed little interest in day-to-day politics, Griffith was a kind of populist who reduced society's problems to heroes and villains. Judging from his films, Griffith distrusted reformers and the wealthy, but had little faith in the poor, who were just as liable to form vigilante posses and mobs as to help their peers. If anything, Griffith apparently believed in a sort of agrarian society that, if it ever existed at all, had disappeared long before the Civil War.

But he knew his audience, and knew that he couldn't go wrong attacking the rich. Moviegoers wanted to see the upper class defeated, or at least blamed for injustice—a formula still in use today.

Griffith's liberal leanings took some courage at the time. They also echoed the feelings of some significant artists at the turn of the twentieth century, among them Frank Norris.

Born in Chicago in 1870, Norris began his career as a newspaper reporter in San Francisco before moving to New York in 1898. In the next five years he published seven novels and two collections of short stories before succumbing to a ruptured appendix in 1902. He was transfixed by the work of Émile Zola, and aimed for a similar realism in his own fiction. By the end of the century he had developed a distinctly American form of naturalism that was both brawny and pitiless. *McTeague* (1899) would be adapted into one of the towering films in the Registry, *Greed* (1925).

After the fatalism of *McTeague*, Norris turned to social activism, to finding solutions rather than just documenting them. At the time of his death he was working on a trilogy about wheat—loosely, its production, distribution, and consumption—from the viewpoint that the American economy was both creating and destroying an underclass. *The Octopus* (1901) dealt with farmers in California whose fortunes were controlled by railroad interests back East. *The Pit* (1903) took place in Chicago's mercantile exchanges.

In *The Pit*, Curtis Jadwin is so profit-driven that he attempts to corner an entire year's wheat market by speculating in wheat futures, an obsession that leads to a nervous breakdown and the possible rupture of his marriage. Norris died in October 1902 before *The Pit* was published. (He never began writing the third novel, *The Wolf*.) Channing Pollock adapted *The Pit* into a play in 1904, which may have been how Griffith became acquainted with it.

Working with a screenwriter—possibly Frank Woods—Griffith tried to merge and condense the two novels, but it was a hopeless task. The best he could do was try to extract noteworthy moments that audience members might recognize. Griffith couldn't hope to explain the financial and psychological subtleties Norris built up over thousands of words. He couldn't even adequately explain who the characters in his film were. The opening shot, for example, includes four people. Readers of *The Octopus* might recognize them as representing a farmer with his father, wife, and daughter, but would others understand their relationships and occupations when Griffith had to paint them with the broadest of brushes?

Griffith was also hampered by the fact that he had little experience with farmers. As a reviewer in the *New York Dramatic Mirror* noted about scenes in which the farmer and his father sow seed, "No wheat would ever come up from the sort of sowing they do, but this slip is lost sight of in the artistic atmosphere of the scene and in the compelling pictures that follow." (It didn't help that a field near Fort Lee, New Jersey, had to stand in for California's San Joaquin Valley.)

The film then cuts to the office of the Wheat King, played by Frank Powell as a dashing and energetic businessman. An intertitle explains that he is "engineering the great corner," but viewers only see an executive ordering underlings around. Griffith later shows a ruined businessman confronting the Wheat King in his crowded office. You can spot him in the group not just from the hand thrust up to his brow, but because he is the only one wearing a hat—a sign that the director was becoming aware of the importance of set and costume design.

The ending retains its power even today. It's a stark image that was imitated directly by the Danish director Carl Dreyer in *Vampyr* (1932), and appropriated by directors for many other movies.

In a sense, the scenes function as illustrations from the novel. The entire film is shot from a stationary camera, but Griffith managed to keep most of the frames filled with motion. By this time his stock company was pretty firmly in place. The cast included many Biograph regulars: his wife Linda Arvidson, Henry B. Walthall, Mack Sennett, Blanche Sweet, Bobby Harron, and Owen Moore.

Griffith perhaps received more credit than he was due for addressing contemporary problems with this work. As social criticism it's pretty weak stuff, offering viewers only the hope that the millionaires who make fortunes from the poor will receive divine retribution, or at least ironic deaths. But at the time it was strong medicine, enough to help get filmmakers as a whole branded as radicals. Encouraged by the positive response, Griffith pursued his social agenda in a number of other films. But his politics were and are difficult to decipher. He became bolder in his attempts to affix blame, until in films like *The Birth of a Nation* and *Intolerance* he was condemning wholesale entire races and cultures.

As Richard Schickel points out in his biography of Griffith, the film marked another milestone in the turn toward quality and respectability. Films had only recently been covered as art instead of technology in the press. Griffith's adaptation of the Robert Browning poem "Pippa Passes" had been released that October, and the *New York Times* pointed to it and to films based on Tolstoy and the Old Testament as proof of cinema's maturity.

White Fawn's Devotion

Pathé Frères, 1910. Silent, B&W, 1.33. 11 minutes.
Cast includes: Red Wing [Lillian St. Cyr].
Credits (offscreen): Written and directed by James Young Deer.
Additional Credits: Released June 18, 1910.
Available: Image Entertainment DVD *Treasures from American Film Archives* (2000). UPC: 0-14381-9706-2-3.

Ethnic stereotypes were staples of early cinema, and filmmakers had little compunction about marketing films designed to either appeal to or mock groups like Asians, blacks, Jews, and the Irish. Characters identified as Indians were filmed by the Edison Company as early as 1894's *Sioux Ghost Dance* and *Buffalo Dance*, which depicted members of Buffalo Bill Cody's "Wild West" show. These early "actuality" films were closer to ethnography

White Fawn (right, played by Lillian St. Cyr) learns that her husband is leaving to claim his inheritance.

than entertainment, but Native Americans soon began to figure in fictional movies. As film historian Scott Simmon has pointed out, many of these films seemed to be based in one form or another on *The Squaw Man*, a play by Edwin Milton Royle. It was first staged in New York City in 1905 in a production that provided an important break for future Western star William S. Hart, and enjoyed periodic revivals over the years. It was adapted into a novel in 1907 and filmed in 1914; it also served as the basis of an unsuccessful musical.

The Squaw Man followed Wynnegate, a disgraced British aristocrat, to the Montana frontier, where he is rescued from death by Nat-u-Ritch, a Native American woman whom he later marries. When Wynnegate is exonerated by his former fiancée, his Indian bride commits suicide so he can return unencumbered to his previous life. Royle was capitalizing on a tendency in serious art to depict Indians as noble savages, romantic members of a doomed race who willingly sacrificed themselves for the very people who were taking their lands. Whites may have been willing to see Indians as tragic figures because, unlike blacks or Asians, they had already been vanquished.

It was this image of Native Americans that became standard in early movies, and not the bloodthirsty killers who dominated dime novels and Wild West shows of the period. In Biograph's *The Broken Doll* (1910) and Pathé's *The Heart of an Indian Maid* (1911), Indians die protecting whites, just as Nat-u-ritch did in *The Squaw Man*. *White Fawn's Devotion* alters the plot of *The Squaw*

Man just enough to avoid litigation, but it too follows the same pattern.

White Fawn's Devotion was directed by James Young Deer, a circus and Wild West show performer who found work at several film studios. Born in Dakota City, Nebraska, Young Deer claimed to be a member of the Ho-Chunk or Winnebago tribe, although documentation is frustratingly sparse. His birthdate is unknown, and he is not listed in the censuses conducted by the Bureau of Indian Affairs. When he remarried in the 1920s, his marriage license listed him as white. However, tribal historian David Smith told film historian Dennis Doros that Young Deer was definitely a Winnebago.

Young Deer married Lillian St. Cyr, a Winnebago who used the stage name Red Wing, in 1906. She was born in 1883 and graduated from the Carlisle Indian Industrial School in 1902. Two years after their marriage, Young Deer and Red Wing were in New York, where she appeared in *The White Squaw* for Kalem. Young Deer also worked at Kalem—as well as at Lubin, Vitagraph, and Biograph—as an actor, writer, and director. In 1910 he was hired by Pathé, a French studio that had opened a branch in the United States. During the next three years he directed over one hundred Pathé titles, at first from its New Jersey studio.

White Fawn's Devotion, one of many Westerns filmed in New Jersey, is fairly typical of its time. The camera almost never moves (it does pan slightly right or left during a chase sequence), and Young Deer stages most of the action on one plane perpendicular to the viewers. Sets are limited (two painted flats pass for a frontier cabin), as are the locations.

Filming was efficient, with the same camera set-ups repeated two or three times for different stages of the story. As Scott Simmon noted, the acting is of the pantomime variety, with many outflung arms and flabbergasted expressions. But Young Deer knew how to build suspense, intercutting a desperate climb down a cliff with an enemy about to sever the rope anchored above. Perhaps only in retrospect is it apparent how vicious the plot can be, and even the happy ending has intimations of violence.

In 1911, Young Deer was named production manager of a new West Coast Pathé studio in Edendale, a suburb of Los Angeles. Along with competing studios, Pathé continued its Indian-themed output. Red Wing was cast by Cecil B. DeMille as Nat-u-Ritch in his 1914 version of *The Squaw Man*, generally regarded as the first feature filmed in Hollywood. That same year D.W. Griffith released *The Battle at Elderbush Gulch*, in which drunken Indians provoke a range war by stealing pet dogs for food. Apart from the occasional sympathetic title like *The Vanishing Race* (1925), the film industry followed Griffith's lead, using Indians as stock villains in hundreds of subsequent movies.

Neither Red Wing's marriage nor her movie career survived the 1920s, but she was an active advocate for Native American rights until her death in 1974. Young Deer's later career was marked by gaps and legal problems. He reportedly made documentaries during World War I, and spent time in Europe after the war. His last film credit was in 1924. He married Helen Gilchrist later in the decade, and died in 1946.

Jeffries-Johnson World's Championship Boxing Contest

The J. and J. Company, 1910. Silent, B&W, 1.33. 120 minutes.
Cast: Jack Johnson, Jim Jeffries.
Credits: Produced by J. Stuart Blackton. Filmed July 4, 1910. Released July 1910.
Available: The Library of Congress. Excerpts from the fight are in *Unforgivable Blackness: The Rise and Fall of Jack Johnson*, directed by Ken Burns. PBS Home Video (2004). ISBN: 1-4157-0744-8. UPC: 0-97368-87454-1.

Boxers were one of the earliest subjects ever filmed by Edison's staff; in 1892, motion picture frames depicting fighters were reproduced in magazines. At the time, boxing and fencing were the easiest sports to film, as they took place in enclosed spaces and featured only two opponents. When Edison began selling films for kinetoscopes, a peephole device, prizefights were among the most popular requests. W.K.L. Dickson and William Heise filmed a staged fight in Edison's Black Maria studio on June 15, 1894, between Michael Leonard and Jack Cushing; this was followed by a film of a fight between James Corbett and Peter Courtney, a nationwide hit.

Boxing movies not only helped popularize the medium with the public, they also began to impact the financing of prizefights. By 1899, a scheduled match between "Pedlar" Palmer and Terry McGovern was postponed a day in order to provide better weather—and lighting—for filmmakers. Corbett continued to appear in films, as did James Jeffries, whose *The Jeffries-Sharkey Fight* (1899) was popular enough to be shown for years.

As Charles Musser noted in *The Emergence of Cinema*, in the early days of film, prizefighting was illegal in every state in the union, a ban often circumvented by billing bouts as exhibitions or contests. Nevada legalized prizefighting in 1897, enabling a match between Corbett and Robert Fitzsimmons that was staged to accommodate filmmakers. The success of *The Corbett-Fitzsimmons Fight* (1897) may have helped relax prohibitions against prizefights in states like New York.

Prizefights also spurred technological advances. A championship fight between Fitzsimmons and Jeffries on June 9, 1899, was scheduled at night, and the American Vitagraph Company planned to film it aided by seventy-five arc lights. (The lights failed, forcing Vitagraph to film a re-creation days later.) *The Jeffries-Sharkey Fight* (1899) was also illuminated by arc lights; what's more, Biograph filmed it on 70mm stock. By showing as many as fifteen consecutive rounds at a time, prizefight films may have conditioned viewers to accept feature-length movies. Another result of the genre's popularity was a rash of pirated, bootlegged, and often fraudulent versions of fights.

Once Corbett's sparring partner, James Jeffries won the heavyweight boxing crown when he defeated Fitzsimmons. According to Dan Streible's book *Fight Pictures*, Jeffries was featured in some twenty movies during his six-year reign as champion. Retiring from the ring in 1905, he took up farming and occasionally refereed fights.

While Jeffries enjoyed his retirement, Jack Johnson was developing a reputation as the preeminent boxer in the world. Born in Texas in 1878, Johnson was the son of a slave who worked as a janitor. Johnson dropped out of grade school and learned the rudiments of fighting while working as a longshoreman. A veteran of "battle royals," he became a professional boxer in 1897, when he knocked out Jim Rocks. Between 1902 and 1908 Johnson fought fifty-seven official fights, defeating world heavyweight champion Tommy Burns in Sydney, Australia, in December 1908.

Johnson still wanted a title fight in the United States. He defeated a series of "Great White Hopes," including future Oscar-winning actor Victor McLaglen. Author Jack London, who reported on the Burns title fight, argued that Jeffries had to come out of retirement to defend his title. "Jeff it's up to you," he wrote. "The White Man must be rescued." When Johnson knocked out middleweight champion Stanley Ketchel in the fall of 1909, Jeffries gave in and began training.

Tex Rickard, a former trail driver and sheriff who promoted his first fight in Alaska, bid $101,000 to stage the championship bout. (Rickard made his stake a few years earlier promoting an interracial fight between Joe Gans and Oscar Nelson in Nevada.) The movie rights were a fundamental part of the deal. The *Johnson-Ketchel* fight had been distributed by the Motion Picture Patents Company (MPPC), an organization formed in an attempt by Edison to control the movie industry through legal threats. William Rock, president of Vitagraph and an MPPC member, and promoter Sid Hester worked out payments for Jeffries and Johnson with Rickard. To film the fight, J. Stuart Blackton, one of the founders of Vitagraph, formed the J. and J. Company. It would use twelve cameramen from Vitagraph, Essanay, and Selig, stationed in a booth overlooking the ring.

The fight was scheduled for July 4, 1910, in San Francisco. Rickard had already built the arena and sold $300,000 in tickets when the governor of California bowed to public pressure and banned the match. Encouraged by Denver S. Dickerson, governor of Nevada, Rickard moved the fight to Reno. Some five hundred journalists, including London, joined the crowds converging there. The fighters were filmed at their separate training camps—Jeffries greeting admirers and sparring, Johnson presiding over a kangaroo court and chasing chickens.

The fight lasted fifteen rounds. Jeffries, his skills eroded, could not keep up with his opponent. Johnson toyed with him, joking with ringside observers. He said later that Jeffries was at his best in the fourth round. Johnson knocked Jeffries down three times in the fifteenth round, causing his seconds to end the fight.

Following the decision, race riots broke out across the country. A Chicago newspaper reported fourteen deaths; twenty-four in San Francisco. Mob violence erupted in Los Angeles, Philadelphia, New Orleans, and other cities. In his book accompanying the Ken Burns documentary *Unforgivable Blackness* (2004), author Geoffrey C. Ward wrote that the United Society of Christian Endeavor started a movement to ban the exhibition of fight films within a day of Johnson's victory. The Hearst press and former President Theodore Roosevelt joined the cause.

Prints of the completed film were ready by July 10th. According to Streible, the movie was shown without incident in New York, Philadelphia, St. Louis, and several other cities. In part this was because exhibitors took precautions to exclude children from the audience, which was also segregated. But as the film was shown in successive cities, opposition to it grew. Public opinion began to turn against Johnson. A film of his next fight, against Jim Flynn, was a financial failure.

In 1912, Congress outlawed the interstate transport of fight films, a direct result of Johnson's dominance in the sport. The law wasn't repealed until 1940, by which time he was no longer a threat.

From the Manger to the Cross

Kalem, 1912. Silent, B&W with tints, 1.33. 71 minutes.
Cast: Robert Henderson-Bland (Jesus, the Man), Percy Dyer (Jesus as a youth), Gene Gauntier (Mary), Alice Hollister (Mary Magdalene), Samuel Morgan (Pilate), James D. Ainsley (John the Baptist).
Credits: Directed by Sidney Olcott. Scenario by Gene Gauntier. Photographed by George K. Hollister. Art direction by Henry Allen Farnham.

Additional Cast: Robert G. Vignola (Judas), George Kellog (Herod), J.P. McGowan (Andrew), Helen Lindroth (Martha), Jack J. Clark (John), Sidney Baber (Lazarus), Montague Sidney (Joseph).
Additional Credits: Produced by Frank J. Marion. Full title: *From the Manger to the Cross; or Jesus of Nazareth.* Also known as *The Life of Christ.* Premiered in New York City on October 14, 1912.
Available: Kino Video VHS (1994). UPC: 7-38329-00806-2.

Acknowledged as one of the first great directors in film, Sidney Olcott was born in Toronto in 1873. After working as a newsboy, he joined amateur theatricals before becoming a professional actor. He entered film in 1904 as an actor, working at Mutoscope (which later became Biograph). When Frank Marion, a Biograph sales manager, formed Kalem with George Kleine and Samuel Long, they hired Olcott as their director.

Olcott's interviews are filled with entertaining tales of trying to shoot a Western without horses (he had cowboys pretend to dust off their clothes as they entered a bar) or of filming a biopic of Henry Hudson in 1908 with a cast of six—three of them Indians who are supposed to attack Hudson's ship, the *Half Moon*. Less amusing to the Kalem owners was his version of *Ben-Hur*, shot in 1907 from a script by Gene Gauntier. It became the subject of a lawsuit that cost Kalem $25,000 and helped establish copyright protection for the estate of *Ben-Hur* author Lew Wallace and for films and scenarios in general.

Gauntier, born Genevieve Liggett in 1885 in Kansas City, wrote for the screen primarily to supplement her income as an actress. (In 1909, when she wrote and starred in *The Girl Spy*, she was making thirty dollars a week as a leading lady, and twenty dollars per script.) Gauntier's 1928 autobiography *Blazing the Trail* is a fascinating and lively account of early filmmaking. She remembers Olcott asking her to write a version of *Tom Sawyer* limited to material he could shoot in one day, and adapted *Ben-Hur* in two days.

Gauntier took credit for the idea of shooting on location in Europe, although Olcott made the same claim. (Kalem did not have a permanent studio until it built a base of sorts in Jacksonville, Florida.) No matter who was responsible, Olcott and Gauntier led a Kalem expedition to Ireland in 1910, where they gave themselves tongue-in-cheek billing as the "O'Kalems" while making films like *A Lad from Old Ireland*. They returned the following summer, spending three months in Dublin. On December 2, 1911, Olcott and Gauntier left on a longer trip, this one to the Mediterranean.

Their original plan had been to shoot adventure films in North Africa and the Middle East. They did make titles like *The Fighting Dervishes* and *Captured by the Bedouins*, as well as the documentaries *Egyptian Sports* and *Ancient Temples of Egypt*. But the locations were so breathtaking that Gauntier began writing *From the Manger to the Cross*. Fortunately

for the filmmakers, the life of Christ included an interlude in Egypt, giving them license to film at the pyramids and in front of the Sphinx.

As filming progressed, they continued to expand the story, eventually making a five-reel film at a time when three reels were considered extravagant. Olcott recruited actors from the London stage to round out the Kalem stock company. In a 1924 interview with *Photoplay*, he spoke about filming with "great precaution lest the sensibilities of the natives be aroused." While shooting Christ entering Jerusalem at St. Stephen's Gate, he claimed that, armed only with a revolver, he fought off an attack by twenty frenzied locals.

Gauntier's script broke Christ's life into ten chapters, using scenes taken from the four gospels (and quoting directly from them for almost all of the intertitles). The screenplay concentrates on familiar material—especially the nativity and passion—and of necessity shortchanges Christ's sermons and parables for depictions of miracles. Hers was a serious attempt to portray the gospels accurately, and refrained from overstatement.

Similarly, Olcott directed with a sense of reverence and a heavy dependence on pantomime. Scenes are staged as tableaus, emphasizing depth and multiple planes of action in the manner of director Edwin S. Porter. Olcott composed frames with strong diagonals that pulled viewers to specific areas in the foreground or background, and moved his actors in arcs that carried them first towards and then away from the camera, depending on the requirements of the scene. When Pilate questions Christ, Olcott uses match cuts that shift the angles of the scene, a daring technique at the time. Cinematographer George Hollister panned his camera across the remarkable landscapes, another advanced technique, and, given the limited film stock and harsh desert lighting, achieved some extraordinary exposures.

The ancient locations, the seriousness of their subject, and the freedom they enjoyed during their expedition clearly exhilarated the filmmakers. *From the Manger to the Cross* shakes off the fustiness and sludgy pacing of its contemporary films, and infuses its material with conviction, authencity, and a bracing sense of immediacy. For many viewers, this was the New Testament brought to life, their first glimpse of the Holy Land, and for some, the first time they saw Christ personified. (It was not the first religious film, or even the first that featured

Christ: Ferdinand Zecca and Lucien Nonguet directed *The Life and Passion of Christ* in 1905.)

From the Manger to the Cross ended up costing Kalem around $25,000. Its world premiere in London occurred on October 3, 1912, before an audience of clergy; the Bishop of London proclaimed it better than the Oberammergau Passion Play. The New York premiere was on October 14, with the general release the following year. By that time Olcott and Gauntier had left Kalem to form their own company, which they eventually brought to Universal. (Gauntier also married cast member Jack C. Clark while they were in Palestine.) Olcott went on to direct Mary Pickford, Marion Davies, and Rudolph Valentino, but Gauntier retired from film in 1918 in order to become a war correspondent.

From the Manger to the Cross was the only feature Kalem released. Vitagraph purchased the Kalem library in 1917. It released an edited version of the film, the basis of copies available today.

The Land Beyond the Sunset

How the other half lived in 1912. Mrs. William Bechtel is playing the grandmother to Joe, a newsboy (Martin Fuller) in *The Land Beyond the Sunset*.

Thomas Edison, 1912. Silent, B&W, 1.33. 14 minutes.

Cast: Martin Fuller (Joe, the newsboy), Mrs. William Bechtel (His grandmother), Bigelow Cooper (The minister), Walter Edwin (The manager of the Fresh Air Fund); Ethel Jewett, Elizabeth Miller, Gladys Du Pell, Mrs. Wallace Erskine [Margery Bonney Erskine] (The Committee).

Credits: Directed by Harold Shaw. Writer: Dorothy G. Shore.

Additional Credits: possibly directed by J. Searle Dawley. Released October 28, 1912.

Available: Image Entertainment DVD *Treasures from American Film Archives* (2000). UPC: 0-14381-9706-2-3.

In *Behind the Mask of Innocence*, Kevin Brownlow provides a detailed history of what he calls "social conscience" films of the silent era, listing them in categories like "divorce," "birth control," and "social diseases." The urge to reform was far more widespread in the early film industry than one might expect, although as film critic Otis Ferguson liked to point out, "Crime doesn't pay—except at the box office."

The Land Beyond the Sunset draws together several strands of film history: advances in filmmaking styles, approaches towards acting and storytelling, and the political and social uses of the medium. If not actually financed by the Fresh Air Fund, the filmmakers of *The Land Beyond the Sunset* were certainly authorized to use the charitable organization's name, aligning this project with other sponsored films. Brownlow places it within his discussion of poverty, with films like Essanay's *Life at Hull-House* (1911) and Vitagraph's *A Silent Plea* (1914). He also cites an Edison film released earlier in 1912, *The Awakening of John Bond*, "produced in co-operation with the American National Association for the Study and Prevention of Tuberculosis," as its publicity material proclaimed. He might also have noted *Children Who Labor*, released by Edison in May of 1912, one of several films that condemned child labor.

Reform advocates like Jane Hull and Jacob A. Riis gave filmmakers models for how to fashion a narrative approach to the topic. Another model was the Fresh Air Fund, founded in 1877 by the Reverend Willard Parsons. His Sherman, Pennsylvania, congregation made homes available for needy children from New York City. It was incorporated in 1888 as "The Tribune Fresh Air Fund Aid Society," and exists today in large part due to funding and support from the *New York Times*. Its goal was and is to bring city children to outdoor environments, either through day trips, summer camps, or residencies with rural families.

Sources credit either Harold M. Shaw or J. Searle Dawley as the director of *The Land Beyond the Sunset*. Shaw was an actor at Edison who appeared in several films directed by Dawley. Born in Tennessee in 1877, he started acting in small parts with the Oakland California Stock Company. He made his screen debut in 1909 at Edison. *The Land Beyond the Sunset* would have been his first directing credit, and although he would go on to helm some fifty films, none approach the artistry of this title.

Dawley, on the other hand, was a veteran director responsible for well-regarded films like *Jack and the Beanstalk* and *The Corsican Brothers* (both 1912). Film historian Eileen Bowser found a 1914 interview Dawley gave for *Motion Picture World* in which he defined the "drama of silence" as "human emotion conveyed by the poetry of movement." Dawley goes on to explain how editing can eliminate "what is called pantomime" from acting, how each filmgoer provides "his own emotions and language for the characters before him on the canvas," and how in the act of watching a film, "the spectator is supplying the thoughts and words of the actor and becomes a part of the performance itself."

These are advanced theories for the time, and *The Land Beyond the Sunset* bears them out. After an opening shot filmed in a studio in which actor Martin Fuller, playing a newsboy, appeals directly to viewers for help, Dawley (or whoever directed the film) dissolves to a live street scene in the Bronx. Passersby ignore Fuller, dressed in rags and holding a sheaf of papers. His home life is even more miserable, with a grandmother who steals his earnings, by implication to buy liquor. This material was shot at the Edison studio on Decatur Avenue and

Oliver Place. Although the walls of the tenement apartment are just painted flats, care has been taken to dress the set with appropriate props, as well as to provide views out the door and window. (Not every filmmaker at that time took these steps.)

Fuller is invited to a Fresh Air Fund picnic, requiring a second set, this time of a train station passenger gate. Dawley then cuts to a park setting, most likely a Bronx location with a view of the Long Island Sound. "His first sight of the world beyond the slums" an intertitle reads, a statement that is still true for many New York children. The games, meals, and storytelling depicted at the picnic are quietly joyous.

When Fuller hears a story about fairies rescuing an abused child and bringing him by boat to a magical land, Dawley dissolves to a dream version of the tale. Filmgoers of the time would have no trouble making the connection between Fuller's real and imaginary life, but the succeeding scenes veer into material that might challenge viewers today. Dorothy G. Shore's scenario rejects liberal pieties, offering a narrative solution that has chilling implications. As the film closes, Dawley has the unknown cinematographer pan and tilt the camera to follow the action, a fairly daring technique at the time. The director holds the final shot, an image that signifies both freedom and mortality, for an entire minute, allowing viewers to read their own interpretations into the story.

It is a powerful and unsettling ending, one that calls to mind such nihilistic films as the Val Lewton–produced *The Seventh Victim* (1943) and François Truffaut's *The Four Hundred Blows* (1959). Film historian William K. Everson called *The Land Beyond the Sunset* "the screen's first genuinely lyrical film," and it is hard to argue with his assessment. Fuller appeared in a few more films, but appears to have stopped acting in 1913. Other cast members continued receiving credits until the Edison studio closed in 1918; Shaw and Bigelow Cooper worked well into the 1920s.

Dawley, born in Colorado in 1877, worked in vaudeville and legitimate theater as an actor, writer, and producer until he was hired by Edwin S. Porter in 1907 to direct *The Nine Lives of a Cat* for Edison. Dawley considered this credit enough to bill himself as "the first motion picture director," and he was certainly one of the first to try to define the medium as art. He directed D.W. Griffith's film debut, *Rescued from an Eagle's Nest* (1908) as well as the first screen *Frankenstein* (1910). In

1913 he followed Porter to Famous Players, where he directed Mary Pickford in *Caprice* (1913). In 1916 he made a *Snow White* that impressed a young Walt Disney, and in the 1920s he oversaw experimental sound shorts for Lee De Forest before embarking on a career in radio.

The Evidence of the Film

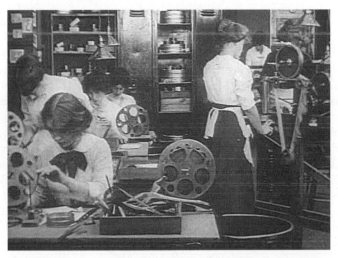

A 1913 editing room becomes a crime lab in *The Evidence of the Film*.

Thanhouser, 1913. Silent, B&W, 1.33. 14 minutes.

Cast: William Garwood (the broker), Marie Eline (messenger boy), Florence LaBadie (sister of little boy), Riley Chamberlin (clerk).

Credits: Directed by Edwin Thanhouser and Lawrence Marston.

Additional Cast: Helen Badgley.

Additional Credits: Released January 10, 1913.

Available: Thanhouser Collection DVD *Volume 5: Thanhouser Kids & Dogs (1912–1915)*, www.thanhouser.org.

Major film studios dominate the history of cinema; as a result, the smaller production companies that flourished in the early twentieth century are often overlooked. In 1909, when actor Edwin Thanhouser opened his own studio, filmmaking in the United States centered around New York City. There were outposts in other cities, such as Lubin in Philadelphia and Selig in Chicago, but the majority of films were shot in the tristate area: New York, New Jersey, and Connecticut.

Thanhouser, who had managed a theater in Wisconsin, converted a skating rink in New Rochelle to a studio. By the time Thanhouser Films went out of business in 1917, it had produced over a thousand shorts, ranging from slapstick comedies and children's films to adaptations of *David Copperfield* and *Dr. Jekyll and Mr. Hyde*. Fewer than two hundred of the films survive today. Thanhouser's grandson Edwin W. ("Ned") Thanhouser formed a company in 1988 to preserve them, as well as posters, scripts, and other ephemera from the studio.

While they are similar in subject and style to work produced by Biograph, Mutual, IMP, and other studios, Thanhouser films in ways both subtle and obvious have their own distinctive qualities. The camerawork, sets, and costumes were all high quality, and the stories generally espoused strong moral values. But watching Thanhouser's work is like finding a new television network on which the stars and supporting casts are unrecognizable.

Studio figures included Thanhouser's wife, the former actress Gertrude Homan, who played key roles as writer, editor, and executive. Marie Eline was "The Thanhouser Kid," even after she left the studio to play Little Eva in a stage adaptation of *Uncle Tom's Cabin*. James Cruze, later famous as the director of films like *The Covered Wagon* (1923) and *Old Ironsides* (1926), had leads in many Thanhouser productions. Both Cruze and Florence LaBadie had key roles in *The Million Dollar Mystery* (1914), a Thanhouser serial.

LaBadie was the most popular Thanhouser star. She was the adopted daughter of a Montreal attorney and his European wife. After schooling in a convent, she began acting. In 1909, her friend Mary Pickford helped her get a job at Biograph. LaBadie moved to Thanhouser in 1911, where she developed a strong following. Her acting was marked by restraint and grace. Coupled with her beauty, in particular her astonishingly expressive eyes, and it's no wonder she was a star. LaBadie died of septicemia after a car accident in 1917.

Tragedy seemed to dog the studio. In 1913, the skating rink studio burned down (prompting its own film, *When the Studio Burned*). Thanhouser had by this time sold his interest in the company to Mutual, which installed Charles J. Hite as president and chief executive officer. Born in 1876 in Ohio, Hite worked in theater in various behind-the-scenes roles. In 1906, he formed his first motion picture company, supplying films he bought from New York distributors to theaters throughout the South. He later ran a film exchange in Chicago and surrounding cities. By 1912, he was in New York, forming the Mutual Film Corporation with Harry Aitken (later associated with D.W. Griffith and *The Birth of a Nation*) and John R. Freuler. Already a millionaire, Hite helped increase Thanhouser's profits with projects like *The Million Dollar Mystery*, at the time the most profitable serial. While driving home to New Rochelle on August 21, 1914, Hite skidded off a viaduct at 155th Street in Manhattan, falling some fifty feet to his death.

In a detailed analysis of *The Evidence of the Film*, Ned Thanhouser broke the movie down to fifty-seven shots, or about four a minute. He also ties the style of the film directly to Griffith, at the time a consultant to the studio, in particular in the use of cross-cutting. The film has relatively simple set-ups: a few street scenes, a broker's office, a courtroom. Henry Watson (William Garwood), a "dishonest" broker, has embezzled $20,000 from his widowed client, Mrs. Caroline Livingston.

Watson plans to pin the crime on a messenger boy (played by a girl, Marie Eline) by having him deliver an envelope filled with newspaper scraps to the widow. First, he has his office staff witness him placing $20,000 into a similar envelope. Then it's just a question of following the boy, knocking him down, and switching envelopes. He does this in front of a film crew shooting on the streets of New Rochelle, a mistake he will come to regret.

When Mrs. Livingston finds out what happens, she has a policeman arrest the boy. He calls his sister (Florence LaBadie) for help, but is still sentenced to jail. Fortunately, his sister is a film editor, and "Some days later," as an intertitle informs us, she happens upon footage that will exonerate her brother if she shows it to detectives. This screening room sequence, which required a matte shot and double exposures, and a few inserts of a strip of film the sister is holding provided the only real technical challenges in the movie. While the angles of the street footage don't make sense, the glimpses into filmmaking, circa 1913, seem entirely accurate. (That's probably co-director Lawrence Marston seen waving a script and stepping behind the camera.)

Even more interesting is a look inside an editing room, where a half dozen women are at work. One is polishing a film with wax, others are rewinding reels, and LaBadie is cutting and splicing at a table. It's a reminder that women did most of the editing work on films at the time.

Ned Thanhouser's D.W. Griffith comparisons seem most apt regarding LaBadie and her "brother." They live in a household that's missing a father, yet they have cheerfully found their way in the world. LaBadie's job as an editor is both working class and glamorous. Her no-nonsense approach to defending her brother puts her squarely with typical Griffith heroines. Other Thanhouser films of the time share Griffith's preoccupation with waifs wrongly accused of crimes, but to be fair, many industry executives felt that was what their audiences wanted.

Matrimony's Speed Limit

Solax Film Company, 1913. Silent, B&W, 1.33. 14 minutes.
Cast: Fraunie Fraunholz, Marian Swayne.
Credits: Produced and directed by Alice Guy-Blaché.
Additional Credits: Released June 11, 1913.
Available: Image Entertainment DVD *Origins of Film* (2001). UPC: 014381980721. The Library of Congress and Smithsonian Video VHS *America's First Women Filmmakers: Alice Guy-Blaché and Lois Weber* (1993). ISBN: 1-57523-003-8; UPC: 7 11027 00033 0.

This modest comedy is one of scores of titles directed by Alice Guy-Blaché, the world's first woman director. Born outside Paris in 1873, she joined Gaumont, a pioneering French film company, in 1896 as a stenographer. When the company switched from making cameras to producing films,

Guy became one of its first directors. Her *La Fée aux Choux* (*The Cabbage Fairy*, 1896) is often credited as the first "story film." (Some sources dispute the year that Guy actually made the film, dating it as late as 1900.) While W.K.L. Dickson and William Heise had been making up characters and sets at Edison since 1893, Guy's achievements in early film can't be overlooked. She experimented with both sound and color, and by 1905 was acting as creative director of the entire Gaumont studio.

In 1907, Guy married Herbert Blaché, a cameraman who operated Gaumont branches in Berlin and London. They moved to New York that same year. Ostensibly they were to set up a Gaumont branch in the United States, but instead they formed their own production company, Solax. At first the company was centered around a former Gaumont print lab in Flushing, but Blaché and his wife soon built a studio in Fort Lee, New Jersey, across the Hudson River from Manhattan. By the end of 1911, Blaché was president of the American branch of Gaumont, while his wife was president of Solax, as well as its chief of production.

Herbert Blaché continued to concentrate on distribution, forming the Exclusive Supply Company in April 1913 to handle films from Solax and other companies. Guy-Blaché, on the other hand, made films, everything from an adaptation of Poe's *The Pit and the Pendulum* (1913) to *Dick Whittington and His Cat*. In May 1913 Solax released the domestic comedy *A House Divided*, starring Fraunie Fraunholz and Marian Swayne. *Matrimony's Speed Limit* came out five weeks later, with the same stars.

Both films deal amusingly with two sides of marriage, and both show Guy-Blaché's strong sense of what stories work best as films. *A House Divided* concerns a middle-class husband and wife who threaten to divorce each other based on a series of mistaken identities. They undergo a trial separation while living in the same house, leading to escalating tensions that presage *The War of the Roses* (1989).

Matrimony's Speed Limit finds Fraunholz facing ruin on the stock market. Swayne, his fiancée, wants to help, but Fraunie, as the intertitles identify him, is too proud to accept. Marian forges a telegram giving Fraunie a fortune, but only if he marries by noon that day. While she corrals a justice of the peace, Fraunie proposes to every woman he meets. The same basic idea would be used by playwright Roi Cooper Megrue in David Belasco's Broadway production of *Seven Chances* (1916), which in turn became a Buster Keaton feature film in 1925. (Even a few of the gags are the same, as when the hero inadvertently proposes to a black woman.) The Keaton film was in turn the basis for *The Bachelor*, a 1999 comedy starring Chris O'Donnell and Renée Zellweger, in a roundabout way making Guy-Blaché a contemporary inspiration.

The direction in *Matrimony's Speed Limit* feels broader than *A House Divided*. Fraunholz, in particular, throws his arms about and pulls his hair with alarming frequency. But Guy-Blaché gets the basic story across with a minimum of fuss (and very few sets). Watch how she changes the camera angle to include a wall clock in Fraunholz's office when time becomes a factor in the plot. That said, the film relies heavily on intertitles, some of which contain the story's best gags.

An added benefit of the film is its brief tour of the streets of Fort Lee, seen as Marian and the justice ride in a car to find Fraunie. Guy-Blaché intercuts Fraunholz's attempts to propose with Marian's drive, throwing in some close-ups of Fraunholz's pocket-watch to increase tension. The most frightening moment watching the film today is a swoony shot as Marian's car turns two corners. Captured by a camera mounted on a car in front of her, the lurching movements can induce motion sickness.

Guy-Blaché continued to direct films, but was forced to give up Solax during the consolidation of studios before 1920. She accepted assignments from Pathé and Metro, but left the country after she divorced Blaché in 1922. (He made films throughout the 1920s.) She was unable to find film work back in France, and fell into obscurity until she was awarded the Legion of Honor in 1953. She moved back to Mahway, New Jersey, near the site of her former studio, in 1964, and died there four years later.

Traffic in Souls

A scene from *Traffic in Souls* reveals the universal gangster code for two sitting ducks.

Universal, 1913. Silent, B&W, 1.33. 87 minutes.

Cast: Jane Gail (Mary Barton), Matt Moore (Officer Larry Burke), Ethel Grandin (Lorna Barton), William Welsh (William Trubus), Howard Crampton (The go-between), Mrs. Hudson Lyston [Millie Liston] (Mrs. Trubus), Irene Wallace (Alice Trubus), William Turner (Isaac Barton), Arthur Hunter (The cadet [procurer]), William Cavanaugh (Bill Bradshaw); Laura Huntley (The country girl), William Burbidge ("Respectable" Smith), William Powers (The emigrant girls' brother).

Credits: Directed by George Loane Tucker [George S. Loane]. Screenplay by Walter MacNamara. Produced by Jack Cohn, Walter MacNamara. Director of photography: Henry Alder Leach. Film editor: Jack Cohn. Produced by IMP [Independent Moving Picture Company].

Additional Cast: George Loane Tucker (Telegraph operator); Jack Poulton, Edward Boring, Walter MacNamara (Cadets); Flora Nason, Vera Hansey (Swedish sisters); Charles Green (Butler).

Additional Credits: Released November 1913.

Available: Flicker Alley DVD *Perils of the New Land* (2008). UPC: 617311673894. Kino Home Video VHS (1994). UPC: 7-38329-00808-6.

In his influential but unreliable *A Million and One Nights*, Terry Ramsaye, one of the earliest film historians, offered a fanciful account of the production of *Traffic in Souls*. He claimed that it was made on the sly in four weeks for $5,000, an amount contributed by George Loane Tucker and fellow directors Herbert Brenon and William Robert Daly, star King Baggot, and editor Jack Cohn. What's more, Carl Laemmle, the future head of Universal and the chief force behind the Independent Moving Picture Company, didn't want to release the finished film, which went on to earn upwards of $500,000.

Film historian Kevin Brownlow later revealed that *Traffic in Souls* actually started with $25,000

put up by theatrical impresario Lee Shubert and former senator Joseph Rhinock, among others. Far from being filmed undercover, this was a major project involving a large cast and locations in two states. Its subject matter—white slavery, a euphemism for sex trafficking—had somewhat inexplicably become one of the raging topics of the day.

Fears about the fates of naive immigrants helped lead to the 1910 White Slave Traffic Act (now known as the Mann Act), which prohibited taking women across state lines for immoral purposes. Entertainers responded with plays like *The Battle* (1909) and *The Lure* (August 1913, produced by Shubert), prostitution melodramas so daring that their productions were raided by the police. Ramsaye wrote that Tucker was familiar with the plays, and saw how the subject could be used on film.

Born in Chicago in 1881, Tucker had desk jobs with railroads before becoming an indifferent actor. With few prospects on the stage, he entered movies in 1908, where he eventually found success directing. According to Brownlow, a more significant figure behind the film was writer and producer Walter MacNamara, a native of Ireland and a former blacksmith, marine engineer, and war correspondent. In 1913, he was a "special photoplay writer," or story editor, at Universal, where he also pitched his own ideas for films. One of them was a police story that hinged on a dictagraph, a recording device. After the success of *The Lure*, which was filmed by Alice Guy-Blaché in 1914, MacNamara added prostitution rings to his cop story, an idea that appealed to Shubert and other investors.

While prostitution had been implied on screen since the turn of the twentieth century, it had generally been treated in comic terms. And while filmmakers the world over had discovered the commercial appeal of women in peril, no one was willing to examine the financial and moral implications of prostitution. The heroines in D.W. Griffith's films may have been menaced by drifters and crooks, but in a narrative sense they were more bystanders than sexual victims.

MacNamara was depicting a different world, an underground network of procurers, pimps, madams, and their prey. They constituted a web of crime that spread throughout New York City, extending to railroads, ocean liners, ferries, trolleys, even legitimate shops and businesses. Women had to be diligently aware of the dangers awaiting them. The well-dressed gentleman offering directions, the pious head of a Citizens' League, the dandy pitching woo with candy and drinks—all could be trying to lure the innocent into sexual slavery.

It was a controversial story, and one that could have used the approval of moral arbiters like John D. Rockefeller, who headed one of the many panels investigating the issue. (The film's publicity campaign bandied Rockefeller's name about, although he had no connection to the project.) By making the police the heroes of the story, MacNamara defused another potential source of criticism. But the writer didn't shy away from accusing charitable organizations of criminal hypocrisy, or suggesting that moralists may have built their riches on sin. MacNamara also didn't forget his audience. It's the smartly dressed businessmen who are the villains of the piece, not hardworking laborers. And while his female victims might be drugged, slapped, and whipped, there are no "clients" in the film, making the story's happy ending more plausible.

At this point in his career, Tucker was a somewhat stodgy director who staged most of the film's interiors in the same monotonous medium shot. With a static frame, set design became whatever furniture and props would fit in front of the camera, with painted flats in the background to suggest either wealth or poverty. What increased the film's sense of realism was Tucker's ability to restrain his cast, in particular the villains, from overacting.

Apart from its subject matter, three qualities set *Traffic in Souls* apart from other films of the time. First, it was a contemporary feature during a time when most lengthy movies were about religious subjects. Second, Henry Alder Leach's remarkable cinematography captured a wide range of New York City locations. His exteriors have striking exposures and angled, stylized compositions.

During shots of a trolley car early in the film, Leach starts to pan the camera to keep the actors in frame. Other cinematographers had been "moving" the camera for years, either because the camera was on a moving object like a train, or to follow action. But about twenty minutes into *Traffic in Souls*, Leach does something extraordinary. He anticipates action, panning the camera from William Powers standing on the shore to Flora Nason and Vera Hansey, two in a crowd of passengers on a ferry pulling into the dock. It was a planned, choreographed shot, one that predicted the future of cinematography. Leach almost topped it at the end of the film with an extended tracking shot down a jail corridor to show that the villains were safely behind bars.

Third, Jack Cohn's editing juggled as many as four story lines at once without confusing viewers or losing sight of the main thrust of the plot. Some critics today complain that *Traffic in Souls* is hard to follow, perhaps because they have seen a battered print that is missing footage and intertitles. (The British copy that Brownlow viewed has additional scenes and a different ending.) But Cohn's vision of the film is always apparent, and his sense of editing is swift, bracing, and confident. While he may have borrowed the cross-cutting climax from Griffith, he built up an enormous amount of tension by delaying action. Cohn's editing is one of the chief reasons why *Traffic in Souls* is still so thrilling today.

Cohn got his younger brother Harry his first job in the film industry; along with Joe Brandt, they would later form Columbia Pictures. *Traffic in Souls* was one of a dozen films George Sloane Tucker made in 1913. He later directed a British version of *The Prisoner of Zenda* (1915); his greatest success, *The Miracle Man* (1919) with Lon Chaney, came two years before his death. *Traffic in Souls* was followed by even more explicit films like *Inside of the White Slave Traffic* (1913) and *The House of Bondage* (1914), but the white slavery cycle was quickly folded into other genres.

Gertie the Dinosaur

Line drawing by Winsor McCay for *Gertie the Dinosaur*.
Courtesy of Milestone Film & Video

Winsor McCay, 1914. Silent, B&W, 1.33. 12 minutes.

Credits: Written and animated by Winsor McCay. Assistant: John A. Fitzsimmons. Premiered in Chicago on February 2, 1914. Distributed theatrically by Vitagraph.

Other Versions: Gertie appeared in McCay's *Gertie on Tour* (1918–21).

Available: Image Entertainment DVD *Winsor McCay: The Master Edition* (2003). UPC: 0-14381-1982-2-5.

Winsor McCay would have been a significant figure in film even if he hadn't made *Gertie the Dinosaur*. He was born Zenas Winsor McKay in either Michigan or Canada, anywhere from 1867 to 1871 (his birth records no longer exist). His father, a realtor, soon changed the family surname to McCay. Winsor grew up in Michigan, near Spring Lake and then in Stanton. From an early age he was obsessed with art. "I couldn't stop drawing anything and everything," he remembered, later dropping out of business school to create advertising posters in Chicago. Two years later he moved to Cincinnati as a commercial illustrator, primarily for carnivals and a dime museum.

For nine years he drew posters. "Missing Link," "Armless Wonder," "Joe-Joe the dog-faced boy," and other oddities and curiosities would return to his imagery throughout his career. Married, and with two children, he took a job in 1898 drawing newspaper cartoons and illustrations for the *Commercial Tribune*. He contributed to a humor magazine and then began drawing color pages for the *Cincinnati Enquirer*. These got him a job at the *New York Herald* and the *Evening Telegram*.

Moving to New York in 1903, McCay began drawing his first comic strips a year later. *Dreams of the Rarebit Fiend* appeared in September 1904; aimed at adults, it presaged surrealism in its depiction of a nightmarish world in which inanimate objects stretched and distorted at will. It was so influential that Edwin S. Porter made a film adaptation in 1906. By then McCay had introduced *Little Nemo in Slumberland*, a spectacularly innovative strip that used color, perspective, depth of field, design, and sequential motion to express both narrative and metaphoric meaning. It had an enormous impact on culture at large, from Edison and Biograph films to popular songs; it was even the subject of a 1908 operetta by Victor Herbert.

McCay's use of movement suggests that he was familiar with motion pictures, in particular the stop-motion animation employed by Porter, J. Stuart Blackton, and other directors. Animator John Canemaker believes McCay was also influenced by the French filmmaker Émile Cohl, whose drawings transformed objects and moved characters into unexpected settings. In *Humorous Phases of Funny Faces* (1906), Blackton filmed himself drawing pictures that he then brought to life through animation. It was a landmark in cinema, and a clear influence on McCay's first efforts in the medium.

In fact, Blackton helped McCay with filming *Little Nemo in Slumberland* at his Vitagraph Studios. McCay combined a live-action prologue with four thousand drawings. The film was released to theaters on April 8, 1911; four days later, McCay started using it in a vaudeville act he had prepared. Later, he had the film hand-colored.

The final *Nemo* strip appeared in July 1911. By then McCay had signed with William Randolph Hearst. He had also started on his second film, *How a Mosquito Operates* (sometimes titled *The Story of a Mosquito*), borrowed from a scene in a 1909 *Rarebit Fiend* strip. According to Canemaker, one of the distinctive features of the film is McCay's ability to give a character, a personality, to the title mosquito.

McCay developed this concept further with his next film, *Gertie the Dinosaur*. Gertie, a pleasantly plump and shy dinosaur who inadvertently gets into trouble because she doesn't know her own strength, has been called by some critics the first anthropomorphic cartoon character. Even with the passage of time, she is certainly one of the most appealing, in part due to McCay's drawings, but also because of his narrative skills. He not only incorporated the film into his vaudeville act, he wrote the plot so that he could interact with Gertie in front of his audience. McCay would appear on stage holding a whip, using it to draw her out from behind some rocks. McCay's timing with Gertie made her seem alive, especially when he "fed" her an apple.

McCay premiered the film at the Palace in Chicago on February 2, 1914. He received glowing reviews there, and again when he brought the act to New York. However, during a performance a stage assistant mistakenly angered Hearst, who then banned mention of McCay's act from his papers. Hearst later ordered McCay to give up his comic strips and animation. Eventually McCay had to cancel his vaudeville engagements.

The artist drew some 25,000 frames for *The Sinking of the "Lusitania"* (1918), a grimly political cartoon, but his later efforts in animation were limited and derivative. Still, it is difficult to find a serious animator alive today who doesn't point to McCay as an influence. Among his innovations was his use of "cycling," or repeating a sequence of movement, to save on drawing new material. To show Gertie breathing, for example, he would film the same sequence of drawings up to fifteen times. Canemaker also credits McCay with inventing "in-betweening," which the artist called the "McCay Split System." He would break motion down into specific poses, draw those, and then later go back and fill in the missing material. McCay's developments would be adopted by the entire animation industry; in fact, John Bray succeeded in stealing many of them and patenting them under his name.

By the time McCay died of a stroke in 1934, his best work had been largely forgotten. But thanks to the efforts of Canemaker and others, his films have been preserved and his reputation restored.

Tess of the Storm Country

Famous Players/Paramount, 1914. Silent, B&W, 1.33. Approximately 55 minutes (5 reels).

Cast: Mary Pickford (Tessibel Skinner), Harold Lockwood (Frederick Graves), Olive Golden (Teola Graves), David Hartford (Daddy Skinner), Louise Dunlap (Old Mother Mol), W.R. Walters (Elias Graves), Richard Garrick (Ben Letts), Eugene Walter (Ezra Longman), Lorraine Thompson (Myra Longman), Jack Henry (Dan Jordan), H.R. Macy (Professor Young), H.L. Griffith (Old Longman).

Credits: Directed by Edwin S. Porter. Assistant director: David Hartford. Scenario: B.P. Schulberg. Based on the novel by Grace Miller White.

Additional Credits: Director of photography: (most likely) Edwin S. Porter. Presented by Daniel Frohman. Produced by Adolph Zukor. Released March 20, 1914.

Other Versions: Pickford starred in a 1922 remake directed by John S. Robertson. It was also remade in 1932, starring Janet Gaynor, and in 1960, starring Diane Baker. *The Secret of the Storm Country* (1917), starring Norma Talmadge and directed by Charles Miller, was a continuation of the story.

Available: The Library of Congress; the Mary Pickford Institute (*www.marypickford.com*).

If any one performer could be singled out for legitimizing the film industry, for influencing its growth and direction, Mary Pickford would be a logical first choice. Born Gladys Smith in Toronto in 1893, she appeared on the stage soon after her father died in 1898. By the time she was ten, she was supporting her sister, brother, and mother. When she was fourteen, she won a part in David Belasco's Broadway production of *The Warrens of Virginia*. (Belasco changed her stage name to "Mary Pickford.") Two years later, in 1909, she persuaded D.W. Griffith to hire her for his Biograph stock company. She appeared as an extra in *Her First Biscuits* (1909) behind Florence Lawrence. It was one of forty-five films Pickford made for Griffith in 1909.

Griffith cast Pickford in thirty-five films the following year, and also hired her brother Jack and sister Lottie so the family could earn more money. Pickford played an astonishing variety of roles in stories that ranged from broad comedies to rural romances and period adventures. Often these were parts that Griffith decided were unsuitable for the Gish sisters, Dorothy and Lillian; many of them were supporting instead of lead roles. Pickford handled them all with the same professionalism and energy.

She understood before most the strengths and drawbacks of the medium, learning how to modulate her acting for the camera, how to become the focal point of a tableau, how to command attention within a frame. She rose above the artificiality of her workplace, with its often shoddy props and costumes, and equally threadbare plot lines and roles. She learned to project an innocence and a belief that the story she was acting could mean something to viewers. To filmgoers, she seemed to believe the emotions she was portraying, believe that she was inhabiting a real world that extended beyond the camera's gaze. On top of whatever qualities her roles demanded, she was impulsive, free-spirited, curious, generous, and down to earth. She was exactly as her fans wanted to see themselves, only blessed with a beauty so overwhelming that it retains its power today. As Griffith cameraman Billy Bitzer wrote, "It was her sincerity, which you couldn't help liking, and it was also how lovely she looked."

Pickford would have been a crucial figure in film solely for her screen work, but she had one of the sharpest business minds in the industry. Her biographers note with admiration her escalating salaries. From $40 a week at Biograph, she went up to $175 a week at IMP, and then $500 a week at Famous Players. By 1916 she was earning $10,000 a week, with a $300,000 signing bonus, and had her own production company. But just as important as money was achieving and maintaining creative control over her product. Pickford was extremely careful about her appearance on screen, doing her own makeup, collaborating with cinematographers, finding and often writing her screenplays, and arguing, at times vehemently, with her directors. She was the only performer to stand up successfully to industry giants like Griffith, Carl Laemmle, and Adolph Zukor. She was also at the forefront of every advance in the industry, from new camera lenses to exploiting trends in literary adaptations to starring in feature-length films.

The actress left Griffith and Biograph in December, 1910, for some forty films at IMP and then Majestic. In 1912 she returned to the stage, starring in *A Good Little Devil* for David Belasco. About that time Adolph Zukor hit upon the phrase "Famous Players in Famous Plays," the start of a production company that would eventually evolve into Paramount Studios. An immigrant from Hungary, Zukor had a successful fur business when he began to experiment with exhibiting movies. He built the equivalent of a modern-day arcade, calling it Automatic Vaudeville, and devoted its second floor to films. He distributed *Queen Elizabeth* (1912), a four-reel film starring Sarah Bernhardt, the reigning stage queen. With partner Daniel Frohman, Zukor began producing film adaptations of Broadway hits like *The Prisoner of Zenda* (1914).

Zukor signed Pickford to a contract in 1913. Her first feature, an adaptation of *A Good Little Devil*, was released in March 1914, although it had been shot the previous May. She starred in a few lost titles, shifting production to the West Coast early in 1914. Zukor gave Pickford a script for *Tess of the Storm Country*, and had to persuade her to consider the lead role.

The script was based on a 1909 novel by Grace Miller White, an author from Ithaca, New York. Born Mary Esther Miller in 1868, she took the name of a younger sister who died in infancy. When her first marriage was failing, she began writing for hire. Between 1907 and 1912 she wrote over fifty novelizations of plays and films, a grueling pace that gave her a full education in making money as an author. She began a series of novels based in the Finger Lakes region of New York, in particular the "storm country" between Ithaca and Lake Cayuga. *Tess of the Storm Country* was extremely popular, leading to a sequel and several other "storm country" novels that essentially duplicated the original's plot. The book was adapted for stage in 1912 by Rupert Hughes; it was this play that B.P Schulberg adapted for his screenplay.

The play and screenplay discard a great deal of White's book, a stew of moral pieties and thick dialect. (Sample dialogue: "I air yer squatter.") What remains is about as pointed and preposterous as melodrama can get: a wealthy town leader evicting squatters, a romance between his daughter and a college rascal, small-town cruelty, snow blowing into crude huts, the rich ordering servants about, hypocrisy exposed during a church service, murder trials, unfair hangings.

Director Edwin S. Porter—the same man behind *The Great Train Robbery* (1903)—was near the end of his career; *Tess* would be the last film on which he received sole directing credit. He had stubbornly held onto antiquated theories about filmmaking, staging tableaus on one plane instead of taking advantage of film's illusion of depth, duplicating actions between shots instead of cutting on movement, and using painted backdrops. As Pickford later told film historian Kevin Brownlow, "He knew nothing about directing. Nothing." Much of *Tess* leans on outmoded theatrics, on exposition delivered in intertitles, on the knowledge filmgoers presumably already had about characters and situations in the story. The camera almost never moves, except to pan across the cliffs of Del Mar, California, standing in (not very persuasively) for the shores of Lake Cayuga.

And yet parts of *Tess* reach across the years, as fresh and appealing now as it must have been back in 1914. Some oddly angled compositions shot in the stark California sunlight have a documentary beauty, in particular a scene in which Frederick is chased off a railroad bridge. The conflict between classes, the sheer injustice of Deacon Graves's edicts, the ineffectualness of the law and the church all make up for the stiff theatrics, like the paint passing for snow and the open-air sets. While the plot is inescapably melodramatic, the film deals honestly with mature themes: children born out of wedlock, men preying on women of the underclass, starvation and death among the poor.

And Pickford, cool, mature, self-possessed even when wrestling with a vase of flowers almost as big as she is, is utterly beguiling. She throws temper tantrums, dreams of love, defends the weak, steals kisses, performs daring stunts, and takes over the screen, no matter how rigidly Porter frames her. As an actress, she is very precise at conveying what she wants audiences to know about her character, toning down her performance for her few close-ups, playing broadly in some cluttered wide shots.

"That was the beginning of my career," Pickford said later. *Tess of the Storm Country* was so successful that it helped turn her into the most popular film star in the world. It established a template for the characters she would play, and positioned Famous Players, and Paramount, at the forefront of the industry. *Tess of the Storm Country* was the only feature Pickford ever re-made. She appeared in a much more expensive and longer version directed by John S. Robertson in 1922.

Lobby card for *Tess of the Storm Country*, Mary Pickford's first filmed version of Grace Miller White's novel. *Courtesy of The Rob Brooks "Mary Pickford Collection," Toronto*

The Perils of Pauline

Pathé-Eclectic, 1914. Silent, B&W, 1.33. 200 minutes (extant version).

Cast: Pearl White (Pauline), Crane Wilbur (Harry Marvin), Paul Panzer (Raymond Owen [named "Koerner" in reissues]), Edward José (Sanford Marvin), Francis Carlyle (Owen's henchman, Hicks), Clifford Bruce (Gypsy leader), Donald MacKenzie (Blinky Bill), Jack Standing (Ensign Summers), Eleanor Woodruff (Lucille), Leroy Baker, Louise Du Pre, Oscar Nye, Sam Ryan, Louis Gasnier, Joe Cuny, Frank Redman, Chief Thunderbird.

Credits: Directed by Louis Gasnier, Donald MacKenzie. Written by Charles W. Goddard, George B. Seitz. Director of photography: Arthur C. Miller. Gowns: Lady Duff Gordon.
Additional Credits: Production began March 23, 1914.
Other Versions: *The Perils of Pauline* (1933), a Universal serial, used a different plot. A 1947 Paramount feature film called *The Perils of Pauline* offered an idealized biography of Pearl White. Universal's *The Perils of Pauline* (1967), starring Pat Boone, has no connection to the original serial.

Available: Grapevine Video DVD (*www.grapevinevideo.com*). UPC: 8-80074-04363-5.

Many viewers today reduce silent film to a shorthand of slapstick and serials. Of the latter, no title is more recognizable than *The Perils of Pauline*. Serials matured as a form in the early twentieth century, and were cross-promoted in newspapers, magazines, and movie theaters. *Perils* was financed by William Randolph Hearst's media empire in part to compete with the success of *The Adventures of Kathlyn*, produced by the Selig Film Manufacturing Company in collaboration with the *Chicago Tribune*. (The first episode of *Kathlyn* was released in December, 1913.) More than just a movie, *The Perils of Pauline* was syndicated to newspapers and then condensed in a novelization that appeared in 1915.

The serial was produced by the French firm Pathé Frères, at the time the largest movie company in the world. Pathé had a presence in the United States as early as 1910, and by 1912 had built a studio at 1 Congress Street, Jersey City, directly across the Hudson River from Manhattan. It was run by J.A. Berst; its director general of production was Louis Gasnier, who had directed films in France. To get around exhibition restrictions imposed by the General Film Company, Pathé established the Eclectic Film Company in 1913. Eclectic could import Pathé's French product unimpeded by General Film, which was in the process of failing in its attempt to monopolize film distribution. Pathé revealed its ownership of Eclectic in 1914, around the time the *Perils* serial began production.

The Perils of Pauline was written by Charles W. Goddard and George B. Seitz. Goddard was solely credited for the novelization of the serial. He was a playwright who had cowritten, with Paul Dickey, *The Ghost Breaker*, a comedy thriller that would later be adapted into vehicles for both Bob Hope (*The Ghost Breakers*, 1940) and Dean Martin and Jerry Lewis (*Scared Stiff*, 1953). Seitz, who would go on to a lengthy career directing B-movies, adapted Goddard's plot line for the screen, and also worked as Gasnier's assistant. Gasnier, whose English was spotty, also had help from Donald MacKenzie, an Edinburgh native. (According to *Perils* cinematographer Arthur C. Miller, Gasnier directed the first ten episodes and McKenzie the final ten. MacKenzie would also claim later that he was the principal director of all the episodes.)

The producers of *The Perils of Pauline* were Leopold and Theodore Wharton, brothers who would later build their own studio in Ithaca, New York. Both had acted before entering movies. Theodore was the first to approach Pearl White about taking the lead in the serial. She was at that point a fairly significant star. When she worked for the Powers Film Company in 1911, it sold calendars with her likeness to theater owners, who would then give them away to customers. That same year she appeared in the New England Exhibitors' Association ball with Paul Panzer, her future costar in *Perils*. Critics cited White's acting for its restraint, and in a film like *The Heart of an Indian Maid*, made by Pathé in 1911, she showed how screen acting would evolve from the pantomime used on stage to a more inward, personal style. (For more about White's background, see *The Exploits of Elaine*, 1914.)

White's character in *The Perils of Pauline* is cheerful, active, and headstrong, an exciting change from the pale, cosseted, Victorian heroines favored by D.W. Griffith. A paradigm of the "new woman" espoused in magazines of the time, she can race a horse, drive a car, and put up a fight when attacked, as she is in *Perils* with dismaying regularity. The plot hinges on whether or not she will marry her boyfriend Harry Marvin (played by Crane Wilbur), but this is not a typical romance. She wants a year off prior to tying the knot to have fun; meanwhile, someone wants to kill her before she inherits her guardian's estate.

Publicity pieces claimed that White did her own stunts, and according to Goddard, she was seriously injured in a scene when Paul Panzer tripped while carrying her upstairs. "I struck on the top of my head, displacing several vertebrae," White said in 1920. "The pain was terrible. For two years I simply lived with osteopaths, and to this day I have some pretty bad times with my back."

One of the delights in watching *Perils* is spotting locations that are largely unchanged today. Miller wrote that the film's locations "were around Fort Lee, Coytesville, and among the rocky cliffs of the Palisades as well as a little farther up the Hudson River in the town of Englewood, where the Morrow and Browning estates were used as homes of characters in the cast." Other endearing qualities about the serial include the high spirits the leads share while exploring the technological wonders of their age, and the filmmakers' sly sense of humor.

Critics of the time, except those employed by Hearst, were not kind to *The Perils of Pauline*. In later years, writers have used terms like "crude and inept," "badly written and badly directed," etc. William K. Everson called Gasnier "one of the worst directors the movies have ever known." But perhaps as a result of Hearst's influence, *The Perils of Pauline* was an enormous success at the box office, far outperforming its competitors. In fact, White became a cultural phenomenon, extolled in magazine articles and popular songs. "Poor Pauline," for example, with words by Charles McCarron and music by Raymond Walker, would be played at theaters exhibiting the serial.

This was the first of nine Pathé serials that White starred in, and she consistently ranked in the top five in motion picture popularity polls. She wrote one of the first movie star autobiographies, *Just Me*, published in 1919. But after World War I, serials featuring White's type of independent,

adventurous women fell out of favor. White tried to switch to feature films, but could not hold on to her audience. The death of her stunt double John Stevenson in an accident during the filming of her last serial, *Plunder* (1922), hastened her departure from the industry. White moved to France, where she died in 1938.

The original twenty chapters of *The Perils of Pauline* have been lost. The current version is derived from a condensed edit prepared for the French market. Some attribute the serial's unintentionally funny intertitles (e.g., "immoral strength" for "immortal strength") to mistakes during translations from English to French and then back to English.

Pearl White crawls through a submarine torpedo tube during a tense moment in *The Perils of Pauline*.

In the Land of the Head Hunters

World Film Corporation, 1914. Silent, B&W with tints and tones, 1.33. 68 minutes.

Cast: Stanley Hunt (Motana, son of Kenada); Margaret Wilson, Sarah [Abaya] Smith Martin, Mrs. George Walkus (Naida, daughter of Chief Waket [played by three actresses]); Bulóotsa (Yaklus), Paddy Maleed (Kenada), Kwa'kwaano [or Haéytlulas, aka "Long Harry"] (Sorcerer).

Credits: Written and directed by Edward S. Curtis. Musical score: John J. Braham. Produced by The Seattle Film Co., Inc.

Additional Cast: Francine Hunt, Bob Wilson, Helen Knox.

Additional Credits: Photography: Edmund August Schwinke. Production manager: George Hunt. Production assistant: Jonathan Hunt. Released December 7, 1914.

Other Versions: The extant footage was re-edited as *In the Land of the War Canoes* (1974).

Available: The 1974 restoration has been released by Milestone Film & Video on the Image Entertainment DVD *In the Land of the War Canoes* (2000). UPC: 0-14381-9361-2-4.

Released in 1914, *In the Land of the Head Hunters* was a financial disappointment for its creator,

Edward S. Curtis, so much so that he sold all rights to the picture to New York's Museum of Natural History eight years later. When the museum lost track of Curtis's material, the film was considered lost until a print surfaced in 1947. Hugo Zeiter, a film collector, donated a tinted and toned, 35mm nitrate print to the Field Museum of Natural History in Chicago. This copy was either destroyed during projection or for safety reasons. Curator George Quimby obtained a 16mm copy, which he brought when he began working at the University of Washington's Burke Museum in 1965.

There Quimby and art historian Bill Holm oversaw a restoration that was completed in 1974. Now titled *In the Land of the War Canoes*, the

Detail of a photograph by Edwin S. Curtis for his film *In the Land of the Head Hunters*.
Courtesy of Milestone Film & Video

forty-seven-minute movie was understood to be the first ethnographic feature and a valuable look at Kwakiutl Indian life. But a new restoration, finished in 2008, provides an entirely different context for the film. Now *In the Land of the Head Hunters* takes its place as the first feature film made with and entirely about Native Americans.

The film was originally seen as a means to finance *The North American Indian*, a twenty-volume history of every extant tribe that occupied three decades in the career of Edward Curtis. Born in 1868, Curtis moved with his father to the Puget Sound area in 1887. Always interested in photography, Curtis mortgaged the family farm after his father's death to buy into a photographic practice. He had his own studio in Seattle by 1897. After encountering a group of explorers on Mount Rainier, he was chosen to accompany the Harriman Expedition to Alaska in 1899 as official photographer. This led to his meeting President Theodore Roosevelt, who in turn introduced him to financier J. Pierpont Morgan. In 1906, Morgan agreed to finance *The North American Indian*, envisioned as a subscription publication along the lines of John James Audubon's *Birds of America*.

Roosevelt wrote the foreword to the first volume, and Morgan continued to pump money into the project until his death in 1913. By that time Curtis had already photographed and filmed Indians throughout the West and Southwest, including Chief Joseph of the Nez Percé, "one of the greatest Indians who ever lived," and one of the inspirations for the entire project. By 1909, with his marriage failing, Curtis had completed only five volumes. A year later he began working with what were known as the Kwakiutl. (Today the tribe is known as the Kwakwaka'wakw.) They were among his favorite Indians; their volume is twice the size of the rest in the series.

In 1911, Curtis tried to make money with what he called The Curtis Indian Picture Opera, a lecture tour complete with lantern slides, films, field recordings, and an orchestra. When this failed, he turned to moviemaking, forming the Continental Film Company in 1912 and appealing to investors with a script he described as "vision quest, love, witchcraft, war, ceremony, revenge, capture, rescue, escape and triumph!"

Although it would feature real Indian rituals, costumes, and locations, *In the Land of the Head Hunters* wasn't conceived as a documentary or ethnographic film but as a fiction film, one of several about Indians that had been commercially successful in recent months. Crucially, Curtis would be working with the cooperation of the Kwakwaka'wakw—in particular, George Hunt, who brokered introductions, acted as interpreter, and secured props. In his photographic work, Curtis implied a pre-contact world for his subjects, at times retouching negatives to eliminate traces of the modern world. He took the same approach for the film, going so far as to reconstruct a native village, building five prop residences and two totem poles.

His plot had traces of Henry Wadsworth Longfellow's poem *The Song of Hiawatha*, and of *Hiawatha*, a film adaptation made in 1913. In Curtis's story, a jealous sorcerer tries to kill Motana in order to steal away his fiancée Naida, daughter of a chief. Motana's violent response leads to war with the sorcerer's brother Yaklus. Most of the filming took place on Deer Island near Fort Rupert, and if for nothing else the picture's images of British Columbia make it worthy of inclusion on the Registry.

But Curtis achieved far more. For one thing, his filmmaking skills were extraordinary. With little training or experience, he staged scenes of notable tension, using a camera that panned and tilted to follow action. He even placed the camera within canoes, offering viewers a subjective view of warriors embarking on a raid. Because at least half of the original film, and all its titles, have been missing, Curtis's technique can seem opaque at times. Given the full plot, it turns out that his narrative instincts were actually quite sound.

Furthermore, Curtis preserved Kwakwaka'wakw rituals and dances that, due to the Canadian Indian Act, natives had been banned from performing. If, as the new restoration points out, some of the dances and situations were fabricated for the film, the Kwakwaka'wakw participated enthusiastically in them, in effect becoming co-producers of their own story.

After spending some $75,000, including commissioning a score by New York composer and conductor John J. Braham, Curtis opened the film in New York City and Seattle in December 1914. Despite excellent reviews, *In the Land of the Head Hunters* was a financial disaster. Distributed by the World Film Corporation, the film earned only $3,269.18 after a year of screenings. After selling his rights, Curtis found work as a researcher and still photographer in Hollywood.

Still, the film had considerable influence on filmmakers, such as Robert Flaherty. Curtis screened his copy for Flaherty in 1915, directly inspiring *Nanook of the North* (1922), another Registry title.

The Exploits of Elaine

Pathé Frères/Eclectic, 1914. Silent, B&W, 1.33. Approximately 270 minutes.

Cast: Pearl White (Elaine Dodge), Arnold Daly (Detective Craig Kennedy), Creighton Hale (Walter Jameson, episodes 1–3), Raymond Owens (Walter Jameson, episodes 4–14), Sheldon Lewis (Perry Bennett), Edwin Arden (Wu Fang), Leroy Baker (The Butler), Bessie Wharton (Aunt Josephine Dodge), William Riley Hatch (President Taylor Dodge), Robin H. Townley (Limpy Red), Floyd Buckley (Michael), M. W. Rale (Wong Long Sin).

Credits: Directed by Louis J. Gasnier, George B. Seitz, Leopold Wharton. Screenplay: Charles W. Goddard, George B. Seitz. Story: Arthur B. Reeve. Produced by Leopold Wharton, Theodore Wharton.

Additional Cast: George B. Seitz, Howard Cody.

Additional Credits: Opened December 29, 1914.

Episodes: 1: "The Clutching Hand"; 2: "The Twilight Sleep"; 3: "The Vanishing Jewels"; 4: "The Frozen Safe"; 5: "The Poisoned Room"; 6: "The Vampire"; 7: "The Double Trap"; 8: "The Hidden Voice"; 9: "The Death Ray"; 10: "The Life Current"; 11: "The Hour of Three"; 12: "The Blood Crystals"; 13: "The Devil Worshippers"); 14: "The Reckoning."

Other Versions: *The New Exploits of Elaine* (1915), *The Romance of Elaine* (1915). *The Clutching Hand* (1936), a fifteen-part serial, was based on an Arthur B. Reeve novel.

Available: Grapevine Video VHS *The Perils of Pauline Episodes 6–9* (1995) contains Chapter 8, "The Hidden Voice." Grapevine Video DVD *Pearl White: Queen of the Serials* contains Chapter 1, "The Clutching Hand" (*www.grapevinevideo.com*).

This fourteen-part serial was the follow-up to *The Perils of Pauline* (1914), an enormously successful serial that featured much of the same creative team. Both starred Pearl White, a pretty, spirited woman whose enthusiastic performances made her a national phenomenon. Both were written in part by George B. Seitz, who would go on to dominate the silent serial field before a long career as a director of sound features.

Serials were an outgrowth of "series" films; both concepts were derived from literature, where authors like Charles Dickens and William Dean Howells serialized their novels in newspapers and magazines before publishing them as books. Series films featured recurring characters like detective Nick Carter or cowboy Broncho Billy Anderson. Serials extended one story line through a dozen or more chapters, much like the daily and weekly comic strips that were growing in popularity around the turn of the twentieth century. A film that didn't end but continued on, that required viewers to return to theaters to find out what happened next, seemed like a gold mine to producers and exhibitors.

What Happened to Mary? (1912, directed by Charles J. Brabin) is sometimes listed as the first serial, although its episodes were not actually connected to each other. Selig's *The Adventures of Kathlyn* (released in December 1913) was the first true serial; its plot was serialized in the *Chicago Tribune* at the same time. The Hearst press countered by serializing and partially financing Pathé's *The Perils of Pauline* in 1914.

These early serials all featured women in the leading roles. These characters rejected old traditions, enjoyed jobs in emerging technologies, took control of their lives, and, in fiction at least, were increasingly the prey of unsavory types.

Pearl White in particular captured moviegoers' fancy, although Ruth Roland and Helen Holmes were also big stars. White was born in Missouri in 1889, and led an uneventful life until she left home at eighteen, against her parents' wishes, to pursue acting. After work in stock companies, she reached New York by 1910. What happened next varies from account to account, and even within her autobiography *Just Me* (1919). She either became a secretary for the small Powers Film Company or turned to acting in films because of her failing voice. Either way, she made scores of shorts between 1910 and 1914 before *The Perils of Pauline* changed her life.

Rushed into production the same year, *The Exploits of Elaine* was based on the writings of Arthur B. Reeve, a mystery writer whose detective, Craig Kennedy, solved crimes through scientific methods and cutting-edge technologies. His inventions included a "Vocaphone" that functioned like an intercom and a machine that could revive the dead (if they weren't dead very long). He is portrayed in *Exploits* and its sequels by Arnold Daly, a balding actor with a tendency to overact. In the story, White plays Elaine Dodge, the daughter of the president of an insurance company. She is threatened by the Clutching Hand, a hunchbacked villain who wears a bandanna over his face as a disguise. Uncovering the Clutching Hand's identity becomes as important a plot device as foiling his many criminal schemes.

The episodes were split between directors Louis J. Gasnier and George B. Seitz, with input from producers and brothers Theodore and Leopold Wharton. Gasnier acted and produced before directing, and is noteworthy for discovering comedian Max Linder. He was sent from France in 1912 to run the American branch of Pathé. Born in Boston in 1888, George Seitz turned to the stage after working as an illustrator. He was hired by Pathé as an actor and screenwriter in 1913.

Pathé faced stiff competition from other studios, who were turning out serials like *The Million Dollar Mystery* (1913). Both *The Perils of Pauline* and *The Exploits of Elaine* have extravagant production values and make use of sophisticated filming styles. Instead of repeating shots from fixed positions, for example, *Exploits* shifts camera angles based on the requirements of the story line. The cameraman also pans and tilts to frame action, a step away from the tableaux style preferred by other filmmakers. The camera is mounted on trucks, trains, boats, and planes, giving *Exploits* a sense of freedom missing from many shorts of the period.

Even so, outlandish plotting makes parts of *Exploits* hard to watch today. Characters fail to recognize voices or even faces, give secrets away at random, fail to hide vital clues, forget to call the police, and seemingly never learn from their mistakes. Elaine isn't allowed to be much more than a victim who escapes one trap to fall promptly into another. Wry humor, such as a doctor's cure of a con artist posing as a cripple, lifts some of the episodes. Hard-edged tension helps others. When criminals throw Elaine onto a library table in one chapter, their violence seems brutal even today. In some shots you can sense the filmmakers pushing toward a new style of cinema: in one instance, the camera starts in close on the Clutching Hand as he sprays a poison gas on the wall of a room, simultaneously panning with him and pulling back to reveal the entire set.

The first episode of *The Exploits of Elaine* ran about thirty minutes; subsequent episodes lasted between eighteen and twenty-two minutes. The serial was a tremendous hit in theaters, with some estimates placing receipts at over a million dollars. Publicity from the Hearst press helped considerably. The serial's episodes were adapted into stories that ran in over four hundred newspapers; they were collected into two illustrated novelizations that were published in 1915. Two sequels, *The New Exploits of Elaine* and *The Romance of Elaine*, appeared within months.

White starred in more serials until she signed a contract with William Fox in 1920 to make feature films. When these proved unsuccessful, she moved to France, where she remained until her death in 1938. Two almost entirely fictional films were made about her, both called *The Perils of Pauline* (1947 and 1967).

Gasnier's career hit its peak during the 1920s. In 1936, he directed *Tell Your Children*, later retitled *Reefer Madness*. Seitz made B-movies and shorts for Columbia and MGM; he also directed all but three of the Andy Hardy entries before dying in 1944.

The Italian

Paramount, 1915. Sound, B&W, 1.33. 70 minutes.
Cast: George Beban (Beppo Donnetti), Clara Williams (Annette Ancello), J. Frank Burke (Trudo Ancello), Fanny Midgley, Leo Willis.
Credits: Written by Thomas H. Ince & C. Gardner Sullivan. Produced by Thomas H. Ince.
Additional Credits: Directed by Reginald Barker.
Available: Flicker Alley DVD *Perils of the New Land* (2008). UPC: 617311673894.

One of the most significant features of the 1910s, *The Italian* had an enormous impact on filmmaking. It starred George Beban, a stage actor famous for his portrayals of Italian characters. Beban had written and starred in a famous vaudeville sketch about an immigrant who is mistaken for a member of the Black Hand criminal gangs. *The Alien* was subsequently filmed by Thomas H. Ince in a format that incorporated an actual live performance by Beban. (Director Raymond West shot footage that theater owners could project if Beban wasn't present.)

Ince and his writing partner C. Gardner Sullivan took credit for the story behind *The Italian*, but as film historian Kevin Brownlow has shown, the basic plot came from a 1913 IMP picture called *The Wop*. Ince had worked at IMP (the Independent Motion Picture Company), which was formed by Carl Laemmle in an attempt to break Edison's control of motion picture patents.

Ince's reputation has fluctuated over the years. Some contemporaries considered him the equal of Griffith, although Mary Pickford was not complimentary about him and William S. Hart, his big discovery, was uncharacteristically closed-mouthed about their relationship. Ince was the son of a comedian-turned-agent, and started performing on stage in 1888, when he was six. He appeared on Broadway before the turn of the twentieth century, and had his own stock company a few years later. He entered films through his wife Elinor Nell Kershaw, a star at Biograph, and began directing as an emergency replacement for an ill colleague.

After joining the New York Motion Picture Company, Ince moved to California, where he built Inceville, a studio near Santa Ynez Canyon. Ince streamlined production methods while reinvigorating the largely moribund Western genre. Overseeing a directing team that included Barker and future notables like Francis Ford, Fred Niblo, and Frank Borzage, he insisted on a complete script before shooting could start, often going so far as to dictate where the camera would be located. Sullivan provided many of these scripts.

Ince did not actually direct most of the films released by New York Motion Picture, although he often took credit for doing so and rarely gave credit to others. This has led some to question his actual input on films, or to suggest that he might better be compared to a "hands on" producer like David O. Selznick. But the best Ince films still have a signature style. They were large-scale productions with expensive sets and costumes and sophisticated camerawork. The Westerns at least were filled with expertly shot action that was not always expertly edited together.

As Brownlow has pointed out, films about the immigrant lower classes—in particular, Italians—constituted a significant genre, in fact almost a cycle. *The Black Hand* (1906), *The Organ Grinder* (1909), and *The Padrone's Ward* (1914) were, along with *The Wop*, just some of the films that focused on Italians. Sullivan's scenario was originally called *The Dago*, and that's how Ince tried to sell it to Charles Beban, who was starring in *The Sign of the Rose* on Broadway. The actor insisted on the title change, as well as a $7000 salary and a percentage of the profits.

The film has an unusual framing device, opening with a scene of Beban in his study reading a copy of a novel called *The Italian*. (Its cover claims that the writers are Ince and Sullivan; insert shots include some examples of amusingly purple prose.) As Beban reads, the screen dissolves to Italy, where the story itself opens. One function of this framing is to elevate the status of the story and its characters while erasing the stigma of their ethnic origins. If Beban, wearing a dressing gown in a well-appointed study, can appreciate *The Italian*, why can't you? The entire sequence—with its smooth camera pans, its inserted close-ups of Beban's eyes and hands, its use of reaction shots, its varied camera angles—is at the upper tier of filmmaking sophistication for 1914.

When the film shifts to Italy, we're suddenly back in the predawn era of filmmaking, with static location shots and actors who fling their arms to the sky. Fortunately, Beban had technique as well as an appealing screen presence, and the longer he appears in frame, the more comfortable director Reginald Barker gets. Beban is Beppo, a happy-go-lucky gondolier who learns that he might lose the farmer's daughter to a wealthy merchant. He travels to New York in steerage in order to become a bootblack, and coincidentally, to secure the Italian ghetto vote for Irish mobster Corrigan. The actor's style is boisterous but grounded in psychological truth. He is also an astute judge of his audience. He knows when to appeal to viewers' sympathies and when to pull back, something that could not always be said about his contemporaries. The cinematography throughout is distinguished by its strong compositions and intricate exposures, with striking silhouette effects and dramatic lighting schemes incorporating broad swaths of shadow.

The Italian glosses over many details, such as how deeply Beban's character is connected to the Irish mob, or how he could afford to send for his fiancée so quickly. Once Annette (played by Clara Williams) arrives, the melodramatic elements of the story kick into gear. But even these are handled with an energy and conviction that is unusual for the time. The filmmakers don't shy away from sensationalistic details—the flies that infest a baby's milk, the slumbering drunks lining the wall of a saloon, the casual brutality of the police—but they provide them for the sake of the story, not just for shock value.

The film falls firmly into a tradition of tolerance that Hollywood continues to preach to this day. Beban's character is the equal of any American he meets, except for a poverty that is not his fault. In fact, his sense of morality and justice is stronger than the people who take advantage of him. This was a difficult message for mainstream America to accept, and far different from the jingoism that would fill the screen during World War I.

The loose, confident style used in *The Italian* was influential as well. It marked a shift away from the "classical" vocabulary employed by D.W. Griffith, and encouraged other filmmakers to develop more nuanced approaches to cinematography and editing. Brownlow notes that the film was not a box-office success, and was not shown in Italy, but its impact has continued over the years. Charlie Chaplin's *The Immigrant* (1917) uses similar shipboard shots. The tenement stairs Beppo climbs are echoed in *7th Heaven* (1927) and *The Cameraman* (1929). The bootblack in Elia Kazan's *America America* (1963) shows the same enthusiasm as Beban, while a shot of Beban in jail bears an uncanny resemblance to shots in Samuel Fuller's *Shock Corridor* (1963).

When *The Italian* was released in January 1915, Ince was still a year away from his signature film *Civilization*, but his producing methods were already changing the film industry. Beban made another Italian-themed film, *One More American* (1918), directed by William deMille, before branching out into writing, producing, and directing. He died in 1928 after a horse-riding accident.

The Birth of a Nation

Epoch Producing Corporation, 1915. Silent, B&W. 1.37. 187 minutes.
Cast includes: Lillian Gish (Elsie Stoneman), Mae Marsh (Flora Cameron), Robert Harron (Tod Stoneman), Henry B. Walthall (Col. Ben Cameron), Miriam Cooper (Margaret Cameron), Walter Long (Gus), Ralph Lewis (Austin Stoneman), Spottiswoode Aitken (Dr. Cameron), Josephine Crowell, Constance Talmadge, Elmer Clifton (Phil Stoneman), Mary Alden (Lydia Brown), George Siegmann (Silas Lynch), Wallace Reid (Jeff [the blacksmith]), J.A. [George] Beranger (Wade Cameron), Josephine Crowell (Mrs. Cameron), Donald Crisp (Gen. Ulysses S. Grant), Raoul Walsh (John Wilkes Booth), Fred Turner, Sam de Grasse, Vera Lewis, Alfred Paget, Seena Owen, Tully Marshall, Elmo Lincoln, John Ford, Howard Gaye, Margery Wilson, Eugene Pallette.
Credits: Directed by D.W. Griffith. Scenario by Griffith, Frank Woods, based on the novel and play *The Clansman* by Thomas Dixon, with additional material from *The Leopard's Spots* by Dixon.
Additional Credits: Director of photography: G.W. Bitzer. Additional cinematography: Karl Brown. Edited by Griffith, Jimmie Smith, Rose Smith. Score: Joseph Carl Breil. Assistants: Raoul Walsh, Christy Cabanne, Erich von Stroheim. Released February 8, 1915.
Available: Kino Video DVD (2002). UPC: 738329026622.

Between 1909 and 1913, D.W. Griffith directed hundreds of one-reel movies for Biograph, including two 1909 Registry titles, *Lady Helen's Escapade* and *A Corner in Wheat.* Chafing under Biograph's limited budgets, and determined to make larger, more important films, he signed a contract with Harry Aitken and took over the Fine Arts studio on Sunset Boulevard in Los Angeles. Like most American filmmakers, he was surprised and influenced by Italian spectacle films like *Cabiria* (1914), and sought a way to incorporate their effects into more familiar material. After experimenting with feature-length films like *Judith of Bethulia* (1914), based on the biblical character,

Griffith searched for a patriotic subject that could support an even larger production. He settled on *The Clansman*, a novel by Thomas Dixon, a former Baptist minister and an unrepentant racist.

Dixon had already adapted his novel, a sequel to *The Leopard's Spots*, for the stage. (Griffith's wife had played in a road company version.) The books and plays were enormous hits, in part because they dealt with the war from a Southern point of view, but also because of their segregationist themes. They coincided neatly with Griffith's beliefs that the South had been betrayed after the war by Northern carpetbaggers.

Griffith had dealt with the war before, notably in *In Old Kentucky* (1909) and *The Informer* (1914), as had other filmmakers, including Thomas Ince with *The Battle of Gettysburg* (1913). But this time Griffith set out to show just what fighting was like, and how awful defeat was for Southern whites. Unfortunately, Griffith's background left him ill-suited to address the racial issues swirling around the plot. Culturally isolated, indifferent to a great deal of contemporary art and criticism, insular to a degree that seems incredible today, he was a nineteenth-century artist working in a twentieth-century medium.

Griffith started *Birth* without a script, although he worked on a treatment with co-scenarist Frank Woods. It's possible that he didn't intend the film to be racist, but for today's sensibilities, the plot he and Woods concocted is appalling. Griffith blamed the North, blacks, and politicians for destroying the Southern way of life, which, in his view, only incidentally included plantations worked by slaves. By reducing characters—no matter how vividly evoked—to stereotypes, and complex situations to political slogans, Griffith refused to deal with the true meaning of the war.

The director said as much in his unpublished autobiography. As biographer Richard Schickel noted, Griffith's main narrative strategy in *Birth* was to get to a point that demanded a "ride to the rescue." (His fame was based in part on his suspenseful cross-cutting and tight editing.) "I could see a chance to do this ride-to-the-rescue on a grand scale," Griffith wrote. "Instead of saving one poor little Nell of the Plains, this ride would be to save a nation."

Griffith cast the film from his stock company favorites, including Mae Marsh, who would figure prominently in his next film, *Intolerance*; here, she's a little too old to be playing a naive daughter on a South Carolina plantation. The other two female leads went to Miriam Cooper, playing Mae Marsh's older sister, and Lillian Gish, who portrayed the daughter of Austin Stoneman (Ralph Lewis), a stand-in for the abolitionist leader Thaddeus Stevens. Silas Lynch, a mulatto and Stevens's underling, was played by George Siegmann, Griffith's chief assistant on this and most of his other films. Henry B. Walthall played a quiet, dignified "Little Colonel" who by accident invented the Ku Klux Klan.

Birth was a sort of launching pad for an entire generation of actors and filmmakers. You can spot Wallace Reid, a major star of the 1920s and later the victim of a drug scandal; Elmo Lincoln, the screen's first Tarzan; Raoul Walsh, here a dashing John Wilkes Booth and the director of Registry films *White Heat* (1949) and *Regeneration* (1915); and future directors John Ford and Christy Cabanne.

Griffith started shooting *Birth* on the Fourth of July in 1914. Filming took place mostly in and around his studio in Los Angeles. Before he finished four months later, Griffith shot about 150,000 feet of film, which he edited down to 13,000. He had a special score compiled by Joseph Carl Breil—a collage of folk tunes, martial melodies, and linking musical passages. The film was released through Epoch Producing Corporation, which was formed specifically for this project. Griffith arranged for sneak previews of *The Clansman* on January 1 and 2, 1915. A month later, the film had its official premiere at Clune's Auditorium in Los Angeles.

Griffith and his backers knew that his film would need massive publicity to make back its budget, let alone a profit. Thomas Dixon managed to get President Woodrow S. Wilson, an old college classmate, to blurb the film. "It is like writing history with Lightning," he said after a special White House screening. Griffith initiated a "road show" style of exhibition, charging premium prices for tickets in a move to equate his work with legitimate theater. Souvenir programs, ushers in period uniforms, and a full orchestra added to the hype. The film played for seven months at Clune's. By the time it reached New York in March, it had its current title, *The Birth of a Nation*.

It also incited controversy that dogs the film to this day. The recently formed National Association for the Advancement of Colored People (NAACP) arranged protests against its exhibition across the country. (It succeeding in getting *Birth* banned in Ohio.) Griffith professed surprise at the reaction, and in a way the rest of his career—especially his next feature, *Intolerance* (1916)—can be seen as a response to how *Birth* was received. He tinkered with the film for months after its opening, adding a prologue, "A Plea for the Art of the Motion Picture," cutting especially inflammatory scenes. He oversaw a revised version that was released in 1921, and a 1930 version with a synchronized score and sound effects.

The big set pieces in the film are still impressive. A prolonged skirmish originally based on the Battle of Petersburg is a remarkable sequence, as is the burning of Atlanta and Lincoln's assassination at Ford's Theatre. But much of *Birth* is meaningless spectacle, Griffith too in love with his footage to shape or even cut it. The acting is disappointing as well; the large gestures Griffith elicited in his Biograph days seem too broad in *Birth*. In ten-minute shorts, one-note acting might be acceptable; for almost three hours, it becomes monotonous.

In the second half of the film, as blacks take over the South, Griffith concocts poisonous reasons for whites to retaliate, mostly based on the threat of interracial sex. In one sequence shot at California's Big Bear Lake, a woman hurls herself from a cliff rather than submit to a soldier (played by a white actor in blackface). The only solution? Robed vigilantes who ride to save Gish from the clutches of a mulatto, and who prevent blacks from voting in the next election.

In Griffith's defense, *Birth* is by no means the only film to treat the KKK kindly. *A Mormon Maid* (1915) has Klan characters, and even Mary Pickford donned robes in *The Heart o' the Hills* (1919). And *The Birth of a Nation* had almost universally excellent reviews. (One smart exception in the *New Republic* was written by Francis Hackett.) It was the first filmgoing experience for many people, and their first indication that film could be treated as an art form equal to other media. By some accounts, it was the most profitable silent feature ever made. And with *Birth*, for better or worse, Griffith established the template for what would become Hollywood's approach to historical incidents: epic in scale, but filled with empty spectacle; grand themes, but simplistic narratives; as much attention paid to promotion as to execution. Griffith's influence resounds in the Biblical epics of the 1950s and '60s, in bloated Westerns like *Duel in the Sun* (1946) and in cheesy historical exploitation like *Alexander* (2004).

Fatty's Tintype Tangle

Mutual, 1915. Silent, B&W, 1.33. 20 minutes.

Cast: Roscoe Arbuckle, Louise Fazenda, Norma Nichols, May Wells, Edgar Kennedy, Frank Hayes, Glen Cavender, Bobby Dunn, John Bordeaux.

Credits: Directed by Roscoe Arbuckle. Produced by Mack Sennett. A Keystone Film Company production. Released July 26, 1915.

Available: Laughsmith Entertainment DVD *The Forgotten Films of Roscoe "Fatty" Arbuckle* (2005).

At the peak of his fame, Roscoe Arbuckle was one of the best-loved comedians in the country. Born in 1887, he was working in theater by the age of eight. After a decade of scrambling for jobs, he went on the road from 1903 to 1913, receiving a broad theatrical training across the United States. He made some film appearances as early at 1909, but it wasn't until he began working at Keystone in 1913 that he devoted himself to the new medium.

Trained by Mack Sennett and Henry "Pathe" Lehrman (who directed his Keystone debut, *The Gangsters*), Arbuckle quickly mastered the basics of silent film comedy. Within a year he had honed his screen persona in a series of almost weekly one-reelers. He started to take control of his films, forming a stock company of actors and technicians, overseeing scripts, and eventually directing his shorts.

Arbuckle was a large but uncommonly graceful man who played his girth for laughs. His skills as a dancer and mime helped him become a leading man, but it was his sense of humor that made him a star. In order to stand out in the flood of screen comedies, Arbuckle needed to brand himself for moviegoers. In his films, his characters were brash but intelligent, outgoing but still shy, inventive but prone to weakness.

With limited budgets and shooting schedules, he was forced to play variations on the same basic situations week after week, sometimes recycling the same sets. Arbuckle often appeared as a worker—a chef or mechanic, for example—but he also played cops and aristocrats. He was one of the few comics who could hold his own on screen with Charlie Chaplin, and in 1914's *The Rounders*, he's arguably the more natural, and funnier, performer. Teamed with Mabel Normand, a talented, exuberant actress who served to make him seem more human, Arbuckle specialized in the sort of henpecked husbands Jackie Gleason would play in *The Honeymooners*—guileless troublemakers and rascals who upset decorum even as they tried to fit into society.

Comedians like Arbuckle and Chaplin helped refine Mack Sennett's knockabout slapstick. The chases and pratfalls were still there, but both comedians emphasized characterizations in their shorts. *Fatty's Tintype Tangle* is typical for its time. It features a philandering husband, a jealous wife, a suspicious mother-in-law, assorted rubes, a suspicious cop, and a sunny day in the park. Sets and props are minimal, the camera is placed functionally, and the story devolves into pratfalls and slapstick at every opportunity. Characters fall into bathtubs, over benches, out of windows and onto telephone wires. But Arbuckle, who at this point in his career was determining the content and style of his films, was careful to establish his characters as individuals with distinct personalities. Unlike many contemporary comedies, the story makes narrative sense, with scenes that build tension as Arbuckle cuts from one story line to another.

The camerawork may be perfunctory, but the look of the film is first-rate, with gags staged clearly and chases put together logically. The performances are restrained by slapstick standards, and the actors are always aware that the characters they are playing are trying to maintain semblances of dignity. Everyone involved seems to be delighted to spin comedy out of the tiniest of plot ideas. Like Arbuckle's best shorts, the joy and excitement in *Fatty's Tintype Tangle* is palpable.

Arbuckle's interests and his approach to comedy can seem a bit peculiar today, but they also make his films more unpredictable and charming than those of many of his rivals. He enjoyed dressing in drag, not to shock viewers, but because women's clothes made him look funnier. He also liked gags that were alternately subversive and violent. His attraction to knockabout slapstick makes sense given his training, but in films like *Good Night, Nurse!* (1918), the humor is frightening and ghoulish.

Like Chaplin, Arbuckle outgrew Sennett's Keystone studio. He moved to New York, where he could film with greater freedom. Producer Joseph Schenck set up the Comique Film Corporation to finance his films. Schenck later worked out a deal with Paramount to star Arbuckle in a half-dozen feature films, the first silent comedian to make such a move. Arbuckle's films for his own studio

were a marked improvement over the Sennett pictures, with a greater attention to plotting and acting. More important, Arbuckle began exploiting the capabilities of film in ways that Sennett would not. He developed intricate cause-and-effect jokes, situations in which a simple pratfall would lead to greater complications, setting off chain reactions that built to hysterical proportions.

He also began a screen partnership in 1917 with Buster Keaton, a move that in itself would assure his place in film history. They paired for almost two dozen shorts before Keaton enlisted in the Army and was sent to Europe during World War I. The collaboration benefited both performers: Keaton learned the ins and outs of filmmaking while Arbuckle learned to restrain his acting and work more on scripts. By the time Keaton returned, Arbuckle had moved beyond shorts, and was preparing his first feature for Paramount.

After completing *Leap Year* (1921), Arbuckle invited friends to a party in a San Francisco hotel suite. At some point a bit actress named Virginia Rappe went into convulsions. She died in a hospital three days later. Arbuckle was charged with manslaughter. The press, led by Hearst papers, exaggerated the party into a full-blown sex-and-sadism orgy. Arbuckle's weight, his tendency to play immature adolescents, and other circumstances surrounding Rappe's death all contributed to a scandal of unprecedented proportions.

Arbuckle's innocence was indisputable, but he was forced to undergo three trials before being acquitted. Revisionists have tried to portray Rappe as the real villain of the story by smearing her reputation. There is no need to demonize her to see the injustice behind Arbuckle's arrest. Most film scholars concede that he had nothing to do with the death, and may not even have known that Rappe was at the party. The jury at his third trial apologized in public for what they called a miscarriage of justice, but the damage had been done.

Leap Year was never officially released in the United States, and Paramount quickly dropped plans for Arbuckle's next three features. He was not only out of work, but would not be hired by any studio in Hollywood. A few performers—notably, Keaton, Mary Pickford, and Eddie Cantor—stood by him, and arranged for him to direct (under pseudonyms) a few shorts and features. It wasn't until the 1930s that Arbuckle was allowed to appear on screen again. He adapted to sound technology fairly well. *Buzzin' Around* (1933), a short he made for Warner Bros., reworks some of the material from his Comique days, with his nephew Al St. John, a member of the Comique troupe, back to help. But his friends could see that he was a broken man. He died of a heart attack within a year.

Regeneration

Fox Film Corporation, 1915. Silent, B&W, 1.33. 72 minutes.

Cast: Rockcliffe Fellowes (Owen), Anna Q. Nilsson (Marie Deering), William Sheer (Skinny), Carl Harbaugh (Ames, the District Attorney), James Marcus (Jim Conway), Maggie Weston (Maggie Conway), John McCann (Owen, age 10), H. McCoy (Owen, age 17).

Credits: Directed by R.A. [Raoul] Walsh. Adapted from Owen Kildare's *My Mamie Rose* by R.A. Walsh, Carl Harbaugh. Produced by William Fox. Photography by George Benoit.

Additional Cast: Peggy Barn.

Additional Credits: Based on the stage adaptation *The Regeneration* by Owen Kildare and Walter C. Hackett. Released September 13, 1915.

Other Versions: Remade by Universal in 1924 as *Fools' Highway*, directed by Irving Cummings.

Available: Image Entertainment DVD (2001). UPC: 0-14381-0510-2-5.

In *Each Man in His Time,* an autobiography filled with tall tales, Raoul Walsh spent more time describing a shot that never existed than the actual impact of what he called the first feature about gangsters, *Regeneration.*

Born in 1887 in New York City, Walsh enjoyed a privileged upbringing in which he met Mark Twain, Buffalo Bill Cody, and Edwin Booth. He left home at an early age, took part in a cattle drive, was a miner, and witnessed a hanging. His first stage job was in an adaptation of Thomas Dixon's *The Clansman.* Returning to New York City, he acted in films for Pathé and Biograph. D.W. Griffith brought him to Hollywood, where he got by as an extra, a stunt man, and a horse wrangler.

Walsh claimed that his first directing effort was *Home from the Sea* in 1915 for a company called Fine Arts, although he is now credited with at least a half-dozen shorts before that. Walsh also worked with industry pioneer Christy Cabanne and screenwriter Frank E. Woods, both of whom would figure in his later career. His most important assignment that year was as assistant director to Griffith on *The Birth of a Nation*, in which he played a small but crucial part as John Wilkes Booth.

In Walsh's version, Winfield Sheehand, a vice-president of the Fox Film Corporation, approached him about a job. Walsh demanded ten times his current salary, and when Sheehand agreed, was suddenly a contract director for William Fox. Walsh's first script for Fox, written with actor and comedian Carl Harbaugh, was an adaptation of *My Mamie Rose*, an autobiography by Owen Kildare. (After writing gags for Buster Keaton and The Little Rascals and directing shorts, Harbaugh appeared in bit parts in Walsh's films up to his death in 1960.)

Kildare, who died in 1911, was an earnest reformer with a strong spiritual streak. He wrote a stage version of his book called *The Regeneration* with Walter Hackett, but that had closed in 1908 after thirty-nine performances. Walsh described the plot to *Regeneration* as "basic": "She falls in love with him. From there, play it by ear."

As you might expect from someone who befriended Jack London and Wyatt Earp, Walsh was always openly dismissive of sentiment, despite resorting to it at every opportunity in his work. The director saw Kildare's story in terms of a William S. Hart plot, with hero Owen as a "good bad man" who just needed a reason—usually female—to drop crime and go straight. Owen is one in a long line of misunderstood, self-sacrificing characters Walsh would use throughout his career. Think of Humphrey Bogart as "Mad Dog" Roy Earle in *High Sierra* (1941), or James Cagney as dentist "Biff" Grimes in *The Strawberry Blonde* (1941), or Wallace Beery as saloon owner Chuck Connors in *The Bowery* (1933)—all brawling, blustering men who fall apart over the first woman who pays them any attention.

This was the film debut for Rockcliffe Fellowes, a tall, dark, handsome type with smoldering eyes (highlighted here with plenty of makeup) and an oddly inexpressive face. Walsh seemed more in tune with the actors playing Owen at younger ages, and with the rogues' gallery of character actors he used to fill in backgrounds. The real casting coup in *Regeneration* was Anna Q. Nilsson. A veteran of some seventy films by the time Walsh was shooting, she had left her birthplace in Sweden to model in New York City, winning her first film role a year later in 1911. Walsh described her as "ravishing," and made good use of her wide, frightened eyes.

Despite the publicity hype surrounding it, *Regeneration* has very little to do with organized crime and a lot to do with personal redemption.

Walsh depicts four criminal incidents in the movie: rolling a drunk, knifing a cop, an attempted rape, and a shooting—but none could be considered gang-related. Set in saloons, tenement slums, and settlement houses, the film assumes a harder edge than do melodramas of the time. Walsh adds a documentary atmosphere to Dickensian scenes of child abuse, but is careful to offer viewers a way out of the dead-end reality that these characters would face in real life. Although the ending is a narrative mess, it does exonerate Owen, making it clear that society is at fault for his misbehavior. *Regeneration* is actually closer in spirit to *Alias Jimmy Valentine*, which was released seven months earlier, than to a genuine gangster movie like Griffith's *The Musketeers of Pig Alley* (1912).

It's clear that Walsh borrowed a lot from Griffith, in particular his cross-cutting among several plot lines at the climax, his symbolic insert shots of nature, and his reverential treatment of women. But Walsh used close-ups in a different manner, to broaden our understanding of his characters rather than to make strictly narrative points. (He even used the equivalent of a zoom, tracking the camera in to a tight shot of child actor John McCann while simultaneously irising in on his face.) The camerawork in *Regeneration* feels freer, more organic, than many movies of the period. When he could, Walsh used real locations with real people, but the majority of the film was shot on sets. The visual centerpiece—a fire aboard a crowded excursion boat—is exciting, even if conceptually it wasn't worked out very well. It also led to one of Walsh's more amusing fibs, this one involving extras without underwear and editors feverishly trying to cover up their bodies on the negative.

The film was a box-office sensation, meriting a re-release four years later and a remake after that. Walsh's career was firmly established, even though he enlisted in the Army Signal Corps after the film's release. He went on to work with Theda Bara, and directed *The Conqueror*, a biopic about Sam Houston that was William Farnum's movie debut. This brought him back into contact with Douglas Fairbanks, leading to *The Thief of Bagdad* (1924).

Even so, *Regeneration* as we now see it could have disappeared forever were it not for archivist David Shepherd, who purchased the only surviving original print when it surfaced in 1976.

The Cheat

Paramount, 1915. Silent, B&W, 1.33. 59 minutes.
Cast: Fannie Ward (Edith Hardy), Sessue Hayakawa (Hishuru Tori/Haka Arakau), Jack Dean (Richard Hardy).
Credits: Scenario by Hector Turnbull and Jeanie Macpherson. Produced by Cecil B. DeMille. Photographed by Alvin Wyckoff. Art director: Wilfred Buckland.
Additional Cast: James Neill (Jones), Utaka Abe (Tori's/Arakau's valet), Dana Ong (District Attorney), Hazel Childers (Mrs. Reynolds), Judge Arthur H. Williams (Courtroom judge).
Additional Credits: Directed by Cecil B. DeMille. Executive producer: Jesse L. Lasky. Edited by Cecil B. DeMille. Released December 13, 1915
Other Versions: Remade in 1923 and 1931; and in 1937 as *Forfaiture*.
Available: Kino Video DVD (2002). UPC: 7-38329-02442-0.

In his autobiography, Cecil B. DeMille described his childhood as equal parts Victorian melodrama and Horatio Alger success story. Those two elements make up a large part of his creative output, and account for much of his popularity as a filmmaker. DeMille's ability to transform anything into the ripest melodrama is the mark of his genius as a showman. His willingness to adapt new technology to the service of hoary plot lines made him one of the most imitated filmmakers of his generation.

Cecil B. DeMille—and to a lesser extent his older brother William—succeeded in theater by aligning themselves with big-pocket producers and by staging theatrical chestnuts as extravaganzas. DeMille's introduction into film was not auspicious. In partnership with Jesse L. Lasky and Samuel Goldfish (later Goldwyn), DeMille traveled to Los Angeles to shoot *The Squaw Man* (released 1914). It became a box-office hit largely as a result of tireless publicity, but was so poor on a technical level that DeMille reshot it four years later. Headquartered in Hollywood, DeMille turned out thirteen films in 1915, including versions of *The Girl of the Golden West*, *The Warrens of Virginia*, *Carmen*, and other "presold" titles, often editing and helping with the screenwriting. He formed lifelong creative relationships, relying on his brother for advice about writing and occasionally about directing.

Cecil took credit for developing Jeanie Macpherson, an actress who became the director's preferred screenwriter for the next twenty-five years. William, in charge of the burgeoning "story department" at the studio, hired Hector Turnbull, a drama critic at the New York *Tribune*, and his sister Margaret. Cecil disliked Turnbull's first script, *Temptation*, but called the scenario for *The Cheat* so superior that "to this day film historians, especially in Europe, regard *The Cheat* as a landmark in the development of cinema."

The Cheat was sensational on every level. Not only did DeMille succeed in casting Fannie Ward—one of studio owner Jesse L. Lasky's contract players—in her biggest screen role, he also turned Sessue Hayakawa into a full-fledged star. Born Kintaro Hayakawa in 1889 in Japan to a family with a samurai heritage, he attempted hara-kiri after being forced out of a naval academy. Hayakawa studied Zen Buddhism at a monastery, then traveled to the United States, where he graduated from the University of Chicago. On returning home, he decided to become an actor after seeing the Japanese Theatre in Los Angeles. His staging of *The Typhoon* won him a film contract with Thomas Ince as well as a wedding with his co-star, Tsuru Aoki.

Hayakawa brought to the screen a technique of restraint and a pride in his racial heritage. He attributed his acting style to his samurai background: "I was always taught that it was disgraceful to show emotion . . . I purposely tried to show nothing by my face." This was only the second film for Fannie Ward, a stage star noted for her youthful beauty and expressive eyes. Her technique here is broad at first, but notice how she scales back her performance once her scenes with Hayakawa take place. (She's also very easy to lip-read.)

At this point in his career DeMille did not deal subtly with actors, but under the white-hot pace of production his grasp of film matured tremendously. In his autobiography he noted that at the time he was directing two films at once. He worked from nine to five on *The Cheat*, ate and rested for three hours, then worked from eight until two in the morning on *The Golden Chance*.

The Cheat boasts an advanced production design courtesy of Wilfred Buckland—like DeMille, a veteran of David Belasco stage plays. The film was made during a period when the industry changed from shooting in sunlight to shooting on roofed, interior sets with artificial light. Buckland's sets worked in sunlight (critics cited their "richness"), but they were just as effective with what became known as "Lasky lighting." Developed in part by cinematographer Alvin Wyckoff, Lasky lighting was low-key, with strong shadows used

for dramatic effect (DeMille called it "Rembrandt lighting," and admitted that it was inspired in part by the work of German stage director Max Reinhardt). For example, Hayakawa is introduced sitting at his desk, lit by a burning brazier that casts sinister shadows on his face. In addition, Wyckoff and DeMille used silhouette lighting for its dramatic effects. They also began moving the camera.

The film had so much impact at the time because DeMille was able to charge modest situations with life-or-death implications. The basic premise is simple: husband Dick Hardy (Jack Dean) is on the verge of a major deal, but his finances are stretched. His flighty wife Edith (Ward) insists on overspending to maintain her social status. She invests charity money on a harebrained get-rich-quick scheme, then turns to unctuous art collector Hishuru Tori (Hayakawa) for a loan when the deal falls through.

DeMille staged the film's most shocking scene carefully. He starts out by showing Tori branding objets d'art with his personal seal. DeMille returns to the seal twice more, telegraphing his big moment fearlessly, aware that viewers were waiting for it. He shot this material with a dexterity missing from the rest of the film, which is as static and flat as most movies of the period. But at this moment, DeMille and his colleagues suddenly reveal film's potential, how mature and complex the medium would quickly become. With its dramatic lighting, a camera following the action by panning and tilting, explicit sexuality, and violence—far more shocking than viewers then or today could expect—it's hard to see how a contemporary filmmaker could improve on DeMille's technique.

The courtroom scene that follows is on many levels sillier than anything that came before, but again DeMille's decisions, his taste and judgment, indicate the future of movies. *The Cheat*'s trial has a courtroom packed with spectators who resemble the mob clamoring at Pilate for blood. After a wonderful pan of the jury and some astute reverse angle shots (and racist jingoism typical of the time), DeMille is willing to concede that perhaps Tori isn't getting a fair trial, and that perhaps no Asian in America could.

The lurid story line, Hayakawa's acting, and the film's lighting and set design all influenced other directors. But staging a climactic spectacle to wipe plot inconsistencies and illogical narratives away was a lesson filmmakers really pounced on. The ending to *The Cheat* would be "borrowed" by everyone from Frank Capra and Alfred Hitchcock to scores of lesser directors. It's no wonder that filmmakers like Abel Gance cite DeMille as inspiration.

The Japanese community objected to *The Cheat* forcefully, so much so that when Paramount re-released the film in 1918, Sessue Hayakawa's Hishuru Tori suddenly turned into Haka Arakau, a "Burmese ivory king." It was still banned in Great Britain and not distributed to Japan. *The Cheat* was remade several times: as a vehicle for Pola Negri in 1923; as a sound film with Tallulah Bankhead in 1931; and in French in 1937 as *Forfaiture*. This version was the basis of an opera by Camille Erlanger, perhaps the first instance of a film being transposed to that medium.

DeMille's post-*Cheat* career is notable for its peaks and valleys. He tried to top himself until no contemporary story could satisfy his needs. He also turned himself into a spokesman for the industry, one of its most celebrated and recognizable figures. (The image of a director wearing jodhpurs and brandishing a megaphone is based largely on DeMille.) He continued making melodramas for the rest of his career, often dressing them in period trappings, while his tolerance evaporated and his politics turned abhorrent—much like the showmen who gave him his start.

Hell's Hinges

Triangle, 1916. Silent, B&W with tints, 1.33. 64 minutes.
Cast: William S. Hart (Blaze Tracy), Clara Williams (Faith Henley), Jack Standing (Reverend Richard Henley), Alfred Hollingsworth (Silk Miller), Louise Glaum (Dolly), Robert McKim (Clergyman), J. Frank Burke (Zeb Taylor).
Credits: Directed by William S. Hart and Charles Swickard. Story and screenplay by C. Gardner Sullivan. Cinematography by Joseph August. Title artist: Mon Randall.
Additional Cast: Robert Korman, Jack Gilbert, Jean Hersholt, Wheeler Oakman.
Additional Credits: Produced by Kay-Bee and by the New York Motion Picture Company. Production dates: September 4 to October 29, 1915. Premiered in New York City on February 3, 1916.
Available: Image Entertainment DVD *Treasures from American Film Archives* (2000). UPC: 0-14381-9706-2-3.

William S. Hart, the lead and co-director of *Hell's Hinges*, was one of the most popular of the silent Western stars. A native of Newburgh, New York, Hart was probably born at the end of the Civil War, although sources range from 1862 to 1872. His father ground millstones, an occupation that led his family throughout the Midwest. Hart grew up on the plains, was conversant in Sioux, and buried a brother in a prairie grave. He experienced firsthand the transformation of the West from buffalo herds on open range to ranches served by railroads.

Hart's father eventually settled in New York, where Hart studied acting with F.F. MacKay. He boarded with Thomas Ince when both were struggling, and became the protégé of Madame Hortense Rhea. At first specializing in Shakespearean roles, Hart had star turns in *The Squaw Man*, *The Trail of the Lonesome Pine*, and *The Virginian*—plays that would later become hit Westerns.

A member of various road companies, Hart ran across Ince again in 1914; his former roommate had become the premiere producer in the film industry. Ince entered movies in 1910 after abandoning vaudeville. Within a year he was directing stars like Mary Pickford. Ince's breakthrough came when he saw how producers could have more control over films than directors. At the time, directors functioned as producers anyway, buying stories, overseeing scriptwriting and casting, arranging for sets to be built, and more. Ince gave up directing (more or less) to concentrate on what he saw as the critical elements in films: scripts and stars. In the process, he helped develop a template for how the studio system would operate.

Ince joined Charlie Chaplin, Mack Sennett, and D.W. Griffith at Triangle, the first motion picture company to go public. Ince bought a Wild West show to have the personnel on hand to film Westerns continuously, and purchased 20,000 acres on which to stage his productions.

Ince gave Hart parts in a couple of Westerns. The actor was dismayed at how the frontier was being depicted in movies. Hart saw the West as harsh, and strove to portray it that way. He paid particular attention to the logistics of life on the frontier. How horses were hitched, for example, or the clothes ranch hands wore. On screen, Hart had a face like granite, and he moved with the deliberate precision of someone trained on the stage. But he understood the value of restraint, of allowing a pose to do the work of an expression. Viewers could read their own thoughts into his visage.

Hart is more noteworthy for the ambiguous characters he portrayed. Having played Messala in a hit Broadway production of *Ben-Hur*, Hart knew how villains could fascinate audiences. Hart's Western heroes had motives that couldn't be fixed. They were men just as likely to fight with a sheriff or judge as with a rustler or card sharp. Unlike earlier straight-arrow Western figures, Hart's characters would drink, smoke, and scuffle. He could be a killer, crook, or fugitive.

During the course of his movies, Hart would be faced with moral choices that called into question his earlier actions. Ultimately Hart would choose good over evil, but even then only on his own terms. It's a role that has figured in Westerns ever since, from John Wayne's gunslinger in *Stagecoach* (1939) to Clint Eastwood's Man with No Name in Sergio Leone's trilogy of spaghetti Westerns.

Hart's formula was very popular at the box office, and at the height of his career he was turning out at many as eleven films a year, often writing as well as directing and starring in them. Even by his standards, *Hell's Hinges* is an unusually austere, even stark, Western. The film's moral tone is apparent right from the opening scenes, as a weak, unworthy minister and his devout sister Faith are exiled to the town of Placer Center, otherwise known as Hell's Hinges—"a good place to ride wide of." Faith's idyllic urban life is replaced by one of hardship and strife on the plains. Her introduction to her new home is a deadly gunfight. In her first encounter with the people of Hell's Hinges, her brother is almost run out of town.

Faith and her brother help set up the film's central conflict, between saloon owner Silk Miller and self-described killer Blaze Tracy. As Tracy, Hart is forced to seek retribution against Faith's persecutors, and it's a mark of the filmmakers' skill that they can evoke Biblical terms so confidently. The firestorm that erupts in the town carries real emotional weight, while delivering all the death and destruction an audience could want.

The film's cast is unusually effective for a period when performances tended toward broad histrionics. Its production values are superb, in particular the camerawork by Joseph August, who would go on to shoot films for John Ford, Howard Hawks, and George Cukor, among others. In its style and tone, if not its actual plot, *Hell's Hinges* points the way to films like *High Plains Drifter* (1973), *Pale Rider* (1985), and other Westerns about moral retribution. Then as now people faced choices about their lives that couldn't be reduced to simple terms like good versus evil.

The film was a highpoint for Hart. His career would enter a swift decline after 1916. He broke with Ince, convinced that the producer was cheating him, and successfully fought a paternity suit that nevertheless took years to settle. While his last film, *Tumbleweeds* (1925), was a success, his grim, humorless character had by then been supplanted by livelier, less stoic stars like Tom Mix and Buck Jones.

In 1924 Ince was fatally injured on a yacht belonging to William Randolph Hearst. Gossip-mongers at the time claimed that Ince was killed due to his relationship with Hearst's mistress Marion Davies, an interpretation amplified in the film *The Cat's Meow* (2001).

Where Are My Children?

Universal, 1916. Silent, B&W with tints, 1.33. 64 minutes.

Cast: Tyrone Power (Richard Walton), Helen Riaume (Mrs. Walton), A.D. Blake (Roger, her brother), Marie Walcamp (Mrs. Carlo [Mrs. Brandt]), Juan De La Cruz (Dr. Herman Malfit), René Rogers (Lillian), Cora Drew (Her mother, the Waltons' housekeeper), C. Norman Hammond (Dr. William Horner), William J. Hope (Eugenic husband), Marjorie Blynn (Eugenic wife), William Haben (Dr. Gilding).

Credits: Produced and directed by Lois Weber and Phillips Smalley. Written by Lois Weber. Based on a story by Lucy Payton and Franklyn Hall. Photographers: Al Siegler, Stephen Norton. A Universal Film Manufacturing Company release.

Additional Credits: Opened April 16, 1916.

Available: Image Entertainment DVD (2007) *Treasures III: Social Issues in American Film, 1900–1934*. ISBN: 978-0-9747009-4-9. UPC: 0-14381-3827-2-3.

"Message dramas" played a significant part in the early film industry. Often tied into reform movements, like *The Land Beyond the Sunset* (1912), they were also closely aligned with purely commercial exploitation. The reform aspects gave the films the imprimatur of social responsibility, but as director Lois Weber readily acknowledged, baser instincts drove the market.

Born in 1882 in Allegheny City, Pennsylvania, Weber was a concert pianist in Charleston, South Carolina, then a singer with the Church Army Workers, an evangelical group centered in New York City. When the Workers disbanded in 1900, Weber went on the stage, appearing in *Why Girls Leave Home*, a hit in 1905. She married the

Helen Riaume, right, listens in on her husband, Tyrone Power (father of the 1940s matinee idol).

manager of the company, Phillips Smalley, a son of the adopted daughter of noted abolitionist and reformer Wendell Phillips.

Three years later, both were working for Herbert Blaché, the husband of pioneer director Alice Guy-Blaché, at the Gaumont Film Studio in Fort Lee, New Jersey. Early on, Weber saw movies as an opportunity to preach to the masses. She got their attention with stories about divorce, promiscuity, and drugs. She was also astute about promoting herself to the industry, placing ads and press releases in industry publications like *Moving Picture World*. Here's a notice from the November 1913, issue: "The Smalleys, who generally crowd several reels of action and plot into one reel, have found a story strong enough for 3 reels. They have called it 'A Jew's Christmas,' and it is a splendid piece of artistry. Released Dec. 18th. Totally different from any Christmas release you ever saw. BOOK IT."

A year later, Weber's *Hypocrites* earned notoriety not just for its nudity, but for being banned in several markets. Those who got a chance to see it would have found a well-meaning but turgid account of ministers past and present whose congregations can't tolerate nudity in art. In subsequent films like *Scandal* (1915), about "the untold misery that arises from gossip mongering," and *Hop "The Devil's Brew"* (1916), "a dramatic portrayal of the secret methods of the opium traffic," Weber continued to exploit contemporary issues in a profitable manner.

Scandal was the first film the Smalleys released through Universal, at the time still a minor player

in the industry. By this point Weber had established the equivalent of her own production company, writing, directing, and producing her projects and relying on a stable of actors. She starred in many of her films, such as *Scandal*, which also featured her husband and Rupert Julian, who would later make a box-office killing imitating the Kaiser in World War I propaganda films. Although the Smalleys shared credit, it was an open secret that Weber was in creative control.

Depending on the source, the Smalleys were making between $3,500 and $5,000 a week at Universal by the time they began production on *Where Are My Children?* Universal head Carl Laemmle said in an interview that Weber "knows the motion picture business as few people do and can drive herself as hard as anyone I have ever known." She acknowledged, "If my message fails to reach someone, I can only blame myself." A *Motion Picture Magazine* profile echoed that attitude: "The public as a whole is sentimental and . . . unless you give them what they want you're not going to make any money."

The script for *Where Are My Children?* was patched together from bits and pieces of several stories, plays, and news items. Moviegoers of the time would have seen parallels between Weber's doctor on trial for publishing a pamphlet on birth control and reformer Margaret Sanger, who endured a similar lawsuit. Weber's idea of a sort of "land of unborn children" seems lifted directly from Maurice Maeterlinck's *The Blue Bird*, an international hit written in 1909. Although the basic plot is simple, reviewers of the time were confused by Weber's cross-cutting, and by the fact that she could not spell out certain story elements too explicitly for fear of censorship. The director's intentions may be clear, but her imagery is sometimes indecipherable.

The film is still remarkably forthright: it would take many decades before movies would be this open again about abortion. Weber didn't concentrate on salacious details, but on the human costs of betrayed relationships, something that many modern-day filmmakers still find uncomfortable. Unfortunately, Weber's technique was trapped in a heavily declamatory style of staging, perhaps a throwback to her street-corner sermonizing. She does little more than place characters within settings, where they portray the most basic emotions. They are either happy or sad, honest or deceitful, without nuance or ambiguity, without even much of a chance to interact with each other.

While Weber had worked with many members of the cast before, it was somewhat of a coup to land Tyrone Power, one of the great matinee idols of his time, as well as his current wife, Helen Riaume. Power, father of the future movie star also named Tyrone Power, would make two other films with Weber.

Universal opened *Where Are My Children?* gingerly, adding introductory titles that tried to spin the film as a lecture on social works. It was still banned in Pennsylvania, where a censor referred to it as "unspeakably vile." When the National Board of Review threatened to withhold its approval, Laemmle got the film endorsed by rabbis, priests, and the noted Presbyterian reformer Dr. Charles H. Parkhurst. Advertisements trumpeted their comments, helping make *Where Are My Children?* one of Universal's biggest performers at the box office.

Laemmle responded by giving Weber her own facilities on the Universal lot in Los Angeles. She made *The Hand That Rocks the Cradle* (1917), in which she appeared with Margaret Sanger, and *The Blot* (1921), her last significant hit. In the 1920s Weber suffered a nervous breakdown after divorcing Smalley and losing her production company. By then her style was so outdated that it was routinely mocked by silent comedians. Laemmle, however, continued to give her work: in the 1930s, Weber directed Universal screen tests, for example. She died in 1939.

Civilization

Thomas H. Ince, 1916. Silent, B&W, 1.33, 86 minutes.

Cast: Herschel Mayall (The King of Wredpryd), Lola May (Queen Eugenie), Howard Hickman (Count Ferdinand), Enid Markey (Katheryn Haldemann), George Fisher (The Christus), J. Frank Burke (Luther Rolfe).

Credits: Directed by Thomas H. Ince, Raymond B. West, Reginald Barker. Photographed by Irvin Willat, Joseph August, Clyde de Vinna.

Additional Cast: Charles K. French (The Prime Minister), J. Barney Sherry (The Blacksmith), Jerome Storm (His son), Ethel Ullman (His daughter).

Additional Credits: Assistant directors: Walter Edwards, David Hartford, Jay Hunt, J. Parker Read. Produced by Thomas Harper Ince. Written by C. Gardner Sullivan. Additional cinematography: Robert S. Newhard, Del Clawson. Edited by Thomas Harper Ince, Le Roy Stone. Score by Victor Schertzinger. Assistants to producer: Raymond B. West, Jay Hunt, Reginald Barker, Irvin Willat, J. Parker Read, Walter Edwards, David M. Hartford. Released April 17, 1916.

Available: Kino Video VHS (1994). UPC: 7-38329-00805-5.

While he is often given credit for directing *Civilization*, Thomas H. Ince most likely left the day-to-day directing chores to his employees Reginald Barker, a Scottish actor who helmed William S. Hart's first features, and Raymond B. West, a special-effects expert. It didn't really matter who did the work or got the credit; the film was an Ince product from start to finish. By 1916, Ince had almost single-handedly developed the assembly-line system of film production that was eventually adopted by the other Hollywood studios.

Ince had opened a Los Angeles branch of the New York Motion Pictures company in 1911. His films were prized by theater owners because of their quality and consistency. They were expensive, but the results were apparent on the screen. Ince developed detailed shooting scripts, writing many himself, at a time when film stories were still scribbled on scrap paper. By controlling story elements, Ince could control his directors, who worked with assigned casts, crews, and sets. He could also make sure that the camerawork, set design, and costumes met his standards. Ince's scripts, which film historian Richard Koszarski compared to blueprints, included everything from when closeups and fades would occur to the order in which scenes would be shot. (To save costs, for example, Ince would have all the scenes that took place in a particular location filmed at one time.)

The year before *Civilization*, Ince moved to the Triangle Film Corporation with D.W. Griffith and

Mack Sennett. It was a short-lived arrangement, but during his time there Ince, perhaps influenced by Griffith, began releasing longer films with more psychological depth than his earlier two-reel Westerns. Crucial support was provided by C. Gardner Sullivan, Ince's chief writer. A former journalist and vaudeville sketch writer, Sullivan broke into the film industry by selling story ideas to Edison. Hired by Ince in 1913, he moved out to California and became the producer's chief writer.

Sullivan received credit on a wide variety of films, from Westerns to message dramas. Sullivan's interest in reform, which was tied to his strong religious beliefs, may have influenced the paths *Civilization* took, but there's little doubt that the screenwriter was expressing Ince's own firmly held political opinions. As were many Americans at the time, Ince was opposed to the United States entering into World War I, and *Civilization* would deliver a message of pacifism he hoped would buttress President Woodrow Wilson's efforts to maintain peace.

Which makes watching the film today all that more baffling. Presented as an allegory, *Civilization* is equal parts majestic spectacle and dated hokum. Set in the mythical European monarchy of Nurma, it shows how a power-hungry king brings his "peaceful, contented" people into war. The film's initial war sequences are impressive, a sort of combination of the Civil War battles shot by Griffith in *The Birth of a Nation* and a vividly realized depiction of trench warfare. Ince doesn't shy away from the horrors of fighting; he shows soldiers firing on civilians, buildings collapsing on troops, dogs rooting around corpses. Ince's battlefields are dustier, murkier, smokier than Griffith's, and they are shown mostly at ground level, not the high-angle view that gave an austere beauty to *The Birth of a Nation*.

When the battles turn against the king, he orders a draft. *Civilization* reaches its most emotional moments as officers tear sons from their mothers' arms, as lovers are separated, as orphaned children stare off at departing soldiers. The king is counting on a new submarine invented by Count Ferdinand. But Ferdinand has converted to pacifism under the influence of his fiancée, a member of a secret anti-war group. Ferdinand sacrifices the crew of his submarine rather than fire on a passenger liner. Pulled from the water, he is worked on by the king's doctors as his soul travels to Hell. There, in front of writhing, naked bodies, Jesus Christ informs Ferdinand that He will assume power over his body in order to preach for peace. In a subsequent scene reminiscent of Dickens, Christ takes the king on a tour of his war to show him the error of his ways.

Ince, or whoever actually directed the film, shows an easy facility with camera placement, with defining the geography of sets and grouping characters within them. He often starts scenes with close-ups, pulling back to show the entire set only if the scene required it. The film's dream sequences are easy to follow, as is some parallel editing that sets up two converging story lines. There is no denying the power of Ince's imagery, or the impact of the giant sets and hundreds of extras. But without reading a synopsis, it's almost impossible to follow the plot.

How valuable are the film's insights? *Civilization* seems to say that if it were up to the little people, war would never occur. It's always easy to blame a king, or his equivalent political construct, especially if you don't provide any context for his decisions. Who wouldn't be against a war presented in this manner?

The choppy editing, with its abrupt transitions and unexplained interpolations, adds to the difficulty. Ince, or Sullivan, not only drops characters, he abandons entire subplots in a rush to get to the pure fantasy sequences. And Ince's attention to detail doesn't extend to his actors, who range in style from smoothly convincing to blunt and obvious.

Critic Edward Wagenknecht saw *Civilization* as a direct response to *The Battle Cry of Peace*, director J. Stuart Blackton's rabble-rousing adaptation of Hudson Maxim's *Defenceless America*. (Henry Ford attacked both book and film, pointing out that war would bolster Maxim's munitions holdings.) Both movies were part of a string of big-budget films that tried to deal with what their directors saw as the major themes of the day. None of them proved successful. Despite the generally positive reviews that *Civilization* received, audiences were more interested in Westerns, comedies, and romances. Ince would return to purely commercial efforts, ones that often seem to lack any personality, until his death in 1924.

Intolerance

Wark Producing Corporation, 1916. Silent, B&W, 1.33. 197 minutes.

Cast includes: Mae Marsh (The Dear One), Lillian Gish (The Woman Who Rocks the Cradle/The Eternal Mother), Robert Harron (The Boy), Fred Turner (The Girl's Father), Sam De Grasse (Arthur Jenkins), Vera Lewis (Mar T. Jenkins), Miriam Cooper (The Friendless One), Walter Long (The Musketeer of the Slums), Tom Wilson (The Kindly Policeman), Ralph Lewis (Governor), Lloyd Ingraham (Judge of the Court), Monte Blue (Strike leader), Marguerite Marsh (Debutante), Howard Gaye (Christ), Lillian Langdon (Mary), Olga Grey (Mary Magdalene), Bessie Love (The Bride of Cana), Margery Wilson (Brown Eyes), Eugene Pallette (Prosper Latour), Spottiswoode Aitken (Brown Eyes's father), Frank Bennett (Charles IX), Josephine Crowell (Catherine de Medici), Georgia Pearce [Constance Talmadge] (Marguerite de Valois/The Mountain Girl), Elmer Clifton (The Rhapsode), Tully Marshall (The High Priest of Bel), Alfred Paget (Belshazzar), Seena Owen (Princess Beloved), George Siegmann (Cyrus), Elmo Lincoln (Bodyguard).

Credits: Written and directed by D.W. Griffith. Titles by Anita Loos. Directors of photography: G.W. Bitzer, Karl Brown.

Additional Cast includes: Wallace Reid, Ted Shawn, Ruth St. Denis, Max Davidson, Grace Wilson, Mildred Harris, George Beranger, Joseph Henabery, Tod Browning, W.S. Van Dyke, Frank Borzage, Donald Crisp, King Vidor, Erich von Stroheim, Gino Corrado.

Additional Credits: Assistant directors include George Siegmann, W.S. Van Dyke, Allan Dwan, Jack Conway, Christy Cabanne, Tod Browning, Monte Blue, Victor Fleming. Set designers: Walter L. Hall, R. Ellis Wales, Frank Wortman. Edited by James Smith, Rose Smith, D.W. Griffith. Production dates: October 17, 1915 to April 1916. Released September 5, 1916.

Available: Kino Video DVD (2002). UPC: 738329026721.

Film epics don't come much stranger than *Intolerance*, D.W. Griffith's follow-up to *The Birth of a Nation* (1915). He had started working on a feature called *The Mother and the Law* before *Birth* was released, and completed a version of the story in the first half of 1915. But after *Birth* became a smash hit, Griffith decided he had to top himself, especially since he finally had the money to fully realize his cinematic dreams. The project gradually expanded to include four separate stories, all loosely tied to the theme of intolerance. Or, "how hatred and intolerance, through all the ages, have battled against love and charity."

The four stories of *Intolerance* (its subtitles include *A Sun Play of the Ages* and *Love's Struggle Throughout the Ages*) take place during different periods, with different casts. Griffith saw the separate stories as "ancient, sacred, medieval, and modern"—or Babylon, the life of Christ, the massacre of the Huguenots, and a modern-day melodrama. The breakthrough tactic in *Intolerance*, and one that worried Griffith considerably before the film was released, was his decision to present the stories in no particular order, and to cut among them whenever he chose.

Griffith filmed each segment in its entirety, starting with reshoots on *The Mother and the Law* while sets for stories about Babylon and the Huguenots were readied. He apparently thought of shooting a version of the life of Christ second, although his version ultimately came down to three episodes: the marriage feast at Cana, Christ's admonition at the temple not to cast the first stone at an adulterer, and bits and pieces of the Passion. Then as now, filmmakers could always rely on Christ to supply a little prestige to their work. Griffith approached the material with the expected reverence, along with more than a little artistic license. (He has the Pharisees quote scripture that hadn't been written yet, and that didn't apply to the wedding feast at Cana anyway.)

The other two segments, ancient and medieval, seem to have sprung from Griffith's viewing of *Cabiria*, a 1914 epic of Roman times from Italy. The medieval section, which concerns the St. Bartholomew's Day massacre of the Huguenots in Paris on August 24, 1572, would be an odd choice for any American director. Griffith and his collaborators did a fairly good job distilling a complex political situation to a few stock figures: the evil Queen Catherine de Medici, the "effeminate" King Charles IX, the lovestruck aristocrat Prosper Latour, and a blameless Huguenot family that included an impossibly beautiful girl known only as "Brown Eyes." Played with surprising delicacy by Margery Wilson, Brown Eyes is about the only affecting aspect of the story until its unexpectedly savage climax.

The Babylon sequence, which shows how Belshazzar lost the city to Cyrus in 538 B.C., was the last to be shot, in part because of the time required to build its enormous sets. These remain among the most remarkable achievements in film, and still have an extraordinary impact today. Imagine how audiences in 1915 must have reacted to the sight of walls and battlements four and five stories high, to courtyards set on three different levels and filled with hundreds of costumed extras, to visuals so expensive it's like they were filmed on and made out of gold.

Cinematographer Billy Bitzer used magnesium flares to capture a night-time battle at the walls of Babylon. When Belshazzar's court was finally finished in the summer of 1915, Griffith and Bitzer tried shooting from a hot-air balloon in order to show the immensity of the sets. The results were too shaky to use. Allan Dwan, a former civil engineer and future director, thought of placing an elevator on a flatbed railroad car, allowing the camera to simultaneously track in and down over the courtyard.

Griffith's version of the fall of Babylon rests on Belshazzar's supposed indifference to defending his city, and the treachery of jealous priests who allow Cyrus to attack through an open gate. It's a fairly muddy example of intolerance, and Griffith doesn't spend much time drawing comparisons to the other stories. He doesn't flesh out the characters, either, apart from a tomboyish Mountain Girl played by Constance Talmadge. It was her first big role, and it introduced her to Loos, subsequently the author of a book about the Talmadge family. (Constance's sister Norma became one of the big movie stars of the 1920s, while her other sister Natalie married Buster Keaton.) The Mountain Girl is a fun part that Constance plays with verve and humor, and it's a mark of her skill that she stands out in a segment filled with orgies, sacrifices, semi-nudity, wild animals, and wholesale destruction.

The first story in the film, set in a modern-day Western city, grew out of *The Mother and the Law*. Reformers are determined to halt the spread of sin—largely, drinking, gambling, and dancing in cafés. They enlist Mary T. Jenkins, the spinster sister of an "autocratic industrial overlord" who runs a factory from his massive but eerily empty office. Griffith suggests that Mary Jenkins takes part in reform out of sexual frustration; or, as an intertitle puts it, "When women cease to attract men they often turn to Reform as a second choice." A strike, a cut in pay, and the next thing you know, a worker known as "Boy" (played by Bobby Harron), has become a gangster, an elderly father dies of a heart attack, reformers take a young baby away to an orphanage, and a heroine is forced into prostitution, leading to a gallows climax that is thrilling and ludicrous at the same time.

Griffith would later release this segment separately under the title *The Mother and the Law*, and it's clearly the strongest material in *Intolerance*. His style of directing is more mature and nuanced than in *Birth* a year earlier, and he employs devices like extreme close-ups with more assurance. He is looser with camera set-ups as well, giving his scenes a more organic and life-like feel. Images in this section seem wider, deeper, more alive. A shot of Boy and Dear One walking on the waterfront on a quiet day off, silhouetted by afternoon sun, is worthy of Walker Evans. During the chase sequence, Griffith had the camera mounted on a locomotive for a striking shot of a train rattling down the tracks. The strike sequence is shocking in its intensity and violence.

Like *The Birth of a Nation*, *Intolerance* boosted the careers of many who worked on it. Griffith's assistants on this film included Sidney Franklin, who would shortly direct Mary Pickford prior to a distinguished career at MGM; and W.S. Van Dyke, who also wound up at MGM directing films like *The Thin Man*. Here he impressed Griffith by his willingness to risk his neck performing stunts, including leaping from the top of the walls of Babylon.

Many see *Intolerance*'s relatively weak showing at the box office as a sign of Griffith's decline. But *Intolerance* didn't lose money, and Griffith's reputation remained strong after its release. Griffith's later problems as a director came from much deeper-rooted problems, including his casting choices, his inability to stay in touch with audiences, and the fact—increasingly apparent over the years—that after hundreds of shorts and two dozen features, he did not have much more of interest to say. But his career stretched on for another fifteen years after *Intolerance*, including one more Registry title, *Broken Blossoms* (1919).

The Curse of Quon Gwon

Mandarin Film Company, 1916. Silent, B&W, 1.33. 35 minutes.
Cast: Violet Wong (Heroine), Harvey Soo Hoo (Groom), Chin Shee (Elder Matron), Marion Wong (Villainess).
Credits: Written and directed by Marion E. Wong. Hair and makeup: Alice Lim.
Title on screen: *The Curse of Quon Gwon when the Far East mingles with the West.*
Available: Preserved by the Academy Film Archive, part of the Academy Foundation, the educational and cultural arm of the Academy of Motion Picture Arts and Sciences (further information: *www.oscars.org/filmarchive*).

A featured bonus on Arthur Dong's documentary *Hollywood Chinese* (2007; further information: *www.hollywoodchinese.com*).

Born around 1895, Marion E. Wong was the niece of Lim Ben, described in a 1916 newspaper article as a "wealthy Chinese merchant and landowner." Wong, who lived in the Oakland, California, area, traveled to China in 1911 and used her trip as inspiration for *The Curse of Quon Gwon*. Regarded as the first Chinese-American feature film, it was written, produced, and directed by Wong, who also had a hand in designing the scenery and costumes.

Asians had been portrayed in film as early as 1894, when W.K.L. Dickson and William Heise photographed the Sarashe Sisters in *Imperial Japanese Dance*. They also filmed Robetta and Phil Doretto [Lauter], who re-created their vaudeville act "Heap Fun Laundry" under the title *Chinese Laundry Scene*—perhaps the earliest film record of Caucasians imitating Asians. Chinese viceroy Li Hung Chang was filmed in 1896, but for the most part Asian-Americans were either ignored or relegated to supporting roles—often derogatory ones, at that. Films were being made in China by 1908, but they were rarely shown abroad.

As an indication of the culture of the time, Wong went to China to meet her future husband, accompanied by two brothers who were looking for wives. In an article for *CineMedusa*, Mara Math wrote that one brother died in China; the second, Albert, married Violet, who would star in *Quon Gwon*. Wong didn't take to her potential spouse, and refused to marry him.

The newspaper article quotes Wong as saying, "I had never seen any Chinese movies so I decided to introduce them to the world. I first wrote the love story. Then I decided that people who are interested in my people and my country would like to see some of the customs and manners of China. So I added to the love drama many scenes depicting these things." Wong may have been inspired by *Madame Butterfly*, a 1915 vehicle for Mary Pickford based on the David Belasco play. She was certainly familiar with Chinese opera, as her plot depicts scenes and incidents that could have been found in many of those productions.

Wong is supposed to have watched Charlie Chaplin filming near Edwin's Cafe, her family's restaurant, and may have met his crew. (The comedian made *A Night Out* and *The Tramp* in the Oakland area early in 1915.) Mara Math believes Wong hired some of Chaplin's crew; this could account for the unusually fluid camerawork in *Quon Gwon*, which tilts and pans to follow characters and at times even anticipates action. The cinematographer provided the most impressive effect in the surviving film, during which a necklace and bracelets dissolve into chains that shackle the heroine.

Contemporary news accounts put the original film at either seven or eight reels long, although all that remains today are reels 4 and 7, and ten additional minutes that had been transferred to 16mm in the 1970s. Also missing are the intertitles, which would have helped explain the relationships among the characters, as well as important plot points. An article in the July 17, 1917 issue of *The Motion Picture World* said the film "deals with the curse of a Chinese god that follows his people because of the influence of western civilization." (Quon Gwon, also spelled Kuan Kung, is a god of war and wealth.)

Violet Wong had a complete copy of the film that lasted into the 1970s. Her daughters Wong Davis and Marcella Wong Yahashiro remembered it as "a very, very sad film but with a happy ending." Gregory Yee Mark, Violet's grandson, credits the film for his career in ethnic studies. Mark, who oversaw the 16mm transfer, believes the film was an attempt to show how the 1911 revolution was changing Chinese culture.

The film was screened at least once in Oakland, but apparently did not receive commercial distribution. In later years, neither Marion Wong nor her sister-in-law Violet would talk about what was apparently considered a financial failure. Wong married Kim Seung Hong in 1917; he was the first Chinese student to graduate from the University of California–Berkeley, and the first Chinese electrical engineer in the country. Marion Wong founded the Singapor Hut restaurant, and toured in vaudeville as a singer and musician. Her daughter Arabella attended Juilliard, and originated the role of Helen Chiao in Rodgers and Hammerstein's *Flower Drum Song* (the 1961 film adaptation is a Registry title).

The Curse of Quon Gwon re-emerged when filmmaker Arthur Dong was researching his documentary *Hollywood Chinese* (2007). Wong Davis and Marcella Wong Yahashiro gave him access to their footage, and authorized him to bring it to the Academy Film Archive for preservation.

Apart from Sessue Hayakawa (*The Cheat*, 1915) and Anna May Wong, Asian-Americans had few opportunities for starring roles in Hollywood movies. (Film historian Tino Balio cites one Cantonese-language feature made in Los Angeles, the 1936 *Sum Hun*.) Although blackface became politically incorrect before World War II, Caucasians like Red Buttons and Mickey Rooney were still impersonating Asians into the 1960s. A performer like Bruce Lee found prospects so limited that he went to Hong Kong to further his career in films like *Enter the Dragon* (1973), another Registry title.

The Poor Little Rich Girl

Mary Pickford in *The Poor Little Rich Girl*.

Artcraft/Paramount, 1917. Silent, B&W, 1.33. 77 minutes.
Cast: Mary Pickford (Gwendolyn), Madeline Traverse (Her mother), Charles Wellesley (Her father), Gladys Fairbanks (Jane), Frank McGlynn (The plumber), Emile LaCroix (The organ grinder), Marcia Harris (Miss Royale), Charles Craig (Thomas), Frank Andrews (Potter), Herbert Prior (The doctor [William Reid Prime]), George Gernon (Johnny Blake), Maxine Hicks (Susie May Squoggs).
Credits: Directed by Maurice Tourneur. Scenario: Frances Marion. Directors of cinematography: John van den Broek, Lucien Andriot. Art director: Ben Carré. Presented by Adolph Zukor.
Additional Credits: Based on the play written by Eleanor Gates and staged on Broadway in 1913. Script: Ralph Spence. Produced by the Mary Pickford Film Corporation. Assistant director: M.N. Litson. Released March 5, 1917.
Other Versions: *The Poor Little Rich Girl* (1936), starring Shirley Temple, was based on short stories written by Eleanor Gates and Ralph Spence.
Available: The Mary Pickford Foundation (*www.marypickford.com*).

Between *Tess of the Storm Country* (1914) and *The Poor Little Rich Girl*, Mary Pickford appeared in twenty features, playing everyone from orphans to princesses, tenement dwellers to backwoods hellions. During that period her salary doubled to $2,000 a week, as well as 50 percent of the profits on her films. These were so popular that Adolph Zukor formed a new company, Artcraft, to distribute them, charging theater owners more than his fees for regular Paramount features. The Artcraft budgets averaged around $170,000, with Pickford receiving $125,000 of that sum.

That left more than enough money to hire the best available talent, including directors Allan Dwan, Sidney Olcott, and, for *The Pride of the Clan* (1917), Maurice Tourneur. Born in France

in 1873, Tourneur spent three years in the military before becoming a book illustrator and interior designer. He became an actor and stage manager in 1900, touring the world with the famous actress Rejane. He began working for Eclair as an assistant to director Émile Chautard. Eclair had opened a branch in the United States in Fort Lee, New Jersey, in 1911. Tourneur was thirty-eight when he left France to run the New Jersey office.

Tourneur directed four films that first year at Eclair. The next year he made seven films at Equitable-World, and six more the following year at Paragon-World. Tourneur's films were marked by modern techniques: close-ups, long tracking shots, single-source lighting, continuity editing. He was anxious to "do something" with film, and collaborated closely with cinematographers like John van den Broek to experiment with the possibilities of film stock.

Pickford, who was twenty-four at the time of filming *The Poor Little Rich Girl*, was determined to assert herself as a filmmaker. Earlier in her career she corrected lighting and compositions on the set. She then realized the importance of surrounding herself with sympathetic and talented workers. Pickford befriended Frances Marion, a divorced artist and actress from San Francisco who had also been a painter, model, and journalist. Trained as a scenarist by the actor, producer, and director

Hobart Bosworth, Marion sold *Mistress Nell* to Pickford in 1915. The two became close friends, discussing what projects Mary should tackle and how to improve them. Marion even wrote a chatty newspaper column under Pickford's name.

Their decision to make *The Poor Little Rich Girl*, in which an eleven-year-old girl almost dies from neglect, may seem odd today, but at the time it was seen as part of a genre that included works by Charles Dickens and Maurice Maeterlinck. Author Eleanor Gates first published the story as a novel in 1912, then staged it on Broadway in 1913 in a production starring Viola Dana. It closed after 160 performances, but proved popular on the road—so much so that Gates could publish the play in 1916. Pickford still had to convince a skeptical Adolph Zukor to let her make the project.

On the set, Pickford and Marion added bits of business to the scenario, confounding Tourneur, who according to every Pickford biographer repeatedly asked, "Where, exactly, do you see that in the script, ladies?" What Tourneur brought to the project was atmosphere and a supple film technique. By using oversized props, by placing tall actors at the foreground of compositions, he could suggest that Pickford, already small in stature, was even tinier than she was. Tourneur understood details about the rich—how they dressed and behaved—better than many American directors who lived more hardscrabble lives. He also preferred restraint in actors' performances, making *The Poor Little Rich Girl* seem more modern than many of Pickford's other features.

Together, Pickford and Marion fashioned a character not nearly as timid and innocent as how society expected children to behave. Pickford's Gwendolyn is a troublemaker who delights in outwitting her guardians, who lies, breaks things, attacks other children, and throws temper tantrums (she throws her clothes out the window during one fit of anger). She is also unmistakably a child, yawning during her lessons, picturing literal bears on Wall Street and "two-faced" women, sobbing in her loneliness and isolation. Biographer Scott Eyman points out that this is one of the few times Pickford played a wealthy character; typically for her, it's still one who struggles against authority. Pickford always sided with the underdog, and it's a measure of her talent and appeal that she could make a child of privilege appear deprived.

Tourneur employed some daring devices while depicting the story. He lights the center of a table during a banquet scene, bathing the diners in an otherworldly glow that ascends upward. He repeats bits of narrative during a fantasy sequence, showing how "real" events are occurring simultaneously with "dream" ones. Death becomes an ominous presence, spelled out in an intertitle not found in the play: "Here in the forest, dark and deep, I offer you, eternal sleep." Pickford is dazzling playing a scene in front of a mirror, but it wouldn't have worked without Tourneur's careful staging. And Pickford has a startling beauty in her close-ups—startling and unsettling, given the role she is playing and her adult age at the time.

In her autobiography, Pickford took credit for discovering how a low reflector could fill out facial features in close-ups, a technique later copied by the entire industry. She describes tormenting Tourneur, "teasing and wheedling and lashing" the director. When Pickford screened *The Poor Little Rich Girl* for Zukor and other Paramount executives, they reacted stonily. It was "one of the blackest days of my life," she wrote later. Worried, she agreed to move to California to work under Cecil B. DeMille, who already had a reputation as a tyrant. They made two films together, neither of which had the impact on moviegoers that *The Poor Little Rich Girl* had. It was such a success that Zukor threw in the towel, and from then on essentially let Pickford do what she wanted.

But success brought its own demands. Fans wanted Pickford to continue playing children, which she did with less and less enthusiasm throughout the 1920s. Trapped in a stereotype that has defined her screen persona to this day, Pickford ultimately retreated from both the film industry and the public in general. Her influence on the rest of the industry, and on American culture in general, was vast. She offered a stronger, feistier archetype for women than D.W. Griffith did with his heroines. She controlled her career to an unprecedented extent, achieving economic independence and creative control that is the envy of stars to this day. Later performers like Janet Gaynor and Shirley Temple established their careers in part by remaking Pickford's films (and, in Temple's case, her look).

Tourneur's next films included an ambitious adaptation of *A Doll's House* (1918) and a screen version of *The Blue Bird* (1918), which essentially allowed him to remake *The Poor Little Rich Girl* the way he wanted to.

The Immigrant

Mutual Film Corporation, 1917. Silent, B&W, 1.33. 20 minutes.

Cast: Charlie Chaplin, Edna Purviance (Immigrants), Eric Campbell (The Head Waiter), Albert Austin (A Diner), Henry Bergman (The Artist).

Credits: Written and directed by Charles Chaplin. Director of photography: Roland Totheroh.

Additional Cast: Tiny Sandford (Cheater), Kitty Bradbury (Mother), Frank J. Coleman (Ship's officer/restaurant owner), John Rand (Diner with no money), William Gillespie (Violinist).

Additional Credits: Edited by Charles Chaplin. Produced by Lone Star Corporation. Released June 17, 1917.

Available: Image Entertainment DVD (1995): *The Chaplin Mutuals Volume 1.* UPC: 0-14381-4100-2-0.

Released in 1917, *The Immigrant* was the twelfth and last film Charlie Chaplin made with the backing of the Lone Star Corporation. Since these dozen titles were distributed by the Mutual Film Corporation, they are generally referred to as "Mutuals." Chaplin made them between 1916 and 1917. At the time, having signed a contract for $670,000, he was not only the highest paid entertainer in the world, but in history. His humble beginnings have been documented extensively in books and biographies. He was born in London in 1889 to music-hall performers who separated when he was a year old. When his mother was institutionalized, Chaplin and his brother Sydney were placed first in a workhouse, then an orphanage.

By the age of eight, Chaplin was a veteran stage performer; ten years later, he joined Syd at the Fred Karno company of acrobats and comics. During a tour of the United States, Chaplin left the company to work for Mack Sennett at Keystone. By his second film, *Kid Auto Races at Venice* (1914), he had already established much of his screen persona. A shabby suit, bowler hat, cane, and greasepaint moustache transformed Chaplin into what became known worldwide as "The Tramp."

Within a year, Chaplin was writing and directing shorts. He was so successful that he left Keystone for Essanay and then for Mutual, his pay rising from $175 to $10,000 a week. He later called his time at Mutual "the happiest period of my career," and the pictures he made there rank with the best comedies ever filmed.

At Mutual, Chaplin had unprecedented creative freedom. He could film whatever subject he wanted, tell whatever story he wanted, with whatever characters he chose to invent. He worked with a hand-picked cast and crew, and with no oversight. There was no one to prevent him from reshooting a scene, or to keep shooting one until he felt he got it right, or to completely alter a finished scene in order to improve a film. He could add or remove characters and situations, or decide not to release a completed film at all.

Explanations for the comedian's style and appeal include his deprived childhood; his physical grace and inventiveness; experiences on stage as a performer in a hit play; training with Karno's acrobats; his growing awareness of the power and limitations of film; his willingness to continually edit his work; his grasp of his audience; his writing, acting, editing, and directing skills; his leftist politics and disdain for the upper classes; his small stature; his gift for pantomime; and his expressive face.

Chaplin's true glory was his compassion—for outsiders and outcasts, for the underprivileged, for those on the margins of society. He not only understood and sided with them, he was one of them. (One of the beauties of *The Immigrant* is that he's literally in the same boat as the teeming masses.) He saw too well that no matter how his screen character succeeded, he would never fit in. Many filmmakers adopted similar stances, but what distinguishes Chaplin is his lack of malice. Chaplin might feel slighted by a wealthy man, but he would never feel inferior to him. He might resent someone's wealth, but not the system that enabled it. It is only luck, not talent or perseverance, that separates him from the successful.

The Immigrant has a setting worthy of Louis Hine or Jacob Riis, but Chaplin uses it not to exploit its squalor, but to give his Tramp a set of problems and obstacles to solve. The passenger steerage stuffed with presumably European immigrants has horrific conditions, with exposed sleeping quarters and questionable food, but Chaplin isn't interested in explaining what is bringing these people to New York City. He wants to show how people cope, retain their humanity, and keep their dreams alive. It was a message that spoke directly to an enormous audience across the world.

On a technical level he had a different set of problems to consider. How to depict the rocking of the boat, for example. Chaplin and cameraman "Rollie" Totheroh used two different methods to show this, both complicated and expensive. In one, the camera was placed on a sort of pendulum device, with the actors pretending to sway back and forth in time with the camera's motion. This procedure has been used so much subsequently that it is often mocked in sci-fi parodies. For the eating scene inside the liner's mess hall, Chaplin built an entire set on rockers just to achieve some gags about bowls and plates sliding back and forth on the galley tables. He then expanded the scene to incorporate some roughhouse tumbling.

Another eating scene makes up most of the second half of the film, this one inside a Skid Row restaurant manned by large, aggressive waiters. Chaplin has found a coin on the sidewalk outside. He slips it into his pocket before entering, but it falls back onto the ground through a hole in his clothes—something we see and he doesn't. The subsequent scene, where he confidently orders food, then notices other patrons beaten and ejected when they can't pay, has a delicious suspense built into it. Chaplin doesn't find out his loss until he has been reacquainted with Edna Purviance, his leading lady for most of the shorts from this period and one of the passengers on the boat. His attempts to delay the inevitable confrontation with Eric Campbell (the "heavy" in many of his films) show the comedian at the height of his powers.

In *Unknown Chaplin*, a fascinating documentary about the comic's working methods, Kevin Brownlow and David Gill combed through outtakes and alternate versions to explain how the restaurant scene was assembled. Chaplin began the sequence with a slightly different cast, then proceeded to work on timing and gags, shooting and reshooting, trying out bits and discarding them, refining other moments, incorporating other actors, all in an effort to improve the material. While it's true that few other filmmakers could afford to work this way, what is remarkable about Chaplin is his drive and dedication. He didn't have to work that hard, but if he hadn't, he wouldn't have been so beloved.

After Mutual, Chaplin signed a million-dollar contract with First National. Within a year, he was one of the founding members of United Artists. His next Registry title is *The Gold Rush* (1925).

Wild and Woolly

Artcraft, 1917. Silent, B&W, 1.33. 56 minutes.
Cast: Douglas Fairbanks (Jeff Hillington), Eileen Percy (Nell Larabee), Charles Stevens (Pedro), Sam De Grasse (Steve Shelby), Calvert Carter (Tom Larabee), Bull Montana, Monte Blue.
Credits: Directed by John Emerson. Produced by John Emerson. Photoplay by Anita Loos. Based on a Story by Horace B. Carpenter. Photography by Victor Fleming.
Additional Cast: Walter Bytell (Collis J. Hillington).
Additional Credits: Released June 24, 1917.
Available: Flicker Alley DVD *Douglas Fairbanks: A Modern Musketeer* (2008), *www.flickeralley.com*. Grapevine Video VHS (1998), *www.grapevinevideo.com*.

Douglas Fairbanks had been a star on Broadway and appeared in almost twenty films by the time he started *Wild and Woolly*. His all-American persona—brash, cocky, athletic, honorable—had been carefully honed over the preceding fifteen years, and positioned Fairbanks as a lighter, carefree alternative to typical male leads. But unlike many silent stars, Fairbanks entered movies fairly late in life. The fact that he was thirty-four when he made *Wild and Woolly* forced some compromises that may be too obvious to viewers today.

Fairbanks was born in 1883 in Denver. He moved to New York with his mother after her divorce, and made his Broadway debut in 1902. But it was his life outside theater that played an essential part in his acting style. In Colorado he had studied at a mining school. Back East he attended Harvard briefly, got to Europe by working on a cattle freighter, and clerked in both a hardware store and a Wall Street firm. On stage and in his films, Fairbanks' characters reflected this broad range of experience. Just as Americans wished they were, he was as comfortable with high society as with hoboes, treating both with dignity and humor. He graduated to larger parts, specializing in excitable juvenile leads, and became known for his broad, even florid, theatrical style. By 1909, when his only son, Douglas, Jr., was born, Fairbanks was ending a five-year theatrical contract. He went to work for his wife's father, but returned to the stage in 1911.

Four years later, he could no longer ignore the money being offered by the film industry. In 1915, he joined other Broadway stars by signing a movie contract, in his case at $2,000 a week with Biograph. D.W. Griffith, who supervised Fairbanks' first movie work, had no idea what to do with him, and the actor's early films are a mélange of somewhat stale Broadway themes adapted for the silent screen.

It wasn't until Fairbanks started working with John Emerson and his soon-to-be-wife Anita Loos that his screen character took shape. Loos had given up acting to write screenplays for Griffith, and she was famous for her sassy story lines and ironic intertitles. Emerson was lured away from becoming an Episcopalian minister to act on stage and then to direct and write. He joined Biograph at roughly the same time as Fairbanks. The trio's first film, *His Picture in the Papers*, was successful, but their next project, *The Mystery of the Leaping Fish* (both released in 1916), marked a strange detour in Fairbanks' career. For one thing, it was a two-reel short, not a feature; for another, it was a comedy about a drug-addicted detective who spends much of the film sniffing or injecting himself with cocaine.

The Americano and *Reaching for the Moon* (both 1917) were more typical of the Emerson-Loos productions. Made the same year, *Wild and Woolly* falls into a similar pattern. By this time Fairbanks was playing a naive or self-centered youth whose outlook was changed or at least broadened by his sudden exposure to a world he never imagined. It was the same sort of role used by comedians—notably, Harold Lloyd and Buster Keaton—and in a sense Fairbanks' popularity both inspired them and legitimized their efforts.

After his first dozen films, Fairbanks was a genuine star, able to form his own production company. He had total control over his projects, from selecting stories to casting, and could work with the directors, writers, and crew he wanted. He expanded the scope of his films, offering stories with larger casts and more scenic locations, and worked more of his trademark stunts into his story lines.

While Fairbanks was clearly too old to be playing juvenile leads, his gusto and exuberance in *Wild and Woolly* are hard to resist. He stars as Jeff Hillington, the Western-mad son of a railroad tycoon. When he's not reading pulp Westerns by a campfire in a bedroom in his father's mansion, he's terrorizing servants and co-workers with his cowboy antics. When his father considers building a spur to a mine near Bitter Creeks, Arizona, Jeff jumps at the chance to scout the project.

But Bitter Creek is no longer a part of the Western frontier—it's a typical twentieth-century small town, with cars and telephones. The mine owners have to convince the townspeople to stage the equivalent of a Wild West festival for Jeff, complete with fake train robberies and square dances. It's a smart story that makes fun of Fairbanks' character while still giving him ample opportunity for stunts and heroism. (It's a shame the film couldn't portray its Indian characters with the same thoughtfulness.) Jeff, like many of the roles Fairbanks played, prefers jumping over tables to walking around them, and in the course of the film he jumps through or off windows, trains, balconies, horses, and at one point the floor of his hotel room. The film makes fun of its viewers' preconceptions about small-town life while at the same time indulging their wish for action and adventure. A clever plot twist—a nefarious Indian agent uses the festival as a cover for a real train robbery—adds another level to the story. All filmgoers had to do was believe that someone like Jeff could actually exist.

Fairbanks cast Sam De Grasse and Charles Stevens, who worked in many of his films, as the chief villains, and seventeen-year-old newcomer Eileen Percy as the spunky heroine, "little Nell." But the film belongs to Doug, who rides through Central Park, does back flips, borrows some rope tricks from Will Rogers, and even dances. He would persist in similar roles until World War I, and his age, made them too improbable. He had by then married Mary Pickford, "America's Sweetheart," and settled into a string of elaborate costume adventures.

The Blue Bird

Famous Players/Lasky, 1918. Silent, B&W with tints, 1.33. 81 Minutes.

Cast: Tula Belle (Mytyl), Robin Macdougall (Tytyl), Edwin E. Reed (Daddy Tyl), Emma Lowry (Mommy Tyl), William J. Gross (Grandfather Tyl), Florence Anderson (Granny Tyl), Edward Elkas (Berlingot), Katherine Bianchi (Berlingot's daughter), Lillian Cook (Berylune), Gertrude McCoy (Light), Lyn Donelson (Night), Charles Ascot (Dog), Tom Corless (Cat), Mary Kennedy (Water), Eleanor Masters (Milk), Charles Craig (Sugar), Sam Blum (Bread), S.E. Potapovitch (Fire), Rosa Rolanda.

Credits: Adapted for the screen by Charles Maigne. Scenic effects by Ben Carré. Photography by John van den Broek. An Artcraft Picture.

Additional Credits: Directed by Maurice Tourneur. Edited by Clarence Brown. Preserved by the George Eastman House as part of the National Endowment for the Arts and the U.S. Park Service's Saving America's Treasures program through the National Film Preservation Foundation. Released March 31, 1918.

Other Versions: Remade in 1940 (directed by Walter Lang) and 1976 (directed by George Cukor).

Available: Kino Video DVD (2005). UPC: 7-38329-04182-3

Maurice Maeterlinck wrote the play *The Blue Bird* in 1909, two years before the Belgian-born poet won the Nobel Prize for Literature. Born in 1862 in Ghent, Maeterlinck was a practicing lawyer when he wrote his first play in 1889. For the next ten years he penned several more plays filled with mystical symbols and references to myths and rituals, among them *Pelléas et Mélisande*. At the turn of the twentieth century he wrote *The Life of the Bee* (published in 1901), a nonfiction work that marked a general lightening in his tone and outlook. The peak of this period was *The Blue Bird*, which became an international hit. Faced with failing eyesight and writer's block, Maeterlinck grew increasingly depressed, and his work reflected his growing preoccupation with mortality. The author moved to the United States in 1940, where he was considered for a job writing for Samuel Goldwyn. He moved back to France after World War II, dying there in 1949.

By then *The Blue Bird* had been filmed three times. The 1910 version was a European production, while the 1940 version—a big-budget Technicolor adaptation starring Shirley Temple—was a financial disappointment. (Some critics felt it compared unfavorably to *The Wizard of Oz*, another Technicolor fantasy released a year earlier. A 1976 Russian co-production, directed by George Cukor and starring Elizabeth Taylor and Jane Fonda, was a notorious failure.)

The 1918 version was directed by Maurice Tourneur, the French immigrant who helmed two of Mary Pickford's best films. Working with her was so difficult that Tourneur formed his own company to produce films without outside interference. He chose ambitious projects: an adaptation of Henrik Ibsen's *A Doll's House*, one of Granville Barker's *Prunella*, and *The Blue Bird*. The screenplay was by Charles Maigne, who also adapted *Prunella*; he would go on to direct his own films, including a 1923 version of *The Trail of the Lonesome Pine*.

Tourneur cast some of the parts with actors he had worked with before. Tula Belle had played a child in *The Doll's House*, for example. Edward Elkas, who plays the widowed neighbor Berlingot, specialized in ethnic parts for much of his career. And while this is Robin Macdougall's only credited film appearance, she gives an especially appealing performance as the young Tytyl.

Tourneur's sensitive direction of his child actors is one of the most satisfying aspects of *The Blue Bird*; his strong pictorial style is another. The film's charming special effects range in complexity from animation combined with live footage and matte paintings to simple paper cut-outs. The set design betrays the story's stage origins, but Tourneur manages to work in location footage along the then unspoiled Hudson River. His style suggested a world beyond the sets, beyond the frame. In one typical shot, Berlingot exits from the Tyl home, then is seen in the same shot hobbling to her house next door through a window in the kitchen wall. Tourneur learned sooner than most the value of underlighting his sets. *The Blue Bird* is filled with silhouettes, with figures lit from below and from sources like windows and lanterns. Working with his steady cameraman John van den Broek, Tourneur separated his characters from the backgrounds of frames, giving depth and realism to the film's shots. Combined with restrained acting and superbly implemented special effects, the cinematography in *The Blue Bird* builds a sense of mystery and wonder that is hard to find in other films of its time.

The story, which sends two young children to a vaguely defined underworld in search of the "blue bird of happiness," owes a lot to *Peter Pan* and *The Wizard of Oz*, particularly in its use of animal characters. Charles Ascot's "dog" moves just like Nana in *Peter Pan*, while his makeup resembles Fred A. Stone's as the Scarecrow in a hit stage version of *Oz*. For that matter, Charles Craig as Sugar is very close to *Oz*'s Tin Man.

The film's opening and closing scenes, set in a poor rural countryside, carry more emotional weight than scenes set in various palaces and cemeteries. While this is one of Maeterlinck's more optimistic stories, modern audiences may be surprised at how much death figures into the plot. A scene in which Mytyl and Tytyl wake up their deceased grandparents, then let them die again, could raise uncomfortable questions from younger viewers. (For that matter, explaining a hall filled with "unborn" children is equally touchy today.) Death permeates the earthbound scenes, with disease and decay literally right around the corner. Despite its upbeat moral, the film can be seen as a somber warning of our mortality, and the fates that await us.

While it received generally positive reviews, *The Blue Bird* was not a financial success. Coupled with the poor box-office performance of *Prunella*, it forced Tourneur to reconsider his opposition to commercial filmmaking methods. He chose less challenging material for his next films, achieving his biggest hit with a 1920 adaptation of Robert Louis Stevenson's *Treasure Island*. That same year he started work on what would become a troubled production of *The Last of the Mohicans*, also a Registry title.

Broken Blossoms

United Artists. Silent, B&W, 1.33. 89 minutes.

Cast: Lillian Gish (Lucy, the girl), Richard Barthelmess (Cheng Huan), Donald Crisp (Battling Burrows), Arthur Howard (Burrows' manager), Edward Pell (Evil Eye), George Beranger (The spying one), Norman Selby (Prize fighter).

Credits: Written and directed by D.W. Griffith. Adapted from a story by Thomas Burke. Director of photography: G.W. Bitzer.

Additional Cast: Moon Kwan (Monk), Ernest Butterworth, Fred Hamer, Geroge Nichols.

Additional Credits: Produced by D.W. Griffith. Based on "The Chink and the Child" from *Limehouse Nights* by Thomas Burke. Film editor: James Smith. Premiered May 13, 1919; general release: October 20, 1920.

Other Versions: Remade in 1936, directed by John Brahm.

Available: Kino Video DVD *Griffith Masterworks* (2002). UPC: 738329027025.

After devoting months to *Intolerance* (1916), D.W. Griffith took almost a year off before turning to smaller projects. He signed a contract with Paramount, and released a half-dozen films through that studio over a three-year period. Two of the films concerned World War I, and featured footage he had shot in trenches in France. In 1919, he was one of the founders of United Artists, along with Mary Pickford, Douglas Fairbanks, and Charlie Chaplin. Because of contractual obligations, he and Chaplin were the only ones supplying films to the company at first. Even though Griffith still owed another film to Paramount, he chose *Broken Blossoms* to be his debut United Artists title.

The film was drawn from a story by the English author Thomas Burke. Born in 1886, Burke grew up in Eltham, at the time a comfortable suburb of London. The *Limehouse Nights* collection was his first book. Situated on the Thames waterfront near London's East End, Limehouse was notorious at the end of the nineteenth century for its bars and opium dens. Filled with immigrants—particularly Asians—it had one of the highest crime rates in London. The success of *Limehouse Nights* led to Burke to write many many more books with Limehouse settings: *Twinkletoes: A Tale of Limehouse*; *A Tea-Shop in Limehouse*; and others. He later wrote travel essays about English inns.

Pickford and Fairbanks, in the midst of an affair but not yet married, passed Burke's book on to Griffith. The first story in the collection, "The Chink and the Child," gives a fair indication of racial sensitivity at the time. Narrated in a style similar to one Damon Runyon would later use, it detailed a perverse triangle. Battling Burrows, a welterweight, is guardian to his illegitimate daughter Lucy. The victim of relentless abuse, Lucy is rescued after Burrows beats her with a dog whip by Cheng Hong, a Chinese merchant and opium addict. Their chaste affair is betrayed by one of Burrows' companions, leading to fatal consequences. The story's bald emotions, downtrodden characters, and morbid plotting appealed to Grififth, who turned it into one of his more carefully prepared productions.

According to Lillian Gish, Griffith had to persuade her to play Lucy Burrows. Gish was in her twenties; the part called for a fifteen-year-old (the girl was twelve in the original story). In other accounts, Griffith considered his protégé and eventual lover Carol Dempster for the part.

While Griffith cast Asians as extras, he never seriously contemplated using one in the lead role. For one thing, there were very few working in film at all. (Sessue Hayakawa, star of 1915's *The Cheat*, had his own production company, and could not work for another studio.) It's unlikely that Griffith could have found an Asian-American actor for the part, even if he tried. He most likely didn't consider casting a Caucasian a problem. He was, after all, a director content to film the waterfront slums of London on an open-air stage off Sunset Boulevard.

Richard Barthelmess was under contract to Dorothy Gish's production company, which made him fair game for Griffith. This was one of his breakthrough roles, in part because he sensed that the part called for rigid restraint. With his eyes taped, his face was almost immobile. To that he added a slight slouch, and a tendency to jut his head forward. It was not a polite or politically correct job, but it was just what Griffith wanted. Gish also found that slouching helped her performance. Her shuffling gait, slumped shoulders, and perpetually widened eyes helped her overcome the age discrepancy.

Griffith and his crew had refined their filmmaking techniques since the epics *Birth of a Nation* (1915) and *Intolerance*. For one thing, the director paid a lot more attention to matching shots. Close-ups were now lit in the same patterns and styles as the wide shots. Griffith tried to match the acting within shots as well, so that a performance would seem consistent throughout a scene. Set decorators had learned to dress views outside doors and windows instead of leaving them black. The goal was to extend the sets past what the camera filmed, building a world beyond the frame.

Broken Blossoms is, as an early intertitle states, "a tale of tears," and Griffith was unrepentent about pulling out all the emotional stops. If the film still works, it is because of his sense of the psychology of the characters. Barthelmess, the "Yellow Man," has fallen into drug addiction as a way to cope with his failure to achieve his goals. (It's telling that Griffith filmed a ten-minute prologue set in China in order to show the Yellow Man's background. Without this lost paradise, the Yellow Man would have seemed weak for falling prey to drugs.) In today's terms, Gish is playing the victim of child abuse, beaten by her father because he is incapable of dealing with the frustrations in his life—a scenario that Griffith seems to understand intuitively. Crisp, an interesting director and an excellent performer who could sometimes overact, captures the nagging shame and self-loathing of the child abuser. He is someone who confirms his own weaknesses by lashing out at victims. Griffith set up the fim's premise so that Gish does not seem masochistic: uneducated, penniless, she has no alternative to her father's abuse.

In fact, all the characters in the film, including Yellow Man's rival Evil Eye and Burrows's manager and opponents, are trapped in the hell of the Limehouse slums. It's something Griffith must have felt himself when he was sleeping in flophouses on the Bowery in New York, unable to find acting work and unable to make a living doing anything else. Griffith's compassion for characters compensates for his melodramatic excesses and Victorian sensibilities. Both Gish and Barthelmess play weirdly presexual characters, adults with adolescent feelings and expressions. With the rampant miscenegation of the time, it would have been too much to expect Griffith to explore an interracial love affair, but the absence of sexual desire takes *Broken Blossoms* out of the realm of reality. It turns what could have been a shattering story into one that seems safely archaic.

Gish had fond memories of working on *Broken Blossoms*. In one interview she spoke about how Karl Brown used a picture postcard and a cutout of a ship to fake a Limehouse waterfront for a shot, and how Griffith hired Norman Selby, a professional fighter, as both an actor and his personal sparring partner. Gish would make only four more films with Griffith before breaking away to sign a contract with MGM. There she starred in a number of expensive but commercially unsuccessful productions, including *The Wind* (1928), a Registry title.

Within Our Gates

Micheaux Film Co., 1920. Silent, B&W, 1.33. 78 minutes.

Cast: Evelyn Preer (Sylvia Landry), Flo Clements (Alma Prichard), James D. Ruffin (Conrad Drebert), Jack Chenault (Larry Prichard), William Smith (Philip Gentry), Charles D. Lucas (Dr. V. Vivian), Bernice Ladd (Mrs. Geraldine Stratton), Mrs. Evelyn (Mrs. Elena Warwick), William Starks (Jasper Landry), Ralph Johnson (Philip Griddlestone), E.G. Tatum (Efrem), Grant Edwards (Emil Landry), Grant Gorman (Armand Griddlestone), Mattie Edwards (Mrs. Landry), S.T. Jacks (Reverend Wilson Jacobs), Jimmie Cook, LaFont Harris.

Credits: Written, produced, and directed by Oscar Micheaux.

Additional Credits: Released January 12, 1920.

Available: Image Entertainment DVD *The Origins of Film* (2001). UPC: 014381980721.

African-Americans appeared on film as early as 1895, at first as objects of ethnic curiosity, and later in the same stereotyped terms used on the stage in minstrel and blackface shows. Titles like *Watermelon Feast* and *Dancing Darkies* (both 1896) fed off prejudice, one of the reasons why historian Thomas Cripps feels that were largely indifferent to early film. Selig's *Something Good—Negro Kiss* (1900), a "Burlesque on the John Rice and May Irwin Kiss," may have tried to approach its audience in a different manner, but for the most part early movies depicted African Americans in harshly unflattering terms.

By 1910, when William Foster began the black-operated Foster Photoplay Company in Chicago, there were over two hundred movie theaters owned by blacks, a number that grew to close to seven hundred within a decade. Foster, later a prominent publicist, specialized in comedies, but the market also included black-oriented newsreels and "race" films produced and financed by whites. The release of *The Birth of a Nation* in 1915 sparked a public outcry against its racism, and became a rallying point for black filmmakers as well as organizations like the National Association for the Advancement of Colored People (NAACP). But while an audience existed for black films, even an established actor like Noble Johnson, a former

Philanthropist Alma Prichard (Flo Clements) advises schoolteacher Sylvia Landry (Evelyn Preer, right) in *Within Our Gates*. *Photo credit: The Film Society of Lincoln Center/The Oscar Micheaux Society*

rodeo star who entered films in 1909, had to struggle for financing. Johnson formed Lincoln Films with his brother George, but relied on parts in Hollywood films to make a living.

Oscar Micheaux took a different approach to movies, one that proved viable for a number of other filmmakers as well. Born on an Illinois farm in 1884, Micheaux worked in Chicago before developing a farm in South Dakota. Details, drawn mostly from his autobiographical novels, are sketchy, but he apparently decided to become an author after seeing a minstrel show in 1909. Around this time he fell in love with the daughter of a white rancher; this thwarted romance became one of the central elements of his fiction. He sold his first book, *The Conquest*, door-to-door through the Midwest and then on a tour of the South. Micheaux used this same method to finance and sell two subsequent novels, writing mainstream stories for a specific audience. Lincoln Films offered to adapt *The Homesteader* (1917), but Micheaux wanted to direct the project himself. He sold shares in the film, which he shot in the Selig studios in Chicago. By touring with the film, especially in the South, Micheaux made a profit of $5,000, enough to start work on another project, *Within Our Gates*.

Micheaux knew that he was not going to sell books, shares, or movie tickets by telling his audience that things were just fine. *Within Our Gates* (even the title is inflammatory) would tackle the most controversial aspects of race head on. At the same time, the director knew he had to cushion viewers and, perhaps more important, censors, from the full impact of his images. He had to surround scenes of lynching and interracial rape with a story line that was as inoffensive as possible, one that implicated his target audience almost as much as society as a whole. It was a difficult balancing act, one that is, for a number of reasons, almost impossible to judge fairly today.

Micheaux's plot revolves around Sylvia Landry (played by Evelyn Preer), a schoolteacher whose engagement to surveyor Conrad Drebert (James D. Ruffin) is ruined by a jealous divorcée and her criminal brother. Sylvia travels south to work at a school for Negroes, but returns to Boston out of a sense of duty to her race. She meets Dr. Vivian, who is "passionately engaged in social questions," and tries to persuade a white philanthropist to finance black education. It's not until almost an hour into the movie that Micheaux unleashes an extended flashback about Sylvia's early life. In it, a wealthy white landowner rapes one of his black workers in a scene that mirrors a black man's assault on Lillian Gish in *The Birth of a Nation*. Micheaux also includes a double lynching, seen for the first time on film from a black viewpoint. Lynching had been shown on film as early as 1904, in *Avenging a Crime*, but Micheaux's version has a matter-of-fact quality that is chilling.

When Micheaux opened the film in Chicago and Detroit in January 1920, he faced immediate criticism from both the white and black press. As with *The Birth of a Nation*, authorities used the threat of race riots to demand cuts. Micheaux, who could afford to print only four copies of the film, had trouble in Shreveport, Louisiana, and Omaha, Nebraska, as well. He didn't even try to exhibit *Within Our Gates* in New York. (He did open his third film, *The Brute*, there, because he could pay for nine prints instead of four.)

The notoriety helped *Within Our Gates* achieve a long life in secondary markets—in churches and schools, for example. Micheaux, meanwhile, continued to make movies, by most counts over forty features in a thirty-year span. Among these are *Body and Soul* (1925), Paul Robeson's film debut, and *The Exile* (1931), his first sound film.

On an aesthetic level, *Within Our Gates* can seem awkward, even unformed. Micheaux's budget—somewhere between $5,000 and $15,000—precluded expensive production values. The acting often seems unrefined, or perhaps under-rehearsed. It may not have been entirely the talent's fault. Evelyn Preer had appeared in Micheaux's *The Homesteader*, and was a member of the Lafayette Players, a well-regarded New York troupe. The differing acting styles may not be entirely Micheaux's fault either, just as the film's chaotic, at times incomprehensible plotting could be the result of other factors.

Recent critics have come up with various rationalizations for Micheaux's "imperfect" cinema, for shots that don't match, gaps in temporal or spatial logic, story lines that career into unexpected tangents. Manthia Diawara, for

one, writes that Micheaux's "loose editing" is like improvisation in jazz, that how the director "misreads and improves upon Hollywood logic is a powerful metaphor for the way in which African-Americans survived . . . within a hostile economic and racist system."

But the *Within Our Gates* we see today is not the version Micheaux showed in 1920. In fact, the film was considered lost for years. The single surviving print, dating probably from the 1920s and retitled *La Negra*, was found in Spain. Only four of the original intertitles remained. Some of the incoherence of the extant film is due to the missing intertitles, as well as the generally poor shape of the materials. Who knows how many people cut or rearranged or duplicated the remaining footage? (*Body and Soul* is the only Micheaux feature with intact intertitles. Working from a translation by Kathleen Newman, Scott Simmon—assisted by Alex Vargas—reconstructed new titles for the restored version of *Within Our Gates*.)

Given these qualifications, Micheaux's achievement is all the more remarkable. The filmmaker could compose and edit wonderful material, like a sequence of Sylvia crossing a Boston street through heavy traffic, the camera providing dynamic angles while quick cutting establishes a jazzy tempo. His characters have a self-awareness that is highly unusual for the period, such as a corrupt preacher who realizes that "Hell is my destiny." To even suggest that blacks faced problems unrelated to racism or oppression from whites was in itself noteworthy. On top of these achievements, Micheaux's biggest contribution may have been proving to others that it was possible to make and exhibit movies independently from the motion picture industry.

One Week

Metro Pictures, 1920. Silent, B&W, 1.33. 19 minutes.

Cast (credited offscreen): Buster Keaton, Sybil Seely, Joe Roberts.

Credits (offscreen): Directed by Buster Keaton, Eddie Cline. Screenplay by Buster Keaton, Eddie Cline. Cinematography: Elgin Lessley. Technical director: Fred Gabourie. Presented by Joseph M. Schenck.

Additional Credits: Released September 1, 1920.

Available: Kino on Video DVD *The Saphead* (2001). UPC: 7-38329-01342-4.

When Buster Keaton was drafted into the Army in 1918, he left behind a burgeoning film career that included co-starring roles in over a dozen shorts with Roscoe "Fatty" Arbuckle. After serving in

Europe during World War I, Keaton returned to the United States to learn that Arbuckle was leaving the Comique Film Corporation for Paramount, where he would be the first silent comedian to switch from shorts to features. Producer Joseph Schenck offered Comique to Keaton, working out a deal with Metro Pictures to release eight Keaton shorts a year.

Keaton not only took over the Comique studio, but got to use Arbuckle's old staff, including cinematographer Elgin Lessley and special effects

Newlyweds Sybil Seely and Buster Keaton outside their new home.

wizard Fred Gabourie. They would remain with Keaton until he moved to MGM in 1929. The comedian then hired Eddie Cline as director. Cline had been with slapstick pioneer Mack Sennett as far back as 1912; more recently he had been making shorts with comedian Slim Summerville at Fox. He received co-directing credit for sixteen of Keaton's nineteen shorts, and while his creative input is unclear, he did helm some significant sound comedies, including the 1940 Registry title *The Bank Dick*.

Making movies was a liberating process for Keaton. On stage he had to perform at his best eight times a week, but on film he only had to get a joke right once. (Furthermore, the "right" wasn't confined by the logic and physics of theater.) Few film performers of the time had as thorough a grounding in physical comedy as Keaton did. In addition, through his collaborations with Arbuckle he learned how to expand the scope and possibilities of material he had been using for years. Perhaps this was why he was disappointed with *The High Sign* (1921), his first completed short. While it had funny moments, it essentially transferred to the screen something that could have been performed just as easily on stage. Keaton was so upset he actually left Comique to take a lead role in the Metro production *The Saphead* before starting in on his next project.

Film historian Kevin Brownlow traced the plot for *One Week* to *Home Made* (1919), one in a series of sponsored films made under the umbrella title *Ford Educational Weekly*. Both films concern the construction of a prefabricated house on a day-by-day basis. Keaton used the plot as the starting point for a series of mistakes, misunderstandings, and deliberate double-crosses. It was also an opportunity to stage jokes on a scale previously unavailable to him, one that encompassed a full-size house that he had built on an empty lot at Metro Studios.

In the story, a jealous boyfriend mislabels the crates holding the parts of a portable house, given to Keaton and his new bride (played by Sybil Seely) as a wedding present. Following the printed instructions leads to a surrealist's dream of a house, with canted angles, a too-small roof, and a door to nowhere on the second floor. The characters could have come from an old Arbuckle short, especially "Handy Hank," played by an unidentified actor who was similar in looks and style to Arbuckle's nephew Al St. John.

But Keaton directed in a markedly different manner than his mentor. He was a patient storyteller, willing to set up jokes early in the film that wouldn't pay off until much later. One small example: The short opens with a calendar shot for Monday the 9th, an insignificant date until Friday rolls around. Keaton restricts views of the house he is building until it is finished, focusing on construction gags that give viewers little glimpses of the disasters awaiting. He is also careful to show how his jokes work so that he doesn't trick and therefore disappoint his audience.

Many of the gags in *One Week* would reappear throughout his movies, reworked, refined, sometimes just copied. At one point a wall of the house falls onto Keaton, who is saved only because of an open second-story window. It was a gag he resurrected from the Arbuckle short *Back Stage* (1919), and one he would stage even more memorably in *Steamboat Bill, Jr.* (1928). In an early scene he takes a fall from the handlebars of a motorcycle, something he would film again in *Sherlock Jr.* (1924, a Registry title). *One Week* also includes astounding stunts that few performers would ever attempt, like a two-story fall onto his back.

One Week doesn't just parody the do-it-yourself ethos of the home mechanic, it extends logic to a degree that is both hilarious and deeply satisfying. If by chance you built your house on the equivalent of a giant turntable, then a gale-force wind will start it spinning like a top. To get inside, you will then be forced, as Keaton is at one point, to somehow match your house's velocity in order to dive through a moving target of a window.

The equanimity with which Keaton solves his problems is one of the most appealing aspects of *One Week*. He may be momentarily puzzled or chagrined, but he doesn't ask for explanations or sympathy, not even when his ingenious solutions backfire. The film received excellent reviews when it was released after Labor Day, with one paper calling it "the comedy sensation of the year." In a sense, Keaton had trained all his life for this moment, and the success of *One Week* vindicated his approach to comedy. In his subsequent shorts he began assembling a stock company, including Joe Roberts (seen briefly here in a bit with a piano) as the heavy and Seely as the ingénue in two more films (she would be replaced by Virginia Fox).

He also began considering the feature-length format, which he tried on an experimental basis with *Three Ages* (1923). His next Registry film is *Cops* (1922).

The Last of the Mohicans

Barbara Bedford as a love-torn Cora Munro in *The Last of the Mohicans*.

Associated Producers, 1920. Silent, B&W, 1.33. 71 minutes.

Cast: Alan Roscoe (Uncas), Barbara Bedford (Cora Munro), Wallace Beery (Magua), Lillian Hall (Alice Munro), Henry Woodward (Major Heyward), James Gordon (Colonel Munro), George Hackathorne (Captain Randolph), Theodore Lerch [Lorch] (Chingachgook), Nelson McDowell (David Gamut), Harry Lorraine (Hawkeye), Sydney Deane (General Webb), Jack F. McDonald (Tamenund), Boris Karloff (Indian), Joseph Singleton.

Credits: Directed by Maurice Tourneur & Clarence Brown. Scenario: Robert A. Dillon. Design: Floyd Mueller. Photography: Philip R. Dubois, Charles van Enger. Presented by Maurice Tourneur.

Additional Credits: Released November 21, 1920.

Other Versions: *The Last of the Mohicans* was filmed in 1911 (Thanhouser Films and Powers Picture Plays), 1932 (Mascot, directed by Ford Beebe and B. Reeves Eason), 1936 (United Artists, directed by George B. Seitz), and 1992 (Twentieth Century-Fox, directed by Michael Mann).

Available: SlingShot Entertainment DVD (1993). ISBN: 1-58448-045-9. UPC: 0-1707-89851-2-2.

Having built a career in France and the United States as an accomplished director with a strong visual style, Maurice Tourneur formed his own production company in order to maintain control over his projects. Films like *The Blue Bird* (1918), although high artistic achievements, proved financially unrewarding. In 1920 he joined several other prominent directors, including Thomas Ince, Allan Dwan, and Mack Sennett, in Associated Producers. (This would soon merge with First National to form Associated First National.)

Tourneur had just finished directing two Robert Louis Stevenson adaptations: *Treasure Island* with Lon Chaney, and *The White Circle* with John Gilbert. Both were thrilling period spectacles aimed at younger viewers, but with enough romance and intrigue to interest adults as well. *The Last of the Mohicans* would repeat the formula, using an American subject instead of European ones.

James Fenimore Cooper's sprawling 1826 novel was set during the French and Indian War of 1767, and based loosely on Captain Robert Rogers, a scout, guide, and later leader of his own irregular militiamen known as "Rogers' Rangers." (He was also the subject of Kenneth Roberts's novel *Northwest Passage*, filmed by King Vidor in 1940). The plot of the novel dealt with the defeat of British troops at Fort William Henry and their retreat to Fort Ann, told from the point of view of two daughters of a British colonel and the Mohicans who are guarding them.

To mainstream viewers, the intricacies of the French and Indian War were not just unfamiliar but hard to explain. Based in Canada, the French were battling the British for control of Lake Champlain and Lake George, the best means of transportation in the area; both sides sought the support of local Indians without really understanding politics among the tribes. The resulting alliances were not only bewildering but highly fluid.

Little of this made any difference to Tourneur, who saw *The Last of the Mohicans* in terms of a Stevenson novel, filled with marauding villains and the few bulwarks who stood against them. Tourneur and his screenwriter Robert Dillon didn't really care about which Indian tribes followed which side in the war: there were just "good" Indians who didn't kill whites and "bad" Indians who wore war paint and raped and pillaged the innocent.

What really interested Tourneur was the idea of a forbidden love affair between a white woman and an Indian man. The director was slightly ambivalent about the benefits or even the possibility of such a union in colonial society, but left no doubts about the sexual attraction between Cora Munro, daughter of a British colonel, and Uncas, son of a Mohican chief. Tourneur's Cora (played by Barbara Bedford) is all heaving breasts and tremulous glances, her dark eyes ringed with makeup to enhance her

hunger. Uncas (played in "redface" by Alan Roscoe) may be noble, but he is also half-naked and given to visiting Cora's bedroom at night, where he casts burning eyes in her direction. Tourneur exaggerated the illicit nature of their relationship, without indicating, as Cooper did in the novel, that Cora had an Indian mother. Furthermore, in the novel she is unattached; here she is unhappily paired with Captain Randolph (George Hackathorne), a coward invented for the film.

Tourneur did not forget his younger audience, giving *The Last of the Mohicans* some of the most thrilling action of the period—fast-paced, brutal, and filled with spectacular imagery. Almost a quarter of the film is given over to the massacre of women and children fleeing Fort William Henry. It is a superbly constructed sequence that starts with carefully composed wide shots of troops marching in parade and gradually descends into the madness of mob hysteria. Hundreds of extras fill out every corner of the frame. At one point a savage, knife clenched in his teeth, advances on a helpless mother and her newborn baby. He's filmed in a shocking close up, heading straight into the lens.

The massacre is based on historical fact, and throughout the film Tourneur and his crew show an attention to detail that is unusual for the industry at the time. But historical accuracy goes only so far. Big Bear Lake, California, substitutes for the shores of Lake George, New York; and Yosemite for the Adirondacks. (Like subsequent film versions of the novel, it proved too expensive and difficult for Tourneur to shoot in New York.)

An accident kept Tourneur off the set for three months, and his assistant Clarence Brown took over, shooting the exteriors according to Tourneur's directions. As Brown told film historian Kevin Brownlow, "Tourneur hated exteriors," leaving them to Brown's unit, which had its own cameraman, Charles van Enger. Brown credited Tourneur and his cinematographer John van der Broek with the most beautiful photography in film. "He painted on the screen," Brown said about Tourneur. "He was a great believer in dark foregrounds. No matter where he set his camera up, he would always have a foreground. On exteriors, we used to carry branches and twigs around with us."

In *The Last of the Mohicans*, Brown created depth through rain and fog effects, and by filming in the mornings and afternoons rather than during the flat light of midday. He also told Brownlow about improvising a dolly by placing the camera on a perambulator fastened to an automobile axle. Brown would go on to become one of the most valued directors at MGM, working with Greta Garbo on a half-dozen films, including *Flesh and the Devil* (1927). ·

Magua was an important role for Wallace Beery, who plays the villain with an exuberance and insolence that were trademarks of his screen persona. Barbara Bedford's obvious screen chemistry with Alan Roscoe led to their marriage in 1922. Roscoe worked in films until his death in 1933. Bedford starred in *The Spoilers* (1923), an Alaskan adventure refilmed many times, and *Tumbleweeds* (1925), William S. Hart's last feature. She appeared in almost two hundred films altogether, largely in bit parts.

Cooper's vision of a perilous frontier filled with savage heathens, stalwart guides, and perfidious soldiers has resonated throughout American culture. He regretted the passing of the wilderness, but saw the benefits of a society that brought law and order to nature. He focused on the lone

hero who bridged the gap between society and wilderness, between citizens and outlaws, between English-based white culture and the "other," signified largely by French and Indian hunters and trappers. His hero evolved over time and books, but whether he was referred to as Natty Bumppo, Hawkeye, or Leatherstocking, he always had the same expert skills and unyielding moral compass. He was a figure who spread throughout entertainment, emulated by everyone from William S. Hart to John Wayne to Clint Eastwood.

When producers chose to remake *The Last of the Mohicans*, they stripped away the moral ambiguities that fascinated Tourneur, concentrating instead on Hawkeye as a savior figure. They found that it was relatively easy to reduce Cooper's plot to a Western formula, and much harder to justify an interracial romance that tried to break away from the double binds of family and patriotism. Tourneur's vision turned out to be considerably more mature than that of many of his followers.

The Making of an American

Turning immigrants into laborers was one of the goals of *The Making of an American.*

The State of Connecticut Department of Americanization, 1920. Silent, B&W, 1.37. 14 minutes.

Credits: Directed by Guy Hedlund. Produced by the Worcester Film Corporation. Presented by the State of Connecticut Department of Americanization, Board of Education.

Additional Credits: Preserved in 1999 by the National Archives of Canada.

Available: Northeast Historic Film DVD (2006). UPC: 7-933130-047900.

The silent film industry was not shy about tackling social issues, and could be counted upon to present a reliably liberal outlook, especially compared to the mainstream press. Registry titles like *The Italian* and *The Immigrant* (both 1915) took a sympathetic attitude toward what many businessmen and civic leaders considered a growing problem: immigration. The post–World War I years saw a tightening of immigration policies, resulting in smaller quotas. That wasn't enough for some leaders—notably Henry Ford, who railed against newcomers who refused to assimilate. "These men of many nations must be taught American ways, the English language, and the right way to live," he said, and he had the Ford Motor Company provide mandatory English language courses for immigrant laborers. U.S. Steel and other companies followed suit.

More than thirty states passed laws regarding the training of immigrants, including funding night-school courses in English. In 1919, Utah passed an Americanization Act authorizing $20,000 in salaries and expenses for educating immigrants. That same year, Connecticut not only funded two years' worth of schooling for immigrants, but formed a Department of Americanization within the State Board of Education. The state also permitted any town to appoint its own Director of Americanization.

Part of that money was paid to the Worcester Film Corporation for *The Making of an American*, an educational short produced in and around Hartford. The Worcester Film Corporation was founded in 1918 in Massachusetts by Floyd A. Ramsdell. In 1919, the *New York Times* noted a screening of *Through Life's Windows* (or *The Tale of a Ray of Light*), written and produced by P.D. Hugdon for Worcester. Hugdon would have been a good candidate for directing this film, but sources credit Guy Hedlund. According to film historian Jan-Christopher Horak, Hedlund had been an actor for Biograph when D.W. Griffith worked there, appearing in films like *Enoch Arden* (1911). Hedlund also starred in Westerns shot at Fort Lee, New Jersey. He may have used the fact that he was a Connecticut native to obtain the directing position for *The Making of an American*.

Although shot on a small budget, the film has sophisticated touches. Hedlund uses cross-cutting when setting up an accident that will injure Peter Bruno, the lead character, and reverse angles to establish a relationship between Pete and the schoolteacher at an English-language course. (The teacher also enunciates so clearly that it is easy to read her lips.) Pete even gets a flashback when interviewing a job hopeful.

The message of the film is that financial security and a better standing in society result when immigrants learn English. Unfortunately, it is a message delivered almost entirely in English, apart from introductory intertitles in Italian, Hungarian, and Polish. While non-English-speaking viewers would be able to follow the plot without much difficulty, they would miss the intertitles' theme of self-improvement: "The way to do a thing is to begin." "Mastery over all good things begins with mastery of self." "Now it's up to you to make good money!"

Hedlund documents Pete's rise from day laborer shoveling in a ditch to the operator of a drill press at a tool and dye plant to an apparently supervisory position at the Hartford Rubber Works. Since it was shot on location, *The Making of an American* offers tantalizing glimpses into everyday life in Hartford in 1920. Connecticut archive documents revealed that the state showed the film to over 112,000 people in 1920.

This is the only directing credit for Hedlund to surface. According to film historian Robert Birchard, the Worcester Film Corporation was operating in New York City in 1927, making industrial, scientific, and educational films. Actor George Duryea appeared in a Worcester short directed by W. Allen Lucey for the National Safety Council; it got him a role in Cecil B. DeMille's *The Godless Girl* (1929). Intriguingly, the Worcester Film Corporation is credited with a thirty-minute film titled *Tools and Rules for Precision Measuring*, produced in 1948 for the Aviation Technician Education Council. The following year, Floyd Ramsdell, as head of the Worcester Film Corporation, applied for patent number 2,650,737, an "apparatus for making film exposures for three-dimensional moving pictures." He retired in 1961 and died in 1983 at the age of ninety-two.

The state of Connecticut dissolved the Department of Americanization in 1921. While researching the Department, Connecticut State Archivist Dr. Mark H. Jones found written material about the project, but the film itself remained lost until 1999. Then Alan Kattelle of Hudson, Massachusetts, donated a 28mm print to the Northeast Historic Film archive, along with newsreels and a copy of another public service film, *Tommy's Troubles*, produced by the Department of Health and the New York Tuberculosis and Health Association.

Immigration, including issues of assimilation and English as a second language, remains a regular topic of debate in current politics.

The Four Horsemen of the Apocalypse

Metro, 1920. Silent, B&W with color and tinted sequences, 1.33. 132 minutes.

Cast: Pomeroy Cannon (Madariaga [the Centaur]), Josef [Joseph] Swickard (Marcelo Desnoyers), Bridgetta Clark (Doña Luisa), Rudolph Valentino (Julio Desnoyers), Virginia Warwick (Chichi), Alan Hale (Karl von Hartrott), Mabel Van Buren (Elena), Stuart Homes (Otto von Hartrott), John Sainpolis (Etienne Laurier), Alice Terry (Marguerite Laurier), Mark Fenton (Senator Lacour), Derrick Ghent (René Lacour), Nigel de Brulier (Tchernoff), Brodwitch [Brodwich] Turner (Argensola), Edward Connelly (Lodgekeeper), Wallace Beery (Lieut. Col. von Richthoffen), Harry Northrup (The General [The Count]), Arthur Hoyt (Lieut. Schnitz).

Credits: Directed and supervised by Rex Ingram. Written for the screen by June Mathis. Based on the novel by Vicente Blasco Ibáñez. Photography by John F. Seitz. Film editor: Grant Whytock. Technical staff: Amos Myers, Joseph Calder. Assistant director: Walter Mayo. Art titles by Jack W. Robson. Produced by Metro Pictures Corporation.

Additional Cast: Brinsley Shaw (Celendonio), Jean Hersholt (Prof. Von Hartrott), Henry Klaus (Heinrick Von Hartrott), Georgia Woodthorpe (Lodgekeeper's wife), Kathleen Key (Georgette), Jacques D'Aurey (Captain D'Aubrey), Curt Rehfeld (Major Blumhardt), Mlle. Dolorez (Mlle. Lucette, The Model), "Bull" Montana (The French butcher), Isabel Keith (The German woman), Jacques Lanoe (Her husband), Noble Johnson (Conquest), Minnehaha (The old nurse), Beatrice Dominguez (Dancer); Richard Arlen, Ramon Samaniego [Ramon Novarro] (extras).

Additional Credits: Film editor: June Mathis. Art direction: Walter Mayo, Kurt Rehfeld. Make-up: Jean Hersholt. Original music: Louis F. Gottschalk. New York premiere March 6, 1921.

Other Versions: Remade in 1962 as *The Four Horsemen of the Apocalypse*, directed by Vicente Minnelli.

Available: The Museum of Modern Art.

Published in 1916 as *Los cuatro jinetes del Apocalipsis* and translated into English in 1918, *The Four Horsemen of the Apocalypse* was the first novel about World War I to find a wide audience in the United States. Written by Vicente Blasco Ibáñez, a Spanish author controversial in his own country for novels thought too realistic and liberal, the book was a multigenerational saga that shifted from cattle ranches in Argentina to the battle trenches of France. Blasco Ibáñez's ultimate message had something to do with maintaining racial purity and with the futility of war, but what most readers took away from it was the perfidy of the German people.

Metro Pictures, run at the time by Marcus Loew, purchased the rights to the novel for $20,000, largely at the urging of screenwriter June Mathis. Born in 1890, she was a stage actress who toured with the famous female impersonator Julian Eltinge before becoming a writer. Winning a screenwriting contest, she signed a contract with Metro in 1915 and moved to Hollywood with her mother. As head of the story department, she exerted considerable authority over the studio's output. For this project, she not only chose director Rex Ingram, but was responsible for casting Rudolph Valentino.

Born Rodolfo Guglielmi in Castellaneta, Italy, on May 6, 1895, Rudolph Valentino reached New York City by 1913. He knocked around as a gardener, waiter, and nightclub dancer, arriving in Los Angeles in 1917 with a faintly unsavory reputation. He found work in films in bit parts, ethnic roles, and as villains, his dark complexion limiting what he was allowed to play. Mathis liked his work in *Eyes of Youth* (1919), where he was a "cabaret parasite," and offered him the role of Julio Desnoyers in *Four Horsemen*. (She also considered Antonio Moreno, who would later take parts Valentino turned down.)

Director Rex Ingram was really Reginald Hitchcock from Dublin. Born in 1893, he studied art at Yale before appearing in Edison films under the name Rex Hitchcock. By 1916 he had finished directing a feature at Universal, but left California to enlist as a flight instructor. Badly wounded in a plane crash, he returned to Universal to find that his staff position had been taken by Erich von Stroheim. (They later became close friends, and Stroheim turned to Ingram to help edit *Greed*.) Ingram labored over a series of unmemorable films, most of them lost, that were described by critics of the time as "high-class horror," "lurid melodramas," and "morbid." But with *Shore Acres* (1920) he assembled what amounted to his own unit, including cinematographer John F. Seitz, editor Grant Whytock, and actress Alice Terry, an ethereal beauty he both discovered and married.

Mathis secured the *Four Horsemen* job for Ingram after working with him on *Hearts Are Trump* (1920), another lost film. They collaborated closely on the script, removing some of the more stridently anti-German touches and building up Valentino's part by adding a tango sequence. Ingram had misgivings about Valentino ("He couldn't be shot with both ears showing," he said later), but when viewing the dailies agreed with Mathis that the actor brought something new to the screen. The writer was on the set every day, coaching Valentino intimately. He called her "little mother" and said, "I could tell by June's face whether she was pleased with the way I was doing a scene."

Intolerance and *Civilization* (both 1916) set high standards for historical epics, even though neither one made much money. Ingram and Mathis aimed a little lower, blending Blasco Ibáñez's artistic pretensions with his shrewd grasp of the marketplace. *Four Horsemen* was a case of having your cake and eating it, too: adulterous passion coupled with guilt and remorse, xenophobic blood-lust tied to pacifist lectures and anti-war slogans. The story's characters shared this dichotomy.

A prologue set in Argentina introduces the wealthy cattle baron Madariaga (Pomeroy Cannon), whose daughters marry a Frenchman and a German respectively. Both families leave the New World for the Old, Karl von Hartrott (Alan Hale) to raise his sons as German soldiers, Marcelo Desnoyers (Josef Swickard) to confront his past as a student rebel and draft dodger. The film criticizes Marcelo for frittering away his share of Madariaga's fortune by collecting antiques, and for losing his moral compass by purchasing a castle on the Marne. But viewers are asked to commiserate with him later when German officers overrun his castle and use his treasures for debauchery.

Without the novel as a guide, the plot to *Four Horsemen* is a ramshackle, unholy mess, with war, rape, adultery, cross-dressing, tangos, fire-breathing dragons, and Death as the Grim Reaper, tinted green and seated atop a horse. Even Christ, disguised as a "stranger" in a third floor garret, puts in an appearance. Ingram had an eye for spectacle, building scenes with hundreds of extras (studio publicity claimed that 12,000 people worked on the film). But he also had a plodding visual style, one that was locked into an earlier age of films as stagebound tableaus.

Cinematographer John F. Seitz, the younger brother of director George B. Seitz, pulls off some impressive effects: a dolly shot during Valentino's tango with dancer Beatrice Dominguez, expressive lighting during love scenes, beautifully composed matte shots. But much of the film feels inert,

despite Grant Whytock's efforts to pull together a story from what he estimated at over a million feet of footage. (Ingram used either twelve or fourteen cameras during one battle sequence; Whytock ended up rejecting almost all of the material.)

Ingram was just as old fashioned with his actors, who employ the stiffened gasps, rolled eyes, and hands-to-the-forehead poses of road-company hams. Left to fend for themselves, Hale and Wallace Beery, two of the most reliable character actors in the early years of sound film, etch strong, riveting individuals (Beery even pulls off a scene in which he takes a bubble bath). Ingram and Mathis saw that the key to Valentino was to make him the most masculine presence in his scenes (apart from parental figures). Ingram gave him a gay friend and put his rival German cousins in spectacles, and kept the star far apart from Beery.

Mathis, whose work had strong spiritualist leanings, took credit for the ending set in a cemetery, which sums up the film as an allegory for, if not exactly war or family ties, then perhaps star power. Like Julio Desnoyers, Valentino was plucked from the sidelines as a dancer, turned into an object of adoration, and ultimately sacrificed on the altar of moral conventions. This film helped make him a star of unprecedented proportions. After one more film with Ingram, he left Metro to join Mathis at Paramount. He would be dead within five years. (His *The Son of the Sheik* from 1926 is also on the Registry.)

Like Marcelo Desnoyers, Ingram left the New World for the Old, setting up a studio in France with Alice Terry. He adapted another Blasco Ibáñez novel, *Mare Nostrum*, in 1926, but lost gradually lost his commercial touch with increasingly exotic pictures. Mathis became one of the principal architects behind *Ben-Hur* (1926), but in 1927 died unexpectedly while attending a play with her mother in New York.

Miss Lulu Bett

Paramount, 1921. Silent, B&W, 1.33. 64 minutes.

Cast: Lois Wilson (Lulu Bett), Theodore Roberts (Dwight Deacon), Milton Sills (Neil Cornish), Mabel Van Buren (Mrs. Dwight Deacon), Clarence Burton (Ninian Deacon), Helen Ferguson (Diana Deacon), Ethel Wales (Grandma Bett), Taylor Graves (Bobby Larkin), May Giraci (Manona Deacon).

Credits: Directed by William deMille. Scenario by Clara Berenger. Based on the novel and play by Zona Gale. Chief Photographer: L. Guy Wilky.

Additional Cast: Charles Ogle (Station agent).

Additional Credits: Presented by Adolph Zukor. Premiered in Los Angeles on November 13, 1921.

Available: Image Entertainment DVD *Why Change Your Wife?* (2005). UPC: 0-14381-1990-2-6.

Three years older than his brother Cecil, William deMille was a successful New York City playwright and theater director in the early twentieth century.

Lois Wilson in the title role of *Miss Lulu Bett*, caught between brother-in-law Theodore Roberts and sister Mabel Van Buren.

Skeptical about movies (as many were at first), he eventually followed Cecil to Hollywood after the success of his brother's *The Squaw Man*. William deMille wrote and directed numerous films at Paramount, many of which have been lost. *Miss Lulu Bett* has been preserved by the Library of Congress.

Based on a novel and play by Zona Gale, and adapted by deMille's future wife Clara Beranger, the movie is a smartly realized and moving Cinderella tale about a lonely, exploited spinster who lives with her overbearing relatives. Miss Lulu Bett (Lois Wilson), as everyone calls her, cooks, cleans, and babysits for her sister Ina (Mabel Van Buren) and her husband Dwight (Theodore Roberts), a tyrannical dentist and justice of the peace. Lulu can't even splurge on posies without receiving a lecture on frugality. Ignored or insulted by her grouchy mother and Ina's two spoiled daughters, worn-down by caring for others, she can no longer imagine what it would take to be happy.

That is, until Dwight's estranged brother Ninian pops up after a twenty-year absence. Full of salesman's pep, he hones in on Lulu, who thrives under his attention. But a scandal drags her back to her sister's house. Shunned by the women at church and gossiped about by men on sidewalks, she seems doomed to bitter and humiliating unhappiness. Unless the local schoolteacher, played by matinee idol Milton Sills, can see through to the real Lulu.

Contemporary audiences would have been well aware of the general outline of *Miss Lulu Bett*, and would have had fewer problems with some of its weaker twists, like a mock wedding that suddenly turns real. Yet the story remains engrossing today. Lulu's choices in love and life are tough: a schoolteacher who's either too timid or too self-absorbed to appreciate her beauty, or a fast-talking traveling salesman whose entire life is a lie; or the endless drudgery of looking after relatives who take her for granted if they notice her at all. Author Zona Gale used gentle humor to soften the story's harshness. Lulu's brother-in-law may think he runs the world, but he can't control his flighty daughters. And her frail mother suddenly regains her strength whenever food appears.

DeMille and Beranger made only modest changes to the play, which Gale claimed to have written in a week. "But as I wasn't satisfied with the last act I held it over from Saturday to Monday to revise. So I can say that it took me ten days, and that doesn't sound quite so bad." Gale did change the novel's ending, but critics and audiences protested so much that she offered a third ending about two weeks into the play's run. This version won the Pulitzer Prize in 1921. After Paramount purchased the film rights, deMille went back to the novel's ending, with Gray's approval.

DeMille's visual style is deceptively simple. Action in the film occurs on one plane, in a steady medium shot, with the camera almost never moving and the actors rarely leaving their marks. But the director provides enough detail to make the story seem real. A close-up of ants crawling across dirty dishes piled high in a kitchen sink makes Lulu's plight something everyone can understand.

Lois Wilson was a former Miss Alabama who oddly leaned toward unglamorous roles in film. Her pale beauty and understated acting give *Miss Lulu*

Bett most of its weight. DeMille had worked with her before, and their collaboration here is marked by restraint. The film's most memorable shot is a tight close-up of Lulu flanked by Dwight and Ina, her eyes darting back and forth as she realizes that she can't escape their hold over her. DeMille's quiet approach suits the story admirably, and Wilson's underplaying keeps the plot from seeming too dated.

Some have tried to portray Lulu's dilemma as an early feminist tract, but that would neglect many of the film's other qualities. For a movie about small-town hypocrisy, *Miss Lulu Bett* ends up embracing much of what it criticizes. Sunday services in a white clapboard church, bower romances, drying dishes by hand after dinner, a buggy ride down a quiet dirt road: *Miss Lulu Bett* celebrates, however inadvertently, a way of life that looks impossibly remote and innocent today. DeMille captures a nostalgic but still clear-eyed view of small-town culture with a grace and dignity that has little in common with his brother's ballyhoo.

Some critics considered William deMille a better filmmaker than Cecil (who spelled his surname DeMille). He worked steadily through the 1920s, but did not adjust well to sound. One of his last credits is as supervisor of the Registry title *The Emperor Jones* (1933). He also wrote a well-regarded autobiography, *Hollywood Saga* (Dutton, 1939).

Tol'able David

First National, 1921. Silent, B&W with tints, 1.33. 94 minutes.
Cast: Richard Barthelmess (David Kinemon), Gladys Hulette (Esther Hatburn), Forrest Robinson (Neighbor [Grandfather] Hatburn), Walter P. Lewis (Iska [Iscah] Hatburn), Ernest Torrence (Luke Hatburn), Ralph Yearsley ("Buzzard" Hatburn), Edmund Gurney (Hunter Kinemon), Marion Abbott (Mrs. Kinemon), Warner Richmond (Allen Kinemon), Patterson Dial (Mrs. Rose Kinemon), Lawrence Eddinger (John Galt [Gault]), Henry Hallam (Doctor).
Credits: Directed by Henry King. Screen adaptation by Edmund Goulding, Henry King. Edited by Duncan Mansfield. Photographed by Henry Cronjager. Presented by Inspiration Pictures, Inc., Charles H. Duell, President.
Additional Credits: Produced by Henry King. Based on the short story by Joseph Hergesheimer. A First National attraction. Released November 21, 1921.
Other Versions: Remade as *Tol'able David* (1930), directed by John G. Blystone.
Available: Kino Video VHS (1998). UPC: 7-38329-01263-2. Image Entertainment DVD (1999). UPC: 014381472929.

Based on a short story by Joseph Hergesheimer, *Tol'able David* was originally planned as a D.W. Griffith production. The director purchased the rights to the story, which appeared in a 1919 collection called *The Happy End*, as a vehicle for actor Richard Barthelmess (*Broken Blossoms*, 1919). With its rural Virginia setting and plot pitting innocent youth against savage bullies, it seemed like ideal material for the director. However, Griffith had been focusing more on heroines rather than heroes, and he chose to make *Orphans of the Storm* (1921) with Lillian and Dorothy Gish instead.

Barthelmess, who had previously been under contract to Lillian Gish, and then to Griffith, decided to go out on his own. He purchased the rights to the "Tol'able David" story for $7,500, and hired Edmund Goulding to write an adaptation. With Goulding's script in hand, Barthelmess sought financing from the independent market, signing with Inspiration Pictures, owned by Charles H. Duell. Duell provided the money, but the studio was really run by Henry King. Born in Virginia in 1888, King grew up on a farm and was studying combustion engineering when he went on the stage in 1902. A decade's worth of knocking around in stock companies and road shows gave him a thorough grounding in entertaining rural audiences. In 1913 he moved to California, where he had leads in several films.

King's career as a director began in 1916 with the Baby Marie Osborne films, in which he appeared opposite one of his acting discoveries. By 1921, when he was hired by Inspiration, he had directed, by his count, over fifty films. At Inspiration he served as director, producer, and head of the scenario department, and it was his decision not only to make *Tol'able David*, but to rewrite Goulding's screenplay. King introduced parts for Gladys Hulette, the highest-paid actor in the production, and for another of his "discoveries," musical comedy veteran Ernest Torrence. The older brother of Broadway star David Torrence, Ernest had studied music in Edinburgh, London, and Stuttgart. King turned him into a psychopathic sadist in the film, typecasting him for the rest of his brief career.

King made several structural changes to Hergesheimer's story while retaining its basic "David versus Goliath" plot line. The film is still a coming-of-age drama about a slight, daydreaming farm boy forced to confront violent interlopers to protect his family, but now David has a girlfriend, and the villains are more explicitly part of a Hatfield/McCoy feud. King rehearsed his cast for a week before bringing them to Crab Bottom (now Blue Grass), Virginia, where the director stayed in the very hotel room where Hergesheimer wrote his story.

The Virginia locations give *Tol'able David* an atmosphere and sense of realism missing from many films of the time. But King's innovations have proved far more wide-ranging. *Tol'able David* employed a three-act structure that became pervasive in the industry. Equally influential was King's use of associative editing, in which he cuts from one character to another for reasons of emotional pull rather than narrative logic. King's sense of humor, based on plenty of animals and broad, cornpone slapstick, connected with rural audiences in a way that more sophisticated directors couldn't. Finally, King's version of David Kinemon helped legitimize what has become a recurring character in American culture: the decent man forced into violence for reasons out of his control.

This avenging figure had been a fixture of Westerns since William S. Hart, but King was canny enough to set the story in contemporary locations, and to modify the plot so that David's violence seemed justified. Audiences feel free to cheer David's actions even as he sinks to the level of the villains he is battling—a formula adopted in everything from *Straw Dogs* (1971) and *The Karate Kid* (1984) to *Die Hard* (1988).

Some critics today refer to *Tol'able David* as Americana, but in 1921, when the rural population was still larger than the urban, it was simply a melodrama with bucolic settings. The difference between King's outlook and that of Griffith or Frank Borzage is telling. In rural stories by the latter directors, the characters were not seen as outsiders—they were basically the same as filmgoers anywhere. They wanted nothing more than to enjoy the amenities of modern life: the clothes, nightclubs, songs, cars, telephones, etc. King depicted his characters as hillbillies, another race in another country, exotic, inscrutable, with incomprehensible beliefs and rituals. It was an approach F.W. Murnau would use in films like *Sunrise* (1927) and *Tabu* (1931). *Tol'able David* also provided inspiration for silent comedians. Some critics see Harold Lloyd's *The Kid Brother* (1927) as simply King's story with gags, while Buster Keaton's *Our Hospitality* (1923) plays with many of the same ideas.

Tol'able David was such a commercial success that it cemented King's reputation as a director. He continued working until 1962, making such notable films as the first *Stella Dallas* (1925), the first *State Fair* (1933), and *In Old Chicago* (1938). His *Twelve O'Clock High* (1949) is also on the Registry. Barthelmess, on the other hand, found himself typecast in boyish roles; one of his last parts was in *Only Angels Have Wings* (1939). Edmund Goulding, upset with the changes King made to his script until the film became a hit, was later a noted director. His *Grand Hotel* (1932), made for MGM, is a Registry title. Torrence was a memorable Captain Hook in the Registry's *Peter Pan* (1924). He died after surgery for gall stones in 1933.

Manhatta

Paul Strand, Charles Sheeler, 1920. Silent, B&W, 1.33. 11 minutes.
Credits: Photographed by Paul Strand and Charles Sheeler.
Additional Credits: Released in 1921.
Available: Image Entertainment DVD *Unseen Cinema: Early American Avant-Garde Film 1894–1941* (2005). UPC: 0-14381-0592-2-9.

One of the first avant-garde films to reach a wide audience, *Manhatta* was a collaboration between two significant artists, Paul Strand and Charles Sheeler. It provides a lyrical vision of Manhattan, from commuters arriving at the Staten Island ferry terminal at South Ferry to the towering skyscrapers of the financial district and midtown. The picture's influence on other filmmakers was enormous, and some consider it the progenitor of the "city symphonies" that appeared in the following decade.

Strand, a New York native, was born in 1890. He studied with the noted reformer and photographer Lewis H. Hine, who introduced him to the work of Alfred Stieglitz. With Stieglitz as his mentor, Strand devoted himself to photography. Influenced by the painters Picasso and Bracque, his early work was marked by geometric abstractions formed from shadows and close-ups. At the same time he developed an interest in candid street photographs, disguising his camera to capture his subjects.

Born in Philadelphia in 1883, Sheeler trained as an artist under William Merritt Chase. Greatly influenced by cubism during a trip to France, he was part of New York's famous Armory show (the International Exhibition of Modern Art) in 1913, where his work was championed by Marcel Duchamp. At the same time Sheeler was developing as a photographer, accepting commercial assignments in part to finance his painting. He returned to Pennsylvania with artist Morton Schamberg, both of them using photography for extra income. In 1917 he took a series of stark, meticulously composed photographs of the interior of an eighteenth-century Quaker farmhouse in Doylestown, Pennsylvania. Shot mostly at night, and employing the principles he had developed in his painting, they set new standards for lighting and composition. Sheeler's precision became a hallmark of his work, whether in photography, painting, or in the fabrics and tableware he designed.

After Schamberg died, Sheeler moved to New York City in 1919. Paintings like *Church Street El* and photographs like *New York, Buildings in Shadow* (both 1920) echo the impressions and effects he was trying to achieve in *Manhatta*. Skyscrapers continued to dominate his work throughout the 1920s. Another hallmark of Sheeler's work was how he would adapt the same piece to different media. A photograph might be reworked as a drawing or painting, for example.

At some point between 1919 and early 1920, Sheeler bought a 35mm motion picture camera, and persuaded Strand to work with him on a film. They shot in and around Manhattan until the fall of 1920. Their resulting film consisted of sixty-five separate shots, arranged from morning views of commuters to a sunset view of Manhattan. While the cinematography is predictably excellent, the film's editing scheme is equally impressive, building narrative scenes by juxtaposing shapes, movements, and shadows.

The film was popular enough to be shown in Europe, but after its initial screenings both Strand and Sheeler lost track of it. The film was considered lost for almost twenty-five years.

Sheeler dropped filmmaking entirely, but still found ways to build from *Manhatta*. When he was filming around Park Row, he was also taking still photographs of buildings. He used one of these photographs for a pencil drawing, *New York* (1920), and then a painting, *Skyscrapers* (1922).

As film historian Bruce Posner notes, *Manhatta* predates similar works by Alberto Cavalcanti, Dziga Vertov, and Walter Ruttman. It was shown throughout Europe: at a dada event in Paris in 1923 along with a Man Ray film, in London in 1927, and at other events and locations. Cavalcanti started *Rien que les heures* in 1926, while Ruttman's *Berlin: Symphony of a City* didn't screen until late 1927. *Manhatta*'s influence in the United States was even stronger. It was followed in short succession by city films from Robert Flaherty, Herman G. Weinberg, Jay Leyda, and others.

With the success of *Manhatta*, Strand purchased an Akeley movie camera and hired himself out as a freelance cinematographer, a strategy that worked well enough until the advent of sound, when freelancers were forced to invest in more expensive equipment. Strand traveled to Mexico instead, where he worked as an official photographer and cinematographer for the Mexican government. He finished *Redes (The Wave)*, an hour-long documentary about a fishing village, in 1934. Strand traveled to Russia, where he met Sergei Eisenstein, before returning to New York City to work on various independent film projects. In fact, Strand's name turns up throughout the Registry, on titles like *The Plow That Broke the Plains* and *The River*. In 1937 he formed Frontier Films with Ralph Steiner and Leo Hurwitz in order to make progressive documentaries, the most significant of which was *Native Land* (1942). Strand became disillusioned with the government after World War II, and moved to France in 1950, living there until his death in 1976.

Sheeler, meanwhile, moved into commercial photography under Edward Steichen at Condé Nast. In 1927, he was commissioned to document the Ford Motor Company's new River Rouge Plant, where the Model A would replace the familiar Model T. It was a crucial assignment that provided the inspiration for some of his greatest paintings, notably *American Landscape* (1930) and *Classic Landscape* (1931), a disturbing composition of cement silos, railroad tracks, and factory smokestacks, all surrounded by the detritus of manufacturing. Sheeler became associated with images of industry, and his streamlined, sharply geometric paintings, often based on photographs, received some criticism for their impersonality. *View of New York* (1931), for example, shows an impeccably painted office interior. A window offers a view of only clouds and sky. A canvas chair sits in a corner. A drafting table, with a camera that is covered by a black cloth, dominates the painting.

His creative career ended after a stroke in 1959. Sheeler died in 1965.

Foolish Wives

Erich von Stroheim, writer, director and star of *Foolish Wives*.
Courtesy of Kino International

Universal, 1922. Silent, B&W, 1.33. 143 minutes.
Cast: Rudolph Christians (Andrew J. Hughes—U.S. Special Envoy to Monaco), Miss DuPont (Helen, his wife), Maude George (Princess Olga Petchnikoff), Mae Busch (Her cousin, Princess Vera Petchnikoff), Erich von Stroheim (Their cousin, Count Sergius Karamzin—Captain 3rd Hussars, Imperial Russian Army), Dale Fuller (Maruschka, a maid), Al Edmundsen (Pavel Pavlich, a butler), Ceasare Gravina (Ceasare Ventucci, a counterfeiter), Malvine Polo (Marietta, his half-witted daughter), C.J. Allen (Albert I, Prince of Monaco), Edward Reinach (Secretary of State of Monaco).
Credits: Directed by Erich von Stroheim. Story and scenario by Erich von Stroheim. Photography: Ben Reynolds, William Daniels. Assistant directors: Edward A. Sowders, Jack R. Proctor. Architects: Elmer Sheely, Capt. Richard Day. Titles: Marian Ainslee, Walter Anthony. Film editor: Arthur Ripley. Score by Sigmund Romberg. A Carl Laemmle presentation.
Additional Cast: Robert Edeson (Andrew J. Hughes), Louise Emmons (Mother Garoupe), Nigel De Brulier (Monk), Mary Philbin (Crippled girl), Harrison Ford (Soldier).
Additional Credits: Technical directors: William Meyers, James Sullivan, George Williams. Wardrobe: Western Costume Company. Props: C. J. Rogers. Production dates: July 12, 1920, to June 15, 1921. Premiered in New York City on January 11, 1922.
Available: Kino DVD (2003). UPC: 7-38329-02472-7.

In a radio tribute to director D.W. Griffith, Erich von Stroheim spoke warmly about his one-time mentor. For his part in Griffith's *Hearts of the World* (1918), Stroheim said, "It meant the chance around the corner. It meant everything." Stroheim got his first breaks in the movie business as an assistant and uncredited bit actor for Griffith. Later he was hired by Douglas Fairbanks, who fired him during a wave of anti-German hysteria brought about by World War I. (For more of Stroheim's background, see the entry for *Greed*, 1924.)

Stroheim used the war to capitalize on his Austrian heritage, embarking on a string of roles as villainous Huns. One thing he learned from Griffith was the value of excess. Both artists viewed excess as a virtue. Stroheim pushed harder and farther than his peers, realizing that a heavy had to earn recognition from viewers just as heroes did. His bad guys didn't just menace women, they tore dresses off with their teeth and tossed wailing infants out windows.

Excess became the key to Stroheim's directing style as well. His stories revolved around debauched aristocrats and the hypocritical nouveau riche, with an occasional saintly innocent thrown in. He added a deviant gloss to the risqué films by Cecil B. DeMille and Ernst Lubitsch, one as close to pornography as mainstream film could get at the time. Stroheim was just as excessive with physical details, constructing enormous sets and ordering expensive costumes. His working methods infuriated studio executives. He would shoot a scene, view the footage, rewrite the script, and shoot the same scene again, repeatedly, adding salacious bits and extravagant props as he went along.

Stroheim sold one of his scripts, *The Pinnacle*, to Carl Laemmle at Universal. In it he played a junior German officer who tries to seduce an American wife. By the time it was released in 1919, Laemmle had retitled it *Blind Husbands*. Stroheim complained about the alteration, but not about the profits the film made. After directing *The Devil's*

Pass Key (1920, a lost film), Stroheim offered Laemmle a similar tale of seduction, this time set in Monte Carlo. The *Foolish Wives* title evoked *Blind Husbands*, but Stroheim upped the ante on every level for his new film. Now he was a Russian aristocrat ensconced with two female "cousins" in a waterfront mansion. His story would unfold on gigantic sets that attempted to reproduce Monte Carlo landmarks, in particular a blindingly white casino that towered over the landscape.

The sets gave *Foolish Wives* a weight, a verisimilitude, that many films of the time lacked. Stroheim showed a generation of filmmakers just how much the medium could achieve given unlimited time and resources. His actors had real spaces to work in, and wore clothes rather than costumes. Today filmmakers strive to shoot in accurate locations, but at the time few directors insisted on seeing an actual ocean outside the window of a set. Stroheim wanted everything real. Like many artists, he was seduced by his tools, by what Orson Welles would refer to as the "toy train" aspect of filmmaking. Stroheim liked to show off the details of his productions, the expensive nooks and crannies, whether they applied to his story or not. He chose visual pleasure over narrative concerns, a significant problem when it came to his sexual fetishes.

Filming on *Foolish Wives* began in July 1920. Eleven months later, Stroheim had shot sixty hours of material, with no end in sight. Irving Thalberg, Laemmle's new production executive, tried to rein Stroheim in, threatening to give the film away to another director. Since he was the lead actor, Stroheim was gambling that he couldn't be replaced as director. Accounts vary, embellished with the passing of time. Threats may have been issued, showdowns either occurred or didn't, and perhaps cameras and equipment were taken off backlot sets and returned to storage. By June 1921, filming was over.

After months of editing, Stroheim handed Thalberg a thirty-reel feature running over six hours. In later interviews and articles, the director claimed that he wanted to exhibit the film in multiple parts, over the course of two nights. "Of course, the moguls that were Irving G. Thalberg could not see that possibility," he wrote. "Many things were cut out." Editor Arthur Ripley was assigned to reduce the running time by half.

Censors asked for more cuts. By the time of its general release, *Foolish Wives* was down to ten reels; even shorter versions came out later.

Not all of the problems associated with *Foolish Wives* were Stroheim's fault. Rudolph Christians, who played the American envoy Andrew Hughes, died of pneumonia on February 7, 1921, seven months into filming. For Christians's remaining scenes, Stroheim used actor Robert Edeson, shooting him from behind. But in truth *Foolish Wives* ended up the way it did because of the director's intransigence in the face of cultural and economic realities. Stroheim knew he was taking too long, spending too much, and filming objectionable material. Griffith did the same thing, and was lauded as a genius.

But Griffith also had a greater understanding of how film narratives worked. In later years Stroheim would learn how to construct scenes, to focus attention within the frame, to build emotions through editing. Here he frequently seems at a loss, cutting from one shot to another for no reason, dawdling over insiginificant moments, botching big scenes like a climactic fire.

Laemmle worked overtime building publicity for *Foolish Wives*, erecting a billboard in Manhattan detailing its expanding budget and even hiring composer Sigmund Romberg to write a score. Scheduled tours brought movie fans to gawk at the life-size re-creations of Café de Paris, Hotel de France, and the casino. *Foolish Wives* had been an attempt on Laemmle's part to burnish his studio's reputation, but the film was ultimately too expensive to be profitable. A July 7, 1921, Universal "Daily Memorandum Picture Costs" listed the total amount spent to date on *Foolish Wives* as $1,053,290.80—more than thirty times the cost of an average feature.

The picture ended up in the top ten performers of the year, but Stroheim would never again enjoy such creative freedom. Thalberg removed him from his next production, *The Merry Go Round* (1923), prompting Stroheim to sign with Samuel Goldwyn to adapt the Frank Norris novel *McTeague*. Ironically, a series of mergers placed Stroheim under Thalberg once more at what became Metro-Goldwyn-Mayer. Their subsequent battle is described in greater detail in *Greed* (1924).

Sky High

Fox Film Corp., 1922. Silent, B&W, 1.33. 47 minutes.

Cast: Tom Mix (Tom Newbury/Grant Newburg), J. Farrell MacDonald (Jim Halloway), Eva Novak (Estelle Halloway), Sid Jordan (Bullet Bates), William Buckley (Victor Castle), Adele Warner (Marguerite), Wynn Mace (Patterson), Pat Chrisman (Pasquale).

Credits: Directed by Lynn Reynolds. Story and screenplay: Lynn Reynolds. Titles: James A. Starr. Produced by William Fox. Director of photography: Ben Kline. Assistant director: George Webster. A William Fox presentation.

Additional Credits: Released January 22, 1922.

Available: Sinister Cinema VHS and DVD (*www.sinistercinema.com*).

William S. Hart and his producer Thomas Ince may have legitimized the Western genre with their series of sober, disciplined films like *The Toll Gate* (1920), but it was up to others to popularize it. Working with actor Harry Carey, John Ford transformed Hart's "good bad man" into a softer, funnier film protagonist. Tom Mix went further, redefining the look and style of the Western hero. As a result, he became one of the most popular movie stars in the country.

Mix was born in Titusville, Pennsylvania, in 1880. The son of a trainer and driver of horses, Mix was an outstanding horseman from an early age. He joined the Army after the start of the Spanish-American War, deserting before the end of his second enlistment in 1902. By 1906 he had married and divorced, served briefly as a Texas Ranger, and was working as a cowboy on the Miller Brothers' 101 Ranch in Oklahoma. There he joined a Wild West show that toured the country; in later press releases he reported winning a national riding and roping championship in 1909. That same year he was hired by the Selig Polyscope company to scout locations and handle cowboy extras for Westerns. Soon he was appearing before the cameras in supporting roles; by 1911 he was a star, often producing and directing his films.

Until Selig went out of business, Mix appeared in as many as 200 one- and two-reel movies. He then signed a contract with William Fox; for the next ten years he had control over his own unit, picking his projects, assembling casts and crews, and to a great extent determining the shape and focus of his career. His films were extremely successful, earning more than enough to justify a salary that was reported to be as high as $18,000 a week. Fox spent an average of $175,000 on a Mix feature; these routinely grossed between $300,000 and $375,000. Mix consistently ranked in the top ten in popularity polls, and he embraced the life of a movie star, buying mansions and cars and throwing extravagant parties.

To a large extent Mix succeeded by repudiating the stiff, moralistic style employed by William S. Hart. Mix's lighthearted, easygoing approach contrasted sharply with Hart's dour demeanor and fire-and-brimstone storytelling. Mix's films were full of action and humor, and at times were paced as fast as slapstick comedies. Although the settings and his occupations changed, he typically played the same character over and over. Often called "Tom," he was a stalwart but fun-loving outdoorsman, chivalrous, respectful of Native Americans and the environment, coolly capable of handling any situation. Right from the start he performed most of his own stunts, not just riding tricks but climbs, jumps, crashes, and falls, all with a minimum of padding or other protection. Mix staged his stunts so filmgoers could see he was performing them, and in the process suffered numerous injuries: a crushed shoulder, broken legs, lost teeth.

Mix dressed in photogenic costumes, favoring tooled-leather cowboy boots, ten-gallon hats, and crisp white shirts. It was a look that would be emulated by a generation of Western actors, but Mix's influence was much more pervasive than clothes. He introduced a Western archetype that would come to dominate movies. Subsequent cowboy stars—Buck Jones, Gene Autry, Roy Rogers—would adopt similar codes of conduct, address similar plot issues, offer similar action and spectacle at the expense of plotting. Commentators at the time complained about Mix's lack of seriousness, saying that his films were aimed at children, but his brand of filmmaking proved to be the most economically viable in Hollywood for the next thirty years.

Many of Mix's films are now lost; some that remain, like his 1925 version of Zane Gray's *Riders of the Purple Sage*, are atypically somber. (According to author and film historian Robert Birchard, a number of Mix films can be found in foreign collections: "By far the largest collection is in the Czech archive.") Mix fans point to *The Great K & A Train Robbery* (1926) and *Just Tony* (1922) as the best of his films. The latter, released eight months after *Sky High*, actually stars Mix's horse Tony (sometimes billed as Tony the

Wonder Horse), and is told from his point of view. Tony, who was retired in 1932, was famous enough to have his footprints imprinted in the sidewalk in front of Grauman's Chinese Theater.

Sky High was shot largely shot in and around the Grand Canyon. Mix plays Tom Newbury (or Grant Newburg—his name changed for different releases), a Deputy Inspector of Immigration. He takes an undercover assignment to find and break a smuggling ring run by Jim Halloway (played by the redoubtable J. Farrell MacDonald). Tom's strategy is to pose as a bouncer in Halloway's saloon, and then worm his way into the smuggling operations. A second story line involves Frazer's niece Estelle (Eva Novak), who stops by the Grand Canyon for a visit. Coincidentally, the floor of the canyon is the highly improbable staging area for the smuggling ring; as might be expected, circumstances throw Tom and Estelle together.

The plot, admittedly absurd, is simply an excuse for the film's action scenes and excellent location photography. *Sky High* is set in the present, with cars and telephones, but the world the characters live in still requires a familiarity with horses, guns, and camping out—and with rock climbing as well, since most of the stunts are set on actual canyon walls and switchbacked trails. If Mix at times looks like he's walking on tiptoes, just remember he's navigating narrow, slanted, rock faces wearing cowboy boots. If you don't believe he is brave, try jumping across a chasm as he does, a stunt that would give Jackie Chan pause.

Sky High was one of nine Tom Mix films released by Fox in 1922. Mix left the studio in 1928, making a half-dozen films for FBO Pictures (later RKO Pictures) before retiring from movies entirely to tour with a circus for three years. In an attempt to finance his own circus, he made nine sound films at Universal, a serial for Mascot, and lent his name to a radio show sponsored by Ralston-Purina. Mix died in a car accident in 1940; Tony was put to sleep in 1942. As author H.F. Hintz pointed out, he was one of the few horse heroes to outlive his master.

The Tom Mix radio show lasted until 1950. Mix's fame extended to a succeeding generation, even if those born after his death did not always understand his accomplishments. Darryl Poniscan made a broken, near-delirious Mix the subject of his 1975 novel, *Tom Mix Died for Your Sins*; in 1988, Bruce Willis played Mix as a glib, insolent movie star in *Sunset*, directed by Blake Edwards.

Cops

First National, 1922. Silent, B&W, 1.33. 18 minutes.

Cast: Buster Keaton, Virginia Fox, Joe Roberts, Eddie Cline.

Credits: Written and directed by Buster Keaton and Eddie Cline. A Joseph M. Schenck presentation of a Comique Film Corporation, Inc., production.

Additional credits: Produced by Joseph M. Schenck. Director of photography: Elgin Lessley. Technical director: Fred Gabourie. Staff editor: J. Sherman Kell. Production dates: December 1921. Copyrighted February 15, 1922; released March 1922.

Available: Kino Video DVD (2001). UPC: 7-38329-01312-7.

Few actors in silent films could claim as much experience as Joseph Keaton, born in Kansas in 1895 and nicknamed "Buster" by magician Harry Houdini. The son of Joseph and Myra Keaton, a song-and-dance team in medicine shows and vaudeville, Keaton was on stage by the time he was three. He soon became the centerpiece of his parents' act, which interspersed knockabout acrobatics with Irish ethnic humor and sentimental songs. Keaton had handles sewn into his clothes to make it easier for his father to toss him around the stage. Their act was so physical and violent that rumors spread that boy was really a midget in disguise.

Medicine shows were the lowest form of show business, and they forced the Keatons to learn how to pull laughs from any kind of audience. Buster found out early on that audiences responded better if he didn't react to his father's roughhousing, the birth of what later became known as his "Great Stone Face." Laughing or taunting his father made it seem as if the young Keaton deserved his punishments, while crying or acting hurt would turn sympathy away from his father. Going on stoically, no matter what happened, coincided neatly with his audience's experience of life. Another lesson: the audience always has to see how the gag works. A man in drag isn't funny unless you know he's a man, just as a pratfall doesn't work without the banana peel.

As he matured, and as his father became more unreliable, Keaton broke up the act and weighed taking a featured spot in a Broadway review. Instead, he met Roscoe "Fatty" Arbuckle, who invited him onto the set of a film he was

Buster Keaton, soon to be the target of every member of the Los Angeles Police Department in the short *Cops*.

making, *The Butcher Boy* (1917). Keaton not only wound up in the film, he gave up the stage to join Arbuckle's Comique Film Corporation. The fifteen shorts they made together marked Keaton's evolution from an accomplished stage clown to an increasingly sophisticated film comedian. Keaton learned how to adjust pacing and timing for the screen, how to establish characters and narrative, how to use cinematography and editing to tell jokes, and how to utilize every part of the screen.

As explained in the entry for *One Week* (1920), when Arbuckle left Comique to make features at Paramount, producer Joseph M. Schenck promoted Keaton to head Comique. There he would make his own shorts, with his own crew. Cinematographer Elgin Lessley and editor J. Sherman Kell were Comique veterans. Fred Gabourie was the technical director, responsible for turning Keaton's ideas into actual sets and special effects. Eddie Cline, who started out with Mack Sennett, received credit as co-writer and co-director on sixteen of Keaton's nineteen shorts. Cline occasionally appeared in the films as well. To replace Arbuckle as a "heavy," Keaton hired Joe Roberts, another former vaudeville knockabout performer who summered near the Keaton family compound on Lake Michigan. For the ingénue role, Keaton signed Virginia Fox, who had worked Charlie Chaplin's half-brother Syd in his "Gussie" comedies for Keystone. (She later married Darryl F. Zanuck.)

Although Keaton was a perfectionist, almost everyone described his productions as fun and easygoing. He liked to play baseball while waiting for inspiration to strike, and didn't mind revising and reshooting material to improve gags. Although he had his own studio (the same one Chaplin used in 1916–17), Keaton preferred working outdoors, on locations that ranged from city streets a few blocks away to the Sierra Nevada mountains. An avid outdoorsman, he used his films as a means to display his physical skills, suffering severe accidents in the process. It became a point of honor for Keaton to perform his own stunts; he was occasionally doubled later in his career, but the jumping, leaping, climbing, back flips, and especially running in *Cops* is all his work. (In the film's most dangerous gag, he effects an escape by grabbing onto a passing car, which pulls him by his arm off his feet and out of the frame.)

Keaton began shooting *Cops* after Arbuckle was arrested for manslaughter after the death of actress Virginia Rappe at a party in San Francisco. Some writers see *Cops* as a response to the incident, which destroyed Arbuckle's career despite his ultimate exoneration. While Keaton frequently used aspects of his personal life in his films, the inspiration behind *Cops* seems purer, or at least more abstract. He seems intent only on making the best possible chase, one freed from the confines of the stage, and even from most narrative demands.

The film has a simple premise: girl rejects boy unless he can get a job. From that narrow perspective Keaton builds a world with mysterious class structures and authority figures, one whose physical laws are puzzles to be mastered, one in which his character is flung about by forces beyond his control. He is complicit in his destiny, first stealing a wad of cash from Joe Roberts's wallet, then "buying" a family's furniture from an obvious con man. Should Keaton have given the swaybacked nag he steals goat glands to run faster? Should he have used an anarchist's bomb as a cigarette lighter? Filmgoers can see the consequences of these decisions looming inexorably over him. Part of the delight *Cops* brings comes from the way Keaton releases this tension in the full-out flight that makes up the last four minutes of the film.

Keaton's best work has a formal beauty and intellectual rigor that has never been surpassed in film. Some writers complain that he lacks emotion, but during this part of his career, at least, what's missing is sentiment. In Keaton's world, sentiment is useless, something either ignored or puzzled over briefly before the next cause-and-effect, chain-reaction gag takes place. It is an attitude that can seem either cold or bracing, but it is one of the reasons why of all the silent clowns his work has dated the least. Another way to account for the timelessness of his work is that he is as superb a filmmaker as he is a performer.

Nanook of the North

A kayak scene from *Nanook of the North*. *Photo courtesy of The Criterion Collection*

Pathé, 1922. Silent, B&W with tinted sequences, 1.33. 78 minutes.
Featuring: Nanook (Allariallak), Nyla, Al Lee, Cunayou, Comock.
Credits: Written, photographed, and directed by Robert Flaherty. Produced by Revillon Frères. Film editor: Charles Gelb. Additional titles: Carl Stearns Clancy. Released in the United States by Pathé Exchange.
Additional Credits: Editing by Robert Flaherty. Premiered in New York City on June 11, 1922.
Available: Criterion Collection DVD (1998). UPC: 7-15515-00982-9.

Born in Michigan in 1884, Robert Flaherty studied at a mining college before embarking on a career as an explorer, surveyor, and prospector. Between 1910 and 1916 he went on several expeditions to the northeast section of Hudson's Bay, searching for iron ore for industrial entrepreneur William Mackenzie. In 1913, Mackenzie authorized Flaherty to purchase a Bell & Howell motion picture camera. Flaherty shot 70,000 feet of 35mm film (over

seventeen hours) about the Inuit living near Baffin Island. A fire in Flaherty's Toronto editing room destroyed the negative; all that was left was a work print of edited material. To Flaherty, the loss wasn't as bad as the realization that his film was a failure. "It was no good," he wrote later, but he resolved to return to the area and film the Inuit properly.

Flaherty received backing from John Revillon, of the prestigious French furriers Revillon Frères. He returned to the Hudson Bay area in 1920 and spent the next two years shooting and editing what would become *Nanook of the North*. Flaherty approached this film differently than his first. For one thing, he brought along the apparatus to both develop and project his film, enabling him to see on the spot what worked and what didn't. As a result, Flaherty could reshoot scenes if he felt they merited better framing and exposures, and he could return to locations if he needed more footage to edit a scene. More crucially, he showed the Inuits what he was shooting, making them participants in shaping the structure and meaning of the film.

The most important difference was in Flaherty's philosophy about his material. From the start he decided to focus on individuals rather than incidents, to tell the story of the Inuit through the people themselves. Having lived with them for years, Flaherty understood the essential elements of their lives, and could zero in on situations that would explain them best to moviegoers. Another distinctive characteristic of Flaherty's work was his eye for composition and editing. He was extraordinarily sensitive to light and perspective, and also to the passage of time. He could imply a temporal unity to footage shot days apart, and he could establish a rhythm and pacing that duplicated those of the subjects he was studying.

Flaherty actively sought out Inuit to play parts in the film, in effect casting his documentary. Nanook was not actually married to the two women, Nyla and Cunayou, who portrayed his wives in the film, and the children shown weren't his either. Flaherty had no qualms about directing his actors; he also used the techniques of Hollywood features to introduce the film's characters, and was confident enough to stage and restage incidents to get what he wanted on film. *Nanook* not only defined what would be called documentaries, but also broke every one of the rules that would be established about the genre. (British writer and filmmaker John Grierson coined the term "documentary" about another Flaherty film, *Moana*, in 1926.) It's perhaps unfair to hold the director to standards that hadn't yet been formulated, but Flaherty always said that he wasn't interested in the external truth of a scene as much as he was in uncovering what he felt was an essential truth about his subject.

To that end, Flaherty altered the reality he was filming to a surprising degree. For scenes shot in the interiors of igloos, for example, the director had the roofs removed to provide more light. In one sequence Nanook hunts a polar bear through a hole in the ice, struggling to hold on to the rope attached to a hook. A harpoon appears and disappears in the sequence, evidence that Flaherty was shooting at different times. (*Nanook Revisted*, a 1990 documentary directed by Claude Massot, claims that

two other Inuit were pulling on the rope through a second, off-camera hole in the ice.) But no matter how much the director manipulated the events in *Nanook*, his film retains an extraordinary charm and innocence. Its most significant achievement may have been how it showed filmgoers that the Inuit were like any other humans, with children and pets and stomach aches.

Flaherty returned to the United States in 1922, but was unable to persuade Hollywood studios to exhibit his film. He finally arranged for Pathé Exchange, an American subsidiary of the French film company, to distribute *Nanook*. Flaherty still had to battle theater owners to show it—that is, until it opened at the Capitol Theater in New York; it quickly became a sensation, opening in Paris and London as well as across the United States. The news that Nanook himself died of starvation two years later only added to the film's mystique.

Flaherty's influence on filmmakers, and on filmmaking, was incalculable. Directors as varied as Leni Riefenstahl, F.W. Murnau, and John Huston cited the importance of his work, while subsequent generations of documentarians used his theories as the basis of their own films. The urge to find more and more remote peoples, more inaccessible places, was followed by Merian C. Cooper and Ernest B. Schoedsack in *Grass* (1925) and *Chang* (1927).

After *Nanook of the North*, Flaherty made some short films in New York City, then accepted an offer from Jesse Lasky at Paramount to direct a feature-length documentary in the South Seas. Shot on Samoa, *Moana* (1926) was the work of a more mature artist. Flaherty stayed in the South Seas to codirect *Tabu* with F.W. Murnau, but the arrangement did not work out. The rest of his career was marked by a struggle to obtain financing for his projects. (United Artists bought *Nanook of the North* in 1947, adding original music by Rudolph Schramm and a commentary written by Ralph Schoolman. It was narrated by Berry Kroeger, a future star of *Gun Crazy*, and ran for three weeks the following year in New York City.)

As his widow, Frances Hubbard Flaherty, said when interviewed by Robert Gardner, "Bob made his films for a general audience. He made them as features, to go out on theatrical screens." But by that time the majority of documentarians had switched their interests from anthropological subjects to political ones. The Flaherty tradition degenerated into soft, sentimental travelogues about how weird foreigners were, like James A. FitzPatrick's *Traveltalks*. It wasn't until the development of lighter, more portable equipment, of faster film stock that required less lighting, and until colleges and universities began subsidizing anthropological research that filmmakers returned to Flaherty's original ideas. John Marshall's *The Hunters* (1957) and Gardner's own *Dead Birds* (1965) used *Moana* and *Nanook of the North* as explicit models.

Salomé

Allied Artists and Distributors, 1923. Silent, B&W with tints and tones, 1.33. 72 minutes.
Cast: Alla Nazimova (Salomé), Mitchell Lewis (Herod Antipas), Rose Dione (Herodias), Arthur Jasmine (The Page of Herodias), Nigel deBrulier (Jokanaan the Prophet), Earl Schenck (Narraboth), Frederick Peters (Namaan the Executioner), Luis Dumer (Tigellius).
Credits: Directed by Charles Bryant. Written for the screen by Peter M. Winters [Alla Nazimova]. Based on the play by Oscar Wilde. Photographed by Charles J. Van Enger. Costumes and settings ("after Aubrey Beardsley") by Natacha Rambova.
Additional Credits: Released February 15, 1923.
Available: Image Entertainment DVD (2003): UPC 0-14381-1995-2-9.

When she entered film in 1916, few actresses could match Alla Nazimova's background and training. Born in Yalta in 1879, she studied with Konstantin Stanislavsky at the Moscow Art Theater. After working with regional theater companies, she joined a St. Petersburg troupe led by Paul Orlenev that toured Europe, ending up in New York City in 1905. There Nazimova appeared in plays by Chekov and Strindberg. Signed by the Shuberts, she learned English over the summer, then stunned theater critics with her performances in *Hedda Gabler* and *A Doll's House*. Largely eschewing stage traditions of the time, Nazimova threw herself into her roles, exploring the background and psychology of her characters, designing costumes, and acting with a freedom and intensity rarely seen on American stages.

Within a few years she was typecast as difficult women, foreigners who were either temperamental or just bizarre. To take control of her career, she toured vaudeville in a one-act play, *War Brides*. Controversial for its pacifist message, it became Nazimova's film debut in 1916 (and the feature debut of Richard Barthelmess as well). The actress followed with a half-dozen equally successful films by a variety of directors. She produced an adaptation of *Camille* in 1921, and the following year wrote and produced *A Doll's House*, with her common-law husband Charles Bryant directing.

Nazimova took an even stronger hand in her next film, an adaptation of Oscar Wilde's *Salomé*. Written in French, and not produced in England until after the author's death, *Salomé* is, in biographer Richard Ellman's opinion, Wilde's most purely decadent work. With its repetitive cadences and themes of incest and violence, it has always been a demanding play for the mainstream. (Richard Strauss's opera, composed in 1905, has perhaps reached a wider audience.)

While Bryant was the nominal director of Nazimova's adaptation, the actress clearly was the dominant creative figure in the film. Although in her forties at the time, Nazimova took the title role as the fourteen-year-old stepdaughter of Herod (played by Mitchell Lewis). Her age is evident in a few shots, but she is remarkably persuasive as a spoiled, petulant teen only dimly aware of the violence and danger around her. Nazimova's eyes are magnetic, and her gestures—in particular, her facial expressions—almost always make psychological sense. She moves her body with the precision of a dancer, and uses her understanding of how the camera operates to simply overpower her fellow performers.

If her acting is exemplary, Nazimova's adaptation is more problematic. Her script condenses Wilde's play to its basic elements, but the frequent use of intertitles does little to explain to viewers exactly what is happening. And to explain the sexual context of the story in mime is beyond her talents, and most likely those of any artist. The film includes frequent shots of Lewis depicting Herod's desire by rolling his eyes, his mouth agape. John the Baptist, here identified as Jokanaan the Prophet, stands wild-eyed and mute, forced to act with his costume. Without spoken dialogue, it is next to impossible to convey Wilde's meaning. Furthermore, Nazimova apparently conceived her adaptation with theater in mind. The film's sets would make sense on a stage; within a movie frame, they seem composed largely of empty space. Black backgrounds, an acceptable theatrical device, destroy the illusion of reality on screen. The stationary camera is always positioned a bit too far away or a bit too close to the actors.

Nazimova had hired set designer Natacha Rambova for *Camille*, and gave her free rein here for the costumes as well. Born Winifred Shaunessy in 1897, Rambova was at the time in the process of almost ruining her husband Rudolph Valentino's film career. Both women cited Aubrey Beardsley (who illustrated *Salomé* when it was published in 1896) as an inspiration, although it's doubtful that Beardsley (or Wilde) would have approved of some of the results: a skullcap with flowers for Herod, a sort of rubber sheath covering the head of Narraboth, a wig festooned with what look like tiny Christmas ornaments for Salomé, leggings with fish scales, a white slave wearing blackface. It's decadence run amok, with little or no attempt to connect average moviegoers.

In his review, the *Variety* critic noted the "effeminacy" of the male actors, and Nazimova was said to have cast homosexuals to achieve a more Wildean tone. That alone would have been enough to deter much of her potential audience. Although the character of Salomé was a popular one in film (a *Dance of the Seven Veils* had been released as early as 1907), this film's source material would have chased away most moviegoers.

How would a typical customer have reacted to Nazimova's performance in 1923? With her scandalous costumes (including a body-hugging silver miniskirt that would raise eyebrows even today) and sexual preening, she could not have been more overt, or more provocative. The same could be said for the film's sexual elements. It's easy to see why Nazimova, who financed the film herself, had trouble finding a distributor.

Salomé was not only a commercial failure, it severely compromised Nazimova's career. She retired from the screen in 1925, and didn't return to movies until 1940. Her last role, filmed shortly before her death in 1945, was a small but significant one in the World War II weepie *Since You Went Away*.

Safety Last!

Harold Lloyd in one of the iconic moments from *Safety Last!*

Pathé Exchange, 1923. Silent, B&W, 1.33. 72 minutes.

Cast: Harold Lloyd (The Boy [Harold]), Mildred Davis (The Girl [Mildred]), Bill Strother (The Pal [Limpy Bill]), Noah Young (The Law [Jim Taylor]), Westcott B. Clarke (The Floorwalker [Stubbs]).

Credits: Directed by Fred Newmeyer and Sam Taylor. Assistant director: Robert A. Golden. Story by Hal Roach, Sam Taylor, and Tim Whelan. Photographed by Walter Lundin. Edited by T[homas].J. Crizer. Titles by H.M. Walker. Technical staff: Fred L. Guiol, C.E. Christensen, and J.L. Murphy.

Additional Cast: Helen Gilmore (Customer), Anna Townsend (Grandmother), Marie Mosquini (Salesgirl), James T. Kelley (Truck driver), Fred C. Newmeyer (Car driver), William Gillespie (Ambulance driver), Mickey Daniels (Newsboy), Roy Brooks (Policeman), Wallace Howe (Photographer), Charles A. Stevenson (Ambulance attendant), Gus Daniels (Office worker).

Additional Credits: Produced by Hal Roach. A Hal Roach Studio presentation. Released April 1, 1923.

Available: New Line Home Entertainment DVD (2005). UPC: 794043844522.

One of the most popular and successful silent film stars, Harold Lloyd was as instantly recognizable on screen as Charlie Chaplin. Born in 1893 in

Burchard, Nebraska, Lloyd and his family moved throughout the Midwest until his parents divorced. Living with his father in Los Angeles, Lloyd dropped out of high school for a career in acting. In his first film, *The Old Monk's Tale* (1913), he played an Indian servant.

After working as an extra at Universal, Lloyd teamed up with Hal Roach, who formed the Rolin Film Company with Dan Linthicum. Lloyd tried a character known as Willie Work, a blatant imitation of Chaplin, but the films didn't sell well. Lloyd left Roach for Mack Sennett's Keystone, then returned in 1915 with the idea for a new character: Lonesome Luke. He worked with the same core group, which included Snub Pollard and Bebe Daniels. Only a dozen or so of the seventy Lonesome Luke films survive; Lloyd filmed the last one in December 1917.

Lloyd's next inspiration was what he referred to as "The Glass Character." "Someone with glasses is generally thought to be studious and an erudite person to a degree," he wrote, "a kind of person who doesn't fight or engage in violence, but I did, so my glasses belied my appearance." Coupled with slicked-back hair and a suit just a shade too tight, the glasses identified Lloyd as an everyman. As film historian Jeffrey Vance explains, "The genius of the character was not that it was extraordinary, but that it was so ordinary, so normal—a store clerk, a fellow next door, a cousin, a brother." The Glass Character conformed to how filmgoers wanted to see themselves—not the lower-class hobo Chaplin often portrayed, or the dreamer Buster Keaton assayed, but a real go-getter, earnest, enthusiastic, peppy. Lloyd admitted to being influenced by Douglas Fairbanks and Charles Ray.

The creative group for this batch of films included cinematographer Walter Lundin (assisted by Henry Kohler) and technical directors Fred Guiol and William MacDonald, responsible for designing stunts and special effects. Gagmen included film editor Thomas Crizer, Frank Terry, future director Sam Taylor, and Jean Havez. Unlike Chaplin, Lloyd relied heavily on writers. He had no training in comedy, no background in music halls or vaudeville to develop timing or physical gags. As one consequence, Lloyd and Roach depended on sneak previews. Lloyd's crew would often shoot multiple takes of a gag and test them with audiences. As the comic put it, "We were going to preview to let the audience actually tell us whether we were on the right track or not,

whether the sequences that we were making were funny or not."

At first Lloyd averaged one short a week, switching to two-reelers after 1919. In August 1919, an accident almost ended his life. A prop bomb blew up during a publicity photo shoot at Witzel Studios. Lloyd's face was burned, and he lost the thumb and forefinger of his right hand. Samuel Goldwyn, who started out as a glovemaker in upstate New York, helped Lloyd find a prosthetic glove that became part of his screen costume from that point on.

By 1921 Lloyd was making $1000 a week, plus 80 percent of the profits on his films. He expanded *A Sailor-Made Man* from a two-reeler to a feature, making back over five times its budget. More features followed, including 1923's *Safety Last!*—the fourth of Lloyd's so-called thrill pictures. (The earlier films, all shorts, were *Look Out Below*, *High and Dizzy*, and *Never Weaken*.)

Safety Last! was inspired by Bill Strother, a "human fly" who climbed skyscrapers as publicity stunts. Lloyd put him under contract, then worked with his writers to devise a plot that would incorporate climbing. The story eventually revolved around Harold as an ambitious department store clerk trying to win a $1000 advertising award by having his roommate Bill climb a downtown office building. But Bill's run-in with cop Noah Young forces Harold to climb the building himself.

No production stills survive to show how Lloyd and his filmmakers achieved their stunts, but Vance and others have used landmarks and period materials to figure out most of the process. Strother, who doubled for Lloyd in the long shots, climbed the International Bank Building in Los Angeles on Sunday, September 17, 1922, covered by four cameras directed by Roach. Lloyd shot his scenes on three different buildings, and on sets constructed on a hill overlooking downtown Los Angeles. With careful framing, cinematographer Lundin could give the impression that Lloyd was much higher off the ground than he actually was. For example, the clock face from which Lloyd hangs is fifteen feet above a padded platform.

This climbing sequence—which takes up almost a half-hour at the end of *Safety Last!*—is a textbook example of how Lloyd's writers developed material for his character. They introduce a drunken bystander (played by Lonesome Luke regular Earl Mohan), who puts into motion the reasons why Harold, and not Bill, ends up climbing the building. Complications pile up as Lloyd ascends the building—pigeons, a mouse, a dog, a flagpole, a tennis net, a photographer's flash—each one realistic enough to persuade viewers that the Glass Character is in danger.

The hour or so of story that appears before the climb was worked over just as carefully. There's a seven-minute sequence in which Harold tries to get to work via trolley, two cars, and an ambulance that contains over a dozen staged gags, jokes with more set-up and pay-off than a simple pratfall. Or a hard-to-stage scene, filled with comic bits, of customers crowding around Lloyd's counter during a sale. (Co-director Sam Taylor liked it so much he used it again in the 1927 Mary Pickford vehicle *My Best Girl*.) But there's not much plot to *Safety Last!*, and what does appear can seem arbitrary, an excuse to veer off into the equivalent of a slapstick one-reeler.

Lloyd's character can seem arbitrary as well, sometimes smart, sometimes dull-witted. There can

be a harsh edge to his jokes, a tinge of cruelty in his use of supporting characters, a racist taint to the Jewish and black figures. By all accounts Lloyd was not racist, and in fact helped make a star out of black actor Sunshine Sammy (Ernest Morrison). He could not have been aware of how his jokes would appear to viewers eighty years later.

Lloyd didn't like being pigeonholed as a "thrill" comic, and most of his other features avoided "high and dizzy" gags. (His competitors feasted on them for years.) But *Safety Last!* did help establish the narrative structure the comic would use almost exclusively for the rest of his career. (Preston Sturges tried to replicate aspects of the film in Lloyd's last feature, 1947's *Mad Wednesday/The Sin of Harold Diddlebock*.) It was the final film for Mildred Davis, who married Lloyd after shooting was completed. *Safety Last!* quickly grossed over ten times its budget, cementing Lloyd's position as a box-office star.

The Thief of Bagdad

Douglas Fairbanks and Julanne Johnston aboard the flying carpet in *The Thief of Bagdad*.

United Artists, 1924. Silent, B&W with tints, 1.33. 154 minutes.
Cast: Douglas Fairbanks (The Thief of Bagdad), Snitz Edwards (His Evil Associate), Charles Belcher (The Holy Man), Julanne Johnston (The Princess), Anna May Wong (The Mongol Slave), Winter-Blossom (The Slave of the Lute), Etta Lee (The Slave of the Sand Board), Brandon Hurst (The Caliph), Tote Du Crow (The Soothsayer), Sojin [Kamiyama] (The Mongol Prince), K. Nambu (His Counselor), Sadakichi Hartmann (His Court Magician), Noble Johnson (The Indian Prince), M. [Mathilde] Comont (The Persian Prince), Charles Stevens (His Awaker), Sam Baker (The Sworder); Jess Weldon, Scotty Mattraw, Charles Sylvester (Eunuchs).
Credits: Directed by Raoul Walsh. Screenplay by Elton Thomas [Douglas Fairbanks]. Scenario editor: Lotta Woods. Photographed by Arthur Edeson. Production design: William Cameron Menzies. Production manager: Robert Fairbanks. Film editor: William Nolan. Costume design: Mitchell Leisen. Assistant director: James T. O'Donohue. Technical advisors: Arthur Woods, Edward Knoblock. A Douglas Fairbanks Pictures production.
Additional Credits: Premiered in New York City on March 18, 1924
Available: Kino Video DVD (2004). UPC: 7-38329-03292-0.

By the beginning of the 1920s, Douglas Fairbanks was among the most popular male stars in movies. Moviegoers loved his distinctively American characters for their "can do" attitude as much as their brawny athleticism. Fairbanks returned the favor by collecting the top writers and craftsmen in the industry; with him as the star, they turned out fast-paced, expensively mounted comedy adventures that were extremely successful at the box office. In the meantime, he wrote self-help books like *Laugh and Live* (1917) and *Whistle and Hoe—Sing as We Go*; became one of the founders of United Artists; and, in 1920, married America's Sweetheart, Mary Pickford.

That same year Fairbanks made his first costume adventure, *The Mark of Zorro*. He followed it with increasingly elaborate spectacles, such as *Robin Hood* (1922), which boasted the largest set ever constructed for movies. By now his character had evolved from a pragmatic but virile businessman who found freedom in the outdoors, last seen in *The Nut* (1921), to a true swashbuckling hero, a champion of the oppressed, a savior of the people, "a fly-by-night missionary in fancy dress," in the words of Alistair Cooke. By some accounts, *Robin Hood* was the most popular film of 1922. It encouraged Fairbanks to expand his vision.

Many film historians point to Paul Leni's *Waxworks* (1924) as inspiration for *The Thief of Bagdad*. Visually, there's a clear connection, although on a narrative level Fairbanks owes as much to the fantasy films by Maurice Tourneur, at the time one of the more respected directors in the industry. The Babylonian sequences in D.W. Griffith's *Intolerance* (1916) may have influenced Fairbanks as well. The story for *The Thief of Bagdad*, written by Fairbanks under the pseudonym Elton Thomas, conflates several themes and characters from *One Thousand and One Nights*.

Fairbanks was forty when he started *The Thief of Bagdad* in 1923. He had been impressed by the stunts in *The Lone Cowboy* (1915), a Tom Mix Western, and sought out its director, Raoul Walsh, who at the time was making *The Conqueror* (1917), a biography of Sam Houston starring William Farnum. Fairbanks liked how Walsh used two cameras to cover action, and how he worked with real weapons. Walsh, whose breakthrough film, *Regeneration* (1915), is on the Registry, had been directing for William Fox. When he signed with agent Harry Wurtzel in 1923, his first job was a loan-out to United Artists.

Many of the sets for *The Thief of Bagdad* had already been built on the stages of the old Samuel Goldwyn studio on Santa Monica Boulevard. In his autobiography Walsh wrote about his amazement while walking through them. "It would be the best picture I had ever directed," he wrote. "That is what one man's genius can do to another man's ego." Fairbanks had hoped to hire Maxfield Parrish to design the film, but Parrish never got beyond a promotional poster. Fairbanks turned to William Cameron Menzies instead. A graduate of Yale and a World War I veteran, Menzies studied at the Art Students League in New York City before entering movies in 1919. His work on *Rosita* (1923), a romance set in 1840s Spain starring Mary Pickford, may have helped persuade Fairbanks to hire him.

Menzies' sets are one of the most striking elements of *The Thief of Bagdad*, which even Walsh called "simple" on a narrative level. Unfortunately, Fairbanks became so enamored of them that he often compromised the dramatic tension of the story in order to spotlight them. Cinematographer Arthur Edeson had to pull the camera back so far that the characters were often dwarfed in the frame. Fairbanks hired hundreds of extras and horses for the crowd scenes, and to get his money's worth he extended their material well beyond what the plot called for.

In fact, for a film so basic that Walsh reduced it to "thief, princess, emir, arch-rival prince," *The Thief of Bagdad* turned out to be a vast, sprawling story filled with digressions and narrative dead-ends. It was spectacle for spectacle's sake, and as far as Walsh was concerned his job was merely technical. He wrote more about how he filmed the flying carpet scenes than about directing Fairbanks. Walsh did take credit for casting Snitz Edwards, a diminutive comic sidekick in scores of films, and the Japanese actor So-Jin as the villainous Mongol prince. This was an important film for Anna May Wong, playing a seductive slave girl; that same year she would play Tiger Lily in *Peter Pan*.

Fairbanks pulled out all the stops for the film's opening engagements, knowing that the only way to make back his investment was to convince moviegoers that they were going to see something extraordinary. Following the grand rituals of ballyhoo, he wrote in the preface for the souvenir program accompanying the film, "Imagery is inherent in the human breast." Critics like the poet Vachel Lindsay and the future playwright Robert E. Sherwood responded enthusiastically. Fans of Fairbanks' earlier films were a bit more muted. Cooke referred to Fairbanks' character as "a boy grotesquely buried in a library of costume," for example.

The actor next turned to a sequel, *Don Q, Son of Zorro* (1925), like *The Thief of Bagdad* a popular hit. His next Registry title is *The Black Pirate* (1927).

Sherlock Jr.

Metro, 1924. Silent, B&W, 1.33. 44 minutes.

Cast: Buster Keaton (Projectionist/Sherlock, Jr.), Kathryn McGuire (The girl in the case), Joe Keaton (Her father), Erwin Connelly (The butler), Ward Crane (The sheik).

Credits: Directed by Buster Keaton. Story by Jean Havez, Joe Mitchell and Clyde Bruckman. Photographed by Elgin Lessley and Byron Houck. Art director: Fred Gabourie. Electrician: Denver Harmon. Distributed by Metro Pictures Corporation. A Joseph M. Schenck presentation. Buster Keaton Productions.

Additional Cast: Jane Connelly (The mother); George Davis, John Patrick, Kewpie Morgan (Conspirators); Ruth Holly (Candy store clerk), Ford West (Theater manager), Doris Deane (Passerby).

Additional Credits: Produced by Joseph M. Schenck. Technical director: Fred Gabourie. Assistant prop master/stunts: Ernie Orsatti. Production dates: January 1924. Released: April 21, 1924.

Available: Kino Video DVD (2001). UPC: 7-38329-01232-8.

In early 1923, with the release of *The Love Nest*, Buster Keaton gave up making shorts. Like his mentor Roscoe Arbuckle, and his comic rivals Charlie Chaplin and Harold Lloyd, Keaton stepped up to feature films, potentially far more lucrative than two-reelers. (Keaton did star in *The Saphead* in 1920, but it was not his production.) For his first feature, *The Three Ages* (1293), he essentially cobbled together three two-reel stories. His second, *Our Hospitality* (1923), was a winsome retelling of *Tol'able David* (1921) with a starring part for his wife, Natalie.

Improvisation, a hallmark of Keaton's shorts, was the first casualty in adjusting to feature-length films. Because the features required larger casts and predetermined sets, Keaton now had to work to a script, usually the result of his collaborating with Jean Havez and Clyde Bruckman. He had to pay more attention to plotting and characterization, and he had to drop the freewheeling, zig-zagging digressions that make his shorts the visual equivalent of jazz. "We had to stop doing impossible gags and what we call cartoon gags," he told Studs Terkel. "They had to be believable or your story wouldn't hold up."

That said, Keaton's third feature, *Sherlock Jr.*, ranks among the most unusual movies ever made. It veers between stage and film, between illusion and reality, between a small-scale romance and an extravagant adventure, in a style so sure-footed and unprecedented as to practically redefine filmmaking. Since it also contains a film within a film, and comments on what Preston Sturges would later call "deep-dish" aspects of narrative forms, it has become a favorite subject of film theorists, who remark on its philosophical depths and surrealist leanings.

Keaton told film historian Kevin Brownlow that one scene inspired the entire picture: a man, in this case a projectionist, tries to enter the movie he is watching. At first he can't; the characters in the film he is watching throw him out of the screen. When he sneaks back in he suddenly finds that he has no control over the narrative: a nighttime scene in a garden cuts without warning to a busy city street, then to a mountain cliff, to a jungle filled with lions, to a desert, etc. It is a scene with the inexorable logic of a nightmare, told with a precision and clarity that is breathtaking. Keaton, his cameramen, and technical director Fred Gabourie filmed it with surveying equipment to align the separate elements. It's not the first time characters in a film related to a movie they were watching; *Tillie's Punctured Romance* (1914) has some pretty funny jokes that take place during a screening. But it may be the first time a filmmaker ever questioned the meaning and function of linear narrative. That Keaton did so in such a light and amusing manner is typical of his comic touch.

Not that Keaton would ever admit to something so arcane. His method of filmmaking was to find a key scene, then the big finish, and have his writers figure out a story to fit around it. Critics of the time complained that *Sherlock Jr.* took forever to start, that Keaton didn't "do" anything for an unconscionably long time. It's true that the film opens with one of the oldest jokes in vaudeville, one that Keaton uses for a half-dozen increasingly adroit variations, and then settles into a small-town romance with a background of stifling conformity.

Keaton does some of his most expressive acting in these sequences. Despite his reputation, his screen persona was not unemotional; instead, he played characters who had to keep their emotions under control. They could show anger, fear, determination, desire, but only as emotions to battle against. Keaton's characters were always trying to hold themselves back. That meant no laughing, or smiling, because nothing in their screen life was ever that funny. Confusing, even perplexing, yes, but not funny. The times when Keaton's characters are their most "human" are when they think no one's watching.

The project was called *The Misfit* when filming began in early 1924. Keaton told later interviewers that he hired Arbuckle to codirect as a favor to his former mentor after his legal troubles. When Arbuckle proved too difficult, Keaton recommended him for *The Red Mill*, a Marion Davies vehicle. *Sherlock Jr.* became one of the few films Keaton for which received sole directing credit.

It also became a tough sell. Preview screenings were so disheartening that Keaton ended up cutting the film down to five reels, almost too short to advertise as a feature. Producer Joseph M. Schenck, Keaton's brother-in-law, didn't want to release it, but relented after demanding a name change to *Sherlock Jr.* Reviews were scathing—*Variety* called it "as unfunny as a hospital operating room"—and while the film made money, Keaton regarded it as a failure.

Today it seems the most modern and accessible of all of Keaton's work, the film that combines his love for the jokes he used on stage as a youth with his appreciation for how cinema could enrich them. In *Sherlock Jr.* he takes the time to show viewers how a quick-change costume stunt is effected, even removing the wall of a set to contain the trick in one shot. He turns a car into a boat, a railroad crossing into an elevator, a one into a four, a man into a woman. He effortlessly doubles and redoubles jokes and entire story lines, pulls off gasp-inducing stunts, and finds a happy ending that is both charming and cryptic.

Keaton learned years later that he broke his neck filming *Sherlock Jr.*, and you can see it happen, right after he runs across the top of a freight train. It's picking up speed, so he grabs onto a water spout. When the last car passes, the spout descends, and the resulting flow of water threw Keaton down to the ground. His head struck a rail, but he still completed the shot, staggering to his feet to watch the topper to the joke as the water knocks over a work crew coming down the track.

You can also see Keaton take a first-rate fall off the back of a motorcycle, replacing his prop man Ernie Orsatti. It sets up a sequence in which Keaton's character rides on the handlebars of the motorcycle, unaware that there is no driver. When critic James Agee wrote his appreciation of silent comedy, he used this sequence to describe the almost algebraic simplicity and appeal of Keaton's humor. In discussing *Sherlock Jr.*, it's hard to resist simply repeating the jokes, each one smarter and harder to perform than the one before. Why ruin the surprise? Of all the films on the Registry, *Sherlock Jr.* deserves to be discovered on its own, without preconceptions.

The Chechahcos

The Alaska Moving Picture Company, 1924. Silent, B&W, 1.33. 87 minutes.
Cast: William Dills ("Horseshoe" Riley), Albert Van Antwerp (Bob Dexter), Eva Gordon (Mrs. Margaret Stanlaw), Baby Margie (Ruth Stanlaw as a child), Alexis B. Luce (Richard Steele), Gladys Johnston (Ruth Stanlaw), Guerney Hays (Pierre), Howard Webster (Professor Stanlaw), H. Miles (Engineer).
Credits: Story and direction by Lewis H. Moomaw. Production manager: George Ed. Lewis. Sets and lighting: Guerney Hays. Photographed by Herbert Brownell and Raymond Johnson.
Additional Credits: Distributed by Pathé. Released in New York City on May 12, 1924.
Available: Image Entertainment DVD *Treasures from American Film Archives* (2000). UPC: 0-14381-9706-2-3.

While it was most likely selected for the Registry because it was the first feature to be filmed entirely within Alaska, *The Chechahcos* has several worthy aspects. It provides a compelling look at frontier life in Alaska, as well as valuable glimpses of pristine mountains and glaciers. Perhaps more interestingly, it is a representative example of what mainstream feature films looked like in the mid-1920s. *The Chechahcos* was the only title produced by the Alaska Moving Picture Corporation, founded by Austin "Cap" Lathrop and George Lewis in 1922.

Born in Michigan in 1865, Lathrop moved to Seattle, where he bought a steamship in 1895 to transport goods and passengers to the Territory of Alaska. His purchase coincided nicely with the Klondike Gold Rush, earning him enough to finance several ventures, including a mining and oil-drilling company. Lathrop was elected mayor of the small town of Cordova in 1911, and from 1920 to 1922 was a member of the House of Representatives for the Alaska Territory. By that time he had converted a clothing store into a movie theater. Lathrop would build or purchase four theaters, as well as Alaska's first two radio stations and a newspaper. At one point he owned two banks and the Healy River Coal Corporation, making him the wealthiest man in the territory.

The Alaska Moving Picture Corporation was not exactly a vanity project, as Lathrop's theaters could always use product, but few independent producers could hope to compete seriously with the increasingly centralized movie industry. Where a major studio had writers, directors, cinematographers, crafts workers, and actors on call, Lathrop and his associates had to pull everything together themselves. According to film historian Scott Simmon's notes on the film, writer and director Lewis S. Moomaw worked for a small production company in Oregon. He had shot some footage in Alaska for *The Golden Trail* (1920), which featured William Dills in its cast. Born in Maine, Alexis Luce was a stage veteran, and apart from Dills gives the most polished performance in the picture. The other actors found limited acting opportunities after this movie; some appeared in *North of Nome* (1925), a lost film.

Lewis may have based parts of his script on Lathrop's life, in particular a long opening section set aboard a steamship. Westerns provided another clear influence. Albert Van Antwerp's stoic engineer Bob Dexter wouldn't have seemed too out of place in a Buck Jones film, for example. The script also bears some resemblance to Rex Beach's novel *The Spoilers*, set in an Alaskan mining town and filmed in 1914 and 1923. The film's focus on generational conflicts and love affairs is reminiscent of Edna Ferber's novels; coincidentally, some believe that Lathrop was a model for her Alaskan epic *Ice Palace*.

It's easy to imagine the Alaska of 1923, when the production took place, as a provincial backwater, which makes the sophistication and skill shown in *The Chechahcos* that much more surprising.

Lewis employs up-to-the-minute techniques: superimpositions, flashbacks, point-of-view shots taken from a moving camera. He juggles several story lines during the climax, cross-cutting among them in a style borrowed from D.W. Griffith. Careful planning went into the production design, and the costumes accurately reflect the characters' psychology and social position in the story.

The camerawork and editing are especially impressive. In an early scene set in the steamship's passenger lounge, Lewis moves from wide shots to close-up inserts, changing angles to swing through the entire set, setting up clear, quick vignettes to introduce a half-dozen or so characters. *The Chechahcos* proves that given the opportunity, just about anyone could make a film that looked as good as Hollywood product.

Turning out enough movies to fill out theater schedules was another matter. Without Hollywood's infrastructure and pool of talent, producers like Lathrop had to start from zero with each new project. That may be why most regional filmmaking of the period was the work of amateurs. In terms of acting, design, cinematography, lighting, editing, and other production values, *The Chechahcos* matches the style and expertise of a movie like Victor Fleming's *Mantrap* (1926), which took place in a similar setting. However, it was easier for Hollywood veterans to make California's Big Bear Lake and Lake Arrowhead look like the Northern frontier than it was to actually shoot there.

Greed

MGM, 1924. Silent, B&W with tinted sequences, 1.33. 130 minutes.
Cast: Zasu Pitts (Trina [Sieppe]), Gibson Gowland ([John] McTeague), Jean Hersholt (Marcus [Schouler]), Dale Fuller (Maria), Tempe Pigott (Mother McTeague), Silvia Ashton ("Mommer" Sieppe), Chester Conklin ("Popper" Sieppe), Joan Standing (Selina).
Credits: Personally directed by Erich von Stroheim. Screen adaptation and scenario by June Mathis and Erich von Stroheim. Edited by Joseph W. Farnham. Settings by Cedric Gibbons. Photography by Ben F. Reynolds and William. H. Daniels. Produced by Metro-Goldwyn-Mayer Corporation.
Cast for Original Version: Gibson Gowland (McTeague), ZaSu Pitts (Trina Sieppe), Jean Hersholt (Marcus Schouler), Frank Hayes (Charles Grannis), Fanny Midgeley (Miss Baker), Dale Fuller (Maria Miranda Macapa), Cesare Gravina (Zerkow), Chester Conklin (Hans Sieppe), Sylvia Ashton (Mrs. Sieppe), Austin Jewel (August [Sieppe]), Oscar & Otto Gotell (Max & Moritz [Sieppe twins]), Joan Standing (Selina), Max Tryon (Uncle Oelbermann), Jack Curtis (McTeague, Sr.), Tempe Piggot (Mother McTeague), Erich von Ritzau (Dr. Painless Potter), Huey Mack (Mr. Heise), E. "Tiny" Jones (Mrs. Heise), J. Aldrich Libbey (Mr. Ryer), Rita Revela (Mrs. Ryer), S.S. Simon (Joe Frenna), Hugh J. McCauley (The Photographer), William Mollenhauer (The Palmist), William Barlow (The Minister), Lon Poff (The Lottery Man), Jack McDonald (The Sheriff), James Fulton (Cribbens).

Additional Credits: Original screenplay by Erich von Stroheim. Titles: June Mathis. Produced by Louis B. Mayer. Cinematography by Ben Reynolds, Ernest B. Schoedsack. Edited by Joseph Farnham, Erich von Stroheim, Rex Ingram, Grant Whytock. Art direction: Erich von Stroheim, Cedric Gibbons, Richard Day. Assistant directors: Eddy Sowders, Louis Germonprez. Production dates: January to October 1923. Released in New York City on December 4, 1924.
Available: Turner Classic Movies VHS (1998).

Example number one in the film industry's battle between art and commerce is usually *Greed*, Erich von Stroheim's troubled adaptation of the Frank Norris novel. Legends swirl around this epic, originally planned as a seven- or eight-hour film to be screened on consecutive nights. From ninety-six hours of footage it was cut down to its current running time of two hours and ten minutes.

Stroheim claimed an aristocratic heritage, and to have served as a career officer in the Austrian military, but he was born the son of a Jewish hatmaker in Vienna in 1885. He emigrated to the United States in his mid-twenties, reaching Hollywood by 1914. There he became an actor, assistant director, and military advisor, working with D.W. Griffith's crew until the start of World War I. Suddenly his strong features, shaven head, military bearing came into demand for roles as German villains. He became "The Man You Love to Hate" until peace was declared in 1919.

Stroheim's breakthrough film was *Blind Husbands* (1919), a romantic triangle he wrote, directed, and starred in (as well as designing the sets). In this and subsequent films he played European officers who threaten the reputations of American women. His attention to detail—both in tiny matters like buttons on uniforms, and in massive sets that replicated entire buildings—helped his budgets skyrocket out of control. His preoccupation, even obsession, with sex and degradation made him the bane of studio executives like Irving Thalberg.

The twenty-three-year-old Thalberg was head of production for Universal when he fired Stroheim midway through the shooting of *Merry-Go-Round*. Stroheim signed a deal with Samuel Goldwyn to make *Greed*; ironically, Goldwyn soon merged companies with Metro and Louis B. Mayer, making Thalberg Stroheim's boss again.

Before the merger, Stroheim had decided to adapt *McTeague*, by Frank Norris, an author whose novels had been used by Griffith for *A Corner in Wheat* in 1909. Norris wrote in a style that could be called "naturalism" rather than "realism," one that used accurate details and real-life incidents, but that adapted events to fit predetermined outlines or plans, such as his belief that greed was poisoning mankind. *McTeague* represented a United States Stroheim knew personally: a hard place of coarse appetites, with violence simmering beneath every relationship. Stroheim shared Norris's romantic outlook as well, one that couldn't resist finding the heroic in the eponymous McTeague's character.

In an unpublished article, Stroheim wrote: "I was going to film stories which would be believable, life-like, even if I had to make them realistic to the Nth degree . . . the motion picture going public had tired of the cinematographic 'chocolate eclairs' which had been stuffed down their throats, and which had in a large degree figuratively ruined their stomachs with this overdose of saccharose in pictures. Now, I felt, they were ready for a large bowl of plebian but honest 'corned beef and cabbage.'" His shooting script ranged from the mining mountains of California to the slums of San Francisco to Death Valley. He ended up filming extensively in San Francisco, even taking over a whole block of buildings to shoot interiors. The Death Valley locations proved especially hard on the cast and crew. Cameramen had to drape wet cloths over film magazines to stop the emulsion from melting away from its backing. The production schedule lasted a staggering 198 days, finally ending in October 1923. Stroheim had enough footage to project continuously for four days.

After months of editing, he handed a nine-hour version to MGM executives. This was screened once in January 1924, and possibly a second time. Stroheim wanted the entire film shown in theaters at once, but wouldn't object to breaking screenings into two nights. Thalberg refused to release the film in either a nine- or a seven-hour cut. Today, viewers are used to miniseries that stretch out over many nights, or to "franchise" films like *The Lord of the Rings* that are essentially nine hours long. But in 1924, such a step would have been commercial suicide. Theater owners couldn't make enough money to pay for booking the film, especially one with a depressing plot and no marketable stars.

After fashioning a five-hour cut, Stroheim felt he couldn't take any more material out. He gave a copy to Rex Ingram, the director and producer of swashbuckling hits like *The Prisoner of Zenda* (1922) and *Scaramouche* (1923). Ingram and his editor Grant Whytock pared the film down to three hours and fifteen minutes. Working with MGM editor Joseph Farnham, Thalberg took another hour out. This is the version that was officially premiered in New York City in December 1924, followed by a national release in January 1925.

Removed from *Greed* were subplots involving several supporting characters, scenes fleshing out the backgrounds of the leads, and long stretches of story line deemed unessential to the film. In the short version, McTeague's father, used by Norris to discuss how heredity affected his characters' fates, disappeared entirely, as did displays of McTeague's almost superhuman strength during his days as a traveling dentist. A love affair between an elderly couple, meant as a counterpoint to McTeague's failed marriage, was deleted. A long plot involving a demented maid vanished. These supporting characters helped provide a context for McTeague and Trina, the woman he loves, a sort of sliding scale of potential destinies awaiting them. (These story lines also explained how Trina and McTeague descend from an apartment to living in a junkman's hovel.)

A greater loss was material that simply filled out the lives of the main characters. In the extant version, their choices and decisions can seem arbitrary. Given time to show what these people were trying to do with their lives, Stroheim could have painted much more nuanced and believable portraits of them. Judging from Stroheim's script, Trina especially could have come off as more human, less shrewish.

The extra footage was destroyed in order to recover its silver. Rumors persisted that the complete version existed for years in MGM vaults, but no additional footage has ever been located.

What story remains is fairly simple. McTeague (played by Gibson Gowland) has a small dental practice on the second floor of a Polk Street apartment building in San Francisco. His best friend Marcus (Jean Hersholt) introduces him to Trina Sieppe (ZaSu Pitts). They fall in love and marry. But a lottery ticket sets off a chain of events that brings them to ruin. McTeague becomes a fugitive, pursued by the vengeful Marcus into the heart of Death Valley.

It's a cold, brutish story told with a sort of sadistic glee by Stroheim. His filmmaking is a curious mixture of archaic and prescient, of Victorian acting and forward-looking camerawork. What makes the film so impressive is the world Stroheim constructed for it. When McTeague looks out his office window, he can watch a trolley passing by. We can too, just as we can see the ocean, the boardwalk, and passersby while McTeague and Marcus argue about love at the Cliff House. These are real people in real locations, and they must have been incredibly liberating to directors used to working in confined sets. This freedom allowed Stroheim to achieve startling effects. A camera set-up about ninety minutes into the film prefigures much of 1950s cinema. It's a close-up of McTeague as he descends a staircase. Over his left shoulder, leaning over a railing, Trina stares down angrily at him. Such deep-focus shots would be considered revolutionary in *Citizen Kane* (1941) fifteen years later. Whether Stroheim's monumental efforts and artistic flourishes are absolutely necessary is the central debate in a commercial medium like film.

Greed got mixed reviews, including one that claimed it was the "filthiest, vilest, most putrid picture in the history of the motion picture business." The critic in *Exceptional Photoplays* commented, "It was never intended to be a pleasant picture. . . . Nobody can complain of being deceived when he goes to see it." The *Variety* review lauded Stroheim's artistic vision, but concluded that the film was a failure because it would never make money. Still, it grossed almost $250,000 at the box office, a healthy amount at the time.

Stroheim's extravagances continued during his next project, *The Merry Widow*, the film that prompted Thalberg to complain, "He doesn't have a foot fetish, he has a footage fetish." Fired from MGM, Stroheim moved to Paramount for *The Wedding March* (1928), a Registry title.

Peter Pan

Paramount, 1924. Silent, B&W with tints and tones, 1.33. 101 minutes.

Cast: George Ali (Nana the dog), Esther Ralston (Mrs. Darling), Cyril Chadwick (Mr. Darling), Mary Brian (Wendy Moira Angela Darling), Jack Murphy (John Napoleon Darling), Philippe de Lacy (Michael Nicholas Darling), Virginia Browne Faire (Tinker Bell), Anna May Wong (Tiger Lily), Betty Bronson (Peter Pan). Members of Peter's Band: Maurice Murphy (Tootles), Mickey McBan (Slightly), George Crane, Jr. (Curly), Winston Doty (First twin), Weston Doty (Second twin), Terence McMillan (Nibs). Pirates: Ernest Torrence (Captain James Hook), Lewis Morrison (Gentleman Starkey), Edward Kipling (Smee), Ralph Yearsley (Italian Cecco), Ed. Jones (Mullins), Percy Barbat (Noodler), Richard Frazier (Giant Blackman), Maurice Cannon (Cookson), Robert Milasch (Kelt), Charles A. Stevenson (Jukes).

Credits: Directed by Herbert Brenon. Screen play by Willis Goldbeck. Photographed by James Howe. Settings by Edward Smith. Assistant director: Roy Pomeroy. Adolph Zukor and Jesse L. Lasky present J.M. Barrie's Peter Pan. An Adolph Zukor and Jesse L. Lasky presentation of a Herbert Brenon production.

Additional Credits: Based on the play by J.M. Barrie. Fencing instructor: Henri Uytennhave. Released December 29, 1924.

Available: Kino Video DVD (1999). UPC: 7-38329-01402-5.

For many of J.M. Barrie's biographers, the key incident in his childhood was the death of his older brother David, his mother's favored son. Barrie, six at the time, spent his formative years trying to replace David, who in his mother's mind remained the "boy who wouldn't grow up." He attended Edinburgh University, and after working as a journalist, moved to London to become a writer. He was the author of several popular novels and plays, including *The Little Minister* (1891) and *The Admirable Crichton* (1902).

Unhappily married, Barrie befriended Arthur and Sylvia Llewellyn Davies and their five sons, George, Jack, Peter, Michael, and Nicholas. The brothers were the inspiration for Barrie's first Peter Pan stories, which were incorporated into *The Little*

White Bird (1902). Barrie continued to tinker with the Peter Pan character, making him the leader of the Lost Boys who lived in Never-Never Land. Barrie sketched out a play he called *The Great White Father* and showed it to producer Charles Frohman in 1904.

Frohman changed the title of the play to *Peter Pan*, and it was his idea to cast a woman in the title role. His motive was to make the casting of the other children easier, because they could now be played by older actors. (Children under fourteen could not appear on stage in England after nine at night.) Nina Boucicault, daughter of the famous playwright and director Dion Boucicault, originated the role in London, where the play opened on December 27, 1904, while Maude Adams first played the part in New York a little less than a year later. The play was an immediate hit on both sides of the Atlantic, but it's important to note that Barrie revised it a number of times, deleting scenes, changing dialogue to fit different actors, adjusting the story to account for World War I and American tastes.

Barrie received his first offer to film *Peter Pan* in 1912, a year after he published *Peter and Wendy*, a prose form of the story. The first film adaptation of his work, *The Little Minister*, appeared in 1915. Cecil B. DeMille directed *Male and Female*, a version of *The Admirable Crichton*, in 1919, and *Sentimental Tommy*, an adaptation of a novel that was a sort of precursor to *Peter Pan*, was released in 1921. In fact, at least fourteen features based on Barrie's work were released during his lifetime.

Barrie attempted to write a screen version of *Peter Pan* himself. He sent a copy to Maude Adams, adding in a letter, "I think it's only worth doing if one can have the many things shown that can't be done on the stage, for we may be sure that what *can* be done on the stage can be done much better than on the screen." Later, he wrote a version with intertitles and several new scenes. When Paramount purchased the screen rights to *Peter Pan* and several other Barrie works, it politely declined his scripts and story notes.

Director Herbert Brenon developed his own script with writer Willis Goldbeck. Brenon was born in Ireland and raised in England. He moved to the United States when he was sixteen, running a nickelodeon before he earned a job as a writer for Carl Laemmle. Although much of his output is lost, Brenon made several important films, including a 1913 version of *Ivanhoe* and pictures starring the swimming sensation Annette Kellerman.

Brenon had his own film company for a time, and also worked for William Fox and Joseph M. Schenck. He signed with Paramount in 1923.

Barrie retained casting approval, and from all the screen tests sent to him in London, he selected Betty Bronson for the title role. Born in Trenton, New Jersey, in 1906, she had been playing bit parts in movies for two years when she met director Victor Fleming, who introduced her to Brenon. Ernest Torrance, a memorable villain in *Tol'able David* (1921), was cast as Captain Hook, while Anna May Wong, fresh from her success in *The Thief of Baghdad* (1924), played Tiger Lily. The only actor to repeat from the stage was George Ali, whose depiction of Nana the dog is one of the film's highlights.

Much of the film was shot on the island of Catalina off the coast of California. Brenon and cinematographer James Wong Howe, his frequent collaborator, were careful to maintain the tone and spirit of the play. What's surprising today is how easily the plot transfers to the silent screen. Barrie is remembered for dialogue that was freighted with hidden meanings, but *Peter Pan* is foremost an adventure of visual splendor. Brenon and Howe take full advantage of the story's fantasy elements, employing a range of tricks from matte shots and double exposures to harnesses and wires similar to those used on the stage. Barrie's words are used in many of the intertitles, but the lack of sound in this version adds a layer of melancholy that is unexpectedly effective.

Barrie didn't much like *Peter Pan*, saying, "It is only repeating what is done on the stage." Brenon's next film, also starring Betty Bronson, was *A Kiss for Cinderella* (1925), based on another Barrie play. Bronson also starred in a comedies like *Are Parents People?* (1925), but her wholesome image seemed out of place in an age of flappers. In 1926, Brenon directed a well-regarded version of *The Great Gatsby* that has since been lost, and an adaptation of *Beau Geste*. He moved to England to start his own film company, but his sound films did not have the same impact as his silent work.

In February 1929, the Great Ormond Street Hospital for Sick Children asked Barrie to lend his name to a fund-raising appeal. He turned them down, but two months later left the hospital all the rights to his Peter Pan plays and books. As a result of the Copyright Designs & Patents Act of 1988, the hospital still collects royalties for performances of the play and use of its characters in the United Kingdom, and until 2023 or the next legislated extension, in the United States as well.

The Lost World

First National Pictures, Inc. 1925. Silent, B&W with toned and tinted sequences, 1.33. 92 minutes.

Cast: Bessie Love (Paula White), Lewis Stone (Sir John Roxton), Wallace Beery (Professor Challenger), Lloyd Hughes (Ed Malone), Alma Bennett (Gladys Hungerford), Arthur Hoyt (Professor Summerlee), Margaret McWade (Mrs. Challenger), Bull Montana (Ape-man), Finch Smiles (Austin), Jules Cowles (Zambo), George Bunny (Colin McArdle), Charles Wellsley (Major Hibbard), Jocko (himself).

Credits: Supervised by Earl Hudson. Screenplay and Editorial Direction: Marion Fairfax. Based on the novel by Sir Arthur Conan Doyle. Dramatic direction: Harry O. Hoyt. Photography: Arthur Edeson. Sets and architecture: Milton Menasco. Film editor: George McGuire. Research and Technical Director: Willis H. O'Brien. Associates: Marcel Delgado, Ralph Hammeras. Chief technician: Fred W. Jackman. Additional technical staff: Homer Scott, J. Devereaux Hennings, Hans Koenekamp, Vernon L. Walker.

Additional Credits: Premiered February 2, 1925.

Available: Image Entertainment, Blackhawk Films DVD. UPC 014381-0319-28. 2001.

Best known today as the creator of Sherlock Holmes, Sir Arthur Conan Doyle wrote scores of other books and plays, including historical adventures, a *History of Spiritualism* (1926), war stories set in the Napoleonic era, and science fiction featuring Professor George Edward Challenger. Doyle wrote the Holmes stories and novels to make money, but his heart was in his adventures. The two Challenger novels, *The Lost World* and *The Poison Belt* (the character appeared in another book as well) marked some of the most invigorating and influential science fiction since H.G. Wells.

The inspiration for *The Lost World* may have come from a lecture delivered at the Royal Geographic Society, where Doyle was a member, about an expedition to a remote mountain plateau in southern Venezuela. Skeleton fossils of dinosaurs had only recently been assembled, and the concept of a prehistoric world was just filtering through to the public. Some scientists speculated that ancient animals isolated by some geographic obstacle might still be alive. Doyle decided to explore what would happen if modern-day man encountered dinosaurs.

To describe his monsters, Doyle relied on Edwin Ray Lankester's pioneering *Extinct Animals* (1905), which Challenger refers to in the novel. Doyle met Roger Casement, the Irish nationalist who had helped expose the harsh conditions in the Belgian Congo. Casement was on his way to Brazil, and Doyle asked him to send back details about his sea voyage, the jungles, and so forth, that he could use in a boys' adventure. As reported in *The Annotated Lost World* by Roy Pilot and Alvin Rodin, the journey the characters take from London to the Amazon and back is remarkably accurate based on conditions at the time.

The irascible Challenger character came from William Rutherford, one of Doyle's college professors. Big-game hunter and explorer Sir John Roxton was likely a sketch of Casement. As he did with Dr. Watson in the Holmes stories, Doyle employed journalist Ed Malone, a wide-eyed amateur much like himself, to chronicle the tale. Rounding out the quartet of adventurers in the novel was Professor Summerlee, used for comic relief and as a straw man for Challenger's lectures.

By the time First National agreed to film *The Lost World*, Doyle was the highest-paid author in the world. Sherlock Holmes had become a phenomenon in print, on stage, and in films. The film version of *The Lost World* would be a big-budget extravaganza featuring an all-star cast and state-of-the-art special effects. Marion Fairfax, an actress-turned-playwright who started writing scripts in 1915, was hired to adapt the Doyle novel for the screen. She had just finished adapting William Gillette's play about Sherlock Holmes for Samuel Goldwyn. Her principal contribution to the script, apart from streamlining Doyle's more expensive ideas, was to add a romantic triangle in the form of Paula White, the daughter of an explorer missing in the Lost World.

Leading the cast was Wallace Beery as Professor Challenger. Born in 1885, Beery tried everything from assisting a circus elephant trainer to producing films in Japan. Breaking into films as a Swedish maid in one-reel comedies, he moved to Hollywood in 1913. Tall and stout, with oversized features, he was typecast as villains until the sound era, when his gravelly voice, cunning eyes, and dominating physical presence made him one of the most popular actors in Hollywood. Lewis Stone, who played Sir Roxton, had an even longer stint in films. His silent career was interrupted by service in World War I, but by the 1920s he was the romantic lead in box-office hits like *The Prisoner of Zenda* (1922). Born in Texas in 1898, Bessie Love had one of the most ingratiating screen personas of any silent actress. She played opposite everyone from William S. Hart to Douglas Fairbanks, but her career was plagued by poor choices. Her appearance in *The Lost World*, limited as it is to modeling gowns and to extreme close-ups of her shocked reactions to various monsters, helped recharge her reputation. She soon starred for Frank Capra in *The Matinee Idol* (1928) and in the first Oscar-winning musical, *The Broadway Melody* (1929).

Harry O. Hoyt was credited with "dramatic direction," or directing the actors, but the real star of the crew was Willis O'Brien. Born in 1886 in Oakland, California, O'Brien became a newspaper cartoonist and sculptor, two pursuits that he combined in developing stop-motion animation. Working first with clay models, then with other inanimate objects, O'Brien learned how to bring anything to life by making it "move" one frame at a time. By adjusting the arm of a ten-inch-high model about an eighth of an inch for each exposed frame, O'Brien could have an allosaurus grab the neck of its prey. It is an extremely time-consuming process requiring enormous amounts of discipline and patience, but the rewards are images of incredible depth and power.

O'Brien made several short comedies with prehistoric creatures before *The Lost World*, but the Doyle adaptation would give him the chance to use his creatures for dramatic effects. Mexican-born sculptor Marcel Delgado fashioned some fifty different dinosaurs, covering his creatures' skeletons with latex to give them more lifelike skins. O'Brien and his crew even added inflatable bladders so the monsters would "breathe," and dabbed gel on their mouths to simulate saliva.

O'Brien moved all the creatures himself, one frame at a time, except for group shots. He used "static" and "traveling" matte shots developed in part by Fred Jackman and Ralph Hammeras to place actors in miniature sets, or the miniature models into life-size sets. He also incorporated regular animation, glass shots, double-exposures, and other techniques. A scene of a brontosaurus on the loose in London convinced Merian C. Cooper that his dream of a giant ape movie would work. He subsequently hired O'Brien and his crew for *King Kong*.

The Lost World's influence spread throughout film. Its journey to the unknown became a staple of the monster genre, as did the animal hijinks, the romantic triangles, and the (regrettably) hostile tribes, here represented by former wrestler Bull Montana, wearing one of the least plausible monkey suits imaginable. *The Lost World* also showed how special effects would be used in later films. Since they were the most expensive part of the budget, O'Brien had to ration their appearance. The first moving dinosaurs don't show up until a half hour into the film, and from there on brief special effects sequences are broken up by much longer sequences involving only the actors.

One of the top ten films of 1925, *The Lost World* helped everyone who worked on it. Doyle, who died in 1930, is said to have enjoyed the movie. (In one release version, he appears in a brief opening clip taken from a Fox Movietone newsreel.) Plans were made for a version with sound, causing the original to be withdrawn from circulation. As a result, a cut-down print running less than an hour was the only version available for decades. When an original print was discovered in a Czech film archive, it became the basis of the current restoration by Serge Bromberg and David Shepard. They used the original shooting script and the 1925 musical score to combine eight different prints into a cut that approximates ninety percent of the original film.

Grass: A Nation's Battle for Life

Paramount, 1925. Silent, B&W with tones, 1.33. 70 minutes.

Cast: Merian C. Cooper, Ernest B. Schoedsack, Marguerite Harrison, Haidar Khan (chief of the Bakhtiari tribe), Lufta (son of Haidar Khan).

Credits: Produced and directed by Merian C. Cooper, Ernest B. Schoedsack, Marguerite Harrison. Photographed and edited by Ernest B. Schoedsack, Merian C. Cooper. Titles and editing: Terry Ramsaye, Richard P. Carver. Presented by Adolph Zukor and Jesse L. Lasky.

Additional Cast: Saladin (Driver), Fettah (Interpreter).

Additional Credits: Theatrical version premiered in New York City on March 20, 1925.

Available: Milestone Film & Video DVD (1999). UPC: 0-14381-5924-2-9.

Few Hollywood filmmakers had a life quite like Merian C. Cooper. Born into a Southern banking family in 1893, he was kicked out of the U.S. Naval Aacademy at Annapolis, but still managed to fight in World War I as a bomber pilot. Crash landing after being ambushed in an air raid, he suffered severe burns to his hands. He recuperated in a German POW hospital while the Army mistakenly sent a death notice to his family. Cooper fought for Poland against Russia after the war, flying seventy missions against the Bolsheviks. Captured and sentenced to death, he escaped and walked from Latvia to Poland and freedom.

Ernest B. Schoedsack, Marguerite Harrison, and Merian C. Cooper
on location for *Grass*. Two guides and interpreters stand to the rear.
Photo courtesy of Milestone Film & Video

After working as a journalist in New York, Cooper signed on to an expedition around the world led by Captain Edward Salisbury. He was joined by Ernest Schoedsack, a runaway from Council Bluffs, Iowa, who became a cameraman for Mack Sennett. Schoedsack was in the Signal Corps during the war, then worked as a freelance newsreel photographer. Cooper and Schoedsack left the expedition when Salisbury's ship was damaged. On their journey to Paris, they decided to film tribes who migrated annually from Persia into Iran. (They originally planned to film the Kurds, but found their culture colorless; some of this footage remains in *Grass*.)

As film historian and distributor Dennis Doros wrote, it was the last great age of exploration, and the first to be extensively filmed. Cooper and Schoedsack were inspired by Robert J. Flaherty's *Nanook of the North* (1922), but also by the adventure films of William Beebe and Martin and Osa Johnson. One of the reasons why they chose the Iran area was that no one else had filmed there at length yet.

While raising funds in New York, Cooper met up again with Marguerite Baker Harrison, a Baltimore widow who had been a journalist and then a spy for the Military Intelligence Department during the war. Posing as a Red Cross nurse, she had come across Cooper while he was a prisoner in Russia. Jailed for a time herself, she turned her experiences into a best-selling travel book. Touring China in 1922, she was arrested again and brought to Moscow, the basis of another hit book once she was freed and returned to New York.

Putting up $5,000, Harrison became the third partner in the *Grass* production company (the other half of the initial $10,000 budget came from Cooper's family). Schoedsack contributed his experience and a lightweight Debrie camera. The three left Angora with 20,000 feet of film stock and no definite plans except to try to photograph the Kurds. Cooper had an idea of building a film around Harrison's search for a "Forgotten People," supposedly a lost race of Asian origin, but it was only by luck that they met up with the Baba Ahmedi tribe.

The opening section of the film covered their initial journey across the Salt Desert, including a stay in a caravansary. They spent Christmas in the city of Konia; the following month, they rented a car in Syria and drove to Baghdad, scouting locations and searching for subjects to film. In Baghdad a British official helped get them permission to join the Bakhtiari migration. After meeting with various princes and tribal leaders, Cooper, Schoedsack, and Harrison found themselves that April camped with Haidar Khan, leader of the Baba Ahmedi tribe.

On April 15, they set out with Haidar and his people to cross the Karun River and climb over a 12,000-foot pass to Zardeh Kuh. Each day, Cooper and Schoedsack would ride on ahead to find vantage points for their camera. The migration took weeks, during which time Cooper and the others lived with the tribe.

If you are not a mountain climber, you may not fully appreciate the difficulty and danger Cooper, Schoedsack, and Harrison faced. *Grass* includes some of the best wilderness cinematography of its time. Schoedsack contrasted majestic landscapes, most never seen by Western viewers, with the struggle of the Bakhtiari to overcome them. What Cooper brought to the project was an unerring sense of showmanship. He knew how to equate the Bakhtiari to moviegoers, how to turn them from exotic case studies into people, primarily by making up jokes about children, animals, costumes. His personality—crude, aggressive, excitable, but also empathetic—seeps into every scene in *Grass*. "I have never seen any other man who so reveled in personal discomfort," Harrison wrote about him in her autobiography. About Schoedsack, she concluded, "I have never seen anyone who was more responsive to beauty in all its forms."

Grass is undeniably beautiful, despite its battered condition today, but it would not have reached as broad an audience without Cooper's skills as a salesman. He and Schoedsack developed their exposed footage themselves in Paris, and edited it together in New York. Its premiere was at the Explorer Club, where Cooper had recently become a member, on January 24, 1925. Cooper continued to show it at lectures and dinner parties; at one of the latter, it was seen by Paramount executive Jesse Lasky.

Lasky inserted additional footage of Cooper and Schoedsack, shot at the Paramount stages in Astoria, to "introduce" them to filmgoers. The film opened to the public that March. Although *Grass* was a "hit," in Cooper's words, Harrison objected to his folksy intertitles and attempts at humor. (In retrospect, Cooper and Schoedsack agreed with her. "I never considered *Grass* a good picture," Cooper later told film historian Kevin Brownlow.) Harrison withdrew from the production company to form the Society of Women Geographers, and continued traveling into her seventies. Cooper and Schoedsack, on the other hand, journeyed to Siam (now Thailand), where they shot their next film, *Chang*. It was another chance to pursue Cooper's ideas about narrative structure, ideas that would soon lead to *King Kong* (1933).

The Gold Rush

United Artists, 1925. Silent, B&W, 1.33. 95 minutes.
Cast: Charlie Chaplin (The Lone Prospector), Mack Swain (Big Jim McKay), Tom Murray (Black Larsen), Malcolm Waite (Jack Cameron), Georgia Hale (The Girl, Georgia), Henry Bergman (Hank Curtis).
Credits: Written and directed by Charlie Chaplin. Assistant directors: H. D'Abbadie D'Arrast, Charles F. Reisner. Photography by Rollie H. Totheroh. Settings by Charles D. Hall.
Additional Cast: Albert Austin (Prospector), Tiny Sandford (Bartender).
Additional Credits: Edited by Charles Chaplin. Production dates: February 7, 1924 to April 16, 1925. Released June 26, 1925.
Available: Warner Home Entertainment DVD (2003) ISBN: 0-7907-8065-8. UPC: 0-85393-79452-1.

By the early 1920s, Charlie Chaplin was the most popular and familiar screen character in the world. He left Mutual, where he made *The Immigrant* (1917), among other shorts, for First National in 1918. Here he wrote and directed his first feature, *The Kid*, in 1921. The transition from two-reelers was not easy for Chaplin. He made two more shorts, then directed *A Woman of Paris* (1923), a feature vehicle for his former leading lady Edna Purviance. While it was not a commercial success, the film showed Chaplin that he had to adjust his directing and acting for a longer format.

Chaplin was also adjusting his approach to his Little Tramp character. Previously the equivalent of a carefree hobo, the Tramp could be reckless because he had no responsibilities or ambitions. But Chaplin was no longer satisfied with knock-about comedy, in part because he could not compete on that level with legions of imitators, and because he wasn't as confident about his physical abilities. In *The Kid* he gave the Tramp a richer emotional life and a job caring for an orphan. In *A Woman of Paris* he experimented with slower pacing, with building characters, with using the camera as a means of expression and not just a recording device.

He began work on *The Gold Rush* in October 1923. Part of his inspiration came from stereopticons of the Klondike gold rush of 1896 that he saw while visiting Mary Pickford and Douglas Fairbanks in October 1923. A second inspiration was a book about the Donner Pass expedition in 1846, an incident marked by starvation and cannibalism. By November, Chaplin had copyrighted "A dramatic composition in three scenes entitled The Gold Rush." It was the first time he started work on a feature with a completed script.

Chaplin cast Mack Swain as Big Jim McKay, one of three "heavies" in the plot. A former vaudevillian,

Charlie Chaplin's prospector seems skeptical of dance-hall star Georgia Hale in *The Gold Rush*.

Swain had worked with both Chaplin and Roscoe Arbuckle at Keystone. Chaplin recruited Eric Campbell from the Fred Karno troupe to pay the villain in his Mutual films, but Campbell was killed in a car accident in 1917. Swain had been starring as "Ambrose" in a series of lackluster shorts when Chaplin hired him to appear in his First National movies. Swain lacked Campbell's training and physical dexterity, but he was an ideal foil nonetheless. This was the last time Chaplin would use a character like Big Jim McKay in his films, another sign that he was evolving from his earlier work.

Shortly after he divorced his first wife, Mildred Harris, Chaplin hired twelve-year-old Lolita MacMurray for a supporting role in *The Kid*. She changed her name to what she hoped was the more movie-friendly Lita Grey, but could not find additional work until Chaplin cast her as a dance-hall girl in *The Gold Rush*.

Filming began near Truckee, California, on February 24, 1924. Not far from the site of the Donner Pass catastrophe, Chaplin re-created Alaska's Chilkoot Pass, hiring six hundred extras to climb up and over a snowy trail ascending the Sugar Bowl. It was an auspicious start to a production that was soon plagued with delays. Lita Grey announced that she was pregnant, forcing Chaplin to halt filming. They married, but Chaplin now needed a new lead. He choose Georgia Hale, a St. Joseph, Missouri, native who had just starred in Josef von Sternberg's *The Salvation Hunters*. Hale was earthier than the typical Chaplin heroine, with a sensuous physicality that was often missing from his films.

Even without the delays caused by Lita Grey, location shooting proved too difficult for Chaplin. The cold restricted his acting; the mountains limited where he could place the camera. He built a massive Alaska set at his Hollywood studio, using flour and salt to stand in for snow.

His plot turns the Tramp into a gold prospector, an entirely plausible situation that Chaplin the screenwriter pays very little attention to. Instead, he is interested in exploring the Tramp's status as an outsider, as a victim of bullies and crooks as well as fate. The film skates between humor and pathos, rescued from the maudlin time and again by Hale's no-nonsense brassiness and by Swain's bewildered double takes. The many set pieces are among the most famous in Chaplin's career, from his frenzied attempts to balance a cabin teetering on the edge of a cliff to the image of the forlorn, isolated Tramp staring through a saloon window at New Year's Eve revelers inside. His "Dance of the Rolls," a bit he developed years earlier with Roscoe Arbuckle, reportedly charmed some audiences so much that projectionists had to re-run it.

On a technical level, *The Gold Rush* is one of Chaplin's most adventurous films. He employs a subtly moving camera during his dances with Hale, uses challenging in-camera dissolves in a famous scene in which he impersonates a chicken, and adopts a battery of special effects tricks, including animation, models, and irises. Paradoxically, he was also stripping away filmic elements, retreating to the same devices he might have used in music halls. The interior of a cabin he shares with Swain and Tom Murray might have been left over from Mary Pickford's painted sets in *Tess of the Storm Country* (1913).

Chaplin's script was so sturdy that it allowed him to focus on individual bits without worrying about how to tie them together. With its three chapters, *The Gold Rush* gave viewers the equivalent of a full night at the movies: first some slapstick, then a romance, and finally an adventure. His vision was so precise, so clear-eyed, that he could work past all the setbacks he faced. His acting, in particular his timing, works so well because his scenes are grounded in emotions that make sense to audiences. Everyone knows the pain of rejection, and can respond when the Tramp is hurt by Georgia. But Chaplin captures fleeting moments just as well. He shares his embarrassment at being caught celebrating the clinching of a date with Georgia with a quick squint and shrug at the audience. The real magic in the scene is the pause he gives just before that gesture.

Nevertheless, he had agonizing doubts, causing shooting to stretch over fifteen months. (Production records show 235 idle days out of a total of 405, leading to a budget over $923,000.) After nine weeks of editing, he premiered the film on June 26 at Grauman's Chinese Theater.

Critical reaction was almost uniformly ecstatic, and the film was a huge commercial success. It also set new standards for other filmmakers and comedians to meet. *The Gold Rush* was especially influential on Buster Keaton, who began to slow down his pacing and to introduce sentimental subplots into his own features. In 1942, Chaplin wrote a musical score and narration for the film, cutting some twenty minutes and tweaking several scenes. It can be disheartening to hear how Chaplin interpreted his material. He delivers his narration, full of flowery, outdated phrasings, with a strident peppiness that is completely at odds with the original narrative. Fortunately, a silent version restored by Kevin Brownlow and David Gill is readily available.

The Freshman

A sudden realization for Harold Lloyd's character in *The Freshman*.

Pathé Exchange, 1925. Sound, B&W, 1.33. 76 minutes.
Cast: Harold Lloyd (The Freshman [Harold "Speedy" Lamb]), Jobyna Ralston (Peggy), Brooks Benedict (The College Cad), James Anderson (The College Hero [Chester A. "Chet" Trask]), Hazel Keener (The College Belle), Joseph Harrington (The College Tailor), Pat Harmon (The Football Coach).
Credits: Directed by Sam Taylor and Fred Newmeyer. Story by Sam Taylor, Ted Wilde, John Grey, Tim Whelan. Photographed by Walter Lundin. Assisted by Henry N. Kohler. Production Manager: John L. Murphy. Assistant Director: Robert A. Golden. Film Editor: Allen McNeil. Art Director: Liell K. Vedder. Technical Director: William MacDonald. Produced by the Harold Lloyd Corporation; William R. Fraser, Gen. Mgr.
Additional Cast: Charles Farrell (Student), Grady Sutton (Student), Gus Leonard (Waiter), May Wallace (Harold's mother), Oscar Smith, Charles A. Stevenson.
Additional Credits: Produced by Harold Lloyd. Titles: Thomas J. Grey. Released September 20, 1925.
Available:New Line Home Entertainment DVD, *The Harold Lloyd Comedy Collection* (2002).

Harold Lloyd ended his relationship with the Hal Roach studio after the release of *Why Worry?* in 1923. He took his new leading lady, Jobyna Ralston, and most of the crew he had assembled and worked with at Roach to his new production company. (The comedian's previous Registry film *Safety Last!* was also released in 1923.) Lloyd released his new films through Pathé, but he kept ownership of his titles.

The comedian had considered playing a college character back in 1915, when he was still imitating Chaplin and had yet to come up with his "Glass Character." *The Freshman* would allow him to capitalize on the increasing prominence of colleges in popular culture while holding onto the fans he had amassed from his earlier work. As he usually did, Lloyd started filming the climax—a football game in a Pasadena stadium—first. As he wrote later, "I think we worked for about two days . . . just somehow the business or the spirit wouldn't come. So we scrapped what we'd shot and went back and did *The Freshman* right from the beginning."

Lloyd's character, Harold Lamb, is the son of a small-town bookkeeper, with all the naïveté the role implies. He's built up an imaginary version of college with self-help books and by studying a motion picture called *The College Hero*. He's even fashioned a signature introduction for himself. "I'm just a regular fellow, step right up and call me 'Speedy,'" he says, extending a hand after a few jig steps. He's ripe for humiliation at the hands of his classmates, and humiliation is the engine that drives the plot. Lloyd's comeuppance and his eventual redemption through heroic action is one of the most durable and popular narrative strategies available to filmmakers.

Oddly, Lloyd doesn't interact much with students in the film. He's forced into delivering a cringe-inducing speech to the student body, and to wasting his money treating hangers-on to ice cream and parties, but for the most part the students are anonymous. Lloyd does his best work with Ralston, playing a sensible maid and the film's love interest; and with Joseph Harrington, an alcoholic tailor who provides the background for the film's strongest laughs.

Harrington's inability to finish Harold's tuxedo in time for the Fall Frolic, the big dance, allows Lloyd to work in some of the jokes left over from *Girl Shy* (1924), where he was a tailor's assistant. The Fall Frolic is structured like Lloyd's old two-reelers; in fact, the sequence could be extracted intact and shown separately. The humor comes from the fact that Harrington has only basted the suit together, which causes it to disintegrate piece by piece despite his efforts to enact on-the-spot repairs. What looks like an inventive, organic scene actually required a lot of re-takes. As Lloyd wrote, "I wanted to be not too old-fashioned and I didn't want to pull my pants off." But after two previews went poorly, his creative team insisted: "Harold, you've got to lose your pants." "So I did and from then on it went fine . . . I had lost everything else and they wanted me to lose my pants."

Lloyd shot bits and pieces of the football game that climaxes the film during an actual game between the University of California–Berkeley, and Stanford University in November 1924. The rest he worked out with his writers and crew, adjusting pieces and adding gags, guided by preview audiences. The end result was Lloyd's most successful film. Shot at a cost of a little over $300,000, it grossed more than $2.6 million, making it one of the top-ranking movies of the year. It was the last title Lloyd distributed through the venerable Pathé studio; the comedian signed a contract with Paramount that gave him 77.5 percent of the domestic gross of his films.

Lloyd made three more silents before turning to sound. After six more features, he ended his screen career with *The Sin of Harold Diddlebock* (1947). Preston Sturges based his script for that film on *The Freshman*, actually incorporating footage from its climax in the opening of the new RKO movie. The story followed Lloyd's character into middle age, ending with some thrill stunts derived in part from *Safety Last!* Production lasted from September 1945, to January 1946, and cost almost $2 million. RKO owner Howard Hughes pulled the film during its initial release, recut it, and released it as *Mad Wednesday* in 1947. Neither version was a box-office success.

Since he retained ownership of *The Freshman*, Lloyd could tinker with it over the years. He issued a new edit of the film in 1953, removing, for example, a scene in which Harold Lamb cries with Peggy after the dance. Lloyd edited it again in 1959, then incorporated it into a compilation film, *Harold Lloyd's Funny Side of Life*, that he released in 1963.

Buster Keaton's *College* (1927) owes a lot to *The Freshman*; it's fascinating to see how the two comics approached similar material in such different manners. Harold "Speedy" Lamb's introductory jig was appropriated by Yasujiro Ozu's characters in *Days of Youth* (1929). In *Horse Feathers* (1932), the Marx Brothers mock much of what Lloyd's character stands for here, even while repeating his football gags. *The Freshman* has proven to be a lasting influence on comedians, both for its characterizations and for its structure.

H.C. Witwer wrote a short story, "The Emancipation of Rodney," in a 1915 issue of *Popular Magazine*. He discussed the piece with Lloyd, an acquaintance, then in 1929 sued the Harold Lloyd Corporation for stealing his story for *The Freshman*. Witwer's widow won a judgment in 1930. It took three more years for the decision to be overturned on Lloyd's appeal.

In November 2000, Suzanne Lloyd Hayes, Lloyd's granddaughter, sued the Walt Disney Co. for $50 million over fifty-six specific similarities between *The Freshman* and *The Waterboy*, a 1998 movie starring Adam Sandler. Since Sandler had made a career out of looting old film ideas (*Little Nicky* from Chaplin's *The Kid*; *Mr. Deeds* from Capra's *Mr. Deeds Goes to Town*; etc.), it seemed to laymen a cut-and-dried case. Sadly, the courts ruled against Hayes and in favor of Disney. As Disney lawyers noted, "Mere ideas are not protected by copyright."

The Phantom of the Opera

An example of the elaborate set design in *The Phantom of the Opera. Courtesy of Milestone Film & Video*

Universal, 1925. Silent, B&W with color sequences, 1.33. 107 minutes.
Cast: Lon Chaney (The Phantom [Erik]), Mary Philbin (Christine Daaé), Norman Kerry (Vicomte Raoul de Chagny), Arthur Edmund Carewe (Ledoux), Gibson Gowland (Simon Buquet), John Sainpolis (Comte Philip de Chagny), Snitz Edwards (Florine Papillon), Virginia Pearson (Carlotta).
Credits: Directed by Rupert Julian. Based on the novel by Gaston Leroux. Presented by Carl Laemmle.
Additional Cast: Edith Yorke (Mama Valerius), Anton Vaverka (Prompter), Bernard Siegel (Joseph Buguet), Olive Ann Alcorn (La Sorelli), Cesare Gravina (Manager), George B. Williams (M. Ricard), Bruce Covington (M. Moncharmin), Edward Cecil (Faust), John Miljan (Valentin), Alexander Bevani (Mephistopheles), Grace Marvin (Martha), Ward Crane (Count Ruboff), Chester Conklin (Orderly), William Tryoler (Director of opera orchestra), Carla Laemmle (Dancer).
Additional Credits: Directing: Edward Sedgwick. Adapted by Raymond Schrock, Elliot J. Clawson. Titles: Tom Reed. Additional writing: Bernard McConville, James Spearing. Director of photography: Virgil Miller. Additional photography: Milton Bridenbecker, Charles J. Van Enger. Film editor: Maurice Pivar. Art director: Charles D. Hall. Consulting artist: Ben Carré. Production dates: October 29 to December 1924. Reshoots: March 1925. Premiered in New York City on September 6, 1925.
Other Versions: Feature film versions include *Phantom of the Opera* (1943), *The Phantom of the Opera* (1962), *The Phantom of the Opera* (1989). The Andrew Lloyd Weber musical was filmed as *The Phantom of the Opera* (2004).

Available: Image Entertainment DVD (2003). UPC: 0-14381-0209-2-2.

Serialized in French and English and published as a novel in 1911, Gaston Leroux's *The Phantom of the Opera* has maintained a persistent hold on the public's imagination. Better known in France for his pioneering journalism, and for popularizing "locked room" mysteries, Leroux always claimed that his novel was based on a true story. Rumors about a "ghost" who inhabited the depths of the Paris Opera House served as good publicity for the building. Finished in 1879, the Opera House featured seventeen stories honeycombed with corridors, stairways, private suites, stables, storage rooms, and a subterranean lake.

A former theater critic, Leroux knew the building's history, including its fatal chandelier accident in 1896. His story, in which a physically monstrous character kidnaps the woman he has secretly desired, was based on ideas and themes from Edgar Allan Poe and especially from Victor Hugo's *Hunchback of Notre Dame*. Leroux's use of Hugo's themes may have sparked Lon Chaney's interest in his novel.

The son of deaf-mutes, Chaney was born in Colorado Springs in 1883. He was eleven when he started working in theater, first as a prop hand, then as a comedian, dancer, actor, stage manager, and ticket handler in vaudeville houses throughout the Southwest. Married and then divorced, Chaney began working in movies in 1913, in part to keep custody of his son Creighton. He appeared in over fifty films between 1913 and 1919, mostly as an extra.

To improve his chances of being hired, Chaney brought his makeup case with him to casting calls. He knew that his theatrical training was strong enough to get him through any film role; his mastery of makeup enabled him to apply for a wide variety of parts. Biographer Michael Blake wrote that during this period, Chaney appeared as Mexicans, French Canadians, elderly men, fishermen, plantation owners, comedians, villains, mounties, miners, thieves, aristocrats, and tramps.

In 1919 Chaney met director Tod Browning, his collaborator on some of his best films. He also had his first "grotesque" part, as "The Frog" in *The Miracle Man*. A con artist who posed as a cripple, The Frog required Chaney to contort his body into painful positions. In the public's mind, the braces, prosthetics, and disfiguring makeup would become the hallmarks of Chaney's acting. Chaney did rely on artificial devices to a distracting extent, but he was first of all an actor with an uncommon ability to communicate to the camera.

Some have suggested that Chaney's upbringing helped make him adept at mime, but as an actor his skill reaches far beyond aping gestures and imitating expressions. Chaney was one of the first film performers to bore into his characters' personalities, to explain their actions through psychology rather than stage conventions. More than almost all of his peers, Chaney thought through his performances, found a way for them to make sense before he committed them to film.

Not all of his roles were grotesque ones, and few of his films could be considered horror, but Chaney's reputation today rests largely on two blockbusters, *The Hunchback of Notre Dame* (1923) and *The Phantom of the Opera* (1925). The former

was overseen by Irving Thalberg when he was still head of production at Universal; Thalberg's decision to reshoot several expensive scenes was a contributing factor in his departure from the studio. But Chaney's creative input was as important as Thalberg's. The actor had a financial investment in the project that gave him some control—over the selection of director Wallace Worsley, for example.

Hunchback was Universal's biggest money maker of 1923. By November of that year Chaney was inquiring about the rights to *The Phantom of the Opera*. He also starred in *He Who Gets Slapped* (1925) for Thalberg at the new MGM studio. Hoping to duplicate the success of *Hunchback*, Laemmle, the head of Universal, was willing to borrow Chaney back and build *The Phantom of the Opera* around him.

While screenwriters Bernard McConville and James Spearing started an adaptation, consulting artist Ben Carré drew two dozen sketches that formed the basis of the film's look. A dozen artists worked on the Opera House interior, the first steel and concrete stage ever built in Hollywood. Rupert Julian was assigned to direct the film. As an actor, he had specialized in imitating Wilhelm II in films like *The Kaiser, Beast of Berlin* (1918). As a director, he took to imitating Erich von Stroheim, whom he had replaced on *Merry-Go-Round* (1923).

Julian brought his own screenwriter, Elliott Clawson, and cast Mary Philbin from *Merry-Go-Round* as the romantic lead. The director did not get along very well with Chaney. As cinematographer Charles Van Enger said later, "Julian would explain to me what he wanted Lon to do, and then I'd go over to Lon and tell him what Julian had said. Then Lon would say to tell him to 'go to hell.'"

Filming started on October 29, 1924, and lasted ten weeks. Chaney was done in November, in time to start one of his best movies, *The Unholy Three* (1925), at MGM. When principal photography was completed, Universal prepared a two-hour version which it previewed in January 1925. Worried by the lackluster response, Laemmle ordered a new ending, and the addition of comic scenes featuring Chester Conklin, these directed by Eddie Sedgwick. The official premiere was on April 26, 1925, in San Francisco.

The film did so poorly that Universal editors recut it immediately, removing much of the comic relief as well as the expensive Technicolor ballet sequences. When it opened again, critics were unimpressed. The public, however, flocked to the film, primarily to see Chaney. His performance found the humanity in the Phantom, elevating the character from a murkily conceived emanation of the subconscious to a figure of real tragedy.

In 1929, Universal prepared a new edit of *Phantom* with a synchronized score. According to film historian Scott MacQueen, several scenes were reshot. Virginia Pearson, who played the opera diva Carlotta in the 1925 version, was transformed into Carlotta's mother for the reissue. Confusingly, a silent version of the 1929 edit was also prepared (for theaters not yet equipped for sound), and it is this version that is most often shown today. The ten-reel, 1925 release exists in a 16mm version reduction made for Universal's "Show-at-Home" consumer line.

Chaney's life was cut short by cancer just as he was about to make the transition to sound movies. The Phantom was seen in several screen incarnations, as well as a long-running musical by Andrew Lloyd Webber.

The Big Parade

Metro-Goldwyn-Mayer, 1925. Silent, B&W, 1.33. 142 minutes.
Cast: John Gilbert (James Apperson), Renée Adorée (Melisande), Hobart Bosworth (Mr. Apperson), Claire McDowell (Mrs. Apperson), Claire Adams (Justyn Reed), Robert Ober (Harry), Tom O'Brien (Bull [O'Hara]), Karl Dane (Slim [Jensen]), Rosita Marstini (French mother)
Credits: Directed by King Vidor. Story by Laurence Stallings. Scenario by Harry Behn. Titles by Joseph W. Farnham. Settings by Cedric Gibbons and James Basevi. Wardrobe designed by Ethel P. Chaffin. Photography by John Arnold. Additional photography: Henrik Sartov. Assistant director: David Howard. Film editor: Hugh Wynn. A King Vidor production of a Metro-Goldwyn-Mayer picture.
Additional Credits: Produced by Irving Thalberg. Premiered in Los Angeles on November 5, 1925.
Available: MGM/UA Turner Entertainment VHS (1988). ISBN 0-7907-5266-2. UPC 012569544130.

The Laurence Stallings and Maxwell Anderson play *What Price Glory* (1924) established a template of sorts for World War I films: some action interspersed with long stretches of humor; a story line oriented more toward the hijinks of its male stars than the romance they were ostensibly seeking. The responses by other studios to the play, eventually filmed by Raoul Walsh for Fox, reflected their differing styles. Paramount's *Wings* (1927) featured up-and-coming male stars in a romantic triangle weighed down by sentimentality. In *All Quiet on the Western Front* (1930), Universal portrayed the war much like the horror films it would soon be producing: grim, depressing, deadly. World War I from MGM's perspective would be posh, relatively comfortable, and drenched with as much sex as censors would allow.

From its inception, MGM positioned itself above other studios by marketing its work as the equivalent of a luxury sedan. It promised more stars than in the heavens, and signed up every veteran director, cameraman, and screenwriter it could. Controlled by a New York City corporation set up by Marcus Loew, the studio made films for largely upscale audiences, since its theaters were concentrated in urban areas.

Head of production Irving Thalberg had actually tried to buy *What Price Glory* while it was on Broadway, but lost out to William Fox. Thalberg bought the next best thing, the co-author of the play, Laurence Stallings, a veteran of the Marines. (Technically, Thalberg bought the rights to Stallings' semi-autobiographical novel *Plumes*, even though its plot dealt only with returning veterans, not the war itself.) Stallings submitted the bare outline about a ne'er-do-well heir who enlists on a whim. Naive Jim Apperson is then torn between a fiancée who lives next door and the lusty French wench in whose hayloft his squad is billeted.

As the title suggests, MGM's war film would be bigger than anyone else's (at least until Howard Hughes entered the battle in 1930 with *Hell's Angels*): more tanks, more soldiers, bigger sets, bigger stars, bigger emotions. But because it was chasing the same audiences as the other studios, *The Big Parade* would also be the same war story as the others, with comedy, romance, some fighting, some teary reunions, and—as Thalberg's boss Louis B. Mayer preferred—a happy ending. Three buddies who go through training together, confront the battlefield, and either survive or expire as the plot requires. (*What Price Glory* showed the value of dual leads in developing comedy, but *The Big Parade* scored a different kind of success by introducing three leads. Now filmmakers could kill off a star without losing the audience's connection to the story.)

John Gilbert, who played the pampered young Jim Apperson, was the son of a noted comedian. He started out in bit parts at the Ince studio, gained attention playing opposite Mary Pickford in *Heart o' the Hills* (1919), and became a popular leading man at Fox in the early 1920s. At MGM he was considered one of the leading lovers of the screen, especially after the death of Rudolph Valentino in 1926. Gilbert was like an all-American version of Valentino—friendly, unthreatening, basically decent. He had a limited range, something Thalberg compensated for by surrounding him with the more accomplished actors Tom O'Brien and Karl Dane. Not just comic relief, these two would do the real acting in Gilbert's scenes, allowing the star to react or just pose comfortably.

Mayer and Thalberg were surprised when they screened director King Vidor's finished version. The film was more than half over before the first casualty, and the fighting had hardly begun before the movie ended. Vidor spent the bulk of his cut on the romance between Jim Apperson and Melisande, played by former Folies Bergères chorine Renée Adorée.

Vidor, a third-generation Texan, broke into the film industry by selling newsreel footage he shot in Galveston. He moved to Hollywood with his wife Florence, who quickly became a major star. Vidor struggled through small-scale comedies and Westerns before signing a contract with Samuel Goldwyn, which, after various mergers and acquisitions, led him to MGM in 1924.

With ten years' experience as a director, Vidor had definite ideas about how to shoot a film. Since much of *The Big Parade* consisted of moving masses of men and material from one side of a frame to another, the director expressed his individuality in small ways. By prolonging the ends of shots as they faded to black, for example. Holding onto the image of an abandoned beer glass on a bar served as a premonition of loss.

Vidor also counted on his performers to carry narratives that other directors might have felt too flimsy. *The Big Parade* features several two-shots in medium close-up in which actors are asked to register an array of shifting emotions without the luxury of cutaways or inserted dialogue. One shot of Gilbert and Adorée sharing chewing gum while falling in love lasts almost four minutes. In a later shot that extends for more than three minutes, Gilbert comforts a soldier in a shell hole as he dies from a wound.

In his autobiography, Vidor wrote about what he called the "silent music" of the film. After studying U.S. Army footage of soldiers and the war, Vidor used a metronome to set a tempo for marching:

> When we filmed the march through Belleau Wood in a small forest near Los Angeles, I used the same metronome, and a drummer with a bass drum amplified the metronomic ticks so that all in a range of several hundred yards could hear. I instructed the men that each step must be taken on a drum beat, each turn of the head, lift of a rifle, pull of a trigger, in short, every physical move must occur on the beat of the drum. Those extras who were veterans of the American Expeditionary Force and had served time in France thought I had gone completely daft and expressed their ridicule most volubly. One British veteran wanted to know if he were performing in "some bloody ballet." I did not say so at the time, but that is exactly what it was—a bloody ballet, a ballet of death.

Ballet or not, the film wasn't enough for Thalberg, who ordered Vidor to return to Texas to shoot more footage. Studio publicists subsequently trumpeted the use of 3,000 soldiers, 200 trucks, 100 airplanes. By increasing the budget some 20 percent, Thalberg ended up with a box-office blockbuster that ran ninety-six weeks at the Astor theater and earned millions of dollars. (Author John Baxter quoted Vidor as saying in 1974 that he didn't like the film: "Today I don't encourage people to see the film. At the time I really believed it was an anti-war movie. Today, if I had to remake it, I would be much more precise.")

As a result of *The Big Parade*, Vidor became the director of choice on the MGM lot, helming some of the studio's biggest successes. He also found the time to make small, personal films that often had a more lasting impact. *The Crowd* (1928) is also a Registry title. Sadly, many in the cast of *The Big Parade* fared poorly. Adorée contracted tuberculosis and died in 1933. Gilbert had well-publicized troubles adjusting to sound films, and died of an alcoholism-induced heart attack in 1936. Born in Copenhagen, Karl Dane enjoyed a solid career in silent comedies in the late 1920s, but could not find work in sound films due to his thick accent; he committed suicide in 1934.

Clash of the Wolves

Warner Brothers, 1925. Silent, B&W, 1.33. 74 minutes.
Cast: Rin-Tin-Tin (Lobo), Charles Farrell (Dave Weston), June Marlowe (May Barstowe), "Heinie" Conklin (Alkali Bill), William Walling (Sam Barstowe), Pat Hartigan (Wm. "Borax" Horton).
Credits: Directed by Noel Mason Smith. Writer: Charles A. Logue. Photography: Alan Thompson and E.B. DuPar. Edited by Clarence Kolster. Art directors: Lewis Geib & Esdras Hartley. Electrical effects: F.N. Murphy. Art titles: Victor Vance. A Warner Brothers presentation.
Additional Credits: Premiered in New York City on November 17, 1925.
Available: Image Entertainment DVD, *More Treasures from American Film Archives.* (2004). ISBN: 0-9747099-1-3. UPC: 0-14381-2271-2-3.

The youngest of twelve siblings, Jack Warner was eleven when his family opened a nickelodeon in 1903. By 1905, Jack and his brothers Harry, Albert, and Sam began to distribute films, and by 1912 they were producing their own shorts. The Warners invested the profits from the hit *My Four Years in Germany* (1917) into a studio in Burbank, California, with Jack as head of production. He campaigned to improve the quality of Warners' movies, initiating a series called "Classics of the Screen" that included an adaptation of Sinclair Lewis's *Main Street* and one of a stage hit, *The Gold Diggers* (both 1923), that would become a long-running franchise for the studio.

Not all of the Warner product was as rarified. *A Dangerous Adventure* (1920), directed by Jack and his brother Sam, was a fifteen-part serial set in a backlot jungle and featuring stunts with circus animals. But in November, 1923, Jack took a step up by signing Rin Tin Tin to appear in *Where the North Begins*.

A German shepherd pup found in a kennel during World War I, Rin Tin Tin was named after a French toy by Captain Lee Duncan, who brought him to Los Angeles. Duncan trained the dog, nicknamed Rinty, and toured with him on vaudeville. In his act, Rinty counted to ten and picked up a coin with his nose. Duncan placed Rin Tin Tin in minor roles in two features, but Jack Warner planned to build a movie around him, in part to compete against Strongheart, a canine star for the rival First National studio.

The key to Rin Tin Tin's screen success was Darryl Zanuck, a new staff screenwriter for Warners. Born in Nebraska and a veteran of World War I, Zanuck was a prizefighter and stevedore before entering pictures. In his first two Warners films, Rin Tin Tin again played subsidiary roles. Zanuck made the dog a star in the same way he did later with Shirley Temple: by turning him into a legitimate fictional character rather than a vaudeville personality who simply performed tricks. Zanuck claimed he wrote a script called *My Buddy* in four days; it later became *Find Your Man* (1924), an adventure with nonstop action.

Zanuck soon moved on to larger assignments, but the studio now had a template for its Rin Tin Tin vehicles. June Marlowe appeared as the romantic lead in five of Rinty's films; she would later star as Miss Crabtree in several *Our Gang* shorts. Chester "Heinie" Conklin often played comic relief, while Pat Hartigan, star of one of the country's first features, *The Life of Moses* (1909), turned up as a villain in five Rinty features.

When *Clash of the Wolves* was filmed, Rin Tin Tin was arguably the biggest star on the Warners lot. Jack called him "the mortgage lifter" because he saved so many theater owners. The dog would be decked out in jeweled collars and fed steak dinners for the benefit of the press, but the studio was just as concerned about Rinty's screen career and committed to his success as it was about its other stars.

What's striking about *Clash of the Wolves* today is how seriously the film treats its audience. Director Noel Mason Smith and writer Charles Logue, both longtime veterans in the industry, expected their moviegoers to be engaged enough with their material to overlook inevitable gaps and compromises in the action scenes—Rin Tin Tin was, after all, only a dog. In return, they provided intensely kinetic chases in stark landscapes, achieved only by employing a variety of difficult camera set-ups.

Similarly, Smith and Logue presumed a certain level of intelligence from viewers. They arranged the meeting between Marlowe's May, a rancher's daughter, and Hartigan's villain Horton in a sophisticated, unsettling manner. Horton stares at May through a window; she notices him and drops her eyes, uncomfortable about men staring at her for the wrong reasons. Horton's piercing gaze is framed in increasingly tight close-ups, while in her reaction shots May seeks silent help from her beau, Dave (played by Charles Farrell), standing just out of the frame. No intertitles are necessary to understand Horton's desires and May's fears.

Clash of the Wolves is a film for adults as much as children. Younger viewers most likely wouldn't understand what happens when a wolf pack attacks its prey, for example, but to older moviegoers, some of the shots here have chilling implications. If Conklin's humor is too broad, if the filmmakers occasionally drop plot elements, the film as a whole displays an admirably high level of skill.

Rin Tin Tin's career ended with his death in 1932, but not before he starred in several more features, on radio, and in a serial (and inspired competitors like RKO's Ace the Wonder Dog). Rin Tin Tin IV starred in a long-running TV series in the 1950s, and his descendants continue to make public appearances.

Lady Windermere's Fan

Warner Brothers, 1925. Silent, B&W, 1.33. 89 minutes.
Cast: Ronald Colman (Lord Darlington), May McAvoy (Lady Windermere), Bert Lytell (Lord Windermere), Irene Rich (Mrs. Erlynne), Edw. [Edward] Martindel (Lord Augustus Lorton), Mme. [Carrie] Daumery (The Duchess of Berwick).
Credits: Directed by Ernst Lubitsch. Adapted to the screen by Julien Josephson. Based on the play by Oscar Wilde. Photography: Charles Van Enger. Assistant directors: George Hippard, Ernst Leammle. Art director: Harold Grieve. Electrical effects: F.N. Murphy. Costumes: Sophie Wachner. Art titles: Victor Vance. Titles by Maude Fulton and Eric Locke. A Warner Brothers presentation of an Ernst Lubitsch production.
Additional Cast: Helen Dunbar (Mrs. Cowper-Cowper), Billie Bennett (Lady Plymdale); Larry Steers, Elinor Vanderveer (Guests).
Additional Credits: Ronald Colman courtesy of Samuel Goldwyn. Assistant camera: Willard Van Enger. Edited by Ernst Lubitsch. A Warner Brothers Classic of the Screen. Production dates: September to October 1925. Released December 26, 1925.
Other Versions: Filmed in English as *Lady Windermere's Fan (1916)*, *The Fan* (1949), *A Good Woman* (2004).
Available: Image Entertainment DVD, *More Treasures from American Film Archives 1894-1931* (2004). ISBN: 0-9747099-1-3. UPC: 0-14381-2271-2-3.

The son of a Berlin tailor, Ernst Lubitsch entered show business surreptitiously, acting in nightclubs and cabarets while working as a bookkeeper for his father. As a member of Max Reinhardt's Deutsches Theater, he advanced from bit parts to leads on stage and, starting in 1913, on screen. He began directing and writing while still an actor, gradually giving up performing entirely. For years his early German films were difficult to see; as they began to emerge from obscurity, many critics were taken aback at how broad and ethnic they could be.

Lubitsch generally alternated between historical epics like *Anna Boleyn* and romantic comedies like *Sumurun* (both 1920). The former was an international hit, and along with *Madame DuBarry* (1919) drew attention from movie executives in the United States. He helped the careers of Pola Negri and Emil Jannings, both of whom would achieve a measure of success in Hollywood, and worked at a headlong pace, completing a dozen feature films between 1919 and 1920.

Hired by Mary Pickford, Lubitsch encountered a wave of anti-German hostility when he reached California. In addition, "Poor Ernst Lubitsch arrived not knowing what kind of demon

I was," as Pickford put it later. He turned down the story she wanted him to make for what became *Rosita* (1923), based on an obscure French play. *Rosita* was one of Pickford's few failures. "It's the worst picture I ever did, it's the worst picture I ever saw," she wrote, but by then Lubitsch had signed with Warner Brothers.

The brothers had been trying to upgrade their studio's image, referring a bit hopefully to films like *Clash of the Wolves* (1925) with Rin Tin Tin as "A Warner Brothers Classic of the Screen." They offered Lubitsch an unusually generous contract that gave him $30,000 a picture, his choice of material, and what amounted to final cut. He responded with *The Marriage Circle* (1924), a comedy of manners that was a huge box-office hit. (He remade it in 1932 as the sound film *One Hour with You*.) But Lubitsch was an expensive craftsman, taking between six to eight weeks to finish a film (the average Warners feature took four weeks).

Lady Windermere's Fan was Lubitsch's fourth project for Warners. It was based on a play by Oscar Wilde, but as he did throughout his career, Lubitsch and his screenwriter Julien Josephson discarded much of the plot, fashioning a new story that was closer in spirit to a soap opera like *Stella Dallas* (1925) than to Wilde's carefully showcased epigrams. Work on the film started in September 1925, with Clive Brook cast as Lord Darlington. According to biographer Scott Eyman, Lubitsch antagonized Brook into departing from the film, replacing him with *Stella Dallas* star Ronald Colman.

Perhaps the director felt that Brook's upper lip was a bit too stiff for what was turning into a far more serious story than the original play. Colman, on the verge of international stardom, was more insouciant, less concerned about "performing" than about maintaining a suave appearance. The actor may have realized that although he was top-billed, the most important role in the movie was that of Mrs. Erlynne, played by Irene Rich.

Born in Buffalo, New York, in 1891, Rich specialized in long-suffering, world-weary, and usually wronged women in a series of popular melodramas like *A Woman Who Sinned*, *A Lost Lady* (both 1924), and *The Wife Who Wasn't Wanted* (1925). She and Lubitsch met during *Rosita*; for this role, he had her dye her hair red to enter into the spirit of the part. He also reshot some of her key scenes at the Vitagraph Studios in Brooklyn.

The director was already famous for what would later be referred to as "the Lubitsch touch." This style couldn't really be detected in the cinematography, which was fairly standard for the time, or in the sets and costume design, which were ornate, even plush, but neither distinctive nor convincing. You can't even pin it down to the acting, which in this film is mostly distraught poses, flared nostrils, darting eyes, and caught breaths. The style is evident in the graceful way the story unfolds, in Lubitsch's willingness to let viewers read the narrative from small details. He structures the film primarily in medium shots and close-ups, moving the camera only to make a point, eliminating anything that doesn't focus on the characters and their feelings.

Early in the film, Lubitsch cuts from a pile of unpaid bills to Irene Rich as Erlynne seated before her desk, biting her thumb and projecting a sense of worry. Cut to Bert Lytell as her son-in-law, Lord Windermere, reaching into an inside pocket for his checkbook. Back to Erlynne, still biting her thumb, a picture of Lady Windermere visible on her desk. She looks up to her son-in-law. An insert shot shows him fumbling open the checkbook. Back to Erlynne, looking away. With the simplest technique and smallest gestures, Lubitsch has encapsulated a troubled relationship while defining for viewers what will drive most of the plot.

But, as Eyman put it, "The critics were not all that impressed." The film turned a profit, but not as much as Lubitsch's earlier efforts. Even worse, it did poorly in Europe, where the Warners expected the director to clean up. Studio executives started referring sarcastically to the "Great Lubitsch" in memos. Jack Warner cabled to his brother Harry, "Small directors making twice money he making." Harry replied, "His pictures are over peoples' heads here." As studio editor Rudi Fehr noted, "Lubitsch had a following, but they weren't coal-miners, they weren't steelworkers." After one more film at Warners, *So This Is Paris* (1926), Lubitsch purchased the remainder of his contract and moved to Paramount. His next Registry title is *Trouble in Paradise* (1932).

Ben-Hur

Metro-Goldwyn-Mayer, 1925. Silent, B&W with color sequences, 1.33. 141 minutes.

Cast: Ramon Novarro ([Judah] Ben-Hur), Francis X. Bushman (Messala), May McAvoy (Esther), Betty Bronson (Mary), Claire McDowell (Princess of Hur), Kathleen Key (Tirzah), Carmel Myers (Iras), Nigel de Brulier (Simonides), Mitchell Lewis (Sheik Ilderim), Leo White (Sanballat), Frank Currier (Arrius), Charles Belcher (Balthazar), Dale Fuller (Amrah), Winter Hall (Joseph).

Credits: Directed by Fred Niblo. Adaptation by June Mathis. Produced from the scenario of Carey Wilson. Continuity by Carey Wilson and Bess Meredyth. Based on the novel by General Lew Wallace, published and copyrighted by Harper and Brothers. Produced by Metro-Goldwyn-Mayer in arrangement with Abraham L. Erlanger, Charles B. Dillingham and Florenz Ziegfeld, Jr. Directorial assistants: Alfred L. Raboch and Reeves Eason. Photography by Rene Guissart, Percy Hilburn, Karl Struss, Clyde DeVinna. Art effects by Ferdinand P. Earle. Settings by Cedric Gibbons and Horace Jackson. Titles by Katharine Hilliker and H.H. Caldwell. Film editor: Lloyd Nosler. Assistant director: Charles Stallings. Costumes by Theaterkunst Hermann J. Kaufmann, Berlin N.54.

Additional Credits: Some footage shot in Rome directed by Charles Brabin. Nativity scene directed by Ferdinand P. Earle. Assistant directors: William Wyler, Christy Cabanne. Film editor in Rome: Aubrey Scotto. Settings: Arnold Gillespie. Production managers: Silas Clegg, Harry Edington, William Wyler. Additional photography: E. Burton Steene, George Meehan, John Boyle, D.W. Martinelli. Production dates: October 1923 to June 1924; August to fall 1924; February 18 to spring 1925; October 1925.

Premiered in New York City on December 30, 1925, New York City. Title on screen: *Ben-Hur A Tale of the Christ*.
Other Versions: *Ben Hur* (1907), *Ben-Hur* (1959).
Available: Warner Home Video DVD (2005). ISBN: 1-4198-1079-0. UPC: 0-12569-87535-3.

Before he was a best-selling novelist, General Lew Wallace was a lawyer in Indiana and a veteran of both the Mexican and the Civil Wars. His first novel, *The Fair God*, a melodrama about the Aztec empire, was based in part on his experiences in Mexico. A chance encounter during a railroad journey with Robert Green Ingersoll, at the time the most famous agnostic in the country, led Wallace to rethink an article he had been writing about the Nativity. Now the Nativity became the opening to a historical novel that Wallace hoped would help prove the divinity of Christ. By the time he finished his research, Wallace had been named governor of the territory of New Mexico. He completed the novel in Santa Fe.

Published in 1880, *Ben-Hur: A Tale of the Christ* was not a popular success at first, but within a decade had sold hundreds of thousands of copies. Sales were helped by playwright William Young's stage adaptation, produced by Klaw & Erlanger in 1899—the first of several versions that grew in size over the years. Sidney Olcott (*From the Manger to the Cross*, 1912) directed the first film version, written by Gene Gauntier and released by Kalem in 1907. It became the center of a legal battle that helped extend copyright protection to motion pictures.

The next attempt to film the novel was overseen by producer Samuel Goldwyn, who put together a project with star Charles Walsh, director Charles Brabin, and writer June Mathis, one of the creative forces behind Rudolph Valentino and *The Four Horsemen of the Apocalypse* (1921). Goldwyn signed a deal promising half of the gross receipts to a theatrical syndicate formed by Klaw & Erlanger. Mathis, Goldwyn's story editor and the impetus behind casting Charles Walsh in the title role, persuaded the producer to shoot the film on location in Italy. Brabin and his crew arrived there in the fall of 1923, and began shooting early in 1924. When Goldwyn's company merged with both Metro Pictures and a company run by Louis B. Mayer, Goldwyn was suddenly out, and Irving Thalberg was put in charge of production for the new Metro-Goldwyn-Mayer.

Thalberg, who was overseeing Erich von Stroheim's *Greed* (1925), wanted to bring the *Ben-Hur* production back to Hollywood. He also rewrote Mathis's script with writers Bess Meredyth and Casey Wilson. Marcus Loew, head of MGM's parent company, brought the writers with him on a trip to Italy, along with actor Ramon Novarro. Born José Ramón Gil Samaniegos in Mexico in 1899, Novarro was a dancer and supporting actor when he was discovered by director Rex Ingram. Perhaps coincidentally, Ingram had just split with Rudolph Valentino, and was looking for a "Latin lover" to replace him. Navarro starred with Ingram's wife Alice Terry in a series of features; now he was going to replace Walsh as Judah Ben-Hur.

Also with Loew was Fred Niblo, a Nebraska native who had directed Valentino in *Blood and Sand* (1922) and Douglas Fairbanks in *The Three Musketeers* (1921). Niblo took over from Brabin (although some of Brabin's footage remained in the final film). As shooting continued, MGM executives became increasingly worried over the balllooning budget. Early in 1925, Loew and Mayer ordered the production back to California. There Thalberg okayed $300,000 to construct a Circus Maximus set that could seat thousands of extras. It became the backdrop of one of silent film's most thrilling sequences, a chariot race staged with extraordinary attention to detail. Filmed with forty cameras, including units equipped with close-up lenses and mounted on trucks, the sheer size of the sequence, with twelve four-horse teams racing seven laps around the course, became a physical reality for moviegoers.

Rightly or wrongly, Thalberg saw *Ben-Hur* in the same terms that he saw King Vidor's *The Big Parade* (1925): as a potential blockbuster whose box-office prospects would improve with the injection of spectacle. The money spent on the chariot sequence would elevate the film above its competition, as would the insertion of Technicolor sequences (nine of these survive). Along with the naval battle, these are the elements of the film that remain vivid, even memorable, today.

In dramatic terms, *Ben-Hur* wasn't much more advanced than *From the Manger to the Cross*. Characters were depicted in black-and-white terms, and acting consisted of broad, histrionic gestures. Like *The Thief of Bagdad* (1924), immense sets were presented as geometric blocks, the equivalent of matte paintings, not as physical space to explore. Thalberg permitted anachronistic touches, especially in the opening scenes, perhaps worried that moviegoers might be intimidated by the subject matter. He did the same thing with *The Big Parade*, betting that some broad humor would help involve viewers in the story. And he made sure that for all the medicine filmgoers would have to swallow, all the sermonizing and piety and Scriptural quotes, they would be rewarded with plenty of sadism and as much sex as he could legally squeeze in.

Another distinguishing aspect of *Ben-Hur* is its guarded presentation of spirituality. Although subtitled *A Tale of the Christ*, this character is seen only from the distance, or as a disembodied hand and arm. The theology presented in the film had been filtered through several sources: Wallace's self-guided research, Mathis's avant-garde concept of masculinity, Thalberg's preoccupation with mass markets, and Mayer's obsession with family life.

That such a seamless story could emerge from so many hands is another surprising element of the film. *Ben-Hur* is more a studio artifact than the work of any one creative vision. If the film lacks the idiosyncrasies of Ingram's *Four Horsemen*, it manages to adapt his innovative camerawork for its own ends, just as it took Mathis's vision of Valentino as screen hero and applied it to Novarro (whose subsequent career was negligible). Thalberg understood that the strengths of film were different from those of theater and literature. He knew how film could expand time, as in a five-minute scene after the chariot race in which Ben-Hur's mother hovers over her sleeping son, wondering whether to wake him. The choices made in the staging and editing of this film were used as a guidebook by the filmmakers who followed.

Ben-Hur was the top box-office draw of 1926, but its budget (close to $4 million), plus the crippling deal with Klaw & Erlanger, placed profits out of reach for MGM—at least for the film's initial run. The production justified for a time Thalberg's approach to moviemaking, and opened up the possibility of religious projects for other studios, such as Paramount's *The King of Kings* (1927) and *Noah's Ark* (1928) from Warner Brothers. *Ben-Hur* helped establish MGM as one of the major players in the industry. The studio would remake the film in 1959, ironically repeating many of the mistakes that plagued the 1925 production.

Hands Up

Paramount, 1926. Silent, B&W, 1.33. 64 minutes.
Cast: Raymond Griffith (Jack, a Confederate spy), Marion Nixon (Mae), Virginia Lee Corbin (Alice Woodstock), Montagu Love (Captain Edward Logan), George Billings (Abraham Lincoln), Mack Swain (Silas Woodstock), Noble Johnson (Sitting Bull), Charles K. French (Brigham Young).
Credits: Directed by Clarence Badger. Screenplay: Monte Brice, Lloyd Corrigan. Story: Reginald Morris. Produced by B.P. Schulberg. Director of photography: H. Kinley Martin. Special effects: Barney Wolff. Presented by Jesse L. Lasky, Adolph Zukor.
Additional Credits: Released January 11, 1926.
Available: Grapevine Video DVD (*www.grapevinevideo.com*).

As one of the most successful movie stars in the world, Charlie Chaplin became the inspiration for a significant number of imitators, including some close enough in looks and style to have their films advertised under Chaplin's name. Smarter, more talented comedians sought to distance themselves from Chaplin's image. Harold Lloyd went from directly imitating his look to donning glasses and tight clothes in opposition to the Tramp's outfit. Roscoe Arbuckle had his girth, Buster Keaton his stone face, Harry Langdon his pre-adolescent persona. Second-tier comics sought different personalities as well. Max Davidson exploited his Jewish ethnicity, Laurel and Hardy adopted upper-class pretensions.

Charley Chase and Raymond Griffith played distinctly middle-class, modern characters. Both were smooth, impeccably dressed, and fully conversant with trends, fads, and changing social mores. Both believed that good manners and civility could get them into or out of any situation. Chase was excitable, often victimized by misunderstandings or by conventions. Griffith, on the other hand,

hovered on the margins of respectability, a con man at times, almost always dismissive of middle-class aspirations.

Born in 1895, he was the son of show people. He lost his voice at a young age (he claimed from yelling on stage, although more likely it was the result of an illness like bronchial pneumonia), ruling out a career on stage but making him a perfect candidate for silent movies. Griffith served two years in the Navy, then trained as an acrobat and mime before touring in vaudeville. His first film credit was in 1915 with the L-KO Motion Picture Kompany, but he did most of his early work at Mack Sennett's studio, writing gags and scenarios as well as appearing in shorts.

In the early 1920s, Griffith joined other screen comics who were graduating from shorts to features. He filmed some at Goldwyn Pictures before signing a contract with Paramount, where he played comic relief in a number of features and leads in some others. *Changing Husbands* (1924) was another of the innuendo-laden domestic comedies popularized by Cecil B. DeMille; *Paths to Paradise* (1925) was a fairly clever adaptation of a play about rival jewel thieves in the style of Ernst Lubitsch's *Trouble in Paradise*.

Hands Up was somewhat atypical for Griffith because it was a period piece about the Civil War. In general filmmakers sided with the South when depicting the War between the States: as defeated underdogs, the Confederacy offered more opportunities for sentiment. Rather than exploit still painful memories evoked by politics, Griffith was more concerned with how to find humor in settings in which violence and death predominated.

One big problem Griffith faced is that he had no distinctive physical skills. He eschewed stunts and pratfalls, was not noticeably dexterous, and rarely took part in daredevil or chase stories. He looked good in clothes, moved with a certain flair, and underplayed in a manner perhaps more appealing today than it was during the 1920s. As a result, he relied more than most comics on the sort of clever, plot-oriented jokes that would give him room to react rather than require him to perform.

Hands Up does have moments of slapstick, some of it surprisingly cold and harsh. Early in the film Griffith's character Jack, a Confederate spy, meets with a general on the battlefield to discuss plans to hijack a shipment of gold from a mine on the western frontier. Griffith keeps a straight face while ducking out of the way of bullets and bombs, ignoring the carnage around him, an attitude Leo McCarey copied for the Marx Brothers in *Duck Soup* (1933).

The rest of the film takes place on a more sober plane. Jack is after the gold in Silas Woodcock's (Mack Swain) mine; so is Captain Edward Logan (Montagu Love), an officious Union officer who, like a foil in a Looney Tunes cartoon, keeps playing by the rules while Jack effortlessly outmaneuvers him. Woodcock's two beautiful daughters provide a gratifyingly risqué element; a befuddled black servant used for some casually cruel gags pins the film to the racism prevalent in the era.

Comparisons between *Hands Up* and Buster Keaton's *The General*, released almost exactly a year later, can be as instructive as they are inevitable. Both films feature cunning Confederate heroes, bumbling Union officers, and pitch-black humor. But whereas Keaton's film has the trajectory of a bullet, with absolutely no digressions, no narrative flab, and no ambiguous moments, Griffith's film is filled with pauses, asides, and narrative dead ends. Keaton's plot hurtles along much as his train speeds down the tracks; Griffith has no compunction about bringing his story to a halt to play, expertly, vaudeville gags unrelated to the plot at hand. *The General* unfolds on an immense and imaginatively detailed canvas; *Hands Up* consists of a half-dozen or so fairly disjointed scenes tied together by a highly improbable story line and some satirical swipes at genre conventions. A long and amusing scene in which Jack teaches an Indian tribe how to Charleston owes a lot to Keaton's 1922 short *The Paleface*. It's an undeniably funny moment, but one that has almost no bearing on the actual outcome of *Hands Up*.

The film got respectable reviews, but it was not a huge box-office hit. Griffith made four more features of varying quality for Paramount, but his screen character was not clicking with moviegoers. (The studio had Adolphe Menjou, a similarly suave, debonair type with a light touch who was also expert at drama.) Griffith broke his contract, married actress Bertha Mann, and honeymooned in Europe for most of 1928. By the time he returned to the United States, the film industry had begun to switch over to sound films. With his raspy voice, the comic was in a difficult position. He made two low-budget sound shorts for Al Christie (in 1929's *The Sleeping Porch* his character has a cold, explaining his hoarseness), and had a silent, unbilled cameo in *All Quiet on the Western Front* (1930) before retiring from the screen.

Griffith continued working as a producer, contributing to several significant Warner Bros. titles before moving to Twentieth Century-Fox. Apart from a few Shirley Temple films, Griffith's most prominent credit there may have been as Associate Producer on John Ford's *Drums Along the Mohawk* (1939). He left film for good in 1940.

The Black Pirate

United Artists, 1926. Silent, color, 1.33. 94 minutes.

Cast: Douglas Fairbanks (The Black Pirate), Billie Dove (The Princess), Tempé Pigott (Duenna), Donald Crisp (MacTavish), Sam De Grasse (Pirate rival), Anders Randolf (Pirate leader), Charles Stevens (Pirate arsonist), John Wallace, Fred Becker, Charles Belcher (Passenger), E.J. Ratcliffe, Nino Cochise.

Credits: Directed by Albert Parker. Story by Elton Thomas [Douglas Fairbanks]. Adapted by Jack Cunningham. Photographed by Henry Sharp. General manager: Robert Fairbanks. Manager of production: Theodore Reed. Photography in Technicolor. Technicolor staff: Arthur Ball, George Cave. Scenario editor: Lotta Woods. Research director: Dr. Arthur Woods. Consultants: Dwight Franklin, Robert Nichols. Supervising art director: Carl Oscar Borg. Associate artists: Edward M. Langley, Jack Holden. Musical score by Mortimer Wilson. Marine technician: P.H.L. Wilson. Film cutter: William Nolan. Stunts: Richard Talmadge. Produced by The Elton Corporation.

Additional Credits: Released March 8, 1926.

Available: Kino on Video DVD (2004). UPC: 7-38329-03302-6.

Child star Jackie Coogan took credit for instigating *The Black Pirate* by telling his neighbor Douglas Fairbanks how much he loved Howard Pyle's *Book of Pirates*. Fairbanks planned a pirate movie after he finished *The Mark of Zorro* (1920), and at one point hoped to have Ernst Lubitsch direct it. But research and the difficulty in finding and making props kept delaying the project. Another factor was Fairbanks' decision to shoot the film in color. Backed in part by MGM, the Technicolor company was trying to prove that its process was suitable for feature films. "The argument is that it tires and distracts the eye," Fairbanks acknowledged, but he added, "I can no longer imagine piracy without color."

With Technicolor's cooperation, Fairbanks and his cameraman Henry Sharp tested the color negative for months, exposing some 50,000 feet of it. Donald Crisp later claimed that he had been hired to direct the movie (something he had done for Fairbanks' *Zorro* sequel *Don Q Son of Zorro*, 1925), but although Crisp had a significant acting part in the film, Albert Parker was listed in trade papers as director as early as June 1925. Parker had once acted on stage with Fairbanks, and had directed some of Doug's earlier features.

The Swedish artist Carl Oscar Borg, famed for his paintings of Native Americans, supervised the production design. For additional help, Fairbanks turned to illustrator Dwight Franklin, an expert on pirates. Franklin not only helped research costumes, he drew the equivalent of storyboards, sketches that showed Fairbanks how individual shots might be composed. According to film historian Rudy Behlmer, Robert Nichols, an English poet, "worked on the orchestration of motion" within scenes.

As director Parker explained later, "*The Black Pirate* story was produced with color in mind, which is to say that we realized that the color must never dominate the narrative. It has been made a story of situations rather than plot, the main narrative being a bare thread." *The Black Pirate* was the first feature specifically designed to take advantage of what Technicolor could do, even if it meant that every prop in the film had to be dyed.

Fairbanks wrote the basic treatment for the story under a pseudonym, then turned it over to Jack Cunningham to flesh out characters and scenes. When Fairbanks purchased *The Curse of Capistrano*, the source material for *The Mark of Zorro*, from pulp writer Johnston McCulley, he also bought its sequel, *The Further Adventures of Zorro*. Material from this novel made its way into *The Black Pirate*, such as the hero's use of a ship's rigging to overcome his foes.

Another important contributor to the film was the Belgian fencing instructor Fred Cavens, who caught Fairbanks' attention for his work on *The Three Must-Get-Theres* (1922), a Three Musketeers parody. Cavens trained Fairbanks and actor Anders Randolf, who had some previous fencing experience. Cavens stood just off camera during the sword duels to offer advice.

Fairbanks cast the film with many of his regular performers, such as Charles Stevens, a fixture at the Fairbanks office, and Sam De Grasse, the villain in Doug's *Wild and Woolly* (1917). Billie Dove was hired in part because she photographed well in the Technicolor Western *Wanderer of the Wasteland* (1924). A former artists' model and Ziegfeld girl, Dove came to Hollywood after marrying director Irvin Willat.

The original plan had been to shoot on the island of Catalina off the coast of California, but it proved too difficult to control lighting. As a result, 95 percent of the film, including shots of the exteriors of various ships, was photographed at the United Artists studio. The production lasted three months, and thanks to surviving outtakes, it's possible to see how Fairbanks carefully planned scenes, yet still allowed for improvised touches.

Fairbanks was more interested in capturing the adventure and excitement of the pirate genre than in telling a story. It doesn't really matter how or why Doug becomes the Black Pirate, for example, or how he ends up protecting a princess from being sold into slavery. The film alludes to all the standard pirate tropes—buried treasure, walking the plank, etc.—but action takes precedence over plot or plausibility. Fairbanks' stunts are among the most exuberant and thrilling sequences in all of silent film. (Adults watching the film today may be surprised at how grisly and coldhearted the action can be.) The two-color Technicolor process adds a charmingly antique look to the film, like the faded pastels from old postcards.

This Technicolor system broke the color spectrum into two components, red/green and blue, that were processed as separate strips of film and then glued together back to back. It was a difficult, time-consuming process prone to shrinkage and scratches, and by 1933 it had been supplanted by a dye-transfer process that was far more lifelike and durable. When Fairbanks donated his film materials to a museum shortly before his death, the color process for *The Black Pirate* was already obsolete. Current color prints have been assembled from alternate takes; these were generally photographed for foreign markets or as a protection negative.

Fairbanks made two more swashbuckling adventures before the advent of sound. His first talkie was an adaptation of *The Taming of the Shrew* (1929), costarring his wife Mary Pickford. But their marriage was crumbling, and Fairbanks, close to fifty, could no longer command the attention of moviegoers. After three more sound films, he retired from the screen.

Theodore Case Sound Tests: Gus Visser and His Singing Duck

Theodore Case, 1924–26. Sound, B&W, 1.33. 90 seconds.

Cast: Gus Visser.

Credits: Directed by Theodore Case or Earl I. Sponable.

Additional Credits: Title supplied later.

Available: Image Entertainment DVD (2004), *More Treasures from American Film Archives, 1894–1931*. ISBN: 0-9747099-1-3. UPC: 0-14381-2271-2-3.

Technicians tried to combine sound with film as early as 1894, with the *Dickson Experimental Sound Film*. The 1900 Paris Universal Exposition featured *Cyrano de Bergerac*, a color film synchronized to a wax cylinder recording. Six years later, George Mendel developed a system that interlocked a projector with a phonograph, resulting in a synchronized sound version of *La Marseillaise* (1907).

Synchronization was one essential element to sound films. It was the only way to provide realistic dialogue, for example. With nonelectric equipment, synchronization was almost impossible, as there was no way to ensure that separate machines would run at exactly the same speed. That was the goal behind Mendel's interlock mechanism, but as long as the sound was separate from the film, it was possible that the two elements would lose synch. This wouldn't matter as much if filmmakers were using sound as an atmospheric device—as background music, for example. But *Singin' in the Rain* (1952) provided a vivid example of what would happen if lines of dialogue suddenly fell out of synch.

Inventors tried two main approaches to synchronized sound films. The first to succeed on a widespread basis was the Vitaphone system developed by Warner Brothers An advancement on Mendel's interlocking mechanism, the Vitaphone system recorded sound onto sixteen-inch shellac platters at 33⅓ rpm. These records would be played on machines linked to film projectors. Proper playback required constant attention from projectionists. If the film broke or the record skipped, synchronization would be lost.

A second approach is often referred to as "sound on film." This used photoelectric cells to transform sound into patterns of light. The resulting patterns or waves were photographed onto a filmstrip of black on white (or clear), with black in one example representing maximum volume and the white or clear area representing silence. Played through a projector equipped with the proper exciter lamp, the wave patterns would be transformed back into sound. The huge advantage this offered over the Vitaphone record system was that the sound and film would never be separated. Even if the film broke, synchronization would remain constant.

The second essential element to sound films was amplification. Without a means of broadcasting music and dialogue to an entire theater, no sound film process would succeed. Amplification required the development of vacuum tubes and speaker horns, a speciality of Western Electric. Ironically, advancements in radio and recording technologies became critical to sound films.

The history of sound-on-film processes is a complicated one marked by competing claims and prolonged lawsuits. Eugene Lauste spent years trying to market his process, which he demonstrated in 1911 and again in 1918. Joseph Tykocinski-Tykociner displayed a variable-density soundtrack in 1922. Lee De Forest, inventor of the Audion vacuum tube, demonstrated his Photophone in 1920. Working for General Electric, Charles A. Hoxie developed an optical sound system for the U.S. Navy. Shortly thereafter, Western Electric technicians invented a "light valve."

De Forest went to Berlin in 1921 on a marketing trip. There he learned about the Tri-Ergon sound-on-film process. About six months later, De Forest announced a new Phonofilm system, one remarkably similar to Tri-Ergon. In April, 1923, De Forest found enough backing to begin filming sound shorts in a Manhattan studio once used by the Talmadge sisters. His subjects included vaudeville stars like Eddie Cantor, Weber and Fields, and Sissle and Blake. Almost a year later, he formed De Forest Phonofilms with Theodore Case and Earl Sponable. He made campaign films, synchronized soundtracks for features, "bouncing ball" cartoons with Max Fleischer, and even experimented with color.

Case and Sponable quit the company in September 1925. Born in Auburn, New York, in 1888, Theodore Case had several inventions to his credit, including a vacuum tube used by the Navy. He had done much of the work for De Forest's labs since 1921, including adapting a movie projector into a sound recorder. After splitting with De Forest, Case continued his work with sound on film. He also struck a deal with William Fox, who purchased the rights to his system. They formed the Fox-Case Corporation in September 1926, with Sponable as head of research. (Fox also purchased rights to the Tri-Ergon process as a precaution.) While lawsuits ensued, Case and Fox prevailed. Within a year, Fox was marketing four Movietone shorts a week, based on the Case technology.

It's unclear when *Gus Visser and His Singing Duck* was filmed, but it was most likely made as a demonstration for Fox investors. According to historian Donald Crafton, Case and Sponable shot it in Fox's New York offices during the summer of 1926, along with a handful of other shorts. As De Forest did, Case and Sponable drew their subjects from vaudeville: Harry Lauder, the famous Scots entertainer; Chic Sale, who parlayed his country bumpkin character into a modest film career; and others. Born in Holland in 1894, Gus Visser had a vaudeville act called "Visser and Company, with Elsie Gelli." According to film historian Scott Simmon, the act included dancing, acrobatics, and "The Original Singing Duck."

Animal acts were a fixture in vaudeville, usually opening shows and then appearing after intermissions. Well-known acts included Swain's Birds, Fink's Mules, and Dubell's Pets, although elephants, sheep, cats, dogs, and pigs were also popular. Barnold's Dog and Monkey Pantomime was one of two acts that featured a "drunken dog." George Burns once worked with Captain Bett's seal. Big Jim, a dancing bear, survived a number of dance crazes.

And then there's Visser's duck, the reluctant performer of "Ma, He's Making Eyes at Me." It was one of several songs written for Eddie Cantor by composer Con Conrad—in this case for a 1921 show called *The Midnight Rounders*. The lyrics were by Sidney Clare ("Please Don't Talk About Me When I'm Gone," "On the Good Ship Lollipop," "Travelin' Light," etc.). "Ma, He's Making Eyes at Me" was later recorded by everyone from Oscar Peterson to Anne-Margret; it was even the title song of a 1940 musical. In the film world at least, Visser's version is unique.

The Son of the Sheik

Paramount, 1926. Silent, B&W, 1.33. 68 minutes.

Cast: Rudolph Valentino (Ahmed and The Sheik), Vilma Banky (Yasmin), George Fawcett (André), Montague Love (Ghabah), Karl Dane (Ramadan); Bull Montana, Binunsky Hyman (Mountebanks); Agnes Ayres (Diana, wife of the Sheik).

Credits: Directed by George Fitzmaurice. Screen adaptation by Frances Marion and Fred de Gresac. Titles: George Marion, Jr. Photography: George Barnes. Settings: William Cameron Menzies.

Additional Credits: Based on *The Sons of the Sheik* by E.M. Hull. Produced by John W. Considine, Jr., Feature Productions. Property master: Irving Sindler. Assistant director: Cullen Tate. Synchronized score added for theatrical rerelease, presented by Emil C. Jenson. Synchronized and arranged by James C. Bradford. Music and orchestrations by Arthur H. Gutman. Turbulent music sequences by Gerard Carbonara. Premiered July 9, 1926.

Available: Kino Video DVD (2000). UPC: 7-38329-01522-0.

In the years following *The Four Horsemen of the Apocalypse* (1920), Rudolph Valentino became one of the most popular stars in the industry, sparking crazes for tangos, "Latin lovers," and exotic costume melodramas. Although his actual record at the box office was surprisingly spotty, in retrospect he has come to represent for many their concept of a 1920s movie star.

After *Four Horsemen*, Valentino teamed with director Rex Ingram and screenwriter June Mathis again in *The Conquering Power*, an adaptation of a Balzac novel. Valentino had a falling out with Ingram, but remained tied to Mathis, who moved to the Famous Players–Lasky studio. In the meantime, Ingram tried to turn Ramon Novarro into the next Valentino.

While filming *Uncharted Seas* in 1921, Valentino met dancer Natacha Rambova, originally Winifred Shaunessy of Salt Lake City. Both Valentino and Rambova were hired for a version

Vilma Banky and Rudolph Valentino in *The Son of the Sheik*.

of *Camille* starring Alla Nazimova (and written by June Mathis). According to biographer Emily Leider, Nazimova and Rambova worked together on changing Valentino's looks. He lost weight and had his eyebrows tweezed, for example. Nazimova, Rambova, and Mathis all shared a taste for the occult, and under their influence Valentino embraced an outré lifestyle that they hoped would enhance his persona as a screen lover.

But two films really solidified Valentino's hold on the public. One was *Blood and Sand* (1922), a bullfighting melodrama that became one of his biggest hits. Even more crucial to his career was *The Sheik*, an adaptation of an Edith M. Hull best-seller that was filmed the year before. In it, Valentino played Sheik Ahmed Ben Hassan, whose kisses and smoldering glances overpower Agnes Ayres, appearing as a virginal, blond British-woman on a tour of the Middle East. The turbans, flowing robes, and petal-strewn beds helped make the film's relatively chaste clinches seem torrid and illicit (although the plot very carefully established the Sheik as honorable, even eligible, before the climax). Rex Ingram answered *The Sheik* with *The Arab*, starring Ramon Novarro.

Within the span of a few films, Valentino's salary went from $250 to $3000 a week. He married Rambova in May 1922, and was briefly jailed for bigamy because he had not received an interlocutory decree from his marriage to Jean Acker. Rambova took charge of his career, but films like *The Young Rajah* (1922) and *Monsieur Beaucaire* (1924) bombed at the box office. What's worse, a backlash was forming against Valentino, and against lounge lizards in general. A notorious

editorial by John Herrick in the Chicago *Tribune* referred to the actor as a "Pink Powder Puff."

Needing a hit, Valentino, who had initiated divorce proceedings against Rambova in 1925, turned to his past—specifically, a sequel to *The Sheik*. Its author, Edith Maude Hull, who was struggling herself, wrote *The Sons of the Sheik* some five years after the original novel. Frances Marion, a screenwriter who had worked with Mary Pickford, wrote an adaptation that streamlined the plot and that focused back on the earlier film—eliminating one of the Sheik's sons in the process. That same year, in addition to writing Frank Borzage's *Lazybones* and an adaptation of *Stella Dallas*, Marion wrote *The Dark Angel* for director George Fitzmaurice. Born in Paris in 1895, Fitzmaurice was a painter and set designer who was building a reputation for visually stylized romances. *The Dark Angel* starred the Hungarian beauty Vilma Banky, a Samuel Goldwyn discovery, and was photographed by George Barnes, both of whom joined the *Son of the Sheik* production. In fact, Fitzmaurice had Marion tailor the role of Yasmin, a street dancer in a gang of pickpockets and thieves, for Banky.

Another key creative addition was William Cameron Menzies, who had worked on set design for Douglas Fairbanks' *The Thief of Bagdad* (1924). *The Son of the Sheik* boasts similarly arched entranceways and false minarets, a Hollywood dream of the desert that would recur in films like *Morocco* (1931).

Valentino played dual roles, happily married father and hellbent son, and it's apparent on screen which part he preferred. In an interview with journalist J. K. Winkler, he complained, "Heaven knows I'm no sheik! Look at this 'sleek black hair.'

Getting a bit thin about the temples, isn't it?" The Valentino of 1926 looks puffier, had circles under his eyes, and as a lover is no more at ease in front of the camera than when he was playing villains and dancers earlier in his career. Marion wrote that Valentino "made no complaint; he was too tired to combat the overwhelming forces that governed his career," and there is an uneasiness about the whole project, a sense that the players aren't sure whether they're in a drama or a comedy.

The star gamely performed several of his own stunts, and Fitzmaurice whipped up a fair amount of action despite the feeble plotting. Everyone made sure that the film delivered what they assumed Valentino's fans wanted: fistfights and woo; the star stripped to the waist, his arms chained overhead to the bars of a cell; the half-naked Banky thrown onto the Sheik's desert bed; derring-do in a tavern as father and son battle overwhelming odds; love thwarted and then refound. The best work came from Banky, who was in the midst of a startling run of hits (she would retire with the advent of sound movies). But *The Son of the Sheik* was playing in a crowded market that also had to support costume adventures from Douglas Fairbanks, Ronald Colman, and others. (Colman's *Beau Geste* would use the same Yuma, Arizona, locations found in *The Son of the Sheik*.)

After filming completed, Valentino signed a three-picture deal with United Artists, planning to appear in a biography of Benvenuto Cellini to be directed by Fitzmaurice. After a successful Los Angeles premiere of *The Son of the Sheik*, Valentino took a cross-country publicity tour by train. He challenged John Merrick to a boxing match, and was filmed boxing in Chicago and New York City. The Gotham premiere was also a success. Valentino went to Atlantic City with vaudeville singer Gus Edwards. On August 14th, he collapsed during a date. He was operated on for acute appendicitis and gastric ulcers. A week later, the peritonitis had spread throughout his body, and he also suffered from pleurisy. He died on August 23rd at the age of thirty-one.

Valentino's body was put on display in New York City, where it was seen by close to 100,000 mourners and curiosity seekers. The official funeral was held in Los Angeles on September 7th. By that time two suicides had been attributed to his death. He was buried in June Mathis's crypt.

Mighty Like a Moose

Pathé, 1926. Silent, B&W, 1.33, 23 minutes.
Cast: Charley Chase (Mr. Moose), Vivien Oakland (Mrs. Moose), Anne Howe "The Radio Girl" (Maid), Charles Clary (Dentist), Gale Henry (Polka dancer), Malcolm Denny, Buddy.
Credits: Directed by Leo McCarey. Titles by H.M. Walker. Produced by Hal Roach. Photographed by Len Powers. Edited by Richard Currier. Supervising director: F. Richard Jones.
Additional Cast: Rolfe Sedan (Nose doctor), Charlie Hall (Shoeshine man), Harry Bowen.
Additional Credits: Written by Charley Chase. Filmed March 20–April 2, 1926. Released July 18, 1926.
Available: Kino Video DVD *The Charley Chase Collection* (2004). UPC: 7-38329-03682-9.

Among the many comedians who could be found at the Hal Roach studio in the 1920s were the Parrott brothers, Charles and James. Born in Baltimore in 1893, Charley was at work by the age of ten, after his father succumbed to drinking. A few years later he was touring in vaudeville, reaching California by 1912. After working for Al Christie at Universal, he moved over to Mack Sennett's Keystone studio, where he had supporting roles in both shorts and features. Without a distinctive look or screen character, Charley began working behind the camera, directing shorts at several studios after leaving Sennett in 1916.

Hal Roach hired Charley as a director in 1920. He worked on comedies starring Snub Pollard, a popular slapstick figure who continued working into the sound era. Charley also worked on shorts with his brother James, who was billed as Paul Parrott. Within a year he was named director general of the studio, with input into all of the Hal Roach product. When Harold Lloyd left the studio in 1923, Roach scrambled to find a replacement. Charley eagerly volunteered, assuming the screen name Charley Chase.

Chase's screen character was an elaboration on the easygoing American Everyman that Harold Lloyd had perfected. Chase was a bright, fun-loving, middle- or upper-class success who sometimes fell afoul of rivals or modern technology, but who generally could hold his own in a difficult world. Tall, angular, with sharp features, he was streamlined in his looks and actions. It was his personality—easygoing or put-upon—that dominated his films, not gags or slapstick.

Chase started out making one-reelers; they proved so popular that within a year Roach promoted

Charley Chase and Vivien Oakland as Mr. and Mrs. Moose in
Mighty Like a Moose. Courtesy of Kino International

him to two-reelers, with larger budgets and a more-or-less solid filmmaking unit. Chase made forty-five shorts with director Leo McCarey, and it is these films that form the basis of his reputation today. The two worked well together, as both were interested in reactions more than punchlines, in expanding and contracting time within scenes, and in improvising on material and situations until they felt they got them right.

Like McCarey's Laurel and Hardy films, the Chase shorts are built around disguises, mistaken identities, impossible premises played out in strictly logical fashion, and the slamming doors of bedroom farce. Chase often finds himself masquerading in his films: as a valet instead of a son in *Mum's the Word* (1926), as an insane rather than normal fiancé in *Crazy Like a Fox* (1926), and in *Mighty Like a Moose*, as an old version of himself instead of the new, improved one. As the plots escalate in speed, Chase could find himself in situations where he had to play two roles simultaneously.

Mighty Like a Moose takes its premise from O. Henry's "The Gift of the Magi," by having a husband and wife make fateful decisions without telling the other spouse. Playing Mr. Moose, Chase has his buck teeth operated on by a dentist. In an adjacent office of the same building, Mrs. Moose (Vivien Westwood) has her nose bobbed. Not recognizing each other, husband and wife start to flirt with their new acquaintances.

Viewers have to set aside disbelief for the story to work (of course major plastic surgery wouldn't heal in the space of an office visit), but McCarey and Chase play the plot as if its situations can and

would occur. Mr. Moose may be cheating on his wife, but he's still a gentleman, which means he has to find a polite way to ditch a wallflower who wants to polka with him at an illicit bootlegging party thrown by his dentist.

Chase and McCarey execute the script's farce elements in an agreeably calm, straightforward manner. McCarey relies on full and medium shots more than close-ups, and lingers on reaction shots rather than emphasizing quick cuts. He was especially fond of some of the routines he and Chase worked out (and, to be completely honest, at times borrowed from vaudeville). Both *Mum's the Word* and *Mighty Like a Moose* include variants on what would become a famous "mirror scene" in *Duck Soup* (1933).

Seen in succession, Chase's shorts betray some of the shortcomings of the Roach studio, such as its limited resources: the same hallway set can be found in film after film. And the level of inspiration in the movies varies, as one would expect when cast and crew are essentially working nonstop. Chase fans argue over which film is his best, with *Limousine Love* (1928) mentioned as frequently as *Mighty Like a Moose*. 1925's *His Wooden Wedding* contains one of the best insert shots in silent film: a letter with the words, "Beware! The woman you are about to marry has a wooden leg! A Friend."

Chase's films were relatively popular and consistently well made, leading some to wonder why he didn't become a bigger star. The comedian made a smooth transition to sound, continuing in his own shorts and appearing as an obnoxious conventioneer in Laurel and Hardy's *Sons of the*

Desert (1933). When Roach let him go in 1936 to concentrate on big-budget features, Chase signed with Columbia, where he starred in two-reelers and directed other comedians. But Chase struggled with alcoholism. His brother James also had an addictive personality, and killed himself in 1939. Chase died of a heart attack in 1940 at the age of forty-six. (McCarey's career is covered in more detail in the entries for *Duck Soup*, 1933, and *The Awful Truth*, 1937.)

The Strong Man

First National, 1926. Silent, B&W, 1.33. 76 minutes.
Cast: Harry Langdon (Paul Bergot), Priscilla Bonner (Mary Brown), Gertrude Astor ("Lily," of Broadway), William V. Mong ("Holy Joe" [Brown]), Robert McKim ("Mike" McDevitt), Arthur Thalasso ("Zandow the Great").
Credits: Directed by Frank Capra. Story by Arthur Ripley. Adapted by Hal Conklin, Robert Eddy. Titles by Reed Heustis. Photographed by Elgin Lessley, Glenn Kershner. Production manager: William H. Jenner. Assistant director: J. Frank Holliday. Technical director: Lloyd Brierly. Lighting by Denver Harmon. Film editor: Harold Young. Produced by Harry Langdon Corporation. A Richard A. Rowland presentation.
Additional Cast: Brooks Benedict (Bus passenger).
Additional Credits: Screenwriting by Harry Langdon, Frank Capra, Tim Whelan. Production dates: May to August 1926. Premiered in New York City on September 5, 1926.
Available: Kino Video DVD (2000). UPC: 7-38329-01732-3.

At his peak, Harry Langdon was considered a contender to Charlie Chaplin as a silent film clown. Subsequent writers reduced him to a sort of idiot savant of comedy: molded into a star by writer and director Frank Capra, and falling back into obscurity once he ignored Capra's advice and tried to succeed on his own. The reality is more complex, but there is no escaping the fact that Langdon's heyday was much shorter than the other major silent stars.

Langdon was born in Council Bluffs, Iowa, in 1884, to a comfortably prosperous family. (In later reports, he described a childhood of poverty, but his father was a successful enough painter that his mother was able to do volunteer work for the Salvation Army.) Stage-struck, he ran away from home to join a medicine show, then a minstrel show, followed by various circuses. He was trained in all aspects of show business, from mime and acrobatics to singing and dancing. Langdon was nineteen when he married Rose Musolff, also a performer. They built a successful vaudeville act around "Johnny's New Car," an evolving routine in which the naive Harry would get in trouble with pedestrians, motorists, and traffic cops.

Langdon was a headline act when Harold Lloyd tried to get him to sign with Hal Roach in 1923. Instead, Langdon went with independent producer Sol Lesser, making at least three shorts for his Principal Pictures. In November of that year he signed with Mack Sennett, and appeared in some routine shorts that had originally been intended for other performers. Within a year he had assembled a filmmaking unit that included director Harry Edwards and writer Arthur Ripley. By the next winter, Frank Capra had joined the team as a gag man.

Langdon's films developed a distinctive pace. The comic slowed everything down—not just the gags but his reactions to them. He changed his vaudeville character from naive to infantile, dressing in undersized clothes to emphasis his tiny frame. Swathing his face in white pancake makeup, he erased his adult features and replaced them with lipstick and mascara, giving himself bee-stung lips, high eyebrows, and rounded eyes. The effect was more presexual than effeminate, emphasized by Langdon's childlike gestures: chewing on his fingers, using a stiff arm to ward off everything from women to spills and accidents.

It was a delicate act that, played the wrong way, could assume unwanted overtones, or even suggest child abuse. Still, Langdon and his crew didn't hesitate to place his character in sexually suggestive situations. Chaplin, Keaton, and to a lesser extent Lloyd all made use of their characters' innocence in the face of "experienced" women. Langdon's character was so naive that when confronted by a femme fatale, he could plausibly reverse gender roles and pretend that his honor was being threatened.

As his shorts became more popular, Langdon began to expand to three reels. He also looked for a better production deal, signing with First National (an arm of Warner Brothers). He took with him Edwards, Capra, Ripley, and other Sennett figures. Before he left, he made a feature for Sennett, *His First Flame* (1927), that remained unreleased until his First National product began coming out. Edwards directed *Tramp, Tramp, Tramp* (1926), which placed Langdon in a cross-country walking race. It was a success, but ran over budget, which gave Capra the opportunity to direct Langdon's next two features, *The Strong Man* and *Long Pants*.

Much of the plot exposition for *The Strong Man* deals with figuring out a way to present Langdon's character, Paul Bergot, in a positive light. This meant explaining behavior that would be seen today as severely dysfunctional. Langdon was surrounded by a typically overbearing heavy (Arthur Thalasso), a pint-size ingénue (Priscilla Bonner), and, oddly, a saloon owner and bootlegger. After a prologue that takes place on a World War I battlefield, his character was sent to Cloverdale, a modern-day Wild West town that William S. Hart might recognize. Once the plot and characters are established, the real heart of the film emerges: three scenes that showcase Langdon's comic style.

In the first, he is seduced by Lily (Gertrude Astor), a no-nonsense Broadway moll who's after a bankroll secreted in Langdon's jacket. It's an eighteen-minute sequence (about the length of a two-reel comedy) that toys with innuendo without veering too far into the tasteless (an overhead shot of Astor grappling with Langdon on a bed comes pretty close). The climax of the film, in which Langdon must appear on stage impersonating a world-renowned weightlifter, is an outstanding comedy situation that would have been played similarly by just about any silent film clown. (In fact, Chaplin incorporated some of Langdon's moves into his song-and-dance routine in *Modern Times*.)

The centerpiece of *The Strong Man* takes place on a sort of combination bus and stagecoach, with Langdon, suffering from a head cold, seated next to an irascible businessman (Brooks Benedict). A battle of wits ensues between two personalities who couldn't be more disparate except for their stubborn streaks. Much of the scene could have been performed on stage, but Capra blocks it out in a manner that would only make sense on film. He pulls the camera in on tight close-ups and two-shots, letting the actors metaphorically lower their volume instead of playing to the balcony. Capra holds the shots for thirty, even forty-five seconds, letting laughs emerge from Langdon's ineptly malevolent expressions, from the incongruity of his attempt to appear mature, from Benedict's deadpan glower. (The staging inadvertently points out the fact that Langdon's jokes don't really register unless an adult is watching—and judging—him.)

In his autobiography, Capra essentially took credit for Langdon's screen persona and box-office success, and blamed the comedian for the rift that led to the director's dismissal after *Long Pants* (1927). Langdon assumed direction of his features, but they were box-office failures. According to Capra, the comedian was forgotten within a few years, but in reality Langdon continued working until his death in 1944, starring in shorts and industrial films, and appearing in supporting roles in features. Like most silent comedians, he had trouble adjusting to sound, in particular how to handle the noise of pratfalls. Forty when he started making films, he was also simply too old to continue acting infantile. Still, he was a significant influence on other comics, especially Stan Laurel, and contributed to the scripts of Laurel and Hardy features. Capra, on the other hand, found himself scrambling for work, and was eventually forced back to Sennett and two-reel comedies. It took a contract with Harry Cohn at Columbia Pictures before he would regain his footing.

Unlikely as it may seem, Harry Langdon is *The Strong Man*.

So's Your Old Man

Paramount, 1926. Silent, B&W, 1.33. 67 minutes.

Cast: W.C. Fields (Sam Bisbee), Alice Joyce (Princess Marie Lescaboura), Charles [Buddy] Rogers (Robert Murchison), Catherine [Kittens] Reichert (Alice Bisbee), Marcia Harris (Mrs. Bisbee), Julia Ralph (Mrs. Murchison), Frank Montgomery (Jeff), Jerry Sinclair (Al).

Credits: Directed by Gregory La Cava. Adapted by Howard Emmett Rogers and Tom J. Geraghty. Screenplay by J. Clarkson Miller. From Julian Street's story, "Mr. Bisbee's Princess." Produced by William Le Baron. Production editor: Ralph Block. Film and title editor: Julian Johnson. Photographed by George Webber. Title decorations by John Held, Jr. Presented by Adolph Zukor, Jesse L. Lasky.

Additional Cast: Walter Walker (Mayor), William "Shorty" Blanche (Caddy), Charles Byer (Prince Lescaboura).

Additional Credits: Released October 25, 1926.

Other Versions: Remade as *You're Telling Me!* (1934).

Available: The Library of Congress.

Once movies took hold in popular culture, they became a financial windfall for many stage performers. Even comics known for their verbal abilities tried starring in features. Will Rogers and Eddie Cantor both made successful silents, although neither had as extensive a pre-talkie career as W.C. Fields.

Fields was a headliner in the Ziegfeld *Follies* when he made his first short, *Pool Sharks*, in 1915, but his film career really began some ten years later. His appearance as Eustace McGargle in the Broadway hit *Poppy* led to a film adaptation, *Sally of the Sawdust* (1925), improbably directed by D.W. Griffith. McGargle was one in a long line of quacks and swindlers that Fields portrayed; his other specialty was the henpecked husband, browbeaten by a domineering wife and ignored or ridiculed by his children. Griffith next directed Fields in *That Royle Girl* (also 1925), but neither film was a commercial success.

Fields left the *Follies* for good in January 1926. Attracted to the easier schedules in filmmaking, he signed a contract with William Le Baron, the de facto head of production at Paramount's East Coast facilities in Astoria, Queens. His first starring feature was *It's the Old Army Game* (1926), based on J.P. McEvoy's *The Comic Supplement*. (Fields remade it in 1934 as *It's a Gift*.) Tom Geraghty, a former newspaper reporter, was hired to adapt the play. "He said all he needed really to make a picture was a set of a door," his daughter Sheila revealed years later. "There is always an air of excitement in a house when the door bell rings."

According to biographer James Curtis, Geraghty couldn't devise a strong enough plot for *It's the Old Army Game*. Fields ended up disliking the film (and its director, Eddie Sutherland) so

much that he insisted on a stronger story for his next vehicle.

"Mr. Bisbee's Princess" had won an O. Henry Award in 1925. Written by Julian Leonard Street, it concerned a small-town businessman whose chance encounter on a train with a European princess leads to turmoil back home. (Street's earlier novel *Rita Coventry* had been turned into a successful film, and the author had a long and productive friendship with writer Booth Tarkington.) Aided by Fields, who always took a strong hand with his scripts, Geraghty worked up an adaptation that he handed over to screenwriter J. Clarkson Miller. (Howard Emmett Rogers added jokes to the material.)

Le Baron assigned Gregory La Cava to direct the project. (La Cava's career is covered in greater detail in *My Man Godfrey*, 1936.) Fields was antagonistic at first, but the two became lifelong friends, and the actor always considered La Cava his favorite director. Fields prepared thirteen pages of notes on the script, but La Cava and his story editor Ralph Block ignored most of them.

Shooting began in August 1926, largely on Long Island locations near the Paramount studio in Astoria. First to be filmed was the climactic golf sequence, a reworking of a bit Fields had introduced in the *Ziegfeld Follies of 1918*, "A Game of Golf." He even brought back his caddy in the act, William "Shorty" Blanche. (Blanche, Fields' valet since 1915, replaced Harry Kelly on stage after Kelly and Fields came to blows over how the caddy should be played.) The scene was shot at the Deepdale Country Club in Great Neck.

Fields could perform the golf routine in his sleep; it was La Cava's job to make sure the gags came across on screen, all the more crucial since the dialogue would be stripped away. La Cava's other big task was to rein in his star, who was notorious for piling on unrelated gags. Fields would use his golf material two mores times in film: for his first talkie, *The Golf Specialist* (1930), and in *You're Telling Me!* (1934).

La Cava's background in comic strips gave him a feel for composition and timing, and his work with comedians like Chic Sales and actors like Richard Dix showed his affinity for small-town life. In *So's Your Old Man* La Cava lingers over young lovers on a backyard swing, the sidewalks where children play, a nearly empty Main Street. A joke where Fields passes around a jug has the clarity of a three-panel strip in a newspaper. A scene outside an apartment building even looks like a cartoon, complete with an ashcan painted with black stripes. And the director tempers Fields' tendency to portray characters as stereotypes, finding the pride and dignity in Louise Carter's harried housewife, for example. La Cava's unhurried pacing, his use of depth within sets, and his empathy for Fields' character all help make *So's Your Old Man* one of the comedian's warmer and affectionate efforts.

Viewers used to Fields' sound films may be surprised by his appearance in *So's Your Old Man*. For one thing, he is thinner and more agile than in his later films. He also sports a patently false cardboard moustache, a slight alteration to those used by Charlie Chaplin and Groucho Marx.

The comedian also scales back his acting to fit the requirement of the plot. *You're Telling Me!*, an almost scene-for-scene remake of *So's Your Old Man*, would zero in on Fields, restaging jokes so that he dominated the screen.

The film was moderately successful, and Fields rushed into his next project, *The Potters*, based on an earlier J.P. McEvoy play. He worked with La Cava on *Running Wild*, the last silent feature made at Paramount's Astoria studio. Fields was then sent to Los Angeles, where Paramount executives teamed him with comic Chester Conklin in three poorly received features that are considered lost. As the film industry switched over to sound, Fields found himself scrambling to reestablish himself on screen. It would take years of shorts and supporting roles before he would star in *You're Telling Me!* One of his last vehicles, *The Bank Dick* (1940), is also on the Registry.

Flesh and the Devil

A scheming Greta Garbo in one of her breakout films, *Flesh and the Devil*.

Metro-Goldwyn-Mayer, 1926. Silent, B&W, 1.33. 112 minutes.
Cast: John Gilbert (Leo von Harden), Greta Garbo (Felicitas), Lars Hanson (Ulrich von Eltz), Barbara Kent (Hertha), William Orlamond (Uncle Kutowski), George Fawcett (Pastor Voss), Eugenie Besserer (Leo's Mother), Marc MacDermott (Count von Rhaden), Marcelle Corday (Minna).
Credits: Directed by Clarence Brown. Screen play by Benjamin F. Glazer. From the novel "The Undying Past" by Hermann Sudermann. Titles by Marian Ainslee. Director of photography: William Daniels. Settings by Cedric Gibbons & Frederic Hope. Wardrobe by [Clement] André-Ani. Film Editor: Lloyd Nosler. Assistant director: Charles Dorian.
Additional Credits: Produced by Irving Thalberg. Production dates: August 9 to September 28, 1926. Released December 25, 1926.
Available: Warner Home Video DVD (2005). ISBN: 1-4198-0958-x. UPC: 0-12569-67472-1.

As a reward for surviving the corporate infighting that led to the formation of Metro-Goldwyn-Mayer, Louis B. Mayer took the equivalent of a victory lap through Europe with his wife Margaret. He went to Italy ostensibly to rein in the out-of-control *Ben-Hur* (1925) production, but Mayer was also checking European market conditions and scouting for talent. In Germany he saw *Gösta Berlings Saga* (1924), a three-hour epic about a defrocked minister directed by Mauritz Stiller. Mayer not only signed Stiller to a contract, but his protégée as well, a nineteen-year-old actress named Greta Garbo.

It was only the second film for Garbo, a former department store clerk who was born Greta Gustafson. She made one more film before arriving in the United States with Stiller in the summer of 1925. Mayer did not expect much from the actress, but in the rushes for *The Torrent* (1926), she caught the eye of Irving Thalberg, Mayer's chief of production. On screen Garbo came across as a new type of feminine character, neither a virgin nor a vamp. She projected a sensuality, a worldly experience that set her apart from the flappers who were dominating popular culture. Garbo was not the first European to star in American films, and she was hardly the first actress to suggest the pleasure to be found in sex. But she was the first Thalberg had the chance to work with, and he set out to make her a star.

Garbo's second MGM project was *The Temptress*. Like her first, it was adapted from a highbrow soap opera by novelist Vicente Blasco Ibáñez, and was originally to be directed by Stiller. But Thalberg didn't like the footage Stiller shot, and replaced him with director Fred Niblo, the same man who had just rescued the floundering *Ben-Hur*. Although Stiller had filmed for two months, Thalberg threw away all of his footage, and had Niblo start anew.

Thalberg's formula for Garbo was to saddle her with a wealthy, usually older lover, then have her fall for a virile, younger man, preferably one with a pencil moustache. In her plots, the actress would get a big build-up to a steamy love scene, then spend the rest of the movie either repeating or paying for her indiscretion. She was bewildered at the parts the studio offered her: "Always the vamp I am, always the woman with no heart." The production of *The Temptress*, which dragged on into October, left her homesick and demoralized. Her sister died of cancer, and her mentor was fired from the studio. She was so uncomfortable with publicity that the studio was forced to make her privacy an aspect of her persona.

Flesh and the Devil was based on *Es War: Roman*, an 1893 novel by playwright Hermann Sudermann (in the words of Garbo biographer Barry Paris, "the German Ibáñez"). It told how a ruthless woman manipulated an aristocratic officer into killing her husband, then married the officer's best friend, provoking another duel of honor. Garbo balked at appearing in the movie until she met her costar, John Gilbert.

The success of *The Big Parade* the year before made Gilbert the biggest male star on the MGM lot. With the death of Rudolph Valentino, he was also one of the screen's most popular lovers. He fell hard for his costar, who soon moved in with him. Garbo, who gave only seventeen interviews in her entire life, said to a Swedish reporter, "I don't know how I should have managed if I had not been cast opposite John Gilbert. Through him I seemed to establish my first real contact with this strange American world. If he had not come into my life at this time, I should probably have come home to Sweden at once."

On the set, Thalberg went out of his way to make Garbo comfortable. (He also had screenwriters essentially repeat the bits that worked in *The Temptress*, notably an attempted strangulation.) The producer cast her *Gösta Berlings Saga* costar Lars Hanson opposite Gilbert, and surrounded Garbo with many of the same technicians she had on *The Temptress*, including cinematographer William Daniels (who is often given credit for teaching her English). Thalberg assigned Clarence Brown to direct the film. Brown gained his experience working with Maurice Tourneur, and had recently proven his ability to work with temperamental actors like Valentino (in *The Eagle*) and Norma Talmadge (*Kiki*).

Mayer's daughter Irene Selznick later wrote that Brown "was a good executive who kept his eyes open and his mouth shut." But the director—and everyone else on the set—could see that Garbo and Gilbert were in love, as would soon become apparent to anyone who watched their footage. Brown later said, "Those two were alone in a world of their own. It seemed to me like an intrusion even yell cut. I used to just motion the crew over to another part of the set and let them finish what they were doing. It was embarrassing."

With the love scenes directing themselves, Brown had to find his inspiration in the margins of the story. He staged a duel in silhouette, showed off MGM's financial prowess by filling the studio's enormous sets with expensively costumed extras, and later built a rhythmic montage to depict Gilbert's character, exiled for a while to Africa, returning to his lover. But for the most part he stayed out of the stars' way. Since he worked so meticulously on her shots, cinematographer Daniels most likely had the closer relationship with Garbo. He designed the film's most famous visual touch by having Gilbert cup a flashlight under his face to simulate lighting a cigarette in a darkened bower.

In the typical MGM style, Brown tended to push everything a bit too much. Scenes linger after they should end, and the characters' emotions surge when restraint might have been more effective. What's most surprising about *Flesh and the Devil* is seeing just how limited an actress Garbo was at this stage of her career. Her part is not a complicated one; in fact, it makes no psychological sense. Gazing implacably at her victims, she is endlessly fascinating. Asked to rend her hair or stalk to her doom, she resorts to risible histrionics, her body and gestures awkward and unconvincing. (MGM would pay closer attention to Garbo's hair and wardrobe in her subsequent films.)

Shooting lasted from August 9 to September 28, including reshoots for an alternate, happier ending. (MGM gave theater owners a choice of which version to screen; in the second, Gilbert is compensated with a friendlier girlfriend.) Accounts differ about an incident about a month into production. As Brown said, "Jack was impetuous and immature at the time, and she had him under her thumb. They were in love, but he was more in love with her than she was with him. He was always proposing to her in front of people." Gilbert apparently believed that she would marry him on September 8, at a double wedding with director King Vidor and actress Eleanor Boardman, but she never showed up. Was Garbo simply playing a role with Gilbert? (His character spends the second half of *Flesh and the Devil* alternately desiring and despising her.) Some reported that Gilbert got into a fight with Mayer that afternoon, and that Mayer subsequently destroyed Gilbert's career. But would Mayer vow vengeance against his biggest star?

Although Garbo refused to marry Gilbert, she lived with him until 1929, when he married actress Ina Claire. *Flesh and the Devil* was a spectacular hit, playing for three weeks at the Capitol Theater in New York City. Playwright and critic Robert Sherwood called Garbo "the official dream princess of the silent drama department of life." The film's success enabled her to stage the equivalent of a wildcat strike, prolonging a dispute with Mayer and Thalberg until April 1927, when she began filming an adaptation of Tolstoy's *Anna Karenina* with Gilbert as her costar. (The studio changed the title, in part so that theater marquees could trumpet, "Garbo and Gilbert in *Love*.")

Gilbert would make two additional films with Garbo, but the actor was unable to hold onto his audience through the sound era. Some attribute his decline to Mayer, although alcoholism, changing public tastes, and poor film choices certainly played bigger roles. He died of a heart attack in 1936. By then Garbo was firmly ensconced as one of the screen's preeminent figures, although her popularity had also peaked with the coming of sound. She would make a total of seven films with Clarence Brown, who prospered for some twenty-five years as one of MGM's most reliable directors.

The General

United Artists, 1927. Silent, B&W, 1.33. 75 minutes.
Cast: Marion Mack (Annabelle Lee), Glen Cavender (Captain Anderson), Jim Farley (General Thatcher), Frederick Vroom (A Southern general), Charles Smith ([Annabelle Lee's] father), Frank Barnes ([Annabelle Lee's] brother); Joe Keaton, Mike Donlin, Tom Nawn (Three Union generals); Buster Keaton (Johnnie Gray).
Credits: Written and directed by Buster Keaton and Clyde Bruckman. Adapted by Al Boasberg & Charles Smith from William Pittenger's *The Great Locomotive Chase*. Produced by Joseph M. Schenck. Photographed by J. Devereux Jennings and Bert Haines. Technical director: Fred Gabourie. Lighting effects: Denver Harmon.
Additional Credits: Edited by Buster Keaton. Production dates: May 27 to September 1926. Premiered in New York City on February 5, 1927.
Other Versions: Some story elements were incorporated into the Red Skelton comedy *A Southern Yankee* (1948). Walt Disney released *The Great Locomotive Chase* (1956), based on the same source material.
Available: *The General* is in the public domain. A David Shepard restoration is available on a Kino Video DVD (2001). UPC: 7-38329-01312-7.

Trains figure into a number of Buster Keaton's movies. A connoisseur of gadgets, he loved depicting the logic and clarity of machines on film. *The General* combines many of his favorite activities: historical research, location shooting, and a massive costar. Biographer Tom Dardis quotes Keaton as saying, "The moment you give me a locomotive and things like that to play with, as a rule I find some way to get laughs out of it." His work resulted in one of the most important Civil War films in cinema.

The idea for *The General* came from a real-life incident in which Union soldiers led by spy James J. Andrews stole a Confederate train in Georgia. They headed north toward Chattanooga, Tennessee, destroying track and bridges along the way, pursued by William Fuller, the Confederate conductor. Fuller managed to nab Andrews before he reached Union lines.

Buster Keaton performed his own stunts, as this frame enlargement from *The General* demonstrates. *Courtesy of Kino International*

Keaton chose to tell the story from the point of view of a Southern engineer, aware that it would make his underdog character more sympathetic to filmgoers. His codirector Clyde Bruckman worked on a screenplay with gag writers Al Boasberg and Charles Smith. Meanwhile, Keaton discussed props and technical issues with his longtime production manager, Fred Gabourie. Keaton strove for authenticity, ordering costumes based on Mathew Brady photographs and assembling his own railroad stock to approximate the engines and cars of the era. He wanted to shoot in the South, but based the production in Oregon instead because that state still had the unspoiled scenery he needed. (Also, his request to use the real-life and still-existing General locomotive was turned down.) Some five hundred National Guard troops appeared as extras, dressing in either Union or Confederate uniforms as the story required.

Most of the production took place near Cottage Grove, Oregon, about thirty miles south of Eugene. The cast and crew arrived on May 27, 1926, and filming began on June 8. Marion Mack, Keaton's costar, had been hired on the recommendation of his sister-in-law's hairdresser. A former Sennett Bathing Beauty, Mack felt "ignored and slighted" by the mostly male filmmakers. She remembered how shooting would be disrupted because "they stopped the train when they saw a place to play baseball." Later, she decided that Keaton was just shy. She was probably unaware of the precarious state of his marriage to Natalie Talmadge.

Keaton's previous features had been produced by his brother-in-law Joseph Schenck and released through MGM. (Schenck's brother Nicholas ran MGM's parent company, Loew's.) But during the filming of *The General*, Schenck became president of United Artists, the production company founded by Mary Pickford and Charlie Chaplin, among others. Money suddenly became more of a factor, especially since Keaton had spent more than twice the original $400,000 budget. (Some have calculated that one shot in *The General* involving a 213-foot-long wooden bridge could have been the single most expensive take in silent film.)

After closing down production due to smoke from forest fires, Keaton filmed for a few weeks in September before editing began. He cut most of the film himself, by hand, holding exposed stock up to daylight rather than using editing machines. The film's New York premiere was delayed several weeks because the run of *Flesh and the Devil* had been extended.

Seen today, *The General* is proof of Keaton's mastery of film technique, from production design to acting and cinematography. To Keaton, there is always a world outside what the camera sees, one his characters must interact with. Keaton paid strict attention to the direction of movement in his films, and he exploited every line, corner, and surface of his settings. In *The General* he enters and exits the frame from every quadrant, building gags on how he gets from one shot to another. Unlike many films of the time, and some films today, there is a logic to *The General*'s world, a sense that laws of physics still apply, that the geography of the frame is crucial.

The plot operates with clockwork precision. On a broad scale, action A—say, the theft of a train—results in action B, the pursuit of the stolen object. On a smaller level, Keaton the engineer jerks on the throttle too quickly, and his passengers fall over. One of the film's most satisfying gags is also one of its purest. A railroad tie has been balanced on a track to derail Keaton's oncoming train. He sits on the cowcatcher holding another tie, unable to scramble back to the cab in time to stop the collision. But he can drop one tie onto the other, using the principal of the lever to get rid of both impediments.

Like the other stunts in the film, the gag took an incredible amount of preparation, from building prop ties that would move the way he wanted to determining the proper speed of the locomotive. Every take required repositioning trains, a cumbersome process. And although Keaton never drew attention to it, this gag and many others in the film were extremely dangerous.

The General moves so logically, so inexorably, that there is little time for diversions. Of all Keaton's features, this has the fewest jokes, and when humor arrives, it is unusually bleak, even black. On the other hand, *The General* compares favorably to any dramatic Civil War movie. In fact, its serious tone and historical context may be why subsequent critics preferred it to the rest of his films. It is the sole Keaton work cited in the *Sight and Sound* best film polls, for example.

Surprisingly, the critical response to the film on its release was largely negative. Robert E. Sherwood, the future Pulitzer Prize–winning playwright, complained that Keaton's jokes about death during battle were tasteless. *Los Angeles Times* writer Katherine Lipke felt that Keaton had made a film "which is neither straight comedy nor is it altogether thrilling drama." *Variety* called it "a flop." *The General* was Keaton's first real box-office failure.

Schenck was dismayed at the theatrical performance of *The General*, and ordered Keaton to scale back his next feature. Perhaps a bit intimidated, Keaton returned to his roots with *College* (1927), playing another juvenile lead and drawing heavily on Harold Lloyd's nonconfrontational style and subject matter for inspiration. Schenck, meanwhile, was in the process of negotiating Keaton's move to MGM, where the comic would gain financial resources at the expense of creative independence. His first MGM project, *The Cameraman* (1929), is also on the Registry.

It

Paramount, 1927. Silent, B&W, 1.33. 72 minutes.

Cast: Clara Bow (Betty Lou Spence), Antonio Moreno (Cyrus Waltham, Jr.), William Austin (Monty Montgomery), Priscilla Bonner (Molly), Jacqueline Gadsden (Adela Van Norman), Julia Swayne Gordon (Mrs. Van Norman), Elinor Glyn (herself).

Credits: Produced and directed by Clarence Badger. Screen play by Hope Loring, Louis D. Lighton. Based on the novel by Elinor Glyn. Titles: George Marion, Jr. Produced by Clarence Badger, Elinor Glyn. Executive producers: Jesse L. Lasky, Adolph Zukor, B.P. Schulberg. Director of photography: H. Kinley Martin. Film editor: E. Lloyd Sheldon. Assistant director: Vernon Keays. A Famous Players–Lasky production.

Additional Cast: Gary Cooper (Newspaper reporter), Dorothy Tree (Sales clerk), Eleanor Lawson (Welfare worker), Rose Tapley (Welfare worker).

Additional Credits: Scenes directed by Josef von Sternberg. Premiered in New York City on February 5, 1927.

Available: Kino Home Video DVD (2001): UPC 7-38329-01952-3. Milestone Film & Video DVD (2004): UPC: 0-14381-19742-6.

The English-born Elinor Glyn was thirty-three when she established her reputation as a writer of daring romances with the novel *Three Weeks* (1907). By then she had written a half-dozen novels about the amorous escapades of the rich and newly rich, books that helped define how movies and magazines would depict vamps. The pearls, feathers, cigarette holders, and tiger skins that decorate silent melodramas, and that seem so silly today, can be traced back to Glyn and her peers. But by the 1920s, when she had moved to the United States, her vision of romance among the aristocrats had been supplanted by the public's appetite for flappers and tomboys.

Paramount producer Jesse Lasky signed Glyn to a contract in 1920, hoping that her once naughty, now accepted brand of sex would translate to the screen. Films like *Beyond the Rocks* (1922), based on her 1906 novel, did respectable business, but after three subsequent flops in a row, she scrambled for a hit. Her solution was *It*, a serialized novel that turned the pronoun into a buzz word. "It" referred to sex, or at least sex appeal, although Glyn coyly covered her tracks by issuing statements like, " 'It' can be a quality of mind as well as physical attraction." Whatever "it" meant, a large part of the popular culture audience became consumed with a guessing game as to who had "it" and who didn't.

Lasky purchased the rights to the novel and promptly assigned Hope Loring and Louis D. Lighton to discard the plot and construct a vehicle

Publicity photo of Clara Bow at Coney Island promoting *It. Courtesy of Milestone Film & Video*

for Clara Bow. The husband-and-wife team had worked on some of Paramount's biggest hits, and were in the process of writing a vehicle for Mary Pickford, *My Best Girl*, that would bear strong resemblances to the shooting script for *It*. Weirdly, although the *It* script basically ignores the novel, it does use the book (and Glyn, who wanders in for a brief cameo about halfway through the movie) as a sort of springboard for its own plot, which concerned a department store clerk with eyes on snaring her boss. Betty Lou, the clerk, projected an aura of hedonism and promiscuity, but would later be revealed to possess strong moral and maternal instincts. In other words, a tramp who's also a virgin, a conundrum perfectly suited for Clara Bow.

Bow was born in Brooklyn in 1905, and escaped a life of extreme poverty at sixteen, when she won a "Fame and Fortune" contest sponsored by a publisher of movie magazines. The prize included a bit part in a movie, which Bow parlayed into appearances in over two dozen films, as well as a contract to producer B.P. Schulberg. When Schulberg became an associate producer at Paramount, he brought Bow with him. Suddenly her movie parts grew more substantial, as the studio groomed her to be their representative flapper, an answer to Colleen Moore in *Flaming Youth* (1923). Bow rose to the challenge, investing her characters in films like *Mantrap* and *Dancing Mothers* (both 1926) with extravagant appetites and boundless energy. In *Kid Boots* that same year, it took the filmmakers about five minutes of screen time to get her into a bathing suit, and although it was

Eddie Cantor's feature debut, Bow was called upon to carry most of the real acting chores.

With her bobbed hair, bee-stung lips, and loose-fitting clothes, Bow became the female personification of the Roaring Twenties. What impressed studio executives, and what drew the public, was her exuberance, her willingness to let herself go on screen, to approximate a state of arousal. Her abandon, so different from the contained sensuality of a Nazimova or Garbo or Anna May Wong, made her seem less intimidating, more accessible. It was a persona later adapted by everyone from Jean Harlow to Carole Lombard.

The scandals that plagued her, in public and in private, added to her mystique. Paramount head Adolph Zukor said that the star "was exactly the same off the screen as on," a subtext to much of the studio's publicity about her. When Glyn magisterially proclaimed that Bow had "it," the novelist was cashing in on a phenomenon. (Glyn also bestowed "it" upon Bow's Spanish-born costar Antonio Moreno and Rex the Wonder Horse, to little effect.)

Much of *It* dances coyly around its central subject of sex. Bow is presented as a sex object, but within the confines of an innocent romantic comedy. (So innocent that the same essential premise could be used that year by Pickford and by Ginger Rogers in 1939's *Bachelor Mother*.) Without Bow's presence, the film wouldn't have gained much more interest than any number of similar titles like *Are Parents People?* (1925), *Irene* (1926), or *Our Dancing Daughters* (1928). What is surprising today is how much the film depends on its intertitles. Title writers like George Marion, Jr., could shape the mood and temperament of a film as much as a soundtrack composer would in the sound era. As well as delivering dialogue and crucial bits of plot, the titles served as captions to help viewers interpret the tone of a scene. *It*'s titles are filled with snappy retorts and insults; it was one of thirty films that Marion worked on that year. *It* is also notable for a brief appearance by Gary Cooper in his last uncredited role.

It was filmed in a month in late 1926 and released in February 1927. That year Bow would make five films, with an important part in *Wings*. But she was spectacularly ill-equipped to handle the fame that engulfed her. Worn down by work and lawsuits, she suffered a number of breakdowns. Bow married cowboy star Rex Bell in 1931, made some ill-advised comeback attempts in sound films, and retired from the public eye in 1933. She died of a heart attack in 1960.

7th Heaven

Fox Film Corporation, 1927. Silent with musical score, B&W, 1.20. 120 minutes.

Cast: Janet Gaynor (Diane Vulmir), Charles Farrell (Chico Robas), Ben Bard (Col. Brissac), David Butler (Gobin), Albert Gran (Papa Boule), Gladys Brockwell (Nana Vulmir), Emile Chautard (Father Chevillon), George Stone (Rat), Jessie Haslett (Aunt Valentine), Lillian West (Arlette), Marie Mosquini (Madame Gobin), Brandon Hurst (Uncle George), Lewis Borzage, Sr. (Streetlighter), Dolly Borzage (Street girl), Sue Borzage (Street girl), Mary Borzage (Woman in bullet factory), Lois Harwick.

Credits: Produced and directed by Frank Borzage. Script: Benjamin [Barney] Glazer. Supervising producer: Sol M. Wurtzel. Titles: Katharine Hilliker, H.H. Caldwell. Based on the play in three acts by Austin Strong. Research: Judith Ann Gilbert. Director of photography: Ernest Palmer. Assistant cameramen: Stanley Little, Harold Schuster. Associate cameraman: Joseph A. Valentine. Assistant associate cameraman: Julian Robinson. Lighting: David Anderson. Art direction: Harry Oliver. Assistant art direction: Fred C. Stoos. Edited: Barney Wolf. Supervising editor: Philip Klein. Assistant directors: Lew Borzage, Jr., Park Frame. French advisor: André Chotin. Costumes: Kathleen Kay. Uniforms: Bert Offord. Makeup: Charles Dudley. Hairdressers: Kitty Thompson, Peggy Chrisman. Script supervisor: Ralph Kaufman. Presented by William Fox. "Diane (I'm In Heaven When I See You Smile)," music by Ernö Rapée, lyrics by Lew Pollack. "Seventh Heaven" by William Perry, Ronn Carroll; orchestration by Samuel L. Rothafel.

Additional Credits: Script revisions: Philip Klein. Initial script: Frances Marion. Second unit directing: John Ford. Matte paintings: Max Borch. Matte supervisor: Fred W. Sersen. Miniatures: Walter Pallman. Miniatures assistants: Fred Morck, Jack Tolkin. Special war effects: Louis Witte. Premiered in Los Angeles on May 6, 1927.

Other Versions: Remade in 1937, directed by Henry King. At least four Chinese versions were filmed. Television version in 1953, directed by Robert St. Aubrey. Stage musical directed on Broadway by John C. Wilson, 1955.

Awards: Oscars for Directing, Actress (Gaynor won for this film and for *Sunrise and Street Angel*), Writing—Adaptation (Glazer).

Available: Twentieth Century Fox Home Entertainment DVD box set *Murnau, Borzage and Fox* (2008).

Remembered as one of the great romances in silent film, *7th Heaven* marked the culmination of director Frank Borzage's career. He won the first Oscar for Best Direction, was the first director to win more than one Academy Award, and was cited as an influence by colleagues as disparate as Sergei M. Eisenstein, Josef von Sternberg, and Samuel Fuller. Borzage was respected by technicians for his planning and understanding of the fundamentals of

film. Actors clamored to work with him. His best films have a vivid pictorial quality and depth, with stories that are unusually focused and driven, even when they veer into the absurd. Borzage's greatest accomplishment may have been his depiction of love as a mystical achievement, a force of destiny as much as an earthly struggle.

Born in 1894 to working-class immigrants, Borzage labored in the construction industry and in silver mines while saving money for acting classes. His training in the theater has Dickensian overtones, with intervals in shantytowns and soup kitchens. He reached Los Angeles at the age of eighteen, where he worked both in front of and behind the camera at a number of studios. Borzage's breakthrough acting role came in Thomas Ince's *The Wrath of the Gods* (1914), in which his sailor character fell in love with a Japanese woman. Altogether, he appeared in some sixty films as an actor.

Biographer Hervé Dumont wrote that Borzage developed his theories of directing from his training as an actor. He wanted situations rather than narratives: "I prefer a thin plot on my pictures. I like to use the majority of the film for characterizations, so I don't like to have to take up too long to unfold a plot. It gets the audience worried about superficialities instead of the real people." As Dumont put it, Borzage's stories "had to be carefully structured, but directed with enough flexibility so that the public would believe the scenes were improvised."

Borzage's first chance to direct was *The Pitch o' Chance* (1915), a story of paired romances that turned on moral choices rather than ideas of good and evil. By 1917 he had given up acting for directing, working at Triangle and, in 1919, for William Randolph Hearst's Cosmopolitan Pictures. Here he had his first triumph, *Humoresque* (1920), written by Frances Marion from a Fannie Hurst novel. At First National he directed Norma Talmadge in a pair of hits, and after working at MGM moved to Fox Film in April 1925. His first contract at Fox gave him $35,000 per film.

7th Heaven was one of eighteen features Borzage directed at Fox between 1925 and 1932. It was based on a play by Austin Strong (grandnephew of Robert Louis Stevenson) that had run for three years on Broadway. A romance with strong religious overtones, it followed an affair in Paris between a sewer worker and a prostitute during World War I. Frances Marion wrote a screenplay version for director Emmett J. Flynn, but West Coast production chief Winfield Sheehan offered the project to Borzage instead. When Marion withdrew from the project, Borzage worked with Irish playwright Benjamin "Barney" Glazer, who had just finished a script for *Flesh and the Devil* for Greta Garbo.

The director resisted Sheehan's efforts to cast his mistress, Madge Bellamy, in the part of Diane, an orphan forced into crime by her cruel sister. Actresses who tested for the part included Mary Pickford, Helen Menken (who originated the part on stage), and Joan Crawford. When Borzage watched Victor Shertzinger direct Janet Gaynor on the set of *The Return of Peter Grimm*, he gave her the part without a screen test. (Born Laura Gainor on October 6, 1906, Gaynor moved from San Francisco to Los Angeles, where she was cast as an extra and in bit parts before signing a contract with Fox.)

John Gilbert was originally slated for Chico, who works his way up from the sewer to cleaning streets. But Gilbert left Fox for MGM in a salary dispute. Joel McCrea tested for the part, and Borzage considered George O'Brien, who ended up in *Sunrise*. Charles Farrell, a burly extra in films like *Old Ironsides*, came to Borzage to pitch his friend Richard Arlen. The director cast Farrell instead, giving the two leads in an important Fox project to relative unknowns.

Shooting was supposed to start in August 1926, but when William Fox persuaded German director F. W. Murnau to come to his studio, everything was suddenly put on hold. All the resources of the studio were devoted to *Sunrise*, Murnau's project, leaving Borzage time to go to Paris with his brother to do research. (Murnau cast Gaynor in *Sunrise*, at Sheehan's request.)

Shooting began on January 24, 1927, with Gaynor alternating between *7th Heaven* and *Sunrise*

until the latter was finished. Comparing the directors later, she said, "With Frank, you responded more with your heart." One contemporary journalist offered this description of Borzage's technique: "When Frank Borzage directed *7th Heaven*, he talked to Janet Gaynor about each scene until his mind and hers were in tune, then he told her to go on the set and think it. The physical reaction he left to her, and she was unconscious of it."

As shooting progressed, Borzage discarded long stretches of the script, but at the same time elaborated on small scenes. He was not concerned about narrative balance, or plausibility—he was trying to pinpoint and capture emotions. He was also unconcerned about technique, unless he could use it to support his goals. Watching *7th Heaven* today, you are drawn into the intricacies of relationships, the shifting balance of power between people falling in love, only to realize with a start that Borzage is playing intimate scenes out in front of hundreds of extras. Director Martin Scorsese described Borzage's manipulation of story as "what I would call lovers' time—every gesture, every exchange of glances, every word *counts*." A sidewalk picnic can last for a half hour, while the whole of World War I is dismissed in half that time.

Borzage's style is perhaps most evident in the film's climax, which intercuts between two plotlines in a manner that renders logic and realism irrelevant. For example, what had been portrayed as a tenement stairwell early in the film suddenly transforms into an ornate, spiral staircase; Borzage films it from an overhead crane that rises over two stories. He was making huge demands on viewers on deeper levels as well. *7th Heaven* tells us that religion, government, and society itself cannot effect our salvation. The only thing worth living for is love, even if we must die to win it.

It was a message that proved irresistible to audiences of the time. William Fox was so impressed that he released *7th Heaven* before *Sunrise*. Within four months of the film's release, the studio prepared a Movietone soundtrack with a score, sound effects, and a pop song, "Diane." The film was a tremendous hit, garnering three Oscars at the first Academy Awards ceremony. Gaynor and Farrell were teamed in eleven more films, and worked with Borzage again on *Street Angel* (1927) and *Lucky Star* (1929). Borzage continued to make distinctive comedies and romances well into the sound era, notably *A Farewell to Arms* (1932) and *History Is Made at Night* (1937). He died in 1962.

Wings

Paramount, 1927. Silent, B&W with color sequences, 1.33. 139 minutes.

Cast: Clara Bow (Mary Preston), Charles Rogers (Jack Powell), Richard Arlen (David Armstrong), Jobyna Ralston (Sylvia Lewis), El Brendel, Richard Tucker, Gary Cooper (Cadet White), Gunboat Smith (Sergeant), Henry B. Walthall (Mr. Armstrong), Roscoe Karns (Lt. Cameron), Julia Swayne Gordon (Mrs. Armstrong), Arlette Marchal (Celeste).

Credits: Directed by William A. Wellman. Story by John Monk Saunders. Screen play by Hope Loring and Louis D. Lighton. Editor-in-chief: E. Lloyd Sheldon. Photographed by Harry Perry. Titles by Julian Johnson. Associate producer: B.P. Schulberg. Presented by Adolph Zukor, Jesse L. Lasky. A Lucien Hubbard production.

Additional Cast: George Irving (Mr. Powell), Hedda Hopper (Mrs. Powell), Margery Chapin, Gloria Wellman.

Additional Credits: Directing by Harry D'Arrast. Assistant directors: Norman Z. McLeod, Dick Johnson, Jim Ewens, E.K. Merritt. Additional camera: Paul Perry, Cliff Blackstone, William Rand, Guy Bennett, E.F.Adams, Albert Myers, Gene O'Donnell, Russell Harlan, Herman Schoop, Al Williams, Bert Baldridge, Frank Cotner, Faxon M. Dean, Ernest Laszlo, Ray Olsen, L. Guy Wilky, Harry Mason, Harry Schapp, Herbert Morris, Art Lane, C.W. Riley, William Clothier. Production dates: January 19 to April 5, 1927. Premiered in New York City on August 12, 1927.

Available: Paramount VHS (1989).

Released just months after Charles Lindbergh's cross-Atlantic flight captivated the nation, *Wings* was also part of a boom in World War I–themed pictures that included *The Big Parade* (1925) and *What Price Glory* (1926). The top-grossing film of the year, it launched several careers, and was also the first to win an Oscar for what would later be called Best Picture.

It was the first big project for director William A. Wellman, a former pilot with the Lafayette Flying Corps (formed as a complement to the Lafayette Escadrille). Born in 1896, Wellman received the nickname "Wild Bill" early in life, dropping out of high school to play minor-league ice hockey. After the start of World War I, he volunteered as an ambulance driver in the French Foreign Legion, becoming a pilot after the United States entered the war. After the war he barnstormed as a stunt pilot, which is how he met and befriended Douglas Fairbanks in 1919. Wellman tried acting, but was more comfortable behind the camera. Within a few years he was directing Westerns and B-movies at Fox.

Wings was based on an unpublished novel by John Monk Saunders, a flight instructor during the war. Saunders never fought overseas, but he did collect stories while studying at Oxford as a Rhodes Scholar. After the phenomenal success of *Wings*, he made a career out of aviation-themed stories, including *The Dawn Patrol* (1930) and *The Last Flight* (1931). (His story "The Dock Walloper" is also the basis of another Registry title, 1928's *The Docks of New York*.) The screenplay adaptation was by the husband-and-wife team of Hope Loring and Louis D. Lighton. Loring would continue as a writer, while Lighton had a significant career as a producer at both Paramount and MGM.

Paramount cast its most promising stars in the film. Charles Rogers, usually billed as "Buddy Rogers," had attracted attention as the male lead in the W.C. Fields comedy *So's Your Old Man* (1926). He learned to fly for his role, something his co-star Richard Arlen already knew how to do. Born Richard Cornelius van Mattimore in 1899, Arlen flew with the Royal Canadian Flying Corps during the war. He started acting in films in 1920, changing his name to Arlen in 1924. *Wings* was his first important role, and it helped establish him as an action hero in a career that stretched into the 1960s. Arlen married his co-star Jobyna Ralston, a WAMPAS Baby Star who appeared in Harold Lloyd features after Lloyd married his former leading lady Mildred Davis.

Gary Cooper, already the veteran of bit parts in scores of films, was given a one-scene cameo to build on his supporting part in *The Winning of Barbara Worth* (1926). Within a year he would be one of the most important stars on the Paramount lot. Top-billed was Clara Bow, famous at the time as the "It" girl. She was already a national phenomenon before she was personally chosen by Elinor Glyn to appear in the screen adaptation of her novella *It* (1927). While it was designed to show off her acting abilities, her role in *Wings* echoed her other roles, only without her characteristic humor and optimism.

Bow plays the flirty next-door neighbor to Rogers, who ignores her because he's chasing Ralston, oblivious to the fact that Ralston and Arlen are in love. That's about as far as character development gets in *Wings*, a fault of Wellman as much as the scriptwriters. Bow is first seen poking her head through lace knickers on her laundry line, and throughout the film she's outfitted in tight sweaters, slinky evening gowns, and at one point lace-up dominatrix boots. Her performance is limited to brash exuberance, tearful gazes, and hoydenish jocularity, a combination of tomboy, Madonna, and whore that was impossible for her to play convincingly. She could act, which she proved in films like *Mantrap* (1926). She just couldn't compete in a film about machines.

Rogers, who had a face like a pug, bulls his way through the film with an insistent energy that can be exhausting. He could act, too. His next part, in the Mary Pickford vehicle *My Best Girl* (1927), showed him to be a subtle comedian, but here he was asked to play over-the-top right from the start. (Rogers went on to marry Pickford in 1937.)

If the characters are simplistic, Wellman seems uncomfortable with other aspects of directing as well. Action is repeated in some cuts, while details about the characters' homes and lives that could help ground the film are largely absent. Wellman has his cameraman experiment with camera angles, leading to odd, intrusive shots taken from a moving swing or up from the floor of a car. When war is declared, Wellman basically stops the film to introduce some weary ethnic humor in the form of El Brendel, one of the most difficult of acquired tastes from the period. With all the thwarted love, Swedish slapstick, family partings, and training sequences, it's fully forty minutes into the film before Wellman offers a flying sequence.

With contributions from some seventeen assistant cameramen, *Wings* contains some of the most thrilling aerial footage every filmed, and Wellman used it brilliantly. He depicted the planes as characters, giving them the sort of precise, detailed introductions other directors would give to their actors. What's even more impressive than the spins, dives, and crashes he and his crew captured was the uniformity he achieved in the look of the flying sequences. Wellman had cameras mounted over the cockpit, which the actors would turn on in mid-flight. It turned out to be a thrilling vantage point. A bonus is the ability to lip-read the actors, including Arlen exclaiming, "Son of a bitch!" as he's fired upon.

The first manned flight had only occurred some twenty years earlier. For many viewers this was the closest they would come to experiencing flying. Wellman gave them everything, from the thrill of take-off to the exhilaration of flying above clouds to the terror of a crash landing. The first dogfight lasts some ten minutes, carefully choreographed so that viewers can tell which side is which. Some of the footage captures the same images that would be seen in war documentaries: bombs dropping on targets, gunners hunched over their sights, the horizon tilting woozily as a pilot pulls out of a turn. That said, some of the shots are so wide that it's impossible to tell what is going on without intertitles.

Wings was a massive production. With location footage shot mostly in Texas, the film included hundreds of extras from the Army's Second Division. Justifiably proud, Wellman at one point has the cameraman pan across a flotilla of some twenty planes waiting to take off. One profligate shot includes machine gunners, a tank spinning left, planes flying overhead, a tree exploding, and a full complement of fighting troops.

A tremendous box-office hit, *Wings* led indirectly to films like *The Air Circus* (1928) and *Hell's Angels* (1930). Today it is credited with winning the first Best Picture Oscar, but at the year of the ceremony there was no actual "Best Picture" award. Instead, there were two "Distinction Awards," one for outstanding production, one for "artistic" production. *Wings* won the former; *Sunrise*, the latter. The following year, the awards were combined into one category.

Sunrise

Fox Film Corporation, 1927. Silent with synchronized score, B&W, 1.20. 94 minutes.

Cast: George O'Brien (The man), Janet Gaynor (The wife), Margaret Livingston (The woman from the city), Bodil Rosing (The maid), J. Farrell McDonald [MacDonald] (The photographer), Ralph Sipperly (The barber), Jane Winton (The manicure girl), Arthur Housman (The obtrusive gentleman), Eddie Boland (The obliging gentleman).

Credits: Directed by F.W. Murnau. Scenario by Carl Mayer. From an original theme by Hermann Sudermann. Photography: Charles Rosher, Karl Struss. Titles by Katherine Hilliker and H.H. Caldwell. Presented by William Fox.

Additional Cast: Sidney Bracey (Dance hall manager), Sally Eilers (Woman in dance hall), Gibson Gowland (Driver).

Additional Credits: Assistant director: Herman Bing. Edited by Katherine Hilliker, H.H. Caldwell. Score by Hugo Riesenfeld. Production design: Rochus Gliese. Assistant art director: Edgar G. Ulmer. Title on screen: *Sunrise A Song of Two Humans*. Production dates: September 1926. Premiered in New York City on September 23, 1927.

Awards: Oscars for Best Artistic Production, Actress (given to Janet Gaynor for her work in this film, *7th Heaven*, and *Street Angel*), Cinematography.

Available: Twentieth Century Fox Home Entertainment DVD (2002). UPC: 0-24543-06858-7.

A key paradox in film is the artifice required to make something look "real" on the screen. From makeup and costumes to set design and lighting, the steps necessary to achieve a natural look increased in complexity as the medium evolved. Trying to attain a psychological realism only increased filmmakers' problems. As the studio system flourished, it became easier to construct sets and costumes that allowed filmmakers to control conditions rather than try to film on location. For a director like Erich von Stroheim, the battle then revolved around whether he could build a reality large enough to fit his vision. In films like *Greed* (1925) and *The Wedding March* (1928), he tried with varying degrees of success to present a larger, more accurate reality than usually found in motion pictures. Other filmmakers imitated his technique, but few were as single-minded in presenting a completely manufactured and romanticized world than F.W. Murnau.

Murnau was born Friedrich Wilhelm Plumpe in Bielefeld, Germany, in 1888. (His adopted surname came from a resort town associated with expressionist artists.) After working in student theater in Heidelberg, he was hired by theatrical impresario Max Reinhardt for his Deutsches Theatre in Berlin. World War I intervened; Murnau, a fighter pilot, spent much of the conflict in a Swiss internment camp. There he began assembling and editing battle footage for German authorities.

In 1919 Murnau formed a movie studio with Conrad Veidt, star of *The Cabinet of Dr. Caligari* (1919), an international sensation. Among his projects, Murnau directed *Janus-Faced* (1920), loosely based on R.L. Stevenson's *Dr. Jekyll and Mr. Hyde*, and *Nosferatu* (1922), an unauthorized adaptation of Bram Stoker's *Dracula*. Although the film barely survived a legal battle with Stoker's widow, it had an enormous influence on filmmakers worldwide.

So did *The Last Laugh* (1924), a psychological drama about how a proud doorman at a luxury hotel reacts to a demotion. A commercial flop when it was released by Universal in the United States, it was critically lauded for Murnau's expressionistic visuals. Mary Pickford was so impressed that she sent her cameraman Charles Rosher to Europe for a year to observe the director's working habits. Murnau had already signed a contract to work for William Fox when he started his last European film, *Faust* (1926).

Murnau's arrival in Hollywood coincided with efforts by William Fox to upgrade his studio. Fox had gone on a buying spree, building up a chain of theaters that would soon number five hundred. He was developing sound movies, based on Theodore Case's new technology, as well as widescreen movies, which would be projected under the Fox Grandeur label. He signed Murnau to a four-picture deal, paying the director $125,000 for the *Sunrise* project.

The script was based on Herman Sudermann's "Die Riese nach Tilsit," also the source of a 1939 German film. Carl Mayer, a screenwriter on *The Cabinet of Dr. Caligari* and *The Last Laugh*, turned the story into the equivalent of a blank-verse tone poem, one that transformed Sudermann's specific characters into moral archetypes. The plot, a romantic triangle that develops after a "city woman" seduces a married farmer, was simple on a narrative level but filled with psychological nuance.

Given an almost unlimited budget, Murnau brought his assistants Herman Bing and Edgar G. Ulmer over from Germany, as well as set designer Rochus Gliese. Gliese's sketches were turned into remarkable sets characterized by foreshortening and sharp angles. For one scene, cameraman Charles Rosher hung tracks from the ceiling, placed the camera on a suspended platform, and had associate Karl Struss operate it upside-down while the platform revolved around the action below.

In another scene, the husband and wife take a trolley from the country to the city. Murnau had a mile of railway track laid near Lake Arrowhead to film the sequence, ending as the trolley enters a city set that reputedly cost $200,000. "There was a great talent," future director Clarence Brown recalled to film historian Kevin Brownlow. "When I saw that set he built at Arrowhead for *Sunrise*, I crawled over it for a day and a half. It was wonderful. We all felt he was great."

In collaboration with Rosher and Struss, Murnau developed a style that relied on long takes, flowing camera movements, and emphatic acting. "The camera is the director's sketching pencil," Murnau wrote. "It must whirl and peep and move from place to place as swiftly as thought itself when it is necessary to exaggerate for the audience the idea or emotion that is uppermost in the mind of a character." Struss called Murnau "the first director I ever worked with who really knew what was going on when he started to move that camera. He knew that you move until you come to a climax, the end of your scene. That's the ultimate, that's what it's all leading up to."

But style was just self-indulgence if it did not serve the story. As splendid as the visuals in *Sunrise* were, they were tied to the narrative, to Murnau's view of his characters and to how he wanted moviegoers to interpret the plot. George O'Brien, who played the farmer, later recalled how Murnau inserted comic relief involving a drunken pig to let both the characters and the audience "take a breath" before a harrowing storm sequence.

Sunrise was the first Fox feature to be released with a Movietone soundtrack. Hugo Riesenfeld's score mirrored the plot's *Sturm und Drang*, and at times pretended to synchronize with action on the screen. It opened in New York accompanied by a Movietone short of Benito Mussolini. Critics praised the film extravagantly, and filmmakers began incorporating Murnau's methods into their work. (John Ford's *Four Sons*, 1928, was shot largely on the village sets left over from Murnau's film.) *Sunrise* won three Oscars at the first Academy Awards ceremony, including the only award ever given for "Artistic Quality of Production."

Sunrise was also a commercial failure. "On Broadway it sank like a stone," as film historian Donald Crafton wrote. (In its defense, *Sunrise* was the third-highest grossing film for Fox that year, after *Street Angel* and *Four Sons*.) Less than three weeks after it opened, Warner Brothers released *The Jazz Singer*, a picture that for better or worse would help make silent films obsolete. Murnau completed two more films for Fox. *The Four Devils* (1928) no longer exists; *Our Daily Bread* was re-edited into *City Girl* (1930). By that time Murnau had left the studio to collaborate with Robert Flaherty on *Tabu* (1931), a Registry title.

The Jazz Singer

Warner Bros., 1927. Silent with synchronized score and sound sequences, B&W, 1.33. 88 minutes.
Cast: Al Jolson (Jakie Rabinowitz), May McAvoy (Mary Dale), Warner Oland (The Cantor), Eugenie Besserer (Sara Rabinowitz), Otto Lederer (Moisha Yudelson), Bobby Gordon (Jakie Rabinowitz at age 13), Richard Tucker (Harry Lee), Cantor Josef Rosenblatt (Concert recital).
Credits: Directed by Alan Crosland. Adaptation: Alfred A. Cohn. Titles: Jack Jarmuth. Photography: Hal Mohr. Edited by Harold McCord. Assistant director: Gordon Hollingshead. Technicians: Fred Jackman, Lewis Geib, Esdras Hartley, F.N. Murphy, "Alpharetta," Victor Vance. Musical score and Vitaphone Orchestra directed by Louis Silvers.
Additional Cast includes: William Demarest (Man dining with Jolson), Myrna Loy (Backstage dancer), Roscoe Karns (Man at train station).
Additional Credits: Production dates: June 11 to August 1927. Premiered in New York City on October 6, 1927.
Other Versions: Remade with Danny Thomas (1952), Jerry Lewis (1959, for television), and Neil Diamond (1980).
Available: Warner Home Video DVD (2007). ISBN: 1-4198-5622-7. UPC: 012569798892.

Although sound had been paired with film as early as 1895, *The Jazz Singer* has become known as the first sound movie. It was certainly the first film to convince both the industry and customers that sound would be an inevitable step. Based on a Broadway play by Samson Raphaelson, *The Jazz Singer* was the culmination of years of effort by Warner Brothers to make talking pictures a reality.

Warners had been using the Vitaphone process for shorts and features since 1926. A scrappy studio built up from one nickelodeon founded near Pittsburgh in 1903, Warners was run by four brothers: Harry, Albert, Sam, and Jack L. After incorporating in 1923, they acquired product from other producers, then merged companies like Vitagraph and First National into their own. Warners had to battle Paramount and Universal for theaters, a significant source of revenue for studios at the time. Warners' theaters tended to be in urban areas, but not in upper-class neighborhoods. This demographic would be reflected in the kinds of films the studio made.

Sam was the Warner who was the most enthusiastic about sound. Earlier attempts at sound failed primarily because speakers weren't loud enough to fill theaters, and because sound was hard to synchronize with a filmed image. The invention of amplifiers, and of electric motors to drive cameras and recording devices in synchronization, as well as refinements in recording technology, solved many of these problems. By the mid-1920s, Theodore Case and later Fox Films developed a method to record sound on film. Warners formed a subsidiary, Vitaphone, to work with Western Electric to develop a sound-on-disc process, betting that records played simultaneously with projectors would be enough to keep sound matched with visuals. It was a strategy doomed to failure, as one skip on the record could throw an entire reel out of synch. (*Singin' in the Rain* gives an example of the potentially disastrous results of falling out of synch.)

With care the process worked excellently. Warners introduced Vitaphone to the public on August 6, 1926, in a program of nine shorts and a feature film, *Don Juan*, to which a synchronized score and sound effects had been added. Other shorts and features followed, until *The Jazz Singer* premiered in New York on October 6, 1927.

It was a somewhat unusual play for the Warner brothers to choose. Most of their earlier sound films had been highbrow. A story about a jazz singer was defiantly lowbrow, and the play's Jewish elements seemed to be angled directly toward the Warners' roots rather than mainstream moviegoers. The film was directed by Alan Crosland, who had a reputation of being able to work with temperamental stars like John Barrymore. George Jessel, who played Jack Robin on Broadway, turned the part down, as did Eddie Cantor. That left the notoriously difficult Al Jolson as the only name star who could fill the role. He was thirty-one at the time (the part called for someone who "should look about twenty-three"), and the harsh lighting and unforgiving film stock required for the Vitaphone process made him look even older in some shots. But Jolson had already worked with sound, in a two-reel short called *Al Jolson in "A Plantation Act"* (1926), where he sang three numbers. He knew how to use the stationary microphone, and to tone down his stage delivery in order to stay within the camera's range.

Jolson was born Asa Yoelson in Srednike, in what would become Lithuania, in 1886. He fled the pogroms with his family, reaching Washington, D.C., in 1894. While his father became a respected cantor, Jolson dropped out of school to sing on street corners. He toured vaudeville with his older brother Harry, then with Joe Palmer, heading out on his own in San Francisco in 1906. By 1912 he was a star in New York, appearing in reviews for the Shuberts. Jolson's act was hard to pin down. He sang popular songs, introduced some new tunes, danced, whistled, and spoke to the audience. Blackface played a large role in his performances, as did his gesture of falling to one knee and extending his arms, almost in supplication. Working in a period before microphones, Jolson had to belt out his lyrics. He emoted his songs, often improvising new lines, holding an audience through sheer determination. Two of his signature songs, "Toot Toot Tootsie, Goodbye" and "My Mammy," appear in *The Jazz Singer*.

Samson Raphaelson based his play on his own short story, "The Day of Atonement," which was inspired by Jolson's life. An advertising executive before he devoted himself to writing, Raphaelson would go on to write the influential romantic comedy *Trouble in Paradise* (1932) as well as

Alfred Hitchcock's *Suspicion* (1941). Alfred A. Cohn, who received an Oscar nomination for his adaptation of Raphaelson's play, oddly would later become Commissioner of Police for the City of Los Angeles. His script adds a prologue and at one point shows the young Jack's discovery by Mary, an actress, in The Happy Hour, a Chicago speakeasy. This material expanded on the play's dialogue. Cohn softens the play's ending somewhat, and fortunately drops a moment when Jack discusses the philosophy of blackface: "Mary, you know if people only knew what it was like to black up like this, I bet everybody would do it. . . . It covers your face and hides everything."

If only *The Jazz Singer* were a better film. Apart from its nine songs, and the 280 or so words of dialogue spoken by Jolson, it's a strictly silent picture, and a pretty dreary one at that. (Raphaelson referred to the play as "heartfelt, corny, and dramatic.") Young Jakie Rabinowitz wants to sing jazz; his father, a cantor in a Lower East Side synagogue in New York, hates jazz so much that he throws Jakie out of his house. Years later, as theatrical star Jack Robin, the son returns home, only to be thrown out again. When his father collapses on his deathbed, Jack must choose between opening night on Broadway, or singing "Kol Nidre" for his father on the Day of Atonement.

Crosland directs the silent sequences in a solemn, maudlin manner, but the sound sequences have the impact of lightning. One of the myths about the transition from silent films to sound is that filmmaking suddenly regressed to the flat, stationary style of the early 1900s. It's true that cameras were difficult to move, that editing had to account for a soundtrack, that the film stock and lighting required for sound weren't as refined, that actors had to group around microphones with very limited ranges. But *The Jazz Singer* proves that with planning, the best techniques of silent film could still be used. The sound segments in *The Jazz Singer* feature everything from post-dubbing to double-exposures to traveling shots. The first extended sound sequence, which occurs three minutes into the film, consists of seventeen shots, including a traveling shot filmed from a truck—as well as an intertitle.

Jolson doesn't get a song until about fifteen minutes into the film, when he sings/intones the tearjerker "Dirty Hands, Dirty Face," then speaks words forever associated with talking movies: "Wait a minute, wait a minute. You ain't heard nothing yet." Throughout the sound segments, Crosland cuts easily between the two cameras used with the phonograph recorders, and to footage shot with silent cameras. He even uses the absence of sound effectively. At one point Jolson pretends to play the piano while singing Irving Berlin's "Blue Skies" to his mother. When the cantor enters and shouts, "Stop!" the soundtrack drops to silence. If the technique of later sound films became more stage-bound, it's not *The Jazz Singer*'s fault.

There It Is

Bowers Comedy Corp., 1928. Silent, B&W, 1.33. 19 minutes.
Cast: Charley Bowers (Charley MacNeesha), Kathryn McGuire (the nurse), Melbourne MacDowell (the Frisbie patriarch), Buster Brodie (the fuzz-faced phantom), Edgar "Blue" Washington (the butler).
Credits: Directed by Harold L. Muller. Written by Charles R. Bowers. Produced by Charles R. Bowers. Director of photography: Harold L. Muller.
Available: Image Entertainment DVD *More Treasures from American Film Archives* (2004). ISBN: 0-9747099-1-3. UPC: 0-14381-2271-2-3.

Even at the height of his popularity, Charley Bowers was a fringe figure in film. He was one of dozens of comedians who appeared in silent shorts at the end of the 1920s, filling in the vacuum left when comics like Chaplin, Keaton, and Lloyd graduated to features. According to one count, almost a thousand comedy shorts were released each year during the 1920s. Slapstick, which required little set-up and almost no dialogue, dominated the market. Clowns struggled to establish an immediately recognizable image. Harry Langdon often perched a peaked felt hat on top of his head to signify his character's pre adolescent mind. Charley Chase, a more urbane, sophisticated character, opted for tailored suits and slicked-back hair. Laurel and Hardy, the fat and the lean, the big and the small, alternated between workday overalls and business suits that suggested higher aspirations.

Bowers, a slight man with curly hair and large, expressive eyes, also wore a bowler, but to it he added oversized jumpsuits or denim overalls and a bow tie. To some he resembled Buster Keaton, especially in his deadpan manner and his obsession with technical details. But his look may have been more closely based on the comic strip characters Mutt and Jeff.

Born in Iowa in 1889, Bowers later claimed to have been kidnapped into the circus at the age of six. He also said he worked as a jockey and horse trainer, and that a circus accident led him to design scenery for theater. As an artist he worked on a series of animated films based on *The Katzenjammer Kids* comic strip, which were originally drawn and directed by Gregory La Cava. In 1916, Bowers obtained the film rights to *Mutt and Jeff*, a popular comic strip by Bud Fisher. (Some have cited the strip as the inspiration for the pairing of Laurel and Hardy.) Teaming with animator Raoul Barré, Bowers formed The Mutt and Jeff Film Company. They hired several animators who would go on to have significant careers with Walt Disney and others, and proceeded to turn out a short film every week. The surviving cartoons are crude but fun, with an emphasis on what could be called cornball humor.

Barré left the company in 1918 on bad terms with Bowers, who was himself fired a year later. Bowers opened his own studio, which lasted until 1921; three years later he signed a contract with Bud Fisher for more *Mutt and Jeff* shorts. When his animators turned against him, Bowers went out on his own, writing and producing a series of two-reel comedies. Using what he called the "Bowers Process," these combined live action with stop-motion animation and line-drawing animation. Bowers' films emphasized gags over structure, often veered into bizarre tangents, and usually featured one or more of his comic inventions, such as a "slipless" banana peel. These were built using complicated, Rube Goldberg–like contraptions that were marvelous examples of his obsessive, detail-oriented imagination.

Bowers made a dozen live-action films in Astoria, Queens, before moving to a larger studio in Los Angeles for *There It Is*. On the eighteen documented films he starred in, he worked with Harold Muller, a cinematographer who received directing credit. But the vision behind the films clearly belonged to Bowers. His stop-motion animation, typically of small, mouse-like creatures, still has the power to entertain today. Bowers did not have distinctive comedic skills as a performer. He didn't have the training in vaudeville or music halls of silent clowns like Keaton and Laurel had, and therefore lacked the ability to judge what would make an audience laugh and for how long, the second sense for rhythm and pacing, for building momentum. It's often easy to reduce a typical Bowers gag to the three panels used in a daily comic strip. In his best films, like *Now You*

Tell One (1926), he managed to tie his jokes to a plot that actually built to a conclusion instead of fizzling to an end.

In *There It Is*, Bowers uses every special effect available to him, from reversing footage to double exposures, from stock footage to stop-motion animation. The California locations, and sunshine, seem to have a liberating effect on the comedian, who is jauntier than in most of his films. It's easy to see how the Buster Keaton of *Sherlock Jr.* (1924) influenced Bowers, as well as Segar's *Popeye* comic strip. The film is unusual in that Bowers plays a fictional character, a Scottish detective, rather than his typical "inventor" type.

There It Is was one of a half-dozen films Bowers released through Educational Film Exchange, a lower-tier distributor. The comedian had a difficult transition to sound films, although the labor-intensive nature of his productions may have been more of a factor than his voice, which like Keaton's had a flat, Midwestern clang. He appeared in a live-action sound short with Lowell Thomas, and made a stop-motion cartoon for Paramount called *Wild Oysters* (1941). He also animated *Pete Roleum*

and His Cousins (1939), a sponsored film about the oil industry that was the first directing credit for Joseph Losey. The director gave a chilling description of Bowers: "He was a small, frail man, a tireless worker, and obviously a first-rate technician. I was struck by his tired, resigned expression, though he was relatively young. His work seemed like terrible endless labor."

In his fifties, Bowers gave up film and returned to drawing cartoons for a newspaper in New Jersey. He died in 1946 at the age of fifty-seven. While the comedian had some champions in the United States, he may have been better appreciated in France, where he was known as Bricolo. In fact, it was up to Raymond Borde, a film historian at the Toulouse Cinemateque, to reignite interest in Bowers. Borde viewed some donated Bricolo films, but couldn't identify the performer until he tracked down a 1928 ad from a small distribution company in Marseilles. With Louise Beaudet at the Montreal Film Library, Borde helped spread the word about Bowers' work. It may be easier to see the comedian's films today than during his prime, but as Borde notes, "Bowers was marginal in all respects."

Pass the Gravy

MGM, 1928. Silent, B&W, 1.33. 23 minutes.

Cast: Max Davidson (Father), [Walter] Spec O'Donnell (Ignatz), Martha Sleeper (Daughter), Bert Sprotte (Schultz), Gene Morgan (Schultz's son).

Credits: Directed by Fred Guiol. Directorial supervision: Leo McCarey. Produced by Hal Roach. Director of photography: George Stevens. Titles: H.M. Walker. Editor: Richard C. Currier. Released January 7, 1928.

Available: The Library of Congress. Excerpted on MGM/UA Home Video VHS (1992), *Laurel & Hardy's Laughing 20's*. ISBN: 0-7928-1035-X. UPC: 0-2761-62418-3-2.

Born in Elmira, New York, in 1892, Hal Roach claimed that he was inspired at an early age by Mark Twain, who summered in the area. Roach left home at seventeen, prospected for gold in Alaska, was a truck driver in Seattle, and worked as an extra in movies when he reached Los Angeles in 1912. Within two years he was directing comedy shorts while building up a stable of talent at what became Hal Roach Studios. After helping establish Harold Lloyd and the Our Gang kids as stars, Roach was on the lookout in the mid-1920s for new comedians. Many received chances, but not unlimited ones.

Almost as important as the performers were the writers, directors, and cameramen behind the

scenes. These included Leo McCarey, Charley Chase, and George Stevens. McCarey had started as a gag writer at Roach Studios in 1923; within three years he was in charge of all comedy shorts. Stevens, the son of actors, entered the film industry in 1921 as an assistant cameraman, and joined Roach in 1927. Within another two years he would be directing his own series of shorts, *The Boy Friends*, before going on to a career in features. Chase, whose *Mighty Like a Moose* (1926) is also in the Registry, was a director and writer as well as a performer. His work with Max Davidson in *Long Fliv the King* (1926) persuaded Roach to give Davidson a shot at starring in his own series of shorts.

Born Max Solomon in Berlin in 1875, Davidson worked as an actor after emigrating to the United States. His first movie may have been D.W. Griffith's *The Narrow Road* in 1912, although his credits are difficult to pin down. He seemingly took every part he was offered, playing everything from tramps and cops to uncredited extras. In 1914 he began a series of Reliance Film Company shorts about the "Izzy" character. These appear to be lost, although other Reliance films of the time in which he played supporting parts, many featuring future director Tod Browning, survive. Davidson also appeared in films starring Tammany Young's "Bill" character; in fact, his credits run close to thirty titles a year until World War I curtailed overall film production.

Davidson alternated between supporting roles in comedy shorts and bit parts in features until 1925, where his work in two films with child star Jackie Coogan, *The Rag Man* and *Old Clothes*, drew attention. Davidson made his first short for Roach, *Don Key (Son of Burro)*, in 1926, working under directors Fred Guiol and James W. Horne, although he continued taking small parts in features in "ethnic" roles.

By this point Davidson was into his fifties, and his wizened, bewhiskered features correlated perfectly to what the film industry saw as Jewish. It was easy for him to play Jewish in a Hollywood fashion: he simply exaggerated the shrugs, grimaces, and double-takes of ragpickers, tailors, restaurateurs and other merchants. In fact, as film historian Ben Model points out, Davidson couldn't really do anything else. He didn't have the youth or physical skills to engage in slapstick, or much training in pantomime. He could only react to situations, and even then in limited ways. The problem confronting filmmakers on a Davidson project was finding something for him to do that was ethnic without being offensive. They also had to surround him with younger performers who would be responsible for performing the physical comedy.

Davidson was playing a caricature, but it was a friendly, good-natured one. His Jews were world-weary but intelligent and relatively optimistic, ready to face the worst. In other words, they were the same as the characters around them, not a sinister race to worry about. In *Long Fliv the King*, Davidson is an American merchant who ends up bewildered by customs in a Ruritarian court. His disdain for the bowing and scraping of royal underlings was more American than Jewish. In his "pilot" film for Roach, *Why Girls Say No* (1927), he insists that his daughter marry a Jewish boy, causing her Gentile boyfriend to don a "Jewish" disguise when he comes over for dinner.

In *Pass the Gravy* he is still playing to type, but the plot ignores his ethnicity, placing him instead in a suburban setting where he falls into the same rivalries that could fit practically any other comic on the Roach lot. Max's fights with next-door neighbor Brigham Schultz (played by Bert Sprotte) have nothing to do with his religion and everything to do with the conventions of comedy shorts. What may be most startling today is how well *Pass the Gravy* predicts the form and content of situation comedies on television. Similar in length, setting, characters, and jokes, *Pass the Gravy* would need only sound to work on television today. It offers the same generic situations and the same easy solutions that leave the underlying conflicts between characters intact. This week Max and Schultz argue over a prize chicken; next week, perhaps a dented car; then maybe a wedding engagement.

The beauty of Leo McCarey's best work is that it is built around silence, around the characters' inability to talk. In *Pass the Gravy* everyone knows something terrible about a celebratory dinner with neighbors except the two patriarchs. It's up to the children to convey what happened to the one father without letting the other find out. They do this by acting out elaborate but silent pantomimes seen through a doorway into another room, a gimmick that also turns up in *His Wooden Wedding* and *Duck Soup*. It works so well because it keeps viewers in on the joke, allowing them to guess at the consequences, only to be outwitted by the ingenuity of Roach's gag writers.

When it was up and running, Roach's system worked so well that it was practically an assembly line, with performers like interchangeable parts in a machine. The same could be said today, with networks and producers relying on a relatively small circle of writers and performers to turn out pilots until one clicks with viewers. The next big hit for Roach didn't come with Davidson but with Laurel and Hardy. Davidson got to star in a few other shorts, notably *Jewish Prudence*, *Don't Tell Everything*, and *Should Second Husbands Come First?* (all 1927), and continued his career into sound films. But within a few years he was back to playing extras and uncredited bits. Davidson died in obscurity in 1950.

The Last Command

Paramount, 1928. Silent, B&W, 1.33. 88 minutes.

Cast: Emil Jannings (Grand Duke Sergius Alexander), Evelyn Brent (Natalie Dabrova), William Powell (Lev Andreyev), Jack Raymond (Assistant director), Nicholas Soussanin (The adjutant), Michael Visaroff (Serge, the valet), Fritz Feld (A revolutionist).

Credits: Directed by Josef von Sternberg. Screen play by John F. Goodrich. Titles by Herman J. Mankiewicz. Story by Lajos Biró. Produced by Adolph Zukor, Jesse L. Lasky. Supervisor: J.G. Bachmann. Cinematography: Bert Glennon. Film editor: William Shea. Art direction: Hans Dreier.

Additional Cast: Harry Semels (Soldier), General Lodijenski (Bit part).

Additional Credits: Story idea: Ernst Lubitsch. Released January 22, 1928.

Awards: Oscar Best Actor (for Jannings' performance here and in *The Way of All Flesh*).

Available: Paramount Home Video VHS (1998).

The inspiration for *The Last Command* came from film director Ernst Lubitsch, who was struck by the story of a General Lodijenski, who fled Russia after World War I and found work in the United States managing a restaurant in New York City. The director encountered Lodijesnki as an extra on the Hollywood set of *The Student Prince of Old Heidelberg* (1927), where the former soldier remarked on the irony of playing a walk-on bit as a Russian general. Lubitsch told the anecdote to Emil Jannings, a German actor who was trying to establish a career in Hollywood film. A few weeks later playwright Lajos Biró told the same story back to Lubitsch, claiming that it came from Jannings.

In director Josef von Sternberg's autobiography, he claimed that he wrote the "manuscript" for what became *The Last Command*, "basing it on a meager but very good idea casually mentioned by Ernst Lubitsch, who thought that it was not good enough for a film." He continued, "I saw an opportunity to deal with the machinery of Hollywood and its callous treatment of the film extra."

It was also an opportunity for Sternberg to work with Emil Jannings, considered by many the premiere dramatic film actor in the world. Born in 1884, one of Jannings' first paying jobs was as a cook on a freighter. He later toured Europe in a theater group before working with Max Reinhardt. Jannings entered films in 1914, and became a star after appearing in three movies directed by Lubitsch. His reputation skyrocketed with *Variety* (1924), directed by E.A. Dupont, and especially after three films by F.W. Murnau, *The Last Laugh* (1924), *Tartuffe* (1926), and *Faust* (1926, playing Mephistopheles). Jannings then joined the parade of German filmmakers emigrating to the United States, signing a contract with Paramount.

A large man with rough features, Jannings was considered a master of makeup as well as a performer who gave himself over completely to his roles. Sternberg called him "shy," but complained that he was difficult to manage. "To direct a child is one thing, but when the youngster weighs close to three hundred pounds it is not easy to laugh at all his pranks." It was Sternberg's idea to structure *The Last Command* as "a film-within-a-film," staging much of the story as a flashback. For that reason, Jannings was actually playing two roles: an officious, ruthless, extremely confident leader of the Russian Army and a broken-down, palsied derelict living in a Hollywood boarding house and subjected to abuse and contempt from everyone he meets. Sternberg wrote that Jannings twisted the two roles together, and that the five weeks it took to shoot the film "seemed like five years."

To play a film director in the modern-day sequences, Sternberg cast William Powell, at the time a veteran of some thirty films and some two hundred stage plays. (*The Last Command* was one of his eight films released in 1928.) Born in Pittsburgh in 1892, Powell studied acting in New York City, and was an established, if not financially successful, performer when he started appearing in films in 1922, playing mostly villains and sidekicks. Sternberg gave Powell's character bits of business he had observed over the years working as an assistant. The actor's presence was strong enough to make him a star in a relatively unsympathetic role, although Sternberg noted that the experience so unpleasant that Powell inserted a clause in his contract prohibiting his working with the director again.

The third lead was taken by Evelyn Brent, another screen veteran who appeared in over a hundred movies during her career. She had starred months earlier in Sternberg's influential gangster movie *Underworld*. Like most of Sternberg's heroines, she is called upon to be both sexually provocative and pure at heart.

Sternberg later prided himself on *The Last Command*'s caustic view of the studio system. "I doubt if anything as savage has ever been said about it," he wrote; he also claimed that executives refused to release the finished film until Paramount investor Otto Kahn insisted on opening it. Hollywood periodically liked to pretend in its movies that filmmaking was a cold, heartless business, but not unless there were happy endings. Two other Registry titles from the same year, *The Life and Death of 9413 A Hollywood Extra* and *Show People*, cover similar territory. The first, an experimental short, is harsh and disillusioned; the second, an MGM comedy, is sunny and upbeat. *Show People* and *The Last Command* even share a similar scene in which the lead approaches an office window to deal with a studio bureaucrat. MGM turns it into the opportunity for some lighthearted gags; in *The Last Command*, it is Jannings' entrance into hell.

Underworld had been an unexpected hit, and Sternberg was given carte blanche for *The Last Command*. He made full use of studio resources, taking its typically lustrous, burnished look for a darkly melodramatic subject. His vision of Russia is pure hokum, yet still luxurious and stimulating.

His portrayal of the psychology of his characters is also hokum, not quite as forgivable today. What is still impressive about *The Last Command* is the dense visual detail Sternberg achieved: the massive sets on Hollywood sound stages, the hundreds of extras who fill shots set both in Russia and the United States, captured by a coolly impassive camera that often glides through a scene.

Jannings won the first Best Acting Oscar for this role and *The Way of All Flesh*. His taste for masochistic characters, and for fetishistic makeup, was given full rein in his next collaboration with Sternberg, *The Blue Angel* (1930), the film that introduced Marlene Dietrich to a world audience. General Lodijenski, meanwhile, was given a bit part in the film; according to film historian Scott Eyman, he "can be observed as a thick-set, middle-aged man with short hair."

The Crowd

Metro-Goldwyn-Mayer, 1928. Silent, B&W, 1.33, 103 minutes.
Cast: Eleanor Boardman (Mary), James Murray (John [Sims]), Bert Roach (Bert), Estelle Clark (Jane), Daniel G. Tomlinson (Jim), Dell Henderson (Dick), Lucy Beaumont (Mother), Freddie Burke Fredericks (Junior), Alice Mildred Puter (Daughter).
Credits: Directed by King Vidor. Screen Play by King Vidor & John V.A. Weaver. Titles by Joe Farnham. Settings by Cedric Gibbons, Arnold Gillespie. Wardrobe by André-Ani. Photographed by Henry Sharp. Film Editor: Hugh Wynn. A Metro-Goldwyn-Mayer presentation of a King Vidor production.
Additional Cast: Sally Eilers.
Additional Credits: Executive producer: Irving Thalberg. Released February 18, 1928.
Available: MGM/UA Home Video VHS (1988).

After the success of MGM's *The Big Parade* in 1925, director King Vidor could shoot almost any project he wanted. He first agreed to guide Lillian Gish through an adaptation of *La Bohème* in 1926, which also featured *Parade* star John Gilbert, then took on *Bardelys the Magnificent*, a Rafael Sabatini swashbuckling vehicle for Gilbert. (Vidor also jettisoned his first wife Florence for the strikingly beautiful Eleanor Boardman, whose career was gathering momentum.)

Vidor later claimed that he came up with the idea for *The Crowd* on the spur of the moment, pitching it to MGM executive Irving Thalberg as *One of the Mob*. Influenced in part by German films like *The Last Laugh*, and by their American counterparts like *7th Heaven* and *Sunrise*, Vidor set out to make a statement about urban life in the twentieth century. His film would deal with the tyranny of the mob, the soullessness of consumer society, implacable fates, and the pitiless odds against success. Or, as he put it in his autobiography, "Objectively, life is like a battle." Raised as a Christian Scientist, Vidor would offer a different form of social commentary than the earnest pessimism of an F.W. Murnau or the Christian-tinged optimism found in Frank Capra films. Vidor's "crowd" would be cold, skeptical, indifferent, and his characters' lives would be determined by forces out of their control. It was a message that infuriated MGM boss Louis B. Mayer and that puzzled Thalberg and other studio executives. Vidor must have had doubts himself, as the film was plagued by delays and reshoots.

Vidor's plot line follows protagonist John Sims from his birth in an upper-middle-class family to his attempts to establish a career in New York City. Determined to make a name for himself, John is instead a cog in the business machine. His illusions of individuality can't protect him from society's temptations: when he should be studying for night school, he goes on a blind date with a secretary, Mary. An advertising placard in a subway car persuades him to propose to her that night. John's dreams of success fall short. Unable to advance himself, he lashes out with increasing frequency at his wife. He ignores his responsibilities, first as a husband, then as a father. A family tragedy throws him into a tailspin from which he may not recover.

Vidor tried to shoot on location as much as possible, although it was difficult to film on the streets of New York without attracting attention. (The crew resorted to hidden cameras at times.) Moments of documentary precision, such as a scene atop a double-decker bus on Fifth Avenue, vie with devices taken straight from German expressionism, as when a young John ascends a staircase built in a stretched perspective. In a similar way, the acting ranges from natural and unforced to overwrought and histrionic. A honeymoon at Niagara Falls shows the mounting ardor between John and Mary in an understated manner that is both charming and psychologically astute. Spats between the two over things like burnt toast and spilt milk have the feel of autobiography. On the other hand, Vidor has trouble depicting the tragic elements in the story, resorting to the sort of semaphore style of acting from a previous generation during moments that called for more restraint.

The problem with *The Crowd* is that Vidor could draw up a plausible premise, but had no idea what to do with it. He could invent a John Sims, but he had no answer for John's problems. There's the nagging sense that Vidor is condescending to his characters. He's sympathetic, of course, but still sees them as poor suckers. But in truth, what insights could Vidor offer to the lives of everyday people? He was a very wealthy film director, someone who sailed to Paris with F. Scott Fitzgerald as his guide, who was carrying on an affair with one of his actresses while attending psychoanalysis sessions six nights a week. Vidor was not only isolated from the lives his customers led, but knew almost nothing about business, about what people who worked for a living had to do every day.

In their biography of the director, authors Raymond Durgnat and Scott Simmon suggest that he was on the verge of a breakdown, citing days in which nothing was filmed while he grappled with a recalcitrant plot that would not permit any but the most depressing of endings. Vidor's indecision is most apparent in the last third of the film, which he reshot repeatedly. (At one point John is about to throw himself off a bridge over a railyard. By the end of the scene he is on a completely different bridge, walking away happily with his son.) In his autobiography Vidor admits to filming three different versions; other writers have claimed as many as seven. Supposedly two versions were offered to exhibitors: a "happy" one and the decidedly ambivalent ending that exists today.

One of the myths surrounding the film asserts that Vidor cast a complete unknown, James Murray, in the lead role of Everyman John Sims. In reality, Murray had already appeared in a number of films, but he was still a risky choice for a part like this. He captures his character's callowness and irresponsibility, but has more trouble exhibiting real emotions as the story turns darker. The role would become a sort of albatross for the actor, who never found another part as significant. However, he did work consistently, with Lon Chaney in *The Big City* the same year as *The Crowd*. He had many jobs in the early 1930s, including the lead in at least one B-movie and supporting roles in Warner Brothers hits like *Baby Face* (1933) and *Havana Widows* (1934). Sadly, Murray could not control his alcoholism, and drowned in the Hudson River in 1936.

Vidor cast his new bride as John's wife Mary. A former WAMPAS star and a model for Kodak, she made a strong impression as an amateur actress in *Souls for Sale* (1923), a surprisingly perceptive romantic comedy with a moviemaking setting. In her early films, Boardman has a serenity and an aloofness unusual for an American star of the period. In *The Crowd* she seems far too sophisticated to play a gum-chewing secretary, and in scenes where she is supposed to be destitute she still exudes a calm beauty that defies her position. Once Vidor divorced her in 1931, her career was essentially over.

Another myth about *The Crowd* is that it was a commercial failure. According to Durgnat and Simmon, the film made back all its costs, although it was certainly not a blockbuster like *The Big Parade*. It was nominated for two Academy Awards, and convinced William Randolph Hearst that Vidor was the man to direct Marion Davies in *The Patsy* and *Show People*. According to biographer Scott Eyman, Louis B. Mayer loathed the film, finding it an "example of everything wrong with 'artistic' filmmaking." *The Crowd* would inspire other filmmakers to tackle similar subjects, such as Frank Capra with *Meet John Doe* (1941), another example of a director unable to find an ending. In a way, *The Crowd* prefigures recent award-winners like *American Beauty* (1999) and *Crash* (2004), fundamentally dishonest films that offer condescending solutions to society's problems.

The Life and Death of 9413 A Hollywood Extra

Robert Florey, 1928. Silent, B&W, 1.33. 13 minutes.
Cast: 9413: Raucourt. [star]: Voya.
Credits: Conceived and realized by Robert Florey and Slavko Vorkapich.
Camera-work: Gregg.
Additional Cast: Jules Raucourt (9413/John Jones), George Voya (The star/15), Adriane Marsh (13), Robert Florey.
Additional Credits: Directed by Robert Florey and Slavko Vorkapich. Director of photography: Gregg Toland. Art direction and editing: Vorkapich. Screened in New York City on June 17, 1928.
Available: Image Entertainment DVD *Unseen Cinema: Early American Avant-Garde Film from 1894–1941* (2005). UPC: 0-14381-0592-2-9.

Making movies on shoestring budgets has a long history stretching back through the drive-in films of the 1950s and exploitation films of the 1930s to the very first efforts in the fledgling medium. *The Life and Death of 9413 A Hollywood Extra* is one of the most famous examples, a film fashioned out of cardboard and mirrors that reputedly cost $97 to make.

The creators of the film were Robert Florey and Slavko Vorkapich. Florey, almost always described as a "French cineaste," fell in love with movies as a youth in France. In his twenties he wrote hundreds of articles for film magazines, as well as gushing biographies of stars like Adolphe Menjou and Douglas Fairbanks. When Florey came to Hollywood in 1921, Fairbanks hired him to handle his European public relations. Two years later Florey wrangled assistant director positions at Fox and MGM. He went to Tiffany, a Poverty Row studio, to direct his debut, *One Hour of Love* (1927), an adaptation of novel *The Broken Gate* that is now lost. But Florey had greater ambitions than directing programmers.

Born in Yugoslavia, Slavko Vorkapich came to the United States after World War I. He found small acting roles, notably under director Rex Ingram, and began working on the editing of Ingram's films. Vorkapich concentrated on dissolves, the effect of one shot blending into another. Dissolves were first done in the camera itself by running the same strip of film past the lens twice, but it was a perilous technique. Make a mistake in one shot, and both are ruined. Furthermore, it was difficult to gauge accurately when one shot should end and the other begin. There was also the possibility of flash frames between shots. Optical printers, which rephotographed two separate shots onto a new film strip, changed the process, making it possible to alter dissolves without destroying the original footage.

Influenced by German expressionism and Russian theorists, Vorkapich developed a strikingly original approach to editing, one that piled images on top of each other in forms that were geometric as well as linear. Vorkapich used jump cuts, shock cuts, and symbolic images to form miniature narratives inside larger films. Vorkapich's work is the most exciting element in *Life and Death*, even though he was years away from perfecting his technique.

When Florey was interviewed by Herman G. Weinberg in *Movie Makers* magazine, he claimed that the inspiration for *Life and Death* came from George Gershwin's *Rhapsody in Blue*. After fashioning a script of sorts with Vorkapich, Florey got financial assistance from Douglas Fairbanks, who gave him film ends (short lengths of unexposed stock that are discarded by cameramen) left over from *The Gaucho*, and access to his editing rooms.

The film was shot by Gregg Toland, at the time an assistant to cinematographer George Barnes at Samuel Goldwyn Studios. Born in Illinois in 1904, Toland grew up fascinated by movies. He built his own motion-picture cameras, and by the age of fifteen was working as an office boy at the Fox studios. Within a year he was an assistant cameraman on two-reelers directed by Al St. John.

For all the talent behind it, *Life and Death* is a surprisingly crude and disjointed effort. Industry insiders had already remarked on the capriciousness of the star system in films like the charming *Souls for Sale* (1923), with Eleanor Boardman as a small-town girl who stumbles into a movie career. Here, John Jones (played by Belgian-born actor Jules Raucourt) comes to Hollywood with dreams of success, money, and celebrity. Identified in a letter of introduction as "an artist," he becomes instead another anonymous extra with the number 9413 written on his forehead. The numbers, with their awful intimation of the Holocaust, turn Jones into a jerky, stuttering marionette babbling nonsense syllables.

It's the do-it-yourself approach that impresses the most today. Florey proves that you can accomplish a lot with few resources. Some of the "sets" consist of nothing more than a table, an old candlestick telephone, two chairs, and a cigar. Hollywood is sometimes depicted by silhouetted

Erector Set models. Not only are some of the shots handheld, but the lighting as well.

The film was called *The Suicide of a Hollywood Extra* when Florey premiered it at a movie club in Los Angeles. Miraculously, it drew the attention of Charlie Chaplin, who screened it for guests at his home. Florey's attitude—thumbing his nose at Hollywood studios—may have attracted Chaplin, who at that point was already disenchanted with many aspects of filmmaking. But Florey and Vorkapich were onto something in their depiction of film acting. Stage-trained actors can seem too broad or blunt on film, their gestures and expressions too pointed. The medium rewards actors whose faces are inscrutable or even blank, letting viewers read what they want into their close-ups. It's the actors who held back—Garbo, Cooper, Keaton—who became the true icons of the screen. After all, with his greasepaint eyebrows and white makeup, Chaplin's Little Tramp is close to being a mask.

Florey was rarely this astute about acting in his subsequent films, and in fact some of the performances in *Life and Death* are distinctly amateurish. But the film became so famous that it was actually picked up by FBO (a predecessor to RKO) and exhibited in commercial theaters. Florey made three other experimental films before returning to features. Like contemporary indie filmmakers, he used his miniscule budgets as a means of getting publicity. In *The Love of Zero* (1929), he even cited the film's total costs—$200—in the opening credits.

The twists and turns in Florey's career are remarkable. He directed the first Marx Brothers film, a stiff and creaky adaptation of their Broadway hit *The Cocoanuts* (1929). He was scheduled to direct *Frankenstein* (1931) at Universal, but the project was given to James Whale. Florey made the atmospheric but disappointing *Murder in the Rue Morgue* (1932) instead. From there his career became a bizarre mélange of B-movies (such as 1937's *Daughter of Shanghai*, a Registry title), assistant directing work, and TV credits like *The Loretta Young Show*.

Vorkapich found his methods adopted widely throughout the industry, although rarely with his intellectual insight or rigor. His own efforts were often buried within lightweight titles. By the 1940s he had essentially left the industry to become head of a film school in Los Angeles. He continued to lecture and write about film, and later in life directed television commercials for clients like Pepsi-Cola.

The Sex Life of a Polyp

Fox Movietone Entertainments, 1929. Sound, B&W, 1.33. 11 minutes.
Cast: Robert Benchley.
Credits: Directed by Thomas Chalmers. Western Electric Equipment. Copyrighted July 25, 1928.
Other Versions: Benchley reworked this material for the MGM short *The Courtship of the Newt* (1938), directed by Roy Rowland.
Available: Kino Video DVD, *Robert Benchley and the Knights of the Algonquin* (2006). UPC: 7-38329-044620-6.

Warner Brothers had been making sound shorts for about two years when the Fox studio decided to compete against Vitaphone with its own proprietary sound system, Movietone. Like Warners did, Fox started out by recording musicians like Raquel Meller and Ben Bernie, who essentially duplicated their stage acts. And like Warners, Fox soon branched out into covering other areas of show business, notably comedians.

Robert Benchley, a charter member of the Algonquin Round Table and drama critic for *Life* magazine, may have seemed an unlikely performer for Movietone, which had previously showcased dancer Ruby Keeler and rube comic Chic Sale. Born in 1889 in Worcester, Massachusetts, Benchley attended Phillips Exeter Academy and Harvard, where he was president of the editorial board of the *Lampoon*. In New York City, he worked as a reporter and then editor of *Vanity Fair*, resigning from the magazine in solidarity when critic Dorothy Parker was fired.

As well as writing and editing drama material for *Life*, Benchley wrote a syndicated column on books and another that focused on humorous subjects. In 1922, he performed a skit for *No Sirree!*, a one-night revue by various members of the Algonquin Round Table. (First known as "The Board," the Round Table met informally in the Rose Room of New York City's Algonquin Hotel. Members included columnist Alexander Woolcott, playwrights George S. Kaufman and Marc Connelly, humorist Franklin P. Adams, and future Hollywood figures Herman Mankiewicz and Donald Ogden Stewart.)

Most of *No Sirree!* consisted of broad parodies of then-current theatrical figures like A.A. Milne

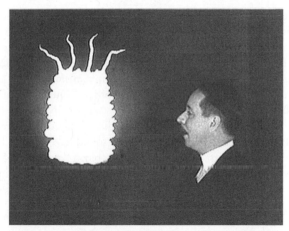

Robert Benchley employs a visual aid during his lecture on
The Sex Life of Polyp.

and Zoe Akins. Benchley chose to rework an after-dinner routine he had started in college. "The Treasurer's Report" was a masterpiece of corporate doublespeak, an effort by someone spectacularly ill-suited at public speaking to explain the finances of a volunteer organization. Projecting a patently false confidence and bonhomie, Benchley's treasurer staggered through a talk that not only made no sense, but that kept veering off into tangents and pointless asides. It was the hit of *No Sirree!*, and songwriter Irving Berlin later persuaded Benchley to perform it in his 1923 production, *Music Box Revue*. He later toured vaudeville with the skit.

At the same time, Benchley's collections of humorous sketches, *Of All Things* and *Love Conquers All*, went through numerous printings. Like many other successful New York authors, Benchley signed a screenwriting contract with Walter Wanger at the Lasky Corporation, part of Paramount. He was supposed to write a vehicle for silent comedian Raymond Griffith (*Hands Up*, 1926), but never completed a script. Next he worked on a musical play with Fred and Adele Astaire called *Smarty*. Although this eventually evolved into the successful Gershwin musical *Funny Face*, Benchley was by then long gone from the project.

Fox executive Thomas Chalmers approached Benchley in 1927 about filming "The Treasurer's Report," but the comedian didn't agree until January 1928. Despite misgivings, he accepted $2,000 to appear before Movietone cameras on a soundstage in Astoria, Queens, and repeat his routine. Directed by Chalmers, the eight-minute short featured a pianist, singer, and extras dressed as dinner guests, a fairly extravagant setting for the comedian. Released that March to Fox theaters equipped for sound, *The Treasurer's Report* was an immediate hit—so much so that Benchley signed a contract to film five additional shorts for $5,000 each at the Fox studio in Los Angeles.

Benchley started his next film, again directed by Chalmers, that spring. It was adapted from a humorous sketch he had written for *Vanity Fair*, "The Social Life of the Newt." (The sketch also appeared in his first book collection, *Of All Things*.) The premise found a learned professor trying to explain reproduction habits to a women's club composed of clueless, giggly matrons. Benchley gives an inspired performance, full of hesitations, self-deprecatory asides, and conspicuously nervous body language, his head bowing and his eyes darting before each "risky" term like "sex life" or "reproduce." His character maintains his good humor throughout, even when forced to confess that the entire talk is pointless: "This tendency to change sex at any moment, while it does save the polyp a great deal of time and expense, nevertheless makes difficult any definite analysis of its sex behavior."

The Sex Life of a Polyp is a sophisticated short for 1928, incorporating animation, back projection, and two different sound sources at a time when Vitaphone was still working out the rudiments of mixing and editing for sound. But apart from technical considerations, the film is a tour de force for Benchley, whose screen work outshines that of most of his Round Table colleagues. His character's dithering, digressive style masks a surprisingly trenchant critique of sexual identity. Benchley's avuncular, beaming expression helps defang the battle of the sexes, even when his disappointed male polyp learns that a female wants to be "just a pal." When Benchley pauses in the middle of the polyp's failed efforts to "bring the lady around to . . . his point of view," he lays clear the meaning of the professor's euphemisms. (The city of Detroit banned the film for its "risqué subject matter.")

The bumbling know-it-all Benchley assayed became a fixture of Broadway and early sound movies. Fellow Round Table members Woolcott and Stewart tried their hand at shorts, while performers like Charlie Ruggles and Charles Butterworth made entire careers out of the type. It was a character Benchley would refine over the next two decades in shorts for Universal, RKO, Paramount, and a long-running series at MGM. These include *How to Sleep* (1935) and *How to Figure Income Tax* (1938). At the same time, he was a popular character actor in films by Alfred Hitchcock, Billy Wilder, Walt Disney, and others. Benchley died in 1945. His son Nathaniel and grandson Peter both became screenwriters and authors.

The Cameraman

Metro-Goldwyn-Mayer, 1928. Silent with synchronized score, B&W, 1.33. 76 minutes.

Cast: Buster Keaton (Buster), Marceline Day (Sally), Harold Goodwin (Stagg), Sidney Bracy [Bracey] (Editor), Harry Gribbon (Cop).

Credits: Directed by Edward Sedgwick. Story by Lew Lipton and Clyde Bruckman. Continuity by Richard Schayer. Titles by Joe Farnham. Directors of photography: Elgin Lessley, Reggie Lanning. Settings by Fred Gabourie. Film editor: Hugh Wynn. Wardrobe by David Cox. A Metro-Goldwyn-Mayer presentation of a Buster Keaton production.

Additional Cast: Edward Brophy (Man in changing room), Vernon Dent (Man in bathing suit), Louise Keaton (Swimming double).

Additional Credits: Producer: Lawrence Weingarten. Story by Byron Morgan. Production manager: William Goetz. Assistant camera: Frank Dugas. Released September 22, 1928.

Other Versions: Loosely remade as *Watch the Birdie* (1950).

Available: Warner Home Video DVD, *Buster Keaton Collection* (2004). ISBN: 0-7927-9712-7. UPC: 0-12569-70092-3.

By running his own production company, Buster Keaton bucked a trend toward consolidation in the film industry at the end of the 1920s, when only two other major silent comedians, Charlie Chaplin and Harold Lloyd, remained truly independent. Keaton relied on his brother-in-law Joseph M. Schenck to handle his finances, and it was Schenck who arranged to release *The General* (1926), *College* (1927), and *Steamboat Bill, Jr.* (1928) through United Artists instead of MGM. Keaton still had control over his projects, but after the mixed reception for *The General*, Schenck began to rein in his budgets. A financial failure, *College* was seen as a rehash of Lloyd's *The Freshman* (1925), and Keaton went way over budget for *Steamboat Bill, Jr.* by staging a cyclone for the film's climax.

By the time Keaton finished filming *Steamboat Bill, Jr.*, Schenck had decided to give up producing in order to take administrative charge of United Artists. He advised Keaton to sign a contract with MGM, controlled at the time by Loew's Incorporated, run by Schenck's brother Nicholas. The comedian later called the move "the worst mistake of my career."

Under production chief Irving Thalberg, MGM resembled a factory, with motion pictures made under almost assembly-line conditions. True, MGM movies were more expensive than other studios', and Thalberg had no qualms about spending additional money to improve individual titles. But schedules were paramount. The Loew's theaters needed product, and Louis B. Mayer wasn't willing to wait while Keaton and his staff put together a project—not while the comedian was earning $150,000 a year.

Keaton was the first true comic hired by MGM, and Thalberg, who had little experience in comedy anyway, was too busy to oversee his work. Thalberg made his brother-in-law Lawrence Weingarten head of Keaton's unit. Edward Sedgwick, Jr. became Keaton's director, working on seven of the eight films the comic made at MGM. He had been one of the "Five Sedgwicks," a vaudeville family act, and had been a film actor and writer, with credits at Fox on Westerns and at Universal with director Rupert Julian.

The comedian kept his core creative group at first, including technical director Fred Gabourie, cinematographer Elgin Lessley, and gag writer Clyde Bruckman. Along with writer Lew Lipton, Bruckman devised a story suggested in part by Keaton. He would play a tintype photographer who becomes a newsreel cameraman in order to pursue a beautiful secretary. (An additional bonus was the opportunity to cross-promote the Hearst International Newsreel, distributed at the time by MGM.)

Keaton hoped to film on location in New York City, but he attracted such large crowds that he gave up after three days. Some location footage remains, such as a shot in which Keaton runs down

56th Street and a scene in Yankee Stadium, but the majority of the film was shot in California. Keaton complained about story elements added by MGM staff writers. "Thalberg wanted me involved with gangsters," he told biographer Rudi Blesh. "That was my fight—to eliminate those extra things." At the same time, he had to persuade studio executives to let him improvise material. As costar Harold Goodwin explained, "The brass wanted to know how they could budget a show if we didn't follow the script. Some thinking!"

One scene devised on the spot involved Keaton and Ed Brophy (making his film debut) trying to change clothes in a cramped dressing room. This was the essence of Keaton's humor since his days with his parents in vaudeville: a character intent on maintaining dignity while trying to solve the often baffling laws of physics—and society. Along with old-fashioned pratfalls, Keaton offered extremely sophisticated jokes, like implying sound during a Tong War sequence, a trick he had used in some earlier films. Other scenes displayed his remarkable grace while running, swimming, balancing, and juggling.

Keaton always drew on his personal life for his humor, making jokes about his conflicts with his father, for example. But *The Cameraman* reflects his real-life experiences to an unprecedented degree. His marriage to the former Natalie Talmadge was failing, he had started drinking heavily, and he was frustrated about working at MGM. It's hard to mistake Keaton's uneasiness around women in *The Cameraman*—in particular, a scene set in the heroine's boarding house. Similarly, it's difficult to interpret a carefully framed shot in which Keaton's heroics are being filmed by a monkey as anything but a comment on his work situation. Given the turmoil behind the production, the biggest surprise today is how sweet-tempered and consistently funny *The Cameraman* is, and how beautifully filmed. Whatever his misgivings about

MGM, Keaton made excellent use of its facilities, especially for an elaborate Chinatown sequence.

The fact that *The Cameraman* was significantly more successful at the box office than his previous three features may be due to MGM's publicity and distributions machines, but the studio saw it as a vindication of its working methods. Keaton's next film, *Spite Marriage* (1929), had flashes of brilliance, but he was increasingly hemmed in by producers, writers, and the rest of the MGM apparatus. In the studio's defense, the comedian was becoming dangerously self-destructive. On the other hand, MGM forced him into wretched vehicles; when his box-office pull declined, it teamed him with the abrasive Jimmy Durante.

Keaton was also growing older, and it was becoming harder and harder to pass himself off as a naive innocent in his films. No longer confident about his choices, in his comedy he returned to what had worked before, to the routines he developed on stage with his parents. When he was suspended and ultimately fired from MGM, he made independent features in France and Mexico, as well as short films for Educational Pictures and Columbia. Keaton continued working in the industry, taking bit parts, writing gags, even directing a musical short. Fortunately, he was still alive when critics began to reappraise his work.

For years, MGM used this title as a sort of training film for its comedians, an example of what they should strive for. The title number from *Singin' in the Rain* (1952) shows that Gene Kelly was keenly aware of *The Cameraman*. In 1950, MGM remade the film, poorly, as *Watch the Birdie*, a vehicle for Red Skelton. The studio also let the original negative deteriorate until it was too worn to salvage. Recent restorations of *The Cameraman* are still missing material, in particular the first, catastrophic newsreel Keaton photographs and screens for his bosses.

The Docks of New York

Paramount, 1928. Silent, B&W, 1.33. 75 minutes.
Cast: George Bancroft (The Stoker), Clyde Cooks (His Pal), Betty Compson (A Girl), Mitchell Lewis (The Third Engineer), [Olga] Baclanova (His Wife), Gustav Von Seyffertitz (Hymn-book Harry), Guy Oliver (The Crimp), May Foster (Mrs. Crimp), Lillian Worth (Steve's girl).
Credits: Directed by Josef von Sternberg. Story and Screen Play by Jules Furthman. Suggested by John Monk Saunders' "The Dock Walloper." Titles by Julian Johnson. Photographed by Harold Rosson. Associate producer: J.G. Bachmann. An Adolph Zukor and Jesse L. Lasky presentation. B.P. Schulberg, General Manager, West Coast Productions.

Additional Credits: Art direction: Hans Dreier. Editing: Helen Lewis. Released September 29, 1928.
Available: Paramount VHS. ISBN: 0-7921-0940-6. UPC: 0-9736-02807-3.

At the height of his fame, many considered Josef von Sternberg the greatest pictorialist in the movies. Born Jonas Sternberg in Vienna in 1894, he traveled with his family between Austria and New

York until his teens. He entered the industry as a patcher, replacing worn-out segments in films, and worked his way up through cutting, editing, writing titles, and assistant directing. He made training films in the Army Signal Corps, then assisted directors in the United States and Europe after armistice. The "von" appeared some time after he moved to Hollywood.

In 1924, Sternberg wrote, produced, and directed *The Salvation Hunters* for under $5,000. Shot on location as a vehicle for British actor George K. Arthur, the film caused a small sensation in Hollywood. An early example of "indie" filmmaking, the picture stood out from industry product for its strong visual style and its avoidance of studio sets. It was picked up by United Artists, and led Sternberg to several canceled projects there and then an eight-picture deal at MGM. The director's autocratic manner and time-consuming methods, as well as his relatively challenging story lines, got him fired almost at once. Charlie Chaplin hired him to direct a film for his former costar Edna Purviance. *A Woman of the Sea*, or *The Sea Gull*, as it is also known, was finished but never released, and is the most significant film in the comedian's career to have vanished. (Oona O'Neill was rumored to have destroyed the sole remaining print in 1991.)

Sternberg took a demotion, working at Paramount as an assistant again, but he impressed executives by completing unfinished scenes in a couple of films, including the Clara Bow breakthrough *It*. As a reward, he was allowed to direct *Underworld* (1927), a gangster film based on a story by Ben Hecht. A bona fide hit, *Underworld* inspired a gangster cycle that lasted almost ten years.

Sternberg's star was George Bancroft, a beefy former stage actor from Philadelphia who made a big impression in Westerns like *The Pony Express* (1922). A few months after *Underworld*, Sternberg and Bancroft made another urban drama together, *The Dragnet*, this one written by the brothers Charles and Jules Furthman. Also a success, *The Dragnet* led to *The Docks of New York*, which was based on a story by John Monk Saunders, at the time the hottest writer at Paramount. (His *Wings* had come out the year before.) Joining Bancroft was Betty Compson, a singularly beautiful blonde who at the time was married to director James Cruze. Compson, a stalwart in Al Christie comedy shorts ten years earlier, had become a true star in the 1920s. She would receive an Oscar nomination

for her next film, *The Barker*. Olga Baclanova, a Russian émigré, would work with Sternberg on two further films. Her most memorable role would be in *Freaks* in 1932. Sternberg cast two industry veterans, Mitchell Lewis and Gustav von Seyffertitz, in key roles as Bancroft's rival and a waterfront preacher, respectively.

When it came to actors, Sternberg was not usually a subtle director, possibly because he saw his characters in such broad terms. Many of the female leads in his films were prostitutes, but prostitutes who were also misunderstood women down on their luck, with hearts of gold hidden beneath tough exteriors. Men on the one hand were tough, even brutish laborers and professionals who kept their feelings to themselves as they were being either redeemed or destroyed by love. The others were wealthy, effete scoundrels who were driven by spite or malice to destroy their rivals.

Sternberg tended to fetishize his depictions of both genders, and while his films were obsessed with sex, it was sex on a weirdly juvenile level. *The Docks of New York* is about desire rather than emotion, about sexual fantasies rather than relationships. He would find his Trilby a few years later with Marlene Dietrich, but for now he turned the sweet, vivacious Betty Compson into the nearest equivalent. Sternberg gave her a frowsy hairdo, kohl-rimmed eyes, and scanty, skin-tight dresses to play Mae, a suicidal prostitute who falls in love with her rescuer, a hotheaded sailor on a tramp freighter. Bancroft, Bill Roberts in the intertitles but simply "The Stoker" in the credits, is first seen half-naked and covered with oil, removing his red-hot stoking rod from a furnace while staring hungrily at graffiti of naked women.

With "The Dock Walloper" as source material, it may be unfair to expect a nuanced story line. Even so, the elemental forces at play in *Docks* remain jarring today. The look on Bancroft's face as he stares at Compson's drenched, writhing torso is unmistakable. So is Baclanova's as she hungrily mauls a dancer's face with kisses. The film, at least in its opening scenes, is more about people staring morosely, angrily, lustfully, at their counterparts than it is about people acting as characters. The glances, stares, and sullen expressions require actors to project attitude, not thought. And once the plot has been established—with the growing relationship between Compson and Bancroft contrasted by a poisonous one between his boss (Mitchell Lewis) and Baclanova, a "dancer"—all Sternberg has to do to keep the story moving is cut from one glowering close-up to another.

Sternberg was part of a wave of European directors infiltrating Hollywood at the time. He was very familiar with German expressionism, and his use of shadows, shafts of light, contorted sets, filters, screens, and scrims all point to UFA and other Berlin film studios. (These techniques were also being used at the time by everyone from John Ford to King Vidor.) But Sternberg's interpretation was curiously American, expressionism without the Teutonic fatalism. The laconic, sarcastic Bancroft is a version of what John Wayne would be ten years later.

Sternberg also brought to the screen a heightened visual awareness of the shape and depth of the frame, as well as a conviction about his material that his stories didn't really warrant. Sternberg's films seem more serious than other Hollywood product. They are slower, more languidly paced, filled with shots that do nothing but evoke atmosphere. Their frames are cluttered with netting, ropes, shadows, lamps, screens, filigree—details that fill up corners and edges and foregrounds often ignored by other directors. Look at Bancroft's introduction: a furnace to his left, a triangular shaft of light filling the right third of the frame, a hanging chain defining the space, a soft glow from another furnace at floor level to the right, and the actor towering over the center of the frame, backlit, the camera gazing up at him. Sternberg had little to say about *Docks* in his autobiography, noting only that he lifted a domestic scene in which Bronson sews a tear in Bancroft's shirt from *Montmarte*, an Ernst Lubitsch film starring Pola Negri.

The cameraman for *The Docks of New York* was Harold Rosson, a member of a remarkable family that included directors Arthur and Richard and actress Helene. After acting in films in New York, he moved to Los Angeles, where he became a camera operator and then a lighting director. He was the cinematographer of choice for such noted directors as Howard Hawks and George Cukor, and later became a fixture at MGM, where he shot *The Wizard of Oz*, among many other films.

Thanks to Rosson and Sternberg, the visual wizardry of *Docks* is on a level with any film of its period. A suicide shown entirely in the reflection of water is worthy of Hitchcock, while a teeming wedding scene evokes Sternberg's *The Blue Angel*, which would come two years later. And if the images seem excessive at times (as when Bancroft carries Compson past distressed fishing nets apparently left over from the previous century), the rewards are a moody romance as involving today as it was eighty years ago.

The Wedding March

Paramount, 1928. Silent, B&W with Technicolor sequences, 1.33. 113 minutes.
Cast: Erich von Stroheim (Nicki), Fay Wray (Mitzi [Schrammell]), ZaSu Pitts (Cecelia [Schweisser]), Mathew Betz (Schani [Eberle]), George Fawcett (Prince [Ottokar] von Wildeliebe-Rauffenburg), Maude George (Princess [Maria] von Wildeliebe-Rauffenburg), George Nichols ([Fortunat] Schweisser), Dale Fuller (Mitzi's mother), Cesare Gravina (Mitzi's father), Hughie Mack (Schani's father).
Credits: "In its entirety an Erich von Stroheim creation." Written by Erich von Stroheim and Harry Carr. An Erich von Stroheim production.
Additional Cast: Sidney Bracey (Naveratil), Anton Vaverka (Franz Joseph I).
Additional Credits: Directed by Erich von Stroheim. Produced by Adolph Zukor, Jesse L. Lasky, P.A. (Pat) Powers. Directors of photography: Hal Mohr, B. Sorenson, Ben Reynolds. Technicolor cameraman: Roy Rennahan. Film editing: Frank E. Hull. Art direction: Richard Day, Erich von Stroheim. Costumes: Max Rée. Production dates: June 1926 to January 1927. Released October 6, 1928.
Available: Paramount Home Video VHS (1987). ISBN: 0-7921-8958-2. UPC: 0-9738-39501-3-4.

After the controversy surrounding *Greed* (1924), Erich von Stroheim was subjected to tighter control for his next film, *The Merry Widow* (1925). Ignoring the libretto by Victor Leon and Leo Stein, and of course constrained from using Franz Lehár's music, Stroheim concocted a sexually explicit look at decadent Hapsburg society, starring John Gilbert and Mae Murray. While it was a critical and financial success, it was the last film Stroheim would make for MGM.

Pat Powers, an independent producer who had worked at Universal in its earliest days, helped Stroheim assemble his next package. *The Wedding March* would be another examination of European aristocrats, this time in Vienna in the court of Franz Joseph I. Powers assured Stroheim that this would be a large-scale, and long, film, and arranged for Paramount to assume the costs.

The project was conceived as a sort of return to the stories and settings that established Stroheim's reputation. He cast himself in the lead role, his first serious acting since *Foolish Wives* in 1922. Opposite him was Fay Wray, a Canadian-born actress who up to that point had parts in several undistinguished Westerns. (Along with Janet Gaynor, Dolores del Rio, Mary Astor, and thirteen others, she was chosen as a WAMPAS Baby Star in 1926.) ZaSu Pitts appeared as a crippled heiress. The other three significant roles were filled by Maude George, George Fawcett, and journeyman actor Mathew Betz. The austerely beautiful Maude George had worked with Stroheim in three of his films, and this was one of her last roles before she retired from movies. Unlike many other actresses, she seemed fully attuned to Stroheim's louche tastes, allowing herself to be filmed in unflattering makeup in early scenes to establish her character's determination and will. Fawcett, who had appeared in *The Merry Widow*, was a stage star in the United States and England at the turn of the twentieth century. He was fifty-five when he made his first film, and became famous for playing uncompromising figures of authority.

George and Fawcett dominate the opening scenes of *The Wedding March*, playing a dissolute couple whose loveless marriage sets the stage for their son Nicki's future unhappiness. They aren't worried about his drinking, or his visits to an extremely posh bordello. But they are intent on marrying him off to the wealthiest possible target, in this case the daughter of the manufacturer of bandages.

As an actor, Stroheim takes a restrained approach to Nicki, his impassive face letting viewers read what they want into his reaction shots. As one of the emperor's mounted guards (or, "First Lieutenant of the Imperial and Royal Life Guard—Mounted"), he is stationed outside St. Stephen's Cathedral on Corpus Christi when he meets Mitzi, the daughter of a violinist who plays at a beer garden. She's accompanied by Schani (Betz), a butcher in a loud checked suit whose frequent spitting represents the vulgarity of the lower classes.

Stroheim does something daring in this scene, playing out a slight flirtation between Mitzi and Nicki for ten minutes, well beyond what other directors would consider necessary. But then, what is necessary for a director to present a realistic vision of the world? How much does a scene require in order to convince viewers that it is actually happening? Did Stroheim need a full choir, a packed church, ornately garbed soldiers, an enormous square built on the backlot for this small moment? Did the camera have to frame his figure in a fetishistic manner for Wray's gaze? Would *The Wedding March* have been as effective without its Technicolor shots of a procession of uniformed soldiers?

A twenty-gun salute upsets Nicki's horse, which tramples Mitzi. Nicki visits her in the hospital, a curiously intimate scene. (Like ZaSu Pitts' Cecelia, Mitzi will walk with a limp for much of the rest of the film.) Later he will watch her play the harp at the beer garden, the reflection on his monocle split into the shape of a cross. Stroheim prided himself on details, and much of *The Wedding March* has the ring of truth. But it's also a world remembered, one softened by dreams and memories.

About an hour into the film, the two leads enter a moonlit apple orchard. Surrounded by apple blossoms, Nicki seduces Mitzi in an abandoned carriage. Stroheim stages the scene so that Mitzi dominates the frame, with Nicki fading into a gray background, a gesture that shows the director was more interested in the film as a whole than in protecting his performance. What makes the scene so remarkable, apart from its glistening cinematography and set design, is its sense of foreboding. Neither Mitzi nor Nicki is truly at fault, but viewers know from earlier intimations that this affair will end poorly.

Subsequent scenes in *The Wedding March* can be as harsh as any in *Greed*, but they are redeemed by Stroheim's more mature view of humanity. Not everyone is a thieving, grasping cheat. People make decisions because of situations, and the people around them, not just on base impulses. Life is unfair, but many are still willing to help those around them. (Even a priest in a confessional, usually targeted as a hypocrite in this kind of film, shows unexpected compassion.) The lost dreams and thwarted opportunities that press down on these characters are what gives *The Wedding March* its power today—that, and a script and directing style that seem more focused, more determined, than Stroheim's other work.

The director filmed from June 1926 until January 1927, an unprecedented schedule for what was meant to be an intimate project. Before shooting was finished studio executives stepped in once again, alarmed at Stroheim's extravagance and painfully slow methods. In editing, Stroheim built scenes far more sophisticated than most of his contemporaries. He blended subjective points of view with majestic crane shots, pared some moments down to impressionistic blurs, and used models and animation in surrealistic flourishes. But the finished film was taken out of his control and broken into two parts. *The Honeymoon*, the second segment, was never released in the United States, and received an extremely limited release in Europe. According to author Robert Birchard, the last known print was destroyed in a fire at the Cinématèque Français.

Stroheim disowned *The Honeymoon*, which was edited by others, and turned to a project funded by Joseph P. Kennedy, soon to be one of the founders of RKO. Kennedy wanted to showcase his mistress, Gloria Swanson, but *Queen Kelly* proved such a disastrous production that it ended Stroheim's directing career. (He helmed one more film for Fox, an adaptation of Dawn Powell's play *Walking Down Broadway*, but it was taken out of his hands, reshot, and released as *Hello Sister*.)

Unable to find work, Stroheim returned to acting, starring as a madman in *The Great Gabbo* (1929) and parodying his image as a maniacal director in *The Lost Squadron* (1931). It wasn't until his role as a German prison warden in Jean Renoir's *Grand Illusion* (1937) that he began to restore his professional reputation.

The Power of the Press

Columbia, 1928. Silent, B&W, 1.33. 65 minutes.
Cast: Douglas Fairbanks, Jr. (Clem Rogers), Jobyna Ralston (Jane Atwill), Mildred Harris (Marie), Robert Edeson (City editor), Dell [Del] Henderson (Johnson), Philo McCullough (Blake), Wheeler Oakman (Van), Edwards Davis (Mr. Atwill).
Credits: Directed by Frank Capra. Written by Frederick A. Thompson, Sonya Levien. Story by Frederick A. Thompson. Adaptation and continuity by Sonya Levien. Produced by Jack Cohn. Photography by Chet Lyons, Ted Tetzlaff. Film editor: Frank Atkinson. Art director: Harrison Wiley. Assistant director: Buddy [Charles C.] Coleman. A Columbia Pictures/Frank R. Capra production.
Additional Cast: Charles Clary (District attorney).
Additional Credits: Released October 31, 1928.
Available: The Library of Congress.

Born in Palermo, Sicily, Frank Capra emigrated with his family to California when he was six. According to his colorful and often unreliable autobiography, *The Name Above the Title*, he had initially planned a career as a chemical engineer, and fell into film by accident. In 1922 he got a job directing an independent production in San Francisco, an adaptation of a Rudyard Kipling poem, with unhappy results. Determined to study the medium, he took every imaginable job in the industry, from processing film to handling props, editing, and writing gags. Fired from the Our Gang comedies at the Hal Roach Studio, he befriended Will Rogers, who helped him get a job with Mack Sennett. Capra's assignment was Harry Langdon, and after several successful shorts and features, he followed the comic when he moved to First National.

When Langdon fired him, Capra continued working for First National, making *For the Love of Mike* in New York with Claudette Colbert. Its failure sent him back to Hollywood, where he accepted a contract with Harry Cohn at Columbia Pictures. It was a step down even from Sennett, as Columbia Pictures, an outgrowth of the CBC Film Sales Company, was considered part of Hollywood's Poverty Row. And Cohn, later

nicknamed "White Fang" by Ben Hecht, had a fearsome reputation.

Nevertheless, Capra made eight features at Columbia in 1928, almost one a month until he took over the production of *Submarine*, a troubled action film. He was looking for a style, experimenting with comedy and drama, working with other screenwriters and occasionally writing material himself. Capra glossed over these films in his autobiography, preferring humorous anecdotes to explanations of how he worked. In fact, he didn't bother to mention *The Power of the Press*.

The plot for the film came from Frederick A. Thompson, a director some ten years earlier (this is his only known writing credit). Screenwriter Sonya Levien was born in Russia in 1895 and received a law degree from New York University. She gave up practicing law to work for Theodore Roosevelt on his *Metropolitan Magazine*, selling enough of her short stories to filmmakers to draw screenwriting offers from Jesse Lasky and others. When her husband Carl Hovey was named a story editor at Paramount, Levien agreed to leave New York for Hollywood.

Levien rarely worked alone, and it's likely that she and Capra developed much of the material in *The Power of the Press* together. In tone and content, the story bears a remarkable resemblance to the films that Capra would make in the 1930s. It features a brash young newspaper reporter (played by Douglas Fairbanks, Jr.) who's willing to bend the rules to get ahead, but who still has a firm sense of morals; a flighty heiress (Jobyna Ralston) looking for a man to anchor her life; and an outwardly stoic and inwardly seething editor (Robert Edeson) who recognizes the hero's talent even as he deplores his abrasive manners.

The characters are trapped in a silly plot about a murdered district attorney, a mayoral campaign, rival reporters, mistaken identities, and love across class lines. You can sense Capra's frustration with not being able to use sound (he would direct the first Columbia talkie for Harry Cohn the following year), but you can also see him developing a visual style. "Don't let the ponderous behind-the-scenes machinery distract from the heroine's fluttering eyelid," he wrote later. "People pay to *hear* Heifetz's violin, not to marvel at his fingers." The cinematography in *The Power of the Press* is simple and direct, with frequent, carefully lit close-ups and frames void of clutter.

It was the point of view Capra chose that made his work distinctive. Another director might have wanted to tell the story through a prize reporter, not a maladroit rookie. When Fairbanks tries to sneak his way into a crime scene, Capra reverses the typical staging to concentrate on the reporter's frustration as he fumes by a doorway, unable to get anyone to take him seriously. And the director takes the time to let the golddigging villainess explain her motives, making her a believable, even sympathetic character instead of just a foil.

The years spent writing and directing comedy gave Capra an excellent sense of timing. *The Power of the Press* doesn't just move quickly, it flows effortlessly from scene to scene. You may wonder why the director inserted a prolonged montage of how a newspaper's front page is revised to incorporate a breaking story, but the sequence never feels like it's slowing down the film. (Capra would make montages like this an important feature of almost all of his films.)

The director had yet to assert himself completely with actors. Ralston, a fixture in Harold Lloyd comedies after the comic married his previous costar, isn't as grounded and sexy as Capra's later heroines. Mildred Harris was famous more for her brief marriage to Charlie Chaplin than for her acting skill, and Capra doesn't bother to use her for much more than window dressing. Fairbanks had become an actor against his father's wishes, and had forged a fairly successful film career by the late 1920s. (This was one of a half-dozen features he made in 1928.) But he was by no means a star, and here he is callow enough to detract from the film.

The success of *Submarine* turned Capra into Columbia's best action director, sidetracking him a bit from his more mainstream goals. He worked with Levien again on *The Younger Generation* (1929), an adaptation of a Fannie Hurst play, but the screenwriter signed a contract with Fox that resulted in Oscar-nominated films like *Cavalcade* and *State Fair* (both 1933). In her long career, Levien worked with directors like Frank Borzage, Henry King, and John Ford, and received an Academy Award for *Interrupted Melody* (1955). Capra, meanwhile, was still some years away from his breakthrough triumph, *It Happened One Night* (1934).

Like most Columbia silents, *The Power of the Press* dropped out of view after sound arrived. The version seen today was restored from a unique print discovered in the collection of John Hampton, which was acquired in 1999 by David W. Packard. An heir to the Hewlett-Packard fortune and president of the Stanford Theatre Foundation, Packard is one of the most significant figures in film preservation.

Show People

Metro-Goldwyn-Mayer, 1928. B&W, 1.33, silent with synchronized musical soundtrack, 80 minutes.

Cast: Marion Davies (Peggy Pepper), William Haines (Billy Boone), Dell Henderson (General Marmaduke Pepper), Paul Ralli (André [Telefair]), Tenen Holtz (Casting director), Harry Gribbon (Comedy director), Sidney Bracey (Dramatic director), Polly Moran (Peggy's maid), Albert Conti (Producer [Mr. Morton]), Rolfe Sedan (Photographer). Cameos: John Gilbert, Charles Chaplin, King Vidor, Elinor Glyn, Douglas Fairbanks, Aileen Pringle, Karl Dane, George K. Arthur, Lew Cody, William S. Hart, Leatrice Joy, Norma Talmadge, Renée Adorée, Rod La Rocque, Claire Windsor, Dorothy Sebastian, Louella Parsons.

Credits: Directed by King Vidor. Written by Agnes Christine Johnson, Wanda Tuchock, Laurence Stallings. Titles: Ralph Spence. Cinematography by John Arnold. Film editor: Hugh Wynn. Art director: Cedric Gibbons. Costume design: Henrietta Frazer. Music: William Axt, David Mendoza. Song: "Crossroads," words by Raymond Klages, music by William Axt and David Mendoza.

Additional Cast: Ray Cooke (Director's assistant), Coy Watson, Jr. (Messenger boy). Additional cameos: Bess Flowers, Estelle Taylor, Bert Roach, Robert Z. Leonard, Marion Davies.

Additional Credits: Produced by Irving Thalberg. Production date: April 1928. Released November 11, 1928.

Available: MGM/UA Home Video VHS (1988).

One result of the success of *The Big Parade* (1925) was the decision by William Randolph Hearst to hire King Vidor to direct three comedies starring Marion Davies. It was an open secret throughout the country that the actress was the married millionaire's mistress. He formed Cosmopolitan Pictures in part to showcase her talents, convinced that he could make her a star the same way he could dictate history.

Hearst met Davies in 1917, well after he established a publishing empire by appealing to the masses with newspaper articles and pictures about sex and crime (and almost single-handedly forcing war between the United States and Spain). Davies was born Marion Cecilia Douras in Brooklyn in 1897, and became a chorus girl when she was sixteen. She made it to the Ziegfeld *Follies* in 1916, and earned a film role the same year she met Hearst. His goal of making her the biggest star in the country was intertwined with his more personal efforts to become a filmmaking mogul. Hollywood, on the other hand, was perfectly willing to let him spend as much money as he wanted while specifying what films it determined to be worthwhile. Hearst never had as much influence on the industry as he thought he did.

Hearst first signed a deal with Paramount to coproduce Cosmopolitan's pictures. These consisted almost exclusively of Davies vehicles. Hearst's tastes ran to highbrow literary adaptations like *When Knighthood Was in Flower* (1922), *Janice Meredith* (1924), and *Quality Street* (1927). Unfortunately, Davies was a better comedienne than actress, and the stiff, artificial movies she starred in almost invariably lost money. By this time Hearst had switched studio affiliation to MGM, where Vidor was under contract.

Vidor directed Davies in *The Patsy* and *Show People* in 1928, and *Not So Dumb*, a sound film adapted from the Marc Connelly/George S. Kaufman play *Dulcy*, in 1930. *The Patsy* showed the public another side of Davies. Unlike her previous films, this one was a modest, charming, and genuinely amusing comedy about sisters battling for the affections of an architect. Vidor surrounded Davies with expert comics like Marie Dressler, and gave the actress the chance to display her talent for impersonations. (She does especially funny, if harsh, takes on Lillian Gish and Mae Marsh, full of mannered gestures and frozen poses.)

Show People expanded on the strengths of *The Patsy* while opening a wider stage for Davies to play on. At the same time, it was a broad satire on Hollywood, filled with easy to spot in-jokes and cameos that would draw in a larger audience than Davies' typical fan base. Originally Thalberg and Mayer had hoped Davies would star in a silent version of the Guy Bolton play *Polly Preferred*, but it proved too difficult to adapt to film. Instead, Vidor

regular Laurence Stallings developed a treatment by Agnes Christine Johnson and Wanda Tuchock about a naive girl trying to break into the picture business. In the final script, Peggy Pepper, the part Davies plays, resembles both Gloria Swanson (who married into royalty just as Polly tries to) and Bebe Daniels. But as critic John Baxter points out, Peggy could just as easily be based on Vidor's first wife Florence, who (like Peggy) drove to Hollywood from Georgia and later graduated from comedies to high-toned dramas. For that matter, why couldn't it be Vidor's second wife Eleanor Boardman, who underwent a similar metamorphosis in 1923's *Souls for Sale*?

Vidor was again careful to protect Davies by surrounding her with an experienced cast. Dell Henderson, playing her father, had appeared in *The Crowd* (1928) and *The Patsy* (again playing her father). William Haines, groomed by MGM as a boyish lead, was a last-minute replacement for James Murray, who was unable to perform due to medical problems. Vidor wrote that he had no problem finding stars to appear in cameos: "It was a Hearst film. They didn't dare refuse." As well as offering candid glimpses of the leading silent stars at the very end of an era, *Show People* provides a wonderful tour of studios like Paramount, Fox, and First National.

The plot maneuvers through a few mistaken identity twists while dropping bromides such as: slapstick is just as important as high art, don't forget the little people, and aristocrats are fakes and impostors. At one point Vidor even mocks one of his own films, *Bardelys the Magnificent* (1926). But for viewers today, the highlights of *Show People* center on Davies herself. In the right hands a generous, uninhibited performer, here she is buoyant and effortless, not afraid to make fun of herself. She doesn't place herself above the material, but is still aware of how wispy it is. A scene in which she tries to show her acting ability to a casting agent by miming ridiculous "moods" shows how much she was willing to satirize herself. (Vidor evidently wanted her to go even farther, but complained that Hearst would not allow Davies to participate in a pie fight.)

While there's no question that Davies appeared in films that did not suit her talents, it's an ironic twist that her reputation today is largely based on Orson Welles' cruel caricature of her in *Citizen Kane* (1941). By almost all accounts, Davies was a warm, loyal figure who valued her relationships. She rallied behind Roscoe Arbuckle, hiring him to direct one of her features even as Hearst's newspapers were destroying his career. When Hearst suffered financial setbacks during the Depression, Davies offered her own money to help him.

By that time Hearst had separated Cosmopolitan Pictures from MGM, moving it to Warner Brothers. Davies starred in a handful of pictures there, but she never established a secure footing in sound movies. She retired in 1937, working as an executive with the Motion Picture Relief Fund. Davies married for the first time after Hearst's death in 1951.

Steamboat Willie

Celebrity Productions, Inc., 1928. Sound, B&W, 1.37. 8 minutes.

Credits: Directed by Walt Disney. Animation: Ub Iwerks. Music: Carl Stalling. Conductor: Carl Edouarde.

Additional Credits: Written by Walt Disney. Animation: Les Clark, Johnny Cannon, Wilfred Jackson, Dick Lundy. Sound effects: Walt Disney. Production dates: June to September 1928. Released November 18, 1928.

Available: Buena Vista Home Entertainment DVD *Walt Disney Treasures— The Adventures of Oswald The Lucky Rabbit* (2007). ISBN: 0-7888-7158-7. UPC: 7-86936-71634-4. *Vintage Mickey* DVD (2005).

Walt Disney was born in Chicago in 1901, but grew up in Missouri, first on a farm, and then in Kansas City. He was encouraged to draw in school, and took classes at the Institute of Art when his family moved back to Chicago. After serving in the Red Cross Ambulance Corps during World War I, Disney returned to Kansas City to pursue a career in art. He befriended Dutch immigrant Ub Iwerks, and worked with him at the Kansas City Film Ad Company, drawing cartoon commercials. In 1922 Disney formed his own company to distribute Laugh-O-Gram films, but went bankrupt. After persuading his brother Roy to invest in a combination of animation and live-action footage released under the umbrella title *Alice in Cartoonland*, Disney went bankrupt again.

Disney moved to Los Angeles in 1923, followed shortly by his brother Roy and Iwerks. The newly formed Disney Brothers Studios featured Walt as the idea man, Roy in charge of money, and Iwerks in charge of the art department. Walt resurrected both the Laugh-O-Gram and Alice films, and in 1927 collaborated with Universal Studios on a new character, Oswald the Rabbit. After over twenty-five cartoons, Oswald was a hit, and Disney approached Universal for better financing terms. Instead, he discovered that Universal owned all rights to Oswald, and was taking over control of the series. In some accounts a chagrined Disney fashioned the Mickey Mouse character on a train ride home from his meeting with Universal executives. (Others point to Ub Iwerks' influence over the mouse's appearance.)

Even a casual comparison shows striking similarities between Oswald and Mickey; it can even be argued that Mickey is simply Oswald with shorter ears. The characters share the same curiosity and sense of humor, the same affinity for trouble-making and practical jokes, the same combination of fear and braggadocio, of optimism and worry. Disney and Iwerks later owned up to copying aspects of Charlie Chaplin and Douglas Fairbanks, but according to his wife Lillian and daughter Diane, Mickey was based primarily on Walt Disney himself.

Mickey's first appearance was in *Plane Crazy*, an extension of a typical Oswald adventure with the same jokes about perspective, the same shifting horizons, the same shrinking and elongating objects. Disney screened the short in at least one theater in Los Angeles, but was unable to convince a studio to distribute it (he came close with MGM). Despite his shrinking finances, Disney had his staff preparing a second Mickey cartoon, *The Gallopin' Gaucho*. But for the third, Disney wanted to use synchronized sound.

Steamboat Willie was not the first sound cartoon; the Fleischer brothers, with De Forest Phonofilm, and Paul Terry, with RCA Photophone, had been making them for five years. But Disney wanted the sound to be a natural adjunct to the visuals, to have characters talk and move in time to music. The new project would use Mickey in a spoof of Buster Keaton's role in *Steamboat Bill, Jr.*

Led by Iwerks, the animation staff prepared footage. In June, Disney projected it while animator Wilfred Jackson (the only employee who knew music) played "Turkey in the Straw" and "Steamboat Bill" on the harmonica. While Iwerks admitted that the artwork was "terrible," the synchronization was sensational. The entire cartoon was redrawn and finished by the end of July, 1928. Now all Disney needed was a sound process.

Two choices were available: sound on disc, pioneered by Vitaphone and Warner Brothers; and sound on film, popularized by Fox. In New York

City that September, Disney signed an agreement with Pat A. Powers, who was hawking Cinephone, a not-quite-legal sound-on-film process. Powers introduced Disney to orchestra conductor Carl Edouarde, and hired musicians for a recording session on September 15. They were working from a score arranged by Carl Stallings, a friend of Disney's from Kansas City. The recording was a disaster, forcing Disney to wire Roy in Los Angeles for money to finance a second, successful session.

Searching for a distributor, Disney screened the finished film for Universal, Paramount, and FBO (which evolved into RKO). He also had Stallings prepare scores for the other four Mickey cartoons (*Steamboat Willie* would be followed by *The Barn Dance*). With money running out, Disney met Harry Reichenbach, a veteran of promotion and at the time manager of the Colony Theater on Broadway. Reichenbach gave Disney $500 to screen *Steamboat Willie* on November 18, 1928.

Unheard of at the time for a cartoon, the film received raves in *Variety*, the *New York Times*, and other publications. It ran for two weeks at the Colony before Pat Powers and his staff started selling it to other locations on states' rights agreements. *Steamboat Willie* was earning money, but after Powers deducted his 10 percent distribution fee, and a royalty fee, and a separate fee for using Cinephone, Disney received very little of it. *Steamboat Willie* made $15,000 within a few months, but Disney was simultaneously borrowing money from friends and relatives to keep the studio going.

Viewers today sometimes complain that *Steamboat Willie* is both primitive and tame. Even by the technical standards of the time it was not remarkably innovative. On a narrative level it was dealing with typical Mickey Mouse (and Oswald the Rabbit) situations. These can seem surprisingly rough today, but anyone who grew up on a farm, like Disney did, was used to barnyard humor. What Disney and his animators did that was so revolutionary was to make sound a part of the art. In *Steamboat Willie* everything dances: smokestacks, water, hillsides, cranes, animal body parts, and, of course, Mickey. Furthermore, Disney achieved a light, effervescent tone that is still charming. Music brings out the jauntiness in Mickey's character just as the stream of gags establishes his humor. Although his appearance would evolve and his character soften, this was essentially the same Mickey who would get into trouble as the Sorcerer's Apprentice in *Fantasia* (1940, a Registry title), who would anchor the Disney studio, and who would go on to become one of the most famous characters in the world. And even at this stage the Disney grace notes, the touches that distinguished the studio's work from its competitors, are evident. The sheet music for "Turkey in the Straw" has a cornball "Hey! Hey!" scrawled on the cover, musical notes emerge from a goat's mouth (and fall to his feet), and at one point Mickey squeezes a duck or goose just like *Gus Visser and His Singing Duck* (1924–1926).

In later years, the studio would remove some thirty seconds of "objectionable" material from the cartoon (recent video releases have reinserted them). But it would always treat *Steamboat Willie* as the turning point in Disney's fortunes.

Fox Movietone News: Jenkins Orphanage Band

Fox Movietone News, 1928. Sound, B&W, 1.37. 11 minutes.

Credits: Photographed by Fox Movietone staff on November 22, 1928, Charleston, South Carolina.

Available: The Fox Movietone News Collection is housed at the University of South Carolina. *Jenkins Orphanage Band* can be viewed there during normal Newsfilm Library hours of operation. More information: *www.sc.edu/library/newsfilm*.

The line between representing and re-creating reality was often ignored by early filmmakers, who presented everything they filmed that wasn't fiction as "real." What we call actuality films today—travelogues, glimpses of celebrities, street scenes, sporting events—at one time dominated the industry.

As early as 1896, films were marketed as news in the same way the press publicized articles about current events. According to film historian Charles Musser, movies about the Spanish-American War, many of them faked, revived the film industry as a whole during a time of economic crisis. Prize fight films proved popular until they were outlawed in 1910. News films were especially profitable in Europe, particularly those by Pathé Frères, a company founded in France by Charles Pathé in 1895.

Historian Raymond Fielding credits the idea for newsreels to Leon Franconi, a Pathé translator stationed in the United States, who after seeing the inauguration of President William Howard Taft urged his employers to think about a weekly news magazine on film. *The Pathé Journal* came out between 1909 and 1910; it was followed quickly by an English version. Imitators like Leon Gaumont produced their own versions of newsreels.

Newsreels, probably Pathé releases imported from France, were screened in the United States by early 1911. The first newsreel to be produced in this country, *Pathé's Weekly*, was released on August 8, 1911. Lasting in one form or another until 1956, it would be the longest-running newsreel in the country. Pathé soon faced competition from Vitagraph, Mutual, and William Randolph Hearst, who attached his name to several film companies in a succession of distribution deals. Hearst is generally credited with first using the term *newsreel* commercially in 1917 (his company later tried to trademark the word).

The first issue of the *Fox News* came out on October 11, 1919. A by-product of William Fox's feature film studio, the newsreel department had a processing laboratory on 55th Street in Manhattan. By 1922, it was receiving 60,000 feet of film a week from 1,008 cameramen stationed around the world. In technical matters, Fox News may have been the most adventurous of the newsreel companies. It was the first to affiliate itself with a wire service, and it was the first to produce a newsreel with sound.

William Fox purchased a sound-on-film process from Theodore Case in 1926 (for more information, see *Theodore Case Sound Tests*, 1924–1926). The resulting Fox-Case Corporation decided to use newsreels to introduce the process to the public through its Fox Movietone Corporation, also formed in 1926. The first Movietone sound newsreel was released on January 21, 1927, but the one that caught the public's attention showed Charles Lindbergh's departure from Long Island on his historic flight to France. Equally important was a ten-minute film of Lindbergh's welcome home ceremony in Washington, D.C.

The first full-fledged Movietone sound newsreel, with four separate segments, came out in October, 1927. By December, the Movietone format had evolved into three sound segments that ranged from sports to celebrity interviews to staged incidents like groundbreaking ceremonies. For a piece on Benito Mussolini, Movietone producer Jack Connolly wrote out the politician's speech on cue cards, and coached his delivery.

The Movietone equipment was so bulky and heavy that it required special trucks to handle the camera, recorder, lights, and generator. Microphones at the time had a narrow range, limiting the kinds of subjects that could be filmed. Sound for a sporting event was often no more than the audience roaring. The search for viable subjects to film naturally led to musicians, but here Movietone faced competition from Vitaphone, which could shoot under controlled conditions on soundstages. Movietone cameramen therefore photographed glee clubs, marching bands, street performers, and other musicians and novelty acts on location.

In the first nine months of 1928, Movietone musical segments included the Pinto Pony Band from Kansas City; the U.S. Navy Band; John Philip Sousa at the Michigan State Fair; a children's band in Santa Barbara; Chee Wee the Singing Dog in Hollywood; and the Georgia Singers Glee Club. November saw films on Virginia banjo player Uncle John Scruggs and Asheville's "Mountaineer Minstrels." On November 21, Eddie Thomas and Carl Scott from Richmond, Virginia, performed on washboard and ukulele.

The following day, a Movietone truck filmed the Jenkins Orphanage Band in Charleston, South Carolina. The Reverend Daniel Jenkins formed the city's first orphanage for blacks in 1891, next to a prison. To purchase farmland, Jenkins organized a brass band, planning to tour the North to secure donations. After playing on the streets of Charleston, the band traveled to New York City and then to London. By 1896 it had a regular schedule of concerts, and within ten years was playing throughout Europe. In 1913, Jenkins formed a second band of apprentice musicians. Soon rival orphanages formed bands, including one in New Orleans that featured Louis Armstrong.

The Jenkins band played traditional brass band numbers by Sousa, but also cakewalks, rags, and, later, jazz. Several important musicians passed through the group, including Jabbo Smith, Cat Anderson, and Freddie Green. According to historian Julie Hubbert, the band started playing "geechie" song from the islands off the South Carolina coast in the 1920s. Derived from the Gullah culture, these songs often featured a dance by a musician. Pianist James P. Johnson turned one of these tunes into "The Charleston," igniting a dance craze that swept the nation. At the insistence of librettist DuBose Heyward, one of the Jenkins bands performed nightly in a production of *Porgy and Bess* on Broadway.

Hubbert believes that jazz historians may have underestimated the impact of the Jenkins Orphanage Band because it did not make professional recordings until the 1940s. The Fox Movietone footage provides a look both at how the band worked, and at how a newsreel segment was put together. Existing outtakes for the segment show how the Fox cinematographer filmed about ten separate shots of dancers, both children and adult. Shot silent, these would be incorporated into the sound material during editing.

With the microphone turned on, the Fox staff filmed the band performing a musical number from start to finish (a car drives past about halfway through the take). The band plays the same song again during the next shot, which pans across the seated front line of musicians and then back across

the second line. In the next set-up, a young boy enters to dance the Charleston. Subsequent takes focus on two young girls dancing, often half out of frame, to the cameraman's frustration. The band continues to play behind every take, each time a bit more listlessly.

When assembling the piece, the editor would have tried intercut the various close-ups and dancing shots with the "master" take. It must have been a tough assignment, as the lighting shifted considerably from the start of the shoot, and some of the younger performers were not that cooperative. In later films, Movietone workers devised several ways to cover up these technical problems, including adding "wild" tracks of ambient tone and sound effects, topped off with a voice-over narration.

The Wind

Metro-Goldwyn-Mayer, 1928. Silent, B&W, 1.33. 78 minutes.

Cast: Lillian Gish (Letty [Mason]), Lars Hanson (Lige [Hightower]), Montagu Love (Roddy [Wirt]), Dorothy Cumming (Cora), Edward Earle (Beverly), William Orlamond (Sourdough); Carmencita Johnson, Leon Ramon, Billy Kent Schaefer (Cora's children).

Credits: Directed by Victor Seastrom. Scenario by Frances Marion. From the Novel by Dorothy Scarborough. Titles by John Colton. Settings by Cedric Gibbons and Edward Withers. Wardrobe by André-Ani. Assistant director Harold S. Bucquet. Photographed by John Arnold. Film Editor: Conrad A. Nervig. A Metro-Goldwyn-Mayer presentation of a Victor Seastrom production.

Additional Credits: Director Victor Sjöström anglicized his name as Seastrom. Production dates: March 29 to May 24, 1927. Released November 23, 1928.

Available: Turner Entertainment Co. VHS (1989). UPC: 02761-61359-33.

When Lillian Gish left D.W. Griffith's company after *Orphans of the Storm* (1921), she was one of the most highly regarded actresses in the industry. Unhappy with her next two films, made for Inspiration Pictures, Gish signed a contract in 1925 with Nicholas Schenck at MGM to make six features. Anxious to procure an actress of her stature, the studio not only gave her control over her projects, but control over who would work on them. Gish chose King Vidor, fresh from his success with *The Big Parade* (1925), to direct her first MGM picture, an adaptation of Henri Murger's book *La Bohème* (1926). For her next film, she had Victor Sjöström direct her in *The Scarlet Letter*, adapted by Frances Marion from Nathaniel Hawthorne's novel. Gish was clearly aiming high, and at first MGM was delighted to show off such a distinguished actress in such glossy productions.

Unfortunately, Gish's films cost twice as much as standard MGM features, half of that money going to the actors, directors, and screenwriters before filming even started. What's worse, her films drew strong reviews but small audiences. Filmgoers seemed to prefer more contemporary stories, or perhaps stories with more modern heroines.

Although born in Sweden in 1879, Victor Sjöström spent some of his childhood in Brooklyn. On the death of his mother he returned to Sweden, then became a professional actor at the age of sixteen. He worked closely with Mauritz Stiller, making his screen debut in one of Stiller's films. But Sjöström became a director as well, gaining international notice with films like *The Outlaw and His Wife* (1918) and *The Phantom Chariot* (1921). When the Swedish film industry went into a decline in the 1920s, Sjöström signed with Samuel Goldwyn's studio. Sjöström therefore found himself under contract at MGM after Goldwyn merged with Metro.

In her autobiography, Gish has little to say about *Annie Laurie* or *The Enemy*, her next two MGM films to be released. But she goes into detail about the filming of *The Wind*, and referred to it in interviews as "[d]efinitely my most uncomfortable experience in pictures." Coming from someone who risked death on an ice floe in *Way Down East* (1920), that statement carries real weight.

Gish wrote that Dorothy Scarborough's novel excited her imagination. Scarborough was a teacher and folklorist in Texas as well as a novelist, and her book caused some controversy for its jaundiced view of frontier life. In it, an orphan from Virginia travels to her cousin's ranch, only to be forced into a marriage with her cousin's neighbor. When she murders a salesman who rapes her, she is driven insane. She is last seen wandering dazed into a prairie dust storm.

Although the story was set around Sweetwater, Texas, Gish and Sjöström decided to film in the Mojave Desert. Conditions there were horrendous. The heat melted the film's emulsion from its celluloid backing. Gish wrote that everyone wore goggles and bandanas to avoid the dust, that the skin on her hand burned off when she grabbed a door knob, and that her hair was ruined in the sun.

So much effort went into just getting the story on film that some of the nuances of the original novel were sacrificed. Screenwriter Frances Marion tended to reduce the settings and themes in *The Wind* to the same ideas found in typical Westerns of the time. There's a comic sidekick named Sourdough, a house party with hillbilly band, and the same sort of leering villain who appears in any Buck Jones B-movie. The central issue in the story is a familiar one as well: frightened, virginal bride; lusty husband; wedding night tears and recriminations. The wedding sequence here lasts over ten minutes, and it's excruciating to watch Gish play the same waif she enacted for Griffith almost fifteen years earlier, here trapped in a situation that becomes increasingly improbable and morose.

In his other films, Sjöström showed a real gift for using nature to comment on his characters' problems. The beginning of *The Wind* is focused and psychologically astute as well, especially in the interplay of a flirting Gish and a confident

Montagu Love aboard a train speeding across the prairie. But when Lars Hanson and William Orlamond start comparing pistols, the film sags under its symbolism. Further drawbacks were Sjöström's decision to shoot *The Wind* like a horror film, and his inability to stop Gish's tics and mannerisms.

Gish wrote that the initial version of *The Wind* "was the best film we had ever done," but Irving Thalberg must have cringed when he screened it. "We have a very artistic film," he told her, which she knew was a harsh criticism. Some writers blame Louis B. Mayer for forcing Sjöström and Gish to shoot a new, happy ending. In *Lion of Hollywood: The Life and Legend of Louis B. Mayer*, Scott Eyman points out that the novel's ending was never in any version of the script and was never shot. Nevertheless, "We all thought the happy ending was morally unjust," Gish said in an introduction to the film's re-issue on video. She did note that "One unhappy ending could ruin your career, and I had had seven." Whatever changes were made had little effect, as the film lost some $87,000.

In a time of flappers and vamps, of European imports and fresh-faced ingénues, Gish was losing her connection to her audience. What viewer would identify or sympathize with the characters she played, helpless women who could only accept or reject the advances of men? This was the last picture she made for MGM, and one of her last leading roles in movies. It was essentially the end of Sjöström's career in Hollywood as well. He made one more film in the United States before returning to Europe. Within a few years he had retired, although he directed a film for Twentieth Century Fox, *Under the Red Robe*, in 1937. Sjöström continued acting, and his last role, in Ingmar Bergman's *Wild Strawberries* (1957), is one of the landmark performances in world cinema.

The Fall of the House of Usher

James Sibley Watson, Jr., 1928. Silent, B&W, 1.33. 13 minutes.
Cast: Herbert Stern (Roderick Usher), Hildegarde Watson (Madeline Usher), Melville Webber (A traveller).
Credits: Produced and directed by James Sibley Watson, Melville Webber. Screenplay by James Sibley Watson, Melville Webber, e.e. cummings. Based on the story by Edgar Allan Poe. Cinematography: James Sibley Watson. Set design: Melville Webber.
Additional Credits: Premiered February 1, 1929.
Other Versions: *La Chute de la maison Usher* (1928, directed by Jean Epstein), *House of Usher* (1960, directed by Roger Corman), *The House of Usher* (1988, directed by Alan Birkinshaw), *Usher* (2002, directed by Curtis Harrington).

Available: Image Entertainment DVD *Treasures from American Film Archives* (2000). UPC: 0-14381-9706-2-3. Image Entertainment DVD *Unseen Cinema: Early American Avant-Garde Film 1894–1941* (2005). UPC: 0-14381-0592-2-9.

By the late 1920s, the film industry was over thirty years old. Its production and distribution methods had been established on the same principles used by factories and other entertainment media, with some room for marketing innovations and technological advances. As a filmmaker, if you were not part of the system, you had almost no chance of finding an audience.

But as film historian Jan-Christopher Horak has detailed, the 1920s saw a growing "amateur" market, one distinct from the home movies that were also becoming more common. Amateurs showed their work in film clubs and art galleries, and wrote manifestos and how-to articles in magazines like *Movie Makers* and *Creative Art*. For some, the goal was to crack the code of the Hollywood system. Robert Florey (*The Life and Death of 9413 A Hollywood Extra*, 1928) made films that on the surface critiqued mainstream movies, but that also served as calling cards, proof that he could deliver a product on a tiny budget. Because the first thing that amateurs discovered was that filmmaking was an incredibly expensive process. As James Sibley Watson, Jr., wrote, "The amateur who tries to compete with the professional producer *on his own ground* is licked from the start by lamps, scenery, and other expensive methods of control."

Born in 1894, Watson had a privileged upbringing. After graduating from medical school, he became interested in filmmaking and began researching related areas, such as optics and X-rays. In 1919, he and his friend Scofield Thayer purchased the magazine *The Dial* from Martyn Johnson. Once edited by transcendentalist Ralph Waldo Emerson, *The Dial* emerged as a literary magazine in January 1920. Its first issue featured works by e.e. cummings and Carl Sandburg. Subsequent issues championed the writings of Edgar Allan Poe while providing a forum for writers as influential as Ezra Pound and T.S. Eliot.

Watson became a member of the board of directors of Eastman Kodak, whose headquarters were located in Rochester, New York. That is where he met Melville Webber, an archeologist and painter who was born in 1895. A bomber pilot during World War I, Webber then taught at Ohio State University, got his master's degree at Harvard, and studied in France before teaching art at the University of Rochester.

Having contributed to *The Dial*, cummings subsequently penned a screenplay for "The Fall of the House of Usher," a story first published in *Burton's Magazine* in 1839. One of Poe's most famous works, it described a visit by an unnamed narrator to the Usher castle, where Roderick and his twin sister Madeline live in illness and gloom. Roderick and the narrator entomb the still-living Madeline;

her escape precipitates the collapse of both the Usher residence and its family tree.

Watson and Webber approached filmmaking as a collaboration, fashioning their own script, one that referred, however obliquely, to new theories about the psychological underpinnings to Poe's work. They were deeply influenced by German expressionist film, in particular *The Cabinet of Dr. Caligari* (1920), whose foreshortened sets and angled compositions forever changed the design of movies. They may also have seen works by F.W. Murnau, in which eerie atmosphere often overwhelmed narratives. The duo worked on their film for two years—in Watson's words, shooting most of it in an empty stable. While Webber designed sets and costumes, Watson built his own optical printer that enabled him to employ sophisticated dissolves and wipes. He wrote later that almost all of the film's seventy scenes were shot three or more times. Watson's wife Hildegarde played the doomed Madeline, while Webber became the mysterious traveler.

The final version had no explanatory intertitles, and made no attempt to provide a context for viewers, who were assumed to be familiar with the original story. As film historian Eileen Bowser wrote, "Its sets and effects dominate over the actors and its atmosphere of doom is the whole meaning of the film."

But even those who had read the story might not have understood what Watson and Webber meant by their shots and editing. As with *Rip Van Winkle* (1896), the intent of the filmmakers here is often obscure. Is their representation of the narrative, founded as it is on artistic and intellectual principles, useless if viewers can't comprehend it? This became the core dilemma in abstract filmmaking, and even Watson seemed to lean on a more accessible narrative approach in his subsequent work.

Conversely, realizing that they couldn't compete with Hollywood production values, filmmakers could choose deliberately subversive subjects for their shock value. (It was a tactic employed by generations of subsequent writers and directors, such as Roger Corman, whose 1960 *House of Usher* is also on the Registry.) Horror, sex, and mockery—Watson tried all three approaches, with varying success. Webber worked with Watson on *Lot in Sodom* (1933); its nudity and sexual suggestiveness made it an art-house favorite for years. But they also collaborated on *The Eyes of Science*

(1930), a sponsored film about Bausch & Lomb lenses (who supplied the prisms and other optics for *The Fall of the House of Usher*).

The Fall of the House of Usher had its first public showing on February 1, 1929, at the Film Arts Guild. Webber later collaborated with Mary Ellen Bute and Ted Nemeth on abstract films in New York City. Watson collaborated with Kenneth R. Edwards on *Highlights and Shadows* (1938), an hour-long promotional film for Kodak.

Big Business

Metro-Goldywn-Mayer, 1929. Silent, B&W, 1.33. 18 minutes.

Cast: Stan Laurel, Oliver Hardy.

Credits: Directed by J. Wesley Horne [James W. Horne]. Supervising director: Leo McCarey. Director of photography: George Stevens. Edited by Richard Currier. Titles by H.M. Walker. A Hal Roach presentation.

Additional Cast: James Finlayson (Homeowner), Stanley (Tiny) Sandford (Policeman), Lyle Tayo (Customer with no husband); Retta Palmer, Charlie Hall (Onlookers).

Additional Credits: Produced at Hal Roach Studios. Production dates: December 18 to 26, 1928. Released April 20, 1929.

Available: Image Entertainment DVD *Slapstick Masters* (2003). UPC: 014381189728.

Few comedy teams have as devoted a following as Laurel and Hardy. Stan Laurel was born Arthur Stanley Jefferson in England in 1890, the son of show business veterans. He appeared onstage as a comedian while still a teenager, and later joined the Fred Karno Company, a group of acrobats and knockabout comics. Laurel roomed with Karno colleague Charlie Chaplin during a 1912 tour of the United States, and like Chaplin decided to remain. He tried vaudeville, made some short comedies, then toured with his common-law wife, Mae Dahlberg. Laurel continued to appear in film, making some popular parodies of hit movies and developing the "Hickory Hiram" character.

When Dahlberg moved to Australia, Laurel took a job with Hal Roach as a gag writer and director. Roach shuffled his large stable of writers and performers about from short to short, trying to duplicate the success of his earlier discoveries like Harold Lloyd and Our Gang. Among the performers was Oliver Norvell Hardy, better known as "Babe." Born in Georgia in 1892, he had some success as a boy soprano before opening his own movie theater in 1910. In Florida he found work as an extra with the Lubin company, eventually moving to California to play heavies and sidekicks in several shorts and features.

Laurel and Hardy had actually worked together in 1917 in *Lucky Dog*, but not as a team. They coincidentally appeared together in some shorts, gradually developing a unique rhythm and style before Roach decided to center films around them. Their characters had not yet been established in their first official film, *Putting Pants on Philip* (1927). But within weeks they had distinctive personalities. Both were impulsive, immature, and unworldly. Hardy was irritable and blustering; Laurel sweet-natured but prone to hysteria. They dressed alike, either in denim overalls or in bowler hats and bow ties.

Film historian Leonard Maltin cites Leo McCarey as the most significant creative force behind the team, quoting cameraman and future director George Stevens: "I think more than anyone else Leo McCarey designed it, because they were doing entirely different kinds of things." McCarey was an expert in prolonging tension in comedy, in delaying punchlines and in building laughs through anticipation. Many other comedians were still relying on Mack Sennett formulas, tearing through material in order to get to a chaotic, free-for-all climax. Under McCarey's guidance, Laurel and Hardy slowed their routines down to a crawl, blissfully unaware of the disasters that viewers knew were awaiting them.

McCarey was also a master of upping the ante on jokes, of pushing a situation to catastrophic but still somehow logical conclusions. In *The Battle of the Century* (1927) he placed Laurel and Hardy in the middle of one of the largest pie fights ever filmed, the result of a single misplaced banana peel. In *Two Tars*, the boys find themselves in a traffic jam that turns into a melee. In *Liberty* (1929), searching for a modest place to change pants leads them to the top of a skyscraper under construction.

The plot of *Big Business* is one of the team's best recipes for disaster as they try to sell Christmas trees in sunny, parched Los Angeles. They receive crucial support from longtime collaborator James Finlayson as an irate customer and from Roach stalwart Tiny Sandford, who plays a remarkably patient cop. As the story progresses, and the destruction mounts, the film feels as if it's one broken vase away from chaos. McCarey stages the slapstick calmly, expertly, simultaneously increasing the stakes while keeping a rein on his characters. Some of the best laughs in *Big Business* come from reaction shots, although in this case it's the lack of a reaction that is so compelling. In fact, the stunned disbelief on the faces of just about everyone in the cast at one point or another could be the real key to the film's success.

Director James Horne was born in San Francisco in 1881. From working on the stage, he joined Kalem in 1912 as an actor and scenario editor, turning to directing in 1915. In the 1920s he was a respected action and comedy director. *Big Business* was the first of twelve movies he helmed for Laurel and Hardy. Most accounts credit Laurel for the small touches that help prolong the laughter—his fluttering hands, for example, or Hardy's withering, baleful glares at the camera. Laurel was

also most likely responsible for the timing of jokes during production. It's easy to spot the team's influence on subsequent films by McCarey (*The Awful Truth*, 1937) and Stevens (*Swing Time*, 1936).

The film was one of an amazing twenty-three shorts the team made between 1928 and 1929. Laurel and Hardy's films were so popular that they were often billed larger in newspaper ads than the features they supported. Because their act relied on timing—really on pauses more than on physical slapstick—they made an almost seamless adjustment to sound. If anything, Hardy's growl and Laurel's whine suited their characters perfectly. By the early 1930s they began appearing in feature-length movies, including some ill-advised operettas that diluted their impact. But they continued to make shorts, such as the Registry title *The Music Box* (1932).

Hallelujah

Metro-Goldwyn-Mayer, 1929. Sound, B&W, 1.37. 100 minutes.
Cast: Daniel L. Haynes (Zeke), Nina Mae McKinney (Chick), William Fountaine (Hot Shot), Harry Gray (Parson), Fanny Belle DeKnight (Mammy), Everett McGarrity (Spunk), Victoria Spivey (Missy Rose); Milton Dickerson, Robert Couch, Walter Tait (Johnson kids); Dixie Jubilee Singers.
Credits: Story and direction by King Vidor. Scenario by Wanda Tuchock. Treatment by Richard Schayer. Dialogue by Ransom Rideout. Recording engineer: Douglas Shearer. Art director: Cedric Gibbons. Wardrobe by Henrietta Frazer. Assistant director: Robert A. Golden. Photographed by Gordon Avil. Film editor: Hugh Wynn. Western Electric sound system.
Additional Credits: Produced by King Vidor, Irving Thalberg. Assistant director: Harold Garrison. Titles for silent version: Marian Ainslee. Songs "Waiting at the End of the Road" and "Swanee Shuffle" by Irving Berlin. Production dates: October 23, 1928 to January 14, 1929. Released August 29, 1929. Nine minutes deleted for the 1939 reissue; this is the current circulating version.
Available: Warner Home Video DVD (2006). ISBN: 1-4198-1712-4. UPC: 0-12569-67676-3.

His career as a director relatively secure after the success of *The Big Parade* (1925), King Vidor alternated between making personal films like *The Crowd* (1928) and more commercial vehicles like *Show People* (1928). (All three are Registry titles.) Vidor envisioned what he originally called *The Negro Story* as a message drama, one based on his experiences growing up in Texas. Eventually titled *Hallelujah*, Vidor's story concerned a sharecropping family whose eldest son is tempted into crime by a honky-tonk singer and dancer. To a certain extent Vidor was drawing on his own relationships: in real life he was in the process of leaving his wife Eleanor Boardman for Wanda Tuchock, a writer who had worked on *Show People* and would receive a writing credit here.

Vidor saw his story in terms of a folk ballad or blues tune, one that fleshed out archetypes with back stories and authentic locations. He later told interviewers that Louis B. Mayer and Irving Thalberg were dead set against a film with an all-black cast, worried about losing the Southern market. Vidor got approval from their boss Nicholas Schenck only after deferring his $100,000 salary.

Budget approval was just the first of several problems Vidor faced. The director scouted locations in Beaumont, Texas, before shooting in Mississippi and Tennessee. He had hoped to cast Paul Robeson as Zeke, the cotton farmer who becomes a preacher out of remorse over his drinking and gambling, but the star turned him down. Vidor hired the next best thing, Daniel L. Haynes, Robeson's understudy in *Show Boat*. He cast Honey Brown, a dancer in *The Blackbirds of 1928*, in the pivotal role of Chick, the woman who brings about Zeke's downfall. Thalberg was not impressed, preferring Nina Mae McKinney, another *Blackbirds* dancer. Vidor used them both, shooting two versions of their location scenes.

Filming began on October 23, 1928, just as the industry was undergoing a major push to sound technology. Just three months earlier, Vidor had told *Motion Picture News*, "Sound pictures, those with dialogue that runs continuously, will do away entirely with the art of motion pictures."

Now he was trying to figure out how to use sound himself: how to gauge the pacing and length of scenes, how to determine what sound effects to use, even how to frame and shoot his actors. He wasn't sure if MGM would be using Western Electric or Movietone equipment, competing processes that required different aspect ratios.

Vidor used silent techniques on location, postponing technical choices until he returned to Los Angeles in November. (By that time MGM had completed its first sound stage. The studio eventually went with the Western Electric sound-on-disc method, which could explain some of Vidor's more awkwardly composed shots.) Vidor finally fired Honey Brown toward the end of November, some six weeks before he finished filming. He had tremendous difficulty synchronizing sound to picture, in part because sound was filmed at a different speed, but also because he neglected to note the dialogue as he was filming, and because he was working with largely untrained actors.

On a technical level, some of what Vidor achieved was remarkable. He shot at difficult locations, such as a working cotton gin and a riverside revival meeting; recorded sound from several sources, including crowd scenes and musical groups; and devised elaborate camera movements, in particular a traveling shot from a wagon working its way down a main street at night, the music shifting as it passes several bars. At one point he uses the song "Going Home" as a transitional device, having Zeke sing it during a travel montage, a strategy that would be adopted throughout the industry.

Like many directors adjusting to sound, Vidor had trouble determining what worked and what didn't, what was clear or confusing, what was too much or not enough. He drags out one death scene for over two minutes, even though the scene is essentially done after a few seconds. People talk when they don't have to, and they talk at length, spelling out feelings and stage directions that are already obvious. The climactic chase goes on forever, with none of the sense of pacing Vidor brought to the death march in *The Big Parade*. At times it's as if Vidor has forgotten the film vocabulary he developed in his silent movies.

An even greater drawback to *Hallelujah* is Vidor's script, worked on by several other writers but basically the director's vision. Vidor depicts the blacks in his film as childlike, with simple appetites and pleasures, unaware of the world at large or the forces keeping them in check. They speak in a fake dialect derived from minstrel shows, blues songs, and plays like *Show Boat*. "I believe you sure is right, Mammy," Zeke drawls early in the film, and the line is as grating as Haynes' delivery of it.

They also behave with an appalling lack of common sense, or memory. What may seem elemental, even inevitable, in the lyrics of a song like "Frankie and Johnnie" looks much different when acted out as slowly and as obviously as it is here. Vidor later regretted his condescending tone, but it's not clear that given the chance he could have improved this far-fetched and repetitive plot.

Vidor's direction falters with many of the performers. Of the cast, only Nina Mae McKinney made much of an impact later. She received a contract from MGM, filmed two musical shorts for Vitaphone, and had specialty numbers in several features. She also costarred with Paul Robeson in *Sanders of the River* (1935). Three years later she began appearing in "race" films produced for the African-American market. This was Victoria Spivey's only feature credit. A blues singer from Texas who started recording in 1926, Spivey played a prominent role in the folk revival of the late 1950s. She was backed by Bob Dylan on her first Spivey Records album, released in 1962.

Hallelujah turned a respectable profit, although it was not the hit Vidor had hoped for. Apart from 1934's *Our Daily Bread*, the director rarely attempted so personal a project again. The film was criticized by some members of the black community, including Robeson, who "loathed" it, according to film historian Scott Eyman. Its reputation is based largely on the fact that it was made at all; some also feel that it is more sincere and ambitious than *Hearts in Dixie*, an all-black film released that March by Fox. *St. Louis Blues*, a Registry title released less than a month after *Hallelujah*, displays a markedly more sophisticated vision of African-American culture.

St. Louis Blues

St. Louis Blues: The great Bessie Smith in her only filmed performance.

RKO, 1929. Sound, B&W, 1.37. 17 minutes.

Cast: Bessie Smith, Jimmy Mordecai, Isabel Washington.

Credits: Story and direction by Dudley Murphy. Choral Arrangements by W.C. Handy and Rosamond Johnson. Cinematographer: Walter Strenge. Edited by Russell Shields. Recordist: George Oschmann. Produced at Gramercy Studio of RCA Photophone, Inc. under the supervision of Dick Currier. Music by W.C. Handy.

Additional Cast: James P. Johnson (piano), Thomas Morris (cornet), Joe Smith (cornet), Hall Johnson Choir, Alec Lovejoy, Shingzie Howard, Johnny Lee.

Additional Credits: Production dates: June 1929. Released September 8, 1929.

Available: Kino Video DVD *Hollywood Rhythm: The Paramount Musical Shorts Volume 1* (2001). UPC: 7-38329-019/2-3.

Techniques for making sound films matured considerably in the three years after Vitaphone was introduced to moviegoers in 1926. Microphones were more sensitive, cameramen returned to tracking and crane shots, and editors could insert close-ups and reaction shots without disturbing the soundtrack. Writers and directors became more adventurous as well. The earliest sound shorts simply recorded performances and were filmed on basic sets. By 1929, some writers would concoct elaborate narrative frames for musical numbers, and directors tried to capture atmosphere as well as the basic work of musicians.

As sound processes spread to more and more theaters, the audience for sound films widened as well. Where the opening Vitaphone program consisted almost exclusively of classical musicians, by 1929, films featured jazz, folk, Western, and Hawaiian styles. It was a market ripe for exploitation, and the major studios vied with each other in attracting vaudeville and nightclub stars before the cameras.

Accounts differ over the genesis of *St. Louis Blues*. According to Bessie Smith's biographer Chris Albertson, W.C. Handy and Kenneth G. Adams wrote a scenario for a short musical which they submitted to RKO, a new studio formed from the FBO studio and the Keith-Albee-Orpheum chain of vaudeville theaters. RKO then assigned the project to director Dudley Murphy, a holdover from FBO. But as Murphy put it in his unpublished memoir, he acquired the rights to Handy's "St. Louis Blues," and persuaded the songwriter to create a special arrangement of the piece. "I got Bessie Smith, the greatest blues singer of all times, to play the part of the St. Louis Woman," Murphy went on, "and wrote a story for the film, suggested by the lyric."

Supporting Murphy's version is the fact that he had been working for years as a writer, producer, and director, specializing in visual interpretations of classical pieces like Debussy's *Prelude to the Afternoon of a Faun*. Along with Fernand Léger, he codirected *Ballet mécanique* (1924), a celebrated experimental short set to music by George Antheil. Murphy's interests took him from collaborations with William Faulkner and Ezra

Pound to casting Bing Crosby in an early musical, and he ranged from bohemian Greenwich Village to Harlem nightclubs, Hollywood, and Paris.

Murphy had trouble finding a stable position within the industry. He worked as an assistant director to Rex Ingram on *Mare Nostrum* (1926), and sold some scripts that were turned into silent comedies. But in 1928, he was renting his personal print of *Ballet mécanique* for $100 a screening to help make ends meet. FBO, soon to be RKO, made a deal with Robert Florey to distribute *The Life and Death of 9413 A Hollywood Extra* (1928, a Registry title), and may have done something similar with Murphy. He wrote and directed two comedies starring "Skeets" Gallagher for FBO that same year, but the new RKO regime put an end to the theatrical distribution of experimental shorts.

Instead, Murphy was hired by playwright Marc Connelly, one of his Algonquin Round Table friends, to film two short sound skits, released by RKO in 1929. He also sold a script for the feature *Jazz Heaven* to the studio. So he was in an excellent position to propose filming a sound short based on "St. Louis Blues." Handy had written the song in 1914, two years after his influential "Memphis Blues," and it was recorded as early as December 1915. By the 1920s it was one of the most popular numbers in the jazz repertoire. In 1925, Bessie Smith recorded what is considered the definitive version, with Louis Armstrong on trumpet and Fred Longshaw on harmonium.

Smith was born in Chattanooga, Tennessee, in 1894, where according to legend she was discovered at the age of eleven by blues singer Ma Rainey. She originally made her mark as a dancer, and throughout her career as a singer she was famous for her strong stage presence. Starting in 1923, she recorded 160 songs for Columbia Records, including some of the finest blues performances ever released. Yet Smith was an inconsistent artist, indifferent about many aspects of her career. She had just made her Broadway debut in a musical roundly panned by critics when the opportunity to make *St. Louis Blues* arose.

Unlike many mainstream filmmakers, Murphy was fully aware of Smith's prominence, and he presented her as a star of great magnitude. The story concocted for the film involves an unfaithful dancer (Jimmy Mordecai), his not-so-secret mistress (Isabel Washington), and Smith as his forlorn and desperate lover. Murphy opens the film with a craps game in a tenement hallway, and within minutes has Mordecai cheating on and beating Smith. She turns to liquor, leading to a performance of the song in a Harlem nightclub, complete with members of Fletcher Henderson's orchestra, the Hall Johnson Choir and an off-screen string section.

Murphy doesn't try to elaborate on the lyrics: this isn't an illustrated, follow-the-bouncing-ball version of the song. In fact, once the director establishes the premise and setting, he leaves the film in the hands of Smith and the tune itself. Murphy shot with four cameras, including one with a close-up lens that resulted in some extremely affecting compositions. Smith was filmed primarily in medium shots that caught her facial expressions as well as the way she moved her body. (They also made it clear she was singing live.) To increase impact, Murphy occasionally moved the camera away from or towards the characters, a technically demanding procedure at the time.

Most sources say the film was shot on a soundstage in Astoria, Queens, but biographer Susan Delson cites a letter from Murphy to Eugene O'Neill describing "a state-of-the-art sound studio in a converted stable near Gramercy Park at 149 E. Twenty-Fourth Street" built by RCA. Murphy wrote that he rehearsed in Harlem before bringing the cast and musicians downtown: "I gave them beer to drink while we set up the cameras and rehearsed in the studio." He had planned to cast Fredi Washington as the other woman, but she was unavailable. Instead, he used her sister Isabel, a chorus dancer who would become the wife of Adam Clayton Powell, Jr.

St. Louis Blues received mixed reviews, but it was popular enough to merit its own advertising in both trade and mainstream press. Murphy next directed *Black and Tan*, an ambitious short featuring Duke Ellington and his orchestra. Murphy's work may have been an important influence on *Applause* (1929), the Rouben Mamoulian musical that came out a few months later.

This is the only film footage of Bessie Smith, who died after a car accident in 1937. For years it was rumored to be lost. The one version that became readily available was an inferior copy re-released by Alfred N. Sack. Murphy's own print, kept with his papers, is of a much higher quality. His adaptation of *The Emperor Jones* (1934) is also on the Registry.

Lambchops

Warner Brothers, 1929. Sound, B&W, 1.33. 8 minutes.

Cast: Burns & Allen [George Burns, Gracie Allen] (themselves).

Credits: Presented by Vitaphone, a subsidiary of Warner Brothers Pictures, Inc. Produced with Western Electric apparatus.

Additional Credits: Possibly directed by Murray Roth. Written by George Burns, Al Boasberg. Song, "Do You Believe Me," by Benny Davis. Released October 1929.

Available: Warner Home Video DVD, *The Jazz Singer* (2007). ISBN: 1-2198-5622-7. UPC: 0-12569-79889-2.

Sound films first became a viable commercial product with the Vitaphone process, described in more detail in the entry for *The Jazz Singer* (1927). To exploit the process, Warner Brothers purchased Vitagraph Studios, which had facilities in Los Angeles and in Brooklyn. On May 24, 1926, at the Manhattan Opera House, they began filming the first Vitaphone short, *The Song of the Volga Boatmen.*

Recording sound on discs required a stable, dust-free environment. Shooting on exterior locations was impossible. Recorders were so primitive that actors couldn't move more than about five feet from the fixed, unidirectional microphones. Post-dubbing and lip-synching had yet to be discovered. A flubbed line, a missed cue, or any other mistake meant that the performers had to start over again from the beginning.

Recording picked up the sound of the motors running the cameras, so cameras had to be enclosed in soundproof booths. As a result, cinematographers could no longer dolly or track, and pans were limited. Editing techniques used in silent films were now out of the question. Establishing shots, reaction shots, inserts, and other devices had to be eliminated. The first solution was to film with multiple cameras, one in a fixed wide shot, the others isolating performers in close-ups.

Vitaphone filmmakers naturally gravitated to musicians, especially those with stage experience, branching out to include comedians and specialty acts. These early Vitaphone performers essentially reenact their stage shows. Performing in a vacuum, without the feedback of a live audience, some seem lost, waiting for reactions that never occur. They don't know which way to look, at times gazing into an indeterminate middle distance.

Audiences of the time could care less about Vitaphone's drawbacks. For many this was their first opportunity to see these performers. The Warners quickly shifted from classical to more popular acts, filming them in Los Angeles by 1927

and back in Brooklyn by 1928. A musician like Roy Smeck might get $350 for a short; Van and Schenck, popular headliners, received $10,000. Fanny Brice, Sophie Tucker, and several jazz bands made films. More than a hundred were shot in the first quarter of 1929.

In August 1929, comedian Fred Allen was scheduled to film a short of his original material. When he had to cancel, the team of Burns & Allen replaced him, using the living room set that had already been built. Burns & Allen had not been a team for very long. New York City native George Burns was born Nathan Birnbaum in 1896. The ninth of twelve children, he was dancing on street corners by the age of seven. He worked without success in several vaudeville acts until he met Gracie Allen in 1923. She was born in San Francisco in anywhere from 1895 to 1906 (her birth records were lost in the 1906 earthquake). The daughter of an Irish clog dancer who abandoned the family when she was five, Allen went to dance school and appeared in an act with her sisters called "The Four Colleens." She quit a dramatic act in Hoboken, New Jersey, then agreed to partner with Burns in what he called "a simple flirtation act."

After opening in Newark, New Jersey, Burns & Allen refined their act, which he called "Dizzy," on the road. First they switched roles: he became the straight man because she was winning more laughs. Allen played a "Dumb Dora," a stock vaudeville figure, the equivalent of a "dumb blonde." It was a difficult part, because she had to appear foolish but still outwit audiences with her punchlines. "What made Gracie different was her sincerity," according to Burns. "She didn't try to be funny." Like their friends and colleagues Jack Benny and Fred Allen, Burns & Allen made the audience a part of their appearances, even to the point of addressing the people in theaters and commenting on the apparatus surrounding their act.

By 1924, they had what Burns called a successful "disappointment act," able to fill in on short notice for performers who fell sick. After touring on the Orpheum circuit, Burns and gag writer Al Boasberg prepared a new skit, "Lamb Chops." They introduced this after Burns wed Allen in January, 1926. For the first time they brought in references to Gracie's relatives, the source of much of their humor in later years. Their two skits resulted in a five-year contract with Keith-Orpheum, as well as a tour of England in 1928.

But talking pictures and radio were death knells for vaudeville. "Gracie and I had the perfect act for radio," Burns wrote. "We talked." (By the mid-1930s they had one of the top-rated shows on the airwaves.) They were also ideally suited for film, requiring not much more than a camera and a microphone to push their act across. For their debut, Burns cut "Lamb Chops" roughly in half to fit the running time for a one-reel Vitaphone short. Burns remembered the director as "an old friend of mine from the Lower East Side, Murray Roth," but he also wrote that *Lambchops* was filmed for Paramount on their Astoria, Queens, soundstages. (Roth did direct the postponed *Fred Allen's Prize Playlets* a month later.)

Shot with two cameras, *Lambchops* provides a glimpse into the heart of vaudeville, circa 1929. Burns and Allen trade a few corny jokes, sing "Do You Believe Me," dance a little, and refer directly to the camera as the audience. "The film allowed us to see ourselves performing for the very first time," Burns wrote, and in fact they modified their act in subsequent films, becoming more conscious of where the camera was, for example. (In much of *Lambchops*, Burns inadvertently obscures his profile.) They signed a contract with Paramount, making $3,500 per short when they had been earning $600 for twelve shows a week. But, writing about their radio performances, Burns noted, "On one show we'd done about half our act; we still had half an act left and only twenty years to fill."

Vaudevillians who had honed their material over the years, nursing it through appearances across the country, might get one chance to film a Vitaphone short. Then what? Few had additional material prepared. For comedians, the need for new jokes became imperative, leading to the formation of writing staffs. Burns & Allen made the problem of mounting shows the centerpiece of their act (as did their friend Jack Benny). On radio and later on television, Burns would discuss the variables of performing with his audience, deconstructing his act before the term was in vogue.

Warners closed the Vitaphone studio in Brooklyn in 1940. In the 1950s, as the studio became more involved in television production, it ceased making Vitaphone shorts altogether. Remnants of the Vitaphone style can still be seen today in music videos and television sitcoms.

Applause

Paramount, 1929. Sound, B&W, 1.37. 78 minutes.
Cast: Helen Morgan (Kitty Darling), Joan Peers (April Darling), Fuller Mellish, Jr. (Hitch Nelson), Jack Cameron (Joe King), Henry Wadsworth (Tony), Dorothy Cumming (Mother Superior), Jack Singer (Dave Holt).
Credits: Directed by Rouben Mamoulian. Story by Beth Brown. Adapted by Garrett Fort. Produced by Monta Bell. Photographed by George Folsey. Western Electric System. Presented by Adolph Zukor and Jesse L. Lasky.
Additional Cast: Mary Gertrude Homes (April Darling as a child), Mack Gray (Eddie Lamont), Roy Hargrove (Slim Lamont), William Stephens (Gus Feinbaum); Florence Dickerson, Lotta Burnell, Madge McLaughlin, June Taylor, Alice Clayton, Claire Rose, May Miller, F. Thomas, Viola Gallo, Sally Panzer, Billie Bernard, Phyliss Bolce, Lois Winters, E. Graniss, Estelle Valentine, A. Stewart (Beef Trust).
Additional Credits: Edited by John Bassler. Sound by Ernest F. Zatorsky. Songs include: "Give Your Little Baby Lots of Loving," by Dolly Morse and Joe Burke; "What Wouldn't I Do for That Man!" by Jay Gorney and E.Y. Harburg. Premiered in New York City on October 7, 1929.
Available: Kino Video DVD (2003). UPC: 7-38329-03232-6.

A box-office disappointment on its release, *Applause* may have failed to find an audience, but it did impress filmmakers who were still grappling with the requirements of shooting with sound. One of a raft of backstage musicals released during the transition to sound, *Applause* was by far the most sordid and depressing—but it was photographed with a freedom that approached anarchy.

The film was based on a 1928 novel by Beth Brown, author of melodramas with show-business settings and once a carnival dancer herself. (She later specialized in anthologies about pets.) Paramount purchased the rights in March 1929 as a possible vehicle for Mae West, but two months later Helen Morgan signed on as the star at $5,000 a week. Morgan was born in South Danville, Illinois, in 1902. Her parents divorced when she was a child, and her first stepfather was later jailed for manslaughter. Morgan became a model, entered a 1923 Miss Montreal contest (she was disqualified because she was American), then moved to Chicago to live with her mother. There she became enough of a celebrity as a nightclub singer to earn a spot in *George White's Scandals of 1925*.

Morgan became one of the premier torch singers in the country, often performing perched atop a piano. At one point four New York City nightclubs were named after her. Although she had no training as an actress, she was offered the

Helen Morgan as Kitty Darling in *Applause*.

part of Julie in the stage *Show Boat*. She delivered definitive versions of "Bill" and "Can't Help Lovin Dat Man," which she also sang in both the 1929 and 1936 film adaptations.

The part of Kitty Darling in *Applause* could have been seen as a variation on Julie in *Show Boat*, or as a fictional account of incidents Morgan had experienced herself. She threw herself enthusiastically into the role, gaining weight and donning a frowsy blonde wig to fit the forty-five-year-old character (Morgan was twenty-six at the time). She gave an incendiary but also largely undisciplined performance that would have dominated any other film of the period.

But *Applause* was also being directed by Rouben Mamoulian, one of the theatrical professionals rounded up by Paramount to help make sound movies. Born in Tiflis, now Tbilisi, Georgia, in 1897, he was a banker's son who studied physics before turning to drama. Rhythm became one of the guiding principles in his career: "Rhythm can have a great power: if it can destroy, it can also build," he wrote. He was recommended by a Russian tenor to George Eastman, who got him a job at The Eastman School at the University of Rochester. English became his seventh language.

Mamoulian failed in a later attempt to establish a dancing school, but was hired by the Theatre Guild to teach drama and, in 1926, to direct *Porgy*. It was a groundbreaking production, not just for DuBose Heyward's book, but for Mamoulian's lighting and staging. Influenced by Stanislavsky, he broke scenes down into beats, and timed every action on the stage to a count. (He would use a similar technique in the 1932 film *Love Me Tonight*.)

Walter Wanger offered Mamoulian a job as a dialogue director at the Paramount studios on Long Island. He spent weeks wandering around sets, observing productions and boning up on film technique. Then he told a bemused Adolph Zukor that he was willing to direct *Applause* for the studio.

In later interviews, Mamoulian described persistent arguments with cinematographer George Folsey about whether or not the camera, trapped inside a soundproof box, could move to follow action. Eventually he had the booth placed on wheels, enabling production assistants to roll it across and through sets. He also fought for two-channel sound, threatening to quit unless he could use two microphones and mix the sound later. Other battles included convincing the wardrobe department to let Morgan appear tattered and bedraggled, and filming on location in Penn Station and the New York subway system.

The very first shot in the film pulls back from a close-up of a store sign to show a grimy, deserted street; on the soundtrack, we can faintly hear a band playing "Hot Time in the Old Town Tonight." At the time it was a startling effect; today, it's hard to overlook how the frame shakes each time the camera turns, or how the lens frequently loses focus. Mamoulian likes his camera to move, whether it needs to or not. Even when it is stationary, it's placed in bizarre locations: behind a pillar in a theater, looking up from a pallet where Kitty had just given birth, looking down on a lecherous comic as he tries to molest Kitty's daughter. The director tried to use sound in as innovative a fashion as the camera. During the sequence at

Penn Station, for example, he had technicians create a fake soundtrack of traffic and crowd noises. Manufactured sound effects like these would soon become an industry standard.

The energy in *Applause* is contagious, if unfocused. Something is always happening, and even if it doesn't make much sense, it's staged in a striking manner. On the minus side, the plot is a tired retread of ideas from *Show Boat*, jammed into morbid, squalid settings, with actors delivering interminable speeches in an old-fashioned, declamatory style. *Applause* is also a musical with almost no music. Morgan gets only two full-fledged production numbers, and she goes into labor during one of them. Immensely appealing during individual songs, she is harder to take over extended lengths as a none-too-bright martyr.

Mamoulian was one of the most outspoken figures in the industry. "No matter how you put it, films for a director are autobiographical," he once wrote. "Films are not as much a reflection of life, as a revelation of life." In another article, he said, "The main *theme* in my films: *Man can overcome* the world and embrace truth." Unfortunately, *Applause* was such a disaster at the box office that it apparently did not receive a full release, skipping Philadelphia, Boston, and other major markets. According to Mamoulian biographer Christopher Connelly, it was booed off the screen in London.

Screenwriter Garrett Fort wrote Helen Morgan's next vehicle, *Roadhouse Nights* (1930), but her career faltered after she was diagnosed with cirrhosis of the liver. Her next Registry film is the 1936 *Show Boat*. Mamoulian had to wait a year to receive another directing assignment, *City Streets* (1931), a gangster film written by Dashiell Hammett. His *Love Me Tonight* is also on the Registry.

H₂O

Frame enlargement from Ralph Steiner's *H₂O*.

Ralph Steiner, 1929. Silent, B&W, 1.33. 13 minutes.

Credits: Filmmaker: Ralph Steiner.

Available: Image Entertainment DVD *Unseen Cinema: Early American Avant-Garde Film 1894–1941* (2005). UPC: 0-14381-0592-2-9.

Born in Cleveland in 1899, Ralph Steiner became interested in photography as a teen. After attending Dartmouth College (the subject of his first book of photographs) he moved to New York City. His early work, which he described as "arty beyond belief," leaned heavily on impressionism, although he quickly moved away from the pictorialism that dominated photography at the time. (Pictorialists tried to make photographs look more like paintings in an effort to legitimize their art form.) After seeing photos by Paul Strand, Steiner turned to a more realistic style, one devoted to everyday objects portrayed without artifice. By the late 1920s he had a significant career as a freelance photographer, shooting both commercial and editorial projects. His unadorned pictures were a major influence on later photographers like Walker Evans.

Steiner's first film *H₂O* is as basic as his photos. It starts with shots of rain; then follows the course of water from eaves to drain pipes to streams, brooks, dams, rivers; and finally, the ocean. As the film progresses, Steiner goes from easily recognizable locations to shots in which planes and depths are impossible to determine. These images are constructed from reflections on the surface of the water, and from the movement of the water itself. Relatively placid scenes allow viewers to pick out objects—pilings, trees, plants, rocks. In the shots of turbulent water, reflections distort and break apart until they become totally abstract.

These swirling images make up the bulk of the film. They are a startling display, evoking everything from sound waveforms to the amoeba shapes used by Jean Arp in his sculpture and painting. But they pose a problem for an editor: How do you cut meaningfully from one abstract image to another?

In assembling his film, Steiner had little concrete to work with—no story, characters, or at times even recognizable images. Without a linear narrative, one in which the shots have causal relationships, Steiner had to construct meaning and pacing through the movements within individual shots. He worked closely with composer Aaron Copland, who helped define the film's rhythms and tempos. Watch how carefully Steiner uses the different currents within his material—some flowing north, some in other directions—as a way to build a rhythm. He also constructs sequences out of the reflections, using their increasing or decreasing speeds as a sort of musical notation. At times physical details—a piece of wood floating by, a building or wall reflected on the water—anchor the film before the abstract montages resume, almost as if to give viewers a chance to catch their collective breath.

Steiner was undoubtedly influenced by earlier films, especially Paul Strand's and Charles Sheeler's *Manhatta* (1921). His short bears some structural resemblances to *Regen*, a tone poem made around the same time by the Dutch filmmaker Joris Ivens. But *H₂O* goes beyond those two works by discarding representation for the abstract.

H₂O was the perfect film for cinema clubs. Not just for its beauty or technical accomplishments, but because it was a film anyone could make. *H₂O* tackled the fundamentals of filmmaking—composition, exposures, subject matter, and, of course, editing—in methods that were easy for nonprofessionals to imitate. Steiner didn't need a studio or a crew. He scouted the locations, shot all the footage, decided all the editing, and made the movie he wanted. The film became an inspiration to countless do-it-yourself amateurs.

And as a matter of fact, the film became available in the midst of a boom in cinema clubs. The American Cinema League, founded in 1926 by Hiram Percy Maxim, an amateur aviator and ham radio operator, encouraged budding filmmakers by publishing *Movie Maker* magazine and by sponsoring an annual filmmaking contest. As Jan-Christopher Horak of George Eastman House wrote, "*H₂O* not only won a prize in *Photoplay*'s contest, but also probably influenced more would-be DeMilles than Eisenstein did; for years the Amateur Cinema League distributed the film to every amateur club in the country."

Steiner made a second film, *Surf and Seaweed*, finishing it in 1930. It took a similar approach as *H₂O* did to the shoreline, but the results seem less magical. Perhaps because he included the shore in most of the shots, the film never attains the same disorienting effects that the earlier one did. Not to mention the fact that *Surf and Seaweed* seems to be repeating earlier discoveries.

At the time, Steiner also was involved peripherally with the formation of the Group Theater. He befriended Paul Strand, and the two would work on *The Plow That Broke the Plains* in 1936. Steiner collaborated with Pare Lorentz and Copland on 1939's *The City*, which was shown at that year's World's Fair in New York City. (Both films are on the Registry.)

After serving in the armed forces during World War II, Steiner accepted an invitation from Louis B. Mayer to work at MGM. But the five years he spent at the studio were unhappy ones, and he returned to New York in the 1950s, where he resumed commercial photography. He also began teaching, and continued making his unassuming personal films and photographs. He was the subject of several retrospectives in the 1970s, and wrote an autobiography, *A Point of View*, in 1978.

All Quiet on the Western Front

Universal, 1930. Sound, B&W, 1.37. 131 minutes.

Cast: Louis Wolheim (Kat [Katczinksy]), Lewis Ayres (Paul [Baumer]), John Wray (Himmelstoss), Arnold Lucy (Kantorek), Ben Alexander (Kemmerick), Scott Kolk (Leer), Owen Davis, Jr. (Peter), Walter Brown Rogers (Behn), William Bakewell (Albert), Russell Gleason (Mueller), Richard Alexander (Westhus), Harold Goodwin (Detering), "Slim" Summerville (Tjaden), Pat Collins (Bertinck), Beryl Mercer (Paul's Mother), Edmund Breese (Herr Meyer).

Credits: Directed by Lewis Milestone. Produced by Carl Laemmle, Jr. Adaptation & dialogue: Maxwell Anderson. Screen Play: George Abbott. Adaptation: Del Andrews. Supervising Story Chief: C. Gardner Sullivan. Synchronization & Score: David Broekman. Supervising film editor: Maurice Pivar. Cinematographer: Arthur Edeson. Film Editor: Edgar Adams. Assistant director: Nate Watat. Art directors: Charles D. Hall, W.R. Schmitt. Recording supervision: C. Roy Hunter.

Additional Cast: Raymond Griffith (Gérard Duval), Ben Alexander, Arthur Garner, Vince Barnett.

Additional Credits: Based on the novel by Erich Maria Remarque. Dialogue director: George Cukor. Production dates: November 11, 1929 to March 1930. Premiered in Los Angeles on April 21, 1930.

Available: Universal Home Video DVD (2001). ISBN: 0-7832-3043-5. UPC: 0-2519-205102-9.

First appearing as a magazine serial in 1928, Erich Maria Remarque's novel *All Quiet on the Western Front* quickly became an international best-seller. By 1931 it had been translated into twenty-five languages, selling over three million copies. Remarque, who was born Erich Paul Remark in Osnabrück in 1898, was eighteen when he was drafted into the German Army. Although stationed near the front, he did not actually fight for the three years he served. He was recuperating from a leg wound when armistice was declared. Remarque wrote his first novel while studying to be a teacher, then held a variety of jobs, including editing a sports magazine, before writing *Im Westen nichts Neues* in 1927. (The German title, literally "In the West, nothing new," is more matter-of-fact than its English equivalent.)

The novel took a logical, dispassionate approach to depicting the war. Narrated by student and then novice soldier Paul Bäumer, it is divided into roughly three sections. In the first, more than half the men in Paul's company are killed. In the second, Paul and his surviving comrades begin to question the meaning of the war. In the third, short vignettes describe the deaths of Paul's companions, and ultimately Paul himself.

Born in Germany in 1867, Carl Laemmle, the head of Universal, had closer ties to the country than did executives at other studios. His Independent Motion Picture Company (IMP) fought against Edison and the Motion Picture Patents Company during the first decade of the twentieth century. After World War I, Laemmle organized and financed many fundraising efforts for Germany. He met Remarque in Germany during a trip in the summer of 1929, when he purchased film rights to the book, and even tried to persuade Remarque to appear in the movie.

Laemmle's son, Carl, Jr., was placed in charge of the project. From the start this was planned as a "prestige" picture, meaning that it had a much larger budget than the ordinary Universal "program" film. The younger Laemmle hired Maxwell Anderson—coauthor of *What Price Glory*, a play that used a war setting to tell a love story—to adapt the novel. Anderson incorporated most of Remarque's motifs, even adhering to his book's ratio of war- to nonwar-related scenes.

Carl Laemmle, Jr., went outside the studio to hire director Lewis Milestone. Born in Russia in 1895, Milestone wanted to be an actor. His disapproving family sent him to Germany to study engineering, but he dropped out and made his way to the United States. After finding a job as a photographer's assistant, he enlisted in the Army in 1917, where he was assigned to the Signal Corps. Here he gained experience dealing with combat footage. After the war he worked for director Henry King, wrote screenplays, and became an assistant director. He made his first feature for Warner Brothers, and two years later won the first (and only) Oscar for Comedy Directing with *Two Arabian Nights*. He had been working for Howard Hughes when he accepted the *All Quiet* assignment. His first step was to demand another screenplay, one that didn't focus on fighting, but concentrated instead on the young characters who would be sent to the front. Both Del Andrews and playwright George Abbott submitted drafts.

Dialogue coach George Cukor recommended Lew Ayres, a musician from Minneapolis who had had one major role before this, in the Greta Garbo vehicle *The Kiss* (1929). Ayres' inexperience as an actor suited his character's naïveté, and Milestone protected him by filling the cast with more experienced actors, notably Louis Wolheim (who was making more than ten times Ayres' salary). Once a fullback at Cornell, Wolheim starred in *The Hairy Ape* on Broadway before embarking on a screen career. He would die of stomach cancer a year after this film. His broken nose and guttural voice made him an excellent choice for the role of "Kat," a hard-bitten sergeant. Slim Summerville, once a Keystone Kop and a director of slapstick shorts for Mack Sennett, specialized in portraying rural bumpkins. He provides what passes for comic relief in *All Quiet*.

Summerville would go on to star in a series of low-budget comedies with ZaSu Pitts, who was originally cast in *All Quiet* as Paul's mother. Preview audiences, used to seeing Pitts in comedies, laughed when she came on screen, forcing Laemmle and Milestone to reshoot her scenes with a different mother, Beryl Mercer. By the time the film was released, Universal had spent almost $1.5 million.

You can see where the money went right in the first shot, a hallway where servants are hard at work cleaning. A front door is opened, revealing a city street bustling with soldiers, marching bands, and onlookers—an artificial world whose expense few producers of the era could justify. Milestone and his cinematographer Arthur Edeson used silent film techniques to free the camera, letting it soar over crowds on a crane, or prowl up the aisles of a high school. At the same time, Milestone mixed sound adroitly, using the marching bands to drown out a teacher's lecture, and constructed montages that gave the effect of delving into characters' thoughts through free association techniques. The aim was to sweep viewers into an experience so real that the horrific events about to unfold could not be denied.

The filmmakers introduced the war itself slowly, first sending a group of recruits through training, then bringing them close to the front lines. Many of the scenes have become clichés in the intervening years, but they retain an almost documentary realism here—partly because the film firmly resists glorifying the war. In *The Birth of a Nation*, an obvious antecedent for many of the battle scenes here, viewers are meant to root for the Southern side. Here there is no one to root for, an especially striking stance considering that for much of the film's audience, Germany was the enemy.

Milestone seems to be quoting *Birth of a Nation* directly in the film's first full-fledged battle scene. The camera ascends on a crane to show a vast battlefield, a vision that still inspires awe. It is followed by the film's single most remarkable shot, with the camera panning along the top of a trench as advancing soldiers are cut down by machine-gun fire.

Milestone and his crew achieved their effects at enormous cost. The cast numbered four thousand, including two thousand veterans. The battle scenes were shot largely at the Irvine Ranch, usually the site of Universal's Westerns. Publicity accounts claim that the production went through twenty tons of powder and ten of dynamite. Cinematographer Edeson was quoted as saying, "Except for not using real bullets, we might as well have been in the war. There were some close calls with explosions. . . . [Lewis Milestone] was hit by some debris from an explosion and was knocked unconscious. He was right by my camera. After that we started wearing those big steel German helmets."

All Quiet won Oscars for Best Picture and Best Director. It was a critical hit, but its budget was too large to help the studio's income. Universal lost over $2 million in 1930, compared to a half-million-dollar profit the year before. If it weren't for its cycle of horror films, starting with *Dracula* and *Frankenstein*, Universal would have gone bankrupt.

When a heavily cut version of *All Quiet* had its premiere in Berlin, it was greeted with stink bombs and walk-outs in a demonstration organized by Joseph Goebbels. The German government quickly banned the film outright. (Ironically, Goebbels' private print was used in a 1984 restoration of the film.) Soon the Nazis would be giving the novel public burnings. His citizenship revoked, Remarque fled to Switzerland, and eventually to the United States, where he worked for a time in Hollywood.

Ayres subsequently enjoyed a successful career, starring in films like *State Fair* (1933) with Will Rogers and *Holiday* (1938) with Katharine Hepburn and Cary Grant. He also played Dr. Kildare in a series of films for MGM. In 1941, largely as a result of his work in *All Quiet on the Western Front*, he declared himself a conscientious objector. Ayres served as an unarmed medical corpsman during the D-Day invasion. He failed to reestablish his film career after the war, although he later directed a documentary about comparative religions, and worked for a time with UNESCO.

Pups Is Pups

Metro-Goldwyn-Mayer, 1930. Sound, B&W, 1.37. 18 minutes.

Cast: Our Gang: Bobby "Wheezer" Hutchins, Allen "Farina" Hoskins, Jackie Cooper, Dorothy DeBorba, Norman "Chubby" Chaney, Mary Ann Jackson, Buddy MacDonald, Werner and Wolfgang Weidler, Allen Tong, the Hill Twins; Charles McAvoy (Cement man), Silas D. Wilcox (Doorman), Lyle Tayo (Dorothy's mother), Dr. H.R. White, Allen Cavan, Charlie Hall (Orchestra leader, violinist), William Gillespie (Bass tuba), Chet Brandenburg, Jack Hill (Crowd extras), Harry Bernard (Officer).

Credits: Produced and directed by Robert F. McGowan. Story by Robert F. McGowan. Dialogue by H.M. Walker. Executive producer: Hal Roach. Director of photography: Art Lloyd. Edited by Richard Currier.

Additional Credits: Music by Leroy Shield. Released August 30, 1930.

Available: Artisan Home Entertainment VHS (1994). ISBN: 1-57492-812-0. UPC: 7-07729-10574-9. RHI Entertainment DVD *The Little Rascals: The Complete Collection* (2008). UPC: 7-96019-81205-4.

***Pups Is Pups* was the 100th entry** in one of the most successful film series in history, the Our Gang comedies. From 1922 to 1944, 221 Our Gang shorts were released, most of them made at the Hal Roach Studio. (In 1938, Roach sold the rights to the series to MGM, which made the last 52 film shorts.)

A former mule skinner and gold prospector in Alaska, Roach was one of the more significant figures in comedy during the 1920s. Hired as a cowboy at Universal in 1912, he had his own production unit by 1914. Roach helped turn Harold Lloyd into a star, and it was as a judge of talent like Lloyd that the producer gained his reputation. His other stars included Snub Pollard, the team of Laurel and Hardy, and Charley Chase. Among the writers and directors Roach hired were Leo McCarey, Frank Capra, George Stevens, Frank Tashlin, Tay Garnett, George Marshall, and Clyde Bruckman.

Roach wasn't the first filmmaker to see the potential in child performers. As early as 1895, Louis Lumière filmed a child playing a prank on a gardener in *L'Arroseur arrosé*. Edwin Porter remade his *Great Train Robbery* as a comedy, with children playing adult characters, in *The Little Train Robbery* (1905). Delinquents and other troublemaking children were the subject of films like *The Terrible Kids* (1906) and *The Truants* (1907). Children and childlike roles, in *The Poor Little Rich Girl* (1917), *Sparrows* (1926) and others, helped make Mary Pickford one of the biggest film stars in the world. Series devoted to children included The Reg'lar Kids, Baby Peggy, Buster Brown, and Micky McGuire, which starred Mickey Rooney. In these comedies, children were usually portrayed as wiser than the adults in charge of them, the source of much of the humor in their plots. Many of the situations and even the actual gags from these early films are still being recycled today.

Lloyd and Pollard had both used Ernie Morrison, a child actor known as Sunshine Sammy, in their shorts, prompting Roach to assemble a film unit devoted to films about children. They were originally going to be referred to as "Hal Roach's Rascals," but theater owners transferred the title of the first film, *Our Gang*, to the series as a whole. The core creative group included Charley Chase, described by film historian Leonard Maltin as a sort of "director-general" and soon to be a star himself; screenwriter Tom McNamara, who once had his own comic strip; H.M. "Beanie" Walker, a cartoonist who wrote intertitles; and Charley Oelze, an assistant director in charge of prop gags.

Fred Newmeyer directed a version of *Our Gang*, but Roach ordered it reshot by Robert McGowan. "Bob" McGowan had been a fireman in Denver until he retired after an accident resulted in gangrene in his foot. McGowan bought a nickelodeon, and became so dissatisfied with the movies he showed that he decided he could do better himself. He started out as Oelze's assistant, then began directing at Al Christie's studio. Chase brought him to the Roach studio, and he is responsible for the best films in the Our Gang series.

The Our Gang films, distributed at the time by Pathé, were extremely popular, in part because they relied on story and character more than gags. The child performers could change from film to film, but a typical Our Gang silent lineup included Mickey Daniels, Johnny Downs, Jackie Condon, Joe Cobb, Mary Kornman, Jay R. Smith, and Allen "Farina" Hoskins.

By 1930, the Roach studio had completed the transition to sound. Since the earlier child actors inevitably outgrew their roles, the new lineup consisted of Allen "Farina" Hoskins, Norman "Chubby" Chaney, Dorothy DeBorba, Mary Ann Jackson, Shirley Jean Rickert, Bobby "Wheezer" Hutchins, Jackie Cooper, Matthew "Stymie" Beard, and Pete the Pup, a pit bull mix characterized by a dark ring around his eye (reputedly a holdover from his appearance as "Tige" in the *Buster Brown* series). One key addition to the crew was composer Leroy Shield, a classically trained pianist whose scores provided an unusually sympathetic backing to the Our Gang films.

Cooper, who had been appearing in film since the age of three, was the most experienced of the new Gang, but he was soon to leave the series to make feature films, at first under the direction of his uncle, Norman Taurog. Hoskins appeared in 105 Our Gang films, more than anyone else. *Pups Is Pups* marked the film debut of DeBorba, who later said she was delighted to learn that her first job was to jump into a mud puddle all day long. But Bobby "Wheezer" Hutchins was arguably the most accomplished performer during this period. He conveyed, with the least artifice, the joy and frequent sorrow of being a child.

As the centennial entry in the series, and the first in the 1930–31 season, *Pups Is Pups* had a larger budget than a typical Our Gang film. (The films generally made a $10,000 profit on a budget of about $20,000.) But in most aspects *Pups Is Pups* is typical, and displays just about all of the reasons why the Our Gang comedies were so popular: simple, unforced acting; believable settings; and uncomplicated jokes that needed little embellishing or special effects.

In later years critics sometimes accused the series of racism in its depiction of its black characters. But as Hoskins pointed out, the white characters were just as broadly drawn. Few other films of the time dealt with the realities of race—or with the Depression, for that matter. The children in the Our Gang films of this period are almost uniformly poor, and it is their resilience in the face of poverty that helps make them so endearing.

With so many characters in each film, Roach's writers had the luxury of pursuing several story lines at once. The premise to *Pups Is Pups* has the kids entering their pets in a snooty downtown dog show. It's mutts, parrots, and pigs versus pedigreed pooches, some of whom are flung into the society orchestra. But the film takes a leisurely, discursive approach to the premise, finding time to linger over several "off story" scenes and moments.

Hutchins dominates the early sound entries. McGowan sensed that he could handle difficult material, and that audiences would relate to him more than to the other children. In *Pups Is Pups* he provides a vivid demonstration of Pavlov's principle: having trained his puppies to respond to a bell, he must find a way to control them when they are lured away by ambulances, ice-cream trucks, sirens, a restaurant triangle, a trained monkey, train whistles, and other distractions. Hutchins' good humor is so endearing that the focus of the film shifts from the other actors over to his desperate attempts to corral his dogs. (The 1931 *Dogs Is Dogs* has Hutchins trapped in a Dickensian setting, physically abused by a stepmother, deprived of food, his dog about to be killed by a neighbor. It's a good example of his acting abilities and of the emotional range the series encompassed.)

When Roach sold the Our Gang rights to MGM, he couldn't anticipate a future market for the shorts. The producer switched his attention to features, made films for the armed forces during World War II, then developed television series in the 1950s. By that time the early Our Gang films had been syndicated to television under the "Little Rascals" name (chosen so as not to compete with the MGM titles). Syndication rights changed hands many times, films were censored or cut to fill time slots, and the brand was diluted by an animated series and a misguided 1994 feature film.

The Big Trail

Fox Film Corporation, 1930. Sound, B&W, 2.13 and 1.33 versions. 116 minutes.

Cast: John Wayne (Breck Coleman), Marguerite Churchill (Ruth Cameron), El Brendel (Gus), Tully Marshall (Zeke), Tyrone Power (Red Flack), David Rollins (Davey Cameron), Frederick Burton (Bascom), Ian Keith (Bill Thorpe), Charles Stevens (Lopez), Louis Carver (Gus's mother in law).

Credits: Directed by Raoul Walsh. Written by Hal G. Evarts. Director of photography: Arthur Edeson (70mm), Lucien Andriot (35mm). Production manager: Archibald Buchanan. Film editor: Jack Dennis. Settings: Harold Miles, Fred Sersen.

Additional Cast includes: Ward Bond (Sid Bascom), Chief John Big Tree (Indian), Marcia Harris (Mrs. Riggs), Marjorie Leet (Mildred Riggs), Helen Parrish (Honey Girl Cameron), Russ Powell (Windy Bill).

Additional Credits: Screenwriting and dialogue by Jack Peabody, Marie Boyle, Florence Postal. Produced by Winfield R. Sheehan. 70mm cinematography by Dave Ragin, Sol Halprin, Curt Fetters, Max Cohn, Harry Smith, Harry Dawe, L. Kunkel. 35mm cinimatography by Don Anderson, Bill McDonald, Roger Sherman, Bobby Mack, Henry Pollack. Art director: Harold Miles. Sound: Bill Brent, Paul Heihly. Makeup: Jack Dawn, Louise Sloane. Premiered in New York City on October 24, 1930.

Available: Twentieth Century Fox Home Entertainment DVD (2008) UPC: 024543519300. Fox Video VHS (1995). ISBN: 0-7939-8691-5. UPC: 0-8616-28691-3-6.

One of the great missed opportunities in cinema, *The Big Trail* was the first widescreen Western, and the first starring role for John Wayne. It was also a box-office failure of such resounding proportions that it exiled Wayne to B-movies for almost a decade, and effectively shut down widescreen films for almost a quarter century. Shot in a 70mm process called Grandeur, the film is by photographic standards a masterpiece. It not only captured an American landscape that is now almost lost, but set a standard for realism in Westerns that has rarely been matched. But no matter how majestic its settings, or how spectacular its hordes of wagons, horses, and cattle, *The Big Trail* may be one of the most poorly written and inconsequential epics ever filmed.

Director Raoul Walsh's career had flourished after he finished *The Thief of Bagdad* (1924) for Douglas Fairbanks. He made *What Price Glory* (1926), a rollicking World War I adventure that inspired many imitators; and wrote, directed, and starred in (with Gloria Swanson) *Sadie Thompson* (1928), an adaptation of W. Somerset Maugham's *Rain*. Walsh was eager to work with sound, and planned to star in as well as direct what would be the first sound Western shot on location, *In Old Arizona* (1929). While he was driving through the desert at night, Walsh's headlights startled a jackrabbit. It jumped through the windshield, blinding Walsh in his right eye and ending his acting career. Warner Baxter replaced him as The Cisco Kid, subsequently winning a Best Acting Oscar for *In Old Arizona*.

For his next project, Walsh decided to document the first wagon train from the Mississippi to Oregon. The scope of the project made it a natural for Grandeur, a widescreen process developed for William Fox by Earl I. Sponable (the same Sponable behind *Gus Visser and His Singing Duck*). Much like Todd-AO decades later, Grandeur was a 70mm system that used Mitchell cameras. Arthur Edeson, a cinematographer who had just finished filming *In Old Arizona* and *All Quiet on the Western Front* (1930), wrote an article in the September 1930 issue of *American Cinematographer* describing his experiences working with Grandeur. Edeson shot about a half-million feet of film over a six-month period, in locations ranging from the Grand Canyon to the Rockies. He and Walsh didn't see rushes until they returned to California at the end of the production, but Edeson described the Grandeur footage as "technically perfect." "Any man who is technically able to do good work on 35mm film should therefore be able to do just as well on wide film," he wrote.

Walsh made some odd choices casting *The Big Trail*. For the chief villain he used Tyrone Power, a famous stage star at the turn of the twentieth century who had made only intermittent film appearances. In this, his only talkie performance, he was almost outdone by his makeup. (This was also Power's last film; he would die the following year, two years before his son Tyrone's film debut.) Nineteen-year-old Marguerite Churchill also had stage experience, but her work here as romantic lead Ruby Cameron was so unimpressive that she could only find later parts in B-movies. Fox contract player El Brendel supplies the comic relief. The son of German immigrants, Brendel developed a vaudeville act around an airhead with a Swedish accent. Inexplicably, he was considered a star until the sci-fi fantasy flop *Just Imagine* (1930), after which his career sank to comedy shorts for Columbia.

The director chose former USC football star Marion Morrison, a prop handler and bit player who had been working in John Ford's unit at Fox, for the lead role. Morrison had recently changed his screen name to John Wayne. *The Big Trail* was not just his first lead, it was his first significant part in film. Already he has the looks and swagger of his later career, and his voice, while thin, is unmistakable. What Wayne lacked at this stage of his career was the confidence and authority that would later command viewers' attention. Here he often seems stiff, frozen in poses, with an awkward awareness of the camera.

Walsh apparently wasn't much help, because none of the acting in the film is very accomplished, with the exception of Tully Marshall. A stage veteran who acted in *Intolerance*, Marshall had an important part in *The Covered Wagon* (1923), an earlier frontier epic with a strikingly similar plot. In *The Big Trail* he plays the sidekick as a grizzled old coot, a strategy that would be duplicated in countless succeeding Westerns. In Walsh's defense, the acting was so stilted because the performers had to bellow their lines so they would register on the microphones. Dreadful dialogue didn't help; imagine Wayne being forced to say, "Yonder stand the great white mountains, and down there is the valley that I've told you about" at any point in his career.

The story includes many of the standard elements of Westerns, from river crossings to shootouts, square dances, and funerals. What's surprising is how little weight Walsh gives to the lives of his characters, and how much attention he pays instead to the mundane details of day-to-day life.

If the plot is a disappointment, the scope of the production is astonishing. Walsh staged the story in the midst of spectacular scenery, and had amazing props to work with. When the Indians attack, and the wagons draw into a circle, Walsh can show off more than forty of them in a single shot. In the most impressive scene, he lowers wagons and people by ropes down a line of sandy bluffs, something as foolhardy to re-create as it must have been for the pioneers to attempt.

Grandeur wasn't the only widescreen system in Hollywood at the time. While experimentation with frame sizes dates back to the nineteenth century, in 1929 Fox was facing direct competition from MGM (which used a system called Realife), United Artists (Magnifilm), and Warner Brothers (Vitascope). Some eleven widescreen features were filmed between 1929 and 1930. Persuading theater owners to buy new projectors and larger screens is a tough sell at any time; in the aftermath of 1929's stock market crash, it was almost impossible. Fox would be able to show the 70mm version of *The Big Trail* on only two screens, one each in New York and Los Angeles.

For his film to be seen in the rest of the country, Walsh had to simultaneously make a version in 35mm (photographed by Lucien Andriot), using the same cast and very similar camera setups. Viewed today, Grandeur is an undisputably stunning process, with exceptional depth of field. Had *The Big Trail* been a success, the history of film might have been quite different. But *Variety* was not fooled by "the simple romance and the silly melodrama." Nor were filmgoers of the time. Walsh's career took a nosedive; like Wayne, he was stuck with nondescript material until 1939, when *The Roaring Twenties* marked a personal comeback of sorts.

The Big Trail would probably have remained a footnote were it not for *John Wayne's America: The Politics of Celebrity*, a 1997 book by historian Garry Wills. In it Wills claimed that *The Big Trail* was an unsung masterpiece that was crucial in defining Wayne's screen persona. Few actors were fortunate enough to reintroduce themselves to the public with the help of a director like John Ford, as Wayne did in *Stagecoach* (1939).

Morocco

Paramount, 1930. Sound, B&W, 1.37. 92 minutes.

Cast: Gary Cooper (Legionnaire Tom Brown), Marlene Dietrich (Mademoiselle Amy Jolly), Adolphe Menjou (Monsieur La Bessiere), Ullrich Haupt (Adjutant Caesar), Eve Southern (Madame Caesar), Francis McDonald (A Sergeant), Paul Porcasi (Lo Tinto).

Credits: Directed by Josef von Sternberg. Adapted by Jules Furthman from the play "Amy Jolly" by Benno Vigny. Photographed by Lee Garmes.

Additional Cast: Emile Chautard, Juliette Compton, Albert Conti, Michael Visaroff.

Additional Credits: Produced by Hector Turnbull. Additional cinematography: Lucien Ballard. Edited by Sam Winston. Art direction: Hans Dreier. Music: Karl Hajos. Songs: "Quand l'amour mourt," music by Octave Crémieux, lyrics by Georges Millandy. "What Am I Bid for My Apple?" music by Karl Hajos, lyrics by Leo Robin. Western Electric Sound System. Premiered in New York City on November 14, 1930.

Available: Universal Studios Home Entertainment DVD *Marlene Dietrich—The Glamour Collection* (2006). ISBN: 1-4170-6995-3. UPC: 0-25192-84552-9.

Like a number of his colleagues, the great German actor Emil Jannings signed a Hollywood contract in the 1920s—in his case, with Paramount. Jannings won the first Best Acting Oscar for *The Way of All Flesh* and *The Last Command*, the latter directed by Josef von Sternberg (and a Registry title). With the advent of sound films, Jannings returned to Germany to work at UFA, the largest German film studio. He persuaded executives there to hire Sternberg for *Der Blaue Engel* (*The Blue Angel*, 1930), an adaptation of the novel *Professor Unrat* by Heinrich Mann. Sternberg cast Marlene

Dietrich in the part of Lola Lola, a heartless cabaret performer who ruins the teacher.

Born Maria Magdalene Dietrich in 1901, the future Marlene worked as a chorus girl before studying acting with impresario Max Reinhardt. Dietrich appeared in more than a dozen movies before Sternberg "discovered" her singing in a nightclub, but there's no question that the director modeled his protégé into a star. *The Blue Angel* was a sensation, prompting Paramount to offer Dietrich a contract. She left Berlin for America the night *The Blue Angel* premiered, leaving behind a husband and daughter.

Sternberg tried to control every aspect of Dietrich's career, restricting press access and placing her on a strict diet-and-exercise regimen. Agent Sam Jaffe said, "I never saw a man who took a piece of clay and so ruthlessly shaped it to his will as Von Sternberg did with Dietrich." Dietrich was a full participant in the shaping of her legend, and in later years always credited Sternberg with creating her screen persona. He in turn seemed unable to reconcile his personal feelings for her with their professional relationship. In his autobiography, he usually referred to her as "that woman."

Dietrich and Sternberg arrived in New York in April 1930. Paramount wanted a Dietrich film ready before *The Blue Angel* opened in the United States, which did not give Sternberg much time. For her first vehicle, he chose a novel by Berlin journalist Benno Vigny, *Amy Jolly, The Woman of Marrakesh*. It was a fairly racy story with wealthy men, fallen women, and colonial attitudes. Paramount had already purchased the rights to the novel, and had assigned Jules Furthman to work on the script. Sternberg told Furthman, a regular collaborator, to change Amy Jolly's trajectory, having her fall in love with a legionnaire in contrast to the similar but more bitter ending of *The Blue Angel*.

Paramount assigned its biggest star, Gary Cooper, to the film. He insisted on top billing, and on changing the title to *Morocco* to deflect attention away from Dietrich. Also cast was Adolphe Menjou, who plays an extremely close approximation of Sternberg himself, down to the hats the director favored. It's a role as demeaning as it was revealing (and completely fabricated, despite Sternberg's innuendos). Cooper's assured performance was singled out for praise by *Variety*, and the director capitalized fully on that star's astonishing physicality. But in truth Sternberg was only interested in his protégé.

The director's infatuation with Dietrich is explicit throughout the film. Compared to her later films, she is relatively unformed—a little stocky, her hair an indeterminate brown, her forehead a bit too prominent. She wears the clothes of a single mother, not a glamorous siren. They were a bit gaudy at times but still practical: filmy, gauzy dresses, but not scandalous or even especially erotic.

Dietrich's appearance varies considerably throughout *Morocco*. In her close-ups she can have an unearthly beauty and allure, coupled with a languorous arousal. In long shots she is occasionally just a hausfrau unsure of her position in the frame. Sternberg is usually credited with the lighting scheme that brought out Dietrich's cheekbones, her stenciled eyebrows, her glossy lips. According to biographer Alexander Walker, cinematographer Lee Garmes actually developed the style: "He at first followed the director's instruction to light her from one side only: but then the daily 'rushes' showed him what this was producing was a second Garbo. Whereupon, without telling Von Sternberg, Garmes reverted to the 'north' lighting he himself preferred."

Sternberg's real influence was on the character Dietrich played. He presents her as an international cabaret star, which she would eventually become, but which at the time was nowhere near the truth. He also presents her as helpless in the face of her desires, a slave to her sexual passions. Again this was wishful thinking on his part, for Dietrich was a dutiful wife and mother. He had to guide her through her scenes, showing her every gesture, every pause, every inflection. (In outtakes you can see her struggling with English, approaching the language as if its words were lyrics to a song.)

Sternberg later claimed that a Moroccan ruler congratulated him on capturing his country so well on film. *Morocco* does cast a spell today, although it is largely the spell of nitrate, with its glowing whites and inky blacks that pulse and throb in an almost tactile way. Sternberg's compositions may be so memorable because he tends to obliterate much of the frame with gauze, shadows, nets, smoke. For someone so visually oriented, he had surprisingly little trouble adjusting to sound, perhaps because he used it sparingly: it takes fifteen minutes before we hear Cooper's first full sentence. Sound was just an accompaniment to Sternberg's images, not their replacement. Unlike many of his contemporaries, he had no trouble moving the camera, blending in tracking shots and pans at a time when MGM pictures, for example, were moribund.

Morocco defines languid; there are only a handful of actual narrative incidents in the story. Most of those are hopelessly, even childishly, romantic. Like Dietrich in a tuxedo and top hat, kissing a woman full on the lips—an unforgettable moment that has nothing to do with the rest of the film. What's striking about *Morocco* today isn't its second-rate plotting, a tired Somerset Maugham amalgam in which the Sahara could just as easily be Malaysia. It is instead the audacity of Sternberg's vision, and Dietrich's willingness to subsume her own personality to achieve it. By pretending that Dietrich was a sexually voracious cabaret star, Sternberg helped form one of cinema's enduring icons.

Released in November 1930, *Morocco* was a smash. *The Blue Angel* opened in the United States three weeks later. By that time Sternberg and Dietrich were already working on their next project, *Dishonored*, which hit theaters in March 1931. The duo would make four more films together, each one more elaborate, each one a little less successful at the box office. After *The Devil*

Is a Woman in 1935, Dietrich never worked with Sternberg again. The director made a pair of mediocre films for Columbia, then went to England for the epic *I, Claudius*. Filming was halted after Merle Oberon was injured in a car crash, and the project was ultimately abandoned. The remainder of Sternberg's career was a sad decline marked by missed opportunities and half-hearted efforts.

From Stump to Ship

Documenting obsolete lumbering practices in Maine: *From Stump to Ship*.

Alfred Ames, 1930. Silent, B&W, 1.37. 27 minutes.
Credits: Produced and directed by Alfred Ames. Written by Alfred Ames, Rufus Fuller. Cinematography by Alfred Ames, Dr. Harold Kane.
Additional Credits: Restoration produced by David Weiss, Karan Sheldon. Narration read by Tim Sample. Music: Sandy Ives, Albert Pelletier, Billy Schubeck. Executive producer and project director: Harry Nevison. Consultants: David C. Smith, Edward Ives, Richard Judd, Jonathan Tankel. Film editors: Harry Nevison, David Weiss. A Project of the University of Maine at Orono and The Northeast Archives of Folklore and Oral History with the support of The Maine Humanities Council and the National Endowment for the Humanities and Champion International Corporation.
Available: Northeast Historic Film DVD (no date): UPC: 7-93313-00019-4. View online or download from *www.windowsonmaine.org*.

Writing in 1930, Alfred Ames traced his family's connection to the lumber business back to 1858, when his father was sent to Whitneyville to run sawmills purchased by the Pope brothers from a Dr. Howard. The Ames family ran the Machias Lumber Company on the seacoast of Maine near the Canadian border until 1930, at which point the operation ceased to be profitable. *From Stump to Ship* was Ames's attempt to document his business, aware that "the long lumber industry in Maine was a thing of the past."

Ames purchased a 16mm camera and set out to cover all the field work of lumbering. He filmed lumber camps in the winter, showing workers cutting down trees and carting them on sleds to landing areas by the Machias River. In the spring, he was there to film logs flowing down the river, showing workers picking apart "points" and log-jams. Dr. Harold Kane, his friend and the owner of a "modern, up-to-date camera," shot footage of millwork at Whitneyville. The final shots in the film show lumber conveyed by the schooners *Lucy Evelyn* and *Bertha B* down the Machias Bay to the Gulf of Maine.

The film was shot silent, but Ames and his nephew Rufus Fuller wrote a script to accompany the footage, which Ames would read during screenings. In the script he took pains to name as many workers as possible, and to point out how difficult and dangerous their jobs were. He adopted a nostalgic tone at times, remembering his first journey up the Machias River in 1879, remarking on how well a stand of trees has grown over twenty-seven years. He and Dr. Kane occasionally wandered into shots, smiling, gentlemanly, and well-dressed (Kane can be seen in knickers at one point).

It's not until the final minutes of the film that Ames reveals his motives behind *From Stump to*

Ship. Commenting on the *Lucy Evelyn*, he says, "Probably this is the last cargo of lumber that I will ever ship." Later, he quotes a somber, poetic farewell from Henry Wadsworth Longfellow, and adds, "This is what I call the twilight of my career as a lumberman." If you know that the Machias Lumber Company was about to close, intimations of change and loss tinge the entire film. Ames points out one worker scrambling over logs in the river, and says that he is now a bellhop in a hotel in Portsmouth.

For the work of a novice filmmaker, *From Stump to Ship* has a surprisingly professional feel. Ames knew the lumber business, of course, so he knew what needed to be covered to convey the breadth of his operations. But he also had to learn how to compose shots, how to determine the best distance to show procedures like felling a pine or riding a bateaux through rapids. He had to learn how to follow action, how to pan smoothly, how to choose angles, how to achieve good exposures in different seasons. The cinematography in *From Stump to Ship*, especially the handheld material, feels both loose and assured. Even if Ames hadn't identified the footage shot by Kane in his script, there is a distinct difference between their camerawork. *From Stump to Ship* fits very comfortably into the type of industrial film exemplified by *Westinghouse Works* (1903).

Ames showed the film at a farewell banquet that year, but he had another motive as well. The film became a promotional tool when he ran for governor in 1932. As Janna Jones, an author and professor who has written extensively about the film, points out, this was not a unique strategy. His opponent, Governor William Gardiner, also showed films during his campaign. Both lost to the Democratic contender, after which Ames apparently showed little further interest in his film. Jones cites a few screenings of *From Stump to Ship* in the 1940s, when Fuller brought it to Rhode Island. In 1970, the family donated it to the University of Maine at Orono.

It wasn't until 1984 that historian David Smith and Henry Nevison, a radio and television producer for the University of Maine's Public Information Office, examined the film carefully. Realizing that it needed to be preserved, they approached Karan Sheldon and David Weiss, commercial film producers who helped obtain some $31,000 to fund the project.

Sheldon and Weiss readily admit that they made crucial mistakes with their restoration, mistakes that point out how important it is to follow standard preservation procedures. First, a commercial lab damaged some of the footage when it tried to make a copy. A second lab made a similar error. Third, Sheldon and Weiss spliced the only original copy onto what are called A and B rolls, a process which is good for printing but irreversibly damaging for archival purposes. They also cut out material, primarily flash frames and other extraneous footage, but still amounting to 180 edits. Finally, in order to include a soundtrack, they sped up the footage from roughly 16 frames per second to 24 fps. What remains of the original *From Stump to Ship*, cut into two hundred pieces, is held at the Fogler Library on the University of Maine's Orono campus.

Little Caesar

Warner Bros., 1931. Sound, B&W, 1.33. 78 minutes.

Cast: Edward G. Robinson (Little Caesar "Rico" Bandello), Douglas Fairbanks, Jr. (Joe Massara), Glenda Farrell (Olga Stassoff), William Collier, Jr. (Tony Passa), Sidney Blackmer ("Big Boy"), Ralph Ince (Pete Montana), Thomas Jackson (Sargeant [sic] Flaherty), Stanley Fields (Sam Vettori), Maurice Black (Little Arnie Lorch), George E. Stone (Otero), Armand Kaliz (De Voss), Nick Bela (Ritz Colonna).

Credits: Directed by Mervyn LeRoy. Novel by W.R. Burnett. Screen version & dialogue by Francis Edward Faragoh. Continuity by Robert N. Lee. Photography by Tony Gaudio. Edited by Ray Curtiss. Art director: Anton Grot. General musical director: Erno Rapee. First National/Vitaphone production.

Additional Cast: Lucille La Verne (Ma Magdalena), Landers Stevens (Alvin McClure).

Additional Credits: Production dates: October to November 1930. Premiered in New York City on January 9, 1931.

Available: Warner Home Video DVD (2005). ISBN: 1-4198-0189, UPC 0-12569-67215-4.

Crime films stretch back at least to *The Burglar on the Roof* in 1898. Gangster films, stories featuring organized crime, arrived early on as well. *The Musketeers of Pig Alley* (1912), a gangster film in all but name, established a template for other films and stories, including *Alias Jimmy Valentine* and *Regeneration* (both 1915). In 1927, Josef von Sternberg turned Ben Hecht's gangster script *Underworld* into a box-office success for Paramount. At Warner Brothers that same year, Bryan Foy was directing the first "100% all-talking" movie, *Lights of New York*, a gangster film with curious similarities to *Little Caesar*.

Edward G. Robinson in his career-making role as *Little Caesar* himself, Rico Bandello.

Born in Ohio in 1899, William Riley Burnett studied journalism at Ohio State University, and then used a political patronage job in a bureau of statistics to write short stories and novels. W.R. Burnett moved to Chicago in 1927, coming into contact with gangster types from his job as a hotel desk clerk. The result was *Little Caesar*, a novel that one critic said was "not literature, but it is a good deal more than journalism." A Literary Guild selection, it became a best-seller as well as the center of a debate over the depiction of gangsters in media.

The novel described the rise and fall of Rico Bandello, a killer who went from petty crook to head of Chicago gangs, partly through gaining control of bootleg liquor during Prohibition. Burnett based Rico in part on Al Capone, at the time the most public figure in organized crime. Burnett wrote his novel as a sort of how-to guide to navigating the world of crime, and what set it apart from other crime stories was Rico's single-minded drive for success. Like a later "master of the universe," Rico allowed nothing to distract him from his goals—not love, friendship, or vices.

Darryl F. Zanuck, head of production at Warners, persuaded the studio to buy the novel, in part to capitalize on its Vitaphone sound process. Although Burnett later complained about how his novel was adapted, the screenplay by Francis Edward Faragoh stayed fairly true to the original story. Directing was Mervyn LeRoy, a former vaudeville actor from San Francisco whose recent work had been film versions of Broadway musicals like *Oh, Kay!* (1928) and *Little Johnny Jones* (1929). As with most successful films, there are conflicting stories about how *Little Caesar* was cast. Jack Warner later said that LeRoy wanted Clark Gable to play Rico. In his autobiographies, LeRoy said that he wanted Gable for Joe Massara's part. In either case, Warner turned Gable down.

Choosing Edward G. Robinson for the starring role looks more risky today that it may have seemed in 1930. Robinson was actually a fairly safe bet. Born in Bucharest, Rumania, in 1893, he moved to New York when he was nine. After studying at the City College of New York, he became an actor. Short, squat, with squashed features and a guttural, snarling voice, he had little chance of playing romantic leads. But he was fluent in six languages, had trained at the American Academy of Dramatic Arts, and brought enthusiasm and commitment to his roles. By the time he starred in *Little Caesar*, the thirty-seven-year-old actor had been in over forty Broadway plays, appeared in silent and sound films, and had been wooed by both Universal and MGM. Robinson had played a gangster in a 1929 Universal film, *Night Ride*, and in Warners' own *The Widow from Chicago* (1930). Perhaps most important, he bore a physical resemblance to Capone.

For whatever the reason he was cast, Robinson completely dominates the film. Chomping on a cigar, leaning into his lines, he exudes menace and a peculiarly reassuring self-confidence. Rico knows when people are condescending to him, and he doesn't mind picking up pointers about his wardrobe and other social skills. He is secure in his brutality, unwavering, implacable, ruthless. It is a startling performance, free from irony and other distancing tactics. Robinson's physicality is a key part of his role. Watch how his hands punctuate his threats, how his cigar becomes a weapon.

Douglas Fairbanks, Jr., who plays Rico's best friend, was the son of one of the biggest stars in silent film, and had established a reputation as a competent second lead in over two dozen silent titles. This was Glenda Farrell's first big film role, and it's one that fails to showcase her true talents. Soon she would be appearing as glib, gum-chewing showgirls, secretaries, or con women in fast-paced Warners comedy-dramas. With a few exceptions, the rest of the cast is made up of the largely face-less performers of early sound film: refugees from the stage too old to start out new in film, or silent actors playing out their career strings.

By the time *Little Caesar* was being filmed, there was enough of a public outcry against how films, radio, and pulp magazines glorified orga-nized crime to make the studio defensive about the project. In fact, the first image in the movie is a leather-bound copy of the book, an attempt to legitimize the entire production. It's followed by a cautionary quote from Scripture, then a gas station holdup, expertly staged in one wide shot. The fol-lowing scene, set in an all-night diner, continues the subconscious Edward Hopper feel.

Unfortunately, LeRoy's command of the mate-rial deserts him throughout most of the rest of the film. The camera moves during montages; other-wise, the film is as stiff and artificial as the worst early sound films. The sets, designed by Anton Grot, are enormous constructions better suited to the stage than to film. An office for Little Arnie Loach has bookcases twenty-five feet high, filled with volumes no casino manager would ever open. A later set showing Pete Montana's apartment has Ruritarian doors that stretch up to the soundstage ceiling and garish furniture grabbed from some failed operetta, a telling indication of what the Warners studio considered "class."

The sets had "pockets" of sound where floor or boom microphones were secreted. Actors clustered around them, leaving wide areas of the frame out of bounds. Because the mikes had narrow ranges, the actors couldn't move from their spots until there was another camera setup. LeRoy tried to disguise this at times by cutting before actors reached their next marks, but it's a very stilted way of making a film. At times it seems as if directing only meant getting the all dialogue recorded. A love scene between Fairbanks and Farrell is cringe-worthy, with excruciating pauses between the lines.

The film has its share of memorable lines of dialogue: "You can dish it out but it's gotten so you can't take it no more" and "The bigger they come, the harder they fall," as well as Rico's final line: "Mother of mercy, is this the end of Rico?" (Rumors that the line was changed from "Mother of God . . ." may be just that, as the shooting script clearly indicates "mercy.") The final sequence, with a downtrodden Rico tracked through an urban wasteland by relentless cops, has a certain grim beauty.

Little Caesar was an enormous hit, not only ensuring the growth of the gangster genre but also typecasting Robinson for years. The actor tried everything from biopics (*Dr. Ehrlich's Magic Bul-let*, 1940) to horror (*The Amazing Dr. Clitterhouse*, 1938) to spoofing his own persona in *The Whole Town's Talking* (1935) and other comedies. But his most effective roles remained criminal ones, much to his chagrin.

The Forgotten Frontier

The Frontier Nursing Service, Inc., 1930. Silent, B&W, 1.33. 59 minutes.
Featuring: Mrs. Mary Breckinridge.
Credits: Filmmaker: [Mary] Marvin Breckinridge.
Additional Credits: Premiered in New York City on January 15, 1931.
Other Versions: Mary Marvin Breckinridge oversaw a condensed sound version in 1986 for which she provided a voice-over narration.
Available: The Library of Congress. Re-edited, twenty-eight-minute sound version: Carousel Film and Video VHS (1986). Footage from the film is used in *Frontier Nursing Service*, a 1984 documentary directed by Anne Lewis and available from Appalshop (*www.appalshop.org*).

Mary Breckinridge was born in 1905 in New York City, a descendant of a vice-president to James Buchanan on her father's side and rubber magnate B.F. Goodrich on her mother's side. Known as Marvin, she led a life of remarkable accomplish-ment. She became interested in still photography at the age of ten and later studied at the Clarence H. White School of Photography. She graduated from Vassar College in 1927, and was one of the first women in the country to receive a pilot's license.

Her cousin, also named Mary Breckinridge, was born in Memphis, Tennessee, in 1881. She was a teacher and mother of two; her second child, born prematurely, died hours after birth. When her first child later died of appendicitis at the age of four, she divorced her husband and devoted herself to nursing. She trained as a nurse in New York City, worked in Europe following World War I, and studied midwifery in England. In 1923, she began a pilot program in eastern Kentucky, focusing on both child health care and on developing a regional health care system. This was an area of widespread poverty, and one that was exceptionally difficult to travel through. In some areas there were no motor roads within sixty miles. Mail and supplies arrived on the backs of mules and horses.

Breckinridge opened her first clinic in Hyden in 1925, and also built what would become her estate, Wendover. By 1928, the Frontier Nursing Service operated a hospital in Hyden and nine outlying clinics. Financing was a constant problem. Breckinridge exhausted her personal fortune before turning to her family for help. She toured urban areas on fund-raising drives. During one of these she suggested that Mary Marvin might study cinematography and make a film about the Frontier Nursing Service.

Mary Marvin traveled to Kentucky in 1928, spending the summer as a volunteer courier for the Frontier Nursing Service. She made three trips in all, covering some six hundred miles on horseback, interviewing families and nurses, and filming in the winter, spring, and summer. Mary Marvin was responsible for transporting her equipment (which included a hand-cranked 35mm camera), setting up and composing her shots, lighting and exposing her scenes, and directing a cast of nonactors who were re-enacting accidents, emergency calls, inoculation drives, and childbirths.

Considering location difficulties, any usable footage at all would have been an achievement. But *The Forgotten Frontier* stands up to any nonfiction film of its period. Mary Marvin displays a full grasp of cinematic technique and an understanding of film form. Apart from the story it tells, which has its own fascinations, *The Forgotten Frontier* is a beautiful, exciting work of carefully edited sequences, stunning landscapes, and a directorial style that brings viewers directly into the action. The film shows just how difficult it was to travel from hamlet to city, but Mary Marvin also captures the beauty of the countryside, the thrill of crossing a river on horseback, the force of weather. The Frontier Nursing Service's various clinics are documented, as is Mrs. Mary Breckinridge's estate

and the recently completed Hyden Hospital. The film highlights the impact of earlier benefactors while reaching out to new donors, an astute strategy when appealing for donations.

Mary Marvin broke the film into segments, first following nurses on their rounds; showing a campaign to inoculate students at a school; focusing on a farmer bringing his ailing twins to a doctor in the city; and finally re-enacting the rescue of a gunshot victim. In a narration she provided years later, she noted with pleasure how the farmer's twins both grew up to marry. However, the gunshot victim was killed two years later in another feud-related shooting.

The Frontier Nursing Service, which still operates, had a direct impact on the health and well-being of the people of eastern Kentucky. Its public health statistics from 1925 to 1954 bettered the country as a whole. For example, in its area of coverage, the Service achieved a maternal mortality rate of 9.1 per 10,000 births, as opposed to 34 per 10,000 for the entire United States.

Mary Marvin Breckinridge received a commission to film *She Goes to Vassar* in 1931. She also made the first professional film of the archaeological site at Chichén Itzá on Mexico's Yucatan Peninsula, as well as films of her journeys to Rhodesia, the Belgian Congo, and South Africa. As a photojournalist, she covered Africa and Europe, including Nazi rallies in Nuremberg, for *Life*, *Look*, *National Geographic*, the *Washington Post*, and other publications. On radio she worked with Edward R. Murrow, delivering over fifty broadcasts on the CBS Radio Network. In 1940, she married Jefferson Patterson, a diplomat and heir to the National Cash Register fortune. As a result, she was forced to leave journalism by the State Department.

Instead, Mary Marvin devoted herself to her husband's career, and, in later years, to philanthropy. She served on several boards, donated a family estate in Maine to Bowdoin College, and turned a farm in Maryland into a park and museum. The MARPAT Foundation, which she founded in 1985, continues to contribute to causes in the Washington, D.C., area. "I've had a rewarding and useful life," she said in the sound version of *The Forgotten Frontier*. That quiet understatement typifies her approach to filmmaking and to journalism as a whole. And her film stands as a testament to addressing and solving problems that still exist today.

City Lights

United Artists, 1931. Sound, B&W, 1.37. 83 minutes.

Cast: Virginia Cherrill (A blind girl), Florence Lee (Her grandmother), Harry Myers (An eccentric millionaire), Allan Garcia (His butler), Hank Mann (A prizefighter), Charlie Chaplin (A tramp).

Credits: A Comedy Romance in Pantomime written and directed by Charles Chaplin. Assistant directors: Harry Crocker, Henry Bergman, Albert Austin. Photographers: Rollie Totheroh, Gordon Pollock. Settings: Charles D. Hall. Music composed by Charles Chaplin. Musical arrangements by Arthur Johnston. Musical direction by Alfred Newman. "La Violetera" by José Padilla.

Additional Cast: Albert Austin (Streetsweeper; Eddie Mason), Henry Bergman (Mayor; Neighbor on ground floor), Victor Alexander (Boxer), Tom Dempsey (Boxer), Willie Keeler (Boxer), Tony Stabeman (Boxer), Eddie Baker (Referee), Ray Erlenborn (Newsboy), Robert Parrish (Newsboy), Austen Jewell (Newsboy), Jean Harlow (Restaurant extra).

Additional Credits: Produced by Charles Chaplin. Edited by Charles Chaplin, Willard Nico. Production manager: Alfred Reeves. Publicist: Harry Crocker. Script supervisor: Della Steele. Premiered in Los Angeles on January 30, 1931.

Available: Warner Home Video DVD (2004). ISBN: 0-7907-7165-9. UPC: 0-85393-76482-1.

After the release of *The Gold Rush* in 1925, it took Charlie Chaplin three years to get his next feature, *The Circus* (1928), into theaters. A delightful, unassuming film, *The Circus* won Chaplin an honorary Oscar, acknowledgment that he was—fifteen years into his career—one of the most significant figures in the industry. Almost at once he started on his next project, which he planned to build around the theme of blindness. Chaplin considered a film about a blind clown, then decided on a story of a blind flower girl and the tramp who makes sacrifices for her.

As usual, Chaplin began shooting with a plot outline and ideas for sketches rather than a completed script. Using his own money, he built an enormous set containing two city blocks and accompanying buildings, which he filled with a full complement of cars, trucks, and costumed extras. As film historians Kevin Brownlow and David Gill showed in the documentary *Unknown Chaplin* (1983), the comedian worked in an organic fashion, building on simple ideas, expanding or discarding gags, using bits of business to define characters and to get in and out of scenes. It is an extremely expensive and pressure-filled way to shoot film, with no guarantee that the finished footage can be used.

For the part of the flower girl, Chaplin first thought about using one of his previous costars. After spotting socialite Virginia Cherrill at a boxing match, he impulsively signed her to the role. Cherrill not only had no training, she was only casually interested in the filmmaking process. After filming started, Chaplin considered replacing her, and at one point did fire her when she left the set for a hairdressing appointment. The director tested Georgia Hale from *The Gold Rush* for the final scene of the film, but reluctantly concluded that he had spent too much time and money to junk what he had already shot.

The *City Lights* production stretched out over two years and eight months, with 179 days devoted to actual filming. Chaplin attributed several hiatuses to illnesses. Judging from outtakes and deleted scenes unearthed by Brownlow and Gill, the actor and director was struggling with every aspect of the film, from Cherrill to the script to the use of sound. (*The Circus* came out almost a year after *The Jazz Singer* was released; since then, every major Hollywood studio had switched over to sound.)

Chaplin knew what he wanted but not how to achieve it. His entire concept for the film was based around its final scene, a delicate, open-ended encounter that forces the two main characters to erase their dreams, step out of their fantasies, and face up to an unforgiving reality. It is a masterful bit of narrative, equal to the highest accomplishments in the medium, and it demanded incredibly sensitive staging. It must have been unnerving to trust the scene to a disinterested, amateur actress who had failed to succumb to his charms. ("Charlie never liked me and I never liked Charlie," Cherrill revealed some fifty years later.)

What could Chaplin have done with a more professional actress? Janet Gaynor had been playing similar roles in a half-dozen films, for example. But as the screen tests for Georgia Hale show, Chaplin was intent on presenting a fantasy image of a woman. Hale was far too practiced, far too mature, to fit into how Chaplin saw the flower girl. In the tests you can see him trying to strip the modernity away from Hale, slowing her down, in the process taking away her individuality. With a Hale or Gaynor in the flower girl's role, the entire film would have collapsed.

If staging the final scene was difficult, it was even harder to get to that point in the narrative. Chaplin was already paring down his approach to filming, eliminating all but the essential ingredients for his gags and staging them in the simplest methods available. Like Buster Keaton did later in his career, Chaplin reached back to what had worked for him before—in his case, the stock figures and situations of the music hall. Chaplin could move the camera when he wanted to, and fully understood the fundamentals of editing, but he was increasingly content to have his characters operate as if behind a stage proscenium.

Much of the plot to *City Lights* could have come from one of the Tramp's early two-reelers for Keystone or Mutual. Chaplin and Roscoe Arbuckle played drunken aristocrats in *The Rounders* (1914), for example, and Chaplin was already toying with boxing in *The Knockout* (1914) and *The Champion* (1915). The director added to and subtracted from the body of *City Lights* as shooting progressed, in one instance constructing a seven-minute comic sequence that ranks with his best pantomime and then cutting it out because it impeded the flow of the story. At times during the film he seems to be using a comic shorthand, setting up gags he never finishes, alluding to familiar situations as if filmgoers already knew the punch lines.

The finished product still bears some signs of Chaplin's desperation. *City Lights* spends some five minutes introducing Chaplin's Tramp character before he meets Cherrill's flower girl. Their introduction required some three hundred takes before Chaplin was satisfied; amateur footage shot on the set shows the director increasingly frustrated with Cherrill's performance, unable to adjust it satisfactorily.

His solution to the scene employed rapid camera pans left and right from a central composition, a technique few other directors have mastered.

The narrative then swings away from the tramp and the flower girl, focusing on subplots involving Harry Myers' alcoholic millionaire and boxing. Unlike Chaplin's earlier films, *City Lights* takes place over a long period of time, a stretch during which the tramp's fortunes visibly decline. When the final scene arrives, Chaplin's decision to use Cherrill pays off: her stiff inexpressiveness and her lack of compassion for Chaplin as a character or employer fit the moment perfectly.

Chaplin realized that he had to provide a soundtrack for *City Lights*, but he worried that filming in English might cut off his foreign markets. Several studios were experimenting with filming in different languages, but Chaplin had never really spoken much in his stage career either, and he was not prepared to give up the pantomime that defined his screen persona. Sound effects pop up intermittently, and Chaplin constructed a score from several of his own themes, as well as "La Violetera" by José Padilla. But *City Lights* is for all purposes a silent film, the last from such a major star.

The film was a critical and financial success, and an influence on subsequent filmmakers like Orson Welles, Federico Fellini, and Stanley Kubrick. Chaplin's next film, *Modern Times*, would not be released until 1936. Cherrill's subsequent movie career was short-lived. In real life, she was the first of Cary Grant's wives.

Dracula

Universal, 1931. Sound, B&W, 1.73. 74 minutes.

Cast: Bela Lugosi ([Count] Dracula), Helen Chandler (Mina [Seward]), David Manners (John [Jonathan] Harker), Frances Dade (Lucy [Western]), Dwight Frye (Renfield), Edward Van Sloan (Dr. Van Helsing), Herbert Bunston (Doctor Seward), Frances Dade (Lucy), Joan Standing (Maid), Charles Gerrard (Martin).

Credits: Directed by Tod Browning. Play script by Garrett Fort. Adaptation and dialogue: Tod Browning. From the play adapted by Hamilton Deane & John Balderston. Based on the play by Hamilton Deane and the novel by Bram Stoker. Produced by Carl Laemmle, Jr., Tod Browning. Director of photography: Karl Freund. Supervising art director: Charles D. Hall. Assistant director: Scott Beal. Recording supervision: C. Roy Hunter. Film editor: Milton Carruth. Supervising film editor: Maurice Pivar.

Additional Cast: Michael Visaroff (Innkeeper), Charles Gerrard (Attendant), Moon Carroll (Maid), Joan Standing (English nurse), Carla Laemmle (Stagecoach passenger); Jeraldine Dvorak, Dorothy Tree, Cornelia Thaw [Mildred Peirce] (Dracula's wives); Anita Harder (Flower girl).

Additional Credits: Special effects: William Davison. Makeup: Jack Pierce. Music director: Heinz Roemheld. Released February 12, 1931.

Cast, Spanish Version: Carlos Villar (Conde Dracula), Lupita Tovar (Eva), Barry Norton (Juan Harker), Pablo Alvarez Rubio (Renfield), Eduardo Arozamena (Van Helsing), José Soriano Viosca (Doctor Seward), Carmen Guerrero (Lucia), Amelia Senisterra (Marta), Manuel Arbo (Martin).

Credits, Spanish Version: Directed by Geoge Melford. Associate producer: Paul Kohner. Spanish version: B. Fernandez Cue. Artistic director: Charles D. Hall. Sound supervisor: C. Roy Hunter. Director of photography: George Robinson. Film editor: Arturo Tavares. Supervising editor: Maurice Pivar.

Other Versions: Universal's first sequel was *Dracula's Daughter* in 1936, followed by *Son of Dracula* in 1943. The character, authorized or not, subsequently appeared in scores of films, television shows, and cartoons.

Available: Universal Studios DVD (1999). IBN: 0-7832-2745-0. UPC: 0-2519-20324-2-4. MCA Universal Home Video VHS (1991). ISBN: 1-55880-468-4. UPC: 0-9689-55003-3-6.

Although vampires are found in almost every culture, our modern fascination with them stems from Bram Stoker's 1897 novel *Dracula*. Stoker led a full but ultimately sad life marked by reversals and disappointments. Born in Dublin in 1847, he wrote freelance theater reviews before meeting and befriending actor Henry Irving in 1876. For over twenty years Stoker labored for the notoriously demanding star, turning aside his own ambitions. Writers like David J. Skal portray an author in thrall to his employer, a monstrous personality who sucked away Stoker's energy.

You can find elements of Irving in the character of Dracula, but the vampire contains a multitude of other traits and antecedents. Skal points out many Shakespearean references—to Macbeth and his three witches, for example, or the fact that Stoker once admitted to basing the vampire on Irving's portrayal of Shylock. Stoker was also influenced by the society surrounding him, such as Oscar Wilde's arrest for homosexuality in 1875, controversy over immigrants from Eastern Europe taking over London neighborhoods, and the spread of venereal diseases like syphilis.

Most critics today agree that Stoker wasn't fully aware of the implications of what he was writing. Reading the novel—actually a series of journal entries and letters written in an ornate style—can be a chore. Reduce the plot to strictly visual terms, take away Stoker's repressed, convoluted writing, and his vision is more clearly terrifying.

Stoker may have been aiming for a dramatic version of the story all along. He directed a staged reading of his own adaptation of the novel within weeks after it had been published, but couldn't convince Irving or anyone else to mount a production. After a series of strokes, Stoker died in 1912. His widow Florence carefully guarded the rights to *Dracula*, almost the only thing of worth in her husband's estate. This meant prosecuting filmmakers and theater producers who tried to adapt her husband's novel, an insurmountable task given that the very word "vampire" had become slang for seductress. A 1920 Hungarian movie escaped her notice, but when F. W. Murnau made *Nosferatu*, a very thinly disguised version of the novel, in 1921, Mrs. Stoker won a legal judgment ordering the film destroyed. (Luckily, prints have survived.)

Mrs. Stoker's next ploy was to authorize theatrical productions, the first of these to family friend Hamilton Deane. He produced a version of *Dracula* in London in 1924, in Skal's words imagining the vampire as a "devilish vaudeville magician in evening dress and an opera cloak." This vision of the character has persisted to this very day, including the high collar on his cape, which helped hide the actor when the vampire "disappeared" through a trap door on stage. An American producer hired John L. Balderston to revise Deane's play for stateside audiences; this production was enough of a hit when it opened in New York City in 1927 that it eventually supported two road companies. The West Coast road company featured Bela Lugosi in the title role.

Several studios, including MGM and Fox Films, negotiated with Mrs. Stoker, Deane, Balderston, and other involved parties for the film rights. Universal, despite head Carl Laemmle's reputed aversion to horror, won, but Lon Chaney, slated for the role, died of cancer before filming could start. A much smaller production was prepared, with the studio playing Bela Lugosi $3,500 for seven weeks' work—the total amount the actor received for a performance so startling and persuasive that it typecast him forever.

The film *Dracula* has several impressively large and detailed sets, and director Tod Browning added sequences that make use of cinematic devices unavailable on stage. But Universal was on the verge of bankruptcy, and the profligate props and extras shown off in *All Quiet on the Western Front* just a few months earlier are nowhere to be found. Instead, an unknown lead actor, minimal special effects, and scenes shot with largely static cameras are the norm. (Universal tried to save even more money by shooting a version in Spanish at night, using the same sets. Directed by George Melford, and starring Carlos Villarias as the Count, this *Dracula* has adherents who claim it is better than the English version. That may be due in part to the fact that the crew for the Spanish version could watch the rushes from the English one before starting their night's work.)

Browning and his crew made several minor changes (the novel's Mina Harker, changed to Lucy Seward in the play, becomes Mina Seward; Lucy Westenra evolves from Weston to Western), but basically followed Deane's play. Mina's fiancé Harker, a crucial figure in the novel, is reduced to a hanger-on in the plays and the film. Unlike the novel, Renfield is the agent who brings Dracula from Transylvania to England, only to be driven insane by the vampire. (Dwight Frye was so memorable as Renfield that he later had trouble finding "normal" roles). Van Helsing becomes the hero, the only person who can stop the vampire (it was the role Deane chose to play on stage instead of Dracula). The doctor would become even more heroic in subsequent films, in 2004 earning his own vehicle, Universal's *Van Helsing*.

The crux of this *Dracula* centers around Mina's virginal sacrifice to the vampire, a sacrifice that makes explicit the perverse sexuality pervading the film. Helen Chandler is shy and withdrawn in the role, making Lugosi's work all that more impressive. He largely directed himself, as Browning had little interest in the film after Chaney died. Lugosi's peculiarly slow, halting speech, icy expressions, and slicked-back hair are so sinister, so macabre, that he became the standard all subsequent vampires had to match.

Cinematographer Karl Freund reportedly disliked Browning so much that he would simply turn on the camera and let it run unattended. Skal points out one shot of Manners, Chandler, and Van Sloan that lasts nearly three minutes; ordinarily it would have been broken down into close-ups and reaction shots, but these were apparently never filmed. Still, for a film of that period the camera moves about relatively freely. Principal photography was finished by mid-November 1930, well under budget. (The final cost was close to a half-million dollars, less than a third of the cost of a top-line studio film.)

Despite mixed reviews, *Dracula* was the top-performing film of the year for Universal.

Its success encouraged Laemmle to put into production John Balderston's screenplay for *Frankenstein*, based on a stage adaptation of Mary Shelley's novel.

Although Universal made several sequels, Lugosi officially appeared as the vampire only one more time. Yet he was so identified with the role that he was buried in a Dracula costume. In 1963, his son Bela Lugosi, Jr., began a suit against Universal, trying to obtain a portion of the ancillary revenue the studio received from licensing his father's image for plastic models, Halloween costumes, card games, candy, jewelry, clothing, records, and many other items. After a long legal battle, the court ruled that the elder Lugosi had entered the public domain after his death.

Universal rereleased *Dracula* theatrically in 1938 and 1947, and, through its subsidiary Screen Gems, to television in 1957. Meanwhile, the vampire's impact spread throughout cinema. The $2 million the film earned at the box office rescued Universal from insolvency (the play made a similar amount), and started a cycle of horror films that introduced characters like Frankenstein's monster and the Invisible Man. Vampires figured in notable films like Carl Theodor Dreyer's *Vampyr*, and Dracula himself (played by Christopher Lee) starred in a series from Hammer Studios.

Tabu

Paramount, 1931. Sound, B&W, 1.37. 81 minutes.
Cast: Matahi (The boy), Reri [Anne Chevalier] (The girl), Jean [William Bambridge] (The policeman), Hitu (The old warrior).
Credits: Directed by F.W. Murnau. Told by F.W. Murnau, R.J. Flaherty. Photographed by Floyd Crosby. Musical setting: Hugo Riesenfeld. Recorded on RCA Photophone. A Murnau-Flaherty production.
Additional Cast: Jules (The captain), Ah Fong (The businessman), Kong Ah (Chinese trader).
Additional Credits: Additional photography: Robert Flaherty. Edited by Arthur Brooks. Associate producer: David Flaherty. Assistant director: William Bambridge. Title on screen: *Tabu: A Story of the South Seas*. Production dates: January to October 1930. Premiered in New York on March 18, 1931, New York City.
Awards: Oscar for Best Cinematography.
Available: Image Entertainment DVD (2002). UPC: 0-14381-5931-2-9.

One of the last of the great silent films, *Tabu* began as a collaboration between F.W. Murnau and Robert Flaherty, regarded by their peers as two of the most accomplished directors in motion pictures. Flaherty, responsible for the groundbreaking documentary *Nanook of the North* (1922), had spent eighteen months filming *Moana* (1926) on the South Sea island of Samoa. (It took him over a year to edit the film.) However, he had trouble adjusting to working within the film industry. He quit an assignment from MGM to codirect *White Shadows in the South Seas* (1928) with W.S. Van Dyke, and the Fox Film Corporation had ceased financing his attempt to film Pueblo Indians in New Mexico.

Murnau was in the process of leaving the Fox studio after relinquishing control of *Our Daily Bread* (released in 1930 as *City Girl*). He bought a yacht and invited Flaherty to sail with him to Tahiti, where they could make a film together. After forming Flaherty-Murnau Productions, Inc., Murnau secured a production deal from Colorart, but this fell apart almost as soon as they arrived in Tahiti.

So did Flaherty's collaboration with Murnau. It became apparent almost at once that Murnau

Lovers Matahi and Reri [Anne Chevalier] in *Tabu*. *Photo courtesy of Milestone Film & Video*

would dictate the shooting. No longer a codirector, Flaherty was still cinematographer. When he started experiencing camera problems, he was forced to send for Floyd Crosby to help him photograph the film. Crosby, who had worked with Flaherty in New Mexico, ended up shooting almost all of *Tabu*. The production lasted from January to October 1930. When filming ended, Flaherty had to sell his share of the picture back to Murnau to settle his debts.

Murnau paid for the film from his own savings, forcing him to rely on improvised shooting techniques and a cast of nonprofessionals instead of the soundstages and trained actors he had used earlier in his career. Yet the look of *Tabu* is as intensely controlled as *Sunrise* (1927), his Hollywood debut. The angles and shadows in both films seem to predict the destinies of the characters, pinning them into confrontations and choices they would rather avoid.

But *Tabu* feels more personal than *Sunrise*, a Registry title. Murnau's distrust of civilization is apparent in both films. Film historian Scott Eyman quotes a letter from the director to his mother: "The thought of cities and all those people is repulsive to me. I want to be alone, [but] I am never 'at home' anywhere." Where *Sunrise* found a solution or cure of sorts in a rural culture, nothing can stop implacable fate in *Tabu*. The film's doomed romance may be an expression of the director's own failed relationships, his inability as a homosexual to find personal happiness in a restrictive, disapproving society.

Few filmmakers have captured a sense of longing and loss as fully and beautifully as Murnau did in *Tabu*. It's tempting to see in Crosby's cinematography something of Flaherty's *Moana*. Both films revel in the glittering reflections and sinuous movement of the ocean. Murnau's vision moves *Tabu* beyond observation into an elemental world of stark emotions. Taken on its own terms, it is perhaps the fullest expression of the art of silent cinema.

Murnau had high hopes for *Tabu*, using the remainder of his Hollywood earnings to hire Hugo Riesenfeld to compose a musical score. (Eyman puts the total budget for *Tabu* at $150,000, an enormous price for a privately financed film.) Murnau also signed a contract with Paramount to distribute the film. Paramount officials suggested to the trade press that Murnau would make additional films for the studio, but the director seemed intent on returning to Tahiti, possibly to shoot an adaptation of Herman Melville's *Typee*. However, he died in a car accident on the Pacific Coast Highway near Santa Barbara a week before *Tabu* opened.

In his notes on *Tabu*, film distributor Dennis Doros wrote that only eleven people, including Greta Garbo, attended Murnau's service in Hollywood. Fritz Lang spoke at a funeral service in Berlin, saying "a pioneer had left us in the midst of his career, a man to whom the cinema owes its fundamental character, artistically as well as technically."

Murnau's death complicated the distribution of *Tabu*, since his contract with Paramount stipulated that the rights to the film return to him after five years. His brother Robert Plumpe took possession of the camera negative in Germany; it was destroyed during World War II. (However, the Austrian Filmmuseum currently holds about ten hours of negative "outtakes," leaving open the possibility that the original negative for *Tabu* still exists.) Rowland and Samuel Brown purchased worldwide rights to *Tabu* in 1940, and released a shortened, censored version in 1948. Murnau's nieces bought the rights back in the 1960s.

Flaherty's subsequent career included stints with John Grierson in Great Britain, as well as the documentary *Man of Aran* (1934). He worked for the U.S. Film Service before accepting a commission from Standard Oil to direct *Louisiana Story* (1948), a Registry title. Crosby traveled through South America in the 1930s, returning to the United States to work on *The River* (1937), a Registry title, with Pare Lorentz.

The actor Jean's real name was William Bambridge; he had a small part in *Mutiny on the Bounty* (1935). Anne Chevalier, who used the name Reri, was sixteen at the time of filming; she would later appear as a dancer in the *Ziegfeld Follies of 1931* and in New York City nightclubs. She visited Murnau's family in Berlin on a tour of Europe that included England and France. In 1934 she starred with her new husband in *Black Pearl*, a Polish film, but after her marriage failed, she returned to the islands. She also had an uncredited part in John Ford's *The Hurricane* (1937), shot in Los Angeles. Chevalier died in 1977.

The Public Enemy

First National Pictures, 1931. Sound, B&W, 1.37. 84 minutes.

Cast: James Cagney (Tom Powers), Jean Harlow (Gwen Allen), Edward Woods (Matt Doyle), Joan Blondell (Mamie), Donald Cook (Mike Powers), Leslie Fenton (Nails Nathan), Beryl Mercer (Ma Powers), Robert O'Connor (Paddy Ryan), Murray Kinnell (Putty Nose).

Credits: Directed by William A. Wellman. Based on the novel *Beer and Blood* by Kubec Glasmon and John Bright. Screen adaptation: Harvey Thew. Photography by Dev Jennings. Art director: Max Parker. Edited by Edw. [Edward] M. McDermott. Wardrobe by Earl Luick. Vitaphone Orchestra conducted by David Mendoza.

Additional Cast: Mae Clarke (Kitty), Snitz Edwards (Poker player/Door watchman), Mia Marvin (Jane), Frankie Darro (Matt Doyle as a boy), Frank Coghlan Jr. (Tom Powers as a boy).

Additional Credits: Produced by Darryl F. Zanuck. Production dates: January to February 1931. Released April 23, 1931.

Available: Warner Home Video DVD (2005). ISBN: 0-7907-9224-9. UPC: 0-12569-69062-2.

The second in an unofficial gangster trilogy that includes *Little Caesar* and *Scarface*, *The Public Enemy* is in many ways the best of the trio. One proponent of that view is director Martin Scorsese, who sees in the film's brutality and realism the seeds of subsequent movies from the Warner Brothers studio. This is the film that made James Cagney a star, that pushed the limits of what was acceptable in movies, and that gave a generation of tough-guy actors standards to live up to.

The film was based on *Beer and Blood*, a novel by Kubec Glasmon and John Bright. (Later editions of the book used the title *The Public Enemy*; many also featured stills from the film.) Darryl F. Zanuck, at the time head of production at Warners, assigned the project to William A. Wellman, known by his nickname "Wild Bill." Accounts vary as to the casting process, but everyone agrees that Edward Woods was originally slated to star as Tom Powers. Whether Zanuck or Wellman or Cagney made the decision or not doesn't matter as much as the fact that Cagney switched roles with Woods shortly before filming began.

Cagney had appeared in four films before this. Born in New York City in 1899, he grew up on the same Lower East Side that nurtured talents like Irving Berlin and George Gershwin before moving to Yorkville, a predominately German neighborhood. In his autobiography, *Cagney by Cagney*, the actor admitted to a rough upbringing filled with street fights. Acting work in Yorkville led to a job in the chorus for a Broadway musical. Cagney also toured in vaudeville with his wife Frances, whom he had met on stage and married in 1922. By 1925 he had carved out a career of sorts in theater. His entry into film came when the play *Penny Arcade* was purchased by Warner Brothers. The studio brought Cagney and his costar Joan Blondell out to Hollywood to reprise their roles in the screen adaptation, *Sinners' Holiday* (1930).

Cagney may have caught Zanuck's attention with his role in *The Millionaire* (1931), a George Arliss vehicle in which the actor played a fast-talking insurance salesman. Tom Powers in *The Public Enemy* was his first starring role, and he positively attacked it. Apart from the bagful of stage, boxing, and other urban tricks he brought to the role, Cagney was alive, present in his scenes in a way his fellow actors were not. (In his autobiography,

Cagney said he based his role on Jack "Dirty Neck" Lafferty, a friend of his father's who ended up in Sing Sing after stealing a car and gunning down its owner.)

Cagney's eyes are always alert, always accurate. In a throwaway scene in which crime boss Paddy Ryan (Robert O'Connor) is describing a new alliance with a brewery owner, his eyes burn through his shots, commanding attention, bringing urgency to a moment that doesn't really deserve it.

The supporting cast seems woefully inadequate today, apart from a few reliable character actors like O'Connor and Snitz Edwards. Cagney overpowers Woods, who plays his childhood pal; and Donald Cook, stuck in a thankless role as the voice of moral authority. Zanuck borrowed Jean Harlow from Howard Hughes as an object of desire for Cagney's character. She had been playing a comic foil for Laurel and Hardy not two years earlier, and her performance as a sexpot in Hughes's *Hell's Angels* did not win her much critical respect. Her screen persona had yet to be defined in *The Public Enemy*; it would take Frank Capra at Columbia—and, more important, the MGM star machinery—to make Harlow a true celebrity. Here she seems awkward, unsure of her lines, as stiff as a mannequin at times.

Joan Blondell, on the other hand, made such a strong impression in a small role as a nightclub pick-up that Warners built several vehicles around her. Blondell had a perfect screen name; enormous eyes that could register desire, skepticism, and humor in equal doses; a voice that pierced through poor miking; and a voluptuous body that the studio exploited as much as the Production Code would allow. (She was also shorter than Cagney, making her an ideal partner for him.) In films like *Havana Widows* (1934), in which she costarred with Glenda Farrell, Blondell ridiculed men, propriety, and morals with an endearing and oddly wholesome glee.

Former dancer Mae Clarke, only months away from lead roles in *Waterloo Bridge* and *Frankenstein*, was one of many unbilled actors in *The Public Enemy*. She shares the film's single most memorable scene with Cagney, the infamous "grapefruit" moment. It's a measure of Cagney's skill that much of his performance seems improvised, and some feel that his impulse to shove half a grapefruit into his girlfriend's face when she complains about his drinking at breakfast caught the crew and director by surprise. Cagney and Clarke may have devised

the bit during rehearsal, but like many other moments in the film it was staged too carefully to be completely off-the-cuff. (Another example of an apparently improvised moment: Cagney reacts angrily when he is refused entry at a speakeasy. He responds by punching his hand through the front door peephole, a moment that surprises no matter how many times you see it. But it couldn't have been improvised, because Cagney would have broken his hand if the prop department hadn't prepared a "flyaway" peephole cover.)

This was a pivotal year for director William Wellman. After drawing attention with *Wings* (1928), he struggled with the transition to sound, making flops like *Chinatown Nights* that are close to unwatchable today. In 1931 he made a total of five films, working with stars like Cagney, Barbara Stanwyck, and Clark Gable. His technique had become so fluid that he could stage an extended dialogue scene on location in a diner, and incorporate a freight train passing right outside the door into the plot (*Other Men's Women*, 1931). Wellman was also paying more attention to the psychological makeup of his characters. He may not have had the best actors to work with, but the roles in *The Public Enemy* make more sense than those in any contemporary gangster film.

The film moves better than most from that period, too. This is partly due to Wellman's experimenting with camera angles, partly due to Dev Jennings's fluid camera work, partly from touches like using live ammunition when Powers flees around a building corner from machine gunners, and partly from a script that eliminates almost all of the material that would explain or condone Cagney's character.

Despite its bleak ending, *The Public Enemy* couldn't help but paint a glamorous picture of life as a gangster. Was it better to toil endlessly as a wage slave, to come back from war a shell-shocked veteran, to face a life of tenement drudgery—or to live it up in nightclubs and penthouse apartments, cosseted by platinum-blond molls, wearing tailored clothes and driving the latest roadsters? While the film doesn't glorify Tom Powers, it does belittles his brother Mike's sanctimonious preaching. As Tom snarls to his brother, still in his Army uniform, "You didn't get those medals holding hands with the Germans."

The Public Enemy hit filmgoers differently than *Little Caesar* and *Scarface*. Edward G. Robinson's Rico Bandello and Paul Muni's Tony Camonte were clearly "other" characters, immigrant, semiliterate Italians who were different from the way most filmgoers perceived themselves. Cagney was an all-American figure, and a callous murderer who showed no remorse for his crimes. (The film was shocking up to a point; these are still fanciful depictions of crooks who dress in coats and ties for breakfast.)

Cagney would spend the rest of his career reacting to this role. Trapped in a seven-year contract at Warners, he learned that he was making less than half the salary of other studio stars. When he wasn't threatening to quit Warners, he found himself in vehicles that placed his urban tough-guy character in interchangeable plots. Although he appeared in musicals, comedies, and even Shakespeare, the public clamored for more gangster roles. Cagney obliged with films like *Angels With Dirty Faces* (1938), *The Roaring Twenties* (1939), and *White Heat* (1949), but he won his Oscar as George M. Cohan in *Yankee Doodle Dandy* (1942). (Cagney also played Lon Chaney in *Man of a Thousand Faces,* 1957.)

Frankenstein

Universal, 1931. Sound, B&W, 1.37. 70 minutes.

Cast: Colin Clive (Henry Frankenstein), Mae Clarke (Elizabeth), John Boles (Victor Moritz), Boris Karloff (The Monster), Edward Van Sloan (Doctor Waldman), Frederick Kerr (Baron Frankenstein), Dwight Frye (Fritz), Lionel Belmore (The Burgomaster), Marilyn Harris (Little Maria).

Credits: Directed by James Whale. Based upon the composition by John L. Balderston. From the novel by Mrs. Percy B. Shelley. Adapted from the play by Peggy Webling. Screen Play: Garrett Fort, Francis Edward Faragoh. Scenario Editor: Richard Schayer. Produced by Carl Laemmle, Jr. Associate producer: E.M. Asher. Recording supervision: C. Roy Hunter. Cinematographer: Arthur Edeson. Film editor: Clarence Kolster. Supervising Film Editor: Maurice Pivar. Art director: Charles D. Hall. Western Electric Sound System.

Additional Cast: Ted Billings, Mary Gordon, Soledad Jiménez.

Additional Credits: Music: Bernhard Kaun. Makeup: Jack Pierce. Set design: Herman Rosse. Special effects: John Fulton, Frank Grove [Frank Graves], Kenneth Strickfaden, Raymond Lindsay. Production dates: August 24 to October 3, 1931. Released November 21, 1931.

Other Versions: Followed by *Bride of Frankenstein* (1935).

Available: Universal Studios DVD (2004). UPC: 25192446122.

Although Universal head Carl Laemmle professed to dislike horror films, after the success of *Dracula* (1931), the studio wasted little time in preparing *Frankenstein*, a novel that grew out of a summer vacation on Lake Geneva. Mary Wollstonecraft, its author, was the daughter of author and publisher William Godwin and noted feminist Mary Wollstonecraft, who died days after her birth. Poet Percy Bysshe Shelley, who was supporting Godwin financially, met Mary Wollstonecraft when she was fifteen. Although he was a married father of two, they fell in love, and Mary traveled with him to Europe when he abandoned his family.

In 1815, Percy and Mary accompanied their friend Jane (later Claire) Clairemont to Switzerland, where they rented a house near Lord Byron. That summer was the coldest in a century, and the friends spent much of their time huddled by a fireplace. It was Byron who suggested they hold a contest to see who could write the scariest story. Mary claimed that the inspiration for her novel came from a dream she had about a sinister laboratory, the first scene she wrote. She was eighteen when she finished *Frankenstein*. Published anonymously in 1818, the novel was an immediate success. Stage adaptations followed, almost two dozen by the turn of the twentieth century.

By that time the name Frankenstein had become part of the cultural consciousness. Most stage adaptations discarded large portions of the novel, which ranged up to the Arctic and back. For the theater, it became most practical to concentrate on Frankenstein's lab and the formation of the monster. Playwrights introduced elements, such as Frankenstein's sinister lab assistant. Meanwhile, the public tended to associate Frankenstein with the monster itself, not the doctor who assembled him from unearthed body parts and cadavers.

The first film version was released by Edison in 1910. Directed by J. Searle Dawley and starring Charles Ogle as the monster, it lasted sixteen minutes. Universal's version came from a 1927 play by Peggy Webling, with Hamilton Deane as the monster. (He had also written and starred in a stage version of *Dracula*.) The play offered a version of the monster as a sort of Hyde to Frankenstein's Jekyll. The project was originally announced for director Robert Florey and Bela Lugosi, the star of the film *Dracula*. For reasons that have never been explained, Universal took the film away from Florey and assigned it to James Whale.

Born in 1893 in a mining town in England, Whale left his working-class background when he enlisted in the British Army at the age of seventeen in World War I. After the war he acted, directed, and designed sets in various London theater companies. *Journey's End*, a blockbuster hit, brought him to Broadway and then to Hollywood, where he also directed the film version of another stage hit, *Waterloo Bridge*.

Whale cast Clive Brook (who had starred in *Journey's End*) as Henry Frankenstein, and Mae Clarke from *Waterloo Bridge* as Frankenstein's fiancée, Elizabeth. Boris Karloff's daughter Sara said that her father was cast as the monster after Whale spotted him eating in the studio commissary. Born William Henry Pratt in England in 1887, the future Karloff emigrated to Canada, where he spent a decade touring with various theater companies, both in that country and in the United States. He made his film debut as an extra in 1916, and by Sara Karloff's count had bit and extra parts in over eighty films before *Frankenstein*.

Makeup for the monster was developed by Jack Pierce, an imperious craftsman who frightened much of the cast. It took three hours each day to apply the monster's mask, a process makeup and special effects expert Rick Baker describes as painful. Pierce used cotton, spirit gum, and collodion (a thick syrup once used to glue on surgical dressings) to "build" the monster's brow and flat forehead, then applied a greenish coating. Mortician's wax held down Karloff's eyelids. (Universal copyrighted Pierce's design for the monster, and the studio has zealously litigated against the unauthorized use of the monster's look.)

Whale worked closely with art director Charles D. Hall in designing the sets, in particular Frankenstein's laboratory, set in a deserted watchtower, and the windmill that provides the fiery climax to the film. Instruments in the lab itself—a huge influence on subsequent horror and science fiction films—were built by Frank Graves, Kenneth Strickfaden, and Raymond Lindsay.

Whale gave the film a distinctly different look than the relatively stagebound *Dracula*. Tod Browning's version of the latter was essentially a silent film with dialogue added, and almost all of the story could have been presented on a stage. From the opening shot of *Frankenstein*—a tight pan across mourners in a cemetery—Whale utilizes all of the techniques available to movies to build an eerie sense of the macabre. The director was comfortable enough with sound to use it with restraint, and adept enough with the camera to abandon the stage proscenium entirely, using all the dimensions of the set to advance the story and enhance its

atmosphere. The sound of dirt hitting the coffin, the glint in Frankenstein's eye as he stares at the funeral party, the black humor as his assistant Fritz wrestles the coffin upright show a director with a sophisticated understanding of the capabilities of the medium.

Unfortunately, much of *Frankenstein* fails to match that level. A third of the film is devoted to stagey exposition, to arguments for and against science, to the same dull talk that clutters many horror films today. As the doddering old Baron Frankenstein, Frederick Kerr shows some awareness of how ridiculous the script is, muttering through his scenes like Popeye. The other leads, especially Universal's resident stiff John Boles, play in a grimly determined style that feels artificial today.

Karloff finally arrives a half hour into the movie, giving one of the central performances in film. Using only his eyes and some stiff gestures, he manages to convey the monster's knowledge of a previous life, knowledge hidden in the haze and pain of his rebirth. He makes the monster sympathetic, an element that distinguishes *Frankenstein* from almost all other horror movies.

The studio embarked on *Frankenstein* under a shroud of secrecy, realizing that the appearance of the monster was the project's strongest calling card. Publicity pitched the monster in the tradition of the studio's other horror films: *The Hunchback of Notre Dame*, *The Phantom of the Opera*, and *Dracula*. The monster was "The walking nightmare that frightened the world." When executives saw the finished film, they almost panicked, ordering Whale to shoot a prologue in which Edward Van Sloan spoke to the audience in an attempt to lighten what was about to follow.

Censors still objected to many elements in the film, notably the encounter between the monster and a farmer's daughter, close-ups of a hypodermic needle, and the extent to which Fritz tortured the monster with fire. Frankenstein's line, "Now I know what it is like to be God," had to be removed when the film was reissued in 1937, as did what happened to Little Maria on the banks of a placid pond.

Universal protected its franchise. It took four years to make a sequel, *Bride of Frankenstein*, although a radio series appeared soon after the initial release. It took many years for the monster to be cheapened into a comic figure.

A Bronx Morning

Jay Leyda, 1931. Silent, B&W, 1.33. 11 minutes.
Credits: Filmmaker: Jay Leyda.
Available: Image Entertainment DVD, *More Treasures from American Film Archives 1894–1931* (2004). ISBN: 0-9747099-1-3. UPC: 0-14381-2271-2-3.

By the time Jay Leyda was shooting *A Bronx Morning*, the city documentary had grown into its own genre. In the ten years since Paul Strand and Charles Sheeler shot *Manhatta* (1921), many other filmmakers had attempted similar films. Both Robert Florey and Robert Flaherty shot films about New York City, *Skyscraper Symphony* (1929) and *24 Dollar Island* (1926) respectively. In Europe, the genre proved a sort of seedbed for filmmakers. *Berlin: Symphony of a City* (1927) helped start the careers of Karl Freund and Carl Mayer. *Menschen am Sontag* (1930), also set in Berlin, featured contributions from no less than five future Hollywood directors: Curt Siodmak, his brother Robert, Edgar G. Ulmer, Fred Zinnemann, and Billy Wilder. Similar films can be found about London, Paris, and other metropolises.

The format for city documentaries was similar throughout the world. The first problem filmmakers encountered was to find a way to give meaning to shots that had none apart from what they were documenting. One shot of a skyscraper is very much like any other: it's what precedes and follows that shot that provides the context for the film. For someone like Flaherty, whose visual sense and grasp of editing rivaled any filmmaker of his time, the city documentary takes on a majesty that is both enormous and alarming. *24 Dollar Island* is an overwhelming assemblage of construction scenes, harbor footage, and skyscraper portraits that resemble nothing so much as high-fashion glamour photography. Built like a hymn to commerce, the film is almost devoid of life, apart from worker drones scurrying around pits filled with mud and rocks. The film's anonymous, towering buildings demand obeisance. Even trees quail and die before them. Flaherty knew what his shots would look like before he filmed them, and the effects he achieved have the earmarks of an artist in full control of his abilities. His film moves with both grace and a sense of dread, and leaves viewers with the queasy sense that the city may have been built for the wrong reasons.

Florey, fresh off the success of his *Life and Death of 9413* (1928), took a much less judgmental attitude toward the city. His *Skyscraper Symphony* is a careful but somewhat lifeless montage of building exteriors, based a bit on the landscape footage in *Entr'acte* (1924). The film has little to say about commerce or society or even architecture, and the fact that it was filmed right around the time Florey was grappling with the Marx Brothers in a Queens studio for their first sound film, *The Cocoanuts*, suggests that more than anything he was looking for a subject that wouldn't talk back.

Leyda was born in Detroit in 1910, and filmed *A Bronx Morning* before his career as a scholar and film historian really began. He had moved to New York in 1929 to work as an assistant to Ralph Steiner, whose H_2O (1929) is as influential as any city documentary. Two years later, Leyda went to Moscow to study film with Sergei Eisenstein, and eventually helped translate much of the Russian director's writings into English. He received a Rockefeller Foundation grant as a film archivist at the Museum of Modern Art, where he worked on a study of D.W. Griffith. He later received a Guggenheim Fellowship to research Emily Dickinson; his two-volume biography on the poet, *The Years and Hours of Emily Dickinson*, was published by the Yale University Press in 1960. Leyda also wrote and edited works on Herman Melville, Sergei Rachmaninoff, Alexander Dovzhenko, and V.I. Pudovkin.

Leyda's career might make *A Bronx Morning* sound forbidding, but the film is like a slight and charming character sketch rather than a weighty tome. Like most city documentaries, it uses transportation to ease into its subject, in Leyda's case an elevated train traveling through a Bronx neighborhood. The first shots are almost abstract, until the tracks of the elevated gradually resolve. Rather than determine what the Bronx means beforehand, Leyda finds his subject through his footage. He holds a shot of a subway car long enough to capture the reflection of a church dome in its window, and exploits his overhead angle to show electrical wires gleaming white against a dark street background.

Once he reaches street level, Leyda finds the Bronx through shop window signs, most of which promise bargains. The full fury of the Depression had yet to hit, but the forecast is ominous. As the film continues, Jewish elements become more predominant, until Leyda frames a woman selling bananas seated in front of a sign in Hebrew. Although its reputation today is still colored by memories of the blighted tenements and gang warfare of the 1980s, at the time the Bronx was where Jewish immigrants went to escape the Manhattan's Lower East Side ghetto.

But if you ignore the clothes and the lack of traffic, life in the Bronx in 1931 is strikingly familiar. Leyda shot in the summer, when, as he put it in his titles, "The Bronx lives on the street." Writers have cited the women and children in *A Bronx Morning* to show how personal the film is, but who else would Leyda have been able to film? The men in the neighborhood are presumably at work. You can also sense the young Leyda's shyness: almost all of the adults are shot from behind or above; or else Leyda shows only their torsos.

He had also studied his Kuleshov, who in 1919 had conducted a famous experiment juxtaposing close-ups of actor Ivan Mozhukhin with a variety of shots to show that editing can affect how viewers interpret acting. How else to explain a sequence in which Leyda cuts together dustbins and garbage cans, a dump truck upending its cargo, and a woman's waist, one hand grasping the neck of her dress? But what could be behind Leyda's fascination with a fruit peddler operating out of a horse-drawn wagon? Five shots in a row, requiring Leyda to changes lenses as well as to pan back and forth—evidence of either great luck or careful planning.

The film ends with a montage of children's games—dice, stickball, wrestling, jump rope, hopscotch, and the like—followed by animals like cats and pigeons juxtaposed with humans. It's clear that Leyda chanced into a lot of his material, but his artistry emerges in how he manipulated what he found. Hollywood craftsmen would kill for his last shot, of a sidewalk pavement across which a discarded newspaper page blows by, artfully off-center.

Freaks

Metro-Goldwyn-Mayer, 1932. Sound, B&W, 1.37. 62 minutes.

Cast: Wallace Ford (Phroso), Leila Hyams (Venus), Olga Baclanova (Cleopatra), Roscoe Ates (Roscoe), Henry Victor (Hercules), Harry Earles (Hans), Daisy Earles (Frieda), Rose Dione (Madame Tetrallini), Daisy Hilton, Violet Hilton (Siamese Twins), Schlitze, Josephine Joseph (Half Woman–Half Man), Johnny Eck (Half Boy), Frances O'Connor (Armless Girl), Peter Robinson (Human Skeleton), Olga Roderick (Bearded Lady), Koo Koo [Minnie Wolsey], [Prince] Randion (The Living Torso), Martha Morris (Armless Girl), Zip & Pip (Pinheads), Elizabeth Green (Bird Girl), Angelo Rossitto (Angeleno) Edward Brophy, Mat McHugh [usually credited Matt McHugh] (Rollo Brothers).

Credits: Suggested by Tod Robbins' story "Spurs." A Metro-Goldwyn-Mayer presentation of a Tod Browning production.

Additional Cast: Murray Kinnell (Sideshow barker), Michael Visaroff (Estate caretaker).

Additional Credits: Directed by Tod Browning. Screenplay by Willis Goldbeck and Leon Gordon. Additional screenwriting: Al Boasberg, Charles MacArthur. Produced by Irving Thalberg. Director of photography: Merritt B. Gerstad. Edited by Basil Wrangell. Art direction: Cedric Gibbons, Merrill Pye. Sound: G.A. Burns. Production dates: November 9 to December 16, 1931. Released February 20, 1932.

Available: Warner Home Video DVD (2004). ISBN: 0-7907-4654-9. UPC: 012569519121.

One of the more difficult films to watch in the National Film Registry is *Freaks*, released by MGM in 1932 in part as a response to Universal Studio's success with the horror genre. Director Tod Browning had left MGM to make *Dracula* (1931) at Universal. Producer Irving Thalberg brought him back with the assignment to make the scariest film possible. Browning came up with a disturbing one instead, possibly the most disturbing fiction feature ever released.

Harry Earles, one of the stars in the two versions of *The Unholy Three* that Browning made (in 1925 and 1930), brought the short story "Spurs" to the director's attention. Born in Germany, Earles traveled the world as a member of the Dancing Dolls family before adopting a new name for film. Browning saw the story—a cruel romantic melodrama involving a trapeze artist, the midget who loves her, and a circus strongman—as a chance to immerse filmgoers in the realm of sideshows.

Born in Kentucky in 1882, Browning ran away from home at sixteen and joined a traveling circus as a clown and contortionist. His fascination with physical abnormality can be traced to his experiences in the circus, and later in vaudeville, although his early career in movies followed a fairly unexceptional path. Browning went from actor to assistant director to screenwriter to director in the span of roughly four years. His early films were largely routine adventures until he directed Lon Chaney in *Outside the Law* (1920). One of the most accomplished actors in movies, Chaney developed a good working relationship with Browning in the 1925 version of *The Unholy Three*. The pair went on to make several movies together, increasingly macabre works that alarmed censors while drawing crowds at the box office.

Browning bought the "Spurs" story as a vehicle for Chaney, but the actor died of cancer just after the release of the 1930 sound remake of *The Unholy Three*. The initial similarities between the two films are striking, especially in the opening scene of *Freaks*, which mimics not only the setting but the lighting, camera placement and editing of the opening to *The Unholy Three*. But the Chaney film was a minor, if enjoyable, tale of a criminal gang, filled with comedy and absurd plot twists. *Freaks* soon becomes something quite different.

Browning had originally planned to open the film with a scene of a half-dozen sideshow oddities having a picnic. There are interrupted by a groundskeeper and the owner of the estate where the picnic is taking place. As his owner gives his permission for the meal to continue, Browning shows the "freaks" in close detail. The camera lingers over a human skeleton, a turtle lady, a bird lady. Most filmgoers had never seen people like this, as they were usually hidden away in circus sideshows. With advances in medicine, many of these conditions can be corrected, so it is even less likely to see individuals like these today. Society no longer views the exploitation of "oddities" as benign, and treats words like "midget" and "pinhead" as offensive.

But it should be noted that the performers in *Freaks* were just that: performers who were well known in their industry, many of them seasoned show business veterans. In fact, the circus and vaudeville offered escapes for many of the freaks in the film, like Daisy and Violet Hilton, Siamese twins sold by their mother after they were born out of wedlock. Of the freaks who appeared in the film, only Olga Roderick, a bearded lady, complained about the movie later.

Judging from the footage, Browning seems to have had a warm, intimate relationship with many of the players. They are not all professional actors, and their performances can seem halting, even amateurish. But there is almost never a sense that they want to be elsewhere.

On the other hand, Browning was not making a documentary. The plot behind *Freaks* is bitter and cruel, a grim, downbeat tale of exploitation, theft, and dismemberment. A beautiful trapeze artist named Cleopatra (played by silent veteran Olga Baclanova) and a strongman (Henry Victor in the part originally envisioned for Chaney) scheme to defraud and then poison Hans, the midget who has fallen in love with her. When the

shocked executives at MGM saw Browning's cut of *Freaks*, they ordered the director to move Hans's story to the beginning of the film, perhaps viewing it as the least objectionable part of the story. But there was no way to remove the sexual innuendo behind his relationship to Cleopatra, made most explicit in a wedding banquet that seems modeled directly on one in Josef von Sternberg's *The Blue Angel* (1930).

By frankly depicting the sexual appetites of the freaks, Browning was trying to make them appear more human. One of the real achievements of *Freaks* is that the characters do develop personalities, that they aren't just curiosities to be gaped at. But with Browning, matters are never simple. The climax, during which the freaks attack the humans at night—in a thunderstorm, crawling through mud with knives clenched in their teeth—presents the freaks as absolute monsters capable of horrific perversions, a reversal of every earlier decent impulse in the film. It is a truly ghastly scene, one that reduces the horror of films like *Dracula* or *Frankenstein* to play-acting, but one whose mixed motives leave viewers queasy, discomfited—participants themselves in the exploitation of unfortunates.

Freaks was an intractable problem for MGM. The studio kept trimming the film until it lasted an hour, but could not find a way to erase or even reduce the story's nightmarish elements. Browning's original ending, a blood-soaked melee, was deemed unreleasable. The director shot three alternate endings, none of which worked very well. The studio tested the film in San Diego in January 1932, then opened it across the country. The advertising campaign, with tag lines like "Can a full grown woman truly love a midget?" didn't pull any punches. Most reviewers were aghast, Louella Parsons excepted. After showing it in New York City that summer, MGM withdrew *Freaks* from circulation. For years, the studio leased the film out to subdistributors like Dwain Esper, who would show it under titles like *Nature's Mistakes*. The film was banned outright in Great Britain for thirty years.

In the United States, the film found a new audience in the 1960s, when the very word "freak" became a countercultural badge of honor. But even those who champion the film are forced to admit that it is at best uneven. David Skal, author of *Dark Carnival: The Secret World of Tod Browning, Hollywood's Master of the Macabre*, felt that Browning never really made the adjustment from silent to sound films. The best sequences in both *Dracula* and *Freaks* have no dialogue, and at times it's readily apparent that the film would have been more powerful as a silent. Browning directed four more movies, including the entertaining *Mark of*

the Vampire (1935) and *The Devil-Doll* (1936), a variation on *The Unholy Three* starring Lionel Barrymore. Although he lived until 1962, Browning never gave an interview about *Freaks*. No one else has made a movie like it.

Scarface

United Artists, 1932. Sound, B&W, 1.37. 93 minutes.

Cast: Paul Muni (Tony [Tony "Scarface" Camonte]), Ann Dvorak (Cesca), Karen Morley (Poppy), Osgood Perkins ([Johnny] Lovo), C. Henry Gordon ([Ben] Guarino), George Raft ([Gino] Rinaldo), Vince Barnett (Angelo), Boris Karloff (Gaffney), Purnell Pratt (Publisher), Tully Marshall (Managing Editor), Inez Palange (Tony's Mother), Edwin Maxwell (Detective Chief).

Credits: Directed by Howard Hawks. Screen story by Ben Hecht. Continuity and dialogue by Seton I. Miller, John Lee Mahin, W.R. Burnett. Co-director: Richard Rosson. Editorial advisor: Douglass Biggs. Directors of photography: Lee Garmes, L.W. O'Connell. Settings: Harry Oliver. Film editor: Edward Curtiss. Sound engineer: William Snyder. Musical directors: Adolph Tandler, Gus Arnheim. Production manager: Charles Stallings.

Additional Cast: Harry J. Vejar (Louie Costillo), Henry Armetta (Pietro), Maurice Black (Hood), Bert Starkey (Epstein), Paul Fix (Gaffney Hood), Hank Mann (Worker), Charles Sullivan, Harry Tenbrook (Bootleggers), John Lee Mahin (MacArthur of the *Tribune*), Howard Hawks (Man in hospital bed), Gus Arnheim (Orchestra leader).

Additional Credits: Produced by Howard Hughes. Continuity and dialogue: Fred Pasley. Based on the novel by Armitage Trail. Art director: Harry Oliver. A Caddo Company/Atlantic Pictures production for United Artists. Production dates: June to October 1931. Premiered in New Orleans on March 31, 1932. Later rated PG.

Other Versions: Remade as *Scarface* (1983).

Available: Universal DVD (2007). UPC: 025195004473.

Like most Howard Hughes projects, *Scarface* came out much later than planned, reaching theaters in 1932, at the tail end of the first cycle of sound gangster films. To compete against box-office hits like *Little Caesar* (1930) and *The Public Enemy* (1931), Hughes felt he had to top them. His movie would have to be more violent, more perverse, more explicit, and more expensive than the competition. As a result, *Scarface* immediately ran into trouble with censors.

To direct, Hughes wanted Howard Hawks, who unfortunately was under contract to Jack Warner at First National (at the time a Warner Brothers subsidiary). Hawks walked out on First National, resulting in a lawsuit that ultimately tied him to Warners for two more years. He had been a professional race car driver, an Army Air Corps pilot during World War I, and a designer of airplanes before he decided to pursue a career in movies. During the 1920s Hawks worked as an editor, casting director, and assistant director before writing, producing, and directing comedy shorts. He wrote and directed his first feature, *The Road to Glory*, in 1925.

Next in was Ben Hecht. He had written the story for *Underworld* (1927), the film that many credited with establishing the gangster cycle. Hawks claimed that he got Hecht interested in the project by comparing Al Capone and his minions to the Borgias. Hecht, who basically turned all of his projects into some variation of a love triangle, was intrigued by Hawks's incest angle. His contribution to the project was a sixty-page treatment that he left in the hands of John Lee Mahin, a former advertising copywriter, and Seton Miller, a writer chosen by Hawks. (Other writers had already submitted scripts, including *Little Caesar*'s W.R. Burnett.) In Hecht's autobiography, *A Child of the Century*, he confessed to a tactic that was ultimately followed by everyone else connected to the film: "[T]here have been several gangster pictures made, and I will double the casualty list of any picture to date, and we'll have twice as good a picture."

Hawks biographer Todd McCarthy suggests that Hecht had a lot to do with casting *Scarface*. Osgood Perkins, who played Johnny Lovo, had played Walter Burns in *The Front Page*. Hecht may have also suggested Paul Muni, an actor who had worked in Yiddish theater for almost twenty years. Born Muni Weisenfreund in 1895 in what was then a part of Austria, Muni moved at a young age to the United States. He followed his theatrical family into Yiddish plays, then reached mainstream theater by replacing Edward G. Robinson in a play called *We Americans*. Three years later he starred in two Fox films, both financial failures, before returning to Broadway. After filming a screen test for Hawks, Muni signed a contract for the lead role.

For Muni's sidekick, Hawks cast George Raft. Born George Ranft in 1895, he grew up in New York City's Hell's Kitchen, and was a boxer and dancer before moving to Broadway and then to Hollywood at the tail end of the silent era. Known for his mob connections, Raft brought some street credibility to the film. Hawks gave him a bit of business flipping a coin that remained with him throughout his career. (Hecht also claimed inspiration for the flip.) Hawks cast Ann Dvorak as Muni's sister after seeing her dance with Raft at a party.

The plot for *Scarface* essentially duplicates *The Public Enemy*, but with more sex, bloodshed, and intimations of smoldering incest. Its three-minute opening shot throws down a gauntlet to other filmmakers by tracking from a close-up of a street sign into the dregs of a political celebration in a dancehall. The camera picks up the shadow of a whistling Camonte (played by Muni), then depicts the off-screen killing of rival gang leader Louis Costillo. Hawks would rarely try such complicated shots later in his career; this one serves as a sort of fanfare for the violence to follow.

Audiences of the time would have been more familiar with the real-life incidents that inspired many of the scenes. The party that Camonte throws when he takes over a gang, for example, had its beginnings in a legendary banquet where Al Capone bludgeoned an underling to death with a baseball bat. The St. Valentine's Day Massacre was notorious enough to receive its own eponymous film, directed by Roger Corman in 1967; it also helped lead off Billy Wilder's *Some Like It Hot* (1959). Here it's just another in a series of slayings tied to the letter *X*. (Hawks offered his crew a bonus if they could invent ways to incorporate *X* into death scenes. Boris Karloff's death in a bowling alley—with his spare *X*ed onto his scorecard—may have been the cleverest.)

Muni plays Scarface almost like a loveable lug, someone who finds most social niceties laughable. With his lumbering gait and exaggerated accent, he separates himself from the role, signaling broadly to audiences that he is "acting." Ben Hecht thought, "He was a make-believe tough guy. You think he's a menace, but he doesn't do anything." Hawks gets better performances from Raft, essentially playing himself, and Dvorak, another in a long line of his tough, independent women.

The film's second selling point is sex, with the camera ogling Dvorak's body as she shakes for Raft in a nightclub scene, and Muni staring openly at Karen Morley as she descends a staircase. Camonte's attraction for his sister is so obvious that no one knew quite what to do with it. *Scarface*'s last half hour is a stew of desire, betrayal, and bloodshed. Its makers might cite Shakespeare, but their motives were far more mercenary.

The Hays Office, the movie industry's assigned censor, wanted Camonte to be depicted as "a cringing coward" when he was killed at the film's end. Hawks came up with a dramatically more satisfying ending before he finished work on the film at the end of October 1931. But this ending was rejected by the Hays Office, forcing Hughes to reopen production so that assistant director Robert Rosson could shoot a scene in which a Muni stand-in is hung by the police.

These steps weren't enough for the Hays Office: it rejected the film outright. Hughes opened *Scarface* anyway, showing the original version in New Orleans at the end of March 1932, and then in other cities and states on an almost case-by-case basis. New York got the hanging version, for example, while the original version showed across the Hudson River in New Jersey.

The hoopla surrounding the film helped make *Scarface* a hit. After the 1940s, it was withdrawn from circulation completely. Apart from 16mm bootleg copies shown at illicit screenings, the film dropped out of sight until 1980, when the rights were purchased by Universal so that Brian De Palma could shoot his 1983 remake. A special presentation at the New York Film Festival marked the first time the original version of *Scarface* was ever screened in the city.

Grand Hotel

Metro-Goldwyn-Mayer, 1932. Sound, B&W, 1.37. 113 minutes.
Cast: Greta Garbo (Grusinskaya . . . the dancer), John Barrymore (The Baron), Joan Crawford (Flaemmchen . . . the stenographer), Wallace Beery (General Director Preysing), Lionel Barrymore (Otto Kringelein), Lewis Stone (Doctor Otternschlag), Jean Hersholt (Senf, the Porter), Robert McWade (Meierheim), Purnell B. Pratt (Zinnowitz), Ferdinand Gottschalk (Pimenov), Rafaela Ottiano (Suzette), Morgan Wallace (Chauffeur), Tully Marshall (Gerstenkorn), Frank Conroy (Rohna), Murray Kinnell (Schweimann), Edwin Maxwell (Dr. Waitz).
Credits: Directed by Edmund Goulding. American play version by William A. Drake. Photographed by William Daniels. Recording director: Douglas Shearer. Art director: Cedric Gibbons. Gowns by Adrian. Film Editor: Blanche Sewell. Western Electric Sound System.
Additional Credits: Produced by Irving Thalberg. Associate producer: Paul Bern. Screenplay: Edmund Goulding. Based on the novel and play *Menschen im Hotel* by Hedwig "Vicki" Baum. Released April 12, 1932.
Other Versions: Remade as *Week-end at the Waldorf* (1945, directed by Robert Z. Leonard). *Menschen im Hotel* (1958, directed by Gottfried Reinhardt).
Awards: Oscar for Best Picture.
Available: Warner Home Video DVD (2004). ISBN: 0-7907-4467-8. UPC: 0-12569-50842-2.

A triumph of style over substance, *Grand Hotel* may be the best example of the work of producer Irving Thalberg. He had been a dominant figure at Universal at the age of twenty, and in conjunction Louis B. Mayer guided MGM, the most prosperous film studio, through the worst years of the Depression. Ambitious, driven, but sickly, he was noted in the industry for his ruthless handling of scripts and his insistence on reshoots after preview screenings. He tended to see individual films as parts of campaigns to increase the prestige of performers and, not incidentally, MGM itself.

The genesis of the project was a 1929 novel by Vicki Baum, *Menschen im Hotel.* Born in Vienna in 1888, the twice-married Baum was a magazine editor who had written a memoir and prize-winning short stories. Serialized in a magazine and later adapted for the stage by Baum herself, *Menschen in Hotel* was a smash hit in Berlin and a Book of the Month Club selection after it was translated into English by Basil Creighton. A maudlin and improbable blend of O. Henry and Fannie Hurst, the novel allowed readers to fantasize about the luxurious lives of the wealthy while being reassured that money didn't buy happiness.

MGM essentially paid for a Broadway production of *Grand Hotel,* written by Charles Drake, in exchange for the film rights. The play was so popular that Thalberg couldn't get around to mounting a film production until 1931. He always envisioned Greta Garbo for the lead role of Grusinskaya, a fading, suicidal ballerina, and Edmund Goulding as the director and (uncredited) screenwriter. The British-born actor and playwright had been working at MGM since 1925, and had directed two previous Garbo vehicles. As a director, he was considered expert in rhythm and pacing, and was known for relying on extended two-shots to increase tension in a scene. (He was also a novelist and composer of songs like "Love, Your Magic Spell Is Everywhere.")

The rest of the cast wasn't settled until just before production started. Goulding suggested Buster Keaton for the role of Kringelein, a milquetoast businessman who was also a potential suicide, but Mayer vetoed the idea. Thalberg considered Clark Gable for the role of the Baron, a jewel thief with a strict sense of morals, but eventually settled on John Barrymore, in part to pair him with his brother Lionel (already under contract to MGM), in part to secure him in a multipicture deal. Thalberg had trouble persuading Wallace Beery to accept the essentially villainous role of Preysing, an unscrupulous business executive. Beery was about to become, for a brief time, one of the studio's biggest stars for his Oscar-winning role as a suicidal boxer in *The Champ* (1932) and his work with Marie Dressler in sentimental comedies.

Thalberg also cast Joan Crawford as Flaemmchen, a stenographer who crosses paths with many of the other characters in the story. It was typical of the working-class parts she was assigned at the studio. As Garbo would gravitate toward esoteric period pieces, Crawford became an important way for the studio to connect with mainstream viewers.

According to film historian Thomas Schatz, Thalberg, Goulding, and Paul Bern, a producer who was about to marry Jean Harlow, met repeatedly for *Grand Hotel* story conferences. Thalberg picked apart Goulding's script (for contractual reasons, only Drake got screen credit), dreamed up new scenes, and delivered prognostications like, "This is a lousy play that succeeded only because it was lousy." Goulding fought for his own ideas—he wanted a murder to be committed with a telephone instead of a revolver—but in the end the story, cast, and even the look and style of the film had all been determined by Thalberg.

"The Lion Tamer," an article by Ruth Biery in the July 1932 *Photoplay*, gives a firsthand account of the shooting of *Grand Hotel*, as well as a very sympathetic portrait of the harried Goulding trying desperately to keep five strong egos focused on the project. In Biery's telling, Crawford sits in her portable dressing room playing Bing Crosby records, Beery keeps calling out for lunch, and John Barrymore forgets his lines. The only professional, disciplined performer is Garbo, who sits meekly in a corner after everyone else has left the set.

Biery wrote about how the cast had to wear felt slippers instead of shoes in order not to scuff the tile floor of the hotel lobby set, but more than the art deco establishing shots, what strikes viewers today are the diffused, smoke-wreathed close-ups by William Daniels, Garbo's preferred cinematographer. This was the height of MGM style, a gauzy version of Mitteleuropan hauteur, with glamorous but lonely people torn between sex and suicide. Goulding began shooting in January 1932, and thanks to Thalberg's planning finished six weeks later without going over his $700,000 budget. Editor Blanche Sewell cut while Goulding was working, giving Thalberg an idea of how the film would look. After previews, he ordered Goulding to reshoot John Barrymore's love scenes with Garbo.

Among the many points Schatz's *The Genius of the System* makes about *Grand Hotel* is the fact that MGM was producing movies for theaters located primarily in upscale, urban neighborhoods. (In the late 1930s, of the 128 theaters owned by Loew's, MGM's parent corporation, 76 were located in and around New York City.) Which meant that MGM movies tended to be about urban, upscale people, whereas Fox, whose theaters were more rural, made movies about rural people, and Warner Brothers, whose theaters were in secondary urban markets, about gangsters and blue-collar workers. MGM essentially cornered the market on society couples in evening clothes sharing cocktails on penthouse balconies or in hotel suites. They hired stars who fit this mold, like the Barrymore brothers and Lewis Stone, or else shoehorned actors like Wallace Beery into tuxedos.

Beery actually gives the strongest, or perhaps the least affected, performance in *Grand Hotel*, fully inhabiting his role without resorting to the actorly tricks used by the rest of the cast. Audiences of the time were most impressed by Garbo in a role that foreshadowed her own increasing reluctance to appear before the camera. Louis B. Mayer, on the other hand, saw how Joan Crawford—hardworking, and far less expensive—could help the studio without the artistic pretensions and production demands that Garbo trailed in her wake.

Grand Hotel was the biggest film of the year for MGM, which unlike the rest of the industry enjoyed tremendous profits in 1932. It enabled Thalberg to renegotiate his contract, taking more of Mayer's share of profits. MGM duplicated his formula almost at once, in *Dinner at Eight*. Crucial differences in this project, produced by Thalberg's rival David O. Selznick, included the use of comedy, and replacing the imperious, aloof Garbo with down-to-earth Jean Harlow. Thalberg, meanwhile, became more and more fallible as his health declined.

The Music Box

Metro-Goldwyn-Mayer, 1932. Sound, B&W, 1.37. 29 minutes.
Cast: Stan Laurel, Oliver Hardy.
Credits: Directed by James Parrott. Director of photography: Len Powers. Edited by Richard Currier. Recording engineer: James Green [Greene]. Dialogue by H.M. Walker.
Additional Cast: Billy Gilbert (Prof. Theodore von Schwartzenhoffen), Charlie Hall (Postman), Lilyan Irene (Nursemaid), Sam Lufkin (Policeman), William Gillespie (Piano salesman), Hazel Howell, Gladys Gale.
Additional Credits: Produced by Hal Roach. Additional photography: Walter Lundin. Production dates: December 7 to 18, 1931. Released April 16, 1932.
Awards: Oscar for Best Short Subject—Comedy.
Available: FHE/Artisan DVD (2003). UPC: 7-07729-14334-3.

The comedy team of Laurel and Hardy made a smooth transition to sound. Working at Hal Roach's studio, they averaged seven shorts a year from 1929 to 1932 (some of these were silent, and some of the sound versions were also shot silent). Roach still had his distribution deal with MGM, which meant that Laurel and Hardy films, along with films starring Our Gang, were shown in the generally upscale Loew's theaters.

The creative personnel that had helped develop the Laurel and Hardy team and its silent shorts had changed. Former supervisor Leo McCarey, the supervisor behind the team's *Big Business* (1929), had moved on to directing features at Paramount. Cinematographer George Stevens had started his own series of comic shorts before signing a contract to direct at RKO. The team was now being photographed by Len Powers (he was assisted by Walter Lundin on this film). *The Music Box* was directed by James Parrott, the brother of silent clown Charley Chase (*Mighty Like a Moose*, 1926).

Roach assigned writers to the films, but story ideas and gags could come from anyone, with Laurel the major creative force behind the scripts. The duo had a rotating stock company working with them. Regulars included James Finlayson, Edgar Kennedy, Charlie Hall, and Sam Lufkin; and, in the sound films, Mae Busch, Thelma Todd, and Billy Gilbert. In addition, after 1928 they had their own theme song, "The Dance of the Cuckoos," or "Ku-Ku," as it is better known. Laurel heard the theme on a radio station, and borrowed it from its composer, T. Marvin Hatley, a musician from Oklahoma. Hatley later became musical director at the Roach studio, and most likely played the piano for the delightful dance that appears halfway through *The Music Box*.

The duo made few alterations to their comic style in adapting to sound. While most sound films reveled in dialogue, Laurel and Hardy barely spoke to each other, or to other characters. *The Music Box* is marked by its minimalist dialogue; many of the lines, as tight and concise as poetry, are repeated by one or more characters. (They were written mostly by Harley "Beanie" Walker, a sports columnist whose byline was "The Wisdom of Blinkey Ben." He wrote almost all the intertitles for Hal Roach films after 1916.) It helped immeasurably that the comics had voices perfectly suited to their screen personas: Laurel's thin and wavering, liable to crack at any moment; Hardy's filled with imperious bluster.

Silence masked much of the violence of slapstick movies; when sound effects were added to pratfalls, they suddenly became painful to watch. Working with sound, Laurel learned he could still get laughs placing a lot of the big falls off-screen. He also made the slapstick "smaller," more realistic. If anything, sound allowed Laurel to slow down the act even further. Much of his humor was built on frustration, on viewers anticipating, waiting for something to happen. Laurel kept delaying his punch lines, or denying them entirely, twisting them into shapes audiences couldn't have expected. In *Hog Wild* (1930), he has Hardy fall off a roof into a fish pond five times, each time adjusting elements of the gag, stripping away extraneous details. According to an interview Roach gave, Laurel would rehearse with Hardy in the morning, seeing how scenes would play. If they didn't work, Laurel and whatever gag man he was working with would try to improve them in time to shoot in the afternoon. That accounts in part for the spontaneous nature of their comedy, its improvisatory feel.

One of the first things studios do with any new technology is to remake whatever old properties they can. In Laurel and Hardy's case, this meant reshooting their most successful silent films, or adapting their best gags to sound. *Sons of the Desert* (1933) incorporates an important gag from *We Faw Down* (1928), for example. *Another Fine Mess* (1931) was a remake of *Duck Soup* (1927). In a sense, the first time a gag was filmed, it was like a rehearsal. The second time, the comics could elaborate, provide variations, improve on the jokes.

The Music Box was based on *Hats Off* (1927), a silent short that is one of the few lost Laurel and Hardy films. Both were filmed in part on Vendome Street in the Silver Lake district of Los Angeles, the site of an outdoor staircase with 131 steps. In *Hats Off* they have to carry a washing machine up the stairs. In *The Music Box*, it's a player piano, recently purchased by a wife for her husband's birthday. Just as the dialogue gains its humor through repetition, the gags grow in power as viewers realize what happened once will happen again. Struggling up the stairs with their crated piano, the boys first encounter a nursemaid with a pram, then a surly professor. They have run-ins with a policeman and a postman. A fish pond figures into three gags, as do misplaced bowler hats.

The film won an Oscar for Best Comedy Short Subject, the only Oscar the team received. (Laurel was given an honorary Oscar in 1960, after Hardy had died). Critics have compared *The Music Box* to Sisyphus and to Beckett, and to half the Warner Brothers cartoons of the 1940s. Leo McCarey thought so highly of the hat gag here that he turned it into a tour de force in 1933's *Duck Soup*. But their influence on others can't explain the charm and innocence of the team.

At the time of *The Music Box*'s release, Laurel and Hardy had already started making feature films. After 1932, their output of shorts dropped rapidly. A dispute with Roach during the filming of *Babes in Toyland* led them to sign contracts with studios like MGM and Twentieth Century-Fox, but by the late 1930s their popularity was slipping. Hardy made some film appearances without Laurel, but had health problems in the 1950s. He died in 1957. Laurel died eight years later. The team never lost the affection of its fans, who are among the most dedicated of all followers of film. The Sons of the Desert may be the most well-known of the Laurel and Hardy appreciation societies.

Love Me Tonight

Paramount, 1932. Sound, B&W, 1.37. 89 minutes.
Cast: Maurice Chevalier (Maurice Courtelin), Jeanette MacDonald (Princess Jeanette), Charlie Ruggles (Vicomte Gilbert de Vareze), Charles Butterworth (Count de Savignac), Myrna Loy (Countess Valentine), C. Aubrey Smith (Duke d'Artelines), Elizabeth Patterson (First aunt), Ethel Griffies (Second aunt), Blanche Frederici (Third aunt), Joseph Cawthorne (Doctor Armand de Pontignac), Robert Greig (Major Domo Flammand), Bert Roach (Emile).
Credits: Directed by Rouben Mamoulian. Screen Play by Samuel Hoffenstein, Waldemar Young, and George Marion, Jr. Based on a play [*Le Tailler au Chateau*] by Leopold Marchand and Paul Armont. Music and lyrics by Richard Rodgers and Lorenz Hart. Photographed by Victor Milner. Western Electric Noiseless Recording.
Additional Cast: Sam Harris (Bridge player), Herbert Munin (Groom), Ethel Wales (Dressmaker), Marion "Peanuts" Byron (Bakery girl), Mary Doran (Mme. Dupont), Cecil Cunningham (Laundress), Tyler Brooke (Composer), Edgar Norton (Valet), Rita Owin (Chambermaid), Clarence Wilson (Shirtmaker), Gordon Westcott (Collector), George Davis (Pierre), Rolfe Sedan (Taxi driver), Tony Merlo (Hatmaker), William H. Turner (Bootmaker), George "Gabby" Hayes (Grocer), George Humbert (Chef).

Additional Credits: Produced and edited by Rouben Mamoulian. Assistant director: William Kaplan. Film cutter: William Shea. Art direction: Hans Dreier. Costume design: Travis Banton, Edith Head. Sound recording: M.M. Paggi. Additional music: John Leipold. Premiered August 13, 1932.
Available: Kino Video DVD (2003). UPC: 7-38329-03222-7.

During the transition from silent to sound films, studios turned to musicals so frequently that they quickly exhausted the genre. Contracts were offered not just to singers and dancers, but to songwriters and directors as well. Composer Richard Rodgers and lyricist Lorenz Hart joined the migration in 1930, after fourteen shows in four years on Broadway and in London (and after theatrical financing dried up as a result of the Wall Street crash of 1929). It was a difficult transition for the team, used to the more collaborative creative process for stage musicals. After working on films like *Heads Up* (1930) and *The Hot Heiress* (1931), they were ready to return to New York.

More than any other figure, director Ernst Lubitsch established the style of musicals at Paramount. Films like *The Love Parade* (1929), *Monte Carlo* (1930), and *The Smiling Lieutenant* (1931) not only made Maurice Chevalier and Jeanette MacDonald movie stars, they transformed the look and content of much of Paramount's product, building an oddly Ruritanian culture of carefree aristocrats who cavorted in castles and chateaus. In 1932, Lubitsch was initially assigned *Love Me Tonight*, a musical based on a French play that would team Chevalier and MacDonald for the third time. In it, a lowly Parisian tailor is mistaken for a wealthy baron. During a weekend at a chateau, he participates in a foxhunt and a dress ball, while falling in love with a demure but secretly hot-blooded princess.

Lubitsch withdrew to concentrate on a melodrama, *The Man I Killed*. When Rouben Mamoulian took over the project, he had directed a total of three films, starting with *Applause* (1929). However, he had worked out an approach to filmmaking that was among the most theoretical in the industry, based in part on his theater experiments in sound and pacing. In his 1927 staging of *Porgy*, for example, he took credit for a "symphony of noises" to provide the atmosphere for Catfish Row. As he explained later, "All the activity, the pounding, tooting, shouting and laughing is done to count. First I use one/two time. Then beat three is a snore . . . beat four silent again . . . then all join in. Then the rhythm changes: four:four to two:four, then six:eight."

Mamoulian duplicated the effect in the opening of *Love Me Tonight*, using rhythm to provide a sweeping view of Paris, from street cleaners and shop workers to philandering aristocrats. As several writers have pointed out, it was not an unprecedented approach: Richard Barrios cites *Sous les toits de Paris* (1930) and *Congress Dances* (1931), while Scott Eyman points to *4 Devils* (1928). But Mamoulian also incorporated his other theories, such as the use of shadows. "Films are not as much a reflection of life, as a revelation of life," he wrote, "the way we would like the world to be."

One of the director's first steps on the production was to replace screenwriter Samson Raphaelson with his own writers, discarding a complicated subplot from the original play in the process. He approached Rodgers and Hart in the early stages of writing, asking them for music that would advance the plot and add depth to the characters. Three songs—"Lover," "Mimi," and "Isn't It Romantic?"—would become standards. Others, like "A Woman Needs Something Like That" and "The Son of a Gun Is Nothing But a Tailor," caused consternation with censors. Hart also worked on rhymed dialogue, a tactic that moved *Love Me Tonight* closer to operettas. Rhymed dialogue would be an important feature of a later Rodgers and Hart musical, *Hallelujah I'm a Bum* (1933).

Rodgers wrote an overture and transitional music, adding up to a total of 114 separate orchestral segments. The songwriters' contributions provide much of the continuity to the story, especially since Mamoulian seemed more interested in his experiments than in the structure of the film. The opening scenes of *Love Me Tonight* are brimming with directorial flourishes. Chevalier performs one song in front of a three-way mirror, providing four different angles in the same shot. Lyrics for the song "Isn't It Romantic?" are carried from Chevalier's customer to a taxi driver, then to a lyricist on a train, marching soldiers, and a gypsy violinist. Similarly, the words to "Mimi" and "The Son of a Gun Is Nothing But a Tailor" get traded among the cast. Many of Mamoulian's effects are charming, but also so specific to this material that they couldn't easily be used again by anyone else.

Or by Mamoulian, for that matter. Apart from a montage at the climax that resembles Russian constructivist filmmaking, most of *Love Me Tonight* settles into the same conventional style used by the director's peers. The film was released on the brink of a more modern musical format, one that eschewed European antecedents. Preston Sturges mocked "Isn't It Romantic?" in *The Palm Beach Story* (1942), while the Marx Brothers parodied elements of this film in *Duck Soup* (1933).

In his forties at the time of filming, Maurice Chevalier was about as atypical as a Hollywood star could get in the 1930s. Born in Ménilmontant, a working-class neighborhood in Paris, he dropped out of school at the age of eleven. After singing in cafés and music halls, his break came when he became the partner and lover of Mistinguett at the Folies-Bergère. Jesse Lasky signed him to a contract at Paramount in 1928. The star did not get along well with Mamoulian, who wrote, "He would come on the set slouching, sit in a corner looking as unhappy and worried as a homeless orphan." When the camera started, "a complete transformation took place—there he was, happy, debonair, truly filled with that joy of living. . . . Then, as I said 'cut,' the light went out of him. He walked back to his corner like a tired man, looking hopelessly miserable, as before."

Censors took quite a toll on the film, although future screenwriter Lamar Trotti, working at the time for Jason Joy at the Production Code office, took pains to note, "This is one of the most delightful scripts I have ever read." In a later interview, Myrna Loy said that her verse of "Mimi" was cut because she was wearing a transparent outfit. The song "The Man for Me" was apparently deleted after the premiere. The film was edited both times Paramount tried to rerelease it. References to the "virgin's spring" disappeared, as did the entire "A Woman Needs Something Like That" number.

This was the last film at Paramount for MacDonald. Like the Marx Brothers, she would head for MGM, where her screen persona underwent the equivalent of pasteurization. Mamoulian directed features with Marlene Dietrich and Greta Garbo before returning to the stage, where he directed a groundbreaking version of *Oklahoma!* in 1945. Within a year, Paramount would be bankrupt.

I Am a Fugitive from a Chain Gang

Warner Brothers, 1932. Sound, B&W, 1.37. 92 minutes.

Cast: Paul Muni (James Allen), Glenda Farrell (Marie [Woods]), Helen Vinson (Helen), Noel Francis (Linda), Preston Foster (Pete), Allen Jenkins (Barney Sykes), Berton Churchill (The Judge), Edward Willis (Bomber Wells), David Landau (The Warden), Hale Hamilton (Rev. [Robert] Allen), Sally Blane (Alice), Louise Carter (Mother), Willard Robertson (Prison Board Chairman), Robert McWade (Attorney), Robert Warwick (Fuller), William LeMaire (A Texan).

Credits: Directed by Mervyn LeRoy. Screenplay by Howard J. Green & Brown Holmes. Based on the autobiography *I Am a Fugitive from a Georgia Chain Gang* by Robert E. Burns. Director of photography: Sol Polito. Edited by William Holmes. Art director: Jack Okey. Gowns by Orry-Kelly. Technical director: S.H. Sullivan. Silks by Cheney Brothers. Vitaphone Orchestra conducted by Leo F. Forbstein.

Additional Cast: Irving Bacon (Barber), Douglas Dumbrille (District Attorney), James Bell (Red), Lew Kelly (Cook), Roscoe Karns (Steve), Jack La Rue (Ackerman).

Additional Credits: Treatment: Robert E. Burns. Screenwriting by Sheridan Gibney, Darryl F. Zanuck. Produced by Hal Wallis. Executive producer: Darryl F. Zanuck. Sound director: Nathan Levinson. Production dates: July 29 to September 7, 1932. Premiered in New York City on October 11, 1932.

Other Versions: Remade as a telemovie, *The Man Who Broke 1,000 Chains* (1987).

Available: Warner Home Video DVD (2005). ISBN: 0-7907-9662-7. UPC: 0-12569-70102-1.

Although it had helped propel the film industry into accepting sound, and had popularized the gangster genre with *Little Caesar* and *The Public Enemy* (both 1931), Warner Brothers was still viewed as an upstart studio by its rivals. The Warners made brash, even brassy films on the cheap, spending much less on their features than RKO or MGM did. Despite a few prestige figures like George Arliss, their stable of actors consisted largely of hungry young faces from New York City, performers who had yet to establish themselves as stars. While the studio would soon embark on a string of energetic musicals, few in Hollywood let Warners forget that it owed much of its success to Rin Tin Tin.

With Harry and Albert in executive positions, brother Jack Warner handled the day-to-day operations at the Burbank studio. (Sam, the fourth brother, died in 1927.) Under Jack were two chief producers, Hal Wallis and Darryl F. Zanuck. After helping turn Rin Tin Tin into a bona fide movie star, Zanuck became studio manager in in 1928, then replaced Wallis as chief of production.

Zanuck set much of the tone for Warners releases, using directors like Michael Curtiz and Archie Mayo to churn out movies as quickly as possible. The studio had gained some momentum with gangster films, but needed a more sophisticated hit to persuade theater owners to carry its product. Jack Warner and Zanuck settled on *I Am a Fugitive from a Chain Gang*, based on an autobiography by Robert E. Burns. It had originally been serialized in

True Detective Mysteries magazine in 1931, and published by Vanguard early in 1932 as *I Am a Fugitive from a Georgia Chain Gang*. By that time Zanuck had already paid Burns for the movie rights.

The story was an incendiary one. Burns, by his own account an underachiever who drifted into the armed services during World War I, personified the downward spiral many underwent during the Depression. A victim of what was called battle fatigue, or shell shock, he roamed the country chasing jobs that would pay the same wages he earned in the war. Down on his luck in Atlanta, he was coerced into a grocery store robbery that netted a little over five dollars. After his arrest, Burns received a sentence of six-to-ten years' hard labor on a chain gang.

Burns's descriptions of life on the chain gang horrified readers. The appalling living conditions, senseless brutality of the guards, poor food, and hard labor itself could be expected. The chains could not. Shackled at the ankles, which were separated by thirteen links of chain, Burns soon had open sores on his legs, and walked in the same hunched shuffle that the other inmates used. A second section of chain was used to tie prisoners to their bunks at night, or to each other during their trips to work. The prison day started at 4:20 a.m., and prisoners wouldn't get back to the barracks until after eight at night.

What made Burns's book truly remarkable was the fact that he escaped, moved to Chicago, and found a job. He was blackmailed into marrying a woman named Emily del Pino, who betrayed him to the police when he tried to divorce her. Assured that he would receive a pardon, Burns returned to Georgia to face the authorities. Instead, he was ordered to serve the remaining nine years of his sentence. Burns somehow managed to escape a second time, and went underground in New Jersey to write his book.

Apart from Zanuck and the Warner brothers themselves, no one at the studio wanted to tackle Burns's story. Director Roy Del Ruth called the book "morbid," and said it would alienate Warners' Southern audiences. But Zanuck assigned staff writer Brown Holmes to the project. Burns, using a pseudonym (as he was still under the threat of arrest), assisted with the first treatments, which were ready by the end of April. Zanuck ordered screenplay drafts from two more writers, offering his own input on the story's structure. References to Georgia were eliminated, as were some speeches against chain gangs. In the meantime Zanuck hired Paul Muni,

who had left Hollywood after starring in *Scarface*, for the lead role. Zanuck also pulled Mervyn LeRoy from the filming of *42nd Street* to direct.

LeRoy's style had become looser and more accomplished since *Little Caesar*, and he was able to utilize sound and camera movement in a less self-conscious manner. He also shot incredibly quickly, averaging over five minutes of material a day. He finished shooting in little over a month, despite the constant presence of Zanuck, who offered advice on everything from where to put the camera to how to direct Muni. The actor was still unused to film, and at times seems less confident than his fellow actors. But Muni was protected in part by the story, which required him to observe and react rather than give many speeches. In a sense his inexperience helped him play someone who, after his escape, was always afraid of being detected.

I Am a Fugitive was a big production by Warners' standards, but it moves with the speed and focus of a nightmare. The script changed the robbery to a hold-up in an all-night diner, handled the trial and sentencing of Jim Allen (Burns's alter ego) in a single scene, then zeroed in on the harsh conditions awaiting in prison. LeRoy makes an occasional statement—Allen notices that the prison's mules are chained together the same way the inmates are—but largely lets the material speak for itself. When he pans down an aisle of bunks, the clatter of chains is all he needs on the soundtrack. Similarly, Allen's encounter after his escape with Linda, a prostitute played by the excellent Noel Francis, has a remarkable power, in part because LeRoy stages it simply and directly, without stopping to comment. The first escape sequence, a violent montage of Allen running through woods, pursued by dogs, builds its tension from the simplest of details: traveling shots so quick they almost blur, matched with the baying of bloodhounds and the prison siren.

Critic and filmmaker Andrew Bergman singled out the film's pessimistic story line as a reason why it still works so well today, writing that it showed "the process by which an individual could move outside the law by standing still." When Allen escapes a second time, he faces a Depression-stricken America in which there are no jobs. The only choice he faces is a life of crime. At one point Allen says, "The state's promise didn't mean anything. It was all lies. . . . Their crimes are worse than mine." He could be talking about the country's failed policies as well as Georgia's prisons. The film's famous closing scene depicts this in a manner that is efficient and heartbreaking at the same time. In his autobiography, LeRoy claimed inspiration for the scene after a fuse blew in the studio, while Zanuck took credit for writing it after the film was previewed in October.

I Am a Fugitive opened in New York in November, nine months after Burns's book was published. It was an immediate sensation, winning the best picture award from the National Board of Review and receiving three Oscar nominations. It also established a precedent for exposé-style filmmaking. Warners would specialize in films about social issues: sharecropping, juvenile delinquency, the Ku Klux Klan, etc. *I Am a Fugitive* also led to many imitations and parodies, from *Sullivan's Travels* to *Cool Hand Luke* to *O Brother, Where Art Thou?* (Warners wasn't above making fun of the film itself, using it for the basis of a bizarre Vitaphone musical comedy short called *20,000 Cheers for the Chain Gang*.) But as Bergman points out, films like *Wild Boys of the Road* (1933), *Black Fury* (1935), *Black Legion* (1936), and *Marked Woman* (1937) all offered solutions—however simplistic—to the problems they addressed. There is no answer to *I Am a Fugitive from a Chain Gang*, no consolation or solace. There is simply the image of Jim Allen confessing to his lover, "I steal," before slipping into the darkness.

Trouble in Paradise

The rapturous expression on Kay Francis's face marks *Trouble in Paradise* as a pre-Code film. *Courtesy of The Criterion Collection*

Paramount, 1932. Sound, B&W, 1.37. 82 minutes.
Cast: Miriam Hopkins (Lily), Kay Francis (Mariette), Herbert Marshall (Gaston), Charlie Ruggles (The Major), Edward Everett Horton (François), C. Aubrey Smith (Giron), Robert Greig (Jacques, the butler).
Credits: Directed by Ernst Lubitsch. Screen play by Samson Raphaelson. Adapted by Grover Jones from the play by Laszlo Aladar. Music by W. Franke Harling. Lyrics by Leo Robin. Photographed by Victor Milner. Gowns by Travis Banton. Western Electric Noiseless Recording.
Additional Cast: Leonid Kinskey (Radical), Rolfe Sedan (Purse salesman), Eva McKenzie (Duchess Chambreau), Luis Alberni (Opera fan), George Humbert (Waiter), Nella Walker (Mme. Bouchet).
Additional Credits: Produced by Ernst Lubitsch. Art direction: Hans Dreier. Sound: M.M. Paggi. Production dates: late July to early September 1932. Opened October 21, 1932.
Available: Criterion Collection DVD (2003). UPC: 7-15515-01312-3.

The films Ernst Lubitsch directed for Warner Brothers in the 1920s were solid but not outstanding performers at the box office. Executives there were nonplussed at how poorly they did in Europe, one reason why the studio hired Lubitsch in the first place. He was gone by 1927, when he signed contracts with MGM and Paramount, and after he persuaded Warners to buy the rights to *The Jazz Singer* (1927). At Paramount Lubitsch made a series of pioneering musicals starring Maurice Chevalier; two of these, *The Smiling Lieutenant* (1931) and *One Hour with You* (1932), had screenwriting contributions by Samson Raphaelson, who had also written *The Jazz Singer*.

Raphaelson liked writing for Lubitsch, calling him "a man of enormous taste." The two worked on nine films together over the next seventeen years, although Raphaelson complained repeatedly about his low salary. His assignment after *One Hour with*

You was adapting *The Honest Finder*, a 1931 Hungarian play by Laszlo Aladar (his name is usually given as Aladar Laszlo). Neither Raphaelson nor Lubitsch seemed interested in the play. Instead, they turned to the life of Georges Manolescu, a famous swindler and thief whose 1907 *Memoirs* had been the basis of two silent films.

In *Trouble in Paradise*, Manolescu became Gaston Monescu, the central figure in a satirical mystery. Lubitsch used contract writer Grover Jones to supply humor, but ended up not needing him. The director and Raphaelson wrote parts specifically for Edward Everett Horton and Charlie Ruggles, two of the most accomplished character actors in Hollywood. A graduate of Columbia, Horton had been a fixture on stage and screen since the 1920s, playing a succession of fussy, irritable, absent-minded bachelors. Ruggles was also popular on stage and in films, usually appearing as an affable but bumbling professional.

Herbert Marshall was cast late in the production. A British actor with a mellifluous voice, he had been in movies since the teens, and had a successful career despite losing a leg in World War I. Miriam Hopkins was born in Georgia and studied ballet before becoming a chorus girl in New York. She signed a contract with Paramount in 1930, when studios were raiding Broadway for talent, and would make a total of three films for Lubitsch. Kay Francis was schooled in a convent, then worked as a secretary while breaking into acting. A tall, glamorous brunette with a slight speech impediment, she appeared in up to a half-dozen films a year before establishing herself at Paramount and then at Warners as the worldly star of "women's" pictures.

Francis and Hopkins had appeared together before in *24 Hours* (1931), a murder drama with a nightclub setting. Francis had also just finished two films with William Powell, including *Jewel Robbery* (1932), a saucy, stylish romantic comedy set in Europe. But where other directors saw Francis as little more than a clothes horse, Lubitsch depicted her as a sexual goddess. Her physical desires, as well as those of Hopkins and Marshall, are what drive the film, not its slow-moving and predictable plot.

"I thought the people in *Trouble in Paradise* were just puppets," Raphaelson said later. His assignment "was just another job and it never occurred to me that I was making history." He finished the script on July 15, 1932; shooting lasted from late July until early September. A possibly apocryphal story has crew members nailing Hopkins' chair to the floor in one scene to prevent her from moving it and upstaging Francis.

Much of the look of the film is due to the German designer Hans Dreier. A World War I veteran, he was working at UFA in Berlin when Lubitsch brought him to the United States in 1924. He was the head of Paramount's art department from 1932 until he retired in 1950. Lubitsch biographer Scott Eyman noted that Dreier treated a set as more than just a background with realistic details; it became a metaphor for the film's characters and their behavior. (Eyman also points out the contributions of costumer Travis Banton, the head costume designer at Paramount from 1928 until 1938.) *Trouble in Paradise*'s luxurious, gleaming art deco and Bauhaus clothing and furniture reflect the streamlined sensuality of the leads, their polite surfaces only hinting at underlying passions.

At one point the project was called *Thieves and Lovers*; it didn't receive its *Trouble in Paradise* title until a week before its preview screenings. The film did not win good reviews. Although it cost only $519,706, much less than Lubitsch's earlier musicals, the movie wound up losing some $135,000.

In subsequent decades, film historians lavished praise on *Trouble in Paradise*, to some degree because they wanted it to represent a pre–Production Code 1930s Hollywood, one of elegantly clothed sexual adventurers dallying in glittering rooms. But moviegoers of the time were less impressed. They preferred the snappy patter of the gangsters at Warner Bros., the insane humor of W.C. Fields and the Marx Brothers, the hothouse sexuality of a Garbo or Dietrich. Even filmmakers had their doubts. F.W. Murnau felt that the director was only "flirting with his great gifts." Josef von Sternberg mocked the sexuality in Lubitsch's films: "No matter what happened, one would always have a twinkle in his eye."

Jim Tully, who wrote the William Wellman–directed *Beggars of Life* (1928), berated Lubitsch for making films aimed at "sophisticated chambermaids and cinema critics." Tully went continued, "Instead of being a great artist, he is merely a merchant like his father. But with this difference . . . his father did not deal in second-hand goods." Lubitsch could have been discussing his own work in an article he wrote for *American Cinematographer* in 1929: "When art begins to be apparent, to show itself as a definite, studied effort to be artistic, it ceases to be art." His next Registry film is *Ninotchka* (1939).

Red Dust

Metro-Goldwyn-Mayer, 1932. Sound, B&W, 1.37. 83 minutes.
Cast: Clark Gable (Dennis Carson), Jean Harlow (Vantine), Gene Raymond (Gary Willis), Mary Astor (Barbara Willis), Donald Crisp (Guidon), Tully Marshall (McQuarg), Forrester Harvey (Limey), Willie Fung (Hoy).
Credits: Produced by Victor Fleming. Screen Play by John [Lee] Mahin. From the play by Wilson Collison. Recording director: Douglas Shearer. Art director: Cedric Gibbons. Gowns by Adrian. Photographed by Harold Rosson. Film Editor: Blanche Sewell. Western Electric Sound System.
Additional Credits: Directed by Victor Fleming. Screenwriting by Donald Ogden Stewart. Produced by Hunt Stromberg, Irving Thalberg. Additional photography: Arthur Edeson. Assistant director: Hugh Boswell. Production dates: August to September 1932. Released October 22, 1932.
Other Versions: Loosely remade as *Mogambo* (1953). *Congo Maisie* (1940) bears enough similarity to *Red Dust* to be referred to as a remake in several sources. However, it was nominally based on another Wilson Collison play.
Available: MGM Home Entertainment VHS (1994).

Based on a 1928 play that closed after eight performances, *Red Dust* was purchased by MGM as a vehicle for Greta Garbo and John Gilbert. When the stars' relationship foundered, production head Irving Thalberg told Paul Bern to develop the piece as a romance for Gilbert and Jean Harlow. Born Harlean Carpenter in Missouri in 1911, Harlow was a newlywed in Los Angeles when she was offered work as an extra at the Fox Studio. Although not especially interested in acting at first, Harlow (she adopted her mother's maiden name professionally) was soon appearing as an extra in comedy shorts and features.

She signed and broke a contract with Hal Roach, divorced her husband, signed a contract with Howard Hughes, and began receiving prominent movie roles in films like *Hell's Angels* (1930) and *The Public Enemy* (1931). Harlow's acting was rudimentary, but she was cast for her looks and personality more than for her ability. Frank Capra found a way to soften her brassiness in *Platinum Blonde* (1931), but it was Paul Bern who first treated her seriously as an actress. Born Paul Levy in 1889, Bern acted, wrote screenplays, and managed movie theaters before moving to Hollywood in 1920, after his mother committed suicide. Introverted, bookish, he was, in the words of author Anita Loos, a "German psycho."

Bern cast Harlow in *The Beast of the City* (1932), a gangster film starring Walter Huston. After her nationwide publicity tour, Loew's president Nick Schenck bought her contract from Hughes for $30,000. (Loew's was the parent company of MGM.) Irving Thalberg cast her in *Red-Headed Woman*, a racy drama about a stenographer who

sleeps her way to the top. The film was a sensation, and at twenty-one years of age, Harlow was a star.

Friends and colleagues were bewildered when Harlow married Bern in July 1932. By then the *Red Dust* project was taking shape. Screenwriter John Lee Mahin took credit for the idea of teaming Harlow with Gable instead of Gilbert. In retrospect the switch to Gable seems intuitive, especially with Gilbert's career in a free fall. The two actors could not be more dissimilar. Gilbert projected a refined, even effete appearance; Gable was masculinity personified. He was born in rural Ohio in 1901, and dropped out of high school to work a succession of labor-intensive jobs. Determined to become an actor, he joined a theater troupe led by actress Josephine Dillon. She took over his career, coaching him in acting and altering his appearance. They married in 1924, but three years later Gable left her and set out on his own.

Gable won leads in two Broadway plays before returning to California. He failed a screen test at MGM, but took a role as the villain in *The Painted Desert* (1931), a Western. By chance, he appeared in *The Secret Six* with Harlow, but it wasn't until *A Free Soul* that same year that Gable's screen persona took full shape. He could play tough, even brutish, but viewers could still believe he was decent. Counter to most of the leading men of the time, he was aggressively masculine, and big enough to physically overpower his costars.

The actor signed a contract with MGM in December 1930, and remained at the studio until 1954. *Red Dust* was one of four films he made in 1932. During filming he formed a bond with director Victor Fleming. A former auto mechanic, Fleming entered films in 1910 as a cinematographer, working under directors like Allan Dwan and D.W. Griffith and with actor Douglas Fairbanks. He was a well-liked but no-nonsense "man's man" who didn't mind following other people's blueprints.

Although shot on MGM's backlot, *Red Dust* has a gritty, feverish feel, emphasized by Fleming in extended tracking shots of a sweaty, stubbled Gable striding purposefully past extras posing as coolies. He's the manager of a rubber plantation in an unspecified Southeast Asian country (the nearest city is apparently Saigon, pronounced "Saygone" by everyone in the cast). One coworker,

Donald Crisp, is a drunken lout; the other, Tully Marshall, acts as Gable's conscience.

Harlow arrives in a filmy dress, an unapologetic prostitute sent upriver to escape moral authorities. She doggedly pursues Gable until he succumbs physically, but he refuses to consider her as a lover. When Mary Astor arrives as the new bride of scientist Gene Raymond, Gable sets out to seduce her, sending her husband to work in a swamp to get him out of the way.

Aided by playwright Donald Ogden Stewart, screenwriter Mahin just manages to squeak the film past censors by engineering a "happy" ending. But there is no mistaking the film's primary focus: sex, illicit sex at that, photographed in a leering but still tastefully diffused manner by Hal Rosson. Many of the bedroom scenes are shot through mosquito netting, giving a warm glow to Astor's patrician beauty. Harlow, meanwhile, is lit like an angel, overhead lanterns softening her deep-set eyes and highlighting her hair. Gable is almost always presented with his face in a sheen—sweat, oil, rain, it doesn't matter, especially with his shirt unbuttoned.

Gene Raymond and Mary Astor later complained about the shoot, especially how the lights heated up the muddy outdoor sets. As Raymond said, "It stank to high heaven. . . . It was not a pleasant picture; it was hard for everybody, but especially the crew." The cast labored on, with Harlow winning the crew's appreciation with her good spirits and lack of airs. (Also for appearing nude in a bathing scene set in a rain barrel.)

Everything fell apart on Labor Day weekend. Bern, who was working on *China Seas*, a future Harlow project, killed himself sometime between Saturday and Sunday. Harlow was briefly considered a suspect, until MGM publicity head Howard Stricklin disclosed a suicide note to the police. Shooting on *Red Dust* resumed on September 7, but without Harlow, who attended Bern's funeral two days later on September 9. The inquest revealed that Bern had been in a common-law relationship with actress Dorothy Millette, who herself had already been married. Weirdly, Millette committed suicide around this time by jumping off a steamship; her body wasn't recovered until September 14. By that time Harlow had returned to the *Red Dust* set, the long hours there a relief from her private life.

With Bern's suicide a lead article in newspapers across the country, Mayer and Thalberg were worried about the film's reception with moviegoers.

Thalberg characteristically tinkered with the final cut, ordering considerable reshooting. (Notice how the liquor bottle label changes during the scene where Gable first gets drunk with Harlow; Gable's haircut changes as well.) Leaks about Bern's tortured private life helped sway public opinion in Harlow's favor, but it was the film itself that did the trick.

Red Dust is both fast-paced and entertaining. As the most polished performer in the cast, Astor is asked to do the heavy lifting, leaving Gable and Harlow free to project attitude. (Poor Donald Crisp's job is to get punched.) Gable does anger better than remorse; Harlow pushes across her lines with a swaggering sexuality. When she kneels down in a negligee and pulls off Gable's boots, the actor leering down at her, *Red Dust* is as explicit as a 1930s film can get.

Hollywood was in the midst of a periodic fixation with prostitutes. Greta Garbo, Marlene Dietrich, Joan Crawford, Bette Davis, Tallulah Bankhead, Mae Clarke, and Barbara Stanwyck all played "fallen" women. What was new and appealing in Harlow's performance was her lack of guilt or shame. Her line of work was just a job, not an opportunity to repent and reform, and she was proud of doing her work well. Harlow didn't mystify or parody sex like Mae West, and she didn't moralize about it either. Audiences loved her straightforward approach, her physicality, her tough wisecracking, her confidence and optimism, and her blazing beauty.

And in the height of the Depression, Harlow was, along with Gable, the best bet MGM had going. Vehicles for the studio's higher paid stars were floundering. *Red-Headed Woman* was a smash; *Red Dust* cost $408,000 to make and grossed over $1.2 million. Harlow and Gable would make four more films together, including her last, *Saratoga* (1937). In the very appealing comedy *Bombshell* (1933), Harlow spoofs her persona as a movie star and her role in *Red Dust*.

Harlow died of kidney failure following a misdiagnosis by a family doctor in 1937. By that time her performances had been greatly restricted by a tightened Production Code, although she never lost the affection of her fans. Gable went on to become one of the most enduring box-office stars in movies. And Fleming continued helming some of the most significant films from MGM, including *Treasure Island* (1934), *Captains Courageous* (1937), and, in 1939, both *The Wizard of Oz* and *Gone with the Wind*.

She Done Him Wrong

Paramount, 1933. Sound, B&W, 1.37. 64 mins.

Cast: Mae West (Lady Lou), Cary Grant (Captain Cummings), Owen Moore (Chick Clark), Gilbert Roland (Serge Stanieff), Noah Beery, Sr. (Gus Jordan), David Landau (Dan Flynn), Rafaela Ottiano (Russian Rita), Dewey Robinson (Spider Kane), Rochelle Hudson (Sally), Tammany Young (Chuck Connors), Fuzzy Knight (Rag Time Kelly), Grace La Rue (Frances), Robert E. Homans (Doheney), Louise Beavers (Pearl).

Credits: Directed by Lowell Sherman. Screenplay by Harvey Thew and John Bright. Based on the play *Diamond Lil* by Mae West. Director of photography: Charles Lang.

Additional Cast: Allan Jenkins (Waiter in saloon), Tom Kennedy (Bartender).

Additional Credits: Produced by Wlliam LeBaron. Film editor: Alexander Hall. Art direction: Robert Usher. Costume designer: Edith Head. "Some of These Days," words and music by Shelton Brooks. "Frankie and Johnny," traditional. "She Done Him Wrong," "A Guy What Takes His Time," words and music by Ralph Rainger. Premiered January 27, 1933.

Available: Universal Studios DVD (2008). UPC: 025192578823. MCA Universal Home Video VHS (1993). ISBN 1-55880-780-2. UPC: 0-9689-80597-3-2.

Paramount Studios entered the Depression in perilous shape. Producer David O. Selznick overhauled its story department, then hired scriptwriting brothers Herman J. and Joseph Mankiewicz and directors George Cukor and John Cromwell. Sam Katz, the head of advertising and distribution, expanded the studio's theater holdings from seven hundred to twelve hundred. (By comparison, Loew's, the parent company of MGM, owned about 120 theaters.) These expensive decisions led to Selznick's departure in 1931; two years later, Jesse Lasky and B.P. Schulberg, holdovers from the studio's earliest days, were forced out. That same year Paramount was forced to declare bankruptcy.

Ironically, the films released by Paramount during this period were among the best in the industry. From the Marx Brothers and W.C. Fields to Marlene Dietrich and Gary Cooper, Paramount films had an effortless polish and sophistication. The studio's filmmakers didn't take their projects too seriously. Their work wasn't art, it was entertainment, and if every now and then something with a little more depth slipped through, so much the better.

Unfortunately, it proved impossible to fill 1,200 theaters week after week with only the promise that something good *might* show up on the screen. Paramount needed hits, both to establish its brand with the public and to persuade theaters to book its product. As many executives have since, Adolph Zukor took the easy way out by pushing sex as much as possible. While Warners would release a few racy films, and some independent producers would try even more risqué material, Paramount

seemed to rely on sex more than any other studio. It played a fundamental role in the Josef von Sternberg/Marlene Dietrich vehicles, and was more promised than delivered in Carole Lombard films like *Love Before Breakfast*. And it was behind the contract offered in 1931 to Mae West.

The daughter of a Brooklyn boxer, livery man, and detective, West was born Mary Jane West in 1892. She played children's roles, notably Little Nell, on stage until she became a teenager, then moved into vaudeville, where she sang and danced while perfecting her image as a vamp. Having rewritten much of her material in Broadway revues, she completed her first play in 1926. Entitled *Sex*, it was a deliberate attempt attract attention by provoking authorities. After performing the play for over a half year, West was arrested for indecency, spending ten days in jail.

Because of censorship pressure, West opened her next play in New Jersey, but 1928's *Diamond Lil* became a Broadway smash. Set on the Bowery during the Gay Nineties, the play defined West's persona—blond, buxom, sexually active, but nobody's fool—for the rest of her career. When her two subsequent plays were closed by the police, West took up the offer from Paramount and moved to the West Coast.

Universal had tried to purchase the rights to *Diamond Lil* in 1930, but Will Hays, head of the Motion Pictures Producers and Distributors of America, placed the piece on a list of restricted plays. As head of what was referred to as the Hays Office, the former postmaster general had been trying to force studios to adhere to his Motion Picture Production Code. Since West insisted on filming *Diamond Lil* as part of her contract, that left Paramount in a difficult situation.

In the meantime, they placed her in a gangster melodrama starring George Raft, fresh off his success in *Scarface*. *Night After Night* (1932) let West recite one of her most famous lines, "Goodness had nothing to do with it," but it was not the box-office smash that the studio had hoped. A sign of the studio's increasing desperation was its announcement that it would film *Diamond Lil* despite the Hays ban.

Lowell Sherman was assigned to direct West's script. A former Broadway star, he had made his film debut in D.W. Griffith's *Way Down East* (1920), and for the next decade starred in sex-heavy comedies and dramas. He started directing after sound came in, and his films, which included *Bachelor Apartment* and *The Royal Bed* (1930), did nothing to ease the Hays Office's concerns. When Hays confronted Paramount executives directly, they assured him that they would not film *Diamond Lil.*

They filmed *She Done Him Wrong* instead. It was the same script, only West's character became Lady Lou instead of Lil. The Hays Office ordered the studio to remove references to white slavery and the Salvation Army, but its influence waned as the Depression deepened. By the time *She Done Him Wrong* finished filming in 1933, Paramount had declared bankruptcy.

No one was fooled when *She Done Him Wrong* opened in February. The *New York Times* called its review "Diamond Lil," while *Variety* said the film was simply a remake of the play. The Roman Catholic Church fumed against the movie, but theater owners were delighted. Budgeted at around $250,000, the film grossed over $2 million in its initial release.

An artifact of the 1930s, the film is a ramshackle affair, confined to a half-dozen sets, featuring the same Paramount character actors who wound up in comedies with W.C. Fields and George Burns and Gracie Allen. On the other hand it is an excellent showcase for West, who preens, sashays, and wobbles serenely throughout the film. By setting her story in a previous generation, she was able to not only parody the melodramas of an earlier time, but get away with more innuendo than a contemporary story could. What's surprising is how affectionately West treats the plots and music she grew up with. Snippets of "When You and I Were Young, Maggie," "After the Ball," and other turn-of-the-century chestnuts can be heard on the soundtrack, and the only real plot, as opposed to shtick, involves protecting a young woman's honor. When a saloon audience bursts into applause after a florid version of "Silver Threads Among the Gold," what is West's target—the people enjoying the song, or us for laughing at them?

Once she arrives, about ten minutes into the film, West rarely relinquishes the screen. Her lines appear like clockwork: "When women go wrong, men go right after them." "It takes two to get one in trouble." West often implied that she discovered Cary Grant, although by the time he was cast in *She Done Him Wrong*, the British-born actor had already appeared in more than a half-dozen films. Still, this was a breakthrough performance for him, if only as the recipient of West's most famous come-on: "Why don't you come up sometime and see me?"

West saves her songs for the end, rolling her eyes for "A Guy What Takes His Time" and dragging "Frankie and Johnnie" out of her past. She doesn't even bother to lip-synch the former. The latter was a well-known number that served as a sort of theme for Jimmie Rodgers; it had also been recorded by poet Carl Sandburg, who referred to it as a "classical gutter song." For that matter, it had been used in Jean Harlow's *Red-Headed Woman* only a few months earlier.

And then the whole thing is over, barely an hour after it starts. (In fact, it is the shortest feature ever nominated for a Best Picture Oscar.) The film's success predictably led to more lascivious movies, many by West herself. It also helped lead to a stronger Production Code, which was implemented in 1934.

West and the film were parodied almost immediately, for example in the Betty Boop cartoon *She Wronged Him Right*. The actress found herself frozen into her role as a Gay Nineties sexpot. *Belle of the Nineties* (1934), *Klondike Annie* (1936), and *My Little Chickadee* (1940) are some of the increasingly neutered signposts in a career that became more and more irrelevant as the years passed. West retired from movies in 1943, revived *Diamond Lil* as a touring show, then appeared in two poorly received films before her death in 1980.

King Kong

RKO, 1933. Sound, B&W, 1.37. 100 minutes.
Cast: Fay Wray (Ann Darrow), Robert Armstrong (Carl Denham), Bruce Cabot (John Driscoll), Frank Reicher (Capt. Englehorn), Sam Hardy (Charles Weston), Noble Johnson (Native chief), Steve Clemento (Witch king), James Flavin (Second mate).
Credits: Produced and directed by Merian C. Cooper and Ernest B. Schoedsack. Screenplay by James Creelman and Ruth Rose. From an idea conceived by Edgar Wallace and Merian C. Cooper. Executive producer: David O. Selznick. Photographed by Eddie Linden, Vernon Walker, J.O. Taylor. Production assistants: Archie F. Marshek, Walter Daniels. Chief technician: Willis H. O'Brien. Art technicians: Mario Larrinaga, Byron L. Crabbe. Technical staff: E.B. Gibson, Marcel Delgado, Fred Reese, Orville Goldner, Carroll Shepphird. Music by Max Steiner. Sound effects: Murray Spivack. Settings by Carroll Clark, Al Herman. Recorded by Earl A. Wolcott. Film editor: Ted Cheesman. Recorded by RCA Photophone System. A Radio Pictures presentation of a Merian C. Cooper and Ernest B. Schoedsack production.

Additional Cast includes: Victor Wong (Lumpy); Fred Behrle, Earl "Hap" Hogan, Walter Kirby, John Northpole, H.R. Warwick, Jack Gallagher, Duke Green, Jockey Haefell, Sam Levine, Sailor Vincent, Kid Wagner, Charles Hall, George Magrill, Van Alder, John Collins, Charles Sewell, Bill Van Vleck, Ralph Bard, T.C. Jacks, Harry Claremont, Art Flavin, Walter Kimpton, Richard McCarew, Jack Perry, Bert O'Malley, Jack Silver, Joe Dill, Leo Beard, Dick Curtis, Jimmy Dime, Tex Duffy, Shorty English, Bill Fisher, Ethan Laidlaw, Hugh Starkey, Bill Dagwell, Roy Brent, Larry Fisher, Walter Taylor, Skeets Noyes, Edward Clark, Blackie Whiteford, Jack Saunders, Harry Walker, Frank Gerrity, Harry Cornbleth, Bud Mason, Charles Sullivan, Al McDonald, James Casey, Tex Higginson (Ship crew members); George Daly, Ernest Schoedsack (Machine gunners); Merian Cooper (Pilot).

Additional Credits: Assistant directors: Ivan Thomas, Doran Cox, Walter Daniels. Production dates: October 10, 1931 to February 1, 1933. Premiered in New York City on March 2, 1933.

Other Versions: Sequel The Son of Kong (1933). Remade as King Kong in 1976 and 2005. Cooper produced and Schoedsack directed Mighty Joe Young in 1949; it featured similar characters and special effects.

Available: Warner Home Video DVD (2005). ISBN: 0-7806-5060-3. UPC: 053939724127.

One of the most memorable characters in all of cinema, King Kong was the invention of producer and director Merian C. Cooper. According to biographer Mark Cotta Vaz, Cooper never got over his fascination with the books on explorations and novels of high adventure he read as a youth. Much of his life reads like one of those tales, and they formed the basis of what would become the film *King Kong*.

Cooper's early years are covered in *Grass* (1925, a Registry title), a documentary he made with his partner Ernest B. Schoedsack. Its success gave the pair carte blanche for their next project. They chose Siam (now Thailand) as the location for *Chang* (1927), a pseudo-documentary about rural villagers. In it, Cooper tried to portray animals as characters with personalities—fun-loving, sentimental troublemakers who could turn violent. Back in the United States, Cooper directed an adaptation of *The Four Feathers* (1929) with Lothar Mendes before retiring from the industry to work in aviation. Cooper was one of the founders of Western Airlines and Pan American Airways.

He was also working on a screenplay about a giant gorilla, perhaps as early as 1929, but definitely by 1930, when he saw an airplane flying above the New York Life Insurance Building and thought of a great ape clinging to its top. Cooper used an expedition to Komodo Island by his friend Douglas Burden for the setting of what would become Skull Island, but from the start he was fascinated by the idea of a prehistoric creature at loose in the heart of Manhattan. Burden helped Cooper work out the technical details of the story—how a film crew could operate on a remote island, for example.

Executives at Paramount and MGM rejected Cooper's story. In June 1931, Cooper met producer David O. Selznick, who had recently quit Paramount and was trying to establish his own production company. Cooper introduced him to investor cousins Cornelius ("Sonny") and John ("Jock") Whitney, and later that year joined Selznick at RKO. At the studio lot in Los Angeles that December, Cooper began experimenting with the special effects for *King Kong*.

Special effects expert Willis O'Brien (*The Lost World*, 1925) had been working on a project called *Creation*, a dinosaur adventure that used stop-motion animation and armature models. Selznick, now head of production, halted the expensive project, then asked Cooper if the footage could be salvaged. Cooper pushed his own story, emphasizing the "ferocious menace" of beasts running through Manhattan, and persuaded the studio to finance tests of a model gorilla.

For the "tests," Cooper built full-scale sets and hired professional actors. He knew Fay Wray from *The Four Feathers*, and cast her by saying she would have "the tallest, darkest leading man in Hollywood." Robert Armstrong was hired as impresario Carl Denham, to some extent because he resembled Cooper. In fact, one of the more amusing aspects of *King Kong* is its close relationship to the actual expeditions Cooper and Schoedsack led.

Before shooting started, O'Brien drew a sketch that crystallized Cooper's approach to the project: a monstrous ape atop the Empire Stage Building, a screaming woman in one fist, fighter planes about to attack. In January 1932, Ernest Schoedsack joined the production as codirector. While working on *King Kong*, he and Cooper started and finished *The Most Dangerous Game* (1932, codirected by Irving Pichel), utilizing Fay Wray and Robert Armstrong again and some of *Kong*'s sets.

As well as being a well-made, exciting adventure, *The Most Dangerous Game* served as a sort of dry run for the dramatic scenes in *Kong*. Editor Archie Marshek remembered Schoedsack timing actors with a stopwatch, speeding up their performances to establish a breathless pace. (Marshek was promoted to production assistant on *Kong*.) At times Schoedsack and Cooper would be overseeing two separate crews at the same time, one shooting *Game*, the other, *Kong*. After *Game* was finished, they continued shooting *Kong* with two crews to save time.

For months *King Kong* didn't have a script, although Selznick had hired mystery writer Edgar Wallace in December 1931, to work on one.

Wallace finished a draft in January 1932, but died of pneumonia the following month. In a memo to Selznick in July of that year, Cooper said the script that existed—called *The Beast*—was his work, executed by staff screenwriter James Creelman. Cooper later said that 90 percent of the dialogue was written by Ruth Rose.

Meanwhile, O'Brien and his crew worked on the special effects shots, using a half-dozen eighteen-inch Kong models and similarly sized dinosaur models; full-scale models of Kong's head, shoulders, paw, and foot; scale puppets of humans to film with the dinosaurs; glass panes painted with jungle details; and rear-projection devices that used cutting-edge cellulose-acetate screens. *Kong* also made use of an optical printer developed by Vernon Walker for RKO.

Late in the production process, Cooper insisted on a new sequence in which Kong attacks an elevated train. He also took the honor of finally killing Kong: he and Schoedsack are in the plane that shoots the ape down. Shortly before the film's release, Selznick left the studio for MGM; Cooper was named to replace him.

Kong opened in New York City on March 2, 1933, days before President Franklin D. Roosevelt called a four-day bank holiday. Critics and moviegoers alike were astonished by the film, which became a worldwide hit. Ever the showman, Cooper had a sequel in theaters before the end of the year.

King Kong has lost little of its power over time, perhaps because its story is adaptable to many different interpretations. To film historian Donald Cripps, it was more than "merely a racist nightmare." Kong was a tragic figure, colonized, enslaved, cut off from his roots. In Germany it was released as *King Kong und die Weisse Frau*. Contemporary critics remember it as a touchstone of their youth. It remains sui generis, a dark, disturbing dream that offers no easy answers, but instead roils society's deepest taboos. We read our own myths into it. Merian Cooper's greatest achievement may have been in his conception of Kong as a figure to be pitied as much as feared.

42nd Street

Warner Bros., 1933. Sound, B&W, 1.37. 90 minutes.

Cast: Warner Baxter (Julian Marsh), Bebe Daniels (Dorothy Brock), George Brent (Pat Denning), Ruby Keeler (Peggy [Sawyer]), Guy Kibbee (Abner Dillon), Una Merkel (Lorraine Fleming), Ginger Rogers (Ann [Lowell]), Ned Sparks ([Thomas] Barry), Dick Powell (Billy Lawler), Allen Jenkins (Mac Elroy), Edward J. Nugent (Terry), Robert McWade (Jones), George E. Stone (Andy Lee).

Credits: Directed by Lloyd Bacon. Dances & ensembles created & staged by Busby Berkeley. Words & music by Al Dubin and Harry Warren. Screen play by Rian James & James Seymour. Based on the novel by Bradford Ropes. Edited by Frank Ware & Thomas Pratt. Art director: Jack Okey. Photography by Sol Polito. Gowns by Orry-Kelly. Silks by Cheney Brothers. Vitaphone Orchestra conducted by Leo F. Forbstein. A Warner Bros. Pictures, Inc. and Vitaphone Corp. presentation.

Additional Cast: Clarence Nordstrom (Groom in "Shuffle Off to Buffalo"), Henry B. Walthall (Actor); Al Dubin, Harry Warren (Songwriters); Toby Wing (Showgirl in "Young and Healthy"), Charles Lane (Playwright), Dave O'Brien (Chorus boy), Rolfe Sedan (Stagehand); Jack La Rue, Tom Kennedy (Thugs); Harry Akst (Jerry), Louise Beavers (Pansy [maid]).

Additional Credits: Produced by Darryl F. Zanuck. Assistant director: Gordon Hollingshead. Sound: Nathan Levinson, Dolph Thomas. Production dates for the Bacon unit: September 28 to October 29, 1932. Reshoots: November 2 and 3. Production dates, Berkeley unit: October 19 to November 16, 1932. Premiered in New York City on March 9, 1933.

Other Versions: Produced by David Merrick as a Broadway musical in 1980, with additional songs and choreography by Gower Champion.

Available: Warner Home Video DVD (2000). ISBN: 0-7907-5014-7. UPC: 0-12569-50012-9.

When production chief Darryl F. Zanuck proposed making *42nd Street* at Warner Brothers, he did it with the knowledge that Harry Warner was dead set against the musical genre. Musicals glutted the market with the coming of sound, and the Warner studio had suffered its share of expensive flops. Zanuck may have fooled Harry and his other brothers into thinking the film would be a drama without songs and dances. He assigned two screenwriters to adapt an unpublished novel by Bradford Ropes about a Broadway director who risks his health to mount a musical.

Director Mervyn LeRoy was equally enthusiastic about *42nd Street*, perhaps because it would be an opportunity to employ Busby Berkeley, a choreographer who had been hired by Samuel Goldwyn to stage the dances in his film version of *Whoopee* (1930). LeRoy had originally been scheduled to direct *42nd Street*, but his work on *I Am a Fugitive from a Chain Gang* (1932) proved too exhausting. Ropes' novel had been published in September, and Zanuck wanted to capitalize on the publicity it had gathered. Unwilling to wait for LeRoy, he assigned staff director Lloyd Bacon to the project.

While preparing the film, Zanuck and LeRoy planned to split the production into two halves. One would cover all the dramatic material; the other would be a separate unit for the musical numbers, with its own soundstages and technicians. Zanuck borrowed Warner Baxter, an Oscar-winning star, from Fox for the role of theater director Julian Marsh, and cast Bebe Daniels, a silent film veteran with extensive stage experience, as the prima donna Dorothy Brock. The crucial supporting roles would be filled by Warner contract players like Guy Kibbee, George Brent, and Dick Powell. *42nd Street* would also be the film debut for Ruby Keeler, who had married one of Warners' biggest stars, Al Jolson.

The film's dramatic scenes have the drive and urban grit of one of Zanuck's gangster pictures, although the script lacks the smart patter Zanuck favored, and Bacon's pacing is slower than most Warners product. Berkeley's musical numbers were what won over moviegoers. While some filmmakers like Rouben Mamoulian and Ernst Lubitsch had experimented with working songs into realistic settings, most directors of the time were content to present numbers as if they were being viewed from a theater stage.

Berkeley, whose early experience had been choreographing parades and marching bands, took a different approach. He wanted the camera to be a part of the number, a "camera that must dance." Rather than give his dancers routines with choreographed steps, he arranged them in geometric patterns and let the camera swoop over them on a crane and crawl under them on a dolly. For purists, this technique was the antithesis of true dance, but in 1933 it seemed fresh, even daring.

42nd Street was backloaded with Berkeley's numbers. Only a few snatches of songs and dances are seen in the first hour of the film, but the final twenty minutes is almost nonstop music. Berkeley takes more chances as the numbers progress. In the buoyant "Shuffle Off to Buffalo," he still pretends that the production could be taking place on a theater stage (he even shows the pit orchestra in one shot). For "Young and Healthy," he abandons that illusion, and by the title tune he has abandoned dance altogether, inserting a story line about battling lovers that ends with death.

On the other hand, seen in strictly dance terms, Berkeley's work wasn't all that different from such stiff, lumbering routines as "Li-Po-Li" from Warners' *The Show of Shows* (1929). Dancers are still marching in unison up bleachers, for example, and the milling about sometimes borders on chaos. But Zanuck was delighted with the finished film, and started work on an unofficial sequel before it was released. The lessons he applied to *Gold Diggers of 1933* included speeding up the pacing, ditching the expensive stars, and adding more production numbers.

By the time *Gold Diggers* started filming, *42nd Street* was one of the genuine box-office hits of the year. But Zanuck was on his way out of the Warners studio, and Berkeley's methods were facing competition from Fred Astaire, who was about to embark on a series of musicals with Ginger Rogers.

Snow-White

Paramount, 1933. Sound, B&W, 1.37. 7 minutes.

Voice Cast: Mae Questel, Cab Calloway.

Credits: Directed by Dave Fleischer. Animated by Roland C. Crandall. Presented by Max Fleischer.

Additional Credits: Produced by Max Fleischer. Songs include "Always in the Way," words and music by Charles K. Harris; "St. James Infirmary," words and music by Joe Primrose; "Tiger Rag," music by the Original Dixieland Jazz Band. Released March 31, 1933.

Available: *Snow-White* is in the public domain. It can be viewed online at the Internet Archive (*www.archive.org*).

Some of the twentieth century's most vibrant art forms collide in *Snow-White*, a cartoon by the Fleischer brothers. Based in New York City, they offered a gritty, sexy alternative to the sunny, rural animation turned out by Walt Disney, MGM, and Warner Brothers.

One of six children, Max Fleischer was born in Vienna in either 1883 or 1885, and emigrated to New York City when he was four. His younger brother Dave was born there in 1894. Although he was a high school dropout, Max was fascinated by gadgetry in general and motion pictures in particular. He was the art editor for *Popular Science* magazine while still in his teens, and patented the rotoscope in 1917. This device allowed artists to turn motion pictures into animation by tracing the outlines of images on film frames from a glass screen, a technique still in use today.

In 1915, Max and Dave made their first film, shooting on top of a rooftop in front of a sheet backdrop. Dave wore a clown costume from his failed attempt to work at Coney Island's Steeplechase Park; this was the source for Ko Ko (also known as Ko-Ko, or KoKo), one of the eeriest cartoon stars

Ko Ko and Betty Boop during the "St. James Infirmary" sequence in *Snow-White*.

of the twentieth century. The brothers made a film for Pathé, then were hired by J.R. Bray to make one short a month for Paramount. During World War I they made instructional films for the armed services. The first in their "Out of the Inkwell" series came out in 1919. These incorporated live footage with animation, and were so successful that two years later the brothers struck out on their own.

Setting up shop first on East Forty-fifth Street in Manhattan, then at 1600 Broadway, and briefly on Long Island, they headed up a staff of animators that grew and shrank depending on income. Max handled financing and contributed story ideas; Dave received directing credit, which in his case meant supervising different units of artists. Along with rotoscoping, the Fleischers developed the position of "in-betweener," and may have been the first to rely on model charts to make their animated characters consistent.

In 1923, Max produced what some consider the first animated features, including an hour-long instructional film called *Einstein's Theory of Relativity*. The Fleischers were at the forefront of synchronized sound movies, working with Lee De Forest on *My Old Kentucky Home*, the first talking cartoon, and introducing "Song Car-Tunes" in 1924. These featured the famous "follow the bouncing ball," which allowed viewers to sing along to lyrics projected onto the screen.

The Fleischers' cartoons were second in popularity only to Otto Messmer's Felix the Cat. Their first independent sound animation came under the umbrella of Talkartoons, starting with *Noah's Lark* in 1929. Initially the Fleischers animated their cartoons to pre-existing recordings, a technique that anticipated the playback system later used by every major studio. When unions objected, they turned to original music, with brother Lou Fleischer doing the arranging. Since there were sixteen frames to a foot, and twenty-four to a second, Lou's arrangements were based on multiples of three or four in order to divide action easily.

From 1927 on, their cartoons were distributed by Paramount, which gave access to the Paramount musical library. That accounts for the prevalence of tunes like "Everyone Says I Love You" in their work. Performers like Louis Armstrong and Cab Calloway would appear in the cartoons at low rates; Paramount would then book their acts in its theaters a week after the cartoons screened.

The sixth Talkartoon, *Dizzy Dishes* (1930), was the first to feature Betty Boop, although in the form of a dog. Animated by Grim Natwick, later one of Disney's star artists, she was based in part on a song-sheet photograph of Helen Kane, a Paramount singer known as the "Boop Oop a Doop Girl." Betty appeared in two more cartoons, including the insanely compelling *Bimbo's Initiation* (1930), before being named in *Betty Coed* (1931). That same year she completed her transformation into a human in *Any Rags*. She was voiced at various times by Margie Hines, Kate Wright, and Little Ann Little, who toured with a Betty Boop vaudeville act. But from 1931 until 1939, the voice and mannerisms of Betty Boop were the work of Mae Questel, a one-time winner of a Helen Kane look-alike contest. (Kane sued the Fleischers in 1934 for stealing her act, but lost.)

Betty Boop was one of the most popular creations in animation, a bright, lively, sexy woman attuned to jazz and other elements of popular culture. Depression-era viewers fell in love with her, and she was soon selling soap, candy, and toys, as well as appearing in a comic strip and on a radio show. Generous, free-spirited, and optimistic, she was an antidote to the bad news permeating the country.

The Fleischers starred her in a total of ninety cartoons, although she also showed up in several others. She was cast in surrealistic mysteries, in variations on a single gag like 1932's *Betty Boop, MD*, and in revamped fairy tales like *Jack and the Beanstalk*. *Snow-White*, the fourteenth Betty Boop cartoon, was also the second of three Fleischer pictures featuring Cab Calloway. It was animated entirely by Roland C. "Doc" Crandall over a period of six months, and included Ko Ko and Bimbo along with Betty.

Today critics like to point out the cartoon's surrealism, its hot jazz elements, and its rotoscoping. Animation historian Michael Barrier also noted the Fleischers' tendency to time their cartoons too monotonously. Everything bounces to the same 3/4

or 4/4 time. The only way to alter this type of pacing was to insert peripheral jokes. According to animator Dave Tendlar, "Dave Fleischer's theory was that every scene should have a gag." As Barrier points out, the easiest way to throw in a joke was to bring an inanimate object to life: a cactus that turns shy, a clock that shouts out a warning, even skeletons and rocks that spring into action—in other words, a fairly prosaic explanation for the Fleischers' pliant, flexible universe so admired by surrealists.

Snow-White stretches Dave Fleischer's gag theory to its limits, in the process combining elements of the familiar fairy tale with "St. James Infirmary," a 1930 song credited to Joe Primrose that can be traced back to the "Gambler's Blues" of the 1890s. (Some sources cite the eighteenth-century English ballad, "The Unfortunate Rake.") While not as bizarrely structured as some Fleischer cartoons, it could not have been made anywhere else. Betty helped introduce another star to the filmgoing public three months later with *Popeye the Sailor*. The Fleischers' *Popeye the Sailor Meets Sindbad the Sailor* (1936) is also on the Registry.

Gold Diggers of 1933

Warner Bros., 1933. Sound, B&W, 1.37. 97 minutes.
Cast: Warren William (Lawrence [J. Lawrence Bradford]), Joan Blondell (Carol [King]), Aline MacMahon (Trixie [Lorraine]), Ruby Keeler (Polly [Parker]), Dick Powell (Brad [Roberts]), Guy Kibbee (Peabody), Ned Sparks (Barney [Hopkins]), Ginger Rogers (Fay [Fortune]).
Credits: Directed by Mervyn LeRoy. Numbers created & directed by Busby Berkeley. Music & lyrics by Harry Warren & Al Dubin. Screen play by Erwin Gelsey & James Seymour. Dialogue by David Boehm & Ben Markson. Based on a play by Avery Hopwood. Edited by George Amy. Art director: Anton Grot. Photography by Sol Polito. Gowns by Orry-Kelly. Vitaphone Orchestra conducted by Leo F. Forbstein.
Additional Cast: Tammany Young (Gigolo Eddie), Billy Barty, Sterling Holloway (Messenger), Charles Lane (Reporter), Etta Moten (Singer).
Additional Credits: Produced by Robert Lord. Production dates: February to April 1933. Released May 27, 1933.
Other Versions: The source play was the basis for *The Gold Diggers* (1923) and *Gold Diggers of Broadway* (1929). Succeeding Gold Diggers include: *Gold Diggers of 1935* (1935), *Gold Diggers of 1937* (1936), *Gold Diggers in Paris* (1938).
Available: Warner Home Video DVD (2006). UPC: 0-12569-67850-7.

The second of three "backstage" musicals released in short order by Warner Brothers, *Gold Diggers of 1933* had been in development before its predecessor, *42nd Street*, finished shooting. In fact, Warners had filmed the story twice before, once as a silent (*The Gold Diggers*, 1923), and in 1929 as the Technicolor feature *Gold Diggers of Broadway*. This last version is unfortunately lost except for its soundtrack, preserved on a set of Vitaphone discs, two reels of footage, and the frantic final minute,

which wraps up various plot strands even as the closing number spins out in the background.

It's not surprising that Jack Warner would choose this project as a remake (or that he would try to keep the production a secret until its release). The 1929 film grossed $4 million, almost as much as MGM's Oscar-winning *The Broadway Melody*. The 1933 version, overseen by chief of production Darryl F. Zanuck, follows the 1929 film fairly closely, albeit with a heavier emphasis on the Depression. Zanuck assigned Mervyn LeRoy, who had been forced to give up directing *42nd Street* due to exhaustion following *I Was a Fugitive from a Chain Gang*, to the project. Also back from *42nd Street* was Busby Berkeley, who again was given his own production unit to stage the musical numbers. In a memo, Zanuck wrote, "I want to retain as much of the old story as possible," and in fact film historian Richard Barrios has correlated almost every lead character in 1933 to the 1929 film.

But where the 1929 version featured a nine-minute "Tip Toe Through the Tulips," sung by Nick Lucas (and, judging from the soundtrack, staged with excruciating stiffness), the 1933 version had five Al Dubin and Harry Warren songs, including the classic "We're in the Money." (Its title was changed to "The Gold Diggers Song" as part of a sheet-music publishing tie-in.) The song opens the film with a bang, and it was moved there by LeRoy and Zanuck, who decided to discard an opening montage of closed theaters called for in the script. Instead, viewers are greeted with the sight of seminude chorines wearing cardboard coins while Ginger Rogers sings Dubin's lyrics in pig latin. For the topper, sheriffs arrive to close down the production and confiscate the props.

Gold Diggers of 1933 follows the same backstage formula as *42nd Street*, only as a comedy, not a drama. In place of an amateur becoming a star, *Gold Diggers* focuses on actresses tricking blue bloods out of their money: Joan Blondell fleecing Warren William, stage veteran Aline MacMahon toying with Guy Kibbee, with ostensible stars Dick Powell and Ruby Keeler fading into the background. LeRoy shot all the dramatic sequences in roughly six weeks, starting in February 1933. Berkeley's musical work began in the first week of March, just before the release of *42nd Street*.

Stopped in its tracks, as it were, the opening number didn't give Berkeley much of a chance to stretch out. "Pettin' in the Park," which appears about a half hour in, lets the choreographer plumb every nuance of Dubin's single entendre lyrics. When Powell takes a can opener to Keeler, sopping wet under a metallic swimsuit, could anyone miss the point? But what meaning can be given to Billy Barty, dressed as an infant, leering up the spread legs of a supine chorus girl? Was anyone at the time fooled into thinking that this was just good, clean fun?

"The Shadow Waltz," which appears after almost an hour of comedy, is a full-blown fantasy of geometrically positioned chorus girls pretending to play neon-lit violins, complete with extension cords. (Barrios reports that dancers narrowly avoided electrocution when the set was struck by an earthquake on March 10.) It's a cartoon come to life, one of those not-very-interesting ones in which ladybugs hop in unison on blades of grass or twirl around flowers that have smiling faces. The patterns have a certain hypnotic fascination, but at almost seven minutes in length, the song reaches a point where the figures cease to be abstract or beautiful and simply blur together.

It takes over forty minutes for William and Kibbee to arrive; once they do, you can sense LeRoy shifting gears in order to showcase the movie's most accomplished actors. This is prototypical Warners humor, with sexy, smart-mouthed women making fools of straitlaced men. The studio would run the formula into the ground in three more *Gold Diggers* films, as well as many spin-offs and variations. A stricter Production Code would eliminate much of the raciness, and appeal, of these follow-ups.

Jack Warner and production supervisor Hal Wallis (replacing Zanuck after the latter left the studio in a salary dispute) insisted on moving "Pettin' in the Park" from the end of the film. Instead, they wanted *Gold Diggers of 1933* to end with "My Forgotten Man," a song of epic chutzpah. In it, Joan Blondell is a streetwalker who comforts homeless World War I veterans with cigarettes. A montage depicts soldiers going off to and returning from battle. A giant set reveals three tiers of men marching in contrasting patterns over arches, plus men marching down bleachers towards the camera, plus lonely women with outstretched arms calling to them from the sides of the frame. As the men halt and stare back at Blondell, she lip syncs the closing lines. It's a triumph of some sort, and it all supposedly takes place on a Broadway stage.

Gold Diggers of 1933 made almost a million dollars more than *42nd Street*. Warners rushed *Footlight Parade* into production, and authorized work on the script for *Dames*, which would be filmed the following February. It also featured songs from the soundtrack in cartoons like *We're in the Money* and *I've Got to Sing a Torch Song*.

Three Little Pigs

United Artists, 1933. Sound, Color, 1.37. 8 minutes.
Voice Cast: Dorothy Compton (Pig with fife), Mary Moder (Pig with fiddle), Pinto Colvig (Practical Pig).
Credits: Directed by Burt Gillett. Produced by Walt Disney. Animation: Fred Moore, Norm Ferguson, Art Babbitt, Dick Lundy. Music: Frank Churchill. Song "Who's Afraid of the Big Bad Wolf?" music and lyrics by Frank Churchill, Ted Sears. Music arranged by Carl Stalling. Color by Technicolor. RCA Sound System.
Additional Credits: Released May 27, 1933.
Other Versions: Sequels: *The Big Bad Wolf* (1934), *Three Little Wolves* (1936), *The Practical Pig* (1939). Footage reedited into *The Thrifty Pig* (1941).
Awards: Oscar for Best Short Subject—Cartoons.

Available: Buena Vista Home Entertainment DVD *Disney's Timeless Tales, Vol. 1*, (2005); *Walt Disney Treasures—Silly Symphonies, 1936*, DVD (2001).

With his Mickey Mouse character firmly established, Walt Disney sought to expand his output by developing a second line of cartoons, one that wouldn't compete with Mickey's titles. Carl Stalling, a friend from his days in Kansas City, brought Disney an idea for what became "Silly Symphonies," cartoons tied to music rather than specific characters. Stalling's goal was to animate music rather than add music to animation. Exhibitors didn't like the first, *The Skeleton Dance* (1929), but Disney was so enamored of it that he started an entire unit devoted solely to Silly Symphonies. To finance them, he worked with Pat Powers, who distributed the Mickey cartoons, to sign a deal with Columbia that would pay the studio roughly $6,000 a title.

Facing a release schedule of up to thirty-six cartoons a year, Disney was forced to add to his staff. Burt Gillett had been working on Felix the Cat cartoons. He brought along animator Ben Sharpsteen, soon to be a mainstay of the studio. Norman Ferguson came from New York; he had worked on a series of "Aesop's Fables" cartoons.

At first Gillett directed Mickey Mouse titles, while Ub Iwerks handled the Silly Symphonies. But Walt and his brother Roy Disney had a falling out with Pat Powers over his accounting methods; Powers had also persuaded Iwerks to leave the Disneys, ostensibly to start his own studio. What's worse, Carl Stalling quit the same week. The only real bargaining chip the Disneys held in order to increase their income was Mickey himself. He proved so popular around the world that Columbia Pictures agreed to extricate the Disneys from their ties to Powers.

In the winter of 1930, Disney hired Ted Sears away from the Fleischer Studio and named him the head of a new Story Department. By that summer Walt had grown disenchanted with Columbia, and through producer Sol Lesser, came to an informal agreement with Joe Schenck, the head of United Artists. By 1932, UA was advancing the studio $15,000 for each Silly Symphony.

Disney used the studio's income to develop new animation techniques, like "pencil tests," or rough drafts that would be screened on a Moviola in a small, dark room dubbed the "sweatbox." This allowed Disney to perfect the jokes and pacing of a cartoon before committing staff to drawing sequences out fully. It was part of a process that also involved Sears and his staff, who wrote and rewrote scripts with greater attention to character and narrative. Character became paramount to Disney, who wanted even inanimate objects like trees and pianos to show feelings. Sears is also often credited with developing the storyboard, a series of drawings that laid out every scene, camera movement, and edit before animators began work. Disney took even more steps to improve his studio. He had instructors give art classes for the staff, commissioned live-action films to examine objects in motion, and experimented with tinting his black-and-white cartoons.

Color became the next hurdle, one that was solved by Technicolor's three-color process. Technicolor needed to get samples of their product out to the public, and offered to help Disney finance color cartoons. Walt became so enthusiastic that he ordered the black-and-white *Flowers and Trees* redrawn in color. The result was so successful that Disney signed a deal giving his studio exclusive animation rights to the process for two years. The first Silly Symphony released after the signing was *Three Little Pigs*.

The film was drawn primarily by Norm Ferguson and Dick Lundy, with assistance by Art Babbitt and Fred Moore. According to Disney biographer Neal Gabler, Ferguson drew the Wolf, Lundy the dance steps, and Babbitt the action. Moore was responsible for animating the pigs, now considered the first flowering of what would become known as the Disney style. Moore not only gave each pig a different personality, he developed them as characters who operated through thought and emotion, and not as the rampaging id Mickey so often expressed.

Crucial to the success of *Three Little Pigs* is the song "Who's Afraid of the Big Bad Wolf?" The music was by staff composer Frank Churchill, aided by voice actor Pinto Colvig; the words came from Ted Sears. What would become an anthem of the Depression was sung by two singers contracted for a recording session for twenty dollars.

The song was simplistic but also light and melodic, attributes that apply to the film as well. Disney preferred a restrained color palette and art design. The frames in *Three Little Pigs* are uncluttered, with broad swaths of soothing greens, blues, and browns. Flowers are grouped as surrogates for the audience, observing the action. Lundy gives the pigs impossible dance steps (look at how long their feet remain off the ground), but they move in perfect time to the music. Disney kept the story clear enough for children to understand, relying on technique and throwaway gags to keep adults interested. (For example, the family portraits hanging on the wall of the brick house, or the cans of "Wolf Proof Paint" sitting around outside.)

Three Little Pigs astonished the country when it was released in May 1933. At a time when features would change twice weekly, theater owners ran the cartoon for weeks. It had an indelible impact on future animators like Chuck Jones, and even curmudgeonly critics bowed to its charms. With a final budget of $15,568, and a print cost of $14,000, *Three Little Pigs* was more expensive than most Disney product. But it was conservatively estimated to earn over $600,000. It legitimized not only Walt Disney's goals and methods, but animation in general. In fact, *Three Little Pigs* may have been the reason why Disney decided to go ahead with his plans to make a feature-length cartoon.

Rabbi J.X. Cohen, director of the American Jewish Congress, was one of several religious leaders who complained about the disguise the wolf adopted when trying to break in to the brick house. Roy Disney defended the scene, even though the wolf was wearing a mask that was intended to show him as a Jewish peddler. The studio reanimated the material when the cartoon was rereleased, depicting the wolf as a Fuller Brush salesman instead.

Baby Face

Barbara Stanwyck ponders life as a "waitress" in her father's speakeasy in *Baby Face*.

Warner Bros., 1933. Sound, B&W, 1.37. 76 minutes.

Cast: Barbara Stanwyck (Lily [Powers/Allen]), George Brent ([Courtland] Trenholm), Donald Cook ([Ned] Stevens), Alphonse Ethier ([Adolf] Cragg), Henry Kolker ([J.R.] Carter), Margaret Lindsay (Ann Carter), Arthur Hohl (Ed Sipple), John Wayne (Jimmy McCoy), Robert Barrat (Nick Powers), Douglas Dumbrille (Brody), Theresa Harris (Chico).

Credits: Directed by Alfred E. Green. Screen play by Gene Markey & Kathryn Scola. Story by Mark Canfield [Darryl F. Zanuck]. Edited by Howard Bretherton. Art director: Anton Grot. Photography by James Van Trees. Gowns by Orry-Kelly. Vitaphone Orchestra conducted by Leo F. Forbstein.

Additional Cast: James Murray (Brakeman), Harry Gribbon (Doorman), Arthur DeKuh (Lutza), Nat Pendleton (Stolvich), Charles Coleman (Hodges), Edward Van Sloan (Jameson), Grace Hayle (Woman at travel desk), Charles Selton (Vandeleur), Spec O'Donnell (Office boy).

Additional Credits: Assistant director: Fred Fox. Sound: Oliver Garretson. Released July 1, 1933.

Other Versions: Warners released an edited version of *Baby Face*, 70 minutes long, after cuts were demanded by the Production Code office. In 2004, the prerelease version was discovered in Library of Congress vaults by George Willeman and Mike Mashon.

Available: Warner Home Video DVD *Forbidden Hollywood Collection Volume One* (2006). ISBN: 1-4198-2638-7. UPC: 0-12569-67964-1.

The Production Code represented the film industry's official view toward vice. Created under former postmaster Will Hays in 1930, it was a largely toothless measure designed to stave off attempts by state and city governments to form independent censorship boards. By officially prohibiting various forms of obscenity (at no time a serious problem with mainstream film), the Production Code gave the major studios leeway to continue releasing the movies they had always been making.

But standards kept changing—lowering, in the eyes of some—and what was prohibited in the early 1920s was passé by the sound era. Still, individual studios promoted separate attitudes. Prostitution was frowned on at Fox and Universal, and treated in a disapproving manner at MGM until producer Irving Thalberg unleashed Jean Harlow in *Red Dust* and *Red-Headed Woman* (both 1932). Paramount took a more favorable opinion in films starring Marlene Dietrich and Mae West. *Blonde Venus* (1932) and *She Done Him Wrong* (1933) didn't explicitly endorse prostitution, but didn't find much fault with it either.

Warner Brothers adopted a moralistic tone in the early sound years. *Safe in Hell* (1931) showed sex as a form of punishment for women, for example. But musicals like *42nd Street* (1933) opened up possibilities the same way that dramas like *Little Caesar* and *The Public Enemy* (both 1931) allowed more graphic crime and violence. *Baby Face* followed the gangster formula established in part by Darryl F. Zanuck. By showing without comment the rewards of organized crime and prostitution, the producer could have his cake and eat it, too. Few viewers of the time mistook the real message behind these films; essentially, "Get it while you can."

Zanuck was quite clear about his intent to do for sex in *Baby Face* what he did for crime in *The Public Enemy*. Adjusted for gender, both films offered the same premise: bright youngster chooses crime as a way out of squalid surroundings. *The Public Enemy* made a star out of James Cagney. For *Baby Face*, Zanuck cast about the only Warners star who could pull off a pose that was sexy, even sultry, but also bitter and cynical: Barbara Stanwyck.

Born in Brooklyn in 1907 and orphaned at the age of four, Stanwyck was a shop clerk and self-taught dancer who worked her way into showman Florenz Ziegfeld's stable, appearing in his midnight shows. She became a stage star when *The Noose* opened on Broadway in 1926. In 1929, she married Frank Fay, a twice-divorced vaudevillian who had carved out a niche as a sarcastic emcee who delivered jokes about acts appearing with him in shows. An alcoholic with a towering ego, Fay brought Stanwyck with him to Hollywood, where he starred in early sound musicals while she struggled in bit parts.

Fay convinced director Frank Capra to watch Stanwyck in a screen test from *The Noose*, beginning a creative relationship that lasted for five films. Capra considered Stanwyck the best actress he ever

worked with, an opinion echoed by many of her other collaborators. But at this point she didn't take films any more seriously than she did dancing. Stanwyck flitted from studio to studio, unable or unwilling to establish a screen persona. She was too ornery and smart to play hard-bitten molls, too angular for ingénues. Stanwyck was cast as the defiant woman, the one who got revenge when she was jailed unjustly, the one who kicked back when she was pushed around by Clark Gable in *Night Nurse* (1931). Competition seemed to inspire her. In *Ladies They Talk About* (1933) she held her own against a cast of professional hams clawing to take over the screen.

Stanwyck collaborated with Zanuck on the story for *Baby Face*, one of his last screenwriting credits (under the pseudonym Mark Canfield). According to notes by screenwriter Howard Smith, they came up with the film's theme—sex is power—together. Stanwyck could draw on her impoverished upbringing to flesh out the early scenes in which her character Lily Powers is prostituted by her father. Zanuck handed a treatment over to contract writers Gene Markey and Kathryn Scola, who submitted a script to the Production Code office in late 1932. Contract director Alfred E. Green shot the film in eighteen days for a budget of $187,000.

Baby Face follows Lily's escape from a steel-town speakeasy to the skyscrapers of Manhattan where, just like a criminal mastermind, she manipulates the system to suit her own aims. Crooks fought their way into society; Stanwyck's character used her body instead. Sex for her was a like a hold-up for Cagney—a stepping-stone to a new life.

Although drenched with sexual liaisons, *Baby Face* is the least erotic of the so-called pre-Code melodramas. For one thing, Lily Powers operates outside her own desires, which are never fully articulated. For another, the newly strengthened Production Code office insisted on edits that neutered much of the story. Some of the changes seem absurd today: *Stanley's Christian Institutions* substitutes for a book by Nietzsche, for example. Most involved minor cuts and dubbed dialogue, because neither Stanwyck nor Brent were available for reshoots. The biggest alterations occurred at the end of the film and in the beginning, where the most sordid aspects of Powers' situation were eliminated.

The Warners studio may have been a target of the Production Code office because of its reputation for rowdy films. (Zanuck was in the process of leaving the studio in a salary dispute; he would take over Twentieth Century with Joseph M. Schenck.) But despite the cuts, the core of *Baby Face* still remained: for unlucky women, sex was commerce, something to be endured. It was not a universally admired attitude, and Stanwyck

paid the price, burning through studios and gritting her teeth in insipid movies. It wasn't until she portrayed a sacrificial mother in a remake of *Stella Dallas* (1937) that viewers really warmed up to her. Stanwyck would rarely play as brazen a character as Lily Powers again, unless it was for comedy, as in *The Lady Eve* (1941), her next Registry title.

The Emperor Jones

United Artists, 1933. Sound, B&W with tints, 1.37. 75 minutes.

Cast: Paul Robeson (Brutus Jones), Dudley Digges (Smithers), Frank Wilson (Jeff), Fredi Washington (Undine), Ruby Elzy (Dolly), George Stamper (Lem).

Credits: Directed by Dudley Murphy. Screen play by Du-Bose [DuBose] Heyward. Based upon the play by Eugene O'Neill. Supervised by William C. de-Mille [deMille]. Incidental music composed and directed by Frank Tours. Photography: Ernest Haller. Art direction: Herman Rosse. Assistant director: Joseph H. Nadel. Sound engineer: Joseph Kane. Production manager: J. Edward Shugrue. Vocal arrangements: J. Rosamond Johnson. Synchronization: Max Manne. Film editor: Grant Whytock. Produced at Eastern Service Studios. Western Electric Noiseless Recording. A John Krimsky and Gifford Cochran presentation.

Additional Cast: Jackie Mabley (Marcella), Blueboy O'Connor (Treasurer), Brandon Evans (Carrington), Taylor Gordon (Stick-Man).

Additional Credits: Produced by John Krimsky, Gifford Cochran. Production dates: May 25 to July 1933. Premiered in New York City on September 19, 1933.

Available: Image Entertainment DVD (2003). UPC: 01438107292.

Aspiring to direct feature films, Dudley Murphy found himself typecast after the success of *St. Louis Blues* (1929), a musical short starring Bessie Smith. His next project, *Black and Tan* (1929), tied a more ambitious story line to the screen debut of Duke Ellington and His Orchestra. He followed that up with another musical short, *He Was Her Man* (1930), based on the song "Frankie and Johnnie" and starring Gilda Gray, known for introducing a dance called the "shimmy" to the public. Murphy was about to sign a contract with Paramount when a married woman was found dead in his apartment. Although the police did not implicate him in the incident, Murphy fled New York for Los Angeles.

There he sold a screenplay and was one of the many writers who worked on *Dracula* (1931). In 1931, he was hired as a codirector on *Confessions of a Co-Ed* and as an associate director on *Twenty-four Hours*. He directed one feature, *The Sport Parade* (1932), but had trouble adjusting to the Hollywood studio system. He abandoned plans for a biopic about magician Harry Houdini, returning instead to New York to tackle *The Emperor Jones*.

Eugene O'Neill's one-act play was staged by the Provincetown Players in New York in 1920, with Charles Gilpin, one of the founders of the

influential Lafayette Players, in the lead role. Possibly based on Vilbrun Guillaume Sam, a president of Haiti who was dismembered during a 1915 revolt, *The Emperor Jones* concerned the bloody end of Brutus Jones, a former Pullman porter who installed himself as ruler of a mythical Caribbean island. Broken into eight scenes, the play's impressionistic flashbacks showed how Jones murdered his friend Jeff, killed a white chain-gang guard, and escaped from a slave ship. Although O'Neill used problematic language and outdated stereotypes, his vision of a black ruler equal to if not better than any white energized and enraged audiences in equal measure.

O'Neill disliked Gilpin's liberties with his script (Gilpin refused to use the word "nigger," for example); when the play opened in London, Paul Robeson was in the lead. Robeson also played Jones in a 1924 revival in New York which transferred to Broadway the following year. Around this time, Murphy contacted O'Neill about adapting the play for film. During the production of *St. Louis Blues* in 1929, Murphy wrote a four-page treatment of *The Emperor Jones* and purchased another O'Neill one-act play, *Before Breakfast*, which he pitched unsuccessfully to RCA Photophone.

In 1933, Murphy got O'Neill's consent to film *The Emperor Jones*; now the director just had to find the money. John Krimsky and Gifford Cochran, Ivy League friends who had made a windfall distributing the German film *Maedchen in Uniform* (1931), were looking for an investment opportunity, and put up $30,000 to acquire the film rights to the play. Murphy and O'Neill both wanted Robeson in the lead. Murphy hired novelist DuBose Heyward to write the script. Heyward had written the novel *Porgy* (1925), and adapted it to the stage two years later with his wife Dorothy. He would later collaborate with George and Ira Gershwin on a musical version called *Porgy and Bess*.

Using Murphy's treatment, Heywood unraveled O'Neill's flashback structure, starting the screenplay when Jones is first hired as a porter. About half of the final script was entirely new material, although based on what O'Neill wrote. It was an expensive decision, for more sets had to be designed and built. Fortunately, Krimsky obtained financing from Western Electric in return for shooting in the Astoria, Queens, studios it had obtained from Paramount.

On Robeson's insistence, the entire film was shot in the New York area, with a chain-gang sequence photographed in New Rochelle and some footage taken at Jones Beach. The cinematographer was Ernest Haller, a Hollywood veteran. Murphy had met editor Grant Whytock on the set of *Mare Nostrum* almost ten years earlier. Credited as supervisor, William deMille was hired as a sort of insurance in case Murphy ran into trouble. DeMille, the director of many features including *Miss Lulu Bett* (1921), later implied that he shot much of the jungle footage, and played a major part in editing.

Film historian Scott MacQueen disputes deMille's account, while acknowledging that Murphy had trouble directing Robeson. The actor later complained about Murphy's "fool notion that negroes had moods," an opinion shared by many white directors at the time (as well as O'Neill himself). Murphy's biographer Susan Delson cites a contemporary interview with King Vidor in which he suggested that blacks didn't understand the technical aspects of acting and filmmaking.

Murphy couldn't have anticipated some of the problems that extended shooting beyond the budgeted schedule. The Hays Office ordered scenes with Fredi Washington reshot because it felt she could be mistaken for a white woman, which meant that she wouldn't be allowed to be seen in the arms of a black man. Nor was Robeson's Jones allowed to be shown killing a white man. The slave ship material was deleted, in Delson's view a crippling compromise of O'Neill's original intentions.

Even so, the film received respectful reviews when it opened in New York on September 19, 1933, and it did strong business in Northern urban centers. The South was another matter, as was the African-American community overall. Although Robeson was an admired figure, O'Neill's language was a major stumbling block, according to articles in the *New York Amsterdam News*.

Whether or not O'Neill was justified in his reiteration of racial slurs, the film veers too often from uncomfortable to offensive. Heywood's contributions, based on Murphy's concepts, constitute the weakest sections of the film. But the jungle sequences that make up the final sixteen minutes of surviving prints were shot with such insight and authority that they almost constitute a separate film. Haller's camera prowls through the sets, the beat of tribal drums provides an ominous backdrop, and Robeson is free to immerse himself in O'Neill's dramaturgy. It is a magnetic performance framed as artfully and sympathetically as possible. In one take that lasts over two minutes, Robeson sits in a small clearing, sings a spiritual, and then tries to talk down his fears, a sustained bit of magic that indicates just how powerful a performer he was.

Krimsky insisted later that *The Emperor Jones* made a small profit, but the film did little to advance Murphy's career. He directed *The Night Is Young* (1935), a musical with operetta ambitions, for MGM, but within a few years was back to directing musical shorts, this time for the Soundies Distribution Corporation. Robeson went to Great Britain to find work in the film *Sanders of the River* (1935). He appeared as Joe in the Universal film *Show Boat* (1936), a Registry title.

Footlight Parade

Warner Bros., 1933. Sound, B&W, 1.37. 102 minutes.

Cast: James Cagney (Chester Kent), Joan Blondell (Nan), Ruby Keeler (Bea), Dick Powell (Scotty), Frank McHugh (Francis), Guy Kibbee (Gould), Ruth Donnelly (Mrs. Gould), Hugh Herbert (Bowers), Claire Dodd (Vivian), Gordon Westcott (Thompson), Arthur Hohl (Frazer), Renee Whitney (Cynthia Kent), Barbara Rogers (Gracie), Paul Porcasi (Appolinaris), Philip Faversham (Joe Grant), Herman Bing (Fralick).

Credits: Directed by Lloyd Bacon. Numbers created and directed by Busby Berkeley. Music and lyrics by Harry Warren and Al Dubin; Sammy Fain and Irving Kahal. Screen Play by Manuel Seff and James Seymour. Dialogue director: William Keighley. Edited by George Amy. Art directors: Anton Grot and Jack Okey. Photographed by George Barnes. Gowns by Milo Anderson. Vitaphone Orchestra directed by Leo F. Forbstein.

Additional Cast includes: Jimmy Conlin, Billy Barty, Pat Wing, George Chandler, Sam McDaniel.

Additional Credits: Story by Robert Lord, Peter Milne. Produced by Robert Lord. Premiered September 30, 1933.

Available: Warner Home Video DVD (2006). UPC: 012569677395.

Crediting *42nd Street* (1933) with rescuing the Warner Brothers studio, which had lost $12 million in

1932, Jack L. Warner announced a slate of big-budget musicals. The first was *Gold Diggers of 1933*, an updating of the Broadway play the studio owned. Key to the success of these films was producer Darryl F. Zanuck, who formed the songwriting team of Al Dubin and Harry Warren, gave Busby Berkeley carte blanche for his musical productions, and took credit for establishing two production units operating simultaneously—one for drama, the other for musical numbers. But Zanuck left the studio in a salary dispute with Warner right as *Footlight Parade* was being prepared. Fortunately the formula was still intact, making this in some ways the best of all the Warners musicals.

The plot mirrors issues the studio was facing. Star James Cagney was in the midst of intense salary disputes with the Warners. A year earlier, he was earning $1,250 a week, compared to $4,000 a week for comparative newcomer Dick Powell—despite the fact that Cagney was clearly the most popular star on the Warners lot. The actor was also seething at being forced to play thugs and hoods. Having started out in a chorus line, he was anxious to broaden his screen image by appearing in a musical comedy.

The premise also echoes real-life events. As the effects of the Depression spread throughout the country, some theater owners turned to "prologues," sort of mini-musicals with live casts and orchestras, to draw audiences. Based on Sunset Boulevard near the Warners studio, Fanchon and Marco produced the most highly regarded of these prologues, sometimes offering condensed versions of famous plays like *Sally*, more often pushing original stories.

Footlight Parade is a fictional account of a Fanchon and Marco producer, one beset by crooked executives, performers with limited abilities, coworkers who steal his ideas, and the constant pressure of having to come up with new shows. It's a chance for Cagney to display swaggering confidence as a good guy rather than a gangster, and he positively jumps at the opportunity to depict a creative businessman who has the same whirlwind energy as a bootlegger. Cagney shows off some of his dance steps throughout the film, and takes a lead role in the final musical number.

Backing up Cagney are familiar faces from the Warner Brothers roster. Joan Blondell had appeared with Cagney in four films so far, and their easygoing chemistry here keeps the often fanciful script grounded. Ruby Keeler had teamed

with Powell in *42nd Street*; if their romance seems slow to start here, it may be because Powell was recovering from pneumonia, and had most of his scenes postponed until late in the shoot. Guy Kibbee may have been Warners' best blowhard. With his bald dome, red face, and wheezy voice, he was a Warners version of the sort of duplicitous but inept rascals played by W.C. Fields. Ruth Donnelly, who plays Kibbee's wife, was at one time a protégé of George M. Cohan. Casting Hugh Herbert as a censor was something of an inside joke. A veteran of theater and vaudeville, he wrote dozens of plays and sketches that almost always crossed the lines of propriety. The reliable Frank McHugh, seen here as an overworked dance director, was a Warners fixture as a second lead—best friend, brother, hanger-on. This was one of sixteen films he appeared in that year. Cagney and McHugh met in 1928 in New York, and remained close friends the rest of their lives.

The presence of so many friends and colleagues may help explain the swift pace of the film, which is at first almost a musical without music. Viewers see snippets of rehearsals, and McHugh and Herbert briefly clown through a romantic duet early on, but it's forty minutes before the first full-fledged number, the listless "Sittin' on a Backyard Fence," appears. But the film is backloaded with three Busby Berkeley numbers that take up some thirty minutes. These were shot by Berkeley and a separate unit, while Lloyd Bacon handled the dramatic scenes on a different sound stage.

Although Berkeley took pains to establish a proscenium (even lifting a curtain at times on the performances), none of the film's prologues could have taken place on a real stage. The prologues aren't really dances, they're processions, or perhaps merely tableaus. In a sense Berkeley is returning to the showmanship of Florenz Ziegfeld, who broke up the variety acts and comics who appeared in his reviews with intricately arranged patterns of chorus girls in revealing costumes while the orchestra vamped on what was hoped would be a new standard.

If the prologues weren't really dances, the songs weren't exactly songs either. Unlike the numbers in the Astaire/Rogers RKO musicals, or later in the Arthur Freed MGM musicals, the songs in these Warner Brothers musicals usually made little or no sense outside the context of the films. None of the songs in *Footlight Parade* became hits, despite efforts by Warners to recycle them in their Merrie Melodies cartoons. Unlike "The Way You Look Tonight" or "Let's Face the Music and Dance," these songs are remembered, if at all, for how they were used in this movie.

"Honeymoon Hotel," the first and least of the three prologues, is a sniggering bit about newlyweds in bridal suites that promises more than it delivers. "Shanghai Lil," the closing number, demonstrates perfectly the highs and lows of the Berkeley style. Cagney takes command of the number effortlessly, whether intoning the lyrics or showing off his peculiarly cocky tap dancing. That's before the chorus line starts displaying animations of Franklin Delano Roosevelt and the National Recovery Administration eagle, before Cagney and Keeler—in soldier drag—march onto a battleship. Berkeley keeps everyone moving so fast that the audience doesn't have time for questions. But there's something impersonal about the whole business. As Cagney would relate later, he never actually met Keeler, but only worked next to her a few days.

The second prologue, "By a Waterfall," is a water ballet of such remarkable proportions that it lifts the entire film into a new form of cinema. Berkeley had toyed with swimming pool shots before in *The Kid from Spain* (1932), but as film historian Richard Barrios points out, filmgoers had never seen anything like this before. Gigantic pools filled with chorines give way to even bigger pools, shown off by overhead views, followed by underwater depictions of synchronized swimming, geometric patterns that resemble digestive tracts, and more skin and spread legs than you could find in a burlesque house. Despite its imitators and parodists, you would be hard-pressed to find anything more exuberantly over the top from that period.

Ironically, films like *Footlight Parade* helped put Fanchon and Marco out of business. What touring company could compete with movie spectacles? This movie also marked a sort of culmination for Busby Berkeley. He had to leave the production early to fulfill his contract with Samuel Goldwyn on the Eddie Cantor vehicle *Roman Scandals*. He returned to Warners to choreograph for musicals like *Dames* and *Wonder Bar* (both 1934), the latter featuring a startlingly racist "Going to Heaven on a Mule." "Lullaby of Broadway" from *Gold Diggers of 1935* won an Oscar for Best Song, but Berkeley himself didn't win for Best Dance Direction. His style was becoming obsolete, and he couldn't adapt to a smaller, more performer-driven choreography that was coming into vogue.

Berkeley tried directing nonmusicals (his *They Made Me a Criminal* in 1939 was a respectable crime melodrama with John Garfield), then moved to MGM, where he worked on a few musicals starring Mickey Rooney and Judy Garland. By the end of the 1940s his work was derided, with Gene Kelly assuming the choreography credit for the Berkeley-directed *Take Me Out to the Ball Game* (1949).

The Invisible Man

Universal, 1933. Sound, B&W, 1.37. 72 minutes.
Cast: Claude Rains (The Invisible One/Man [Jack Griffin]), Gloria Stuart (Flora Cranley), William Harrigan ([Arthur] Kemp), Henry Travers (Cranley), Una O'Connor (Mrs. [Jenny] Hall), Forrester Harvey (Mr. [Herbert] Hall), Holmes Herbert (Chief of police), E.E. Clive (Jaffers), Dudley Digges (Chief of detectives), Harry Stubbs (Inspector Bird), Donald Stuart (Inspector Lane), Merle Tottenham (Milly).
Credits: Directed by James Whale. Screenplay R.C. Sherriff. Produced by Carl Laemmle, Jr. Art director: Charles D. Hall. Special effects: John P. Fulton. Camera: Arthur Edeson. Film editor: Ted Kent. Western Electric Noiseless Recording.
Additional Cast: John Carradine (Villager), Walter Brennan (Bicycle owner), Dwight Frye (Reporter), Tom Ricketts (Farmer), Bob Reeves (Detective Hogan), Robert Adair (Detective Thompson), Bert Young (Switchman).
Additional Credits: Writing by Preston Sturges, Philip Wylie. Based on the novel by H.G. Wells. Music: Heinz Roemheld. Makeup: Jack P. Pierce. Sound: William Hedgcock. Visual effects supervisor: Frank D. Williams. A Carl Laemmle presentation. Production dates: June to August 1933. Released November 13, 1933.
Other Versions: Universal's sequels include *The Invisible Man Returns* (1940), *The Invisible Woman* (1940), *The Invisible Agent* (1942), *The Invisible Man's Return* (1944), and *Abbott and Costello Meet the Invisible Man* (1951). The character appeared briefly in other films, and in two Universal-financed television series.
Available: Universal Studios DVD (2004). UPC: 251925454298. MCA Universal VHS (1991) ISBN: 1-55880-448-X. UPC: 0-9689-80398-3-3.

Casting about for a monster to follow up on the success of *Dracula* and *Frankenstein* (both 1931), Universal production chief Carl Laemmle, Jr., settled on *The Invisible Man*, an 1897 novel by H.G. Wells. After years of struggle, Wells had made his reputation with a series of works in what would eventually be called science fiction, including *The Time Machine*, *The Island of Dr. Moreau*, and *The War of the Worlds*, all filmed numerous times. Like those books, *The Invisible Man* combined grisly set pieces with extended passages in which Wells had his characters debate scientific, philosophical, and moral issues. But there were drawbacks to turning it into a film. Unlike a vampire or mummy, the Invisible Man was a scientist without superhuman powers. He was capable of practical jokes and general mischief, but posed more of an abstract than supernatural threat.

Adapting the novel proved too difficult for contract screenwriter Preston Sturges, who tried setting the story in Russia. Another draft commissioned by Universal incorporated Martians, an idea Wells had used to better effect in *The War of the Worlds*. Writers and *Dracula* veterans Garrett Fort and John Balderston eventually gave up on the project, as did assigned director Robert Florey. James Whale had worked with Boris Karloff, selected by Universal to star in the production, in both *Frankenstein* and *The Old Dark House* (1932). He agreed to take on the film in part to avoid directing a *Frankenstein* sequel.

Whale brought in screenwriter R.C. Sherriff, a British playwright known for the morose World War I drama *Journey's End*. (Whale had directed the play in London in 1928.) Sherriff retained many of the elements of Wells's novel, most enjoyably arguments among characters about the limitations faced by invisible scientist Jack Griffin. (He can't operate undetected in rainy conditions, for example, or for an hour after eating.) Guided by Whale, Sherriff rearranged and simplified the plot so that it more closely resembled the film *Frankenstein*, down to an ornate lab set and a dismayed girlfriend (played by Gloria Stuart).

In line with his approach to *The Old Dark House*, Whale also added several comic touches, particularly for the role of Jenny Hall, an innkeeper's wife who encounters the Invisible Man when he tries to hide in the rural village of Iping. Played to perfection by Una O'Connor, she delighted Wells, who otherwise objected to much of the film. Whale brought back many of the villager types who populated *Frankenstein*, and who would show up as comic relief in *Bride of Frankenstein* (1935).

The title role had originally been intended for Karloff, but by the time production started he was unavailable. Whale argued for Claude Rains over Colin Clive, who had been Laemmle's suggestion. Born in London in 1889, Rains, the son of an actor, was on stage by the age of eleven. He worked in the United States until serving in World War I, then taught acting at the Royal Academy (with Laurence Olivier and John Gielgud among his students). Rains was back on Broadway by 1927, where he starred in some twenty plays.

The actor was reluctant to take on the Invisible Man, in part because he didn't want to be typecast in horror roles, but also because his face would not be seen by moviegoers until the closing scenes. That didn't stop him from trying to upstage Stuart. In an amusing essay she wrote called "In Love with a Man Who Had Lost His Mind," Stuart described how Rains tried to angle her out of a two-shot, even after Whale admonished him to stop.

No one could do much with the script—not Rains with his mellifluous voice, not Whale with his black humor, not even the screeching O'Connor. *The Invisible Man* is a patchwork of music-hall slapstick, the occasional violent catastrophe, and special effects. These last were overseen by John P. Fulton, who revealed many of his secrets in an article for *The American Cinematographer* in September 1934. Essentially he updated the same matte and double-exposure tricks that had been in use since *Princess Nicotine* (1909) and earlier. Fulton had the walls and floor of a bare set lined with black velvet, and outfitted Rains head to toe in black velvet as well. Over this bodystocking Rains would wear the garments that on screen would seem to be covering an invisible body. This footage would then be optically printed with what had been filmed on the normal set.

Fulton not only had to match the lighting used by cinematographer Arthur Edeson, he also had to correct "the various little imperfections, such as eye holes, etc., which were naturally picked up by the camera. This latter was done by retouching the film, frame by frame, with a brush and opaque dye. We photographed thousands of feet of film in the many 'takes' of the different scenes, and approximately 4,000 feet of the film received individual hand-work treatment in some degree."

All this effort is evident in the final print, which at times still has the ability to startle viewers. If only the rest of the film had been as imaginative. A character like Griffin should have been able to range far and wide, but he seems content merely to scare charwomen and vandalize pubs. If you were invisible, would you waste your time knocking mugs of beer off bars? Rains begged out of the inevitable sequels, replaced at first by Vincent Price. But after important roles in such Registry titles as *Mr. Smith Goes to Washington* (1939), *Casablanca*, and *Now, Voyager* (both 1942), Rains returned to the horror genre in a remake of *The Phantom of the Opera* (1943). Whale's next Registry title, *Bride of Frankenstein*, marked for many the peak of his style of filmmaking.

Duck Soup

Groucho Marx doesn't mind addressing moviegoers directly in *Duck Soup*.

Paramount, 1933. Sound, B&W, 1.33. 70 minutes.

Cast: The Marx Brothers: Groucho (Rufus T. Firefly), Harpo (Pinky), Chico (Chicolini), Zeppo (Bob Roland); Margaret Dumont (Mrs. [Gloria] Teasdale), Louis Calhern (Trentino), Raquel Torres (Vera Marcal), Edgar Kennedy (Vendor), Edmund Breese (Zander), Charles B. Middleton (Prosecutor).

Credits: Directed by Leo McCarey. Screenplay by Bert Kalmar and Harry Ruby. Additional dialogue: Arthur Sheekman, Nat Perrin. Director of photography: Henry Sharp. Music and lyrics: Bert Kalmar and Harry Ruby.

Additional Cast: William Worthington (First Minister of Finance), Edwin Maxwell (Secretary of War), Leonid Kinsky (Agitator), Verna Hillie (Secretary), George MacQuarrie (First judge), Fred Sullivan (Second judge), Davison Clark (Second Minister of Finance), Eric Mayne (Third judge).

Additional Credits: Based in part on a script called *Cracked Ice* by Grover Jones, Bert Kalmar, and Harry Ruby, supervised by Herman J. Mankiewicz. Edited by LeRoy Stone. Art direction: Hans Dreier, Wiard B. Ihnen. Music direction: Arthur Johnston. Recording engineer: H.M. Lindgren. Released November 17, 1933.

Available: Universal Studios Home Entertainment DVD (2004). UPC: 025192125027.

The five Marx Brothers—Leonard (Chico), Adolph (Harpo), Julius (Groucho), Milton (Gummo), and Herbert (Zeppo)—grew up in New York City. (A sixth brother, Manfred, died in infancy.) The sons of Jewish immigrants from Eastern Europe, they were related on their mother Minnie's side to Al Shean, half of a famous vaudeville team, Gallagher & Shean. With no other connections and few marketable skills, the brothers, urged on by Minnie, entered show business. Since their musicianship was rudimentary, they formed a comedy act.

Like their uncle, the brothers relied on ethnic humor at first, but as they toured the country in an act called *Skool Daze*, they began to develop different characters, exaggerating their qualities until they became caricatures. Chico, the eldest, took Italian dialect comedy to extremes, while Groucho's con man went beyond Jewish humor into a fantasy world of greasepaint mustaches and flamboyant insults. Unable to compete with his brothers' quips and ad libs, Harpo retreated into silence, relying on pantomime and music to communicate. Zeppo and Gummo were essentially straight men in an act that didn't need any, since Groucho proved to be the perfect foil to both Chico and Harpo. Gummo stuck around until they reached Broadway with a revue called *I'll Say She Is*. Zeppo was a pleasant but bland presence in the brothers' first five films, but dropped out after *Duck Soup* to become a talent agent.

While *I'll Say She Is* was a success, the brothers' real break was their next Broadway show, *The Cocoanuts*. With a book by George S. Kaufman and songs by Irving Berlin, it was a tremendous hit. The brothers signed a contract with Paramount to film an adaptation of *The Cocoanuts*, which they did simultaneously while appearing in their next Broadway hit, *Animal Crackers*. *The Cocoanuts* (1929) and *Animal Crackers* (1930) were both filmed at the Paramount soundstages in Astoria. For their first original screen story, *Monkey Business* (1931), the brothers moved to Los Angeles. By the time *Horsefeathers* (1932) came out, the Marxes had swept the nation, hosting their own radio shows and appearing on the cover of *Time*.

The brothers' progress over their first five films is fascinating. *The Cocoanuts* was loosely tied to scandals involving Florida real estate speculation. Although billed first, the brothers were essentially comic relief in a traditional Broadway musical romance. On stage they were known to discard their lines and improvise at will, infuriating playwright Kaufman, but the film version freezes them in supporting roles to the exceedingly uninteresting leads. *Animal Crackers* is more of the same, set on Long Island. But the romantic leads were relegated to the background, giving the brothers more time for their specialties. Groucho was now a phony explorer and big-game hunter who used insults to silence his skeptics, while Harpo and Chico were small-time hoods completely unphased by their high-society surroundings.

Monkey Business, their first original film, mocked Hollywood gangster movies, while *Horsefeathers* took on college sports. The brothers' vaudeville roots were still detectable, but the trappings of Broadway musicals had almost completely disappeared. By now the brothers had solidified their roles. Harpo, for all purposes a homeless tramp, chased women, played harps, and disrupted rituals for reasons that remained indecipherable. Chico was a cheat, a gambler, and a piano player whose dialect enabled him to slip out of any commitments. Groucho assumed higher and higher positions in society, although he was clearly a fraud and charlatan with no education or skills. Film author Joe Adamson points out that in five films, Groucho rose from con artist to president of Fredonia.

Mocking Hollywood's penchant for films about fictional Eastern European monarchies, *Duck Soup* concerns an unnecessary war founded on Groucho's dislike of a dignitary from the neighboring country of Sylvania. Appointed president by the woman whose money keeps the country afloat, Groucho quickly makes a shambles of his administration, hiring his brothers as spies or cabinet officials. The idea for the script evolved over several drafts, with contributions from songwriters Bert Kalmar and Harry Ruby, producer Herman J. Mankiewicz, and gag writers Arthur Sheekman and Nat Perrin (who had written scripts for a radio show starring Groucho and Chico).

The Marxes' earlier films had been directed by well-meaning journeymen who essentially got out of the brothers' way. *Duck Soup* was directed by Leo McCarey, a veteran of silent comedy who had worked with Laurel and Hardy and other slapstick stars. McCarey, a bit against his will, found himself typecast as a comedy director at Paramount, in direct competition with studio head Ernst Lubitsch (whose films were the object of much of *Duck Soup*'s satire). He was the only director with the confidence and experience to challenge the Marxes to edit themselves.

McCarey saw that the Marxes' humor was based, much like W.C. Fields' and Laurel and Hardy's, on hostility. Unlike those comedians, the Marxes were deliberately, insanely hostile, more interested in provoking fights than in winning them. International politics was the perfect playground for them. Their casual dismissal of diplomacy, legislation, and all the other workings of government gave them the opportunity to expose everyone—presidents, generals, philanthropists, ministers—as petty, narrow-minded, and irrational people fueled by emotions rather than patriotism. But with puns and pratfalls.

In *Duck Soup*, McCarey stripped away the piano and harp interludes featured in all of the brothers' other films, eliminated romantic subplots, and rejected anything that would soften the brothers' characters. Without irrelevant musical numbers and courtship chit-chat, *Duck Soup* was all good parts, no filler. (McCarey even got talented actors, including Louis Calhern and Margaret Dumont, Groucho's favorite foil, to help.)

McCarey showed little interest in some details of filmmaking, like matching shots (i.e., making sure that elements remain constant throughout a scene). *Duck Soup* is filled with moments when characters who should be sitting are suddenly standing, or pants that should be rolled up are rolled down. The director occasionally allowed the pacing to lag, and saw nothing wrong with repeating gags two or three times. But his comic background made *Duck Soup* more visual than other Marx Brothers films, including a magical bit, played in complete silence, featuring a broken mirror and three brothers, each trying to play Groucho. McCarey may have borrowed it from *Sittin' Pretty* (1924), a silent short he directed starring the brothers Charley Chase and James Parrott, although writers have traced the bit back to both Max Linder and various vaudeville acts.

Harpo and Chico also have extended routines with Edgar Kennedy, master of the slow burn and double take. Playing a lemonade salesman, Kennedy paticipates in the sort of escalating violence found in Laurel and Hardy's *Big Business* (1928), a short supervised by McCarey. These bits, with their almost complete lack of dialogue and their ruthless, relentless logic, are unique in the Marx canon—and, in fact, in 1930s comedy in general. Only Fields tried such lengthy displays of frustration, something he had perfected in vaudeville.

Duck Soup was not a success. Its message—leaders can't be trusted, war is a sham, politics thoroughly corrupt, justice futile—may not have been exactly what audiences wanted at the height of the Depression. In the film's defense, Paramount was on the verge of bankruptcy, and marketing and advertising suffered as a result. With five films in as many years, the brothers may have saturated their market. Paramount's other stars, like Fields and Marlene Dietrich, were also making excellent films that failed at the box office. The studio decided not to renew the Marx Brothers' contract. When the act re-emerged with *A Night at the Opera* (1935), it was under the guidance of MGM producer Irving Thalberg, and without Zeppo.

It Happened One Night

Columbia, 1934. Sound, B&W, 1.37. 105 minutes.

Cast: Clark Gable (Peter [Warne]), Claudette Colbert (Ellie [Ellen Andrews]), Walter Connolly (Andrews), Roscoe Karns ([Oscar] Shapeley), Jameson Thomas ([King] Westley), Alan Hale (Danker), Arthur Hoyt (Zeke), Blanche Friderici (Zeke's Wife), Charles C. Wilson (Gordon).

Credits: Directed by Frank Capra. Screen Play by Robert Riskin. Based on the short story by Samuel Hopkins Adams. Photography: Joseph Walker. Film Editor: Gene Havlick. Musical Director: Louis Silvers. Western Electric Noiseless Recording.

Additional Cast includes: Ward Bond (Bus driver), Eddie Chandler (Bus driver), James Burke (Detective), Irving Bacon (Gas attendant).

Additional Credits: Assistant director: C.C. Coleman. Produced by Harry Cohn. Art director: Stephen Goosson. Sound: E.L. Bernds. Production dates: November 13 to December 22, 1933; reshoots January 1934. Premiered in New York City on February 22, 1934.

Awards: Oscars for Best Picture, Director, Writing—Adaptation, Actor, Actress.

Other Versions: Remade as *You Can't Run Away From It* (1956).

Available: Columbia TriStar Home Video DVD (1999). ISBN: 0-7678-3660-X. UPC: 0-43396-03949-0.

In his autobiography *The Name Above the Title*, director Frank Capra described the making of *It Happened One Night* as a series of battles. But then Capra saw life itself, especially life inside the film industry, as a battle. When the dust cleared at the Oscar ceremonies in 1935, and *It Happened One Night* wound up winning the five top awards, few rushed forward to claim credit for its success—one indication of how difficult the entire project had been.

Under contract to Harry Cohn at Columbia, Capra had gained considerable notice for his previous film, *Lady for a Day*, at the time the most successful adaptation of a Damon Runyon story to make it onto the screen. Capra fully expected to win the Best Directing Oscar for the film, and wrote that his follow-up movie was more or less a fluke. He had read the short story "Night Bus" in *Cosmopolitan* magazine, asked Cohn to buy it, and promptly forgot about it until he was scrambling for a story after a proposed project at MGM fell through.

It's a dramatic account worthy of a movie, but probably not completely true. Samuel Hopkins Adams, the author of "Night Bus" was an extremely well-known figure who had been in the public eye since the early 1900s, when his muckraking articles about patent medicines caused a sensation. Adams coined the phrase "Flaming Youth" to describe the 1920s, and his novel of that name and others of his works were adapted into movies. Not only was the Adams story likely film material from the start, but similar stories had already been released by Universal and MGM.

Working with screenwriter Robert Riskin, Capra transformed the elements of "Night Bus" into one of the most durable formulas in Hollywood. (Capra credits writer Myles Connolly with providing the keys to the adaptation: changing what had been a starving artist into a newspaper writer with a chip on his shoulder, and turning the narrative engine into an updated *Taming of the Shrew*.) Madcap heiress, rebel journalist, thwarted love, forced engagements, mean cops, honest workers, and a romance played out in public: it was a formula Capra and his many imitators returned to again and again throughout the 1930s. Elements would change, but the essential struggle between enemies who become lovers would remain. (To see what "Night Bus" might have become, watch 1941's *Double Wedding*, an MGM adaptation of Ferenc Molnár's *Great Love*: heiress and starving artist meet and fall in love, this time in a trailer.)

Capra suggests that his abortive project at MGM is what led to Clark Gable being loaned to Columbia for the film. MGM owed Columbia a star for one movie, and Louis B. Mayer sent Gable in punishment for the actor's salary demands and general carousing. Claudette Colbert was also against working in the film. When approached, she doubled her going rate for a picture to $50,000, and insisted that shooting be completed in a month. When Cohn and Capra readily agreed, the actress was trapped.

You can see the leads' hesitation about the film in their opening scenes, in which both play characters who are furious about their fates but powerless to change them. Colbert is the married daughter of a tycoon, depicted in full bluster by Walter Connolly. He's in the process of getting her marriage to foppish aviator King Westley annulled; she responds with a hunger strike aboard his yacht near Miami. When that doesn't work, she dives overboard, determined to join up with Westley in New York. Gable is reporter Peter Warne, first seen in a phone booth in the Miami bus terminal, drunkenly telling off his editor in New York. It's as if the two leads are acting out their displeasure at being stuck in a tired plot with an upstart director at a studio notorious for its cheapness.

Conversely, Capra could have been adroitly manipulating his actors' unhappiness. How appealing would it have been for Gable to mock his MGM persona as a gangster or gigolo? (The actor's first shot in the film, a high-angle close-up as he snarls into the phone, shows more polish and care than he had ever received in his MGM films.) Or how appealing for Colbert to shriek at all the male authority figures in her life? The director capitalizes on this animosity throughout the film, allowing first one, then the other to erupt angrily at the plot twists that confront them.

Twists are about all the plot offers. A bag is stolen, a ticket is lost, a bus swerves off the road. Money goes missing, rewards are offered, a car needs gas, rain washes out a bridge. Capra knows that the real story is behind the plot's events. It's in the way Colbert wears Gable's scarf, in the way Gable protects her from predators. All Capra needed to do was define the space around them, give them the opportunity to let their screen personalities emerge and take over the story.

Critics have had seventy years to dissect *It Happened One Night*. Some use it to tackle screwball comedy, some to examine feminism, some to complain that they just don't make them like that anymore. But Hollywood didn't make movies like this back in 1934, either, or at least not intentionally. *It Happened One Night* is filled with gaffes: food that appears or disappears at a breakfast table,

drivers who switch places in the middle of scenes, scarves that change position from shot to shot. In several scenes you can see actors mouthing dialogue that was subsequently erased from the soundtrack. Capra even repeats action in one scene, cutting from a shot of Colbert bolting to her left to a different angle of Colbert bolting to her left.

What's also surprising is how little actual comedy is in the film. Capra essentially plays the story straight, throwing in the occasional dig at cops or bosses, but never suggesting that there are jokes in the script. In fact, the gags generally go to the character actors, including a resplendent Roscoe Karns as a clueless Lothario and Alan Hale as the most annoying driver in the world. Gable and Colbert spend most of their time proclaiming their indifference to each other. Foreplay in their case consists of fooling the people around them, of getting away with a ruse.

Fans remember moments from this film—the "walls of Jericho," the bus sing-along, the hitchhiking lessons—but tend to forget the expertise behind them. Capra fills his frames with extras, with props and windows and weather. His tactics (and Joseph Walker's cinematography) gave his films an immediacy that his rivals' lacked. Events in a Capra film, no matter how far-fetched, actually seem to be taking place somewhere in real life. These weren't just actors on a set, they came across as real people.

Capra didn't write much about Joe Walker, his cinematographer in all of his films from *Flight* in 1929 to *Mr. Smith Goes to Washington* ten years later. But Walker's work was crucial to the mood of the film. He frequently backlights Colbert, silhouetting her in a golden aura that is far more erotic than the actual situations she's playing. He shoots Gable in a darkly romantic fashion that became the standard for other photographers to emulate. And he takes more care with the important scenes on buses and in terminals and motor courts than with the "wealthy" sets at the climax.

It Happened One Night received mediocre reviews, and opened to mixed business. But as word of mouth spread the film never stopped playing. What endeared Capra to audiences was the way he presented their country. This was the way Americans wanted to feel about themselves, snappy, can-do types who could handle any situation. The Depression was only a momentary drawback, a bit of adversity that just needed someone with a scheme or gimmick to make it go away.

After sweeping the major Oscars (a feat not duplicated until *One Flew Over the Cuckoo's Nest* in 1975), *It Happened One Night* became the film to beat at other studios. It influenced everyone from Preston Sturges (who wrote a half-dozen variations on it) to Richard Donner (whose *Bird on a Wire* from 1990 showed how debauched the premise could become). For better or worse, it confirmed the validity of depicting relationships in film as a war between the sexes.

Tarzan and His Mate

Metro-Goldwyn-Mayer, 1934. Sound, B&W, 1.37. 104 minutes.

Cast: Johnny Weissmuller (Tarzan), Maureen O'Sullivan (Jane Parker), Neil Hamilton (Harry Holt), Paul Cavanaugh (Martin Arlington), Forrester Harvey (Beamish), Nathan Curry (Saidi).

Credits: Directed by Cedric Gibbons. Based upon the characters created by Edgar Rice Burroughs. Screen play by James Kevin McGuinness. Adaptation by Howard Emmett Rogers and Leon Gordon. Produced by Bernard H. Hyman. Recording director: Douglas Shearer. Art director: Arnold Gillespie. Photographed by Charles G. Clarke, Clyde DeVinna. Film Editor: Tom Held. Western Electric Sound System. A Metro-Goldwyn-Mayer presentation.

Additional Cast: Yola d'Avril (Mrs. Feronde), William Slack (Tom Pierce), Desmond Roberts (Henry Van Ness), Jiggs (Cheetah).

Additional Credits: Co-director: Jack Conway. Screenwriting: C. Gardner Sullivan. Sound mixing: C.S. Pratt. Second unit directing: Nick Grinde. Lion, monkey, and hippo scenes staged by James McKay. Animal supervision: George Emerson, Louis Roth and Louis Goebel. Special effects director: James Basevi. Art effects: Warren Newcombe. Photographic effects: Irving Ries. Sound effects: T.B. Hoffman, James Graham, Michael Steinore. Music: George Richelavie, Fritz Stahlberg, Paul Marquardt, Dr. William Axt. Maureen O'Sullivan's swimming double: Josephine McKim. Production dates: August 2, 1933 to February 28, 1934. Reshoots: March 1934. Released April 20, 1934.

Other Versions: Sequel to *Tarzan the Ape Man* (1932). Followed by *Tarzan Escapes* (1936).

Available: Warner Home Video DVD The Tarzan Collection (2004). UPC: 012569599529.

For much of the twentieth century, Tarzan was one of the most recognized fictional creations in America. Invented in 1911 by Edgar Rice Burroughs, he became the subject of best-selling novels, comic books, radio serials, and movies. An orphan raised by apes, Tarzan was a combination of ideas inspired by Romulus and Remus, Rudyard Kipling's Mowgli, and the country's fascination with Africa. "I was mainly interested in playing with the idea of a contest between heredity and environment," Burroughs explained in 1931. He was also looking for a hit, having failed to succeed in his other endeavors.

The son of a major in the Civil War, Burroughs was born in 1875 in Chicago. He worked in stationery, for his father's battery company, and for Sears, Roebuck and Co., and was living on a ranch in California when he wrote what was published as *A Princess of Mars*. *Tarzan of the Apes* was his second story, and it made him independently wealthy. He astutely held onto rights for the character, licensing them on a case-by-case basis. Tarzan sold bread, ice cream, and bathing suits, for example.

In 1916, Burroughs signed a deal for the first Tarzan movie with William Parsons, head of the National Film Corporation. (He had already sold the rights to *The Lad and the Lion*, a non-Tarzan story, to William Selig in 1914.) Financial problems and World War I delayed the production, which finished shooting in January 1918. Roughly a third of this version of *Tarzan of the Apes* survives, enough to prove that Elmo Lincoln was too stiff and burly for a King of the Jungle. Paying customers liked the film a lot more than critics did. In private, Burroughs complained about the changes to his plot.

In the 1920s, Tarzan appeared in a fifteen-episode serial, *The Son of Tarzan* (1920); in a Goldwyn Pictures release *The Revenge of Tarzan* that same year; in a serial called *The Adventures of Tarzan* (starring Elmo Lincoln again); in *Tarzan and the Golden Lion* (1927), where he was played by James Pierce; and in a Universal serial, *Tarzan the Mighty* (1928), this time played by Frank Merrill.

On April 15, 1931, Burroughs signed with MGM to make a talking picture called *Tarzan the Ape Man*. Producer Irving Thalberg had previously authorized an expedition to Africa to shoot an adaptation of *Trader Horn*, a 1927 best-seller—ignoring the problems that location shooting in Italy had brought to *Ben-Hur* (1925). Although director W.S. Van Dyke procured exciting animal footage, the production was an expensive disaster that required reshoots on MGM's backlot. The film was a hit when it was finally released in 1931, but Thalberg was convinced that the studio could shoot an "African" movie right at home, using some of the material left over from *Trader Horn*.

Significantly, Burroughs sold the rights to the character, not to his plots, so MGM was free to dream up its own Tarzan story. In fact, *Tarzan the Ape Man* was really a version of *Trader Horn* with different character names. Screenwriter Cyril Hume is credited with discovering Johnny Weissmuller at the Hollywood Athletic Club. Van Dyke enthusiastically agreed that the former Olympic swimming champion would be perfect as Tarzan.

Weissmuller was actually born in Romania in 1904; his family immigrated to Pennsylvania the following year, then to Chicago. He started swimming competitively in 1920, and won a national championship the following year. From that point, he never lost a race until he retired in 1928. For two generations of moviegoers, he became the definitive screen Tarzan.

Meanwhile, Burroughs learned that a contract he had signed in 1929 had been purchased by producer Sol Lesser, who committed to making a Tarzan serial despite MGM's plans. A lawsuit postponed but did not stop Lesser's serial.

Tarzan the Ape Man was one of the top box-office draws of 1932, in part due to the chemistry between Weissmuller and his costar, Maureen O'Sullivan, in part because MGM made it a big-budget spectacular, with more animals, dangerous stunts, and exotic thrills than any rival film. The film also introduced the chimpanzee Cheetah, one of the crucial characters in subsequent entries in the series.

Other elements of the film would be repeated as well, in particular Tarzan's yell. Studio publicists insisted that it was derived from a variety of sounds edited together, although biographer John Taliaferro wrote that, "the noise was nothing more than Weissmuller's own yodel." MGM always intended on producing a sequel, but Thalberg wanted to wait to exploit public demand for the character. That's when Sol Lesser stepped in with *Tarzan the Fearless* (1933), an odd combination of feature and serial starring swimmer Buster Crabbe as the King of the Jungle.

MGM pumped more than a million dollars into *Tarzan and His Mate*, in every aspect the finest film version of the character. The nominal producer was again Bernard Hyman, although with a budget this big every executive, including Thalberg and Louis B. Mayer, had some input. Oddly, the film was assigned to Cedric Gibbons to direct. At the time the head of the studio's art department, Gibbons was acknowledged as an excellent production designer. Originally, he was to be assisted by Van Dyke, but during the actual production Jack Conway worked with Gibbons, and today Conway is generally thought to have directed most of the film.

Whoever directed *Tarzan and His Mate*, it was a complicated, difficult production that stretched out for six months. Taliaferro attributes many of the scenes to the influence of films like *Bird of Paradise* (1932), *Ecstasy*, and *King Kong* (both 1933). A sequence in which Tarzan swims with a clearly naked Jane caused so much consternation that the Hays Office censors demanded its deletion. The newly strengthened Production Code was now being enforced, and Jane's subsequent outfits would be far less skimpy. MGM compromised by offering three different versions of the scene. It wasn't until 1991 that the offending footage was restored.

Although principal photography was officially finished, footage was still being shot as late as March 1934. After previews, MGM removed some fourteen minutes from the film. How much of this was due to censorship is unclear, but for decades the film ran ninety-three minutes. When Ted Turner purchased the MGM film library, a longer cut was found, and this is the version available today.

Tarzan was a mainstay at MGM until 1942. By that time Thalberg was dead, and the temptation to cut corners had reduced budgets for the series. O'Sullivan's decision to stop playing Jane persuaded executives to sell Weissmuller's contract to Sol Lesser, who brought the series over to RKO. When Weissmuller could no longer convincingly play Tarzan, he became Jungle Jim in a series that lasted for twenty films. Other Tarzans followed—Lex Barker, Gordon Scott, Denny Miller, Jock Mahoney—but no one matched Weissmuller's appeal.

The Thin Man

Metro-Goldwyn-Mayer, 1934. Sound, B&W, 1.37. 91 minutes.
Cast: William Powell (Nick [Charles]), Myrna Loy (Nora [Charles]), Maureen O'Sullivan (Dorothy [Wynant]), Nat Pendleton (Guild), Minna Gombell (Mimi [Wynant Jorgenson]), Porter Hall (MacCaulay), Henry Wadsworth (Tommy), William Henry (Gilbert [Wynant]), Harold Huber (Nunheim), Cesar Romero (Chris [Jorgenson]), Natalie Moorehead (Julia Wolf), Edward Brophy ([Joe] Morelli), Edward Ellis ([Clyde] Wynant), Cyril Thornton (Tanner).

Credits: Directed by W.S. Van Dyke. Screen Play by Albert Hackett and Frances Goodrich. From the novel by Dashiell Hammett. Produced by Hunt Stromberg. Musical score by Dr. William Axt. Recording director: Douglas Shearer. Art director: Cedric Gibbons. Associate art directors: David Townsend, Edwin B. Willis. Wardrobe by Dolly Tree. Photographed by James Wong Howe. Film editor: Robert J. Kern. Western Electric Sound System. A Cosmopolitan production of a Metro-Goldwyn-Mayer presentation.

Additional Cast: Asta [the dog], Ruth Channing (Mrs. Jorgenson), Gertrude Short (Marion), Clay Clement (Quinn), Robert E. Homans (Bill), Raymond Brown (Dr. Walton); Douglas Walton, Sherry Hall (Taxi drivers); Polly Bailey (Janitress); Arthur Belasco, Garry Owen, Edward Hearn (Detectives); Fred Malatesta (Head waiter); Rolfe Sedan, Leo White (Waiters); Walter Long (Stutsy), Kenneth Gibson (Apartment clerk), Tul Lorraine (Stenographer), Bert Roach (Foster), Huey White (Tefler), Ben Taggart (Police captain), Charles Williams (Fight manager); Phil Tead, Thomas Jackson, Nick Copeland, Creighton Hale, Dink Templeton (Reporters); John Larkin (Porter).

Additional Credits: Assistant director: Les Selander. Production dates: April 9 to 27, 1934. Released May 25, 1934.

Other Versions: *After the Thin Man* (1936), *Another Thin Man* (1939), *Shadow of the Thin Man* (1941), *The Thin Man Goes Home* (1943), *Song of the Thin Man* (1947).

Available: Warner Home Video DVD (2005). ISBN: 1-4198-1325-0. UPC: 0-12569-67568-1.

The last completed novel by Dashiell Hammett, *The Thin Man* was dedicated to Lillian Hellman, a playwright he met in Hollywood in 1930. Published in January 1934, it was optioned by MGM, although as a murder mystery with comic overtones, it was not thought of highly by production head Louis B. Mayer. When director W.S. Van Dyke persisted, Mayer okayed the project as the studio's equivalent of a B-picture. (For years, the studio insisted that it made only "A" movies.)

The son of Judge W.S. Van Dyke of San Diego, Woodbridge Strong Van Dyke did not learn about his family's illustrious past until he was a teenager. His father died while he was still an infant, and his mother took to the stage, despite strenuous objections from the family. Van Dyke also acted, as well as working as a lumberjack, miner, and newspaper reporter. When he reached Hollywood, he took extra parts until he found work as a director's assistant. Hired by D.W. Griffith, he helped stage the extraordinary shots of carriages careening on top of the walls of Babylon in *Intolerance* (1916).

Like many other directors, he learned his trade making Westerns. Van Dyke's starred Tim McCoy and Buck Jones, and they carried him through the 1920s. He signed on as co-director of *White Shadows in the South Seas* (1928), shot largely on location in the South Pacific, and took over the film from director Robert Flaherty when the project ran into scheduling trouble. Now thought of as someone who could shoot on location, Van Dyke was assigned to *Trader Horn* (1931), a troubled film whose production he detailed in the jaundiced but amusing nonfiction book *Horning into Africa*.

Trader Horn led to *Tarzan the Ape Man* (1932), the first entry in a highly successful MGM franchise. Van Dyke met Myrna Loy while directing *Penthouse* (1933), in some ways a precursor to *The Thin Man*. Although the plot was a crime melodrama, Van Dyke staged it as a fast-paced comedy, with Loy playing a witty, cynical call girl opposite the unfortunately stiff and self-important Warner Baxter. Van Dyke cast her with Clark Gable and William Powell in *Manhattan Melodrama* (1934), a ponderous crime drama put together by David O. Selznick. (Van Dyke and Selznick first met in 1927 on a Tim McCoy Western.) Shot quickly and cheaply, it turned into an enormous hit for the studio, giving Van Dyke more leeway with *The Thin Man*.

The studio was going through a transitional stage. Former wunderkind Irving Thalberg found his duties split with Selznick and lesser producers like Hunt Stromberg. Selznick's pictures turned out to be a lot more profitable than Thalberg's; Stromberg specialized in working out Selznick's formulas in cheaper settings. Thus Powell and Loy were reunited in a quickie project that used largely contract players and pre-existing sets. Both had gone through career difficulties. Powell had played mostly villains in the silent era (cf. *The Last Command*, 1928). His detached, almost supercilious acting was ideally suited to talkies. Viewers loved him as long as he didn't take his material seriously. By *Jewel Robbery* (1932), he had developed a sophistication and urbanity that he would hone over the next two decades as one of the industry's major stars.

Loy had started out as a dancer, and after breaking into movies in 1925 found herself typecast as exotic foreign types and nymphomaniacs. Only a few months earlier she had taped up her eyelids to play Fu Manchu's sadistic daughter in *The Mask of Fu Manchu* (1932). Van Dyke turned her somewhat limited acting range into an advantage by making her a "normal" character: middle-class, all-American, grounded, sensible, but still physical and fun-loving. Loy became an alternative to MGM's stable of highbrow divas like Greta Garbo, Norma Shearer, and Joan Crawford. Within two years of *The Thin Man*, she was the number one female box-office star in the country.

Van Dyke shot *The Thin Man* in sixteen days, a breakneck pace at a time when most features took thirty to forty days. Fellow director George Sidney said admiringly, "If he figured a close-up would only run for three feet, that's all he shot. He knew cutting." On the other hand, actress Ann Rutherford once confided, "If you got half the words right, he would say, 'Print it!'" "It's just a technical job," Van Dyke said. "You have to possess some power of visualization, imagination, but that's not genius." He once wrote an article for actors in which he advised, "Figure out how you would naturally do a thing and then do it naturally some other way."

But plenty of hacks make films in three weeks, and they are almost all disappointing. *The Thin Man* worked not because it was glib and quick, but because Powell and Loy portrayed married life as something wonderful. According to Van Dyke, he told screenwriters Albert Hackett and Frances Goodrich that he wanted "eight scenes of marital felicity" in the script; they were more important than the often preposterous plot twists that drove the murder mystery. (Hammett was on the set, and may have contributed to the writing; Hackett and Goodrich, one of Hollywood's best married writing teams, later worked on *It's a Wonderful Life*, 1946.) As Nick and Nora Charles, Powell and Loy offered viewers a vision of domesticity that was both glamorous and flippant, and undeniably sexy.

When not basking in the alcohol-sodden moments that serve as foreplay between Nick and Nora, Van Dyke reveled in crooks, leeches, dysfunctional families, and hangers-on, turning the MGM soundstages into the equivalent of an after-hours party. Rowdy supporting actors like Ed Brophy bring *The Thin Man* closer to a Warner Bros. gangster flick than typical MGM product.

The film was so popular that it spawned instant imitators, as well as five sequels, radio and television series, and a Broadway musical. It was also a crucial factor in the burgeoning screwball comedy genre. Powell and Loy would team up in thirteen films overall, most of them easygoing comedies in which they played mildly bickering spouses. Van Dyke worked uncredited on *Naughty Marietta* (1936), a Registry title. He served in the Marines, and set up a recruiting station at MGM prior to World War II. Van Dyke died of cancer and heart disease in 1943.

William Powell and Myrna Loy as Nick and Nora Charles confront a midnight intruder in *The Thin Man*.

Little Miss Marker

Paramount, 1934. Sound, B&W, 1.37. 79 minutes.

Cast: Shirley Temple (Little Miss Marker), Adolphe Menjou (Sorrowful Jones), Charles Bickford (Big Steve), Dorothy Dell (Bangles Carson), Lynne Overman (Regret), Warren Hymer (Sore Toe), Sam Hardy (Bennie the Gouge), John Kelly (Canvas Back), Frank McGlynn, Sr. (Doc Chesley), Jack Sheehan (Sun Rise), Frank Conroy (Dr. Ingalls).

Credits: Directed by Alexander Hall. Screenplay by William Lipman, Sam Hellman, Gladys Lehman. Based on a short story by Damon Runyon. Produced by B.P. Schulberg. Music by Ralph Rainger. Lyrics by Leo Robin. Photographed by Alfred Gilks. Western Electric Noiseless Recording.

Additional Cast: Gary Owen (Grinder), Willie Best (Dizzy Memphis), Puggy White (Eddie), James Burke (Detective Reardon), Edward Earle (Father), Mildred Gover (Sarah), Tammany Young (Buggs).

Additional Credits: Edited by William Shea. Art direction: Hans Dreier, John B. Goodman. Released June 1, 1934.

Other Versions: Remade as *Sorrowful Jones* (1949), directed by Sidney Lanfield, starring Bob Hope; *Forty Pounds of Trouble* (1962), directed by Norman Jewison, starring Tony Curtis; *Little Miss Marker* (1980), directed by Walter Bernstein, starring Walter Matthau, Julie Andrews, Sara Stimson.

Available: Universal Home Video VHS (1996). ISBN: 0-7832-1751-X. UPC: 0-9689-82711-3-4. Universal Home Video DVD (2005). UPC: 025192594120.

The child star by whom all others are judged, Shirley Temple was born in Santa Monica, California, in 1928. Her father was a bank teller; her mother, Gertrude, had her taking dancing lessons when she was three. Inspired in part by the success of the Our Gang movies, the two made the rounds of studios looking for work for Shirley in bit parts or as an extra. Temple was chosen to appear in *Baby Burlesks*, a series of shorts in which child actors imitated adult stars. From there she graduated to bit parts in films at Warners, Universal, and Paramount. At the end of 1933, she signed a short-term contract with the Fox Film Corporation, singing "Baby Take a Bow" in the Depression-themed variety show *Stand Up and Cheer*. On the basis of this performance, Winifred Sheehan, a general manager at Fox, extended her contract for seven years.

While waiting for her next Fox project, Temple auditioned for Alexander Hall, who was directing *Little Miss Marker* for Paramount. A former actor, World War I veteran, and film editor, Hall gave Temple the part because she could carry off the script's gangland slang. *Little Miss Marker* was based on a short story by Damon Runyon, a sports writer and humorist whose *Lady for a Day* had been a successful film the year before for Frank Capra. *Little Miss Marker* was another variation on Runyon's favorite theme, the hearts of gold that tick inside the gangsters, con men, and petty crooks who lived and worked in and around New York's Times Square. Runyon's benign take on hustlers, thieves, and prostitutes can make parents cringe today, but at the time it was seen as more realistic, or perhaps more honest, than the thinly disguised hero worship found in the Warners gangster cycle.

In pairing Temple with seasoned screen actors like Adolphe Menjou and Charles Bickford, Hall was well aware that viewers' sympathies would lean toward the child. Although she was almost six at the time, Temple "played" much younger, and the most compelling aspect of the film today is its casual treatment of the peril her character faces. Temple is a de facto marker, left with Menjou as a gambling IOU. The world into which she is thrust includes doped racehorses, suicide, bootleg liquor, and kept women. Although a child, Temple's Marker has an uncanny insight into the adult mind, an insight Runyon suggests was earned through hard experience. The plot boils down to a love story between Marker and bookie Sorrowful Jones (Adolphe Menjou), and Hall has the two actors play their scenes like bickering newlyweds staking out their territory. It may be impossible for viewers today to avoid the story's uncomfortable sexual implications.

In her autobiography, Temple wrote guardedly about Menjou's antipathy toward her, saving her real wrath for Hall, who pretended that her mother had been kidnapped to elicit tears in one scene. Menjou works hard to divert attention away from Temple, but in every scene the viewer's eyes go straight to the child. Temple can be guileless and manipulative at the same time. Like a high-wire act in a circus, a large part of Temple's appeal comes from her brinksmanship, from viewers willing her to finish a line, a scene, her part without collapsing. When she sings "Laugh You Son of a Gun," her only song in the film, the tension comes from whether or not she can make it through the lyrics without faltering.

Novelist and critic Graham Greene found a more unsavory explanation for Temple's popularity, one that was "a little depraved, with an appeal interestingly decadent." In a famous libel case, Greene was fined for comparing Temple to Claudette Colbert and Marlene Dietrich, and for questioning the motives of the "middle-aged men and clergymen" who watched her movies. Given the explicitness of Temple's *Baby Burlesks*, this was not a completely unwarranted accusation. (Her character in one short was named "Morelegs Sweettrick.") Greene lost the case, which bankrupted the magazine that printed his reviews. For decades he was prohibited from reprinting his words. Temple quoted them herself in her autobiography, aware of the issue, if unwilling to discuss it fully.

This was Temple's first starring role, although *Stand Up and Cheer!* took the country by storm when it was released a few weeks before *Little Miss Marker*. Temple followed them with four more features that year, including *Baby Take a Bow* and *Bright Eyes*. Her talent and optimism won her extraordinary affection from moviegoers, and proved a godsend to an industry reeling from the Depression. Temple was the number one box-office star for four years' running, the recipient of an honorary Oscar in 1934, and the center of a consumer empire that included dolls, clothes, and books.

Temple starred in two or three musicals a year; their budgets averaged between $200,000 and $300,000, and they reliably grossed over a million dollars each. As she aged, she mined the classics of an earlier generation: *Daddy Long Legs* (released as *Curly Top* in 1935), *Poor Little Rich Girl* (1936), *Wee Willie Winkie* and *Heidi* (1937), *Rebecca of Sunnybrook Farm* (1938), *The Little Princess* (1939). By 1940, and the expensive failure of *The Blue Bird*, her film career was essentially over. She appeared in a dozen more features, no longer as a child star, and without much impact.

But her influence was pervasive—in animation, in music, in fiction, and, of course, in movies. Anne Edwards, a Temple biographer, makes an interesting case that the opening of *The Littlest Rebel* (1935), during which a girl's birthday party on a Southern plantation is broken up by news of the start of the Civil War, influenced Margaret Mitchell's *Gone With the Wind*. Other studios sought their own child stars. Jack Warner hired Sybil Jason, for example, and placed her in vehicles that clearly aped Temple's. Director Peter Bogdanovich presented an anti–Shirley Temple in *Paper Moon* (1973), which won Tatum O'Neal an Oscar, but the plot was essentially a Temple story adjusted for modern tastes with cigarettes and vulgarities.

As the years passed, and her films became more difficult to see, Temple's career was defined by generalities and misconceptions. Her duets with Bill Robinson were famous; less noted was the fact that her character got along better with butlers, maids, cooks, and other servants than with her own relatives. Temple's mother Gertrude was tagged as the archetypal "stage mother." As Allan Dwan, who directed Shirley in three films, said, "Shirley was the product of her mother. Shirley was the instrument on which her mother played. I don't know why the mother was like that—but I'd seen it before with Mary Pickford and her domineering mother."

In a Hollywood plot, Temple's faltering film career should have led to a breakdown of some sort before an unexpected twist inspired her to make a comeback. In real life, Temple married television executive Charles Black in 1950, and was known subsequently as Shirley Temple Black. She has had a distinguished career as a diplomat, humanitarian, and author. Her adult life is as exemplary as was her success as a child performer.

Punch Drunks

Columbia, 1934. Sound, B&W, 1.37. 18 minutes.

Cast: The Three Stooges (Moe [Howard], Larry [Fine], Curley [Howard]), Dorothy Granger.

Credits: Directed by Lou Breslow. Screen Play: Jack Cluett. Story: Jerry Howard, Larry Fine, Moe Howard. Photography: Henry Freulich. Film editor: Robert Carlisle.

Additional Cast: Oscar Hendrian, Frank Moran, Max Rosenbloom (Plug Uglies); Casey Colombo (Mr. McGurn), Chuck Callahan (Waiter), Al Hill (Killer Kilduff), Larry McGrath (Referee).

Additional Credits: Produced by Jules White. Production dates: May 2 to 5, 1934. Released July 13, 1934.

Available: Columbia TriStar Home Entertainment DVD, *The Three Stooges: Goofs on the Loose* (2004). ISBN: 1-4049-5616-6. UPC: 043396051010.

The sound era brought an abrupt end to a classic age of silent slapstick. Some historians claimed that silent comedians were unable to adjust to sound. In reality, most of them adjusted quite well. Laurel and Hardy didn't win their Oscar until well into sound films. Buster Keaton found his greatest financial success working at MGM. Charlie Chaplin persisted in making silent films until 1936, but his popularity hardly waned in the 1930s. Harold Lloyd made several successful sound films, working until World War II.

What had changed was that silent stars had aged, and could no longer perform the stunts that made their reputations. The comics who succeeded in early sound films—the Marx Brothers, W.C. Fields, Wheeler & Woolsey—were new to filmgoers. They were largely urban, as were their new fans. A more important point was that silent slapstick was just that—silent. The often violent chases and falls were pillowed by silence, cushioned from reality. With the addition of sound, the blows, pratfalls, slips, crashes suddenly could be heard. A sound film couldn't deny or hide the pain of slapstick. For many viewers, there was nothing funny about a performer crying or groaning as he fell down a fight of stairs.

Unless, of course, viewers understand there is no chance of real harm. One thing the Three Stooges accomplished was to eliminate the pain from live-action slapstick. Their slaps, eye gouges, head bops, hair pulling, shin kicks, and blows from sledgehammers—accompanied on the soundtrack by amplified splats, gongs, and claps—exaggerated violence to a point where it was disconnected from reality. In a Keaton or Lloyd film, the falls were designed to be risky but survivable. No one could survive the falls in a Three Stooges film.

229

Their gags and films were closer to cartoons than to silent comedies.

The Stooges themselves came from a vaudeville act put together by Ted Healy, a fast-talking, hard-drinking comedian who was eventually killed in a barroom brawl in 1937. Healy, born Clarence Earnest Lee Nash in 1896, started out in an acrobat act, switched to a blackface routine, then returned to a tumbling bit. Needing a replacement in 1922, he hired his childhood friend, the nonacrobatic Moe Howard, as a stooge, or sort of audience heckler. Sometimes called a rube, the stooge was a fixture in vaudeville and in early film. Today stooge characters supplant the comics themselves in many films.

Moe was joined by his brother Shemp, and then by Larry Fine in 1925. The Stooges quit Healy's act over his alcoholism, rejoined him briefly when he signed motion-picture deals with Fox and MGM, then quit again in 1934 when it became apparent that Healy would not stop drinking.

Moe Howard, whose real name was Harry Moses Horwitz, took over the act. (Moe claimed to have acted in Vitagraph shorts before 1910, but the films apparently do not survive.) With his younger brother Curly (at first spelled "Curley"; his real name was Jerome) and Fine (really Louis Feinberg), Moe signed a contract at Columbia Pictures for a series of two-reel comedies. Moe essentially took over Healy's role in the act, playing the "brains" of the team. Larry was a harmless bystander who wandered into trouble the way Stan Laurel did, while Curly was raging id—part Harpo Marx, part Donald Duck.

Punch Drunks was the second of 190 films the comics shot at the studio, a stretch of almost twenty-five years that made them the longest-running team in movies. In fact, they were the last comics to make two-reel shorts at all. In *Punch Drunks*, the Stooges' plot formula is already in place, even though the characters are still gestating. Moe plays a miserly fight manager, Curly a waiter in a greasy spoon, and Larry a traveling musician. Moe is eating with his fighters when Larry arrives, willing to entertain restaurant customers for either $200 or a bowl of soup. When Larry plays "Pop Goes the Weasel" on his violin, it sends Curly into a homicidal rage. Seeing his fighters knocked unconscious, Moe signs Curly to a contract.

Training involves the three flirting with Dorothy Granger, whom they spot when her car gets a flat tire. Curly starts winning his fights, shown by a conspicuously skimpy montage of headlines. But at the championship bout, Curly accidentally smashes Larry's violin. Curly is beaten senseless by his opponent while Larry runs through the town looking for a record of "Pop Goes the Weasel."

Directed by the journeyman Lou Breslow and written by the Stooges themselves, *Punch Drunks* is a low-budget effort from a studio that was considered the cheapest of the majors. The cast and crew filmed outside, or on existing sets, and used stock footage and back projection as much as possible. Under the guidance of producer Jules White, retakes were kept to a minimum. (Born in Budapest in 1900, White would direct and write screenplays as well as produce. As head of short subjects at Columbia, he had enormous control over the films of the Stooges, as well as those by other comics under contract to Columbia, like Buster Keaton.) When you are shooting your entire film in three days, and releasing it six weeks later, you don't have time for retakes.

The Stooges in *Punch Drunks* and their other early films, like the Oscar-nominated *Men in Black*, are harsher, more remote characters than they would become later on. The gags are closer to burlesque than to vaudeville, with jokes about tapeworms, midgets who hand out cigars, and punches as fallback gags. But even at the beginning of their shorts, they excelled in lifting ideas from their screen predecessors.

Everyone in comedy steals. Comics like Milton Berle even made taking other people's jokes a part of their act. The Stooges took themes, premises, plots, and jokes from silent comedies, reworking them for sound (and for smaller budgets). The boxing background used in *Punch Drunks* was a favorite in silent films, notably in Keaton's *Battling Buster*. The Stooges' *An Ache in Every Stake* (1941) was based on Laurel and Hardy's *The Music Box* (1932), and *The Sitter-Downers* (1937) owes a lot to Keaton's *One Week* (1920).

The Stooges also borrowed from themselves, remaking many of their shorts as cast members changed. (Curly retired after a stroke, replaced by his older brother Shemp. When Shemp died in 1955, his part was taken first by Joe Besser, then "Curly Joe" DeRita.) When the series stopped in 1958, Columbia sold their shorts to television through its subsidiary, Screen Gems. The Stooges became a mainstay of afternoon children's shows and baseball rain delays, winning an entirely new audience. They parlayed their new success into a few negligible feature films, like *Snow White and the Three Stooges* (1961). The Stooges continued to work, making a television pilot that wasn't picked up and announcing film projects that were never produced. But when Moe died of lung cancer in 1975, the team officially came to an end.

A company formed in part by Moe, Comedy III Productions, Inc., keeps a tight rein on the Stooges' reputation. *U.S. News & World Report* noted that in 1997, there were more than two hundred licensed Stooges' products. Mel Gibson, a fan of the team, used Curly's shtick in *Lethal Weapon* (1987), and in 2000 produced a television biopic entitled *The Three Stooges*.

Imitation of Life

Universal, 1934. Sound, B&W, 1.37. 111 minutes.

Cast: Claudette Colbert (Beatrice Pullman), Warren William (Stephen Archer), Rochelle Hudson (Jessie Pullman), Ned Sparks (Elmer Smith), Louise Beavers (Delilah), Fredi Washington (Peola), Baby Jane [Juanita Quigley] (Baby Jessie), Alan Hale (The furniture man), Henry Armetta (The painter), Wyndham Standing (The butler).

Credits: Directed by John M. Stahl. Screenplay: William Hurlbut. From the novel by Fannie Hurst. Produced by Carl Laemmle, Jr. Art director: Charles D. Hall. Musical director: Heinz Roemheld. Photography: Merritt Gerstad. Special effects: John P. Fulton. Film editors: Philip Chan, Maurice Wright. Western Electric Noiseless Recording.

Additional Cast: Marilyn Knowles (Jessie Pullman, aged 8), Sebie Hendricks (Peola Johnson, aged 4), Dorothy Black (Peola Johnson, aged 9), Clarence Hummel Wilson (Landlord), Henry Kolker (Doctor Preston), G.P. Huntley, Jr. (James), Paul Porcasi (Café manager), Paullyin Garner (Mrs. Ramsey), Alice Ardell (French maid), Walter Walker (Hugh), Noel Francis (Mrs. Eden), Franklin Pangborn (Mr. Carven), Tyler Brooke (Tipsy man), William Austin (Englishman), Edgar Norton (Butler), Alma Tell (Mrs. Carven), Lenita Lane (Mrs. Dale), Barry Norton (Young man), Joyce Compton (Young woman), Reverend Gregg (Black minister), Edna Bowdoin (Black secretary), Daisy Bufford (Black waitress); Ethel Sykes, Monya Andre (Party women); Curry Lee (Black chauffeur); Claire McDowell, Norma Drew (Teachers); Stuart Johnston (Undertaker); Hattie McDaniel (Funeral onlooker).

Additional Credits: Additional dialogue: Victor Heerman, Finley Peter Dunne, Jr. Screenwriting: Arthur Richman, Preston Sturges, Walter Ferris, Bianca Gilchrist, Samuel Ornitz, Sarah Y. Mason. Assistant directors: Scott Beal, Fred Frank. Associate producer: Henry Henigson. Supervising film editor: Maurice Pivar. Sound supervisor: Gilbert Kurland. Makeup: William Ely. Production dates: June 27 to September 11, 1934. Released November 26, 1934.

Other Versions: Remade as *Imitation of Life* (1950), directed by Douglas Sirk.

Available: Universal Home Video DVD (2003). ISBN: 0-7832-8706-2. UPC: 0-25192-42332-1.

When Universal made *Back Street* in 1932, Fannie Hurst was a proven commodity, with over a dozen of her stories and novels adapted to the screen. Born in Ohio in 1887, Hurst began writing short stories as a teenager, and later wrote and acted in plays. Her breakthrough came with the *Saturday Evening Post*, which published twenty of her stories by 1914. Hollywood began using her material a few years later, with director Frank Borzage achieving success with *Humoresque* (1920) and *Back Pay* (1922). Borzage would later develop a more nuanced approach to "tearjerkers," one that incorporated spiritual faith into realistic settings.

Hurst, meanwhile, turned to novels in which her heroines grappled with social issues like the exploitation of domestic workers and the double standard regarding to adultery. During the 1920s, her work was filmed by companies like William Randolph Hearst's Cosmopolitan Pictures. Carl Laemmle, Jr., had signed John Stahl to direct *A Lady Surrenders* (1930) for Universal; with the success of that film, and of *Strictly Dishonorable* (1931), an adaptation of a Preston Sturges play, Stahl was given a contract to direct three more "specials" for the studio. The first of these, based on Hurst's *Back Street*, was one of the biggest hits of the year for Universal, still known primarily for horror pictures and cheap Westerns.

Born in 1886 in New York City, Stahl began acting in legitimate theater and vaudeville as a teenager. In an interview with *Hollywood Reporter* in 1932, he said that his first film as a director was *The Boy and the Law* (1914) for Vitagraph, but his career didn't take off until he began working for Louis B. Mayer, an independent producer who would be one of the founders of MGM. Stahl quit Mayer to form Tiffany Stahl Productions with M.H. Hoffman and L.A. Young; he was head of production for the independent studio until 1929. (Tiffany later devolved into one of the least reputable of the "Poverty Row" studios.)

Stahl's first "domestic drama" was *Wives of Men* in 1917, "and I have been writing and directing domestic dramas ever since." He quoted Mayer approvingly as saying, "John Stahl couldn't direct a picture without a bed in it," but Stahl was simply exploiting a niche that accounted for a growing portion of the audience. All of the major studios released "women's pictures," with Paramount and MGM focusing on the usually lighthearted problems of young adults and Warners and Fox opting for heavier fare like *Safe in Hell* (1930) and *7th Heaven* (1927).

Back Street concerned a mistress, played by Irene Dunne, who remains "faithful" to her married lover for twenty years. While it ran into some trouble with censors and the office of the Production Code, it was embraced wholeheartedly by mainstream moviegoers, in part because of Stahl's straightforward, nonjudgmental style, but also because the director toned down the potentially objectionable elements of Hurst's plot. "The reality that women approve in fiction is not palatable to them on screen. They edit as they read, eliminating from their imaginations the sordidness and squalor of modern fiction," he wrote. "Harshness and bad taste must be blue-penciled by the director." If not, women "would run miles from the theater."

Stahl's next film, *Only Yesterday* (1933), based on a novel by Frederick Lewis Allen, depicted the plight of an unwed mother in sympathetic terms. It marked the film debut of Margaret Sullavan, and gave Stahl another hit. For *Imitation of Life*, which Laemmle purchased for $25,000, Stahl would get to work with an even bigger star, Claudette Colbert, borrowed from Paramount for $90,000. The plot to the novel was so controversial that Stahl ended up using nine screenwriters, including Preston Sturges, to iron it out.

Gone were the heroine's loveless marriage to a boarder in her father's rooming house, a tragic love triangle, and an interracial marriage. In their place was a dual plot line about two single mothers who were disappointed by their daughters. Colbert's role involved casually seducing and bilking a half-dozen or so admirers before falling for a playboy ichthyologist (Warren William), only to find heartbreak at the hands of her daughter (Rochelle Hudson).

"Direction, to my way of thinking, is more a matter of 'feeling' than anything else," Stahl once wrote. "Certainly it doesn't consist of telling an actor to come onto the set and speak the lines called for in the scenario." Other directors, notably Borzage and Leo McCarey, would follow their instincts as well. Like some of their films, *Imitation of Life* is more a collection of emotional moments than a coherent story. Stahl isn't concerned about matching action in shots or what happens in the background of the frame or even structuring scenes plausibly. He wants to get to the diffused close-up of the weepy heroine.

This may be why *Imitation of Life* seems so bifurcated today. Colbert's haughty, even icy screen demeanor did not do "weepy" well, and her story line creaks and groans. (Pulp writer James M. Cain would make better use of this story line in *Mildred Pierce*, filmed in 1945.)

The second plot, which involves Colbert's black maid Delilah (Louise Beavers) and her light-skinned daughter Peola (Fredi Washington), seems to take place in an alternative universe, one in which life is harsh and pain is real. Hurst, who counted Zora Neale Hurston among her friends, was serious about the problem of racial inequality, and Peola's efforts to "pass" in white society have a startling directness, both in the book and on the screen.

Washington's background as a actress plays into her performance in *Imitation of Life*. (When she appeared in *The Emperor Jones*, 1934, she was ordered to wear darker makeup so audiences wouldn't mistake her for a white woman.) Washington's acting speaks to us across the years, making it clear that race is something that can't be glossed over with cocktails and wisecracks. "You don't know what it is to look white and be black," she says at one point, and who could deny that her life would have been easier if she had "passed." Reviewers singled out Washington and Beavers for praise.

Imitation of Life was one of the top-grossing films of the year, but at a huge price. Universal spent almost $200,000 before Stahl even started shooting, and he filmed for three months, using up enough time and money for three horror pictures. Stahl would go through almost a million dollars on his next feature, *Magnificent Obsession* (1935); by the time it was released, Laemmle and his father were ousted from the studio.

Naughty Marietta

Metro-Goldwyn-Mayer, 1935. Sound, B&W, 1.37. 104 minutes.

Cast: Jeanette MacDonald (Marietta), Nelson Eddy (Warrington), Frank Morgan (Governor d'Annard), Elsa Lanchester (Madame d'Annard), Douglas Dumbrille (Uncle), Joseph Cawthorne (Herr Schuman), Cecilia Parker (Julie), Walter Kingsford (Don Carlos), Greta Meyer (Frau Schuman), Akim Tamiroff (Rudolphe), Harold Huber (Abe), Edward Brophy (Zeke).

Credits: Book and Lyrics by Rida Johnson Young. Screen Play by John Lee Mahin, Frances Goodrich and Albert Hackett. Produced by Hunt Stromberg. Music by Victor Herbert. Musical adaptation by Herbert Stothart. Photographed by William Daniels. Additional lyrics: Gus Kahn. Recording director: Douglas Shearer. Gowns by Adrian. Art director: Cedric Gibbons. Associate art directors: Arnold Gillespie, Edwin B. Willis. Film editor: Blanche Sewell. Western Electric Sound System.

Additional Cast: Cora Sue Collins (Felice), Harry Cording (Pirate), William Burress (Bouget), Billy Dooley (Drunk).

Additional Credits: Directed by W.S. Van Dyke, Robert Z. Leonard. Produced by Hunt Stromberg. Production dates: December 4, 1934 to February 7, 1935. Premiered in Washington, D.C., on March 8, 1935.

Available: MGM/UA Home Video VHS (1992). ISBN: 0-7928-1554-8. UPC: 0-2761-60371-3-8.

Once a real factor in popular culture, light operas have now dwindled into a niche market. Even when it was released, *Naughty Marietta* was considered old fashioned. Victor Herbert's operetta premiered in 1910, and twenty-five years later its tale of disguised princesses and inept pirates would seem to have little relevance for Depression audiences. Remarkably, this adaptation proved so popular that it led to a series of musicals starring Jeanette MacDonald and Nelson Eddy.

MacDonald had already proven herself a star in films like *Love Me Tonight* (1932). She had recently reteamed with Maurice Chevalier in *The Merry Widow*, directed by Ernst Lubitsch for MGM, prior to signing a contract with the studio at Louis B. Mayer's behest. Mayer was the one executive there with a real taste for light opera, and he saw *Naughty Marietta* as a way to standardize the formula Lubitsch (and producer Irving Thalberg) established with *Merry Widow*. Typically, Mayer first sought to cut costs. The choice of the operetta itself saved money, as it was an attempt to salvage a project first announced at the studio years earlier. Mayer assigned it to producer Hunt Stromberg, a Thalberg protégé who had recently succeeded with *The Thin Man* (1934). A former sports writer, Stromberg had a good working relationship with W.S. Van Dyke, in part because "One-Take Woody" wasted neither time nor money when shooting a film. But the producer had a reputation for withdrawing into silence when confronted by less confident talent. During his career he managed to alienate writers like Aldous Huxley and F. Scott Fitzgerald (although it should be noted that their work for the studio rarely met professional standards). Here the assigned director, Robert Z. Leonard, left after one day's work. Van Dyke filled in for the duration, but this is one of two MGM features released without a director's credit (the other was *Hollywood Party* in 1934).

Van Dyke's apparent indifference to the material may be one reason why *Naughty Marietta* can seem slipshod and chaotic. Shots often don't match, and even within individual scenes cinematography can range from polished to erratic. But the real drawback to the film is not its rushed production schedule or its dated script; it is instead MacDonald's costar Nelson Eddy. A former telephone operator from Providence, Rhode Island, Eddy attracted attention after winning a Gilbert and Sullivan competition in 1922. He studied grand opera, performing in Europe as well as with the Philadelphia Civic Opera. Eddy then toured the country as a concert singer, and gathered more fans through extensive radio appearances. He signed with MGM in 1933, waiting two years for his breakthrough role.

From today's vantage point, Eddy's singing seems competent but emotionally bland, while his acting can only be described as stiff. As a result, those around him overcompensate, giving veteran scene-stealers like Frank Morgan the chance to really ham it up. As another compensation, Herbert's tunes arrive like clockwork, every ten minutes or so, and they are given a big-budget treatment. "Tramp, Tramp, Tramp" and "Ah, Sweet Mystery of Life" are probably the most recognizable tunes today; MacDonald duets with Eddy in the latter and in the "Italian Street Song." Paradoxically, presenting the songs—in fact, the entire story—in a realistic manner instead of a theatrical one emphasizes the banality and silliness of the material.

That same year, MGM's *A Night at the Opera* mocked music much like this, but *Naughty Marietta* was still a commercial hit, and even received a Best Picture nomination. Dubbed "Singing Sweethearts," MacDonald and Eddy appeared together in seven more movies. Van Dyke would become a mainstay in MacDonald's career until she left the studio in 1942. (The director would die a year later at the age of fifty-six.) But in popular culture, light opera was being replaced by musicals. The same year *Naughty Marietta* was released, films starring Fred Astaire and Ginger Rogers, Bing Crosby, Eleanor Powell, Frances Langford, Alice Faye, George Raft, Maurice Chevalier, Al Jolson, Dick Powell, and Gene Autry, among others, came out, with songs by composers like Jerome Kern, Irving Berlin, Cole Porter, and the other tunesmiths responsible for what became known as the Great American Songbook.

Bride of Frankenstein

Universal, 1935. Sound, B&W, 1.37. 75 minutes.

Cast: [Boris] Karloff (The Monster), Colin Clive (Henry Frankenstein), Valerie Hobson (Elizabeth), Ernest Thesiger (Doctor Pretorius), Elsa Lanchester (Mary Wollstonecraft Shelley), Gavin Gordon (Lord Byron), Douglas Walton (Percy Bysshe Shelley), Una O'Connor (Minnie), E.E. Clive (Burgomaster), Lucien Prival (Butler), O.P. Heggie (Hermit), Dwight Frye (Karl), Reginald Barlow (Hans), Mary Gordon (Hans' Wife), Ann Darling (Shepherdess), Ted Billings (Ludwig), Elsa Lanchester (The Monster's Mate).

Credits: Directed by James Whale. Screenplay: William Hurlbut. Suggested by the original story written in 1816 by Mary Wollstonecraft Shelley and Adapted by William Hurlbut, John Balderston. Produced by Carl Laemmle, Jr. Musical score: Franz Waxman. Art director: Charles D. Hall. Photographer: John J. Mescall. Photographic effects: John P. Fulton. Orchestra conductor: Bakaleinikoff. Film editor: Ted Kent. Western Electric Noiseless Recording. A Carl Laemmle presentation of a James Whale production.

Additional Cast includes: Neil Fitzgerald, Rollo Lloyd, Walter Brennan (Neighbor), Billy Barty (Baby); Robert A'Dair, Jack Curtis, Frank Terry, John Carradine (Hunters); Tempe Pigott (Auntie Glutz); Gunnis Davis (Uncle Glutz); Edwin Mordant (Coroner), Sarah Schwartz (Marta), Josephine McKim (Mermaid).

Additional Credits: Screenwriting by Tom Reed. Makeup: Jack Pierce, Otto Lederer. Sound supervisor: Gilbert Kurland. Production dates: January 2 to March 7, 1935. Released April 22, 1935.

Other Versions: Sequel to *Frankenstein* (1931).

Available: Universal Home Video DVD (2004). ISBN: 0783288204.

Universal Studios waited four years to make the sequel to *Frankenstein*, in part because director James Whale and star Boris Karloff were unwilling to try to top what had been one of the most successful films in the studio's history. Fourth-billed in the original film, Karloff became an international celebrity on the strength of his performance as the monster. The actor signed a contract with Universal that started out at $750 a week and quickly rose to almost five times that amount, but still found himself playing small, unbilled parts in forgettable movies. Universal built *The Mummy* (1932), a quasi-remake of *Dracula*, for Karloff, and then teamed him with Whale again that same year for *The Old Dark House*. But for the most part he made stronger impressions in loan-outs to MGM (*The Mask of Fu Manchu*, 1932) and RKO (*The Lost Patrol*, 1934) than he did in Universal pictures.

Whale, meanwhile, was trying to establish himself as an "A" director, someone capable of serious drama like *Waterloo Bridge* (1931). Faced with a project like *The Old Dark House*, one of the seminal haunted-house movies, he discarded much of J.B. Priestley's original novel *Benighted* to concentrate on atmosphere and acting. Along with Karloff, the film starred Charles Laughton (in his American movie debut) and Ernest Thesiger, two actors not known for restraint. Whale also pushed comic elements in *The Invisible Man* (1933), an adaptation of the H.G. Wells novel that gave plenty of screen time to character actor Una O'Connor.

O'Connor and Thesiger also appear in *Bride of Frankenstein*, which is essentially a grander, more peculiar remake of *Frankenstein*. It's as if Whale approached the project as a chance to do what time and budget restrictions prevented him from accomplishing in the first film. The sets, again by Charles "Danny" Hall, duplicate *Frankenstein*'s dank, dark look, but on a larger, more lavish scale. Whale helped design the forest scenes, which evolve from lush greenery and waterfalls to a scarred landscape of burnt, limbless trees and jumbled boulders, with painted backdrops for skies. Much of *Bride of Frankenstein* looks as though it could be taking place on a World War I battlefield.

Whale also insisted on a five-minute prologue featuring Mary Wollstonecraft Shelley, her husband Percy Shelley, and Lord Byron discussing the gestation of her novel. Gavin Gordon's over-the-top performance as Byron sets the tone for the film: broad, even flamboyant, darkly comic, with jokes pitched slightly higher than middlebrow.

The bulk of the film picks up where *Frankenstein* left off, starting at the burned-out watermill where the monster supposedly met his doom. The first murders occur almost at once, but notice how prominent O'Connor's part is in the opening, and how Whale uses sight gags to offset the horror, as if hinting to the audience that it's okay not to take the story seriously. The arrival of Thesiger, playing a scientist even madder than Frankenstein, is a further signal to relax in what has become an alternate universe to the original film. (There's also the sad truth, too little noted in Frankenstein films, that the monster is too slow and awkward to be an actual menace. You practically have to stand still for him to catch you.)

Whale's touch greatly influenced other filmmakers. Early in the story Thesiger displays the results of his previous experiments: tiny humans he keeps in bell jars. This memorable conceit would fuel *The Devil-Doll*, an MGM horror film made not two years later, as well as comic books and science fiction films over the following decades. Thesiger's ripe delivery of lines like, "Do you like gin? It is my only weakness," or his toast, "To a new world of gods and monsters" spoke to a different audience, one that saw the outsider status of many of the characters in *Bride* as a code for homosexuality.

Colin Clive, his features visibly softened from the original film, would drink himself to death two years after finishing *Bride*. He had also broken his leg horseback riding shortly before production began, explaining why he plays much of the picture seated. Biographers describe Whale's many efforts to increase the actor's involvement with the film, but there is a hollow quality to his performance. Mae Clarke, who played his fiancée in the original film, was replaced by the seventeen-year-old Valerie Hobson. Whale found a way to include a role for Dwight Frye, whose Igor character was killed in *Frankenstein*. Nevertheless, most of Frye's part, which at one point involved two murders and an inquest, was cut. John Carradine, who would have a long and somewhat reluctant career in horror, appears as a hunter who sets the monster off on a murderous rampage.

Karloff resisted one of Whale's innovations, a scene in which a blind hermit teaches the monster to talk. The actor realized that this would reduce sympathy for the monster, as well as take away some of the terror associated with him. For if the monster can talk, he can reason, making it harder to explain away his outbursts of violence. (In the novel, the monster is articulate enough to debate philosophy with Dr. Frankenstein.) The film's single most affecting moment may be Karloff's silent reaction as the monster overhears how it had been constructed from dead body parts.

Whale had met Elsa Lanchester in London, and had directed her husband Charles Laughton in *The Old Dark House*. The director knew the relatively petite actress well enough to cast her as a seven-foot-tall monster. She later claimed that hissing swans from a London park were the inspiration for her monster's vocalisms, but what could have prompted her brilliant physical gestures, the furtive, feline movements of her head, the way she flings her arms up when aghast? It is such a visually and emotionally powerful performance that it's always surprising to realize how short her time is on screen.

Whale pushed the religious imagery in the film so strongly that censors objected. The monster at one point was to identify with a figure of Christ on a crucifix; this scene was changed, but another in which the monster is strung up in a Christ-like pose was retained. In another explicit reference, the soundtrack swells with the strains of Schubert's "Ave Maria" as the hermit and the monster cement their friendship. (This was the first Hollywood credit for composer Franz Waxman, whose use of musical motifs for each of the main characters became a hallmark of his best scores.)

By the time Whale gets around to creating a new monster, the film itself has fallen into the worst sort of scientific mumbo-jumbo. Unlike *Frankenstein*, which uses electricity fancifully but logically, *Bride* can't explain how its science works. There's a telephone straight out of *The Exploits of Elaine* (1914) and tricks with flinging bodies that can be found in *The Great Train Robbery* (1903). Whale may have had more money to spend, but in the end he didn't have much more to say about life and the creation of it. He would soon be turning his attention to directing *Show Boat* (1936).

Karloff played Frankenstein again in *Son of Frankenstein* (1939), and the character was used in a number of other films, each one a little more prosaic, a little less frightening, than the last.

Top Hat

RKO, 1935. Sound, B&W, 1.37. 100 minutes.

Cast: Fred Astaire (Jerry Travers), Ginger Rogers (Dale Tremont), Edward Everett Horton (Horace Hardwick), Erik Rhodes (Alberto Beddini), Eric Blore (Bates), Helen Broderick (Madge Hardwick).

Credits: Directed by Mark Sandrich. Screen play by Dwight Taylor and Allan Scott. Story by Dwight Taylor. Music and lyrics by Irving Berlin. Musical director: Max Steiner. Gowns by Bernard Newman. Photographed by David Abel. Photographic effects by Vernon Walker. Ensembles staged by Hermes Pan. Art director: Van Nest Polglase. Associate art director: Carroll Clark. Set dressing by Thomas Little. Recorded by Hugh McDowell, Jr. Music recorded by P.J. Faulkner, Jr. Sound cutter: George Marsh. Edited by William Hamilton. Recorded by RCA Victor system. A Radio Pictures presentation of a Pandro S. Berman production.

Additional Cast: Donald Meek (Curate), Florence Roberts (Curate's wife), Gino Corrado (Lido hotel manager), Peter Hobbes (Call boy), Leonard Mudie (Flower shop owner), Lucille Ball (Flower shop clerk), Robert Adair (Assistant hotel manager), Bud Flanagan (Man in elevator), Ben Holmes, Nick Thompson, Tom Costello, John Impolite, Genaro Spagnoli, Rita Rozelle, Phyllis Coghlan, Charles Hall, Anya Taranda, Henry Mowbray, Tom Ricketts, Tom Brandon, Roy Brent, Tito Blasco, Rosette Rosalie.

Additional Credits: Orchestrations: Edward Powell. Dance director: William Hetzler. Production dates: April 8 to June 5, 1935. Premiered in New York City on August 29, 1935.

Available: Warner Home Video DVD (2005). ISBN: 0-7806-3989-8. UPC: 0-53939-65902-3.

As an art form defined by motion, dance is ideally suited to film. Some of the most popular early Edison films were dances, including fan and serpentine dances performed by Carmencita and by Annabelle Whitford. Dance gained new attention with the coming of sound. In films like *Whoopee!* (1930) and later *42nd Street* (1933), Busby Berkeley offered an approach to choreography that turned dance into geometric patterns. That approach changed with Fred Astaire.

Astaire was born in Omaha, Nebraska, in 1899, the younger brother of dance prodigy Adele Astaire. He followed his sister to New York City in 1904, where they trained at a school run by Claude Alvienne. A year later Fred and Adele were performing professionally in vaudeville, and by 1907 Fred was incorporating his own choreography into the act. With an occasional hiatus, they continued to perform as a vaudeville act until 1917, when they moved to the musical stage. Over the next fifteen years, they appeared in ten Broadway shows, performing songs by Gershwins and Howard Dietz, among others. They also toured England. The act broke up when Adele married Charles Cavendish, a son of the Duke of Devonshire.

Fred Astaire's first solo performance was in *Gay Divorce*, with songs by Cole Porter. While it wasn't a flop, it wasn't a huge success either. Leland Hayward, Astaire's agent, got him a film contract at RKO. (He was first loaned out to MGM for *Dancing Lady* in 1933.) In his autobiography, *Steps in Time*, Astaire, perhaps bitter over how his theatrical career ended, wrote, "I found working before the camera much more interesting than theatre appearances."

For his first RKO film, *Flying Down to Rio* (1933), Astaire was billed fifth, just below Ginger Rogers. Fortunately for his career, the film was a hit, and he was singled out for praise by reviewers. Pandro Berman, now Astaire's producer and chief backer, promptly purchased the rights to *Gay Divorce* and *Roberta* for him. Ginger Rogers at this stage was considered more a comic foil than a dancing partner, and Astaire at first resisted becoming part of a new team. But their duet to "The Carioca," as well as Rogers' previous experience in film, persuaded Berman to build the newly retitled *The Gay Divorcee* (1934) around them.

"Night and Day" helped *The Gay Divorcee* become a box-office hit, and also established Astaire and Rogers as one of the premiere romantic duos in film. Nevertheless, they played supporting roles in their next film, *Roberta* (1935), another

huge success. By this time Astaire was working with Hermes Pan, billed as "Assistant Dance Director." The son of the Greek consul to Nashville, Pan moved to New York when he was fourteen, appearing in the chorus of Rogers' first musical show. He became Astaire's dance partner.

"I would play Rogers for the first two weeks. I know how she dances and what she expects from Astaire," Pan said. "We just fool around, just fool around for hours." What Pan called "fooling around" would be an intense workout for anyone else. "Astaire and Rogers use at least eight weeks blocking out the routines and practicing them. At the end of those eight weeks, the filming begins," Pan explained. "Some of the smoothest dances would be shot even as much as forty times before the perfect one came along."

For Astaire, "Each dance had to spring somehow out of a character or situation." He was also intimately involved with how his work looked on screen. It was crucial for the audience to see that he and Rogers were performing their routines whole, that they weren't assembled out of bits and pieces of film shot at separate times and then cut together. In that sense Astaire was like a musician who was determined to master his performance as a piece. The payoff in film was that Astaire only had to get it perfect once, not night after night. It took Astaire a while to persuade producers and directors that his approach would work—even as late as *Swing Time* (1936), director George Stevens was inserting cutaways into numbers. But eventually RKO technicians developed a crab dolly that could unobtrusively follow Astaire and Rogers around a set in precisely designed compositions.

Top Hat was the first script written specifically for the team, and typically Astaire hated it. "It is a series of events patterned *too closely* after *Gay Divorce*, without the originality & suspense of that play," he wrote to the studio. "I am cast as a *straight juvenile* & rather a cocky and arrogant one at that—a sort of objectionable young man without any charm or sympathy or humor." Even so, critic Arlene Croce felt that Dwight Taylor's screenplay crystallized all the elements that define an Astaire/Rogers film—especially how the act of dancing brought them together romantically. (It's not surprising that many of those elements can also be found in *The Gay Divorcee*, as Taylor wrote the original book for the musical.)

To answer Astaire's objections, Allan Scott, a Rhodes Scholar and playwright for the Theatre

Guild, rewrote Taylor's draft, working with director Mark Sandrich. (Scott would receive credit on six of the team's films.) At the same time, songwriter Irving Berlin, who had been contracted to write six songs for the film, worked from Taylor's script and Astaire's suggestions. This was Berlin's first score for Astaire, and his first film work since 1930. He wrote the title tune based in part on a routine Astaire had performed in the 1930 Flo Ziegfeld show, *Smiles*. He tried out other songs for the team while they were working on the set of *Roberta*.

The eventual score to *Top Hat* is one of the most beguiling and popular of the 1930s. "No Strings," "Isn't This a Lovely Day," "Top Hat," "Cheek to Cheek," and "The Piccolino" were not only popular hits at the time, but have become enduring entries in what some refer to as the Great American Songbook. (Berlin's sixth song, "Get Thee Behind Me Satan," ended up in the team's next film, *Follow the Fleet*.) Astaire became lifelong friends with the composer.

"At the studio the work was fun," Astaire wrote. "Ginger and I never failed to find plenty to laugh about." "You would be surprised how much she adds to the numbers," Sandrich said. "Fred arranges them, and then, when they get to rehearsing, Ginger puts in her own suggestions." Rogers waited until 1966 to offer her opinion: there was "no loafing on the job of an Astaire picture, and no cutting corners."

Top Hat was the last Astaire/Rogers film in which the music was recorded live, with a fifty-piece orchestra performing to the side of the stage. "Some people say that *Top Hat* was my best picture," he wrote. "But I think *Top Hat* was good for its period, just as our Broadway show *Lady, Be Good!* was for its time." About his movies he added, "It's rather appalling to me to think that they may still be running a hundred years from now."

Critic John Mueller, who has meticulously timed every Astaire film, notes that only 26 of the film's 100 minutes include dancing. Fortunately for viewers, the dancing in *Top Hat* is among the highest quality ever achieved in the movies. Audiences at the time responded ecstatically, making the film the number two box-office performer of the year worldwide. Astaire and Rogers made six more films together at RKO, including *Swing Time*, a Registry title.

A Night at the Opera

Metro Goldwyn Mayer, 1935. Sound, B&W, 1.37. 91 minutes.

Cast: Groucho Marx (Otis B. Driftwood), Chico Marx (Fiorello), Harpo Marx (Tomasso), Kitty Carlisle (Rosa), Allan Jones (Ricardo [Barone]), Walter [Wolf] King ([Rudolfo] Lassparri), Siegfried Rumann ([Herman] Gottlieb), Margaret Dumont (Mrs. Claypool), Edward Keane (Captain), Robert Emmet [Emmett] O'Connor (Henderson), Lorraine Bridges (Louisa).

Credits: Directed by Sam Wood. Screenplay by George S. Kaufman and Morrie Ryskind. From a story by James Kevin McGuinness. Director of photography: Merritt B. Gerstad. Recording director: Douglas Shearer. Art director: Cedric Gibbons. Associate art directors: Ben Carre, Edwin B. Willis. Film editor: William LeVanway. Wardrobe by Dolly Tree. Musical score: Herbert Stothart. "Alone," music by Nacio Herb Brown, lyrics by Arthur Freed. "Cosi-Cosa," music by Kaper and Jurmann, lyrics by Ned Washington. Dances by Chester Hale.

Additional Cast: Rita and Rubin (Dancers), Billy Gilbert (Conductor), Jonathan Hale (Stage manager), Alan Bridge (Immigration inspector), James Wolfe (*Il Trovatore* soloist), Fanchon and Marco (Dancers).

Additional Credits: Produced by Irving G. Thalberg. Assistant director: Lesley Selander. Additional script material: Al Boasberg. "(All I Do the Whole Day Through Is) Dream of You," music Nacio Herb Brown. Production dates: June 14 to August 1935. Released November 15, 1935.

Available: Warner Home Video DVD (2004): ISBN: 0-7907-9031-9. UPC: 0-12569-59692-2.

After the box-office failure of *Duck Soup* (1933), the Marx Brothers left Paramount to sign a contract with Irving G. Thalberg at MGM. No longer the "boy wonder" of producers, Thalberg was now one of many executives on the MGM lot. But he still had his astute feel for what film audiences wanted. He decided to take the Marxes back to their roots, hiring George S. Kaufman and Morrie Ryskind to fashion the equivalent of a Broadway musical comedy in which the Marxes would again supply comic relief to a romantic couple.

Thalberg reasoned that by returning the Marxes to roles as clowns in clown costumes they would no longer appear threatening to moviegoers. In their Paramount films, the Marxes were much closer to the con men, sullen immigrants, and wily hoboes that Depression-era Americans faced every day. In *A Night at the Opera*, they were stripped of menace, of the possibility that they could cheat and rob you. Here, and for the rest of their careers, they would only cheat and rob themselves, and occasionally buffoonish villains.

By deliberately softening the characters the Marxes played, Thalberg turned them into just another comedy act. Graced with a tremendous script and Thalberg's personal supervision, the Marxes made the most of *A Night at the Opera*.

But the film established a formula that the Marxes followed in picture after picture, despite diminishing returns. In Thalberg's defense, the Marxes still found a way to threaten certain proprieties. Their mere appearance was designed to offend, to say nothing of their behavior. As a comparison, update their characters to modern-day movies. Could a screenwriter comfortably work a mute homeless person into a Jim Carrey or Adam Sandler vehicle?

The Marxes themselves had lost none of their personal hostilities, and their practical jokes at the time had a bitter undertone. It was a period when Groucho might sign his autograph "Greta Garbo." Feeling underappreciated at MGM, they barricaded themselves in Thalberg's office, stripped naked, and roasted potatoes in his fireplace. Their gripes worked, as Thalberg, never known as a good judge of comedy, devoted more attention than usual to the production.

Setting the Marxes loose in the world of opera was both a brilliant inspiration and a compromise. Before their targets included viewers themselves, or at least anyone who wanted to make a killing in real estate, thought colleges provided education, and believed in the role government took in society. In *A Night at the Opera*, the Marxes would be lampooning a genre of music and a high-society caste that mainstream moviegoers felt deserved ridicule but knew next to nothing about.

But since this was an MGM film, and MGM was a studio with pretensions to quality, the Marxes could only mock a specific type of opera, that sung by villains. Unlike *Monkey Business* (1931), which made fun of all highbrow music, *A Night at the Opera* devotes considerable screen time to Kitty Carlisle and Allan Jones, who sing bland love songs and a sort of bowdlerized form of opera arranged to be palatable for novice listeners.

Thalberg also decided to allow the brothers to try out their material on the road, another brilliant stroke. In cities like Seattle, Portland, and Salt Lake City, the brothers could simultaneously hone their material and reintroduce themselves to an audience that had rejected *Duck Soup*. The tour not only tightened the pacing of the film's big comic scenes, it gave the Marxes the confidence to play for laughs on the set, having already worked out the timing of their lines on stage.

The Marxes brought their usual hijinks to the production, but the atmosphere at MGM was different than at Paramount. Also, the brothers were fighting for their careers. (Zeppo had dropped out of the act to become an agent; Allan Jones, working in his second film, plays a variant on Zeppo's role as a straight man.) Kitty Carlisle, who later married playwright Moss Hart, remembered a deadly serious Groucho trying out his gags on her on the set first thing in the morning. She saw him as a lonely, insecure comic, despite being intelligent and articulate.

A Night at the Opera was a resounding hit, with critics and moviegoers responding enthusiastically to the new, softer Marxes. According to biographer Joe Adamson, during World War II several minutes of footage were cut from the camera negative to take out references to Italians; an opening montage was also deleted.

Thalberg died before the brothers completed their next film, *A Day at the Races* (1937). They missed his input, and as the years passed they lost more and more control over their pictures. Although he also toured with a band and hosted radio shows, Chico's gambling habit compelled the act to keep making films. Groucho took roles in dead-end projects like *Copacabana* (1947), but seemed to lose interest in movies entirely. (Late in his life, he had a couple of cameos in otherwise forgettable pictures.) He devoted his energy to his writing, penning several books of light comedy, and to *You Bet Your Life*, a long-running and extremely popular quiz show. Happily married, Harpo went on being Harpo, writing an autobiography, recording an album, and appearing on occasional TV shows.

Modern Times

United Artists, 1936. Sound, B&W, 1.37. 83 minutes.

Cast: Principal characters: Charlie Chaplin (A factory worker), Paulette Goddard (A gamin [Ellen Peterson]). Supported by Henry Bergman (A cafe proprietor), Stanley Sandford (Burglar/Big Bill), Chester Conklin (A mechanic), Hank Mann (Burglar), Stanley Blystone (Sheriff Couler), Allan Garcia (President of Electro Steel Corp.), Dick Alexander (A convict), Cecil Reynolds (The chaplain), Myra McKinney (The chaplain's wife), Murdoch McQuarrie, Wilfred Lucas, Ed Le Sainte, Fred Malatesta, Sam Stein, Juana Sutton, Ted Oliver.

Credits: Produced, written, and directed by Charlie Chaplin. Assistant director: Carter De Haven. Photography by Rollie Totheroh, Ira Morgan. Settings by Charles D. Hall, Russell Spencer. Music composed by Charlie Chaplin. Conducted by Alfred Newman. Arranged by Edward Powell, David Raksin. Recorded by Paul Neal, Frank Maher. Use of popular musical numbers by special permission. Western Electric Noiseless Recording.

Additional Cast: Louis Natheaux (Burglar/Addict), Lloyd Ingraham (The governor), John Rand (Crook), Heinie Conklin (A workman).

Additional Credits: Assistant director: Henry Bergman. Edited by Charlie Chaplin. Art director: Danny Hall. Premiered February 5, 1936.

Available: Warner Home Video DVD (2003). UPC: 085393765125.

After the release of *City Lights* (1931), Charlie Chaplin left the United States on a world tour with his brother Sidney. He returned to Los Angeles in late 1933, shaken by the rise of fascism he witnessed in Europe, encouraged by his encounters with natives in the South Seas. He no longer felt compelled to make films, no longer needed money or acclaim. Unlike most of his contemporaries he was in a position to wait until inspiration struck. In an interview with the *New York Times* after the release of the film, Chaplin gave this version for the genesis of *Modern Times*: "I was riding in my car one day and saw a mass of people coming out of a factory, punching time-clocks, and was overwhelmed with the knowledge that the theme note of modern times is mass production. I wondered what would happen to the progress of the mechanical age if one person decided to act like a bull in a china shop."

The main problem Chaplin faced was one that vexed his United Artists partners Mary Pickford and Douglas Fairbanks—and, in fact, all silent stars. Not just how to adjust to sound, but how to adapt his screen persona to a changing culture. Chaplin developed his Little Tramp character out of raw desperation, needing to establish himself at once as an economically viable screen performer. In his early days the Tramp was ruthless, amoral, and ravenous—pure id. It was only later that Chaplin felt comfortable refining the character, giving him a background that implied some breeding and education, as well as ambitions that stretched beyond mere appetite. But the Tramp was still a tramp, fearful and disdainful of authority, with no special labor or social skills and few prospects of succeeding in society.

As his filmmaking technique matured, Chaplin continued to refine the Tramp, making him liberal, sentimental, a friend to the underclass. He took on more responsibilities: a child in *The Kid* (1921), a military mission in *Shoulder Arms* (1918). But hijinks and practical jokes that seemed like a lark in the teens became less amusing in the 1920s. The Tramp was no longer an iconoclast, someone who chose to be carefree; now he was just obstinate and unemployable, someone who had failed to find a path in life. Like the other silent comedians,

Chaplin also had to adjust to his advancing age. Better film stock, lenses, and lighting paradoxically made it harder for him to hide his years.

All these factors helped delay the production of *Modern Times*, which like his other films proceeded in fits and starts. Chaplin at one point intended to use dialogue throughout the film, and wrote a script in which the Tramp and his "gamin" girlfriend talk back and forth, as in the following exchange. Girl: "I'm just pouring the juice of the steak on roast potatoes." Tramp: "On the roast potatoes, uh?" Girl: "It's ready." Tramp: "Already?" Page after page of the same discouraging talk—talk that states what is already seen, talk about anything and everything, talk as pointed as a sermon.

Chaplin's problem wasn't sound, it was dialogue. An expert mime, he could convey what he needed with gestures and intertitles. So although he scheduled recording sessions, as the *Modern Times* project progressed, Chaplin gradually stripped away dialogue and sound. He allowed his character and the gamin (played by his companion at the time, Paulette Goddard)—and, in fact, all of the "little people" in the film—to continue to exist in the silent era. Only the film's villains—technocrats, industrial magnates—were given sound dialogue. Even so, they can only be heard through microphones or on records. When Chaplin's Tramp finally does speak, in the film's closing moments, he uses a nonsense language.

The director was so demanding about the sound for *Modern Times* that both conductor Alfred Newman and composer David Raksin quit. Newman had to be replaced by Edward Powell, but Raksin agreed to return to help Chaplin interpolate songs like "Hallelujah, I'm a Bum," "The Prisoner's Song," and "Titine" into the score. Chaplin's own theme for "Smile" became a pop hit when John Turner and Geoffrey Parsons added lyrics to it in 1954.

Modern Times opens with some facile shots comparing subway commuters and herds of sheep, and finds dark humor in assembly lines and other time-saving devices. But for much of the film Chaplin went back to his past, to material that he had worked with before, at times incorporating bits he admired from other performers. He resurrected a roller skating routine from *The Rink* (1916), gliding so gracefully that you may not even notice the scene's complicated special effects. He slipped in some prison mess-hall gags that wouldn't have been out of place in *The*

Immigrant (1917), and some business in a shanty that could have fit into *The Gold Rush* (1925). He even brought in his old Keystone colleague Chester Conklin for a very polished skit about machinery repairmen. If Chaplin's character had a voice, none of these gags would work.

Chaplin also gave a considerable portion of the story over to Goddard, whom he had met after his world tour. She had been a model, a Ziegfeld Girl (under the stage name "Peaches"), and briefly the wife of a wealthy lumberman before winning a contract at Hal Roach's studio. Chaplin not only bought out her contract, but married her secretly in 1933. She is arguably the most mature and independent of all his post-Keystone screen heroines.

Modern Times is filled with impressive, even audacious moments. At one point a red construction flag drops off the back of a passing truck. The Tramp picks it up, hoping to return it, only to find himself leading a parade of strikers down the street. The camera pulls back on a crane to show riot police arriving to break up the demonstration. In one take Chaplin brings viewers from the harmless slapstick of an earlier age to the brutality of the present.

Before the film opened, Chaplin had to make five cuts to appease Production Code censor Joseph Breen. For timing purposes, Chaplin took out a scene in which the Tramp has a misunderstanding with a traffic cop, and also cut the final verse of his performance of "Titine." (These outtakes can be seen in a digitally restored rerelease.) Some critics at the time saw a resemblance between the assembly line scenes in *Modern Times* and those in *Á nous la liberté* (1929) by René Clair. Films Sonores Tobis sued Chaplin for plagiarism, persisting in the suit until Chaplin's studio paid a modest settlement in 1947.

Chaplin had a different ending in mind when he started *Modern Times*, and actually filmed a version in which Goddard enters a convent after the Tramp is hospitalized. His revision, considerably more open-ended, preserves the possibility of a happier future for the Tramp. This was the Tramp's last screen appearance, and Chaplin's last truly funny film.

Flash Gordon

Jean Rogers as Dale Arden in *Flash Gordon*.

Universal, 1936. Sound, B&W, 1.37. 249 minutes.
Cast: Larry "Buster" Crabbe (Flash Gordon), Jean Rogers (Dale Arden), Priscilla Lawson (Princess Aura), Charles Middleton (Emperor Ming), Frank Shannon (Doctor Zarkov), Richard Alexander (Prince Barin), John Lipson (King Vultan), Theodore Lorch (High priest), Richard Tucker (Professor Gordon), George Cleveland (Professor Hensley), James Pierce (Prince Thun), Duke York Jr. (King Kala), Muriel Goodspeed (Zona), Earl Askam (Officer Torch), House Peters, Jr. (Shark man).

Credits: Directed by Frederick Stephani. Screenplay: Frederick Stephani, George Plympton, Basil Dickey, Ella O'Neill. Based on the newspaper feature entitled *Flash Gordon* [by Alex Raymond] owned and copyrighted by King Features Syndicate. Produced by Henry MacRae. Art director: Ralph Berger. Photography: Jerry Ash, Richard Fryer. Electrical effects: Norman Dewes. Special properties: Elmer A. Johnson. Edited by Saul Goodkind, Edward Todd, Alvin Todd, Louis Sackin. Recorded by R.C.A. Victor "High Fidelity" Sound System. A Henry MacRae production.

Additional Cast: Lane Chandler, Cap Somers, Jerry Frank (Shark men); William Desmond, John Bagni (Hawk men); Glenn Strange, Fred Kohler, Jr. (Robots); Bull Montana, Constantine Romanoff (Monkey men).
Additional Credits: Assistant director: Ray Taylor. Special effects: Kenneth Strickfaden. Theme music: Clifford Vaughan. Production dates: October to December 1935. Opened April 6, 1936.
Other Versions: Sequels *Flash Gordon's Trip to Mars* (1938), *Flash Gordon Conquers the Universe* (1940). Edited into seventy-two-minute feature version entitled *Flash Gordon*. A feature-length *Flash Gordon* (1980) was directed by Mike Hodges.
Available: Image Entertainment DVD *Flash Gordon Space Soldiers* (1996). UPC: 0-14381-8961-2-1.

One of the dirty secrets of the film industry is that its most profitable products are often its most disreputable ones. Although Carl Laemmle resisted efforts by producer Irving Thalberg to upgrade his Universal releases, Laemmle's son, Carl, Jr., went in the opposite direction, pouring money into prestige projects like *All Quiet on the Western Front* (1930) and *Show Boat* (1936). That last film helped hasten the departure of both Laemmles from the studio, which was newly resolute in its intention to concentrate on Westerns, horror films, and serials.

Serials had been around since the early 1910s, at first featuring a series of plucky heroines. They were almost always promoted in connection with newspaper and magazine series, and, in the case of *The Exploits of Elaine* (1913, a Registry title), tie-ins with novels. While the first serials focused on women, men soon took over the genre; everyone from Francis Ford (director John Ford's older brother) and William Desmond to boxer Jack Dempsey starred in them. In the early years of sound films, serials tended to have Western themes, although one, *The Phantom Empire* (1934), managed to combine Western and sci-fi genres with Gene Autry's popular radio broadcasts.

Serials were an early attempt to deal with long-form narratives in film. As such they served as laboratories for writers, directors, and editors who were trying to figure out the best ways to show action and increase tension. For production designers and producers, serials provided training in how to cut costs—to repurpose sets, to save on props and on cast salaries. Serials became so profitable that Universal set up an entire unit devoted to them under Henry MacRae. The studio released over sixty serials before the transition to sound; between 1929 and 1936, another thirty came out with music and dialogue.

With competition from Columbia, Republic, and other studios, Universal faced the real possibility of killing a golden goose unless it could elevate the status of its serials. 1934's *Tailspin Tommy*, based on a comic strip, was so lucrative that the studio made a deal with the King Features Syndicate to develop other serials based on comic strips. A year earlier, King Features had asked cartoonist Alex Raymond to come up with an idea that could compete with *Buck Rogers*, a science-fiction strip. Raymond's first *Flash Gordon* was printed on January 7, 1934. It quickly outgrew *Buck Rogers* in popularity.

Universal made plans to turn *Buck Rogers* and two of Raymond's other strips—*Secret Agent X-9* and *Jungle Jim*—into serials. (The latter two came out in 1937.) To differentiate *Flash Gordon* from other serials, MacRae assigned it a budget of $350,000, three times the normal cost for serials at that time. He still cut corners wherever he could, purchasing Zarkov's rocketship and supporting footage from Fox's 1930 sci-fi film *Just Imagine*. MacRae had music recycled from horror films like *The Invisible Man* (1933) and *Werewolf of London* (1935). Meanwhile, art designer Ralph Berger found new ways to use sets constructed for films like *The Mummy* (1932) and *Bride of Frankenstein* (1935).

MacRae assigned four screenwriters to the project, which would wind up consisting of thirteen chapters. According to film historian Raymond William Stedman, the writers basically copied the first year of Alex Raymond's strip, down to his costume designs. The plot started with an expedition by Flash Gordon, his girlfriend Dale Arden, and mentor Dr. Zarkov to fly an untested spaceship to the planet Mongo, where they would battle the emperor Ming's plan to destroy humanity through deadly rays.

Buster Crabbe, a recent graduate of the University of Southern California and a contract player at Paramount, met MacRae after reading a casting call for *Flash Gordon* in a trade paper. Crabbe had already appeared in the serial *Tarzan the Fearless* (1933), so he knew what he was getting into, although he would later complain that the Flash Gordon role typecast him for the rest of his career. Playing Ming was Charles Middleton, a villain in scores of Westerns, and here, crowned by a bald cap, delightfully imperious.

Raymond's strip was directed toward adults as much as children, with romantic subplots that veered into provocative areas. MacRae pitched the serial to the same audience, as the casting of nineteen-year-old Jean Rogers as Dale Arden and Priscilla Lawson as Princess Aura proved. Stedman, who saw *Flash Gordon* as a child, never forgot how a menacing villain corners Rogers, her heaving chest covered only by a flimsy halter top, at the end of Chapter 5.

Like the strips themselves, the individual serial chapters managed the feat of saying nothing at great length. Cost-cutting extended to using stock footage whenever possible, and repeating scenes from previous episodes. A twenty-minute chapter might include two minutes of repeat or wraparound material. To complete the thirteen chapters in the six weeks MacRae allotted, filming lasted fifteen hours a day, six or seven days a week.

Today the serial's uneven acting, preposterous cliff-hanging situations, absurd sets, and thin

plotting practically define camp. Still, *Flash Gordon* had an outsized impact on movies. Even in subliminal ways, bits and pieces of the serial emerge in unlikely places. The appearance of Ming on his throne, the positioning of his guards, even the style of rocket ships come into play in *Star Wars* (1977), for example.

Flash Gordon was so popular that some theaters showed episodes at night as well as during weekend matinees. In fact, it was Universal's second-highest-grossing film of the year (*Three Smart Girls*, a musical starring Deanna Durbin, was first). Crabbe appeared in two sequels, and also portrayed Buck Rogers in a 1939 serial.

The Plow That Broke the Plains

Poverty as art: depicting the effects of drought in *The Plow That Broke the Plains*.

U.S. Resettlement Administration, 1936. Sound, B&W, 1.37. 25 minutes.
Credits: Written and directed by Pare Lorentz. Photographers: Ralph Steiner, Paul Ivano, Paul Strand, Leo T. Hurwitz. Film editor: Leo Zochling. Music composed by Virgil Thomson. Conducted by Alexander Smallens. Narrator: Thomas Chalmers. Research editor: John Franklin Carter, Jr. Sound technician: Joseph Kane.
Additional Credits: Western Electric Noiseless Recording. Recorded by Eastern Service Studios, New York. Produced by the Office of Information, Resettlement Administration. John Franklin Carter, director. Premiered May 10, 1936.
Available: Image Entertainment DVD *Our Daily Bread and Other Films of the Great Depression* (1999). UPC: 0-14381-4671-2-3.

Coined by British filmmaker and critic John Grierson in 1926, "documentary" at first referred to any nonfiction film. For Pare Lorentz, a documentary was "a factual film which is dramatic," a definition that eliminated most travelogues, newsreels, and educational films. Although they included

staged scenes, Robert Flaherty's features—*Nanook of the North* (1922), *Moana* (1926)—indicated one direction for documentaries. Grierson, Lorentz, and their colleagues wanted to take a new approach, fact-oriented, but more along the lines of commentary than the mere reporting found in newsreels. At the same time, many civil servants were asking the question: How is the government to inform and educate the public when the commercial media choose not to?

Historian Robert L. Snyder traces the first U.S. government–financed film to 1908, a record of an airplane flight by Wright brothers. A 1911 film about the Pima Indian Reservation in Arizona marked the first public release of a government-financed film. Eventually films were released by several branches of the government: the Department of Agriculture, the War Department, the Department of the Interior, and others. Some titles were farmed out to commercial producers, like Edison and the Bray Company. By 1935, more than four hundred government films, most of them of poor quality, were available.

Born in West Virginia in 1905, Pare Lorentz was writing for The New Yorker by 1925. He worked for trade publications, then became the film critic for Judge magazine. He went to Washington, D.C., with six other reporters to write for the Hearst syndicate, but was fired almost immediately. But after writing the text for a book of photographs of President Franklin D. Roosevelt, Lorentz met Secretary of State Henry A. Wallace. This led to introductions to Dr. Rexford Guy Tugwell, a former economics professor at Columbia University, and to John Franklin Carter, the chief of the Office of Information for the Resettlement Administration. Tugwell was looking for subjects for films; Lorentz suggested the Dust Bowl, which he had observed while driving to his wife's family in Des Moines, Iowa.

Formed in 1935, at the height of the Depression, the Resettlement Administration was primarily a relief agency, with a budget of over $300 million. Ron Stryker, the chief of the photographic staff, hired such eminent still photographers as Dorothea Lange and Walker Evans. Lorentz, who had already written about the Dust Bowl for Newsweek, received a budget of $6,000 to make a documentary. Lorentz had to compete with commercial product released by Hollywood, but he couldn't afford actors or a filming stage, and he couldn't record sound on location. These restrictions helped shape what would become The Plow That Broke the Plains.

While the storms that wracked the Midwest and the migration of "Okies" had been covered in newsreels, Lorentz wanted to explain the causes and consequences of the prolonged drought that was threatening to cripple agriculture. He hired cameramen Ralph Steiner (H₂O, 1929), Paul Strand (The Wave, 1936), and Leo Hurwitz (who had shot footage for the WPA and on the "Scottsboro Boys" trials). Without a script, they started shooting in Montana in September 1935. After filming in Wyoming, Colorado, Kansas, and Texas, everyone realized that some sort of script had to be hammered out. Personal conflicts grew so heated

that Steiner later refused to join Frontier Films because it was founded by Strand and Hurwitz.

Lorentz rejected a screenplay written by Strand and Hurwitz because "they wanted it all to be about human greed and how lousy our social system was. And I couldn't see what this had to do with dust storms." Lorentz was more interested in a lyrical approach to the subject, along the lines that Grierson took with his Night Mail (1934). By this time Lorentz was in Hollywood, trying to get stock footage and the use of editing rooms for free. (Director King Vidor eventually helped him.) Assisted by Dorothea Lange, Paul Ivano shot one additional day of material at a migrant camp.

In Night Mail, Grierson built up rhythm and pacing through narration, notably an evocative list of town names intoned magisterially on the soundtrack. Lorentz took the same approach, but wanted to structure The Plow That Broke the Plains around a musical score first. After interviewing a dozen composers, he hired Virgil Thomson on the basis of his knowledge of folk music. The two worked closely together, Thomson timing out songs on the piano while screening footage, Lorentz editing scenes based on the score. Thomson persuaded Alexander Smallens to conduct his score in a studio in Astoria, Queens.

Lorentz wrote the narration after the film had been cut to thirty minutes. Having just read Antoine de Saint-Exupéry's Night Flight, he aimed for a minimum of words, repeated in rhythm to Thomson's music. "My intent," he wrote later, "was to have the pictures tell the story." Breaking with accepted procedures, he did not let Thomas Hardie Chalmers watch the film when he was reciting the narration. Lorentz based some of the voice-over on captions for Dorothea Lange photographs (e.g., "Blown out, baked out and broke").

The entire film ended up costing $19,260. On May 10, 1936, the Museum of Modern Art sponsored a screening at the Mayflower Hotel in Washington, D.C., of The Plow That Broke the Plains, along with Len Lye's Color Box and excerpts from Leni Riefenstahl's Triumph of the Will. On May 28, the film opened at the Rialto Theatre in Times Square, with Florida Special, starring Jack Oakie and Sally Eilers. After playing in three thousand theaters, the film entered the "federal" circuit, where it was shown at Army posts, CCC camps, on Navy vessels, and in Sunday schools and cinema clubs.

Lorentz managed to review his own film, writing that it was "an unusual motion picture which might have been a really great one had the story and the construction been up to the rest of the workmanship." While the camerawork and editing owe a little to the Soviet style of filmmaking (big skies, stalwart workers, machines moving in phalanxes), the movie overall is a surprisingly graceful and involving work that doesn't try to talk down to or mislead its audience. Thomson's score adds enormous gravity to the film, which at the time seemed to herald a new style of documentary. Strand and Hurwitz would collaborate with Lorentz on *The City* (1939), a Registry title; Lorentz's next film, *The River* (1937), is also on the Registry.

Show Boat

Universal, 1936. Sound, B&W, 1.37. 113 minutes.

Cast: Irene Dunne (Magnolia), Allan Jones ([Gaylord] Ravenal), Charles Winninger (Cap'n Andy Hawks), Paul Robeson (Joe), Helen Morgan (Julie [LaVerne]), Helen Westley (Mrs. Parthy Hawks), Queenie Smith (Elly), Sammy White (Frank [Schultz]), Donald Cook (Steve [Baker]), Hattie McDaniel (Queenie), Francis X. Mahoney (Rubber Face [Smith]), Marilyn Knowlden (Kim as a girl), Sunnie O'Dea (Kim at sixteen), Arthur Hohl (Pete [Gavanaugh]), Charles Middleton ([Sheriff] Vallon), J. Farrell McDonald (Windy), Clarence Muse ([Sam,] Janitor).

Credits: Directed by James Whale. Produced by Carl Laemmle, Jr. Stageplay, screenplay, and lyrics by Oscar Hammerstein II. Based on the novel by Edna Ferber. Music by Jerome Kern. Director of photography: John J. Mescall. Special cinematographer: John P. Fulton. Art director: Charles D. Hall. Film editors: Ted Kent, Bernard Burton. Musical director: Victor Baraballe. Dance numbers staged by LeRoy Prinz. Costumes designed by Doris Zinkeisen. Costumes executed by Vera West. Assistant director: Joseph A. McDonough. Technical director: Leighton Brill. Sound supervisor: Gilbert Kurland.

Additional Cast: Patsy Barry (Kim, as a baby), Charles Wilson (Jim Green), Mae Beatty (Landlady), Stanley Fields (Jeb, hillbilly patron), Stanley J. Sandford (Backwoodsman), Tom Ricketts (Minister), Gunnis Davis (Doctor), Harry Barris (Jake, pianist), Elspeth Dudgeon (Mother Superior), E.E. Clive (English theater producer), LeRoy Prinz (Dance director), Eddie Anderson (Onlooker).

Additional Credits: Assistant directors: Harry Mieneke, Joe Torillo. Story: Billie Burke. Contributing writer: Zoë Akins. Additional lyrics: P.G. Wodehouse. Second camera: Alan Jones. Editor supervisor: Maurice Pivar. Musical arrangement: Russell Bennett. Recording of music: Mike McLaughlin. Recording of production: William Hedgecock. Hair: Doris Carico. Makeup: Jack Pierce, Charles Gorman. Wardrobe: Carl Leas. Production dates: December 9, 1935 to March 11, 1936. Released May 14, 1936.

Other Versions: Remade as: *Show Boat* (1951), directed by George Sidney, starring Kathryn Grayson, Ava Gardner, Howard Keel, Joe E. Brown.

Available: MGM/UA Home Video VHS (1990). ISBN: 0-7928-0189-x. UPC: 0-2761-61757-3-1.

One of the landmarks of American musical theater, *Show Boat* was arguably the first Broadway musical to deal seriously with issues like racism and miscegenation. In exposing the inner workings of show business, from touring companies not far removed from medicine shows to vaudeville and "legitimate" theater, it reveled in double meanings, mirrored roles, and the irony of performers posing as performers. Written by Jerome Kern and Oscar Hammerstein, II, *Show Boat* also boasts some of the most enduring melodies and sophisticated lyrics of the twentieth century.

Hammerstein based the play on a 1926 Edna Ferber novel, discarding some of the book's melodramatic turns and concentrating more on the antebellum plot than on the contemporary material. Intent on bringing realistic characters and situations to musical theater, Kern and Hammerstein were breaking new ground. *Show Boat* opened at the Ziegfeld Theatre on December 27, 1927, and ran for 572 performances.

Carl Laemmle at Universal had purchased the film rights to Ferber's novel shortly after it was published, and began a silent production with Laura La Plante and Joseph Schildkraut. When the musical *Show Boat* became a Broadway success, Laemmle inserted some musical numbers (not by Kern and Hammerstein) into his film. By the time the Universal *Show Boat* was ready to be released in 1929, the score from the play had become too firmly entrenched in the cultural landscape for moviegoers to accept different songs. Laemmle was forced to pay Florenz Ziegfeld $100,000 for the rights to the Kern-Hammerstein score. Unwilling to reshoot the entire film, Laemmle inserted some dubbed versions of songs into the silent footage, and also had a sound prologue added, featuring performances by Tess Gardella (billed as "Aunt Jemima") and Helen Morgan, who sang "Can't Help Lovin' Dat Man" and "Bill." (Paul Robeson was cast as Joe in the original production, but dropped out after the opening was delayed. He didn't appear in the part until 1932.)

Encouraged by the box-office success of *Imitation of Life* (1934) and *Bride of Frankenstein* (1935), Carl Laemmle, Jr., Universal's head of production, decided to continue making big-budget, high-profile films that would compete directly with studios like MGM. He okayed a remake of *Show Boat* to be directed by James Whale, and featuring Robeson, Morgan, and Charles Winninger (who originated the role of Cap'n Andy Hawks on Broadway). For the leads, he cast Irene Dunne (also appearing in the studio's *Magnificent Obsession*) and Allan Jones, a newcomer who made a big impression in *A Night at the Opera* (1935).

Laemmle, Jr., also paid for new Kern and Hammerstein songs, including one written especially for Robeson, "Ah Stills Suits Me." Cast and director salaries now approached $400,000, with another $130,000 for sets and wardrobe.

Director James Whale's background was in set decoration and macabre *Frankenstein* adaptations, but he was serious about musical comedy. He elicited strong performances from Irene Dunne and especially from Paul Robeson, while allowing genial hams like Charles Winninger and Helen Westley full rein. But he worked much too slowly, driving up the cost of the film. According to film historian Thomas Schatz, Whale was spending over $16,000 a day on *Show Boat* where his *Bride of Frankenstein* had averaged $8,630 a day. Whale ultimately lost control of the film, forcing editors to make do with footage that didn't match, with poor process work, with performances that needed more rehearsing.

This was Robeson's last Hollywood role before he went to England to make movies. At ease, confident in a way his costar Hattie McQueen couldn't match, he imparts a dignity and intelligence to a character some might have found demeaning. Robeson understood the layers of the film, could see how Irene Dunne wearing blackface and imitating a "darky" cakewalk was commenting on racism, not condoning it. He was forever associated with "Ol' Man River," and Whale's staging of the song was respectful to the performer, but also inventive. Whale started with a 360-degree crane shot around Robeson, who was seated on a dock pier, ending with a tight closeup of the actor's face as he intoned the lyrics. German expressionism and Russian constructivism creep in when Whale cuts to an artificial cotton field in forced perspective, and to blacks pushing bales of cotton up a silhouetted diagonal.

"Bill" is staged more simply, but just as carefully. This was also Helen Morgan's last Hollywood feature, after a career in which her alcoholism and problems with gangsters were open knowledge with her admirers. Morgan's florid, almost sobbing singing style has been out of fashion for some seventy-five years, as has her method of heavily emoting her lyrics. Whale had to find a way to convey her close connection to the song's narrative without letting her sink into bathos. He constructed a sequence of twenty-seven shots, starting with a pan across a large theater set before narrowing in on the three main characters in the scene: Julie LaVerne (Morgan), a mixed-blood singer at the end of her career; Jim Green (Charles Wilson), a hard-bitten impresario; and Jake (real-life songwriter Harry Barris), a saloon pianist. Whale had six main takes of Morgan performing the song to work with; he alternated those with medium shots of the three and reaction shots for the first verse, then cut away to onlookers in the theater—dancers, bartenders, janitors—listening to Julie sing the second verse. He saved the extreme close ups of Morgan for the most intimate lyrics, but relied on a medium shot of the singer for most of the performance. These captured the hand gestures and facial expressions that Morgan used as part of her act.

By framing the song so carefully Whale could showcase how powerful Morgan's performance was. He even helped shape the emotional responses of filmgoers, by cutting away to the subdued onlookers during the entire second verse, for example. On the other hand, Morgan was lip-synching to a prerecorded music track, and Whale simply didn't have the patience or the authority to coax her acting to match the level of her vocals. In her close-ups, she doesn't come close to her recorded breathing. (Whale also had to fudge one of the cuts, requiring an audible edit in the soundtrack.) In the cutaways, some of the extras are listless, not paying attention. These imperfections wouldn't have been allowed on an Astaire set at RKO, or in an MGM or Warners musical. But the younger Laemmle was stuck. He had already put the studio into hock to pay for *Show Boat*. As shooting dragged on into March, he and his father were ousted by East Coast interests from the company the senior Laemmle founded.

The film was finally released in May 1936 at a cost of over $1.2 million. It received positive reviews and did well at the box office, but it was too late to save the Laemmles—or Whale, for that matter; this was his last big-budget project. MGM acquired the rights to the film in 1946, when it financed a Broadway revival of the play prior to starting its own film version in 1950. The complicated rights situation has made difficult to see the Universal *Show Boat*. For all its flaws, it is by far the best film adaptation of the property.

Fury

Metro-Goldwyn-Mayer, 1936. Sound, B&W, 1.37. 92 minutes.

Cast: Sylvia Sidney (Katherine Grant), Spencer Tracy (Joe Wilson), Walter Abel (District Attorney), Bruce Cabot (Kirby Dawson), Edward Ellis (Sheriff), Walter Brennan ("Bugs" Meyer), Frank Albertson (Charlie [Wilson]), George Walcott (Tom [Wilson]), Arthur Stone (Durkin), Morgan Wallace (Fred Garrett), George Chandler (Milton Jackson), Roger Gray (Stranger), Edwin Maxwell (Vickery), Howard Hickman (Governor), Jonathan Hale (Defense Attorney), Leila Bennett (Edna Hooper), Esther Dale (Mrs. Whipple), Helen Flint (Franchette).

Credits: Directed by Fritz Lang. Screen Play by Bartlett Cormack and Fritz Lang. Based on a story by Norman Krasna. Produced by Joseph L. Mankiewicz. Musical Score by Franz Waxman. Recording director: Douglas Shearer. Art director: Cedric Gibbons. Associate art directors: William A. Horning, Edwin B. Willis. Wardrobe by Dolly Tree. Photographed by Joseph Ruttenberg. Film editor: Frank Sullivan.

Additional Cast: Clarence Kolb (Mr. Pippin), Harry Hayden (Jailer), Edward La Saint (Doctor), Ben Hall (Goofy); Murdock MacQuarrie, Al Herman (Dawson's friends); Esther Muir, Raymond Hatton (Hector), Ward Bond (Theater patron), Minerva Urecal (Fanny).

Additional Credits: Production dates: January 20 to April 25, 1936. Released May 29, 1936.

Available: Warner Home Video DVD (2005): ISBN 0-7907-9215-X. UPC: 0-12569-69042-4.

Few directors in Hollywood could claim a background as exciting as Fritz Lang's. The son of a middle-class architect in Vienna, Lang dropped out of school in 1910 to roam the world, supporting himself by drawing. He was exhibiting his paintings in Paris when World War I was declared. Joining the Austrian Army, he was sent to the front, where he was wounded three times. He began writing for films when he was hospitalized for a year (losing the use of one eye). Hired by director Joe May, he wrote scripts and acted before directing his first film in 1919. A year later he formed a partnership with screenwriter Thea von Harbou, eventually marrying her in 1924.

Lang's German films include some of the masterpieces of world cinema. He concentrated on cynical, paranoid adventures and mysteries (*Die Spinnen/The Spiders*; the *Dr. Mabuse* series, etc.), and on lavish, big-budget adaptations like *Die Nibelungen*, a two-part version of the same legend used by Richard Wagner in *Der Ring des Nibelungen*. In *Metropolis* (1927) he presented a delirious vision of the future as a mechanistic world divided into haves and have-nots. Two years later, in *Frau im Mond/The Woman in the Moon*, he invented the countdown still used today before rocket launches. *M* (1931), his first sound film, depicted a citywide manhunt for a serial killer played by Peter Lorre. *Das Testament des Dr. Mabuse* (1933) was banned by the Nazis, but it brought Lang an offer from Dr. Joseph Goebbels to supervise the making of Nazi films.

Lang fled Germany that night, leaving behind a fortune and a soon-to-be ex-wife. After directing a film in France, he went to the United States, where he was hired by David O. Selznick for a one-picture deal at MGM. Lang was not happy in his new position. It took him almost two years to find a project the studio would accept, time he used to learn English by reading comic strips. He was given a four-page outline by studio executive Eddie Mannix called "Mob Rule" by Norman Krasna. Working with MGM staff writer Bartlett Cormack, Lang combined the outline with a real-life lynching that occurred in San Jose, California, two years previously. The story would show how prejudice and bigotry could turn ordinary people into a violent mob.

In early drafts of the script, *Fury* concerned a lawyer mistakenly arrested for a murder. Citizens in the small town, roused to action by gossip and lies, attack the jail where he is being held, determined to lynch him. Lang later claimed that he wanted the lawyer to be guilty, a twist too challenging for the industry to accept. (Six years later, Lamar Trotti and William Wellman would have to finesse a similar situation in *The Ox-Bow Incident*.) Lang also took credit for changing the lawyer to Joe Wilson, an auto mechanic played by Spencer Tracy. Speaking years later, the director said he wanted the protagonist to be a working man who couldn't express himself. Citing comic strips, he commented that everything happens to "'John Doe'—you and me, not the wealthy."

By all accounts a demanding perfectionist, Lang is never described as a "nice" person, and stories about his tantrums and tirades are widespread. How he even managed to get *Fury* made at MGM is something of a mystery. Selznick by this time had left the studio to form his own production company. Louis B. Mayer had hired Sam Katz from Paramount to head a musical production unit. Katz in turn hired screenwriter Joseph L. Mankiewicz, who wanted to direct but who ended up producing. None seemed likely to back a lynching melodrama.

And *Fury* does not offer easy answers. Lang and his colleagues establish their story carefully, introducing sweethearts Joe Allen and Katherine Grant (played by Sylvia Sidney, the prototypical

Depression heroine) as ordinary people, giving Joe stricter morals than his brothers, and taking pains to explain why Joe doesn't understand the potential danger following his arrest for a kidnapping and murder. Lang documents the growing hysteria surrounding Joe's imprisonment with the same cool paranoia he brought to *M* and his *Dr. Mabuse* films, at the same time singling out lawyers and the media for criticism decades before films like *Ace in the Hole*. There are some notable cracks in *Fury's* logic, especially concerning Joe's alibi, but the first hour of the movie shows a small-town America that had never been seen on the screen before. (To viewers today, it's all the more startling to see character actors who normally portrayed kind-hearted small-towners in films by Frank Capra and Preston Sturges playing bloodthirsty vigilantes.) *Fury* derails in its second half as Joe concocts a far-fetched revenge scheme. Until then, the story's inexorable drive makes it among the more powerful movies of its period.

Manckiewicz would later take credit for almost every aspect of *Fury*, from helping Krasna rewrite his outline to hiring screenwriter Bart Cormack to casting Spencer Tracy, a newcomer to MGM, as the star. Mankiewicz was also partially responsible for spreading stories about Lang's behavior on the set, including fighting with Tracy over when to break for lunch and with cinematographer Joseph Ruttenberg over lighting. Mankiewicz's biography describes an incident in which Lang injured actor Bruce Cabot with a smoke pot and an attempt by disgruntled stagehands to kill the director by dropping lights on him.

Whatever the truth, Lang refused to shake hands with Mankiewicz after the film's opening, and wouldn't work at MGM again until 1955's *Moonfleet*. Although it received positive reviews, *Fury* was not a popular picture. (Filmed for about $600,000, it eventually showed a profit of close to $250,000.) It did not look like a typical MGM movie, either in its cast or its production design, and certainly not in its moral. The studio generally avoided message dramas, and wouldn't directly address social issues again until 1949's *Intruder in the Dust*.

Swing Time

"Bojangles of Harlem," Fred Astaire's tribute to Bill Robinson, from *Swing Time*.

RKO, 1936. Sound, B&W, 1.37. 103 minutes.

Cast: Fred Astaire (John "Lucky" Garnett), Ginger Rogers (Penelope "Penny" Carrol), Victor Moore (Everett "Pop" Cardetti), Helen Broderick (Mabel Anderson), Eric Blore (Gordon), Betty Furness (Margaret Watson), Georges Metaxa (Ricardo "Ricky" Romero).

Credits: Directed by George Stevens. Music by Jerome Kern. Lyrics by Dorothy Fields. Screen play by Howard Lindsay and Allan Scott. From a story by Erwin Gelsey. Musical director: Nathaniel Shilkret. Art director: Van Nest Polglase. Associate art director: Carroll Clark. "Silver Sandal" set and "Bojangles" costumes by John Harkrider. Photographed by David Abel. Photographic effects by Vernon Walker. Set dressing by Darrell Silvera. Dance director: Hermes Pan. Gowns by Bernard Newman. Recorded by Hugh McDowell, Jr. Sound cutter: George Marsh. Edited by Henry Berman. Recorded by RCA Victor System. A Radio Pictures presentation of a Pandro S. Berman production.

Additional Cast: Landers Stevens (Judge Watson), John Harrington (Raymond), Pierre Watkin (Simpson), Abe Reynolds (Schmidt), Gerald Hamer (Eric Lacanistram), Edgar Dearing (Policeman); Harry Bowen, Harry Bernard (Stagehands); Frank Jenks (Red); Jack Good, Donald Kerr, Ted O'Shea, Frank Edmunds, Bill Brande (Dancers); Ralph Byrd (Hotel clerk), Charles Hall (Taxi driver), Jean Perry (Roulette dealer), Olin Francis (Muggsy), Floyd Shackelford (Romero's butler), Ferdinand Munier (Minister), Joey Ray (Announcer), Fern Emmett (Watsons' maid), Jack Rice (Wedding guest), Frank Mills, Bob O'Connor, Tom Curran, Martin Chichy, Sam Lufkin, Frank Hammond, D.A. McDonald, Sailor Vincent.

Additional Credits: Orchestrations: Edward Powell. Rehearsal pianist: Hal Borne. "Waltz in Swing Time" by Robert Russell Bennett. Assistant director: Argyle Nelson. Dialogue director: Ben Holmes. Screenwriting by Dorothy Yost, Ben Holmes, Anthony Veiller, Rian James. Produced by Pandro S. Berman. Second camera: Joe Biroc. Hair stylist: Louise Sloan. Makeup: Louis Hippe. Production dates: May 11 to July 31, 1936. Premiered in New York City on August 27, 1936.

Awards: Oscar for Best Music—Original Song ("The Way You Look Tonight").

Available: Warner Home Video DVD (2005). ISBN: 0-7806-3988-X. UPC: 0-53939-65712-8.

The Fred Astaire/Ginger Rogers musicals were so profitable for RKO that the studio couldn't afford not to make them. However, both Fred and Ginger began to chafe at the demands of turning out two new films every year. While the budgets increased, the formula didn't vary much. Both leads generally played dancers or entertainers romantically attached to other people. Sometimes the settings were posh, as in *Top Hat*'s Hollywood versions of London and Venice. Almost all of the team's previous films took place abroad; *Follow the Fleet*, the sole exception, ended with a casino number that was pure Monte Carlo.

Swing Time was conceived along populist lines, as a way of connecting Astaire to a less elite, more working-class audience. It became a valentine to New York City, glamorous despite its Depression settings. *Swing Time* makes passing references to picket lines and work stoppages, but its New York is pure fantasy. Gleaming snow falls on quaint gazebos in rustic parks, nightclubs are enormous playgrounds for the wealthy. Despite the modernist trappings, it's still a city similar to the one in which both Astaire and Rogers matured as artists only a few years before. (Among the several in-jokes in the script: Helen Broderick takes Astaire to a broken-down inn called the New Amsterdam, the name of the theater where they both performed in *The Band Wagon* a decade earlier.)

Despite new settings, the Astaire/Rogers formula still applied. They would annoy each other at first, he would pursue her fitfully, they would realize that they loved each other when they danced, and complications would keep them apart until the last reel. Much of the supporting cast was the same, with vaudeville veteran Victor Moore taking over from *Top Hat*'s Edward Everett Horton as Astaire's sidekick. Returning creative personnel included Astaire's choreography partner Hermes Pan, producer Pandro S. Berman, screenwriter Allan Scott, and art director Van Nest Polglase. If so much was the same, what makes *Swing Time* among the finest musicals ever filmed?

Some credit should go to director George Stevens. The one-time cinematographer for Laurel and Hardy had developed his own series of comedy shorts, "The Boy Friends," before working for Universal and then RKO. Directors had been glorified traffic cops on previous Astaire/Rogers films: the input from choreographers and songwriters determined how much of the plots would be played, and even the actors considered the comic relief skits to be filler. But Stevens understood the value of slowing scenes down until genuine emotions emerged from the contrived patter. In *Alice Adams* (1935) he juggled comedy and drama through mood and atmosphere. He would do the same here, giving *Swing Time* a depth that other musicals of the time lacked. Stevens was probably responsible for playing up Astaire's resemblance to Stan Laurel, most noticeably in the song "A Fine Romance." He also took the idea of spontaneous laughter at the film's climax from Laurel and Hardy, such as their *Leave 'Em Laughing* (1928).

Composer Jerome Kern and lyricist Dorothy Fields also deserve praise. Their score proved astonishingly rich, both melodically and verbally, with some of the most memorable songs in Astaire's entire career. The dances draw out every emotional nuance of Kern's wistful tunes, just as Fields' lyrics showcase the hope and vulnerability of the leads. "Pick Yourself Up" was a witty rejoinder to the Depression; "A Fine Romance" ached with rue and loss. As critic Arlene Croce pointed out, "The songs are more tightly interwoven with the script—and with each other—than in any other Astaire-Rogers film." Not only are the lyrics self-referential, numbers like "A Fine Romance" and "The Way You Look Tonight" are sung in counterpoint, a strategy so satisfying as to seem magical.

The routines devised by Astaire and Pan include some of the best dancing ever filmed. There may be no better tap duet on celluloid than "Pick Yourself Up," two minutes of energy and invention that is faultlessly executed and ridiculously engaging. Astaire's big set piece, "Bojangles of Harlem," makes use of chorus lines (dismissing Busby Berkeley in a few easy glides); adds double exposures and trick photography so he can dance with and against his own shadows; and throws in a syncopated finish that casually takes apart and reassembles the tune. It is also performed in blackface, the only such number in Astaire's oeuvre, and has consequently come under attack in some circles. It is difficult to detect any offensive intent in the routine, which is clearly meant to honor dancer Bill "Bojangles" Robinson. It is the best showcase in the film for Astaire's sheer musicality, his ability to animate every nook and cranny of a melody.

The pivotal duet in *Swing Time*, "Never Gonna Dance," takes place in a deserted nightclub flanked by two staircases. The routine incorporates both "The Way You Look Tonight" and the "Waltz in Swing Time," as well as several pauses and half-starts that build into a dance suffused with loss. It ends with a crane shot that follows Astaire and Rogers up the facing staircases. It reputedly required forty-seven takes to achieve, and left Rogers' feet bleeding at the end of the day.

Also critical to the success of the film was Hal Borne, Astaire's rehearsal pianist, who played the doctored and vamped piano in "Bojangles"; Nathaniel Shilkret, a talented bandleader who conducted the RKO orchestra; and Robert Russell Bennett, who pulled together the "Waltz in Swing Time" from assorted Kern themes.

The script came from "Portrait of John Garnett," a story RKO owned. Pandro S. Berman assigned Howard Lindsay, who directed Astaire's *Gay Divorce* on Broadway, to write a draft. Allan Scott rewrote this version, working with Stevens after filming started. "The old cycle kept rolling on," was how Astaire described the project in his autobiography, *Steps in Time*. "It was difficult for any of us to make a decision about breaking up the format." *Swing Time* took longer to shoot than the team's previous films, and required considerably more fiddling in postproduction. One number, "It's All in the Cards," was cut out completely, as were some scenes with Astaire and Moore.

Astaire was somewhat dismissive of the movie after its release. Although it finished in the box-office top ten for the year, it was not as profitable as *Top Hat* or *Follow the Fleet*. The team's next film, *Shall We Dance* (1937), with a score by George and Ira Gershwin, made even less money. After the team split up in 1939, both Astaire and Rogers would go on to long and distinguished careers. George Stevens is next represented in the Registry by *Gunga Din* (1939); Astaire, by *The Band Wagon* (1953).

My Man Godfrey

Universal, 1936. Sound, B&W, 1.37. 93 minutes.
Cast: William Powell (Godfrey), Carole Lombard (Irene Bullock), Alice Brady (Angelica Bullock), Gail Patrick (Cornelia Bullock), Jean Dixon (Molly), Eugene Pallette (Alexander Bullock), Alan Mowbray (Tommy Gray), Mischa Auer (Carlo), Pat Flaherty (Mike), Robert Light (Faithful George).
Credits: Directed by Gregory La Cava. Screen play by Morrie Ryskind, Eric Hatch. Based on the novel by Eric Hatch. Executive producer: Charles R. Rogers. Photographer: Ted Tetzlaff. Musical director: Charles Previn. Special effects: John P. Fulton. Sound supervisor: Homer G. Tasker. Film editors: Ted Russell, Kent Schoengarth. Miss Lombard's gowns by Travis Banton. Art director: Charles D. Hall. Western Electric Noiseless Recording. A Universal presentation.
Additional Cast: Grady Sutton (Van Rumple), Selmer Jackson (Guest), Franklin Pangborn (Master of ceremonies); Edward Gargan, James Flavin (Detectives); Robert Perry (Doorman); Grace Fields, Katherine Perry, Harley Wood, David Horsley, Phillip Merrick (Socialites); Ernie Adams (Forgotten man).
Additional Credits: Produced by Gregory La Cava. Screenwriters: Robert Presnell, Zoë Akins. Wardrobe: Brymer. Assistant directors: Scott R. Beal, Fred Frank, Nate Slott. Production dates: April 15 to May 27, 1936; reshoots in June 1936. Released September 6, 1936.
Other Versions: Remade in 1957, directed by Henry Koster, starring David Niven and June Allyson.
Available: Criterion Collection DVD (2001). UPC: 7-15515-01192-1.

Although critics trace its antecedents back to Mozart and Shakespeare, screwball comedy was a distinctively American form that flourished during the height of the Depression in the 1930s. It almost invariably involved broad comedy in highbrow settings, and often concerned the clash of "old money" with modern-day economic realities. Old money usually took a drubbing in screwball comedies, which extolled common-sense solutions to problems like unemployment and romance across class lines. Many credit Frank Capra with popularizing the form with *It Happened One Night* (1934), although every Hollywood studio had been developing projects along similar lines.

Universal was slow to join the party, in part because it derived so much of its revenue from monsters and cowboys, in part because Carl Laemmle, Jr., made enough disastrous choices to be removed, along with his father, from management. In the aftermath of their departure, budgets for Universal features were slashed. *Show Boat* (1936) had cost over $1.2 million; the original budget for *My Man Godfrey* was $586,000. The script, based on a novel by Eric Hatch called *1101 Park Avenue* (it was later retitled *My Man Godfrey*), was a topical farce about a homeless man who becomes butler to a family of wealthy eccentrics. Hatch wrote a screenplay from his book, but the script was really the work of Morrie Ryskind and Gregory La Cava.

Born in 1895 in New York City, Ryskind, the son of Russian Jewish immigrants, showed early promise as a writer. He assisted playwright George S. Kaufman before being expelled from Columbia for a satirical editorial, then became Kaufman's partner on *Cocoanuts* and *Animal Crackers*, groundbreaking plays starring the Marx Brothers that were adopted into hit movies. Ryskind won a Pulitzer for his work on *Of Thee I Sing* with the Gershwin brothers, then wrote *A Night at the Opera* (1935) with Kaufman. He preferred revising scripts until the moment of shooting, and sought opinions from as many people as possible about his material.

Ryskind's working methods coincided neatly with La Cava's. Born in Towanda, Pennsylvania, in 1892, La Cava was a newspaper cartoonist before entering the film industry as an animator on "Mutt and Jeff" cartoons, a training ground for artists like Walter Lantz. La Cava became head of cartoons for the Hearst company, then switched to live-action comedies. By the end of the silent era, he was directing features starring W.C. Fields and Richard Dix on Paramount's New York stages. His sound films could feel heavy-handed, as producers reined in his habit of improvising on the set.

Moving to California, he worked first for Paramount, then for First National, where he was fired after the failure of *Saturday's Children* in 1929. He burned bridges at several other studios, notably Twentieth Century, before turning independent. La Cava approached Universal with the package for *My Man Godfrey*, and he insisted on William Powell for the lead role. Powell, under contract with MGM at the time, accepted the offer with one condition: his ex-wife Carole Lombard had to be his costar.

One of the best-loved stars of the golden age of Hollywood, Lombard was born Jane Alice Peters in Fort Wayne, Indiana, in 1908. She made her first screen appearance at the age of twelve; four years later, she signed a contract with Fox that ended when she was in a disfiguring car crash. In 1927 she signed with Mack Sennett, becoming expert in slapstick comedy in a series of two-reelers. She became a bona fide star playing opposite John Barrymore in *Twentieth Century* (1934), a screwball

precursor directed by Howard Hawks. Despite her great beauty, Lombard projected a down-to-earth quality that endeared her to moviegoers.

The younger Laemmle had hoped to cast contract player Constance Bennett; with Lombard on board, the budget for *My Man Godfrey* threatened to balloon out of control. But as film historian Thomas Schatz pointed out, La Cava was an unusually frugal filmmaker. He shot quickly and confidently, eschewing multiple angles and unnecessary master shots. A director like John Stahl, one of the stalwarts of the Universal staff, could shoot 500,000 feet of film for a project like *Magnificent Obsession* (1935); La Cava shot 110,000 for *My Man Godfrey*.

The film was an unexpected hit, the first to be nominated for Oscars in all four acting categories. Universal, now under the control of J. Cheever Cowdin, a perfect screwball name, was happy with the revenue. But Cowdin had already shifted the studio's focus to cheaper productions, such as serials like *Secret Agent X-9* (1937), which could be completed on a quarter of *Godfrey*'s budget.

Many of the filmmakers who followed La Cava learned the wrong lessons from *My Mad Godfrey*. They thought screwball comedies meant oddball characters engaged in frivolous pursuits in wealthy settings. Hollywood comedies from the late 1930s are filled with madcap heiresses, aristocrats disguised as servants, trivial chases—*The Mad Miss Manton* (1938), for example, starring Henry Fonda and Barbara Stanwyck. But *My Man Godfrey* wasn't about how eccentric its characters were; it was about their struggle for happiness, a struggle impeded by social forces. The film couldn't be pigeonholed easily—it wasn't exactly detailing a class war, but more the realization that wealth ultimately provided little satisfaction. It was in service to society that an individual found meaning in life.

La Cava's next film, *Stage Door* (1937), dealt with the same issues in starker terms. Based on the Edna Ferber–George S. Kaufman hit play, and adapted by Morrie Ryskind, the film followed the travails of largely unemployed actresses in a boarding house. As in *My Man Godfrey*, the characters were more interested in work than in money, in getting the chance to fulfill their destinies. Unemployed, the actresses felt worthless, no better than the prostitutes some of them would become, either suicidal or deluded, forced to do their acting for their roommates.

What's remarkable about La Cava's films is that even at their most wrongheaded they still project a warm, optimistic view of humanity. Not the saccharine bromides of Andy Hardy movies—La Cava was more clearheaded than that. But even in the midst of the emotional torment that makes up most of a film like *Primrose Path* (1940), a bowdlerized account of a girl forced into prostitution, La Cava and his characters never despair. They believe, however foolishly, that fate will give them their chance.

Socialite Rene Bullock (Carole Lombard) has a crush on her butler (William Powell) in *My Man Godfrey*.

Dodsworth

Samuel Goldwyn, 1936. Sound, B&W, 1.37. 101 minutes.

Cast: Walter Huston (Sam Dodsworth), Ruth Chatterton (Fran Dodsworth), Paul Lukas (Arnold Iselin), Mary Astor (Edith Cortright), David Niven (Captain Lockert), Gregory Gaye (Kurt von Obersdorf), Mme. Maria Ouspenskaya (Baroness von Obersdorf), Odette Myrtil (Renée De Penable), Spring Byington (Matey Pearson), Harlan Briggs (Tubby Pearson), Kathryn Marlowe (Emily), John Howard Payne (Harry).

Credits: Directed by Samuel Goldwyn. Based upon the novel written by Sinclair Lewis and dramatized by Sidney Howard. As produced for the stage by Max Gordon. Screen play by Sidney Howard. Produced by Samuel Goldwyn. Art direction: Richard Day. Musical direction: Alfred Newman. Photography: Rudolph Maté. Costumes: Omar Kiam. Film editor: Daniel Mandell. Sound recordist: Oscar Lagerstrom. Western Electric Wide Range Noiseless Recording. A Samuel Goldwyn presentation.

Additional Cast: Beatrice Maude (Mary, the maid), Charles Halton (Hazzard), Gino Corrado (American Express clerk), Ines Palange (Edith's housekeeper), William Wyler (Violinist).

Additional Credits: Special effects: Ray Binger. Opened in New York City on September 18, 1936. Distributed by United Artists.

Awards: Oscar for Best Art Direction (Richard Day).

Available: MGM Home Entertainment DVD (2001). ISBN: 0-7928-5161-7. UPC: 0-27616-86937-1.

Sinclair Lewis started writing *Dodsworth* in 1927, having already won and rejected a Pulitzer Prize for *Arrowsmith*. *Dodsworth*, about a middle-aged industrialist from the Midwest who travels to Europe with his wife, had some parallels with the author's life. After achieving remarkable commercial success with novels like *Main Street* and *Babbitt*, he became increasingly dissatisfied. He traveled to Europe with his wife Grace Hegger in 1925; it was the beginning of the end of their marriage.

Published in 1929, *Dodsworth* is dedicated to Dorothy Thompson, a journalist who married Lewis in 1928 after his divorce from Hegger. A year later, Lewis accepted the first Nobel Prize for Literature awarded to an American. John Ford directed a version of *Arrowsmith* for producer Samuel Goldwyn in 1931. It was written by playwright Sidney Howard, who tipped Goldwyn off about Lewis's new novel, saying that the rights were available for $20,000. The producer was reputed to reply, "You can't sell a middle-age love story. Who the hell cares about a middle-age love story? Nobody. Not even middle-age people are interested in a middle-age love story."

Undeterred, Howard, himself a Pulitzer Prize winner in 1925, wrote a stage version of *Dodsworth* starring Walter Huston and Fay Bainter that opened on Broadway to glowing reviews. When Goldwyn went to purchase the rights, Howard's price was now $160,000. The producer assigned William Wyler to direct the project.

Ruth Chatterton confronts her husband (played by Walter Huston) in *Dodsworth*.

Born in Alsace, then a part of Germany, in 1902, Wyler was studying the violin when he was offered a job by Carl Laemmle, a distant cousin and head of Universal. Wyler worked his way up from the bottom, translating press releases, handling props, editing scripts, casting, and finally assistant directing. From there he was promoted to directing low-budget "Blue Blazes" Westerns. After more than forty of these, he earned the right to make well-regarded dramas like *Counsellor-at-Law* (1933), based on an Elmer Rice play and starring John Barrymore. Wyler started working for Goldwyn in 1936, the year he divorced actress Margaret Sullavan. The producer was so happy with *These Three* (1936) that he offered Wyler both *Dodsworth* and *Dead End*, another stage hit.

Goldwyn fell extremely ill during a sea voyage to Europe while Wyler was working with Howard on the script for *Dodsworth*. The entire project was in jeopardy, although the producer made a full recovery. "He had written a good script," Wyler said of Howard. "I wanted to loosen it up a little more." In reality, the director needed to soften the depiction of Fran Dodsworth, a flighty wife who has a fling with a European aristocrat. Wyler needed to "make Fran less of a bitch at the outset," especially since she was being played by Ruth Chatterton. A noted beauty in silent films, Chatterton hated playing "a woman trying to hold onto her youth," as Mary Astor put it.

Astor, appearing as a sympathetic widow who befriends Sam Dodsworth, had her own problems to cope with—notably, a child custody trial that exposed her affair with playwright George

S. Kaufman. Both Goldwyn and Wyler defended Astor for the duration of what was one of the most notorious divorce scandals of the 1930s.

Since Walter Huston had a penalty clause in his stage contract, no one else could realistically be considered for the part of Sam Dodsworth. But few actors had both the technique and the insight that Huston brought to the project. The actor had returned to Broadway after a run of indifferent films in California. "I was certainly a better actor after my five years in Hollywood. I had learned to be natural—never to exaggerate," he said. Wyler was delighted with his performance. "No acting ruses, no acting devices," he commented, "just the convincing power that comes from complete understanding of a role."

Huston's Dodsworth is one of the landmark performances of the 1930s, fully fleshed out, with complications and contradictions intact. A deeply sympathetic man despite his flaws, Dodsworth is also increasingly attuned to his wife's limitations, and to the emptiness of his own life. Wyler, financed by Goldwyn, surrounded Huston with the sort of support an actor dreams of, paying close attention to every possible detail of the film. He sent a film crew to Europe, giving detailed instructions about the footage he wanted. He drove actors like David Niven insane by insisting on repeated takes of scenes. Wyler spent an afternoon filming a scrap of paper blowing along a sidewalk. (He can also be seen playing the violin in an orchestra about an hour into the movie.)

The result was one of the most intelligent, if rueful, depictions of marriage ever committed to film. Cruel at times, it is also as honest as Hollywood in general—and Goldwyn, in particular—could get. "Do you ever think you'll get me out of your blood?" Chatterton warns when Huston threatens to walk out on her. Wyler shoots this long, intricate, and crucial scene first in calm wide shots, then in steadily tighter close-ups that echo the characters' jagged emotions. Since it takes place aboard a passenger liner, the actors are also surrounded by dozens of constantly changing extras. It's tour de force

direction, but give Goldwyn credit for mounting it so expansively.

Even though the novel's ending had been changed significantly, Sinclair Lewis was delighted, wiring the producer, "I do not see how a better motion picture could have been made from both the play and the novel." Although the film received seven Oscar nominations, Goldwyn complained, "I lost my goddamn shirt. I'm not saying it wasn't a fine picture. It was a *great* picture, but nobody wanted to see it. In *droves*."

Popeye the Sailor Meets Sindbad the Sailor

Immortal enemies Popeye and Bluto (here performing as Sindbad) in their two-reel extravaganza, *Popeye the Sailor Meets Sindbad the Sailor.*

Paramount, 1936. Sound, color, 1.37. 16 minutes.
Cast: Voices of Jack Mercer (Popeye, the spinach eating sailor), Mae Questel (Olive Oyl, the irresistible damsel), Gus Wickie (Sindbad the Sailor, "the most remarkable fellow"). Other characters—J. Wellington Wimpy, the hamburger fiend; Boola, the two headed giant; Rokh, the mighty eagle—voiced by various Fleischer employees.
Credits: Directed by Dave Fleischer. Produced by Max Fleischer. Animation: Willard Bowsky, George Germanetti, Edward Nolan. Music and lyrics: Sammy Timberg, Bob Rothberg, Sammy Lerner. Western Electric Noiseless Recording.
Additional Credits: Writers for Popeye in the 1930s included Jack Mercer, Bill Turner, Joe Stoltz, Ed Watkins, Dave Fleischer, Seymour Kneitel, Warren Foster, Ted Pierce, Izzy Sparber. Released November 27, 1936.
Available: Warner Home Video DVD *Popeye the Sailor 1933–1938* (2007). UPC: 012569797963.

Popeye first appeared in *Thimble Theater*, a comic strip started in 1919 by E.C. (Elzie Crisler) Segar. Born in 1894, Segar was a musician and film projectionist before he decided to become a cartoonist. Moving to Chicago, he sold two strips, one about Charlie Chaplin, before switching to

King Features Syndicate in New York. The original characters in *Thimble Theater* were Olive Oyl, her brother Castor Oyl, and her boyfriend Ham Gravy. Popeye arrived when Olive needed to sail to Dice Island. He wore a cap and smoked a corncob pipe, and usually squinted shut his right eye. (Some historians think that Segar based Popeye on Frank "Rocky" Fiegle, a short, obstreperous man who worked in a bar in Chester, Illinois, Segar's birthplace.) Within a few months he had so completely taken over the strip that Segar renamed it after him.

With money to spare after the success of Betty Boop cartoons, Fleischer Studios licensed Popeye's character from King Features. Betty introduced Popeye to the screen in 1933 in *Popeye the Sailor Man*. The character was a sensation, so popular that Paramount (the Fleischers' distributor) eventually released about one short a month. Since the Fleischers were located in New York, the Popeye cartoons tended to have a grittier, more urban feel than cartoons from Disney or Warners. The animation was not as rich or full: often only one or two elements moved in a shot. But the artists employed by the Fleischers for Popeye were encouraged to expand animation beyond physical reality into the same giddy surrealism that graced Betty Boop's cartoons. In addition, Popeye scripts were unusually literate, filled with puns and double entendres. This was partly due to the fact that the dialogue was added after the drawing was completed; voice actors like Jack Mercer were free to ad lib as timing permitted. That's why Popeye and his nemesis Bluto mumble so much without moving their mouths.

Music was an important element on screen; Popeye's theme song, "I'm Popeye the Sailor Man," figured into every one of the cartoons. It was written by Sammy Lerner, one of the staff musicians at the studio. Another musician was Sammy Timberg, who had been working in New York as a songwriter on Rudy Vallee shorts. Once a vaudevillian, Timberg would go on to compose songs for Superman and Betty Boop cartoons, as well as pop tunes like "Help Yourself to My Heart," covered by Frank Sinatra. Timberg later became a talent agent, and died in 1992 at the age of eighty-nine. He wrote Sindbad's song in this cartoon, a prime example of a melody so indelible it can become irritating.

Bluto, the character who "plays" Sindbad, had appeared only once in the print comic strip. He became a recurring figure in the cartoons, an oversized villain whose nefarious schemes usually had an element of genuine sadism. In the same way, it was the Fleischers who made spinach such an important weapon in Popeye's arsenal; the vegetable was rarely mentioned by Segar. The Fleischers incorporated other characters from the strip into their cartoons, including Wimpy, whose insatiable appetite for hamburgers became one of the series' most enduring gags, and Poopdeck Pappy, Popeye's father. Alice the Goon may have helped popularize the use of "goon" in slang.

By 1936, Popeye had brought so much revenue into the studio that the Fleischers began plans for a feature-length cartoon. As a sort of trial run, they okayed Popeye Color Specials, Technicolor cartoons that would be about twice as long as the regular black-and-whites. *Popeye the Sailor*

Meets Sindbad the Sailor was the first. It incorporated another Fleischer invention, 3-D sets. Artists would construct elaborate backgrounds—mountains, caves, walls, and the like—out of solid materials, building them on a large turntable that could revolve at any desired speed. When characters moved through a scene, the backgrounds, with real surfaces and shadows, moved with them.

Popeye was originally voiced by William "Billy" Costello, a vaudevillian whose stage name was Red Pepper Sam. According to animation historian Jerry Berg, Costello based his signature growling, guttural voice in part on a rival, Cliff Edwards. (Also known as "Ukulele Ike," Edwards covered a number of pop songs, including "Singin' in the Rain"; appeared in dozens of movies; and hosted a radio show. He also played Jiminy Cricket in 1940's *Pinocchio*.) By 1935, Costello proved too difficult to work with, and was replaced by in-betweener and future writer Jack Mercer.

Olive Oyl has been voiced by many actresses, most notably by Mae Questel (who also did Betty Boop for a time). Questel later said that she based Olive's voice in part on ZaSu Pitts. Questel does Olive's voice here; she could also fill in as Popeye when Mercer wasn't available. Questel continued to appear in films until 1989, and voiced Betty Boop in *Who Framed Roger Rabbit* (1988). She died ten years later. Bluto was voiced by Gus Wickie in this film, and by other actors throughout the run of the series.

Popeye the Sailor Meets Sindbad the Sailor was a phenomenal hit when it was released in November 1936. Some theaters even ran the cartoon as the featured attraction. The Fleischers were encouraged enough to schedule two more color specials, *Popeye the Sailor Meets Ali Baba's Forty Thieves* (1937) and *Aladdin and His Wonderful Lamp* (1939). They also decided to move their studio to Miami, Florida, in response to a strike and the threat of unionization. Jack Mercer made the move with them, although Questel elected to remain in New York. But after the tepid reaction to the Fleischer feature cartoons *Gulliver's Travels* (1939) and *Mr. Bug Goes to Town* (1941), Paramount took over the studio, renaming it Famous Studios. The Fleischers were soon forced out of the company they founded.

Between 1933 and 1957, 234 Popeye cartoons were released to theaters. Paramount then sold them to Associated Artists Productions (AAP), who replaced most of the opening titles and syndicated them to television. Popeye proved so successful with a new generation of children that King Features made 220 more cartoons. In 1970, the Hanna-Barbera studio offered *The All New Popeye Hour* (aka *The Continuing Adventures of Popeye*); *Popeye & Son* came out in 1987. Robert Altman directed a singularly poor live-action *Popeye*, starring Robin Williams and Shelley Duvall, in 1980.

One end result of the various sales and syndications is that the original Popeye cartoons for years were almost impossible to see. Thirty-four of the films, including *Popeye the Sailor Meets Sindbad the Sailor*, are in the public domain, and are available in generally poor condition on numerous DVDs and Internet websites. While various entities have owned the cartoon titles, King Features Syndicate (now a part of the Hearst Entertainment and Syndication Group) retained rights to the characters, who are the company's "intellectual property." In June 2006, it reached an agreement with Warner Home Video to restore all of the cartoons for DVD release in 2007. This release is a wonderful opportunity for a new generation of children to be enthralled by one of the smartest, funniest, and most lovable of all cartoon characters.

Rose Hobart

Joseph Cornell, 1936. Sound, B&W with tones, 1.37. 19 minutes.
Credits: Constructed by Joseph Cornell.
Additional Credits: Made up primarily of footage from the Universal feature *East Of Borneo* (1931), starring Rose Hobart, Charles Bickford, George Renavent, Lupita Tovar, Noble Johnson. Directed by George Melford. Director of photography: George Robinson. Music for Cornell's construction by Nesto Amaral and his Orchestra.
Available: Image Entertainment DVD *Treasures from American Film Archives* (2000). UPC: 0-14381-9706-2-3.

Born in Nyack, New York, in 1903, Joseph Cornell attended Phillips Academy in Andover, Massachusetts. However, the death of his father in 1917 forced his mother to move to a less wealthy neighborhood in Flushing, Queens. Cornell worked as a salesman and textile designer while helping care for his partially paralyzed brother Robert, who was confined to a wheelchair. In 1929, the family moved to Utopia Parkway, and Cornell lived in this same house until his death in 1972.

Best known as a collagist, Cornell collected everything from magazines and records to watch springs, photographs, souvenir ephemera, and toys. Unable to draw, he used these objects in boxes he constructed in his basement and then stored in an unplugged refrigerator. Starting in 1929, he began assembling paper collages, which he displayed in a show at the Julien Levy Gallery in 1932.

Cornell also collected a wide variety 16mm film: newsreels, novelty films, comedies, and movies by the Lumière brothers, D.W. Griffith, Georges Méliès, and Louis Feuillade. *Rose Hobart* has a few bits and pieces from this collection, but was primarily made up of shots culled from *East of Borneo*, a 1931 Universal feature directed by George Melford and photographed by George Robinson.

In *Rose Hobart*, named after the star of the film, Cornell reduced the plot of *East of Borneo* to a series of erotic situations and gazes, turning an improbable jungle melodrama into a story of thwarted desire. Time and space no longer mattered, or made sense; characters remained ciphers; and the "story" became whatever viewers thought about the people and settings they were seeing on the screen.

Rose Hobart was screened at the Julien Levy Gallery starting in December 1936. Cornell projected it at 16 frames per second instead of 24, slowing down the motion. To further increase the film's dreamlike qualities, he showed it through a deep-blue filter, approximating the tones used for nighttime scenes in silent films. In the background he played songs like "Forte Allegre" and "Belem Bayonne" from *Holiday in Brazil* by Nesto Amaral and his Orchestra.

In his memoir, gallery owner Julien Levy wrote that after a screening of *Rose Hobart* in 1937, surrealist artist Salvador Dali furiously kicked over the projector, complaining, "It isn't that I could say Cornell stole my idea. I never wrote it or told anyone, but it is as *if* he had stolen it." According to Levy, Cornell was aghast, and was reluctant to show his film again. But in a 1980 *New York Times* article, Donald Windham wrote that Cornell's embargo on screenings was a "myth fabricated by the New York art world to cover up its long indifference to his cinema." Windham agreed that Cornell did not spend much time on film after the Levy show, but by 1948 was showing his works to anyone who would watch them, from Gypsy Rose Lee to Montgomery Clift.

Among his viewers were experimental filmmakers like Stan Brakhage, Ken Jacobs, Jack Smith, and Larry Jordan. Cornell would collaborate with some of them in the 1950s, refashioning footage that Brakhage shot, for example. But Cornell was not interested in making films in the traditional sense; he found cameras too technical to operate. As biographer Deborah Solomon pointed out, Cornell had similar fears about ballet, one of his other obsessions. The actual experience of attending a ballet performance was too overwhelming for him; he preferred to stay at home and fantasize about it.

Solomon cites Cornell's influence on artists as diverse as Robert Rauschenberg and Octavio Paz, but there is another side to Cornell that has discomfited many writers. James Fenton felt that Cornell feared the subconscious, and wrote that even his most devoted admirers "must sometimes turn away from a certain shadow box wishing they had not seen it, or experience acute anxiety in seeing one of his short films." (Fenton noted that Audrey Hepburn returned the box Cornell made for her.) Su Friedrich complained about critics who "pick sufficiently obscure artists and praise them so insistently, so uncritically, so vaguely, for so long, that people were bound to give them a place in the pantheon of the art gods."

No one can say with certainty how intent Cornell was upon disturbing "spatial and temporal continuities," or whether he wanted "to divest the images of narrative causality and to imbue them with paradoxes and contradictions," or even if he felt he was turning *East of Borneo* into "a rich tincture of feminine angst and unrequited desire." To some there will always be the nagging suspicion that he was simply isolating and repeating the "good parts" from one of his celluloid fantasies.

Rose Hobart's career was marked by several reversals, which she detailed in an engaging memoir, *A Steady Digression to a Fixed Point* (1994). "I've been accused of being everything from a Communist to a lesbian," she wrote in the introduction, "but I was only interested in making things better for people." She depicted Frank Borzage as an unyielding tyrant who refused to rehearse her for the thirty-six takes her death scene required in *Liliom* (1930), her film debut. Hobart had roles in several movies in the 1930s and '40s, and was also named to the board of directors of the Screen Actors Guild. Although she signed an affidavit in 1947 stating that she was not a member of the Communist Party, she refused to answer questions before a Congressional hearing the following year. *Red Channels* magazine placed her at a Communist rally in Mexico City the same night she was giving birth. In November, 1949 she was named a Communist by Lee J. Cobb and subsequently blacklisted. Her last film was *Bride of Vengeance* (1949); some twenty years later she was able to find minor parts on television. She died in 2000.

Master Hands

Jam Handy Productions for The Chevrolet Motor Company, 1936. Sound, B&W, 1.37. 33 minutes.

Credits: Photography: Gordon Avil. Orchestral Score: Samuel Benavie. Rendition: Detroit Philharmonic Orchestra. Film Editing: Vincent Herman. Produced by The Jam Handy Organization.

Additional Credits: Executive producer: Henry Jamison Handy.

Available: The Internet Archive (*www.archive.org*). Flicker Alley DVD *Saved from the Flames* (2008). ISBN: 1893967-34-4. UPC: 6-17311-67349-8.

Released during an agonizing period for American labor, *Master Hands* depicts work in a Chevrolet assembly plant in Flint, Michigan, as a heroic endeavor. Produced by the Jam Handy Organization, possibly for a shareholder meeting, it was later used as a morale-booster during World War II and then as a training film. While it cannot be said to have inspired Charlie Chaplin, portions of the film do dovetail nicely with his *Modern Times* (1936). Just a year later, a similar setting would be the site of a controversial "Memorial Day massacre" covered in the *Republic Steel Strike Riots Newsreel Footage*, also a Registry title.

The Jam Handy Organization was formed by Henry Jamison Handy, an Olympic swimmer who was suspended from the University of Michigan after writing a tongue-in-cheek article about one of his professors. Hired by the *Chicago Tribune*, Handy became fascinated by advertising techniques. He composed lectures that used slides and slogans to energize salesmen, then hired animators to turn his illustrations into cartoons. By 1916, he was working at The Bray Studio, the pioneering New York animation company that at one time or another employed Max Fleischer, Gregory La Cava, and Walter Lantz. A large proportion of Bray's revenue came from sponsored films, financed by the government, the auto industry, and other clients. Handy was

This crane shot in *Master Hands* evokes one in *Westinghouse Works* some thirty years earlier.

named head of a new Bray branch office covering Chicago and Detroit.

When the company faced financial setbacks, Handy won a breach of contract suit in 1921, and used part of his settlement to form Diamond Productions in Chicago. This evolved into the Jam Handy Organization, with offices in Detroit, three blocks away from the new General Motors headquarters. The auto giant became one of Jam Handy's most important clients, and as General Motors grew, more and more money became available for promotion and advertising. *General Motors Around the World* (1927), filmed by Handy's Newspapers Film Corporation, boasted footage from twenty-five countries and five continents. It was screened for journalists and potential investors, and was covered in the *New York Times*.

Famed for his eccentric practices, such as eschewing business desks and pockets on his suits, Handy created a line of "Direct Mass Selling" films in 1935, the heyday of Detroit filmmaking. Direct Mass Selling grew to over a hundred titles, including commercial-quality cartoons directed by Max Fleischer, among others, and automobile safety films. Many of these have been preserved by archivist Rick Prelinger.

Prelinger noted a marked European influence on the Jam Handy cartoons, and this same influence is obvious in *Master Hands*. Married to a Germanic soundtrack composed by Samuel Benavie, the images in *Master Hands* assume an importance and gravity not usually associated with assembly line work. The subject matter and even individual camera set-ups are strikingly similar to the *Westinghouse Works* series (1904), but Handy's film goes further to portray work in a Chevrolet plant as a clanging, clashing battle to turn raw iron and steel into automobiles. Cinematographer Gordon Avil, who would go on to a long career in film and on television, was familiar with the work of industrial still photographers like Margaret Bourke-White. Many of his compositions have the same striking lighting and geometric designs.

Only three years later, in films like *The City*, similar footage would be used to condemn factory work as physically dangerous and economically enslaving. General Motors, meanwhile, turned its attention to the general public by ordering films that promoted its research, importance to American business, safety record, and other issues. As Prelinger and other writers have pointed out, this had something to do with the fact that the corporation had been forced to recognize the United Auto Workers union. A film like *From Dawn to Sunset* (1937) took as its goal showing how important GM workers were for local businesses.

The Jam Handy Organization continued producing films well into the 1960s. Handy, who died in 1983 at the age of ninety-seven, estimated that his company released over 7,000 titles. Among these were training movies and commercials for Campbell's Soup, Monsanto, Bristol-Myers, the United Way, and Pittsburgh Paints. In 1971, the Jam Handy Organization's movie production operations were spun off into The Bill Sandy

Company, which at first concentrated on the auto industry but later accumulated several Fortune 100 clients. This company became the Sandy Corporation in 1985, and was acquired in 1996 by Automatic Data Processing. In January 2007,

Sandy Corporation was acquired by General Physics Corporation, described on its website as "a global provider of technical training, training administration solutions, and other performance-improvement services."

Hindenburg Disaster Newsreel Footage

Various, 1937. Silent, B&W, 1.37. Most versions run between 2 and 5 minutes.

Credits: Cinematography by Al Gold, Larry Kenney, Deon De Titta (Fox Movietone News); James A. Seeley ([Hearst's] News of the Day); Bill Deekes (Pathé News); Al Mingalone (Paramount). Sound by Addison Tice (Fox Movietone News). Editing by Max Klein (Paramount).

Available: Pathé footage and footage licensed by Eugene Castle for his home-market newsreel *News Parade* can be viewed at the Internet Archive (*www.archive.org*). The Pathé newsreel can be licensed from ITN Source (*www.itnsourc.com*). Home movie footage of the *Hindenburg* in 1936 can be found on the Image Entertainment DVD *Treasures from American Film Archives* (2000). UPC: 0-14381-9706-2-3.

Much like today's televised news, newsreels in the 1930s were geared toward three subjects: celebrities, sports, and disasters. Most of the former consisted of staged photo opportunities featuring movie stars, politicians, and other familiar faces. Apart from sports, it was hard to find a story that could be told in purely visual terms, just as it was hard to plan for a natural disaster. Newsreel footage of floods, earthquakes, fires, and the like was filmed on assignment, usually after the fact, or else submitted by freelancers lucky enough to capture a newsworthy situation.

One popular spot to catch celebrities was as they boarded or disembarked from ocean liners. Air terminals were a distant second, at least in the 1930s, when air travel often veered into the "disaster" category. Nevertheless, dirigible flights were routinely covered by the five major producers of newsreels, and on May 6, 1937, crews from each of the five were sent to Lakehurst, New Jersey, to film the landing of the *Hindenburg*.

Count Ferdinand von Zeppelin is credited with the idea for a rigid airship assembled around a frame of compartments holding a lighter-than-air gas like hydrogen or helium. The first practical dirigible flew on July 2, 1901. Zeppelin formed a passenger airline with Hugo Eckener in 1909. Airships were used during World War I for reconnaissance and bombing missions. After the war larger airships were built, with passenger promenades and restaurants. The *Graf Zeppelin* became the first airship to circumnavigate the globe. Construction on the *Hindenburg*, which was similar in style and

size to the two *Zeppelin* models, began in May 1933. The dirigible was finished in March 1936, and made its first flight two months later.

The *Hindenburg* made ten transatlantic flights in 1936, some to South America, some to Lakehurst (the closest landing spot to New York City). It carried seventy-two passengers, over thirty crew members, and mail, cargo, and livestock. Transatlantic tickets cost $400 one way and $700 round trip, and all flights were fully booked. The *Hindenburg*, after all, was faster and quieter than steamships, and had a perfect safety record. The rest of the industry wasn't as fortunate. In 1933, for example, a total of seventy-five people died in the crash of the U.S.S. *Akron* off the coast of New Jersey.

During the winter of 1936, workers added ten more cabins to the *Hindenburg*; the ship could carry more weight because it was filled with hydrogen, which was more buoyant—and dangerous—than helium. Eighteen flights to Lakehurst were scheduled during the 1937 season. The first began on May 3, when the *Hindenburg* departed Frankfurt. Persistent headwinds delayed its crossing. When the ship reached Maine and then Boston, it was almost twelve hours late. The *Hindenburg* flew over Manhattan around 4:00 p.m., its passing filmed by cameramen in airplanes. A storm delayed its landing at Lakehurst until about half past seven.

John Iannaccone, a member of the landing crew, remembered workers grabbing the two landing lines dropped from the ship. "Six men were ordered up into the bow section" to distribute weight. "Suddenly there was a very strong shock going through the ship and I could see people running away." A fire started four minutes after the landing lines were dropped. It exploded through the entire ship in only thirty-two seconds. Thirty-six people died, including thirteen passengers and one member of the landing crew. Remarkably, sixty-two people on the ship survived, most by jumping to the ground.

The newsreel cameramen were positioned close to each other. (The Universal cinematographer had left earlier to attend a Broadway play.) Consequently, the surviving footage is roughly similar. It was all sensational, a record of destruction so vivid and awful that it helped hasten the end of commercial dirigible flights. Film historian Raymond Fielding has identified Al Gold's footage as the version most often seen today. In an article, Gold wrote that Larry Kennedy and his assistant Deon De Titta "had gotten many of the marvelous shots you saw on the screen in the Movietone News special. I was the only one given screen credit but many of the great shots in our release were photographed by Kennedy." In a hearing about the disaster, Gold testified, "I could hear only the grinding of my camera. Whatever other sounds were around the blazing pile never came to my ken."

Broadcast announcer Herbert Morrison of WLS in Chicago was recording the *Hindenburg* landing with his engineer Charles Nelson when the ship burst into flames. His was the first on-site account of a full-scale disaster to be heard by the public. The NBC radio network reversed its prohibition of prerecorded programs to broadcast Morrison's words that night. His emotional reporting—"It's broken into flames! It's flashing . . . flashing! It's flashing terrible . . . oh, oh, oh! . . . It's burst into flames! . . . Oh my, this is terrible, oh my, get out of the way please! It is burning, bursting into flames and is falling. . . . Oh! This is one of the worst catastrophes in the world! . . . Oh! It's a terrible sight. . . . Oh! And the humanity and all the passengers. . . !"—is now inextricably tied to the newsreel footage.

Republic Steel Strike Newsreel Footage

Paramount, 1937. Sound, B&W, 1.37. 20 minutes.
Credits: Photographed by Orlando Lippert. Produced by Paramount News, A.J. Richard, editor.
Available: The National Archives.

By one count, ten thousand strikes involving over five million workers took place between 1933 and 1937. Freelance newsreel cameramen quickly learned that footage of picket lines was valuable. For example, a dockworkers' strike in San Francisco in early 1936 was covered by all the major newsreel organizations, including Fox Movietone, Pathé, and Paramount.

Several laws passed as a part of the New Deal encouraged union organizing in the early 1930s. In June 1936 the Steelworkers Organizing Committee (SWOC) began in Pittsburgh, Pennsylvania, with Philip Murray as director. Less than a year later, the SWOC, representing a half-million workers, signed a collective bargaining agreement with Carnegie-Illinois and other subsidiaries of U.S. Steel. This first agreement established a $5-a-day wage, an eight-hour day, and paid overtime.

Independent foundries, often referred to as "Little Steel," resisted labor's attempts to organize. These companies included Bethlehem Steel, Youngstown Sheet and Tube Company, American Rolling Mills, and Republic Steel. Founded in 1899, by the 1930s Republic Steel consisted of several plants scattered across Ohio, Indiana, and Illinois. Tom Girdler, its chairman, was vehemently antiunion. As the SWOC

targeted "Little Steel," Girdler hired strikebreakers and built up arsenals of rifles, tear gas, and other weapons in the Republic plants.

The SWOC called a strike for May 26, 1937. Some 85,000 workers took part. Most plants, including Youngstown Sheet and Tube, closed down completely, willing to wait until the strikers' benefits ran out. But the Republic Steel South Chicago plant remained open. That Thursday about half of the plant's 2,200 employees walked out, gathering outside the plant gate on Burley Avenue. Captain James Mooney of the Chicago Police Department ordered over two hundred policemen to push the strikers away from the gate. Twenty-three workers were arrested.

SWOC organizers headquartered in Sam's Place, a closed tavern some six blocks away. Assured by Chicago Mayor Edward Kelly that peaceful picketing would be allowed, on Friday, May 27, the strikers attempted to march to the plant gate. They were turned back. That evening three hundred strikers tried again. This time fighting broke out, and the strikers were forced to retreat again. SWOC District Director Nick Fontecchio announced a mass meeting on Sunday, May 30. Mooney, warned that the strikers intended to invade the plant, called for 264 policemen to assemble that same day.

Some 1,500 strikers from other plants and their supporters arrived at the SWOC headquarters

Sunday morning. After speeches, about 1,000 people marched across a field toward the gate at 117th Street and Burley Avenue.

Although several newspaper and magazine reporters and still photographers covered the event, Orlando Lippert was the only newsreel photographer present. (Other newsreel companies chose to cover the nearby Indianapolis 500.) Lippert planted his camera on a sound truck outside the plant gates. He photographed the handful of picketers there, as well as policemen milling about by the side of the road. Facing north, he filmed the advancing marchers, occasionally recording brief bursts of sound. The strikers converged on a double line of policemen at the edge of the field. Lippert later testified that he was changing lenses when violence erupted.

Hurriedly catching up, Lippert panned his camera across a wave of policemen surging into the body of the marchers. Rifles and tear gas canisters explode on the soundtrack. Lippert pans from right to left and then back, echoing the chaos and fear of unrestrained conflict. As the workers try to retreat, Lippert films policemen swinging at them with billy clubs.

In the aftermath of the violence, Lippert switched lenses at times to provide a closer look at individuals. In this footage, policemen prowl over the field, poking at the grass with their billy clubs. Strikers lie prone on the ground, or sit dazed, heads in hands. The police have to carry some strikers to paddy wagons. At one point they push an elderly man who is grasping the back of his head into a van.

Policemen carry a motionless striker in a white shirt toward the camera. As they place him on the ground, streaks of blood are evident across the back of his shirt. Later two men worriedly check his pulse. Finally he is carried to a makeshift ambulance. Lippert took six shots of the incident, obviously concerned about what had happened. The cameraman then panned across the field until his film ran out.

Press accounts initially portrayed the strikers as an angry mob. *New York Times* headlines claimed that "Strikers Fight Police" and "Steel Mob Halted." But gradually different details emerged. Four strikers were killed by gunfire that day; six more subsequently died. Seven of the ten dead had been shot in the back. Thirty others were wounded by gunfire; over sixty strikers required emergency medical treatment. (Thirty-five policemen reported minor wounds; three of them spent the night in a hospital.)

In early June the Paramount newsreel staff began to work on Lippert's footage, preparing the opening title: "Conflict between police and strikers near the South Chicago plant of the Republic Steel Co., Memorial Day, 1937." But by the end of the month Paul Anderson of the *St. Louis Post-Dispatch* was reporting that the film had been suppressed. In an article entitled "Frightful Film," *Time* magazine quoted Paramount News Editor A.J. Richard explaining the decision not to distribute the film by saying, "We show to a public gathered in groups averaging 1,000 or more and therefore subject to crowd hysteria."

Anderson's article about the film was due to his friendship with Wisconsin Senator Robert La Follette, head of a Congressional Civil Liberties Committee. La Follette subpoenaed the film for hearings in July about what was now being referred to as the Memorial Day Massacre. Several police testified at the hearings, as did victims of the beatings. On the last day of the hearings, La Follette screened the film for an audience of about seven hundred. First came Lippert's unedited footage. The senator then had the footage shown at silent speed (a version of slow motion), freezing the action a dozen times to highlight evidence of police brutality.

La Follette's committee concluded that the police were wrong to prevent marchers from picketing the Republic plant, and that they used excessive and illegal force against the strikers. But the violence continued, in Youngstown, Massillon, and Cleveland. A total of sixteen workers were killed outside Republic plants. The SWOC was forced to call off the strike, turning to the National Labor Relations Board for help instead. Girdler resigned under pressure, but "Little Steel" did not sign union contracts until 1942.

After the hearings, Paramount released the newsreel footage to theaters (it was immediately banned in Chicago). But as a *Time* reporter noted, the film seemed anticlimactic. The reporter complained that there were no close-ups, and that Lippert shot only from behind police lines. The article concluded, "Audiences last week did not begin to hiss, boo and shout until they had seen close-ups of the dead, dying and wounded."

The footage La Follette used in his hearings is available for viewing at the National Archives, but the actual Paramount newsreel is harder to locate. The Paramount newsreel library was sold to Gruen in 2003. Gruen went bankrupt in 2004, and it's unclear who presently holds the rights to the film.

Lippert continued to work in newsreels and sponsored films. He shares a cinematography credit with George Hoover on *Singing Wheels* (1937), an instructional short about the trucking industry sponsored by the Motor Truck Committee of the Automobile Manufacturers Association.

The Life of Emile Zola

Warner Bros., 1937. Sound, B&W, 1.37. 116 minutes.
Cast: Paul Muni (Emile [Émile] Zola), Gale Sondergaard (Lucie Dreyfus), Joseph Schildkraut (Capt. Alfred Dreyfus), Gloria Holden (Alexandrine Zola), Donald Crisp (Maitre Labori), Erin O'Brien Moore (Nana), John Litel (Charpentier), Henry O'Neill (Colonel Picquart), Morris Carnovsky (Anatole France), Louis Calhern (Major Dort), Ralph Morgan (Commander of Paris), Robert Barrat (Major Walsin-Esterhazy), Vladimir Sokoloff (Paul Cezanne), Grant Mitchell (Georges Clemenceau), Harry Davenport (Chief of Staff), Robert Warwick (Major Henry), Charles Richman (M. Delagorgue), Gilbert Emery (Minister of War), Walter Kingsford (Colonel Sandherr), Paul Everton (Assistant Chief of Staff), Montagu Love (M. Cavaignac), Frank Sheridan (M. Van Cassell), Lumsden Hare (Mr. Richards), Marcia Mae Jones (Helen Richards), Florence Roberts (Madame Zola), Dickie Moore (Pierre Dreyfus), Rolla Gourvitch (Jeanne Dreyfus).
Credits: Directed by William Dieterle. Screen play by Norman Reilly Raine, Heinz Herald, Geza Herczeg. Story by Heinz Herald and Geza Herczeg. Source material: Matthew Josephson's *Zola and His Time*. Music by Max Steiner. Dialogue director: Irving Rapper. Photography: Tony Gaudio. Film editor: Warren Low. Art director: Anton Grot. Costumes by Milo Anderson, Ali Hubert. Makeup artist: Perc Westmore. Musical director: Leo F. Forbstein.
Additional Cast includes: Frank Mayo (General Pelleux), Iphigenie Castiglioni (Mme. Charpentier), Bonita Granville (Violet), Ferdinand Gottschalk (La Rue), Irving Pichel (Mathieu Dreyfus).
Additional Credits: Produced by Hal Wallis, Henry Blanke. Production dates: February to May 10, 1937. Premiered in New York City on August 11, 1937.
Awards: Oscars for Best Picture, Writing—Screenplay, Actor in a Supporting Role (Schildkraut).
Available: Warner Home Video VHS (2000). ISBN: 0-7907-4752-9. UPC: 0-12569-52393-2. Warner Home Video DVD (2005): UPC 012569692527.

In the mid-1930s, most Warner Brothers films fell into three categories: musicals, generally with Dick Powell; action films, predominately starring James Cagney; and "prestige" films. These latter were an attempt by Warners to burnish its brand name with expensive, high-profile movies that would get good reviews. In earlier years George Arliss would appear in biographies like *Disraeli*. In 1935, Warners released a star-studded version of *A Midsummer Night's Dream* codirected by German émigré Max Reinhardt. That same year Paul Muni won a Best Actor Oscar in *The Story of Louis Pasteur*, which also won for Best Screenplay and Original Story. It was directed by William Dieterle, a former actor who had worked with Reinhardt in Berlin and who codirected *A Midsummer Night's Dream* with him.

Born in Ludwigshafen, Germany, in 1893, Dieterle moved to the United States in 1930, having directed and starred in several German films. He became one of a half-dozen or so staff directors at Warners, earning $1,000 a week to churn out five or six films a year. Dieterle had little input into his assignments other than to adhere to their strict schedules and budgets. The real creative control over Warners films lay in the hands of production executive Hal Wallis and, in the case of the biographies, supervisor Henry Blanke. Another German, Blanke had worked on Fritz Lang's *Metropolis* before joining Warners, first in Berlin and then overseeing the studio's foreign productions in Hollywood.

In 1936, literary agent Heinz Herald pitched a story about author Émile Zola's defense of Alfred Dreyfus. Working with another German, Geza Herczeg, Herald submitted a treatment that tried to shape the story as another *Louis Pasteur*. Wallis got Jack Warner to agree to pay for a script, which was finished in November and then rewritten by staff writer Norman Reilly Raine. By February 1937, Blanke had a "final" script ready.

Wallis doubled the *Pasteur* budget, but argued with Blanke over several elements in the film. For one thing, this was the third film in a row in which Muni was playing a bearded Frenchman, and Wallis did not want the expensive actor's face obscured by makeup. Blanke threatened to quit over the film's costumes, finally winning approval to hire designer Ali Hubert. Blanke also insisted on replacing Ben Weldon, who was cast as Paul Cézanne, with Vladimir Sokoloff, even though it meant reshooting the film's opening scenes.

When Dieterle finished shooting on May 10, 1937, the film still didn't have a name. *The Life of Emile Zola* was a curious choice, as Zola's life is barely alluded to in the story. The first half-hour speeds through Zola's early years, showing him rooming with Cézanne in a freezing Parisian garret, interviewing a prostitute for his breakthrough novel *Nana*, then adjusting to fame as the titles of his books pass by in a montage. Muni portrays the author as a sort of idiot savant, stammering in the face of wealth, mumbling to himself in the rain, squeezing his eyes in concentration, oblivious to his saintly wife whenever inspiration strikes. In the classic Warners style, things keep happening: Nana no sooner opens her autographed copy of Zola's book than soldiers march off to Germany, resulting in *The Downfall*, another novel that angers French authorities.

All this is true to a point, but the film basically ignores Zola's style of naturalism or theories on heredity or work as a playwright. Instead, the picture focuses on the case of Alfred Dreyfus, played by Joseph Schildkraut. The son of Rudolph Schildkraut, a famous star in Berlin and on Broadway, Joseph had also worked with Reinhardt before moving to Broadway plays and films, mostly in Hollywood.

The script does a relatively good job explaining the Dreyfus Affair in the simplest terms possible, even though the word "Jew" is never uttered in the film. A French Army captain, Dreyfus was accused in 1894 of giving military secrets to the Germans. Convicted, he was stripped of his rank and sentenced to Devil's Island. His family—represented here by his wife Lucie (played by Gale Sondergaard)—campaigned for his innocence, aided by Lt. Col. Marie Georges Picquart (Henry O'Neill), who accused Major Walsin-Esterhazy (Robert Barrat) of being the real traitor. When Esterhazy was acquitted in a court-martial in 1898, the Dreyfus campaign seemed doomed.

The film presents these facts from Zola's point of view, as the author resists various efforts to get him involved in the campaign to exonerate Dreyfus. Periodically we see Dreyfus himself, withering away in a concrete cell, his hair the saintly white of a religious hermit. Or the French military conspirators, including an exuberantly oily Louis Calhern in the same sort of role he played in *Duck Soup*. When Zola agrees to take on the case, he writes his famous *J'Accuse!*—the 1898 article that leads to his arrest for libel. Sporting the world's only Scots-French accent, Donald Crisp arrives to defend him.

Zola's trial justifiably occupies the center of the film, and it is handled in a manner intended to rouse audiences against French authorities and their injustices. Not that the film absolves the French public, which is usually seen as a snarling mob rioting outside the courtroom or burning Zola's books—a gesture that could not have failed to evoke the political climate in contemporary Germany. The studio may not have been willing to address the anti-Semitism that fueled the Dreyfus Affair, but there's no questioning the pride cast and crew took in the film—in particular Paul Muni, once a Yiddish actor with the name Muni Weisenfreund.

On film Muni can seem too broad, too willing to use gestures, makeup, and accents as theatrical devices or crutches. Here he subordinates himself to the character, but allows his own sense of outrage at what occurred, at what was occurring, to emerge. The centerpiece of his performance is Zola's final statement to the jury, a speech that was filmed in a single shot lasting almost five minutes. For once you can sense how spellbinding Muni must have been on stage, in his preparation, his understanding of his role, and his delivery.

Unfortunately, the Dreyfus Affair lacked the tidy ending movies prefer. Zola didn't die the day Dreyfus was reinstated, as is implied in the film, nor was the author accidentally killed by his wife. For that matter, Dreyfus was never acquitted; he was pardoned instead by the French President. The film tacks on a largely pointless funeral for Zola, and here it's evident that while Dieterle could elicit good performances, he had little sense of rhythm or pacing. The director would soon leave Warners for RKO, where he made a respectable version of *The Hunchback of Notre Dame* and a brilliant piece of Americana, *The Devil and Daniel Webster*. He also directed *Portrait of Jennie*, a troubled project produced by David Selznick. During the Communist witch hunts, Dieterle was tainted by his association with Bertolt Brecht and Kurt Weill, and left the U.S. in the early 1950s to work in Europe. He never regained his cinematic footing.

The Prisoner of Zenda

United Artists, 1937. Sound, B&W, 1.37. 101 Minutes.
Cast: Ronald Colman (Rudolf Rassendyll/King Rudolf V), Madeleine Carroll (Princess Flavia), C. Aubrey Smith (Col. Zapt), Raymond Massey (Black Michael), Mary Astor (Antoinette de Mauban), David Niven (Capt. Fritz von Tarlenheim), Douglas Fairbanks, Jr. (Rupert of Hentzau), Montagu Love (Detchard), Wilhelm von Brincken (Krafstein), Philip Sleeman (Albert von Lauengram), Eleanor Wesselhoeft (Frau Holf), Alexander D'Arcy (De Gautet).
Crew: Directed by John Cromwell. Screen play by John L. Balderston. Based on the novel by Anthony Hope [Hawkins] and the play by Edward

Rose. Adaptation by Wells Root. Additional dialogue: Donald Ogden Stewart. Produced by David O. Selznick. Assistant producer: William H. Wright. Director of photography: James Wong Howe. Musical score: Alfred Newman. Art Director: Lyle Wheeler. Interior Decoration: Casey Roberts. Special effects: Jack Cosgrove. Technical advisors: Prince Sigvard Bernadotte, Colonel Ivar Enhorning. Costumes: Ernst Dryden. Supervising Film Editor: Hal C. Kern. Film Editor: James E. Newcom. Recorder: Oscar Lagerstrom. Assistant Director: Frederick A. Spencer. A Selznick International presentation.

Additional Cast includes: Florence Roberts (Duenna), Torben Meyer (Black Michael's butler), Ralph Faulkner (Bersonin), Ian MacLaren (Cardinal), Byron Foulger (Master Johann), Howard Lang (Josef).

Additional Credits: Scenes directed by W.S. Van Dyke, George Cukor. Screenwriting by Ben Hecht. Initial director of photography: Bert Glennon. Premiered in New York City on September 2, 1937.

Other Versions: MGM remade the film in color in 1952 with Stewart Granger, Deborah Kerr, and James Mason in the lead roles. Peter Sellers starred in a comic version in 1979, Malcolm Sinclair in a BBC TV miniseries in 1984. Hope's *Rupert of Hentzau* (published 1898) has also been filmed, as a silent in 1922 and for TV in 1964.

Available: Warner Home Video DVD (2007). UPC: 012569795129. MGM/UA Home Video VHS (1990): ISBN: 0-7928-0079-6. UPC: 0-2761-61644-3-8.

An international hit when it was published in 1894, *The Prisoner of Zenda* brought the spirit and élan of Rafael Sabatini's swashbucklers into the Victorian era. Written in a month by Anthony Hope Hawkins, a part-time lawyer, it helped establish an adventure genre that enriched novelists Sir Arthur Conan Doyle, H. Rider Haggard, and John Buchan. The novel introduced Ruritania to the language, made its insouciant public school protagonist the hero of choice for a generation of readers and filmgoers, and spawned numerous imitations and parodies. In its first year of publication, the novel sold over thirty thousand copies in the United States and Great Britain. Within forty years, it had sold over a half-million copies, and it has never gone out of print.

Hope based his plot on what he called the "ancient" device of mistaken identity, and the complications that ensue when an Englishman impersonates a Balkan king take on a Shakespearean resonance by the novel's climax. *The Prisoner of Zenda* was escapist entertainment, written with flair and wit as well as a keen sense of what the audience wanted. In that sense it was the perfect project for David O. Selznick, arguably the most significant producer in Hollywood during the late 1930s.

Selznick's father Lewis had been head of his own movie studio before being forced out of the industry in 1923. That same year Selznick made two exploitation films before moving from New York to Hollywood. There he was hired by Louis B. Mayer, and within a few years had married Mayer's daughter Irene (leading to the famous quip, "The son-in-law also rises."). Selznick worked for a time at Paramount, and was head of production at RKO

in 1933 when Mayer asked him back to MGM to stand in for the ailing Irving Thalberg. Over the next three years Selznick continued Thalberg's tradition of quality by producing stylish, sophisticated, but also entertaining adaptations of plays and novels like *Dinner at Eight* (1933), *David Copperfield* (1934), and *A Tale of Two Cities* (1935). Like Thalberg, Selznick was a hands-on producer who took control over scripting, casting, and, if necessary, reshoots.

Selznick set out on his own in 1936, forming Selznick International Pictures and signing a deal with Technicolor to produce color movies. Fueled by cigars and Benzedrine, he accomplished more in the next ten years than many do in a lifetime. While putting together Technicolor projects like *Nothing Sacred* and *A Star Is Born* (both 1937), Selznick brought Ingrid Bergmann and Alfred Hitchcock to Hollywood, in the meantime shepherding *Gone With the Wind* to the screen.

The Prisoner of Zenda was an in-between project for Selznick, something to keep his company occupied before *Nothing Sacred* started shooting. He bought the rights and several drafts of treatments and screenplays from MGM for $100,000, hoping that the recent abdication of Edward VIII would bring free publicity to a story about kings and coronations. *Zenda* was already a proven hit, having been adapted to the stage by 1896 and filmed three times before. Selznick cast Ronald Colman, who had worked with him in *A Tale of Two Cities*, and Madeleine Carroll, a British actress who had been the heroine of Hitchcock's *The 39 Steps* (1935), in the leads.

Colman, a British orphan and veteran of World War I, had important parts in several significant silent films—notably, *The Winning of Barbara Worth* in 1926—and became one of the biggest stars in Hollywood in the sound era. He specialized in suave, self-sacrificing roles, losing the girl in such big-budget hits as *Arrowsmith* (1932), *A Tale of Two Cities*, and Frank Capra's *Lost Horizon*. Even when his screen romances didn't founder, Colman spent much of his time either misinterpreting or actively fighting off the advances of women, a tactic Cary Grant would use to great effect in the late 1940s. Carroll, a regally beautiful blonde, had moved to Hollywood the year before to make films for Twentieth Century-Fox. She essentially gave up her career after her sister was killed in the blitz of London during World War II. The film was an important break for Douglas Fairbanks, Jr., the son of the screen swashbuckler. His career had faltered in the early 1930s, and his role here as Rupert of Hentzau was his first real attempt to follow directly in his father's footsteps.

Born in Ohio in 1888, John Cromwell became an actor before he was twenty, eventually reaching Broadway as a director and producer as well. He joined the wave of emigrants to wash over Hollywood in 1928, when the industry was switching to sound films; there he concentrated on directing instead of acting. He was better-known for his sensitivity guiding stars like Irene Dunne, Katharine Hepburn, Bette Davis, and Barbara Stanwyck than for a facility with swashbuckling, and when the original production was finished Selznick would hire Woody Van Dyke to punch up *Zenda*'s action in reshoots.

Although Selznick hired Donald Ogden Stewart to write the screenplay, Stewart only got an "additional dialogue" credit by the time the film was released. Selznick incorporated ideas from drafts by Ben Hecht, Wells Root, and Jules Furthman, and contributed lines himself. He started out with cinematographer Bert Glennon, soon to shoot *Stagecoach* (1939), but replaced him with James Wong Howe. All during the production Selznick was under pressure to begin *Nothing Sacred*, which still didn't have a script. And the weight of *Gone With the Wind* must have been a tremendous burden. Still, Selznick made sure to get the details right with *Zenda*, even if it meant hiring more collaborators and abandoning finished material.

Zenda's script is surprisingly close to the novel. The film dispenses with most of Hope's descriptive scenes, as they would have been too expensive to film. A coronation parade through the streets of the Ruritanian capital was discarded, for example, as well as long chases through the countryside. The movie speeds up the romance between Rassendyll and Flavia, lowers the body count early on, and adds more business for Rupert of Hentzau, a villain so compelling that Hope gave him his own sequel. The most impressive production sequence is a ball that takes place on a gargantuan set, captured in a stately crane shot, while the best acting in the film could be by Mary Astor, playing a mistress forced to betray her lover in an attempt to save his life. The reshot swordfights are marred by some obvious doubling and undercranking, but also feature some intricately backlit compositions. *Zenda* even includes some understated special effects, such as a split-screen shot in which Colman shakes hands with himself.

Opening at New York's Radio City Music Hall in September, *Zenda* was a solid hit with critics and audiences. *Variety* called it "hokum of the 24-carat variety," and hard-to-please Otis Ferguson called it "one of the best things in its class," in part because it treated its hokum "with dignity." (He also pointed out that "They throw in everything but the War of the Roses and elephants.") With its moats, drawbridges, secret passages, drugged wine, waltzes, moonlit trysts, secret writs, and hidden daggers, *Zenda* does seem to encompass every possibility of the genre. But the combination of carefully opulent production values, appealing actors, and a rousing if far-fetched story is hard to resist. And in a way it's reassuring to learn that glib one-liners in action films didn't start with Bruce Willis or Arnold Schwarzenegger. Handling a knife that just missed his head, Colman tosses off the line at his departing enemy, "If at first you don't succeed. . . ."

The Awful Truth

Columbia, 1937. Sound, B&W, 1.37. 91 minutes.

Cast: Irene Dunne (Lucy Warriner), Cary Grant (Jerry Warriner), Ralph Bellamy (Daniel Leeson), Alexander D'Arcy (Armand Duvalle), Cecil Cunningham (Aunt Patsy), Molly Lamont (Barbara Vance), Esther Dale (Mrs. Leeson), Joyce Compton (Dixie Belle Lee), Robert Allen (Frank Randall), Robert Warwick (Mr. Vance), Mary Forbes (Mrs. Vance).

Credits: Directed by Leo McCarey. Screen Play: Viña Delmar. Based on a play by Arthur Richman. Associate producer: Everett Riskin. Photography: Joseph Walker. Film Editor: Al Clark. Art directors: Stephen Goossón, Lionel Banks. Interior Decorations: Babs Johnstone. Musical director: Morris Stoloff. Music: Ben Oakland. Lyrics: Milton Drake. Gowns by Kalloch. Western Electric Mirrophonic Recording. A Columbia Pictures Corporation presentation of a Leo McCarey production.

Additional Cast: Claud Allister (Lord Fabian), Zita Moulton (Lady Fabian), Scott Colton (Mr. Barnsley), Wyn Cahoon (Mrs. Barnsley), Paul Stanton (Judge), Leonard Carey (Butler), Byron Foulger (Secretary), Bess Flowers (Viola Hearth); Edgar Dearing, Al Bridge (Motorcycle cops); Mitchell Harris (Attorney), Miki Morita (Servant), George Pearce (Caretaker), Frank Wilson (Master of Ceremonies), Vernon Dent (Police sergeant), Bobby Watson (Hotel clerk), Kathryn Curry (Celeste), Edward Pell, Sr. (Bailiff), John Tyrell (Hank), Edmund Mortimer (Attorney), Skippy (Mr. Smith).

Additional Credits: Produced by Leo McCarey. Screenplay draft by Dwight Taylor. Production dates: June 21 to August 1937. Released October 21, 1937.

Awards: Oscar for Best Director.

Other Versions: Filmed in 1925 and 1929. Remade as *Let's Do It Again* (1953), with Jane Wyman, Ray Milland.

Available: Columbia Pictures Home Video DVD (2003). ISBN: 0-7678-8149-4. UPC: 0-43396-07763-8.

Often cited as one of the key screwball comedies of the 1930s, *The Awful Truth* has a long history. A successful play in the 1920s, it was filmed in 1925 as a silent feature starring Agnes Ayres and Warner Baxter. Marshall Neilan directed an early sound version for Pathé starring stage veteran Ina Claire. The man who purchased the screen rights for this version, D.A. Doran, became an executive at Columbia, which bought Pathé's scripts after that company folded. Doran revived the project in 1937, just as studio head Harry Cohn was hiring director Leo McCarey as a replacement for the departing director Frank Capra.

McCarey's previous film, the heartbreaking *Make Way for Tomorrow* (1937), failed to find an audience, and led to the termination of his contract at Paramount. But Cohn was hiring him for his comedy skills. The son of a promoter of prize fights in California, McCarey tried everything from boxing to mining to the law before entering films as a third assistant director in 1918. A gag writer for Hal Roach in 1923, within three years he had worked his way up to vice president. He wrote and directed some of Laurel and Hardy's best silent shorts, but really hit his stride during the sound era. He worked with some of the best comedians in the industry, including Eddie Cantor, the Marx Brothers (for their best movie, *Duck Soup*, 1933), Burns and Allen, W.C. Fields, Mae West, and Harold Lloyd.

Comics respected McCarey because he humanized them, giving them bits of business that endeared them to viewers. His training in silent comedies made him a master of escalating tension within a scene through reaction shots rather than dialogue. He wasn't afraid of holding a shot until the laughs came, or of expanding a seemingly small moment like ordering a drink or answering a phone into a long scene. He also knew that frustration was at the core of the great comedians' success.

For *The Awful Truth*, McCarey retained the basics of the original play, which centered around an estranged husband's doubts over his wife's relationship with another man. But he dropped almost all of the plot incidents, which dealt with mining interests, a fire in an apartment building, and a midnight assignation at a luxurious mountain camp. McCarey focused instead on the key element in all of Hollywood's romantic comedies: sex. Or, more correctly, the inability of the leads to make love to each other. Hollywood romances resorted to endless variations on why men and women couldn't "get together": another spouse, a disapproving parent, a previous engagement, even amnesia. But in *The Awful Truth*, Lucy and Jerry Warriner are married, and remain married for almost all of the movie. By having them remain husband and wife, McCarey removed all the plot twists and embroideries that other directors rely on. For him, it's only pride keeping Lucy and Jerry apart, and few human failings are funnier.

The three leads were played by Irene Dunne, Cary Grant, and Ralph Bellamy. Dunne had proven her light comedy credentials in *Theodora Goes Wild* (1936), but she did not want to appear in the film because McCarey was still working on a new version of the story with playwright and novelist Viña Delmar. In fact, Dunne later said that she never saw a complete script for the film.

Grant, a contract player at Paramount since the beginning of the decade, had recently taken the daring step of jettisoning ties to the studio in order to freelance. He signed individual contracts for four pictures each at RKO and Columbia. He had just finished the comedy-fantasy hit *Topper* (1937) for Columbia when Cohn assigned him to *The Awful Truth*.

According to writer and director Peter Bogdanovich, this is the film in which Grant came into his own. He had been more or less window dressing before that, although some of his insouciant wit occasionally came through in movies like *Sylvia Scarlet* (1935) and *Topper*. While he subsequently made a handful of poor pictures, after *The Awful Truth* he became one of Hollywood's most incandescent stars. No one else made so many successful films so consistently, or retained the affection of his audience for such a long time.

McCarey was famous for improvising on the set, often doodling on a piano until inspiration struck. With the right performers, his technique made his films seem more natural and lifelike than almost anything else coming out of Hollywood. But it was a delicate balancing act: one wrong step could make a mood, even an entire film, collapse. McCarey trusted his instincts more than his scripts, and therefore often stumbled into material too arch or coy to stand up, notably some treacly business with a cuckoo clock that closes the film.

Grant did not like improvising, and was appalled at McCarey's habit of scribbling lines and scenes on scraps of paper. He appealed to Cohn to take him off the film, or at least let him switch parts with Bellamy, but Cohn refused. Part of the actor's frustration seeps into his performance. Grant's Jerry Warriner often seems fed up with the people around him. He also realizes his mistakes even as he's making them. Grant's ability to portray more than one layer of his characters to filmgoers became a hallmark of his acting.

The plot that McCarey and Delmar settled on mimicked stage musicals, and in a sense the film is closer to *Top Hat* (1935) and its ilk than to screwball comedies. McCarey even staged sequences like musical numbers, with little bits of libretto to tie them together. One drawback to the director's methods was an inattention to detail that can be its own source of humor. McCarey went for the emotional moment rather than one that fit the narrative, and alert viewers can almost always spot rafts of gaffes in his films. Watch how Cary Grant seems to be standing and sitting at the same time during the courtroom scene, for example.

McCarey wasn't afraid to go back to his silent roots either. Grant's bit with a bowler hat was based on a fundamental Laurel and Hardy gag; McCarey also worked wonders with the hat in an essentially silent bit with Edgar Kennedy and Harpo and Chico Marx in *Duck Soup*.

Despite McCarey's apparently lackadaisical methods, he finished the film on time and under budget. *The Awful Truth* turned a profit within months. It received six Oscar nominations, with McCarey winning for Best Director. Ralph Bellamy, nominated for Best Supporting Actor, was typecast for years as a result of his work here (he was even mocked by name in *His Girl Friday*). Dunne and Grant teamed in two more films, including another McCarey project, *My Favorite Wife* (1940), a variation on *Enoch Arden* that wound up repeating many of the comic situations from this film. McCarey would also direct Dunne memorably in *Love Affair* (1939), coincidentally remade later by McCarey as *An Affair to Remember* (1957) with Cary Grant. Dunne's career included significant films like *Anna and the King of Siam* (1946), *Life with Father* (1947), and *I Remember Mama* (1948). She retired from movies in 1952, devoting her time to politics and charity.

The River

Farm Security Administration, USDA, 1937. Sound, B&W, 1.37. 31 minutes.
Credits: Written and directed by Pare Lorentz. Photography: Floyd Crosby, Stacy Woodard, Willard Van Dyke. Music composed by Virgil Thomson. Conductor: Alexander Smallens. Narrated by Thomas Chalmers. Narration written by Pare Lorentz. Research editor: A.A. Mercey. Film editors: Leo Zochling, Lloyd Nosler. Sound technician: Al Dillinger. Presented by the Farm Security Administration with the cooperation of the Public Works Administration, Tennessee Valley Authority, Civilian Conservation Corps, and the Army Engineers. Western Electric Mirrophonic Recording. Recorded at General Service Studios.
Additional credits: Production dates: Fall 1936, to March 1, 1937. Premiered October 29, 1937.
Available: Image Entertainment DVD *Our Daily Bread and Other Films of the Great Depression* (1999). UPC: 0-14381-4671-2-3.

After the success of *The Plow That Broke the Plains* (1936), Pare Lorentz searched for a subject that was as equally pressing and nonideological as the Dust Bowl, one that the government wouldn't mind sponsoring. At a funeral for Louis Howe, Lorentz told Dr. Rexford Tugwell, an advisor to President Franklin Delano Roosevelt, that he could make a film about the Mississippi River Valley for $50,000. Tugwell got Roosevelt's approval a half-hour later. The film actually cost $49,500, more than double the budget for *The Plow*. Lorentz also wrangled a raise, from $25 to $30 a day.

Inspiration for the project came from the *Mississippi River Valley Committee Report*. Lorentz planned a geographical survey of the Mississippi, concentrating more on its tributaries than the river itself. He referred to Army engineering "blueprints" of the river, learned the pronunciations of names from the Bureau of Indian Affairs, and asked for research from the Interior Department and the U.S. Geological Survey. As with his previous film, he set out without a completed script, although as the production advanced, crew members helped prepare shot lists.

Shooting started in the fall of 1936, and eventually covered fourteen states (compared to five for *The Plow*). Lorentz hired cinematographers Stacy and Horace Woodard, brothers who made Oscarwinning nature films for a series called *The Struggle of Life*. They went to West Virginia, shooting footage of what had been Lorentz's grandfather's land. Horace left the project early on; Stacy left at the end of December. Lorentz replaced them with Willard Van Dyke and Floyd Crosby. More details about Van Dyke can be found in the entry for *The City* (1939). Crosby, recommended to Lorentz by director King Vidor, had won an Oscar shooting *Tabu* (1931), then spent years on *Matto Grosso* (1933), an ill-fated documentary set in the jungles of Brazil. Crosby shot with an eye to later editing needs, giving Lorentz enough material to piece together a sequence of loading bales of hay onto steamships, for example.

January 16, 1937, was supposed to be the last day of shooting, but heavy flooding convinced Lorentz to bring Crosby and Van Dyke to Memphis, Tennessee a week later. The flood provided publicity for the film, and also tied in with the government's efforts to win approval for Tennessee Valley Authority projects. Filming ended on March 1 in Ironton, Ohio.

Lorentz wrote an article on the flood for *McCall's* magazine, and used this as the basis for the script for *The River*. He worked with editor Lloyd Nosler (another Vidor recommendation) in structuring his footage. At the same time he was collaborating with Virgil Thomson on the musical score. Thomson wrote loud, direct music for the flood material, keeping it simple so it wouldn't detract from the powerful images. But Lorentz fought bitterly with the composer over the music for a steamboat sequence, until Thomson finally threatened to quit.

Two problems arose. First, how could Lorentz incorporate the Civil War into the history of the river without offending either Northern or Southern sensibilities? Second, how could he incorporate the flood footage without drawing attention away from the other problems he wanted to cover? In other words, how could he keep *The River* from resembling any other newsreel? There was never any question in his mind about advocacy versus objectivity. He saw documentaries as the opportunity to provide commentary on subjects, not the reporting role taken by newsreels.

The *Mississippi River Valley Committee Report* stressed the problem of water runoff in highlands, and this became the theme of the movie. In broad strokes, Lorentz showed how the Mississippi was fed by tributaries; how man ruined the valley with agriculture and industry—with cotton, the Civil War, lumber, and steel; and how resulting floods threatened to displace the population. This close relationship of water, land, and people needed a savior, and that would be the Tennessee Valley Authority.

The River is more self-conscious than *The Plow*. The voice-over drew from Ernest Hemingway as well as John Grierson, with narrator Thomas

Chalmers repeating catch-phrases and lists of trees, rivers, cities, states, and the like. Similarly, the photography was studied, with angular compositions that seemed more European than American. Documentaries like Joris Ivens' *Regen* (1929) and Grierson's *Night Mail* (1934) showed Lorentz how to structure scenes, and also what type of footage to obtain.

Lorentz arranged for Roosevelt to see a print of the finished film after a showing of *Thin Ice* with Sonja Henie. He also screened it for Secretary of State Henry Wallace, who complained, "There's no corn in it." (Wallace was from Iowa.) Lorentz was worried because Senator Harry Byrd had started an investigation into budgets for government films. Furthermore, the Resettlement Administration had been judged unconstitutional, and Lorentz's supporters there had been replaced.

The director decided to distribute the film himself, opening it in New Orleans on October 29, 1937, a month after Roosevelt saw it. Roark Bradford, author of stories that evolved into the play and movie *Green Pastures*, and writer Lyle Saxon helped Lorentz get the film booked into an independent theater with a Walt Disney cartoon (Disney was experiencing labor problems of his own). Roark's response to the one sequence: "That's a real levee outfit of mules. Look at that old gray mule slacking back in the harness, letting the black mule take all the weight."

The Washington, D.C., premiere took placed on December 7, 1937. A *Christian Science Monitor* review astutely noted, "Some of the sequences are masterpieces of oblique suggestion, and all drive home the central philosophy or 'propaganda' . . . that what man has wrecked can be put together again—by TVA dams, let us say." The propaganda complaint surfaced in other reviews as well, but the film's run was extended in Chicago. When it opened in New York City in February, it was held over longer than the accompanying feature, *Scandal Street*. As a result, Paramount took over distribution of the film, offering it to theaters for free except for shipping costs. That August, *The River* won an award for the best documentary film at the International Film Festival in Venice, beating out Leni Riefenstahl's *Olympiad*.

By that time, Lorentz was planning his next film—*Ecce Homo!*—about unemployment. He was named head of the U.S. Film Service in August 1938. He contributed to *The City* (1939), directed *The Fight for Life* (1940), and oversaw *Power and the Land* (Joris Ivens, 1940) and *The Land* (Robert Flaherty, 1941), But World War II swept aside his plans, and Lorentz found his approach to documentaries replaced by a more direct form of propaganda promulgated by Frank Capra in the *Why We Fight* series (1943–45).

When the government is financing your film on the problem of flooding in the Mississippi River Valley, dams may be the solution. From *The River*.

Snow White and the Seven Dwarfs

RKO, 1937. Sound, color, 1.37. 83 minutes.

Credits: Supervising director: David Hand. Sequence directors: Perce Pearce, William Cottrell, Larry Morey, Wilfred Jackson, Ben Sharpsteen. Supervising animators: Hamilton Luske, Fred Moore, Vladimir [Bill] Tytla, Norman Ferguson. Assistant directors: Hal Adelquist, Carl Fallberg. Mike Holoboff. Adapted from Grimms' Fairy Tales. Technicolor. Recorded by RCA Victor "High Fidelity" Sound System. A Walt Disney Feature Production. Story adaptation: Ted Sears, Richard Creedon, Otto Englander, Dick Rickard, Earl Hurd, Merrill De Maris, Dorothy Ann Blank, Webb Smith. Character designers: Albert Hurter, Joe Grant. Music: Frank Churchill, Leigh Harline, Paul Smith. Art directors: Charles Philippi, Tom Codrick, Hugh Hennesy, Gustaf Tenggren, Terrell Stapp, Kenneth Anderson, McLaren Stewart, Kendall O'Connor, Harold Miles, Hazel Sewell. Backgrounds: Samuel Armstrong, Mique Nelson, Phil Dike, Merle Cox, Ray Lockrem, Claude Coats, Maurice Noble. Animators: Frank Thomas, Les Clark, Dick Lundy, Fred Spencer, Arthur Babbitt, Bill Roberts, Eric Larson, Bernard Garbutt, Milton Kahl, Grim Natwick, Robert Stokes, Jack Campbell, James Algar, Marvin Woodward, Al Eugster, James Culhane, Cy Young, Stan Quackenbush, Joshua Meador, Ward Kimball, Ugo D'Orsi, Woolie Reitherman, George Rowley, Robert Martsch.

Featuring the voices of: Adriana Caselotti (Snow White), Harry Stockwell (Prince), Lucille La Verne (Wicked Queen), Moroni Olsen (Magic Mirror), Billy Gilbert (Sneezy), Otis Harlan (Happy), Scotty Mattraw (Bashful), Pinto Colvig (Grumpy, Sleepy), Atwell (Doc), Steve Buchanan (Humbert).

Additional Credits: Produced by Walt Disney. Assistant director: Ford Beebe. Additional animation: John McManus, Hugh Fraser, Sandy Strother, Paul Busch, Marc Davis, Louie Schmitt, Cornett Wood, Campbell Grant, Amby Pallwoda, Riley Thomson. Premiered December 12, 1937.

Awards: Walt Disney received an honorary Oscar in 1939.

Available: Buena Vista Home Entertainment DVD (2001). ISBN: 0-7888-2812-6. UPC: 7-86936-15060-5.

One of the formative films from Walt Disney's youth was *Snow White*, a 1916 feature starring Marguerite Clark and directed by J. Searle Dawley. It made such a vivid impression on Disney that he chose the same subject for his first feature film. After a financially rocky start, Disney's cartoon studio had seen unprecedented success since the coming of sound. Mickey Mouse was by some accounts the most popular film star in the world, and the Silly Symphonies series had blockbuster hits as well, such as *Three Little Pigs* (1933, a Registry title). The studio was known for its technical innovations, making a transition to Technicolor years before other animation houses were allowed to use the process, and incorporating the multiplane camera, a device that gave the illusion of the camera moving through animated backgrounds.

But Disney wasn't satisfied with making cartoon shorts. For one thing, they were not especially profitable. The studio released a report in 1934 stating that *Three Little Pigs* earned $64,000, a tidy sum for a cartoon. But it had cost $60,000 to make, effectively wiping out profits. Disney hoped that a feature-length film would earn more money;

he may have also hoped that a feature cartoon would give his company more prestige.

Although he had no financing for a feature film, Disney had a staff member register the *Snow White* title in 1933. He bought the rights to a play by Winthrop Ames that had been the basis of the 1916 film, and in the winter of 1934 he began to act out the story as he saw it to his animators. While meeting with writers that fall, he abandoned the idea of writing a complete script. Instead, individual scenes were assigned to different groups. These scenes would be refined dozens of times, with gags and other ideas added and subtracted. He also insisted that his animators attend art classes conducted at the studio.

It wasn't until November 1935 that Disney felt confident enough to schedule work on the feature. He severely underestimated the time *Snow White* would require, but then no one had tried animation on this scale before. Especially not with Disney's perfectionist streak. He chose animators for specific scenes and moments—Fred Moore and Hamilton Luske handled the introductory material with the dwarfs, for example, while Norm Ferguson did most of the Queen's scenes. Ferguson, Luske, Moore, and Bill Tytla became the four supervising animators. Dave Hand, the nominal director, was assisted by several other animators, who divided the film's thirty-two scenes among themselves.

While Disney was very much a hands on administrator, he gave free rein to his writers and artists. His biggest contribution to the script of *Snow White* may have been his realization that the lead character needed to be surrounded by vivid supporting roles, preferably comic. (It was the same approach Warner Brothers would take toward its Errol Flynn vehicles.) He had the dwarfs christened with names like "Dopey" and "Sneezy," clues that would define how the characters would behave in the story. (Disney even contributed one of the names, "Grumpy.")

The actual animation work started in February 1936, although the schedules weren't set until that September. The "rough" drawings would be screened and corrected repeatedly before they were approved for "clean-up." Disney kept adding story ideas, like turning the forest through which Snow White tries to escape into a living beast. "It would

be good for her to be caught in the bushes showing these grotesque hands," he wrote.

One immediate problem was how to depict Snow White. Disney had never been satisfied with the studio's human characters. Now he turned to Grim Natwick, an animator who had helped turn Betty Boop into a star when he was working at the Fleischer studio. Natwick used Marjorie Belcher, who later married and performed with dancer Gower Champion, as a model. (The Prince gets only two scenes because Disney was unhappy with how he looked.)

Disney started casting the voice actors in 1936. Some, like Pinto Colvig, came from the studio ranks; others, like Billy Gilbert (who voiced Sneezy), were stars on their own. Equally important was the music. Frank Churchill, who wrote "Who's Afraid of the Big Bad Wolf" for *Three Little Pigs*, joined two other composers for the score. "Someday My Prince Will Come" became for a time a popular standard, but "Whistle While You Work" was the real standout from the score. (Viewers today may be surprised by the country inflections to some of the songs; Disney always fancied yodeling.)

Also in 1936, Disney and his brother Roy switched distributors, from United Artists to RKO. The latter studio had access to more theaters, but also increased pressure on Disney to meet his deadline of December 1937. Recording the animation onto film didn't begin until March 1937. In order to finish on time, Disney authorized the use of rotoscoping, or drawing outlines from live footage. The budget grew to over a million dollars, forcing Disney to mortgage his studio.

Photography finally finished on December 1, 1937, a week before the first sneak preview. According to biographer Neal Gabler, Charlie Chaplin stepped in before the film opened with advice for Disney on what fees and rentals he should be asking. When it premiered on December 12, the film was an immediate success. But Disney was unhappy about what he perceived as several flaws in the animation. Even years later, he still complained about the Prince.

Walt Disney's drive and dedication helped make the studio's next features, *Fantasia* and *Pinocchio* (both 1940, and both Registry titles), even greater artistic achievements.

Daughter of Shanghai

Paramount, 1937. Sound, B&W, 1.37. 62 minutes.

Cast: Anna May Wong (Lan Ying Lin), Charles Bickford (Otto Hartman), Larry [Buster] Crabbe (Andrew Sleete), Cecil Cunningham (Mrs. Mary Hunt), J. Carrol Naish (Frank Barden), Anthony Quinn (Harry Morgan), John Patterson (James Lang), Evelyn Brent (Olga Derey), Philip Ahn (Kim Lee), Fred Kohler (Captain [D.] Gulner), Guy Bates Post (Lloyd Burket), Virginia Dabney (Rita, a dancer).

Credits: Directed by Robert Florey. Screen Play by Gladys Unger and Garnett Weston. Based on a story by Garnett Weston. Photographed by Charles Schoenbaum. Art direction by Hans Dreier and Robert Odell. Edited by Ellsworth Hoagland. Sound recording: Charles Hisserich and Richard Olson. Interior decorations by A.E. Freudeman. Musical direction by Boris Morros. Western Electric Mirrophonic Recording. Presented by Adolph Zukor.

Additional Cast: Ching Wah Lee (Quan Lin), Frank Sully (Jake Kelly), Ernest Whitman (Sam Blike), Mrs. Wong (Amah), Paul Fix (Miles), Gwen Kenyon (Switchboard), Charles Wilson (Schwartz), John Hart (Sailor), Michael Wu (Yung Woo), Mae Busch (Lil), William Powell (Carib waiter); Carmen Bailey, Paulita Arvizu, Carmen La Roux, Tina Menard (Dancers); Gino Corrado (Interpreter); Alex Woloshin, Agostino Borgato (Gypsies); Harry Strang (Sailor), Lee Shumway (Ship's officer), Pierre Watkin (L.T. Yorkland).

Additional Credits: Additional dialogue: William Hurlbut. Produced by Edward T. Lowe. Executive producer: William LeBaron. Assistant director: Stanley Goldsmith. Released December 17, 1937.

Available: The Library of Congress.

Hollywood studios liked to promote their big-budget, star-driven films, but B-movies were their real bread and butter. The "A" films were lavished with expensive sets and crews, and received publicity and advertising that simply weren't available to films with lower budgets. But B-movies were often the difference between profit and loss for a studio. They kept contract players and salaried crew members at work. They helped justify the purchase of costly equipment and props, and kept backlots and soundstages operating. They provided product for movie theaters, which at this time were owned in large part by the studios themselves. They allowed filmmakers to experiment with new techniques, gave aspiring actors a showcase to demonstrate their skills, and in some cases allowed studios to rework stories they already owned in different time frames and formats. Since B-movies did not have to appeal to as broad an audience as big-budget films, they could target niche groups: children, action fans, mystery buffs.

The trade publication *Variety* often referred to B-movies as "programmers" because that's how studio executives thought of them, as material to be inserted into a movie theater's program for the night, fodder with no pretense to art or originality. Even a poor B-movie can show viewers today something about cultural tastes and filmmaking styles of the time. Under the right circumstances, a low-budget film could rise above its limitations, like *Daughter of Shanghai*, a skilled and enjoyable thriller.

The script was based on a relatively timely premise: smuggling illegal aliens into San Francisco. In the hands of screenwriters Gladys Unger and Garnett Wilson, the issue boiled down to an isolated gang of crooks and thugs, something that could be solved with a few arrests rather than a correcting wider societal ills. For producers Harold Hurley and Edward T. Lowe, Jr., the script was an opportunity to cast Anna May Wong, a veteran star who was trying to reestablish her career in the United States after appearing in a series of European films. For director Robert Florey, who codirected *The Life and Death of 9413 A Hollywood Extra* (1928), it was a chance to experiment with the staff and equipment at Paramount, and perhaps graduate to a more expensive project.

For most of the cast, *Daughter of Shanghai* was a paycheck. It was one of six films Anthony Quinn made that year. He had just married Katherine DeMille, director Cecil B. DeMille's daughter, and he was still years away from leading roles. Quinn, who had two small scenes, didn't bother to mention the film in his autobiography. Cecil Cunningham appeared in eight films in 1937, including a Jack Benny comedy, *Artists & Models*, and the Leo McCarey hit *The Awful Truth*. Tall, angular, with short white hair, on screen she fell somewhere between Edna Mae Oliver and Eve Arden. Given the chance, she could be ruthless, charming, or distracted. J. Carrol Naish played largely ethnic villains in some two hundred films; Gino Corrado, who appears in the film's Caribbean section, had over three hundred credits.

The film is unusual, but not unprecedented, in its use of Asian characters. What distinguished *Daughter of Shanghai* from a big-budget movie like MGM's *The Good Earth* (made that same year) was the fact that actual Asian actors were playing the Asian roles. Philip Ahn, for example, was a member of an acting family with roots in Korea. He mostly had to content himself with playing houseboys and villains. It was unusual for him to appear as a government agent, just as it was unusual to give the lead role in a film to Wong. More a striking presence than an accomplished actress, she was too exotic to play mundane parts.

Here she reprises a dance from *Piccadilly* (1929), a British silent directed by E.A. Dupont, only without the veil of silence or the incandescent beauty of her youth to protect her. (She appears in two other Registry titles, *The Thief of Bagdad* and *Peter Pan*, both from 1924.)

Florey had been working in Hollywood since the 1920s, which may explain the presence of so many silent stars in *Daughter of Shanghai*. Mae Busch, for example, had once acted in Keystone films, and starred in Erich von Stroheim's *Foolish Wives* (1922). Fred Kohler's career went back even further, to 1911; he appeared in Josef von Sternberg's silents, in the Technicolor Western musical *Under a Texas Moon* (1930), and in numerous other Westerns. Evelyn Brent had once been a leading lady in silent films (*The Last Command*, 1928), and had worked with Kohler in *Underworld* (1927). Florey not only gave jobs to these actors, he gave them space within the film to develop characters beyond the stereotypes depicted in the script. Florey's European background could account for the unusually diverse cast and settings. Mandarin, Spanish, and French are used in the film, which takes a sympathetic attitude toward people trying to enter the country. (A fanciful one as well, as the seaplanes used to dodge government officials were more expensive than the cargo they delivered.) It was a viewpoint that would be repeated in other Registry titles like *America America* (1963) and *El Norte* (1983).

Daughter of Shanghai uses all the tricks available to a studio film of the period: stock footage of planes and ships, montages of newspaper headlines, back-projected scenes set aboard freighters, model shots of seaplanes landing in water tanks, matte shots and other special effects, and some set design that evokes the heady days of *Blonde Venus* and *Morocco*. The story includes bump-and-grind dances, fistfights in tight quarters, cold-blooded shootings, villains in disguise, undercover cops, and former leading man Charles Bickford wearing a fake beard and chasing a dame away "before I crack your neck."

B-movies could use material that might have been questioned in films with bigger budgets. Within the restrictions of the Production Code, *Daughter of Shanghai* gets away with implying or actually showing adultery, bondage, lesbianism, and interracial sex. There is no mistaking the leers imprisoned sailors give Wong, decked out in drag in the hold of a tramp steamer. Or the looks she receives during her musical number in a filthy banana republic saloon. (It's hard to believe one plot could contain such a whirlwind of activity, but *Daught of Shanghai* pulls it off with genuine panache.)

It may not be fair to criticize a 1937 B-movie for failing to give Wong a legitimate love story, for prohibiting Ahn's character from winning a fight without help from a white man, or for suggesting that immigration as a problem was simply an issue of arresting a few bad eggs. *Daughter of Shanghai* presented Asian characters in positive terms, without condescension. It also toyed with the boundaries of acceptable screen behavior, gave work to a number of film veterans, exploited Paramount's technical capabilities, and offered moviegoers an hour or so of swift, painless entertainment—exactly what a B-movie should do.

Inside Nazi Germany

RKO Pathé, 1938. Sound, B&W, 1.37. 16 minutes.
Credits: Directed by Jack Glenn. Written by James L. Shute. Produced by Louis de Rochemont.
Additional Credits: Released January 21, 1938.
Available: The Library of Congress.

By the mid-1930s, every Hollywood studio except Warner Bros. had a newsreel department. Newsreels were considered a vital part of a movie theater program, and one survey estimated that at least 90 percent of theaters regularly scheduled them. Studios set up newsreel offices throughout the country, staffing them with salaried and freelance cameramen. At its height, Fox Movietone had thirty trucks equipped with cameras and sound recording equipment.

Louis de Rochemont was at one time the director of short subjects for Fox Movietone News. Born in Chelsea, Massachusetts, in 1899, de Rochemont was fascinated by photography at an early age, making his own camera from a design he saw in *Popular Mechanics*. He sold footage to local theaters under the title *See Yourself As Others See You*, and made his mark as a freelance cameraman when he staged a re-enactment of the arrest of a suspect who tried to bomb a bridge between Maine and Canada in 1915. He enlisted in the Navy during World War I, and shot recruiting films in Istanbul in 1922. He continued to work under contract to the Navy after leaving the service.

De Rochemont financed and produced *The Cry of the World*, a documentary compiled from stock footage in newsreel archives. So by the time he was hired by Movietone, he was familiar with re-enactments, with obtaining the cooperation of government agencies, and with compilation films. He oversaw two series for Movietone: "The Magic Carpet of Movietone" and "The March of the Years," the latter a clear forerunner of "The March of Time."

De Rochemont was not the first to come up with the idea for The March of Time. David O. Selznick suggested turning a CBS radio show with that title into a newsreel soon after it debuted in March 6, 1931. The radio show was developed by Roy Larsen, since 1922 the circulation editor for *Time* magazine, and Fred Smith. The show used actors like Orson Welles, Agnes Moorehead, and Art Carney to dramatize news stories. Starting in 1933, Westbrook Van Voorhis became "The Voice of Time" for the series.

With the success of *Fortune* and *Life* magazines, Larsen had the financing available to spread publicity about the Henry Luce empire on film as well as radio, but he balked at what he thought would be exorbitant production costs for re-enacting news stories on camera. De Rochemont showed him that costs could be contained by using archival or actuality footage, available in some cases for as little as a dollar a foot.

De Rochemont quit Movietone to work for Larsen, opening an office in June 1934 with a staff of six. De Rochemont hired writers and editors, but no cameramen. While the radio show used an article in that week's *Time* magazine as the basis for each episode, de Rochemont wanted the films to be independent of the magazine. His first format divided a ten-minute newsreel, or "issue," into five two-minute segments. In its first year, The March of Time covered the rearming of Germany, Father Coughlin's Social Justice movement, and Huey Long, then the governor of Louisiana.

De Rochemont quickly discovered that in most cases nonactors had not yet learned how they would appear on screen. Huey Long happily cooperated with what turned out to be a highly critical piece, for example. De Rochemont shaped Long's footage through narration, which told viewers how to respond to what they were seeing. De Rochemont's willingness to color or even contradict actuality footage through voice-overs may be his most significant contribution to documentaries.

Henry Luce called the series "fakery in allegiance to the truth," and de Rochemont had no qualms about staging scenes, even hiring actors to impersonate figures like President Franklin Delano Roosevelt. He described March of Time segments as symbols of events, just as newspaper reporters used words as symbols. The series was enormously popular, seen by an estimated twenty million people a week, and shown in nine thousand theaters. The March of Time was rewarded a special Oscar in 1936 "for having revolutionized" newsreels.

Inside Nazi Germany was envisioned as a "single subject" or "special issue" episode, one story that would occupy the entire newsreel. It starts with pictures of an innocent Germany, one with happy citizens, captured travelogue-style in cafés and amusement parks. Gradually a darker element is introduced: the loss of religious freedom, discrimination against Jews, the increasing militarization of the country, efforts to indoctrinate youth to the Nazi cause.

The initial footage, some of it shot by Julien Bryan (*Siege*, 1940), seems innocuous. It is the voice-over that provides meaning. "The child ceases to be an individual," the narrator intones over German propaganda footage of children at play. "He is denied the right to strike, or even ask his employer for a raise" is spoken over stock scenes of factory workers. (At the same time, newsreels were documenting violent confrontations in the United States—at Republic Steel, for example—when workers tried to strike.) The narration defines the images, which otherwise could have had a different impact.

Bryan's material, and the scenes taken without compensation from German sources, were deemed too bland by director Jack Glenn. He and de Rochemont shot staged footage in Hoboken, New Jersey, and in Manhattan. It was designed to highlight sensational details. Cleaning ladies from the March of Time offices impersonated imprisoned nuns sitting forlornly behind bars (which were made of cardboard). Anti-German activists portrayed "typical" German families at home, forced to contribute food and money to Nazi Youth. Glenn even inserted an execution by guillotine into a discussion of widespread arrests.

Although its methods would be considered irresponsible today, *Inside Nazi Germany* was one of the first films to investigate the political regime. For millions, it was irrefutable proof that something terrible was happening in Europe. De Rochemont also drew a direct connection between Nazi Germany and the German American Bund, led at the time by Fritz Kuhn. (A participant in the filming, Kuhn later claimed that he had been double-crossed.)

Inside Nazi Germany was released in January 1938 as Issue 6, Volume 4. A firestorm of criticism resulted. Harry Warner, somehow perceiving a pro-German bias, banned the film from Warner Bros. theaters. The film was also banned for a time in Chicago and in several individual theaters. De Rochemont exploited the controversy, taking out ads that promised "uncensored" prints and listing positive quotes from celebrities like Walter Winchell and Dorothy Thompson. The film was subsequently reissued several times.

Bringing Up Baby

RKO, 1938. Sound, B&W, 1.33. 102 minutes.
Cast: Katharine Hepburn (Susan), Cary Grant (David [Huxley]), Charlie Ruggles (Major [Horace] Applegate), Walter Catlett ([Constable] Slocum), Barry Fitzgerald (Mr. [Aloysius] Gogarty), May Robson (Aunt Elizabeth), Fritz Feld (Dr. [Fritz] Lehman), Leona Roberts (Mrs. [Hannah] Gogarty), George Irving (Mr. Peabody), Tala Birell (Mrs. Lehman), Virginia Walker (Alice Swallow), John Kelly (Elmer).
Credits: Directed by Howard Hawks. Screen Play by Dudley Nichols & Hagar Wilde from the story by Hagar Wilde. Associate producer: Cliff Reid. Photographed by Russell Metty, A.S.C. Musical Director: Roy Webb. Art director: Van Nest Polglase. Associate art director: Perry Ferguson. Special effects by Vernon L. Walker, A.S.C. Gowns by Howard Greer. Recorded by John L. Cass. Set dressing by Darrell Silvera. Edited by George Hively. Assistant director: Edward Donahue. Recorded by RCA Victor System.
Additional Cast: Jack Carson (Circus roustabout), Richard Lane (Circus manager), Ward Bond (Motorcycle cop), George Humbert (Louis, the headwaiter), Ernest Cossart (Joe, the bartender), Stan Blystone (Porter), Asta [Skippy] (George, the dog), Nissa (Baby, the leopard).
Additional Credits: Produced by Howard Hawks. Leopard trainer: Madame Olga Celeste. "I Can't Give You Anything but Love, Baby," lyrics by Dorothy Fields, music by Jimmy McHugh. Released February 18, 1938.
Available: Warner Bros. Home Video DVD (2005). ISBN: 0-7907-6535-7. UPC: 053939640724 Turner Home Entertainment VHS (1996). ISBN: 0780615530.

Touted today as one of the key screwball comedies, *Bringing Up Baby* was not a success when it was released. In fact, it was not the film that director Howard Hawks wanted to make when he signed with RKO in 1937. Hawks instead had been working on *Gunga Din* (1939), contributing some of the elements that ended up in that film's shooting script. But the project bogged down in casting problems, and Hawks decided to move on.

The director read a short story in *Collier's* magazine by Hagar Wilde about a paleontologist, an heiress, and her pet leopard, and told the studio he was interested in it. RKO's story department agreed, and Hawks soon started work on a script with Wilde. Since Wilde was not a professional screenwriter, Hawks hired Dudley Nichols to help out. Born in 1895, Nichols enlisted in the Navy in World War I, ultimately working on a minesweeper. He worked as a newspaper journalist for ten years, then turned to screenwriting. His first film was John Ford's *Men Without Women* (1930), and he went on to work on fourteen films with the director. He refused to accept his Oscar for *The Informer* (1935) for political reasons. At the time Nichols was working on *Bringing Up Baby*, he was also helping form the Screen Writers' Guild. *Baby* was his only full-fledged comedy.

Pandro Berman, one of the leading RKO producers, pushed Katharine Hepburn for the female role, so Hawks and his writers tailored the Susan Vance part for her. The male lead was turned down by everyone from Ronald Colman to Ray Milland. Cary Grant agreed to the part once Hawks explained to him that the way to play it was in the style of comedian Harold Lloyd.

When filming started, the budget stood at almost $800,000, a huge amount at the time for what was a modest comedy. Hawks worked slowly as well, especially with Hepburn, who had never acted in a screwball comedy before. Walter Catlett, a vaudeville and stage veteran famous for his Ziegfeld *Follies* appearances, eventually had to show Hepburn how to play comedy, although Grant's advice to always look depressed before taking a pratfall was a big help. (Catlett, who plays Constable Slocum, has the best timing in the film. Watch his hands as he interrogates Hepburn and Grant in jail: he's giving them the tempo of the scene.)

Hawks' style of filmmaking was anathema to the studio system. Although he is acknowledged as a superior director today, at the time he was seen as an iconoclast who made expensive, unprofitable movies. With Howard Hughes supplying the money, Hawks didn't need a studio's backing for *Scarface*, but many of the director's following films were indifferent genre pieces. Today film writers accept his *Twentieth Century* (1934) as one of the forerunners of the screwball style. At the time it was significant more for its daring, blatant cynicism. *Twentieth Century* reveled in its characters' thirst for fame and delusions about their careers. It was a sharp antidote to the blandly moralistic or mildly satirical films of the day.

Hawks' characters are always bluffing stoicism or bravery in an attempt to hide their true feelings. The director probably felt that since viewers could see the bluffs, his characters were realistic, even honest. But it's one thing to repress your feelings; it's another to lie about them by pretending they don't affect you. In *Twentieth Century* or the profoundly cynical masterpiece *His Girl Friday* (1940), this disconnect proves immensely entertaining. In a supposedly more realistic and somber piece like *Only Angels Have Wings* (1939), it can seem weirdly inauthentic.

As he did with other genres, Hawks was approaching screwball comedy fairly late in the game. And, like *Scarface*, Hawks was determined to push the envelope of what was permissible. Susan Vance and David Huxley, the characters played by Hepburn and Grant, are so repressed that they're almost psychotic. Grant, first seen wrapped in a lab coat and being denied sex by his future wife, is unsure of his masculinity. Hepburn is an immature liar who likes to start fights, and the 1930s equivalent of a stalker.

This is the second of four films Hepburn and Grant made together, films that document a relationship with deep undercurrents of suspicion and desire. Fred Astaire and Ginger Rogers surrounded their sexuality with both a forbidding virtuosity and the coy denial that desire existed; William Powell and Myrna Loy presented a relationship past that giddy introductory stage, smoldering rather than aflame. Hepburn and Grant are like the king and queen of the prom, still shuffling for position, for power, staking out their territory, but too perfectly suited for each other to deny love.

Hawks was astute enough to let the two stars discover each other on screen. The first half of *Bringing Up Baby* is like eavesdropping on a budding relationship. While the world portrayed is familiar from other films about the wealthy—golf courses, mansions, nightclubs, museums, country estates—it's a weirdly depopulated one in which only Hepburn and Grant make any difference. After the introductory scenes, Hawks allows almost

ten minutes to pass in which the two are the only characters in the film. It's remarkable that the director can sustain their breezy, bantering tone so long, especially considering how passive-aggressive they are.

Unfortunately, the second half of *Bringing Up Baby* turns into a sort of homecoming week for hams. Large chunks of screen time are handed over to old-timers performing dialect humor or retrieving stage routines from earlier in their careers. Hawks and his writers resort to surprisingly weak plot twists—not one but two leopards; not one, but two emasculating Amazons; not two but three tiny blowhards—upping the ante of ridiculousness until nothing in the story matters anymore. The dirty jokes sprinkled around are so blunt they resemble schoolboy graffiti: a bone in a box, Grant in a negligee, the back of a dress ripped off.

Hawks shot for ninety-one days, forty days over schedule, increasing the budget by almost 50 percent (and consequently triggering several costly penalty payments to the stars). On its release it was a failure, both critically and commercially. (In his biography on Howard Hawks, writer Todd McCarthy argues that the film did well in several markets, but not New York. He does note that the studio ultimately lost $365,000 on the film.) *Bringing Up Baby* not only helped kill the screwball genre, it sent Hepburn back to the New York stage, the epithet "box office poison" trailing behind her like a stained stole. Hawks' costly delays were partially responsible for his losing the *Gunga Din* job. He left RKO, making his next film at Columbia. Only Grant emerged unscathed. He would make two more films with Hepburn, and three with Hawks.

The elevated reputation today for *Bringing Up Baby* may be due to the fact that it was an easy film to see when more striking films were not. The RKO library was sold to television early on, and circulating prints were always available for repertory theaters. Hepburn and Grant went on to become much bigger stars, spurring interest in their earlier careers and how they developed. Pauline Kael championed the film, inspiring a generation of her acolytes to study it. While arguments can be made for *Bringing Up Baby*'s superior acting and dialogue, its unapologetic tone and dark palette, the truth is almost everyone connected with the film did better work elsewhere.

The Adventures of Robin Hood

Warner Bros., 1938. Sound, color, 1.37. 102 minutes.
Cast: Errol Flynn (Robin Hood), Olivia de Havilland (Maid Marian), Basil Rathbone (Sir Guy of Gisbourne), Claude Rains (Prince John), Patrick Knowles (Will Scarlett), Eugene Pallette (Friar Tuck), Alan Hale (Little John), Melville Cooper (High Sheriff of Nottingham), Ian Hunter (King Richard the Lion-Heart), Una O'Connor (Bess), Herbert Mundin (Much), Montagu Love (Bishop of the Black Canons), Leonard Willey (Sir Essex), Robert Noble (Sir Ralf), Kenneth Hunter (Sir Mortimer), Robert Warwick (Sir Geoffrey), Colin Kenny (Sir Baldwin), Lester Matthews (Sir Ivor), Harry Cording (Dickon Malbete), Howard Hill (Captain of Archers), Ivan Simpson (Proprietor of Kent Road Tavern).
Credits: Directed by Michael Curtiz and William Keighley. Original screen play by Norman Reilly Raine and Seton I. Miller. Based upon ancient Robin Hood legends. Music by Erich Wolfgang Korngold. Dialogue director: Irving Rapper. Photography by Tony Gaudio, Sol Polito. Film editor: Ralph Dawson. Art director: Carl Jules Weyl. Costumes by Milo Anderson. Makeup artist: Perc Westmore. Sound by C.A. Riggs. Technicolor photography: W. Howard Greene. Technicolor color director: Natalie Kalmus. Technicolor associate: Morgan Padelford. Technical advisor: Louis Van Den Ecker. Orchestral arrangements: Hugo Friedhofer. Musical director: Leo F. Forbstein. Photographed in Technicolor. A First National picture.
Additional Cast includes: Charles McNaughton (Crippen), Lionel Belmore (Humility Prin), Austin Fairman (Sir Nigel), Crauford Kent (Sir Norbert), Reginald Sheffield (Herald), Wilfred Lucas (Archery official), Holmes Herbert (Archery referee), Jack Deery, Paul Power, Leonard Mudie, Edward Dew, Sidney Baron, Olaf Hytten, Val Stanton, Ernie Stanton, Alec Harford, Peter Hobbes, Halliwell Hobbes, Martin Lamont, Hal Brazeale, Ivo Henderson, John Sutton.
Additional Credits: Directing: William Dieterle, B. Reeves Eason. Produced by Hal Wallis. Associate producer: Henry Blanke. Screenwriting: Rowland Leigh. Special effects: Byron Haskins. Dialogue director: Colin Campbell. Archery consultant: Howard Hill. Fencing consultant: Fred Cavens. Production dates: September 26, 1937 to January 14, 1938. Premiered April 25, 1938.
Awards: Oscars for Best Music–Original Score, Editing, Art Direction.
Available: Warner Home Video DVD (2002). ISBN: 0-7907-4541-0. UPC: 0-12569-51312-9.

Warner Bros. executives were toying with the idea of a feature about Robin Hood as early as 1935, when Dwight Franklin proposed James Cagney for the role to Jack Warner. Franklin, who was working on *Captain Blood* (1935) at the time, promised that it would be "entirely different" from the 1922 *Robin Hood* with Douglas Fairbanks, although it's peculiar that he hadn't thought that *Blood* star Errol Flynn would make a good Robin. The dashing Flynn, an Australian who had been a sailor and writer before brief work as an actor brought him to London and then to Hollywood, would soon be seen as a successor to Fairbanks. He would also personify a new side of Warner Brothers, one entirely different from its beginnings as a scruffy, urban-oriented studio that churned out gangsters flicks and musicals.

The quest for legitimacy, for parity with studios like MGM and Paramount, persuaded Jack Warner to turn away, however slowly, from vehicles for Cagney, Edward G. Robinson, and other tough-guy contractees. On the musical front, the studio's *Gold Diggers* series had devolved into weak vehicles for Dick Powell, whose popularity was slipping even as he matured out of juvenile lead roles.

As an alternative, Hal Wallis, a replacement for former production chief Darryl Zanuck, initiated a series of profitable biopics, including the Registry title *The Life of Emile Zola* (1937). He was behind the Robin Hood project, but with very definite opinions. "You cannot have the maid or anyone else reading lines such as, 'Oh, M'Lord, tarry not too long for, I fear, in her remorse, she may fling herself from the window,'" he warned in 1937, after Rowland Leigh turned in a draft that eliminated Maid Marion entirely. Wallis later assigned writers Norman Reilly Raine and Seton I. Miller to the film.

On some levels, the Robin Hood project would be a continuation of the *Captain Blood* formula. Like that film and *The Charge of the Light Brigade* (1936, written in part by Raine), Flynn would costar with Olivia de Havilland, and ultimately be directed by Michael Curtiz. William Keighley, a former actor and theater director who came to Warners in 1932, was the original director, possibly because he had worked well with Flynn in *The Prince and the Pauper* (1937). But after shooting for weeks on location with cinematographer Tony Gaudio, Keighley turned in footage—"thousands of feet of film with hundreds of people"—that in Wallis's opinion couldn't be used.

Curtiz was Wallis's favorite director; he helmed more than twenty pictures for the producer. His résumé included *Under a Texas Moon* (1930), the first location Western filmed in an earlier Technicolor process, and one that featured a vaguely Robin Hood–like hero. But after his dictatorial style on *Captain Blood* and *The Charge of the Light Brigade*, Curtiz was not well liked by Flynn. The actor was also worried about his wigs and outfits. But Flynn rehearsed diligently with fencing instructor Fred Cavens, who would work on all of the star's swashbuckling pictures. The final swordfight in *The Adventures of Robin Hood* between Flynn and Basil Rathbone (playing the villainous Sir Guy of Gisbourne) is one of the best filmed duels of the era.

Wallis did warn associate producer Henry Blanke that Curtiz "is, of course, more likely to go overboard than any one else, because he just loves to work with mobs and props of this kind." An additional difficulty was that this was the first Technicolor feature for many involved, with complicated lighting, costume, and makeup requirements. The studio was throwing so much money into the project that Wallis eventually had several other directors filming material. In fact, as many as three crews were working at once, some reshooting material that had already been filmed and discarded for various reasons.

The producer and his staff had to persuade composer Erich Wolfgang Korngold to write the score for *Robin Hood*. According to film historian Rudy Behlmer, Korngold refused the project after he saw a rough cut. The worsening political situation in Austria, where Korngold's property was soon confiscated, forced the composer to secure financing to help get his family and relatives out of the country. He accepted the assignment; experts consider his score one of the best of the period.

At slightly over $2 million, *The Adventures of Robin Hood* was the most expensive Warners production to date. The first preview in Pomona, California, convinced studio executives that they had a hit. Behlmer noted that no significant changes were needed before its general release, and the film became one of the studio's biggest crowd pleasers. Warners rushed Flynn into a romantic melodrama, *The Sisters*, and a remake of *The Dawn Patrol* (both 1938) while preparing his next big vehicle, *Dodge City* (1939), a Technicolor Western that also featured de Havilland. They would appear together in a total of eight features. De Havilland also starred in the Registry title *The Heiress* (1949).

Love Finds Andy Hardy

MGM, 1938. Sound, B&W, 1.37. 91 minutes.

Cast: Lewis Stone (Judge James K. Hardy), Mickey Rooney (Andrew Hardy), Fay Holden (Emily Hardy), Cecilia Parker (Marian Hardy), Judy Garland (Betsy Booth), Lana Turner (Cynthia Potter), Ann Rutherford (Polly Benedict), Mary Howard (Mrs. Tompkins), Gene Reynolds (Jimmy MacMahon), Don Castle (Dennis Hunt), Betty Ross Clarke (Aunt Millie), Marie Blake (Augusta), George Breakston ("Beezy"), Raymond Hatton (Peter Dugan), Frank Darien (Bill Collector).

Credits: Directed by George B. Seitz. Screen play by William Ludwig. From the stories by Vivien R. Bretherton. Based upon the characters created by Aurania Rouverol. Recording director: Douglas Shearer. Art director: Cedric Gibbons. Associates: Stan Rogers, Edwin B. Willis. Wardrobe by Jeanne. Photographed by Lester White. Film editor: Ben Lewis. Songs: "Meet the Beat of My Heart," "It Never Rains But What It Pours," words and music by Mack Gordon and Harry Revel. "In-Between," words and music by Roger Edens. Vocal arrangements by Roger Edens. Musical score by David Snell.

Additional Credits: Produced by J.J. Cohn. Associate producer: Lou Ostrow. Assistant director: Tom Andre. Script supervisor: Carey Wilson. Sound: Ralph Shugart. Makeup: John Dawn. Production dates: May to June 1938. Released July 22, 1938.

Available: Warner Home Video DVD (2004). ISBN: 0-7907-8975-2. UPC: 0-12569-59062-5.

While child performers have always been popular in films, in the 1930s movies about adolescents were more problematic. Apart from the occasional nod to classics like *Huckleberry Finn* or *Tom Sawyer*, adolescents were either ignored or presented as problems, as in the juvenile delinquent melodrama *Wild Boys of the Road* (1933). A plush adaptation of Eugene O'Neill's nostalgic coming-of-age play *Ah, Wilderness!* was a success for MGM in 1935. Lionel Barrymore and Spring Byington played the warm, loving parents, while Mickey Rooney had an important part as a younger brother.

Born into a vaudeville family in 1920, Rooney became a part of the act and entered films when he was six. He changed his name from Joe Yule, Jr., to Mickey McGuire while starring in a series of films based on the McGuire comic-strip character, then to Mickey Rooney when he graduated to feature film roles in 1932. Rooney signed with MGM in 1934. After playing Puck in *A Midsummer Night's Dream* for Warners in 1935, Rooney had roles in prestige projects like *Ah, Wilderness!* and *Captains Courageous* (1937).

Perhaps in response to downbeat films like *Dead End* (1937), which portrayed teens as semiliterate gang members on their way to the gas chamber or electric chair, MGM head Louis B. Mayer actively sought out a project which would present family life in more pleasant terms. He also wanted to showcase Rooney, who had been forced to play down his gift for clowning and dancing in his previous features. Equally as important, Mayer was looking for stories that were cheap and easy to film. One project under development was an adaptation of the Broadway play *Skidding* by Aurania Rouverol, originally envisioned as a courtroom vehicle for Lionel Barrymore. Mayer had screenwriter Kay Van Riper build up a subsidiary role for Rooney. The result, *A Family Affair*, was enough of a hit that Mayer okayed a series of films based on the characters.

To keep costs down, Barrymore and Byington were replaced by contract employees Lewis Stone and Fay Holden. Cecilia Parker—another veteran of *Ah, Wilderness!*—continued her role as Andy's sometimes snobby older sister Marion. Assorted MGM ingénues, including Kathryn Grayson, Donna Reed, and Esther Williams, would appear as Andy's love interests. The stories would revolve around adolescent concerns: dates, cars, school, part-time jobs, vacation trips. By keeping the focus of the scripts narrow, producers J.J. Cohn and Lou Ostrow would be able to film cheaply on mostly pre-existing sets. Usually working with director George B. Seitz, they could shoot a Hardy film in a month, and have it in theaters a month later.

As film historian Thomas Schatz noted in *The Genius of the System*, *Love Finds Andy Hardy*, the fourth film in the series, "was put together virtually overnight." Rooney had appeared with Judy Garland in *Thoroughbreds Don't Cry* the previous year, and this installment in the Hardy series would be as much a showcase for her as for him. Both were committed to bigger films that summer, *Boys Town* and *The Wizard of Oz*, respectively, so shooting had to proceed quickly. As a result, screenwriter William Ludwig had to replace Van Riper, who was on another assignment, and Betty Ross Clark filled in for Sara Haden as Aunt Millie. Ludwig turned a *Cosmopolitan* magazine short story by Vivien R. Bretherton into a screenplay by late April 1938. Shooting started on May 16 and lasted twenty days, including one day for retakes. Garland's three musical numbers were filmed at the end of June. The film was previewed during the Fourth of July weekend, and opened in New York and Los Angeles on July 13.

Love Finds Andy Hardy was a solid hit, and MGM continued pairing Rooney and Garland. She would appear in two more Hardy films, but they began to blur together into a separate series of teen musicals with titles like *Babes in Arms* (1939), *Strike Up the Band* (1940), and *Babes on Broadway* (1941). Mayer and other studio executives couldn't help but notice that Rooney's low-budget films were making as much or more than big productions like *The Wizard of Oz* and *The Women*. In fact, Rooney was the top box-office star in the country from 1939 through 1941. Along with Deanna Durbin, Rooney was awarded a special Oscar in 1938 for "significant contribution in bringing to the screen the spirit and personification of youth, and as a juvenile player setting a high standard of ability and achievement." The Andy Hardy series won a special Oscar in 1942 "for its achievement in representing the American Way of Life."

Today it's difficult to understand all the fuss. The Hardy films can seem simple-minded and artificial when they're not focusing on Rooney, at which point they often become grating and overbearing. By this time a veteran with over ten years in the industry, Rooney had too many tricks to fall back on in his acting. He was always older than the part he was playing, and he always let viewers know it. His nervous tics—how he shook his hair or bugged out his eyes or bobbed his head—showed audiences that acting was just a game, that Rooney wasn't like Andy Hardy—or Jimmy or Terry or Whitey or his other roles—in real life. (In real life he married Ava Gardner, albeit briefly.)

Nor is the filmmaking in the Hardy series especially noteworthy. Director Seitz moves his actors around briskly, but can't disguise how threadbare the Hardy plots are. Or how tight his budget is, judging from how often he resorts to back-projection. Hardy premises are simple: the family goes on a vacation, or Emily visits her ailing mother, or Judge Hardy hears a minor case. Each film had one or two heart-to-heart, man-to-man talks between Andy and his father (here Andy has to confess that he put money down on a car). And each film featured Andy first flirting with and then angering a girl. *Love Finds Andy Hardy* has three thwarted romances: Regular girlfriend Polly Benedict (series regular Ann Rutherford) comes back unexpectedly from a vacation; local mantrap Cynthia Potter (Lana Turner, a few years away from true stardom) proves too demanding; and the visiting Betsy Booth (Judy Garland), the daughter of a musical comedy star, lacks the "glamour" necessary to keep Andy interested. Plot twists hinge on telegrams, phone calls, letters, and other hoary devices. Every half-hour or so the film stops so Garland can belt out a mediocre tune from the MGM song library.

Is it fair to hold the Andy Hardy films up to the same standards as more serious movies? The Hardy series functioned the way TV series do today. Viewers found the films reassuring because the characters never really changed no matter what problems they faced. (When Rooney did change—i.e., grew older—the series quickly fell out of favor.) The Hardy formula, altered slightly, endured throughout the 1950s, in the *Gidget* and *Beach Blanket Bingo* series, for example, but also in Elvis Presley's musicals. Although we compliment ourselves on our increased sophistication today, are television series like *Dawson's Creek* or *Gilmore Girls* really all that different from Andy Hardy?

Porky in Wackyland

Warner Bros., 1938. Sound, B&W, 1.37. 7 minutes.
Credits: Supervision: Robert Clampett. Produced by Leon Schlesinger. Animation: Norman McCabe and I. [Izzy] Ellis. Musical direction: Carl W. Stalling.
Additional Credits: Voice actor: Mel Blanc. Writing: Warren Foster. Writing and sound effects: Treg Brown. Released September 24, 1938.
Other Versions: Remade in color as *Dough for the Do-Do* (1949, directed by Friz Freleng). Clampett's *Tin Pan Alley Cats* (1943, Warner Bros.) and Tex Avery's *The Cat That Hated People* (1948, MGM) used elements from the original story line.
Available: Warner Home Video DVD, *Looney Tunes Golden Collection Volume 2* (2004). ISBN: 0-7907-8650-8. UPC: 0-85393-12842-5.

The Warner Brothers animation department produced the loudest, brashest, and most consistently funny cartoons of any major studio. It developed the largest stable of cartoon stars, employed some of the most significant artists in the industry, and left a legacy that continues to influence both humor and filmmaking. It was formed in late 1929 to cash in on the success of Walt Disney's cartoon shorts. Directors Hugh Harman, Rudolf Ising, and Isadore "Friz" Freleng had all worked for Disney. They approached producer Leon Schlesinger, who was running Pacific Art and Title. He arranged a deal with Warners to distribute what Harman and Ising called "Looney Tunes."

The series was a play on Disney's own Silly Symphonies, just like their first character, Bosko, resembled a rubbery version of Mickey Mouse. The first Bosko Looney Tune, *Sinkin' in the Bathtub*, came out in April 1930. Warners ordered a second series, "Merrie Melodies," designed to exploit its music library, in 1931. Ising headed this series, while Harmon concentrated on Looney Tunes. Harmon and Ising left in a budget dispute in 1933; Schlesinger replaced them by promoting animators Freleng and Bob Clampett.

In 1934 Schlesinger switched the Merrie Melodies series to color (Looney Tunes remained black-and-white until 1944). He also hired Tex Avery, who brought a new concern for characterization and for the structure and pacing of gags. (Avery's career is covered in *Magical Maestro*, 1952.) Other key hires included animator Chuck Jones, sound effects specialist Treg Brown, and voice actor Mel Blanc. (For more about Jones, see *One Froggy Evening*, 1956.) In Avery's first film for Warners, *Gold Diggers of '49* (January, 1936) he introduced an early version of a character who would become Porky Pig.

Frank Tashlin, another new director, helped refine Porky's screen persona, making him a clumsy, irritable middle-class home-owner as well as a stuttering pig. Porky became the first legitimate Warners cartoon star, and he was a strong enough character to retain his personality even though he was being handled by four different directors. This was partly due to Blanc, a radio performer whose vocal interpretations were both nuanced and vivid. But much of the style and "feel" of Warner Bros. cartoons was due to another hire: Carl Stalling.

Born in 1891 in Missouri, Stalling had played organ for silent films in Kansas City, where he also conducted orchestras in theaters. He had worked on the groundbreaking *Steamboat Willie* (1928), and then scored "Flip the Frog" cartoons for Ub Iwerks. It was Stalling who chose the theme songs for Looney Tunes ("The Merry-Go-Round Broke Down") and Merrie Melodies ("Merrily We Roll Along"), and developed the trademark "boinngg!" sound heard throughout the Warners canon.

But it was Stalling's encyclopedic knowledge of pop tunes that made his work so distinctive. "He developed a memory which related to the titles, so if you had a woman with a red dress on, he always played 'The Lady in Red,'" Chuck Jones remembered. "It didn't mean anything because nobody in the world knew the songs even then." But by adopting, squishing, chopping up, distorting, and dismembering pop chestnuts, Stalling was appealing to older, more educated viewers by adding a self-reflexive layer of irony only they would understand.

Although all the Warner Bros. cartoon directors took a hand at defining Porky, film critic Leonard Maltin credits Robert Clampett with the most inventive work. Clampett, who started working at Warners at the age of seventeen, directed ten cartoons in 1938, all but one of them starring Porky. Even by Warners' standards, *Porky in Wackyland* stands out. Ostensibly a story about Porky's search for the Dodo Bird, it's really an excuse for a series of blackout skits that gives free rein to the imaginations of animators and gag writers.

Some of the jokes are cultural references, like a duck repeating the word "Mammy!" in the style of Al Jolson, or a take-off on the Sinclair Lewis novel *It Can't Happen Here*. Others are the stuff of nightmares, especially since Clampett has stripped away familiar backgrounds. *Porky in Wackyland* looks more like a Dali or de Chirico landscape than a bit of middle America, and it was as fully populated at times as a Brueghel depiction of hell. If its visual style was aggressive, its content was positively subversive, especially in the context of the cartoons surrounding it.

Porky in Wackyland did little to alter or advance its characters, but it had a much larger influence on animators than one might suspect. Historian Michael Barrier considers this the first true Clampett cartoon, as he had essentially been teaming with Chuck Jones on his earlier films. Warners remade it twice, as *Tin Pan Alley Cats* in 1943, and again in color as *Dough for the Do-Do* in 1948. That same year Tex Avery, then at MGM, offered his own version of the story in *The Cat That Hated People*. *Porky in Wackyland* became a favorite of underground comic book artists of the late 1960s. They plundered its look and jokes repeatedly in "head" comics that surfaced at the time.

Clampett directed dozens of cartoons for Warners. He teamed Porky with Daffy Duck, helping ensure the latter's stardom; gave Porky the famous "That's all folks!" sign-off (stolen from the early Bosko cartoons); introduced an early version of Tweety Bird; and directed one of the most notorious of the Warners cartoons, *Coal Black and De Sebben Dwarfs* (1943). Clampett left Warners in 1946 for Screen Gems, where he worked on stories rather than directing.

Our Day

Wallace Kelly, 1938. Silent, B&W, 1.37. 12 minutes.
Featuring: Mrs. Oliver Kelly, Mabel G. Kelly, Oliver Kelly, Lady Luck. [Wallace Kelly also appears. Mrs. Oliver Kelly is Mattie Kelly, widow of Oliver Kelly, Sr., and mother to Oliver Jr. and Wallace. Mabel Kelly, née Graham, is Wallace's wife. Oliver Kelly, Jr., is Wallace's older brother and the editor and publisher of *The Lebanon Enterprise*. Lady Luck is the family wirehair terrier.]
Credits. Filmmaker: Wallace Kelly.
Available: The Internet Archive (*www.archive.org*).

An example of home movies from 1938, *Our Day* is both sophisticated and charming, a grab bag of cinematic devices and tricks in the employ of a "documentary" of a day in the life of the Kelly family. Filmed in 16mm by Wallace Kelly, and featuring his family and dog, it is further proof that the language of cinema is flexible enough for almost any purpose.

In the 1930s it did not take much technical expertise to crack the code of Hollywood filmmaking. With minimal training and the right equipment, just about anyone could obtain decent focus and exposures. What most home moviemakers lack is an understanding of the structure of film: what story to tell, what scenes to include, how to move from one scene to another, even how scenes are assembled in the first place. Wallace Kelly's background in art and journalism gave him an advantage over other amateur filmmakers. He knew both the elements of composition, and how to tell a story.

Kelly was born in Lebanon, Kentucky, about sixty miles southeast of Louisville, in 1910. After studying at the Cincinnati Art Academy, he moved to New York City in 1929 to work as a book illustrator. There he purchased a movie camera, skipping lunch for a year to pay for it, according to his daughter Martha. His first film, made in 1929–30, was about his life in New York. He also won the lead in *The Story of Astoria*, a commissioned film advertising the Queens neighborhood. Kelly auditioned for the Provincetown Players and was accepted into the company, but had to return to Lebanon to see to his ailing father. The stock-market crash in October 1929 contributed to the disbanding of the Provincetown Players.

By that time Kelly's father had died, and he remained at home to help his older brother Oliver run *The Lebanon Enterprise*, the family-owned newspaper. He continued to make motion pictures, and with his fiancée Mabel Graham, still photographs. In 1935, the two won first prize in the Newspaper National Snapshot Awards. They used their prize money to marry and then to study portrait photography in New York City.

Kelly and his wife opened a photographic studio in Lebanon (it can be seen in portions of *Our Day*). He also wrote a novel, *Days Are as Grass*, which was awarded the first Alfred A. Knopf Fellowship in 1940. During World War II he was a medic in the South Pacific. From 1946 to 1950, he made movies grouped as the "Baby Martha" series about his newborn daughter. After closing his photo studio, he devoted himself to painting, woodcuts, and other graphic arts.

According to Martha Kelly, her father made about twenty-five movies. His subjects included "family trips, the 1933 Century of Progress, friends and family in day-to-day activities (making a model airplane, playing tennis, riding a horse, singing Christmas carols), and his mother's flower garden. He tried some 'trick' photography such as fake car crashes and sinking ships and some animation." Only two of the films, *Our Day* and *The Enterprise Goes to Press*, had scripts, but Wallace added titles to some of the travel films.

"It was lonely," the daughter told a reporter about her father's life as an artist. Author Garry Barker referred to Kelly as an "ethical and classical" artist, "one who thought as much about art as he worked at producing it." Kelly's sophistication is obvious throughout *Our Day*, from the easy, natural performances he elicited from his family to his consistently inventive framing.

What really impresses viewers today is how well Kelly could mimic mainstream Hollywood filmmaking. He was especially adept at choosing the proper camera angle to advance his story. Most amateur filmmakers take a head-on approach to their subjects. Kelly used reverse angles, over-the-shoulder shots, and shifting points of view to generate a sense of seamless motion. "He did what a Hollywood director would have done at the time," said Dwight Swanson, one of the founders of The Center for Home Movies (*www.centerforhomemovies.org*).

Since 2003, the Center for Home Movies has helped coordinate Home Movie Days across the country. Martha Kelly and her husband Roger Bardwell read about a Home Movie Day in New York City in a "Talk of the Town" article in *The New Yorker*. They brought two of Kelly's films to an event in 2007. "*Our Day* was almost not shown because they thought it was an old episode of *Our Gang*," she remembered.

Dan Streible, an associate professor at NYU Cinema Studies and a founder of the Orphan Film Symposium, arranged for a DVD of *Our Day* to be screened at a National Film Preservation Board meeting, which helped lead to its selection to the Registry. Russ Suniewick restored the film and oversaw its blowup from the original 16mm to 35mm. Through his Colorlab, and a grant from Dwight Swanson, Suniewick is working on four more Wallace Kelly films. The new print of *Our Day* was first shown to the public at an Orphan Film Symposium screening on March 29, 2008.

Gunga Din

RKO, 1939. Sound, B&W, 1.37. 117 minutes.

Cast: Cary Grant ([Archibald] Cutter), Victor McLaglen (MacChesney), Douglas Fairbanks, Jr. ([Tommy] Ballantine), Sam Jaffe (Gunga Din), Eduardo Ciannelli (Guru), Joan Fontaine (Emmy [Stebbins]), Montagu Love (Colonel Weed), Robert Coote ([Bertie] Higginbotham), Abner Biberman (Chota), Lumsden Hare (Major Mitchell).

Credits: Produced and directed by George Stevens. Screenplay by Joel Sayer & Fred Guiol. Story by Ben Hecht & Charles MacArthur. From Rudyard Kipling's poem "Gunga Din." Music by Alfred Newman. Technical advisors: Sir Robert Erskin Holland, Captain Clive Morgan, Sergeant Major William Briers. Photography by Joseph H. August, A.S.C. Art director: Van Nest Polglase. Associate art director: Perry Ferguson. Special effects by Vernon L. Walker, A.S.C. Set decorations by Darrell Silvera. Gowns by Edward Stevenson. Recorded by John E. Tribby & James Stewart. Edited by Henry Berman & John Lockert. Assistant directors: Edward Killy & Dewey Starkey. Recorded by RCA Victor System. Pandro S. Berman in charge of production.

Additional Cast includes: Cecil Kellaway (Mr. Stebbins), Reginald Sheffield, Charles Bennett.

Additional Credits: Screenwriting by Anthony Veiller, William Faulkner, Dudley Nichols, Lester Cohen, John Colton, Vincent Lawrence. Editing by John Sturges. Production dates: June 24 to October 19, 1938. Premiered in Los Angeles on January 29, 1939.

Other Versions: Remade as *Sergeants 3* (1962).

Available: Warner Home Video DVD (2004). ISBN: 0-7806-4871-4. UPC: 0-53939-68362-2. Turner Home Entertainment VHS (1993).

The archetypal Hollywood adventure film, *Gunga Din* had a circuitous path to the screen. Nobel Prize–winning poet and author Rudyard Kipling originally wrote "Gunga Din" in 1890; it was collected in *Barrack-Room Ballads* in 1892. Set in the heart of the British colonial system, the poem extols the bravery of a water-carrier who yearned to become a real soldier. Producer Edward Small optioned the rights to the poem in 1936, shortly before joining RKO. Studio staff writers Lester Cohen and John Colton began a screen adaptation. After disagreeing with Samuel Goldwyn over *Come and Get It* (1936), director Howard Hawks also came to RKO. Excited about *Gunga Din*, he went to New York to work on a new draft with Ben Hecht and Charles MacArthur, the authors of *The Front Page*. As Todd McCarthy notes in his biography of Howard Hawks, the three turned to *Soldiers Three*, a collection of Kipling short stories, as well as to *The Front Page* itself for inspiration. In their version, Din is reduced to a subsidiary character. The real focus is on three friends, a Cockney, a Scot, and an Irishman, and their adventures battling a thuggee cult.

By early 1937, Hawks had turned the script over to Dudley Nichols, while RKO producer Sam Briskin asked MGM for the use of Clark Gable, Spencer Tracy, and Franchot Tone for the three leads. When the casting process dragged on too long, Hawks and Nichols went to work on a project that would become *Bringing Up Baby* (1938). By the time Hawks finished that film, Pandro S. Berman, head of his own production unit at RKO, had taken over *Gunga Din*. He ordered writer Anthony Veiller to cut down the existing script, which was close to three hundred pages. After meeting with Hawks over the project, he had RKO terminate its contract with the director.

Berman turned to George Stevens, who after *Swing Time* (1936) had worked with Fred Astaire and Ginger Rogers separately on movies. There was little in Stevens' career to indicate that he was suitable for what was going to be the most expensive RKO picture ever made, but the choice proved an astute one.

In later interviews, Stevens claimed that he thought up the idea of adding a third soldier to what had been a romantic triangle. He hired Joel Sayer (once with *The New Yorker*) and Fred Guiol (a former gag writer for Hal Roach) to come up with a new script in three weeks, complaining that the previous one was "all dialogue" and "there were no outside scenes." (According to Tom Dardis in *Some Time in the Sun*, William Faulkner also worked on the script, but received no screen credit.)

The cast now included Victor McLaglen, a burly Irishman who won an Oscar for *The Informer* (1935); Cary Grant, who was searching for a way to broaden his appeal from romances and comedies; and Douglas Fairbanks, Jr., who had made a splash in *The Prisoner of Zenda* (1937). Fairbanks would later claim that he and Grant switched roles on a coin toss, but Berman said that Grant insisted on taking the comic, rather than the romantic, lead. The title role went to Sam Jaffe. Already in his forties, he had started out in Yiddish theater with his mother Ada Steinberg Jaffe, and had just appeared as an ancient guru in Frank Capra's *Lost Horizon* (1937). The other big ethnic roles were filled by the Italian Eduardo Ciannelli and future

TV director Abner Biberman. Thrown in as well were silent star Montagu Love and nineteen-year-old Joan Fontaine, just about the only woman on a set of hundreds of men.

Almost all of the filming took place in Lone Pine, California, in the foothills of the Sierras. Stevens began shooting without a completed script, and said later that he was working a day ahead of the writers. In fact, his first scene was an improvised meeting between Grant and Jaffe, played out next to extras practicing drill formations. If Berman hoped that Stevens would work faster than Hawks, he was quickly disappointed. Stevens spent ten days constructing an action sequence that is the centerpiece of the film, but which placed the project irrevocably behind schedule and over budget.

This sequence, which sends McLaglen, Grant, and Fairbanks to the remote village of Tantrapur to investigate an ominously silent telegraph station, is one of the most exhilarating in film. Credit should go to the stars, who bring a brio, a bracing derring-do, and stout humor to their roles. The exceptional cinematography and set design are also factors, as is the outstanding stunt work. But it is Stevens who deserves the real accolades. His command of pacing is extraordinary. The scene builds from silent, cautious prowls through a deserted village of sunlit shacks, then bursts into action after armed thugs are discovered hiding in a gloomy shed. Stevens brews the scene slowly, adding more villains, then more firepower, to the mix. The shots are designed so clearly that viewers can sense the action flowing through the village. As the violence escalates the camera climbs as well, pulling up from streets to rooftops to the edge of a precipice.

Stevens' methods caused the film to go twenty days over the ten days alloted, but Berman was helpless to stop him without losing the studio's investment. *Gunga Din* eventually cost close to $2 million, an amount that was probably close to what Hawks would have spent. (He was busy planning his own action film, *Only Angels Have Wings*, which also starred Cary Grant.)

This is one of the few films Grant plays in uniform, but he proved that he was up to the demands of the adventure genre by broadening his Cockney accent and by emphasizing the comedy in his dialogue. Confronting a temple filled with assassins, he strolls to the center of the frame and says in a bantering tone, "Now you're all under arrest." (His background as an acrobat enabled him to keep his character's movements light and graceful.) McLaglen, excellent at portraying an aggrieved decorum, was equally good in an important role as the head of the trio, the one whose word carried the most weight among the three. McLaglen's dyspeptic sergeant gave Grant the chance to be irresponsible and get away with it.

The film's casual depiction of racism has raised some hackles over the years, but Stevens and his writers finessed part of the problem by making the villains thugs, and not Indian society as a whole. The film endorses the soldiers' behavior, but not the politics that put them there. (Stevens also gets away with a "damn" from Montagu Love as he recites the end of Kipling's poem. David O. Selznick took on the censors for the same problem in *Gone With the Wind*; the producer often found himself fighting battles other people had already won.)

Gunga Din's impact resonated throughout subsequent Hollywood action films. Released in January 1939, it became the second-highest grossing film of the year (number one was *Gone With the Wind*). Its influence can be seen in everything from *Butch Cassidy and the Sundance Kid* to the *Indiana Jones* films to action blockbusters like the *Die Hard* and *Terminator* series. *Butch Cassidy* screenwriter William Goldman said flatly, "Nothing ever in my life had the impact of *Gunga Din*. Nothing."

Stagecoach

The shot that helped make John Wayne a star: his introduction as The Ringo Kid in *Stagecoach*.

United Artists, 1939. Sound, B&W, 1.37. 96 minutes.

Cast: Claire Trevor (Dallas), John Wayne (Ringo Kid), Andy Devine (Buck), John Carradine (Hatfield), Thomas Mitchell (Doc [Josiah] Boone), Louise Platt (Lucy Mallory), George Bancroft ([Marshal] Curley [Wilcox]), Donald Meek (Peacock), Berton Churchill (Gatewood), Tim Holt (Lieutenant [Blanchard]), Tom Tyler (Luke Plummer).

Credits: Directed by John Ford. Original story: Ernest Haycox. Screenplay: Dudley Nichols. Art direction: Alexander Toluboff. Associate art director: Wiard B. Ihnen. Director of photography: Bert Glennon. Musical direction: Boris Morros. Musical score based on American Folk Songs adapted by Richard Hageman, Louis Gruenberg, Franke Harling, John Leipold, Leo Shuken. Film editors: Otho Lovering, Dorothy Spencer. Costumes: Walter Plunkett. Sound: Frank Maher. Assistant director: Wingate Smith. Western Electric Mirrophonic recording. A Walter Wanger presentation.

Additional Cast: Chris Martin (Chris), Cornelius Keefe (Captain Whitney), Elvira Rios (Yakeema), Francis Ford (Sgt. Billy Pickett), Florence Lake (Mrs. Nancy Whitney), Marga Ann Daighton (Mrs. Pickett), Walter McGrail (Captain Sickle), Paul McVey (Express agent), Brenda Fowler (Mrs. Gatewood), Chief Big Tree (Indian scout), Yakima Canutt (Cavalry scout), Chief White Horse (Indian leader), Bryant Washburn (Cavalry captain), Duke Lee (Lordsburg sheriff), Kent Odell (Billy Pickett, Jr.), Harry Tenbrook (Telegrapher), Louis Mason (Sheriff), Joe Rickson (Ike Plummer), Vester Pegg (Hank Plummer), William Hopper (Cavalry sergeant), Ed Brady (Saloonkeeper), Jim Mason (Jim), Franklyn Farnum (Deputy); Buddy Roosevelt, Bill Cody, Jr. (Ranchers); Helen Gibson (Dance hall girl), Steve Clemente.

Additional Credits: Produced by Walter Wanger. Stunt choreography: Yakima Canutt. Production dates: November 1938 to January 7, 1939. Released March 3, 1939.

Awards: Oscars for Best Actor in a Supporting Role (Mitchell), Best Music—Scoring.

Other Versions: Remade as *Stagecoach* in 1966 (directed by Gordon Douglas) and 1986 (directed by Ted Post).

Available: Warner Home Video DVD (2006). ISBN: 1-4198-2472-4. UPC: 0-12569-7899-3.

Including shorts and television shows, John Ford directed 137 films, and supervised 87 documentaries. He won four Best Directing Oscars, was a founding member of the Director's Guild of America, and was held in high regard by his peers. Although he suffered through a string of disappointing films in the late 1930s, when he began filming *Stagecoach*, he was arguably the most accomplished and talented director in America.

Born the son of Irish immigrants in 1895, Sean O'Feeney grew up in Portland, Maine, although he returned frequently with his family to Ireland. A theater usher as a teenager, he became interested in film after his older brother Francis became an actor. Francis changed his surname to Ford, entered the film industry in 1909, and quickly became a notable star and director. When he got John a job at Universal in 1914, his younger brother also adopted the Ford surname.

Within three years, John Ford had worked his way up from property master to director. He started a series of Western features starring Harry Carey, variants on the films William S. Hart was making. Some of these have resurfaced in recent years, and already display Ford's talent for distilling narrative events to quick, forceful visual images. Ford moved to William Fox's studio in the 1920s, where he mastered both large-scale epics like *The Iron Horse* (1924) and low-key, easygoing comedies like *Riley the Cop* (1928).

Ford was skilled at every aspect of filmmaking, from costume design and art direction to cinematography and editing. He knew how to tell a story without dialogue, how to move crowds and focus action, and how to stage fights and slapstick. His eye for composition and for staging dramatic material has never been bettered in film. He was drawn to American themes, often in the Western frontier, and to stories about the moral issues that shaped the country. In his later years, Ford's viewpoints could curdle into blind patriotism, but even then he was willing to question authority.

When interviewed, Ford liked to tell tall tales, entertaining but often unreliable, about his films. He claimed that Westerns were passé when he set out to make *Stagecoach* in 1937. The truth is, Westerns made up almost a third of all movies filmed in Hollywood, and supplied most of the revenue for the industry. Performers in Westerns could make far more money for their studios at the box office than stars with higher salaries. Buck Jones helped keep Universal afloat during the Depression, while Gene Autry almost singlehandedly invented the entire singing cowboy genre. Studio executives may have looked down on Westerns, but when *Stagecoach* was released, it was competing against *Union Pacific*, *The Oklahoma Kid*, *Frontier Marshal*, *Santa Fe Trail*, *Destry Rides Again*, *Virginia City*, *Jesse James*, and several other big-budget Westerns.

Ford also claimed that *Stagecoach* was based on Guy de Maupassant's "Boule de Suif," the unofficial source for *Shanghai Express*, *The Bridge at San Luis Rey*, and any number of other films and books. The script really came from "Stage to Lordsburg" by Ernest Haycox, a short story about a gunman who falls in love with a prostitute while on his way to a shoot-out. Screenwriter Dudley Nichols changed some plot elements, added and subtracted characters, but essentially followed the basics of Haycox's plot. The final script places a group of disparate characters into a perilous situation, then watches how they react to pressure. In this case it's a largely self-exiled group: a Confederate soldier, an absconding banker, an alcoholic doctor, a wanted criminal, a prostitute forced out of town.

Ford met producer Merian C. Cooper when they were both working at RKO in the early 1930s. By this time Cooper, the man behind *Grass* (1925) and *King Kong* (1933), and an early advocate of Technicolor, had a production deal with David O. Selznick. He and Ford hoped to make *Stagecoach* as a large-scale color epic, but Ford had already promised the lead roles in the film to John Wayne and Claire Trevor. When Selznick demurred, Cooper also dropped out (he would work with Ford again after World War II). Ford ended up with Walter Wanger at United Artists, a move that severely cut back his budget.

Wayne had been kicking around in bit parts and B-Westerns ever since *The Big Trail* flopped back in 1930. (Tom Tyler, his one-time partner in "The Three Mesquiteers" series, shows up here as villain Luke Plummer.) Ford knew the Ringo Kid was a star-making role, and he also knew that Wayne had matured to the point where he could carry it. The actor credited stunt man Yakima Canutt, another Three Mesquiteers veteran, for much of his style. "I spent weeks studying the way Yakima Canutt walked and talked," he said. "I noticed that the angrier he got, the lower his voice, the slower his tempo. I try to say my lines low and strong and slow, the way Yak did."

Canutt, who won the world rodeo championship three years in a row, was responsible for many of the film's stunts. (This was the only time he worked on a Ford production.) The chases in particular were so impressive that they are being copied to this day. These scenes were photographed in California, as were the film's interiors. But to many viewers the film is inextricably linked to Monument Valley. This was the first time Ford used the location, and he would return more than a half-dozen times. *Stagecoach*'s images of majestic buttes, far-flung horizons, and immense skies are so stately that they still evoke feelings of pride and grandeur. Ford also established long-term relationships with the Navajo in the area. The tribe gave him the name Natani Nez, or Tall Leader, and the director would go on to use them in several more films.

While *Stagecoach* features all the expected elements of a Western—Indian attacks, chases, shoot-outs, gunfights—the characters set the film apart from the fillers and programmers that made up much of the genre. By treating his story and characters seriously, Ford helped elevate the Western in general, proving that it could accommodate adult situations. (Wayne and Claire Trevor were so popular a screen couple that they appeared together again almost immediately in *Allegheny Territory*.)

The camera negative to *Stagecoach* is gone, lost to nitrate decomposition and to the decision to extract sections for trailers. Most of the prints in circulation during the 1950s and '60s were battered and splicy. The current available version of *Stagecoach* comes from a preservation negative made from John Wayne's personal copy. *Stagecoach* has proven an enormous influence over filmmakers ranging from Orson Welles, who screened it repeatedly before starting *Citizen Kane* (1941), to Joss Whedon, creator of the television series *Firefly* and its film version, *Serenity* (2005). "I'm not going to make any bones about it, *Stagecoach* was the model for this as much as any other single thing," he said in an interview.

Ford's next film on the Registry, *Young Abe Lincoln*, was made the same year.

Verbena Tragica

Columbia, 1938. Sound, B&W, 1.33. 71 minutes.

Cast: Fernando Soler (Mateo Vargas), Luana de Alcañiz (Blanca), Juan Torena (Claudio), Pilar Arcos (Mamita), Cecilia Callejo (Lola), Jorge [George] Mari (Pepito), Carlos Villarías (Manuel), Romualdo Tirado (Perez), Sergio de Karlo (Luis), Leonor Turich (Tensita), Danton Ferrero (Doctor), Lou Hicks (Pat), Carlos Ruffino (Tomara), Israel Garcia (Jose), Fred Gonzalez (Ventura), Pedro Viñas (Vendedor de Globos).

Credits: Dirigida por Charles Lamont. Argumento original y adaptación cinematográfica de Jean Bart. Producida por Jaime Del Amo. Gerente de Producción: Frederick A. Spencer. Fotografía: Arthur Martinelli. Sonido: William R. Fox. Compilación: Guy V. Thayer. Escenografía: Edward Jewell. Supervisión musical: Lee Zahler. Version española de Miguel de Zárraga. Canciones originales "El Patrón," "El Coronel," Sergio de Karlo. "Gitanerías," Pilar Arcos. Ayudante director: Ralph Slosser. Western Electric Sound System. Una producción Cantabria Films.

Credits in English: Directed by Charles Lamont. Story and screenplay by Jean Bart. Produced by Jaime Del Amo. Production manager: Frederick A. Spencer. Photographed by Arthur Martinelli. Sound: William R. Fox. Edited by Guy V. Thayer. Art direction: Edward Jewell. Musical supervisor: Lee Zahler. Spanish translation: Miguel de Zárraga. Assistant director: Ralph Slosser. Songs "El Patrón," "El Coronel," words and music by Sergio de Karlo. "Gitanerías," words and music by Pilar Arcos.

Additional Credits: Filmed May–June 1938. Released March 12, 1939.

Available: The Library of Congress.

When the film industry switched from silent to sound movies, the foreign market—a significant portion of Hollywood's income—was suddenly in jeopardy. Cutters could change the intertitles used in silents from English to any language without affecting the film as a whole, but spoken dialogue presented unprecedented problems. Subtitling was expensive, and with the equipment of the time could degrade cinematography. Dubbing required a new cast of voice actors who needed rehearsal time. No matter how hard they tried, their voices would never match the movements of mouths on screen. A third approach involved filming the same story in different languages. Again, this was expensive, and the resulting films could differ from each other in terms of acting, pacing, and even lighting.

This third approach was the preferred method in the transitional period from silent to sound, and it's possible today to compare the English version of *Dracula* with its Spanish counterpart, or an English and German *Anna Christie*. It was a small but notable step from duplicating an English-language film to producing an original story in another language. Warners made films in French and German; Universal financed some shorts made in Germany; Fox Films released German features. But writing and shooting films for European audiences, in countries with established film industries, did not make much sense in California. On the other hand, Los Angeles had a sizable Spanish-speaking population, with Mexico and Central and South America not far away.

All of the major studios distributed Spanish-language films, about 150 of them between 1930 and 1938, according to film historian Gary D. Keller. Katz counted thirty features in 1930, and over forty in 1931, but noted that production dropped rapidly through the balance of the decade. *Primavera en otoño* (1933, Fox), *Contra la corriente* (1936, RKO), and *Sucedió en La Habana* (1938, Republic) all starred Luana Alcañiz, a Spanish-born actress whose regal bearing made her ideal for playing both wives and mistresses.

Even a lower-tier studio like Columbia dabbled in the Hispanic market. It released four such films in 1931, and while the numbers declined over the decade, continued sending out features to Spanish-language theaters: *La Noche del Pecado* (1933), *La Sombra de Pancho Villa* (1934), *En Agua en el Suelo* (1935), etc. Like most of Columbia's product, these were low-budget melodramas with accordingly limited production values. *Cruz Diablo* (1935) aimed a little higher, and featured Julian Soler in a supporting role.

Soler, who appeared in two other Columbia features, was one of four brothers who acted in movies. (There were eight children in all; a sister, Mercedes, appeared in dozens of movies.) The eldest brother was born Fernando Díaz Pavía in 1896. His first screen credit was *The Spanish Jade* (1915), but he came into his own in the 1930s, playing brusque but good-natured leads in dramas and affable buffoons in comedies. Soler worked in Mexico and also for Cinexport Distributing, a U.S. company that specialized in Spanish-language films.

Verbena Tragica (or Tragic Festival) was a change of pace for Soler. Written in English by Jean Bart, a playwright also responsible for *The Man Who Reclaimed His Head* (1934), the story takes place in New York City over the Columbus Day holiday, with a street fair as the backdrop. Soler plays Mateo, a Spanish-born boxer who is ending an eight-month jail sentence for fighting with a policeman. Waiting for him are his mother (Pilar Arcos, a Cuban singer), his young brother Pepito (George Mari), and his wife Blanca (Alcañiz). Rounding out the cast are his manager Manuel (Carlos Villarías, who starred in the Spanish version of *Dracula*), a neighbor Claudio (played by the Filipino Juan Torena), and a sister Lola (Cecilia Callejo). The story takes place over the course of one day, on three main sets: Mateo's apartment, a neighborhood saloon, and the street outside. A sense of claustrophobia enhances the tragic aspect of the story, as the characters have nowhere to hide once their secrets unfold.

This was the second and final project for Cantabria Films, a company run by Jaime Del Amo. But apart from the language, *Verbena Tragica* was in all respects a typical Columbia picture. The crew included those working their way up from independent films, like composer Lee Zahler and art director Edward Jewell (both had contributed to the tawdry *Rebellious Daughters* in 1938). Cinematographer Arthur Martinelli had already shot a Spanish-language film, *Mis dos amores* (1938), for Paramount. Assistant director Ralph Slosser worked on the second unit for *Gone With the Wind* (1939), but titles like *House of Dracula* (1945) are more typical of his projects. *Verbena Tragica* was directed by Charles Lamont, a Mack Sennett veteran whose previous titles included *Oh, Duchess!* (1936), *Knee Action* (1937), and the Buster Keaton short *Love Nest on Wheels*. Lamont's presence behind the camera may explain the film's reliance on literal slapstick, with child actor George Mari bearing the brunt of the slaps. Lamont keeps a steady pace, pausing only for jokes and three songs, trusting the actors to deliver even if he didn't understand what they were saying.

Columbia approached the Hays Office for approval to shoot the project as *Block Party*, and was warned that the story's elements of adultery would have to be handled carefully. That may be one reason why an English-language version was never filmed. (It may also be the reason why *Verbena Tragica* was never copyrighted, despite a copyright notice in the opening credits.) Journalist Miguel de Zárraga translated Bart's script into Spanish, and may be responsible for some of the film's cultural flavor. The characters drink wine instead of beer, and have paella for dinner, but in most respects could be of any ethnicity. They wear coats and ties or dresses, smoke cigarettes, sit at the same tables and hit the same marks that their English counterparts did. They even banter with a typical New York Irish cop, even though this one happens to speak Spanish.

Politics would hasten the decline of Hollywood Spanish-language films, but they were replaced by product from a burgeoning Mexico studio system. That same year Soler and Alcañiz moved to Mexico, Soler to begin directing and producing as well as starring in films. Luis Buñuel cast him in *El Gran Calavera* (1949) and *Susana* (1951). He continued working until his death in 1979. Cecilia Callejo found small parts in English-language films like *Only Angels Have Wings* (1939), and even worked with Lamont again in *Salome Where She Danced* (1945). Later in his career, Lamont helmed several films featuring Abbott and Costello, Ma and Pa Kettle, and Judy Canova, as well as Technicolor costume adventures starring Maureen O'Hara and Yvonne de Carlo. These last helped gain him a cult following. Lamont died in 1993.

Marian Anderson: The Lincoln Memorial Concert

Hearst Metrotone/MGM, 1939. Sound, B&W, 1.37. 8 minutes.
Featuring: Marian Anderson, Kosti Vehanen, Harold Ickes.
Credits: Combined from an NBC radio broadcast and Hearst Metrotone newsreel footage by archivists Blaine Bartell and Jeffrey Bickel at the UCLA Film and Television Archive. Filmed and recorded Easter Sunday, April 9, 1939.
Available: The first portion of the concert appears on Image Entertainment DVD *Treasures from American Film Archives* (2000). UPC: 0-14381-9706-2-3.

Marian Anderson's career was largely, and unfairly, defined by race. Born in 1897 in Philadelphia, she was twelve years old when her father died. The oldest of three daughters, Anderson by then had been singing with the Union Baptist Church choir for six years. She attracted enough attention for the church to take up a collection for her education, but she was prevented from attending a Philadelphia music school because she was black. While her mother took in laundry, Anderson scrubbed floors to help pay for private music lessons. She applied to Yale, but couldn't afford the tuition when she was accepted.

Anderson won a singing contest with the New York Philharmonic, began recording spirituals for Victor, and gave a concert at New York's Town Hall, but had trouble advancing her career. She studied and performed in London, then used a fellowship to tour Europe. During the 1933 season, she gave over a hundred concerts, and in the following years performed in Russia, France, Spain, and Austria. After a concert in Salzburg, conductor Arturo Toscanini exclaimed, "What I have heard today one is privileged to hear only once in a hundred years."

Impresario Sol Hurok offered Anderson the opportunity to return to the United States in 1935. Her comeback concert at Town Hall was a triumph, leading to performances on records, radio, and in movie shorts, as well as a grueling but highly profitable touring schedule. Although she could sing for Eleanor and Franklin Delano Roosevelt in the White House, she still faced segregation in the South. In 1938, the only Southern state where Anderson could perform was Texas.

To broaden her audience, Hurok tried to book an Easter Sunday concert at Constitution Hall, a 4,000-seat auditorium in Washington, D.C., that was owned by the Daughters of the American Revolution (DAR). Theaters were still segregated in Washington. At the National Theater, blacks were allowed to perform on stage, but couldn't sit in the audience. The DAR policy at Constitution Hall prohibited them from performing on stage (although they were allowed to sit in balconies). When booking manager Fred E. Hand turned down the concert, Hurok brought the DAR's policy to the attention of the press.

Although Eleanor Roosevelt resigned from the DAR in protest, the ban against Anderson was not rescinded. Working through the NAACP, Hurok broached the idea for a racially integrated concert to be held outdoors. Secretary of the Interior Harold Ickes authorized the use of the plaza in front of the Lincoln Memorial.

When the concert began shortly after 5:00 p.m., official estimates placed the size of the crowd at 75,000. Ickes opened the program with a stirring introduction, insisting that "Genius draws no color line." Backed by her longtime accompanist, Finnish pianist Kosti Vehanen, Anderson sang seven songs, starting with "America" and encoring with the popular spiritual "Nobody Knows the Trouble I've Seen."

The concert was broadcast on the NBC Blue radio network, and filmed in part by Hearst Metrotone News. According to UCLA archivist Blaine Bartell, Fox Movietone, Warner Pathe, and Paramount may also have filmed portions of the concert. The Hearst cameramen stopped shooting Anderson after the first verse of "America," and didn't resume until her third number, Schubert's "Ave Maria." Excerpts from the Hearst footage were used in a story called "Nation's capital gets a lesson in tolerance," released through MGM in *News of the Day*, volume 10, number 259. UCLA has preserved that episode and the Hearst outtakes.

At UCLA's Ninth Festival of Preservation in 1998, Bartell and fellow archivist Jeffrey Bickel presented Hearst footage that had been synched to the NBC radio broadcast. "We began this project with three different sources for sound, all of which were recorded at slightly different speeds," Bartell wrote. "We used digital technology to work on the sound track, and photochemical labs for the picture. This meant we were able to maintain proper pitch as we intercut elements but could not maintain a constant tempo." Recent advances in digital technologies could address problems Bartell faced earlier. He has also located additional footage of the concert, but added that "at present we do not have the funds needed to proceed."

The DAR's ban against black performers continued until 1952. Among the other artists affected were Paul Robeson, Harry Belafonte, and Hazel Scott. Anderson finally performed in Constitution Hall in 1953. By that time she was "an international figure of the highest importance," in the words of one reporter. She toured Japan with Eleanor Roosevelt, made her debut at the Metropolitan Opera in 1955, was a goodwill ambassador for the U.S. State Department, and sang at two presidential inaugurations. She was awarded more than twenty honorary degrees and, in 1963, the Presidential Medal of Freedom. Anderson died on April 8, 1993.

Wuthering Heights

United Artists, 1939. Sound, B&W, 1.33. 104 minutes.
Cast: Merle Oberon (Cathy), Laurence Olivier (Heathcliff), David Niven (Edgar), Flora Robson (Ellen), Donald Crisp (Dr. Kenneth), Geraldine Fitzgerald (Isabella), Hugh Williams (Hindley), Leo G. Carroll (Joseph), Miles Mander (Lockwood), Cecil Kellaway (Earnshaw), Cecil Humphreys (Judge Linton), Sarita Wooten (Cathy as a child), Rex Downing (Heathcliff as a child), Douglas Scott (Hindley as a child).
Credits: Directed by William Wyler. Screen play by Charles MacArthur and Ben Hecht. From the novel by Emily Brontë. Produced by Samuel Goldwyn. Photography: Gregg Toland. Art direction: James Basevi. Music: Alfred Newman. Costumes: Omar Kiam. Film editor: Daniel Mandell. Sound recorder: Paul Neal. Makeup artist: Blagoe [Robert] Stephanoff. Assistant director: Walter Mayo. Western Electric Recording. A Samuel Goldwyn presentation.
Additional Cast: Alice Ehlers (Harpsichordist).
Additional Credits: Screenwriting by John Huston. Released April 13, 1939.
Awards: Oscar for Best Cinematography, Black-and-White.
Other Versions: *Abismos de pasión* (1954, directed by Luis Buñuel); *Wuthering Heights* (1970, directed by Robert Fuest); *Wuthering Heights* (1978, TV miniseries directed by Peter Hammond); *Hurlevent* (1985, directed by Jacques Rivette); *Arashi ga oka* (1988, directed by Yoshishige Yoshida); *Wuthering Heights* (1992, directed by Peter Kosminsky); *Wuthering Heights* (1998, television, directed by David Skynner); *Wuthering Heights* (2003, television, directed by Suri Krishnamma); *Cime tempestose* (2004, television, directed by Fabrizio Costa).
Available: MGM Home Entertainment VHS (2000). ISBN: 0-7928-4598-6. UPC: 0-27616-00132-0.

Published in 1847 under the pseudonym Ellis Bell, *Wuthering Heights* was a popular rather than critical success, and the only novel by Emily Brontë, who died the following year. When Hollywood went on a mid-1930s binge of adapting the classics, screenwriters Charles MacArthur and Ben Hecht finished a draft that retained the novel's gothic elements and complicated flashback structure, but that stripped away almost half the plot. Their new version focused on the affair between Cathy Earnshaw and Heathcliff, an orphan found on the streets of Liverpool by her father, and ended with the lovers' deaths.

Director William Wyler may have found out about the script from Sylvia Sidney, who had starred in his *Dead End* (1937), and may have tricked producer Samuel Goldwyn into buying it by claiming that Walter Wanger was going to make it. What's clear is that Goldwyn, who based the reputation of his studio on the prestige of its output, needed a story like *Wuthering Heights* to compete with similar films from MGM (*Pride and Prejudice*, 1940), David O. Selznick (*Gone With the Wind*, 1939), and Warner Brothers (Wyler's own *Jezebel*, 1938). Goldwyn also needed a project for Merle Oberon, the Indian-born British actress whose contract he had purchased from her future husband Alexander Korda.

Wyler, who was also under contract to Goldwyn, sailed to England in 1938 to research the Yorkshire moors and to find a cast for his film. He signed Flora Robson, a distinguished actress who had appeared with Oberon in the unfinished *I, Claudius* (1937). On the recommendation of Hecht, he sought out Laurence Olivier, who had starred with Oberon in *The Divorce of Lady X* (1938). Olivier, hired and then fired from *Queen Christina* (1933) with Greta Garbo, had professed disdain for Hollywood, preferring the British stage. He was also in the midst of a tempestuous affair with Vivien Leigh (both were married to others at the time), and suggested that if she were cast as Cathy he might reconsider. Wyler, who also tested Robert Newton for Heathcliff, eventually won Olivier over. Leigh accompanied him to California, where she was quickly cast as Scarlett O'Hara in *Gone With the Wind*.

Wyler reworked the script with an uncredited John Huston, but the two couldn't alter the fact that the story as Wyler could film it was little more than a series of entrances and exits surrounding the same basic emotional conflict played out obsessively and repetitively. (*Abismo de pasión*, an excellent 1954 Mexican version directed by Luis Buñuel, was far more frank about the novel's themes of incest and necrophilia.) What Wyler needed to do was find a way to make the characters in the story, and the world surrounding them, seem real. He started by filling out the rest of the cast from the ranks of British actors living in Los Angeles. David Niven, who had appeared in *Dodsworth* (1936), was hesitant to work with Wyler again, but the director swore that he had changed from the prior tyrant who demanded take after take.

But Wyler hadn't changed. Niven recalled that the director required forty takes for a simple shot in which he merely had to enter a room. Wyler drove everyone in the cast to distraction by shooting the same gesture, the same line of dialogue, the same movement over and over. Many of the performers who worked with the director accused him of sadism or worse, but Wyler's tactics had logical roots. Bette Davis recalled watching rushes with Wyler, and seeing her performance change from rehearsed and mannered to passionate and unfettered as the takes mounted up.

Wyler was trying to achieve the absence of artifice, a psychological reality that looked and felt spontaneous rather than willed. If that meant fostering an antagonism between Olivier and Oberon, or allowing the headstrong Olivier to become a figure of scorn on the set, or driving Oberon into the hospital after filming her hysterical breakdown, Wyler didn't mind. He was confident in his approach, and believed his methods would help the technicians on the set reach the same level of automatic proficiency as the actors. In a scene set in the Grange, the home of the Linton family, Niven stands over Oberon, who is seated before her needlepoint stand. At one point he leans towards her, then straightens again. The camera almost imperceptibly follows his movement down and up, mirroring his indecision, an effect that could only be the result of repeated practicing. (This was the third complete film that Wyler made with Gregg Toland, one of the most respected cinematographers in the industry.)

Production notes emphasized the other efforts Wyler and Goldwyn made toward realism, including stripping hundreds of acres of vegetation from the hills surrounding Chatsworth, California, and importing a thousand heather plants to simulate the English moors. On the other hand, Goldwyn insisted on changing the time frame of the novel from the turn of the nineteenth century to the 1840s so Oberon and Geraldine Fitzgerald (who played her sister-in-law Isabella) could wear off-the-shoulder dresses.

In addition, Goldwyn wanted a happy ending. As Wyler put it, "He didn't want to look at a corpse at the fadeout." When Wyler refused to comply, Goldwyn hired H.C. Potter to direct the closing shot, which used doubles for Olivier and Oberon to reunite their characters in the afterlife. (Producer Darryl F. Zanuck would demand something similar for his adaptation of *How Green Was My Valley*, a project that Wyler started working on, but that John Ford actually directed.)

Wuthering Heights opened to respectful reviews, but the film did not break even until Goldwyn rereleased it some years later. It did help make Olivier a star; his next movie in Hollywood was *Rebecca* (1940). Wyler continued working with Goldwyn until he enlisted in the service during World War II. At the end of the war, the two reunited for *The Best Years of Their Lives*, their last project together.

The City

Civic Films, Inc., 1939. Sound, B&W, 1.37. 44 minutes.

Credits: Directed and photographed by Ralph Steiner, Willard Van Dyke. Produced by American Documentary Films, Inc. Associate in production: Henwar Rodakiewicz. Original outline: Pare Lorentz. Scenario: Henwar Rodakiewicz. Commentary: Lewis Mumford. Narrated by Morris Carnovsky. Photographed by Ralph Steiner, Willard Van Dyke. Film editor: Theodore Lawrence. Original music by Aaron Copland. Associate cameramen: Roger Barlow, Edward Anhalt, Rudolph Bretz. Musical conductor: Max Goberman. Production manager: John Flory. Supervised by Oscar Serlin. Recorded by RCA. Made possible from a grant from the Carnegie Corporation of New York. A presentation of The American Institute of Planners through Civic Films, Inc.

Additional Credits: Premiered at the New York World's Fair on May 26, 1939. **Available:** The Internet Archive (*www.archive.org*).

Backed by a somber, stately theme by Aaron Copland, *The City* opens with a written thesis: "We must remould our old cities and build new communities better suited to our needs." To prove that point, directors and cinematographers Ralph Steiner and Willard Van Dyke offer five segments that explore different aspects of city life, from rural

One of the reasons why *The City* argues for urban planning.

New England with its town meetings to planned communities in the suburbs.

Van Dyke shot and directed the opening and closing segments. His idyllic view of life in an agrarian New England community—sunny weather, water wheels, and pleasant town meetings—ignores the isolation, poor transporation, backbreaking labor, and fragile health that dominated life in the eighteenth century. Van Dyke's meticulous cinematography presents a world that is calm, self-contained, and exquisitely beautiful. Watch how he frames a magnificent tree behind a blacksmith working the metal rim of a broken wheel. While Henwar Rodakiewicz and Lewis Mumford are given credit for the screenplay and narration, Pare Lorentz's influence is unmistakable, from the use of repetition to poetic phrases like, "We used our hands and mastered what our hands did for us."

The second segment, shot by Ralph Steiner, documents the squalid living conditions in the tenements surrounding steel mills in Pittsburgh. This is real advocacy filmmaking, capturing appalling conditions and presenting them to an audience whose diet of Hollywood films may have left them unprepared for such realism. Steiner leads viewers into the material by cutting from the eighteenth-century blacksmith's forge to workers tapping a modern-day furnace of molten steel. With Copland adding the rhythm of a railroad to the score, Steiner follows freight trains from the factory yard to a vast industrial landscape. As Morris Carnovsky intones, "Pillars of smoke by day, pillars of fire by night," Steiner begins shifting the focus from work to home, now using smoke as a visual motif. Steiner concentrates on children

and the elderly—those most at risk from their surroundings—and through editing suggests that these conditions are endemic to industrial cities. It's a masterful segment, as troubling today as it was in 1939.

Steiner is also responsible for the next two sections, one dealing with Manhattan, another with traffic congestion in and around cities. The Manhattan footage evokes an earlier era of city symphonies, with skyscrapers reduced to abstract geometric forms and juxtaposed with masses of anonymous workers on streets, trains, and ferries. What distinguishes Steiner's approach is how he gradually starts mixing staged footage in with actuality footage, until in his segment on traffic jams, almost all of the material is scripted.

The final section, by Van Dyke, is also scripted, although some of the footage that ended up in the film was improvised. Shot in Radburn, New Jersey, and Greenbelt, Maryland, the segment depicts life in a planned community as a series of bike rides and ball games on treeless, landscaped fields outside austere concrete and cinderblock buildings. It's a sobering and not very convincing vision of the new frontier as a sort of prefabricated hive filled with happy drones. Just as with Lorentz's *The River* (1937), the solutions offered here—highways, cloverleafs, and what Archer Winsten called "factories that look like the Museum of Modern Art"—might be considered problems today.

This was Van Dyke's first attempt at directing. Born in Colorado in 1906, he became an accomplished still photographer, forming the influential f/64 group in San Francisco in 1932 with Edward Weston, Ansel Adams, and others. He was one of three cinematographers on Pare Lorentz's *The*

River (1937). Steiner, whose H_2O (1929) is in the Registry, also worked with Lorentz on *The Plow That Broke the Plains* (1936). Both were members of Frontier Films, the left-wing group formed in part as a reaction to "The March of Time." *The City* had originally been planned for Frontier Films, but when Steiner and Van Dyke quit the group over political differences, they took the project with them.

The City was sponsored by the newly named American Institute of Planners (AIP), an organization of professional city planners. It was an outgrowth of The American City Planning Institute (ACPI), formed in 1917 with Frederick Law Olmstead, Jr., as president. In addition to certifying city planners, the ACPI tried to influence public policy and legislation, and to persuade the public of the need for city planning. Frederick J. Adams and Flavel Shurtleff, both on the faculty of the Massachusetts Institute of Technology, were significant members, the former editing the ACPI *Planners' Journal*. They saw *The City* as an opportunity for the American Institute of Planners to make its case directly to the public attending the 1939 World's Fair in New York City. It was shown daily at the Theatre of the Science and Education Building on the World's Fair site in Flushing, where it was seen by thousands.

While critics were generally positive in their reviews, they were fully aware of what Winsten, a writer for the *New York Post*, referred to as "the dreamy aspect of wishful thinking." British filmmaker John Grierson wrote, "There is something wrong about the Steiner–Van Dyke paradise . . . I do not believe Steiner and Van Dyke believe a word of it any more than I do. . . . Their cameras get an edge and defeat their theories."

World War II disrupted American Documentary Films. Lorentz became head of the U.S. Film Service, while Van Dyke went overseas for the Office of War Information. His subsequent career consisted almost entirely of work on sponsored films, followed by a stint at the Museum of Modern Art and one as vice president of the International Federation of Film Archives. After World War II, Steiner was hired briefly at MGM, but could not adjust to working within the studio system. He later concentrated on experimental films, financing them with his commercial photography.

In 1978, the AIP merged with the American Society of Planning Officials to become the American Planning Association, "a nonprofit public interest and research organization representing 39,000 practicing planners, officials, and citizens involved with urban and rural planning issues."

Young Mr. Lincoln

Twentieth Century-Fox, 1939. Sound, B&W, 1.37. 100 minutes.

Cast: Henry Fonda (Abraham Lincoln), Alice Brady (Abigail Clay), Marjorie Weaver (Mary Todd), Arleen Whelan (Hannah Clay), Eddie Collins (Efe [Turner]), Pauline Moore (Ann Rutledge), Richard Cromwell (Matt Clay), Donald Meek (John Felder), Judith Dickens (Carrie Sue), Eddie Quillan (Adam Clay), Spencer Charters (Judge Herbert A. Bell), Ward Bond (J. Palmer Cass).

Credits: Directed by John Ford. Original screen play by Lamar Trotti. Associate producer: Kenneth Macgowan. Music by Alfred Newman. Photography: Bert Glennon. Art direction: Richard Day, Mark-Lee Kirk. Set decorations: Thomas Little. Film editor: Walter Thompson. Costumes: Royer. Sound: Eugene Grossman, Roger Heman. Western Electric Mirrophonic Recording. A Twentieth Century-Fox presentation of a Darryl F. Zanuck and Cosmopolitan production.

Additional Credits: Produced by Darryl F. Zanuck. Assistant director: Wingate Smith. Additional cinematography: Arthur Miller. Musical direction: Louis Silvers. Production dates: March–April 1939. Premiered in Springfield, Illinois on May 30, 1939.

Additional Cast: Milburn Stone (Stephen A. Douglas), Cliff Clark (Sheriff Billings); Stephen Randall, Robert Lowery (Jurors); Charles Tannen (Ninian Edwards), Francis Ford (Frank Ford), Fred Kohler, Jr. (Scrub White), Kay Linaker (Mrs. Edwards), Russell Simpson (Woolridge), Edwin Maxwell (John T. Stuart), Charles Halton (Hawthorne), Harry Tyler (Barber), Clarence Hummel Wilson (Dr. Mason), Eddy Waller (Father), Jack Kelly (Matt Clay as a boy), Dickie Jones (Adam Clay as a boy), Robert Homans (Mr. Clay), Louis Mason (Clerk), Jack Pennick (Big Buck).

Available: Criterion Collection DVD (2006). UPC: 7-15515-01672-8.

As one of the heroes of the country, President Abraham Lincoln has figured in many feature films. D. W. Griffith's *The Birth of a Nation* (1915) included a version of his assassination; John Ford's *The Prisoner of Shark Island* (1936) dealt with the aftermath of his death. Lincoln played a pivotal role in the 1938 melodrama *Of Human Hearts*, and turned up in many other films, whether necessary to the plot or not. As David O. Selznick began work on *Gone With the Wind* (1939), competing moguls sought their own bit of Americana to exploit. That and the increasing risk of war may have contributed to not one but two big-budget biographies of Lincoln that were put into development in 1939. Released in 1940 by RKO, *Abe Lincoln in Illinois* was based on a Pulitzer Prize–winning play by Robert Sherwood. Directed by John Cromwell, it was a straightforward biography emphasizing the love affair between Lincoln (played by Raymond Massey) and his wife Mary Todd (Ruth Gordon).

Young Mr. Lincoln took a different tack, showing a brief period in Lincoln's life, before he became a politician, let alone president. It was one of three films to be directed that year by John Ford, and all three were attempts on his part to uncover or explain the country's past. More than just celebrating the nation's heritage, Ford was interested in depicting heroes before they became heroes, at the moments when their actions decided their futures. The Ringo Kid in *Stagecoach*, for example, at the crossroads between good and evil, or the farmer Gilbert Martin in *Drums Along the Mohawk*, called upon to fight in a war.

Ford's Lincoln was not the Great Emancipator, or even the rail-splitter studying by candlelight in his log cabin. As written by Lamar Trotti, this Lincoln was close to a rascal. He tricks two clients out of their money in the opening scene, is not above threatening physical violence, wins a tug-of-war by cheating, and is brusque to the point of rudeness to what passes for high society in 1830s Illinois. Still, as Ford told interviewer Peter Bogdanovich, he wanted the picture "to give the feeling that even as a young man you could sense that there was going to be something great."

The project began as a 1935 script by Howard Estabrook, but producer Darryl F. Zanuck didn't become interested until Sherwood's play became a success. Ford and Henry Fonda both gave fanciful accounts of how the latter was cast as Lincoln. In his autobiography, Fonda credits Ford as being the first person in Hollywood to capture his imagination. An amateur actor from Omaha, Nebraska, Fonda was playing in summer stock when he joined the University Players with James Stewart and Margaret Sullavan, whom he married in 1931. He signed a contract at Twentieth Century-Fox in 1935, but made little impact on the public before he played Frank James in the Western *Jesse James* (1938). Fonda didn't think he could play Lincoln until Ford shamed him into the production, calling the part a "jake-legged lawyer in Springfield, for Christ's sake!"

Zanuck kept a close eye on the project, ordering Trotti to add characters and rearrange events in the script. After viewing Ford's rushes, he complained, "Do you feel that at times the tempo is apt to be a little slow?" (Much later, on a film with director Elia Kazan, Zanuck described what Ford did "when he is stuck and has run out of plot: somebody always sings and you cut to an extreme long shot with slanting shadows.") Ford protected himself from editors and interfering producers by intentionally "crossing the line" with his camera. In the classic studio style, it was considered bad form to move beyond 180 degrees in setting up shots. From the reverse angle, characters might exit on the "wrong" side of the frame. Ford did it on purpose, as cinematographer Winton C. Hoch told biographer Joseph McBride, because editors wouldn't be able to cut on action. They would have to include Ford's entire shot, at the pacing the director intended.

McBride saw *Young Mr. Lincoln* as an attempt to explain how the future president learned politics—specifically, how he learned to bring opposing sides together through compromise. For Ford it was also a way to refine sentimental ideas from his earlier films. Screenwriter Trotti had collaborated with Ford on two Will Rogers pictures earlier in the decade, and here he reworked situations and dialogue from one of them, *Judge Priest* (1934). (Trotti also based the closing courtroom trial on a case he covered as a newspaper reporter in Georgia.) A moment when Lincoln "talks" to the deceased Ann Rutledge at her grave would be echoed in *My Darling Clementine* (1946), as would the peculiar, stiff-legged dance Fonda used here.

But *Young Mr. Lincoln* was really a Zanuck film, and Ford a hired gun with limited opportunities to express himself. You can sense the battle between what the director wanted and what the Fox studio style permitted. Ford got some wonderful chiaroscuro effects, with Lincoln's eyes burning beneath the brim of his stovepipe hat, for example. Ford included a scene for his brother Francis, one in a series of degrading moments the younger brother foisted on the elder. But the crowd scenes are typical big-budget Fox circa the late 1930s, and there isn't much that Ford can do with them. As history, *Young Mr. Lincoln* is unreliable at best. But the picture reassured moviegoers that the country could wage a war without losing its values. Ford's next Registry film, *The Grapes of Wrath* (1940), would call those values into question with an authority rarely matched in cinema.

The Wizard of Oz

MGM, 1939. Sound, color with B&W sequences, 1.37. 101 minutes.

Cast: Judy Garland (Dorothy [Gale]), Frank Morgan (Professor Marvel), Ray Bolger (Hunk), Bert Lahr (Zeke), Jack Haley (Hickory), Billie Burke (Glinda), Margaret Hamilton (Miss Gulch), Charley Grapewin (Uncle Henry), Pat Walshe (Nikko), Clara Blandick (Auntie Em), Toto, The Munchkins [The Singer Midgets].

Credits: Directed by Victor Fleming. Screenplay by Noel Langley, Florence Ryerson, and Edgar Allan Woolf. Adaptation by Noel Langley. From the book by L. Frank Baum. Produced by Mervyn LeRoy. Musical adaptation: Herbert Stothart. Lyrics: E.Y. Harburg. Music: Harold Arlen. Associate conductor: George Stoll. Orchestral and vocal arrangements: George Bassman, Murray Cutter, Paul Marquardt, Ken Darby. Musical numbers staged by Bobby Connolly. Photographed in Technicolor by Harold Rosson. Photography associate: Allen Davey. Technicolor color director: Natalie Kalmus. Technicolor associate: Henri Jaffa. Recording director: Douglas Shearer. Art director: Cedric Gibbons. Associate art director: William A. Hornung. Set decorations: Edwin B. Willis. Special effects: Arnold Gillespie. Costumes by Adrian. Character makeups created by Jack Dwan. Film editor: Blanche Sewell.

Additional Cast includes: Mitchell Lewis (Guard), Lois January (Woman with cat); Prince Denis, Lady Ethel, Jerry Maren (Munchkins); Donna Massing (Hairdresser), The Debutantes, The King's Men Octet, St. Joseph's Choir, Tyler Brooke, Rolfe Sedan, Charles Irwin, Charles Oliver Smith, Bobby Watson, George Beranger.

Additional Credits: Footage directed by King Vidor, George Cukor, Richard Thorpe. Screenwriting: Herman Mankiewicz, Irv Brecher, Ogden Nash, Herbert Fields, Robert Pirosh, George Seaton, Samuel Hoffenstein, Jack Mintz, Sid Silvers, John Lee Mahin. Assistant directors: Al Shenberg, Wallace Worsley. Assistant producer: Arthur Freed. Matte paintings: Warren Newcombe. Production dates: October 13, 1938 to March 1939. Premiered August 12, 1939.

Awards: Oscars for Best Music—Original Score, Best Music—Original Song ("Over the Rainbow").

Other Versions: *The Wonderful Wizard of Oz* (1910), *Wizard of Oz* (1925). Sequel: *Return to Oz* (1985).

Available: Warner Home Video DVD (2005). ISBN: 1-4198-1859-7. UPC: 0-12569-67705-0.

When MGM decided to turn *The Wonderful Wizard of Oz* into a Technicolor musical, L. Frank Baum's novel was already part of the most successful fantasy franchise in American history. The best-selling novel was not only the first in a series of fourteen illustrated children's books, but Baum's own stage adaptation was a hit on Broadway and across the country, running in various forms from 1902 to 1911. The original show incorporated motion picture footage filmed for the production, and from 1902 on Baum tried many times to transfer his work to the screen. He licensed the rights to the characters to Selig Polyscope, which released a 1910 version of *The Wonderful Wizard of Oz*, the oldest surviving Oz film.

Baum formed the Oz Film Manufacturing Company in 1914, and adapted an aborted musical project into *The Patchwork Girl of Oz* (1914), the first of six features made by the company. After Baum's death in 1919, his son Frank wrote the screenplay for a 1925 *Wizard of Oz* starring

slapstick comedian Larry Semon. Oliver Hardy, later to team with Stan Laurel, played the Tin Woodman. A 1933 cartoon version ran into legal problems, after which the rights to the books and characters were purchased by Samuel Goldwyn.

Film historian Hugh Fordin places the genesis of the MGM *Wizard of Oz* at a meeting between songwriter Arthur Freed and studio head Louis B. Mayer. Freed wanted to move into producing, and saw *Oz* as a vehicle for Judy Garland. He was seconded by Mervyn LeRoy, a former Warner Bros. producer recently hired by Mayer. On the one hand it was a commercial move by Mayer, who was looking to cash in on the success of Walt Disney's *Snow White and the Seven Dwarfs* (1937). Other studios would release fantasy films, notably *The Blue Bird* (1940), a Shirley Temple vehicle put out by Twentieth Century-Fox. But Mayer made an economic commitment to the project that was far larger than the revenues he could hope to recoup. His backing helped make *The Wizard of Oz* a much greater film.

The production has been covered extensively in a number of books and documentaries; it was even the subject of *Under the Rainbow*, a 1981 comedy starring Chevy Chase. Aljean Harmetz's groundbreaking *The Making of "The Wizard of Oz"* went into extensive detail about the many screenwriters, composers, directors, cameramen, and other crew members who contributed to the film. *The Wizard of Oz* pushed the limits of technology with special effects and cinematography, gave career-defining roles to its cast members, and introduced several hit songs.

The Wizard of Oz has been explained as a political allegory about Populism as exemplified by the Greenback and Progressive parties; as an argument against the prevailing monetary policies of Baum's time; as the search for psychological unity (with the Scarecrow, Tin Woodman, and Cowardly Lion representing elements of personality that Dorothy must acquire); and with many other arguments. That Baum's book can successfully support so many readings is a sign of his skill as a writer. Although some critics have tried to align the MGM version with world events of 1939, finding a political subtext in a battle between a tyrannical witch and a benevolent wizard, what may be more instructive is how the studio adapted old, familiar material for a new audience.

Through Freed, LeRoy, and other creative personnel, MGM developed a two-pronged approach to *Oz*, making sure that through spectacle, comedy, and adventure it would entertain young viewers who might be unfamiliar with the plot and characters. To this end, over a dozen screenwriters simplified Baum's novel, eliminating characters and incidents, focusing on the element of homesickness as a theme for the movie.

To keep adults interested, MGM added a score by Harold Arlen and E.Y. "Yip" Harburg, songwriters responsible for hits like "It's Only a Paper Moon." It cast vaudevillians like Ray Bolger and Bert Lahr, stage veterans like Frank Morgan and Billie Burke—performers who had proven their appeal over the decades. Crucially, MGM played the film straight, without the irony that could have deflated the story's whimsy.

It was in some respects a disastrous production. Buddy Ebsen, originally cast as the Scarecrow, switched parts with Ray Bolger and became the Tin Woodman. He was hospitalized after breathing in dust from his aluminum-based makeup. Margaret Hamilton, forever associated with her role as the Wicked Witch of the West, was seriously burned when a special-effects fire ignited too soon. Betty Danko, her stunt double, was also hospitalized after an explosion.

Several scenes were excised from the various scripts, including a bit about the Munchkin fire department. An entire production number built around a song called "The Jitterbug" was cut before the film was released. Mayer tried to delete "Over the Rainbow" from the final version, but was overruled by Freed. (A reprise of the song was filmed, then excised after it brought both Garland and crew members to tears on the soundstage.) But in spite of the turmoil, the accidents, the changes in cast and crew, *The Wizard of Oz* succeeded as no other film fantasy had. Credit should go to the MGM studio as much as to any one individual.

An expensive production, *The Wizard of Oz* did well at the box office, but not enough to pay off its budget. The film turned a profit when it was rereleased in 1948, but by 1983 had still earned only $6 million theatrically. The film's hold on the public really began with a series of televised broadcasts, first on CBS, then on NBC. Each time it aired after its initial showing in 1956, its audience grew. By 1983, and its twenty-fifth consecutive showing, it was back on CBS.

But that year *The Wizard of Oz* was also a best-selling videotape, having been released to the home market in 1980. One of the paradoxes of owning a copy of a film is that you never have to actually watch it. If your copy is always available, watching the film during an annual broadcast is no longer a special occasion. And if, as is the case now, *The Wizard of Oz* is shown several times a year on different cable channels, is there ever any urgency to see it? It will be interesting to see how well the film can exert its magic on a new generation of viewers.

The Women

MGM, 1939. Sound, B&W with one color sequence, 1.37. 133 minutes.

Cast: Norma Shearer (Mrs. Stephen [Mary] Haines), Joan Crawford (Crystal Allen), Rosalind Russell (Mrs. Howard [Sylvia] Fowler), Mary Boland (Flora, the Countess De Lave), Paulette Goddard (Miriam Aarons), Joan Fontaine (Mrs. John [Peggy] Day), Lucile Watson (Mrs. Morehead), Phyllis Povah (Mrs. Phelps [Edith] Potter), Virginia Weidler (Little Mary [Haines]), Marjorie Main (Lucy), Virginia Grey (Pat), Ruth Hussey (Miss Watts), Muriel Hutchison (Jane), Hedda Hopper (Dolly DePuyster), Florence Nash (Nancy Blake), Cora Witherspoon (Mrs. Van Adams), Ann Morriss (Exercise instructress), Dennie Moore (Olga), Mary Cecil (Maggie), Mary Beth Hughes (Miss Trimmerback).

Credits: Directed by George Cukor. Screen play by Anita Loos and Jane Murfin. From the play by Clare Boothe [Luce]. By arrangement with Max Gordon Plays and Pictures Corporation. Produced by Hunt Stromberg. Directors of photography: Oliver T. Marsh, Joseph Ruttenberg. Musical score: Edward Ward and David Snell. Recording director: Douglas Shearer. Art Director: Cedric Gibbons. Associate: Wade B. Rubottom. Set decorations: Edwin B. Willis. Gowns and fashion show by Adrian. Hair stylist: Sydney Guilaroff. Film editor: Robert J. Kern. Color sequence in Technicolor. Western Electric Sound System. A Metro-Goldwyn-Mayer presentation.

Additional Cast: Butterfly McQueen (Lulu), Margaret Dumont (Mrs. Wagstaff), Barbara Jo Allen (Receptionist), Aileen Pringle (Saleslady), Judith Allen (Corset model), Dorothy Sebastian (Saleswoman), Gertrude Astor (Nurse), Lilian Bond (Mrs. Erskine), Betty Blythe (Mrs. South), Dorothy Adams (Miss Atkinson), Suzanne Kaaren (Tamara), Peggy Shannon (Mrs. Jones).

Additional Credits: Originally staged at the Ethel Barrymore Theatre, New York City, December 26, 1936. Screenwriting by Donald Ogden Stewart. Production dates: April 25 to July 7, 1939. Released September 1, 1939.

Other Versions: Remade as *The Opposite Sex* (1956) and as *The Women* (2008).

Available: Warner Home Video DVD (2005). UPC: 012569675407.

Few studios were as flush with funds at the end of the 1930s as MGM, which could afford to dangle a project like *The Women* at director George Cukor as a sort of consolation prize for giving up *Ninotchka* (1939). Written by Clare Boothe Luce, the wife of *Time* magazine publisher Henry Luce, *The Women* had a successful run on Broadway starting in December 1936. The following year producer Max Gordon hired director Gregory La Cava to direct a film version to star Claudette Colbert and Ilka Chase, the original Sylvia Fowler on stage. When this project failed to materialize, MGM bought the play in 1938 for Norma Shearer.

Born in 1903 into an unconventional household, Clare Boothe failed in her bid to become an actress. She met millionaire George Tuttle Brokaw on a voyage to Europe, and married him in 1923. Brokaw's drinking and Boothe's conflicts with his family led to their divorce in 1929, with Boothe going to Reno, Nevada, to await the settlement. Back in New York City, she became a writer and editor at *Vanity Fair*, introducing the feature, "We Nominate for Oblivion." Boothe left the magazine in 1934, the same year she met Luce. He divorced his wife and married Boothe in November 1935, the month her first play, *Abide With Me*, opened on Broadway to poor reviews.

A year later she was back on Broadway with *The Women*, a satirical look at the frivolous, gossip-ridden lives of idle rich wives and the women who want to join them. In Boothe's view, it was a jungle out there, and she had the personal history to back up her bitterness. What she didn't have was much expertise at playwriting, and some have suggested that she used George S. Kaufman not just as a model for her plot and characters, but as an unacknowledged script doctor. *The Women* won over playgoers then, and still does today, by reassuring everyone that the rich are just as flighty, ill-mannered, and inept at love as we want them to be.

Norma Shearer had never been the most profitable star at MGM, but by marrying the boss she assured herself of first dibs at choice roles. But Irving Thalberg died in 1936, and as his widow, Shearer's power started to decline. Seriously misguided flops like *Marie Antoinette* (1938) didn't help. *The Women* would be her swan song as a major star, her last significant film at the studio where she had worked from its start. She would star in only three more movies before retiring in 1942. Shearer had never appeared in a film with Joan Crawford, who insisted on sharing star billing. Ironically, Crawford would leave the studio

in 1942 as well, the victim of poor choices and a changing marketplace. Possibly the best performance in the film comes from Rosalind Russell, who also fought for star billing. Playing Sylvia Fowler, she provides most of the spark in a film that is glittering but often empty.

The studio's press department trumpeted the "135 speaking roles" in the film (far more than on stage)—some of them real surprises, like an uncredited Butterfly McQueen in her film debut. Actresses pulled over from the play included Beatrice Cole, Mary Cecil, Beryl Wallace, Marjorie Main, and Phyllis Povah, who had worked with Cukor back in his days as a theater director in Rochester, New York.

Cukor didn't bother shooting the Technicolor fashion show that pops up almost an hour into the film. (MGM inserted a similar piece into the Marx Brothers' *A Day at the Races* in 1938.) In fact, biographer Patrick McGilligan faults the director for his lackadaisical approach to *The Women*, which started shooting almost exactly a month after he was fired from *Gone With the Wind*. In his defense, Cukor had to compensate for a script stripped of much of its bite by censors. He kept screenwriter Anita Loos on the set to come up with substitute lines, and also called on playwright Donald Ogden Stewart for help.

Cukor couldn't do much with Shearer, whose acting is regrettably broad, or with a plot line that required Shearer's character to sink to the level of those around her to get back her man. It is a relief when the veteran character actress Mary Boland shows up to lament the husband who pushed her off a mountain in the Alps or the cowboy singer she is bankrolling on the radio.

The Women is frequently revived, almost always with severe modifications to Boothe's original script. (In the 2008 film version, most of the wives have jobs, for example.) She wrote another comedy, *Kiss the Boys Goodbye*, which ridiculed Hollywood, and which was filmed as a musical in 1941. By then Boothe was immersed in her new career as a war correspondent, having written the nonfiction *Europe in the Spring* in 1940. She later served in the House of Representatives and as Ambassador to Italy.

Mr. Smith Goes to Washington

Columbia, 1939. Sound, B&W, 1.37. 130 minutes.

Cast: Jean Arthur ([Clarissa] Saunders), James Stewart (Jefferson Stewart), Claude Rains (Senator Joseph Paine), Edward Arnold (Jim Taylor), Guy Kibbee (Governor [Hubert] Hopper), Thomas Mitchell (Diz Moore), Eugene Pallette (Chick McGann), Beulah Bondi (Ma Smith), H.B. Warner (Senate Majority Leader), Harry Carey (President of the Senate), Astrid Allwyn (Susan Paine), Ruth Donnelly (Mrs. [Emma] Hopper), Grant Mitchell (Senator MacPherson), Porter Hall (Senator Monroe), Baby Dumpling (Hopper Boy), H.V. Kaltenborn (Himself), Pierre Watkin (Senate Minority Leader), Charles Lane (Nosey), William Demarest (Bill Griffith), Dick Elliott (Carl Cook); Billy Watson, Delmar Watson, John Russell, Harry Watson, Gary Watson (Hopper Boys).

Credits: Directed by Frank Capra. Screenplay by Sidney Buchman. Story by Lewis R. Foster. Director of photography: Joseph Walker. Film editors: Gene Havlick, Al Clark. Art direction: Lionel Banks. Montage effects by Slavko Vorkapich. Assistant director: Arthur S. Black. Gowns by Kalloch. Musical score by Dimitri Tiomkin. Musical direction: M.W. Stoloff. Western Electric Mirrophonic Recording. A Columbia Pictures Corporation presentation.

Additional Cast includes: Jack Carson (Sweeney), Joe King (Summers), Paul Stanton (Flood), Russell Simpson (Allen), Stanley Andrews (Senator Hodges), Walter Soderling (Senator Pickett), Frank Jaquet (Senator Byron), Ferris Taylor (Senator Carlisle), Carl Stockdale (Senator Burdette), Wright Kramer (Senator Carlton), Alan Bridge (Senator Dwight), Edmund Cobb (Senator Gower), Arthur Loft (Chief clerk), Frederick Burton (Senator Dearborn), Harry Bailey (Senator Hammett), Wyndham Standing (Senator Ashman), Robert Walker (Senator Holland), Victor Travers (Senator Grainger), John Ince (Senator Fernwick), Sam Ash (Senator Lancaster), Ed Mortimer (Senator Agnew), Philo McCullough (Senator Albert), Frank O'Connor (Senator Alfred), Harry Stafford (Senator Atwater), Jack Richardson (Senator Manchester), Vera Lewis (Mrs. Edwards), Dora Clement (Mrs. McGann), Laura Treadwell (Mrs. Taylor); Helen Jerome Eddy, Ann Doran, Beatrice Curtis (Paine secretaries); Byron Foulger (Hopper's secretary), Frank Otto (Fiske), Jack Rice (Lang); Eddie Fetherston, Ed Randolph, Milt Kibbee, Vernon Dent, Michael Gale, Anne Cornwall, James Millican, Mabel Forrest, Nick Copeland, Dulcie Day (Senate reporters); Clyde Dilson, William Newell, George Chandler, George Morgan, George McKay, Matt McHugh, Evalyn Knapp, Dub Taylor, Jack Gardner, Donald Kerr, Eddie Kane, William Arnold, Hal Cooke, James McNamara, Jack Egan, Eddy Chandler, Dick Fiske, Billy Wayne (Reporters).

Additional Credits: Contributor to story construction and dialogue: Myles Connolly. Produced by Frank Capra. Technical advisor: James Preston. Sound engineer: Edward Bernds. Set design: Walter Holscher. Hair stylists: Helen Hunt, Faye Hanlin. Makeup: William Knight, Fred Phillips. Special effects: Fred Jackman, Jr. Premiered in Washington, D.C. on October 17, 1939.

Awards: Oscar for Best Writing—Original Story (Foster).

Remakes: *Billy Jack Goes to Washington* (1977, directed by Tom Laughlin). The film was the basis of a television series in 1962.

Available: Columbia/TriStar Home Video DVD (1999). ISBN: 0-7678-2801-1. UPC: 0-43396-27969-8.

After the unprecedented

After the unprecedented critical and commercial success of *It Happened One Night* (1934), Frank Capra became one of the most influential and recognizable directors in the industry. Under contract to Harry Cohn at Columbia, Capra turned out a series of extraordinarily popular movies, all written in part by Robert Riskin. *Mr. Deeds Goes to Town* (1936) crystallized the Capra-Riskin formula, pitting a naive but moral individual against society's corrupt elite. It was followed by *Lost Horizon* (1937), an adaptation of the James Hilton best-seller about Shangri La, and *You Can't Take It With You* (1938), a film version of a George S. Kaufman and Moss Hart play that won a Best Picture Oscar.

You Can't Take It With You was the last collaboration between Capra and Riskin, apart from their troubled *Meet John Doe* in 1941. Biographer Joseph McBride suggests that Capra, who often took a screenwriting credit on his films, was jealous of the acclaim Riskin was receiving, especially after the writer signed a lucrative deal with Samuel Goldwyn. Riskin's first project with Goldwyn was *The Real Glory* (1939), a war adventure set in the Pacific and starring Gary Cooper.

The *Mr. Smith* project originated with a story by Lewis R. Foster called "The Gentleman from Montana" that had been optioned in 1937. When director Rouben Mamoulian expressed interest, he said that Capra traded him Clifford Odets' *Golden Boy* for it. In his autobiography, Capra wrote that he decided to make "The Man from Montana" before he finished reading it. (McBride points out the similarities between the story and a Pulitzer Prize–winning play *Both Your Houses* by Maxwell Anderson. Columbia ended up optioning it to avoid potential legal difficulties.) With Riskin gone, Capra turned to screenwriter Sidney Buchman, who had worked uncredited on *Broadway Bill* (1933). Buchman would receive sole screenwriting credit, although Capra also had his friend Myles Connolly work on the script. No matter who the writer was, Capra exerted considerable influence over the outcome.

Over the years the Capra hero had been refined from the brash, abrasive reporter played by the likes of Douglas Fairbanks, Jr., and Clark Gable to a sort of guileless innocent surrounded by treachery. Capra shifted the brassiness over to the heroine—often Jean Arthur in this period—and surrounded the leads with veteran character actors like Lionel Stander, Charles Lane (who gets the opening shot here), and Thomas Mitchell. These actors supplied the exposition that explained plot points to the viewers, as well as the cynical wit necessary to keep Capra's stories from curdling under the weight of their sentiment.

Mr. Smith was a critical project for Capra, who had been trying to mount a biography of Chopin. This would be his last film for Columbia, and in a sense he was summing up his career at the studio, reworking the themes and characters from his most successful earlier films, this time setting them on a national scale. The director also turned to the past for casting. He had worked with most of the principals before, and summoned supporting actors from all corners of his career. Always loyal, he gave an important part here to Harry Carey, a star of silent Westerns who had helped him find work in the early 1910s.

This was the breakthrough year in James Stewart's career after a half decade of mostly supporting roles and second leads. Capra originally envisioned the part of Jefferson Smith for Gary Cooper, and only signed Stewart in January 1939, three months before shooting started. Stewart brought a conviction to the role that Cooper may have lacked, and the choices his character made in the film played a part in the actor's decision to enlist in the Air Force after the start of World War II.

Capra brought the principals to Washington, D.C., to shoot some location footage, but had carpenters build a duplicate of the Senate chamber on a Columbia soundstage for the bulk of the filming. Capra incorporated several technical innovations into *Mr. Smith*. He filmed with multiple cameras, resurrecting a technique from the early sound era when cameras were too bulky to move easily. This meant he could run through entire scenes instead of repeating portions for close-up insert shots. When close-ups were necessary, he used projecting equipment to play back dialogue, instead of having a continuity person feed lines to actors. Capra and editor Gene Havlick fine-tuned the editing of *Mr. Smith* by listening to the recorded responses of filmgoers at sneak previews, adding timing intervals for laughs, for example.

Shooting ended on July 7, 1939, over schedule by a week and almost $300,000 over budget. By the time *Mr. Smith* was ready for its October 17 premiere at the National Press Club in Washington, Capra was fending off charges from conservative media that his film attacked the country's political system. In fact, the director was so cautious about the story that the film never identified Jefferson Smith's home state, or whether he was a Democrat or Republican. (Smith's seat was on the Democrats' side of the aisle.)

As far as screenwriter Sidney Buchman was concerned, Capra was a simplistic political thinker who believed in fairy tales. "I really believe he never knew what *Mr. Smith* was actually saying," he told Bernard Tavernier in a 1969 interview. A member of the Communist Party at the time he wrote the script, Buchman may have been responsible for some of the film's unexpected cynicism. On the other hand, Capra himself had become more cynical, less willing to believe in happy endings, no matter how loudly he espoused them. Expert at constructing dead-end traps for his heroes, he was finding it harder and harder to extricate them when it came time for the closing credits. *Mr. Smith*'s climax hinges on a suicide, as would Capra's next two serious films, *Meet John Doe* and *It's a Wonderful Life*. War broke out in Europe as the director was editing *Mr. Smith*, adding to the sense that something close to despair was seeping into Capra's view of the world.

Ninotchka

MGM, 1939. Sound, B&W, 1.37. 110 minutes.

Cast: Greta Garbo (Ninotchka), Melvyn Douglas (Leon [Count d'Algout]), Ina Claire (Swana), Bela Lugosi (Razinin), Sig Rumann ([Mischa] Iranoff), Felix Bressart (Buljanoff), Alexander Granach (Kopalski), Gregory Gaye (Rakonin), Rolfe Sedan (Hotel Manager), Edwin Maxwell (Mercier), Richard Carle (Gaston).

Credits: Directed by Ernst Lubitsch. Screen Play by Charles Brackett, Billy Wilder, and Walter Reisch. Based on the Original Story by Melchior Lengyel. Musical Score: Werner R. Heymann. Recording Director: Douglas Shearer. Art Director: Cedric Gibbons. Associate: Randall Duell. Set decorations: Edwin B. Willis. Gowns by Adrian. Make-Up Created by Jack Dawn. Hair Styles for Miss Claire by Sydney Guilaroff. Director of photography: William Daniels, A.S.C. Film editor: Gene Ruggiero. Western Electric Sound System.

Additional Cast: George Tobias (Russian visa official), Dorothy Adams (Swana's maid, Jacqueline), Lawrence Grant (General Savitzky), Charles Judel (Père Mathieu, café owner), Frank Reicher (lawyer), Edwin Stanley (lawyer), Peggy Moran (French maid), Marek Windheim (manager), Mary Forbes (Lady Lavenham), Alexander Schonberg (Bearded man), George Davis (Porter), Armand Kaliz (Louis, headwaiter), Wolfgang Zilzer (Taxi driver), Tamara Shayne (Anna), William Irving (Bartender), Bess Flowers (Gossip), Elizabeth Williams (Indignant woman), Paul Weigel (Vladimir), Harry Semels (Neighbor-spy), Jody Gilbert (Streetcar conductress), Florence Shirley (Marianne).

Additional Credits: Production dates: May 31 to August 11, 1939. Released November 3, 1939.

Other Versions: Remade as *Silk Stockings* (1957).

Available: MGM/UA Home Video VHS (1999). Warner Home Video DVD (2005): ISBN: 1419807749. UPC: 012569566828.

MGM advertised *Ninotchka* with the tagline "Garbo Laughs," as if the prospect of their biggest star merely acting wasn't enough to draw viewers to theaters. Since her arrival at the studio in 1925, Garbo had been one of the studio's most important, and protected, stars. Mayer and Irving Thalberg delayed her first sound movie—an adaptation of Eugene O'Neill's *Anna Christie*—until 1930, years after the rest of the industry had converted. (Of the major stars, only Chaplin waited longer to used sound.) The studio built *Grand Hotel* (1932) around her, then featured her in a series of extravagant costume melodramas like *Queen Christina* (1933), *Anna Karenina* (1935), and *Camille* (1937).

Garbo was a critics' favorite while remaining something of a mystery to mass audiences. Unlike her rival Marlene Dietrich, whose physicality was always a crucial element of her appeal, Garbo was harder to plumb. Like the best movie stars, her face remained something of an immobile mask, impossible to read with certainty. Viewers could impose their own thoughts and feelings onto her expressions, and in that way become a part of her stories. But plush, highbrow romances like *Conquest* (1937) failed to find sizeable audiences, leading Garbo to be branded "box office poison" by Harry Brand, president of the Independent Theater Owners of America.

Mayer decided that the imperially aloof Garbo needed to be "humanized," or at least brought down to the level of Americans. (Dietrich was undergoing a similar transformation by appearing as a hell-raising saloon singer in the Universal Western *Destry Rides Again*.) George Cukor, who had directed Garbo in *Camille*, was originally assigned to the project, but he was involved in the preliminary production details of David O. Selznick's *Gone With the Wind*. Meanwhile, Ernst Lubitsch, back at the studio for the first time since *The Merry Widow* in 1934, had been assigned *The Women*, much to his regret. When Cukor was dropped from *Gone With the Wind*, he switched assignments with Lubitsch, taking on the filming of *The Women*.

Lubitsch offered a *Ninotchka* treatment by the Hungarian writer Melchior Lengyel to screenwriters Charles Brackett and Billy Wilder, who were fresh off the success of *Midnight* (1939), a breezy Paramount comedy that had a similar European setting. (Austrian screenwriter Walter Reisch also worked on the script, and as always Lubitsch added his own comic bits and dialogue.) Brackett and Wilder's biggest contribution to the story, apart from their typically biting jokes, was to shape *Ninotchka* as a Cinderella tale and to develop the roles of three low-level Russian envoys. Much as Dorothy in *The Wizard of Oz* was guided by a trio of friends, the envoys here would bring Ninotchka

to Paris, introduce her to a French lover, and then arrange for the story's happy ending. Brackett and Wilder also supplied much of the film's consistently marvelous dialogue. Even the throwaway bits are impressive. When Ninotchka orders raw carrots and beets for lunch, an appalled restaurateur replies, "This is a restaurant, not a meadow."

The vaunted Lubitsch touch can feel oppressive at times. He was famous enough at this point in his career to receive his own shot in the film's trailer, although he had not had a hit movie for over five years. Scenes not included in the published screenplay are heavy-handed and obvious, such as Kopalski (played by Alexander Granach) walking a picket line at the end of the film. Some bits played out in front of and behind a hotel room door evoke *Trouble in Paradise* (1932). But for the most part Lubitsch remains discreet, giving the actors plenty of room, letting the story unfold at an unforced pace, using an unobtrusive camera and quiet fades to punctuate scenes. His greatest trick may have been successfully portraying Garbo as earthier than her romantic rival Ina Claire, playing a Grand Duchess.

But then this is more a Garbo film than a Lubitsch one. Reviewers at the time appreciated her willingness to spoof her screen persona, especially the robotic monotone she uses to deliver her lines in her opening scenes. Garbo plays Ninotchka as an utter naïf, and her bewilderment at the consumer charms of Paris, her consternation at how easily her comrades are corrupted, and her gradual thawing in the face of love show how accomplished a performer she was. Her more romantic scenes, the ones in which she wears ill-advised evening gowns while succumbing to Melvyn Douglas's wooing, aren't nearly as enjoyable. Making fun of the Garbo aura is one thing, reducing it to the level of other romantic comedy actresses is another.

It was a dilemma neither the actress nor her studio could resolve. Her next film, *Two-Faced Woman* (1941), also offered two Garbos, a stiff European one and a bubbly "American" one. It was a notorious failure. Although only in her late thirties, Garbo found it impossible to connect to a younger film audience. She didn't retire so much as simply withdraw from the screen and from public life. She considered a number of roles in later years, but apart from a 1949 screen test photographed by James Wong Howe did not appear on film again. Garbo received an honorary Academy Award in 1954, a year after she moved to New York City. She died there in 1990.

Destry Rides Again

Universal, 1939. Sound, B&W, 1.33. 94 minutes.

Cast: Marlene Dietrich (Frenchy), James Stewart (Tom Destry, Jr.), Mischa Auer (Boris), Charles Winninger (Washington Dimsdale), Brian Donlevy (Kent), Allen Jenkins (Gyp Watson), Warren Hymer (Bugs Watson), Irene Hervey (Janice Tyndall), Una Merkel (Lily Belle), Billy Gilbert (Loupgerou), Samuel S. Hinds (Judge Slade), Jack Carson (Jack Tyndall), Tom Fadden (Lem Claggett), Virginia Brissac (Sophie Claggett), Edmund Macdonald (Rockwell), Lillian Yarbo (Clara), Joe King (Sheriff Keogh), Joe King (Claggett Boy), Ann Todd (Claggett Girl).

Credits: Directed by George Marshall. Screen Play: Felix Jackson, Gertrude Purcell, Henry Myers. Original story by Felix Jackson. Suggested by Max Brand's novel "Destry Rides Again." Produced by Joe Pasternak. Director of photography: Hal Mohr. Art director: Jack Otterson. Associate art director: Martin Obzina. Associate producer: Islin Auster. Film Editor: Milton Carruth. Set decorations: R.A. Gausman. Gowns: Vera West. Assistant director: Vernon Keays. Musical director: Charles Previn. Musical score: Frank Skinner. Songs: Lyrics by Frank Loesser. Music by Frederick Hollander. Sound supervisor: Bernard B. Brown. Technician: Robert Pritchard. Western Electric Recording. A Universal presentation of a Joe Pasternak production.

Additional Cast includes: Dickie Jones (Eli Whitney Claggett), Carmen D'Antonio (Dancer), Harry Cording (Rowdy), Minerva Urecal (Mrs. DeWitt), Bob McKenzie (Doctor), Billy Bletcher (Pianist), Lloyd Ingraham (Turner).

Additional Credits: Production dates: September to October 1939. Opened in New York City on November 30, 1939.

Other Versions: Max Brand's novel was the source for *Destry Rides Again* (1932). *Frenchie* (1950) used a similar plot line. Remade as *Destry* (1954).

Available: Universal Home Video DVD (2003). ISBN: 0-7832-5504-7. UPC: 0-25192-12092-3.

Often described as Hollywood's *annus mirabilis*, the year 1939 also marked a turning point in the careers of many movie veterans. With *Ninotchka*, Greta Garbo was asked to become a comedienne in an attempt shore up her fan base. Marlene Dietrich, her most significant counterpart, underwent a similar transformation from an exotic European vamp to a lusty American wench in *Destry Rides Again*.

Since debuting in the United States with *Morocco* in 1930, Dietrich had elaborated on her screen persona in five more films directed by her Svengali, Josef von Sternberg. Each one defined her as an object of sexual desire, inscrutable, unknowable, bedecked in increasingly complex layers of feathers, gauze, and veils. As her stories grew more fanciful, her audiences dwindled. Like Garbo, Dietrich played spies, mistresses, and historical figures, and like Garbo, she seemed increasingly remote and irrelevant to filmgoers. Worried, Paramount first removed her from Sternberg's influence, teaming her fruitlessly with Frank Borzage in *Desire* (1936) and Ernst Lubitsch in *Angel* (1937). (Sandwiched between was an abandoned film, *I Loved a Soldier*, a remake of the Pola Negri vehicle *Hotel Imperial* that had been started by Henry Hathaway.) Especially in retrospect, these films had their virtues, but they failed to draw viewers. Like Garbo, Katharine Hepburn, and Joan Crawford, Dietrich was labeled "box office poison."

Dietrich's prospects were not good. The market for sophisticated European-style dramas had shrunk in this country, while political unrest had closed off much of the European market. In June 1939, she became an American citizen, just before sailing to Europe to secure the safety of her family. (The German press had by this time taken to referring to her as a "traitress.") But producer Joe Pasternak offered a potential solution.

Born in Hungary in 1901, Pasternak worked his way up from busboy and waiter at the Paramount commissary in Los Angeles to second assistant director. Switching to Universal, he created a job that took him to Berlin, where he produced films for cabaret star Franciska Gaal, among others, but also looked for properties that could be transformed into Hollywood movies. For example, Gaal's *Kleine Mutter* became the Ginger Rogers comedy *Bachelor Mother*. With the rise of Nazism, Pasternak returned to Hollywood, bringing with him film director Henry Koster, screenwriter Felix Joachimsohn, and his brother-in-law S.Z. "Cuddles" Sakall, soon to be a popular character actor.

After he helped develop Deanna Durbin into a star for Universal, Pasternak's talent for "repurposing" properties came into play. Universal had the rights to *Destry Rides Again*, a novel by Max Brand that had been filmed with Tom Mix in 1932. Working with Joachimsohn (now Felix Jackson), Pasternak turned a fairly dour story of revenge into a lighthearted Western comedy. Instead of focusing on an innocent man who becomes a killer when he is framed, this version of *Destry* centered on his son, a pacifist who eschews the use of guns. It also featured a saloon singer who went from being a crook's mistress to saving the hero at the cost of her own life. Pasternak reached Dietrich in Europe with an offer of $75,000, about half of her normal fee, for the part.

Dietrich embraced the role, realizing that it could expose her to an entirely new audience. Pasternak assigned director George Marshall to the project. A former bit player and screenwriter, Marshall was noted for his work with comedians like Laurel and Hardy, W.C. Fields, and Will Rogers, and for his facility with Westerns. Opposite Dietrich was James Stewart, a rising star in his first full-fledged Western. Filling out the cast were some of the more accomplished character actors in Hollywood, including Brian Donlevy as the heavy, Mischa Auer in a comic relief role more developed than his bit in *My Man Godfrey*, and Una Merkel as Dietrich's female adversary.

Marshall built the film like a series of two-reelers, or even one-reelers. The first twenty minutes are devoted to Dietrich, who gets to perform two songs, and to her surroundings—mostly an extraordinarily large saloon filled with more customers than most frontier towns had as residents. Without Paramount's technicians to protect her, Dietrich is vulnerable at times to unflattering close-ups. This is partly due to the new image given to her by Universal's makeup and costume department. Dietrich's eyebrows were lowered, her cheeks given more rouge, and her lips made fuller. As Alexander Walker wrote in his book about the star, Dietrich was also asked to sacrifice her mystery, her hint of sexual perversion, her European sensibilities, and, most tellingly, her dignity. Her first song ends with a (dubbed-in) yodel, and at one point she's subjected to a catfight with Merkel. Dietrich used to be pitiless; here, she's just another Wild West dame who cheats at cards and stuffs coins down her cleavage. (Today it seems careless that an obviously German woman is called "Frenchy," but the growing hostility toward Germany was a distinct factor in 1939.)

Stewart arrives late in the film, riding in a stagecoach with Jack Carson and Irene Hervey. It takes almost an hour for Stewart's first real scene with Dietrich, one in which he further "humanizes" her by trying to remove her makeup. Stewart approaches his role lightly, sliding so comfortably into Western traditions that the genre would become the focus of his later career. But the two leads wind up handing their screen time over to hams like Charles Winninger, playing the sort of alcoholic lawman that Howard Hawks would rely on in films like *Rio Bravo*. This being a Universal effort, perhaps it's understandable for the film to end in a paroxysm of mob violence, just like the Frankenstein movies.

It's easy to see *Destry*'s influence on subsequent Westerns. It was such a popular success that it was remade as *Frenchie* in 1950 and as *Destry* in 1954 with Audie Murphy. "Americanizing" Dietrich worked in a way that it didn't for Garbo. While Garbo refused to make another film, Dietrich basically repeated variations on this role in a variety of settings until after World War II. At that point she began playing herself, an international cabaret star who occasionally found herself in dramatic situations. She toured the world with a nightclub act, made a few more film appearances, notably the Registry title *Touch of Evil* (1958), then slowly withdrew from the public.

Cologne: From the Diary of Ray and Esther

Raymond and Esther Dowidat, 1939. Silent, B&W, 1.37. 14 minutes.
Featuring: Esther Dowidat, "Old Man" Guettler, Hans Guettler, Bill Guettler, Henry Mohlbacher.
Credits: Photographed and edited by Raymond William Dowidat.
Available: Image Entertainment DVD *Treasures from American Film Archives* (2000). UPC: 0-14381-9706-2-3.

A home movie in the form of a diary, *Cologne* is a fascinating example of amateur filmmaking from the 1930s. It was made by Dr. Raymond William Dowidat, a general practitioner in rural Minnesota. Born in 1909 in Hennepin County, Dowidat and his wife Esther moved to Cologne in 1937. At the time it was a mill and dairy town forty miles southwest of Minneapolis. With about 350 residents, it was not a bustling metropolis.

Dowidat opened and closed his film with shots of the Cologne water tower. Much of the subsequent movie is dedicated to landscape shots. Some were taken from the top of a mill, others from a church steeple, and still others perhaps from the tower itself. Cologne is revealed as a compact and tidy town bounded by a pond, train tracks, and farms.

After the introductory shots, Dowidat cuts to Esther writing in a diary. In a second cut, he shows an insert shot of a lined page from the diary, a technique he uses to include explanatory titles. Curiously, he employs them in the style of silent films from the early teens—that is, his titles describe what the following shots will show. It's an old-fashioned technique somewhat at odds with the rest of the movie, which uses film grammar in a sophisticated manner.

For example, the opening titles feature both a superimposition and a dissolve, difficult to achieve with a home-movie camera. At times Dowidat "cheats" by inserting material shot earlier, repurposing it to fit his new story. The physical edits in the film are obvious due to the nature of splicing from frame to frame. But many of the sequences were edited in the camera, which meant that Dowidat had a preconceived notion of how he was going to present material; he wasn't just filming at random. With that in mind, viewers today can discern a subtle bias underneath the movie's simple structure. From a bird's-eye view of the town, remote and almost abstract, Dowidat zeroes in on the two factors that control Cologne's economy: grain and milk. Churches and shops are seen or mentioned in passing, while schools and local government are ignored.

Dowidat also shows the railroad, and his inclusion of The Flyer, a passenger train that doesn't stop in Cologne, has a wistfulness that adds a bite to his narrative. In fourteen minutes, Dowidat has covered everything of importance in the town; imagine living there for two years. One intertitle refers mysteriously to memories both "pleasant and bitter," adding a different tinge to shots of townspeople miming fights in saloons. Like the best art, Dowidat's film asks more questions than it answers.

Dowidat's daughter Adele came across *Cologne* in her mother's attic, but had no means of viewing it until she and her husband Richard Johnson had the film transferred to videotape. She brought it to the Minnesota Historical Society, where sound and visual collection curator Bonnie Wilson watched it. "It was a well-made amateur film," Wilson told reporter Brooks Boliek later. "I see hundreds of these a year, and to get something that isn't just shooting relatives coming out the door is special."

Preserved with a grant from the National Film Preservation Foundation, the film has subsequently been screened at the Museum of Modern Art and on Turner Classic Movies. It underscores the importance of saving other amateur films, which are today often classified under the umbrella of "orphan films." Not every amateur film is as sophisticated as this, but who can determine what is and isn't important enough to preserve? How many family records are decaying in attics and basements, victims of neglect and obsolescent technologies?

Gone With the Wind

Selznick International/MGM, 1939. Sound, color, 1.33. 226 minutes.

Cast: Clark Gable (Rhett Butler), Vivien Leigh (Scarlett O'Hara), Leslie Howard (Ashley Wilkes), Olivia de Haviland (Melanie Hamilton). The Players at Tara, the O'Hara Plantation in Georgia: Thomas Mitchell (Gerald O'Hara), Barbara O'Neill (Ellen, his wife), Vivien Leigh (Scarlett), Evelyn Keyes (Suellen), Ann Rutherford (Carreen); Scarlett's beaux: George Reeves (Brent Tarleton), Fred Crane (Stuart Tarleton). The house servants: Hattie McDaniel (Mammy), Oscar Polk (Pork), Butterfly McQueen (Prissy); in the fields: Victor Jory (Jonas Wilderson, the overseer), Everett Brown (Big Sam, the foreman). At Twelve Oaks, the nearby Wilkes plantation: Howard Hickman (John Wilkes), Alicia Rhett (India, his daughter), Leslie Howard (Ashley, his son), Olivia de Havilland (Melanie Hamilton, their cousin), Rand Brooks (Charles Hamilton, her brother), Carroll Nye (Frank Kennedy, a guest), Clark Gable (Rhett Butler, a visitor from Charleston). In Atlanta: Laura Hope Crews (Aunt "Pittypat" Hamilton), Eddie Anderson (Uncle Peter, her coachman), Harry Davenport (Dr. Meade), Leona Roberts (Mrs. Meade), Jane Darwell (Mrs. Merriwether), Ona Munson (Belle Watling). And: Paul Hurst, Cammie King, J.M. Kerrigan, Jackie Moran, L. Kemble Cooper, Marcella Martin, Mickey Kuhn, Irving Bacon, William Bakewell, Isabel Jewell, Eric Linden, Ward Bond, Cliff Edwards, Yakima Canutt, Louis Jena Heydt, Olin Howland, Robert Elliott, Mary Anderson.

Credits: Directed by Victor Fleming. Produced by David O. Selznick. Screen Play by Sidney Howard. Director of photography: Ernest Haller. Special photographic effects: Jack Cosgrove. Technicolor associates: Ray Rennahan, Wilfrid M. Cline. Production design: William Cameron Menzies. Musical Score by Max Steiner. Art direction by Lyle Wheeler. Interiors by Joseph B. Platt. Interior decoration by Edward G. Boyle. Costumes designed by Walter Plunkett. Supervising film editor: Hal C. Kern. Associate film editor: James E. Newcom. Scenario assistant: Barbara Keon. Production manager: Raymond A. Klune. Assistant director: Eric G. Stacey. Recorder: Frank Maher. Technicolor Co. supervision:

Natalie Kalmus. Assistant musical director: Lou Forbes. Historian: Wilbur G. Kurtz. Technical advisors: Susan Myrick, Will Price. Western Electric Sound System.

Additional Credits: Directing by George Cukor, Sam Wood. Screenplay contributions: Ben Hecht, Jo Swerling, Charles MacArthur, John Van Druten, Oliver H.P. Garrett, F. Scott Fitzgerald. Based on the novel by Margaret Mitchell. Initial cinematography: Lee Garmes. Stunt work: Yakima Canutt. Production dates: December 10, 1938; January 26 to February 15, 1939; March 2 to July 1, 1939; additional shooting between July and November 1939. Premiered in Atlanta on December 15, 1939.

Awards: Oscars for Best Picture, Director, Writing—Screenplay, Actress, Actress in a Supporting Role (McDaniel), Cinematography—Color, Film Editing, Art Direction.

Available: Warner Home Video DVD (2004). ISBN: 0-7907-9049-1. UPC: 0-12569-59172-1.

Like *The Birth of a Nation* (1915) before it, *Gone With the Wind* once stood as a benchmark in film: the biggest, most expensive, most technologically advanced, longest, most awarded, and the most profitable of all American films. While it has since been superseded in those categories, it remains the standard to which an older generation of filmgoers compares everything that followed. Released on the eve of World War II, *Gone With the Wind* marks a dividing point in American film, from a past of silent epics to a future of weekly blockbusters.

Based on the novel by Margaret Mitchell, it became the subject of a famously prolonged and publicized production that has been detailed at length in everything from *Memo From David O. Selznick* to fan scrapbooks.

Selznick had worked at RKO and MGM before forming Selznick International in the mid-1930s, counting on his friend Jock Whitney for financial backing and on his connections with Technicolor for a production edge. He was familiar with the process of adapting literary properties, having turned out well-regarded versions of *David Copperfield*, *A Tale of Two Cities* (both 1935), and *The Prisoner of Zenda* (1937). Mitchell's book was published in June 1936, but Katharine Brown, the head of Selznick's New York City story department, saw a draft in May and urged her boss to buy it. Selznick paid $50,000 for the rights in July. Even though it was many months before he would actually read the book, he could see at once that a film adaptation would face considerable structural difficulties. The producer considered starting at the halfway point in the story, as he did with *David Copperfield*; he also thought about releasing the film in two parts, as Erich von Stroheim had hoped to do with *Greed* (1924).

Selznick asked Mitchell to work on a screenplay, but she refused. The producer then turned to Sidney Howard, a playwright known for his skill at plotting. Howard won the right to work on his farm in Tyringham, Massachusetts, where he spent six weeks turning out a four-hundred-page script. His version stripped away many characters, such as Scarlett's child by her first husband and her relatives in Charleston and Savannah, as well as a long stretch of material about the O'Hara family before Tara.

Many subsequent writers worked on the script, including, for two weeks, F. Scott Fitzgerald. All complained about the producer's interference, and on his insistence that they could only use dialogue that Mitchell herself employed. Meanwhile, Selznick assembled a crew for preproduction, including production designer William Cameron Menzies and cinematographer Lee Garmes. He assigned George Cukor to direct, and cast many of the supporting roles. Olivia de Haviland, a fixture at Warner Brothers, was anxious to expand on her image as Errol Flynn's screen girlfriend, and embraced the relatively unrewarding role of Melanie Wilkes. Leslie Howard at first could not be persuaded to play Ashley Wilkes, rightly seeing it as a continuation of the effete, diffident parts he had acted many times before. Selznick got his cooperation by agreeing to give him a producing credit on *Intermezzo* (1939). The actor then underwent weeks of screen tests until Selznick was satisfied with his makeup and hairpiece.

The two lead roles, Rhett Butler and Scarlett O'Hara, remained unfilled when Selznick was forced to begin filming in December 1938, some thirty months after the producer's initial investment. Opinion polls insisted that no one but Clark Gable could play Butler, but the actor was uncomfortable taking on a character the public seemed to have already defined. The real catch was Louis B. Mayer, who as the head of MGM held the rights to Gable's contract. Mayer released Gable only on the condition that MGM distribute the film.

Casting Scarlett was more complicated. Selznick tested just about every available actress, most of whom were eager to play the mercurial, headstrong heroine. (Bette Davis even made *Jezebel*, a sort of feature-length screen test that incurred Selznick's wrath when Warners released it in 1938.) The producer seemed to be most serious about Paulette Goddard, although he had Jean Arthur film many scenes. The probably apocryphal version is too good to resist repeating. Selznick's brother Myron was one of Hollywood's leading agents. He allegedly brought Vivien Leigh to his brother the night the burning of Atlanta was staged, saying, "Here is your Scarlett." After some tests, Selznick agreed, although he complained throughout production about the size of her breasts.

The burning of Atlanta was the first footage shot for *Gone With the Wind*, and it marked the scope of Selznick's ambition. The RKO backlot was sacrificed for the event, including the giant gates of *King Kong*. All seven of the Technicolor cameras then in existence were there to record the scene. Stunt doubles filled in for Rhett and Scarlett as they fled by horse and carriage through the flames.

George Cukor began filming in January 1939, and immediately ran into trouble. His first scene was a ball in Charleston, and it required the increasingly unhappy Gable to not only dance but to deliver flowery dialogue in a mock-chivalrous style. Although all involved were circumspect about details afterward, Selznick fired Cukor after two weeks, replacing him with Victor Fleming. Gable was happy with the macho, casually profane Fleming, while Leigh and de Havilland continued to consult with Cukor off the set about their performances.

Fleming refused to work until Selznick gave him a final script. Selznick hired Ben Hecht and sequestered himself with Fleming and the author for five days, acting out parts until a screenplay was finally finished. Selznick himself wrote the famous closing lines for Rhett Butler, adding "Frankly" to "My dear, I don't give a damn."

It would be inconceivable today to start a film this massive in scope without a script, a cast, or even a secure director, but Selznick counted on his benzedrine-fueled drive to pull him through. The chaos surrounding the production was magnified by the use of Technicolor, still a relatively experimental process, and by Selznick's seemingly arbitrary decisions. He replaced cinematographer Lee Garmes with Ernest Haller because he was unsatisfied with the dark hues Garmes was obtaining. Even so, much of the finished film has surprisingly muted colors, reflecting the story's increasingly elegiac mood.

Selznick also had to deal with the public controversy surrounding the book. Bowing to pressure from the NAACP, he deleted the "n-word" and references to the Ku Klux Klan. He also took special care with the story's African-American characters, although actors like Hattie McDaniel still were forced to justify their work to often angry colleagues. The film takes a more nuanced approach to slavery than the book, and almost manages to avoid naming the enemy North entirely. But Selznick fought the Hays Office to keep Rhett's mild curse and loose morals.

The producer's style became so oppressive that Fleming quit well into production. Selznick replaced him with MGM journeyman director Sam Wood, keeping Wood on when Fleming returned two weeks later. Wood shot in the morning; Fleming, the afternoon, as Selznick pushed to the end of filming.

After months of postproduction, which included deleting barbecue scenes and Scarlett's wedding night with Charles Hamilton, Selznick prepared for the film's premiere in Atlanta on December 15, 1939, charging ten dollars a ticket in a benefit for the Atlanta Community Fund.

As the film opened in other cities, critics were forced to bow before the magnitude of Selznick's achievement. A few complained that *Gone With the Wind* was hokum on a grand scale, but most embraced the film just as eagerly as the public did. Today it seems the most intimate of epics, a story of vast upheaval that often seems to be taking place with two or three people in a small, dark room. When the canvas opens the effect is magisterial, even when individual shots and scenes are gaudy, or at times faked.

The film marked the beginning of the end of Gable's carefree, swaggering power. From this role on his work was darker, less mocking. Leigh also had trouble living up to Scarlett, and did not achieve the same impact in film until *A Streetcar Named Desire* over a decade later. Both director Elia Kazan and playwright Tennessee Williams were well aware of Scarlett during the staging of *Streetcar*, and the resemblance between the two roles was almost certainly intentional. Blanche DuBois is a Scarlett without a protector in Rhett, a Scarlett who can no longer forge her own way on the strength of her family's past, a Scarlett reduced to the kindness of strangers.

Tevye

Maymon Films, 1939. Sound, B&W, 1.37. 96 minutes.
Cast: Maurice Schwartz (Teyva), Miriam Riselle (Chavah), Rebecca Weintraub (Goldie), Paula Lubelski (Zeitel), Leon Liebgold (Fedya), Vicki Marcus (Shloimele), Betty Marcus (Perele), Julius Adler (Priest), David Makarenko (Mikita), Helen Grossman (Mikita's Wife), Morris Srossberg (Starosta), Al Harris (Zazuli), Louis Weisberg (Shtarsina), Boas Young (Uradnick [Officer]).
Credits: Directed by Maurice Schwartz. Screenplay by Maurice Schwartz. Adaptation by Marcy Klauber. Based on writings by Sholom Aleichem. English subtitles: Leon Chrystal. Produced by Henry Ziskin. Director of photography: Larry Williams. Edited by Sam Citron. Settings by William Saulter. Sound recorded by Paul Robillard. RCA Sound System. Music by Sholom Secunda.
Additional Credits: Released December 21, 1939.
Available: National Center for Jewish Film at Brandeis University (www.jewishfilm.org). ISBN: 1-58587-189-3. UPC: 800821021006. Ergo Media, Inc., VHS (1990). ISBN: 1-56082-007-1.

Yiddish theater played a vibrant, if largely hidden, role in early twentieth-century culture. By one estimate, there were over two hundred Yiddish theaters and touring groups in the United States between 1890 and 1940. Many were centered in New York City, especially along Manhattan's Second Avenue. There plays by Ibsen and Shaw were performed before their English-language debuts on Broadway. Stars like Jacob Adler, Bertha Kalich, and Molly Picon had large followings. Set designers like Boris Aronson, who worked on some of the most important plays of the 1940s and '50s, started out in New York on Second Avenue.

Yiddish film, on the other hand, can be traced to 1911, and in subsequent years found three centers of production: Russia, Poland, and New York. According to historian J. Hoberman, Yiddish films in the United States were largely based on plays presented on the Lower East Side. The first Yiddish film with synchronized sound appeared eighteen months after *The Jazz Singer*.

Maurice Schwartz formed the Yiddish Art Theatre in 1918. Born in the Ukraine, Schwartz as a child of eleven was stranded in Liverpool, England, while his family made its way to New York. He had to live in the streets until his parents could send for him. As an adult, Schwartz and his partner Max Wilner took over a former German theater on East Fourteenth Street, where they staged plays by Strindberg and Schnitzler, among others. Schwartz produced, starred in, and often directed the plays, including a 1919 production of *Tevye*. It was based on a character created by Sholom Aleichem, the pseudonym used by Sholom Rabinowitz, in a series of eight monologues published separately and then in a collection of stories. (Rabinowitz's son-in-law I.D. Berkowitz originally adapted *Tevye der Milkhauer* for the stage.)

Schwartz appeared in his first film, *Visker*, in 1924, and starred in and codirected *Uncle Moses* in 1930. He first proposed making *Tevye* in 1936, but couldn't secure financing for the project until 1938. Schwartz wrote the screenplay for the film, with songwriter Marcy Klauber ("I Get the Blues When It Rains") given credit for the adaptation. The script combined plots from "Chava" (1906) and "Lekh-Lekho" (1916), with some humor added from the first monologue, "Tevye Strikes It."

The same monologues formed the basis of the Broadway musical (and movie) *Fiddler on the Roof*, but *Tevye* is an entirely different story. Schwartz added new characters while eliminating many of the familiar figures from the musical. His version opens as Tevye's widowed daughter Zeitel returns home with her two children. Tevye's other daughter Chavah is enmeshed in a romance with Fedya, the gentile son of a wealthy landowner. The father is dead set against Chavah marrying outside of her faith, and cuts her off when she elopes. The marriage precipitates a series of tragedies that could destroy Tevye's family.

(As critic Jan Lisa Huttner notes, transliterating from Hebrew to Yiddish to English can result in potentially confusing variant spellings. Chavah, Tevye's daughter, can easily become Chava, and just as easily Khave. Tevye is also spelled Tevya, and the other daughter in the film can be spelled Tseytl, Tzeitel, or Zeitel.)

Schwartz's Tevye is strikingly different from the one portrayed by Zero Mostel on Broadway (and Topol on film). Although resigned to the gentile world, this Tevye, a Russian farmer who has run a dairy for fifty years, has managed to maintain his faith and his integrity, masking his bitterness with humor and erudition. Schwartz avoids resorting to anger or other emotional outbursts, investing his part with a strength and pride that is as inspiring today as it was in 1939.

Produced by restaurateur Harry Ziskin for $70,000 (at the time roughly one-tenth of a typical Hollywood "A" feature), *Tevye* was filmed largely on location on a potato farm in Jericho, Long Island, after three weeks of rehearsals at the Yiddish Art Theater. With such a small budget, Schwartz had to keep his crowd scenes to a minimum, and could not afford the luxuries of in-depth rehearsals. But the cast was so familiar with the material that the acting overall feels easy and assured. Cinematographer Lawrence Williams, a veteran with over twenty years' experience, was more concerned with capturing the action than in composing striking compositions, but his work is sympathetic to the material. Occasionally, as Tevye whips his horse past his scorned daughter, for example, Williams devises rough, gripping camera pans and tilts.

At the time, some Yiddish critics objected to Schwartz's portrayal of the story's Christian characters. They vote to expel Tevye from the village in order to profit from his farm, and some steal from him during an enforced auction of his belongings. But Schwartz is careful to include sympathetic farmers, as well as a police officer scorned by Christian and Jew alike. *Tevye* may not be especially balanced, but it is honest and, in light of the political climate of the time, daring. Other critics complained that Schwartz misinterpreted the meaning of Aleichem's writings. But the film, which opened at New York's Continental Theater during the Christmas season, was a solid hit. It played for five weeks on Broadway when most films could barely muster a single week.

Tevye was an important part of what *Variety* called a "boom" in Yiddish and black films. It was one of twenty-three Yiddish features to open in

New York since 1937, a period Hoberman refers to as the "zenith" of Yiddish films.

Schwartz was not the only director of Yiddish-language films in the 1930s. Edgar G. Ulmer, whose *Detour* is in the Registry, was shooting Yiddish musicals at the same time. But as the Jewish audience assimilated or aged, the demand for Yiddish films inevitably declined. Ironically, some writers trace the rise of Method Acting to The Group Theatre, formed in 1931 in part in response to Yiddish theater. Stella Adler, along with Lee Strasberg one of the founders of The Group Theatre, was the daughter of Yiddish theater fixture Jacob Adler, and got her start in Yiddish plays.

The National Center for Jewish Film at Brandeis University offers "the most comprehensive collection of Jewish-themed film and video in the world." It has preserved the best available copy of *Tevye* from a 35mm print with English subtitles.

Trance and Dance in Bali

Gregory Bateson, Margaret Mead, 1936–39. Silent with sound added later, B&W, 1.33. 22 minutes.

Credits: Photography by Gregory Bateson and Jane Belo. Edited by Josef Bohmer. Music arranged by Colin McPhee. Written and Narrated by Margaret Mead. Produced by Gregory Bateson and Margaret Mead with assistance from Committee for Research in Dementia Praecox, supported through the 33rd Degree Scottish Rite, North Masonic Jurisdiction; Cambridge University; The American Museum of Natural History; Department of Child Study, Vassar College.

Additional Credits: Directed by Gregory Bateson, Margaret Mead. Edited and scored in 1952. Copyright controlled by the Institute for Intercultural Studies.

Available: Audio-Visual Services, Pennsylvania State University, VHS (1988): *http://mediasales.psu.edu.*

Between March 1936, and March 1938, Margaret Mead and Gregory Bateson conducted fieldwork in Bali. (They spent an additional six-week period there in February and March 1939.) Mead, born in 1901 in Philadelphia, had studied under Franz Boas, the dominant figure in American anthropology, at Columbia University. Although she had recently married seminarian Luther Cressman, she convinced her father to finance an expedition to Samoa after she earned her master's degree. Her book *Coming of Age in Samoa* was a sensation when it was published in 1928; that same year she married the New Zealand anthropologist Reo Fortune, and continued fieldwork with him.

Bateson, born in 1904, was the son of a famous geneticist, William Bateson. Gregory studied biology and natural history at Cambridge before heading to Polynesia. His first book, *Naven*, came out in 1936. By that point he had not only met Mead and Fortune, but combined his research efforts with theirs. Bateson and Mead were wed in Singapore in 1936.

In June of that year, the two anthropologists set up research quarters in the village of Bajoeng Gedé near the famous ruins of Kintamani in the district of Bangli. That November they established a second camp in the palace of a former rajah; the following year, they erected a third camp in the village of Batoean. Financing for their expedition came in part from the Committee for Research in Dementia Praecox (referred to today as schizophrenia). Mead believed that religious cultures built around trance rituals experienced the same psychological effects as schizophrenics, and her work was an attempt to prove this hypothesis.

As anthropologist Andrew Lakoff later pointed out, Bateson and Mead operated under several other premises as well. They asserted that scientists could diagnose a culture's psychic structure, flaws and all, from analyzing members' bodies. They also believed scientists could do this at a distance simply by examining photographs and films. And, as Lakoff wrote in 1996, "According to Mead and Bateson's theory, Balinese personality is characteristically withdrawn as a result of consistently frustrating relations between mother and child." They would try to prove this by taking some 25,000 photographs and shooting 22,000 feet of film.

Working with translator Madé Kalér, Mead and Bateson documented as much of Balinese culture as they were permitted to observe. Bateson and Mead were sometimes aided by Katharane Mershon and by Jane Belo, who later worked with Zora Neale Hurston on the *Commandment Keeper Church* project. As they described in their 1942 book *Balinese Character: A Photographic Analysis*, Mead would take verbal notes while Bateson, armed with two cameras, moved among the Balinese. "We tried to use the still and the moving-picture cameras to get a record of Balinese behavior, and this is a very different matter from the preparation of 'documentary' films or photographs," they wrote. "We tried to shoot what happened normally and spontaneously, rather than to decide upon the norms and then get Balinese to go through these behaviors in suitable lighting."

The resulting films were not the first ethnographic movies. Filmmaker Jean Rouch wrote that an aborigine dance filmed in Australia by Baldwin Spencer in April 1901 might deserve that honor. They were not even the first movies to be shot in the South Pacific. Gaston Méliès, brother of film pioneer Georges Méliès, was filming in Tahiti in 1912. Robert Flaherty brought his family with him to Samoa during the filming of *Moana* (1926), and was one of the participants in F. W. Murnau's *Tabu* (1931), filmed in various South Pacific locations. Charlie Chaplin and his brother Sydney visited Bali in 1932 during their world tour, and filmed a *kris* dance. The Chaplins didn't attempt to provide a greater narrative meaning to their footage, but were still smart enough filmmakers to capture the important elements of the performance.

Trance and Dance in Bali was not screened for the public until 1952, by which time Bateson had divorced Mead. She wrote a narration that provided a cultural background for the footage, which had been edited down to three sequences. In the first, a masked witch has her disciples spread plague through the land. The second sequence involves followers of the king's dragon who are placed into a trance by the witch. Revived by the dragon, they turn their ceremonial kris knives on themselves. The third sequence shows the dancers reviving from their trances.

The dancers were filmed with two cameras. Footage from the first, which had a standard lens and was placed on a tripod, resembles any travelogue film—the Chaplins', for example. Bateson used a close-up lens on the second camera, which was generally handheld, and occasionally filmed in slow motion. This material has an extraordinary intimacy that evokes Flaherty's work.

Mead wrote in 1977, "Many years before I had seen some films of trance dancing," but Flaherty's films—in particular, *Moana*—were the primary influence on Bateson and Mead. Just as Flaherty's objectivity was questioned in later years, some writers have challenged *Trance and Dance in Bali* and the other films in the Mead and Bateson collection. Mead didn't like the country, while Bateson called its people "penny wise" and "pound foolish." "The Balinese are markedly dependent on

spatial orientation," he wrote. Driven in a car on a winding road, a Balinese "may become severely disoriented and unable to act (*e.g.*, a dancer may be unable to dance) until he has got back his orientation by seeing some important landmark." The same might be said of a Finn or an Afgahni, or indeed anyone driven somewhere unknown.

Furthermore, Mead was paid to find evidence of schizophrenia in the Balinese; consciously or not, this must have affected what she what she chose to document. What Chaplin filmed as lively and slightly risqué came across as sour and menacing in Mead's interpretation. Even Bateson was at odds with Mead over her methods and conclusions. As late as 1976, they were still arguing vehemently over handheld filming versus using a tripod, how long shots should last, how close to get to subjects, and so on. Although most ethnographic filmmakers would disagree today, Mead insisted there was nothing wrong in staging scenes, or in paying the Balinese to perform. "We created the *context* in which the notes and photographs were taken, e.g., by paying for the dance," she insisted.

As far as a political context, Bali was controlled by the Dutch at the time, and in the view of many writers, Mead and Bateson ignored evidence of brutalities inflicted on the Balinese. In *The Third Eye: Race, Cinema and Ethnographic Spectacle*, Fatimah Tobing Rony wrote that natives were ordered to perform for the cameras. "Madé Kalér, Mead and Bateson's main informant, said people were angry at being forced to pose nude, but would be arrested if they refused."

Trance and Dance in Bali was one of six films in a series called "Character Formation in Different Cultures." Mead re-edited the footage for CBS, which broadcast it in 1953 as part of its "Adventure" series. Archivists are still cataloging the other Bateson and Mead films; *Learning to Dance in Bali*, filmed in 1936, became available for public screening only in the 1970s, for example. Later in his life, Bateson became involved with cybernetics, and along with Stewart Brand and California governor Jerry Brown, Jr., was influential in E.F. Schumacher's "small is beautiful" movement. Mead's continuing influence in anthropology is buttressed in part by the Margaret Mead Film Festival, which annually screens documentaries and ethnographic films.

His Girl Friday

Columbia, 1940. Sound, B&W, 1.37. 92 minutes.

Cast: Cary Grant (Walter Burns), Rosalind Russell (Hildy Johnson), Ralph Bellamy (Bruce Baldwin), Gene Lockhart (Sheriff Hartwell), Porter Hall (Murphy), Ernest Truex (Bensinger), Cliff Edwards (Endicott), Clarence Kolb (Mayor), Roscoe Karns (McCue), Frank Jenks (Wilson), Regis Toomey (Sanders), Abner Biberman (Louie), Frank Orth (Duffy), John Qualen (Earl Williams), Helen Mack (Mollie Malloy), Alma Kruger (Mrs. Baldwin), Billy Gilbert (Joe Pettibone), Pat West (Warden Cooley), Edwin Maxwell (Dr. Egelhoffer).

Credits: Directed by Howard Hawks. Screen play by Charles Lederer. From the play *The Front Page* by Ben Hecht and Charles MacArthur, as produced by Jed Harris. Director of photography: Joseph Walker. Film Editor: Gene Havlick. Art direction: Lionel Banks. Gowns by [Robert M.] Kalloch. Musical director: M.W. Stoloff. Western Electric Mirrophonic Recording.

Additional Credits: Produced by Howard Hawks. Screenwriting by Ben Hecht, Morrie Ryskind. Second unit director: Arthur Rosson. Assistant director: Cliff Broughton. Sound: Lodge Cunningham. Production dates: September 27 to November 21, 1939. Premiered in New York City on January 12, 1940.

Other Versions: *His Girl Friday* is a remake of *The Front Page*, 1931, directed by Lewis Milestone and starring Pat O'Brien and Adolphe Menjou. Billy Wilder directed *The Front Page*, starring Walter Matthau and Jack Lemmon, in 1974. Ted Kotcheff directed *Switching Channels*, an adaptation of *His Girl Friday* set in a television station and starring Burt Reynolds, in 1988.

Available: Columbia TriStar Home Video DVD (2000). ISBN: 0-7678-2803-8. UPC: 0-43396-26709-1.

No one has been able to determine the identity of the young woman who read Hildy Johnson's part in *The Front Page* one night with director Howard Hawks. Written by former reporters Ben Hecht and Charles MacArthur, it is one of the best American plays, as fully alive and relevant today as when it was first staged in 1928. Central to the Hecht/MacArthur canon, *The Front Page* described a love story between two men, editor Walter Burns and reporter Hildy Johnson, professionals who define themselves through their work. All Hawks would admit to later was, "I said it's better with a girl playing the part of the reporter than a man." It was a brilliant choice, perhaps the most important element the director added to the film.

Hawks had already filmed another Hecht/MacArthur stage hit, *Twentieth Century*, and he had invested considerable energy in developing a version of *Gunga Din* to be written by the pair, one whose plot would make heavy use of *The Front Page*. That may have inspired his interest in remaking the play, which had been a hit when it was filmed by Lewis Milestone in 1931. Hawks had just started filming *Only Angels Have Wings* at Columbia when he convinced studio head Harry Cohn to secure the rights to *The Front Page*, recently held by Howard Hughes.

Hecht was working on *Gone With the Wind*, and could provide only temporary help on the project. He and Charles Lederer worked together on a draft, with Lederer providing a crucial element: Hildy would be Walter Burns's ex-wife, a move that heightened the tension—sexual and professional—of their scenes together. Born in 1910, Lederer was raised by his aunt, Marion Davies; he would continue to collaborate with Hecht throughout the 1940s.

Lederer wrote a total of three drafts by July 1939. Hawks then hired veteran playwright Morrie Ryskind for further script work. By the time a shooting script was ready, over half the original dialogue from the play had been rewritten. Hildy's gender required some new characters, including her fiancé Bruce Baldwin. New scenes included a lengthy introduction which establishes the bickering relationship between Hildy and Burns, and a restaurant scene in which Burns evaluates how much of a romantic threat Baldwin might be.

Hawks had always planned to cast Cary Grant as Walter Burns, and the actor, at the time a lead in *Only Angels Have Wings*, agreed readily. Finding Hildy proved more difficult. Columbia head Harry Cohn wanted to cast Jean Arthur, one of his contract players, but after her treatment in *Only Angels* she didn't want to work with Hawks again. Carole Lombard and Irene Dunne also turned down the part. Rosalind Russell was a last-minute decision.

Born in 1908 in Connecticut, Russell worked first on the stage before signing a contract with MGM in 1934. She was consigned to "other women" roles until *The Women*, where she turned in a sensational performance as a brittle, unstable gossip. Russell approached Hawks warily, well aware that she wasn't his first choice. More than the director, Grant was the one who gave her confidence after principal photography began on September 27, 1939. Shooting went relatively quickly, at least for a Hawks film. One scene in a restaurant proved so difficult that it took four days instead of two to shoot, but when filming was done, Hawks was only seven days over schedule.

Hawks's changes had the paradoxical effect of making the film truer to the spirit of the play. As a director, Hawks seems to get out of the way, to let the actors and script blossom by themselves.

His choices are questions of taste, of emphasis, of providing viewers with the clearest possible version of the material. In a way he is reverting to the old-fashioned "best seat in the house" theory, but a seat that can move among the reporters in the press room, settling on the characters who count. The camera moves freely, but almost always in the same mid-level, medium-shot frame. Hawks switches the plane of action only during a few dramatic highpoints: Hildy interviewing Earl Johnson in his isolation cell, for example, or the reporters peering out a window at Molly's body below. Stage techniques color some of the characters. Baldwin always has a raincoat and umbrella with him, props that separate him from the world of journalism.

"I tried to make my dialogue go fast—perhaps 20% faster than most pictures," Hawks told Richard Schickel later. Hawks also took credit for padding the dialogue so the characters could continue talking without stepping on laugh lines or important information. "Sometimes we put a few unnecessary words at the front of a sentence and a few at the end so people can overlap in their talking and you still get everything they wanted to say," he said. Hawks biographer Todd McCarthy cites one study that rated the actors at 240 words per minute (compared to an average speaking rate of 150 wpm). Hawks always said that *The Front Page* had the "finest modern dialogue that had been written," and by having the cast deliver it so quickly, he was offering a dream version of America in which everyone was smart, sophisticated, and hyperarticulate. The result is like watching pros so afraid of losing the spotlight that they keep talking until they run out of air.

In-jokes delight audiences today: Grant uses his real name, Archie Leach, when referring to a crook, and compares Bellamy to "that fellow in the pictures—you know, what's his name—Ralph Bellamy." Aficionados also exclaim over the work by the brilliant character actors, figures who reappear throughout the National Film Registry titles and

who brought so much humor and depth to countless movies. The excitable Billy Gilbert, a mainstay of comic two-reelers; Abner Biberman, a memorable villain in *Gunga Din*; Roscoe Karns, a glib fast-talker in everything from *All Quiet on the Western Front* to *It Happened One Night*; Cliff "Ukulele Ike" Clifford, later memorialized as Jiminy Cricket in *Pinocchio*; Porter Hall, a frequent player in Preston Sturges films; Clarence Kolb, an expert at cold, cigar-wielding executives—they were professionals playing professionals, and Hawks gave them all a warm showcase.

Perfectly matched, Grant and Russell relish their roles, so much so that Russell hired her own writer to give them more gag lines. Their give-and-take feels authentic, organic, perhaps because they are willing to risk losing audience sympathy. Every comedy Grant made subsequently is colored by his work here, by the fact that he could very easily be the totally amoral rascal he was as Walter Burns. Russell, meanwhile, found herself trapped in a series of "career girl" roles until she was finally forced to return to the stage, where her starring turn in *Auntie Mame* gave her a new strait-jacket. (One side result: Grant introduced Russell to her future husband, Frederick Brisson, and was best man at their wedding.)

One impressive element of *His Girl Friday* today is its breathtaking cynicism. The politicians, reporters and policemen who populate *The Front Page* and *His Girl Friday* use crime for their own purposes: to sell papers, to win elections, to thwart the will of the public. The only decent characters in the story, the only ones who can be trusted, are a naive insurance salesman, a prostitute, and an unhinged killer. It's a vision of America more ruthless and hard-hearted than any other film of its time, and the fact that it's delivered as a glib farce only makes it more chilling. When Walter Burns snarls, "I ought to know better than to hire anyone with a disease," the statement's sting remains after the laughter fades.

The Shop Around the Corner

MGM, 1940. Sound, B&W, 1.37. 99 minutes.

Cast: Margaret Sullavan (Klara Novak), James Stewart (Alfred Kralik), Frank Morgan (Hugo Matuschek), Joseph Schildkraut (Ferencz Vadas), Sara Haden (Flora), Felix Bressart (Pirovitch), William Tracy (Pepi Katona), Inez Courtney (Ilona), Sarah Edwards (Woman customer), Edwin Maxwell (Doctor), Charles Halton (Detective), Charles Smith (Rudy).

Credits: Produced and Directed by Ernst Lubitsch. Screen play by Samson Raphaelson. Based on a play by Nikolaus Laszlo. Musical score: Werner R. Heymann. Recording engineer: Douglas Shearer. Art director: Cedric

Gibbons. Associate art director: Wade B. Rubottom. Set decorations: Edwin B. Willis. Hair styles for Miss Sullavan by Sydney Guilaroff. Director of photography: William Daniels. Film editor: Gene Ruggiero. Western Electric Sound System. A Metro-Goldwyn-Mayer presentation of a Loew's Incorporated and Ernst Lubitsch production.

Additional Cast: Grace Hayle (Plump woman), Charlie Arnt (Policeman), Gertrude Simpson (Customer), William Edmunds (Waiter), Mary Carr (Grandmother), Mabel Colcord (Aunt Anna); Renie Riano, Claire Du Brey, Ruth Warren, Joan Blair, Mira McKinney (Customers).

Additional Credits: Laszlo is also credited as "Miklós László." Unit production manager: Arthur Rose. Production dates: November to December 5, 1939. Released January 12, 1940.
Other Versions: Remade as *In the Good Old Summertime* (1949) and the Broadway musical *She Loves Me* (1962); inspiration for *You've Got Mail* (1998).
Available: Warner Home Video DVD (2002). ISBN: 0-7907-7147-0. UPC: 0-12569-56692-7.

Originally a Hungarian play called *Parfumerie*, *The Shop Around the Corner* was translated into English by Steffie Trondle and purchased by director Ernest Lubitsch in July 1938. He planned it as a vehicle for Dolly Haas, a German actress who was trying to build a career in Hollywood.

After establishing his reputation in Germany and then at Warner Brothers, Lubitsch made *One Hour with You*, *Trouble in Paradise* (both 1932), and other hits at Paramount. With much fanfare, he was named chief of production at the studio in 1935, the first filmmaker in the sound era to run one of the majors. It was a difficult period for the studio and the director, and the failure at the box office of *Bluebeard's Eighth Wife* in March 1938 led to his dismissal. He formed Ernst Lubitsch Productions in order to make *The Shop Around the Corner* in October 1938, but eventually chose not to produce the film himself. (His biographer Scott Eyman called the decision "a loss of nerve.")

Instead, Lubitsch signed with MGM to direct *Ninotchka* (1939), at the request of its star, Greta Garbo. As part of the deal, the studio paid him $62,500 for *The Shop Around the Corner* (he had paid $16,500 for the story), and agreed to cast Margaret Sullavan and James Stewart—provided he finish *Ninotchka* first. The Garbo film, her first comedy, was her biggest hit in years, and gave Lubitsch the freedom to make *The Shop Around the Corner* on his own terms.

While Metro researcher Henry Noerdlinger compiled an inventory of an actual Budapest leather store (the setting for almost all of the play), Lubitsch worked with his longtime collaborator Samson Raphaelson on the screenplay. (Raphaelson had started on the project back in 1938.) They revised the play by cutting lengthy speeches and changing a few plot elements. For example, in the movie Margaret Sullavan applies for a job; in the play, her character is already working in the store.

In trying to define "the Lubitsch touch," most writers point to his Paramount films, Eurocentric musicals and romances filled with suave characters.

But *The Shop Around the Corner* reveals the best aspects of the director's work and personality. As Eyman noted, he does not condescend to any of the story's characters, not the supercilious errand boy, the haughty customers, or even the deceitful clerk. Unusually for the director, it is a film solidly entrenched in the working class, and one that treats its problems with insight and compassion. "I have known just such a little shop in Budapest," he said in an interview in New York after the film opened, and it's clear that he knew exactly how the people in it behaved.

Lubitsch treated their romantic foibles with the same serious intent he gave to the counts and countesses in his earlier films, but even more than in *Ninotchka*, he displayed a new warmth and tenderness for his characters—admittedly, while putting them through unbearable emotional turmoil. This is a romantic comedy that features suicide, betrayal, and the cruelest of practical jokes, as well as a holiday season that dissolves into double-crosses and deceptions.

The director credited James Stewart for much of the film's success, saying that "he holds his public by his very lack of handsome face or suave manner." The actor would win a Best Supporting Actor Oscar for *The Philadelphia Story* that year, but this was the first film in which he displayed the full range of his skill, the first in which he showed the cunning and sometimes mean-spirited edge he would bring to more mature roles in the postwar 1940s. He was also working with Margaret Sullavan, a friend from his days with the University Players and the wife of another friend, actor Henry Fonda. Their easy intimacy adds to *The Shop Around the Corner*'s lasting charm. (They would also team in their next film, Frank Borzage's *The Mortal Storm*, released the same year.)

The film was shot in sequence in twenty-seven days, a rare occurrence at the time, but not as difficult here because of its limited sets. By shooting the story in order from start to finish, Lubitsch and the actors developed strikingly rich moods and emotions, and built a rapport that was difficult to achieve on other productions. Seen as a modest, unexceptional movie when it was released, *The Shop Around the Corner* has grown in stature over the years. Despite remakes and variations, no one has yet been able to match its delicacy and sincerity.

The Grapes of Wrath

Twentieth Century-Fox, 1940. Sound, B&W, 1.37. 129 minutes.

Cast: Henry Fonda (Tom Joad), Jane Darwell (Ma Joad), John Carradine (Casy), Charley Grapewin (Grandpa), Dorris Bowdon (Rosasharn), Russell Simpson (Pa Joad), O.Z. Whitehead (Al), John Qualen (Muley), Eddie Quillan (Connie), Zeffie Tilbury (Grandma), Frank Sully (Noah), Frank Darien (Uncle John), Darryl Hickman (Winfield), Shirley Mills (Ruth Joad), Roger Imhof (Thomas), Grant Mitchell (Caretaker), Charles D. Brown (Wilkie), John Arledge (Davis), Ward Bond (Policeman), Harry Tyler (Bert), William Pawley (Bill), Charles Tannen (Joe), Selmar Jackson (Inspection officer), Charles Middleton (Leader), Eddie Waller (Proprietor), Paul Guilfoyle (Floyd), David Hughes (Frank), Cliff Clark (City man), Joseph Sawyer (Bookkeeper), Frank Faylen (Tim), Adrian Morris (Agent), Hollis Jewell (Muley's Son), Robert Homans (Spencer), Irving Bacon (Driver), Kitty McHugh (Mae).

Credits: Directed by John Ford. Screen play by Nunnally Johnson. Based on the novel by John Steinbeck. Produced by Darryl F. Zanuck. Associate producer: Nunnally Johnson. Director of photography: Gregg Toland. Technical director: Tom Collins. Musical direction: Alfred Newman. Art direction: Richard Day, Mark-Lee Kirk. Set decorations: Thomas Little. Film editor: Robert Simpson. Costumes: Gwen Wakeling. Sound: George Leverett, Roger Heman. Western Electric Recording. A Twentieth Century-Fox presentation.

Additional Credits: Accordion music: Danny Borzage. Production dates: October 4 to November 16, 1939. Premiered January 24, 1940.

Awards: Oscars for Best Directing, Actress in a Supporting Role (Darwell).

Other Versions: *The Grapes of Wrath* (1991), directed by Kirk Browning and Frank Galati (a videotaped version the Steppenwolf Theatre Company stage production).

Available: Twentieth Century Fox Home Entertainment DVD (2004). UPC: 0-24543-10330-1

John Steinbeck's novel *The Grapes of Wrath* won the Pulitzer Prize when it was published in 1939. It was the author's third book about agriculture and labor, following *In Dubious Battle* (1936) and *Of Mice and Men* (1937). Steinbeck dramatized the latter for a successful stage production, then began two aborted attempts to turn his research—including his observations of a flood at a migrant camp in Visalia—into a novel. His third effort, which he finished in a five-month stretch, focused on an individual family and its journey from Oklahoma to California. He alternated the story of the Joads with accounts of nature and with political and economic incidents.

While controversial, the novel was an immediate best-seller, dominating literary debate as well as making an impact on the culture at large. Twentieth Century-Fox studio head Darryl F. Zanuck paid Steinbeck $100,000 for the movie rights, calling the book "a stirring indictment of conditions which I think are a disgrace and ought to be remedied." It was a risky move on Zanuck's part, not only because he knew moviegoers preferred lighter entertainment, but because Steinbeck directly accused banks of exploiting migrants, potentially angering Fox's chief investors at Chase National Bank.

Zanuck considered directors Clarence Brown and John Cromwell for the film before assigning John Ford to the project. Documentary filmmaker Pare Lorentz had introduced Steinbeck to screenwriter Nunnally Johnson earlier, and Johnson was the only person Zanuck wanted to adapt the novel. Born in 1897 in Columbus, Georgia, he served in the cavalry in World War I, worked as a journalist in New York, and moved to Hollywood in 1932. He wrote some of the most successful Fox films during the 1930s, and had worked with Ford before. Johnson made several significant changes to the novel, not just eliminating material that would never have passed the censors, but rearranging plot incidents. In particular, Johnson provided the semblance of a happy ending where the novel offered little but starvation and death.

Ford's contributions were just as important to the film's ultimate success. The director had always shown an appreciation for family and heritage, for connection to the land, and the film adds several moments that amplify this. A scene in which Ma Joad, going through family heirlooms, finds a pair of earrings from her past was original to the film. Ford had a feel for grit, for poverty and desperation, that other directors lacked. His vision was focused, stark, and unforgiving. He also added an Irish sentimentality that was often at odds with Steinbeck's message, but which made the film a bit more palatable to audiences.

What Ford and Johnson removed from the book was just about any concrete criticism of police, politicians, and especially evangelists, the subject of Ma Joad's scorn. This made the film more a story of the Joads' struggle to survive than an indictment of a society dependent on exploiting the lower classes. If anyone is condemned, it is the filmgoer for not helping change conditions. Oddly, the film depicts work only once, as Tom Joad and others dig a ditch, and even that scene isn't farmwork.

But when it came to capturing the novel's harshness, the filmmakers didn't hold back. They took Casy the preacher's bleak message—"There ain't no sin and there ain't no virtue. There's just what people do."—directly from the novel. They included Tom Joad's crucial question, "What is a red anyway?" They showed poverty—on the roads, in cities, and in migrant camps—when just about all of Hollywood had turned away. The film is suffused with both hunger and injustice, even if specific instances Steinbeck imagined in the novel are missing.

One false note is how isolated the stoic Okies seem. The film portrays them almost as frontiersmen from the nineteenth century unable to adapt to modern life. The real Okies knew all about contemporary culture; indeed, they coveted it—the movies, the clothes, the cars, the makeup. They wanted nightclubs and big band music, despite the forlorn "Red River Valley" used by Alfred Newman to anchor the soundtrack.

Zanuck borrowed cinematographer Gregg Toland from Samuel Goldwyn. It was the first time Toland worked with Ford. He found a visual equivalent for Ford's (and Steinbeck's) lyrical view of nature, but he adopted documentary techniques to portray conditions as realistically as possible. He also pushed the boundaries of what was considered acceptable cinematography. Especially in its opening, much of *The Grapes of Wrath* is shrouded in darkness, with characters mere suggestions in the frame, or highlighted in chiaroscuro.

Most of the dialogue scenes were shot on soundstages or on the Fox backlot, although second units photographed in Oklahoma, Texas, and in migrant camps in California. Zanuck took credit for one of the film's most impressive moments, an extended traveling shot from the highway into a squalid camp. With its tilted angles, jarring turns, parched ground, and tar-paper shacks, the camera makes California look like a Third World refugee camp. Simply by exposing these conditions to a mainstream audience primed for romance and comedy, the film achieved everything Steinbeck set out to do.

Zanuck dictated that the actors avoid makeup, but it was Ford who got them to forgo vanity. Tom Joad is one of Henry Fonda's signature roles, notable as much for his restraint as his sincerity. In order to get the part, he had to sign a seven-year contract with Fox. Jane Darwell had to persuade Ford to cast her as Ma Joad. The director had wanted Beulah Bondi, but Darwell brought to the role a necessary craftiness and need. John Carradine (as Casy the preacher) and John Qualen (as Muley, a displaced farmer) both have troubling, almost mystical speeches that are among the highlights of their careers. (Dorris Bowdon, who played the pregnant Rosasharn, married Nunnally Johnson after the film opened.)

Working with a budget of $750,000, Ford began shooting on October 4, 1939, and finished forty-three days later on November 16. Editing took about a month. Steinbeck viewed the finished film in December 1939, and wrote, "Zanuck has more than kept his word. He has a hard, straight picture in which the actors are submerged so completely that it looks and feels like a documentary film. . . . No punches are pulled." As a film, *The Grapes of Wrath* was "a harsher thing than the book, by far. It seems unbelievable but it is true."

The film premiered in January 1940, and was Fox's biggest moneymaker of the year. It was strong medicine for mainstream America. Not since *I Am a Fugitive from a Chain Gang* (1932) did a Hollywood film deal so unflinchingly, and with such pessimism, about social issues. Some, especially on the left, found fault with the movie's sentimentality, complaining that lines like "Maybe one guy with a million acres and a thousand farmers starving" did not adequately address society's problems. Nevertheless, *The Grapes of Wrath* received six Oscar nominations, winning the award for Best Direction. It was the second win for Ford, who at this point in his career had been directing for over twenty years. He was especially proud of Toland's cinematography and of the soundtrack—not just Newman's score but the subtle sound effects of birds and crickets, too.

Looking back, how much have conditions improved? What is the solution to poverty, to the injustices of capitalism, to the oppression of the weak? For Ford, especially after his experiences in World War II, the answer came in the lonely vigilantism of Wyatt Earp in *My Darling Clementine* (1946). For Zanuck, the answer was in the people, the same people who were coming to his movies, the same people who would band together to defeat tyranny in *The Longest Day* (1962). Rather than try to provide answers, Steinbeck expanded the scope of the questions; after World War II, he worked on a Mexican production of his novella *The Pearl* (1948).

Pinocchio

RKO, 1940. Sound, color, 1.33. 88 minutes.

Voice Cast: Dickie Jones (Pinocchio), Cliff Edwards (Jiminy Cricket), Christian Rub (Geppetto), Walter Catlett (Honest John), Frankie Darro (Lampwick), Evelyn Venable (The Blue Fairy), Charles Judels (Coachman), Don Brodie (Carnival barker), Mel Blanc (Cleo, Figaro the, Gideon the cat, additional voices).

Credits: Supervising directors: Ben Sharpsteen, Hamilton Luske. Sequence directors: Bill Roberts, Norman Ferguson, Jack Kinney, Wilfred Jackson, T. Hee. Animation directors: Fred Moore, Franklin Thomas, Milton Kahl, Vladimir Tytla, Ward Kimball, Arthur Babbitt, Eric Larson, Woolie Reitherman. Story adaptation: Ted Sears, Otto Englander, Webb Smith, William Cottrell, Joseph Sabo, Erdman Penner, Aurelius Battaglia. Character designs: Joe Grant, Albert Hurter, John P. Miller, Campbell Grant, Martin Provensen, John Walbridge. Music and lyrics: Leigh Harline, Ned Washington, Paul J. Smith. Art direction: Charles Philippi, Hugh Hennesy, Kenneth Anderson, Dick Kelsey, Kendall O'Connor, Terrell Stapp, Thor Putnam, John Hubley, McLaren Stewart, Al Zinnen. Backgrounds: Claude Coats, Merle Cox, Ed Starr, Ray Huffine. Animation: Jack Campbell, Oliver M. Johnston, Berny Wolf, Don Towsley, Don Lusk, John Lounsbery, Norman Tate, John Bradbury, Lynn Karp, Charles Nichols, Art Palmer, Joshua Meador, Don Tobin, Robert Martsch, George Rowley, John McManus, Don Patterson, Preston Blair, Les Clark, Marvin Woodward, Hugh Fraser, John Elliotte.

Additional Credits: Premiered February 7, 1940. Released by RKO until 1954, then by Buena Vista.

Awards: Oscars for Best Music, Original Score; Music, Original Song—"When You Wish Upon a Star."

Other Versions: Collodi's book has been the basis of numerous film adaptations, including *Pinocchio* (1968; made-for-TV); *Le Avventure di Pinocchio* (1972; TV miniseries); *Pinocchio* (1976; made-for-TV), *The Adventures of Pinocchio* (1996; directed by Steve Barron); *Pinocchio* (2002; directed by and starring Robert Benigni).

Available: Buena Vista Entertainment DVD (2009). UPC: 7869367 85951. Disney Home Video DVD (1999). UPC: 717951005793. VHS (1999).

The success of *Snow White and the Seven Dwarfs* (1937) allowed Walt Disney to start his staff on *Bambi*. But when script problems for that project proved intractable, Disney decided to develop *Pinocchio* instead. *The Adventures of Pinocchio*, published in 1883, collected some thirty-five articles by Carlo Collodi that had been serialized in newspapers. Collodi was the pen name for Carlo Lorenzini (1826–90), a former journalist born in Florence who fought for Italy in two wars. He became a civil servant in education, wrote fiction and nonfiction, and translated French fairy tales so well that he was asked to write his own. His story about a wooden puppet who yearns to become a real-life boy was immensely popular throughout the world, and its potential for animation was obvious. But *Pinocchio* was also a fanciful and at times frightening book that dealt openly with grisly topics like dismemberment and death.

Staff writers started working on the project in the fall of 1938. Disney soon discovered other problems with adapting the novel into a film. Collodi's plot lacked a clear, straightforward story line. Assembled from bits and pieces, the book is repetitive, inconsistent, and without the unity and logical flow that Disney preferred. Furthermore, Pinocchio keeps backsliding, and must learn the same moral lessons over and over again. Even while Disney's writers were struggling over the script, animators started fleshing out individual sequences. As he did with *Fantasia* (which was in simultaneous development), Disney assigned animators and directors to individual characters and even individual movements in *Pinocchio*. But by July 1939, he realized that the script wasn't working. Pinocchio was too unlikable a character. It wasn't until Disney focused on Jiminy Cricket that the project gathered momentum. In the opening chapters of the book, Pinocchio actually kills a talking cricket with a mallet, but Disney saw that they could use the insect as the puppet's conscience, a moral center, throughout the story.

In September 1939 Disney decided that Jiminy would narrate the film, which meant he needed to turn the insect into a more appealing figure. Animator Ward Kimball was assigned the job, but Disney complained about his work. "I kept eliminating all the appendages, the sawtooth legs and arms," Kimball said. The end result was essentially a tiny humanoid. "He was a cricket because we called him a cricket," Kimball admitted.

In contrast to his previous productions, Disney sought out celebrities to provide voices for the animated characters in *Pinocchio*. Jiminy Cricket was voiced by Cliff "Ukulele Ike" Edwards, a former vaudevillian who had appeared in a number of early sound films at MGM. Edwards had lost some popularity during the Depression, but he was still known for introducing songs like "Fascinating Rhythm." Before *Pinocchio*, his most recent hit had been "It's Only a Paper Moon." Edwards' warm personality came through in his voice; this film was the start of an association with the Disney studio that lasted until his death in 1971.

Joining Edwards was another vaudevillian, Walter Catlett, who voiced the fox Honest John and sang "An Actor's Life for Me." Catlett's timing was impeccable (as it was in *Bringing Up Baby* two years earlier). He and Edwards borrowed a page from the Fleischer studio by improvising asides on the soundtrack. Lampwick, a young boy who befriends Pinocchio, was acted by Frankie Darro, a child star in silent films. Voicing Pinocchio was a career highlight for Dickie Jones, who had a long career in bit parts and in Westerns, in particular with Gene Autry. This was one of the last film roles for Evelyn Venable, a stage actress who had some success at RKO in the mid-1930s. Her role as the Blue Fairy relied heavily on rotoscoping, the process of drawing an outline of a human figure developed at the Fleischer Studio.

Also in contrast to *Snow White*, Disney began work on *Pinocchio* before the musical score was set. Both Paul J. Smith and Leigh Harline had both worked on the previous film; Harline was the head of the Walt Disney Studio Music Department. The lyrics that wound up in the film were written by Ned Washington, a newcomer to the studio but an established and extremely successful songwriter responsible for hits like "Love Me Tonight" and "I Don't Stand a Ghost of a Chance With You." Born in Scranton, Pennsylvania, in 1901, Washington entered show business as a master of ceremonies in vaudeville, then as a lyricist for everyone from Bing Crosby and Jimmy McHugh to Max Steiner, and later, Dimitri Tiomkin. He had worked at MGM and Paramount before signing a contract with Disney.

The songs in *Pinocchio* show a marked improvement over those in *Snow White*. "When You Wish Upon a Star," almost thrown away in the opening credits, won an Oscar, was a hit for Glenn Miller and many other musicians, and became Walt Disney's de facto theme song. Evoking the ethnic humor of vaudeville, "I've Got No Strings" goes through three variations: Dutch, French, and Russian. In the film it is a tour de force of animation artistry, seamlessly melding several types of movement, from dancing marionettes to Pinocchio's awkward gestures to Stromboli's sweeping arms.

But then *Pinocchio* is filled with tour de force sequences. The artists were aided at times by scale models, following a suggestion by animator Joe Grant. They also had the luxury of experimenting with effects, with discarding months of work, with exploring new techniques until Disney was satisfied with the results. An article in the January

1940 issue of *Popular Mechanics* describes some of the effort that went into animating Monstro the whale, following the process from pencil drawings to chalk on colored paper to "a tracing-dyeing-photographing process on a newly developed type of sensitive film." Animators could refer to a five-foot whale model complete with artificial lungs.

Just as important was the work Disney's writers had done on the script. The film removed most of the book's violence. For example, Collodi burned Pinocchio's feet off and later hung him by the neck on a tree overnight. But the writers actually made some sequences more frightening. The film Pinocchio encounters drinking, smoking, and gambling on Pleasure Island, details missing from the book. The screenwriters condensed the puppet's five-month stay on the island into one terrifying night, giving the film a narrative momentum that's often missing from *Snow White*. Stromboli is a much more horrific presence in the film than the book's Showman, while Monstro the whale (originally a giant shark) is one of the unforgettable monsters in animation.

Disney had hoped to open *Pinocchio* at Radio City Music Hall in December 1939, but the workload was so enormous that he had to reschedule the release. Even the February date meant that the staff had to work overtime, including Christmas Eve. Critics were stunned when they finally saw the film. In the *New York Times*, Frank Nugent wrote that it was the "best cartoon ever made." Otis Ferguson thought that it "brings the cartoon to a level of perfection that the word cartoon will not cover." Moviegoers were not as enthusiastic. *Pinocchio* cost $2.7 million to make, but took in only $2 million in its original release. (The studio got about half of that amount.) Some have argued that the film appealed to children rather than adults, or that it was too demanding for children, or that it couldn't compete against the recently released *Gone With the Wind*, or pointed to the loss of European markets due to World War II. With hindsight it has become apparent that *Pinocchio* is the richest, most rewarding feature Walt Disney ever produced. In fact, it is difficult to name a better feature-length cartoon, making its initial box-office problems all that more inexplicable.

Siege

Julien Bryan (behind windshield) watches as his interpretor deals with a Warsaw policeman. Bryan was the director of *Siege*. *Photo courtesy Sam Bryan/The International Film Foundation*

RKO/Pathé, 1940. Sound, B&W, 1.37. 10 minutes.

Credits: Photographed and described by Julien H. Bryan. Produced and edited by Frederic Ullman, Jr., and Frank Donovan.

Additional Credits: Photographed September 7 to 21, 1939. Released February, 1940.

Available: The Steven Spielberg Film and Video Archive at the United States Holocaust Memorial Museum (http://resources.ushmm.org). For DVD copies, contact Sam Bryan at samkbryan@aol.com or *www.internationalfilmfoundation.com.*

Newsreels played an increasingly important role as the war in Europe spread during the 1930s, even as access to battleground sites became more restricted. Propaganda was always available, but unfiltered reporting was almost impossible to find. For one thing, newsreel cinematography was an expensive process, one that required elaborate equipment. The act of filming drew attention to itself, so much so that filmmakers almost always needed the cooperation of local authorities before they could begin shooting. Processing, editing, and transporting film that depicted controversial information could result in arrest and imprisonment. In *Siege*, Julien Bryan managed to document the German invasion of Poland, and spirit the footage out of Europe right under the noses of Nazi officials.

Author, photographer, and public speaker Julien Hequembourg Bryan was born in Titusville, Pennsylvania, in 1899, to an elder in a Presbyterian church. He grew up listening to missionaries lecturing about distant lands and people, and developed a passion for travel. After high school he joined the American Field Service, driving an ambulance with the French Army during World War I. This became the basis of a book of essays and photographs, *Ambulance 464*, published in 1918. After graduating from Princeton University, he began shooting and selling film footage collected on his travels through Russia and Europe. He also gave lectures to help offset the costs of his journeys.

Bryan purchased a 35mm motion picture camera sometime before his first trip to the Soviet Union in 1930. While he was closely guided by Soviet authorities, few American filmmakers had such free rein inside Russia. Bryan also shot footage in Germany that would be incorporated into in the *March of Time* special issue *Inside Nazi Germany* (1938, a Registry title). He used this material, as well as his still photographs, on a lecture tour in 1938 and 1939. (Bryan's footage appeared in eleven different March of Time episodes.)

According to his son Sam, in the summer of 1939 Bryan filmed travelogue material in Switzerland and the Netherlands. (This footage may have been commissioned by or sold to Kodak for its home education market.) The German invasion of Poland began on September 1. Bryan arrived in Warsaw on the seventh day of the war, bringing with him 6,000 feet of unexposed 35mm film. The Polish government had already fled the city; its military was retreating from German and Russian

Ten-year-old Kazimiera Mika mourns the death of her older sister, killed during a German air raid. *Photo by Julien Bryan, courtesy Sam Bryan/The International Film Foundation*

advances in three directions. Bryan was the last journalist from a neutral country in Warsaw.

Having experienced fighting on the front in Verdun in 1917, Bryan assumed that the new conflict would be similar, with an emphasis on trench warfare. He didn't anticipate the total warfare unleashed by the Germans, a strategy that targeted civilians as much as the military. Warsaw mayor Stefan Starzynski gave Bryan permission to film the invasion, and supplied him with a car and interpreters. For the next two weeks, until September 21, Bryan filmed day and night, interiors and exteriors, documenting efforts by the Poles to barricade the city, German air attacks, fires, injuries, and deaths. He showed men digging trenches across streets and stacking trolley tracks in defensive barriers. He filmed a church that had been bombed during a Sunday Mass, and a maternity hospital where infants and mothers huddled in basement corridors. In what he called the most tragic scene he ever photographed, Bryan showed peasants digging for potatoes in the same field where seven women had been machine gunned to death moments before.

Bryan's footage provided irrefutable visual evidence of the catastrophic effects of the invasion. Although he relied on the cooperation of local authorities, and occasionally composed shots, he focused on facts, on incidents he witnessed firsthand. Issues of diplomacy and political maneuvering became irrelevant to the visual proof of the horror and brutality of war.

After September 21, Bryan was allowed to travel to Koenigsberg, Germany, with other citizens from neutral countries. He hid his film inside a gas mask canister that a fellow American had purchased as a souvenir. Bryan got the footage back six weeks later in New York. He licensed it to the RKO Pathé newsreel department, where it was edited by Frederic Ullman, Jr., and Frank Donovan. They had put together a number of shorts for RKO, and shaped the footage in the style of their previous work. But Bryan exerted considerable influence on the film's structure through his narration.

The resulting film, *Siege*, followed generally accepted rules for newsreels: no blood or close-ups of corpses, for example, and no severe brutality. (Bryan's outtakes are much harsher.) The film's restraint broadened its potential audience. For many viewers, this was their first chance to see the results of the Blitzkrieg. Bryan never pretended that he was being impartial: he blamed the Nazis and defended the Poles. But his evidence could not have been more precise or damning.

The film's structure makes an effective argument against German actions. From relatively impersonal accounts of defense strategies, it moves to the effects of the Nazi air attacks, and gradually zeroes in on the personal toll. (Ullman and Donovan added music and a few sound effects—notably, burning sounds for the fire sequences and engine noises as planes flew over the city.) By the end of the film Bryan is focusing squarely on the victims, shown in a series of devastating portraits. He calls their faces "magnificent," and they are. They are also doomed, the unspoken but inescapable message behind this movie.

Siege had an enormous impact on documentary filmmaking, not in the least for its daredevil aspects.

To this day war correspondents hope for a situation similar to the one Bryan faced: the only reporter left to tell the truth. Bryan's measured but impassioned narration was crucial as well, reminiscent of Edward R. Murrow's radio broadcasts from the roofs of London. Bryan wrote an accompanying book, also called *Siege*. (He returned to Warsaw in 1958 for another book, revisiting survivors of the invasion.)

After the film's release, Bryan was hired by the Office of Coordinator of Inter-American Affairs for a series of short films on Latin America, part of the War Department's attempt to enlist civilian support for the coming war. These films came to the attention of the Davella Mills Foundation, a nonprofit organization founded by David Bloss and Ella Mills to deter war. Bryan received a $300,000 grant for a film company, and formed the International Film Foundation in 1945.

Over two hundred films were released by the IFF, some shot by Bryan's son Sam. Julien Bryan continued working until his death in 1974. One of his last projects was a 16mm reissue of *Siege*. According to Sam Bryan, one good copy of the original 35mm material remains.

Commandment Keeper Church

Zora Neal Hurston, 1940. Silent, B&W, 1.37. 42 minutes.
Featuring: Rev. George Washington, Izora Robinson, Hugh Washington, May Belle Washington, Carrie Belle Washington, Hattie Mae Washington, Julia Jones, Henry Moore, Reuben Stephenson, Willie Robinson, Frank Bates, Carrie Roberts, Zora Neale Hurston.
Credits: Onsite project director: Zora Neale Hurston. Project organizer: Jane Belo. Cinematographers: Lou Brandt, Bob Lawrence. Sound: Norman Chalfin.
Additional Credits: Full Title: *Seventh Day Church of God, South Carolina, May 1940. Commandment Keeper Church, Beaufort field footage. Margaret Mead collection.*
Available: The Library of Congress.

One of the goals of the National Film Registry is to publicize the existence of films produced outside the studio system. As well as experimental and sponsored films, these include films made for educational or research purposes. The Margaret Mead and Gregory Bateson *Trance and Dance in Bali* (1938) documented Balinese rituals to support scientific hypotheses. *Commandment Keeper Church* arose from similar motives.

Mead had been working with anthropologist Jane Belo on comparing religious trances in various cultures. (Belo's findings would be published as *The Trance in Bali* in 1960.) Belo hired Zora Neale Hurston in March 1940 to investigate trances, or religious ecstasies, in church settings in the South. Hurston, at that point the author of three novels and a central figure in the Harlem Renaissance, had studied in New York under anthropologist Franz Boas. She had done extensive fieldwork in Florida and the Caribbean, collecting songs and folklore that she often incorporated into her fiction.

In April Hurston met Belo in Beaufort, South Carolina, the urban center of Gullah culture, to study the Commandment Keeper Seventh Day Church of God. ("Gullah," a possible derivation from "Angola," refers to language, foods, and customs stretching back to the origins of the slave trade in South Carolina's Low Country.) Led by Rev. George Washington, the Commandment Keeper Church based its services on sermons and music performed on guitars and various percussion instruments. Members of the small congregation occasionally went into trances. It was exactly what Belo was looking for.

She returned to New York to marry Frank Tannenbaum. There she arranged to send Norman Chalfin, Lou Brandt, and Bob Lawrence to Beaufort to film and record the services. Hurston, who had her own designs on the Commandment Keeper Church, wrote to Paul Green at the University of North Carolina to ask for recording equipment. Hurston envisioned using the church's songs, some of them spirituals concerning modern-day events, in a Biblical play she had proposed writing with Green. "I don't want them to get ahold of certain tunes which I have earmarked," she wrote.

The three New York filmmakers arrived in Beaufort in mid-May. Chalfin, a graduate student at Columbia University, was responsible for recording the church services from microphones onto disks. Brandt (an assistant director to Edgar G. Ulmer and others on Yiddish-language features) and Lawrence handled the camera. Plans to record the congregants in synchronized sound were dashed because the church was not wired for electricity. Chalfin ended up running cables some six hundred feet to a farmhouse to power his recording equipment. Brandt and Lawrence hand-cranked their camera, or used a winding mechanism for shorter, 100-foot lengths rather than full magazines.

The filmmakers shot four different sequences: a service on Friday night, May 17, a Saturday morning river baptism, a Saturday evening service, and Sunday services. Chalfin recorded over 150 disks. In addition, Brandt and Lawrence shot some exterior footage. Returning to New York, Chalfin and the others used these recordings in various projects, broadcasting some of them on WNYC. Hurston remained behind, supervising her own recordings, but by Labor Day she, too, was in New York. Beaufort was "a nice quiet place to work, but insufferably dull. I want to see and feel," she wrote. She began working on her autobiography, *Dust Tracks on a Road* (published 1942), and spent time in 1941 as a staff writer at Paramount.

After Jane Belo's death in 1968, the films ended up with Margaret Mead's papers. While searching the Margaret Mead/South Pacific Ethnographic Archives Collection at the Library of Congress, Kristy Andersen and Arlene Balkansky came across four reels of film that turned out to be the Beaufort footage. Balkansky located Norman Chalfin, by that time a patent attorney at the NASA Jet Propulsion Lab. He had run a recording and transcription service during World War II, and had copies of the Beaufort field recordings as well as some additional film footage shot by Lou Brandt. (Brandt worked as a film and stage producer until his death in 1971.)

Balkansky has inventoried over an hour's worth of music and sound from Chalfin's disks.

In 2002, Ken Weissman at the Library of Congress began trying to synchronize the sound with the Beaufort film footage. Until that project is completed, the silent footage can be viewed at the Library of Congress. Much of the material has a raw feel, as if the filmmakers could barely contain their subjects. Lights and cables are visible in the background, the congregants sometimes stare quizzically at the lens, and exposures and pans are often imprecise. Additional material—of a carpenter at work, of children on a sidewalk—indicates that Hurston may have had more than research in mind for the project. She can be seen in many of the shots, dancing, praying, and playing a conga drum.

The footage that documents Rev. Washington and his congregation singing and preaching into microphones feels incomplete without sound. But the film still provides an unprecedented look into life in Beaufort in 1940. This is a world that Hollywood could never show, that filmgoers of the time could never see. The church services, both inside and out, have a severe beauty and contagious energy, but what may be most surprising is a shot filmed from the passenger's seat of a car driving down the highway leading into Beaufort. For over a minute the camera floats like a ghost over a two-lane road that winds through a vanished landscape of trees, billboards and gas stations—a small but priceless window into a lost world.

Dance, Girl, Dance

RKO, 1940. Sound, B&W, 1.37. 90 minutes.

Cast: Maureen O'Hara (Judy [O'Brien]), Louis Hayward (Jimmy Harris), Lucille Ball (Bubbles [Tiger Lily White]), Virginia Field (Elinor Harris), Ralph Bellamy (Steve Adams), Mary Carlisle (Sally), Katharine Alexander (Miss Olmstead), Edward Brophy (Dwarfie), Walter Abel (Judge), Harold Huber (Hoboken Gent), Maria Ouspenskaya (Madame Basilova), Ernest Truex (Bailey #1), Chester Clute (Bailey #2), Lorraine Krueger (Dolly), Emma Dunn (Daisy), Sidney Blackmer (Puss in Boots), Vivian Fay (The Ballerina), Ludwig Stossel (Caesar), Erno Verebes (Fitch).

Credits: Directed by Dorothy Arzner. Screenplay by Tess Slesinger and Frank Davis. Story by Vicki Baum. Produced by Erich Pommer. Executive producer: Harry E. Edington. Director of photography: Russell Metty. Special effects by Vernon L. Walker. Art director: Van Nest Polglase. Associate art director: Al Herman. Set decorations by Darrell Silvera. Gowns by Edward Stevenson. Recorded by Hugh McDowell, Jr. Edited by Robert Wise. Assistant director: James H. Anderson. RCA Recording System. An RKO Radio Pictures, Inc., presentation. Musical director: Edward Ward. Dances staged by Ernst Matray. "Morning Star" and "Jitterbug Bite," music by Edward Ward, lyrics by Chester Forrest and Robert Wright. "Mother, What Do I Do Now?" music and lyrics by Chester Forrest and Robert Wright.

Additional Cast: Jeanne Lafayette (Nanette the maid), Robert Emmett O'Connor (Policeman at Palais Royale), Dewey Robinson (Palais Royale manager).

Additional Credits: Cinematography: Joseph H. August. Production dates: April 15 to July 1940. Released August 30, 1940.

Available: Warner Home Video DVD (2007). ISBN: 1-4198-4803-8. UPC: 0-53939-78222-6.

A troubled production that saw a title change and shifts in personnel, *Dance, Girl, Dance* had little impact when it was released in 1940. It was viewed by RKO studio executives as another opportunity to exploit Maureen O'Hara, a Dublin-born actress brought over from England for the 1939 version of *The Hunchback of Notre Dame*. The studio had rushed her into a remake of *A Bill of Divorcement* (which had served as Katharine Hepburn's film debut in 1933) before telling the press that she would appear in *Have It Your Way*, based on a story by Vicki Baum and to be directed by Roy Del Ruth.

The "gaze" as demonstrated by Harold Huber in *Dance, Girl, Dance*.

O'Hara, who had spent the previous film fending off the advances of director John Farrow, was relieved to be working again with producer Erich Pommer after both had labored on Alfred Hitchcock's *Jamaica Inn* (1939). Pommer had been behind almost every significant German film of the 1920s. After the Nazis came into power he became a producer in France and England. But his health was poor, and he was unfamiliar with working methods in Hollywood. He clashed with Del Ruth, a journeyman director who had been struggling to establish a new career after leaving Warner Brothers. Del Ruth evidently saw the project as a romantic triangle rather than a vehicle for O'Hara, and left after a few weeks.

Pommer replaced him with Dorothy Arzner, famous today as the only female director in Hollywood during the 1930s. But at the time Arzner was known more for her sense of story and structure than her directing. She was born in San Francisco in 1900, but grew up in Los Angeles, where her father owned a restaurant. Arzner studied premed at USC, then volunteered for an ambulance corps during World War I. When she returned to the United States, she entered the film industry by typing scripts for director and writer William deMille. She switched to editing, becoming the chief editor at Realart (a Paramount production arm) and embellishing her reputation by saving *Blood and Sand* (a 1922 Rudolph Valentino bullfighting melodrama) from costly reshoots. She edited *The Covered Wagon* (1923) for director James Cruze, and wrote and edited his historical epic *Old Ironsides* (1926).

When she threatened to leave Paramount for Columbia, she was given the opportunity to direct Esther Ralston, an important studio asset, in *Fashions for Women* (1927). Arzner later worked with stars like Clara Bow, Claudette Colbert, and Ruth Chatterton; gave an assist to the career of Fredric March; and after leaving Paramount in 1933, directed Katharine Hepburn in a feminist film, *Christopher Strong* (1933). Arzner played down her gender with contemporary journalists, and even in later years did not regard her accomplishments as noteworthy. "I was not dependent on the movies for my living," she said, "so I was always ready to give the picture over to some other director if I couldn't make it the way I wanted."

The ideas behind Arzner's films are generally more interesting than the movies themselves, and her real strength was in conceptualizing what would or wouldn't work on celluloid. Filmmaker Ally Acker credits Arzner with developing the story for and producing *Theodora Goes Wild* (1936), the film that established Irene Dunne as a comedienne. Arzner was not especially adroit with actors, at least judging by the films she directed. While impressed with the director's background, for example, O'Hara was upset at Arzner's disinterest in blocking out action.

It was up to the actors to supply whatever energy came through in *Dance, Girl, Dance*. Nominal leads Ralph Bellamy (as a ballet impresario) and Louis Hayward (as a stinking rich playboy) assert almost no personality at all, while Edward Brophy is typically brash and abrasive in a part that he might have written himself. Lucille Ball, still a decade away from her dominance as a television sitcom star, made a much greater impression in standard programmers like *Five Came Back* (1939) than as Bubbles/Lily White/Tiger Lily, the golddigging stripper she plays here. Poor O'Hara, one of the fieriest and most beautiful stars of her time, fades into the background as a timid ballerina forced into burlesque.

Not that *Dance, Girl, Dance* is a chore to sit through. It is a typically polished studio product of its era, midway between a B-movie and a big-budget film, with a cast of distinctive supporting actors who push across the hoariest material. What's immediately noticeable about the movie is its eccentric pacing, its extra beats and odd insert shots, as well as the melancholy tone that threatens to overwhelm the story. Although it is a musical with three commissioned songs, Arzner stages the half-dozen production numbers indifferently, rarely bothering to move the camera or adjust the viewing angle.

Arzner treats some of the supporting characters, in particular the playboy's ex-wife Elinor (played by Virginia Field), with a consideration unusual for the genre, and the script develops Elinor's subplot along unexpected and satisfying lines. Another standout is Maria Ouspenskaya, whose role shows the consequences of a lifetime devoted to art.

Still, *Dance, Girl, Dance* would likely have dropped out of sight had it not been for a wave of revisionist thinking about Hollywood in the 1970s. Feminists championed the film and Arzner's career, expounding on how a woman brought a different point of view to a story about the conflict between love and work, art and commerce, stripping and ballet. Some argued that *Dance, Girl, Dance* was about the "gaze," about how men view women, how moviegoers view film, and even how women look at women. The "gaze" explains the close-ups of Harold Huber staring listlessly at O'Hara's hula dance, then puffing excitedly on his cigar as Ball sashays across the floor. It is also the reason for O'Hara's impassioned lecture to her burlesque audience (and by extension, filmgoers) to stop treating bump-and-grind strippers so disrespectfully. "Go ahead and stare, I'm not ashamed," the aspiring ballerina shouts. "I know you want me to tear my clothes off."

It would have helped revisionist thinkers if Arzner hadn't undermined the film's radical theories with a pointless catfight played for laughs, or if censorship standards hadn't rendered moot the differences between Bellamy's high-art ballet and Ball's routines. And if Arzner's gender is the crucial factor here, why is Leo McCarey's version of stripping in *The Awful Truth* (1937) simultaneously more erotic, funnier, and less judgmental?

Arzner would direct one more feature, *First Comes Courage* (1943), a slow-paced anti-Nazi espionage yarn starring Merle Oberon, before retiring from Hollywood for health reasons. In later years she taught filmmaking at UCLA and directed Pepsi commercials for Joan Crawford. O'Hara, who by this point needed a hit, made a poorly received musical, then was called to a meeting with John Ford, who was casting *How Green Was My Valley*.

Knute Rockne All American

Warner Bros., 1940. B&W, 1.33, 97 minutes.

Cast: Pat O'Brien (Knute Rockne), Gale Page (Bonnie Skiles Rockne), Ronald Reagan (George Gipp), Donald Crisp (Father John Callahan, C.S.C.), Albert Basserman (Father Julius Nieuwland), Owen Davis, Jr., (Gus Dorais); Nick Lukats, Kane Richmond, William Marshall, William Byrne ("The Four Horsemen"); The Moreau Choir of Notre Dame.

Credits: Directed by Lloyd Bacon. Original Screen Play by Robert Buckner. "Based upon the private papers of Mrs. Rockne, and reports of Rockne's intimate associates and friends." Executive producer: Hal B. Wallis. Associate producer: Robert Fellows. Director of photography: Tony Gaudio. Film editor: Ralph Dawson. Art director: Robert Haas. Sound by Charles Lang. Gowns by Milo Anderson. Special effects by Byron Haskin, Rex Wimpy. Makeup artist: Perc Westmore. Technical advisors: Nick Lukats, J.A. Haley. Orchestral arrangements: Ray Heindorf. Musical director: Leo F. Forbstein. RCA Sound System.

Additional Cast: John Litel (Committee chairman), Henry O'Neill (Doctor), John Qualen (Lars Knudson Rockne), Dorothy Tree (Martha Rockne), John Sheffield (Knute at age 7), George Reeves (Player in locker room at halftime); Howard Jones, Glenn "Pop" Warner, Alonzo Staff, William "Bill" Spaulding (Themselves).

Additional Credits: Montage editing: Don Siegel. Released October 4, 1940.
Available: Warner Home Video DVD (2006): UPC: 012569791183. MGM/UA Home Video VHS (1988): ISBN: 0-7928-1119-4. UPC: 0-2761-60555-3-8.

Few critics have ever tried to defend *Knute Rockne All American* on artistic grounds. As a morale-builder during World War II, the film proved popular enough with viewers willing to accept its themes of teamwork and sacrifice. Later it became famous for providing future President Ronald Reagan with one of his signature film roles. Today it is an example of Warner Brothers filmmaking at its most efficient and anonymous.

The studio had played out a string of inspirational films based on men of science and politics, such as *The Life of Emile Zola* (1937). Capitalizing on a sudden spurt of filmmaking brought about in part by the country's entrance into war, it now sought movies about more contemporary characters. Knute Rockne, a bona fide sports celebrity with no taint of controversy, was an easy choice. His life of hard work, success, and tragic death fit the biopic formula to a "T."

Rockne was born in Voss, Norway, in 1888. His family moved to Chicago, where as a teen he dropped out of high school to work in the post office. Rockne entered Notre Dame University when he was twenty-two, and failed to make the football team until his sophomore year. He became an assistant coach at Notre Dame after graduating. By 1917 he was head coach, and had his first unbeaten season in 1919. Ultimately he would coach five unbeaten teams. He is credited with popularizing two football innovations—the forward pass and the backfield shift—but is perhaps best known for a halftime speech he gave during a 1928 game against Army.

The coach had always claimed that George Gipp was the most gifted athlete he worked with, despite the fact that Gipp gambled, missed practice, and disobeyed orders on the field. As a senior, Gipp contracted pneumonia, and died in December 1920. Trying to rally his players against a stronger Army team in 1928, Rockne recited what he called Gipp's deathbed speech. It appears in the movie in this form: "I've got to go, Rock. It's all right, I'm not afraid. Some time, Rock, when the team is up against it, when things are wrong and the breaks are beating the boys, tell them to go in there with all they've got and win just one for the Gipper. I don't know where I'll be then, Rock, but I'll know about it, and I'll be happy."

The speech, delivered twice in the film, is the focal point of an otherwise antiseptic biopic that glosses over much of Rockne's life, such as the fact that he converted to Roman Catholicism in part in order to become Notre Dame's athletic director, or that he published a novel, *The Four Winners*, that same year. Also neglected are Rockne's newspaper columns, frequent appearances in newsreels, and career as a motivational speaker for the Studebaker Corporation. The screenwriters use phlebitis to explain away his breakdown in 1929. Perhaps most tellingly, the film fails to note the reason why Rockne took his fatal airplane flight in 1931: he was heading to Los Angeles to sign a motion-picture contract.

The film's Rockne is happily married, hard-working, and obsessed with football. Watching a line of chorus girls inspires him to devise his backfield shift, for example. *Knute Rockne All American* is paced so breathlessly that it barely has time for any biographical facts (or any punctuation, although most sources throw a comma or dash into the title today). Most of the movie seems to be montages, constructed by future hard-boiled director Don Siegel, that pass by in a blur. The games are stitched together from newsreel footage, backlot shots, and special effects utilizing back projection and other techniques, while the progress of Rockne's team is explained by cheering crowds, newspaper headlines, and trains hurtling across the screen. At least three times, screenwriter Robert Buckner resorts to the hopeful line, "This will revolutionize football." But there's no time to stop for more than the opening of Grantland Rice's famous newspaper article—"Against a gray October sky the Four Horsemen ride again"—let alone introduce the Horsemen themselves. This is a film that essentially dispenses with drama.

At the time Lloyd Bacon was one of the highest-paid directors on the Warners lot, having established his reputation with musicals like *42nd Street* and *Footlight Parade* (both 1933). Here he seems content to sit back and watch, allowing Pat O'Brien full rein in his performance as Rockne. Born in Wisconsin in 1899, O'Brien was a devout Catholic who gave up law school at Marquette University to pursue acting. He came to New York in 1920, persuading his friend Spencer Tracy to join him there, and started out as a chorus boy. He became a movie star as reporter Hildy Johnson in the first film version of *The Front Page* (1930). His square features helped typecast him as the voice of probity in dozens of films, often as a priest, and often opposite his friend James Cagney.

O'Brien studied Rockne's voice patterns and physical mannerisms for his role, and buried his face in prosthetic makeup to mimic the coach's large nose and thinning hair. It's a careful, honest interpretation that means very little to viewers no longer familiar with Rockne's characteristics. O'Brien's work is overshadowed today by Ronald Reagan, who appears after a half hour as the lazy, rebellious Gipp. Reagan's in the film for less than ten minutes, but it was some of the best work of his career. He almost didn't get the part, as the role had been offered to Dennis Morgan, among others. For that matter, Jack L. Warner and screenwriter Buckner lobbied seriously for James Cagney to play Rockne. However, both Notre Dame and the coach's widow Bonnie, who had approval over casting, insisted on O'Brien.

When his career faltered in the 1950s, O'Brien would claim that he was victim of a "reverse blacklist" for his conservative views. But he found work on stage and television, and toward the end of his life was reunited with Cagney in *Ragtime* (1981). Reagan's definitive screen role came in *King's Row* (1942), a polished slice of soap opera hokum that gave him the line he later used for the title of his autobiography: "Where's the rest of me?"

The Great Dictator

United Artists, 1940. Sound, B&W, 1.37. 120 minutes.
Cast: People of the Palace: Charles Chaplin (Hynkel, Dictator of Tomania), Jack Oakie (Napaloni, Dictator of Bacteria), Reginald Gardiner (Schultz), Henry Daniell (Garbitsch), Billy Gilbert (Herring), Grace Hayle (Madame Napaloni), Carter De Haven (Bacterian Ambassador). People of the Ghetto: Charles Chaplin (A Jewish barber), Paulette Goddard (Hannah), Maurice Moscovich (Mr. Jaeckel), Emma Dunn (Mrs. Jaeckel), Bernard Gorcey (Mr. Mann), Paul Weigel (Mr. Agar). With: Chester Conklin (Barbershop customer), Esther Michelson, Hank Mann (Storm trooper), Florence Wright (Secretary), Eddie Gribbon (Storm trooper), Robert O. Davis [Rudolph Anders] (Commandant), Eddie Dunn (Storm trooper), Nita Pike (Secretary), Peter [George] Lynn (Storm trooper).
Credits: Written & directed by Charles Chaplin. Assistant directors: Dan James, Wheeler Dryden, Bob Meltzer. Directors of photography: Karl Struss, Roland Totheroh. Art director: J. Russell Spencer. Film editor: Willard Nico. Musical direction: Meredith Willson. Sound: Percy Townsend, Glenn Rominger. RCA Sound System. A Charles Chaplin production.
Additional Cast: Sig Arno, Don Brodie, Gino Corrado, Tiny Sandford.
Additional Credits: Released October 15, 1940.
Available: Warner Home Entertainment DVD (2003). ISBN: 0-7907-8064-X. UPC: 0-85393-79442-2.

The Hollywood film industry responded slowly to the rise of totalitarianism in the 1930s, but it did respond. In films subtle and broad, in symbol-laden melodramas and slapstick comedies, filmmakers argued in basically liberal terms for personal freedom, for open government, and against tyranny. In hindsight it is easy to criticize studio heads for not attacking fascism earlier. In their defense, they were concerned about eliminating a considerable portion of their world audience (MGM had an office in Berlin until the summer of 1940, for example).

Filmmakers in a position to control their own projects had to choose how to address fascism. In a personal drama, as Frank Borzage tried in *Three Comrades* (1938)? As black comedy, like Leo McCarey's *Duck Soup* (1933)? Dispensing with narrative niceties, Charles Chaplin opted to attack Adolf Hitler and Benito Mussolini head on, questioning their personalities as well as their goals.

Chaplin was in a unique position to make *The Great Dictator*. His reputation and fortune assured after almost twenty-five years in the film industry, he was under no pressure to release product unless he wanted to. His last two features, *City Lights* (1931) and *Modern Times* (1936), had been received rapturously. He made *The Great Dictator* solely to take a stand against what he saw as a worsening political climate.

The script gave Chaplin dual roles: as Hynkel, a Hitler-like tyrant, and as a Jewish barber who falls victim to anti-Semitism. According to film historian Kevin Brownlow, "Chaplin considered Hitler one of the greatest actors he had ever seen," and the comedian went to great lengths to impersonate him correctly. He also relied on newsreel footage to recreate parody versions of Albert Speer's architectural designs, and based other scenes on material from Leni Riefenstahl's feature-length documentary about Nazism, *Triumph of the Will* (1935). Equally important was Chaplin's attention to detail for the ghetto scenes. Here he again incorporated ideas from newsreels, although he later confessed that he was unaware of the full extent of Nazi atrocities.

When Chaplin announced to the press his plans to film a parody of Hitler, he was criticized in private by a number of industry executives. Presidential aide Harry Hopkins reportedly contacted Chaplin to indicate Franklin D. Roosevelt's approval of the project. Chaplin assembled a cast and crew on his studio lot, where carpenters constructed a ghetto consisting of some three blocks of building fronts. Filming started on September 9, just days after the outbreak of fighting in Europe. Chaplin filmed as he always had since he became his own producer: shooting take after take, reworking material, adding and discarding scenes, changing the cast, and, when inspiration failed, simply shutting down production. His half brother Syd took behind-the-scenes color footage with a handheld 16mm camera. In it Chaplin can be seen experimenting, clowning, getting frustrated and then angry.

Current events forced Chaplin to revise shooting as he went along. He abandoned his original ending, a sort of slapdash free-for-all in which soldiers drop their weapons and engage in folk dancing. Instead, he wrote a six-minute speech that he would deliver to troops and, by extension, to the audience. As Brownlow points out, this is the first time Chaplin speaks to filmgoers as himself—not as Hynkel the tyrant or as the Tramp. Handwritten notes show the concepts he was grappling with: reason, happiness, kindness, beauty, imagination, grandness, freedom, adventure, love.

On one level this closing speech was an admission of defeat on Chaplin's part. He had hoped to use humor to expose the fundamental fallacies and illogic of totalitarianism, but as Axis control spread across Europe he felt he had to make a more direct plea to his audience. Chaplin's speech is full of noble and brave sentiments which he delivered as passionately as Hynkel's nonsense diatribes, an irony filmgoers at the time overlooked. (*Variety* did note that "the preachment is strong" in its review.)

Production stretched out over an unimaginable 559 days, 391 of those "idle" ones in which no shooting took place. Chaplin's difficulty in completing the film may have been due to his increasing awareness of the inadequacy of his project. The sad truth was that the Tramp was no match for Hitler. Chaplin himself was a reduced figure, working outside the mainstream of the industry, no longer able to shape popular culture as he had twenty years earlier, no longer open to cinematic innovations. (He proudly showed a crane he purchased for the production to director Lewis Milestone, only to be told that cranes had been standard in the industry for over a decade.) Perhaps saddest of all, the Little Tramp was no longer funny. Chaplin has to work hard to keep up with Jack Oakie, who plays his parody of Mussolini with disarming simplicity.

The Great Dictator is also a testament to Chaplin's growing grandiosity. As a cousin noted, "He became more and more important to himself." He would direct only four more features, each one slower, fustier, less funny. It may be unreasonable to expect anyone to maintain the white-hot creativity Chaplin showed earlier in his career. And it's important to note that Chaplin was taking a stand when most of his colleagues were resorting to euphemisms. In *The Great Dictator*, storm troopers persecute and kill Jews who have been confined to a ghetto. In most other films, the word "Jew" never appeared. Hitler and Mussolini are depicted as clods, buffoons—dangerous but inept, blinded by rage and self-importance. It took daring and courage for Chaplin—who backed his words with his own money—to make this film.

The Great Dictator opened simultaneously in two New York theaters on October 15, 1940. According to Brownlow, it became Chaplin's biggest moneymaker, even with a wide swath of Europe closed off to him. It was the last time the Tramp character appeared on film.

Tacoma Narrows Bridge Collapse

Barney Elliott, 1940. Silent, color, 1.37. 8 minutes.

Credits: Photographed by Barney Elliott, Harbine Monroe.

Additional Credits: Filmed November 7, 1940.

Available: The Camera Shop (www.camerashoptacoma.com). Black-and-white excerpts can be viewed at the Internet Archive (*www.archive.org*).

Designed in part by Leon Moisseiff, the Tacoma Narrows Bridge was the third-longest suspension bridge in the world when it opened on July 1, 1940. Moisseiff, who was born in Latvia and received a degree in civil engineering at Columbia University, established his reputation by helping to design several bridges in New York City and the Delaware River Bridge in Philadelphia. He helped popularize a "deflection theory" that essentially stated that longer bridges could be more flexible than previously thought.

Suspension bridges have a long history; engineer and author Henry Petroski traces them back to well before the seventeenth century, when the Chinese are believed to have built the first iron-chain examples. An iron-chain suspension bridge was built in England in 1741. Petroski cites several catastrophic collapses of suspension bridges in the nineteenth century, due to stampeding livestock, soldiers marching in step, the weight of railroads, and the like. But with continuing modifications, the length of suspension bridges expanded, from the Brooklyn Bridge's 1,500 feet to over 4,000 for the Golden Gate Bridge.

But, as Petroski points out, "Successful designs do not necessarily tell us very much about how close to failure they are." John Roebling designed the Brooklyn Bridge with stay-cables to stiffen the main support cables. Subsequent designers began to eliminate stay-cables. Bridges with wide, heavy decks, or roadways, worked fine without them, as shown by New York City's Manhattan and Williamsburg Bridges. But bridges designed by Othmar Ammann and David Steinman began to sway as soon as they were completed. (Ammann had to add diagonal stays to his 1939 Bronx Whitestone Bridge, while Steinman needed supplementary cables on his Deer Isle Bridge in Michigan.)

Moisseiff worked for twelve years as a draftsman and assistant designer for the New York Department of Bridges before forming his own firm in 1915. As early as 1889, the people of Tacoma, Washington, had researched a bridge to connect their town with the Kitsap peninsula. The state of Washington financed a bridge study through toll revenues, and in 1937 engineer Clark Eldridge submitted a fairly conventional design. Moisseiff's competing design for a cheaper, narrower bridge won out in 1938. Since the bridge was federally funded in part, consulting engineer Theodore L. Condron was required to check Moisseiff's design. He decided that the bridge was, in Petroski's words, "inadvisably narrow for its length."

Moisseiff's reputation was strong enough to overrule Condron's objections, and construction began that November. But when the bridge opened in July 1940, it would sway in the slightest wind, earning the nickname "Galloping Gertie." It became a tourist attraction of sorts, as well as a site for experiments conducted by University of Washington engineering professor F.B. Farquharson, hired with others to attempt to reduce the bridge's movements.

Farquharson was one of many observers on November 7, 1940, when wind began to make the bridge buckle. He was equipped with a still camera and a 16mm motion picture camera. James Bashford also took still photographs. Barney Elliott and Harbine Monroe were freelance newsreel photographers who had opened The Camera Shop three years earlier. They photographed the bridge with a 16mm Bell & Howell camera, using Kodachrome stock. Their footage has the startling logic and clarity of a bad dream. Once seen, images of the destruction of the bridge are unforgettable.

Elliott licensed the film to Universal Newsreel, among other companies. In order to incorporate it into its weekly newsreel, Universal blew the footage up to 35mm, and processed it in black-and-white. These excerpts, which are in the public domain, have come to stand for all the Tacoma Narrows footage. However, Ed Elliott, Barney's son, still retains rights to his father's footage. You can purchase copies from his website, named after his father's Camera Shop. Professor Farquharson's film and photographs are held by the Department of Civil Engineering at the University of Washington.

The bridge was rebuilt with a new design in 1950. But, as Petroski points out, major bridge failures occur roughly every thirty years, perhaps the time it takes for a new generation of engineers to forget the lessons learned by its predecessors. Bridge designs tend to be based on earlier bridges, only longer and larger. The flaws hidden within these designs emerge as the spans grow. "Failure drives successful design," Petroski wrote. "The essential lesson of the Tacoma Narrows Bride is not that it fell but that it fell in an atmosphere of confidence that it would not, and in a manner that was not anticipated."

The Tacoma Narrows Bridge in the process of collapsing.

Fantasia

Walt Disney Studio, 1940. Sound, color, 1.37. 124 minutes.

(Note: The original release had no on-screen credits.)

Cast: Leopold Stokowski, Deems Taylor.

Credits: Directed by James Algar, Samuel Armstrong, Ford Beebe, Norman Ferguson, Jim Handley, T. Hee, Wilfred Jackson, Hamilton Luske, Bill Roberts, Paul Satterfield, Ben Sharpsteen. Produced by Walt Disney.

Written by Lee Blair, Elmer Plummer, Phil Dike, Sylvia Moberly-Holland, Norman Wright, Albert Heath, Bianca Majolie, Graham Heid, Perce Pearce, Carl Fallberg, William Martin, Leo Thiele, Robert Sterner, John McLeish, Otto Englander, Webb Smith, Erdman Penner, Joseph Sabo, Bill Peet, Vernon Stallings, Campbell Grant, Arthur Heinemann, Phil Dike.

Art direction: Ken Anderson, Bruce Bushman, Arthur Byram, Tom Codrick, Robert Cormack, Harold Doughty, Yale Gracey, Hugh Hennesy, John Hubley, Dick Kelsey, J. Gordon Legg, Kay Nielsen, Lance Nolley, Ernie Nordli, Kendall O'Connor, Charles Payzant, Curtiss D. Perkins, Charles Philippi, Thor Putnam, Herbert Ryman, Zack Schwartz, Terrell Stapp, McLaren Stewart, Al Zinnen. Visual effects: Dan McManus, Joshua Meador, Gail Papineau, Leonard Pickley, Miles E. Pike, John F. Reed.

Supervising animators: Norman Ferguson, Ollie Johnston, Ward Kimball, Eric Larson, Joshua Meador, Fred Moore, Vladimir Tytla.

Animation and background art: Edwin Aardal, Art Babbitt, Preston Blair, James Bodrero, Jack Bradbury, Paul Busch, Jack Campbell, Nino Carbe, Bob Carlson, Les Clark, Claude Coats, Charles Conner, Merle Cox, Al Dempster, Ugo D'Orsi, Phil Duncan, Art Elliott, John Elliotte, Jules Engel, Roy Forkum, Hugh Fraser, Franklin Grundeen, Harry Hamsel, Eric Hansen, John Hench, Ray Huffine, Earl Hurd, Bill Justice, Lynn Karp, Walt Kelly, Paul B. Kossoff, Ethel Kulsar, Ed Levitt, Ray Lockrem, Hicks Lokey, John Lounsbery, Ed Love, Don Lusk, Brice Mack, Dan MacManus, Murray McClellan, John McManus, John P. Miller, James Moore, Milt Neil, Gerald Nevius, Lester Novros, Art Palmer, Don Patterson, Martin Provensen, Wolfgang Reitherman, Art Riley, George Rowley, William Shull, Grant Simmons, Lorna S. Soderstrom, Stan Spohn, Joe Stahley, Ed Starr, Robert Stokes, Robert Storms, David Swift, Howard Swift, Norman Tate, Frank Thomas, Riley Thomson, Don Tobin, Harvey Toombs, Don Towsley, John Walbridge, Bernard Wolf, Cornett Wood, Marvin Woodward, Cy Young, Robert W. Youngquist.

Additional Cast: Nigel De Brulier (Sorcerer model), Walt Disney (Voice of Mickey Mouse), Marge Champion (Dance model), James MacDonald (Percussionist), Paul J. Smith (Violinist), Corey Burton (Dubbing for Deems Taylor).

Additional Credits: Premiered in New York City on November 13, 1940.

Awards: Honorary Oscars to Walt Disney, William E. Garity, J.N.A. Hawkins for sound; to Leopold Stokowski for "widening the scope of the motion picture as entertainment."

Sequel: *Fantasia/2000* (1999), with new material directed by Gaëtan Brizzi, Paul Brizzi, Hendel Butoy, Francis Glebas, Eric Goldberg, Don Hahn, Pixote Hunt.

Available: Disney DVD (2000). ISBN: 0-7888-1806-6. UPC: 7-17951-00461-1.

Walt Disney first met conductor Leopold Stokowski at Chasen's restaurant in Los Angeles. Stokowski, who led the Philadelphia Orchestra, may have been the most famous conductor in America at the time. While a strong advocate of modern composers, he was also committed to bringing classical music to a wider audience, through series like "Youth Programs." Stokowski was a champion of new technology. He was recording as early as 1917, and appeared as himself in films like *100 Men and a Girl* (1937), a Deanna Durbin vehicle. Disney, on the other hand, was an early proponent of combining music and animation, for example, through his *Silly Symphonies* series.

The meeting between the two led to a cartoon short with Mickey Mouse set to "The Sorcerer's Apprentice" by Paul Dukas. For the soundtrack, Stokowski conducted an orchestra of eighty-five freelance musicians in January 1938, recording between midnight and three in the morning. Disney and his brother Roy knew they could never recoup the cost of the cartoon, which was three times an average Mickey budget. Searching for a way to justify its costs indirectly led to *Fantasia*.

In another sense, the real genesis of *Fantasia* was the financial and critical success of *Snow White and the Seven Dwarfs* (1937), which gave Disney the freedom to pursue a more expansive project. For three weeks in the fall of 1938, Disney, Stokowski, and Deems Taylor, a composer and music critic, winnowed down the classical repertoire to a half-dozen or so numbers that might be able to support animation. Stokowski then recorded these with the Philadelphia Orchestra.

The *Concert Feature*, as it was referred to at the time, proved unexpectedly demanding. When the studio's writers hit a wall with *Pinocchio*, Disney pulled animators off it to work on the concert film. Much as Irving Thalberg had done at MGM, Disney kept throwing different people at problems until they were solved. He hired the German animator Oskar Fischinger, for example, who prepared test footage for Stokowski's arrangement of Bach's "Toccata and Fugue in D Minor." It was intended to be abstract, but Disney became uncomfortable with Fischinger's total immersion into geometric shapes. Instead, the piece was "softened" by turning some shapes into objects like violin bows, or by providing clouds, a horizon, and other representational elements. A disgruntled Fischinger left the studio.

Disney also abandoned the story line for Tchaikovsky's "Nutcracker Suite," which was turned into the equivalent of a "Four Seasons Suite." In fact, the "Sorcerer's Apprentice" sequence was the only one that didn't change the "story" behind its music. What changed in that sequence was Mickey Mouse himself; thanks to work by animator Fred Moore, the new Mickey had a larger head, eyes with pupils, and a pear-shaped body, modifications that made it easier for animators to show the character's emotions.

The most daring choice of music was Igor Stravinsky's *The Rite of Spring*, which had provoked riots at its premiere only some twenty-five years earlier. The Disney team reimagined the composer's score for Serge Diaghilev's *Ballets Russes* as a creation story that started in the mists of the cosmos, dabbled in molecular biology, then showed the rise and fall of dinosaurs. John Hubley was one of the animators who helped achieve such striking effects in the sequence. Stravinsky, the only *Fantasia* composer alive at the time of filming, came to the studio to watch "The Sorcerer's Apprentice." He also sold the rights to *The Firebird* to Disney.

Beethoven's Symphony Number 6, the "Pastoral," wasn't the original music for the "pagan" sequence. Disney had intended to use Gabriel Pierné's music for the ballet *Cydalise and the Goat-Foot*, envisioning it as the backdrop to a dance involving fauns, centaurs, and "centaurettes." As work proceeded, Disney decided to drop Pierné for the Pastoral, reassured when Deems Taylor told him, "Beethoven was a good deal of a pagan himself, and would have liked nothing better than to meet up with a gang of fauns and centaurettes."

The Pastoral segment illustrated the fundamental problem with supplying a story to music. By reducing Beethoven's work to a plotline, you are limiting what his music can represent. You are also forced to supply an explanation or narrative to all the piece's themes and melodies. *Fantasia* is a battleground in which viewers have to decide what is more important—the visuals or the music. Contemporary reviewers singled the Pastoral sequence out for the harshest criticism, and seen today it is the one segment that throws the tastes and standards of the entire project into question.

Spoofing the "Dance of the Hours" from Amilcare Ponchielli's opera *La Giaconda* cleverly sidestepped critics. The expected human dancers were replaced by ostriches, hippos, elephants, and alligators. Layout artist Ken O'Connor staged the sequence as an actual ballet with complex visual motifs. The final sequence combined portions of Modest Mussorgsky's "A Night on Bald Mountain" with Franz Schubert's "Ave Maria," featuring new English lyrics by Rachel Field. A journey from the profane to the sacred, it features some truly terrifying effects by animator Vladimir Tytla as well as the

longest single shot ever attempted in animation up to that point. Using a horizontal multiplane camera, it lasted 217 feet. Technicians needed three tries to capture the shot, one of which was ruined by an earthquake. Work on it finished only four hours before the film's premiere.

By that time interstitial live-action footage had been shot (by premiere cinematographer James Wong Howe) and the soundtrack recorded onto a new, six-channel process Disney dubbed Fantasound. A precursor of the stereo sound that would be adopted widely in the 1950s, Fantasound was so expensive (it cost $85,000 to outfit a theater with the necessary equipment) that at first only two theaters could offer it, one in New York and one in Los Angeles. The studio positioned *Fantasia* an event, an experience different from going to a normal movie. As Griffith did with *The Birth of a Nation*, Disney publicized the film as a "road show" with programs, reserved seating, and specially trained ushers.

Disney wanted *Fantasia* to seem more like a concert than a film, and omitted credits on the screen. He even thought of altering the structure of the film, rearranging, adding, and deleting segments as time passed. RKO, the studio that distributed Disney's films, refused to handle *Fantasia*, so Walt and his brother Roy had to lease theaters in New York and Los Angeles themselves. The film ran for a year in both cities, and for eight months in San Francisco, but as animator and film historian John Canemaker notes, it "was not a success for a variety of reasons." All in all, the film was shown in only twelve theaters with Fantasound, and only sixteen prints were prepared.

If critics were unkind to *Fantasia*, the public was largely indifferent. In January 1941, RKO agreed to distribute the film, but on its terms. *Fantasia* was cut from 124 minutes to 84 minutes, with the Deems Taylor footage the first to go. Disney had always planned for a sequel, and even started in on a version of Claude Debussy's "Claire de Lune" and other segments. The studio did release other music-oriented films: *Make Mine Music* and *Melody Time*, for example. But in a later interview, Disney referred to *Fantasia* as an "artistic success, financial failure." Film critic Leonard Maltin said that Disney "never really got over it," and it's true that—in creative terms, at least—the studio's output became increasingly conservative after *Fantasia*.

Melody Ranch

Gene Autry singing the theme to *Melody Ranch*.

Republic, 1940. Sound, B&W, 1.37. 84 minutes.

Cast: Gene Autry (Himself), Jimmy Durante (Cornelius J. Courtney), Ann Miller (Julie Shelton), Barton MacLane (Mark Wildhack), Barbara [Jo] Allen [Vera Vague] (Veronica Whipple), George "Gabby" Hayes (Pop Laramie), Jerome Cowan (Tommy Summerville), Mary Lee (Penny), Joseph Sawyer (Jasper Wildhack), Horace MacMahon [McMahon] (Bud Wildhack), Clarence Wilson (Judge "Skinny" Henderson), William Benedict (Slim).

Credits: Directed by Joseph Santley. Original screenplay: Jack Moffitt, F. Hugh Herbert, Bradford Ropes, Betty Burbridge. Special comedy sequences: Sid Kuller, Ray Golden. Associate producer: Sol C. Siegel. Production manager: Al Wilson. Photography: Joseph August. Supervising editor: Murray Seldeen. Film editor: Lester Orlebeck. Art director: John Victor MacKay. Musical director: Raoul Kraushaar. Special music and lyrics: Jule Styne, Eddie Cherkose. Wardrobe by Adele Palmer. RCA Sound System. A Republic Production.

Additional Cast: Veda Ann Borg (Receptionist), Horace Murphy (Loco), Tom London (Joe), John Merton (Wildhack cohort), Dick Elliott (Sheriff Barstow), Lloyd Ingraham (Ed); Jack Ingram, Horace Murphy, Jack Kirk, Frankie Marvin (Radio singers); George Chandler (Cab driver), Edmund Cobb (Intimidated voter), Ray Teal (Gambler), Wally West (Classroom spectator), Frank Hagney (Door guard), John Merton (Alarmist), Tex Cooper (Race bettor); Ruth Gifford, Maxine Ardell (Majorettes); Slim Whitaker, Jim Corey (Ranchers); Gerald Oliver Smith (KRL spectator), Art Mix (Rider); Art Dillard, Chick Hannon (Outlaws); Curley Dresdon, George Chesebro, Merrill McCormack, Billy Bletcher, Herman Hack, Carl Cotner, Tiny Jones, Tom Smith (Extras); Champion.

Additional Credits: Assistant director: George Blair. Production dates: September to October 1940. Released November 15, 1940.

Available: Image Entertainment DVD (2003). UPC: 0-14381-3994-2-4.

Gene Autry was born in Texas in 1907, but grew up in Oklahoma, where he sang in the choir for his grandfather's Baptist church. He hoped for a career in baseball, working in a railroad telegraph office in his spare time. As Autry related in his memoir, Will Rogers entered the office one day, heard Autry singing, and advised him to move to New York to pursue show business. Autry did leave work in 1928 for New York, where he consulted with fellow Oklahomans

Johnny and Frankie Marvin, who were appearing in vaudeville and making records for Victor.

The Marvins urged Autry to change his singing style from pop-oriented to blues—in other words, copy singers like Jimmie Rodgers instead of big stars like Al Jolson. Autry's breakthrough came with a song he wrote with Jimmy Long, a friend from Oklahoma, "That Silver Haired Daddy of Mine." Distributed by Sears, Roebuck on ARC Records, the tune became a nationwide hit, leading to a spot on the WLS *Barn Dance* in Chicago, at the time the biggest showcase for country music on radio. As a corollary to appearing on the show, Autry positioned himself for the first time as a "singing cowboy," donning the Western duds he would continue to wear throughout the rest of his career.

"Singing cowboys" were a Hollywood invention, not a reality of the frontier. Some songs did originate with the cattle drives of the late nineteenth century, or in ranch bunkhouses, but the Hollywood version of a guitar-strumming cowboy in fancy duds singing a Tin Pan Alley song about Western skies is about as credible as Hollywood calling Dick Powell a jazz singer. Ken Maynard is credited as film's first singing cowboy for his appearance in *Sons of the Saddle* (1930), although several country-and-western musicians preceded him on screen.

Contemporary accounts describe Maynard as especially difficult. Studios routinely replaced him with less recalcitrant actors, and by 1934 Maynard found himself working for Nat Levine at Mascot

Pictures, one of the "Poverty Row" studios. By that time Autry had befriended Herbert Yates, the owner of both ARC Records and a film processing lab. Yates often invested in pictures, including those produced by Nat Levine. He engineered a meeting between Levine and Autry, earning Autry a supporting role in the Maynard vehicle *In Old Santa Fe*. That same year Autry appeared in a Maynard serial, *Mystery Mountain*.

Autry did well enough for Levine to substitute him for Maynard in the serial *The Phantom Empire*, a delirious mix of science fiction and the Wild West, with Gene hosting his own radio show above the entrance to a subterranean civilization. The combination of his hit records, radio show, and movie appearances gave Autry unprecedented popularity. His first starring feature, *Tumbling Tumbleweeds* (1935), only increased his fame.

By the mid-1930s Autry had refined his singing style, removing its blues and country inflections. He didn't sing authentic Western songs, he sang carefully modulated versions of pop tunes or artfully constructed modern tunes with traditional themes. In films, he didn't play characters, he played himself, Gene Autry, as a befuddled but good-hearted rube uneasy with his celebrity status. His movies took place in an incongruous modern frontier with buses and trucks and telephones; on the other hand, one not far removed from the Oklahoma where he grew up. And his stories concerned present-day problems: the dam failing, wealthy landowners cheating the poor, someone stealing valuable trees. He featured a code of ethics in his films and books, and insisted that his material be suitable for all ages. In his stories, he often tried to help troubled youths.

Autry took his job seriously. His films were made quickly and cheaply, but he did not cut corners. "There wasn't too much pre-production," he said in a later interview. "You'd take your script, and then you'd start reading it, and you'd start going over certain situations where songs would fit in, and then you'd begin trying to find songs that would fit. And, if you couldn't get that particular song, why you'd have to come up and write one that would fit." At the same time the director and cameraman would be scouting locations, often near Lone Pine, California. Autry made between six and eight features a year; combined with his weekly radio broadcasts, his heavy recording schedule, and sponsoring a rodeo that toured the country annually, it was a crushing work load.

Melody Ranch was Autry's forty-third feature for Republic Pictures, which absorbed Mascot in 1935. It was in some ways a consolation to Autry, who had walked out on his contract after learning that Republic owner Herbert Yates had essentially been short-changing him. (Until he returned under new terms, Republic replaced Autry with Roy Rogers, who enjoyed his own remarkable career.) *Melody Ranch* featured a higher budget than most Republic pictures, and borrowed vaudeville and radio star Jimmy Durante and future MGM supporting star Ann Miller to fill out the cast. The film would also cross-promote Gene's CBS radio show, conveniently named *Melody Ranch*. By 1940, the actor was the highest-rated cowboy star at the box office, and the number four star overall.

Autry had great fun mocking himself on screen and radio. There are several pointed barbs in *Melody Ranch* about his commercial endorsements. The "Nose Posse" he's shilling in the film isn't far removed from Wrigley's gum, an Autry sponsor for decades. His introduction to the children of Torpedo, where he's agreed to appear as an honorary sheriff during "Frontier Days" celebrations, shows him half-conscious and sprawled in the dirt. At one point bad guys Joe Sawyer and Horace McMahon (even the villains were upgrades) sing a surprisingly astute parody of Autry's theme song, "Back in the Saddle Again."

The star is at his best singing numbers like "Call of the Canyon" or "We Never Dream the Same Dream Twice," the latter a duet with Ann Miller that he wrote with Fred Rose. Polished but not fussy, sincere but not self-righteous, Autry is as smooth and accomplished as any screen singer of his time. He was also loyal to the people who helped him earlier in his career. He made Smiley Burnette, a colleague from Chicago, his sidekick in over sixty films, put Frankie Marvin on his payroll (Marvin can be seen in the opening number), and gave so much attention to his back-up trio that all three eventually won movie and recording contracts of their own.

Autry served in the Air Transport Command during World War II, then left Republic to found his own production company in 1947. He switched to television in the 1950s, and withdrew from public performances after 1956. By that time he had earned enough from his movies and hit songs like "Here Comes Santa Claus" and "Rudolph the Red-Nosed Reindeer" to purchase the California Angels, a major league baseball team. He died in 1998, four years before the Angels won their first World Series.

The Bank Dick

Grady Sutton, left, listens to W.C. Fields in *The Bank Dick*.

Universal, 1940. Sound, B&W, 1.37. 72 minutes.

Cast: W.C. Fields (Egbert Sousé), Una Merkel (Myrtle Sousé), Franklin Pangborn (J. Pinkerton Snoopington), Shemp Howard (Joe Guelpe), Jessie Ralph (Mrs. Hermisillo Brunch), Richard Purcell (Mackley Q. Greene), Cora Witherspoon (Agatha Sousé), Grady Sutton (Og Oggilby), Evelyn Del Rio (Elsie Mae Adele Brunch Sousé), Russell Hicks (J. Frothingham Waterbury), Pierre Watkin (Mr. Skinner), Al Hill (Filthy McNasty), George Moran (Cozy Cochran), Bill Wolfe (Otis), Jack Norton (A. Pismo Clam), Pat West (Assistant director), Reed Hadley (Francois), Heather Wilde (Miss Plupp), Harlan Briggs (Doctor Stall), Bill Alston (Mr. Cheek).

Credits: Directed by Edward Cline. Original screen play: Mahatma Kane Jeeves [W.C. Fields]. Director of photography: Milton Krasner. Art director: Jack Otterson. Associate art director: Richard Riedel. Film editor: Arthur Hilton. Musical director: Charles Previn. Collaborating director: Ralph Ceder. Sound supervisor: Bernard B. Brown. Technician: William Hedgcock. Gowns: Vera West. Set decorations: R.A. Gausman. Western Electric Mirrophonic Recording.

Additional Cast: Fay Adler (Secretary), Jan Duggan (Customer in bank), Bobby Larson (Boy in bank).

Additional Credits: Writing by Richard Carroll. Executive producer: Cliff Work. Associate producer: Jack J. Gross. Music: Frank Skinner. Production dates: September to October 22, 1940. Released November 29, 1940.

Available: Universal Studios DVD *W.C. Fields Comedy Collection* (2004). ISBN: 1-4170-1574-8. UPC: 0-25192-57812-0.

One of the unlikeliest of movie stars, W.C. Fields appeared on screen as a curmudgeon, a henpecked hedonist, a conniving coward, and at times a sentimental parent. "Just a great big frightened bully," was how he described his screen persona, but he sustained a connection with audiences for almost fifty years, and earned the respect of his fellow performers. As a teenager he developed skills that eventually turned him into a stage and vaudeville star around the world. This early work, including some of his silent films, has been lost to the ages, depriving us of the opportunity to see him in his physical prime. (One exception is the Registry title *So's Your Old Man*, 1926.) Today he is often thought of as the prematurely old, somewhat frail man he became in his later years.

Fields had a famously unhappy upbringing, offering as his epitaph, "I would rather be living in Philadelphia." Born William Claude Dukenfield in 1879, he left home at the age of eleven, becoming an expert pool player and juggler in an itinerant life of hard knocks. His juggling act took him through Europe, South Africa, and Australia. By his second world tour, Fields made the quips he improvised during juggling mishaps a part of his act. Eventually the humor took over from the juggling, and when he appeared as a headliner in the Ziegfeld *Follies*, it was as a comedian in skits with props and supporting characters.

In one form or another, these skits sustained Fields throughout the rest of his career. He used one in his first film, *Pool Sharks* (1915), and adapted them into many of his later features. The routines allowed Fields to introduce characters who expanded his view of society, a view that was strikingly cynical, even misanthropic. The world Fields inhabited was one of surly shopkeepers, shrewish wives, belligerent children, dead-end jobs, grinding poverty, bad food in threadbare boarding houses. His skits and later his films delighted in exploring grandiloquent frauds and con artists, as well as the abjectly stupid and bitter.

Fields' language grew more and more ornate over the years, a combination of Biblical phrasing and the flowery pronouncements of politicians, dotted with obscure, sometimes invented proper names and private phrases that stood in for curses. His orotund acting style tended to mock not only teetotalers, reformers, straitlaced prudes, and authority figures in general, but the very melodramatic plots in which he was appearing.

Some of Fields' films were ramshackle affairs, shot quickly and cheaply, cast with cronies from vaudeville rather than movie stars. But he also worked with directors like D.W. Griffith, Gregory La Cava, and Leo McCarey. A series of early sound shorts produced by Mack Sennett, like *The Dentist* (1932) and *The Fatal Glass of Beer* (1933), show an unbridled Fields on the verge of anarchy, attacking decorum with a glee that is palpable.

Fields was in his forties by the time he started making sound films. No longer a leading man, he took supporting roles at the start of the 1930s, or appeared in omnibus films, until he connected with a new audience. It didn't take long. He appeared in five films in 1934, showing off his juggling in *The Old Fashioned Way*, and remaking his silent feature *It's the Old Army Game* (1926) as *It's a Gift*, for most fans his masterpiece. He was a memorable Micawber in the MGM production of *David Copperfield* (1935), and costarred with Bing Crosby in *Mississippi* that same year.

A new career as a radio star, combined with personal difficulties—including a worsening problem with alcohol—affected Fields' film output at the end of the 1930s. In an effort to make a new start, he signed a contract with Universal. *The Bank Dick* was his second production with the studio. He submitted a fifty-three-page treatment on June 12, 1940. Biographers have cited his early stage skits, including *The Potters*, as well as portions of *It's a Gift*, for elements of the plot. Uncredited screenwriter Dick Carroll helped structure Fields' storyline.

The ultimate credit for the script went to Mahatma Kane Jeeves, one of Fields' more elaborate pseudonyms. (Biographer James Curtis traces it to the "Jeeves" stories by P.G. Wodehouse: "My hat, my cane, Jeeves!") He invented roles for character actors Grady Sutton (a standout in 1935's

Man on the Flying Trapeze) and Franklin Pangborn, playing a fussy bank examiner. Now in his sixties, Fields had trouble keeping control over his project, especially after Universal assigned contract writer Charles Grayson to revise the script.

But when it came time to film, director Eddie Cline jettisoned most of the studio script and allowed Fields to use his own material. Cline, a veteran of silent comedies, also inserted gags he improvised while blocking scenes. The five-minute car chase that ends the film took second unit director Ralph Cedar two weeks to shoot. (Universal would borrow the footage for chase scenes in numerous other movies.) When filming his scenes for a special-effects process, Fields accidentally threw a steering wheel through a back-projection screen. Cinematographer Milton Krasner said, "You could rest assured that when you did a picture with Fields you had a long picture." Krasner also admitted to using a special filter to disguise Fields' nose, which daily turned red from drinking.

Despite his ailing health, Fields approached his comedy seriously. After a preview in November, he sent the studio detailed notes about how to elicit or stretch out laughs. "The twenty dollar bill gag was cut so short it did not register" was one example. Curtis notes that the Production Code requested the elimination of the line, "Looks not unlike the Mona Lisa, only a little heavier," but made no objections to the name "Black Pussy Cat" for a saloon or to Fields' frequent swearing.

While it received glowing reviews, *The Bank Dick* fared poorly at the box office, perhaps because Fields was competing with films from Charlie Chaplin, the Marx Brothers, and Jack Benny and Fred Allen. Fields wrote and starred in one more feature, *Never Give a Sucker an Even Break* (1941) before bad health caught up with him. Limited largely to cameos in his final years, he died in a sanitarium on Christmas Day, 1946. His humor has had a lasting impact on our culture, from the self-loathing Archie Bunker in television's *All in the Family* to Steve Martin's parade of exasperated screen parents to the defiantly rude cartoon character Homer Simpson.

The Philadelphia Story

MGM, 1940. Sound, B&W, 1.37. 112 minutes.

Cast: Cary Grant (C.K. Dexter Haven), Katharine Hepburn (Tracy Lord), James Stewart (Macaulay Connor), Ruth Hussey (Elizabeth Imbrie), John Howard (George Kittredge), Roland Young (Uncle Willie), John Halliday (Seth Lord), Mary Nash (Margaret Lord), Virginia Weidler (Dinah Lord), Henry Daniell (Sidney Kidd), Lionel Pape (Edward), Rex Evans (Thomas).

Credits: Directed by George Cukor. Screen play by Donald Ogden Stewart. Based on the play by Philip Barry, produced by the Theatre Guild, Inc. Produced by Joseph L. Mankiewicz. Director of photography: Joseph Ruttenberg. Musical score: Franz Waxman. Film editor: Frank Sullivan. Art director: Cedric Gibbons. Associate art director: Wade B. Rubottom. Set decorations: Edwin B. Willis. Gowns by Adrian. Hair styles by Sydney Guilaroff. Recording director: Douglas Shearer. Western Electric Sound System.

Additional Cast includes: Russ Clark (John), Hilda Plowright (Librarian), Lita Chevret (Manicurist), Lee Phelps (Bartender), David Clyde (Mac), Claude King (Willie's butler), Robert de Bruce (Dr. Parsons), Veda Buckland (Elsie).

Additional Credits: Assistant director: Edward Woehler. Production dates: July to August 14, 1940. Premiered in New York City on December 27, 1940.

Awards: Oscars for Best Actor (Stewart), Screenplay.

Other Versions: Remade as *High Society* (1956) with Bing Crosby, Grace Kelly, Frank Sinatra.

Available: Warner Home Video DVD (2005). ISBN: 0-7907-9576-0. UPC: 0-12569-69902-1.

Tarred in 1938 (along with several other actresses) as "box office poison," Katharine Hepburn realized she could not salvage her career at RKO when executives there cast her in *Mother Carey's Chickens*. The headstrong star instead bought out the rest of her contract and returned to the East Coast, determined to reestablish herself as a stage actress. She was in a better position to do so than most of her peers, since she had the financial backing of Howard Hughes and the affection of several significant theatrical figures.

One of these was Philip Barry, one of the most highly respected playwrights working in New York. A World War I veteran and graduate of Yale, Barry had spent the 1920s honing a brand of brittle, pointed comedies, usually about the inability of the upper classes to relate to the modern world. In *Holiday* (1928), Barry developed the kind of heroine Hepburn would specialize in for years to come, and in fact she starred in the 1938 film version with Cary Grant. The "Barry girl" disdained tradition and her wealthy background, searching instead for a life of meaning and relevance. After the death of his infant daughter in 1934, Barry wrote a series of gloomy pieces that failed at the box office. He needed a hit, and when Hepburn approached him looking for a vehicle, he offered her two treatments to consider. She chose what would become *The Philadelphia Story*.

The story concerned the pending marriage of Tracy Lord, a divorced society heiress, to George Kittredge, a noveau riche industrialist. Complicating matters are two reporters for a gossip magazine who arrive to cover the wedding, as well as Tracy's ex-husband, C.K. Dexter Haven, whose presence causes her to question her choices and principles. Hepburn and Barry worked closely together during the writing. Barry based Hepburn's Tracy Lord character in large part on the star herself, or at least how the public and the actress perceived the star's personal life to be.

The Philadelphia Story opened at the Shubert Theatre in March 1939, with Joseph Cotten, Van Heflin, Frank Fenton, and Philip Foster among those supporting Hepburn. It was an immediate hit, running for a year before going on tour. Every studio in Hollywood wanted to adapt it, but Hepburn, with Hughes's help, had already retained the movie rights for herself. She sold them to Louis B. Mayer at MGM for $250,000, with the stipulation that she not only star, but retain control over many aspects of the production, including cast approval. Hepburn originally asked for Clark Gable and Spencer Tracy as her costars. She eventually gave up top billing to Cary Grant, who only agreed to appear after Barry's play underwent restructuring. James Stewart, one of the hottest stars in the country after starring in *Mr. Smith Goes to Washington*, *Destry Rides Again*, and *The Shop Around the Corner*, took the important but smaller part of Macaulay Connor, a journalist with a low impression of high society. Mayer assigned Joseph L. Mankiewicz as producer.

Hepburn also asked for director George Cukor and screenwriter Donald Ogden Stewart. She wanted the same sense of security she found while making her last film, *Holiday* (1938), a Philip Barry play starring Grant, directed by Cukor, and adapted by Stewart. Born in 1894, Stewart was one of the few members of the Algonquin Round Table to succeed as a Hollywood screenwriter. He had first made a name for himself writing literary parodies in the 1920s after befriending F. Scott Fitzgerald. Stewart traveled in Europe with Ernest Hemingway, and became the model for Bill Gorton in the novel *The Sun Also Rises*.

Stewart acted in the 1928 stage version of *Holiday* in order to improve his own dialogue writing, and wrote the screenplay for *Laughter* (1930), considered by some a prototype for screwball comedies. But he didn't start work on *The Philadelphia Story* screenplay until Mankiewicz had spent some time on his own version. Mankiewicz, who recorded the stage production in order to find its laugh lines, added some visual gags, notably an adroit opening scene involving golf clubs. His most important contribution was to combine the character of Tracy Lord's brother with her ex-husband, C.K. Dexter Haven. This gave Haven (and Cary Grant) better lines and more scenes, but it also added a layer of hurt and remorse that the play lacked.

Stewart claimed that *The Philadelphia Story* was one of his easiest jobs because Barry's play was so good. But the screenwriter succeeded in opening up what had been a two-set production into a story that flowed through a variety of locations, adding some new material that captured Barry's own voice. Cukor, meanwhile, approached the project with his own set of concerns. Still smarting over being fired from *Gone With the Wind*, he had just finished directing two play adaptations, *The Women* and *Susan and God*. Cukor had worked with Hepburn and Grant together twice before, so he was confident about them. But he was worried about maintaining Barry's tone on screen. "You want to give the illusion that it's improvised," he said later about the film. But he realized that he couldn't just film the stage version, that he had to find a consistent rhythm and pacing that complemented the story. He allowed Grant and James Stewart to improvise a scene in which Stewart, drunk on champagne, expounds on Hepburn's character. It is one of several moments in the film in which life breaks through the boundaries of the play.

As for Hepburn, she saw the film as perhaps her last chance in Hollywood. She had won a Best Actress Oscar in only her third film, *Morning Glory*

(1933). But when she stopped playing herself—that is, a privileged, possibly spoiled actress with pretensions to grandeur—audiences lost all interest in her. Acting outside her range—a bonnie lass in *The Little Minister*, an aviatrix in *Christopher Strong*—she works too hard, falling back on mannerisms that would harden into clichés. But in *Stage Door*, essentially playing herself, *Bringing Up Baby* (a ditzy version of herself), and *Holiday* (a softer, more romantic version of herself), she seems less artificial, more accessible.

More than any of her peers, Hepburn sought stories in which her characters underwent dramatic changes in personality. These were comeuppance roles, parts in which she is tamed, brought down to earth. You wouldn't see Irene Dunne or Bette Davis or Jean Arthur playing women who had to be humanized, reduced, lessened. But Hepburn insisted on forcing her persona as a screen star and celebrity to its knees. Tracy Lord in *The Philadelphia Story* would be the ultimate Hepburn role, the ultimate roman à clef. After all the rumor and gossip about her private life, Hepburn would expose it on stage and screen, showing eager audiences the unhappiness and sordid underside to wealth that they always imagined. Hepburn's Tracy is mannered, self-centered, insensitive, but audiences forgave her because she wanted to be kind, and because at the end of the story she apologized for being who she was. Her closing lines, after submitting to insults from almost every member of the cast, are, "You know how I feel? Like a human, like a human being."

Audiences flocked to *The Philadelphia Story* for reassurance that being wealthy isn't all that great, in the process handing MGM over a million dollars in profit. Hepburn would go on to star in the Registry title *Woman of the Year* (1942), while Grant used a more sinister version of his character here in *Notorious* (1946).

The Blood of Jesus

Sack Amusement Enterprises, 1941. Sound, B&W, 1.37. 57 minutes.
Cast: Cathryn Caviness (Martha Ann Jackson), Spencer Williams (Razz Jackson), Juanita Riley (Sister Jenkins), Reather Hardeman (Sister Ellerby), Rogenia Goldthwaite (The Angel), Jas. B. Jones (Satan), Frank H. McClennan (Judas Green), Eddie De Base (Rufus Brown), Alva Fuller (Luke Willows), Rev. R.L. Robertson and The Heavenly Choir.
Credits: Written and directed by Spencer Williams. Produced by Alfred N. Sack. Director of photography: Jack Whitman. Sound recording: R.E. Byers. An Amegro Films presentation.
Additional Credits: Opened January 1941.
Available: The Internet Archive (*www.archive.org*). Battered copies are available from many sources; a good version is included as an extra on

the Wellspring DVD *Movies of Color: Black Southern Cinema* (2002). ISBN: 0-7942-0285-3. UPC: 7-20917-31662-8.

With the surge in filmmaking in the 1930s, it became economically feasible for producers to target niche markets. Yiddish, Ukrainian, and Spanish films were made and shown wherever populations were dense enough to support renting a theater, typically a second- or third-run houses in urban locations.

Black cinema developed in similar circumstances, but for different reasons. African-Americans had been featured in film since its earliest days, but they were usually portrayed by white performers in blackface. Black characters were almost always relegated to minor roles as servants, porters, cooks, and the like. Some historians trace the birth of black cinema—stories with, by, and about black characters—to the backlash caused by *The Birth of a Nation* (1915). Films like *The Birth of a Race* (1918) tried to counter narratives by D.W. Griffith and others that were construed as racist. Filmmakers like Oscar Micheaux and performers like Paul Robeson helped grow an infrastructure devoted to black films.

The arrival of sound threatened this structure. Independent filmmakers had limited access to the new technology, which also forced producers to come up with more capital to finance productions. Some all-black sound shorts from 1928 and 1929 were actually financed by film veteran Al Christie, a writer and director whose career stretched back to 1909. While directing his own features, Christie saw a market for musical shorts, and adapted "Darktown Birmingham," stories by Octavus Roy Cohen that ran in the *Saturday Evening Post*, into a series of films starring performers from Harlem's Lafayette Players Stock Company.

One of the stars in this series was Spencer Williams. Born in 1893 in Vidalia, Louisiana, the large, gregarious Williams was working as a sound technician when Christie tapped him to write and perform. He played the lead in *Music Hath Harms* (1929) and the comic relief in four Herb Jeffries musical Westerns (getting cowriting credit for 1939's *Harlem Rides the Range*). Williams may have become acquainted with Alfred N. Sack through the Jeffries films. Sack, a theater owner and exhibitor from Dallas, Texas, distributed black films throughout the South, and was looking to produce his own movies. The two recognized an unfulfilled market in religious films, which led to *The Blood of Jesus*, shot in Texas on a budget of about $5,000. (Most black features of the time cost between $10,000 and $15,000.)

Williams not only wrote the film and starred in it, but directed as well. For that kind of money he could not afford much experimentation—or much rehearsal, for that matter. His plot concerns a newly baptized wife, her nonreligious husband, and an accident with a hunting rifle that leaves her near death. An angel tells the wife, Martha Ann Jackson (played by the beautiful Cathryn Caviness in her only film role), that she must decide between heaven and hell.

Satan (James B. Jones) lures her to a nightclub, where she witnesses drinking and dancing. The smooth talking Rufus Brown (Eddie De Base) offers her a job in what looks like a thinly disguised bordello; when she flees, she collapses at an actual crossroads between Zion and hell. A crucifix bleeds on her face, bringing her back to life. Williams fills out the film with many spirituals and hymns, a riverside baptism, some adroitly delivered comedy, and extensive footage of dancers and singers, shot live in front of enthusiastic clubgoers.

Williams knew his audience, and after over a decade in the industry, knew filmmaking as well. Critics today often complain about how "primitive" *The Blood of Jesus* is. It's true that in terms of sound, lighting, and set design, Williams didn't have much to work with. But given the chance he could construct cunning scenes and coax convincing performances from obvious amateurs. The shooting accident is a sophisticated mix of close-up inserts, animation, and off-screen sound effects. Martha Ann's dead-end fate at Brown's hands is a stark, frightening display of the wages of sin. The comic relief from Juanita Riley and Reather Hardeman is pointed and timely enough to fit into a contemporary sitcom.

The film presents urban society as evil and decadent, and agrarian life as religious and pure, and it does so with larger-than-life incidents and symbols drawn from the music and sermons its viewers would have known well. (They may have appreciated the irony of decidedly urban filmmakers visualizing hymns and Biblical passages in rural terms.) In one sense, the film was capturing a life that was already gone; in another, it was providing a persuasive, modern-day version of familiar and well-loved religious themes.

The Blood of Jesus played not only at the six hundred or so movie theaters that showed black films, but in churches and schools. Williams continued to write, star in, and direct films for Sack, including *Go Down, Death!* (1944), an adaptation of the poem by James Weldon Johnson. In that film he cut right to the chase, starting out with the drinking, gambling, and dancing before focusing on religious material. By the end of the decade, Williams was making more genre-oriented films like *Dirty Gertie from Harlem, U.S.A.* (1946), a broad adaptation of *Rain*; and *Juke Joint* (1947), a comedy of morals set in a nightclub. In the 1950s, Williams played Andrew Hogg Brown in seventy-eight episodes of *Amos'n'Andy* on television. (The

actor and director Williams is often mistaken for songwriter Spencer Williams [1889–1965], composer of "I Ain't Got Nobody," "Basin Street Blues," and others.)

The Lady Eve

Herpetologist Charles Pike (Henry Fonda) in the clutches of con artist Jean Harrington (Barbara Stanwyck), from *The Lady Eve. Courtesy of The Criterion Collection*

Paramount, 1941. Sound, B&W, 1.37. 94 minutes.

Cast: Barbara Stanwyck (Jean [Harrington/Lady Eve Sidwich]), Henry Fonda (Charles [Poncefort Pike]), Charles Coburn ("Colonel" Harrington), Eugene Pallette (Mr. Pike), William Demarest (Muggsy), Eric Blore (Sir Alfred McGlennan Keith [Pearly]), Melville Cooper (Gerald), Martha O'Driscoll (Martha), Janet Beecher (Mrs. Pike), Robert Greig (Burrows), Dora Clement (Gertrude), Luis Alberni (Chef).

Credits: Written and directed by Preston Sturges. Based on a story by Monckton Hoffe. Produced by Paul Jones. Director of photography: Victor Milner. Edited by Stuart Gilmore. Art direction: Hans Dreier, Ernst Fegté. Musical director: Sigmund Krumgold. Costumes by Edith Head. Sound recording: Harry Lindgren, Don Johnson. Western Electric Mirrophonic Recording.

Additional Cast: Frank Moran (Bartender, party), Pat West (Bartender, ship), Wilson Benge (Butler), Harry Rosenthal (Piano tuner), Abdullah Abbas (Florist), Norman Ainsley (Sir Alfred's manservant), Arthur Hoyt (Lawyer); Jimmy Conlin, Al Bridge, Vic Potel (Stewards); Reginald Sheffield (Professor Jones); Wanda McKay, Betty Farrington, Nell Craig, Robert Dudley (Ship passengers); Torben Meyer (Purser).

Additional Credits: Executive producer: William LeBaron. Production dates: October 21, 1940 to December 5, 1940. Premiered in New York City on February 25, 1941.

Other Versions: Remade as *The Birds and the Bees* (1956).

Available: Criterion Collection DVD (2001). UPC: 7-15515-01162-4.

Preston Sturges wrote and directed eight films between 1940 and 1944, one of the most astonishing bursts of creativity in the history of the medium. Uniquely among these eight, *The Lady Eve*, his third directing effort, arose from a story by another author, in this case the Irish writer Monckton Hoffe. But, like all of the director's best work, *Eve* was based in part on his own life.

Born Edmond Biden in Chicago in 1898, Sturges was raised largely in Europe by his mother Mary, a singer and artist who befriended the dancer Isadora Duncan. In 1901, Mary married Solomon Sturges, a Chicago stockbroker, but she still spent at least half the year in Europe, where Sturges was schooled. He was managing his mother's cosmetics store in Deauville, France, when she sent him home after the outbreak of World War I. Sturges ran the New York branch of the firm, growing it from a storefront to a factory in Brooklyn and adding his own inventions to the line. He married his first wife Estelle, a divorcée, in 1923. That same year his mother returned and took the cosmetics company away from him.

Estelle left Sturges in 1927, taking with her his primary means of support. Sturges returned to cosmetics; he also tried songwriting on the side. When appendicitis left him in the hospital for six weeks, he experimented with playwriting. He had one enormous hit, *Strictly Dishonorable*, which was filmed in 1931. Its success propelled him back into the demimonde inhabited by his mother. He married heiress Eleanor Post Hutton in 1930, but she was unhappy almost from the start and fled to

Europe. He followed her there, but could not win her back.

In short, Sturges had firsthand knowledge of the world he depicted in his scripts. He really was that starstruck inventor who dogged his disapproving wife to Florida in *The Palm Beach Story* (1942). He really was the penniless writer who struck it rich in *Christmas in July* (1940). What's more, he knew this world as an insider, not as a bitter gigolo like his Paramount colleague Billy Wilder. Sturges genuinely liked the mountebanks, card sharps, clueless dreamers, hard-edged financiers, smothering mothers, and cynical valets in his stories, and he cast them with some of the most distinctive character actors in movies: Eugene Pallette, Eric Blore, Edgar Kennedy, and the like. Unusually for the time, he wrote supporting parts with specific actors in mind, especially William Demarest, a former vaudevillian who could wrap his penetrating urban growl around the most tongue-twisting dialogue.

When Sturges returned to the United States in 1932, he followed many other New York writers in taking a Hollywood job, in his case with Universal. He wrote several scripts, contributed to others, and adapted plays and novels. He signed a contract with Paramount in 1936, working on notable films like *Easy Living* (1937) and *If I Were King* (1938). After his mistress left him, Sturges married another divorcée in Reno, Nevada in November 1938, at the time he was working on the Monckton Hoffe story.

Sturges was so disappointed with how Mitchell Leisen directed his script for *Remember the Night* (1940) that he offered to sell Paramount an original screenplay for one dollar, provided he could direct. (Leisen also drove Billy Wilder to directing after he changed the script for *Midnight*, 1939.) That story, written in 1933 as *The Vagrant*, was released in 1940 as *The Great McGinty*. It was the first Oscar ever awarded for Original Screenplay.

Although he kept a few plot elements from Hoffe's story (which was also reworked by Jeanne Bartlett), Sturges essentially wrote an entirely new script for what became *The Lady Eve*; about all he

retained was the concept of a woman disappointed in love who poses as another person to get revenge on the man. Producer Albert Lewin recommended that Sturges almost completely revise the draft he submitted to Paramount, and his specific advice pinpointed the problems Sturges had. The writer put the script away while he directed *The Great McGinty* and *Christmas in July*, returning to it in 1940 with two box-office successes under his belt.

Now he could pressure Paramount into giving him Barbara Stanwyck and Henry Fonda (under contract at Twentieth Century-Fox) for his leads. Stanwyck had starred in *Remember the Night*, and was enthusiastic about working with Sturges. She was also one of the highest-paid actresses in the world, and her presence made everything about the project bigger. She had twenty-five costume changes, for example, all designed by Edith Head. Photography started in October 1940.

Stanwyck called the shooting of *The Lady Eve* a "carnival," compared to the "cathedral" she later experienced on Frank Capra's *Meet John Doe* (1941). That sense of joy and spontaneity comes through in the final film. Breathless pacing characterizes much of Sturges's work, but he is also open and accessible in a distinctly American manner. Sturges will try anything, from the lowliest pratfall to wispy allusions and convoluted puns, showing more trust in his audience than almost any of his peers. In one medium shot, a horse threatens to knock Fonda right out of the frame; Sturges punctuates the moment with a snippet from "With The Wind And The Rain In Your Hair," a best-selling pop tune of the time.

With writing this intelligent, the temptation is to simply quote as many lines as possible. Sturges offered more than just jokes, however. He pushed the story's snake symbolism as far as he could, resulting in a stateroom scene that stretched the Production Code to its limits. Jean Harrington became one of Stanwyck's defining roles, and the commercial success of the film freed Sturges to take on increasingly risky projects. His next movie, *Sullivan's Travels* (1941), is also on the Registry.

Sergeant York

Warner Bros., 1941. Sound, B&W, 1.37. 134 minutes.

Cast: Gary Cooper (Alvin C. York), Walter Brennan (Pastor Rosier Pile), Joan Leslie (Gracie Williams), George Tobias ("Pusher" Ross), Stanley Ridges (Major Buxton), Margaret Wycherly (Mother York), Ward Bond (Ike Botkin), Noah Beery, Jr. (Buck Lipscomb), June Lockhart (Rosie York), Dickie Moore (George York), Clem Bevans (Zeke), Howard Da Silva (Lem), Charles Trowbridge (Cordell Hull), Harvey Stephens (Captain Danforth), David Bruce (Bert Thomas), Charles Esmond (German Major), Joseph Sawyer (Sergeant Early), Pat Flaherty (Sergeant Harry Parsons), Robert Porterfield (Zeb Andrews), Erville Alderson (Nate Tompkins).

Credits: Directed by Howard Hawks. Screen play by Abem Finkel and Harry Chandlee and Howard Koch and John Huston. Based upon the

Diary of Sergeant York as edited by Tom Skeykill. Produced by Jesse L. Lasky and Hall B. Wallis. Music by Max Steiner. Director of photography: Sol Polito. Battle sequences photographed by Arthur Edeson. Film editor: William Holmes. Art director: John Hughes. Technical advisors: Donoho Hall; Paul Walters, Capt., F.A.R.; William Yetter. Sound by Oliver S. Garretson. Makeup artist: Perc Westmore. Orchestral arrangements by Hugo Friedhofer. Musical director: Leo F. Forbstein. RCA Sound System. A Warner Bros. Pictures presentation of a Warner Bros.—First National Picture.

Additional Cast includes: Frank Wilcox (Sergeant), Donald Douglas (Captain Tillman), Lane Chandler (Corporal Savage), Frank Marlowe (Beardsley), Jack Pennick (Corporal Cutting), James Anderson (Eb), Guy Wilkerson (Tom), Tully Marshall (Uncle Lige), Lee "Lasses" White (Luke), Charles Middleton (Mountaineer), Elisha Cook Jr. (Piano player).

Additional Credits: Scenes directed by Vincent Sherman, B. Reeves Eason. Screenwriting and research by Julien Josephson. Based on *Sergeant York and His People* by Sam K. Cowan; *Sergeant York: Last of The Long Hunters*, by Tom Skeykill; *Sergeant York: His Own Life Story and War Diary*, edited by Tom Skeykill. Production dates: February to May 1941. Premiered in New York City on July 2, 1941; general release September 27, 1941.

Awards: Oscars for Best Actor, Film Editing.

Available: Warner Home Video DVD (2006). UPC: 012569793750.

As one of the most decorated soldiers in American history, Alvin C. York was a natural subject for a film biography. Raised in rural Tennessee, York was a wayward youth until he turned to religion. Drafted during World War I, he registered as a conscientious objector. After debating with himself on a mountaintop near his home, he decided to fight, becoming a member of Company G of the Second Battalion, 328th Infantry. On October 8, 1918, during the Meuse-Argonne offensive, York and his company were pinned down by machine-gun fire behind German lines. Drawing on his hunting and shooting experiences in Tennessee, York killed over twenty German soldiers. With the surviving members of his company, he captured a total of 132 German prisoners. For his exploits he received the Congressional Medal of Honor, as well as awards from France and Italy.

York refused to cash in on his success, despite offers from showman Florenz Ziegfeld and Paramount producer Jesse L. Lasky. But Lasky persisted over the years, despite losing his fortune after being forced out of Paramount. In early 1940, Lasky finally persuaded York to sign over his rights for a biopic by appealing to his patriotism. (York assigned his profits to a local school.) Lasky also optioned the rights to three books relating to York.

York's story was a good fit at Warner Brothers, which in the 1930s helped establish a cycle of biographies (for example, *The Life of Emile Zola*, 1937, a Registry title). The studio had also found great success with large-scale Technicolor blockbusters like *The Adventures of Robin Hood* (1938, a Registry title), which gave its craftspeople experience with filming large crowds on location. With the looming war, it was time to concentrate on patriotic subjects. James Cagney was about to embark on *Yankee Doodle Dandy* (1942, a Registry title), a musical about George M. Cohan. Harry and Jack Warner jumped at the York project, assigning producer Hal B. Wallis to the film.

Lasky hired screenwriters Harry Chandlee and Julien Josephson (soon replaced by Abem Finkel) to research York's friends and family in Tennessee. Lasky and Wallis both wanted Gary Cooper to play York. The actor had to be persuaded by York himself to take the role (it was also offered to Henry Fonda, James Stewart, and Ronald Reagan). To sign Cooper, who was under contract to Samuel Goldwyn, the Warners had to give up Bette Davis for *The Little Foxes* (1941).

Howard Hawks was not the first choice for director. Victor Fleming, King Vidor, Henry King and others either had commitments or weren't interested. Hawks had just been fired from *The Outlaw*, a Howard Hughes project (finally released in 1943); had already tangled with Wallis during *Ceiling Zero* (1936); and had likewise burned bridges at most studios. He somehow persuaded Lasky that he could finish the film under budget, as long as he could hire John Huston to rewrite the script. (Wallis was responsible for pairing Huston with screenwriter Howard Koch.)

Hawks later took credit for several elements of the screenplay, notably correlating an early turkey shoot with the shooting of several German soldiers. But Huston told film critic and historian Todd McCarthy that he tried to inject humor into the story because "York was a very amusing fellow." Huston considered the movie lightweight, and thought it "absurd to want to try to find an overall moral in it." (Finkel complained at length about the script's "blundering stupidities," objecting in particular to the depiction of York and his cronies as hillbillies.)

Typically for the director, he was four days behind schedule after the first week of work. The studio was at its peak of production in March 1941, with eight features filming at once. Art director John Hughes oversaw construction of a revolving mountain and farmland set that enabled cameraman Sol Polito to set up shooting angles for several different scenes. But bad weather, recalcitrant animals, assorted illnesses, and the director's habit of changing dialogue added to the delays. As the production expanded into a twelve-week schedule, Wallis assigned B. Reeves Eason to direct battle sequences on location in the San Fernando Valley.

Hawks reshot some of Eason's footage in late April, but left the production on May 1 to go to the Kentucky Derby. Warner contract director Vincent Sherman oversaw the final days of shooting. With the nominal director gone, Wallis supervised editor William Holmes, who assembled a 150-minute preview version that was screened in June. It took another two weeks to prepare the final cut for the world premiere on July 1.

A variety of factors helped make *Sergeant York* the biggest hit in Hawks' career, among them Cooper's natural, unforced performance (winning him his first Oscar), and a thoughtful script that addressed viewers' fears head on. While clearly propaganda, *Sergeant York* didn't set up villains so much as try to answer questions. York, a religious pacifist, was the perfect surrogate for an audience worried about war and killing. The film was credible and graphic about fighting, and ultimately treated its main subjects—reconciling religion and war—seriously. (Cameraman Arthur Edeson, who replaced the ailing Polito, had also worked on *All Quiet on the Western Front*, 1930, and the two films share some of the horrors of trench warfare.) It tried to show that our country could emerge from battle with morals and homespun values intact.

Sergeant York was somewhat of an anomaly for Hawks, both in style and subject matter. It was the only full-fledged biography he undertook, and the one film in his career that evinced a studio rather than personal style. But on other levels this was a typical Hawks production. As a director, he tended to respond rather than innovate, to try to top existing works rather than forge new ones. *Scarface* (1932, a Registry title) could be seen as a response to the Warner cycle of gangster films; *Bringing Up Baby* (1938, a Registry title) to the screwball genre. *Sergeant York* was Hawks' take on Americana, on films like John Ford's *Young Mr. Lincoln* (1939, a Registry title). To *York* he brought his characteristic interests: a tough, sexy brunette (played by Joan Leslie in a role Hawks envisioned for Jane Russell); cornpone humor that condescended to hicks; and laconic, tough-guy heroics (notably from former child star Dickie Moore).

Hawks continued his association with Warners until 1946's *The Big Sleep*. Cooper, meanwhile, became the most successful actor in the industry, working with Hawks again in *Ball of Fire* (1941) before playing Lou Gehrig in *The Pride of the Yankees* (1942). He is also represented on the Registry by *High Noon* (1952). Audie Murphy, in some ways York's World War II equivalent, played himself in the autobiographical *To Hell and Back* (1955). Preston Sturges mocked some of the elements of *Sergeant York* in *Hail the Conquering Hero* (1944), while Clint Eastwood's *Flags of Our Fathers* (2006) offers a different viewpoint on the consequences of heroism.

Citizen Kane

RKO, 1941. Sound, B&W, 1.37. 119 minutes.
Cast: Joseph Cotten (Jedediah Leland), Dorothy Comingore (Susan Alexander Kane), Agnes Moorehead (Mary, Kane's mother), Ruth Warrick (Emily Monroe Norton Kane), Ray Collins (Jim W. Gettys), Erskine Sanford (Herbert Carter), Everett Sloane (Mr. Bernstein), William Alland (Jerry Thompson), Paul Stewart (Raymond), George Coulouris (Walter Parks Thatcher), Fortunio Bonanova (Matiste), Gus Schilling (The Headwaiter), Philip Van Zandt (Mr. Rawlston), Georgia Backus (Miss Anderson), Harry Shannon (Kane's Father), Sonny Bupp (Kane III), Buddy Swan (Kane, age eight), Orson Welles ([Charles Foster] Kane).
Credits: Produced and directed by Orson Welles. Original Screen Play: Herman J. Mankiewicz, Orson Welles. Photography: Gregg Toland. Music composed and conducted by Bernard Herrmann. Special effects: Vernon L. Walker. Art director: Van Nest Polglase. Associate art director: Perry Ferguson. Editing: Robert Wise. Recording: Bailey Fesler, James G. Stewart. Costumes: Edward Stevenson. RCA Sound System. A Mercury production.
Additional Cast includes: Gino Corrado (Gino, waiter at El Rancho); Alan Ladd, Richard Wilson, Arthur O'Connell (Reporters).
Additional Credits: Writing: John Houseman, Roger Denny, Molly Kent. Photography: Russell Metty, Harry Wild. Editorial assistant: Mark Robson. Makeup: Maurice Seiderman. Singing voice for Susan Kane: Jane Forward. Production dates: June 29 to October 23, 1940; reshoots: October 1940 through January 1941. Released September 5, 1941.

Awards: Oscar for Best Writing—Original Screenplay.
Available: Warner Home Video DVD (2001). ISBN: 0-7806-3520-5. UPC: 0-53939-65652-7.

When *Sight and Sound* magazine conducted its Ten Best Films of the Decade polls, starting in 1952, the first winner was *Citizen Kane*, the debut feature by writer and director Orson Welles. *Kane* for a time became the de facto Great American Film, displacing such aspirants as *The Birth of a Nation* and *Greed*, but its reputation has dimmed recently. It is easier to see now on television, which shrinks Welles's vision and tames his effects, than on the screen. The techniques that made *Citizen Kane* seem so fresh have been assimilated into the mainstream, and the people it mocked are no longer familiar. If *Citizen Kane* can't shock the way it once did, it can still entertain. As Pauline Kael noted, of all the screen classics, it may be the most fun to watch.

Welles enraged many Hollywood old-timers when he "burst" onto the scene in 1939, signing a contract with RKO that gave him an almost unprecedented degree of control over his films. (He didn't win over professionals when, after given a tour of the RKO studio, he referred to it as "the biggest electric train a boy ever had.") But the boy wonder's career stretched back farther than many had imagined.

Like his contemporary Preston Sturges, Welles had a privileged upbringing in the Midwest. He was groomed from an early age for great achievements in the arts, and he took that training seriously. He attended the Todd School, toured Europe, then moved to New York, where he set out to make a name for himself. He did this partly by surrounding himself with a new generation of actors, writers, and producers—John Houseman, for one, would go on to a long and distinguished career in plays, films, and television; and extraordinary actors like Agnes Moorehead and Joseph Cotten, performers with strong technical skills and the willingness to experiment. They formed the backbone of the Mercury Theater, founded in 1937.

Welles experimented with independent film, directing *Hearts of the Age* in 1934. His other projects clamored for attention from the public: an all-black *Macbeth*, staged in 1936; a 1938 radio adaptation of H.G. Wells' *The War of the Worlds*, so convincing that it spread panic among listeners.

After signing with RKO, Welles brought the Mercury Theater with him to Hollywood. He suggested several projects that met with opposition from studio executives. One idea that was approved was a roman à clef about William Randolph Hearst. Welles knew that a thinly disguised film about a Hearst counterpart whose political ambitions were ruined by his affair with an actress would not arrive unnoticed in the marketplace.

Working with screenwriter Herman J. Mankiewicz, Welles fashioned a story that used a convoluted flashback structure to examine different aspects of the wealthiest and most influential American in the early part of the twentieth century, one whose life was plagued by unhappiness and who died with his dreams unfulfilled. It was an audacious take on the American success story. That Welles built the title role for himself says something about his ambivalence about his own desires and motives.

Pauline Kael wrote an essay, later expanded into a book, that attributed most of the inspiration for *Kane* to Mankiewicz, an otherwise underwhelming screenwriter noted more for his drinking and scabrous social skills than for his resume. Mankiewicz was a drama critic in New York who left for Hollywood in the mid-1920s. He sent a famous telegram to Ben Hecht tipping him off to working in movies: "Millions are to be grabbed out here, and your only competition is idiots." He wrote intertitles for silents, scripts for generally lackluster early sound films, then signed for a time with MGM. He spent more energy on drinking and gambling than on establishing a style or reputation as a writer.

But Mankiewicz had entry into Hearst's world, something denied Welles, and he had an eye for singling out the flaws in the people he took the time to study. His observations, as well as his skill at screenplay structure, were invaluable. He was also pointlessly cruel, as in his caricature of Hearst's well-liked mistress, Marion Davies, as a talentless nag devoted to jigsaw puzzles.

Kane's structure owes something to Preston Sturges's *The Power and the Glory*, a turgid biography of a thwarted, unhappy industrialist that was filmed at Paramount in 1933. But Welles borrowed liberally from other sources, notably *Time* magazine and *The March of Time* newsreels (more popular in New York than the Hearst media), adopting their snappy, jaundiced, superficial take on celebrity. He also fished through the growing collection of Hollywood scandals, changing details enough to protect himself from legal retribution.

Before shooting started, Welles screened *Stagecoach* (1939) over and over, and quizzed technicians at length about what he could and could not do in film. His background on the stage helped him achieve the brisk editing style he employed in *Kane*. In theater Welles used lighting and free-form sets to glide almost imperceptibly between scenes. In *Kane* he got the same effects the same way, through lighting shifts and with sets whose walls could magically float away. He gave free rein to cinematographer Gregg Toland, who developed a method of deep-focus photography that kept every element of the frame sharp.

Welles was entranced with filmmaking tricks, and *Kane* is a compendium of models, miniatures, mattes, optical printing, animation, sets lifted from *King Kong* and *The Hunchback of Notre Dame*, and every other possible device. Examining a print of

Kane on a Moviola some twenty years later, editor Aram Avakian marveled at how many trick cuts Welles and his editor Robert Wise devised. Avakian claimed that there was not one straight cut in the entire film.

Welles disguised many of his intentions during filming by identifying his footage as "tests," and he fooled Hearst's gossip columnist Louella Parsons by claiming that his film had nothing to do with her boss. When the film was finally screened for Hearst's lawyers, the mogul tried to have his friends at MGM buy it outright. Twentieth Century-Fox and Warner Brothers theaters refused to book it, and mention of it was banned from the Hearst press. Hearst's heavy-handed attempt to quash the film worked to a certain extent, for *Kane* never received widespread booking. However, *Citizen Kane* did make a profit, and it also won an Oscar for Original Screenplay. (Ironically, Mankiewicz had to fight Welles for a screenplay credit, taking his case to the Writers Guild for arbitration.)

Kane was a boon for almost every technician associated with it, from Wise to composer Bernard Herrmann and producer Houseman. Its leading cast members found instant footing in Hollywood. Still, the film was not the success Welles hoped it would be, and its poor box-office reception tarnished the luster of the boy wonder. He was already hard at work on *The Magnificent Ambersons*, a film in many ways superior to *Kane*. Still, *Citizen Kane*'s influence was phenomenal. Welles showed Hollywood how its arsenal could dazzle filmgoers, and within the next few years movies of all types began to include ceilings, deep focus, and overlapping sound. *Kane* shifted the emphasis of creativity from producers to directors. Suddenly the vision of a film relied more on the man calling "cut" than on the producer who bought the project and assembled everyone on the set.

The film also proved a terrible millstone for Welles, who was faced with the prospect of topping it with every new project. Although he went through ups and downs typical to any artist's career, his later work was largely a shambles. Bad choices, unfinished films, unnecessary arguments, divorces, squabbles, and inadequate funding dogged Welles until he went into exile.

The Maltese Falcon

Humphrey Bogart as Sam Spade, facing a decisive moment in *The Maltese Falcon*.

Warner Bros., 1941. Sound, B&W, 1.37. 100 minutes.
Cast: Humphrey Bogart (Sam Spade), Mary Astor (Brigid O'Shaughnessy), Gladys George (Iva Archer), Peter Lorre (Joel Cairo), Barton MacLane (Lt. of Detectives Dundy), Lee Patrick (Effie Perine), Sydney Greenstreet (Kaspar Gutman), Ward Bond (Detective Tom Polhaus), Jerome Cowan (Miles Archer), Elisha Cook, Jr. (Wilmer Cook), James Burke (Luke), Murray Alper (Frank Richman), John Hamilton (Bryan).

Credits: Directed by John Huston. Screen play by John Huston. Based upon the novel by Dashiell Hammett. Executive producer: Hal B. Wallis. Associate producer: Henry Blanke. Director of photography: Arthur Edeson. Dialogue director: Robert Foulk. Film editor: Thomas Richards. Art director: Robert Haas. Sound by Oliver S. Garretson. Gowns by Orry-Kelly. Makeup artist: Perc Westmore. Music by Adolph Deutsch. Musical director: Leo F. Forbstein. RCA Sound System.

Additional Cast: Walter Huston (Captain Jacoby), Emory Parnell (Mate, *La Paloma*), Robert Homans (Policeman), Creighton Hale (Stenographer); Charles Drake, Bill Hopper, Hank Mann (Reporters).

Additional Credits: Production dates: June 9 to July 18, 1941. Reshoots: August and September 1941. Premiered in New York City on October 3, 1941.

Other Versions: *The Maltese Falcon* (1931, directed by Roy Del Ruth), *Satan Met a Lady* (1936, directed by William Dieterle). *The Black Bird* (1975, directed by David Giler) is a parody sequel.

Available: Warner Home Video DVD (2006). UPC: 0-12569-79488-7.

Published in February 1930, *The Maltese Falcon* was Dashiell Hammett's third novel, and the second to be optioned for the movies. Warner Brothers purchased the rights that June, by which time Hammett was writing sporadically for Paramount and struggling with what would be his last novel, *The Thin Man*. A spare, hard-edged story of corruption and betrayal, *The Maltese Falcon* earned excellent reviews and helped legitimize the type of thriller writing found in pulp magazines like *Black Mask*.

What set Hammett apart from other pulp authors was his authenticity and his pitiless judgment. Before illness forced him to retire, Hammett had been a detective with the Pinkerton agency. Out of professional necessity, he learned the ins and outs of the criminal class, and knew how to pin characters down with a few indelible images. During mining strikes in Montana he experienced firsthand how power and violence could twist morality. His actions there as a strikebreaker haunted him throughout his life.

Sam Spade, the private eye in *The Maltese Falcon*, evolved from Hammett's earlier protagonist, The Continental Op. A loner who operated under his own rules, Spade in the novel is a dark, menacing figure often described in Satanic terms. Released in May 1931, the first film version of *The Maltese Falcon* (directed by Roy Del Ruth and starring Ricardo Cortez) succeeded in capturing some of the novel's moral ambiguities. A second version, *Satan Met a Lady* (1936), was played largely for laughs. By 1941, Hammett had joined the Communist Party, been fired from MGM, and had missed deadlines for a contracted novel.

John Huston had been one of the Warner studio's best and most versatile screenwriters for the previous five years. He had just collaborated with novelist W.R. Burnett on *The High Sierra* (1941), a hard-boiled gangster picture that helped catapult Humphrey Bogart to stardom. His contract gave him the right to direct a film for Warners. By selecting *The Maltese Falcon*, a property the studio already owned, and one that required a minimal number of cheap sets, Huston may have been opting to "fail low." He was delighted when George Raft turned down the lead role, opening it up for Bogart.

Although this was his debut as a film director, Huston was not exactly a novice. His father Walter was one of the most famous actors of his era (he appears in an unbilled cameo in *The Maltese Falcon* as a ship captain), and John had both acted and directed on stage. In his autobiography he describes preparing for his feature debut by sketching out each scene beforehand and consulting with William Wyler for advice.

Along with Bogart and his father, Huston assembled a dream cast of character actors: Peter Lorre, who achieved international prominence as a pedophile and serial killer in Fritz Lang's *M* (1931); Sydney Greenstreet, an esteemed stage actor making his film debut; and Elisha Cook, Jr., promoted here from his usual walk-on role as messenger boy or elevator operator. Mary Astor's scandalous past made her especially effective as Brigid O'Shaughnessy, the story's femme fatale.

Huston was watched closely by producer Henry Blanke, who reported back to studio head Jack Warner. Viewing the rushes, Warner complained that Huston's pacing was too slow; despite assurances from the director that the story would pick up, Warner continued to press for faster timing throughout the production. Huston had the luxury of rehearsing the film's climactic scenes a full day before shooting. As a result, Huston and cinematographer Arthur Edeson were able to work out complex shots that reframed action without resorting to cutting. "I don't remember exactly how many dolly moves were made," Huston wrote, "but the number twenty-six comes to mind."

After thirty-four days of shooting, principal photography was finished in July, two days ahead of schedule and $54,000 under budget. To Huston's surprise, both Warner and producer Hal Wallis attended the first preview in Pasadena. As a result of that screening, Huston reshot three brief scenes and the film's ending.

The Maltese Falcon was an enormous success, cementing Bogart's new celebrity status, propelling Huston to the top ranks of Warners directors, and prompting a one-volume reissue of Hammett's five novels. Bogart and Huston would team up for five more films, including *The Treasure of the Sierra Madre* (1948).

"One reason Huston is so good is he makes the book," Bogart said later. "He doesn't write in new characters or themes. That's what he did

Mary Astor as cornered femme fatale Brigid O'Shaughnessy in *The Maltese Falcon*.

with *The Maltese Falcon*." But Huston's work went beyond simply staging scenes from the novel. He recognized the queasy underside to Hammett's plot, the allure of thievery, of getting away with sleeping with your partner's wife, of double-crossing your putative partners, of pulling one over on the cops. The con game raises (perhaps even causes) the physical passion between Spade and Brigid O'Shaughnessy, just as it allows Kaspar Gutman (Greenstreet) to betray his lover.

Huston's genius was in seeing that he didn't have to comment on Hammett's story as long as he presented it honestly. Hammett wasn't interested in mysteries per se, and the "solutions" to his novels are often laughable. As a writer, he learned that suspense didn't come from chases or shoot-outs or fistfights, but from the way relationships between characters changed. He also found that it was better not to tell readers what his characters were thinking, or how they felt, other than external details like whether or not they were cold or tired. We have to read into Spade's motives: they aren't spelled out for us. It's possible that he is honorable and above-board, but it's just as possible that he is an unscrupulous villain taking sexual advantage of one client while extorting money from others.

In a way Huston's approach was the key to Bogart's acting: to hold back what he was thinking from the audience. Earlier in his career he had been broad, even hammy, in a succession of ill-fitting juvenile roles. By the time he appeared in *The Petrified Forest* (1936) he had honed his menacing posture to a sharp point, but still tried too hard, projecting to the back rows. It was while working with Edward G. Robinson and James Cagney in films like *The Roaring Twenties* (1939) that he saw the value of underacting, in part to offset his costars' blazing screen personas. Directors like Raoul Walsh (*High Sierra*) and Huston, men who were skeptical of Hollywood's high opinion of itself, who knew that only a crisis could prove strength, helped Bogart perfect his mask of indifference.

The Maltese Falcon marks one of the most auspicious directorial debuts in movies. Almost immediately, it became the subject of imitations and parodies. Jack Warner pursued the idea of a sequel until he found out how much Hammett wanted to charge. The film's real legacy may be how it helped Hollywood reach a new degree of psychological honesty. Huston's next Registry film is the World War II documentary *The Battle of San Pietro* (1944).

How Green Was My Valley

Twentieth Century-Fox, 1941. Sound, B&W, 1.37. 119 minutes.

Cast: Walter Pidgeon (Mr. Gruffydd), Maureen O'Hara (Angharad), Donald Crisp (Mr. Morgan), Anna Lee (Brownyn), John Loder (Ianto), Sara Allgood (Mrs. Morgan), Barry Fitzgerald (Cyfartha), Patric Knowles (Ivor), Roddy McDowall (Huw), Welsh Singers, Morton Lowry (Mr. Jonas), Arthur Shields (Mr. Parry), Ann Todd (Ceinwen), Frederick Worlock (Dr. Richards), Richard Fraser (Davy), Evan S. Evans (Gwilym), James Monk (Owen), Rhys Williams (Dai Bando), Lionel Pape (Evans), Ethel Griffies (Mrs. Nicholas), Marten Lamont (Iestyn Evans).

Credits: Directed by John Ford. Screen play by Philip Dunne. Based on the novel by Richard Llewellyn. Produced by Darryl F. Zanuck. Music: Alfred Newman. Director of photography: Arthur Miller. Art direction:

Richard Day, Nathan Juran. Set decorations: Thomas Little. Film editor: James B. Clark. Costumes: Gwen Wakeling. Sound: Eugene Grossman, Roger Heman. Makeup artist: Guy Pearce. Western Electric Mirrophonic Recording.

Additional Cast: Clifford Severn (Mervyn), Dennis Hoey (Motshell), Eve March (Meillyn Lewis), Tudor Williams (Singer), Herbert Evans (Postman), Mary Field (Eve), Tiny Jones (Shopkeeper), Jack Pennick (Mine superintendent), Mary Gordon, Will Lewis, Lewis Rees, Owen Thomas, Phillip Dare, Edward Davies, Reese Williams, Gomer Morgan, Emlyn Jones, Ellis James, John C. Thomas, Caradac Rees, Jack Griffiths, Gwilym Isaac, Jack Owen, Joseph T. Jones, Hugh Thomas, Howell A. Jones, David Jones, Stewart Bair, Robert Bradford, Allan Watson, Jan Williams, Cyril Clare, Arthur Pritchard, Robert B. Williams, David J. Reed, Leonard Clare, Alice A. Jones, Helen Davies, Arvonia Jones, Anne McCullough, E.W. Davies.

Additional Credits: Assistant directors: Gene Bryant, Edward O'Fearna. Technical advisors: Rhys Williams, Idwal Jones. Production manager: William Koenig. Narration read by Irving Pichel. Production dates: June 10 to August 12, 1941. Premiered in New York City on October 28, 1941.

Awards: Oscars for Best Picture, Director, Actor in a Supporting Role (Crisp), Cinematography—Black-and-White, Art Direction–Interior Direction—Black-and-White.

Other Versions: Llewellyn's novel was the basis of a 1975 TV miniseries.

Available: Twentieth Century Fox Home Entertainment DVD (2002). UPC: 024543060734.

In 1939, producer Darryl F. Zanuck purchased the rights to Richard Llewellyn's *How Green Was My Valley* for $300,000, a high price even then for the best-selling book. Zanuck originally envisioned the book as a way to compete with David O. Selznick's *Gone With the Wind* (1939), but as screenwriter Philip Dunne pointed out, "The book had no structure, so one of the difficult things was to find out how to arrange the scenes." Nevertheless, Zanuck called for a four-hour film to be shot on location in Wales, in Technicolor. His proposed cast included Laurence Olivier, Tyrone Power, and Katharine Hepburn.

Zanuck hired William Wyler to direct; at the time, Wyler was one of the most prestigious directors in the industry. Ernest Pascal, the original screenwriter and president of the Screen Writers Guild, had already been fired because he turned the book "into a labor story and sociological problem story," as Zanuck later complained. Zanuck may not have been aware at the time that Phillip Dunne, Pascal's replacement, was even more left-wing.

Dunne started working in July 1940, on what was still planned as a four-hour film. World War II eliminated the possibility of shooting in Wales, and Fox executives told Zanuck that if he shot the film in the United States it would have to be in black-and-white. Zanuck ordered Dunne to shorten the script to two hours. The writer went with Wyler to Lake Arrowhead, where they tried to make sense out of the story by transposing scenes. "Willy couldn't write a line, but he knew what *you*

could do and he *made* you do it," Dunne wrote in his memoir. "I worked harder on scenes for Willy than I ever worked in my life."

The solution to adapting the novel was to discard most of the plot, which was narrated by Huw Morgan as he ages from ten to sixty. Dunne and Wyler decided to limit the time frame of the script to Huw as a ten-year-old. This not only eliminated potentially sticky scenes of Huw losing his virginity, it allowed the story to unfold from the point of view of a young child not fully aware of the larger political and social structures affecting his family. Furthermore, Huw could now participate in the choices and actions of adults without appreciating their consequences.

Llewellyn's basic story remained intact. *How Green Was My Valley* documents how social changes bring about the dissolution of the Morgan family, proud coal miners in a Welsh village loosely based on Gilfach Goch. Now that it was to be filmed in California, Wyler oversaw construction of a mining village near Malibu while Zanuck tinkered with the script. Dunne noted how Zanuck kept pushing details about labor unrest into the background, focusing on an affair between Gruffydd and Angharad Morgan as "the only halfway happy love story we have in our entire film."

Fox executives in New York withheld approval for the project for so long that Wyler left to shoot *The Little Foxes*. By that time he had cast Roddy McDowall as Huw. McDowall, a child star in British films, found work in Hollywood almost immediately after he was evacuated from Great Britain during the London Blitz. Dunne, for one, considered McDowall "the real auteur of the picture."

When Zanuck threatened to quit over *How Green Was My Valley*, Fox executives agreed to John Ford as the director, and a million-dollar budget. Dunne wrote that Ford didn't alter his script, but the director's presence on the project unavoidably brought out the story's resemblance to *The Grapes of Wrath* (1940). Ford had a hand in casting, rejecting Zanuck's choice of Gene Tierney for Angharad. Instead, he picked Maureen O'Hara, the Irish actress who had made a strong impression with audiences in *The Hunchback of Notre Dame* (1939). (She also starred in 1940's *Dance, Girl, Dance*, a Registry title.)

Ford's own childhood echoed many of the incidents in *How Green Was My Valley*, one reason why the film's emotions seem so heartfelt. Like the Joads in *The Grapes of Wrath*, the close-knit

Morgans enjoy living and working surrounded by beauty, only to have it all taken away from them by forces out of their control. Ford won't offer any solutions to the problems in the story. Work is dangerous and unfair. Management can't be trusted. Unions become corrupt. Churches feud among themselves. Emigration tears apart families and communities. Love sours, loyalty erodes, faith weakens. The downward arc of *How Green Was My Valley*, from sunny mountainsides to dank mines, from family happiness to a diaspora, from love to hate, from life to death, is as hopeless as any in American film.

Even the addition of a happy ending à la *Wuthering Heights* (1939) did little to blunt *How Green Was My Valley*'s message. To his credit,

Zanuck remained dedicated to the film throughout the production. On its release, it proved to be a surprising commercial success. Critics were more cautious in their support, and to this day many argue that *Citizen Kane* deserved the Academy Award that year for Best Picture. *Kane* was a delightful stunt with the appeal of an eager puppy; for all its sentimental touches and melodramatic twists, *How Green Was My Valley* called on viewers to question their fundamental beliefs about society. It was a film of courage and honesty, especially as the country was drawn inexorably into war. By the time it won five Oscars, Ford was in the Navy making educational and propaganda films and documentaries. His next Registry feature is *My Darling Clementine* (1946).

Sullivan's Travels

Two in a diner, neither willing to face up to the truth. Veronica Lake and Joel McCrea in *Sullivan's Travels*. *Courtesy of The Criterion Collection*

Paramount, 1941. Sound, B&W, 1.37. 90 minutes.

Cast: Joel McCrea (John L. Sullivan), Veronica Lake (The Girl), Robert Warwick (Mr. LeBrand), William Demarest (Mr. Jones), Margaret Hayes (Secretary), Porter Hall (Mr. Hadrian), Robert Greig (Sullivan's Butler [Burrows]), Franklin Pangborn (Mr. Casalsis), Eric Blore (Sullivan's Valet), Georges Renavent (Old Tramp), Harry Rosenthal (The Trombenick), Byron Foulger (Mr. Valdelle), Torben Meyer (The Doctor), Victor Potel (The Cameraman), Richard Webb (Radio Man), Charles Moore (Colored Chef), Almira Sessions (Ursula), Esther Howard (Miz Zeffie), Frank Moran (Tough Chauffeur), Alan Bridge (The Mister), Jimmy Conlin (The Trusty), Jan Buckingham (Mrs. Sullivan), Robert Winkler (Bud), Chick Collins (Capital), Jimmie Dundee (Labor).

Credits: Written and directed by Preston Sturges. Associate producer: Paul Jones. Director of photography: John Seitz. Process photography: Farciot Edouart. Art direction: Hans Dreier and Earl Hedrick. Musical direction: Sigmund Krumgold. Music score: Leo Shuken and Charles Bradshaw. Edited by Stuart Gilmore. Costumes: Edith Head. Makeup artist: Wally Westmore. Sound recording by Harry Mills and Walter Oberst. Western Electric Mirrophonic Recording.

Additional Cast: Harry Hayden (Mr. Carson), Willard Robertson (Judge), Pat West (Counterman), J. Farrell MacDonald (Desk sergeant), Roscoe Ates (Diner cook, Owl Wagon), Paul Newlan (Truck driver), Arthur Hoyt (Preacher), Gus Reed (Mission cook), George Anderson (Sullivan's manager), Monte Blue (Slum cop), Dewey Robinson (Sheriff), Madame Sui-Te-Wan (Harmonium player), Jess Lee Brooks (Black preacher), Chester Conklin (Old bum).

Additional Credits: Produced by Preston Sturges. Executive producer: Buddy DeSylva. Production dates: May 12, 1941 to July 22, 1941. Screened December 1941. Released January 28, 1942.

Available: Criterion Collection DVD (2001). UPC: 7-15515-01212-6.

Preston Sturges finished filming *The Lady Eve* in November 1940, in debt to Darryl Zanuck at Twentieth Century-Fox for having borrowed one of his stars, Henry Fonda. To repay his obligation, Sturges offered Zanuck *Song of Joy*, a script he had worked on while writing *Diamond Jim* in 1935. The story concerned an opera singer signed to a Hollywood contract. Through a bureaucratic mix-up, the fictional studio has only four weeks to invent, film, and finish her starring vehicle.

According to Sturges historian Brian Henderson, *Song of Joy* was a self-referential, deconstructionist parody of the Hollywood studio system, finished well before those terms were in vogue. Zanuck hated it, correctly referring to it as "something out of Preston's trunk," but perhaps unaware that Sturges revised many of his projects over several years. Henderson considers the script a more adventurous look at movies than *Sullivan's Travels* became, although it was probably the jumping off point for the film. Sturges began writing *Sullivan's Travels* in February 1941, and finished a third draft a few days after he started filming that May.

The script and film are ramshackle affairs that undergo severe shifts in mood. The growing consensus among critics was that Sturges's films had expert dialogue but were a bit stiff visually. Here he tried to compensate with broad physical comedy: undercranked chases, elaborate pratfalls, an oil portrait whose expression changes. More often than not, the slapstick falls flat. But a few miscalculated jokes matter little to the overall picture. *Sullivan's Travels* was then and is now the single most captivating film about filmmaking to come out of a Hollywood studio.

Sturges made a stab at correlating his script to Jonathan Swift's *Gulliver's Travels*. Like Gulliver, director John L. Sullivan embarks on several journeys intended to teach him about different aspects of both humanity and morality. Sturges quickly dropped direct parallels to the novel, but some self-referential flashes remain in Sullivan's exasperation over the failure of his first three "travels."

The gist of the film is contained in a four-minute scene done in one take. *Sullivan's Travels* actually begins at the end, the end of a clichéd adventure movie featuring a fight to the finish on top of a speeding train. In a takeoff on a similar opening in *Citizen Kane* (1941), Sturges cuts to a smoky screening room, where John L. Sullivan (played by Joel McCrea) is trying to persuade studio executives LeBrand (Robert Warwick, a political fixer in 1940's *The Great McGinty*) and Hadrian (Porter Hall, a justice of the peace in 1944's *The Miracle of Morgan's Creek*) to fund his adaptation of the novel *O Brother, Where Art Thou?* (Filmmakers Joel and Ethan Coen used this title for their 2000 comedy set in the Depression-era South. The novel was supposedly written by "Sinclair Beckstein," a play on Sinclair Lewis and John Steinbeck.)

An argument over art versus commerce ensues, spilling over into LeBrand's adjoining office. Sullivan believes that "with grim Death gargling at you from every corner," it is his responsibility to address social issues like poverty. LeBrand and Hadrian want him to make a sequel to *Ants in Your Pants of 1939*, offering him an extravagant budget and every star on the Paramount lot. Their back-and-forth is informed, sharp, and just as relevant today as it was in the 1940s. The dialogue, alternately affectionate and cynical, distills Sturges's own beliefs into a persuasive stand for mainstream entertainment and against what he later refers to as "deep-dish" art.

Sullivan is determined to find out what it's like to be poor, and he sets out like any successful Hollywood director would: with a support staff publicizing his every move. Now directing his fourth film, Sturges could expand his repertory company of character actors, spotlighting everyone from Frank Moran (who mutters in a tough-guy growl, "It's what you call a paraphrase") to Jimmy Conlin, playing a diminutive trusty in a prison camp reminiscent of *I Was a Fugitive from a Chain Gang* (1932). Sturges was lucky to cast Joel McCrea, an affable, undemanding performer who would go on to work in two more films with him. Veronica Lake was still considered a starlet as production started. She was also pregnant, necessitating some changes in her wardrobe and shooting schedule. Within a year she would be one of the most popular stars in the country.

With *Sullivan's Travels*, Sturges broadened his scope, exploring characters and settings new to his work: lunch wagons, shanty towns, corrupt cops, petty crooks. At the peak of his powers as a writer, his touch was so light and assured that some viewers never caught on to how he was spoon-feeding them the very material he mocked in his opening. He also fiddled with his script up to and during shooting. He took out an extended sequence in which a sheriff threatens Sullivan with vagrancy, for example, replacing it with the second of three scenes about watching movies. (Sullivan's theater experiences mirror his descent in society, while the films he watches increase in quality. The last clip is from Walt Disney's 1934 cartoon *Playful Pluto*, chosen after Charlie Chaplin refused to allow Sturges to use *The Gold Rush*.)

Like novels about writing, movies about filmmaking are just too tempting for some artists to ignore. Few have matched the friendly, breezy quality of *Sullivan's Travels*. How much of its visual style was attributable to Sturges, and how much to the experienced craftsmen at Paramount, is open to debate. A silent, seven-minute montage in the second half of the film is unique in his work; for that matter, unique to any other Hollywood feature of the time as well. But no one wrote like Sturges, and no one managed to deal with such big themes in such an open, unintimidating, and satisfying manner. If his touch occasionally faltered, as in the mildly racist humor toward the opening, he at least put on the screen people who weren't ordinarily seen in Hollywood movies. Sturges's next Registry title is *The Miracle of Morgan's Creek* (1944).

Kannapolis, NC

H. Lee Waters, 1940–41. Silent, Color and B&W, 1.37. 137 minutes.
Credits: Directed, photographed, and edited by H. Lee Waters.
Available: Rare Book, Manuscript, and Special Collections Library, Duke University Libraries.

One of the first discoveries filmmakers made was how much people liked to see themselves on screen. At the end of the nineteenth century, J. Stuart Blackton and others went on tours, filming townspeople during the day and then projecting the movies at night. Twenty years later, Pare Lorentz broke into the industry by filming locals for northeast movie houses. Twenty years after Lorentz, Ivan Besse filmed 2½ hours of footage of the residents of Britton, South Dakota, exhibiting it at the Strand Cinema, where he was the projectionist. About the same time Arthur J. Higgins worked as an itinerant filmmaker in California and other states.

H. Lee Waters was born in 1902 in South Carolina. In 1917, his family moved to Lexington, North Carolina, where his parents worked in a textile mill. Waters worked there as well, but started as an apprentice in a photography shop in 1925. A year later, his mother helped him buy the shop. Waters did the standard portrait and commercial work of any small-town photography business, but he also documented the town itself, along with its surroundings, selling postcards of local buildings and businesses.

In 1936, Waters supplemented his still photography equipment with a Kodak Cine Special 16mm camera and began traveling from town to town, over a hundred of them, in North and South Carolina, Virginia, and Tennessee. In each town he would negotiate with the manager of the local movie theater to rent the building for a night for what he called *Movies of Local People*. The manager would help advertise the day Waters would be photographing in the town. Waters would bring the processed film back about two weeks later.

In order to get the largest possible audience, Waters needed to film as many people as he could. He typically shot at schools, outside mills and factories, and along main streets. Waters made a point of filming businesses as well, hoping their owners would recognize the value of advertising. When it came time to show the films to his customers, Waters used a state-of-the-art Bell & Howell FilmO Arc projector with a rectifier, a set-up that would give his work a professional look that compared favorably to Hollywood product.

According to documentarian Tom Whiteside, Waters projected everything he filmed, editing only in the sense that he was splicing rolls of film together, or to remove footage that was exposed improperly. Every screening was like a Hollywood preview: Waters was right there with the audience, discovering what they liked and didn't like, what worked and didn't work. Waters' style evolved as he went from town to town. He began to use trick photography, like reversing action or speeding it up, and to incorporate flourishes like dissolves.

Waters' great strength was his understanding of people, his feel for individuals and their defining characteristics. He grew up with millworkers and could gain their trust; he also knew how to deal with professionals, local politicians, policemen, and businessmen. And from his portrait work he knew how to depict his customers at their best. What is most striking about his films may be the trust his subjects share with him. Some people are embarrassed, hurrying past the camera with their faces hidden, but almost no one displays any annoyance or impatience.

Whiteside, who directed *The Cameraman Has Visited Our Town* (1989), a documentary about Waters, has noted that for most people in these towns, this was their first opportunity to see themselves on film. They display an openness and curiosity about Waters and what he is doing. The schoolchildren, shot in close-ups that would have placed Waters and his camera in their midst, are especially appealing. But all of the footage has a hypnotic quality, a sense that we are being given a window into a past stripped of cynicism and pretense. The automobiles, billboards, window displays, and other glimpses of day-to-day life are fascinating in their own right, but it is the people—parents, children, workers, students—who give Waters' films their flavor and charm.

Waters shot mostly in black-and-white, with color used sparingly because of its expense and exposure requirements. He also shot mostly outside, in sunlight. He preferred shooting in smaller towns, like Pittsboro or Scotland Neck, North Carolina. In a big city like Durham, Waters would have to compete with a half-dozen or so movie theaters.

About thirty miles from Charlotte, Kannapolis grew up around the Cannon Mills, in the 1930s a world leader in home textile products. It was a company town, with the hospital and police department provided by the Cannon family. (Cannon merged with Fieldcrest in 1985; Fieldcrest Cannon was purchased by the Pillowtex Corporation in 1997. Pillowtex closed the Kannapolis mill in 2003, laying off some 4,800 workers. The mill itself was demolished in 2006.) While he was there, Waters shot over two hours of film, about a third of it in color. He filmed in what was called "Fishtown," a predominately black area; this material makes up almost a third of the footage. Since Kannapolis was segregated, Waters showed his film in both white and black theaters.

Waters retained the rights to his films, but many of them were scattered by the time of his death in 1997. Several have been collected at the Duke University Rare Book, Manuscript, and Special Collections Library. Visual Materials Archivist Karen Glynn said that $100,000 is needed to archive and preserve Waters' films, some of which are still turning up.

Woman of the Year

MGM, 1942. Sound, B&W, 1.37. 114 minutes.

Cast: Spencer Tracy (Sam Craig), Katharine Hepburn (Tess Harding), Fay Bainter (Ellen Whitcomb), Reginald Owen (Clayton), Minor Watson (William J. Harding), William Bendix ("Pinkie" Peters), Gladys Blake (Flo Peters), Dan Tobin (Gerald Howe), Roscoe Karns (Phil Whittaker), William Tannen (Ellis), Ludwig Stossel (Dr. Lubbeck), Sara Haden (Matron), Edith Evanson (Alma), George Kezas (Chris).

Credits: Directed by George Stevens. Original screen play by Ring Lardner, Jr., and Michael Kanin. Produced by Joseph L. Mankiewicz. Director of photography: Joseph Ruttenberg. Musical score: Franz Waxman. Recording director: Douglas Shearer. Art director: Cedric Gibbons. Associate art director: Randall Duell. Set decorations: Edwin B. Willis. Gowns by Adrian. Hair styles by Sydney Guilaroff. Film editor: Frank Sullivan. Western Electric Sound System.

Additional Cast: Jack Carr (Baseball spectator), Jimmy Conlin (Reporter), Ben Lessy (Punchy).

Additional Credits: Screenwriting by John Lee Mahin. Production dates: August 27 to October 21, 1941; additional scenes: December 1941. Premiered in New York City on February 5, 1942.

Awards: Oscar for Best Screenplay—Original Writing.

Other Versions: Remade as *Woman of the Year* (1976), directed by Jud Taylor, starring Joseph Bologna and Renée Taylor; adapted into the Broadway musical *Woman of the Year* (1984).

Available: Warner Home Video DVD (2000). ISBN: 0-7907-4491-0. UPC: 0-12569-50972-6.

When *The Philadelphia Story* turned out to be MGM's biggest film of 1940, Katharine Hepburn, its star, signed a contract with the studio that gave her control over her cast, directors, and even her projects. She showed an outline for a script to Louis B. Mayer, who asked producer Joseph L. Mankiewicz for his opinion. Mankiewicz thought it was good enough to have been ghostwritten by Ben Hecht and Charles MacArthur, and advised Mayer to pay the $100,000 Hepburn was asking.

Ring Lardner, Jr., and Michael Kanin received screenwriting credits for *Woman of the Year*, but Hepburn said that the idea for the story came from Kanin's younger brother Garson. He had struck upon a formula for Hepburn movies: "A high-class, or stuck-up, or hoity-toity girl is brought down to earth by an earthly type or a lowbrow or a diamond in the rough, or a cataclysmic situation." He thought the formula could be applied to a character like journalist Dorothy Thompson, but he was preparing to enter the Signal Corps (he later made documentaries for the Office of Strategic Services), and did not have time to write a screenplay. Michael Kanin had been a commercial artist and musician before becoming a screenwriter for RKO. Lardner, the son of a noted journalist and the brother of three writers, all of whom died young, dropped out of college to see the world. He ended up studying at the University of Moscow before returning to New York, where he became a reporter. A job as a publicist for David O. Selznick turned into script-writing assignments on films like *A Star Is Born* and *Nothing Sacred* (both 1937). That same year, Lardner officially joined the Communist Party.

The script Lardner and Kanin turned in to MGM was a literate, contemporary, adult romance that dealt with the balance of power in relationships; at the same time, it gave its leads plenty of opportunities for glamorous outfits, physical slapstick, and movie idol close-ups. For Hepburn, *Woman of the Year* was almost a continuation of *The Philadelphia Story*. While she would never again play a society heiress, her Tess Harding is the equivalent of an heiress who either out of duty or necessity is working for a living.

To direct *Woman of the Year*, Hepburn chose George Stevens. They had worked together before on *Alice Adams* (1935), perhaps the best of Hepburn's early films. Stevens was developing a style of long takes and tight close-ups that resulted in a physical frankness and seductiveness that was far beyond the work of his peers. Stevens had found out how to depict people who were attracted to each other. A sense of intimacy, of yearning, is pervasive in his films of this period. As his son, George Stevens, Jr., has noted, "My father never wanted to work at MGM. He thought it was a producer's studio where the department heads decided what the photography was going to be like. Hepburn called him and asked him to do it, so he did it as a one-shot for Kate." What Stevens gave Hepburn was the chance to act without holding back, without the reserve she displayed with other directors. Hepburn could be as unappealing, as mean as she wanted, knowing that Stevens wouldn't let the audience hate her. (Stevens is also responsible for the excellent supporting work done by a rogues' gallery of character actors, including William Bendix as a slaphappy bartender and Roscoe Karns and Jimmy Conlin as caustic reporters.)

Hepburn had wanted to work with Spencer Tracy in *The Philadelphia Story*, and asked for him again as *Woman of the Year* was being prepared. But he was committed to *The Yearling*, an adaptation of the Marjorie Kinnan Rawlings novel. When that production was postponed (for another five years), Tracy agreed to Hepburn's project. A number of versions of their first meeting have circulated through the years. The Hepburn-authorized account has Mankiewicz and Hepburn walking out of the Thalberg Building and bumping into Tracy. "Mr. Tracy, I think you're a little short for me," Hepburn said. "Don't worry, Kate," quipped Mankiewicz, "he'll cut you down to size."

Cutting Hepburn down to size was the entire point of *Woman of the Year*, as it was for most of her successful vehicles. What no one expected was the affair that sprung up between Tracy and Hepburn, an attraction that was palpable on screen. Even though "Spencer thought I had dirty fingernails," as Hepburn commented later, theirs became one of the most enduring and popular relationships in Hollywood, an open secret (since Tracy remained married) for over twenty-seven years (and eight more films).

Hepburn received another Oscar nomination for Best Actress, while Lardner and Kanin won for Best Writing—Original Screenplay. At the awards ceremony they refused to acknowledge Mankiewicz, who in their opinion had cheapened their script by hiring John Lee Mahin to write a new ending. In the original, Hepburn reconciles with Tracy by writing a sentimental, apologetic article under his byline. In the new version, Hepburn tries to cook Tracy breakfast, failing miserably. Stevens directed it as the equivalent of a one-reel silent comedy, as in his old Laurel and Hardy days.

Kanin worked with Lardner again, but predominately collaborated with his wife, Fay Mitchell, on plays and screenplays. Stevens would direct *The More the Merrier* (1943) before entering the armed services. Lardner entered the Army Signal Corps, and after the war signed a contract with Fox. He was blacklisted after refusing to cooperate with the House Un-American Activities Committee.

Knowing Lardner's career, is it possible to read something more into *Woman of the Year*? Does the arrival of a Greek orphan refugee send a message? Is it subversive to suggest that celebrity might not be satisfying? "Responsibility," one of the bywords of the film—is that subversive as well? At one point, Fay Bainter, playing a spinster aunt, says to Hepburn, "You can't live alone in this world, Tess. It's no fun." Decoding lines like this for evidence of Communist propaganda shows how misguided the witch hunt could be.

Woman of the Year was remade as a television movie in 1976, and adapted into a Broadway musical. But its real influence was on the romantic comedies that followed. Garson Kanin returned to the subject and style with *Adam's Rib* (1949, a Registry title). Even as inconsequential a film as *The Egg and I* (1947) worked on the principle of cutting its star, Claudette Colbert, down to size.

Tulips Shall Grow

Tulips Shall Grow: In George Pal's stop-motion method, each facial expression required a different sculpture.

Paramount, 1942. Sound, color, 1.37. 7 minutes.
Credits: Directed by George Pal.
Additional Credits: Released January 26, 1942.
Available: Image Entertainment DVD, *The Puppetoon Movie* (2000).
UPC: 0-14381-5865-2-7.

Before computers, animated film came in two versions: hand-drawn and stop-motion. Hand-drawn films were necessarily labor intensive, although various time-saving techniques and devices took hold over the years. They offered several advantages over stop-motion. For one thing, animators could draw anything they wanted to. They weren't limited by the size and number of characters or sets, by the difficulty in changing perspectives, by lighting or production design or all the other demands of real-life cinematography. Another bonus: if an individual drawing or even a sequence of motion didn't work, the animator could replace it fairly easily.

Stop-motion animation worked on a different principle. It basically took moving pictures back to its origins as still photography, using a succession of single exposures in which elements were adjusted slightly in each frame to simulate movement. It was the method behind the earliest trick and novelty films, and can be seen in everything from *The Great Train Robbery* (1903) to time-lapse photography collages like *Koyaanisqatsi* (1983). Once filmmakers learned that they could use stop motion to move inanimate objects like desks and automobiles, it was a small step to utilizing the process to animate cutouts and puppets.

In films like *The Cameraman's Revenge* (1912), the Polish animator Ladislas Starevich made wonderful, intricate fantasies that moved costumed insects through miniature sets. His work was shown throughout Europe, and influenced artists like the German-born Lotte Reiniger, whose *The Adventures of Prince Achmed* (1926) is considered by some the first feature-length animated film; and Oskar Fischinger, whose career is covered in *Motion Painting No. 1* (1947).

George Pal was born in Cegléd, Hungary, in 1908. The son of noted Hungarian actors, he studied architecture before becoming a commercial artist. At the Hunnia Films studio in Budapest, Pal learned about animation from an American editor, George Feld. In 1930, he married Zsoka Grandjean; the following year they moved to Berlin, where Pal became head of the animation department at the UFA studio. He made his first animation featuring puppets, a cigarette ad, in 1932. Pal fled Germany before the Nazis came to power, opening an animation studio in Holland in 1935. There he made advertising films for Philips Radio and Horlicks Malted Milk, among other clients.

Pal's films used handmade puppets positioned on painted plywood sets. The bodies were carved from wood, the limbs fashioned out of rubber. Since the puppets at first were solid, with no moving parts, individual models had to be built for each stage of whatever action they had to perform, including changing facial expressions. Generally Pal needed twenty-eight versions of each character. When you consider that up to thirty-eight different puppet characters might appear at the same time, the work involved in filming Pal's advertisements was staggering. But the results were astonishing. Pal's films had a solid, physical reality missing from hand-drawn cartoons, yet they shared the same buoyant humor and pacing found in Walt Disney's *Silly Symphonies* series.

Animator Walter Lantz helped Pal obtain U.S. citizenship when he was hired by Paramount in December 1939. Pal built a staff of twenty-five effects artists, including at one time or another Willis O'Brien and Ray Harryhausen. His goal was to produce between four and six Puppetoons a year. Each one took six weeks of preparation, six weeks of shooting, and six weeks of postproduction. By now he was working with armature puppets, which made it easier to position and move their arms and legs. However, he was also paying stricter attention to synchronized dialogue. Each word a character said might require nine different heads, and each main role might need between one hundred and two hundred heads.

Scripts would be worked out by Pal and story sketch artist Jack Miller. While the musical score was composed and recorded, sketches would be filmed to give woodworkers a guide for carving figures. The puppets were then animated against cardboard and papier-mâché sets. At first each Puppetoon was a "one-shot" film, with new characters and sets. Then Pal introduced recurring characters, like Jasper, "a black version of Huckleberry Finn" who starred in fourteen films. Among the most famous of the Puppetoon characters is *Tubby the Tuba* (1947), based on the 1945 hit song written by Paul Tripp and George Kleinsinger and performed by Danny Kaye.

Tulips Shall Grow was unusual for its time because it took such a strong political stand. "I made *Tulips Shall Grow* because I was furious at the Nazis for what they did to Holland," Pal said later. As to why the film didn't receive an Oscar, he explained, "In those days, they thought cartoons and Puppetoons had to be funny. I didn't think it was necessary to be funny—it could be meaningful." The Screwball Army from *Tulips Shall Grow* made a second appearance in *Bravo Mr. Strauss* (1943), in which the composer takes a Pied Piper role to protect the Vienna Woods.

Pal did receive an honorary Oscar in 1943 "for the development of novel methods and technique in the production of short subjects known as Puppetoons." However, it was as a live-action filmmaker that he is best known today. He won five Oscars as a producer, director, and special effects supervisor, and is regarded by some as "the father of science fiction" for his work on films like *Destination Moon* (1950), *War of the Worlds* (1953), and *The Time Machine* (1960).

Some of the forty-two Puppetoons, including *Tulips Shall Grow*, have been preserved by the UCLA Film & Television Archive.

Jam Session

Soundies Distributing Corporation, 1942. Sound, B&W, 1.37. 3 minutes.

Featuring: Duke Ellington and His Orchestra: Ray Nance (violin), Rex Stewart (trumpet), Ben Webster (saxophone), Joe Nanton (trombone), Barney Bigard (clarinet), Sonny Greer (drums), Fred Guy (guitar), Jimmy Blanton (bass), Duke Ellington (piano).

Credits: Directed by Joseph [Josef] Berne. Produced by Sam Coslow. An R.C.M. Production. Song "C Jam Blues" written by Duke Ellington and Barney Bigard.

Additional Credits: Musical director: Lud Gluskin. Casting director: Ben Chapman. Production manager: Herman Webber. Released February 16, 1942.

Available: The Library of Congress. The five Ellington Soundies are featured on *Duke Ellington: Early Tracks from the Master of Swing*, A CDCard Company DVD (2004, www.collectordirect.com).

Producers have tried to connect musicians and filmmakers since the earliest days of sound movies. In fact, musicians initially did more to popularize sound technology than dramatic features did. By 1929, every major studio and several independent production houses were making musical shorts featuring nightclub, radio, and recording artists.

In their history of the Soundies Distributing Corporation, Maurice Terenzio, Scott MacGillivray, and Ted Okuda cite a dentist in Los Angeles who in 1938 developed the "Cinematone," the first attempt to combine jukeboxes with movie projectors. Two years later, the Mills Novelty Company, the country's largest jukebox manufacturer, and James Roosevelt, the son of President Franklin Delano Roosevelt, formed Globe-Mills Productions to market the "Panoram."

The Panoram was a tall, wooden cabinet that housed a 16mm RCA projector. It ran eight hundred feet of film, enough for roughly eight three-minute songs, on a loop. The movies were reflected off two mirrors and then back-projected onto a ground-glass screen. Each performance cost a dime, although customers had to cycle through all eight songs rather than pick a particular number. Globe-Mills rather optimistically hoped to sell 100,000 Panorams to bars and restaurants; at the height of its popularity, there were approximately 4,500 Panorams operating commercially.

Globe-Mills split into two production companies in 1940, with Roosevelt operating under Globe Productions and the Mills's film company renamed "The Soundies Distributing Corporation of America." The Soundies program of eight songs would be changed once and sometimes twice a week. There was consequently tremendous pressure for material, especially since competitors like Vis-o-graph and Phonofilms started marketing their own proprietary jukebox systems.

Soundies were produced by Cinemasters (later Minoco Productions) in New York City; and by two companies, Fredrick Fehler Productions and Cameo Productions, in Los Angeles. The latter used two main directors, Roy Mack and Josef Berne, and was managed by Sam Coslow, a fairly well-known songwriter. (Among his compositions were "Just One More Chance" and "My Old Flame.") When Roosevelt joined the Marine Corps in 1941, Coslow became the major salesman for Soundies.

Only seven Soundies were filmed in 1940. By the end of 1941, eight new Soundies were available every week. Few were photographed live. The standard procedure was to record the music in the morning, then film the performers lip-synching lyrics and miming the playing of their instruments in the afternoon. Unless the musicians were major stars, sets and costumes were necessarily utilitarian, and little attempt was made to provide a narrative framework for the numbers.

The war effort, with its demand for raw materials, damaged plans to expand Soundies. Even worse was the ban on recorded music announced by James Petrillo, president of the American Federation of Musicians, to start in August 1942. Earlier in 1942, Coslow formed R.C.M. Productions with James Roosevelt and Gordon Mills. The staff included Berne and Dudley Murphy, who had directed the Registry films like *St. Louis Blues* (1929) and *The Emperor Jones* (1934).

Murphy also directed *Black and Tan* (1929), Duke Ellington's first film appearance. Born Edward Kennedy Ellington in 1899, the Duke was by 1942 one of the most highly regarded jazz musicians in the country. He was also the veteran of several movie appearances in shorts and features. He had met Coslow as early as 1926, when both were working with agent Irving Mills, and at some point in 1941 agreed to make five Soundies.

Jazz fans consider the first, *Hot Chocolate*, released on December 31, 1941, to be the best; it featured a performance of "Cottontail" and dancing by Arthur White's Lindy Hoppers. Ellington made two Soundies on January 5, 1942: *Bli-Blip*, extracted by his musical revue *Jump for Joy*, and *Flamingo*. Vocalist Ivie Anderson was featured in January 19's *I Got It Bad and That Ain't Good*. *Jam Session* came out about a month later, and showcased Ellington and a half-dozen of his musicians playing the instrumental "C-Jam Blues." The band had recorded the studio version of the song in Chicago on January 21, so the film was an opportunity to cross-promote the record release. Like *Hot Chocolate*, *Jam Session* offers fans tantalizing glimpses of what many consider the best band line-up Ellington ever led. Ellington's band would appear on screen again, notably in *Cabin in the Sky* (1943), but the Soundies performances are crucial for portraying the musicians in more relaxed, lifelike settings.

R.C.M. would win an Oscar in 1943 for *Heavenly Music*, a celestial debate between classical and jazz musicians, and Soundies would continue to be produced until the end of 1946. But the process could never compete successfully with music jukeboxes, which patrons used primarily for dancing and romancing. You had to watch Soundies, and you often had to wait to see the song you wanted. When television began making inroads in bars, Panorams were doomed.

Ironically, 1950s processes like the Snader and Studio Telescriptions adapted Soundies methods for television broadcasts. A decade later, Scopitone briefly revived the idea of video jukeboxes. For musical historians, these shorts sometimes provide the only visual record of performers. A few Soundies were repackaged as feature films, but the more obscure titles are extremely difficult to track down. Country songs and ethnic titles, including Hawaiian music and polkas, are especially hard to find.

To Be or Not to Be

United Artists, 1942. Sound, B&W, 1.37. 99 minutes
Cast: Carole Lombard (Maria Tura), Jack Benny (Joseph Tura), Robert Stack (Lieut. Stanislav Sobinski), Felix Bressart (Greenberg), Lionel Atwill (Rawitch), Stanley Ridges (Professor Siletsky), Sig Ruman (Col. Ehrhardt), Tom Dugan (Bronski), Charles Halton (Producer Dobosh), George Lynn (Actor-Adjutant), Henry Victor (Capt. Schultz), Maude Eburne (Anna), Halliwell Hobbes (Gen. Armstrong), Miles Mander (Major Cunningham).
Credits: Produced and directed by Ernst Lubitsch. Screenplay by Edwin Justus Mayer. Original story by Melchior Lengyel. Executive producer: Alexander Korda. Photographed by Rudolph Maté. Production designed by Vincent Korda. Musical score by Werner R. Heymann. Production manager: Walter Mayo. Technical supervision: Richard Ordynski. Special effects by Lawrence Butler. Interior decoration: Julia Heron. Associate art director: J. MacMillan Johnson. Miss Lombard's costumes: Irene. Sound: Frank Maher. Film editor: Dorothy Spencer. Makeup artist: Gordon Bau. Casting director: Victor Stuker. Assistant directors: William Tummel, William McGarry. Western Electric Recording.
Additional Cast: James Finlayson (Scottish farmer), Helmut Dantine (Co-pilot).
Additional Credits: Opened March 6, 1942.
Other Versions: Remade as *To Be or Not to Be* (1983), starring Mel Brooks, Anne Bancroft.
Available: Warner Home Video DVD (2005). ISBN: 0-7907-9003-3. UPC: 0-85393-19762-9.

After finishing *The Shop Around the Corner* (1940) at MGM, director Ernst Lubitsch formed a production company with Sol Lesser, a producer best known for a series of Westerns starring George O'Brien. Lesser in turn signed a five-picture deal with United Artists, which was contingent on delivering a Lubitsch picture. They started with *That Uncertain Feeling*, a remake of one of Lubitsch's silent films, but it was not a happy experience for the director. When the film did poorly at the box office, Lubitsch signed a contract with Twentieth Century-Fox in March 1941.

He still owed a film to United Artists, and turned to a script he had started working on with Melchior Lengyel, his collaborator on *Ninotchka*. Lubitsch originally saw *To Be or Not To Be* as a comeback vehicle for Maurice Chevalier, a French singer and actor who had had a short career in Hollywood at the beginning of the sound era. When it became clear that Chevalier could not leave France, Lubitsch turned his attention to Jack Benny.

Born Benjamin Kubelsky in 1894, Benny played violin in a vaudeville theater orchestra after he was thrown out of high school. He toured the country in two vaudeville acts before entering the Navy for a year. By that point he was concentrating on comedy more than music, deriving his humor from the pauses in his delivery. By the end of the 1920s he was a top vaudeville performer. He married Sadie Marks in 1927; as "Mary Livingstone," she became a crucial part of his later act.

Benny appeared in a few film shorts and features, but he was a surprisingly unappealing presence on screen. It was only after he started a radio show in 1932 that he perfected the "Jack Benny" character. As writer Ted Sennett noted, Benny's persona was almost entirely negative. He played a vain, insecure skinflint who was thoughtless or cruel to everyone around him; a relentlessly demanding blowhard and coward who was easily taken advantage of by dates, shopkeepers, and his own staff. Lubitsch saw him as a Polish ham, a talentless, cuckolded actor working in Warsaw on the eve of the Nazi invasion.

Having broken with his longtime collaborator Samson Raphaelson, Lubitsch hired Edwin Justus Mayer, who had worked on his *Desire* in 1936, to rewrite the script. Mayer brought a more sophisticated world view than Raphaelson, but this was clearly Lubitsch's project, and his input was considerable.

Lubitsch cast Miriam Hopkins to play Benny's wife, but she objected to what she perceived as a small part. Benny pushed for Carole Lombard, who was anxious to work with Lubitsch. One of Hollywood's biggest stars, Lombard slowed her career when she married Clark Gable in 1939. She threw herself wholeheartedly into *To Be or Not To Be*, endearing herself to the cast and crew with her spontaneity and warmth. As Maria Tura, wife of "that great, great Polish actor Joseph Tura," she is essentially playing a grown-up version of the spoiled, deceitful actress in *Twentieth Century* (1934), someone who thinks that a provocative evening gown is appropriate attire for a play about concentration camps.

Lubitsch gave Robert Stack, a relative newcomer, an important role as Lombard's admirer. A child of Hollywood, he had known Lombard for years. He later described Benny as innocent and insecure, worriedly trying out his lines on anyone who would listen. "He'd always ask me, 'Is it funny?' and I'd say, 'Jesus, don't ask me.' 'But you're an actor,' he'd say." The rest of the cast was filled with familiar character actors like Sig Ruman and Charles Halton. As in *The Shop Around the Corner*, it was the supporting players who got most of the laugh lines, and, in the case of Felix Bressart, the emotional moments as well.

Filming was scheduled to start in October 1941, with Lubitsch aiming to end by Thanksgiving. Because of the switch to Lombard, production didn't begin until early November. When Pearl Harbor was attacked on December 6, the entire project was suddenly in jeopardy. But Lubitsch insisted that American audiences could still appreciate a satire of Nazi aggression, even one that joked that a Gestapo officer was nicknamed "Concentration Camp Ehrhardt." Lubitsch shot for forty-two days; the most demanding may have been the day Benny needed thirty takes to perfect his reaction to finding Stack in Lombard's bed.

Lombard's last day on the project was New Year's Eve, when she sat for publicity photographs. She promised to appear on Benny's radio program before leaving with her mother on a bond-selling tour. On January 16, 1942, their plane left Indianapolis. It crashed outside Las Vegas that evening, with no survivors.

To Be or Not To Be was released in March 1942, the only change required being the deletion of a line by Lombard, "What could happen on a plane?" It received decidedly mixed reviews, with many critics objecting to the film's humorous treatment of Nazis and war in general. (In hindsight, *To Be or Not To Be* has many of the same gung-ho qualities as most of Hollywood's war efforts.) Stung, Lubitsch wrote a defensive article that appeared in the *New York Times* on March 29, 1942. "I was tired of the two established, recognized recipes," he wrote. "Drama with comedy relief and comedy with dramatic relief. I made up my mind to make a picture with no attempt to relieve anybody from anything at any time." He cited the W.C. Fields comedy *It's a Gift* (1934), which included a priceless bit with a blind-and-deaf customer in a grocery store. "I laughed and laughed," he wrote. "Then I realized there can be no rules. It must depend on how it is done."

This was the last significant film from Lubitsch. He directed two more entertaining trifles, then suffered a fatal heart attack while filming *That Lady in Ermine* in 1947. (It was finished by Otto Preminger.) Benny's film career, never spectacular, sputtered out in the 1940s, apart from occasional cameos. But he continued to enjoy remarkable success with his radio shows, which he transferred to a television series that lasted in various forms from 1950 to 1965. One of the most beloved comedians of his generation, Benny died at the age of eighty in 1974.

Yankee Doodle Dandy

Warner Bros., 1942. Sound, B&W, 1.37. 126 minutes.

Cast: James Cagney (George M. Cohan), Joan Leslie (Mary), Walter Huston (Jerry Cohan), Richard Whorf (Sam Harris), Irene Manning (Fay Templeton), George Tobias (Dietz), Rosemary DeCamp (Nellie Cohan), Jeanne Cagney (Josie Cohan), Frances Langford (Singer [Nora Bayes]), George Barbier (Erlanger), S.Z. Sakall (Schwab), Walter Catlett (Theater manager), Douglas Croft (George M. Cohan, as a boy of 13), Minor Watson (Albee), Eddie Foy, Jr. (Eddie Foy), Chester Clute (Goff), Odette Myrtil (Madame Bartholdi), Patsy Lee Parsons (Josie Cohan, as a girl of 12), Capt. Jack Young (The President).

Credits: Directed by Michael Curtiz. Screen play by Robert Buckner and Edmund Joseph. Original story by Robert Buckner. Based on the story of George M. Cohan. Lyrics and music by George M. Cohan. Executive producer: Hal B. Wallis. Associate producer: William Cagney. Director of photography: James Wong Howe. Dialogue director: Hugh MacMullan. Film editor: George Amy. Art director: Carl Jules Weyl. Montages by Don Siegel. Dance numbers staged and directed by Leroy Prinz and Seymour Felix. James Cagney's dances routined by John Boyle. Technical advisor: William Collier, Sr. Sound by Everett A. Brown. Makeup artist: Perc Westmore. Gowns by Milo Anderson. Orchestral arrangements: Ray Heindorf. Musical director: Leo F. Forbstein. RCA Sound System. A Warner Bros. Pictures presentation of a Warner Bros.–First National Picture.

Additional Cast: Pat Flaherty (White House guard), Henry Blair (George M. Cohan, age 7), Jo Ann Marlowe (Josie Cohen, age 6), Frank Faylen (Sergeant), Georgia Caine (Boarder); George Meeker, Frank Mayo (Hotel clerks); Creighton Hale (Telegraph operator); Spencer Charters, Thomas Jackson, William Davidson (Stage managers); Eddie Acuff, Walter Brooke, Bill Edwards, William Hopper (Reporters).

Additional Credits: Executive producer: Jack L. Warner. Screenwriting: Julius and Philip Epstein. Additional photography: Sol Polito. Sound recording: Nathan Levinson. Scoring: Heinz Roemheld. Production dates: December 3, 1941, to February 10, 1942. Premiered in New York City on May 29, 1942. General release: January 2, 1943.

Awards: Oscars for Best Actor, Music—Scoring of a Musical Picture, Sound—Recording.

Available: Warner Home Video DVD (2003). UPC: 012569504127.

Meant as a tribute to George M. Cohan, *Yankee Doodle Dandy* now functions as a showcase for its star, James Cagney. The subject may have seemed like a natural for Warner Brothers, which had gained prestige as well as revenue with biopics like *The Life of Emile Zola* (1936). As World War II occupied a larger part of the country's culture, Warners switched to American subjects like *Knute Rockne All American* (1940), which enabled the studio to make money and at the same time contribute to the war effort by boosting morale. But Cohan proved unexpectedly difficult to work with.

Born in 1878, Cohan was arguably America's first musical comedy star. He not only danced, sang, and acted, he wrote self-consciously American songs and plays about American subjects, although his reputation as a patriotic flag-waver has been blown out of proportion (largely by this film). From 1902 to 1921, he starred in and produced a string of successful Broadway plays, and was the prime inspiration for a generation of song-and-dance men.

James Cagney saw Cohan perform only once, and was turned down by the star when he auditioned for a show, but Cagney was so impressed that later in his career he trained with Cohan's occasional choreographer, Johnny Boyle. Few moviegoers in the 1930s thought of Cagney as a hoofer, although that's how the actor made his name on the New York stage. He was always intent on breaking free from his gangster persona, to the extent that he risked suspension from Warners to make a low-budget musical for its competitor Grand National.

Cohan had turned down earlier appeals to make a film of his life, but by 1940, dying of intestinal cancer, he tried to persuade Samuel Goldwyn to produce a biography starring Fred Astaire. When that failed, he signed a contract with Jack Warner, first getting assurances that Cagney could sing and dance. Warner assigned producer Hal Wallis, but according to Cagney biographer John McCabe, associate producer William Cagney (the actor's brother) took on most of the producing duties.

The first screenwriter, Robert Buckner, worked with Cohan for months on a script. (Cohan submitted his own screenplay as well.) Buckner wrote Wallis that he was flummoxed, both by Cohan's demands and by the lack of conflict in his life. Cohan prohibited details about his personal life (his first wife sued Warners for invasion of privacy anyway), finally agreeing to include a fictional "Mary" who could stand in for his various romances. Buckner characterized Cohan's public life as "very dull" in narrative terms. "The main feature of these years is simply that Cohan coined a fortune."

Buckner was even reluctant to concentrate on Cohan's plays, "purely products of their periods and all followed the same simple story formula—'A young man gets rich between 8:30 and 11 p.m.'" He fashioned a story line that showed Cohan's early life dancing with his family in The Four Cohans, and worked up a suitably patriotic ending. But Cagney was disappointed with the script, and insisted that Julius and Philip Epstein, the

Oscar-winning twins who helped write Casablanca (1942), work on it. (They received help from gag-writer Edmund Joseph, and negotiated for his screen credit.)

In the end, Cagney resisted a story about Cohan's life, opting to concentrate on his work instead. The film ignores Cohan's widely disliked antiunion stance, for example, and limits other personal information because, as Cagney put it, "It was a sad story."

The actor rehearsed his dancing with the cast for three weeks before production started. The first day of filming was December 8, 1941, the day President Roosevelt declared war. Although director Michael Curtiz had a reputation for pushing actors around, Joan Leslie, cast as Cohan's love interest "Mary" and seventeen at the time, remembers Cagney taking control of the set. The actor would rewrite scenes on the spot, choreograph routines with her, and defend other cast members from the director's outbursts.

As he wrote in his autobiography Cagney by Cagney, the actor's favorite scene in the film was a re-creation from Little Johnny Jones, featuring a version of "Give My Regards to Broadway." But the most demanding was a scene in which Cohan bids his dying father goodbye. (Walter Huston played the father; he had starred in a Cohan production, Elmer the Great, in the 1920s, and called Cohan one of the best stage directors he ever worked with.) Cagney was so effective that director Curtiz burst into tears behind the camera. The actor then had to repeat the moment five more times for close-ups and covering shots. At least one take was ruined when the script girl started sobbing. When the finished film was shown to Cohan's lawyer, Edward C. Raftery, for his approval, he started crying as well.

When Cohan screened Yankee Doodle Dandy, he said to his son, "My God, what an act to follow." The film's premiere, a benefit for war bonds, earned almost $5 million in one night. The critical response was overwhelmingly positive, and it went on to become one of the top-grossing movies of the year. Although Cagney won an Oscar for his performance, in one sense it was the end of his career as a movie star. He left Warners for his own production company, and his output dropped off markedly. (He did reprise his Cohan role briefly in The Seven Little Foys in 1955.) It wasn't until 1949 and White Heat, a Registry title, that he appeared in another significant film.

The Magnificent Ambersons

RKO, 1942. Sound, B&W, 1.33. 88 minutes.

Cast: Joseph Cotten (Eugene Morgan), Dolores Costello (Isabel Amberson), Anne Baxter (Lucy Morgan), Tim Holt (George Minafer), Agnes Moorehead (Fanny Minafer), Ray Collins ([Uncle] Jack Amberson), Richard Bennett (Major Amberson), Erskine Sanford (Roger Bronson), J. Louis Johnson (Sam the butler), Don Dillaway (Wilbur Minafer), Charles Phipps (Uncle John Minafer).

Credits: Written and directed by Orson Welles. Based on the novel by Booth Tarkington. Director of photography: Stanley Cortez. Set design: Mark-Lee Kirk. Set dresser: Al Fields. Film editor: Robert Wise. Assistant director: Freddie Fleck. Ladies' wardrobe: Edward Stevenson. Special effects: Vernon L. Walker. Sound recording: Bailey Fesler with James G. Stewart. RCA Sound System.

Additional Cast: Dorothy Vaughn (Mrs. Johnson), Ann O'Neal (Mrs. Foster); Elmer Jerome, Maynard Holmes, Edwin August, Jack Baxley, Harry Humphrey (Townspeople outside Amberson mansion); Jack Santoro (Barber); Lyle Clement, Joe Whitehead, Del Lawrence (Men in barber shop); Katherine Sheldon, Georgia Backus (Women in sewing room); Bobby Cooper (George as a boy), Heenan Elliott ("Terrorized" laborer); Drew Roddy (Elijah); Bert LeBaron, Jim Fawcet, Gil Perkins (Men idling in sunshine); Henry Rocquemore (Man in apron); Nina Gilbert, John Elliott (Guests at ball); Helen Thurston (Lucy's stunt person), Dave Sharp (George's stunt person), Jess Graves (Servant in dining room scene), Olive Ball (Mary the maid), Gus Schilling (Drugstore clerk), James Westerfield (Irish policeman), William Blees (Young driver at accident), Philip Morris (Second policeman), Orson Welles (Narrator).

Additional Credits: Produced by Orson Welles. Associate producers: Jack Moss, Richardson Wilson. Additional editing: Mark Robson. Music by Bernard Herrmann. Additional music: Roy Webb. Additional footage directed by Norman Foster, Robert Wise, Freddie Fleck, Joseph Cotten, Jack Moss. Makeup: Maurice Seiderman. Released July 10, 1942.

Other Versions: *The Magnificent Ambersons* (2002), a television version based on Welles' script and directed by Alfonso Arau.

Available: Turner Home Entertainment VHS (1996). ISBN: 0-7806-1430-5. UPC: 0-53939-63853-0.

As a follow-up to *Citizen Kane*, Orson Welles chose a novel by Booth Tarkington, *The Magnificent Ambersons*. Welles claimed that his father and the author were friends, and felt that characters in the novel referred to his own family. Although it exists only in a truncated form, the film is in many respects a more impressive work than *Kane*. It was also the last that Welles made under a contract with RKO that promised him complete artistic freedom.

Welles had already staged the novel in 1939 as an hour-long radio show starring himself, Walter Huston, and Huston's wife Nan Sunderland. RKO agreed to finance the film based in part on the radio show, and in part on the fact that the project that Welles had originally planned to make, an adaptation of Eric Ambler's spy thriller *Journey Into Fear*, was nowhere near ready to film. Welles's script for *Ambersons* was surprisingly faithful to the novel; he changed it primarily toward the end, assuming a darker tone than Tarkington had intended.

Robert L. Carringer, author of *The Magnificent Ambersons: A Reconstruction*, suggests that

Welles was uncomfortable playing George Amberson Minafer because the part was too close to his own life. He cast Tim Holt, a likable second lead who was the son of silent action star Jack Holt, instead. (At one point in *Ambersons* Holt passes in front of a poster for one of his father's films). Opposite him, as Lucy Morgan, Welles cast Anne Baxter, a relative newcomer to film. The granddaughter of architect Frank Lloyd Wright, Baxter was especially adept at capturing the coldness behind Lucy's flirtatious nature, a quality she shares with many other women in Welles' films. Dolores Costello, a silent star who was once married to John Barrymore, plays George Minafer's mother Isabel with a faded grace that presages her fate in the story. Agnes Moorehead, a Mercury Theater regular, appeared as George's spinster aunt Fanny. Her work is perhaps the most open and moving in the film, and Welles often makes her the focal point of compositions, even when she is not the center of a scene.

Welles used many of the same technicians from *Kane*, with the notable exception of Gregg Toland, who had enlisted in the Naval Photographic Service. Replacing him as cinematographer was Stanley Cortez, the brother of actor Ricardo Cortez; he had started out in still photography as an assistant to Edward Steichen. It was his first big-budget picture, which makes the film's complex visual scheme all the more remarkable.

Welles biographer Simon Callow points out that as filming on *Ambersons* started on October 28, 1941, Welles was also overseeing production in Mexico of a short film called *Bonito the Bull,* as well as appearing on a CBS radio series, *The Lady Esther Show.* At times, Welles resorted to recording his directions to actors on disc, to be played back when he was absent. But he devoted his full attention to the film's centerpiece, a twenty-minute ball sequence that took nine days to shoot. Both Welles and Cortez claimed inspiration for the idea to film the ball as "a symphony of movement." The camera (remarkably for the time, a handheld one) glides in and out of sets, up and down stairs, between and around actors, giddy like everyone at the crush and opulence of the ball, but still determined to keep a graceful reserve. Welles needed a crew of over a hundred to capture the scene.

Yet it's the simple moments in *Ambersons* that have the most resonance. A kitchen scene in which Moorehead exposes her character's delusions while Holt gamely eats cake is as stark as Ingmar Bergman. Welles' narration (taken at times word-for-word from the novel) is marked by loss and melancholy, by regret and remorse. The shift from sunny frivolity, from a Currier and Ives–hued nostalgia for the past, to a grimy, dystopian present, is one reason why *Ambersons* has always had trouble finding an audience.

A month after filming started, Welles showed an hour of footage to RKO chief George Schaefer, who was so impressed that he scheduled *The Magnificent Ambersons* to open at Radio City Music Hall over the Easter weekend in 1942. But after the attack on Pearl Harbor, and the country's subsequent entry into war, the atmosphere at the studio changed. When RKO ordered filming to start on *Journey Into Fear*, it meant many of the *Ambersons* cast and crew would be working on two pictures a day. Principal photography was completed on January 22, 1942. Welles finally finished work on *Ambersons* on February 5, 1942, when he recorded the narration in a studio in Miami. Then he left the country for Brazil to make a film for the war effort, ostensibly leaving Jack Moss, formerly a manager with the Mercury Theater, in charge of the film. Welles hoped to be able to oversee Robert Wise's editing through cables and telephone calls.

By the end of February *The Magnificent Ambersons* had yet to be edited, even though it was scheduled to be released in the beginning of April. *Kane* had lost money, RKO's other big films at the time had lost money, and the studio badly needed a hit. From a continent away, Welles slowly lost control of the film. In March, studio executives ran a sneak preview of a 131-minute version in Pomona, California, following an Eddie Bracken musical, *The Fleet's In*. Reaction was overwhelmingly negative. As Schaefer wrote to Welles, "It was like getting one sock in the jaw after another for over two hours."

Carringer argues that Welles deliberately sabotaged the project. Immediately before the Pomona screening, he ordered Wise to remove thirteen crucial minutes from the movie, and to shoot a new scene to cover the omission. What Welles wanted out was the material that made most explicit George's Oedipal conflict with his mother and Eugene. In Carringer's opinion, the scenes were too close to Welles' own childhood for the public to see. The second preview screening in Pasadena came off much better than the first; by that time, Wise had reinserted as much of the footage as he dared.

In the eyes of Schaefer, nothing worked. It wasn't just audiences and studio executives who disliked the film. Wise complained at length about its faults, and even Joseph Cotten felt it was "more Chekhov than Tarkington." A new ending was shot, much of Bernard Herrmann's score was replaced by RKO composer Roy Webb, and in the end the film ran a mere eighty-eight minutes. RKO released it as the second-half of a double bill with *Mexican Spitfire Sees a Ghost*, starring Lupe Velez.

Parts of the film today seem prosaic, especially the tacked-on, inconsequential ending. But there is no denying the power of *The Magnificent Ambersons*—in particular, the sense of bitterness and loss that pervades the film. It stands today as the most mature, the least cynical or manipulative, of all Welles' films. It cost close to a million dollars to make; RKO later wrote it off as a $625,000 loss. Schaefer was forced out of his job; Welles would never again be given complete control of a Hollywood film.

Now, Voyager

Warner Bros., 1942. Sound, B&W, 1.37. 117 minutes.

Cast: Bette Davis (Charlotte Vale), Paul Henreid (Jeremiah "J.D." Durrance), Claude Rains (Dr. Jaquith), Gladys Cooper (Mrs. Henry Vale), Bonita Granville (June Vale), John Loder (Elliot Livingston), Ilka Chase (Lisa Vale) Lee Patrick (Deb McIntyre), Franklin Pangborn (Thompson), Katherine [Katharine] Alexander (Miss Trask), James Rennie (Frank McIntyre), Mary Wickes (Nurse Dora Pickford).

Credits: Directed by Irving Rapper. Screenplay by Casey Robinson. From the novel by Olive Higgins Prouty. A Hal B. Wallis production. Director of photography: Sol Polito. Music by Max Steiner. Dialogue director: Edward Blatt. Film editor: Warren Low. Sound by Robert B. Lee. Art director: Robert Haas.

Special effects: Willard Van Enger. Montages by Don Siegel. Set decorations by Fred M. MacLean. Gowns by Orry-Kelly. Makeup artist: Perc Westmore. Orchestral arrangements: Hugo Friedhofer. Musical director: Leo F. Forbstein. RCA Sound System. A Warner Bros./First National Picture.

Additional Cast: Charles Drake (Leslie Trotter), Lester Matthews (Captain), Frank Puglia (Giuseppe/Manoel).

Additional Credits: Production dates: April 7 to June 23, 1942. Reshoots: July 1942. Released October 31, 1942.

Awards: Oscar for Best Music—Scoring of a Dramatic or Comedy Picture.

Available: Warner Home Video DVD (2005). ISBN: 1-4198-1086-3. UPC: 0-12569-67539-1.

By the start of World War II, Warner Brothers was one of the most efficient of the Hollywood studios, turning out musicals, comedies, Westerns, thrillers, and romances that found favor with moviegoers, if not always with critics. Once you have the machine up and running, how do you keep supplying product to theaters? Like most studios, Warners used brute force in the early 1930s, insisting that contract players appear in vehicle after vehicle, no matter what the quality. Few actors were as vehemently, openly rebellious to Warners tactics than James Cagney and Bette Davis, both of whom were suspended for failing to appear in scheduled productions. Cagney even left the studio for a while, while Davis fled to England to avoid working in subpar movies.

Forced back to Warners by a court decision, Davis still tried to exert control over her career. She began working with Casey Robinson, a writer who had been one of the architects of the successful swashbuckler *The Sea Hawk* (1935). Robinson had grown in importance at the studio until he could advise producer Hal Wallis on casting, editing, and dealing with Joseph Breen at the Production Office. Robinson worked on several of the films that brought Davis new acclaim, in particular *Dark Victory* and *The Old Maid*. (They did a total of six together.)

If they could, Warner executives would have sold the same film over and over again. Instead they sought material that was the same, only different—stories in which Davis could play a victim while still falling in love and modeling the latest fashions. Warners' readers turned to plays and novels for ideas, aware that other studios were doing the same for stars like Norma Shearer, Irene Dunne, and Ginger Rogers. (In fact, all three stars were considered at one time or another for this project.)

Now, Voyager was based on a novel by Olive Higgins Prouty, whose *Stella Dallas* had been a success both as silent and sound films. The book starts with Charlotte Vale (played by Davis) emerging as a social butterfly after years of mental abuse at the hands of her mother (Gladys Cooper), matriarch of a prominent Boston family. Prouty suggested filming the book as a partial silent, with subtitles and a male narrator, to handle a plot riddled with flashbacks. Robinson, himself an expert in flashbacks, discarded Prouty's suggestions and played the story relatively straight.

Prouty and Robinson used psychiatry as a plot device, a toy that enabled them to justify the cruel emotional manipulations that Charlotte undergoes. Offering the mother as a villain was a new narrative twist. Emphasizing the mother, expertly played by Gladys Cooper, allowed the filmmakers to disguise the fact that Charlotte enters into an adulterous affair with J.D. Durrance (Henreid), a married architect, a potentially censorable plot development.

The title of the novel and film came from the Walt Whitman poem "The Untold Want." ("Now, voyager, sail thou forth, to seek and find.") Prouty chose it because she felt it would make the novel easier to sell, not out of any affinity for the poet or his themes. That same combination of innocence and pretension marks the film itself, which simultaneously wants to be a serious drama and a heavy-breathing potboiler.

According to a 1982 interview with director Irving Rapper, the film was originally planned for Michael Curtiz, who fell ill. (Edmund Goulding had worked on a screenplay in hopes of directing it himself.) Born in London in 1898, Rapper moved as a youth to New York City and was on stage by the age of eight. He entered films as a dialogue coach for Curtiz and William Dieterle, who "liked to consult astrological charts to see how a scene should be played." Rapper's first assignment as a director was *Shining Victory* (1941), based on an A.J. Cronin novel. After *One Foot in Heaven* (1941), adapted by Casey Robinson, Rapper worried that he would be typecast as a director of "inspirational" material. But it received a Best Picture Oscar nomination, and indicated that Rapper might have the stamina to handle the mercurial Davis.

"I immediately recast some of the parts," Rapper said after getting the assignment. He replaced Dame May Whitty with Cooper, added Ilka Chase and Bonita Granville, and tried to hire Charles Boyer instead of Henreid. Shooting took place largely on sets left over from other Warners films. (Many of the actors seem like leftovers as well: Sam Spade's secretary shows up on a liner to Rio, and the Casablanca chief of police opens a sanitarium in Vermont.) In a May 5, 1942, memo to Hal Wallis, Robinson suggested reshooting several scenes, in particular a moment in which Charlotte accepts Durrance despite his marriage. Wallis agreed, and further reshoots took place on July 3, after the main production had wrapped.

When it was released, the film received mixed reviews. *Time* called it "Warner Bros.' solemn contribution to the study of the mother complex," adding "the picture often succeeds (in the course of two hours) in looking like the moving and intelligent drama it thinks it is." It was a commercial success in one of the industry's best years, and it has been embraced in subsequent years by several groups of fans. For homosexuals, it became an example of the coded context of secret affairs, of hidden pasts and closeted love. Feminists describe the film as an "initiation" or "coming of age" story. Semiologists decode the use of cigarettes as sexual signifier.

Cigarettes are both a substitute for and an indication of sex in *Now, Voyager*, and the film's signature moment—Henreid lighting two cigarettes at once—has sparked its own controversy. Prouty had a cigarette-lighting ritual in the novel that was too cumbersome to film. Actor George Brent said he was taught the gesture Henreid used by director Alfred Green for *The Rich Are Always With Us* (1932). In interviews, Rapper said that the

idea might have been stolen from an Allan Dwan silent. Coupled with the film's famous closing line, "Don't let's ask for the moon—we have the stars," it is a gesture both foolish and morosely romantic.

One more cog in the Warners studio machinery was composer Max Steiner. Although Davis later complained about his score for *Now, Voyager*, calling it too intrusive, Steiner's music had the effect of tying the material together, making it seem like the railroad station set and the passenger liner set and the poor back projection and the overstuffed Boston interiors were all part of the same world. He could also add color and emotion to footage that wouldn't ordinarily make much of an impact. His subtle tropical melodies playing under a restaurant scene between Davis and Henreid do more to cement their moment together than the dialogue or staging. Steiner won an Oscar. Davis, Robinson, and Rapper would reteam for *The Grass Is Green* in 1944.

Road to Morocco

Paramount, 1942. Sound, B&W, 1.37. 82 minutes.
Cast: Bing Crosby (Jeff Peters), Bob Hope (Orville "Turkey" Jackson/Aunt Lucy), Dorothy Lamour (Princess Shalmar), Anthony Quinn (Mullay Kasim), Dona Drake (Mihirmah), Vladimir Sokoloff (Hyder Khan), Mikhail Rasumny (Ahmed Fey), George Givot (Neb Jolla).
Credits: Directed by David Butler. Written by Frank Butler, Don Hartman. Produced by Paul Jones. Director of photography: William C. Mellor. Film Editor: Irene Morra. Art direction: Hans Dreier, Robert Usher. Costume design: Edith Head. Makeup: Wally Westmore. Special effects by Farciot Edouart, Gordon Jennings. Musical director: Victor Young. Music advisor: Arthur Franklin. Songs: lyrics by Johnny Burke, music by Jimmy Van Heusen. Choreography: Paul Oscard. Sound: Earl Hayman, Walter Oberst, Loren L. Ryder.
Additional Cast includes: Andrew Tombes (Oso Bucco), Leon Belasco (Yusef), Yvonne De Carlo (Handmaiden), Stanley Price (Idiot), Rita Christiani (Specialty dancer).
Additional Credits: Executive producer: B.G. DeSylva. Production dates: February 23 to April 23, 1942. Opened in New York City on November 10, 1942.
Available: Universal Home Video DVD (2002). ISBN: 0-7832-55241-1. UPC: 0-25192-12292-7.

Road to Morocco was the third of seven Paramount Pictures "Road" movies starring Bing Crosby, Bob Hope and Dorothy Lamour. The first, *Road to Singapore* (1940), had originally been intended for George Burns and Gracie Allen, and then for Fred MacMurray and Jack Oakie. Friends in real life, Crosby and Hope brought an informal quality to their ad hoc teaming that proved infectious. The initial *Road* movies were so successful that they encouraged other studios to follow suit. Warner Brothers, for example, quickly paired singer Dennis Morgan with beefy funnyman Jack Carson in

a series of self-referential comedies, many of them directed by David Butler.

Butler's career stretched back to 1897, when he appeared on stage at the age of three in a play directed by his father. After acting in films, he began directing at Fox in 1927. Throughout the 1930s he made musicals and Shirley Temple vehicles, and had just finished directing Hope in *Caught in the Draft* (1941). The comedian was embarking on an unprecedented series of hit films. Born Leslie Townes Hope in England in 1903, he grew up in Cleveland, where he performed as a singer and dancer in amateur shows. He formed a vaudeville act that eventually brought him to New York, where he appeared in plays like *Roberta*. Hope made some negligible comedy shorts; it was his successful radio program that won him a contract at Paramount for the feature *The Big Broadcast of 1938*. In that film he introduced his theme song, "Thanks for the Memory."

Hope's subsequent films were a mixed lot, but by now he had learned the value of writing, and built up a library of gags that he replenished constantly. He also honed his screen persona as a glib but cowardly con artist usually done in by his own machinations. Gags meant everything for Hope, and he would do anything to make them work, including stepping out of character or punctuating punchlines with growls, barks, and squeaks.

Crosby, meanwhile, was the pre-eminent popular singer in America. He was born Harry Lillis Crosby in Tacoma, Washington, in 1903, and received a Catholic education in Spokane. Plans to study law gave way to playing drums and singing in a band. Then he formed a duo with Al Rinker, whose sister Mildred Bailey was a successful vaudevillian singer. With her help Crosby and Rinker became established in Los Angeles, adding Harry Barris to become The Rhythm Boys, a trio featured in *The King of Jazz* (1930). Crosby soon went out on his own, winning a CBS radio show after starring in the 1931 short *I Surrender Dear* (which included the title song). The show was an enormous success, and his records, on the Columbia label, sold millions.

Signing with Paramount, the singer made a number of popular but generally undistinguished musical comedies. Exceptions, including *Mississippi* (1935) with W.C. Fields and *Rhythm on the Range* (1936) with Mary Martin, showed him to be an affable, unpretentious actor with a rare talent for underplaying. But poor vehicles damaged his appeal to filmgoers, and by the end of the 1930s his film career had become tenuous.

The first two *Road* pictures were directed by Victor Schertzinger, a former violinist and orchestra conductor who composed a musical score for *Civilization* (1916), and were written in part by Frank Butler, a former actor from Oxford, England, who had worked on films starring Harold Lloyd and Laurel and Hardy, as well as some of weaker Crosby and Hope movies of the 1930s.

Road to Singapore (1940) and *Road to Zanzibar* (1941) were light, easygoing, escapist comedies with a few tunes and some romance in the form of Dorothy Lamour. The glamorous, beautiful Lamour, a former Miss New Orleans, was cast to a great degree because she looked so alluring wearing sarongs in films like *Jungle Princess* (1936) and *The Hurricane* (1937).

After two movies, the *Road* production unit had developed an unhurried, friendly working style. Director David Butler added a willingness to push the zanier aspects of the story, and to let his stars appear to ad lib. (Almost all of the asides, in-jokes, and quick retorts were in fact scripted.) Talking camels, obviously fake sets, pop culture references, and ridiculous plot twists became the norm. Ancient gags—dribble cups, whoopee cushions, exploding cigars—evoked the days of vaudeville. The only certainties were that the three leads would sing, and that Bing would end up with Lamour. *Road to Morocco* also featured possibly the best song in the series, "Moonlight Becomes You," which became yet another blockbuster Crosby recording.

Road to Morocco revitalized Crosby's film career, and he eventually began appearing in non-singing roles. For Hope, it solidified his position as one of the top-ten moneymaking actors. He was a viable movie star into the 1960s, and also became one of the most enduring and best-loved of television celebrities. He wrote or contributed to several memoirs, hosted a golf tournament that collected millions for charity, and was renowned for visiting troops overseas. He died at the age of 100 in 2003.

Casablanca

Warner Bros., 1942. Sound, B&W, 1.37. 103 minutes.

Cast: Humphrey Bogart (Rick Blaine), Ingrid Bergman (Ilsa Lund), Paul Henreid (Victor Laszlo), Claude Rains (Louis Renault), Conrad Veidt (Major Strasser), Sydney Greenstreet (Ferrari), Peter Lorre (Ugarte), S.K. [S.Z.] Sakall (Carl), Madeleine LeBeau (Yvonne), Dooley Wilson (Sam), Joy Page (Annina Brandel), John Qualen (Berger), Leonid Kinskey (Sascha), Curt Bois (Dark European).

Credits: Directed by Michael Curtiz. Produced by Hal B. Wallis. Screen play by Julius J. and Philip G. Epstein and Howard Koch. From a play by Murray Burnett and Joan Alison. Music by Max Steiner. Director of photography: Arthur Edeson. Dialogue director: Hugh MacMullan. Film editor: Owen Marks. Art director: Carl Jules Weyl. Technical advisor: Robert Aisner. Montages by Don Siegel and James Leicester. Sound by Francis J. Scheid. Special effects by Lawrence Butler, director, and Willard Van Enger. Set decorations by George James Hopkins. Gowns by Orry-Kelly. Makeup artist: Perc Westmore. Songs by M.K. Jerome and Jack Scholl. Orchestral arrangements: Hugo Friedhofer. Musical director: Leo F. Forbstein. RCA Sound System. A Warner Bros. Pictures presentation of a Warner Bros.–First National picture and a Hal B. Wallis production.

Additional Cast: Helmut Dantine (Jan Brandel), Marcel Dalio (Croupier), Ludwig Stossel (Mr. Leuchtag), Ilka Gruning (Mrs. Leuchtag), Dan Seymour (Abdul), Jean Del Val (Police officer), Creighton Hale (Customer), Monte Blue (American), Leon Belasco (Dealer), Paul Irving, Torben Meyer.

Additional Credits: Screenwriting: Wally Klein, Aeneas MacKenzie, Lenore Coffee, Casey Robinson. Executive producer: Jack L. Warner. Unit manager: Al Alleborn. Production dates: May 25 to August 3, 1942. Opened in New York City on November 25, 1942. General release: January 23, 1942.

Awards: Oscars for Best Picture, Director, Screenplay.

Available: Warner Home Video DVD (2003). ISBN: 0-7907-7230-2. UPC: 0-12569-56812-9.

For two generations *Casablanca* stood as the definitive American movie romance, one built on regret and a new awareness of how world events impacted individuals. Its reputation has dimmed in recent years as memories of World War II fade, but its catch phrases and gauzy clinches have remained part of our cultural vocabulary. Each new group of viewers gets to interpret the film in different ways: as a stand against fascism, an example of star machinery, proof (or refutation) of the auteur theory. On more fundamental levels, *Casablanca* shows better than many films exactly how the studio system worked.

The source material for the film was an unproduced play called *Everybody Comes to Rick's*, written by Murray Bennett and Joan Alison. It was one of scores of projects purchased by Warner Brothers, who, like the other major studios, stockpiled as many stories as possible. Producer Hal Wallis, who had just signed a six-picture deal with Warners, selected the play from the studio library, along with titles like *Now, Voyager* (1942). Several employees got involved with the project, such as story editor Irene Lee, who recommended it, and screenwriter Robert Buckner, who didn't. He called Rick "two-parts Hemingway, one-part Scott Fitzgerald, and a dash of café Christ." Buckner departed for *Yankee Doodle Dandy* (1942); Wallis assigned Julius and Philip Epstein to write the script instead.

Twins born in New York City in 1909, the Epsteins were in the top tier of Warners' screen writers. Julius was unbelievably fecund in the 1930s, writing hundreds of scripts, treatments, and story ideas. Together, the brothers were adept at a style of writing that supplanted the tough patter of earlier Warners musicals and gangster movies. Warners pictures were now cynical, world-weary, but still witty, with a slightly higher class of characters wrapped up in slightly more urbane problems.

The earliest models cited for *Casablanca* in studio memos were *Algiers* (1938), a swoony remake of a French melodrama, and *Grand Hotel* (1933), the MGM all-star extravaganza. Wallis even tried to cast Hedy Lamarr, one of the stars of *Algiers*, before deciding that Warner contract player Ann Sheridan would be more cost effective. Humphrey Bogart, a bona fide star after *The Maltese Falcon* and *High Sierra* (both 1941), was picked for Rick as early as February 1942, although other names for the part surfaced regularly before filming started.

The rest of the cast was a combination of contract players and independent actors who signed on for the project. Peter Lorre and Sydney Greenstreet had appeared with Bogart in *The Maltese Falcon*; Claude Rains and Paul Henreid had just finished the Bette Davis vehicle *Now, Voyager*. Wallis wasn't sure if Sam, the piano player in Rick's bar, would be a man, such as Clarence Muse, or a woman—perhaps Hazel Scott or Lena Horne. As filming approached, he settled on Dooley Wilson, a singer and drummer under contract to Paramount.

Many of the stories surrounding the production concern revisions to the script before and during filming. In particular, the ending of the story was alleged to have been decided on the spot. However, the ending to *Casablanca* remained unchanged from the play through the many drafts required for the shooting script. What did change were individual lines, some of them spur-of-the-moment inspirations like "Round up the usual suspects," and the romance between Rick and Ilsa, punched up by Casey Robinson after finishing his *Now, Voyager* assignment.

Ilsa was now being played by Ingrid Bergman, borrowed from David O. Selznick in return for the use of Olivia de Havilland. Bergman may have been perplexed about her role because Ilsa's relationship with Rick was changing, as were certain key scenes. This may have led to a hesitancy in her acting, a quality that ended up contributing to the film's sense of impermanence, of a world changing for the worse. While the doomed romance between Rick and Ilsa gives *Casablanca* a tragic appeal, what really won over viewers was the gradual transformation of Rick from disinterested, even apathetic, bystander to committed patriot. It was how moviegoers wanted to believe they would act under similar circumstances.

Director Michael Curtiz kept the production moving briskly, but his work was watched over by Wallis and, at a greater remove, Jack Warner. Wallis told photographer Arthur Edeson that he was taking too long to light one of the Parisian scenes, for example. Unit manager Al Alleborn reported arguments and delays to Wallis, and complained that by shooting an airport scene for *Desert Song*, director Robert Florey was preventing the *Casablanca* unit from using the same set. Wallis gave advice to Max Steiner on how to score certain scenes, added dialogue (including the film's famous closing line), and wrote detailed memos about editing. All this while overseeing development of other films in his contract, including *Air Force* and *Watch on the Rhine* (both 1943).

Wallis was in some ways the major creative force behind *Casablanca*, even though Julius Epstein said that story editor Irene Lee "was much smarter than Wallis [and was] the one who assigned us to write it." Perhaps the real "author" of *Casablanca* was the Warner Bros. studio itself, a factory with the actors, crew, props, sets and equipment necessary to put together this film along with scores of others. The picture may have resonated so well with the public because it was given a limited release just days after Allied forces invaded the city of Casablanca. The film got an additional boost during its general release some five months later when the city hosted an Allied summit with Franklin D. Roosevelt, Winston Churchill, and Joseph Stalin. Plans for a sequel started almost immediately, but Wallis severed his relationship with the studio after Jack Warner grabbed the film's Best Picture Oscar during the Academy Awards ceremonies.

Cat People

A past curse weighs on Simone Simon in *Cat People*.

RKO, 1942. Sound, B&W, 1.37. 73 minutes.

Cast: Simone Simon (Irene Dubrovna), Kent Smith (Oliver Reed), Tom Conway (Dr. Louis Judd), Jane Randolph (Alice Moore), Jack Holt (Commodore).

Credits: Directed by Jacques Tourneur. Written by DeWitt Bodeen. Produced by Val Lewton. Music by Roy Webb. Musical director: C. Bakaleinikoff. Director of photography: Nicholas Musuraca. Art directors: Albert S. D'Agostino, Walter E. Keller. Set decorations: Darrell Silvera, Al Fields. Gowns by Renié. Recorded by John L. Cass. Edited by Mark Robson. Assistant director: Doran Cox. RCA Sound System.

Additional Cast: Alan Napier (Carver), Elizabeth Dunne (Miss Plunkett), Elizabeth Russell (The Cat Woman), Mary Halsey (Blondie), Alec Craig (Zookeeper), George Ford (Policeman), Betty Roadman (Mrs. Hansen), Dot Farley (Mrs. Agnew), Charles Jordan (Bus driver), Lon Kerr (Taxi driver), Leda Nicova (Patient), Theresa Harris (Minnie), John Piffle (Café proprietor), Murdock MacQuarrie (Shepherd), Bud Geary (Mounted policeman), Eddie Dew (Street policeman), Connie Leon, Henrietta Burnside.

Additional Credits: Supervising producer: Lou Ostrow. Special effects: Vernon Walker. Production dates: July 28 to August 21, 1942. Premiered in New York City on December 6, 1942.

Other Versions: *The Curse of the Cat People* (1944), while not a sequel, features much of the same cast and crew. Paul Schrader directed a remake, *Cat People* (1982).

Available: Warner Home Video DVD (2005). ISBN: 0-7806-5063-8. UPC: 0-53939-72442-4.

When Orson Welles departed from RKO, he left behind two commercial disappointments—*Citizen Kane* (1941) and *The Magnificent Ambersons* (1942)—and several expensive sets. He also cost production chief George Schaefer, a major supporter, his job. The new RKO regime focused on low-budget pictures that could be paired in double-bills. Chosen to head one of the new production units was Val Lewton.

Born Vladimir Leventon in Yalta in 1904, Lewton and his immediate family were brought to New York City by his aunt, the actress Alla Nazimova. (She starred in the 1922 Registry title *Salome*.) According to biographer Edmund G. Bansak, Lewton grew up with a fear of cats, an aversion to being touched, and a photographic memory for plots. He dropped out of college to become a reporter, sold short stories to magazines, and by his twenties had already published mysteries, historical novels, and pornography. In 1926 he took a job with Howard Dietz reading books and screenplays for MGM. He continued writing, including a 1930 short story called "The Bagheeta," about a beautiful woman who turns into a leopard.

In 1932, producer David O. Selznick, who also started as a reader at MGM, hired Lewton as a secretary; his functions ranged from script analysis to directing the second unit on films like *A Tale of Two Cities* (1935). Lewton contributed to the screenplay of *Gone With the Wind* (1939), a book he called "ponderous trash," but he was also forced into demeaning jobs, like timing rest room patrons to determine how long the intermission should be. When tax problems forced Selznick to break up his company, Lewton accepted an offer to make B-movies from Charles Koerner at RKO.

Koerner had specific rules: budgets of $150,000 per film; Lewton had to use pretested titles; and no film could last longer than seventy-five minutes. Lewton's first step was to hire DeWitt Bodeen, a playwright who had just assisted Aldous Huxley on a draft of *Jane Eyre* (1944).

Given the title *Cat People*, Lewton first came up with a story about Balkan villagers who turn into cats at night to fight the Nazis. Budget demands persuaded Lewton to narrow the plot and settings. With New Yorkers for characters, Lewton could simplify research and writing; he could also use existing sets rather than build new ones. Bodeen eventually focused the script on one woman, a commercial illustrator in New York City who fears that she has been cursed by an ancient evil that will transform her into a predatory cat.

While the script came together, Lewton assembled a crew that included cinematographer Nicholas Musuraca and editor Mark Robson. Robson had worked with editor Robert Wise on *The Magnificent Ambersons* and, like Wise, he would graduate to directing under Lewton. To direct this project, Lewton chose his former collaborator Jacques Tourneur, the son of noted silent director Maurice Tourneur (*The Blue Bird*, 1918). The younger Tourneur had worked for his father upon his return to Europe in the late 1920s, and began directing features in France in 1931. He moved to Hollywood in 1934 to direct short films for MGM. Along with Lewton, he headed the second unit for *A Tale of Two Cities*. (Tourneur and cinematographer Musuraca would work together on the 1947 Registry title *Out of the Past*.)

Lewton cast Simone Simon after seeing her in *The Devil and Daniel Webster* (1941). A French actress who shuttled between the United States and Europe, Simon's presence required Bodeen to revise his script to account for her accent. Robson took credit for spotting Jane Randolph in *The Falcon's Brother* (1942); Lewton not only gave her a lead role, but found one for her costar Tom Conway as a psychiatrist. As with his crew, Lewton would use the same actors in several of his films.

The unit became expert at re-purposing materials. Apart from a grand staircase built for *The Magnificent Ambersons*, most of the sets for *Cat People* came from *The Devil and Miss Jones* (1941). Lewton used a café soundstage in three different ways: as a coffee shop, a pet shop, and a restaurant. (The same sets and similar characters would reappear in Lewton's subsequent films; viewed sequentially, they have the disorienting effect of offering different angles of the same constricted world.)

The Lewton crew also became expert at achieving effects through the basic fundamentals of filmmaking, such as sound and montage. One of *Cat People*'s most famous sequences consists of shots of Jane Randolph and then Simone Simon walking across sets of sidewalks at night. Their footsteps, and some rustling bushes, are the only sounds. By altering the tempo of cuts, by juxtaposing wide shots and close-ups, Mark Robson builds tension out of thin air. A sudden noise becomes the equivalent of a shriek.

Jarring noises became a fixture of the Lewton films, and of almost all horror films to follow. But what's more striking about *Cat People* is how quiet it is. In other films of the time, characters broadcast their lines and personalities, confident in who they are and what they represent, their roles fixed by script and shooting styles. Here, crucial plot twists are spoken quietly, almost in whispers, a symptom of insecurity and self-doubt. Lewton's characters were plagued by psychological problems, by worries that they were secretly unworthy, even evil. The leads in this film and the Lewton films to follow know something is wrong with their lives, even if they can't pin down what it is. *Cat People* is, on the surface, about a murderous predator, but it is really about sexual dysfunction, about jealousy forced into the open, about crippling neuroses as a way of life.

The search for an answer to these problems is the driving force behind Lewton's films, and to an unusual extent his characters exhibit a free will that is at odds with much of the entertainment of the time. Their choices are their own, not the result of demands for a happy ending or a solution to a mystery. They may operate within rigid plots, but they change in ways that melodramatic conventions—and moviegoers—can't anticipate. The most shocking aspect of Lewton's films may be how many of his characters choose death over life, shattering the worlds of those around them.

Press screenings for *Cat People* were held in November 1942, and the film opened in December on a double-bill with *Gorilla Man*. Selznick wrote to Lewton that the film "is in every way a much better picture than ninety percent of the 'A' product that I have seen in recent months." It earned some $4 million on a budget of $134,959.

RKO announced the second film from the unit—*I Walked with a Zombie* (1942)—before shooting even started on *Cat People*. *Zombie*, an unacknowledged version of *Jane Eyre*, continued Lewton's obsession with mortality, focusing on those who "court death," in Edmund Bansak's words. *The Leopard Man* (1943) followed a group of Southwestern artists and villagers who are marked for death; while Lewton's masterpiece, *The Seventh Victim* (also 1943), was about people who, in the words of John Donne, "run to death." By any standard they are extraordinary films—the fact that they were made under such tight restrictions makes them even more remarkable.

Lewton oversaw a total of eleven films for RKO, but when Koerner died the producer's remaining projects were cancelled, forcing him to leave the studio. He completed three more films at other studios, but his spirit was broken. He died of a heart attack in 1951.

Shadow of a Doubt

Universal, 1943. Sound, B&W, 1.37. 108 minutes.

Cast: Teresa Wright (Young Charlie [Newton]), Joseph Cotten (Uncle Charlie [Oakley]), Macdonald Carey (Jack Graham), Henry Travers (Joseph Newton), Patricia Collinge (Emma [Spencer Oakley] Newton), Hume Cronyn (Herbie Hawkins), Wallace Ford (Fred Saunders), Edna May Wonacott (Ann Newton), Charles Bates (Roger Newton), Irving Bacon (Station master), Clarence Muse (Pullman porter), Janet Shaw (Louise [Finch]), Estelle Jewell (Catherine).

Credits: Directed by Alfred Hitchcock. Screenplay by Thornton Wilder, Sally Benson, Alma Reville. (Wilder receives an additional screen credit: "We wish to acknowledge the contribution of Mr. Thornton Wilder to the preparation of this production.") From an original story by Gordon McDonell. Produced by Jack H. Skirball. Director of photography: Joseph Valentine. Original musical score; Dimitri Tiomkin. Art director: John B. Goodman. Associate art director: Robert Boyle. Director of sound: Bernard B. Brown. Technician: Robert Pritchard. Set decorations: R.A. Gausman. Associate set decorator: E.R. Robinson. Musical director: Charles Previn. Set continuity: Adele Cannon. Film editor: Milton Carruth. Assistant director: William Tummel. Teresa Wright's gowns by Adrian. Costumes: Vera West. Western Electric Recording. A Skirball Productions presentation.

Additional Cast: Alfred Hitchcock (Card player), Minerva Urecal (Mrs. Henderson), Isabel Randolph (Mrs. Margaret Green), Earle S. Dewey (Mr. Norton), Elly Malyon (Librarian), Edward Fielding (Doctor), Sarah Edwards (Wife of doctor), Vaughan Glaser (Dr. Phillips), Virginia Brissac (Mrs. Phillips), Ruth Lee (Mrs. MacCurdy), Grandon Rhodes (Reverend MacCurdy), Edwin Stanely (Mr. Green), Frances Carson (Mrs. Potter); Byron Shores, John McGuire (Detectives); Constance Purdy (Mrs. Martin), Shirley Mills (Young girl).

Additional Credits: Assistant director: William Tummel. Production dates: August to November 1942. Released January 12, 1943.

Other Versions: Remade as *Step Down to Terror* (1958) and for television as *Shadow of a Doubt* (1991).

Available: Universal Studios DVD (2000). ISBN: 0-7832-5469-5. UPC: 0-2519-20672-2-8. Universal Studios DVD (2006). UPC: 025192831324.

After the international success of *The Lady Vanishes* (1938), Alfred Hitchcock set his sights on working in Hollywood, anxious to take advantage of the resources of the American film industry. In 1939 he moved to the United States, lured by the promise of working with David O. Selznick, considered at the time the most prestigious producer in the industry. Their relationship was marked by creative conflicts both small and large, and resulted in such noteworthy films as *Rebecca* (1940) and *Spellbound* (1945). Preoccupied with *Gone With the Wind* (1939) and with reorganizing Selznick International into David O. Selznick, Inc., the producer loaned Hitchcock out to other studios: United Artists for *Foreign Correspondent* (1940), RKO, and then Universal. There Hitchcock worked with producer Jack H. Skirball on *Saboteur* (1942).

For his next project Hitchcock turned to Margaret McDonell, the head of Selznick's story department. Her husband Gordon gave Hitchcock a verbal pitch for an idea called "Uncle Charlie." Based on a real-life incident in Hanford, California, in 1938, the story concerned the relationship between a niece and her visiting uncle, who is revealed to be a suspect in a series of particularly brutal murders. Hitchcock persuaded playwright Thornton Wilder, whose *Our Town* had recently won a Pulitzer, to turn McDonell's story into a screenplay. Hitchcock felt that Wilder displayed special insights into small-town life in his writings. Before production began, Hitchcock refined Wilder's script with his wife Alma Reville and with

Sally Benson, who would later contribute to the screenplay for *Meet Me in St. Louis* (1944).

Hitchcock told actor Hume Cronyn that the production would be an opportunity to enjoy themselves in the California wine country outside Santa Rosa. It was Cronyn's debut in film, and in his memoir he wrote about Hitchcock's unerring sense of the frame. "The camera lies, you know—not always, but sometimes. You have to learn to accommodate it when it does," the director explained when asking the actor to move in a specific direction. (Cronyn also wrote about how three martinis would put Hitchcock to sleep before dinner.) Hitchcock borrowed Teresa Wright and Joseph Cotten from Samuel Goldwyn. In a letter, Selznick later complained bitterly that Goldwyn tried to steal Hitchcock from him, that "you told Hitch that he shouldn't be wasting his talents on stories like *Shadow of a Doubt*, and that this wouldn't be the case if he were working for you."

The director and Skirball signed a one-picture contract for *Shadow of a Doubt* in April 1942. The main shooting took place in Santa Rosa that August, followed by a month of interior work in Hollywood. Afterward Wright marveled at how Hitchcock knew every aspect of the film before he started shooting. He was so precise in his descriptions to the cast and crew that when she finally attended a screening, it was if she "had seen the movie already."

Hitchcock's mastery of technical details was already evident in films like *Saboteur*. *Shadow of a Doubt* marked the first time in America that his subject matter lived up to his filmmaking skills. Consequently, he often referred to it as his favorite. But *Shadow of a Doubt* built on themes the director had already broached in his British films, like the creepy sterility of village life, a thick, inhospitable atmosphere that at any moment could mutate into violence.

On a narrative level, the most interesting accomplishment in *Shadow of a Doubt* was Hitchcock's ability to connect the commonplace to evil. Franz Lehár's light, lilting "The Merry Widow Waltz" becomes the theme song for murder. Joseph Cotten, a kindly, reassuring presence in Orson Welles' films, becomes a possible serial killer. (Hitchcock had a knack for bringing out the hidden evil in leading men like Ray Milland, Robert Walker, and, perhaps most famously, Anthony Perkins.) Lesser directors relegated crime and brutality to dark alleys and slums; Hitchcock saw it in the day-to-day life of sunny California.

The director may have gotten the idea for the waltz from composer Dimitri Tiomkin, who gave a fascinating account of a preview screening. Dismayed when studio executives fell asleep, he became even more worried at the rest of the audience: "They giggled through my sinister waltz harmonies and laughed loudly in moments of terror." He found Hitchcock serenely sipping a brandy at the bar. "The laughs were a sign that the picture had them on edge," he explained. "American audiences will break into nervous laughter when they are overwrought, a good sign for a suspense picture." Tiomkin's variations on Lehár's melody are complex, psychologically motivated, yet easy to overlook—just like Joseph Valentine's meticulous yet unfussy cinematography.

World War II interrupted the careers of many involved in the film. Wilder enlisted in the Army before shooting started. Gordon McDonell later wrote the story for *They Won't Believe Me* (1947), a thriller similar in style to *Shadow of a Doubt*. Cronyn, who married actress Jessica Tandy in November 1942, continued to collaborate with Hitchcock, acting in *Lifeboat* (1944) and helping write *Rope* (1948) and *Under Capricorn* (1949). Wright appeared in another Registry work, *The Best Years of Their Lives* (1946). Hitchcock finished two propaganda films before returning to Selznick to make *Spellbound*. His next Registry film is *Notorious* (1946).

The Ox-Bow Incident

Twentieth Century-Fox, 1943. Sound, B&W, 1.37. 75 minutes.

Cast: Henry Fonda (Gil Carter), Dana Andrews (Donald Martin), Mary Beth Hughes (Rose Mapen), Anthony Quinn (Francisco Morez), William Eythe (Gerald Tetley), Henry Morgan (Art Croft), Jane Darwell (Jenny Grier), Matt Briggs (Judge Daniel Tyler), Harry Davenport (Arthur Davies), Frank Conroy (Major Tetley), Marc Lawrence (Jeff Farnley), Paul Hurst (Monty Smith), Victor Kilian (Darby), Chris-Pin Martin (Pancho), Willard Robertson (Sheriff Risley), Ted North (Joyce).

Credits: Directed by William A. Wellman. Produced and written for the screen by Lamar Trotti. From the novel by Walter Van Tilburg Clark. Director of photography: Arthur Miller. Art direction: Richard Day, James Baseyi. Set decorations: Thomas Little, Frank E. Hughes. Film editor: Allen McNeil. Costumes: Earl Luck. Makeup artist: Guy Pearce. Sound: Alfred Bruzlin, Roger Heman. Music: Cyril J. Mockridge. Western Electric Recording.

Additional Cast: George Meeker (Mr. Swanson), Almira Sessions (Miss Swanson), Margaret Hamilton (Mrs. Larch), Dick Rich (Butch Mapes),·

Francis Ford (Alva Hardwick), Stanley Andrews (Bartlett), Billy Benedict (Greene), Rondo Hatton (Gabe Hart), Paul Burns (Winder), Leigh Whipper (Reynolds), George Lloyd (Moore), George Chandler (Jimmy Carnes), Hank Bell (Red), Forrest Dillon (Mark).

Additional Credits: Production dates: June to August 1942. Released May 21, 1943.

Available: Twentieth Century Fox Home Entertainment DVD (2003). UPC: 0-24543-06106-9.

Born in a log cabin in Maine in 1909, Walter Van Tilburg Clark grew up in Reno, where his father was president of the University of Nevada. Although he gained a knowledge of the physical West through extensive hiking, Clark was a serious student, earning two master's degrees and publishing a book of poetry while teaching in Vermont. He taught in Cazenovia in central New York State while working on short stories and his first novel, published in 1940. A straightforward, unadorned account of the lynching of three men accused of cattle rustling, it was praised by reviewers for its intellectual aspirations as much as for its literary qualities.

The book was a tough sell in Hollywood, where Paramount producer Harold Hurley bought the rights but couldn't interest his studio in an adaptation. When he was fired, he sold the book to director William Wellman, whose reputation had grown after leaving Warner Brothers to write and direct *A Star Is Born* (1937) for David O. Selznick. Wellman had since worked at Paramount before reuniting with Darryl F. Zanuck at Twentieth Century-Fox. Here he worked for the first time with screenwriter Lamar Trotti, one of the most reliably liberal voices at the studio. Wellman had a handshake deal with Zanuck to make *The Ox-Bow Incident*; he also had to agree to direct two more Fox projects.

They had collaborated on *The Public Enemy* (1931); the director referred to the Fox studio head as "the hardest-working little guy you have ever seen in all your life." "Zanuck was the only one with guts to do an out-of-the-ordinary story for the prestige rather than the dough," Wellman wrote in his autobiography, and it seemed clear to everyone involved that a film of *The Ox-Bow Incident* would not be a moneymaker. (Zanuck called the novel "too bitter and sunless.") But Trotti wanted to be involved, as did Henry Fonda, in Wellman's words, the most dedicated actor he ever worked with. "Six weeks before we started *The Ox-Bow Incident*, he wardrobed himself, had me okay it, and then lived and probably slept in it," Wellman wrote. "The boots, the Levi's, the hat, the shirt, the bandanas, became part of Gil Carter."

Fonda, Trotti, and even Zanuck may have been hoping for another film along the lines of *The Grapes of Wrath* (1940), but when Zanuck left the studio to join the war effort, his replacement, Bill Goetz, said Wellman's budget was too high. Zanuck ordered Goetz to honor his commitment to Wellman, but the limited funding is obvious in the finished film, which recycled sets and locations from other Fox properties. (Even the soundtrack, with its accordion version of "Red River Valley," feels lifted from *The Grapes of Wrath*.)

Clark found only two significant changes between his novel and the film (one was the reading of a letter; the other, the singing of a spiritual), but other critics have pointed out many alterations in tone and meaning from the original book. For one thing, Trotti had to find a solution to a story that verged on despair over the human condition. Writing about social-issue films like this one, Pauline Kael concluded that Hollywood wanted to "give the public a happy ending so they won't have to think about it afterwards."

The film also left out Clark's dim opinion of the justice system, reducing the theme of the story to a condemnation of mob violence. Historian Thomas Cripps criticized the fact that one character was turned into a phony rather than real Confederate. In his 1957 study *Novels Into Film*, George Bluestone noted how Trotti dropped a few of Clark's characters, and built up the Gil Carter role played by Fonda. While still a rough, hard-bitten cowpuncher, Carter became the moral center of the story, a guide to how to behave. Trotti also made some characters less guilty than they appeared in the novel. Wellman made his own changes. He took out a bloody ending devised by Trotti, finding it more effective to keep the violence off-screen.

Dore Schary, who within a decade would be running MGM, had this to say about Wellman's work: "Good direction must seem like no direction at all. Bill's whole effort is to wipe away all traces of his own participation so that the eventual scene looks as though a roving camera had poked in and caught the people unaware." The absence of style became the film's style—it was a report as straightforward and hard to dismiss as a newsreel.

For a wartime release, *The Ox-Bow Incident* offered a bleak message that ran counter to much of the propaganda being churned out by the studio system. It was essentially ignored by moviegoers, although it received respectful reviews. Despite its genuine accomplishments, there is a self-congratulatory air about the film, a sense that simply bringing up the problem of vigilantes somehow solved it. Michael Wood quotes writer Charles Higham: "[The] anti-lynching argument would surely have been reinforced had one of them been guilty." Wood goes on to find fault with the film's somber plot twists: "This heavy irony seems to imply not so much that we ought not to lynch people as that we ought to check our facts out properly before we do."

In hindsight, it's easy to criticize choices made by entertainers in another era. The year Wellman filmed *The Ox-Bow Incident*, six blacks were lynched in the United States. Three more were lynched in 1943, when the film was released.

Fonda enlisted in the Navy as soon as he finished this project, returning to film with *My Darling Clementine* (1946), a Registry title. In 1954, Wellman directed *Track of the Cat*, an adaptation of the last significant work of fiction Clark wrote.

Stormy Weather

Twentieth Century-Fox, 1943. Sound, B&W, 1.37. 78 minutes.

Cast: Lena Horne (Selina Rogers), Bill Robinson (Bill Williamson), Cab Calloway (Himself), Katherine Dunham (Herself), Fats Waller (Himself), Fayard Nicholas, Harold Nicholas (as The Nicholas Brothers), Ada Brown (Herself), Dooley Wilson (Gabe Tucker).

Credits: Directed by Andrew Stone. Screenplay by Frederick Jackson, Ted Koehler. Adaptation by H.S. Kraft. From an original story by Jerry Horwin, Seymour B. Robinson. Produced by William Le Baron. Assistant to the producer: Irving Mills. Director of photography: Leon Shamroy, A.S.C. Art Direction: James Basevi, Joseph C. Wright. Set Decorations: Thomas Little, Fred J. Rode. Film Editor: James B. Clark. Makeup Artist: Guy Pearce. Special Photographic Effects by Fred Sersen. Sound: Alfred Bruzlin, Roger Herman. Musical Direction: Emil Newman. Musical Sequences: Dances Staged by Clarence Robinson. Costumes Designed by Helen Rose. Supervised by Fanchon. Western Electric Recording.

Additional Cast: Ernest "Bubbles" Whitman, Leo Watson, Zutty Singleton, Benny Carter, Alton Moore, Gene Porter, Irving Ashby, Slam Stewart.

Additional Credits: Released July 21, 1943.

Available: Twentieth Century Fox Home Video DVD (2005). UPC: 0-24543-22183-8. VHS (1991).ISBN: 0-7939-1168-0. UPC: 0-8616-21168-3-4

Composer Harold Arlen and lyricist Ted Koehler originally wrote "Stormy Weather" for Cab Calloway, who at the time was appearing in a series of revues at Harlem's Cotton Club. Arlen's own recording of the song became a hit, making "Stormy Weather" the biggest song of 1933. It helped bring both Arlen and Koehler to Hollywood, although the songwriting team soon parted amicably. The film *Stormy Weather* reunited them briefly, with Koehler also receiving a screenwriting credit. In the interim he had worked on musicals at various studios, contributing to songs like "Animal Crackers in My Soup," "Out in the Cold Again," and "Don't Worry 'bout Me."

Arlen, meanwhile, had become one of the country's top composers. Born Hyman Arluck in Buffalo, New York, in 1905, Arlen started out singing at his father's synagogue. In a life reminiscent of *The Jazz Singer*, he founded a ragtime band, moved to New York City, and tried to succeed as a performer, meeting Koehler and writing "Get

Happy" and other songs with him. In Hollywood he wrote for Eddie Cantor and Al Jolson, then was hired with Yip Harburg for MGM's *The Wizard of Oz*. During World War II he teamed with lyricist and vocalist Johnny Mercer for hits like "That Old Black Magic" and "Happiness Is (Just) a Thing Called Joe," the latter appearing in the film *Cabin in the Sky* (1943).

With a cast that included Eddie "Rochester" Anderson and Ethel Waters, *Cabin in the Sky* was one of the first all-black musicals released by a major studio. It was preceded by *The Green Pastures* (1936), an adaptation of Marc Connelly's Broadway Biblical fantasy, and even earlier by King Vidor's *Hallelujah* (1929), another religious-themed story set in the South. Unlike those films, *Stormy Weather* was defiantly of the moment, a fictionalized account of the life of one of its stars, Bill Robinson.

Born in Virginia in 1878, Robinson claimed he was dancing for a living at the age of six. Changing his name from Luther to Bill, he toured as a child actor, then as part of a vaudeville team with George C. Cooper. Robinson stayed with the team until 1914, when he developed a solo act with the help of agent Marty Forkins. Despite the racism of the time, Robinson was a popular performer who danced at training camps during World War I and toured Europe as well.

Robinson began appearing in theatrical revues and in films, including *Harlem Is Heaven* (1933), an independent film financed by blacks, and *Black Orchids* (1934), a Vitaphone short. Working with Shirley Temple at Fox helped bring his dancing to a new audience.

His costar in *Stormy Weather* was Lena Horne. Born in Brooklyn in 1917, she came from a privileged family. Her grandmother graduated from Atlanta University in 1881, and was active in the NAACP. Her uncle advised President Franklin D. Roosevelt on race relations. At sixteen, Horne got a job in the Cotton Club chorus line. That led to various singing and dancing engagements, with Noble Sissle's Society Orchestra for a time, and after marrying Louis J. Jones in 1937, at functions in Pittsburgh. She starred in a low-budget musical, *The Duke Is Tops* (1938), then joined Charlie Barnet's Orchestra in 1940. Horne continued to sing with a variety of musicians in New York, convinced that she was being discriminated against because she was light-skinned.

MGM's Roger Edens saw Horne performing with Katherine Dunham and her dancers, and arranged for an audition at the studio. Horne had to be persuaded by figures like Count Basie and Paul Robeson to sign a contract there, and refused to play the maid roles usually offered to blacks. Worried about offending white customers in the South, MGM positioned her musical numbers so that they could be edited out easily. But the studio still found it difficult to find enough work for Horne. After *Cabin in the Sky*, Horne was loaned out to Fox for *Stormy Weather*.

The script, which called for a romance between Horne and Robinson, forty years her senior, was merely a thin framework for a series of songs and dances. Chief among these are two numbers by Fats Waller, including a disarming rendition of his signature song, "Ain't Misbehavin' "; an appearance by Cab Calloway strikingly similar to his work in Betty Boop cartoons ten years earlier; and "The Jumpin' Jive," a showpiece for the Nicholas Brothers. Horne sings "Diga Diga Do" and the title tune (also used for a performance by Katherine Dunham and her dancers), and dances occasionally with Robinson. He is seen to best advantage in "My My, Ain't That Somethin'," where he performs a bit of his famous staircase dance. Horne would be associated with the song "Stormy Weather" for the rest of her career.

Stormy Weather may strike some viewers today as racist. Robinson dresses up as an African native for a jungle number, and the appearance on the soundtrack of songs like "The Darktown Strutters Ball" carries connotations that were perhaps not so evident in 1943. But unlike most Hollywood features with all-black casts, *Stormy Weather* didn't make excuses for its characters. They were not figures in a religious fantasy or caricatures meant to entertain whites. They were simply people, the same as the singers, dancers, musicians, and comedians who appeared in other Fox musicals. (They didn't get the same budget: there are some notably shaky crane shots in *Stormy Weather*, and in at least one scene you can see the shadow of a boom mike over Robinson's head.) That alone sets *Stormy Weather* apart from other musicals of the 1940s. The chance to see entertainers like Robinson, Horne, Waller, and the Nicholas Brothers is, of course, just as good a reason to watch the film today.

Lassie Come Home

MGM, 1943. Sound, color, 1.37. 89 minutes.

Cast: Roddy McDowall (Joe Carraclough), Donald Crisp (Sam Carraclough), Dame May Whitty (Dally), Edmund Gwenn (Rowlie), Nigel Bruce (Duke of Rudling), Elsa Lanchester (Mrs. Carraclough), Elizabeth Taylor (Priscilla), Ben Webster (Dan'l Fadden), J. Patrick O'Malley (Hynes), Alan Napier (Jock), Arthur Shields (Andrew), John Rogers (Snickers), Alec Craig (Buckles), Lassie [Pal].

Credits: Directed by Fred M. Wilcox. Screen Play by Hugo Butler. Based on the novel by Eric Knight. Produced by Samuel Marx. Director of Photography: Leonard Smith, A.S.C. Technicolor director: Natalie Kalmus. Associate: Henri Jaffa. Musical Score: Daniele Amfitheatrof. Recording director: Douglas Shearer. Art director: Cedric Gibbons. Associate: Paul Groesse. Set Decorations: Edwin B. Willis. Associate: Mildred Griffiths. Make-up: Jack Dawn. Special effects: Warren Newcombe. Film editor: Ben Lewis. Western Electric Sound System.

Additional Credits: Produced by Harry Rapf. Executive producer: Dore Schary. Production dates: September to October 1942. Premiered in New York City on October 7, 1943. Later rated G.

Other Versions: *Son of Lassie* (1945), *Courage of Lassie* (1946), *Lassie* (1947 ABC radio show), *Hills of Home* (1948), *The Sun Comes Up* (1949), *Challenge to Lassie* (1950), *The Painted Hills* (1951), *Gypsy Colt* (1954 remake), *Lassie* (1954 TV series), *Lassie's Great Adventure* (1964 TV compilation), *The Magic of Lassie* (1978), *The New Lassie* (1989 TV series), *Lassie* (1994), *Lassie* (1997 TV series), *Lassie* (2005).

Available: Warner Home Video DVD (2004). ISBN: 0-7907-7551-4. UPC: 0-12569-5742-3.

Author Eric Knight first wrote about Lassie, the loyal Yorkshire collie, in a short story for the *Saturday Evening Post*. It was so popular that he expanded it into a novel, *Lassie Come-Home*, which was published in 1940. Born in 1897 in Yorkshire, Knight dropped out of school when he was twelve to work in a textile factory when his family suffered economic reversals. Reunited with his mother in the United States in 1912, he soon gave up school again to fight in World War I for the Canadian Infantry. After the war Knight wrote film reviews, then moved to Los Angeles as a screenwriter. Unhappy with the industry, he moved out of the city to concentrate on novels. *Lassie*, his third, was one of the best-selling books of 1940. It drew heavily on his childhood, not only in its portrayal of the Yorkshire landscape, but in terms of the guarded interaction between the upper and lower classes.

MGM purchased the rights to the novel after it was published, hoping to expand on its B-movie slate by offering a popular title aimed at younger viewers. Dore Schary, then the head of MGM's low-budget projects, assigned Sam Marx, the studio's former story editor, to produce the film. Marx cast Roddy McDowall as Joe Carraclough, the youngster affected most when his pet collie is sold to a local duke, and Donald Crisp as his father. The two actors had appeared together in *How Green Was My Valley* (1941), which may have been why Crisp was given a role that called for someone much younger. McDowall played an almost identical role in *My Friend Flicka*, which was released six months before *Lassie Come Home*.

Long-time professionals filled important roles. Dame May Whitty, perhaps best known today for her role as Mrs. Froy in Alfred Hitchcock's *The Lady Vanishes* (1938), was in her late seventies; it had been over twenty years since she was named Dame Commander for her volunteer work during World War I. This was her first screen appearance with her husband Ben Webster since they made a version of *Enoch Arden* in 1914. Edmund Gwenn had worked on both sides of the Atlantic until the start of World War II, when he became a fixture in American films as kindly, fun-loving old gentlemen. His most famous role was as Santa Claus in *Miracle on 34th Street* (1947, a Registry title). Born in Mexico in 1895, Nigel Bruce turned to acting after being seriously wounded fighting for Great Britain in World War I. He reached Hollywood in 1934, where he specialized in gruff, bumbling Englishmen until his breakthrough role as Dr. Watson in a series of Sherlock Holmes films starring Basil Rathbone. Lassie was played by Pal, a male collie who beat out some three hundred competitors in auditions.

The one bona fide discovery in *Lassie Come Home* was Elizabeth Taylor. She grew up in London to American parents who returned to the United States at the start of World War II. Although she appeared in a Universal comedy the year before, this was the start of a career at MGM that lasted twenty years.

Covering as it does a dog's four-hundred-mile journey from northern Scotland to Greenall Bridge in Yorkshire, the plot of *Lassie Come Home* is tied closely to a landscape of highlands, lochs, and moors. With the outbreak of war, MGM filmmakers would not be able to work in Great Britain; instead, they sought locations in California that would approximate the novel's settings. Big Bear Lake, Lake Arrowhead, and Monterey may not have resembled Inverness, Loch Lomand, or Glasgow, but they still looked stunning in Technicolor. The Carracloughs' little cottage on a lane leading up the hill from the village has been transformed, MGM-style, into a near-mansion overlooking a sweeping vista of parched valleys and distant mountains. *Lassie Come Home* had a budget of $564,000, making it MGM's highest-priced B-movie of the year. Since the costs for the cast and crew were negligible (there were no top stars, Elizabeth Taylor was making $75 a week, and this was director Fred Wilcox's feature debut), most of the money wound up on the screen.

For a children's story, both book and film spend an unexpected amount of time on unemployment, class friction, brutality, and death. The movie stints on a few of the novel's scenes, most likely for budgetary reasons, but includes moments that must have been puzzling to viewers who hadn't read the book, such as armed shepherds who consider shooting the dog as it crosses a field. Even much of the class-conscious dialogue comes straight from the pages of Eric Knight.

Filming lasted from September to October 1942. By that time an adaptation of Knight's novel *This Above All* starring Tyrone Power and Joan Fontaine had already been released by Twentieth Century-Fox, and Knight had been recruited to work in the Army film unit run by Frank Capra. After a test screening of *Lassie Come Home* on February 9, 1943, one of Schary's first moves was to extend Elizabeth Taylor's contract.

Two weeks before that screening, Knight, by then a major in the Special Services, was killed in the crash of a transport plane off Surinam in South America. This posed a dilemma for MGM, which did not want to be seen as capitalizing on the death of a war hero. An opening credit explaining that Knight died in the line of duty was added to the film, and its general release was delayed until December of that year.

Lassie Come Home performed well enough at the box office for MGM to order a string of sequels. *Son of Lassie* appeared in 1945, and by the end of the decade the collie was starring in a radio series as well. A television series lasted almost twenty years, from 1954 to 1972. It was followed by an animated series, a feature cobbled together from four TV shows, a 1978 musical starring James Stewart, and a 1994 drama aimed at young children. The latest incarnation, a 2005 feature shot in Scotland, Ireland, and the Isle of Man, returned to Knight's original novel. Starring Peter O'Toole, Samantha Morton, and John Lynch, and written and directed by Charles Sturridge, it is a beautiful and moving account of the story.

Meshes of the Afternoon

Maya Deren, Alexander Hammid, 1943. Silent, B&W, 1.37. 14 minutes.
Featuring: Maya Deren, Alexander Hammid.
Credits: Directed by Maya Deren, Alexander Hammid. Cinematography by Alexander Hammid. Edited by Maya Deren.
Additional Credits: Original music by Teiji Ito, added by Deren in 1959.
Available: Mystic Fire DVD *Maya Deren Experimental Films* (2002, *www. mysticfire.com*). UPC: 715098764931.

Born in Russia in 1917 and raised in New York, Maya Deren studied journalism and literature at New York University and Smith College. She was a secretary and publicist for dancer Katherine Dunham when she met cinematographer Alexander Hammid in Hollywood in 1942. Ten years her senior, Hammid (born Alexander Hackenschmied) had worked in Europe and the United States, primarily on documentaries and experimental films. "Sasha" Hammid took credit for giving Deren the name "Maya," the mother of Buddha (she was born Eleanora).

Hammid's film expertise opened up a new world for Deren, who had middling success as a poet and dancer. She felt that part of her problem was that she "thought in images." A bemused Dunham spoke about how "drums took her over. She was possessed by rhythm." "In film I can make the world dance," Deren said, but that was only one of her theoretical approaches to cinema. She also described her work as "the films of a woman, and the time quality is the time of a woman. A woman has strength to wait. Time is built into her body." She sought a "constant metamorphosis, each image . . . always becoming another."

Deren was also conversant with psychoanalytic theory, and as critic Scott MacDonald writes, it's tempting to read *Meshes of the Afternoon* "as a psychodramatization of Deren's resistance to conventional marriage and domesticity." On the surface the record of a dream, or "trance" as she referred to it later, *Meshes of the Afternoon* is also a catalog of symbols, both obvious and obscure. After decades of pop-culture psychiatry, the shots of flowers, purses, keys, doorways, and steps are fairly easy to decipher, as are the slow-motion and jump-cut sequences that repeat or distort activity. Other passages resist quick interpretation.

What was most apparent to viewers of the time was how different *Meshes of the Afternoon* was from other movies. Critic P. Adams Sitney has suggested that Deren's film was the logical successor to Luis Buñuel's *Un chien Andalou* (1928), as if experimental films had languished in limbo for fifteen years. On the other hand, historians like Jan-Christopher Horak and Bruce Posner assert that several independent, experimental filmmakers preceded Deren in the United States as well as Europe. For that matter, dream sequences were used in many features and shorts, and visual symbols were widespread in cinema, especially in animation.

That said, *Meshes* had a distinctive visual look and editing scheme that for the time were tremendously exciting. Previous experimental films had been shot with professional equipment and 35mm film stock, largely on sets. Here, the Los Angeles sunlight gives a sharp definition to the exterior walkways and foliage, while the 16mm camera moves in gyrating patterns and quick bursts that would not have been possible in mainstream movies. (Filmmaker Stan Brakhage attributes much of the visual style to Hammid's cinematography.) Even more startling was Deren's physical presence. With her lush, full body and defiantly unruly hair, she was the opposite of the typical airbrushed and de-ethnicized Hollywood actress. Wearing pants and a plain top, Deren moved with a dancer's grace that belied the spartan, often threadbare locations around her.

Hammid and Deren moved to New York City after filming *Meshes of the Afternoon*. There their lives took on the stereotyped messiness of the Bohemian culture. Deren began film projects and then abandoned them. She helped Hammid make *The Private Life of a Cat*, but spent more time publicizing her own work. She rented the Provincetown Playhouse in Greenwich Village to screen *Meshes of the Afternoon*, *At Land* (1944), and *A Study in Choreography for Camera* (1945, codirected with choreographer Talley Beatty), calling the event "Three Abandoned Films." She wrote *An Anagram of Art, Form and Film*, won a Guggenheim Fellowship, and in 1947 won an experimental film award at the Cannes Film Festival. She also divorced Hammid, who subsequently married Deren's roommate.

Deren's impact on filmmakers like Brakhage and Amos Vogel was enormous, on one level because she showed how an independent, experimental cinema could exist in a commercial marketplace. What few acknowledged is how cleverly Deren appropriated Hollywood's tactics and applied them to her work. Despite its artistic trappings, *Meshes of the Afternoon* is just as reliant on star power as a Garbo or Dietrich feature. Deren's face and body became the dominant factor in her films, not their time schemes or symbolic blossoms. A close-up of Deren could excuse poor production values, choppy editing, the lack of narrative meaning around her. (Equally exciting to some viewers were the glimpses of hipster life at the edges of the frame: daybeds disguised as couches, paint peeling off the walls, hand-me-down sofas and easy chairs, jeans and T-shirts.)

Deren spent the last fifteen years of her life trying to construct an artistic framework for her films, at the same time embellishing the cult of personality that grew around her. Solipsistic in the extreme, she argued that the flaws and weaknesses in her films were planned, the result of how women perceived time or her insights into dream theory or the manifestation of trance and ritual. She adopted pseudo-religious iconography, explored alternative philosophies, and took a fifteen-year-old lover, Teiji Ito. Deren spent two years filming in Haiti, amassing 18,000 feet of exposed film which she was then unable to edit into shape. When she died of a cerebral hemorrhage in 1961, she had completed seven films, and left five unfinished. Her work has given many filmmakers the confidence to pursue their own vision. They have also imitated Deren's refusal to "communicate" with viewers, except in oblique, self-referential ways.

The Miracle of Morgan's Creek

Paramount, 1944. Sound, B&W, 1.37, 98 minutes.

Cast: Eddie Bracken (Norval Jones), Betty Hutton (Trudy Kockenlocker), Diana Lynn (Emmy Kockenlocker), William Demarest (Officer Kockenlocker), Porter Hall (Justice of the Peace), Emory Parnell (Mr. Tuerck), Alan Bridge (E.L. Johnson), Julius Tannen (Mr. Rafferty), Victor Potel (Newspaper editor).

Credits: Written and directed by Preston Sturges. Director of photography: John F. Seitz. Music score by Leo Shuken, Charles Bradshaw. Musical direction: Sigmund Krumgold. Art direction: Hans Dreier, Ernst Fegté. Edited by Stuart Gilmore. Costumes: Edith Head. Makeup artist: Wally Westmore. Sound recording by Hugo Grenzbach, Walter Oberst. Set decoration: Stephen Seymour. Western Electric Mirrophonic Recording.

Additional Cast: Brian Donlevy ("McGinty"), Akim Tamiroff ("The Boss"), Almira Sessions (Wife of Justice of the Peace), Esther Howard (Sally), J. Farrell MacDonald (Sheriff); Frank Moran, Bud Fine (Military police); Connie Tompkins (Cecilia), Georgia Caine (Mrs. Johnson), Torben Meyer (Doctor), George Melford (U.S. marshal), Jimmy Conlin (Mayor), Harry Rosenthal (Mr. Schwartz), Chester Conklin (Pete); Byron Foulger, Arthur Hoyt ("McGinty's" secretaries); Nora Cecil (Head nurse), Jack Norton (Man with champagne), Joe Devlin (Mussolini), Bobby Watson (Hitler), Len Hendry (Soldier who wants everyone to marry).

Additional Credits: Executive producer: Buddy DeSylva. Assistant director: Edmund Bernoudy. Filming dates: October 21, 1942 to December 1942. Reshoots: February 25, 1943. Premiered in New York City on January 19, 1944.

Other Versions: Remade as *Rock-a-Bye Baby* (1958), written and directed by Frank Tashlin, with Dean Martin and Jerry Lewis.

Available: Paramount DVD (2005). ISBN: 1-4157-1371-5. UPC: 0-97360-43124-7.

After completing *The Palm Beach Story* (1942), a comedy about infidelity, writer and director Preston Sturges turned to a pet project: *Triumph Over Pain*. Based on a book by René Fülöp-Miller, it was the biography of Dr. William T.G. Morton, a Boston dentist who discovered anesthesia. Staunchly opposed to the idea, Paramount head Buddy DeSylva re-edited the finished film and released it as *The Great Moment* (1944). Its failure at the box office helped persuade Sturges to leave Paramount for a contract with Howard Hughes, a move that many feel contributed to his artistic decline.

First Sturges had two more projects to finish at Paramount. One was a script about hero worship called *The Little Marine*; it was released in the middle of 1944 as *Hail the Conquering Hero*. Sturges had begun work on the other script, *The Miracle of Morgan's Creek*, in July 1942. As historian Brian Henderson has shown, Sturges tinkered with the idea in fits and starts, sometimes writing out scenes with dialogue, sometimes paraphrasing the story in prose, sometimes listing plot points and questions. Sturges apparently always had the end of the story in mind, but it took considerable work to find characters and plotting that could get him to that point.

By 1942 the war effort had seeped into almost every aspect of popular culture. Movies, books,

Dealing with the aftermath of a messy scandal: Alan Bridge, William Demarest, Betty Hutton and Diana Lynn in *The Miracle of Morgan's Creek*.

magazines, newspapers, plays, and radio extolled men in uniform and the sacrifices necessary by civilians to support them. What Sturges set out to do in his last two Paramount films would have been audacious enough in peacetime, but in the face of an overwhelming propaganda machine must have seemed positively foolhardy. He was going to attack not only hero worship, but the sanctity of motherhood.

That July Sturges was writing one of the lead roles in *The Miracle of Morgan's Creek* for Eddie Bracken, one of Paramount's biggest stars. Born in 1915 in Astoria, Queens, Bracken had worked in vaudeville as a child and acted in several comedy shorts in a style stolen from Hal Roach's *Our Gang*. He played Henry Aldrich on Broadway in *What a Life!* and also starred in the stage version of *Brother Rat*. His shtick as a shy, stammering juvenile prone to hysterical outbursts won him a contract at Paramount, where he appeared in comedies and musicals.

Betty Hutton was cast as the other lead, Trudy Kockenlocker. Born in Battle Creek, Michigan, in 1921, she had been a singer with the Vincent Lopez band before her Broadway debut in 1940. The rest of the cast was filled with faces familiar from Sturges's other films: William Demarest, Al Bridge, Porter Hall, and Esther Howard, among others. Returning in the story's framing scenes were Brian Donlevy and Akim Tamiroff from Sturges's first directorial effort, *The Great McGinty* (1940).

First Sturges had to get a script finished that would pass the censors. Because he was depicting soldiers, he also needed approval from the Office

of War Information (OWI). Shooting was supposed to start on October 21, but that September Sturges was still figuring out how to present the "miracle" that occurs to Trudy. On October 21, Paramount received seven pages of objections from Joseph Breen of the Hays Office; he was primarily concerned about whether or not Trudy is drunk when she agrees to get married at a dance for departing soldiers.

Trudy soon realizes that she is pregnant; what's worse, she can't remember the name of the soldier she married ("Ratzkiwatzki" is as close as she can get). She could get a divorce, but she needs a wedding license first. Trudy asks milquetoast bank clerk Norval Jones, the Bracken role, to impersonate Ratzkiwatzki before a nearby justice of the peace. The complications that ensue leave Trudy alone and pregnant on Christmas Eve, in effect turning the film into a contemporary retelling of the Nativity. The "miracle" in the title becomes even more blasphemous with the final twist in the plot, one so clever that it ultimately couldn't be censored.

The film's subject matter, Hutton's casual physicality, and not-so-suble touches like the name "Kockenlocker" led film critic James Agee to write in *The Nation* that the Hays Office "has been raped in its sleep." Even so, Sturges had to recut and even reshoot material to pass OWI censors after a screening in February 1943. Henderson cites a typical OWI directive: "Sequence should be of three or four clean cut and fresh looking soldiers in uniforms in barracks saying in morning how they had a swell time last night, but with no reference to drinking, and that now they are ready for duty and departure for war."

Larger meanings aside, *The Miracle of Morgan's Creek* is strong evidence of Sturges's growth as a filmmaker. The rap against him was that he wasn't a visual stylist. Here he stages a prolonged conversation between Trudy and Norval as they walk down a city street, at the time one of the most difficult scenes to accomplish (and consequently, one that ambitious filmmakers try to stage to this day). But the "look" of the film is also a reflection of how homogenized the medium had become. There was little variation at this point between Paramount and Warner Brothers or any other major studio. They all had roughly the same equipment, the same level of technical expertise in their staffs, the same wartime restrictions regarding lighting and the construction of sets.

What other filmmakers didn't have was Sturges's dazzling command of language, his ability to define and explore character through personality, his willingness to question conventions, his impeccable plotting, and his extraordinary freedom as both writer and director, creator and interpretor. Who else would have written Demarest this speech to complain about his daughters? "They're a mess no matter how you look at 'em . . . a headache 'till they get married . . . or else, they're so homely you can't get rid of them at all and they hang around the house like Spanish moss and shame you into an early grave." Who else would have held onto a moment that had almost nothing to do with the plot, just to give Demarest the chance to shine? And who else has the talent to fill his movies with such a profusion of equally brilliant moments?

The Miracle of Morgan's Creek was a legitimate box-office hit when it was finally released in January 1944. Sturges ran into censorship trouble making *Hail the Conquering Hero* as well, but it was nothing compared to the creative difficulties he had working for Howard Hughes. While some critics defend the two films he completed with Hughes— *The Sin of Harold Diddlebock* (1947) and *Unfaithfully Yours* (1948)—nothing he did later in his life matched his accomplishments at Paramount.

The Memphis Belle

U.S. Army Eighth Air Force/Paramount, 1944. Sound, color, 1.37. 42 minutes.
Featuring: Captain Robert K. Morgan (Pilot), Captain James A. Verinis (Co-pilot), Captain Vincent B. Evans (Bombardier), Captain Charles B. Leighton (Navigator), Technical Sergeant Robert J. Hanson (Radio operator), Technical Sergeant Harold P. Loch (Engineer, Top turret gunner), Staff Sergeant Casimer A. Nastal (Waist gunner), Staff Sergeant Clarence E. Winchell (Waist gunner), Staff Sergeant Cecil H. Scott (Ball turret gunner), Staff Sergeant John P. Quinlan (Tail gunner), King George VI, Queen Elizabeth.
Credits: Directed by Lt. Col. William Wyler. Cinematographers include: Maj. William C. Clothier, Lt. Harold Tannenbaum. Edited by John Sturges. Narration written by Sgt. Lester Koenig. Narrated by Edgar Kern. Music by Gail Kubik. "All aerial combat film was exposed during air battles over enemy territory."
Additional Credits: Alternate title: *The Memphis Belle: A Story of a Flying Fortress.* Military liaison: Lt. Col. Beirne Lay. Theatrical premiere: April 15, 1944.
Available: The Internet Archive (www.archive.org). United American Video Corporation VHS (1990). UPC: 0-84296-04078-0.

Throughout World War II, the U.S. government financed hundreds of documentaries for both military and civilian audiences. They were shown in public theaters as well as in screening halls on military bases, airfields, and ships at sea. A series like *Why We Fight* educated viewers about the political reasons for fighting, and about the enemy himself. Many documentaries were more purely instructional, like *How to Build a Trestle Bridge*; others functioned as what we call propaganda today.

These titles presented soldiers, politicians, and civilian volunteers as part of an effort to preserve and spread freedom. Within this group were films about combat, always a delicate subject due to the inevitability of death and carnage. The military's goal—to uplift viewers by showing them how the war was being won—was often at odds with how individual filmmakers perceived actual fighting.

Capturing combat footage became a badge of honor for the many Hollywood filmmakers who joined the military. John Ford's *Battle of Midway* (1942), Darryl F. Zanuck's *At the Front in North Africa* (1943) and John Huston's *Report from the Aleutians* (both 1943) all showed viewers at home how their troops responded in battle. William Wyler enlisted after winning a directing Oscar for *Mrs. Miniver* (1942), about the effects of the war on an English family. His first military film was *The Memphis Belle*, released in 1944. It concerned the crew of a B-17, a massive bomber known as a "Flying Fortress" that was used for long-range bombing runs over German territory.

The crew of the *Memphis Belle* had flown twenty-three successful missions when Wyler chose the plane as the subject of his film. (The director had started following another plane whose crew was led by Captain Oscar O'Neill, but it was shot down over Germany in the spring of 1943.) Before they could start filming, Wyler and his small, four-man crew had to attend training schools in England. "We had to learn how to take a machine gun apart and put it back together, because we had to be able to take over the machine gun in case one of the gunners got hurt," he said in a 1975 interview. Wyler also spoke at length about the difficulty of shooting in a sub-zero environment with hand-wound 16mm cameras, under fire from enemy planes, unable to match exposures when filming from different sides of the plane.

It was only by participating in raids that Wyler could envision the shape of the film. (The director flew in five missions.) Inspiration came from a 1941 British documentary, *Target for Tonight*, a sober, reserved account of a Royal Air Force bombing raid on Germany, and *Phyllis Was a Fortress*, about a mission over France. But that film included staged footage and scripted dialogue, some shot in a studio. Wyler insisted on using only genuine footage and soldiers, which made his task of fashioning a story all the more difficult.

Born in 1911, editor John Sturges started out at RKO, then worked as a production assistant for David O. Selznick before becoming an editor. Enlisting in the Army, he was assigned to the Air Corps, where he edited over forty documentaries and training films. He worked closely with Wyler, helping fashion a tremendous amount of footage into a comprehensible story. The two worked in the United States for six months to trim over 20,000 feet to forty-two minutes. They frequently had to "cheat" in *The Memphis Belle*, using footage shot from other planes in order to present a clear picture of the *Belle's* squadron and its targets. Sound for the film had to be recorded separately; the engines roaring on the soundtrack could have come from any plane, for example. The filmmakers used footage from different missions; in fact, the mission depicted here as the *Belle's* twenty-fifth was actually its twenty-fourth, because Wyler felt it more dramatic. (The *Belle* was retired from combat missions after the twenty-fifth.)

None of this denies the authenticity of the film, however, or the skill Wyler and his crew showed in capturing the details necessary to convey a sense of what it was like to participate in a bombing mission. Wyler's determination to show the truth is apparent throughout the film, even when it covers injuries and death, something civilian audiences at the time were not used to seeing. What's still striking today is how beautiful some of the cinematography is, and how influential. Shots that appear here would be copied for decades by other filmmakers, some of whom would also insert Wyler's actual footage into their movies.

Wyler originally planned a two-reel short (a little over twenty minutes), but after consulting with military brass in London, he received permission to expand his film to five reels. Wyler hired Lester Koenig to write a new script. (Koenig's grandparents had been Oscar-winning screenwriters at RKO, but his early writing work at Paramount had been unrewarding.) Wyler later said that "in large measure it was Koenig's superlative commentary and the ideas expressed in it" that made film a success. Editing took place at the Hal Roach Studios, and a rough cut was ready by December 1943. Wyler wanted the film to be shown theatrically, and received a boost from President Franklin D. Roosevelt. Seeing it in February 1944, the President responded, "This has to be shown right away, everywhere." Paramount agreed to distribute five hundred prints to 10,000 theaters.

The film's quiet, matter-of-fact tone proved more effective than more hyperbolic documentaries. As Wyler put it, "The situation was dramatic in itself. You didn't have to dramatize it. You could just show a gunner or a navigator looking around, waving and grinning at the camera, and you'd say, 'This is Jim Jones from such-and-such a place in Iowa. He's dead now.'"

Wyler's next project, codirected with Sturges, was *Thunderbolt*, which dealt with P-47s fighting in Italy. Sturges would go on to become a significant director, with titles like *Bad Day at Black Rock* (1955) and *The Great Escape* (1963) to his credit. Wyler flew four combat missions in all, suffering the loss of hearing in one ear as a result. As it was for so many, the war was a transformative experience for the director. His first postwar feature project was *The Best Years of Our Lives* (1946), which attempted to depict what awaited veterans—much like the ones we see in *The Memphis Belle*—when they returned home.

Double Indemnity

Paramount, 1944. Sound, B&W, 1.37. 107 minutes.
Cast: Fred MacMurray (Walter Neff), Barbara Stanwyck (Phyllis Dietrichson), Edward G. Robinson (Barton Keyes), Porter Hall (Mr. Jackson), Jean Heather (Lola Dietrichson), Tom Powers (Mr. Dietrichson), Byron Barr (Nino Zachette), Richard Gaines (Mr. Norton), Fortunio Bonanova (Sam Gorlopis), John Philliber (Joe Peters).
Credits: Directed by Billy Wilder. Screenplay by Billy Wilder and Raymond Chandler. From the novel by James M. Cain. Director of photography: John Seitz. Editorial supervision: Doane Harrison. Music score: Miklós Rózsa. Art direction: Hans Dreier, Hal Pereira. Process photography: Farciot Edouart. Costumes by Edith Head. Makeup artist: Wally Westmore. Sound recording by Stanley Cooley, Walter Oberst. Set decoration: Bertram Granger. Western Electric Mirrophonic Recording.
Additional cast: Bess Flowers (Secretary), Kernan Cripps (Conductor), Betty Farrington (Nettie, maid), Sam McDaniel (Garage attendant), Judith Gibson (Telephone operator), Miriam Franklin (Keyes' secretary).
Additional Credits: Produced by Joseph Sistrom. Executive producer: Buddy G. DeSylva. Assistant editor: Lee Hall. Production dates: September 27 to November 24, 1943. Released April 24, 1944.
Other Versions: Remade as the television film *Double Indemnity* (1973, directed by Jack Smight).
Available: Universal Studios Home Entertainment DVD (2006). ISBN: 1-4170-7251-2. UPC: 0-25192-90/82-1.

One of the cornerstones of the film noir genre, *Double Indemnity* had a tortuous journey from book to screen. The original story was written in the summer of 1935 by James M. Cain, at the time a middling screenwriter at Universal. It was based in part on a notorious 1927 case involving Ruth Snyder and Judd Gray, who murdered her husband Albert Snyder—although the author always insisted that the genesis of the plot came from a newspaper proofreader who was so bored with his job that he allowed a dirty headline to slip through.

Cain had worked briefly for an insurance company, and could write authoritatively about an insurance salesman who concocts the perfect murder with the help of a bored, unhappy housewife, only to be outwitted by jealousy, greed, and an insistent claims checker. Cain tried to sell it to the movies, but the Production Code office objected to the story's themes of adultery, incest, and murder. Instead, it was serialized in *Liberty* magazine. Cain later claimed that his story increased the magazine's circulation by millions.

Double Indemnity was the only story that had not yet been filmed when it appeared part of Cain's 1943 anthology *Three of a Kind*. Paramount executive Joe Sistrom brought it to Billy Wilder's attention, just as he had helped find Wilder's first directing project, *The Major and the Minor* (1942). Charles Brackett, Wilder's normal writing partner, refused to have anything to do with the project, and Cain was unavailable to work on it himself.

Either Sistrom or William Dozier, an MGM executive, recommended Raymond Chandler. (Sistrom made a chance remark that impressed Cain so much he used it in his own screenwriting efforts: "All characters in B pictures are too smart.")

Chandler was not well known at the time. Born in Chicago in 1888, but educated in England, he turned to writing for pulp magazines out of desperation after losing his job with a California oil company. He distilled his disdain for hardboiled writing and for Los Angeles in general into the character of Philip Marlowe, a private eye whose integrity, even nobility, set him apart from other detectives. Almost twenty years older than Wilder, Chandler had not worked on many screenplays—or novels, for that matter. As Wilder said, "Chandler had no idea about the structure of a picture nor the structure of a novel—it always ends somewhere with millions of questions, it is not tidy. But the descriptions, the dialogue, are absolutely first-rate."

Wilder and Chandler discarded much of Cain's plot, which wound up in a delirious suicide pact on an ocean liner. Chandler, who was too naive to negotiate his screenwriting contract through an agent, also discovered that Cain's dialogue wouldn't work on screen. "It doesn't quite play," he said, despite extensive rehearsals. "For the screen, everything has to be sharpened and pointed and wherever possible elided." Cain readily agreed.

The collaboration between Chandler and Wilder was unpleasant (as it would be between Chandler and Alfred Hitchcock on *Strangers on a Train*), but it resulted in an extremely tight and focused screenplay that bristled with tough-guy patter and sexual innuendo. The story's three main characters—salesman Walter Neff, too smart and sure of himself to realize he's in over his head; Phyllis Dietrichson, a blond, amoral femme fatale; and Barton Keyes, a brilliant, calculating detective figure—would resound throughout 1940s thrillers.

Wilder had trouble casting all three parts. Alan Ladd, James Cagney, and others turned down the Neff role. The director had to bully Fred MacMurray into the job. MacMurray, a former big band singer and saxophonist, usually played soft, amiable types in comedies. "I fought a long losing fight against taking the role," he said later. "I didn't want to admit that I was refusing the part because I was afraid of it, because I feared that a guy who had played nothing but comedy roles would find this part too heavy to handle."

Barbara Stanwyck was also hesitant, especially after Wilder dressed her in a blond wig and form-fitting clothes in an effort to make her look as "sleazy" as possible. At that point she was the highest-paid actress in the country, whereas Wilder had directed only two relatively minor Hollywood features. But she praised the script, as well as Wilder's direction and the moody cinematography by John Seitz. "For an actress, let me tell you the way those sets were lit, the house, Walter's apartment, those dark shadows, those slivers of harsh light at strange angles—all that helped my performance," she said in a 1987 interview. "The way Billy staged it and John Seitz lit it, it was all one sensational mood."

In a sense, Wilder may have been capitalizing on *Remember the Night*, a 1940 romance written by Preston Sturges and directed by Mitchell Leisen. In it, Stanwyck played a career criminal, and Mac-Murray a New York City prosecuting attorney who jeopardizes his career when he falls for her. Neff could very well have been that attorney years later, anonymous and disillusioned in sunny Los Angeles, just as the thief Stanwyck played could have settled into an unhappy marriage. Wilder and Chandler certainly drew from John Huston's version of *The Maltese Falcon* (1941), in particular that film's cold-blooded Brigid O'Shaughnessy.

But several elements set *Double Indemnity* apart from previous films: the palpable glee Wilder took in his characters' foibles, the inexorable downward pull of the story, the carefully chiseled dialogue, the use of actual Los Angeles locations, and Edward G. Robinson, Little Caesar himself in the crucial role of Barton Keyes. More than one writer has pointed out that *Double Indemnity* is as much a love story between Neff and Keyes as it is a murder thriller. Robinson, his vest jammed with pencils, cigars, and pocket protectors, gives a thoroughly convincing depiction of a brilliant but socially inept theoretician, and each of his half-dozen or so scenes provides an extra jolt, a new layer of menace, to the film. It was the first time

since he had become a star that he didn't receive top billing in a film.

Double Indemnity has its flaws. Its middle section, what Joe Breen's Production Code office described as "a blueprint for murder," often bogs down in inconsequential logistical details: alibis, doorbells, witnesses, lucky breaks, cars that won't start. (Chandler would incorporate many of these devices into his script for *Strangers on a Train*, only abetted there by Hitchcock's dark humor.) Stanwyck's blond wig makes her startlingly unattractive at times, while Neff's relationship with Phyllis's stepdaughter Lola skirts with the queasy sexual perversions Cain favored in his novels.

In its best scenes, though, the film is as shocking as a slap in the face. Robinson's showboating account of actuarial tables about suicide is one of the highlights of his career, while the steamy double entendres in Neff's initial meeting with Phyllis set a standard that has rarely been matched. Even so, Wilder had tremendous difficulty with the film's ending, a recurring problem in his career. He filmed a scene set in an execution chamber, only to delete it after previews. (The scene, which can be found in the published screenplay, would have provided an unnecessarily maudlin and pointed moral to the story.)

Double Indemnity was an immediate hit. Cain wrote, "It's the only picture I ever saw made from my books that had things in it I wish I had thought of." Wilder next made an Oscar-winning drama about alcoholism, *The Lost Weekend* (1945), inspired perhaps by working with Chandler. A chronic alcoholic, the novelist fell off the wagon and wrote "Writers in Hollywood," a bitter essay about his experience, for the *Atlantic Monthly*; on the other hand, more adaptations of his work reached the screen, such as *The Big Sleep* (1946).

Double Indemnity would resonate through Wilder's subsequent films, often in unexpected ways. Nino Zachette, here an ex-con lured into an affair with an older woman, surfaces as failed screenwriter Joe Gillis in *Sunset Boulevard*, for example. As Woody Allen once told interviewer Eric Lax about *Double Indemnity*, "It's Billy Wilder's best movie—but practically anyone's best movie."

Going My Way

Paramount, 1944. Sound, B&W, 1.37. 126 minutes.

Cast: Bing Crosby (Father Charles Francis Patrick O'Malley), Barry Fitzgerald (Father Fitzgibbon), Frank McHugh (Father Timothy O'Dowd), James Brown (Ted Haines, Jr.), Gene Lockhart (Ted Haines, Sr.), Jean Heather (Carol James), Porter Hall (Mr. Belknap), Fortunio Bonanova (Tomaso Bozanni), Eily Malyon (Mrs. Carmody), Robert Mitchell Boychoir, Risë Stevens (Genevieve [Jenny] Linden).

Credits: Produced and directed by Leo McCarey. Screen play by Frank Butler and Frank Cavett. Story by Leo McCarey. Music direction: Robert Emmett Dolan. Vocal arrangements: Joseph J. Liley. Music associate: Troy Sanders. New songs: lyrics by Johnny Burke; music by James Van Heusen. Director of photography: Lionel Lindon. Art direction: Hans Dreier, William Flannery. Special photographic effects: Gordon Jennings. Edited by LeRoy Stone. Costumes: Edith Head. Makeup artist: Wally Westmore. Sound recording by Gene Merrit, John Cope. Set decoration: Steve Seymour. Western Electric Mirrophonic Recording.

Additional Cast: George Nokes (Pee-Wee Belknap), Tom P. Dillon (Officer Patrick McCarthy), Stanley Clements (Tony Scaponi), Carl Switzer (Herman Langerhanke), Bill Henry (Intern), Hugh Maguire (Pitch Pipe), Robert Tafur (Don Jose), Martin Garralaga (Zuniga), Sybyl Lewis (Jenny Linden's maid), George McKay (Mr. Van Heusen), William Frawley (Max [song publisher]), Jack Norton (Mr. Lilley), Anita Bolster (Mrs. Hattie Quimp), Jimmie Dundee (Fireman).

Additional Credits: Production dates: August 16 to October 22, 1943. Premiered in New York City on May 3, 1944.

Awards: Oscars for Best Picture, Director, Actor, Supporting Actor (Fitzgerald), Writing—Original Story, Writing—Screenplay, Music—Original Song ("Swinging on a Star").

Other Versions: McCarey directed the sequel *The Bells of St. Mary's* (1945), starring Bing Crosby and Ingrid Bergman. Basis for a television series in 1962.

Available: Universal Studios Home Entertainment DVD (2007). UPC: 0-25193-23692-0.

When he began *Going My Way*, Leo McCarey was one of the most successful and admired directors in Hollywood. He had already won an Oscar for *The Awful Truth* (1937), one of the signature screwball comedies, and had worked with almost every significant screen comedian except Charlie Chaplin and Buster Keaton. McCarey's vision was distinctively American, and many of his personal projects dealt with the clash between European and American sensitivities. *Ruggles of Red Gap* (1935) brought a proper British manservant to the Western frontier, for example, while *Love Affair* (1937) examined a relationship between an American career woman and a European playboy.

Studio executives have always been reluctant to back religious films. Religion is a notoriously touchy subject, and a film that actively promoted Catholicism over, for example, Methodism could potentially offend a large portion of the movie-going audience. It was safer to finance films that remained ambiguous about religious creeds, that were based on history like *The Ten Commandments* (1923) or *Ben-Hur* (1925), or that offered a sort of nondenominational "spirituality."

So McCarey was taking a significant risk with *Going My Way*, which focused squarely on priests in a troubled New York City parish. His method for disarming antagonistic studio executives, as well as paying customers, was a return in a way to *Ruggles of Red Gap*: he didn't try to pretend that the priests were the same as everyone else, but showed how they tried to adapt to the world around them while retaining their religious identities.

McCarey was lucky to land Bing Crosby in the title role. At the time Crosby was the top male star in films, as well as on radio and records. As a result of carefully calculated career moves, he was the personification of everyday America: an easygoing, golf-playing husband and father who was patriotic and religious without being ostentatious. Crosby's personal life was considerably more complex, but there's little reason to doubt that he subscribed to the sentiments in *Going My Way*.

Crosby's presence also meant that the musical aspect of McCarey's original story would have to be beefed up. Songs had always played an important part in the director's work, but someone of Crosby's caliber demanded the participation of experts—in this case, lyricist Johnny Burke. The author of hits like "Pennies from Heaven" and "The Moon Got in My Eyes," Burke signed with Paramount in 1936, and was Crosby's chief lyricist for almost twenty years. In 1940, he arranged for Paramount to sign composer Jimmy van Heusen. They had worked together on a few films before *Going My Way*, including *Road to Morocco* (1942), which featured "Moonlight Becomes You." "Swinging on a Star," one of two songs they wrote for *Going My Way*, would win an Oscar for Best Song.

The music in the film operates on several levels. For one thing, moviegoers would expect songs in a Bing Crosby picture. But McCarey used the tunes to both personalize and develop Crosby's character. They became moral lessons as well as examples of how Crosby's Father O'Malley solved problems. McCarey delivered these problems and lessons in a manner so smooth and ingratiating that many mistook them for entertainment. One of the real charms in watching the film today is trying to pinpoint exactly when McCarey is advancing the plot, and not just exploring parables and vignettes, or wandering down improvisatory paths.

Released during the height of World War II, *Going My Way* was a major box-office hit. It was the first film to win Oscars for writing, directing, song, and best picture. It also caused a change in voting rules for the Academy of Motion Picture Arts and Sciences when Barry Fitzgerald was nominated in both the Best Actor and Best Supporting Actor categories. *Going My Way* gave Crosby some of the signature tunes in his career, not just "Swinging on a Star," but "Too-Ra-Loo-Ra-Loo-Ra" and "The Day After Forever." The picture was so popular that within months McCarey and Crosby were filming a sequel, *The Bells of St. Mary's* (1945). Costarring Ingrid Bergman, the film essentially repeated the original, only with a new element of sex. McCarey carefully tamped down any possibility of an affair between Father O'Malley and Bergman's Sister Mary Benedict, but still filmed their scenes as if they were taking place in a romantic drama.

Because many of McCarey's subsequent films embraced a staunch conservatism, it has been fashionable to belittle his work. But at the peak of his career, directors esteemed him as much as Ernst Lubitsch. Writer Ephraim Katz quotes Jean Renoir as saying, "Leo McCarey is one of the few directors in Hollywood who understands human beings." Certainly few directors could portray such emotionally charged scenes with such simplicity and grace. Sentimental as they are, films like *Love Affair* and *Going My Way* seem honest in a way that other directors have trouble matching.

Jammin' the Blues

The President, Lester Young, about to play in *Jammin' the Blues*.

Warner Bros., 1944. Sound, B&W, 1.37. 10 minutes.

Featuring: Lester Young, Red Callender, Harry Edison, Marlowe Morris, Sidney Catlett, Barney Kessel, Joe Jones, John Simmons, Illinois Jacquet, Marie Bryant, Archie Savage.

Credits: Directed by Gjon Mili. Produced by Gordon Hollingshead. Photographed by Robert Burks. Technical director: Norman Granz. Film editor: Everett Dodd. Sound by Charles David Forrest. Art director: Roland Hill. RCA Sound System.

Additional Credits: "Jammin' the Blues" and "Midnight Symphony" by Lester Young. "On the Sunny Side of the Street," lyrics by Dorothy Fields, music by Jimmy McHugh. Copyrighted May 5, 1944.

Available: Warner Home Video DVD *Passage to Marseille* (2006). UPC: 0-12569-67990-0. Eagle Rock Entertainment DVD *Improvisation* (2007). UPC: 801213906093.

From 1926—when Warner Bros. started using the Vitaphone process to introduce sound to moviegoers—until World War II, the format for musical shorts had changed in only minor ways. The earliest musical shorts were strictly representational, capturing performances as if they were being given on stage in a theater. Occasionally the setting changed—from garden bower to parlor, for example, or from bandstand to arena—but cumbersome cameras and inadequate microphones limited the ability of directors to change perspectives. Once postdubbing freed cameramen from stationary positions, musical shorts took on more of a narrative framework. Writers made up stories about the performers, explaining why they were in front of the camera, or introduced fictional characters who acted out songs or placed them within plots.

Second features, the undercards of double-bills, were usually fifty to sixty minutes long. They assumed some of the functions of musical shorts, giving screen time to up-and-coming radio performers, for example. By World War II, Warner Brothers had closed its Vitaphone studio in Brooklyn. Now all the studio's shorts were being produced in Hollywood under producer Gordon Hollingshead. His department preferred miniature dramas, many with Western settings, and many directed by Crane Wilbur, a former star of silent serials.

Apart from cartoons and documentaries, Warners released about one short a month in 1944. These included the Westerns *Gun to Gun*, *Trailin' West*, and *Trial by Trigger*, but also musical performance pieces like *Sunny Dunham and His Orchestra*, *Harry Owens and His Royal Hawaiians*, and *Bob Wills and His Texas Playboys*. *Jammin' the Blues* was different from most musical shorts, in part because it was directed by Gjon Mili, a freelance still photographer for *Life* magazine who had helped develop the use of flash and strobe lights to capture dance and athletics.

But the ringer in the crew for *Jammin' the Blues* was Norman Granz, at the time a twenty-six-year-old Army veteran who was working as an editor at MGM. As a teenager in Los Angeles, Granz became obsessed with jazz. He befriended drummer Lee Young, whose brother Lester was one of the most celebrated saxophone players in the country. Lester Young had made his reputation first in Kansas City, then as a sideman for Count Basie, and finally as a musical collaborator with vocalist Billie Holiday. Lester formed a band with Lee, which brought him into contact with Granz, who recorded the Lester Young Trio around this time.

Granz had started promoting jazz concerts in Los Angeles nightclubs, insisting on integrated audiences and—because he wanted customers to pay attention to the music—no dancing. At some point he hit upon the idea of staging "jam sessions" for the public. "Battle of the bands" nights had been a familiar feature at concert venues for years, but jam sessions, which took place in after-hours clubs and back rooms, were necessarily private. Granz rightly guessed that the public would like to see musical stars pair up with peers in a concert setting.

Jammin' the Blues would serve as free publicity for Granz's project, which debuted at the Los Angeles Philharmonic Auditorium two months after the film was finished. At one point or another, "Jazz at the Philharmonic," the umbrella title for the series, featured all of the musicians in *Jammin' the Blues*, as well as other jazz stars like Charlie Parker, Ella Fitzgerald, and Ben Webster. The series lasted until 1957, by which time Granz had helped form the influential jazz label Verve Records.

Early musical shorts assumed that viewers knew what they were watching, but *Jammin' the Blues* adopts the pedantic tone of an educational film. We could be watching a lecture about cave paintings or ethnic dance, delivered in the hushed tones of a museum tour guide. By dressing it with modernist flourishes, *Jammin' the Blues* wants to enshrine jazz as high art. Fortunately, Granz and Mili love the music as much as its musicians, and are acutely aware of how best to frame them. (The cinematography was by Robert Burks, who would shoot several features for Alfred Hitchcock.)

Lit and framed as towering, almost mythical figures, the musicians in *Jammin' the Blues* make the music they are playing seem mysterious and romantic, even if they are miming to prerecorded tracks. Lester Young becomes a moody, film noir figure wreathed in cigarette smoke. Harry Edison delivers his trumpet solos oblivious to the motion around him (or the camera, for that matter). For better or worse, many future jazz artists used these performances as models, slipping into similar roles both on- and off-stage.

Film historian Leonard Maltin cites the 1939 *Symphony of Swing* with Artie Shaw as a predecessor to *Jammin' the Blues*, but the style Mili used was too complex and time-consuming for other filmmakers to emulate successfully. Mili and Granz collaborated again in 1950 on a film about jazz improvisation. It was never completed, but sections of it were released in 2007 with other jazz films under the title *Improvisation*.

Laura

Twentieth Century-Fox, 1944. Sound, color, 1.37. 87 minutes.
Cast: Gene Tierney (Laura Hunt), Dana Andrews (Mark McPherson), Clifton Webb (Waldo Lydecker), Vincent Price (Shelby Carpenter), Judith Anderson (Ann Treadwell).

Credits: Produced and directed by Otto Preminger. Screen Play by Jay Dratler and Samuel Hoffenstein, and Betty Reinhardt. Music by David Raksin. Musical direction: Emil Newman. Director of photography: Joseph LaShelle. Art direction: Lyle Wheeler, Leland Fuller. Set decorations:

Thomas Little. Associate: Paul S. Fox. Film editor: Louis Loeffler. Costumes: Bonnie Cashin. Makeup artist: Guy Pearce. Special photographic effects: Fred Sersen. Sound: E. Clayton Ward, Harry M. Leonard. Western Electric Recording. A Twentieth Century-Fox presentation.

Additional Cast: Dorothy Adams (Bessie Clary), James Flavin (McAvity), Clyde Fillmore (Bullitt), Ralph Dunn (Fred Callahan), Grant Mitchell (Corey [scenes deleted]), Kathleen Howard (Louise), Lee Tung Foo (Servant), Cy Kendall (Inspector); Harold Schlickenmayer, Harry Strang, Lane Chandler (Detectives); Frank La Rue (Hairdresser), Buster Miles (Office boy), Jane Nigh (Secretary), John Dexter (Jacoby).

Additional Credits: Contributing screenwriters: Ring Lardner, Jr., Jerome Cady, Robert Spencer Carr, George Bricke, Philip Lewis. Original cinematographer: Lucien Ballard. Production dates: April 27, 1944 to June 1944. Opened in New York City on October 11, 1944.

Awards: Oscar for Best Cinematography.

Available: Twentieth Century Fox Home Entertainment DVD (2004). UPC: 0-24543-0602-6.

One of the signature film noirs of the 1940s, *Laura* boasts several milestones. It was director Otto Preminger's first significant feature in a career that stretched over several decades. David Raksin's theme music became an enduring pop standard. The film helped popularize the film noir genre, solidified Dana Andrews' stardom, and brought Clifton Webb back to the screen after almost two decades on the stage. *Laura*'s flashback structure and use of voice-over became emblematic of the genre, as did its rain-swept streets and looming nighttime shadows. The film was also a textbook example of how the studio system worked, circa 1944.

Like *Casablanca* at Warner Brothers, *Laura* was a film made by committee. It bore the creative stamps of everyone from Darryl F. Zanuck to cinematographer Lucien Ballard and writer Ring Lardner, Jr., although many contributions to the project went uncredited, and some were actually discarded. The story originated with Vera Caspary, who wrote a play called *Ring Twice for Lora* in 1939. Her agent showed it to Otto Preminger, who at the time was pursuing a theatrical career.

Born in Vienna in 1906, Preminger acted in and produced and directed plays in Austria, working with Max Reinhardt among others. In 1935, he was invited to the United States to direct *Libel!* an English-language version of a play he had mounted in Austria. This led to a contract at Twentieth Century-Fox; there Preminger argued with production head Darryl F. Zanuck over *Kidnapped* (1938). Fired, Preminger returned to New York in need of work.

"He wanted to make it a conventional detective story," Caspary said after Preminger offered to help her adapt *Laura* for the stage. She turned him down, and, failing to find a producer, refitted the story into two novels. Fox bought them both and the play for $30,000, and William Goetz, subbing for Zanuck,

assigned them to Preminger. (The director was back on the Fox lot only because Zanuck had left Hollywood to participate in the war effort.)

Preminger oversaw a draft by the three credited screenwriters, stripping away the multiple narrators Caspary used. (She complained later that he had weakened the ending of the novel, and had a poor understanding of the title character.) By that point Zanuck had returned to the Fox lot. He agreed to let Preminger produce *Laura*, but didn't want him directing what had been elevated into a big-budget film. (Instead, Preminger directed *In the Meantime, Darling*, a romantic drama originally called *Army Wives*.)

Zanuck added considerable input into the *Laura* project, from casting and budget suggestions to script doctoring. Zanuck approved Rouben Mamoulian for director, despite his spotty box-office record, and he approved Mamoulian's casting of Gene Tierney and Dana Andrews, two Fox contract players. The original Laura was to have been Jennifer Jones, then under contract to David O. Selznick. She refused to report to the set, and as suits and countersuits proceeded, the part was given to Tierney. Against Zanuck's wishes, Preminger hired Clifton Webb in the crucial role of columnist Waldo Lydecker.

One of the great creations of the 1940s, Waldo personified a bracing hauteur that represented to the rest of the country the New York City breed of cultural arbiters. What Webb added to the part, along with years of stage experience and a facility for delivering urbane dialogue, was his homosexuality, an open secret in the industry. Ring Lardner, Jr., ended up writing most of his dialogue, and lines like, "I don't use a pen—I write with a goose quill dipped in venom" have become some of the most memorable elements of the film.

Preminger was at first the only one who wanted Webb, and he shot the screen test that persuaded Zanuck to agree hire him. That fact may have helped the studio chief when it came time to replace Mamoulian, whom Preminger accused of sabotaging the material. Finally given control of shooting, Preminger scuttled the eighteen days' worth of footage Mamoulian oversaw. He started over again with a new cinematographer, Joseph LaShelle, although Mamoulian later said that some of his material, photographed by Lucien Ballard, made it into the final print.

Vincent Price, who enjoyed Mamoulian's restrained personal style, had trouble adjusting to

Preminger, who would soon get a reputation as a directorial tyrant. But he quickly realized that Preminger's approach made sense. "The New York society depicted in the film are all darlings, sweet and charming and clever and bright—on the surface," Price said years later. "But underneath they're evil. And Otto understood this in a way that Mamoulian did not."

Preminger also knew how set decoration, lighting, and music could contribute to or detract from mood and atmosphere. He and LaShelle devised long, elaborate tracking shots that showed off sets filled with props. He also gave leeway to David Raksin, hired when Fox's other composers turned *Laura* down. Raksin had a weekend to prove himself by writing a theme that could replace Duke Ellington's "Sophisticated Lady," Preminger's first choice for the film. It was the same weekend his wife informed him that she was leaving him. Raksin poured his feelings of unrequited love into a melody that became one of the biggest pop hits of the 1940s.

Raksin's "Laura" theme, Webb's acerbic humor, and Tierney's unearthly beauty are what earned *Laura* its reputation as a film noir, but Raksin, among others, saw that "it was not a detective story but a love story in a detective story milieu." Zanuck wanted something like *The Maltese Falcon*, filmed by John Huston in 1941. "It wasn't the plot" that made *The Maltese Falcon*, he said, "it was the amazing characters." In *Laura*, the details of the murder don't really matter. Nor do the ostensible clues: a cigarette case, a bottle of Black Pony scotch, two clocks (these last Zanuck's substitute for a lethal walking stick). For Preminger, the real heart of *Laura* is found in glimpses of skewed relationships, of thwarted desires, not in evidence of crimes. He wanted viewers to determine guilt or innocence based on what they saw of lifestyles and class behaviors. He hoped they would ignore the illogical flashbacks and the kind of theatrical staging that left party guests stranded like potted plants in the backgrounds of shots.

Laura was a substantial hit, earning about twice its budget of $1 million. Although Preminger tried to expand into musicals and comedies, his greatest successes for the next decade were in film noir. He is also represented on the Registry by *Carmen Jones* (1954). In 1990, Fox restored to *Laura* a portion of a flashback delivered by Waldo Lydecker that the studio deleted before the official opening.

Meet Me in St. Louis

MGM, 1944. Sound, color, 1.37. 113 minutes.

Cast: Judy Garland (Esther Smith), Margaret O'Brien ("Tootie" Smith), Mary Astor (Mrs. Anna Smith), Lucille Bremer (Rose Smith), Leon Ames (Alonzo Smith), Tom Drake (John Truett), Marjorie Main (Katie), Henry Davenport (Grandpa), June Lockhart (Lucille Ballard), Henry H. Daniels, Jr. (Lon Smith, Jr.), Joan Carroll (Agnes Smith), Hugh Marlowe (Colonel Darly), Robert Sully (Warren Sheffield), Chill Wills (Mr. Neely).

Credits: Directed by Vincente Minnelli. Screenplay by Irving Brecher and Fred F. Finklehoff. Based on the book by Sally Benson. Produced by Arthur Freed. Lyrics and music: Hugh Martin and Ralph Blane. Director of photography: George Folsey. Color director: Natalie Kalmus. Color associate: Henry Jaffa. Film editor: Albert Akst. Musical adaptation: Roger Edens. Musical direction: George Stoll. Orchestrations: Conrad Salinger. Dance director: Charles Walters. Recording director: Douglas Shearer. Art direction: Cedric Gibbons, Lemuel Ayers, Jack Martin Smith. Set decorations: Edwin B. Willis and Paul Huldschinsky. Costume supervision: Irene. Costumes designed by Irene Sharaff. Make-up created by Jack Dawn. Technicolor. A Metro-Goldwyn-Mayer presentation.

Additional Cast: Donald Curtis (Dr. Girard), Mary Jo Ellis (Ida Boothby), Ken Wilson (Quentin), Robert E. O'Connor (Motorman), Darryl Hickman (Johnny Tevis), Leonard Walker (Conductor), Victor Kilian (Baggage man), John Phipps (Mailman), Major Sam Harris (Mr. March), Mayo Newhall (Mr. Braukoff), Belle Mitchell (Mrs. Braukoff), Sidney Barnes (Hugo Borvis), Myron Tobias (George), Victor Cox (Driver).

Additional Credits: Screenwriting by Sally Benson, Doris Gilbert, Sarah Y. Mason, Victor Heerman, William Ludwig. Songs by Hugh Martin and Ralph Blane; Arthur Freed and Nacio Herb Brown; Robert Cole and J. Rosamond Johnson. Premiered in St. Louis on November 22, 1944.

Available: Warner Home Video DVD (2004). ISBN: 0790744767. UPC: 012569508927.

The distinctive MGM style of musical was due in large part to producer Arthur Freed. He was born in South Carolina in 1894, and served in World War I as a sergeant in the Army. He entered show business by playing piano for a music publisher in Chicago, then by touring in vaudeville, where he appeared with acts like The Marx Brothers and Gus Edwards. He became a songwriter, often working with Nacio Herb Brown, composing hits like "I Cried for You," "You Are My Lucky Star," "All I Do Is Dream of You," and "Temptation." Freed was not an especially sophisticated writer, and even his standards have a sing-song quality to them. But he was a hard worker, and he staked out a position for himself at MGM during its critical transition from silents to talkies. Freed and Brown wrote the songs for *The Broadway Melody* (1929), the first musical to win a Best Picture Oscar, and they worked on several other early sound films.

Freed got his own unit after he served as associate producer on *The Wizard of Oz* in 1939.

He had certain predilections, some a result of the talent he had to work with, some a result of studio politics. For example, Freed tried to recycle songs already owned by the studio, not coincidentally many of them his own. The producer tailored his musicals for performers, of which Judy Garland was the most significant. He had helped her in her career-making role as Dorothy Gale in *The Wizard of Oz* (1939), developed her talent in Mickey Rooney vehicles, and guided her through her first mature part in *Little Nellie Kelly* (1940). Esther Smith is probably Garland's best post-*Oz* role, due in part to the winning story surrounding her.

That story came from Sally Benson's autobiographical sketches about growing up in St. Louis, Missouri, at the turn of the twentieth century. Born Sara Mahala Redway Smith in 1900, Benson moved with her family to New York City in 1911. She entered journalism in 1919, after marrying and divorcing Reynolds Benson, progressing from celebrity interviews to book and film reviews. She sold her first short story to *The New Yorker*, and in subsequent fiction became known for sharp, acerbic satires. A series of softer stories about the teen Judy Graves led to a best-selling book, *Junior Miss*, which later became a hit radio series, a Broadway play, and a movie.

Benson's next project was based on her sister's diaries about the 1904 St. Louis World's Fair. Published in 1942 as *Meet Me in St. Louis*, it was purchased by Freed, who had a hard time convincing MGM executives that a film could be fashioned from it. It wasn't contemporary, it wasn't a love story, and in fact wasn't much of a story at all, but a series of twelve nostalgic recollections about a middle-class suburban family enjoying the World's Fair before preparing to move to New York. Freed worked with a half-dozen writers to fashion a plot from the reminiscences. He thought the key was the Smith children's reluctance to be uprooted. The prospect of losing friends, memories, and a way of life proved enormously resonant in the midst of World War II.

Garland had to be persuaded to take the role, reluctant to play another teenager. Both Lucille Bremer, a singer who had a brief career in movies, and Henry H. Daniels were making their film debuts. While sets were built on the MGM backlot, Blane and Martin worked on the score. The book's title forced the use of the song "Meet Me in St. Louis, Louis," written by Andrew B. Sterling and Kerry Mills to celebrate the 1904 fair. Freed used the song to introduce the Smith family one by one as they sing snatches of its lyrics, Freed himself dubbing for Leon Ames.

In an oft-told story, Freed insisted that Blane and Martin write a song about a trolley. At first the duo tried songs set on trolleys, or including trolleys in the lyrics, but Freed was adamant that the song had to be about the trolley itself. Blane got out of the jam when he spotted a newspaper picture of a trolley with the caption "Clang clang clang went the trolley." "The Trolley Song" became a pop hit and one of Garland's signature numbers. As did "Have Yourself a Merry Little Christmas," a bleak holiday tune that fit the wartime spirit. Sung by Garland with heartbreaking resignation to Margaret O'Brien, playing the younger sister Tootie, it is the strongest emotional point in the film, and a moment of despair that the film never really recovers from.

Freed gave the project to Vincente Minnelli, a Broadway veteran who had heretofore directed bits and pieces of other films and an all-black musical produced by Freed, *Cabin in the Sky*. Minnelli already had a reputation for expressionistic flourishes, and he would go on to become one of the most visually extravagant directors on the lot. He had a knack for capturing the fragile emotions that roil relationships as they are starting, that moment when the inexperienced go from timid to yearning. It was something that Garland excelled in as well, which made their work together easier. The two would eventually marry, after working together on *The Clock*.

St. Louis's Halloween sequence allowed Minnelli the most room to stretch out. It is a scene composed almost entirely of subjective shots, as Tootie becomes increasingly frightened walking down a dark street. O'Brien's other stand-out moment is her duet with Garland to "Under the Bamboo Tree," a popular hit in 1902. It is a sequence that wouldn't have been out of place in an Andy Hardy film, but overall there are darker emotions here, problems that would disrupt the family. That the film doesn't solve these conflicts, at least not the way Benson's book did, can be seen as a masterstroke by Freed, at that time one of the most astute judges of the audience in the industry.

Not all the shooting went smoothly. Garland was already known as a temperamental actress, and she was "sick" a great deal during the production, which lasted five months. But she wasn't the only one. Astor, her career revitalized after *The Maltese*

Falcon some three years earlier, suffered from a virus that kept her off the set. O'Brien went on strike, or its equivalent, a work stoppage, until she received a significant pay raise. Delays helped raise the film's budget to $1.5 million, but it grossed well over four times that figure.

The film ends as the family visits the fair, represented by matte paintings and back projection. It is a grand finish to an often troubling story. It's amusing to think that the Smith family might be on its way to see the Registry title *Westinghouse Works* (1904), a sensation that year at the fair.

National Velvet

Elizabeth Taylor riding Piebald (played by King Charles) in *National Velvet*.

MGM, 1944. Sound, color, 1.37. 123 minutes.

Cast: Mickey Rooney (Mi Taylor), Donald Crisp (Mr. Brown), Elizabeth Taylor (Velvet Brown), Anne Revere (Mrs. Brown), Angela Lansbury (Edwina Brown), Jackie Jenkins (Donald Brown), Juanita Quigley (Malvolia Brown), Arthur Treacher (Race patron), Reginald Owen (Farmer Ede), Norma Varden (Miss Sims), Terry Kilburn (Ted), Arthur Shields (Mr. Hallam), Aubrey Mather (Entry official), Alec Craig (Tim), Eugene Loring (I. Taski), Dennis Hoey (Mr. Greenfield), Matthew Boulton (Entry official), Gerald Oliver Smith (Photographer).

Credits: Directed by Clarence Brown. Screen play by Theodore Reeves and Helen Deutsch. Based on the novel *National Velvet* by Enid Bagnold. Produced by Pandro S. Berman. Photographed in Technicolor. Director of photography: Leonard Smith. Technicolor color consultant: Natalie Kalmus. Technicolor associate: Henri Jaffa. Musical score: Herbert Stothart. Recording director: Douglas Shearer. Art direction: Cedric Gibbons, Urie McCleary. Set decorations: Edwin B. Willis. Set decorations associate: Mildred Griffiths. Special effects: Warren Newcombe. Costume supervision: Irene. Costume associate: Kay Dean. Men's wardrobe: Valles. Makeup created by Jack Dawn. Film editor: Robert J. Kern. Western Electric Sound System. A Metro-Goldwyn-Mayer presentation of a Clarence Brown production.

Additional Cast includes: Howard Taylor, Moyna MacGill, Billy Bevan.

Additional Credits: Production dates: Mid-January to June 26, 1944. Premiered in New York City on December 14, 1944. National release: April, 1945. Rated G in 1971.

Awards: Best Actress in a Supporting Role (Anne Revere), Film Editing.

Other Versions: *National Velvet*, an NBC television series, ran 1960–62. *International Velvet* (1978, directed by Bryan Forbes), featured a character who played Velvet Brown's niece.

Available: Warner Home Video DVD (1999). ISBN: 0-7907-4416-3. UPC: 0-12569-50632-9.

Often regarded as a milestone in the career of Elizabeth Taylor, *National Velvet* is just as notable as the prototypical MGM product of its time. Enid Bagnold's novel was published in the United States in 1935. Producer Pandro S. Berman, then with RKO, tried to buy the rights as a possible project for Katharine Hepburn. Instead, Paramount bought them, selling the novel to MGM two years later. The studio announced many plans for the book, but with the outbreak of war and the closing of European markets, the project was put on hold. When Berman signed a contract with MGM in 1941, he renewed development of an adaptation, seeing it in the vein of *The Wizard of Oz*, a family film with family themes. Tests were shot of numerous actors, but Berman wasn't satisfied with them, or with the script.

The tenor of the production changed when Berman replaced director Mervyn LeRoy with Clarence Brown, who renewed his contract with the studio in November 1943. A former engineer and car salesman, Brown was once a protégé of director Maurice Tourneur. He was famous as

"Garbo's director," having helmed seven of her movies. But more indicative of Brown's sensibility was *Ah, Wilderness!* (1935), his adaptation of the Eugene O'Neill play. A true ensemble piece, it was also Americana at its finest: nostalgic, sweet-tempered, but still critical and realistic.

Brown rewrote the script for *National Velvet,* building up a role for juvenile actor Jackie Jenkins, who had appeared in the director's *The Human Comedy* (1943), an adaptation of the William Saroyan play that also starred Mickey Rooney. Like that film, Brown saw *National Velvet* as a celebration of the family, and devoted much of the film to Velvet Brown's parents and siblings. The father, a butcher played by screen veteran Donald Crisp, is blustering and wrongheaded in the manner of television sitcom dads, but Brown is careful to show that he always ends up making the right decisions. The mother, played by Anne Revere in an Oscar-winning performance, is an improbable but highly appealing combination of strength and sensitivity, the core of the family as well as the arbiter of its problems. Judith Anderson had once been considered for the part; she shared with Revere an indomitable spirit that could easily tip over into pathological.

Ah, Wilderness! had helped launch Mickey Rooney's career at MGM. As the star of the Andy Hardy films, he was one of the most valuable actors at the studio. Rooney was also transitioning from teenager to adult, and had adopted a more restrained acting style under Brown's guidance in *The Human Comedy.* But there is no question that the film owes much of its appeal to Elizabeth Taylor, at the time a British twelve-year-old who was signed to a contract at MGM on the basis of a screen test directed by Fred Zinnemann. While not as technically accomplished as peers like Virginia Weidler, Taylor was blessed with an ethereal beauty and an innocent, almost naive screen persona. How much of her acting here is attributable to Brown is open for debate, but he achieved a similar effect with Claude Jarman in his next film, *The Yearling.*

National Velvet is much more than an accumulation of performances, however. Brown chose the film's locations, which included the surreal seascapes near Monterey, California. Using his engineering background, he approached the production as a series of problems that had to be solved in the most efficient manner. As a result, he turned to state-of-the-art technology: matte paintings, double exposures, back projection, and other special effects, to say nothing of the still balky Technicolor process.

While *National Velvet* has a reputation as a horse movie, very little screen time actually centers on Piebald, or "The Pie," played in the film by King Charles. The climactic Grand National race takes up only seven minutes of screen time, for example. Critics of the day singled out the sequence, which contributed to an Oscar win for editor Robert Kern, but Brown also deserves praise for overcoming daunting production problems. He told the press he wanted to film the race with no sound at all—no dialogue, no background noise—but the footage seemed too unreal when viewed totally silent. Even so, the sound is extremely spare: crowd noises, the beat of hooves, the thwacking of brush. Brown also had to figure out how to place Taylor in the race convincingly. He ended up limiting her to three close-ups shot with back projection. Most of the race is shown in wide shots, making camera angles and editing all the more important to maintain pacing. The infrequent close-ups and moving shots add a pounding intensity to the sequence.

Some directors might have ended the film with the race and the novel's satisfying plot twist on it. But Brown, like Enid Bagnold, realized the importance of ending Velvet Brown's fantasy properly. The final fifteen minutes of the film let viewers celebrate the young girl's accomplishments, but they also raise moral questions about wealth and celebrity that few other movies of the time bothered mentioning. As *The Wizard of Oz* did, *National Velvet* concludes that there is no place like home, but Brown also shows how constricting that home is, and how it is fracturing.

What happens when home is a dirt-floor shack became the focus of Brown's adaptation of Marjorie Kinnan Rawlings' novel *The Yearling* (1946). Closely aligned with Louis B. Mayer, Brown would lose interest in filmmaking after Mayer was forced out of MGM. Elizabeth Taylor very quickly matured into one of the studio's most glamorous and profitable stars. She would appear with Anne Revere again in the Registry title *A Place in the Sun* (1951).

Mom and Dad

Hallmark Productions, 1945. Sound, B&W, 1.37, 97 minutes.

Cast: Hardie Albright (Carl Blackburn), Lois Austin (Sarah Blake), George Eldredge (Dan Blake), June Carlson (Joan Blake), Jimmy Clark (Dave Blake), Bob Lowell (Jack Griffith), Jimmy Zaner (Allen Curtis), Jane Isbell (Mary Lou), Virginia Vann (Virginia), Willa Pearl Curtis (Junella), Robert Filmer (School superintendent), Forrest Taylor (Dr. Ashley), John Hamilton (Dr. Burrell), Jack Roper (School coach), Wheeler Oakman (Salesman), Francis Ford (Country doctor), Betty Sinclair (Waitress), Lucille Vance (Women's Club president), Kay Renard (Nightclub singer), The Liphams (Young acrobats).

Credits: Directed by William Beaudine. Original screenplay by Mildred Horn. Produced by J.S. Jossey and Kroger Babb. Under the personal supervision of Barney A. Sarecky. Associate producer: Lewis G. Dow. Cameraman: Marcel LePicard. Musical director: Eddie Kay. Special effects: Ray Mercer. Set dresser: John Sturtevant. Make-up artist: Ted Edlin. Film editor: Lloyd Friedgen. Sound engineer: Glen Glenn. Assistant director: Arthur Hamburger. Executive assistant: Betty Sinclair A Hygenic Productions production.

Additional Credits: Story by Kroger Babb and Mildred Horn. "Where Shall We Dream Tonight?" and "That's What You Do": words and music by Edward Kay and Eddie Cherkose. Premiered in Oklahoma City on January 3, 1945. Rated R in 1969.

Available: Movies Unlimited VHS (*www.moviesunlimited.com*).

The goal of all commercial filmmakers is to separate customers from their money. How best to do that has puzzled everyone from Thomas Edison and his staff to present-day producers and distributors. Much of the focus of this quest has been on the product itself: Do moviegoers want comedy or drama? Documentary or fiction? Stars or actors? Original material or adaptations?

A different approach concentrates more on publicity and advertising than on creative elements. RKO producer Val Lewton was handed film titles chosen by surveys of potential customers, for example, and then had to find projects to fit them. Mastering what used to be called ballyhoo required a keen understanding of the marketplace and a knowledge of tried-and-true gimmicks stretching back to circuses and medicine shows. One of the expert promoters in the 1940s was Kroger Babb, who took a disreputable genre and fashioned from it what some consider to be the most profitable exploitation movie ever made.

While every showman knew that sex was an easy sell, the problem was finding a way to sell it without offending authorities, both local and national. One solution was the "sex hygiene" story, which surrounded titillating material with a moral framework. The 1913 play *Damaged Goods* was able to discuss intercourse by condemning syphilis; its film adaptation reputedly earned $2 million. Similar films followed: *Crusade of the Innocent* (1922), *The Solitary Sin* (1924), *The Miracle of*

Life (1926), and fifteen more cautionary sex tales between 1927 and 1929. These were made by independent companies and distributed through "four-walling," a practice of renting a movie theater outright, providing all prints and advertising, and then reaping all the profits.

Howard Babb was born in 1906 in Lees Creek, Ohio, and took the nickname "Kroger" from a midwestern grocery chain. A reporter in the 1920s, he started out in show business as the public relations director for a chain of movie theaters. He joined Howard Russell Cox and Howard Underwood to distribute *Dust to Dust*, a retitled version of *Child Bride* (1938). Something of an anomaly, *Dust to Dust* ranked with high-budget exploitation films like *The Birth of a Baby* (1938) and *Child Bride* (1941). Kroger came up with the idea of making and marketing the most expensive exploitation film of its era, and funded it by asking twenty individual investors to contribute to the newly formed Hygenic Productions.

Babb ended up with a budget of $63,000 for *Mom and Dad* (many exploitations films were shot for under $20,000). With his future wife Mildred Horn, he fashioned a screenplay based closely on *High School Girl* (1934). Through J.S. Jossey, one of the investors and an executive at Monogram Pictures, he obtained access to Monogram sound-stages for one week. He hired director William Beaudine, an industry veteran who had worked with Mack Sennett, D.W. Griffith, and Mary Pickford, and who was known for his speed. They pulled together a crew primarily from the Monogram staff.

The basic plot of *Mom and Dad* describes how high school student Joan Blake is swept off her feet by a visiting pilot. She's soon "in trouble," but is afraid to tell her sternly disapproving mother. A kindly schoolteacher, hounded out of his job for trying to teach sex education, is the first to help her. Reinstated, he brings experts to school to screen sex-education films for his students.

Although they may seem harmless today, these sex-education films-within-a-film were the raison d'être for *Mom and Dad*. Babb assembled them almost out of thin air, splicing legitimate medical footage with hokey staged re-enactments. One film showed the normal delivery of a baby; a second showed one delivered through caesarian section. The third film used government footage that documented advanced cases of syphilis and gonorrhea. Uncomfortable to watch, even gruesome, these films shocked a generation of moviegoers who had no real experience with pornography.

The explicit footage could also be edited into or out of the film without difficulty, thus skirting local censorship boards. Crucially, the body of *Mom and Dad* never mentioned "pregnancy," "intercourse," or other hot-button words. To obtain permission to screen his film, Babb would send up to six front men out to meet with town leaders. They would be armed with "cold" or clean versions of *Mom and Dad*, as well as letters of recommendation from often fraudulent politicians and doctors.

Babb's contract insisted on gender-segregated showings (women only at 2:00 and 7:00 p.m.; men at 9:00 p.m.), and with nurses in attendance at every showing. Booking agent Joe Solomon later revealed what you may have already guessed: "They weren't really nurses but nobody knew the difference." Also present at every show: Elliot Forbes, an "eminent sexual hygiene commentator" who would hawk books like Hildegarde Esper's *Facts of Life* or *Your Sex Questions Answered*. Forbes was another fake, but his presence helped sell an enormous number of books. At one point Babb had twenty-five out-of-work vaudevillians acting as Forbes across the country.

Time magazine reported that by 1949, *Mom and Dad* had earned $8 million, and had been seen by twenty million customers. The publication in 1948 of Alfred Kinsey's *Sexual Behavior in the Human Male* proved to be excellent publicity for the film, so much so that knockoffs like *Street Corner* and *Because of Eve* came out that same year. *Mom and Dad* became the focus of a censorship battle that wasn't settled until 1956, when the Appellate Division of the New York State Supreme Court overturned the New York State Censor Board by saying that the depiction of human birth was not "indecent."

Later handled by Modern Film Distributors, *Mom and Dad* proved profitable well into the 1960s, although its niche was gradually replaced by legitimate sex-education films designed for and marketed to public schools. Babb had another hit when he picked up the rights to the anti-marijuana drama *Wild Weed* (1949), and in 1953 released a re-edited version of Ingmar Bergman's *Summer with Monika* as the sex film *Monika, the Story of a Bad Girl*. According to film historian Eric Schaefer, Babb's personal productions were box-office failures. He died of heart failure in 1980.

The Battle of San Pietro

U.S. Army Pictorial Services, 1945. Sound, B&W, 1.37. 33 minutes.
Credits: Produced by the Army Pictorial Service. Music: The Army Air Force Orchestra, the Mormon Tabernacle Choir, St. Brendan's Boys Choir. A War Department presentation.
Additional Credits: Written and directed by John Huston. Narration by John Huston. Cinematography: Jules Buck, John Huston, additional U.S. Army Signal Corps cameramen. Editing: Gene Fowler, Jr. Music: Dmitri Tiomkin. Filmed primarily in December 1943. Released theatrically in May 1945. Note: The title on most prints is *San Pietro*.
Available: The Internet Archive (www.archive.org). Image Entertainment DVD, *Treasures from American Film Archives* (2000). UPC: 0-14381-9706-2-3.

One of the most powerful documentaries about World War II, *The Battle of San Pietro* was the second of three films made by John Huston after he left Hollywood to join the U.S. Army Signal Corps. The first, *Report from the Aleutians* (1943), was nominated for an Oscar. The second began when he was in London in the fall of 1943. He was asked to film the Allied campaign to Rome; accompanying him there were novelist Eric Ambler and photographer Jules Buck (the latter had worked on the *Aleutians* film). Coincidentally, Huston had been writing a screenplay adaptation of Ambler's *Journey Into Fear* when he left for Alaska.

The advance on Rome was delayed by many factors. Huston, Ambler, and a crew of six found themselves in Naples, searching for a subject to film. In his memoirs, Ambler wrote this about the structure of their planned project: "Our best plan would be to move into a small town immediately after the enemy had left, and then make a film of what happened next to its inhabitants."

San Pietro, a town of some 1,400 that was the strategic key to the Liri Valley, became the focus of the film. Hemmed in by mountains, it was heavily fortified by German defenses. In his autobiography, *An Open Book*, Huston devoted a chapter to the battle, which involved primarily the 143rd Infantry Regiment of the 36th Texas Infantry Division. Fighting began on December 8 and stretched

Candid glimpse of a soldier in *The Battle of San Pietro*.

out over days, with troops repeatedly repulsed by Germans in fortified defensive positions. Huston and his crew often found themselves too far ahead of Allied lines, and had to take cover with natives hiding in mountain caves.

Or at least that's how the director described the filming. But as it turned out, Huston didn't reach the Liri Valley until the last day of fighting. In 1989, Lance Bertelsen, a professor at the University of Texas, published "*San Pietro* and the 'Art' of War," in which he analyzed unedited footage from the film. Bertelsen determined that most of the film "was restaged between late December and late February using troops from the 36th Division." Captain Joel Westbrook, who had actually fought in the battle, was assigned to assist Huston. Soldiers were given concussion grenades to use during filming. Westbrook and Huston positioned them according to maps of the battle, after Huston had decided what situations to re-create.

Huston filmed some of the material himself, along with Buck and other Signal Corps cameramen, and their footage has a directness and immediacy missing from most wartime documentaries. Huston wrote about one photographer who was shaking too much to film the 360-degree pan the director wanted: "Then I had him do it a third time and he was as steady as a rock." In the finished film you can see how the concussions from exploding howitzers jar cameras, how soldiers leap for cover, how some appear to be killed by bullets and shells.

The structure of the film may have been decided by Ambler and Huston, but the director was responsible for its narration, which he delivered himself. Apart from the occasional purple passage (a career-long problem with Huston), it is a model of clarity and restraint. Like the still photographs by Robert Capa, whom Huston admired, there was no separation between artist and soldier in *The Battle of San Pietro*, no pontificating from a position of safety, no moralizing about the rights or wrongs of one side or another. There was just the war itself, dirty and deadly, with its endless problems to solve.

Huston returned to Astoria soundstages outside New York City, and eventually to Hollywood, to edit the footage. He prepared a five-reel version that even he realized went too far. Soldiers interviewed about home life were later seen as corpses, and Huston claimed that he included shots of dismembered body parts. Although Captain Westbrook felt that Huston depicted the battle accurately, a consensus was forming among Army officials not to release the film at all. After a special screening, General George C. Marshall declared that every soldier going into combat should see it. Huston cut some twenty minutes from the original version, and agreed to tack on a superfluous prologue read by General Mark Clark.

The shorter version of *The Battle of San Pietro* is all that remains today, but it ranks with *The Memphis Belle* (1944) as one of the most honest and respectful of battle documentaries. Dense with information, it is also extremely easy to follow, thanks to Huston's use of maps and the startling cinematography, strong enough to sustain several extended silent passages. Especially impressive is the director's coda: shots of natives emerging from caves to deal with the rubble of their homes, and then a sequence focusing on children. Here, without words, Huston shows viewers precisely why we were fighting.

Film critic James Agee called *The Battle of San Pietro* "as good a war film as I have seen." (He would later work with Huston on *The African Queen*, 1951.) The director's next documentary, *Let There Be Light*, dealt with the rehabilitation of soldiers blinded in battle. The Army considered it so disturbing that it prohibited its release. It wasn't screened publicly until Ronald Haver, then the curator of the Los Angeles County Museum of Art, included it in a 1980 retrospective of Huston's films. Producer Ray Stark, MPAA executive Jack Valenti, and Vice President Walter Mondale were instrumental in persuading Secretary of the Army Clifford Alexander to declassify *Let There Be Light* and *Report from the Aleutians*. At the time, Huston shrugged off the controversy; he had already returned to working on a pet project, an adaptation of *The Treasure of the Sierra Madre* (1948).

The House I Live In

RKO, 1945. Sound, B&W, 1.37. 11 minutes.

Cast: Frank Sinatra.

Credits: Directed by Mervyn LeRoy. Written by Albert Maltz. Produced by Mervyn Leroy, Frank Ross. Director of photography: Robert De Grasse. Film editor: Philip Martin, Jr. Musical director: Axel Stordahl. "The House I Live In," music by Earl Robinson; words by Lewis Allan. "If You Are But a Dream" composed by Moe Jaffe, Jack Fulton, Nat Bonx. A Frank Ross and Mervyn LeRoy presentation. Copyright Frank Ross Productions, Ltd. RCA Recording System.

Additional Cast: Axel Stordahl, Harry McKim, Teddy Infuhr, Merrill Rodin.

Additional Credits: "If You Are But a Dream" incorporates a musical theme from Anton Rubinstein's Romance No. 1 in E-Flat. Released September 11, 1945.

Available: The Internet Archive (*www.archive.org*). Grapevine DVD *Calendar Girl* (*www.grapevinevideo.com*).

In 1945, Frank Sinatra was at the height of his popularity as a singer. Born in Hoboken, New Jersey, in 1915, he entered show business after winning a radio contest on the *Major Bowes Amateur Hour*. A featured singer in bands led by Harry James and Tommy Dorsey, Sinatra was idolized by legions of bobby-soxers. He went solo in the 1940s, appearing as a singer in minor musical films and getting his first acting role in *Higher and Higher* (1943).

Throughout his career, Sinatra was committed to racial and religious equality, having experienced taunting as a youth about his Italian heritage. Several anecdotes describe how he would physically fight reporters, bartenders, and others who insulted blacks and Jews. When he recorded "Ol' Man River," Sinatra changed the lyrics "Here darkies work" to, "Here we all work." In 1944, he pledged to President Franklin D. Roosevelt to address the youth of the country about tolerance.

In 1945, Sinatra made thirty speaking appearances, including a World Youth Rally at Carnegie Hall. Director Mervyn LeRoy approached the singer about filming a short on the topic, the equivalent of a modern-day public service announcement. To sugar-coat the message, Sinatra would perform two songs in the film, a reprise of his January pop hit "If You Are But a Dream" and "The House I Live In."

Written by Earl Robinson and Lewis Allan (a pseudonym for Abel Meeropol), "The House I Live In (That's America to Me)" had been recorded by Paul Robeson and Conrad Thibault. The Delta Rhythm Boys sang it in Universal Studio's 1944 propaganda musical *Follow the Boys*. Sinatra recorded his movie version on May 8, 1945. Allan, who also wrote the lyrics to the anti-lynching song "Strange Fruit," was upset that some of his lines were omitted. The second verse, which started "My neighbors white and black," was cut, as was a line that referred to "the worker and the farmer."

Leftist playwright Albert Maltz wrote the screenplay, which reworked some of the material Sinatra was already using in his public addresses. Maltz, also a novelist and short story writer, had worked on documentaries after moving to California in 1941. He would soon be imprisoned as one of the "Hollywood Ten" and blacklisted for twenty years.

Reportedly shot in two days, the film opens in a recording studio, where Sinatra and Axel Stordahl, his arranger at the time, are finishing a take of "If You Are But a Dream." Sinatra steps out into an alleyway, the second of the film's two sets, for a cigarette. Spying a group of boys picking on another, the singer interrupts to talk about racial and religious diversity as cornerstones of the struggle for freedom. Simplistic but still sincere, it was a controversial statement for Sinatra to make. And while the film's budget was small, LeRoy and producer Frank Ross (at the time an RKO vice president) did not skimp on the production, which featured crane shots, a full studio orchestra, a polished editing scheme, and even a war montage composed of stock footage.

During an August 15, 1945, radio performance with Bing Crosby, Sinatra sang "The House I Live In," receiving an extended ovation. Sheet music with Sinatra's portrait and a still from the film went on sale. The movie opened on September 11 in New York, and was reviewed favorably by both *Variety* and *Downbeat*. Sinatra continued his speaking tour, publicly admonishing white businessmen after a high school race riot in Gary, Indiana. Future jazz saxophonist Sonny Rollins remembered how an appearance by Sinatra at Harlem's Benjamin Franklin High helped quiet tensions at his school: "After that things got better, and the rioting stopped."

As a "tolerance short subject," *The House I Live In* received an honorary Academy Award at the 1946 ceremonies. Sinatra continued to make the song a part of his act, including it in his appearance at Caesar's Palace in 1974 and on his only authorized live release. (For a time after the terrorist attacks of 9/11, comedian Bill Cosby used it to open his shows.) Ironically, the movie caught the attention of the FBI, which increased its surveillance of Sinatra. Along with Maltz, songwriters Robinson and Allan were also members of the Communist Party. Under his real surname of Meeropol, Allan later adopted the children of Julius and Ethel Rosenberg after their parents were executed.

Mildred Pierce

Warner Bros., 1945. Sound, B&W, 1.37. 111 minutes.
Cast: Joan Crawford (Mildred Pierce Baragon), Jack Carson (Wally Fay), Zachary Scott (Monte Baragon), Eve Arden (Ida Corwin), Ann Blyth (Veda Pierce Forrester), Bruce Bennett ([Albert] Bert Pierce), Lee Patrick (Mrs. Maggie Biederhof), Moroni Olsen (Peterson), Veda Ann Borg (Miriam Ellis), Jo Ann Marlowe (Kay Pierce).
Credits: Directed by Michael Curtiz. Screen play by Ranald MacDougall. Based on the novel by James M. Cain. Produced by Jerry Wald. Executive producer: Jack L. Warner. Director of photography: Ernest Haller. Film editor: David Weisbart. Art director: Anton Grot. Music by Max Steiner. Montages by James Leicester. Sound by Oliver S. Garretson. Set decorations by George James Hopkins. Dialogue director: Herschel Daugherty. Special effects by Willard van Enger. Wardrobe by Milo Anderson. Makeup artist Pere Westmore. Orchestral arrangements: Hugo Friedhofer. Musical director: Leo F. Forbstein.
Additional Cast: John Compton (Ted Forrester), Barbara Brown (Mrs. Forrester), Butterfly McQueen (Lottie), George Tobias, Charles Trowbridge.
Additional Credits: Screenwriting by James M. Cain, Thames Williamson, Catherine Tunney, Albert Maltz, William Faulkner. Premiered September 24, 1945.
Awards: Oscar for Best Actress.
Available: Warner Home Video DVD (2005). ISBN: 1-4198-1085-5. UPC: 0-12569-67538-4.

The term *film noir* has been traced to French critic Nino Frank in 1946, and its definition is elastic enough to include *Mildred Pierce*. At the time no one working on the film would have called it that, however. They thought they were shooting a star vehicle for Joan Crawford, who had been under contract for two years at Warner Brothers without yet starting a film.

Crawford had spent eighteen years at MGM, outlasting her rivals Greta Garbo and Norma Shearer, but was reduced in the end to demeaning parts in pedestrian films. Born in 1906 in Oklahoma, she was a chorus girl in Chicago and a dancer for hire in New York when MGM producer Harry Rapf signed her to a contract in 1925. The studio held a nationwide contest to change her birth name, Lucille Fay Le Sueur, then tried her out in over two dozen films, ranging from Westerns to horror to slapstick. Crawford would do anything to become a star, but nothing seemed to work until she played an uninhibited flapper in *Our Dancing Daughters* (1928). Even F. Scott Fitzgerald was impressed, writing about her "laughing a great deal with wide, hurt eyes."

Crawford became one of MGM's most durable and dependable stars, and the studio responded by cultivating her image in a series of plushly mounted comedies and dramas in which she usually played ambitious working girls—reporters, dancers, stenographers, models. (The studio also tried to protect the actress from assorted scandals, including a hit-and-run automobile accident and ruining a West Point cadet's career, but gossip persistently circulated around her.) Crawford aligned herself with anyone she felt could help her professionally, including William Haines, Douglas Fairbanks, Jr. (her first husband), Clark Gable, Franchot Tone (husband number two), Joseph Mankiewicz, and George Cukor. Her MGM formula lost its relevance as World War II commenced, and the studio released her from her contract in 1943.

Jack Warner signed Crawford almost at once, possibly in order to bring contract player Bette Davis into line. Davis had already turned down *Mildred Pierce*, as had Rosalind Russell, but Crawford saw that the project was really an extension of the parts she had played the previous decade. In the story, Mildred dumps her ineffectual, unemployed husband to start what would become a chain of restaurants. The plot essentially picked up from where the "happily ever after" endings of many of her MGM films left off.

The source material was a 1941 novel by James M. Cain, one of the hottest pulp novelists in Hollywood on the basis of books like *Double Indemnity* and *The Postman Always Rings Twice*. But the project would never have passed the Production Code until Warners producer Jerry Wald provided a flashback structure for the plot. (A similar trick was used in Paramount's adaptation of *Double Indemnity*.) The flashback allowed the filmmakers to "punish" the villains in a way that the novel didn't, although Production Code authority Joseph Breen still felt the script was "sordid and repellent."

Wald hired Cain to work on a script, replaced him with story analyst Thames Williamson, assigned screenwriter Catherine Tunney to the project, and used Albert Maltz to punch up the murder plot. When he persuaded Michael Curtiz, Warners' most successful director at the moment, to take on the project, Ranald MacDougall came on to rework the script. Wald and Curtiz were responsible for the cast, which included mostly Warners contract players like Eve Arden and Jack Carson.

With a budget of $1,342,000 and a nine-week shooting schedule, Wald became nervous as December 13, the first day of production, approached. He hired three more writers, including William Faulkner, to tweak the script, but there was no finished screenplay as filming started. Curtiz took his time shooting, roiling studio head Jack Warner, who threatened to close down the film. (In Warner's words, "Technical perfection does not necessarily mean the success of a picture.") Curtiz shot mostly in sequence, using a restaurant he owned and his Malibu house for some locations. Filming was finished in late February, but Wald refused to release the picture for seven months, after the end of World War II.

Mildred Pierce struck an immediate chord with filmgoers. A tantalizing mix of sex and crime served up as a cautionary tale, the film also tapped into many of the concerns of working women and returning veterans. Curtiz, cinematographer Ernest Haller, and the numerous adaptors of James M. Cain provided many of the visual and narrative tropes of what would become film noir. The jagged angles, the half-hidden faces, the shadows that seep across many of the frames all reach back to German expressionism, but they also refer to the graphic art found in pulps—how Zachary Scott's corpse splays out in a diagonal receding from the camera, for example.

Much of the picture plays out like any domestic melodrama—in fact, like Crawford's MGM movies from a decade earlier. The characters may be seething underneath, but on the surface they are all good manners. Even the love scenes are dispassionate, rote. It's only when the violence erupts that the turmoil within the plot can be glimpsed. Curtiz films the shooting and the slaps in a sensual style, the camera darting toward the bodies involved.

Crawford won the Academy Award for Best Actress, legitimizing her move to Warners and cementing her new screen persona. For the rest of her career, she would specialize in playing women who had reached a level of success, but were now threatened by unimagined fears and unintended consequences: a philandering husband or boyfriend, ungrateful relatives, unscrupulous business partners. Ultimately, these threats came from psychopaths, killers, and finally actual monsters. Crawford herself never gave up—not when her audience deserted her, not when her face froze into a painted mask, not when her film vehicles descended into muck, not even when her adopted daughter accused her of abuse.

Christina Crawford's *Mommie Dearest* (1978) helped inaugurate an entire genre of tell-all biographies exposing the faults and failings of famous parents. Looking back now, it's difficult not to read something more into Crawford's performance in *Mildred Pierce* as a self-sacrificing mother beset by a deceitful daughter.

Detour

Producers Releasing Corporation, 1945. Sound, B&W, 1.37. 68 minutes. **Cast:** Tom Neal (Al Roberts), Ann Savage (Vera), Claudia Drake (Sue Harvey), Edmund MacDonald (Charles Haskell, Jr.), Tim Ryan (Nevada Diner proprietor), Esther Howard (Diner waitress), Pat Gleason (Joe, trucker at diner). **Credits:** Directed by Edgar G. Ulmer. Screen play and original story: Martin Goldsmith. Produced by Leon Fromkess. Associate producer: Martin Mooney. Director of photography: Benjamin H. Kline. Film editor: George McGuire. Production manager: Raoul Pagel. Assistant director: William A. Calihan, Jr. Art director: Edward C. Jewell. Set decorator: Glenn P. Thompson. Director of make-up: Bud Westmore. Wardrobe designer: Mona Barry. Sound engineer: Max Hutchinson. Dialogue director: Ben Coleman. Musical score: [Leo] Erdody. Western Electric Sound System.

A grim Tom Neal stares into the future in *Detour*.

Additional Cast: Don Brodie (Used car salesman), Roger Clark (Cop), Eddie Hall (Used car mechanic), Harry Strang (California Border Patrol).

Additional Credits: Screenwriting by Martin Mooney. "I Can't Believe That You're in Love with Me," music by Jimmy McHugh, words by Clarence Gaskill. "I'm Always Chasing Rainbows," music by Harry Carroll, words by Joseph McCarthy. Filmed June 25 to 30, 1945. Released November 30, 1945.

Other Versions: Remade as *Detour* (1992), directed by Wade Williams, starring Tom Neal, Jr.

Available: The Internet Archive (www.archive.org), and, among many other sources, Questar Entertainment DVD (2004). ISBN: 1-59464-068-8. UPC: 0-33937-03501-2.

Edgar G. Ulmer had an enviably eclectic career that included horror films, Yiddish and Ukrainian films, musicals, instructional films, and *Detour*, the most elemental and hopeless of all film noirs. Ulmer, born in Vienna in 1904, studied architecture before becoming a stage actor, set designer, and assistant director. While still a teenager, he came to New York to design sets for Broadway shows, then returned to Berlin to work as an assistant to F.W. Murnau. On films like *The Last Laugh* (1924), Ulmer received a thorough training in lighting, camera angles, and other cinema fundamentals. Ulmer accompanied Murnau to Hollywood, where he worked on two Registry titles, *Sunrise* (1927) and *Tabu* (1931).

Under contract at Universal, Ulmer directed several Westerns in a unit that included William Wyler; he was also an art director at Warner Brothers and MGM, working for directors like Ernst Lubitsch, Cecil B. DeMille, and Erich von Stroheim. He was in Berlin in 1929 to codirect the famous "street symphony" *Menschen am Sonntag* (1929) with Robert Siodmak; Billy Wilder and Fred Zinnemann also contributed to the film. It's hard to find a significant film figure Ulmer *didn't* work with.

Ulmer came back to the United States as an art director, but convinced Harry Cohn at Columbia to let him direct *Damaged Goods* (1933), a scandalous cautionary film about syphilis. He then talked his way into helming *The Black Cat* (1934), a Universal horror film that teamed Boris Karloff and Bela Lugosi for the first time. It was his first A-movie budget, most of which he devoted to lavish, Bauhaus sets. Although *The Black Cat* was a financial success, it would be the last film he would direct for a major studio. Ulmer fell in love with Shirley Castle Alexander, who was married to a nephew of Universal head Carl Laemmle. He was blacklisted from Universal, although he married Shirley, who worked with him the rest of his career.

For the next decade Ulmer directed an astonishing variety of films, producing and cowriting many of them: *Green Fields/Greene Felde* (1937), *The Singing Blacksmith/Yankel Dem Schmidt* (1938), both in Yiddish; the all-black *Moon Over Harlem* (1939); the Ukrainian *Cossacks in Exile/Zaprosh za Dunayem* (1939); the Spanish-language *Cloud in the Sky* (1940); government-sponsored films like *Goodbye, Mr. Germ* (1940); and a serial-killer film starring John Carradine, *Bluebeard* (1944).

By this time Ulmer was working at Producers Releasing Corporation, one of the "Poverty Row" studios in Hollywood. He shot most of his PRC films in six days, sometimes with eighty camera setups a day. (Each time the camera's position is moved is considered a set-up.) Ulmer's best trick in low-budget films was to leave one wall of a set blank: no windows, pictures, or props. He could place essentially any actor in the story there to film close-ups for any part of the plot. "I would say 'Look camera left; look camera right,'" he told writer and director Peter Bogdanovich. He didn't even bother to slate the shots: "I had to cut with the camera, because I was only allowed fifteen thousand feet for a feature, no more: two to one, nothing more." (This is an astonishingly low ratio of printed takes for a commercial production. A director like William Wyler might film thirty or forty takes of a shot.)

PRC was considered the cheapest of the low-budget studios. It churned out product indiscriminately. In November, 1945, the month *Detour* was released, PRC sent out six other films, including another Ulmer title, *Club Havana*. The company was formed in 1939 by Ben Judell; it 1940 it was absorbed into the Pathé Corporation. Leon Fromkess, once a treasurer at Monogram Pictures, became production supervisor and, in 1944, president. He left the company in September 1945, although he still received a producing credit on *Detour*.

The story came from a novel by Martin Goldsmith, a brother-in-law of Anthony Quinn. Ulmer referred to the book as "very bad," and had Martin Mooney, a PRC publicist, rewrite Goldsmith's script. Tom Neal, a boxer in college and a graduate of the Harvard Law School, was cast in the lead role as a piano player who falls into one of cinema's worst losing streaks. Neal's sullen good looks and limited acting abilities made him perfect as a down-on-his-luck hero who holds the same grim expression at each new blow. Claudia Drake plays what *Variety* used to call the "thrush" role, but the film really belongs to Ann Savage as Vera, film noir's archetypal vituperative nag. It's a fearless, relentlessly nasty performance that in its own way defines the near-shrieking tone studios like PRC felt forced to adopt to gain attention.

Detour is such an archetypal film noir in large part because Ulmer stripped away extraneous elements: the complicated plots, detectives, crooks, and schemes of other thrillers are all missing here. *Detour* has a good girl, a bad girl, and a loser, and it traps them all in a bitter nightmare that unfolds in an anonymous, indifferent city, or on an equally anonymous road. Ulmer's direction is cold, precise,

and focused. Every shot advances the story, every scene cements the hero's fate. The dialogue is terse, hard-bitten: "There ought to be a law against dames with claws." "You give a lift to a tomato, you expect her to be nice." "That's life—whichever way you turn, fate sticks out a foot to trip you." Early on, Neal refers to a ten-dollar bill as "a piece of paper with germs crawling on it."

Rumors persist that *Detour* is one of the cheapest films ever made, but Ulmer insisted on a some complicated shots with more extras, props, and lighting than were usually found in such low-budget films. PRC uncharacteristically agreed to spring for the rights to two songs, and Ulmer treated them in a fresh, vigorous manner. As he sits in the Nevada Diner, an unshaven Neal complains when a trucker plays "I Can't Believe That You're In Love With Me" on the jukebox. In a single take, Ulmer tracks in on Neal's face, switches the lighting scheme as the actor begins a voice-over, pulls back to reveal an oversized prop coffee mug, then glides over to the jukebox to start the film's first flashback: Claudia Drake singing the song in front of a big band.

Ulmer's exuberance and visual agility are what stand out in *Detour*, not the cramped sets or the increasingly tortured plot. (Or some glaring errors; to maintain Neal's east-to-west, right-to-left movements on the screen, Ulmer had to flip footage during early hitchhiking sequences. As a result, vehicles have steering wheels on the right, and drive on the wrong side of the road.) The film did exceptionally well for a low-budget thriller, winning a grudgingly admiring review from *Variety*. But Ulmer would soon leave PRC, spending the next twenty years flitting from project to project until strokes forced him to stop directing. Tom Neal's career was damaged when he got into a fracas that gave actor Franchot Tone a concussion. He was later convicted of involuntary manslaughter in the death of his third wife, Gale. He died in 1971, less than a year after being released from prison.

Topaz

Dave Tatsuno, 1943–45. Silent, color, 1.37. 48 minutes.

Credits: The *Topaz* collection consists of nine 8mm Kodachrome rolls photographed by Dave Tatsuno.

Available: The *Topaz* films are archived at The Japanese American National Museum (www.janm.org). Excerpts from the films, and an interview with Tatsuno, are included on *Return to the Valley: The Japanese-American Experience After WWII*, produced by KTEH, Silicon Valley Public Television (2003). More information: *www.returntothevalley.org.*

Immediately after the bombing of Pearl Harbor on December 7, 1941, the United States government began restricting the movement of Japanese Americans living in the country. Within forty-eight hours, over twelve hundred Japanese Americans were in custody. President Franklin D. Roosevelt signed Executive Order 9066 on February 19, 1942, authorizing any measures to secure the West Coast. From April to October, Japanese Americans were brought to assembly centers in Washington, Oregon, California, and Arizona. Some had less than two days' notice. From there they were assigned to one of ten relocation centers, or internment camps.

The relocation centers were spread out across California, Idaho, Utah, Arizona, Wyoming, and Arkansas. They consisted of barracks housing, a common mess hall, shower facilities, and few other amenities. The government supplied seed and equipment for inmates to farm their own crops and livestock, although some camps were located in deserts and were not suited to agriculture.

The Topaz internment camp, officially the Central Utah Relocation Center, covered almost 20,000 acres in Millard County, about 140 miles south of Salt Lake City. It opened on September 11, 1942, and at its peak held 8,130 inmates. Most came from Alameda and San Francisco. Among them was Dave Tatsuno and his family.

Born Masaharu Tatsuno in 1913, he grew up in San Francisco, adopting the name Dave in high school. After graduating from the University of California–Berkeley in 1936, he considered a career as a Presbyterian minister, but was asked to help with the family business. (His father had opened the Nichi Bei Bussan store in 1902.) Tatsuno became fascinated by film after he saw a home movie of a friend who had recently died. He bought a Bell & Howell 8mm camera and began making his own movies.

The Tatsunos were significant enough in the Oakland Japanese American community that their relocation was covered by photographers like Dorothea Lange. Dave Tatsuno's Bell & Howell camera was classified contraband, along with radios, swords, and other items, so he left it with a friend. At Topaz, Tatsuno became the manager of the dry-goods division of the War Relocation Authority's Co-op. Walter Honderick, his supervisor, was also a fan of home movies. He had Tatsuno's camera sent to the camp under his name. In later years, Tatsuno always singled out Honderick for his help.

As a manager, Tatsuno was allowed to travel across the country to purchase merchandise. "Back east people didn't know about the camps," he said. In Chicago and other cities he would buy rolls of Kodachrome color film. Processing the film required smuggling it out to his brother, a student

at the University of Utah. When his wife Alice sent for a sewing machine, Tatsuno had a friend include a projector in the package. (Sixty years later, Tatsuno was still protective of the people involved, refusing to identify those who helped him, apart from Honderick.)

Tatsuno's Topaz footage is the only color film documenting life inside an internment camp. What he shot was "not a documentary," he insisted. "I was merely taking family shots." He noted that Kodachrome made the camp look "more colorful than the bleak, dusty, and arid wasteland that it was." And many of his shots seemed "peaceful and almost happy because whenever I took shots of evacuees, they would ham it up and smile." In Tatsuno's view, his films were missing "the fear, the loneliness, the despair and the bitterness that we felt."

Tatsuno captured many of the same moments that any amateur filmmaker would: church services, birthdays, holidays, fellow workers, family members. But with a limited amount of film, he had to pick and choose what he covered, pre-editing what to shoot. In Delta, the nearest town, he photographed the main street, a reverend and his family, a hotel that served steak dinners. In the camp he covered traditional methods for making *moji* cakes, and students in a class in public speaking that he taught. He filmed weather: dust storms, snow, striking sunsets. A smooth, carefully composed landscape filmed from a bus window evokes a similar moment in *Commandment Keeper Church* (1940). "You're a movie man and you like to take beautiful shots," he explained.

But *Topaz* is also a documentary record of a terrible injustice, one reason why it should be seen by the widest possible audience. "The most telling shot in *Topaz* is my brother coming in to visit us in an American uniform," Tatsuno said. A draftee, the brother was supposed to fight in Europe, but the war there had ended. Instead, he trained in counterintelligence. Although a member of the armed forces, "he had to come to an American guard to visit his family," Tatsuno remembered. "What a travesty."

After the war Tatsuno reopened the family store and moved to San Jose. He seemed to lose interest in the internment films. When he saw Jacques Cousteau's *The Silent World* (1956), he became one of the first scuba divers in the Bay Area, and he devoted himself to underwater photography. Karen Ishizuka, at the time a curator at the

Japanese American National Museum, uncovered the films after talking with members of the family. They were screened at the museum in 1994, and chosen for the Registry two years later. Ishizuka also incorporated some of the footage into her documentary *Something Strong Within* (1994). In it, Tatsuno offers a modest theme for of his work: "I hope you see the spirit of the people trying to reconstruct a community despite overwhelming obstacles." He died at the age of 92 in 2006.

Why We Fight

U.S. Army Signal Corps, 1943–45. Sound, B&W, 1.37.
Titles: (1) *Prelude to War* (1943), 53 minutes. (2) *The Nazis Strike* (1943), 41 minutes. (3) *Divide and Conquer* (1943), 57 minutes. (4) *The Battle of Britain* (1943), 54 minutes. (5) *The Battle of Russia* (1943), 83 minutes. (6) *The Battle of China* (1944), 65 minutes. (7) *War Comes to America* (1945), 70 minutes.
Credits: Directed by Frank Capra, Anatole Litvak. Written by Anthony Veiller, Robert Heller, Leonard Spiegelgass, James Hilton, Allen Rivkin, William Shirer, Billy Henry, Frank Capra. Produced by Frank Capra. Edited by William Hornbeck. Music (in part) by Alfred Newman, Dimitri Tiomkin, Meredith Willson. Music performed by the Army Air Force Orchestra. Narrated by Walter Huston, Anthony Veiller, Lloyd Nolan, John Litel, Paul Stewart. Research: Edgar Peterson, Richard Griffith. Production assistant: Lyman Munson. Animation: Walt Disney Studios.
Additional Credits: Screenwriters include: John Huston, Theodor S. Geisel, Jo Swerling, Ben Hecht, Lillian Hellman, Marc Connelly, John Cheever, Irwin Shaw, Irving Wallace, Frances Goodrich and Albert Hackett, William Saroyan, Carl Foreman, Robert Stevenson, Valentine Davies, Gene Fowler, John Gunther. Editors include: Henry Berman, John Hoffman, Merrill White, Rex McAdam, Arthur Kramer, William Lyon, Marcel Cohen.
Awards: *Prelude to War*, Oscar for Best Documentary, 1943.
Available: Rhino Home Video VHS (1998). Goodtimes DVD (2001). UPC: 018713830166.

In his autobiography *The Name Above the Title*, director Frank Capra described how frightened he was after screening *Triumph of the Will*, Leni Riefenstahl's "terrifying" documentary about Nazism. As he put it, "Satan couldn't have devised a more blood-chilling super-spectacle." Like many in the film industry, Capra volunteered his services to the armed forces after the United States entered World War II. He completed *Arsenic and Old Lace* for Warner Brothers (due to contractual obligations it was held from release until 1944), then traveled to Washington, D.C., and New York City. Working out of offices in the Department of the Interior, he assembled a team that included British writers like Eric Knight and fellow director Anatole Litvak. (Born in Russia in 1902, the Jewish Litvak fled Germany after the rise of Nazism. In 1936, he directed the French romance *Mayerling*, which led to a contract at Warners. There he directed an early anti-fascist feature, *Confessions of a Nazi Spy*.)

Capra's mission, as described to him by Chief of Staff General George C. Marshall, was to make the case for war that could be understood by the general serviceman. Capra had to tailor his message to people who might not see newsreels or read newspapers. He had every means at hand except time. This precluded filming almost any original material, but it gave him the inspiration to base the project on newsreel footage taken from the Axis powers—or, as Capra put it, "use the enemy's own films to expose their enslaving ends."

After Capra and his team accumulated footage from various government agencies, he opened production offices in an obsolete Twentieth Century-Fox studio on Western Avenue in Los Angeles. In his book, Capra named dozens of helpers on the "Why We Fight" series; the unit was also responsible for "Know Your Ally" and "Know Your Enemy" series (a total of ten released features) and for the *Army-Navy Screen Magazine*, which had some fifty entries. It's difficult to assign credits to what was a collaborative effort, but the one person singled out by everyone for his work was editor William Hornbeck. Once the supervising editor for Mack Sennett, Hornbeck moved to Great Britain at the start of sound movies, returning to the United States to take part in the war effort.

Hornbeck oversaw an editing staff that at one point numbered twenty-five. They waded through hundreds of thousands of feet of film, selecting material on the basis of rough outlines prepared by writers. Hornbeck tried to establish geographic unity by having the Axis forces move from right to left and the Allies from left to right. Graphics associated the Axis with an evil black, while the Allies attacked on the backs of white arrows. The "Why We Fight" films offer a staggering amount of montage: guns, planes, explosions; marching, factories, arsenals; soldiers, machine guns, corpses.

The footage was stronger than that allowed in Hollywood films. In *The Battle of China* a rifleman shoots point-blank two kneeling Chinese prisoners, their hands tied behind their backs. In the same film bound prisoners are herded into a mass grave and shot. Such graphic material could support an exaggerated narration, and in "Why We Fight" Walter Huston is often called upon to question the entire German and Japanese races. "The Germans have an inborn national love of regimentation and harsh discipline," he says in *Prelude to War*. In *Divide and Conquer* he compares Adolf Hitler to John Dillinger, and there on the screen is a shot of Dillinger's corpse.

At the time such comparisons were considered fair game. So was the use of doctored film. "Why We Fight" incorporated German and Japanese newsreel footage along with material from *Triumph of the Will*, but rewrote the narration to change the meaning of the scenes. "Why We Fight" made extensive use of American documentaries like *The River*, *The City*, and *Siege*, which might be expected. Also present in the series were clips from several fiction films. Capra biographer Joseph McBride lists material from the following films, none of it identified in the series as fiction: *America*, *Drums Along the Mohawk*, *The Cross of Lorraine*, *Penny Serenade*, *Confessions of a Nazi Spy*,

A Tale of Two Cities, *All Quiet on the Western Front*, *Sergeant York*, *The Good Earth*, and more.

Marshall ordered that every serviceman see all seven entries in "Why We Fight." Capra screened *Prelude to War* for President Franklin Delano Roosevelt, who asked why it couldn't be shown in theaters. Capra received access to a lot of footage by promising it wouldn't be shown commercially, and butted heads with officials in the Office of War Information, which had negotiated with theater owners to have its own shorts represent the government. But *Prelude to War* and *The Battle of Russia* did receive theatrical releases; the former won an Oscar, although it did not attract a large audience.

The Battle of Russia was the source of some controversy after the war, while *The Battle of China* faced considerable opposition within military circles during its production. Today these are two of the more striking entries in the series, far superior to episodes like the meandering *War Comes to America*.

Notorious

Cary Grant and Ingrid Bergman in *Notorious*. *Courtesy of The Criterion Collection*

RKO, 1946. Sound, B&W, 1.37. 102 minutes.
Cast: Cary Grant ([T.R.] Devlin), Ingrid Berman (Alicia Huberman), Claude Rains (Alexander Sebastian), Louis Calhern (Paul Prescott), Madame [Leopoldine] Konstantin (Mme. [Anna] Sebastian), Reinhold Schunzel ("Dr. Anderson" [Otto Rensler]), Moroni Olsen (Walter Beardsley), Ivan Triesault (Eric Mathis), Alex Minotis (Joseph), Wally Brown (Mr. Hopkins), Sir Charles Mendl (Commodore), Richard Costa (Dr. Barbosa), Eberhard Krumschmidt (Hupka), Fay Baker (Ethel).
Credits: Directed by Alfred Hitchcock. Written by Ben Hecht. Production assistant: Barbara Keon. Director of photography: Ted Tetzlaff. Special effects by Vernon L. Walker, Paul Eagler. Art directors: Albert S. D'Agostino, Carroll Clark. Set decorations: Darrell Silvera, Claude Carpenter. Music by Roy Webb. Musical Director: C. Bakaleinikoff.

Orchestral arrangements: Gil Grau. Edited by Theron Warth. Sound by John E. Tribby, Terry Kellum. Miss Ingrid Bergman's gowns designed by Edith Head. Assistant director: William Dorfman. RCA Sound System. An RKO Radio Pictures, Inc., presentation, by arrangement with David O. Selznick.
Additional Cast: Alfred Hitchcock (Guest), Gavin Gordon (Ernest Weylin), Antonio Moreno (Seno Ortiza), Frederick Ledebur (Knerr), William Gordon (Adams), Charles D. Brown (Judge), Peter Von Zerneck (Rossner), Fred Nurney (John Huberman), Herbert Wyndham (Mr. Cook), Aileen Carlyle (Guest), Harry Hayden (Defense Council), Dink Trout (Court clerk); John Vosper, Eddie Bruce, Don Kerr, Ben Erway, Emmett Vogan, Paul Bryar, Alan Ward, James Logan (Reporters); Howard Negley, Frank Marlowe, George Lynn (Photographers); Gary Owen, Lester Dorr

(Motorcycle policemen); Patricia Smart (Mrs. Jackson); Candido Bonsato, Ted Kelly (Waiters); Frank Wilcox (FBI agent).

Additional Credits: Screenwriting by Clifford Odets. Produced by Alfred Hitchcock. Opened in New York City on August 15, 1946.

Other Versions: Remade as a television movie in 1992, directed by Colin Bucksey.

Available: Criterion Collection DVD (2001). ISBN: 1-55940-925-8. UPC: 7-15515-0127-2-0.

Pigeonholed as the "Master of Suspense," director Alfred Hitchcock's best work actually concerned troubled relationships, none more moving, or complicated, as the love affair between Ingrid Bergman and Cary Grant in *Notorious*. A major box-office hit on its release, it remains one of Hitchcock's most accomplished films, with three of the best performances the director ever elicited.

The genesis of the script was a story by John Taintor Foote, "The Song of the Dragon," published in the *Saturday Evening Post* in 1921. In August 1939, producer David O. Selznick was considering developing the story as a vehicle for Vivien Leigh, as well as for Alfred Hitchcock, both of whom were under contract with him. Selznick was only interested in one aspect of the story: the heroine sleeping with the villain in order to break up a spy ring. Ingrid Bergman expressed enthusiasm for the project in late 1941, provided Hitchcock was the director.

Hitchcock told François Truffaut that he and scriptwriter Ben Hecht updated the story to the Nazi era and switched its setting from New York to Latin America. (Hecht was officially hired in 1944.) They toyed with the idea of the Nazis setting up a secret army, "But we couldn't figure out what they were going to do with the army once it was organized." Hitchcock needed a "MacGuffin," a device that would propel the plot without necessarily adding any narrative meaning. He chose uranium, which, at least by his account, brought the director under the surveillance of government agents protecting atomic secrets.

Selznick insisted on changes that were incorporated into the more than a half-dozen screenplay drafts that Hecht and Hitchcock submitted. For one thing, the producer wanted a "happy ending." For another, he had to deal with objections to the story, especially the characterization of Alicia as "a grossly immoral woman," from Joseph Breen at the Production Code Administration. J. Edgar Hoover complained about the story's depiction of FBI agents.

After announcing his retirement to the press with the release of *Night and Day* (1946), a Cole Porter biopic, Cary Grant changed his mind two weeks later and accepted the lead role in *Notorious*. He persuaded Hitchcock to hire Clifford Odets; the playwright turned in a draft on September 18, 1945. According to studio notes, the final version was written between October 10, 1945, and January 22, 1946. By this point Selznick was immersed in *Duel in the Sun*, a large-scale Western starring Gregory Peck and Jennifer Jones. The producer ended up selling the entire *Notorious* package—script, stars, and director—to RKO (by some accounts making a $500,000 profit).

After several revisions, Hecht had given Hitchcock fully detailed characters with rich psychological backgrounds. Alicia (Ingrid Bergman), the wealthy but disillusioned daughter of a man convicted of treason, has thrown herself into a life of dissipation. Devlin (Grant), a cynical government agent, has to get Alicia to prostitute herself for the same country that imprisoned her father. Their target was Alexander Sebastian (Claude Rains), a wealthy Nazi investor living with his deeply suspicious mother in an isolated South American mansion.

Although Alicia falls in love with Devlin, she agrees to seduce Sebastian, hoping that Devlin will stop her. How far the hard-hearted Devlin will make her go to prove her love becomes the central issue of the film. It's a story that has almost nothing to do with espionage or the war effort; instead, it dissects its romantic angles with clinical accuracy. Hitchcock turns Devlin (and by implication, the moviegoer) into a voyeur, one who manipulates Alicia like a puppet.

In the 1940s, Bergman and Grant were two of the most appealing performers in film, and Hitchcock highlights their almost impossible beauty at every opportunity. Grant is dark, angular, rarely smiling; Bergman starts out lush and carefree, drinking and showing as much skin as censors could stand. They share a drawn-out kiss that caused consternation at the time for its length (to skirt Production Code restrictions, Hitchcock keeps the camera locked on their faces as they walk from one room to another). But Hitchcock devotes just as much of the film to depicting the lovers' suspicion and distrust, drawing viewers in on an emotional level that few movies of the time would attempt.

Of course, the director has his showboating moments, including a two-story crane shot that sweeps across a majestic staircase down through a lobby into a tight close-up of Bergman's hand clutching a key. That same staircase figured into one of the most suspenseful scenes in Hitchcock's entire output, with four characters each facing the deciding moments in their lives. (Hitchcock filmed the best of four possible scripted versions of the sequence.)

The director included unusually complicated matte shots and back projection, by his account angering cinematographer Ted Tetzlaff with lighting suggestions. He placed Rains on boxes to act with the taller Bergman, and ended up eliminating several scenes that he felt overstated the story's themes. Some viewers may not notice his more difficult work, including a series of complicated tracking shots that hold the characters in frame as they negotiate potential emotional landmines.

And yet he told Truffaut that he was proudest of the film's simplicity, and its lack of violence. About Cary Grant's character he said, "One can hardly blame him for seeming bitter throughout the story." Claude Rains, on the other hand, "is a rather appealing figure, both because his confidence is being betrayed and because his love for Ingrid Bergman is probably deeper than Cary Grant's." The emotional paradoxes at the heart of *Notorious* are what help make it resonate so deeply today, not its silly espionage capers, and not even Hitchcock's technical flourishes. It was the career highlight for almost everyone involved, and one of Hollywood's most troubling love stories.

Grant and Bergman appeared together again in Stanley Donen's *Indiscreet* (1958), a step in the rehabilitation of her film career after the scandal surrounding her affair with director Roberto Rossellini. Grant's next film with Hitchcock was *To Catch a Thief* (1955); they also collaborated on *North by Northwest* (1959). Hitchcock's next Registry title is *Rear Window* (1954).

The Big Sleep

Warner Bros., 1946. Sound, B&W, 1.37. 114 minutes.

Cast: Humphrey Bogart (Philip Marlow), Lauren Bacall (Vivian Sternwood Rutledge), John Ridgely (Eddie Mars), Martha Vickers (Carmen Sternwood), Dorothy Malone (Bookshop girl), Peggy Knudsen (Mona Mars), Regis Toomey (Bernie Ohls), Charles Waldron (General Sternwood), Charles D. Brown (Norris, the butler), Bob Steele (Canino), Elisha Cook, Jr. (Harry Jones), Louis Jean Heydt (Joe Brody), Sonia Darrin (Agnes Lowzier), Theodore von Eltz (Arthur Gwynne Geiger), Tom Rafferty (Carol Lundgren), James Flavin (Captain Cronjager), Joseph Crehan (Medical Examiner), Joy Barlowe (Taxi driver), Tom Fadden (Sidney), Ben Welden (Pete), Trevor Bardette (Art Huck), Emmet Vogan (Ed, the deputy), Forbes Murray (Furtive man), Pete Kooy (Motorcycle cop), Carole Douglas (Librarian), Jack Chefe (Croupier), Paul Weber, Jack Perry, Wally Walker (Mars' thugs), Lorraine Miller (Hatcheck girl), Shelby Payne (Cigarette girl); Janis Chandler, Deannie Bert (Waitresses); Marc Lawrence.

Credits: Directed by Howard Hawks. Screen play by William Faulkner, Leigh Brackett & Jules Furthman. From the novel by Raymond Chandler. Director of photography: Sid Hickox. Music by Max Steiner. Film editor: Christian Nyby. Special effects: E. Roy Davidson, director; Warren E. Lynch. Art director: Carl Jules Weyl. Sound by Robert B. Lee. Set decorations by Fred M. MacLean. Wardrobe by Leah Rhodes. Makeup artist: Perc Westmore. Musical director: Leo F. Forbstein. RCA Sound System.

Additional Cast: Pat Clark (Mona Mars in first version).

Additional Credits: Screenwriting by Philip Epstein. Executive producer: Jack L. Warner. Unit production manager: Chuck Hansen. Production dates: October 10, 1944 to January 12, 1945; reshoots in January 1946. Premiered in New York City on August 23, 1946.

Other Versions: *The Big Sleep* (1978), directed by Michael Winner, starring Robert Mitchum.

Available: Warner Home Video DVD (2000): ISBN: 0-7907-4698-0. UPC: 0-12569-50262-8.

Fresh from his success with *To Have and Have Not* (1944) for Warner Brothers, Howard Hawks suggested Raymond Chandler's *The Big Sleep* as a follow-up for Humphrey Bogart and Lauren Bacall. Chandler's reputation had grown since his days toiling for pulp magazines. He had co-written the screenplay for *Double Indemnity* (1944), a recent hit for Paramount, and his *Farewell, My Lovely* was currently being filmed at RKO (it would be released that year as *Murder My Sweet*). Jack Warner was enthusiastic about reteaming Bogart and Bacall, and approved the project. Since Chandler was under contract to Paramount (where he was writing *The Blue Dahlia*), Hawks turned to William Faulkner to adapt the novel.

Faulkner had also worked on *To Have and Have Not*, earning less than a quarter of what co-writer Jules Furthman received, and was souring on Hollywood as a whole. Hawks had read a pulp mystery called *No Good from a Corpse*, and hired its author to help Faulkner. He was surprised to learn that Leigh Brackett was a twenty-eight-year-old "she," and not a "he," but took her on at $125 a week.

Hawks had little interest in remaining faithful to Chandler's novel. Since it involved drugs, prostitution, pornography, and intimations of incest, a straight adaptation would never get past censors anyway. But he wanted Faulkner and Brackett to remain true to the spirit of the novel, which meant that the future Nobel Prize-winner, and a future *Star Wars* screenwriter, had to figure out Chandler's notoriously complicated plot, jerry-rigged from four short stories he had written for pulp magazines. (Per Faulkner's wishes, the two worked on alternate chapters, and never compared notes, a procedure that must have increased confusion.) One famous anecdote has Hawks and Bogart asking the writers who killed Owen Taylor, a chauffeur in the story. When neither could answer, Hawks wired Chandler, who confessed that he didn't know either.

But as Hawks biographer Todd McCarthy points out, the script does solve this mystery: Taylor was killed by Brody, who had been following him in order to steal compromising photographs. Hawks even shot a scene explaining this, but as Warners ordered changes to the film, it was ultimately discarded.

Still, the movie somehow managed to follow the general outline of the novel. Wealthy General Sternwood hires private eye Philip Marlowe to straighten out his daughter Carmen's gambling debts. Marlowe learns that she is mixed up in a blackmail plot that leads to two murders. Sternwood then asks him to find his other daughter Vivian's missing husband, who, it turns out, has also been murdered. Faulkner and Brackett finished their first draft in two weeks, and a revised draft two weeks later. Hawks still wasn't satisfied with the ending, but decided to start shooting and figure the script out later.

Chandler imagined Marlowe as a chivalrous knight; Hawks envisioned him as a cynical Lothario beset on all sides by man-hungry women. He pumped up subsidiary roles, emphasizing sexual hunger whenever he could, as with a cabbie (Joy Barlowe) and a bookstore clerk (nineteen-year-old Dorothy Malone). The Sternwood sisters were played by newcomer Martha Vickers (formerly Martha MacVicar) as Carmen and Bacall as Vivian.

The shoot, which started on October 10, 1944, was fraught. Bogart and Bacall had fallen in love during their previous film, but Bogart had since returned to his wife Mayo. Hawks was in love with Bacall, and became furious when he saw that she was falling for Bogart again. Bogart missed a day of shooting due to his wife's drinking, and since he was in almost every scene and shot, Hawks was stuck until he returned. Production was supposed to end on November 28, but by that point Hawks hadn't gotten halfway through the script. When Faulkner left Hollywood for his home in Mississippi, Hawks hired Jules Furthman to help tighten the rest of the script. He finally finished shooting on January 12, 1945, thirty-four days behind schedule.

The film was previewed in February; Bogart and Bacall announced their engagement a month later. *To Have and Have Not*, which opened in October 1944, was an enormous hit. Warners rushed Bacall into *Confidential Agent*, a spy thriller based on a Graham Greene novel which was a critical and box-office disappointment when it opened in October 1945.

That fall Charles K. Feldman, Bacall's agent, approached Jack Warner with the idea of reshooting *The Big Sleep* to emphasize the relationship between Bogart and Bacall. Warner agreed immediately. Philip Epstein wrote new material, including a famous scene in which the duo use horse-racing terms as sexual banter. Bacall was also given sexier outfits and more glamorous lighting for her close-ups.

A total of eighteen minutes changed from the first, pre-release version to the second, although the former is only two minutes longer than the latter. What came out was much of the explanation for the plot, such as who killed Owen Taylor. Todd McCarthy sees an even greater loss. Hawks would later admit, "During the making of *The Big Sleep* I found out for the first time that you don't have to be too logical, you should just make good scenes." McCarthy finds in this second version a willingness on Hawks' part to sacrifice logic and consistency for "scenes" that emphasized star power or visual flourishes.

For example, in the first version, Bogart hears a gunshot outside the blackmailer's house. He enters through French doors, sees a corpse, recognizes Carmen Sternwood slumped in a chair, then discovers both drugged liquor and a hidden camera used in blackmailing the girl. It's a tightly compressed scene that conveys a lot of information in a short time, but Hawks cut out most of it in the second version. He didn't mind sacrificing exposition and even characters to increase the entertainment factor of the film. (He even changed the actress playing Eddie Mars' wife from Pat Clark to Peggy Knudsen.)

(Robert Gitt at the UCLA Film & Television Archives restored the 1945 version in 1996; both versions are now available on DVD.)

What's striking about *The Big Sleep* at this remove is how little sense it makes as a whole. It's just Bogart wandering around a dark, wet Los Angeles, bombarded by sexpots and occasionally knocking a thug around. The murders, including a chilling office killing, don't really add up. Hawks has the settings down pat—he captures the tough guy attitude and patois. But the director keeps throwing dames at Bogart instead of actually working out a plot.

Plotting would be a problem on Hawks' next film, *Red River* (1948), as well. Bogart and Bacall would make only two more films together, although their relationship endured as one of the great Hollywood romances. Faulkner worked with Hawks on one more film, 1955's *Land of the Pharaohs*, but the author was essentially finished with screenwriting. Brackett, on the other hand, collaborated with Hawks on several of his late Westerns. Her final screenplay credit was for *The Empire Strikes Back* in 1980.

The Killers

Burt Lancaster and Ava Gardner in *The Killers*. Courtesy of *The Criterion Collection*

Universal-International, 1946. Sound, B&W, 1.37. 102 minutes.

Cast: Burt Lancaster (Ole Anderson, aka Pete Lund), Ava Gardner (Kitty Collins), Edmond O'Brien (James Reardon), Albert Dekker (Big Jim Colfax), Sam Levene (Lt. Sam Lubinsky), Vince Barnett (Charleston), Virginia Christine (Lily Harmon), Jack Lambert (Dum-Dum Clarke), Charles D. Brown (Packy Robinson), Charles McGraw (Al), William Conrad (Max).

Credits: Directed by Robert Siodmak. Screenplay by Anthony Veiller. From the story by Ernest Hemingway. Produced by Mark Hellinger. Director of photography: Woody Bredell. Music: Miklos Rozsa. Assistant to the producer: Jules Buck. Film editor: Arthur Hilton. Art direction: Jack Otterson, Martin Obzina. Set decorations: Russell A. Gausman, E.R. Robinson. Special photography by D.S. Horsley. Director of sound: Bernard B. Brown. Sound technician: William Hedgcock. Gown supervision: Vera West. Hair stylist: Carmen Dirigo. Director of make-up: Jack P. Pierce. Assistant director: Melville Shyer. Song "The More I Know of Love," lyrics by Jack Brooks, music by Miklos Rozsa. Western Electric Recording. A Mark Hellinger Productions, Inc., presentation.

Additional Cast: Donald McBride (Kenyon), John Miljan (Jake), Phil Brown (Nick Adams), Queenie Smith (Mary Ellen "Queenie" Doherty), Garry Owen (Joe), Harry Hayden (George), Bill Walker (Sam), Jeff Corey (Blinky Franklin), Charles Middleton (Farmer Brown).

Additional Credits: Title on screen: *Ernest Hemingway's The Killers*. Production dates: April 29 to June, 1946. Released August 28, 1946.

Other Versions: Remade as *The Killers* (1964, directed by Don Siegel).

Available: Criterion Collection DVD (2003). UPC: 7-15515-01332-1.

At the end of World War II, Ernest Hemingway was a household name, a novelist, short story writer, and war correspondent who had a profound influence on early twentieth-century literature. He was also in poor health and chronic debt. Movies provided an enviable source of income while requiring almost no labor on his part. Claiming to disdain Hollywood, Hemingway couldn't afford to reject its offers. Howard Hawks directed an adaptation of *To Have and Have Not* (1944) that brought together Humphrey Bogart and Lauren Bacall. It followed *For Whom the Bell Tolls* (1943), starring Gary Cooper and Ingrid Bergman. In the works: *The Macomber Affair* (1947), starring Gregory Peck and Joan Bennett.

Former newspaper columnist and scriptwriter Mark Hellinger spent part of the war in the South Pacific, returning to sign a contract with Universal. (More of his biography can be found in the entry for *The Naked City*, 1948.) He wanted to start at Universal with a splash, choosing "The Killers," a Hemingway short story that had been published in *Scribner's* magazine in 1927. "The exploitation values are little short of gigantic," was how Hellinger pitched it to Universal executive Bob Sparks.

Hellinger faced two immediate problems. "The Killers" was a well-known story about two hit men who take over a diner to ambush their target, a boxer known only as "the Swede." Hellinger had to use that situation because readers and critics would expect it, but he also had to come up with enough new material to fill out a feature film. The producer hired novelist Richard Brooks, who introduced an insurance investigator looking into the crime; and then John Huston, the screenwriter and director of *The Maltese Falcon* (1941). (Under contract at the time to Warner Brothers, Huston gave his screen credit to Anthony Veiller, his collaborator.) Together, Huston and Veiller constructed a story filled with elaborate flashbacks that fleshed out backgrounds for the Swede and his enemies. (Hellinger added his own touches, including a deathbed confession based on one he had heard from gangster Dutch Schultz.)

The Killers wasn't created in a vacuum. Huston had a fascination with heists and their aftermaths, a theme he used in *The Maltese Falcon* and *High Sierra* (1941); he would explore it at length in *The Asphalt Jungle* (1950). James Reardon, an insurance investigator played by Edmond O'Brien, may have been inspired by Edward G. Robinson's character in the highly successful *Double Indemnity* (1944). Orson Welles used a similar flashback structure in *Citizen Kane* (1940), as did Otto Preminger in *Laura* (1944). *The Killers* could be seen as simply reworking the types and situations that were beginning to define the film noir genre.

But Hellinger's two leads lifted *The Killers* out of the ordinary. This was the film debut for Burt Lancaster, a one-time circus performer who had entertained troops during the war. Hellinger had seen him in the Broadway flop *A Sound of Hunting*, and realized that the actor's physical presence could boost what was actually a fairly limited role as the Swede. Young, virile, aggressive, Lancaster was part of a new crop of film actors who were starting to replace the aging stars of the 1930s. It was also the first significant film appearance for Ava Gardner, signed to an MGM contract after modeling for a New York City photographer. Uncredited bits and minor roles in dozens of films were leading her nowhere, while her tumultuous personal life threatened to overwhelm her career. But Hellinger saw enough in her performance in *Whistle Stop* (1946), a backwoods soap opera, to

offer her the part of Kitty Collins. One of the classic femme fatales in film noir, the cold, calculating Collins was perfectly suited to Gardner, a guarded actress who was at the time uncomfortable with expressing emotion in front of a camera.

The real key to the success of *The Killers* may have been director Robert Siodmak. Born in Memphis, Tennessee, but raised in Germany, Siodmak was the son of a Jewish banker. He tried acting and banking before working behind the cameras, first as an editor, then translating intertitles. After a stint at the UFA studio, he co-directed the influential *Menschen am Sonntag* (1929) with Edgar G. Ulmer. He began to specialize in thrillers, but when Joseph Goebbels attacked *Burning Secret* (1933), an adaptation of a Stefan Zwieg story, Siodmak fled the country. After directing the noir-like *Pieges* (*Snares*, 1939) in France, he signed a two-year contract with Paramount.

Siodmak's first seven American films were "hack work," he said later. Their villains were "Japs, Germans, or Italians so I could make them as wicked as I wanted." He pushed his brother Curt, a screenwriter, out of the *Son of Dracula* (1943) project at Universal, winning a seven-year contract in the process. Siodmak credited meeting producer Joan Harrison, once Alfred Hitchcock's assistant, with revitalizing his career. Although a B-movie, *Phantom Lady* (1944), their first project, became one of the iconic film noirs of the 1940s. Based on a Cornell Woolrich story, it offered a compelling and seductive visual equivalent to pulp thrillers, and was imitated throughout the industry.

Siodmak used *Phantom Lady*'s cameraman, Elwood Bredell, on *The Killers*. In an *American Cinematographer* article, Bredell rejoiced in being able to "take a crack at a show where nothing had to be beautiful." He cut back drastically on lighting, limiting the number of arc lamps for night scenes and foregoing fill light in others. As for Gardner's unearthly good looks, "All we did was rub a little Vaseline into her skin for a sheen effect." Bredell based the visual scheme for the entire film around Gardner's flesh tones, creating an "out of balance lighting" that pushed the contrast between white and black to extremes.

The Killers contains several notable set pieces, some borrowed from *Phantom Lady* and other noirs, some that would reappear in subsequent films. *Gun Crazy* (1949) elaborated on Siodmak's staging of a robbery, which he filmed in one take from a crane stationed near the Universal studio gate. (The "Danger Ahead" theme from Miklos Rozsa's score was subsequently used for the *Dragnet* TV series.) The most arresting material in the film may be its opening twenty minutes, lifted intact from the Hemingway story. (This diner scene makes excellent use of two future noir stalwarts, actors Jim Conrad and Charles McGraw.) If the later plot developments in the film lack the nightmarish logic of the best thrillers, Siodmak could always return to the ferocious carnal energy between Lancaster and Gardner.

Even Hemingway liked *The Killers*, which opened to tremendous acclaim and long lines at the box office. Hellinger produced another film with Lancaster, the hard-edged prison drama *Brute Force* (1947), before returning to New York to make *The Naked City*. Lancaster, a full-fledged star after *The Killers*, made two more films with Siodmak, including the praised noir *Criss Cross* (1948). His next Registry title is *From Here to Eternity* (1953). Siodmak also worked with Gardner again, but her subsequent career was shaped to an unusual degree by incidents in her private life. The director returned to Germany in the late 1950s, where he continued to make brisk, efficient thrillers.

My Darling Clementine

Henry Fonda as Wyatt Earp in *My Darling Clementine*.

Twentieth Century-Fox, 1946. Sound, B&W, 1.37. 97 minutes.

Cast: Henry Fonda (Wyatt Earp), Linda Darnell (Chihuahua), Victor Mature (Doc Holliday), Cathy Downs (Clementine Carter), Walter Brennan (Old Man Clanton), Tim Holt (Virgil Earp), Ward Bond (Morgan Earp), Alan Mowbray (Granville Thorndyke), John Ireland (Billy Clanton), Roy Roberts (Mayor), Jane Darwell (Kate), Grant Withers (Ike Clanton), J. Farrell MacDonald (Mac [Bartender]), Russell Simpson (John Simpson).

Credits: Directed by John Ford. Screen play by Samuel G. Engel and Winston Miller. From a story by Sam Hellman. Based on a book [*Wyatt Earp: Frontier Marshal*] by Stuart N. Lake. Produced by Samuel G. Engel. Musical direction: Alfred Newman. Music: Cyril Mockridge. Orchestral arrangements: Edward Powell. Director of photography: Joe MacDonald. Art direction: James Basevi, Lyle Wheeler. Set decorations: Thomas Little. Associate set decorator: Fred J. Rode. Film editor: Dorothy Spencer. Costumes: René Hubert. Makeup artist: Ben Nye. Special photographic effects: Fred Sersen. Sound: Eugene Grossman, Roger Heman. Western Electric Recording. A Darryl F. Zanuck presentation.

Additional Cast: Don Garner (James Earp), Francis Ford (Dad), Ben Hall (Barber), Arthur Walsh (Hotel clerk), Louis Mercier (François), Mickey Simpson (Sam Clanton), Fred Libby (Phin Clanton), William B. Davidson (Owner, Oriental Saloon), Earle Foxe (Gambler), Aleth Hansen (Guitar player), Dan Borzage (Accordion player), Don Barclay (Owner, Opera House), Harry Woods (Marshal), Charles Stevens (Indian Charlie), Frank Conlan (Piano player), Robert Adler (Stagecoach driver), Charles E. Anderson, Duke Lee, Margaret Martin, Frances Rey.

Additional Credits: Assistant director: Edward O'Fearna. Additional directing: Lloyd Bacon. Production dates: April to June 1946. Reshoots: July and September 1946. Prerelease version: 103 minutes. World premiere: October 16, 1946.

Other Versions: *Frontier Marshal* (1934, directed by Lewis Seiler), *Frontier Marshal* (1939, directed by Allan Dwan), *Powder River* (1953, directed by Louis King).

Available: Twentieth Century Fox Home Entertainment DVD (2003). UPC: 0-24543-10318-9.

When John Ford returned to Hollywood after World War II, he was one of the most honored directors in the industry. He had won three directing Oscars, most recently for *How Green Was My Valley* (1941). Two of his wartime documentaries, *The Battle of Midway* and *December 7th*, received Oscars as well. Coming home meant an opportunity to address the issues that preoccupied him during the war, as well as offer his vision of American society. Ford was technically still in the Navy when he directed *They Were Expendable* (1945), a war film obsessed with death. Almost all of his remaining films would be Westerns or period dramas. "Making Western pictures of that era has been a crusade with me since the war," he told an interviewer in 1949.

Ford was under contract to deliver one more feature to Twentieth Century-Fox. Production chief Darryl F. Zanuck suggested a story that had been filmed many times before, twice at Fox. Stuart N. Lake's biography *Wyatt Earp: Frontier Marshal* gave a whitewashed version of the famous sheriff's career. With input from Earp himself, it glossed over his career as a gambler, and downplayed his reputation as a gunslinger. It was filmed in 1934 with George O'Brien, and again in 1939, this time directed by Allan Dwan and starring Randolph Scott as Earp and Cesar Romero as Doc Holliday.

After seeing Dwan's film, Ford thought it should be remade in Technicolor with Fonda as Earp; he agreed with Zanuck that Victor Mature would make a good Holliday. Aided by ideas from Ford and Zanuck, writer Winston Miller worked from Sam Hellman's original screenplay used by Dwan. Ford wanted to end the film in a graveyard; it was Zanuck who suggested the scene that was used, a poignant parting between Earp and Clementine, the story's heroine.

Fonda described the filming of *My Darling Clementine* as one filled with nostalgia. "It was like being a child again at camp," he said. The actor told director Lindsay Anderson that he was endlessly amazed at Ford's direction, how he devised ideas "at the moment, just little pieces of business, sometimes little pieces of dialogue that were so right on." One of the best remembered from this film is how Fonda's Earp sat balancing a chair on the porch in front of a hotel.

Equally important to the film is Ford's focus on the day-to-day realities of life on the frontier—how horses were handled, for example, or how the dead were buried. Small details—the oil lamps, the burritos for sale at a theater, the sparks flying from a gun barrel—give *My Darling Clementine* an authority missing from most films of its time.

In later years, Ford claimed that he was friends with Earp, and based the film's climactic "gunfight at the O.K. Corral" on what Earp told him had really happened. That the biographical facts in *My Darling Clementine* are almost entirely made up—gunfight and all—shouldn't be surprising. Ford was aiming for a larger canvas than the travails of a gambler-turned-sportswriter who wanted to justify his disreputable background. He was trying to define in his own terms the passing of the Western frontier, a pivotal moment in history. To do so, he stripped down the Western genre to its most basic elements.

My Darling Clementine is built around archetypal conflicts: between the entrenched evil symbolized by the Clanton family and the lesser evil of the Earp brothers; between Eastern culture in the form of Boston exile Doc Holliday and itinerant actor Granville Thorndyke and a more rough-hewn frontier style of living; between church and state, friendship and duty, even handgun and rifle. Ford stages these in a landscape of staggering solitude, in night shadows that evoke Rembrandt, in the most powerful and compelling close-ups yet seen in film.

Ford tells a story of cattle rustling, murder, crooked gambling, consumption, and revenge in dispassionate terms. His Earp is a vain, cold character, interested only in avenging his brother. (Fonda brings some warmth to the role, but—tellingly—his most sentimental touches were added by another director.) Each meeting is fraught with danger, and the film's violence is raw, shocking. Yet *My Darling Clementine* also contains hope in the form of one of Ford's great set pieces, a church service that turns into a social.

If *My Darling Clementine* is free of the blarney that afflicted many of Ford's later films, the credit might be due to Zanuck. In July, Ford handed in a preview cut that was almost two hours long, and displayed no interest when Zanuck asked him to cut it down. Zanuck wrote in a memo that the film needed a "major and radical cutting job," and hired Lloyd Bacon to direct additional material when Ford refused. Zanuck mostly tried to speed up the pace of the film. In a few scenes he added more (and louder) music, and at one point he inserted a variation on a scene that Ford had used in *Young Mr. Lincoln* (1939). The biggest change came at the very end of the film, where Bacon put in a shot that was, in Zanuck's words, "honest, legitimate, and reasonable." That wasn't filmed until September, just a month before the world premiere.

My Darling Clementine was a significant hit at the box office, although Ford tended to play down its importance, perhaps due to Zanuck's intervention. Its influence on subsequent filmmakers is unmistakable. It's hard to imagine the work of Akira

Kurosawa or Sergio Leone, for example, without acknowledging Ford's indelible landscapes, his monumental close-ups, his almost geometric groupings of characters. An entire school of spaghetti Westerns springs forth from the dusty Tombstone streets in *My Darling Clementine*. In Ford's film, even clichés feel like they're being seen for the first time.

About halfway through *My Darling Clementine*, Ford stops the story to focus on Granville Thorndyke, star of the frontier equivalent of a medicine show (he's played to plummy perfection by veteran ham Alan Mowbray). Thorndyke's scenes serve several narrative functions: to escalate the tension between the Clantons and the Earps,

to indicate how cultured Holliday is, to tighten his bond with Wyatt, and so on. But still, why bother to take viewers into a theatrical setting? Perhaps because Ford sees his characters as stage performers, players in a tragedy they can neither steer nor stop. Their dialogue is as simple and pointed as lyrics from a ballad. Ford's version of Earp, Holliday, and the people surrounding them is more direct, more appealing, more incisive than the truth. The director's unofficial motto—"When the legend becomes fact, print the legend"—makes more sense applied here than when he formulated it for *The Man Who Shot Liberty Valance* (1962). That film and *The Searchers* (1956) are also on the Registry.

The Best Years of Our Lives

Hoagy Carmichael (left) plays "Up the Lazy River" for returning war veteran Harold Russell in *The Best Years of Our Lives*.

Samuel Goldwyn, 1946. Sound, B&W, 1.37. 169 minutes.

Cast: Myrna Loy (Milly Stephenson), Fredric March (Al Stephenson), Dana Andrews (Fred Derry), Teresa Wright (Peggy Stephenson), Virginia Mayo (Marie Derry), Cathy O'Donnell (Wilma Cameron), Hoagy Carmichael (Butch Engle), Gladys George (Hortense Derry), Harold Russell (Homer Parrish), Roman Bohnen (Pat Derry), Ray Collins (Mr. Milton), Victor Cutler (Woody), Minna Gombell (Mrs. Parrish), Walter Baldwin (Mr. Parrish), Steve Cochran (Cliff), Dorothy Adams (Mrs. Cameron), Marlene Aames (Luella Parrish), Charles Halton (Prew), Ray Teal (Mr. Mollett), Howard Chamberlin (Thorpe), Dean White (Novak), Erskine Sanford (Bullard), Michael Hall (Rob Stephenson).

Credits: Directed by William Wyler. Screen Play by Robert E. Sherwood. From a novel by MacKinlay Kantor. Produced by Samuel Goldwyn. Director of photography: Gregg Toland. Art direction: Perry Ferguson, George Jenkins. Film editor: Daniel Mandell. Costume designer: [Irene] Sharaff. Set decorations: Julia Heron. Makeup: Robert Stephanoff. Hair stylist: Marie Clark. Sound recorder: Richard DeWeese. Music: Hugo Friedhofer. Musical direction: Emil Newman. Western Electric Recording. A Samuel Goldwyn presentation.

Additional Cast: Clancy Cooper (Taxi driver), Hal K. Dawson (Man at airport), Ralph Sanford (George H. Gibbons), Robert Karnes (Technical Sergeant), Blake Edwards (Corporal), John Tyrrell (Gus), Donald Kerr (Steve), Heinie Conklin (Customer), Alan Bridge (Superintendent).

Additional Credits: Aerial photography: Paul Mantz. Production dates: April 15 to August 9, 1946. Premiered in New York City on November 21, 1946.

Other Versions: Remade for television as *Returning Home* (1975, directed by Daniel Petrie). Goldwyn oversaw the release of a "widescreen" version in 1954.

Awards: Oscars for Best Picture, Director, Writing—Screenplay, Actor (March), Actor in a Supporting Role (Russell), Film Editing, Music—Scoring of a Dramatic or Comedy Picture. Russell also received an Honorary Award.

Available: MGM Home Entertainment DVD (2000). ISBN: 0-7928-4613-3. UPC: 0-27616-85013-3.

Like several of his colleagues, William Wyler returned from World War II deeply changed. As a member of the Information Division of Special Services, he flew in bombing missions which damaged his hearing. Having documented the heroism of a B-17 crew in *The Memphis Belle* (1944), Wyler also had firsthand experience with the less savory side of the war effort. He was almost discharged after punching a doorman at the Statler Hotel over an anti-Semitic remark, and he had run-ins with many of his commanding officers.

Wyler resumed his Hollywood career as one of the most honored directors in the business. Of the seven feature films he made between 1936 and 1941, six had been nominated for best picture, and five for best director. He decided to partner with director Frank Capra and producer Samuel Briskin in Liberty Films, but he still owed one more picture to producer Samuel Goldwyn. The producer wanted Wyler to take on *The Bishop's Wife* (1947), a Christmas fantasy that wound up being directed by Henry Koster. But Wyler was more interested in *Glory for Me*, a story in free verse about the problems soldiers were having adjusting to civilian life. It was written in January 1945 by MacKinlay Kantor, a prolific novelist who flew with the Eighth Air Force as an overseas correspondent.

Goldwyn commissioned Kantor to write the piece after the producer's wife showed him a *Time* magazine article about returning veterans. The treatment, which Kantor later turned into a novel, concerned three soldiers of different backgrounds who meet when coming home to Boone City (based on Cincinnati). Fred Derry was a former soda jerk and newlywed when he left for the war; Alton Stephenson, an assistant vice president at a bank, was coming back to a wife and two children; and Homer Wermels (later Homer Parrish), once engaged to his childhood sweetheart, was now a hopeless spastic.

Wyler and Goldwyn agreed that Robert Sherwood, a three-time Pulitzer Prize winner, was the best candidate for adapting Kantor's impressionistic and overwhelmingly bitter story into a screenplay. Sherwood took some persuading, but began working on the script at the end of 1945. His breakthrough came when he changed Derry's story and fleshed out a part for Peggy, Stephenson's daughter. Goldwyn cast the film with his contract players: Dana Andrews for Derry, Farley Granger for Homer, and Teresa Wright for Peggy. Fred MacMurray and Olivia de Haviland turned down the roles of Peggy's parents. They were filled by Fredric March and Myrna Loy, a fan of Kantor's novel.

Wyler remembered screening *Diary of a Sergeant* (1945), a Signal Corps film about Harold Russell, who lost both his hands in an accidental explosion at an Army training camp in Georgia. With Goldwyn's approval, Sherwood rewrote Homer's part to fit Russell. In a 1946 interview, Wyler admitted that Russell "had no acting technique," but still exclaimed over his performance. "I didn't try to teach him to act. I concentrated on guiding his thinking more than his actions, because I reasoned that if he was thinking along the right lines he just couldn't do anything wrong." Russell is unforgettable in the film, easily transcending any possibility of "stunt" casting.

Shooting began on April 15, 1946, and continued for one hundred days. This was the sixth and last picture Wyler made with Gregg Toland, one of the best cinematographers in the industry. He agreed with the director that the film would use deep focus instead of diffused backgrounds and glamorous close-ups. According to Wyler, the approach meant that, "I can have action and reaction in the same shot without having to cut back and forth from individual cuts of the characters." Wyler told *The New York Times*, "By letting the camera turn with the actors it caught their actions and reactions. In that way the players did their own cutting." French theoretician André Bazin referred to Wyler's "invisible style," which allowed the viewer to pick out what part of the frame to concentrate on.

But deep focus was a time-consuming process. Every inch of the set had to be lit, and all the actors in scenes had to hit their marks. The result was a film that seemed more realistic, weightier, than normal Hollywood product. The earned experience Wyler brought to the project added to the movie's depth. A key scene set in the nose cone of a decommissioned B-17 worked because Wyler had been there himself in flight. But the scene had even more impact because the director was willing to trust Dana Andrews to carry the moment without dialogue, with only the soundtrack to provide narrative meaning.

Months into the shoot, Wyler was still trying to alter the script, worried that the film would be too long. The evolving shape of the plot is evident in the final film. Its first hour is the equal of anything Wyler directed, but the picture loses focus as it devolves into a familiar romantic drama. During the shoot, Wyler met with editor Daniel Mandell every morning to go over rushes. As a result, a rough cut was ready only a few weeks after the end of photography. A preview screening in Long Beach, California, on October 17 convinced

Goldwyn and Wyler to release a version that was close to three hours long.

Goldwyn spent $400,000 advertising *The Best Years of Our Lives*, which was promoted on Hoagy Carmichael's radio show, in the House of Representatives, in *Reader's Digest*, and at numerous other venues. It received ecstatic reviews, grossed almost ten million dollars in a year, and won seven Oscars, including Best Picture. Billy Wilder called it "the best-directed film I've ever seen in my life," and it helped open the floodgates for other films about returning veterans. His commitment to Goldwyn fulfilled, Wyler left for Liberty Pictures, a company soon to fall to financial pressures. His next Registry film, *The Heiress* (1949), was released by Paramount.

It's a Wonderful Life

RKO, 1946. Sound, B&W, 1.37. 130 minutes.
Cast: James Stewart (George Bailey), Donna Reed (Mary Hatch [Bailey]), Lionel Barrymore (Mr. Potter), Thomas Mitchell (Uncle Billy), Henry Travers (Clarence), Beulah Bondi (Mrs. Bailey), Frank Faylen (Ernie), Ward Bond (Bert), Gloria Grahame (Violet), H.B. Warner (Mr. Gower), Todd Karns (Harry Bailey), Samuel S. Hinds (Pa Bailey), Mary Treen (Cousin Tilly), Virginia Patton (Ruth Dakin), Frank Albertson (Sam Wainwright), Charles Williams (Cousin Eustace), Sara Edwards (Mrs. Hatch), Bill Edmunds (Mr. Martini), Lillian Randolph (Annie), Argentina Brunetti (Mrs. Martinia), Bobbie Anderson (Little George), Ronnie Ralph (Little Sam), Jean Gale (Little Mary), Jeanine Ann Roose (Little Violet), Danny Mummert (Little Marty Hatch), Georgie Nokes (Little Harry Bailey), Sheldon Leonard (Nick), Frank Hagney (Potter's bodyguard), Ray Walker (Joe, luggage shop), Charlie Lane (Real estate salesman), Edward Kean [Keane] (Tom, Bldg. & Loan), Carol Coomes [Coombs] (Janie Bailey), Karolyn Grimes (Zuzu Bailey), Larry Simms (Pete Bailey), Jimmy Hawkins (Tommy Bailey).
Credits: Produced and directed by Frank Capra. Screen Play by Frances Goodrich, Albert Hackett and Frank Capra. Additional scenes by Jo Swerling. Based on a story by Philip Van Doren Stern. Musical score written and directed by Dimitri Tiomkin. Directors of photography: Joseph Walker, Joseph Biroc. Special photographic effects: Russell A. Cully. Art director: Jack Okey. Set decorations: Emile Kuri. Makeup supervision: Gordon Bau. Film editor: William Hornbeck. Sound by Richard Van Hessen, Clem Portman. Costumes by Edward Stevenson. Assistant director: Arthur S. Black. RCA Sound System. A Liberty Films presentation.
Additional Cast: Stanley Andrews (Mr. Welch), Al Bridge (Sheriff), Ellen Corby (Miss Davis), Dick Elliott (Man on porch), Tom Fadden (Toll collector), Charles Halton (Mr. Carter [bank examiner]), J. Farrell Mac-Donald (Homeowner), Carl "Alfalfa" Switzer (Freddie).
Additional Credits: Screenplay: Dalton Trumbo, Clifford Odets, Marc Connelly, Michael Wilson, Dorothy Parker. Director of photography: Victor Milner. Premiered in New York City on December 20, 1946.
Available: Republic Entertainment VHS (1995). ISBN: 0-7820-0509-8. UPC. 0-17153-20713-2. Republic Entertainment DVD (2001). ISBN: 0-7820-1003-2. UPC: 0-17153-20712-5. Paramount DVD (2007). UPC: 097361313849.

When Frank Capra returned to Hollywood after World War II, he had been away from the film industry for four years. Having severed ties with Harry Cohn at Columbia Pictures, where he had enjoyed his greatest success, and with screenwriter Robert Riskin, perhaps his most influential collaborator, Capra was uncharacteristically tentative about his next move. Like other directors returning to work after volunteering in the war effort, Capra felt the need to make a statement about the war and how it affected the people of the United States.

First he had to find a replacement for Columbia Pictures. With Sam Briskin, a former Cohn underling, Capra formed Liberty Pictures, a production company that he hoped would give directors full creative freedom. He was joined there by William Wyler, who was shooting *The Best Years of Their Lives* (1946), and later by George Stevens. Capra couldn't decide on his next project, and was considering a Western, a remake of one of his early Columbia films, even an adaptation of the stage hit *Harvey*.

In 1939 Capra directed a radio program called *Can We Forget?* as a benefit for the Motion Picture Relief Fund. In the show a widow considers suicide at Christmastime, but is persuaded by her husband's ghost to continue living. A year earlier, author and historian Philip Van Doren Stern got the idea for a story about a man who is saved from suicide by his guardian angel, who shows how the lives of those around him would have changed for the worse had he died. Stern finished "The Greatest Gift" in 1943. Unable to sell it, he printed two hundred copies to distribute to his friends. Shirley Collier, his agent, was then able to sell the film rights to RKO for $10,000.

The studio intended the story for Cary Grant, who later made a different Christmas film, *The Bishop's Wife* (1947). By that time Dalton Trumbo had finished a screenplay adaptation, which was revised by Clifford Odets and Marc Connelly. Capra bought the rights and the script from RKO in September 1945. The director hired Frances Goodrich and Albert Hackett, the screenwriting team responsible for hits like *The Thin Man* (1934). They were infuriated when Capra gave their work to Jo Swerling and then to Dorothy Parker for polishing. Capra took a writing credit himself (for the last time in his career), and files indicate that he and Swerling reworked about a quarter of the script. Several of these writers would go on to suffer from blacklisting (Trumbo went to jail), and according to Capra biographer Joseph McBride, as production approached lines were being drawn between liberals and conservatives.

Capra made arrangements with John Ford to secure the services of arch-conservative Ward Bond, who was appearing in *My Darling Clementine* (1946). He also wanted Anne Revere to play Ma Bailey; she had just won a supporting Oscar for *National Velvet* (1944). Revere's career was seriously damaged when she was blacklisted in 1951. (The part went to Beulah Bondi, who had played James Stewart's mother in three previous movies.)

The director had wanted Stewart, a fighter pilot during the war, from the start, but the actor was thinking of retiring to his hometown in Pennsylvania. In later years Stewart credited Lionel Barrymore with giving him the motivation to tackle the part. The role of George Bailey was a difficult one that carried the actor through some twenty years, from student to father. It also required Stewart to portray a suicidal despair missing from his pre-war work. This was the beginning of a string of superb performances from the actor, who became one of the iconic figures in American film in the 1950s.

Barrymore had not been the first choice for the villainous Mr. Potter; Capra also thought about Claude Rains and Charles Coburn. For Mary, George's long-suffering wife, the director decided on Donna Reed only after Jean Arthur turned down the part. Capra's loyalty to character actors is evident throughout the film, from H.B. Warner (*Lost Horizon*, 1937) to Alfalfa Switzer and J. Farrell MacDonald.

McBride has traced elements in the final script for *It's a Wonderful Life* to various writers. Trumbo, for example, was responsible for the line about an angel receiving wings every time a bell rings. But the film itself is unmistakably a product of Capra's imagination. It shares with his Columbia work in the 1930s an assured grasp of film language, brought up to date by his documentary work during the war. (Capra fired initial cinematographer Victor Milner during the shoot. His replacement, Joseph Walker, had to leave due to a previous commitment, and trained camera operator Joseph Biroc to take over for him.) Capra had more resources available to him than before the war. He could shoot exteriors at night, for example, on a massive city set erected on an RKO lot in Encino. He was also conscious of the directions in which the industry was moving. Portions of *It's a Wonderful Life* resemble film noir, or newsreels, both of which were growing in popularity.

And Capra was still a master of manipulating emotions. *It's a Wonderful Life* contains some of his most grating effects and corniest humor, but it also cuts closer to doubt and desperation than he had ever come before. Two scenes in particular show a new maturity and sympathy. Thwarted once again in his attempts to leave home, George Bailey (Stewart) visits Mary Hatch (Reed), ostensibly the girlfriend of another man. In an emotionally charged monologue, Bailey rails against the hopeless future closing in on him. And for two minutes straight, Capra holds him in a tight two-shot with Mary, the director confident in the power of image and words. Much later in the film Bailey sits in a bar facing utter ruin. Capra slowly moves the camera in until his face fills the frame, a close-up as iconic as those used by John Ford. Originally Stewart was supposed to recite the Lord's Prayer, but RKO officials objected. The harrowing prayer Stewart does deliver is actually more effective for being less predictable.

It's a Wonderful Life has a reputation now as a Yuletide fantasy, but the film's dream sequence runs a mere seventeen minutes (out of over two hours). And as Capra would admit later, the plot is honeycombed with glaring holes and flaws in logic. The film's final five minutes, ostensibly a paean to small-town life, aims for the climactic intensity of his great 1930s Columbia films. But there is no happy ending here. The money for the Building and Loan is still missing, the thief is still plotting against happiness, and Bailey is still dreaming of escaping the chains of Bedford Falls. You can sense Capra like a conductor in the background, energetically waving his arms, hoping the brass band and choir will drown out the bleakness of Bailey's life. It was a sensational performance on the director's part, even though the film failed to find an audience at the time.

It was also Capra's last full-fledged masterpiece. He subsequently made entertaining movies, but none of them matched the scope and ambition of this one. The film's poor showing at the box office led to Capra's selling Liberty to Paramount. The subsequent tangled chain of ownership resulted in the film falling into the public domain in 1974, an excuse for every television station in the country to run increasingly battered and edited prints during holiday seasons. More than any other factor, this probably accounts for the film's huge audience over the past three decades. Following the precedent set by the

Sheldon Abend/*Rear Window* court case, Republic Pictures used the underlying rights to the short story to reassert copyright control over the film.

It will be interesting to see whether future viewers, now limited to sanctioned screenings, will grow as attached to *It's a Wonderful Life*.

George Stevens World War II Footage

Director George Stevens in France in a shot from his World War II footage.

George Stevens, 1944–46. Silent and sound, color and B&W, 1.37. Approximately 420 minutes.

Credits: Directed by George Stevens. Cameramen include Stevens, Ken Marthey, Jack Muth, Dick Kent, William Mellor. Sound: Bill Hamilton. Assistant director: Hollingsworth Morse. Writers: Irwin Shaw, William Saroyan, Ivan Moffat.

Additional Notes: The Library of Congress collection includes: 304 minutes of color footage; 54 minutes of silent black-and-white footage; 32 minutes of sound interviews of Dachau survivors; *D Day to D+1*, a 33-minute, edited and narrated documentary presented by the "SHAEF [Supreme Headquarters Allied Expeditionary Force] Public Relations Division."

Available: Library of Congress. Footage edited by George Stevens, Jr., in the compilations *George Stevens: A Filmmaker's Journey* (1984) and *George Stevens: D-Day to Berlin* (1994).

Leni Riefenstahl's *Triumph of the Will* (1935) impressed and frightened those Hollywood directors who screened it. In it, Riefenstahl presented Adolf Hitler as a god-like Aryan who could lead Germany back to its rightful place as a world leader. Frank Capra wrote in his autobiography, "Seeing it practically paralyzed my own will." George Stevens told his son, "That film influenced my life more than any I would ever see."

Hollywood filmmakers responded in characteristic ways. In the *Why We Fight* series, Capra portrayed the Allies as unwilling but determined participants in a war of ideas. John Ford immersed himself in the dirty work of propaganda, filming educational pieces for the Army before heading

to the South Pacific to cover front-line action. William Wyler attached himself to fighter pilots conducting long-range aerial attacks on Germany. John Huston sought out stories of individuals in difficult terrain, people who were challenged both physically and emotionally.

In the 1930s, George Stevens, a former cameraman and director of slapstick shorts and B-Westerns, had quietly built a reputation as an artist who could handle a broad range of material, and who had a deep rapport with actors. His prior Registry titles include *Swing Time* (1936), one of the finest American musicals, and *Gunga Din* (1939), the premiere boys' adventure. After finishing *The More the Merrier* (1943), Sevens gave up his Hollywood career to join the Special Coverage Unit of the Allied Expeditionary Force.

Stevens may have lucked into his eventual assignment, or he may have just insisted on it. Coworkers and actors alike marveled at his ability to get his own way. He went to London, where he gathered a group of a dozen or so cameramen, writers, and support personnel dubbed the "Stevens Irregulars." As novelist Irwin Shaw noted later, the Irregulars were generally too old for military service. They also shared a belief in liberal, even pacifist, values. All would be tested severely in the coming months.

During preparations for Operation Overlord, the massive campaign to invade Normandy from Great Britain, General Dwight Eisenhower ordered that film crews provide material for a documentary film that would meet industry standards. Stevens took charge of the assignment. His men filmed D-Day activities on 35mm black-and-white stock. However, Stevens also brought along his own 16mm camera, as well as a cache of Kodachrome color film.

After filming the Normandy landing, Stevens set up a base camp between the Utah and Omaha beaches. As the Army progressed inland, he moved to a camp about a kilometer from the front lines. While his men filmed soldiers and settings that would be used in newsreels and documentaries, Stevens took a more personal tone with his home movies. At this stage the war was still something of an adventure, one marked by camaraderie and "roughing it" with mess kits around camp fires. Stevens had staged similar scenes in *Gunga Din*. But as the days passed, and they made their way into the interior of France, the tone and tenor of the film changed.

None of them had seen destruction on this level before, whole villages blown apart, the dead left where they lay in streets and ditches. With a practiced eye for composition, how would Stevens exploit the dead and dying? Can devastation be depicted in artistic terms? A new sense of caution marks this footage, a realization of responsibility toward the victims being filmed and the viewers who would watch later.

These issues could be put aside briefly during the liberation of Paris. Stevens said that August 25, 1944, was the best day of his life, and a giddiness prevails despite the sniper attacks and a parade of German prisoners his cameramen captured on film. Stevens and his crew continued working during the Battle of the Bulge and on through the winter of 1944. In the spring of 1945 they crossed the Rhine River and inspected the underground slave labor factories in Nordhausen. A week later they linked with the 1st Ukrainian Army Group at Torgau on the Elbe River.

According to his son, Stevens "received urgent orders to move south through Germany to Bavaria." They were present at the liberation of Dachau, documenting the subsequent plague of typhus and the first religious service after the fall of the Nazis. Their footage reflects the stunned anger they must have felt. Again they were faced with the dilemma of using artistic methods to depict monstrous crimes. After Dachau, Stevens and his remaining Irregulars reached Berlin, ironically shooting in the wreckage of buildings used by Riefenstahl in *Triumph of the Will* and *Olympiade*.

Stevens and his Irregulars were changed forever by their war experiences. Shaw wrote what is regarded as the first World War II novel, *The Young Lions*, published in 1948. Moffat worked on the screenplay of Stevens' *Giant* (1956, also a Registry title). William Mellor won Oscars for cinematography on two Stevens films, *A Place in the Sun* (1951) and *The Diary of Anne Frank* (1959). Stevens returned to Hollywood with *I Remember Mama* (1948), a film that was in part about what it meant to be an American.

Stevens kept his war films in a Bekins Storage facility on Ventura Boulevard in Los Angeles for decades. His son, George, Jr., edited the material in two compilations, *A Filmmaker's Journey* and *From D-Day to Berlin*. Asked how viewing the footage affected his interpretation of his father's other films, he answered, "I don't think it changed as much as enlarged my understanding of my father as a man, seeing him in that footage and understanding what an extraordinary experience he lived in those years."

The compilations are an excellent introduction to the work that Stevens did during the war. Viewing the entire collection of footage, available at the Library of Congress, provides another angle on his time in Europe. The unedited films are more clearly home movies. They include off moments, down time, after-hours clowning, and a preoccupation with transportation. Convoys, trucks and jeeps mired in mud, bridges built or destroyed, tanks, carts, boats, donkeys, and bicycles all come under the camera's gaze. In Africa and in Paris, Stevens films predictable tourist attractions: pyramids, the Eiffel Tower.

The Dachau material is considerably more extensive, and disturbing. Black-and-white films are part of the collection as well, and they include sound interviews with camp survivors. Stevens and his crew examined every corner of the camp. No matter how difficult it was to film, they knew they were responsible for bearing witness.

One of the more interesting pieces of the collection is a secret D-Day film presented by the SHAEF Public Relations Division. Edited in part from Stevens' color footage, it begins on June 4, as the Allies prepare for the invasion. The minimal narration and absence of a soundtrack score give the film a modern air. From a critical standpoint, this film and the others in the collection document a change in the director's attitude toward his work. When you have lived through a war, and seen its results, what other story could seem important? Stevens would never direct another comedy, but instead searched for stories that dealt with moral issues.

Miracle on 34th Street

Twentieth Century-Fox, 1947. Sound, B&W, 1.37. 96 minutes.
Cast: Maureen O'Hara (Doris Walker), John Payne (Fred Gailey), Edmund Gwenn (Kris Kringle), Gene Lockhart (Judge Henry X. Harper), Natalie Wood (Susan Walker), Porter Hall (Granville Sawyer), William Frawley (Charles Halloran), Jerome Cowan (Thomas Mara), Philip Tonge (Julian Shellhammer).
Credits: Directed by George Seaton. Written for the screen by George Seaton. Story by Valentine Davies. Produced by William Perlberg. Musical direction: Alfred Newman. Music: Cyril Mockridge. Orchestral arrangements: Edward Powell. Directors of photography: Charles Clarke, Lloyd Ahern. Art direction: Richard Day, Richard Irvine. Set decorations: Thomas Little, Ernest Lansing. Film editor: Robert Simpson. Wardrobe direction: Charles Le Maire. Costumes designed by Kay Nelson. Makeup artist: Ben Nye. Special photographic effects: Fred Sersen. Sound: Arthur L. Kirbach, Roger Heman. Western Electric Recording.
Additional Cast: Harry Antrim (R.H. Macy), Lela Bliss (Mrs. Shellhammer), Alvin Greenman (Alfred), James Seay (Dr. Pierce), Robert Hyatt (Tommy Mara), Marlene Lyden (Dutch girl), Mary Field (Dutch girl's adoptive mother), Percy Helton (Santa Claus in parade), Herbert Heyes (Mr. Gimbel), Mae Marsh (Woman in line), "Snub" Pollard (Court officer), Ann Staunton (Mrs. Mara), Thelma Ritter (Peter's mother), Anthony Sydes (Peter), Jack Albertson (Mail sorter).
Additional Credits: Production dates: October 26, 1946 to March 1947. Released May 2, 1947.
Awards: Best Actor in a Supporting Role (Gwenn), Writing—Original Story (Davies), Writing—Screenplay (Seaton).
Other Versions: Remade as *The Miracle on 34th Street* (1955, TV), *Miracle on 34th Street* (1959, TV), *Miracle on 34th Street* (1975), *Miracle on 34th Street* (1994).
Available: 20th Century Fox Home Entertainment DVD (2006). UPC: 024543381723.

While it remains one of film's enduring Christmas fantasies, *Miracle on 34th Street* was also a canny example of how the movie industry developed its prospects. During World War II, Valentine Davies, a veteran screenwriter and playwright serving in the Coast Guard, became disillusioned with the increasing commercialization of the Christmas season, and Santa Claus in particular. He outlined "This Is the Time," a story about Kris Kringle living in an old-age home on Long Island. Kringle fills in for an incapacitated Santa at the Macy's Thanksgiving Day Parade, and later is hired to be the store's Claus. Davies' treatment included Doris Walker, a single mother; Susan Walker, her young daughter; and Frederick Gailey, a lawyer and their neighbor. The climax involved a courtroom trial to determine Kringle's sanity, which required Gailey to prove the existence of Santa Claus.

Davies sent his treatment, now called "Kris Kringle," to George Seaton, whom he had known at the University of Michigan. Born in Indiana in 1911, Seaton had also entered film as a screenwriter, contributing to titles like the Marx Brothers' *A Day at the Races* (1937) and *The Song of Bernadette* (1943), a prototype for a wave of religious movies. Seaton had worked at MGM and Paramount before moving to Twentieth Century-Fox in 1941. His first directing effort was *Diamond Horseshoe*, an extravagant Betty Grable musical.

Seaton's producer on that film was William Perlberg, who like Seaton moved to Fox from Columbia when studio chief Darryl F. Zanuck decided to involve himself more deeply in the war effort. For this project, they cast Maureen O'Hara as Doris Walker; she had contracts with both RKO and Fox, but was growing unhappy over the escapist fare she was being offered after *How Green Was My Valley* (1941). Her costar John Payne was also seeking a new direction for his career after appearing as the love interest in numerous Fox musicals. The Welsh actor Edmund Gwenn's career stretched back to the early twentieth century, when he was admired by George Bernard Shaw. His relatively small physical stature complemented his low-key interpretation of Kris Kringle.

Miracle on 34th Street was always seen as an ensemble piece, with significant roles for employees, customers, and authorities. Seaton and Perlberg cast familiar character actors as a human resources executive (Porter Hall), a judge (Gene Lockhart), his assistant (William Frawley, Fox's answer to William Demarest), and a prosecuting attorney (Jerome Cowan). This was the film debut for Thelma Ritter, whose brief but memorable bit as a pleased customer helped launch a long career.

The film was also seen as both a publishing tie-in and a chance to promote Macy's Department Store. While Seaton began filming in November 1946, Davies was busy expanding his treatment into a short novel, to be published by Harcourt, Brace and Company. Fox made arrangements with Macy's to have Gwenn appear as Santa Claus in the Thanksgiving Day Parade, a New York City tradition since 1924. Macy's insisted that filming not interrupt the parade, so Gwenn performed with no prior publicity. (Newspapers announced his role the following day.) Seaton and his crew also grabbed several location shots with O'Hara and Philip Tonge, and shot inside the store itself. Most of these were establishing shots that would be combined with soundstage footage photographed back in Hollywood, although Gwenn did perform a scene with Alvin Greenman, playing a Macy's janitor, in the store's employee locker room.

Critical to the success of the film was the part of Susan Walker, a little girl who has been raised to be skeptical of fairy tales. Nine-year-old Natalie Wood was cast as Susan. Born Natasha Gurdin to Russian émigré parents, she had appeared the previous year with Claudette Colbert and Orson Welles in the weepie *Tomorrow Is Forever*. In her early performances, Wood often projected a hard-earned maturity that can be heartbreaking. She brought a gravity and a suggestion of personal loss and pain to her part here that adds immeasurably to the film's somber tone.

Like the best fantasies, *Miracle on 34th Street* succeeds so well because no one connected with it was "playing down" to the audience. By avoiding special effects, by focusing on personal relationships, and by developing the plot along realistic lines, the filmmakers allowed viewers to form their own opinions about what happens in the story. The revelations here are small ones, and the rewards in scale with what a postwar audience might expect.

Filming ended in February 1947, but an industry strike left Fox with a shortage of titles to distribute that spring. Zanuck, never a strong supporter of the film, put it into limited release in May 1947. That meant Davies and his publishers had to scramble to meet the new release date, as the book featured advertisements for the film on its dust jacket. The book was a tremendous success, with over 400,000 copies in print by the end of the year. (A facsimile edition was published in 2001.) The film was equally successful, especially after its broad release that September.

Payne wanted O'Hara to appear in a sequel with him, and even wrote a screenplay that remains unproduced. Seaton and Davies joined forces with Natalie Wood again on *Chicken Every Sunday* (1949), a turn-of-the-twentieth-century bit of Americana. Seaton moved to Paramount and later to Universal, where he directed the influential disaster epic *Airport* (1970). Davies, meanwhile, received an Academy Award nomination for the baseball film *It Happens Every Spring* (1949), for which he also wrote a novel. He wrote and directed *The Benny Goodman Story* (1955), and was president of the Academy of Motion Picture Arts and Sciences when he died in 1961 at the age of fifty-five.

Out of the Past

RKO, 1947. Sound, B&W, 1.37. 97 minutes.

Cast: Robert Mitchum (Jeff [Bailey/Markham]), Jane Greer (Kathie [Moffat]), Kirk Douglas (Whit [Sterling]), Rhonda Fleming (Meta Carson), Richard Webb (Jim), Steve Brodie ([Jack] Fisher), Virginia Huston (Ann [Miller]), Paul Valentine (Joe [Stephanos]), Dickie Moore (The kid), Ken Niles ([Leonard] Eels).

Credits: Directed by Jacques Tourneur. Screen Play by Geoffrey Homes, based on his novel *Build My Gallows High*. Produced by Warren Duff. Executive producer Robert Sparks. Director of photography: Nicholas Musuraca. Art directors: Albert S. D'Agostino, Jack Okey. Special effects by Russell A. Cully. Set decorations: Darrell Silvera. Makeup supervision: Gordon Bau. Music by Roy Webb. Musical director: C. Bakaleinikoff. Film editor: Samuel E. Beetley. Sound by Francis M. Sarver, Clem Portman. Gowns by Edward Stevenson. Assistant director: Harry Mancke. RCA Sound System.

Additional Cast: Wallace Scott (Petey), Tony Roux (Jose Rodriguez), Oliver Blake (Tillotson), Theresa Harris (Eunice Leonard), Mary Field (Marny), Harry Hayden (Canby Miller), John Kellogg (Lou Baylord).

Additional Credits: Screenwriting: Frank Fenton, James M. Cain. Song "The First Time I Saw You" composed by Nathaniel Shilkret. Released November 13, 1947.

Other Versions: Remade as *Against All Odds* (1984).

Available: Warner Home Video DVD (2004). ISBN: 0-7806-4672-X. UPC: 0-53939-67592-2.

Released during the same postwar trend that saw films like *The Killers* and *The Strange Love of Martha Ivers* (both 1946), *Out of the Past* displays many of the characteristics of the film noir genre: an untrustworthy femme fatale, a worn-out antihero, shadowy lighting, flashbacks, a doom-laden voiceover. But *Out of the Past* stands apart by virtue of its striking settings and its unusually convincing characters, the latter the result of an adroit script by pulp author Geoffrey Homes, and an exceptionally sympathetic cast. But much of the credit should go to director Jacques Tourneur.

This was Tourneur's first "A" budget film after toiling for years in B-movies and short subjects, and you can sense the director's excitement and relief at being able to work with real actors, real sets, on real locations. A graduate of the Val Lewton unit at

The heavy-lidded Robert Mitchum calculates his chances in *Out of the Past*.

RKO, Tourneur excelled at establishing mood with simple strokes, and at conveying complicated plotting with a minimum of fuss. But more than that he prized underplaying by his actors. Faced with directing lower-tier performers in the Lewton films, Tourneur slowed them down, pulled them back, and held them in check, in the process keeping them within their abilities. In *Out of the Past* every major character is hiding something, forcing each of them to erase emotions and freeze expressions. Jane Greer, playing one of the iconic bad girls in film noir, said that Tourneur had her act as impassively as possible, partly to hide her villainy from the audience, but also so filmgoers would be able to read their own emotions into her performance.

Greer had appeared in a couple of low-budget mysteries and in *They Won't Believe Me*, an interesting thriller that came out a few months before this film. More than her acting, her real life may have contributed to her performance in *Out of the Past*. Prodded by a determined mother, Greer, born in Washington, D.C., in 1924, was a beauty pageant contestant and professional model before she entered her teens. She dropped out of school to sing in a nightclub, signed a contract with Howard Hughes, married singer Rudy Vallee, and within a year was divorced and unemployed. Asked to dissemble and manipulate men as Kathie Moffat, Greer had only to call upon her own experiences.

By the time *Out of the Past* was shooting, Robert Mitchum was a veteran of over thirty films. Born in Connecticut in 1917, he was a teen runaway who bummed across the country in a succession of laboring jobs (he also spent time on a Georgia chain gang). Married and working at a Lockheed Aircraft factory in California, he joined a theater group with his sister, and within months was playing bit parts, mostly in low-budget Westerns. His résumé includes eighteen films in 1943 alone. While he received an Oscar nomination for *The Story of G.I. Joe* (1945), his role here as a drifter with a sordid past—someone he had come close to playing in real life—is the one that established him as a major box-office star.

Unlike tough guys from an earlier decade, Mitchum was a big man unbowed by his life's hard knocks. His sullen, insolent style was the opposite of the energy showed by a James Cagney or Edward G. Robinson, and even compared to contemporaries like Burt Lancaster, he seemed indifferent to his craft and to celebrity in general. His cynicism fit the mood of the country, and helped make him a dominant star for the next thirty years.

The third lead went to Kirk Douglas. This was only his third film role, but he had worked on stage and radio since 1941 (with time out for service in the Navy during World War II). Douglas was still a year or so away from his career-defining role as an unscrupulous boxer in *Champion* (1949), but in later years he would rarely underplay as effectively as he does here. Adding strong support is former child star Dickie Moore, appearing as a deaf mute who befriends Mitchum. (He later cynically claimed that this was his favorite role because he had no lines.)

The plot to *Out of the Past* is one of the most bitter and hopeless of all film noirs, remarkably cruel in the moments of happiness it allots its characters. Screenwriter Geoffrey Homes was a pseudonym for Daniel Mainwaring, a former detective, journalist, and studio publicist who grew up on a farm in the Sierra Nevadas. He published his first novel in 1933, then focused on two separate mystery series featuring detectives and crime-solving journalists. Mainwaring set many of his stories in northern California, and paid attention to developing realistic characters and situations. By the time he wrote *Build My Gallows High*, his final novel, in 1947, Mainwaring had started working on screenplays, finishing six in the first year of one of his studio contracts. Most were unapologetically pulp and of little consequence, but a new contract with RKO gave him entry to more sophisticated, and expensive, productions.

Mainwaring adapted his own novel, changing minor details but generally keeping close to the original. (Red Bailey becomes Jeff Bailey, for example.) Like a number of noirs with flashbacks, *Out of the Past* is episodic, with each new episode signaling a shift in atmosphere. The opening, set in Bridgeport, some eighty miles from Lake Tahoe, is sunny and bucolic, a feeling amplified by location photography of pristine rivers perfect for fishing. A sequence in Acapulco is also sunny, but the light is now oppressive, menacing, the scenes set mostly in bars and cantinas. By the time the story switches back to the Sierras and San Francisco, the scenes almost all take place at night. The settings become confined cabins, mob-run nightclubs, darkened bedrooms. Even the back seat of a taxi cab holds its own dangers.

The dialogue is filled with noir gems. "If I have to, I'm going to die last," Mitchum's Jeff says at one point. There are also several cunning, unexpected plot twists that keep the story's outcome in doubt. But more than the hard-boiled quips and sudden reversals, *Out of the Past* offers complex characters with fully worked-out psychological histories. These feel like real people, perhaps tougher or more glamorous than we're used to, but people we could still recognize today. They are cut off from their moorings, adrift in a world in which morality doesn't seem to matter. As the story proceeds their choices, their chances at happiness, are eliminated one by one until the only choice left is to die. A despairing message, but one that more and more filmgoers felt was an accurate reflection of postwar society.

The film changed Mitchum's life (as did his conviction for possession of marijuana the following year). Formerly seen as a comical heavy or a good-natured lunk, he was now the actor of choice for downbeat thrillers and melodramas. His later career was marked by ups and downs, but he always remained a star—perhaps because being a celebrity didn't seem to matter to him. Tourneur's *Berlin Express* (1948) caught some of the mood of *The Third Man* (1949), and *Stars in My Crown* (1950) found the director doing very well with a religious-tinged memoir set in the nineteenth-century West. He eventually turned to television work. Mainwaring wrote several first-rate screenplays before teaming with Don Siegel on *Invasion of the Body Snatchers* (1956), a Registry title.

Motion Painting No. 1

Oskar Fischinger, 1947. Sound, color, 1.37. 11 minutes.
Credits: Photographed and painted by Oskar Fischinger.
Additional Credits: Title on Screen: *Motion-Painting I.*
Available: Center for Visual Music DVD (2006, *www.centerforvisual music.org*). ISBN: 0-9764320-1-3. UPC: 9-780976-432012.

One of the key figures in animation, Oskar Fischinger was born in Geinhuasen, Germany, in 1900. At the age of fifteen, he spent a year as a carpenter constructing pipe organs; the following year he worked as a draftsman in an architect's office. His interest in music and drawing led him to a meeting in 1920 with Dr. Bernhard Diebold, who encouraged him to pursue filmmaking. Fischinger saw Walter Ruttmann's influential abstract film *Lichtspiel Opus 1* in 1921, but had already begun his own film work.

Over the next several years Fischinger experimented with every known aspect and technique of animation, using cutouts and silhouettes, line drawing, painted cels, wax figures, negative imagery, tints and toning, altering photographed footage, and screening with multiple projectors. He synchronized film footage to records, using a slide rule to determine how to move his figures. (These were used as advertisements for the recordings.) He created special effects for films like Fritz Lang's *Frau im Mond* (1928), invented both a projection device and a machine for slicing wax, and with the Hungarian chemist Bela Gaspar helped develop Gasparcolor, the first European three-strip process. Fischinger started using color for advertising, animating commercials for cigarettes and toothpaste.

Advertising allowed Fischinger to work with abstract narratives and forms, an area that was increasingly proscribed by Nazi officials as "decadent" or "degenerate" art. Fischinger used a commercial for cigarettes, *Muratti Greift Ein* (*Muratti Gets in the Act*, 1934), as the basis for the purely abstract *Composition in Blue* (1935). When the film was screened at the Venice Film Festival, Fischinger was pressured to leave Germany. His commercials won him a job at Paramount, where he was asked to draw an animated sequence for *The Big Broadcast of 1937*, a Jack Benny comedy. Fischinger completed the sequence in color, but the film was being shot in black-and-white. Fired when he refused to change his work (which was cut from the finished film), Fischinger was hired by MGM for *An Optical Poem* (1937), an abstract animation set to Liszt's Second Hungarian Rhapsody. (John Cage served as his assistant.) He was then hired to work on Walt Disney's new feature film.

Fischinger once claimed that years earlier he had discussed making an animated feature film tied to classical music with Leopold Stokowski. He felt betrayed when he found out that Stokowski had teamed with Disney for *Fantasia*. Nevertheless, Fischinger started on a sequence based on Bach's Toccata and Fugue in B Minor. He was dismayed to learn that other artists were adding representational forms—clouds, water, and the like—to his purely abstract drawings, and quit the studio after nine months.

Orson Welles put Fischinger on his staff. The director had vague plans of making an animated tribute to Louis Armstrong which never came to fruition. Fischinger met Baroness Hilla von Rebay, curator of The Museum of Non-Objective Painting (Guggenheim Foundation), who helped him with financial grants. Fischinger purchased his animation back from Paramount and reworked it as *Allegretto* (1943), a charming and extremely influential attempt to animate music. At the same time he began work on a larger project which would be tied to Bach's Second Brandenburg Concerto.

Fischinger had purchased the performance rights for the piece from his friend, conductor Otto Furtwangler, in 1934. He tried many approaches to the film, at one point envisioning a three-projector system similar to what would become Cinerama. He also considered anamorphic lenses and 70mm film stock. Dissatisfied with his results, and with his grant money almost expended, Fischinger took a new tack. Working with oil paints, he began abstract figures on an upright easel, photographing his work frame-by-frame on 35mm Technicolor. When paint on the original board became too thick, he covered it with a clear plexiglass sheet and continued. (He used six sheets in all.)

Remarkably, Fischinger painted for months with no assurance that his approach would succeed. He could test his processed footage to make sure his exposures were correct, but he could not screen it. "I only saw the film when the first color composite release print was ready," he wrote later. Through his friendship with Ub Iwerks, he was able to surreptitiously obtain a half-dozen 16mm prints from the Disney lab.

Fischinger wrote, "Searching for the last 13 years to find the ideal solution to the problem of the absolute color film, I truly believe to have found it now, and my new, forthcoming work will show it." Unfortunately, Rebay hated the finished film, referring to it as "awful little spaghettis." She refused to finance anything else by the artist.

Others felt differently. Seemingly shot in one eleven-minute take, *Motion Painting No. 1* is an overwhelming accomplishment dense with ideas about color, sound, and movement; about rhythm and form; about the meaning and purpose of animation. It inspired animators like Norman McLaren, Jordan Belson, and Harry Smith, who said the only film he "ever gave a real title to was *Homage to Oskar Fischinger* (*Film No. 5*, in the current scheme of things). I learned concentration from him."

Motion Painting No. 1 won the Grand Prize at the Brussels Experimental Film Competition in 1949, but Fischinger never got the opportunity to see it screened in 35mm, as he could not afford to pay for a print to be struck. He subsequently invented the Lumigraph, an instrument for playing light images, and experimented briefly with 3-D film. Intriguingly, he also worked with synthesized sound, drawing notes and tones on paper to be photographed onto optical soundtracks. But apart from some advertising work for television, he never completed another film. Instead, he concentrated on painting, completing scores of abstract oils. (His work is exhibited by Jack Rutberg Fine Arts in Hollywood.) Fischinger died of a heart attack in 1967.

In 1970, Dr. William Moritz began working with Fischinger's widow Elfriede to catalog and restore the animator's films. Moritz's appreciation of Fischinger in a special 1974 issue of *Film Culture* became the basis of a biography, *Optical Poetry: The Life and Work of Oskar Fischinger*, published by the Indiana University Press in 2004, and the source of most of the information in this article. Moritz stressed the spiritual aspect of Fischinger's work, noting that the animator used music at first as a

sort of short-cut for audiences skeptical of abstraction, and did not want to be known as a "music illustrator." Moritz, an accomplished writer, educator, and animator, died in 2004.

Before her death in 1999, Elfriede Fischinger helped establish The Fischinger Archive in Long Beach, California.

The Treasure of the Sierra Madre

Warner Bros., 1948. Sound, B&W, 1.37. 126 minutes.

Cast: Humphrey Bogart ([Fred C.] Dobbs), Walter Huston (Howard), Tim Holt (Curtin), Bruce Bennett (Cody), Barton MacLane (McCormick), Alfonso Bedoya (Gold Hat), A. Soto Rangel (Presidente), Manuel Donde (El Jefe), Jose Torvay (Pablo), Margarito Luna (Pancho).

Credits: Directed by John Huston. Screen play by John Huston. Based on the novel by B. Traven. Produced by Henry Blanke. Executive producer: Jack L. Warner. Director of photography: Ted McCord. Music by Max Steiner. Art director: John Hughes. Film editor: Owen Marks. Sound by Robert B. Lee. Technical advisors: Ernesto A. Romero and Antonio Arriaga. Set decorations by Fred M. MacLean. Special effects by William McGann, H.F. Koenekamp. Makeup artist: Perc Westmore. Orchestral arrangements: Murray Cutter. Musical director: Leo F. Forbstein. RCA Sound System. A Warner Bros.—First National Picture.

Additional Cast: Jacqueline Dalya (Flashy girl), Bobby Blake (Mexican boy), Spencer Chan (Proprietor), Julián Rivero (Barber), John Huston (White Suit), Harry Vejar (Bartender), Pat Flaherty (Customer), Guillermo Calles (Mexican storekeeper), Robert Cañedo (Lieutenant); Ernesto Escoto, Ignacio Villalbazo (Bandits); Ildefonso Vega, Francisco Islas, Alberto Valdespino (Indians); Manuel Bautista (Indian child), Sabino García Pérez (Escort), Mario Garralaga (Railroad conductor), Clifton Young, Jack Holt, Ralph Dunn.

Additional Credits: Assistant directors: Dick Mayberry, John Prettyman. Technical advisor: Hal Croves. Production manager: Luis Sanchez Tello. Wardrobe: Robert Odell, Ted Schultz. Production dates: March to July 18, 1947. Released January 24, 1948.

Awards: Oscars for Best Director, Writing, Actor in a Supporting Role (Walter Huston).

Available: Warner Home Video DVD (2003). ISBN: 0-7907-8344-4. UPC: 0-12569-58162-3.

Part of the appeal of *The Treasure of the Sierra Madre* lies in the mystery behind its creator, B. Traven. A *New York Times* article in 1990 identified him as Ret Marut, a German actor who may have been born in San Francisco in 1882. Marut was deported from Great Britain in 1923 as a "German communist," while Traven arrived in Mexico in 1924. Some thirty years later, he acquired a Mexican passport that identified him as Traven Torsvan, born in Chicago in 1890. He used many other pseudonyms throughout his life.

Traven's books began appearing in Germany in the 1920s, and were printed in the United States a decade later. It's not clear in what language they were written, although the manuscripts contain distinctly German allusions. *The Treasure of the Sierra Madre*, Traven's third novel, was published in Germany in 1927, and in the United States in

1935. It used the travails of down-and-out laborers who become gold prospectors as a metaphor for the greed that corrupts humanity. Traven meanwhile was in the midst of a cycle of six "jungle" novels that describe the Mexican Revolution largely from the point of view of native Americans.

In his autobiography, director John Huston wrote how incidents in *The Treasure of the Sierra Madre* paralleled his own experiences in Mexico. He shared an agent, Paul Kohner, with Traven, and helped persuade Warner Brothers to begin efforts to purchase the screen rights (for $6500) in late 1941. (Contract negotiations were difficult, as Traven refused to meet with lawyers or to use his full name.) When Huston joined the war effort, Warners assigned screenwriter Robert Rossen to adapt the novel, but the project was dropped until 1946. That's when Huston began exchanging letters with Traven, eventually sending the novelist his own version of the script.

At Traven's suggestion, Huston stripped away much of the background material from the novel, in the process exaggerating the story's tragic overtones. He also built up some characters, notably the bandit Gold Hat (played by Alfonso Bedoya). Mentioned only once in the novel, Gold Hat haunts much of the film, and gets to deliver its signature line, "I don't have to show you any stinkin' badges."

Huston finished one draft on August 21, 1946, and a second on January 10, 1947. In between, he traveled to Acapulco, where he met Hal Croves, a translator he thought for a time was really Traven. Huston hired him as a technical advisor. After receiving an approved budget from Warners producer Henry Blanke, Huston and his art director John Hughes scouted Mexico for locations, choosing Tampico and the mountains surrounding Jungapeo. He returned with Humphrey Bogart, Tim Holt, and his father Walter Huston for principal photography in April 1947. He described the shooting in his autobiography as a series of practical jokes and sullen arguments.

Much of the film is concerned with craft, with the particulars of surviving on the bum in a foreign country. *Treasure* is like a textbook for panhandling in its opening scenes; later, it provides concrete details about supplying prospecting expeditions, about building sluices, about coping with the elements. Most directors didn't bother with this level of storytelling, but it's something Huston clearly delighted in. By revealing these tips and secrets, the director was making a statement about his own life, with all its hard knocks and reversals. He took a similiar approach when making films about robbing banks (*The Asphalt Jungle*), waging war (*The Red Badge of Courage*, 1951), and hunting for whales (*Moby Dick*, 1956).

Many believe that Bogart did his best acting as Fred C. Dobbs. Certainly it was his most aggressive film performance, without any appeal to sympathy or forgiveness, *Casablanca*'s Rick reduced to a snarling dog. Adding a layer of humanity and heroism to the same basic character helped Bogart win an Oscar in *The African Queen* (1951, a Registry title). The showiest acting in *The Treasure of the Sierra Madre* is from Huston's father Walter. Expanding on the shrewd and deceptively corn-pone Scratch he played in *The Devil and Daniel Webster* (1941), Walter Huston summoned up a lifetime on stage and screen to deliver an utterly beguiling master class in hamminess. Tim Holt, at the time the star of his own series of B-Westerns at RKO, proved a perfect foil for both the elder Huston and Bogart.

While it won four Oscars, *The Treasure of the Sierra Madre* was an expensive failure at the box office. The film drew out a streak of pessimistic determinism from Huston the director, one that would see a fuller flowering in *The Asphalt Jungle* (1950). Like Traven's writing, the film is grimly downbeat, oppressively condemnatory, offering hope only in the return to a pre-industrial utopia of native rituals. For Huston, it was "one of the few pictures I don't turn the dial away from when I come across it on television."

Director Paul Thomas Anderson studied it repeatedly while writing *There Will Be Blood* (2007). "All of life's questions and answers are in *The Treasure of the Sierra Madre*," he told *New York Times* reporter Lynn Hirschberg. "It's about greed and ambition and paranoia and looking at the worst parts of yourself." It would take Huston several more decades, including periods of self-imposed exile in Ireland and Mexico, before he would offer a more complicated world view in films like *Wise Blood* (1980) and *The Dead* (1987).

The Pearl

Aguila Films/Asociados Mexico-Americanos/RKO, 1947. Sound, B&W, 1.37. 77 minutes.

Cast: Pedro Armendáriz (Quino), María Elena Marqués (Juana), Fernando Wagner, Charles Rooner (Doctor), Alfonso Bedoya (Godfather of Juanito), Gilberto González (Gachupin), Juan Garciá (Sapo).

Credits: Directed by Emilio Fernández. Screen play by John Steinbeck, Emilio Fernández, Jack [Jackson] Wagner. Original story by John Steinbeck. Produced by Óscar Dancigers. Director of photography: Gabriel Figueroa. Music by Antonio Diaz Conde. Film editor: Gloria Schoemann. Director of sound: James L. Fields. Sound by Nicolas de la Rosa, Clem Portman. Unit manager: Federico Amérigo. Art director: Javier Torres Torija. RCA Sound System. Shot at Studios Churubosco. An RKO Radio Pictures, Inc., presentation of a Film Asociados Mexico-Americanos/Aguila Films production.

Additional Cast: Enedina Díaz de Léon (Medicine woman), Raúl Lechuga, Max Langler, Pepito Morillo, Guillermo "Indio" Calles, Columba Domínguez, Enriqueta Reza, Beatriz Ramos, Luz Alba, Victoria Sastre, Margarito Luna, Carlos Rodríguez, Irma Torres, Andres Huesca y sus Costeños.

Additional Credits: Assistant director: Ignacio Villarreal. Unit manager: Federico Amérigo. Production manager: Alberto A. Ferrer. Lighting: Daniel Lopez. Camera operators: Ignacio Romero, Paul Rivers. Sound director: James L. Fields. Sound editing: Victor Lewis. Makeup: Armando Meyer. U.S. premiere February 17, 1948.

Other Versions: Remade in 2001, written and directed by Alfredo Zacarias.

Available: The Library of Congress.

While Hollywood stopped making Spanish-language movies at the end of the 1930s, the start of World War II saw the federal government encouraging the film industry to prop up a "Good Neighbor" policy. Nelson D. Rockefeller's Office for Coordination of Inter-American Affairs involved Walt Disney, Orson Welles, and others in projects like *The Three Caballeros* (1942) and *It All Came True* (begun but abandoned by Welles). Even a mainstream Fox musical like *Springtime in the Rockies* (1942) found room for Carmen Miranda and a climactic "Pan-Americana Jubilee" production number. Fox later specialized in Technicolor musicals with Latin American settings, while Republic released *Song of Mexico* (1944) in a Spanish-language version, *La canción de México*. After the war, Spanish-influenced musicals continued from Universal (*Cuban Pete*, 1946, with Desi Arnaz), Paramount (*Road to Rio*, 1947), and in numerous B-Westerns. Dramas were harder to find, although Anthony Mann's *Border Incident* (1949) portrayed the plight of illegal aliens in noirish terms.

A Medal for Benny (1945), directed by Irving Pichel, was a comedy about the posthumous awarding of a Medal of Honor. It was based on a short story by John Steinbeck, who also worked on the screenplay. After the release of *The Grapes of Wrath* (1940), Steinbeck found himself conflicted by his new wealth and celebrity. He divorced and remarried, covered the war as a journalist, cowrote the nonfiction *Sea of Cortez*, and wrote a war novel set in Norway. He also wrote a script for *The Forgotten Village* (1941), an independently produced documentary about the dangers of superstitions in a small Mexican village.

Steinbeck worked with Jack Wagner on the script for *A Medal for Benny*, and collaborated with him again for what became *The Pearl*. Wagner's career went all the way back to working as an assistant cameraman for D.W. Griffith; he served in the Army Signal Corps during World War I. Steinbeck had heard the story for *The Pearl* during one of his trips to Baja California, and made several attempts to write it as a fable. A version called *Pearl of the World* was serialized in the *Women's Home Companion* starting in December 1945. Steinbeck's final version was published in 1947.

Their third collaborator was Emilio "El Indio" Fernández, one of the more fascinating figures in Mexican film. Born in 1904 in Coahuila, Fernández grew up a violent supporter of nationalism. He sided with General Adolfo de la Huerta in a failed rebellion against President Alvaro Obregón, receiving a prison sentence of twenty years. Fernández fled to Los Angeles, where he worked as an extra in Hollywood. He returned to Mexico in 1934 under a general amnesty, working as a screenwriter and occasional actor. He earned his nickname from his Indian looks, which won him roles as bandits and cowboys.

Fernández's debut as a director was *Lá Isla de la pasión* (1942), for which he also wrote the script. It was his first collaboration with Pedro Armendáriz, a graduate of the Polytechnic Institute of San Luis Obispo and an insurance salesman and guide in Mexico City before becoming an actor. A year later Fernández formed another creative bond with Gabriel Figueroa, a cinematographer who had worked with noted cameraman Edward Tisse on Sergei Eisenstein's aborted *¡Que viva Mexico!* (1932).

Financing for *The Pearl* came from Óscar Dancigers, a producer who fled France during the war. Dancigers became the head of Eagle Films Productions, hiring Fernández when the director was fired from his previous studio. With the participation of Steinbeck, *The Pearl* became an expensive prestige project for Dancigers, who arranged to share some of the production costs with RKO. As a result, both Spanish- and English-language versions were filmed.

Mexican sources insist that filming started in October 1945, with interiors shot in a studio in Mexico City and exteriors in Acapulco. Hollywood trade publications reported that some scenes were shot in California in 1946, and that Steinbeck went to Mexico in August 1946 to put the final touches on the project. (*The New York Times* reported in January, 1947, that Steinbeck had the score changed to include more "folk" elements.) Both versions were finished for under $400,000, a very low budget for a Hollywood production. The Spanish version was about ten minutes longer, and did not include the song "Huapango." The U.S. premiere took place on February 17, 1948. *The Pearl* marked the first Mexican-made English-language picture released in the United States.

As far as the plot went, Fernández and Steinbeck shared a somewhat naive vision of the purity of native peoples and the inevitably corrupting influence of civilization. Much of *The Pearl* could have been filmed by the Soviets. Armendáriz plays Quino, a poor but happy fisherman who faces a crisis when his infant son is bitten by a scorpion and the doctor refuses to treat him. Quino's real problems begin when he finds an enormous pearl, setting into motion a tragic series of events determined by greed and jealousy. The message that the modern world leads to corruption and death could not be more deterministic, or less convincing.

Armendáriz and the rest of the cast act in a solemn, stately manner befitting Steinbeck's heavily moralistic writing. (It's surprising how the future Nobel Prize winner could resort to such potboiler clichés to resolve the story. He drags Quino from ocean to swamp to desert to mountain, leaving a trail of blood behind.) Life creeps into the film through the boisterous fireworks and folk songs that mark a village festival, and through Figueroa's remarkable cinematography. His work on the beach next to Armendáriz's village has a formal beauty and compositional strength that evokes Floyd Crosby's photography in *Tabu* (1931). (Gloria Schoemann's structurally concise editing adds considerable gravity to these images.) A true visionary, Figueroa would later be hired by John Ford and Luis Buñuel. Armendáriz

would also be used by Ford in a number of Westerns, while Fernández would go on to a long career as one of the most significant figures in the Mexican film industry.

The Naked City

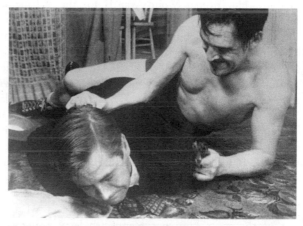

Homicide cop Jimmy Halloran (Don Taylor) is manhandled by suspect Willie Garzah (Ted de Corsia) in *The Naked City*.
Photo courtesy of The Criterion Collection

Universal International, 1948. Sound, B&W, 1:37. 96 minutes.
Cast: Barry Fitzgerald (Lt. Daniel Muldoon), Howard Duff (Frank Niles), Dorothy Hart (Ruth Morrison), Don Taylor (Jimmy Halloran), Ted de Corsia ([Willie] Garzah), Frank Conroy (Captain Donahue), House Jameson (Dr. [Lawrence] Stoneman), Anne Sargent (Mrs. Halloran), Adelaide Klein (Mrs. Batory), Grover Burgess (Mr. Batory), Tom Pedi (Detective Perelli), Enid Markey (Mrs. Hylton).
Credits: Directed by Jules Dassin. Screenplay by Albert Maltz & Malvin Wald. Story by Malvin Wald. Produced and narrated by Mark Hellinger. Associate producer: Jules Buck. Director of photography: William Daniels. Art direction: John F. DeCuir. Film editor: Paul Weatherwax. Original music by Miklós Rózsa and Frank Skinner. Musical supervision: Milton Schwarzwald. Sound: Leslie I. Carey, Vernon W. Kramer. Set decorations: Russell A. Gausman, Oliver Emert. Gowns by Grace Houston. Hair stylist: Carmen Dirigo. Make-up: Bud Westmore. Assistant director: Fred Frank. Dress shop: Jay Thorpse. Western Electric Recording. Released March 1948.
Additional Cast: David Opatoshu (Dave Miller), James Gregory (Albert Hicks), Walter Burke (Peter Backalis), Paul Ford (Henry Fowler), Arthur O'Connell (Shaeffer), Virginia Mullen (Martha Swenson), Molly Picon, Kathleen Freeman, Nehemiah Persoff.
Awards: Oscars for Best Cinematography, Black-and-White; Film Editing.
Other Versions: Basis for *Naked City* (TV series, 1958).
Available: Criterion DVD (2007). ISBN: 1-934121-31-2, UPC: 7-15515-02292-7. Kino Video VHS (1998). UPC: 7-38329-02013-2.

Sometimes cited as the first film noir shot on location in New York City, *The Naked City* is actually closer to a police procedural than a thriller. As such it can be seen as an outgrowth of MGM's series of "Crime Does Not Pay" shorts, or the Inspector Maigret novels by Georges Simenon. Its legacy is found throughout television, from series like *Dragnet* and

Hill Street Blues to the more contemporary *Law & Order* and *CSI* franchises. (The movie inspired its own long-running TV series, which used the same closing lines, "There are eight million stories in the naked city. This has been one of them.") In film, *The Naked City* is part of a post–World War II continuum from stage-bound dramas produced in Hollywood to location movies, made possible by new technology and the creative influence of Italian neo-realism. *The House on 92nd Street*, for example, took a documentary approach to an FBI investigation some three years before *The Naked City*, and was filmed in New York City locations.

But *The Naked City* could boast an impeccable New York City pedigree. As author Luc Sante has pointed out in his essay on the film, the genesis of the project was a 1945 book by tabloid photographer Arthur Fellig, better known as Weegee, called *Naked City*. The photos captured New Yorkers in distinctly New York locations: in seedy taverns on the Bowery, on the subway, on a crowded Coney Island beach.

When producer Mark Hellinger saw the book, he immediately changed the name of his current project, *Homicide*, and hired Weegee as a unit photographer. Born in 1903 in New York,

Hellinger was a newspaper reporter and columnist who counted Damon Runyon as a colleague. From producing plays on Broadway, he became a screenwriter in Hollywood, working with Frank Capra and Raoul Walsh, among others. He signed with Warner Brothers in 1937, and was named a producer after the success of *The Roaring Twenties* (1939), for which he wrote the story. Hellinger quit when Hal Wallis started interfering with his productions. He covered World War II for the Hearst news syndicate.

In August 1945, Hellinger signed a deal with Nathan Blumberg at Universal. His first Universal project, *The Killers* (1946, a Registry title), made a star of Burt Lancaster, who also appeared in Hellinger's tough prison drama, *Brute Force* (1947). The latter was directed by Jules Dassin, who was born in Connecticut in 1911, but grew up in the Bronx. Dassin worked in the Yiddish theater, wrote radio scripts, and broke into the film industry by shooting shorts for MGM. He left that studio after directing a half-dozen negligible features.

Homicide had been written by Malvin Wald, brother of the more famous screenwriter Jerry Wald. He was joined by Albert Maltz, who had won an Oscar for *The House I Live In* (1945), but who was also proficient at hard-boiled thrillers like *This Gun for Hire* (1942). However, the plot to *The Naked City*, which involves a murdered blond model and a burglary ring, took a back seat to the production itself, which ranged over wide swaths of Manhattan, with some of Queens thrown in as well. (The script was cynical enough to acknowledge that the film was as disposable as the tabloids swept into the trash in its closing shot.)

Barry Fitzgerald was hesitant to take the lead role of Lt. Dan Muldoon, but agreed when Hellinger assured him that his part had no physical demands. Howard Duff had been in *Brute Force*; Dorothy Hart was a contract player at Universal; and Don Taylor had been playing affable supporting leads at MGM. Dassin used his background

in New York theater to cast local actors in several parts. Molly Picon was a fixture on the Yiddish stage, and the Brooklyn-born Ted de Corsia had worked in radio and on stage.

The actors are consistently upstaged by the film's locations. Studios were reluctant to shoot in New York because it was so expensive. Adding to costs was the fact that passersby would ruin takes by staring at the camera or interrupting actors. Cinematographer William Daniels, who had made his reputation on films directed by Erich von Stroheim or starring Greta Garbo, used various subterfuges to hide his camera, including shooting out of the side of a truck. Fortunately, many of the scenes were written so that pedestrians could participate. Daniels also used back projection when exterior scenes demanded close-ups.

Live sound was still a problem, as portable tape recorders were not in widespread use. Sante believes this is the reason why Hellinger chose to narrate the film. The producer could simply relate what was happening in scenes, or even explain what the actors were thinking. He was also saving a lot of money, as actors with speaking parts required higher wages.

Although it won two Oscars, *The Naked City* was not an especially successful film. This may be due to the industry's growing hostility toward liberal politics. Maltz was arrested during the production, and later was imprisoned as one of the Hollywood Ten. Dassin, named as a Communist in House Un-American Activities Committee hearings, went into exile in Europe, where he eventually married Melina Mercouri, and where he directed the well-regarded heist film *Rififi* (1955). Sadly, *The Naked City* was Hellinger's last film. He died of a heart attack before it was released.

The Naked City's biggest impact may have been on other filmmakers. Within months writers were incorporating accounts of police working methods into stories like *White Heat* (1949), while producers and directors were scouting their own New York City locations.

Letter from an Unknown Woman

Universal International, 1948. Sound, B&W, 1.37. 87 minutes.

Cast: Joan Fontaine (Lisa Berndle), Louis Jourdan (Stefan Brand), Mady Christians (Frau Berndle), Marcel Journet (Johann Stauffer), Art Smith (John), Carol Yorke (Marie), Howard Freeman (Herr Kastner), John Good (Lt. Leopold von Kaltnegger), Leo B. Pessin (Stefan, Jr.), Erskine Sanford (Porter), Otto Waldis (Concierge), Sonja Bryden (Frau Spitzer).

Credits: Directed by Max Opuls [Ophüls]. Screen play by Howard Koch. From the story by Stefan Zweig. Produced by John Houseman. Director of photography: Frank [Franz] Planer. Coordinator of production: John Hambleton. Art direction: Alexander Golitzen. Film editor: Ted J. Kent. Musical score: Daniele Amfitheatrof. Orchestrations: David Tamkin. Sound: Leslie I. Carey, Glenn F. Anderson. Gowns: Travis Banton.

Technical adviser: Paul Elbogen. Set decorations: Russell A. Gausman, Ruby R. Levitt. Hair stylist: Carmen Dirigo. Make-up: Bud Westmore. Assistant director: John F. Sherwood. A Western Electric Recording.

Additional Cast: Audrey Young (Pretty), William Trenk (Fritz), Fred Nurney (Officer on street), Torben Meyer (Carriage driver), Hermine Sterler (Mother Superior), C. Ramsey Hill (Col. Steindorf), Will Lee, William Hall (Movers), Lotte Stein (Woman musician), Ilka Gruning (ticket Ticket collector), Paul E. Burns (Concierge), Roland Varno (Second), Celia Lovsky (Flower vendor), Lester Sharpe (Critic), Michael Mark (Café customer), Lisa Golm (Woman musician), Rex Lease (Station attendant), Edmund Cobb (Carriage driver), Betty Blythe (Frau Kohner), Arthur Lovejoy (Footman), Guy L. Shaw (Café customer), June Wood (Cashier), Jean Ransome (Maid), Judith Woodbury (Model), Manuel Paris (Baron's second), John McCullum (Store helper), Robert W. Brown (First Officer), Leo Mostovoy, Shimen Ruskin.

Additional Credits: Executive producer: William Dozier for Rampart Productions. Production dates: August to October 1947. Released April 28, 1948.

Available: Republic Home Video VHS (1998). ISBN: 0-7820-0847-X. UPC: 0-17153-53863-2.

The prolific Austrian author Stefan Zweig wrote the novella *Brief einer Unbekanten* in 1922, a year after Max Oppenheimer gave up journalism for acting and changed his name to Ophüls. Born into a wealthy German family, Ophüls became a theatrical producer and director in Vienna and then throughout Germany, where he directed films at UFA before fleeing the country in 1932. After working in France and Switzerland, Ophüls reached the United States in 1941, one of several wartime émigrés struggling for a foothold in Hollywood. Writer and director Preston Sturges recommended Ophüls to his then-boss Howard Hughes, who hired him to work on what would become *Vendetta*. Fired (as was Sturges), Ophüls directed a negligible costume adventure before he was approached by Rampart Productions for *Letter from an Unknown Woman*.

Rampart was founded by Joan Fontaine and her second husband William Dozier, a producer. Fontaine was born Joan de Beauvoir de Havilland in Tokyo in 1917, and spent much of her career in the shadow of her sister Olivia de Havilland. Fontaine's two big breaks were *A Damsel in Distress*, a 1937 Fred Astaire musical with a score by the George and Ira Gershwin, and *Gunga Din* (1939, a Registry title), in which she was the only woman of consequence in the cast. She then made two films for Alfred Hitchcock in which she played shy, retiring women who were menaced by glamorous leading men, winning a Best Actress Oscar for the second, *Suspicion* (1941).

But Fontaine did not have the protection her sister, under contract to Warner Brothers, enjoyed. During World War II Fontaine realized she had to nurture her career herself, even if it meant mounting her own vehicles. Rampart hired Howard

Koch, who had just worked uncredited on *The Best Years of Our Lives*, to adapt Zweig's novella. In expanding the plot, Koch changed the hero from a writer to a classical pianist, a move which enabled Daniele Amfitheatrof to fill his score with lush, romantic musical themes.

Ophüls proved a singularly astute choice for director, not just for his fond memories of Vienna. The director took an unusual interest in his female characters, finding in them motives and strengths that took them beyond the stereotypes found in most women's pictures. In *Letter* this was amplified by Fontaine's own interest in the story, but Ophüls found a cinematic style that captured the feelings of his characters in subtle and effective ways. Foremost was his use of extended tracking shots.

Working with Franz Planer, Ophüls devised complicated moving shots that traveled in and out of rooms, up and down staircases, and throughout large soundstages. Sustaining a shot through a changing space heightens the reality of scenes, as directors like Erich von Stroheim, Orson Welles, and Hitchcock had already discovered. But Ophüls went further, keeping his characters in medium or even close-up compositions while the camera continued to move, the sweeping frame behind them echoing their emotions. It is a method so effective, so seductive, that it has been adopted by virtually every director working today.

Of course, simply moving the camera can't account for the film's delicacy and subtlety. Ophüls paid close attention to sets and costumes, but especially to sound: the squeak of a door as Fontaine enters a study, birds singing quietly when she first meets Jourdan. *Letter* captures an Austria that was already lost in 1948, one of horse-drawn carriages, duels at dawn, military bands in a town square. Planer (a German who had worked for years in Europe) and Ophüls were attuned to the details of day-to-day life, giving the actors a realistic world in which to operate. Fontaine is superb in what may be her best role, ranging from love-smitten teen to conflicted mother. Jourdan is equally accomplished in a difficult role, earning sympathy as a disillusioned Lothario. (A Resistance fighter during World War II, Jourdan was brought to Hollywood by David O. Selznick to work with Hitchcock in *The Paradine Case*.)

It's tempting to lump *Letter* in with a cycle of tearjerkers filled with self-sacrificing single mothers like *Stella Dallas* and de Havilland's own *To Have and to Hold*. But *Letter* has subtle differences.

Fontaine makes her own choices throughout the film: to leave home for a job as a model, to pursue Jourdan until he realizes he can have her, to abandon the husband who cares for her and who clearly loves her. Unlike many soap opera heroines, she has a measure of control over her life. It is not the church or society or poverty that does her in, but her own willful mistakes. This pessimism, the sense that the best one can hope for is a few moments of fleeting happiness, was a startling touch in Zweig's time and remains so today. It is a rare movie that forces its characters to confront the emptiness and loss that make up their lives.

Ophüls made two more films in America, absorbing thrillers that found small but appreciative audiences, before returning to Europe. Adapting Arthur Schnitzler in *La Ronde* (1950) and Guy de Maupassant in *Le Plaisir* (1951), Ophüls could continue exploring a lost past of aristocratic foibles, of doomed affairs and restless lovers. He died of heart disease in 1957, but not before he was singled out by writers like François Truffaut as a proof of the *auteur* theory. His son Marcel, who had worked on his father's film crews, became famous as the director of documentaries like *The Sorrow and the Pity* (1971) and *Hotel Terminus: Klaus Barbie—His Life and Times* (1988), for which he won an Oscar.

Abbott and Costello Meet Frankenstein

Universal-International, 1948. Sound, B&W, 1.33. 83 minutes.

Cast: Bud Abbott (Chick), Lou Costello (Wilbur), Lon Chaney, Jr. (Lawrence Talbot), Bela Lugosi (Dracula), Glenn Strange (Monster), Lenore Aubert (Sandra Mornay), Jane Randolph (Joan Raymond), Frank Ferguson (Mr. McDougal), Charles Bradstreet (Dr. Stevens).

Credits: Directed by Charles T. Barton. Original screenplay by Robert Lees, Frederic I. Rinaldo, John Grant. Produced by Robert Arthur. Director of photography: Charles Van Enger. Art direction: Bernard Herzbrun, Hilyard Brown. Film editor: Frank Gross. Sound: Leslie I. Carey, Robert Pritchard. Set decorations: Russell A. Gausman, Oliver Emert. Music: Frank Skinner. Orchestrations: David Tamkin. Gowns: Grace Houston. Hair stylist: Carmen Dirigo. Make-up: Bud Westmore. Special photography: David S. Horsley, Jerome Ash. Assistant director: Joseph E. Kenny. Western Electric Recording.

Additional Cast: Vincent Price (voice of The Invisible Man).

Additional Credits: Title animation: Walter Lantz. Title on screen: *Bud Abbott Lou Costello Meet Frankenstein*. Production dates: February 5 to March 26, 1948. Released June 15, 1948.

Available: Universal Home Video DVD (2000). UPC: 251920572294.

By the late 1940s, Universal Studios had almost exhausted its horror franchises. Dracula, Frankenstein's monster, The Wolf Man, and The Invisible Man had appeared separately and in various combinations in over a dozen films, each one seemingly more threadbare and desperate than the one before. Roles that had been played by Bela Lugosi and Boris Karloff were now being filled by Glenn Strange and Lon Chaney, Jr. With the monsters' ability to scare viewers increasingly in doubt, the studio decided to exploit them in a comedy. It had the perfect comic team to use: Abbott and Costello.

William "Bud" Abbott, the straight man who always got first billing in the team, was born in 1895 or 1898 in New Jersey or New York, the son of circus employees. Like his father, Abbott entered the business end of show business, organizing tours and then managing a string of theaters that went bankrupt. Born Louis Cristillo in Paterson, New Jersey, in 1906, Lou Costello had a more conventional childhood but a more adventurous career. A fairly successful athlete in school, he traveled to Hollywood to break into movies, eventually doing stunt work for the likes of Joan Crawford and Delores Del Rio. Costello then formed a comic duo that performed in vaudeville; he apparently teamed up with Abbott when his own partner failed to appear one night.

Abbott and Costello worked steadily in the dying years of vaudeville, switching to burlesque as bookings dried up. (They always performed "clean.") They essentially played to type, with Abbott a surly, mean-spirited con artist, and Costello a whiny, naive patsy. Their forte was dialogue, patter delivered quickly and precisely. With the help of writers like John Grant, they developed a handful of sure-fire routines performed over and over again until they ran like clockwork. "Mustard," "Crazy House," and especially "Who's On First?" became their signature bits.

The team broke into radio in 1938, and by 1940 were regulars on Kate Smith's show, where they were required to perform "Who's On First?" once a month. The previous year they were a hit in *Streets of Paris*, a stage revue in which they played two comics who wandered onstage to do burlesque skits. In 1940 they appeared in their first film for Universal, *One Night in the Tropics*. The following year their *Buck Privates*, reputedly made for $90,000, grossed some $10 million. Abbott and Costello were suddenly the third highest money-making stars in the country.

Universal hurried them through a string of service and genre comedies; the team also appeared in some MGM titles. With their background in burlesque, Abbott and Costello relied almost exclusively on dialogue humor, playing the same basic roles over and over. They had limited physical abilities: they couldn't sing or dance, and rarely tried to act. In his earlier days, Costello was known for his pratfalls, but by the time they starred in films both men were old enough to require stunt doubles.

After some two dozen films, including a couple of independent productions, the team lost much of its appeal. Offered a project called *The Brain of Frankenstein*, Costello reportedly replied, "My five-year-old daughter can write something better than that." But with a $50,000 bonus and the hiring of director Charles Barton and screenwriter John Grant, longtime collaborators, Costello agreed to participate.

Boris Karloff, however, refused to don the monster makeup he wore in *Frankenstein*. The monster's part was played by Glenn Strange, who had done the same in both *House of Frankenstein* (1944) and *House of Dracula* (1945). Chaney repeated his performance as The Wolf Man (and doubled as the Frankenstein monster in some scenes when Strange broke his leg). According to some references, Lugosi wasn't considered at first for Dracula. The actor was in the midst of a downward spiral that would lead to his death in 1956. Makeup could not disguise the deterioration since his original portrayal of the vampire years earlier.

Abbott and Costello play two baggage clerks in Florida who unwittingly help Dracula in his plan to revive Frankenstein's monster. Most of the script concentrates on their bickering, with the backstage, real-life conflicts between the two simmering just beneath the surface of the story. At times the writers repeat bits from earlier Abbott and Costello movies, notably *Hold That Ghost* (1941). The script also repeats gags from other horror comedies, everything from Bob Hope's *The Ghost Breakers* (1940) to *The Old Dark House* (1932) to Three Stooges bits.

Given the right dialogue, Costello can shine. At one point Chaney, playing the tormented Lawrence Talbot, warns the duo that he will turn into a wolf when the moon rises. "You and twenty million other guys," Costello mutters. Abbott tells him not to be scared of a wax dummy. "Dummy nothing," Costello replies. "It was smart enough to scare me." One of his dates had so much bridgework on her teeth that "every time I kissed her I had to pay a toll."

The comic also gets some nice physical bits, especially with The Wolf Man. Just as in *Hold That Ghost*, he is oblivious at first to danger, then rendered speechless by fright. As a result, he just misses capture by various monsters, then can't tell anyone what happened. (It helps that the monsters here are generally too slow to catch up to anyone, making the hairsbreadth escapes slightly more credible. Hong Kong filmmakers would use the same principle in a series of extremely funny 1980s horror movies about "hopping vampires.")

Still, it's hard to overlook the fact that the magic is gone from much of the proceedings. The monsters can't match the mystery and terror of their earlier incarnations, while Abbott and Costello at times are just going through the motions. The film's cheesiness is part of its modest charm, and it was Universal's biggest smash in three years. It led to four more monster teamings: *Abbott and Costello Meet The Killer, Boris Karloff* (1949), *Abbott and Costello Meet the Invisible Man* (1951), *Abbott and Costello Meet Dr. Jekyll and Mr. Hyde* (1953, again with Boris Karloff), and *Abbott and Costello Meet the Mummy* (1955)—the last in series, and the team's last for Universal.

Abbott and Costello broke up in 1957. Both players attempted some legitimate roles, but Costello died two years later at the age of fifty-three. Abbott passed away in 1974. By financial standards, they were extremely successful movie stars. Today they are more likely to be remembered for their baseball routine in which "Who's on first, What's on second, and I-Don't-Know's on third."

Red River

United Artists, 1948. Sound, B&W, 1.37. 133 minutes.

Cast: John Wayne (Tom Dunson), Montgomery Clift (Matthew Garth), Joanne Dru (Tess Millay), Walter Brennan (Groot Nadine), Coleen Gray (Fen), Harry Carey, Sr. (Melville), John Ireland (Cherry Valance), Noah Beery, Jr. (Buster McGee), Harry Carey, Jr. (Dan Latimer), Chief Yowlatchie (Quo), Paul Fix (Teeler Yacey), Hank Worden (Simms), Mickey Kuhn (Matthew as a boy), Ray Hyke (Walt Jergens), Hal Talliaferro (Old Leather), Ivan Parry (Bunk Kenneally).

Credits: Directed and produced by Howard Hawks. Screenplay by Borden Chase and Charles Schnee. From the *Saturday Evening Post* story by Borden Chase. Music composed and directed by Dimitri Tiomkin. Co-director: Arthur Rosson. Photographed by Russell Harlan. Film editor: Christian Nyby. Art director: John Datu Arensma. Sound: Richard DeWeese. Music recorder: Vinton Vernon. Makeup: Lee Greenway. Special effects: Donald Steward. Assistant director: William McGarry. The song "Settle Down" by Dimitri Tiomkin. Special photographic effects: Allan Thompson. Production manager: Norman Cook. Western Electric Recording. Monterey Productions.

Additional Cast: Paul Fiero (Fernandez), William Self (Wounded wrangler), Dan White (Laredo), Tom Tyler (Quitter), Lane Chandler (Colonel), Glenn Strange (Naylor), Shelley Winters (Dance-Hall girl).

Additional Credits: Executive producer: Charles K. Feldman. Production dates: September 5 to December, 1946; additional scenes: April 1947. Premiered August 26, 1948.

Other Versions: Remade for television in 1988.

Available: MGM Home Entertainment DVD (1997). ISBN: 0-7928-3742-8. UPC: 0-27616-6042-2-4.

After the financial success of *The Big Sleep*, Howard Hawks felt he had earned the right to make his own movies, without studio interference. Like many directors returning to work after World War II, he formed his own production company, Monterey Productions, with his wife Slim and his agent Charles Feldman. Although Hawks owned the rights to many literary properties, his first project to secure financing was "The Chisholm Trail," a serial by Borden Chase that appeared in *The Saturday Evening Post*. It was a fictional account of the first of the nation's great cattle drives.

Born under the name Frank Fowler in 1900, Chase led a hardscrabble life that provided the inspiration for several action scripts in the 1930s. He started on a script of "The Chisholm Trail" for Hawks, but the director found him too difficult to work with, and replaced him with Charles Schnee, a Yale Law School graduate who had only started writing scripts the year before. Chase left behind a screenplay very similar to the serial and subsequent published novel. In it, Tom Dunson and his adopted son Matthew Garth start a ranch in Texas. After years of work, Dunson stands to lose everything unless he can find a market for his cattle. His only hope is to drive them to Missouri. Garth, returning from the Civil War, joins the drive, in part to protect his own interests. Halfway through the journey, Garth takes the herd away from the increasingly tyrannical Dunson, and heads off to Abilene, Kansas. There Garth faces Dunson in a showdown.

Under Hawks's guidance, Schnee made several changes to Chase's script, in particular adding a prologue and revising the ending. Hawks approached stars like Cary Grant and Gary Cooper, but no one was willing to take on the starkly unsympathetic role of Dunson. Feldman suggested his client John Wayne, at the time a respectable performer in middle-tier Westerns and war movies. No one suspected that Wayne would be capable of delivering a nuanced and unvarnished version of Dunson. Montgomery Clift was suggested by theatrical impresario Leland Hayward (ironically in the middle of an affair with Hawks' wife). Hayward got his client a salary on par with Wayne's. Hawks cast Joanne Dru only after his other choices fell through, and in later interviews expressed regret over her work. The rest of the cast included Hawks regulars like Walter Brennan, stalwart character actors like Noah Beery, Jr., and a true Western icon, Harry Carey, Sr. *Red River* would be one of his last film appearances. Although they didn't share any scenes, this is the only film in which he appeared with his son, Harry Carey, Jr.

Hawks wasn't allowed to use his photographer of choice, Gregg Toland, who was under contract to Samuel Goldwyn. Instead, he hired Russell Harlan, a former stuntman who had shot a string of B-Westerns. (The two would go on to work together on seven films.) Principal photography took place on a ranch in southern Arizona, with the interiors shot on soundstages in Hollywood. Work was supposed to start by August 26, 1946, but it was delayed until after Labor Day.

The production was a constant battle. Hawks had trouble finding enough cattle, and more trouble trying to move them around. Clift had prepared carefully for his first movie role, but did not feel comfortable about Hawks or Wayne. John Ireland, playing gunslinger Cherry Valance, was too undisciplined for the director. Bad weather, actors off on drinking sprees in nearby Tucson, and Hawks' characteristically slow working methods helped lengthen the shooting schedule and double the budget.

Hawks and the leads left for Hollywood in November, shooting the interiors on Samuel Goldwyn's soundstages. Meanwhile, assistant director Arthur Rosson stayed behind to shoot the stampede sequence. When filming finally ended, Hawks realized that he had gone too far over budget to make any profit over his salary on the film. He was forced to sign on to direct *A Song Is Born*, a remake of his *Ball of Fire* starring Danny Kaye and Virginia Mayo. Perhaps understandably, it was one of his more uninspired films, as he was anxiously working on *Red River* with his longtime editor Christian Nyby. Due to various legal problems, a release print wasn't ready until the summer of 1948. That's when Howard Hughes sued his one-time employee for stealing the ending of his Western *The Outlaw* (1943).

As biographer Todd McCarthy points out, Hawks frequently lifted ideas and material from his earlier films. The roles of Fen and Tess here could be compared to the two roles Frances Farmer played in *Come and Get It* (1936), for example. But even Hawks had to admit that the ending in *Red River*, always a problem for the director and Schnee, is almost identical to *The Outlaw*, on which he had worked. (It's an amusing irony that the endings to both films are among their weakest aspects.)

Also around this period a second version of *Red River* emerged. The first cut, supervised by Hawks, uses a diary format for transitions, with pages from the handwritten *Early Tales of Texas* bridging various scenes. The second version, shorter by about seven minutes, uses a voice-over by Walter Brennan. Some of its scenes, notably during the climax, are more condensed, and it is the version Hawks ultimately preferred. But by this time the director was on his way to Europe to film *I Was a Male War Bride*, so the correct release version was never clearly established.

Borden Chase would go on to write several significant screenplays, among them *Winchester '73* and *Bend of the River*. He always complained about what Hawks did to his material—in particular, *Red River*'s ending. But the film proved extremely popular with moviegoers, ending up the third best performing film of the year. In fact, with *Red River* and *A Song Is Born*, at one point Hawks had the two top-grossing films in the country.

There are undeniable flaws in the film: the use of back projection in some of dialogue exchanges, the fact that the same mountain can be seen on the horizon throughout the drive, Dru's shaky command of her character, and so on. Perhaps most glaring is the way Hawks relied on the cattle drive itself to provide a story line. In *The Far Country* or *Lonesome Dove*, for just two examples, a cattle drive provides a background to compelling dramatic incidents taking place in the foreground. The nuts and bolts of real cattle drives simply aren't that interesting, no matter how prettily they are photographed.

For some critics, this was Hawks' last personal film. It was certainly the last time he invested his own money, and in a way the last time he took filmmaking seriously. From this point on in his career, he shot primarily remakes, soft musicals, and Westerns that were far less ambitious. He also became self-deprecating in interviews, claiming that his films didn't mean anything, that he was only interested in entertaining moviegoers. He was clearly aiming for more in *Red River*, trying to match the efforts of the directors who went off to war and came back with something to say. John Ford, Frank Capra, and George Stevens were embracing large themes, determined to show why the country won the war, or at least deserved to win it. Hawks, on the other hand, was glorifying the stuff of B-movies, of singing cowboys with their ballads about trail wranglers who died tragically. Were it not for Harlan's cinematography, and Wayne's fearless performance, *Red River* would not be such a prominent Western today.

Louisiana Story

Lopert Films, Inc., 1948. Sound, B&W, 1.37. 79 minutes.

Cast: Joseph Boudreaux (The boy [Alexander Latour]), Lionel Le Blanc (His father [Jean Latour]), Mrs. E. Bienvenu (His mother), Frank Hardy (The driller [Tom]), C.P. Guedry (His boilerman).

Credits: Produced and directed by Robert Flaherty. Story by Frances and Robert Flaherty. Narration written and spoken by Robert Flaherty. Associate producers: Richard Leacock, Helen van Dongen. Photography: Richard Leacock. Editor: Helen van Dongen. Music by Virgil Thomson. Performed by Members of the Philadelphia Orchestra, Eugene Ormandy conducting. Sound: Benjamin Doniger. Sound assistant: Leonard Stark. Editorial assistant: Ralph Rosenblum. Technical assistant for music: Henry Brant. Music recording: Bob Fine. Re-recording: Dick Vorisek. Reeves Sound Studio. Western Electric Recording. A Lopert Films, Inc., presentation of a Robert Flaherty Productions production for Standard Oil of New Jersey.

Additional Credits: Released September 28, 1948.

Awards: Pulitzer Prize for Music (Thomson).

Available: Home Vision Entertainment DVD (2003). ISBN: 0-7800-2479-6. UPC: 0-37429-16382-5.

After releasing *Moana* (1926), a documentary shot in Western Samoa, director Robert Flaherty worked on two Hollywood films set in the South Pacific, leaving both of them over creative differences. He spent almost a decade in Europe, where he completed *Man of Aran* (1934) and codirected *Elephant Boy* (1937), a fiction feature. He returned to the United States to shoot *The Land* (made in 1940 but not officially released) for the United States Department of Agriculture. During World War II he worked on films for the Army.

In April 1944, Roy Stryker, manager of public relations for Standard Oil of New Jersey,

Lionel Le Blanc in *Louisiana Story*.

approached Flaherty about making a film for the company. As Flaherty's widow Frances later told Robert Gardner, Standard Oil (which would evolve into ExxonMobil) was very specific about what it wanted: "a permanent artistic record of the contribution which the oil industry has made to civilization" that would "present the story of oil with the dignity, epic sweep it deserves." Flaherty signed a contract with Standard Oil in December 1944. In exchange for a budget of $175,000, he would provide a feature film called *The Christmas Tree* and two shorter nature documentaries. (A "Christmas tree" is an assembly of valves fitted onto the tubing of a well rig.)

Flaherty took a skeleton crew consisting of his wife, cinematographer Richard Leacock, and editor Helen van Dongen to Louisiana, where they set up headquarters in Abbeville, about twenty miles from Lafayette. (They were joined during production by sound engineer Benji Doniger and his assistant Leonard Stark.) Born in London in 1921, Leacock studied physics at Harvard before joining Paul Strand at Frontier Films, a documentary organization centered in New York City. He had worked for years as a combat photographer in Asia for the Army Signal Corps, and now left a pregnant wife at home in New York for an assignment that turned out to be much longer than anyone expected. He brought with him an Arriflex 35mm camera, and believes that *Louisiana Story* was the first feature shot on that equipment.

Helen van Dongen was born in Amsterdam in 1909, where she became a founding member of an influential avant-garde film group. She assisted the Dutch documentarian Joris Ivens on groundbreaking films like *De Brug* (1928) and *Regen* (1929),

then became an assistant editor. She studied in Paris, at UFA in Berlin, and with Sergei Eisenstein in Russia before moving to New York City, where she worked with Ernest Hemingway on *The Spanish Earth* (1937). She met Flaherty in 1939, and worked with him on *The Land*.

Both Leacock and van Dongen remembered arguing at length with Flaherty over the focus and scope of the film—even what they would be shooting. Leacock exulted in the freedom of testing filters and film effects, worried over fogged and scratched footage, and wrote to his wife that Flaherty would film anything at all except what was written in the script. They found the film's lead actor, Joseph Boudreaux, one night in a café, well after they had started shooting, and were still casting and finding locations months after they arrived.

Van Dongen's diary noted that this was the first time Flaherty attempted to incorporate sound into how he intended to shoot his story, and wrote about consulting with him regarding filming coverage for his dramatic scenes and viewing rushes to make sure he had enough footage. Both van Dongen and Leacock agreed that the shoot verged on chaos. But when Standard Oil executives visited the location, and viewed footage prepared for them, they were so pleased that they kept increasing the budget, which eventually topped $250,000.

Since this was a sponsored film, Flaherty spent considerable time shooting on an oil derrick. Leacock and van Dongen completed a long sequence documenting how the derrick operated, footage that the executives approved. Then Flaherty told them he wanted to start over and shoot the material at night. Although furious at first, Leacock realized the director was right when he saw the new rushes.

It's difficult to determine how much of an impact van Dongen had on the film. According to historian Richard Barsam, she gave *Louisiana Story* its "clarity, coherence, structure, and rhythm." On the other hand, the film clearly reflects Flaherty's vision; its most closest precedent may be his *Moana*. In his earlier career, Flaherty had been an organic filmmaker, adjusting what he wanted his stories to be only after accumulating thousands of feet of material. Despite working from a script, Flaherty was constantly broadening the scope of *Louisiana Story*, even while neglecting its narrative structure. He ended up shooting on a 37-to-1 ratio, some 300,000 feet, or 138 hours, of material. Filming finally ended in December 1947.

To edit the footage, van Dongen was forced to hire assistants, including Ralph Rosenblum, whose later credits include several Woody Allen films. She wrote that she worked closely with composer Virgil Thomson on the score, and was largely responsible for the film's sound design, compiled from live sound recorded on site onto acetate disks. Thomson broke the score into three sections: Cajun folk music; "scenery" music inspired by Mendelssohn, Debussy, and other classical composers; and "noise" shaped by van Dongen—for example, a nine-minute oil derrick sequence. Thomson's music won a Pulitzer Prize, the only one awarded to a film score. He later adapted the score into two concert suites, *Acadian Songs and Dances* and *Louisiana Story*.

The final sound mixing was finished toward the end of May 1948. Although the film technically belonged to Standard Oil, both the company and Flaherty had always planned to release it theatrically. The director complained later about the contract he signed with Lopert Films; he also signed over rights to the Army for $12,500, a move he regretted. The film was shown at the Venice Film Festival, earned an Oscar nomination, and received an excellent review from *Variety*, but it failed to do much business.

Frances Flaherty always resisted attempts to classify *Louisiana Story* as a "documentary." She referred to it as an autobiography, or alternately as a fantasy of her husband's early life on the mining frontiers of Michigan. She described the film's stunning opening passage, a ten-minute scene in which Boudreaux drifts through a lush bayou landscape on his pirogue, in terms of three haikus her husband admired. Through Leacock, Flaherty achieved a visual style of almost supernatural beauty, a serene, glowing version of a nature filled with mortal danger. Through van Dongen he built a story of soft, watery interludes interrupted by scenes of remarkable tension.

Louisiana Story is less of a documentary than *Moana* or even *Nanook of the North* (1922), another Flaherty film on the Registry. Its scenes are created, not found. Flaherty directs Boudreaux to look frightened of supposedly nearby alligators, even though the boy was never in danger. He was constructing an emotional state that could exist in theory, but not then and there as the camera rolled. At the same time, Flaherty was leaning on the different set of rules used for documentaries. If a shot was out of focus, if the camera moved, if the acting was amateurish, it was because the story was "real," not fiction.

But *Louisiana Story* has an emotional and intellectual truth that separated it from mainstream Hollywood product. Its digressions, its view of nature, its version of bayou life are so seductive, so persuasive, that their impact continues to be felt—in *Modesta* (1956), for example, a film that seems to based directly on this (it was directed by Benji Doniger). Or in *The Night of the Hunter* (1955), which uses water in the same dreamy fashion. While van Dongen retired from film in 1950 after marrying Kenneth Durant, Leacock went on to become the most influential documentarian of the period (e.g., *Primary*, 1960). *Louisiana Story* was the last feature Flaherty directed. He died in 1951.

Force of Evil

MGM, 1948. Sound, B&W 1.33. 78 minutes.
Cast: John Garfield (Joe Morse), Thomas Gomez (Leo Morse), Marie Windsor (Edna Tucker), Howland Chamberlin (Freddie Bauer), Roy Roberts (Ben Tucker), Paul Fix (Bill Ficco), Stanley Prager (Wally), Barry Kelley (Detective Egan), Paul McVey, Beatrice Pearson (Doris Lowry), Georgia Backus (Sylvia Morse).
Credits: Directed by Abraham Polonsky. Screenplay by Abraham Polonsky, Ira Wolfert. Based on the novel *Tucker's People* by Ira Wolfert. Produced by Bob Roberts. Director of photography: George Barnes. Operative cameraman: Jack Warren. Music by David Raksin. Art direction: Richard Day. Editorial supervision: Walter Thompson. Film editor: Arthur Seid. Assistant film editor: Howard Lee Paul. Executive production manger: Joseph C. Gilpin. Assistant director: Robert Aldrich. Musical director: Rudolph Polk. Casting director: Jack Baur. Set decoration: Edward G. Boyle. Head grip: Carl Gibson. Makeup supervision: Gus Norin. Hair stylist: Lillian Lashin. Wardrobe supervision: Louise Wilson. Hats by Kenneth Hopkins. Dialogue director: Don Weis. Sound engineer: Frank Webster.

Additional Cast includes: Beau Bridges (Frankie Tucker), Jack Overman (Juice), Tim Ryan (Johnson), Barbara Woodell (Mary), Raymond Largay (Bunte).

Additional Credits: Production dates: June 2 to July 1948; reshoots, November 1948. Premiered in New York City on December 25, 1948.

Available: Republic Pictures DVD (2004). UPC: 0-17153-13428-5.

Force of Evil was largely ignored when it was released by MGM on the bottom half of a double bill at the end of 1948. The film was based on *Tucker's People*, a 1943 novel by Ira Wolfert. A war correspondent, he won a Pulitzer for articles collected in two books, *Battle in the Solomons* (1943) and *American Guerilla in the Philippines* (1945). The latter became the basis for a 1950 Tyrone Power vehicle directed by Fritz Lang. But *Tucker's People* attracted little attention until Abraham Polonsky chose it for his directing debut.

Born in New York City in 1910, Polonsky had been a teacher, labor organizer, and practicing lawyer when he was asked to provide legal details for a radio script. He quickly gave up law for writing. As demand for his work grew, Polonsky also started writing novels. He served in the OSS during World War II, then worked briefly at Paramount before joining with director Robert Rossen for *Body and Soul* (1947), a drama about boxing that starred John Garfield. All three men—Polonsky, Rossen, and Garfield—would become victims of the anti-Communist blacklist that was just taking hold in Hollywood.

Garfield, born Julius Garfinkel in New York City in 1913, lived a hardscrabble life battling with Bronx street gangs until he won a scholarship in a debating contest. Giving up ambitions to be a fighter, he studied acting. After crossing the country as a hobo, he joined the Group Theatre in New York in 1932. His first real break on stage was a starring role in *Awake and Sing!*, which led to a seven-year contract with Warner Brothers. The studio was looking for a replacement for its aging tough guys, and cast Garfield in a series of remakes and variations on the films that made stars like James Cagney famous. Garfield drew more attention as a doomed, fatalistic lover in the romantic melodrama *Four Daughters* (1938), a movie that brought out the wounded underside to his rebellious exterior. During World War II he gave strong performances in films like *Air Force* (1943) and *Destination Tokyo* (1944), and portrayed a blind war hero in *Pride of the Marines* (1945). Garfield also became one of the leading actors in film noir by appearing in *The Fallen Sparrow* (1943), based

on a Dorothy Hughes novel, and *The Postman Always Rings Twice* (1946), a wildly popular James M. Cain adaptation costarring Lana Turner.

By this time Garfield was operating without a studio contract. He formed a production company with producer Bob Roberts, and also explored returning to the New York stage. Garfield tended to ignore the heart condition that had prevented him from entering the armed forces; as a consequence, he suffered his second heart attack during the filming of *Body and Soul*. Impressed by Polonsky, who doctored the *Body and Soul* script on the set with Rossen, Garfield encouraged the writer to turn to directing, asking him to start with *Tucker's People*.

Polonsky later said that in his script for *Force of Evil*, "my early New York life and my thrashing about in Hollywood came together in a personal and political way." When shooting started, the director faced more immediate concerns, as the budget for the film was too small to allow expensive sets or improvisation. Polonsky and cinematographer George Barnes had to grab their location shots in New York City whenever they could get them. An off-hours shot of Garfield staggering through a deserted Wall Street district has an eerie tone, as do shots on the Hudson River waterfront, the George Washington Bridge hulking in the background. Barnes tried some ambitious use of shadows and angled sets, but for the most part *Force of Evil* is straightforward and unadorned.

Playing a crooked lawyer, Garfield slipped right into Polonsky's ornate dialogue, using a flood of words to distract himself and others from the moral implications of his actions. As Joe Morse, he and mobster Ben Tucker (Roy Roberts) plan to take over the numbers racket, bankrupting "mom and pop" operations by fixing a number everyone plays on the Fourth of July. The only problem is that Joe's brother Leo (Thomas Gomez) runs one of those backroom operations. Leo became a crook so that Joe could receive an education, and now wants no part of the organized crime that Tucker represents.

The clash between the two brothers is the driving force behind *Force of Evil*, not the romantic subplots involving Leo's secretary (played by newcomer Beatrice Pearson in her only significant film role) and Tucker's wife (noir icon Marie Windsor), nor the explicit criticism of an economic system that makes such corruption inevitable. Garfield embodies the gnawing guilt and disdain for conventions that would become mainstays of rebel actors in the following decade. It is a brave performance typical of an actor who tried to remain true to his beliefs.

But by the time filming was completed, Garfield's production company was bankrupt, forcing him to sell *Force of Evil* to MGM, a studio more comfortable with Arthur Freed musicals than with a downbeat drama in which no one emerges unscathed. Released with almost no fanfare, the film was dismissed by *The New Yorker* as "dull," while *Variety* complained that it wasn't "hard-hitting" enough. Polonsky had one more screenplay credit, *I Can Get It for You Wholesale* (1951), before he was blacklisted. An unapologetic Communist, he was forced to use "fronts" for his work for almost twenty years. It wasn't until Don Siegel's *Madigan* in 1968 that Polonsky's name could appear again on screen. He was then hired by Robert Redford to write and direct the Western *Tell Them Willie Boy Is Here* (1970), but it was far

too late for Polonsky to re-establish his career. He spent decades trying to mount an adaptation of Thomas Mann's *Mario the Magician*, but worked infrequently in film before his death in 1999 at the age of eighty-eight.

Garfield was also hounded by anti-Communist hysteria. Although never a member of the party, he was forced to appear before the House Un-American Activities Committee in 1951. When he refused to name names, his film career was ended. Garfield died the following year at the age of thirty-nine; his friends insisted that the blacklisting contributed to his heart failure.

Force of Evil's reputation grew over the years, and its influence is readily apparent in the work of directors like Francis Ford Coppola (whose *Godfather* films also examine gangsters in terms of their business practices) and Martin Scorsese, who has cited the film's importance to his own work.

In the Street

Helen Levitt, 1948. Silent, B&W, 1.37. 18 minutes.
Credits: Photographed by Helen Levitt, Janice Loeb, James Agee.
Additional Credits: Directed and edited by Helen Levitt. Levitt released a re-edited version in 1952. This included a musical score by Arthur Kleiner.
Available: The Museum of Modern Art. A videocassette released by Arthouse is currently out of print.

Born in Brooklyn in 1913, Helen Levitt dropped out of high school to work for a commercial photographer in the Bronx. While she was always interested in photography, a show by Henri Cartier-Bresson changed her approach to the medium. She not only befriended the photographer, she bought a Leica similar to the one he used. "He let me watch him shoot once," Levitt told *New York Times* reporter Sarah Boxer in 2004. "He went to the Brooklyn waterfront. I never saw any of the pictures. I don't remember anything. Just tagging along."

Levitt has always been taciturn about her work, but in acknowledging Cartier-Bresson's influence, she offered an insight into her creative process. In one of his few interviews, Cartier-Bresson advised, "Basically, you have to get people to forget the camera." Levitt took the same approach, disguising her camera when taking to the streets of Spanish Harlem. There she photographed pedestrians, bystanders, and especially children. Her work was featured in a one-person show at New York's Museum of Modern Art in 1943.

Around 1938, Levitt met author James Agee through her friend Walker Evans, another noted still photographer. Agee wrote an introductory essay to *A Way of Seeing*, one of Levitt's earliest published collections of photographs. In 1945, Levitt and Agee, joined by her sister-in-law Janice Loeb, set out to make the motion picture equivalent of her still photographs. They shot primarily on East 103rd Street in Spanish (or East) Harlem, using a Cine-Kodak hand-wound 16mm camera. Like the old Brownie cameras, the Cine-Kodak could be focused from waist level through a right-angle viewfinder. This made it possible for Levitt to hide her camera inside a box and adjust her compositions without her subjects noticing.

Like Cartier-Bresson and Evans, Levitt was trying to capture life unscripted, without preconceptions or biases. She hid her camera not to trick her subjects, but to remove their defenses, their poses. One constant throughout her work is the respect she has for the private lives of her subjects. She does not exploit the emotions of the people she photographs, she documents them, her compassion always evident.

Agee's work on *In the Street* was primarily as a companion and possible bodyguard. Levitt performed a similar function with Evans when he made a series of still photographs in the New York subways. "I would just sit next to him, so we were just two people in the subway, so people wouldn't stare at him," she explained. Agee also helped Levitt organize her material, as he did with her books, and provided some bombastic introductory titles.

Unlike Pare Lorentz (*The River*, 1937) or George Sidney (*All My Babies*, 1953), documentarians who told you how to interpret their films, Levitt avoided attaching any meaning to her work. *In the Street* evokes urban tone poems like *Manhatta* (1921) and *A Bronx Morning* (1931), only without their roughly chronological frameworks. Instead, Levitt structures her film around events like Halloween, or makes comparisons between apparently random moments. Time is fragmentary; plotting, tenuous. Scenes are built from the smallest details: a cat in a window, a dog on a sidewalk. Children will suddenly start fighting, milling across the street; Levitt then cuts to a boy crying, then another. Are they connected? Was there a reason for the melee?

At roughly the same time they were making *In the Street*, Levitt, Loeb, and Agee collaborated with Sidney Meyers and Richard Bagley on *The Quiet One* (1949), a quasi-documentary account of a young runaway from the Wiltwyck home for troubled boys. In 1952, Levitt released a slightly different cut of *In the Street*, this one with a spare musical score by Arthur Kleiner, a Viennese pianist and composer who was the Musical Director of The Museum of Modern Art Film Department from 1939 to 1967. (Kleiner also worked with George Balanchine and Agnes de Mille, among others.)

Levitt's films tied into a Hollywood trend toward using location footage rather than working on soundstages. They also showed other filmmakers that the material for movies could be found anywhere. Artists as diverse as Stan Brakhage (*Dog Star Man*, 1964) and Morris Engel (*The Little Fugitive*, 1953) took inspiration from *In the Street*.

John Szarkowski, director emeritus of the Department of Photography at the Museum of Modern Art, credits Levitt with legitimizing an entirely new genre of street photography. She received two Guggenheim grants to revisit the scenes of her earlier work; when many of these photographs were stolen in 1970, she started over again. She is the author of *In the Street: Chalk Drawings and Messages New York City 1938–1948* (1965, reprinted in 1987), *Crosstown* (2001), and *Slide Show* (2005), among others.

White Heat

James Cagney made a triumphant return to the gangster genre in *White Heat*.

Warner Bros., 1949. Sound, B&W, 1.37. 114 minutes.
Cast: James Cagney (Cody Jarrett), Virginia Mayo (Verna Jarrett), Edmond O'Brien (Hank Fallon/Vic Pardo), Margaret Wycherly (Ma Jarrett), Steve Cochran ("Big Ed" Somers), John Archer (Phillip Evans), Wally Cassell (Cotton Valetti), Fred Clark (Daniel Winston/The Trader).

Credits: Directed by Raoul Walsh. Screen play by Ivan Goff and Ben Roberts. Suggested by a story by Virginia Kellogg. Produced by Louis F. Edelman. Director of photography: Sid Hickox. Art director: Edward Carrere. Film editor: Owen Marks. Music by Max Steiner. Sound by Leslie G. Hewitt. Set decorator: Fred M. MacLean. Wardrobe by Leah Rhodes. Special effects by Roy Davidson (director), H.F. Koenekamp.

Orchestrations: Murray Cutter. Makeup artist: Perc Westmore. RCA sound system. A Warner Bros.—First National Picture.

Additional Cast: Mickey Knox (Het Kohler), G. Pat Collins (Herbert/The Reader), Paul Guilfoyle (Roy Parker), Fred Coby (Happy Taylor), Ford Rainey (Zuckie Hommell), Robert Osterloh (Tommy Ryley), Ian MacDonald (Bo Creel), Marshall Bradford (Chief of Police), Ray Montgomery (Ernie Trent), George Taylor (Police surgeon), Milton Parsons (Willie Rolf) Jim Toney (Brakeman), Leo Cleary (Fireman), Murray Leonard (Engineer).

Additional Credits: Production dates: May 5 to June 1949. Released September 2, 1949.

Available: Warner Home Video DVD (2005). ISBN: 1-4198-0311-5. UPC: 0-12569-67235-2.

After he won an acting Oscar for *Yankee Doodle Dandy* (1942), James Cagney left Warner Brothers to form his own production company with his brother William. On his own, the star appeared in four films, including a thriller for Twentieth Century-Fox and a well-regarded but financially disastrous adaptation of William Saroyan's *The Time of Your Life* (1948). Needing money, the brothers returned to the Warner "factory," which was now missing a former adversary, producer Hal Wallis. Cagney's new contract gave him $250,000 on a schedule of one film per year, plus script approval and the opportunity to develop projects for his company.

Cagney knew he had to make a splash in his comeback film, and settled on *White Heat*, a crime story. For years the star had resisted gangster roles, choosing musicals, Westerns, comedies, and stage adaptations to avoid typecasting. But every time he felt his earning power waning, he returned to the genre. Cagney was also encouraged by the recent success of big-budget film noirs like *Out of the Past*, *The Killers*, and *The Strange Love of Martha Ivers*, movies that helped make stars out of Robert Mitchum, Burt Lancaster, and Kirk Douglas respectively. These films also took sex and violence to new levels. Cagney consequently upped his character's brutality and psychosis.

The star knew what the public wanted, and he also knew how to spin the project to make it seem that he was making a positive sociological statement. Here was how he was quoted in a press release: "We are trying to make a gangster picture that will be a *good* gangster picture, a picture that will pay its way by helping deter crime." The "redeeming" qualities of the film—its tendency to play up police work in heroic terms, and to show state-of-the-art technology—turn out to be its biggest flaws today.

Writers Ivan Goff and Ben Roberts worked from a story by Virginia Kellogg, but Roberts later admitted that the film was about Ma Barker, a bank robber who raised her sons as criminals. The writers reduced Barker's four sons to one, Cody Jarrett, a psychopath with a mother fixation and crippling migraines. The writers never explain the source or meaning of Cody's illness. A T-man at one point mentions that insanity runs in Cody's family, but in truth Cody's disease is simply a plot device, a means to allow Cagney to be crueler than he had ever been on screen before.

The script also toys with Cody's mother fixation, implying more than the filmmakers could show. But apart from its edgy elements, the script is notable for reworking almost all of the themes and memorable bits from Cagney's earlier Warners films. In *The Public Enemy* he smashed a grapefruit into Mae Clarke's face; here he kicks Virginia Mayo off a chair. In *Each Dawn I Die* he suffered through a prison sentence; here he throws a memorable tantrum in a prison mess hall. In *The Roaring Twenties* he fought with rival gangsters; here he stalks double-crossing Steve Cochran, playing the duplicitous "Big Ed."

Cody Jarrett's struggles manage to turn him into a heroic character, despite his viciousness and psychological flaws. Cody may be ruthless, but as the film shows, that is the only way a gangster can survive. He is right to be paranoid, to shoot first, abandon wounded colleagues, and trust no one but his mother. Cody is a natural evolution of Cagney's earlier criminal roles. Had any of them survived, they might be in similar circumstances, surrounded by no-talent petty crooks, hounded by the police, threatened by new security devices. As director Raoul Walsh had already proved in *High Sierra* (1941), and Sam Peckinpah would show in *The Wild Bunch* (1969), criminals are more sympathetic as they age and the odds mount against them.

This was the third time Cagney had worked with Walsh, his director on *The Roaring Twenties* (1939) and on the charming period romance *The Strawberry Blonde* (1941). A film veteran who prided himself on his image as a man's man, Walsh wrote in his autobiography that Cagney was the best actor he ever directed. But the actor was unhappy during shooting, in part because Warners refused to let him cast his friend Frank McHugh, in part because the studio kept trying to cut corners.

Walsh preferred quick, unfussy pacing in his films, and he liked actors who didn't cause trouble. Virginia Mayo, a contract actress who plays Cody's trampy wife Verna, spoke about Cagney's intensity and his willingness to help her and the rest of the cast, but she preferred not to talk about Walsh. The director, who was John Wilkes Booth in *The Birth of a Nation* (1915), never lost his fondness for D.W. Griffith's style of acting, with its exaggerated gestures and pointed reactions. Also apparent is Walsh's disregard for the details of filmmaking. Cagney, Mayo, and Margaret Wycherly received careful direction, but the other actors were left to fend for themselves. Watch how badly Fred Clark, a mainstay of television sitcoms in the coming decade, overacts. You can see a stuntman bounce off a mattress after one jump, and editors had to optically reprint shots that Walsh failed to cover correctly.

The tension between glorifying law and order and dwelling on the "good parts"—violence and crime—prevents *White Heat* from attaining the maniacal intensity of Cagney's earlier films. "Spectographs," "oscillators," and other laughable crime-fighting devices dominate long stretches of

the film, and the action scenes can seem slow and predictable compared to a movie like *Gun Crazy* (1950). Cagney also had to face the fact that he was no longer young. His typical expression here is anxious and weary. His eyes are still penetrating, but his face is puffy, his body stiff, stocky. Bits of his old fire pop up—when he casually shoots an enemy while munching on a chicken leg, for example—but Cagney had taken his gangster character as far as he could go.

White Heat was a financial and critical success, so much so that imitations inevitably appeared. Walsh's use of locations was picked up on almost immediately. Edmond O'Brien would find himself in similar warehouses and factories within the year in *D.O.A.*, a Registry title. The film set a new standard for its followers: now screen crooks had to be rougher, more ruthless, more psychotic. Endings became more incendiary, more explosive, until *Kiss Me Deadly* (1955) went atomic.

The Heiress

Paramount, 1949. Sound, B&W, 1.37. 115 minutes.

Cast: Olivia de Havilland (Catherine Sloper), Montgomery Clift (Morris Townsend), Ralph Richardson (Dr. Austin Sloper), Miriam Hopkins (Lavinia Penniman), Vanessa Brown (Maria), Mona Freeman (Marian Almond), Ray Collins (Jefferson Almond), Betty Linley (Mrs. Montgomery), Selena Royle (Elizabeth Almond), Paul Lees (Arthur Townsend), Harry Antrim (Mr. Abeel), Russ Conway (Quintus), David Thursby (Geier).

Credits: Produced and directed by William Wyler. Written for the screen by Ruth and Augustus Goetz from their play *The Heiress*. Suggested by the Henry James novel *Washington Square*. Associate producers: Lester Koenig, Robert Wyler. Music by Aaron Copland. Production designed by Harry Horner. Costumes: Edith Head. Director of photography: Leo Tover. Art direction: John Meehan. Set decoration: Emile Kuri. Special photographic effects: Gordon Jennings. Assistant director: C.C. Coleman, Jr. Edited by William Hornbeck. Sound supervision: Leon Becker. Sound recording by Hugo Grenzbach and John Cope. Makeup supervision: Wally Westmore. Men's wardrobe: Gile Steele. Western Electric Recording.

Additional Cast: Donald Kerr (Fish peddler), Harry Pipe (Mr. Gebhardt), Una Mortished (Chambermaid), Ralph Sanford (*Castle Queen* Captain), Lester Door (Groom), Franklyn Farnum (Dr. Isaacs), Douglas Spencer (Minister).

Additional Credits: Men's wardrobe: Gile Steele. Set decoration: Harry Horner. Released October 6, 1949.

Awards: Oscars for Best Actress; Costume Design, Black-and-White; Music, Scoring of a Dramatic or Comedy Picture; Art Direction—Set Decoration, Black-and-White.

Other Versions: *Washington Square* (1997), directed by Agnieszka Holland.

Available: Universal DVD (2007). UPC: 0-25193-23672-2.

Published in 1881, after Henry James had moved to Europe, *Washington Square* concerns a domineering father, his homely daughter, and the fortune hunter who tries to marry her. James apparently did not think much of the piece, which was based

on an anecdote told to him by actress Fanny Kemble, and deleted it from a collected edition of his works. But the public embraced it, making it one of the most popular of his twenty novels.

Ruth Goodman, the daughter of a theatrical producer, was a story editor and costume designer when she married aspiring author Augustus Goetz. Together they wrote *One-Man Show* (1945), a drama that centered on a conflicted father-daughter relationship. They returned to this theme in an adaptation of *Washington Square*, focusing much of their play on Dr. Austin Sloper's distaste for his daughter Catherine. (Ironically, James tried for several years to succeed as a playwright, but ultimately was forced to abandon the stage.) "I'm always amused when people say we simply took everything from the original," Ruth Goetz said later. "It's not true. The James story doesn't have the jilt in it. We also found the key to the story: the cruel fact that Catherine is a child her father didn't love." They condensed the novel's time frame and, on the advice of producers, provided a happy ending. When this was poorly received, they reverted to their original ending and renamed the play *The Heiress*. It opened on Broadway in 1947, with Wendy Hiller, Basil Rathbone, and Peter Cookson in the lead parts.

Director Lewis Milestone urged actress Olivia de Havilland to see the play. An Oscar winner for *To Each His Own* (1946), de Havilland was also nominated for *The Snake Pit* (1948) for a part that required her to abandon her glamorous image. She was so taken with *The Heiress* that she asked William Wyler to consider directing it. He was also enthusiastic about the project, and hired the Goetzes to write a screenplay adaptation.

While the Goetzes went to work, Wyler started casting. He considered Errol Flynn for the role of Morris Townsend. Flynn had costarred with de Havilland in nine films, and their pairing would have given *The Heiress* emotional shadings that were missing from the play. But Wyler felt that Flynn was too attractive to plausibly pursue the plain Catherine Sloper. Montgomery Clift, on the other hand, was one of the hottest actors in movies, having starred in *Red River* and *The Search* (both 1948). His casting may have been the result of commercial calculations, as he was ill-suited for this sort of period role. Perhaps Wyler sensed that Clift's difficulty connecting to de Havilland personally would add to the ambiguity of his screen character. (Clift did much better in his next Registry film, *A Place in the Sun*, 1951.)

The crucial role of Austin Sloper was filled by Ralph Richardson, suggested to Wyler by Laurence Olivier. One of the most accomplished actors in England, Richardson originated the role of Sloper in the play's London production. He had just completed work in one of the best British films of the decade, *The Fallen Idol* (1948), directed by Carol Reed from a Graham Greene play and screenplay. In terms of technique, Richardson was far superior to his costars, something Wyler exploited during the production of *The Heiress*, just as he exploited Clift's disdain for de Havilland. She feared being upstaged by Richardson, and in fact it is difficult to watch anyone else when he is on screen.

This is partly due to Wyler's careful treatment of his character. Austin Sloper is typically shot from a low angle to increase his physical and intellectual dominance over the other characters. Richardson is very specific about making eye contact with de Havilland and Clift, and he has Sloper turn away from his daughter whenever he is about to say something hurtful. Often he is positioned in the foreground of the frame, where his haughty reactions can register more strongly. At other times he hovers in the background, his disapproval silent but obvious. It is a brilliant performance, easily the best

in the film, and the only person to come close to him is Betty Linley, who originated her role as Mrs. Montgomery on Broadway.

Wyler was delighted by Richardson's skills. On the other hand, he was disappointed by Clift, by the actor's personality and also by his working habits. Clift's voice was too modern for his part, and he seemed unwilling to immerse himself completely into what was an admittedly detestable character. On the other hand, Wyler knew that de Havilland could not meet the demands of her role on her own. The director cut one of her speeches, saying, "Olivia cannot do it. She hasn't got it." (He also filled a prop suitcase with weights to get the expression of exertion he wanted from her as she carries it up a staircase.)

De Havilland had spent much of the preceding decade trying to break free from her ingénue status of the 1930s, throwing herself into a variety of roles. She was rewarded for playing someone she wasn't—a tomboy in *The Strawberry Blonde* (1941), an unwed mother in *To Each His Own*, a mental patient in *The Snake Pit*. As a homely heiress, she acts with her makeup: heavy eyebrows, circles under her eyes, hair in tight, unflattering braids. Moviegoers knew that underneath was the same gorgeous, tremulous girl who fell for Flynn in picture after picture.

Wyler protected her in *The Heiress*, enough so that she won her second Best Actress Oscar. This was not the director's best or most difficult work (the same could be said of Aaron Copland's score, which rehashes a handful of nineteenth century songs). The relationships in *Dodsworth* (1936) and *Wuthering Heights* (1939) are far more complicated, far less schematic. Some scenes here evoke *The Letter* (1940) and *The Little Foxes* (1941), particularly in Wyler's use of deep-focus photography to isolate and trap characters within large sets. Still, Wyler's technique is subtle and engrossing. He shoots as a novelist would write, using long shots and quick cuts for descriptive passages, then pulling in on extended closeups for the dramatic confrontations. He holds these shots for a minute, two minutes at a time, achieving an emotional reality that would have been dashed by cutting. Wyler would use the same approach in his next film, *Detective Story* (1951), another play adaptation. By the time of his next Registry film, *Roman Holiday* (1953), these devices had been subsumed into a polished, almost anonymous style of filmmaking which left the emphasis strictly on the characters and story, not on his technical dexterity.

All the King's Men

Columbia, 1949. Sound, B&W, 1.37. 110 minutes.

Cast: Broderick Crawford (Willie Stark), John Ireland (Jack Burden), Joanne Dru (Anne Stanton), John Derek (Tom Stark), Mercedes McCambridge (Sadie Burke), Shepperd Strudwick (Adam Stanton), Ralph Dumke (Tiny Duffy), Anne Seymour (Lucy Stark), Katharine Warren (Mrs. Burden), Raymond Greenleaf (Judge Stanton), Walter Burke (Sugar Boy), Will Wright (Dolph Pillsbury), Grandon Rhodes (Floyd McEvoy).

Credits: Written for the screen and directed by Robert Rossen. Based upon the Pulitzer Prize novel *All the King's Men* by Robert Penn Warren. Director of photography: Burnett Guffey. Art director: Sturges Carne. Film editor: Al Clark. Editorial adviser: Robert Parrish. Set decorator: Louis Diage. Montages: Donald W. Starling. Gowns by Jean Louis. Assistant director: Sam Nelson. Makeup by Clay Campbell. Hair styles by Helen Hunt. Sound engineer: Frank Goodwin. Musical score by Louis Gruenberg. Musical director: Morris Stoloff. Assistant to the producer: Shirley Miller. Western Electric Recording. A Columbia Pictures Corporation presentation of a Robert Rossen production.

Additional Cast: H.C. Miller (Pa Stark), Richard Hale (Hale), William Bruce (Commissioner), A.C. Tillman (Sheriff), Houseley Stevenson (Madison), Truett Myers (Minister), Phil Tully (Football coach), Helene Stanley (Helene Hale), Reba Watterson (Receptionist), George Farmer (Bus man), John Giles (Young boy), Ted French (Dance caller); William Cottrell, King Donovan (Reporters); Paul Maxey (Local chairman), Frank McClure (Doctor), Irving Smith (Butler), Louis Mason (Minister), John "Skins" Miller (Drunk), Edwin Chandler (Radio announcer); Wheaton Chambers, Marshall Bradford, Avery Graves, Nolan Leary, William Green (Senators); Glen Thompson, Al Wyatt (State troopers); Harold Miller (Speaker of the House), Mary Bear (File clerk), Stephen Chase (Puckett); Richard Gordon, Tom Ferrandini, Judd Holdren, George Taylor, James Linn, Pat O'Malley (Politicians); Earl Dewey, Roy Darmour, Charles Sherlock (Harrison politicians); Robert Filmer, Bert Hanlon (Editors); William Tannen, Anthony Merrill (Men in city bar); Al Thompson, Charles Haefele (Men in cheap bar).

Additional Credits: Produced by Robert Rossen. Screenplay: Norman Corwin. Editorial assistant: Frank Keller. Second unit director: Don Siegel. Premiered in New York City on November 8, 1949.

Awards: Oscars for Best Picture, Actor (Crawford), Actress in a Supporting Role (McCambridge).

Other Versions: *All the King's Men* (2006), written and directed by Steve Zaillian.

Available: Columbia TriStar Home Entertainment DVD (2001). SIBN: 0-7678-2788-0. UPC: 0-43396-05889-7. Sony Pictures DVD (2006). UPC: 043396130524.

When it was published in 1946, *All the King's Men* was widely seen as a commentary on the life of Louisiana governor Huey Long. The second novel by Robert Penn Warren, the story followed three main characters: Jack Burden, an effete journalist seduced by wealth and celebrity; Anne Stanton, the beautiful daughter of Old South money; and Willie Stark, an ignorant, uncouth politician who rises from rural poverty to control his state through bribes and corruption. More a poet than a novelist, Warren wove their stories into dense, allusive prose that evoked the South of William Faulkner. It was so rich in detail, so convoluted in structure, that even without its hot-potato subject matter it seemed impossible to film.

It was a challenge that appealed to Robert Rossen, at the time one of the more promising

writers and directors in Hollywood. He was born in 1908 in New York City's Lower East Side, and grew up poor. After attending New York University, he focused on theater, directing, and writing message dramas, invariably critical of society. He earned a screenwriting contract at Warner Brothers in 1936, a year before he joined the Communist Party. Rossen started out in the industry writing gangster and crime movies, notably Raoul Walsh's *The Roaring Twenties* (1939), then became disillusioned with both Hollywood and the Party. He left California for New York, returning after World War II, when he collaborated with director Lewis Milestone on films like *The Strange Love of Martha Ivers* (1946).

Rossen directed one of the classic boxing films, *Body and Soul* (1947), written by Abraham Polonsky and starring John Garfield. In May of 1947, Rossen was one of nineteen "unfriendly" witnesses called to appear before the House Un-American Activities Committee (HUAC). Inexplicably, the committee stopped questioning after the first ten, the "Hollywood Ten." The following year, Rossen wrote a letter to Columbia head Harry Cohn saying that he did not belong to the Party. That was enough for Cohn to let Rossen write and direct *All the King's Men*. Looking for a "prestige" project, the studio had purchased film rights for the novel for $250,000.

It was a torturous process, despite Rossen's frequent consultations with Warren. The director faced more severe censorship restrictions than the novelist did, as well as the demands of the marketplace. He especially struggled over the ending, writing to Warren, "When you are dealing with American movies you can forget, when you get to the end, anything like what you call irony—then it's cops and robbers, cowboys and Indians." Rossen wrote at least ten drafts, but according to cast members and Don Siegel, hired as the second unit director, no one ever saw a complete version. In his autobiography, Siegel described the shooting of *All the King's Men* as a drunken blur. As to how he staged and photographed Willie Stark on the stump: "I leafed through the book and found a suitable passage for him to use as one of his political speeches."

"Him" was Broderick Crawford, a former vaudevillian and radio actor who originated the role of Lenny in John Steinbeck's *Of Mice and Men* on Broadway. Crawford had been making films since 1937, in largely unrewarding supporting parts as tough guys and thugs, perfect for his rough voice and overbearing screen persona. Rossen is reputed to have offered the part to an angry, antagonistic John Wayne, but it's hard to imagine a better actor at the time than Crawford for the bullheaded Stark. Mercedes McCambridge may also have been hired for her voice; Orson Welles called her "the world's greatest living radio actress." This was her screen debut.

Rossen shot much of the location footage in and around Stockton, California. According to Cohn biographer Bob Thomas, he had by that point completely discarded the script, and was shooting directly from the book, emulating the style of Italian neorealists. As Rossen noted later, "*Open City, The Bicycle Thief,* and so on marked me deeply, and I even thought, when I became a director, that that was the way of making films."

Studio executives were appalled at the footage they screened back in Los Angeles. Overexposed, grainy, it looked more like a documentary than a Columbia feature. Furthermore, it was difficult to distinguish a theme or style from what Rossen shot. Even after Rossen and editor Al Clark assembled the footage, the film did not make sense. Preview audiences hated it. Clark and his assistant Frank Keller recut the film and rerecorded the soundtrack, to no avail.

Cohn reluctantly agreed to let Rossen shoot more footage to build up McCambridge's role. The director also added new material for Broderick Crawford, but nothing seemed to work. Cohn asked editor Robert Parrish to help. When Parrish screened *The Roaring Twenties,* he found it more a series of impressions than a conventionally structured narrative. He tried the same approach with Rossen's new film. "We decided to take each scene in *All the King's Men,* roll it down on the synchronizer, find the center, or climax of the scene, roll it back a hundred feet, cut—then roll forward from the center a hundred feet and cut, arbitrarily," he explained.

The new version was "like an exciting 106-minute montage." Parrish and Rossen had to re-insert three minutes of material, but the next preview received a "rousing" reception. When it was released, critics and moviegoers responded immediately, making the film one of the year's box-office hits. It won three Oscars.

Despite some poor performances, *All the King's Men* remains tough, relevant, and uncompromising today. It reaches beyond abstract principles to involve viewers on a personal level. Where Frank Capra would choose a comfortable surrogate, a Longfellow Deeds or a Jefferson Smith, to carry his stories, *All the King's Men* is told from a position of privilege. Capra places us on the outside looking in, where we see the foibles of the great outlined in relief. But on the inside looking out, the way Rossen did it, we can understand better the psychology driving the powerful, the pressures besetting them.

As a director, Rossen was so skeptical and determined that he could barely control his story. Like the book, his film is bursting with angles and details, tangents and diatribes. Something so seething was new to postwar American movies, although in hindsight it's easier to see the debt owed to *Citizen Kane* as well as to Capra himself.

Rossen ignored the advice of one of the film's characters: "For heaven's sake, don't try to improve their minds." But he was in trouble politically. While lawyers at Columbia tried to break his contract, Rossen hid in Europe and Mexico before agreeing to testify before the HUAC in 1951. After two more years without work, he confirmed the names of fifty-seven Communist sympathizers in a 1953 hearing. It was a decision that made him, in actress Jean Seberg's words, "an agonized man." His 1963 film *The Hustler* is also on the Registry.

Adam's Rib

MGM, 1949. Sound, B&W, 1.37. 101 minutes.

Cast: Spencer Tracy (Adam Bonner), Katharine Hepburn (Amanda Bonner), Judy Holliday (Doris Attinger), Tom Ewell (Warren Attinger), David Wayne (Kip Lurie), Jean Hagen (Beryl Caighn), Hope Emerson (Olympia La Pere), Eve March (Grace), Clarence Kolb (Judge Reiser), Emerson Treacy (Jules Frikke), Polly Moran (Mrs. McGrath), Will Wright (Judge Marcasson), Elizabeth Flournoy (Dr. Margaret Brodeigh).

Credits: Directed by George Cukor. Screen Play by Ruth Gordon and Garson Kanin. Produced by Lawrence Weingarten. Director of photography: George J. Folsey. Music by Miklós Rózsa. Song: "Farewell, Amanda" by Cole Porter. Art directors: Cedric Gibbons, William Ferrari. Film editor: George Boemler. Recording supervisor: Douglas Shearer. Set decorations: Edwin B. Willis. Associate: Henry W. Grace. Special effects: A. Arnold Gillespie. Miss Hepburn's costumes by Walter Plunkett. Hair

styles designed by Sydney Guilaroff. Make-up created by Jack Dawn. Western Electric Recording.
Additional Cast: Janna deLoos (Mary), Paula Raymond (Emerald), Anna Q. Nilsson (Mrs. Poynter), Tom Noonan (Reporter).
Additional Credits: Produced by Loew's Incorporated. Released November 18, 1949.
Available: Warner Home Video DVD (2000). ISBN: 0-7907-4393-0. UPC: 0-12569-50552-0.

The talented overachiever Garson Kanin was born in Rochester in 1912, where he became interested at a young age in acting by watching movies in a theater his father owned. He dropped out of high school in 1929, working as a musician while attending acting school. A middling actor, he had better success as an assistant, first to Broadway director George Abbott, then to Samuel Goldwyn in 1937. Still in his twenties, he was directing stars like John Barrymore, Ginger Rogers, and Cary Grant at RKO when the war intervened. Drafted into the army, he made documentary and instructional shorts, winning an Oscar with Carol Reed for *The True Glory* (1945). His first postwar play, *Born Yesterday*, became one of the enduring hits on the Broadway stage, and made a star of Judy Holliday.

Kanin had met director George Cukor in 1939; in fact, the director introduced him to his future wife, actress Ruth Gordon. After *Born Yesterday*, Kanin began collaborating with his wife on a screenplay which became *A Double Life* (1947). Directed by Cukor, it won an Oscar for its star, Ronald Colman. Cukor, who had been mired in unrewarding thrillers, felt rejuvenated, and would work on six more projects with the couple.

Kanin had come up with the idea for *Woman of the Year* (1942), the first teaming of Spencer Tracy and Katharine Hepburn; now he and Gordon plotted a comedy tailored specifically for the stars. *Adam's Rib* became the sixth of nine Tracy/Hepburn pairings (he always got top billing), and it is the one that most accurately captured how moviegoers believed the two behaved in real life. It is also the last full-fledged film they made together. Their subsequent teamings—1952's *Pat and Mike* (also directed by Cukor and written by Kanin and Gordon), *Desk Set* (1957), and *Guess Who's Coming to Dinner?* (1967)—have the air of stunts, publicity coups rather than serious films.

Kanin's scripts (and the films he directed at RKO) have a clocklike precision, an enjoyably mechanical feel, as if he were building machines to test hypotheses. He was also expert in exploiting the personalities of actors. He and Gordon used their insiders' knowledge of the lives of stars like Tracy and Hepburn to ground their stories with the sort of personal details that gave them the ring of truth. Tracy may not have been the successful lawyer he portrayed in *Adam's Rib*, but viewers felt that he probably would wake up grouchy and disheveled the way he did in the film.

Cukor was not a director who concerned himself with technical matters. Biographer Patrick McGilligan described how Cukor would rely on production designer Harry Horner to help him compose shots, while editor Robert Parrish waited on sets to tell the director how long to let scenes run. Someone more attuned to technical issues would have noticed the boom shadow crossing over Tracy's bed during his opening shot, for example.

Cukor's real concern was with acting, which ranged in experience on *Adam's Rib* from veteran to novice. He was familiar with Hepburn, having directed her screen debut as well as five other features, and knew how to rein in her "actressy excesses." She preferred to mold her performance through many takes, whereas Tracy wanted everything done in one take. Tracy also refused to rehearse with Hepburn ("Never. Not once. Ever," she said), forcing Cukor to devise ad hoc methods to get through their scenes. But Cukor and Tracy were also close friends, and Cukor had directed him in five films, so the shooting proceeded smoothly.

Adam's Rib featured a number of performers who would figure in significant films in the 1950s. This was Jean Hagen's screen debut; she would employ her squeaky voice memorably in *Singin' in the Rain* (1952). David Wayne became a familiar face at Twentieth Century-Fox and later on television. Tom Ewell had his screen breakthrough in Billy Wilder's *The Seven Year Itch* (1955). Judy Holliday had a small part in Cukor's *Winged Victory* (1944); at the time of filming, she was still starring on Broadway in Kanin's *Born Yesterday*. During *Adam's Rib*, Hepburn ceded her screen space to Holliday in an attempt to convince Columbia head Harry Cohn to hire her for the screen version of *Born Yesterday* (1950).

In 1989, Kanin wrote an article in which he said the inspiration for Adam and Amanda Bonner came from Dorothy and William Dwight Whitney, friends of Gordon. They were lawyers who handled the divorce of actor Raymond Massey and Adrianne Allen, only to subsequently get divorced themselves and marry their clients. He also wrote that he changed the name of Hepburn's character from Madelaine to Amanda because Cole Porter refused to write a song for a Madelaine. Porter donated profits for "Farewell, Amanda" to the Runyon Cancer Fund.

Twelve O'Clock High

Twentieth Century-Fox, 1949. Sound, B&W, 1.37. 132 minutes.

Cast: Gregory Peck (General [Frank] Savage), Hugh Marlowe (Lt. Col. Ben Gately), Gary Merrill (Col. [Keith] Davenport), Millard Mitchell (General Pritchard), Dean Jagger (Major [Harvey] Stovall), Robert Arthur (Sgt. Mellhenny), Paul Stewart (Capt. "Doc" Kaiser), John Kellogg (Major Cobb), Bob Patten (Lt. Bishop), Sam Edwards (Birdwell), Roger Anderson (Interrogation Officer).

Credits: Directed by Henry King. Screen Play by Sy Bartlett and Beirne Lay, Jr. Based on the Novel by Beirne Lay, Jr. and Sy Bartlett. Produced by Darryl F. Zanuck. Music: Alfred Newman. Orchestration: Edward Powell. Director of photography: Leon Shamroy. Art Direction: Lyle Wheeler, Maurice Ransford. Set Decorations: Thomas Little, Bruce Macdonald. Film Editor: Barbara McLean. Makeup Artist: Ben Nye. Special photographic effects: Fred Sersen. Sound: W.D. Flick, Roger Heman. Air Force Technical Advisor: John H. deRussy, Colonel, U.S.A.F., Group Operations Officer, 305th Bomb Group, Chelveston, England, 1942. Western Electric Recording.

Additional Cast: Joyce MacKenzie, Don Hicks, Lee MacGregor, Lawrence Dobkin (Capt. Twombley), Kenneth Tobey (Sgt. Keller).

Additional Credits: Technical advisor: Major Johnny McKee. Presented by Darryl F. Zanuck. Released in Los Angeles on December 21, 1949.

Awards: Oscars for Best Supporting Actor (Jagger), Sound.

Other Versions: Basis for *12 O'Clock High* (TV series, 1964).

Available: 20th Century Fox Home Entertainment DVD (2001). UPC: 0-24543-03007-2.

After World War II, those Hollywood moguls who served in the armed forces returned to business with a renewed sense of purpose. Darryl F. Zanuck, a reserve lieutenant colonel in the Signal Corps, reasserted his control of Twentieth Century-Fox with a series of films that were hard-hitting for their time: *Gentlemen's Agreement*, about anti-Semitism; *The Snake Pit*, about insane asylums; and *Pinky*, about racial prejudice. All were based on novels, the preferred source of material at all the major studios. Louis Lighton, a screenwriter turned Fox producer, was the first to suggest buying the screen rights to *Twelve O'Clock High*.

Written by two veterans, the novel was a fictionalized account of Colonel Frank A. Armstrong, a former minor league baseball player and law student who enlisted in the U.S. Army Air Corps in 1928. During the early months of the war he was a combat observer with the Royal Air Force. In July 1942, Armstrong took over the 97th Bomb Group, leading many combat missions, including the first daylight raid over Axis territory by the United States. Promoted to brigadier general that same year, he later led raids over Japan.

In the book, Armstrong becomes Brigadier General Frank Savage, who is assigned to the 306th bomb group. Stationed in Britain, the 306th suffers from low morale and loose discipline thanks to severe casualties. Savage must not only replace his friend, Col. Keith Davenport, but whip surly,

antagonistic pilots into fighting shape. Sy Bartlett and Beirne Lay, Jr., the original authors, wrote a screenplay that failed to interest anyone, including Gregory Peck, who turned it down.

Peck, classified 4-F due to a back injury, was at the time Fox's brightest star. Born in La Jolla, California, in 1916, he gravitated toward acting against the wishes of his pharmacist father. Peck studied in New York with Martha Graham, among others, and debuted on Broadway in 1942. Two years later he made his first film, the undistinguished *Days of Glory*. But after working with Alfred Hitchcock in two films, and on MGM's *The Yearling*, he was one of the most popular stars in the country.

Fox executives were reluctant to pursue *Twelve O'Clock High*, feeling that it was too close to MGM's *Command Decision* (1948)—let alone *The Dawn Patrol* from an earlier war. It wasn't until Zanuck fired Lighton and took over the adaptation himself that any progress was made. Zanuck had almost all of the supporting characters and subplots stripped away, focusing the story almost entirely on Savage and his mental deterioration.

Zanuck offered the script to director Henry King, one of the mainstays at Fox. (More about King's career can be found in the entry for *Tol'able David*, 1921.) During the 1930s King worked with Fox's biggest stars: Will Rogers, Alice Faye, Tyrone Power, Henry Fonda, and others. His films were marked by a brisk competence that emphasized story over style. An aviator himself, he approached *Twelve O'Clock High* eagerly.

Peck wasn't so optimistic, worried about portraying a military officer. But he enjoyed working with King, describing their collaboration as a give-and-take between father and son, or brothers. In his career, Peck would work more often with King than any other director.

Zanuck received the cooperation of the Air Force in securing planes and in the use of the Eglin Air Force Base in Florida, which stood in for the base in Britain. In return, he had to tone down Savage's character, who originally suffered a nervous breakdown. Filming lasted a little over two months. Editing the footage was more difficult than usual, as Barbara McLean had to incorporate aerial footage taken by Allied and Axis planes during actual combat.

The finished product is one of the more realistic postwar films to deal with combat. In part this is due to the structure of the screenplay, which zeroes in closely on a half-dozen characters who must cope with unrelieved stress. After a dramatic opening that alludes cryptically to the physical consequences of aerial combat, the film avoids flying sequences altogether. Instead, it concentrates on how Savage, replacing a popular officer, gains the respect and trust of the young pilots of the 918 Bomb Group. He does this primarily by being a strict disciplinarian—canceling passes, closing the base bar, etc. During a briefing, he advises his pilots, "Consider yourself already dead." This being a Hollywood film, Savage will grow to identify with pilots as they learn to trust and respect him. But *Twelve O'Clock High* is distinguished by its tone of quiet professionalism, both behind and in front of the camera. From Dean Jagger, who plays Savage's adjutant, to Gary Merrill, the colonel Savage replaces, the acting is understated, even deferential.

In an especially effective tactic, King refrains from showing combat footage until almost two hours into the film. Many civilians had yet to see footage like this, and the sight of planes exploding, clearly killing all aboard, was a sobering one. King wisely realized that sprinkling combat footage throughout *Twelve O'Clock High* would not only lessen its impact, but could be seen as exploitative.

Instead, the film received mostly rapturous reviews on its release. Peck made the cover of *Life* magazine, and received a Best Actor Oscar nomination, his fourth in five years. The film was also nominated for Best Picture. It was not only successfully rereleased in 1955, but became the basis of a television series in 1964. Peck and King went back to work together on *The Gunfighter*, a 1950 Western that tackled some of the same subjects in *Twelve O'Clock High*. One sign of Peck's new clout: his fee per picture went from $45,000 to $100,000.

Gun Crazy

United Artists, 1950. Sound, B&W, 1.37. 87 minutes.

Cast: Peggy Cummins (Annie Laurie Starr), John Dall (Bart Tare), Berry Kroeger (Packett), Morris Carnovsky (Judge), Anabel Shaw (Ruby Tare Flagler), Harry Lewis (Sheriff Clyde Boston), Nedrick Young (Dave Allister), Rusty Tamblyn (Bart Tare at fourteen).

Credits: Directed by Joseph H. Lewis. Screenplay by MacKinlay Kantor, Millard Kaufman. From the *Saturday Evening Post* story by MacKinlay Kantor. Produced by Maurice King, Frank King. Assistant to the producers: Arthur Gardner. Director of photography: Russell Harlan. Film editor: Harry Gerstad. Music by Victor Young. Song: "Mad About You," music by Victor Young, lyrics by Ned Washington. Sound engineer: Tom Lambert. Production designed by Gordon Wiles. Music editor: Stuart Frye. Orchestrations by Leo Shuken, Sidney Cutner. Assistant director: Frank S. Heath. Production manager: Raymond Boltz, Jr. Dialogue coach: Madeleine Robinson. Script continuity by Jack Herzberg. Technical advisor: Herman King. Miss Cummins' wardrobe by Norma [Koch]. Western Electric Recording. Pioneer Pictures Corp.

Additional Cast: Don Beddoe (Driver), Virginia Farmer (Teacher), Frances Irwin (Band singer), Anne O'Neal (Augustine), Stanley Prager (Bluey-Bluey), Robert Osterloh (Policeman), Mickey Little (Bart at seven).

Additional Credits: Millard Kaufman was fronting for screenwriter Dalton Trumbo. Production dates: May 2 to June 1949. Released January 20, 1950.

Available: Warner Home Video DVD (2004). ISBN: 0-7907-8320-1. UPC: 0-85393-19712-4.

MacKinlay Kantor's short story "Gun Crazy," published in the *Saturday Evening Post* in 1940, was one of dozens of pulp works he wrote while struggling to support himself as a writer. It was told from the point of view of newspaper editor Dave Allister as he followed the criminal career of his childhood friend Nelson Tare on teletype reports. Kantor became a war correspondent for the *Post* in 1943, and turned his experiences into *Glory for Me*, a novel in verse. It became the basis for *The Best Years of Our Lives* (1946), one of the most honored of postwar movies, raising the value of Kantor's other works. Even so, "Gun Crazy," which explicitly connected crime with sex, was not an easy choice for film.

The story was purchased by the King brothers, three producers who had started out in low-budget film in the early 1940s under their family name, Kozinsky. Working at Monogram and PRC (Producers Releasing Corporation), they specialized in gritty crime dramas like *Dillinger* (1945), films that drew attention more for their provocative subject matter than their quality. Maurice and Frank King (the third brother, Herman, received a "technical advisor" credit) assigned the *Gun Crazy* project to director Joseph H. Lewis.

Born in New York City in 1900, Lewis had wanted to be an actor, but instead became a camera assistant at MGM, where his brother Ben was an editor. Lewis learned the craft of filmmaking after bluffing his way into the chief editor position at the newly formed Republic Studios, although he later claimed to Peter Bogdanovich that "I never cut a picture in my life." Lewis was determined to become an artist, which he pursued by learning how to shoot anything "with appeal." Lewis signed a deal to direct B-Westerns at Universal, and in 1937 finished seven films.

Even with seven-day shooting schedules, Lewis tried to inject a distinctive visual style into his films. He placed wagon wheels in the foreground to break up the monotony of his Westerns, put a camera on a polo horse, and once shot through a spinning roulette wheel. He also learned how to "suggest" a location with minimal sets and props. During World War II he directed instructional films like *Shooting the M-1 Rifle* (1943) in the Signal Corps. After the war, his *My Name Is Julia Ross* established Lewis as a director of real promise.

The script for *Gun Crazy* was credited to Kantor, who according to Lewis turned in an unfilmmable draft 375 pages long, and Millard Kaufman. It was one of Kaufman's first screen credits, but as was revealed later, he was fronting for Dalton Trumbo, who had been blacklisted after his 1947 appearance before the House Un-American Activities Committee. In the script Nelson Tare's name was changed to Bart Tare, and his girlfriend, Annie Laurie Starr, suddenly developed a British background to accommodate actress Peggy Cummins.

Born in Wales, Cummins had been brought to the United States by Fox to star in *Forever Amber* (1947), but she was replaced by Zanuck favorite Linda Darnell. Cummins tended to play more sophisticated roles than Annie Laurie, but she brings an unexpected verve and bite to her part as an amoral killer who uses sex to control the men around her. Her costar John Dall had similarly limited experience. Born in New York City, he made his screen debut in *The Corn Is Green* (1946), earning an Academy Award nomination in a sympathetic role. In Alfred Hitchcock's *Rope* (1948) he played a thrill killer. Something about Dall—the squint in his eye, his crooked smile, the way he carried himself—made him seem hard to trust, perhaps one of the reasons why he made only eight films.

Rope provides another connection, because in that film Hitchcock gave the illusion that everything was occurring in one long take. The most fascinating elements of *Gun Crazy* today are its two "real-time" robberies, shot on location, with live sound, the first done in one take. Lewis went to great lengths to achieve these scenes, filming a test of the first robbery on 16mm to prove to his cinematographer Russell Harlan that it could be done. Harlan and his crew removed the back from a stretch Cadillac to fit in a 35mm camera, mounted on a greased board so that it could pull up to the side window when Cummins steps out of the car. Dall and Cummins then drove through the town of Montrose, California, turning up and down blocks, parking in front of a bank, the camera capturing a small-town landscape out the windshield while the two share jittery small talk. Dall parks the car; Cummins waits while he enters the bank. The camera waits, too, never blinking as a cop walks up to question Cummins just as Dall returns with the loot. What had been seventeen pages of script became one harrowing feat of brinksmanship.

Filmmakers had used long takes before, but nothing from Hollywood had ever seemed this raw and real. At other times in the movie it's as if the camera can barely contain the action. Real life seems to explode around the edges of the frame, threatening everything Hollywood stood for. New, lighter camera and sound equipment made the shots possible, as did filmgoers' familiarity with documentary footage. Audiences didn't mind a rougher look if the material was sensational enough.

Gun Crazy also tapped into the gloomy foreboding of postwar film noir. By now the rules of noir had been established, but Lewis sped past a lot of them, itching to get to the good parts, not really that interested in who Bart Tare was or why he became a killer. The long takes and location shooting were brilliant strokes, but judging from the director's comments later, they were apparently completely intuitive. Film historian Glenn Erickson believes that the ersatz psychology that opens the film—a long scene in which a judge sentences the young Bart Tare to reform school—saved it from the censors, who otherwise would have objected to *Gun Crazy*'s relentless, sexually charged crime spree.

Gun Crazy was released with a new title, *Deadly Is the Female*, in January 1950. It attracted so little notice that the Kings tried releasing it again that summer under its original title, to no avail. But the film was influential within the industry, and it became a prime example of what critic Manny Farber called "termite art." Jean-Luc Godard praised *Gun Crazy*, and borrowed from it liberally in *A bout de souffle* (1960). The sweater-and-beret ensemble that Cummins wore as a getaway outfit turned up on Faye Dunaway in *Bonnie and Clyde* (1967).

But *Gun Crazy* was influenced itself by the films that came before it—by the lunch wagon scene in *Scarface*, for example, or the carnival in *Freaks* (both 1932). It joined a long line of doomed-lovers-on-the-run films, from *You Only Live Once* (1937) to *They Live By Night* (1949) through to *Thieves Like Us* (1974). Among other titles, Lewis directed a violent but undistinguished gangster film, *The Big Combo* (1955), and a bizarre Western, *Terror in a Texas Town* (1958), then spent the rest of his career in television, directing episodes of *The Rifleman*, *The Big Valley*, and other series.

D.O.A.

United Artists, 1950. Sound, B&W, 1.37. 83 minutes.

Cast: Edmond O'Brien (Frank Bigelow), Pamela Britton (Paula Gibson), Luther Adler (Majak), Beverly Campbell (Miss Foster), Neville Brand (Chester), Lynn Bagget (Mrs. Philips), William Ching (Halliday), Henry Hart (Stanley Philips), Laurette Luez (Marla Rakubian), Jess Kirkpatrick (Sam), Cay Forrester (Sue), Fred Jaquet (Dr. Matson), Larry Dobkin (Dr. Schaefer), Frank Gerstle (Dr. MacDonald), Carol Hughes (Kitty), Michael Ross (Dave), Donna Sanborn (Nurse).

Credits: Directed by Rudolph Maté. Story and screenplay: Russell Rouse, Clarence Green. Produced by Leo C. Popkin. Executive producer: Harry M. Popkin. Associate producer: Joseph H. Nadel. Director of photography: Ernest Laszlo. Art director: Duncan Cramer. Film editor: Arthur H. Nadel. Music written and directed by Dimitri Tiomkin. Set decorations: Al Orenbach. Assistant director: Marty Moss. Costumes by Maria Donovan. Makeup: Irving Berns. Sound recording: Ben Winkler, Mac Dalgleish. RCA Sound System.

Additional Cast: Jadie Carson (Bandleader), Shifty Henry (Bassist), Ray Laurie (Pianist), Teddy Buckner (Trumpeter), Van Streeter (Saxophonist), Peter Leeds (Leo, bartender), Virginia Lee (Jeanie), Roy Engel (Police captain), George Lynn (Homicide detective), Hugh O'Brian (Fan), Jerry Paris (Bellhop), Ivan Tiiesault (Photographer), Philip Pines (Angelo), Frank Cady (Bartender).

Additional Credits: Technical adviser: Dr. Edward F. Dunne. Production dates: August to September 1949. Released April 30, 1950.

Other Versions: *Color Me Dead* (1969), directed by Eddie Davis, with Tom Tryon, Carolyn Jones; *D.O.A.* (1988), directed by Annabel Jankel and Rocky Morton, with Dennis Quaid, Meg Ryan.

Available: The Internet Archive (*www.archive.org*). Questar DVD (2004). ISBN: 1-59464-068-8. UPC: 0-33937-03501-2. Bridgestone Multimedia VHS (1998). ISBN: 1-56371-536-8. UPC: 0-95163-98843-2.

In the 1920s and '30s, Rudolph Maté was a cinematographer for noted directors like René Clair, Fritz Lang, and especially Carl Dreyer, for whom he shot *The Passion of Joan of Arc* (1928) and *Vampyr* (1932). Born in 1898 in Krakow, Poland, he started out in film working as an assistant cameraman for Alexander Korda in Budapest and as an apprentice to Karl Freund in Berlin. Like so many of his peers, Maté left Europe for Hollywood, arriving in 1935. There he worked with William Wyler, Leo McCarey, Alfred Hitchcock, Ernst Lubitsch, and other directors, amassing five Academy Award nominations between 1940 and 1944. After World War II, he gave up cinematography for directing, starting with an innocuous Ginger Rogers comedy, *It Had to Be You* (1947).

Whether by design or because he had no other offers, Maté leaned toward unsophisticated genre pieces: Westerns, costume melodramas, and a science-fiction fantasy, *When Worlds Collide* (1951), that won an Oscar for special effects. More typical was *The Black Shield of Falworth* (1954), in which Tony Curtis uttered his immortal line, "Yonder lies the castle of my father." But Maté's first solo effort, *The Dark Past* (1949), was a sharply executed suspense film with a compelling plot. Maté followed it with *No Sad Songs for Me* (1950), a soap opera with an equally strong story line: a mother dying of cancer must break the news to her family.

Maté directed those films for Columbia, and at a different time might have stayed with the studio. But in 1950 the entire movie industry was in a state of upheaval, and directors like Maté had to scramble for work. For his next project, he turned to Cardinal Pictures, a production company that specialized in offbeat thrillers and comedies with slightly faded stars. Brothers Harry and Leo Popkin started out in B-level crime films in the 1930s; now they were giving the team of Russell Rouse and Clarence Greene the opportunity to develop screenplays. Rouse and Greene both came from New York City; Rouse, who was five years older, was the idea man, while Greene would later become the team's producer.

Their script for *D.O.A.* had one of the most original story hooks in all of film noir: an accountant from Banning, California, goes to San Francisco for a vacation. After a night in a bar, he learns that he has been fatally poisoned. For the remainder of the film, he tries to find out who killed him, and why. It was such a sterling idea that no one seemed to spend much time working out the rest of the story.

With a title like *D.O.A.*, audiences knew what to expect. Once Edmond O'Brien, who plays the accountant Frank Bigelow, announces to homicide detectives that he's been "murdered," and once the film goes into an extended flashback, every character introduced in the story is a potential suspect. Maté and his cinematographer Ernst

Lazslo could concentrate on atmospheric touches, confident that viewers would put up with a lot to learn the solution to the plot. (Lazslo, another Hungarian émigré, had spent a decade at Paramount as a camera operator. *D.O.A.* was his first Cardinal picture, but he would work with Rouse and Greene again in the coming years.)

D.O.A. has some strong visual flourishes and good use of locations in San Francisco and Los Angeles. The cinematography in *Double Indemnity* is an obvious inspiration, especially when Neville Brand chases O'Brien into a drug store, or when O'Brien investigates an office in the Bradbury Building in downtown Los Angeles. But the limited budget clearly hampered the filmmakers. For every traveling shot down a city street, we are given shabby, flatly lit interiors. Nor would the Popkins pay much for actors. Even by 1950s B-movie standards, this was an undistinguished cast. The stocky, stolid O'Brien, who had an important role in the previous year's *White Heat*, would have been the most recognizable name. This was Neville Brand's film debut. Born in 1921, the Illinois native spent ten years in the Army, where he became interested in acting after appearing in training films. He saw considerable action, and was heavily decorated. He studied acting after his

discharge, and appeared on Broadway, but harsh features and a rough voice made him a perfect tough guy on film. Brand's performance here owes a lot to the Richard Widmark of *Kiss of Death* (1947), but in later years he developed his own version of heavies, one that allowed intelligence and humor to sneak in. Luther Adler, who played the mysterious Majak, probably had the best acting résumé. He was the son of Jacob Adler, a star of Yiddish theater in New York City, and the brother of Stella Adler, the famous acting teacher. Luther Adler had a long career as a stage actor and director, but made less of an impact in film.

The film did well at the box office, although the press treated it as more of a gimmick than a genuine thriller. Rouse and Greene continued their collaborations, with *The Well* (1951), for example, which Rouse codirected with Leo Popkin. The writers would win an Oscar for writing the story for *Pillow Talk* (1959). O'Brien would earn an Oscar as well, as Best Supporting Actor in *The Barefoot Contessa* (1954). The story for *D.O.A.* resonated with other filmmakers. The film has been remade twice, as *Color Me Dead* in 1969 and as *D.O.A.* in 1998, but it is the unacknowledged inspiration for a number of other movies as well, such as *Crank* (2006).

In a Lonely Place

Columbia, 1950. Sound, B&W, 1.37. 93 minutes.
Cast: Humphrey Bogart (Dixon Steele), Gloria Grahame (Laurel Gray), Frank Lovejoy (Brub Nicolai), Carl Benton Reid (Captain Lochner), Art Smith (Mel Lippman), Jeff Donnell (Sylvia Nicolai), Martha Stewart (Mildred Atkinson), Robert Warwick (Charlie Waterman), Morris Ankrum (Lloyd Barnes), William Ching (Ted Barton), Steven Geray (Paul), Hadda Brooks (Singer).
Credits: Directed by Nicholas Ray. Screen play by Andrew Solt. Adaptation by Edmund H. North. Based upon a story by Dorothy B. Hughes. Produced by Robert Lord. Director of photography: Burnett Guffey. Art director: Robert Peterson. Film editor: Viola Lawrence. Set decorator: William Kiernan. Musical score by George Antheil. Musical director: Morris Stoloff. Assistant director: Earl Bellamy. Gowns by Jean Louis. Makeup by Clay Campbell. Hair styles by Helen Hunt. Sound engineer: Howard Fogetti. Technical adviser: Rodney Amateau. Associate producer: Henry S. Kesler. Western Electric Recording. A Columbia Pictures Corporation presentation of a Santana Production.
Additional Cast: Alice Talton (Frances Randolph), Jack Reynolds (Henry Kesler), Ruth Warren (Effie), Ruth Gillette (Martha), Guy Beach (Swan), Lewis Howard (Junior), Arno Frey (Joe), Pat Barton (Hatcheck girl), Cosmo Sardo (Bartender), Don Hamin (Driver), George Davis (Waiter), Frank Marlowe (Attendant), Billy Gray (Young boy), Melinda Erickson (Tough girl), Jack Jahries (Officer), David Bond (Dr. Richards), Myron Healey (Post Office clerk), Robert Lowell (Airline Clerk), Robert Davis (Flower shop custodian).
Additional Credits: "I Hadn't Anyone Till You," composed by Ray Noble. Released May 17, 1950.
Available: Sony Pictures DVD (2003). UPC: 043396078963. Columbia TriStar Home Video VHS (1989).

Usually listed as a film noir (albeit one of the finest examples from the 1950s), *In a Lonely Place* is a movie that can't be pigeonholed so easily. On the surface a murder mystery, it is far more coherent, and satisfying, if seen as an account of an affair between two people so psychologically damaged that they don't believe they can love again. It is a story in which faith and loyalty supplant desire, character becomes destiny, and outside forces thwart the best intentions. It was the product of intense collaboration between director Nicholas Ray and his cast and crew, utilizing the resources of a studio system that was crumbling around them. If it is not Humphrey Bogart's best performance, it is certainly his most penetrating.

After marrying Lauren Bacall, his costar in three films, Bogart formed his own production company, Santana Productions, testing the free agent market as many other actors of the time did. His partner at Santana was Robert Lord, a prolific screenwriter at Warner Brothers during the 1930s as well as a producer of lower-tier product. Bogart's previous two films—*The Treasure of the Sierra Madre* and *Key Largo* (both 1948)—had been prestigious successes. For his first Santana film, *Knock on Any Door* (1949), Bogart played a lawyer trying to save a misunderstood hoodlum from the electric chair. It was directed by Nicholas Ray, chosen by Bogart because of his work on a moody crime melodrama, *They Live by Night* (1948).

Bogart and Lord had purchased the rights to the 1947 novel *In a Lonely Place* by Dorothy B. Hughes. Largely forgotten today, Hughes had a proven track record at the time as the source for two exceptional film thrillers, *The Fallen Sparrow* (1943) and *Ride the Pink Horse* (1947). Her best novels concern deeply troubled characters who try to fight their true personalities. There was never any question of filming the original plot of *In a Lonely Place*, which was narrated from the point of view of a serial killer who impersonated a screenwriter in part to find his victims. What interested the producers of *In a Lonely Place* was the novel's Hollywood background and the concept of a violent, unstable man who may or may not be a murderer.

Like Alfred Hitchcock would do with Patricia Highsmith's novel *Strangers on a Train*, Lord had Edmund H. North discard much of Hughes's plot in his adaptation. When Ray signed on as director, he in turn threw out North's script, working with Andrew Solt on a new draft. Ray's version of *In a Lonely Place* shared with his later film *Rebel Without a Cause* (1956) a sullen, misunderstood protagonist who defends strays and who falls in love reluctantly. True to the real Bogart, screenwriter Dixon Steele is prone to heavy drinking and violent outbursts. Even his remorseful apologies are clouded by his misanthropy.

Cast as Bogart's love interest was Ray's wife Gloria Grahame. The director met the actress on the set of *A Woman's Secret* (1949); they married as soon as she divorced her husband Stanley Clements, but theirs was an unhappy relationship marked by bitter arguments. They were in the process of splitting up as filming started on *In a Lonely Place*, prompting peculiar contractual clauses in which Grahame had to agree not to argue with or otherwise question her husband on the set. (She later married one of Ray's sons from a previous marriage.)

Although her career includes several superior performances, Grahame never became an A-list movie star, perhaps because she never hid her indifference for the industry and for most of the roles assigned to her. On screen she comes across as cocky and rebellious, unmindful of her looks and unconcerned about winning over viewers. She is also coolly, completely in control of herself in a way that eluded most of her peers. Some critics complained that her part in *In a Lonely Place* would have been better suited to Lauren Bacall, but then Bacall would have been forced to redeem Bogart's character (and she was also under contract to Warners). Grahame allows the paranoia and sexual hostility in the story (which she was experiencing at the time with Ray) to emerge unchecked.

In her book *Lulu in Hollywood*, Louise Brooks wrote, "Unlike most technical actors, Humphrey was extremely sensitive to his director. But like most actors from the theatre, he was slow in building a mood and grimly serious about maintaining it." There was a showboating quality to his role as Dobbs, the unscrupulous prospector in *The Treasure of the Sierra Madre*. As Dixon Steele, Bogart has nowhere to hide, no tricks to play, no way to soften his character. He battles his personal demons for our entertainment, rescued only by a last-minute improvisation worked out on the set by Ray.

Santana would last for only a half-dozen or so pictures before Bogart sold it to Harry Cohn at Columbia for a million dollars. His next Registry film is *The African Queen* (1951), a change of pace with a vengeance. In 1952, Grahame worked with Josef von Sternberg in *Macao*, Cecil B. DeMille in *The Greatest Show on Earth*, and Vincente Minnelli in *The Bad and the Beautiful*, a Registry title. In his next films, Ray experimented with stars both big (John Wayne, Joan Crawford) and small, finally hitting commercial paydirt with *Rebel Without a Cause*. But he never again directed a film as focused, revealing, and determined as *In a Lonely Place*. He called it one of his favorite pictures, noting "It's a very personal film: the place in which it was filmed was the first place I lived in Hollywood."

The Asphalt Jungle

MGM, 1950. Sound, B&W, 1.37. 112 minutes.

Cast: Sterling Hayden (Dix Handley), Louis Calhern (Alonzo D. Emmerich), Jean Hagen (Doll Conovan), James Whitmore (Gus Minissi), Sam Jaffe (Doc Erwin Riedenschneider), John McIntire (Police Commissioner Hardy), Marc Lawrence (Cobby), Barry Kelley (Lt. Ditrich [Dietrich]), Anthony Caruso (Louis Ciavelli), Teresa Celli (Maria Ciavelli), Marilyn Monroe (Angela Phinlay), William Davis (Timmons), Dorothy Tree (May Emmerich), Brad Dexter (Bob Brannom), John Maxwell (Dr. Swanson).

Credits: Directed by John Huston. Screenplay by Ben Maddow and John Huston. From a novel by W.R. Burnett. Produced by Arthur Hornblow, Jr. Director of photography: Harold Rosson. Art directors: Cedric Gibbons and Randall Duell. Film editor: George Boemler. Music by Miklos Rozsa. Recording supervisor: Douglas Shearer. Set decorations: Edwin B. Willis. Associate set decorator: Jack D. Moore. Hair styles created by Sydney Guilaroff. Make-up created by Jack Dawn. Western Electric Sound System.

Additional Cast includes: Alex Gerry (Maxwell), Thomas Browne Henry (James X. Connery), James Seay (Janocek), Don Haggerty (Andrews), Henry Rowland (Franz Schurz), Strother Martin (Karl Anton Smith), Henry Corden (William Doldy), Gene Evans (Policeman), Fred Marlowe (Reporter).

Additional Credits: Production dates: October 31 to December 1949. Released in New York City on June 8, 1950.

Other Versions: Remade as *The Badlanders* (1958), *Cairo* (1963), *Cool Breeze* (1972).

Available: Warner Home Video DVD (2004). ISBN: 0-7907-8965-5. UPC: 0-12569-59032-8.

Novelist W.R. Burnett had a low opinion of movies, despite selling many of his books to the industry and earning a lucrative living screenwriting. "Writing for pictures isn't writing," he once complained. "It's rewriting." In another interview, he said, "Novel writing was what I was interested in—not pictures. I was actually subsidizing myself so I could write novels." One of Burnett's many fans was writer and director John Huston, who adapted *High Sierra* (1941), a breakout film for Humphrey Bogart. Having severed ties with Warner Brothers, where he had worked many years, with *Key Largo* (1948), Huston directed the disappointing melodrama *We Were Strangers* (1949) at Columbia before signing a two-picture deal with MGM.

Huston's first assignment was supposed to be *Quo Vadis* with producer Arthur Hornblow, Jr., but when he came up with a script that alluded to the Holocaust, he was replaced (the film was eventually released in 1951 under Mervyn LeRoy's direction). In his autobiography, Huston wrote that he was delighted to learn that studio executive Dore Schary had purchased *The Asphalt Jungle*, published by Alfred A. Knopf in 1949. To assist with the adaptation, Hornblow assigned MGM contract writer Ben Maddow.

Born in Passaic, New Jersey, in 1909, Maddow was a social worker when he joined Frontier Films, a leftist documentary group formed by Ralph Steiner and others. Maddow wrote voice-over narrations for several films before being drafted into the Army's First Motion Picture Unit during World War II. He began writing for feature films after the war, with two Glenn Ford vehicles helping lead to *Intruder in the Dust* (1949), an MGM version of a William Faulkner story. For *The Asphalt Jungle*, Maddow endured Huston's practical jokes and "reverse snobbery," later calling him "an intellectual amateur."

Their script followed Burnett's novel closely. They eliminated a newspaper reporter who functioned as a framing device in the novel, and played down one character's obsession with young prostitutes. But for the most part they transferred Burnett's scenes and words intact, much as Huston had done ten years earlier in his adaptation of *The Maltese Falcon* (1941). Set in a nameless Midwestern industrial city, *The Asphalt Jungle* details a jewelry store robbery from several points of view: "Doc" Riedenschneider (played by Sam Jaffe), the ex-con who masterminds the heist; Dix Handley (Sterling Hayden), a "hooligan" who provides the muscle; Lon Emmerich (Louis Calhern), a crooked lawyer; and assorted cohorts.

Burnett wrote short, edgy chapters filled with hard-boiled dialogue and occasionally mushy analysis. He spent considerable time detailing how corrupt the local police were, and came up with psychological insights that today seem superficial and unsatisfying. Huston and Maddow stripped the extraneous material away, focusing almost exclusively on the crooks and their immediate surroundings. As with *The Maltese Falcon*, Huston would depend on the cast to make the story work.

Huston wanted to use nonactors like artist Ludwig Bemelmans; it was Hornblow who came up with Calhern and Jaffe, the most accomplished and nuanced performers in the film. Huston did insist on Sterling Hayden, an actor who had washed out of his contract at Paramount after freezing in front of the camera. The director protected Hayden throughout the film, pairing him with professionally trained actors like Jaffe or Jean Hagen who would feed him lines and set the timing for scenes. But he also wanted a Dix who wasn't intellectual, who instead was borderline stupid, and to achieve this he exploited Hayden's insecurities, eliciting an awkward, haunting performance full of pauses and stumbles.

Another coup was the casting of Marilyn Monroe in one of her first significant roles. She had been on the verge of giving up acting after "knocking around, and I mean knocking around, for about six years." Monroe later called Huston the first genius she'd ever met. Darryl F. Zanuck, who had let her contract lapse at Twentieth Century-Fox, renewed it after seeing *The Asphalt Jungle*.

Huston's interests had not changed much since *The Maltese Falcon*, but he started paying much more attention to the visual style of his films after his documentary work during World War II. In *The Asphalt Jungle*, he embraced both location shooting and the deep-focus cinematography that were coming into favor throughout the industry. With cinematographer Harold Rosson, he devised close-ups of pitiless intensity, noirish industrial landscapes, and group shots that allowed actors to range freely over sets.

The director credited objections from censors for helping him improve a suicide. "It turned out to be a better scene for the change," he wrote. The film remains surprisingly mature for its time, with frank depictions of drugs, sex, and violence. Huston got away with it primarily because he didn't call attention to the story's seamier elements. In fact, once he established how he wanted his actors to interpret their characters and set the tone and pacing he wanted, Huston could get out of the way of the material and performers. "It was easy to make because the people were so good," he said later. "Everything was fine-tuned."

Huston embellished Burnett's version of the heist at the center of the plot, adding bits with nitroglycerine and an electric eye that quickly became genre clichés. *The Asphalt Jungle* had an enormous impact on filmmakers, inspiring a raft of heist films in the United States and Europe. It had an especially strong impact on Stanley Kubrick, who used Hayden in his own version of a heist film, *The Killing* (1956).

The Asphalt Jungle marked another dividing line in the House Un-American Activities Commission hearings. Jaffe and Maddow would soon be blacklisted, while Hayden would later suffer remorse over naming names. It also set MGM head Louis B. Mayer on edge. "I wouldn't walk across the room to see a thing like that," he said, complaining that it was "full of nasty, ugly people doing nasty, ugly things." When Huston started on his next project for the studio, an adaptation of Stephen Crane's *The Red Badge of Courage*, Mayer objected strenuously. As detailed in Lillian Ross's extremely entertaining book *Picture*, *The Red Badge of Courage* led indirectly to Mayer's dismissal from the studio and Huston's self-imposed exile to Europe.

Sunset Boulevard

Paramount, 1950. Sound, B&W, 1.37. 110 minutes.

Cast: William Holden (Joe Gillis), Gloria Swanson (Norma Desmond), Erich von Stroheim (Max Von Mayerling), Nancy Olson (Betty Schaefer), Fred Clark (Sheldrake), Lloyd Gough (Morino), Jack Webb (Artie Green), Franklyn Farnum (Undertaker), Larry Blake (1st finance man), Charles Dayton (2nd finance man); Cecil B. DeMille, Hedda Hopper, Buster Keaton, Anna Q. Nilsson, H.B. Warner, Ray Evans, Jay Livingston (themselves).

Credits: Directed by Billy Wilder. Written by Charles Brackett, Billy Wilder, D.M. Marshman, Jr. Produced by Charles Brackett. Music score by Franz Waxman. Director of photography: John F. Seitz. Art direction: Hans Dreier and John Meehan. Special photographic effects: Gordon Jennings. Process photography: Farciot Edouart. Set decoration: Sam Comer and Ray Moyer. Editorial supervision: Doane Harrison. Costumes: Edith Head. Edited by Arthur Schmidt. Makeup supervision: Wally Westmore. Sound recording by Harry Lindgren and John Cope. Assistant director: C.C. Coleman, Jr. Western Electric Recording.

Additional Cast: Sidney Skolsky, Eddie Dew (Assistant coroner), Roy Thompson (Shoeshine boy), Michael Brandon (Salesman), Kenneth Gibson (Salesman), Peter Drynan (Tailor), Ruth Clifford (Sheldrake's secretary), Bert Moorhouse (Gordon Cole), E. Mason Hopper (Doctor), Gertrude Astor (Courtier), Eva Novak (Courtier), Julia Faye (Hisham).

Additional Credits: Produced between April 18 and June 11, 1949. Reshoots: June 18, June 21–23, July 7, 1949; January 5, 1950. Released August 4, 1950. Title on screen: *Sunset Blvd*.

Awards: Oscars for Best Art Direction–Set Decoration—Black and White, Music, Scoring for a Dramatic or Comedy Picture, Writing—Story and Screenplay.

Other Versions: A stage musical with a score by Andrew Lloyd Webber was produced in London in 1993 and in New York in 1994.

Available: Paramount DVD (2002). ISBN: 0-7921-7286-8. UPC: 0-97360-49274-3.

Like novelists writing about writing, filmmakers have turned the camera on themselves throughout the history of the medium. The resulting movies have generally been comedies like *Show People* (1928) or *Boy Meets Girl* (1938), affectionate stories with an occasional hint of sarcasm. Paramount took a notably more hard-edged approach, with its unofficial trilogy of *The Last Command* (1928), *Sullivan's Travels* (1941), and *Sunset Boulevard* offering some of the darkest accounts of the industry on film.

After successive hits with *Double Indemnity* (1944) and *The Lost Weekend* (1945), writer and director Billy Wilder hit a rough patch creatively. His writing partner Charles Brackett wanted to do a comedy centering on a movie star who had lost her hold on the box office. He envisioned a sympathetic story about "the woman who had been given the brush by 30 million fans," but Wilder wasn't enthused until one of his bridge cronies, D. M. Marshman, Jr., came up with an angle involving a Midwest screenwriter who becomes a sort of paid escort to the star. This was something Wilder understood, given his background as a gigolo and screenwriter himself.

While still a comedy of sorts, the story now became something dark and sordid, with elements of horror and film noir mixed in. Writing on the script proceeded slowly. Wilder had fewer than thirty pages to show when trying to cast the film. Mae West refused the part, not wanting to play someone "old." So did Pola Negri and Mary Pickford, the latter at that time close to a recluse herself. George Cukor recommended Gloria Swanson, then hosting a local talk show on television in New York.

Born in 1897, Swanson was an Army brat who entered the industry through Chicago's Essanay Film Company. There she met her future husband Wallace Beery; when he got a job with Mack Sennett's Keystone Film in Los Angeles, she accompanied him there. Her career didn't take off until she appeared in a series of steamy marital melodramas for Cecil B. DeMille at Paramount. Films like *Male and Female* (1919) and *Why Change Your Wife?* (1920) made her a celebrity, a role she pursued as avidly as any of her movie parts. She left Paramount in 1926, embarking on a series of troubled independent productions financed by Joseph P. Kennedy. She ended up firing director Erich von Stroheim from *Queen Kelly* (1928), which did not receive a theatrical release in the United States.

Swanson was one of many silent stars unable to make the transition to sound films, due more to her age and her overly expressive acting than to her voice. With his typical cruelty, Wilder seized on these elements in his depiction of faded star Norma Desmond. To her credit, Swanson jumped into the project wholeheartedly, offering her photographs and mementos to help dress sets, and allowing Wilder to use a clip from *Queen Kelly*—especially appropriate as Stroheim was hired as Desmond's butler.

Wilder cast Montgomery Clift as the doomed screenwriter. According to Wilder biographer Kevin Lally, Clift dropped out of the project two weeks before shooting, worried about the story's similarities to his then-affair with torch singer Libby Holman. Instead, Joe Gillis became a huge break for William Holden, who had been typecast as affable romantic leads after becoming a star in *Golden Boy* (1939). The actor was worried that he didn't have the experience to play the part, but Wilder famously told him, "Do you know Bill Holden? . . . Then you know Joe Gillis."

Desmond's part may have been based on Mae Busch, an actress many considered delusional. Then again, Greta Garbo, a notorious recluse, hadn't made a film since 1941, while Pickford retired from the screen in 1933. (Aficionados point to Marie Prevost, a former Mack Sennett Bathing Beauty who came to a grisly end.) Whoever the inspiration for Desmond was, it seems probable that Betty Schaefer, the script reader who tries to save Gillis, was based on Audrey Young, an actress Wilder met during *The Lost Weekend*. (She became his second wife during the production of *Sunset Boulevard*.) Nancy Olson, at the time still a student at UCLA, was cast in the part. She told Lally later, "That girl is not someone who truly interests him."

There is just enough truth to the story and characters in *Sunset Boulevard* to keep viewers unsettled. Whether incorporating the Paramount lot, where Cecil B. DeMille was filming *Samson and Delilah*, or featuring real stars of the silent era as the "Waxworks" bridge players, Wilder was using reality in a way that the industry as a whole wasn't prepared for. (The film especially enraged MGM head Louis B. Mayer.) But more than the accuracy of the sets and props, Wilder achieved a psychological honesty about his characters that was as ghastly as it was transfixing. Which made the Grand Guignol effects he slathered on a bit too calculated and cynical. The film's rats, haunted mansion, slashed wrists, even the fact that the story is narrated by a ghost, all helped distance the audience from what was really occurring. The effects reduced *Sunset Boulevard* at times to a horror film or a *film à clef*, disguising the withering tale of disillusionment and self-loathing at its core.

As he had in *Double Indemnity*, Wilder overplayed his hand, filming a prologue set in a morgue that left preview audiences laughing. Once he cut the scene, *Sunset Boulevard* became tougher, meaner, scarier, and a box-office hit. It inspired other filmmakers to try their hand at exposes: Joseph Mankiewicz with *All About Eve*, Vincente Minnelli with *The Bad and the Beautiful*, for example. (It also sundered Wilder's working relationship with Charles Brackett, who was privately appalled at the tone of the film.) Wilder may have taken the wrong message from his success, making his next film, *Ace in the Hole* (1951) even more cynical. He quickly learned that filmgoers preferred light to bitter. His next film on the Registry is the romantic comedy *Sabrina* (1954).

All About Eve

Twentieth Century-Fox, 1950. Sound, B&W, 1.37. 138 minutes.

Cast: Bette Davis (Margo [Channing]), Anne Baxter (Eve [Harrington]), George Sanders (Addison DeWitt), Celeste Holm (Karen [Richards]), Gary Merrill (Bill Simpson [Sampson]), Hugh Marlowe (Lloyd Richards), Gregory Ratoff (Max Fabian), Thelma Ritter (Birdie [Coonan]), Marilyn Monroe (Miss Casswell), Barbara Bates (Phoebe), Walter Hampden (Aged actor), Randy Stuart (Girl), Craig Hill (Leading man), Leland Harris (Doorman), Barbara White (Autograph seeker), Eddie Fisher (Stage manager [scenes deleted]), William Pullen (Clerk), Claude Stroud (Pianist), Eugene Borden (Frenchman), Helen Mowery (Reporter), Steve Geray (Captain of waiters).

Credits: Written and directed by Joseph L. Mankiewicz. Produced by Darryl F. Zanuck. Director of photography: Milton Krasner. Music: Alfred Newman. Art direction: Lyle Wheeler, George W. Davis. Set decorations: Thomas Little, Walter M. Scott. Film editor: Barbara McLean. Wardrobe direction: Charles LeMaire. Costumes for Miss Bette Davis designed by Edith Head. Orchestration: Edward Powell. Special photographic effects: Fred Sersen. Makeup artist: Ben Nye. Sound: W.D. Flick, Roger Heman. Western Electric Recording. A Darryl F. Zanuck presentation.

Additional Credits: Based on "The Wisdom of Eve" by Mary Orr. Production dates: April 10, 1950, to June 7, 1950. Premiered October 13, 1950.

Awards: Oscars for Best Picture; Director; Writing, Screenplay; Actor in a Supporting Role (Sanders); Costume Design, Black-and-White; Sound, Recording.

Other Versions: Adapted into the stage musical *Applause* (1970). Book by Betty Comden and Adolph Green; score by Charles Strouse and Lee Adams.

Available: Twentieth Century Fox Home Entertainment DVD (1999). UPC: 0-8612-12621-5. DVD (2003) UPC: 024543060673.

Based on a May 1946 *Cosmopolitan* magazine short story by part-time actress Mary Orr, *All About Eve* has become the quintessential Hollywood film about Broadway, or more specifically Broadway actors. Written and directed by Joseph Mankiewicz, the film received a then-record fourteen Academy Award nominations, winning six Oscars. Thanks to an outsized performance by Bette Davis and a script crammed with sarcastic one-liners, *All About Eve* remains almost as popular today as when it was released.

After a successful career as a screenwriter, Joseph Mankiewicz switched to producing in the 1930s, first for MGM and then Twentieth Century-Fox. At Fox he argued successfully for the chance to direct, making his debut with *Dragonwyck* (1946), before embarking on a series of comedies and thrillers.

NBC Radio's *City Playhouse* had already broadcast an adaptation of Orr's "The Wisdom of Eve" by the time Mankiewicz started writing a script called *Best Performance*. After Fox purchased the rights from Orr, Mankiewicz made several key changes to her story. In print, Margolo Cranston, 45, is happily married; in the script, Margo Channing, 40, is single. The ending of the film is different, and Mankiewicz added the part of Birdie Coonan for Thelma Ritter.

Biographer Kenneth L. Geist ties Mankiewicz's interest in the original story to his rivalry with his older brother Herman Mankiewicz, a screenwriter of *Citizen Kane* (1941). That film's fascination with journalism is mirrored by *All About Eve*'s with the theater, but the closer connection is the contrast between a fading former star and his, or her, younger replacement. By 1950, Herman was essentially unemployable, while Joseph had just won Oscars for writing and directing *A Letter to Three Wives* (1949).

A Letter to Three Wives offers another key to understanding *All About Eve*. Like *Wives*, *Eve* focuses on three female roles: the aging star Margo, her understudy Eve Harrington, and Margo's friend Karen, an actress in the story but a "civilian" in the movie. And like *Wives*, *Eve* is told in flashback through a voice-over narration. Celeste Holm, cast as the comparatively rational Karen, has said, "To me, *All About Eve* was not all about the character of Eve, but it was 'All About Women.' Joe meant that there are aspects of each other in Eve, Margo and Karen."

Mankiewicz originally wrote the story with Susan Hayward in mind, but agreed with Fox production chief Darryl F. Zanuck that Claudette Colbert was more suitable—that is, older. But Colbert quit when she injured her back. Everyone from Marlene Dietrich to Gertrude Lawrence was considered as a replacement until Zanuck personally persuaded Bette Davis to take the part. (The two had feuded at Warner Brothers years earlier.) Davis's career had dimmed since World War II, and she had not received serious film offers since her contract at Warners ended the previous year.

Holm for one found Davis difficult to work with, although the star became so enamored of her on-screen partner Gary Merrill that she married him after shooting. Mankiewicz also had his hands full with Marilyn Monroe, still on the verge of stardom and unused to working with this caliber of actors. Gary Merrill claimed that Monroe needed twenty-five takes to complete a short scene with George Sanders in a theater lobby.

Sanders and Gregory Ratoff were the most experienced male members of the cast. Born in Russia, Ratoff had been a member of the czar's army before acting in New York with the Yiddish Players. He can be seen in several early sound films, and was also a competent director. Sanders was also born in Russia, although he was raised primarily in England. He abandoned business for the stage, started appearing in British films, and by 1937 had landed in Hollywood. There he starred in two suspense series, *The Saint* and *The Falcon*, replaced in the latter by his brother Tom Conway.

The other actors were generally Fox contract players, and are the weakest aspect of the film today. Zanuck had wanted Jeanne Crain to play Eve; Anne Baxter was cast when Crain became pregnant. Although Baxter had appeared in *The Magnificent Ambersons* (1942), her subsequent roles in the 1940s were disappointing, apart from winning a Supporting Actress Oscar for *The Razor's Edge* (1947). She never remarked on Mankiewicz's conception of Eve as a lesbian.

Mankiewicz later admitted that the characters in *All About Eve* were "perhaps a little overwritten, but bear in mind that these were all new characters then, and I had to make sure people caught on." As a result, the script requires several hard-bitten theater types to fall immediately for the cunning Eve, failing to see through her patently melodramatic ploys. On the one hand theater people are brilliant, driven, glamorous; on the other, they're dopes.

This distrust of the audience extends to Mankiewicz's direction as well: the film frequently grinds to a halt so he can insert heavy-handed reaction shots. Typically they're of Baxter, her eyes narrowed, her shoulders slumped, her voice breathy. (Baxter contradicts the effect by making sure her audience doesn't mistake her for the character she is playing.)

Shooting lasted six weeks. When Mankiewicz delivered his rough cut to Zanuck, the producer re-edited the long party sequence that featured Davis's signature line: "Fasten your seat belts. It's going to be a bumpy night." Mankiewicz had tried to structure the scene from several alternating viewpoints. Zanuck's efforts to simplify the narrative flow helped lead to some inconsistencies, such as how flashbacks and voice-overs switch from one character to another.

Mankiewicz later said he based Margo on Peg Woffington, an eighteenth-century actress, possibly to deter guessing games about who the "real" Margo was. Many thought of Tallulah Bankhead anyway; Sam Staggs—who wrote *All About "All About Eve"*—posits European actress Elisabeth Bergner, also mentioned at one time by Mary Orr.

Ultimately, what endeared *All About Eve* to moviegoers was the optimism underlying Mankiewicz's cynicism, the sense that things would ultimately work out for the best. It was a view far more romantic than that of Billy Wilder's *Sunset Boulevard* (1950), and as a result *All About Eve* won many more awards. Mankiewicz earned repeat dual Oscars (after *A Letter to Three Wives*) for writing and directing, the last significant Academy Award he or anyone else in the cast would receive. Some critics believe that Davis and Baxter, both up for the same Oscar, split their votes, thereby losing Best Actress to Judy Holliday for *Born Yesterday*.

Davis, like Gloria Swanson in *Sunset Boulevard*, subsequently became trapped in a downward spiral of tawdry melodramas based on her characters' age and fragile mental state. Orr, whose short story ended quite differently, retained the theatrical rights to "The Wisdom of Eve," preventing Mankiewicz from pursuing a stage version. She also visited the characters again in "More About Eve," published in the July 1951 issue of *Cosmopolitan*.

Gerald McBoing Boing

UPA's simplified animation style evident in *Gerald McBoing Boing*.

Columbia, 1951. Sound, color, 1.37. 7 minutes.
Credits: Director: Robert Cannon. Story: Dr. Seuss [Theodore Geisel]. Story adaptation: Bill Scott, Phil Eastman. Design: Bill Hurtz. Music: Gail Kubik. Animation: Bill Melendez, Rudy Larriva, Pat Matthews, Willis Pyle, Frank Smith. Color: Herb Klynn, Jules Engel. Story told by Marvin Miller. Executive producer: Stephen Bosustow. Supervising director: John Hubley. Production manager: Adrian Woolery. Produced by United Productions of America.
Additional Credits: Released January 25, 1951.
Other Versions: UPA produced three immediate sequels—*Gerald McBoing Boing's Symphony* (1953), *How Now Gerald McBoing Boing* (1954), and *Gerald McBoing Boing on the Planet Moo* (1955)—and a short-lived television series, *The Gerald McBoing Boing Show* (1956).
Awards: Oscar for Best Short Subject—Cartoons.
Available: Bonus feature on two-disc special edition of *Hellboy*, Columbia/TriStar Home Entertainment DVD (2004). ISBN: 1-4049-3592-4. UPC: 0-43396-01317-9. Sony Pictures DVD *Cartoon Adventures Starring Gerald McBoing Boing* (2006). UPC: 043396130685.

The distinctive style of *Gerald McBoing Boing* helped redirect the animation industry in the 1950s. It was released through Columbia Pictures by UPA, an independent animation house. United Productions of America was formed when Zachary Schwartz from Screen Gems and Dave Hilberman from Graphic Films rented a painting studio together. Stephen Bosustow, who was working at Hughes Aircraft, was looking for help preparing a filmstrip on plant safety. Turned down by Graphic Films, he used Schwartz and Hilberman instead.

As Industrial Films and Poster Service, the three oversaw the production of *Hell Bent for Election* (1944), a campaign film for Franklin Delano Roosevelt that was directed by Chuck Jones. With music by Earl Robinson and lyrics by E.Y. Yip Harburg, and artistic contributions from John Hubley and Bill Hurtz, it was a critical success.

Two subsequent cartoons, *Flat Hatting* for the Navy and *Brotherhood of Man* for the United Auto Workers, indicated a new method of animation art, with flat backgrounds and stylized characters. In 1946, Schwartz and Hilberman sold their interest in the company to Bosustow; they formed Tempo Productions, while Bosustow renamed his company UPA.

According to film historian Leonard Maltin, "Virtually all of UPA's staff had received its animation training at the Walt Disney studio." Some of the employees were holdovers from Screen Gems, where Frank Tashlin was briefly in charge in 1941. During a Disney strike, he hired away artists like Ted Parmelee and John Hubley. But Columbia grew increasingly dissatisfied with Screen Gems cartoons, closing it in 1948 and signing a contract with Bosustow, who promised to continue using studio characters like Fox and Crow.

Along with Hubley and Hurtz, the UPA team included director and animator Robert "Bobe" Cannon and production manager Adrian Woolery. Two early UPA films for Columbia were nominated for Academy Awards; *The Magic Fluke* (1949), which finds Fox having trouble directing a symphony orchestra, was a probable influence on Tex Avery's Registry cartoon *Magical Maestro* (1952). Hubley's biggest coup for UPA may have been inventing the Mister Magoo character, a nearsighted curmudgeon with a faint resemblance to W.C. Fields.

Gerald McBoing Boing, filmed in 1950 and released in January 1951, was the culmination of UPA's efforts to break away from the traditional animation exemplified by Walt Disney and Warner Brothers. The story concerned a young boy who could only speak in sound effects. It was written by Dr. Seuss, who had also written several of UPA's cartoons for the Armed Forces during World War II. His rhyming dialogue would become his trademark in children's books like *The Cat in the Hat*. According to Maltin, the portions of his script that could be addressed in purely visual terms were discarded; Gerald's later radio career was invented by Bill Scott and Phil Eastman, credited with "story adaptation."

Maltin quotes designer Bill Hurtz many years later: "In *Gerald McBoing Boing*, we were trying for absolute simplicity—how few lines could be in this picture? How elemental could it get?" Hurtz wanted to make a cartoon that followed a continuous path, without cuts or dissolves. Characters in the foreground would remain constant, while backgrounds would change to indicate new settings. "We thought of this as a picture without walls," Hurtz said, and in much of *Gerald McBoing Boing* there is no distinction between wall and floor. A train station might be shown by a horizontal line for the platform, with parallel lines receding to the horizon for the railway. A living room could be indicated by a floor lamp, a couple of chairs, and a picture window. Sometimes swaths of color stood in for backgrounds. These took on psychological significance, indicating Gerald's moods during the story.

UPA's animation style was "a breath of fresh air," in the words of animator Bill Melendez. *Gerald McBoing Boing* won an Oscar for animation, defeating an MGM Tom and Jerry cartoon and another entry from UPA. Both Disney and Warners were shut out, an omen that no one in the industry could ignore. Throughout the 1950s, UPA turned out several noteworthy cartoons, including the even more visually impressive *The Tell-Tale Heart* (1953, a Registry title). Although Bosustow sold out in 1959, the studio's style continued into the 1960s, notably with the *Rocky and Bullwinkle* series, which featured Parmelee, Hurtz, and other former UPA employees.

The Thing from Another World

RKO, 1951. Sound, B&W, 1.37. 87 minutes

Cast: Margaret Sheridan (Nikki), Kenneth Tobey (Captain Patrick Hendry), Robert Cornthwaite (Dr. Carrington), Douglas Spencer (Scotty), James Young (Lt. Eddie Dykes), Dewey Martin (Crew Chief), Robert Nichols (Lt. Ken Erickson), William Self (Corporal Barnes), Eduard Franz (Dr. Stern), Sally Creighton (Mrs. Chapman), James Arness ("The Thing").

Credits: Directed by Christian Nyby. Screen play by Charles Lederer. Based on the story "Who Goes There?" by John W. Campbell, Jr. Produced by Howard Hawks. Associate producer: Edward Lasker. Director of photography: Russell Harlan. Special effects by Donald Steward. Film editor: Roland Gross. Music composed and directed by Dimitri Tiomkin. Art directors: Albert S. D'Agostino, John J. Hughes. Set decorations: Darrell Silvera, William Stevens. Ladies' wardrobe by Michael Woulfe. Makeup supervision: Lee Greenway. Hair stylist: Larry Germain. Special photographic effects: Linwood Dunn. Sound by Phil Brigandi, Clem Portman. RCA Sound System. A Winchester Pictures Corp. presentation.

Additional Cast: George Fenneman (Dr. Redding), John Dierkes (Dr. Chapman), David McMahon (Brig. Gen. Fogarty), Lee Tung Foo (Cook), Robert Stevenson (Capt. Fred Smith).

Additional Credits: Screenwriting by Ben Hecht. Production dates: October 25, 1950 to March 3, 1951. Released April 6, 1951. Also known as *The Thing*.

Other Versions: Remade as *The Thing* (1982), directed by John Carpenter.

Available: Warner Home Video DVD (2003). ISBN: 0-7806-4345-3. UPC: 0-53939-66862-9.

John W. Campbell, Jr., wrote "Who Goes There?" under the pseudonym Don Stuart. Howard Hawks read the story, which was published in 1938, while he was directing *I Was a Male War Bride* (1949). He paid $900 for the story, which was about a shapeshifting alien attacking scientists in Antarctica. According to Hawks biographer Todd McCarthy, the director needed a project to pitch to RKO while he assembled what would become *The Big Sky* (1952). Hawks hired screenwriters Ben Hecht and Charles Lederer to rework the story; only the latter received a screen credit.

The Thing was not the first science-fiction film, but in McCarthy's view it was the first significant film to combine sci-fi and horror formulas. It was also one of the first sci-fi movies to take place in a realistic setting, not the future or another planet. The first half of the script concentrates on technical and logistical details: how planes land on ice, the layout of the Arctic compound, radio communications, etc. The filmmakers changed the location from Antarctica to the North Pole in part to suggest the nearby Russian threat. They also introduced themes and conflicts that have become staples of the genre: man as prey versus alien killers, science versus the military, and others.

Hawks considered hiring Lederer to direct the project, but instead turned it over to editor

Christian Nyby, who had played a major role in reshaping the original cut of *Red River* (1948). This was still Hawks' project, produced under his Winchester Pictures banner, with Hawks hand-selecting the cast and crew. (He even kept almost 90 percent of Nyby's directing fee.) Hawks had promised Kenneth Tobey a lead role after he appeared in *I Was a Male War Bride*; here he is Captain Patrick Hendry, the alpha male in a testosterone-heavy cast. Margaret Sheridan, who plays the sassy love interest, was a Hawks discovery. He saw her in a *Vogue* ad and signed her to a personal contract in 1945, enrolling her in a regimen of classes that included dance and drama. He had hoped to use her in *Red River*, but she married and became pregnant before shooting started. "She wasn't the same girl," Hawks said later about her appearance in *The Thing*. "If she'd only done *Red River*, she'd have been a big star." Nyby took the credit for casting George Fenneman, later Groucho Marx's straight man on *You Bet Your Life*, and James Arness, who would anchor the long-running television series *Gunsmoke*.

Shooting was supposed to begin on October 25, 1950, but Hawks and his crew wasted seven weeks on location in Montana waiting for snow that never arrived. Almost all the exteriors were shot instead at the RKO ranch in the San Fernando Valley, the actors suffering through stifling weather in their Arctic apparel. Interiors were shot in an icehouse in downtown Los Angeles because Hawks wanted to see vapor when the actors breathed. Sets there were kept at a constant 25 degrees.

Hawks didn't claim the directing credit perhaps because the genre was still considered low class, perhaps because apart from the dialogue there wasn't that much to do. A lot of the movie is establishing shots of characters getting into and out of planes or rooms. A lot more is devoted to introductions, to brief science discussions, and to exposition delivered at breakneck pace so viewers won't realize how foolish it is. Themes and situations from other Hawks films pop up: the brotherhood of aviators and hostile locations from *Only Angels Have Wings* (1939) and *Air Force* (1943), the grace-under-pressure camaraderie from *His Girl Friday* (1940), the antagonistic romance subplot and insolent, wisecracking feminine lead from almost any Hawks title. But unlike those films, little is at stake for the characters here—beyond mere survival, of course.

Accounts vary as to who actually directed the film. In later interviews, most of the actors agreed that work wouldn't commence on the set unless Hawks was present. His method was to rewrite the script in the morning and shoot the revisions in the afternoon; as a result, what was supposed to be a modest, nine-week shoot actually took almost five months to finish. Some insist that Nyby is the real director, but his post-*Thing* career was negligible; he claimed that he was only offered low-budget horror films until he moved into television.

For a low-budget, black-and-white sci-fi film with a no-name cast and primitive special effects, *The Thing* was surprisingly successful. (RKO lengthened its title to *The Thing from Another World* to avoid comparisons to "The Thing," a Phil Harris novelty song.) Hawks' reputation was a major part of the film's publicity, helping it gain more attention than other low-budget items.

But *The Thing* was also a blast to watch, an extremely entertaining movie full of confidence, even swagger. It was one of the best, and most influential, sci-fi films of the 1950s. Its canny mingling of Universal horror tricks and up-to-the-minute scientific mumbo jumbo connected directly to audiences. Like the old *Frankenstein* and *Wolf Man* films, *The Thing* introduces its monster in brief spurts, gradually allowing the full horror of the character to emerge. The introductory half hour lulls viewers into a false sense of complacency, as characters exchange banter and viewers watch a plane land three times. But as the film proceeds, the jolts—many of them caused by human error—come with increasing frequency. The filmmakers are adept at other horror tropes: the musical sting, the shock cut, the countdown to increase tension (aided here by the use of a clicking, blinking Geiger counter). Hawks' brisk, no-nonsense pacing and level-headed characters add greatly to the film's breezy, insouciant tone.

Todd McCarthy cites a number of authors and filmmakers who were influenced by *The Thing*: Michael Crichton, Arthur C. Clarke, John Frankenheimer, Ridley Scott. Films like *Alien* (1979) or even *Close Encounters of the Third Kind* (1977) would not have been the same without *The Thing*. It is a "first contact" story that helped set the tone for a decade fraught with political hysteria and with fear of the unknown. And although he declined credit for it, *The Thing* was on many levels the last of Howard Hawks' great films.

A Place in the Sun

Paramount, 1951. Sound, B&W, 1.37. 122 minutes.

Cast: Montgomery Clift (George Eastman), Elizabeth Taylor (Angela Vickers), Shelley Winters (Alice Tripp), Anne Revere (Hannah Eastman), Keefe Brasselle (Earl Eastman), Fred Clark (Bellows), Raymond Burr (Frank Marlowe), Herbert Heyes (Charles Eastman), Shepperd Strudwick (Anthony Vickers), Frieda Inescourt (Mrs. Vickers), Kathryn Givney (Louise Eastman), Walter Sande (Jansen), Ted de Corsia (Judge), John Ridgley (Coroner), Lois Chartrand (Marsha Eastman), Paul Frees (Morrison).

Credits: Produced and directed by George Stevens. Screenplay by Michael Wilson and Harry Brown. Based on the novel *An American Tragedy* by Theodore Dreiser and the Patrick Kearney play adapted from the novel. Music score: Franz Waxman. Director of photography: William C. Mellor. Special photographic effects: Gordon Jennings. Process photography: Farciot Edouart, Loyal Griggs. Edited by William Hornbeck. Associate producer: Ivan Moffat. Associate director: Fred Guiol. Art direction: Hans Dreier and Walter Tyler. Set decoration: Emile Kuri. Costumes: Edith Head. Makeup supervision: Wally Westmore. Assistant director: C.C. Coleman, Jr. Assistant to the producer: Howie Horwitz. Sound recording by Gene Merritt and Gene Garvin. Western Electric Recording.

Additional Cast: William R. Murphy (Mr. Whiting), Douglas Spencer ("Bear Bait" [Boatkeeper]), Josephine Whittell (Margaret [Secretary]), Frank Yaconelli (Truck driver), Ralph Dunn (Policeman), Bob Anderson (Eagle Scout); Lisa Golm, Frances Driver (Maids); Mary Kent (Mrs. Roberts), Ken Christy (Warden), Kathleen Freeman (Martha), Wallace Scott (Factory guard); Hans Moebus, Eric Wilton (Butlers); Mike Mahoney (Motorcycle cop), Al Ferguson (Bailiff), James W. Horne (Tom Tipton), Laura Eliott (Miss Harper).

Additional Credits: Production began October 1949. Opened in Los Angeles on August 15, 1951.

Other Versions: Dreiser's novel was adapted as *An American Tragedy* (1931), directed by Josef von Sternberg.

Awards: Oscars for Best Director, Writing—Screenplay, Cinematography—Black-and-White, Film Editing, Music—Scoring of a Dramatic or Comedy Picture, Costume Design—Black-and-White.

Available: Paramount DVD (2001). ISBN: 0-7921-7284-1. UPC: 0-9736-05815-4-6.

Director George Stevens' war experiences (covered in the entry for *George Stevens: World War II Footage, 1944–46*) changed the tone and tenor of the films he made when he returned to Hollywood. The war also gave him new collaborators, such as associate producer Ivan Moffat and cinematographer William Mellor, veterans of "Stevens' Irregulars." Like many other leading directors, Stevens now wanted to make a statement about America and what it meant to live there. He first chose to adapt *I Remember Mama* (1948), a memoir about an immigrant family in San Francisco at the turn of the twentieth century.

During this period, Stevens joined with Frank Capra and William Wyler in Liberty Films, an independent production company that the directors hoped would give them greater control over their work. The reality of the marketplace forced them to retreat to the financial safety of the Hollywood majors. They sold the company, along with their projects, to Paramount. That's where Stevens hoped to make a new, updated version of the Theodore Dreiser novel *An American Tragedy*.

First published in 1925, the novel was based on the 1906 murder of factory worker Grace Brown in New York's Adirondack Mountains. She was drowned by Chester Gillette in Big Moose Lake, and his subsequent trial drew the attention of the national press. Writing over a decade later, Dreiser presented the crime as emblematic of American society, especially its conflict between upward mobility and rigid class lines. The novel earned Dreiser some of the best reviews of his career.

Patrick Kearney adapted the novel into a play which opened on Broadway in 1926. Four years later, Russian director Sergei Eisenstein announced plans to film the novel as his first Hollywood project at Paramount. Executives there balked at the size of his script, taking the project away from Eisenstein and assigning it to Josef von Sternberg. Dreiser was so angry about Sternberg's 1931 version that he initiated a lawsuit against the studio.

Since Paramount still owned the rights to the novel and play, Stevens thought he would have no trouble with a new adaptation. Instead, he had to fight for at least two years to get approval, in part because Sternberg's film had been such a resounding flop. While battling executives, Stevens worked with screenwriters Michael Wilson and Harry Brown to update the novel from the 1920s to the postwar period. Stevens wanted to show a society that promised freedom and advancement for returning veterans, yet offered the same poor wages and limited chances that characterized the Depression. Another new element: the sexual enticements increasingly prevalent in culture, in particular suggestive advertising and passionate romantic movies.

Stevens cast Shelley Winters as doomed factory worker Alice Tripp after she dressed herself in a dowdy fashion for an audition. Previously branding herself as a sexpot, Winters was so effective as a shrewish nag that it became part of her screen persona. (Charles Laughton exploited this same quality after he cast her in *The Night of the Hunter*, 1955.) Montgomery Clift was anxious to play the role of George Eastman, the son of religious zealots who were distant relations to an upper-crust manufacturing family. But he started to criticize Stevens, referring to him as a "craftsman" instead of an artist. "George preconceives everything through a viewfinder," he said, turning to acting coach Mira Rostova for advice. (According to author Sam Kashner, she wound up ruining many takes by sitting too close to the camera.)

This was the first of three films Clift made with Elizabeth Taylor. Seventeen at the time, she had been growing up on screen at MGM, where she was cast as beautiful and plucky in a series of undemanding roles. (*National Velvet*, 1944, is on the Registry.) She worried about her lack of technique at first, but later realized how Stevens manipulated her naïveté and emotions in her scenes with Clift. His dedication impressed her. "For the first time in my life I started to take acting seriously," she said later. "I started to listen."

Stevens shot a tremendous amount of material, discarding some and compressing other scenes into extended dissolves that hovered on the edge of montage. This was a new stylistic device in his work, and while it enabled him to make easy contrasts—between the Eastmans' wealth and the hard lives endured by downtrodden workers, for example—it also limited the way viewers could interpret what they were seeing.

A former cinematographer, Stevens was exacting about the information in the frame. The film's compositions are so strong that they can outweigh the impact of dialogue and acting. His tendency to shoot more than he needed, more than he could use, meant that when it was time to edit the film, the narrative structure often bent out of shape. While *A Place in the Sun* follows the general outline of *An American Tragedy*, Stevens strips away almost all of George Eastman's background, and most of Tripp's story as well.

What he concentrates on is the relationship between Eastman and Angela Vickers—in particular, their brief moments of passion. The extreme close-ups of Taylor and Clift nuzzling were as erotic as mainstream cinema could offer, and they threw all the other elements of the film out of whack. Stevens returned to these shots repeatedly during the narrative, whether or not the plot required them, and they became an almost subconscious part of American culture, an idealization, even a guide for moviegoers who might not even know what they were yearning for. "It just happened," Taylor said about the kisses. "There was no direction, I wasn't told what to do, I just kissed him instinctively."

Taylor might have believed that, but she had to be coaxed into an environment that would enable her instincts to emerge. The framing, the lighting, her relationship with Clift—encouraged and shaped by Stevens—all contributed to what transpired in the scene. The tragedy in the director's eyes seemed to be that these two impossibly beautiful people couldn't wind up together. But what was keeping them apart? Society? Work? Heredity? Stevens couldn't answer these questions any more than anyone else could. What he could do was catch an inchoate desire and fix it on the screen.

Moviegoers of the time were won over by the film's solid craftsmanship and by its occasional swipes at social issues. Most of all they were entranced by Taylor, who became an icon of beauty for the 1950s. When *A Place in the Sun* won six Oscars, including one for directing, Stevens may have reached the wrong conclusions. Like John L. Sullivan in *Sullivan's Travels* (1941), Stevens was determined to make meaningful films where his true strengths lay in knockabout comedy. His pictures would grow increasingly ponderous and self-important, starting with *Shane* in 1953.

The Day the Earth Stood Still

Twentieth Century-Fox, 1951. Sound, B&W, 1.37. 92 minutes.

Cast: Michael Rennie (Klaatu/Carpenter), Patricia Neal (Helen Benson), Hugh Marlowe (Tom Stevens), Sam Jaffe (Jacob Barnhardt), Billy Gray (Bobby Benson), Frances Bavier (Mrs. Barley), Lock Martin (Gort), Elmer Davis (Himself), H.V. Kaltenborn (Himself), Drew Pearson (Himself), Gabriel Heatter (Himself; heard on radio).

Credits: Directed by Robert Wise. Screen play by Edmund H. North. Based on a story by Harry Bates. Produced by Julian Blaustein. Music: Bernard Herrmann. Director of photography: Leo Tover. Art direction: Lyle Wheeler, Addison Hehr. Set decorations: Thomas Little, Claude Carpenter. Film editor: William Reynolds. Wardrobe direction: Charles Le Maire. Klaatu's costume designed by Perkins Bailey. Costumes designed by Travilla. Makeup artist: Ben Nye. Special photographic effects: Fred Sersen. Sound: Arthur L. Kirbach, Harry M. Leonard. Western Electric Recording.

Additional Cast: Frank Conroy (Harley, Secretary to the President), John Brown (George Barley), Marjorie Crossland (Hilda, Barnhardt's housekeeper), Edith Evanson (Mrs. Crockett).

Additional Credits: Production dates: April 9 to May 23, 1951. Opened in New York City on September 18, 1951.

Other Versions: Remade by Twentieth Century Fox in 2008, directed by Scott Derrickson.

Available: Twentieth Century Fox Home Entertainment DVD (2002). UPC: 0-24543-05005-6.

Yin to *The Thing from Another World*'s yang, *The Day the Earth Stood Still* distilled Cold War hysteria to a science-fiction allegory with religious overtones.

Quiet, measured, and "friendly" where *The Thing* was fast, edgy, and "mean," *The Day* presents a world where it is too late to contain our enemies, where science bests the military, and where compromise rather than war is the answer. While the film exploited a craze for flying saucers and spacemen, its serious, documentary approach has been a pervasive influence on subsequent sci-fi and suspense films, even as most viewers remain oblivious to its crypto-fascist message.

The Day was put together by Julian Blaustein, a contract producer at Twentieth Century-Fox. Born in New York City in 1913, and educated at Harvard, Blaustein was, like Val Lewton, vastly overqualified for his first job as a reader at Universal. Promoted to story editor, he later headed the story department at Paramount before working, as Lewton did, for David O. Selznick. After serving in the Army during World War II, he was signed by Darryl F. Zanuck at Fox.

Years spent amassing and decoding stories gave Blaustein an enviable sense of what narratives worked and didn't work in film, while his reactions to the war and his time in the Army fomented his sense of social justice. His first producing credit, *Broken Arrow* (1950), dealt with the betrayal of Indians, and was ghost-written by the blacklisted Albert Maltz. Blaustein's subsequent films almost always espoused a moralistic point of view, and in interviews he spoke often about filmmakers' responsibility to uplift their audiences.

The producer said that the inspiration for *The Day* came from newspaper stories about efforts to control postwar politics through the United Nations—in particular, the headline phrase "peace offensive." Blaustein was disturbed by a "negative" ambience in coverage of the UN, and wanted to prove that "peace is a five-letter word, not a dirty word." He knew a science-fiction framework could disguise didactic intentions, and had Fox readers search for a story he could adapt to his purposes. In interviews he claimed to have read over two hundred stories and scripts before settling on "Farewell to the Master," a pulp story by Harry Bates published in the October 1940 issue of *Astounding Stories* magazine.

Blaustein assigned screenwriter Edmund H. North to the project, specifying changes in the plot and fleshing out the characters with the author. The son of vaudeville performers, North, born in 1911, wrote modestly successful screenplays before making training films in the Army Signal Corps during World War II. After the war he worked on three noteworthy films, including an estimable adaptation of Dorothy Hughes' pulp novel *In a Lonely Place* (1950), before starting Blaustein's project.

The producer selected Robert Wise, in the midst of a six-picture deal with Fox, to direct. Wise had been a film editor at RKO, with *Citizen Kane* and *The Magnificent Ambersons* to his credit, and started working with producer Val Lewton in the aftermath of the Orson Welles debacle surrounding those two films. Lewton gave Wise his first directing credit on *The Curse of the Cat People* (1944), having him replace Gunther von Fritsch after production had started. "The experience with Val was one of the high points of my career," Wise said later, and his films have in common with Lewton's a narrative focus and expertise with technical effects that show a thorough understanding of the power and complexity of film.

Wise claimed not to have tampered much with North's first draft other than tightening it. But the film is distinctly different from other Fox movies of the time, even though it shares with them a greater use of location footage and realistic details, such as the appearance here of four real-life journalists who deliver exposition.

Zanuck had wanted Spencer Tracy to play the part of the alien Klaatu, a suggestion that dismayed everyone else on the project. (Wise wanted Claude Rains, an equally dubious choice.) On the other hand, Zanuck did find Michael Rennie, a newcomer to American films and an astute choice for the alien. Patricia Neal earned the enmity of sci-fi fans by claiming later that she couldn't deliver her lines without cracking up. Lock Martin, a doorman at Grauman's Chinese Theater, was chosen to play the robot Gort because of his extreme height. The robot is controlled at one point by the phrase "Klaatu verata niktu," one of the most familiar quotes in sci-fi movies.

Trained in B-movies, Wise had no trouble staying under Zanuck's $1 million limit for *The Day*. Wise not only used stock footage and existing sets, he turned to models and mattes for many of the special effects. Other effects were achieved with devices as simple as flashlights. One of the alien's big tricks—turning off power across the planet—required almost no effort to show convincingly. In fact, much of the film is made up of montages, essentially silent sequences tied together more by associative editing and voice-over narration than by what the shots themselves mean.

Wise always claimed not to have noticed the script's religious overtones, such as the alien adopting the name "Carpenter," or a scene in which a potential savior dies for humanity's sins and then is resurrected. Wise doesn't go so far as to linger on crosses, but the story does contain a Judas and a Pilate, as well as what could pass for a Sermon on the Mount. "You have faith," the alien tells Sam Jaffe, comforting a troubled actor who would soon be blacklisted. "You have power over life and death?" another character asks.

More troubling today is the script's insistence that peace can only be achieved by giving up freedom. No one at the time could have mistaken the references to the Soviet Union throughout the film, especially in the implied threat of the robot Gort. Weirdly, the alien proposes a totalitarian regime as the solution to society's problems. By ceding power to robots, the aliens "live in peace . . . secure in the knowledge that we are free of aggression or war." Wise's film offers the same threat as *The Thing*: Our planet can be destroyed by aliens. Or, as Klaatu puts it, "This Earth of yours will be reduced to a burned-out cinder." The films' responses could not be more diametrically opposed, and they played out in diverging strands of sci-fi films throughout the 1950s: *The War of the Worlds* (1953) on the one hand, *Forbidden Planet* (1956) on the other.

This was an important credit for soundtrack composer Bernard Herrmann. He used two theremins to help achieve the ominous mood that marks nighttime scenes around Klaatu's flying saucer. North's later career was marked by several Westerns and an Oscar for *Patton* (1970), cowritten with Francis Ford Coppola. Blaustein continued producing movies through the 1960s. And Wise went on to direct such blockbusters as *West Side Story* (1961) and *The Sound of Music* (1965), both Registry titles.

A Streetcar Named Desire

Warner Bros., 1951. Sound, B&W, 1.37. 125 minutes.

Cast: Vivien Leigh (Blanche [DuBois]), Marlon Brando (Stanley [Kowalski]), Kim Hunter (Stella [Kowalski]), Karl Malden (Mitch [Mitchell]), Rudy Bond (Steve [Hubbell]), Nick Dennis (Pablo [Gonzalez]), Peg Hillian (Eunice), Wright King (A Collector), Richard Garrick (A Doctor), Ann Dere (The Matron), Edna Thomas (The Mexican Woman), Mickey Kuhn (A Sailor).

Credits: Directed by Elia Kazan. Screen Play by Tennessee Williams. Adaptation by Oscar Saul. Based upon the Original Play *A Streetcar Named Desire* by Tennessee Williams, as presented on the stage by Irene Mayer Selznick. Produced by Charles K. Feldman. Director of photography Harry Stradling. Art Director: Richard Day. Film Editor: David Weisbart. Original Music by Alex North. Musical Direction by Ray Heindorf. Sound by C.A. Riggs. Set Decorator: George James Hopkins. Wardrobe by Lucinda Ballard. Makeup Artist: Gordon Bau. RCA Sound System.

Additional Credits: Production dates: August to October 1950. Premiered in New York City on September 19, 1951.

Awards: Oscars for Best Actress (Leigh), Supporting Actor (Malden), Supporting Actress (Hunter), Art Direction–Set Decoration—Black-and-White, Costume Design—Black-and-White.

Available: Warner Home Video DVD (2006). ISBN: 0-7907-9580-9. UPC: 0-85393-89322-4.

Based on Tennessee Williams' Pulitzer Prize–winning play, the film version of *A Streetcar Named Desire* marked a generational dividing line, defined in large part by Marlon Brando's performance as Stanley Kowalski. Born in Omaha, Nebraska, in 1924, Brando reached New York in 1943, a high-school dropout. Studying at the Actors' Studio, he became a devotee of "method" acting, making his Broadway debut in the sentimental memoir *I Remember Mama*. He earned Elia Kazan's attention in the failed *Truckline Café*, which also featured Karl Malden.

Kazan had just mounted Arthur Miller's *All My Sons*, and would win a directing Oscar for *Gentlemen's Agreement* (1947). Playwright Tennessee Williams had enjoyed critical and financial success with *The Glass Menagerie* in 1944, but this had followed years of struggle and would be followed in turn by several unsuccessful projects. By the time he finished *Streetcar* (which he pulled together from several one-act plays), his agent Audrey Wood had run out of producers willing to back it. Wood sent the play to Irene Mayer Selznick, the daughter of MGM chief Louis B. Mayer and the ex-wife of producer David O. Selznick. To the surprise of everyone involved, she agreed to finance the play, and chose Kazan as the director.

John Garfield was considered for the role of Stanley, but his contract demands were too steep. Williams became enthusiastic about Brando after Kazan sent the actor to meet him on Cape Cod. Writer, actor, and director Hume Cronyn staged the one-act version in Los Angeles as a sort of audition for his wife, Jessica Tandy, who won the Broadway role of Blanche DuBois. Selznick chose Kim Hunter as the innocent sister of the psychologically damaged heroine. Kazan cast his friend Malden as Mitch Mitchell, Blanche's putative suitor. From rehearsals on, Brando dominated the production, egged on in part by Williams, who, according to Kazan, had a crush on the actor.

After it opened on December 3, 1947, critics singled out Tandy for praise, mentioned Brando in passing, and gave mixed, unenthusiastic reviews for the play itself. But *Streetcar* was a solid hit with audiences, running for two years on Broadway and then opening in road productions.

Producer Charles K. Feldman bought the movie rights to the play, getting Warner Brothers to back him only if he found a bigger star than Tandy. Vivien Leigh was familiar with the role of Blanche, having just played her for six months in a London production directed by her then-husband Laurence Olivier. In later interviews, Karl Malden described the slight changes to the role that Leigh insisted on, but noted how easily the cast adapted to her. (He claimed to prefer Tandy's Blanche, and said that Brando liked Leigh better.)

Kazan agreed to direct the film on Williams' behalf, bringing along most of the creative team behind the stage production. He thought about opening up the play, setting scenes at Belle Reve, the ancestral mansion in Auriol, Mississippi, that Blanche claims was lost to creditors in the first act. Williams and Oscar Saul, hired to help with the screenwriting, objected strenuously. Kazan altered the play in more profound ways instead. He had always felt that the plot was thrown out of balance by Brando's dominating performance on the stage, and sought to shift the emphasis to Leigh.

He could do this by refining scenes with the camera, essentially restaging the story. Kazan could keep the camera on Leigh's face as Brando delivered a line, for example, or move the camera closer to or farther away from the actors. He could insert reaction shots, pulling viewers from one actor to another. Cinematographer Harry Stradling painted almost every scene with thick shadows, adding another way for Kazan to offer his own interpretation of the material. The film version had several new scenes, and switched locations of others.

Kazan wrote that what excited him about directing was the chance to explore "dangerous" and "unusual" situations and emotions, which generally translated to sex and violence. Billy Wilder's *Sunset Boulevard* (1950) gave filmmakers new license to take advantage of actresses. Like that movie, much of *Streetcar* looks like a horror film today, with Kazan exploiting Leigh's deteriorating looks and mental health for shock value. (She would make only two more films before her death.) In his notes, Kazan wrote that he saw Blanche as incompetent, a streetwalker.

Leigh brought more than that to her acting. Watch her disdain as Mitch makes love to her, her realization of how easy he is to toy with. She is equally good in her encounter with a young newspaper boy, using her hands and arms as well as her whispery voice to lure him to her side.

But what struck the film world was Brando's performance. His Stanley reshaped film acting, not always for the better. Many mistook his sexual swagger and slurred line readings as keys to his success. But it was the actor's ability to invest Stanley with humor, remorse, even tenderness, that rescued the character (albeit at the expense of some psychological credibility). He later claimed to loathe the part, but he would never fully escape its shadow.

Before filming started, the office overseeing the enforcement of the Production Code, run at this time by Joseph Breen, objected to Blanche's marriage to a homosexual and her ostensible nymphomania; Stanley raping Blanche without being punished for it; and Stella remaining with Stanley despite his assault on her sister. The filmmakers gave in on the last point, and changed the cause of Blanche's husband's suicide from homosexuality to "poetry." The rape remained, although censors insisted on further cuts amounting to about four minutes of screen time. The trimmed footage was discovered intact in the early 1990s and restored to prints in 1993.

Shooting took place on two stages at the Warners studio, one for the interior of the Kowalski apartment, one for the courtyard exterior. This enabled Kazan to not only rehearse with the cast throughout the production, but to shoot the script in chronological order. Filming ended in the fall of 1950, slightly behind schedule. *Streetcar*'s release was held up by censorship problems until Kazan and Brando finished their next project, *Viva Zapata!* When it finally opened, in September 1951, *Streetcar* received cautiously positive reviews. But it was a sensation at the box office, earning over $4 million and eight Oscar nominations. Brando, who was never again so free of artifice in his screen acting, was overlooked at the Academy Awards, while Leigh, Malden, and Hunter all won. "Winning did nothing for my film career," Hunter said later, "because I was blacklisted." Three weeks after the Oscar ceremony, Kazan testified as a friendly witness before the House Un-American Activities Committee.

An American in Paris

MGM, 1951. Sound, color, 1.37. 113 minutes.
Cast: Gene Kelly (Jerry Mulligan), Leslie Caron (Lise Bourvier), Oscar Levant (Adam Roberts), Georges Guetary (Henri Baurel), Nina Foch (Milo Roberts), Eugene Borden (Georges Mattieu), Martha Bamattre (Mathilde Mattieu), Mary Young (Old woman dancer), Ann Codee (Thérèse), George Davis (François), Hayden Rorke (Tommy Baldwin), Paul Maxey (John McDowd), Dick Wessel (Ben Macrow).
Credits: Directed by Vincente Minnelli. Screenplay: Alan Jay Lerner, based on his story. Produced by Arthur Freed. Director of photography: Alfred Gilks. Ballet photography: John Alton. Art direction: Cedric Gibbons, Preston Ames. Set decoration: Edwin B. Willis. Associate set decorator: Keogh Gleason. Music: George Gershwin. Lyrics: Ira Gershwin. Musical direction: Johnny Green, Saul Chaplin. Orchestrations: Conrad Salinger. Choreography: Gene Kelly. Assistant choreographer: Carol Haney. Edited by Adrienne Fazan. Montage sequences: Peter Ballbusch. Special effects: Warren Newcombe, Irving G. Ries. Costume design: Orry-Kelly. Beaux Arts Ball costumes: Walter Plunkett. Ballet costumes: Irene Sharaff. Technicolor direction: Henri Jaffa, James Gooch. Recording direction: Douglas Shearer. Makeup: William Tuttle. Hair stylist: Sydney Guilaroff. Gene Kelly's paintings by Gene Grant. Technicolor. Western Electric Sound System.
Additional Credits: Production dates: August 1950 to January 1951. Premiered in New York City on October 4, 1951.
Awards: Oscars for Best Picture, Writing—Story and Screenplay, Cinematography—Color, Art Direction–Set Decoration—Color, Costume Design—Color, Music—Scoring of a Musical Picture.
Available: Warner Home Video DVD (1999). ISBN: 0-7907-4441-1. UPC: 0-12569-50692-3.

Arthur Freed, MGM's most reliable producer of musicals, was following a Hollywood trend when he developed *Words and Music* (1948), a biopic about the songwriting duo of Richard Rodgers and Lorenz Hart. But films about songwriters generally had boring plots, especially when their story lines had to be cleaned up. With *Easter Parade* that same year, Freed solved the problem by building new story lines around existing songs. He used Irving Berlin songs in *Easter Parade*, and his own, cowritten with Nacio Herb Brown, in *Singin' in the Rain* (1952). For *An American in Paris*, he nabbed what was at the time the most valued library of songs available: those written by George and Ira Gershwin.

Freed paid over $150,000 for the film rights to the songs, with an additional $60,000 to Ira Gershwin for his help on the project. He assigned the film to Vincente Minnelli, who was originally scheduled to direct *Easter Parade* until various accidents and crises threatened to derail the project. With Gene Kelly aboard in the lead, Freed hired Alan Jay Lerner for the script. Lerner had been writing for advertising and radio while working on Broadway musicals with Frederick Loewe. In 1947, the smash hit *Brigadoon* established their reputation.

The seventeen-minute ballet that ends the film was always a part of the project, as Freed had

been impressed with the British film *The Red Shoes*. The Paris setting was therefore a given, since the "American in Paris" suite was the only Gershwin piece left that was long enough to support a ballet. (Warner Brothers had already released a Gershwin biopic under the title *Rhapsody in Blue*.) What Lerner supplied was the idea of two romantic triangles that threatened to keep the leads apart from each other. The first consisted of Jerry Mulligan (Gene Kelly), a World War II veteran struggling to establish himself as a painter in Paris; Milo Roberts (Nina Foch), a wealthy heiress with a succession of kept men; and Lise Bourvier (Leslie Caron), a clerk in a parfumerie.

Lise is also being kept in a way, by music hall star Henri Baurel (Georges Guetary), who hopes, à la *Daddy Long Legs*, to marry her. Jerry befriends Henri through composer Adam Roberts (Oscar Levant); neither one realizes they are both after the same woman. Underneath the colorful surface gaiety of *An American in Paris* runs a deep strain of melancholy. Perhaps not so coincidentally, given the bulk of Minnelli's work, the lovers here find more solace in their work than in their relationships.

Freed had hoped to lure Maurice Chevalier back to American movies for the role of Henri, but feared possible political controversy. Instead, he hired Georges Guetary, an actor in minor French films who had been appearing on Broadway in *Arms and the Girl*. Freed thought of Cyd Charisse or Vera-Ellen for Lise, but Kelly remembered seeing Leslie Caron dancing in Paris with the Ballets des Champs Elysées. He flew there to film her screen test. Caron was seventeen when she arrived in the United States.

Lerner submitted a draft of the script in February 1950. Shooting started that August, although the script for the ballet wasn't finished until September. While workers prepared the ballet sets, Minnelli directed *Father's Little Dividend*, a sequel to the successful comedy *Father of the Bride*.

Some MGM executives wanted to release *An American in Paris* without the closing ballet, but according to Lerner, Louis B. Mayer fought for the extra $500,000 needed to complete the film. He would soon be ousted from the studio. The ballet was a fairly daring idea, although not unprecedented. (George Balanchine had ended *On* the Town with the "Slaughter on Tenth Avenue" ballet.) It would become a crucial part of the Freed formula, showing up in *Singin' in the Rain* and *The Band Wagon* (1953).

The ballet consisted of eight sections loosely tied together by Kelly's pursuit of Caron. It should more properly be referred to as a dance suite, as few actual ballet steps are used, and the plot is almost nonexistent. The sets and dances were inspired in part by the art of Dufy, Rousseau, Rodin, and Toulouse-Lautrec, but also by George M. Cohan and *On the Town*. It's a weird hybrid that often teeters on the edge of vulgarity.

The screen is swathed in bold colors: red, blue, the "Minnelli yellow" that had to be specially mixed for his sets. The characters are elegant, brittle, always a step away from despair. Minnelli's camera swoops and swirls, even for an inconsequential moment when Henri enters a café. But finding a consistent artistic vision in the film can be difficult. For example, Kelly—not Minnelli—directed the scene in which Caron's character is introduced via a series of vignettes. Minnelli used a different cinematographer, John Alton, for the ballet. Hal Rosson reshot the "I Got Rhythm" number after a sneak preview in the spring of 1951. At least three numbers were cut from the film: Kelly singing "I've Got a Crush on You," and Guetary doing "Love Walked In" and "But Not for Me." Perhaps Freed deserves the most credit for the ultimate shape of the film.

He could deserve the blame, too. As critic Stephen Harvey pointed out, the film is marred by inexplicable choices. Bad Gershwin songs like "By Strauss" receive even worse staging. Kelly spends more time dancing with men than with Caron. In his mind, this was his ideal screen persona—as Harvey wrote, "the lovable, regular guy who just happens to be a genius." The Paris in the film seems more suited to the 1920s, to *7th Heaven* and the Lost Generation of American expatriates, than to the 1950s. The film looks glossy enough to be medicinal—as if MGM were delivering art to the masses in sugarcoated, bite-size drops.

The masses of the time lapped it up. *An American in Paris* grossed over $8 million and earned eight Oscar nominations, winning six of them, including Best Picture. But in recent years its reputation has declined compared to the ebullient *Singin' in the Rain* and the rueful *The Band Wagon*. Here once again is an opportunity to cite the steady influence of Buster Keaton on MGM performers. (A persistent rumor is that the studio used Keaton's *The Cameraman* as a sort of textbook for comedy, screening it for all of its performers and filmmakers.) In his opening scene, Kelly moves through his cramped quarters like Keaton and Arbuckle did in their short films, using Rube Goldberg-devices to make more room, while in a dream sequence Oscar Levant plays all the musicians in an orchestra—and the entire audience, as well—just as Keaton did in *The Playhouse*.

Duck and Cover

Federal Civil Defense Administration, 1951. Sound, B&W, 1.37. 9 minutes.
Cast: Vincent Bohan, Leo "Hitch" Langlois III, Ray W. Mauer.
Credits: Directed by Anthony Rizzo. Screenplay by Ray J. Mauer. Executive Producer: Leo M. Langlois. Director of photography: Drummond Drury. Art director: Lars E. Calonius. Music arrangement: Dave Lambert. Produced by Archer Productions, Inc., for the Federal Civil Defense Administration in consultation with the Safety Commission of the National Education Administration.
Additional Credits: Song "Duck and Cover" by Leo Carr, Leon Corday, Leo Langlois. Narration spoken by Robert Middleton. Voice of Bert the Turtle: Carl Ritchie. Copyrighted 1951.
Available: The National Archives. Online: Internet Archive (*www.archive.org*). Bear Family CD box set *Atomic Platters: Cold War Music from the Golden Age of Homeland Security* (2005). ISBN: 3-89916-141-6.

One of the most famous government films ever made, *Duck and Cover* was screened for millions of schoolchildren as training for how to respond in the event of a nuclear attack. It was one of nine Federal Civil Defense movies made in 1951, when

fear of nuclear war fueled anxieties over the Iron Curtain. After the Soviets detonated an atom bomb in 1949, the U.S. government formed the Federal Civil Defense Administration (FCDA), precursor to today's Department of Homeland Security, to help calm a worried populace.

Howard R.H. Johnson, chief of motion pictures for the FCDA, and Dallas Halverstadt, Special Assistant to the Assistant of the President, brokered a deal with educational film companies to make the nine civil defense films at no cost to the government. Profits would be earned by selling prints of the films to schools and libraries. The distributor, usually James M. Franey's Castle Films, would retain the bulk of this money, while the producer would earn a royalty on each print

How to animate a nuclear explosion, from *Duck and Cover*.

sold. Franey brought information about the film projects to Archer Productions, at the time the premier broadcast ad agency in New York.

Archer had been formed by advertising veteran Leo Langlois in part to promote the work of his brother-in-law Lars Calonius, a former Disney animator who moved to New York to cash in on television commercials. Langlois met with government officials in Washington, and returned to New York with vague outlines for a film about "what to do when you see the big flash," one that would "eliminate any panic possibilities." A second film would cover the aftermath of a nuclear attack; this was released as *Our Cities Must Fight*.

In May 1951, Langlois and copy writer Ray J. Mauer met with officials of the National Education Administration to hash out details of the scripts. The premise for *Duck and Cover* came from Helen Seth-Smith, an assistant headmistress of The Potomac School in Virginia. When she told the meeting about her school's "duck and cover" drills, the phrase resonated with Mauer, Langlois, and ultimately Howard R.H. Johnson. While Mauer worked on scripts for *Duck and Cover* and *Our Cities Must Fight*, Langlois hired Anthony Rizzo, a television director from Chicago, to helm the two films.

Mauer's first script introduced Bert the Turtle, the perfect animal metaphor for the film's theme. By the second draft, Calonius was contributing sketches that would be animated and interspersed with live action. P.S. 152 in Astoria, Queens, was used for the classroom scenes. Despite the best efforts of historians Ken Sitz, Bill Geerhart, and Curtis Samson, who have written extensively about the film, the only person positively identified from this material is teacher Vincent Bohan. (Langlois' son Hitch and Mauer have cameos later in the story.) The live-action shooting took two weeks.

The theme song for *Duck and Cover* was written by Leo Carr and Leon Corday, along with Langlois, who were also responsible for the famous jingle "See the U.S.A. in Your Chevrolet." Musical arranger Dave Lambert later was a member of the jazz trio Lambert, Hendricks & Ross. In addition to the film, Bert appeared in a fourteen-minute radio show that was distributed across the country; on a commercial recording by Dick "Two Ton" Baker, released on Coral Records; in a color pamphlet (three million copies were handed out at schools); and in a newspaper comic strip.

The film was part of the FCDA's Alert America Convoy, which toured the country starting in January 1952. Later that month it was screened for educators in New York City. *Duck and Cover* was broadcast on television as early as February 23, 1952; the first classroom screening was in New York city on March 6. The film became a public service announcement fixture for the rest of the decade.

But Archer Productions was doomed when Langlois failed to secure financing for *American Almanac*, a planned television series. Archer was forced to sell rights to the two FCDA films back to the government for $13,000 (a loss of $12,000). Rizzo and Mauer found other jobs in advertising, while Langlois became an assistant director on television shows in California.

The unstated goal of *Duck and Cover* was to both instill and defuse fear. "Always remember, the flash of an atomic bomb can come at any time, no matter where you may be," narrator Robert Middleton warns. A sense of free-floating dread permeated 1950s culture in America, erupting in unlikely places: country songs, pulp novels, movies like *My Son John* (1952). It was up to the government to channel this angst before it turned to hysteria. Although no one with nuclear experience believed Middleton's statement, "Even a thin cloth can protect you," some form of concrete advice had to be presented to the public. "We must obey the civil defense worker" was really the only solution this film, or the FCDA in general, could offer.

The government continued to instruct the public about nuclear dangers throughout the 1950s. *The House in the Middle* (1954) is also on the Registry.

The African Queen

United Artists, 1951. Sound, color, 1.37. 105 minutes.

Cast: Humphrey Bogart (Charlie Allnutt), Katharine Hepburn (Rose Sayer), Robert Morley (The Brother [Rev. Samuel Sayer]), Peter Bull (German captain), Theodore Bikel (German first officer), Walter Gotell (German second officer), Peter Swanwick (German officer at Shona), Richard Marner (German officer at Shona).

Credits: Directed by John Huston. Based on the novel *The African Queen* by C.S. Forester. Adapted for the screen by James Agee & John Huston. Produced by S.P. Eagle [Sam Spiegel]. Director of photography: Jack Cardiff. Art director: Wilfred Shingleton. Second unit photography by Ted Scaife. Music composed by Allan Gray. Played by The Royal Philharmonic Orchestra conducted by Norman Del Mar. Editor: Ralph Kemplen. Production managers: Leigh Aman, T.S. Lyndon-Haynes. Assistant director: Guy Hamilton. Assistant art director: John Hoesli. Camera operator: Ted Moore. Make-up: George Frost. Hairdresser: Eileen Bates. Miss Hepburn's costumes designed by Doris Langley Moore. Other clothes by Connie De Pinna. Wardrobe mistress: Vi Murray. Continuity: Angela Allen. Special effects: Cliff Richardson. Sound recordist: John Mitchell. Sound editor: Eric Wood. Western Electric Recording. Color by Technicolor. A Romulus–Horizon production. Distribution controlled by Independent Film Distributors, Ltd.

Additional Credits: Screenwriting by Peter Viertel. Production dates: May to August, 1951. Released in Los Angeles on December 23, 1951.

Awards: Oscar for Best Actor.

Available: Twentieth Century Fox VHS (1997).

After directing *The Treasure of the Sierra Madre* in 1948, John Huston made one more film for Warner Brothers before deciding with his producer Sam Spiegel to test the independent market. He directed *We Were Strangers* at Columbia, then two films at MGM, including *The Red Badge of Courage* (1951). During the editing process for *Red Badge,* Huston worked in Santa Barbara on his next project with film critic and screenwriter James Agee.

Born in Cairo in 1899 but raised in London, C.S. Forester was an indifferent poet and an author who eked out a living writing biographies until he hit the jackpot with *Payment Deferred*, a hit on stage and screen for Charles Laughton. Forester's *The African Queen* was published in Great Britain in 1932 and in the United States in 1935, with a different ending. At one point it was purchased by Columbia as a vehicle for Laughton and his wife Elsa Lanchester, then by Warners. More daunting than the novel's plot—which involved a suicidal downriver journey by the reprobate captain of a thirty-foot steamer and an orphaned missionary—was its location in the Congo. Huston found the prospect of shooting on location in Africa immensely appealing, and convinced Spiegel to borrow the $50,000 needed to get the rights from Warners.

Spiegel ultimately secured financing for the film from Romulus, a British production company run by the brothers John and James Woolf. By all accounts, casting was a snap. This was the fifth film Humphrey Bogart made with Huston, and although the actor was dubious about location work, he was eager to work with the director again. Charlie Allnutt was his first entirely sympathetic role since early in his career, one that allowed him to play drunk and slovenly yet still heroic.

Katharine Hepburn, who was cast as the spinster Rose Sayer, saw the production as a sort of respite from her relationship with Spencer Tracy. She became alarmed at the state of the screenplay, and at Huston's apparent indifference to discussing the project, but in later years she credited the director with giving her the best acting advice she ever received. Hepburn had been portraying Rose the way Forester had written her: "She would not allow herself to show weakness. She shut her mouth like a trap into its usual hard line." "Have you ever seen Mrs. [Eleanor] Roosevelt visit the soldiers in the hospitals?" Huston asked her after shooting started. She "felt she was ugly," he explained, and "always put on her society smile." Hepburn suddenly saw a better way to play Rose. "I was his from there on in," she wrote later.

The script was in trouble because Agee had suffered a heart attack in California before he and Huston had decided on an ending. Huston brought screenwriter, novelist, and playwright Peter Viertel with him to Africa. Viertel was the son of Salka Viertel, a screenwriter herself and a famous confidante of Greta Garbo. Huston had known Peter as a child, and had worked with him on *We Were Strangers* (1948). Like Hepburn, Viertel found Huston's drinking and attempts at big-game hunting juvenile. His novel *White Hunter, Black Heart* is a thinly disguised account of his experiences in Africa. (The novel was filmed by Clint Eastwood in 1990.)

Viertel and Huston worked out two possible endings, both of which differed from the novel's. A bigger change was a ten-minute scene that opened the movie. The novel starts after the Germans have destroyed a missionary camp, but Huston and Agee take the time to show how the camp operated first, in the process mocking the missionaries' religious fervor and coarsening Forester's characters. In the film, the natives don't know the words to the hymns they are singing and abandon Samuel's service at the first distraction. Allnutt, brisk and efficient in the novel, is introduced in the movie as a sort of stumbling buffoon. Forester kills off Samuel in the opening pages, while Agee and Huston give actor Robert Morley considerable space to skewer the missionary's pretensions. Some changes were definite improvements. Rose—in Forester's hands, driven and relatively humorless—blossoms into a warm, appealing heroine in the film.

In general, however, Huston followed his instincts, which, as in his earlier adaptations of novels, meant trusting the material. Forester's book works in part because of its matter-of-fact tone, and in the film Huston used a similar emotional distance that allowed the majestic scenery and wildlife to overpower Bogart and Hepburn. Like the book, the film dwells on details: how to fire up a steam engine, where to find fuel, how to replace a drive shaft. These are matters that interested Huston throughout his career. (In *Picture*, Lillian Ross included a fascinating portrait of Agee expounding on the symbolic nature of the relationship between Allnutt and Rose: "'Tell me something I can understand,' Huston replied. 'People on the screen are gods and goddesses. They're not real, they're symbols. You can't have symbolism within symbolism, Jim.'")

The simple, unambiguous nature of the story and characters connected directly with moviegoers. The part of Allnutt won Bogart his only Oscar, while Rose Sayer helped shape Hepburn's subsequent film choices; she would play similar spinsters to great effect in *Summertime* (1955) and *The Rainmaker* (1956). Huston himself returned to a two-character story with *Heaven Knows, Mr. Allison* (1957). He and Bogart teamed up for one more film, *Beat the Devil* (1953), a disastrous injoke parody that severed their relationship.

The production of *The African Queen* has been described in entertaining detail by several of the participants, including Huston, Hepburn, and Lauren Bacall, who accompanied Bogart. Rampant illness, poor weather, recalcitrant wildlife, a boat that sank, drunken binges, Huston's frequent hunting expeditions, a chronic lack of funds, and Bogart's increasing disenchantment made it one of the more difficult productions of its day. (Bogart was still unhappy when the production shifted to London to shoot interiors and water tank footage, especially when Huston asked him to work with real leeches. By the way, all of Morley's scenes were shot in England.)

Forester was living in Berkeley, California, while Huston was shooting in Africa. The novelist would achieve his greatest acclaim in a series of eleven books featuring the naval officer Horatio Hornblower. Huston would embark on a self-imposed exile, living first in Ireland and then Mexico. His filmmaking declined during the 1960s, but his final works—including *Wise Blood* (1979) and *The Dead* (1987)—marked a triumphant return to form.

Magical Maestro

MGM, 1952. Sound, Technicolor, 1.37. 7 minutes.
Credits: Directed by Tex Avery. Produced by Fred Quimby. Animation: Grant Simmons, Michael Lah, Walter Clinton. Story: Rich Hogan. Musical direction: Scott Bradley. Western Electric Sound Recording.
Additional Credits: Vocal Talent: Daws Butler (Mysto the Magician), Carlos Ramirez (Poochini). Released February 9, 1952.
Available: MGM/UA Home Video VHS *Tex Avery's Screwball Classics* (1988). UPC: 0-2761-63852-3-9.

Fred "Tex" Avery was one of the most distinctive directors from the golden age of animation. According to historian Greg Ford, Avery was the one who gave Warner Brothers cartoons their frantic pacing. Leonard Maltin credits Avery with "some of the greatest cartoons ever made." And animators Joe Adamson and John Canemaker both devoted books to Avery's creations.

A distant relative of Judge Roy Bean, Avery was born in Texas in 1908. After studying at the

Chicago Art Institute, he traveled to California in 1929, where he joined the Walter Lantz studio, first as an inker and painter, then as an in-betweener. Avery worked on Oswald the Rabbit cartoons, including titles like *Ham and Eggs* (1933). Given the opportunity to experiment, he extended standard gags by adding variations and toppers to them. By the time he left Lantz, he been promoted to director.

Leon Schlesinger at Warners hired Avery in 1935, naming him the head of an animation unit that included Robert Clampett and Chuck Jones. Avery's first film, *Gold Diggers of '49*, released in January 1936, made use of a character that had appeared in *I Haven't Got a Hat* (1935), Porky Pig. Avery also directed the cartoon that introduced Daffy Duck (*Porky's Duck Hunt*, 1937) and the first cartoon that indicated what the Bugs Bunny character would become (*A Wild Hare*, 1940). One of Avery's best cartoons at Warners was the black-and-white *Porky's Preview* (1941), a dizzying parody of film in general, and animation in particular, with Porky screening his own drawings for an audience of barnyard animals. Its stick figures, scratched-out sketches, disruptive music, and distorted perspectives were especially harsh on the pretensions of the Disney studio.

Avery left Warners for MGM that same year, bringing with him a vision of animation as a collection of gags stacked frantically, even recklessly, on top of each other. His first MGM short, *The Blitz Wolf* (1942), retold the Three Little Pigs in World War II terms. He invented deliberately obnoxious characters like Screwy Squirrel and the bears George and Junior, and in 1943's *Dumb-Hounded* introduced the grating Droopy the Dog. But Avery wasn't as interested in developing characters as he was with sticking familiar figures into chaotic stories that unreeled too furiously for viewers to realize exactly what was happening. Avery told Joe Adamson that all it took for a "guaranteed laugh" was to put a character into an impossible situation—that is, one in which it would be killed. "Because they cannot do it live!" Avery exclaimed. He also told Adamson that the eye can register action in as little as five frames, or roughly a fifth of a second "from the screen to your eye to the brain." In Avery's world, an anvil would land on a character's head after four or five frames, without showing its full descent from the sky. It was a lesson that liberated other animators as well.

Many consider *King-Size Canary* (1947) and *Bad Luck Blackie* (1949)—two stories that take logical premises to hysterical extremes—as Avery's best work at MGM. *Magical Maestro*, initially a fairly sedate reworking of ideas that dated back to vaudeville, displays Avery's weaknesses as well as his strengths: a sometimes faulty story structure; a racial and cultural insensitivity that would allow uncomfortable digs at blacks, hillbillies, and South Seas natives; and a short attention span that left characters and subplots unresolved. Even at seven minutes, the piece feels like it's running out of ideas.

On the other hand, Avery sets up the story with a simplicity and grace that is astonishing, using a flash-forward to dispense with dialogue after the opening scene. *Magical Maestro* features three main characters, and they were all variations on stalwart figures in MGM cartoons: a version of Avery's own Droopy Dog, an evolution of the wolf who appeared in many of his adult fairy tales, and a bulldog who was often the third leg of MGM's slapstick triangles. You might consider them character actors, supporting players as opposed to top-billed stars like Tom and Jerry.

The bulk of the film is Avery's take on the "Largo al factotum" tune from Rossini's opera *The Barber of Seville*. The familiar refrain "Figaro, Figaro" was a favorite target of animators. It had been used in *You Ought to Be in Pictures* (1940), with Porky Pig and Daffy Duck; *Barber of Seville* (1944), with Woody Woodpecker; and *Long-Haired Hare* (1948) and *Rabbit of Seville* (1949), both with Bugs Bunny. For Avery it was an opportunity to play with the fundamentals of narrative.

Like Buster Keaton's projectionist in *Sherlock Jr.* and Daffy Duck in *Duck Amuck* (both Registry titles), Poochini, "the world's greatest baritone," finds himself trapped in a plot that has no logic. Through a magic wand, his enemy, Mysto the Magician, can dress Poochini as anything: a toddler, Carmen Miranda, a coolie, a square dance caller. Wearing a tutu, Poochini has to dance en pointe; in chaps and spurs he's forced to sing "Oh My Darling, Clementine." Part of *Magical Maestro*'s fun comes from the "show must go on" desperation that was a fixture of vaudeville comedy, but for the most part the humor depends on Avery's imagination. Animator Irven Spence said about Avery, "He would take your extremes and go over them a little bit. At the time you felt like you were animating something that was really exaggerated, but then Tex would take it and *double* it!"

In Avery's world, if one gag doesn't work, another will replace it within seconds. Avery's concept of modeling, what some refer to as the plasticity of his animation, continues to surprise and delight. His willingness to bend, squeeze, block, slice, chop, and otherwise distort his characters, the settings they are in, even the film we are watching sets his cartoons on an entirely different plane from his contemporaries.

According to Spence, Avery came up with the ideas for his cartoons, did the rough layouts for animators, altered their tests, and then continued editing when the drawing was finished. Michael Lah, one of three credited animators on *Magical Maestro*, talked about throwing drawings out after test reels were animated. "Some of that pacing was so fast that you didn't need any in-betweens or drawings to carry out the action."

Avery's professional pace was so wearying that he retired from the studio for a year in 1950. When he returned, he promoted Lah to codirector; Lah took his place when Avery left MGM for good in 1953. Avery went back to the Lantz studio, where he directed four more cartoons, two of them starring Chilly Willy. Avery quit Lantz in a salary dispute in 1955, and never worked on another theatrical cartoon. He died in 1980.

Singin' in the Rain

Gene Kelly's hoofer runs into the irresistible force that is Cyd Charisse in *Singin' in the Rain*.

MGM, 1951. Color, sound, 1.33. 103 minutes

Cast: Gene Kelly (Don Lockwood), Donald O'Connor (Cosmo Brown), Debbie Reynolds (Kathy Selden), Jean Hagen (Lina Lamont), Millard Mitchell (R.F. Simpson), Douglas Fowley (Roscoe Dexter), Cyd Charisse (Dream Ballet dancer), Rita Moreno (Zelda Zanders).

Credits: Directed by Gene Kelly, Stanley Donen. Script: Betty Comden, Adolph Green. Suggested by the song "Singin' in the Rain." Produced by Arthur Freed. Associate producer: Roger Edens. Director of photography: Harold Rosson. Special effects: Warren Newcombe, Irving G. Ries. Edited: Adrienne Fazan. Art directors: Cedric Gibbons, Randall Duell. Set decorators: Edwin B. Willis, Jacque [Jacques] Mapes. Costumes: Walter Plunkett. Choreographers: Gene Kelly, Stanley Donen. Musical director: Lennie Hayton. Orchestrations: Conrad Salinger, Wally Heglin, Skip Martin. Vocal arrangements: Jeff Alexander. Costumes designed by Walter Plunkett. Hair styles designed by Sydney Guilaroff. Make-up created by William Tuttle. Sound recordist: Douglas Shearer. Technicolor. Western Electric Sound System.

Additional Cast: Madge Blake (Dora Bailey), King Donovan (Rod), Kathleen Freeman (Phoebe Dinsmore), Jimmie Thompson ("Beautiful Girl" singer); Patricia Denise, Jeanne Coyne (Girl dancers); Bill Chatham, Ernest Flatt, Don Hulbert, Robert Dayo (Male dancing quartet); David Kasday (Kid), Bobby Watson (Diction coach), Julius Tannen (Sound process demonstrator), Brick Sullivan (Policeman, "Singin' in the Rain" number), Snub Pollard (Pedestrian, "Singin' in the Rain" number), Judy Landon (Olga Mara).

Additional Credits: Songs by Nacio Herb Brown, Arthur Freed; Al Hoffman, Al Goodhart; Roger Edens, Adolph Green, Betty Comden. Jean Hagen dubbed Debbie Reynolds' lines when she was pretending to dub Lina Lamont's dialogue. Betty Noyes dubbed Debbie Reynolds' singing voice when she was pretending to dub Lina Lamont's singing. Released March 27, 1952.

Available: Warner Home Video DVD (2000). ISBN: 0-7907-4422-8. UPC: 0-12569-50202-4.

Producer Arthur Freed was considering a *Singin' in the Rain* project as early as March of 1949, as a vehicle for tap dancer Ann Miller. He sold his song library to MGM the following year, then tried to get contract screenwriters Adolph Green and Betty Comden to build a script around it. Most of the tunes had been written with Nacio Herb Brown in the late 1920s and early '30s, and some had become quite famous: "You Were Meant for Me," "All I Do Is Dream of You," "You Are My Lucky Star." Freed and Brown did the score for *The Broadway Melody* (1929), the first all-talking musical and the first to win an Oscar for Best Picture.

Comden and Green weren't interested in Freed's project until they set the story in the same period that the songs became hits. The transition from silent films to talkies gave them their plot. Hollywood lore was filled with stories about the casualties of sound; just as many newcomers got their start because of the new technology. As the screenplay took shape, it became an affectionate satire, filled with stories, some apocryphal, some experienced by Freed and Brown themselves. Their characters were brittle, self-deluding show-biz types who pretended to be impervious to rejection and humiliation while embracing the hedonism and adulation that came with stardom. The script mocked everyone from Clara Bow to Richard Barthelmess, whose *Weary River* (1929) was an early example of a star's singing voice being dubbed. Part of the fun is guessing which real-life figures the characters represented. R.F. Simpson (played by Millard Mitchell) is close to Freed himself, while Roscoe Dexter (Douglas Fowley) is usually seen as a Busby Berkeley stand-in.

Director Stanley Donen was attached to the project at an early stage. Comden and Green feared that Howard Keel might be cast as the lead, but were delighted when Gene Kelly came aboard. Donen may not have been as happy, as he would now have to share directing and choreography credits with Kelly. The director waited until after Kelly's death to describe their working relationship, offering two definitions of "codirecting": "The first is 'With great difficulty.' And the second, which I used to joke about, is 'If you substitute the word "fight" for "codirect," then you have it,'" he said.

Born in Pittsburgh in 1912, Kelly worked in dance schools before attending college. Then he worked odd jobs until he got into a Broadway chorus in 1938. Two years later he was starring in *Pal Joey* and choreographing other Broadway shows. He debuted in film opposite Judy Garland in *For Me and My Gal* (1942). After serving in the Navy during World War II, he worked in a series of increasingly adventurous musicals like *On the Town* (1949). He also acted in several dramatic films, developing a screen persona inspired by Douglas Fairbanks, Sr.

Donen screened *Bombshell* (1933), a perceptive Jean Harlow comedy about filmmaking, for the cast. By now it included Jean Hagen, an MGM contract player who had recently toured in the play *Born Yesterday* and who had impressed Louis B. Mayer's wife Lorena in the studio's *Adam's Rib*. Oscar Levant had been considered for Kelly's sidekick, and an early draft of the script had a segment built around him. Donald O'Connor, on loan from Universal for $50,000, got the part instead. Born in 1925, O'Connor was the son of a circus strongman and an acrobat, and toured vaudeville with his mother after his father died. He made his first film in 1937 with two of his brothers, and continued on a solo film career through the 1940s (he also served in World War II). He soldiered through titles like *Feudin', Fussin', and A-Fightin'* (1948) and six of the seven "Francis the Talking Mule" entries, and was an early performer on television. O'Connor's background allowed Donen and Kelly to use a more knockabout style of dance.

While the sets were built in April 1951, costume designer Walter Plunkett worked on the five hundred or so costumes the film required. He admits that he parodied some of his work for silent star Lilyan Tashman. Art director Randall Duell and set decorator Jacques Mapes unearthed many of the film's props from MGM's vast holdings. Don Lockwood's home is furnished with items from *Flesh and the Devil* (1927), for example.

Shooting started on June 18, 1951. After a week, the directors replaced cinematographer John Alton with Harold Rosson. Reynolds fainted after shooting "Good Morning," and O'Connor needed two days off after "Make 'Em Laugh." (The only new Brown and Freed number in the film, it so closely resembled Cole Porter's "Be a Clown" from 1948's *The Pirate* that it became a source of embarrassment for the producer.) It took one and a half days to shoot the "Singin' in the Rain" number, but many more to choreograph and rehearse. Snub Pollard, a silent-screen veteran who had once teamed with Harold Lloyd, has a bit part in the sequence. Kelly said later that handling the umbrella was one of the hardest parts of the number. He never acknowledged how close in style and content the scene is to one in Buster Keaton's *The Cameraman* (1929), often cited as a training film for MGM comics.

The "Broadway Rhythm" ballet toward the end of the film was originally budgeted at $80,000. By the time Kelly and Donen had finished, the cost had risen to over $600,000, almost exactly the amount the film went over its entire budget. The loosely plotted ballet strings together speakeasies, gangsters, and chorus lines, but is notable primarily as a showcase for dancer Cyd Charisse. Whether consciously or not, in one routine the dancer slows down many of the steps Reynolds danced earlier in "All I Do Is Dream of You." Charisse shows how charged, how voluptuous, those moves could be.

Filming ended on August 28. The first cut was ready a week later, and music and sound were added in October. Some numbers were cut, including Kelly singing "All I Do Is Dream of You" and Reynolds' "You Are My Lucky Star." A number planned for Rita Moreno was also discarded; her part was whittled down to a single line near the end of the film. Minor corrections were made after a preview in December. The film opened at New York City's Radio City Music Hall on March 27, 1952.

Reviews were extremely positive, although *Variety* noted that the "ballet bit" could be eliminated. But while the film was financially successful, it didn't attain its "classic" status for many years. By the 1960s the film was a regular feature in all-time top ten lists. It became such an icon that Stanley Kubrick aped it in *A Clockwork Orange* (1971). The dour Donen claimed not to like the film, saying that it was too long, and that only Jean Hagen's character was fully fleshed out.

As Donen knew, *Singin' in the Rain* is not the best musical ever filmed, but it is one of the easiest to like. Comden and Green found how rewarding it was to mock the efforts of an earlier generation, even as they duplicated those efforts on screen. "We really hadn't advanced that far ourselves," Donen noted. "We were still using discs for the musical playback. We hadn't even gone to tape yet."

Comden and Green didn't mind mocking the present, either. The script, and Donen's direction, capture Kelly's egotism, his blinding grin and frightening self-absorption. "I'm such a ham," he says at one point, and no one bothers to dispute him. But what has always won viewers over to *Singin' in the Rain* is the film's easy exuberance, its sense that nothing could be more fun than making movies, a sense captured best by the Donen's sweeping crane shot as Kelly strides, arms outstretched, into the middle of a rain-drenched street.

High Noon

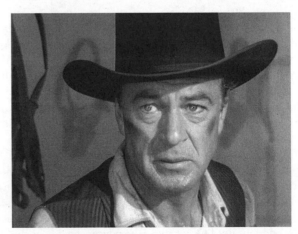

Gary Cooper in his Oscar-winning performance as Sheriff Will Kane in *High Noon*.

United Artists, 1952. Sound, B&W, 1.33. 85 minutes.

Cast: Gary Cooper (Will Kane), Thomas Mitchell (Jonas Henderson), Lloyd Bridges (Harvey Pell), Katy Jurado (Helen Ramirez), Grace Kelly (Amy Fowler Kane), Otto Kruger (Judge Percy Mettrick), Lon Chaney [Jr.] (Martin Howe), Henry Morgan (Sam Fuller), Ian MacDonald (Frank Miller), Eve McVeagh (Mildred Fuller), Morgan Farley (Minister), Harry Shannon (Cooper), Lee Van Cleef (Jack Colby), Robert Wilke (James Pierce), Sheb Wooley (Ben Miller).

Credits: Directed by Fred Zinnemann. Screenplay by Carl Foreman. Based on the Magazine Story "The Tin Star" by John W. Cunningham. Director of photography: Floyd Crosby. Editorial supervision: Harry Gerstad. Production supervisor: Clem Beauchamp. Production design by Rudolph Sternad. Music composed and directed by Dimitri Tiomkin. Ballad "High Noon" ["Do Not Forsake Me"] by Dimitri Tiomkin, lyrics by Ned Washington, sung by Tex Ritter. Unit manager: Percy Ikerd. Art director: Ben Hayne. Assistant director: Emmett Emerson. Men's wardrobe: Joe

King. Ladies' wardrobe: Ann Peck. Set decorations: Murray Waite. Sound engineer: Jean Speak. Film editor: Elmo Williams. Makeup by Gustaf Norin. Hair stylist: Louise Miehle. Head grip: Morris Rosen. Script clerk: Sam Freedle. Music editor: George Emick. Western Electric Recording. Magnetic recording by Sound Services, Inc.

Additional Cast: Tom London (Sam), Ted Stanhope (Station master), Larry Blake (Gillis), William Phillips (Barber), Jeanne Blackford (Mrs. Henderson), James Millican (Baker), Cliff Clark (Weaver), Ralph Reed (Johnny), William Newell (Jimmy), Lucien Prival (Bartender), Guy Beach (Fred), Howland Chamberlin (Hotel clerk), Virginia Christine (Mrs. Simpson), Virginia Farmer (Mrs. Fletcher), Jack Elam (Charlie), Paul Dubov (Scott), Harry Harvey (Coy), Tim Graham (Sawyer), Nolan Leary (Lewis), Tom Greenway (Ezra), Dick Elliott (Kibbee), John Doucette (Trumbull).

Additional Credits: Associate producer: Carl Foreman. "The Tin Star" appeared in *Collier's*, December 6, 1947. Filmed September 5 to October 13, 1951. Opened in New York City on July 24, 1952.

Awards: Oscars for Best Actor, Editing, Scoring of a Dramatic or Comedy Picture, Song.

Other versions: *High Noon, Part II: The Return of Will Kane* (CBS television movie, 1980, directed by Jerry Jameson); *High Noon* (TBS television movie, 2000, directed by Ron Hardy).

Available: Artisan Home Entertainment DVD (2002). UPC: 0-17153-12571-9.

The mournful theme to *High Noon* wafts insistently through the picture, the most respected of the socially conscious Westerns that began to appear after World War II. As sung by Tex Ritter, a political science student and cowboy star of the 1930s, "Do Not Forsake Me" encapsulates the strengths and weaknesses of *High Noon*. Both song and film are piously simple and restrained, both fulfill superbly the demands of their genres, and both deliver blunt, artificial "messages."

Screenwriter Carl Foreman said he came up with the idea of a lone sheriff battling four villains in 1947 (although the concept is one of the hallmarks of Westerns). Foreman's background as a publicist and carnival promoter, and later as a screenwriter for Bowery Boys comedies, gave little indication of his true ambitions. After the war, he joined producer Stanley Kramer in a series of increasingly pointed social dramas under the aegis of Screen Plays, Inc. The war was a turning point for Kramer, a New York City native who had completed little of merit in the film industry previously. But titles like *Home of the Brave* and *The Men*, the latter directed by Fred Zinnemann, earned publicity and positive reviews by tackling "hot-button" topics like racism and veterans.

Zinnemann, born in Vienna in 1907, signed a three-picture deal with Kramer that would include *The Member of the Wedding* (1952) as well as *High Noon*. (He would helm *From Here to Eternity*, also on the Registry and filmed in part on the same backlot.) In his career he worked with everyone from Robert Siodmak and Billy Wilder in Berlin to Robert Flaherty and Busby Berkeley in Hollywood. He codirected *The Wave*, a documentary filmed in Mexico, before embarking on "Pete Smith Specialties" and "Crime Does Not Pay" shorts for MGM. Shooting on confined sets, with small budgets, helped him when it came time to preplan what he called "jigsaw puzzle pictures" like *High Noon*.

In his autobiography, Zinnemann noted approvingly that Kramer was among the first of the postwar producers to seek financing from outside the industry, in *High Noon*'s case from a lettuce grower in Salinas, California. In a later interview, Foreman's son Jonathan said that most of the money for the film came from Bruce Church, a Republican businessman and friend of Gary Cooper.

For legal protection, Kramer bought the rights to "The Tin Star," a short story with a premise similar to Foreman's script. He signed Grace Kelly after seeing her in an off-Broadway play. Katy Jurado had been a star for years in Mexican cinema; this was her first important Hollywood part. Lloyd Bridges had been in *Home of the Brave*; like many other people on the film, he was coming under increasing scrutiny for his political views. Zinnemann had a hand in casting as well, choosing Sheb Wooley as one of the three villains waiting for the noon train to deliver their leader. Wooley, who enjoyed a long career in country-and-western music, ironically beat out another country singer, Don Gibson. Zinnemann picked Lon Chaney, Jr., for his "flat voice." This was the feature debut for Lee Van Cleef, the first person seen in the film.

Zinnemann had a close relationship with cinematographer Floyd Crosby, who was also under political investigation. They agreed on a washed-out, "documentary" look for the film, based in part on photographs by Matthew Brady. Crosby tried some adventurous traveling shots and one impressive overhead shot on a crane Zinnemann borrowed from director George Stevens. But for the most part the pace of the production was so grueling that he had to grab whatever he could. With a budget of $750,000 and a twenty-eight-day shooting schedule, there was little margin for error.

The director later said that the film was driven by three themes: the looming threat to retiring sheriff Will Kane, symbolized by a static shot of empty railroad tracks; a victim searching for help, in constant movement but finding no one; and time, shown in a succession of clocks and timepieces that gradually grow larger in the frame. These were visual ideas that could be easily grasped by just about any filmgoer; when wed to Dimitri Tiomkin's "clip-clop" score, the film itself became a sort of metronome. (The music also helped hide how many corners the filmmakers were cutting.)

Kramer and Zinnemann ordered two extraneous subplots eliminated after a disastrous preview. For a while the film was used as a textbook example of "real time" editing, until film professors had to acknowledge that almost nothing in the movie occurs in real time. Instead, Elmo Williams, who won an Oscar for editing, manipulated scenes, stretching or condensing them according to the narrative demands of the plot. The final scene, thirteen minutes long and almost wordless, has been emulated too many times to count.

Cooper was cast as Sheriff Will Kane despite misgivings from studio executives. Cooper may have been awarded his second Oscar for this portrayal, but he was capable of far more nuanced acting—in *The Westerner* (1940), for example, where his character expertly navigated perilous political waters. In a sense, he extended the role some four years later in *Friendly Persuasion* (1956), where he has become a full-fledged Quaker and is not just married to one. His moral choices in that film were far more challenging, and satisfying.

At the time, Kramer insisted that *High Noon* had no political implications, even though Foreman exiled himself to England before the end of shooting. It's true that the parallels to the Communist witch-hunt are somewhat shaky. But few could fail to connect the film with the prevailing climate.

High Noon set a new standard for Westerns by stripping away almost all the requisites of the genre. Chases, Indian attacks, a siege on the jail—the movie dutifully rejects them all, replacing them with sermons, moralizing, and a sort of shorthand form of symbolism. So many filmmakers followed its formula that a backlash developed. Directors like Anthony Mann and Budd Boetticher set out to make "real" Westerns in which the theme was revealed through action, while Howard Hawks and John Wayne answered *High Noon*'s "moral cowardice" with *Rio Bravo* (1959). But the marketplace was still flooded with moody, black-and-white Westerns featuring tortured heroes and ersatz folk theme songs. The formula worked even better on television. The narrative engine of just about every episode of *Gunsmoke*, for a while the longest-running fiction series on television, can be traced back to *High Noon*.

This Is Cinerama

Cinerama Productions, 1952. Sound, color, 2.59. 120 minutes.
Featuring: Lowell Thomas (Host and narrator).
Credits: Produced by Merian C. Cooper, Robert L. Bendick. Executive producers: Lowell Thomas, Michael Todd, Louis B. Mayer. Production executive: Louis B. Mayer. Associate producer: Michael Todd. Musical director: Louis Forbes. Cameraman: Harry Squire. Assistant cameraman: Jack Priestley. Camera technician: Coleman Thomas Conroy, Jr. Grip: Marty Philbin. Sound: Richard J. Pietschmann, Jr. Sound assistant: Fred Bosch. Film editor: Bill Henry. Sound effects: Reeves Sound Studios. Cinerama research and development: Fred Waller, Hazard E. Reeves, Walter Hicks, Wentworth Fling, Karl Vogel, Dr. Ernest Hare, Fred Koppler, Michael Chitty, Ernest Franck, Norman Prisament, Otto Popelka, Emil Neroda, Richard Vorisek, Ed Schmidt, Richard J. Pietschmann, Jr., C. Robert Fine, Larry Davee, Lyman Wiggins, S.J. (Joe) Begun, Col. Richard Ranger. European sequences and roller coaster sequence supervisors: Michael Todd, Michael Todd, Jr. Prolog supervisor: Walter Thompson. "America the Beautiful" supervisor: Fred Rickey. Pilot: Paul Mantz. Additional sequence supervisors: Merian C. Cooper, Michael Todd. Music performed by Cinerama Philharmonic Orchestra, Salt Lake City Tabernacle Choir, Vienna Philharmonic, Vienna Boys Choir, Long Island Choral Society.
Additional Credits: Directed by Merian C. Cooper, Gunther von Fritsch, Michael Todd, Jr. Score includes music by Max Steiner, Alfred Newman, David Raksin, Morton Gould. The title *This Is Cinerama* doesn't appear on prints released to theaters, but the film was copyrighted under that name. Advertisements originally referred to the film as *Cinerama*. Premiered in New York City on September 30, 1952.
Available: *This Is Cinerama* receives periodic screenings at three Cinerama-equipped theaters: The National Media Museum in Bradford, England (*www.nationalmediamuseum.org.uk*); the Seattle Cinerama Theater in Seattle, Washington (*www.seattlecinerama.com/*); and the Cinerama Dome in Los Angeles (*www.arclightcinemas.com*). Excerpts from the film appear in the documentary *Cinerama Adventure* (2002), directed by David Strohmaier.

Faced with a box-office attendance that dropped almost in half between 1948 and 1952, panicked Hollywood executives looked for something to distinguish movies from other forms of entertainment—specifically, television. Typically, some executives turned to the past. Processes that had been rejected twenty and thirty years earlier suddenly seemed viable. Color became more prominent, 3-D was re-introduced to moviegoers, and the shape of the screen itself changed.

Widescreen movies had been exhibited as early as 1897, and it wasn't until ten years later that the industry settled on the standard aspect ratio used for the next forty years. The Great Depression is blamed for ending experiments with widescreen and 70mm films at the end of the 1920s. But Fred Waller continued to tinker with a device that would record what the normal eye could see and ears could hear.

Born in Brooklyn in 1886, Waller was educated as an engineer. He parlayed his interest in film techniques and equipment into a job as head of special effects for Paramount in the 1920s. Working out of an indoor tennis court in Oyster Bay, Long Island, Waller developed Vitarama, an eleven-camera system that was a hit at the 1939 New York World's Fair. (Waller filmed one segment on another of his patented inventions, waterskis.)

Vitarama was an elaborate process that had to be tailored to individual theaters. In addition, the light beams from the eleven separate projectors interfered with each other when shone on a screen. Curving the screen solved some, but not all, of the problem. Waller next built a new device that used five cameras and a soundtrack that viewers listened to through headphones. Like Hale's Tours at the turn of the twentieth century, his Flexible Gunnery Trainer tried to immerse viewers in all-encompassing visuals, above, below, and to either side as well as straight ahead. He sold it as a flight simulation device to the armed services during World War II. Waller and his company installed seventy-five trainers in the United States and Great Britain.

The gunnery trainers worked fine in confined spaces, but were impractical in movie theaters. Waller continued his experiments, determined to find a way to mimic human vision on screen. He decided that a sense of depth, achieved in three-dimensional processes, was not as important as including and engaging peripheral vision. Waller wanted to fill the entire field of vision the human eye took in, which he calculated at approximately 160 degrees wide and, in a theater setting, sixty feet tall. Cinerama, the name for his three-camera system, worked out to 146 degrees wide and fifty-five feet tall.

Waller had dropped the two overhead cameras because of problems with reflections. These problems continued with the three-camera system until a new screen was designed, one made up of over a thousand vertical strips that were arranged like louvers on a window blind. Waller also contacted Hazard "Buzz" Reeves, who since 1933 had been building specialty recording equipment for the film industry. (Reeves was also instrumental in developing what was marketed as the Waring Blender.) The two had worked together at the World's Fair; now Reeves applied his work in sound reproduction to the Cinerama process. He came up with a seven-channel directional stereo soundtrack which was played back from 35mm film stock that had been coated with magnetic oxide. (This was adapted into the 35mm mag stripe, an industry standard until the introduction of digital sound.) By positioning speakers throughout the theater, Reeves built the first true surround-sound experience.

Reeves was named president of Cinerama after he invested money to keep the company afloat. Meanwhile, Waller had test footage shot from the Rockaways' Playland "Atom Smasher" roller coaster in Queens, using a mount that held three cameras equipped with 27mm lenses and shooting at 26 frames per second. Another segment featured a Long Island choir singing excerpts from Handel's *Messiah*. Although Hollywood executives were noncommittal, Reeves hired showman Michael Todd as a producer for the company.

While Todd and his son Michael Todd, Jr., went to Europe to film material, newsman and radio commentator Lowell Thomas became involved with the process. Famed for narrating Fox Movietone newsreels and for making T.E. Lawrence (better known as Lawrence of Arabia) a celebrity, Thomas became an indefatigable backer of Cinerama. He also helped engineer the removal of Todd from the staff, replacing him with Merian C. Cooper, the filmmaker behind such milestones as *Grass* and *King Kong*. (Todd went on to develop a rival widescreen system, Todd-AO.)

Cooper was ultimately responsible for the final structure of *This Is Cinerama*, which included newly filmed color versions of the original roller coaster ride, Todd's European footage, and a closing "America the Beautiful" sequence taken from a B-25 fighter flown by pilot Paul Mantz. *This Is Cinerama* was photographed by Harry Squire, a cinematographer who started out at the Edison studio before working at Fox Movietone and later on the Frank Buck feature *Bring 'em Back Alive* (1932).

The film premiered in New York City on September 30, 1952. The Cinerama company sold what was called a "hard ticket"—that is, reserved, assigned seats—in an effort to distinguish *This Is Cinerama* from the rest of the film industry's product. The company installed a slit screen, the seven-channel sound system, and three separate projector booths aligned with the screen into New York City's Broadway Theatre. A fourth booth held the sound engineer, who mixed sound for each screening on the fly. A fifth technician ran the curtain and lights. There were no reel changeovers during screenings: each projector reel initially held some eighty minutes' worth of film. As a result, *This Is Cinerama* required an intermission so projectors could be rethreaded.

Like the early Vitaphone sound shorts, *This Is Cinerama* was a mix of the virtuously highbrow (bagpipers in Edinburgh, the Vienna Boys Choir) and the stridently commercial, rendered palatable by Cooper's flair for showmanship. The film brought viewers to La Scala, to Crater Lake, to the Cypress Gardens in Florida, and—in perhaps its most memorable shot—under the Golden Gate Bridge from the nose of a B-25. The premiere was covered on the front page of the *New York Times*, and *This Is Cinerama* went on become the top-grossing film of the year (it played in the same theater for almost two years).

Over the next six years, the company made a total of five Cinerama travelogues, and expanded to fourteen theaters. By then competing studios had introduced several other widescreen processes (the Soviets introduced their version of Cinerama, Kino Panorama, in Brussels in 1958). Cooper, who by this time had dissociated himself from the company, always insisted that the process would be seen as a fad unless it was used for feature films. MGM and Cinerama signed a two-picture deal to do just that, resulting in *The Wonderful World of the Brothers Grimm* and *How the West Was Won* (both 1962).

Retired projectionist John Harvey was a major factor in getting both *This Is Cinerama* and *How the West Was Won* named to the National Film Registry. Unlike the other travelogues, color separations were made for *This Is Cinerama*, and the soundtrack remained in good shape, enabling film preservationists to oversee a better-than-average restoration that became available in time for the film's fiftieth anniversary screening. Due to equipment demands, this is one of the most difficult films in the Registry to see. David Strohmaier helped develop what he calls a "smileybox" format that approximates the shape of the Cinerama screen, enabling him to excerpt segments from *This Is Cinerama* for his documentary *Cinerama Adventure*. But to anyone who has had the opportunity to see it, there is no comparison between normal widescreen projection and true Cinerama.

The Bad and the Beautiful

MGM, 1952. Sound, B&W, 1.37. 118 minutes.

Cast: Lana Turner (Georgia Lorrison), Kirk Douglas (Jonathan Shields), Walter Pidgeon (Harry Pebbel), Dick Powell (James Lee Bartlow), Barry Sullivan (Fred Amiel), Gloria Grahame (Rosemary Bartlow), Gilbert Roland (Victor "Gaucho" Ribera), Leo G. Carroll (Henry Whitfield), Vanessa Brown (Kay Amiel), Paul Stewart (Syd), Sammy White (Gus), Elaine Stewart (Lila), Ivan Triesault (Von Ellstein).

Credits: Directed by Vincente Minnelli. Screen play by Charles Schnee. Based on a story by George Bradshaw. Produced by John Houseman. Director of photography: Robert Surtees. Art directors: Cedric Gibbons, Edward Carfagno. Film editor: Conrad A. Nervig. Music by David Raksin. Assistant director: Jerry Thorpe. Recording supervisor: Douglas Shearer. Set decorations: Edwin B. Willis, Keogh Gleason. Special effects: A. Arnold Gillespie, Warren Newcombe. Women's costumes designed by Helen Rose. Hair styles by Sydney Guilaroff. Make-up by William Tuttle. Western Electric Sound System.

Additional Cast: Barbara Billingsley (Evelyn Lucien), Francis X. Bushman (Eulogist), Sandy Descher (Screaming girl on movie set), Kathleen Freeman (Miss March), Ned Glass (Wardrobe man), Peggy King (Singer).

Additional Credits: Production dates: April to June 1952. Premiered in Los Angeles on December 25, 1952, Los Angeles.

Awards: Oscars for Best Actress in a Supporting Role (Grahame), Art Direction–Set Direction—Black and White, Cinematography—Black and White, Writing—Screenplay.

Other Versions: While not strictly a sequel, *Two Weeks in Another Town* (1962, directed by Minnelli) has a similar milieu, and incorporates footage from this movie into its story.

Available: Warner Home Video DVD (2001). ISBN: 0-7907-4756-1. UPC: 0-12569-52402-6.

Dore Schary met John Houseman when they were both working at RKO after World War II. Schary replaced Louis B. Mayer as head of MGM in 1951, the same year Houseman signed a contract to produce at the studio. His first project was *Holiday for Sinners*, a negligible Gig Young vehicle. Houseman's next film came from a short story in the February 1951 *Ladies' Home Journal*: "Memorial to a Bad Man" by George Bradshaw. In it, a Broadway producer (loosely based on Jed Harris) sends letters to three of his protégés from his deathbed. Its structure recalled both *Citizen Kane* (1941) and *A Letter to Three Wives* (1949), for which Joseph Mankiewicz had won a screenplay Oscar.

Houseman bought the story and another, "Of Good and Evil," for $11,500. Perhaps inspired by the success of *Sunset Boulevard* (1950), Houseman switched the locale of Bradshaw's story from New York City to Hollywood. He assigned the project to screenwriter Charles Schnee, a former lawyer who had worked on Houseman's *They Live by Night* (1949). With input from Houseman, Schnee reimagined the main character as the ruthlessly ambitious movie producer and director Jonathan

Shields. His career is detailed in a series of flashbacks in which he betrays his friends and professional colleagues; ironically, he is now appealing to them for help with his latest movie. Schnee suggested that Shields was driven by a desire to avenge the reputation of his father, whose career was destroyed by studio executives. This was close enough to the life of David O. Selznick that the producer initiated a lawsuit against the project, which he later dropped.

Schnee, Houseman, and later Vincente Minnelli, when he joined the production as director, sprinkled clues about other real-life celebrities throughout the story. Shields and his directing partner Fred Amiel (played by Barry Sullivan) make names for themselves by directing low-budget horror movies that resemble Val Lewton's RKO hits a decade earlier. Two other directors in the story could have real-life counterparts. The German tyrant Von Ellstein (Ivan Triesault) has characteristics of both Erich von Stroheim and Josef von Sternberg, while Henry Whitfield (Leo G. Carroll) is clearly meant to represent Alfred Hitchcock, down to his Alma Reville like companion (Kathleen Freeman).

Houseman and Minnelli insisted on Kirk Douglas for the lead, even though he was not under contract and had not yet shown the ability to carry a film. Lana Turner was a somewhat surprising choice for Georgia Lorrison, the troubled movie star, but Minnelli managed to coax from her what many fans consider her strongest screen performance. Barry Sullivan was originally scheduled to play James Lee Bartlow, the script's version of a sober, cleaned-up William Faulkner. But when Dick Powell wanted the part, Sullivan was given the smaller role of Fred Amiel, undergoing a fate similar to his character's. Houseman knew Gloria Grahame from RKO; Nicholas Ray, her husband at the time, had directed *They Live by Night* for him. She made the most of her relatively small role as Bartlow's wife.

Called *Tribute to a Bad Man*, the production fell between two musicals directed by Minnelli, *An American in Paris* (1951) and *The Band Wagon* (1953). Shooting started on April 9, 1952, one day after his divorce from Judy Garland was finalized. Like many of the characters in his films did, Minnelli threw himself into work to counter personal setbacks. Building on the style he developed in his previous dramas, he staged some of the scenes here as if they were musical numbers, choreographing the actors to beats. Minnelli devotees point to Georgia Lorrison's nervous breakdown while driving along a rainswept highway as one of the film's highlights, although the scene doesn't make much sense either psychologically or as an example of defensive driving. In fact, Lorrison's character as a whole doesn't bear much examining. The script implies she is an alcoholic and prostitute because her father was, but filmgoers at the time were probably associating the part with Turner herself, by that time already married three times and the victim of several scandals.

Working for the first time with cinematographer Robert Surtees, Minnelli moves the camera adroitly, gliding over the improbable twists in the plot, singling out Charles Schnee's stinging quips with angled close-ups. Shooting ended in June, with a final budget slightly over $1.5 million. Over Houseman's objections, the studio jettisoned the title in favor of one concocted by publicist Howard Dietz, who felt filmgoers would associate the "beautiful" in *The Bad and the Beautiful* with Turner. (*Tribute to a Bad Man* was later used as the title for a 1956 James Cagney Western.) Posters for *The Proud Land*, the film that nearly destroys Shields's career here, can be seen in Minnelli's *The Band Wagon*.

The Bad and the Beautiful proved popular with filmgoers, who felt they were getting an inside look at the movie industry. Joseph Mankiewicz saw it differently. He called it "a slick machine-made entertainment that has some good savage moments in it, that looks good, but never gets to the point. . . . Any picture that eight men have to approve is sure to be a piece of crap."

The film is an interesting companion piece to Paramount's *Sunset Boulevard*, the latter filled with cobwebs, walking ghosts, and streams of self-loathing, while Minnelli and company present an ultimately upbeat view of moviemaking as a collaborative process among quirky but talented artists. Paramount and MGM offered equally contrasting versions of the industry back in the late 1920s, with *The Last Command* hell to *Show People*'s sunny heaven. In a final irony, the real-life Lana Turner underwent career and personal reversals similar to those her Georgia Lorrison character suffers through here.

All My Babies

Georgia Department of Health, 1953. Sound, B&W, 1.37. 53 minutes.

Featuring: Mary Frances Coley, Mattie Mansfield, Martha Sapp, Alvin Sapp, Harriet Godbee (Miss Penny).

Credits: Written, directed and produced by George C. Stoney for the Medical Audio-Visual Institute of the Association of American Medical Colleges. Director of photography: Peaslee Bond. Asst. cameraman: Robert Galbraith. Sound engineer: Walter Winn. Assistant: Jack Brown. Chief electrician: Robert Downey. Sound Service: McGeary-Smith, Inc. Edited by Sylvia K. Cummins. Musical director: Louis Applebaum. Music performed by The Musical Art Chorus, Othello C. Wilson, director. Filmed under the technical supervision of Certified Nurse-Midwives: Marian F. Cadwallader, R.N., B.S., and Hannah D. Mitchell, R.N., M.P.H. Introduced by Wm. A. Mason, M.D., M.P.H. Made in Albany, Georgia. Copyright 1952, Georgia Dept. of Health.

Additional Credits: Title on screen: *All My Babies . . . A Midwife's Own Story.*

Available: Image Entertainment DVD (2007). UPC: 014381384529.

The documentarian and educator George C. Stoney was born in 1916 in Winston-Salem, North Carolina. He studied journalism at the University of North Carolina and at New York University. One of his early projects was fieldwork on sociologist Gunnar Myrdal's *An American Dilemma*, an influential survey of black life. Stoney worked as a freelance writer and then as an information officer for the Farm Security Administration. During World War II he served as a photo intelligence officer. Interested in community activism, he joined the Southern Educational Film Service in 1946 as a writer and director. He also formed Stoney Associates, one of the key documentary production companies of the 1950s.

One of his first films was *Palmour Street* (1949), made for the Georgia Department of Public Health. Through dramatic re-creations, Stoney addressed various problems in family relations, following a checklist provided by department doctors. *All My Babies* had a similar genesis. It was a sponsored instructional film that had to cover specific medical points—118 by Stoney's count. It was also intended for a specific audience: rural black midwives, some of whom were presumed to be illiterate. The Department of Health's goal was to teach good hygiene practices in order to lower what it considered to be a high infant mortality rate on deliveries performed by "granny midwives." It was up to Stoney to find a way to get this message across.

In 1925, there were 9,000 licensed midwives in Georgia, and they delivered close to half the babies in the state each year. As the number of hospitals and obstetricians rose, and the medical costs of childbirth fell, the number of midwives also declined. By the time Stoney began his project, there were fewer than 2,200 midwives, and they catered to a largely rural and poor clientele.

Stoney could have made a purely functional instructional film, recording a lecture from a doctor, for example. He decided that his audience would respond better to a film that resembled the actual movies they were seeing. He also felt that the themes of the film should be told from a peer's point of view, someone who could present the film's message in a manner the audience could relate to personally.

Research was key. Stoney spent months looking for the right midwife. In Albany he met Mary Coley, at the time a fifty-year-old mother of eleven. In cooperation with the local health department, she had been delivering babies—by her count, close to 3,000—since 1929. Stoney rejected Coley at first because she was short and weighed close to three hundred pounds. "I hate to confess this," he told an interviewer years later, "but I knew the camera would make her appear larger, and I didn't want to perpetuate the Aunt Jemima stereotype."

Stoney could not find a better candidate, however, and returned to observe Coley for three months in 1951. He began shooting in January 1952. In his script he planned to show three different pregnancies. One would be an ideal home delivery, with a cooperative mother in a supportive household. For this he chose Martha Sapp, who agreed to deliver her child without anesthesia before Stoney's camera. The second would show a more difficult pregnancy in which the mother was not able to follow guidelines regarding health and hygiene. The third example would be a case too difficult for Coley to handle. Early on in the pregnancy she would advise this client to go to a doctor.

In later years Stoney described the tense racial climate in which he worked. A white man filming a black woman behind closed doors was too great a taboo in some parts of rural Georgia. A sheriff halted filming at one location; Stoney had to explain what he was trying to do before he received permission to continue. Whites are almost completely absent from the film, as are most traces of modern life.

Stoney shot most of the film silent, adding spirituals sung by a choir and a voice-over from

Coley for sound. Even so, he ran over his $75,000 budget, and had to sell some of his family's real estate in North Carolina to complete the film. Coley proved to be an excellent choice. Solid, even stocky, she came across as calm, experienced, and utterly trustworthy. For viewers today, her scripted narration—"Of course I had foretold Ida what they was going to do"—may seem condescending. However, Stoney's respect for her and the other figures in the film is unmistakable.

When it was released, *All My Babies* proved so popular that it began to be used by out-of-state medical schools. UNESCO and the World Health Organization chose it for training midwives. The film became a staple of high school and elementary school classes, in part because it showed a human birth in a manner that teachers felt students could handle. Although shot in a matter-of-fact style, the fifteen-minute sequence is still startling today.

Stoney continued to make instructional films throughout the following two decades, but he is perhaps better known for helping to introduce public access television to the United States. From 1966 to 1970, he was a director of the Challenge for Change project, which produced documentaries for the National Film Board of Canada, but which also took steps in opening up public access to its facilities. In 1971, Stoney helped found the Alternative Media Center in New York City; it made the tools of broadcasting available to everyone. While teaching at New York University, he cofounded the National Federation of Local Cable Programmers. He also continued to make documentaries, including *The Uprising of '34* (1995), about the 1934 textile workers' strike.

Coley died of diabetes in 1966. Over the years some of her descendants assumed that Stoney had exploited her for profit. As Bernard Coley, a grandson, said, "We heard that this man came down from the North and got rich and famous off Grandma." A telecom entrepreneur in Palo Alto, California, Bernard Coley met with Stoney in New York to learn the truth. The result was a sequel to *All My Babies*, filmed by Stoney in Dougherty County, Georgia, in the summer of 2007. It featured a reunion, arranged in part by Bernard Coley, of many of the survivors of the 1952 film.

The Naked Spur

James Stewart on location for *The Naked Spur*.

MGM, 1953. Sound, color, 1.37. 92 minutes.

Cast: James Stewart (Howard Kemp), Janet Leigh (Lina Patch), Robert Ryan (Ben Vandergroat), Ralph Meeker (Roy Anderson), Millard Mitchell (Jesse Tate).

Credits: Directed by Anthony Mann. Written by Sam Rolfe and Harold Jack Bloom. Produced by William H. Wright. Director of photography: William Mellor. Technicolor color consultants: Henri Jaffa, Robert Brower. Art directors: Cedric Gibbons and Malcolm Brown. Film editor: George White. Assistant director: Howard W. Koch. Music by Bronislau Kaper. Recording supervisor: Douglas Shearer. Set decorations: Edwin B. Willis. Special effects: Warren Newcombe. Make-up created by William Tuttle. Western Electric Sound System. Color by Technicolor.

Additional Credits: Production dates: May to June 30, 1952. Released February 6, 1953.

Available: Warner Home Video DVD (2006). ISBN: 1-4198-3393-6. UPC: 0-12569-79246-3.

In the 1940s and '50s, Westerns dominated American culture to an extent hard to fathom today. Singing cowboys like Gene Autry cracked the box-office top ten, while the genre as a whole proved a godsend both to actors aging out of leading roles and newcomers trying to gain attention. Many Westerns were uninspired, using violence and music to cover up threadbare plots and simplistic characters. They had also been targeted at younger viewers, but this market was growing up and increasingly rejecting movies for television.

Critics tended to look down on Westerns, unless, like Fred Zinnemann's *High Noon* (1952) and Henry King's *The Gunfighter* (1950), they concerned "serious" topics. As a result, the five Westerns made by director Anthony Mann and star James Stewart have often been underappreciated. They looked just like "real" Westerns, with rugged outdoors scenery and plenty of violence. But they cut a lot deeper. Stewart was a different actor after his experiences as a bomber pilot during World War II. And Anthony Mann had developed an unusually acute feel for the depravity underlying modern society. Tied to his strong storytelling skills, it gave their films together a psychological realism unusual for the time.

The partnership between Mann and Stewart came about in part due to the actor's pioneering gross percentage deal arranged by agent Lew Wasserman. It was a deal that guaranteed Stewart 50 percent of his films' profits, as well as star billing and approval over cast and director. The contract went into play with *Harvey* (1950), a financial failure, but the first Stewart film released under the new system was *Winchester '73* (1950), a lean, cold-blooded Western directed by Mann.

Mann was born Emil Bundsmann in San Diego in 1906. At ten, after his family had moved to New York City, Mann became obsessed with acting. He dropped out of high school to work in theater, eventually forming his own company, the Red Barn Playhouse. He changed his name to Mann when he earned his first Broadway directing credit. Mann worked for producer David O. Selznick as a sort of talent scout, helping find Broadway actors to cast in films like *Gone With the Wind* (1939). He was an assistant director for Preston Sturges at Paramount, where he later began to direct distinctively shot and edited film noirs. He replaced Fritz Lang on *Winchester '73*, bringing a sense of period accuracy and a greater understanding of the Western landscape to the project. Stewart and Mann followed *Winchester '73* with *Bend of the River* (1952), a vivid revenge adventure set in Oregon in the 1840s.

Their third collaboration was *The Naked Spur*, written by Sam Rolfe and Harold Jack Bloom. Like the other Mann/Stewart Westerns, the story involved a journey through a perilous landscape. Farmer Howard Kemp (played by Stewart) is escorting wanted criminal Ben Vandergroat (Robert Ryan, borrowed from RKO) back to justice, and not incidentally a sizable bounty. Accompanying him are Ben's mistress Lina (Janet Leigh), the prospector Jesse Tate (Millard Mitchell), and Roy Anderson (Ralph Meeker), just out of the Army.

It's a simple premise, but one fraught with moral land mines. Ben, exceedingly clever, plays his captors against each other, reminding them, "Money splits two ways better than it does with three." The story's journey framework allows Mann to reveal aspects of the characters gradually, through their physical actions, but also through their choices and conversations. And the Colorado Rockies settings gives the film a realism missing from most contemporary Westerns.

"I don't like to shoot in a studio," Mann told Charles Bitsch and Claude Chabrol in a 1957 interview. Actual landscapes gave him new ideas for staging scenes, but a more important reason was, "Actors get much more authentic on location. In a studio, everything is quiet, everything is built for the scene. . . . But if an actor has to play the scene on a mountaintop, alongside a river, or in a forest, there is wind, dust, snow, the crackling of branches—all this interrupts the actor and forces him to give more, and he becomes more alive." *The Naked Spur* bears out this theory beautifully. Arguing with Leigh, Stewart really struggles to be heard above the roar of a river. In another scene, Mann sets the camera so viewers know the actor really is climbing the cliffs holding him back from his goals.

But the film offers more than action, breathtaking settings, and strong acting. Mann presents a world in which good and evil are no longer black and white. Choices have consequences, motives can change, and what once seemed right thing to do might no longer make sense. It was a view perfectly attuned to a newly skeptical society, a changed culture in which Indians could no longer be treated as target practice, and women deserved more than subsidiary roles.

Shooting lasted six weeks in the spring of 1952. The film opened the following year in order to avoid a glut of Stewart films (and Westerns).

Mann and the actor next collaborated on *The Glenn Miller Story* (1953), a biography that turned out to be their biggest hit, but their best work together was in the Western genre. The informal partnership ended in 1957 when Mann decided to make *The Tin Star* with Henry Fonda instead of *Night Passage* with Stewart and Audie Murphy. Mann's later films, big-budget epics like *El Cid* (1961) and *The Fall of the Roman Empire* (1964), were critical and financial failures. He died of a heart attack in 1967, during the shooting of *A Dandy in Aspic* (released in 1968).

Duck Amuck

Warner Bros., 1953. Sound, color, 1.37. 7 minutes.

Credits: Directed by Charles M. Jones. Story: Michael Maltese. Animation: Ken Harris, Ben Washam, Lloyd Vaughan. Layouts: Maurice Noble. Backgrounds: Philip De Guard. Voice characterizations: Mel Blanc. Musical direction: Carl Stalling. Color by Technicolor.

Additional Credits: Released February 28, 1953.

Other Versions: *Rabbit Rampage* (1955, directed by Jones) reworked the plot with Bugs Bunny as the star.

Available: Warner Home Video DVD, *Looney Tunes Golden Collection, Volume 2* (2003). ISBN: 0-7907-8176-X. UPC: 0-85392-79182-8.

Of all the directors of Warner Brothers cartoons, Charles "Chuck" Jones has the highest critical reputation. Four Warners cartoons are included on the Registry, and Jones directed three of them. *Duck Amuck* comes from the post–World War II period, when Warners was the undisputed king of cartoon shorts.

Born in Spokane, Washington, in 1912, Jones studied at the Chouinard Art Institute (now the California Institute of the Arts), hoping for a job in commercial art. Instead, he was hired by Ub Iwerks as a "cel washer" for " Flip the Frog" cartoons. Jones eventually found a home at Warners, working with Robert Clampett in an animation unit headed by Tex Avery; Jones also worked under Frank Tashlin. He cites Avery and Friz Freleng as his principal inspirations. During World War II he collaborated with Theodore Geisel (better known as Dr. Seuss) on "Private Snafu" cartoons for the armed services.

After the war, Jones headed his own unit, which included writer Mike Maltese and animator Ben Washam. According to animation historian Michael Barrier, these three were the creative team behind *Duck Amuck*, along with layout artist Maurice Noble. The cartoon began with a premise Jones dreamed up: What if Daffy Duck ran out of background? Daffy made his film debut in Tex Avery's *Porky's Duck Hunt* (1937), where Clampett as animator helped define his character. By the time *Duck Amuck* was being drawn, Daffy was the second most popular cartoon character at Warners. Unlike the unflappable Bugs Bunny, Daffy was highly excitable. By this point in his career he was also extremely paranoid—in other words, the perfect actor for *Duck Amuck*.

It's hard to talk about the cartoon without using terms like "self-reflexive" and "deconstructive," as *Duck Amuck* is all about isolating and distorting the elements that make up animation. As film historian Leonard Maltin has pointed out, there was a self-reflexive aspect of animation from its earliest days. In a film like *Gertie the Dinosaur* (1914), animator Winsor McKay interacted with his drawings; the Felix the Cat cartoons of the 1920s had the star taking his children to a movie theater to watch him on screen. In *Comicalamities* (1928), Felix even talks back to his animator. The Fleischer Brothers also broke the barrier between drawing and live action in their "Out of the Inkwell" cartoons (and 1924's *Cartoon Factory* introduced a premise very similar to this film). Popeye and Bugs Bunny periodically spoke to the audience in their films, and at times even jumped out of the frame.

What sets *Duck Amuck* apart from these earlier examples is its malevolent animator. A film like Buster Keaton's *Sherlock Jr.* (1924) asked what happened if a character lost control over elements of the movie he was in. What if a mountain suddenly turned into the ocean, or night into day? *Duck Amuck* raises similar questions, but it's really about how a mean-spirited creator can torment his creation. Daffy, as usual primed for work and eager to please, is ready to appear in what he believes is a swashbuckling adventure. When the background art changes, Daffy tries to change, too, switching costumes and acting styles. His frustration is the chief source of humor in the film, that and Carl Stalling's ability to meld songs as disparate as "Aloha Oe," "Jingle Bells," and "Old MacDonald" on the soundtrack.

Jones credited animator Ben Washam for much of the success of the cartoon, although they argued vigorously over how Daffy's monologues should be played. Washam was known for character animation rather than action, crucial in a film that is basically Daffy talking for six minutes. One notable aspect of the film is how Jones and his staff felt comfortable recycling gags from earlier shorts. Clampett and writer Warren Foster used an eraser to "rub out" Daffy back in *The Great Piggy Bank Robbery* (1946), for example, while the poorly drawn background scenery that pops up at one point looks just like that in Tex Avery's *Porky's Preview* (1941).

John Kricfalusi, the creator and director of television's *The Ren & Stimpy Show*, said this about Jones: "He's a very good director, but his directing is in front of the characters. His characters are victims of the direction. When something happens to Daffy Duck in those Bugs and Daffy cartoons like *Rabbit Seasoning*, it's really not fair to Daffy. I feel sorry for him. Bugs Bunny is not winning those cartoons on his own. Daffy Duck has no choice but to lose, it's preordained that he is going to lose, for no reason. I never feel that from a Clampett cartoon. . . . [His characters] don't feel like they're being pushed around by the director."

When Clampett and Avery left Warners, Jones by default became the studio's most visible animator. He was responsible for several important characters, perhaps none more famous that the Road Runner and Wile E. Coyote. His next Registry title is *One Froggy Evening* (1956).

Shane

Paramount, 1953. Sound, color, 1.37. 118 minutes.

Cast: Alan Ladd (Shane), Jean Arthur (Marian Starrett), Van Heflin (Joe Starrett), Brandon De Wilde (Joey Starrett), Walter Jack Palance (Jack Wilson), Ben Johnson (Chris Calloway), Edgar Buchanan (Fred Lewis), Emile Meyer (Rufe Ryker), Elisha Cook, Jr. (Stonewall Torrey), Douglas Spencer (Shipstead), John Dierkes (Morgan), Ellen Corby (Mrs. Torrey), Paul McVey (Sam Grafton), John Miller (Atkey), Edith Evanson (Mrs. Shipstead), Leonard Strong (Ernie Wright), Ray Spiker (Axel Johnson), Janice Carroll (Susan Lewis), Martin Mason (Ed Howells), Helen Brown (Martha Lewis), Nancy Kulp (Mrs. Howells).

Credits: Produced and directed by George Stevens. Screenplay by A.B. Guthrie, Jr. Additional dialogue by Jack Sher. Based on the novel by Jack Schaefer. Director of photography: Loyal Griggs. Music score: Victor Young. Associate producer: Ivan Moffat. Associate director: Fred Guiol. Edited by William Hornbeck and Tom McAdoo. Art direction: Hal Pereira and Walter Tyler. Set decoration: Emile Kuri. Second unit photography: Irmin Roberts. Special photographic effects: Gordon Jennings. Process photography: Farciot Edouart. Costumes: Edith Head. Technical advisor: Joe DeYong [de Young]. Makeup supervision: Wally Westmore. Assistant director: John Coonan. Assistant to the producer: Howie Horwitz. Sound recording by Harry Lindgren, Gene Garvin. Western Electric Recording. Color by Technicolor. Technicolor color consultant: Richard Mueller.

Additional Cast: Will Simmonds, Bill Dyer, Steve Raines (Homesteaders); Howard J. Negley (Pete); Beverly Washburn (Ruth Lewis); George Lewis, Bill Cartledge, Jack Sterling, Henry Wills, Rex Moore, Ewing Brown (Ryker's Men).

Additional Credits: Production dates: July to October 1951. Premiered April 23, 1953, New York City.

Awards: Oscars for Best Cinematography—Color.

Available: Paramount DVD (2000). ISBN: 0-7921-6371-0. UPC: 0-9736-06522-4-6.

Jack Schaefer was a reporter, teacher, and editor before he became a novelist. Born in Cleveland in 1907, he spent most of his career on the East Coast. His first novel, *Shane*, published in 1949, was also his most famous. He seemed a bit nonplussed when it became a fixture in middle- and high-school literature courses. "I have never deliberately written stories for children," he wrote in 1989. The novel became a best-seller in part because it was so simple, elemental. Schaefer rearranged the facts of the Johnson County range war in 1892 Wyoming, reducing them to a series of confrontations: between a gunslinger and an admiring boy, between a stranger and a farmer trying to eke out a frontier ranch, between cattlemen and shepherds.

Paramount bought the book the year it was published, intending it for either Alan Ladd or Ray Milland. The project lay dormant until George Stevens' son read the novel and recommended it for his father. Stevens had avoided Westerns throughout his career (his *Annie Oakley* in 1935 had Western elements, but was really a biography). He tried to interest Montgomery Clift, his star in *A Place in the Sun* (1951), but the actor did not want to work with him again. A possibly apocryphal story has Stevens, pressured by Paramount head Y. Frank Freeman to start production, picking the three leads from a list of the studio's contract players.

Stevens was too controlling a director to base a film on rash decisions. He realized early in the process that Alan Ladd's personality fit that of the book's title character. Both Ladd and Shane were quiet, even passive types who were reaching the ends of their careers. Ladd was an unlikely action hero. Born in 1913, he spent years on the fringes of the film industry, playing extras and bit parts in movies like *Hold 'Em Navy* (1937) and *Citizen Kane* (1941). His role as a hit man in *This Gun for Hire* (1942) made him a star, although his subsequent films were largely lackluster. But even in his weakest vehicles, he came across as a sensitive, intelligent man who wasn't quite sure how to respond to situations.

This was the first film for Jean Arthur since Billy Wilder's *A Foreign Affair* in 1948, and it would be her last. She had worked with Stevens before, most memorably in *The More the Merrier* (1943), and appreciated his consideration for her shyness. Like Ladd, Arthur gave the impression of being intelligent on screen, but in the wrong hands could seem shrill and aggressive. Stevens was able to mold her performance without causing her to question her decisions. William Holden had been penciled in for the third lead, but was replaced by Van Heflin just before production started.

Howard Hawks took credit for persuading Stevens to hire novelist A.B. Guthrie, Jr., as screenwriter. Guthrie had never written for movies, but Hawks had just finished filming his breakthrough novel, *The Big Sky* (1952). Born in Indiana in 1901, but raised in Montana, Guthrie wrote some of the best Western novels of his time. He was especially adept at portraying flawed characters and in foregrounding confrontations. Stevens and Guthrie collaborated on a screenplay that remained true to the spirit of Schaefer's novel while also commenting upon the entire genre of Western films.

Shane serves as Stevens' summing-up of Westerns. Like most of his contemporaries, he felt that the genre had largely been defined by John Ford, and *Shane* contains many shots, scenes, and even characters that are derived from or based on Ford's landmark films. Stevens also had something to say about "message" Westerns like *High Noon* (1952). Made at the same time as *High Noon*, *Shane* can be seen as an answer to that film, or a variation with decidedly different politics. In its depiction of the relationship between Shane and young Joey Starrett, the film can even be seen as a corollary to Gene Autry pictures. The fact that *Shane* can sustain so many interpretations is a mark of Stevens' storytelling skill.

The film had an enormous impact on the public imagination. It was a time of flux for the industry, and *Shane* was clearly addressing the passing of an era—not just of the West, of the frontier now tamed, but of movies as well. As mentioned above, Arthur retired from the screen after this film, and Ladd never again found a comparable part. Filmmakers as disparate as Woody Allen and Clint Eastwood found inspiration from the film. Allen considers it one of the great American films, and has spoken at length about Stevens' skill at portraying relationships and staging action. Eastwood directed a virtual remake, *Pale Rider*, in 1985.

Although filmed in the traditional 1.37 screen ratio, *Shane* was finished on the cusp of the widescreen era. Cinematographer Loyal Griggs complained bitterly when Paramount released a "widescreen" version that simply lopped off the tops and bottoms of his frames. (Today's prints are full frame.) Stevens' next film, *Giant* (1956), is also on the Registry.

The Hitch-Hiker

RKO, 1953. Sound, B&W, 71 minutes.

Cast: Edmond O'Brien (Roy Collins), Frank Lovejoy (Gilbert Bowen), William Talman (Emmett Myers), Jose Torvay (Captain Alvarado), Sam Hayes (Himself/Radio announcer), Wendel Niles (Himself/Radio announcer), Jean Del Val (Inspector General), Clark Howat (Government agent), Natividad Vacio (José).

Credits: Directed by Ida Lupino. Screen Play by Collier Young and Ida Lupino. Adaptation by Robert Joseph. Produced by Collier Young. Associate producer: Christian Nyby. Music by Leith Stevens. Director of photography: Nicholas Musuraca. Photographic effects by Harold E. Wellman. Art directors: Albert S. D'Agostino, Walter E. Keller. Musical director: C. Bakaleinikoff. Film editor: Douglas Stewart. Set decorations: Darrell Silvera, Harley Miller. Sound by Roy Meadows, Clem Portman. Makeup artist: Mel Berns. Assistants to producers: James Anderson, Robert Eggenweiler. Assistant director: William Dorfman. RCA Sound System. Distributed by RKO Radio Pictures, Inc.

Additional Cast: Rodney Bell (Proprietor), Martin Garralaga (Bartender), Tony Roux (Gas station owner), Jerry Lawrence (News broadcaster); Felipe Turich, Rosa Turich (Mexicans in car); Orlando Veltran, George Navarro (Barkers); Joe Dominguez (Man outside store), June Dineen (Waitress), Al Ferrara (Gas station attendant), Henry Escalante (Mexican guard), Taylor Flaniken (Mexican policeman), Wade Crosby (Joe, bartender), Kathy Riggins (Child), Gordon Barnes (Hendrickson), Ed Hinton (Chief of Police), Larry Hudson (FBI agent).

Additional Credits: Story by Daniel Mainwaring. Shooting dates: June 24 to July 1952. Released May 21, 1953.

Available: Kino Video DVD (1998). UPC: 7-38329-01442-1.

Between 1949 and 1954, Ida Lupino wrote and directed six features for The Filmakers, a production company she formed with her husband Collier Young. During the same period, she starred in seven other films. At the time she was the only woman directing features in Hollywood, a job she later described as one she fell into.

Lupino was born in London in 1918, the daughter of music hall comedian Stanley Lupino and actress Connie Emerald. (Stanley's brother Lupino Lane was an internationally successful film comedian.) She entered the Royal Academy of Dramatic Art at the age of thirteen, and made her film debut two years later. A contract with

William Talman, one of the stalwarts of film noir, in *The Hitch-Hiker*. *Courtesy of Kino International*

Paramount brought her to Hollywood, where she languished in ingénue roles. When she played a prostitute in *The Light That Failed* (1939) and a killer in *They Drive by Night* (1940), she won a contract at Warner Brothers. She spent the 1940s in a succession of demanding roles that taught her the commercial value of exploitation. By the end of the decade, she realized that her future career depended on finding her own projects.

The stated goal of The Filmakers was to tackle themes of social interest in low-budget movies that could be marketed cheaply. The first of these, *Not Wanted* (1949), was supposed to have been directed by Elmer Clifton. When he suffered a heart attack, Lupino filled in for him, uncredited. As she put it later, she was on an eighteen-month suspension from RKO and "I had to do something to fill up my time."

Critics like to refer to *The Hitch-Hiker* as a film noir, but it more closely resembles a Western, from its mountain and desert locations near Lone Pine, California, to its elemental plot line which pits two friends against the outlaw holding them hostage. The plot was reputedly based on Billy Cook, who while hitchhiking in 1950 went on a killing spree that left six dead. It was also based on a story by Daniel Mainwaring, the screenwriter of *Out of the Past* (1947) and *Invasion of the Body Snatchers* (1956). Howard Hughes, at the time the head of RKO, which distributed Filmakers' titles, refused to give Mainwaring a credit. Hughes used anti-Communist hysteria as his reason, although some have suggested there was personal animosity between the two.

Lupino and Young ultimately received screenwriting credit, and feminist scholars have searched both the script and the film for characteristics they could ascribe to Lupino's gender, rather than her talent. Late in her career, Lupino belittled feminists, but took private pride in her professionalism. Describing her working methods, she said, "You don't tell a man, you suggest to them. 'Let's try something crazy here—that is, if it's comfortable for you, love.'"

Still, what's notable about the overall feel of *The Hitch-Hiker* is how easily it fits into the RKO studio style. The story, cinematography, music, and editing were all by veteran RKO hands. Given a restrictive budget and a tight shooting schedule, Lupino was more worried about getting the film finished than adding personal touches. She solves some problems by setting scenes at night, which limited the time it took to light scenes; by setting different exterior scenes in the same general locations, a trick also employed by directors like Budd Boetticher; and by using back projection in the car scenes, which make up the bulk of the movie.

There are adroit visual flourishes in *The Hitch-Hiker*, like a smooth, quick pan by cinematographer Nicholas Musuraca from a tight two-shot of Edmond O'Brien and Frank Lovejoy to the gun in William Talman's hand. All three actors were familiar noir figures: O'Brien was in *White Heat* (1949) and *D.O.A.* (1950); Lovejoy had an important role in *In a Lonely Place* (1950). Talman's parts ranged from cop parts to villains; his portrayal here of sadist Emmett Myers is one of the highlights of his career, although he was better known as the district attorney on the *Perry Mason* television series.

According to writer Richard Koszarski, what Lupino brought as a director to *The Hitch-Hiker* and to *The Bigamist*, her subsequent film, was an ability "to reduce the male to the same sort of dangerous, irrational force that women represented in most male-directed examples of Hollywood film noir." Today we can see that Lupino was struggling to differentiate her film from other noirs despite working with the exact same elements. Portions of *The Hitch-Hiker* are uncannily similar to movies like *Ride the Pink Horse* (1947) or *On Dangerous Ground* (1952), in which she starred. Other scenes in *The Hitch-Hiker* are mired in the same either/or situations found in many film noirs. "Cat and mouse" is the verbal shorthand for a strategy that allows storytellers to repeat essentially the same situation over and over. Either the outlaw kills his captives, or he doesn't—everything else just delays the ultimate outcome. (Dashiell Hammett addressed this very problem in *The Maltese Falcon* back in 1930.)

Lupino fills out this material by indicating how sadistic Myers is—an astute commercial move but not a very rewarding narrative one. *The Hitch-Hiker* becomes more implausible as it progresses. A killer this vicious and cruel would have dispatched his hostages rather than try to cross a desert on foot with them. (Myers himself sums up the plot fairly early on: "You guys are gonna die, that's all. It's just a question of when.")

O'Brien also starred in *The Bigamist*, a Filmakers project that included Joan Fontaine and Lupino herself. By that time she had divorced Collier Young, who rather inconveniently married Joan Fontaine a month before the release of *The Bigamist*. Lupino wed actor Howard Duff a year previously; after The Filmakers stopped production in 1955, she concentrated primarily on directing episodes of television series.

From Here to Eternity

Columbia, 1953. Sound, B&W, 1.33. 118 minutes.

Cast: Burt Lancaster (1st Sgt. Milton Warden), Montgomery Clift (Robert E. Lee Prewitt), Deborah Kerr (Karen Holmes), Donna Reed (Lorene/Alma), Frank Sinatra (Angelo Maggio), Philip Ober (Capt. Dana Holmes), Mickey Shaughnessy (Sgt. Leva), Harry Bellaver (Mazzioli), Ernest Borgnine (Staff Sgt. James R. "Fatso" Judson), Jack Warden (Cpl. Buckley), John Dennis (Sgt. Ike Galovitch), Merle Travis (Sal Anderson), Tim Ryan (Sgt. Pete Karelsen), Arthur Keegan (Treadwell), Barbara Morrison (Mrs. Kipfer).

Credits: Directed by Fred Zinnemann. Screen play by Daniel Taradash. Based upon the novel by James Jones. Produced by Buddy Adler. Director of photography: Burnett Guffey. Art director: Cary Odell. Film editor: William Lyon. Set decorator: Frank Tuttle. Assistant director: Earl Bellamy. Technical advisor: Brig. Gen. Kendall J. Fiedler, Ret. Gowns by Jean Louis. Musical director: Morris Stolof. Background music by George Duning. Song: "Re-enlistment Blues" by James Jones, Fred Karger, Robert Wells. Makeup by Clay Campbell. Hair styles by Helen Hunt. Sound Engineer: Lodge Cunningham. Orchestrations by Arthur Morton. Western Electric Recording. A Columbia Pictures Corporation presentation.

Additional Cast: Jean Willes (Annette), Claude Akins (Sgt. Baldy Dhom), Robert Karnes (Sgt. Turp Thornhill), Robert Wilke (Sgt. Henderson), Douglas Henderson (Cpl. Champ Wilson), George Reeves (Sgt. Maylon Stark), Don Dubbins (Friday Clark), John Cason (Cpl. Paluso), Kristine Miller (Georgette), John Bryant (Capt. Ross), Joan Shawlee (Sandra), Angela Stevens (Jean), Mary Carver (Nancy), Vicki Bakken (Suzanne), Margaret Barstow (Roxanne), Della Salvi (Billie), Willis Bouchey (Lieutenant Colonel), Al Sargent (Nair), William Lundmark (Bill), Weaver Levy (Bartender), Tyler McVey (Maj. Stern), Brick Sullivan (Military guard), Carleton Young (Col. Ayres), Fay Roope (Gen. Slater), Moana Gleason (Rose), Freeman Lusk (Col. Wood), Robert Pike (Maj. Bonds); Patrick Miller, Robert Healy, Norman Wayne, Joe Sargent, Mack Chandler, Edward Laguna, John D. Veitch, John Davis, Carey Leverette (Soldiers).

Additional Credits: Cinematography: Floyd Crosby. Bugle tutor: Manny Klein. Technical advisor: Sgt. Bill Mullen. Sound recording: John P. Livadary. Opened in New York City on August 5, 1953.

Other Versions: The film was remade twice for television, as a miniseries in 1979 (directed by Buzz Kulik), and in 1980 (directed by Ray Austin, Rick Hauser). *The Thin Red Line* (also filmed twice, in 1964 and 1998) is based on James Jones's 1962 sequel to his novel.

Awards: Academy Awards for Best Picture, Director, Writing—Screenplay, Actor in a Supporting Role (Sinatra), Actress in a Supporting Role (Reed), Cinematography, Film Editing, Sound—Recording.

Available: Columbia TriStar Home Entertainment DVD (2003). ISBN: 1-4049-3069-8. UPC: 0-43396-00868-7.

Published in 1951, *From Here to Eternity* was an immediate best-seller and later a National Book Award winner. Author James Jones based much of the novel on his experiences in the peacetime Army before World War II, depicting a world of rigid social lines, mind-numbing routines, and empty lives. Sex and sadism drove the plot, which focused on four infantrymen, their officers, and the women attracted to them. Harry Cohn purchased the screen rights for $82,000, an enormous sum given the censorship problems inherent to the eight-hundred-page book. Jones tried to adapt it as a screenplay but failed, as did other writers.

It was up to Daniel Taradash, a graduate of Harvard Law School who had worked on the boxing movie *Golden Boy* (1939), to solve the book's plot problems. His main inspiration was to separate the lead character, Robert E. Lee "Prew" Prewitt, from "Fatso" Judson, a vicious sergeant in control of the Stockade at the Schofield Army Barracks near Pearl Harbor. In the novel, Prewitt becomes a victim of Judson, but Taradash had Judson attack Angelo Maggio, a hapless private from New Jersey, instead. Taradash also condensed Prewitt's background, making him more recognizably heroic than the character in the novel.

At first an advertising copywriter, producer Buddy Adler had made award-winning shorts at MGM before entering the Signal Corps during World War II. He left as a lieutenant colonel; he also maintained a number of contacts at the Pentagon. They were crucial in obtaining the Army's cooperation during the film. The Army insisted on two changes to the script. Director Fred Zinnemann felt the first—eliminating beatings in the Stockade—an improvement over the screenplay. The second, which forces a sort of happy ending for one plot line where Jones had employed irony and sarcasm instead, was more upsetting. Zinnemann later wrote, "It makes me sick every time I see it."

Zinnemann and Cohn clashed frequently over casting. Cohn wanted Aldo Ray, a burly, gruff-voiced contract player, for Prewitt; Zinnemann insisted on Montgomery Clift, whom he had worked with on the Berlin-based postwar movie *The Search* (1948). After all, Zinnemann argued, Jones had written than Prewitt was a "deceptively slim young man." Cohn wanted Joan Crawford to play Karen Holmes, the barren, promiscuous wife of the G Company captain; the star even did wardrobe tests. Backed by Taradash and Adler, Zinnemann got Deborah Kerr, whose previous roles had been limited to well-mannered ladies. Zinnemann was against casting Donna Reed as Lorene, a prostitute in a brothel in the novel and a hired dancing partner in a private club in the film. But Cohn had Reed appear in three screen tests, eventually winning over the director.

Eli Wallach had been everyone's idea for Maggio, and he, too, made tests for the studio. But his previous commitment to Elia Kazan left the role open as the start of shooting approached. Frank Sinatra campaigned assiduously for the role. The singer had suffered career reversals, and his troubled marriage to Ava Gardner was fodder for the tabloid press. Nervous tensions weakened his singing voice, affecting his recording contract and nightclub appearances. And in the McCarthy era, Sinatra's overtly liberal politics were viewed as a handicap.

Sinatra found out that the role was open while he was in Africa, where Gardner was appearing in *Mogambo* for director John Ford. The singer (or

Gardner) paid his own fare back to Hollywood for a screen test, and he later accepted a paltry $8000 (plus star billing) for the role. Maggio, a sacrificial martyr who is beaten to death for daring to stand up to injustice, could not have been a better choice for rehabilitating Sinatra's career. While his role doesn't make much psychological sense (few parts in the film do), Sinatra performed it with such conviction, and obvious desperation, that he won an Academy Award.

Clift was earnest as well, although he was frankly less believable as a bugler and boxer than he was as a cowboy in *Red River* (1948). (Despite the use of stunt doubles, Zinnemann had considerable trouble with Clift's one big boxing scene, shooting it four different times, including back in Hollywood.) But he and Zinnemann understood that the role of Prewitt, like Maggio another martyr, really played off the other people in the story. Prewitt remains passive until others open up to him, and even then he is withdrawn from events and feelings. The real star of the story is 1st Sergeant Warden, played by Burt Lancaster in a performance that offers finely calibrated expressions of repressed anger, self-loathing, and tamped-down desire. (To get him, Cohn had to pay producer Hal Wallis $150,000, plus money for the script and stars of *Bad for Each Other*, a stalled Wallis project.)

Zinnemann shot the film in forty-one days, mostly in Hawaii, but also on the same backlot where he filmed *High Noon*. Given such a tight schedule, he was forced to adopt a utilitarian style, relying on depth of field to stage scenes on several planes of action. Zinnemann brought the camera in tight on the actors during their love scenes, including one on a beach near Diamond Head that has become one of the hallmarks of 1950s screen erotica. Kerr in a bikini and Lancaster in swimming trunks embracing in the pounding surf was a greater threat to censors of the time than the fact that she was playing a married woman. The wet hair, hungry kisses, and Lancaster's chiseled, acrobat's body looming over the aroused Kerr— this was as hot as commercial movies got at the time. A later scene on a nightclub patio is more subdued but even more passionate. In a softly diffused close-up, Kerr, her mouth parted, positively twists with desire in Lancaster's arms.

Few moviegoers at the time were fooled by the film's ostensible themes of lost innocence, the futility of life, how perverse rules corrupted the Army, etc. They went to see the stars, the illicit sex, the Japanese attack on Pearl Harbor (shown in a combination of stock footage, model shots, and patently false re-enactments), and, incidentally, the Hawaiian landscape. (Cohn also threw them country music phenomenon Merle Travis, who sings the minor pop hit "Re-enlistment Blues" twice.) Rambling, lurid, dramatically unbalanced, *From Here to Eternity* seemed illuminating and sophisticated at the time because it flirted with adult themes while still providing what the masses wanted. Prewitt takes a stand against sadism, then has a switchblade fight in an alley.

After battles before and during production, Cohn earned further enmity from Zinnemann by insisting on a running time under two hours. Cut were scenes in which Clift's character fears that the Germans were attacking Hawaii, and a sort of improvised blues song in the barracks. But Cohn never doubted the value of the finished film. For the New York opening, he used his name for the first time in advertisements in a personal appeal to viewers. The film opened to tremendous business, earning almost $20 million (on a budget of around $2.5 million) and becoming the biggest moneymaker in Columbia's history. All five stars were nominated for Academy Awards; the film eventually won eight Oscars, tying the record for *Gone With the Wind* (1939).

The Band Wagon

Jack Buchanan and Fred Astaire performing "I Guess I'll Have to Change My Plan" in *The Band Wagon*.

MGM, 1953. Sound, color, 1.33. 112 minutes.
Cast: Fred Astaire (Tony Hunter), Cyd Charisse (Gabrielle Gerard), Oscar Levant (Lester Marton), Jack Buchanan (Jeffrey Cordova), Nanette Fabray (Lily Marton), James Mitchell (Paul Byrd), Robert Gist (Hal Benton).
Credits: Directed by Vincente Minnelli. Story and screenplay: Betty Comden, Adolph Green. Adapted from the Broadway revue *The Band Wagon* (1931) with songs by Howard Dietz and Arthur Schwartz. Produced by Arthur Freed. Associate producer: Roger Edens. Directors of photography: Harry Jackson, George Folsey. Art direction: Cedric Gibbons, Preston Ames. Set decoration: Edwin B. Willis, Keogh Gleason. Musical numbers designed by Oliver Smith. Musical direction: Adolph Deutsch. Orchestrations: Conrad Salinger, Skip Martin, Alexander Courage. Dances and Musical Numbers Staged by Michael Kidd. Edited by Albert Akst. Special effects: Warren Newcombe. Costumes: Mary Ann Nyberg. Technicolor color consultants: Henri Jaffa, Robert Brower. Print process: Ansco Color. Recording supervisor: Douglas Shearer. Makeup: William Tuttle. Hairstylist: Sydney Guilaroff. Assistant director: Jerry Thorpe. Western Electric Sound System.
Additional Cast: Thurston Hall (Colonel Tripp), Ava Gardner (Herself), LeRoy Daniels (Shoeshine man), Madge Blake (Gushy woman), Sue Casey (Tall woman in penny arcade), Matt Mattox (Specialty dancer), Dee Trunell and Jimmie Thompson (Troupe members), Steve Forrest (Man), Dee and Eden Hartford, Julie Newmar (Girls in "Private Eye" number).
Additional Credits: Cyd Charisse's vocals dubbed by India Adams. Released August 7, 1953.
Available: Warner Home Video DVD (2005). ISBN: 0-7907-9566-3. UPC: 0-12569-69842-0.

The last of the unequivocally great Arthur Freed musicals, *The Band Wagon* came together almost by accident. Having scored a windfall exploiting his song library in *Singin' in the Rain* (1952), Freed was determined to do the same favor for Howard Dietz, a part-time lyricist and full-time MGM publicist who is given credit for coming up with the studio's Leo the Lion logo. Dietz had started out writing lyrics for revues back in New York, generally but not always with composer Arthur

Schwartz. *The Band Wagon*, originally staged in 1931, marked the last time Fred Astaire and his sister Adele appeared together in a show.

Music from the revue had been used as recently as 1949 in the Twentieth Century-Fox musical *Dancing in the Dark*, which may have been the inspiration behind Freed's project. He tried to marry the score to "Strategy of Love," a short story by Peter Viertel, but gave up after a few months. Then he asked Betty Comden and Adolph Green, the screenwriters for *Singin' in the Rain*, to come up with a story based on the ersatz oompah tune "I Love Louisa." The writers, avid theater movie fans since their days as sketch artists known as "The Revuers," concocted a story about putting on a Broadway show, from financing and casting to rehearsals to out-of-town tryouts to opening night. They based several of their characters on real-life artists. Maniacal stage director Jeffrey Cordova (played by Jack Buchanan) was a combination of Orson Welles, Norman Bel Geddes, and José Ferrer. The playwright team of Lily and Lester Marton (Nanette Fabray and Oscar Levant) could have been Comden and Green themselves, or Garson Kanin and Ruth Gordon, or even Oscar Levant and his wife June.

Comden and Green wrote their lead character Tony Hunter specifically for Fred Astaire. They built in semi-affectionate jibes about the dancer's well-known phobias: his height, his dislike of lifting dancing partners, his early career. What gave their portrayal real bite was the fact that Hunter, like Astaire himself, was considered something of a dinosaur. Astaire had just finished *The Belle of New York*, an expensive flop set at the turn of the century, and was wary of anything that reeked of fantasy or the past. It had been over fifteen years since *Top Hat*, and yet the dancer was still associated with elegant clothes in black-and-white settings, with what one character refers to as *Swinging Down to Panama*.

Astaire's films were predominantly romances, with his role as a hoofer either an impediment or a boon to love, but not the central point of the story. But *The Band Wagon* has so much plot that there is little time for a love affair. Perhaps as a result, Astaire has only one traditional production number with his dancing partner, Cyd Charisse. This was a breakthrough role for Charisse—in the previous year's *Singin' in the Rain*, she wasn't even allowed to speak. Her character here, Gabrielle Gerard, has connections to Charisse's real life. Both had

training in ballet, and both fell in love with their teachers; Charisse ended up marrying hers.

Actor Clifton Webb, a song-and-dance man in Dietz/Schwartz revues before he became famous as a bilious curmudgeon in films like *Laura* (1944), was originally a candidate for the part of Jeffrey Cordova. He suggested Jack Buchanan, a fixture in West End musicals and an occasional performer in films. Buchanan delivers a finely calibrated performance, playing someone egotistical but not conceited, pretentious but also talented.

Director Vincente Minnelli brought to *The Band Wagon* an arsenal of tracking and crane shots, and a willingness to shoot everything possible in one long take. He may also be responsible for the shrill performances from Oscar Levant, MGM's house hypochondriac, and Nanette Fabray, the star of several Broadway plays. This was her first adult film role, and, surprisingly, her only musical one.

Shooting started in September 1952, and lasted until the following January. Minnelli's methods drove Astaire to a minor and temporary breakdown during the scene that leads into "I Love Louisa." When he apologized, Minnelli responded, "Oh, that's perfectly all right, Fred, I drive everybody crazy."

Choreographer Michael Kidd was working on his second film after a successful decade on Broadway. In his study of Astaire's dances, John Mueller dismissed Kidd as "a choreographer with a predilection for acrobatics and sight gags," and it's true that there are very few "straight" numbers in the film. Of these, none is straighter than "I Guess I'll Have to Change My Plans," an ingratiating soft-shoe routine with Astaire and Buchanan both in top hat and tails, and the only number in the film that could actually work on a stage.

The first version of *The Band Wagon* ran almost two-and-a-half hours, causing Freed to order four numbers to be cut. Oscar Levant's piano solo was deleted, as was a tantalizing Astaire solo to "Got a Bran' New Suit," which had previously been danced to by Eleanor Powell. Charisse's "Two-Faced Woman" was also cut, although a version of it exists as a DVD extra.

The twelve-minute "Girl Hunt Ballet" remained intact. A gigantic closing production number had become de rigueur in Freed films. Perhaps because it is narrated, the "Girl Hunt Ballet" has more of a plot than the closing numbers in *An American in Paris* and *Singin' in the Rain*. Astaire is game, but the piece seems more Kidd's work than his. Opening with a reference to *42nd Street*, the piece soon devolves into parodies of Mickey Spillane's hard-boiled prose set to dance. When Cyd Charisse shows up in a Louise Brooks bob, shimmying in a skin-tight, beaded, fringed, and slit red dress, you can see exactly why the Legion of Decency rated *The Band Wagon* "Morally objectionable in part for all."

Released on August 7, 1953, *The Band Wagon* earned some $5 million on a budget of approximately $2 million. It received generally good reviews and was nominated for three Oscars, but the immediate perception was that it didn't live up to *Singin' in the Rain*. In his autobiography, *Steps in Time*, Astaire explained the film's style with,

"Our intention was more or less to rib the theatrical side of this story mercilessly in the playing." Remarkably self-effacing, he also wrote, "I liked it although it had some flaws, I suppose. The New York critics raved about it but the Hollywood boys did not." Only later did it become apparent that for many of the people involved, this was their last masterpiece. For better or worse, its most famous numbers today are "Triplets," a novelty song that was painful for the three dancers involved to perform, and "That's Entertainment," a spur-of-the-moment bit Dietz and Schwartz tossed off to help advance the plot. It has since become a sort of signature song for MGM, which used it as the title of three compilation films.

Roman Holiday

Paramount, 1953. Sound, B&W, 1.37. 118 minutes.

Cast: Gregory Peck (Joe Bradley), Audrey Hepburn (Princess Anne/Anya "Smitty" Smith), Eddie Albert (Irving Radovich), Hartley Power (Mr. Hennessy), Margaret Rawlings (Countess Vereberg), Tullio Carminati (General Provno), Paolo Carlini (Mario Delani), Claudio Ermelli (Giovanni), Paolo Borboni (Charwoman), Alfredo Rizzo (Taxi driver), Laura Solari (Secretary), Gorella Gori (Shoe seller).

Credits: Produced and directed by William Wyler. Associate producer: Robert Wyler. Screenplay by Ian McLellan Hunter and John Dighton. Story by Dalton Trumbo. Music score by Georges Auric. Directors of photography: Frank F. Planer, Henri Alekan. Art directors: Hal Pereira, Walter Tyler. Edited by Robert Swink. Costumes: Edith Head. Assistant directors: Herbert Coleman, Piero Musetta. Make-up supervision: Wally Westmore, Alberto De Rossi. Sound recording by Joseph De Bretagne. Western Electric Recording. Filmed at Cinecittà Studios, Rome.

Additional Cast: Heinz Heindrich (Dr. Bonnachoven), John Horne (Master of ceremonies); Count Andrea Eszterhazy, Col. Ugo Ballernini, Ugo De Pascale, Bruno Baschiera (Embassy aides); Princess Alma Cattaneo, Diana Lante (Ladies in waiting); John Fostini, George Higgins, Alfred Brown, John Cortay, Richard McNamara, Sidney Gordon (Reporters at poker game); Tania Weber (Irving's model), Gildo Bocci (Flower seller); Piero Scanziani, Kurt Klinger, Maurice Montabre, Sytskey Galema, Jacques Ferrier, Otto Gross, Julian Cortes Cavanillas, Friedhelm Lampe, Juilo Moriones, Stephen House, Ferdinanad De Aldislo (Reporters at press conference).

Additional credits: Screenwriting by Ben Hecht, Preston Sturges, Valentine Davies. The Screenwriters Guild restored Trumbo's credits in 1992. Production dates: June 23 to October 11, 1952. Premiered in New York City on August 27, 1953.

Awards: Oscars for Best Actress, Costume Design—Black-and-White, Writing—Motion Picture Story (originally awarded to Ian McLellan Hunter, and posthumously in 1993 to Dalton Trumbo).

Other Versions: Remade for television in 1987 (directed by Noel Nosseck).

Available: Paramount DVD (2002). ISBN: 0-7921-7216-5. UPC: 0-97360-62044-3.

The idea for *Roman Holiday* dates to 1948, when Dalton Trumbo wrote a script about a princess fleeing her obligations and a reporter who plans to sell her story to the press. Once Trumbo was blacklisted, the script was sold to Frank Capra under fronting author Ian McLellan Hunter's name. Trumbo's

idea made use of the hoopla surrounding the romance of Great Britain's Princess Margaret with a divorced commoner, but his premise was really a variation on everything from Mark Twain's *The Prince and the Pauper* to *The Poor Little Rich Girl* (1917). It is always gratifying when audiences learn that royalty, heads of state, and the ultra-wealthy yearn to be little people just like them, and it was this aspect of the story that appealed to Capra. He was thinking about Cary Grant and Elizabeth Taylor in the lead roles, but he was also thinking about returning to stories along the lines of *It Happened One Night* (1934). Imagine a younger Clark Gable playing newspaperman Joe Bradley, or Claudette Colbert as the runaway princess, and you can see the approach Capra might have taken with the story.

When Capra's Liberty Films, formed along with colleagues George Stevens and William Wyler, proved too difficult to sustain, he sold the company to Paramount. Executives there balked at his proposed budget for *Roman Holiday*. Capra ended up transferring the script (and one for *Friendly Persuasion*) to William Wyler.

According to Wyler's biographer Jan Herman, one reason the director took on the project was to enjoy the tax advantages of living outside the United States for eighteen months (a reason why Gregory Peck agreed to participate as well).

Paramount agreed to let Wyler shoot in Rome primarily because postwar laws had frozen its profits in various European countries. Wyler tried to cast Taylor and Jean Simmons, then went with newcomer Audrey Hepburn. Born Edda Van Heernstra Hepburn-Ruston in Belgium in 1929, Hepburn studied dance, but also suffered severe privations during World War II. After the war she was cast in bit parts in a few British films, then won the approval of Colette to play the title role in the stage version *Gigi*. She was such a hit on Broadway that Paramount had to pay the play's producers $50,000 to secure her release.

Wyler claimed that Gregory Peck originally didn't want to play reporter Joe Bradley, worried that his part was not as important as Hepburn's. Peck disputed that version in Gary Fishgall's biography. This would not only be his first comic role; Peck was also in the process of starting an affair with nineteen-year-old journalist Veronique Passani.

Wyler liked his movies slower than Capra's often frantic pacing, and he let *Roman Holiday* unfold in a leisurely manner that suggested a production schedule with idle afternoons at outdoor cafés and late-night suppers that stretched into early morning hours. His princess wasn't as haughty as Capra's might have been, and his newspaperman's innate decency was obvious from the start, which meant that the drama in the story had to arise solely from their interaction with each other. The key to his approach was to strip the two lead characters of their resources and strengths.

Unhappy with the script, Wyler hired British writer John Dighton to work on a new version. (Wyler went through several other writers as well.) Dighton continued writing straight through the production, revising scenes and lines on the spot. Shooting began in Rome in June 1952, accompanied by hordes of fans. Wyler shot in expected tourist locations like the Forum and the Pantheon, but he also received access to piazzas, churches, and palaces. A scene at the Palazzo Brancaccio featured genuine aristocrats as extras, just as Wyler cast working journalists for the princess's press conference.

Wyler and Dighton added comic details to emphasize Peck's innocent intentions, and staged many scenes as if they were silent comedy. The delicacy of Wyler's touch was crucial—especially his decisions on how far to take the suggestive scenes, how far to push the romance, how to cope with Hepburn's limited technique. As a director, Wyler favored an eye-level point of view and limited visual flourishes. The camera moves only when it to, pulling ahead ahead of Peck as he walks away from a press conference that has irrevocably altered

his life, for example. *Roman Holiday* catches Wyler just before his style started to congeal. As Peck put it, "He sensed the interplay between actors. There's a whole parade of moments, with nuances and subtexts. He understood them. This was the 'Wyler touch.'"

Peck was so impressed by Hepburn's performance that he insisted that she share top billing with him. He didn't mind Wyler's notoriously slow working methods, saying later, "I don't really see the point in settling for two takes, or three takes, if you can get it better on the thirty-second." The actor and director grew so close that when Peck formed his own production company, he asked Wyler to direct its first project, *The Big Country*.

Hepburn was not quite so open to Wyler's tactics, recalling how he bullied and yelled at her to elicit tears during an important scene. For the most part Wyler was careful with the actress, turning her artless line readings into part of her character's naïveté. Hepburn's light, natural performance is one of the most appealing aspects of the film today—that, and a story line that refuses to press for deeper meanings. *Roman Holiday* is just that: a vacation from movies that browbeat viewers into condemning corruption or bigotry or other postwar vices.

Herman wrote that Wyler viewed *Roman Holiday* as a fairy tale, and most viewers won't have trouble making connections to its Cinderella aspects. For youngsters, the lure of the film can be found in its settings, its fancy dress ball and outdoor dance, and the way the leads keep getting away with childish things. Who wouldn't fall in love under those circumstances? For adults, the story gains weight from the pang of its inevitable outcome. Wyler's instincts really pay off when the film quietly shows the choices its characters make.

Roman Holiday didn't open until the end of August 1953, almost a year after shooting ended. It was an immediate hit, and Hepburn a sensation. At the time Wyler earned his actors more Oscar nominations than any other director. Hepburn continued the tradition, winning an Oscar for her first Hollywood film. *Roman Holiday* also won an Oscar for Best Writing—Motion Picture Story. During the 1954 ceremonies, this was awarded to Ian McLellan Hunter. It wasn't until 1993 that Dalton Trumbo received a posthumous Oscar for his work on the original premise to the script. The restored version of the film, completed in 2002, includes Trumbo's name in the credits.

Little Fugitive

Richie Andrusco as Joey in *Little Fugitive*.

Joseph Burstyn, Inc., 1953. Sound, B&W, 1.37. 81 minutes.

Cast: Richard Brewster (Lennie), Winifred Cushing (Mother), Jay Williams (Pony ride man), Will Lee (Photographer), Charley Moss (Harry), Tommy DeCanio (Charley), Richie Andrusco (Joey).

Credits: Written and directed by Ray Ashley, Morris Engel, Ruth Orkin. Screen play by Ray Ashley. Produced by Ray Ashley, Morris Engel. Photographed by Morris Engel. Music composed and performed by Eddy Manson. Edited by Ruth Orkin and Lester Troob. Sound and music supervised by Lester Troob. Sound effects: Harold Johnson. Sound cutting: Ruth Longwell. Camera design by Charles Woodruff and Morris Engel. Presented by Morris Engel and Ray Ashley.

Additional Cast: Ruth Orkin (Mother on beach).

Additional Credits: Filming dates: July 5 to September 1952. Opened in New York City on October 6, 1953.

Other Versions: Remade in 2006 as *Little Fugitive*, directed by Joanna Lipper.

Available: Kino International DVD *The Films of Morris Engel* (2008). UPC: 738329060923.

Shot on a shoestring budget and released without the help of major distributors, *Little Fugitive* proved that independent filmmaking could make economic as well as creative sense. The film succeeded in part because its creative collaborators saw how to update established movie styles with new technical developments, and because they correctly identified both a workable subject matter and a potential audience. But the real reason why *Little Fugitive* has remained so important lies in its more elusive qualities: a discerning photographic eye, an understanding of the experience of childhood, and unmistakable charm.

Morris Engel, a producer and director as well as cinematographer, was born in Brooklyn in 1918 and raised in Williamsburg and Coney Island. A devotee of Westerns as a child, he decided against attending college in order to join the Photo League, a cooperative group founded in 1936 by Sid Grossman and Sol Libsohn. Engel worked as a cinematographer on Paul Strand's *Native Land* (1939), where he formed an aversion to the heavy tripods needed to steady cameras. As a still photographer, he was on the staff of *PM* magazine, taking many of its cover shots. He joined the Navy during World War II, and was assigned to the Combat Photo Unit 8 under Edward Steichen.

In the Navy Engel met Charles Woodruff, an engineer who adapted the Cunningham Combat Cameras used in the armed services so they could be handheld. By holding the camera against his chest and using a strap around his neck as a brace, Engel could achieve the smooth, steady look of a Hollywood feature film without using a tripod.

After the war Engel met another freelance photographer, Ruth Orkin. Born in California in 1921, she had struggled for years to break into the film industry, working as a messenger at MGM and trying unsuccessfully to land a job in a union. Moving to New York City in 1943, she alternated between taking baby portraits and photos in nightclubs until she eked out a career doing features for magazines like *Life* and *Ladies Home Journal*. Orkin and Engel married in 1952, the same year they made *Little Fugitive*.

The third collaborator was Ray Ashley, a pseudonym for Raymond Abrashkin, a former editor at *PM* magazine and the coauthor of a syndicated comic strip. Ashley also wrote for Young People's Records and developed the "Danny Dunn" series of children's books. Ashley's expertise with children coincided with Engel's background in street photography in and around Coney Island. With a budget of about $30,000, they set out to make a movie about a young boy who runs away from home and ends up on the Coney Island boardwalk.

"Too many of our friends said, 'You don't really have a story' again and again and again," Engel remembered later. He admitted, "It's a super simple story, but there's a great purity to it." Consulting with child psychologists helped them keep plot incidents to a certain level of realism, but what ultimately entranced viewers was the film's honesty and perception about what it meant to be a child. As Engel put it, children can be mean, they will lie and cheat and steal, and it doesn't make sense to ignore those qualities. But *Little Fugitive* still finds and exults in the innocence behind their actions. Like *In the Street* (1948), the film is not so much timeless as out of time altogether. In some ways *Little Fugitive* fleshes out the same situations found in *In the Street*; both films manage to depict childhood without the filter of adult irony or condescension.

A large share of the credit for the film's success should go to seven-year-old Richie Andrusco, found one afternoon on a Coney Island carousel. It took some time for Andrusco to adapt to the presence of the camera, but overall his performance is as unforced and persuasive as any other child actor of his time. But an even more important factor was Engel's cinematography. He would talk later about the freedom his modified camera gave him, but it was his eye for composition that helped make the film so haunting. "I did shoot *Little Fugitive* to a degree as if I was doing stills," he said. "I spent a lot of time at Coney Island shooting candid still photographs and it wasn't all that different."

Filming started on July 5, 1952, and lasted until around Labor Day. While they were working from a script outline, many of the scenes were improvised, or based on small suggestions. The filmmakers had hired a professional editor, but after shooting started he refused to assemble dailies into a rough cut. In desperation Engel turned to Orkin, who originally was only going to put the footage in order. She came up with a cut that daringly lingered over moments and situations that would have been removed from most mainstream product. (Orkin also had a small role in the film, filling in when Engel needed an actress for a scene on the beach.)

The filmmakers could not find anyone to distribute their picture until Joseph Burstyn agreed to open it at the Normandie Theater in Manhattan. "If you wanted to kill a picture in those days, you put it in the Normandie," Engel complained later, adding that it was "a tremendously large handicap" for the film to overcome. When Burstyn, who had been importing features from Italy, died on a flight to Paris, his office manager took over distribution. Remarkably, *Little Fugitive* played for fourteen weeks in New York City, and got over 5,000 bookings across the country.

Filmmakers as disparate as John Cassavetes and François Truffaut championed *Little Fugitive*, and it's easy to trace the film's influence on movies like Truffault's *The Four Hundred Blows* (1959). Documentary filmmaker DA Pennebaker (*Dont Look Back*, 1967) was inspired by the simplicity behind the film. "There were no lights, no sound man, nothing," he said. "I thought that's the way these films are going to go, they're going to go into the cities and into the streets and they're going to really be films about where they are."

Engel and Orkin collaborated on the equally well received *Lovers and Lollipops* (1955). Engel also directed *Weddings and Babies* (1958), starring Viveca Lindfors. But few were willing to follow his appreciation for ordinary, day-to-day life. Engel filmed commercials in the 1960s, then, as Orkin did, returned to still photography. Orkin succumbed to cancer in 1985. Engel, to the end a welcoming and generous filmmaker, died in 2005.

The Living Desert

Walt Disney Productions, 1953. Sound, color, 1.37. 69 minutes.

Credits: Directed by James Algar. Script by James Algar, Winston Hibler, Ted Sears. Associate producer: Ben Sharpsteen. Musical director: Paul Smith. Orchestration: Edward Plumb. Photographed by N. Paul Kenworthy, Jr. and Robert H. Crandall. Additional photography by Stuart V. Jewell, Jack C. Couffer, Don Arlen, Tad Nichols. Narrated by Winston Hibler. Animation effects: Joshua Meador, John Hench, Art Riley. Special process: Ub Iwerks. Sound director: C.O. Slyfield. Sound recording: Harold J. Steck. Film editor: Norman Palmer. Print by Technicolor. RCA Sound System.

Additional Credits: Kenworthy and Crandall photographed all of the material except: bat sequence (Couffer), time-lapse of flowers (Jewell), Colorado River flash flood (Nichols), mud puddles (Arlen). Released November 10, 1953.
Awards: Oscar for Best Documentary—Features.
Available: Walt Disney Video DVD *Walt Disney Legacy Collection—True Life Adventures Vol. 2* (2006). UPC: 786936710236.

The postwar period was one of creative turmoil for Walt Disney and his studio. The propaganda market had dried up, ending Disney's lucrative films made for the government. The studio was still recovering from an animators' strike that led to the formation of a rival company, UPA. Disney toyed with making educational films and filmstrips, but decided that they were not profitable enough. With features like *Song of the South* (1946) and *So Dear to My Heart* (1949), he began moving the studio toward live-action films, which would dominate its output in the coming decades. He also saw promise in the area of nature films. Against his brother Roy's wishes, he authorized the husband-and-wife team of Alfred and Elma Milotte to shoot documentary footage in Alaska. They sent back 100,000 feet of film, most of which Disney turned down. "Too many mines. Too many roads. More animals. More Eskimos," he wired back.

The Milottes then spent a year filming seals on the Pribilof Islands, material that Disney found fascinating. What had been planned as a feature-length documentary on Alaska became *Seal Island* (1948), a half-hour nature film that won an Oscar for Best Short Subject. Other shorts followed, gathered under the umbrella of True-Life Adventures. These were not the first nature documentaries, but they established or refined formulas that would soon be imitated by the rest of the industry.

Most of the True-Life Adventures were directed by James Algar. He could probably be viewed as an editorial supervisor, since the nature footage came from several freelancers as well as staff cameramen. The films were as heavily scored as Disney's cartoons, and in fact Algar used music to help fashion the documentary footage into stories. The True-Life Adventures tended to anthropomorphize animals, through the music but also through the narration, delivered by Disney veteran Winston Hibler. By identifying birds and insects as courting or married couples, and by timing their motions to tangos and square dances, the films turned their subjects into the equivalent of live-action cartoon characters.

In 1949, Disney completed his first completely live-action feature, *Treasure Island*, a hit for a studio that industry experts had judged as floundering. Encouraged, Disney put into action long-standing plans for what would become Disneyland, continued with the production of the animation feature *Peter Pan* (1953), and considered a television series that could make use of his True-Life Adventures shorts.

One of the freelance submissions to the True-Life Adventures series showed a battle between a wasp and a tarantula that was part of research for a doctoral thesis by UCLA graduate student N. Paul Kenworthy, Jr. He filmed on three-walled, waist-high sets built to accommodate his lights and cameras. Because Kenworthy was able to light the sets so carefully, his close-up cinematography captured its subjects in extraordinary detail. Disney hired Kenworthy to photograph more footage, and this makes up the bulk of what became the studio's first feature-length documentary, *The Living Desert*.

Algar combined Kenworthy's material with other freelance footage shot specifically for the script he wrote with Ted Sears and Winston Hibler. To sugarcoat the documentary for moviegoers, and also to brand it as a Disney product, Algar opened the film with animated sequences, and later used animation as a transition between scenes. Hibler's narration was criticized at the time, although it fit the style of other documentary voice-overs such as the "Pete Smith Specialties" at MGM. Hibler used a light, easygoing tone that aimed for informative rather than pompous. Portraying insects and animals as stock figures in a drawing room comedy enabled him to gloss over details about the life-and-death struggles unfolding on the screen.

While Kenworthy's footage was the most complicated in the film, other contributors offered astonishing images, such as the sight of a bobcat perched atop a saguaro, or a coatimundi munching on a scorpion. True, some of the footage was manipulated, and even run in reverse, to make it seem as if insects were dancing. A long sequence of Salton Sea mud puddles bursting in time to a humorous score was neither science nor entertainment. And comments like, "Coatis are born bandits, even to the masks on their faces" diluted the educational value of the film.

The studio's films had been distributed by RKO since the early 1930s. Now owned by Howard Hughes, RKO wanted no part of *The Living Desert*, causing the Disney brothers to form Buena Vista Film Distribution. They released *The Living Desert* as a package with the cartoon *Ben and Me* and the live-action short *Stormy*. Some critics took offense with the documentary, but it was a financial success and an Oscar winner. Disney followed it with *The Vanishing Prairie* (1954), another Oscar winner, and four more features. In all, the series won eight Oscars. The same combination of music, narration, and location cinematography marks most of the nature documentaries being made today.

The Tell-Tale Heart

Columbia, 1953. Sound, color, 1.37. 8 minutes.

Credits: Directed by Ted Parmelee. Story adaptation by Bill Scott, Fred Grable. Produced by Stephen Bosustow. Design and color by Paul Julian. Animation by Pat Matthews. Music by Boris Kremenliev. Camera Work by Jack Eckes. Production manager: Herbert Klynn. As narrated by James Mason. Technicolor. United Productions of America.

Additional Credits: Based on the story by Edgar Allan Poe. Released December 17, 1953.

Available: Learning Corporation of America VHS. Bonus feature on special edition of *Hellboy*, Columbia/TriStar Home Entertainment DVD (2004). ISBN: 1-4049-3592-4. UPC: 0-43396-01317-9.

Made in 1953, when United Productions of America (UPA) was operating at its peak, *The Tell-Tale Heart* was distinct from mainstream animation because it attempted to tell a serious story in a serious manner, without jokes or humor. Documentaries and instructional films had used animation for noncomedic purposes, but cartoons as a whole were considered light or frivolous. Even an "adult" feature like *Fantasia* was leavened with gags and slapstick.

And while an organization like UPA, which considered itself an "anti-Disney" company, might experiment with graphic and musical styles, to step outside the humor genre entirely was a definite risk. Through its distribution deal with Columbia, UPA was assured that *The Tell-Tale Heart* would reach a mainstream audience. However, Columbia would be reluctant to finance unpopular animation, no matter how weighty its message. (UPA head Stephen Bosustow had only recently persuaded Columbia to raise budgets for individual cartoons from $27,000 to $35,000.)

UPA might be making a serious project, but it could still hedge its bet. For one thing, Edgar Allan Poe's "The Tell-Tale Heart" was in the public domain, which meant that writers Bill Scott and Fred Grable could adapt it without cost. Poe's stories had a built-in recognition factor: almost every student in the country would come across his work at one time or another. And while the author had a permanent place in the literary canon, his macabre tales could be potboilers, exploitation stories designed to elicit no more than chills and shrieks. In fact, Poe's story, written in late 1842, was rejected by the *Boston Miscellany* magazine, whose editor asked for "more quiet articles." The story was eventually accepted in *The Boston Pioneer*; its editor, James Russell Lowell, wrote of the author as "three-fifths of him genius and two-fifths sheer fudge."

Poe probably based the story on a robbery and murder committed in 1830 and successfully prosecuted by Daniel Webster. A short story by Charles Dickens, "A Confession Found in a Prison in the Time of Charles the Second," may have been another inspiration. Poe's genius was to adopt the point of view of the criminal, and to present his thoughts in a monologue that resembles the stream of consciousness style employed by twentieth-century writers. The monologue format made the story a favorite of actors, and the insanity that permeates the piece attracted filmmakers as early as 1928, when Charles F. Klein directed *The Telltale Heart* as a short.

Director Ted Parmelee had been a graphic designer at one point, which helps explain why the UPA version of *The Tell-Tale Heart* has such a strong visual style. The film expands on the "one set" strategy used in UPA's earlier *Gerald McBoing-Boing* (1951, a Registry title), adopting a flowing design in which locations and times are suggested by adding or subtracting visual elements, not by cutting or dissolving. Jagged lines indicating the veins of an eyeball will extend across the frame until they represent a broken pitcher on a floor. Rectangular panels will change a staircase into a room. The frame will shift from wide-shot to close-up depending on which visual element is emphasized. (A trade publication at the time suggested that the visual style came from the work of scenic designer Eugene Berman at New York's Metropolitan Opera.)

All of the visual strategies are tied to the psychology of the story, right from the angular, distorted credit sequence that mirrors the mind of the narrator. The film's other elements were just as carefully considered. UPA did not have an in-house musical director, but hired composers on a project-by-project basis. Boris Kremenliev, who supplied the effective score here, was a Bulgarian émigré who taught composition and ethnic music at UCLA. The narration, which lifts several lines directly from the story, was delivered by James Mason, a British actor who had just started work on *A Star Is Born*. With titles like *Odd Man Out* (1947) and *The Man Between* (1953) to his credit, he was an important figure to be doing voice work. He would play a similarly untrustworthy narrator in *Lolita* (1962).

Mason's presence helped assure that *The Tell-Tale Heart* would be treated seriously by reviewers. Still, Bosustow remembers audiences, conditioned by years of cartoon viewing, laughing at the film when it first came out. Critic and historian Leonard Maltin has written that the only fault with the film today is that "it moves too quickly to realize the full potential of its eerie narrative." Although UPA's work had a direct influence on the formation of Zagreb Animation Studios in Yugoslavia, the company struggled financially. By the end of the decade, most of its creative personnel had left. Ted Parmelee, for example, found work directing episodes of *Rocky and Bullwinkle* for Jay Ward Productions.

Eaux d'Artifice

Kenneth Anger, 1953. Sound, B&W with tints and hand coloring, 1.37. 13 minutes.

Cast: Carmillo Salvatorelli (The Water Witch).

Credits: Conceived, directed, photographed, and edited by Kenneth Anger. Camera assistants: Thad and Charles Lovatt. Filmed in the Garden of the Villa D'Este, Tivoli.

Available: Fantoma DVD *The Films of Kenneth Anger, Volume One* (2007). UPC: 6-95026-70482-9. 16m prints from Canyon Cinema (*www.canyoncinema.com*).

Born In Santa Monica, California, in 1932, Kenneth Anger grew up in the heart of an illusory Hollywood, one that shaped his life and career. By his account, he attended dance school with Shirley Temple and was an extra in *A Midsummer Night's Dream* (1935), although he is not listed in Warner Brothers records. He also told interviewers that he made his first film, *Who Has Been Rocking My Dreamboat*, in 1941, at the age of nine. Anger's early films have long been unavailable, although he described them in *Film Culture 31*. For example, *Prisoner of Mars* (1942) was a "science-fiction rendering of the Minotaur myth." In *The Nest* (1943), "a brother and sister relate to mirrors and each other until a third party breaks the balance."

Anger starred as "The Dreamer" in *Fireworks* (1947), a fifteen-minute exploration of gay rape fantasies that quickly became a favorite of underground film societies. He moved to France after graduating from high school; *Fireworks* got him introductions to Jean Cocteau and Anais Nin, and the opportunity to re-edit Sergei Eisenstein's *Que Viva Mexico* (1932). He started his only 35mm film, *Rabbit Moon* (1950), in the Parisian studio Cocteau had used, but didn't edit the footage until 1971. He also began several projects that he was forced to cancel in the face of censorship and financial problems.

Anger's next "official" film was *Eaux d'Artifice*, or "Water Works." (The title is also a pun on *Feux d'Artifice*, or "Fireworks.") Anger received permission to shoot at the Garden of the Villa D'Este, commissioned in 1560 by Cardinal Ippolito II d'Este, and restored in the nineteenth century and again after World War II. He used the garden, famed for its ornate fountains, as the backdrop for what critic P. Adams Sitney called "a single-image film" that culminated in a "union between protagonist and landscape." The protagonist in this case is a Water Witch played by Carmillo Salvatorelli, a circus performer recommended by Italian director Federico Fellini.

For a background score, Anger chose passages from Antonio Vivaldi's *The Four Seasons*, music that was not only appropriate to his classical settings and style, but that provided a rhythmic framework for editing. As Oskar Fischinger did with Bach in *Motion Painting No. 1* (1947), Anger used Vivaldi as both a metronome and as a narrative guide. When Vivaldi's passages increased in speed and urgency, for example, Anger could build tension by cutting his imagery in a rapid pattern. He could also edit in a sort of counterpoint, at times anticipating the music, at times behind the score.

Furthermore, Anger could time his pans and tilts to match the beat of the score. His cinematography ranges from strictly representational to abstract, from easily deciphered wide shots of the garden to close-ups of water, backlit and shot in slow motion until they resemble gleaming jewels arcing across the screen. He employs double-exposures, montages, and dissolves to add narrative connections to his shots. Close-ups of the faces of statues seem to stare menacingly at the Water Witch as she strides through the garden. (Much of the eerie beauty of the film comes from the fact that it was shot on infrared stock and printed with a cyan filter, mimicking the voluptuous look of nitrate.)

In editing the film, Anger used a range of approaches, from a shot-countershot scheme that could be found in any conventional Hollywood feature to a more ambiguous montage that was based on emotion and atmosphere. How much of an artistic leap it was to connect the stormy passages of *The Four Seasons* to water flowing down garden troughs may depend on how ripe for cliché you find Vivaldi. Anger's title, with its multiple puns, could be a sort of pre-emptive strike against such strictly literal interpretations. Perhaps Anger's film is about desire and pursuit, a story about men staring at a begowned figure who is unable to avoid their liquid eruptions. When he originally released the film through Cinema 16, a New York film society, he alluded to "a Firbank heroine lost in a baroque labyrinth." (The largely forgotten Ronald Firbank wrote novels and plays in the early twentieth century that writer Susan Sontag assigned to "the canon of camp.")

Anger returned to the United States to settle an inheritance, which he used to finance *Inauguration of the Pleasure Dome* (1954). His most famous film may be *Scorpio Rising* (1964), which used rock'n'roll music and amateur performers to comment on leather-clad motorcyclists and their culture. Later film projects, like *Kustom Kar Kommandos* and *Lucifer Rising*, fell prey to bizarre twists. Anger is perhaps best known to the public for the books *Hollywood Babylon* and *Hollywood Babylon II*, compendia of scandals, rumors, half-truths, and gossip about Hollywood celebrities.

Salt of the Earth

Independent Productions Corporation, 1954. Sound, B&W, 1.37. 92 minutes.

Cast: Rosaura Revueltas (Esperanza Quintero), Juan Chacón (Ramón Quintero), Will Geer (Sheriff), David Wolfe (Barton), David Sarvis (Hartwell), Mervin Williams (Alexander), Henrietta Williams (Teresa Vidal), Ernest Velásquez (Charley Vidal), Angela Sánchez (Consuelo Ruíz), Joe T. Morales (Sal Ruíz), Clorinda Alderette (Luz Morales), Charles Coleman (Antonio Morales), Clinton Jencks (Frank Barnes), Virginia Jencks (Ruth Barnes), E.A. Rockwell (Vance), William Rockwell (Kimbrough), Frank Talavera (Luis Quintero [Ramón's son]), Mary Lou Castillo (Estella Quintero [Ramón's daughter], Floyd Bostick (Jenkins), Victor Torres (Sebastian Prieto), E.S. Conerly (Kalinsky), Elvira Molano (Mrs. Salazar); Adolfo Barela, Albert Muñoz (Miners), and the Brothers and Sisters of Local 890, International Union of Mine, Mill, and Smelter Workers, Bayard, New Mexico.

Credits: Directed by Herbert J. Biberman. Written by Michael Wilson. Produced by Paul Jarrico. Photography by Stanley Meredith, Leonard Stark. Music by Sol Kaplan. Editing by Joan Laird, Ed Spiegel. Sound: Dick Stanton, Harry Smith. Associate producers: Sonja Dahl Biberman, Adolfo Barela. Assistant directors: Jules Schwerin, David Wolfe. Production manager: Jules Schwerin. Coordinator: Paul Perlin. Expeditor: Irving Fajans. Technicians: Robert Ames, Irving Hentschel, Harry Reif, Herman Lipney, Fred Hudson, John Matthias, Marcia Endore, Mel Kells. An Independent Productions Corporation and International Union of Mine, Mill, and Smelter Workers presentation.

Additional Credits: Initial editing: Barton Hayes. Production dates: December 1952 to March 1953. Premiered in New York City on March 14, 1954.

Available: Pioneer DVD (1999). UPC: 013023002593. MPA Home Video VHS (1987). UPC: 0-38306-13603-5.

Loosely based on a prolonged strike at a New Mexico zinc mine, *Salt of the Earth* brought Hollywood methods to a leftist, anti-capitalist, and pro-union story. Made largely by blacklisted filmmakers, it used real locations and nonactors along with a professional cast and crew. Filming was completed despite the arrest of lead actress Rosaura Revueltas and threats from local mobs. While the film was made available to union groups, churches, and schools, it never received a full-fledged, 35mm, theatrical release.

The actual strike against the Empire Zinc Company lasted some fifteen months through 1951 and 1952. When members of Local 890 of the International Union of Mine, Mill, and Smelter Workers were prohibited by a court order from participating in a picket line, their wives took their place. And when more than eighty-five women were arrested, they brought their young children along with them to jail. Blacklisted writer Paul Jarrico visited Bayard, New Mexico, during the strike, and spoke to Clinton Jencks, representative of Local 890, about turning the incident into a film. He was followed by screenwriter Michael Wilson, who spent five weeks with the workers while preparing a plot outline. Despite winning an Oscar for *A Place in the Sun* (1951), Wilson was also blacklisted.

Jarrico, born in 1915 in Los Angeles, joined the Communist Party during the 1930s, around the time he began writing B-movie scripts for Columbia. Apart from serving in the Merchant Marines and Navy during World War II, he worked steadily at RKO and other studios during the 1940s. Named by his former writing partner Richard Collins and by Budd Schulberg to the House Un-American Activities Committee, Jarrico was barred from the RKO lot by studio owner Howard Hughes. Unlike some of his peers, Jarrico fought back, suing the state of California. He was also determined to keep working, outside the system if necessary.

Jarrico formed Independent Productions Corporation, financed by Simon Lazarus, a California theater owner. Their third partner was Herbert Biberman. He worked in his family's textile business before studying drama at Yale, then joined the Theatre Guild in 1928, directing and acting in its first production, *Red Rust*. Biberman also directed *Green Grow the Lilacs* (the precursor to *Oklahoma!*) before making a few B-movies in Hollywood. He refused to testify at a 1947 hearing, and was named as a Communist by Budd Schulberg in 1950. As one of the original "Hollywood Ten," he spent over a year in jail.

Biberman married Oscar-winning actress Gale Sondergaard in 1930. Another blacklisting victim, she took part in preproduction for *Salt of the Earth*, reading Wilson's script to Bayard workers in March 1952. With the approval of local residents, the story recounted major incidents in the strike, but also focused on two main themes: discrimination against minority workers, and discrimination against women.

The former was not unexpected. In the May 1953 issue of *Frontier*, journalist Elizabeth Kerby noted that the chief of the New Mexico State Police and a local sheriff had both spent a year in jail for torturing a black prisoner. Ninety-seven percent of Local 890 was Mexican-American. Kerby quoted cast member Joe T. Morales: "During war we're Americans. During election, we're Spanish-Americans. The rest of the time we're just damn Mexicans."

But the script's feminist bent was more surprising. In a casting call sent to Mexico in 1952, the producers wrote, "The woman is a doubly oppressed individual . . . not only as a member of this cultural minority, but also as a woman." It was a message that appealed to Revueltas, a respected actress in the Mexican film industry. "I had waited all my life to do this picture," she wrote at the time, happy at the opportunity "to play a role that would honor my people."

Filming started in January on a ranch owned by Alford Roos, a local mining engineer. Days went by without trouble, despite a February 12 article by syndicated columnist Victor Riesel condemning the film as Communist propaganda. But on February 23, Immigration Service officials confiscated Revueltas's passport and visa. The next day, Congressman Donald Jackson, a Republican from California, blasted the production on the floor of the House as "a new weapon for Russia." Revueltas was arrested; she later left the country voluntarily. The cast and crew were threatened when they tried to film in the town of Central. At least one crew member was beaten. Tensions escalated until the State Police arrived. After the filmmakers left on March 7, a local cast member's house burned down in a suspicious fire.

Postproduction proved difficult. Jarrico had to set up secret editing rooms in Topanga Canyon, in Burbank, and in the ladies' room of a Pasadena theater. Editor Barton Hayes turned out to be an government informer, and was forced to quit. Jarrico was afraid to let musicians see the film as they recorded the score. It took more than a year before a release print was ready. Then Jarrico learned that no theater owner would book the film.

Salt of the Earth finally opened at the 86th Street Grande Theatre in New York City on March 14, 1954, almost a year after the screenplay was published in the *California Quarterly*. It received respectful reviews. *Time* said, "The film, within the propagandistic limits it sets, is a work of vigorous art." *Variety* thought it was a "[g]ood, highly dramatic and emotion-charged piece," although its commercial prospects were "practically nil." Jarrico later wrote that the film played in a total of thirteen theaters in the United States. By that time he had left the country for Europe, where *Salt of the Earth* received a more pronounced welcome.

The film had a vigorous afterlife when it was championed in the 1960s by a new generation of critics, and when its creators were allowed to return to the industry. Its impact can be seen in films like *Modesta* (1956), which borrowed its production techniques, and *Harlan County U.S.A.* (1976), which echoed some of its themes in a documentary setting. While it's difficult at times to overlook the picture's condescending attitudes, *Salt of the Earth* marks a crucial step in the evolution of independent filmmaking.

The House in the Middle

National Paint, Varnish and Lacquer Association, 1954. Sound, color, 1.37. 13 minutes.

Credits: Production company: Robert J. Enders, Inc. Sponsored by the National Paint, Varnish and Lacquer Association. Produced by The National Clean Up—Paint Up—Fix Up Bureau, with the cooperation of the Federal Civil Defense Administration. Copyrighted May 3, 1954.

Available: The National Archives. Online at the Internet Archive (*www. archive.org*).

Aimed at an older audience than *Duck and Cover* (1952), *The House in the Middle* attempted to reassure viewers about nuclear warfare, believed to be a real possibility in the 1950s. The film adopts the techniques of advertising, documentaries, and fiction features, blending these styles in a way that inadvertently reveals more than intended about cultural attitudes of the time. Like the other titles produced either by or with the cooperation of the Federal Civil Defense Administration, *The House in the Middle* had a dual purpose: to simultaneously frighten the public about nuclear bombs, and to show how it could survive an attack.

An atom bomb explodes in the opening shot of the film, only to be tamed by the title and credits superimposed over the mushroom cloud. Viewers were told that the film was produced by "The National Clean Up—Paint Up—Fix Up Bureau," an ostensibly impartial organization that presumably had no mandate to distort or twist the facts. The "bureau" was actually a campaign to encourage neighborhood pride through house painting—and, not incidentally, sell house paint—started in 1912 by the National Paint, Oil, and Varnish Association. In 1933 the name of the organization was changed to the National Paint, Varnish, and Lacquer Association, and it was this group that financed the film. (Now known as the National Paint and Coatings Association, its mission in part is to serve as "the industry's chief advocate and spokesperson before the government and public.")

The film itself was produced by Robert J. Enders, Inc., an advertising agency founded by Enders, who also produced largely patriotic radio shows like *Our Land Be Bright* (1947–48). The impact of the film is dependent on its narration, which serves to interpret and define the stock footage that makes up almost all of the running time. Apart from a few pick-up shots of urban houses and some closing shots of various spruce-up efforts, the only original material in the film was filmed on a single office set. There the narrator sits at a desk, a file cabinet with the triangular Civil Defense logo toward the left of the frame, and six photographs of houses used in the nuclear test to the right. It was the same basic set-up used in commercials whenever an expert was about to deliver "facts." In this case, that narrator warns viewers,

"A house that's neglected may be a house that's doomed—in the atomic age."

The bulk of *House* consists of film taken by the government at the Nevada Proving Grounds (later named the Nevada Test Site) that intends to prove just that. Fixed cameras document the destruction of numerous props after the detonation of an atomic bomb. "Rundown," "untidy" "eyesores" burst into flame. "Spick and span" houses survive. This point is repeated through three separate tests, each one a bit more frightening.

While the film may be misguided, even duplicitous, about the actual effects of an atomic blast, at the time *The House in the Middle* was serving other purposes besides shocking viewers into buying paint and sweeping up the yard. The sheer number of nuclear blasts documented here and elsewhere was proof of the power of the government and a warning to other countries. The narrator's references to filthy slums and alleys separated viewers from the "others" who threatened danger. Not just subversives who left magazines and newspapers scattered across their living rooms, but anyone who didn't conform: immigrants, non-whites, potential Communists.

Unfortunately for the filmmakers, the house pointed to as well-kept in one test actually suffered more damage than the rundown one. Even more dumbfounding than trying to claim that paint will protect homes from atom bombs is the effort the government took to prove the point.

In 1956, Enders produced another film for the Federal Civil Defense Administration, this one directed by Robert L. Friend, written by Will H. Connelly, and financed by the Burroughs Corporation. The National Archives holds copies of a second version of *The House in the Middle*, one that is in black-and-white and is six minutes long. It contains the same footage of nuclear testing, but has a different actor and office set. This version identified the experiment as "Operation Doorstep," and urged viewers to obtain free copies of the government pamphlet *Fire Fighting for Householders*. Without the financial backing of the National Paint, Varnish and Lacquer Association, its conclusion was slightly different: "Be prepared if disaster strikes! Remember, Civil Defense housekeeping saved the house in the middle."

Johnny Guitar

Republic, 1954. Sound, Color, 1.37. 110 minutes.

Cast: Joan Crawford (Vienna), Sterling Hayden (Johnny Guitar/Johnny Logan), Mercedes McCambridge (Emma Small), Scott Brady (Dancin' Kid), Ward Bond (John McIvers), Ben Cooper (Turkey Ralston), Ernest Borgnine (Bart Lonergan), John Carradine (Old Tom), Royal Dano (Corey), Frank Ferguson (Marshal Williams), Paul Fix (Eddie), Rhys Williams (Andrews), Ian MacDonald (Pete).

Credits: Directed by Nicholas Ray. Screen Play by Philip Yordan. Based on the novel by Roy Chanslor. Music: Victor Young. Song "Johnny Guitar" by Peggy Lee and Victor Young. Sung by Peggy Lee. Director of photography: Harry Stradling. Art director: James Sullivan. Assistant director: Herb Mendelson. Sound: T.A. Carman, Howard Wilson. Costumes designed by Sheila O'Brien. Set decorations: John McCarthy, Edward G. Boyle. Special effects: Howard and Theodore Lydecker. Film editor: Richard L. Van Enger. Makeup supervision: Bob Mark. Hair stylist: Peggy Gray. Optical effects: Consolidated Film Industries. Trucolor by Consolidated. RCA Sound System. A Herbert J. Yates presentation.

Additional Cast: Will Wright (Ned), John Maxwell (Jake), Robert Osterloh (Sam), Frank Marlowe (Frank), Trevor Bardette (Jenks); Sumner Williams, Sheb Wooley, Denver Pyle, Clem Harvey (Posse).

Additional Credits: Screenwriting by Ben Maddow (fronted by Philip Yordan) and Nicholas Ray. Produced by Nicholas Ray. Production dates: October to December 1953. Premiered in New York City on May 26, 1954.

Available: Republic Entertainment Inc. VHS (1995). ISBN: 0-7820-0297-8. UPC: 0-17153-21273-0.

A film that came about through a peculiar confluence of events and people, *Johnny Guitar* is a defiantly off-kilter Western with an ardent cult following. It has been interpreted as an anti–McCarthy tract, a subversively feminine reading of the Western genre, and a bluntly Freudian take on the frontier ethos. On its release, it failed to please any of its creators, or the public at large, for that matter.

The source novel was written by Roy Chanslor, a former newspaper reporter who had worked on dozens of largely undistinguished films in the 1930s and 1940s. In addition to screenwriting, he turned to pulp novels after World War II. Chanslor dedicated *Johnny Guitar* to Joan Crawford, who optioned the rights; the project ended up at Republic Studios, with Nicholas Ray attached to direct. Chanslor wrote a draft of a screenplay with Ray which he handed in on June 10, 1953. This was later revised by Ray and Ben Maddow, who had been blacklisted shortly after working on *The Asphalt Jungle* (1950). Philip Yordan, who was working at the time on his own Western, the Oscar-winning *Broken Lance* (1954), fronted for Maddow and reportedly split his screenwriting fee.

Simon and Schuster printed the novel in 1953; a year later, it was reissued in paperback by Pocket Books, complete with a signed testimonial on the back cover from Crawford. The actress had burned through studio contracts at MGM and Warner Brothers, and like many of her contemporaries was basically freelancing her way through the 1950s. Crawford's screen persona remained fixed despite changing times. She was almost invariably cast as a career woman lusted after and betrayed by male leads, and as she aged the list of occupations available to her became increasingly sordid. In a few years she would be reduced to demeaning roles in low-budget horror films. *Johnny Guitar* was her only film for Republic Pictures.

The Republic studio was largely the work of Herbert Yates, a salesman who was instrumental in the film careers of Gene Autry, Roy Rogers, and John Wayne. Consolidated Film Industries, the processing lab of choice for independent studios, was owned by Yates, and he used it as a springboard for merging companies like Mascot and Monogram into Republic. The studio profited from serials and B-movies, almost exclusively Westerns. The cheapest were shot in seven days for $30,000; "deluxe" Republics had budgets of $300,000, with a three-week schedule.

But Yates wanted the prestige associated with a major studio, and periodically sank huge budgets into "A" pictures like Allan Dwan's *Sands of Iwo Jima* (1949) and John Ford's *The Quiet Man* (1952). He also tried to make his wife Vera Hruba Ralston a star, casting her in twenty films, only two of which turned a profit. Republic stockholders sued Yates over Ralston; meanwhile, both Autry and Rogers sued Yates when he sold their films to television. The real death knell for the studio was the collapse of the B-movie market as younger filmgoers switched to watching TV. *Johnny Guitar* would be Republic's last "A" picture, and the last in Consolidated's Trucolor process.

For Ray, a former folklorist and student of Frank Lloyd Wright, *Johnny Guitar* would be his first opportunity to work in the Western genre, as well as his first feature job after the end of his contract at RKO. Ray had no real affinity for Westerns and did not think much of the project or of Crawford. But he was fascinated with injecting psychological symbolism into his work, and was developing a sort of mannered, loping style of filming in which close-ups and insert shots register as statements or examples of character strengths and flaws. At times he brought a new spin to stock Western situations—how a bartender would slide a mug of beer down a saloon bar, for example. Ray turned the bit into a juggling act that showed off the dexterity of the story's gunslinger, Johnny Guitar.

The plot concerns a broken love affair between Vienna, a saloon hostess, and Johnny Guitar, aka Johnny Logan. They encounter each other again in the middle of a sort of range war among ranchers, miners, and the railroad, played out before the towering red rocks of Sedona, Arizona. Arson, lynching, and a bank robbery propel the characters to deadly confrontations. Chases and fistfights were the meat and potatoes of Republic Westerns, and Ray had to include them whether he wanted to or not. The fact that he staged them in so perfunctory a manner may have been a result of budgetary limitations or just plain indifference. Ray exploited the personal animosity between Crawford and costar Mercedes McCambridge, goading McCambridge in particular into a wooden, stilted parody of a sexually repressed spinster.

Crawford, who had hoped to cast Claire Trevor in the McCambridge role, insisted that her close-ups be shot on a soundstage rather than on location, adding another level of artificiality to the movie. Her face frozen in a Kabuki-like mask, her lips a vivid slash of red, Crawford makes no allowances for the Western settings—she could have just come off the set of *Mildred Pierce* (1945).

Ray had to find a way to surround this immovable object with some semblance of life. He tried color, splashing bright reds across the screen, and architecture, fashioning bizarrely inappropriate interiors. He introduced homosexual subtexts, and delighted in screenwriter Maddow's thinly veiled references to the McCarthy witch hunts. The script portrayed vigilante justice as inherently evil, and forced Ward Bond, one of the most right-wing actors in Hollywood, into implicitly rejecting the findings of the House Un-American Activities Committee hearings through his screen character. The fact that Sterling Hayden named names may have tempted Ray to let the actor struggle through a bad John Wayne imitation without comment or guidance.

Johnny Guitar doesn't look or sound like any other Western of its era, but "different" doesn't necessarily mean good. Writing and acting can still be bad despite highbrow intentions and stylistic daring. The film's fans tend to be those who dislike Westerns to begin with, or who delight in Crawford's camp appeal. On the other hand, filmmaker Martin Scorsese considers *Johnny Guitar* "one of the great operatic works of the cinema," and Bernardo Bertolucci cited its influence in his screenplay for Sergio Leone's *Once Upon a Time in the West* (1968). Ray's next Registry film is *Rebel Without a Cause* (1955).

Seven Brides for Seven Brothers

MGM, 1954. Color, sound, 2.55. 101 minutes.
Cast: The Pontipee Brothers: Howard Keel (Adam), Jeff Richards (Benjamin), Russ Tamblyn (Gideon), Tommy Rall (Frank), Marc Platt (Daniel), Matt Mattox (Caleb), Jacques d'Amboise (Courtesy New York City Ballet) (Ephraim). The Brides: Jane Powell (Milly), Julie Newmeyer [Newmar] (Dorcas), Nancy Kilgas (Alice), Betty Carr (Sarah), Virginia Gibson (Liza), Ruta Kilmonis [Lee] (Ruth), Norma Doggett (Martha). The Townspeople: Ian Wolfe (Rev. Elcott), Howard Petrie (Pete Perkins), Earl Barton (Harry), Dante DiPaolo (Matt), Kelly Brown (Carl), Matt Moore (Ruth's Uncle), Dick Rich (Dorcas' Father), Marjorie Wood (Mrs. Bixby), Russell Simpson (Mr. Bixby).
Credits: Directed by Stanley Donen. Screen Play by Albert Hackett & Frances Goodrich and Dorothy Kingsley. Based on the story "The Sobbin' Women" by Stephen Vincent Benet. Produced by Jack Cummings. Director of photography: George Folsey. Art directors: Cedric Gibbons, Urie McCleary. Film editor: Ralph E. Winters. Color by Ansco. Color consultant: Alvord Eiseman. Assistant director: Ridgeway Callow. Costumes designed by Walter Plunkett. Recording supervisor: Douglas Shearer. Set decorations: Edwin B. Willis, Hugh Hunt. Special effects: A. Arnold Gillespie, Warren Newcombe. Hair styles by Sydney Guilaroff. Make-up created by William Tuttle. Song lyrics by Johnny Mercer, music by Gene de Paul. Musical direction: Adolph Deutsch. Musical supervision: Saul Chaplin. Dances and musical numbers staged by Michael Kidd. Orchestrations: Alexander Courage, Conrad Salinger, Leo Arnaud.
Additional Cast: Anna Q. Nilsson (Mrs. Elcott), Larry Blake (Drunk), Walter Beaver (Lem).

Additional Credits: Production dates: November 30, 1953 to February 2, 1954. Premiered in Houston, Texas, on July 15, 1954.
Awards: Oscar for Best Music—Scoring of a Musical Picture (Adolph Deutsch, Saul Chaplin).
Available: Warner Home Video DVD (2000). ISBN: 0-7907-4421-X. UPC: 0-12569-50652-7.

The impetus for *Seven Brides for Seven Brothers* came from Jack Cummings, a nephew of MGM studio head Louis B. Mayer. Cummings started out as a script clerk, working his way up to short subject director and then to producer of films like *Born to Dance*, *Broadway Melody of 1938*, and *Kiss Me Kate*. He purchased the screen rights to Stephen Vincent Benet's short story "The Sobbin' Women" from Joshua Logan for $40,000, then assigned the screenwriting team of Frances Goodrich and Albert Hackett to write an adaptation. He also selected director Stanley Donen, who had shot two mediocre films after codirecting *Singin' in the Rain* with Gene Kelly.

This was a chance for Donen to prove himself apart from Kelly, who was working on the same lot on an adaptation of the Broadway musical *Brigadoon*. But Donen faced serious problems. First, he would have to shoot in CinemaScope, a widescreen process that was still considered experimental. The studio was so worried that it ordered Donen to shoot simultaneously a "flat" version with normal cameras; this version has resurfaced as an extra on some DVD reissues.

Mayer had been ousted from the studio a few years earlier; Dore Schary, his replacement, decided to commit more funds to *Brigadoon* than to *Brides*. Donen's budget was halved, meaning that he could no longer shoot on location. Unfortunately, the CinemaScope process made it quite apparent to viewers that Donen was using painted backdrops. "The backdrops always hurt the picture," he said later. The director also hoped to hire composer Harold Arlen to work with lyricist Johnny Mercer on the score, but Mercer's schedule forced Donen to accept Gene de Paul instead. "Cummings wanted to use old American country songs," he said, an approach that might have been more rewarding than de Paul's tunes.

Howard Keel, cast as the lead by Cummings after they worked together on *Kiss Me Kate*, tried to get Donen fired for George Sidney. "I loved working with Jack," Keel said later. "He was the hero behind *Seven Brides for Seven Brothers*. That movie was made in 34 days, and Jack set it up so well that *I* could have shot it." Keel may have been miffed because his character is absent from large portions of the film, but no one on the film could have been happy with the way the studio was handling the project.

One move everyone agreed on was hiring choreographer Michael Kidd. Exhausted after working on the stage musical *Can-Can*, Kidd had to be persuaded to take on the project. He agreed only on the provision that there would be no production numbers. "I'll stage the songs as *scenes*," he insisted. "There is to be no dancing in the movie." Kidd choreographed the songs by himself, searching for the plot points in the songs, working out routines for each brother, before rehearsing with the cast.

He broke his own rule for the film's centerpiece, the barnstorming sequence in which the brothers compete against townsfolk over potential "brides." Kidd had propmen spread construction props like lumber and barrels over an empty soundstage, then started experimenting with them. Donen pointed out that since Keel's character was already married, and contract player Jeff Richards couldn't dance, the sequence needed only five of the brothers. But with five rivals and five women, that still meant Kidd had to account for fifteen dancers. It took three weeks to prepare the sequence, and three days to shoot it. Russ Tamblyn, trained as a gymnast, started competing with Tommy Rall over who could perform the more daring stunt, adding to the sequence's sense of derring-do. Some critics consider this an athletic high point of dance on film.

Kidd switched the setting for "I'm a Lonesome Polecat" from the bunkhouse to a wintry forest, and persuaded Donen to shoot the entire number in a single take, a risky maneuver. His efforts to challenge the style and restrictions of the musical form were largely offset by the other elements of the film—notably, weak songs, a script lacking in character development, and the artificial gloss MGM typically applied to costumes, sets, and orchestrations. In their defense, Kidd and Donen were hamstrung by a plot with too many characters—almost every action in the script had to be multiplied six times. But the most difficult aspect of the film to come to grips with today is its casually contemptuous treatment of women. *Seven Brides* takes modern-day concerns like stalking, date rape, abduction, and incest, wraps them up in motherhood and patriotism, and offers them as musical comedy. After the advances achieved in musicals like *Oklahoma!* and *Carousel*, *Seven Brides* seems today a regrettable regression. "I'm disappointed with the physical look of it," Donen would admit years later, but the "look" of the film is hardly its most significant flaw.

Filming wrapped on February 2, 1954, at a cost of a little over $2.5 million. *Seven Brides* opened at New York City's Radio City Music Hall on July 22. Although the studio did not put much effort into advertising and publicity, the film grossed over $4 million in its initial release, a far better return than *Brigadoon*. Reviews were generally positive, and the barnstorming sequence became the favorite clip for anyone preparing a dance documentary. The participants may not have realized it at the time, but the musical genre had already started its decline.

On the Waterfront

Rod Steiger and Marlon Brando in *On the Waterfront*.

Columbia, 1954. Sound, B&W, 1.37. 108 minutes.

Cast: Marlon Brando (Terry Malloy), Karl Malden (Father Barry), Lee J. Cobb (John Friendly), Rod Steiger (Charley Malloy), Pat Henning (Timothy Dugan), Leif Erickson (Glover [Crime Commission investigator]), James Westerfield (Big Mac), Tony Galento (Truck [bodyguard]), Tami Mauriello (Tullio [bodyguard]), John Hamilton ("Pop" Doyle), John Heldabrand (Mutt), Rudy Bond (Moose), Don Blackman (Luke), Arthur Keegan (Jimmy), Abe Simon (Barney), Eva Marie Saint (Edie Doyle).

Credits: Directed by Elia Kazan. Screenplay by Budd Schulberg. Based upon an original story by Budd Schulberg. Suggested by articles by Malcolm Johnson. Produced by Sam Spiegel. Director of photography: Boris Kaufman. Art director: Richard Day. Film editor: Gene Milford. Music by Leonard Bernstein. Production manager: George Justin. Assistant director: Charles H. Maguire. Sound: James Shields. Script supervisor: Roberta Hodes. Dialogue supervisor: Guy Thomajan. Wardrobe supervision: Anna Hill Johnstone. Wardrobe mistress: Flo Transfield. Hair stylist: Mary Roche. Make-up supervision: Fred Ryle.

Additional Cast: Barry Macollum (Loanshark), Mike O'Dowd (Specs), Martin Balsam (Gilette [Crime Commission investigator]), Fred Gwynne (Slim), Thomas Handley (Tommy Collins), Anne Hegira (Mrs. Collins), Pat Hingle (Jocko [bartender]), Nehemiah Persoff (Cabdriver).

Additional Credits: Premiered in New York City on July 28, 1954.

Awards: Oscars for Best Picture, Actor (Brando), Supporting Actress (Saint), Director, Writing—Story and Screenplay, Editing, Cinematography—Black and White, Art direction—Black and White.

Available: Columbia Home Video DVD (2001). ISBN: 0-7678-0427-9. UPC: 0-43396-78409-3.

In his autobiography, Elia Kazan described how the growing hysteria over the possible Communist infiltration of the movie industry led his collaborator, playwright Arthur Miller, to abandon *The Hook*, a drama set on the New York waterfront. Miller had been researching his idea since 1947; he and Kazan pitched the idea in Hollywood in 1951, while Kazan was preparing *Viva Zapata!* Roy Brewer, a "representative" of the the International Alliance of Theatrical and Stage Employees, so spooked Miller at a meeting with Columbia head Harry Cohn that he withdrew his script.

During the same period Budd Schulberg was also working on a "waterfront" screenplay. He based his project on a Pulitzer Prize–winning series of newspaper articles by Malcolm Johnson, and in fact early drafts of the screenplay centered on an investigative reporter exposing corruption in the longshoremen's union.

Johnson was accused of being a Communist—at the time, the surest method of silencing an opponent—by union head Joseph P. Ryan. Ironically, both Kazan and Schulberg testified as friendly witnesses before the House Un-American Activities Committee (HUAC); both "named names." This decision colors every aspect of what ultimately became *On the Waterfront*, a film that depicts informing in heroic terms.

Kazan's testimony before the HUAC made him a pariah in certain film and theater circles; Schulberg already was one, on the basis of his best-selling novel *What Makes Sammy Run?* His father, B.P. Schulberg, had been the victim of studio politics at Paramount at the end of the silent era; some have seen in his son's career an attempt to respond to his father's problems, and to his own trouble working within the studio system.

Kazan worked closely with Schulberg on the many drafts of *Waterfront*, helping refine the characters and situations. The director's last film—*Man on a Tightrope* (1953), a melodrama about a circus escaping a Communist regime in Europe—had been a box-office failure, and he had trouble selling this idea to studio heads in Hollywood. When Darryl F. Zanuck—a logical choice considering his muckraking films of the 1930s—turned them down, Schulberg got the script to Sam Spiegel, the producer of *The African Queen* (1952).

Frank Sinatra campaigned for the lead role, and may have been cast by Spiegel, but the singer was considered a box-office liability at the time. Kazan then cast Marlon Brando, leaving Spiegel to mollify Sinatra. The director also cast his close collaborator Karl Malden in a pivotal role as Father Barry, based on the real-life Father John Corridan, a priest whose meetings helped expose the corruption in the longshoremen's union. Lee J. Cobb, whose career seemed to have stalled after he starred in Kazan's stage production of *Death of a Salesman*, played John Friendly, the mobster controlling the union. Eva Marie Saint, found according to Kazan from her listing in the *Players' Directory*, was chosen over Elizabeth Montgomery and Joanne Woodward. Appearing in his second film as Terry Malloy's brother Charley was Rod Steiger, a World War II veteran who previously had performed impressively on stage and television.

Kazan's autobiography describes a demanding thirty-six-day shoot in a harsh Hoboken, New Jersey, winter. The cold and the largely location shooting made the actors "miserable-looking human beings." But despite the difficulties, "It's as close as I came to making a film exactly as I wanted." This was the first Hollywood film for cinematographer Boris Kaufman. The brother of Russian film director Dziga Vertov, Kaufman had shot all of Jean Vigo's films, joined the French Army, then emigrated to the United States in 1942. Kaufman had been shooting documentaries before Kazan tapped him for *Waterfront*. His work here, although influenced by the neorealism popular in Europe, is perhaps more remarkable for its meticulously exposed landscapes.

The centerpiece of *On the Waterfront* is a five-minute scene in the back of a taxicab between Brando and Steiger. In it, Steiger warns his brother Brando not to testify against the union. In turn, Brando accuses Steiger of sabotaging his boxing career. It is a landmark moment from 1950s films, often used in classes and acting textbooks. Kazan was uncharacteristically modest about the scene, noting only that the budget limited them to one cramped

back seat in the shell of a car; Kaufman played with lights to give the illusion that the car was moving. It was shot in a day; five camera set-ups, seven takes, and twenty-one edits are in the finished film.

In his autobiography, Brando complained that Steiger kept ruining takes by crying. For his part, Steiger held a grudge against Brando for decades for leaving the set after his lines were shot, an extreme breach of etiquette. Kazan had to feed Steiger his lines off-camera for his close-up, which Kazan cut to four times in the film.

Although it's tempting to view *On the Waterfront* as groundbreaking, it actually fits easily into the creative elite's growing disillusionment with postwar society. Kazan and Schulberg deserve credit for addressing union corruption, but they were hardly the first filmmakers to do so. After all, they originally approached Zanuck because of his predilection for "message" films. *Waterfront* should perhaps be seen in the tradition of the 1930s social realist films from Warner Brothers, films which exposed problems and offered solutions, however simpleminded. Kazan was working with a new generation of actors, and with equipment that made location shooting a reality. Otherwise, he was using the same narrative formulas from twenty years earlier, formulas that let Hollywood pat itself on its back for making "tough," "adult" films. In fact, it's not that hard to transform *Waterfront* into a typical 1950s Western, in which a neurotic hero goes up against the corrupt rancher who is terrorizing the countryside. Or even a William S. Hart morality story, with Terry Malloy another "good bad man" who won't get involved until after a personal tragedy.

Arguments have never stopped as to what *On the Waterfront* ultimately means. For Kazan, the theme was simple: "When Brando, at the end, yells at Lee Cobb, the mob boss, 'I'm glad what I done—you hear me?—glad what I done!' that was me saying, with identical heat, that I was glad I'd testified as I had." Brando, who was unhappy about his performance, wrote that the film was Kazan's and Schulberg's justification for finking on their friends. (The actor thought that he was "in and out" of character in the film, although in the script itself Terry Malloy switches from inarticulate, even preliterate, to poetic with alarming ease.) Steiger said that Kazan betrayed his "family" of filmmaking colleagues by informing. By the time they made these statements, both actors had conveniently forgotten that Kazan testified some eighteen months before *Waterfront* began.

Whether a courageous drama or an apologia for snitches, *On the Waterfront* was a box-office sensation, earning almost $10 million in its initial release. It also performed impressively at the Oscars, winning eight awards and earning four other nominations. And Brando's plaintive lines, "I could've had class, I could've been a contender, I could've been somebody" have passed into American folklore.

Rear Window

Paramount, 1954. Sound, color, 1.66. 114 Minutes.

Cast: James Stewart (L.B. "Jeff" Jeffries), Grace Kelly (Lisa Carol Fremont), Wendell Corey (Thomas J. Doyle), Thelma Ritter (Stella), Raymond Burr (Lars Thorwald), Judith Evelyn ("Miss Lonelyhearts"), Ross Bagdasarian (Composer), Georgine Darcy ("Miss Torso"), Jesslyn Fax ("Miss Hearing Aid"), Rand Harper (Newlywed), Irene Winston (Anna Thorwald), Havis Davenport (Newlywed), Sara Berner (Woman on fire escape), Frank Cady (Man on fire escape).

Credits: Directed by Alfred Hitchcock. Screenplay by John Michael Hayes, based on the short story "It Had to Be Murder" by Cornell Woolrich. Director of photography: Robert Burks, A.S.C. Technicolor Color Consultant: Richard Mueller. Art Direction: Hal Pereira and Joseph MacMillan Johnson. Special Photographic Effects: John P. Fulton, A.S.C. Edited by George Tomasini. Music Score by Franz Waxman. Costumes: Edith Head.

Additional Cast includes: Marla English, Kathryn Grandstaff [Grant] (Partygoers); Alan Lee (Landlord); Anthony Warde, Fred Graham, Edwin Parker, Don Dunning (Detectives); Benny Bartlett (Friend of "Miss Torso"), Harry Landers, Dick Simmons, Iphigenie Castiglioni, Ralph Smiley, Len Hendry, Mike Mahoney, Alfred Hitchcock.

Additional Credits: Produced by Alfred Hitchcock. Sound director: Loren L. Ryder. Production dates: November 13, 1953 to January 14, 1954. Premiered in New York City on August 1, 1954. Rated PG in 1983.

Other Versions: Remade for television in 1988.

Available: Universal Studios DVD (2008). UPC: 025195018258.

Throughout his career, director Alfred Hitchcock loved to pose and then solve technical problems. In *Lifeboat*, he staged an entire film in a boat in the open sea. *Rope* takes place almost entirely within one apartment. For *Rear Window*, he chose another story that took place on one set, but with an added complication. Hitchcock tried to show an entire film through one point of view, in this case that of photographer "Jeff" Jefferies. Audiences could only see what Jefferies could see, and in theory at least would experience only what he experienced.

To up the ante, Jefferies is hobbled by a broken leg and confined to a wheelchair in a cramped Greenwich Village apartment. Lulled by the torpor of the long summer days, he stares voyeuristically out his window into neighboring apartments. He begins to suspect that Thorwald, who lives across the courtyard, has murdered his bedridden wife. Since Jefferies is unable to move, it's up to his girlfriend Lisa, a beautiful model, and his hard-bitten nurse to help him unravel the mystery.

The script for *Rear Window* was based on "It Had to Be Murder," a short story by Cornell Woolrich. He may not be as familiar today as some of his pulp colleagues, but Woolrich had an incalculable impact on film noir. He found premises that were uniquely suited to the genre, and invented unusually well-rounded female characters; in fact, the women often took the lead from the generally ineffectual heroes. "It Had to Be Murder" originally appeared in *Dime* magazine in February 1942, and then as "Rear Window" in a 1944 collection called *After-Dinner Story* by William Irish, one of Woolrich's pseudonyms.

Theater director Joshua Logan turned Woolrich's story into a thirteen-page treatment, introducing a romantic element into the plot. John Michael Hayes, previously a writer for radio, used Logan's blueprint for his own treatment, which he started in June 1953. He finished that September while Hitchcock was wrapping up his 3-D movie *Dial M for Murder*. Hayes worked on further drafts for two months, then continued to fine-tune the script throughout the shoot.

The set, which included a courtyard, the backs of three apartment buildings, an alley, and even a portion of the street beyond, was one of the largest interior sets ever constructed. The flats stretched from the basement of Paramount's Stage 18 to the ceiling, and required so many lights that the studio had to borrow them from its rivals.

Shooting started on November 13, 1953, and wrapped two months later. By this time Hitchcock had worked with his key creative personnel on several films. *Rear Window* was his first widescreen film, and contains several complicated shots that seem so effortless that it's easy to miss how difficult they were to achieve. One notable technical aspect of the film is the fact that it contains no dissolves between shots or scenes. This was potentially a big handicap: filmmakers rely on dissolves not just as transitions between scenes, but to smooth out shots that might seem jarring if simply cut together. Remarkably, the fades to black between scenes were done in camera rather than optically in the lab, an even bigger handicap that left no margin for error within a shot, or later during scoring and editing.

It's like working without a net, proof of Hitchcock's assurance and confidence in his methods.

Hitchcock was equally confident about the story, which dealt with several of his favorite themes. There's the cool but sexually charged blonde, the hero powerless to stop a pending disaster, and a villain with sympathetic qualities. By keeping the characters in the facing apartments at a distance, Hitchcock entices viewers into sharing Stewart's voyeurism, then implicates them in the violence that results.

Since the apartment characters are so far from the camera, they have to rely on the oversized gestures of an earlier generation of actors to compensate. You can spot Hitchcock employing these silent film techniques in his cameo as a visitor fiddling with a clock in the apartment of a composer (played by real-life writer Ross Bagdasarian).

The voyeuristic element of the film extends to Stewart and Kelly's relationship, a relationship that even today seems frank and mature. It was the second time Hitchcock worked with Grace Kelly. She more or less plays herself—that is, if she had been attracted to an older photographer rather than a prince. Her patrician ease, her casual physicality, and her remarkable looks all contributed to make this role one of the most appealing women in Hitchcock's oeuvre. Stewart had worked with Hitchcock before in *Rope*, another trick film that was a contrived and largely unenjoyable variation

on the Leopold and Loeb murder case. By this time Stewart had perfected his middle-age angst, and was unafraid of showing his characters as self-involved, misguided, and at times unfair. He was also in the middle of a series of taut, first-rate Westerns with director Anthony Mann, and spent the balance of his film work in the 1950s bringing an "everyman" quality to heroic roles: SAC pilot, FBI agent, munitions expert.

Hitchcock worked with Stewart two more times, and with Kelly on the lighthearted caper thriller, *To Catch a Thief* during the filming of which she met her future husband, the Prince of Monaco. She would make only two more films before retiring from acting.

Rear Window went slightly over its $1 million budget, but earned some $10 million in box-office receipts by 1956. Unlike some other Hitchcock films, it never really lost its popularity. It was rereleased in 1962 (to capitalize on the success of *Psycho*) and in 1983. In 1995, film historians Robert Harris and James Katz embarked on a full-scale restoration of the movie. For release prints, they used the Technicolor dye transfer process, resurrected for the first time since 1974. Unlike the original Eastmancolor prints, the Technicolor process could fully exploit the film's color and lighting schemes. Now it's possible to make out Raymond Burr's face as he puffs on a cigar in his darkened apartment.

Sabrina

Paramount, 1954. Sound, B&W, 1.33. 114 minutes.
Cast: Humphrey Bogart (Linus Larrabee), Audrey Hepburn (Sabrina Fairchild), William Holden (David Larrabee), Walter Hampden (Oliver Larrabee), John Williams (Thomas Fairchild), Martha Hyer (Elizabeth Tyson), Joan Vohs (Gretchen Van Horn), Marcel Dalio (Baron), Marcel Hillaire (The Professor), Nella Walker (Maude Larrabee), Francis X. Bushman (Mr. Tyson), Ellen Corby (Miss McCardle).
Credits: Produced and directed by Billy Wilder. Written for the screen by Billy Wilder, Samuel Taylor, Ernest Lehman. From the play by Samuel Taylor. Songs adapted and music composed by Frederick Hollander. Director of photography: Charles Lang. Editorial advisor: Doane Harrison. Art direction: Hal Pereira and Walter Tyler. Process photography: Farcio Edouart. Special photographic effects: John P. Fulton. Set decoration: Sam Comer and Ray Moyer. Edited by Arthur Schmidt. Costumer supervision: Edith Head. Assistant director: C.C. Coleman, Jr. Makeup supervision: Wally Westmore. Sound recording by Harold Lewis and John Cope. Western Electric Recording.
Additional Cast: Marjorie Bennett (Margaret, cook), Emory Parnell (Charles, butler), Kay Riehl (Mrs. Tyson), Nancy Kulp (Jenny), Kay Kuter (Houseman), Paul Harvey (Dr. Calaway); Emmett Vogan, Colin Campbell (Board members); Harvey Dunn (Man with tray), Marion Ross (Girlfriend), Charley Harvey (Party guest), Otto Forrest (Elevator operator), David Ahdar (Ship steward), Grey Stafford, Bill Neff).
Additional Credits: Costume design: Hubert de Givenchy. Released September 23, 1954.

Awards: Oscar for Best Costume Design—Black and White.
Other Versions: Remade as *Sabrina* (1995, directed by Sydney Pollack).
Available: Paramount DVD (2001). ISBN: 0-7921-7210-8. UPC: 0-9736-05402-4-6.

Billy Wilder followed *Sunset Boulevard* (1950) with two dark, cynical dramas that were essentially about how gullible mobs—and, by extension, moviegoers—were. *Sabrina* would mark a return to his roots as a writer of romantic comedies. Paramount executives, searching for a vehicle for Audrey Hepburn after *Roman Holiday* (1953), purchased the rights to *Sabrina Fair*, an unproduced play by Samuel Taylor. (Some accounts have Hepburn finding the property; in others, Wilder tries to option it.)

Born in 1912 in Chicago, Taylor entered theater as a script reader and "play doctor" for

Audrey Hepburn as a Long Island Cinderella in *Sabrina*.

playwright Sidney Howard. He worked on *What a Life*, a 1938 play by Clifford Goldsmith that evolved into the highly successful "Henry Aldrich" series on radio and at Paramount. (Wilder and his then-partner Charles Brackett wrote the screenplay for *What a Life*, released in 1939.) After working on many radio shows, Taylor found his next big success in adapting short stories by Robert Fontaine into the 1950 Broadway hit *The Happy Time* (later a successful film starring Charles Boyer).

Taylor's contract with Paramount prevented the studio from opening the film until after the stage version had premiered. The studio assigned the project to Wilder, and gave Taylor the chance to adapt his work with the director. The playwright quit after a few weeks, appalled at the liberties Wilder was taking with his plot. In fact, the film and stage versions of *Sabrina* bear almost no resemblance to each other, apart from basic settings and characters. Both stories concern the daughter of a chauffeur who becomes involved with two of the wealthiest brothers on Long Island. But the stage Sabrina is an expert in international affairs who recites Milton and who fled Paris to avoid romantic entanglements. She is skittish about marriage and indifferent to both brothers at first, and in fact has to be thawed before her true feelings emerge.

The film Sabrina is a fairy-tale character, a Cinderella who's been kept from the ball by class lines instead of by a witch. It was the second "princess" role in a row for Hepburn, who had won an Oscar in *Roman Holiday*, and the second time she was romantically paired with older actors. Wilder tailored the part carefully for Hepburn's

talents, emphasizing her fragility, beauty, and wistful expressions. It takes all of four minutes for the director to feature the first of many admiring close-ups the actress would receive, well before her other two leads even reach the screen.

Her role as Sabrina solidified Hepburn's stardom, and helped make her one of the fashion icons of the 1950s. Ironically, although Edith Head won the Oscar for costume design, Hubert de Givenchy was actually responsible for Hepburn's dresses and gowns after her character's return from Paris.

This was the third film Wilder made with William Holden, who like Hepburn had received an Oscar in his previous role (as a cynical prisoner-of-war in *Stalag 17*). Holden's debt to Wilder may be why he agreed to the part of the playboy David Larrabee, an unappealing as well as undemanding role, and why he wore such unflattering hair dye. Samuel Taylor saw Linus Larrabee, the responsible Larrabee brother, as a sophisticated type. (He was played by Joseph Cotten on stage.) Wilder thought he had Cary Grant cast as Linus, but Grant dropped out just before filming started.

Grant's emergency replacement was Humphrey Bogart, fresh off *The Caine Mutiny* (1954). Perhaps aware that the role was too much of a stretch for him, Bogart lashed out about the film to the press. He dismissed Wilder as a "Prussian German with a riding crop. He's the type of director I don't like to work with." He also complained that Hepburn required too many takes. On the other hand, the actress later revealed that Wilder asked her to slow down the filming process so he could finish the script.

To replace Samuel Taylor, Wilder borrowed Ernest Lehman from MGM, where he had been adapting *Executive Suite* (1954) for Holden, among others. Wilder's methods drove Lehman to a physical collapse (in the director's defense, Lehman had a tendency to collapse on other projects as well). The writer called the director "crude," and there is something uncomfortable about Wilder's willingness to use emotional extremes as narrative tricks. Suicide, for example, functions as a sort of neurotic foreplay in *Sunset Boulevard*; here, it is the basis for a weird bit of comedy for Hepburn that is never resolved. Bogart's character claims to be suicidal as well.

But Wilder's commercial instincts were sound. He not only rearranged elements from Taylor's play, he introduced plot lines that gave the story tension and momentum, and that called into question the characters' motives. Sabrina doesn't mind breaking up David Larrabee's engagement, for example. And Linus wants to see his brother married to protect a plastics deal he has been engineering.

Lehman admitted later that the script wasn't finished when shooting began, but Wilder couldn't wait any longer without losing his cast. Sitting in a studio office, the writer found himself unable to complete a last scene, distracted by a touch football game led by Dean Martin and Jerry Lewis on the lawn outside his window. He later worked the incident into one of his short stories, "The Small Sound of Applause." Lehman refused to collaborate with Wilder again, although he did work with Charles Brackett, the director's former writing partner, on *The King and I* (1956). He was on the brink of a new level of success, marked by Registry titles like *Sweet Smell of Success* (1957).

This was the last film at Paramount for Wilder, who had started working there during the 1930s. He gave a little publicity for his next project, an adaptation of the stage hit *The Seven Year Itch*, by mentioning it twice in this film. He worked with Hepburn again in *Love in the Afternoon* (1957), another May–December romance. (She married actor Mel Ferrer the week *Sabrina* opened.) Wilder's next Registry title is *Some Like It Hot* (1959).

A Star Is Born

Tommy Noonan and Judy Garland in the third version filmed of "The Man That Got Away" from *A Star Is Born*.

Warner Bros., 1954. Sound, color, 2.55. 175 minutes.
Cast: Judy Garland (Vicki Lester/Esther Blodgett), James Mason (Norman Maine), Jack Carson (Matt Libby), Charles Bickford (Oliver Niles), Tom Noonan (Danny McGuire), Lucy Marlow (Lola Lavery), Amanda Blake (Susan Ettinger), Irving Bacon (Graves), Hazel Shermet (Libby's secretary).
Credits: Directed by George Cukor. Screen play by Moss Hart. Based on the Dorothy Parker, Alan Campbell, Robert Carson screen play. From a story by William A. Wellman and Robert Carson. Produced by Sidney Luft. Director of photography: Sam Leavitt. New songs: Music by Harold Arlen, lyrics by Ira Gershwin. Dances created and staged by Richard Barstow. Musical direction by Ray Heindorf. Art director: Malcolm Bert. Film editor: Folmar Blangsted. Sound by Charles B. Lang, David Forrest. Set decorator: George James Hopkins. Special effects by H.F. Koenekamp. Vocal arrangements by Jack Cathcart. Orchestrations by Skip Martin. Song: "Born in a Trunk," music and lyrics by Leonard Gershe. Associate producer: Vern Alves. Special color design adviser: [George] Hoyningen-Huene. Technicolor color consultant: Mitchell G. Kovaleski. Makeup artist: Gordon Bau. Miss Garland's makeup created by Del Armstrong. Miss Garland's hair styles by Helen Young. Associate directors: Earl Bellamy, Edward Graham, Russell Llewellyn. Art direction and costumes for "Born in a Trunk" by Irene Sharaff. Production design by Gene Allen. Costumes designed by Jean Louis, Mary Ann Nyberg. RCA Sound System. A CinemaScope Picture. Color by Technicolor. A Warner Bros. presentation of a Transcona Enterprises production.
Additional Cast: George Fisher, Joan Shawlee (Announcers); James Brown (Glenn Williams), Frank Puglia (Bruno), Dub Taylor (Driver), Lotus Robb (Miss Markham), Blythe Daly (Miss Fusselow), Leonard Penn

(Director), Emerson Treacy (Justice of the Peace), Strother Martin (Express man), Grady Sutton (Artie Carver), Rex Evans (Emcee), Sam Colt (Sam), Paul Bryar (Bartender), Frank Ferguson (Judge), Percy Helton (Gregory).

Additional Credits: Cinematography by Harry Stradling, Winston Hoch, Milton Krasner, Harold Rossen. Production dates: October 12, 1953 to February 13, 1954; additional shooting in June and July 1954. Premiered in Los Angeles on September 29, 1954. Original running time: 181 minutes.

Other Versions: Filmed in 1937 (directed by William Wellman), 1976 (directed by Frank R. Pierson).

Available: Warner Home Video DVD (2000). ISBN: 0-7907-4345-0. UPC: 0-85391-75882-2.

Despite her years of success at MGM, Judy Garland's career at the studio was marked by turmoil that has been extensively documented in books and articles. Indeed, for many of her followers, Garland's problems are as compelling as her accomplishments. They have added a quality of doomed bravado to her work, one that can help excuse her personal and creative decisions.

Dropped from the production of *Annie Get Your Gun* (1950), Garland made her last full appearance at MGM in *Summer Stock* (1950), a mid-tier musical with one blazing bit of old-fashioned magic in her routine for the song "Get Happy." After leaving MGM, the singer attempted suicide; suffered a nervous breakdown; divorced her second husband, director Vincente Minnelli; and married Sidney Luft, a former test pilot and B-movie producer. Luft arranged a series of concerts for Garland in London and New York. He also plotted her comeback in movies with *A Star Is Born.*

David O. Selznick had produced a nonmusical version of the story in 1937, starring Janet Gaynor and Fredric March as two halves of a Hollywood couple, Gaynor's on the rise, March's in an alcoholic, suicidal decline. The screenplay also bore a resemblance to *What Price Hollywood?* (1932), a drama also produced by Selznick that helped put director George Cukor on the map. Rights to *A Star Is Born* had been purchased by producer Ed Alperson; along with Luft, Garland, and investor Ted Law, he formed Transcona Enterprises to finance and market a new musical version built around Garland.

Alperson sold the project to Jack Warner at Warner Bros.; *A Star Is Born* became part of a nine-picture deal which would give Luft a year or so to package the Garland vehicle. The Warners studio announced to the press that it would finance and distribute *A Star Is Born* in September 1952. The budget was set at $1.5 million, with $100,000 going to Garland. Hired as screenwriter was Moss Hart, a

Pulitzer Prize–winning playwright who had won an Oscar for writing *Gentlemen's Agreement* (1947).

Composer Harold Arlen and lyricist Ira Gershwin were hired to provide songs for the film. Arlen had worked with Garland before, notably on *The Wizard of Oz* (1939). In his first drafts, Hart changed the beginning of the 1937 movie, updating some details and altering aspects of the Esther Blodgett role to fit Garland's experiences. (The finished film would subtly reflect Garland's own career, from her early days to stardom.) He included room for a half-dozen or so songs, giving Arlen and Gershwin their themes and positions. Within two weeks, the team had come up with two pieces, including "The Man That Got Away," one of Garland's signature numbers for the rest of her career.

Luft had hoped to land Cary Grant for the part of Norman Maine, the egomaniacal actor who becomes involved with the unknown Esther Blodgett. Instead, British actor James Mason took the part. About his career at the time, he said, "I was not getting anywhere very fast." But Mason was used to taking risks, and his performance helped ground a film that was threatening to spin out of control. George Cukor was hired in part because he helped refine Garland's screen image in *The Wizard of Oz.*

Production officially started on August 13, 1953, when Richard Barstow began dance rehearsals. Garland started recording her songs about a week later. Shooting was supposed to start on September 1, but a week later cast members were still being hired, like Charles Bickford, a wonderfully gruff, no-nonsense presence whose career in film started with Cecil B. DeMille's *Dynamite* in 1929.

As delays continued, director of photography Harry Stradling left the production. He was replaced by Winston Hoch. The first shooting took place on October 12; a few days later, Jack Warner decided to switch the production from the still experimental WarnerScope process to CinemaScope. The initial footage would have to be reshot, including "The Man That Got Away." By this time Winston Hoch had been fired, replaced by Milton Krasner, on loan from Twentieth Century-Fox. Finally, Luft hired Sam Leavitt, who had just finished filming the 3-D *Southwest Passage* (1954).

Sickness prolonged the shoot, as did the decision to refilm as many as a dozen scenes. As the production extended into February, and then March, Garland's behavior became more erratic. A rough cut was screened on March 25, 1954. Three weeks later, Cukor directed six days of reshoots. He left California on April 28 for a vacation, even though Ira Gershwin, among others, felt that the film needed another musical number. Working with Roger Edens, her old colleague at MGM, Garland came up with a medley sequence called "Born in a Trunk."

When she auditioned the number for Jack Warner, he enthusiastically agreed to open the production again for the two weeks required to shoot it. Once this sequence was inserted into the film, *A Star Is Born* ran three hours and two minutes. Adding to the difficulty in marketing the film of that length was a lawsuit started by David O. Selznick, who insisted that he had retained exhibition rights from the original *A Star Is Born*.

Bad luck plagued the entire project. Luft and Garland could not have anticipated the problems new technologies would bring. Cukor's predisposition for slower pacing and extended takes resulted in a film much longer than the script indicated. The saddest aspect of *A Star Is Born* may be Garland's failure to adapt to the times. She was still playing the starstruck, naive kid she had portrayed almost twenty years earlier. Garland was a divorced mother of two, and the gulf between who she was in real life and the role she was playing had become too great.

The film opened in Hollywood on September 29, 1954, and in New York City two days later.

Although reviews were positive, word of mouth was troubling. For example, director Elia Kazan wrote these comments to Moss Hart: "Everything had been blown up or glamorized. Numbers which were supposed to be the essence of informality were informal on such a huge scale! I also thought [Cukor] had put too much self-pity into the feelings of the two leads." "It dragged interminably," said Noël Coward. "I found myself wishing that dear enchanting Judy was at the bottom of the sea. The picture ran for three hours; if it had been cut down to two, it would have been really exciting."

Harry Warner felt the same way, and ordered his younger brother Jack to shorten *A Star Is Born*. Twenty-seven minutes were removed, but the film still performed poorly at the box office. Historian Ronald Haver estimates that the Warner studio lost at least $2 million just on production costs. Garland's career as a movie star was over, although she appeared in a few more films. She began incorporating her age and her increasingly fragile mental state into her live performances, which took on the ghoulish air of a tightrope act. She died of an overdose of sleeping pills in 1969.

Haver oversaw a restoration in 1983, after a search turned up some of the missing soundtrack and film footage. In 2008, digital technicians began work on a 6K resolution transfer. Ned Price, vice-president of mastering at Warner Bros. Technical Operations, promised, "Our expectation is that the restoration would live for easily 100 years."

Carmen Jones

Twentieth Century-Fox, 1954. Sound, color, 2.55. 105 minutes.
Cast: Harry Belafonte (Joe), Dorothy Dandridge (Carmen Jones), Pearl Bailey (Frankie), Olga James (Cindy Lou), Joe Adams (Husky Miller), Broc [Brock] Peters (Sergeant Brown), Roy Glenn (Rum Daniels), Nick Stewart (Dink Franklin), Diahann Carroll (Myrt), Madame Sui-Te-Wan (Grandmother), Sandy Lewis (T-Bone). Singing voices: Le Vern [LeVern] Hutcherson (Joe), Marilynn [Marilyn] Horne (Carmen Jones), Marvin Hayes (Husky Miller).
Credits: Produced and directed by Otto Preminger. Book & lyrics by Oscar Hammerstein 2nd. Music by Georges Bizet. Based on Billy Rose's Broadway production of the musical play *Carmen Jones*. Screenplay by Harry Kleiner. Director of photography: Sam Leavitt. Film editor: Louis R. Loeffler. Art direction: Edward L. Ilou. Set decoration: Claude E. Carpenter. Costume design: Mary Ann Nyberg. Musical direction: Herschel Burke Gilbert. Associate: Ted Dale. Music recording: Vinton Vernon, Murray Spivack. Music editors: Leon Birnbaum and George Brand. Sound: Roger Heman and Arthur L. Kirbach. Camera operator: Albert Myers. Production manager: Herman E. Webber. Production assistant: Maximilian Slater. Assistant director: David Silver. Casting consultant: Lina Abarbanell. Fights staged by John Indrisano. Titles designed by Saul Bass. Photographed in CinemaScope. Color by De Luxe Laboratories. Western Electric Recording.
Additional Cast: Brock Peters (singing voice for Rum Daniels).

Additional Credits: Production dates: June to July 1954. Premiered in New York City on October 28, 1954.
Available: Twentieth Century-Fox Home Video DVD (2002). UPC: 0-24543-01883-4.

Although it received mixed reviews when it premiered in Paris in 1875, Georges Bizet's *Carmen*, based on a story by Prosper Mérimée and with a libretto by Henri Meilhac and Ludovic Halévy, has become one of the most famous operas in the world. One sign of its popularity is the number of adaptations and parodies that have resulted; in film alone, everything from a *Burlesque on Carmen* (1915) starring Charlie Chaplin to *U-Carmen* (2005), a South African film performed in Xhosa.

After the success of *Show Boat*, for which he wrote the book and lyrics, Oscar Hammerstein II spent most of the 1930s working in Hollywood. He returned to New York in 1942 for the stage show *Carmen Jones*, which was being mounted by impresario Billy Rose. Hammerstein worked from Bizet's music, adapting the setting and characters of the opera to the modern-day American South. Carmen, who originally worked in a tobacco factory, now worked in a parachute plant. Joe (played in the film by Harry Belafonte), her new infatuation, became a member of the military police and a candidate for flight school. Carmen would betray Joe with prize fighter Husky Miller instead of bullfighter Escamillo.

Hammerstein's growing political consciousness may have been behind his decision to make *Carmen Jones* an all-black play. It opened on December 2, 1943, at the Broadway Theatre, with Muriel Smith, Inez Matthews, and Luther Saxon in the leads. The play received excellent reviews and ran for 502 performances. But after the poor showing at the box office of all-black musical films like *Cabin in the Sky* and *Stormy Weather* (both 1943), there seemed little hope of adapting *Carmen Jones* to the screen. Hammerstein meanwhile embarked on a partnership with Richard Rodgers that led to musical landmarks like *Oklahoma!* (1943), *Carousel* (1945), and *South Pacific* (1949).

Since the 1930s Otto Preminger had endured many ups and downs with Twentieth Century-Fox head Darryl F. Zanuck. He had also developed into an actor of some note, playing villainous Germans in World War II propaganda films, and had continued his earlier career of directing stage productions, notably *The Moon Is Blue*. Preminger formed his own production company to make the screen version of *The Moon Is Blue*, one of the first films to directly challenge the Production Code. Rejected by studios like United Artists, he returned to Zanuck and Fox for the $800,000 needed to produce the screen version of *Carmen Jones*.

Preminger considered a number of actresses for the lead role, but cast Dorothy Dandridge on the strength of a screen test she made with actor James Edwards. Born in 1922, Dandridge spent a hardscrabble youth in Los Angeles while her mother Ruby eked out a living in bit parts. Dorothy and her older sister Vivian formed a singing trio with Etta Jones, landing a spot at the Cotton Club in Harlem. Dorothy made her film debut in *A Day at the Races* (1937) and appeared in other musicals and shorts in the 1940s. She suffered through an unhappy marriage to Harold

Nicholas before starting a successful career as a nightclub performer, and had begun acting again in films when she persuaded Preminger to make her Carmen.

Preminger and Zanuck both believed that the project required classically trained singers. Katherine Hilgenberg was hired to dub Dandridge's singing voice, but she sparred so nastily with Preminger that she quit. Her replacement was nineteen-year-old Jackie Horne, a USC student who had been singing cover songs for Tops Records. As Marilyn Horne, she would become one of the most respected voices in opera.

Most of the filming, which began on June 30, 1954, took place on RKO soundstages. Dandridge, who by this time had entered into a romantic relationship with Preminger, was appalled at his treatment of actors. "He had no view of himself at all," she wrote in her autobiography, and described walking off the set after he screamed at Roy Glenn. Three weeks' rehearsal time allowed Preminger and cinematographer Sam Leavitt to adjust the compositions of the extremely wide CinemaScope frames, and to plan surprisingly elaborate and extended shots. At the same time, Horne and the other singers were recording the score at the Twentieth Century-Fox studio.

It's difficult to fault the sincerity the cast and crew brought to *Carmen Jones*, but many aspects of the film have dated poorly—in particular, Hammerstein's idiomatic lyrics. Much of the story takes place in a weirdly idealized South (a "fantasy," as Preminger wrote later); Hammerstein doesn't seem fully comfortable until the film reaches a nightclub scene filled with familiar musical types, including an especially entertaining Pearl Bailey as Frankie. Bizet's music is almost like a straightjacket at times, while Preminger also has to struggle against Production Code restrictions.

One indisputable success in the film is Dandridge, whose beauty and power startled filmgoers. She portrayed an authority and knowingness that had not been previously permitted to black actresses in mainstream film, and her seduction of Harry Belafonte's Joe crackles with an unexpected energy and eroticism. She was the first African-American to receive a Best Actress nomination, but was unable to resolve the conflicts in her personal life. Her affair with Preminger ended badly, her daughter from her first marriage was institutionalized, and Dandridge was abused by her second husband. She was nearly destitute when she died in 1965.

A Time Out of War

Left: Alan Cohen before he changed his name to Corey Allen. Center: Robert Sherry, along with Cohen a UCLA theater student. Across the river: Barry Atwater, at the time the head of the UCLA Motion Picture Division's sound department.
Courtesy of Terry Sanders

Carnival Productions, 1954. Sound, B&W, 1.37. 22 minutes.

Cast: Barry Atwater (Craig), Robert Sherry (Alden), Alan Cohen (Connor).

Credits: Written and directed by Denis Sanders. Based on the short story "Pickets" by Robert W. Chambers. Produced by Denis and Terry Sanders. Cinematography by Terry Sanders. Music by Frank Hamilton. Script supervisor: Ray Pearson. Assistant director: Rita Montgomery. Camera Operator: Morris Green. Unit manager: Steve Brody. Sound: Tony Gorsline, Barry Eddy. Sound effects. Robert Lloyd. Produced with the cooperation of the University of California at Los Angeles Department of Theatre Arts.

Awards: Oscar for Best Short Subject—Two Reels.

Available: American Film Foundation (*www.americanfilmfoundation.com*).

The first student film to win an Oscar, *A Time Out of War* also helped launch the careers of Denis and Terry Sanders. Denis Sanders persuaded his younger brother Terry to switch schools in order join him in the film program at UCLA. They shot their first film, *Subject: Narcotics* (1952), sponsored by the Narcotic Educational Foundation of America, on a budget of $1200, dividing the producing, directing, and editing credits.

For Denis's thesis project, the brothers were determined to make a dramatic film in 35mm, and they wanted it to be about the Civil War. "We read all the Ambrose Bierce stories but decided they were too well known," Terry Sanders said in an interview. "Since we had no money to purchase literary rights, the story had to be copyrighted 1895 or earlier, the cut-off for 'public domain.' Denis disappeared into the UCLA library, where he proceeded to read every obscure Civil War story

he could find. Ten days later, he emerged with 'Pickets' by Robert W. Chambers, which he found in an 1895 issue of *McClure's* magazine."

Chambers was a much better known author in the early twentieth century, when at least two dozen films were adapted from his works. (Among them were *America*, filmed by D.W. Griffith in 1924, and the Marion Davies vehicle *Operator 13*, adapted from *Secret Service Operator 13* in 1934.) Born in 1865, he wrote a dozen volumes of short stories, and as many novels, over a career that stretched more than thirty years. "Pickets" was also published in an 1898 collection called *The Haunts of Men.* Heavily indebted to Bierce, the story focused on three soldiers—two Union, one Confederate—stationed on opposite sides of a river. Craig, the Confederate soldier, proposes an hour's truce. The three meet warily on opposite banks of the river, curiosity overcoming caution. Given its war background, the plot for "Pickets" was filled with foreboding, with the sense that betrayal and violence could occur at any moment. Its tension built from the basic identities of the characters and their physical relationship to one another; in other words, it was perfect material for film.

With a total budget of $2000, the Sanders brothers did not have the luxury of a long production. Terry remembers auditioning UCLA theater students for the two Northerner roles. "For Craig, the Southerner, Denis chose Barry Eddy (later he changed his acting name to Barry Atwater) who was head of the UCLA Film School sound department. This killed two birds with one stone, getting us great access to sound equipment." Terry, who handled the cinematography, used a 35mm French Eclair reflex camera he borrowed from an importer and dealer. "I think this was the first use of the camera in the U.S. We shot on 'short ends,' throwaway film we could get from the studio for a penny or two a foot."

Filming took place along the Santa Ynez River near Santa Barbara. "We carefully excluded from the frame everything that couldn't pass for the Deep South," Terry said. He remembers waiting anxiously for wind to ruffle the surface of the water, the only way he could suggest that the river was flowing, and not the shallow, stagnant backwater they found.

The Sanders brothers followed the story closely, to the point of copying dialogue verbatim. During one key exchange the camera remains behind Craig, allowing his posture to define his emotions. Here's how Chambers described the moment: "He paused in his examination and remained motionless on the bank, head bent. Presently he looked up and asked Alden if he had made a mistake."

What the brothers expanded on was the physical world the soldiers inhabited: the stream Chambers described in his story, the brush on the banks, the fishing rod Connor, a Northerner, fashions. To this Terry Sanders could add the waning light of late afternoon, sunlight reflecting on water, reeds swaying in the breeze, clouds banked over a meadow. When married to a spare musical accompaniment by Frank Hamilton, the effect was haunting and deeply evocative.

In fact, *A Time out of War* is so technically accomplished that it easily transcends categorization as a "student film." The brothers entered it in the Venice Film Festival, where it won first prize for Live Action Short Film. Encouraged, the brothers formed Carnival Productions with their agent Jules Goldstone in order to give the film a commercial release and thereby qualify for an Academy Award. It opened at the El Rey Theater on a double-bill with an Italian production of *Romeo and Juliet*, and that spring won an Oscar, besting entries from Warner Brothers and Twentieth Century-Fox. Terry remembers being congratulated by a "puzzled looking" Walt Disney, whose own *Siam* lost. After the win, the film was distributed nationally by Universal.

Terry was hired as second unit director for Charles Laughton's *The Night of the Hunter* (1955), and both brothers collaborated with Laughton on an adaptation of Norman Mailer's *The Naked and the Dead*. Laughton abandoned the project after the box-office failure of *The Night of the Hunter*. The brothers worked together on *War Hunt*, a 1962 feature and Robert Redford's film debut, but relied on commissioned films for income. Terry Sanders made several documentaries for the USIA, including *A Meeting with America*, *In Pursuit of Peace*, and *Portrait of Zubin Mehta*. He was a founder of the American Film Foundation, and with fellow filmmaker Freida Lee Mock has distributed numerous documentaries. Their *Maya Lin: A Clear Strong Vision* (1994) won the Oscar for Best Documentary—Features. His most recent film, *Fighting for Life* (2008), concerns the medical treatment of soldiers wounded in the Iraq war.

Denis Sanders also worked for the USIA, notably on *Czechoslovakia 1918–1968*, another Registry title.

Marty

United Artists, 1955. Sound, B&W, 1.37. 89 minutes.
Cast: Ernest Borgnine (Marty [Piletti]), Betsy Blair (Clara [Snyder]), Esther Minciotti (Mrs. Piletti), Augusta Ciolli (Aunt Catherine), Joe Mantell (Angie), Karen Steele (Virginia), Jerry Paris (Tommy).
Credits: Directed by Delbert Mann. Story and screenplay by Paddy Chayefsky. Produced by Harold Hecht. Associate producer: Paddy Chayefsky. Photography by Joseph LaShelle. Art direction: Edward S. Haworth, Walter Simonds. Editorial supervision: Alan Crosland, Jr. Costume design: Norma [Koch]. Assistant director: Paul Helmick. Music & effects editor: Robert Carlisle. Makeup: Robert Schiffer. Hair styles: Agnes Flanagan. Set decorator: Robert Priestley. Sound recording: John Keen, Roger Heman. Casting supervision: Betty Pagel. Music by Roy Webb. Song "Marty" by Harry Warren. Additional music by George Bassman. Western Electric Recording. A Hecht–Lancaster presentation.

Additional Cast: Frank Sutton (Ralph), Robin Morse (Joe), Charles Cane (Lou), James Bell (Mr. Snyder), Minerva Urecal (Mrs. Rosari), Walter Kelley (The Kid).
Additional Credits: Production dates: September to October 1954. Opened April 12, 1955.
Awards: Oscars for Best Picture, Director, Writing—Screenplay, Actor.
Available: MGM Home Video DVD (2001). ISBN: 0-7928-5012-2. UPC: 0-27616-86292-1.

Marty marked the first time a television drama was adapted to the big screen. It was the result of a relatively brief flowering of serious writing on television, a medium still feeling its way with audiences.

TV offered more visual possibilities than theater, but could not compete with film spectacles. For producers like Fred Coe, that meant it was best suited for small-scale character sketches, stories with modest themes and low-key resolutions.

One of Coe's favorite writers was the short, argumentative Paddy Chayefsky. Born Sidney Chayefsky in 1923 in the Bronx, he got his nickname in the Army. While recuperating from wounds received in World War II, he was selected by filmmaker Garson Kanin to work with Carol Reed on *The True Glory*. Still in the service, he wrote the book and lyrics to a musical show that brought him to the attention of producer Joshua Logan. Despite his connections, Chayefsky had trouble finding work after the war, until Kanin and his wife Ruth Gordon gave him $500 to write a play. Chayefsky traveled to Hollywood, where he worked briefly as an actor, met Harold Hecht and Betsy Blair, and sold a script that later became *As Young As You Feel* (1951).

Back in New York City, Chayefsky wrote radio scripts for CBS, leading to work on *Danger*, a television series developed by Yul Brynner and Sidney Lumet. Hired by Fred Coe for a show that was sponsored alternately by Philco and Goodyear, Chayefsky insisted on attending rehearsals and observing productions. Some rehearsals were held in the ballroom of the Abbey Hotel, also the site for Friday night meetings of the "Friendship Club." A sign on the wall asking women to dance with men because "they have feelings too" was the original inspiration for *Marty*.

"I set out in *Marty* to write a love story, the most ordinary love story in the world," Chayefsky wrote later. He used an Italian ethnic setting because he had written about Jewish characters for three pieces in a row. Chayefsky and director Delbert Mann had wanted to cast Martin Ritt as Marty Piletti, a lonely, homely butcher. Because of Ritt's problems with the blacklist they hired Rod Steiger instead. Chayefsky referred to the script as a "character satire," but was chagrined to notice during rehearsals that "no one was laughing." The show was broadcast live on May 24, 1953.

Critical reaction was enthusiastic. As CBS producer Sandy Fox wrote, "Audiences were so used to seeing shows about 'the winners,' the beautiful. What Paddy gave us that night was a story about 'the losers.'" Harold Hecht saw the broadcast, and wanted to make a film version as part of a three-picture deal he had with United Artists.

When Arthur B. Krim and Robert Benjamin took over the nearly moribund United Artists studio in 1951, it was distributing primarily European films and low-budget independent movies. Krim and Benjamin made a deal with Hecht–Lancaster Productions that resulted in box-office hits like *The Flame and the Arrow* (1950) and *The Crimson Pirate (1952)*, Burt Lancaster adventure vehicles. Hecht, at one time an actor and dancer, became an agent in 1934; Lancaster was first his client, and then his partner in one of the first actor-driven independent production companies since the silent days.

The film *Marty* was Hecht's project; Lancaster was busy preparing *Trapeze* and *The Kentuckian*, which he was also directing. The budget for *Trapeze* was $1,000,000; for *Marty*, $150,000. Chayefsky got $13,000 of that, plus final script approval, choice of director (he insisted on Delbert Mann), and an assistant director credit (he settled for "Associate Producer"). When his feature script was finished, Chayefsky said, "I honestly feel that *Marty* in film form is a better play than it was on TV."

Casting was difficult. Rod Steiger turned down the film role because he didn't want to sign a long-term contract with Hecht–Lancaster. Burt Lancaster took credit for suggesting Ernest Borgnine, who was working with him on *Vera Cruz*. However, Borgnine said that *Vera Cruz* director Robert Aldrich told Delbert Mann about him. Betsy Blair campaigned for the role of Clara Snyder (played by Nancy Marchand on TV), but Hecht worried about her rumored "leftist" sympathies. Gene Kelly, her husband at the time, ordered MGM head Dore Schary to clear his wife's name so she could be hired.

Rehearsals began in September 1954. The cast and crew had three days to shoot all the exteriors in the Bronx. Then United Artists threatened to close down the production. Hecht obtained a loan in October from Bankers Trust to finish the project, and formed Steven Productions with Lancaster solely for *Marty*. Hecht also mortgaged his house to pay for shooting one new scene and reshooting another. The final budget was close to $343,000.

When *Marty* opened in New York City on April 12, 1955, it did strong business. However, box office elsewhere was disastrous until the film won the Palme d'Or at the Cannes Film Festival. That prompted an ad campaign featuring Burt Lancaster that was estimated to cost $400,000, or more than the entire film. *Marty* later won Oscars for Best Picture, Actor, and Screenplay.

By that time the film was a smash, earning some $3 million, and the line "What do you wanna do tonight?" had become a familiar catchphrase.

The film version of *Marty* cemented Chayefsky's reputation as a poet of the "little people," despite his often condescending tone. Chayefsky moves his characters around like chess pieces, their conversations and interactions part of worked-out designs. He is the type of screenwriter who doesn't let viewers think for themselves, one self-consciously proud of depicting "ugly" people, "real" people. But Hollywood had made movies like this before; in fact, the romances of society's marginal characters had been a fixture of the industry since the days of Mary Pickford. *Broken Blossoms* (1919), *Miss Lulu Bett* (1921), *The Shop Around the Corner* (1940), even *A Streetcar Named Desire* (1951), to name four films from the Registry, all deal with the troubled affairs of shopkeepers, spinsters, and blue-collar workers.

The success of *Marty* led to a flood of features based on television dramas: *Requiem for a Heavyweight*, *Twelve Angry Men* (also a Registry title), *The Rainmaker*, *The Bachelor Party*, and *The Catered Affair*, the last two written by Chayefsky. While the film did little for Blair, who divorced Kelly in 1957 and moved to Europe, it helped make Borgnine a fixture in films and on television. He and director Delbert Mann hoped to make a sequel, but Chayefsky refused permission. However, in 1965 Chayefsky and Hecht pitched *Marty* as a TV series, and shot a pilot with Tom Bosley. By that time Chayefsky had abandoned television and film to concentrate on stage plays, but he was to make a triumphant return to movies with *The Hospital* in 1971. (Some television prints removed a five-minute scene in which Clara tells her parents about her date with Marty. According to Mann, this was a syndication issue; this shorter version has been supplanting the uncut release.)

Kiss Me Deadly

Ralph Meeker as Mickey Spillane's Mike Hammer in *Kiss Me Deadly*.

United Artists, 1955. Sound, B&W, 1.66. 106 minutes.

Cast: Ralph Meeker (Mike Hammer), Albert Dekker (Dr. G.E. Soberin), Paul Stewart (Carl Evello), Juano Hernandez (Eddie Yeager), Wesley Addy (Capt. Pat Murphy), Marion Carr (Friday), Marjorie Bennett (Apartment manager), Mort Marshall (Ray Diker), Fortunio Bonanova (Carmen Trivaco), Strother Martin (Harvey Wallace), Madi Comfort (Singer), James McCallion (Horace), Robert Cornthwaite (FBI agent), Silvio Minciotti (Moving man), Nick Dennis (Nick), Ben Morris, Jack Elam (Charlie Max), Paul Richards (Man with switchblade), Jesslyn Fax (Horace's wife), James Seay (FBI agent), Percy Helton (Doc Kennedy), Leigh Snowden (Girl at pool), Jack Lambert (Sugar Smallhouse), Jerry Zinneman (Sammy), Maxine Cooper (Velda [Wickman]), Cloris Leachman (Christina [Bailey], Gaby Rodgers ([Lily] Carver/Gabrielle), Sam Balter (Radio announcer).

Credits: Produced and directed by Robert Aldrich. Screenplay by A.I. Bezzerides. Photographed by Ernest Laszlo. Production supervisor: Jack R. Berne. Art director: William Glasgow. Set decorator: Howard Bristol.

Film editor: Michael Luciano. Assistant director: Robert Justman. Assistant to the producer: Robert Sherman. Sound: Jack Solomon. Casting supervisor: Jack Murton. Make-up: Bob Schiffer. Music composed and conducted by Frank DeVol. Orchestrations by Albert Harris. "Rather Have the Blues" sung by Nat "King" Cole, Kitty White. Glen Glenn Sound Co. Recording. Photographic effects & title: Complete Film Service. A Victor Saville presentation of a Parklane Pictures production.

Additional Cast: Joe Hernandez (Radio announcer); Trude Wyler, Mara McAfee (Nurses).

Additional Credits: Released May 18, 1955.

Available: MGM Home Entertainment DVD (2001). ISBN: 0-7928-5011-4. UPC: 0-27616-86291-4.

Film noir as a genre tended toward obsessively moody and downbeat stories; few got as apocalyptic as *Kiss Me Deadly*. Based on a Mike Hammer novel by

Mickey Spillane, the film was presented by Victor Saville, a British director and producer who had released film versions of two earlier Spillane novels through Parklane Pictures.

Spillane was born in Brooklyn in 1918. He was writing for pulp magazines and comic books when he became a fighter pilot flight instructor during World War II. After the war, he pitched a "Mike Danger, Private Eye" project to the comics, but couldn't find a taker. He sold it as a novel to E.P. Dutton instead. When *I, the Jury*, a so-so seller as a hardcover in 1947, came out as a Signet paperback in 1948, it sold millions of copies. Spillane quickly churned out six more tough mysteries, five of them featuring Mike Hammer. Although deplored by most critics, the books were commercial blockbusters. The Hammer character became the star of a radio show, two televisions series, a comic strip, and many motion pictures.

The Hammer books both simplified and coarsened the private eye genre, primarily by raising levels of sex and violence—in particular, sadistic violence. Spillane's motives were more commercial than literary, leading to formulaic and repetitive plotting. Much of *Kiss Me Deadly*, published in 1952, consisted of people walking in and out of rooms. Women threw themselves at Mike Hammer, but the big, lumbering alter ego seemed befuddled by their interest. Spillane's use of phrases like "hot kisses" and "sledgehammer blows" set the mood readers wanted, but the stories hardly made sense, and could barely be considered mysteries.

Thriller author Lawrence Block found Spillane's work in comics crucial to his novel writing. "The new generation of readers who embraced Spillane had read comic books before they read novels. They were used to the pace, the frame-by-frame rhythm," Block wrote. "The fast cuts, the in-your-face immediacy, and the clear-cut, no-shades-of-gray, good v. evil story lines of the Mike Hammer novels come straight out of the comic-book world." At the same time, Spillane crystallized a pervasive Cold War hysteria, coming down on a deeply conservative, "might is right" side that appealed to his core audience.

Robert Aldrich, on the other hand, embodied the chaos sweeping through the movie industry during the 1950s. Born in Rhode Island in 1918, he broke into the film industry in 1941 as a production clerk at RKO. Working up the ladder, he assisted such notable directors as William Wellman, Lewis Milestone, and Charles Chaplin. Next came producing, then writing and directing episodes for television series. He directed his first feature in 1953, incorporating both the techniques he had learned from master directors as well as the shortcuts necessary in TV production. This combination of highbrow pretension and lowbrow tactics stayed with Aldrich throughout his career.

The script for *Kiss Me Deadly* was written by A.I. Bezzerides, a Turkish-born author who entered the industry after his novel *Long Haul* was adapted into *They Drive by Night* (1940). The year before, Bezzerides had written an ambitious screenplay for *Track of the Cat* (1954), based on a Walter Van Tilburg Clark novel. He considered Mickey Spillane a comedown, and in interviews later admitted that his *Kiss Me Deadly* script mocked Spillane and the whole tough-guy school of writing. "I wrote it fast because I had contempt for it," he said. The novel was set in New York City and centered around $2 million missing from drug deals. Bezzerides dropped the money element and added a lot of classical allusions that would have baffled the book Mike Hammer. The plot was now about the "great whatsit," as Hammer's girlfriend Velda referred to it.

Bezzerides depicted the private eye as bullheaded, vicious, and oblivious to the scope and meaning of his case. Bezzerides was relieved to learn that Aldrich agreed with him. As a result, *Kiss Me Deadly* has some of the worst detective work on film, with Hammer routinely missing or ignoring clues and repeatedly placing himself and his companions in jeopardy.

Aldrich wasn't interested in narrative logic as much as delivering shocks, right from the opening shots of an underclad Cloris Leachman racing barefoot down a nighttime highway. He also didn't have the budget to correct mistakes. Few of the shots within scenes "match." Leachman is in the middle of the road in her close-ups, for example, and on the side in her long shots. Aldrich mixed real locations with sets and back projection; actors from *Citizen Kane* with newcomers like Leachman; classical Hollywood editing with a newfangled, jangly style of quick cuts and elisions; ersatz jazz with a traditionally bombastic score that he hoped added meaning and tension to otherwise prosaic shots. A meaningless phone conversation might feature a complicated overhead crane shot. On the other hand, one murder is shown with three unrelated shots lasting a second or so each.

Film editor and historian Glenn Erickson credits Aldrich's fast, cheap, and blunt style—as coarse in its way as Spillane's writing—with influencing

French New Wave filmmakers, who inserted jump cuts and sloppy set-ups into their movies. They may not have realized that Aldrich left out so much material because he couldn't afford to shoot it, and that he cut so quickly because he didn't have coverage. Erickson and Alain Silver were largely responsible for restoring the film's original ending. For years, viewers assumed that *Kiss Me Deadly* ended with special effects shots awkwardly edited together. But the Bezzerides script featured another scene, some of which appeared in the film's trailer. The footage, about sixty-five seconds, turned up in Aldrich's private print held by the Directors' Guild. It has been reinserted back into circulating copies.

Kiss Me Deadly was not a success at the box office, and essentially dropped out of sight until writers resurrected the film noir genre in the 1970s. Its influence on more modern attempts at film noir, such as John Boorman's *Point Blank* (1967), is unmistakable. Aldrich went on to invent one of the most durable genres in recent years, horror films exploiting outdated actresses, such as *What Ever Happened to Baby Jane?* (1962). He also directed *The Dirty Dozen*, a box-office bonanza in 1967. Performers like Leachman and Strother Martin went on to significant movie careers, while Spillane himself played Hammer in a 1963 film, *The Girl Hunter*.

The Night of the Hunter

United Artists, 1955. Sound, B&W, 1.37. 93 minutes.

Cast: Robert Mitchum (Preacher Harry Powell), Shelley Winters (Willa Harper), Lillian Gish (Rachel), James Gleason (Birdie [Steptoe]), Evelyn Varden (Icey [Spoon]), Peter Graves (Ben Harper), Don Beddoe (Walt [Spoon]), Billy Chapin (John [Harper]), Gloria Castilo [Castillo] (Ruby), Sally Jane Bruce (Pearl [Harper]).

Credits: Directed by Charles Laughton. Screen play by James Agee. From the novel by Davis Grubb. Produced by Paul Gregory. Photography by Stanley Cortez, A.S.C. Art direction by Hilyard Brown. Assistant director: Milton Carter. Film editor: Robert Golden, A.C.E. Music by Walter Schumann. Production manager: Ruby Rosenberg. Set decoration: Al Spencer. Wardrobe: Jerry Bos. Assisted by Evelyn Carruth. Makeup: Don Cash. Hair stylist: Kay Shea. Sound: Stanford Naughton. Property man: Joe La Bella. Special photographic effects: Jack Rabin, Louis De Witt. Western Electric Recording.

Additional Cast: Mary Ellen Clemons (Clary), Cheryl Callaway (Mary), Gloria Pall (Burlesque dancer), Paul Bryar (Bart the hangman), Kay La Velle (Miz Cunningham); Corey Allen, Michael Chapin (Teenage boys); John Hamilton (Rancher), James Griffith (District Attorney).

Additional Credits: Screenwriting by Charles Laughton. Second unit directors: Terry Sanders, Denis Sanders. Production dates: August 18 to October 7, 1954. Premiered in Des Moines, Iowa, on July 26, 1955.

Other Versions: Remade for television in 1991.

Available: MGM Home Entertainment DVD (2000). ISBN: 0-7928-4336-3. UPC: 0-27616-7994-2-5.

The only feature directed by Charles Laughton, *The Night of the Hunter* embraces every genre from children's film to thriller, every style from German expressionism to documentary. Although its influence was widespread, to date no one has succeeded in recapturing its unique combination of artful and artless.

Laughton was one of the most respected stage and film actors of his time. Born in England in 1899, he was headed for a career as a hotelier when World War I intervened. As a returning veteran, he was drawn to the stage. After studying in London, he made his West End debut in 1926. Laughton appeared in comedy shorts with another stage newcomer, Elsa Lanchester, marrying her in 1929, the same year he had a memorable cameo in his first feature, *Piccadilly*. Within five years he was the biggest star in British film, and an increasingly familiar presence in Hollywood.

A large, even overbearing figure, Laughton combined faultless technique with an astonishing ability to inhabit the characters he played. He was a difficult, demanding man, plagued by self-doubt but withering in his criticism of others. Complaining about the actors he faced in one movie, he told the director, "A fencing master cannot fence with amateurs."

In between films, he toured the United States and England, giving staged readings of Shaw's *Don Juan in Hell* and Stephen Vincent Benet's *John Brown's Body* (which he also edited and directed). He helped run an acting school in Los Angeles, where he directed more stage productions. While appearing in a Georges Simenon adaptation that would eventually be released as *The Man on the Eiffel Tower* (1949), Laughton helped the director, his friend and costar Burgess Meredith, by directing the scenes in which Meredith appeared. The actor later took over direction of Herman Wouk's stage adaptation of his novel *The Caine Mutiny Court-Martial* from Dick Powell.

In 1953, Laughton and his manager Paul Gregory optioned the first novel by Davis Grubb, a writer from West Virginia. *The Night of the Hunter* was an attempt at a modern-day folk story, tinged with poetic lyricism that has not dated well. In it, a psychopathic criminal known as the Preacher chases two children who hold the key to a fortune hidden by their dead father.

Gregory secured financing for the project from United Artists. Laughton sent the book to Robert Mitchum, who agreed to the part before work began on a script. Laughton also cast Shelley Winters and Lillian Gish in key roles. He then hired Pulitzer Prize-winner James Agee to write the screenplay adaptation. According to Laughton's biographer Charles Higham, the alcoholic Agee submitted an overlong script set in a too-specific Depression-era South of breadlines and soup kitchens. Laughton let it be known that he rewrote Agee's work, but other accounts give the screenwriter more credit for the final script. (Agee died of a heart attack in New York City that May; he was awarded a posthumous Pulitzer Prize in 1958 for *A Death in the Family*.)

Cinematographer Stanley Cortez met Laughton during the filming of *The Man on the Eiffel Tower*. Laughton had admired Cortez's remarkable work on *The Magnificent Ambersons* (1942), and the two collaborated closely on the new project. As a result, *The Night of the Hunter* has a look unique in Hollywood films of its period. In later interviews Cortez described elaborate efforts to get Shelley Winters' hair to unfold properly underwater; the triangular compositions of a shot depicting a murder; the forced perspective used when the children hide in a hayloft: "The figure moving against the horizon wasn't Mitchum at all. It was a midget on a little pony."

Mitchum had reached a point in his career where moviemaking had lost it glamour for him. He had already undergone an arrest for possession of marijuana and appeared in several negligible movies (*My Forbidden Past*, *White Witch Doctor*, etc.) without denting his appeal to the public. But Laughton somehow persuaded the actor to approach this part seriously. Mitchum has never been as menacing, as psychologically astute, or as fearless as in this role. He is a monster brought to life, a force of pure id, and one of the most frightening figures in 1950s cinema. Today we would reduce a similar character to labels like "serial killer." But Mitchum is far more intriguing, a man whose intelligence and wry humor allow him to justify anything.

Mitchum reportedly did not get along with Winters, and her performance is the weakest in a movie of wildly unbalanced acting. If Mitchum had trouble relating to his costar, Laughton had enormous difficulty eliciting naturalistic performances from the two child actors cast in the film. Billy Chapin by that time had been in the industry

for nearly ten years, and both his brother and sister also worked as actors. Sally Jane Bruce, on the other hand, apparently never worked in film again.

Shooting began on August 14, 1954, and included work on the Republic Studios lot as well as on Rowland V. Lee's ranch. Outtakes show just how cleverly and patiently Laughton elicited performances from both his untrained and professional cast. As the takes mount up, Laughton coaxes and shapes the actors until they provide what he has been looking for.

Laughton's willingness to experiment, to push boundaries, is the most unexpected aspect of the film today. The risks he took later became a hallmark of independent filmmaking. He was just as eager to change the shape of the frame as he was to experiment with a subjective camera, combining silent film techniques with more modern ideas. His film had a clear vision, one uncompromised by studio interference.

However, the director was reluctant to carry the story to its logical conclusion. It would take a heartless director to endanger the children in the film any further, but it would take a more logical and disciplined one to avoid the novel's sudden shift into Sunday school fantasy. Lillian Gish's informal orphanage could be the outgrowth of a Mary Pickford film like *Sparrows*. The last third of the film is almost a throwback to an earlier age, when films abandoned plotting for scenes of visual splendor and moments of piercing tenderness. What grounds *The Night of the Hunter* is its pitiless honesty, like Gish's offhand observation, "It's a hard world for little things."

At the time it was released, with rock and roll music just starting to dominate radio, with widescreen and color film processes seen as antidotes to television's increasing dominance, this small, personal, troubling film was doomed to failure. *Variety* astutely complained about "offbeat touches that have a misty effect," well aware that *The Night of the Hunter* couldn't compete in the cultural marketplace. Laughton started work on an adaptation of Norman Mailer's *The Naked and the Dead* with Terry and Denis Sanders, and sent Stanley Cortez to Hawaii to scout locations while they struggled over the script. But the project was eventually taken away from him. (Raoul Walsh wound up directing a version in 1958.) Laughton never had another serious opportunity to make a film, and in fact acted in only a handful of movies before his death in 1962.

Oklahoma!

Magna Theatre Corp., 1955. Sound, color, 2.20. 148 minutes.

Cast: Gordon MacRae (Curly), Gloria Grahame (Ado Annie), Gene Nelson (Will Parker), Charlotte Greenwood (Aunt Eller), Eddie Albert (Ali Hakim), James Whitmore (Mr. Carnes [Judge Andrew Carnes]), Shirley Jones (Laurey), Rod Steiger (Jud Fry), Barbara Lawrence (Gertie), Jay C. Flippen (Skidmore), Roy Barcroft (Marshal), James Mitchell (Dream Curley), Bambi Linn (Dream Laurey).

The Dancers: James Mitchell, Jennie Workman, Kelly Brown, Lizanne Truex, Bambi Linn, Virginia Bosler, Evelyn Taylor, Jane Fischer, Marc Platt.

Credits: Directed by Fred Zinnemann. Music by Richard Rodgers. Book and lyrics by Oscar Hammerstein II. Screen play by Sonya Levien and William Ludwig. Adapted from Rodgers and Hammerstein's Musical Play Based Upon a Dramatic Play by Lynn Riggs. Originally produced on the stage by The Theatre Guild. Produced by Arthur Hornblow, Jr. Dances staged by Agnes de Mille. Production designed by Oliver Smith. Art direction by Joseph Wright. Music conducted and supervised by Jay Blackton. Musical arrangements by Robert Russell Bennett. Background music adapted and conducted by Adolph Deutsch. Director of photography: Robert Surtees. Costumes by Orry Kelly and Motley. Production executive: Barney Briskin. Set decoration: Keogh Gleason. Color consultant: Alvord Eiseman. Production aide: John Fearnley. Todd-AO technician: Schuyler A. Sanford. Film editor: Gene Ruggiero. Assistant director: Arthur Black, Jr. Music coordinator: Robert Helfer. Recording supervisor: Fred Hynes. Make-up: Ben Lane. Hair stylist: Annabell. Wardrobe: Frank Beetson and Ann Peck. Westrex recording system. A Rodgers & Hammerstein production of a Magna release.

Additional Cast includes: Ben Johnson (Cowboy at depot).

Additional Credits: Based on the play *Green Grow the Lilacs* by Lynn Riggs. Sound editor: Milo Lory. Music editor: Ralph Ives. Sound recording: Joseph I. Kane. Second unit cameraman: Floyd Crosby. Production dates: July 14, 1954, to December 6, 1954. Premiered in New York City on October 13, 1955.

Awards: Oscars for Best Music—Scoring of a Musical Picture (Robert Russell Bennett, Jay Blackton, Adolph Deutsch); Sound—Recording.

Other Versions: Simultaneously filmed in a CinemaScope version with different credits and a running time of 138 minutes. Magna distributed the Todd-AO version; RKO, the CinemaScope version until 1956, when distribution was taken over by Twentieth Century-Fox.

Available: Twentieth Century Fox Home Entertainment DVD (2005). UPC: 0-24543-20843-3.

In the preface to his play *Green Grow the Lilacs*, Lynn Riggs wrote that he was trying to "recapture in a kind of nostalgic glow . . . the old folk songs and ballads I used to hear in my Oklahoma childhood." Riggs was born in 1899 near Claremore in what was then called the Cherokee Nation Indian Territory. He set his play around 1900, seven years before Oklahoma became a state, and two years before his mother, who was one-eighth Cherokee, died. Like the old tales he remembered, the play dealt with outsized characters: a rambunctious cowboy, his headstrong girlfriend, an angry farmhand. On stage *Green Grow the Lilacs* was filled with music, and even featured a hoedown complete with fiddlers.

Produced by the Theatre Guild and directed by Herbert J. Biberman (*Salt of the Earth*, 1954), the play starred Franchot Tone and June Walker.

Also in the cast were future acting teacher Lee Strasberg and Woodward Ritter, better known today as cowboy star Tex Ritter. Although the play was not a success, it impressed composer Richard Rodgers when the Theatre Guild approached him to work on a musical update. Rodgers was enjoying the success of *By Jupiter*, what would be his longest-running production with his collaborator Lorenz Hart, but Hart refused to work on what was tentatively called *Away We Go!* Oscar Hammerstein II, hired to write the book, became lyricist as well, initiating one of the most successful songwriting teams in Broadway history.

When it opened on March 31, 1943, at the St. James Theatre in New York, *Oklahoma!* had as big an impact on musical theater as *Show Boat* had some fifteen years earlier. Music and dance were integrated into the book instead of presented as separate performances. The psychology behind the characters became an important element in the plot, which presented its rural settings as worthy of serious consideration rather than fodder for jokes. Directed by Rouben Mamoulian, with dances by Agnes de Mille, *Oklahoma!* ran for over two thousand shows, influencing every musical that followed.

Although the play had been financed in part by Harry Cohn at Columbia, Rodgers and Hammerstein resisted efforts to adapt it to movies, afraid to cannibalize the audience for many profitable touring productions of *Oklahoma!* It wasn't until producer Michael Todd approached them with test footage from a new process that they considered a film version. Todd had been an early proponent of Cinerama; when he was forced out of that company by the other investors, he began searching for a rival process, one that wouldn't require three projectors, one in which "everything comes out of one hole."

Todd hired Dr. Brian O'Brien at the University of Rochester, who became head of research at the American Optical Company. He oversaw development of 65mm film, with a negative image four times larger than standard 35mm film and with a six-channel magnetic soundtrack. (Sound requirements made the final print size 70mm.) Todd hired director Fred Zinnemann, who had participated in Cinerama tests, to shoot footage in what was called Todd-AO. When Rodgers and Hammerstein viewed the footage, they not only gave permission to adapt *Oklahoma!*, they set up their own production company to maintain control over the production. Magna—the company formed to distribute *Oklahoma!*—included former Paramount producer Arthur Hornblow, Jr., and former Fox chief Joseph Schenck. (Todd was eventually forced out of the production.)

The original leads were now too old for the film version. Zinnemann gave some thought to Paul Newman or James Dean for the role of Curly, but agreed with the composers that the part required a true singer. Gordon MacRae had been a big-band singer before joining the Army Air Corps. After World War II, he appeared on Broadway and on radio, became a recording star, and made several films at Warner Brothers, notably teaming with Doris Day in musicals like *Tea for Two* (1950). Shirley Jones was discovered by Rodgers & Hammerstein talent scout John Fearnley; she had been singing in the chorus of an *Oklahoma!* touring company.

Rod Steiger had been suggested to Rodgers and Hammerstein by Zinnemann; although untrained, he did his own singing and dancing (as did Gloria Grahame). In his autobiography, Zinnemann praised Steiger's talent for exploring Jud Fry's motives: "He emerged as a disturbed, isolated person shunned by everyone, and this seduced the audience into a kind of reluctant pity."

Filming was unusually complicated, not in the least because of poor weather on location in Nogales, Arizona. (Zinnemann nixed shooting in Oklahoma because "too many oil wells were marring the landscape.") This was the first attempt to film in Todd-AO; the process was so new that only one wide-angle lens for it existed in the world. To protect their investment, Magna executives ordered Zinnemann to shoot two versions simultaneously, one in CinemaScope. (The CinemaScope prints would be the source of 35mm reduction prints for theaters that could only handle "flat" films.)

There are subtle differences in the two versions. The Todd-AO 2.20 aspect ratio offered a slightly looser, more open frame, whereas CinemaScope, at 2.55, was longer, narrower. Some scenes were shot with the cameras side by side, like shots involving moving trains; some were filmed one after the other, like MacRae's rendition of "Surrey with the Fringe on Top." Interior and nighttime scenes were shot on MGM soundstages back in Los Angeles. (MGM also supplied much of the technical crew, like cinematographer Robert Surtees.)

Zinnemann had no experience directing musical films, but he had made the award-winning *High Noon* (1952) and *From Here to Eternity* (1953). He took a calm, measured approach to the material, avoiding camera tricks for the most part (aside from a few "you are there" shots during the runaway wagon sequence). He could emphasize an element of dance or music in ways that couldn't be accomplished on stage, by drawing the camera in or cutting to a different angle. Zinnemann felt confident enough in the music, the performances, and de Mille's choreography to let some shots run on for ninety seconds or more, even if it meant breaking a cardinal rule about cutting the dancers' feet out of the frame.

Magna executives wanted the experience of viewing the Todd-AO *Oklahoma!* to be as close to attending a theatrical performance as possible. Filmgoers had to order reserved seats in advance, and no popcorn was sold during shows. Some forty theaters were renovated to accommodate the larger screen required for Todd-AO projection.

Paradoxically, the decade or so it took to bring *Oklahoma!* to the screen made it seem a bit old fashioned by the time it opened. Other plays and films had caught up—for example, it's unlikely that *Seven Brides for Seven Brothers* (1954) would have looked the same without *Oklahoma!* Like their later collaborations, such as *The Sound of Music* (1965), Rodgers and Hammerstein front-loaded *Oklahoma!* with their best material, leaving a second half of reprises and hasty plot twists. But few filmed musicals can boast an opening as galvanizing as MacRae's version of "Oh What a Beautiful Mornin'," a sequence as subtly erotic as "The Surrey with the Fringe on Top," or any of a dozen other elements that make *Oklahoma!* so distinctive.

Rebel Without a Cause

Warner Bros., 1955. Sound, color, 2.55. 111 minutes.

Cast: James Dean (Jim Stark), Natalie Wood (Judy), Sal Mineo (John "Plato" Crawford), Jim Backus (Frank Stark), Ann Doran (Mrs. Stark), Corey Allen (Buzz Gunderson), William Hopper (Judy's father), Rochelle Hudson (Judy's mother), Dennis Hopper (Goon), Edward Platt (Ray Fremick), Steffi Sidney (Mil), Marietta Canty (Plato's nurse), Virginia Brissac (Mrs. Stark), Beverly Long (Helen), Ian Wolfe (Dr. Minton, lecturer at planetarium), Frank Mazzola (Crunch), Robert Foulk (Gene), Jack Simmons (Cookie), Tom Bernard (Harry), Nick Adams (Chick), Jack Grinnage (Moose), Clifford Morris (Cliff).

Credits: Directed by Nicholas Ray. Produced by David Weisbart. Screen Play by Stewart Stern. Adaptation by Irving Shulman. From a story by Nicholas Ray. Director of photography: Ernest Haller. Art director: Malcolm Bert. Film Editor: William Ziegler. Music by Leonard Rosenman. Sound by Stanley Jones. Set decorator: William Wallace. Costumes designed by Moss Marry. Makeup supervisor: Gordon Bau. Dialogue supervisor: Dennis Stock. Assistant directors: Don Page, Robert Farfan. RCA Sound System.

Additional Cast: Dorothy Abbott (Nurse), Jimmy Baird (Bean, Judy's brother), Paul Birch (Police Chief), Paul Bryar (Desk Sergeant #2), Louise Lane (Policewoman), Nelson Leigh (Desk Sergeant #1), David McMahon (Crunch's father), Peter Miller (Hoodlum), Bruce Noonan (Monitor), House Peters, Jr. (Police officer), Stephanie Pond-Smith (Girl), Gus Schilling (Attendant), Almira Sessions (Teacher), Dick Wessel (Planetarium guide), Robert Williams (Ed, Moose's father).

Additional Credits: Executive producer: Steve Trilling. Production design: Malcolm C. Bert. Art direction: Malcolm C. Bert. Production dates: March 28 to May 26, 1955. Premiered in New York City on October 27, 1955. Rated PG-13 in 2005.

Available: Warner Home Video DVD (1999). ISBN: 0-7907-3742-6. UPC: 0-85391-40692-1.

One of the sources of *Rebel Without a Cause* was a 1944 book of that title by psychologist Robert Lindner, a specialist in "hypnotic therapy." Warner Brothers purchased the book in 1946, perhaps as a gesture toward the hard-hitting message films the studio used to make in the 1930s. The book remained unused until 1954, when director Nicholas Ray submitted a seventeen-page treatment called "The Blind Run." Ray's story was, in his words, "without dramatic structure but with a point of view." Like Lindner's book, it dealt with juvenile delinquency, a problem that always existed but that now had a new name and a new set of explanations.

Ray was not an expert on the subject, although he believed in the connection between psychology and creativity. He was born Raymond Nichols Kienzle in 1911 in Wisconsin. His father died when he was fifteen. Ray earned a college scholarship, studied with Frank Lloyd Wright at Taliesin, and moved to New York City to work with the Group Theatre. He built a career in radio, specializing in folklore, before he became an assistant director to Elia Kazan for *A Tree Grows in Brooklyn*. He directed his first feature, an adaptation of the

pulp crime novel *Thieves Like Us*, in 1947; it was released in 1949 under the title *They Live by Night*. Working at a furious pace, Ray directed fourteen films in ten years, including the cult Western *Johnny Guitar* (1954, a Registry title) and *Knock on Any Door* (1949), an earnest melodrama about juvenile delinquency.

When Ray made it clear that he did not want to use Lindner's book, Warners assigned Leon Uris, better known today as the author of best-selling novels like *Exodus* (1957) and *Topaz* (1967), to work with him on developing "The Blind Run" into a script. The two interviewed social workers, teenagers, and policemen, and Uris even did volunteer work with disaffected youth. As Ray wrote later, "All told similar stories—divorced parents, parents who could not guide or understand, who were indifferent or simply 'criticized,' parents who needed a scapegoat in the family." But the director wasn't satisfied with Uris's work. Warners then assigned Irving Shulman, whose novel *The Amboy Dukes* (1947) was also about juvenile delinquency. Shulman came up with the idea for the film's "chickie run," or drag race, but according to Ray, the writer didn't get along with James Dean. (Shulman was allowed to turn his screenplay into the 1956 novel *Children of the Dark*.)

Ray had met with Dean in New York to show him a portion of the script, and wrote later that they had a handshake deal to make the movie. Born in Indiana in 1931, Dean studied at the University of California, landing bit parts on TV shows and in commercials. Actor James Whitmore introduced Dean to method acting, and encouraged him to pursue it further at the Actors Studio in New York City. There he got a screen test with Kazan for *East of Eden* (1955), a generational melodrama based on a John O'Hara novel. Dean's performance received some harsh reviews, but by the film's release, Warners was already committed to *Rebel*.

Ray and producer David Weisbart, formerly an editor on films like *A Streetcar Named Desire* (1951), continued to work on the project, coming up with the idea of setting the film's climax at the Griffith Park Observatory. Stewart Stern, the third writer on the project, was an infantryman in the Battle of the Bulge. He had written a screenplay for *Teresa* (1951), a film noted at the time for its psychological realism and acuity. He became close friends with Dean, and referred to the film as "a modern day *Peter Pan*: three kids inventing a world of their own." As far as Ray was concerned, the script boiled down to one of his script notes: "A boy wants to be a man, quick."

Apart from nabbing Dean, casting was a drawn-out process involving protracted auditions and screen tests. Corey Allen's open hostility helped him win the important part of Buzz. Real-life gang member Frank Mazzola became Crunch. Dennis Hopper was a candidate for the role of Plato, but Ray cast Sal Mineo instead after his screen test with Dean and Natalie Wood. A native of the Bronx, Mineo had appeared in several Broadway productions. It was his openness and vulnerability that won him the part as much as his chemistry with Dean. This was the first important "serious" role for former child-star Wood; one of the popular rumors surrounding the film is that she didn't persuade Ray to cast her until she was involved in an automobile accident with Hopper.

The behind-the-scenes histrionics are in some ways more interesting than the dutiful storytelling that winds up in the film. In later interviews, Mineo claimed that he was directed to perform Plato as a homosexual attracted to Dean's Jim Stark. The alleged affair Ray, in his forties at the time, had with the teenaged Wood pales beside the fact that his wife Gloria Grahame had recently left him for his son. Dean bewildered his fellow actors by taking so much time preparing for his scenes. Jim Backus, a comedian cast to play Dean's father, spoke about him shadow boxing and climbing up and down a stage ladder to get into the proper mood.

Dean was trying to remove the artifices of acting, to find an emotional honesty to his character that would be stronger than technique. Like Marlon Brando, to whom he was often compared, Dean was willing to expose his emotions in ways that would have been unthinkable to many of his contemporaries. In hindsight it is difficult to say that his work is any more honest than a "classical" star like James Cagney or Henry Fonda, especially since his three screen vehicles have aged so poorly. But at the time he was considered revolutionary.

So revolutionary that four days after filming started, studio head Jack Warner ordered Ray to start the project over again and upgrade to color. (That is one rumor; another is that the studio's contract with CinemaScope insisted that the film couldn't be in black-and-white.) That meant working out a new budget, resulting in fewer extras and switching the time frame from Christmas to Easter to make set decoration easier. It also rendered the film's original opening scene—in which a father bringing Christmas presents home is mugged by delinquents—meaningless. The current opening credits, with a drunken Dean encountering a wind-up monkey, is a remnant of the lost scene.

Jack Warner was willing to spend more on *Rebel* in part because he was excited by the film's treatment of delinquency. *Rebel* was following in the tradition of troubled youth movies like *The Wild One* (1953) and *Blackboard Jungle*, which opened right before Ray started filming, and in the tradition of the studio's own "ripped from the headlines" problem films. In common with most Hollywood films, *Rebel* attempted to explain or solve juvenile delinquency by reducing it to a single problem that required a simple solution. What Warner hadn't counted on was the way the film showed viewers how easy and attractive delinquency could be. Even more troubling to parents, Dean, Wood, and Mineo weren't playing motorcycle thugs or inner-city hoodlums; they were playing wealthy, even privileged, teens (or at least older versions of them). It didn't take long for fans to adopt their clothes, their mannerisms, and their tortured attitudes.

Filming finished on May 26, 1955, eleven days behind schedule. Dean went to work at once on *Giant*. Mineo would join him there, while Wood's next film was *The Searchers* with John Wayne. *Rebel Without a Cause* was ready for screening on October 3, 1955, three days after Dean died in a car crash. The film received three Oscar nominations, but its true legacy is the impact it left on youth culture. Not just the rash of teen-oriented films and television shows that followed, but even "serious" art like *West Side Story*. Or, for that matter, such touchstones as *Easy Rider* and *American Graffiti*. When Wood drowned in 1981, four years after Mineo was murdered, *Rebel Without a Cause* could even claim a morbid cult following.

All That Heaven Allows

Universal International, 1955. Sound, color, 1.77. 89 minutes.
Cast: Jane Wyman (Cary Scott), Rock Hudson (Rob Kirby), Agnes Moorehead (Sara Warren), Conrad Nagel (Harvey), Virginia Grey (Alida), Gloria Talbott (Kay [Scott]), William Reynolds (Ned [Scott]), Charles Drake (Mick Anderson), Hayden Rorke (Dr. Hennessy), Jacqueline de Wit (Mona Plash), Leigh Snowden (Jo-Ann), Donald Curtis (Howard Hoffer), Alex Gerry (George Warren), Nestor Paiva (Manuel), Forrest Lewis (Mr. Weeks), Tol Avery (Tom Allenby), Merry Anders (Mary Ann).
Credits: Directed by Douglas Sirk. Screenplay by Peg Fenwick. Based on the story by Edna L. Lee and Harry Lee. Produced by Ross Hunter. Director of photography: Russell Metty. Technicolor color consultant: William Fritzsche. Music: Frank Skinner. Music supervision: Joseph Gershenson. Art direction: Alexander Golitzen, Eric Orbom. Set decorations: Russell A. Gausman, Julia Heron. Sound: Leslie I. Carey, Joe Lapis. Film editor: Frank Gross. Gowns: Bill Thomas. Hair stylist: Joan St. Oegger. Make-up: Bud Westmore. Assistant director: Joseph E. Kenny. Western Electric Recording. Copyright 1954. Print by Technicolor.
Additional Credits: Production dates: January 5 to February 1955. Opened December, 1955.
Other Versions: Remade as *Angst essen Seele auf Ali/Ali: Fear Eats the Soul* (1974, directed by Rainer Werner Fassbinder).
Available: Criterion Collection DVD (2001). UPC: 7-15515-01142-6.

Director Douglas Sirk preferred calling the string of soap operas he made for Universal in the 1950s "melodramas." At the time they were referred to as women's pictures, but they were very different from the women's pictures of the 1930s and '40s. Actresses like Bette Davis, Barbara Stanwyck, Claudette Colbert, and Joan Crawford made their mark playing victims of prejudice, intolerance, and, for Davis in *Dark Victory* (1939), disease. The punishment in most of these films concerned family: the heroines were prevented from having or taken away from their spouses and children. Suggestions that families might be the problem, and not the reward or solution, were usually limited to comedies, thrillers, or "serious" films like *The Magnificent Ambersons* (1942). *All That Heaven Allows* has a more subversive message: not only could families cause misery, but the entire search for happiness in American society might be misguided.

Born Claus Detlev Sirk in Denmark in 1900, Sirk changed his name to Detlef Sierck when he moved to Germany in his teens. A leftist intellectual, he switched from theater to film to deter persecution by the Nazis. With his Jewish wife, he fled Germany in 1937, ending up in Hollywood in 1939 with the name Douglas Sirk and with an offer from Warner Brothers to remake one of his German films. When that project fell through, he directed the zero-budget *Hitler's Madman* for Producers Releasing Corporation in 1943. After directing a half-dozen independent films, he signed

with Universal, where he was assigned a submarine melodrama and a 3-D Western.

Sirk not only felt superior to his assignments, he had a growing disdain for American society. But it wasn't until he was teamed with producer Ross Hunter that the director found an outlet for his true opinions. Hunter started as an actor in films like *Hit the Hay* (1946), and wisely switched to producing in the early 1950s. Initially his specialty was adding color and a modern spin to old Universal properties like *Magnificent Obsession*, previously filmed in 1935. Directed by Sirk, and starring Hunter's friend Rock Hudson and Jane Wyman, the 1954 release was such a hit at the box office that Universal quickly okayed another film with the same essential team.

Sirk typically thought little of *All That Heaven Allows*, a novel written by journalist Harry J. Lee, Jr., and his mother Edna. (Edna Lee also wrote *Queen Bee*, which became a vehicle for Joan Crawford.) In a 1979 interview for the BBC, he said, "In spite of a poor story, a nothing of a story, I put a lot of my own into that film. My mirrors, my symbols, my statues, my literary knowledge about Thoreau and so forth. I was trying to give that cheap stuff a meaning." The director focused on the look and sound of the film rather than on its plot, or its acting. Drawing on his background in German expressionism, Sirk had cameraman Russell Metty wash the sets with primary colors, vivid blues and reds that were meant to echo the characters' psychological states. Frank Skinner provided a soothing orchestral soundtrack with vaguely classical overtones.

The story concerns a love affair between a recent widow and mother of two young adults, played by Jane Wyman, and her gardener (Rock Hudson), actually a tree surgeon with plans to open his own nursery. The children, a psychology-obsessed coed (Gloria Talbott) and her prig of a brother (William Reynolds), are indifferent to their mother until she steps outside how they are willing to see her. Friends in Wyman's country club set are openly hostile, except for a radiant Agnes Moorehead, her head aflame with red tints.

Wyman won an Oscar playing a deaf mute in *Johnny Belinda* (1948), and she is an even more passive character here. Her blank features

508

almost never betray emotion, although her eyes can't hide her inner fears, even when she is smiling. Sirk presents her character as a stick figure in a lopsided argument against materialism, tapping into an increasingly popular vision of suburbia as hell, albeit a pricey one filled with consumer goods. The idea of questioning economic values is a worthy one, but Sirk doesn't bother to present it very cogently. It's as if Wyman's character had no existence outside this movie, that she came to life the moment the camera rolled. Her children and friends are strangers to her, she has no outside interests—no bridge or garden club, no charities, no religion, no taste in art, no apparent appetites. She wears what she finds in her closet, does what she is told to do, and agonizes over the happy ending that is staring her in the face.

It's a frustrating role and performance, much like the rest of the film. German director Rainer Werner Fassbinder once criticized Sirk's work by writing, "You leave his films feeling somehow dissatisfied." For every astutely judged scene, there is one filled with blunt psychological forebodings, or clichés like, "To thine own self be true." Yet Sirk somehow maintains a balance between compassion and criticism, between a happy ending and a blanket condemnation, keeping the film's underlying tensions and contradictions in check. (To see how effective Sirk's direction was, compare *All That Heaven Allows* to Todd Haynes' modern-day homage, *Far From Heaven*, released in 2002. By making explicit what Sirk and his colleagues left unstated, Haynes reduced his film to a pastiche.)

To viewers today, the movie's most glaring contradiction is Rock Hudson's performance as a love interest. This film and *Magnificent Obsession* helped establish him as a credible dramatic actor, even though *Variety*'s critic found him "handsome and somewhat wooden." As a closeted homosexual, Hudson necessarily kept his true emotions in check. The disconnect between his true life and the character he plays gives *All That Heaven Allows* a poignancy Sirk could not have intended.

The director continued to work with Hudson, as well as with Robert Stack and Dorothy Malone, but within four years Sirk had given up filmmaking for good, retiring with his wife to Munich. Wyman, her steely resolve intact, would later become a fixture on television, which is depicted here as an alien invader of households, "the last refuge of lonely women."

One Froggy Evening

Warner Bros., 1955. Sound, color, 1.37. 7 minutes.
Credits: Directed by Charles M. Jones. Story: Michael Maltese. Animation: Abe Levitow, Richard Thomson, Ken Harris, Ben Washam. Layouts: Robert Gribbroek. Backgrounds: Philip De Guard. Musical direction: Milt Franklyn.
Additional Credits: Vocals by Bill Roberts.
Available: Warner Home Video DVD, *Looney Tunes Golden Collection Volume 2* (2004). ISBN: 0-7907-8650-8. UPC: 0-85393-12842-5.

Director Chuck Jones and writer Michael Maltese spent much of the 1950s refining their approach toward animation. The way they pared away background clutter and detailed animation was partly a result of changing artistic styles, evidenced in cartoons like *Gerald McBoing Boing* (1951, a Registy title). But it was also due to tighter budgets. At Warner Brothers, producer Leon Schlesinger had long since been replaced by Edward Selzer, an executive with little interest in animation. Required to turn out a short every five weeks, Jones found himself manipulating budgets in order to sneak personal projects through. He would finish a Road Runner piece in three weeks, for example, in order to spend more time on another film.

The idea for *One Froggy Evening* came from Maltese, who gave Jones a brief premise: a construction worker discovers a singing frog. The two then collaborated on the full script, with Jones struggling to understand the frog's character. "To me, looking back on it, it is a very touching story," he said later. "I really felt sorry for the frog and the man." Critics have subsequently cast the film as a parable about greed and frustration, but at the time Jones was more concerned with what the frog would sing.

Since the frog is discovered during the demolition of an 1892 building, Jones and composer Milt Franklyn searched for popular tunes from that era. They came up with examples like "Hello, Ma Baby" from 1899 and "Come Back to Erin" from 1866, but also "I'm Just Wild About Harry," a 1921 hit by Eubie Blake and Noble Sissle. How did the frog learn the song? For that matter, how did he learn "The Michigan Rag," penned by Jones, Maltese, and Franklyn especially for this film?

Film historian Michael Barrier credits much of the film's animation to Ben Washam, an acknowledged master of characterization. Strikingly, there is no dialogue in the film apart from song lyrics and the occasional crowd noise, so Washam's treatment of the construction worker was critical. Other workers at Warners have told critics that Ken Harris did the frog's high-stepping dance numbers. Historian Keith Scott discovered that the vocals were by Bill Roberts, a nightclub singer in Hollywood who had previously worked with Tex Avery on the cartoon *Little Tinker* (1947).

Jones and his staff included several in-jokes, not the least of which were two more entries in the ever-expanding Acme business directory. The most touching may have been the building erected in 1955, named for Warners sound effects specialist Tregoweth "Treg" Brown.

It wasn't until decades after the release of *One Froggy Evening* that the star received his name, Michigan J. Frog. In the 1970s, Jones needed to identify the character for a television show; the "Michigan" came from "The Michigan Rag." The middle initial came from *Time* film critic Jay Cocks, who along with animation critic Charles Solomon considers *One Froggy Evening* a "perfect" cartoon. This was the frog's sole screen appearance, although he later became the mascot of the short-lived WB television network.

Perfect or not, *One Froggy Evening* exemplifies what was happening to animation in general and to the Warner Brothers animation department in particular. Directors like Avery and Robert Clampett had departed years earlier, Avery for other studios and eventually to make commercials, Clampett to produce puppetry on television. Maltese was about to leave to work for the new Hanna Barbera company, where he would write for *Huckleberry Hound*, among other TV shows. Jones himself had left Warners during a brief strike, and would soon be modifying his old cartoons for television. Before that happened, he finished another Registry title, *What's Opera, Doc?* (1957).

The Court Jester

Paramount, 1956. Sound, color, 2.35. 101 minutes.

Cast: Danny Kaye (Hubert Hawkins), Glynis Johns (Maid Jean), Basil Rathbone (Sir Ravenhurst), Angela Lansbury (Princess Gwendolyn), Cecil Parker (King Roderick I), Mildred Natwick (Griselda), Robert Middleton (Sir Griswold), Michael Pate (Sir Locksley), Herbert Rudley (Captain of the Guard), Noel Drayton (Fergus), John Carradine (Giacomo), Edward Ashley (The Black Fox), Alan Napier (Sir Brockhurst), Lewis Martin (Sir Finsdale), Patrick Aherne (Sir Pertwee), Richard Kean (Archbishop), Hermine's Midgets, The American Legion Zouaves (of Richard F. Smith Post No. 29, Jackson, Michigan).

Credits: Written, produced and directed by Norman Panama and Melvin Frank. Director of photography: Ray June. Technicolor color consultant: Richard Mueller. Art direction: Hal Pereira, Roland Anderson. Edited by Tom McAdoo. Assistant to the producers: Hal C. Kern. Music scored and conducted by Victor Schoen. Songs by Sylvia Fine and Sammy Cahn except "The Maladjusted Jester," by Sylvia Fine. Choreography: James Starbuck. Second unit director: William Watson. Special photographic effects: John P. Fulton, Irmin Roberts. Process photography: Farciot Edouart. Set decoration: Sam Comer, Arthur Krams. Costumes: Edith Head, Yvonne Wood. Assistant director: John Coonan. Technical advisor: D.R.O. Hatswell. Makeup supervision: Wally Westmore. Sound recording by Harry Lindgren, John Cope.

Additional Credits: Production dates: November 1954 to February 1955; reshoots: February and March 1955. Opened February 2, 1956.

Available: Paramount DVD (1999). ISBN: 0-7921-5519-X. UPC: 0-9736-05512-7-3.

When Danny Kaye started production on *The Court Jester*, he had just received an honorary Oscar "for his unique talents, his service to the Academy, the motion picture industry, and the American people." Born David Kaminski in Brooklyn in 1913, he dropped out of school to work in the "Borscht Belt," in vaudeville, and in nightclubs. He appeared in a few comedy shorts, but was struggling to make headway when he met Sylvia Fine in 1939. (They married a year later.) Also born in 1913, she was a college graduate who had written the score for a musical adaptation of George Bernard Shaw's *Arms and the Man* with her cousin, future novelist Irwin Shaw. Fine began composing specialty numbers for Kaye at Camp Tamiment, a resort in the Pennsylvania Poconos. Songs like "Anatole of Paris" and "Stanislavsky," intricate tongue twisters filled with rapid-fire puns, became a mainstay of his act, and later part of his Broadway debut with Imogene Coca in *The Straw Hat Review*. This led to a supporting role in Moss Hart's play *Lady in the Dark*, in which he sang "Tchaikovsky," a Fine patter number in which he rattled off some fifty Russian names in little more than half a minute.

Producer Samuel Goldwyn had seen Kaye performing his nightclub act, and pursued him for two years before the comic finally signed a movie contract. Goldwyn perhaps saw in Kaye the opportunity to recycle the films he had made some ten years earlier with comedians like Eddie Cantor; according to Fine, he used to greet Kaye with a cheery "Hello, Eddie!" Fine's vision of her husband's stage and screen persona was very precise: he wasn't cruel, bombastic, or a "nebbish," he was an "eager beaver" who would "trip himself up in enthusiasm." Goldwyn starred Kaye in *Up in Arms* (1944; based on the source material for the Cantor play and movie *Whoopee!*), for which Fine worked in two of her specialty numbers. Goldwyn paired Kaye with movie newcomer Virginia Mayo in *Wonder Man* (1945), *The Kid from Brooklyn* (1946, a remake of a Harold Lloyd film), *The Secret Life of Walter Mitty* (1947, based on the James Thurber short story), and *A Song Is Born* (1948; a remake of Howard Hawks' *Ball of Fire*).

Kaye's films were so successful that he quickly became Goldwyn's top box-office draw, but he was dismayed at parts that he felt restricted his abilities. He left for Warner Brothers at the end of his contract, reteaming with Goldwyn for the hit *Hans Christian Andersen* (1952). Kaye and Fine formed Dena Productions, named after their daughter, for *Knock on Wood* (1954); like *White Christmas*, in which he appeared with Bing Crosby in a reworking of *Holiday Inn*, it was released by Paramount. That same year, Kaye was named ambassador-at-large for UNICEF, the United Nations Children's Fund.

Knock on Wood was also Kaye's first film with the team of Melvin Frank and Norman Panama. The two had met at the University of Chicago, moving to Hollywood to write for Bob Hope's radio show. Soon they were writing Hope's movie scripts, including *Monsieur Beaucaire* (1946), which sent up some of the same situations found in *The Court Jester*. In fact, Hope proved Kaye's best model: the aggressive coward that Hope perfected in the 1940s became a sort of prototype for Kaye's own parts. *Knock on Wood* played off Hope's espionage comedies, while *The Court Jester* alluded to Hope vehicles like *The Princess and the Pirate* (1944) as well as *Monsieur Beaucaire*.

Frank and Panama also had to work within a structure devised over the years by Fine and Kaye. That meant more musical numbers than Hope would use, a prolonged patter sequence, some dialect routines, and opportunities for Kaye to dance and mime. As in many of his movies, Kaye plays several roles: as Hubert Hawkins, a shy acolyte of the Robin Hood–like Black Fox; as the Fox himself in a musical number; as Giacomo, an Italian jester; and, thanks to a witch's spell, as a master swordsman and assassin.

Fine worked with songwriter Sammy Cahn for most of the score, writing Kaye's patter routine, "The Maladjusted Jester," herself. Her lyrics could be delightfully intricate and multilayered: "For a jester's chief employment is to kill himself for your enjoyment and a jester unemployed is nobody's fool." Cahn, who had just won an Oscar for the title song to *Three Coins in the Fountain*, would soon begin a long working relationship with Frank Sinatra. Like everyone else on the film, he embraced a philosophy espoused in a number Kaye sings over the opening credits: "Each tried and true effect for the umpteenth time we'll resurrect." Frank and Panama deserve credit for the film's most famous patter routine, "No, the pellet with the poison's in the vessel with the pestle."

With its large cast, elaborate sets and costumes, and copious special effects, *The Court Jester* ended up the most expensive film comedy of its era. It was popular with moviegoers, although critics were more reserved. *The New Yorker*'s John McCarten complained about Kaye's "cuteness," writing that "Danny's a big boy now, and a big-league comedian, and he ought to cut out that sort of thing." He thought the film "wasn't half as funny as the things it tries to spoof." *Variety* noted that the film's "timeworn" clichés received a "not-so-subtle treatment." Unlike Hope's best vehicles, Kaye's films have not aged well, perhaps because of their campy, theatrical quality. It's clear that the comedian feels superior to his material, and to the people who like it. The only things he takes seriously in *The Court Jester* are his frivolous songs and dances.

The Court Jester was the last unqualified success in Kaye's film career. He would only appear in five more titles, although he also hosted an Emmy-winning television series in the 1960s prior to returning to the Broadway stage for *Two by Two* (1970). Kaye died in 1987 of complications after heart surgery, four years before his wife.

Frank and Panama followed *The Court Jester* with a Broadway musical, *Li'l Abner*, based on the Al Capp comic strip. They continued working for Hope on vehicles like *The Facts of Life* (1960), but broke up the team in the 1960s, their brand of humor a victim of changing tastes. Oddly, comedies about the age of chivalry have grown more popular in recent years, inspired perhaps by Richard Lester's swashbuckling *Three Musketeers* series (starting in 1974). *Monty Python and the Holy Grail* (1975), *The Princess Bride* (1987), *Robin Hood: Men in Tights* (1993), and even *Shrek* (2001) all cover much of the same territory as *The Court Jester*.

Invasion of the Body Snatchers

Allied Artists, 1956. Sound, B&W, 2.00. 80 minutes.

Cast: Kevin McCarthy (Dr. Miles Bennell), Dana Wynter (Becky Driscoll), Larry Gates (Dr. Danny Kauffman), King Donovan (Jack Belicec), Carolyn Jones (Theodora "Teddy" Belicec), Jean Willes (Sally), Ralph Dumke (Nick), Virginia Christine (Wilma), Tom Fadden (Ira), Kenneth Patterson (Kenneth Driscoll), Guy Way (Sam), Eileen Stevens (Anne Grimaldi), Beatrice Maude (Grandma Grimaldi), Jean Andren (Aunt Eleda), Bobby Clark (Jimmy Grimaldi), Everett Glass (Dr. Pursey), Dabbs Greer (Max Lomax), Pat O'Malley (Baggage man), Guy Rennie (Proprietor), Marie Selland (Martha Lomax), Sam Peckinpah (Charlie Buckholtz, gas meter reader), Harry J. Vejar.

Credits: Directed by Don Siegel. Screenplay by Daniel Mainwaring. Based on the *Collier's Magazine* serial by Jack Finney. Produced by Walter Wanger Pictures, Inc. Director of photography: Ellsworth Fredericks. Production design: Edward Haworth. Production manager: Allen K. Wood. Assistant directors: Richard Maybery, Bill Beaudine, Jr. Film editor: Robert S. Eisen. Sound: Ralph Butler. Music composed and conducted by Carmen Dragon. Sound editor: Del Harris. Music editor: Jerry Irvin. Special effects: Milt Rice. Set decorator: Joseph Kish. Make-up: Emile LaVigne. Hairdresser: Mary Westmoreland. Script supervisor: Irva Ross. Western Electric Recording. Produced in Superscope. An Allied Pictures Corporation presentation.

Additional Cast: Whit Bissell (Dr. Hill), Richard Deacon (Dr. Harvey Bassett), Robert Osterloh (Ambulance Driver), Frank Hagney.

Additional Credits: Dialogue director: Sam Peckinpah. Released February 5, 1956. Jack Finney's *The Body Snatchers* serialized in *Collier's Magazine* from November 26 to December 24, 1954.

Other Versions: *Invasion of the Body Snatchers* (1978, directed by Philip Kaufman), *Body Snatchers* (1993, directed by Abel Ferrara), *The Invasion* (2007, directed by Oliver Hirschbiegel).

Available: Artisan Home Entertainment/Republic Pictures DVD (1998). ISBN: 0782009980.

With a story line so potent it has been remade repeatedly, *Invasion of the Body Snatchers* remains one of the most influential horror movies of the 1950s. It succeeds so well in part because it isn't really a horror movie at all. If anything, it is closer to a murder mystery, or a film noir from the previous decade. Given that its screenwriter was responsible for thrillers like *Out of the Past* (1947), the film's grim, shadowy qualities shouldn't be so surprising. But an equally important factor behind *Invasion of the Body Snatchers* was its director, Don Siegel.

Born in Chicago in 1912, Siegel had a peripatetic upbringing, attending schools in New York and London as well as performing in vaudeville as a mandolinist and as a drummer in a ship's orchestra. An uncle who was a film editor got him a job at Warner Brothers, where he cataloged the studio's stock library. This ground-floor approach to editing gave him an unusually deep understanding of the different parts of a movie and how they related to each other. He graduated to assembling montage sequences for films as varied as *Yankee Doodle Dandy*, *Casablanca* and *Now, Voyager* (all 1942, and all in the Registry). From that position, he became a second unit director, fleshing out feature films with location footage, stunts, and everything else the main director didn't shoot personally.

Siegel won an Academy Award for *Star in the Night* (1945), a short parable. He left Warners to direct at other studios, including RKO and Universal. In 1954, he made *Riot in Cell Block 11* for Allied Artists, an outgrowth of Monogram Pictures. Producer Walter Wanger, who made the film in part to expose conditions he experienced while serving a sentence for shooting an agent he suspected was romancing his wife, was impressed with the way Siegel could combine a personal drama with the action scenes demanded by the genre.

Screenwriter Daniel Mainwaring had worked with Siegel before, on *The Big Steal* (1949), a stylish but improbable crime story starring Robert Mitchum, and the previous year on *An Annapolis Story*, a routine cadet tale that featured Kevin McCarthy in a supporting role. Wanger hired Mainwaring to adapt Jack Finney's *The Body Snatchers*, which ran as a serial in *Collier's Magazine* before being published as a novel in 1955.

Both Wanger and Siegel agreed that the project would differ from other horror films. There would be few special effects, no monsters, and almost no violence. Mainwaring structured the story like a mystery, but one that had no real solution. Where implacable fate was the source of Jeff Bailey's problems in *Out of the Past*, here society itself was to blame, that and the "mass hysteria" engendered by an unknown force operating somewhere in the cosmos.

Finney's story was set in Santa Mira, California (Mill Valley, in later editions of the novel). Something is affecting the people there, something that Dr. Miles Bennell (Kevin McCarthy) learns are seed pods that replace human personalities with alien ones. With former friends trying to turn him into an alien, he must flee town with his girlfriend, Becky Driscoll (Dana Wynter).

Everyone associated with the film denied there were any political implications to the story. McCarthy said later, "I thought this was about people who work on Madison Avenue. They have no hearts." But it's clear that Bennell and Becky are being pursued because they refuse to conform to society. Both are divorced iconoclasts at odds with the townspeople in Santa Mira (and Becky just got back from an unexplained stay in Europe). Both have intellectual tastes and expensive clothes. Both are ill-equipped to deal with the new, Cold War world.

Siegel shot much of the film in Sierra Madre and in various locations in and around Los Angeles, with cinematographer Ellsworth Fredericks employing the same slatted shadows and distorted angles that could be found in noirs like *Double Indemnity*. Siegel's background as a montage editor is evident in the film's crisp, confident pacing, especially during the chase sequences. *Invasion of the Body Snatchers* offered its many imitators a blueprint for how to generate shocks. A four-minute sequence in which Bennell breaks into a basement is an expertly assembled collection of tracking shots, red herrings, and trick jolts, all wreathed in gloomy, menacing shadows.

Siegel's low-key, realistic style is crucial to the impact of the story, as is Mainwaring's gradual elimination of everything that could help Bennell and Becky. Wanger and other Allied Artists executives eventually decided that Mainwaring's story was too hopeless, and insisted on adding opening and closing scenes that softened the story. Even so, the happy ending Finney invented for the novel was discarded.

After ten days for rehearsals, the film was shot in nineteen days for a budget of $300,000. Because Allied Artists had a poor distribution system, the film did not have much immediate impact on its release. However, word of mouth turned it into a hit, and filmmakers who ransacked its ideas burnished its reputation. Apart from its acknowledged remakes, *Invasion of the Body Snatchers* had a widespread influence over the horror genre. Half the episodes of TV's *The Twilight Zone* seem based on its premise.

Mainwaring and Siegel worked on two more projects together, but the director's reputation today is due in large part to his work with Clint Eastwood. McCarthy, the brother of author Mary McCarthy, briefly reprised his part here in the 1978 remake. Several other Jack Finney works were also filmed, including the ghastly *Maxie* (1985) with Glenn Close. Producer Walter Wanger spent years on his last project, a version of *Cleopatra* (1963) that became one of the notorious disasters of the 1960s.

The Searchers

Warner Bros., 1956. Sound, color, 1.75. 119 minutes.

Cast: John Wayne (Ethan Edwards), Jeffrey Hunter (Martin Pawley), Vera Miles (Laurie Jorgenson), Ward Bond (Capt. Rev. Samuel Johnson Clayton), Natalie Wood (Debbie Edwards), John Qualen (Lars Jorgensen), Olive Carey (Mrs. Jorgensen), Henry Brandon (Chief Scar), Ken Curtis (Charlie McCorry), Harry Carey, Jr. (Brad Jorgensen), Antonio Moreno (Emilio Figueroa), Hank Worden (Mose Harper), Beulah Archuletta (Look), Walter Coy (Aaron Edwards), Dorothy Jordan (Martha Edwards), Pippa Scott (Lucy Edwards), Pat Wayne (Lt. Greenhill), Lana Wood (Debbie Edwards as a child).

Credits: Directed by John Ford. Screenplay by Frank S. Nugent. Based on the novel by Alan LeMay. Executive producer: Merian C. Cooper. Associate producer: Patrick Ford. Photographed by Winton C. Hoch in VistaVision. Music by Max Steiner. Song "The Searchers" by Stan Jones. Production supervisor: Lowell J. Farrell. Art directors: Frank Hotaling and James Basevi. Second unit photography: Alfred Gilks. Technicolor color consultant: James Gooch. Assistant director: Wingate Smith. Film editor: Jack Murray. Orchestrations: Murray Cutter. Sound: Hugh McDowell and Howard Wilson. Men's wardrobe: Frank Beeton. Women's wardrobe: Ann Peck. Make-up: Web Overlander. Hair dresser: Fae Smith. Special effects: George Brown. Properties: Dudley Holmes. Set decorator: Victor Gangelin. Script supervisor: Robert Gary. RCA Sound Recording.

Additional Cast: Robert Lyden (Ben Edwards), Bill Steele (Ed Nesby), Cliff Lyons (Col. Greenhill), Jack Pennick (Army sergeant), Peter Mamakos (Jerem Futterman); Away Luna, Billy Yellow, Bob Many Mules, Exactly Sonnie Betsule, Feather Hat, Jr., Harry Black Horse, Jack Tin Horn, Many Mules Son, Percy Shooting Star, Pete Gray Eyes, Pipe Line Begishe, Smile White Sheep (Comanche); Ruth Clifford (Crazed woman), Dan Borzage (Accordion player).

Additional Credits: Production dates: Winter 1955; June to August 1955. Released May 26, 1956.

Available: Warner Home Video DVD (1997). ISBN: 0-7907-3306-4. UPC: 0-85391-46512-6. 50th Anniversary Collector's Edition in the *John Wayne/John Ford Film Collection* box set, Warner Home Video (2006). UPC: 012569843813. Warner Home Video DVD, *John Wayne Collection* (2007). UPC: 085391158653.

After working on *This Is Cinerama* **(1952),** producer Merian C. Cooper formed C.V. Whitney Pictures with socialite and venture capitalist "Sonny" Whitney. Their stated intention was to make an "American Series" of patriotic films, starting with *The Valiant Virginians* by James Warner Bellah and *The Searchers* by Alan LeMay. Cooper had previously teamed with director John Ford in Argosy Pictures, a company that dissolved in 1956 after a dispute with Republic Pictures. Ford signed with Whitney in 1954 to direct *The Searchers*, and began working on the script with screenwriter Frank Nugent in March 1955.

LeMay's novel, which first appeared as the serial *The Avenging Texans* in *The Saturday Evening Post*, opened in the aftermath of an Indian raid led by Scar that results in the kidnapping of a ten-year-old girl. Martin Pauley (Pawley in the film), a foster brother who was orphaned in a previous raid, joins Amos Edwards (Ethan Edwards in the film), an uncle, on a quest to find her. Their five-year journey takes them to the snow-covered north, to the Comancheros in New Mexico, to Army fort and Indian village. It was a perfect vehicle for Ford to explore the physical and social expanses of the West, and to examine themes basic to all his films: what is family, how does one belong to society, what distinguishes the committed from the obsessive, and, finally, what is justice?

Told almost exclusively from the point of view of Martin Pawley, the novel is as hard and bare-boned as its settings. In adapting the book, Ford and screenwriter Frank S. Nugent softened it in some areas. LeMay's story made it clear, for example, that the Edwardses were pressing their luck by ranging where they did—most of their neighbors had already been killed in raids. Pawley's guilt drives the book. It makes him put up with Ethan's bigotry and surliness as a means to an end, it lets him ignore his one chance at a happy life, it forgives his violence and treachery during the long years of his quest.

Pawley is a subsidiary character in the film, one of the commercial changes Ford and Nugent made to the book. Nugent expanded and sanitized the Amos/Ethan role for John Wayne, who at the time was at the height of his career (largely as a result of Ford's mentoring over the previous two decades). The book's Ethan was a tougher character than Ford or Wayne were willing to show. Still, few performances in Westerns are as complex and hard to read as Wayne's Ethan, a man driven by a combination of rage and desire that frightens and bewilders him. Wayne acted without vanity, and was startling in his directness. He wouldn't attempt a role this harsh, this unforgiving, again.

Although he had recently been fired from *Mister Roberts* (1955), Ford was at a point in his career where he was too sure of himself to listen to advice, too headstrong to edit himself, and too enamored of his earlier successes to permit innovation. Unlike *Stagecoach* (1939) or *My Darling Clementine* (1946), two earlier Registry Westerns, *The Searchers* has an expansive feel. Ford gives himself plenty of time to fool around, to indulge in antics like fisticuffs and donnybrooks. Ultimately, his fed-up women and tongue-tied beaus feel forced, artificial.

Ford cast his son-in-law Ken Curtis in the role of Charlie McCorry, a deadly serious role in the book but one that's played for laughs in the film. Much of the cast had worked with Ford many times, like Ward Bond, John Qualen, and Harry Carey, Jr. Dorothy Jordan, the first person seen in the film, had retired from movies in 1933 when she married Merian C. Cooper. Olive Carey, who played Martin's adopted mother, was the widow of Harry Carey, one of Ford's earliest collaborators. (Wayne self-consciously echoed one of Harry Carey's habitual poses in the final shot of *The Searchers*.)

Jeffrey Hunter took the pivotal role of Martin Pawley, further undermining the novel's strengths. One of the class of pretty but callow leading men under studio contracts in the 1950s, Hunter lacked the depth or the technique to play the part the way LeMay had imagined it. Ford deserves some of the blame; he had trouble judging the performances of other younger actors at this stage of his career. It's as if he could no longer see what worked and what was affected in his protégés. But picture Robert Wagner or George Hamilton or any number of contemporaneous juvenile leads in the role and you can see Ford's problem.

There are great set pieces in the book that don't survive in the picture—notably, a blizzard on the plains that would have been too expensive to film. In place of these Ford and Nugent added a deeply moving part for Hank Worden as a mentally unstable cowboy, and quiet displays of family dynamics that are precise and heartbreaking. Ford and Nugent simplify the climax as well. A four-way chase in the novel becomes a narrower, more focused sequence in the film. Rangers and the Army have been systematically destroying Comanche tribes. Martin and Ethan must find Scar and his village before their fellow whites butcher them. As they enter the village, Ford stays with Ethan, forcing viewers to contemplate at close hand his anger and bigotry.

The Searchers was a complicated production, broken into two parts in the winter and summer of 1955. Principal photography began on June 16 in Monument Valley, and ultimately included locations in Canada and Colorado. Despite some compromises and miscalculations, what Ford accomplished ranks with the best work in the Western genre. *The Searchers* is a film so visually clear and precise that it requires no dialogue. With only the simplest of devices, like the door that frames the opening and closing shots, Ford conveyed a range of emotions, and of narrative ambiguity, that was astonishing.

Ford's vision of the West is as profound and troubling as any in cinema. Which makes the film's initially guarded critical reception hard to understand. *The Searchers* failed to receive a single Oscar nomination, and while it did well enough at the box office, it was by no means a blockbuster. However, its influence reverberated through culture. Buddy Holly picked up on one of Ethan Edwards' catchphrases and turned it into the pop

hit "That'll Be the Day." A 1962 poll in *Cahiers du Cinéma* placed *The Searchers* among the best American sound films. Peter Bogdanovich used its opening and closing shots to frame his 1971 documentary *Directed by John Ford*. Many critics today consider *The Searchers* not only Wayne's best work, but one of the finest Westerns ever filmed.

Giant

Warner Bros., 1956. Sound, color, 1.66. 201 mins.

Cast: Elizabeth Taylor (Leslie Lynnton Benedict), Rock Hudson (Jordan "Bick" Benedict, Jr.), James Dean (Jett Rink), Carroll Baker (Luz Benedict II), Jane Withers (Vashti Snythe), Chill Wills (Uncle Bawley), Mercedes McCambridge (Luz Benedict), Dennis Hopper (Jordan "Jordy" Benedict III), Sal Mineo (Angel Obregon II), Rodney Taylor (David Karfrey), Judith Evelyn (Mrs. Nancy Lynnton), Earl Holliman (Robert "Bob" Dace), Robert Nichols (Mort "Pinky" Snythe), Paul Fix (Dr. Horace Lynnton), Alexander Scourby (Polo), Fran Bennett (Judy Benedict), Charles Watts (Judge Oliver Whiteside), Elsa Cardenas (Juana Guerra Benedict), Carolyn Craig (Lacey Lynnton), Monte Hale (Bale Clinch), Sheb Wooley (Gabe Target), Mary Ann Edwards (Adarene Clinch), Victor Millan (Angel Obregon, Sr.), Mickey Simpson (Sarge), Pilar Del Rey (Mrs. Obregon), Maurice Jara (Dr. Guerra), Noreen Nash (Lona Lane), Ray Whitley (Watts), Napoleon Whiting (Jefferson Swazey).

Credits: Directed by George Stevens. Screen Play by Fred Guiol and Ivan Moffat. Based on the novel by Edna Ferber. Produced by George Stevens and Henry Ginsberg. Director of photography: William C. Mellor. Production designed by Boris Leven. Editing by William Hornbeck. Associate film editors: Phil Anderson, Fred Bohanan. Sound by Earl Crain, Sr. Set decorator: Ralph Hurst. Second unit director: Fred Guiol. Second unit assistant director: Russ Llewellyn. Second unit photography by Edwin DuPar. Music composed and conducted by Dimitri Tiomkin. Songs: "Giant," "There's Never Been Anyone Else But You," lyrics by Paul Francis Webster, music by Dimitri Tiomkin. Costumes designed by Marjorie Best. Miss Taylor's costumes designed by Moss Mabry. Makeup supervisor: Gordon Bau. Assistant director: Joe Rickards. Production manager: Tom Andre. RCA Sound Recording. Copyright 1956 by Giant Productions.

Additional Credits: Premiered in New York City on October 10, 1956.

Awards: Oscar for Best Director.

Available: Warner Home Video DVD (2003). ISBN: 0-7907-7148-9. UPC: 0-85392-32212-1.

When Edna Ferber's novel *Giant* was published in 1952, critics treated it—not very kindly—as a satirical comedy. Ferber had written generational sagas before, notably *Cimarron* (1930) and *Come and Get It* (1935). These works, as well as the plays she wrote with George S. Kaufman (including *Dinner at Eight*, 1932, and *Stage Door*, 1936), helped make her one of the most-read woman authors of her time.

Director George Stevens had won an Oscar for *A Place in the Sun* (1951), and was nominated for the Western *Shane* (1953). After 1954, he would make only four more movies, spending an increasing amount of time on each one. He worked on the screenplay for *Giant* with Ivan Moffat and Fred Guiol, the same creative team who had worked on his two previous films. (Stevens met Moffat, who

was related to Max Beerbohm, during World War II, and knew Guiol from his days at the Hal Roach Studio. Guiol started out as a cameraman and technical director, working on many of Harold Lloyd's films, and then directed shorts for Roach.)

Stevens was meticulous about the look of *Giant*. He built the mansion that is the centerpiece of the film on the desolate plains outside Marfa, Texas, filming there through the bad weather that plagued the production. Further problems were caused by Elizabeth Taylor's pregnancy and by the death of James Dean in a car accident two weeks before the production wrapped.

This was the third and final starring role for Dean, and the first in which he was required to play someone older than his age. Stevens was clearly enamored of the actor, cutting to him as frequently as the story would allow, and using his improvised moments to punctuate scenes. The most resonant image from the film is a photo of Dean taken by Floyd McCarty. Wearing jeans, boots, and a cowboy hat, and clutching work gloves, the actor is stretched out in the back seat of a convertible limousine, the Marfa mansion etched in deep focus against the horizon.

Dean didn't have as high an opinion of Stevens, as he confided to gossip columnist Hedda Hopper in an interview she chose not to print. The director's pace had slowed considerably since his days on *Swing Time* (1936) and *Gunga Din* (1939). Something else had changed as well. Audiences embraced Stevens's prewar films for their characters, mostly positive thinkers who believed in society and who stood up to oppression. Liberals took to Stevens's style of populism, and even conservatives had trouble opposing the director's viewpoints, so full of common sense and a belief in the dignity of the individual. Filmgoers enjoyed Stevens's films because of their sunny optimism, but also because they wanted to believe they could be lighter than air like Fred Astaire and Ginger Rogers, articulate and sympathetic like Ronald Colman in *Talk of the Town*, brave and gallant like Cary Grant in *Gunga Din*.

After the war, Stevens understandably lost much of his optimism. But he also adopted an insistent, preaching tone, no longer convinced that mainstream audiences could comprehend the true meaning of his films. It's hard to argue with the social and political viewpoints of the characters in *Giant*, but it's also hard to like these characters. This is partly due to Ferber's novel, which reworks bits and pieces of her better plots without reaching a satisfying conclusion, and without establishing truly tragic dimensions. The central conflict in *Giant*—both novel and film—boils down to which of two crass, insensitive Texans should be allowed to have more money. The rest of the immense story is a generational saga only in the sense that things keep happening, whether or not they apply to the plot.

How else can one explain the film's many unrewarding sidetracks and digressions? The screen time devoted to Mercedes McCambridge, badly overplaying her role, for example. Stevens seems oddly unwilling to explore the sexual subtext of the story, such as Ferber's implication that Dean's character is illegitimate. The director also has trouble figuring out Elizabeth Taylor. She drifts through her role serenely unconcerned, delivering her dialogue like a substitute schoolteacher.

Rock Hudson did not fare much better. In his earlier films he had played Indians, villains, and largely untrustworthy lovers—in other words, roles built around artifice and deception, in which "bad" acting could have been seen as a creative choice. Asked to play a "real" person like Bick Benedict, Hudson was out of his depth. Dean, too, did not have the technical training nor the emotional experience to play the bitter, disillusioned drunk that Jett Rink becomes. (Dean couldn't throw a punch, either, rendering his fistfights unintentionally funny.) He resorts to outsized gestures, and, in the first half of the film at least, to imitating Walter Brennan. Critics like to conjecture about what Dean's career would have been like had he survived. The more interesting question is how well he could have stood up to a genuine movie star.

Being a producer as well as a director meant that Stevens could afford to wait for the weather he wanted, such as the muted dawn that illuminates a coffin by the railroad siding. But the director's touch deserts him during the subsequent funeral, which features on a choir of robed schoolchildren singing the national anthem. Stevens keeps pushing themes and morals in the film, like the jukebox that plays "The Yellow Rose of Texas" as Hudson gets beaten up in a diner for defending his Mexican progeny. (Viewers at the time would have been more aware of the song's ugly racial history.)

At the same time, this is as mainstream as Hollywood filmmaking of the period gets. It was like attending a posh, comfortable church to hear a sermon that, over the course of three hours, reached some glancing truths about the trials and disappointments of raising a family. A pious, even heartfelt, sermon, but not a very demanding one.

Giant became the "road show" movie that Warner Brothers could use to compete against *Oklahoma!* and other spectacles then in vogue. Dean's death, and the cult that grew around him, added to the film's notoriety. It became the single most successful movie in Warners' history until *Superman* in 1978, and won for Stevens his second directing Oscar. It also led, indirectly, to a seriously misguided remake of Ferber's *Cimarron* (1960) starring Glenn Ford and Mercedes McCambridge.

The Ten Commandments

Paramount, 1956. Color, sound, 2.35. 231 minutes. Rated G
Cast: Charlton Heston (Moses), Yul Brynner (Rameses), Anne Baxter (Nefretiri), Edward G. Robinson (Dathan), Yvonne De Carlo (Sephora), Debra Paget (Lilia), John Derek (Joshua), Sir Cedric Hardwicke (Sethi), Nina Foch (Bithiah), Martha Scott (Yochabel), Judith Anderson (Memnet), Vincent Price (Baka), John Carradine (Aaron), Olive Deering (Miriam), Douglass Dumbrille (Jannes), Frank DeKova (Abiram), Henry Wilcoxon (Pentaur), Eduard Franz (Jethro), Donald Curtis (Mered), Lawrence Dobkin (Hur Ben Caleb), H.B. Warner (Amminadab), Julia Faye (Elisheba); Lisa Mitchell, Noelle Williams, Joanna Merlin, Pat Richard, Joyce Vanderveen, Diane Hall (Jethro's daughters); Abbas el Boughdadly (Rameses' Charioteer), Cavalry Corps Egyptian Armed Forces (Pharaoh's chariot host), Fraser Heston (the infant Moses), John Miljan (the blind one), Francis J. McDonald (Simon), Ian Keith (Rameses I), Paul De Rolf (Eleazar), Woodrow Strode (King of Ethiopia), Tommy Duran (Gershom), Eugene Mazzola (Rameses' son), Ramsay Hill (Korah), Joan Woodbury (Korah's wife), Esther Brown (Princess Tharbis), Rushti Abaza, Dorothy Adams, Eric Alden, E.J. Andre, Babette Bain, Baynes Barron, Kay Bell, Mary Benoit, Henry Brandon, Robert Carson, Robert Clark, Rus Conklin, Touch Connors, Henry Corden, Edna May Cooper, Kem Dibbs, Maude Fealy, Mimi Gibson, Diane Gump, Nancy Hale, June Jocelyn, Richard Kean, Gail Kobe,

Fred Kohler, Jr., Kenneth MacDonald, Peter Mamakos, Irene Martin, George Melford, John Merton, Amena Mohamed, Paula Morgan, Dorothy Neumann, John Parrish, Rodd Redwing, Addison Richards, Keith Richards, Marcoreta Starr, Onslow Stevens, Clint Walker, Amada Webb, Frank Wilcox, Jeane Wood.

Credits: Produced and directed by Cecil B. DeMille. Written for the screen by Acncas MacKenzie, Jesse L. Lasky, Jr., Jack Gariss, Fredric M. Frank. ("This work was compiled from many sources and contains material from the books: *Prince of Egypt* by Dorothy Clarke Wilson; *Pillar of Fire* by Rev. J.H. Ingraham; *On Eagle's Wings* by Rev. A.E. Southon.") Associate producer: Henry Wilcoxon. Photographed in VistaVision. Color by Technicolor. Director of photography: Loyal Griggs. Additional photography: J. Peverell Marley, John Warren, Wallace Kelley. Technicolor color consultant: Richard Mueller. Special photographic effects: John P. Fulton. Optical photography: Paul Lerpae. Process photography: Farciot Edouart. Art direction: Hal Pereira, Walter Tyler, Albert Nozaki. Set decoration: Same Comer, Ray Moyer. Music by Elmer Bernstein. Edited by Anne Bauchens. Set construction: Jerry Cook. Properties: Gordon Cole, Robert Goodstein. Choreography: Leroy Prinz, Ruth Godfrey. Dialogue supervision: Frances Dawson, Donald MacLean. Makeup supervisor: Wally Westmore. Makeup: Frank Westmore, Frank McCoy. Hair stylist: Nellie Manley. Sound recording supervisor: Louis H. Mesenkop. Sound recording: Harry Lindgren, Gene Garvin. A Western Electric Recording. Costumes: Edith Head, Ralph Jester, John Jensen, Dorothy Jeakins, Arnold Friberg. Unit director: Arthur Rosson. Research: Henry Noerdlinger, Gladys Percey. Assistant directors: Francisco Day, Michael Moore, Edward Salven, Daniel McCauley, Fouad Aref (Egypt). Production management: Frank Caffey, Kenneth DeLand, Donald Robb. "Acknowledgment for valuable cooperation is given to: Dr. William C. Hayes (Metropolitan Museum of Art, New York); Dr. Labib Habachi (Department of Antiquities, Luxor, Egypt); Dr. Keith C. Seele, Dr. Ralph Marcus, Dr. George R. Hughes (Oriental Institute, University of Chicago); Rabbi Rudolph Lupo (Jewish Community Library, Los Angeles)."

Additional Cast: Herb Albert, Frankie Darro, Richard Farnsworth, Dustin Farnum, Michael Moore, Jon Peters.

Additional Credits: Production dates: October 13 to December 3, 1958 (Egypt); March to August 1955 (Hollywood). Premiered in New York City on November 8, 1956.

Awards: Oscar for Best Effects—Special Effects.

Other Versions: DeMille filmed *The Ten Commandments* in 1923.

Available: Paramount DVD (2006). UPC: 097360412246.

At some point in the 1920s, Cecil B. DeMille lost interest in the present. The director found a winning formula with *The Ten Commandments* (1923) and *The King of Kings* (1927); apart from a handful of contemporary projects, he concentrated on period films for the rest of his life. In his autobiography, DeMille claimed that his first *Ten Commandments* was made in response to a wave of scandals plaguing the film industry in the early 1920s. It was a weird hybrid of religious spectacle and sin-laden thriller, one half set in Egypt as Moses leads the enslaved Israelites to freedom, one half in a modern-day San Francisco of adultery, corruption, leprosy, and crashing motorboats.

After helping to centralize moviemaking in Hollywood, and after cementing Paramount's position at the top of the industry, DeMille was forced out of the studio at the end of 1924. He made some films under his own production company, signed a contract with MGM, and returned to Paramount in 1932. In *The Sign of the Cross* (1932) and *Cleopatra* (1934), he embellished his

proclivity for visual spectacle while delivering as much pre–Production Code sensuality as he could get away with. When tastes (and production codes) changed, DeMille switched to Westerns, the same genre that provided his start in film. But DeMille had trouble topping himself in stories that called for parched, hardscrabble sets and faded, worn costumes. To much of the public, he was better known as the host of the Lux Radio Theatre, but he was forced off the air in a union dispute. He returned to Biblical storytelling with *Samson and Delilah* in 1949, helping to inaugurate a string of religious films from other studios who realized that while sin must be punished, under the cover of Scripture it could be shown in lascivious detail first.

As DeMille's films grew in size, they took longer and longer to complete. *The Greatest Show on Earth* wasn't released until 1952, three years after *Samson and Delilah*. Once known for his ability to turn anything into a rousing adventure, DeMille began to pontificate. His politics began to sour. He took a leading role in ferreting out agents of the Red Menace, and at one point tried to assume control of the Directors Guild.

The Ten Commandments remake would be the biggest film DeMille ever attempted, five years in the making, with a cast of thousands (25,000 by one count), shot on location in Egypt. He discarded the "contemporary" half of his earlier script and expanded on its Biblical passages, adding much more about the life of Moses and the fate of the Israelites under the Egyptians. He sought out experts about costumes and architecture, built massive sets with the cooperation of Egyptian authorities, and essentially took over the entire Paramount studio to shoot the film's interiors. He even brought back rocks from Mount Sinai to add authenticity to the soundstage set.

DeMille claimed that people "from all over the world" had been urging him to remake *The Ten Commandments*, but that he wasn't sure the film would work until he cast Charlton Heston as Moses. The two had worked together before in *The Greatest Show on Earth*, but Heston was not an obvious choice to play the Biblical patriarch in what was becoming one of the most expensive movies of all time. A native of Illinois and an Air Force veteran, Heston worked on the stage and in amateur films, but gained most of his attention by appearing on television. After *The Greatest Show* he was cast in a series of mediocre Westerns and action films. *The Ten Commandments* would be a turning point in his career.

Heston's uncertainty about his acting is apparent in the early scenes of the film. He gains more stature as the film progresses, although that may also be a function of the increasingly heavy robes and beards he is asked to don. DeMille later wrote, "On the sands of the Egyptian desert or on the rocky slopes of Sinai, before each of his big scenes he would go off by himself for a half-hour, in costume, and walk up and down, in solitary thought."

Yul Brynner was also a relative newcomer to film. Born in Russia (according to his son, in 1920), Brynner was a trapeze artist in Paris before turning to acting after a serious fall. He spent World War II making radio broadcasts in French for the U.S. Army, then worked in stage and on TV in New York. In 1951 he was cast as the lead in Rodgers and Hammerstein's *The King and I*, a part he would play off and on for the rest of his life. (He won an Oscar for the film version, released in 1956.) *The Ten Commandments* was his third film, and his version of the Egyptian pharaoh Rameses is the most physically imposing performance in the film.

Critics at the time lambasted DeMille's choice of Anne Baxter as Nefretiri, and today her acting stands out as the most forced and artificial in the cast. But what could any actress do with lines like, "Oh Moses, Moses, you stubborn splendid adorable mule"? The rest of the cast betrayed DeMille's unique mix of high-minded sincerity and crass commercialism. Distinguished actors like Edward G. Robinson and Judith Anderson appeared next to contract players and starlets who would soon wind up in television series or exploitation films. DeMille reserved parts for friends who had worked with him for decades, like Julia Faye, H.B. Warner, and Henry Wilcoxon. "The greatest single problem in *The Ten Commandments* was the Voice of God," he wrote. (Heston's voice was used during the burning bush sequence, and a mix of several voices at other times.)

The director suffered a serious heart attack while filming in Egypt, and continued work against the advice of his doctors. By the time the film was finished, he had spent over thirteen million dollars, a large portion of that going to the enormous sets built at Beni Youssef and to the special effects, in particular the parting of the Red Sea. (DeMille tried to keep secret the methods for achieving the parting. In 1923, special effects technicians used gelatin molds to add a throbbing effect to "walls" of water. In 1956, most of the sequence relied on double exposures and footage shot in reverse.)

As far as the filmgoing audience was concerned, *The Ten Commandments* would be more than a movie; it would be an experience, complete with an overture, entr'acte, exit music, and souvenir programs. DeMille even appeared in an introduction to explain how solemn his motives were, and provided the film's intermittent narration. One can admire the breadth of the director's vision without necessarily agreeing with his methods, or his interpretation of Scripture. *The Ten Commandments* evokes a period before even DeMille started making movies, when directors would assemble elaborate tableaus of historical events and photograph them as if they were tapestries or murals. No matter how many extras crowd the backgrounds of his compositions, the film still feels leaden, inert. *Variety* complained that it was "too long," "too much," and "conventional."

Nevertheless, *The Ten Commandments* was an extraordinary success at the box office. Within three years it had grossed over $80 million, and had been seen by close to a hundred million people. The film received seven Oscar nominations, winning for Best Special Effects. It became an Eastertime staple on television, as well as a template of sorts for subsequent epics like *Ben Hur* and *Cleopatra*. It would also be the last film DeMille would complete. He died of heart disease in January 1959.

Disneyland Dream

Robbins Barstow, 1956. Sound, color, 1.37. 35 minutes.
Featuring: Robbins Barstow, Meg Barstow, Mary Barstow, David Barstow, Daniel Barstow.
Credits: Filmed, Directed, Written, Edited, and Narrated by Robbins Barstow. BTA Films & Video, Wethersfield, Connecticut, USA.
Additional Cast: Steve Martin.
Additional Credits: Sound and narration recorded in 1995.
Available: Internet Archive (*www.archive.org*). Contact Robbins Barstow at RobbinsB@aol.com.

Born in 1920, Robbins Barstow started making movies at the age of twelve, "family chronicles, travelogs, and other documentaries," as he wrote to blogger Cory Doctorow in 2008. In 1936, he filmed *Tarzan and the Rocky Gorge*, a twelve-minute fiction short starring himself, two younger brothers, and

Comedian Steve Martin believes he is the youth wearing the top hat in this frame enlargement from *Disneyland Dream. Courtesy of Robbins Barstow*

three neighbors. He was by that time a member of the Amateur Cinema League, and a devoted fan of Hollywood movies. Given the limitations of available equipment and amateur acting, Robbins' Tarzan short shows a sophisticated understanding of camera angles and composition, structuring scenes, and editing.

In a biographical essay, he wrote, "All my life I have had two primary aims in my movie and video making: create meaningful records of people, places, and events; and to share these 'moving images' with other people. I edited my films to make them meaningful, and I projected them to limited, on-the-spot audiences, in homes or auditoriums, to share them." Barstow also married, raised a family of three, and worked for thirty-four years as director of professional development for the Connecticut Educational Association.

Disneyland Dream, which features Barstow along with his wife Meg and children Mary (eleven at the time), David (eight), and Danny (four), came about as the result of a 1956 contest sponsored by 3M's "Scotch Brand Cellophane Tape." Every family member entered the contest, with Danny's entry winning one of twenty-five grand prizes, a week's vacation at Disneyland.

In *Disneyland Dream,* Barstow provides an amusing narrative frame for the trip, documenting the submission of entries, how family members "fainted" on learning of Danny's win, and their flight from Connecticut to California. He employs tricks like reversing footage, using stop motion, and inserting associative footage like fireworks

into the storyline. Throughout the film he is an indefatigable performer, his wife and children enthusiastic accomplices.

The film displays many of the characteristics and some of the drawbacks to home movies. Barstow's handheld, 16mm camera cannot record scenes as clearly as more expensive equipment, especially without the support of tripods and dollies. He did not have the luxury of preplanning many of his shots, was not able to film second or third takes on location, and had to use existing light. The opening scenes at the family home in Wethersfield, Connecticut, where Barstow was able to control his actors and settings, and stage written scenes, are more carefully composed and photographed than the later Disneyland material.

Most home movies share some key elements. Due to the nature of the equipment—the time it takes to set up, for example—home filmmakers tend to gather their subjects in familiar tableaus. For example, around the Christmas tree, exiting the front door, entering the car, seated around a picnic table. Few filmmakers proceed beyond these initial points, because they are just recording their families, not involving them in stories, and because the equipment prevents them from taking part in the festivities they are filming. Another staple of home movies is modes of transportation. Arrivals and departures, by car, train, bike, boat, or plane, may account for more footage than blowing out candles on birthday cakes.

Disneyland Dream has its share of tableaus and tarmacs, but Barstow graces them with a point of view and an understanding of how to shoot and put together scenes. He was also lucky enough to visit Disneyland when the theme park was only a year old—in fact, not entirely completed. At the time, the Disney staff made its own films about the amusement park, which have recently been released through the *Walt Disney Treasures* series. Bright and professional, they are like Hollywood product, promising beauty and excitement. Barstow's film gives a much better approximation of what the Disneyland experience was like for an average tourist.

Barstow continued filming in 16mm until 1985, when he switched first to 8mm and then to video. The new processes enabled him to record live commentary (and were considerably cheaper). While converting his old 16mm stock, Barstow was able to add soundtracks and narrations. Over seven decades, he has amassed more than one hundred amateur video productions, which he has shown to church groups, historical societies, and a growing number of film organizations, including Northeast Historic Film (*www.oldfilm.org*) and Home Movie Day (*www.homemovieday.com*). He has also donated twelve of his works to the Library of Congress.

Soon after *Disneyland Dream* was named to the National Film Registry in December 2008, Barstow received an e-mail from comedian Steve Martin. As reported by Susan Dunne in *The Hartford Courant*, Martin recognized himself in the film: "At age eleven I worked at Disneyland. I sold guidebooks at the park from 1956 to about 1958. I am as positive as one can be that I appear about 20:20 into your film, low in the frame, dressed in a top hat, vest, and striped pink shirt, moving from left to right, holding a guidebook out for sale."

Modesta

Film Unit of the Division of Community Education, 1956. Sound, B&W, 1.37. 36 minutes.
Cast: Juan Ortiz Jiménez, Antonia Hidalgo (Modesta), Barrio Sonadora community.
Credits: Directed by Benji Doniger. Written by Benji Doniger, Luis. A. Maisonet, René Marqués. Based on a story by Domingo Silas Ortiz. Produced by Otoniel Vila Pintado. Director of photography: Luis A. Maisonet. Edited by Paul V. Falkenberg. Sound: José Raúl Ramirez. Original music by Héctor Campos Parsi. "Una mujer en mi vida" courtesy Flor Morales Ramos (Ramito). A presentation of Departamento de Instruccion Pública División de Educación de la Comunidad.
Available: The Library of Congress.

Film historian Gary D. Keller dates the beginnings of the Puerto Rican film industry to 1916, when the Sociedad Industrial Cine Puerto Rico was formed. Its three documented features are believed lost. Subsequent production companies included the Tropical Film Company and Porto Rico Photoplays. In the 1920s, Juan Emilio Viguié Cajas worked as a freelance newsreel cameraman for commercial companies as well as the government. He is credited with the first Puerto Rican sound feature, *Romance tropical* (1934), also believed lost.

After World War II, the Committee on Parks and Public Entertainment financed some half-dozen documentary shorts. In 1949, Luiz Muñoz Marin became the first popularly elected governor of Puerto Rico, a position he held for sixteen years. One of his early actions in office was the establishment of the División de Educación de la Comunidad (Division of Community Education), responsible for producing radio shows, lectures, books, and pamphlets in support of reform. Under the jurisdiction of the Departmento de Instrucción Pública, the Division of Community Education also produced some sixty-five short films and two features between 1950 and 1975. These films featured Puerto Rican performers and artists, as well as filmmakers from mainland United States, including director Willard Van Dyke, screenwriter Edwin Rosskam, and Benjamin Doniger, a cinematographer who worked with Robert Flaherty on *Louisiana Story* (1949).

Films made under the Division of Community Education were largely aimed at a *jíbaro*, or rural, audience. These were the people Muñoz Marin had to win over in order to put his policies in place. Films like *El puente* (1954), directed by Amílcar Tirado, stressed the importance of community solidarity and cooperation. It showed how a village overcame isolation by building a bridge. *Los Peloteros* (1951), directed by Jack Delano, was the Division's first feature and is generally cited as its best film. In it, children trying to buy baseball uniforms taught the adults around them the value of working together.

Many Division films were based on actual characters and events. Most were shot on location, using nonactors in many of the roles. But Division filmmakers also adapted literary works. *Ignacio* (1956), directed by Angel F. Rivera, was adapted from *Los Casos de Ignacio y Santiago* by the short-story author and playwright René Marqués. That same year Marqués helped director Doniger and his cameraman Luis A. Maisonet adapt a short story by Domingo Silas Ortiz about a woman in a poor barrio who stands up to her abusive husband. Again the overarching theme was cooperation, but with its intimations of *Lysistrata*, *Modesta* made feminist issues its central concern.

Befitting its title, *Modesta* is a small, careful film marked by moderation. As Flaherty did in *Louisiana Story*, Doniger spends considerable time on the countryside of Puerto Rico itself, documenting both its beauty and harshness. Its characters are revealed as much by their actions as their dialogue, which is terse, even blunt. Doniger is matter-of-fact about the grinding poverty in rural communities; just detailing the demanding chores and tasks women faced is commentary enough.

Doniger and his crew display an easy familiarity with film technique, incorporating an unobtrusive and amusing flashback in the opening scenes, cross-cutting between a cockfight and Modesta's day-to-day routine to make political and social points, using a pop song by Ramito to illustrate their themes. Doniger elicits commendable performances from his mostly amateur cast, while Maisonet makes excellent use of dawn and dusk lighting. *Modesta* is not nearly as aggressive as *Salt of the Earth* (1954), with which it shares several scenes and ideas, but in its way it is just as effective. Its closing shots, with the villagers heading home guided by candlelight, and a cantina owner closing up shop for the night, are especially satisfying.

Modesta was popular worldwide, winning an award at the 1956 Venice Film Festival. Doniger worked on several other Division films, as did Maisonet, who directed *Gena la de Blas* in 1964. Marqués wrote *Juan sin seso* (1959), a satire of advertising, as well as an influential documentary, *¿Qué opina la mujer?* (1957), which interviewed First Lady Inés Mendoza de Muñoz Marin and other figures about the treatment of women in Puerto Rican society.

Early Abstractions

Harry Smith, 1939–56. Silent, color and B&W. 1.37. 23 minutes.

Credits: Painted, animated, and photographed by Harry Smith.

Titles (with Smith's timing and dating): *No. 1*, 5 minutes, 1939?–47; *No. 2*, 10 minutes, 1940–42?; *No. 3*, 10 minutes, 1942–47; *No. 4*, 6 minutes, 1950; *No. 5*, 6 minutes, 1950; *No. 6*, 20 minutes, 1951; *No. 7*, 15 minutes, 1951; *No. 8*, 5 minutes, 1954 (longer version became *No. 12*); *No. 9*, 10 minutes, 1954; *No. 10*, 10 minutes, 1956 (study for *No. 11*). Numbers 6, 8, and 9 no longer exist.

Available: Harry Smith Archives DVD and VHS, *Early Abstractions & Mirror Animations* (*www.harrysmitharchives.com*).

Born in Portland, Oregon, in 1923, Harry Smith grew up familiar with a variety of spiritual beliefs, from Freemasonry to the religious practices of the Indian tribes around the Puget Sound. After studying anthropology at the University of Washington, Smith moved to San Francisco, where he became a fixture of the avant-garde community. While amassing a collection of 78 rpm records, he also began painting intricate, geometric canvases in the style of Kandinsky.

Smith dates his first attempts at filmmaking to 1939, explaining that they were the result of his transcribing Indian dialects and rituals. "In an effort to write down dances, I developed certain techniques of transcription. Then I got interested in the designs in relation to the music."

He later grouped his films into four categories: "batiked abstractions made directly on film between 1939 and 1946; optically printed non-objective studies composed around 1950; semi-realistic animated collages made as part of my alchemical labors of 1957 to 1962; and chronologically superimposed photographs of actualities formed since the latter year."

Smith started out by drawing directly onto the film, a process that was labor-intensive but not nearly as complex as his technique for film *No. 2*: "The second one was made with Come-Clean gum dots, adhesive dots that Dick Foster got for me. . . . The film was painted over with a brush to make it wet, then with a mouth-type spray gun, dye was sprayed onto the film. When that dried the whole film was greased with vaseline. . . . With a pair of tweezers, the dots were pulled off. That's where those coloured balls drop and that sort of stuff . . . then color was sprayed onto where the dot had been. After that dried, the whole film was cleaned with carbon tetrachloride." Film *No. 3* took some five years to complete. Smith applied pieces of masking tape directly to film, and then cut them into shapes with a razor and ruler, "picking off all those little squares that are revolving around."

When projected, the films' abstract and geometric shapes jiggled, danced, merged and split, changed colors, and slid into and out of the frame, according to a rhythm and pace that Smith later attributed to various drugs and hallucinogens. Collector Luis Kemnitzer remembers Smith setting one of his paintings on an easel and playing a jazz record. "He would then stand to one side of the painting, long pointer in hand, slightly huddled over, and formally point to one small area after another in succession as the music progressed. He announced that this was a new art form. Time and events were in a linear progression and happening all at once at the same time."

The first films in effect animate this theory. Smith would screen them for jazz musicians and record their improvisations. "By comparing these tapes with each other and with the films it has been possible to make a start toward an investigation of intuitive creation," he wrote. At first Smith was unaware of the work of animators like Len Lye who used similar techniques. Later, he would seek out screenings of films by Oskar Fischinger (*Motion Painting No. 1*, 1947) and others.

No. 4, according to Smith shot in one night, shows Fischinger's influence, as well as that of jazz musicians. No longer drawing, Smith was now using lights on a reflective surface to duplicate the patterned movements of his earlier films. Historian Jamie Sexton connects *No. 4* to *Manteca*, a 1950 Smith painting that was named after a Dizzy

Gillespie recording. Smith dedicated *No. 5* to Fischinger; it continues the techniques used in *No. 4*, only in color instead of black-and-white. *No. 7* develops along the same lines, but also plays with shifting background colors. Or, as Smith described it in a catalog, "Optically printed Pythagoreanism in four movements supported on squares, circles, grillworks and triangles with an interlude concerning an experiment."

No. 10 adopts an entirely different animation technique. Here Smith took cut-out images and moved them across a background, building up collages that swirled and expanded into outer space. As Smith put it, "The final scene shows Aquaric mushrooms (not in *No. 11*) growing on the moon while the Hero and Heroine row by on a cerebrum."

By this point Smith had moved to New York City, where he received a grant from Hilla Rebay at the Guggenheim. He also persuaded Moses Asch at Folkways Records to release the *Anthology of American Folk Music*, an eighty-four-song collection that remains his most famous achievement. In it, Smith constructed the equivalent of an alternate universe for American culture—one in which blues, country, and folk music all existed on the same plane and discussed the same subjects.

Smith continued to make films, including *Mahagonny* (1980) and an animated version of *The Wizard of Oz* that was never completed. He was also known for his collections of Ukrainian Easter eggs and paper airplanes, the latter donated to the Smithsonian Institution. Smith died in 1991, the same year he received a Chairman's Merit Award at the Grammy ceremony.

Early Abstractions filmmaker Harry Smith, photographed by John Palmer.

On the Bowery

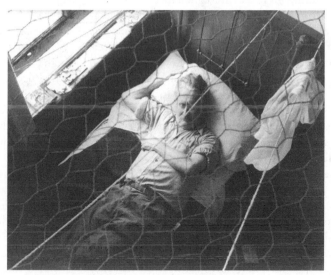

Gorman Hendricks in a Bowery flophouse. Photo from *On the Bowery*. *Courtesy of Milestone Film & Video*

Film Representations, 1957. Sound, B&W, 1.37. 63 minutes.

Cast: Men of the Bowery: Ray Salyer, Gorman Hendricks, Frank Matthews.

Credits: Produced and directed by Lionel Rogosin in collaboration with Richard Bagley, Mark Sufrin. Technical staff: Newton Avrutis, Darwin Deen, Lucy Sabsay, Greg Zilboorg, Jr., Martin Garcia. Edited by Carl Lerner. Music by Charles [Borromeo] Mills. Conducted by Harold Gomberg. Copyright 1956 Lionel Rogosin Productions, Inc. Dedication: To Gorman Hendricks.

Additional Cast: Reverend George L. Bolton, superintendent, Bowery Mission.

Additional Credits: Director of photography: Richard Bagley. Released March 18, 1957.

Available: Milestone Film & Video DVD.

The heyday of the Bowery, a Manhattan thoroughfare that has become shorthand for Skid Row, may have been the late eighteenth century, but its notoriety began a century later, when it became a center of nightlife and the setting for several songs and plays. Most of these dealt with the brothels and flophouses that lined the streets, or the saloon owners and street gangs who preyed on hapless visitors. They tended toward the comic, like a song called "The Bowery," written by Charles H. Hoyt and Percy Gaunt for the play *A Trip to Chinatown* (1892), or the Edison short *How They Do Things on the Bowery* (1902).

Life on the Bowery was far harsher. It was where Stephen Foster drank himself to death, where prostitutes killed themselves with carbolic acid at McGurk's "Suicide Hall," and where the "Bowery Boys" attacked the homeless. One source estimated that 25,000 men lived in Bowery flophouses in 1907. The area was so bad that missionaries came from abroad to help. *The Christian Herald*, based on a British weekly, started publishing in 1878. The following year Rev. and Mrs. Albert G. Ruliffson established the Bowery Mission as a shelter for the homeless. It was purchased by the Christian Herald Association in 1895, and moved to its present location at 227–229 Bowery.

The Mission plays an important role in *On The Bowery*, a landmark in both documentary and independent filmmaking. It was the first film by Lionel Rogosin, born in New York City in 1924 and educated at Yale. After serving in the Navy during World War II, he entered the corporate world as a chemical engineer, earning enough within a decade as a textile magnate to finance his own feature. In later interviews he cited the work of Robert Flaherty and Vittorio De Sica as inspirations, as well as *All Quiet on the Western Front* (1930).

According to his son Michael, Rogosin's original plan was to make a film about apartheid, something he had experienced touring Africa after the war. He began searching for a project to practice on in New York City, and even tried his hand shooting with a 16mm Bolex. Rogosin had $30,000 and a two-page outline when he started *On the Bowery*, but he had also researched the area for six months.

"That's the primary thing for that kind of film—to spend a lot of time on-location with the subject," he told interviewer Eric Brietbart.

During his research, Rogosin met screenwriter Mark Sufrin, who introduced him to cinematographer Richard Bagley. The three formed the creative team behind *On the Bowery*. They interviewed physicians at Yale and at Bellevue Hospital, and obtained the cooperation of Bowery Mission officials. As Michael Rogosin put it, they became obsessed with their subject, turning it into a crusade. "It's clear that this was meant to be a condemnation of capitalist society," he wrote about his father's intentions. "What brutal world created these broken lives?"

As Lionel Rogosin put it, they wanted to show how "the alienation generally at work in American society" led to "drink and senseless violence." They would not be blaming the people on the Bowery so much as the system that betrayed them into "loneliness, ignorance and futility." Sufrin wrote that they tried "to extract a simple story from Bowery itself. Not a 'typical' or 'symbolic' story, but an essence of truth of the place to expose (not dramatize)."

Rogosin knew the general direction his story would take, as well as the tone he wanted—one that stripped away the artifice of fiction filmmaking, forcing viewers to confront directly the squalor of life on the Bowery. As Sufrin put it in an article for *Sight and Sound*, "Our actors were taken from the street and would speak in their own argot, with guides of what to say only for story purposes. Direction on our part would try to define the action, but not gesture or inflection."

Key to the success of the film was Rogosin's understanding of and sympathy for his cast. He found Kentucky native Ray Salyer scrambling for day-labor jobs on a street corner. "We were amazed and delighted with the almost exact duplication of his story to ours," Sufrin wrote. Some of his scenes were scripted, but Salyer's sincerity is unmistakable. Gorman Hendricks, an older man who both helps and betrays Salyer, was a longtime Bowery denizen who died of cirrhosis shortly after filming. As a sort of surrogate for viewers, he gave Rogosin the opportunity to take his camera inside flophouses and other Bowery locations.

Sufrin wrote at length about the difficulties the crew faced during the three-month production: cast members would be arrested and return with shaves and haircuts, making it difficult to match them with material already filmed. Or they would just "disappear." The police would interfere. Construction crews started demolishing the Third Avenue el and widening the streets. Shooting at night, without lights, was especially difficult.

As a cinematographer, Bagley had worked on industrials and the groundbreaking documentary *The Quiet One* (1948). He was also an alcoholic, "so he was very close to the subject of *On the Bowery*," Rogosin said. (Bagley died of alcoholism five years later.) Impromptu encounters shot from the back seat of a car are composed as thoughtfully as those in Hollywood moviemaking. A scene of three men in an alley straining Sterno into a paper cup, seemingly caught on the fly, features a half-dozen carefully considered camera angles.

Bagley hid his 35mm Arriflex camera under a bundle to film inside some bars. "We became part of the smell, the gargoyle faces, the wine sores, the sleeping and retching," Sufrin wrote, and the footage is as shocking as any film of the time. Rogosin planned the film's "mad scene," which Sufrin called "a three-day nightmare," before he met his colleagues. It was conceived, shot and edited in a way to mimic the sense of helplessness, the loss of control that drunkenness brings. It is a powerful corrective to decades of romanticizing alcohol in mainstream culture, particularly Hollywood films.

Rogosin said that it took six months to edit the film. "It should have taken three," he admitted, "but none of us knew what we were doing, until I hired Carl Lerner." Lerner helped tie the disparate material together, using dissolves to connect scenes and locations, at other times crosscutting among the three principal characters to provide a cross-section of the Bowery. The spare score was by Charles Borromeo Mills, a composer from Asheville, North Carolina, who had won a Guggenheim Fellowship in 1952.

The director had considerable difficulty getting his film to the public. "*On the Bowery* just had no commercial appeal," Rogosin said. "Most distributors saw it, threw up their hands and said, 'Who's going to show this?'" A dismissive (and misguided) review by *New York Times* critic Bosley Crowther didn't help. Rogosin subsequently founded the Bleecker Street Cinema, and later, Impact Films, in part to give a platform to independent filmmakers. "It was clear that I couldn't go through the system," he said.

On the Bowery remains one of the most sensitive and incisive looks at alcoholism on record. Its influence spread to features as well as documentaries. John Cassavetes was a fan of Rogosin's work, for example, and Shirley Clarke employed many of the same strategies in *The Cool World* (1963). Rogosin's next project was an anti-apartheid story, *Come Back Africa* (1960), filmed on location in South Africa. He died in 2000.

The Tall T

Randolph Scott, left, beginning to discover the extent of Richard Boone's villainy in *The Tall T.*

Columbia, 1957. Sound, color, 1.66. 78 minutes.

Cast: Randolph Scott (Pat Brennan), Richard Boone (Frank Usher), Maureen O'Sullivan (Doretta Mims), Arthur Hunnicutt (Ed Rintoon), Skip Homeier (Billy Jack), Henry Silva (Chink), John Hubbard (Willard Mims), Robert Burton (Tenvoorde).

Credits: Directed by Budd Boetticher. Screen Play by Burt Kennedy. Based on a story ["The Captives"] by Elmore Leonard. Produced by Harry Joe Brown. Associate producer: Randolph Scott. Assistant to producer: David Breen. Director of photography: Charles Lawton, Jr. Technicolor color consultant: Henry Jaffa. Music composed and conducted by Heinz Roemheld. Art director: George Brooks. Film editor: Al Clark. Set decoration: Frank A. Tuttle. Assistant director: Sam Nelson. Sound: Ferol [Ferrol] Redd. Technicolor. RCA Recording. A Columbia Pictures Corporation presentation of a Scott-Brown production.

Additional Cast: Robert Anderson (Jace), Fred E. Sherman (Hank Parker), Chris Olsen (Jeff Parker).

Additional Credits: Filmed July 20 to August 8, 1956. Released April 1957.

Available: Sony Pictures Home Entertainment DVD *The Films of Budd Boetticher* (2008). ISBN: 1-4248-8728-3. UPC: 043396228856. Goodtimes Home Video VHS (1990). ISBN: 1-55510-356-1. UPC: 018713044945.

Budd Boetticher first worked with Randolph Scott on *The Desperadoes* (1943), a Western from Columbia Pictures produced by Harry Joe Brown. Born in 1892, Brown studied law before becoming a director and producer in the 1920s. After helping to develop Ken Maynard as a star, he met Scott on the set of *Union Station* (1939), a Fritz Lang Western. The two became friends and later formed the Producers-Actors Corporation. By the late 1940s Scott, a onetime star of romances, musicals, and comedies, had given up contemporary roles to concentrate solely on Westerns.

Boetticher had broken into film as a technical advisor on *Blood and Sand* (1941), Rouben Mamoulian's remake of a Rudolph Valentino silent about bullfighting. Born in Chicago in 1916, Boetticher was adopted by a wealthy Midwesterner who had married a woman thirty-four years younger than him. Boetticher told critic Dave Kehr years later, "It wasn't a great youth. I was spoiled rotten and I had to get over that my mother and father weren't my parents." Typical to his stoic, tough-guy persona, he added, "When I found out I was adopted I was delighted."

His knee ruined playing football, Boetticher drove to Mexico to recuperate. There he fell under the spell of bullfighting, and studied seriously to become a matador. But working with Mamoulian made him want to direct, and after years as an assistant he was allowed to helm five B-movies at Columbia, mostly Boston Blackie quickies. Cast off by Columbia, Boetticher made low-budget thrillers for Eagle Lion and for Monogram. While filming *Killer Shark* (1950), he befriended Andrew McLaglen, the second assistant director and also the son of the actor Victor McLaglen. Boetticher showed him the script for what became *Bullfighter and the Lady* (1951); McLaglen helped persuade Batjac, a production company owned by John Wayne, to finance the film.

The story behind the troubled production and release of *Bullfighter and the Lady* has many different versions, but one result was that Boetticher got a directing contract at Universal, one he says he deliberately sabotaged while making *Wings of the Hawk* (1953). In 1956, when Batjac was trying to develop *Seven Men from Now* by first-time screenwriter Burt Kennedy, Boetticher and Randolph were paired again. Made cheaply but professionally, the film convinced Scott to ask Boetticher to join his company.

The Tall T, their next film, was produced by Harry Joe Brown. The collaborators were all industry veterans (even Burt Kennedy, who had been writing for radio and television), and they all had similar ideas about what made a good Western. Scott had settled into a screen persona as a weather-beaten stoic—tough, laconic, but unfailingly moral. "He had something very few people today have," Boetticher said. "He had class." He also had limitations as an actor. While an excellent rider, Scott was in his fifties, and too old for extended action scenes. That meant his films had to rely more on conversation, on the give-and-take between good guys and villains (since romance for the hero was basically out of the question).

Scott's characters were tight-lipped because the actor was not that proficient with dialogue. That meant exposition would be handled by costars, and they included young actors like James Coburn and Lee Marvin who were just starting out in film. Brown's budgets limited Boetticher to eighteen-day shooting schedules, which meant that he had to shoot quickly and precisely, especially difficult since he often picked remote locations near Lone Pine, California. There was no fooling around on his sets or in his movies, unless it helped the story. Everything had a purpose, and everyone was expected to perform on cue.

Critic Andrew Sarris referred to the Boetticher/Scott films as "floating poker games" because they consisted of physical and moral standoffs in which it's unclear who has the upper hand. Scott's motives often seem ambiguous, while the villains crafted by Boetticher and his screenwriters are intelligent, helpful, even charming. Women in these films are traded back and forth as their value escalates or diminishes. In the best films in the series, Scott and his adversaries play out their battles during journeys across harsh, unforgiving landscapes—ones photographed with breathtaking beauty. (Boetticher liked to use either Lucien Ballard or Charles Lawton, Jr., as his cameraman.) In *The Tall T*, Scott's Pat Brennan spends much of the film a prisoner of amoral crooks who have lucked onto a valuable hostage: the newlywed daughter of the area's richest man. Brennan knows he will be killed as soon as her ransom arrives.

The Boetticher/Scott films are stripped of frivolities, of metaphors and judgments, of subtexts and niceties. They didn't "mean" anything, they were just Westerns about embattled people trying to survive on the frontier. Today they appear are so fundamental, so tough and hard in their acting, storytelling, and directing, that they outshine almost all other Westerns of their time. *The Tall T* is not the best in the series, although it was the first film adapted from an Elmore Leonard story, and it helped win Richard Boone win the lead in *Have Gun, Will Travel*, an immensely popular television series that started in 1957. The real gems in the Ranown films (the name Scott and Brown adopted for their company after *The Tall T*) are *Ride Lonesome* (1959) and *Comanche Station* (1960), two taut, compelling stories filmed in a style as well-worn as a comfortable saddle. The wide, Cinema-Scope frame used in *Comanche Station* gives an even more isolated feel to the story and characters.

Scott retired after *Comanche Station*, although he later agreed to make one more film, *Ride the High Country*, a Registry title, in 1962. Harry Joe Brown retired with him, apart from a late Western with Glenn Ford. Boetticher filmed the pilot and opening episodes for *Maverick*, an enduring television series starring James Garner. He then embarked on a quest to make a film about the Mexican matador Carlos Arruza, one he would never complete satisfactorily. After Arruza died in a car accident on May 20, 1966, Boetticher lost everything: his wife, his money, and his health, ending up for a time in a mental institution. When he returned to Hollywood, he was essentially unemployable.

It's easy to get caught up in the Boetticher myth: his tales of standing up to authority figures like Harry Cohn at Columbia, his attempt to blow up the Universal backlot to get out of a contract, the lost years he spent pursuing a quixotic epic. As Clint Eastwood pointed out to Dave Kehr, there's little doubt that Boetticher—antagonistic, belligerent—was the cause of many of his problems. When I met him he was unfailingly polite and generous, although by then his stories had been repeated so many times that they felt like stage routines.

In each of them, he fought valiantly, sometimes futilely, to present his vision of reality.

But Eastwood is also quick to praise Boetticher's style. "That kind of filmmaking is very subtle, there's no razzmatazz," he said. To Eastwood, Boetticher was "more influential than the mainstream guys. I must say I've stolen a lot of that over the years."

Boetticher was fortunate to be making Westerns during a time when the genre dominated American culture. He was also fortunate to be able to work with professionals like Scott, Brown, Kennedy, Ballard, and others who were proud of their craft. Those conditions may never arise again, so any opportunity to enjoy the Ranown films is one to be savored.

12 Angry Men

United Artists, 1957. Sound, B&W, 1.66. 95 minutes.
Cast: Henry Fonda (Juror #8 [Davis]), Lee J. Cobb (Juror #3), Ed Begley (Juror #10), E.G. Marshall (Juror #4), Jack Warden (Juror #7), Martin Balsam (Juror #1), John Fiedler (Juror #2), Jack Klugman (Juror #5), Edward Binns (Juror #6), Joseph Sweeney (Juror #9), George Voskovec (Juror #11), Robert Webber (Juror #12).
Credits: Directed by Sidney Lumet. Story and screenplay by Reginald Rose. Produced by Henry Fonda and Reginald Rose. Associate producer: George Justin. Director of photography: Boris Kaufman. Music composed and conducted by Kenyon Hopkins. Film editor: Carl Lerner. Art director: Robert Markel. Assistant director: Donald Kranze. Operative cameraman: Saul Midwall. Sound: James A. Gleason. Script supervisor: Faith Elliott. Makeup: Herman Buchman. A United Artists presentation of an Orion-Nova production.
Additional Cast: Rudy Bond (Judge), James Kelly (Guard), Billy Nelson (Court clerk), John Savoca (Accused).
Additional Credits: Premiered in Los Angeles on April 10, 1957.
Other Versions: Remake of a "Studio One" presentation broadcast September 20, 1954 and directed by Franklin J. Schaffner.
Available: MGM Home Entertainment DVD (2001). ISBN: 0-7928-4922-1. UPC: 0-27616-85900-6. MGM Video DVD (2008). UPC: 027616097101.

When *Marty* (1955) won a Best Picture Oscar, it helped persuade studio executives that television shows were a legitimate source of material for features. Two more Paddy Chayefsky television dramas, *The Catered Affair* (1956) and *The Bachelor Party* (1957), quickly became movies. For actor Henry Fonda, adapting a television drama was an opportunity to take further control over his career. After he returned from World War II, Fonda made three films with John Ford and three other negligible features. By 1948, fed up with the political climate in Hollywood and distraught over a failing marriage that would end with his wife's suicide in 1950, he retreated to New York City and the stage. For the next seven years, Fonda concentrated on live acting, mostly in and around New York City.

His screen comeback was in an adaptation of his Broadway hit *Mister Roberts* (1955), but it was an unhappy experience during which he was forced to fire director John Ford. After starring in *The Wrong Man* (1956), an uncharacteristic flop by Alfred Hitchcock, Fonda took what was for him the unprecedented step of producing his own film. He chose *12 Angry Men*, an Emmy–winning

drama by Reginald Rose that had been broadcast in 1954. It was a story that appealed to his liberal politics, one in which he could build on a screen persona as a strong, silent moral arbiter in the tradition of *The Grapes of Wrath*'s Tom Joad and *My Darling Clementine*'s Wyatt Earp.

Rose's story was a cunning fit for live television, consisting of a single set and twelve main actors. He wrote it after sitting on a jury in a manslaughter case. As he explained in a 1997 interview, "We got into this terrific, furious, eight-hour argument in the jury room. I was writing one-hour dramas for 'Studio One' then and I thought, wow, what a setting for a drama." Born in New York in 1920, Rose served in World War II after college, then started writing for television. His work had a strong moralistic bent, and his 1953 play *Thunder on Sycamore Street* stirred considerable controversy before it was censored by television executives.

What Rose learned from television writing was how narrow the scope of TV cameras was, and how he could use dialogue to focus attention. His lines are so precise and pointed that they provide the equivalent of a blueprint for directors. In *12 Angry Men* each actor has a showboating monologue that cries out for a close-up; several side conversations allow for two-shots; and the back-and-forth arguing lets directors build tension through crosscutting. It was "the most intricate plot of anything I've ever written," he said. Franklin J. Schaffner, represented on the Registry with *Planet of the Apes* (1968) and *Patton* (1970), directed the television show, broadcast on September 20, 1954. It starred Franchot Tone, Norman Fell, and others; two cast members, Joseph Sweeney and George Voskovec, repeated their roles in the film.

Fonda and Rose chose Sidney Lumet to direct the film version. Born in Philadelphia in 1924, Lumet was on stage at the age of four, acting in Yiddish theater and later on Broadway. After serving in India during World War II, Lumet returned to New York to start his own theater group. By 1950 he was working as a director for CBS, collaborating with Yul Brynner on the *Danger* series. Fonda was impressed by his work on several dramatic anthology series; he also knew that Lumet's television experience would have prepared him for shooting on a tight, nineteen-day schedule.

Lumet hired cinematographer Boris Kaufman, an Oscar winner for *On the Waterfront* (1954). "I don't know of another cameraman who has the sense of dramatic interpretation that Boris has," Lumet told filmmaker Peter Bogdanovich. Together they devised a number of carefully choreographed sequences, such as a seven-minute crane shot that introduces the jurors, and a three-minute shot that isolates Ed Begley from the other jurors. As Lumet recounted in his book *Making Movies*, he had Kaufman adjust lighting and lenses as the story progressed, letting the visual scheme evolve from a detached, overhead view to claustrophobic close-ups. He also rehearsed the actors steadily without cameras until they mastered their lines.

The cast included both veterans and newcomers. Lee J. Cobb originated the role of Willy Loman in *Death of a Salesman*; here, he holds back nothing in a demanding part. Like Cobb, Martin Balsam had also appeared in *On the Waterfront*. As with Jack

Klugman, Jack Warden, and Ed Binns, most of his experience had been on television. All responded to Lumet's direction by delivering intense, focused, and complementary performances.

A bracing, confrontational film, *12 Angry Men* was the triumph of liberal ideals played out in the microcosm of a stereotypical cross-section of society. Although lip service is paid to "do-gooders" whose bleeding hearts help promote juvenile delinquency, Rose's script never wavers in its support of progressive, left-wing beliefs. While not especially balanced, his story builds a persuasive case by picking apart rather than attacking bigotry and prejudice. Rose is even generous enough to find excuses for the villains, one of the reasons why *12 Angry Men* has remained so popular over the years.

Ironically, while the film received generally good reviews when it opened, it was not a box-office success, something Henry Fonda attributed to the release scheme employed by United Artists. It was the last time Fonda would produce a film. He did star in Lumet's next feature, *Stage Struck* (1958); the director, meanwhile, returned to television and directing for the stage before establishing himself in the 1960s as one of the foremost interpreters of New York City on the screen. His next Registry film is *King . . . A Filmed Record . . . Montgomery to Memphis* (1970).

A Face in the Crowd

Warner Bros., 1957. Sound, B&W, 1.85. 126 minutes.
Cast: Andy Griffith (Larry "Lonesome" Rhodes), Patricia Neal (Marcia Jeffries), Anthony Franciosa (Joey de Palma), Walter Matthau (Mel Miller), Lee Remick (Betty Lou Fleckum), Percy Waram (Gen. Hainseworth), Paul McGrath (Macey), Rod Brasfield (Beanie), Marshall Neilan (Senator Worthington Fuller), Alexander Kirkland (Jim Collier), Charles Irving (S. J. Luffler), Howard Smith (J.B. Jeffries), Kay Medford (Mrs. Rhodes), Big Jeff Bess (Sheriff Big Jeff Bess), Henry Sharp (Abe Steiner).
Credits: Directed by Elia Kazan. Story and screenplay by Budd Schulberg. Directors of photography: Harry Stradling, Gayne Rescher. Songs by Tom Glazer and Budd Schulberg. Score composed by Tom Glazer. Film editor: Gene Milford. Production manager: George Justin. Assistant director: Charles H. Maguire. Art directors: Richard Sylbert, Paul Sylbert. Costume designer: Anna Hill Johnstone. Special assistant: Charles Irving. Sound: Ernest Zatorsky. Sound editor: Don Olson. Wardrobe: Florence Transfield. Makeup: Robert E. Jiras. Hairdresser: Willis Hanchett. Script & continuity: Roberta Hodes. RCA Sound System.
Additional Cast includes: Rip Torn (Barry Mills), Lois Nettleton (Macey's nurse), John Cameron Swayze, Earl Wilson, Mike Wallace, Walter Winchell, Faye Emerson, Sam Levenson, Burl Ives, Virginia Graham, Bennett Cerf, Betty Furness.
Additional Credits: Produced by Elia Kazan for Newtown Productions. Production dates: August 13 to November 1956. Premiered in New York City on May 28, 1957.
Available: Warner Home Video DVD (2005). ISBN: 0-7907-9213-3. UPC: 0-85393-35262-2.

Some years after it was released, Budd Schulberg told an interviewer that the inspiration for *A Face in the Crowd* was a drunken tirade Will Rogers, Jr., delivered against his father, at the time of his death one of the most beloved celebrities in the country. Schulberg typically revealed the anecdote after Rogers, Jr., was no longer around to defend himself. "Your Arkansas Traveller," published in the short story collection *Some Faces in the Crowd*, elaborated on the idea of a hillbilly performer whose homespun observations strike a chord with his rural audience. Discovered in a small-town jail by an ambitious radio producer, Lonesome Rhodes rises from vagrant to host of a televised variety show, in the process reaping a fortune in advertising endorsements and influencing national politics.

Like most of the cultural elite, Schulberg and director Elia Kazan, reteaming after their collaboration on *On the Waterfront* (1954), shared a distaste for country music without really bothering to understand it. Their Rhodes not only can't sing, he has no real songs to perform either—yet his act is lapped up by screaming fans. "Pity the fools who actually like this stuff," the film seems to be saying.

The fictional Rhodes shared characteristics with several performers of the time, from stars like Arthur Godfrey and Tennessee Ernie Ford to the more obscure Red Foley and Cliffie Stone. But Rhodes is also a liar, cheat, drunk, and lech, someone with contempt for both the highbrow and for his hick followers. Kazan had Andy Griffith, in his film debut, play him as a grating, overbearing blowhard who bellows his lines, leers at the opposite sex, and eats with his hands. He's not only dangerous—a "demagogue in denim," as one character puts it—but venal, as shown by his political advice in a senatorial campaign and an affair with a high school cheerleader (played by Lee Remick in her film debut).

Rhodes' rise and fall is meant as a cautionary tale, but exactly what is Kazan's target? Business? Politics? Entertainment? The director is perhaps most harsh in his criticism of television advertising, a subject that takes up most of the second half of the film. Movies had made fun of ads for years. Preston Sturges built *Christmas in July* (1940) around an advertising campaign for coffee, while Joseph L. Mankiewicz wove a subtle critique of advertising through his Oscar-winning script for *A Letter to Three Wives* (1949). Kazan took what might be called a sledgehammer approach to ads, delivering a montage of commercial parodies so crude and garish that they would never have been approved for broadcast.

Biographer Richard Schickel quotes Kazan's script notes: "This has to be Daumier," he wrote. "This has to be directed in anger," even if it meant forcing Jack Daniels on Griffith to get him through a scene. After a short career as a stand-up comedian, Griffith made his mark on Broadway in 1955 in *No Time for Sergeants*, playing a country bumpkin who ends up in the Air Force. (Ironically, it was first performed as a live television drama.) By his own admission, Griffith wasn't much of an actor. "While I was on that picture, I became Lonesome Rhodes," he said. "I was not a very nice man."

The premise to *A Face in the Crowd* bears a strong resemblance to *Meet John Doe* (1941), a film that flummoxed director Frank Capra so much he had to shoot multiple endings. (For that matter, Rhodes goes through a similar trajectory as Willie Stark in the Registry title *All the King's Men*, 1949.) Kazan's film can be seen as a sexed-up, dumbed-down version of Capra's plot, one in which relationships are physical conquests and politics purely personal.

Capra famously never found a satisfactory ending to *Meet John Doe*. Kazan at one point thought about using an ending Capra rejected as too downbeat, but his real problem with *A Face in the Crowd* was his distaste for the mainstream. Who can stop the redneck demagogues, the Madison Avenue hucksters? Not the audience, in Rhodes' words "stupid idiots" and "miserable slobs." Not politicians, embodied here by erstwhile director of silent features Marshall Neilan as a spineless Senator. Even Marcia Jeffries, Patricia Neal's ostensible heroine, has cloudy motives. No, it was up to well-dressed but skeptical intellectuals to see through the phony pretensions of advertising executives and hillbilly singers. In this film as least, Kazan's idea of heaven is a Manhattan bar where "real" celebrities gather to chatter while a piano tinkles cocktail jazz in the background. There Walter Matthau, nattily clad in a suit and tie, brandishes a pipe, sips martinis, and delivers bromides about integrity. All the while Kazan has been leaning toward what looks like fascism. "The mass had to be guided by a strong hand, by the responsible elite," says one plutocrat, words put into practice by the film itself.

A Face in the Crowd has moments of startling prescience. The teens who crowd the tarmac when Rhodes' plane lands would show up in force for the Beatles a few years later. The collusion between entertainers and politicians is a given in campaigns today. Even the way Rhodes exposes the artifice of broadcasting—pointing out cameras, showing viewers the edges of sets—has become common practice.

Speaking about the movie later, Kazan claimed that he was among the first to expose television as "a terrible hypnotic force." But just as he missed how country music was giving way to rock and roll, Kazan didn't really see how television differed from film. You can sense his bewildered jealousy of a teen audience that preferred Elvis Presley and TV over Burl Ives and movies. The same director who was winning Oscars a few years earlier could no longer command the box office. He would only be allowed to direct a half-dozen more features, none of them substantial hits.

Sour and self-satisfied, *A Face in the Crowd* annoys more than illuminates. Like *Quiz Show* (1994), it mocks its viewers, condemning them for wanting to be entertained. (Kazan was soon appealing to directly to an audience of "stupid idiots" in overwrought melodramas like 1961's *Splendor in the Grass*.) Some critics today praise *A Face in the Crowd*

because it confirms what they already believe: country music is awful, consumers are idiots, and only the cultural elite knows what's good for the country. A much more mature and persuasive account of manipulating the masses can be found in *Sweet Smell of Success*, released the same year. Kazan's next film, *Wild River* (1960), is also on the Registry.

Sweet Smell of Success

Press agent Sidney Falco (Tony Curtis, left) eyes columnist J.J. Hunsecker (Burt Lancaster) warily in *Sweet Smell of Success*.

United Artists, 1957. Sound, B&W, 1.85. 96 minutes.

Cast: Burt Lancaster (J.J. Hunsecker), Tony Curtis (Sidney Falco), Susan Harrison (Susie Hunsecker), Marty Milner (Steve Dallas), Jeff Donnell (Sally), Sam Levene (Frank D'Angelo), Joe Frisco (Herbie Temple), Barbara Nichols (Rita), Emile Meyer (Harry Kello), Edith Atwater (Mary), The Chico Hamilton Quintet [Chico Hamilton, Paul Horn, Carson Smith, Fred Katz].

Credits: Directed by Alexander Mackendrick. Screenplay by Clifford Odets and Ernest Lehman. From the novelette by Ernest Lehman. Produced by James Hill. Photographed by James Wong Howe. Music scored and conducted by Elmer Bernstein. Art director: Edward Carrere. Editorial supervision: Alan Crosland, Jr. Songs by Chico Hamilton and Fred Katz. Production manager: Richard McWhorter. Assistant director: Richard Mayberry. Costumes designed by Mary Grant. Set decorator: Edward Boyle. Makeup: Robert Schiffer. Effects editor: Robert Carlisle. Music editor: Lloyd Young. Sound recording: Jack Solomon. Westrex Recording System. A Hecht, Hill and Lancaster presentation of a Norma–Curtleigh Productions picture.

Additional Cast: William Forrest (Senator Harvey Walker), Joseph Leon (Joe Robard), David White (Otis Elwell), Lawrence Dobkin (Leo Bartha), Lurene Tuttle (Loretta Bartha), Queenie Smith (Mildred Tam), Autumn Russell (Linda James), Jay Adler (Manny Davis), Lewis Charles (Al Evans), Philip Van Zandt (Radio Director); James Hill, Clifford Odets (Theater Bystanders).

Additional Credits: Released June 24, 1957.

Other Versions: Ernest Lehman oversaw a Broadway musical adaptation in 2002, written by John Guare and directed by Nicholas Hytner.

Available: MGM Home Entertainment DVD (2001). ISBN: 0-7928-5016-5. UPC: 0-27616-86296-9.

Filmmakers generally treated journalism kindly in the 1930s, apart from the occasional sour diatribe like

Five Star Final (1931). Gossip columnists, often portrayed by fast-talking Lee Tracy, were comic relief, perhaps nuisances but mostly harmless. Concurrent with the Red Scare, the 1950s saw a consolidation of power in the gossip industry. Columnists like Walter Winchell and Ed Sullivan accumulated enough influence to make or break careers. At the same time, magazines like *Confidential* made smears their staple product.

Born in 1915 on Long Island, New York, Ernest Lehman tried to make a living as a freelance writer before becoming a copywriter and publicist for a theatrical agency; he later fed items and tips to *Hollywood Reporter* columnist Irving Hoffman. Judging from his later fiction, it was a life that filled him with self-loathing. The lies, manipulations, and betrayals endemic to the industry became the subjects of short stories he wrote for magazines like *Cosmopolitan*.

Gossip columnist J.J. Hunsecker, a Winchell type with an unhealthy attachment to his mentally fragile sister Susie, first appeared in the short story "Hunsecker Fights the World." Also in the plot was Sidney Falco, a publicity flack afflicted with a guilty conscience and ulcers. Falco was Lehman's greatest fictional creation, an alter ego who allowed the author to criticize the gossip industry by assuming the guise of its guiltiest practitioner. The 1950 "novelette" "Tell Me About It Tomorrow!" (later retitled "Sweet Smell of Success") continued Hunsecker's and Falco's sagas. This time the two conspire to wreck Susie's imminent marriage to jazz musician Steve Dallas. The real point of the story was whether Falco, its narrator, would redeem his soul, or allow his conscience to be overcome by the desire for a place were "the air would be scented with the sweet smell of success."

Lehman reached Hollywood on the strength of "The Comedian," a vitriolic roman à clef about a television star who resembled Milton Berle, Jackie Gleason, and Sid Caesar. (Like the columnists he criticized, Lehman was an expert at blind items that could apply to more than one person.) His writing is caustic but not especially realistic, despite frequent allusions to real-life people and places. "Panic stabbed at my insides," a line from "The Comedian," is typical of his style. Lehman got a writing contract at Paramount, but his first job was adapting *Executive Suite* (1954), a bloated boardroom melodrama at MGM.

Rod Serling's 1957 television adaptation of "The Comedian" won an Emmy, and made adapting "Sweet Smell of Success" seem more plausible to Hecht, Hill, and Lancaster, an independent production company founded around star Burt Lancaster. Lehman was dubious about working with the company, but its first project, *Marty* (1955), won a Best Picture Oscar. The relatively happy experiences of its writer, Paddy Chayefsky, persuaded Lehman to option his story, provided that he direct the picture.

Lehman not only didn't direct, he didn't finish the screenplay, which was handed over to playwright Clifford Odets. On the tail end of a once-promising career, Odets had tackled very similar material in a Hollywood tell-all drama called *The Big Knife* (1955). Here he had to be goaded into working, perhaps because he was given very precise orders about what to do with Lehman's script. Odets cleaned up material ripe for censoring, rearranged plot elements, added his trademark pointed dialogue. "You're a cookie full of arsenic," J.J. tells Falco.

But in reshaping the story, Odets eliminated a great deal of its ambiguity. "Sally, you ought to know me by now," Falco says to his secretary. "Hunsecker's the golden ladder to the place I want to get." Odets may as well have inserted an intertitle, or cut to a billboard alerting viewers that "Here is the plot." Lehman could barely contain his bile in his novelette, which proceded like a stream-of-consciousness rant, but to Odets, each scene had to make a point, no matter how obvious. Like J.J.'s secretary complaining that Falco is "immersed in a theology of making a fast buck."

Tony Curtis's performance as Falco, full of desperate cunning and sweaty remorse, is the high point of his career. "I should have done *Sweet Smell* the first movie I ever made," he said. "In all the films I've done, I've never lost Sidney. And I don't want to lose him." Even so, there is an element of reserve in his acting. Curtis strains to show the toll Falco's ruthless behavior extracts. He wants viewers to see that underneath the deceit there is a core of decency. Lancaster, on the other hand, is focused, relentless, unconcerned about what audiences think of him. His anger and repression are startling, both for that period and for today.

"I really sank into the depths when I decided to work with them," Lehman said about Lancaster's company. Of the other two partners, Harold Hecht was a former dancer who named names, and James Hill had been an MGM screenwriter. Soundtrack composer Elmer Bernstein later told director James Mangold. "The combination of people in that movie—Hecht, Lancaster, Odets—was a snake pit. Burt was really scary. He was a dangerous guy, he had a short fuse, he was very physical. You thought you might get punched out."

Lancaster was as ruthless a producer as his J.J. Hunsecker was a columnist. Lehman was quickly fired as director and replaced by Alexander Mackendrick, a Scottish-born director who had previously been known for whimsical comedies like *Whisky Galore* (1949) and *The Ladykillers* (1955). "There was never a final shooting script for the movie. . . . It was all still being revised, even on the last day of principal photography. It was a shambles of a document," he said later. Mackendrick had a keen sense of irony and an ability to invert expectations. In his films, a little old lady staves off cold-blooded killers, or children outwit pirates, or farmers defeat revenuers.

Whimsy was the last thing Lancaster wanted. *Sweet Smell of Success* hurtles along like a rush-hour subway train, its cars jammed with the anxious and hopped-up. Mackendrick captured the scent of cigarettes and spilled drinks, of dirty clothes and cramped offices, getting a New York feel even though much of the film was shot in Hollywood. Credit should also go to cinematographer James Wong Howe, who framed the film's many villains with pitiless accuracy. He shot the film's exteriors on location in Manhattan during a bitterly cold December 1956, and January 1957. Director Sidney Pollack was especially impressed with the way Howe used telephoto lenses for wide shots, and wide angle lenses for close-ups, a method that emphasized the buildings surrounding the characters. "These techniques create an overall effect, in which moviegoers feel oppressed by the city, without necessarily understanding why," he said.

But the director was stymied by the film's weak links, Martin Milner and Susan Harrison as the innocent, square lovers, and by a script that insisted on comeuppance for the two leads. In a *Vanity Fair* article, author Sam Kashner suggested that Harrison, suicidal in real life, was overwhelmed by the larger-than-life personalities around her. She made only one more feature. Milner, on the other hand, had a relatively prominent career in television series.

Sweet Smell of Success got some respectful reviews, but was ignored at the box office. (According to Kashner, the film may have lost as much as $500,000.) As a result, Lancaster and Curtis retreated to more likable roles: a heroic submarine officer in *Run Silent, Run Deep* (1958), a musician on the lam in *Some Like It Hot* (1959), respectively. Lancaster ended up firing Mackendrick from *The Devil's Disciple* (1959); the director's later films were not commercially popular, but he was greatly admired as a teacher at the California Institute of the Arts. Odets' last feature while he was alive was a vehicle for Elvis Presley, *Wild in the Country* (1961). Although he was pushed out of his own project, Lehman embarked on a series of spectacular screenwriting successes, including *North by Northwest* (1959).

What's Opera, Doc?

Warner Bros., 1957. Color, sound, 1.37. 7 minutes.

Credits: Directed by Chuck Jones. Story: Michael Maltese. Animation: Ken Harris, Abe Levitow, Richard Thompson. Layouts: Maurice Noble. Backgrounds: Philip DeGuard. Film editor: Treg Brown. Voice Characterization: Mel Blanc. Musical arrangement: Milt Franklyn. Song "Return My Love," lyrics by Michael Maltese.

Additional Credits: Voice of Elmer Fudd: Arthur Q. Bryan. Released July 6, 1957.

Available: Warner Home Video DVD, *Looney Tunes Golden Collection Volume 2* (2004). ISBN: 0-7907-8650-8. UPC: 0-85393-12842-5.

Almost as soon as sound was applied to animation, filmmakers turned to classical music for both inspiration and jokes. In 1929, for example, Carl Stalling used *Danse Macabre* by Saint-Saëns for one of Walt Disney's earliest "Silly Symphonies" cartoons. Animators relied on classical motifs as shorthand for dawn, storms, and nature in general. An outstanding use of opera was the 1944 Woody Woodpecker cartoon *The Barber of Seville*; Porky Pig mocked the same music in *Notes to You* (1941), and Bugs Bunny tackled it later in *Rabbit of Seville* (1950).

Cartoons with classical music tended to show respect for musicians' craftsmanship and skill, but little tolerance for what was perceived as diva-ish behavior. But as animation historian Daniel Goldmark has pointed out, the characters in these cartoons were almost always portrayed as performers.

Like Disney's *Fantasia* (1940), what set *What's Opera, Doc?* apart was the sense that its characters were living within a world of music—in this case one created by Richard Wagner. Bugs Bunny and his nemesis Elmer Fudd are thus bound by the rules Wagner established, forced to deal with a world of magical helmets, towering landscapes, and oversized emotions.

Like the Marx Brothers in *A Night at the Opera* (1935), Jones had a grudging respect for opera and classical music in general, as well as a professional appreciation for its comic potential. It did not take much to make opera look absurd—simply casting Bugs and Elmer was enough. Writer Michael Maltese had already explored the subject in *Herr Meets Hare*, a 1945 propaganda cartoon directed by Friz Freleng. There Bugs seduced "Fatso Goering" by disguising himself as Brunhilde, riding up to him on an enormous white horse. (Carl Stalling used music by Strauss and other composers during the sequence.)

What's Opera, Doc? repeats that sequence but expands on it as well, after an opening sequence that makes fun of *Fantasia* and another that places Elmer Fudd and his quest for Bugs Bunny within the context of Wagner's universe. Historian Jerry

Beck credits much of the success of the film to lay-out artist Maurice Noble, who was responsible for the cartoon's vivid background designs. Noble had worked with Jones and Maltese earlier in his career; this piece marked a reunion of sorts, one far more ambitious than ordinary Warner Brothers shorts. As film critic Leonard Maltin wrote, standard cartoons of the time had around sixty backgrounds; *What's Opera, Doc?* had 104, many of them highly stylized. Noble's work, in addition to mocking the Disney studio's artistic pretensions, also showed the influence of the simpler, more line-oriented style of drawing used by the UPA studio.

The music for *What's Opera, Doc?*, arranged by Milt Franklyn, used several motifs from Wagner's *Der Ring des Niebelungen* cycle, especially "The Ride of the Valkyries" from *Die Walküre* and the overture and "Pilgrim's Chorus" from *Tannhäuser*. (Jones proudly claimed that he took "the entire fourteen hours and squashed it down to six minutes.") Franklyn worked with a fifty-piece orchestra under contract to Warners, a luxury almost unimaginable today.

At the time of its release, *What's Opera, Doc?* received little attention. Ironically, the very pretensions Jones and his crew were mocking eventually helped elevate its status. *What's Opera, Doc?* was a cartoon for people who didn't like cartoons, who were put off by the rough-and-tumble slapstick of ordinary Bugs and Elmer encounters, who could congratulate themselves on recognizing allusions to classical music and modern art. (It was the first cartoon selected for the Registry.) Viewed as a cartoon, and not as an artistic statement, *What's Opera, Doc?* doesn't compare favorably to the best Bugs versus Elmer encounters. Normally preternaturally fleet, here they are often frozen into poses and situations, waiting for musical themes to play out.

Beck saw another problem with the cartoon, and Jones's career—namely, "how to reconcile his three-dimensional characters with what Noble called 'designed flat forms.'" Jones's characters were losing their physical reality, forcing the director to rely more on expressing their thoughts and emotions. In other words, they were becoming too self-conscious, and were working too hard to win over viewers through "personality." What had seemed effortless fifteen or twenty years before was becoming studied and precious.

The Warner animation studio closed in 1963. Jones made "Tom and Jerry" cartoons at MGM, then reunited with Theodore Geisel to adapt the Dr. Seuss book *How the Grinch Stole Christmas* (1966). He died in 2002.

Will Success Spoil Rock Hunter?

The star of *Will Success Spoil Rock Hunter?*, Jayne Mansfield, a willing participant in a film that mocked her celebrity.

Twentieth Century-Fox, 1957. Sound, color, 2.35. 93 minutes.
Cast: Tony Randall (Rockwell Hunter), Jayne Mansfield (Rita Marlowe), Betsy Drake (Jenny Wells), Joan Blondell (Violet), John Williams (Irving LaSalle, Jr.), Henry Jones (Henry Rufus), Lili Gentle (April Hunter), Mickey Hargitay (Bobo Branigansky), Georgia Carr (Calypso singer).
Credits: Written and directed by Frank Tashlin. Screen story by Frank Tashlin. Based on the play by George Axelrod, produced on the stage by Jule Styne. Produced by Frank Tashlin. Director of photography: Joe MacDonald. Music: Cyril J. Mockridge. Conducted by Lionel Newman. Vocal supervision: Ken Darby. Song "You've Got It Made" by Bobby Troup; orchestration by Edward B. Powell. Art directors: Lyle R. Wheeler, Leland Fuller. Set decorations: Walter M. Scott, Bertram Granger. Special photographic effects: L.B. Abbott. Film editor: Hugh S. Fowler. Executive wardrobe designer: Charles LeMaire. Makeup by Ben Nye. Hair styles by Helen Turpin. Assistant director: Joseph E. Rickards. Sound: E. Clayton Ward, Frank Moran. CinemaScope lenses: Bausch & Lomb. Color by DeLuxe. Color consultant: Leonard Doss. Westrex Recording System.
Additional Cast: Groucho Marx (George Schmidlap), Barbara Eden, Minta Durfee.
Additional Credits: Released July 29, 1957.

Available: Twentieth Century Fox Home Entertainment DVD (2006). UPC: 024543228318

Film has always been tied to the advertising industry, and a significant portion of early movies were themselves ads. Actors played ad men in films and on stage, but the possibility that advertising might have a pernicious effect on culture didn't become a widespread theme until the 1950s. Novels like Sloan Wilson's *The Man in the Gray Flannel Suit* (filmed in 1956) began to question not only the postwar work ethic, but an entire social class built around New York City media, especially Madison Avenue ad agencies.

For a brief period in the mid-1950s, George Axelrod was considered an expert in casting these issues in comic terms. A sometime-novelist and journeyman author for TV and radio, he found success with *The Seven Year Itch*, a 1952 play that became a film vehicle for Marilyn Monroe in 1955. His next play—*Will Success Spoil Rock Hunter?*—reworked *Faust* on Madison Avenue. Opening on October 13, 1955, it starred Jayne Mansfield, Orson Bean, Martin Gabel, Walter Matthau, and Tina Louise.

The curvaceous Mansfield did not mind exploiting her looks or her slight resemblance to Marilyn Monroe. Born Vera Jayne Palmer in 1933, she was a veteran of beauty contests before appearing in bit parts in films. Axelrod's mildly risqué play, and relentless publicity, catapulted her to fame, although no one knew what to do with her apart from displaying her body at every opportunity. Frank Tashlin did just that in *The Girl Can't Help It* (1956), which paired her with *Seven Year Itch* star Tom Ewell. Remembered today more for its stellar rock 'n' roll music than its hit-or-miss humor, the ramshackle *Girl Can't Help It* was an indirect catalyst for *Will Success Spoil Rock Hunter?*

A grammar-school dropout, Tashlin worked for several animation studios while also drawing his own daily comic strip, *Van Boring*. He sold gags to Hal Roach, was a story editor for Walt Disney, and directed cartoons at Warner Brothers. In the 1940s he gave up animation for live-action features, writing and then directing comedies for Bob Hope, Red Skelton, and Dean Martin and Jerry Lewis. In taking on *Will Success Spoil Rock Hunter?* Tashlin dropped almost all of Axelrod's script, concocting instead a plot about an ad writer who tries to get a movie star to endorse a brand of lipstick.

Cast with Mansfield was Tony Randall, a more open and rueful personality than the dyspeptic Orson Bean was on stage. This was his second film after extensive radio and television work, and he made excellent use of the befuddled and slightly irate expression that would become his trademark. Playing his boss was Henry Jones, a stage veteran and reliable character actor on film; he was also in *The Girl Can't Help It*. The English-born John Williams, who appears as the ad agency president, is perhaps most famous for playing the inspector in *Dial M for Murder* on the stage, in film, and on television. Mansfield's secretary Violet was one of Joan Blondell's comeback film roles after a hiatus for stage work. Like Williams, she has an unexpectedly poignant monologue about the missed opportunities in her life.

Like Axelrod did in his plays, Tashlin fully expected moviegoers to make the connections between the characters on the screen and their real-life counterparts. Although Mansfield is playing a movie star named Rita Marlowe, the role is clearly based on the actress's life (albeit one in which she is considerably more famous). Many viewers would have been familiar with Blondell's career, and would have known that she was in some ways a 1930s version of Mansfield. Mickey Hargitay, cast here as the movie star's spurned lover, was involved in an off-screen affair with Mansfield that eventually led to their marriage. The actress would appear that year in *Kiss Them for Me*, starring Cary Grant. *Success* was Betsy Drake's first film in five years; she would soon divorce Grant in real life.

Tashlin was fond of breaking the wall between the screen and viewers, having Tony Randall address the audience, inserting a fake intermission "for TV fans," fooling with the shape of the CinemaScope screen, and even playing around with the Twentieth Century-Fox fanfare at the opening of the film. (He did something similar in *Porky's Romance*, a 1937 Warners cartoon.)

Among the real and imagined products and personalities mentioned in the film: Shelton's Beer, Tres Chic shampoo, the Dandy Electric Shaver, Crunchy Crispies breakfast cereal, Frank's Vacuum-Packed Peanut Butter, Flake-Off face peel, NBC, Idlewild Airport, *TV Guide*. The Fox movies *A Hatful of Rain*, *Love Me Tender*, *Love Is a Many Splendored Thing*, *The King and I*, *The Girl Can't Help It*, *Kiss Them for Me*, and *The Wayward Bus* (the last three supposedly starring Rita Marlowe). Also Spencer Tracy, Errol Flynn, Clark Gable, Debbie Reynolds, Eddie Fisher, Elvis Presley, Louella Parsons, Earl Wilson, Ed Sullivan, Bennett

Cerf, Ed Murrow, Bill Holden, Jennifer Jones, and Stayput Lipstick, the product that drives the entire movie. To say nothing of Jayne Mansfield, reduced to a generic brand of "blond bombshell." The term *walking cartoon* also applies, although to be fair every character in the film seems lifted from comic strips.

Mansfield is a good sport throughout, even as the film mocks her real-life ambitions. A Movietone News team filmed the actress promoting the movie in Washington, D.C., and apart from the production values, *Nation's Capital Scene of Texan Get-Together* could have been outtakes from *Success*. What limits the film to its time period is a script that is filled with bright gags and energetic premises, but with almost no insights into its subjects. Tashlin's sense of timing is impeccable, and

he elicits uniformly strong performances from a cast of widely varying abilities. But making fun of Madison Avenue is not the same as making sense of it. (Tashlin could also have used a gag-writer, and a third act.)

The director went on to some well-liked Jerry Lewis vehicles, Danny Kaye's last film comedy, and a couple of indifferent Doris Day titles. Tashlin was a big influence on animators like Chuck Jones, and played a large role in defining mainstream film humor in the 1950s, but he has been regarded more highly in Europe than the United States. He died in 1972. Mansfield had trouble maintaining a film career, and had been reduced to exploitation movies at the time of her death in a car accident. Randall's career blossomed on television, where he won an Emmy as Felix Unger in *The Odd Couple*.

Jailhouse Rock

MGM, 1957. Sound, B&W, 2.35. 97 minutes.
Cast: Elvis Presley (Vince Everett), Judy Tyler (Peggy Van Alden), Mickey Shaughnessy (Hunk Houghton), Vaughn Taylor (Mr. Shores), Jennifer Holden (Sherry Wilson), Dean Jones (Teddy Talbot), Anne Neyland (Laury Jackson).
Credits: Directed by Richard Thorpe. Screen play by Guy Trosper, based on a story by Ned Young. Produced by Pandro S. Berman. Director of photography: Robert Bronner. Art directors: William A. Horning, Randall Duell. Set decorations: Henry Grace, Keogh Gleason. Special effects: A. Arnold Gillespie. Assistant director: Robert E. Relyea. Make-up by William Tuttle. Associate producer: Kathryn Hereford. Film editor: Ralph E. Winters. Music supervised by Jeff Alexander. Songs by Mike Stoller and Jerry Leiber; Sid Tepper and Roy C. Bennett; Abner Silver and Aaron Schroeder; Aaron Schroeder and Ben Weisman. Recording supervisor: Dr. Wesley C. Miller. Technical advisor: Colonel Tom Parker. Process lenses by Panavision. Westrex Recording System. Perspecta sound. In CinemaScope. A Metro-Goldwyn-Mayer presentation of an Avon Production.
Additional Cast: The Jordanaires, Hugh Sanders (Warden), Percy Helton (Sam Brewster), Peter Adams (Jack Lease), William Forrest (Studio head), George Cisar (Bartender), Robin Raymond (Dotty), Dick Rich (Guard), Glenn Strange (Simpson), Gloria Pall, Walter Johnson (Shorty), Wilson Wood (Record engineer), Don Burnett (Mickey Alba), Francis DeSales (Surgeon).
Additional Credits: Production dates: May 13 to June 14, 1957. Premiered in Memphis, Tennessee, on October 17, 1957.
Available: Warner Home Video DVD (2000). ISBN: 0-7907-4411-2. UPC: 0-12569-50612-1.

The third film Elvis Presley appeared in, *Jailhouse Rock* was also the last one he took seriously in a movie career that stretched over three decades. Born in Tupelo, Mississippi, in 1935, Presley grew up in and around Memphis, where he absorbed gospel, rhythm and blues, and country music. He was driving a truck when he was signed by record producer Sam Phillips, the head of Sun Records. A year later, in August 1955, Col. Tom Parker became his manager. Parker placed the singer

on television shows and helped negotiate a new recording contract with RCA Victor Records.

By 1956, songs like "Heartbreak Hotel" and "Don't Be Cruel" helped make Presley the most popular teen singer in the country, and the center of a storm of controversy over his music and hip-shaking "gyrations." Frank Sinatra, for example, called Elvis's style of rock and roll "the most brutal, ugly, desperate, vicious form of expression it has been my misfortune to hear." (Sinatra dueted with Presley on television in 1960.)

Since Elvis had conquered records, radio, and television, Parker reasoned that films were the next step. Three weeks after the release of his first album, Presley filmed a screen test for Paramount; days later, Parker signed a seven-year contract with producer Hal Wallis at Paramount. Presley's first film was on a loan-out to Twentieth Century-Fox. He played a supporting role in *Love Me Tender* (1956), a Western. Although top-billed in his next film, *Loving You* (1957), a cleaned-up account of a truck driver-turned-pop star, Presley was again in a subordinate role.

Jailhouse Rock was made at MGM under producer Pandro S. Berman, a no-nonsense veteran who worked at RKO in the 1930s. Again the story was a coming-of-age tale, but this time closer to the facts in Elvis's life, and without the antiseptic whitewash of his earlier movies. The songwriting team of Jerry Leiber and Mike Stoller provided four songs and helped produce the soundtrack recording sessions. (Stoller can also be seen playing piano in the movie.) Known for R&B hits like "Hound Dog" and "I'm a Hog for You Baby," the songwriters were dubious about working with Presley at first, but his talent and commitment won them over.

The songs were recorded over three sessions in April and May 1957, two months before the release of *Loving You*. Presley used his regular backup band of Scotty Moore (guitar), Bill Black (bass), and D.J. Fontana (drums), augmented by either Stoller or Dudley Brooks on piano. (These musicians can also be seen at times during the film.)

Filming took place from May to June 1957. A former vaudeville performer, director Richard Thorpe had started out making Westerns in the silent era, and more recently had helmed several second-tier musicals at MGM. Efficient but noncommittal, he was more concerned with finishing the film rather than making it artistic. Presley is often credited with creating the choreography for the title tune, but as his biographer Peter Guralnick noted, Alex Romero actually worked out the routine based on how the singer moved.

Guralnick also described how Presley studied his rushes every night, trying to improve his performance. Whether from Thorpe's indifference or a tight budget, the musical routines in *Jailhouse Rock* are the film's weakest element. They are shot in a stale, unimaginative manner, with almost no attempt to either dramatize the material or present it realistically. Elvis has trouble lip-synching to his recordings, a problem that would plague him throughout his career. Even the vaunted "Jailhouse Rock" number suffers from choppy transitions, garish Las Vegas touches, and overdubs that negate the song's crude energy.

Still, this is the Ur-text for Elvis films, the one that showed both his potential and his decline. It provides an unguarded look at the early, sullen performer, the one who electrified youth by showing such contempt for education, authority, adults, culture, and propriety. "It's the beast in me," he says as he forces himself on a pretty record promoter. When she fights him off, he consoles himself with blondes in bathing suits who gather by his new swimming pool. *Jailhouse Rock* offers an uncanny prediction of how Presley's career would evolve, seduced by money and Hollywood and fame, surrounding himself with sycophantic flunkies, ignoring his responsibilities, disdaining emotional relationships, agreeing to sing trashy songs in an endless parade of lackluster movies (thirty-one fiction features in all).

At the same time, it gave viewers what Col. Tom Parker thought they deserved: Elvis drinking and fighting; Elvis loving and singing; Elvis stripped to the waist and beaten by sadistic prison guards. He starts out inspired by country music (there are pictures of Hank Williams and Ernest Tubb on the wall of his jail cell), but selling out is inevitable. When he's ready for his recording contract, the pictures behind him include Perry Como and Hugo Winterhalter. The film presents a jaundiced view of the entire music industry: A&R men steal songs, DJs accept sex to play records, customers laugh during performances, and everyone wants a piece of the star.

Critics chide Elvis for giving up on the promise showed in *Jailhouse Rock*, pointing to his long list of popcorn movies as well as forgettable pop songs as proof that he squandered his talent. But Elvis's abilities as an actor limited him to playing himself, and it's not as if starring in thinly disguised, reproving autobiographies was fun. How many times could he make a film about a mean-spirited, conceited artist who alienates his friends and destroys his life by pursuing mindless hedonism at the expense of genuine art? Which would you rather do—portray yourself as a snarling, loveless egoist who ends up in prison or in a hospital, or a race car driver/helicopter pilot/carnival roustabout/priest so happy with life that you spontaneously burst into songs like "Do the Clam"? Having confirmed to the world how miserable a celebrity's life could be in *Jailhouse Rock*, Elvis chose the latter.

The film, which premiered at the same Memphis movie theater where Elvis once ushered, was a significant hit, adding to Presley's luster. His next film, *King Creole* (1958), follows another singer menaced by crooks and women on his way to fame. Based on *A Stone for Danny Fisher* by Harold Robbins, it was directed by Michael Curtiz.

The Bridge on the River Kwai

Columbia, 1957. Sound, color, 2.55. 161 minutes.

Cast: William Holden (Shears), Alec Guinness (Colonel Nicholson), Jack Hawkins (Major Warden), Sessue Hayakawa (Colonel Saito), James Donald (Major Clipton), Geoffrey Horne (Lieutenant Joyce), Andre Morell (Colonel Green), Peter Williams (Captain Reeves), John Boxer (Major Hughes), Percy Herbert (Grogan), Harold Goodwin (Baker), Ann Sears (Nurse), Henry Okawa (Captain Kanematsu), Keiichiro Katsumoto (Lieutenant Miura), M.R.B. Chakrabandhu ([Col. Broome] Yai); Vilaiwan Seeboonreaung, Ngamta Suphaphongs, Javanart Punynchoti, Kannikar Dowklee (Siamese Girls).

Credits: Directed by David Lean. Screenplay by Pierre Boulle [see additional credits]. Produced by Sam Spiegel. Director of photography: Jack Hildyard. Music by Malcolm Arnold. Played by the Royal Philharmonic Orchestra. Chief editor: Peter Taylor. Chief sound editor: Winston Ryder. Art director: Donald M. Ashton. Assistant art director: Geoffrey Drake. Production manager: Cecil Ford. Technical adviser: Major-General L.E.M. Perowne. Construction manager: Peter Dukelow. Consulting engineers for the bridge: Husband & Co. of Sheffield. Constructed by Equipment and Construction Co. of Ceylon. Camera operator: Peter Newbrook. Assistant directors: Gus Agosti, Ted Sturgis. Sound: John Cox, John Mitchell. Continuity: Angela Martelli. Chief electrician: Archie Dansie. Make-up: Stuart Freeborn, George Partleton. Wardrobe: John Apperson. RCA Sound Recording. A Horizon Picture photographed in CinemaScope.

Additional Credits: Screenplay by Michael Wilson and Carl Foreman. Based on the novel by Pierre Boulle. Second unit camera: Freddy Ford. Construction engineer: Keith Best. Production dates: November 1956 to May, 1957. Filmed in Sri Lanka. Premiered in New York City on December 18, 1957. Rated PG.

Awards: Oscars for Best Picture, Director, Writing—Screenplay Based on Material for Another Medium, Actor (Guinness), Cinematography, Editing, Music—Scoring.

Available: Columbia TriStar Home Video DVD (2000). ISBN: 0-7678-5873-5. UPC: 0-43396-05747-0.

For novelist Pierre Boulle, *The Bridge on the River Kwai* was a black comedy that satirized a British mania for following rules. For blacklisted screenwriter Carl Foreman, the tale was a high-spirited adventure involving submarines, wisecracking spies, and romance. It took director David Lean to see the epic scope of the story, as well as its tragic aspects.

Born in Avignon, France, in 1912, Boulle worked for British companies in Malaya in the 1930s. He was a spy for the Free French Forces during World War II, and spent two years in a prisoner of war camp. Returning to France, he became a writer of novels based on his experiences in Southeast Asia. *Le Pont de la rivière Kwai*, his third novel, was published in 1952 and translated into English two years later. Set in a prisoner of war camp in the Burmese jungle, it focused on Colonel Nicholson, a by-the-books disciplinarian with a narcissistic martyr complex. When the Japanese Colonel Saito orders the prisoners to build a strategically vital railroad bridge, they respond with sabotage. But to prove British superiority over the Japanese, Nicholson takes command of the project, overseeing the construction of a structurally advanced bridge.

Carl Foreman, blacklisted after writing *High Noon* (1952), was working at the time for London Films, a company run by Alexander Korda. Korda was incensed when Foreman optioned *The Bridge on the River Kwai*, primarily because the novel showed British soldiers cooperating with the Japanese. He sold the novel to Sam Spiegel, a producer who formed a partnership with Foreman to develop the book. Spiegel, who had just worked on the Oscar-winning *On the Waterfront* (1954), offered the project to several top-tier directors, including Howard Hawks and John Ford. (Ford turned it down because he couldn't make sense of Nicholson's character.) Stars as varied as Cary Grant, Spencer Tracy, and Humphrey Bogart were approached for roles.

David Lean attracted Spiegel's attention with *Summertime* (1955), a bittersweet romance set in Venice and starring Katharine Hepburn. Lean's film career stretched back to the 1920s. Born in 1908, he dropped out of a Quaker school, worked briefly as an accountant, then took entry-level jobs at film studios. At the transition to sound films, he was editing newsreels, then features, often uncredited. After cutting two films for director Michael Powell, he codirected his first feature, *In Which We Serve* (1942), with Noël Coward. Lean made two more films based on Coward works, then in 1945 directed *Brief Encounter*, a quintessentially British melodrama of thwarted romance. After two adaptations of books by Charles Dickens, including the internationally successful *Great Expectations* (1946), Lean helmed films of varying quality. Following *Hobson's Choice* (1954), he would complete only six more features, none of them set in England.

According to biographer Kevin Brownlow, Lean was appalled when he read Foreman's script for *The Bridge on the River Kwai*. He saw Nicholson as a figure of Shakespearean tragedy, and the plot as "a tremendous clash of wills." Key to the project's success was finding a way to get viewers to "understand and admire" Nicholson. Lean and his collaborator Norman Spencer wrote a treatment in March 1956. A week later he signed a contract to direct the project.

Preproduction began almost at once, with art director Don Ashton finding appropriately mountainous locations near the village of Kitulgala in Ceylon. By June, Lean had engineered the firing of Foreman, who recommended Michael Wilson to replace him. Another blacklisted screenwriter, Wilson had written *A Place in the Sun* (1951) and *Salt of the Earth* (1954). He was asked to invent material for an American character that Spiegel and Columbia Pictures insisted on adding (the studio also demanded a love scene that Lean later described as "bloody awful.")

Although he has a comparatively small role, William Holden, at the time the biggest star in the industry, guaranteed that the film would be made. After much persuasion, Alec Guinness accepted the lead role of Nicholson. He later complained about Lean's lack of humor, and during the shoot the director feuded with most of the other British actors as well.

The production was more demanding than any of Lean's previous films. Brownlow reported the accidental deaths of two crew members, but the six months of oppressive heat in the jungles took their toll as well. Leeches, dysentery, and deadly river currents added to Lean's problems. So did the fact that the shoot was running wildly over schedule, with no possible additional funds from Columbia. Principal photography finally finished in April 1957 after some six months. Unable to return to Great Britain because of tax laws, Lean worked in Paris with editor Peter Taylor, finishing a rough cut that August.

Despite the recalcitrant crews and difficult conditions, Lean managed to wrest out of the jungle a vision of war in microcosm as a battle between two arrogant, wrongheaded, but not unsympathetic military officers. Lean's directorial style, honed after years of editing and translating literature to the screen, gave a depth and structure to what could have been a straightforward adventure. The metaphorical implications emerge gradually, organically, almost as if unintended. Lean's greatest achievement may have been to make such an epic story seem so intimate and personal. Previous war films like *The Big Parade* (1925) and *All Quiet on the Western Front* (1930) are cumbersome, pointed, and unpersuasive by comparison.

Lean received two unpleasant surprises when he saw the release print. First, Sam Spiegel put his name on the credits before Lean's. Second, the screenplay was credited to Pierre Boulle, not to Lean or to Michael Wilson. Lean's displeasure increased when Boulle, who did not speak English, won an Oscar for Best Screenplay. Foreman spread the word that he actually wrote the script, stirring more dissension. He and Wilson received Oscars posthumously, in 1985; their screenwriting credits were restored in 2000.

The Bridge on the River Kwai was an international blockbuster, making fortunes for Spiegel and for William Holden. (Even its theme song, the "Colonel Bogey March," became a hit.) It influenced a generation of filmmakers, and sustained the prisoner of war genre well into the 1960s. Many took the narrative engine of the story for their own, like Michael Cimino (in *The Deer Hunter*, 1978) and writer and director James Cameron. In both *Rambo: First Blood Part II* (1985) and *Aliens* (1986), Cameron used Holden's role to construct plot lines in which characters escaped from horrible situations through tremendous effort, only to be sent right back to their nightmares.

The movie gave Lean the economic freedom to pick and choose his projects; it also put him in the position of having to top himself with each subsequent project. His next film, *Lawrence of Arabia* (1962) is also on the Registry.

Paths of Glory

United Artists, 1957. Sound, B&W, 1.37. 86 minutes.

Cast: Kirk Douglas (Colonel Dax), Ralph Meeker (Corporal Paris), Adolphe Menjou (General Broulard), George Macready (General Mireau), Wayne Morris (Lieutenant Roget), Richard Anderson (Major Saint-Auben), Joseph Turkel (Private Arnaud), Susanne Christian (German girl), Jerry Hausner (Tavern owner), Peter Capell (Colonel Judge), Emile Meyer (Priest), Bert Freed (Sergeant Boulanger), Ken Dibbs (Private LeJeune), Timothy Carey (Private Ferol), Fred Bell (Shell-shocked soldier), John Stein (Captain Rousseau), Harold Benedict (Captain Nichols).

Credits: Directed by Stanley Kubrick. Screenplay by Stanley Kubrick, Calder Willingham and Jim Thompson. Based on the novel by Humphrey Cobb. Produced by James B. Harris. Photographed by George Krause.

Art director: Ludwig Reiber. Film editor: Eva Kroll. Music: Gerald Fried. Camera operator: Hannes Staudinger. American production manager: John Pommer. German production manager: George von Block. Unit manager: Helmut Ringelmann. Assistant directors: Hans Stumpf, Dixie Sensburg, Franz-Josef Spieker. Script clerk: Trudy von Trotha. Sound: Martin Müller. Costume designer: Ilse Dubois. Special effects: Erwin Lange. Military advisor: Baron von Waldenfels. Assistant editor: Helene Fischer. Camera grip: Hans Elsinger. Makeup: Arthur Schramm. Produced at Bavaria-Filmkunst Studios Munich. A Bryna Productions presentation of a Harris-Kubrick Pictures Corporation production.

Additional Credits: Production dates: January to March 1957. Released December 25, 1957.

Available: MGM Home Entertainment DVD (1999). ISBN: 0-7928-4140-9. UPC: 0-27616-7674-2-4.

The problem with making an anti-war film isn't getting a liberal audience to agree with you but in winning over those who are not against war to begin with. It requires building an argument so logical and compelling that no one can fault it. Erich Maria Remarque's *All Quiet on the Western Front* (filmed in 1930) tried to show the futility of war through the experiences of an "everyman" who is at first disillusioned and then killed during World War I. Humphrey Cobb, a Canadian Army veteran who was wounded and gassed in the conflict, was inspired to write *Paths of Glory* after reading newspaper articles about financial compensation to the families of soldiers unjustly executed during the war. (The title refers to Thomas Gray's "Elegy Written in a Country Courtyard": "The paths of glory lead but to the grave.") Cobb focused on a political rather than personal angle. Published in 1935, his *Paths of Glory* was successful enough to be adapted for the stage that September by Pulitzer Prize–winning playwright Sidney Howard. Cobb's message proved unpalatable to the mainstream public, and the play closed within a month.

Cobb did find work in Hollywood, contributing to the prison melodrama *San Quentin* (1937), but his novel proved too controversial for film until the mid-1950s, when director Stanley Kubrick and his producer James B. Harris stumbled across the book, then owned by MGM. Born in the Bronx in 1926, Kubrick was a staff photographer for *Look* magazine while still in high school. He was twenty-two when he made his first film, a documentary about a prize fight, and twenty-five when he finished his first feature, *Fear and Desire* (1953). He financed this and *Killer's Kiss* (1955) largely through relatives and friends, not only writing and directing, but photographing and editing them. In 1954 he formed a partnership with James B. Harris; his next film, *The Killing* (1956), while still an independent production, featured a larger budget and a professional cast.

In adapting *Paths of Glory*, Kubrick collaborated with Calder Willingham, a novelist and playwright from Georgia whose first book, *End as a Man* (1948), dealt with hypocrisy in a military academy. Willingham adapted it for the screen as *The Strange One* (1957). As he did with *The Killing*, Kubrick asked pulp author Jim Thompson to polish the dialogue. Thompson's distinctive voice can be heard in fiery, vituperative rants directed at officers.

Studios rejected the script until Kirk Douglas became attached to the project. While he was fully aware of its questionable commercial prospects, Douglas helped arrange financing through his Bryna Productions. (In his autobiography, he quotes himself as saying, "Stanley, I don't think this picture will ever make a nickel, but we *have* to make it.") As part of his deal for the big-budget adventure *The Vikings*, Douglas got United Artists to agree to release *Paths of Glory* on a budget of about a million dollars.

Kubrick enlarged the role of Colonel Dax, the character Douglas would play, but otherwise followed Cobb's novel fairly closely. Both book and film are divided into three parts: a prologue in which generals decide to attack an enemy-held position (called the "Pimple" in the book and the "Anthill" in the film); the battle itself; and a court-martial after the French soldiers fail to secure the position. The script strips away supporting material, concentrating almost entirely on pure narrative, in the process avoiding appeals to sentiment. Orders are given, positions are scouted, and the battle ensues, with no consideration for whether either side is right or wrong.

Shooting took place in Germany at the Geiselgasteig Studios. For the big battle scene, the filmmakers rented a 5,000-square-yard farm pasture, where eight cranes and some sixty crew members helped prepare the terrain, planting explosives among the shell holes. An extensive layout of trenches was built, modified from original designs to fit camera tracks. Most of the interiors were shot on soundstages, although the climactic court-martial was filmed in the Schleissheim Castle.

Douglas was impressed by Kubrick's preparation. The director made heavy demands on his cast and crew, but the result was footage with the immediacy of a newsreel. In lieu of editing to a shot/reaction shot pattern, Kubrick constructed many scenes with characters moving around the sets, first one, then another occupying the dominant position in the frame. This not only made lighting difficult, it forced actors to perform with each other rather than wait for their close-ups. (He also tested the limits of film stock, in some shots deliberately washing out highlights for a harsh effect.) He devised several extended tracking shots, often with the camera moving in reverse. These have the effect of drawing viewers into the soldiers' world, making their environment feel real. Since portable microphones weren't available, recording sound was also difficult, especially since Kubrick preferred live sound to postdubbing.

Despite these obstacles Kubrick achieved a remarkable look and feel for *Paths of Glory*. The script hurtles forward with a ghastly momentum; the camera and sound ground viewers in a nightmare of violence and death. Unlike *All Quiet on the Western Front*, there is no escape from the war, no higher reason to appeal to, no relief from death. The ensemble acting is unusually effective, with veteran stars like Wayne Morris (a World War II Navy fighter pilot) willing to risk their careers to play unlikable roles. (Only George Macready, whose real-life facial scar suited his part as General Mireau, seemed to be overacting.) At the same time, Kubrick's technical mastery is unmistakable. For the battle, Kubrick follows the French soldiers' advance in a tracking shot that progresses from right to left. When he cuts to a longer lens, he pulls viewers shockingly close to the action, trapping them in the same inexorable march to doom.

Directors as varied as King Vidor and John Huston had tried to achieve similar effects, but Kubrick had the equipment and persistence to succeed to an unprecedented extent.

Kubrick's touch faltered only in the film's closing moments, as battle-hardened soldiers sitting in a café find themselves sympathizing with a young girl singing "The Faithful Hussar" in German. Kubrick undercuts the sentiment with sarcastic editing and some of the few zoom shots in the film, a premonition of the more heavy-handed efforts to come. (Kubrick married the actress, Susanne Christian, shortly after filming.)

Paths of Glory was not a box-office success, despite admiring reviews. In fact, it was banned for years in France, Spain, and other countries. Kubrick had trouble finding work, and in a sense was rescued by Douglas when he was hired to replace Anthony Mann on *Spartacus* (1960). Kubrick made two more war films, *Dr. Strangelove* (1964, a Registry title) and *Full Metal Jacket* (1987).

Glimpse of the Garden

Marie Menken, 1957. Sound, color, 1.33. 5 minutes.
Credits: Directed by Marie Menken. Photography and editing by Marie Menken.
Available: The Film-Makers' Cooperative (*www.film-makerscoop.com*), Canyon Cinema (*www.canyoncinema.com*).

Born in 1909, Marie Menken grew up in New York City in a family of four children. She became interested in art at an early age. To finance her painting, she worked as a secretary for the Guggenheim family, and later as an assistant curator at the Guggenheim Foundation. She received a grant to attend the Yaddo art colony, where Willard Maas was working on his writing. The son of a wealthy railroad baron, Maas taught literature at Wagner College on Staten Island, wrote poetry, pursued left-wing politics, and was the divorced father of a son. Menken married Maas in 1937, and remained with him after he determined he was homosexual.

Menken shot Maas's *Geography of the Body*, a 1943 experimental work that used extreme close-ups and lyrical editing to turn images of a body into art. During World War II, she worked in special effects for Signal Corps movies, shooting macrophotography and helping animate graphics for instructional films. She performed a similar function on *The Seasons*, a ballet by Merce

Cunningham and John Cage. It was an experience that encouraged her to make her own movies. As she put it, Cunningham "was entertained and delighted. So was I. It was fun. All art should be fun in a sense and give one a kick."

Menken's first significant solo film was *Visual Variations on Noguchi* (1945), which she made in the sculptor Isamu Noguchi's studio. She later told filmmaker Stan Brakhage that she was trying to approximate the "flying spirit of movement" within Noguchi's pieces, "how they made me feel." Brakhage was astonished by her handheld camera, writing that it liberated him and other filmmakers from the feeling that "we have to imitate the Hollywood dolly shot . . . that the smooth pan and dolly was the only acceptable thing."

Brakhage also extolled the "grubbiness" of Menken's work, the fact that you could see her splices and could tell how she was holding the camera. "She would hang the film strips on clothespins and, after much meditation and often without running them through a viewer at all, would cut them together." This do-it-yourself approach extended to her subject matter as well. Menken edited together stock footage of spermatozoa for *Hurry! Hurry!* (1957), and constructed film portraits of people like Kenneth Anger and Dwight Ripley by editing together pictures of objects they liked.

Glimpse of the Garden was filmed in Ripley's garden. A wealthy alcoholic, he had been one of Maas's boyfriends. Brakhage called it "one of the toughest of Marie's works" because it was based more on rhythm and editing than on its ostensible visual subject, a collection of rare flowering plants. The film opens with two establishing shots of the garden grounds, then moves into close-ups of flowers and plants. Menken tilts and whirls the camera at times; she also walks through bushes, uses jump cuts to draw closer to blooms, and alternates between static shots of individual blossoms and pans so fast the objects blur.

When Jonas Mekas screened the film at the Cinemathèque Française in 1963, he reported that the French laughed derisively at it, mocking its simplicity and apparent lack of metaphoric meaning. Back in the United States, Menken had influential admirers, despite or perhaps because of her abrasive lifestyle. On the night he met Menken and Maas, Brakhage watched aghast as Maas's boyfriend left Maas bloody and beaten on a Brooklyn sidewalk. Playwright Edward Albee acknowledged that Menken and Maas were inspirations for Martha and George in *Who's Afraid of Virginia Woolf?* Andy Warhol was impressed by the parties Menken and Maas threw in their Brooklyn Heights penthouse. "Their friends called them scholarly drunks," he wrote.

Warhol liked the fact that Menken was not only saying that anyone could make art, that technique wasn't necessary or even desired, but that anything could be art. He adopted her handheld style in his early films, made her the subject of one of his screen tests, and allowed her to film *Andy Warhol* (1965), which also showed the artist Gerard Malanga at work in the Factory. She had the title role in Warhol's *The Life of Juanita Castro* (1965).

Menken continued to make films throughout the 1960s, including *Notebook*, which she was still working on when she died on December 29, 1970. Maas died four days later, "probably the only romantic thing he ever did in his relationship with Marie Menken," according to Brakhage.

The Hunters

The Film Study Center, Peabody Museum, Harvard University, 1957. Sound, color, 1,37, 73 minutes.

Credits: Written and directed by John Marshall. Produced by the Film Study Center of the Peabody Museum at Harvard University. Photography: John Marshall. Ethnography: Lorna Marshall. Field sound recording: Daniel Blitz. Edited by John Marshall with the assistance of Robert Gardner. Photographed on a Peabody Museum, Harvard University/Smithsonian Institute expedition led by Laurence Marshall.

Available: Documentary Educational Resources DVD (*www.der.org*).

Born in 1932 in Cambridge, Massachusetts, John Marshall turned a childhood fascination with Africa into a lifelong career documenting the !Kung tribes of the Kalahari Desert. His father Laurence Marshall, a business executive, retired in 1950 to devote time to his family. He turned an expedition to South West Africa (now Namibia) into a family project, with his wife Lorna assigned to ethnography, his daughter Elizabeth to writing a book, and John to documenting their experiences on film. Laurence Marshall approached the Peabody Museum at Harvard and the Smithsonian Institution for help in setting up the expedition. The main thrust of the trip was to have been a search for lost cities, but on their second expedition they met Bushmen in a remote desert setting.

The tribes had had no direct contact with whites, or with modern civilization. Basically communities of hunters and gatherers, they subsisted on whatever roots and berries the women found and whatever game the men caught. John Marshall gained the trust of the Ju/'hoansi tribe, learning their language and spending weeks at a time in their villages.

Working at first with a handheld Bell & Howell 16mm camera and Kodak color film stock, he shot hundreds of rolls of film of the !Kung between 1950 and 1952. Five years later, with the help of Robert Gardner, he edited the footage into a seventy-three-minute feature.

Marshall shaped his material into a narrative form rather than a scientific one. He explained certain aspects of life within the !Kung villages, but was more intent on providing an easily understandable story line for filmgoers whose knowledge of the Kalahari was limited. The "plot" became the hunt for food, the single most important need the tribes faced.

Randomly shot footage of tribesmen and their activities now had a theme that could tie it together.

!Kung hunter with poison-tipped arrows. Photograph for *The Hunters* from the Marshall family collection. *Courtesy of Documentary Educational Resources*

From the footage Marshall developed personalities within the tribes, describing their feelings and emotions in a narration he wrote and delivered. He also now had a framework for the centerpiece of the film, an account of a five-day hunt by four tribesmen for a giraffe. The narration may give the illusion of objectivity, but Marshall offers unsupported interpretations of his characters' thoughts, and is not above inserting extraneous footage into a scene to provide transitions. Modern-day documentarians disavow these methods, but in spite of them, *The Hunters* is a surprisingly graceful and moving film, filled with unexpected humor and tension, as well as with compositions that impart a grave beauty to a harsh landscape. Marshall succeeds in presenting an approximation of what it must be like to live in the Kalahari.

Marshall's observation of the giraffe hunt resulted in some graphic and gruesome footage that helped make *The Hunters* a favorite of teachers trying to interest their students in anthropology. The footage also raised questions about Marshall's participation in !Kung life. Should he have given supplies to help them? Should he have aided in the hunt? Should he have somehow deterred them from poisoning and then spearing a female giraffe to death?

While some ethnographic filmmakers have been accused of exploiting their subjects, Marshall's personal commitment to the Ju/'hoansi tribe has never been questioned. His empathy with the tribe members is palpable, and their willingness to have him accompany them is an indication of their feelings for him. Marshall repaid that trust by returning to the Ju/'hoansi tribe for the next fifty years, shooting hundreds of thousands of feet of footage documenting their lives. His series of films on the !Kung total over twenty-five titles, including the monumental, six-hour, five-part series, *A Kalahari Family*, completed in 2001.

To help support this project, Marshall hired himself out as a cameraman, shooting footage of the civil war in Cyprus for NBC. He also worked with Richard Leacock and DA Pennebaker on cinema verité projects, and was the cinematographer on *Titicut Follies* (1967), Frederick Wiseman's debut documentary. Between 1968 and 1971, he shot and released the "Pittsburgh Police Series," an influential cinema verité examination of the Pittsburgh Police Department that consisted of twenty short black-and-white films.

Due to the political tensions surrounding apartheid, Marshall was not permitted to enter the Kalahari from the early 1960s until 1978, when he made *N!ai, The Story of a !Kung Woman*. The intervening years had had a dreadful impact on the bushmen. While Marshall later repudiated some of the strategies he used in *The Hunters*, deciding that they were too personal and artistic, he devoted the last thirty years of his life to political activism, much of it on the behalf of the !Kung. He died in 2005.

Let's All Go to the Lobby

Filmack, 1957. Sound, color, 1.37. 60 seconds.

Credits: Produced by Filmack Studios.

Available: *Let's All Go to the Lobby* and other Filmack trailers are for sale only to theater owners. A shortened version of the film can be viewed on the Filmack Studios website (*www.filmack.com*).

Coming attractions for movies have a long history that stretches back to the silent era. What are referred to in the industry as "snipes" have an even longer tradition, as they were variations on a form of advertising used in music halls and in lantern shows. In film, snipes are material that is not part of the feature presentation, such as ads for local businesses, notices of future shows, courtesy requests, and information about concessions. Film historian Scott Simmon traces advertising films back to 1897, when William Heise made the thirty-second-long *Admiral Cigarette*. The Vitaphone short *The Happy Hottentots* (1930) shows what a small-town theater of the period looked like, with business ads stitched onto the stage curtain.

Founded in 1919 as the Filmack Trailer Company, Filmack Studios carved out a niche for itself as a producer and distributor of trailers. Based in Chicago, the studio started by filming newsreels as well as promotional material for theaters. Irving Mack, a former newspaperman, hired animator Walt Disney in the 1920s and Dave Fleischer in 1953. By that time concessions like popcorn and candy were a significant portion of a typical theater's revenue. Filmack commissioned a series of trailers to capitalize on this trend, including *Let's All Go to the Lobby*.

Robbie Mack, the third generation of Macks to run the studio, believes the film was produced around 1955, although work may have started on it in 1953. Consisting of six shots, the film employs fundamental animation techniques. In one shot, four animated concessions—gum, popcorn, a box of candy, and a soda—walk from right to left behind a drawing of theatergoers in the foreground, an illusion of depth that was perfected in the 1930s by both Disney and the Fleischer brothers. Another shot which depicts four happy consumers uses the same theory of sequential action employed by Winsor McCay in *Gertie the Dinosaur* (1914).

The melody for the background music was identified at the time as "We Won't Be Home Until Morning," but is known under several titles, such as "The Bear Went Over the Mountain," and "Malbrouk" or "Malbrough." Music historians Roger Lax and Frederick Smith trace the tune back to 1783's "For He's a Jolly Good Fellow," but note that it may date from the Crusades. Beethoven used it in his 1813 "Battle Symphony," Marie Antoinette sang it as a lullaby, and Napoleon was rumored to have been humming it as he started his Russian campaign.

With its simple, repetitive lyrics and streamlined animation, *Let's All Go to the Lobby* has a hypnotic pull that is as compelling today as it was fifty years ago. The decision to use animation instead of photography eliminated any worries about showing brand names, but it also made the entire idea of concessions abstract instead of realistic. Filmack could make the experience happy rather than mercenary; depicting popcorn, candy, and soda as living, even jaunty, characters made purchasing concessions seem like a great opportunity to make new friends.

Whether Fleischer animated *Let's All Go to the Lobby*, and who performed the score's sprightly new lyrics, are questions that may never be answered satisfactorily. "I wasn't around at the time," explained Robbie Mack, adding that production records from the 1950s disappeared many years earlier. However, a page in *Inspiration*, a Filmack catalog disguised as a magazine, offers a slightly different version of *Let's All Go to the Lobby* as *Trailer Number 1*, in Technicolor, at $11.25 a print. The copy notes, "Both trailers were produced EXCLUSIVELY for Filmack by Dave Fleischer, Famous Producer of POPEYE and other Cartoon Greats!" (The trailer costs $135 today, still a bargain.)

Coming up with a figure of how many prints have been struck is basically guesswork. Mack believes that up to 80 percent of independent theaters screened the film at one point or another. Filmack still sells between fifty and one hundred copies a year. Conservatively, considering replacement copies, thousands of prints may have been struck. How many viewers have seen *Let's All Go to the Lobby*? Consider that the film may have been screened three or four times a day, in hundreds of theaters, for decades.

Filmack had even more success, at least at drive-ins, with its *Variety Show*, available in five- or ten-minute versions. A countdown to the start of a feature film, it had dancing concessions, a hot dog snuggling suggestively into a bun, and repeated warnings that the major attraction was about to start. Another tantalizing hint that Fleischer may have animated these trailers is *Ain't She Sweet*, a "follow the bouncing ball" short he made in 1933. It, too, features a gag in which hot dogs jump eagerly into buns.

As times changed, Filmack added new trailers. It now offers three animated "No Smoking" clips; *Clapboard Crossplug Datestrip*, which can customize "Coming Soon" and "Now Showing" alerts for individual theaters; various *Courtesy Trailers* ("Turn Off Phones & Beepers," "Refrain from Talking," etc.); *Public Service Trailers*; and a number of *Feature Presentation* trailers, available in CinemaScope as well as "flat" formats.

Rather than renting its trailers, Filmack sells its prints outright, a practice that goes back to the earliest days of motion pictures. Watching a Filmack trailer connects viewers to a time when the industry was controlled by a handful of entrepreneurs. In fact, Filmack is very likely the oldest company in the industry that has been run by one family.

Touch of Evil

A monstrous Orson Welles as a monstrous police detective in *Touch of Evil*.

Universal International, 1958. Sound, B&W, 1.85. 109 minutes.
Cast: Charlton Heston ("Mike" Vargas), Janet Leigh (Susan Vargas), Orson Welles (Hank Quinlan), Joseph Calleia (Pete Menzies), Akim Tamiroff (Joe Grandi), Joanna Moore (Marcia Linnekar), Ray Collins (Adair), Dennis Weaver (The night man), Valentin De Vargas (Pancho), Mort Mills (Schwartz), Victor Millan (Manuelo Sanchez), Lalo Rios (Risto), Michael Sargent (Pretty Boy), Phil Harvey (Blaine), Joi Lansing (Blonde), Harry Shannon (Gould), Marlene Dietrich (Tana), Zsa Zsa Gabor (Strip-club owner).
Credits: Directed by Orson Welles. Screenplay by Orson Welles. Based on the novel *Badge of Evil* by Whit Masterson. Produced by Albert Zugsmith. Director of photography: Russell Metty. Music: Henry Mancini. Music supervision by Joseph Gershenson. Art direction: Alexander Golitzen, Robert Clatworthy. Set decorations: Russell A. Gausman, John P. Austin. Sound: Leslie I. Carey, Frank Wilkinson. Film editors: Virgil Vogel, Aaron Stell. Gowns: Bill Thomas. Make-up: Bud Westmore. Assistant director: Phil Bowles. Westrex Recording System.
Additional Cast: Joseph Cotten (Coroner), Rusty Wescoatt (Casey); Mercedes McCambridge, Wayne Taylor, Ken Miller, Raymond Rodriguez (Gang members); Arlene McQuade (Ginnie), Domenick Delgarde (Lackey), Joe Basulto (Delinquent), Jennie Dias (Jackie), Yolanda Bojorquez (Bobbie), Eleanor Dorado (Lia), Gus Schilling (Ex-con), Keenan Wynn.
Additional Credits: Material directed by Harry Keller. Screenwriting: Paul Monash. Camera operator: Phil Lathrop. Production dates: February 18 to April 1957. Released February 1958. Original running time: 95 minutes. Restoration produced by Rick Schmidlin. Edited by Walter Murch. Consultant: Jonathan Rosenbaum. Rated PG-13 in 1998.
Available: Universal Home Video DVD (2008). UPC: 025195027809.

After the commercial failure of *The Lady from Shanghai* (1948), a stylishly lurid but weakly plotted thriller, Orson Welles went into a more-or-less self-imposed exile. On the one hand, no Hollywood studio would hire him; on the other, Europe, where he spent most of the next ten years, still considered him a genius. Welles's next few films, with time out for occasional appearances in trashy epics like *Prince of Foxes* (1949), consisted of virtual remakes of *Citizen Kane* and adaptations of Shakespeare, pieced together helter-skelter over the years with borrowed actors and equipment.

Welles usually looked on his acting assignments as ways to finance his independent films.

For his part in *Man in the Shadow* (1957), he rewrote his material, with the approval of Universal executives. They then offered him one of the lead roles as a corrupt sheriff in an adaptation of *Badge of Evil*, a pulp novel by Whit Masterson. (The name was a pseudonym for Robert Wade and H. William Miller, who coauthored several crime novels.) With Welles on board, the studio approached Charlton Heston to play a narcotics cop threatened by the sheriff. Heston agreed only on the condition that Welles be allowed to direct. Universal production head Edward Muhl restricted Welles to an $825,000 budget and thirty-eight-day shooting schedule. (According to a later interview, Heston said that Welles came in at $900,000 and thirty-nine days.)

Given the opportunity to direct within the studio system once more, Welles decided to pull out all the stops. *Touch of Evil* would not just cast America's Moses as a Mexican cop, complete with swarthy makeup and a bad accent; it would throw the heretofore virginal Janet Leigh into extreme sexual peril in a story of rampant corruption on the Mexican border. With access once more to cranes, lighting, craftsmen, and the rest of the enormous resources of Universal Studios, Welles concocted an elaborately choreographed opening shot that spread out over several city blocks in Venice, California. For other scenes he employed the choppy, disjointed editing that had become a necessity in his European productions. Dark, jazzy, bitter, and swaggering, *Touch of Evil* put the final nail in the coffin of his mainstream ambitions.

Welles rewrote the script optioned by producer Albert Zugsmith, changing the ethnic identity of Heston's character, beefing up parts for Marlene Dietrich and Mercedes McCambridge, and adding Dennis Weaver into the plot after admiring the actor's work on TV's *Gunsmoke*. Also in the film were familiar Welles figures like Joseph Cotten and Akim Tamiroff.

Much of *Touch of Evil* was filmed at night, in part to avoid studio interference, but also because the story demanded it. The most famous shot in the film is the opening, which follows the progress of a bomb planted in a car near a border crossing. Welles had intended to score the shot with incidental music from car radios and nightclub jukeboxes, but as with many of his plans, the outcome was quite different.

Welles was preparing a rough cut when he left the country to scout locations for what he hoped would be his next production, an adaptation of *Don Quixote*. When Universal executives screened the cut, they took over the film, prohibiting Welles from further editing and from shooting necessary retakes. Despite objections from Heston and Leigh, veteran director Harry Keller was hired to handle the reshoots.

What Welles envisioned as a two-hour feature was cut to ninety-five minutes. Credits were placed over the opening shot, along with theme music by Henry Mancini. Welles wrote Muhl a fifty-eight-page memo outlining changes he thought would improve the Universal cut, but it was ignored. *Touch of Evil* was finally released as the second-half of a double feature, appearing with Harry Keller's *The Female Animal* (1958). It was a box-office failure in the United States, although it was received enthusiastically in Europe. Welles never had another chance to direct in Hollywood.

Some critics see *Touch of Evil*'s influence in the work of French New Wave directors, although the French probably viewed the film simply as a continuation of Welles's European titles. Writers have also suggested that Dennis Weaver's character had some bearing on the part played by Anthony Perkins in Alfred Hitchcock's *Psycho* (1960). It seems more likely that Hitchcock saw how he could use Janet Leigh. Welles merely threatened her with rape and drug addiction; Hitchcock would have her character handled much worse.

Heston kept a copy of Welles's memo to Muhl. It became the basis of a restoration undertaken in 1998 by producer Rick Schmidlin and editor Walter Murch. They removed the opening credits with Mancini's music and when possible removed Keller's scenes. Welles by that time had been dead for thirteen years, so it is impossible to determine what he would have wanted restored. In his later years he professed to be happy with *Touch of Evil*, Keller's scenes and all.

Seen in the context of *Journey into Fear* (1943) and *The Stranger* (1946), *Touch of Evil* is a snappy, fast-paced cop thriller with perverse overtones. But viewed alongside *Citizen Kane* (1941) or *The Third Man* (1949), the film shows just how much Welles had lowered his standards. *Variety* wrote, "*Touch of Evil* smacks of brilliance but ultimately flounders in it." While the film carried more heft than much of its competition at the time, it was clearly an attempt to cash in by someone with a dim grasp of the market. Aficionados relish its cameos and in-jokes, as well as the moments when Welles unleashed his still formidable filmmaking skills. But the title of *Touch of Evil* is too apt:

Welles was just toying with the genre. Like many of his films, he pulled away before it was finished, giving himself an excuse for its eventual failure.

Vertigo

Paramount, 1958. Sound, color, 1.85. 129 minutes.

Cast: James Stewart (Det. John "Scottie" Ferguson), Kim Novak (Madeleine Elster/Judy Barton), Barbara Bel Geddes (Midge Wood), Tom Helmore (Gavin Elster), Henry Jones (Official), Raymond Bailey (Doctor), Ellen Corby (Manageress), Konstantin Shayne (Pop Leibel), Lee Patrick (Woman mistaken for another).

Credits: Directed by Alfred Hitchcock. Screenplay by Alec Coppel & Samuel Taylor. Based upon the novel *D'Entre les Morts* by Pierre Boileau and Thomas Narcejac. Associate producer: Herbert Coleman. Director of photography: Robert Burks. Technicolor color consultant: Richard Mueller. Music by Bernard Herrmann. Conducted by Muir Mathieson. Costumes: Edith Head. Special sequence by John Ferren. Art direction: Hal Pereira & Henry Bumstead. Special photographic effects: John P. Fulton. Process photography: Farciot Edouart & Wallace Kelley. Set decoration: Sam Comer & Frank McKelvy. Titles designed by Saul Bass. Edited by George Tomasini. Assistant director: Daniel McCauley. Makeup supervision: Wally Westmore. Hair style supervision: Nellie Manley. Sound recording by Harold Lewis & Winston Leverett. Westrex Recording System.

Additional Cast: Alfred Hitchcock (Man by shipyard), Paul Bryar (Captain Hansen), Margaret Brayton (Saleswoman), William Remick (Jury foreman), Julian Petruzzi (Flower vendor); Sara Taft, Margaret Bacon, Catherine Howard (Nuns); Fred Graham (Policeman), Mollie Dodd (Beauty salon operator); Don Giovanni, John Benson (Salesmen); Roxann Delmar (Model), Bruno Santina (Waiter); Dori Simmons, Nina Shipman, Ezelle Poule (Women mistaken for another); Ed Stevlingson (Attorney), Joanne Genthon (Woman in portrait), Roland Gotti (Maitre d'), Victor Gotti (Customer at Ernie's), Carlo Dotto (Bartender), Jack Richardson (Male escort),; June Jocelyn (Miss Woods), Miliza Milo (Saleswoman), Buck Harrington (Gateman), Bert Scully (Art gallery attendant), Steve Conte (Burglar); Lyle Moraine, Kathy Reed (Patrons); David Ahdar (Priest), Bess Flowers (Diner at Ernie's).

Additional Credits: Second unit director: Herbert Coleman. Second unit camera: Irmin Roberts. Production manager: Frank Caffey. Titles animated by John H. Whitney. Production dates: September 30 to December 19, 1957. Premiered in San Francisco on May 9, 1958.

Available: Universal Home Video DVD (1998). ISBN: 0-7832-2605-5. UPC: 0-2519-20183-2-9.

Often described today as Alfred Hitchcock's most personal film, *Vertigo* was also one of his biggest disappointments. During his interview sessions with François Truffaut (published in English in 1967), the director seemed surprised to learn that the source novel, *D'Entre les Morts*, had been written specifically for him. ("What if I hadn't bought it?" he asked.) Pierre Boileau and Pierre Ayraud (also known as Thomas Narcejac) had previously written *Celle qui n'était plus*, filmed as *Les Diaboliques* in 1955. *D'Entre les Morts* ("From Among the Dead") focused on an acrophobic private eye who falls in love with the woman he is tailing. His vertigo prevents him from rescuing her when she apparently falls to her death from a tower. The private eye then tries to mold another woman into the image of his lost love.

Both Hitchcock and James Stewart, with whom he had recently worked on *Rear Window* (1954) and *The Man Who Knew Too Much* (1956), loved the novel. The director saw it as an opportunity for Vera Miles, and he later seemed to carry a grudge against the actress when she revealed that she was pregnant. "I believed the artistic success of *Vertigo* was dependent on Vera Miles," he said later. "The wardrobe tests with her were brilliant." At least that was his official version. Dan Auiler, author of *"Vertigo": The Making of a Hitchcock Classic*, believes that the director was interested in hiring Kim Novak before Miles's screen tests. On some levels Novak was a sensible choice. After all, she was named the number one female star of 1956 by *Box Office* magazine. Stewart had to agree to make two films at Columbia to secure Novak's services from Harry Cohn.

Hitchcock was also unhappy with a script turned in by playwright Maxwell Anderson called *Listen Darkling*. (Anderson had written Hitchcock's previous film, *The Wrong Man*, 1956). Another version, by Paramount contract writer Alec Coppel, proved equally unappealing, although Coppel later received screen credit. It wasn't until Samuel Taylor, the playwright behind *Sabrina Fair* (1954), tackled the project that Hitchcock and Stewart were satisfied.

While Taylor scouted locations in northern California, Hitchcock recovered from colitis and a hernia operation. When they could work together, they fashioned an unusually complex story line that gave away several key plot twists far earlier than other filmmakers would have. Taylor's version included a role he had written for Barbara Bel Geddes, who plays a designer with an unrequited love for Stewart's Scottie Ferguson. As Midge Wood, she offers a counterpoint to Novak's Madeleine, although as the characters evolve, reflections multiply, and the plot begins to circle back on itself, it becomes increasingly difficult to determine exactly who any of the actors is portraying.

According to biographer Patrick McGilligan, Novak annoyed the director, from her wardrobe demands to her insistent pleas for help. After Hitchcock refused to tell her how to do scenes, she remembers asking Stewart, "What do you think he wants me to do?" Hitchcock's indifference toward her may have been an attempt to keep her off guard, possibly enhancing the uncertainty her character faces. Taylor thought that an actress with better technique might not have been as convincing in the part.

Filming took place in tourist spots in and around San Francisco. For one shot, Hitchcock had cinematographer Robert Burks and second-unit cameraman Irmin Roberts use a combination of a forward zoom with a reverse dolly to achieve a disorienting effect of shifting perspectives. It has since become known as "the *Vertigo* shot," and has been used in films like *Jaws* (1975). Hitchcock gleefully told Truffaut that he saved over $80,000 for the effect by using a model; it still took $19,000 to pull off.

For a fee of $17,500, Bernard Herrmann wrote the score for *Vertigo* in one month and thirteen days. Hitchcock was determined to control the sound in his film as closely as the visuals. He took out the pop songs Taylor included in his script (as Scottie tails Madeleine, for example), and gave very specific directions to Herrmann for individual scenes and even shots. "As Madeleine approaches Scottie and becomes a big head, we should take all the sounds of the restaurant away," he wrote in his postproduction notes, leaving room for Herrmann to insert another rendition of "Madeleine's Theme." "We'll just have the camera and you," the director told Herrmann for the film's crucial ten-minute centerpiece. Herrmann wanted to conduct the score himself, but was prevented by a musicians'

strike. Hitchcock had to use the Scottish conductor Muir Mathieson and a pickup orchestra in London. When they quit in support of the American strike, recording resumed in Vienna. (Herrmann thought *Vertigo* should have been set in New Orleans with Charles Boyer instead of James Stewart.)

When it was finished, *Vertigo* didn't look or sound like any other Hitchcock film. (In fact, after an early preview, some Paramount executives demanded changes to the score as well as to the visuals.) There were no real set pieces, no displays of dazzling technique, no chases and villains to resolve the story. For once in his career, Hitchcock didn't mind confusing his audience. As he explained to Truffaut, "That's perfectly natural since we're telling the story from the viewpoint of a man who's in an emotional crisis." The director complained about minor flaws in logic in the plot, but readily admitted that his hero "wants to go to bed with a woman who's dead. He is indulging in a form of necrophilia."

Neither critics nor audiences responded with the enthusiasm Hitchcock expected. *Vertigo* was not a financial failure, but it wasn't a hit, either. Stewart brought an unprecedented emotional and sexual vulnerability to his performance. But he had also invested in the project, and never worked with Hitchcock again. When the rights reverted to the director in the 1970s, he pulled the film from circulation. Perhaps as a result, it gained an aura over the years. Most critics today consider it Hitchcock's masterpiece, although mainstream audiences have remained cool to the film. Hitchcock immediately retreated to the formulas that had worked for him earlier. His next Registry film is *North by Northwest* (1959).

Gigi

MGM, 1958. Sound, color, 1.85. 116 minutes.

Cast: Leslie Caron (Gigi), Maurice Chevalier (Honoré Lachaille), Louis Jourdan (Gaston Lachaille), Hermione Gingold (Mme. Alvarez), Eva Gabor (Liane d'Exelmans), Jacques Bergerac (Sandomir), Isabel Jeans (Aunt Alicia), John Abbott (Manuel).

Credits: Directed by Vincente Minnelli. Screenplay: Alan Jay Lerner, from the novel by Colette. Produced by Arthur Freed. Assistant directors: William McGarry, William Shanks. Director of photography: Joseph Ruttenberg. Art direction: William A. Horning, Preston Ames. Costumes, scenery, production design: Cecil Beaton. Set decoration: Henry Grace, Keogh Gleason. Film editor: Adrienne Fazan. Music: Frederick Loewe. Lyrics by Alan Jay Lerner. Musical direction: André Previn. Orchestrations: Conrad Salinger. Vocal supervision: Robert Tucker. Color consultant: Charles K. Hagedon. Print process: Metrocolor. Recording supervisor: Dr. Wesley C. Miller. Makeup: William

Tuttle, Charles Parker. Hair stylists: Guillaume, Sydney Guilaroff. In CinemaScope and Metrocolor.

Additional Cast: Edwin Jerome (Charles, the butler), Lydia Stevens (Simone), Maurice Marsac (Prince Berensky), Monique Van Vooren (Showgirl), Dorothy Neumann (Designer), Maruja Ploss (Mannequin), Richard Bean (Harlequin), Marilyn Sims (Redhead), Pat Sheehan (Blonde).

Additional Credits: Leslie Caron's vocals dubbed by Betty Wand. Scenes directed by Charles Walters. Additional cinematography: Ray June. Assistant editor: Margaret Booth. Production dates: August 5 to October 30, 1957; reshoots February 1958. Premiered in New York City on May 15, 1958. Rated G in 1975.

Awards: Oscars for Best Picture, Director, Writing—Screenplay based on Another Medium, Music—Scoring of a Musical Picture (Previn), Music—Original Song ("Gigi"), Cinematography—Color, Art Direction—Set Decoration, Costume Design, Film Editing.

Available: Warner Home Video DVD (1999). ISBN: 0-7907-4407-4. UPC: 0-12569-50602-2.

Defiantly old-fashioned, *Gigi* was a sort of last stand for the traditional musical as developed by Metro-Goldwyn-Mayer. It was also the last significant credit for producer Arthur Freed, who for almost twenty years oversaw some of MGM's most important titles.

The original story, written by Colette during the Nazi occupation of France, was serialized starting in 1944. Two years later it was translated into English for *Harper's Bazaar*. Colette wrote the script for a 1949 French film directed by Jacqueline Audry and starring Danièle Delorme. Three years later Audrey Hepburn starred on Broadway in an adaptation by Anita Loos; Colette translated this version back into French. The French play opened in Paris in February 1954, seven months before Colette's death.

Arthur Freed had a chance to obtain the film rights to *Gigi* in 1951, but it wasn't until Anita Loos tried turning her play into a musical that the producer seriously considered the project. The studio negotiated for two years with the Production Code office to obtain clearances for the story, which concerned training a schoolgirl to become a courtesan. Approval came after the studio insisted that the basic plot was "the triumph of an apparently naive little girl who simply wants no part of this shabby way of life."

Freed spent $200,000 paying off Loos and the Colette estate, then hired Alan Jay Lerner to write a new script. In France, Lerner approached Maurice Chevalier, who knew and liked Colette and the original film. A fan of *My Fair Lady*, a show Lerner wrote with Frederick Loewe, Chevalier signed on for $100,000. Lerner also signed Leslie Caron, who was starring in the title role in a London production.

Loewe at first was reluctant to compose for the film, but he joined Lerner and Minnelli in Paris in the spring of 1957. By May they had only a six-page synopsis, perhaps half the score, and no real sense of a shooting budget. Loewe made Honoré Lachaille (Chevalier's role) Gaston's uncle, and not his father, removing a potentially sticky incestuous subplot. Isabel Jeans, who gives the film's richest, plumiest performance as Aunt Alicia, was suggested to Freed separately by both George Cukor and Cecil Beaton. (Beaton, a photographer and designer, was hired as a sort of production designer, responsible for costumes and scenery and the general "look" of the film.)

The leads, now joined by Louis Jourdan as Gaston, recorded the score in a Paris studio, singing to André Previn's piano. (The orchestra parts were added months later in Hollywood.) Shooting started on August 5, 1957, at the Bois de Boulogne, sight of the opening and closing number, "Thank Heaven for Little Girls," and the Battle of the Flowers.

Bad weather forced changes in the schedule; a scene planned at the beach resort of Trouville was canceled. Four days at Maxim's restaurant passed in a chaotic blur of broken props and extras fainting from the heat. Benny Thau wired Freed from Culver City, insisting that the project, already a half million dollars over budget, return to the studio. There Minnelli and his crew shot the remaining interiors, including the newly written "The Night They Invented Champagne," and some exteriors. The beach at Venice, California, substituted for Trouville, for example.

After some reshoots, the production finished on October 30, 1957. Minnelli and his cameraman Jim Ruttenberg left immediately for Europe to shoot *The Reluctant Debutante*. Adrienne Fazan began editing, assisted by Margaret Booth, who according to Fazan "cut all the warmth out of it."

Lerner called the first preview of *Gigi* on January 20, 1958, "a total disaster." Thau and the other MGM executives reluctantly put up $300,000 for nine days of reshoots starting February 11. Accounts differ as to what actually changed. In Lerner's autobiography, he wrote that Charles Walters directed Chevalier's "I Remember It Well," but Chevalier was not scheduled for any of the reshoots. At Lerner's request, Walters did shoot a slower version of Jourdan's "Soliloquy." Fazan said that she replaced a new version of "The Parisians" with Minnelli's original.

Freed contracted with the Shuberts to open *Gigi* at the Royale Theatre on Broadway, determined to give the film the cachet of a stage musical. The gimmick worked: starting on May 15, 1958, it ran there for a year. Although the final budget topped $3 million, the film was an enormous hit, grossing over $13 million in two releases.

Gigi owes a great deal to *My Fair Lady*, even in its score. "The Night They Invented Champagne" is a can-can to *My Fair Lady's* flamenco "The Rain in Spain," while *Gigi's* "Say a Prayer for Me Tonight" was originally written for Eliza in *My Fair Lady*. Both stories involve training a woman to please a man, an angle that has tempered enthusiasm for *Gigi* in recent years. A feeling of déjà vu permeates the film. Hollywood craftsmen working for Freed had figured out everything years earlier: how to assemble scenes, how to stage numbers, etc. In a sense all Minnelli could do was repeat earlier films in color, on a wider frame, with more cranes, and with Louis Jordan instead of Fred Astaire. (The dancer had just finished a musical version of *Daddy Long Legs*, another account of training a naive young girl for marriage.)

As well, Minnelli had to skirt around the central theme of the plot: preparing Gigi for her deflowering. His directorial touches dismayed Cecil Beaton, who wrote, "As soon as we had a swan in the backlot—it looked like a backlot."

Even the ostensibly foolproof "I Remember It Well" is punctuated by a donkey gag. (Critic Dave Kehr has remarked on how closely Minnelli followed the 1949 film, "often scene by scene and frequently line by line.")

Yet despite the recherché roués and mistresses that populate *Gigi*, the film itself follows a well-worn Hollywood formula: a girl pretends to be something she's not; it's only when she acts "natural" that her romance succeeds. Gigi holds out until Gaston proposes, the basic narrative ploy of almost every romance ever filmed. And at the end, she is the same awful type Gaston has been complaining about for the entire movie, while Colette's plot has been neutered by marriage.

The 7th Voyage of Sinbad

Columbia, 1958. Sound, color, 1.85. 88 minutes.
Cast: Kerwin Mathews (Sinbad), Kathryn Grant (Princess Parisa), Richard Eyer ([Baronni] The Genie), Torin Thatcher (Sokurah), Alec Mango (Caliph), Danny Green (Karim), Harold Kasket (Sultan), Alfred Brown (Harufa), Nana de Herrera (Sadi), Nino Falanga (Sailor), Luis Guedes (Crew member), Virgilio Teixeira (Ali).
Credits: Directed by Nathan Juran. Written by Kenneth Kolb. Produced by Charles H. Schneer. Director of photography: Wilkie Cooper. Special visual effects created by Ray Harryhausen. Music composed by Bernard Herrmann. Production supervisor: Luis Roberts. Art director: Gil Parrendo. Film editors: Edwin Bryant, Jerome Thoms. Assistant directors: Eugenio Martin, Pedro de Juan. Technical assistant: George Lofgren. Recording supervisor: John Livadary. Stunt supervisor: Enzo Musumeci-Greco. Main titles by Bob Gill. Technicolor color consultant: Henri Jaffa. Titles: Bob Gill. In Technicolor and Dynamation. Westrex Recording System. A Morningside production.
Additional Credits: Production dates: August 12, 1957 to March 7, 1958. Premiered in New York City on December 23, 1958.
Other Versions: Harryhausen used the Sinbad character in *The Golden Voyage of Sinbad* (1974) and *Sinbad and the Eye of the Tiger* (1977).
Available: Columbia TriStar Home Video DVD (1999). ISBN: 0-7678-2780-5. UPC: 0-43396-01149-6.

Soon after George Pal left cartoons for feature films, Ray Harryhausen, once one of his animators, made the switch as well. Born in 1920 in Los Angeles, Harryhausen cited a screening of *King Kong* (1933) as a key influence on his career. The film's stop-motion animation "changed my life," Harryhausen said later. "You know it is not real, but it looks real. It's like a nightmare or something in a dream." With the help of his parents he began experimenting with the technique, building creatures with armatures from old clothes and clay. He became adept enough to be hired as an animator by Pal for his Puppetoons series at Paramount.

Harryhausen enlisted at the start of World War II, serving in the Information Services division of the Signal Corps under Frank Capra. He worked on instructional films like *How to Bridge a Gorge* (1942), and contributed special effects to Capra's *Why We Fight* series. When he left the army, he concentrated on building puppets for a series of short films based on Mother Goose characters, while also making some commercials and sponsored films. Then he was hired by Willis O'Brien to work on *Mighty Joe Young* (1949), a sort of updated version of *King Kong*. O'Brien, the same man whose work Harryhausen had admired in *Kong*, was by that point a mentor and friend to the younger animator.

Harryhausen completed four shorts, which he sold to school districts as *The Mother Goose Stories* (1946). By 1953 he had finished four more fairy tales, including versions of "Rapunzel" and "King Midas." In 1951, he was hired to animate *The Beast From 20,000 Fathoms* (released 1953), for which he devised a split screen technique that could sandwich effects into pre-existing footage. Harryhausen followed this with *It Came from Beneath the Sea* (1955), based on an idea by producer Charles Schneer about a giant octopus that pulls down the Golden Gate Bridge. But Harryhausen was already thinking about moving from monsters back into fairy tales and myths. In 1950, for example, he worked on a project called *The Lost City*, which would have been "based purely on Greek mythology." For it he drew sketches of a horseback rider fighting a giant Cyclops, a scene which would eventually emerge in a changed form in *The 7th Voyage of Sinbad*.

It Came from Beneath the Sea cemented a working relationship between Harryhausen and producer Charles Schneer that was to last for decades. "*The 7th Voyage of Sinbad* started with a dozen drawings Ray had done some years before I met him," Schneer told an interviewer. The producer sold the idea to Columbia for a budget of about $650,000, provided that the film was made in color. Assigned as director was Nathan Juran, a low-budget specialist who had worked with Schneer and Harryhausen on *20 Million Miles to Earth* (1957). Schneer based the production in Spain, partly because of lower filming costs, but also to take advantage of locations like the Alhambra Palace in Granada. He cast Kerwin Mathews, a Columbia contract player, in the title role.

Mathews remembers his first scene taking place in the palace, where he was supposed to be talking to a princess some four inches high. "I spent the rest of the film looking for little Kathy Crosby or great big monsters," he recalled later. Billed as Kathryn Grant, the actress had entered movies after competing in beauty pageants, and had extensive work both in films and on television. She married Bing Crosby in October of 1957, about six weeks after filming started.

The 7th Voyage of Sinbad is only very loosely connected with the exploits of the Arabian Nights character, or with the Registry title *Popeye the Sailor Meets Sindbad the Sailor* (1936), for that matter. Instead, the film deals with monsters and situations similar to those that appear throughout Harryhausen's career. A swordfight with a skeleton shows up in an expanded form in *Jason and the Argonauts* (1963), and a two-headed roc resembles the oversized Phororhacos in *Mysterious Island* (1961).

Harryhausen's tastes were formed from the work of Willis O'Brien, and by extension Merian C. Cooper, and by such artists as Gustave Doré. Like O'Brien, Harryhausen learned early in his work how important it was to develop personalities for his characters—how the Cyclops pulls over a bench to sit and watch his dinner cooking, for example. One crucial difference with Harryhausen is that he pitched his stories at younger viewers, determined to entertain them instead of their parents. As a result, acting can sometimes suffer in his films, and plot lines can be disappointingly superficial.

Like Hitchcock, Harryhausen could imagine a fascinating situation, but not a plausible narrative that would lead to it. Writing about *The 7th Voyage of Sinbad*, he admitted, "The turning point was a key or concept of Sinbad fighting a skeleton on the top of a ruined spiral staircase. Initially, the choice of Sinbad was almost incidental: it was the skeleton that I wanted to animate." Mathews attributes part of the success of the sequence to fencing instructor Enzo Musumeci-Greco. "We were choreographing things exactly as you would choreograph a dance sequence, in counts of eight," he said in an interview. "With Bernard Herrmann's music, it's almost a dance sequence."

Still, the film's special effects retain their power to surprise and delight to this day. Harryhausen's obsessive attention to detail and his uncanny ability to impart personality to fur and clay made a tremendous impression on young filmgoers. Peter Jackson, who directed his own version of *King Kong* (2005), is an enthusiastic fan, and it's not hard to spot Harryhausen's ideas running through the adventure films of George Lucas and Steven Spielberg. Harryhausen and Schneer both considered the similarly themed *Jason and the Argonauts* their best work together.

A Movie

Canyon Cinema, 1958. Sound, B&W, 1.37. 12 minutes.
Credits: Filmmaker: Bruce Conner.
Available: Canyon Cinema (*www.canyoncinema.com*).

The first of over a dozen experimental shorts directed by Bruce Conner, *A Movie* is a collection of found footage held together by a repurposed musical score and by Conner's joke-filled editing. Similar to but more lighthearted than the reverential *Rose Hobart* (1936), *A Movie* is an avant-garde film that mainstream viewers have no trouble appreciating.

Conner was born in Kansas in 1933 and studied art at the Kansas City Art Institute, the University of Nebraska, the Brooklyn Museum Art School, and the University of Colorado. He moved with his wife Jean to San Francisco in 1957, where he became part of an arts community that included Joan Brown, Jay DeFeo, and Lawrence Ferlinghetti. Conner worked in a variety of media, including painting, drawing, watercolor, printmaking, photography, film, wood engraving, and collage. He first drew attention with a series of assemblages: sculptures of found objects—stockings, costume jewelry, broken dolls—shrouded with nylon. He also began splicing footage together from 16mm films he found or bought from thrift shops. His sources included newsreels, documentaries, educational films, features, interstitial footage, and stag films.

Twelve minutes long, *A Movie* begins with Conner's name in white over a black background, shown full-frame for a considerable length of time. Countdown leaders, a title for "End of part four," and a title of "The End" appear before a credits sequence consisting of separate frames announcing "A" "Movie" "by" "Bruce Conner." (It will be repeated four more times during the course of the film, just as "The End" returns unexpectedly.)

The first "real" footage is from a stag film, showing a seated, topless blonde removing her stockings. Conner then cuts to a montage of scenes lifted from Westerns, primarily chases involving Indians and Conestoga wagons. One shot features a wagon driving directly over a camera planted on the ground; Conner uses it for a match cut to a tank hurtling over an embankment, a thrilling shift in time.

A segment features newsreel footage of race cars spinning around dirt tracks, some then involved in crashes. Longer and longer stretches of black leader reduce the frame to nothingness. Gradually the footage shifts to the air: a biplane soaring over clouds, a pair of acrobats on a tightrope over a city street, the *Hindenburg* about to moor.

In the film's baldest joke, a submarine commander looks through a periscope to "see" a bikini-ed Marilyn Monroe lolling on a bed. Torpedoes are fired from the nose of the sub. A mushroom cloud, perhaps from the Bikini Atoll, rises into the sky. Before the film ends, Conner will introduce images that include, among others, the Pope, the exploding *Hindenburg*, piles of war dead, a "resurrected" *Hindenburg* (achieved by running the footage in reverse), the Tacoma Narrows Bridge collapsing, natives dismembering a dead elephant, and Teddy Roosevelt pretending to deliver a speech. The film ends with footage appropriated from a Jacques Cousteau documentary of a scuba diver disappearing into the open hatch of an underwater wreck.

Viewers of *A Movie* inevitably try to construct a story from the footage. All the individual shots "mean" something initially, and are all easy to decipher. Conditioned by years of exposure to narrative films, we are trained to extrapolate additional meanings when one shot is spliced to another. Conner toys with these expectations, but the essential question remains: Can *A Movie* be reduced to a plot, a theme, a message?

Critic P. Adams Sitney detects "intellectual rhythms" in the work "which move between the terrible and the ridiculous, part of a general interior drift." He and other writers have found images of hope alternating with images of destruction. Author Amei Wallach called the atom bomb the "protagonist" of *A Movie*, and wrote that Conner's prime motivation was to "undermine": "Conner wants the eye to be in constant movement and so misled by the next thing it sees that, when it returns to the first, it sees something altogether different." On the other hand, Conner may just be filling in footage to match his soundtrack music (a version of "The Pines of Rome" by Respighi), searching for images that will satisfy the score's increasingly dramatic demands. Did Conner improve what he borrowed? Could he construct a scene as well as the filmmakers he quoted, or was he just making jokes at their expense?

Conner followed *A Movie* with *Cosmic Ray* (1961), another assemblage film that cut a nude dancer and a cannon to images of Mickey Mouse while Ray Charles sings "What'd I Say" on the soundtrack. Later he collaborated with early MTV stars like Devo and David Byrne. He resisted being pinned down to any one genre or style. "I've already been typecast as a filmmaker and sculptor," he told a *New York Times* interviewer. "What I want to do is change." He taught filmmaking, life drawing, painting, and sculpture, and participated in scores of individual and group exhibitions. In 1998 he declared himself an "Anonymous Artist."

A show at the Walker Art Center, *2000 BC: The Bruce Conner Story, Part II,* was labeled by Conner "Not A Retrospective." It filled galleries with his assemblages, mandala drawings from the 1960s, inkblot drawings from the 1990s, collages made from turn-of-the-nineteenth-century engravings, and "photograms," but included only one of his more than three hundred paintings.

Conner had conflicts with museums and galleries trying to show his work, and seemed ambivalent about his films, prohibiting the distribution of many of them on video. (He may also have been unable to pursue or obtain copyright clearances for the work he appropriated.) While it's relatively easy to find in libraries and museums, *A Movie* is often offered for sale in used copies at $1,000 a print. Connor died in 2008.

Some Like It Hot

United Artists, 1959. Sound, B&W, 1.85. 120 minutes.

Cast: Marilyn Monroe (Sugar Kane Kowalczyk), Tony Curtis (Joe/Josephine/Junior), Jack Lemmon (Jerry/Daphne), George Raft (Spats Colombo), Pat O'Brien (Detective Mulligan), Joe E. Brown (Osgood Fielding III), Nehemiah Persoff (Little Bonaparte), Joan Shawlee (Sweet Sue), Billy Gray (Sig Poliakoff), George E. Stone (Toothpick Charlie), Dave Barry (Bienstock); Mike Mazurki, Harry Wilson (Henchmen); Beverly Wills (Dolores), Barbara Drew (Nellie), Edward G. Robinson, Jr. (Johnny Paradise).

Credits: Produced and directed by Billy Wilder. Screenplay by Billy Wilder and I.A.L. Diamond. Suggested by a story by R. Thoeren and M. Logan. Director of photography: Charles Lang, Jr. Associate producers: Doane Harrison, I.A.L. Diamond. Miss Monroe's gowns by Orry-Kelly. Background score: Adolph Deutsch. Songs supervised by Matty Malneck. Art director: Ted Haworth. Set decorator: Edward G. Boyle. Property: Tom Plews. Special effects: Milt Rice. Film editor: Arthur P. Schmidt. Script continuity: John Franco. Makeup artist: Emile LaVigne. Hair styles: Alice Monte, Agnes Flanagan. Production manager: Allen K. Wood. Assistant director: Sam Nelson. Wardrobe: Bert Henrikson. Music editor: Eve Newman. Sound: Fred Lau. Westrex Recording System.

Additional Cast: Joan Fields (Band member), Paul Frees (Funeral director), Tom Kennedy (Bouncer), Jack McClure (Henchman).

Additional Credits: Based on *Fanfaren der Liebe* (1951), directed by Kurt Hoffman; written by Heinz Pauck; based on a story by Robert Thoeren and Michael Logan. Curtis's voice as "Josephine" was dubbed in part by Paul Frees. Production dates: August 4 to November 6, 1958. Released March 29, 1959.

Awards: Oscar for Best Costume Design—Black and White.

Other Versions: Adapted into the stage musical *Sugar!* (later retitled *Some Like It Hot*).

Available: MGM Home Entertainment DVD (2001). UPC: 0-27616 86038-5. MGM/Sony Pictures Collector's Edition DVD (2006). UPC: 0-27616-15120-9.

After working for most of his Hollywood career at Paramount, Billy Wilder spent the last half of the 1950s trying to secure a position as a director even as the studio system was crumbling around him. In a span of five years, he made films at five different studios, including a significant financial flop at Warners (*The Spirit of St. Louis*, 1957) and a movie that didn't make enough money at Allied Artists (*Love in the Afternoon*, 1957). With the decade winding down, Wilder was in a summing up stage. He also needed a commercial hit. It came in the unlikely form of a German musical comedy from 1951, *Fanfaren der Liebe*.

In later years Wilder would deride *Fanfaren der Liebe* as dreck, a "heavy-handed Bavarian *Charley's Aunt*, replete with dirndls and lederhosen." The film is actually a smooth, satisfying comedy about two unemployed musicians who go to any lengths to find work, including disguising themselves as gypsies and blacks. Dressing in drag to join an all-women orchestra, they travel by train to a resort hotel for an extended engagement. Both fall for the band's singer while fending off advances from clueless but determined men.

Wilder grabbed the drag idea, but realized that it needed an extra angle to sustain a feature film. His current writing partner, I.A.L. Diamond, made a crucial point: drag comedies work better as period pieces; that way, costumes for both men and women are uniformly peculiar. That gave Wilder the idea to tie the plot to the St. Valentine's Day Massacre in 1929 Chicago. The gangster connection would provide a strong impetus for his musicians, now a saxophonist named Joe and a bassist named Jerry, to get into drag and stay there.

Wilder and Diamond retained much of the plot of *Fanfaren der Liebe*, but their additions and alterations—in particular their snappy, vivid dialogue—are telling. The train rides in both films rely on quick costume changes for jokes, but with Pullman berths instead of separate compartments, Wilder and Diamond could indulge in much more intimate situations. A hotel manager in the German film became millionaire and yacht owner Osgood Fielding III, a part that drew vaudeville clown Joe E. Brown out of retirement. Gaby, the German heroine, was a cool, sophisticated brunette who quickly figured out the truth behind the cross-dressing. Wilder originally envisioned Mitzi Gaynor as the heroine for *Some Like It Hot*. But when Marilyn Monroe, the star of Wilder's Fox hit *The Seven Year Itch* (1955), expressed interest, the writers quickly beefed up the part of Sugar Kane Kowalczyk, a blonde singer whose bad luck with men gave her a drinking problem.

Wilder had considerable trouble directing Monroe four years earlier. Now, in the midst of a tempestuous marriage to playwright Arthur Miller, she was even harder to handle. Like the fish that got away, Wilder's accounts of Monroe's working habits became more and more exaggerated over the years. A scene in which Monroe was to say, "It's me, Sugar" required forty-seven takes in one account. By the time biographer Kevin Lally interviewed Wilder in 1994, it was up to eighty-three takes. (After the film was released, Wilder got into a feud with Miller, who accused the director of indirectly causing his wife's second miscarriage.)

The rest of the casting was much easier. Wilder always said that Jack Lemmon was his first choice for the bassist Jerry; Lemmon had to extend his contract at Columbia to take the part.

Lemmon and Tony Curtis each received $100,000 to Monroe's $300,000. Wilder filled the other roles with familiar faces from the past: George Raft (who earlier had turned down the lead in *Double Indemnity*), Pat O'Brien, and tough-guy character actors like Mike Mazurki and Tom Kennedy.

Although Monroe was contractually obligated to appear only in Technicolor, the color tests for *Some Like It Hot* were so garish (in particular the drag makeup) that everyone agreed black-and-white was necessary. In later interviews, Jack Lemmon spoke in glowing terms about Wilder, although at the time he was unsure about some of the director's choices. "The only way to play it was to let it all hang out and just go, trusting that Wilder would say 'Cut' if it got out of bounds," he told Don Widener. Over the years Curtis has changed his account of the British accent he used while impersonating "Junior," a Shell Oil millionaire. At first he said it was just British, then admitted that he based it on Cary Grant.

What the actors didn't know was that Wilder and Diamond were still working on the script after filming started in August 1958. Diamond's widow Barbara told Lally that the writers "hadn't the faintest idea how they were going to end it" until two days before the finale was shot. Filming wrapped on November 6, several weeks late and a half-million over budget.

Lemmon said that the preview for *Some Like It Hot* was the worst of his career, but that Wilder's only change was to eliminate a scene on the train between Joe and Jerry. Reviews were generally positive, and the film went on to make some $15 million, enough for United Artists to propose a television series spin-off to NBC. The film's reputation has continued to grow over the years, in part for its broadly tolerant view of sexuality, and in part because it was Monroe's last successful role.

For Wilder, it was a chance to examine and evaluate his film career, and the industry in general. Like Alfred Hitchcock's *North by Northwest*, *Some Like It Hot* looked back to the past, reworking old bits with modern technology and gently mocking faded styles and customs. Both films give the current viewer a way of seeing the 1950s, with Hitchcock finding something sinister in streamlined technology and wide open spaces, Wilder seeing the contradictions between lust and repression in popular culture. He seemed to be reverting to his past as a gigolo and taxi dancer, giving moviegoers of 1959 a whiff of decadence, a glimpse of perversion, the thrill of smut, before calling everything a joke and sending moviegoers home to their spouses. Today it's easier to see how cruel Curtis's seduction of Monroe is, how lost the actress was, how hard it was for her to make eye contact.

Interestingly, both Hitchcock and Wilder immediately made radical changes in their filmmaking styles, turning to darker, meaner, and cheaper projects, Hitchcock with *Psycho* and Wilder with *The Apartment*.

North by Northwest

MGM, 1959. Sound, color, 1.75. 136 minutes.

Cast: Cary Grant (Roger O. Thornhill), Eva Marie Saint (Eve Kendall), James Mason (Phillip Vandamm), Jessie Royce Landis (Clara Thornhill), Leo G. Carroll (Professor), Josephine Hutchinson ("Mrs. Townsend"), Philip Ober (Lester Townsend), Martin Landau (Leonard), Adam Williams (Valerian), Robert Ellenstein (Licht), Philip Coolidge (Dr. Cross), Edward Binns (Captain Junket), Edward Platt (Victor Larrabee), Les Tremayne (Auctioneer); Patrick McVey, Ken Lynch (Chicago policemen).

Credits: Directed by Alfred Hitchcock. Written by Ernest Lehman. Associate producer: Herbert Coleman. Music by Bernard Herrmann. Director of photography: Robert Burks. Production designed by Robert Boyle. Art directors: William A. Horning & Merrill Pye. Set decorations: Henry Grace & Frank McKelvey. Special effects: A. Arnold Gillespie & Lee LeBlanc. Titles designed by Saul Bass. Film editor: George Tomasini. Color consultant: Charles K. Hagedon. Recording supervisor: Franklin Milton. Hair styles by Sydney Guilaroff. Make-up by William Tuttle. Assistant director: Robert Saunders. Westrex Recording System. In VistaVision and Technicolor. A Metro-Goldwyn-Mayer presentation.

Additional Cast: Alfred Hitchcock, John Beradino (Sgt. Emile Klinger), Nora Marlowe (Housekeeper), Doreen Lang (Maggie), Alexander Lockwood (Judge Anson B. Flynn), Harvey Stephens (Stockbroker), Walter Coy (Reporter), Madge Kennedy (Mrs. Finlay), Frank Wilcox (Weltner), Robert Shayne (Larry Wade), Carleton Young (Fanning Nelson), Olan Soule (Assistant auctioneer), Wilson Wood (Photographer), Patricia Cutts (Hospital patient).

Additional Credits: Produced by Alfred Hitchcock. Production dates: August 26, 1958 to December 19, 1958. Premiered in Chicago on July 9, 1959.

Available: Warner Home Video DVD (2004). ISBN: 0-7907-9993-6. UPC: 0-12569-67099-0.

After the poor box-office performance of Vertigo (1958), perhaps Alfred Hitchcock's most deeply felt film, the director retreated to a plot line that had worked for him in the past: a picaresque journey involving a wronged man who is trying to clear his name. Hitchcock had worked variations on this theme throughout his career, from *The Thirty-Nine Steps* (1935) through *Saboteur* (1942) to his recent remake of *The Man Who Knew Too Much* (1956), starring James Stewart. Signing a one-picture deal

Asked, "What does the 'O' stand for?" in his monogram, Roger Thornhill replies, "Nothing." From the first train sequence in *North by Northwest*.

with MGM, the director set out to make the ultimate escapist entertainment.

Hitchcock considered filming the novel *The Wreck of the Mary Deare* by Hammond Innes, and even commissioned screenwriter Ernest Lehman to work on a draft. (It was eventually filmed in 1959, starring Gary Cooper, and with a script by Eric Ambler.) But as early as 1955, Hitchcock was working on what would become *North by Northwest*, first with screenwriter John Michael Hayes (*Rear Window*, 1954), then with *New York Tribune* editor Otis Guernsey, who wrote a treatment that was later discarded.

The director's original plan had been to take the characters from the United Nations in New York City to Alaska, stopping at representative landmarks along the way. Hitchcock had already thought up a sequence at Mount Rushmore. As Hayes explained in a 1984 interview, "What Hitch really wanted to do was develop a story on which he could hang the Mount Rushmore scene and a few other unrelated ideas." Hayes and other writers often complained about Hitchcock's method of working backward from visual moments, trying to find a plot that could tie them together. The director once told Peter Bogdanovich, "As far as I am concerned, you see, the content is secondary to the handling; the effect I can produce on an audience rather than the subject matter."

Hitchcock also told Bogdanovich that he cast Cary Grant in the lead role because the actor "enables the audience to identify with the main character . . . Cary Grant represents a man we know. He's not a stranger." Grant's initial salary was supposed to be $450,000, but with bonuses and delay clauses, it came closer to $750,000. The actor wanted Sophia Loren, his costar in two previous films, to play opposite him, while MGM suggested contract player Cyd Charisse. Hitchcock chose instead Eva Marie Saint, another in a long line of icy, independent blondes in his films. The director offered the role of Phillip Vandamm, the chief villain, to James Mason, because he wanted someone "smooth and distinguished." As he told director François Truffaut, "The difficulty was how we could make him seem threatening at the same time. So what we did was to split this evil character into three people: James Mason, who is attractive and suave; his sinister-looking secretary ["Leonard," played by Martin Landau]; and the third spy, who is crude and brutal." (Hitchcock was referring to "Valerian," played by Adam Williams, although Robert Ellenstein's "Licht" fits as well.)

By this time Ernest Lehman has proceeded through drafts of what he originally called *In a Northwesterly Direction*. The title *North by Northwest* (believed by some to be a reference to *Hamlet*: "I am but mad north-north-west") was suggested by MGM story editor Kenneth MacKenna.

The plot involves the kidnapping of advertising executive Roger O. Thornhill. He then goes on the run when he is accused of murdering a diplomat. Like Humbert Humbert in *Lolita* (a part Grant turned down), Thornhill is exposed to an America he had never seen, one of crop-dusters, national monuments, pine forests, high-end auctions, and urbane killers. In the process, he sheds his narcissism and matures into someone capable of love.

Thornhill also learns that the government has invented a false identity to fool foreign agents, and reluctantly participates in a scheme to trap an international something-or-other. This is as much of an explanation as Hitchcock is willing to give viewers, and in a telling touch he has the roar of airplane engines drown out Leo G. Carroll when his character gets down to specific details. *North by Northwest* is really about a handful of encounters, some apparently dead-end plot twists, and Hitchcock's mastery of the full arsenal of studio resources and trickery. He not only had the number-one box-office star of 1958, an Oscar-winning actress, and the screenwriter of *Sweet Smell of Success* (1957), he had Saul Bass to create the opening credits and Bernard Herrmann to write the score (his fifth for Hitchcock).

Years later, Saint still seemed a bit bewildered by the director's technique. "We didn't have any rehearsal," she said. Hitchcock introduced them with, "This is Cary Grant, you're going to fall in love with him, this is Eva Marie, you're going to fall in love with her." "And you start," the actress added. Actors were just a piece of the filmmaking puzzle.

Hitchcock was justifiably proud of the crop-dusting sequence, a seven-minute chase without dialogue or music, and of models constructed for the United Nations (which refused permission to film in its interiors). He was equally pleased with the naughty double entendres he slipped in, but he regretted omitting a sequence on a Detroit car assembly line. (Steven Spielberg later used a similar idea in *Minority Report*, 2002).

North by Northwest was a resounding hit, and moviegoers were delighted by a film so smart and eager to please. It was the last movie Grant and Hitchcock made together. Perhaps emboldened by his success, Hitchcock took an abrupt shift in tone and content for his next film, *Psycho* (1960), also on the Registry.

Pull My Daisy

G-String Productions, 1959. Sound, B&W, 1.37. 27 minutes.

Cast: Mooney Peebles (Bishop), Alan [Allen] Ginsberg (Alan), Gregory Corso (Gregory), Peter Orlofsky [Orlovsky] (Peter), Larry Rivers (Milo), Beltiane (Milo's wife), David Amram (Mez McGillicuddy), Alice Neal (Bishop's mother), Sally Gross (Bishop's sister), Denise Parker (Girl in bed), Pablo Frank (Little boy).

Credits: Adapted, photographed, and directed by Robert Frank, Alfred Leslie. Written and narrated by Jack Kerouac. Edited by Leon Prochnik, Robert Frank, Alfred Leslie. Music composed and conducted by David Amram. "The Crazy Daisy," lyrics by Alan [Allen] Ginsberg, Jack Kerouac. Performed by Anita Ellis. A G-String Enterprise.

Additional Cast: Richard Bellamy was "Mooney Peebles," the Bishop; Delphine Seyrig was "Beltiane," Milo's wife.

Additional Credits: Based in part on *The Beat Generation* by Jack Kerouac. Sometimes released under the title *The Beat Generation*. Premiered in New York City on November 11, 1959.

Available: The Library of Congress. Steidl, Gerhard Druckerei und Verlag DVD *Robert Frank: The Complete Film Works* (2008). ISBN: 3865213650.

The defining film of the late 1950s counterculture, *Pull My Daisy* collected the leading "Beat" figures in a Bowery loft to play out the final act of an unproduced Jack Kerouac play called *The Beat Generation*. *Pull My Daisy* is unmatched as a document of an era which at the time was rapidly disappearing. As a film, it is an oddity, a curio defended by a shrinking number of beatnik fans. Shot in 1959, it received its theatrical premiere in New York City on a double bill with John Cassavetes' *Shadows*. It has subsequently surfaced in museum retrospectives, on occasional television broadcasts, and in infrequent theatrical showings.

According to biographer Gerald Nicosia, Kerouac wrote the play in one night after returning to New York City in 1957 from a trip to Florida. It focused on a drug- and alcohol-filled day in the life of Jack Duluoz, an alter ego for the author. He hoped to have it staged off-Broadway by producer Leo Gavin, but despite the efforts of his agent Sterling Lord, *The Beat Generation* was never published or performed in his lifetime. (The play was rediscovered in a warehouse in 2004 and subsequently published by Thunders Mouth Press.)

Robert Frank had been working in photography since he was a teenager, at first in his native Switzerland, then, after 1947, in New York City. Tired of commercial work, he traveled through South America and Europe. In 1955, he received a grant from the John Simon Guggenheim Memorial Foundation for a project that eventually became *The Americans*, one of the most influential books of photographs in the last century. It consisted of 83 images Frank edited down from the close to 28,000 pictures he took during a car journey through half the states in the union. The book was published in France in 1958 and the following year, with an introduction by Kerouac, in the United States.

Frank was unprepared for the furor *The Americans* raised, although the book has subsequently been accepted as a classic. "I think I always had a cold eye," Frank said in an interview. "I always saw things realistically. But, it's also easier to show the darkness than the joy of life." He had already decided to give up still photography when he began collaborating with his neighbor, painter Alfred Leslie, on the film project proposed by Kerouac. Part of the second wave of abstract expressionism in the 1950s, Leslie was in the process of abandoning abstraction for representational painting.

Kerouac based his play on his friend Neal Cassady, in particular on a day Cassady's wife Carolyn invited a bishop over for dinner, a meal disrupted by the arrival of several friends. Painter Larry Rivers became "Milo," a stand-in for Cassady. Milo was supposed to be a railroad brakeman and reformed drug user, although Rivers wears the uniform of a passenger conductor. A former saxophonist with jazz bands, Rivers was a leading figure in New York art circles in the 1950s, collaborating with poet Frank O'Hara on a stage production, and, as the decade turned, briefly embracing Pop Art.

His wife was played by Delphine Seyrig, a Lebanese-born French actress making her film debut. She had been studying at the Actors Studio and had appeared on television; after *Pull My Daisy*, she returned to France, where she became one of the iconic figures of European cinema during the 1960s. Seyrig subsequently worked with Alain Resnais, François Truffaut, Luis Buñuel, Chantal Akerman, and Marguerite Duras.

Appearing as the disruptive friends were poets Gregory Corso, Allen Ginsberg, and Peter Orlovsky. Ginsberg and Orlovsky had accompanied Kerouac on the night of the bishop's fateful visit, and in theory would add a level of realism to the proceedings. Kerouac also wanted to perform, but Frank barred him from the set after he arrived drunk one day. Corso was cast in his place.

For plot, *Pull My Daisy* offers the misogynistic, anti-social antics of four dropouts who pride themselves on mocking propriety. Their targets include long-suffering wives and ministers, precisely the people who least needed criticizing. In his dispassionate direction, Frank may be mocking "free spirits" who drink, take drugs, pretend to play music, and repair to the nearest bar at the first sign of trouble. Or he may be endorsing it. The philosophy Kerouac, Ginsberg, and the others were promoting had already entered into the mainstream. In fact, their attitudes had been ridiculed in cartoons, and twisted into melodramas about juvenile delinquency, B-movie fodder for drive-ins. Kerouac wanted to release the film under his original title *The Beat Generation*, but that name had been taken by MGM for a low-budget exploitation vehicle for Mamie Van Doren.

Critics at the time acclaimed *Pull My Daisy* for its loose, improvisational feel, but as Leslie revealed years later, the film was scripted, rehearsed, and shot on a constructed set. So when characters are positioned at the edges of frames, when the focus is soft, when lights flare into the lens, that was what Frank intended. Critic Ray Carney noted that Kerouac's "ad-libbed" narration was also prepared in advance. (He performed it four times, and the final version was mixed from three takes.) When Kerouac intones, "Peanut butter cockroaches, cockroach, cockroach cockroach of the eyes," he was reciting a text, not responding to the visuals on the screen.

Kerouac died in 1969, by most accounts a bitter, disillusioned, and isolated alcoholic. Frank continued to make films, including *The Sin of Jesus* (1961; it was described by Jonas Mekas as "one of those few movies which test the audience."), *Me and My Brother* (1969, starring Peter Orlovsky, his brother Julius, and Allen Ginsberg), and a notorious documentary of a 1972 Rolling Stones tour that was the subject of a protracted legal battle. Frank eventually returned to still photography. A revised edition of *The Americans* was published in 1986. He has also directed music videos for artists such as Patti Smith and New Order.

Shadows

Lion International, 1959. Sound, B&W, 1.37. 81 minutes.

Cast: Ben Carruthers, Lelia Goldoni, Hugh Hurd, Anthony Ray, Dennis Sallas, Tom Allen, David Pokitillow, Rupert Crosse, Davey Jones, Pir Marini, Victoria Vargas, Jack Ackerman, Jacqueline Walcott, Cliff Carnell, Jay Crecco, Ronald Maccone, Bob Reeh, Joyce Miles, Nancy Deale, Gigi Brooks, Lynn Hamelton, Marilyn Clark, Joanne Sages, Jed McGarvey, Greta Thyssen.

Credits: Directed by John Cassavetes. Produced by Maurice McEndree. Cameraman: Erich Kollmar. Supervising film editor: Len Appelson. Editor: Maurice McEndree. Lighting: David Simon. Assistant to lighting: Cliff Carnell. Assistant to camera: Al Ruban. Sets by Randy Liles, Bob Reeh. Assistant director: Al Giglio. Production manager: Wray Bevins. Production staff: Maxine Arnolds, Anne Draper, Mary Anne Ehle, Ellen Paulos, Leslie Reed, Judy Kaufman. Saxophone solos: Shafi Hadi

[Curtis Porter]. Additional music: Charles Mingus. Song: "Beautiful" by Jack Ackerman, Hunt Stevens, Eleanor Winters. Sound: Jay Crecco. Recorded at Titra. Associate producer: Seymour Cassel. Presented by Jean Shepherd's *Night People*.

Additional Credits: Additional editing: Wray Bevins. Final version premiered in New York City on November 11, 1959.

Available: Criterion Collection/HVE/Castle Hill Productions DVD (2004). UPC: 0-37429-18772-2.

Technological advances helped liberate filmmakers in the late 1950s. 16mm cameras, faster film stocks, portable Nagra tape decks all gave directors the freedom to shoot in locations and situations that were previously too difficult. But equipment was still expensive, limiting opportunities to work independently. A bona fide star who alternated between Hollywood and experimental theater in New York, John Cassavetes found a different route to making a feature.

Born in 1929 to a Greek father, Cassavetes was a troubled, underachieving youth who turned to acting as a sort of last resort. He attended the American Academy of Dramatic Arts in New York City, met Virginia Rowlands at the end of 1953, and married her some four months later. Cassavetes found work in live television dramas, where he gained recognition as a serious, intense actor. He appeared in some eighty roles in two years, becoming successful enough to sign a contract with MGM, where his wife Gena also worked.

Cassavetes had a deep suspicion of the studio system, as well as a disdain for most Hollywood product. He wanted actors to live, not act; thought life itself was artificial; sought a way to break the "masks" that people assumed; and expressed contempt for Method acting. With his friend Burt Lane (father of actress Diane Lane), Cassavetes founded an acting workshop at a rehearsal space on West 46th Street in Manhattan. The students included Lelia Goldoni, Ben Carruthers, Hugh Hurd, and Tony Ray—the core group in *Shadows*.

While fooling around one afternoon, Cassavetes came up with the premise for an improvisation. He told Goldoni, Carruthers, and Hurd that they were children of black parents. Ray, chosen as Goldoni's boyfriend, finds out for the first time about her mixed race. It was an exciting idea because there was no "right" way to play the scene, no one answer or solution to the situation. The results were so powerful that Cassavetes decided to turn the exercise into a film.

Cassavetes later admitted to being inspired by Morris Engel's *Little Fugitive* (1953), by *On the Bowery* (1957), and by independent filmmaker Shirley Clarke, whose equipment he borrowed. In a way, live television drama, with its insistence on tight close-ups and with cameras that could pan and roll swiftly through sets, was another inspiration. In putting together a film, Cassavetes was also counting on his reputation as a New York City hipster with ties to the jazz community. You couldn't get much hipper than Charles Mingus, who contributed to the soundtrack.

Guessing that he could shoot the film for $5,000 (the final budget was closer to $40,000), Cassavetes appealed to everyone he knew for donations. Among those who contributed were director William Wyler, playwright Reginald Rose, and gossip columnist Hedda Hopper. Cassavetes, a frequent guest on *Night People*, a radio show hosted by Jean Shepherd, asked listeners there for money, promising a free screening of the finished movie in return.

The closing credit for *Shadows* proudly proclaims, "The film you have just seen was an improvisation." But according to film professor Ray Carney, the film was almost entirely scripted and planned by Cassavetes and Maurice McEndree. As Cassavetes said later, "I invented, or conceived, the characters of *Shadows* rather than a storyline. The idea of the story fitting the characters instead of the character fitting the story is perhaps the main different point about the film." Cassavetes grabbed what he could for the film's exterior shots, at times hiding the camera in the back seat of a taxi cab. But the extended scenes in apartments were the result of considerable rehearsal and reshaping. Some sets were built in the workshop space; Cassavetes also shot in the penthouse he shared with Gena Rowlands.

The director knew what he wanted, but not how to get it. Whether due to opaque directing or the limited skills of the performers, some scenes simply do not work. A fight between Hugh Hurd and Tony Russell, for example, is bristling with emotions that feel honest and hard-earned. But the script lets them down and leaves Cassavetes trapped, unable to resolve something that doesn't quite make sense, but also unable to move forward unless the conflict takes place.

The shoot was troubled. Lelia Goldoni, eighteen at the time, described the process as "a gigantic free-for-all." Cassavetes fought with Burt Lane, with cameraman Erich Kollmar, and with the actors. Filming ended in May 1957, followed by eighteen months of editing. Here Cassavetes discovered exactly what he didn't know about film-making. Most of the sound couldn't be used. Cassavetes forgot to have someone take notes during the shoot, so no two takes matched, either with each other or with the rest of the film. Charles Mingus was hired to score the film during back-to-back recording sessions amounting to three hours. He came up with fewer than three minutes of music.

Cassavetes scheduled three midnight screenings of *Shadows* at the Paris Theater in November 1958. Many in attendance left before the film's end, convincing the director more editing was needed. But since Cassavetes had burned all the outtakes, that meant reshooting the needed material. He borrowed $5,000 from future Andy Warhol collaborator Nikos Papatakis, who would appear in the new footage. Cassavetes replaced almost two-thirds of the film, infuriating many of the actors and crew members.

The new version of *Shadows* was blown up to 35mm and shown on November 11, 1959, with *Pull My Daisy*. Unable to find a domestic distributor, Cassavetes signed with British Lion, then insisted on an ill-conceived campaign to bring *Shadows* to a blue-collar audience. The new distribution deal cut most of the participants out of any share of profits, prompting a class action lawsuit against Cassavetes. David Pokitillow, "deceived and embarrassed" by the director, and Erich Kollmar were never paid anything while Cassavetes was alive.

Watching *Shadows* today, you can sense Cassavetes' talent, but you can also see that he is still trying to find his technique, fumbling at times with the realities of directing a feature, trying to stake out his own place in the same gritty New York streets occupied by *Sweet Smell of Success* (1957). *Shadows* is a sort of trial run for *Faces* (1968), his next independent film and a much more ambitious project. Cassavetes starred in it himself, perhaps realizing that it was time to exploit the marquee value of his name.

Cassavetes' abilities grew immensely over the next three decades. Ironically, his hipster credentials vanished almost at once. The world of be-bop, of jazz nightclubs and bongo parties, or picking up "chicks" in Times Square bars, of shiny suits and skinny ties and sunglasses worn at night, gave way to a generation more interested in sock hops and hot rods, in rumbles and rock 'n' roll. Cassavetes found his muse in Gena Rowlands, and shifted his focus—as he did in his own life—to exploring personal relationships rather than the world surrounding them.

For years the first version of *Shadows* was assumed lost after Cassavetes misplaced his last copy. Ray Carney subsequently found a copy, but alleges that he has been prevented from distributing or even screening it by the Cassavetes estate.

Ben-Hur

MGM, 1959. Sound, color, 2.20. 233 minutes.
Cast: Charlton Heston (Judah Ben-Hur), Jack Hawkins (Quintus Arrius), Haya Harareet (Esther), Stephen Boyd (Messala), Hugh Griffith (Sheik Ilderim), Martha Scott (Miriam), Cathy O'Donnell (Tirzah), Sam Jaffe (Simonides), Finlay Currie (Balthasar), Frank Thring (Pontius Pilate), Terence Longdon (Drusus), George Relph (Tiberius), André Morell (Sextus).
Credits: Directed by William Wyler. Produced by Sam Zimbalist. Screen play by Karl Tunberg. Based on the novel *Ben-Hur: A Tale of the Christ* by General Lew Wallace. Director of photography: Robert L. Surtees. Additional photography: Harold E. Wellman and Pietro Portalupi. Music by Miklos Rozsa. Art directors: William A. Horning and Edward Carfagno. Set decorations: Hugh Hunt. Special photographic effects: A. Arnold Gillespie, Lee LeBlanc, and Robert R. Hoag. Color consultant–settings: Charles H. Hagedon. Film editors: Ralph E. Winters, John D. Dunning. 2nd unit directors: Andrew Marton, Yakima Canutt. Assistant directors: Gus Agosti, Alberto Cardone. Make-up by Charles Parker. Unit production manager: Edward Woehler. Recording supervisor: Franklin Milton. Sound recordists: Sash Fisher, William Steinkamp. Costumes designed by Elizabeth Haffenden. Color consultant–costumes: Joan Bridge. Hair styles by Gabriella Borzelli. Photographed in MGM Camera 65. Photographic lenses by Panavision. Technicolor. Westrex Recording System.
Additional Cast includes: Marina Berti (Flavia), Adi Berber (Malluch), Laurence Payne (Joseph), Stella Vitelleschi (Amrah), Jose Greci (Mary), Claude Heater (Christ), Mino Doro (Gratus), Howard Lang (Hortator).

Additional Credits: Screenwriters: Christopher Fry, Gore Vidal, Maxwell Anderson, S.N. Behrman. Executive producers: Joseph R. Vogel, Sol C. Siegel. Produced by J.J. Cohn. (Producer Sam Zimbalist died of a heart attack November 4, 1958.) Film editor: Margaret Booth. Production dates: May 18, 1958 to January 30, 1959. Filmed at Cinecittá Studios. Premiered in New York City on November 18, 1959.
Awards: Oscars for Best Picture, Director, Actor, Supporting Actor (Hugh Griffith), Cinematography—Color, Film Editing, Music—Scoring of a Dramatic or Comedy Picture, Sound (Franklin Milton), Costume Design—Color (Elizabeth Haffenden), Art Direction–Set Decoration—Color, Effects—Special Effects (A. Arnold Gillespie, Robert MacDonald, Milo B. Lory).
Other Versions: Filmed in 1907 and 1925.
Available: Warner Home Video DVD (2005). ISBN: 1-4198-1079-0. UPC: 0-12569-87535-3.

By the end of the 1950s, the founding figures at MGM were all gone. Marcus Loew had died in 1927, and Irving Thalberg in 1936. Louis B. Mayer was forced out of his office in 1951, to be replaced by Dore Schary and then a succession of production heads, while Nicholas Schenck had to leave Loew's in 1956. Joseph Vogel became head of Loew's, MGM's parent company, in 1957. He soon announced to the press plans to remake the 1925 version of *Ben-Hur*.

Sam Zimbalist, who ultimately received producer's credit on the new *Ben-Hur*, had wanted to remake the film as early as 1954, after the success of other MGM epics like *Quo Vadis?* (1951). Paramount's enormous profits from *The Ten Commandments* (1956), Cecil B. DeMille's remake of his own 1923 film, was another incentive. Zimbalist hired several writers, including playwrights Maxwell Anderson and S.N. Behrman, to hack at the General Lew Wallace novel, and planned to use Sidney Franklin, for years one of the studio's most reliable directors. When Franklin proved too ill to work on the project, Zimbalist hired William Wyler.

Wyler had just finished *The Big Country* (1958), an oversized Western starring Gregory Peck and Charlton Heston. The director later gave several reasons why he took the assignment, such as wanting to "out DeMille DeMille," and working again in Rome, the site of his earlier hit, *Roman Holiday*. Money must have been a factor: he was guaranteed either 8 percent of the gross or 3 percent of the profits, on top of $350,000. *Ben-Hur* would ensure the director's financial stability for the rest of his life.

When Burt Lancaster and Rock Hudson turned down the title role of Judah Ben-Hur, Wyler offered it to Heston. No doubt his having just played Moses in *The Ten Commandments* was another consideration, but Wyler had originally wanted Heston to play Messala, the villain in the story. Stephen Boyd, born in Northern Ireland and a contract player at Twentieth Century-Fox, took Messala's part instead.

Filming took place at the Cinecittà studios in Rome. By the time production started, the budget had more than doubled to $15 million. Wyler was unhappy with the draft of a screenplay by Karl Tunberg. Novelist Gore Vidal worked on the project as a way to get out of the rest of his MGM contract. In later years, he insisted that he played up the story's homosexual subtext without Wyler's awareness. Talking about Judah Ben-Hur and Messala, Vidal wrote, "There is something emotional between these two . . . it's a love scene gone wrong."

Wyler and Heston both professed ignorance of Vidal's designs. The director said he discarded the novelist's draft, preferring to work with British playwright Christopher Fry, who remained on the set throughout the shoot. Heston agreed with Wyler's account. "Whatever was good in the dialogue was Fry's," he said. It was a halfhearted endorsement at best, since the plot still remained. As the shooting progressed, Wyler had to drop his focus on improving the script and simply get the film done.

An added problem with the production was the use of 65mm cameras. Only six cameras were in existence; Wyler had two of them, and second unit director Andrew Marton had three of the others. Wyler hated the 65mm process, saying, "Nothing is *out* of the picture, and you can't fill it. You either have a lot of empty space, or you have two people talking and a flock of others surrounding them who have nothing to do with the scene."

After the shoot, Wyler spoke privately about his "disappointment" with Heston's performance. "Willy was a very *wise* director, but he didn't empathize with actors as artists," Heston said in return. "He was just not interested in making you feel good. He was only interested in making you *be* good." Wyler may have had high standards with his actors, but it was clear that he was willing to settle in other areas.

In the thirty years or so since the silent *Ben-Hur*, storytelling methods had matured as much as the more technical aspects of filmmaking had. Wyler is more restrained in his depiction of characters than previous director Fred Niblo was, for example. Wyler's Roman soldiers aren't thieving, lying thugs who berate and molest innocent women, and his version of the Nativity strips away the gauzy, greeting card imagery used in the silent. But restraint isn't much of a strategy when dealing with a story this fraught with melodrama. Wyler's choices are too often hokey and corny in ways he never was earlier in his career. The silent *Ben-Hur* had eerie premonitions of Nazi Germany. In Wyler's version, when Messala threatens, "Extinction for your people," it's fifteen years after the Holocaust, and the director was pushing a more obvious meaning.

Wyler knew his work would be scorned by intellectuals. "I was completely written off as a serious director by the avant-garde, which had considered me a favorite for years," he admitted later. *Ben-Hur*'s reputation was based more on its size than its creative accomplishments. A million pounds of plaster, 40,000 cubic feet of lumber,

40,000 tons of white sand from Mediterranean beaches, 300 sets, 6,000 extras: the statistics pile up like items on an accounting sheet. Missing was the confidence and assurance of the 1925 version. Back then, MGM built real boats and burned them up; in 1958, Wyler had to content himself with models in a water tank.

Yakima Canutt, the industry's most honored stuntman, masterminded the new chariot sequence, the best-remembered part of the film. It featured nine four-horse teams circling a life-size track, and took five weeks to shoot at a cost of a million dollars. Canutt's son Joe doubled for Heston, but according to Marton, Heston and Boyd did everything "except for two stunts." The crucifixion scene, shot in January 1959, marked the end of principle photography. Six months of

postproduction followed, as well as an avalanche of publicity. *Ben-Hur* toys, candy bars, and perfumes assaulted the public.

Meanwhile, Tunberg got into a public spat with Fry over screenplay credits. Some believe this is the reason why *Ben-Hur* did not win a writing Oscar, even as it was breaking records by winning eleven other Academy Awards. A box-office phenomenon, the film's legacy was felt in a raft of Biblical and pseudo-Biblical epics.

Wyler gave MGM what it wanted—a mammoth, bloated epic—but he did not believe in what he was doing. Who could take a story seriously that treated the Passion as an anticlimax? The director never regained his reputation or his form. His final films were occasionally diverting, but not commercially successful.

Wild River

Twentieth Century-Fox, 1960. Sound, color, 2.35. 110 minutes.

Cast: Montgomery Clift (Chuck Glover), Lee Remick (Carol Garth Baldwin), Jo Van Fleet (Ella Garth), Albert Salmi (R.J. Bailey), Jay C. Flippen (Hamilton Garth), James Westerfield (Cal Garth), Barbara Loden (Betty Jackson), Frank Overton (Walter Clark), Malcolm Atterbury (Sy Moore).

Credits: Produced and directed by Elia Kazan. Screenplay by Paul Osborn. Based on the novels *Mud in the Stars* by William Bradford Huie and *Dunbar's Cove* by Borden Deal. Director of photography: Ellsworth Fredericks. Film editor: William Reynolds. Art direction: Lyle R. Wheeler, Herman A. Blumenthal. Set decorations: Walter M. Scott, Joseph Kish. Costumes designed by Anna Hill Johnstone. Makeup by Ben Nye. Hair styles by Helen Turpin. Music composed and conducted by Kenyon Hopkins. Assistant director: Charles Maguire. Sound: Eugene Grossman, Richard Vorisek. Color by DeLuxe. Color consultant: Leonard Doss. Westrex Recording System.

Additional Cast: Big Jeff Bess (Joe John Garth), Robert Earl Jones (Ben), Bruce Dern (Jack Roper).

Additional Credits: Released March 26, 1960.

Available: The Library of Congress.

After his relatively unhappy experiences adapting a John Steinbeck novel into the 1955 film *East of Eden*, director Elia Kazan wrote, "I'd decided I'd no longer wait for authors to send me their plays or for film producers to propose movies I might direct. I'd initiate my own projects . . . I'd take an active role in organizing . . . even in the writing."

Persuading Twentieth Century-Fox to purchase the novel *Mud on the Stars* by William Bradford Huie, Kazan started a screenplay about an elderly woman who resists attempts by the Tennessee Valley Authority to buy her farm. Kazan was returning to the milieu of his first movie, the documentary *People of the Cumberland* (1937), produced and released by Frontier Films. In fact,

the finished *Wild River* opens with documentary footage of floods, then cuts to the sort of "man in the street" interviews popular with newsreels of the time. The opening not only alludes to *The River* (1937), but succeeding scenes will comment directly on Pare Lorentz's documentary.

Kazan soon discovered, "The screenwriter's craft was more difficult than I'd believed." After three drafts, he asked Paul Osborn to help. Osborn had been an unsuccessful playwright in the 1930s (*Morning's at Seven*) until he adapted a novel into the Broadway hit *On Borrowed Time*. This led to his reputation as someone who could adapt heavyweight material for stage and screen: *Madame Curie* for MGM in 1943, *A Bell for Adano* on Broadway in 1945, and *East of Eden* for Kazan. Osborn had his own ideas for the project, and wouldn't agree to work on it for some time. At some point in the writing process, Fox also purchased the rights to *Dunbar's Cove*, a novel by Borden Deal whose plot closely paralleled what would become *Wild River*.

Kazan claims in his autobiography that he had originally intended *Wild River* as an homage to the New Deal. But he was surprised to realize his sympathies had shifted. He was now on the side of Ella Garth, forced off her island farm in the Tennessee River to make way for a dam that would supply hydroelectric power to the region. "Perhaps I was beginning to feel humanly, not think ideologically," he wrote, although by that point in his career his identification with the underdog had become automatic. Kazan was not a deep thinker but a passionate one. He saw Ella as one more lone warrior standing up to injustice, an approach that appealed to his sense of himself but that ultimately disrupted the plot he had chosen.

For Ella to resist the TVA, she not only has to deny progress and common sense (her farm will be flooded whether she leaves it or not), she also has to side with what Kazan called "'reactionary' country people," a class he depicted as ignorant, racist, violent, and inbred. Opposing Ella is Chuck Glover, a liberal, effete Northeasterner who drops in by plane, tries to integrate the workforce, and departs as soon as he can.

For Glover, Kazan cast Montgomery Clift, an actor who had specialized in playing effete liberals who turn themselves into martyrs by standing up to authority. Clift's career at this point was in a tailspin after a car accident during the filming of *Raintree County* (1957) permanently altered his face. Kazan wrote that Fox executive Spyros Skouras pushed Clift for the part. "In some way or another he was a cripple. And he also drank. I can't stand drunken actors."

Kazan expressed this attitude during the shoot by socially and sexually emasculating Glover. "Monty's sexuality was that of a child waiting for his mother to put her arms around him," he wrote. He had Lee Remick play the aggressor in their scenes. Remick, who had debuted in Kazan's *A Face in the Crowd* (1957) as a sexually charged high-school cheerleader, was playing a variant on Eva Marie Saint's role in *On the Waterfront* (1954)—a pretty, available blonde waiting for someone to take her away. As Carol Baldwin, Ella Garth's granddaughter, Remick repeatedly describes her love for the land and its people, yet abandons them at the first opportunity.

Ella Garth was played by Jo Van Fleet, who won an Oscar in her first film, *East of Eden*. Thirty-seven at the time, she was playing someone twice her age. "Full of unconstrained violence," Kazan wrote, "she'd eat Clift alive, and I was prepared to let her." Van Fleet has only three or four significant scenes, but she is the centerpiece of the film.

Although it is slower and more guarded than his earlier films, *Wild River* can be seen as another attempt on Kazan's part to justify his actions during the McCarthy period. Typically, he blamed Skouras and the rest of the Fox staff for its poor showing at the box office. The director seemed unwilling to face up to the film's confused politics, or the inadequacies of his style. The period details in *Wild River*—a couple of posters, some radio show clips—seem like afterthoughts. The musical score is an odd combination of folk and easy listening. The camerawork is stiff, stoic, a throwback to 1930s filmmaking. The actors' close-ups seem to be shot in entirely different time periods, and almost no one ever makes eye contact. Even the sex scenes seem slow and slack.

The film has several showboating moments. Carol enters her dead husband's house and finds leaves and dust on their marriage bed. She brushes them off, is overcome, strips off the cover, sinks to her knees. This is the kind of acting Kazan loves: the scene as exercise, as a way to pretend your life is ruined. But in its way the moment is as much of a stunt as Van Fleet's dyed hair and fake age spots. Clift, on the other hand, recedes into the frame, letting the others do all the work.

Both Ella Garth and Chuck Glover appear as metaphors for Christ during the film. Ella's parable about selling a dog, delivered to poor black tenant farmers who gaze up at her with undisguised admiration, is smart and condescending at the same time. Glover, taunted and beaten by the Depression-era equivalent of Roman centurions, splayed on his bed in a crucified pose, undergoes his own resurrection by the film's end. It's an odd counterpart to the film's peculiar sex scenes and erratic social commentary.

"This is one of my favorites, possibly because of its social ambivalence," Kazan wrote. "I hope the negative is safe in one of Fox's vaults, although I've heard a rumor that it was destroyed to make space for more successful films." Fox spokespeople insist that the film's elements are safe. It is available on home video in other territories, but its release in the United States has been delayed due to underlying rights issues.

Jazz on a Summer's Day

Galaxy Attractions, 1960. Sound, color, 1.37. 81 minutes.

Featuring: Louis Armstrong, Mahalia Jackson, Gerry Mulligan, Dinah Washington, Chico Hamilton, Anita O'Day, George Shearing, Jimmy Guiffre, Chuck Berry, Jack Teagarden, Thelonious Monk, Big Maybelle, Sonny Stitt, Eli's Chosen Six, David Bailey, Danny Barcelona, Bob Brookmeyer, Buck Clayton, Bill Crow, Eric Dolphy, Art Farmer, Harold Gaylon, Nathan Gershman, Terry Gibbs, Urbie Green, Henry Grimes, Jim Hall, Peanuts Hucko, Jo Jones, Ray Mosca, Armando Peraza, Max Roach, Rudy Rutherford, Sal Salvador, Willis Conover.

Credits: Cameramen: Bert Stern, Courtney Hafela, Ray Phealan. Script and continuity: Arnold Perl, Albert D'Annibale. Assistant cameramen: Mike Cuesta, Jack Schatz, Pierre Streit. Musical director: George Avakian. In charge of production: Allan Green. Associate producer: Harvey Kahn. Edited by Aram Avakian. Assistant editors: John B. Welsh, Bill Grossman. Script girls: Judi Schoenback, Lily Fenichel. Sound by Columbia Records, Elliot Gruskin. Optical effects by Film Opticals, Inc. Color by Deluxe.

Additional Credits: Produced and directed by Bert Stern. Production dates: July to August 1958. Opened in New York City on March 28, 1960.

Available: New Yorker Video DVD (2000). ISBN: 1-56730-214-9. UPC: 717119165048.

Like Stanley Kubrick, Bert Stern came to film through commercial photography. Born in 1930 in Brooklyn, Stern was a cameraman in the Army during the early 1950s, where he learned how to use the compact, almost indestructible Eyemo 35 millimeter camera. Like Kubrick, Stern found work at *Look* magazine. In interviews, Stern has pointed to Kubrick's early films as the primary inspiration behind *Jazz on a Summer's Day*. (Stern also took the iconic photograph of Sue Lyon in heart-shaped sunglasses that was used in the advertising campaign for Kubrick's 1962 adaptation of *Lolita*.)

George Wein, the owner of a jazz club and record label, started the Newport Jazz Festival in 1954. Elaine Lorillard, with her husband Louis a significant backer of the festival, invited Stern to document it. By 1958 one of the most recognized commercial photographers in the world, Stern felt that making a feature was the best way to advance his career. He arrived in Newport with a cast and crew and began rehearsals for a fiction film, a romance that would use the festival as a backdrop. But after a few days' work, Stern abandoned the project, citing at various times an inadequate script, problems with the cast, and his own shortcomings as a filmmaker.

Stern still had permission to shoot on the festival grounds, and switched his focus to covering the musicians performing there. In the director's words, earlier film documentaries about jazz were usually "black and white, kind of depressing, and in little downstairs nightclubs. This brought jazz out into the sun." Just as important was Stern's decision to entrust the sound recording to Columbia Records executive George Avakian. Having one master source for music, rather than assembling piecemeal takes, assured that the final film would have a consistently high-quality sound.

Stern, who admitted that he didn't know much about jazz, also relied on Avakian to determine which performers to shoot. ("The only person I had heard was Chico Hamilton," he said later.) So although the Festival lasted four days, and showcased musicians like Duke Ellington, Benny Goodman, and Miles Davis, Stern and his crew only shot performances on Saturday and Sunday.

Stern had as many as five cameras going at once. He preferred shooting from the foot or the side of the stage, about thirty feet from the performers, using telephoto lenses so that the musicians' faces would fill the screen. Much was made subsequently about his aiming into stage lights or mixing up camera angles, supposedly breaking the "rules" of documentary filmmaking. But Stern was simply trying to capture what he could from positions that were not conducive to classical styles of cinematography.

Far more revolutionary was his decision to cut away from musicians to unrelated shots of waterfront scenes, yachting, tourists, etc. At times Stern's photography provides an abstract counterpoint to the music on the soundtrack; at other times, he offers what could be interpreted as a "narrative" for a song. These tactics became mainstays of the musical documentary genre. Concert films today are unthinkable without shots of concertgoers, of arenas before and after shows, of candid interviews and freewheeling montages of settings and surroundings.

George Avakian's younger brother Aram edited the film. Born in 1926, Aram attended both Yale and the Sorbonne before working as an editor on the CBS documentary series *See It Now*, hosted by Edward R. Murrow. In the years following the release of *Jazz on a Summer's Day*, some have asserted that Aram deserves a director's credit for helping Stern shape the material as he was shooting it. Stern agrees that Avakian was "the most experienced filmmaker on the set," but insists that "*Jazz on a Summer's Day* is not directed. It was produced and filmed." (On the other hand, Stern also claims that 90 percent of the film is his.)

There's no question that Aram Avakian was a crucial component to the film's success. Stern received some financial help from Elaine Lorillard, but essentially paid for the shoot himself. He also had to come up with the money for editing, which was a six-month process. Avakian whittled 80,000 feet of film down to 8,000, preparing short segments that Stern would show to prospective investors. (Some sources claim that Stern shot up to 130,000 feet.) The strategy persuaded Chicago lawyer Milton Gordon to put up the $30,000–$40,000 Stern needed to complete the film. (Gordon formed Galaxy Attractions after making millions by syndicating "Charlie Chan" and "Ramar of the Jungle" films to television.)

Some of Stern's decisions can be questioned today, such as following a Dixieland band through the streets of Newport, editing out passages of songs, adding transitional footage shot later on Long Island, or cutting away from Thelonious Monk to show part of the America's Cup trials. But Stern's eye for composition offset many of the obstacles he faced filming, and also prefigure many of the documentary techniques that have become more familiar in recent years. The lack of a voice-over narration, a commonplace approach in the 1960s, seems especially daring here. And Stern and his crew captured some incredible performances with an intimacy and immediacy missing from earlier documentaries, giving viewers new insights into well-known figures like Louis Armstrong.

Stern shot the performances before getting clearances from the musicians, then had to negotiate rights with them individually. At $25,000, almost a quarter of the entire budget, Armstrong was the most expensive. One of the great artists of the twentieth century, Armstrong is in fine form here, even though this was material he had been performing for up to thirty years. Equally impressive is Mahalia Jackson, another Columbia Records artist, who closes the film's performances.

Jazz on a Summer's Day can also be treasured for the serendipitous moments Stern captured. Like Chuck Berry, looking impossibly young and handsome, bulling his way through "Sweet Little Sixteen" while jazz stalwarts like Jack Teagarden look on bemusedly. When Berry has to pause for a clarinet solo in the middle of his rock-and-roll anthem, you get a sense of how out of place he must have felt.

Stern went on to direct three short films about Twiggy, the 1960s model, but his importance as a filmmaker rests on *Jazz on a Summer's Day*, the precursor to a generation of films like *Monterey Pop* (1969) and *Woodstock* (1970).

Psycho

Paramount, 1960. Sound, B&W, 1.85. 108 minutes.
Cast: Anthony Perkins (Norman Bates), Vera Miles (Lila Crane), John Gavin (Sam Loomis), Martin Balsam (Milton Arbogast), John McIntire (Al Chambers), Simon Oakland (Dr. Richmond), Vaughn Taylor (George Lowery), Frank Albertson (Tom Cassidy), Lurene Tuttle (Mrs. Chambers), Pat Hitchcock (Caroline), John Anderson (Charlie), Mort Mills (Highway patrolman), Janet Leigh (Marion Crane).
Credits: Directed by Alfred Hitchcock. Music by Bernard Herrmann. Assistant director: Hilton A. Green. Pictorial consultant: Saul Bass. Screenplay by Joseph Stefano. Based on the novel by Robert Bloch. Director of photography: John L. Russell. Art direction: Joseph Hurley & Robert Clatworthy. Set decorator: George Milo. Unit manager: Lew Leary. Titles designed by Saul Bass. Edited by George Tomasini. Costume supervision: Helen Colvig. Make-up supervision: Jack Barron & Robert Dawn. Hairstylist: Florence Bush. Special effects: Clarence Champagne. Sound recording by Waldon O. Watson & William Russell. Westrex Recording System. Shamley Productions.
Additional Cast: Alfred Hitchcock, Helen Wallace (Customer), Frank Killmond (Bob Summerfield), Don Ross (Mechanic), Francis De Sales (Deputy District Attorney Alan Deats), Sam Flint (County Sheriff), Pat McCaffrie (Police guard), George Eldredge (Chief of Police James Mitchell); Ted Knight, Fletcher Allen (Policemen).
Additional Credits: Produced by Alfred Hitchcock. Production dates: November 30, 1959 to February 1, 1960. Reshoots: February 15 and March 1, 1960. Opened June 16, 1960. Rated M in 1968 and R in 1984.
Other Versions: *Psycho II* (1983), *Psycho III* (1986), *Psycho IV* (made-for-TV, 1990). A remake of *Psycho* directed by Gus Van Sant was released in 1998.

Available: Universal DVD (1999). ISBN: 0-7832-2584-9. UPC: 0-2519-20251-2-9.

While North by Northwest (1959) was a commercial success, it was also the most expensive film Alfred Hitchcock had ever made. As a producer, he must have been aware of the cycle of low-budget horror movies geared toward younger viewers. And as the creative force behind *Alfred Hitchcock Presents*, which premiered on CBS in 1955, he saw the potential of adapting television techniques to motion picture filmmaking. He realized that with the right story, cheap sets, flat lighting, and fast shooting didn't matter. And with censorship standards weakening, stories could be more explicit in terms of sex and violence.

In 1959, Hitchcock read a *New York Times* book review of *Psycho*, a novel by Robert Bloch, and eventually purchased the rights for $9,000. A protégé of horror writer H.P. Lovecraft, Bloch sold his first short story to *Weird Tales* in 1933. In the 1950s, Bloch was living in Wisconsin, not far from Plainfield, the home of serial killer Ed Gein. When Gein was arrested in 1957, Bloch found the subject for his next novel: how a friendly neighbor could actually be a homicidal maniac.

Paramount had already rejected the novel when Hitchcock proposed adapting it for his next film. The studio agreed to distribute *Psycho* only under the condition that Hitchcock finance it himself, through his Shamley Productions. (Paramount ended up paying some crew salaries in order to preserve their union benefits.) All these considerations helped fashion what *Psycho* would eventually become. For example, Hitchcock said later that he made the film in black-and-white because color would have made the blood seem too gory. However, black-and-white was also a considerably cheaper process. The low budget helped determine the cast: Vera Miles because she was under contract to Hitchcock; John Gavin instead of a more expensive actor like Cliff Robertson; Janet Leigh, a friend of Hitchcock and his wife, because she agreed to a salary cut to $25,000 in exchange for working only three weeks.

Hitchcock saved money by using crew members from his television series, like cinematographer John Russell and set designer George Milo. Assistant director Hilton Green, who worked on *North by Northwest*, oversaw filming the location footage. Saul Bass provided storyboards for one of the murder scenes. Bernard Herrmann, who apart from Hitchcock gets the largest credit in the film, provided a score composed solely for strings.

Persistent rumors have dogged the production. Although Bass tried to take credit for *Psycho*'s first murder sequence, Leigh and several crew members insist that it was the work of Hitchcock, and that he was beside the camera for each of the seven days it took to film. Consisting of some seventy shots, the forty-five second sequence is among the most famous, and most imitated, in all cinema. Hitchcock referred to it as "pure film," and in a sense it evokes the theories of montage promulgated by Sergei Eisenstein. Some of its details—the rings holding up the shower curtain, the blood flowing to a drain—approach a visual poetry even as they document the passing of a life.

It was also a depiction of graphic violence of the type Hitchcock had largely avoided during his career. His films were always known for their vivid set pieces, but these usually involved chases, attempts to evade detection, accidents, and the like—not cold-blooded murder. (Even the killing in *Strangers on a Train* is seen reflected through broken eyeglasses.) *Psycho* upped the ante for everyone—filmmakers as well as filmgoers.

Trying to discuss the sequence without giving it away for anyone who hasn't seen the movie brings up the issue of Hitchcock's "MacGuffin." Building a suspense story around a secret means that once the secret is revealed, there is no reason to wait around to see what else happens. *Psycho*'s "secret" became common knowledge fairly early in the movie's release. Not only could subsequent viewers prepare themselves for the shower sequence, they could dismiss what happened in the rest of the film.

Unlike the earlier Hitchcock masterpieces, which examined faith and loyalty in relationships, the transference of guilt, and other potentially absorbing issues, *Psycho* was all about how best to scare people. And if the best method turned out to be a succession of jolts, of shocking sounds and images that could be delivered through the low-budget television tricks, without the apparatus of a Hollywood studio system, then what was the point of making movies? Was the future of cinema a race to the bottom? More and more grotesque violence to impress increasingly jaded viewers?

"I feel it's tremendously satisfying for us to be able to use the cinematic art to achieve something of a mass emotion," Hitchcock told French director François Truffaut. But *Psycho* was the last time he fully connected with a mass audience. The MacGuffin became an increasingly onerous sticking point in his subsequent films. In *The Birds*, he tried to pretend that there wasn't one, or at least refused to provide an answer for it. In *Family Plot*, he switched stories halfway through, opening up an entirely new narrative in much the same way he did in *Psycho*. By *Frenzy* he was reduced to the same strategies of the filmmakers around him, who by this time had assimilated all of his tricks.

Psycho received mixed reviews when it was first released, although many critics placed it on their "best of the year" lists. It was a phenomenal commercial success, in part because of Hitchcock's adroit publicity campaigns. He appeared in the film's trailer, which avoided showing any footage from the actual release, and he prohibited entry in theaters after the film had started. (He also never worked with Paramount again.) By 1966 it was estimated to have made $14.3 million on a budget of a little more than $800,000.

The film also inspired imitators determined to outdo each other in terms of sex and violence. *Homicidal* (1961), directed by William Castle, may have been the first, but it was followed by many others (including a few based on Robert Bloch's works, like *Strait-Jacket* in 1964). Some have traced the entire slasher film genre from *Psycho*, in part because of Ed Gein, but also because of the flat, affectless style Hitchcock employed. Whether *Psycho* should be blamed for something like *Saw V* (2008) is open to debate, but there is no questioning *Psycho*'s profound impact on pop culture.

House of Usher

American International Pictures, 1960. Sound, color, 2.35. 79 minutes.
Cast: Vincent Price (Roderick Usher), Mark Damon (Philip Winthrop), Myrna Fahey (Madeline Usher), Harry Ellerbe (Bristol).
Credits: Produced and directed by Roger Corman. Screenplay by Richard Matheson. Based on Edgar Allan Poe's "The Fall of the House of Usher." Executive producer: James H. Nicholson. Music by Les Baxter. Director of photography: Floyd Crosby. Production design by Daniel Haller. Film editor: Anthony Carras. Process photography directed by Larry Butler. Special effects: Pat Dinga. Photographic effects: Ray Mercer. Music editor: Eve Newman. Sound editor: Al Bird. Paintings by Burt Schoenberg. Assistant director: Jack Bohrer. Sound: Phil Mitchell. Makeup: Fred Phillips. Wardrobe: Marjorie Corso. Properties: Dick Rubeu. Alta Vista productions. Sound recorded by Ryder Sound Services. In Cinemascope and Color. A James H. Nicholson & Samuel Z. Arkoff presentation of an American International Picture production.
Additional Cast: Bill Borzage, Mike Jordon, Nadajan, Ruth Oklander, George Paul, David Andar, Eleanor Le Faber, Geraldine Paulette, Phil Sylvestre, John Zimeas.
Additional Credits: Assistant director: Larry Knowland. Title on screen: *Edgar Allan Poe's House of Usher*. Production dates: January 1960. Premiered June 18, 1960.
Other Versions: *The Fall of the House of Usher* (1928, directed by James Sibley Watson, Melville Webber), *The Fall of the House of Usher* (1928, directed by Jean Epstein), *The Fall of the House of Usher* (1949, directed by Ivan Barnett), *The House of Usher* (1988, directed by Alan Birkinshaw).
Available: MGM DVD (2005). UPC: 027616910875.

The first color film by producer and director Roger Corman, *House of Usher* initiated a highly profitable series of Edgar Allan Poe adaptations released by American International Pictures. Born in Detroit in 1926, Corman moved with his family to Beverly Hills when his father found work as an engineer in Los Angeles. After serving in the Navy, Corman became a script reader in 1948. His first break came when he sold the story *The House in the Sea* to Allied Artists. It was filmed as *Highway Dragnet* (1954), and earned Corman an associate producer credit.

Corman found his best customers at American Releasing Corporation, renamed American International Pictures, Inc., and run by James H. Nicholson and Samuel Z. Arkoff. The first film they distributed by Corman was *The Fast and the Furious* in 1954. Since it was released as the second half of a double bill, it received less money than the top-billed film. That inspired Corman to package his own double features, which he turned out at a dizzying pace. Here's a typical passage from his autobiography: "*Blood Island* was finished on a Saturday and I started *Last Woman* on Monday. Two Saturdays later we wrapped *Last Woman* and were ready to start *Creature* the following Monday."

At AIP, quantity trumped quality, and Corman found himself scrambling to solve technical and logistical problems rather than addressing mise en scène. In later years he boasted of doubling sets (using them for more than one movie), cheating with stock footage, grabbing scenes without permits or full staffs. He found ingenious methods to bypass expensive special effects, but his tightfisted filming style meant that he sometimes had to settle for flat acting and stale staging.

Double features stopped making economic sense for AIP at the end of the 1950s. Corman proposed a risky project to Nicholson and Arkoff, an adaptation of Edgar Allan Poe's "The Fall of the House of Usher." "Poe has a built-in audience," Corman argued. "He's read in every high school." The AIP executives kept looking for a monster in Richard Matheson's script. "The house is the monster," Corman replied. Quoting, "The house lives, the house breathes," he wrote, "That's the line that allowed us to make the movie."

Nicholson and Arkoff okayed roughly $300,000 for a fifteen-day shoot. About $100,000 of that went to Vincent Price, the biggest star Corman had worked with to that point. Two years earlier, Price had scorned horror films, saying that he had trouble keeping a straight face during the shooting of *The Fly* (1958). But he wasn't being offered anything else, and for the rest of his career he would play variations on twisted, demonic madmen and twisted, misunderstood scientists.

In his autobiography, Corman credited production designer Daniel Haller for the look of *House of Usher*, calling him "the real star of the show." Haller bought $2,500 worth of stock sets and scenery from Universal, transforming them into rooms and corridors that looked more elaborate and sturdy than they actually were. Another key figure was cinematographer Floyd Crosby, who achieved sophisticated tracking shots with minimal fuss. Les Baxter, a musician better known for his easy listening arrangements of popular chestnuts, composed a score that complemented the look of the film.

Corman brought his own interpretation of the horror genre to the project, one he and screenwriter Robert Towne had worked out with a Beverly Hills psychiatrist. One of his conclusions: "The classic horror sequence is the equivalent of the sexual act." Another was the belief that a moving camera and a subjective point of view were the keys to tension. Translated to *House of Usher*, this meant that "The house can be seen as a woman's body with its openings—windows, doors, arches. The corridor becomes a woman's vagina." Fear came from subconscious taboos as well as from rats, cobwebs, creaking doors, and thunder and lightning. "The film was about decay and madness," Corman concluded.

"I told my cast and crew: I never wanted to see 'reality' in any of these scenes," the director wrote later. A recent forest fire in the Hollywood Hills provided the charred, misshapen trees seen in the film's few exteriors. Covered by two cameras, an old barn in Orange County became the burning mansion in the film's climactic scene. "Since one roaring blaze looks as good as another in a long shot, I cut the *Usher* sequence into the other films," Corman acknowledged later.

House of Usher was a bona fide hit for AIP, earning $1 million in rentals that summer alone. Nicholson and Arkoff wanted another Poe film, so Corman gave them *Pit and the Pendulum* (1961). Shot with the same basic crew but with a bigger budget, it resembled a new and improved *House of Usher*, with a cast upgrade in the form of horror queen Barbara Steele. Five more Poe films followed, all dealing in one way or another with incest and premature burial. Corman noted, "*The Terror* began as a challenge: to shoot most of a gothic film in two days using leftover sets from *The Raven*." Details like these led Vincent Price to this observation: "Roger had a quiet authority and a definite psychological approach to the Poe films. His energy was mystifying."

Corman directed over 50 low-budget indies, and produced and/or directed another 250 features for New World Pictures and Concorde/New Horizons. His pictures are remembered today more for the opportunities they gave to budding filmmakers than for their quality. The list of those who worked for Corman is staggering: Francis Ford Coppola, Peter Bogdanovich, Jonathan Demme, Martin Scorsese, Ron Howard, John Sayles, James Cameron, and many more. Robert Towne sold his first script to Corman. Jack Nicholson sold Corman three screenplays, and appeared in eight of his films. By providing a training ground for so many talented artists, and by making low-budget movies more acceptable to mainstream audiences, Corman arguably had a larger cultural impact than many better-known filmmakers.

The Apartment

United Artists, 1960. Sound, B&W, 2.35. 125 minutes.

Cast: Jack Lemmon (C.C. Baxter), Shirley MacLaine (Fran Kubelik), Fred MacMurray (J.D. Sheldrake), Ray Walston (Joe Dobisch), Jack Kruschen (Dr. Dreyfuss), David Lewis (Al Kirkeby), Hope Holiday (Margie MacDougall), Joan Shawlee (Sylvia), Naomi Stevens (Mrs. Mildred Dreyfuss), Johnny Seven (Karl Matuschka), Joyce Jameson (The blonde), Willard Waterman (Mr. Vanderhof), David White (Mr. Eichelberger), Edie Adams (Miss Olsen).

Credits: Produced and directed by Billy Wilder. Written by Billy Wilder and I.A.L. Diamond. Associate producers: I.A.L. Diamond, Doane Harrison. Director of photography: Joseph LaShelle. Filmed in Panavision. Art director: Alexander Trauner. Music by Adolph Deutsch. Film editor: Daniel Mandell. Assistant director: Hal Polaire. Set decorator: Edward G. Boyle. Sound: Fred Lau. Script continuity: May Wale. Property: Tom Plews. Production manager: Allen K. Wood. Special effects: Milt Rice. Makeup: Harry Ray. Music editor: Sid Sidney. Sound effects editor: Del Harris. Westrex Recording System. A Mirisch Company, Inc., presentation.

Additional Cast: Frances Weintraub Lax (Mrs. Lieberman), Benny Burt (Bartender), Hal Smith (Santa Claus), Joe Palma (Janitor).

Additional Credits: "Theme from *The Apartment*" was a new title for "Jealous Lover," a song by Charles Williams. Production dates: November 1959 to February 1960. Premiered in Los Angeles on June 21, 1960.

Awards: Oscars for Best Picture, Director, Writing: Story and Screenplay—Written Directly for the Screen; Film Editing; Art Direction–Set Decoration—Black and White.

Other Versions: Produced as a stage musical, *Promises, Promises*, in 1968.

Available: Twentieth Century Fox Home Entertainment DVD (2007). UPC: 8-83904-10080-5-50.

Writer and director Billy Wilder finished the 1950s with two box-office hits, *Witness for the Prosecution* (1958) and *Some Like It Hot* (1959), but they followed box-office and critical failures like *The Spirit of St. Louis* (1957). *The Apartment* in some ways sums up both the decade and Wilder's career.

The bowler hat and tight shirt connect Jack Lemmon's character in *The Apartment* to silent film comedians.

It offered his most scathing account of corporate America, one he had been refining since *Ace in the Hole* (1951). It could be seen as a dark, brooding variation on *The Seven Year Itch* (1955), complete with a cruel parody of Marilyn Monroe.

Biographer Kevin Lally traces *The Apartment* back to Wilder's screening of *Brief Encounter* (1945), David Lean's stiff-upper-lip romance about a thwarted affair between two people married to others. Wilder wasn't as interested in the lovers as he was in the "others," like the husband waiting at home for his wife to return. He told Lally that he often found the lead characters in stories like these "tedious." A germ of the story came from a real-life incident in which producer Walter Wanger shot agent Jennings Lang for sleeping with his wife, Joan Bennett. According to Wilder's writing partner, I.A.L. Diamond, another element came from a story about a woman who committed suicide in a man's apartment as revenge for being wronged.

The idea of setting *The Apartment* in corporate New York City may have been Wilder's master stroke. After all, the director was partly responsible for promoting the hedonistic bachelor lifestyle that dominated so much of American popular culture in the 1950s, from a leering Tom Ewell trying to cheat on his wife in *The Seven Year Itch* to an equally randy Tony Curtis trying to bed Monroe in *Some Like It Hot*. *The Apartment* takes a clinical look at that phenomenon, twisting the conventions of bedroom farces to show exactly what was at stake behind all the office parties, supper clubs, and assignations. Like *The Crowd* (1928), work in *The Apartment* is meaningless, soulless, but life outside work is just as bad: demeaning, corrupting, ultimately hollow.

Wilder knew this was a depressing message for a film, but he had several secret weapons. Foremost among them was Jack Lemmon, who was making the transition from dependable supporting actor to leading man. *The Apartment* may be his best showcase, because his part consists of a series of demanding acting exercises. He is called on to play sick, to play drunk, to work with props like shaving cream or a bowler hat, to do physical and verbal comedy, to suggest unrequited love and to accept rejection. Lemmon would later become typecast as a victim in corporate nightmares, but in *The Apartment* he seems to be experiencing treachery and betrayal for the first time.

Shirley MacLaine was still finding her way as an actress, and in later interviews described clashing with Wilder over scene interpretations and individual line readings. Some of the fighting may have been a psychological ploy on the director's part, because he extracted a performance that manages to disguise emotional vulnerability with false bravado. The third main role, personnel manager Sheldrake, had originally been intended for Paul Douglas. When he died, Fred MacMurray reluctantly filled in, fully aware of how the role might damage his new screen and television persona as an amiable dad. (Wilder had persuaded MacMurray to play "bad" many years earlier, in 1944's *Double Indemnity*.)

Apart from a few cheap digs at television, Wilder and Diamond's script is unusually focused, even by their standards. Their preferred method is indirection: characters become aware of their circumstances through dropped asides, misplaced props, overheard phone calls. Less nuanced writers would have had their characters tell each other everything. Like Arthur Schnitzler's play *La Ronde* (filmed by Max Ophüls in 1950), the chain of events set off by each sexual conquest in *The Apartment* never really ends, but instead circles back to ensnare new victims. But for once, Wilder's cynicism seems justified, and for once it is tempered by sympathy for his characters.

An office Christmas party shows just how accomplished Wilder had become as a director. Much of the scene takes place in the glass-walled office of Lemmon's C.C. Baxter as he tries to persuade MacLaine's Fran Kubelik to go out with him. Baxter is following proper dating etiquette, but everything he says has the opposite effect on Kubelik, who has just found out that her lover has been lying to her. She can't stop Baxter, and she can't tell him the truth. She also doesn't understand why his attitude suddenly changes, because he can't tell her how her cosmetics case reveals another side of her character. Written with unerring precision, the scene is directed with a delicacy not often seen in Wilder's previous films.

Some critics complained that *The Apartment* was sordid and immoral (a provocative advertising campaign that gave a seriously skewed impression of the film couldn't have helped much). But for the most part the film was praised, and it went on to win five Oscars. Lemmon would make a total of seven films with Wilder, who also worked with MacLaine again in *Irma la Douce* (1963). Wilder continued directing films until 1981, but he never again matched the intensity and insight of *The Apartment*.

Primary

Drew Associates/Time-Life Broadcast, 1960. Sound, B&W, 1.33. 53 minutes.

Featuring: John F. Kennedy, Jacqueline Kennedy, Robert Kennedy, Hubert H. Humphrey, Muriel Buck Humphrey.

Credits: Conceived and produced by Robert Drew for Time-Life Broadcast. Photographers: Richard Leacock, D A Pennebaker, Terrence McCartney-Filgate, Albert Maysles. Managing editor: Robert Drew. Sequence editors: Richard Leacock, D A Pennebaker, Terrence McCartney-Filgate. Assembly editor: Robert Farren. Writer: Robert Drew. Narrator: Joseph Julian. Music by courtesy of the candidates.

Additional Credits: Camera: Bill Knoll.

Available: Docurama DVD (1999). ISBN: 0-7670-5757-0. UPC: 7-67685-95623-6.

Born in Toledo, Ohio, in 1924, Robert Drew was a fighter jet pilot in the Air Force when he was struck by the idea of making films in a new, direct manner. He became a journalist and editor at *Life* magazine, where he specialized in photo essays, all the while working toward a new kind of documentary. "Real life never got onto film, never got onto television," he said, pointing out that when he worked on a film with photographer Allan Grant about architect Philip Johnson, it took two people to carry a camera tripod, let alone the other equipment required to make documentaries. With the right equipment and strategy, a small crew could tackle any subject, shoot in any location, without interfering with the reality being portrayed.

As a Nieman Fellow at Harvard University, Drew studied storytelling and film editing. He decided that the documentaries he had worked on were word-logic based, or lectures with pictures. He wanted "theater without actors, plays without playwrights, reporting without summary and opinion."

In a way he was following the Russian filmmaker Dziga Vertov, whose *Kino-Pravda* promised to depict the world without human subjectivity. Drew was also extending the ideas of Louis de Rochemont and his *March of Time*. In fact, like de Rochemont, Drew sold his idea to Time-Life executives as a way to extend the reach of their magazines to viewers of the five local television stations owned by the organization. The first project would be a show about the Democratic Presidential Primary contest in Wisconsin between Senators Hubert H. Humphrey and John F. Kennedy.

Drew assembled a staff that included Richard Leacock, a cameraman on Robert Flaherty's *Louisiana Story* (1948) who had also worked with de Rochemont and Willard Van Dyke; Albert Maysles, who would later work with his brother David on a series of influential documentaries; and D A Pennebaker, a retired businessman who had been photographing experimental documentaries. All were World War II veterans, and all had been working on equipment that would permit synchronized sound without cables. Cables were the big stumbling block to intimate filmmaking. They required the sound technician to remain tethered to the cameraman, doubling the space the film crew needed in any given location.

Drew and his colleagues filmed for five days and nights. Leacock had the only synch-sound camera; the others used everything from tiny hand-wound cameras to Arriflexes. They received full cooperation from the candidates, even filming in their hotel rooms as returns came in. Drew allowed the cameramen to edit their own footage, culling some 40,000 feet of film down to an hour's length. Because of a faulty synch cable, Drew had to rely on a hand-cranked editing machine invented by Loren Ryder to match sound with film.

In Drew's words, the reaction to the broadcast of *Primary* was "overwhelming silence." But when the film started receiving awards from documentary festivals, and accolades from documentarians like John Grierson, both Time-Life and ABC offered him additional work. Drew ended up producing five one-hour documentaries for ABC's *Close-Up!* series.

Speaking fifty years later, Pennebaker (who only worked one day on the film) remembers Drew forming his candid film group because Time-Life was considering purchasing ABC. More intriguing were the reasons why the filmmakers chose to cover the primary. "Bob and all of us saw Kennedy as a kind of helmsman of a new adventure. Win or lose we assumed he was the new voice, the new generation," Pennebaker said. "The hope of the film was to do something with Kennedy."

Primary makes this bias obvious throughout by contrasting an isolated, somewhat forlorn Humphrey with the youthful, energetic Kennedy, almost always surrounded by noisy crowds. The opening shots of the movie, which place Humphrey opposite a frankly unintelligible farmer in overalls, signals a new approach to documentaries. No more "man in the street" interviews with carefully coached "bystanders" recorded and photographed like a feature film. *Primary* would catch people off guard, in truthful poses, speaking from their hearts and not from a script.

That was the goal, at least. "No interviews," Drew ordered. "Never ask anybody to do anything. Never ask someone to repeat a line. Never ask someone to repeat an action." It's a tactic that works fine when your subjects are articulate, but not so well with the tongue-tied. And with Humphrey and Kennedy, Drew was documenting longtime politicians adept at handling awkward situations. Watch how Humphrey takes over the direction of a television show from his seat in front of the camera. (Drew broke one of his rules in the film, interviewing a radio announcer after a Humphrey broadcast on a small-town station.)

"We all saw him as kind of a nerd," Pennebaker said about Humphrey. "That was part of his appeal to farmers. He didn't understand television at all." Kennedy, who ran as a sort of celebrity, did. Humphrey's campaign song was a corny reworking of the "Ballad of Davy Crockett"; Kennedy had Frank Sinatra swinging a revamped "High Hopes." Still, the filmmakers develop a grudging respect for Humphrey, an affable, straight-talking pol who wins over anyone who bothers to listen.

Seen today, the weaknesses in *Primary* are largely due to the technical limitations faced by the filmmakers. The sound is poor throughout, and is noticeably out of synch in many shots. The filmmakers were limited by how noisy their cameras were, and how large. Pennebaker complained about not having enough film to capture entire events. Four-hundred-foot rolls would have allowed them to film for ten or eleven minutes at a stretch. "Time is axiomatic for producing a scene, instead of a medley of tiny shots." Too many moments in *Primary* feel as if we are peering over the shoulders of people who are blocking our view, catching the tail ends of conversations.

On the other hand, consider the first time we see Kennedy in *Primary*. In one thirty-second take, the camera follows him through a surging crowd of well-wishers, through a side door and up a short flight of stairs onto a stage, where he joins his wife and then turns to an ecstatic audience. No one had seen footage like this before. If Drew cheated the sound on some shots, or suggested that scenes were occurring simultaneously when they weren't, or took unnecessary jabs at Humphrey, he was still opening up a political process that for most Americans had been hidden. Television viewers of the time may not have realized it, but Drew and his colleagues were irrevocably changing the way documentaries would be made. They were also helping to alter politics, forcing candidates to make their appearance part of their campaigns.

Kennedy was so pleased with the film that he gave Drew permission to film in the White House for *Crisis* (1963), a documentary about a racial conflict involving the President and George Wallace, governor of Alabama. Drew's third film about Kennedy, *Faces of November* (1964), dealt with the aftermath of his assassination. Pennebaker (*Dont Look Back*, 1967) and Maysles (*Salesman*, 1969) are also represented on the Registry.

A Raisin in the Sun

Sidney Poitier in *A Raisin in the Sun.*

Columbia, 1961. Sound, B&W, 1.85. 128 minutes.

Cast: Sidney Poitier (Walter Lee Younger), Claudia McNeil (Lena Younger), Ruby Dee (Ruth Younger), Diana Sands (Beneatha Younger), Ivan Dixon ([Joseph] Asagai), John Fiedler (Mark Lindner), Louis Gossett (George Murchison), Stephen Perry (Travis Younger), Joel Fluellen (Bobo), Louis Terkel (Herman), Roy Glenn (Willie Harris).

Credits: Directed by Daniel Petrie. Produced by David Susskind and Philip Rose. Screen play by Lorraine Hansberry. Based on the play by Lorraine Hansberry. Produced on the stage by Philip Rose and David J. Cogan. Director of photography: Charles Lawton, Jr. Art director: Carl Anderson. Film editors: William A. Lyon, Paul Weatherwax. Set decorator: Louis Diage. Assistant director: Sam Nelson. Make-up supervision: Ben Lane. Hair styles by Helen Hunt. Music by Laurence Rosenthal. Sound supervision: Charles J. Rice. Sound: George Cooper. Orchestrations: Arthur Morton. A Paman-Doris production. RCA Sound Recording.

Additional Credits: Released May 29, 1961.

Other Versions: A television adaptation starring Danny Glover and Esther Rolle and directed by Bill Duke and Harold Scott was filmed in 1989. A filmed version of a 2004 Broadway revival starring Sean Combs, Phylicia Rashad, and Audra McDonald and directed by Kenny Leon was broadcast in 2008.

Available: Columbia TriStar Home Video DVD (1999). ISBN: 0-7678-2806-2. UPC: 0-43396-00919-6.

Columbia Pictures was so worried about filming *A Raisin in the Sun* that it insisted on measures to limit its budget to $1.5 million. For one thing, playwright Lorraine Hansberry wasn't allowed to "open up" the original story by setting scenes on location. For another, she had to cut almost an hour's worth of material, conversations that she felt addressed the social and philosophical issues at the core of her play.

Hansberry's family was at the forefront of the struggle for racial equality in the 1930 and '40s. Her father Carl, a realtor and prominent member of the NAACP, moved into an all-white neighborhood in Chicago in 1938 to challenge restrictive real estate covenants. The case reached the Supreme Court, which in 1940 outlawed restrictive covenants. Tellingly, Hansberry's father later became disillusioned by the slow progress of real estate reform, and considered leaving the country.

Hansberry grew up on speaking terms with the leading African-Americans in the country, including Paul Robeson, Duke Ellington, and Jesse Owens. She dropped out of college after two years, but not before becoming interested in drama. She moved to New York, where she was a reporter and editor for Paul Robeson's newspaper *Freedom*. She married songwriter and intellectual Robert Nemiroff; when he cowrote a pop hit, she could concentrate full-time on her personal writing. She finished *A Raisin in the Sun* in 1957.

The title came from "Harlem," a poem by Langston Hughes: a dream deferred will "dry up/ like a raisin in the sun." Nemiroff took the play to Philip Rose, a classically trained singer who had become a theatrical producer. Rose sent the script to Sidney Poitier, who was "overwhelmed" by the material. The actor's decision to commit to a six-month contract helped Rose and his producing partner David J. Cogan secure enough financing to open the play in New Haven.

Poitier also found the original stage director, Lloyd Richards, a well-regarded actor who would later tackle the plays of Athol Fugard and August Wilson, as well as head the Yale School of Drama for an unprecedented twelve years.

Rehearsals started in December 1958. Poitier was arguably the dominant black actor of the period, but the rest of the cast was talented as well. Ruby Dee had been a member of the American Negro Theater, and had prominent roles in films like *No Way Out* (1950) and *Edge of the City* (1957). This was the Broadway debut for Louis Gossett, Jr., who would win a Best Supporting Actor Oscar twenty years later. Diana Sands made important strides by appearing in plays by Shakespeare and Shaw. (Like Hansberry, Sands died of cancer in her thirties.)

A Raisin in the Sun opened in Philadelphia and Chicago before it reached Broadway. It was a sensation in New York, running for over five hundred performances and winning the New York Drama Critics Award. Columbia bought the screen rights for the play for $300,000, with another $50,000 for Hansberry to write the screenplay. A Columbia publicist acknowledged in an interview with the *New York Times* that the film was a "risky project for the studio. With a budget of $1.5 million, the worldwide gross will have to double that to break even. We have to write off most of the Southern market because of the theme. . . . If it's just good, it won't make a dime."

For director, Columbia chose Daniel Petrie, a Glace Bay, Nova Scotia, native who had acted on Broadway before directing in television. Petrie agreed that the stage cast should remain intact for the film. Gossett, for one, championed the director. "He was one of the earliest pioneers," the actor said. "At a time when other directors wouldn't take the risk, Dan did [the play] justice." Asked about dealing with actors, Petrie later said, "You have to create an atmosphere for them to work without imposing on them." He saw acting in basic terms: "All the actor has to do is think the thoughts of the character."

In producing the film, Rose was joined by David Susskind, a television producer and talk-show host who would win over two dozen Emmys in his career. Susskind later commented on "pretty extensive" problems during shooting, which lasted from July 6 to September 7, 1960. The filmmakers weren't allowed to use a fraternity's name, or to shoot certain houses as locations. Susskind was surprised by the bigotry he encountered.

The budgetary restrictions the filmmakers faced are obvious today. The film essentially takes place on one set, with a few largely extraneous exterior shots thrown in. Petrie maintains the illusion of a "fourth wall" between viewers and the action on stage for much of the film, breaking the plane primarily during Poitier's more impassioned speeches. The actor's pent-up energy is apparent in the way in which he paces the set, frustrated, angry, embittered. It must have been a relief for Poitier to play such a role. He had characteristically been cast as the conscience of his race, and the opportunity to explore a flawed, damaged hero inspired the actor to greater passion than he had previously displayed on screen.

Hansberry's theatrical devices, like the houseplant that needs more light, may be more obvious today than when the play opened. Petrie saw *A Raisin in the Sun* as "black America's *Death of a Salesman*," but Hansberry herself cited *Juno and the Paycock* as the reason why she decided to write drama. Sean O'Casey's play is a decided influence here—at least until the final act, when the piece suddenly becomes a message drama about social justice. The inexorable tragedy of the opening, with the characters trapped by their own shortcomings as well as by discrimination, is replaced by speeches filled with determination and uplift. Robert Nemiroff, for one, was unhappy with the film, writing about "the drastically cut and largely one-dimensional 1961 movie version—which, affecting and pioneering though it may have been, reflected little of the greatness of the original stage performances."

What gives the play, and the film, its power today is the breadth of Hansberry's interests. The morality of alcohol, chauvinism, Afrocentrism, jazz versus folk music, abortion, theft, and betrayal are just some of the themes Hansberry addresses, in speeches that are simultaneously earthy and philosophical. The author had only one other play produced before she succumbed to cancer. *To Be Young, Gifted, and Black*, adapted by her husband, was the most significant of her posthumous works.

The Hustler

Twentieth Century-Fox, 1961. Sound, B&W, 2.35. 135 minutes.

Cast: Paul Newman (Eddie Felson), Jackie Gleason (Minnesota Fats), Piper Laurie (Sarah Packard), George C. Scott (Bert Gordon), Myron McCormick (Charlie Burns), Murray Hamilton (Findley), Michael Constantine (Big John), Stefan Gierasch (Preacher), Cliff Pellow (Turk), Jake LaMotta (Bartender), Gordon B. Clarke (Cashier), Alexander Rose (Score Keeper), Carolyn Coates (Waitress), Carl York (Young Hustler), Vincent Gardenia (Bartender).

Credits: Produced and directed by Robert Rossen. Screenplay by Sydney Carroll and Robert Rossen. Based on the novel by Walter S. Tevis. Director of photography Eugene Shuftan [Eugen Schüfftan]. Film editor: Dede Allen. Production design by Harry Horner. Production manager: John Graham. Associate art director: Albert Brenner. Assistant director: Charles Maguire. Technical advisor: Willie Mosconi. Set decorator: Gene Callahan. Music: Kenyon Hopkins. Camera operator: Saul Midwall. Sound: James Shields, Richard Vorisek. Costumes designed by Ruth Morley. Makeup by Robert Jiras. Hairstyles by Donoene. Script supervisor: Marguerite James. Still photographs by Muky. Chief electrician: David Colden. Chief grip: Martin Nallan, Jr. Assistant cameraman: William Cronjager. Assistant film editor: Richard Stone. Sound editor: Edward Beyer. Music editor: Angelo Ross. "Louisville," music by Dan Terry. Optical effects: Film Opticals. A Twentieth Century-Fox presentation.

Additional Cast: Tom Ahearne (Bartender), Charles Dierkop (Pool room observer), Willie Mosconi (Willie), Charles Mosconi.

Additonal Credits: Premiered in New York City on September 25, 1961.

Awards: Oscars for Best Cinematography—Black and White, Art Direction–Set Direction—Black and White.

Other Versions: Sequel: *The Color of Money* (1986), starring Paul Newman and Tom Cruise, directed by Martin Scorsese.

Available: Twentieth Century Fox Home Entertainment DVD (2007). UPC: 0-24543-37226-4.

Robert Rossen had been scheduled to testify before the House Un-American Activities Committee in 1947, but the hearings inexplicably stopped after the "Hollywood Ten" appeared. During another round of hearings in 1951, Rossen testified without naming names. But his career had come to a standstill. In 1953 he petitioned the committee to testify again. This time he named fifty-seven people whose names were supplied by the committee, confirming their connection to the Communist Party. It was a move that haunted the writer, producer, and director for the rest of his life.

Rossen directed five films after *All the King's Men* (1949), but not one was a success. He was still tinkering with the Western *They Came to Cordura* (1959) for years after its release. In 1960, he also attempted a stage adaptation of Warren Miller's novel *The Cool World*, but it closed after two performances. One of his earlier playwriting efforts, *Corner Pocket*, concerned pool, and may have influenced his interest in *The Hustler*, a novel by Walter Tevis.

Expanded from a short story, the novel focuses on Fast Eddie Felson, a talented but undisciplined pool player whose sole ambition is to defeat Minnesota Fats, the reigning champion of pool halls. But to Rossen, "The film is really about the obstacles he encounters in attempting to fulfill himself as a human being." Rossen and screenwriter Sydney Carroll stripped away much of the background in Tevis's novel. (Also known as Sidney, Carroll worked predominately in TV.)

In the film, Felson no longer owns a pool hall, but is caught in mid-flight on a journey across America to confront Minnesota Fats. The alcohol that tormented him in the novel (and Tevis in real life) becomes a plot device, a shortcut for identifying winners and losers, in the film. As he did with *All the King's Men*, Rossen changed the ending of *The Hustler*, in this case a concession to star Paul Newman as much as to the expectations of mainstream filmgoers.

Born in Cleveland in 1925, Newman had been an unexceptional sailor during World War II and an indifferent college student before studying drama at Yale and at the Actors Studio in New York. A strong performance in the stage version of *Picnic* led to a movie contract and a succession of roles in high-profile films like *The Long Hot Summer* (1958) and *Exodus* (1960). But Newman also appeared in several duds, at the same time losing credibility with critics for what were perceived as safe, commercial choices. Like his Billy the Kid in *The Left Handed Gun* (1958), Fast Eddie would be another chance for Newman to explore fame and celebrity, topics he returned to again and again throughout his career.

Fame and celebrity meant something entirely different to Rossen, who believed that success in a capitalist society inevitably led to corruption. Fast Eddie's competitive drive was his "tragedy," a message that many filmgoers may have missed. The politics behind *The Hustler* didn't hold much interest for Jackie Gleason, a TV star who was entertained by his own hobbies. Gleason, who had had a hard upbringing, knew his way around pool halls, but he also understood the psychology and style of his character, Minnesota Fats. Years of work in vaudeville and nightclubs had taught Gleason how to pin down a role with a few direct touches and gestures. Unprecedented success on television gave him the confidence to underplay his part.

George C. Scott had different opinions as to what constituted success in acting, and he wasn't afraid to criticize Newman's work as showy and lacking in technique. This was Scott's third film role after years of struggling in summer stock and TV series. Since the plot called for his character—a perverse, even sadistic "manager" named Bert Gordon—to treat Fast Eddie with disdain bordering on disgust, Scott may have been simply taking his part home with him. In a similar way, Piper Laurie, cast as the ambiguous love interest Sarah Packard, had ambivalent feelings about her career, and would retire after this film for fifteen years. Her performance swings from unguarded and emotionally vulnerable to indifferent, perhaps realizing in the end that Sarah was more a symbol than a person. As Rossen said later, "If I think about this world of today, I cannot keep from seeing in it a great number of cripples."

Newman praised Rossen later, admiring how the director would let actors mold scenes during the three weeks of rehearsals before shooting. The actor saw himself as a hustler in his career as well as in this movie, bluffing his way into situations he wasn't qualified to handle. He was also afraid of being seen as a pretty boy, and consequently enjoyed toying with his screen persona—carefully, so as not to damage his appeal, but still questioning the ultimate value of his work. Willie Mosconi, the greatest pool player of his generation, trained Newman, placed the pool balls for each take, and made at least one of the shots himself. (In an unbilled part in the film, he also holds the stake for one of the games.)

Rossen's past in social realism found a new outlet with lighter, more flexible equipment. Much of *The Hustler* was filmed in and around New York City, including the Ames Billiard Academy on 44th Street and Broadway in Manhattan. Rossen had the good fortune to work with Eugen Schüfftan, a world-class cinematographer expert at lighting and shooting complex, shifting compositions in deep focus. Schüfftan won an Oscar, as did Harry Horner and Gene Callahan for art and set decoration. This was an important credit for editor Dede Allen, who remembers Rossen warning her, "Don't forget kid, it's not about pool, it's about character."

Rossen could also take advantage of relaxed censorship standards. There is no doubt that Fast Eddie and Sarah are living with each other, for example, and while the film does not make the story's homosexual context explicit, it is unmistakable nevertheless. Less obvious to viewers of the time was how closely *The Hustler*'s plot resembled gunslinger Westerns of the previous decade, ones that discussed morality in earnest tones. Much of the action takes place in the equivalent of saloons, and many of the exterior locations show streets as deserted as those in a shoot-out. *The Hustler* can also be reduced to a coming-of-age tale, a harsh, grim one in which Fast Eddie must experience violence and death to mature.

Apart from Newman, Gleason, and Scott, few emerged unscathed from the film. Rossen, terminally ill, completed one more screen project. Schüfftan shot that and a few international productions, but his career was essentially over. Laurie's next screen work was in *Carrie* in 1976. Walter Tevis's next novel, *The Man Who Fell to Earth* (published in 1963), became a cult film starring David Bowie in 1976, but the author fell victim to alcoholism and did not publish again until 1980. He died four years later, after writing *The Color of Money*, a sequel to *The Hustler*.

West Side Story

United Artists, 1961. Sound, color, 2.20. 151 minutes.
Cast: Natalie Wood (Maria), Richard Beymer (Tony), Russ Tamblyn (Riff), Rita Moreno (Anita), George Chakiris (Bernardo), Simon Oakland (Lt. Schrank), Ned Glass (Doc), William Bramley (Officer Krupke), Tucker Smith (Ice), Tony Mordente (Action), David Winters (A-rab), Eliot Feld (Baby John), Bert Michaels (Snowboy), David Bean (Tiger), Robert Banas (Joyboy), [Anthony] Scooter Teague (Big Deal), Harvey Hohnecker [Evans] (Mouthpiece), Tommy Abbott (Gee-Tar), Susan Oakes (Anybodys), Gina Trikonis (Graziella), Carole D'Andrea (Velma), Jose De Vega (Chino), Jay Norman (Pepe), Gus Trikonis (Indio), Eddie Verso (Juano), Jaime Rogers (Loco), Larry Roquemore (Rocco), Robert Thompson (Luis), Nick Covacevich [Navarro] (Toro), Rudy Del Campo (Del Campo), Andre Tayir (Chile), Yvonne Othon [Wilder] (Consuelo), Suzie Kaye (Rosalia), Joanne Miya (Francisca).

Credits: Directed by Robert Wise and Jerome Robbins. Screenplay by Ernest Lehman. Music by Leonard Bernstein. Lyrics by Stephen Sondheim. Choreography by Jerome Robbins. Associate producer: Saul Chaplin. Music conducted by Johnny Green. Production designed by Boris Leven. Director of photography: Daniel L. Fapp. Costumes designed by Irene Sharaff. Assistant director: Robert E. Relyea. Dance assistants: Tommy Abbott, Margaret Banks, Howard Jeffrey, Tony Mordente. Film editor: Thomas Stanford. Music editor: Richard Carruth. Photographic effects: Linwood Dunn, Film Effects of Hollywood. Orchestrations by Sid Ramin, Irwin Kostal. Sound by Murray Spivack, Fred Lau, Vinton Vernon. Sound editor: Gilbert D. Marchant. Musical assistant: Betty Walberg. Vocal coach: Bobby Tucker. Musical supervision by Saul Chaplin, Johnny Green, Sid Ramin, Irwin Kostal. Titles & visual consultation by Saul Bass. Production artist: M. Zuberano.

Set decorator: Victor Gangelin. Make-up: Emile La Vigne. Hairdresser: Alice Monte. Wardrobe: Bert Henrikson. Casting: Stalmaster-Lister Co. Based upon the stage play produced by Robert E. Griffith and Harold S. Prince, by arrangement with Roger L. Stevens; book by Arthur Laurents; play conceived, directed and choreographed by Jerome Robbins. A Mirisch Pictures, Inc., presentation, in association with Seven Arts Productions, Inc., of a Beta Production. A Robert Wise production. Technicolor, Panavision 70.

Additional Cast: John Astin (Glad Hand), Penny Santon (Madam Lucia), Marni Nixon (Singing voice for Maria), Jimmy Bryant (Singing voice for Tony), Betty Wand (Singing voice for Anita).

Additional Credits: The 70mm prints featured a 6-track Westrex soundtrack. Assistant director: Ulu Grosbard. Opened in New York City on October 18, 1961.

Awards: Oscars for Best Motion Picture, Director, Actor in a Supporting Role (Chakiris), Actress in a Supporting Role (Moreno), Art Direction–Set Decoration—Color, Cinematography—Color, Costume Design—Color, Film Editing, Music—Scoring of a Musical Picture (Saul Chaplin, Johnny Green, Sid Ramin, Irwin Kostal), Sound (Fred Hynes, Todd-AO; Gordon E. Sawyer, Samuel Goldwyn Studio Sound Department).

Available: MGM Home Entertainment DVD (2003). UPC: 027616898807.

The idea for *West Side Story* originated with Jerome Robbins. Born Jerome Rabinowitz in New York City, he was raised in Weehawken, New Jersey, where his father ran a corset manufacturing company. Dropping out of school at the height of the Depression, he danced in burlesque sketches and in chorus lines on Broadway. At the same time he studied ballet and danced in shows choreographed by George Balanchine and Agnes de Mille. Robbins' first attempt at choreography was *Fancy Free* in 1944, with a score by Leonard Bernstein. This later evolved into the Broadway and MGM hit *On the Town* (1949).

Robbins began working on what would become *West Side Story* in 1949, while he was immersed in choreographing hit plays like *The King and I.* Collaborating with playwright Arthur Laurents and composer Leonard Bernstein, Robbins set out to update *Romeo and Juliet* to modern-day New York City. A draft of "East Side Story" focused on a star-crossed romance between a Jewish girl and a Roman Catholic. Robbins and Laurents switched the setting to a gang war between the Anglo Jets and the Puerto Rican Sharks, with a doomed romance between Maria, who works in a Puerto Rican bridal shop, and Tony, an Italian who helps out at a soda fountain.

The play's gestation period was unusually long because Robbins and Bernstein were working on so many other projects, but also because Robbins chose to name names at an HUAC hearing. Bernstein finished *Candide* in 1956, the same year he signed a recording contract with Columbia Records. This led to his famous "Young People's Concerts" on CBS television, for which he won an Emmy. He also accepted the role as principal conductor for the New York Philharmonic for the 1957 season—all of this while writing the score for *West Side Story* and participating in casting and production meetings. "All the peering and agony and postponement and re-re-rewriting turn out to have been worth it," he wrote later.

Bernstein's goal was to compose a tragic musical without relying on styles and formulas derived from opera. Larry Kert and Carol Lawrence were cast as the leads, Bernstein insisting that the show needed real kids more than stars. The spring of 1957 brought more delays when the show's producer, Cheryl Crawford, quit suddenly. Robbins, overburdened by his directing duties, tried to hire choreographer Herbert Ross, but that idea was vetoed by the show's new producers, Harold Prince and Robert Griffith.

With a New York theater booked and five weeks of tryouts scheduled, Bernstein and lyricist Stephen Sondheim were still adding to the score in the summer of 1957. They borrowed the music from "Quintet" to create "Tonight," which replaced "Somewhere" in the balcony scene. Bernstein pulled the music for "Gee, Officer Krupke" from *Candide*; meanwhile, Sondheim's "millions of lyrics to insanely fast music" were dropped from the opening number. The pressure was intense, and personality clashes ensued. Bernstein wrote to his wife, "Jerry continues to be—well, Jerry: moody, demanding, hurting."

"Something's Coming," sung by Tony as he prepares for the dance, wasn't written until August (and appears to have been borrowed from Laurents' writing). "It's really going to save his character," Bernstein wrote. "It gives Tony balls—so that he doesn't emerge as just a euphoric dreamer." Sondheim, on the other hand, worried about the play. "The whole piece trembles on the brink of self-conscious pretentiousness."

At least one critic, Harold Clurman, concurred after *West Side Story* opened on Broadway on September 26, 1957. He called it "phoney," and accused Robbins et al. of slumming. That didn't stop the play from winning two Tonys and running for over seven hundred performances. Film rights were snatched up by Seven Arts Productions, a partnership between producer Eliot Hyman and agent Ray Stark. When their distribution deal with United Artists foundered, the studio turned to the Mirisch Company to develop this and two other projects.

After seeing the play, producer Walter Mirisch was intent on using Jerome Robbins as director, and equally intent on hiring Robert Wise as protection. Wise brought in Ernest Lehman, his screenwriter on *Executive Suite* (1954). As he did with *The Sound of Music* (1965), Lehman "opened up" the play by placing scenes within real locations. He positioned the "Gee, Officer Krupke" song in the first act instead of after the gang murders, a decision Sondheim later objected to, and moved "I Feel Pretty" and "Cool" as well.

Mirisch rejected Kert and Lawrence as "too old" for the movie. Natalie Wood was considered, dropped, and then cast again as Maria. During the production she believed that her singing would end up in the film, but her songs were dubbed by Marni Nixon. No one seemed very happy with hiring Richard Beymer, who had been working primarily in television. (His voice was dubbed by Jim Bryant.) Apart from Wood and Rita Moreno, the latter typecast as the hot-blooded Anita, Russ Tamblyn was the most recognizable face in the cast. Playing Riff, he was given several opportunities to show off his acrobatic skills.

Robbins didn't like the idea of filming on real locations until he saw the crumbling tenements at the future site of New York's Lincoln Center. Now he wanted everything done outside. Bernstein wrote a new "Prologue" that introduced the Jets and Sharks prowling the streets, playgrounds, and vacant lots of Manhattan's West Side.

These opening scenes are the most incongruous moments in the film today. The sight of clean-cut, well-dressed "hoodlums" pirouetting on building rubble, or carefully faking fistfights, gives the first few minutes of *West Side Story* an artificiality that is hard to overcome. Robbins later insisted on intrusive lighting techniques in some of the numbers. These isolated Maria and Tony in frames otherwise crowded with dancers, or surrounded the couple with a golden, fuzzy glow. (Similar tricks were being used in *The Music Man*, 1961, perhaps inspired by the film of *South Pacific*, 1958.)

But when it works, *West Side Story* is as dazzling a combination of music, lyrics, and dance as the musical form can achieve. Robbins ended up filming only four sequences—the "Prologue," "Cool," "America," and "I Feel Pretty"—before he was fired by Walter Mirisch and his brother Harold. (His choreography was used for the other numbers.) Wise and Lehman would incorporate much of what they learned here in filming *The Sound of Music* (1965), notably opening the film by descending from the heavens.

The film opened at the Rivoli Theater in New York on October 18, 1961. Its view of troubled teens who only need guidance to find happiness was exactly what old-line critics wanted to see. *Variety* trumpeted an "emotion-ridden and violent musical." "Here is juvenile delinquency in its worst and most dangerous sense," the review added, although other writers bemoaned the film's "frenzied hokum." *West Side Story* won a total of ten Academy Awards. Its soundtrack spawned three pop hits on AM radio. Productions of the play continue around the world.

Flower Drum Song

Universal International, 1961. Sound, color, 2.35. 131 minutes.
Cast: Nancy Kwan (Linda Low), James Shigeta (Wang Ta), Benson Fong (Wang Chi-Yang), Jack Soo (Sammy Fong), Juanita Hall (Madame Liang), Reiko Sato (Helen Chao), Patrick Adiarte (Wang San), Kam Tong (Doctor Li), Victor Sen Yung (Frankie Wing), Soo Yong (Madame Ten Fong), Ching Wah Lee (Professor), James Hong (Headwaiter), Miyoshi Umeki (Mei Li).
Credits: Directed by Henry Koster. Screenplay by Joseph Fields. Based on the novel *The Flower Drum Song* by C.Y. Lee. Produced by Ross Hunter. Music by Richard Rodgers. Lyrics by Oscar Hammerstein, 2nd. Director of photography: Russell Metty. Costumes: Irene Sharaff. Choreography by Hermes Pan. Original title paintings by Dong Kingman. Music supervised and conducted by Alfred Newman. Associate: Ken Darby. Art directors: Alexander Golitzen, Joseph Wright. Set decorations: Howard Bristol. Technical advisors: H.K. Wong, Albert Lim. Sound: Waldon O. Watson, Joe Lapis. Unit production manager: Norman Deming. Produced in association with Fields Productions. Dialogue coach: Leon Charles. Script supervisor: Marshall Wolins. Film editor: Milton Carruth. Make-up: Bud Westmore. Hair stylist: Larry Germain. Assistant director: Phil Bowles. Photographic lenses by Panavision. Titles executed by Pacific Title. Westrex Recording System.

Technicolor. A Universal-International presentation of a Ross Hunter production, in association with Joseph Fields.
Additional Cast: Spencer Chan (Dr. Chou), Arthur Song (Dr. Fong), Weaver Levy (Policeman), Herman Rudin (Holdup man), Robert Kino (Bank manager), Jon Fong (Square dance caller).
Additional Credits: Premiered in New York City on November 9, 1961.
Available: Universal DVD (2006). ISBN: 0-7832-9995-8. UPC: 0-25192-41902-7.

Born in Hunan, China, in 1917, Chin Yang Lee came to the United States as a foreign exchange student and graduated from the Yale Drama School. He moved to San Francisco's Chinatown, where he edited a Cantonese newspaper while living in a small room over a Filipino nightclub. After winning a short story contest, he was able to sell his first novel, *The Flower Drum Song*. According to playwright

David Henry Hwang, it was the first Chinese American-novel to be released by an established publishing house, and represented "the birth of a new literary genre."

The Flower Drum Song detailed the clash of cultures and generations, the loss of tradition, and the pangs of assimilation, but it also told the stories of authentic, appealing Chinese Americans grappling with day-to-day life. By turns funny, caustic, and sensual, it brought a new world of Chinese art and folklore to mainstream readers.

Lee's agent Ann Elmo sold rights to the book to theatrical producer Joseph Fields, one of three children of veteran stage performer Lew Fields. (Joseph's brother Herbert contributed books for such notable plays as Up in Central Park and Annie Get Your Gun; his sister Dorothy was the first woman to win a songwriting Oscar, for Swing Time's "The Way You Look Tonight") He brought the project to Oscar Hammerstein II, who agreed to collaborate on a stage adaptation. Hammerstein also showed it to his partner Richard Rodgers, who had worked with both Herbert and Dorothy Fields back in his days with Lorenz Hart.

The three changed the novel considerably, introducing the character of Sammy Fong, a wisecracking gambler and owner of the Celestial Gardens nightclub, and changing Linda Low from a flighty party girl to a showgirl dating Sammy. The central plot remained similar: Americanized college student Wang Ta chases women while his conservative father wants him to settle down and marry a girl from the Chinese mainland. Love comes in the form of Mei Li, a servant in the book and a stowaway and "picture bride" in the play.

All three of the collaborators were seriously ill during the writing of Flower Drum Song. Fields suffered a heart attack in October 1958, a month after rehearsals began. Hammerstein had both his gall bladder and his prostate removed. Rodgers was recovering from a breakdown, and his wife was in a hospital due to alcoholism. The toll is evident in both the book and the score. For much of the play, C.Y. Lee's incisive writing is turned into ethnic humor that wouldn't have been out of place in a Weber and Fields skit. While Rodgers and Hammerstein continued the research into Asian music they had begun in The King and I, they also returned to styles and ideas that had worked for them before. Bits and pieces of Oklahoma!, South Pacific and Carousel swirl in and out of Flower Drum Song, whch at other times seems like a dry run for The Sound of Music.

In Rodgers' autobiography, you can sense his frustration at the compromises reached for the play. None of the leads was Chinese American, perhaps because of the attitude expressed by casting director Eddie Blum: "The problem is that Asians are generally very poor actors because they are too shy." Rodgers wanted Yul Brynner to direct the play, but hired Gene Kelly because of Brynner's film commitments. "It wasn't one of Rodgers and Hammerstein's best shows," Kelly said later, deciding that he had to cram it full of "every joke and gimmick in the book." While the play ran on Broadway for six hundred performances, it received mixed reviews.

Rodgers thought Miyoshi Umeki, who played Mei Li, had "a slight but adequate voice." She was one of the few stage actors signed to the film version, which didn't begin until after the Broadway run of the play had ended. (Juanita Hall, an African-American who played the imperious Madame Laing, and Patrick Adiarte as Ta's baseball-enthused younger brother were two other veterans of the stage production. Hall had also played Bloody Mary in South Pacific.)

Producer Ross Hunter suggested casting Nancy Kwan as Linda Low. A Hong Kong native, Kwan studied ballet in England, where she was discovered by Ray Stark, who cast her in The World of Suzie Wong (1960). Kwan's singing voice was dubbed by B.J. Baker. Singing for Reiko Sato, who played seamstress Helen Chao, was future opera star Marilyn Horne. James Shigeta was born in Hawaii to Japanese parents. He was a star in Japanese musicals, and had parts in Hollywood thrillers before being cast as Wang Ta. This was comedian Jack Soo's film debut; he would go on to a long career on television.

On stage, Kelly had worked with choreographer Carol Haney. For the film version, Hunter and director Henry Koster turned to Hermes Pan, Fred Astaire's longtime collaborator. Pan may account for the long, uninterrupted takes in the production numbers, a characteristic of the work he did with Astaire. Koster was born in Berlin in 1905, and fled Germany during the rise of Nazism. Along with friend and producer Joe Pasternak, he played a key role in the career of singer Deanna Durbin. He also directed the first CinemaScope feature, The Robe (1953), so he was well suited for both musical and widescreen directing.

For a young David Henry Hwang, who wrote an updated stage version of Flower Drum Song that opened on Broadway in 2002, the movie was a guilty pleasure. On its release, the *Variety* critic complained about the "sheer opulence and glamour" in an otherwise "unaffecting, unstable, and rather undistinguished experience."

Rodgers didn't bother to mention the film in his autobiography, and the best songs in the score— "I Enjoy Being a Girl," "Love Look Away," and "Don't Marry Me"—became famous in other settings.

The Man Who Shot Liberty Valance

Strother Martin, left, and Lee Marvin, unapologetic villains in *The Man Who Shot Liberty Valance*.

Paramount, 1962. Sound, B&W, 1.66. 123 minutes.

Cast: John Wayne (Tom Doniphon), James Stewart (Ransom Stoddard), Vera Miles (Hallie), Lee Marvin (Liberty Valance), Edmond O'Brien (Dutton Peabody), Andy Devine (Link Appleyard), Ken Murray (Doc Willoughby), John Carradine (Cassius Starbuckle), Jeanette Nolan (Nola Ericson), John Qualen (Peter Ericson), Willis Bouchey (Jason Tully), Carleton Young (Maxwell Scott), Woody Strode (Pompey), Denver Pyle (Amos Carruthers), Strother Martin (Floyd), Lee Van Cleef (Reese), Robert F. Simon (Handy Strong), O.Z. Whitehead (Ben Carruthers), Paul Birch (Mayor Winder), Joseph Hoover (Hasbrouck).

Credits: Directed by John Ford. Screenplay by James Warner Bellah and Willis Goldbeck. Based on the story by Dorothy M. Johnson. Produced by Willis Goldbeck. Director of photography: William H. Clothier. Music scored by Cyril Mockridge. Conducted by Irvin Talbot. Art direction: Hal Pereira, Eddie Imazu. Edited by Otho Lovering. Process photography: Farcio Edouart. Set decoration: Sam Comer, Darrell Silvera. Assistant director: Wingate Smith. Costumes by Edith Head. Makeup supervision: Wally Westmore. Hair style supervision: Nellie Manley. Sound recording by Philip Mitchell, Charles Grenzbach. Westrex Recording System.

Additional Cast: Jack Pennick (Bartender), Anna Lee (Stagecoach passenger), Charles Seel (Election Council president), Shug Fisher (Drunk), Danny Borzage.

Additional Credits: Music from *Young Mr. Lincoln*: Alfred Newman. Released April 22, 1962.

Available: Paramount DVD (2001). ISBN: 0-7921-7266-3. UPC: 0-9736-06114-4-1.

According to biographer Joseph McBride, director John Ford purchased the rights to the short story "The Man Who Shot Liberty Valance" by Dorothy M. Johnson for $7,500, assigning screenwriters James Warner Bellah and Willis Goldbeck to adapt it in March 1961. Johnson was one of the most highly regarded Western writers of the time; her novella "The Hanging Tree" had been filmed

successfully in 1959. "Liberty Valance," which appeared in *Cosmopolitan* in 1949 and which was anthologized in *Indian Country* in 1953, was a stark morality tale in which one man accepts the rewards for another's actions, in the process ruining the true hero's life. Told in short, spare vignettes, the story captured a frontier world with few absolutes besides evil and death, one in which consequences haunt anyone with a conscience.

Coming from a wealthy background, Bellah taught English at Columbia, won fencing titles in Europe, crewed on the first regular mail flights, and wrote fast-paced, brittle adventures. His short stories formed the basis of all three films in Ford's "cavalry trilogy," but as his son James, Jr., told McBride, "I think my father had great contempt for Ford, not as an artist but from a social standpoint." (He also said his father was "a fascist, a racist, and a world-class bigot.") Bellah wrote some screenplays for Ford, but the director usually had other writers rework them, often reversing Bellah's original themes.

Willis Goldbeck entered films in the 1920s as a screenwriter, adapting the 1924 version of *Peter Pan*. He later wrote several entries in MGM's "Dr. Kildare" series. An occasional director and producer, he was nearing retirement when he teamed with Bellah for Ford's *Sergeant Rutledge* (1960).

Working under Ford's close supervision, Goldbeck and Bellah fleshed out Johnson's story with several roles for the director's stock characters, notably a heavy drinking newspaper editor and a black servant. They also added a veneer of Irish sentimentality that marred many of Ford's films.

For *Liberty Valance*, the director wanted John Wayne to play Tom Doniphon (Bert Barricune in Johnson's story), the rancher whose dreams are thwarted when he reluctantly helps a stranger. That meant placing the project at Paramount, where Wayne had just signed a contract. The studio put up half of the $3.2 million budget. James Stewart, whose Ransom Stoddard eventually becomes a Senator, received less than half of Wayne's salary in return for half ownership of the film and first billing in all advertising. (The screenwriters elevated the status of Stewart's character, who is a near-penniless drifter in Johnson's story.)

The other actors had either worked with Ford before (like Andy Devine, John Carradine, Vera Miles, Woody Strode, and John Qualen), or were replacing performers who were no longer available (e.g., Edmond O'Brien giving an impersonation of Thomas Mitchell). Or they were part of a younger generation of character actors who specialized in bad guys, like Lee Van Cleef, Strother Martin, and the outstanding Lee Marvin. (Marvin had starred in *The Missouri Traveler*, a 1958 coming-of-age drama produced by Ford's son Patrick.)

It had been six years since Ford directed *The Searchers*, and while he made three subsequent Westerns, *The Man Who Shot Liberty Valance* would be his way of summing up the genre that gave him his start back in 1917. It is a film about artifice, about shaping myths by discarding facts, about the price our society paid for "taming" the wilderness. It is also, sadly, the work of an elderly man. Ford worked almost entirely on sets and the Paramount backlot. He filmed in black-and-white instead of color, telling interviewers later that he wanted the shadows and darkness that the process brought. In reality, black-and-white was much cheaper, and would disguise the extensive makeup required by the stars to play young men.

The most famous line in the film was delivered by Carleton Young, playing editor Maxwell Scott: "This is the West, sir. When the legend becomes fact, print the legend." As director and writer Peter Bogdanovich pointed out, Ford is doing the opposite in this film, "printing" the fact and not the legend behind Ranse Stoddard's life. It's an arbitrary distinction, as both Ford and Dorothy Johnson were more interested in story rather than history, using facts as details, not as plotlines.

Like many other directors of his age (he was sixty-seven at time of filming), Ford knew what he wanted but had lost confidence in his artistic judgment. He returned to his earlier successes, even if it meant retreating to the stiff staging and acting of a previous generation. He even eschewed the title song, replacing it with a musical theme from *Young Mr. Lincoln* (1939). ("The Man Who Shot Liberty Valance," written by Burt Bacharach and Hal David, became a pop hit for Gene Pitney.) The world had changed around Ford. A film like *Ride the High Country*, released a few months later, served as more of a valedictory than Ford's ornery, angular take on the frontier. (It also featured color, exteriors, and stars acting their age.)

Critics were dismissive of *The Man Who Shot Liberty Valance* (*Variety* said that the filmmakers "overplayed their hands."), although it did well enough at the box office. It was only after writers reached a consensus on Ford's importance as a director that the film was re-evaluated. Now, according to McBride, it is "the most important American film of the 1960s." It is certainly one of the most melancholy, suffused with remorse and the sense of imminent mortality.

Ride the High Country

MGM, 1962. Sound, color, 2.35. 94 minutes.

Cast: Randolph Scott (Gil Westrum), Joel McCrea (Steve Judd), Mariette Hartley (Elsa Knudsen), Ron Starr (Heck Longtree), Edgar Buchanan (Judge Tolliver), R.G. Armstrong (Joshua Knudsen), Jenie Jackson (Kate), James Drury (Billy Hammond), L.Q. Jones (Sylvus Hammond), John Anderson (Elder Hammond), John Davis Chandler (Jimmy Hammond), Warren Oates (Henry Hammond).

Credits: Directed by Sam Peckinpah. Written by N.B. Stone, Jr. Produced by Richard E. Lyons. Music composed and conducted by George Bassman. Director of photography: Lucien Ballard. Art direction: George W. Davis and Leroy Coleman. Set decoration: Henry Grace, Otto Siegel. Color consultant: Charles K. Hagedon. Film editor: Frank Santillo. Assistant director: Hal Polaire. Hair styles by Mary Keats. Make-up by William Tuttle. Recording supervisor: Franklin Milton. Photographic lenses by Panavision. In CinemaScope and Metrocolor. Westrex Recording System.

Additional Cast: Carmen Phillips (Saloon girl), Percy Helton (Luther Sampson).

Additional Credits: Screenwriting: Robert Creighton Williams, Sam Peckinpah. Released May 1962.

Randolph Scott and Joel McCrea in Sam Peckinpah's Western *Ride the High Country*.

Available: Warner Home Video DVD (2006). ISBN: 0-7907-9229-x. UPC: 0-12569-69072-1.

When it was released in 1962, *Ride the High Country* was the second feature in a double bill with *The Tartars*, a long-forgotten Italian swordfighting epic. Good reviews and festival awards helped the film's prospects, but *Ride the High Country* suffered from MGM's weak advertising and from a market that was shifting away from Westerns. Later it was championed as a sort of elegy for the entire genre, part of a cycle of movies that questioned the meaning and purpose of Westerns. *Lonely Are the Brave* and *The Man Who Shot Liberty Valance* appeared the same year; the year before, John Huston and playwright Arthur Miller tried to demolish Western stereotypes with *The Misfits*.

Ride the High Country does have its elegiac elements, including valedictory performances from Joel McCrea and Randolph Scott that rank among the best in their careers, and a story filled with anger and regret over aging. But it is just as notable as perhaps the best film by maverick director Sam Peckinpah. Born in Fresno, California, in 1926, Peckinpah came from a distinguished background, but his youth was marked by violent outbursts and incipient alcoholism. After serving with the Marines in China during World War II, he received a master degree in drama at the University of Southern California.

Peckinpah had menial jobs in television before he was hired as a dialogue director by Don Siegel. Always ambitious, he offered to rewrite scripts, and even appeared as a meter reader in *Invasion of the Body Snatchers* (1956). As many did during that unsettled period, Peckinpah shifted from films back to television, where he wrote scripts and directed episodes for *Gunsmoke*, *The Westerner* (a series he helped create), and others. When *The Westerner*

was canceled, one of its stars helped Peckinpah get a job directing his first feature, an unremarkable Western called *The Deadly Companions* (1961).

Peckinpah then read *Guns in the Afternoon*, a screenplay being packaged by Richard Lyons. Lyons had produced four B-Westerns for Twentieth Century-Fox, but *Guns in the Afternoon* was different, a strong story about two aging lawmen who escort a gold shipment from a mining town in the mountains back to the city. After working with writers N.B. Stone, Jr., and Robert Creighton Williams, Lyons sent the script out to Joel McCrea and Randolph Scott.

Scott later said he got the script through his friend and collaborator Burt Kennedy, who had worked with him on his previous film, *Comanche Station* (1960). McCrea was hesitant about accepting the project. "If I was going to make one more picture," he told his biographer, "I wasn't going to destroy my image with it." One of the enduring stars of Hollywood, McCrea made romances and comedies in the 1930s and '40s (notably *Sullivan's Travels* in 1941), followed by straightforward, uncomplicated roles as decent men in generally undistinguished Westerns. The two stars ended up switching their parts, with Scott basically playing a continuation of the grizzled, unpredictable characters from his series of Ranown films directed by Budd Boetticher (such as *The Tall T*, 1957).

Lyons hired Peckinpah (for $12,000) after screening episodes of *The Westerner*. He agreed to let the director rewrite the script; as a result, *Ride the High Country* is filled with names, people, and incidents from the director's life and his family history. The budget was set at $800,000, leaving Peckinpah very little elbow room on a twenty-four-day shooting schedule. However, the low priority the studio gave the film also meant Peckinpah would not be supervised very closely.

With Lyons' support, he pulled together a cast and crew that included colleagues from television, like Warren Oates. They shot for four days in the Sierras near Mammoth Lakes before weather forced them to return to Los Angeles.

A crucial difference between Peckinpah and earlier directors was his background in television, where he learned to use multiple cameras. More than one camera made editing much easier, especially when a director wasn't sure what he wanted. John Ford or Alfred Hitchcock would work out scenes beforehand and shoot only what was needed. Peckinpah preferred shooting from as many angles as possible, and then editing scenes together from the best footage. As biographer David Weddle noted, the final shootout in *Ride the High Country* required 150 separate camera set-ups, and took six days to film.

A by-product of this approach was Peckinpah's willingness to cut closer and quicker than prevailing styles. Margaret Booth, the chief editor at MGM, complained that his footage couldn't be edited, but Lyons arranged for Peckinpah to supervise his own version with editor Frank Santillo—who was perfectly willing to pare down to one-frame cuts. "You make the sequence move by allowing the audience to fill in the gaps," he told biographer Garner Simmons. "Some of the shots were only six frames long, and I said to Sam that even at that length some of them would appear too long on the screen." These "flash cuts" became a hallmark of Peckinpah's career. On the other hand, Lyons complained years later that, "If he had his way, Peckinpah'd still be cutting that show this week."

MGM's management changed during post-production of *Ride the High Country*, and president Joseph Vogel wound up hating the film so much that he barred Peckinpah from the studio. Lyons finished work on it and supervised what is generally regarded as an overly intrusive score.

But the more perceptive critics could see something in *Ride the High Country* that was missing from most other Westerns of the period. The story acknowledged the passing of the West, and by implication the passing of a previous generation of performers and filmmakers. But it still believed in the basic truths of the genre: issues of morality, the necessity for hard choices, the temptations of evil. To say nothing of the power of the landscape, the professionalism and grace of iconic Western stars, and the satisfaction of the Western's basic narrative elements. Peckinpah's respect for the genre and its intricacies may be the most surprising element of the film today. If *Ride the High Country* is elegiac, recalling all the extraordinary Westerns of the past, it is also satisfying in a manner Peckinpah never achieved again. It is a film of unexpected emotional turmoil, and what can be seen as a deep, committed spirituality. Much of his future work would address similar topics, such as *The Wild Bunch* (1969).

McCrea would appear in four more Westerns, but in producer Walter Mirisch's opinion, by that time he was more interested in his ranch than in movies. This was Scott's last film. After a career that stretched back to silent movies, he removed himself completely from the industry.

The Music Man

Warner Bros., 1962. Sound, color, 2.00. 151 minutes.

Cast: Robert Preston (Prof. Harold Hill), Shirley Jones (Marian Paroo), Buddy Hackett (Marcellus Washburn), Hermione Gingold (Eulalie MacKenzie Shinn), Paul Ford (Mayor Shinn), Pert Kelton (Mrs. Paroo); The Buffalo Bills (Themselves): Al Shea (Ewart Dunlop), Wayne Ward (Oliver Hix), Vern Reed (Jacey Squires), Bill Spangenberg (Olin Britt); Timmy Everett (Tommy Djilas), Susan Luckey (Zaneeta Shinn), Ronny Howard (Winthrop Paroo), Harry Hickox (Charlie Cowell), Charles Lane (Constable Locke), Mary Wickes (Mrs. Squires), Monique Vermont (Amaryllis Paroo); Sara Seegar, Adnia Rice, Peggy Mondo (Townswomen).

Credits: Produced and directed by Morton Da Costa. Based on Meredith Willson's *The Music Man* with his music and lyrics. Book written in collaboration with Franklin Lacey. Stage play produced by Kermit Bloomgarden with Herbert Greene, in association with Frank Productions, Inc. Screenplay by Marion Hargrove. Director of photography: Robert Burks. Art director: Paul Groesse. Film editor: William Ziegler. Assistant director: Russell Llewellyn. Production supervisor: Joel Freeman. Music supervised and conducted by Ray Heindorf. Choreography by Onna White. Assistant choreographer: Tom Panko. Sound: M.A. Merrick, Dolph Thomas. Set decorator: George James Hopkins. Vocal arrangements: Charles Henderson. Orchestrations: Ray Heindorf, Frank Comstock, Gus Leven. Costume design: Dorothy Jeakins. Makeup supervisor: Gordon Bau. Supervising hair stylist: Jean Burt Reilly. Miss Jones' hair styles: Myrl Stoltz. A Warner Bros. Pictures presentation. Filmed in Technirama [Super Technirama 70] and Technicolor. RCA Sound Recording.

Additional Cast: Ronnie Dapo (Norbert Smith), Jesslyn Fax (Avis Grubb), Patty Lee Hilka (Gracie Shinn), Garry Potter (Dewey), J. Delos Jewkes (Harley MacCauley), Ray Kellogg (Harry Joseph), William Fawcett (Lester Lonnergan), Rance Howard (Oscar Jackson), Roy Dean (Gilbert Hawthorne), David Swain (Chet Glanville), Arthur Mills (Herbert Malthouse), Rand Barker (Duncan Shyball), Jeannine Burnier (Jessie Shyball), Shirley Claire (Amy Dakin), Natalie Core (Truthful Smith),

Shirley Jones and Robert Preston in *The Music Man*.

Therese Lyon (Dolly Higgins), Penelope Martin (Lila O'Brink), Barbara Pepper (Feril Hawkes), Anne Loos (Stella Jackson), Peggy Wynne (Ada Nutting), Hank Worden (Undertaker), Milton Parsons (Farmer), Natalie Masters (Farmer's wife), Maudie Prickett (Townswoman), Percy Helton (Conductor); Casey Adams, Charles Perchesky (Salesmen).

Additional Credits: Full Title: *Meredith Willson's The Music Man*. Sound supervisor: George R. Groves. Casting: Hoyt Bowers. Opened June 19, 1962.

Awards: Oscar for Best Music—Scoring of Music, Adaptation or Treatment (Ray Heindorf).

Other Versions: Remade for television in 2003, directed by Jeff Bleckner.

Available: Warner Home Video DVD (1999). ISBN: 0-7907-?815-5. UPC: 0-85391-67682-9.

Born in Mason City, Iowa, in 1902, Meredith Willson entered the music business playing the piccolo in the John Philip Sousa Band, a story he recounted at length in his memoirs. But Willson also attended what later became the Juilliard School of Music and played the flute with the Philharmonic Society of New York under Arturo Toscanini. In the 1930s, he conducted several radio orchestras while writing soundtracks for movies, including Chaplin's *The Great Dictator* (1940). During World War II, he was the head of the music division for the Armed Forces Radio Service. He also composed the best-selling pop hits "May the Good Lord Bless You and Keep You" and "You and I."

Willson spent eight years writing *The Music Man*, an affectionate, comic musical about a con artist operating in River City, a place much like his hometown. While he received encouragement and financial help from composer Frank Loesser, Willson wrote the music, lyrics, libretto, and a great deal of the story himself. "I had never tried to write a musical comedy, and it didn't come easy," he said in 1980. "I guess I must have done 30 or 40 full rewrites before I got it right." (Loesser's Frank Productions invested in the play; his Frank Music published Willson's songs.)

The writing may have been difficult, but not the subject matter. "I didn't have to make anything up for *The Music Man*," Willson said. "All I had to do was remember." He drew on everything from ragtime to Irish jigs in his musical vision of America. Many of the show's songs have entered the fabric of our culture: not just the brash "Seventy Six Trombones," but the tour de force "Trouble (in River City)" and the soaring "Till There Was You" (covered by the Beatles, among others).

Willson had considered appearing in the play himself. He also thought about centering the plot around a music teacher. The eventual story, with its blustering politicians, gossiping wives, and burned-out drummers, found its inspiration as much from plays like N. Richard Nash's *The Rainmaker* as from Willson's own life. (He did base the librarian Marian Peroo on his mother.)

Opening on December 19, 1957, *The Music Man* was an immediate hit, running for 1,375 performances and winning several Tonys. One of those Tonys went to star Robert Preston, who like Willson was in his first Broadway musical. His role as Prof. Harold Hill was the breakthrough Preston had been seeking since he dropped out of school at sixteen to study acting. A contract player at Paramount during the 1930s, Preston had been relegated to second leads and supporting roles, sometimes in Cecil B. DeMille's big-budget movies, more often in programmers. After serving in the Air Force during World War II, he turned increasingly to television and to the New York stage. *The Music Man* was a gamble for Preston and for the show's producers, but critics agreed that he captured the slick, deceptive side of Harold Hill as well as the con artist's sentimental core. (Danny Kaye and Gene Kelly had been among those considered for the part.)

The play was a gamble for Warner Brothers as well. The studio, which had missed out on the trend for road show productions, saw *The Music Man* as its chance to show off its resources in a project with a high recognition factor. To buttress their investment, studio executives wanted to cast Frank Sinatra (the actor had also tried to purchase the screen rights himself). Willson, whose contract gave him unusual control over filming, insisted on retaining Preston.

Coming over from the play were choreographer Onna White and director Morton Da Costa. Born in Philadelphia in 1914, Da Costa had been an actor in the 1940s before moving to directing. His project on Broadway before *The Music Man* was *Auntie Mame*; he also directed the 1958 movie version. Although they didn't originate their parts, both Paul Ford and Susan Luckey had played them on stage. The Buffalo Bills, a barbershop quartet, were in the Broadway production, as was Pert Kelton (playing Marian Peroo's mother). The original Alice Kramden on Jackie Gleason's "The Honeymooners," Kelton made her vaudeville debut in 1917, at the age of three. She was a welcome presence in early sound films like Raoul Walsh's *The Bowery* (1933); she had retired from both stage and screen until *The Music Man*.

Shirley Jones, a star in *Oklahoma!* (1955), replaced stage performer Barbara Cook in the film. (The choreography in *Oklahoma!* was an unmistakable influence on Onna White.) In later interviews, Jones marveled over moving from a prostitute in *Elmer Gantry* (1960) to Marian the librarian in this film; she also recalled trying to hide her pregnancy through a series of corsets and carefully designed dresses as production dragged on.

Rehearsals and shooting lasted nine months, in part because some of the routines were so complicated, in part because Da Costa experimented with film techniques that hadn't been seen since the heyday of Busby Berkeley. The big production numbers in *The Music Man* feature hundreds of extras, stretch out over blocks of the studio backlot, and involve several stanzas of tongue-twisting lyrics like, "He's a barefaced double-shuffle two-bit thimble-rigger." Add in Da Costa's use of crane shots and complex tracking schemes, and the fact that neither Preston nor Jones were trained dancers, and the delays involved in completing *The Music Man* are more understandable.

When the film premiered in Mason City, Jones remembered a publicity campaign that evoked the same ballyhoo that the film did, with box socials, fireworks, and marching bands. *The Music Man* was the most successful film of the year for Warners, and one of the last gasps of the big-budget musical—although its success did persuade the studio to embark on an adaptation of *My Fair Lady* (1964). Just a few years later, *Hello, Dolly!* (1969) would fail at the box office, despite settings and songs similar to *The Music Man*. Willson's play, meanwhile, has become a favorite of amateur and dinner-theater groups. It was revived on Broadway in 1980 and 2001.

The Manchurian Candidate

United Artists, 1962. Sound, B&W, 1.85. 126 minutes.

Cast: Frank Sinatra (Maj. Bennett Marco), Laurence Harvey (Raymond Shaw), Janet Leigh (Eugenie Rose Chaney), Angela Lansbury (Eleanor Iselin), Henry Silva (Chun Jin), James Gregory (Sen. John Iselin), Leslie Parrish (Jocelyn Jordan), John McGiver (Sen. Thomas Jordan), Khigh Dhiegh (Dr. Yen Lo), James Edwards (Cpl. Allen Melvin), Douglas Henderson (Col. Milt), Albert Paulsen (Zilkov), Barry Kelley, Lloyd Corrigan (Holborn Gaines), Madame Spivy (Berezovo).

Credits: Directed by John Frankenheimer. Screenplay: George Axelrod. Based upon a Novel by Richard Condon. Produced by George Axelrod and John Frankenheimer. Executive producer: Howard W. Koch. Director of photography: Lionel Lindon. Production designer: Richard Sylbert. Film editor: Ferris Webster. Music composed and conducted by David Amram. Assistant director: Joseph Behm. Assistant film editor: Carl Mahakian. Costumes by Moss Mabry. Janet Leigh's hair styles by Gene Shacove. Assistant art director: Philip M. Jefferies. Set decorator: George R. Nelson. Dialogue coach: Thom Conroy. Operative cameraman: John Mehl. Costumer: Wesley V. Jefferies. Property master: Arden Cripe. Hair stylist: Mary Westmoreland. Makeup artists: Bernard Ponedel, Jack Freeman, Ron Berkeley. Special effects: Paul Pollard. Sound mixer: Joe Edmondson. Script supervisor: Amalia Wade. Sound effects editor: Del Harris. Music editor: Richard Carruth. Re-recording: Buddy Myers. Music recording: Vinton Vernon. Photographic effects: Howard Anderson Co.

Additional Cast: Merritt Bohn (Jilly), Mimi Dillard (Mrs. Melvin), Helen Kleeb (Mrs. Henry Whitaker), Richard LePore (Pvt. Edmund Mavole), Tom Lowell (Pvt. Bobby Lembeck).

Additional Credits: Released October 24, 1962. Rated PG-13 in 1988.

Other Versions: *The Manchurian Candidate* (2004), directed by Jonathan Demme. John Lahr wrote a play adaptation that was staged in England in 1991.

Available: MGM Home Entertainment DVD (2004). ISBN: 0-7928-6158-2. UPC: 0-27616-91113-1.

Richard Condon's career included stints as a hotel clerk, waiter, and five years as a publicist for Walt Disney Pictures. Ulcers made him drop out of the publicity profession after two decades. Then, at the age of forty-two, he wrote his first novel. His second book, *The Manchurian Candidate*, was published in 1959 to strong reviews. A best-seller, it disguised relatively serious themes of political corruption, consumer and military brainwashing, and Cold War espionage with lurid sexual subplots and sadistic violence. Condon considered the book a satire; he also said his fast-paced plotting and visual writing style were the result of having screened 10,000 films.

Hollywood for the most part ignored the book, which had many censorable elements. But screenwriter George Axelrod, who had just earned an Academy Award nomination for adapting Truman Capote's *Breakfast at Tiffany's* (1962), persuaded director John Frankenheimer that it was a novel worth pursuing. The two put up $10,000 to option the screen rights. Frankenheimer thought that the story captured the hysteria that gripped politics during the McCarthy era, and wanted those parallels within Condon's book emphasized.

Frankenheimer, born in 1930, began working in film while still in the Air Force. After contributing to documentaries, he joined CBS as an assistant director. He replaced Sidney Lumet on *You Are There*, and built a reputation as one of the most exciting directors in live television. As director William Friedkin said later, "He invented the way live television drama was shot and no one ever did it better than him." The commercial success of *Birdman of Alcatraz* (1962) gave him leeway to take on a more controversial project.

It was up to Frank Sinatra to secure financing for the film. The singer had appeared in a string of poorly received movies, many involving his "Rat Pack" friends, but he still had a contract with United Artists and the muscle to push nervous executives into agreeing to the film. Sinatra later suggested that he received approval from President John F. Kennedy, a fan of the book, saying that Kennedy wanted to know who would play the mother. According to film historian Rob Nixon, Sinatra thought the role should go to Lucille Ball.

Instead, Frankenheimer and Axelrod cast Angela Lansbury, an accomplished stage and screen veteran whose biggest problem during her film career was the ease with which she stole scenes from higher billed costars. Although she was only three years older than Laurence Harvey, she played his mother with an authority and conviction that were mesmerizing. Against her initial wishes, she agreed to Frankenheimer's request to kiss Harvey full on the lips in their last scene. Axelrod was leery of incorporating the book's explicit incest (a prevalent theme in best-sellers of the time). As Sinatra

said, "She put a period onto the whole idea, 'Is she or isn't she?'—the whole point" of the book.

Axelrod was stymied by many aspects of the novel, and found himself resorting to screenwriting techniques he didn't like: voice-overs, flashbacks, etc. Sinatra was key here as well. When he demanded to see a script, Axelrod had to finish some sixty pages over a weekend. Axelrod and Frankenheimer agreed that some changes—removing the mother's heroin addiction, for example, adding a black character to the platoon in the story, and altering the ending to make Harvey's character more heroic—were necessary. However, as Frankenheimer said years later, "We set out to do Dick Condon's book, and that's what we did."

Frankenheimer was forced to shoot Sinatra's material first, since the actor was available for only fifteen days. The director wanted a documentary look, and staged several shots in cars and at Madison Square Garden with handheld cameras. He also had Harvey jump into the boat pond at Central Park on one of the coldest days of the winter. But Frankenheimer didn't mind fudging material when it helped his film. He combined shots from Madison Square Garden with others taken in an arena in Los Angeles, where he had more extras to work with.

Like the book, which careens through several writing styles, Frankenheimer employed a variety of techniques in making the film. A pre-credit Army patrol and a Congressional hearing later in the story are filmed with documentary precision. A brainwashing sequence early in the movie features a 360-degree pan, remarkable enough in itself, but even more impressive because Frankenheimer uses it to dismember reality. The scene ends up incorporating three different versions of "truth," then starts to bleed one into the other until it seems as if everything is a hallucination. Frankenheimer employs jarring jump cuts and montages, but also lets scenes play out in single takes that can last over a minute. As Lansbury said, "He loved using every trick of the trade, he relished that." For deep-focus shots, "it was terribly important that we understood that we were in this position" in the frame. "John was not a Method director, but he directed with such passion that you couldn't help but be drawn into his web of enthusiasm."

The director drew explicit connections between Senator Johnny Iselin (played by James Gregory) and Senator Joe McCarthy, having the actor imitate McCarthy's blustering bravado and repeat his catch phrases. Other themes were treated more subtly—the suggestion that society is being brainwashed by television, for example. Alfred Hitchcock was an admitted influence on Frankenheimer; so was Jean-Luc Godard. But his style in *The Manchurian Candidate* ends up being his own. Frankenheimer and Axelrod offer a nightmare world rooted in realistic detail, one whose savvy about how society operates was far more advanced that what Hollywood usually presented in its social critiques. Not even Hitchcock wanted to be this cynical.

The film received good reviews when it opened, but it was not a popular success (Lansbury did win a Best Supporting Actress nomination). A year later, after the assassination of President Kennedy, the film became a liability rather than an asset. United Artists withdrew it from circulation, and although it was later broadcast on television, the film became extremely difficult to see. Details about what actually happened to it are murky. One biography claims that Sinatra bought the rights in 1972 and withdrew the film completely in 1975. In 1988 the singer authorized a commercial rerelease, and also gave the remake rights to his daughter Tina, who was a producer of the 2004 version.

Of the people associated with the film, Angela Lansbury fared the best. Her role revitalized her career, which later extended into television and triumphant stage appearances. Harvey died of a heart attack at the age of forty-five, Sinatra had trouble establishing a career in serious films, and Frankenheimer suffered through several years of alcoholism.

How the West Was Won

MGM, 1962. Sound, color, 2.59. 164 minutes.

Cast: Carroll Baker (Eve Prescott Rawlings), Lee J. Cobb (Marshal Lou Ramsey), Henry Fonda (Jethro Stuart), Carolyn Jones (Julie Rawlings), Karl Malden (Zeb Prescott), Gregory Peck (Cleve van Valen), George Peppard (Zeb Rawlings II), Robert Preston (Roger Morgan), Debbie Reynolds (Lilith "Lily" Prescott), James Stewart (Linus Rawlings), Eli Wallach (Charlie Gant), John Wayne (Gen. William Tecumseh Sherman), Richard Widmark (Mike King), Brigid Bazlen (Dora Hawkins), Walter Brennan (Col. Jeb Hawkins), David Brian (Attorney), Andy Devine (Cpl. Peterson), Raymond Massey (Abraham Lincoln), Agnes Moorehead (Rebecca Prescott), Henry (Harry) Morgan (Gen. Ulysses S. Grant), Thelma Ritter (Agatha "Aggie" Clegg), Mickey Shaughnessy (Deputy), Russ Tamblyn (Confederate spy). Narrated by Spencer Tracy.

Credits: "The Civil War" directed by John Ford. "The Railroad" directed by George Marshall. "The Rivers," "The Plains" directed by Henry Hathaway. Written by James R. Webb. Suggested by the series "How the West Was Won" which appeared in *Life* magazine. Produced by Bernard Smith. Directors of photography: William H. Daniels ("The Plains"), Milton Krasner ("The Outlaws"), Charles Lang, Jr. ("The Rivers"), Joseph LaShelle ("The Civil War," "The Railroad"). Art direction: George W. Davis, William Ferrari, Addison Hehr. Set decoration: Henry Grace, Don Greenwood, Jr., Jack Mills. Color consultant: Charles K. Hagedon. Film editor: Harold F. Kress. 2nd unit photography: Harold E. Wellman. Assistant directors: George Marshall, Jr., William McGarry, Robert Saunders, William Shanks, Wingate Smith. Production supervisor for Cinerama: Thomas Conroy. Special visual effects: A. Arnold Gillespie, Robert R. Hoag. Costumes by Walter Plunkett. Hair styles by Sydney Guilaroff. Make-up created by William Tuttle. Music: Alfred Newman. Associate: Ken Darby. Songs: Music by Alfred Newman. "How the West Was Won," lyrics by Ken Darby. "Home in the Meadow," lyrics by Sammy Cahn. "Raise a Ruckus," "Wait for the Hoedown," "What Was Your Name in the States?" lyrics adapted by Johnny Mercer. Folk Singing by Dave Guard and the Whiskeyhill Singers. Music Co-ordinator: Robert Emmett Dolan. Recording supervisor: Franklin Milton. In Metrocolor.

Additional Cast includes: Lee Van Cleef, Ken Curtis, Jay C. Flippen, Harry Dean Stanton, Joe Sawyer, William Wellman Jr.

Additional Credits: Footage directed by Richard Thorpe. Production dates: May 26 to November 30, 1961. Opened February 20, 1963.

Awards: Oscars for Best Writing—Story and Screenplay Written Directly for the Screen, Sound, Film Editing.

Available: Warner Home Video DVD (1999). ISBN: 0-7907-4469-4. UPC: 0-12569-50852-1.

Introduced to the public in 1952, by 1960 the widescreen Cinerama process had been used for a total of five travelogues. While the films were popular, only twelve theaters in the entire country could project them. Cinerama was also competing against other widescreen processes, ones that were substantially cheaper to both film and project. Right from the start the company was in serious danger of folding.

Travelogues were not what producer Merian C. Cooper envisioned for Cinerama. A vice-president and early investor in the company, he wanted the process to revolutionize the film industry the same way Technicolor did. After the opening of *This Is Cinerama* (1952), Cooper even announced to the press that the next Cinerama release would be a Civil War film directed by John Ford (another investor in the company). The rest of the board didn't match his enthusiasm; since *This Is Cinerama* ran for more than two years, they were content to fund more films like it. But by the end of the decade, everyone associated with the company realized that the only way to expand the Cinerama franchise was to produce feature films.

Although he had left the company, Cooper helped engineer a deal with MGM to make four features using Cinerama. What story could stand up to the process itself, could fill that enormous screen and hold viewers' attention? One possibility came from singer Bing Crosby. In 1959, he optioned a collection of articles in *Life* magazine about settling the West, hoping to turn it into a television series to benefit St. John's Hospital in Santa Monica. When the television series proved too complicated, Crosby sold the idea to MGM, with the provision that the studio would honor his commitment to St. John's.

Sol Siegel, the production chief at MGM at the time, planned *How the West Was Won* as the first in the studio's four-picture deal with Cinerama. (He simultaneously started production on *The Wonderful World of the Brothers Grimm*, which ended up opening first). He assigned the project to producer Bernard Smith, an editor-in-chief at Alfred A. Knopf before becoming a story editor for Samuel Goldwyn Pictures. Smith hired screenwriter James R. Webb. Born in 1909, Webb wrote magazine articles before becoming a screenwriter in Hollywood in the 1930s. At first he specialized in Roy Rogers vehicles, but after World War II he took on bigger assignments like *Vera Cruz* (1954) and *The Big Country* (1958).

Webb's crucial contribution was to focus the *Life* articles' vague observations about frontier life onto a single family, the Prescotts. His script followed three generations as they encountered just about every significant incident in the Wild West. Webb reduced the basic plot to six segments: riverboat transportation, the covered wagon migration, the Civil War, how the railroad tamed the frontier, cattle drives, and the rise and fall of gunfighters. (The cattle drives proved too expensive, and were dropped.)

Smith hired the film's three directors. John Ford shot the Civil War material; George Marshall, the railroad; and Henry Hathaway the remaining three. (Richard Thorpe added some transitional footage, but wasn't credited.) Casting was handled by St. John's boosters, who persuaded stars to appear at a fixed salary of $5,000 per week. In a certain sense, this was the best cast that money could buy in 1962. On the other hand, most of the performers were screen veterans who agreed to help out because they had already worked with each other; almost all of them were too old for their roles. Debbie Reynolds, the film's love interest and a dance hall singer, had been playing similar parts for over a decade. According to his biographer Gary Fishgall, Gregory Peck, who was lured into the project by Irene Dunne, was instrumental in getting MGM to raise St. John's profit participation from 5 to 10 percent. John Wayne appeared out of deference to his one-time mentor, John Ford; Wayne's role as General Sherman is extremely small, and he has only a handful of lines.

Most of the footage in the film was directed by Henry Hathaway, like his codirectors Ford and Marshall, a one-time prop boy at Universal. Born in 1898 in Sacramento, Hathaway, the son of an actress, entered film as a child actor in Westerns. After serving in the military during World War I, he worked as an assistant director for a decade before helming B-Westerns. Hathaway built his reputation by working fast and without ostentation. His best films, like *The Dark Corner* (1946) and *Kiss of Death* (1947), were simple, direct, and very successful with mainstream audiences. He had just completed the burly *North to Alaska* (1960) with John Wayne and Stewart Granger, and would subsequently direct Wayne in his Oscar-winning performance in *True Grit* (1969).

Since directing *Destry Rides Again* in 1939, George Marshall had gone on to a solid career specializing in musicals and comedies. Like most veteran directors, he turned increasingly to Westerns in the 1950s, including a remake, *Destry* (1954), with Audie Murphy. He directed *West's* closing sequence, which combined elements of *High Noon* (1952) and *3:10 to Yuma* (1957) with a rousing climax on a runaway train. Along with a similar sequence in Hathaway's "River" segment, in which a raft splits apart descending white-water rapids, and the justly acclaimed buffalo stampede, the train footage made the best use of Cinerama's visual strengths.

At twenty-two minutes, Ford's sequence is the darkest in the film. He shot it in May and June of 1961, both on location near Paducah, Kentucky, and at the MGM ranch in Simi Valley. Ford worked with cinematographer Joseph LaShelle to counteract one of the most visually obtrusive aspects of Cinerama, the two vertical lines that marked where the images from the three projectors overlapped. Ford used fence posts, trees, and other vertical elements to try to block out the lines. He also set most of the story, which concerns the Battle of Shiloh, at night, which further disguised the frame marks.

Ford's sequence emphasized the main weakness of *How the West Was Won*, the lack of a fully developed plot. Each segment in the movie feels truncated, almost as if the story was being told in shorthand, with characters and situations that bordered on cliché. MGM, which had committed $15 million to the budget, had its publicity department trumpet the movie's logistics: 5,000 costumes, 77 sets, 12,000 cast members, 630 horses, 150 mules, 2000 buffalo, 203 wranglers, hoping the sheer size of the project would impress moviegoers.

Peck enjoyed working with Hathaway, but had a low opinion of the entire project. He was quoted as saying, "I found it impossible to act realistically in front of that giant machine with three lenses." For one thing, many of the actors in a scene couldn't maintain eye contact with each other. Because the Cinerama screen curved so much, performers had to be angled away from each other to give the illusion that they were talking face-to-face. It was also very difficult to pan or tilt the cameras without distorting vertical elements in the frame. In other words, trees and buildings would appear to "bend" when the cameras passed by them. Generally, directors could only move the Cinerama rig forward or backward.

Filming began in May 1961, with Ford's sequence, and lasted until the following January, covering locations in nine states. It premiered in London in November 1962, and in Los Angeles the following February. Critics were decidedly mixed when the film opened, but audiences loved *How the West Was Won*, making it the top-grossing release of 1963. It also had a strong impact on director Sergio Leone, who cast Eli Wallach in *The Good, the Bad, and the Ugly* (1966) based on his performance here. And Leone's *Once Upon a Time in the West* (1968) borrows some of the visual motifs from Marshall's "Railroad" sequence, among others.

This is the last Cinerama feature to date, and there is little likelihood that another will be made. Although it still has fans, the process has been superceded by other, easier widescreen methods, such as the single-projector Cinerama system employed in 1963's *It's a Mad, Mad, Mad, Mad World*.

Lawrence of Arabia

Columbia, 1962. Sound, color, 2.20. 227 minutes.

Cast: Peter O'Toole ([T.E.] Lawrence), Alec Guinness (Prince Feisal), Anthony Quinn (Auda Abu Tayi), Jack Hawkins (General Allenby), Jose [José] Ferrer (Turkish bey), Anthony Quayle (Colonel [Harry] Brighton), Claude Rains (Mr. Dryden), Arthur Kennedy (Jackson Bentley), I.S. Johar (Gasim), Gamil Ratib (Majid), Michael Ray (Farraj), Zia Mohyeddin (Tafas), John Dimech (Daud), Donald Wolfit (General Murray), Omar Sharif (Sherif Ali [Ibn el Kharish]), Howard Marion Crawford (Medical officer), Jack Gwillim (Club secretary), Hugh Miller (RAMC Colonel).

Credits: Directed by David Lean. Screenplay by Robert Bolt [and Michael Wilson]. Produced by Sam Spiegel. Director of photography: F.A. [Freddie] Young. Music composed by Maurice Jarre. Orchestrations by Gerard Schurmann. Played by The London Philharmonic Orchestra. Conductor: Sir Adrian Boult. Production designed by John Box. Art director: John Stoll. Costume designer: Phyllis Dalton. Editor: Anne V. Coates. Sound editor: Winston Ryder. Second unit direction: Andre Smagghe, Noel Howard. Second unit photography: Skeets Kelly, Nicolas Roeg, Peter Newbrook. Production manager: John Palmer. Location manager: Douglas Twiddy. Casting director: Maude Spector. Set dresser: Dario Simoni. Wardrobe: John Wilson-Appleson. Assistant art directors: R. Rossotte, G. Richardson, E. Marsh, A. Himmington. Property master: Eddie Fowlie. Chief electrician: Archie Dansie. Camera operator: Ernest Day. Assistant director: Roy Stevens. Continuity: Barbara Cole. Sound recording: Paddy Cunningham. Sound dubbing: John Cox. Makeup: Charles Parker. Hairdresser: A.G. Scott. Construction manager: Peter Dukelow. Construction assistant: Fred Bennett. Special effects: Cliff Richardson. Photographed in Super-Panavision 70 and Technicolor. Produced by Horizon Pictures (G.B.) Ltd. Released through Columbia Pictures Corporation.

Additional Cast: Kenneth Fortescue (Allenby's aide), Stuart Saunders (Regimental Sergeant-Major), Fernando Sancho (Turkish Sergeant), Henry Oscar (Reciter), Norman Rossington (Corporal Jenkins), John Ruddock (Elder Harith), M. Cher Kaoui (Khitan), Mohammed Habachi (Talal), Harry Fowler (William Potter), Jack Hedley (Reporter).

Additional Credits: Screenwriting: Beverley Cross, David Garnett. Michael Wilson received posthumous credit after arbitration in 1995. Second unit direction: André De Toth. Filming dates: May 15, 1961 to October 1962. Premiered in New York City on December 16, 1962.

Rated G in 1971, PG in 1988. Reconstructed and restored by Robert A. Harris in 1989.

Awards: Oscars for Best Picture, Director, Cinematography—Color, Film Editing, Music—Score (Substantially Original), Sound, Art Direction–Set Direction—Color.

Available: Columbia/TriStar Home Entertainment VHS (2001). ISBN: 0-7678-7049-2. UPC: 0-43396-06755-4.

After the worldwide success of *The Bridge on the River Kwai* (1957), director David Lean divorced his third wife, actress Ann Todd, and married his fourth, Leila Matkar. While searching for his next film subject, he considered a biopic on Mahatma Gandhi. Instead, he settled on T.E. Lawrence, a World War I hero who led an Arab army into Damascus. Lawrence's exploits were documented by journalist Lowell Thomas, whose book *With Lawrence in Arabia* helped make the soldier a legend in the United States. Lawrence's own books, in particular *Seven Pillars of Wisdom*, burnished his reputation.

Several filmmakers tried to adapt Lawrence and his books to the screen, including director Rex Ingram and producer Alexander Korda. Actors mentioned for the lead role ranged from Leslie Howard, Robert Donat, Burgess Meredith, and Alan Ladd. David Lean expressed interest in the project as early as 1952, when the rights to Lawrence's life were held by Korda and Columbia Pictures.

Producer Sam Spiegel became involved around 1955, the same time playwright Terrence Rattigan was trying to mount a production that would focus on Lawrence's homosexuality. He hired Michael Wilson, a screenwriter who had been blacklisted from the film industry in the United States since his appearance before an HUAC hearing. Wilson had worked on *The Bridge on the River Kwai*, and the treatment he wrote for the project helped Spiegel procure the movie rights from Lawrence's younger brother, A.W. (Lawrence himself had died in a motorcycle accident in 1935.)

Spiegel held a press conference about the upcoming production in 1960; a few months later, Rattigan mounted his production of *Ross*, starring Alec Guinness, which another producer threatened to turn into a film starring Laurence Harvey. By that time Lean was in Jordan, scouting locations with production manager John Palmer. That summer, he shot screen tests of Albert Finney, who ultimately turned down the role of Lawrence. Lean then cast Peter O'Toole after seeing him in *The Day They Robbed the Bank of England* (1960). A native of Ireland, O'Toole had served in the British Navy before attending the Royal Academy of Dramatic Art. Of his experience on the film, he said later, "The most important influence in my life has been David Lean."

Wilson wrote three drafts of a screenplay for Lean, who found fault with all of them. Wilson quit the project, and as a result did not receive screen credit until a 1995 arbitration hearing acknowledged his contributions. He was replaced by Robert Bolt, whose play *A Man for All Seasons* had been seen by Spiegel. Lean was already preparing to film in Jordan when Bolt started writing.

Lean cast Omar Sharif in the crucial role of Lawrence's friend Ali after considering several other actors. "He would have a preponderant influence over my career," Sharif wrote in his memoirs. Lean hired playwright Beverley Cross to work on battle scenes in the story. (David Garnett also worked in London on a screenplay.) Bolt finally arrived in Jordan and began writing from Spiegel's yacht, the *Malahne*. He condensed material from *Seven Pillars*, combining characters into archetypal figures, and made more explicit Lawrence's sadomasochism. Bolt was about halfway through his draft when Lean began shooting on May 15, 1961.

Lean biographer Kevin Brownlow gives a vivid account of the production in the Jordanian desert: extreme heat, primitive conditions, cumbersome 65mm cameras that had to be protected from dust and dirt, animals, extras, language problems. Furthermore, Lean couldn't view any of the footage shot in Jordan until weeks later. He had to trust cinematographer Freddie Young and his own judgment. With costs mounting, Spiegel shut down the production on September 28, 1961, after Lean had been shooting for 117 days. Despite the director's objections, Spiegel moved the production to Spain, where filming resumed that December.

Former feature director André De Toth and future director Nicolas Roeg joined the production there. John Box rebuilt the town of Aqaba so it could be photographed from above in what became the most exciting shot in the film, as Lawrence and his followers gallop from the desert through the city to the sea. Four months of filming took place in Morocco. After two years and three months, the production was finally finished.

Spiegel announced to the press that the film would be shown to the Queen of England on December 10, 1962, giving Lean an unbreakable deadline for editing. Lean, who had started out in the industry as an editor, worked closely with Anne Coates, who had been assembling the rushes into a rough cut all along. He told her, "It's what you take out which makes the movie, not necessarily what you leave in."

Maurice Jarre had been the third choice for composer; Spiegel had tried and failed to get Aram Khatchaturian and Benjamin Britten (he also momentarily thought of using Richard Rodgers). Jarre's score became one of the most recognizable of its time, even though it was composed and recorded in only six weeks.

After the screening for the Queen, *Lawrence of Arabia* opened in New York City on December 16, 1962. A.W. Lawrence hated the film, denouncing it to the press in England and America. Reviews in the United States were mixed, but the film did outstanding business at the box office. Even so, Lean was dissatisfied with it almost immediately after its release. Like others, he thought it was too long, and dramatically unbalanced, with the pacing in the second half too rushed. He blamed the fact that he had started shooting before the script was finished; shortly after the opening run, he deleted some twenty minutes of material.

Lawrence of Arabia shows both the strengths and weaknesses of the "epic" genre. As a film it is stupendous, larger-than-life in acting and cinematic technique—at least in individual moments. Bolt's script works on an intellectual level, but not an emotional one. The size of the production became a crutch to lean on, a diversion for viewers when characters and plotting were lacking. The immensity of the desert *is* the story for much of the film's first hour, that and how slowly Lean unfolds the plot. With so many actors and extras, so many animals and props, so many magnificent locations,

Lean may have felt forced into using them all, whether the story required them or not.

The film established O'Toole as an international star, and its influence on directors as disparate as Sergio Leone and Steven Spielberg is unmistakable. It would be the last time Lean worked with Spiegel. However, his next two films, *Dr. Zhivago* (1965) and *Ryan's Daughter* (1970), were both scripted by Robert Bolt.

To Kill a Mockingbird

Atticus Finch (Gregory Peck) delivering his closing argument in *To Kill a Mockingbird*.

Universal International, 1962. Sound, B&W, 1.85. 129 minutes.

Cast: Gregory Peck (Atticus Finch), John Megna (Charles Baker "Dill" Harris), Frank Overton (Sheriff Heck Tate), Rosemary Murphy (Miss Maudie Atkinson), Ruth White (Mrs. Dubose), Brock Peters (Tom Robinson), Estelle Evans (Calpurnia), Paul Fix (Judge Taylor), Collin Wilcox (Mayella Violet Ewell), James Anderson (Robert E. Lee Ewell), Alice Ghostley (Stephanie Crawford), Robert Duvall (Arthur "Boo" Radley), William Windom (Gilmer), Crahan Denton (Walter Cunningham), Richard Hale (Mr. Radley), Mary Badham ([Jean Louise] Scout [Finch]), Phillip Alford ([Jeremy Atticus] Jem [Finch]).

Credits: Directed by Robert Mulligan. Screenplay by Horton Foote. Based upon Harper Lee's novel *To Kill a Mockingbird*. Produced by Alan J. Pakula. Music: Elmer Bernstein. Director of photography: Russell Harlan. Art director: Henry Bumstead. Set decorations: Oliver Emert. Sound: Waldon O. Watson, Corson Jowett. Production manager: Ernest B. Wehmeyer. Assistant to producer: Isabel Halliburton. Film editor: Aaron Stell. Costumes by Rosemary Odell. Men's wardrobe: Seth Banks. Make-up: Bud Westmore. Hair stylist: Larry Germain. Script supervisor: Meta Rebner. Assistant director: Joseph Kenny. Main titles designed by Stephen Frankfurt.

Additional Cast: Steve Condit (Walter Cunningham Jr.), Bill Walker (Reverend Sykes), Hugh Sanders (Dr. Reynolds), Pauline Myers (Jessie), Jester Hairston (Spence Robinson), Jamie Forster (Hiram Townsend), Nancy Marshall (Schoolteacher), Kim Hamilton (Helen Robinson), Kelly Thordsen (Burly man), David Crawford (David Robinson), Kim Hector (Cecil Jacobs), Barry Seltzer (Schoolboy), Guy Wilkerson (Jury foreman), Charles Fredericks (Court clerk), Jay Sullivan (Court reporter).

Additional Credits: Art direction: Alexander Golitzen. Narration spoken by Kim Stanley. Edward Muhl in charge of production for Universal

International. A production of Pakula-Mulligan Productions, Inc. and Brentwood Productions. Production dates: February 12 to May 3, 1962. Limited opening on December 25, 1962.

Awards: Oscars for Best Actor, Writing—Screenplay Based on Material from Another Medium, Art Direction–Set Decoration–Black-and-White.

Available: Universal Studios Home Entertainment DVD (2005). UPC: 025192786624.

Harper Lee's first, and to date sole, novel, *To Kill a Mockingbird* not only won a Pulitzer Prize, but was an unexpected best-seller when it was published in 1960. Born in Monroeville, Alabama, in 1926, Lee was working as a airlines reservation clerk in New York City when she submitted several short stories to agent Annie Laurie Williams. Her husband, Maurice Craine, encouraged Lee to write a novel instead. As a Christmas present in 1956, the couple gave her a stipend that would allow her to work on her writing full-time. Craine submitted Lee's draft, called *Atticus*, to J.B. Lippincott, where editor Theresa von Hohoff took on the project. She helped Lee shape the novel that was to become *To Kill a Mockingbird*.

While much of the novel was autobiographical in detail, Lee brought a poetic vision and quiet wit to a plot that was equal parts coming-of-age story and courtroom melodrama. The character of Atticus Finch, a moral, upright lawyer, was based on her father, A.C. Lee, a publisher, banker, and politician. Jean Louise, the tomboy nicknamed Scout, was based on Lee herself. Dill, a next-door neighbor, came from Truman Capote, Lee's childhood friend.

In the novel, Atticus is called on to defend Tom Robinson, a black sharecropper accused of raping a white woman. Lee most likely based this on a 1933 incident in which the white Naomi Lowery accused the black Walter Lett of raping her. When Lett was sentenced to death, Monroeville citizens mounted a campaign to reopen his case. Lett's sentence was commuted to life imprisonment; he died four years later in a mental hospital.

The bulk of the novel concerns three children—Scout, her older brother Jem, and Dill—and their adventures in the Depression-era South. Lee took a strategy of relating the novel from two points of view: the six-year-old Scout, and the mature Jean Louise. This combination of both childlike simplicity and rueful nostalgia gives the novel much of its emotional power.

The publication of *To Kill a Mockingbird* changed Lee's life. Ordinarily shy and retiring, she faced relentless publicity demands after her book sold a half-million copies in six months. Hollywood approached Williams, her screen rights agent, with offers to adapt the book for Gary Cooper and Bette Davis. Williams held out for Alan Pakula and Robert Mulligan, partners in a new production company.

Pakula had abandoned his family's printing business to work as a production assistant at Paramount. His first big success was *Fear Strikes Out* (1957), a biopic about the mentally unstable outfielder Jimmy Piersall. It was directed by Mulligan, a Bronx native who served in the Marines during World War II before finding a job at CBS as a messenger. Within a few years he was one of the more respected directors of live drama on the network. While Mulligan finished work on *The Spiral Road* (1962), a lurid Rock Hudson adventure set in the tropics, Pakula met with Lee and scouted Monroeville for locations.

Universal pushed for Rock Hudson to play Atticus, but agreed to Pakula's choice, Gregory Peck. Peck's involvement was predicated on forming his own company, Brentwood Productions, with Pakula and Mulligan. (Lee started her own company, Atticus Productions, as a tax shelter.) The actor also insisted on input with casting and rewriting. Since Lee refused to work on an adaptation, Pakula turned to Horton Foote.

At the time Foote had sold only one previous film script, *Storm Fear* (1955), but had built a reputation from his plays and television work. Foote's small-town Texas background connected him with Lee, and his experience as an actor in the 1940s helped make his dialogue seem realistic, even everyday. Under Pakula's guidance, Foote compressed the novel's time frame, removed several characters, and added a potential love interest for Atticus. Mulligan worried that Foote was shifting attention away from the child characters.

In casting the other roles, Pakula and Mulligan searched for new faces, finding many of them on the New York stage and television. Foote had been impressed by Robert Duvall's work in his play *The Midnight Caller*, for example. Scout and Jem were cast after open auditions in Birmingham, Alabama. Mary Badham, nine at the time, had appeared on a single *Twilight Zone* episode, while Phillip Alford had even less experience. John Megna, who played Dill, had been on the Broadway stage in *All the Way Home*. Mulligan rehearsed with the children for over a month to get them used to the presence of cameras.

Interiors were shot in Revue Studios soundstages on the Universal lot. The exteriors were assembled by art directors Alexander Golitzen and Henry Bumstead from frame houses near Chavez Ravine that had been condemned in preparation for building Dodger Stadium. (A.C. Lee died that April.)

In June, and again in July, Peck sent memos to Universal executives complaining about Mulligan's editing, writing that the movie now spent too much time on the children and not enough on Atticus. The actor's stance led to the deletion of several scenes, including one in which Jem reads to a dying Mrs. Dubose. As a result, *To Kill a Mockingbird* can seem weirdly bifurcated, half children's story, half Perry Mason episode.

Peck told his biographer Gary Fishgall that he practiced his climactic courtroom speech two- or three-hundred times. Although Mulligan cuts away twice to brief reaction shots, Peck delivered his speech in one take lasting almost seven minutes. Mulligan staged the speech so Peck would hit four marks, in effect changing the shot from a wide angle to a medium close-up and back without having to move the camera.

While technically demanding, the scene also points out what many critics perceived as fundamental problems with *To Kill a Mockingbird*. Atticus doesn't use legal arguments to argue his client's innocence, he uses his moral revulsion against racism to try to exonerate Tom Robinson. Layer on Elmer Bernstein's overly emphatic score, and *To Kill a Mockingbird* takes on an aura of piety that can be discomfiting. Critic Pauline Kael complained about Peck's "virtuously dull" performance, while Andrew Sarris wrote, "This is not much of a movie even by purely formal standards."

Moviegoers embraced the picture, making it one of the top box-office performers of 1963. (The film received a limited opening in December 1962 to qualify for the Oscars.) The role of Atticus Finch distilled Peck's screen persona to that of a quiet, decent, firm father and liberal. Harper Lee wrote, "In that film, the man and the part met."

Mulligan's future work mirrored his interest with small-scale, personal, nostalgic dramas, such as *Summer of '42* (1971) and *Same Time, Next Year* (1978). Pakula, on the other hand, turned to political and social themes when he became a director: *The Parallax View* (1974), *All the President's Men* (1976), *The Devil's Own* (1997).

What impresses most about *To Kill a Mockingbird* today is the acting of the children, in particular Mary Badham, whose chemistry with Peck is unmistakable. Their scenes together get to the heart of what Lee achieved as a novelist, a profound glimpse of love tinged with sorrow.

The Nutty Professor

Paramount, 1963. Sound, color, 1.85. 107 minutes.

Cast: Jerry Lewis (Professor Julius Kelp/Buddy Love), Stella Stevens (Stella Purdy), Del Moore (Dr. Mortimer Warfield), Kathleen Freeman (Miss Lemmon), Med Flory (Student football player), Norman Alden (Student football player), Howard Morris (Elmer Kelp), Elvia Allman (Edwina Kelp), Milton Frome (Dr. M. Sheppard Leevee), Buddy Lester (Bartender), Marvin Kaplan (Nightclub patron), David Landfield (Student), Skip Ward (Student football player), Julie Parrish (Student), Henry Gibson (Gibson [student]), Les Brown and his Band of Renown.

Credits: Directed by Jerry Lewis. Written by Jerry Lewis and Bill Richmond. Produced by Ernest D. Glucksman. Associate producer: Arthur P. Schmidt. Director of photography: W. Wallace Kelley. Art direction: Hal Pereira and Walter Tyler. Edited by John Woodcock. Music scored and conducted by Walter Scharf. Song: "We've Got a World That Swings," lyrics by Lil Mathis, music by Louis Yule Brown. Assistant director: Ralph Axness. Set decoration: Sam Comer and Robert Benton. Makeup supervision: Wally Westmore. Makeup artist: Jack Stone. Hair style supervision: Nellie Manley. Men's Wardrobe: Sy Devore, Nat Wise. Costumes: Edith Head. Production manager: Bill Davidson. Assistant production manager: Hal Bell. Dialogue coach: Marvin Weldon. Script supervision: Dorothy Yutz. Property master: Martin Pendleton. Filmed in Technicolor. Technicolor color consultant: Richard Mueller. Assistant to the producer: Marshall Katz. Special photographic effects: Paul K. Lerpae. Sound recording by Hugo Grenzbach and Charles Grenzbach. Copyright 1963 by Jerry Lewis Enterprises, Inc.

Additional Cast: Richard Kiel (Bodybuilder).

Additional Credits: Premiered in Houston, Texas, on June 4, 1963.

Other Versions: *The Nutty Professor* (1996, directed by Tom Shadyac and starring Eddie Murphy), *Nutty Professor II: The Klumps* (2000, directed by Peter Segal and starring Eddie Murphy).

Available: Paramount Home Video DVD (2004). ISBN: 1-4157-0380-9. UPC: 0-97360-56364-1.

Jerry Lewis had written, produced, directed, and/or starred in dozens of films before *The Nutty Professor*, by critical consensus his most successful work. Born Joseph Levitch in Newark, New Jersey, in 1926, Lewis dropped out of high school to be a performer like his parents. He had established a tenuous foothold in the "Borscht Belt" in the Catskills when he teamed with baritone Dean Martin in 1946. Their subsequent nightclub act was a smash, and within three years they were major stars on stage, screen, and radio. Id to Martin's ego, Lewis specialized in loud, undisciplined clowning, using squeaky voices, costumes, and pratfalls to try to draw attention away from Martin's persona as a smooth crooner and ladies' man.

The act broke up bitterly in 1956, with Martin pursuing a successful career as a singer, movie star, and television host. Working largely in movies, Lewis often produced, wrote, and directed his vehicles, becoming one of Paramount's most profitable contract players of the period. He looked to the past rather than the future, adapting older films and plays and drawing inspiration from silent comedians like Chaplin and Keaton and vaudeville stars like Lou Costello. Lewis credits director Frank Tashlin with teaching him the possibilities of film as a medium, but it's Lewis himself who was largely responsible for the look and style of his projects.

In later interviews, the comedian named the 1941 MGM version of *Dr. Jekyll and Mr. Hyde*, starring Spencer Tracy, as the prime inspiration for *The Nutty Professor*. Lewis began working on the project in 1956; after writing "eight or nine" drafts he hired screenwriter Bill Richmond to assist him. They went back and revised the first draft for filming.

Lewis felt comfortable working with familiar faces. Richmond had worked on two of his previous films, composer Walter Scharf on many more. Kathleen Freeman, who plays a secretary, was a veteran of thirteen Lewis films; Del Moore, here an officious college dean, was Lewis's close friend. But the comedian was proud of his ability to spot talent. He says he promoted W. Wallace Kelley from the special effects department to be the director of cinematography on *The Nutty Professor* (Kelley did have a half-dozen prior DP credits). This was a significant appearance for Stella Stevens (née Estelle Egglestone), a blond bombshell whose biggest role before this was as Elvis Presley's love interest in *Girls! Girls! Girls!* (1962).

Shooting started on October 9, 1962, with several days devoted to rehearsals and a week's worth of shooting taking place at Arizona State in Tempe. At this stage in his career Lewis was extremely confident about his abilities, and was unconcerned about dropping scenes he had already filmed and altering those he had yet to shoot. Gags were added or changed on the spot, and retakes were often needed when cast members couldn't keep straight faces.

Where a movie like *The Errand Boy* (1961) was marked by dead-end skits, blackouts, and non sequiturs, *The Nutty Professor* was Lewis's bid to appeal to an older, more sophisticated audience, one that expected stories to make sense and characters to mature or at least change over the course of a film. It was also an opportunity for Lewis to adopt the pathos Chaplin employed in *Limelight* (1952), to associate himself with the struggles and consequences of celebrity and the creative process.

But this is, after all, a Jerry Lewis movie, so he is introduced with a gag that wouldn't have been out of place in a Three Stooges short. For most of the film he wears a dental appliance that gives him buck teeth, and speaks in a high-pitched whine he says he adopted from a man he observed on a train in 1956. Add greasy hair, black-framed spectacles, hunched shoulders, a mincing gait, and you have Lewis's impression of a nerd, Professor Kelp.

Kelp pines for his buxom student Stella Purdy (Stevens), prompting him to concoct a potion that turns him into the suave, cigarette-smoking ladies' man Buddy Love. Some viewers try to connect Love to Dean Martin, but Lewis and his colleagues have always claimed that Love is a part of Lewis's own personality. Whatever his source, Love alternates with Kelp in a plot that roughly parallels the original Robert Louis Stevenson story, albeit one without rape, murder, and dismemberment.

The Nutty Professor is a strikingly insular film. There are only eight major sets and one exterior location, all of them cheap to construct or dress. Although there are dozens of extras, there are only four main parts, two of those played by Lewis. It is a prime example of the kind of quick, efficient moviemaking Lewis excelled at. Not counting crosscutting between situations, the film has about a dozen scenes, some of them running ten to twelve minutes. Some situations reach back to burlesque and even vaudeville for inspiration, notably a scene in which Buddy Love has Dr. Warfield audition for *Hamlet*.

Lewis was especially proud of another scene in Warfield's office, one in which the doctor berates Professor Kelp for causing an explosion. The laughs were supposed to come as a result of Kelp's helpless silence in the face of scorn, but today it's hard to find the humor in the humiliation of an ugly person. For the rest of his career, Lewis would persist in glorifying the abject (as did Chaplin and, to a lesser extent, Keaton). It's the insistent demands on the sympathies of his audience that has dated Lewis's comedy the most.

The final cost of *The Nutty Professor* was just under $2 million, some $380,000 over budget. The film brought in over $3.3 million in its original release, even though it was competing against rereleases of Lewis's earlier Paramount films. (Convinced that Paramount was undermining his work, Lewis sued the studio in 1966 for its rerelease and television sales policies.) The studio could reliably count on $2.5–3.5 million for each Lewis film at the time, but *The Nutty Professor* marked a turning point in the comedian's career. Before it was released in 1963 (backed by a massive, seven-week, nationwide publicity tour), Lewis signed a contract with ABC to create eighty hours of live TV each season. At $50,000 a show, he became the highest-paid performer on television. At the same time, box-office returns on his films started declining. By the end of the decade he was gone from Paramount; in the 1970s he appeared in only two films, one of which remains unreleased.

Lewis kept in the public eye largely through his Muscular Dystrophy telethons and occasional guest host appearances on talk shows. Always championed by the French, he regained some critical attention by appearing in a straight dramatic role in Martin Scorsese's *The King of Comedy* (1983). In recent years he has made some sporadic comeback attempts and battled several life-threatening illnesses; he also wrote an autobiography and a book-length appreciation of Dean Martin.

Shock Corridor

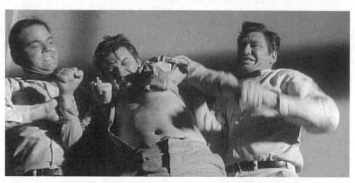

Guards manhandle Johnny Barrett (Peter Breck) in *Shock Corridor*.
Courtesy of The Criterion Collection

Allied Artists Pictures Corporation, 1963. Sound, B&W with color sequences, 1.85. 100 minutes.

Cast: Peter Breck (Johnny Barrett), Constance Towers (Cathy), Gene Evans (Boden), James Best (Stuart), Hari Rhodes (Trent), Larry Tucker (Pagliacci), Paul Dubov (Dr. Menkin), Chuck Roberson (Wilkes), Neyle Morrow (Psycho), John Matthews (Dr. Cristo), William Zuckert (Swanee), John Craig (Lloyd), Philip Ahn (Dr. Fong), Frank Gerstle (Police Lieutenant), Rachel Romen, Barbara Perry, Marlene Manners, Linda Randolph, Lucille Curtis, Jeanette Dana, Marie Devereux, Karen Conrad, Allison Daniell, Chuck Hicks, Wally Campo, Ray Baxter, Linda Barrett, Harry Fleer.

Credits: Written, produced, and directed by Samuel Fuller. Executive producers: Sam Firks, Leon Frumkess. Director of photography: Stanley Cortez. Art director: Eugene Lourie. Production manager: Rudolph Flothow. Film editor: Jerome Thoms. Set decorator: Charles Thompson. Music by Paul Dunlap. Assistant director: Floyd Joyer. Assistant to Leon Frumkess: Herbert Luft. Make-up Supervision: Dan Greenway. Costumer: Einar H. Bourman. Recording supervisor: Phil Mitchell. Choreography: Jon Gregory. Special Optical Effects: Lynn Dunn. Special effects: Charles Duncan. Script Supervisor: Mary Chaffe [Chaffee]. Titles: Ray Mercer. Sound by Ryder Sound Services. Music and sound effects supervisor: Gordon Zahler. Music Editor: Jack Lowry. Sound Effects Editor: Josef von Stroheim. Copyright 1963 F&F Productions, Inc.

Additional Credits: Color sequences photographed by Samuel Fuller for the films *House of Bamboo* (1955) and *Tigrero* (never completed). Premiered in New York City on September 11, 1963.

Available: Criterion Collection DVD (1998). UPC: 0-37429-12592-2.

Samuel Fuller's life was as diverse and adventurous as any of his movies. Born in Massachusetts in 1911, he spent his teen years with New York City newspapers, selling them on the streets, working as a copyboy, dropping out of school to become a crime reporter and cartoonist. His early experiences led to a finely detailed movie about print journalism, *Park Row* (1952), that starred Gene Evans. He left New York in the 1930s, crossing the country on freight trains and writing dispatches from the road for various papers. Lurid pulp novels like *Burn, Baby, Burn!* (1935) helped land him a job as a screenwriter; he scratched out work in Hollywood until 1942, when he was drafted.

Fuller served in the First Infantry Division, earning the Bronze and Silver Stars while participating in three amphibious assaults and the liberation of a concentration camp. After the war, Fuller sold a novel to Howard Hawks and worked on several unproduced screenplays. His breakthrough film was *I Shot Jesse James* (1949), made on the cheap for producer Robert Lippert. Fuller's style and attitude—abrasive, punchy, aggressively lowbrow—made his work stand out from other B-moviemakers, and drew the attention of Darryl F. Zanuck at Twentieth Century-Fox.

The director made his most polished films at Fox, but titles like *Fixed Bayonets!* (1951) and *House of Bamboo* (1955) were still distinguished by their rapid pacing and harsh brutality. Fuller was a two-fisted writer and director, determined to make an impact even at the expense of coherence and credibility. His most personal projects, like *Park Row*, were financially unsuccessful, but he managed to inject his own style and interests into routine programmers, turning *Pickup on South Street* (1953) into something extraordinary.

With the film industry essentially falling apart at the end of the 1950s, Fuller again had to scramble for work. He formed his own production company, Globe Enterprises, releasing films through Universal or Columbia. With his market and budgets shrinking, Fuller needed story angles he knew he could sell to theater owners. He was also competing with filmmakers like Roger Corman and William Castle who could crank out youth-oriented films on miniscule budgets. Fuller pitched his films to a slightly different audience, older males with a taste for exploitation. The director filled his stories with drugs, strippers, and violence, pushing the limits of the Production Code. Fuller got away with his excesses by branding his films with themes or "messages" that gave them a soupçon of legitimacy.

Shock Corridor promised its audience almost everything an exploitation title could offer in 1963: sex, drugs, violence, and of course insanity. Filmmakers had been using mental illness as a subject since the dawn of cinema; in fact, it's hard to think of a movie villain who isn't unbalanced in some way. *The Snake Pit* (1948), *A Child Is Waiting* (1961), and even the horror-oriented *Bedlam* (1946) all tried to deal seriously with mental institutions. Fuller may have been influenced by Ken Kesey's novel *One Flew Over the Cuckoo's Nest*, which had been published the year before.

In his script, the director used a journalism angle to bring viewers into an asylum. The film opens with a deception, as a psychiatrist (played by the distinguished Asian actor Philip Ahn) and Johnny Barrett (Peter Breck), a newspaper reporter, role-play parts in a scheme to trick state doctors into accepting Barrett as a patient. Fuller opens up the scene to reveal two other observers: Barrett's boss, and his girlfriend Cathy (Constance Towers), a stripper filled with foreboding about his plan.

What is his plan? Fuller barely bothers to reveal the actual premise of the film—that Barrett is going undercover into the asylum to solve an unsolved murder by questioning three inmate witnesses. As the title suggests, the goal of the film is to shock viewers, something a straightforward murder investigation was not going to do. Fuller concentrates instead on a simplistic, clichéd, but admittedly exciting view of asylum life, one with hydrotherapy, shock treatments, and, behind an unlocked door, nymphomaniacs ready to pounce en masse on unsuspecting males. But Fuller's ideas, interesting in the abstract, could seem ludicrous when worked out on the screen. Could a black man be exposed to so much bigotry that he becomes a racist himself? Of course. Would he hate other blacks and want to join the Ku Klux Klan, even fashioning a Klan hood out of his pillowcase, as Hari Rhodes does here? Outside of Fuller's world, a lot less likely.

Shooting *Shock Corridor* was Stanley Cortez, the same cinematographer who worked with Orson Welles on *The Magnificent Ambersons* and with Charles Laughton on *The Night of the Hunter*. (For the film's three, brief color sequences, Fuller used footage he had shot for *House of Bamboo* and *Tigrero*, a movie set in South America that was never completed.) Cortez's inventive lighting helped deal with the project's budget limitations. He adjusted shadows to make the same set look like two different offices, for example, or altered the tone and meaning of a scene simply by using a high or low camera angle. For a film with no exteriors, Cortez managed to vary the visuals enough to keep them interesting.

Fuller drew his cast largely from television performers, although he had worked many years before with Gene Evans. Constance Towers was actually a classically trained singer who had appeared on stage as well as in two John Ford Westerns. She would also star in Fuller's subsequent film, *The Naked Kiss* (1964).

The Naked Kiss was the last true Fuller film until *The Big Red One* (1980), an account of his experiences during World War II which was taken out of his hands and slashed of over an hour's worth of footage. (Most of the excised material was restored when the film was rereleased in 2005.) Fuller's toehold in Hollywood had always been tenuous, but he remained a popular figure in Europe and in film schools, even as he found it more and more difficult to mount his own productions. He was not a subtle writer or director, but his ability to work with low budgets, and to transfer his nightmares to the screen, proved enormously influential with younger filmmakers. Tim Robbins, for example, directed an amusing documentary, *The Typewriter, the Rifle & the Movie Camera* (1996), featuring tall tales from Fuller himself, as well as interviews with admirers like Jim Jarmusch and Quentin Tarantino.

Zapruder Film of the Kennedy Assassination

Abraham Zapruder, 1963. Silent, color, 8mm. 26 seconds.

Credits: Photographed by Abraham Zapruder.

Available: MPI Home Video DVD *Image of an Assassination: A New Look at the Zapruder Film* (1998, www.mpihomevideo.com). UPC: 0-30306-7282-2-3. Also online at *www.assassinationresearch.com/zfilm/*.

Abraham Zapruder was born in Kovel, Russia, in 1905. He he received four years' education in Hebrew school before emigrating in 1920 to the United States, where he found work in New York

City as a fabric pattern maker. After marrying Lillian Shapovnick in 1933, Zapruder moved to Texas in 1941 to work for Nardis of Dallas, a clothing company. With his partner Irwin Schwartz, Zapruder later formed his own dress labels, Chalet and Jennifer Juniors. Schwartz and Zapruder worked out of the Dal-Tex Building, across the street from the Texas School Book Depository and near Dealey Plaza.

On November 22, 1963, Zapruder and his secretary, Marilyn Sitzman, went to Elm Street to watch President John F. Kennedy's motorcade pass. Supported by Sitzman, Zapruder climbed a concrete parapet next to a staircase for a better view. Using an 8mm Bell & Howell Zoomatic camera and Kodak Kodachrome II film, Zapruder photographed the motorcade from the moment it turned onto Elm from Houston Street until it went under a railroad bridge. President Kennedy was mortally wounded by a rifle shot as his limousine was almost immediately in front of Zapruder.

Returning to his office, Zapruder encountered *Dallas Morning News* reporter Harry McCormick, who contacted Secret Service agent Forrest Sorrels. The three brought the film to television station WFAA, where Zapruder appeared on air to describe what he saw around 3:00 p.m. At the same time, the film and three copies were processed at a local Eastman Kodak plant. Sorrels sent two copies to Washington, D.C.

On November 23, Zapruder sold his film and copy to *Life* magazine, with the provision that frame 313, showing the fatal impact wound, would not be published. Individual frames from the film were published in black-and-white in the November 29 issue of *Life*, and in color in subsequent issues. By this point a number of frames had been damaged and deleted. *Life* ordered 16mm and 35mm copies made in 1967 and 1968. A copy was used in the 1969 trial of Clay Shaw, and was shown ten times by prosecutor Jim Garrison. Zapruder died on August 30, 1970, of cancer.

In March 1975, ABC's *Good Night America*, hosted by Geraldo Rivera, broadcast an apparently bootleg copy. It was the first time the film was seen on television. When the Zapruder family initiated a lawsuit over royalties, Time, Inc., the owner of *Life*, sold the footage back to them a month later.

In 1978, the Zapruder family asked the National Archives to store the footage. For the next seventeen years, the archives kept the film in a security cabinet inside a refrigerated vault. Director Oliver Stone paid $85,000 to use the footage in *JFK* (1991). A year later, President George H.W. Bush signed a law that designated the footage an "assassination record" under the control of the government. In 1999, the federal government purchased the film from the Zapruder estate for $16 million. In December of that year, the estate donated its copyright to the Sixth Floor Museum at the Texas School Book Depository. The museum currently controls all rights to the footage.

In 1997, LMH, a company formed by the Zapruders to manage the footage, authorized a digital preservation. After warming up the film to 50 degrees for twenty-four hours, Joseph Barabe of McCrone Associates photographed each individual frame onto Kodak 6121 4x5 transparency film. Barabe included the entire film strip, capturing more visual information around the sprocket holes than had previously been seen by the public. The 4x5 transparencies were scanned into a computer at 1500 dpi. With the original information preserved, further enhancements could be made to the computer record. Scratches were removed, for example. Motion stabilization placed each frame on the same horizontal plane, making the film easier to follow visually.

The Zapruder film is not the only record of the assassination—some thirty-two photographers and filmmakers who covered Dealey Plaza on the day of the motorcade have been identified. Orville Nix, an air-conditioning engineer, filmed the motorcade from a reverse angle from Zapruder, for example. Footage shot by George Jeffries of Kennedy in his limousine moments before the assassination surfaced in 2007.

However, the Zapruder footage remains the most authoritative visual record of the assassination. It is a difficult film to watch, not just for its brutal violence, but for the effect the killing had on Kennedy's family and on society as a whole. Zapruder never got over what he saw. To his credit, and that of his heirs, he never stopped trying to protect the footage from commercial exploitation.

America America

Warner Bros., 1963. Sound, B&W, 1.37. 168 minutes.

Cast: Stathis Giallelis (Stavros Topouzoglou), Frank Wolff (Vartan Dama-dian), Harry Davis (Isaac Topouzoglou), Elena Karam (Vasso Topouzo-glou), Estelle Hemsley (Grandmother Topouzoglou), Gregory Rozakis (Hohannes Gardashian), Lou Antonio (Abdul), Salem Ludwig (Odys-seus Topouzoglou), John Marley (Garabet), Joanna Frank (Vartuhi), Paul Mann (Aleko Sinnikoglou), Linda Marsh (Thomna Sinnikoglou), Robert H. Harris (Aratoon Kebabian), Katharine Balfour (Sophia Keba-bian), Giorgos Foundas, Dimitris Nikolaidis, Dimos Starenios.

Credits: Written, produced and directed by Elia Kazan. Director of pho-tography: Haskell Wexler. Film editor: Dede Allen. Production design: Gene Callahan. Costumes by Anna Hill Johnstone. Music by Manos Hadjidakis. Lyrics by Nikos Gatsos. Associate producer: Charles H. Maguire. Chief Grip: Cesare Onorati. Chief electrician: Massimo Mas-simi. Make-up: Emilio Trani. Production assistant: Burtt Harris. Sound mixer: Leroy Robbins. Script continuity: Marie Kenney. Camera opera-tor: Harlowe Stengel. Assistant cameraman: Ralph Gerling. Liaison in Greece for Athena Enterprises Corporation: Theodore Kritas. Rerecord-ing mixer: Richard Vorisek. Head sound editor: Edward Beyer. Sound editors: Jean Bagley, John Fitzstephens. Music editor: Stanley Buetens. Assistant film editor: Peter Grivas. Optical effects by film Opticals, Inc. Filmed at the Alfa Studios in Athens, Greece.

Additional Credits: Opened December 15, 1963.

Other Versions: Kazan's 1966 novel *The Arrangement* continues the stories of some of the characters in *America America*; Kazan directed the screen adaptation in 1969.

Awards: Oscar for Best Art Direction–Set Decoration—Black and White.

Available: Warner Home Video VHS (1994). ISBN: 0-7907-2100-7. UPC: 0-85393-57943-2.

As early as 1956, Elia Kazan was telling interviewers that he wanted to write the story of his family's passage from Turkey to the United States. The director was born in Istanbul in 1909; his parents moved briefly to Berlin before arriving in New York, where an uncle had established a rug busi-ness. *America America* (Kazan did not use a comma in the title, although almost all other sources do) told the story of this uncle, named Stavros in the book and movie.

Kazan wrote the script for the film in New York in 1960, after his father died. He relied a great deal on stories told to him by his grand-mother when he was a child. Although involved in a theater program at New York City's Lincoln Center, he traveled to Turkey with his pregnant mistress, Barbara Loden, to scout locations for a film. Meanwhile, his wife Molly sent his script and notes to Sol Stein, who was establishing the pub-lishing house of Stein and Day. Adapted into novel form by Molly and Stein, *America America* became the firm's first book.

Kazan's previous films had not done well at the box office, and the studios he showed his latest script to were not interested in backing an immigrant saga with no famous stars. Kazan's attorney Bill Fitelson arranged a production deal with Seven Arts, recently started by former agent Ray Stark, who gave the film a budget of $1.5 mil-lion. As Kazan recounts in his autobiography, he was drinking with his crew at a hotel bar in Turkey when he learned that Seven Arts had reneged on its deal. Kazan believed it was because he had cast Stathis Giallelis, a Greek he had seen sweeping up in a producer's office, in the lead role. Fitelson man-aged to set up a deal with Warner Brothers instead.

Kazan shot for a week in Turkey when Charles Maguire, the director's longtime production man-ager and assistant director, told him they had to leave immediately. With Turkish government censors closing in on them, Maguire smuggled the exposed footage out of the country. A disap-pointed Kazan shot the rest of the film in Greece. He did not get along with Haskell Wexler, his cinematographer, although he recognized Wexler's talent. "I didn't like him personally," Kazan wrote later, adding that Wexler took the job only because he knew the film would boost his résumé. (Wexler, on the other hand, said that Kazan felt that gener-osity was "a sign of weakness. It was typical of him to put people in their places. If you knock them down a little, it makes you the director of life.")

The frequent arguments over camera positions and frame compositions may have helped give *America America* its untamed look and immediacy. Wexler was adept at shooting with a handheld camera, allowing him to work in tighter locations than cinematographers tied down to tripods. At this point in his career Kazan was confident enough in his abilities as a director to stage entire scenes with the camera moving constantly. Wide shots suddenly transform into medium shots of two characters talking, then evolve again to reveal a third character's reactions.

Kazan was also shooting on a budget so tight that he couldn't—or didn't bother to—match shots. Isaac's (Stavros' father, played by Harry Davis) hair changes from one moment to the next, for example. But the director was in full com-mand of what he needed to tell a story. A scene in a church shows two families arranging a betrothal almost entirely in close-ups of eyes. Kazan leaves out information that doesn't interest him—what happens to certain characters, or how people get from one spot to another. All he needs to show are the parched, overwhelming landscapes, or a delicate, tentative fiancée, to convey the fear and yearning his uncle faced.

This was an important credit for editor Dede Allen, whose next film would be the groundbreaking *Bonnie and Clyde*. Kazan wrote about how composer Manos Hadjidakis helped him sort out his footage after the shoot by providing a preliminary score to help tie scenes together. But sound—dialogue and effects as well as music—is just as important to Allen in her editing scheme. She often pulls up sound from a succeeding scene to use as transitions from one sequence to another, or uses a musical motif to define the mood and direction of a scene. At other times she cuts the action abruptly, finding a visual equivalent for Kazan's pushy, insistent voice.

America America is unlike most immigrant stories, which generally begin shortly before or after characters arrive in their new land. It takes Kazan almost two hours of screen time to get Stavros on a boat to the United States. It is a measure of the director's talent that the film rarely feels slow, or long. And it is a measure of Kazan's personality that the film at times feels like one more justification for his political choices. "Look at where I came from," he seems to be saying. Stavros' behavior, his willingness to do anything to get his family to America, can be seen as an attempt to place Kazan's betrayal of his colleagues in perspective.

Difficult, uncompromising, but rewarding, *America America* received some glowing reviews, but was a box-office failure. It was the last entirely personal and successful film Kazan would make.

Point of Order

Filmed from television screens, kinescopes tended to smear visual details, as in this shot of Senator Joseph McCarthy in *Point of Order*.

Continental Distributing, Inc., 1964. Sound, B&W, 1.37. 97 minutes.

Featuring: Robert T. Stevens, John G. Adams, Joseph N. Welch, Gen. Walter B. Smith, Sen. Karl E. Mundt, Ray H. Jenkins, Sen. John L. McClellan, Sen. Stuart Symington, Joseph McCarthy, Roy M. Cohn, Gen. C.E. Ryan, Francis P. Carr, James Juliana, Sen. Henry Jackson, Robert Collier.

Credits: Editorial director: Emile de Antonio. From an idea by: Daniel Talbot. Produced by Emile de Antonio, Daniel Talbot. Executive producer: Eliot D. Pratt. Consultant: Daniel Drasin. Processing: Movielab. Associate producers: Henry Rosenberg, Robert Duncan.

Additional Credits: Edited by Robert Duncan. Original television material directed by Ed Sherer for WMAL-TV, an ABC affiliate in Washington, D.C. Premiered at the New York Film Festival, September 1963. Opened theatrically on January 14, 1964.

Available: New Yorker Video DVD (2005). ISBN: 1-56730-385-4. UPC: 7-17119-06854-7.

A turning point in the career of Senator Joseph McCarthy, the Army-McCarthy hearings were the first nationally televised congressional inquiry. The purpose of the hearings, held between March 16 and June 17, 1954, was to determine if McCarthy and his aide Roy Cohn improperly influenced the Army concerning Private G. David Schine. With his accusations that the armed forces, the State Department, the CIA, and the nuclear industry had been infiltrated by Communists, McCarthy wielded enormous influence over national politics.

While not entirely responsible for the anti-Communist hysteria that swept the country at the time, he became a figurehead for the witch-hunt mentality that destroyed so many careers in politics and show business.

Public sessions of the hearings, conducted by the Senate Subcommittee on Investigations, began on April 22. At first all four existing national broadcasting networks planned to televise the hearings, but NBC and CBS, unwilling to give up daytime programming revenue, later opted to air highlights edited from pool footage. ABC, struggling to establish itself as a national network, broadcast all thirty-six days of the public hearings, a total of 188 hours of sessions. Some estimates place the audience for the hearings at twenty million.

Among the figures who questioned McCarthy and forty-four other witnesses in the public hearings were Joseph N. Welch, a Boston lawyer hired as special counsel for the Army; committee counsel Ray H. Jenkins; and Senator Stuart Symington. Welch played a key part in testimony on June 9, 1954, goading Cohn to produce a list of purported Communists "before sundown." In retaliation, McCarthy accused Fred Fisher, a lawyer with Welch's firm of Hale & Dorr, of having belonged to a Communist front organization. Welch's reply—"Have you no decency, sir, at long last? Have you left no sense of decency?"—is widely regarded today as the beginning of McCarthy's downfall. Perhaps equally telling was Symington's retort when McCarthy claimed, "You're not fooling anyone." Getting up to leave the hearing, Symington said, "Senator, the American people have had a look at you now for six weeks. You're not fooling anyone, either."

The following December, the Senate voted to censure McCarthy. However, the effects of the blacklist continued to be felt for years, impacting everything from foreign relations to the casting of movies and television shows. When Daniel Talbot and Emile de Antonio were considering using television materials to make a feature film, McCarthyism was still a factor in the entertainment industry.

Talbot, who ran the New Yorker Theater in Manhattan, was looking for alternative programming to fill in gaps in his schedule. De Antonio, the son of a Scranton physician, had a background in modern art before forming G String Productions to distribute *Pull My Daisy* (1958). He had also produced the folk music protest short *Sunday*

(1961). The two agreed that the McCarthy hearings had the historical significance and drama to draw moviegoers. They purchased the entire 188 hours, which were available from CBS on 16mm kinescopes. (In the days before videotape, kinescopes were made by filming directly from television monitors. These filmed records could then be used for later broadcasts.)

After screening all of the footage, Talbot and de Antonio selected the twelve most interesting hours. "We thought we might book this stopgap film into local theaters (in effect, converting each theater into a local TV set) and charge $1 an hour or $5 for viewing this 12-hour film in its entirety," Talbot wrote in *The New York Times*. Another option was using the material in a conventional documentary. They hired German editor Paul Falkenberg to shape the footage, which they planned to accompany with music and a narration by journalist Mike Wallace.

De Antonio and Talbot soon abandoned this approach, instead hiring filmmaker Robert Duncan as an editor. By now they were down to three hours of footage; they had also run out of money. De Antonio took over the project, providing notes for Duncan as he finished each sequence. De Antonio decided to dispense with a narrator, apart from an opening statement that would provide a context for the hearings. This was read by de Antonio himself over a black screen.

Since he no longer had to provide a chronological history of the hearings, de Antonio could concentrate specifically on the material he found the most dramatic. He and Duncan focused on six incidents or "scenes" from the hearing: McCarthy's claims that Army charts were false; thirteen minutes devoted to whether or not a photograph had been cropped; a letter from President Dwight D. Eisenhower ordering the end of testimony by members of the executive branch of the government; almost twenty minutes on the debate over a forged letter from J. Edgar Hoover; McCarthy's accusations against Fisher; and an argument between Symington and McCarthy over the handling of classified files. (De Antonio later added explanatory material about the various charges and countercharges, and identified the key players.)

The lack of a narration gave viewers the illusion that de Antonio and Talbot were showing them an unbiased account, but neither ever denied that they selected material that would portray McCarthy in the worst possible light. Far from being objective, they had a definite point of view towards the senator, which their movie clearly reflected. Few viewers at the time realized that de Antonio and Talbot were also manipulating the chronology of the hearings, switching around footage to suit narrative purposes.

In a 2001 article, film historian Vance Kepley, Jr., analyzed the footage for each segment. The sixteen minutes devoted to the debate over Fred Fisher used material from June 9, 1954, then from June 7, and ended with a segment from May 31. The "Army Charts" sequence started on May 11, and ended on April 26. Careful viewers could tell that material came from different days by the clothes the participants were wearing, but without access to more information could not determine the precise sequence of events.

Do the ends justify the means in documentary filmmaking? Did turning McCarthy into a villain justify the shortcuts de Antonio took? Does *Point of Order* present a deceptive account of the hearings? Or do de Antonio's methods offer a clear,

coherent story line, and a plausible explanation for McCarthy's downfall? First seen in a position of power, essentially controlling the hearings, by his own words and methods he is revealed to be a duplicitous blowhard. In the film's telling at least, when his career collapses, McCarthy is never sure what hit him.

Point of Order was shown at the first New York Film Festival in September 1963, and immediately afterward at the Museum of Modern Art. Talbot opened the film commercially on January 14, 1964, adding an exclamation point to its title. The following year he formed New Yorker Films, which for four decades has been a highly regarded independent distribution company. (New Yorker Films folded in 2009.) De Antonio's next feature, *Rush to Judgment* (1966), took a critical look at the investigation into the assassination of President John F. Kennedy. He also directed *In the Year of the Pig* (1968), one of the first feature documentaries to question the Vietnam War. De Antonio died in 1989.

Dr. Strangelove or: How I Learned to Stop Worrying and Love the Bomb

Columbia, 1963. Sound, B&W, 1.66. 95 minutes.

Cast: Peter Sellers (Group Captain Lionel Mandrake/President Merkin Muffley/Dr. Strangelove), George C. Scott (Gen. Buck Turgidson), Sterling Hayden (Brig. Gen. Jack D. Ripper), Keenan Wynn (Col. Bat Guano), Slim Pickens (Maj. T.J. "King" Kong), Peter Bull (Alexi DeSadesky), James Earl Jones (Lt. Lothar Zogg), Tracy Reed (Miss Scott), Jack Creley (Staines), Frank Berry (Lt. H.R. Dietrich), Glen[n] Beck (Lt. W.D. Kivel), Shane Rimmer (Capt. G.A. "Ace" Owens), Paul Tamarin (Lt. B. Goldberg), Gordon Tanner (Gen. Faceman), Robert O'Neil (Adm. Randolph), Roy Stephens (Frank); Hall Galili, Laurence Herder, John McCarthy (Burpelson soldiers).

Credits: Directed and produced by Stanley Kubrick. Screenplay by Stanley Kubrick, Terry Southern & Peter George. Base[d] on the book *Red Alert* by Peter George. Associate producer: Victor Lyndon. Director of photography: Gilbert Taylor. Production designer: Ken Adam. Film editor: Anthony Harvey. Music: Laurie Johnson. Art director: Peter Murton. Production manager: Clifton Brandon. Assistant director: Eric Rattray. Camera operator: Kelvin Pike. Camera assistant: Bernard Ford. Continuity: Pamela Carlton. Wardrobe: Bridget Sellers. Special effects: Willy Veevers. Travelling matte: Vic Margutti. Recordist: Richard Bird. Sound supervisor: John Cox. Dubbing mixer: John Aldred. Sound editor: Leslie Hodgson. Assistant editor: Ray Lovejoy. Assembly editor: Geoffrey Fry. Make-up: Stewart Freeborn. Hairdresser: Barbara Ritchie. Aviation advisor: Capt. John Crewdson. Main title by Pablo Ferro. A Columbia Pictures Corporation presentation of a Stanley Kubrick production.

Additional Credits: Executive producer: Lee Minoff. Filmed at Shepperton Studios, England. Premiered in New York City on January 29, 1964.

Available: Columbia Pictures Home Entertainment DVD (2004). ISBN: 1-4049-4616-0. UPC: 0-43396-0261602.

While the unfounded optimism of a film like *Duck and Cover* (1951) can seem quaint today, for those

growing up in the 1950s and '60s, the threat of nuclear annihilation was a very real possibility. Nuclear gamesmanship became a preoccupation of director Stanley Kubrick, especially after the Cuban Missile Crisis of 1962. He read dozens of books on the topic, but it was a 1958 thriller called *Red Alert* by Peter Bryant (a pseudonym for Peter George) that he ended up buying. The novel introduced a delusional Air Force officer who tries to instigate a nuclear war with Russia.

Kubrick, his producing partner James Harris, and Peter George, hired to write the screenplay, had trouble finding the right approach to the story. (Harris left the project, and his partnership with Kubrick, to direct his own films.) An early draft titled *The Delicate Balance of Terror* had extraterrestrials investigating a post-apocalyptic Earth. At some point in the writing process, Kubrick realized that he wanted to tell the story as a comedy. He hired Terry Southern, the author of cult novels like *Candy* and *The Magic Christian*, for a two-month stretch. Accounts vary as to who contributed what to the final screenplay, but judging from his other writing, Southern was probably responsible for the characters' punning names and for much of the film's sexual sarcasm. Kubrick, on the other hand, was drawn to the ironies inherent to George's plot—how viewers could root for the crew of a B-52 to simultaneously succeed and fail, for example. He was also energized by the possibility of juggling three separate story lines at once.

The director claimed in interviews that he shot the film in England because comic Peter Sellers was going through a divorce and couldn't leave the country. But Kubrick preferred working as far away from Hollywood as possible. Filming at Shepperton Studios gave Kubrick that much more control over the production. He originally cast Sellers, who played an important role in his previous film, an adaptation of Vladimir Nabokov's *Lolita* (1962), in four roles. Born in 1925, Sellers, a key figure on *The Goon Show* and a fixture in British comedics in the 1950s, had played three roles in Jack Arnold's *The Mouse That Roared* (1959). Here he does Group Captain Lionel Mandrake as a by-the-book British officer psychologically damaged by an injury from World War II; President Merkin Muffley as an Adlai Stevenson type, the film's blandly rational voice of reason; and Dr. Strangelove as a crippled, crypto-Fascist. (He modeled the voice for this last role on famous still photographer Arthur "Weegee" Fellig.) Sellers had also intended playing "King" Kong, pilot of a B-52 fighter jet, but was never satisfied with the accent he devised for the character. The estimable Slim Pickens, a mainstay of Hollywood Westerns, ended up playing Kong without a trace of irony— exactly what the part needed.

Kubrick cast George C. Scott and James Earl Jones after seeing them in a Central Park production of *The Merchant of Venice*, using his background as an amateur chess fanatic to keep the normally recalcitrant George C. Scott in check. According to Jones, Scott's occasionally over-the-top performance was a result of manipulations by the director, who used takes he promised were just experiments. Sterling Hayden, who had appeared in Kubrick's *The Killing* (1956), came out of retirement to play the delusional Turgidson.

This was the first time Kubrick worked with Ken Adam, who would later win an Oscar for *Barry Lyndon* (1975). Adam said that his background as an RAF pilot in World War II fascinated the director. Since the military refused to cooperate with the production, art director Peter Murton had to construct the cockpit of the B-52 from photos he found in a paperback book called *Strategic Air Command* by Mel Hunter. The exterior of the plane was a series of models filmed over second unit footage taken in the Arctic. Adam was responsible for the War Room, one of his typically stunning giant-size sets.

The director also appropriated effects from outside sources. The opening credits unfold over stock footage of refueling planes; the film closes with stock footage as well. By incorporating brand names like Coca-Cola and Bell Telephone, the director could add an extra veneer of reality. A narration adopts the tone of a serious, government-sponsored piece of propaganda; footage inside the B-52 could have been taken from a military training film. An attack on an airfield is shot with handheld telephoto lenses that mimic battleground documentaries—or reports to come from Vietnam. (Kubrick was a cameraman for the attack sequence.) No matter what his influences, Kubrick's technique is extraordinary through *Dr. Strangelove*. He shows an explosion inside an airplane with eight shots in ten seconds, allowing the soundtrack to distort and the film stock to flare before adding a tracking shot that pulls viewers into the action, letting them sense what is happening even if they don't absorb all the details. It's a sequence filmmakers are still copying.

Kubrick fanatics obsessively pore over the details of his films, finding hidden meanings in maps, lamps, bathrooms, and other supposed "trademarks." One of their most sought-after Kubrick pieces is the original ending to the film, an eleven-minute pie-fight sequence in the War Room. Kubrick wisely jettisoned it before the opening, which was scheduled for December 1963. It had to be moved to the following year because of the assassination of President John F. Kennedy (a line of dialogue referring to Dallas had to be redubbed as well).

It is difficult to imagine today the impact *Dr. Strangelove* had on contemporary viewers. The rival film *Fail-Safe* (1964) treated the subject with deadly seriousness; Kubrick neatly finessed that film by turning nuclear war into a chess game that no one could win. In a farce marked by empty posturing and fatal logic, audiences have nowhere to turn for relief. In retrospect he may not have needed Terry Southern. The film's smutty names and jokes about orgasms are the stuff of a schoolboy's daydream. But the best parts of *Dr. Strangelove* move with the inexorable drive of *Paths of Glory* (1957) and with the deadpan brilliance of a Buster Keaton short. The film showed the world the insanity of a policy of Mutual Assured Destruction without once bogging down into the particulars of right or wrong, of United States versus Russia. This towering work was Kubrick's last completely successful film, and is arguably the best of his career.

The Cool World

Cinema V, 1964. Sound, B&W, 1.37. 104 minutes.

Cast: Hampton Clanton (Duke), Carl Lee (Priest), Yolanda Rodriguez (Luanne), Clarence Williams (Blood), Gary Bolling (Littleman), Bostic Felton (Rod), Gloria Foster (Mrs. Custis), John Marriot (Hurst), Georgia Burke (Grandma), Marilyn Cox (Miss Dewpont), Jerome Raphael (Mr. Shapiro), Mel Stewart (Con-man), Joseph Dennis (Douglas Thurston). The Kids: Ronald Perry (Savage), Charles Richardson (Beepbop), Bruce Edwards (Warrior), Lloyd Edwards (Foxy), Ted McCain (Saint), Joe Oliver (Angel), Claude Cave (Hardy), Maurice Sneed (Rocky). With: William Ford (Ace), Ken Sutherland (Big Jeff), J.C. Lee (1st Coolie), Bert Donaldson (Forty-five), Billy Taylor (Mission), Riley Mac (Mac), Alfred Collymore (China). Adults: George W. Goodman (Newscaster), Richard Ward (Street speaker), Jay Brooks (Littleman's father); Val Besoglio, Vic Ramano (Gangsters); Ted Butler (Mr. Osborne), Pheta Canegata (Pheta), William Canegata (Cop). Sandra McPherson (Coney Island girl), Wilbur Green (Priest's buddy), Nettie Avery (Big Daddy), Esther Bodie, Irma Williams (The two ladies).

Credits: Directed & edited by Shirley Clarke. Screenplay by Shirley Clarke, Carl Lee. From the novel by Warren Miller and the play by Warren Miller & Robert Rossen. Producer: Frederick Wiseman. Director of photography: Baird Bryant. Sound mixer: Richard Vorisek. Sound editor: Hugh A. Robertson, Jr. 1st assistant editor: Laurence Solomon. Assistant editors: Richard Preston, John Oettinger. Set design: Roger Furman. Additional footage: Leroy McLucas. Script consultant: Edward Bland. Sound: Dave Jones. Music composed & arranged by Mal Waldron. Jazz group: Dizzy Gillespie, Yuseff Lateef, Mal Waldron, Aaron Bell, Art Taylor. Rock & Roll Group: Hal Singer, Charles Jackson, Julian Evell, Herbie Lovelle. Calliope: Stan Free. Gospel music: Barbara Webb. Music recording: William Blachly. Assistant to the cameraman: Jane Bryant. Interior lighting: Tom Mangravite. Assistant director: Alex Goitein. Wardrobe mistress: Gertha Brock. Casting & dialogue director: Carl Lee. Production manager & assistant to the producer: Dorothy Oshlag. Continuity & assistant to the director: Madeline Anderson. Associate editor: Peggy Lawson. Print by Movielab. A Wiseman Film Company Production.

Additional Credits: Opened in New York City onApril 20, 1964.

Available: Zipporah Films (*www.zipporah.com*).

The second feature by Shirley Clarke, *The Cool World* was a deliberate attempt to provoke filmgoers grown complacent on a diet of Hollywood movies. A six-minute pre-credit sequence shot on the streets of Harlem sets the tone: as a sidewalk preacher delivers a withering anti-white sermon ("The white man is the devil . . . we have known slavery not only of the body but of the very soul. . . ."), a teenage gang member tries to buy a handgun before embarking on a class trip down Fifth Avenue to Wall Street. The pulsing jazz on the soundtrack and the documentary-like camerawork assaulted viewers, most of whom had never seen this world before.

Music and documentaries played important roles in Clarke's professional life. Born in 1925 in New York City, she started out as an avant-garde dancer, turning to film in order to document choreographer Daniel Nagrin's *Dance in the Sun* (1953). Clarke explored theories of rhythm and movement in other short pieces, and joined with experimental filmmakers Stan Brakhage and Jonas Mekas in the Independent Filmmakers of America, an attempt to form a distribution network for alternative films. Along with Willard Van Dyke, DA Pennebaker, and Richard Leacock, she was part of a team that shot shorts for the United States Pavilion at the 1958 World's Fair in Brussels. Clarke used her leftover footage for *Bridges-Go-Round* (1958), a significant example of Abstract Expressionism in film.

Clarke's first feature, *The Connection* (1960), commented on the spread of cinema verité among documentarians. In it, heroin addicts react to the presence of a motion-picture camera while waiting for a dealer to arrive with their next fix. The film sparked a legal battle against state censorship boards that reached the Supreme Court, with Clarke ultimately winning the right to use language that was in violation of obscenity laws.

Clarke's decision to adapt *The Cool World* came about through her collaborator, Carl Lee. Originally a 1959 novel by Warren Miller, *The Cool World* had been adapted for the stage by the author and Robert Rossen, an Oscar-winning screenwriter and director. The play opened on Broadway in February 1960 and featured some significant actors, among them James Earl Jones, Cicely Tyson, and Raymond St. Jacques. It was Rossen's first play since 1935, but it ran for only two performances. (His next project was *The Hustler*, filmed in 1961 with Paul Newman.)

The son of Canada Lee, a boxer and actor who was blacklisted in the 1950s for his views on desegregation, Carl Lee rehearsed with gang members to refashion the novel into something that would more closely approximate actual conditions on the streets of Harlem. Lee, who had also appeared in *The Connection*, took the role of Priest, a small-time pimp and con artist who gets into trouble with the downtown mob. As Duke Custis, a role played on stage by Billy Dee Williams, Clarke cast Hampton "Rony" Clanton, a teenager from North Carolina. Clanton remarked later on the trouble he had keeping a straight face during his love scenes.

Duke's goal in *The Cool World* is to get enough money to buy a Colt handgun from Priest, something he feels will win him the presidency of the Royal Pythons gang. Duke wants passersby to say of him, "It's a cold killer," an ambition that continues to be glorified in some areas of pop culture. For much of the film, Clarke follows the outlines of Miller's novel, but she can shift the focus of the story in ways that weren't available on stage. When Duke and his girlfriend Luanne (Yolanda Rodriguez) go to Coney Island, for example, Clarke can slow the pace down to dwell on boardwalk arcade games, the empty beach, and the only truly open sky in the film. Scenes set in the Python clubhouse have the uncertain timing and unfocused conversations of real life, the result of extensive improvisations and rehearsals.

By the time *The Cool World* was released, rival independent films like John Cassavetes' *Shadows* (1959) had already opened theatrically. But Cassavetes was still using actors to tell actorly stories about love and jealousy and show business ambition. Viewers saw in *West Side Story* (1961) a sanitized Harlem in which gangs danced in chorus lines and teen lovers inadvertently acted out Shakespeare. *The Cool World*, with its sprawling gang rumbles and sadistic sex, was like a slap to both schools of filmmaking.

Several actors in *The Cool World* had long-term careers. Lee appeared in *Superfly* (1972); Clarence Williams in TV's *The Mod Squad*); Gloria Foster in *Nothing But a Man* (1964) and *The Matrix* (1999); and Val Besoglio on HBO's *The Sopranos*. Clarke would make only one more feature, the controversial *Portrait of Jason* (1967). After an unsatisfying experience in Hollywood, she turned to video for pieces like *Ornette: Made in America* (1986). Frederick Wiseman, the film's producer, turned to directing documentaries like *Titicut Follies* (1967) and *High School* (1968, a Registry title).

Empire

Andy Warhol, 1964. Silent, B&W, 1.37. 486 minutes.
Credits: Directed by Andy Warhol. Photographed by Jonas Mekas.
Available: The Museum of Modern Art.

According to Gerard Malanga, an artist and photographer who worked closely with Andy Warhol at the time, "It was John Palmer who came up with the idea for *Empire*." Malanga knew Palmer through Wagner College; Palmer knew Henry Romney, vice-president of the Rockefeller Foundation, headquartered in New York City. Romney's office, on the forty-fourth floor of the Time-Life Building, had an unobstructed view of the Empire State Building sixteen blocks to the south. On July 25, 1964, Warhol, accompanied by Malanga, Palmer, cinematographer Jonas Mekas, and Marie Desert, went to Romney's office.

Mekas set up an Auricon 16mm sound camera and pointed it at the Empire State Building. From 8:06 p.m. until 2:42 the following morning, he filmed the building in one unchanging shot. The Auricon held 1,200 feet of film in one magazine, roughly thirty-five minutes, necessitating fourteen magazine or "reel" changes. During these reel changes, Warhol occasionally left the lights in

Romney's office on; on these occasions, you can see the filmmakers' reflections in the office windows.

What else do you see in *Empire*? A better question might be, "What do you watch?" Viewers quickly exhaust the visual information in the *Empire* frame; after a few minutes, they have nothing left to "read" or interpret. They can concentrate on the changes in the frame—building lights that blink on and off, the flash frames caught on reel changes, the streaks made during film processing—but inevitably will find their minds wandering, unable to concentrate fully on an image that doesn't merit full attention. The building may start to lose its iconic power, to become a backdrop, a scenic element, something seen but not noticed outside a window.

Who would watch a single, basically unchanging shot for eight hours? Warhol offered some answers about *Empire* and his other films. He said that he was interested in investigating the difference between "real" and "reel" time, for example. He was in the process of redefining what could and couldn't be "art." On a more practical level, he was still establishing a reputation as an underground, rather than commercial, artist. It was imperative

601

for Warhol to position himself as far from the mainstream as possible, while still presenting work that was instantly recognizable, that required no training in art appreciation. At the same time, he had to distinguish his work from other, more "reputable" independent artists. He was not willing to be the next Bruce Conner.

Born Andrew Warhola in Pittsburgh, Pennsylvania, in 1928, he studied painting at the Carnegie Institute of Technology. He moved to New York in 1949, where he became a financially successful commercial artist. He had his first New York exhibition in 1952, bought a townhouse in 1959, and became interested in experimental film through the Film-Makers' Cooperative, founded by Jonas Mekas in 1960. Warhol bought his first motion picture camera, a 16mm Bolex, in 1963.

One of his first movies, *Sleep*, was planned as an eight-hour film, although the actual running time is some three hours shorter. *Empire* can be seen as a natural outgrowth of *Sleep*. Mekas shot at twenty-four frames per second, but Warhol had the film projected at silent speed, sixteen frames per second, giving the film a softer, more dreamlike quality, and not incidentally padding its running time by some two hours.

It's tempting to treat Warhol's early movies as jokes, although several critics have made serious defenses of them. But Warhol was an indisputably talented draftsman and a wizard as a promoter, so it's difficult to simply dismiss outright his choices or inspirations. It may be impossible to determine

how sincere he was about his film work. (One of his next films was a seventy-minute shot of Taylor Mead's rear end.) But the splash he made in the 1960s had an enormous influence on popular culture. In the films that followed, like *Chelsea Girls* (1966), Warhol began to experiment with sound and image, with size and shape of the frame, with acting and directing.

Nevertheless, he began to withdraw from film, especially after he was shot by Valerie Solanas. Paul Morrissey and others assumed the technical duties of actually shooting the movies. By that point, like Dali, Warhol had become a brand name. And like most independent filmmakers, he discovered that exploitation films were the path to profit. With X-rated titles like *Trash* (1970) and *Andy Warhol's Frankenstein* (1973), he found the mainstream audience that had eluded him earlier.

While he was alive, Warhol resisted attempts to edit or otherwise condense *Empire*. As a result, it is one of the most difficult titles to see from the National Film Registry. No commercial theater would risk showing it, despite Warhol's wishes. The work is too ungainly for most museums to show as well. The Museum of Modern Art, which has the original film elements, does screen it on occasion—most recently in September 2006. The museum also showed a two-hour excerpt during the exhibition *Out of Time: A Contemporary View* in 2006 and 2007. A one-hour excerpt showed up on *Andy Warhol: Four Silent Movies*, an Italian bootleg DVD on the Raro Video label.

Nothing But a Man

Cinema V, 1964. Sound, B&W, 1.37. 92 minutes.

Cast: Ivan Dixon (Duff [Anderson]), Abbey Lincoln (Josie), Julius Harris (Will [Anderson]), Gloria Foster (Lee), Martin Priest (Mill worker), Leonard Parker (Frankie), Yaphet Kotto (Jocko), Stanley Greene (Rev. Dawson), Helen Lounck (Effi), Helene Arrindell (Doris), Walter Wilson (Car owner), Milton Williams (Pop), Melvin Stewart (Riddick), Rev. Marshal Tompkin (Revivalist), Alfred Puryear (Barney), Charles McRae (Joe), Ed Rowan (Willie), Tom Ligon, William Jordon (Teenagers), Dorothy Hall (Soloist), Gertrude Jeanette (Mrs. Dawson), Gil Rogers (Mill foreman), Richard Webber (Garage owner), Eugene Wood (Superintendent), Jim Wright (Barman), Arland Schubert (Hiring boss), Peter Carew (Store keeper), Bill Riola (Ginn foreman), Jay Brooks (Undertaker), Robert Berger (Desk clerk), Jary Banks (Bessie), Richard Ward, Moses Gunn (Mill hands), Mark Shapiro, William Phillipps (Car passengers), Sylvia Ray, Esther Rolle, Evelyn Davis (Church women).

Credits: Directed by Michael Roemer. Written by Michael Roemer and Robert Young. Produced by Robert Young, Michael Roemer, Robert Rubin. Photographed by Robert Young. Assistant cameraman: Peter Vollstadt. Electrician: Frank Sukosd. Edited by Luke Bennett. Associate editor: Robert Machover. Assistant editor: Peter Gessner. Unit manager: William Rhodes. Sound: Robert Rubin. Sound mixer: Albert Gramaglia.

Harmonica: Wilbur Kirk. Location manager: Philip Clarkson. Assistant: Clayton Riley. Costumes: Nancy Ruffing. Secretary: Sandi Nelson. Services: Cal Penny. Titles: F. Hillsberg, Inc. Musical artists by arrangement with Motown Record Corporation. Music performed by: Mary Wells, The Gospel Stars, Martha and the Vandellas, the Miracles, Holland-Dozier, Little Stevie Wonder, The Marvelettes. A Roemer-Young Du Art production. Produced in Association with Du Art Film Laboratories. By arrangement with Bay State Film Productions, Inc.

Additional Credits: Production dates: June to September 1964. Opened in New York City on November 27, 1964.

Available: New Video Group DVD (2004). ISBN: 0-7670-2616-0. UPC: 7-67685-94613-8.

Filmed during a period of extreme racial tension, *Nothing But a Man* tried to show in personal terms how racism affected the lives of blacks in the rural South. The fact that it was written, photographed, and directed by white Harvard graduates with backgrounds in documentaries may have been a factor in the film's limited success during its initial release.

Born in Berlin in 1928, writer and director Michael Roemer experienced Kristallnacht as a frightened ten-year-old. His family fled to England; after World War II, he entered Harvard. Roemer met Robert Young while making *A Touch of the Times*, a student film. Young, born in 1931, had dropped out of MIT to serve in the Navy as a photographer's mate. About the war, he later said, "I developed a strong identification with the underdog."

After college, Young went to NBC to film and assemble documentaries like *Sit-In*, which covered the efforts by Fisk College students to integrate a Nashville lunch counter. Fired after working for eight years with newsreel pioneer Louis de Rochemont, Roemer joined Young at NBC. The team filmed *Cortile Cascino*, a documentary about Sicily, for the network's "White Paper" series. Two days before it was to air, executives pulled it from the schedule. Devastated, Young said that he and Roemer decided to "never make anything that anyone could take away from us . . . we said 'Let's go South.'"

Young's previous work with African-Americans, and a letter from Roy Wilkins, the head of the NAACP, gave the filmmakers entry to a society on the verge of momentous change. Traveling from South Carolina to New Orleans, they gathered research and film footage that they would later fashion into the script for *Nothing But a Man*. Their script would focus on Duff Anderson, a laborer on a railroad section gang, and his relationship with Josie Dawson, a twenty-six-year-old schoolteacher living with her father, a minister, and her stepmother. With few family ties and an independent, well-paying job, Duff has been immune to much of the segregation endured by less transient blacks. Faced with the new responsibilities and the pervasive injustice in a world where he was a second-class citizen, Duff could have fled the region for the North. But Young and Roemer were adamant about cutting off this option: they wanted Duff to solve his problems without running away, or losing his dignity.

Today, Roemer readily admits that whites shouldn't have been making a film like *Nothing But a Man*. But, "This was a story we were allowed to tell . . . no one else was telling it." As he said to one cast member, "This is not about black people necessarily. This is about oppression." Given the filmmakers' backgrounds, the documentary realism

and understated acting styles could be expected. Not so the prescient script, which addresses issues that are still critical to the black community today. The lack of a family structure, the use of coded words, the place of religion, the impact of poverty: all are worked into a romance that is depicted with sensitivity and insight. As Young said, "There was not much rhetoric in it," an important point for a project that was initially greeted with skepticism.

Charles Gordone, a playwright who won a Pulitzer for *No Place to Be Somebody*, suggested three principal cast members: Ivan Dixon, Abbey Lincoln, and Julius Harris. Born in New York in 1931, Dixon studied acting before making his debut on Broadway in *The Cave Dwellers* in 1957. He sometimes doubled for Sidney Poitier in films, and appeared in a supporting role in both the play and film versions of *A Raisin in the Sun*. This was his first starring film role. Born Anna Marie Wooldridge in Chicago in 1939, Abbey Lincoln was a successful supper-club singer who recorded with Benny Carter in 1956. That same year she appeared as herself in Frank Tashlin's *The Girl Can't Help It*, singing "Spread the Word." By the time of *Nothing But a Man*, Lincoln had married drummer Max Roach. This was the film debut for Julius Harris, a nurse-turned-actor who had also been a boxer and musician, as it was for Yaphet Kotto, Esther Rolle, Mel Stewart, Leonard Parker, and Moses Gunn.

Shooting took place between June and September 1963, mostly in Cape May, New Jersey, with Atlantic City filling in for Birmingham, Alabama. During that period, Medgar Evers was shot dead in Jackson, Mississippi. The March on Washington took place in August; there Dr. Martin Luther King, Jr., delivered his "I Have a Dream" speech. On September 15, a bomb killed four girls at the Sixteenth Street Baptist Church in Birmingham. Meanwhile, black cast members of *Nothing But a Man* had to stay in a segregated hotel, and chafed when they weren't allowed to attend the March on Washington. Dixon even quit temporarily, talked back onto the set by assistant Clayton Riley.

By the end of the shoot, Roemer and Young's crew was down to one grip. Roemer remembers using a boat trailer to improvise tracking shots. Remarkably, the director received permission to use songs from Motown Records from his college friend George Schiffer, then an attorney for Motown head Berry Gordy, Jr.

The film was chosen for the Venice Film Festival in 1964, and screened at the New York Film Festival that same year. It opened commercially at New York's Cinema V, and at a few art-house theaters in other cities. But it never found much of an audience. About the first screenings, Roemer said, "Everybody walked out. People just looked depressed." Professional distributors thought the film unsuitable for whites because of its black subject matter. And many theater owners were wary about advertising to black filmgoers. *Nothing But a Man*'s reputation grew through an underground movement of cinema clubs and church groups.

Roemer expresses regrets about the film today. The relative lack of humor, for example, or the wish that he had introduced Duff's character as an angrier person. About the shooting, he said, "I made serious mistakes. There were tensions between the white component and the African-American component." Dixon for one has spoken about Roemer as a "director who used actors as puppets." Roemer would give the cast inflections, even expressions he wanted them to use. As Lincoln described it, "*Nothing But a Man* was the same as the music, really. It was brilliantly conceived. Precise, too. Michael Roemer knew what key he wanted things in. You couldn't do just anything you wanted to do."

Restraint and indirection mark the film, both in Roemer's work and Young's cinematography. *Nothing But a Man* is filled with difficult shots. One pans from the backseat of a speeding car, the sun rising through a forest seen through windows, to a child sleeping in the front seat. A scene of Duff departing a church service at night has the formal purity of German expressionism. Yet Young never calls attention to his work, which is all about capturing honest performances within realistic settings.

The film broke taboos just by showing Abbey Lincoln brushing her teeth, or kissing Ivan Dixon. But Roemer's strongest effects came from what he didn't show, by what the characters don't say. The fact that Duff doesn't know where or when his father was born, for example. A shot of Josie's wedding that ends just as her father, the minister, glares at her. For much of the film, Roemer's characteristic reaction shot is of nothing: the school superintendent closing a door behind him, Duff's back turned when Josie questions him about his son.

Roemer's next film, *The Plot Against Harry*, shot by Young in 1969, was not released until 1989. Roemer also taught film at Yale. Young has had an extensive career as a writer, director, and producer. Ivan Dixon also became a director after working as an actor in television. Abbey Lincoln appeared with Sidney Poitier in *For Love of Ivy* (1968), but her political activism may have restricted her acting opportunities. Gloria Foster, so memorable here as Will Anderson's girlfriend, married actor and director Clarence Williams III. She gained a new generation of fans as The Oracle in *The Matrix* (1999), and died of diabetes while filming *The Matrix Reloaded* (2003).

The T.A.M.I. Show

Electronovision/AIP, 1964. Sound, B&W, 1.66. 111 minutes.

Featuring: Jan and Dean ("Here They Come," "The Little Old Lady from Pasadena," Sidewalk Surfin'"), Chuck Berry ("Johnny B. Goode," "Sweet Little Sixteen," "Nadine," Maybellene"), Gerry and the Pacemakers ("Maybellene," "Don't Let the Sun Catch You Crying," "It's Gonna Be Alright," "How Do You Do It?" "I Like It"), Smokey Robinson and the Miracles ("That's What Love Is Made Of," "You Really Got a Hold on Me," "Mickey's Monkey"), Marvin Gaye with the Blossoms ("Stubborn Kind of Fellow," "Pride and Joy," "Can I Get a Witness," "Hitchhike"), Lesley Gore ("Maybe I Know," "You Don't Own Me," "It's My Turn," "Judy's Turn to Cry"), The Beach Boys ("Surfin' U.S.A." "Surfer Girl," "Dance Dance Dance," "I Get Around"), Billy J. Kramer and the Dakotas ("Little Children," "I'll Keep You Satisfied," "Bad to Me," "From a Window"), The Supremes ("When the Lovelight Starts Shining Through His Eyes," "Run Run Run," "Baby Love," "Where Did Our Love Go?"), The Barbarians ("Hey Little Bird"), James Brown and the Fabulous Flames ("Out of Sight," "Prisoner of Love," "Please Please Please," "Night Train"), The Rolling Stones ("Around and Around," "Off the Hook," "Time Is On My Side," "It's All Right").

Credits: Directed by Steve Binder. Producer: Lee Savin. Executive producer: William Sargent, Jr. Director of photography: James E. Kilgore. Production designer: Frank Swig. Special material: Digby Wolfe.

Production manager: Del Jack. Post production supervisor: S. Richard Krown. Production coordinator: John Rougeot. Technical supervisor: Robert J. Ringer. Technical director: Charles W. La Force, Jr. Video engineer: Carl Hanseman. Audio engineer Lionel St. Peter. Audio consultant: David Hassinger. Camera operators: John Braislin, Ernie Hall, Ken Lampkin, Gary Stanton. Film editors: Bruce Pierce, Kent Mac Kenzie. Sound editor: Ronnie Ashcroft. Associate director: George Turpin. Music arranged and conducted by Jack Nitsche [Nitzsche]. Theme song "Here They Come" written by Steve Barri, Phil Sloan. Associate producer: Al Ham. Choreography: David Winters. Assisted by Toni Basil. Production assistant: Nannette Eiland. Costumer: Wallace A. Harton. Talent consultant: Amanda Bluth. Fashions from Corky Hale, Hollywood. Producers assistant: Carol Bartlett. Technical facilities by Mark Armistead T.V. Inc. under the supervision of Joseph E. Bluth. Electronic film recording by RCA. Film processing by Technicolor. Recorded at the Santa Monica Civic Auditorium, Santa Monica, California, on October 28 and 29, 1964. A Theatrofilm by Electronovision in association with Screen Entertainment Co.

Additional Cast: Teri Garr.

Additional Credits: Alternate title: *Teenage Command Performance*. Released December 29, 1964.

Other Versions: Sequel *The Big T.N.T. Show* (1966, directed by Larry Peerce and produced by Phil Spector). The two films were edited together for the home video market under the title *That Was Rock* (1984).

Available: The Library of Congress. "Out of Sight" by James Brown is excerpted on the Shout Factory DVD *I Got the Feelin': James Brown in the '60s* (2008). UPC: 8-26663-10879-8.

With movie attendance in a freefall in the late 1950s, desperate studio executives turned to alternative processes to draw television viewers back into theaters. Color, stereo sound, and widescreen formats worked for a time, but movies were still failing to connect with younger audiences. Producers like James Nicholson and Samuel Arkoff at American International Pictures were among the first to tap into rock music as a means to attract teenagers. But the early rock 'n' roll films tended to be weak updatings of old-fashioned musical formulas, with singers limited to lip-synching to prerecorded tracks. It was a technique that worked fine for Elvis Presley, a performer groomed for the movies, but one that could not adjust to a pop market that was breaking new acts every week.

Electronovision, the brainchild of H. William "Bill" Sargent, Jr., wasn't designed for rock music, but as a cheap method of distributing Broadway plays to a nationwide audience. Born in 1927 in Oklahoma, Sargent was a self-taught electronics wizard who held some four hundred patents for tape heads, amplifiers, camera components, and other devices. He made enough money installing public address systems to move to Los Angeles in 1959. There he started the Home Entertainment Company (HEC), which specialized in closed-circuit television broadcasts. He produced a boxing match featuring Cassius Clay (Muhammad Ali) that prefigured the pay-per-view market.

Sargent sold HEC to found Electronovision, promising presentations of live performances featuring better quality video-to-film transfers. His first production, Richard Burton performing *Hamlet* on Broadway, earned millions of dollars. Sargent then hired Steve Binder to put together a rock concert featuring the best available groups. They had worked together a few years earlier on a benefit for the NAACP.

In 2004, Binder told reporter Steve Rosen that Sargent had serious plans for his rock movie. The concert was staged for something called T.A.M.I., which stood for either Teen Age Music International or Teenage Awards Music International, described in a souvenir pamphlet as "an international nonprofit organization" that was going to help teenagers "establish a position of respect in their communities." In a foreshadowing of today's *American Idol*, teens were supposed to vote on their favorite musicians who were competing for awards.

Sargent's plans fell apart when he lost control of the project to AIP. He continued packaging events, including *Give 'em Hell Harry* (1975), a version of James Whitmore's one-man show about Harry S. Truman, and *Richard Pryor Live in Concert* (1979), the first in a series of films of performances by stand-up comedians. He invested in *Beatlemania*, a long-running stage piece consisting of covers of Beatles songs that was the subject of considerable legal wrangling with the group. "I'm always being sued," Mr. Sargent said later.

The T.A.M.I. Show offered a surprisingly broad cross-section of rock 'n' roll acts. Some areas were underrepresented: pop music from Philadelphia and from New York City's Brill Building, garage rock from the Pacific Northwest, soul from Memphis. Still, three of Motown's hottest acts (at the time in the midst of a package tour) were there, as were two surf groups, one of them The Beach Boys, arguably the most popular band in the United States at the time. (The Boys, either miffed at not being the closing act, or aware of how poorly their performance compared to the other musicians, had their segment removed when the film was rereleased.) "British Invasion" groups like Gerry and the Pacemakers were overshadowed by The Rolling Stones, still without a solid hit in the States but on the verge of stardom.

The Stones are the most interesting group to watch in the film. They had appeared frequently on British television, but had yet to work out their stage personalities for American audiences. (They had debuted on *The Ed Sullivan Show* just a few days earlier.) You can see rhythm guitarist Brian Jones calculating what expressions to use, just as you can sense Binder and his cameramen experimenting with how to capture the group. The Stones had been afraid to appear after James Brown, a dynamic stage performer whose act ended with a literal showstopper, but received encouragement from Marvin Gaye. "Just go out there and do your thing," he told them. Brown later called the movie "a masterpiece and the beginning of my career in one way. I'd been getting that kind of response for a long time, but white people didn't get to see me because they didn't go to the venues I was playing at."

Which was exactly Sargent's point. *The T.A.M.I. Show* was a chance for suburban teenagers to see

Brown and Motown acts, as well as British groups who characteristically had very limited Stateside tours. Brown's "Papa's Got a Brand New Bag" was a tremendous hit a few weeks later, broadening his audience immeasurably. This was also a turning point of sorts for The Supremes, under Berry Gordy's guidance an extremely polished singing trio. They were soon to become two singers backing up Diana Ross, due in part to her remarkable connection to the camera. Chuck Berry's offhand performance, in which he discarded lyrics and threw off the house band's timing, may have been an indication of his declining sales, or his disdain at the fact that all the rock groups in the movie had stolen his music.

The production was also a chance for technicians to hone their skills in filming rock acts: how to follow the music, when to cut to close-ups, what backdrops to use, how to incorporate prerecorded tracks into live performances, how to sweeten audience sounds. Most of *The T.A.M.I.* show relies on a three-camera set-up used by television for sitcoms, although Binder also had a crane to work with. When two cameras positioned behind the Stones shoot out into the audience, they provide some of the most exciting footage in the movie. Future filmmakers would use the same vantage points in *Monterey Pop* (1969) and *Woodstock* (1970).

Those concert films helped sound the death knell for Sargent's original plans. Television itself, which incorporated the look and style of *The T.A.M.I. Show* into series like *Shindig* and *Hullaballoo*, was another factor. Still, there is a palpable thrill to *The T.A.M.I. Show*, a sense that both musicians and filmmakers were discovering themselves, that is largely missing from what followed. An edited version was briefly available on home video, but rights to the film are now held by Dick Clark Productions, which has no plans to rerelease it.

Dog Star Man

Stan Brakhage, 1961–64. Silent, color, 1.37. 74 minutes.

Credits: Filmmaker: Stan Brakhage.

Sections: *Prelude* (25 minutes), *Part 1* (30 minutes), *Part 2* (5 minutes), *Part 3* (7 minutes), *Part 4* (6 minutes).

Other Versions: *The Art of Vision* (1965).

Available: 16mm prints from Canyon Cinema (*www.canyoncinema.com*) and Film-Makers' Cooperative (*www.film-makerscoop.com*). Criterion Collection DVD (2003). UPC: 7-15515-01402-1.

The most prolific and influential of experimental filmmakers, Stan Brakhage was born Robert Sanders in a Kansas City orphanage in 1933. Adopted three weeks after his birth, he grew up in Denver, where he appeared on radio as a boy soprano. Influenced by Sergei Eisenstein and Jean Cocteau, Brakhage dropped out of Dartmouth to make films. His first, *Interim* (1952), detailed an encounter between teenagers in an Italian neorealist style. Brakhage moved to San Francisco and then to New York, in both cities allying himself with avant-garde artists like Maya Deren, John Cage, and Joseph Cornell, with whom he collaborated on short films. Ill and destitute, he returned to Denver in 1957, where he married.

Brakhage continued to struggle financially, directing commercials, industrials, and sponsored films, and later teaching film history for three decades. But his output as a filmmaker was extraordinary—over four hundred films, ranging from shorts less than ten seconds long to collections and cycles that could run over four hours.

Film critic Fred Camper finds in Brakhage's work a "quest for 'moving visual thinking' that doesn't depend on language." Brakhage told interviewer Scott MacDonald that an optician identified his eyesight as having abnormally rapid saccadic movements—in other words, he tended to scan and assemble pictures in his head rather than seeing them whole. "I wasn't trying to invent new ways of being a filmmaker, that was just a byproduct of my struggle to come to a sense of sight," he said.

Brakhage's exposure to artists like Cornell, his perceived physical limitations, and his maturing theories of filmmaking led him to abandon conventional narrative techniques. Instead, he adopted a variety of methods to alter the way we see and interact with movies. He scratched the emulsion, for example, painted directly on celluloid, and sandwiched physical objects like grass and moths between clear strips of film. He superimposed images on top of each other, flipped exposed stock, ran footage backward and upside-down.

He also largely discarded what he called "oppositional editing"—the traditional shot/reaction shot used by filmmakers almost since the medium was invented. As Camper explains, "opposition is a form of affirmation because it accepts the terms of what is being opposed." Instead, some of Brakhage's editing consists of "lateral moves," attempts to shift the grammar of film. Viewers comfortable with mainstream narrative techniques can often feel at a loss when confronted with Brakhage's dense layers of imagery. For some contemporaries, the experience had ties to improvisatory jazz, beat poetry, or abstract painting.

On a more fundamental basis, Brakhage was also trying to shift the meaning of film, expanding what a movie could show, or what it could be about. *Desistfilm* (1954) used a lurching, handheld camera to try to mimic the effects of inebriation. *The Act of Seeing With One's Own Eyes* (1971) included clinical autopsies and open-heart surgery. *Mothlight* (1963) was made without a camera, using found objects.

Brakhage began *Dog Star Man* around the same time he was writing *Metaphors on Vision*, which explained his theories about film. The film cycle consists of four parts and a prelude made between 1961 and 1964. What the cycle "means" is open to interpretation, although some clues are available. Sirius, the Dog Star, is the brightest star in the sky apart from the sun; it was also the name of Brakhage's pet dog. According to critic P. Adams Sitney, the four parts occur during a single day, with the *Prelude* depicting "dreams of the preceding night." The four parts can be broken down roughly into seasons. Camper describes the plot as: a woodsman (played by Brakhage) attempts to chop down a tree on top of a mountain during a blizzard.

Technically, *Part 1* consisted of a single film; *Part 2* had two rolls of film superimposed over each other; *Part 3* used three rolls of film, one of Brakhage, one of his wife at the time, and one of viscera; *Part 4*, a continuation of *Part 1*, consisted of four strips of film superimposed over each other. In *The Art of Vision* (1965), Brakhage projected each element of *Dog Star Man* separately and sequentially over a roughly four-hour period.

Many filmmakers have copied the "look" of Brakhage's films, but few have matched his conceptual rigor. His ideas have been assimilated into mainstream culture, in everything from music videos to feature films. A persistent rumor makes Brakhage the cinematographer of one of the iconic ads of the 1960s, in which a bottle of Downey Fabric Softener falls in slow motion onto a pile of folded towels. Records of the On Film ad agency in Princeton, where Brakhage was an employee, have been lost, and the filmmaker's widow Marilyn believes the commercial may have been for Scott Tissue. Whatever ads Brakhage may have been responsible for, his ways of seeing have had an enormous impact on film and on our culture as a whole. He contracted bladder cancer in 1966, possibly as a result of dyes he used to paint his films, and died of the disease in 2003.

The March

USIA, 1964. Sound, B&W, 1.37. 32 minutes.
Credits: Directed by James Blue.
Additional Credits: Produced by George Stevens, Jr. A News of the Day production. Title on screen: *The March in Washington*.
Available: National Archives DVD (*www.archives.gov*). UPC: 8-83629-57016-7.

The March on Washington for Jobs and Freedom, a landmark in the civil rights movement, took place on August 28, 1963. It was initiated by A. Philip Randolph, who had suggested a similar march in 1941, and was organized by several civil rights leaders, including Bayard Rustin, John Lewis, and Dr. Martin Luther King, Jr. Over 200,000 people took part, arriving in chartered buses, trains, and airplanes. Their route led from the Washington Monument to the Lincoln Memorial, where a podium was erected for speakers and performers.

Marian Anderson, whose 1939 concert at the Lincoln Memorial is also on the Registry, was supposed to lead the opening National Anthem, but could not reach the stage through the crush of the crowd. She sang "He's Got the Whole World in His Hands" later in the program. Other performers included Eva Jessye, Joan Baez, and Mahalia Jackson. Randolph, Lewis, Mrs. Medger Evers, and Roy Wilkins were among those who spoke, but today the march is remembered best as the setting for King's "I Have a Dream" speech, one of the most recognizable pieces of oratory in the country's history. Remarkably, King extemporized the final portion of the speech, in some accounts after Mahalia Jackson urged him to "Tell them about the dream, Martin."

Some 1,600 press passes were issued by organizers, and the march was covered extensively by both print and broadcast journalists. CBS broadcast the Lincoln Memorial segment live, and the three major networks led with the story on their nightly news programs. (Surprisingly, few of the initial accounts dealt with King's speech.) Such wide coverage, both in this country and abroad, would have discouraged many documentarians from covering the subject. But George Stevens, Jr., at the time the director of the Motion Picture Service at the United States Information Agency (USIA), felt that a film about the march was essential to the mission of the agency.

"There was some opposition to it in the USIA, fearing that it would simply highlight the fact that the US had racial division," he wrote recently. "I saw it as an opportunity to show that in our kind of democracy, protest was part of the system and that the values represented would present a positive picture of the United States."

Stevens, who had been hired by Edward R. Murrow, was twenty-eight when he arrived in Washington, D.C., in February 1962. His background included directing for television and working as an associate producer and second unit director for his father, George, Sr., on features like *The Diary of Anne Frank* (1959). For his first USIA project, he wanted to cover First Lady Jacqueline Kennedy's trip to India and Pakistan. He discovered a significant problem with USIA funding—notably, that he had to accept the lowest bids on contracts for making films.

Stevens established a relationship with the Hearst newsreel company, persuading it to hire documentarian Leo Seltzer. He also recruited film school students, or filmmakers just starting their careers—Charles Guggenheim, who owned a production company in St. Louis, for example, as well as Bruce Herschensohn, Kent Mackenzie, Carroll Ballard, Ed Emshwiller, Tibor Hirsch, and Terry Sanders. Stevens discovered James Blue at the Cannes Film Festival, where he was showing *The Olive Tree of Justice*, a story about the war in Algeria.

An Oklahoma native, Blue studied drama at Oregon University. After military duty, he received a Fulbright Scholarship to study at the Institut des Hautes Études Cinématographiques film school in Paris, where he graduated at the top of his class in 1958. A brief spell at a New York City ad agency led to his return to Europe, where he made seven shorts for Studio Africa. Stevens hired him to work on films for the Alliance of Progress in South America. Blue completed three ten-minute films for the USIA, including *The School at Rincon Santo* (1963), about a schoolhouse built by Colombians with U.S. materials.

As director of the Motion Picture Service, Stevens allowed his staff considerable creative freedom, maintaining control over USIA product through the selection of creative personnel, as well as his approval over treatment, script, and final cuts. He would present filmmakers with a list of potential subjects, asking what appealed to them. "Here were all these young men who had given up jobs to get behind JFK," he told writer Richard Dyer McCann. "It was an exciting atmosphere of fresh thought and action, of energy, of youth."

According to Stevens, Blue came late to the *March* project. "We hired many 35mm cameramen through Hearst News and covered the event thoroughly," he said. "I think it was afterward that I asked Jim Blue to become involved. No one at Hearst could craft the kind of film we wanted." Stevens was looking for a new kind of documentary, one that avoided commentary. "I liked to respect the audience and let them develop their own conclusions wherever possible," he wrote recently. As he told McCann, "We don't want to depend too heavily on narration. We try never to have a voice-of-doom narrator, for example."

Since Stevens didn't want to rely on a voice-over to establish a context for *The March*, he needed material that "spoke" for itself—imagery so strong and vivid that it would outweigh the absence of historical or background information. Tying the various elements of *The March* together was music, especially the unofficial theme songs of the civil rights movement, like "Eyes on the Prize" and "We Shall Overcome." Like King himself, the music, combined with shots of the milling crowds, preached a kind of nonviolence. As a result, both liberals and conservatives found something to complain about with *The March*. There was no mention of violent repression in the South, or of segregation in the North. The *Phoenix Gazette*, on the other hand, complained that the film endorsed "mob action." Secretary of State Dean Rusk was reported to be "greatly disturbed" by the film.

Today, Stevens remembers a slightly different response to the film. "It was, for the most part, wonderfully received by USIA posts overseas, but a few complained. Congressman John Rooney of New York, the chair of the appropriations subcommittee that governed USIA, asked us to screen the film for his committee in a conference room on the Hill. Rooney asked me 'If I got a security clearance on my star.'"

James Blue's *A Few Notes on Our Food Problem* (1968) received an Oscar nomination. He taught at the University of Buffalo, and oversaw a five-part collaborative televions series in Houston called *The Invisible City* (1979). Throughout his career, he taped hundreds of hours of interviews with noted film directors from around the world. Blue died in 1980.

Stevens was the founder of the American Film Institute, and cocreator and producer of the Kennedy Center Honors. He has also written, produced, and directed television specials and dramas. His play *Thurgood,* the story of civil rights pioneer and Supreme Court Justice Thurgood Marshall, opened on Broadway in 2008 with Laurence Fishburne in the title role. His book *Conversations with the Great Filmmakers of Hollywood's Golden Age* was published by Alfred A. Knopf in 2007.

Buses arriving in Washington for *The March*.

The Sound of Music

Twentieth Century-Fox, 1965. Sound, color, 2.20. 174 minutes.
Cast: Julie Andrews (Maria), Christopher Plummer (Captain von Trapp), Eleanor Parker ("The Baroness"), Richard Haydn (Max Detweiler), Peggy Wood (Mother Abbess), Anna Lee (Sister Margaretta), Portia Nelson (Sister Berthe), Ben Wright (Herr Zeller), Daniel Truhitte (Rolfe), Norma Varden (Frau Schmidt), Marni Nixon (Sister Sophia), Gil Stuart (Franz), Evadne Baker (Sister Bernice), Doris Lloyd (Baroness Ebberfeld). The children: Charmian Carr (Liesl), Nicholas Hammond (Friedrich), Heather Menzies (Louisa), Duane Chase (Kurt), Angela Cartwright (Brigitta), Debbie Turner (Marta), Kym Karath (Gretl).
Credits: Produced and directed by Robert Wise. Screenplay by Ernest Lehman. Based on the stage musical with music and lyrics by Richard Rodgers and Oscar Hammerstein II, book by Howard Lindsay and Russell Crouse. Produced on the stage by Leland Hayward, Richard Halliday, Richard Rodgers and Oscar Hammerstein II. With the partial use of ideas by Georg Hurdalek. Associate producer: Saul Chaplin. Music by Richard Rodgers. Lyrics by Oscar Hammerstein II. Additional words and music by Richard Rodgers ["I Have Confidence in Me" and "Something Good"]. Music supervised, arranged, and conducted by Irwin Kostal. Production designed by Boris Leven. Director of photography: Ted McCord. Choreography by Marc Breaux and Dee Dee Wood [Breaux]. Costumes designed by Dorothy Jeakins. Puppeteers: Bil Baird and Cora Baird. Second unit supervision: Maurice Zuberano. Vocal supervision: Robert Tucker. Film editor: William Reynolds. Additional photography: Paul Beeson. Sound: Murray Spivack, Bernard Freericks. Unit production manager: Saul Wurtzel. Assistant director: Ridgeway Callow. Dialogue coach: Pamela Danova. Music editor: Robert Mayer. Set decorations: Walter M. Scott, Ruby Levitt. Special photographic effects: L.B. Abbott, Emil Kosa, Jr. Sound recording supervised by Fred Hynes, James Corcoran. Makeup: Ben Nye. Hair styles: Margaret Donovan. Produced in Todd-AO. Color by De Luxe. Westrex Recording System. An Argyle Enterprises, Inc., production.
Additional Credits: From the book *The Story of the Trapp Family Singers* by Maria von Trapp. Continuity sketches: Maurice Zuberano. Sound: Douglas O. Williams, Eugene Grossman. Men's wardrobe: Richard James. Women's wardrobe: Josephine Brown. Julie Andrews' makeup: Willard Buell. Titles: Pacific Title & Art Studio. Aerial sequences in Superpanorama 70. Premiered in New York City on March 2, 1965.
Other versions: Remake of *Die Trapp-familie* (Germany, 1956). This film and its sequel, *Die Trapp-familie in Amerika* (1958), were edited into the Twentieth Century-Fox release *The Trapp Family* (1961).
Awards: Oscars for Best Picture, Director, Film Editing, Sound, Music—Scoring of Music, Adaptation, or Treatment.
Available: Twentieth Century Fox Home Entertainment DVD (2005). UPC: 0-24543-20838-9.

One of the most popular films of the last fifty years, *The Sound of Music* had its beginnings in a Broadway stage hit and, before that, in the real-life experiences of the Trapp family. Much of the plot, written for the play by Howard Lindsay and Russell Crouse, was based on truth: Maria Kutschera was a novitiate at the Nonnberg Abbey in Salzburg when she was hired as a governess by Captain Georg von Trapp, a widower, to look after his seven children. Maria and Georg married in 1937. The family turned to music after a bank failure wiped out von Trapp's savings, and fled Austria shortly after the Anschluss in 1938.

The play and film stop at this point, although the family enjoyed considerable success in the United States, touring the country and later establishing the Trapp Family Lodge near Stowe, Vermont. Georg died in 1947. Maria's memoir, *The Story of the Trapp Family Singers*, was published in 1949. The group disbanded in 1956; by that time, the lodge was undergoing conversion to a ski resort. That same year Maria sold the movie rights to her book to German producers for $9,000. Wolfgang Liebeneiner directed two fiction features adapted from the book: *Die Trapp-Familie* (1956, written by Georg Hurdalek) and *Die Trapp-Familie in Amerika* (1958). In 1961, Twentieth Century-Fox released a re-edited version of the two films in the United States as *The Trapp Family*.

By this time Fox had already purchased the film rights to the Broadway play for $1.25 million. Oscar Hammerstein II later wrote to a friend that Mary Martin, for two decades one of the reigning queens of Broadway musicals, read Maria von Trapp's book and campaigned to have it adapted. In Laurence Maslon's account, Paramount asked stage director Vincent J. Donehue to view the German films to see if they should be adapted into English versions. Donehue screened them for Martin and her husband Richard Halliday, who quickly involved agent and *South Pacific* producer Leland Hayward.

Hayward hired Lindsay and Crouse to write the adaptation, which was not yet going to be a musical. But as the story's musical background took on a more integral part in the plot, Hayward enlisted the songwriting team of Richard Rodgers and Oscar Hammerstein II, who became involved in the project in early 1959. Their contributions became the defining element of what was now called *The Sound of Music*.

With Martin and Theodore Bikel in the leads, the play opened on November 16, 1959, to generally lackluster reviews. Commercially, however, it was a sensation, running 1,443 performances, winning six Tony awards, and spawning road and international productions. Throw in the money from Fox and the receipts from the best-selling cast

recording, and *The Sound of Music* became one of the most profitable musicals ever staged.

The Fox studio, meanwhile, was in severe financial trouble. It wasn't until Darryl F. Zanuck's *The Longest Day* was a hit in 1962 that the studio began seriously developing the project. Zanuck hired screenwriter Ernest Lehman, who over the course of several drafts "opened up" the play by incorporating real-life locations into the script. His most significant contribution may have been to switch the order of two songs. Now "My Favorite Things" preceded "The Lonely Goatherd," a move that gave more emotional weight to Maria's introduction to the Trapp family.

Zanuck considered several directors, including William Wyler, who actually traveled to Austria to scout locations. Biographer Jan Herman wrote that Wyler told his wife, "I just can't bear to make a picture about all those nice Nazis." Lehman had worked with Robert Wise on *West Side Story* (1961), for which Wise shared a Best Directing Oscar, and since the director's next project, *The Sand Pebbles*, was delayed, he signed a contract in November 1963 to direct *The Sound of Music*.

Wise cast Julie Andrews after screening *Mary Poppins*, her first film, which had yet to be released. While Andrews was a significant star of stage and television, Fox was taking a real risk in placing a big-budget musical on her shoulders. Wyler had wanted Rex Harrison, who costarred on stage with Andrews in *My Fair Lady*, for Captain von Trapp; Fox suggested Bing Crosby. Yul Brynner also lobbied for the part, but Wise chose Christopher Plummer, a classically trained Canadian actor who was at first indifferent to the project. Plummer signed after persuading Lehman to add more humor to the captain's part. Of the children, Liesl proved the most difficult to cast, with Mia Farrow and Teri Garr among those who took screen tests. Charmian Farnon (her name was changed to Carr) was hired two weeks after filming started.

The shooting of *The Sound of Music* has been extensively documented: bad weather, practical jokes, technical problems, on-set accidents. Richard Rodgers agreed to contribute two new songs, "I Have Confidence" and "Something Good," the latter replacing the stage show's "An Ordinary Couple." (Hammerstein passed away in 1960.) "My Favorite Things" was the first material filmed, starting on March 26, 1964. The last shot before previews was taken on August 20. Wise screened the film in Tulsa, Oklahoma, and Minneapolis,

Minnesota. The premiere took place the following March in New York City.

Again, the reviews were predominately negative, while box-office receipts set records. Critic Pauline Kael's comments, which included wondering if the Trapp children vomited on stage, led to her dismissal from *McCall's* magazine. Other writers made unkind comparisons to Rodgers and Hammerstein's previous musicals; some brought up the resemblances between "Getting to Know You" and "Do Re Mi," between "You'll Never Walk Alone" and "Climb Ev'ry Mountain." Almost everyone was disappointed by the second half of the movie, which basically reprised the songs from the first. In a rock 'n' roll era that included hit films like *A Hard Day's Night*, *The Sound of Music* seemed hopelessly outdated to many.

So what accounts for the film's enormous popularity? (According to Maslon, adjusted for inflation, *The Sound of Music* ranks third in the all-time box-office list, behind *Gone with the Wind* and *Star Wars*.) It remains an old-fashioned musical, constructed according to Broadway principles that even then were disappearing. But perhaps craft and expertise are the real hallmarks to the film. At its best, the score is effortlessly melodic, the lyrics open and direct. The film is technically superb, from the opulent production design to the bright cinematography and lush sound.

Director Robert Wise was nothing if not a traditionalist. The editor of *Citizen Kane* (1941), he also directed *Curse of the Cat People* (1944), and the influence of both Orson Welles and Val Lewton is evident throughout *The Sound of Music*—in the exquisite Laendler dance and ballroom sequences, for example, or in the way Wise manipulates sound during a scene set in a graveyard. Cast members later marveled at how the director could piece together shots taken miles and even continents apart, but even more impressive was Wise's vision of the film as a whole. Starting with the pre-credit descent from heaven to Andrews on a mountain summit singing the title tune, the director gave moviegoers a stream of sound and imagery that was both splendid and comforting, exotic and reassuring. Wise would never achieve the same results on screen again.

The Pawnbroker

Landau Releasing Organization/American International Pictures/Allied Artists, 1965, Sound, B&W, 1.37, 115 minutes

Cast: Rod Steiger (Sol Nazerman), Brock Peters (Rodriguez), Jaime Sanchez (Jesus Ortiz), Thelma Oliver (Ortiz' girl), Marketa Kimbrell (Tessie), Baruch Lumet (Mendel), Juano Hernandez (Mr. Smith), Linda Geiser (Ruth), Nancy R. Pollock (Bertha), Geraldine Fitzgerald (Marilyn Birchfield), Raymond St. Jacques (Tangee), John McCurry (Buck), Ed Morehouse (Robinson), Eusebia Cosme (Mrs. Ortiz), Warren Finnerty (Savarese).

Credits: Directed by Sidney Lumet. Screenplay: Morton Fine, David Friedkin. Based on the novel by Edward Lewis Wallant. Produced by Roger Lewis, Philip Langner. An Ely Landau production. Executive producer: Worthington Miner. In charge of production: Alfred Markim. Associate producer: Joseph Manduke. Music: Quincy Jones. Production designer: Richard Sylbert. Director of photography: Boris Kaufman. Film editor: Ralph Rosenblum. Costumes: Anna Hill Johnstone. Orchestrations: William Byers, Quincy Jones. Assistant director: Dan Eriksen. Unit manager: Ulu Grosbard. Sound editors: Jack Fitzstephens, Alan Heim. Sound: Dennis Maitland. Sound mix: James Gleason. Makeup: Bill Herman. Hairdresser: Ed Callaghan. Wardrobe: George Newman, Marilyn Putnam. Casting: Jessica Levy. Optical effects: Film Opticals, Inc. Titles: F. Hillsberg, inc. Print by Movielab. An Ely Landau and Herbert R. Steinmann presentation.

Additional Cast includes: Jack Ader (Morton), E.M. Margolese (Papa), Marianne Kanter (Joan), Ed Morehouse (Robinson), Marc Alexander (Rubin).

Additional Credits: Production dates: October to December 1963. Released April 20, 1965.

Available: Artisan Entertainment/Republic Pictures DVD (2003): UPC: 0-17153-14587-8.

A veteran of the Navy during World War II, Edward Lewis Wallant worked as a graphic designer while writing in his spare time. The success of his second novel, *The Pawnbroker*, allowed him to devote himself to writing full time. Like his other works, it was a story of personal redemption, focusing on Sol Nazerman, a Holocaust survivor who endures a series of crises over Easter weekend. Sadly, Wallant died of an aneurysm in 1962, shortly after completing his third novel.

The book was purchased by MGM, which planned to shoot it in London to take advantage of tax loopholes. A bemused Sidney Lumet, hired to direct two weeks before the scheduled start of shooting, insisted on returning to the book's locations in New York City's Spanish Harlem. He cast most of the actors, apart from Rod Steiger, who was already attached as the lead.

Lumet wrote later that he eliminated the more overt religious aspects of the book. With editor Ralph Rosenblum, he also devised a way to incorporate Nazerman's past, depicted as dreams in Wallant's book, into his present. Both were equally significant to the pawnbroker; in fact, the past threatened to overwhelm his day-to-day life. Lumet used what he called "shock cuts" to blend the two time periods. Subliminal advertising was

Rod Steiger as Sol Nazerman in *The Pawnbroker*.

a fad at the time, and the director enjoyed experimenting with how short a shot could be and still register with viewers. "The old idea was that it took three frames for an image to register on the eye," he wrote. But with Rosenblum he used "one frame, two frame, three frame cuts of increasing rapidity, finally up to six frame cuts and then eventually into a sequence."

Apart from its editing, *The Pawnbroker* was revolutionary on several other levels. It was the first mainstream feature in the United States to feature a Holocaust survivor as the main character, and the first to use nudity for dramatic purposes. Cinematographer Boris Kaufman shot in difficult conditions, at night without lights, for example. (His next project was 1965's *Film*, written by Samuel Beckett and starring Buster Keaton.) This was the first Hollywood feature scored by an African-American, and the first film credit for Quincy Jones, a former trumpet player, arranger, producer, and songwriter who subsequently left the music industry to work in Los Angeles. There he scored over thirty other movies, and in time returned to producing and arranging for musicians.

The Pawnbroker pit Steiger's depiction of Nazerman as harsh, unyielding, and brutal against characters like the young Ortiz, trapped by poverty, goaded by friends into crime. The film's uncompromising story line and downbeat tone frightened studio executives. Although his next film, *Fail-Safe* (1964), would be a critical and commercial success, Lumet and producer Ely Landau could not find a distributor until *The Pawnbroker* opened in England and won two awards at the Berlin International Film Festival.

The Pawnbroker received generally respectful reviews when it finally opened. Critics singled out Rod Steiger for praise; he said later that it was his best work. However, the film also raised controversy. Both blacks and Jews of the time complained about characters and settings in the film. Some writers felt that the flashbacks were either inaccurate or in poor taste. Critic Stanley Kaufman objected to portraying Nazerman as necessarily dysfunctional, as if x amount of brutality would result in y amount of social paralysis. In his book *Screening the Holocaust*, Israeli-born critic Ilan Avisar criticized a plotline that had Nazerman redeemed, or "Christianized," by the sacrificial death of a worker conveniently named "Jesus."

Scholar Alan Mintz was also offended by the film's insistence on eternal Jewish suffering and redemptive Christian love. In addition, Mintz believed the film was an attempt on Lumet's part to compare and contrast the Holocaust with the racial unrest of the civil rights era. Incidents in the present provoke flashbacks to similar situations Nazerman experienced in the past. Was it fair for Lumet to compare the Harlem of the 1960s to Nazi Germany, a comparison he later denied? ("There was certainly no attempt to show Harlem as a modern concentration camp—it's quite the reverse, Harlem in the film is meant to have an enormous life about it with all its sadness," he wrote.)

"The worthiness of [Lumet's] message is taken for granted," Mintz wrote, and despite its occasional missteps *The Pawnbroker* managed to address complex topics with taste and sensitivity. Steiger's work may be admirable, but Wallant's original conception and Lumet's incisive directing placed his performance within a credible and disturbing context. "The basic line taken in *The Pawnbroker* is that regardless of how brutal life is one must go on," Lumet wrote at the time. But the director admitted to teacher and author Joanna E. Rapf in 2003, "I know if I had to do the movie over again I would not do it," citing an article by Elie Wiesel that criticized the exploitation of the Holocaust for art.

With producer Ely Landau, Lumet co-directed the documentary *King: A Filmed Record . . . Montgomery to Memphis* (1969), a Registry title. His *Network* (1976) is also on the Registry.

Dead Birds

Dead Birds: Skirmish line in a ritual war. Photograph by Michael Rockefeller. *Copyright Peabody Museum, Harvard University*

Robert Gardner, 1964. Sound, color, 1.37. 85 minutes.

Featuring: Weyak, Pua.

Credits: Directed by Robert Gardner. Cinematography by Robert Gardner. Sound by Michael C. Rockefeller. Sound editing by Joyce Chopra.

Available: Documentary Educational Resources DVD (*www.der.org*).

Filmed in the highlands of New Guinea, *Dead Birds* became one of the most influential ethnographic movies of the 1960s. It is about the Dugum Dani, one of the peoples of West New Guinea. They live in an isolated, three-hundred-square-mile valley cut off by mountains from the coast. By 1961, the Dutch New Guinea government had "pacified" wide areas of the valley. But direct contact with the Dani had only recently been made, and they were essentially still living in a Stone Age world. They hunted with spears and bows and arrows, farmed with sticks, and lived in thatched huts in villages of between thirty to forty people. The men wore dried, hollowed gourds; the women, nets woven from plants.

Gardner received permission to mount an expedition to the area from Dr. Victor J. DeBruyn, head of the Native Affairs Office in Dutch New Guinea. Inspiration for the film came from *The Hunters* (1957, a Registry title), which examined tribesmen in the Kalahari Desert of Africa. Gardner's goals for the expedition included a documentary film, a scientific book, a popular book, a book of photographs, and a series of sound recordings. He saw the various *Dead Birds* projects as second in an anthropological trilogy, with *The Hunters* (1957) covering hunting societies, *Dead Birds* agricultural groups, and a third study for what Gardner called "pastoral groups." Financed in part by the Film Study Center of the Peabody Museum at Harvard, he put together a crew that included anthropologist Kurt Heider, who did the major research and writing; wilderness author Peter Matthiessen, who documented the expedition in *Under the Mountain Wall: A Chronicle of Two Seasons in the Stone Age* (1962); sociologist Jan Broekhuyse, who had researched similar highland groups; still photographer Eliot Elisofon; and Michael Rockefeller, who worked as a sound recordist and still photographer. (Rockefeller would drown a few months later off the southern coast of New Guinea while on assignment for the Museum of Primitive Art.)

The expedition came to the Dani with a native translator and with gifts, principally seashells prized by the tribe, but also salt, steel axes, and knives. Finding it difficult to gain the trust of the Dani women, Gardner focused on two men: Weyak, a farmer and warrior, and Pua, a young swineherd. As a result, *Dead Birds* presents a somewhat skewed version of Dani life, as Gardner acknowledged later when writing about his film. "Film, because it is a medium in time, is a way to unfold something. It can be about how fire is made by one warrior or it can be about an entire neighborhood of Dani living a complex existence capable of evoking an immense range of meanings and moods." He also noted, "In deciding to focus on the topic of violence, I was well aware that much of Dani existence would elude me."

The filmmakers pretended to the natives that their cameras were the equivalent of eyeglasses, machines that enabled them to see better. They wouldn't show the tribesmen any photographs or films. Because members of the expedition remained among the Dani for twenty-six months, Gardner worried about the ultimate impact his crew would have on the tribesmen.

Filming lasted from February to September 1961, with Gardner shooting color 16mm stock in an Arriflex camera. Critical of other documentaries ("I have sat through hours of murky and meaningless ethnographic film because the principal virtue of photography . . . had been completely overlooked."), the director had a framework and point of view in mind before he started. He began the narration by reciting a Dani folk tale with the moral that "all men like birds must die," and then depicts a society engulfed in an endless and meaningless war.

When working with Weyak or Pua, Gardner can film in extreme close-up. Pua at first shows some signs of wariness, his eyes darting to the director and then away again, but he eventually adapts to the presence of the camera. The subjects become so cooperative that they repeat actions so Gardner can capture them from different angles. In showing the rest of the villagers, Gardner has to retreat at first to higher ground. He documents the small farming lots that dot the valley, the no-man's-land that marks the frontier between the warring tribes, and the watchtowers built from poles and vines.

Much of *Dead Birds* concerns itself with day-to-day life: gardening, weaving, building fires, cooking, games, magic, medicine. Gardner also addresses feasts, dancing, religion, and the afterlife. But the narration—omniscient and ominous—colors all the material. The first shot we see of the Dani includes a corpse, and battles are seemingly always imminent. In a way, the warfare makes the more mundane aspects of anthropology palatable, and gives viewers a reason to sit through an educational presentation of Dani rituals and practices.

Gardner is adroit at manipulating time, especially when suggesting that events filmed days apart are occurring simultaneously. (He also tries to synchronize sound to image, although he was filming silent.) The narration helps tie scenes together. But to documentary purists, he was distorting the truth of what he recorded. Gardner was reaching back to the techniques and strategies developed by Robert Flaherty in the 1920s, in particular the way Flaherty read into the thoughts of his subjects. Gardner describing someone as "stunned and angry" seems fair enough. But is a statement like, "They go to war because of ghosts, and because they like to," based on fact or supposition?

Dead Birds does finally deliver on the violence it had been promising. A warrior is shot in the buttocks, the barbed arrow dug out with twigs in front of the camera. A doctor sucks another arrow from a fighter's chest. A child is killed by the Aikhe River. An enemy is killed trying to steal pigs. The battles are difficult to watch, if only because they remind us how little modern society has advanced from prehistoric times. Gardner shoots them from a distance at first, but later, he is in the midst of the warriors. "The fighting is not very enthusiastic," he complains at one point. "Many are worried that the rain will ruin their hair or feathers."

The film had an enormous impact when it was released, with everyone from Margaret Mead to Robert Lowell to Stan Brakhage attesting to its artistry. Its legacy is not entirely spotless. Gardner pushed the boundaries of what was acceptable in documentaries, both in their filming techniques and in what they showed. Within a decade, anthropologists like Napoleon Chagnon went beyond those limits, in the minds of some provoking violence among natives to spice up their books and films.

Gardner continued to make films: *Rivers of Sand* (1974), *Forest of Bliss* (1984), and many shorts. He was the Director of the Film Study Center at Harvard from 1957 to 1997, and collaborated on numerous books. In 2006 he wrote an autobiography, *The Impulse to Preseve: Reflections of a Filmmaker.*

The Endless Summer

Bruce Brown Films, 1966. Sound, color, 1.33. 92 minutes.
Featuring: Robert August, Mike Hynson, Terence Bullen, Wayne Miyata, Butch Van Artsdalen, Nat Young.
Credits: Photographed, edited, and narrated by Bruce Brown. Assistant photographers: R. Paul Allen, Paul Witzig, Bob Bagley. "Endless Summer" musical theme by The Sandals. A Bruce Brown Films presentation.
Additional Credits: Released theatrically June 15, 1966.
Other Versions: Sequels *The Endless Summer 2* (1994), directed by Bruce Brown; *Step Into Liquid* (2003), directed by Dana Brown.
Available: Image Entertainment DVD (2000). UPC: 0-14381-8790-2-5. Website: *www.brucebrownfims.com.*

Fueled by a surfing craze he played a large part in forming, filmmaker Bruce Brown set out in 1965 to make a feature film about the sport. *The Endless Summer* became one of the most successful documentaries of the 1960s, and helped establish a filmmaking formula that is still being followed today.

Born in San Francisco in 1937, Brown describes his childhood as an idyllic period of more surfing than schooling. He enlisted in the Navy after high school in part to surf in Hawaii, and was working as a lifeguard when Dale Velzy, at the time the "World's Largest Manufacturer" of surfboards and the proprietor of a famous surfing shop, offered him $5,000 to document the Velzy surfing team. "That covered the cost of the camera, travel and a year's living expenses," Brown said.

Slippery When Wet (1958) showed surfing from California to Hawaii, and established Brown as one of the sport's best cinematographers. (He has always credited Bud Browne, Greg Noll, and John Severson as influential predecessors and colleagues.) For the next eight years, Brown would film surfers in the fall and winter, edit the footage in the spring, and scramble both to arrange screenings of his finished work, and to finance the next film.

At first he would narrate the footage live at screenings. Next he began to take advantage of a burgeoning craze in surf music to fashion ad-hoc soundtracks. He has also described a fluid process of editing in which his films would change from screening to screening, depending on the reactions of the most recent audiences. "We had rewinds and viewers in the back of the van and I would actually edit the stuff while we were traveling," he told surfing historian Tim Ryan.

Brown had convinced himself that he needed to attend film school, but realized after completing five surfing documentaries he had already taught himself what he needed to know. His next goal was to set his work apart from competition, which

by the mid-1960s time included "beach blanket" feature films and television coverage, notably on ABC's *Wide World of Sports. Waterlogged* (1962), a compilation of footage from his previous four films, gave him the freedom he needed to make a feature on a more relaxed schedule. With a budget of $50,000, Brown embarked on a world tour with Robert August and Mike Hynson, two of the most respected surfers in the sport.

Brown filmed the two surfers with a Bolex 16mm camera equipped with a zoom lens and a waterproof plexiglass container. As a filmmaker, he eschewed fancy effects, and rarely shifted his camera once he found a good viewing point. His audience wasn't interested in fussy techniques or elaborate montages; they wanted surfing unobstructed by cinematic tricks. When not in the water, he almost always used a tripod. Years of experience gave him the ability to follow surfers smoothly, despite using a long lens.

The main selling point for *The Endless Summer* was its location footage. Brown shot August and Hynson surfing in Senegal, Nigeria, South Africa, New Zealand, Tahiti, and other areas. As he reminded his viewers repeatedly, no one had ever surfed in many of these waters. For the film's framework, Brown imitated a travelogue style that stretched back to the earliest days of the medium. The film's glimpses of flora and fauna, of natives at work and play, of tourist landmarks like Table Mountain and Waikiki, could have come from any episode of *John Nesbitt's Passing Parade.* Brown's "cool daddy-o" narration can sound corny today, but at the time it spoke to an audience suspicious of a more traditional style of documentary, one they associated with instructional or educational films. (By today's standards, the narration has its cringe-worthy moments when it refers to Africans, but Brown's sensibility is clearly not racist.)

Brown considers 1964 the release date for *The Endless Summer* because he began screening it that year. Unable to persuade studios to distribute the film, he rented theaters himself, a practice known as "four-walling," with assistant cinematographer R. Paul Allen as publicist. "We went to Wichita, Kansas, in January," he said. "It showed for two weeks and sold out its entire run, breaking the record of *My Fair Lady.*" Allen then arranged a press screening at a theater in Kips Bay, Manhattan. Reviews were so positive, and subsequent attendance so strong, that the film ran for a year.

In 1966, Cinema V picked up the film for distribution in the United States and eventually worldwide. Brown's figures put the film's receipts at over $20 million, a substantial return on his original $50,000 budget. He used some of his profits on his next feature, *On Any Sunday* (1970). Coproduced by Steve McQueen, the documentary brought dirt bikes to the theatrical marketplace. In 1992, Brown came out of semiretirement to direct *The Endless Summer 2*, but criticized the way it was handled by New Line Cinema. The first *Endless Summer* has become so culturally entrenched that Brown's company sells tie-in memorabilia that ranges from T-shirts to restaurant franchises.

Castro Street

Canyon Cinema, 1966. Sound, color, 1.33. 10 minutes.
Credit: A film by Bruce Baillie.
Available: Canyon Cinema, *www.canyoncinema.com.*

Some of Bruce Baillie's films are characterized as an extension of the lyrical style Stan Brakhage developed in the 1950s. Critics also remark on his "social awareness," as if it existed separate from his aesthetic strategies. In discussing Baillie's work, there is a temptation to focus on either its beauty or its social commentary. The choices he has made, both in his life and his work, are not that simple.

Baillie was born in Aberdeen, South Dakota, in 1931. He served in the Navy during the Korean War, then attended college in both Minnesota and at the University of California at Berkeley. After a year at the London School of Film Technique, he worked for Will Hindle on a CBS talk show, *PM West*, and for Marvin Becker Films, a San Francisco company that produced—among other films—a compilation of highlights from the VIII Winter Olympic Games in Squaw Valley, California.

In 1960, Baillie began working on his first film, *On Sundays*, which he described as a combination of documentary and fantasy. Subsequent films were shorter, with Baillie experimenting with both narrative strategies and with the process of filmmaking. He began shooting with filters, gauzes, and mattes, as well as with different film stocks, trying to approximate with homemade devices effects achieved by optical printers. But Baillie's goals were different than the dissolves and wipes optical printers typically produce. He was more interested in layering or superimposing images on top of each other in rhythmic patterns, in isolating elements of landscapes until they were no longer immediately comprehensible, and in constructing meaning out of a succession of abstract forms.

His films became abstract in content as well as style, often with no discernible narrative, and with soundtracks that consisted of collages of industrial noise or "found" sound. Academics could read many "meanings" into his films. P. Adams Sitney discussed the "ironic pessimism" of a film like *A Hurrah for Soldiers* (1962–63), and saw in *To Parsifal* (1963) how Baillie was beginning to "elaborate his equivocal relationship to technology by employing the train both as a symbol of the waste land and the heroic thrust of the Grail quester."

How much do you have to know beforehand to appreciate Baillie's films? Commentators familiar with his work can view the pieces in context, can compare shots and sequences and films to others. Those who don't know what Baillie has done are left to decide if what they are seeing has meaning or beauty or whatever they feel constitutes a movie.

Castro Street, one of a half-dozen or so films Baillie released in 1966, offers no credits, no narrative, no explanation. Ten minutes long, it serves as a sort of travelogue of a Castro Street in Richmond, California—an industrial setting near Oakland. The street was the site of a Standard Oil refinery and well as a freight railroad switching yard. According to film critic Scott MacDonald, this stretch marked the "most difficult dimension of Bay Area life to come to terms with aesthetically." Baillie shows both sides of the street simultaneously, going up one side and down the other.

Making the film "blew my fuses for life," Baillie said later. MacDonald quotes the artist's description of preparing for the shoot as grabbing prisms and glasses from his mother's kitchen, previsualizing how to combine color and black-and-white film stocks, and then calculating when to go to negative images, when to superimpose, when to use mattes. As he told MacDonald, "I was making mattes by using high contract black-and-white film that was used normally for making titles. I kept my mind available so that as much as one can know, I knew about the scene I had just shot when I made the next color shot. What was white would be black in my negative, and that would allow me to matte the reversal color so that the two layers would not be superimposed but combined."

Baillie's images, often appearing in high-contrast color, almost always distorted (the longest stretch without superimpositions is a fifteen-second shot of a field), look as if they are throbbing with some undefined inner pulse. Objects come into and out of focus, become recognizable and then not, and are accompanied by the sounds of railroads, radios, a piano played in a nearby room. Rhythm could be established somewhat by the industrial noise soundtrack, but it mostly relied on Baillie's sense of timing as he panned and tilted his camera. Trains functioned as a narrative framework, but the structure of *Castro Street* is based more on imagery than a traditional plot.

When it's possible to pick the 1966 pop song "Good Lovin'" by the Young Rascals out of the surrounding noise, is it because Baillie wants to fix his film in a specific time? Because that's what was on the radio when he was shooting? Because the song has a connection to the images? Should you know that Baillie considered the "simpler, steady color" shots feminine, and the shorter railroad shots masculine?

Ultimately, the viewer has to decide what *Castro Street* means, and whether or not it is a "movie" or simply a string of images and sounds. Watch *Castro Street* intently enough, and you may look at every subsequent industrial landscape, perhaps any landscape at all, in a different manner.

At the same time Baillie was making *On Sundays* in 1960, he was organizing impromptu screenings in his backyard of works by local independent filmmakers. This grew into a "floating cinematheque" that shifted from Canyon to Berkeley and then to San Francisco. The screenings eventually fell under the Canyon Cinema label. In 1967, artists including Bruce Conner and Robert Nelson joined Baillie in founding Canyon Cinema, Inc., a film distribution company operating on a cooperative basis. Described as "a democratic, artist-run organization," it has seen its library grow from 40 titles to over 3,700, and lists almost four hundred members worldwide.

Baillie is the recipient of several awards and grants. He has taught film at Rice University and Bard College while continuing to make films like *Quick Billy* (1967–70).

Through Navajo Eyes

Sol Worth and John Adair, 1966. Silent, B&W, 1.33. Series of seven films, 117 minutes.

Titles (as originally listed in the Appendix to the book *Through Navajo Eyes*): (1) *A Navajo Weaver*, directed by Susan Benally, 20 minutes. (2) *The Navajo Silversmith*, directed by Johnny Nelson, 20 minutes. (3) *The Spirit of the Navajo*, directed by Maxine and Mary Jane Tsosie, 20 minutes. (4) *The Shallow Well*, directed by Johnny Nelson, 20 minutes. (5) *Old Antolope Lake*, directed by Mike Anderson, 15 minutes. (6) *Intrepid Shadows*, directed by Al Clah, 15 minutes. (7) *Untitled Film*, directed by Alta Kahn, 10 minutes.

Corrected titles with new timings: (1) *A Navajo Weaver*, directed by Susie K. Benally, 22 minutes. (2) *Navajo Silversmith*, directed by John Nelson, 22 minutes. (3) *The Spirit of the Navajo*, directed by Maxine and Mary Jane Tsosie, 21 minutes. (4) *The Shallow Well*, directed by Johnny Nelson, 14 minutes. (5) *Old Antolope Lake*, directed by Mike Anderson, 11 minutes. (6) *Intrepid Shadows*, directed by Al Clah, 18 minutes. (7) *Second Weaver*, directed by Susie Benally, 9 minutes.

Cast includes: Alta Kahn, Johnny Nelson (The intruder), Sam Yazzie (Medicine man), Richard Chalfen (Patient).

Additional Credits: Financed by National Science Foundation and Annenberg School of Communication, University of Pennsylvania. Directors of research: John Adair, Professor of Anthropology San Francisco State College; Sol Worth, Associate Professor of Communications, Annenberg School of Communication. Research assistant: Richard Chalfen, Annenberg School of Communication.

Available: The Museum of Modern Art.

John Adair was born in Memphis, Tennessee, in 1913, and studied at the University of Wisconsin. While doing fieldwork in New Mexico, he became interested in Navajo and Pueblo culture. Adair studied silversmiths, photographing a documentary short, *Southwestern Indian Silversmiths* (1939) and publishing a book on the subject in 1944. He also managed the Navajo Arts and Crafts Guild, designed to help artists achieve economic independence, in Window Rock, Arizona. After serving in World War II, he received his doctorate in anthropology from the University of New Mexico. Hired by Cornell University in 1948, he ran a series of field seminars in New Mexico and Arizona that focused on health issues. He became Professor of Anthropology at San Francisco State University in 1964.

Sol Worth, born in 1922 in New York City, was a painter and photographer who studied at the University of Iowa before serving in the Navy during the war. He then worked at the Goold Studios in New York while taking courses in filmmaking. He received a Fulbright Lectureship in 1956 to teach and make a documentary in Helsinki. *Teatteri*, the resulting film, earned him a position at the Annenberg School of Communications at the University of Pennsylvania.

In 1966 Worth received a grant from the National Science Foundation to test his theses about visual communication. He partnered with Adair because of Adair's extensive fieldwork with the Navajo. The two also collaborated on a book about their research: *Through Navajo Eyes: An Exploration in Film Communication and Anthropology*, published by the Indiana University Press in 1972. In it, the authors presented a theory of film as a language. It was their belief that, taught the basic skills of filmmaking, an ethnic culture would develop a language of film distinctive from that used by Hollywood.

Worth and Adair, along with their assistant Richard Chalfen, went to Pine Springs, Arizona, where Adair was already acquainted with many of the Navajo. They spent two days teaching a half-dozen or so natives how to use handheld 16mm cameras, covering technical details like focus, exposure, but also ideas about narrative and editing: what wide shots "meant" as opposed to close-ups, what shots are needed to tell a story, how to transition between scenes, and so forth.

The Navajo filmmakers started with eight "practice" films of about 100 feet, or two to three minutes, in length. Al Clah, an artist who had studied at the Institute of American Indian Life in Sante Fe, explored concepts of motion, especially circular rather than linear motion. Sisters Maxine and Mary Jane Tsosie took a strictly literal approach, filming John Adair hanging his laundry. Johnny Nelson filmed a story about a field thirsty for rain. The Navajo then started on their longer projects.

In *A Navajo Weaver*, Susie Benally filmed her mother, Alta Kahn, weaving a rug. Most of the film concerned preparation: washing wool, making dye, etc. In structure it is similar to "how-to" films and television shows about cooking, painting, or other physical activities. But Benally had a quick, jittery style that employed short shots and jump cuts. She shot in bursts, the way Jonas Mekas would in *Reminiscences of a Journey to Lithuania* (1971–72), giving a modern, almost disjointed feel to a craft that had not changed much in two hundred years.

In *The Navajo Silversmith*, Johnny Nelson not only took the time to create credits carved onto a rock for his film, but also conceptualized a story with a sophisticated editing scheme featuring flashbacks and associative cutting. From a studio workbench, Nelson cut to the artist prospecting and mining silver in the desert. (In their book, the surprised Worth and Adair point out that no mining had ever taken place on this particular reservation.) Shots were carefully composed, the editing at times almost subliminal, the story a convincing account of the artistic process, from inspiration to creation. *The Navajo Silversmith* proves above all that it does not require much training or experience for a filmmaker's personality to emerge.

The Spirit of the Navajo is a portrait of medicine man Sam Yazzie by his granddaughters, the Tsosie sisters. Although clearly uncomfortable in front of the camera, Yazzie shows how various rituals were performed, even practicing on a game Chalfen. *The Shallow Well*, the second film by Nelson, is a fairly straightforward document of a construction project. Nelson had been foreman on other well-digging jobs, and so was familiar with each stage of the project. Like typical instructional films of the time, Nelson presented a problem, a process, and a solution. Water from standing pools was dirty and hard to use. Digging a well was hard work requiring cooperation from many people. The result was clean, reliable water running through a system of pipes. As Worth and Adair point out, this is the only film in the series that is set in an unavoidable present, with workers leaving the site in pickup trucks.

Old Antelope Lake (spelled *Antolope* in the title) is a travelogue of sorts, a look at how the Navajo use a body of water on the reservation. Boys throw rocks into the water, men fish, others ride horses into the lake, sheep graze by the shore. About halfway through, director Mike Anderson introduces a young boy who uses lake water to wash clothes at a fire pit, a subtle call for the improved conditions brought about by *The Shallow Well*.

According to Worth and Adair, *The Intrepid Shadows* was the film least understood by the Navajo when it was screened for them. You might be confused as well unless you remember to take the title seriously. Alfred Klah's work is an ambitious attempt to explain landscape in terms of narrative archetypes. This is one film in the series that suffers from technical limitations: a faulty close-up lens and some imprecise exposure settings, for example. But pacing and f-stops can be learned through experience. What's unmistakable is Klah's sense of story, of how to combine imagery to provide meaning, of how changing angles can affect how we interpret a location. Klah faced the same problems any filmmaker faces: How do you make viewers see what you want them to see? How do you tell a story? He solved these questions through pure filmmaking, without the need for dialogue or narration.

The final film in the series, now called *Second Weaver*, was the only one made without credits. Worth and Adair wrote that it was filmed by Alta Kahn, but in a revised edition of *Through Navajo Eyes* published in 1997, it was suggested that her daughter Susie Benally was the real filmmaker. *Second Weaver* might be seen as an alternate version of *A Navajo Weaver*, one that is shorter and more pointed.

The most revealing aspect of the films may be how easily the Navajo adapted to the process of making movies, and how quickly they asserted their personalities. Nelson was playful, curious; Benally was anxious to capture everything; Al Klah was spiritual and a bit obscure. What we don't see is almost as interesting. The filmmakers edited out

almost all of the modern world. A basketball court, a few vehicles, some tools, and overhead wires in the background of one shot are the extent of the twentieth century. How the Navajo live, where they shop, the details of divorce, unemployment—are missing. We get instead glimpses into past arts, past rituals—perhaps what the Navajo thought the filmmakers wanted to see.

These are case studies in a way, similar to what Adair and Worth would have filmed had they been holding the cameras. In a review of the book, Margaret Mead complained that "the filming process was presented to the Navajo didactically, so it is not surprising that all of the Navajos but one—the artist—made didactic films." She wondered what the results would have been if the Navajo approached filmmaking as an attempt "to produce a flow of movement."

Then again, Mead also wrote, "The way frames could be combined to make cademes, and cademes edited into edemes was conceptualized as a linear process of the linguistic type which has script as its model." Fortunately, the films in *Through Navajo Eyes* require no academic justification, no pigeonholing through jargon. They stand on their own as fully formed works of art.

David Holzman's Diary

Direct Cinema Limited, 1967. Sound, B&W, 1.37. 73 minutes.
Cast: L.M. Kit Carson (David Holzman), Eileen Dietz (Penny Wohl), Lorenzo Mans (Pepe), Louise Levine (Sandra), Fern McBride (Woman on subway), Michael Levine (Sandra's boy friend), Bob Lesser (Max), Jack Baran (Policeman).
Credits: Produced and directed by Jim McBride. Screenplay: Jim McBride, L.M. Kit Carson. Director of photography: Michael Wadley [Wadleigh]. Additional photography: Paul Goldsmith, Paul Glickman. Edited by Jim McBride. A Paradigm production.
Additional Credits: Screened in film festivals in 1967.
Available: Fox Lorber Home Video VHS (1993).

By the late 1960s, cracks began to appear in the critical support for cinema verité, or "direct cinema" as it was often referred to in English. What had once seemed an objective means of presenting unfiltered truth on screen was now viewed with more skepticism. Banned from using the full arsenal of documentary techniques, verité directors were forced to compensate by finding personalities strong enough to dominate their films. For many documentarians, that meant focusing on show business or politics. A filmmaker like Frederick Wiseman, who could interpret an entire institution in terms of its personality, was rare. Critics

also became more aware that editing, an inherently subjective process, was the primary means of shaping a cinema verité documentary. Editing extended to the camera itself, in what the cinematographer chose to shoot. In fact, by selecting a topic, a director was already introducing a bias into supposedly objective reporting.

At the same time, film equipment became progressively more portable, easier to handle, with film stocks letting cameramen get away with less lighting. A battery-powered Nagra reel-to-reel tape deck that could provide synchronized sound was the perfect complement to a 16mm Eclair or Bolex camera.

An Eclair NPR (Noiseless Portable Reflex) camera with an Angenieux 9.5 to 95mm zoom lens is what David Holzman proudly shows off at the beginning of *David Holzman's Diary*. Filming from his Upper West Side apartment in New York City, Holzman speaks into a $195.00 Miniature Lavalier Microphone (model #649B), announcing to the audience his intention of filming a diary of his life, now that he's lost his job and has been reclassified 1-A by the draft board. Holzman photographs his apartment carefully, pointing the Eclair at his makeshift editing table as he fiddles with the Nagra to the left of the frame. A wall mirror reflects the camera, which sits on a tripod like a baleful eye. Holzman promises an unvarnished look at his life, including his crumbling relationship with Penny, a model. He lets stray noises intrude on the soundtrack, allows the processing marks to show at the ends of reels, and constantly reminds viewers of the apparatus of filmmaking.

Solipsism doesn't get much more self-centered than *David Holzman's Diary*. Despite some handheld tours of the streets and sidewalks of the Upper West Side, most of the film zeroes in on Holzman himself. And here is where the cracks in cinema verite become gaping fissures.

Because what do you show when nothing is happening? What do you record when you have nothing to say? How can you film someone who doesn't want to be filmed, as Penny makes painfully clear? Holzman instead photographs his friend Pepe, standing in front of a pop art mural. "Some people's lives are good movies and some people's lives are bad movies," he says, reducing the entire philosophy behind cinema verité to a flip of the coin. "I'm sure you can write a better script," he adds.

The centerpiece of the film is a stationary shot of Holzman seated in a desk chair fingering his lavalier mike. For seven minutes, he sips a Pepsi, shifts in the chair, and teeters on the edge of a breakdown. Statements in his stream of consciousness monologue include, "I don't know what you're waiting for, I've got nothing to say" and "I thought I could control it, I could rearrange it, my life. . . . I could see what it was supposed to do. That's—that's not what happened." He ends the shot with an obscenity before shutting off the camera.

Director Jim McBride was born in 1941 in New York City and graduated from the film school at New York University after transferring from Kenyon College. While working as an editor for Michael Wadleigh, he finalized the screenplay for *David Holzman's Diary* with classmate L.M. Kit Carson. McBride's goal was to make the most attention-getting film he could for no money (the final budget totaled around $2,500). If cinema verité was demolished in the process, so be it.

McBride shot most of *David Holzman's Diary* in April 1967, filming all of the Holzman apartment interiors over a four-day stretch. If you've gotten this far, it's not giving too much away to state that *David Holzman's Diary* was a hoax, a carefully scripted faux documentary in which every flub, every out-of-focus shot, every soundtrack distortion was intentional.

Which isn't to say that *David Holzman's Diary* doesn't have serious intentions. McBride name-checks everyone from Vincente Minnelli to Jean-Luc Godard, from Herman Melville to Norman Mailer. (Critic Scott MacDonald has written that McBride based the Holzman character on experimental filmmaker Andrew Noren.) Cinematographer Michael Wadleigh, later the director of *Woodstock* (1970), adds a droll wit to many of his compositions. Cary Grant, in a poster for *Suspicion*, towers menacingly over Penny; Wadleigh's awkward zooms approximate Holzman's nervous voyeurism. A stop-motion distillation of an entire night's television broadcasting prefigures a school of film advertising. McBride fills the soundtrack with pop ephemera like "I'm a Man" by the Spencer Davis Group, but the radio background to Holzman's life also has news reports of rioting in Newark and casualty totals from Vietnam. If only all cinema verité works looked and sounded so good.

And there are legitimate documentary aspects to the film. McBride nails the details of life in New York City—cramped apartments, bizarre eating routines, urban views into and out of windows, belligerent but curious pedestrians, instant judgments and fights with strangers. In a later interview, McBride claimed that a scene on a sidewalk featuring a pre-op transsexual was totally impromptu.

Once editing was completed, McBride could not find a distributor willing to give *David Holzman's Diary* a theatrical release. It gained some notoriety at film festival screenings, but it wasn't until 1973 that it received a public exhibition at the Whitney Museum of American Art in New York. (New Yorker Films then showed it commercially in a few art-house theaters.) By that time McBride had made two other features, received an AFI grant, signed a contract with BBS Productions, saw his plans for *Gone Beaver* with Vanessa Redgrave fall apart when the $1.5 million project was canceled, and was back in New York City driving a cab. His career did not recover momentum until he directed a loose remake of Jean-Luc Godard's *Breathless* in 1983. Carson's subsequent career includes a documentary about Dennis Hopper (*The American Dreamer*, 1971), a writing credit for Wim Wenders' *Paris, Texas* (1984), and an acting role in Sidney Lumet's *Running on Empty* (1988).

A Time for Burning

Ernie Chambers, the future Nebraska state senator, in *A Time for Burning*.

Lutheran Film Associates & Quest Productions, Inc./Contemporary Films, 1967. Sound, B&W, 1.37. 56 minutes.

Featuring: L. William Youngdahl, Ernie Chambers, Ted Backstrom, Ray Christensen, Gene Zimmerman, Earle Persons, Alexander V. Sorensen.

Credits: Conceived, directed and edited by Barbara Connell, William C. Jersey. Produced by William C. Jersey. Executive producer: Robert E.A. Lee. Photographed by William C. Jersey. Sound by Barbara Connell. Assistant cameraman, assistant editor: Justus Taylor. Lyrics and music: Tom Paxton. Arranged by B.G. Kornfeld. Sung by Ronnie Gilbert. Produced by Quest Productions, Inc., for Lutheran Film Associates.

Additional Credits: Released January 1967.

Available: Docurama DVD (2005). ISBN: 0-7670-8596-5. UPC: 7-67685-97523-7.

Lutheran Church Productions was founded in 1952 as part of an outreach program of the Evangelical Lutheran Church in America and The Lutheran Church–Missouri Synod. Its goal was to finance and distribute motion pictures that upheld the morals and principles of the Lutheran Church. The first project, *Martin Luther*, was proposed by the National Lutheran Council and leaders of the United Lutheran Church in America. Directed by Irving Pichel, it premiered in Minneapolis, Minnesota, in May 1953. (Earlier films sponsored by the Lutheran Church included *The Way of Peace*, a 1947 cartoon written and directed by Frank Tashlin.)

In the early 1960s, Lutheran Church Productions merged with other film-oriented organizations into Lutheran Film Associates. Robert E.A. Lee, director the group from 1954 through 1988, authorized funding a proposal from filmmakers Bill Jersey and Barbara Connell. They had met L. William Youngdahl, a Lutheran minister in New Jersey recently named pastor of Augustana Lutheran Church in Omaha, Nebraska. Youngdahl was committed to connecting his white parish with black Lutheran congregations in Omaha. "When I talked to him, I told him he how he could end up," Jersey said later. "I made a figure of the cross, and that's the way it happened."

Jersey, a follower of cinema verité, approached filming without a script. "If you don't have a script, you don't cut yourself off from what happens," he said. "The risk is tremendous because nothing may happen." It's not clear that anyone involved with *A Time for Burning* knew what would result, certainly not Lee and the Lutheran Film Associates. Judging from the race riots that plagued urban centers like Detroit and Newark, Jersey felt confident that the material he and Connell were about to capture would at least be timely. He was grateful that the church never wavered in its support of the project.

Although he used cinema verité principles, Jersey also broke the "rules" of direct cinema. For one thing, *A Time for Burning* uses two narrators, Youngdahl himself and Ray Christensen.

For another, Jersey and Connell added music, in particular a mild but still intrusive protest song written by Tom Paxton over the closing credits. As a cameraman and coeditor, Jersey could not resist commenting on the material. He shoots some of the inflammatory news clippings posted on the wall of a barber shop, but ends the brief montage with a drawing of John F. Kennedy, as if suggesting a way out of racial controversies.

Cinema verite's shortcomings are easy to spot in *A Time for Burning*. It's clear that the presence of Jersey and Connell affect the participants of the meetings they filmed. Their subjects are cautious when making statements, overly deferential. Some switch to an oratorical mode when the camera is on them. They perhaps pre-censor their comments. As a cameraman, Jersey sometimes plays catch-up to events, missing opening statements of speeches, for example. (When necessary, he will cover a line or phrase with a wide shot that doesn't require synch sound.)

Another aspect of cinema verité—the need for personalities—is evident as well. Jersey and Connell found a gold mine with Ernie Chambers, a barber and activist whose soft-spoken demeanor hid bitter, cynical, deeply divisive attitudes. Chambers, a rhetorical bully more interested in agitating than in genuine debate, dominates his scenes. Jersey shoots him in tight close-ups, whereas the Lutheran leaders are more frequently placed against backgrounds that fix them firmly in a middle-class suburbia.

Heroes and villains are easy to spot in *A Time for Burning*, although viewers today might be surprised at how articulate these figures are. As the film opens, Youngdahl is trying to persuade his congregation to sponsor visits from a neighboring black church. He knows he is in for a fight, but neither he nor the filmmakers could predict the reactions the integration outreach would engender. Parish members struggle with the issue. As could be expected, there are extremists on either side: voices of caution and restraint, but also rebels who want to forge ahead. Simply getting a vote from a parish council requires elaborate arguments.

These arguments, while heartfelt, sound cold and empty with the benefit of hindsight. "The timing is not good," one minister keeps repeating. Another talks of deteriorating property values. Forty years later, we feel we know better answers.

As Ray Christensen, who emerges as an unexpected leader in the course of the film, asks, "How many years do I have to prepare myself to talk to another person?" To another member, he points out that their church is behind the business world in terms of racial equality. As we might be today, Ray seems dumbfounded that his parish can't see the obvious.

The biggest drawback to cinema verité may be the style's inability to provide a context for filmed material. When Frederick Wiseman is filming an operation in *Hospital* (1970), a wider context may not be necessary. But how useful would it be to know that the National Guard was called out to stop rioting in North Omaha the same year Jersey and Connell were filming? Or that both Dr. Martin Luther King, Jr., and Malcolm X felt the need to deliver speeches in Omaha? Jersey and Connell did not identify any of the figures in the film, allowing the "villains" to remain cloaked in anonymity. But when Alexander V. Sorensen, the mayor of Omaha, delivers an impassioned speech demanding equal rights for all, why shouldn't he be named?

Jersey later pointed to the cinema verité style as a primary reason why broadcast networks refused to air *A Time for Burning* (it was eventually shown on public television, and later distributed to theaters). Networks more likely shied away from the film because it lacked a tidy ending. Today the film is a sad reminder that good intentions are not enough, as well as a vivid snapshot of a different generation.

Based in San Francisco, Jersey has enjoyed a long career making documentaries on subjects like religious fundamentalism (*The Glory and the Power*). He credited Robert E.A. Lee, who died in February 2009, as the most important force behind the film. "*A Time for Burning* would never have happened without Robert Lee," Jersey said, still marveling years later over the producer's integrity. "He has this trial by fire with others within the church who say, 'We're making a film about the church's failure?' He says, 'We should do it.'" Youngdahl went on to hold pulpits in several parishes around the country. Chambers served as state senator in the Nebraska legislature for over thirty years. Lutheran Film Associates continues to fund films, notably *The Joy of Bach* (1980).

Dont Look Back

Bob Dylan and D A Pennebaker in 1966, a year after *Dont Look Back. Courtesy Pennebaker Hegedus Films*

Leacock Pennebaker, Inc., 1967. Sound, B&W, 1.37. 96 minutes.
Featuring: Bob Dylan, Albert Grossman, Bob Neuwirth, Joan Baez, Alan Price, Tito Burns, Donovan, Derroll Adams.
Credits: Directed by D A Pennebaker. Produced by Albert Grossman, John Court. Camera by D A Pennebaker. Assistant camera: Howard Alk. Sound: Jones Alk, D A Pennebaker. Concert recordings: J. Robert Van Dyke. A Leacock Pennebaker, Inc., presentation.
Also Featuring: Allen Ginsberg, Horace Judson, Marianne Faithful.
Additional Credits: Photography by Ed Emshwiller. Filmed in April and May 1965. Premiered in San Francisco on May 17, 1967.
Other Versions: Footage from the same tour is incorporated into the documentary *65 Revisited* (2007).
Available: Docurama DVD (1999). ISBN: 0-7670-2216-5. UPC: 7-67685-944/3-8. *Bob Dylan Dont Look Back 1965 Tour Deluxe Edition*, Docurama DVD (2007). UPC: 767685982433.

A folksinger who helped transform pop music in the 1960s, Bob Dylan was a flashpoint for the mainstream media and a messiah figure for a rapidly growing alternative press. By turns elusive and outgoing, cryptic and verbose, he was a new style of celebrity, one looked on with misgivings by adults and embraced by the baby boomer generation.

Originally Bobby Zimmerman, a nondescript teenager from Hibbing, Minnesota, Dylan developed a look based equal parts on his singing hero Woody Guthrie and on movie star James Dean. Dylan's evolution from scruffy folksinger crashing in Greenwich Village apartments to spokesperson for a generation was so fascinating because it occurred largely in public. As filmmaker D A Pennebaker put it, "He was kind of inventing himself as he went along."

Donn Alan Pennebaker was born in Illinois in 1925. A veteran of World War II, he studied mechanical engineering at Yale. While photographing experimental documentaries, he began working on a way to synchronize 16mm cameras with tape recording equipment. Pennebaker joined Drew Associates in 1959, working for one day on what would become *Primary* (1960) and on five subsequent *Living Camera* documentaries for ABC. In 1964, Pennebaker and veteran filmmaker Richard Leacock formed Leacock Pennebaker, Inc. Pennebaker began to focus on music and musicians with a film about jazz singer and songwriter Dave Lambert.

By 1965, Dylan had recorded three albums for Columbia Records, two of them best-sellers. (Record company profits were significantly higher from albums than singles, and Dylan was one of the pioneers in shifting popular tastes towards the album format.) With songs like "Chimes of Freedom," "Blowin' in the Wind," and "Mr. Tambourine Man," his value to Columbia had reached a point where the label was willing to invest in a tour of England. Albert Grossman, Dylan's manager, approached Pennebaker about documenting the tour.

Pennebaker accompanied Dylan for almost a month, starting in April 1965. It was the singer's last acoustic tour, eight shows in seven venues in cities like Sheffield, Birmingham, and Manchester. Pennebaker shot about twenty hours of film; for the last two shows in London's Royal Albert Hall, he hired Howard and Jones Alk to film additional concert material.

Dylan had already been filmed performing at the Newport Folk Festival, and he had learned how to use the camera to his benefit. Apart from the concert material, which was photographed in a straightforward manner, Dylan and Pennebaker cooperated on what would be filmed. Perhaps unconsciously, their model was *A Hard Day's Night* (1964), a musical comedy starring The Beatles. Several scenes and individual shots in *Dont Look Back* mirror the Beatles' film, from encountering fans outside music halls to dealing with journalists at press conferences. Even the look of the film, with its gritty, sometimes washed-out black-and-white stock, echoes *A Hard Day's Night*.

"Dylan is sort of acting throughout the film," Pennebaker acknowledged. What may not be so apparent is how carefully both the director and the musician crafted what would end up in the final cut. Called upon to cite his influences, Dylan sings two Hank Williams songs, choices that consciously aligned him with a mainstream America his fans had rejected. (Dylan would later record a country music–tinged album in Nashville.) The film opens with a promotional piece for the song "Subterranean Homesick Blues," one of three versions Pennebaker filmed in New York City. It was designed to introduce fans to the new "electric" Dylan, one who hoped to break out of a folkie niche and into a rock audience.

One of the more memorable sequences in *Dont Look Back* is Dylan's encounter with *Time* magazine reporter Horace Judson. Pennebaker edited this incident into an angry diatribe about the meaning of "truth" and the usefulness of mainstream media. The goal was to position Dylan as someone who could toy with clueless journalists, whose withering sarcasm defended him from the frustrations of modern life. Many critics of the time used the moment to condemn what they saw as Dylan's anger or meanness. But according to eyewitness Anthea Joseph, the musician was fully justified in his attack. Judson was "abusive," poorly prepared, someone who didn't think the musician was "a serious artist."

Pennebaker eschewed a voice-over narration, explanatory titles, or any other attempt to provide a context for the material he was filming. "I wanted it to be like an Ibsen play," Pennebaker said later. At another point, he explained, "What I wanted to do was just be present when Dylan enacted his whole life and show you what he deals with and what interests him." The director also left out almost all of the music from the tour. "I hadn't been trying to make *Dont Look Back* a concert film," he said. "I wanted it to be about Dylan, so I had cut the songs down. I figured if people wanted to hear the music they had the records." Pennebaker collected a dozen songs from the outtakes into the 2007 documentary *65 Revisited*.

In the two years it took to edit and release the film, Dylan had gone electric—to the consternation of many of his die-hard folk fans. After a life-threatening motorcycle accident, he then withdrew from the public, but continued his interest in film. Pennebaker helped shoot *Eat This Document*, about Dylan's 1966 tour of England with The Hawks. Dylan appeared as an actor in Sam Peckinpah's *Pat Garrett & Billy the Kid* (1973), and later directed films like *Renaldo and Clara* (1978). Pennebaker was one of the directors of the influential concert film *Monterey Pop* (1969), and continues to be a significant voice in documentary film.

In the Heat of the Night

United Artists, 1967. Sound, color, 1.85. 110 minutes.

Cast: Sidney Poitier (Virgil Tibbs), Rod Steiger ([Bill] Gillespie), Warren Oates (Sam Wood), Lee Grant (Mrs. [Leslie] Colbert), Larry Gates ([Eric] Endicott), James Patterson (Mr. Purdy), William Schallert (Mayor Schubert), Beah Richards (Mama Caleba), Peter Whitney (Courtney), Kermit Murdock (Henderson), Larry D. Mann (Watkins), Matt Clark (Packy), Arthur Malet (Ulam), Fred Stewart (Dr. Stuart), Quentin Dean (Delores [Purdy]), Scott Wilson (Harvey Oberst), Anthony James (Ralph), Timothy Scott (Shagbag), William C. Watson (McNeil), Eldon Quick (Charles Hawthorne), Stuart Nisbet (Shuie), Khalil Bezaleel (Jess), Peter Masterson (Fryer), Jester Hairston (Butler), Phil Adams (1st tough), Nikita Knatz (2nd tough), Sam Reese (Clerk).

Credits: Directed by Norman Jewison. Screenplay by Stirling Silliphant. Based on a novel by John Ball. Produced by Walter Mirisch. Director of photography: Haskell Wexler. Music by Quincy Jones. Song: "In the Heat of the Night" sung by Ray Charles. Art director: Paul Groesse. Film editor: Hal Ashby. Set decorator: Robert Priestley. Music editor: Richard Carruth. Sound editor: James Richard. Sound: Walter Goss. Rerecording: Clem Portman. Song lyrics by: Alan & Marilyn Bergman. Titles: Murray Naidich. Production supervisor: Allen K. Wood. Production manager: James E. Henderling. Unit production manager: J. Howard Joslin. Script supervisor: Meta Rebner. Makeup: Del Armstrong. Men's costumer: Alan Levine. Casting by Lynn Stalmaster. Assistant to the producer: Hal Ashby. Westrex Sound. A Mirisch Corporation presentation of a Norman Jewison–Walter Mirisch production.

Additional Credits: Writing: Robert Alan Aurthur. Production dates: September to December 1966. Premiered in New York City on August 2, 1967.

Awards: Oscars for Best Picture, Actor (Steiger), Writing—Screenplay Based on Material from Another Medium, Editing, Sound.

Other Versions: Sequels *They Call Me MISTER Tibbs!* (1970), *The Organization* (1971). Settings and characters used for the television series *In the Heat of the Night* and four made-for-TV movies.

Available: MGM Home Entertainment DVD (2001). ISNB: 0-7928-4836-5. UPC: 0 27616-85792-7.

Author John Ball struggled for years to succeed as a writer. Born in Schenectady, New York, but raised in Milwaukee, he worked at *Fortune* magazine in the late 1930s, then became a music critic. For over a decade he wrote liner notes on record albums and reviews for newspapers in Brooklyn and New York, as well as two music industry–oriented books. An interest in aviation (he held a pilot's license) brought him to the Institute of Aerospace Sciences, where he was a director of public relations. Ball dabbled in science fiction and wrote books about flying; he also worked on a mystery novel about an African-American detective who teams up with a racist Southern cop to solve a murder.

Ball later wrote that the idea for *In the Heat of the Night* came to him in the 1930s. "I couldn't have written it then," he said. "I wasn't a good enough writer to do the idea justice." Published in 1965, *In the Heat of the Night* drew attention from actor Sidney Poitier, whose agent submitted it to Walter Mirisch. Planning to produce it through United Artists, where he had a development deal, Mirisch asked screenwriter Robert Alan Aurthur to adapt the book. Aurthur contributed a treatment before leaving for France to work on *Grand Prix* (1966). Mirisch replaced him with Stirling Silliphant.

Silliphant had been a publicist at Twentieth Century-Fox before producing a low-budget feature on boxer Joe Louis and writing three fast-paced thrillers, including *Nightfall*, in the 1950s. He also helped build two hit television series: *Naked City*, based on the 1948 Jules Dassin film, and *Route 66*, which sent two friends to a different locale each week to encounter romance and drama. Silliphant met Poitier while writing *The Slender Thread*, a fact-based melodrama about a suicide prevention hotline.

Mirisch, Poitier, and Silliphant worked together on a script, changing elements of Ball's novel to facilitate filming. A character in the story who had been an orchestra conductor became a real estate developer, for example. George C. Scott was originally cast as small-town sheriff Bill Gillespie, but he was committed to a Broadway play. Mirisch replaced him with Rod Steiger, whose previous

films ranged from Sidney Lumet's Holocaust-tinged drama *The Pawnbroker* (1964) to David Lean's sweeping epic *Doctor Zhivago* (1965).

Steiger was such a dedicated actor that he brought to the foreground the central problem with the script. While presented as a murder mystery, *In the Heat of the Night* was really a story "about tolerance, about understanding between the races," as Mirisch put it later. Steiger didn't want to play a stereotype in a polemic about race, and struggled to find a way to bring Gillespie to life.

The actor fusses and fidgets throughout the film, a physical manifestation of Gillespie's self-doubts, but Steiger also resists cheap tricks and easy solutions. He didn't want to smoke cigars or chew tobacco, lazy shortcuts other actors often chose in portraying rednecks. Chewing gum made the sheriff more approachable, harder for viewers to pigeonhole. Told to fashion his part after Bull Connor, a notoriously racist Southern sheriff, Steiger instead focused on Gillespie's skills, knowing that it was easy to dismiss an outright racist, more difficult to acknowledge the innate racism in society.

In the Heat of the Night asked a lot of moviegoers of the time. In the throes of the civil rights movement, it was positing a black man as the intellectual and moral superior to whites in the film. Virgil Tibbs was Poitier's first truly mainstream part, one that didn't make excuses about his race or protect him with plot contrivances like blindness, nuns, or suicide threats. It was a role that would be difficult for many to accept. According to Mirisch's autobiography, United Artists executives were ready to sacrifice the entire Southern market rather than face the possibility of picketing or other disturbances.

Mirisch assigned the project to Norman Jewison, a former television director who had done well with one of the producer's previous films, *The Russians Are Coming the Russians Are Coming* (1966). Jewison didn't have much time to establish a directorial style: with a schedule of only forty days, he and cinematographer Haskell Wexler had to grab whatever material they could. The production filmed most of the location footage in Sparta, Illinois, a small town near the Missouri boarder. It was the closest Northern equivalent to the Deep South scouts could find. Jewison insisted on at least some "real" Southern footage, including views of cotton fields. Both Poitier and Steiger remembered their three days of filming in Tennessee as distinctly uncomfortable, complete with threats from shotgun-wielding rednecks.

A hit on its release, *In the Heat of the Night* went on to receive five Oscars. It solidified Poitier's box-office standing; he repeated the Virgil Tibbs role in two sequels. The Gillespie character and the story's settings were later used in a television series, as well as a half-dozen novels by John Ball. *In the Heat of the Night* may not have solved racism, but its matter-of-fact depiction of equality within the framework of an exciting thriller was at least a step in the right direction.

Bonnie and Clyde

Warner Bros., 1967. Sound, color, 1.78. 111 minutes.

Cast: Warren Beatty (Clyde Barrow), Faye Dunaway (Bonnie Parker), Michael J. Pollard (C.W. Moss), Gene Hackman (Buck Barrow), Estelle Parsons (Blanche), Denver Pyle (Frank Hamer), Dub Taylor (Ivan Moss), Evans Evans (Velma Davis), Gene Wilder (Eugene Grizzard).

Credits: Directed by Arthur Penn. Written by David Newman & Robert Benton. Produced by Warren Beatty. Director of photography: Burnett Guffey. Film editor: Dede Allen. Music composed by Charles Strouse. Art director: Dean Tavoularis. Costumes designed by Theadora Van Runkle. Special consultant: Robert Towne. Assistant to the producer: Elaine Michea. Production manager: Russ Saunders. Assistant director: Jack N. Reddish. Script supervisor: John Dutton. Makeup created by Robert Jiras. Sound by Francis E. Stahl. Set decorator: Raymond Paul. Special effects: Danny Lee. Hair stylist: Gladys Witten. Miss Dunaway's cosmetics by Warner Bros. Cosmetics. Men's wardrobe: Andy Matyasi. Women's wardrobe: Norma Brown. "Foggy Mountain Breakdown" written by Earl Scruggs, performed by Flatt & Scruggs & the Foggy Mountain Boys. Technicolor. A Warner Bros. Pictures presentation of a Tatira-Hiller production.

Additional Cast: James Stiver (Grocery store owner), Harry Appling (Bonnie's uncle), Mabel Cavitt (Bonnie's mother), Ann Palmer (Bonnie's sister); Ada Waugh, Frances Fisher (Bonnie's aunts); Gary Goodgion (Billy).

Additional Credits: Titles: Wayne Fitzgerald. Production dates: October to December 1966. Premiered in New York City on August 13, 1967. Rated R in 2007.

Awards: Oscars for Best Actress in a Supporting Role (Estelle Parsons), Cinematography.

Available: Warner Home Video DVD (2008). ISBN: 1-4178-5624-3. UPC: 0-85391-16789-3.

A turning point in the depiction of violence on screen, *Bonnie and Clyde* was also a distillation of competing trends in cinema during the 1960s. A biography of sorts of real-life criminals Bonnie Parker and Clyde Barrow, the film updated the gangster genre perfected by Warner Brothers in the 1930s for a new generation. Screenwriters David Newman and Robert Benton were inspired by the French New Wave, and used elements of films like *Breathless* (1959) in their script. Commercially, the producers took advantage of several marketing opportunities, with the result that gangster fashions briefly dominated the clothing industry and bluegrass music enjoyed a widespread popularity. For better or worse, *Bonnie and Clyde* introduced the tricks and devices of underground horror and drive-in movies to a mainstream audience, lowering standards for what was considered permissible to show on screen.

Coworkers at *Esquire* magazine in New York City, Newman and Benton worked on a treatment of the story after reading John Toland's *The Dillinger Days*. Benton, who grew up in Texas, was familiar with Barrow and Parker, who had already been the basis of Fritz Lang's *You Only Live Once* (1937) and *The Bonnie Parker Story* (1958). (Benton's father attended the criminals' funerals.) Newman and Benton wrote together and separately, Flatt and Scruggs and the Foggy Mountain Boys providing a musical background to their labors.

Elinor Wright Jones, wife of one of the creators of *The Fantastiks*, read their seventy-five-page treatment and sent it to Arthur Penn. A former TV director, Penn made his feature debut directing Paul Newman in a revisionist Billy the Kid drama, *The Left Handed Gun* (1958). When it failed commercially, Penn focused on theater. He directed five Broadway hits in three years, including *The Miracle Worker*, whose success in turn revived his film career.

Newman and Benton completed a screenplay in 1963. They met with François Truffaut about the project in March 1964. He gave them advice about manipulating time, about using montage to condense scenes, and about depicting the sexual relationship between Bonnie and Clyde. (Screening the 1949 *Gun Crazy* also helped the writers.) Truffaut came tantalizingly close to committing to the project several times; so did Jean-Luc Godard, but both directors turned down the project after reading a revised script in September.

By now Elinor Jones and Norton Wright were the producers. They estimated the budget at $1.3 million. Warren Beatty, who was filming *Mickey One* with Penn in Chicago, also became interested in producing after he read the script. He waited until the option Jones and Wright had on the property expired in November 1965, then purchased it himself for $75,000.

Beatty went back to Penn, persuading him to direct. Having helmed two flops—*Mickey One* (1965) and a dreadful melodrama called *The Chase* (1966)—Penn wasn't in much of a position to argue. He originally saw the film in terms of the gritty, black-and-white photographs of Walker Evans. In time he agreed with Beatty to adopt a more romanticized view of the Depression-era Dust Bowl. In these choices, Penn and Beatty were concurring with Newman, who said of the criminals, "The thing about them that made them so appealing and relevant, and so threatening to society, was that they were aesthetic revolutionaries."

The lighthearted tone ultimately used by the filmmakers was somewhat at odds with the screenwriters' original conception of Bonnie and Clyde as not just outlaws, but outcasts. In 1967 you could not have found much more glamorous outcasts than Warren Beatty and Faye Dunaway (chosen after Beatty considered a half-dozen other actresses). Similarly, positioning Beatty as a sexually confused, stupidly violent hick ran so contrary to the public's perception of him as to reduce his performance to a parody.

Although it may have gone over the heads of most filmgoers, the makers of *Bonnie and Clyde* were mocking the bluegrass music ultimately used on the soundtrack, just as they condescended to their rural characters. Bluegrass was not even recognized as a genre of music until 1946; Bonnie and Clyde and their peers were more likely to have listened to big-band and pop music, to have aspired to the penthouses and limousines they saw in movies and magazines. The musical soundtrack turned the characters into cartoons, and made them easier to laugh off.

Location filming took place in Texas, far away from possible interference by Warner Brothers executives. The cast by now included veterans from television and Broadway, like Gene Hackman, who had worked with Beatty in *Lilith* (1964). (It was the screen debut for Gene Wilder.) Also on location was screenwriter Robert Towne. Beatty and Towne shared psychotherapists, and had started working together on a modern-day version of William Wycherley's *The Country Wife*, which would later be filmed as *Shampoo* (1975).

Leisurely and amiable for most of its length, *Bonnie and Clyde* suddenly demanded that filmgoers take the material seriously during its climactic bloodbath. Many critics of the time decried the film, asserting that it was inappropriate for mainstream entertainment, that it glorified criminals, and that it made violence exciting, even beautiful. Penn responded by evoking the assassination of John F. Kennedy and the Vietnam War, adding that "I would have to say that I think violence is a part of the American character." Years later, Benton would talk about "the aesthetic of violence," saying that "*Bonnie and Clyde* took it from *Yojimbo* and *Seven Samurai*, so if you're going to hang somebody hang Kurosawa, don't hang Arthur Penn." He added, "We made Bonnie and Clyde so ordinary, and that's what's disturbing."

Jack Warner hated the film so much that he tried to dump it, despite its positive reception at the Montreal Film Festival. (Warner was in the process of turning the studio over to Seven Arts.) When Pauline Kael's rave review was turned down by the *New Republic*, she took it to *The New Yorker*, the beginning of her long and influential career as the magazine's film critic. "We don't take our stories straight anymore," she wrote. "*Bonnie and Clyde* needs violence; violence is its meaning."

The controversy helped fuel interest in the film, but not enough to stop Warners from pulling it from the market. Beatty kept pushing the movie, eventually meeting with Seven Arts head Eliot Hyman and convincing the studio to give it another shot. When *Bonnie and Clyde* was rereleased in early 1968, it became a box-office phenomenon.

Cool Hand Luke

Warner Bros., 1967. Sound, color, 2.35. 126 minutes.

Cast: Paul Newman (Luke), George Kennedy (Dragline), J.D. Cannon (Society Red), Lou Antonio (Koko), Robert Drivas (Loudmouth Steve), Strother Martin (Captain), Jo Van Fleet (Arletta), Clifton James (Carr), Morgan Woodward (Boss Godfrey), Luke Askew (Boss Paul), Marc Cavell (Rabbitt), Richard Davalos (Blind Dick), Robert Donner (Boss Shorty), Warren Finnerty (Tattoo), Dennis Hopper (Babalugats), John McLiam (Boss Keen), Wayne Rogers (Gambler), [Harry] Dean Stanton (Tramp), Charles Tyner (Boss Higgins), Ralph Waite (Alibi), Anthony Zerbe (Dog Boy), Buck Kartalian (Dynamite), Joy Harmon (The girl).

Credits: Directed by Stuart Rosenberg. Screenplay by Donn Pearce and Frank R. Pierson. Based on the novel by Donn Pearce. Produced by Gordon Carroll. Director of photography: Conrad Hall. Art director: Cary Odell. Film editor: Sam O'Steen. Music by Lalo Schifrin. Assistant director: Hank Moonjean. Associate producer: Carter DeHaven, Jr. Unit manager: Arthur Newman. Sound: Larry Jost. Set decorator: Fred Price. Costumes designed by Howard Shoup. Makeup supervisor: Gordon Bau. Supervising hair stylist: Jean Burt Reilly. Technicolor, Panavision. A Warner Bros. Pictures presentation of a Jalem production.

Additional Cast: Donn Pearce, Rance Howard, James Gammon, Joe Don Baker.

Additional Credits: Opened November 1, 1967. Rated GP in 1970.

Awards: Oscar for Best Actor in a Supporting Role (Kennedy).

Available: Warner Home Video DVD (1997). ISBN: 0-7907-3150-9. UPC: 0-85391 10372-1.

Born in 1928, author Donn Pearce led what was once known as a "colorful" life. He was still a minor when he enlisted in the Army in 1944, and ended up in the Merchant Marine after going AWOL. Pearce had trouble with authorities in France and Italy, made his way back to the United States through Canada, and moved to Florida. He told reporters later that he worked with a partner as a safecracker, and was arrested and convicted of breaking and entering and grand larceny when he tried to go out on his own.

Pearce's two years in the Florida State Prison were spent mostly on a chain gang doing road work. He began writing what would become *Cool Hand Luke* in the evening, before lights out. When the book was released, reviewers pointed to safecracker Donald Graham Garrison as the inspiration for the title character. (Garrison was released from prison in 1980.) But in later years Pearce implied that he himself was Cool Hand Luke—or at least that Paul Newman wasn't.

After his release, Pearce worked through several drafts of *Cool Hand Luke* before selling it as a paperback original. (It was later printed in a hardbound edition.) The book did not attract much interest, but Pearce did manage to sell it to Warner Brothers for $80,000, with an additional $15,000 for writing a screenplay adaptation. Pearce was also present during shooting, and can be seen as an extra in the film, but his recollections of the production were not pleasant.

The screenplay was developed in part by Jalem, a production company formed by actor Jack Lemmon. After Pearce's initial draft, Frank R. Pierson was assigned to the project. A Harvard–educated reporter for *Time*, Pierson became a story editor for the TV series *Have Gun, Will Travel*. He wrote for that and other shows until 1965, when he collaborated with Walter Newman on the Western parody *Cat Ballou*. Pierson followed Pearce's episodic plot fairly closely, although he made the story's religious symbolism more explicit and added what became the film's catchphrase, "What we've got here is failure to communicate," delivered by the prison camp Captain (Strother Martin). "It's a stupid line," Pearce always said, adding that guards were rednecks, not pseudo-intellectuals.

Director Stuart Rosenberg also had a background in television. Born in 1927 in Brooklyn, he taught at New York University before directing hundreds of episodes for a variety of TV series like *The Untouchables*. He had to abandon his first feature project due to an actors' strike, then directed a message drama in Germany for producer Louis de Rochemont. *Cool Hand Luke* was his first Hollywood project.

Much of the cast also came from television, with roles divided between old-line actors like George Kennedy and a younger generation symbolized by Dennis Hopper. Kennedy, a World War II veteran with a larger-than-life presence, had been building his career in supporting parts in television and movies, primarily Westerns. This was his breakthrough role, and he approached it doggedly, giving Rosenberg exactly what the director wanted. Hopper, on the other hand, while also experienced in television and films, was increasingly fed up with the studio system. His disdain for his slightly comic role in *Cool Hand Luke* is all too obvious. Hopper was about to make history by directing *Easy Rider* (1969).

The movie gave important exposure to Harry Dean Stanton, Wayne Rogers, and especially Strother Martin, a former swimming champion who spent a decade trying to advance from uncredited bit parts. Almost fifty when he filmed *Cool Hand Luke*, Martin could seem much older on screen. He specialized in wizened, garrulous sidekicks who could be buffoonish or, as here, menacing. This was the first of four films that Martin made with Paul Newman.

By the end of the 1960s Newman had been nominated for two Oscars, and had established himself as one of the top box-office draws in the country. He had just finished working with Alfred Hitchcock in *Torn Curtain* (1966) and with Martin Ritt on *Hombre* (1967), an adaptation of an Elmore Leonard Western. He came fairly late to the project, which he called one of the best scripts he had read in years. Publicity reports quote him as saying, "Luke is detached and indifferent, but he can't beat the system he scoffs at." On a more fundamental level, Newman saw the role as a continuation of the anti-establishment loners he played in *The Hustler* (1961) and *Hud* (1963). Or, as publicists put it, "Luke is The Hustler without a dream of victory, Harper without a moral mission, Hud without a father to defy."

Exteriors for the film were shot in Stockton, California, where crews reconstructed a prison site, complete with barracks and kennels. The photography by Conrad Hall evoked the classic Hollywood style of the 1930s, with the notable addition of zoom lenses. Several shots in *Cool Hand Luke* could have come from *I Am a Fugitive from a Chain Gang* (1932), although the films could not be farther apart in their messages. *Cool Hand Luke* sets up Lucas Jackson, a war hero arrested for vandalism, as a Christ figure, someone who refuses to conform to society's regulations, who leads by example, who teaches his followers through parables and miracles (like eating fifty eggs in one sitting). It accepts as a given that chain gangs and the guards who run them are bad, but has nothing coherent to say about the prison system as a whole.

Exactly what Luke is rebelling against is never made clear in the script. Society in the form of brutal, vicious prison guards may be bad, but it is not the reason why Luke was imprisoned. Jo Van Fleet shows up as Luke's mother (she was six years Newman's senior) in another of her scene-stealing performances, but she adds almost nothing to our understanding of his character. "Sometimes nothing can be a real cool hand," Luke says at one point, and it's as if the filmmakers used that as their guiding principle.

Audiences didn't care what Luke stood for, or against, they just wanted to be entertained by Newman's good looks and swagger. (Pearce insisted that Newman was too small for the part, and would never have survived in a prison camp.) For all its squalid settings and implied injustices, *Cool Hand Luke* presented prison as a series of poker games, sing-alongs, and happy-go-lucky japes. It was exactly how filmgoers wanted to see chain gangs.

In Cold Blood

Columbia, 1967. Sound, B&W, 2.35. 134 minutes.

Cast: Robert Blake (Perry Smith), Scott Wilson (Dick Hickock), John Forsythe (Alvin Dewey), Paul Stewart (Jensen), Gerald S. O'Loughlin (Harold Nye), Jeff Corey (Mr. Hickock), John Gallaudet (Roy Church), James Flavin (Clarence Duntz), Charles McGraw (Tex Smith), Will Geer (Prosecuting attorney), John McLiam (Herbert Clutter), Ruth Storey (Bonnie Clutter), Brenda C. Currin (Nancy Clutter), Paul Hough (Kenyon Clutter), Vaughn Taylor ("Good Samaritan"), Duke Hobbie (Reporter), Sheldon Allman (Rev. Jim Post), Sammy Thurman (Flo Smith), Raymond Hatton (Elderly hitchhiker), Sadie Truitt (Herself), Myrtle Clare (Herself), Teddy Eccles (Young hitchhiker), Al Christy (Sheriff), Don Sollars (Luke Sharpe), Harriet Levitt (Mrs. Hartman), Ronda [Rhonda] Fultz (Nancy's friend), Mary-Linda Rapelye (Susan Kidwell).

Credits: Written for the screen and directed by Richard Brooks. Based on the book by Truman Capote. Director of photography: Conrad Hall. Music: Quincy Jones. Assistant director: Tom Shaw. Art director: Robert Boyle. Film editor: Peter Zinner. Script supervisor: John Franco. Public relations: Al Horwits. Sound: Wm. Randall, Jr., Dick Tyler, A. [Arthur] Piantadosi. Sound effects: John H. Newman. Set decorator: Jack Ahern. Special effects: Chuck Gaspar. Wardrobe: Jack Martell. Make-up: Gary Morris. Optical effects: Pacific Title. Filmed in Panavision. Prints by Technicolor. Filmed with the cooperation of the People and Law Enforcement Agencies of Kansas, Missouri, Colorado, Nevada, Texas, Mexico. Acknowledgment for Technical Assistance to Dr. Joseph Satten and the Division of Law and Psychiatry, The Menninger Foundation. Copyright Pax Enterprises.

Additional Cast includes: Richard Kelton (Nancy's boyfriend), John Collins (Judge Roland Tate), Bowman Upchurch (Andy).

Additional Credits: Produced by Richard Brooks. Camera operator: Jordan Cronenweth. Production dates: March to June 1967. Opened December 14, 1967. Rated R in 1970.

Other Versions: Remade as a television miniseries in 1996. The films *Capote* (2005) and *Infamous* (2006) both deal with the writing of *In Cold Blood*.

Available: Columbia TriStar Home Entertainment DVD (2003). ISBN: 0-7678-7128-6. UPC: 0-43396-06831-5.

A milestone in nonfiction literature, Truman Capote's *In Cold Blood* has also been dogged by questions about its accuracy. Inspired by a 1959 newspaper account of the murders of four members of the Clutter family in Holcomb, Kansas, Capote spent years researching the crime, going so far as to establish personal relationships with Perry Smith and Dick Hickock, the two drifters arrested and later executed in the case. He did not tape-record his interviews or take notes, believing they would distract his subjects. He told George Plimpton, "I could get within 95 percent of absolute accuracy, which is as close as you need" by simply relying on his memory. Capote altered some scenes and characters, imagined the thoughts of people he never interviewed, and made up an ending that echoed the one in his novel *The Grass Harp*.

He also publicized his work relentlessly, quipping, "A boy's got to hustle his book." *In Cold Blood* was serialized in four parts in *The New Yorker* before being published by Random House. Despite questions about the propriety of exploiting the deaths of six people, the book became a phenomenon. Capote earned a reported $700,000 for paperback rights, and sold the film rights to Columbia for a million dollars.

The novelist had experience as a screenwriter in the 1950s, and some have seen the influence of movies in the writing of *In Cold Blood*. Capote used the equivalent of cross-cutting and dissolves to draw connections among his characters. Flashbacks fleshed out backgrounds but also served to build suspense. Some scenes were constructed in a style similar to narrative filmmaking, with establishing shots, point-of-view shots, and reaction shots.

Capote showed little interest in adapting his book for film, and once the property was sold had almost no control over how it would be shot. However, he did approve the hiring of director Richard Brooks, a former playwright and screenwriter. Brooks' previous film had been *The Professionals* (1966), a solid Western similar in tone to Sam Peckinpah's *The Wild Bunch* (1969). But much of Brooks' earlier work, starting with his novel *The Brick Foxhole* (1945), had a strong streak of social criticism. (The novel helped him get a contract to write an adaptation of *The Killers*, 1946.) Brooks believed he had a responsibility to grapple with problems. "When I was in college, if a public official was corrupt, we went after him," he told writer John Mariani. "The kids today have been burned, left without heroes by Vietnam."

In filming *In Cold Blood*, Brooks strained for realism, using the Clutters' family photographs, shooting on actual locations, hiring neighbors, members of the jury, even the executioner. He adopted many of Capote's methods, such as cutting from farmer and father Herbert Clutter shaving in his bathroom to ex-con Perry Smith washing in the men's room of a bus terminal. But he also changed elements of the book, not always to Capote's liking.

Brooks introduced a reporter played by Paul Stewart who functioned as a sort of alter ego for Capote. Stewart brought a voice of moral wisdom to the story that was largely absent from the book. Asked what will happen in the wake of the crime, he intones, "More laws will be passed. Everybody will pass the buck. And then, next month, next year, the same thing will happen again." (Much of Stewart's material came from the director's research at the Menninger Foundation.) Brooks also concentrated on the killers instead of their victims, opening himself to charges of romanticizing the criminals.

There's no question the director exploited the details of the actual crime. In his essay "Pornoviolence," author Tom Wolfe criticized Capote's intentions: "The book is neither a who-done-it nor a will-they-be-caught, since the answers to both questions are known from the outset. . . . Instead, the book's suspense is based largely on a totally new idea in detective stories: the promise of gory details, and the withholding of them until the end." Brooks did exactly the same thing, building up to and then lingering over uncomfortably vivid images designed to tease and shock viewers.

In the film's opening, Brooks adopted a jazzy, updated film-noir style, editing Conrad Hall's evocative cinematography with Quincy Jones' score to suggest characters hurtling to an inevitable fate. But when it came to depicting the murders, Brooks limited the soundtrack to a moaning wind and staged shots in a flat, affectless manner, as if the situation were too serious to turn into art. Other filmmakers quickly took the same tone to justify violence that was more and more unsettling. George Romero copied the staging of several shots in Brooks' film for his *Night of the Living Dead* (1968), as did Terrence Malick in *Badlands* (1973).

The film's cast reflected the director's focus. The police investigators, townspeople, and victims were largely drawn from real life or television; John Forsythe, perhaps the biggest name at the time, had starred in *Bachelor Father* for five years, and would later anchor *Dynasty*. But Brooks was considerably more careful with his two lead actors. Scott Wilson bore a marked resemblance to Richard Hickock, and his performance as a killer without remorse was so precise that it may have affected his subsequent career. Robert Blake, who plays Hickock's partner Perry Smith, had been a child actor in the 1930s and '40s, including a turn as a street urchin in *The Treasure of the Sierra Madre* (1948), which his character cites twice in this film. Blake made explicit the homoerotic undertones of Capote's book, with Brooks' encouragement offering sexual confusion as a motive for Smith's actions.

Blake's troubled life, in particular his arrest in 2001 for the murder of his second wife Bonnie Bakley, brings another somber note to *In Cold Blood*, which received generally good reviews but failed to capture a broad audience. Brooks directed another true crime story, *Looking for Mr. Goodbar* (1977), among his half-dozen or so post–*In Cold Blood* features.

The Graduate

Embassy Pictures, 1967. Sound, color, 2.35. 106 minutes.

Cast: Anne Bancroft (Mrs. Robinson), Dustin Hoffman (Ben Braddock), Katharine Ross (Elaine Robinson), William Daniels (Mr. Braddock), Murray Hamilton (Mr. Robinson), Elizabeth Wilson (Mrs. Braddock), Buck Henry (Room clerk), Brian Avery (Carl Smith), Walter Brooke (Mr. McGuire), Norman Fell (Mr. McCleery), Alice Ghostley (Mrs. Single-man), Marion Lorne (Miss DeWitte), Eddra Gale (Woman on bus).

Credits: Directed by Mike Nichols. Screenplay by Calder Willingham and Buck Henry. Based on the novel by Charles Webb. Produced by Lawrence Turman. Director of photography: Robert Surtees. Production designer: Richard Sylbert. Film editor: Sam O'Steen. Costumes by Patricia Zipprodt. Hair styles by Sydney Guilaroff. Songs by Paul Simon. Sung by Simon and Garfunkel. Additional music by Dave Grusin. Production supervision by George Justin. Assistant director: Don Kranze. Sound: Jack Solomon. Assistant film editor: Bob Wyman. Set decorator: George Nelson. Script supervisor: Meta Rebner. Makeup: Harry Maret. Hair dresser: Sherry Wilson. Casting consultant: Lynn Stalmaster. Filmed in Panavision. Color by Technicolor. A Joseph E. Levine presentation of a Mike Nichols–Lawrence Turman production.

Additional Cast: Elisabeth Fraser (Lady #2), Harry Holcombe (Minister), Lainie Miller (Nightclub stripper), Mike Farrell (Bellhop), Richard Dreyfuss (Boarder).

Additional Credits: Production dates: March 13 to August 5, 1967. Premiered in New York City on December 21, 1967.

Awards: Oscar for Best Director.

Available: Twentieth Century Fox Home Entertainment DVD (2007). UPC: 02761607503150.

Published in 1963 by the New American Library, *The Graduate* was based on an incident in novelist Charles Webb's life when his college girlfriend had an abortion. Producer Lawrence Turman was intrigued by a review that compared Benjamin Braddock, the novel's protagonist, to Holden Caulfield from J. D. Salinger's *The Catcher in the Rye*. Having previously partnered with Stuart Millar, Turman invested his own money to option the novel as his first solo project.

Turman hired William Hanley to adapt the novel and offered Mike Nichols the directing position. Nichols had just helped turn a Neil Simon play called *Nobody Loves Me* into the Broadway hit *Barefoot in the Park*, starring Robert Redford. Before that he was one-half of a comedy team with Elaine May; their act, directed by Arthur Penn, had been a Broadway smash in 1960 as *An Evening with Mike Nichols and Elaine May*. With a background in improvisation, they fashioned sharp, edgy skits that not only influenced their peers, but that resonated throughout their later careers.

While Turman tried to finance his production, Nichols continued to direct stage plays, including the Tony–winning *Luv* and *The Knack*, a British comedy. Turman eventually interested someone he called "the king of the schlockmeisters," Joseph E. Levine, whose Embassy Pictures put up the budget

for *The Graduate*. By that time Nichols had signed a contract to direct the screen version of Edward Albee's *Who's Afraid of Virginia Woolf?* (1966), to be written and produced by Ernest Lehman. (He also won his third consecutive Tony award for directing *The Odd Couple*.)

Turman hired novelist and screenwriter Calder Willingham to begin a new adaptation, but neither he nor Nichols was satisfied with the result. "It was in every way unacceptable," Nichols recalled, adding that the writing was "vulgar." Peter Nelson also wrote a screenplay that was quickly rejected. Nichols had befriended Buck Henry during the difficult and protracted shooting of *Who's Afraid of Virginia Woolf?* and asked him to read the novel.

The son of silent movie star Ruth Taylor, Henry had worked in improv and written for television; *Get Smart*, a project he developed with Mel Brooks, was currently a hit sitcom. While Henry had reservations about the novel's main character—"I had a feeling that in real life, Benjamin Braddock was not a person you'd want to know"—he also connected with the novel, saying, "I think Larry Turman and Mike and I *all* thought that we were the protagonist." Working with Nichols, he stripped away much of the plot, removing a long hitchhiking sequence, a firefighting adventure, instances of homophobia, and Braddock's encounters with prostitutes.

What remained was a black comedy about a confused, alienated college graduate who starts an affair with a married woman and then falls in love with her daughter. Henry and Nichols understood that Braddock's indecision and guilt over Mrs. Robinson mirrored the younger generation's love-hate relationship both with their parents and with what they saw as an outdated, unworkable culture. For most viewers, the film distilled the argument down to a single word: "plastics," given as business advice to Braddock at a party of his parents' friends. (The scene was one of Henry's most significant contributions to the story; another was his deadpan performance as a hotel clerk.)

Nichols credits his reading of *The Beast in the Jungle* by Henry James with helping him take a radical approach to casting Braddock, portrayed in the novel as blond and handsome. Robert Redford wanted to play the part, and Turman had considered Steve McQueen and Walter Beatty. But when Nichols auditioned Dustin Hoffman, he saw the value in reversing expectations about Braddock. "He couldn't be a blond, blue-eyed person, because then why is he having trouble in the country of the blond, blue-eyed people?" the director reasoned.

Hoffman, who felt he had done poorly in the audition, had to be persuaded to take the role. He was still making a name for himself on the New York stage, and did not see himself as a movie star. Nichols' decision "took enormous artistic courage," the actor said later. Nichols cast and then fired Hoffman's roommate Gene Hackman three weeks into rehearsals, explaining that the part needed someone who was of a different generation. "Mike is ruthless when it comes to artistic decisions," Buck Henry said. Hackman's part as Mr. Robinson was given to Murray Hamilton.

Casting Anne Bancroft was another risky move. Only six years older than Hoffman, she would be playing ten years past her age. Born Anna Maria Louisa Italiano in 1931, Bancroft had been working in film and television from the age of twenty, giving up Hollywood in the late 1950s to build her reputation on stage. Her role as Annie Sullivan in *The Miracle Worker* (filmed in 1962) helped rejuvenate her career. Bancroft's intelligence shines through on the screen, giving her portrayal of Mrs. Robinson considerably more nuance and emotional depth than the script suggested. She made what could have been a frat boy's dirty joke the only character in the

film who had an understanding of her world. As Hoffman put it, "Anne and Mike Nichols made a very critical decision—which was not to judge the character."

Nichols also made sure the film would be accepted by a mainstream audience by treating the plot's potentially sordid elements discreetly. *The Graduate* remains middlebrow in message, style, and technique. Yes, Nichols calls for some elaborate camera trickery, skirts tastefully around some sexual encounters, gently ribs middle-class suburbia, and lards the soundtrack with folk-rock tunes. But his film never challenges the status quo—it ultimately accepts it.

Although marketed as counterculture heroes, Simon and Garfunkel, who perform four songs for the film, were about as far away from the hippie revolution as you could get. Nichols had hired Simon to compose film-specific scores, but the songwriter repeatedly missed his deadlines. Nichols seized on "Mrs. Roosevelt," a wistful song about the past, and changed it to "Mrs. Robinson." Simon won a Grammy for the song and for the film's soundtrack album, helping solidify the film's commercial success.

The Graduate became the top-grossing film of 1968, propelling Hoffman to a long career as a movie star and making Nichols a sought-after director. Once seen as defining the zeitgeist, today *The Graduate* seems mildly titillating, bright, even garish, and aimed squarely at the broadest possible audience.

Planet of the Apes

Twentieth Century-Fox, 1968. Sound, color, 2.35. 112 minutes.

Cast: Charlton Heston (George Taylor), Roddy McDowall (Cornelius), Kim Hunter (Zira), Maurice Evans (Dr. Zaius), James Whitmore (President of the Assembly), James Daly (Honorious), Linda Harrison (Nova), Robert Gunner (Landon), Lou Wagner (Lucius), Woodrow Parfrey (Maximus), Jeff Burton (Dodge), Buck Kartalian (Julius), Norman Burton (Hunt leader), Wright King (Dr. Galen), Paul Lambert (Minister).

Credits: Directed by Franklin J. Schaffner. Screenplay by Michael Wilson and Rod Serling. Based on the novel by Pierre Boulle. Produced by Arthur P. Jacobs. Associate producer: Mort Abrahams. Music: Jerry Goldsmith. Creative makeup design: John Chambers. Director of photography: Leon Shamroy. Art direction: Jack Martin Smith, William Creber. Set decorations: Walter M. Scott, Norman Rockett. Special photographic effects: L.B. Abbott, Art Cruickshank, Emil Kosa, Jr. Film editor: Hugh S. Fowler. Unit production manager: William Eckhardt. Assistant director: William Kissel. Sound: Herman Lewis, David Dochendorf. Costumes designed by Morton Haack. Makeup by Ben Nye, Dan Striepeke. Hairstyling: Edith Lindon. Orchestration: Arthur Morton. Filmed in Panavision. Color by De Luxe. Westrex Recording System. Produced by APJAC Productions, Inc., and released by Twentieth Century-Fox Film Corporation.

Additional Credits: Production dates: May 21 to August 10, 1967. Opened in New York City on February 8, 1968.

Awards: Honorary Oscar to John Chambers for "outstanding make-up achievement."

Other Versions: Sequels: *Beneath the Planet of the Apes* (1970), *Escape from the Planet of the Apes* (1971), *Conquest of the Planet of the Apes* (1972), *Battle for the Planet of the Apes* (1973). Basis for a television series in 1974. Remade as *Planet of the Apes* (2001).

Available: Twentieth Century Fox Home Entertainment DVD (2006). UPC: 0-24543-22974-2.

Pierre Boulle's novel *Planet of the Apes* was published in France in 1963 (and in the United States as *Monkey Planet*). The book told about a space expedition gone awry, leading to a crash landing. Crew members find themselves on a world where apes rule and humans are considered animals without basic rights. Based in part on his track record with

The Bridge on the River Kwai (1957), Boulle had little trouble selling the movie rights to producer Arthur P. Jacobs. At the time affiliated with Warner Brothers, Jacobs planned an adaptation to be directed by Blake Edwards. Rod Serling, a prolific writer and creator of television's *Twilight Zone*, was hired to write the screenplay. Serling made his reputation with live television dramas like *Requiem for a Heavyweight*, but he was especially adept at science fiction with O. Henry–style twist endings, like the one in Boulle's book. In fact, he wrote "The Odyssey of Flight 33," a story that echoed many of Boulle's devices; in 1961 it became one of the more memorable *Twilight Zone* episodes.

Serling submitted his script in November 1964, but four months later Warners postponed the project. Jacobs held onto the novel and formed APJAC, an independent production company. In 1966 he signed a deal to film *Planet of the Apes* with Twentieth Century-Fox, which had hesitated over the project until *Fantastic Voyage* (1966) proved that the science fiction genre could attract moviegoers. Michael Wilson, a victim of the blacklist, was hired to revise the Serling draft. He added a courtroom scene that provided the best joke in the film: a "see no evil, hear no evil, speak no evil" tableau of primate judges.

Meanwhile, Jacobs conducted experiments with makeup expert John Chambers to make sure that the simian actors would appear realistic. Edward G. Robinson, who was originally cast as Dr. Zaius, made a screen test with Charlton Heston, Jacobs' first choice for Taylor, the astronaut leader. Robinson had to drop out of the project due to poor health. What Heston brought to the role, apart from his screen history as Moses and Ben-Hur, was his relationship with Franklin J. Schaffner, his director on *The War Lord* (1965).

Born in Tokyo in 1920, Schaffner was the child of missionaries, and lived in Japan until he was six. When his father died, his mother moved back to the United States. Schaffner attended grade school in Lancaster, Pennsylvania, and enlisted in the Navy after college. Unable to find work as an actor, he became an assistant director at *The March of Time* before moving to CBS. There he worked on sports and campaign coverage before spending two years directing episodes of *Playhouse 90*. That background, and his success directing the Broadway play *Advise and Consent*, got him a contract at Twentieth Century-Fox. His first feature was *The Stripper* (1963) with Joanne Woodward.

The War Lord proved that Schaffner could handle a big-budget project that fit into the Fox style and philosophy: in other words, lavish but mainstream, mildly provocative but ultimately conservative in outlook. *Planet of the Apes* was also representative of movies in general in the late 1960s. The actors had longer hair than a few years earlier, and were more disrespectful of authority. But fundamentally they were familiar stereotypes who would not have been that far out of place in *Voyage to the Bottom of the Sea*, a 1961 Fox feature.

Planet of the Apes boasts an amusingly clunky production design. The Concorde-like spaceship has its equipment stashed inconveniently down corridors and up towers. The astronauts don metal backpacks when they set out on hikes, and drink from brightly colored thermoses. Boulle's novel was set in a roughly contemporary 1960s, but Fox couldn't afford the expensive sets that period would entail. Instead, the movie takes place in a sort of pre-industrial society filled with inexplicable anachronisms.

Serling's trick-ending stories typically played out in about twenty minutes. With almost two hours to fill, Schaffner has plenty of time for long chases, many of them without dialogue, and for monologues delivered by an uncharacteristically surly Heston. Veteran cinematographer Leon Shamroy is called on to use zoom lenses to make ironic points, while composer Jerry Goldsmith leans too heavily on musical stings to drive across shocks. Despite its drawbacks, the film was a substantial hit, leading to four sequels and a remake. With make-up problems solved and cheap sets established, additional episodes rolled off a studio assembly line. *Planet of the Apes* also helped trap Charlton Heston, who appeared in the first sequel, in a sci-fi ghetto of films like *The Omega Man* (1971) and *Soylent Green* (1973).

The Producers

Embassy Pictures, 1968. Sound, color, 1.85. 90 minutes. Rated PG.

Cast: Zero Mostel (Max Bialystock), Gene Wilder (Leo Bloom), Dick Shawn (L.S.D. [Lorenzo Saint DuBois]), Kenneth Mars (Franz Liebkind), Estelle Winwood ("Hold Me Touch Me"), Christopher Hewitt (Roger De Bris), Lee Meredith (Ulla), Renée Taylor (Eva Braun), Andreas Voutsinas (Carmen Giya), Bill Hickey (Drunk in bar), David Patch (Goebbels), Barney Martin (Goering), Madlyn Cates (Concierge), Shimen Ruskin (Landlord), Frank Campanella (Bartender), Josip Elic (Violinist), John Zoller (Drama critic), Brutus Peck (Hot dog vendor). The Ladies: Anne Ives, Amelie Barleon, Elsie Kirk, Nell Harrison, Mary Love.

Credits: Written and directed by Mel Brooks. Produced by Sidney Glazier. Associate producer: Jack Grossberg. Director of photography: Joseph Coffey. Music composed and conducted by John Morris. Original songs: "Love Power," music by Norman Blagman, lyrics by Herb Hartig. "We're Prisoners of Love," "Springtime for Hitler," words and music by Mel Brooks. Edited by Ralph Rosenblum. Assistant director: Michael Hertzberg. Production designer: Charles Rosen. Costume designer: Gene Coffin. Titles designed by Elinor Bunin. Choreographer: Alan Johnson. Music supervisor: Felix Giglio. Unit manager: Louis A. Stroller. Casting director: Alfa-Betty Olsen. Production supervisor for Embassy Pictures & Universal Marion Corporation: Robert Porter. 2nd assistant director: Martin Danzig. Script supervisor: Betty Todd. Production secretary: Connie Schoenberg. Camera operator: Edward Brown. Set decorator: James Dalton. Gaffer: Morton Novak. Set grip: Edward Engels. Construction: Joseph Williams. Scenic artist: Shelly Bartolini. Carpenter: Eli Aharoni. Production sound: Willard Goodman. Makeup: Irving Buchman. Assistant editor: Michael Breddan. Sound editor: Alan Heim. Opticals: Creative Opticals, Inc. Wardrobe: Celia Bryant. Assistant to producer: Robert Buchman. Prints by Pathe. A Joseph E. Levine presentation of a Sidney Glazier production.

Additional Cast: Bill Macy (Jury foreman).

Additional Credits: Opened in New York City on March 18, 1968.

Awards: Oscar for Best Story and Screenplay Written Directly for the Screen.

Other Versions: Staged as a Broadway musical in 2001. Stage version adapted for film as *The Producers* (2005, directed by Susan Stroman).

Available: Sony Pictures Home Entertainment DVD (2005). ISBN: 1-4049-1367-X. UPC: 0-27616-13042-6.

The first of three Mel Brooks films on the Registry, *The Producers* is closest to the show business traditions the writer, director, and comedian grew up on. Born in Brooklyn in 1926, Brooks escaped what he described as Jewish slums through entertainment. As a teen he worked in the Borscht Belt, a group of resort hotels in the Catskills, where he washed dishes as well as played the drums and worked on a comedy act. He enlisted in the Army during World War II, seeing action on the front in Europe. He told writer John Lahr about trying to cope with the carnage he witnessed: "Along the roadside, you'd see bodies wrapped up in mattress covers and stacked in a ditch, and those would be Americans, that could be me. I sang all the time."

Returning to Catskill resorts, he befriended comedian Sid Caesar, who later hired him for his writing staff on *Your Show of Shows* and *Caesar's Hour*. Brooks' writing competition included Woody Allen, Neil Simon, and Carl Reiner. On

their own, Brooks and Reiner developed a "Two-Thousand-Year-Old Man" routine that became a hit comedy album. At a time when many comedians played down ethnicity, Brooks embraced his Judaism, making it a central component of his humor. Another key element was his affection for performers who didn't succeed. Like George Burns before him, Brooks reveled in stories of inept, talentless individuals who doggedly pursued show biz careers.

Brooks won an Oscar in 1963 for the short film *The Critic*, in which a puzzled filmgoer tries to decipher a European art film suspiciously reminiscent of Ingmar Bergman. Later in the decade his career was in jeopardy, after a failed marriage, a Broadway flop for which he wrote the book, and a screenplay he couldn't sell. He told friends like Larry Gelbart that he was writing a novel called *Springtime for Hitler*, based on a producer he once knew who seduced elderly women for money. The story didn't work as a book because "there was too much talk and not enough action," and it didn't make sense as a play either because "there were too many sets." He turned it into a screenplay, but had trouble persuading a studio to finance a film with "Hitler" in the title. (By this time the plot centered around a scheme to find the world's worst play, and then sell 25,000 percent of what would be nonexistent profits to investors.)

An agent introduced Brooks to producer Barry Glazier, who grew up in a Jewish orphanage in Philadelphia before becoming a movie usher. After World War II, Glazier worked briefly in the jewelry business, then procured a position in one of Eleanor Franklin's charitable foundations. After her death, he secured $90,000 to make *The Eleanor Roosevelt Story* (1965), which won an Oscar for feature documentary. "Nobody would go near Mel for a feature picture," Glazier said later, but the producer amassed $1 million, half of that from Joseph E. Levine, a producer and distributor who had made a fortune importing foreign Godzilla and Hercules movies. Levine was intent on upgrading the image of his company, Embassy Pictures (soon to be purchased and turned into AVCO Embassy).

Brooks by now had married actress Anne Bancroft, and it was through her that he met Gene Wilder, who in 1963 was performing in Brecht's

Mother Courage. Trained for a time at the Old Vic in England, and at the Actors Studio, Wilder had made his film debut in *Bonnie and Clyde* (1967) a few months earlier. Glazier suggested Zero Mostel, a former nightclub entertainer whose career as a movie thug was ruined by the blacklist. Mostel couldn't even find stage work until 1958, but starred in a trio of Broadway hits in the 1960s: *Rhinoceros, Fiddler on the Roof,* and *A Funny Thing Happened on the Way to the Forum.* The film version of the latter play marked his return to the screen in 1966.

Glazier called Mostel "an absolute horror," and also related how Levine hated the rushes from *The Producers,* the film's new title. A preview screening in Philadelphia in November 1967 was memorably disastrous. Levine pointed to a bag lady in the audience and said to Brooks, "Look, even she fell asleep." Critics were equally unkind when the film finally opened a year later. Andrew Sarris complained that the Nazi era was still too recent to joke about. Also, "Things didn't work cinematically. It wasn't well-made. It was more like specialized cinematic vaudeville. The bad taste wasn't just about Hitler and gays, it was about women, too."

Casting director Alfa-Betty Olsen attributed the initial response to Brooks' aggressive, "in your face" humor. Supporters have since cited films like *Million Dollar Legs* (1932) and *Duck Soup* (1933) as forerunners of *The Producers'* loud, frantic style, although those earlier titles were also box-office failures. But Brooks still needed to learn how to stage and pace his jokes, and how to edit himself as a writer. (He also borrowed from vaudeville the idea that no joke is too dirty or too offensive if it is delivered by sexually neutered comics.) The succession of women Mostel must cajole out of their money seems endless, as do the small-minded jokes about homosexuals, the burlesque asides of biki-nied dancers, and the grating interplay between Mostel and Wilder.

Whatever his faults, Brooks achieves something magical with the five minutes that make up the opening number of *Springtime for Hitler.* Not just a monument to bad taste, it helps reduce Nazism to an object of scorn, as Ernst Lubitsch did in *To Be or Not to Be* (1942, remade by Brooks in 1983). It also demolishes Broadway and movie musical clichés in a manner as affectionate as it is devastating. Released on its own, *Springtime for Hitler* would have challenged viewers in way that the film as a whole can't. Brooks would make musical interludes like this a staple of his later films, including his two other Registry titles, *Blazing Saddles* and *Young Frankenstein* (both 1974).

2001: A Space Odyssey

MGM, 1968. Sound, color, 2.20. 149 minutes.

Cast: Keir Dullea (David Bowman), Gary Lockwood (Frank Poole), William Sylvester (Dr. Heywood Floyd), Daniel Richter (Moonwatcher), Leonard Rossiter (Dr. Smyslov), Margaret Tyzack (Elena), Robert Beatty (Halvorsen), Sean Sullivan (Michaels), Douglas Rain (Voice of HAL 9000), Frank Miller (Mission controller), Glenn Beck, Edwina Carroll (Stewardess), Bill Weston, Alan Gifford (Poole's father), Penny Brahms (Stewardess), Mike Lovell, Edward Bishop, Ann Gillis, Heather Downham, John Ashley, Jimmy Bell, David Charkham, Simon Davis, Jonathan Daw, Peter Delmar, Terry Duggan, David Fleetwood, Danny Grover, Brian Hawley, David Hines, Tony Jackson, John Jordan, Scott Mackee, Laurence Marchant, Darryl Paes, Joe Refalo, Andy Wallace, Bob Wilyman, Richard Wood.

Credits: Produced and directed by Stanley Kubrick. Screenplay by Stanley Kubrick and Arthur C. Clarke. Director of photography: Geoffrey Unsworth. Additional photography: John Alcott. Film editor: Ray Lovejoy. Special effects designed and directed by Stanley Kubrick. Special effects supervisors: Wally Veevers, Douglas Trumbull, Con Pederson, Tom Howard. Production designers: Tony Masters, Harry Lange, Ernest Archer. Wardrobe: Hardy Amies. Music by Aram Khatchaturian ("Gayaneh Ballet Suite"), György Ligeti ("Atmospheres," "Lux Aeterna," "Requiem"), Johann Strauss ("The Blue Danube"), Richard Strauss ("Thus Spoke Zarathustra"). First assistant director: Derek Cracknell. Special photographic effects unit: Colin J. Cantwell, Bryan Loftus, Frederick Martin, Bruce Logan, David Osborne, John Jack Malick. Camera operator: Kelvin Pike. Art director: John Hoesli. Sound editor: Winston Ryder. Makeup: Stuart Freeborn. Editorial assistant: David De Wilde.

Sound supervisor: A.W. Watkins. Sound mixer: H. L. Bird. Scientific consultant: Frederick I. Ordway III. Filmed in Super Panavision. Made at MGM British Studios Ltd., Borehamwood, England. Metrocolor. A Stanley Kubrick production.

Additional Cast: Vivian Kubrick ("Squirt," Floyd's daughter).

Additional Credits: Based on the Arthur C. Clarke story "The Sentinel." Additional photography: Gilbert Taylor. Line producer: Victor Lyndon. Production dates: January 28, 1965 to March 10, 1968. Premiered in New York City on April 4, 1968.

Awards: Oscar for Special Visual Effects.

Other Versions: Sequel, *2010* (1984), directed by Peter Hyams.

Available: Warner Home Video DVD (2007). UPC: 0-12569-64776-9.

Director Stanley Kubrick first began work on what would become *2001: A Space Odyssey* in February 1964, when he told Columbia Pictures publicist Roger Caras that he was "fascinated with the possibility of extra-terrestrials." Caras introduced Kubrick to Arthur C. Clarke, at the time a relatively obscure science fiction writer whose most significant achievement was the predication of geo-synchronous communications satellites. Kubrick read Clarke's 1954 novel *Childhood's End*, but Clarke pushed his 1948 short story "The Sentinel" instead. It concerned a slab discovered on the Moon that turned out to be a warning beacon.

Kubrick and Clarke saw a short film called *To the Moon and Beyond* at the 1964 New York World's Fair. The special effects in the film prompted Kubrick to hire Douglas Trumbull. From *Universe*, a 1959 film released by the National Film Board of Canada, Kubrick hired Walley Gentelman and Con Pederson. Gentelman shot some experimental 65mm footage in New York before withdrawing from the project. On May 17, Clarke signed a contract to write what was then called "How the Solar System Was Won." Kubrick wanted a "mythological documentary," which Clarke interpreted to mean a sci-fi version of *How the West Was Won* (1962). He finished a version near the end of 1964.

MGM president Richard O'Brien approved the script with some qualifications, such as asking Kubrick to shoot in 70mm Super Panavision rather than Cinerama. The studio announced the project, now called *Journey Beyond the Stars*, in February 1965. (It was changed to *2001: A Space Odyssey* that April.) Kubrick was given $6 million for special effects, out of a total budget of $10.5 million.

According to biographer Alexander Walker, Kubrick wasn't interested in the science-fiction aspects of the story so much as concepts of intelligence and communication. Walker also saw a connection between *Dr. Strangelove* (1964), Kubrick's previous film, and *2001*. A computer had a minor role in the earlier film; now Kubrick was casting a computer in a major part—in fact, the lead of the entire movie. In Clarke's early drafts, the computer, known as Athena, was programmed to lie to crew members about the purpose of a mission to Jupiter. Gradually Kubrick changed the computer into HAL 9000, which overreacts because it made a mistake. (Douglas Rain, who also narrated *Universe*, provided the voice of HAL.)

Not including the scriptwriting, *2001* took almost three years to film. Kubrick spent six months in preproduction. Starting on December 29, 1965, he filmed with the live cast for four and a half months. He then spent eighteen months working on 205 special-effects shots, based on work by his crew as well as consultations with scientists and designers at universities and aerospace companies. Along with state-of-the-art techniques,

Kubrick made some more prosaic choices. The mission goes to Jupiter instead of Saturn because Kubrick wasn't satisfied with how Saturn's rings looked on film.

Up until the middle of 1965, Clarke's script had an extensive voice-over that explained what was happening in the story. Gradually Kubrick decided that mainstream viewers would never understand the science in *2001*, and dropped the voice-over entirely. Throughout his career, Kubrick had guided his viewers carefully, precisely, feeding just the information he wanted in the manner of an unfolding chess game. Now it no longer mattered what a shot meant, just how it looked. Similarly, the story was just material to interpret. Kubrick and Clarke knew what the plot in *2001* was, so individual scenes still made sense to them. Moviegoers, on the other hand, were cast adrift. How could they know that in the end of Clarke's story a Star Child detonated hydrogen bombs that destroyed the Earth because mankind had evolved into a higher life form? Or that in one sequence Kubrick was trying to mimic phosphenes, the phenomenon of "seeing" lights behind closed eyelids?

The only exterior shots in the film were of the Moonwatcher smashing a tapir skeleton and throwing a club into the air, photographed on a Borehamwood backlot. The rest of *2001* was a triumph of production design and special effects. The final third was the most difficult to film, and it was the only section Trumbull worked on. (Biographer John Baxter wrote that Trumbull took most of his ideas from experimental animators Jordan Belson and John Whitney.) Production designer Ken Adam, who worked with Kubrick on *Barry Lyndon* (1975), said, "Wally Veevers was responsible for 85 percent of the effects on *2001: A Space Odyssey*. There were no computers and digital stuff. Wally did it all with worm gears, the old-fashioned way." Other contributors included Andrew Birkin, who shot footage of the Outer Hebrides, and Bob Gaffney, who filmed in Arizona.

But the key to *2001* was in its editing. Kubrick told Walker, "I love editing. Everything that precedes editing is merely a way of producing film to edit." *2001* contains one of the medium's iconic jump cuts, from prehistoric man to the space age, but just as influential was the way Kubrick matched sound and music to visuals. He used Mendelssohn and Vaughan Williams while screening footage for MGM executives, and considered hiring composer Carl Orff. (MGM insisted on Alex North instead, but his score wasn't used.) Kubrick was inspired to use Richard Strauss's "Also Sprach Zarathustra" after hearing it in a Time-Life documentary about World War I. Johann Strauss's "Blue Danube" waltz may have been suggested by Andrew Birkin or by Kubrick's wife Christiane. It was used in a space station docking sequence that became one of the most remembered moments in the film.

Previews took place in March 1968. After a screening in Washington, D.C., Kubrick deleted interviews with real-life scientists from the opening of the film. The premiere took place on April 4, 1968, in New York City. The very next day, Kubrick cut out nineteen minutes of material. After informal polls of moviegoers, MGM switched its advertising campaign to reflect the druggier aspects of the film, using a blurb from the *Christian Science Monitor*: "*2001* is the ultimate trip." The movie became a fixture on college campuses, but Kubrick had already turned to research on a biography of Napoleon, an unrealized project. His next film would be *A Clockwork Orange* (1971).

High School

OSTI, Inc., 1968. Sound, B&W, 1.37. 74 minutes..

Credits: Produced and directed by Frederick Wiseman. Photographed by Richard Leiterman. Assistant camera: David Eames. Edited by Frederick Wiseman. Associate editor: Carter Howard. Dedicated to Katherine Taylor and the New World Foundation.

Other Versions: Sequel, *High School II* (1994).

Available: Zipporah Films (*www.zipporah.com*).

The cinema verité style championed in the early 1960s by Richard Drew and the Maysles brothers in films like *Primary* (1960) and *Salesman* (1968) fell out of favor fairly quickly. Filmmakers chafed at the style's restrictions—in particular, the elimination of narrations that could help explain stories or put situations into context. It became increasingly obvious that verité only worked when the subjects being filmed had to ignore the presence of the camera and sound equipment. For a politician trying to win votes, for a salesman trying to sell Bibles, documentary crews were of secondary importance. Movie stars, television performers, pop singers, and stage actors all were used to operating in public, and could both adjust to the presence of cameras and even exploit them for their own purposes.

If you didn't want to film celebrities, how could you use cinema verité? Frederick Wiseman's solution was to concentrate on the basic building blocks of society—as he put it, to "discover what kind of power relationships exist and differences between ideology and the practice in terms of the way people are treated." In his early films he sought out institutions—mental asylums, hospitals, welfare courts—in which decisions had to be made whether or not a camera was watching. *High School*, his second documentary, examined a public school, focusing primarily on the interaction between students and adult disciplinarians.

Born in Boston in 1930, Wiseman studied law at Yale, was drafted into and served in the Army, lived for two years in Paris, and taught at the Institute of Law and Medicine at Boston University. Unfulfilled, he pursued an interest in movies, producing *The Cool World* (1964, a Registry title) before deciding to make his own films. *Titicut Follies* (1967) was filmed in the Massachusetts Correctional Institution at Bridgewater, a prison for the criminally insane. Those who got to see it at the time drew connections to reformers from Charles Dickens to Jacob Riis. It was muckraking of the highest order, rigorous in its approach because Wiseman did not want anyone questioning his facts.

Titicut Follies was banned in Massachusetts as an invasion of the privacy of the inmates filmed, and remained banned until 1991. For his next project, Wiseman chose a less controversial setting, Northeast High School in Philadelphia. With some 4,500 students, it was considered an above-average public school that attracted largely middle-class families.

Wiseman was given access to the entire school: classrooms, offices, cafeteria, auditorium, club rooms, the gym, and even lounges. He worked unobtrusively, shooting on 16mm black-and-white film, without lights, and with a single-track tape recorder. This enabled him to work in smaller, tighter, more difficult locations than other documentarians. It also allowed him to capture candid moments that might not have taken place before a larger crew. For this project he hired Canadian cinematographer Richard Leiterman, and it's Leiterman who should be given some credit for what became identified as Wiseman's style. The filmmakers favored tight close-ups of faces, hands, fingers, often panning from one subject to a second during the course of a conversation. The use of zoom lenses was limited. Reverse angles, reaction shots, inserts, and other techniques of feature films were avoided. The close-ups could be used for coverage when Wiseman had to edit sound or when the camera ran out of film. Corridors, empty classrooms, and other "landscape" shots could be used for transitions between scenes.

Wiseman recorded the sound himself, sometimes directing Leiterman with his microphone. But the real directing came before the camera started. Wiseman was expert at gaining the trust of his subjects, at convincing them that he wasn't interrupting or altering their behavior. His main tactic was patience, waiting for a clarifying moment to emerge, for a character to be defined. Once he saw what he wanted he pounced, covering up the fact that Leiterman sometimes missed the start of scenes by pulling sound up over the ending of the preceding scene.

Shaping the material was almost as crucial as filming it. *High School* is more pointed than most of Wiseman's work, and he makes many of his points through juxtaposing scenes. One teacher tries to convince his students that their lives are determined by the principal of cause and effect; the next will be teaching about Jean-Paul Sartre and existentialism. A teacher recites "Casey at the Bat," followed by girls hitting softballs in a gym class. A hall monitor looks through a door window; the next shot, presumably from his viewpoint, is of girls performing calisthenics.

Although it's against the "rules" of cinema verité, Wiseman uses music throughout the film. Otis Redding's "Sittin' on the Dock of the Bay" backs up the opening traveling shots that show the neighborhoods around the school. "Simple Simon Says," a bubblegum pop song by the 1910 Fruitgum Company, plays during the calisthenics, a scene shot so adroitly that Wiseman can cut directly to the lyrics. Simon and Garfunkel's "The Dangling Conversation" becomes the focus of a discussion in a poetry class; "Hey, Look Me Over" is performed by the marching band.

What is the picture of high school that Wiseman ultimately assembles? "In our judgment at the time, it was a totally negative portrayal," Bill Jones, a public information officer for the Philadelphia school system, said in an interview. Jones screened the film with schools superintendent Mark Shed,

who agreed to authorize its release. But Richardson Dilworth, head of the school board, was "incensed by the film." He threatened Wiseman with a lawsuit. Still smarting over the reaction to *Titicut Follies*, the director agreed to a settlement that prohibited the exhibition of *High School* within a specified radius of Philadelphia. The first "legal" showing of *High School* in the Philadelphia area was on a PBS broadcast in 2001.

The critical consensus of the time was that Wiseman was siding with the students, and critiquing teachers and administrators. But *High School* is not so easy to pin down. It's true that much of the school seems irrelevant to students' needs. But are the students blameless? In a later interview, Wiseman said, "When critics comment about the first *High School*, they often write about the indifference or insensitivity of the faculty, but the passivity of the students was just as striking to me."

Are the students really even the focus? Wiseman devotes more screen time to adults, people he may understand better. He is also selective about what class material he shows. There is no algebra or chemistry in *High School*, no geology or biology because they concern facts that can taught largely through drills. The classes Wiseman shows are "discussion" groups in which students are supposed to form and deliver opinions. In the examples presented here at least, if not also in the experience of most filmgoers, attempts by teachers to "connect" are largely futile.

High School is most effective in documenting the difficulty in communicating—between teacher and student, between parent and child, between artist and audience. The best scenes are not about teaching or being a student, but about the negotiations between disciplinarians and those who must obey. As Wiseman said about his work later, "The theme that unites the films is the relationship of people to authority."

Yes, there are discouraging messages in the film. "You can't have what you want when you want it." "It's nice to be individualistic, but there are certain places to do it." Should principles like these be taught? Do alternative methods—at the time, pretending Paul Simon lyrics were poetry—work, or are they just as depressing as rote learning? On the other hand, seen today, in the context of reduced funding for education, of increased violence in schools, of lowered test scores, *High School* presents an almost idyllic vision of education. However wrongheaded, the teachers and administrators seem committed to delivering the means and skills for students to survive in the world.

Wiseman returned to the subject with *High School II* (1994), shot at Central Park East, a progressive New York City school. After the original *High School*, he began making films under contract to WNET, the New York City public television outlet at the time. One subsequent film, *Hospital* (1970), was also selected for the Registry.

Night of the Living Dead

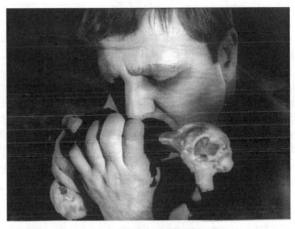

What zombies do in *Night of the Living Dead*.

Continental Distribution/Walter Reade Organization, 1968. Sound, B&W, 1.37. 96 minutes.

Cast: Duane Jones (Ben), Judith O'Dea (Barbra), Karl Hardman (Harry [Cooper]), Marilyn Eastman (Helen [Cooper]), Keith Wayne (Tom), Judith Ridley (Judy), Kyra Schon (Karen Cooper), Charles Craig (Newscaster), Bill Heinzman [William Hinzman] (Cemetery ghoul), George Kosana (Sheriff McClelland), Frank Doak (Scientist), Bill "Chilly Billy" Cardille (Reporter), Samuel R. Solito (Ghoul), Mark Ricci (Scientist), Lee Hartman (Reporter); Jack Givens, R. J. Ricci, Paula Richards, John Simpson, Herbert Summer, Richard Ricci, William Burchinal, Ross Harris, Al Croft, Jason Richards, Dave James, Sharon Carroll, William Mogush, Steve Hutso, Joann Michaels, Phillip Smith, Ella Mae Smith, Randy Burr (Ghouls).

Credits: Directed by George A. Romero. Screenplay by John Russo, George Romero. Produced by Russell W. Streiner, Karl Hardman. Photographed by The Latent Image, Inc. [George A. Romero] Production director: Vincent Survinski. Production manager: George Kosana. Sound engineers: Gary R. Streiner, Marshall Booth. Special effects: Regis Survinski, Tony Pantanello. Make-up: Hardman Assoc., Inc. [Karl Hardman] Props: Charles O'Dato. Title sequence: The Animators. Script coordination: Jacqueline Streiner. Continuity: Betty Ellen Haughey. Hair styles: Bruce Capristo. Lighting supervisor: Joseph Unitas. Laboratory: W.R.S. Motion Picture Lab. Produced through the facilities of: The Latent Image, Inc., and Hardman Associates, Inc., Pittsburgh, Pa.

Additional Cast: George A. Romero (Reporter), John A. Russo (Military reporter), Russell Streiner (Johnny), Vincent D. Survinski (Vince).

Additional Credits: Executive producer: Russell W. Streiner. Edited by George A. Romero. Premiered in Pittsburgh on October 1, 1968.

Other Versions: Sequels: *Dawn of the Dead* (1978), *Day of the Dead* (1985), *Land of the Dead* (2005), *Diary of the Dead* (2007), *Survival of the Dead* 2009), all directed by George A. Romero. Remakes and spin-offs: *Night of the Living Dead* (1990, directed by Tom Savini), *The Return of the Living Dead* (1985, directed by Dan O'Bannon), *Dawn of the Dead* (2004, directed by Zack Snyder), *Night of the Living Dead 3D* (2006, directed by Jeff Broadstreet).

Available: Elite Entertainment DVD (2002). UPC: 7-90594-11172-4.

Few films on the Registry provoked as much controversy on its release as *Night of the Living Dead*, the first of several horror films directed by Bronx native George A. Romero. According to press notes for the 1990 version of *Night of the Living Dead*, Romero was arrested at the age of fourteen for throwing a burning dummy from a rooftop while making *The Man From the Meteor* (1954). The same notes stated that he was a grip and assistant cameraman on such mainstream Hollywood films as *Peyton Place* (1957) and *North by Northwest* (1959).

After graduating from the Carnegie Institute of Technology in Pittsburgh, he helped form The Latent Image, an advertising agency. His clients included Calgon, Iron City Beer, and local Chevrolet dealers. Other members of the Latent team included Russell Streiner, Karl Hardman, Marilyn Eastman, and John Russo, all of whom became involved in a feature film project.

According to Russo, the Latent Image creative personnel incorporated Image Ten Productions to make a horror film. The first idea was for a comedy about a monster from outer space, but that proved too expensive. Russo's image of a boy running away from home and stumbling across a demented graveyard helped inspire Romero to write the first half of what would become *Night of the Living Dead*, referred to at various times as *Night of the Anubis* or *Night of the Flesh Eaters*. Romero also drew ideas from *I Am Legend*, a science fiction novel by Richard Matheson. Russo wrote the second half after consulting with the other Image Ten members.

The project was filmed in between commercial assignments over a nine-month period. Romero rented a farmhouse in Evans City (about twenty-five miles from Pittsburgh) for the central location. The only professional actors hired were Duane Jones and Judith O'Rea. Jones's part was originally a redneck truck driver, but "Ben" became more refined due to the actor's personality. Russo and Romero also altered the parts played by Keith Wayne and Judith Ridley after they were cast. The third and most important change was to decide who would survive to the end of the film, an issue debated by all the Image Ten members.

Romero and his fellow filmmakers were following a time-honored method for breaking into the industry through the horror genre. They could attract media attention only by provoking outrage, which meant upping the ante on violence and gore. Without completely turning off mainstream filmgoers, the Image Ten crew tried to break as many taboos as possible. Among these were placing a black hero in racially and sexually charged situations, as well as making cannibalism explicit rather than implied. Patricide, dismemberment, death by bludgeoning, and some discreet nudity were icing on the cake. Distinctive to Romero's approach to the material was the absence of a narrative frame. Characters had no real back stories, and the only explanations for the zombie hordes who attack the protagonists were muddled and incomplete. Like computer shooter games a generation later, the only point to *Night of the Living Dead* was its violence.

After the film was completed, Romero and his partners were unable to find commercial distributors until they persuaded the Walter Reade Organization to take on the project. The world premiere was at Pittsburgh's Fulton Theater on October 1, 1968. Marilyn Eastman wrote that Romero cut the film significantly after this screening—especially footage of the closing bonfire.

Romero would later make higher claims for the movie. In a 1990 interview, he said, "Truthfully,

all we were trying to do was make a film that was more than just blood and violence . . . a film that does have a conscience, that does have a message. And that message is simply that because of man's inability to communicate, mankind will never successfully deal with any type of holocaust, any kind of major threat."

Other critics weren't so understanding. *Variety* called it an "unrelieved orgy of sadism." Sniffing that it was "made by some people in Pittsburgh," *New York Times* critic Vincent Canby complained about actors who "stagger around, stiff-legged, pretending to be flesh-eating ghouls." For a 1981 screening, critic Kelly Greene wrote that the film was pornography "that had merely substituted violence for sex."

Greene also pointed out the immediate influence on *Night of the Living Dead*: Florida filmmaker Herschell Gordon Lewis, whose *Blood Feast* (1963) and *Two Thousand Maniacs* (1964) offered unprecedented imagery of gore. Worried about alienating his audience, Romero tamped down Lewis's violence, depicting it in shadowy black and white and limiting it to two or three gross-out sequences. For other scenes, he lifted from Alfred Hitchcock, in particular *Psycho* (1960), the wellspring of many horror films of the last forty years. When Barbra (Judith O'Rea) first ascends the farmhouse staircase, for example, Romero employs an overhead angle similar to a *Psycho* scene featuring Martin Balsam. Romero adds a fashionable jump cut to a shot that lasts about a second, then cuts to a reverse angle shot of a decomposing skull, zooming in on the eyes to pump up the effect.

Romero's technique is not nearly so concise in the rest of the film. Scary but illogical scenes are followed by protracted blocks of exposition delivered by television news announcers, or endless debates among the survivors of the zombie plague. The canned soundtrack music, licensed for $1,500 from Capitol Records, helped focus attention on the film's limited sets, poor lighting, and unprofessional acting.

Just as he did in his commercial work, Romero would learn to focus on the "money shots" in his future films. After abortive attempts to work in other genres, he focused on increasingly explicit horror films, finding success in variations on the *Night of the Living Dead* franchise. He also had to mount a battle for control of the original film, mistakenly believed to have fallen into public domain, which explains the myriad bad dupes and edited versions that were once available.

In a 1993 article, reporter Susan Wloszczyna tracked down many of the cast members. Duane Jones, a longtime acting teacher, died in 1989. Karl Hardman was running a Pittsburgh production studio with his wife, Marilyn Eastman. Romero continues to write and direct features.

Bullitt

Warner Bros.–Seven Arts, 1968. Sound, color, 1.85. 114 minutes. Rated M.

Cast: Steve McQueen ([Frank] Bullitt), Robert Vaughn (Chalmers), Jacqueline Bisset (Cathy), Don Gordon (Delgetti), Robert Duvall (Weissberg), Simon Oakland (Captain [Sam] Bennet), Norman Fell ([Captain] Baker), Georg Stanford Brown (Dr. Willard), Justin Tarr (Eddy), Carl Reindel (Stanton), Felice Orlandi (Renick), Victor Tayback (Pete Ross), Robert Lipton (Aide), Ed Peck (Westcott), Pat Renella (John Ross), Paul Genge (Mike), Al Checco (Desk clerk), Bill Hickman (Phil), John Aprea (Killer).

Credits: Directed by Peter Yates. Screenplay by Alan R. Trustman and Harry Kleiner. Based on the novel *Mute Witness* by Robert L. Pike [Robert L. Fish]. Produced by Philip D'Antoni. Executive producer: Robert E. Relyea. Director of photography: William A. Fraker. Art director: Albert Brenner. Film editor: Frank P. Keller. Production manager: Jack N Reddish. Titles by Pablo Ferro Films. Music by Lalo Schifrin. Costume designer: Theadora Van Runkle. Unit manager: Joe L. Cramer. Assistant director: Tim Zinnemann. Sound: John K. Kean. Set decorators: Phillip Abramson, Ralph S. Hurst. Assistant editor: Ralph H. Martin. Special effects: Saul Bedig. Script supervisor: Marshall J. Wolins. Costumer: Alan Levine. Make-up: Emile LaVigne. Hair stylist: Pat Davey. Technicolor. A Warner Bros.–Seven Arts presentation of a Solar production.

Additional Cast includes: Joanna Cassidy, Suzanne Somers.

Additional Credits: Stunts: Carey Loftin, Bill Hickman, Bud Ekins. Opened in New York City on October 17, 1968, New York City. Re-rated PG.

Awards: Academy Award for Best Editing.

Available: Warner Home Video DVD (2005). ISBN: 0-7907-9567-1. UPC: 0-85393-89262-3.

Remembered today mostly for its car chase through the streets of San Francisco, *Bullitt* was part of a resurgence in cop thrillers in the late 1960s. In a sense *Bullitt* was following a formula established by films like *In the Heat of the Night* (1967) and *Madigan* (1968), which starred Sidney Poitier and Henry Fonda, respectively. They all made use of actual locations instead of backlots, and real police technology instead of the hunches and coincidences that propelled cop films of an earlier generation. The first two took a decidedly more downbeat tone than the heroic optimism that had been a staple of the genre. *Bullitt* added some new elements to the cop formula.

The film was a based on a novel by Robert Fish, a civil engineer who was born in Cleveland in 1912. While working for a plastics firm in Brazil, Fish began several series of thriller novels centered around characters like Captain José da Silva, a Brazilian intelligence officer, and Kek Huuygens, a smuggler. Another creation, Lt. Clancy, was a hard-bitten New York City cop plagued by bad luck. Written under his pseudonym Robert L. Pike, *Mute Witness*, a 1963 Clancy novel, was originally purchased by television producer Philip D'Antoni as a possible vehicle for Spencer Tracy. With an aging star and New York settings, the resulting film might have been another *Madigan*.

But when Steve McQueen became involved, the project switched into an entirely new sphere. Born in Indianapolis in 1930 (some sources give Slater, Missouri, as his birthplace), McQueen was a troubled youth who did time in a reform school in Chino, California. Odd jobs took him around the country. He learned about automobiles in the Marines, and used the G.I. Bill to pay for acting school in New York. After some stage experience and the lead in *The Blob* (1958), a low-budget horror film, McQueen built up his reputation starring as a bounty hunter in the TV series *Wanted: Dead or Alive*. As one of the seven hired killers in *The Magnificent Seven*, McQueen held his own with costars like Yul Brynner and James Coburn. His performance in *The Great Escape* (1963), another ensemble piece set during World War II, cemented his stardom.

McQueen won his following by playing cool in an age that valued cool above all else. His characters would wait until everyone else in a scene had spoken, and acted. The typical McQueen response was silence, his face set in a defiant, skeptical pose, until his opponents went too far. McQueen's acting style changed the Clancy character from someone who suffered through bad luck to someone who never expected anything else, and who was determined not to show how bad luck affected him. In a time when real-life heroes were likely to be assassinated, when racial and military struggles were tearing the country apart, an actor like McQueen gained fans by refusing to let chaos intimidate him.

Screenwriters Alan R. Trustman, a Boston lawyer and investor, and Harry Kleiner, a producer and writer for Otto Preminger and Samuel Fuller as well as for TV's *The Virginian*, switched the locale of *Mute Witness* to San Francisco (the setting for another series of Fish's cop procedurals). McQueen, whose clout had grown after starring in the large-scale war melodrama *The Sand Pebbles* (1966), insisted on shooting on location. He had worked with Trustman before on *The Thomas Crown Affair* (1968), as well as with actor Robert Vaughn. McQueen had to "convince" Vaughn to take an unsympathetic part by having the studio increase its salary offers. Rather than go with an established American director, McQueen wanted to use Peter Yates. A longtime assistant director in Great Britain, Yates had just directed and cowritten *Robbery* (1967), a British crime thriller that opened with a prolonged car chase.

Yates asked to use new, lightweight Arriflex cameras that allowed more flexible shooting arrangements. Veteran cinematographer William Fraker had no trouble adjusting to the longer takes and more realistic lighting Yates preferred. *Bullitt* was covering familiar territory as far as cop thrillers went. Similar scenes and locations could be found in everything from *The Maltese Falcon* (1941) to *D.O.A.* (1950) and *Vertigo* (1958). Yates and Fraker understood how much of an advantage it was to shoot on location, with live sound if possible. They didn't want to resort to back projection footage shot by second unit directors. Their actors would be in the actual buildings, on the streets, and in the cars seen in the film.

With real locations, Yates had to get the particulars of the plot right, and it seems at times as if the film is obsessed with details. How cops split up stakeout duties, how evidence is tagged, how a trigger is squeezed on a pump-action shotgun, how intensive care doctors treat cardiac arrest, how to fit a stretcher into a small elevator—*Bullitt* shows all this and more, even how to break into a newspaper vending machine. But Yates also delights in showing how details can go horribly wrong.

The car chase remains the centerpiece of the film, and like the ten-minute bank robbery in *Gun Crazy* (1949) it's more noteworthy for its realism than for cinematic trickery. Shot and edited in a relatively straightforward manner, it succeeds in making viewers part of the action by alternating objective and subjective viewpoints. Shots of a grimly determined McQueen behind the wheel of his Ford Mustang, or of noted stunt driver Bill Hickman (playing "Phil," a hit man's accomplice) in his Dodge Charger, alternate with shots of the streets they are traveling as if viewers were seeing them through windshields. The filmmakers skew the geography of San Francisco, and repeat some incidents from different angles (which is why a green Volkswagen Beetle keeps reappearing), but the sequence builds in a logical fashion. Should you be involved in a high-speed chase, this is how you would want to drive. (McQueen is noticeable in several of the shots, although he was also doubled by stunt driver Bud Ekins.)

The same rationale applies to the rest of the film. McQueen's Frank Bullitt may have been a simple updating of Sam Spade (with the same trenchcoat, no less). But for viewers of the time, he handled himself the way they wanted a detective to: a persistent cop and a pretty good shot who wouldn't let bad guys or wealthy snobs push him around. In 1968 terms, that also means someone who wears blue turtlenecks with brown tweed blazers, who likes trendy restaurants and ersatz jazz, and who is casually dismissive of his girlfriend's art aspirations and her hesitations about his career. Frank Bullitt was more dogged than intelligent, but he was a straight talker at a time when honesty seemed to be in short supply.

Especially in the movies. That meant the San Francisco skylines, the Mustangs, the facsimile machines, even the unexpectedly involved medical scenes all made *Bullitt* more honest than other Hollywood movies and television shows. Honesty was perhaps the key component to being "cool," and it was a quality McQueen lost his hold on fairly quickly. The disaster blockbuster *The Towering Inferno* six years later was his last bona fide commercial success, and in another six years he would be dead from cancer at the age of fifty.

For a time *Bullitt* was the cop film to beat, and several directors tried—Don Siegel with *Dirty Harry* (1971), for example, and William Friedkin with *The French Connection* (1971).

OffOn

Scott Bartlett, 1968. Sound, color, 1.37. 9 minutes.

Credits: Directed and edited by Scott Bartlett. Additional footage: Tom DeWitt. Vidio [Video]: Michael MacNamee. Sound composition: Manny Meyer.

Available: Image Entertainment DVD, *Treasures from American Film Archives* (2000). UPC: 0-14381-9706-2-3.

On the cover of one of his catalogs, filmmaker Scott Bartlett poses naked, brandishing a spear. Like his movies, it was a defiant image, at once threatening and playful, evoking multiple cultural meanings. He was born in Atlanta on November 2, 1943, "1:04 a.m., Scorpio with Leo rising," as he noted on his résumé, and was a graduate of the Illinois Institute of Technology. He moved to San Francisco during the 1960s, where he taught at the University of California at Berkeley, and formed the Film Arts Foundation, a nonprofit organization that remains one of the country's media arts leaders.

Bartlett made his first film, *Metanomen*, in 1966 while studying at San Francisco State College. The following year, as he told film historian Gene Youngblood, "Television sort of found me. I had been superficially exposed to it, as my friend Tom DeWitt was in the TV department at school. That summer another friend, Michael MacNamee of Washington State University, said he could set up a TV studio situation for me at a station in Sacramento."

Aided by DeWitt, MacNamee and Manny Meyer, Bartlett approached his three-hour block of studio time with the intent of exploring and exploiting video technology in ways to supplement what he could accomplish on film. Released in 1968, *OffOn* is regarded as the first serious artistic use of video in film. In their conversations Bartlett and Youngblood expounded on Bartlett's intentions in terms that veered into mysticism. "The visual form of *OffOn* is too pure to make exclusively personal," Bartlett said. Youngblood felt that, "The pulsating blue-red eyeball which opens the film is more than just an eye; it's the Third Eye, the mystic pineal gland, which sees within you and without you."

"*OffOn* speaks a total language of synergistic impulses," Youngblood continued. Bartlett reduced the concrete to abstract by focusing on isolated elements and repeating them in various permutations. The mantra Youngblood cites is, "Repeat & purify, repeat & reduce, repeat & synthesize." But *OffOn* is far more complex than Bartlett originally suggested.

In later interviews, he explained how he made the film. "I filmed the images in black & white & made 16mm loops of them." (*OffOn* used twenty of these loops, shot with DeWitt for a light show called *Timecycle*.) He went on,

> The black & white loop information was sent into a TV switcher. The color was induced by electronic television circuitry cross-feeding white information in competition with itself where white light breaks into colors: spectral breakdown.
>
> Simultaneously we projected film loops on a rear screen on the studio floor and a television camera filmed that. The rear screen photage was constructed with a bank of projectors which included a lot of moire patterns & liquids. That composite image was pumped into the system & crossbred with film chains. Usually the same image on both. Then a second camera is recording the transmission of that combination. It filmed a television monitor on the control room floor.

Once the film was developed, Bartlett rolled it by hand through a trough filled with food coloring, a process that took all night. "A yoga dedication" was how he described the work. The finished film opened with the image of an eye, and in other sections included seagulls, a motorcycle that the "electronic gods" clipped into studio circuits, as well as body parts that throb, pulse, and mutate in time with the electronic soundtrack. It was what used to be called psychedelic: a succession of distorted images meant to inspire meditative thoughts. The trick with psychedelia is to find a greater meaning for the visuals other than sheer razzle-dazzle. In this case the key word was synergy—between real and abstract, between film and video, even between male and female.

OffOn won an award at the 1968 Yale Film Festival, and was popular on the university circuit. Bartlett used similar techniques to make *A Trip to the Moon* in 1968; he refilmed this as *Moon* the following year.

Bartlett's impact as a filmmaker was immediate in the Bay Area. George Lucas, for one, noted, "I grew up knowing the underground of Scott Bartlett and Bruce Connor and the whole gang of underground filmmakers in San Francisco." Bartlett's style was imitated in light shows for rock concerts, and later incorporated into mainstream art and commercials. Aside from filmmaking, Bartlett remained closely involved with the Film Arts Foundation. He wrote a rock opera called *Atlantic Rising* that for a time was in development at Francis Ford Coppola's Zoetrope studio, and did special effects for big-budget films like *Starman* and *Altered States*. He died in 1990 from complications following a kidney and liver transplant.

Why Man Creates

Kaiser Aluminum and Chemical Corporation, 1968. Sound, color, 1.37. 23 minutes.

Credits: Directed by Saul Bass. Written by Saul Bass, Margo Simon. Produced by Saul Bass & Associates. Cinematography: Erik Daarstad. Film editors: Albert Naipas, Ken Mackenzie, Cliffe Oland. Music: Jeff Alexander. Staff: Elaine Bass, Kaye Dyal, Morrie Marsh, Mavis Terroni. Animation: Art Goodman & Pantomime. With the cooperation of: Dr. Paul Saltman: University of Calif. at LaJolla; Dr. James Bonner and Dr. Jesse Greenstein: California Institute of Technology; Dr. Renato Dulbecco: The Salk Institute; The Los Angeles County Museum of Art; The Museum of Primitive Art: New York; The Museum of Modern Art: New York. Presented by Kaiser Aluminum & Chemical Corporation.

Additional Credits: Camera operator: George Lucas.

Awards: Oscar for Documentary—Short Subject.

Available: Pyramid Direct Films DVD, *http://pyramiddirect.com*.

Sponsored films extend back to the earliest days of cinema. They generally served two purposes: straight advertising for products and services, and publicity for companies, like the *Westinghouse Works* series (1903, a Registry title). During World War II, propaganda films reached new levels of subtlety by exploiting psychological strategies, and these ideas gradually spread to the corporate community. Now advertising didn't have to be about a specific product or service—it could be an attempt to place a company, an occupation, even a trend or goal within a welcoming, comforting environment. Conversely, anything could be reduced to a brand: a company, an artist, a song, a movie.

Saul Bass flourished at the crossroads of corporate and creative communities. Until a Supreme Court decision against block booking helped start the breakup of traditional Hollywood studios, a corporation like MGM or Warner Brothers was the identifying brand behind films. Each studio had introductory logos and theme music, and a "house style" for credits. Consumers who learned studio brand identities might be at a loss when it came to independently produced and released films. Bass was one of the first to develop a "brand" for individual films, a specific graphic design that would be featured in all the publicity surrounding a movie. Posters, titles, soundtrack albums, and print advertising for a film like *The Man with the Golden Arm* (1955) all contained the same distinctive "logo," in that case dismembered body parts shaped into a rectangle.

For the first two decades of the sound era, studios paid little attention to credit design. Very occasionally titles might be supported by illustrations or even animation. As optical processes improved, the cost of titles dropped, leaving more room for creative titling. Bass was one of the innovators in the area, devising opening titles that reflected not just the meaning, but the psychological tone of the films that followed. The perpendicular lines that converge and separate in the opening credits of *North by Northwest* (1959) foretell the many criss-cross patterns that operate within the movie.

Bass was also a pioneer in "corporate identity," which tried to tie diverse elements of large corporations into easily recognizable symbols. "You have to communicate what the company is and at the same time say where the company is going," he said. "It is telling the story of a corporation's life on a postage stamp." Bass's work included logos for AT&T, Minolta, Honda, Exxon, and the YWCA.

In interviews, Bass described a childhood of struggle. Born in 1920 to immigrant parents, he left high school at fifteen to take painting classes. He later studied under Gyorgy Kepes at Brooklyn College before apprenticing at New York design firms, using the two-hour commute to continue studying on his own. He moved to Los Angeles in 1946, working in advertising.

Bass opened his own studio in 1952. His first important titling job was in 1954, for Otto Preminger's *Carmen Jones*. Soon he was working on films for William Wyler, Alfred Hitchcock, and Stanley Kubrick, often in collaboration with his assistant Elaine Makatura. They married in 1962, the year Bass completed his first short, *Apples and Oranges*. He then made *From Here to There* (1964) for United Airlines, and *The Searching Eye* (1964) for Kodak. The latter was exhibited at the New York World's Fair.

Author Douglas Sandberg has written that his father Robert A. Sandberg, an author and teacher, was instrumental in hiring Bass for *Why Man Creates*. At the time the elder Sandberg was a vice president for public affairs and advertising at the Kaiser Aluminum and Chemical Corporation; he and his colleague Don Fabun were responsible for *Kaiser Aluminum News*, an award-winning periodical issued by the company. Its articles sometimes covered topics like economic education and creativity. According to his son, Sandberg convinced Kaiser executives to put up $250,000 for the budget of the film.

Bass broke his film, which he called "a series of explorations, episodes & comments on creativity," into eight parts, each shot in a different manner. "The Edifice" is a two-minute history of the world animated in the manner of Saul Steinberg, notable for its quick, clever jokes and its concept of history as an ever-rising skyscraper. Other parts include "Fooling Around," "The Process," "Judgment," "A Parable," "Digression," "The Search," and "The Mark." Bass used the full complement of film technology available to him, from collage, stock footage, stop-motion animation, and live-action footage which he doctored in various ways. His technique of combining animation, collage, and live action was especially influential—notably, on future Monty Python work by Terry Gilliam.

The film's breadth of reference is impressive. Bass cites everyone from Euclid to Alfred Nobel, Voltaire, and Robert Burns, and everything from the invention of mathematics to Balinese sculpture to the destructive influence of critics. Just as engaging is the tone of the movie: erudite but accessible, clever without undue irony, quick but not glib.

Teachers appreciated Bass's very open definition of creativity, and of the examples he offered. Equally important was his conviction that creativity is an essential part of humanity. The film ends with an answer to its title: "That urge to look into oneself and out at the world, and say, 'I am unique. I am here. I am.'" It also helped that the structure of the film could be adapted very easily to a syllabus. As a result *Why Man Creates* became a staple in classrooms. It also won an Oscar for Bass, who went on to direct a number of other films, including the 1974 science-fiction feature *Phase IV*. His style of titling fell out of favor in the 1970s, but Bass enjoyed a resurgence in popularity in the 1990s, designing credits for four Martin Scorsese films before his death from non-Hodgkin's lymphoma in 1996.

Midnight Cowboy

United Artists, 1969. Sound, color, 1.85. 113 minutes. Rated X.

Cast: Dustin Hoffman (Ratso), Jon Voight (Joe Buck), Brenda Vaccaro (Shirley), John McGiver (Mr. O'Daniel), Ruth White (Sally Buck), Sylvia Miles (Cass), Barnard Hughes (Towny), Jennifer Salt ([Crazy] Annie), Bob Balaban (The young student), Georgann Johnson (Rich lady), Jan Tice (Freaked-out lady), Jonathan Kramer (Jackie), Viva (Gretel McAlbertson), Ultra Violet, Anthony Holland, Gastone Rossilli (Hansel McAlbertson). Texas: Gil Rankin (Woodsy Niles), Gary Owens (Little Joe), T. Tom Marlow, George Eppersen (Ralph), Al Scott (Cafeteria manager), Linda Davis (Mother on the bus), J.T. Masters (Old cow-hand), Arlene Reeder (The old lady). New York: Anthony Holland (TV Bishop), Paul Benjamin (Bartender), Peter Scalia, Vito Siracusa (Vegetable grocers), Peter Zamagias (Hat shop owner), Arthur Anderson (Hotel clerk), Tina Scala, Alma Felix (Laundromat ladies), Richard Clarke (Escort service man), Ann Thomas (The frantic lady). The Party: Paul Jabara, International Velvet, Cecelia Lipson, Taylor Mead, Paul Morrissey. Florida: Joan Murphy (The waitress), Al Stetson (Bus driver).

Credits: Directed by John Schlesinger. Screenplay by Waldo Salt. Based on the novel by James Leo Herlihy. Produced by Jerome Hellman. Director of photography: Adam Holender. Production designer: John Robert Lloyd. Film Editor: Hugh A. Robertson. Sound editors: Jack Fitzstephens, Vincent Connelly. Sound mixer: Dick Vorisek. Graphic effects: Pablo Ferro. Creative consultant: Jim Clark. Costume designer: Ann Roth. Associate producer: Kenneth Utt. 2nd unit director: Burtt Harris. Production manager: Hal Schaffel. Assistant production manager: Fred Caruso. Assistant art director: Willis Conner. Assistant to the director: Michael Childers. Set decorator: Phil Smith. Camera operator: Dick Katrina. Continuity: Nick Sgarro. Sound: Abe Seidman. Assistant editors: Edward Rothkowitz, Leonard Saltzberg, Richard Cirinicone. Special lighting effects: Joshua Light Show. Chief electricians: Willie Meyerhoff, Norman Leigh. Key grip: Mike Mahony. Construction grip: William J. Gerrity. Head carpenter: Ed Swanson. Master scenic artist: Ed Carzero. Make-up consultant: Dick Smith. Make-up: Irving Buchman. Hairdressing: Bob Grimaldi. Wardrobe supervisor: Max Solomon. Musical production: Toxev French. Musical supervision: John Barry. "Everybody's Talkin'," words and music by Fred Neil; arranged and conducted by George Tipton; sung by [Harry] Nilsson. Harmonica played by Jean "Toots" Thielemans. "A Famous Myth," "Tears and Joy" by J. Comanor; sung by The Groop. "He Quit Me" by W. Zevon; sung by Lesley Miller. Arranged and conducted by Garry Sherman. "Jungle Jim at the Zoo," "Old Man Willow" produced by Wes Farrell for Buddah Records. Sung by Elephants Memory. Electronic music by Sear Electronic Music Production. Color by De Luxe. Filmed at Filmways Studio, New York City.

Additional Cast: Waldo Salt (Joe Pyne).

Additional Credits: Original music by John Barry. Casting: Marion Dougherty. Premiered May 25, 1969. Re-rated R in 1971.

Awards: Oscars for Best Picture, Director, and Writing—Screenplay Based on Material from Another Medium.

Available: Sony Pictures Home Entertainment DVD (2006). ISBN: 1-4248-0005-6. UPC: 0-27616-13598-8.

Born in 1927, James Leo Herlihy grew up in Detroit, served in the Navy during World War II, and studied acting and playwriting at the Pasadena Playhouse College. He cowrote *Blue Denim*, an abortion message drama which ran on Broadway before being adapted to film in 1959. His 1960 novel *All Fall Down* was adapted by William Inge into a 1962 movie starring Warren Beatty and Eva Marie Saint. *Midnight Cowboy* was published in 1965, and received generally positive reviews.

John Schlesinger read the novel while he was directing *Darling* (1965), his Oscar-winning look at the life of a British model. Born in London in 1926, he performed a magic act for fellow servicemen during World War II, and had small roles in plays and film during the 1950s. He directed documentaries for the BBC, winning a prize for *Terminus* in 1961. His debut feature, *A Kind of Loving* (1962), was grouped with the "kitchen sink" school of small-scale, downbeat British dramas, but in this and subsequent films Schlesinger developed a reputation for eliciting strong performances and for capturing settings with documentary precision.

Schlesinger's partner Michael Childers later described how anxious the director was to film in the United States. *Midnight Cowboy*, which dealt with a deluded male prostitute who drifts into destitution in New York City, could hardly have been a less likely mainstream movie. But Jerome Hellman, a former agent who had produced two previous features, took on the project. He had read a short piece on draft dodgers by Waldo Salt, and hired him to adapt the novel. A middling screenwriter during and after World War II, Salt had been blacklisted after 1951. This was his first important project in twenty years. (Salt can be seen briefly in the film; his daughter Jennifer has a larger role.)

Schlesinger and Hellman collaborated with Salt on the script while casting and scouting locations. They condensed much of the novel's unwieldy background material into impressionistic flashbacks that they scattered throughout the film. More critically, they changed one central character, Ratso Rizzo, from a youngster to an adult, making more explicit the homosexual content of the plot. Hellman and Childers have described the audition process as grueling. Both Dustin Hoffman and Jon Voight explained how they had to convince Schlesinger to cast them, in Voight's case through a series of screen tests that helped shape his role.

Hellman credited casting director Marion Dougherty for suggesting Brenda Vaccaro and Barnard Hughes. Newcomers in the cast included Sylvia Miles, whose flamboyant, six-minute scene won her an Oscar nomination, and Bob Balaban, at the time still a college student. Childers said that Schlesinger saw something in John McGiver

that persuaded him that the actor, previously typecast in "responsible" roles, could play the part of a religious zealot. The main cast participated in almost a month of rehearsals marked by extensive improvisations overseen by Schlesinger. These became sources for Salt's lines of dialogue, "the last thing to come into a scene," his daughter said. "So much of what was discovered in *Midnight Cowboy* came from the rehearsal room," Hoffman said.

Shooting began in May 1968 in New York City. Schlesinger, fascinated by American culture, shot as much as possible in real locations, although Rizzo's condemned apartment had to be re-created on a soundstage at Filmways Studios in the Bronx. (Shooting also took place in Texas and Florida.) For a scene in what was meant to approximate The Factory, Schlesinger got help from Andy Warhol, who loaned art and helped dress the set. As he did in *Terminus*, Schlesinger preferred using a telephoto lens for street scenes, which enabled him to set the camera as far as three blocks away from the performers. Voight and Hoffman, both still relatively unknown, could be filmed walking through crowds without eliciting reactions from pedestrians.

John Barry's haunting musical theme, played primarily on a harmonica, proved crucial to the finished film. It set a tone of nostalgia and lost innocence that helped soften the often sordid settings. "Everybody's Talkin'," a 1966 song by Fred Neil, was just as invaluable. Neil, a songwriter and performer who started his career writing a hit for Roy Orbison, had been a fixture in the New York City folk scene of the 1960s. Tellingly, Schlesinger preferred Harry Nilsson's cover version, a smoother, more pop-oriented arrangement, to the original.

The Motion Picture Association of America rated the original release of *Midnight Cowboy* "X," the first time it had used the rating for a mainstream film. Hellman agreed with Schlesinger that nothing in the film would be changed before its release. Childers describes how MPAA officials later begged Schlesinger to cut a few frames so the organization could give the film an R rating. Schlesinger refused, but the film was re-rated R anyway.

A critical and commercial success, *Midnight Cowboy* was another in a series of films that drew a dividing line between "old" and "new" Hollywood. Its influence on other filmmakers was immediate, both in terms of subject matter and in Schlesinger's improvisatory, freewheeling style. His use of flash-forwards, associative editing, and mixed film stocks gained traction in more commercial movies. But what distinguished *Midnight Cowboy*, then and today, was Schlesinger's compassion for its characters. Other films dealt with similarly deprived people, but few asked viewers to understand and love them. Although Hoffman's Rizzo can be seen as a continuation of Chaplin's Little Tramp, Schlesinger adamantly resists the easy sentimentality of films like *City Lights* (1931). (Voight also evokes Chaplin in one scene as he stares hungrily through the window of a diner.) It is a mark of his accomplishment that *Midnight Cowboy* manages to be uplifting rather than either maudlin or sordid. "If I have a criticism of *Cowboy*," Schlesinger told Ian Buruma in 1999, "it's that I think it's terribly snazzy in the way it's cut. I wonder if I were approaching it now whether I wouldn't do it in a simpler fashion."

For all its wacky supporting characters and incidents both funny and sad, *Midnight Cowboy* boils down to a love story between two flawed, doomed characters. The fact that they were men

raised the hackles of conservative thinkers. The fact that Schlesinger made both men not just sympathetic, but appealing, may be the greatest accomplishment of the film. *Midnight Cowboy* ultimately transcends its sordid settings, its sexual issues, its trendy allusions and stylistic excesses. It is one of the great film romances of the 1960s.

Schlesinger's next film, *Sunday, Bloody Sunday* (1971) was equally impressive, but his subsequent work was disappointing, both artistically and financially. He died in 2003. Hoffman and Voight have enjoyed distinguished careers, while Salt would win another Oscar for *Coming Home* (1978). Herlihy objected to some of the changes to his novel when the film was released, in particular Voight's scenes with Barnard Hughes and Bob Balaban. But he admitted that if he himself had worked on it, "I'd have messed it up." Herlihy wrote one more novel, *The Season of the Witch* (1971), and pursued an acting career into the 1980s, but committed suicide in 1993.

The Wild Bunch

Warner Bros., 1969. Sound, color, 2.35. 145 minutes. Rated R.

Cast: William Holden (Pike Bishop), Ernest Borgnine (Dutch Engstrom), Robert Ryan (Deke Thornton), Edmond O'Brien (Sykes), Warren Oates (Lyle Gorch), Jaime Sanchez (Angel), Ben Johnson (Tector Gorch), Emilio Fernandez (Mapache), Strother Martin (Coffer), L.Q. Jones (T.C.), Albert Dekker (Pat Harrigan), Bo Hopkins (Crazy Lee), Dub Taylor (Wainscoat), Jorge Russek (Lieutenant Zamorra), Alfonso Arau (Herrera), Chano Urueta (Don José), Sonia Amelio (Teresa), Aurora Clavel (Aurora), Elsa Cardenas (Elsa), Paul Harper (Ross), Bill Hart (Jess), Rayford Barnes (Buck), Steve Ferry (Sergeant McHale), Enrique Lucero (Ignacio), Elizabeth Dupeyron (Rocio), Yolanda Ponce (Yolis), Jose Chavez (Juan Jose), Rene Dupeyron (Juan), Pedro Galvan (Benson), Graciela Doring (Emma), Major Perez (Perez), Fernando Wagner (Mohr), Jorge Rado (Ernst), Ivan Scott (Paymaster), Sra. Madero (Margaret), Margarito Luna (Luna), Chalo Gonzalez (Gonzalez), Lilia Castillo (Lilia), Elizabeth Unda (Carmen), Julio Corona (Julio)

Credits: Directed by Sam Peckinpah. Screenplay by Walon Green and Sam Peckinpah. Story by Walon Green and Roy N. Sickner. Produced by Phil Feldman. Director of photography: Lucien Ballard. Music by Jerry Fielding. Art director: Edward Carrere. Associate producer: Roy N. Sickner. Wardrobe supervisor: Gordon Dawson. Film editor: Louis Lombardo. Production manager: William Faralla. Assistant directors: Cliff Coleman, Fred Gammon. Second unit director: Buzz Henry. Special effects: Bud Hulburd. Associate film editor: Robert L. Wolfe. Key grip: Bud Gaunt. Makeup: Al Greenway. Sound: Robert J. Miller. Script supervisor: Crayton Smith. Music supervised by Sonny Burke. Filmed in Panavision and Technicolor. A Warner Bros.—Seven Arts presentation of a Phil Feldman production.

Additional Credits: Production dates: March to June 1968. World premiere: June 28, 1969.

Available: Warner Home Video DVD (1997). ISBN: 0-7907-3103-7. UPC: 0-85391-40342-5.

The release of Sam Peckinpah's Western *Ride the High Country* (1962) was seriously mismanaged by MGM. However, the film impressed actor

Charlton Heston enough to recommend the director for *Major Dundee* (1965), a post–Civil War epic. Peckinpah and Heston clashed on the set, and the director later asked to have his name removed from the credits. While waiting for a chance at another feature, he worked in television, notably on an adaptation of Katherine Anne Porter's *Noon Wine* (1966) starring Jason Robards, Jr.

Phil Feldman, part of an independent production company, Seven Arts, that had just purchased much of Warner Brothers, brought Peckinpah *The Diamond Story*, a heist script set in Africa. Instead, Peckinpah pushed a script written by Roy Sickner, a stuntman who knew Lee Marvin, and Walon Green. Heavily influenced by spaghetti Westerns, *The Wild Bunch* was little more than a series of shoot-outs.

Much of the industry at the time was consumed with the bidding frenzy for William Goldman's *Butch Cassidy and the Sundance Kid* (1969). Cassidy's gang was known as "The Wild Bunch," although Green's ninety-six-page screenplay for *The Wild Bunch* concerned a different set of outlaws. The script's resemblances to Lee Marvin's recent *The Professionals* (1966), and the possibility of Marvin's participation, helped Feldman and

Seven Arts head Ken Hyman hire Peckinpah to rewrite and direct the project.

Peckinpah asked his frequent writing partner Jim Silke to help with the script, but Silke saw the story as an old-fashioned Western: "The outlaw with the heart of gold." (In the story, hardened criminals donate some of their loot to Mexican rebels, then sacrifice their lives to rescue a rebel captive.) Silke helped Peckinpah realize that the key to the plot was outlaw leader Pike Bishop's realization that his criminal life was a betrayal of his moral beliefs.

When Marvin dropped out to make *Paint Your Wagon* (1969), Feldman and Hyman cast William Holden as Pike Bishop and Robert Ryan as his nemesis Deke Thornton. The aging actors were inspired choices, as their lives and careers meshed into the parts they were playing. Many other cast members had worked with Peckinpah before, such as Warren Oates, Dub Taylor and Ben Johnson. Lucien Ballard, the cinematographer for *Ride the High Country*, went over period newsreels with Peckinpah in order to pin down visual details.

Filming took place on location in Mexico, starting on March 25, 1968, after a week of rehearsals. It was not an easy shoot. Twenty-two crew members were fired during production. Peckinpah's goal was to "bury *Bonnie and Clyde*" according to wardrobe supervisor Gordon Dawson. For some scenes, Peckinpah demanded up to 230 actors and 53 horses. Over 90,000 rounds of blank ammunition were used. According to biographer David Weddle, Peckinpah used over 25,000 feet of film and required 131 camera set-ups in the first week of shooting. The final shootout required 10,000 squibs, or blood packs, and took six more days than the nineteen that had been allotted. Filming finished after eighty days of work. All told, Peckinpah exposed over 333,000 feet of negative, almost a third over his budget.

Peckinpah spent six months editing with Lou Lombardo, according to Feldman arguing over individual frames. The first rough cut, almost four hours long, was ready by September 1968. While Peckinpah left to shoot *The Ballad of Cable Hogue*, Lombardo and Feldman reduced the film to two hours, forty-five minutes; Peckinpah later took out another twenty minutes. At two hours and thirty-one minutes, *The Wild Bunch* had 3,642 edits, more than five times the Hollywood average for a feature. More edits were required by the MPAA and by Warner executives, but Peckinpah felt that the final film was 96 percent "his."

Montage this dense hadn't been attempted since Sergei Eisenstein back in the 1920s. Lombardo persuaded Peckinpah to film the major shootouts with up to six cameras, some operating at different speeds. The editor would then intercut normal motion and slow motion, expanding time at some points and contracting it at others. Take a sequence in the opening bank robbery in which a wounded bounty hunter falls from a roof to the street. In the first set-up, taken from behind, the bounty hunter is shot, a blood pack detonating on his back. The next shot, a reverse angle, repeats the action of the bullet's impact. Lombardo and Peckinpah cut away to a blurry shot of Holden fleeing the bank, then return to the roof to show the hunter falling over the parapet. The fifth shot is a close view of Ernest Borgnine firing his pistol, the sixth is of two different two bounty hunters hiding on a roof, the seventh shows a corner window of the bank with a robber firing out. The eighth shot is a wide view looking up to a stunt man's fall from the roof to the street. The fall is interrupted by the corner shot of the bank, another shot of the rooftop bounty hunters, one of Jaime Sanchez fleeing the bank. Back to the fall for six frames, then to the rooftop, then another angle of the roof showing Robert Ryan. In the fifteenth shot the fall ends. Total time: eight seconds.

Peckinpah was working on the limits of what moviegoers could comprehend, providing more information, and at a faster pace, than the average mind could absorb. By overwhelming viewers, Peckinpah hoped to disarm their normal defenses—"it's only a movie"—and immerse them in the experience of violence and death. Exactly why he wanted to expose mainstream audiences to such relentless violence was never clear. Violence "is in all of us, as the film shows," he said. When filmgoers objected, it was because "[t]hey can't turn their faces away and that makes them mad." In press conferences, Holden and Borgnine gamely tried to connect *The Wild Bunch* to the Vietnam War and the race riots that swept the country in 1968. Left unanswered was what Peckinpah ultimately hoped to accomplish with his movie.

In fact, the point of *The Wild Bunch* was right there in the opening credits, which spelled out the futility of religion, the corruption of authority figures, the inherent cruelty of mankind, the loss of morality in modern society. Peckinpah added to these his characteristic sentimental flourishes, gratuitous violence, and blunt ironic touches, but he essentially had nothing more complex to say during the rest of the film. Some critics viewed the entire movie as a somewhat distasteful exercise in exploitation; others drew their own metaphors with modern society. Just about everyone could appreciate Peckinpah's stunning technique; fewer saw that it had been applied to less-than-worthy material.

The general public avoided the film. When Steve Ross purchased Warners in 1969 and fired Hyman, Feldman was ordered to cut another ten minutes from the picture. Peckinpah spent the rest of his career fighting battles with studio executives, family, and friends, but he never made another film that matched the power of *The Wild Bunch*. He died in 1984 of heart failure.

Easy Rider

Dennis Hopper and Peter Fonda in *Easy Rider*.

Columbia, 1969. Sound, color, 1.85. 95 minutes. Rated R.

Cast: Peter Fonda (Wyatt), Dennis Hopper (Billy), Luana Anders (Lisa), Luke Askew (Stranger on Highway), Toni Basil (Mary), Karen Black (Karen), Warren Finnerty (Rancher), Sabrina Scharf (Sarah), Robert Walker (Jack), Jack Nicholson (George Hanson), Antonio Mendoza (Jesus), Phil Spector (Connection), Mac Mashourian (Bodyguard), Tita Colorado (Rancher's wife). Commune: Sandy Wyeth (Joanne), Robert Ball (Mime #1), Carmen Phillips (Mime #2), Ellie Walker (Mime #3), Michael Pataki (Mime #4). Jail: George Fowler, Jr. (Guard), Keith Green (Sheriff). Café: Hayward Robillard (Cat Man), Arnold Hess, Jr. (Deputy), Buddy Causey, Jr. (Customer #1), Duffy Lafont (Customer #2), Blase M. Dawson (Customer #3), Paul Guedry, Jr. (Customer #4), Suzie Ramagos (Girl #1), Elida Ann Hebert (Girl #2), Rose LeBlanc (Girl #3), Mary Kaye Hebert (Girl #4), Cynthia Grezaffi (Girl #5), Colette Purpera (Girl #6). House of Blue Lights: Lea Marmer (Madame), Cathé Cozzi (Dancing girl), Thea Salerno (Hooker #1), Anne McClain (Hooker #2), Beatriz Monteil (Hooker #3), Marcia Bowman (Hooker #4). Pickup truck: David C. Billodeau, Johnny David.

Credits: Directed by Dennis Hopper. Written by Peter Fonda, Dennis Hopper, Terry Southern. Produced by Peter Fonda. Executive producer: Bert Schneider. Director of photography: Laszlo Kovacs. Associate producer: William L. Hayward. Production manager: Paul Lewis. Film editor: Donn Cambern. Assistant editor: Stanley Siegel. Consultant: Henry Jaglom. Sound effects: Edit-Rite, Inc. Music editing: Synchrofilm, Inc. Re-recording: Producers Sound Service, Inc. Sound: Ryder Sound Service, Inc. Titles: Cinefx. Color processing: Consolidated Film Industries. Post production: Marilyn Schlossberg. Art director: Jerry Kay. Assistant cameraman: Peter Heiser, Jr. Sound mixer: Le Roy Robbins. Script supervisor: Joyce King. Location manager: Tony Vorno. Make-up: Virgil Frye. Special effects: Steve Karkus. A Pando Company presentation in association with Raybert Productions.

Additional Credits: Additional cinematography: Les Blank, Baird Bryant, Barry Feinstein. Production dates: February 23 to April 1968. Premiered in New York City on July 14, 1969.

Available: Columbia TriStar Home Video DVD (1999). ISBN: 0-8001-4178-4. UPC: 0-43396-01749-8.

Before *Easy Rider*, youth-oriented movies were either made by or sanctioned by adults. From Shirley Temple and Andy Hardy right up to the beach party pictures with Annette Funicello and Frankie Avalon, mainstream youth movies followed predictable formulas that had been established by the major studios. In the later 1950s and early '60s, exploitation films by Roger Corman, Arch Hall, and others began to tilt the balance of power over to teenagers and performers in their twenties. With *Easy Rider*, that power shifted completely over to the young.

Young in this case did not preclude professional. Almost everyone in the cast and crew of *Easy Rider* had experience or industry connections, starting with Peter Fonda. He was the son of Hollywood icon Henry Fonda, of course, but he was also the star of several motorcycle exploitation flicks put out by American International Pictures (AIP). In his autobiography *Don't Tell Dad*, Fonda wrote that the inspiration for *Easy Rider* came from a photograph in which he stands in front of motorcycles with his friend and fellow actor Bruce Dern. While visiting his sister Jane in France, where she was making a film with Roger Vadim, Fonda convinced the novelist and screenwriter Terry Southern to work on the motorcycle script.

Dennis Hopper, the third collaborator, made his film debut in *Rebel Without a Cause* (1955). He had worked with Fonda in *The Trip* (1967), a Roger Corman film written by Jack Nicholson. Hopper's reputation as a difficult personality had sidelined his career, but a rebellious attitude and a predilection for recreational drugs were entry-level qualifications for this film. Fonda, Hopper, and Southern approached AIP with a story about Wyatt (or Captain America) and Billy, two bikers who score a major cocaine deal in order to ride across the country and retire in Florida. It was an update of *The Searchers* (1956); "America would be our Natalie Wood," Fonda wrote.

When Sam Arkoff and Jim Nicholson at AIP objected to the script, Jack Nicholson steered the project to Raybert, an independent production company founded by Bert Schneider and Bob Rafelson. Schneider's father Abe was head of Columbia Pictures; his son had worked in television on the East Coast before resettling in California to join his friend Rafelson. They came up with the idea for *The Monkees*, a television series knockoff of The Beatles' *A Hard Day's Night* (1964). Although scorned by rock fans for manufacturing a musical group composed of actors, Schneider and Rafelson made a fortune from both the show and Monkees records. They used some of this money to pay for *Head* (1968), a feature-length Monkees movie, and budgeted $360,000 for Hopper and Fonda's project.

Hopper began shooting in New Orleans on 16mm, without a completed script or most of the cast. They shot for six days, with Fonda concluding that Hopper was "a little fascist freak." Back in Los Angeles, they replaced cinematographer Barry Feinstein with Laszlo Kovacs. Hopper's wife left him, and he faced legal troubles over a speeding ticket. Fonda met Southern in New York to finish the script. Hopper flew there, encountering actor Rip Torn in a restaurant. Torn had been cast as George Hanson, a Southern lawyer who befriends Wyatt and Billy. There are several differing accounts of what happened next, all involving threats and knives. Undisputed was the fact that Torn was out of the movie. He subsequently won a $900,000 judgment against Hopper for defamation, and,

years later, a retraction from *The New York Times Magazine* for repeating rumors about the incident.

Torn was replaced by Jack Nicholson, who could then serve as a sort of cop on location for Schneider and Rafelson. Also new to the production was producer Bill Hayward. Tension continued between Fonda and Hopper, especially when Hopper insisted on improvising situations with nonactors. At the end of the shoot, the motorcycles were stolen. Hopper and Fonda then had to reassemble a crew to shoot a crucial scene that had been forgotten.

Hopper edited the film for twenty-two weeks, winding up with a cut over four hours long. Schneider ultimately bribed Hopper to leave for Taos, New Mexico, then brought together a team to get the film down to a manageable length. Schneider took a print to the Cannes Film Festival, where it received an award, before opening it in New York on July 14, 1969. When it earned close to $20 million on a final budget of just over $500,000, the film had a profound impact on the industry. It was also roundly condemned by moral arbiters.

It may seem laughable today that the issues of hair and clothes could have seemed in any way dangerous. But the hippie lifestyle shown in the film, romanticized as it was, did frighten what Richard Nixon called the silent majority. (It's a measure of Southern's skill that the commune in *Easy Rider* looks absolutely ghastly, a combination of bad food, worse hygiene, and cavorting mimes.)

The film encapsulated a cultural divide in a way that previous biker and rock movies didn't. *Easy Rider*'s hippies and bikers weren't all that threatening; for that matter, neither were the plot or music. That made the movie all the more appealing to younger viewers anxious to jump onto the countercultural bandwagon. Also, Fonda and Hopper, perhaps unconsciously, appropriated the arguments and strategies of the civil rights movement for their plot. In fact, had their characters been black, the film would have made considerably more sense.

The sense of privilege hanging over *Easy Rider* can be galling. Few hippies then had the money or time to determine if New Mexico was better than New Orleans, for example. Or to fly to France to solicit writing help. Apart from Rip Torn, just about everyone associated with the movie did well. Soundtrack sales bolstered the sagging fortunes of The Byrds. Bert Schneider and Bob Rafelson embarked on a string of landmark films, including *The Last Picture Show* (1971), also on the Registry.

Hopper was allowed to ruin his career with the self-indulgent *The Last Movie* (1971). Fonda could make tight-lipped, skin-deep films like *Wanda Nevada* (1979). Both actors rehabilitated their reputations, Hopper with *Blue Velvet* and

Hoosiers (both 1986), Fonda with *Ulee's Gold* (1997). Perhaps no one benefited as much as Jack Nicholson, who found in George Hanson the template for his career. For years he appeared in similar roles, rootless failures searching for father figures, like Bobby Dupea in *Five Easy Pieces* (1970, a Registry title).

The Learning Tree

Warner Bros., 1969. Sound, color, 2.35. 107 minutes. Rated PG.

Cast: Kyle Johnson (Newt [Winger]), Alex Clarke (Marcus), Estelle Evans (Sarah), Dana Elcar (Kirky), Mira Waters (Arcella), Joel Fluellen (Uncle Rob), Malcolm Atterbury (Silas Newhall), Richard Ward (Booker Savage), Russell Thorson (Judge Cavanaugh), Peggy Rea (Miss McClintock), Carole Lamond (Big Mabel), Kevin Hagen (Doc Tim Cravens), James [Jimmy] Rushing (Chappie Logan), Dub Taylor (Spikey), Felix Nelson (Jack Winger), George Mitchell (Jake Kiner), Saundra Sharp (Prissy), Stephen Perry (Jappy), Don Dubbins (Harley Davis), Jon Lormer (McCormack), Morgan Sterne (Mr. Hall), Thomas Anderson (Pastor Broadnap), Philip Roye (Pete Winger), Hope Summers (Mrs. Kiner), Carter Vinnegar (Seansy), Bobby Goss (Skunk).

Credits: Written for the screen, produced and directed by Gordon Parks. Based on the novel *The Learning Tree* by Gordon Parks. Associate producer: James Lydon. Director of photography: Burnett Guffey. Art director: Ed Engoron. Film editor: George R. Rohrs. Set decorator: Joanne MacDougall. Story consultant: Genevieve Young. Sound by Robert Miller. Unit production manager: Russell Llewellyn. Music by Gordon Parks. Music orchestrated and conducted by Tom McIntosh. Special photographic effects: Albert Whitlock. Assistant directors: Jack Aldworth, Fred Giles. Music supervised by Sonny Burke. Makeup supervision: Gordon Bau. Supervising hair stylist: Jean Burt Reilly. Administrative assistant to Mr. Parks: Suzanne Crayson. Title Song "The Learning Tree" sung by O. C. Smith.

Additional Credits: Released August 9, 1969.

Available: Warner Home Video VHS (1987).

Notable at the time of its release as the first feature film directed by an African-American that was financed by a Hollywood studio, *The Learning Tree* may be more significant today for the ease with which it fits into the tradition of black filmmaking. For his first feature project, the esteemed photographer and writer Gordon Parks, Sr., chose his own autobiographical novel. Set in rural Kansas in the 1920s, the film, like the book, is a coming-of-age story about a youth whose relatively sheltered upbringing has not prepared him for the realities of racism. In a way, Parks is following in the footsteps of filmmakers like Oscar Micheaux and Spencer Williams, men who experienced racism firsthand, and who could report on it with more verisimilitude than a white director, no matter how well-intentioned.

The opening scene, which finds the adolescent Newt Winger (Kyle Johnson) fighting for his life during a tornado, offers an oblique commentary on *The Wizard of Oz*. Unlike L. Frank Baum's poor

but benign Kansas, Parks' Kansas is a world in which moonshiners abuse their children and sex is an open topic. It's also a world in which Kirky (Dana Elcar), a white sheriff, can shoot a black man in the back with impunity. Parks' matter-of-fact treatment of brutality is a direct affront to Hollywood's earlier attempts to define a place for blacks in society. The gloves are off in *The Learning Tree*; Parks isn't worried about offending sensibilities, and he's not interested in softening his imagery.

But he's also not interested in starting a war. As Parks told one newspaper reporter, "I have a right to be bitter, but I would not let bitterness destroy me. As I tell young black people, you can fight back, but do it in a way to help yourself and not destroy yourself." What makes *The Learning Tree* distinctive may be the way Newt maintains his dignity, despite the prejudice and injustice that confront him daily.

Parks led a remarkable life before becoming a filmmaker. The youngest of fifteen children born into a sharecropper's family in Fort Scott, Kansas, Gordon Roger Alexander Buchanan Parks was living on the streets by the time he was a teenager. After a stint as a porter and waiter on a railroad, he forged a career for himself as a photographer. His 1942 portrait of cleaning woman Ella Watson standing before an American flag is a good example of his abilities: technically accomplished; direct, even confrontational in subject matter; unassailably honest. Parks was hired as the first black staff photographer for *Life* magazine. His 1961 photo essay on Flavio Da Silva, an asthmatic youth from the slums of Rio de Janeiro, led to his first film, a documentary called *Flavio* (1964).

Further documentaries followed; by this time Parks had also embarked on a writing career that would include memoirs, poetry, and several novels. After some three hundred assignments for *Life*,

Parks left the magazine. He wrote, "I found myself on a plateau of loneliness, not knowing really where I belonged. In one world I was a social oddity. In the other I was almost a stranger." The need to create came as a result of "a desperate search for security within a society that held me inferior simply because I was black. . . . It was a constant inner rebellion against failure."

Parks was unable to break into Hollywood ranks until actor, screenwriter, and director John Cassavetes introduced him to Ken Hyman at Warner Brothers. Parks signed a contract that included writing and scoring as well as directing *The Learning Tree.*

The downside to the deal with Warners was a low budget that precluded big stars. Most of the performers came from television, and for a large portion of them, this would be the most significant entry on their résumés. Parks did cast two wily veterans, Dana Elcar and Dub Taylor, in important supporting roles. Elcar, a fixture on television until he went blind due to glaucoma, does a very credible job as the racist sheriff. Taylor, a mainstay of Westerns in the 1940s, appears as a sideshow carny who organizes a fight competition at a county fair; that same year he appeared in the Sam Peckinpah Western *The Wild Bunch* and a George C. Scott comedy, *The Flim-Flam Man.*

In his autobiography *Voices in the Mirror* (1990), Parks gives a vivid description of the pressure he felt shooting *The Learning Tree.* He had three months to not only write the screenplay, but coordinate all of the crew members and resolve hundreds of minor details. How many wind machines to order, for example, and what livestock would be required for the tornado scene that opens the story. Shooting took another three months, some of which was spent persuading the initially hostile Fort Scott townspeople to cooperate with the project. Parks took another three months to edit and score the film.

By keeping the narrative rich in incident, and by framing everything in the wonder of the natural world, Parks may hope you will overlook the sometimes poor acting and dialogue. As could be expected, the film's cinematography, by Burnett Guffey, is lush and evocative. Parks knows how to use devices like slow motion, filters, and fades to black, just as his narrative sense—his knowledge of the story and what each moment means—informs the editing. *The Learning Tree* is a demanding film with troubling messages, but it is not an accusatory or despairing one. Parks himself is proof that it is possible to escape from the restrictions imposed by society. More important, he did so while still retaining his dignity, his earthy humor, and respect for others.

The Learning Tree received respectful reviews but was a mediocre box-office performer. (The film did have a long afterlife in schools, churches, and at family film festivals.) Like Micheaux and Williams before him, Parks turned to a more commercial project for his next film, giving up rural settings and family themes for *Shaft* (1971), one of the progenitors of the "blaxploitation" movement.

Medium Cool

Paramount, 1969. Sound, color, 1.85. 110 minutes. Rated X.

Cast: Robert Forster (John), Verna Bloom (Eileen), Peter Bonerz (Gus), Marianna Hill (Ruth), Harold Blankenship (Harold), Charles Geary (Harold's father), Sid McCoy (Frank Baker), Christine Bergstrom (Dede), William Sickingen (News director), Robert McAndrew (Pennybaker), Marrian Walters (Social worker), Beverly Younger (Rich lady), Edward Croke (Plain-clothesman), Doug Kimball (Newscaster), Peter Boyle (Gun clinic manager), Georgia Todda (Secretary), Sandra Ann Roberts (Blonde in car), Janet Langhart (Maid); Jeff Donaldson, Bill Sharp, Robert Paige, Richard Abrams, Walter Bradford, Russell Davis, Felton Perry, Val Grey, Livingston Lewis, Barbara Jones, John Jackson (Black militants); Linda Handelman, Marla Friedman, Kathryn Schubert, Barbara Brydenthal, Elizabeth Molsant, Rose Bormacher (Gun clinic ladies). With: China Lee, Roger Phillips, Robert Blankenship. James Jacobs, Spence Jackson, Dorlen Suhr, Kenneth Whitener, Connie Fleischauer, Mary Smith, Nancy Noble (Kennedy students); Simone Zorn, Madeleine Marcou, Mickey Pallas, Morris Bleckman, Lestre Brownlee, Linn Ehrlich, Wally Wright, Sam Ventura, George Bouillet (Media people).

Credits: Written and directed by Haskell Wexler. Produced by Tully Friedman, Haskell Wexler. Director of photography: Haskell Wexler. Camera operators: Haskell Wexler, Mike Margulies. Camera assistant: Ron Vargas. Editor: Verna Fields. Assistant editor: Marsha Griffin. Editorial consultant: Paul Golding. Art director: Leon Erickson. Sound: Chris Newman. Sound editor: Kay Rose. Gaffer: Tom Ryan. Script supervisor: Meta Rebner. Assistant director: Wendell Franklin. Associate producers: Michael Philip Butler, Steven North. Assistant to the producer: Jonathan Haze. Production assistant: William Schwartz. Our man in Chicago: Studs Terkel. Titles: James Talbot. Color by Technicolor. Music scored by Mike Bloomfield. Music performed by Paul Butterfield, Michael Bloomfield, Marcus Doubleday, Bob Jones, Noel Jukes, John Kahn, Ira Kamin, Fred Olson, Jerry Oshita, Brother Bones. Incidental music: Mothers of Invention.

Additional Credits: Released August 27, 1969. Re-rated R in 1970.

Available: Paramount DVD (2001). ISBN: 0-7921-7741-x. UPC: 0-9736-06907-4-3. VHS (1994). ISBN: 0-7921-3323-4.

Haskell Wexler had directed one film, an hour-long documentary on civil rights called *The Bus* (1965), when he approached Paramount Pictures about adapting *The Concrete Wilderness*, a 1967 novel by Jack Couffer about a boy from Appalachia who has trouble adjusting to living in Chicago. Wexler had just won an Oscar for his cinematography on *Who's Afraid of Virginia Woolf?* (1966), and his reputation was built almost exclusively on his work as a cameraman. But he felt so strongly about the project that he invested $800,000 of his own money into the production.

He even started filming *The Concrete Wilderness*, shooting scenes involving twelve-year-old Harold (Harold Blankenship, an amateur from West Virginia) and his single mother Eileen, played by Verna Bloom. Little of this story made it onto the screen; you can see bits and pieces of the original idea in scenes involving Harold's homing pigeons. Instead, Wexler's movie evolved into a near-documentary examination of the political situation in Chicago in 1968. A year after the "summer of love," worries about the Vietnam War, civil rights, drugs, and assassinations permeated society. Tensions between parents and children, between an older generation seen as a ruling class and a younger one depicted as rebels and delinquents, between haves and have-nots, erupted into riots across the country that spring. Since Chicago would be the site of the Democratic National Convention in late August, both the police and protestors prepared for a showdown.

By his own account, Wexler knew that something was stirring. He shifted the focus of his film to a television news cameraman who would undergo a political awakening through his work. Wexler hoped to cast John Cassavetes in the part, but used Robert Forster instead. Forster had worked on stage and television, but had had limited exposure in film, notably a lead in a Gregory Peck Western, *The Stalking Moon* (1968). Wexler gave Forster an Eclair 16mm camera with no film in it as a prop.

Forster's partner Gus, a soundman, was played by Peter Bonerz, later a fixture on television as both an actor and a director. Marianna Hill, who has a small role as a nurse, also had TV experience; coincidentally, she and Verna Bloom would both end up in a Clint Eastwood film, *High Plains Drifter* (1973). Wexler used Peter Boyle as a manager of a gun clinic; it was one of his first credited film appearances. Like Boyle, most of the other actors who appeared in *Medium Cool* were essentially unknowns, adding to the documentary feel of the movie.

Aided by Paul Golding, Wexler restructured his original concept of the film, in some cases shifting footage out of its intended chronology. *Medium Cool* opens with Forster and Bonerz filming a car accident on a freeway. Dispassionate, uninvolved, they wait until they've gotten the material they want before radioing an ambulance for help. Even when photographing National Guard volunteers at riot exercise, Forster is strictly professional. A chance encounter with Bloom and her son, who live in a tenement, sparks Forster's realization that he cannot remain detached from his surroundings. By the end of the film, Forster and Bloom are reluctant participants in the riots that marked the Democratic convention.

Wexler and Golding have admitted that Jean-Luc Godard was their favorite filmmaker, and the finished *Medium Cool* may be the closest thing to a Godard film ever released by a major Hollywood studio. (The two cite Peter Watkins' fake documentary *The War Game* as another influence.) The shambling structure, use of pop music and graphics, and digressions into political debates marked the movie as distinctly anti-Establishment. It didn't even offer the classical narrative style of *Easy Rider* (although it was closer to the spirit of the times than most Hollywood attempts to deal with the "youth culture"). What made *Medium Cool* especially demanding was its mixture of truth and fiction, of documentary and feature. The movie is perhaps most famous today for its footage of actual riots, including a shot in which police throw tear gas canisters at Wexler and his camera. On the soundtrack you can hear someone calling, "Look out, Haskell, it's real," a line cited by reviewers at the time as proof of the film's authenticity. But the line was dubbed in later by an actor.

Wexler and his crew were allowed to film the National Guard in Michigan, and briefly had permission to enter the convention headquarters. The cinematography features Wexler's typically fluid, handheld shots and natural lighting, made all the more remarkable by the fact that almost the entire film was done on 35mm. (Wexler has said that the only 16mm footage was taken inside the convention.)

It took Wexler and his editorial crew almost half a year to finish *Medium Cool*. It received an X rating, in part for a brief sequence with full frontal nudity, but in Wexler's opinion more for the film's uncompromising political views. (The rating was later adjusted to R.) But apart from its politics, the film raises challenging questions. How much should we involve ourselves in the problems of society? Can a documentary ever be truly objective? How does the media affect our behavior? In asking these, Wexler should perhaps be forgiven for some of the film's cheap broadsides and forced irony, including an ending constructed more for aesthetics than narrative logic.

Although it received generally positive reviews (*Variety* complained that it was "confusing" and its

motives "difficult to fathom"), the film was a box-office failure. Wexler was so disillusioned by the process that he has limited his subsequent directing primarily to documentaries. He did, however, continue to work as a cinematographer on many mainstream Hollywood films, including the Registry title *One Flew Over the Cuckoo's Nest* (1975). He received a second Oscar for the cinematography on 1976's *Bound for Glory*, and was the subject of a documentary directed by his son Mark Wexler, *Tell Them Who You Are* (2004).

Butch Cassidy and the Sundance Kid

Twentieth Century-Fox, 1969. Sound, color, 1.85. 110 minutes. Rated M.

Cast: Paul Newman (Butch Cassidy), Robert Redford (The Sundance Kid), Katharine Ross (Etta Place), Strother Martin (Percy Garris), Henry Jones (Bike salesman), Jeff Corey (Sheriff Bledsoe), George Furth (Woodcock), Cloris Leachman (Agnes), Ted Cassidy (Harvey Logan), Kenneth Mars (Marshal), Donnelly Rhodes (Macon), Jody Gilbert (Large woman), Timothy Scott (News Carver), Don Keefer (Fireman), Charles Dierkop (Flat Nose Curry), Francisco Cordova (Bank manager), Nelson Olmstead (Photographer), Paul Bryar (Card player #1), Sam Elliott (Card player #2), Charles Akins (Bank teller), Eric Sinclair (Tiffany's salesman).

Credits: Directed by George Roy Hill. Written by William Goldman. Produced by John Foreman. Executive producer: Paul Monash. Director of photography Conrad Hall. Art direction: Jack Martin Smith, Philip Jefferies. Set decoration: Walter M. Scott, Chester L. Bayhi. Special photographic effects: L.B. Abbott, Art Cruickshank. Main title: Glen Advertising, Inc. Music composed and conducted by Burt Bacharach. "Raindrops Keep Fallin' on My Head," performed by B.J. Thomas. Lyrics by Hal David, music by Burt Bacharach. Film editors: John C. Howard, Richard C. Meyer. Unit production manager: Lloyd Anderson. Assistant director: Steven Bernhardt. Sound: William F. Edmonson, David E. Dockendorf. Orchestration: Leo Shuken, Jack Hayes. Costumes by Edith Head. Makeup by Dan Striepeke. Hairstyling by Edith Lindon. Special still photography: Lawrence Schiller. Graphic montage by John Neuhart. Second unit director: Michael Moore. Second unit photographer: Harold E. Wellman. Assistant to producer: Ron Preissman. Dialogue coach: Robert Crawford, Jr. Filmed in Panavision. Color by De Luxe. A George Roy Hill, Paul Monash production. A Newman-Foreman presentation. Produced by Campanile Productions, Inc., and released by Twentieth Century-Fox Film Corporation.

Additional Cast: Percy Helton (Sweetface).

Additional Credits: Production dates: September 16, 1968 to March 13, 1969. Released September 24, 1969. Re-rated PG in 1974.

Other Versions: Prequel: *Butch and Sundance: The Early Days* (1979, directed Richard Lester). *The Legend of Butch & Sundance* (2004, directed Sergio Mimica-Gezzan).

Awards: Oscars for Best Cinematography, Original Score, Original Song, and Writing—Screenplay Based on Material from Another Medium.

Available: Twentieth Century Fox Home Entertainment DVD (2006). UPC: 0-23543-24457-8.

"Most of what follows is true." That opening title from screenwriter William Goldman clued in filmgoers that *Butch Cassidy and the Sundance Kid* was a different kind of Western. The genre in 1969 might not have been dead, but it was increasingly irrelevant to the younger viewers who were making up a growing part of the film audience. The

hip, ironic tone employed by Goldman separated *Butch Cassidy* from dull, lumbering epics starring Charlton Heston or Gregory Peck; this film aimed for the lighthearted style of *Cat Ballou*, a box-office surprise in 1965. Like that film, *Butch Cassidy* understood the function of celebrity in the Wild West. As *The Wild Bunch* (1969) did, *Butch Cassidy* also set out to deconstruct the genre by adding Brechtian elements, by pushing the limits of censorship, and by eliminating many of the staples of previous Westerns. It was in the eyes of Goldman and director George Roy Hill a postmodern Western.

How revolutionary was it? Hindsight reveals just how heavily Goldman leaned on earlier stories—not just *Cat Ballou*, but less obvious inspirations, like playwright Neil Simon. Goldman's pairing of the loud, swaggering Butch Cassidy with the tight-lipped, repressed Sundance Kid echoed the set-up for Simon's *The Odd Couple* (filmed in 1968). For that matter, it replayed the central basis of Henry King's *Jesse James* (1939): two major stars, a name screenwriter, a name director, and real-life crooks equal box-office smash. The battling, comic duo can even be traced back to the Flagg and Quirk team in *What Price Glory* (a play by Laurence Stallings and Maxwell Anderson that was filmed in 1926). Like Butch and Sundance, they skirted the laws of society, were attracted to the same women, and had a love-hate relationship marked by quips and practical jokes.

What *Butch Cassidy* did well was update the most popular and successful elements of Westerns to the *Easy Rider* (1969) era. It gave younger viewers a Western with widescreen color, better sound, rougher language, bloodier violence, young stars, and pop music. Both Goldman and director George Roy Hill saw Butch and Sundance as modern characters in a period piece, an approach that solidified the film's appeal for the young. But the basic roles, the situations, even the plot remained the same as in the old formulas. Outlaws portrayed as romantic rebels; saloons, card games, holdups, chases on horseback; the passing of the West, the closing of the frontier, outlaws hemmed in by changing society—*Butch Cassidy* was treading the same territory as *My Darling Clementine* (1946).

For better or worse, Goldman revolutionized the screenplay format. He injected himself into what was previously a formal, impersonal, even stiff style of writing. He offered advice, criticism, opinions about what was happening in his story, how to film it, how to act it. A leap from a cliff—something Goldman lifted from *Gunga Din*—became in his style the biggest leap in the world, the highest cliff, the scariest jump. A posse wasn't just a posse, it was the scariest posse ever formed, a superposse.

Goldman got $400,000 for what was initially called *The Sundance Kid and Butch Cassidy*. It was up to Twentieth Century-Fox to make sure the money wasn't wasted, which meant the studio was committed to a big-budget film. As with almost every big-budget film of the time, overtures were made to Marlon Brando for the lead role. At one point Steve McQueen was interested, but Newman and his producing partner Paul Monash committed first. Newman was intent on playing Butch—as written, the role with the best lines. The lines allowed the actor to explore celebrity and the price of fame, as he had in *The Hustler* (1961). When the other possible actors lost interest, Newman and director George Roy Hill cast Robert Redford as the Sundance Kid. Fox agreed, with the proviso that the title be switched to *Butch Cassidy and the Sundance Kid*.

Redford had previously done his best work on television. In film, he had generally been cast as a love interest or secondary lead. Speaking later about *Butch Cassidy*, he said, "This unquestionably was the film that put me in a new place. It changed my life." It was not an easy process. In a "making of" documentary he later donated to Yale, Hill remarked repeatedly on the trouble he had directing both Redford and Katharine Ross, an ingénue whose biggest impact had been in *The Graduate* (1967). As for Newman, he said, "I played him [Butch] loose. I usually keep a very tight rein on

my characters. But I thought for Butch, I wasn't going to make any judgments about him. I used a good deal of myself in the part."

Hill rehearsed the cast for two weeks on the Fox lot before shooting started in Colorado on September 16, 1968. Other locations included an abandoned Mormon settlement near Zion National Park and Mexico, which doubled for Bolivia. Hill had Goldman write three montage scenes to give Ross more footage; the director treated them as musical interludes. He had hoped to use the New York City sets prepared on the Fox backlot for *Hello Dolly*, but studio executives refused. By employing period photographs as mattes on an animation stand, Hill could pretend that the three leads were in New York for considerably less money than it would have cost to actually shoot scenes there. Hill didn't want what he called a traditional Western score, turning to pop composer Burt Bacharach for his "semi-modern sound." (Hill may not have realized that he was simply going back to the "semi-modern" scores used in most Westerns during the 1950s.) Hill pointed out that only twelve minutes of the film are scored, almost none of it with dialogue.

"I wanted a kind of washed out, desaturated look to the film," Hill said. He allowed cinematographer Conrad Hall, who helped scout locations, to overexpose, typically by two f-stops. Hall relied on backlighting, clouds of dust, and other devices to obscure the visuals. The film's most spectacular stunt—a leap into a river gorge—was accomplished by combining footage shot in Colorado with work by stuntmen at Fox's Malibu ranch, along with matte work by special effects expert Bill Abbott.

Butch Cassidy received mixed reviews when it was released in September 1969. Roger Ebert called it "slow and disappointing" despite "several good laughs and three sound performances." Still, audiences flocked to theaters, and the film subsequently won four Oscars. It set the standard for "buddy" pictures. Everything from *Midnight Cowboy* (1969) and *Harry and Walter Go to New York* (1976) to *Lethal Weapon* (1987) and *Midnight Run* (1988) sought to recapture Newman and Redford's screen chemistry. The roles had a lasting impact on the stars. Newman named his children's camp after the film's Hole in the Wall Gang, while Redford turned his Sundance Film Festival into a major force in independent film. The two stars and director Hill would reteam once more in 1973's *The Sting*.

Czechoslovakia 1918–1968

USIA, 1969. Sound, color, 1.37. 15 minutes.
Credits: Written, produced and directed by Denis Sanders, Robert Fresco. Edited by Marvin Walowitz. Music by Charles Bernstein. Graphic Design: Norman Gollin. A Film by Sanders/Fresco Film Makers.
Awards: Oscar for Best Documentary—Short Subjects.
Available: The National Archives (*www.archives.gov*). Special order through Terry Sanders at the American Film Foundation (*www.americanfilm foundation.com*).

Formed in August 1953, the United States Information Agency was intended to explain and promulgate the government's policies abroad, as well as provide a record or history for foreigners. (The agency was called the United States Information Service in other countries.) Perhaps best known for radio programs like the Voice of America and Radio Marti, the USIA also funded some 17,000 films and 2,000 video productions, which it offered free of charge to foreign broadcast outlets. According to the provisions of the 1948 Smith-Mundt Act, passed in response to use of propaganda during World War II, it was against the law to distribute these films domestically.

In 1961, President John F. Kennedy named journalist Edward R. Murrow head of the USIA. The following year, Murrow chose George Stevens, Jr., to head the USIA's Motion Picture and Television Service. It became a place where filmmakers were free to experiment with documentary forms and styles. In 1964, the agency released its first feature-length documentary, *John F. Kennedy: Years of Lightning, Day of Drums*, which won an Academy Award. (A law had to be passed to allow its exhibition within the United States.)

Frank J. Shakespeare was named director in 1969. By that time, Denis Sanders and Robert Fresco had made a number of films for the Agency, including a survey of West Point and three profiles of Adlai Stevenson. The last, *Adlai Stevenson: The Ambassador*, took the team, based in Los Angeles, over ten months to complete. After USIA officials watched it, they summoned the filmmakers to Washington, D.C.

There, Fresco recalled screening about two hours of fine-grain 35mm black-and-white footage of the Russian invasion of Czechoslovakia in the spring of 1968. The Czechs had taken "every camera they had" from both the Barrandov studios and from private sources to document the invasion. "They filmed their own rape," was how Fresco put it. The processed footage was brought to Prague

embassies, and then smuggled out of the country in diplomatic pouches.

USIA officials were not sure what to do with the footage. Fresco returned to California and wrote what he called a seven-page "libretto" that used visual terms to explain the history of Czechoslovakia from its inception in 1918 to the invasion. No dialogue would be necessary. After working for David L. Wolper on the ABC documentary series *Story of . . .*, Fresco had grown to hate voice-over narrations; by making a film that had no dialogue, he would also avoid problems with dubbing and subtitling.

The USIA purchased Fresco's treatment, but offered no comments until the spring of 1969, when it told Sanders and Fresco that it wanted a documentary finished by the anniversary of the invasion. "We didn't sleep a wink for six weeks," Fresco said. He and Sanders had to find visual material to cover the forty-nine years leading up to the invasion, and edit that and the two hours of smuggled footage down to a one-reel short. Fresco remembered obtaining photographs from Sovfoto, the Soviet stock photography agency, telling officials there that he needed it for an "educational film."

Working with editor Marvin Walowitz, Sanders and Fresco cut the material to old Czech recordings. The only original material consisted of shots of a slide projector, used to provide dates. During the invasion sequence, they laid in a version of "It's a Long Way to Tipperary" sung by the Red Army Chorus. When they viewed a rough cut in Washington, USIA officials complained that the film was "too upsetting," but Shakespeare threatened to resign if the film wasn't released. "It was an honest agency," Fresco said, adding that he and Sanders were never asked to alter any of their USIA films.

The final step was to add a score, which Fresco remembered Charles Bernstein composing almost overnight. Trade screenings in Los Angeles earned the film an Academy Award nomination. Although it was illegal to exhibit the film commercially, *Czechoslovakia 1918–1968* still won the Oscar. After receiving his statuette from Bob Hope and Fred Astaire, Fresco thanked the Czechs who had risked their lives to provide the footage.

The USIA was dissolved in 1999. Smith-Mundt was amended to permit access to USIA films and other materials twelve years after their production. Although it was championed by former New York Senator James L. Buckley, *Czechoslovakia 1918–1968* unfortunately remains a difficult film to see.

A sophisticated editing scheme is only one of the reasons why *Czechoslovakia 1918–1968* remains so powerful today. Sanders and Fresco moved from still photographs to motion picture clips, from wide and pastoral to intimate and deadly, in a manner so adroit it is almost imperceptible. Without browbeating viewers, they conveyed the horror of the Nazi occupation as well as the hope of the Prague Spring. Color added an emotional component—yellow for prosperity, red for danger, black-and-white for

reality. Along with Bernstein's score, Sanders and Fresco used a montage of sounds as complex and pointed as their visual edits.

But it is the Czech footage that ultimately makes the film so memorable. One shot was taken from the back seat of a car driving through the streets of Prague. Visually seductive, it glides through the city, the speed of the car drawing the eye to a view of a stone wall topped by foliage drifting by lazily. The road turns, and then you see the tanks—thirteen of them, lined up one after another, with helmeted soldiers in the turrets awaiting orders. The shot goes on for thirty seconds, a terrible risk on the part of someone desperate to show the world what was happening.

Salesman

Paul Brennan in *Salesman. Courtesy of The Criterion Collection*

Maysles Films, 1968. Sound, B&W, 1.33. 91 minutes.

Featuring: Paul Brennan (The Badger), Charles McDevitt (The Gipper), James Baker ("The Rabbit"), Raymond Martos ("The Bull"), Kennie Turner, Melbourne T. Feltman, Margaret McCarron.

Credits: Directed by Albert Maysles, David Maysles, Charlotte Zwerin. Photography: Albert Maysles. Editing: David Maysles and Charlotte Zwerin. Contributing film editor: Ellen Giffard. Assistant editor: Barbara Jarvis. Sound mixer: Dick Vorisek. A Maysles Films, Inc., production.

Additional Credits: Sound: David Maysles. Research: David Maysles.

Available: Criterion Collection DVD (2001). ISBN: 0-78002-428-1. UPC: 0-37429-1589-2-0.

The Maysles brothers objected to grouping their films with the cinema verité movement, preferring the term "cinema direct." "There's nothing between us and the subject," David explained to critic Jack Kroll in a 1969 interview. Albert Maysles, the older

brother, was born in Boston in 1926, and started making films in 1955 after teaching psychology. His first documentary concerned psychiatric patients in Russia. David, born in 1931, also studied psychology, and after serving in World War II worked for a time in Hollywood. He joined Albert on a motorcycle trip from Munich to Moscow, and first collaborated with him on the documentary short *Youth in Poland* (1957).

The Maysles were in the forefront of documentary filmmaking during the shift to lighter, more portable equipment that occurred in the late 1950s. Albert worked on *Primary* (1960), and with David filmed an hour-long portrait of film producer Joseph E. Levine (*Showman*, 1962). Unlike Frederick Wiseman, who concentrated on documenting institutions, the Maysles brothers gravitated toward personalities like The Beatles, Marlon Brando, and Truman Capote. For *Meet Marlon Brando* (1965) and *Love from Truman* (1966), the brothers worked with editor Charlotte Zwerin. Born in Detroit in 1931, she had been a film librarian and editor for CBS before forming her own production company, winning an Academy Award for *Robert Frost: A Lover's Quarrel with the World* (1963). She met the Maysles when she was working at Drew Associates.

In 1967, the Maysles began searching for a subject that would allow them to document the area where they grew up. Since they had both worked as door-to-door salesmen, David looked for companies that would let them follow employees with a camera. As he put it, "We were looking for salesmen who would be interesting, who would be on the road, who would be sort of O'Neill type of characters."

The Mid-American Bible Company agreed, as did four of their representative Bible salesmen. The Maysles followed them through two stretches, one outside Boston, the other in Florida. Albert handled the 16mm camera, while David carried a synch-sound tape recorder. The Boston scenes capture the weary monotony of a New England winter: snow, slush, cinderblock motel rooms, block after block of row houses. Florida comes as a relief of sorts, until the salesmen try to navigate the faux Middle Eastern streets of Opa-Locka. Halfway through the film the salesmen attend a conference in Chicago, where pep talks alternate with threats of firings. It is David Mamet, specifically *Glengarry Glen Ross*, brought to life.

The brothers insisted later that "We don't doctor situations." That said, the Maysles were hardly trying to be objective. With David actively seeking out Eugene O'Neill types, a specific point of view had already formed before shooting started: the salesman as a tragic figure. In deciding which characters and scenes to film, the brothers pursued what they hoped would be photogenic and compelling, not necessarily informative or explanatory. They didn't shoot one encounter because "The housewife didn't look that interesting," as David put it. As filming progressed, they concentrated on Paul Brennan, a middle-aged sales veteran who was undergoing a crisis of faith. "Paul Brennan is very much like my father," Albert said, but he was important to the film because he fulfilled the brothers' vision of a doomed character.

The emphasis on Brennan was due in part to Charlotte Zwerin, who edited the raw footage with no previous knowledge or expertise in the subject. "I think this removal from the scene," she said, "helped my judgment and helped me to understand more clearly what the viewer would feel." Working with David, she helped shape the material, constructing scenes from snippets and pickup shots, building a plot that turned the salesmen's work into a game or battle. Without this contest structure, without a suggestion of winners and losers, why would mainstream viewers watch *Salesman*? It had no overview like traditional documentaries or newsreels, nothing to show or teach except a pervasive discontent with society.

The brothers agreed that some of the scenes they filmed made them uncomfortable—in particular, when Brennan is seen pressuring a housewife into paying off a contract, telling her that her husband already signed it. In fact, Albert felt that everything the salesmen did was "just on the other side of the border" of what was morally acceptable. "We actually believe we can come to situations without materially affecting them," he said. "We know very well that that equipment is not going to change things." But the truth is the brothers' presence had a significant impact on the people they were filming. Some customers can be seen glancing warily at the camera; others clearly relish performing. Did some purchase Bibles simply to be included in the film? Did the presence of a film crew give greater authority and credibility to the salesmen? Should the Maysles have warned housewives that they were being fleeced?

For their next project, *Gimme Shelter* (1970), a feature about the 1969 Rolling Stones tour of the United States, the three filmmakers could turn these questions around, confronting members of the group about a murder that occurred during a concert at Altamont. But by the time the Maysles made *Grey Gardens* (1976), a documentary about Edith Bouvier Beale and her daughter "Little Edie," it was hard to avoid charges of exploitation.

The Maysles collaborated frequently with the artist Christo and his wife Jeanne-Claude on documenting their large-scale artworks. They also financed their work by shooting numerous commercials for clients like Citibank and *Sports Illustrated*. David died in 1987; as of this writing, Albert's most recent work was as a cinematographer on *Shine a Light* (2008), Martin Scorsese's documentary on the Rolling Stones.

MASH

Twentieth Century-Fox, 1970. Sound, color, 2.35. 116 minutes. Rated R.
Cast: Donald Sutherland (Capt. "Hawkeye" Pierce), Elliott Gould (Capt. "Trapper" John McIntyre), Tom Skerritt (Capt. "Duke" Forrest), Sally Kellerman (Major Margaret "Hot Lips" Houlihan), Robert Duvall (Major Frank Burns), Roger Bowen (Col. Henry Blake), René Auberjonois (Father Mulcahy), David Arkin (Sgt. Vollmer), Jo Ann Pflug (Lt. "Dish" Schneider), Gary Burghoff (Cpl. "Radar" O'Reilly), Fred Williamson (Capt. Oliver Harmon "Spearchucker" Jones), Michael Murphy (Capt. "Me Lay" Marston), Indus Arthur (Lt. Leslie), Ken Prymus (Pvt. Seidman), Bobby Troup (Sgt. Gorman), Kim Atwood (Ho-Jon), Tim Brown (Cpl. Judson), John Schuck (Capt. Walter "Painless" Waldowski), Dawne Damon (Lt. Storch), Carl Gottlieb (Capt. Black), Tamara Horrocks (Capt. Bridget "Knocko" McCarthy), G. Wood (Gen. Charlie Hammond), Bud Cort (Pvt. Boone), Danny Goldman (Capt. Murrhardt), Corey Fischer (Capt. Bandini).

Credits: Directed by Robert Altman. Screenplay by Ring Lardner, Jr. From the novel by Richard Hooker. Produced by Ingo Preminger. Music by Johnny Mandel. Song "Suicide Is Painless," music by Johnny Mandel, lyrics by Mike Altman. Director of photography: Harold E. Stine. Art direction: Jack Martin Smith, Arthur Lonergan. Set decoration: Stuart A. Reiss, Walter M. Scott. Orchestration: Herbert Spencer. Film editor: Danford B. Greene. Sound: Bernard Freericks, John Spack. Special photographic effects: L.B. Abbot, Art Cruickshank. Associate producer: Leon Erickson. Unit production manager: Norman A. Cook. Assistant director: Ray Taylor, Jr. Medical advisor: Dr. David Sachs. Makeup supervision: Dan Striepeke. Hairstyling by Edith Lindon. Titles by Pacific Title. Filmed in Panavision. Color by De Luxe. Westrex Recording System.

Additional cast includes: J. B. Douglas (Col. Wallace C. Merrill), Yoko Young (Japanese servant); Fran Tarkenton, Ben Davidson, Tommy Brown, Tom Woodeschick (Football players).

Additional Credits: Writing: John T. Kelly. Editorial consultant: Louis Lombardo. Additional editing: Graeme Clifford. Production dates: April 14 to June 1969. Premiered in New York City on January 25, 1970.

Awards: Oscar for Best Writing—Screenplay Based on Material from Another Medium.

Other Versions. Television series *M*A*S*H* (1972–83).

Available: Twentieth Century Fox Home Entertainment DVD (2005). UPC: 0-24543-22456-3.

According to biographer Jan Stuart, the defining moment in Robert Altman's life was when he almost lost his life in a training incident aboard an Air Force twin-engine plane in 1945. From that point on, rules were different for him, something to be bested or avoided. Born in Kansas City in 1925, he had dropped out of Wentworth Military Academy to enlist. After serving as a copilot on bombing runs in the South Pacific, Altman returned to Los Angeles with the hopes of being an actor. Instead, he contributed story ideas to three low-budget features before going back to Kansas City.

Altman found work directing industrial and educational films for the Calvin Company, one of the largest producers of sponsored movies in the country. By biographer Patrick McGilligan's count, Altman directed at least sixty titles, including *The Magic Bond* (1955, about the Veterans of Foreign Wars) and *Honeymoon for Harriet* (sponsored by International Harvester). His first feature, *The Delinquents* (1957), got him a job directing episodes of *Alfred Hitchcock Presents* on television, which he parlayed into steady work on other shows like *Hawaiian Eye*, *Bonanza*, and *Combat*. Here Altman met many of the actors he would cast later; he also earned the enmity of a growing number of executives. He completed four additional feature films before getting the opportunity to direct *MASH*.

The script for *MASH* evolved in an unusually roundabout fashion. In 1963, W.C. Heinz, one of the most respected journalists of the World War II era, wrote a novel called *The Surgeon* whose subject was a thoracic specialist. It drew the attention of H. Richard Hornberger, who wanted help writing about his experiences as a doctor during the Korean War. Under the pseudonym Richard Hooker, they wrote the 1968 novel *MASH*. When they asked Ring Lardner, Jr., to write a blurb for it, he passed it on to his former agent Ingo Preminger, who had a development deal at Twentieth Century-Fox. Preminger convinced Fox executives Richard Zanuck and David Brown to finance the film, with Lardner as writer.

Lardner, an Oscar-winning screenwriter (*Woman of the Year*, 1942), had spent a year in jail as one of the Hollywood Ten, and was just re-emerging from twenty years of being blacklisted. His new agent, George Litto, also represented Altman, which is how the director got an early draft of Lardner's script. Several other directors, including Sidney Lumet, Stanley Kubrick, George Roy Hill, and Bud Yorkin, turned the project down. Altman got the job almost by default.

The director feuded with Preminger from the start, in particular over casting. "There's a weakness in Altman," Preminger said later. "He loves unattractive people." The producer won over Altman with Sally Kellerman, Donald Sutherland, and Elliott Gould. Altman did manage to cast veterans of his earlier work, including Tom Skerritt, Michael Murphy, and Robert Duvall. Many cast members were making their feature debuts, such as former football star Fred Williamson and Bud Cort, soon to star in *Harold and Maude* (1971).

Once filming started, Altman insisted that his cinematographer use zoom lenses, hoping for both a documentary look and to catch actors unaware, before they started "acting." "The zoom was a great help when you're dealing with actors," he said in an interview. "No one was ever quite sure exactly what was happening." After arguing for a week, Altman replaced the Fox cinematographer with Harold Stine, who had worked with him at Warner Brothers.

MASH took place on a far larger scale than Altman had used before—with up to three hundred extras, an entire front-line hospital, and all the accompanying military hardware. To compensate for a potentially intimidating atmosphere, the director tried to establish a spirit of camaraderie by hosting parties, fostering an "us against them" atmosphere that not everyone appreciated. Sutherland, for one, said, "I never understood exactly what he wanted." Gould erupted furiously during one lunch, and, along with Sutherland, later tried to have Altman replaced.

Because of his shooting methods, Altman had a great deal of trouble editing the film. Danford Greene spent weeks editing the football game that makes up the end of the film, aware that Altman was consulting other editors about how to shape the rest of the material. It was screenwriter John T. Kelly, a friend of Altman's from his television days, who came up with one key for the film by writing the closing credits in the form of press notes for a movie release. Altman amplified this notion with a running commentary of announcements delivered over the hospital intercom. By simply cutting to a close-up of a loudspeaker, Altman could find his way in and out of scenes.

When they saw a rough cut, Zanuck and Brown wanted to re-edit the film to take out its nudity and gore. Preminger defended Altman's work, and preview screenings confirmed his opinion. *MASH* became one of Fox's most profitable films, outgrossing such big-budget blockbusters as *Tora! Tora! Tora!* (1970) and *Hello, Dolly!* (1969). It was the first war movie that echoed the country's

disenchantment with Vietnam, even if it did so by humiliating women, denigrating homosexuals, and mocking the sincerity and work ethic of individuals like Major Frank Burns (played by Robert Duvall). Altman's vision glorified the louche, the dissolute, the self-styled mavericks and iconoclasts, his leads modern-day equivalents to the Marx Brothers.

MASH's success led to a long-running television series, as well as several novels written by Hornberger and others. (The acronym stands for Mobile Army Surgical Hospital; the asterisks between the letters were a later addition.) Altman responded poorly to his new celebrity, complaining to Preminger that he deserved more money. A year after *MASH* was released, he told *New York Times* writer Aljean Harmetz that Lardner's script had been a "disaster," and that the director was responsible for "the basic concept, the philosophy, the style, the casting . . . plus all the jokes" in the film. Later, Altman amplified his comments, saying he "disliked" Lardner's script, calling it "hawkish" and a "rough outline."

According to McGilligan, almost all of the elements of the final film were in Lardner's script. Altman did add anti-clerical bits, as well as staging what Lardner called a "stag banquet" as Da Vinci's *The Last Supper* (an idea taken from Luis Buñuel's *Viridiana*, 1960). But the director's treatment of Lardner became untenable for Litto and Preminger. When Altman asked the producer for a share of the film's profits, it was easy to turn him down, especially since the director had just insulted the Fox studio in the press. The experience of making *MASH* was so disillusioning that Preminger produced only one more film.

Speaking after he appeared in *Nashville* (1975, a Registry title), actor Ned Beatty said, "If you took Bobby Duvall's performance out of *MASH*, you'd see a mess, a lot of behavior that is totally without sense." Altman's next film, *Brewster McCloud* (1970), was even more chaotic, both in front of and behind the cameras.

Hospital

OSTI, Inc., 1970. Sound, B&W, 1.33. 73 minutes.

Credits: Produced and directed by Frederick Wiseman. Photographed by William Brayne. Edited by Frederick Wiseman. Associate editor: Carter Stanton-Abbott. Sound mixer: Richard Vorisek. Camera assistant: David Martin. Assistant editor: Susan Primm. Production assistants: Robbin Mason, Margit Andersson. An OSTI Film. Copyright OSTI Inc. 1969. Production note: "*Hospital* was made at Metropolitan Hospital Center

in New York through the cooperation of the Department of Hospitals, administrators, staff and patients."

Additional Credits: Released February 2, 1970.

Awards: Emmy for Outstanding Achievement in News Documentary Programming—Individuals (Wiseman, director) and Outstanding Achievement in News Documentary Programming—Programs.

Available: Zipporah Films (*www.zipporah.com*).

After his first two documentaries, *Titicut Follies* (1967) and *High School* (1968), resulted in lawsuits, Frederick Wiseman began to make films under contract to WNET, at the time the public television outlet in New York City. One reason for this new arrangement was to ensure that his films would not fall victim to censorship for what he perceived to be political or personal reasons. The arrangement also freed Wiseman from some of the difficulties of securing financing for his work.

Wiseman did not change his approach to filmmaking, nor his interest in showing how institutions operated. However, he did change cinematographers, hiring William Brayne, who had worked on *Warrendale* (1967), a documentary directed by Allan King that received a theatrical release after it was banned from Canadian television. Brayne would go on to shoot eight films with Wiseman, helping solidify the filmmaker's style. The first of these films was *Law and Order* (1969), a look at the Kansas City police department. It won an Emmy for Outstanding Achievement in News Documentary Programming.

In interviews Wiseman sometimes expressed discomfort for the explicitly polemical stance he took in *Titicut Follies*. He has also defended the particular institutions he has chosen to portray. *High School*'s Northeast High School was considered one of the jewels of Philadelphia's public school system; the Kansas City police department didn't face the charges of racism and corruption found in other cities.

Metropolitan Hospital, the setting for *Hospital*, was and is part of the New York City hospital system. It is located in East Harlem in Manhattan (specifically, 1901 First Avenue, adjacent to the East River and the FDR Drive). Since 1875 it has also been affiliated with the New York Medical College, a private institution with about 1,700 students and 1,300 faculty members. The doctors depicted in *Hospital* were largely graduates of the New York Medical College, which meant that they should have been among the best qualified emergency room doctors in the city.

Although Wiseman was given free access to the hospital, most of his film takes place in and around the emergency rooms. As just about every medical television show and movie has found out, this is where the action is, where split-second decisions are made about patients who may have no case histories to help doctors make choices. For that reason alone, *Hospital* stands in contrast

to *Titicut Follies*, whose patients have often been trapped for years in a sort of medical limbo. *Hospital* is a bit different visually as well, with Brayne employing a freer camera style with more movement. And, as Wiseman noted, "I always think in terms of the relationship between one movie and another. And I'm always thinking about how one scene may parallel another, because the films are a natural frame of reference for me. I'm interested in a variety of points of view—the similarities and differences between different places, and the same or different ways of expressing the same values."

Wiseman and Brayne cannot resist showing some of the Grand Guignol aspects of a hospital, including autopsies, operations, and, in one class, a doctor slicing into a cadaver's brain held in his hand. The urban setting gives them more opportunities to shock viewers. Blood streams down the shirt of one emergency room visitor. Another has to be tied into a wheelchair. Patients lie unattended on gurneys in corridors, or wander around waiting rooms.

Wiseman is also a smart enough filmmaker to realize that he is not in a position to show or explain long-term illnesses, elective procedures, or many other day-to-day problems and procedures that make up the bulk of time spent by the hospital staff. Instead, the crux of the film is the conversations the doctors have about patients and their families. These can be moving or frightening: a daughter who tearfully admits that she doesn't know what medications her grievously ill mother is taking, an overdose patient who begs a doctor not to let him die.

The most painful conversations are those conducted over telephones. In one, an emergency room physician complains that a second hospital has been dumping its patients. A psychiatrist pleads with a government official to place a suicidal patient on welfare. A nurse tries to find authorization to keep a young abuse victim at the hospital overnight. Although everyone speaks in a civil tone, these are life-and-death negotiations with no clear resolutions. Tellingly for a Wiseman film, the "villains" are all off camera. No professional on screen is ever less than concerned and sympathetic.

Wiseman fashions his material into a story in the editing room. Here he adopted a more serious tone than he did in *High School*, with few of that film's editing jokes. Once facile touch has Wiseman cutting from a church service to traffic on the FDR Drive outside. The cut pulls us away from the activity within the hospital, as Wiseman intended, but is it also implicating us in our passive indifference to the misery just beyond our cars?

Critics at the time remarked on Wiseman's generous attitude toward the people in *Hospital*, as if in his earlier films he had set out to do hatchet jobs. Some complained that he wasn't being objective, but as he replied, "To me, it is so utterly obvious that this kind of filmmaking isn't objective, that there is always a process of selection taking place, that I don't feel I have to educate on that issue. It's not an issue that's related solely to documentary film. Anybody who's asked to write about something does so from his or her point of view."

The other question always asked of the filmmaker is how involved he gets with situations and subjects. Wiseman finds his scenes by first winning the trust of those he is filming. "I try to present myself very directly, very honestly. In the same way that I'm trying to size up the situation, to figure out what to shoot, the participants are making some kind of instinctive judgment as to whether they can trust me or not. There's a kind of a mutual sizing up that's going on." *Hospital* is one of the few films in which Wiseman remembers stepping out of his role as filmmaker, in this case to help a Hispanic automobile accident victim.

Hospital was broadcast on WNET on February 2, 1970, and won two Emmys that year. Seen today, what may be most astonishing about the film is how patiently and clearly it lays bare the workings of the health care system. *Hospital* doesn't try to solve the problems facing public health policy, but it does provide a context for discussing them.

By 2009, Wiseman had completed over thirty documentaries covering everything from New York's Central Park to the Panama Canal Zone to Belfast, Maine.

Patton

Twentieth Century-Fox, 1970. Sound, color, 2.20. 172 minutes. Rated M.
Cast: George C. Scott (General George S. Patton), Karl Malden (General Omar N. Bradley), Michael Bates (Field Marshal Sir Bernard Law Montgomery), Edward Binns (Maj. General Walter Bedell Smith), Lawrence Dobkin (Col. Gaston Bell), John Doucette (Maj. General Lucian K. Truscott), James Edwards (Sgt. William George Meeks), Frank Latimore (Lt. Col. Henry Davenport), Richard Muench (Col. Gen. Alfred Jodl), Morgan Paull (Capt. Richard N. Jenson), Siegfried Rauch (Capt. Oskar Steiger), Paul Stevens (Lt. Col. Charles R. Codman), Michael Strong (Brigadier General Hobart Carver), Karl Michael Vogler (Field Marshal Erwin Rommel), Stephen Young (Captain Chester B. Hansen), Abraxas Aaran (Willy), Peter Barkworth (Col. John Welkin), John Barrie (Air Vice-Marshal Sir Arthur Coningham), David Bauer (Lt. Gen. Harry Buford), Tim Considine (Soldier who gets slapped), Albert Dumortier (Moroccan minister), Gerald Flood (Air Chief Marshal Sir Arthur Tedder), Jack Gwillim (Gen. Sir Harold Alexander), David Healy (Clergyman), Bill Hickman (Patton's driver), Sandy Kevin (Correspondent), Cary Loftin (Bradley's driver), Alan MacNaughtan (British briefing officer), Lionel Murton (Third Army Chaplain), Clint Ritchie (Tank Captain), Douglas Wilmer (Maj. Gen. Francis de Guingand), Patrick J. Zurica (1st Lt. Alexander Stiller).
Credits: Directed by Franklin J. Schaffner. Produced by Frank McCarthy. Screen story and screenplay by Francis Ford Coppola and Edmund H. North. Based on factual material from *Patton: Ordeal and Triumph* by Ladislas Farago and *A Soldier's Story* by Omar N. Bradley. Senior military advisor: General of the Army Omar N. Bradley, USA. Directory of photography: Fred Koenekamp. Music: Jerry Goldsmith. Art direction: Urie McCleary, Gil Parrando. Set decoration: Antonio Mateos, Pierre-Louis Thevenet. Special photographic effects: L.B. Abbott, Art Cruickshank. Makeup supervision: Dan Striepeke. Makeup artist: Del Acevedo. Action coordinator: Joe Canutt. Film editor: Hugh Fowler. Unit production managers: Francisco Day, Eduardo G. Maroto, Tadeo Villalba. Assistant directors: Eli Dunn, Jose Lopez Rodero. Second unit cameramen: Clifford Stine, Cecilio Paniagua. Orchestration: Arthur Morton. Mechanical effects: Alex Weldon. Associate producer: Frank Caffey. Technical advisors: General Paul D. Harkins, USA, Ret., Colonel Glover S. Johns, USA, Ret. Second unit direction: Michael Moore. Sound supervision: James Corcoran. Sound, production: Don Bassman, Douglas Williams. Sound, rerecording: Murray Spivack, Ted Soderberg. Photographed in Dimension 150. Process consultants: Richard Vetter, Carl Williams. Color by De Luxe. Titles by Pacific Title. Westrex Recording System. A Twentieth Century-Fox presentation of a Frank McCarthy–Franklin J. Schaffner production.

Additional Credits: Filming dates: February 3 to August 1969. Opened in New York City on February 4, 1970. Re-rated PG.
Awards: Oscars for Best Picture, Director, Actor, Editing, Writing—Story and Screenplay Based on Factual Material or Material Not Previously Published or Produced, Sound, Art Direction–Set Direction.
Other Versions: *The Last Days of Patton* (1986), directed by Delbert Mann.
Available: Twentieth Century Fox Home Entertainment DVD (2006). UPC: 024543234692.

Ladislas Farago's biography of General George S. Patton, *Patton: Ordeal and Triumph*, was published in 1964. At the time, producer Frank McCarthy was working at Universal, after spending over a decade at Twentieth Century-Fox. When McCarthy returned to Fox in 1965, he pursued a film about Patton which would be based on the Farago book. Born in 1912 in Richmond, Virginia, McCarthy attended the Virginia Military Institute, and was an aide to General George C. Marshall during World War II. In that position, he had firsthand knowledge of Patton's strengths and weaknesses.

Several directors turned down the project, in part because McCarthy didn't have a workable script, but also because of Patton's reputation as a right-wing hawk. To solve the screenplay problem, McCarthy hired Francis Ford Coppola, most likely because Coppola worked with Gore Vidal on the script for *Is Paris Burning?*, a World War II movie released in 1966. Coppola's reaction to Patton after reading the biography was, "Wait a minute, this guy was obviously nuts." He began writing with the intent of showing both Patton's military genius and his psychological flaws, the only way he saw a film succeeding with broad audiences. He pulled incidents, stories, and quotes from his research sources and ordered them on cards.

Coppola decided that Patton's most important qualities were his training in history and literature, and his upbringing as a Southern gentleman. He wrote an opening monologue during which Patton talks directly to the movie audience, culled from a half dozen of his actual speeches. Coppola believes that this scene got him fired from the project, although at the time McCarthy told the press that he left to direct *You're a Big Boy Now* (1967). McCarthy replaced Coppola with Edmund North, a veteran writer whose work includes the Registry titles *In a Lonely Place* (1950) and *The Day the Earth Stood Still* (1951).

William Wyler was scheduled to direct *Patton*, but left because of script delays to make *Funny Girl* (1968). Franklin Schaffner was hired on the basis of the box-office success of his *Planet of the Apes* (1968), and because he was friends with McCarthy. By this point Fox had acquired rights to *A Soldier's Story* by General Omar N. Bradley, which made Bradley a technical advisor on the film and also eased potential criticism from the military. Bradley conducted McCarthy, Schaffner, and North on a tour of battle sites in Tunisia, Normandy, and Belgium; according to McCarthy, "His wife was a big help, too; she was a screen writer herself under the name of Kitty Buhler."

McCarthy, Schaffner, and North met with George C. Scott, whose technique and physical attributes made him a natural for Patton, in New York and later in Hollywood to revise the script. Once filming began on February 3, 1969, Scott continued to insist on changes to the screenplay. When these were rejected, the actor refused to work. While praising Scott to the press later, McCarthy admitted, "There is no denying that he can be a very difficult man. I will say this for him: he never got drunk except for cause."

When Scott went missing for a day, "Franklin always had something else to shoot," McCarthy continued. Schaffner was seduced by the enormity of his canvas, often staging conversations in extreme long shots to show off his locations and props. "He did it the hard way," McCarthy said. "There is not a single optical in the whole picture, except for the fade-in and fade-out at the beginning and end of each act. Frank didn't use a single miniature, blue-backing or process shot. Everything was life-size."

As the film's technical advisor, General Paul Harkins, Patton's deputy chief of staff, helped lay out the battles. Due to bad weather, production became an issue of logistics, of getting scenes on film rather than trying to finesse individual shots. Schaffner fought similar battles on *Planet of the Apes*, but here he had an additional problem. Despite North's efforts, the script was still a series of vignettes that failed to offer a coherent "take" on Patton. The film's massive battle scenes certainly looked expensive, but they lacked the focus and subtext of previous World War II blockbusters.

In North's defense, much of his work was deleted—some ninety minutes from the first rough cut. Schaffner and editor Hugh Fowler worked on the film for almost eight months, carving it down to roughly three hours. Even at that length, *Patton* was a surprise hit at the box office and with critics. *Variety* summed it up by saying, "It is 100% American, in every way: sometimes ennobling, sometimes disgusting, always vital."

Patton was an even greater success at the Oscars. Scott famously refused to accept his Best Actor award, comparing the ceremonies to a "meat contest." He reprised his role some fifteen years later for a television movie. Coppola, meanwhile, was surprised to discover much of his script made it into the final cut of *Patton*. He credits the screenwriting Oscar he shared with North for preventing him from being fired from *The Godfather* (1972). *Patton's* connections to Coppola's later work, in particular, *Apocalypse Now* (1979), are obvious.

King . . . A Filmed Record . . . Montgomery to Memphis

Commonwealth United, 1970. Sound, B&W, 1.33. 185 minutes.
Contributing Talents: Harry Belafonte, Ruby Dee, Ben Gazzara, Charlton Heston, James Earl Jones, Burt Lancaster, Sidney Lumet, Joseph L. Mankiewicz, Paul Newman, Anthony Quinn, Clarence Williams III, Joanne Woodward.

Credits: Conceived and produced by Ely Landau. Associate producer: Richard Kaplan. Editors: John Carter, Lora Hays. Assisted by Hank Greenberg, Steve Roberts, Jack Sholder. Continuity: Ely Landau. Music selected by Coleridge Taylor Perkinson. Sound editing: Filmsound, Bill Franz, Ross-Gaffney. Sound Mix: Recording Studios, Inc. Gary Leiman,

Joe Dalisera, Al Gramaglia. Research and production staff: John Anthony, Diane Asselin, David Boehm, Kathy Collins, Ronald Gold, Mitchell Grayson, Kermit Kahn, Joseph Liss. Music coordinated through Frank Music Corporation. Music rights were granted to the production by Ark Music Corporation; Moses Asch (Folkways Records); Joan Baez; Blue Note Records; Donald Byrd; ESP-Dish; Everest Records; Freedom Singers; Jasper Music Publishing Co.; Abbey Lincoln & Max Roach; Milna Publishing Company; NCA Strand Productions & Enterprises; Newport Folk Foundation; Nisandy Music; Odetta; Allan Ribbach; Ryerson Music; Nina Simone; Tradition Records; Vanguard Recording Society, Inc.; Verve/Forecast Records; Andy Williams. Literary rights granted to the production by Ralph Ellison; Dick Gregory; Robert Hayden; Langston Hughes Estate; Alfred A. Knopf, Inc.; October House, Inc.; Charles Scribner's Sons. Literary rights coordinated through Joan Daves.

Additional Credits: Directorial services: Joseph L. Mankiewicz, Sidney Lumet. Screened March 24, 1970.

Other Versions: *King* was edited to 104 minutes and released to the home market. Richard Kaplan later produced and directed *Legacy of a Dream* for the Martin Luther King Foundation.

Available: Two-disc special commemorative edition (2009): *http://afilmed record.com*. Also available from Richard Kaplan Productions (*http:// richardkaplanproductions.com/king*). Edited version from Fox/Lorber Associates, Inc.; Pacific Arts Video VHS (1988). Also available from The King Center, 449 Auburn Avenue NE, Atlanta, GA 30312.

Ely Landau was one of the first producers to try to combine theater and film with television. Born in 1920 in New York City, he served in the Air Force during World War II, then produced and directed television shows. In 1953 he helped found National Telefilm Associates, which at one time or another owned most of the Twentieth Century-Fox and Republic Pictures feature film libraries, as well as Paramount's short-subject library.

One of the television series Landau helped produce was *Play of the Week*, established to offer faithful interpretations of stage works. In 1962, Landau produced a film version of Eugene O'Neill's *Long Day's Journey into Night*, directed by Sidney Lumet. Landau's subsequent pictures, like *The Pawnbroker* (1964), marked him as an adventurous, socially responsible, and politically conscious producer who insisted on quality.

When Dr. Martin Luther King, Jr., was assassinated in Memphis, Tennessee, on April 4, 1968, he left behind a visual and aural legacy of records, tape recordings, photographs, and film. He was one of the first public figures whose entire career had been documented. An astute judge of media, he knew how to exploit his celebrity to further his message.

King's public work coincided with the transition from movie newsreels to television news broadcasts. As a result, he was filmed more on location than in the studio: behind lecterns and podiums; in the midst of demonstrations and peace marches; in front of and, memorably, inside jails. As he evolved from small-town minister to national spokesman, his sense of how to carry himself, how to project his voice, what expressions to use evolved as well. This documentary helps show King's growth into one of the towering figures in the civil rights movement; inadvertently, it also shows how he became a media icon.

In a way, King's work in and with the media provided a template for everyone who followed. King and his colleagues had to learn how to control the film or television frame. In the documentary's early clips, he is often a face in a crowd, not the center of focus. Even during his most famous speech, what is now referred to as "I Have a Dream," King is framed with irrelevant and at times distracting figures, including a policeman who adjusts a row of microphones and people in the background who are not always paying attention.

Later in his career, King was more often filmed from a slightly low angle looking up at his left side, a medium close-up with no distracting figures or patterns in the background. It is a set-up used by politicians to this day. At the same time, King knew the value of location footage. Reporters interview him while he is marching down highways or toward city halls, and as the cameras follow, often on trucks, the visuals build a sense of momentum that makes King's victories seem inevitable.

Originally Landau approached associate producer Richard Kaplan with an idea for a ten-minute film tribute to King. Kaplan had volunteered in the civil rights movement, and would work with Landau at the American Film Theater. He would go on to produce and direct many documentaries, and was one of the founders of the Documentary Center at Columbia University. The two producers and their editors John Carter and Lora Hays had only recordings and still photographs to work with for the early material. They supplement these with explanatory footage taken from newsreels and television, occasionally adding sound effects and switching the chronology of footage. By focusing on King, the filmmakers lose some sense of context. The Vietnam War is barely mentioned, while urban riots are seen as King reacted to them, not as events on their own. On the other hand, King is one of the crucial figures of the twentieth century, and a strong enough figure to make this documentary consistently engrossing.

King is seen taking a central role in the 1955 bus boycott in Montgomery, Alabama, enduring arrest and the bombing of his house while insisting on a strategy of nonviolence. He participates in the "Freedom Rides," trying to end interstate segregation. He is arrested in Birmingham, resulting in the "Letter from a Birmingham Jail." These are some of the most shameful and yet uplifting incidents in our country's history.

For the most part the film adopts King's restrained tone. Juxtaposing the reverend with Bull Connor, seen spouting racist doggerel, is about as pointed as the filmmakers will get. (The editors do insert a jarring and not completely effective eight-second montage of Ku Klux Klan members, burning crosses, and explosions early on.) The problem was to condense King's life without losing his message. This meant assembling and collating footage, rebuilding moments and scenes from a variety of sources and viewpoints. Kaplan noted that the first edit ran ten hours.

The reconstruction of King's "I Have a Dream" speech in Washington in 1963 is typical of their efforts. The eight-minute segment contains almost the entire speech, even though Landau and his staff were forced to rely on footage that was badly scratched. The full flowering of King's rhetoric can be appreciated best in the triumphant closing passages, and the film includes four reaction shots to allow for the fifteen seconds of applause that follows it. (The speech is also the centerpiece of *The March*, 1964, a Registry title.)

Before the speech, footage shows the arrival of celebrities at the rally. They were filmed because they helped prove the importance of the event to reporters and cameramen. In a similar strategy, Landau had directors Joseph L. Mankiewicz and Sidney Lumet film a dozen or so movie stars reciting poetry and prose on soundstages, inserting the footage at various stages into the documentary. Even at the time, critics considered their appearance a distraction. The *New York Times* complained that the film was "too long, exactly to the extent that it includes a number of cameo guest appearances by such stars as Paul Newman, Burt Lancaster, James Earl Jones and others who mostly look at the camera and very sincerely recite verse."

With stars, the film's total running time reached 185 minutes. Landau scheduled a one-night-only presentation of the film in which proceeds from the $5 admission charge would benefit the Martin Luther King, Jr. Special Fund. In New York City some fifty theaters were rented on March 24, 1970. *Time* magazine reported a few weeks later that the limited showing of *King* raised some $3.5 million. The film was also shown on a special television broadcast with limited commercial interruptions. When it was released on videotape, the celebrity interludes were removed, apart from that of Harry Belafonte, who appears after the opening credits.

The experience of making *King* helped persuade Ely Landau to form the American Film Theatre in 1972. In the next two years he produced fourteen filmed adaptations of plays ranging from *The Iceman Cometh* to *Rhinoceros*, with stars like Katharine Hepburn, Lee Marvin, and Zero Mostel. Landau's last credit was in 1985, eight years before his death.

James Earl Jones delivers a dramatic reading of "What Ever Happens to the Least" from Dick Gregory's autobiography prior to the "Selma" segment of *King*. *Courtesy of Richard Kaplan*

Woodstock

Warner Bros., 1970. Sound, color, 2.35. 223 minutes, rated R.

Featuring: Richie Havens; Joan Baez; The Who; Sha Na Na; Joe Cocker; Country Joe and the Fish; Arlo Guthrie; Crosby, Stills and Nash; Ten Years After; John Sebastian; Santana; Sly & the Family Stone; Canned Heat; Jefferson Airplane; Janis Joplin; Jimi Hendrix.

Credits: Directed by Michael Wadleigh. Produced by Bob Maurice. Editor and assistant director: T. [Thelma] Schoonmaker. Associate producer: Dale Bell. Photographed by Michael Wadleigh, David Myers, Richard Pearce, Don Lenzer, Al Wertheimer. Sound and music and assistant to the director: Larry Johnson. Music advisor, coordinator: Eric Blackstead. Sound engineer: Lee Osborne. Music mixer: Dan Wallin. Editor and assistant director: Martin Scorsese. Editors: Stan Warnow, Yeu-Bun Yee, Jere Huggins. Production managers: Sonya Polonsky, Lewis Teague. Location unit supervisor: John Binder. Location music engineers: Eddie Kramer, Lee Osborne. Dubbing supervisor: Graham Lee Mahin. Additional photography: Ed Lynch, Chuck Levey, Ted Churchill, Fred Underhill, Richard Chew, Bob Danneman, Stan Warnow. "Going Up the Country" sung by Canned Heat. The song "Woodstock" written by Joni Mitchell. Original 16mm processing and printing: J. & D. Labs, New York City. Titles by Charles Cirigliano. Color by Technicolor. A Wadleigh–Maurice, Ltd., production. A Warner Bros. presentation. A film by Michael Wadleigh.

Additional Credits: Title on screen: *Woodstock: 3 Days of Peace & Music.* Production dates: August 1969. Opened March 26, 1970.

Awards: Oscar for Best Documentary—Features.

Available: Warner Home Video DVD (1997). ISBN: 0-7907-2935-0. UPC: 0-85391-35492-5.

The Woodstock music festival was first planned as a benefit concert to help build a recording studio in Woodstock, New York. The four original promoters hoped for an audience of between 50,000 and 100,000. (The promoters were Michael Lang, who had worked on the Miami Pop Festival; Artie Kornfeld, an executive at Capitol Records; Joel Rosenman, a lawyer from Long Island; and John Roberts, an investor.) The idea gradually evolved into a music festival along the lines of the Monterey International Pop Music Festival, held in June 1967. The four promoters hoped their festival would be annual.

Forming Woodstock Ventures, they began searching for a site for the concert, settling at the last moment on a location near Bethel, NY. By the time they leased land from farmer Max Yasgur, they had already sold over a half-million dollars' worth of tickets. Woodstock, with its official slogan "Three Days of Peace and Music . . . An Aquarian Exposition" and official dove-and-guitar logo designed by Arnold Skolnick, was being promoted as a brand, a "happening," rather than a concert with individual groups. While the Woodstock Ventures principals could not have expected the over 400,000 people who eventually showed up at the concert site, they were fully aware of the financial potential in filming and recording the event. Eddie Kramer, an engineer for acts like The Beatles, The Rolling Stones, and Led Zeppelin, was one of the engineers hired to record the Woodstock performances.

Remembering the critical success of films like *Jazz on a Summer's Day* (1960), *Festival* (1967), and *Monterey Pop* (1968), Roberts and Rosenman made a deal with Wadleigh-Maurice Productions to film the concert. "Wadleigh" was Michael Wadleigh, born in 1941 in Akron, Ohio, and previously known as cinematographer "Michael Wadley" on *David Holzman's Diary* and *Who's That Knocking at My Door?* (both 1967). Wadleigh and producer Bob Maurice talked the Woodstock Ventures principles into allowing them to film the concert at their own expense, then try to sell the completed movie to a distributor. Woodstock Ventures would receive 50 percent of the producer's royalty (minus the distributor's cut), with Wadleigh-Maurice Productions receiving 30 percent of that amount. As the opening of the concert approached, Wadleigh and Maurice tried to renegotiate the deal, asking for $100,000 in return for giving up a share of the profits, but John Roberts refused.

A dozen or so cinematographers ended up working at the concert site (the finished film also used some television news footage). As the scope of the event became apparent, cameramen shifted their focus from the stage to the audience, interviewing numerous attendees and officials, as well as people from surrounding towns. By including footage of cooking and sanitation facilities, food supplies airlifted in by Army helicopters, and impromptu camping and swimming arrangements, the filmmakers could showcase the event itself as much as the musicians who performed there.

Woodstock became famous for being gigantic; the larger it grew, the prouder its participants got. Bad weather marred much of the proceedings, and traffic congestion disrupted the concert schedule even further. Several performers chose not to be included in the film, or were edited out of the final cut, including Creedence Clearwater Revival, Johnny Winter, the Grateful Dead, and the Incredible String Band. Other bands never made it to the concert: the Jeff Beck Group broke up just before Woodstock began.

By the time Wadleigh was ready to edit his footage, Woodstock had become a touchstone for a generation of hippies and hippie manqués. The director was sitting on a gold mine, and had the opportunity to make as large, as excessive a film as he wanted. Among the editors he hired were Thelma Schoonmaker and Martin Scorsese, whom he had met during the making of *Who's That Knocking at My Door?* (Both were credited as assistant directors as well.) They approached the material chronologically, from constructing the stage to the postconcert clean-up. They had a wide screen to play with, but also had to compensate for footage that was often sub par: underlit, out of focus, shaky. As a solution, they split the frame into multiple sections. That way they could offset "bad" footage with what in other documentaries would be cutaways: shots of audience members, roadies, weather, etc.

Splitting the frame could also be used for creative effects, such as freezing a shot or doubling or mirroring performers. They could edit each musical act differently in order to highlight or comment on the musicians' various styles, not just to compensate for inadequate or missing footage. (It also meant they could work with multiple sound sources. In the film's opening they use the sound of helicopters flying overhead in one shot to aid in the editing of interviews on the opposite side of the screen.) The earlier groups, shot in daylight with a limited number of cameras, did not benefit from this approach as much as the stars who performed later. By the time The Who and Sly and the Family Stone appear, the film makes full use of any and all editing effects.

Before *Woodstock* the film was released, The Rolling Stones had appeared at the Altamont Speedway Free Festival in California. The film of that concert, included in *Gimme Shelter* (directed by Albert and David Maysles and Charlotte Zwerin), provides a sobering counterpoint to *Woodstock*, and examines in greater detail the relationship between performer and audience. *Gimme Shelter* was released in December 1970; by that time *Woodstock*, the film and the record album, was a commercial phenomenon. Over the years Wadleigh continued to tinker with the film, until in 1994 he offered an expanded version with some forty additional minutes of footage. He also released a stand-alone version of Jimi Hendrix's performance, *Jimi Hendrix: Live at Woodstock* (1999).

Five Easy Pieces

Columbia, 1970. Sound, color, 1.85. 98 minutes. Rated R.

Cast: Jack Nicholson (Robert Eroica Dupea), Karen Black (Rayette Dipesto), Susan Anspach (Catherine Van Oost), Lois Smith (Partita Dupea), Ralph Waite (Carl Fidelio Dupea), Billy "Green" Bush (Elton), Irene Dailey (Samia Glavia), Toni Basil (Terry Grouse), Lorna Thayer (Waitress), Richard Stahl (Recording engineer), Helen Kallianiotes (Palm Apodaca), William Challee (Nicholas Dupea), John Ryan (Spicer), Fannie Flagg (Stoney), Marlena MacGuire (Twinky), Sally Ann Struthers (Betty).

Credits: Directed by Bob Rafelson. Screen play by Adrien Joyce [Carole Eastman]. Story by Bob Rafelson and Adrien Joyce. Produced by Bob Rafelson, Richard Wechsler. Executive producer: Bert Schneider. Director of photography: Laszlo Kovacs. Interior designer: Toby Rafelson. Associate producer: Harold Schneider. Film editors: Christopher Holmes, Gerald Shepard. Sound effects: Edit-Rite, Inc. Assistant editors: Pete Denenberg, Harold Hazen. Re-recording: Producer's Sound Service, Inc. Sound: Audio Tran. Color processing: MGM Laboratories. Sound mixer: Charles Knight. Script supervisor: Terry Terrill. Assistant director: Sheldon Schrager. Production coordinator: Marilyn Schlossberg. Casting: Fred Roos. Wardrobe: Bucky Rous. BBS Productions. Songs Performed by Tammy Wynette: "Stand by Your Man," by Billy Sherrill and Tammy Wynette; "D-I-V-O-R-C-E," B. Braddock, C. Putnam; "Don't Touch Me," Hank Cochran; "When There's a Fire in Your Heart," Merle Kilgore, S. Williams. Piano Performed by Pearl Kaufman: Fantasy in F Minor, Op. 49, Chopin; Chromatic Fantasy & Fugue, Bach; Concerto in E-Flat Major, K. 271, Mozart; Prelude in E Minor, Op. 28, Chopin; Fantasy in D Minor, K. 397, Mozart.

Additional Credits: Production dates: November 10, 1969 to January 3, 1970. Opened in New York City on September 11, 1970.

Available: Columbia TriStar Home Video DVD (1999). ISBN: 0-7678-2805-4. UPC: 0-43396-09659-2.

The success of *Easy Rider* (1969) vindicated the approach that Bert Schneider and Bob Rafelson were taking toward moviemaking. It also gave BBS the money to pursue any project the producers wanted. (Raybert, the original company, evolved into BBS with the addition of Steve Blauner.) Schneider okayed a picture that Rafelson wanted to direct, and in order to secure Jack Nicholson in the lead role, promised that the actor could direct an adaptation of Jeremy Larner's novel *Drive, He Said*.

Nicholson was responsible for pairing Rafelson with screenwriter Carole Eastman, who used the pseudonym "Adrien Joyce." She had worked on the screenplay of *The Shooting* (1967), one of two low-budget Westerns the actor had filmed back-to-back under director Monte Hellman. Rafelson wanted the story to be about a failed concert pianist, a sort of prodigy turned prodigal son, who returns home when his father is struck by illness. Eastman's script contained most of what ended up in the film, although Rafelson did make some changes, notably to the ending. The screenwriter was reputedly furious when Rafelson took a "story by" credit.

From Rafelson's bare-bones premise, Eastman fashioned a plotline that ranged from the oil fields of Bakersfield, California, to the rain-drenched islands of Puget Sound, from trailer park trash and country-and-western music to the self-important salons of the intelligentsia. Guiding moviegoers through this landscape was Nicholson's Bobby Dupea, who staves off his existential angst in a series of sexual conquests. According to screenwriter Rober Towne, Eastman may have based Dupea on her brother Charlie, who was "very particular, very quirky, very much like his sister." Eastman added political allusions (the script originally ended with a Chappaquiddick-like car accident), but her story operated primarily on psychological terms: What drove Bobby Dupea? What was the source of his unhappiness?

Five Easy Pieces doesn't try to answer these questions. Instead, it offers situations and characters for viewers to decipher. Eastman invented a gallery of fascinating women, including Bobby's adoring and love-starved sister Partita (played by Lois Smith), the coldly manipulative Catherine Van Oost (Susan Anspach), and Rayette (Karen Black), a coffee shop waitress who dreams of a singing career. Eastman's men, on the other hand, were all crippled—either physically, or, in Bobby's case, emotionally. "I don't have any inner feelings," he tells his brother's mistress, and while he knows he's lying, it's still something he wants to believe.

Equally important to the story were its settings. The young filmgoers who were BBS's target audience had little patience for redneck society, and even less for the silent majority they probably believed made up most of the upper class. But *Five Easy Pieces*, while still critical, found worth and even beauty in both cultures. It was not mocking Tammy Wynette any more than it mocked Chopin; anyway, its real concern was why Bobby Dupea could not connect to either world.

From the start, Rafelson intended to bring a European sensibility to the film, incorporating the ideas behind the French New Wave without losing his own point of view, using a style that is modest, even self-deprecating. A traffic jam early in the film evokes Jean-Luc Godard's *Week End* (1967), but in style and tone *Five Easy Pieces* is closer to the work of François Truffaut or Eric Rohmer. It was also a much better-made movie than *Easy Rider*, especially in the often handheld camerawork by Laszlo Kovacs. The film's imagery is perceptive, insightful, locating beauty in an oil derrick as well as a ferry plowing across choppy, gray water. Kovacs rarely calls attention to his work. His most flamboyant shot, a 360-degree pan as Dupea plays one of the "five easy pieces" on the piano, reveals more about Dupea's background than about the cinematographer's technical prowess.

Rafelson filmed roughly in sequence, starting in Bakersfield on November 10, 1969, and winding up in British Columbia on January 3, 1970. He spent some six months editing the material, embellishing his growing reputation as a perfectionist. When the film opened in September 1970, it was seen as a corrective to both the superficial rebellion of *Easy Rider* and the big-budget, creatively moribund "A" movies still being made by the studios. At the time, filmgoers embraced Nicholson's character, especially during his encounter with an antagonistic waitress in a coffee shop. Few were as critical about Dupea as he was about himself. The film may try to blame his self-destructive tendencies a little too easily on his dysfunctional family, but Rafelson and his colleagues do capture that family vividly and convincingly.

Nicholson worked with Rafelson in *The King of Marvin Gardens* (1972) and, years later, in *Blood and Wine* (1996). The Dupea role echoed throughout his career, perhaps most tellingly in *The Passenger* (1975). The actor's next Registry film is *Chinatown* (1974).

Multiple SIDosis

Sid Laverents, 1970. Sound, color, 1.37. 9 minutes.
Cast: Sid Laverents, Adelaide Laverents.
Credits: Written, photographed, edited, and directed by Sid Laverents. Assistant camera operators: Adelaide Laverents, Lin and Louise Brown. Song "Nola" by Felix Arndt.
Available: *Multiple SIDosis* is deeded to the UCLA Film & Television Archive, which plans a wider release in the future.

Former vaudevillian Sid Laverents made *Multiple SIDosis* while a member of the San Diego Amateur Film Club. First screened for the club in 1970, the film developed an underground reputation as a home movie tour de force. In recent years it has been championed by a new generation of musicians and filmmakers.

Born in 1908, Laverents made a name for himself in vaudeville as a one-man band, following a tradition that can be traced back to the fourteenth century. While still a teenager, he was heading for New York City and possible fame with his first wife Sue when they were trapped in a flood. According to *The Sid Saga*, an ongoing autobiographical film started in 1985, after the breakup of his marriage he turned to a succession of jobs: sign painter, salesman, metal worker. Drafted, he spent much of the 1940s in Calcutta. In 1949, after divorcing his second wife, he met and married Adelaide, settled in California, and worked as an airplane engineer.

In 1959, Laverents bought a Bolex 16mm camera and used it to film a vacation in Canada, screening the footage for the San Diego Amateur Film Club. Founded in 1949, the club was part of a groundswell of amateur filmmaking that began in the 1920s and reached its peak during the Depression; at that time some 250 clubs numbered perhaps 250,000 members. In addition to his personal films, Laverents also made industrial and promotional films, as well as three titles in a series he called "Wonders That Surround Us." *Snails* (1966) was purchased by the California Department of Education for use in classrooms; biographer Jake Austen called it "one of Sid's weirdest and best films."

Two years earlier, Laverents made *The One-Man Band*, which re-created his vaudeville act. His first film to use synchronized sound, it incorporated an elaborate credit sequence, one of the trademarks of his later works. In it he performed "St. Louis Blues," "Tiger Rag," and "The Washington and Lee Swing" on drums, kazoos, slide whistles, cymbals, a bike horn, and a banjo.

The One-Man Band was a warm-up for *Multiple SIDosis*, a dizzying display of double-tracking inspired in part by the 1950s recordings of Les Paul and Mary Ford. The film opens on Christmas, as Laverents unwraps a two-track reel-to-reel tape recorder given to him by his wife. Like the best magicians, Laverents lays out all the details of the trick he is about to perform for viewers. Seated before a microphone in his study, he turns on a metronome and begins to record the tracks of a song.

The tune Laverents chose was the infectious "Nola," written in 1916 by Felix Arndt and later the theme song for Victor Lopez's orchestra. It was recorded many times, including a version by whistler Elmo Tanner, and lyrics were added later by Sunny Skylar. Laverents' version allowed him to incorporate many of his one-man band instruments.

Laverents added a cinematic twist to his musical performance, one that mirrored his use of multitrack recording. Through multiple exposures, he filmed himself playing a banjo, ukulele, bottles, jaw harp—portraying up to eleven musicians at once, all in time with a metronome clicking in the upper left corner of the frame. According to reporter Matt Haber, it took four years to complete the film. In an interview, Laverents said that it took him three to four months to record each track. For a studio film, the multiple exposures would have been accomplished with an optical printer, but Laverents did them all in camera, using a technique similar to what Buster Keaton employed when filming *The Play House* in 1921.

While solving the technical issues clearly fascinated Laverents, the film itself was more than a question of timing problems. Laverents went to the trouble to invent different characters for each musician, changing his hair, clothes, and at one point donning Mickey Mouse ears. This attention to detail helps make *Multiple SIDosis* one of the most ingratiating works on the Registry.

While writing a dissertation on amateur film clubs in California, Melinda Stone came across the San Diego Amateur Film Club and the movies by Laverents. She was so impressed that "I just started hounding people, calling the Smithsonian, calling the Getty, just anybody I knew who had an interest in folk-film culture." Invited to a summit meeting of archivists, she showed *Multiple SIDosis* to Library of Congress official Pat Loughney. As she told the *LA Weekly*, "Within eight months it was on the Registry."

Film preservationist Ross Lipman oversaw the restoration of *Multiple SIDosis*, and its blowup to 35mm. On August 7, 2008, Lipman helped arrange a centennial birthday party for Laverents at the James Bridges Theater at UCLA. Screened at the party were both *Multiple SIDosis* and *The Sid Saga*. Laverents succumbed to pneumonia in May 2009.

Serene Velocity

Frame enlargements from *Serene Velocity*. *Courtesy of Ernie Gehr*

Ernie Gehr, 1970. Color, silent, 1.33. 23 minutes at 16 fps; 15 minutes at 24 fps.

Credits: Filmmaker: Ernie Gehr.

Available: Canyon Cinema (*www.canyoncinema.com*).

The best way to screen *Serene Velocity* is not to know anything about it beforehand. Facts lessen the film's otherworldly pull, and could cause viewers to look for what they might not otherwise notice. There will be plenty of time after the film has ended to search for the "tricks" behind it. As critic Gilberto Perez wrote, "Part of the pleasure, part of the mystery, of watching an Ernie Gehr film is trying to figure out how he does it."

Hypnotic is an adjective critics often use to describe Gehr's work. Born in 1943, he was raised in Milwaukee after his parents fled Nazism in Germany. He told interviewers that after serving in the Army, he "stumbled across" a Stan Brakhage film being screened in a makeshift theater in New York City. That night inspired him to become a filmmaker.

Gehr completed a half-dozen short films before *Serene Velocity*. P. Adams Sitney gives this description for *Reverberation* (1969): "By refilming these shots through an optical printer he distended the time of human action so that the integrity of the couple's gestures dissolves in the prolonged gaps between the frames of the original shots."

On some levels *Serene Velocity* is even more theoretically rigid. The film was shot in one night in the corridor of a classroom building at the State University of New York at Binghamton. With the camera fixed on a tripod and pointing down the hallway, Gehr composed a frame in which the lines marking the ceiling and floor extended to a vanishing point in the center of the frame, forming an "X." The other elements in the shot include ceiling lights and emergency exit signs which are also reflected on the waxed tile floor; doorways along the walls of the corridor; and a black space in the center of the frame that resolves as the film progresses.

Serene Velocity is composed of still shots, each four frames, or a quarter of a second, long. (Gehr intended the film to be projected at the silent speed of sixteen frames per second, but as he wrote, "At this point in time 16mm silent speed projectors run at 18 fps, that is the speed at which the film is projected most of the time, and I accept that.") "There might be a mistake here and there," he told an interviewer in 1980, "but generally it's four frames. It's still to still to still." Gehr changes the exposure on a cyclical pattern that repeats every four frames. And after every four frames, he adjusts the focal length of the lens, minutely at first (50mm to 55mm and back), then gradually expanding the difference between lens lengths. At first the film pulses and hums; by the end, it throbs almost violently.

As Gehr wrote in program notes introducing the film, "In *Serene Velocity* the optical and psychological factors—persistence of vision/reciprocal tension—that allow for the movie illusion of motion and space became the initial subject of the film itself." That description cannot do justice to the experience of actually watching the film. Writing in *The Yale Review*, Gilberto Perez pointed out that "five movies are going on at once in *Serene Velocity*: we can watch the fluorescent lights and red exit signs on the ceiling, or watch the reflections on the floor, or watch either of the two walls and the new objects—doors, water fountains, hanging ashtrays—coming into view from the sides as the focal length changes (coming into view only to be abruptly yanked back and come in again the next

moment), or we can focus on the center, the sets of double doors halfway down the corridor and all the way at the far end."

Again, explanations, whether poetic or technical, cannot convey the visual stimulation the movie generates. How the intermittent black doorways on the corridor walls make the sides of the frame bulge and retract, how reflections blur into stripes, how the film seems to mutate from a photograph to a loop of cascading shapes, how the coming dawn solves the mystery at the center of the frame. As critic Scott MacDonald pointed out, Gehr managed to transform one of the dullest locations of contemporary life into a place of magic.

Gehr's later films continued his interest in structuralism. *Still* (1969–71) compiles double exposures taken through a window onto Lexington Avenue in New York City. *Signal—Germany on the Air* (1982–85) used footage from a camera he stationed at a traffic intersection in Berlin. *Side/Walk/Shuttle* (1991) was filmed in an outdoor elevator at the Fairmont Hotel on Nob Hill in San Francisco. *Passage* (2003) intercut before-and-after shots of Berlin's S-Bahn to comment on the fall of the Berlin Wall. Gehr remains an adventurous, challenging artist, but he is also one of the more accessible and enjoyable of experimental filmmakers.

Shaft

MGM, 1971. Sound, color, 1.85. 100 minutes. Rated R.
Cast: Richard Roundtree (John Shaft), Moses Gunn (Bumpy Jonas), Charles Cioffi (Vic Androzzi), Christopher St. John (Ben Buford), Gwenn Mitchell (Ellie Moore), Lawrence Pressman (Tom Hannon), Victor Arnold (Charlie), Sherri Brewer (Marcy), Rex Robbins (Rollie), Camille Yarbrough (Dina Greene), Margaret Warncke (Linda), Joseph Leon (Byron Leibowitz), Arnold Johnson (Cul), Dominic Barto (Patsy), George Strus (Carmen), Edmund Hashim (Lee), Drew Bundini Brown (Willy), Tommy Lane (Leroy), Al Kirk (Sims), Shimen Ruskin (Dr. Sam), Antonio Fargas (Bunky), Gertrude Jeannette (Old lady), Lee Steele (Blind vendor), Damu King (Mal), Donny Burks (Remmy), Tony King (Davies), Benjamin R. Rixson (Bey Newfield), Ricardo Brown (Tully), Alan Weeks (Gus), Glenn Johnson (Char), Dennis Tate (Dotts), Adam Wade (Brother #1), James Hainesworth (Brother #2), Clee Burtonya (Sonny), Ed Bernard (Peerce), Ed Barth (Tony), Joe Pronto (Dom), Robin Nolan (Waitress), Ron Tannas (Billy), Betty Bresler (Mrs. Androzzi), Gonzalo Madurga (Counterman), Paul Nevens (Elevator man), Jon Richards (Elevator starter).
Credits: Directed by Gordon Parks. Screenplay by Ernest Tidyman and John D.F. Black. Based on the novel by Ernest Tidyman. Produced by Joel Freeman. Associate producer: David Golden. Director of photography: Urs Furrer. Art director: Emanuel Gerard. Unit production manager: Steven Skloot. Assistant director: Ted Zachary. Film editor: Hugh A. Robertson. Sound: Lee Bost, Hal Watkins. Costume designer: Joe Aulisi. Set decoration: Robert Drumheller. Casting: Judith Lamb. Make-up by Martin Bell. Technical assistant to composer: Tom McIntosh. Metrocolor. Music by Isaac Hayes. Rhythm by The Bar-Kays and Movement. A Metro-Goldwyn-Mayer presentation of a Stirling Silliphant/Roger Lewis production.

Additional Cast: Gordon Parks (Harlem resident).
Additional Credits: Production dates: January 18 to March 12, 1971. Premiered in Los Angeles on June 25, 1971.
Awards: Oscar for Best Music—Song ("Theme from *Shaft*").
Other Versions: Sequels *Shaft's Big Score!* (1972), *Shaft in Africa* (1973). Roundtree starred as John Shaft in seven made-for-TV movies broadcast on CBS in 1973 and 1974. In 2000, Samuel L. Jackson starred in an updated version of *Shaft*.
Available: Warner Home Video DVD (2000). ISBN: 0-7907-4375-2. UPC: 012569505124.

In his autobiography *Voices in a Mirror*, Gordon Parks explained that the critical praise for *The Learning Tree* (1969, a Registry title) won him his second feature assignment, *Shaft*, at MGM. "Frankly, I didn't hold great expectations for its success, but it offered me a chance to expand my knowledge of directing," he wrote years later, although at the time he was more enthusiastic about the opportunity to make what amounted to a black version of *The French Connection* (1971, a Registry title).

Like *The French Connection*, *Shaft* had a screenplay by Ernest Tidyman. It was also the first of seven novels the former *New York Times* editor wrote about John Shaft, an African-American private eye working in Manhattan. Parks credited John D.F. Black for the final shooting script, and acknowledged that actor Richard Roundtree contributed to how the Shaft character would be portrayed. Roundtree was a native of New Rochelle, NY, who attended Southern Illinois University on a football scholarship. He was a model and clothes salesman in New York City while studying acting with the Negro Ensemble Company.

MGM set up numerous obstacles for Gordon and producer Joel Freeman. The studio wanted the production moved from New York City to Los Angeles; Parks had to fly to a meeting with studio heads to persuade them that he could film in Manhattan and stay under budget. Freeman wanted Roundtree to shave off his moustache—"A moustache on a black leading man was just *too* macho" was how Parks put it—but the director and actor prevailed. Parks also succeeded in doubling the previous number of blacks working on his crew to a dozen or so.

Parks and cinematographer Urs Furrer exult in their New York City locations, giving *Shaft* a gritty, urban feel that would be copied in a series of black-oriented action films. The movie captures a Times Square that has long since vanished, one that Parks knew well from his work on *Life* magazine. It was a world of grindhouse movies, hot dog stands, and blind newsies, dirtier and more desperate than *Sweet Smell of Success* (1957), but with the same insider passwords and shabby offices.

This was the director's chance to play with private eye conventions developed over three or four decades of filmmaking, and to pulp fans much of *Shaft* will be as comfortable as a B-movie from the 1940s. With corrupt cops, a client hiding information, confrontations plagued by double-crosses, and frequent chases and beatings, the plot adheres to the tried-and-true. When Parks chooses to make a racial point, it is usually a subtle one—the way a cab driver refuses to pick up Shaft, for example. For the most part, the film deals with race by ignoring it. When an Italian hood uses the "n" word for the first time, over an hour into the film, it comes as a shock.

Parks and Roundtree were still proud of the opportunity to place a black man within a previously whites-only role; this pride may account for the film's occasionally slow pace and digressions. *Shaft* doesn't have the focus and clarity of *The Maltese Falcon* (1941); instead, it's more like an exercise in style along the lines of Howard Hawks' *The Big Sleep* (1946). Adding immeasurably to that style is the score by Isaac Hayes. A former session musician and songwriter at Stax Records, he had become the label's most important performer after the release of his *Hot Buttered Soul* album in 1969. Hayes had auditioned for the part of Shaft, and his title song was crucial in establishing Shaft's character.

The "Theme from *Shaft*" would go on to win an Academy Award, the first awarded to a black composer. By that time *Shaft* was an enormous box-office success, prompting two sequels and enough imitators to help coin the term "blaxploitation." Parks directed *Shaft's Big Score* (1972), but dissociated himself from *Shaft in Africa* (1973), worried that he would be typecast as a blaxploitation director. Instead, he made *The Super Cops* (1974), a fast-paced action film about white policemen in a black neighborhood of Brooklyn. Parks' disputes with Paramount over the distribution of *Leadbelly* (1976), a biography of the blues musician, forced him to essentially withdraw from the film industry.

Roundtree found himself typecast as well. Trying to avoid action films, he worked in television, developing a career as a character actor. He also suffered a serious bout with breast cancer, and has become a spokesman for detection and prevention of the disease. Both Parks and Roundtree had roles in the 2000 feature film update of *Shaft*.

The Last Picture Show

Columbia, 1971. Sound, B&W, 1.85. 126 minutes. Rated R.
Cast: Timothy Bottoms (Sonny Crawford), Jeff Bridges (Duane Jackson), Cybill Shepherd (Jacy Farrow), Ben Johnson (Sam the Lion), Cloris Leachman (Ruth Popper), Ellen Burstyn (Lois Farrow), Eileen Brennan (Genevieve), Clu Gulager (Abilene), Sam Bottoms (Billy), Sharon Taggart (Charlene Duggs), Randy Quaid (Lester Marlow), Joe Heathcock (The sheriff), Bill Thurman (Coach Popper), Barc Doyle (Joe Bob Blanton), Jessie Lee Fulton (Miss Mosey), Gary Brockette (Bobby Sheen), Helena Humann (Jimmie Sue), Loyd Catlett (Leroy), Robert Glenn (Gene Farrow), John Hillerman (Teacher), Janice O'Malley (Mrs. Clarg), Floyd Mahaney (Oklahoma patrolman), Kimberly Hyde (Annie Annie Martin), Noble Willingham (Chester), Marjorie Jay (Winnie Snips), Joye Hash (Mrs. Jackson), Pamela Keller (Jackie Lee French), Gordon Hurst (Monroe), Mike Hosford (Johnny), Faye Jordon (Nurse),

Ben Johnson won a Best Supporting Actor Oscar as Sam the Lion in *The Last Picture Show*.

Charles Seybert (Andy Fanner), Grover Lewis (Mr. Crawford), Rebecca Ulrick (Marlene), Merrill Shepherd (Agnes), Buddy Wood (Bud), Kenny Wood (Ken), Leon Brown (Cowboy in café), Bobby McGriff (Truck driver), Jack Mueller (Oil pumper), Robert Arnold (Brother Blanton), Frank Marshall (Tommy Logan), Tom Martin (Larry), Otis Elmore (1st mechanic), Charles Salmon (Roughneck driver), George Gaulden (Cowboy), Will Morris Hannis (Gas station man), The Leon Miller Band.

Credits: Directed by Peter Bogdanovich. Screenplay by Larry McMurtry and Peter Bogdanovich. Based on the novel by Larry McMurtry. Executive producer: Bert Schneider. Produced by Stephen J. Friedman. Design: Polly Platt. Director of photography: Robert Surtees. Associate producer: Harold Schneider. Art director: Walter Scott Herndon. Editor: Donn Cambern. Unit production manager: Don Guest. Assistant director: Robert Rubin. Design assistant: Vincent Cresciman. Casting: Ross Brown. Production coordinator: Marilyn LaSalandra. Assistant to the director: Gary Chason. Location manager: Frank Marshall. 2nd assistant director: William Morrison. Script supervisor: Marshall Schlom. Mixer: Tom Overton. Production assistant: Mae Woods. Wardrobe: Mickey Sherrard, Nancy McArdle. Sound effects: Edit-Rite, Inc. Re-recording: Producers Sound Service, Inc. A BBS production.

Additional Credits: Originally 118 minutes. Opened in New York City on October 3, 1971, New York City.

Awards: Oscars for Best Supporting Actor (Johnson), Supporting Actress (Leachman).

Other Versions: Sequel: *Texasville* (1990).

Available: Columbia TriStar Home Video DVD (1999): ISBN 0-7678-2790-2. UPC: 0-43396-50429-5.

One of the most technically assured films of the 1970s, *The Last Picture Show* follows the lives of the inhabitants of the fictional small town of Anarene, Texas, in the late 1950s. Expanding from a coming-of-age story about two high school seniors, the film encompasses a cross-section of society, from rich to poor, old to young, hopeful to despairing. With meticulous black-and-white cinematography, an influential country-and-western-tinged soundtrack, and uniformly excellent ensemble acting, *The Last Picture Show* is both an elegy for the past and a warning for the future. Apart from the occasional self-conscious allusion to John Ford or Howard Hawks, and some overripe dialogue, it is one of the sparest and least dated works of the decade.

A film programmer at a New York movie theater and occasional critic and reviewer, Peter Bogdanovich championed the careers of Hollywood's Golden Age directors during the early 1960s. He and his wife Polly Platt, a production designer, moved to Los Angeles in 1964 to break into the industry. He was assistant director on *The Wild Angels* (1966), a Roger Corman motorcycle flick, then produced, wrote and directed *Targets* (1968), a tawdry, low-budget thriller that featured a desiccated Boris Karloff in one of his final roles. Bert Schneider, who with Bob Rafelson and Steve Blauner ran the BBS production company, was impressed enough by *Targets* to offer to back whatever project Bogdanovich wanted. (BBS was awash in money after the success of 1969's *Easy Rider*.)

Actor Sal Mineo had given Platt Larry McMurtry's third novel, called *The Last Picture Show*. It was not a commercial success: four years after it was published, it had sold only 1,500 copies. Still, Schneider gave Bogdanovich a million-dollar budget and an eight-week shooting schedule. He also agreed to let McMurtry work on the screenplay. As McMurtry wrote in *Film Flam*, "It was immediately clear to them that I knew nothing about writing screenplays, and just as immediately clear to me that they knew nothing about Texas." McMurtry thought his novel was "a flatly written book," and regretted that at the time he hadn't concentrated more on the novel's older characters. But he was impressed with Bogdanovich's commitment to the material. "Something like thirty percent of the script of *The Last Picture Show* had to be altered once production started, because the scenes were playing longer than anyone had expected them to." Among the changes: a class trip to San Francisco was scrapped as too expensive, and a comic basketball game was dropped for a more introspective scene about Joe Bob, the preacher's son.

Bogdanovich saw model Cybill Shepherd on the cover of *Glamour*, and over the objections of his producers cast her in a leading role. They began an affair during the shoot that perhaps unconsciously mirrored part of the film's plot. As he later told journalist Peter Biskind, "It was one of those times when life just takes over, and you don't really have control." Bogdanovich ended up divorcing Platt, and although Shepherd starred in three more of his movies, their affair also ended. Biskind details the soap opera antics behind the shoot at length in *Easy Riders, Raging Bulls*.

In interviews, Bogdanovich said that director John Ford urged Ben Johnson, a stalwart presence in many Westerns of the 1950s, to accept the part that ultimately won him a supporting Oscar. In its gravitas and depth of experience, Johnson's performance places the other roles and the rest of the story in perspective. Cloris Leachman does much the same as Ruth Popper. She had worked in films for some fifteen years (she can be seen in the opening credits of 1955's *Kiss Me Deadly*), but this was her breakthrough performance, winning her a supporting actress Oscar. Both Jeff Bridges and Ellen Burstyn received nominations as well.

While the actors were outstanding, they were also showcased with unusual care and precision by Bogdanovich. The director's affection for classic cinema styles is obvious throughout the film, but *The Last Picture Show* is more notable for his understatement. At a time when popular media was dominated by counterculture music and movies, Bogdanovich was offering a bracing, sympathetic look at the people who are left behind. As McMurtry wrote, it was "a movie about living-in-spite-of-or-in-the-teeth-of-defeat, a superb thing for any work of art to try to be about." The author gave this explanation for the approach both he and Bogdanovich took: "Narrative is not, finally, memorable; one forgets stories and even outcomes and remembers moments, just as in life one forgets years, even decades, and remembers—moments."

Moments in *The Last Picture Show* achieve the depth and artistry of the films Bogdanovich loved growing up as a child. They also anchor a world lost to time, one many were not sorry to see go. McMurtry provided the characters and settings, but Bogdanovich captured the loneliness and discontent lurking beneath those bleak, dusty skies.

The Last Picture Show premiered at the New York Film Festival in 1971 (along with another Bogdanovich film, the documentary *Directed by John Ford*), and went on to garner eight Academy Award nominations. Apart from *Paper Moon* (1973) and *Mask* (1985), Bogdanovich never regained his box-office touch. McMurtry, on the other hand, has had a strong impact on popular culture. Best-selling novels like *Terms of Endearment* and *Lonesome Dove* became hit movies and miniseries. He also wrote two sequels to *The Last Picture Show*: *Texasville* and *Duane's Depressed*. Bogdanovich directed a warm and accomplished adaptation of *Texasville* in 1990, assembling much of the original cast.

The French Connection

Twentieth Century-Fox, 1971. Sound, color, 1.85. 104 minutes. Rated R.

Cast: Gene Hackman (Jimmy Doyle), Fernando Rey (Alain Charnier), Roy Scheider (Buddy Russo), Tony Lo Bianco (Sal Boca), Marcel Bozzuffi (Pierre Nicoli), Frederic De Pasquale (Devereaux), Bill Hickman (Mulderig), Ann Rebbot (Marie Charnier), Harold Gary ([Joel] Weinstock), Arlene Farber (Angie Boca), Eddie Egan (Simonson), Andre Ernotte (La Valle), Sonny Grosso (Klein), Benny Marino (Lou Boca), Pat McDermott (Chemist), Alan Weeks (Pusher), Al Fann (Informant), Irving Abrahams (Police mechanic), Randy Jurgensen (Police sergeant), William Coke (Motorman), The Three Degrees.

Credits: Directed by William Friedkin. Screenplay by Ernest Tidyman. Based on the book by Robin Moore. Produced by Philip D'Antoni. Executive producer: G. David Schine. Music composed and conducted by Don Ellis. Director of photography: Owen Roizman. Film editor: Jerry Greenberg. Associate producer: Kenneth Utt. Art director: Ben Kazaskow. Set decorator: Ed Garzero. Sound: Chris Newman, Theodore Soderberg. Technical consultants: Eddie Egan, Sonny Grosso. Unit production manager: Paul Ganapoler. Assistant directors: William G. Gerrity, Terry Donnelly. Special effects: Sass Bedig. Stunt coordinator: Bill Hickman.

Location consultant: Fat Thomas. Makeup artist: Irving Buchman. Wardrobe: Joseph W. Dehn, Florence Foy. Casting: Robert Weiner. Color by De Luxe. Titles: Pacific Title. Westrex Recording System. A Philip D'Antoni Production in association with Schine-Moore Productions.

Additional Credits: Sound design: Don Hall. Production dates: November 1970 to March 1971. Premiered in New York City and Los Angeles on October 7, 1971.

Awards: Oscars for Best Picture, Director, Actor (Hackman), Writing—Screenplay Based on Material from Another Medium, Editing.

Other Versions: The sequel *French Connection II* (1975) starred Hackman and Ray was directed by John Frankenheimer. *The Seven-Ups* (1973) was a spin-off featuring Roy Scheider.

Available: Twentieth Century Fox Home Entertainment DVD (2005). UPC: 0-24543-22581-2.

The Best Foreign Film Oscar for 1969 went to *Z*, a political thriller directed by Costa-Gavras. Its style was derived in part from *The Battle of Algiers*

(1966), a pseudo-documentary about terrorism and torture during the Algerian uprising against the French. Both films used handheld cameras, live sound, and nonactors to simulate a newsreel style, one that viewers would perceive as more honest or true than fiction features. *Z* also won an Oscar for Best Editing, and it is that aspect of the movie that may have impressed director William Friedkin the most.

Born in what he called a slum in Chicago in 1935, Friedkin lived a rough life that included an arrest for armed robbery. He became obsessed with movies, and broke into the industry through the mailroom of a local Chicago television station. Friedkin worked his way up to directing television shows; although his abrasive personality got him fired from every station in town, he still received job offers, including one from producer David Wolper that brought him out to California in 1965. After working in episodic television, he directed four feature films that were critical and commercial failures. A lunch with director Howard Hawks convinced Friedkin that he was on the wrong track, and that he should be making pictures for mainstream audiences.

That opportunity came with *The French Connection*, a project based on a 1969 nonfiction book by Robin Moore that followed a heroin deal from Marseilles to New York City. Its heroes were real-life cops Eddie Egan and Sonny Grosso, who through stakeouts and street work realize that French businessman Jean Jehan is masterminding a multi-million-dollar drug sale. Producer Philip D'Antoni (*Bullitt*, 1968) optioned the rights, planning to make an adaptation at National General Films. In an article for the *DGA Quarterly*, Friedkin wrote that he spent a year working on two unsuccessful screenplays with D'Antoni, who then hired Ernest Tidyman on the basis of his *Shaft* novels to write a draft. (Friedkin told another interviewer that he ignored the script and let the actors improvise much of the dialogue.) The final script altered a number of details from the book. For one thing, Jehan's name was changed to Alain Charnier and Egan's to James "Popeye" Doyle; for another, shootings result in several deaths in the film, whereas no one was killed in the actual case.

The National General deal fell through, and other studios turned down the project until Richard Zanuck at Twentieth Century-Fox offered Friedkin and D'Antoni a budget of less than $2 million. However, Friedkin didn't want to use Gene Hackman, eventually cast by D'Antoni as Popeye Doyle. Jackie Gleason and newspaper columnist Jimmy Breslin had each been considered. Breslin was turned down because he couldn't drive, and actor Peter Boyle accepted the part but later dropped out on the advice of his agent.

Years later, Friedkin told an interviewer, "For me, so much of filmmaking is in the casting. If the roles are cast well, and you've talked to the actors about what you want to do, they express what they see, and you reach a kind of consensus about how it should be played. One of the ways I was able to get naturalistic acting, and still do, is that I really don't rehearse."

Hackman and Roy Scheider, who played Buddy Russo, who was based on Grosso, spent weeks going on patrols with New York policemen; they also used the time to find ways to suggest the personal bond between Doyle and Russo. (Egan and Grosso were advisors on the set, and also took small roles.) Friedkin later admitted that he cast Fernando Rey by mistake; he had asked for an actor he had seen in a Luis Buñuel film whose name he didn't know. He got Rey instead of Francisco Rabal.

Hackman's fierce, unapologetic portrayal of Doyle would win him an Oscar and cement his reputation as one of the most talented actors in film. With its furious bursts of energy, his work was reminiscent of an early James Cagney. Watch how he tries to wheedle Russo into an all-night stakeout with the line, "Come on, just for fun," or the venomous glare when he learns a rival Fed has been assigned to his case.

By showing how stakeouts operated, how cops rousted druggies, how dealers tested the purity of drugs, even where crooks ate, the film brought the criminal culture to life in ways that hadn't been seen on the screen before. This was partly due to advances in technology that enabled Friedkin to use live sound and shoot in locations that would have been impossible a few years earlier. But it was also due to the director's willingness to submerge viewers in a gritty, hostile world far removed from the reassuring authority of other cop films.

The centerpiece of *The French Connection* is its car chase. Friedkin's job was to top the chase in *Bullitt*, and he did it by changing the rules. As he wrote in the *DGA Quarterly*, "I felt that we shouldn't have one car chasing another car. We had to come up with something different; something that not only fulfilled the needs of the story, but that also defined the character of the man who was going to be doing the chasing." Friedkin and D'Antoni worked out a story line in which Doyle drove a car after an elevated train with one of the French crooks inside.

Filming the sequence took five weeks, in part because the crew was only allowed to shoot for roughly five hours a day. The script called for five main stunts involving a brown Pontiac that Doyle commandeers from a civilian driver. Friedkin and cinematographer Owen Roizman used up to three cameras mounted on and in Doyle's car. Multiple cameras were used for exteriors as well. Since they were relying on actual pedestrians and traffic, the cameras couldn't be undercranked, and the speed of the cars couldn't be faked. Friedkin said that Hackman drove through much of the sequence,

and that stunt driver Bill Hickman at times approached speeds of ninety miles an hour.

Despite all the work required to film the sequence, Friedkin credits its ultimate success to sound designer Don Hall and editor Jerry Greenberg. The sound of the train wasn't recorded until several months after principal photography, while the car noises were created at the Fox studio in California. "The cutting and mixing were enormously difficult," Friedkin wrote, but the result was one of the signature sequences of the 1970s.

The French Connection was a phenomenal commercial success, leading to a sequel and a spin-off. Friedkin's next film, *The Exorcist* (1973), was an even bigger box-office hit.

The Hospital

United Artists, 1971. Sound, color, 1.85. 102 minutes. Rated GP.
Cast: George C. Scott (Dr. [Herb] Bock), Diana Rigg (Barbara [Drummond]), Barnard Hughes (Drummond), Richard A. Dysart (Dr. Wellbeck), Stephen Elliott (Dr. Sundstrom), Donald Harron (Milton Mead), Andrew Duncan (William Mead), Nancy Marchand (Mrs. Christie), Jordan Charney (Hitchcock), Roberts Blossom (Guernsey), Lenny Baker (Dr. Schaefer), Richard Hamilton (Dr. Ronald Casey), Arthur Junaluska (Mr. Blacktree), Kate Harrington (Nurse Dunne), Katherine Helmond (Marilyn Mead), David Hooks (Dr. Einhorn), Frances Sternhagen (Mrs. Cushing), Robert Walden (Dr. Brubaker), William Perlow, M.D. (Cardiac Arrest doctor), Bette Henritze (Operating Room nurse), Rehn Scofield (Dr. Spezio), Dora Weissman (Lady in the hospital), Carolyn Krigbaum (Dr. Bock's secretary).
Credits: Directed by Arthur Hiller. Written by Paddy Chayefsky. Produced by Howard Gottfried. Associate producer: Jack Grossberg. Director of photography: Victor J. Kemper. Production designed by Gene Rudolf. Costumes designed by Frank Thompson. Music composed and conducted by Morris Surdin. Film editor: Eric Albertson. 1st assistant director: Peter Scoppa. Casting: Marion Dougherty Assoc. Production associate: Florence Nerlinger. Extra casting: Sybil Reich. Sound effects and music editing: Edit Inter, Ltd. Camera operator: Edward Gold. Gaffer: Richard Quinlan. Key grip: James Finnerty. Script supervisor: Barbara Robinson. 2nd assistant director: Larry Albucher. Scenic artist: Bruno Robotti. Titles designed by Bond Record. Set decorator: Herbert Mulligan. Set dresser: Robert Reilly. Sound mixer: Dennis Maitland. Makeup: Vincent Callaghan. Wardrobe supervisor: Martin Gaiptman. Construction grip: Walter Way. Master carpenter: Harry Lynott. Technical advisor: Evelyn Woerner. Transportation captain: William Curry. Opticals by Imagic, Inc. Color by Deluxe. Camera and lenses by Panavision. A Howard Gottfried/Paddy Chayefsky production in association with Arthur Hiller.
Additional Cast: Paddy Chayefsky (Narrator), Christopher Guest (Resident), Stockard Channing (Nurse in Emergency Room).
Additional Credits: Premiered December 14, 1971. Re-rated PG-13 in 1997.
Awards: Oscar for Best Writing—Story and Screenplay Based on Factual Material or Material not Previously Published or Produced (Chayefsky).
Available: MGM Home Entertainment VHS (2000). ISBN: 0-7928-0982-3. UPC: 0-27616-2361-3-5. DVD (2003): UPC: 0-27616-8955-2-3.

After the poor reception for *The Americanization of Emily* (1964), Paddy Chayefsky changed his focus from films to the theater. Success eluded him there as well, although it did bring him into contact with people he would use in his later projects. It was

a period of turmoil in his personal life. His wife Susan suffered from a painful neurological disorder. Chayefsky considered the people treating her "dismissive," and was inspired to begin a story he believed would serve "as a microcosm for all the ills of contemporary society." His son said later that Chayefsky was drinking heavily and suicidal, elements that surfaced in the character he created to carry the story, Dr. Herman Bock. He pitched his premise to David Picker at United Artists. Picker and fellow executive Arthur Krim then offered Chayefsky a two-picture deal.

Chayefsky partnered with Howard Gottfried, a former executive producer for television, to form Simcha Productions. Once he read it, Krim felt that Chayefsky's script was too long, "with an overemphasis on medical technology." The screenwriter changed a few elements, notably the ending, but on the whole retained the original's style and tone. What he did do before shooting started was pare down its length. From the initial 170 pages, the script shrank to 137 pages, of which 128 scenes were finally shot.

United Artists gave Simcha a $2.5 million budget, asking for Burt Lancaster or Walter Matthau in the lead. Chayefsky held out for George C. Scott, who had just won a Best Acting Oscar for *Patton* (1970). Where UA asked for Jane Fonda as the romantic lead, Chayefsky chose Diana Rigg instead. She had been appearing on Broadway with Barnard Hughes in *Abelard and Heloise*, so Hughes also received an important part in *The Hospital*.

Chayefsky received permission to shoot in Metropolitan Hospital in Manhattan's Upper East Side, the same institution covered by Frederick Wiseman in his documentary *Hospital* (1970).

Scott's salary, along with the Simcha costs, made it impossible to hire Chayefsky's first choice for director, Arthur Hiller. Instead, Michael Ritchie (*Smile*, 1975) started the shoot. But after realizing what Ritchie's plans for the movie were, Chayefsky insisted that Picker hire Hiller. *Smile* took a sarcastic look at beauty pageants, but Ritchie's tone in that film was soft-hearted, even affectionate, not hectoring or disapproving. Chayefsky's take on the public health system was bitter, rancid, and he watched over Hiller to make sure that vision remained intact.

Rigg, a classically trained British accent who had a cult following from her role as Mrs. Emma Peel on the television series *The Avengers*, remembered a difficult shoot due to extensive dialogue and a camera that had to navigate through narrow spaces. (On unmatted prints you can see sound and lighting technicians jammed under desks or crouched down next to file cabinets.) Scott compounded problems by arriving late and then drinking heavily through the early days of the shoot.

"George's great talent is his sense of rage," Gottfried said. Once the actor and screenwriter staked out their territories, Scott turned in an exceptional performance. One of Bock's suicidal rants covered six pages of dialogue and took up over three minutes of screen time; Scott nailed it in three takes. It was one of the actor's last serious film roles, one of the last times on screen that he invested himself fully in a character rather than blustering his way through a part.

Chayefsky oversaw the sound mixing for the film, which necessitated several last-minute rescues on the parts of other crew members. *The Hospital* opened in December to mixed reviews but good box office. Critics at the time complained about the movie's quick shifts in mood, from thriller to comedy to romance to satire. In retrospect they were probably put off by the more distasteful narrative strategies Chayefsky employed, as well as his towering misanthropy.

Frederick Wiseman's 1970 documentary offers a fascinating contrast to Chayefsky's drama. Some of the shots in the two films were almost identical, especially those taken in corridors and in the emergency room. But where Wiseman refused to supply a context for his scenes, or a narration to explain what was happening, Chayefsky provided both. Wiseman's depiction of doctors and their staffs performing heroically despite daunting legal and financial restrictions is a polar opposite of Chayefsky's world, where doctors and nurses routinely mangle and maim their patients, where accounting is more important than health, and where the outside world is made up of immature protesters who are the voice of a catastrophically ill society. Chayefsky's booze-sodden hero represents the last hope for humanity, a concept typical of the author's overheated and belligerent view of the world.

Chayefsky's original audience was solidly urban and middle class, those who preferred television to stage and cinema. The author never lost his compulsion to explain life to them, to hector and rail at the injustices he was a victim to since childhood. In Scott, Chayefsky found the perfect outlet for his rage, although once the curses and self-loathing subside, neither writer nor actor can provide much of a resolution to *The Hospital*'s plot. Rape as therapy for midlife crises? Using murder to solve organizational problems? Invective as defense? Chayefsky seems to advocate all that and more. When *The Hospital* works, such as in a fifteen-minute scene between Scott and Rigg in a doctor's office at night that bristles with electricity, the film has an immediacy that is both seductive and persuasive. But when Scott intones that "Someone's got to be responsible" for the "whole wounded madhouse of our times," it's hard to avoid the feeling that you are being lectured to. The thrill of opening up an institution to insult drives *The Hospital*, but it is Chayefsky's anger and revenge that make it so hard to watch today.

Harold and Maude

Paramount, 1971. Sound, color, 1.85. 91 minutes. Rated GP.

Cast: Ruth Gordon (Maude), Bud Cort (Harold), Vivian Pickles (Mrs. Chasen), Cyril Cusack (Glaucus), Charles Tyner (Uncle Victor [Ball]), Ellen Geer (Sunshine Doré), Eric Christmas (Priest), G. Wood (Psychiatrist), Judy Engles (Candy Gulf), Shari Summers (Edith Phern), M. Borman (Motorcycle officer), Susan Madigan (Girlfriend); Ray Goman, Gordon DeVol, Harvey Brumfield (Police officers); Henry Dieckoff (Butler), Philip Schultz (Doctor), Sonia Sorrell (Head nurse), Margot Jones (Student nurse), Barry Higgins (Intern); Jerry Randall, Pam Bebermeyer, Joe Hooker (Stunt doubles).

Credits: Directed by Hal Ashby. Written by Colin Higgins. Produced by Colin Higgins and Charles B. Mulvehill. Executive producer: Mildred

Lewis. Director of photography: John Alonzo. Film editing: William A. Sawyer, Edward Warschilka. Songs composed and performed by Cat Stevens (Courtesy of Island Records and A&M Records). Recordings supervised by Paul Samwell-Smith. Camera operator: Jose Marquette, Jr. Head grip: Charles Record. Gaffer: Richard Hart. Costume designer: William Theiss. Wardrobe supervisor: Andrea Weaver. Make up: Bob Stein. Hair stylist: Kathryn Blondell. Production designer: Michael Haller. Unit production manager: Wes McAfee. Special effects: A.D. Flowers. Production associate: Steve Silver. Production assistant: Jeff Wexler. 1st assistant director: Michael Dmytryk. 2nd assistant director: Robert Enrietto. Set dresser: James Cane. Stunt co-ordinator: Joe Hooker. Music editor: Ken Johnson. Editorial apprentices: Don Zimmerman, Sam Gemette. Titles by Pablo Ferro. Casting: Lynn Stalmaster. Sound: William Randall. Re-recording: Richard Portman. Sound editors: James A. Richards, Frank Warner. Color by Technicolor. A Mildred Lewis–Colin Higgins production.

Additional Cast: Cat Stevens (at cemetery), Hal Ashby (in arcade), Marjorie Morley Eaton (Madame Arouet), William Lucking (Policeman).

Additional Credits: Opened in New York on December 20, 1971. Re-rated PG in 1978.

Available: Paramount DVD (2000). ISBN: 0-7921-6508-X. UPC: 0-9736-08042-4-9.

Peter Bart, a former film executive and currently a journalist at *Variety*, once called the 1970s "the last great time for pictures that expanded the idea of what could be done with pictures." It was also a period of severely declining revenues for studios, who in desperation turned to projects and filmmakers that would have been rejected in earlier years. The resulting movies were hit-or-miss commercially, although some executives tried to take the sting out of the losers by calling them "cult films."

One of the projects that Bart, at the time vice-president of production at Paramount, had was *Harold and Maude*, expanded from the script for a planned twenty-minute short by UCLA film student Colin Higgins. Born on the island of New Caledonia in the South Pacific, Higgins attended Stanford University and volunteered for the Army before settling in Los Angeles. Mildred Lewis, his landlady and an aspiring producer, helped place the script with Paramount. It was Bart's idea to send the project to Hal Ashby.

Born in 1929, Ashby dropped out of high school and was a divorced painter of bridges when he decided to move from Wyoming to California. He endured a hard life before finding a toehold as an assistant editor at Republic, Disney, and MGM. Known for his phenomenal memory and relentless schedule, Ashby became disillusioned after working on several Norman Jewison projects (winning an Oscar for editing *In the Heat of the Night*, 1967). Jewison encouraged Ashby to direct *The Landlord* (1970), which impressed Bart enough to offer him *Harold and Maude*.

Higgins's script concerned a fabulously wealthy twenty-year-old who stages mock suicides and attends funerals "for fun." He falls in love with Maude, a seventy-nine-year-old free spirit who teaches him the meaning of life. Ashby, a committed hippie, civil rights defender and anti-war demonstrator, asked Bart to hire Charles Mulvehill as producer. Mulvehill had previously been working for the Mirisch Company, where he befriended Ashby during the making of *The Russians Are Coming The Russians Are Coming* (1966).

Mulvehill and Ashby wrangled a $1.2 million budget and cast Bud Cort and Ruth Gordon in the title roles. Born in 1948 in New Rochelle, Cort dropped out of NYU to pursue acting, appearing in commercials and on television shows while also performing in a comedy act. He was "discovered" by director Robert Altman, who gave him a small part in *MASH* (1970). Cort was the star of Altman's next film, *Brewster McCloud* (1970), a black comedy set in Houston that flopped at the box office. Altman reputedly warned Cort that appearing in *Harold and Maude* would typecast him as a kook.

Ruth Gordon had given up film acting in the 1940s, after she married writer Garson Kanin. Together they wrote several films for director George Cukor, including *Adam's Rib* (1949). Gordon returned to the screen in 1965, now playing elderly eccentrics, some evil, some merely demented.

Harold and Maude depicts seven suicide attempts (nine if you include those by other characters), and Ashby's deadpan staging of them is the highlight of the film. Otherwise this determinedly offbeat coming-of-age story can seem painfully trite and self-indulgent. (The *Variety* review said it "has all the fun and gaiety of a burning orphanage.") Ashby and Higgins mock such tired subjects as macho soldiers, sexually perverse priests, and the filthy rich, advocating instead alcohol, dope, driving fast, and listening to Cat Stevens songs. Unnecessarily cruel toward its characters, in particular Harold's mother (played at a perfect pitch by British actress Vivian Pickles), it is also marred by broad ironic strokes and kitschy self-help slogans.

One of the most elaborate shots in *Harold and Maude* is the very first, a single take almost four minutes long that shows Harold preparing to hang himself. It's a stunt with death as a gag line, and it showed that Ashby and cinematographer John Alonzo, a former acting student and cameraman for animal documentaries, were willing to sacrifice clarity and comprehension for the sake of an effect.

Insistently nonconformist, *Harold and Maude* spoke to a generation of filmgoers who didn't want to watch what their parents were watching, who thought that a portrait of Richard Nixon on the wall of an office was automatically funny, and who had been listening to "Trouble" on alternative rock stations. They were not enough at first to rescue the film, which was savaged by critics and ignored in theaters. "You couldn't drag people in," said Mulvehill. "The idea of a twenty-year old boy with an eighty-year-old woman just made people want to vomit."

But then *Harold and Maude* was embraced as a cult film by the same audience that made *King of Hearts* (1966) an inexplicable hit. *Harold and Maude* played in one theater for three years, and became a steady performer in repertory programs (often billed with *King of Hearts*). Ashby went on to direct such commercial blockbusters as *The Last Detail* (1973) and *Shampoo* (1975), but his career suffered in the 1980s. He died of pancreatic cancer in 1988.

It took Higgins more time, but within a few years he was one of the more bankable writers and directors on the basis of box-office hits like *Foul Play* (1978) and *Nine to Five* (1980). Higgins died of AIDS four months before Ashby. Cort has had an extensive career in film and television, but has never been able to shake his association with *Harold and Maude*. Cat Stevens, born Steven Demetre Georgiou in 1948, changed his name to Yusuf Islam when he converted in 1977. He now performs under the name Yusuf.

Bud Cort and Vivian Pickles in *Harold and Maude*.

(nostalgia)

Hollis Frampton, 1971. Sound, B&W, 1.33. 36 minutes.

Cast: Michael Snow (Hollis Frampton).

Credits: Filmmaker: Hollis Frampton.

Available: Image Entertainment DVD *Treasures IV: American Avant Garde Film 1947–1986*. ISBN: 978-0-9747099-5-6. UPC: 0-14381-4737-2-8. The Film-Makers' Cooperative (*www.film-makerscoop.com*).

A photographer, author, teacher, and critic, Hollis Frampton was often grouped, against his wishes, with structural filmmakers. Born in 1936 in Ohio, he never graduated from high school or college, although he did study at Phillips Academy and Western Reserve University. He befriended the artists Carl Andre and Frank Stella at Phillips, and worked briefly for an elderly Ezra Pound. Moving to New York City, he sculpted and wrote poetry before switching his attention to still photography. He also worked as a technician in a film laboratory, which he used as an opportunity to explore the intricacies of film stocks. While not financially successful, Frampton used his connections to photograph artists and artworks for various magazines and catalogs.

Frampton began making films in the fall of 1962, but "the first films I will publicly admit to making came in early 1966." These early works are lost or destroyed, but Frampton used them as training. *Word Pictures* (1962), for example, became the basis for *Zorn's Lemma*. Frampton bought a Bolex 16mm camera in 1966 and began teaching film at the Free University of New York. He would later teach at Hunter College, Cooper Union, and other schools.

He finished *Zorn's Lemma* in 1970. Based in part on a text by Carl Andre, it used mathematical

(nostalgia) by Hollis Frampton (1971, preserved by the Museum of Modern Art).

formulas to determine the length of shots. In the second of three sections, twenty-four individual letters are shown for one second—or twenty-four frames—each. They are replaced by images that either contain or refer to the letters. Gradually these sets are replaced by moving, "wordless" images. It was one of the first experimental films to be screened at the New York Film Festival, where it delighted audiences used to more mainstream material.

Frampton next started a seven-part series of films collected under the title *Hapax Legomena*. (The title refers to a word or group of words that appears only once in a language.) Released in 1971, *(nostalgia)* was the first in the series. It is made up of a few fundamental elements: a voice-over narration, ostensibly autobiographical musings by Frampton, but delivered by his friend and colleague Michael Snow; footage of twelve black-and-white still photographs, shot from an immobile, overhead camera; and black leader. The narration explains when, where, and why Frampton took the photographs, what they mean to him artistically, and how he regards them today. Since the photographs are resting on an electric hot plate, they slowly burn and disintegrate before the camera. Black leader is placed between the footage of each photograph. At the risk of giving away a crucial plot point, the narration and visuals don't coincide: Frampton, through the voice of Snow, is talking about the next image we are about to see.

(nostalgia) is both playful and curiously tense. By filming a photograph, Frampton has taken the "moving" out of "moving pictures." At the same time, the burning photos do "move." In fact, they curl, writhe, float, and collapse in on themselves, and their destruction is as haunting as the lost lives and locations they document. In his narration, Frampton displays the poet's knack for verbal imagery, for telling psychological details, and for a heightened awareness of the gulf between speaker and listener. By disconnecting sound from image, Frampton forces the viewer into the impossible task of visualizing what is about to come, while remembering what is disappearing from the frame, at the same time trying to appreciate, or make sense of, the juxtaposition of the images and sounds being screened. (Why precisely twelve photographs, for example. Do they represent months? Hours? Years? Disciples?) It's hard to imagine a more direct, precise way to challenge viewers about memory and how it operates. Or about the definition of film. It is only when *(nostalgia)* is over that it's structure becomes clear.

On its release, some accused *(nostalgia)* of being no more than a stunt. In *Wide Angle Saxon* (1976), filmmaker George Landow (a pseudonym for Owen Land) included a film-within-a-film called "Regrettable Redding Condescension" in which he poured red paint over a hot plate while repeating Michael Snow's recitation of "Do you see what I see?" from this film. (Landow called his fictional filmmaker Al Rutcurts, an anagram for "structural.") And in Frampton's other films, there is the sense that his intellect is so far advanced that he is just toying with filmgoers.

His writing can be equally dense and demanding. P. Adams Sitney quotes this sentence from an article called "A Pentagram for Conjuring the Narrative": "'I' is the English familiar name by which an unspeakably intricate network of colloidal circuits—or, as some reason, the garrulous temporary inhabitant of the nexus—addresses itself." However, much of Frampton's writing is as solid and useful as any about art. For example, his observations about science as "cold and unfeeling" and art as "warm and emotional": "Scientists think of the sciences as straightforward and arts as abounding in mystery. And none of these things is true. In the sciences in particular, and in the queen of the sciences—mathematics—and, indeed, in the almost celestial, clumsily named intellectual entity computer science, which has already made mathematics a kind of subset of its interests, nothing is quite as rampant as a sort of undefined gut aestheticization."

He agreed that sculpture "affected my handling of film as a physical material. My experience of sculpture has had a lot to do with my relative willingness to take up film in hand as a physical material and work with it. Without it, I might have been tempted to more literary ways of using film, or more abstract ways of using film."

The other entries in *Hapax Legomena* include *Poetic Justice, Critical Mass, Travelling Matte, Ordinary Matter, Remote Control*, and *Special Effects*. For his final project, the *Magellan* cycle, he planned a film with a running time of about thirty-six hours, to be viewed over the course of 371 days. Most of the films would be as short as the early Lumière titles, less than a minute. On important days, such as solstices, longer films would be screened. He completed about eight hours of the planned total. During this period, Frampton became a professor at the State University of New York at Buffalo, where he helped form the Center for Visual Study. He also worked on developing two computer languages to deal with sound and graphics. Frampton died of lung cancer on March 30, 1984, at the age of forty-eight.

Tom, Tom, the Piper's Son

Ken Jacobs, 1969–71. Silent, color and B&W, 1.37. 115 minutes

Credits: Filmmaker: Ken Jacobs, from a 1905 Biograph film photographed by G.W. Bitzer. Cinematography assistant: Jordan Meyers. Negative-matching assistance: Judy Dauterman. Original print rescued by Kemp Niver.

Other Versions: Sequel: *A Tom Tom Chaser* (2002, 10 minutes).

Available: The Filmmakers' Coop (*www.film-makerscoop.com*). Projected quarterly at The Anthology Film Archives, New York City (*www.anthologyfilmarchives.org*).

In February 1905, Biograph released *Tom, Tom, the Piper's Son*, an eight-scene elaboration on the nursery rhyme. Its opening shot, a crowded tableau of a street fair based on a Hogarth print entitled "Southward Fair," featured acrobats, jugglers, and musicians performing for onlookers. In the corner of the frame, Tom steals a pig, initiating a fight and chase.

Tom and his father bring the pig inside their cottage, pursued by twenty or so angry citizens. The thieves and their pig are forced to flee into a hearth and up the chimney, after which their pursuers dutifully climb out of the chimney and either jump or fall from the thatched roof. Tom hides in a pile of hay on the floor of a barn. The pursuers climb a ladder to the loft; Tom then knocks the ladder aside and escapes through a fence and into a farmhouse. His followers jump from the loft into the hay, then break through the farmhouse door. Tom and his pig climb through a window out into a courtyard, where they hide in a well. There they are captured.

Running about eight minutes, the film was a typically well-shot and produced Biograph effort, featuring a large cast, detailed costumes, and seven different sets. Like many comedies of the time, it is essentially an extended chase, made longer by the number of participants involved. Starting in 1969, filmmaker Ken Jacobs began experimenting with a print of the film, rephotographing it from a screen and via a homemade optical printer.

Jacobs' film begins with a full version of the original movie, followed by his elaboration on the footage. He starts by blowing up a portion of the frame, showing only the legs of the actors in the first scene. From there Jacobs examines every aspect of the print, looping segments so movements are repeated, slowing down and speeding up footage and shutters, allowing processing marks to appear, inserting black leader between sections, adjusting the size of the frame by blocking parts of it out with mattes, freezing on facial expressions, filming the footage at an angle, doubling it with split screens, removing it from the shutter mechanism, even filming the beam of the projector lens.

In *Visionary Film*, avant-garde historian P. Adams Sitney wrote about viewing three different versions of *Tom, Tom, The Piper's Son*. In the second, Jacobs introduced color footage, primarily of house plants backlit behind a hanging bedsheet.

Jacobs inserted these passages as a means of "relaxing" viewers, although Sitney objected to their "disorienting" quality. The third version of *Tom, Tom* includes what may be the acid test for mainstream viewers: a long segment in which the film is shown "by hand," wound back and forth without a shutter so that it is impossible to discern individual frames. The effect is like flipping the pages of a book too fast to pick out any words. This section is almost as disconcerting as one that examines patterns of grain in the whites of the Biograph film, blown up to fill the entire frame.

Viewers are always struggling to supply a meaning to what they see. At times Jacobs' film actually clarifies action that was obscure in the original. He singles out actors and reveals facial expressions that otherwise would have been too difficult to see. Three onlookers stand to the side of the frame and watch in amusement at the train of sixteen people who follow Tom and his father out of the chimney. By zooming in on them, Jacobs reveals that one man is also pinching snuff. Jacobs has changed how we will now view the original film, adding a meaning to it that was not apparent before.

At other times, Jacobs turns the original imagery into something entirely new, a kind of cinematic Rorschach test. Blown up to the right size, a window frame can look like bars on a cell, and a blurred figure in a background can take on ominous, even satanic, overtones. Optically enlarged, costumes form black-and-white patterns that resolve into shapes—a wolf's head, for example, or horns. Jacobs toys with the flickering effect from mistimed shutters, something the cinematographers of the time fought hard to overcome. The result can provoke nausea in viewers.

In a film like *Serene Velocity* (1970, a Registry title), time becomes a means of suspense, a threat to the narrative. But time means nothing to Jacobs. It is just another element to manipulate, speed up or slow down, reverse, even render meaningless once the shutter is gone. When you can't tell what you are seeing, does it make any difference how long a shot lasts? But didn't the original film hold shots far longer than necessary, and expand the cast beyond all narrative purpose simply to make the story run longer?

Tom, Tom asks viewers to determine how long effects, shots, scenes, even movies should be. For Jacobs, his film was about "the whole bizarre human phenomena of story-telling itself" and "the fantasy of reading any bygone time out of the visual crudities of film." He was specific in his instructions to projectionists: "Please allow clear tail to pass completely through projector, show projector beam without film for another 20 seconds before stopping projector. Allow at least 20 seconds of darkness before turning up auditorium lights. Thanks!"

Jacobs returned to the project in 2002 when digitizing the film for video transfer. Born in Williamsburg, Brooklyn, in 1933, he grew up in what he described as a broken home. He developed a love of art as a teenager, and after serving in the U.S. Coast Guard studied painting and filmmaking. In 1956 he became friends with filmmaker Jack Smith, who starred in *Blonde Cobra* (released in 1963). Jacobs later developed what he called "The Nervous System" in which he experimented with simultaneously projecting two films to provide a 3-D effect. Many of these projects carry warnings for epileptics.

Among his other accomplishment, Jacobs invented "The Nervous Magic Lantern," which uses a projector but no film or video. In 1986 he released *Perfect Film*, a reprint of discarded footage he found, and in 1991 *Keaton's Cops*, a version of the Buster Keaton film in which only the bottom quarter of the frame is visible. Some consider *Star Spangled to Death* (2004), a seven-hour combination of found footage and original material which he began shooting in 1957, to be his masterpiece.

Cabaret

Allied Artists, 1972. Sound, color, 1.85. 124 minutes. Rated PG.

Cast: Liza Minnelli (Sally Bowles), Michael York (Brian Roberts), Helmut Griem (Maximilian von Heune), Joel Grey (Master of Ceremonies), Fritz Wepper (Fritz Wendel), Marisa Berenson (Natalia Landauer), Elisabeth Neumann-Viertel (Fraulein Schneider), Helen Vita (Fraulein Kost), Sigrid Von Richtofen (Fraulein Mayr), Gerd Vespermann (Bobby), Ralf Wolter (Herr Ludwig), Georg Hartmann (Willi), Ricky Renee (Elke), Estrongo Nachama (Cantor); Kathryn Doby, Inge Jaeger, Angelika Koch, Helen Velkovorska, Gitta Schmidt and Louise Quick (The Kit-Kat Dancers); "Heirat" sung by Greta Keller.

Credits: Directed by Bob Fosse. Screenplay by Jay [Presson] Allen. Research consultant: Hugh Wheeler. Based on the musical play *Cabaret*, book by Joe Masteroff, music by John Kander, lyrics by Fred Ebb. Based on the play [*I Am a Camera*] by John Van Druten and stories by Christopher Isherwood. Produced by Cy Feuer. Produced on the New York stage by Harold Prince. Dances and musical numbers staged by Bob

Fosse. Music supervised, arranged and conducted by Ralph Burns. Additional songs by John Kander and Fred Ebb. Associate producer: Harold Nebenzal. Photographed by Geoffrey Unsworth. Editor: David Bretherton. Choreographic music associate: Fred Werner. Production manager: Pia Arnold. Production designer: Rolf Zehetbauer. Costume designer: Charlotte Flemming. Make-up and hairstyling: Raimund Stangl, Susi Krause. Sound: David Hildyard. Titles: Modern Film Effects. Gaffer: Herbert Fischer. Art direction: Jurgen Kiebach [Hans Jürgen Kiebach]. Set dresser: Herbert Strabl [Strabel]. Filmed on location in West Berlin and at Bavaria Atelier Gesellschaft mbH, Munich, West Germany. An Allied Artists Pictures Corporation and ABC Pictures Corp. presentation of an ABC Pictures Corporation production.

Additional Credits: Executive producer: Martin Baum. Production dates: March to July 1971. Opened February 13, 1972.

Awards: Oscars for Best Director, Actress, Actor in a Supporting Role (Grey), Cinematography, Film Editing, Art Direction—Set Decoration (Rolf Zehetbauer, Hans Jürgen Kiebach, Herbert Strabel), Music—Scoring Original Song Score and/or Adaptation (Ralph Burns), Sound (Robert Knudson, David Hildyard).

Available: Warner Home Video DVD (2003). ISBN: 0-7907-8222-7. UPC: 0-85392-79862-9.

The origins of *Cabaret* extend back to author Christopher Isherwood's four-year sojourn in Berlin during the early 1930s. He had planned a novel, *The Lost*, about his experiences, but never completed it. Sections of his Berlin writings were published, however, including "Sally Bowles" (1937) and "Goodbye to Berlin" (1939), both later collected in *Berlin Stories* (1954). Autobiographical in tone (Isherwood even began using his name in the stories), they presented a vivid picture of Germany on the verge of Nazism. Playwright John Van Druten adapted Isherwood's stories into *I Am a Camera*, which had a successful run in 1951 and later became a 1955 movie starring Julie Harris and Laurence Harvey.

Composer Sandy Wilson, whose play *The Boy Friend* was a hit in 1954, was the first to try to adapt *I Am a Camera* into a musical. When his option on the material expired, producer Harold Prince hired writer Joe Masteroff and the composing team of John Kander and Fred Ebb for the project. Masteroff, a World War II veteran who shifted from acting to writing, had written the book for the musical *Little Me*. Kander, born in 1927, had been a piano accompanist and arranger when he met Prince in 1962. Ebb, born in 1935, had been writing for nightclub acts and revues when he teamed up with Kander in 1963. Prince hired them to write the songs for *Flora, The Red Menace*, a 1965 musical that won Liza Minnelli a Tony award.

Minnelli, the daughter of singer Judy Garland and director Vincente Minnelli, auditioned for the Sally Bowles part in *Cabaret*, but was turned down. (Jill Haworth starred on Broadway in the role.) The play opened on November 20, 1966, and ran for almost three years, winning Tonys for Best Musical and for Kander and Ebb's score. It was so successful

that a film version became prohibitively expensive for Cinerama, Inc., which owned the rights for a time. Manny Wolf of Allied Artists purchased the rights for $1.5 million, which he later split with Martin Baum at ABC Film Corporation. Wolf and Baum hired longtime show business veteran Cy Feuer to produce, and Jay Presson Allen to work on the script. They approached Prince about directing the film, but Prince was busy rehearsing the new Stephen Sondheim show, *A Little Night Music*.

Bob Fosse was Prince's most accomplished professional rival. Born in Chicago in 1927, he was on stage in vaudeville and burlesque before he was a teenager. He had a nightclub act with his first wife, appeared as a dancer in Hollywood movies, choreographed *The Pajama Game* and *Damn Yankees* on stage and screen, and had made his film debut as director with *Sweet Charity*. Fosse's meticulous, time-consuming methods doubled the budget for the film, which contributed to its failure at the box office.

By this time Feuer had much of the *Cabaret* package in place, including Allen's script, Liza Minnelli to star as Sally Bowles, and Joel Grey to reprise his role as "Master of Ceremonies" of the Kit-Kat Klub. Fosse was hired with the understanding that Baum would be watching the budget—at the time $5 million—closely. Baum agreed that the film would have to be shot on location in Germany.

Fosse "wanted to make a brand new statement," according to Grey, who had to appeal to Baum to keep his part. (Grey was the son of singer and comedian Mickey Katz. Like Fosse, he was thoroughly familiar with the seedier aspects of show business, which he incorporated into his performance.) After his friends Neil Simon and Paddy Chayefsky agreed that Allen's script was weak, Fosse hired Hugh Wheeler to rewrite it (Wheeler received a "research" credit). They dropped the play's subplot about a romance between a landlady and a Jewish grocer, as well as all the songs from the play that didn't occur in the nightclub. ("Tomorrow Belongs to Me," often mistaken for a genuine German song, was retained even though it was sung in a *biergarten*. Fosse later said that he regretted including the number.) New to the film version was a romance between a salesman and a wealthy Jewish heiress, played by former model Marisa Berenson. The biggest change may have been the new character of Baron Maximilian von Heune, the center of a romantic triangle that turned writer Brian Roberts into a bisexual.

Fosse rehearsed with Minnelli, Grey, and the other principals for six weeks, reworking Minnelli's screen appearance as well as her approach to her songs. Replacing the discarded tunes were three new numbers: "Mein Herr," "The Money Song," and "Maybe This Time," the last inspired by a request from Fosse for something to fit Bowles' character after she falls in love.

When Fosse was prohibited from using Robert Surtees as cinematographer, he held a grudge against Feuer for the rest of his life. He insisted on working within the restrictions of a ten-by-fourteen-foot stage. "I never used more than six girls," he said about his choreography. "I tried to make the dances look not as if they were done by me, Bob Fosse, but by some guy who is down and out."

Minnelli was the true key to the success of the film. Earlier, Ebb had played an important part in establishing what and how she performed; Fosse brought a new emphasis on how she moved. Unspoken among all her collaborators was the influence of her mother. Like Judy Garland, Minnelli the actress can't stop seeking the approval of her audience. Without much acting technique to draw on, she tends to force her characters' lines and emotions. Accepting her as a performer means accepting her as a person more than an actress.

Fosse (and many of her other directors) used Minnelli not only for her connection to her notoriously unstable mother, but for her emotional vulnerability, her inner turmoil, the suggestion that she was always on the verge of a breakdown. It was a cruel way to exploit her, but one that Minnelli participated in fully. The tragedy of Sally Bowles is how deluded she is, a problem Garland's characters never had to face, whatever other shortcomings they may have possessed.

Like Minnelli, Fosse sought approval, too. He was addicted to razzle-dazzle, afraid of boring viewers, determined to nail down every step and nuance of the film. Faced with Minnelli's limited dancing ability, he broke her steps down into pieces, shards, using a half-dozen or more takes and camera angles to assemble a routine. He filmed from within the cabaret audience, from behind the curtain looking out over the stage, from below and above, circling around Minnelli, filling the frame with her garishly made-up face, surrounding her with props and chorus dancers, isolating her in cold spotlights, cutting away to onlookers both aroused and bored. The musical numbers in *Cabaret* are intentionally jarring and discontinuous, even at the expense of the performers (for example, the on-screen Minnelli is often out of synch with her soundtrack singing in her climactic number). Fosse's choreography—inspired at the time partly by the need to protect nondancers—became an industry standard. Abandoned was Fred Astaire's method of showing a dancer's entire body and filming in one take.

Fosse's directorial style was forceful, even intrusive. He inserted quick shots of external violence in some of the songs, used brown-shirted Nazis to pump up melodrama, tried to illustrate Ebb's lyrics with cutaway shots, and pitched some scenes at the point of hysteria. Seen today, *Cabaret* is both self-congratulatory and nervous: proud of its daring subjects and settings, worried that viewers might not appreciate how daring it is. Despite all its flouting of sexual norms, *Cabaret* is closer in style to *Hello, Dolly!* (1969) than it is to the more youth-oriented musicals that would follow.

But in 1972, it was a sensation, earning some $20 million and winning eight Oscars. Fosse completed a remarkable hat trick that year, also winning an Emmy for directing *Liza with a Z* on television and a Tony for directing *Pippin* on stage. For better or worse, the movie established Minnelli as the star who belted showstoppers. Fosse, Kander, and Ebb collaborated on the hit show *Chicago*, while the songwriters worked with Minnelli again on Martin Scorsese's *New York New York* (1977).

The Godfather

Paramount, 1972. Sound, color, 1.85. 175 minutes. Rated R.
Cast: Marlon Brando (Don Vito Corleone), Al Pacino (Michael Corleone), James Caan (Sonny Corleone), Richard Castellano (Peter Clemenza), Robert Duvall (Tom Hagen), Sterling Hayden (Capt. McCluskey), John Marley (Jack Woltz), Richard Conte (Don Emilio Barzini), Al Lettieri (Virgil Sollozzo), Diane Keaton (Kay Adams), Abe Vigoda (Sal Tessio), Talia Shire (Connie Corleone), Gianni Russo (Carlo Rizzi), John Cazale (Fredo Corleone), Rudy Bond (Don Carmine Cuneo), Al Martino (Johnny Fontane), Morgana King (Mama Corleone), Lenny Montana (Luca Brasi), John Martino (Paulie Gatto), Salvatore Corsitto (Bonasera), Richard Bright (Al Neri), Alex Rocco (Moe Green), Tony Giorgio (Bruno Tattaglia), Vito Scotti (Nazorine), Tere Livrano (Theresa Hagen), Victor Rendina (Philip Tattaglia), Jeannie Linero (Lucy Mancini), Julie Gregg (Sandra Corleone), Ardell Sheridan (Mrs. Clemenza), Simonetta Stefanelli (Apollonia), Angelo Infanti (Fabrizio), Corrado Gaipa (Don Tommasino), Franco Citti (Calo), Saro Urzì (Vitelli).

Credits: Directed by Francis Ford Coppola. Screenplay by Mario Puzo and Francis Ford Coppola. Produced by Albert S. Ruddy. Director of photography: Gordon Willis. Production designer: Dean Tavoularis. Costume designer: Anna Hill Johnstone. Edited by William Reynolds and Peter Zinner. Associate producer: Gray Frederickson. Music composed by Nino Rota. Conducted by Carlo Savina. Additional music, Mall wedding sequence: Carmine Coppola. Art director: Warren Clymer. Set decorator: Philip Smith. Casting: Fred Roos, Andrea Eastman, Louis DiGiaimo. Postproduction consultant: Walter Murch. Makeup: Dick Smith, Philip Rhodes. Hair stylist: Phil Leto. Wardrobe supervisor: George Newman. Camera operator: Michael Chapman. Script continuity: Nancy Tonery. Production recording: Christopher Newman. Re-recording: Bud Grenzbach, Richard Portman. Color by Technicolor. An Albert S. Ruddy production.

Additional Credits: Title on screen: *Mario Puzo's The Godfather.* Additional screenwriting: Robert Towne. Production dates: March 29 to August 1971. Premiered in New York City on March 15, 1972.

Awards: Oscars for Best Picture, Actor (Marlon Brando), Writing—Screenplay Based on Material from Another Medium.

Other Versions: Sequels: *The Godfather Part II* (1974), *The Godfather Part III* (1980).

Available: Paramount Home Entertainment DVD (2004). ISBN: 0-7921-7329-5. UPC: 0-97360-80494-2.

Everyone likes to take credit for the success of *The Godfather*, at one point the most profitable film ever made. Looking back, what's surprising is how close its close its key participants were to failure. Novelist Mario Puzo, for example, was ready to give up on writing. A New York City native, he attended college on the G.I. Bill after serving in World War II. He wrote his first novel in 1955, then spent ten years working for pulp magazines while finishing his second. A Putnam editor offered him an advance for a Mafia novel after hearing Puzo's stories about the mob. "I was forty five years old and tired of being an artist," he wrote later. *The Godfather* might be his last chance at a best-seller.

Puzo knew his market, and enough about the Mafia, to write a complex, generational saga filled with sex and violence. He gave his characters recognizably human qualities and placed them within intricate, soap-opera plot lines. An immense undertaking, it was also a popular phenomenon, outselling rival novels like *Love Story* and *The Exorcist*. "I wrote below my gifts," Puzo confessed, but he was delighted when the book was sold to the movies.

A former reporter and aspiring novelist himself, Peter Bart was a vice-president at Paramount when he received sixty pages of Puzo's manuscript, called *Mafia* at the time. Bart, who had been hired by production head Robert Evans, was skeptical about the book's subject matter, especially since Paramount had lost a bundle on *The Brotherhood* (1968). But Bart was riveted by Puzo's treatment; he wrote later that the option rights gave Puzo enough financial security to finish the novel. In any event Paramount committed to the work before the novel was published.

Francis Ford Coppola was not an obvious choice to direct. *Finian's Rainbow* (1968) had been a creative disaster, and his follow-up, *The Rain People* (1969), failed at the box office, despite some supportive reviews. His only other recent screen credit had been as a screenwriter for *Patton* (1970). On top of that, Coppola was not interested in adapting a large-scale novel—he had been intent on developing his own material. But he needed to repay a loan Warner Brothers had given him to form American Zoetrope, his San Francisco production company. (Warners would end up getting most of Coppola's salary.) He agreed to meet with producer Al Ruddy and the Paramount executives. At that point everyone envisioned a small film.

When the novel stayed on the best-seller list for over a year, the film project ballooned. Suddenly everyone had opinions about Coppola's choices. Evans was against casting Al Pacino, who had appeared in two minor films, in one as a heroin addict. Nobody wanted Marlon Brando except Puzo and Coppola, who at first had considered Laurence Olivier and George C. Scott. Brando had just turned down a role in *The Conversation* (1974), a script Coppola was developing. "I thought Marlon was this strange, moody titan," he said, "but he turned out to be very simple, direct."

When shooting started, some executives started complaining that rushes by cinematographer Gordon Willis were too dark. Willis had argued on the set with Coppola, who was convinced that editor Aram Avakian was angling to replace him. (Avakian was fired and replaced himself by William Reynolds and Peter Zinner.) Ruddy had to deal with complaints from Italian-American associations; Charles Bludhorn, head of Paramount, fired Stanley Jaffe. Bart heard rumors that Elia Kazan was going to take over the movie. Coppola believes the only reason he was kept on the film was because he won a screenwriting Oscar for *Patton*.

Brando's scenes took six weeks to film. Crew members had to hide cue cards for him throughout the sets. Brando wore facial prosthetics designed by Dick Smith and Phil Rhodes: a mouthpiece, latex rubber on his face, and earplugs; he also placed weights in shoes. According to biographer Patricia Bosworth, screenwriter Robert Towne helped write one scene, and it was Brando himself who came up with the idea of making a joke with an orange rind.

The director had his father Carmine hired to write incidental music, but Nino Rota ended up composing some of the most distinctive musical themes of the decade. Combined with Willis's superlative cinematography, the music helped turn potentially stock characters into complicated, believable people. While Coppola generally adhered to the novel's plot, he focused in on several key moments of loyalty and betrayal, allowing them to build in intensity. These moments are what viewers remember from the film, not the story's more melodramatic contrivances.

After editing in San Francisco, Coppola delivered a cut that was almost three hours long. "I took a pulpy, salacious novel and turned it into a movie about a bunch of guys sitting in a dark room talking," he said later. According to Ruddy, Bludhorn went "crazy," insisting that Coppola take out thirty minutes. He did, but Evans argued persuasively for the longer version. (Evans also angered Coppola by insinuating that he "rescued" the film himself in the editing room.)

Bart wrote that part of the success for *The Godfather* was due to Frank Yablans, Paramount's head of distribution, who made the decision to open the film "wide," at four hundred theaters, rather than showcasing it. Along with *Love Story*, *The Godfather* resuscitated Paramount, even though Ruddy described the production as "a hideous experience." Puzo was faced with the task of topping himself, while Coppola frankly admitted, "I wasn't prepared for what happened when the movie opened." In his opinion, the film's success distorted his life and almost destroyed his career. "It would make me a hero and a prisoner of my own mythology," he said to Bart.

Deliverance

Warner Bros., 1972. Sound, color, 2.35. 109 minutes. Rated R.

Cast: Jon Voight (Ed), Burt Reynolds (Lewis), Ned Beatty (Bobby), Ronny Cox (Drew), Bill McKinney (Mountain man), Herbert "Cowboy" Coward (Toothless man), James Dickey (Sheriff Bullard), Ed Ramey ("Old Man"), Billy Redden (Lonnie), Seamon Glass (First Griner), Randall Deal (Second Griner), Lewis Crone (First Deputy), Ken Keener (Second Deputy), Johnny Popwell (Ambulance driver), John Fowler (Doctor), Kathy Rickman (Nurse), Louise Coldren (Mrs. Biddiford), Pete Ware (Taxi driver), Macon McCalman (Deputy Queen), Hoyt Pollard (Boy at gas station), Belinha Beatty (Martha Gentry), Charlie Boorman (Ed's boy).

Credits: Produced and directed by John Boorman. Screenplay by James Dickey. Based on his novel. Director of photography: Vilmos Zsigmond. Editor: Tom Priestly [Priestley]. Art director: Fred Harpman. Property master: Syd Greenwood. Script supervisor: Ray Quiroz. Technical advisors: Charles Wiggin, E. Lewis King. Production supervisor: Wallace Worsely. Assistant directors: Al Jennings, Miles Middough. Production secretary: Sue Dwiggins. Special effects: Marcel Vercoutere. Wardrobe master: Bucky Rous. Makeup: Michael Handcock. Hair stylist: Donoene McKay. Sound mixer: Walter Goss. Sound editor: Jim Atkinson. Dubbing mixer: Doug Turner. Assistant editor: Ian Rakoff. 2nd unit photography: Bill Butler. Creative associate: Rospo Pallenberg. Casting: Lynn Stalmaster. "Dueling Banjos" arranged and played by Eric Weissberg with Steve Mandel. The song "Dueling Banjos" is an arrangement of the song entitled "Feudin' Banjos," copyright owner: Combine Music Corp. Filmed in Panavision and Technicolor.

Additional Credits: Production dates: May to August 1971. Premiered in New York City on July 30, 1972.

Available: Warner Home Video DVD (2007). UPC: 085391165125. Warner Home Video DVD (1999). ISBN: 0-7907-3726-4. UPC: 0-85391-5442-4.

Based on a best-selling novel by James Dickey, *Deliverance* became one of the top box-office films of 1973, a year after it originally opened. Born in 1923, Dickey was a combat pilot during World War II and the Korean War, a teacher, and a copywriter with McCann Erickson in New York City before establishing a reputation as a poet. He received a Guggenheim fellowship in 1960, and won a National Book Award for *Buckdancer's Choice* in 1965. Dickey's style, heavily dependent on rhythm and meter, focused on nature, violence, and sex, and the need for mankind to connect with its animal impulses.

Deliverance, his first novel, placed three inexperienced businessmen and one woodsman poseur on a canoe trip down the Cahulawassee River. Halfway through their journey they are attacked by hunters, and must learn to kill to survive. It was a *Boys' Life* adventure for adults, suffused with sex, religious symbolism, and what passed at the time for social commentary. Elemental enough to be grasped by the dimmest reader, it became a financial gold mine and the basis of cultural debates about the innate savagery in man.

Warner Brothers story editor Barry Beckerman persuaded production head John Calley to purchase the novel before it was published. Dickey, who had written "two small documentaries for the government in California," was hired to adapt his novel. As he recounted later, "The writer quickly discovers that . . . his opinion, after a certain quickly-reached point, will not count for much." The author argued vehemently and at length with director John Boorman, usually to no avail. Given Dickey's style of script writing—"A single hand comes in, and seems to hover over the paper in what is at the same time an authoritative and yet almost a ceremonial way"—it's probably a good thing he lost.

A former documentarian in Great Britain, Boorman was hired to direct the Dave Clark Five in *Catch Us If You Can* (1965, also known as *Having a Wild Weekend*), one of the many knockoffs of The Beatles' *A Hard Day's Night* (1964). Two years later he directed Lee Marvin in *Point Blank*, a gratuitously ugly and vicious thriller that was embraced by some critics after it failed at the box office. Boorman's next film, the similarly ugly *Hell in the Pacific* (1968), left his commercial reputation in tatters. With *Deliverance* he set out to make the equivalent of a modern-day Western, one that focused on adventure at the expense of narrative depth.

According to the director, *Deliverance* was an attempt to explain how urban life and its separation from nature was "very dangerous and destructive." As it appeared on screen, however, the film was more easily seen as a battle between the liberal elite and the silent majority, or in this case comfortably well-off businessmen and the inbred, predatory cretins who want to rape, kill, and dismember them. In Boorman's hands, the four canoeists have almost no personalities or backgrounds, and no clear-cut moral stances on issues like hunting. They, like the liberals who were blindsided by President Richard Nixon's rise to power, were sitting ducks for the furtive crooks who actually controlled the country.

On one level *Deliverance* simply replaced the bloodthirsty Indians of an earlier era of Westerns with redneck hillbillies, an equally insulting characterization. Boorman added two qualities that set his film apart. Unlike most previous adventures, which presented Nature as awesome but essentially neutral, Boorman depicted the Georgia woods and rivers as ominous deathtraps. Second, he filmed entirely on location on the Chattooga River, something that would have been impossible even a few years earlier.

Working with ace cinematographer Vilmos Zsigmond, Boorman devised a visual style that matched the script's dark, foreboding forests and rocky gorges. The Chattooga itself "was too benign; I wanted something nightmarish." He worked with Technicolor for months on desaturating color levels, and at one point in the story resorted to solarizing the film to reflect a character's emotional turmoil.

This was the film debut for both Ronny Cox and Ned Beatty, a Louisville native who had worked for years in regional theater. His characteristically fearless performance was the start of a distinguished career on screen and television. His other Registry titles include *Nashville* (1975) and *Network* (1976). (Ironically, given his part as a canoeing novice, Beatty had the most river experience of the actors.) Beatty became a close friend of Burt Reynolds, whose role here was instrumental in making him one of the top box-office stars of the 1970s.

A former college football star, Reynolds had been working in film and television for over a decade; this was his first substantial role. Throughout his subsequent career he tried repeatedly to establish himself as a serious leading man, but it was only when he adopted a good-ol'-boy persona that he found success on film. Reynolds portrayed private eyes, athletes, and assorted con artists in titles like *Gator* (1976) and *Smokey and the Bandit* (1977), forming a sort of redneck Rat Pack that began to bottom out in *Stroker Ace* (1983) and its ilk. (Boorman originally wanted Lee Marvin and Marlon Brando in the two lead roles.)

Deliverance was such a hit that it gave Boorman carte blanche for extravagantly bizarre projects like *Zardoz* (1974), a fantasy filmed in Ireland, and *The Emerald Forest* (1985), an adventure set in the Amazon jungle. Some critics were drawn to his overemphatic style, but his lower-key films, like the semi-autobiographical *Hope and Glory* (1987) and the fact-based *The General* (1998), are better examples of what he could accomplish as a director.

Dickey, who appeared in a small part as a sheriff investigating the incident, never matched the commercial success of *Deliverance*. The last three decades of his life were marked by turmoil; he died of fibrosis of the lungs in 1997. Dickey had hoped to use "Buckdancer's Choice," an old Southern fiddle tune that had been adapted to twelve-string guitar, on the movie's soundtrack. Instead, Warner Brothers opted for a song called "Dueling Banjos," played by Eric Weissberg on the banjo with Steve Mandel on guitar. The song, and Billy Reddin, the local student who played the banjo-playing Lonnie, became shorthand icons for the movie.

As the studio soon discovered, "Dueling Banjos" was actually taken from "Feudin' Banjos," written by Arthur Smith, a prominent musician and host of nationally televised variety show. His "Guitar Boogie" had sold over a million copies. (Smith recorded "Feudin' Banjos" in 1955 with bluegrass virtuoso Don Reno.) Smith won a significant copyright infringement suit against the studio.

According to a memoir by his son Christopher Dickey, the author had originally wanted Sam Peckinpah to direct his script. Along with films like Peckinpah's *Straw Dogs* (1971), *Deliverance* helped usher in a new era of vigilante films, one that gave moviegoers the vicarious power to strike back at their perceived enemies. The genre reached its culmination in a series of *Death Wish* (1974) films that eventually managed to repulse even hard-core action fans.

Peege

Phoenix Learning Group, Inc., 1972. Sound, color, 1.37. 28 minutes.

Cast: Bruce Davison (Greg), Jeanette Nolan (Peege), William Schallert (Father), Barry Livingston (Damien), David Alan Bailey, Lilyan MacBride [Lillian McBride], Kirk Scott, Susan Granof, Charles Mayer, Robin Sloane, David Brennan, Barbara Rush (Mother).

Credits: Written and directed by Randal Kleiser. Produced by David Knapp and Leonard S. Berman. Cinematography: Douglas Knapp. Associate producer: Paul Woodville. Lighting director: Harry Winer. Script supervisor: Sybil Scotford. Art director: Joan Dierkop. Music: Charles Albertine. Sound: Ken Robinson, Les Rumsey. Makeup: Herb Balkind. Miss Nolan's makeup: Louis LaCava. Editor: Randal Kleiser. Assistant editors: Richard Gibb, Andrew London, Debbie Dozier. Title design: Peter Mackey. A David Knapp presentation, in association with Bedford Productions.

Additional Credits: Premiered August 7, 1972.

Available: Phoenix Learning Group, Inc. DVD (*www.PhoenixLearning Group.com*).

Instructional films make up a large but mostly hidden part of the movie world. In an admittedly arbitrary distinction from educational and industrial films, instructionals include how-to movies, training films, and those designed to promote discussion in group settings. Filmmakers as celebrated as John Ford and the Fleischer brothers tackled the genre, which remains a viable way to break into the industry.

A Pennsylvania native who attended high school on Philadelphia's Main Line, Randal Kleiser came to USC to study film when he was eighteen. In addition to his classes, Kleiser made something of a career as an actor in commercials and as a stand-in. In a 1974 interview, he described the work as "an excellent way to learn about lighting and staging." He completed seven student films, including the award-winning *Hands in Innocence* (1969).

The Directors Guild Foundation helped finance *Peege*, which was based on incidents in Kleiser's life in 1972. He used a visit he made with his family to his ailing grandmother in a nursing home as the basis for a half-hour screenplay. Casting director Joel Thurm got the script to Bruce Davison, who had run track with Kleiser at Radnor High School. As the star of *Willard* (1971), a horror movie that was a surprise box-office hit, Davison was a legitimate celebrity, and his decision to act in *Peege* made casting the rest of the film considerably easier.

The title role went to Jeanette Nolan, a veteran actress whose film debut was as Lady Macbeth in Orson Welles' *Macbeth* (1948). She played a fictional version of Kleiser's grandmother during five different time periods. In a later interview, Kleiser remembered how Nolan researched blindness to enact Peege's last days, and decided to remove her false teeth at times to adjust her physical appearance. Barbara Rush, who played the mother in the family, also had a significant film career, having starred with actors like Paul Newman and Marlon Brando. Kleiser remembers casting William Schallert after seeing him as the father on TV's *The Patty Duke Show*; similarly, Barry Livingston was cast as one of the sons in part because of his recurring role on TV's *My Three Sons*.

Financing suddenly became easier as well. Kleiser met David Knapp, an ambitious associate producer who was looking for a producing credit. He was working on *Something Evil* (1971), a TV movie directed by Steven Spielberg, and had extra office space he made available to Kleiser. Eventually the producer and director assembled enough financing to hire a forty-man crew. But even though they were shooting on 16mm instead of costlier 35mm, Kleiser had to cut corners as much as possible.

Locations included an apartment lobby, which was disguised as a nursing home waiting room at Christmas time, and actor Scott Glenn's home, borrowed for a flashback scene that needed a working fireplace. Topanga Canyon passed for suburban Philadelphia. The main location was a Veterans Administration facility that was facing demolition. This became the nursing home bedroom where Greg (Davison), a college student visiting from California, first realizes how much his grandmother's health has deteriorated.

The core of *Peege* is a private encounter in which Greg draws out his grandmother, who has become frail and nonresponsive, by summoning up their shared memories. Kleiser shot much of the scene in a tight two-shot, a set-up Davison recalled using in one of his later films, *Longtime Companion* (1990). Throughout *Peege*, Kleiser isolates details—a catheter tube, crumbs on a floor—without commenting on them, building an atmosphere of polite dread. In a half-hour span he worked in five unobtrusive flashbacks (one of which actually covers three separate time periods). Kleiser's most sophisticated work comes when Greg leaves Peege's room, and, by extension, her life. Here, as in other scenes, the moving camera adopts a subjective viewpoint that draws viewers into the moment.

Peege premiered at a repertory theater in Los Angeles, and attracted enough attention to get Kleiser representation at the Creative Management Associates talent agency. CMA took the film to Universal, which declined to distribute it, but the studio did offer Kleiser a nonexclusive contract. His first professional employment was directing an episode of *Marcus Welby, M.D.*

Kleiser entered *Peege* in the Atlanta Film Festival, where it was seen by Barbara Bryant and Heinz Gelles. They had just formed Phoenix Films & Video, dedicated to supplying films to libraries, universities, and special interest groups. They offered to distribute *Peege*, and according to Kleiser, have been responsible for getting the film to a surprisingly wide audience. They also helped finance a sequel of sorts, *Portrait of Grandpa Doc* (1977), a fictional account of Kleiser's paternal grandfather.

Over the years the film has been used in medical schools, hospitals, nursing homes, and high schools and universities as a way of introducing points of discussion in gerontology studies. Professors have developed detailed analyses of the film's characters and their motives in study aids. Kleiser, on the other hand, was more interested in recapturing a moment in his life than in presenting a case study that covered educational issues. Production photos show how intently he mimicked specific visual details from his home and family.

Now centered in St. Louis, the Phoenix Learning Group, Inc., still distributes both *Peege* and *Portrait of Grandpa Doc*. Kleiser's career has included such box-office hits as *Grease* (1978) as well as *Honey, I Shrunk the Audience* (1994), a site-specific 3-D short shown at Disneyland.

Film Portrait

Jerome Hill, 1972. Sound, Color and B&W, 1.37. 81 minutes.

Credits: Written and directed by Jerome Hill. Produced by Barbara Stone, David C. Stone. Photographed by Jerome Hill. Additional cinematography: Antoine Vernier, William Stevenson, William Reilly, Eric D. Andersen, Gayne Raescher, Lloyd Ahern, C. Redington Barrett. Edited by Henry Sundquist. Sound: Robert C. Fine. Music by Jerome Hill. Music direction: Milton Kaye, Samuel Baron. Includes songs written or recorded by Alec Wilder, Alan Downs. Assistant director: Antoine Vernier. A Heptagon Film presentation.

Additional Credits: Includes material from *Train Arriving at La Ciotat Station* (Auguste & Louis Lumière, 1896), *Knight of Black Art* (Georges Méliès, 1908), *The Magic Umbrella* (Jerome Hill, 1927), *La Cartomancienne* (Jerome Hill, 1932).

Available: The Film-Makers' Cooperative (*www.film-makerscoop.com*).

Written in the form of a chatty, digressive essay, *Film Portrait* documents the life of Jerome Hill, an heir to a Minnesota railway fortune who became an artist, writer, and filmmaker. He was born in St. Paul in 1905, attended Yale, served in the Army, and chose to live in France on the basis of a map of Paris his aunt once showed him. As Hill notes in his narration to *Film Portrait*, almost everyone in his family had a camera, so he had a wealth of archival material to choose from in assembling his film.

Hill's career included directing *Grandma Moses* (1950), a sponsored biography of the primitive painter written by poet Archibald Macleish, and *Albert Schweitzer* (1957), written and narrated in part by the humanitarian and Nobel Peace Prize winner. The latter won an Academy Award for Documentary (Features). Hill began, but never released, a biography of Carl Gustav Jung made in cooperation with the psychiatrist, and directed two fiction films, *The Sand Castle* (1961) and *Open the Door and See All the People* (1964), which he says were inspired by conversations with Jung.

During the 1960s Hill experimented with painting directly onto film celluloid, an approach he explores freely in *Film Portrait*. Hill also uses several other animation techniques, including collage, stop-motion, and cut-outs. *Film Portrait* makes liberal use of freeze-frames, optically printed zooms, negative imagery, jump cuts, slow motion and reverse photography, and associative or stream-of-consciousness editing. Hill elaborates on these techniques by composing a score that alternately complements and contradicts the visuals, and by writing a narration that is not always completely reliable.

Hill's grandfather founded one of the few Midwest railroads that did not go bankrupt during the Depression. His family had access to wealth that seems unimaginable today. The Hill children were the subject of Pathé travelogues as early as 1909, and had their own film library while growing up, one that included works by D.W. Griffith and Georges Méliès. As Hill remarks, "What a privilege to learn films by heart, as if they were pieces of music." Hill says that as a child he developed a taste for the dramatic and spectacular, as well as an obsession with the world of illusion.

When home movie equipment became available, members of the Hill family began documenting their gatherings, vacations, and other events. Hill describes an effort in the 1920s to shoot an amateur version of "The Pied Piper of Hamelin" in a suburb of Rome. The clips he provides of this film and the earlier Pathé and home movie efforts comprise the most fascinating moments of *Film Portrait*.

Hill became absorbed with technical properties of film. He once shot an entire story with the actors performing backward; by filming them in reverse, and then projecting the result normally, the actors would appear to be moving forward. Hill was influenced by art deco and surrealism, and his *La Cartomancienne*, which he shows in its entirety, fits in comfortably beside the films of Jean Epstein and René Clair.

Like many memoirs or personal essays, *Film Portrait* can be exasperating, a grab bag of ideas that are developed haphazardly or not at all. Hill's concept of time, of how cinema depicts the past and future, merits more explication than the few offhand comments he provides. "Isn't voyeurism at the core of the cinematic experience?" he asks at one point, but he is more interested in moving to the next epigram, the next breezy quip, than in discussing the topic seriously. Hill's cool, detached, ironic tone takes getting used to as well. He can come off as a dilettante, a dabbler with the means to finance his whims. Viewers watching this would learn nothing about his influence on other filmmakers. Stan Brakhage made Hill a central figure in *Song XIII* (1965), for example, and dedicated *American Thirties Song* (1969) to him.

Film Portrait contains shots of unearthly beauty, like skiers moving in reverse who erase their figure-eight patterns from a white mountain slope, or Maude Oakes, an actress in many of his films, ascending a set of stone stairs in dazzling sunlight. It also documents lost moments, like native dances by Blackfoot Indians (Hill was an honorary member of the tribe), and even effectively restages one of the seminal Lumière films. If the director remains an elusive figure in his own autobiography, what is apparent throughout *Film Portrait* is his inquisitiveness, pronounced sense of aesthetics, firm moral tone, and lighthearted humor. Hill died in November 1972, before his friend Jonas Mekas could release the film through the Anthology Film Archives.

Reminiscences of a Journey to Lithuania

Jonas Mekas, 1971–72. Sound, color and B&W, 1.37. 82 minutes.

Featuring: Jonas Mekas, Adolfas Mekas, Pola Mekas, Petrus Mekas, Peter Kubelka, Hermann Nitsch, Annette Michelson, Ken Jacobs.

Credits: Photographed, edited, and directed by Jonas Mekas. Sound by Jonas Mekas. Produced by Vaughan Films, Ltd., and Norddeutscher Rundfunk.

Additional Credits: Screened at the New York Film Festival on October 4, 1972.

Available: The Film-Makers' Cooperative (*www.film-makerscoop.com*); Canyon Cinema (*www.canyoncinema.com*).

Jonas Mekas was born in 1922 on a farm near Semeniskiai, Lithuania. With his brother Adolfas, he became a resistance fighter against the Soviets. Forced to flee the country, they were imprisoned in a forced labor camp near Manburg. After the World War II, the brothers began studying film at a displaced persons camp before they were allowed to emigrate to the United States. They settled in New York City, where Jonas became the founder and editor of *Film Culture* magazine and a critic at *The Village Voice*. He also shot footage with a handheld 16mm Bolex camera.

Jonas Mekas was crucial to the postwar experimental film community. He helped found the Film-Makers' Cooperative, which set up a distribution scheme for independent filmmakers, and the Anthology Film Archives, which houses and screens one of the most significant collections of avant-garde films in the world. He has been tireless in his efforts to educate filmgoers about the medium, in mentoring filmmakers and writers, and in pursuing his theories about movies.

Reminiscences of a Journey to Lithuania is broken into three parts. As Mekas has written in his program notes for the film, "The first part is made up of footage I shot with my first Bolex, during my first years in America, mostly from 1950–1953. It shows me and my brother Adolfas, how we looked in those days; miscellaneous footage of immigrants in Brooklyn, picnicking, dancing, singing; the streets of Williamsburg." The footage, mostly black-and-white, is accompanied only by Mekas's autobiographical musings and an occasional piano accompaniment on the soundtrack. His observations, coupled with the shifting tones of black-and-white and color stock, give a ghostly aura to the images. "They looked like sad animals who didn't know where they were," Mekas says of Lithuanian exiles at an outdoor picnic.

Mekas wrote, "The second part was shot in August 1971, in Lithuania. Almost all of the footage comes from Semeniskiai, the village I was born in. You see the old house, my mother (born 1887), all the brothers, goofing, celebrating our homecoming." This material, all in color, was shot in a style Mekas had been developing since the 1950s. He would film in bursts, editing action in the camera as it was occurring. "On some days I shot ten frames, on others ten seconds, still on others ten minutes. Or I shoot nothing." The effect can be fragmented, scattershot, elliptical, or as P. Adams Sitney describes it, "pixilated."

The style can also seem exclusionary, as viewers are limited in how much of a scene they are permitted to observe. On a more practical level, the strategy allowed Mekas to husband his unexposed footage, to stretch out his raw material. Mainstream filmmaking has subsequently caught up to Mekas. In feature films and especially in advertising, individual shots are often doctored to remove "boring" sections or to maintain a consistent pace.

Mekas was also circumscribed in what he was allowed to film in Lithuania. He doesn't explain the background for the second part of *Reminiscences* in the film, but in a 2006 interview he spoke about the conditions under which he was permitted to return to Lithuania. In New York City, Mekas arranged for an editor of *Pravda* to meet the poet Allen Ginsberg. The next time Mekas attended the Moscow Film Festival, he received permission to return to his birthplace for the first time in twenty-seven years. While he was happy to be reunited with his family, Mekas was keenly aware of the ambivalence the other Lithuanians felt toward him. "To them, I could just as easily be an American spy as a Soviet spy. After all, how come I was permitted to visit Lithuania?"

When they saw what he shot, Soviet authorities wanted Mekas to destroy the film. They had expected a typically pro-Soviet portrait of Lithuania, not an opaque diary. "It was done in a very personal way," Mekas said. "I was just going by myself with my Bolex. You don't really see how Lithuania is today: you see it only through the memories of a Displaced Person."

In the third and shortest section of the film, Mekas returns to the labor camp where he was imprisoned. Then he visits with friends, including the filmmakers Peter Kubelka and Ken Jacobs, and the performance artist Hermann Nitsch. From examining the library of a monastery, Mekas cuts to a fire that destroyed a Vienna market in August 1971.

Reminiscences can be seen as the middle of a trilogy of "diary" films that began with *Diaries Notes and Sketches* (1969) and concludes with *Lost Lost Lost* (1976). But nostalgia, the sense of exile, the lack of a true home are central to all of Mekas's work. It's interesting that once he began working in video, where raw tape is cheap and plentiful, he abandoned his pixilated shooting methods. Mekas has also expanded his collaboration with his audience, turning strips of film into artwork exhibited in galleries and continuing to write poetry. And he has not stopped releasing films: *Self Portrait* (1990), *As I Was Moving Ahead Occasionally I Saw Brief Glimpses of Beauty* (2000), *A Letter from Greenpoint* (2005), and others.

Frank Film

Frank Mouris Productions, 1973. Sound, color, 1.33. 9 minutes.
Credits: Written, produced, photographed, and directed by Frank Mouris, Caroline Mouris. Sound: Tony Schwartz. Narration: Frank Mouris.
Additional Credits: Released in New York City on April 13, 1973. Rated G in 1976.
Awards: Oscar for Best Short Subject—Animated Films.

Available: Direct Cinema Limited 16mm and VHS (*www.directcinema.com*).

Collage played a significant role in the work of artists like Joseph Cornell, but it had a more limited impact in film—perhaps for technical reasons, as assembling collages could require many successive generations of duped film stock, more likely for the fact that it is an extremely labor-intensive activity.

In one sense, all optical editing is a form of collage, since dissolves involve superimposing one image on another. Animation filmed with a multiplane camera could also be regarded as collage, although filmmakers almost always combined different pictorial elements to give the illusion that they formed one picture.

Frank Mouris and his wife Caroline Ahlfors Mouris used an animation stand to create *Frank Film*, a collage work that took three years to assemble. They researched, cut out, and glued onto acetate cells 11,592 images—photographs, illustrations, and other graphic work—arranging them in geometric patterns that cascade up, down, and across the frame, timed to both an internal rhyme scheme (pies beget desserts, televisions beget other appliances) and to the soundtrack. Composed of two separate narrations overlaid on each other, the soundtrack itself is a form of collage, mixed by Tony Schwartz so that one channel generally predominates over the other, but at times too dense to fully comprehend. One voice-over is a dry, self-deprecating autobiography of Frank Mouris, delivered by Mouris himself. The other, also voiced by Mouris, is a free-form, stream-of-consciousness monologue that plays off images on the screen as well as details of Mouris's life.

Overload is the operative word for *Frank Film*, which offers a dizzying and ultimately depressing snapshot of consumer goods in the second half of the twentieth century. The film may not explicitly criticize the consequences of capitalism, but the material on display can't help but evoke themes of greed and gluttony. While the film charts the gradual maturation of Mouris, who moves from narcissism to an interest in sexuality to attempts at socialization, the underlying mood is one of insecurity. His autobiography isn't significant to stand by itself, and is periodically drowned out by irrelevant data. Similarly, one image isn't interesting or worthwhile enough to hold the screen, it has to be duplicated, mirrored, contrasted with others.

Mouris insists that he had no ulterior motive in mind when creating the film. Instead, he saw *Frank Film* as the 1970s equivalent of a calling card movie—a work designed to attract further work. In an interview with Heather Kenyon, he said, "Caroline and I did *Frank Film* just to do that one personal film that you do to get the artistic inclinations out of your system before going commercial. Then we planned to join the industry, as you call it, armed with her MBA and my MFA." That may explain Mouris's comical insistence on self-identification throughout the film, although he wryly notes that his tactic backfired.

When *Frank Film* won an Oscar in 1973 for animated short subject, the Mourises may have expected the instant celebrity Frank describes at one point on the soundtrack. What happened was a bit more prosaic. The film received some theatrical distribution through a deal with United Artists (the studio blew the original 16mm up to 35mm), but most of the income for the film came from the usual sources: museums, universities and other schools, and especially libraries. Like almost all independent films at the time, *Frank Film* in its 16mm form was distributed by Pyramid Films, and the tattered prints you are likely to encounter generally bear the Pyramid logo.

The Mourises received enough awards and grants to finance subsequent films, including *Frankly Caroline* (1999), another collage effort focusing on the other half of the Mouris household. However, Mouris says that as a result of winning an Oscar, "we became fiercely independent filmmakers, only interested in doing new films, whatever the genre, and not just repeating ourselves in one area of film." They followed the advice of fellow animator John Hubley, who accepted commercial work with the intention of completing his own personal films during summers. To finance their projects, the Mourises shot television commercials for Levi's Shirts, Nickelodeon Toys, and other products. They also did freelance animation work for MTV, VH1, HBO Comedy, Nick at Nite, PETA, the Cartoon Network, Nickelodeon, and *Sesame Street*. They maintain a production office in Nassau on Long Island.

American Graffiti

Universal, 1973. Sound, color, 2.35. 112 minutes. Rated PG.

Cast: Richard Dreyfuss (Curt), Ronny Howard (Steve), Paul Le Mat (John), Charlie Martin Smith (Terry), Candy Clark (Debbie), Mackenzie Phillips (Carol), Cindy Williams (Laurie), Wolfman Jack (Disc jockey), Bo Hopkins (Joe), Harrison Ford (Bob Falfa), Manuel Padilla, Jr. (Carlos), Beau Gentry (Ants), Jim Bohan (Holstein), Jana Bellan (Budda), Deby Celiz (Wendy), Lynn Marie Stewart (Bobbie), Terry McGovern (Mr. Wolfe), Kathy Quinlan (Peg), Tim Crowley (Eddie), Scott Beach (Mr. Gordon), John Brent (Car salesman), Gordon Analla (Bozo), John Bracci (Station attendant), Jody Carlson (Girl in Studebaker), Del Close (Man at bar—Guy), Charles Dorsett (Man at accident), Stephen Knox (Kid at accident), Joseph Miksak (Man at liquor store), George Meyer (Bum at liquor store), James Cranna (Thief), Johnny Weissmuller, Jr. (Badass #1), William Niven (Clerk at liquor store), Al Nalbandian (Hank), Bob Pasaak (Dale), Chris Pray (Al), Susan Richardson (Judy), Fred Ross (Ferber), Jan Dunn (Old woman), Charlie Murphy (Old man), Ed Greenberg (Kip), Lisa Herman (Girl in Dodge), Irving Israel (Mr. Kroot), Kay Ann Kemper (Jane), Caprice Schmidt (Announcer at dance), Joe Spano (Vic), Debralee Scott (Falfa's girl), Ron Vincent (Jeff), Donna Wehr (Carhop), Cam Whitman (Balloon Girl), Jan Wilson (Girl at dance), Suzanne Somers (Blonde in T-bird), Flash Cadillac and the Continental Kids (Herby & the Heartbeats).

Credits: Directed by George Lucas. Written by George Lucas and Gloria Katz & Willard Huyck. Produced by Francis Ford Coppola. Co-produced by Gary Kurtz. Visual consultant: Haskell Wexler. Film editors: Verna Fields, Marcia Lucas. Sound montage and re-recording: Walter Murch. Casting: Fred Roos, Mike Fenton. Assistant to the producer: Beverly Walker. Design consultant: Al Locatelli. Directors of photography: Ron Eveslage, Jan D'Alquen. Art director: Dennis Clark. Costume designer: Aggie Guerard Rodgers. Production manager: James Hogan. Gaffer: William Maley. Key grip: Ken Phelps. Production sound: Arthur Rochester. Set decorator: Douglas Freeman. Key hair stylists: Gerry Leetch, Betty Iverson. Script supervisor: Christina Crowley. Choreographer: Toni Basil. Sound editing: James Nelson. Music coordinator: Karin Green. Titles & optical effects: Universal Title. Color by Technicolor. Filmed in Marin and Sonoma Counties, California, and completed at American Zoetrope Studios, San Francisco. A Lucasfilm, Ltd./Coppola Co. production.

Additional Credits: Production dates: June to July, 1972. Opened August, 1973.

Other Versions: Sequel *More American Graffiti* (1979), directed by Bill L. Norton.

Available: Universal Home Video DVD (1998) UPC: 025192422324.

One of the most influential and successful filmmakers of his generation, George Lucas was born in 1944 in Modesto, California, the son of an office supplies salesman and walnut farmer. Lucas preferred racing cars to school, and in June 1962, before graduating high school, was involved in a car accident that left him with crushed lungs. While building race cars later, he met cinematographer Haskell Wexler, who helped him get into the film program at the University of Southern California. Of the eight student films he made there, *THX-1138: 4EB (Electric Labyrinth)* won first prize at the National Student Film Festival.

After USC, Lucas worked as a cameraman for Saul Bass, as an editor for the USIA, shot portions of the Rolling Stones concert at Altamont that were used in the documentary *Gimme Shelter* (1970), and married film editor Marcia Griffin. Lucas then won an internship from Warner Brothers, where he met director Francis Ford Coppola. They formed American Zoetrope, an independent production company in San Francisco. The company's first project, released by Warners, was *THX 1138* (1971), a feature version of Lucas's student film.

A financial and critical failure, the film forced Lucas to rethink his goals. He targeted his next project squarely at a demographic he felt was being ignored by Hollywood, fashioning an autobiographical coming-of-age story centered around one night in the lives of several teenagers in a small town much like Modesto. "*Graffiti* was for sixteen-year-olds," he said later. By setting the story in 1962, Lucas could avoid much of the turmoil surrounding civil rights, the Vietnam War, drug use, the hippie culture, etc., while still dealing with a recognizable pop culture.

Like Steven Spielberg later, Lucas was intent on re-creating a critical period in his life, the last time he felt comfortable with the world and his position in it. In a sense he had been guessing about the characters in *THX 1138*, imagining their society and how they operated in it; on the other hand, he felt he knew the 1960s—the clothes, the songs, the hobbies and cars. The characters in *American Graffiti* were for the most part on the verge of sexual knowledge, a condition Lucas has repeated in his films to this day. (The story could be occurring just at the time Lucas had his car accident.)

The script was submitted in a treatment form that Lucas prepared with the help of newlyweds Gloria Katz and Willard Huyck. (Lucas had Richard Walters work out a full screenplay, but rejected it. Katz and Huyck eventually turned in a 180-page script.) The only studio that showed any interest in the project was Universal, where executive Ned Tanen eventually oversaw a deal that paid the director $20,000 out of a budget of roughly $750,000. (It was the last in Universal's plan to catch up with *Easy Rider* by making five cheap, youth-oriented films.) Lucas reluctantly accepted Francis Ford Coppola as his producer. According to Katz and Huyck, Coppola was responsible for hiring casting director Fred Roos, who played a major part in finding actors for the film.

Lucas had only twenty-nine days to shoot *Graffiti*, a tight schedule for a story that took place almost exclusively at night. He edited the film with his wife Marcia and Verna Fields, an industry veteran who had worked on three Peter Bogdanovich movies. Structurally an ensemble piece, *American Graffiti* was assembled like a jigsaw puzzle, with dramatic moments alternating between slapstick and action.

In later interviews, Lucas claimed that *Graffiti* was the first film to make extensive use of rock music, which would come as a surprise to the makers of *The Girl Can't Help It* (1956), *Jamboree* (1957), *A Hard Day's Night* (1964), and dozens of other teen-oriented movies. Lucas also said that *Graffiti* was the first time a film featured four separate but interlocking story lines; he might as well have taken credit for *Intolerance* (1916) and *The Rules of the Game* (1939) while he was at it.

The film previewed in San Francisco on January 28, 1973, a legendary screening that saw an angry Ned Tanen threatening to bury the picture and an equally angry Coppola offering to buy it outright from Universal. The studio paid more attention to another Tanen project, *Jesus Christ Superstar*, than it did to *Graffiti*. But Lucas's film proved a phenomenal hit, earning over $100 million in its initial release and spawning an entire nostalgia industry.

Lucas had nothing to do with the sequel, *More American Graffiti*, or with the television knock-offs like *Happy Days* and *Laverne & Shirley*. (The director did add three deleted scenes and about two minutes additional screen time to reissues and video releases in order to highlight actors like Harrison Ford. He also digitally altered the shot of Mel's Drive-In in the opening credits.) Lucas didn't even get much credit for helping establish an entire generation of movie stars. *American Graffiti* was the first, or most important, résumé entry for a surprising number of actors and crew members. The film also contributed to the rupture between Lucas and Coppola, who angered the director by cutting Haskell Wexler and coproducer Gary Kurtz out of profit-sharing arrangements. Lucas and Coppola in turn both shunned Universal as a result of Tanen's behavior, thus depriving the studio of the *Star Wars* gold mine that would come later.

Critics at the time saw *Graffiti* as a warm, nostalgic look at an era that had barely ended. It may be easier today to recognize how subversive Lucas's vision was. *Graffiti* isn't about mainstream characters, the normal people who trudged through high school on their way to boring careers. And it isn't about the athletes, cheerleaders, and student council members who are consistently mocked in the course of the film. *Graffiti* is about loners, misfits, and outcasts, the nerds who couldn't get dates, the gang leaders who had no gangs, the borderline tramps with bad reputations. Lucas understood that, in terms of drama, more things happen to these people than to the mainstream. He also sensed that moviegoers could simultaneously relate to and feel superior to outsiders. It's a lesson that helped drive the plot to *Star Wars*.

The vignettes of minor rebellion and fumblings toward love, efforts that in real life would usually lead to failure, Lucas wraps up in a series of happy endings. He undercuts these a bit with some pointed postscripts (a device that quickly became such an annoying cliché that it was satirized in *National Lampoon's Animal House*), but even they can't destroy the film's resolutely feel-good vibes. Sentimental, manipulative, *American Graffiti* is also fundamentally false. Even its soundtrack is out of date, at times by ten years. Nevertheless, it paved the way for one of the most successful careers in the industry.

Enter the Dragon

Warner Bros., 1973. Sound, color, 2.35. 98 minutes. Rated R.

Cast: Bruce Lee (Lee), John Saxon (Roper), Ahna Capri (Tania), Shih Kien (Han), Bob Wall (Oharra), Angela Mao Ying (Su Lin), Betty Chung (Mei Ling), Geoffrey Weeks (Braithwaite), Yang Sze [Bolo Yeung] (Bolo), Peter Archer (Parsons), Jim Kelly (Williams), Ho Lee Yan (Old man), Marlene Clark (Secretary), Allan Kent (Golfer); William Keller, Mickey Caruso (L.A. cops); Pat Johnson, Darnell Garcia, Mike Bissell (Hoods).

Credits: Directed by Robert Clouse. Written by Michael Allin. Produced by Fred Weintraub & Paul Heller. Associate producer: Raymond Chow. Director of photography: Gilbert Hubbs. Film edited by Kurt Hirschler and George Watters. Fighting sequences staged by Bruce Lee. Music: Lalo Schifrin. Assistants to the producers: Jeffrey Schechtman, Andre Morgan. Production manager: Louis Sit. Assistant director: Chaplin Chang. Costume designer: Louis Sheng. Makeup: Sheung Sun, John Hung. Hairdresser: Lai Chun. Sound mixer: Robert Lin. Music editor: Gene Marks. Panavision. Technicolor. A Warner Bros. Inc.–Concord Productions Inc. production.

Additional Cast includes: Sammo Hung (Sparring partner), Roy Chiao (Shaolin Abbot); Jackie Chan, Yuen Wah, Yuen Biao (Fighters).

Additional Credits: Production dates: January 25 to April 1973. Opened in New York City on August 17, 1973.

Bruce Lee in a hall of mirrors sequence deleted from the original American release of *Enter the Dragon*.

Other Versions: A 1998 reissue added four minutes of material cut from the original release.

Available: Warner Home Video DVD (1998). ISBN: 0-7907-3557-1. UPC: 0-85391-59212-9.

Martial arts was represented on film as early as *Romance of the West Chamber* (1927), directed in Shanghai by Hou Yao and based on a play dating to the thirteenth century. As an important part of Chinese culture, martial arts played a major presence in Asian film throughout the twentieth century, although in Hollywood techniques like judo or karate were generally treated as magic or comedy. The foremost proponent of martial arts in the latter half of the century, Bruce Lee not only reinvigorated a national movie industry, but helped legitimize an entire genre of film.

Born in 1940 in San Francisco, but raised in Hong Kong, Lee was the son of a Chinese opera performer. He had small roles in Hong Kong films as a child, then studied dance and kung fu as a teenager. He also became involved in street gangs, a reason why his parents sent him back to the United States for his education. He studied philosophy at the University of Washington, where he waited on tables and gave dance and kung fu lessons. In 1964 he opened the first of three martial arts schools. He also began pursuing acting seriously, winning a supporting part in the television series *The Green Hornet*.

In the show, which was based on a 1930s radio series, Lee played Kato, a chauffeur and houseboy. Although Lee did have a few opportunities to display his martial arts skills, the role was not that different from those given to Asians for decades. After a brief but mesmerizing appearance in *Marlowe* (1969), Lee decided that his prospects in film were stronger in Hong Kong. He moved there with his family in 1971.

Lee signed a two-picture deal with Raymond Chow, who had formed Golden Harvest after working at a studio run by the Shaw Brothers. The first, *Fists of Fury* (1971), was a box-office sensation. *The Chinese Connection* in 1972 was even more popular. Lee's inimitable athleticism transferred especially well to the screen. He was not only exceptionally well trained, but had a strong sense of how to maximize his fighting style on screen. "Most Chinese movies followed the Japanese," he said. "There were too many weapons—especially swords. So we used a minimum of weapons and made it a better film. I mean people like films that are more than just one long, armed hassle."

Lee's film characterizations were proud, forceful, unapologetic, but still respectful of tradition and legitimate authority. In his movies he stood up to bullies and thieves, holding his own with other races rather than acting subservient. He developed an enormous following worldwide, and formed his own company, Concord Productions, to make his next film. Shot partially in Rome, *The Return of the Dragon* (1972) featured Chuck Norris in a supporting role. It continued Lee's attempt to make a "multilevel" film, "the kind of movie where you can just watch the surface story, if you like, or can look deeper into it."

Hoping to cash in on Lee's popularity, Warners prepared a script for Lee that essentially placed him in a kung fu version of *Dr. No* (1962): a secret agent infiltrates a martial arts tournament held on an island in order to uncover the crime ring operating there. Producer Fred Weintraub had worked with Lee in the United States on a concept that eventually became the television series *Kung Fu* with David Carradine. Lee embraced the Warner film project, which was financed jointly with Concord and Golden Harvest, and even allowed

Warners to assign a Caucasian director, Robert Clouse. But Lee substantially revised the script, and maintained a tight control over how his action scenes were filmed.

With a heritage stretching back centuries, martial arts offers numerous schools and regimens to follow. Lee trained in Wing Chun as a teenager, and also studied jujitsu, Western boxing, and fencing. In the United States, he developed his own style, Jeet Kune Do, sometimes translated as "the way of intercepting fist." As the result of his intensive training, he was capable of remarkable physical feats. He approached the filming of martial arts scenes as if they were routines to be choreographed. He drew from earlier kung fu movies, but he used a rhythm-oriented soundtrack to help edit his fights. The score helped the fights build in tempo and intensity, a strategy adopted by many subsequent martial arts filmmakers. In some ways, *Enter the Dragon*

resembles a musical in which fluff and filler surround numbers of startling inventiveness and skill.

Lee's influence has been pervasive in Hong Kong and in action films in general. The fact that he died of a cerebral edema three weeks before *Enter the Dragon* opened in the United States only added to his legend. Lee imitators appeared in Hong Kong films almost at once, as did pieced-together documentaries about the fighter. Lee helped bring kung fu movies in general, and the Hong Kong film industry as a whole, to the attention of the world. Several extras and supporting actors in *Enter the Dragon* went on to significant film careers: Jackie Chan, Sammo Hung, Yuen Wah, Yuen Biao, etc. *Enter the Dragon* ended up grossing over $100 million, one reason why action choreography in everything from James Bond to Batman films now incorporates a wider range of leaps, kicks, and martial arts-inspired stunts.

Mean Streets

Warner Bros., 1973. Sound, color, 1.85. 112 minutes. Rated R.

Cast: Robert De Niro (Johnny Boy), Harvey Keitel (Charlie), David Proval (Tony), Amy Robinson (Teresa), Richard Romanus (Michael), Cesare Danova (Giovanni), Victor Argo (Marlo), Jeannie Bell (Diane), David Carradine (Drunk), Robert Carradine (Boy with gun), George Memmoli (Joey), Murray Mosten (Oscar), Harry Northup (Soldier), Lenny Scaletta (Jimmy), Ken Sinclair (Sammy), Lois Waldon (Jewish Girl), Robert Wilder (Benton), Dino Seragusa (Old man), D'Mitch Davis (Cop), Peter Fain (George), Julie Andleman (Girl at party), Jaime Alba (Young boy #1), Ken Konstantin (Young boy #2), Nicki "Ack" Aquilino (Man on docks), B. Mitchell Reed (Disc jockey).

Credits: Directed by Martin Scorsese. Screen play: Martin Scorsese and Mardik Martin. Story: Martin Scorsese. Produced by Jonathan T. Taplin. Executive producer: E. Lee Perry. Director of photography: Kent Wakeford. Additional photography: Norman Gerard. Edited by Sidney Levin. Pre- and post-production coordinator: Sandra Weintraub. Production manager: Paul Rapp. Sound mixer: Don Johnson. Visual consultant: David Nichols. Titles, opticals & processing: Consolidated Film Industries. Sound: Glen Glenn. Sound effects: Angel Editorial. Taplin-Perry-Scorsese Productions.

Additional Cast: Catherine Scorsese (Woman in hallway), Martin Scorsese (Jimmy Shorts).

Additional Credits: Production dates: April to June 1973. Premiered at the New York Film Festival on October 2, 1973.

Available: Warner Home Video DVD (2001). ISBN: 0-7907-5839-3. UPC: 0-85391-91272-9.

Born in Flushing, New York, in 1942, Martin Scorsese grew up in the Little Italy section of lower Manhattan. Afflicted with asthma, he was isolated from much of the culture and day-to-day life in his Italian-American community. Instead, with his father, he became immersed in movies. A devout Roman Catholic, Scorsese studied to become a priest, but failed an entrance exam to divinity school at Fordham College. At New York University, he took film courses and began making his first 16mm films.

With no connections to the film industry, Scorsese needed to make himself noticed. He did this by exploiting his religious and cultural backgrounds, but primarily by pushing the limits of acceptability—a time-honored method for outsiders trying to be heard. He made two 16mm shorts, one an adaptation of a horror story, the other a comic monologue about a small-time gangster. His first feature project, *Who's That Knocking at My Door?* (1964–69), was part of a projected trilogy about a character named J.R. or Charlie, a loose alter ego for the director. Scorsese completed an hour-long version starring Harvey Keitel; NYU instructor Haig Manoogian convinced him to rewrite the script and shoot it again. Keitel was the only holdover from the original cast.

The final version of *Who's That Knocking at My Door?* included many of the themes and devices Scorsese would use throughout his career. Keitel's J.R. is torn between religious piety and worldly temptations. Although loneliness compels him to connect with others, his obsessions and neuroses keep him apart from the people he reaches out to. Like Jean-Luc Godard, Scorsese uses pop cultural references—songs, clothes, advertising—to both fix the characters in a time and place and to provide an ironic commentary on their actions. Unlike Godard, Scorsese had a lifetime of film history to draw on, an understanding of how Golden Age film directors handled dramatic situations, a firm grasp of the often rigid editing schemes of classic Hollywood movies. By merging French New Wave sensibilities with mainstream Hollywood crafts-manship, Scorsese gave his New York characters and subjects a unique look and style.

While working toward a directorial career, Scorsese taught at NYU, edited films like *Woodstock* (1970), directed a short called *The Big Shave* (1967, financed in part by a grant), and assisted on *Street Scenes* (1970), a collaborative political documentary. He also developed many friendships and associations that would be constants throughout his movies, among them editor Thelma Schoonmaker, screenwriter Mardik Martin, and critic Jay Cocks. But he had yet to crack the mainstream.

The director's first Hollywood offer came from Roger Corman, who produced the Depression-era exploitation film *Boxcar Bertha* (1972). Despite its explicit religious symbolism, the film had little to do with Scorsese's interests. He returned to New York determined to make a movie that expressed and perhaps explained his background. *Mean Streets* was the second part of his J.R./Charlie trilogy, one that would refine his dual impulses: religious leanings and the lure of evil. (The title is a reference to pulp writer Raymond Chandler, who used the phrase in describing his private detective Philip Marlowe.)

The semi autobiographical script was a collaboration between Scorsese and his NYU friend Mardik Martin. In part they were attempting to answer Francis Ford Coppola's adaptation of *The Godfather* (1972). "We wanted to tell the story about real gangsters," Mardik said. Scorsese got $300,000 for the project from Jonathan Taplin, a one-time road manager of the rock group The Band. The budget was so small that Scorsese was forced to shoot much of the film in Los Angeles. Apart from a few exceptions, the exteriors were shot in New York City; the interiors, in Los Angeles.

Scorsese wanted to make the San Gennaro street festival part of the film, which meant that he had to start shooting without a complete cast. He offered the lead role of Charlie to Jon Voight, and then as filming approached to Harvey Keitel. An ex-Marine who grew up in Brooklyn, Keitel was a logical choice, as *Mean Streets* picked up right where *Who's That Knocking at My Door?* left off. Scorsese gave Robert De Niro the choice of four roles in the film. De Niro had wanted the lead, but agreed to play Johnny Boy, the most demanding and volatile part in the film. This was the first of eight films the director and actor made together. "Bob gets to do the things I would like to do I guess," Scorsese said in an interview. "I think he enjoys playing out those aspects of the character and, there's no doubt about it, it's almost like a catharsis of going through moments that he feels are emotional truths."

Mean Streets introduces a large cast of characters and follows several story lines, but the film boils down to the need for Charlie, conflicted about his life, to redeem the self-destructive Johnny Boy. The film has a deliberately raw feel, a corrective to the slick style of *The Godfather*. But Scorsese also self-consciously evokes the films and filmmakers who inspired him. He includes clips from John Ford's *The Searchers* (1956) and Roger Corman's *The Tomb of Ligeia* (1964), as well as shots and scenes that refer to everyone from Godard to Abbott and Costello.

Scorsese was also developing a recognizable style, one that contrasted long tracking and handheld shots with angled jump cuts, timed to soundtracks rich with rock songs and Italian pop. Actors welcomed his willingness to improvise and collaborate, while crew members were grateful for his thorough planning and understanding of technical matters. Although *Mean Streets* was not a financial success, it is in some ways a template for Scorsese's future work. He would refine and replay situations from this movie in *Taxi Driver* (1976) and *GoodFellas* (1990), both Registry titles. Even his more mainstream pieces like *Alice Doesn't Live Here Anymore* (1974) have thematic and stylistic resemblances.

Badlands

Warner Bros., 1973. Sound, color, 1.85. 94 minutes. Rated PG.

Cast: Martin Sheen (Kit), Sissy Spacek (Holly), Warren Oates (Father), Ramon Bieri (Cato), Alan Vint (Deputy), Gary Littlejohn (Sheriff), John Carter (Rich man), Bryan Montgomery (Boy), Gail Threlkeld (Girl), Charles Fitzpatrick (Clerk), Howard Ragsdale (Boss), John Womack, Jr. (Trooper), Dona Baldwin (Maid), Ben Braco (Gas attendant).

Credits: Written, produced and directed by Terrence Malick. Executive producer: Edward R. Pressman. Directors of photography: Brian Probyn, Tak Fujimoto, Stevan Larner. Editor: Robert Estrin. Associate editor: William Weber. Assistant editor: Marion Segal. Art director: Jack Fisk. Associate art director: Ed Richardson. Production manager: William Scott. Sound effects: Sam Shaw. Associate producer: Lou Stroller. Original music composed and conducted by George Tipton. Hair/wardrobe:

Dona Baldwin. Casting: Diane Derfner. Assistant directors: John Broderick, Carl Olsen. Production mixer: Maury Harris. Assistant camera: Tony Palmieri. Artwork: Joan Mocine. Autos: Gary Littlejohn. Stunts: George Fisher. Music editor: Erma Levin. Titles, opticals and processing by Consolidated Film Industries. Recorded by Glen Glenn Sound.
Additional Cast: Terrence Malick (Architect).
Additional Credits: Production dates: May to July 1973. Opened in New York City on October 15, 1973.
Available: Warner Home Video DVD (1999). ISBN: 0-7907-3924-0. UPC: 0-85391-60862-2.

As controversial today as when it was released, *Badlands* marks a dividing line between films intended as art and movies made as commerce. In writing, producing, and directing the project, Terrence Malick was issuing a challenge to his contemporaries, one answered in titles as disparate as *The Sugarland Express* (1974) and *Heaven's Gate* (1980). *Badlands* was far more influential with filmmakers than it was successful with critics or audiences. In the thirty years since its release, Malick's style and technique have been appropriated by makers of commercials and music videos; his approach to narrative, arguably the most significant factor in *Badlands*, has been more difficult to emulate.

Born in 1943 in Illinois, Malick was a Harvard graduate, Rhodes scholar, freelance journalist for *Newsweek* and *The New Yorker*, and philosophy professor at MIT. Writer Peter Biskind attributes the suicide of his younger brother to the theme of guilt that runs through Malick's work. Malick was one of the early students at the American Film Institute, where he made *Lanton Mills* (1969), a Western parody he appeared in along with Warren Oates and Harry Dean Stanton. At AFI, Malick made important contacts, such as Jack Nicholson, who hired him to revise his script for *Drive, He Said* (1971). (He also contributed to the script for *Dirty Harry*, although his work did not reach the screen.)

Malick wrote the screenplay for *Deadhead Miles* (1972), a trucker comedy, and *Pocket Money* (1972), an unclassifiable buddy Western starring Paul Newman and Lee Marvin, but his intent had always been to direct. Screenwriter Jacob Brackman introduced Malick to Edward R. Pressman, a fledgling producer whose *Sisters* (1973), directed by Brian De Palma, had become an unexpected hit. Pressman agreed to finance *Badlands*, a script Malick had written about a 1958 killing spree by Charlie Starkweather and Caril Ann Fugate.

With a budget of $350,000, Malick was limited to shooting entirely in Colorado, although his story ranged over a great deal of the Midwest. Even so, the budget wouldn't cover screening dailies. According to Biskind, Jill Jakes, Malick's wife at the time, balked at paying for an injured crewmember's helicopter flight to a hospital. Malick reportedly ran out of money but continued to shoot with whatever crew he could assemble; he was also forced to fill in when an actor failed to show up on time.

This was an important film for both Martin Sheen and Sissy Spacek. Sheen, born Ramon Estevez in 1940, had worked extensively on stage and television, and had appeared in supporting roles in a half-dozen or so features. Kit was his first opportunity at a big screen role, which he won in part for his youthful good looks and slight resemblance to James Dean. (He was thirty-two during the shoot, playing someone seven years younger.) Spacek, born in Texas in 1949, also specialized in playing younger than her age. She lived with her cousin Rip Torn and his then-wife Geraldine Page when she moved to New York City. Spacek won cheesecake roles in two features before playing Holly, a fifteen-year-old cheerleader, in *Badlands*.

Although based on the Starkweather killings, Malick's script for *Badlands* took several liberties with the factual record. For example, while it's true that Starkweather was a garbageman, he killed both of Fugate's parents, not just her father. Malick's vision of the story was not tied to facts, just as his approach to filmmaking paid little attention to tradition. The director was working in a popular genre loosely codified as "couples on the run" whose origins stretched back to the earliest days of cinema. Movies like *You Only Live Once* (1937), *They Live by Night* (1949), *Bonnie and Clyde* (1967), and *Thieves Like Us* (1974) presented their runaways in romantic terms, as victims of capitalism or society or even sexual dysfunction.

In *Badlands* Malick doesn't blame anyone or anything for his young killers, who are indifferent to their fate. There are no back stories for these characters: they exist solely as we see them. (Malick is just as restrictive in what he shows viewers of the time period.) By using deliberately trite narration delivered in an affectless voice-over by Spacek, by refusing to dramatize the story's violence, by equating the killers to cycles in nature, Malick seems to be exonerating Kit and Holly, to be suggesting that they were a natural outgrowth of the 1950s. They were simply taking their hero worship of James Dean, and of movies and pop culture in general, to its logical conclusion. Kit and Holly are inspired by comic books that omit the true consequences of violence, by rock songs they don't know how to dance to, by a sense of rebellion tied to nothing in particular and everything at once. Whether this is a valuable insight or an abdication of responsibility on Malick's part will depend on your willingness to decipher his directing technique as well as his writing.

Some critics were appalled at the violence in *Badlands*; others were bored by the film's languid pacing and digressive style. Malick's next finished film, *Days of Heaven* (1978, a Registry title), expanded on his preoccupation with visuals. It was the last film he would direct until 1998's *The Thin Red Line*. (Malick moved to France in 1979, remaining there for some fifteen years. He also edited art books under the pseudonym David Whitney.) Sheen's next important film would be *Apocalypse Now* (1979). Spacek married *Badlands* art director Jack Fisk after filming was completed. Her commercial breakthrough came as the heroine in Brian De Palma's adaptation of Stephen King's *Carrie* (1976).

Sissy Spacek in *Badlands*.

The Sting

Universal, 1973. Sound, color, 1.85. 129 minutes. Rated PG.

Cast: Paul Newman (Henry Gondorff), Robert Redford (Johnny Hooker), Robert Shaw (Doyle Lonnegan), Charles Durning (Lt. Wm. [William] Snyder), Ray Walston (J.J. Singleton), Eileen Brennan (Billie), Harold Gould (Kid Twist), John Heffernan (Eddie Niles), Dana Elcar (F.B.I. Agent Polk), Jack Kehoe (Erie Kid), Dimitra Arliss (Loretta), Robertearl [Robert Earl] Jones (Luther Coleman), James S. Sloyan (Mottola), Charles Dierkop (Floyd—bodyguard), Lee Paul (Bodyguard), Sally Kirkland (Crystal), Avon Long (Benny Garfield), Arch Johnson (Combs), Ed Bakey (Granger), Brad Sullivan (Cole), John Quade (Riley), Larry D. Mann (Train conductor), Leonard Barr (Burlesque house comedian), Paulene Myers (Alva Coleman), Joe Tornatore (Black gloved gunman), Jack Collins (Duke Boudreau), Tom Spratley (Curly Jackson), Kenneth O'Brien (Greer), Ken Sansom (Western Union executive), Ta-Tanisha (Louise Coleman), William Benedict (Roulette dealer).

Credits: Directed by George Roy Hill. Written by David S. Ward. Produced by Tony Bill and Michael and Julia Phillips. A Richard D. Zanuck/David Brown production. Associate producer: Robert L. Crawford. Director of photography: Robert Surtees. Film editor: William Reynolds. Art director: Henry Bumstead. Set decorations: James Payne. Music adapted by Marvin Hamlisch. Piano rags by Scott Joplin. Costumes by Edith Head. Sound: Robert Bertrand, Ronald Pierce. Production manager: Ernest B. Wehmeyer. First assistant director: Ray Gosnell. Second assistant director: Charles Dismukes. Special photographic effects: Albert Whitlock. Technical consultant: John Scarne. Script supervisor: Charlsie Bryant. Cosmetics by Cinematique. Titles & optical effects: Universal Title. Title artwork: Jaroslav Gebr. Title & graphic design: Keleidoscope Films, Ltd. Casting by Marion Dougherty Associates. Westrex Recording System. Color by Technicolor.

Additional Credits: Production dates: January to April 1973. Premiered in New York City on December 25, 1973.

Awards: Oscars for Best Picture, Director, Writing—Story and Screenplay Based on Factual Material or Material Not Previously Published or Produced, Music—Scoring Original Song Score and/or Adaptation, Editing, Costume Design, Art Direction—Set Decoration.

Other Versions: Sequel *The Sting II* (1983).

Available: Universal Home Entertainment DVD (2005). ISBN: 1-4170-5387-9. UPC: 0-25192-79022-5.

Con men and grifters have been fixtures in film since the earliest narratives. *Rubes in the Theatre* (1901) and *How They Do Things in the Bowery* (1902) are just two of a series of films Edwin S. Porter made about hapless victims of confidence games. Con men abound in the slapstick films of Mack Sennett, and most of the stars in Hal Roach's films could be viewed as fakes or frauds. Ernst Lubitsch, the Marx Brothers, Billy Wilder, and Preston Sturges made great use of them throughout their careers. In *Lady for a Day* (1933) and its remake, *A Pocketful of Miracles* (1961), Frank Capra offered sentimental accounts that presaged *The Sting*.

In interviews, screenwriter David S. Ward claims that he found out about confidence men while researching pickpockets. "Since I had never seen a film about a confidence man before, I said I gotta do this." It's possible that Ward never saw *The Rainmaker* (1956), *The Flim-Flam Man* (1967), *Putney Swope* (1969), or any of the dozens of other films that were clear antecedents for *The Sting*. But in a way he was right. The audience he was reaching for wasn't in school yet when *A Pocketful of Miracles* or *Ocean's Eleven* (1960) were playing in theaters. As George Lucas and Steven Spielberg were doing, Ward was reworking old models for a new generation, playing them out on a wider canvas, one that didn't have to skirt around racial and sexual issues.

One key to plots about con men is that film-goers want to feel they are in on the trick. They don't have to know how a scheme works, and they don't mind a twist or two, but it's important for the story to feature clearly recognizable "good" and "bad" characters. It took Ward a year to correctly adjust this aspect of the script, to figure out how much information he could hold back from the audience while still making the leads sympathetic. He went back to the same milieu Damon Runyon (and Capra) employed, imagining an underground brotherhood of crooks and thieves who assemble for a big operation and then melt away after the "mark" has been taken. This is the fable Ward pitched to Tony Bill.

As an actor, Bill had appeared in supporting roles in *Come Blow Your Horn* (1963, starring Frank Sinatra) and *You're a Big Boy Now* (1966, directed by Francis Coppola). He wanted to direct as well as produce, but his previous film, *Dead-head Miles* (1972), was deemed unreleasable. Bill teamed with Michael and Julia Phillips to buy two of Ward's scripts, *Steelyard Blues* and *The Sting*. They attracted a cast including David Sutherland and Jane Fonda to the former, a whimsical story about dropouts who team up to restore an airplane. It was a box-office flop.

In its early drafts, *The Sting* was a darker, more revenge-driven drama. As more people became involved with the project, it assumed a sunnier tone. Robert Redford committed to the film early on, before Phillips and Bill had a firm studio deal. They ended up with Richard Zanuck and David Brown, executives who had recently left Warner Brothers for Universal. Redford and George Roy Hill had been trying to finance a film

about barnstorming aviators, what would become *The Great Waldo Pepper* (1975), giving Hill an inside shot at directing *The Sting* after Zanuck and Brown rejected Ward as a director.

Hill sent the script to Paul Newman, who was reluctant to play "an older guy handing off the scepter to a younger one." It was only after Ward beefed up what had been a supporting role, and after the producers agreed to give Newman top billing, $500,000, and a percentage of the profits, that he signed on. Newman actually needed a hit: his last five films had been box-office disappointments. Everyone behind *The Sting* began hoping for another *Butch Cassidy and the Sundance Kid* (1969).

Ward said he listened to blues records from the 1930s when writing the script, and complained when Hill decided to base the soundtrack for *The Sting* on piano pieces by Scott Joplin, predominantly his rags. (Hill had probably been influenced by two volumes of Joplin's piano music recorded in 1970 and 1972 by Joshua Rifkin; they were unexpected hits for Nonesuch Records.) Ragtime flourished in the early 1900s; *The Sting* was set in 1936. Ward said that Hill told him, "David, you may be one of five people who sees this movie who knows that."

Marvin Hamlisch, who adapted the Joplin pieces for the film, exclaimed about the "tongue-in-cheek" aspect of ragtime. "It's fun, it's rhythmic, it's sassy." These qualities dismayed Ward, who saw *The Sting* in heavier terms, but Hill told Julia Phillips that he wanted to make a 1930s film. To that end he incorporated a variety of optical wipes, borrowed introductory credits from the old Warners house style, and had artist Jaroslav Gebr come up some ersatz Norman Rockwell paintings to use as chapter headings. Characteristically, Hill's added details were close, but naggingly not quite accurate, to the period.

Phillips wrote that Hill wanted Richard Boone for the part of the villain, Doyle Lonnegan. To her relief, Newman, shooting *The Mackintosh Man* in Ireland, gave a copy of the script to costar Robert Shaw, who signed on enthusiastically as Lonnegan. A handball accident before the start of shooting was the reason for his distinctive limp in the movie.

Newman doesn't appear until almost a half hour into *The Sting*, and for most of the film he takes a back seat to Redford, a reversal of their status in *Butch Cassidy and the Sundance Kid*. Since *Butch*, Redford had alternated between contemporary and period pictures, and had become considerably more comfortable at being a box-office sensation. He brings emotional depth to the sometimes formulaic scenes set in diners, overnight trains, and tenements.

It was most likely the team of Newman and Redford that got *The Sting* off to a good start on its release, but it was Hill's commercial instincts that made it one of the most successful films of the year. Schlocky adaptations of "The Entertainer" swept through popular culture, designers prepared for a return of Depression-era fashions, and audiences kept lining up for the film. Viewers today may be surprised at how brightly lit the film is (and how easy it is to spot where the lights were located), how long it takes for Hill to tell the story, and how Ward's plot depended on so many improbable events occurring at the same time. But *The Sting* was such a comfortable, professional experience that filmgoers didn't mind being conned. When *The Sting II*, also written by David S. Ward, came out ten years later, audiences weren't so forgiving.

Blazing Saddles

Warner Bros., 1974. Sound, color, 2.35. 93 minutes. Rated R.

Cast: Cleavon Little (Bart), Gene Wilder (Jim [The Waco Kid]), Slim Pickens (Taggart), Harvey Korman (Hedley Lamarr), Madeline Kahn (Lili Von Shtupp), Mel Brooks (Governor Lepetomane/Indian Chief), David Huddleston (Olson Johnson), Liam Dunn (Rev. Johnson), Alex Karras (Mongo), John Hillerman (Howard Johnson), George Furth (Van Johnson), Claude Ennis Starrett, Jr. (Gabby Johnson), Carol Arthur (Harriett Johnson), Richard Collier (Dr. Sam Johnson), Charles McGregor (Charlie), Don Megowan (Gum chewer), Robyn Hilton, Karl Lucas, Dom DeLuise, Burton Gilliam (Lyle), Count Basie.

Credits: Directed by Mel Brooks. Screenplay by Mel Brooks, Norman Steinberg, Andrew Bergman, Richard Pryor, Alan Uger. Story by Andrew Bergman. Produced by Michael Hertzberg. Director of photography: Joseph Biroc. Production design: Peter Wooley. Choreography by Alan Johnson. Music composed and conducted by John Morris. Original songs "I'm Tired," "The French Mistake," "The Ballad of Rock Ridge," music and lyrics by Mel Brooks. "Blazing Saddles," music by John Morris, lyrics by Mel Brooks, performed by Frankie Laine. Film editors: John C. Howard, Danford Greene. Title design: Anthony Goldschmidt. Sound: Gene S. Cantamessa. Rerecording: Arthur Piantadosi, Richard Tyle, Les Fresholtz. Set decorator: Morey Hoffman. Property master: Sam Gordon. Casting: Nessa Hyams. Unit production manager: William P. Owens. Special costumes designed by Nino Novarese. Wardrobe: Tom Dawson. Makeup: Al Fama, Terry Miles. Hairdresser: Lola "Skip" McNally. Script supervisor: Julie Pitkanen. First assistant director: John C. Chuylay. Special effects: Douglas Pettibone. A Crossbow Production. Filmed in Panavision and Technicolor.

Additional Credits: Production dates: January to March 1973. Promotional premiere on February 6, 1974. Opened wide on February 7, 1974.

Other Versions: Brooks prepared a TV series, *Black Bart* (1975).

Available: Warner Home Video DVD (2004). ISBN: 0-7907-5735-4. UPC: 0-85391-89592-3.

After the critical success of *The Producers* (1967), Mel Brooks turned to *The Twelve Chairs* (1970), based on a Ukrainian novel that had been filmed twice before, once in 1945 with Jack Benny and Fred Allen. Its plot concerned a manic search for missing treasure, a premise so popular that a Russian version was being filmed even while Brooks and his crew were shooting in Yugoslavia. *The Twelve Chairs* received some positive reviews, but performed so poorly at the box office that it placed Brooks' career as a director in jeopardy. In fact, he didn't get another offer until a chance encounter with David Begelman, at the time an agent, who told him about *Tex X*, a screenplay in development at Warner Brothers.

Written by Andrew Bergman, a film student who had written a breezy history of Depression-era movies, *We're in the Money*, *Tex X* placed a black hipster from Harlem in a traditional Western, finding humor in his reaction to genre clichés. Brooks was reluctant to take on the project, telling one reporter later that the original script had better situations than dialogue. But Brooks needed a hit, which he hoped to find by returning to methods that had worked for him years earlier, when he was a staff writer for Sid Caesar's television show.

Brooks assembled a staff of writers, including his friends Norman Steinberg and Alan Uger, as well as Bergman and Richard Pryor. As a nationally known African-American comedian, Pryor's presence would presumably defuse any charges of racism. (According to Brooks, Pryor was more interested in writing jokes for the "Mongo" character than in okaying the "black" gags.) They spent months expanding Bergman's story. Discussing their work, biographer James Robert Parrish wrote, "Their rule of thumb was 'Go for broke.'" Brooks told the press, "We're trying to use every Western cliché in the book—in the hope that we'll kill them off in the process." The brainstorming produced a 412-page script, which was cut to 275 pages.

After Warners approved the script, now called *Black Bart*, Brooks continued tinkering with it, taking out several characters and subplots. A servant based on Erich von Stroheim's character in *Sunset Boulevard* (1950) disappeared, for example. So did a joke involving Tony Martin singing "The Tenement Symphony," and references to Walt Disney and the Jolly Green Giant.

The gags that did remain were a disorganized hodgepodge of cultural references, riffs on earlier Westerns, and skits that wouldn't have been out of place on Caesar's show, or in vaudeville, for that matter. The style and pacing were so close to Warner cartoons that Brooks appropriated the Looney Tunes musical tag at one point. The scatological tone, evident right in the film's title, may have been Brooks' biggest contribution to the film.

Warners objected to the casting of Richard Pryor in the lead role, perhaps wary of his controversial reputation. When James Earl Jones couldn't fit the schedule, Brooks cast Cleavon Little, a television actor with limited film experience, in the role of Bart. For his sidekick, the Waco Kid, an alcoholic gunslinger, Brooks hoped to use Dan Dailey. When Dailey turned him down, Brooks hired Gig Young. When Young proved unable to perform after shooting started, Brooks replaced him with Gene Wilder, the costar of *The Producers*.

The real casting coup in the film was Madeline Kahn, who delivered a sensational parody of Marlene Dietrich. She had recently completed important roles in two Peter Bogdanovich movies; for Brooks she unleashed a comic sensibility that went beyond delivering gags to exploring the psychological underpinnings of her character. Asked about Brooks, she said later, "For a funny man he's very serious."

Filming started in January 1973, extending for about ten weeks on the Warner Brothers backlot and other locations. Editing took nine months, during which Brooks deleted a considerable amount of material. He whittled down his own role, for example. Bart's practical jokes on Mongo, a massive killer played by former football star Alex Karras, were largely eliminated, as was a bit about an evangelical baptism. Nine months of fiddling may explain why the film seems so poorly paced today, with jokes that fail to build momentum and too many scenes that dwindle into blackouts.

Despite objections by studio executives, Brooks kept in what would become a notorious scene in which cowboys break wind around a campfire. Talking about it later, he said, "It was a broad, brave truth that had always been on the back of everyone's tongue when they were watching straight Westerns."

Brooks also said, "The movie has got to be about something." In other words, he needed a structure to play off, a story line so clear and obvious that viewers could concentrate on the jokes instead of the plot. At the time, Westerns were still familiar enough that no one needed to be told about saloons, stagecoaches, or shoot-outs. Some of Brooks' other allusions weren't quite as clear, such as the appearance of the Count Basie Orchestra in the middle of the desert, or how Brooks based his portrayal of Governor Lepetomane on Groucho Marx in *Duck Soup* (1933). What the film lacked was a coherent plot; Brooks' approach was too scattershot to do much damage to the genre.

Reviews for *Blazing Saddles* were mixed. *The Wall Street Journal* called it "an undisciplined mess," and Pauline Kael wrote that it was "just dirty TV." Brooks, on the other hand, said, "I think in ten years, and I'm tooting my own horn now, *Blazing Saddles* will be recognized as the funniest film ever made." The film did well enough with moviegoers to boost Brooks' standing in the industry. His next film, *Young Frankenstein* (1974), is also on the Registry.

. . . no lies

Direct Cinema Limited, 1973. Sound, color, 1.37. 16 minutes. Rated R.

Cast: Shelby Leverington (The woman), Alec Hirschfeld (The filmmaker).

Credits: Produced and directed by Mitchell Block. Photography: Alec Hirschfeld. Editor: Ray Anne School. Assistant cameraman: Ronald Levitus. Gaffer & key grip: Jim McCalmont. Sound recordist: Jenny Goldberg. Title design: Gene Samuelson. With special acknowledgment to: Gregg Clapp, Camera Service Center; Editors Corner, Phil Haultcoeur, Tim Timpanaro, EUE Opticals; Haig P. Manoogian, Muffie Meyer, Emil Neroda, The Sound Shop; The Rape Tape.

Additional Credits: Written by Mitchell Block. Released February 24, 1974. A 35mm version released theatrically was rated R by the MPAA. The home video version is unrated.

Available: Direct Cinema Limited DVD (*www.directcinemalimited.com*). ISBN: 978-1-55974-746-2. UPC: 9-781559-747462.

When it was first screened at film festivals and symposia, Mitchell Block's . . . *no lies* provoked controversy far out of proportion to most student films. Shot in a cinema verité style, the movie purported to show a conversation between a cameraman and a woman while she dressed in her apartment for a date. As the cameraman, who is shooting a school assignment, questions her, she gradually reveals that she was recently raped, and describes her subsequent experiences with the police. Egged on and then badgered by the cameraman, she bursts into tears, a cinematic metaphor for her physical rape. The tics of the verité style—zooming in tight to focus, lurching to keep a walking character in frame—add to the movie's realism, as does the fact that it appears to be filmed in one continuous take.

Only nothing about the film is as it appears. Closing credits reveal that the woman is being played by an actress. There are actually two edits in the film, and at least one point when a line of dialogue had to be redubbed. As director Mitchell Block wrote later, the entire piece was rehearsed over a six-week period and was recorded on video prior to shooting. On the day of production, Block staged another run-through before shooting on 16mm color stock. While . . . *no lies* did not have fully scripted dialogue, story points were prepared to guide the cast. These were refined during rehearsals, enhancing the performances in the final production. The set, a friend's apartment, was also altered slightly in order to ease filming. (Block has included two rehearsal takes recorded on video for the Direct Cinema home release.)

Block made the film as his graduate thesis project at NYU's film school. Since he had been working as a line producer on *Mean Streets* (1973), he needed an "easy" story, one with a limited number of sets and actors, that would require few props, and that didn't need the polished look of a fiction film. Verité filmmakers made a virtue out of shaky camerawork, marginal lighting and sound, of exposing the artifice of moviemaking. Built around a supposedly off-the-cuff conversation that had built-in surprise revelations, . . . *no lies* fit the bill perfectly.

Some viewers felt betrayed when the closing credits revealed that . . . *no lies* was fiction. (Others perhaps weren't paying as much attention, as the film is still used to train police and social workers.) Block was unapologetic about fooling filmgoers. In a 2006 article, "The Truth about *No Lies* (If You Can Believe It)," he cited several other false documentaries as inspiration—in particular, the Registry title *David Holzman's Diary* (1967). "Without *David Holzman*, there would be no . . . *no lies*," he wrote. "I believed it. I loved the film. I was taken in by [L.M. Kit] Carson's Holzman character."

Block also wrote at length about the relationship between filmmakers and subjects, and filmmakers and audiences. "In . . . *no lies*, I abuse (a) the subject [Leverington] with an insensitive filmmaker [Hirschfeld], (b) undermine the audience's relationship with the filmmaker, by making him unlikable and unethical and (c) abuse the spectator by pretending to present the truth and lying." He continued: ". . . *no lies* is really about the filmmaker manipulating the audience. ALL filmmakers in both dramatic and non-fiction forms do this."

. . . *no lies* wasn't just a criticism of cinema verité, but of documentaries as a whole. Another inspiration Block mentioned was *An American Family*, a twelve-part series about the Louds, a Santa Barbara family that was broadcast on PBS in 1973. One of Block's NYU professors had resigned from the project, concerned about the ethics of exploiting the Louds. Block had other objections. He thought that documentaries were forced to manipulate and exploit their subjects "because 'reality' is slow and not usually dramatic and filmmakers are almost never filmmaking at the 'right' moment." Editing not only shapes material, it makes the story move faster, and disguises the fact that "most of the time, filmmakers miss key moments; the documentary film is always rushing to catch up with the story."

Block's insights into the fundamental dishonesty of the verité format are even more pertinent today, in an age where shaky camerawork signifies "honesty" in television advertising and actors speak directly to viewers instead of pretending to ignore them. "Spectators [need to] become more sophisticated reading the film text being presented," Block wrote. "They need to understand how easy it is to manipulate the form so that it appears to be the 'truth' when it is not."

After NYU, Block and Hirschfeld made *Speeding?* (1974), a more lighthearted fake documentary that featured appearances by director Martin Brest and Roger Corman-perennial Dick Miller along with actual police and California Highway Patrolmen. Hirschfeld has since been a camera operator and cinematographer for many New York–based films and television series. Block formed Direct Cinema Limited, a distributor of documentaries, live-action shorts, and animated films, twenty-three of which have won Oscars. He conceived and was the executive producer for *Carrier* (2008), a ten-hour documentary series broadcast on PBS.

Special mention should be made of Shelby Leverington, whose work in . . . *no lies* achieved an enviable combination of sincerity and ambiguity. She had worked with Block and Hirschfeld before, on the low-budget horror film *Death by Invitation* (1971). Block based her role here on *The Rape Tape* (1972), a video diary by Jenny Goldberg that documented actual victims of rape. Leverington used their accounts to fashion a moving story that felt true on every level. The fact that it wasn't adds an uneasy quality to her performance, making viewers feel guilty for questioning her even though they are right to do so. It was a brilliant balancing act, one of several in . . . *no lies*. Leverington has since appeared in numerous films and television shows.

Shelby Leverington from . . . *no lies* ©2008 directcinema.com. All Rights. Reserved Photo courtesy Direct Cinema Limited

The Conversation

Paramount, 1974. Sound, color, 1.85. 113 minutes. Rated R.

Cast: Gene Hackman (Harry Caul), John Cazale (Stan), Allen Garfield (Bernie Moran), Frederic Forrest (Mark), Cindy Williams (Ann), Michael Higgins (Paul), Elizabeth MacRae (Meredith), Teri Garr (Amy), Harrison Ford (Martin Stett), Mark Wheeler (Receptionist), Robert Shields (The Mime), Phoebe Alexander (Lurleen).

Credits: Produced and directed by Francis Ford Coppola. Written by Francis Ford Coppola. Co-producer: Fred Roos. Associate producer: Mona Skager. Director of photography: Bill Butler. Music: David Shire. Production designer: Dean Tavoularis. Supervising editor, sound montage & re-recording: Walter Murch. Property master: Ted Moehnke. Editor: Richard Chew. Set decoration: Doug Von Koss. Script supervisor: Nancy Tonery. Costumer: Aggie Guerard Rodgers. Production manager: Clark Paylow. Assistant director: Chuck Myers. Casting: Jennifer Shull. Title by Wayne Fitzgerald. Production recording: Art Rochester, Nat Boxer, Mike Evje. Technical advisors: Hal Lipset, Leo Jones. Color by Technicolor. A Directors Company presentation of a Coppola Company production.

Additional Cast: Robert Duvall (Director).

Additional Credits: Cinematography by Haskell Wexler. Production dates: November 27, 1972 to March 1973. Opened April 7, 1974, New York City.

Available: Paramount Home Video DVD (2000). ISBN: 0-7921-6087-8. UPC: 0-9736-02307-4-1.

On some levels the most successful filmmaker of his generation, Francis Ford Coppola has endured numerous ups and downs in his career, many tied to an elemental struggle between art and commerce. Born in Detroit in 1939, Coppola was the son of an actress and a concert flutist. He contracted polio at the age of nine, and the year he spent as an invalid fed into the script that would eventually become *The Conversation*. Coppola became a technology geek, going so far as to bug his parents' house and telephone, before developing an interest in filmmaking in high school. He founded a film workshop in college, then moved to California to attend film school at UCLA.

While struggling for a foothold in the industry, Coppola tried everything, including directing a soft-core exploitation feature (*Tonight for Sure*, 1961) and a three-day, $40,000 horror quickie for Roger Corman (*Dementia 13*, 1963). The exuberant comedy *You're a Big Boy Now* (1966) ended up being his thesis project for UCLA. The release of that film, plus Coppola's growing reputation as a script doctor, got him his first big-budget feature, *Finian's Rainbow* (1968), starring Fred Astaire.

Coppola readily admitted later that he was not talented or knowledgeable enough at the time to direct an adaptation of a Broadway musical.

Finian's Rainbow was a resounding flop, but the director had already assembled the elements of his next film. Based on his own screenplay, *The Rain People* (1969) was a quiet, unpredictable road picture with appealing characters and a confident directing style. Together with George Lucas, he formed American Zoetrope, a production company based in San Francisco. Coppola's Oscar-winning script work on *Patton* (1970) was instrumental in getting the assignment to direct *The Godfather*.

Work on the script for *The Conversation* started in the late 1960s, after Coppola had seen Michelangelo Antonioni's *Blowup* (1966), a thriller about a photographer who unwittingly records evidence of a crime. Coppola had hoped to film *The Conversation* after *The Rain People*, but found himself scrambling for money to support American Zoetrope. He continued to tinker with the script, which combined his interests in Herman Hesse's *Steppenwolf* and New Wave European filmmaking with more commercial movies. Editor Walter Murch described the project as Coppola's attempt "to make an alloy of Hesse and Hitchcock."

The success of *The Godfather* gave Coppola the freedom to devote his time to a small-scale, personal project, which he did under the aegis of the Directors Company, which he formed with Peter Bogdanovich and William Friedkin. He used crew members from his earlier films notably, production designer Dean Tavoularis, composer David Shire, and sound designer Walter Murch—and picked much of the cast from previous collaborations as well. Gene Hackman had made a commitment to the project years earlier, and although he had since won an Oscar for *The French Connection* (1971), he worked for his previous rates in the lead role as Harry Caul.

"It's a depressing and difficult part to play," Hackman told the press at the time, "because it's so low key." Caul is an intensely private individual who is also intensely proud of his profession in audio espionage. Although he resembles a private eye, Caul thinks that he can distance himself intellectually and emotionally from his work planting bugs and recording surreptitious meetings. In *The Conversation* he encounters a situation that questions both his skills and his beliefs.

Coppola may have been a fan of New Wave films, but he was not slavishly addicted to copying European styles. *The Conversation* has a genuine plot as well as something to say about society and culture, and at this stage of his career the director

was skilled enough to make his points in a clear, forceful manner. Remarkably prescient in its treatment of wiretapping, *The Conversation* is also one of the most visually and aurally seductive movies of its time, one whose layers of artistry continue to unfold with repeated viewings.

According to biographer Michael Schumacher, it was not an easy shoot, in part because of extensive location filming in spots like San Francisco's Union Square, but also because Coppola was busy preparing *The Godfather Part II* (1974). At one point Coppola shut down the production for ten days in order to replace cinematographer Haskell Wexler with Bill Butler. (Ironically, the same thing would happen the following year on *One Flew Over the Cuckoo's Nest*.)

Coppola had worked with Murch on *The Rain People*, and hired him as supervising editor because, "although the film was about privacy, sound would be the core element in it." Murch told interviewer Michael Ondaatje that Coppola ran out of money during the production, and therefore couldn't shoot about fifteen pages of the script. Murch was forced to find a way to work around the missing footage during the post-production process, which required eleven months. To balance two plot lines, Caul's personal evolution and a murder mystery, Murch hid the meaning of a line of dialogue that was explicit in the script. "There were many screenings we had along the way where the audience was completely flummoxed!" he recalled. Delaying a crucial clue actually confirmed Coppola's original notes about the murder suspects: "They are important only because someone is listening." The first cut of *The Conversation* was over four hours long; remarkably, Murch edited the film during the day while mixing *American Graffiti* (1973) at night.

Despite some respectful reviews on its release, *The Conversation* was not a commercial success. Coppola blamed Paramount's promotion; the studio devoted much more attention to *The Great Gatsby* (1974), to no avail, as it turned out. But *The Conversation* was a demanding film for mainstream moviegoers, one that offered questions but few answers, and one that refused to give its characters easy ways out of their problems. Over the years it has become one of the touchstones of 1970s cinema, an example of a director at the height of his powers fashioning what would turn out to be his most accomplished film. It was the last time for many years that Coppola would try such a personal project on such an intimate scale. His next Registry film is *The Godfather Part II* (1974).

Chinatown

Paramount, 1974. Sound, color, 2.35. 130 minutes. Rated R.

Cast: Jack Nicholson (J.J. Gittes), Faye Dunaway (Evelyn Mulwray), John Hillerman (Yelburton), Perry Lopez (Escobar), Burt Young (Curly), Bruce Glover (Duffy), Joe Mantell (Walsh), Roy Jenson (Mulvihill), Diane Ladd (Ida Sessions), Dick Bakalyan (Loach), John Huston (Noah Cross), Darrell Zwerling (Hollis Mulwray), James Hong (Evelyn's butler), Cecil Elliott (Emma Dill), Beulah Quo (Maid), Federico Roberto (Cross' butler), Allan Warnick (Clerk), John Rogers (Mr. Palmer), Roman Polanski (Man with knife), Nandu Hinds (Sophie), James O'Reare (Lawyer), Jerry Fujikawa (Gardener), Belinda Palmer (Katherine), Roy Roberts (Major Bagby); Noble Willingham, Elliott Montgomery (Councilmen); Rance Howard (Irate farmer), George Justin (Barber), Doc Erickson (Customer), Fritzi Burr (Mulwray's secretary), Charles Knapp (Mortician), Claudio Martinez (Boy on horseback); John Holland, Jesse Vint, Jim Burke, Denny Arnold (Farmers in the valley); Elizabeth Harding (Curly's wife); Paul Jenkins, Lee De Broux, Bob Golden (Policemen).

Credits: Directed by Roman Polanski. Written by Robert Towne. Produced by Robert Evans. Director of photography: John A. Alonzo. Associate producer: C.O. Erickson. Music: Jerry Goldsmith. Production designer: Richard Sylbert. Film Editor: Sam O'Steen. Costume designer: Anthea Sylvert. Assistant director: Howard W. Koch. Unit production manager: C.O. Erickson. Art director: W. Stewart Campbell. Sound mixer: Larry Jost. Set designers: Gabe Resh, Robert Resh. Script supervisor: May Wale Brown. Special effects: Logan Frazee. Titles: Wayne Fitzgerald. Re-recording: Bud Grenzbach. Makeup: Hank Edds, Lee Harmon. Hairstylists: Susan Germaine, Vivienne Walker. Wardrobe: Richard Bruno, Jean Merrick. Casting by Mike Fenton–Jane Feinberg. Color by Technicolor. Filmed in Panavision.

Additional Credits: Premiered in Los Angeles on June 20, 1974.

Awards: Oscar for Best Writing—Original Screenplay.

Other Versions: Sequel *The Two Jakes* (1990), directed by Jack Nicholson.

Available: Paramount DVD (2007). ISBN: 1-4157-2903-4. UPC: 097361224442.

In the early 1960s, screenwriter Robert Towne and actor Jack Nicholson both took acting courses from Jeff Corey, who turned to teaching after being blacklisted in the 1950s, and their paths continued to cross as their careers advanced. Both used their work for Roger Corman as a stepping-stone to bigger projects. While Nicholson became an increasingly bankable star in films like *Easy Rider* (1969) and *Five Easy Pieces* (1970), Towne built a reputation as a script doctor, working behind the scenes on hits like *Bonnie and Clyde* (1967). Towne did a revision of Nicholson's script for *Drive, He Said* (1971), and took a part in the film as Karen Black's husband.

It was during the production of *Drive, He Said* that Towne thought of the idea for *Chinatown*. With Nicholson in mind, Towne invented a private eye who gets involved with a real-life incident in the Los Angeles of the 1930s. He pitched it to Robert Evans, a Paramount executive who had helped develop *The Godfather* (1972). Evans saw the project as a potential vehicle for his girlfriend at the time, Ali MacGraw. He also thought of Roman Polanski as the director.

Born in Paris in 1933, Polanski grew up in Poland during the rise of Nazism. He spent much of World War II hiding with Catholic families or fending for himself; his mother was killed at Auschwitz. After the war he went to art school, acted on radio, and won a place in the directors' course at the Lodz Film School. Exquisitely crafted shorts like *Two Men and a Wardrobe* (1958) won him recognition throughout Europe. The success of his feature debut *Knife in the Water* (1962), a dark, unsparing thriller, led to *Repulsion* (1965), starring Catherine Deneuve and filmed in England. His first film in the United States, *Rosemary's Baby* (1968), was an unqualified commercial success.

In 1969, Polanski's pregnant wife Sharon Tate was murdered by Charles Manson and his followers, a notorious crime that sent the director into an emotional tailspin. He was living in Rome when Evans contacted him to work on *Chinatown*. By that point Nicholson and production designer Richard Sylbert had committed to the project. (According to biographer Dennis McDougal, Nicholson at one point gave Towne $10,000 to help him finish the script.) Polanski remained ambivalent about accepting the job when he first arrived in Los Angeles.

Towne thought of the project as an homage to the film noir genre of the 1940s, and he followed many of its conventions and formulas. But he also set out to tackle what he saw as contradictions or weaknesses in detective stories. He made his private eye, J.J. Gittes, specialize in divorce cases because fictional detectives always complained about them. The plot was built around a real-life land grab in which city engineer William Mulholland built an aqueduct that allowed Los Angeles to expand at the expense of Owens Valley, an agricultural center. "I figure I do a detective movie and do it about a real crime," Towne said, "rather than stealing a jewel-encrusted falcon."

Towne pulled apart Agatha Christie stories trying to see how she plotted, wrote almost two dozen treatments, and finally handed in a 250-page screenplay that dismayed Polanski. "It was terribly long and convoluted," the director said later. Towne and Polanski sparred over several elements of the script, most notably the ending. Towne had written a long sequence that evoked the tragic endings of films like *Out of the Past* (1947). Polanski instead shot a cryptic but violent scene that opened up an entirely new, and cruel, story line. It took years for the screenwriter to accept this ending, although he subsequently wrote that Polanski improved on his vision.

Polanski may have upset Towne, but he drove Faye Dunaway—cast in a lead role as Evelyn Mulwray after Jane Fonda turned it down—to hysterics. Their fights ultimately had to be brokered by Evans. At one point Polanski smashed a television set in Nicholson's trailer, but he still won the actor's affections. The casting of John Huston as Noah Cross, a patriarch and potential client for Gittes, added another layer of intensity to the film. Nicholson had begun a relationship with Huston's daughter Anjelica, a model at the time. When Cross's character asks, "Are you sleeping with my daughter?" the line resonates in an eerie manner.

Huston's brief performance is only one of the many factors that make *Chinatown* so extraordinary. His admonition to "Just find the girl, Mr. Gittes" in retrospect carries as much weight as Polanski's turn as a switchblade-wielding enforcer. The violence in *Chinatown* is stark and searing, a harsh corrective to the relatively painless beatings and assaults of scores of earlier detective movies. Similarly, the crimes revealed in the film have terrifying implications. But it is the emotional toll that is the most haunting element.

Anchoring the film is Nicholson's performance, a thoughtful, assured take on a complex, not entirely likable character. *Chinatown* is not only set in the past, it is *about* the past, and the efforts by Gittes to forget or dismiss what has happened to him before the story starts. No matter what his motives, his search for peace is doomed—at least in the world that Polanski envisioned.

Chinatown's voluptuous visual style both fetishized and elaborated on the look of film noir. Sylbert later explained that he keyed his production design to the line "Find the girl." Colors went from dusty browns to strong blues as clues emerged; period props and architecture accentuated the social standing of the characters. Cinematographer John Alonzo tried to avoid zooming more than 5mm in any one shot in order to enhance the period feel. He replaced Stanley Cortez, thought by Polanski to be too slow, on short notice. (While he received an Oscar nomination, Alonzo always gave credit to Cortez, saying that he worked from Cortez's detailed notes.)

Towne conceived of *Chinatown* as the first part of a trilogy. *The Two Jakes* would take Gittes to 1948 and the rise of oil and gas companies; *Cloverleaf* would be set in 1959, as the freeway system transformed Los Angeles. He, Evans, and Nicholson retained rights to the characters, preventing anyone else from making a sequel. After several disputes and cancellations, Nicholson directed *The Two Jakes* in 1990. *Chinatown* is the last film to date directed in the United States by Polanski, who fled to Europe after pleading guilty to a charge of unlawful sex with an underage girl.

Chinatown remains one of the landmark films of the 1970s, as well as the most successful example of film noir since the genre's postwar heyday. It was also the culmination of a cinema of personal freedom and expression. *Chinatown* marked a time when young filmmakers had a common goal of cinema as art, rather than movies as commodity, as well as the sudden means to achieve it. A short time later the release of *Jaws* (1975) and *Star Wars* (1977) changed the mechanics of movie distribution. Movies were now about profit, not art, spectacle over content. Industry executives felt justified in admiring *Chinatown* while rejecting similar projects because "it didn't make much money."

Antonia: A Portrait of the Woman

Rocky Mountain Productions, 1974. Sound, color, 1.37. 57 minutes.

Featuring: Antonia Brico, members of the Brico Symphony Orchestra and The Rocky Mountain Concert Choir, The South Denver High School Concert Choir, Beverly Christiansen, Trudy Hines, Helen Palacas, Judy Collins.

Credits: Directed by Judy Collins, Jill Godmilow. Produced by Judy Collins. Director of Photography: Coulter Watt. Editing: Jill Godmilow. Sound recording: Nigel Noble, Jerry Bruck. Mixing engineer: Tom Dillinger. Animated sequence—Design: Irene Trivas. Animation: Ed Smith. Tympani: Phil Kraus. Camera: Coulter Watt. Second camera: Paul Ryan, Bill Troutfeather. Assistants: Bill Schwartz, Roger

Carter, Peter Hedgeman. Location manager: Eugenia Morrison. Production secretary: Billie Green. Special thanks to the American Federation of Musicians.

Additional Credits: Opened September 18, 1974.

Available: Pioneer Artists DVD, release PA-11982 (2003). UPC: 013023198296.

Born in Rotterdam in 1902, and raised by foster parents in California, Antonia Brico gained worldwide attention by being the first woman to conduct the Berlin Philharmonic and numerous other symphony orchestras. Her foster mother, an ardent believer in spiritualism, brought her along to séances, where, as she laughingly related later, she was encouraged by Liszt and Beethoven to pursue music. Brico studied piano, but was intent on becoming a conductor, relishing the chance to work with a broader palette. Brico always described her childhood as "unhappy," and moved away from her parents when she was still a teenager. She supported herself by selling sheet music in a department store and by playing music in restaurants.

Brico studied in Germany under Karl Muck and at the Berlin State Academy of Music. She made her conducting debut with the Berlin Philharmonic in 1930, then returned to the United States to conduct orchestras in San Francisco and Los Angeles. But Brico was unable to find steady employment until she returned to Europe, where she worked in Germany, Poland, Finland, and other countries. The worsening economic and political landscape there forced her to return to New York in late 1932.

Society connections helped her obtain an engagement at the Metropolitan Opera House. This led to other concerts, first with the Musicians' Symphony Orchestra in 1933, then with other groups across the country. Brico's next step was to form the New York Women's Symphony Orchestra, which was renamed the Brico Symphony Orchestra when she added male musicians in 1939. The orchestra appeared at New York's Town Hall and later at Carnegie Hall. The group disbanded after the start of World War II.

While guesting for various orchestras, Brico applied for the conducting post at the Denver Civic Symphony Orchestra. Convinced after an interview that she had won the position, she moved to Denver, only to learn that a man had been hired instead. Brico stayed in the city, turning to teaching to support herself and later taking over what would become the Brico Symphony Orchestra. But for the rest of her life Brico remained bitter over what she perceived as snubs based on her gender.

Singer-songwriter Judy Collins, once a student of Brico's, was fascinated by the conductor's background. Born in 1939, Collins was a child prodigy on the piano. She turned to folk music as a teenager, releasing her first album when she was twenty-two. Throughout the 1960s she was famous as an interpreter of other songwriters like Joni Mitchell and Leonard Cohen. Her most well-known hits were versions of Mitchell's "Both Sides Now" and Stephen Sondheim's "Send in the Clowns."

In 1972, at the height of her popularity, Collins set out to record Brico on film. Along with Jill Godmilow, an independent filmmaker who worked primarily in documentaries, Collins scheduled three shoots in Denver with a small crew from New York City. The singer left most of the technical considerations to the crew, concentrating on eliciting stories from her former teacher. Godmilow remembers Spartan shooting conditions, working with Lowell lighting kits and at most two microphones. The filmmakers decided to shoot Brico rehearsing her orchestra and teaching her students, a move that wouldn't draw attention to possible mistakes or flubs. They intercut these scenes with some performance footage. The pieces included Schubert's Symphony No. 7 in C Major and the Schumann Piano Concerto, played by sixteen-year-old Helen Palacas. As Godmilow points out, it's a mark of Brico's timing and discipline that the disparate musical material could be cut together so seamlessly.

But the interviews with Brico are what make up the heart of this warm, affectionate film. Collins, already aware of most of Brico's stories, carefully guides the conductor through biographical details, waiting for signs of her teacher's humor, determination, and sense of outrage to emerge. The interviews, conducted around Brico's kitchen table or in the study of her modest Denver home, never pretend to be impartial. Collins is in many of the shots, laughing at jokes or prodding Brico about particular points. Most of the anecdotes were well-rehearsed. As early as 1935, in a *New Yorker* "Talk of the Town" piece, Brico is telling how she took piano lessons to stop biting her fingernails, or how at an early age she was impressed by conductor Paul Steindorff's "magic wand." Toward the end of the movie, the filmmakers stage scenes of Brico clowning around, accompanying herself on barrelhouse piano as she sings "After You've Gone." "I'm not so sure I want that in public," she says cautiously, one of the few signs of hesitation from an obviously powerful character. Watch how she directs the crew when she wants them to notice a photograph on her wall. Or when she rails over her limited opportunities as an assistant tries to adjust a lighting scrim.

Collins and Godmilow used clips from Fox Movietone newsreels about Brico to cover much of her early career. Photographs and newspaper clippings proved useful as well, allowing the filmmakers to suggest some points Brico may not have been willing to admit—for example, her implied feud with conductor José Iturbi during the 1940s. The film also includes an animated sequence called "The Great Kettledrum War of 1937 or A Film Maker's Fantasy of a Contest that Never Took Place." In it, a slender woman in an evening gown outlasts a stout gentleman in a tuxedo in a tympani duel. (The filmmakers' feminist stance might have been more effective if the tympani parts on the soundtrack hadn't been played by a man.)

Antonia: A Portrait of the Woman received a fairly wide theatrical release, due in part to Collins's celebrity, and was nominated for Best Feature Documentary Oscar. Brico died in 1989.

A Woman Under the Influence

Gena Rowlands received an Oscar nomination for her work in *A Woman Under the Influence. Courtesy of The Criterion Collection*

Faces Distribution Corporation, 1974. Sound, color, 1.85. 147 minutes. Rated R.

Cast: Peter Falk (Nick Longhetti), Gena Rowlands (Mabel Longhetti), Fred Draper (George Mortensen), Lady Rowlands (Martha Mortensen), Katherine Cassavetes (Mama Longhetti), Matthew Laborteaux (Angelo Longhetti), Matthew Cassel (Tony Longhetti), Christina Grisanti (Maria Longhetti). O.G. Dunn (Garson Cross), Mario Gallo (Harold Jensen), Eddie Shaw (Dr. Zepp), Angelo Grisanti (Vito Grimaldi), Charles Horvath (Eddie), James Joyce (Bowman), John Finnegan (Clancy), Vince Barbi (Gino), Cliff Carnell (Aldo), Frank Richards (Adolph), Hugh Hurd (Willie Johnson), Leon Wagner (Billy Tidrow), Dominique Davalos (Dominique Jensen), Xan Cassavetes (Adrienne Jensen), Pancho Meisenheimer (John Jensen), Sonny Aprile (Aldo), Ellen Davalos (Nancy), Joanne Moore Jordan (Muriel), John Hawker (Joseph Morton), Sil Words (James Turner), Elizabeth Deering (Angela), Jackie Peters (Tina), Elsie Ames (Principal), N.J. Cassavetes (Adolph).

Credits: Written and directed by John Cassavetes. Produced by Sam Shaw. Camera operators: Mike Ferris, David Nowell. In Charge of Lighting: Mitchell Breit. Lighting crew: Chris Taylor, Bo Taylor, Merv Dayan. Additional photography: Caleb Deschanel. Additional camera: Gary Graver. Art director: Phedon Papamichael. Wardrobe, production secretary: Carole Smith. Props: Kevin Joyce. Graphics: Steve Hitter. Supervising editor: Tom Cornwell. Editors: David Armstrong, Sheila Viseltear, Beth Bergeron. Music: Bo Harwood. Mix: Henry Michael Denecke. First assistant director: Jack Corrick. Second assistant director: Roger Slager. Associate producer: Paul Donnelly. Color by MGM Labs, Inc.

Additional Credits: Production dates: November 1, 1972 to January 24, 1973; additional shooting: March 1973. Screened at the New York Film Festival, September 20, 1974.

Available: Criterion Collection DVD (2004). ISBN: 0-18002-920-8. UPC: 0 37429-19892-6.

After the delayed release of his first film, the Registry title *Shadows*, John Cassavetes had an uneven career through the 1960s. Unhappy with two studio features he directed, *Too Late Blues* (1962) and *A Child Is Waiting* (1963), he also had trouble re-establishing his acting career. It wasn't until he received a Best Supporting Actor nomination for the box-office hit *The Dirty Dozen* (1967) that he had the financial freedom to pursue his vision of independent filmmaking. But *Faces* (1968), *Husbands* (1970), and, in particular, *Minnie and Moskowitz* (1971), were unsuccessful commercially. And by concentrating on directing, Cassavetes lost momentum with acting, his main source of income.

Cassavetes turned to writing plays, completing three interlocking pieces between the summer of 1971 and the winter of 1972. He combined and revised them into a film script in August, 1972, planning it as a feature with a budget of $250,000. The story focused on the marital and mental problems affecting a blue-collar family. It fit into a cycle of novels and films, like Francis Ford Coppola's underappreciated *The Rain People* (1969) and the trashy *Diary of a Mad Housewife* (1970), that saw insanity as a by-product, or perhaps end result, of intractable cultural problems. Cassavetes considered playing the father, a construction worker, himself. But he gave the part of Nick Longhetti instead to his friend Peter Falk, riding a wave of popularity after the success of his television series *Columbo*. Gena Rowlands played Nick's troubled wife Mabel.

Falk put up half of the original budget; Cassavetes, the other half. (The final budget was closer to $1,000,000.) In a cost-cutting measure, the director offered his services to the American Film Institute as a "filmmaker-in-residence." This not only gave him access to equipment, but to a free crew of AFI students. He saved more money by putting the cast—which included his wife Gena, two of his children, his mother Katherine, and his mother-in-law Lady Rowlands—on deferred salaries. Cassavetes rented a house on Taft Avenue in Hollywood and proceeded to rehearse and shoot from November 1, 1972, to January 24, 1973. (He shot more footage that March.)

Cassavetes selected AFI student Caleb Deschanel as cinematographer. It was Deschanel's big break, the start of a career that would include noted work in films like *The Black Stallion* (1979, a Registry title). But he was fired a week into the shoot. Most of the crew quit in sympathy. Cassavetes replaced him with Michael Ferris, like soundtrack composer Bo Harwood a complete neophyte.

By now Cassavetes had developed a distinct visual style, one that employed long takes, little concern for lighting, and handheld cameras. "I want everything to go fast and use long focal lenses and a set that has some depth," he said. "What's important to me is just that you convince the audience and yourself that what's on the screen is really happening." About half the film was shot with telephoto lenses, a strategy that kept the camera at a distance from the actors, but that also resulted in a narrow depth-of-field and an often grainy look. Focus was especially hard to judge, as the actors could move where they wanted and didn't have to hit "marks."

Cassavetes had also honed his approach to writing and directing. "In replacing the narrative, you need an idea," he said about the script. "And the idea in *A Woman Under the Influence* was a concept of how much you have to pay for love." In directing, he tried to establish an atmosphere of comfort and authenticity for the actors, but he adamantly refused to help them understand their characters. Gena Rowlands often felt adrift, and the shoot was marked by the same violent disagreements and fights that fill the film. Cassavetes never called "action" or "cut," and often left the cameras rolling without the actors' knowledge. He would also jump into takes, or call out suggestions, trying to keep the cast off-balance.

Editing on the almost 120 hours of footage started in February 1973. By that November, Cassavetes had a four-hour cut. By the time the film premiered at the New York Film Festival the following fall, the film was 155 minutes. Eight more minutes came out before its commercial release. Cassavetes decided to distribute the film himself, booking theaters, ordering prints, overseeing publicity and advertising. *A Woman Under the Influence* was by any standard a commercial success, grossing $6 million domestically and $6 million more abroad. Gena Rowlands received an Oscar nomination for her performance.

But the critical backlash was immediate and surprisingly virulent. John Simon savaged the film with the words "muddle-headed, pretentious, and interminable." Some writers called it self-indulgent and misguided. Pauline Kael, a long-time Cassavetes enemy, called Rowland's character "a symbolic victim." In retaliation, Cassavetes would offer quips like, "I hate entertainment. There's nothing I despise more than being entertained." Or, "At what point do I reveal what's going to happen? My system is *never* to reveal it." Describing *The Godfather Part II*, which he was competing against at the Oscars, he said, "It's really boring, and I personally think that gangsters are really boring people." (His next project, *The Killing of a Chinese Bookie* in 1976, was a gangster film.)

A Woman Under the Influence remains divisive today. To some, this is the pinnacle of independent filmmaking in the 1970s, a film with harrowing glimpses into societal ills and two definitive performances from gifted actors. To others, it is sloppy, overlong, a grab bag of weird decisions and actorly tics. Falk and Rowlands are too intelligent to sink into these characters, and as a result often seem to be playing down to their roles. The real face of madness is never this beautiful, this refined, this sophisticated.

What is clear today is that Cassavetes isn't interested in what is wrong with his characters as much as he is in humiliating them, forcing them into situations in which they have no defenses, browbeating them into states of hysteria. Viewers can mistake the rage and misogyny behind *A Woman Under the Influence* as wisdom or insight, or feel that depicting an abusive relationship somehow explains it.

The box office for the film led to an offer for Cassavetes to direct *One Flew Over the Cuckoo's Nest*, although he left the project over script and casting differences. He directed four more films and acted in many others, but none of his later work matched the impact of *A Woman Under the Influence*. Cassavetes died of cirrhosis of the liver at the age of fifty-nine in 1989. A few years later, the elements for *A Woman Under the Influence* burned in a warehouse fire. The only prints available today feature a new soundtrack mixed by Al Ruban, a longtime Cassavetes collaborator.

The Godfather Part II

Paramount, 1974. Sound, color, 1.85. 201 minutes. Rated R.

Cast: Al Pacino (Michael [Corleone]), Robert Duvall (Tom Hagen), Diane Keaton (Kay), Robert De Niro (Vito Corleone), John Cazale (Fredo Corleone), Talia Shire (Connie Corleone), Lee Strasberg (Hyman Roth), Michael V. Gazzo (Frankie Pentangeli), G.D. Spradlin (Senator Pat Geary), Richard Bright (Al Neri), Gaston Moschin (Fanuc), Tom Rosqui (Rocco Lampone), B. [Bruno] Kirby, Jr. (Young Clemenza), Frank Sivero (Genco), Francesca de Sapio (Young Mama Corleone), Morgana King (Mama Corleone), Mariana [Marianna] Hill (Deanna Corleone), Leopoldo Trieste (Signor Roberto), Dominic Chianese (Johnny Ola), Amerigo Tot (Michael's bodyguard), Troy Donahue (Merle Johnson), John Aprea (Young Tessio), Joe Spinell (Willi Cicci), Abe Vigoda (Tessio), Tere Livrano (Theresa Hagen), Gianni Russo (Carlo), Maria Carta (Vito's mother), Oresta Baldini (Vito Andolini as a boy), Giuseppe Sillato (Don Francesco), Mario Cotone (Don Tommasino), James Gounaris (Anthony Corleone), Fay Spain (Mrs. Marcia Roth), Harry Dean Stanton (F.B.I. man #1), David Baker (F.B.I. man #2), Carmine Caridi (Carmine Rosato), Danny Aiello (Tony Rosato), Carmine Foresta (Policeman), Nick Discenza (Bartender), Father Joseph Medeglia (Father Carmelo), William Bowers (Senate committee chairman), Joe Della Sorte (Michael's buttonman #1), Carmen Argenziano (Michael's buttonman #2), Joe Lo Grippo (Michael's buttonman #3), Ezio Flagello (Impressario), Livio Giorgi (Tenor in *Senza Mamma*), Kathy Beller (Girl in *Senza Mamma*), Saveria Mazzola (Signora Colombo), Tito Alba (Cuban president), Johnny Naranjo (Cuban translator), Elda Maida (Pentangeli's wife), Salvatore Po (Pentangeli's brother), Ignazio Pappalardo (Mosca), Andrea Maugeri (Strollo), Peer LaCorte (Signor Abbandando), Vincent Coppola (Street vendor), Peter Donat (Questadt), Tom Dahlgren (Fred Corngold), Paul R. Brown (Senator Ream), Phil Feldman (Senator #1), Roger Corman (Senator #2), Yvonne Coll (Yolanda), J.D. Nicola (Attendant at brothel), Edward Van Sickle (Ellis Island doctor), Gabria Belloni (Ellis Island nurse), Richard Watson (Custom official), Venancia Grangerard (Cuban nurse), Erica Yohn (Governess), Theresa Tirelli (Midwife).

Credits: Produced and directed by Francis Ford Coppola. Screenplay by Francis Ford Coppola & Mario Puzo. Based on the novel *The Godfather* by Mario Puzo. Co-produced by Gray Frederickson & Fred Roos. Director of photography: Gordon Willis. Production designer: Dean Tavoularis. Editors: Peter Zinner, Barry Malkin, Richard Marks. Costume designer: Theadora Van Runkle. Associate producer: Mona Skager. Music composed by Nino Rota. Conducted by Carmine Coppola. Additional music composed by Carmine Coppola. Sound montage & re-recording: Walter Murch. Art director: Angelo Graham. Set decorator: George R. Nelson. Makeup artists: Dick Smith, Charles Schram. Production manager: Michael S. Glick. Assistant director: Newton Arnold. Casting: Michael Fenton, Jane Feinberg, Vic Ramos. Title by Wayne Fitzgerald. Hair stylist: Naomi Cavin. Special effects: A.D. Flowers, Joe Lombardi. Production recording: Chuck Wilborn, Nathan Boxer. Script supervisors: John Franco, B.J. Bachman. Color by Technicolor. A Coppola Company production.

Additional Cast: James Caan (Sonny Corleone).

Additional Credits: Title on screen: *Mario Puzo's The Godfather Part II.* Production dates October 1, 1973 to June 1974. Premiered in New York City on December 12, 1974.

Other Versions: Sequel to *The Godfather* (1972). Followed by *The Godfather Part III* (1980).

Awards: Oscars for Best Picture, Director, Actor in a Supporting Role (De Niro), Writing—Screenplay Adapted from Other Material, Music—Original Dramatic Score, Art Direction–Set Decoration.

Available: Paramount Home Entertainment DVD (2005). ISBMN: 0-7921 7331-7. UPC: 0-97360-84594-5.

Paramount executives quietly assembled a team to produce a sequel to *The Godfather* (1972) even before the original film was released. Mario Puzo signed a contract to write a screenplay in August 1971. After extended negotiations, Francis Ford Coppola agreed to terms to rewrite Puzo's screenplay, produce, and direct the project. Paramount announced the sequel in July 1972, stating that the new film would open on March 27, 1974.

According to producer Al Ruddy, 85 percent of the first *Godfather* was the work of Puzo. Coppola was preoccupied during much of the preproduction of *The Godfather Part II*. He was in the midst of editing *The Conversation* (1974, another Registry title), was on a real-estate buying spree in San Francisco, hoped to open an informal acting school, purchased *City* magazine, and was running the offices of Zoetrope, his production company. He also wrote a script for *The Great Gatsby* (1974) and broke off his business relationship with George Lucas over producers' salaries for *American Graffiti* (1973).

It's unclear just how much Coppola's staggering workload contributed to the making of *The Godfather Part II*. Certainly the deadlines imposed by the studio and the pressures to top what was becoming the most successful film in history were factors in how the sequel was assembled. Despite the demands on Coppola's time, *Part II* became the culmination of one of the most astonishing bursts of creative energy in cinema.

"The idea of a sequel seemed horrible to me," he said about the project. At first he agreed only to produce the film, suggesting that Martin Scorsese direct it. Then he saw a different approach to a sequel, one that sidestepped the issue of making a movie that was simply more of the same. Instead, he would expand on the original story, taking it into both the past and the future. "This time I really set out to destroy the family," he said in an interview. "Yet I wanted to destroy it in the way that I think is most profound—from the inside. The movie is meant to be like *The Oresteia*, showing how evil reverberates over a period of generations."

Puzo's draft was called *The Death of Michael Corleone*. Coppola, working separately, was more interested in contrasting the rise of an earlier generation's Vito Corleone with Michael's corruption. Coppola would "kill" Michael Corleone by destroying his family and isolating him from his colleagues. "I would have showed Michael at the height of his power," Puzo argued. "Everything is great with him. He's the only one who knows what's happening to him." Puzo felt that the final film version was "too much on the nose, too blatant."

Comparing turn-of-the-twentieth-century New York City with the organized crime empire of the late 1950s gave Coppola the chance to construct two opposite but equally compelling worlds, ones divorced in large part from the corrupt, mundane modern world he depicted in *The Conversation*. *The Godfather Part II* ranges from a romanticized Little Italy to a sumptuous Lake Tahoe and a glitteringly decadent Havana, all captured brilliantly by Dean Tavoularis's production design and Gordon Willis's cinematography.

Coppola's decision to intercut Vito's and Michael's stories together perplexed some critics at the time. Today filmmakers feel more comfortable mixing plot lines and even time frames, but when Coppola was filming *Part II*, some worried that mainstream viewers would have trouble keeping up with was essentially two films running concurrently. Coppola was more worried about the fact that he had written a crucial scene for Marlon Brando, but the actor was asking for more money than anyone wanted to pay. The director finessed the problem by turning the scene into a surprise birthday party for the elderly Vito Corleone.

Richard Castellano was also left out of the sequel over money issues. He was replaced by Michael Gazzo, playing the new character of Frankie Pentangeli. Coppola had to persuade Pacino to return to his role; the actor ended up with a salary some twenty times what he had earned earlier. The director had auditioned Robert De Niro for the original *Godfather*; after seeing his performance in Scorsese's *Mean Streets* (1973), he chose him to play the young Vito. Both De Niro and Pacino had studied with Lee Strasberg at the Actors Studio; now their teacher was taking his first film role in decades as the gangster Hyman Roth.

Shooting began on October 1, 1973, at Lake Tahoe. Pacino contracted pneumonia in February 1974, forcing Coppola to switch to the Vito Corleone story line. Here the decision to cast De Niro paid off. Through his extensive research, the actor was able to build on Brando's Oscar-winning performance and make Vito's role his own. Perhaps just as moving was the work by John Cazale as Fredo Corleone, a part expanded from the original film by Puzo and Coppola. Filming didn't end until June 1974, by which point Coppola had enough material for a six-hour movie.

The first rough cut ran close to five hours. By the first public sneak preview, on November 27, he had edited the film down to a little over three hours. Editor Barry Malkin remembered making some eighty cuts to the film between the sneak and the official premiere in December. Early reviews were mixed, with the *New York Times*' Vincent Canby calling it "a Frankenstein's monster stitched together from leftover parts." *The New Yorker*'s Pauline Kael may have been the first critic to point out the film's resemblance to opera.

Coppola has continued to fiddle with the *Godfather* movies, cutting and reassembling them in different collections, adding and deleting sequences, rearranging the soundtrack. As with many operas, there may never be a definitive version. Coppola recently spent a year restoring the first two *Godfather* films with Robert A. Harris and Joanne Lawson. Preservationists discovered that the original negatives had been damaged in the 1980s, and that the films' dissolves no longer timed out correctly. While Gordon Willis is pleased with the overall restoration, he said, "I'm the first to admit that the darker material, especially in *Part II*, is difficult to reproduce properly." *The Godfather Part II* was the last feature whose release prints were made using Technicolor's dye-transfer process. As Willis noted, "It was beautiful on dye-transfer, but at the moment, the positive available isn't doing the job we all hoped for."

Young Frankenstein

Twentieth Century-Fox, 1974. Sound, B&W, 1.85. 106 minutes. Rated PG.

Cast: Gene Wilder (Dr. Frankenstein), Peter Boyle (The Monster), Marty Feldman (Igor), Madeline Kahn (Elizabeth), Cloris Leachman (Frau Blücher), Teri Garr (Inga), Kenneth Mars (Inspector Kemp), Richard Haydn (Herr Falkstein), Liam Dunn (Mr. Hilltop), Danny Goldman (Medical student), Oscar Beregi (Sadistic jailor), Arthur Malet (Village elder), Anne Beesley (Little Girl); Monte Landis, Rusty Blitz (Gravediggers); John Madison, John Dennis, Rick Norman, Rolfe Sedan, Terence Pushman, Randolph Dobbs, Norbert Schiller, Patrick O'Hara, Michael Fox, Lidia Kristen, Richard Roth (Insp. Kemp's aide), Gene Hackman (Blind man).

Credits: Directed by Mel Brooks. Screen story and screenplay by Gene Wilder and Mel Brooks. Produced by Michael Gruskoff. Director of photography: Gerald Hirschfeld. Music composed and conducted by John Morris. Film editor: John C. Howard. Unit production manager: Frank Baur. Assistant director: Marvin Miller. Production designer: Dale Hennesy. Set decorator: Bob de Vestel. Title and graphic design: Anthony Goldschmidt. Casting by Mike Fenton, Jane Feinberg. Makeup created by William Tuttle. Men's wardrobe: Dick James, Ed Wynigear. Women's wardrobe: Phyllis Garr, Carolyn Ewart. Makeup artist: Ed Butterworth. Costumes by Dorothy Jeakins. Hairdresser: Mary Keats. Special effects: Henry Millar, Jr., Hal Millar. Script supervisor: Ray Quiroz. Production mixer: Gene Cantamessa. Sound editor: Don Hall. Special thanks to Kenneth Strickfaden for original Frankenstein laboratory equipment. Filmed with Panavision equipment. Prints by DeLuxe. Westrex Recording System. A Gruskoff/Venture Films, Crossbow Productions, Inc., and Jouer Limited production.

Additional Credits: Production dates: February 26 to May 1974. Released December 15, 1974.

Other Versions: Produced as a Broadway musical in 2007.

Available: Twentieth Century Fox Home Entertainment DVD (2006). UPC: 024543371571.

Actor Gene Wilder brought the idea for *Young Frankenstein* to Mel Brooks while Brooks was editing his Western satire *Blazing Saddles* (1974). Wilder later explained that the script "sort of goes along with where I was in life at the time." Over seven years of therapy had changed the actor from a "sheep" to a self-professed wild man filled with "rage at my first wife." He began writing *Young Frankenstein* on a lined pad of yellow legal paper, finishing a scene set at the Transylvania train station, and showing the resulting two pages to Brooks.

"I'd written one screenplay called *Hesitation Waltz*," Wilder recalled. "It wasn't any good." Brooks supervised Wilder with his new idea; the actor completed a total of three drafts that imagined how Dr. Frankenstein's grandson would react if he inherited the family castle. "Mel would come in from *Blazing Saddles* and make me add or change things," Wilder told an interviewer. "He'd say, 'You have no villain, you just have a burgermeister.'" Finally Wilder had a 150-page script to show studios. Columbia Pictures expressed interest in the draft, but Twentieth Century-Fox offered Brooks a larger budget and final cut.

Brooks and Wilder collaborated on a fourth draft. As Wilder put it, "My job was to make him more subtle. His job was to make me more broad. I would say, 'I don't want this to be *Blazing Frankenstein.*'" At the same time, Brooks offered the actor valuable lessons, "He taught me never to be afraid of offending. It's when you worry about offending people that you get in trouble."

Mike Medavoy, Wilder's agent at the time, helped package the script with two of his other clients: Marty Feldman as the hunchbacked lab assistant Igor, and Peter Boyle as the monster. Medavoy also got the script to producer Michael Gruskoff. Brooks wrote the part of Frau Blücher specifically for Cloris Leachman, remembering her work from their days in television. The director had originally cast Teri Garr as Frankenstein's fiancée, but gave the part to Madeline Kahn after her work in *Blazing Saddles*. Garr became Frankenstein's fetching lab assistant Inga instead. (Garr's mother worked in wardrobe on the film.)

Brooks located some of the original props designed by Ken Strickfaden for the 1931 film *Frankenstein* (a Registry title). The director remembered suffering from recurring nightmares after seeing James Whale's film as a child, and later said that exorcising these demons was one reason why he made *Young Frankenstein*. He also remembered entertaining friends by singing "Puttin' on the Ritz" in the voice of Boris Karloff, although he demurred when Wilder wanted to film a similar scene. Wilder fortunately won out, and the resulting scene is the funniest moment in the film.

Filming took fifty-four days that most in the cast and crew remembered fondly. Gene Hackman took an uncredited role as a blind hermit simply to find out what a Brooks set was like. Kahn later pointed out one of the difficulties in working with the director, notably "tension because everyone wanted to please him, so they felt they had to be funny." Winding up with a three-hour cut, Brooks spent six months editing the film. He dropped a song by the gravediggers, a sequence in which the monster is taught how to play musical instruments, and "literary jokes, not cinematic." After twelve complete cuts, Brooks had to relinquish the film in order to make his opening day deadline. He also faced arbitration by the Writers Guild of

America, which decided that Wilder deserved a cowriting credit.

Much of the success for *Young Frankenstein* is due to the filmmakers' reverence for the original material. Key scenes are played straight, not for laughs, and the performances by Wilder, Garr, and especially Boyle are free of an irony that might have deflated the film's tone. As Brooks put it, "You can't keep winking because it diminishes the melodrama. The melodrama has to be there." Biographer James Robert Parish believes that the solid structure of Wilder's script helped rein in Brooks' tendency to excess. Having a concrete story line to follow, rather than simply mocking a broad genre, made *Young Frankenstein*

more palatable to mainstream audiences. The film earned more than ten times its budget in its initial release.

Mocking the horror genre was nothing new, as the Registry title *Abbott and Costello Meet Frankenstein* (1948) proves. Some critics believe that Whale's own *Bride of Frankenstein* (1935) was a parody of his earlier film. The box-office success of *Young Frankenstein* helped lead to a string of largely ineffectual parodies of monster films, including *Love at First Bite* (1979) and Brooks' own *Dracula: Dead and Loving It* (1995). As he did with *The Producers*, Brooks later oversaw the transformation of *Young Frankenstein* into a Broadway musical directed by Susan Stroman.

Fuji

Robert Breer, 1974. Sound, color, 1.37. 9 minutes.

Credits: Photographed, edited, and directed by Robert Breer.

Available: The Film-Makers' Cooperative (*www.film-makerscoop.com*); Canyon Cinema (*www.canyoncinema.com*).

Robert Breer was born in Detroit in 1926, the son of a prominent engineer. After attending Stanford University in California and serving in the Army during World War II, he lived for a decade in Paris, at first intending to be a painter. It was by documenting his art work with his father's 16mm Bolex that he became interested in film. His early work followed in the "graphic cinema" tradition of European artists like Hans Richter and Fernand Léger, although at the time he had little knowledge of avant-garde film history. Like the Austrian filmmaker Peter Kubelka, he tried to apply various art theories to a single frame of film. "I'm interested in the domain between motion and still pictures," he wrote. "The single frame is the basic unit of film, just as bricks are the basic unit of brick houses."

After *Form Phases* (1952–54) and *Image by Images* (1954–56), Breer began experimenting with collages of objects, later combining them with images of abstract geometric forms. When he returned to the United States in 1959, he continued making his version of animated films, conscious that his work was in direct opposition to what was traditionally considered animation. After applying concepts of pop and minimalist art to his films, he began tackling what he saw as the fundamental issues of animation in *66* (1966), *69* (1969), and *70* (1970). In these films he

explored basic tenets like motion, which he would variously freeze, invert, speed up, or repeat; color, shown in alternating fields or selected from color wheels; depth, which he would imply or deny by rotating or flattening objects; and drawing itself, changing the thickness and edges of lines, switching from abstract to representational. At the same time Breer was building what amounted to solid animation: abstract, motorized sculptures whose motion was barely perceptible. He also experimented with mechanical "pre-cinema" devices like thaumatropes that operated on the margins of still and motion photography.

During the 1970s Breer began using still photographs and motion picture clips in his films. For *Fuji*, he used footage of the Japanese mountain taken inside a passenger railroad car as a starting point for animation. Breer inserts color fields and abstract images into the frame, but he also rotoscopes the image, outlining figures and at times coloring them. It's the same process developed by the Fleischer brothers in the 1920s, but instead of using it as an animation short-cut, Breer uses it to restructure the content of the frame. His rotoscoping might isolate a geometric pattern, provide illusory depth to a figure, or break figures into shards of color. "Found" railroad sounds provides a tempo for the animation.

For filmgoers, the "narrative" or plot becomes an attempt to decode the meaning of the images, to see what the footage really is without its animated overlays. Breer repeats the same shots over and over, adding or subtracting elements, transforming the content into different shapes and abstractions. The viewer has to decide what it "means." Breer's only hint is the film's title. Viewers need to already have an understanding about the mountain and its place in Japanese culture. Those who know how the Japanese have used Fuji's image in art will be able to appreciate better Breer's allusions to watercolors and prints from Japanese history. If not, they are left to contemplate the jittery beauty of the images themselves.

Fuji also comments on the experience of rail travel, how car windows reduce landscapes to abstract blocks or frames, how landscapes can repeat themselves in daily commutes or through comparison to similar geographic patterns. Just as the railway circles around the mountain, the film circles around its subject, offering different angles, colors, and interpretations of the same object.

In the tradition of Stan Brakhage and similar artists, Breer's films turn what is usually an illusion, a play of light and shadows, into a concrete medium that can be drawn or painted on. In that same tradition, he shows us that anything can become art: a conductor, a window, the back of a head. *Fuji* is as rewarding as it is challenging, a jazzy, free-spirited exercise that can be interpreted anew with each screening. Breer now lives in upstate New York; his daughter Emily is also an animator.

Nashville

Ronee Blakley performing as Barbara Jean in *Nashville*.

Paramount, 1975. Sound, color, 2.35. 160 minutes. Rated R.
Cast: David Arkin (Norman), Barbara Baxley (Lady Pearl), Ned Beatty (Delbert Reese), Karen Black (Connie White), Ronee Blakley (Barbara Jean), Timothy Brown (Tommy Brown), Keith Carradine (Tom Frank), Geraldine Chaplin (Opal), Robert DoQui (Wade Cooley), Shelley Duvall (L.A. Joan [Marthe]), Allen Garfield (Barnett), Henry Gibson (Haven Hamilton), Scott Glenn (Pfc. Glenn Kelly), Jeff Goldblum (Tricycle man), Barbara Harris (Albuquerque), David Hayward (Kenny Frasier), Michael Murphy (John Triplette), Allan Nicholls (Bill), Dave Peel (Bud Hamilton), Cristina Raines (Mary), Bert Remsen (Star), Lily Tomlin (Linnea Reese), Gwen Welles (Sueleen Gay), Keenan Wynn (Mr. Green), James Dan Calvert (Jimmy Reese), Donna Denton (Donna Reese), Merle Kilgore (Trout), Carol McGinnis (Jewel); Sheila Bailey, Patti Bryant (Smokey Mountain Laurels); Richard Baskin (Frog), Jonnie Barnett, Vassar Clements, Sue Barton, Elliott Gould, Julie Christie.
Credits: Produced and directed by Robert Altman. Written by Joan Tewkesbury. Executive producers: Martin Starger, Jerry Weintraub. Director of photography: Paul Lohmann. Associate producers: Robert Eggenweiler, Scott Bushnell. Music arranged and supervised by Richard Baskin. Political campaign: Thomas Hal Phillips. Edited by Sidney Levin, Dennis Hill. Assistant directors: Tommy Thompson, Alan Rudolph. Production coordinator: Kelly Marshall. Assistant to the producer: Jac Cashin. Sound: Jim Webb, Chris McLaughlin. Sound system: Lion's Gate 8 Track Sound. Re-recording mixer: Richard Portman. Sound editor: William A. Sawyer. Assistant sound editor: Randy Kelley. Music recorded by Gene Eichelberger and Johnny Rosen. Assistant editors: Tony Lombardo, Tom Walls. Script supervision: Joyce King. Hair stylist: Ann Wadlington. Makeup: Tommy Thompson. Wardrobe: Jules Melillo. Title design: Dan Perri. Filmed in Panavision. Color by MGM Film Laboratories. Chem-tone process by TVC Lab. An ABC Entertainment presentation of a Jerry Weintraub production.
Additional Credits: Production dates: July to August 31, 1974. Premiered in New York City on June 11, 1975.
Awards: Oscar for Best Music—Original Song ("I'm Easy" by Keith Carradine).
Available: Paramount DVD (2000). ISBN: 0-7921-6499-7. UPC: 0-9736-08821-4-8.

After the international success of *MASH* (1970), director Robert Altman had carte blanche to develop any project he wanted. He used this freedom to make a series of films that commented on the genres he worked in while learning his craft in industrial films, B-movies and television series. His revisionist Western (*McCabe & Mrs. Miller*, 1971), psychological thriller (*Images*, 1972), detective story (*The Long Goodbye*, 1973), and Depression-era melodrama (*Thieves Like Us*, 1974) won critical praise despite shrinking box-office returns.

Altman needed a subject that would connect him with mainstream filmgoers, and he thought he found it in Nashville, Tennessee, the center of much of the country music industry. Actor Keith Carradine made his film debut in *McCabe & Mrs. Miller* and was one of the leads in *Thieves Like Us*. During the production of that film, he sang two of his own compositions for Altman, "I'm Easy," and "It Don't Worry Me" (the latter written for but not used in *Emperor of the North Pole*, 1973). "When I heard them I knew I wanted to plan a whole movie around them," Altman said later. The director may have found an equal amount of inspiration from *The Great Southern Amusement Company*, a script United Artists wanted him to make with singer Tom Jones.

Altman sent screenwriter Joan Tewkesbury to research Nashville. Jerry Weintraub, a producer of tours for singers like Frank Sinatra and Elvis Presley, was trying to break into movies; he helped Altman secure a deal with Martin Starger at ABC for a film budgeted at $2.2 million. Altman then asked Tewkesbury to start a new script built around the breakup of a trio similar to one made up of John Denver and Bill and Taffy Danoff, all clients of Weintraub's. The only story element Altman demanded was that the script end with an assassination that missed its intended political target and killed a singer instead.

Tewkesbury's script originally used authentic country music, like Merle Haggard's "Okie from Muskogee." But "it became too expensive," Altman explained, adding, "This wasn't about how good the songs were." Instead, the actors would write and perform their own music, a decision that further removed *Nashville* the movie from the reality of Nashville the city. The music score was arranged by Richard Baskin, son of an ice cream magnate and an indifferent actor and songwriter. His take on the music: "Much of country-western music is a parody of itself. The truly great music, if you go back twenty years, is kind of saccharine and trite."

Baskin was friends with Ronee Blakley, a backup singer for Hoyt Axton; she was cast as troubled country star Barbara Jean after Altman fired Susan Anspach. Henry Gibson, a *Laugh-In* alumnus who had a minor role in *The Long Goodbye*, became Haven Hamilton, a strait-laced conservative singer loosely based on Hank Snow and Roy Acuff. This was the film debut for Lily Tomlin, another *Laugh-In* comic; her part was originally written for Louise Fletcher.

Some cast members had misgivings about their roles. Barbara Harris, who played an amateur trying to break into the industry, said about Keith Carradine, "We would weep every night with our parts. 'I hate being a masher,' he'd go. 'I hate being psychotic,' I'd go." Harris prepared material with songwriter Shel Silverstein, but Altman refused to use most of it. Geraldine Chaplin remembered "the cruel side of Bob" in his "total hate relationship" with Harris. He made her sing an extra forty-five minutes at the final scene at the Parthenon, even though there was no film in the cameras. "And he was laughing," Chaplin added.

Filming took place in July and August of 1974, with Altman organizing several set pieces that involved all twenty-four of the film's cast members. Along with multiple cameras, the director also relied on multitrack sound recording. Sound designer Jim Webb came by recommendation of cinematographer Paul Lohmann. Webb, who had handled sound for rock documentaries, gave all the actors radio microphones, and developed a "sound zoom" technique that mirrored the effect of Lohmann's moving camera.

Altman had 200,000 feet (about sixteen hours) of material when he left Nashville in the beginning of September. He contemplated cutting two entire movies, *Nashville Red* and *Nashville Blue*. They would tell the same story, but from different perspectives, with different characters emphasized in each version. He was talked out of this plan, although as publicity for the film built, he spoke with ABC about broadcasting a ten-hour miniseries version on television.

After three months, Altman had a three-hour version. Film critic Pauline Kael saw this rough cut in January 1975, and wrote a glowing review in the March 3 issue of *The New Yorker*, calling it an "orgy for movie-lovers." Her article prompted more *Nashville* stories, including a spread on Ronee Blakley in *Vogue* and a cover in *Newsweek*. Altman cut eleven more minutes from the film before its official opening on June 8, 1975.

On the whole, critics praised *Nashville*. Roger Ebert wrote, "I felt I understood more about people. I felt somehow wiser." The public, on the other hand, ignored it. By the time it opened in Nashville that August, Altman was defending it by criticizing more successful country-oriented films like *Payday* (1973) and *W.W. and the Dixie Dancekings* (1975). Country music stars were dismissive. "I'd rather see *Bambi*," Loretta Lynn said, while

Minnie Pearl, one of the most respected spokespersons for the industry, opined, "I'm afraid a lot of people who love our music will be offended by the film. The music was terrible." "Not merely bad country songs, but fake country songs," as writer Nick Tosches put it.

Altman wasn't interested in country music itself, except as a target of scorn. He wanted his cross-section of Nashville to stand in for the country as a whole. Where he employed a generational divide in his previous movies, here he was constructing a cultural one. In his eyes, and those of many critics, it was "us against them," the intellectual elite against the great unwashed. The director had no trouble ennobling Lily Tomlin's character because her children were deaf and she sang with a black choir, but he couldn't find any humanity in Henry Gibson's caricature or his music. *Nashville* espoused the same attitude as Elia Kazan's *A Face in the* Crowd (1957),

where Walter Matthau, representing an urbane Manhattanite, smoked a pipe and sipped martinis while tsk-tsking about hillbillies.

It was a glib, cruel argument that ignored history and tradition, but that spoke directly to a narrow wedge of society. It's telling that not a single legitimate country star participated in the movie; when Altman wanted some celebrity cameos to add a touch of realism, he had to turn to Julie Christie and Elliott Gould.

To studio executives, *Nashville* was yet more proof that Altman was commercial poison. Not even his devoted critics wanted to defend his next film, *Buffalo Bill and the Indians, or Sitting Bull's History Lesson* (1976); with its box-office failure, and that of his following films, Altman found his career in jeopardy. It wasn't until his satire of Hollywood, *The Player* (1992), that he began to regain a reputation as a maverick filmmaker.

Jaws

Universal, 1975. Sound, color, 2.35. 134 minutes. Rated PG.

Cast: Roy Scheider (Brody), Robert Shaw (Quint), Richard Dreyfuss ([Matt] Hooper), Lorraine Gary (Ellen Brody), Murray Hamilton (Vaughn), Carl Gottlieb (Meadows), Jeffrey C. Kramer (Hendricks), Susan Backlinie (Chrissie), Jonathan Filley (Cassidy), Ted Grossman (Estuary victim), Chris Rebello (Michael Brody), Jay Mello (Sean Brody), Lee Fierro (Mrs. Kintner), Jeffrey Voorhees (Alex Kintner), Craig Kingsbury (Ben Gardner), Dr. Robert Nevin (Medical Examiner), Peter Benchley (Interviewer).

Credits: Directed by Steven Spielberg. Screenplay by Peter Benchley and Carl Gottlieb. Based upon the novel by Peter Benchley. Produced by Richard D. Zanuck and David Brown. Director of photography: Bill Butler. Film editor: Verna Fields. Music by John Williams. Production designer: Joseph Alves, Jr. Special effects: Robert A. Mattey. Production executive: William S. Gilmore, Jr. Underwater photography: Rexford Metz. Camera operator: Michael Chapman. Sound: John R. Carter, Robert Hoyt. Unit production manager: Jim Fargo. First assistant director: Tom Joyner. Script supervisor: Charlsie Bryant. Set decorations: John M. Dwyer. Technical advisor: Manfred Zendar. Cosmetics by Cinematique. Titles & optical effects: Universal Title. Westrex Recording System. Live shark footage filmed by Ron and Valerie Taylor. Filmed in Panavision. Color by Technicolor. A Zanuck/Brown production.

Awards: Oscars for Film Editing, Music—Original Score, Sound.

Additional Credits: Screenwriting by Howard Sackler, John Milius, Robert Shaw. Sound: Roger Heman, Jr., Earl Madery. Production dates: May 2 to September 15, 1974; additional photography October to December 1974. Opened June 20, 1975.

Other Versions: Sequels *Jaws 2* (1978), *Jaws 3-D* (1983), *Jaws: The Revenge* (1987).

Available: Universal Studios DVD (2000). ISBN: 0-7832-4439-8. UPC: 0-25192-09122-3.

By 1974, Steven Spielberg's career as a director was so secure that he could risk moving out of television. Born in 1946, Spielberg devoted much of his adolescence to making movies, first on Super 8, then on 16mm. While he was infatuated with

motion pictures, his interest stemmed in part from his desire to recreate them on his own terms. His projects escalated in size until he began working in 35mm. He started but left unfinished *Slipstream*, a science fiction feature, in 1967. *Amblin'*, a short he made the following year, helped get him a job at Universal. There his first assignment was "Eyes," an episode in a three-part pilot for Rod Serling's new television series, *Night Gallery*.

Spielberg filmed more *Night Gallery* episodes, as well as entries for series like *Marcus Welby, M.D.* and *Columbo*. *Duel* (1971), a near-wordless thriller made for TV, was so successful that an expanded version was released theatrically in Europe. His feature film debut was *The Sugarland Express* (1974), an elaboration on a real-life Texas manhunt. It began his collaboration with producers David Brown and Richard Zanuck. Lew Wasserman, at the time the head of Universal's parent company MCA, wrote off the film as a "downer," but it confirmed Spielberg's filmmaking talent and ability to control a large production.

Spielberg had hoped to make *Watch the Skies*, a science-fiction script that eventually became *Close Encounters of the Third Kind* (1977); when financing efforts stalled, he pursued *Jaws*, a novel by Peter Benchley that he had seen in Richard Zanuck's office. Inspired by a 1964 newspaper article about a shark hunter, and the graphic documentary *Blue Water, White Death*, Benchley started writing his best-seller the year the documentary was released, 1971. Galleys of the book prompted a bidding war among Hollywood studios in 1973; Universal prevailed, with Zanuck and Brown as the producers.

Spielberg was not the first choice to direct *Jaws*, but his work on *The Sugarland Express* persuaded Zanuck and Brown to take a chance on him. The director wavered about the project, trying to quit at one point to film *Lucky Lady* (1975) instead. "I have very mixed feelings about my work on that picture," Spielberg admitted two years later. "*Jaws* is almost like I'm directing the audience with an electric cattle prod."

"I was a prostitute," was how Richard Dreyfuss explained why he joined the cast of *Jaws*. Spielberg called him "my alter ego," but his first choice for ichthyologist Matt Hooper had been Jon Voight. Dreyfuss's energetic underdog became a surrogate for moviegoers, a way for them to enter into the story. Roy Scheider was cast as small-town police chief Brody largely on the basis of his performance in *The French Connection* (1971). Robert Duvall had asked to play legendary shark hunter Captain Quint, but Spielberg turned him down. Robert Shaw, a British actor who had worked for Brown and Zanuck in *The Sting* (1973), was hired after Lee Marvin refused the role.

The producers hired Ron and Valerie Taylor, the photographers of *Blue Water, White Death*, to film footage of great white sharks in Australia. When a shark attacked their boat, it inspired Spielberg to insert new scenes for Dreyfuss' character. Meanwhile, Benchley submitted two screenplay drafts. Although Spielberg kept much of his plot, he wasn't satisfied with the dialogue or action. Playwright Howard Sackler wrote an uncredited draft that introduced the story about the sinking in 1944 of the USS *Indianapolis*, one of the most vivid scenes in the finished film. Carl Gottlieb helped Spielberg revise the script throughout the shoot.

Several written accounts of the production have described it as a nightmare. What was supposed to take 55 days took almost 160 instead, with a corresponding increase in the budget. The decision to shoot much of the film on actual boats in the Atlantic contributed to many of the delays. Uncooperative weather and the sheer physical burden of filming on the ocean made the production far more difficult than anyone expected. That, and

the fact that the three mechanical sharks (nicknamed "Bruce") built for the production would not work properly.

While Universal executives generally supported Spielberg, there was talk about moving or even stopping the film. "Every day we were over schedule, they wanted to take the movie out of Martha's Vineyard and move it to the Bahamas, to Florida," producer David Brown told director Gary Fleder years later. "I kept saying to Steven, 'Never take the film out of the camera. If you do, it may not go back in the camera.'"

In the long run, the trouble with the mechanical sharks actually helped make *Jaws* a better movie. Since the props looked fake or didn't work, Spielberg had to work out ways to keep the shark hidden from the audience. That way the viewers' imaginations can come into play. In an interview for *Take One*, Spielberg said, "You're so limited being on a boat that I find myself running out of shots; I found myself out of shots really the third day at sea." The director resorted to a full complement of other cinematic devices, such as a combination zoom-and-dolly shot from *Vertigo* (1958). He also found a sympathetic editor in Verna Fields, who helped pare some 400,000 feet of footage down to 11,000, in the process hitting upon a way to marry the visuals to John Williams's famously ominous score.

Early sneak previews convinced Universal executives that they had a hit. They spent $2.5 million promoting the film, over a million more than typical movies of the time. Much of this went to television ads. Crucially, Wasserman told Zanuck to limit the number of opening theaters. Zanuck had booked 600 theaters, but *Jaws* opened in only 469, raising interest and demand among moviegoers. *Variety* correctly labeled it "an artistic and commercial smash." The film turned a profit within two weeks; by the end of the summer, it was the most profitable movie ever made.

For updating previously successful filmmaking strategies, and for finding a way to connect them to a burgeoning baby boomer audience, Spielberg deserves much of the credit for *Jaws*. Should he then be criticized for the film's pairing of sex and violence? Should he have placed his talents in the service of a film that, as he said during filming, "will scare the hell out of anyone who's ever swum in the ocean"?

Some writers have accused Spielberg of being responsible for what they perceive as a subsequent "dumbing down" of motion pictures. After *Jaws*, "every studio movie became a B movie," wrote critic Peter Biskind. *Orca* (1977), *Alligator* (1980), *Tentacles* (1977), and *Piranha* (1978) were just some of the *Jaws* knockoffs. (Universal itself contributed with three unnecessary sequels.) In the book *Open Wide*, authors Dade Hayes and Jonathan Bing make the intriguing case that *Jaws* may have simply repeated a formula for summer blockbusters established by Warner Brothers back in 1953 with *The Beast from 20,000 Fathoms*.

The Rocky Horror Picture Show

Twentieth Century-Fox, 1975. Sound, color, 1.85. 98 minutes. Rated R.

Cast: Tim Curry (Dr. Frank-n-furter), Susan Sarandon (Janet Weiss), Barry Bostwick (Brad Majors), Richard O'Brien (Riff Raff), Patricia Quinn (Magenta), Little Nell [Campbell] (Columbia), Jonathan Adams (Dr. Everett V. Scott), Peter Hinwood (Rocky Horror), Meat Loaf (Eddie), Charles Gray (The Criminologist), Jeremy Newson (Ralph Hapschatt), Hilary Labow (Betty Munroe). The Transylvanians: Perry Bedden, Christopher Biggins, Gaye Brown, Ishaq Bux, Stephen Calcutt, Hugh Cecil, Imogen Claire, Tony Cowan, Sadie Corre, Fran Fullenwider, Lindsay Ingram, Peggy Ledger, Annabelle Leventon, Anthony Milner, Pamela Obermeyer, Tony Then, Kimi Wong, Henry Woolf. Principal musicians: Count Ian Blair, Mick Grabham, David Wintour, B.J. Wilson, Phil Kenzie, Rabbit [John Bundrick], Richard Hartley.

Credits: Directed by Jim Sharman. Screenplay by Jim Sharman and Richard O'Brien. Original musical play music and lyrics by Richard O'Brien. Produced by Michael White. Executive producer: Lou Adler. Associate producer: John Goldstone. Musical direction and arrangements by Richard Hartley. Director of photography: Peter Suschitzky. Film and music editor: Graeme Clifford. Design by Brian Thomson. Original costume design by Sue Blane. Incidental music by Richard Hartley. Dances staged by David Toguri. Sound recordist: Ron Barron. Music recording: Keith Grant. Dubbing mixer: Bill Rowe. Dubbing editor: Ian Fuller. Art director: Terry Ackland-Snow. Set dresser: Ian Whittaker. Make-up: Peter Robb-King. Based on original make-up designs created by Pierre La Roche. Hairdresser: Ramon Gow. Wardrobe: Richard Pointing, Gillian Dods. Production manager: John Comfort. Continuity: Sue Merry. Special effects: Wally Veever, Colin Chilvers. Title sequences by Camera Effects, Ltd. Made on location and at Bray Studios, Berkshire, England. Post production at EMI-Elmstree Studios, England. Prints by De Luxe. A Twentieth Century-Fox presentation of a Lou Adler–Michael White production.

Additional Credits: Production dates: October 21 to December 19, 1974. Released September 25, 1975.

Other Versions: *Shock Treatment* (1981), directed by Jim Sharman and written by Richard O'Brien, uses many of the same characters and actors.

Available: Twentieth Century Fox Home Entertainment DVD (2000). UPC: 024543005759.

A box-office failure in its initial release, *The Rocky Horror Picture Show* became a phenomenon when it was re-released specifically for midnight screenings. A relatively short-lived fad, midnight movies grew out of a practice by television stations of airing horror and exploitation films in late-night slots. For theater owners, midnight was an opportunity to screen films that were defiantly out of the mainstream. *El Topo* (1969) and *Pink Flamingos* (1972) were notorious and successful not because they were good, but because they were marketed as too outré for middlebrow audiences.

The Rocky Horror Picture Show was based on a stage play, *The Rocky Horror Show*, by Richard O'Brien, an actor who appeared in the 1972 British stage production of *Jesus Christ Superstar*. Composers Andrew Lloyd Webber and Tim Rice chose the Australian Jim Sharman, who had also directed a version of *Hair*, to head the London production of *Superstar*. Sharman and O'Brien later worked together on a staging of Sam Shepard's *The Unseen Hand*, at which point O'Brien showed the director songs he had prepared for a musical parody of science fiction and horror films. Sharman brought "Little Nell" Campbell into the project, as well as his production designer Brian Thomson. He also gave the play its title.

The Rocky Horror Show opened in a tiny, sixty-seat theater in June 1973. It ran for almost three thousand performances, moving to larger theaters to accommodate crowds. Versions of it ran in Los Angeles and New York, and in other countries. Tim Curry, a classically trained actor, originated the lead role of Dr. Frank-n-furter, and starred in the first two U.S. productions.

Curry signed on for the film, as did several other *Rocky Horror Show* veterans: O'Brien, Campbell, Patricia Quinn, and costume designer Sue Blane. For commercial reasons, Twentieth Century-Fox wanted Americans in the cast, which explains the presence of Susan Sarandon and Barry Bostwick as Janet and Brad, naive lovers who accidentally wander into a mansion where a Transylvania convention is being held. Sharman and O'Brien retained much of the original stage show, including the music and the general design for the sets. They opened up the first act, adding a wedding scene not found in the play, and eliminated a murder that resulted in cannibalism. Some of their ideas, like shooting the opening third of the film in black-and-white, and including clips from a half-dozen or so cult movies, proved too expensive to execute. The filmmakers added the equivalent of a chorus in the form of convention attendees; they acted as a sort of laugh track during the dialogue scenes. Filming took place from October 21, 1974, to December 19, 1974.

The Rocky Horror Picture Show opened in Westwood, Los Angeles, on September 25, 1975, to generally lackluster reviews (*Variety* called it "obvious" and "flat"). A planned New York opening on Halloween was canceled; instead, the film was offered on a double bill with *Phantom of the Paradise*, another rock musical. Credit for booking it as a midnight movie has been taken by a number of people. The midnight screenings started on April 1, 1976, in New York City's Waverly Theater. According to an official Fox studio timeline, audience members began to participate in screenings by that September, and by the following year were bringing costumes and props to shows.

Audience participation was the one element that distinguished *Rocky Horror* from other midnight movies. Audiences felt comfortable responding verbally to films like *Pink Flamingos*, but *Rocky Horror* inspired greater devotion. The movie's slow pacing and blockheaded characters gave viewers plenty of opportunities to mock the proceedings on the screen—or imitate them. As costumes and rituals inside the theater grew more elaborate, fan clubs sprouted, and screenings spread to other cities. Fox had more than two-hundred prints for midnight screenings circulating at one point.

Even its most devoted fans never tried to argue that *The Rocky Horror Picture Show* was a "good" movie in the normal sense of the word. Mistakes, flimsy plotting, slapdash choreography, tuneless songs and woeful acting were all explained away as intentional, "camp," part of the coded subtext of the film. Talent and skill no longer mattered; style and transgression did. Those who objected to clumsy sex jokes as old as vaudeville just "didn't get it." Participants in theaters relished the fact that they were just as bad, or good, as the performers on the screen.

Outré is a tough niche for studio executives to master. It's no wonder the film was initially a flop: its target audience preferred loft parties to movie cineplexes. Fortunately for the filmmakers, and Fox, the do-it-yourself ethos surrounding *The Rocky Horror Picture Show* quickly became more important than the picture itself. Recapturing that phenomenon was especially difficult, however. Sharman and O'Brien collaborated on *Shock Treatment* (1981), which grew out of experimental sequels to the original *Rocky Horror* stage play. The film was a critical and commercial disaster; what's worse, the entire midnight movie circuit was beginning to collapse, rendered irrelevant by cable and home video. The *Rocky Horror* cult is still thriving, with productions of the play opening periodically around the world. But now that anyone can see the film at home, costumed extravaganzas at movie theaters are increasingly rare.

The Buffalo Creek Flood: An Act of Man

Appalshop, 1975. Sound, B&W, 1.37. 40 minutes.

Featuring: Shirley Marcum, W.A. Wahler, Thomas N. Bethell, Kathy Bryant, Rev. Jim Somerville.

Credits: Produced, directed and edited by Mimi Pickering. Cinematography: Robert Gates, Gene DuBey, Scott Faulkner, Mimi Pickering, Alida Herrick, Marty Newell, Ben Zickafoose, Angie DeBord, Mike Stanton (flood footage). Video: Dave Miller, Mimi Pickering. Still photography: Don Stillman, Ford Reid, Earl Dotter, Mimi Pickering, Larry Craft, Gene DuBey, Jeanne Rasmussen, Dave Miller. Dam graphics: W.A. Wahler & Associates. Assistant editor: Alida Herrick. Sound: Herb E. Smith, Bill Richardson, Mimi Pickering, Gary Slemp. Technical assistance: Roland Brown, Gene DuBey. Music: "The Buffalo Creek Flood" by Doug Yarrow & Ruth Yarrow. Performed by Jack Wright. Special thanks: Brenda Mahoney, David Massey, Stanley Majka, The Mountain Eagle, Bill & Josephine Richardson. This film was made possible by a grant from the Abelard Foundation. Funded in part by the National Endowment for the Arts and Cineric, Inc.

Additional Credits: Released October 1975.

Other Versions: *Buffalo Creek Revisited* (1985), a sequel directed by Mimi Pickering.

Available: Appalshop DVD (2006). UPC: 8-37101-19167-8.

Buffalo Creek follows a narrow mountain valley in Logan County, West Virginia, that in 1972 was home to more than sixteen small coal-mining communities. A tipple, an assemblage of machines and conveyors that separates coal from impurities, operated at the headwaters of Buffalo Creek since 1946. It served eight separates mines, and was purchased in 1970 by the Pittston Company, the largest independent coal-mining organization in the country. Pittston, headquartered in New York City, had signed a lucrative contract with the Japanese steel industry that guaranteed a market for as much coal as the company could produce.

Waste materials, as much as a quarter of every ton mined, are an inevitable by-product of any tipple. At first mine owners simply piled up the waste, but as stricter environmental laws were passed, they turned to other procedures. Earthen dams were built at the headwaters of Buffalo Creek

Buffalo Creek Flood: Wreckage from the flood. *Courtesy of Mimi Pickering*

as early as 1964. By 1970, three separate dams, constructed from earth and mine debris, held back 21 million cubic tons of water.

Heavy rains in February 1972 alarmed Steve Dasovich, Pittston's local mine boss. He and Jack Kent, supervisor of local strip-mining operations, inspected the dams on February 24, including an area that had given way the previous February. Water continued to rise, and at 4:30 on the morning of the February 26, it was clear to both men that it would reach the tops of the dams. Dasovich ordered a drainage ditch dug with a bulldozer, but at eight that morning, the dams gave way. Millions of tons of water swept through the valley, killing 125 and injuring 1,100. Seven hundred homes were destroyed or condemned.

Chairman of the Pittston Company was Joe Routh, one of the pioneers of strip-mining in West Virginia. In 1969, he hired Nicholas Carmicia to run the company. According to Thomas N. Bethell, a research director of the United Mine Workers of America, Pittston had the second-worst safety record of any mining company in the country, with 9 fatalities and 734 serious accidents in 1971. Three government agencies issued reports faulting the design of the dams, which was in violation of state and federal laws. At the time when Pittston was selling its coal for $125 a ton, the high-end estimate for constructing a safe dam was around $200,000. Carmicia called the dams' failure an act of God, and at first refused to accept damage and injury claims. In Bethel's opinion, Pittston engaged in "obstruction and opposition to the law just on the principle of opposing it."

Mainstream media gave extensive coverage to the disaster. The *New York Times* noted that the Department of the Interior had warned the industry five years earlier that accepted practices could duplicate a coal waste accident in Aberfan, Wales, that killed 116 schoolchildren in 1966. Pressure from reporters during press conferences may have persuaded Pittston to adopt a more conciliatory tone. It later settled out of court for $13 million. But who represented the victims of the disaster? How could their voices be heard?

Appalshop, a nonprofit multi-disciplinary arts and education center in Whitesburg, Kentucky, was formed in 1969 as an economic development project of the War on Poverty. Originally dedicated to activism on a local level, the organization has grown to encompass theater, video, radio, books, and recordings. Its films included *UMWA 1970: A House Divided* (1970, directed by Ben Zickafoose and Dan Mohn), which cross-cut between a speech given by United Mine Workers president Tony Boyle, then under indictment for misuse of funds, and interviews with antagonistic miners. That same year, Zickafoose directed *Coal Miner: Frank Jackson*, a twelve-minute portrait of Jackson as he worked. In 1973, Gene DuBey directed *Strip Mining in Appalachia*, another example of Appalshop's commitment to activist filmmaking. Both Zickafoose and DuBey worked on *The Buffalo Creek Flood: An Act of Man*, as did the rest of the Appalshop staff.

Mimi Pickering joined Appalshop in 1971. Born in California, she attended Antioch, then interned with the West Virginia Black Lung

Association. She completed her first film, *The Struggle of Coon Branch Mountain* (1971), in West Virginia before moving to Kentucky. She was in West Virginia on the day of the disaster, and later was asked to document the hearings of the Citizens' Commission to Investigate the Buffalo Creek Disaster, formed shortly after the flood.

In March 1972 Pickering and David Miller interviewed survivors at an emergency shelter set up at the Man High School, taping them with a video Portapak. Whenever funds became available, Pickering continued filming in the area, documenting the aftermath of the flood and interviewing experts like Bethell. She followed the hearings and reports of the Citizens' Commission, caught Carmicia on camera at an impromptu press conference, and viewed film and photographs donated to the project. She eventually combined all of these elements into a single documentary.

The Buffalo Creek Flood adopts a functional style, avoiding fancy graphics and camerawork.

Pickering's intent is to convey information in as clear a manner as possible, without obvious bias. Her technique is subtle: contrasting the proud, stoic voices of the survivors with the corporate doublespeak practiced by Pittston; having Bethell recite sobering statistics over devastating footage of wrecked cars and homes. A filmmaker coming to the region to document the disaster could not have understood the people and geography of the region as well as Pickering did. Her point of view is from the inside out, from someone who lived in the area and, like other residents, was affected by corporate decisions. This is advocacy filmmaking at its most basic, and effective.

Pickering returned to the subject in 1985, examining efforts to rebuild Buffalo Creek communities. Her other films include *Chemical Valley* (1991), broadcast on PBS, and *Hazel Dickens: It's Hard to Tell the Singer From the Song* (2001). She is also the director of the Appalshop Community Media Initiative, which teaches media strategies to grassroots organizations.

One Flew Over the Cuckoo's Nest

Louise Fletcher won an Oscar for her performance as Nurse Ratched in *One Flew Over the Cuckoo's Nest*.

United Artists, 1975. Sound, color, 1.85. 138 minutes. Rated R.

Cast: Jack Nicholson (Randle P. McMurphy), Louise Fletcher (Nurse Ratched), William Redfield (Harding), Dean Brooks (Dr. Spivey), Scatman Crothers (Turkle), Danny DeVito (Martini), William Duell (Sefelt), Brad Dourif (Billy Bibbit), Sydney Lassick (Cheswick), Christopher Lloyd (Taber), Will Sampson (Chief Bromden), Vincent Schiavelli (Frederickson), Delos V. Smith, Jr. (Scanlon), Marya Small (Candy), Louisa Moritz (Rose), Mimi Sarkisian (Nurse Pilbow), Nathan George (Washington), Michael Berryman (Ellis), Peter Brocco (Col. Matterson), Alonzo Brown (Miller), Mwako Cumbuka (Warren), Josip Elic (Bancini), Lan Fendors (Nurse Itsu), Ken Kenny (Beans Garfield), Mel Lambert (Harbormaster), Kay Lee (Night supervisor), Dwight Marfield (Ellsworth), Ted Markland (Hap Arlich), Phil Roth (Woolsey), Tin Welch (Ruckley).

Credits: Directed by Milos Forman. Screenplay by Lawrence Hauben and Bo Goldman. Based on the novel by Ken Kesey. Produced by Saul Zaentz & Michael Douglas. Director of photography: Haskell Wexler. Additional photography by Bill Butler. Original music composed by Jack Nitzsche. Supervising film editor: Richard Chew. Associate producer: Martin Fink. Production designer: Paul Sylbert. Additional photography: William Fraker. Unit production manager: Joel Douglas. Art director: Edwin O'Donovan. First assistant director: Irby Smith. Film editors: Lynzee Klingman, Sheldon Kahn. Sound recordist: Lawrence Jost. Costumer: Agnes Rodgers. Make-up: Fred Phillips. Hairdresser: Gerry Leetch. Script supervisor: Natalie Drache. Post-production sound director: Mark Berger. Music editor: Ted Whitfield. Title by Wayne Fitzgerald. Casting: Mike Fenton & Jane Feinberg. A Fantasy Films presentation.

Additional Credits: Title on screen: *One flew over the cuckoo's nest.* Production dates: January 6 to March 1975. Premiered in New York City on November 19, 1975.

Awards: Oscars for Best Picture, Director, Actor, Actress, Writing—Screenplay Adapted from Other Material.

Available: Warner Home Video DVD (1997). UPC: 085393622220. Warner Home Video Special Edition DVD (2002). UPC: 085393746322.

When Ken Kesey's novel *One Flew Over the Cuckoo's Nest* was published in 1962, several actors and producers expressed interest in the movie rights. Kirk Douglas ended up purchasing them, but could not convince a studio to back the project. Determined to make a film from the book, he first hired playwright Dale Wasserman to write a stage adaptation. Despite Douglas in the lead role, the production closed after eighty-two performances, making his quest for movie financing that much more difficult.

Born in 1944, Michael Douglas, the actor's son, studied acting and appeared in Off-Broadway shows before signing a contract with CBS. He starred in a handful of films before his role on the television series *The Streets of San Francisco* made him a celebrity. With the financial security to pursue producing, Douglas took over the rights to *Cuckoo's Nest* in 1970 (his father retained a percentage). The younger Douglas had just as much trouble attracting financing, and eventually formed a partnership with Saul Zaentz, a San Francisco–based jazz and rock producer and manager whose Fantasy Records provided much of the backing for the film.

Kesey was hired to write a screenplay, but his work was judged unsuitable. In the ensuing years since *Cuckoo's Nest* was published, he had written the favorably received *Sometimes a Great Notion* (filmed in 1971), but gained more notoriety for leading what became known as the Merry Pranksters on a drug-addled cross-country bus trip. Kesey was a centerpiece of Tom Wolfe's nonfiction book *The Electric Kool-Aid Acid Test*, and became a spokesman of sorts for LSD. His dismissal from the *Cuckoo's Nest* project eventually led to a lawsuit; to his dying day, he insisted that he never saw the film.

Douglas's friend Lawrence Hauben wrote a draft while the producers searched for a director. John Cassavetes was one prospect; he later claimed that he quit over script problems. Several other directors turned down the project. Czech exile Milos Forman couldn't afford to; he was living on the verge of destitution in New York City's Chelsea Hotel. With a background in documentaries made for the state-sponsored film industry in Czechoslovakia, Forman had an international hit with the bittersweet romance *Loves of a Blonde* (1965). His American directing debut, *Taking Off* (1971), had been a box-office disaster, but his approach to filmmaking meshed nicely with the European-influenced features Douglas had starred in.

The producers hired screenwriter Bo Goldman to work with Forman on a revised draft. "I was going to give up and go back out to Long Island with my wife and run a fish store in Sagaponack," Goldman remembered. Instead, he worked for two months with Forman while Douglas and Zaentz tried fruitlessly to get studios to invest in the project.

Director Hal Ashby recommended the actor Jack Nicholson for the lead role. (Nicholson later told interviewers that he had tried to option the novel back in 1963.) As arguably the hottest actor in the industry on the strength of hits like *Easy Rider* (1969), *Five Easy Pieces* (1970) and *The Last Detail* (1973), Nicholson's presence legitimized the *Cuckoo's Nest* project. (His million-dollar salary also helped double the film's budget.) United Artists, which had turned down the movie earlier, now agreed to distribute it.

Accounts differ as to the casting of Louise Fletcher in the pivotal role of Nurse Ratched. Nicholson remembered recommending her for her performance as a Depression-era killer in *Thieves Like Us* (1974); Forman said he had been considering Shelley Duvall from the same movie until he saw Fletcher's performance. She, too, had been close to leaving show business, especially after being promised a part in *Nashville* that wound up going to Lily Tomlin.

Filming took place at the Oregon State Hospital for the Insane in Salem, apparently the only institution that would permit a movie crew to work on its premises. Asylum head Dr. Dean Brooks appeared in the film as Dr. Spivey, giving a very persuasive performance in scenes that were largely improvised with Nicholson. Brooks also convinced the producers to use inmates and workers as extras and crew members.

As Randle P. McMurphy, Nicholson added to his repertoire of defiantly offbeat characterizations. The role could be seen as a logical extension of those he played in *Five Easy Pieces* and *The Last Detail*. In a 1980s interview, he said that McMurphy's "tragic flaw" was that "he knows he's irresistible to women and in reality he expects Nurse Ratched to be seduced by him." The clash of wills between McMurphy and Ratched is the most distinctive aspect of the film today. Interestingly, Forman has at times expressed regret at the way Ratched was depicted in the film.

Several writers have described the production as tumultuous. Early on, cinematographer Haskell Wexler was replaced by Bill Butler, who had shot Nicholson's directing debut, *Drive, He Said* (1971). The depressing settings understandably preyed on the cast and crew. Nicholson told *Women's Wear Daily* that on the shoot he was "basically being an inmate, with dinner privileges out."

Cuckoo's allegorical overtones were an obvious factor in the film's success with both critics and viewers. Forman was careful not to spell out too clearly what the story and McMurphy's character "meant," but it was easy enough to draw connections, to politics, for example. "The book is about what I just left—the totalitarian system,"

the director once said. Like *Cool Hand Luke* (1967), the plot is structured after World War II prisoner-of-war movies, complete with breakouts and detentions in isolation cells. (Nicholson even dresses like Steve McQueen in 1963's *The Great Escape*.) Does that make Nurse Ratched a symbol of fascism? And what should viewers see in the film's religious symbolism? McMurphy gathers a band of disciples, performs "miracles" (getting the dumb to talk, for example) and is sacrificed for his beliefs. Viewers can read their own interpretations into the material. although the film does offer a persuasive argument against electroshock therapy.

The film won the five top Oscars at the March 1976 ceremonies, the first film to do so since Frank Capra's *It Happened One Night* in 1934. Forman would win another directing Oscar for *Amadeus* (1984), produced by Zaentz. Douglas returned to acting with *Coma* (1978), and later won an acting Oscar for *Wall Street* (1987).

Think of Me First as a Person

Dwight Core, Sr., 1960–1975. Sound, color and B&W, 1.37. 8 minutes.
Featuring: Dwight Core, Jr.
Credits: Directed by George Ingmire & Dwight Core, Sr. Camera and narration: Dwight Core, Sr. Editing: George Ingmire & Dwight Core, Sr.
Available: Copies may be purchased from *www.thinkofmefirstasaperson.com*.

Dwight L. Core was a World War II veteran and civil servant who worked as a photographer for the Norfolk Naval Shipyard in Portsmouth, Virginia, while raising a family of five children in nearby Bayview. As an amateur filmmaker, he shot nature documentaries, commercials and home-made murder mysteries. His fifth child and first son, Dwight, Jr., was born in 1960.

Like many parents, Core filmed his son in a variety of situations over the next two decades: birthday parties, opening Christmas presents, bathing, playing on a swing set. Unlike most families, Core worked with a 16mm camera, which gave his photography a clarity missing from the 8mm and Super8 film used in many homes at the time. He also understood how to structure shots to form scenes. One other quality distinguished his work from other home movies: Dwight, Jr., had Down syndrome.

Core decided to institutionalize his son in 1966, sending him to a training school in

Lynchburg, Virginia, that provided the background for the grimmest material in the completed movie. Although after attending the school, Dwight, Jr., showed "marked improvements in his functional skills," as his father noted, the separation was traumatic for both parents and children.

According to his children, Core battled alcoholism during this period. It wasn't until the 1980s that he found a narrative approach to his son's story. He prepared a voice-over based on "Think of Me First as a Person," a poem by Rita Dranginis. Some of the situations described by Dranginis meshed easily with Core's footage, but he abandoned the project well before he died of emphysema in 1995.

Core's grandson George Ingmire inherited a box containing the family's collection of films. A high school student at the time, he didn't examine the footage for almost a decade. He was looking for one of Core's murder mysteries to prepare as a family Christmas present when he found an audiotape describing Dwight, Jr. After finding footage that seemed to correlate with the audio, Ingmire set out to complete his grandfather's project.

While the basic outline of the piece had been set by Core, Ingmire was faced with establishing a pace and tone that would complement what his grandfather photographed. Ingmire structured the film as a series of vignettes, adding subtle sound effects to reinforce Core's narration. The first two minutes and the final scene of the finished film use the Dranginis poem, rearranged to correspond to Core's footage. The central section of the film is a more personal look at Dwight, Jr. The final result is a seamless and deeply moving collaboration among three disparate but still connected people.

Society has resorted to a series of euphemisms to describe people like Dwight, Jr. Developmentally challenged, learning disabled, and similar phrases serve to turn individuals into abstractions. As Dranginis and Core realized, the most important step is to turn statistics into people, to provide a human face for the challenged or disabled. The temptation in this approach is to appeal to sympathy, to make readers or viewers feel sorry for the subjects. *Think of Me First as a Person* doesn't ask for pity, but presents a portrait of Dwight Core, Jr., that is dignified and appealing.

"My goal when I first discovered it was very mundane," Ingmire told reporter Brooks Boliek. "My aspirations were to give it to family members as gifts, and maybe show it at a couple of film festivals." Ingmire screened his cut of *Think of Me First as a Person* at the Home Move Night in New Orleans in August 2006. It attracted the attention of archivist Dwight Swanson, who brought a copy to a film festival in Alaska. Since then the film has been shown at the Black Maria Film and Video Festival, the 6th Orphan Film Symposium, and other events.

Ingmire works as both a teacher and in media production. He has filmed documentaries and commercials in the New Orleans area, recorded sound for feature films, and received an Artist Fellowship for his radio documentaries. Dwight, Jr., passed away in October, 2008, at the age of forty-eight.

Taxi Driver

Robert De Niro as Travis Bickle, the eponymous *Taxi Driver*.

Columbia, 1976. Color, sound, 1.85. 114 minutes. Rated R.

Cast: Robert De Niro (Travis Bickle), Jodie Foster (Iris [Steensma]), Albert Brooks (Tom), Harvey Keitel (Sport), Leonard Harris (Charles Palantine), Peter Boyle (Wizard), Cybill Shepherd (Betsy), Diahnne Abbot (Concession girl), Frank Adu (Angry black man), Vic Argo (Melio), Gino Aroito (Policeman at rally), Garth Avery (Iris' friend), Harry Cohn (Cabbie in Belmore), Copper Cunningham (Hooker in cab), Brenda Dickson (Soap opera woman), Harry Fischler (Dispatcher), Nat Grant (Stick-up man), Richard Higgs (Tall Secret Service man), Beau Kayser (Soap opera man), Vig Magnotta (Secret Service photographer), Robert Maroff (Mafioso), Norman Matlock (Charlie T.), Bill Minkin (Tom's assistant), Murray Mosten (Iris' time keeper), Harry Northup (Doughboy), Gene Palma (Street drummer), Carey Poe (Campaign worker), Steven Prince (Andy, gun salesman), Peter Savage (The John), Martin Scorsese (Passenger watching silhouette), Robert Shields (Palantine aide), Ralph Singleton (T.V. interviewer), Joe Spinell (Personnel officer), Maria Turner (Angry hooker on street), Robin Utt (Campaign worker).

Credits: Directed by Martin Scorsese. Written by Paul Schrader. Produced by Michael Phillips and Julia Phillips. Director of photography: Michael Chapman. Visual consultant: David Nichols. Creative consultant: Sandra Weintraub. Special makeup: Dick Smith. Supervising film editor: Marcia Lucas. Film editors: Tom Rolf, Melvin Shapiro. Music by Bernard Herrmann. Associate producer: Phillip M. Goldfarb. Art director: Charles Rosen. Assistant director: Peter R. Scoppa. Script supervisor: Kay Chapin. Special effects: Tony Parmelee. Costume designer: Ruth Morley. Make-up: Irving Buchman. Hairdresser: Mona Orr. Mixer: Les Lazarowitz. Recorder: Roger Pietschman. Supervising sound effects editor: Frank E. Warner. Casting: Juliet Taylor. Title design: Dan Perri. A Columbia Pictures presentation of a Bill/Phillips production.

Additional Credits: Production dates: June to September 1975. Released February 8, 1976.

Available: Sony Pictures Home Entertainment DVD (2007). ISBN: 1-4248-4061-9. UPC: 0-43396-17404-7.

By 1975, Martin Scorsese had been working in film for over ten years. His Hollywood productions had been disappointments on a creative level. His independent films failed to fulfill his vision, in part because of their small budgets, but also because Scorsese was still developing his style. *Taxi Driver* would be different. By now Scorsese and his cast and crew were all veterans who knew how to use the machinery of moviemaking. As he said later, "It was the first time in New York that I actually shot a film the right way."

Taxi Driver was a convergence of several talented individuals committed to the same vision. Scorsese had worked with Harvey Keitel on a number of films, with Robert De Niro on *Mean Streets* (1973), and with Jodie Foster on *Alice Doesn't Live Here Anymore* (1974). This was his first project with Paul Schrader, a Calvinist film theoretician who had been burnishing his reputation by spreading rumors that he slept with a handgun under his pillow.

Born in Grand Rapids, Michigan, in 1946, Schrader attended film school at UCLA, then briefly became a film critic. He wrote an academic treatise on film directors Bresson, Ozu, and Dreyer (*Transcendental Style in Film*) before collaborating with his brother Leonard on *The Yakuza* (1974), a trashy but commercial gangster film set in Japan. *Taxi Driver* was written during a period of prolonged depression in which he was living in a car and frequenting all-night porn theaters for a place to sit. After an ulcer led him to a hospital emergency room, he finished a draft in ten days, tying his own experiences to a fairly conventional romantic formula.

Schrader later described the plot as a sort of existential conundrum for cabbie Travis Bickle, who is attracted to a woman he can't have and dismissive of the woman who is available. "The taxicab was a metaphor for loneliness," he wrote later, but what excited movie executives who read *Taxi Driver* was the transgressive nature of the story. Schrader not only filled his script with porn theaters, but made a central character a twelve-year-old prostitute.

Producers Julia and Michael Phillips got a copy of the script from director Brian De Palma, who hoped to direct it himself. (Instead, he helmed Schrader's next script, a variation on *Vertigo* called *Obsession*, 1976.) The Phillipses separated after setting up deals with David Begelman at Columbia Pictures for three movies: *Taxi Driver, Close Encounters of the Third Kind*, and *Fear of Flying*. They considered other directors, including Lamont Johnson and even their producing partner Tony Bill. Scorsese was hired when his attempt to adapt *Bury My Heart at Wounded Knee*, to star Marlon Brando, stalled.

Schrader's preoccupation with guilt and redemption fed into Scorsese's own obsessions. Schrader wasn't afraid to tackle taboos. By placing politically incorrect profanities into the mouths of monsters, he could get away with figurative murder. Scorsese had done the same thing in *Mean Streets*, but this was a more focused story that dissected its themes more precisely.

De Niro typically threw himself into research, driving a cab at nights and talking with other drivers. Keitel's research included interviewing a pimp. Julia Phillips had hoped to cast Farrah Fawcett in the part of Betsy, but Scorsese was intent on Cybill Shepherd. He used her the way Peter Bogdanovich did in *The Last Picture Show* (1972), as an icy, unobtainable object of desire. Despite the empowerment themes in *Alice Doesn't Live Here Anymore*, Scorsese wasn't interested in the female characters in *Taxi Driver*. This was a film about lonely men, how they deluded themselves about women, how in their eyes the search for a personal connection was debasing and ultimately hopeless.

Scorsese later remembered the filming, which started in the summer of 1975, as hot and difficult. Inadvertently, he and his crew were capturing a New York City that was rapidly disappearing. The 42nd Street that Travis frequents, a strip of third-run and porn movie houses, has since been replaced by legitimate theaters and chain restaurants. The Belmore Cafeteria and Variety Photoplays are gone, both now sites for residential towers. Even Checker cabs have been retired.

But in other, more fundamental ways, *Taxi Driver* shows a New York that has always existed, one with the same grit and desperation of *Traffic in Souls* (1913) and *Sweet Smell of Success* (1957). This was partly due to the extraordinary cinematography by Michael Chapman, hired for his work on *The Last Detail* (1973). Now considered one of the premier visual interpreters of New York, Chapman has a brilliant grasp of lighting, especially in difficult circumstances, and an ability to find visual equivalents for narrative situations.

Credit should also be given to Bernard Herrmann, whose score added a depth and poignancy previously missing from Scorsese's work. Herrmann had essentially been forgotten by the industry until the film school generation rediscovered his pioneering work with Orson Welles and Alfred Hitchcock. This would be his last completed score; he died after recording it.

According to Julia Phillips, Marcia Lucas was of crucial help in determining the final shape of the film. Scorsese had been having trouble piecing together a version following Schrader's script. It wasn't until Scorsese decided that the film was unfolding in Travis Bickle's mind that the film began to make sense. "Everything in *Taxi Driver* is from Travis's point of view," he said. "He's in everyone's light but alone, over the shoulder."

Taxi Driver polarized both industry insiders and filmgoers. (Surprisingly, Scorsese had little trouble with censors.) Critics like Pauline Kael championed the movie, but others pointed to what they perceived as its misogyny, violence, and other exploitative aspects. Scorsese later defended the violence in his films by saying that it mirrored what he witnessed in his childhood. But he had had enough Catholic training to know that there is always a choice: succumb to temptation, or take the moral path. As the Reverend Francis Principe, one of his high school teachers, put it, "Too much Good Friday, Marty, not enough Easter Sunday."

The film not only confirmed Robert De Niro's stardom, it influenced a subsequent generation of filmmakers. *Taxi Driver* has been parodied frequently, in particular Bickle's "You talking to me?" speech to his mirror. (De Niro took his own whacks at it on *Saturday Night Live* and in *The Adventures of Rocky & Bullwinkle*, 2000.) It has also proved a millstone of sorts for Scorsese, who has felt compelled to return to its themes and stylistic devices in many of his subsequent films.

The Outlaw Josey Wales

Warner Bros., 1976. Sound, color, 2.35. 136 minutes. Rated PG.
Cast: Clint Eastwood (Josey Wales), Chief Dan George (Lone Watie), Sondra Locke (Laura Lee), Bill McKinney (Terrill), John Vernon (Fletcher), Paula Trueman (Grandma Sarah), Sam Bottoms (Jamie), Geraldine Keams (Little Moonlight), Woodrow Parfrey (Carpetbagger), Joyce Jameson (Rose), Sheb Wooley (Travis Cobb), Royal Dano (Ten Spot), Matt Clarke (Kelly), John Verros (Chato), Will Sampson (Ten Bears), William O'Connell (Sim Carstairs), John Quade (Comanchero leader), Frank Schofield (Senator Lane), Buck Kartalian (Shopkeeper), Len Lesser (Abe), Doug McGrath (Lige), John Russell (Bloody Bill Anderson), Charles Tyner (Zukie Limmer), Bruce M. Fischer (Yoke), John Mitchum (Al), John Chandler (First bounty hunter), Tom Roy Lowe (Second bounty hunter), Clay Tanner (First Texas Ranger), Bob Hoy (Second Texas Ranger), Madeline T. Holmes (Grannie Hawkins), Erik Holland (Union Army sergeant), Cissy Wellman (Josey's wife), Faye Hamblin (Grandpa), Danny Green (Lemuel).
Credits: Directed by Clint Eastwood. Screenplay by Phil Kaufman and Sonia Chernus. From the book *Gone to Texas* by Forrest Carter. Produced by Robert Daley. Director of photography: Bruce Surtees. Associate producers: Jim Fargo, John G. Wilson. Music by Jerry Fielding. Film editor: Ferris Webster. Assistant to the producer: Fritz Manes. Unit production manager: John G. Wilson. Assistant director: Jim Fargo. Casting: Jack Kosslyn. Production designer: Tambi Larsen. Set decoration: Chuck Pierce. Sound editor: Keith Stafford. Stunt coordinator: Walter Scott. Sound: Bert Hallberg. Re-recording mixer: Tex Rudloff. Makeup supervision: Joe McKinney. Hairstylist: Lorraine Roberson. Costume supervisor: Glenn Wright. Titles & optical effects: Pacific Title. Filmed in Panavision. Color by De Luxe. A Malpaso Company film.
Additional Cast: Kyle Eastwood (Josie's son), Richard Farnsworth (Comanchero).
Additional Credits: Released June 30, 1976.
Other Versions: Sequel *The Return of Josey Wales* (1986), directed by and starring Michael Parks.
Available: Warner Home Video DVD (1999). ISBN: 0-7907-4134-2. UPC: 0-85391-25882-7.

Of the movie stars of the modern era, no one has had as much impact as Clint Eastwood. This dismayed many critics, who for some thirty years denigrated much of his work as an actor and director. Eastwood was at the forefront of the spaghetti Western genre, an international phenomenon in the 1960s, and originated one of the most indelible roles of the 1970s, Dirty Harry. He almost single-handedly kept the Western film tradition alive in the 1980s and 1990s, and he is one of the last adherents to the classical filmmaking style embodied by directors like Don Siegel (a personal friend).

Eastwood was born in San Francisco in 1930 and grew up in various towns along the West Coast. After a series of odd jobs and four years in the Army, he moved to Los Angeles to pursue acting. He was a contract player at Universal at a time when the category was being phased out, earning bit parts in a string of largely forgettable films. For eight seasons he played Rowdy Yates on the *Rawhide* television series, where he caught the attention of Italian director Sergio Leone. Their "Man with No Name" trilogy of Westerns made Eastwood a star. He returned to Hollywood to make a Western, *Hang 'em High*, and a cop thriller with Western overtones, *Coogan's Bluff* (both 1968). The latter began his working relationship with Siegel.

Siegel had a cameo in Eastwood's first feature as a director, *Play Misty for Me* (1973), and has been an acknowledged inspiration in his subsequent films. Eastwood had just finished directing *The Eiger Sanction* (1975), a troubled production that saw the accidental death of a stuntman, when his office received *The Rebel Outlaw: Josey Wales*, a novel purportedly written by Forrest Carter. Producer Robert Daley was taken by the story's scope and characters, and passed it on to Eastwood. He liked the book as well, and agreed to let Sonia Chernus, a former reader at CBS who was now story editor for Eastwood's Malpaso production company, write a screenplay adaptation.

(Later it was revealed that Forrest Carter was really Asa Carter, a Ku Klux Klan member and speechwriter for segregationist governor George Wallace. Carter had also written *The Education of Little Tree* in 1976; that book became embroiled in a controversy after it was republished in 1991.)

Eastwood hired Philip Kaufman to rewrite Chernus's script. A former law student, Kaufman had written and directed a revisionist Western, *The Great Northfield Minnesota Raid* (1972). His key contribution was to include the presence of Redlegs, the chief villains early in the story, throughout the film. What had been an arbitrary plotline now had the sweep of an epic Western. Redlegs destroy Wales's home and family, forcing him into a life of revenge during the Civil War. When the South surrenders, Wales heads West, searching for peace and hounded by his enemies.

After scouting locations in Arizona, Utah, and California, Kaufman began directing what was now called *The Outlaw Josey Wales*. In Eastwood's opinion, the director was catastrophically slow and indecisive. After two weeks, the actor decided to replace Kaufman with himself. (This later prompted a change in Directors' Guild of America rules to prevent a similar occurrence in the future.) The film was also notable for introducing

Eastwood to Sondra Locke, his costar in several future films.

A quick, efficient filmmaker, Eastwood rarely indulges in complicated camera tricks or editing schemes. Like Siegel, he prefers straightforward narrative devices, striving first for clarity. From Leone, he took an appreciation for landscapes and an eye for offbeat character actors. The faces in *The Outlaw Josey Wales* are as memorable as the film's expansive vistas. Critics at the time complained about the acting in Eastwood's films, but in *Josey Wales* he displays both sympathy and affection for his cast, in particular Chief Dan George.

Critics also complained about the brutality and violence in Eastwood's films, and after the release of *Dirty Harry* (1971) he was often accused of fascist tendencies, and worse. Leone's films could veer into morally despicable moments; similarly, in his early pictures, Eastwood could misjudge the meaning and impact of his fistfights and shootouts. But *Josey Wales* offers a reasoned and for its time fairly liberal response to violence.

The Outlaw Josey Wales is the work of a talented, confident filmmaker, one as aware of the plot's similarities to John Ford's *The Searchers* (1956) as of its critique of the Vietnam War. Eastwood occasionally pushes the material too strongly, and at times doesn't exploit situations fully. He also shows a weakness for glib one-liners to sum up situations. (Still, few filmmakers could resist threats like "Dying ain't much of a living.") It's clear throughout the film that Eastwood respects the story, his actors, and, perhaps most important, his audience. By the time he made *Unforgiven* (1992, a Registry title), a film that is in some ways an elaboration of themes presented in *The Outlaw Josey Wales*, most critics had caught on to how skilled he really was.

To Fly!

Lawrence Associates, 1976. Sound, color, 1.44. 27 minutes.

Credits: Directed, photographed, and edited by Greg MacGillivray and Jim Freeman. Produced by Greg MacGillivray and Jim Freeman. Executive producer: Byron McKinney. Associate producer: Jeff Blyth. Written by Francis Thompson, Greg MacGillivray, Jim Freeman, Robert Young, Arthur Zegart. Narration written by Tom McGrath. Editing supervisor: Alexander Hammid. Sound editing: Sam Shaw. Music editing: Richard R. McCurdy. Music composed, conducted, and arranged by Bernardo Segáll. Production coordinator: Barbara Smith. Production assistant: Cindy Huston. Assistant cameraman: Philip D. Schwartz. Space sequence filmed in cooperation with Graphic Films Corp. Special effects supervision: Jeff Blyth. Grip: Rae Troutman. Gaffer: Pat Gilluly. Aerial

acrobatic pilots: Art Scholl, Frank Tallman. Balloonist: Peter Walker. Helicopter pilots: George Nolan, Chuck Phillips, Adrian Brooks. Hang Glider pilot: Bob Wills. Thanks: The Blue Angels. A Francis Thompson Inc., Production. Sponsored by the Smithsonian Institution and Conoco, Inc., a DuPont company. Released by Lawrence Associates.

Additional Credits: Premiered July 1, 1976. Press materials refer to the title as *TO FLY!*

Other Versions: MacGillivray Freeman Films' film *Flyers* (1982) had a similar aerial theme.

Available: Screened periodically at the IMAX Theatre at the National Air and Space Museum, Smithsonian Institution. Reduction prints available at the Library of Congress.

Starting in the 1950s, when Hollywood fought television for viewers, the film industry tried many tactics to lure customers back into theaters, including color, stereo sound, and widescreen formats. Todd-AO, championed by showman Michael Todd, used 65mm film stock to achieve an image four times larger than standard 35mm film. VistaVision, a rival technology pushed by Paramount, ran 35mm film stock horizontally through cameras and projectors to achieve a larger image size. IMAX, developed in Canada by Graeme Ferguson, Roman Kroitor, Robert Kerr, and William C. Shaw, essentially combined Todd-AO and VistaVision by running 65mm stock horizontally through cameras. This gave their process a negative area equal to three standard 65mm frames—in others words, a very big picture.

Tiger Child, the first IMAX film, premiered at Expo '70 in Osaka, Japan. Sixteen IMAX and OMNIMAX (which projected onto a concave, instead, of flat, screen) titles were released between 1970 and 1976, when Greg MacGillivray and Jim Freeman made *To Fly!*

Born in 1945, MacGillivray became a surfing fanatic at the age of twelve. After surfing with his father in Corona del Mar, California, he moved to Laguna Beach as a teenager. Soon he was filming his companions as well as riding waves. While studying physics at the University of California at Santa Barbara, he began exhibiting his amateur surfing films, projecting them to a cassette of Beach Boys songs while improvising a live narration. For his second movie, *The Performers* (1965), MacGillivray anchored cameras underwater, filming in slow motion that brought out the grace and agility of surfing. "Surfing taught me how to be patient," he said about his filmmaking style. "The surf is only good about once a week. By learning that, I was able to learn the idea of patience with film."

In the early 1960s, MacGillivray met Jim Freeman, another surfer who had been trying to film the sport. They became partners, working together for the first time on *Free and Easy* (1967), which examined surfing cultures in California and Hawaii; filming television commercials; and in 1972 releasing the compilation film *Five Summer Stories*, a feature-length documentary that ran in theaters for seven straight years. They became adept at aerial photography, especially from helicopters. They photographed *Sentinels of Silence* (1971), an eighteen-minute short that was essentially a helicopter tour of Mexico. It won Academy Awards for both Best Documentary—Short Subject and Short Subject—Live Action. The MacGillivray Freeman company shot crucial aerial footage for *Jonathan Livingston Seagull* (1973) and for *The Towering Inferno* (1974). The company also made corporate films and experimented with sound systems and widescreen processes.

MacGillivray Freeman was perfectly positioned to win a commission from the Smithsonian Institution, which wanted a film to open its new National Air and Space Museum, timed to coincide with the nation's bicentennial. The museum's setting and historic occasion helped determine the shape of the film, which would provide an account of the history of aviation. Work started in 1974, with 1976 as the deadline.

The film opens on a majestic bank of clouds, showing off all the strengths of the IMAX system, then introduces a hot-air balloon ride, supposedly taking place in 1831. While the writing here and throughout the film is perfunctory, the cinematography is stunning. Since earlier IMAX viewers complained of motion sickness, the filmmakers here refrained from quick cutting and from rapid camera movement. "You want the shots to last a long time," MacGillivray said later. "The audience wants to be there."

The point of view in *To Fly!* is stately, processional, celebrating the American landscape while remaining distant from it. At least until a scene in which the camera, peering downward, seems to float above a river, and then extends out and over the edge of a tumbling waterfall that fills the entire frame. Even in smaller formats, it's a breathtaking shot, one that induced gasps from viewers.

The rest of the film, whether consciously or not, mimics the closing section of *This Is Cinerama* (1952). Like that film, *To Fly!* tours the country, showing scenic vistas without having much to say about them, apart from stirring up some patriotic empathy. Conestoga wagons, trains, cars and biplanes slide by as the film journeys from coast to coast. At about twelve minutes into the film, the frame splits into multiple frames in order to include non-IMAX footage, now a standard practice in large-format films. (Blown up to IMAX proportions, normal footage would appear too blurry and out-of-focus.)

To Fly! was an immediate success, and helped legitimize large-format films, IMAX in particular. Two days before its premiere, Jim Freeman died in a helicopter crash while scouting locations in California. MacGillivray is still working as a producer, director, and cinematographer. His company, "the world's largest independent producer and distributor of giant screen films," has released such popular titles as *Everest* (1998) and *The Alps* (2007). MacGillivray continues to grow as an artist. Films like *Grand Canyon Adventure: River at Risk* (2008), shot in both flat and 3-D versions, not only boast exceptional cinematography, they deal in concrete issues like water conservation in a style that is illuminating as well as entertaining.

Thirty years later, *To Fly!* still screens regularly at the National Air and Space Museum. It is the second-highest grossing large-format documentary ever made. IMAX, meanwhile, has expanded its screens from museums to some two hundred commercial movie theaters in North America.

Harlan County U.S.A.

Director Barbara Kopple during the filming of *Harlan County U.S.A. Courtesy of The Criterion Collection*

Cinema 5, 1976. Sound, color and B&W, 1.78. 104 minutes.

Featuring (in order of appearance): Nimrod Workman, E.B. Allen, Bessie Lou Cornett, Jim Thomas, Jerry Wynn, Mickey Messer, Bob Davis, Nanny Rainey, Lois Scott, Joe Dougher, Tom Pysell, Jerry Johnson, Frieda, Sudie Crusenberry, Tommy Fergerson, Dorothy Johnson, Bill Worthington, Betty Eldridge, Crystal Fergerson, Ron Curtis, Barry Spielberg, Bill Doan, Polly Jones, Farmington Widows, Diane Jones, Phyllis Bowens, Otis King, Florence Reese, Mary Lou Fergerson.

Credits: Produced and directed by Barbara Kopple. Director of editing: Nancy Baker. Associate director: Anne Lewis. Principal cinematographer: Hart Perry. Cinematography: Kevin Keating. Additional cinematography: Phil Parmet, Flip McCarthy, Tom Hurwitz. Assistant camera: Anne Lewis, Shane Zarintash, Dick Donovan, Michael Hamilton, Alex Lukman. Sound recordist: Barbara Kopple. Additional sound: Tim Colman, Bob Gates, John Walz. Production manager (during Miller-Boyle campaign): Marc N. Weiss. Editors: Nancy Baker, Mary Lampson. Assistant editors: John Walz, Judy Rabinovitz, Helene Susman, Bette Fried. Consulting editor: Lora Hays. Contributing editor: Mirra Bank. Sound editor: Josh Waletzky. Mixer: Lee Dichter. Opticals: Hart Perry, Michael Hamilton. Titles: Jean Bertl, Jose Gallardo. Main title artwork: Cecelia Grobla Waletzky. A Cabin Creek Film production.

Additional Credits: Screened at the New York Film Festival on October 15, 1976.

Awards: Oscar for Best Documentary—Features.

Available: Criterion DVD (2006). ISBN: 0-78003-016-8. UPC: 0-37429-20832-8.

By the early 1970s it became difficult to ignore the drawbacks to cinema verité, in particular its illusion of objectivity. By discarding voice-over narratives, the give-and-take of interviews, and attempts to provide or explain context, direct cinema practitioners found themselves limited to covering celebrities, institutions, or civic disasters. Released in 1976, *Harlan County U.S.A.* showed how the style would be forced to evolve in the coming years.

In the 1960s, the United Mine Workers of America was controlled by its president Tony Boyle. When he was challenged by Joseph "Jock" Yablonski, Boyle eventually took a contract out on his rival's life. Yablonski was murdered along with his wife and daughter in his home in Washington, Pennsylvania, near Pittsburgh. This incident captured the attention of Barbara Kopple. Born in New York City in 1946, she started out in film by working for Albert and David Maysles, first as an office assistant, then in their editing rooms. She gradually branched out to other aspects of production.

The Yablonski murders sparked what would become *Harlan County U.S.A.*, but a strike at the Brookside mine in Kentucky provided the angle Kopple needed to tell the story. She began her film with a straightforward account of mining conditions in 1973, gradually widening the focus to provide a context for the strike. The Harlan County area had a history of labor problems stretching back to the 1930s, when it was routinely referred to as Bloody Harlan County. Kopple filmed many of the survivors of that era, and their wizened faces and tales of lifelong poverty are a direct condemnation of the mining industry. Kopple is anything but an objective reporter. When the workers at the Brookside mine go on strike against Duke Power and its subsidiary, the Eastover Mining Co., she is clear about who is right and who is wrong. Or, as Florence Reese asks in the film's unofficial theme song, "Which Side Are You On?"

The director relied heavily on music to provide a sort of narrative for the film. In a way, the film is structured like a protest song, which in the Appalachian tradition used individual incidents to comment on larger problems. For some it was an approach that limited or blunted the film's attack. Not everyone in Harlan County was a bluegrass aficionado: some more likely listened to Waylon Jennings than Hazel Dickens. Kopple depicted the strikers as isolated, rural, timeless, just as John Ford tried to portray the Joads in *The Grapes of Wrath* (1940).

By design, the film that *Harlan County U.S.A.* grew most to resemble was *Salt of the Earth* (1954), Herbert Biberman's fictional account of a strike in New Mexico. Kopple even screened a 16mm print of the film in a community center. "We got a bunch of ideas about what we could do with our strike," recalls Jerry Johnson, one of the strikers. (He can be seen picketing Duke Power headquarters in New York City, where he engages in a friendly dialogue with a city cop.)

In a recent interview, Johnson said that the strike started because Norman Yarborough, the president of Eastover, wouldn't allow miners to equip their homes with running water. It's an issue alluded to very briefly in the film because Kopple never quite captured anyone saying it. Johnson also said that he worked in the mines because Eastover paid better ($33 a day, with some benefits) than sawmills, the only other jobs available in the area.

A voice-over narration might have helped explain the background of the strike to viewers.

Kopple's skills as an editor allow her to present a clear, direct account of the strike itself, which lasted thirteen months. The film shows the arrival of strikebreakers ("It took a while to get them all out of prison," Johnson said), the increasing tensions between the strikers and their bosses, the arrest of many of the miners' wives, the disillusionment as the months drag on, and escalating violence that culminates in the murder of Lawrence Jones, one of the strikers. (The murder remains unsolved because a grand jury refused to indict the primary suspect.)

Kopple pulled together material from many sources, including television broadcasts, press conferences, and newsreels. (She is not above fiddling with this footage, for example, adding sound effects to shots of trucks and jeeps patrolling streets.) Sometimes the story was waiting there for her to record, such as her first, tentative encounter with Basil Collins, a line foreman hired as an enforcer for the strikebreakers. At other times she filmed at personal risk, putting herself and her crew in danger in order to document injustices against the strikers.

Harlan County U.S.A. is partisan filmmaking at a vivid, close-up level. Kopple's defiance becomes one the film's endearing traits. The scenes where she is fired upon, where her cameraman is knocked to the ground, where she helps women on the picket line stand down "gun thugs" are moving and inspiring in ways that mainstream documentaries couldn't equal. But the film also marks a dead end of sorts for direct cinema. You can hear Kopple breaking out of its straitjacket as she questions people on camera, and see it when she is forced to use explanatory titles.

The film was preserved in 2004 by the Women's Preservation Fund of New York Women in Film and Television and The Academy Film Archive. Watching it today is a disheartening experience. Nothing much has changed for the miners; in fact, many of the strikers in the film were blacklisted and forced to leave the area to find work. (In Johnson's case, he moved to Ohio.) In January 2006, twelve miners died in a cave-in at the Sago Mine in West Virginia; the mine had accumulated hundreds of safety violations in the previous year. In May 2006, five more miners died in an explosion in Darby Mine No. 1 in Harlan County. The probable cause of the explosion was coal dust, and

Kentucky Darby LLC, the owner of the mine, had been cited forty-one times for failing to clean up coal dust adequately. Inadequate emergency equipment may have led to the suffocation of three of the victims.

Kopple covered another strike, this time concerning the meat-packing industry, in *American Dream* (1990). While she continues to direct documentaries, including 2006's *Shut Up and Sing*, she has also worked in fiction filmmaking.

Rocky

United Artists, 1976. Sound, color, 1.85. 119 minutes. Rated PG.

Cast: Sylvester Stallone (Rocky [Balboa]), Talia Shire (Adrian), Burt Young (Paulie), Carl Weathers (Apollo [Creed]), Thayer David (Jergens), Joe Spinell (Gazzo), Jimmy Gambina (Mike), George Memmoli (Ice rink attendant), Bill Baldwin (Fight announcer), Billy Sands (Club fight announcer), Don Sherman (Bartender), Shirley O'Hara (Secretary), Arnold Johnson, Tony Burton (Apollo's trainer), Jodi Letizia (Marie), Burgess Meredith (Mickey), Al Salvani [Silvani] (Cut man), Diana Lewis (TV commentator), George O'Hanlon (TV commentator), Larry Carroll (TV interviewer), Stan Shaw (Dipper), Pedro Lovell (Club fighter [Spider Rico]), DeForest Covan (Apollo's corner), Simmy Bow (Club corner man), Hank Rolike (Apollo corner man), Kathleen Parker (Paulie's date), Frank Stallone (Timekeeper), Lloyd Kaufman (Drunk), Jane Marla Robbins (Owner of pet shop), Jack Hollander (Fats), Joe Sorbello (Bodyguard), Christopher Avildsen (Chiptooth), Frankie Van (Club fight referee), Lou Fillipo (Championship fight announcer), Paris Eagle (Fighter); Frank Stallone, Jr., Robert L. Tangrea, Peter Glassberg, William E. Ring, Joseph C. Giambelluc (Streetcorner singers); Joe Frazier (Himself).

Credits: Directed by John G. Avildsen. Written by Sylvester Stallone. Produced by Irwin Winkler and Robert Chartoff. Executive producer: Gene Kirkwood. Director of photography: James Crabe. Music: Bill Conti. Art director: James H. Spencer. Edited by Richard Halsey. Executive in charge of production: Hal Polaire. Production manager: Ted Swanson. Casting by Caro Jones. Production design by Bill Cassidy. Visual consultant: David Nichols. Make-up created by Mike Westmore. Film editor: Scott Conrad. Assistant film editors: Geoffrey Rowland, Janice Hampton. Post-production sound: Ray Alba, Burt Schoenfeld. Music editor: Joseph Tuley, Jr. Boxing choreography: Sylvester Stallone. Technical advisor: Jimmy Gambina. Sound: Harry W. Tetrick. Sound mixer: B. Eugene Ashbrook. Set decorator: Raymond Molyneaux. Costume supervisor: Joanne Hutchinson. Costumer: Robert Cambel. Titles: MGM. Prints by Deluxe. Color by Technicolor. A Robert Chartoff–Irwin Winkler production of a John G. Avildsen film.

Additional Credits: Premiered in New York City on November 21, 1976.

Other Versions: Sequels: *Rocky II* (1979), *Rocky III* (1982), *Rocky IV* (1985), *Rocky V* (1990), and *Rocky Balboa* (2006).

Awards: Academy Awards for Best Picture, Director, Film Editing.

Available: Twentieth Century Fox Home Entertainment DVD (2006). UPC: 0-27616-06025-9.

Boxing has played a part in film since the earliest days of the medium, and in fact was a prime force in making movies commercially viable. In the 1920s, it provided a setting for comedies by Charlie Chaplin, Buster Keaton, Harold Lloyd, and other silent stars. The prizefight milieu energized early talkies and even gave boxers like Max Baer acting roles; he starred in *The Prizefighter and the Lady* (1933) with Myrna Loy.

By the end of the 1930s boxing had taken on more melodramatic shadings in downbeat films like *Golden Boy* (1939) with William Holden and *City for Conquest* (1940) with James Cagney. In the 1940s, fight films were primarily about corruption, personal betrayals, and pointless battles. *Body and Soul* (1947), *The Set-Up*, *Champion* (both 1949), and later *The Harder They Fall* (1956) left little room for optimism.

Rocky either ignored the darker aspects of the sport, or played them for laughs. In doing so it both revitalized the genre and made Sylvester Stallone a star. Born in 1946 in New York City, Stallone had an unstable upbringing in Maryland and Philadelphia. He dropped out of college to become an actor, taking odd jobs while scrounging for bit parts. He made an impression in *The Lords of Flatbush* (1974), a period piece about gangs in Brooklyn, partly by helping rewrite the script, but was unable to find work afterward. With a pregnant wife and few career prospects, he decided to bet everything on a personal project.

Stallone based the premise of his script on Chuck Wepner, a journeyman fighter who in March 1975 went almost fifteen rounds with champ Muhammad Ali. Publicists claimed that Stallone wrote the first draft in three days, but he later admitted that he had been working on the idea for much longer. Unstated but patently obvious in the script and film was the connection between Rocky's attempts to be a prizefighter and Stallone's efforts to find a foothold in the film business. He sold the script to producers Irwin Winkler and Robert Chartoff, taking a small fee with the proviso that he star. The producers, who were working at United Artists at the time, agreed to the deal, in the process retaining rights to sequels.

The film was made for twenty-eight days on a budget of roughly a million dollars. It was not a schedule with much padding, but *Rocky* was a small-scale project with limited, and cheap, locations. Stallone, who carried the brunt of the story, knew what he wanted, and knew how he was going to play the title character. It was up to director John G. Avildsen to hold the other pieces of the production together.

Avildsen was born in Oak Park, Illinois, in 1935, and went to New York University. He worked several different jobs in the industry while making his own shorts and commercials. The tendentious anti-hippie melodrama *Joe* (1970), which he also shot, was a surprise hit, and got him assignments working with Jack Lemmon and Burt Reynolds. Avildsen's strengths were in coaxing extroverted performances from introverted stars, in surrounding leads with sympathetic supporting players, and in establishing atmosphere. Through James Crabe's moody cinematography, *Rocky* achieved a vivid sense of dank, dead-end fear.

The filmmakers asked David Shire to score the picture. He turned them down, but his then-wife Talia Shire took the opportunity to audition for the part of Adrian, the shy pet-shop clerk who forms a relationship with Rocky. "When I did *Rocky*, I felt I had finally come into my own," she said later. "Adrian was me. That whole syndrome. Please God, don't notice me, but won't somebody notice me?" The film helped legitimize her career as an actress outside the influence of her brother, Francis Ford Coppola. As for David Shire's replacement, composer Bill Conti earned a Grammy for the *Rocky* soundtrack album, and his "Gonna Fly Now" became a number one pop hit. The fighter's fanfare, adapted from a Baroque composition, for a time was ubiquitous at sporting events.

Rocky proved extraordinarily popular at the box office, despite some dismissive reviews. Stallone judged his underdog theme astutely, and tied his film in with the nation's upbeat celebrations (as well as with numerous product placements). By simplifying the genre, stripping it of its associations to corruption and crime, and by placing it in what amounted to a nostalgic setting, he made prize-fighting seem harmless. (It also helped that he kept the actual fight footage to under fifteen minutes of the film.)

Stallone's vision, which included such anachronisms street-corner doo-wop performers some twenty years after the fact, was extremely influential, both in this country and internationally. Chartoff and Winkler may not have otherwise agreed to produce *Raging Bull* (1983), seen by most critics as a corrective to *Rocky*. Matt Damon and Ben Affleck used Stallone and his film as a model while writing *Good Will Hunting* (1997). Jackie Chan has cited the importance of *Rocky* to his own work. Stallone introduced another equally successful franchise, his *Rambo* films, which were originally based on the novel *First Blood* by David Morrell. Rambo is the flip side of Rocky Balboa, someone who never finds his emotional footing in a redemptive relationship. Figures supplied by Stallone's publicists total the grosses for the Rambo and Rocky films at over $3 billion.

Efforts by Stallone to extend his screen persona beyond these characters have been less successful. He has produced, written, and directed movies and television shows, both for himself and others, and has starred in comedies, remakes, musicals, and children's films, all without winning a larger audience. (Along the way, he has given important career boosts to artists like James Cameron.) In portraying the angst of the inarticulate, Stallone has been trapped in a narrow niche. He can be Rocky or Rambo forever, it seems, but moviegoers aren't willing to buy him as anything else.

Network

MGM/United Artists, 1976. Sound, color, 1.85. 121 minutes. Rated R.
Cast: Faye Dunaway (Diana Christensen), William Holden (Max Schumacher), Peter Finch (Howard Beale), Robert Duvall (Frank Hackett), Wesley Addy (Nelson Chaney), Ned Beatty (Arthur Jensen), Jordan Charney (Harry Hunter), Conchata Ferrell (Barbara Schlesinger), Darryl Hickman (Bill Herron), Roy Poole (Sam Haywood), William Prince (Edward George Ruddy), Beatrice Straight (Louise Schumacher), Marlene Warfield (Laureen Hobbs), Arthur Burghardt (Great Ahmed Kahn), Bill Burrows (TV director), John Carpenter (George Bosch), Kathy Cronkite (Mary Ann Gifford), Ed Crowley (Joe Donnelly), Jerome Dempsey (Walter C. Amundsen), Gene Gross (Milton K. Steinman), Stanley Grover (Jack Snowden), Cindy Grover (Caroline Schumacher), Mitchell Jason (Arthur Zangwill), Paul Jenkins (TV stage manager), Ken Kercheval (Merrill Grant), Kenneth Kimmins (Associate producer), Lynn Klugman (TV production assistant), Carolyn Krigbaum (Max's secretary), Zane Lasky (Audio man), Michael Lipton (Tommy Pellegrino), Michael Lombard (Willie Stein), Pirie MacDonald (Herb Thackeray), Russ Petranto (TV associate director), Bernard Pollock (Lou), Sasha von Scherler (Helen Miggs), Lane Smith (Robert McDonough), Theodore Sorel (Giannini), Fred Stuthman (Mosaic figure), Cameron Thomas (TV technical director), Lydia Wilen (Hunter's secretary), Lee Richardson (Narrator).
Credits: Directed by Sidney Lumet. [Screenplay] By Paddy Chayefsky. Produced by Howard Gottfried. Director of photography: Owen Roizman. Production designer: Philip Rosenberg. Costume designer: Theoni V. Aldredge. Editor: Alan Heim. Associate producer: Fred Caruso. Original music composed and conducted by Elliot Lawrence. Casting: Juliet Taylor. Sound editors: Jack Fitzstephens, Sanford Rackow, Marc M. Laub. Re-recordist: Dick Vorisek. Sound mixer: James Sabat. Set decorator: Edward Stewart. Ms. Dunaway's Make-up: Lee Harman. Make-up artist: John Alese. Hair stylist: Phil Leto. Costumers: George Newman, Marilyn Putnam. Filmed in Panavision. Prints in Metrocolor. A Howard Gottfried/Paddy Chayefsky production.
Additional Credits: Released in New York City on November 27, 1976.

Awards: Oscars for Best Actor (Finch), Actress (Dunaway), Supporting Actress (Straight), Writing—Screenplay Written Directly for the Screen.
Available: Warner Home Video DVD (2006). ISBN: 0-7907-9305-9. UPC: 0-12569-69242-8.

Just as *The Hospital* **(1971)** was prompted by Paddy Chayefsky's experience while visiting his ailing wife, *Network* came about as a result of the author's futile attempts to pitch story ideas to television executives. Later Chayefsky spoke about the desensitizing nature of network news programs and the dangers of turning news departments into profit centers. But at the time he was smarting over NBC's rejection of a proposed series about singles starring James Coco, as well as his lawsuit against United Artists for trying to package *The Hospital* for sale to ABC.

Chayefsky's producing partner Howard Gottfried (the "Howard" in Howard Beale's name) helped assemble a $50,000 deal that gave United Artists executives the chance to read the script for *Network*. After researching the NBC news department with Dave Tebet, Chayefsky turned in a draft in April 1974. When UA head Arthur Krim expressed reservations, Gottfried took back the script, selling it to MGM over a year later. (United Artists eventually coproduced the film with MGM.)

According to Gottfried, Chayefsky's contract gave him almost unlimited control over the film. Especially important to him was the "By Paddy Chayefsky" credit, instead of the more typical "Screenplay by." Director Sidney Lumet collaborated with the author for two months on rewrites. (Lumet had worked on Yul Brynner's *Danger* television series, for which Chayefsky sold his first script.) Despite its timely, satirical subject matter, *Network* was really built around the same themes and ideas that drove *The Hospital*, in particular "male menopause" and the overall malaise and dehumanization brought about by modern society.

The film also fell into a cycle of movies that attempt to explain why television is evil and dangerous, going back to Bela Lugosi in *Murder by Television* (1935). *Network* shares with *A Face in the Crowd* (1957) a bewildered exasperation about how people can let themselves be hoodwinked by television; both movies chalk it up to a sort of mass hypnosis that is ultimately inexplicable.

Lumet's reputation and Chayefsky's previous successes facilitated the casting process. The director warned Faye Dunaway, chosen in September 1975, that he would edit out any attempts on her part to make her role sympathetic. He insisted that Dunaway play programming executive Diana Christensen without any vulnerability. During rehearsals, Lumet had to coax William Holden into making eye contact with his fellow actors. Once Holden did, Lumet was so startled by the depth of the actor's emotions that he told him to pull back until they were ready to shoot.

Howard Beale, the insane newscaster whose threats to commit suicide on air set off a nationwide political movement, was turned down by everyone from George C. Scott and Paul Newman to Henry Fonda, who had a strong "personal distaste" for the material. Peter Finch had to audition for the part to persuade the filmmakers that he could handle an American accent. Born in London but raised in Australia, Finch was brought to England in 1949 as Laurence Olivier's protégé. He was a mainstay of British films in the 1950s and '60s.

Lumet thought of casting Robert Duvall as the cutthroat executive Frank Hackett. "What's fascinating about Duvall is how funny he is," Lumet said later. (Watch how Duvall keeps trying to smooth his hair when he gets angry.) Ned Beatty was cast as network head Arthur Jensen on the recommendation of director Robert Altman, after the original actor proved incapable of performing up to Lumet's standards. Beatty had one night to prepare a four-page speech, and was finished after one day's shooting. Although she had been in films since 1952, Beatrice Straight established her reputation on stage, winning a Tony in Arthur Miller's *The Crucible*. Playing Holden's wife, she essentially had one scene in *Network* (although she appears in others). That was enough for her to win a Best Supporting Actress Oscar.

After two weeks of rehearsals, shooting started in Toronto in January 1976. According to editor Alan Heim, Chayefsky was on the set every day, and watched dailies at night. Arguments arose over how certain scenes should be played, and the filmmakers had to threaten to fire Dunaway before she agreed to her nude scene. Finch's famous "mad as hell" speech was pieced together from two takes, all that Lumet felt comfortable requesting from him.

Lumet and cinematographer Owen Roizman worked out a complicated lighting scheme that in the director's words would "corrupt the camera." At first lit in a naturalistic style, the film evolved as the story progressed, resembling more and more the slick look of television commercials. Only

Holden remained lit in a realistic style. Roizman achieved some impressive visual effects, such as showing television cameras honing in relentlessly on Beale like robotic monsters. The implication was that film provided a truer version of reality than television, even though it used the same technical devices. (Lumet would reveal television cameras and lights to his viewers, but not the equipment he was using to film.)

Network received some scathing reviews when it was released in November 1976. Critic John Simon referred to its "pedestrian plot and shopworn prose," for example. But Chayefsky's unbridled combination of sex, profanity, and satire caught on with the public, making the film a pop culture phenomenon. Today *Network* seems equal parts prescient and dunderheaded, sympathetic toward its old, dying characters and needlessly cruel to everyone else.

Chayefsky's solutions, whether tongue in cheek or not, have little practical use. "Turn off your TV," Beale urges repeatedly, but how does cutting off information help anyone? Beale also exhorts his viewers to send postcards to the White House, as if the collective will of voters cannot be thwarted. Ultimately, Chayefsky throws up his hands in despair, using a vaguely racist subplot about revolutionaries to stage an ending that answers nothing. He would make one more film, the troubled *Altered States* (1980), before dying of cancer. Sadly, Finch died of a heart attack while promoting *Network* in Los Angeles.

Hollywood continues to congratulate itself on its superiority to television. Films like *Quiz Show* (1994) and *Ed TV* (1999) berate moviegoers for their obsessive viewing habits, even though television has long since become the financial engine for the movie industry.

Chulas Fronteras

Flaco Jiménez (left) and Fred Ojeda performing "Un mojado sin licencia" ("A Wetback Without a License") in *Chulas Fronteras.*
Photo by Nelson Allen, courtesy Brazos Films

Brazos Films, 1976. Sound, color, 1.37. 58 minutes.

Featuring: Los Pinguinos del Norte, Narciso Martínez, Lydia Mendoza, Willie López, Diddy Fuentes, Salomé Gutiérrez, Flaco Jiménez, Fred Ojeda, David Jiménez, Santiago Jiménez, Los Alegres del Terán.

Credits: Camera and editing: Les Blank. Conceived and produced by Chris Strachwitz. Assistant editing: Maureen Gosling. Consultant: Guillermo Hernández. Interpreter: Pacho Lane. Sound: Chris Strachwitz. A film by Les Blank. A Brazos Films presentation.

Additional Credits: Directed by Les Blank. Released December 30, 1976.

Available: Brazos Films DVD BF–104 (2003), *www.arhoolie.com and www.lesblank.com.* UPC: 7-94819-01049-6.

Eulalio González, better known as El Piporro, sang "Chulas Fronteras" in the 1963 Mexican film

El bracero del año. He later recorded it for ORO Records, a label owned by Willie López. It became the theme song for López's "Chulas Fronteras" radio program, broadcast to an audience along the border of Texas and Mexico. It's also one of over a dozen *norteña* songs featured in *Chulas Fronteras,* a vivid introduction to Tex-Mex music filmed by Les Blank.

Born in Florida in 1939, Blank attended Phillips Academy, where his classmates included filmmaker Hollis Frampton (*nostalgia*, 1971), artist Frank

Stella, and composer Fred Rzewski. He graduated from Tulane University with a Master of Fine Arts in Theatre Arts, attended film school for two years at USC, then wrote, shot, and edited documentaries for the Army and Navy, while making educational and advertising films.

Moving his base to New Orleans, Blank began examining Cajun culture by following his interests in food and music. He also developed an improvisatory style of filmmaking, one in which he attempted to capture moments and feelings rather than simply deliver information. With his commercial background, he was adept with the more traditional "talking heads" documentary style, and his best interviews are marked by his subjects' apparent openness in front of the camera.

"I'm a cultural peeping tom," he said in an interview. "I find my own cultural heritage to be a bit thin." He admitted to being influenced more by Ingmar Bergman and Federico Fellini than by documentary filmmakers. "I felt more of an urge to convey emotion and to tell a story than to report on reality."

Financing was a persistent problem. Blank made commercials and industrial films for clients as varied as Holly Farms Poultry, The California Almond Growers' Exchange, Archway Cookies, and the National Wildlife Federation. In 1965 he released a short film about jazz musician Dizzy Gillespie; he made his first independent film in 1967. *The Blues According to Lightnin' Hopkins*, released in 1968, offered unprecedented insight into a largely neglected musical genre. He started shooting Mardi Gras material for *Easy Rider* (1969), but was replaced when the production turned to an all-union crew. Blank met Chris Strachwitz while finishing *The Blues According to Lightnin' Hopkins*, and used Strachwitz's recordings of one of his discoveries, the East Texas artist/sharecropper Mance Lipscomb, for the documentary *A Well Spent Life* (1971).

Blank was less than enthusiastic about a project on musician Leon Russell in 1972, but admitted, "Whenever a film is about to get started I'm overcome with a complete dread, an apprehension just wondering what, of all the many things that go wrong, is going to go wrong this time." *A Poem Is a Naked Person* (1974), the resulting feature-length documentary, has never been released commercially, and has been screened only a handful of times. *Washington Post* critic Tom Zito proclaimed it the best film ever made about rock and roll.

According to a 1992 interview, Chris Strachwitz then had to coax Blank out of a severe depression by suggesting the *Chulas Fronteras* project.

One of the key figures in folk and indigenous music, Strachwitz was born in Silesia, Germany, in 1931. Displaced after World War II, Strachwitz and his family moved to Nevada in 1947, from which point on he could indulge his love for American music, at first hillbilly and country, then jazz and blues. He experimented with recording before serving in the Army after becoming a U.S. citizen. While teaching in high school, he formed his own record label, Arhoolie Records, in 1960—as he wrote, "inspired by hearing Lightnin' Hopkins perform in a Houston beer joint." Mance Lipscomb, discovered during his first Texas field trip, became the first artist released on the Arhoolie label. Strachwitz branched out into country, Cajun, Zydeco, and gospel, and later produced pioneering releases and reissues of Texas swing, Hawaiian, and early Mexican music.

"I first became fascinated with Mexican music while still in high school in Santa Barbara. It was a small station further south in Santa Paula when I heard mostly mariachi ranchera. But I also vividly recall the sound of accordion or conjunto music," Strachwitz told interviewer Larry Benicewicz. He wasn't interested in preserving mariachi or pop music, but in presenting Tejano conjunto and Mexican *norteña* music to a wider audience. His first Mexican release was *Conjuntos Nortenos* (1970) by Los Pinguinos del Norte, who appear in *Chulas Fronteras*.

Also appearing are Lydia Mendoza and Flaco Jiménez, two of the most storied Tex-Mex musicians. Mendoza, who made her first recordings in 1928, is seen cooking for a Christmas party as well as singing in a music hall. Blank and Strachwitz offer one of her earliest hits over a montage of photographs from her life. Jiménez's father and son both play accordion in the film, but the opportunity to see Flaco perform two songs in the prime of his career is one reason why *Chulas Fronteras* is so valuable.

Another reason to treasure the project is for the glimpses Blank provides into a way of life that had never been documented properly in an American film. The musicians, farmers, workers, and families in *Chulas Fronteras* are trying to carve out an identity in a society that doesn't want them to have one, to preserve their traditions rather than assimilate. And then there is the music in *Chulas Fronteras*—an insistent, driving mix of accordion and baja sexto that is one of the glories of the Tex-Mex culture. Thanks in part to Blank and Strachwitz, the influence of norteña music persists to this day in Grammy-winning artists like Los Tigres del Norte. The film helped revitalize Blank's career. It was the first of nine of his films selected for the Telluride Film Festival. His *Garlic Is As Good As Ten Mothers* (1980) is also on the Registry.

Killer of Sheep

One of the extraordinary images caught offhand in *Killer of Sheep*. *Courtesy of Milestone Film & Video*

Charles Burnett, 1977. Sound, B&W, 1.37. 80 minutes.

Cast: Henry Gayle Sanders (Stan), Kaycee Moore (Stan's wife), Charles Bracy (Bracy), Angela Burnett (Stan's daughter), Eugene Cherry (Eugene), Jack Drummond (Stan's son), Slim, Delores Farley, Dorothy Stengel, Tobar Mayo, Chris Terrill, Lawrence Pierott, Russell Miles, Homer Jai, Johnny Smoke, Paul Reed, Steven Lee, Charles Davis, Cecil Davis, Carlos Davis, Dorothy Daniels, Jannie Whitsey, Bill Williams, Calvin Walker, Sammy Kay, Le Roy Seibert, Cassandra Wright, Junior Blaylock, Charles Cody, Sheila Johnson, Lisa Johnson, 300 lbs, Menorie Davis, Tony Davis, Carl Davis, Roderick Johnson, Crystal Davis, Peggy Corban, Vincent Smith, Susan Williams, Soul Thompson, Pat Johnson, Bobby Cox, Cadillac, Arthur Williams, Jr., Calvin Williams, Alvin Williams, Patricia Williams, Brenda Williams, Bruce Warren, Dian Cherry, Latishia Cherry, Jonathan Cherry, Vernell Cherry, Margrenet Clark, Ronnie Burnett, Regina Batiste, Henry Andrews, Danny Andrews, Marcus Hamlin, Divinoni Hamlin, Ricky Walsh, Gentry Walsh, Michael Harp, Derek Harp, Reggie Williams, Robert Thompson, Ray Cherry, Verrane Tucker.

Credits: A film by Charles Burnett. Sound: Charles Bracy. Assistant sound: Willie Bell, Larry Clark, Christine Penick, Andy Burnett. Thanks to: Earl's Columbia Liquor Store, Solano Meat Co., Louis B. Mayer Foundation.

Additional Credits: Written, directed, filmed, edited, and produced by Charles Burnett. Production dates: 1975 to 1977.

Available: Milestone Film & Video DVD (2007). UPC: 78418010748.

Given the chance, most filmmakers opt for the mainstream. Even dedicated leftists like the creators of *Salt of the Earth* (1954) used commercial styles and techniques to speak to a broad audience. Charles Burnett, the writer and director of *Killer of Sheep*, took a different approach to the marketplace, one that valued vision over compromise, and that sacrificed quick profits for artistic integrity.

Born in Vicksburg, Mississippi, in 1944, Burnett grew up in the Watts section of Los Angeles. Like Chicago and Detroit, it was an endpoint in the World War II migration of African-Americans from the South. He attended film school at UCLA, joining fellow students like Larry Clark (*Passing Through*, 1977) and Julie Dash (*Daughters of the Dust*, 1991). Burnett cites Elyseo Taylor, who created the Ethno-Communications department, and documentarian Basil Wright (*Night Mail*, 1936) as professors who influenced him.

Starting with *Several Friends* (1969), Burnett's short films show how he developed a personal style, one that focused in tightly on individuals, allowing their characters to emerge through long, digressive conversations in kitchens, parking lots, and on porches. Music, ranging from blues and jazz to contemporary soul, acts as both commentary on and counterpoint to their lives. *Killer of Sheep*, which drew on similar characters and situations from *Several Friends*, became Burnett's master's thesis at UCLA.

On a budget of about $10,000 (much of that grant money) Burnett filmed in and around his neighborhood, using a largely nonprofessional cast, shooting on weekends in friends' homes. Henry Gayle Sanders, who plays Stan, the lead role, was a Vietnam veteran who had written an autobiographical novel before studying film and then acting. Kaycee Moore, who appears as Stan's wife, had limited theater experience before *Killer of Sheep*. Friends performed double duties. Charles Bracy, for example, appeared as an actor, and also recorded sound.

Burnett worked from a screenplay and occasionally from storyboards, but he was open to improvisation as well. Moore, in particular, delivered some of her best moments extemporaneously. Since he was working with children, Burnett had to be adaptable to unexpected situations. At other times, he was intent on simply getting his material on film. Sanders later remembered how he and Burnett were the only two present to film scenes in a slaughterhouse.

On a superficial level, Burnett's films combine his interests in ethnic issues, Southern myths, and documentary realism. But efforts to pigeonhole his work can reduce its meaning. Burnett may draw on recognizable traditions in Italian neorealist and nonfiction film, but he adds an empathy and compassion that distinguish him from other writers and directors. He understands his characters without condescending to them—or excusing their faults. At the time, distributors couldn't classify him with either lowbrow "blaxploitation" filmmakers or with the sort of highbrow, human-interest oriented artists who were turning up on public television.

"There wasn't any notion of getting a theatrical release," he said in an interview years later. "What we were doing was basically a reaction about how some films are made about the working class and the working poor and how the problems were always so simple and clear-cut and easily solved. I came from an environment where there was no one solution." In trying to find and connect with moviegoers, Burnett in a way re-created the marketing strategies of an earlier generation. He brought *Killer of Sheep* to church groups, social action committees, community meetings. Over time the film developed a grassroots reputation.

Without a theatrical distributor, *Killer of Sheep* won a critics' award at the 1981 Berlin International Film Festival. Burnett, meanwhile, photographed *Bush Mama* (1979, directed by Haile Gerima), and wrote and photographed *Bless Their Little Hearts* (1984, directed by Billy Woodbury). He finished photography on his next feature project, *My Brother's Wedding* (1983), but was unable to edit it satisfactorily until 2007. A grant from the John D. and Catherine T. MacArthur Foundation gave Burnett the financial freedom to continue working in film. As his reputation grew, he was able to assemble bigger stars and larger budgets on films like *To Sleep with Anger* (1990). A recent short, *Quiet as Kept* (2005), takes Burnett's style and preoccupations and applies them to the aftermath of Hurricane Katrina.

Annie Hall

United Artists, 1977. Sound, color, 1.85. 94 minutes. Rated PG.
Cast: Woody Allen (Alvy Singer), Diane Keaton (Annie Hall), Tony Roberts (Rob), Carol Kane (Allison), Paul Simon (Tony Lacey), Shelley Duvall (Pam), Janet Margolin (Robin), Christopher Walken (Duane Hall), Colleen Dewhurst (Mom Hall). Featured cast: Mordecai Lawner (Alvy's Dad), Donald Symington (Dad Hall), Joan Newman (Alvy's Mom), John Glover (Actor Boy Friend), Jonathan Munk (Alvy, Age 9), Russell Horton (Man in Theatre Line), Christine Jones (Dorrie), Mary Boylan (Miss Reed), Marshall McLuhan (Himself). With: Helen Ludlam (Grammy Hall), Ruth Volner (Alvy's Aunt), Martin Rosenblatt (Alvy's Uncle), Hy Ansel (Joey Nichols), Rashel Novikoff (Aunt Tessie), Wendy Girard (Janet), John Doumanian (Coke Fiend), Bob Maroff (Man #1 Outside Theatre), Rick Petrucelli (Man #2 Outside Theatre), Lee Callahan (Ticket Seller at Theatre), Chris Gampel (Doctor), Dick Cavett (Himself), Mark Lenard (Navy Officer), Dan Ruskin (Comedian at Rally), Bernie Styles (Comic's Agent), Johnny Haymer (Comic), Ved Bandhu (Maharishi), John Dennis Johnston (L.A. Policeman), Lauri Bird (Tony Lacey's Girlfriend); Jim McKrell, Jeff Goldblum, William Callaway, Roger Newman, Alan Landers, Jean Sarah Frost (Lacey Party Guests); Vince O'Brien (Hotel Doctor), Humphrey Davis (Alvy's Psychiatrist), Veronica Radburn (Annie's Psychiatrist), Robin Mary Paris (Actress in Rehearsal), Charles Levin (Actor in Rehearsal), Wayne Carson (Rehearsal Stage Manager), Michael Karm (Rehearsal Director), Petronia Johnson (Tony's Date at Nightclub), Shaun Casey (Tony's Date at Nightclub), Ricardo Bertoni (Waiter #1 at Nightclub), Michael Aronin (Waiter #2 at Nightclub); Lou Picetti, Loretta Tupper, James Burge, Shelly Hack, Albert Ottenheimer, Paula Trueman (Street Strangers); Beverly D'Angelo (Actress in Rob's T.V. Show), Tracey Walter (Actor in Rob's T.V. Show); Davie Wier, Keith Dentice, Susan Mellinger, Hamit Perezic, James Balter, Eric Gould, Amy Levitan (Alvy's Classmates); Gary Allen, Frank Vohs, Sybil Bowan, Margaretta Warwick (School Teachers); Lucy Lee Flippen (Waitress at Health Food Restaurant), Gary Muledeer (Man at Health Food Restaurant), Sigourney Weaver (Alvy's Date Outside Theatre), Walter Bernstein (Annie's Date Outside Theatre).
Credits: Directed by Woody Allen. Written by Woody Allen and Marshall Brickman. Produced by Charles H. Joffe. Executive producer: Robert Greenhut. Associate producer: Fred T. Gallo. Director of photography: Gordon Willis. Edited by Ralph Rosenblum. Art director: Mel Bourne. Costume designer: Ruth Morley. Casting: Juliet Taylor/MDA. Production Manager: Robert Greenhut. 1st assistant director: Fred T. Gallo.

2nd assistant director: Fred Blankfein. Location manager: Martin Danzig. Script supervisor: Kay Chapin. Sound mixer: James Sabat. Rerecording mixer: Jack Higgins. Camera operator: Fred Schuler. 1st assistant cameraman: Thomas Priestley. Gaffer: Dusty Wallace. Key grip: Robert Ward. Wardrobe supervisors: George Newman, Marilyn Putnam. Makeup artist: Fern Buchner. Hair stylist: Romaine Green. Set decorators: Robert Drumheller, Justin Scoppa, Jr. Film editor: Wendy Green Bricmont. Animated sequences: Chris Ishii. Sound editing: Dan Sable/Magnofex. "Seems Like Old Times," music by Carmen Lombardo, lyrics by John Jacob Loeb. "It Had To Be You," music by Isham Jones, lyrics by Gus Kahn. Performed by Diane Keaton; accompanist, Artie Butler. Titles: Computer Opticals. Camera and lenses by Panavision. Prints by Deluxe. A Jack Rollins–Charles H. Joffe Production. Released April 20, 1977.

Additional Credits: Production dates: May 19, 1976 to February 1977. Opened April 20, 1977.

Awards: Oscars for Best Picture, Director, Screenplay, Actress (Keaton).

Available: MGM Home Entertainment DVD (2000). ISBN: 0-7928-3847-5. UPC: 0-27616-6559-2-9.

One of the distinctive aspects of Woody Allen's career is how much his personal life plays into his humor. Comedians have always drawn from their lives for their jokes, but almost all of them performed as characters, not as themselves. The miserly "Jack Benny" who appeared on radio and in films was a character created for the public, not the real-life husband and father. But when stars like Frank Sinatra began to erase the boundaries between public and private in the 1950s, comics like Lenny Bruce and Mort Sahl followed suit, no longer pitching their jokes as if they were being delivered by someone separate from themselves.

Born in 1935 in the Bronx, raised in Brooklyn, Allen grew up interested in sports and comic books. Married while still a teenager, he was also by that time selling jokes to newspaper columnists like Earl Wilson. A job in a writer's development program at NBC led to his writing jokes for television stars like Sid Caesar. Allen could have gone on to a career like fellow Caesar writers Mel Brooks and Larry Gelbart. Instead, he signed with talent managers Jack Rollins and Charles Joffe, who encouraged him to perform his material before live audiences.

Allen worked elements of his life into his act, exaggerating his physical limitations by coughing, whining, and stuttering during his delivery, making jokes about his divorce in 1962 (which led to a lawsuit settled out of court). Intellectual pretensions became a part of Allen's act. His name-dropping and references to philosophy made audiences feel smart, even if they were laughing at punch lines with roots in Borscht Belt humor. Seen as a sort of apolitical, nonthreatening version of Lenny Bruce, Allen made a smooth transition to television. He also transferred his act to hit records and wrote comic articles that were eventually collected into books.

In 1965, Allen broke into movies writing and acting in *What's New, Pussycat?*, a dreadful youth-oriented sex comedy. He vowed to take full control over his film career. He provided a comic soundtrack to a re-edited Japanese spy thriller, *What's Up, Tiger Lily?* (1966), then wrote two Broadway plays. In 1969, he wrote and starred in his directorial effort, *Take the Money and Run* (1969). In it and his succeeding films, Allen employed a broad, slapstick style filled with pop-culture allusions and in-jokes. Spoofing self-help books, science fiction, Russian literature, even Humphrey Bogart, Allen became one of the most reliable comic performers of the 1970s.

Annie Hall started as *Anhedonia*, a Greek term for the inability to experience joy. It was intended to be a surrealist version of the inner workings of the protagonist's mind, one that would slide from scene to scene in a stream-of-consciousness style. In the press notes for the film, Allen wrote, "It was a major turning point for me. I had the courage to abandon the safety of broad comedy. I said to myself: 'I think I'll try and make some deeper film.'" It was also the first of his films to fully embrace his personal life. Allen would play Alvy Singer, a stand-up comedian who rose from humble origins to write gags for other comics, become a stand-up star, and appear on television. It was also the first of his films to make use of realistic New York locations, carefully photographed by Gordon Willis.

Allen wrote the script with Marshall Brickman, devising many of the scenes as they walked the streets of New York. They came up with a parody of *Invasion of the Body Snatchers* (1956), set scenes in the French Resistance, placed Franz Kafka in a professional basketball game, and more, resulting in a rough cut well over two hours long. It was while editing this material with Ralph Rosenblum that Allen saw the core of the film: Alvy's relationship with the flighty Annie Hall.

Hall was played by Diane Keaton, for a time his real-life romantic partner. (Keaton's real name is Diane Hall.) By stripping the film down to Alvy's scenes with Annie, Allen found a foil for his screen persona, as well as a way to make an emotional connection with filmgoers. But aspects of his original vision remain in the finished film. *Annie Hall*'s structure is a marvel of shifting time spans, digressions, and jokes that break the wall between screen and viewers. An incident will spark a flashback that is then invaded by characters from the present, who comment on the action like a Greek chorus.

Allen cloaks this fluid use of time with a barrage of asides, one-liners, and an arsenal of filmmaking tricks ranging from animation to superimpositions, split screens, subtitles, and documentary footage. But technique is secondary to content, to the flattering portrait of Diane Keaton that, of course, reflects favorably on Allen himself. In the film's opening he quotes a Groucho Marx quip about not wanting to join a club that would have him as a member, but the film is in a sense the opposite of that joke. In other words, Allen must be doing something right to have had a girlfriend like Keaton.

Although he could be ponderous and hectoring in his later movies, in *Annie Hall* Allen captured

a nostalgia tinged with melancholy that moviegoers of the time found endearing. Allen included them in his jokes, even as he mocked their counterparts in the film. And unlike his later movies, *Annie Hall* unfolded in apartments and restaurants and nightclubs that felt real and accessible.

The film affected fashion to a surprising degree, with United Artists licensing an "Annie Hall" look to designers. It helped solidify Keaton's status as a star, and gave important breaks to several other performers: Sigourney Weaver, Beverly D'Angelo, Gary Muledeer, etc. Allen would work with Brickman, Keaton, and Willis on his next New York–based comedy, *Manhattan* (1979), also a Registry title.

Star Wars

Twentieth Century-Fox, 1977. Sound, color, 2.35. 121 minutes.
Cast: Mark Hamill (Luke Skywalker), Harrison Ford (Han Solo), Carrie Fisher (Princess Leia Organa), Peter Cushing (Grand Moff Tarkin), Alec Guinness (Ben [Obi-Wan] Kenobi), Anthony Daniels (See Threepio [C3PO]), Kenny Baker (Artoo-Detoo [R2-D2]), Peter Mayhew (Chewbacca), David Prowse (Lord Darth Vader), Jack Purvis (Chief Jawa), Eddie Byrne (General Willard), Phil Brown (Uncle Owen), Shelagh Fraser (Aunt Beru), Alex McCrindle (General Dodonna), Drewe Henley (Red leader), Dennis Lawson (Red Two [Wedge]), Garrick Hagon (Red Three [Biggs]), Jack Klaff (Red Four [John "D"]), William Hootkins (Red Six [Perkins]), Angus McInnus (Gold leader), Jeremy Sinden (Gold Two), Graham Ashley (Gold Five), Don Henderson (General Taggi), Richard LeParmentier (General Motti), Leslie Schofield (Commander #1).
Credits: Written and directed by George Lucas. Produced by Gary Kurtz. Production designer: John Barry. Director of photography: Gilbert Taylor. Music by John Williams. Performed by the London Symphony Orchestra. Special photographic effects supervisor: John Dykstra. Special production & mechanical effects supervisor: John Stears. Film editors: Paul Hirsch, Marcia Lucas, Richard Chew. Production supervisor: Robert Watts. Costume designer: John Mollo. Art directors: Norman Reynolds, Leslie Dilley. Make up supervisor: Stuart Freeborn. Production sound mixer: Derek Ball. Casting: Irene Lamb, Diane Crittenden, Vic Ramos. Supervising sound editor: Sam Shaw. Supervising music editor: Kenneth Wannberg. Dolby sound consultant: Stephen Katz. Continuity: Ann Skinner. Titles: Dan Perri. Panavision. Technicolor. Prints by DeLuxe. Dolby System noise reduction.
Additional Credits: Voice of Darth Vader: James Earl Jones. Second unit photography includes: Carroll Ballard. Second unit make up includes: Rick Baker. Production dates: March 22, 1976 to June 1976; reshoots: January, 1977. Photographed in Tunisia, Tikai National Park, Guatemala, Death Valley National Monument, EMI Elstree Studios, Borehamwood, England. Opened May 25, 1977.
Awards: Oscars for Best Film Editing, Music—Original Score, Sound, Effects—Visual Effects, Art Direction–Set Decoration, Costume Design.
Other Versions: *Star Wars: Episode V—The Empire Strikes Back* (1980), *Star Wars: Episode VI—Return of the Jedi* (1983), *Star Wars: Episode I—The Phantom Menace* (1999), *Star Wars: Episode II—Attack of the Clones* (2002), *Star Wars: Episode III—Revenge of the Sith* (2005).
Available: Twentieth Century Fox Home Entertainment DVD (2006). UPC: 024542263739.

Movies, television shows, and books all helped inspire George Lucas to write *Star Wars*, but in an interview he gave a more immediate reason for tackling

the project. "When I did [*American*] *Graffiti*, I discovered that making a positive film is exhilarating," he said. "I saw that kids today don't have any fantasy life the way we had—they don't have Westerns, they don't have pirate movies." Given the financial success of *American Graffiti*, "I thought, 'Maybe I should make a film like this for even younger kids.'"

In 1972, while the national release of *Graffiti* was being prepared, Lucas began channeling his research into fairy tales and myths. A year later, he had a thirteen-page treatment that writer Peter Biskind called "virtual gobbledygook." Most Hollywood executives were skeptical of the project, but not Alan Ladd, Jr., head of production at Twentieth Century-Fox. He understood that Lucas was trying to combine science fiction with swashbucklers, and agreed to a $3.5 million budget. Lucas held on to music and merchandising rights, as well as control over sequels.

Lucas tinkered with the script for almost three years, expanding and contracting scenes, adding and deleting characters, working out a cosmology that owed equal allegiance to *The Wizard of Oz* and *The Lord of the Rings*, as told by Joseph Campbell. (His plot was also so close to *The Hidden Fortress*, a 1958 film by Akira Kurosawa, that he wondered if he should secure remake rights.) Ultimately, his friends Willard Huyck and Gloria Katz polished his work. At the same time, Lucas poured money into Industrial Light and Magic (ILM), a special effects production house he formed for the film.

Unable to hire Douglas Trumbull, who worked on Stanley Kubrick's *2001: A Space Odyssey* (1968), Lucas did the next best thing and hired his assistant, John Dykstra.

Dykstra brought to ILM a camera whose motions were controlled by computer. This meant that the same shots could be filmed over and over again in perfect registration, enabling technicians to add special effects with very little difficulty. The opening shot of *Star Wars* shows off this new capability, incorporating a tilt across moving objects that would have been almost impossible to obtain a few years earlier.

Lucas cast *Star Wars* in the same room with director Brian De Palma, who was casting *Carrie*. Amy Irving went to the latter film; the more prim and youthful Carrie Fisher, daughter of movie star Debbie Reynolds, to the former. "This is a Disney movie," Lucas kept telling everyone, setting his targets on a pre-teen audience. He gave the lead role of Luke Skywalker to the relatively callow Mark Hamill, for example, reserving Harrison Ford for a supporting role as daredevil mercenary Han Solo.

Filming started in Tunisia for desert scenes and then England at the Elstree Studios. Most accounts describe it as a dispiriting time for Lucas, and in fact it was more than twenty years before he would direct again. Worried about the footage, he asked his wife Marcia to help edit it. She worked on the project until an emergency brought her to Martin Scorsese's *New York, New York*.

Few of the special effects were ready for the first screening early in 1977. Lucas spliced in black-and-white battle footage from World War II movies; the film was also missing John Williams' bombastic score. Afterward the screening, Marcia Lucas decried the film as "the *At Long Last Love* of science fiction." Brian De Palma told Lucas that moviegoers wouldn't understand his plot. Spielberg, on the other hand, predicted that it would make $100 million.

Lucas may not have been optimistic about *Star Wars*, but he knew what he was supposed to do as a filmmaker. He insisted that the soundtrack be recorded in Dolby Stereo, an expensive step, but one that helped popularize the process throughout the industry. A year before the film opened, Lucas made a slide-show presentation before the Comic-Con convention, building an audience of young boys. They would help turn the movie into a cultural phenomenon.

Star Wars opened on May 25, 1977, to strong business, but what startled executives was how often moviegoers returned to see it again. Novelist Jonathan Lethem, thirteen that summer, traveled from Brooklyn to Times Square twenty-one times to watch it. Alec Guinness met a twelve-year-old who had seen it a hundred times. The fans were so obsessive that they formed clubs, edited newsletters, and later created web sites devoted to the film and its characters. Jack Sorenson, president of the subsequently formed LucasArts, explained the film's pull in this way: "*Star Wars* is the mythology of a nonsectarian world. It describes how people want to live."

It has proven to be an extremely durable mythology. Lucas expanded his original vision to encompass two separate trilogies, a feature-length cartoon, a televised Christmas special, novelizations, video games, and some of the most profitable ancillary materials ever put on sale. In the process he helped change how movies are made and marketed.

Star Wars did not earn Lucas much critical respect—at least not until the money started pouring in. (By 1997, *Star Wars* merchandising had earned over $3 billion in license fees.) Writers then had to figure out how Lucas did it. According to Biskind, "Lucas and Spielberg returned the '70s audience, grown sophisticated on a diet of European and New Hollywood films, to the simplicities of the pre-'60s Golden Age of movies." Others accused Lucas of neo-Fascism by emulating Leni Riefenstahl's *Triumph of the Will*. But wasn't Lucas siding with the underdog Rebel Alliance? Or was he just finding a way to update the clichés he watched on television as a child?

Lucas has never stopped working on *Star Wars*, either by producing and occasionally directing sequels, but also by retrofitting the original film with new special effects. A 1997 re-release was digitally altered, and a 2004 version offered computer-generated special effects and scenes pulled together from unused material. In 1981, Lucas officially changed the title of the film to *Star Wars: Episode IV—A New Hope*, reflecting the film's position within the Star Wars marketing empire.

Eraserhead

David Lynch/AFI, 1977. Sound, B&W, 1.85. 89 minutes.

Cast: John Nance (Henry Spencer), Charlotte Stewart (Mary X), Allen Joseph (Mr. X), Jeanne Bates (Mrs. X), Judith Anna Roberts (Beautiful girl across the hall), Laurel Near (Lady in the radiator), V. Phipps-Wilson (Landlady), Jack Fisk (Man in the planet), Jean Lange (Grandmother), Thomas Coulson (The boy), John Monez (Bum), Darwin Joston (The boss), Hal Landon, Jr. (Pencil machine operator).

Credits: Written, produced and directed by David Lynch. Camera and lighting: Frederick Elmes, Herbert Cardwell. Location sound and re-recording: Alan R. Splet. Assistant to the director: Catherine Coulson. Production manager: Doreen G. Small. Picture editing: David Lynch. Sound editing: Alan R. Splet. Sound effects: David Lynch, Alan R. Splet. "Lady in the Radiator" song composed and sung by Peter Ivers. Pipe organ by "Fats" Waller. Crew: Jeanne Field, Michael Grody, Stephen Grody, Toby Keeler, Roger Lundy, John Lynch, Dennis Nance, Anatol Pacanowsky, Carol Schreder. Production design and special effects: David Lynch. Special effects photography: Frederick Elmes. Assistant camera: Catherine Coulson. Thanks: Jack Fisk, Sissy Spacek, George Stevens, Jr. Produced with the cooperation of The American Film Institute Center for Advanced Film Studies. Copyright 1976 by David Lynch.

Additional Cast notes: The following performers were cut from final version: Jennifer Lynch (Little girl), Brad Keeler (Little boy), Peggy Lynch, Doddie Keeler (People digging in the alley), Gill Dennis (Man with cigar), Toby Keeler (Man fighting), Raymond [Jack] Walsh (Mr. Roundheels).

Additional Credits: Opened theatrically September 28, 1977.

Available: Absurda/Subversive DVD (2006). UPC: 858334001039.

Born in Missoula, Montana, in 1946, David Lynch became interested in film while attending art school in Philadelphia in the 1960s. "I wanted my paintings to move," he said in an interview, and to achieve that goal he completed three abstract shorts, one of which won him an AFI grant. *The Grandmother*, the third, was his entree to study at the Institute itself in Los Angeles. There he began writing *Gardenback*, a screenplay about an adulterous couple. Placing this couple in a nightmare landscape gave him *Eraserhead*.

"It all came from Philadelphia," Lynch told another interviewer when asked about the visual style for the film. He called it "my most spiritual film," and revealed that he first started meditating at some point during the five-year shoot.

Since Lynch had submitted a twenty-two-page script to his AFI instructors, he was told to make a forty-two minute film. He holed up in the former stables on the Institute property, where he built many of the props and sets for the film. His production equipment consisted of two Eclair cameras, video cameras, and a lighting package. He filmed *Eraserhead* primarily at night, with a budget of $20,000, working with a tiny crew and a handful of actors.

Classmate David Lindeman recommended actor Jack Nance for the part of Henry Spencer, a civil service drone who is roped into marriage.

Nance obligingly kept his character's frizzed-up hairdo over the five years of shooting. The only performer in the cast with extensive professional experience was Charlotte Stewart, a friend of production manager Doreen Small. Lynch warned Stewart, a veteran of TV's *Little House on the Prairie*, that he'd have to "frump her up."

"The rest of the world disappeared," he said about the shoot. Cameraman Herbert Cardwell worked for nine months on the film; he was replaced by Frederick Elmes, who shot for three years. Filming started in June 1972 and proceeded on a trial-and-error basis, with Lynch reshooting much of the material, adding minor variations. Financial and moral support came from Jack Fisk, a production designer who appeared as "The Man in the Planet," and his wife-to-be, actress Sissy Spacek.

Eraserhead unfolds in a few claustrophobic sets. The plot concerns Henry Spencer's attempts to cope with his dysfunctional marriage and its offspring, an equally dysfunctional alien fetus. Hints of sexual perversity linger on the edges of scenes, which are punctuated by non sequiturs or by the suggestion of gore in the form of ketchup, chocolate sauce, soup, rice pudding, and baked Cornish game hens that eject black goo when sliced. As far as the AFI staff was concerned, the *Eraserhead* project was about crazy guys building creepy sets in an abandoned barn, making actors look ugly and trying to concoct gross-out imagery. In 1976, George Stevens, Jr., then the AFI head, ordered Lynch to leave the grounds, and had editing machines installed in his former living quarters. Jack Fisk's sister Mary helped raise the money needed to complete the film elsewhere.

Once filming was finished, Lynch oversaw a monaural sound mix compiled onto magnetic track salvaged from discard bins at Warner Bros. The soundtrack to *Eraserhead* is an astonishing collage of industrial noise and jaunty organ instrumentals from old Fats Waller records; it became a template for future horror and torture porn filmmakers. Lynch brought the completed film, twelve reels of sound and twelve of picture, to New York, hoping to enter it in the Cannes Film Festival. Instead, it premiered at FilmEx 77, a commercial film market. By this time Lynch had a composite print (with picture and sound together). After the first screening, he cut out approximately twenty minutes of material. "I loved them as little scenes, but they didn't belong in the film," he said of the elisions.

One person who was impressed by the film was Ben Barenholtz, a former theater manager who was a crucial figure in what became known as "midnight movies." Among the films he exhibited were *El Topo* (1970) by Alexander Jodorowsky and *Pink Flamingos* (1972) by John Waters. Barenholtz opened *Eraserhead* at the Cinema Village in New York in the fall of 1977. According to Lynch, twenty-six people attended the first screening. Critic J. Hoberman called it "a murky piece of post-nuclear guignol," while *Variety* said it was "a sickening bad-taste exercise."

Word-of-mouth and an ubiquitous ad campaign featuring a crazed-looking Nance turned *Eraserhead* into a niche success. It played the midnight circuit in seventeen cities over a four-year period, and launched Lynch's career as a director. He has resolutely refused to offer an interpretation of the plot or explanations for *Eraserhead*'s visual style, but has admitted that, "No critic or viewer has given an interpretation that has been my interpretation in the twenty-five years that it has been out."

Often overlooked is how astute a marketer Lynch is. Better than many of his contemporaries, he understood how to publicize himself and his works. Lynch's carefully cultivated image as an eccentric is always good copy, and he has managed to attract and exploit upper-tier talent to his projects, even though apart from *Blue Velvet* and the television series *Twin Peaks*, they have been commercial and artistic failures.

He also understood the basics of filmmaking in ways that more ambitious artists didn't. Lynch knew that it was cheaper to film in black and white instead of color, to use model sets rather than build life-size ones, to film at night and not day, to use stop-motion rather than hand-drawn animation. He saw that it was easier to market a horror film than an experimental one, and that he stood a better chance of making a profit if he could turn screenings of *Eraserhead* into events rather than simply the next scheduled showing at a multiplex.

Lynch was following in the footsteps of exploitation filmmakers like Ed Wood, William Castle, and Val Lewton, and in fact you can see traces of all three filmmakers' works in *Eraserhead*. For younger audiences of the time, the film became a rite of passage, proof that they could stomach anything thrown at them. Lynch's cult following expands and contracts, but his core fans remain obsessively devoted to him. His latest release is *Inland Empire* (2006), a three-hour meditation on identity, the visual quality of video, and the use of obscurity in narrative.

Close Encounters of the Third Kind

Columbia Pictures, 1977. Sound, color, 2.35. 135 minutes. Rated PG.
Cast: Richard Dreyfuss (Roy Neary), François Truffaut (Claude Lacombe), Teri Garr (Ronnie Neary), Melinda Dillon (Jillian Guiler), Gary Guffey (Barry Guiler), Bob Balaban (David Laughlin), Roberts Blossom (Farmer), Merrill Connally (Team leader), George DiCenzo (Major Benchley), Lance Henriksen (Robert), Warren Kemmerling (Wild Bill), J. Patrick McNamara (Project leader), Philip Dodds (Jean Claude), Shawn Bishop (Brad Neary), Adrienne Campbell (Silvia Neary), Justin Dreyfuss (Toby Neary); Amy Douglass, Alexander Lockwood (Implantees); Gene Dynarski (Ike), Mary Gafrey (Mrs. Harris), Norman Bartold (Ohio Tolls), Josef Sommer (Larry Butler), Rev. Michael J. Dyer (Himself), Roger Ernest (Highway patrolman), Carl Weathers (Military police), F.J. O'Neil (ARP Project member), Randy Hermann (Returnee #1, Flt. 19), Hal Barwood (Returnee #2, Flt. 19), Matthew Robbins (Returnee #3, Flt. 19); David Anderson, Richard L. Hawkins, Craig Shreeve, Bill Thurman (Air traffic controllers); Roy E. Richards (Air East pilot), Gene Rader (Hawker); Eumenio Blanco, Daniel Nunez, Chuy Franco, Luis Contreras (Federales); James Keane, Dennis McMullen, Cy Young, Tom Howard (Radio telescope team); Richard Stuart (Truck dispatcher), Bob Westmoreland (Load dispatcher), Matt Emery (Support leader); Galen Thompson, John Dennis Johnston (Special forces); John Ewing (Dirty Tricks #1), Kevin Atkinson (Dirty Tricks #2), Robert Broyles (Dirty Tricks #3), Kirk Raymond (Dirty Tricks #4).
Credits: Written and directed by Steven Spielberg. Produced by Julia Phillips & Michael Phillips. Director of photography: Vilmos Zsigmond. Director of photography of additional American scenes: William A. Fraker. Director of photography of India sequence: Douglas Slocombe. Production designer: Joe Alves. Special photographic effects: Douglas Trumbull. Music by John Williams. Film editor: Michael Kahn. Associate producer: Clark Paylow. Visual effects concepts: Steven Spielberg. Unit production manager: Clark Paylow. Additional directors of photography: John Alonzo, Laszlo Kovacs. Technical advisor: Dr. J. Allen Hynek. Set decoration: Phil Abramson. Realization of "extraterrestrial" by Carlo Rambaldi. Art director: Dan Lomino. Assistant director Chuck Myers. Music editor: Kenneth Wannberg. Supervising sound effects editor: Frank Warner. Supervising dialogue editor: Jack Schrader. Production sound mixer: Gene Cantamesa. Production illustrator: George Jensen. Make-up supervisor: Bob Westmoreland. Hairdresser: Edie Panda. Casting: Shari Rhodes, Juliette Taylor. Title design: Dan Perri. Panavision. Metrocolor. A Columbia presentation, in association with EMI, of a Julia Phillips & Michael Phillips production.
Additional Credits: Screenwriting by Paul Schrader, Hal Barwood, Matthew Robbins, John Hill, David Giler, Jerry Belson. Director of photography: Frank Stanley. Premiered in New York City on November 15, 1977.
Available: Sony Pictures DVD (2007). UPC: 043396212688.

After the unprecedented success of *Jaws* (1975), director Steven Spielberg had his choice of projects. He returned to his childhood fascination with science fiction, coincidentally the genre George Lucas was also exploring in *Star Wars*. Where Lucas imagined a future as an extension of *Flash Gordon* serials, Spielberg reduced the scope of his project to a deeply personal present. While critics have subsequently concentrated on Spielberg's mastery of film technique, his real genius may be in his ability to present complex story lines from the point of view of someone very similar to the suburban Phoenix youth he once was. It was a sensibility shared by a vast audience of maturing baby boomers, and more than any other director of his time, Spielberg was keyed into their fears and desires, their cultural references, their prolonged adolescence, their largely absent parents.

While still a teenager, Spielberg filmed *Firelight*, his first feature, and one that received considerable local attention when it premiered in 1964. By then he had seen *It Came from Outer Space* (1953) a half-dozen times, and he later told author Ray Bradbury that that film (adapted from a Bradbury story) was the primary inspiration for *Close Encounters*. After the film opened, he even asked Bradbury, "How do you like *your* film?"

Before he started filming *Jaws*, Spielberg had signed a development deal for something called *Watch the Skies* (the closing words from *The Thing from Another World*, 1951), based on a short story he wrote in 1970 called "Experiences." In the summer of 1973, producer Michael Phillips (*The Sting*) started talking about science fiction films with Spielberg, and it was Phillips and his wife Julia who set up the deal with David Begelman at Columbia Pictures. Paul Schrader was hired to write the script in December 1973.

Not surprisingly, Schrader's Calvinist vision did not mesh well with Spielberg's suburban optimism. (He called Schrader's draft "one of the most embarrassing screenplays ever professionally turned in to a major studio or director.") Schrader cited St. Paul and *King Lear* when talking about his version. On the other hand, Spielberg had his constantly growing knowledge of film history to bank on, as well as help from several colleagues. Biographer Jim McBride lists Hal Barwood, Matthew Robbins, John Hill, David Giler, and Jerry Belson as contributors to the script. (The "Close Encounters" phrase came from Dr. J. Allen Hynek, a technical advisor on the film and a former consultant to the Air Force. He gave three degrees to "encounters," the third being actual contact with aliens.)

Spielberg not only shaped the screenplay, he spent a year determining the visual design of the film. George Jensen prepared thousands of drawings covering seven major sequences, in particular the closing visual extravaganza. Even so, Spielberg had to film the actors without knowing exactly what Douglas Trumbull's special effects would look like. Trumbull, who worked on *2001: A Space Odyssey*, had just turned down Lucas's *Star Wars*. One key to the success of his effects here was the Electronic Motion Control System, which enabled technicians to repeat camera movements precisely enough to combine several layers of material shot at different times. Still, the effects had to be "lit" on the set, when spaceships passed by, for example, a time-consuming process. The final film contained some two hundred special-effects shots.

The first live take took place on December 29, 1975, in order for the studio to write off tax shelter claims. The bulk of the production started in May 1976, much of it in an airplane hanger in Alabama. By then the budget had almost doubled to $11.5 million. (Trumbull's special effects added up to $3.3 million. Final budget estimates range as high as $20 million.) Spielberg later said that the *Close Encounters* production was even worse than *Jaws*, in part because of financial pressure from a studio on the verge of bankruptcy. Julia Phillips tried to replace cinematographer Vlimos Zgimond, and succeeded in hiring other cameramen for the additional footage needed. Phillips herself was forced off the production in the summer of 1977.

By that time *Star Wars* had opened to unprecedented business, putting even more pressure on Spielberg. Columbia insisted on opening *Close Encounters* in November, some two weeks after sneak previews in Dallas. One of the last decisions Spielberg made was to eliminate the song "When You Wish Upon a Star" from the closing credits. But he always referred to the first release of *Close Encounters* as a "work in progress." He would continue to tinker with the film, adding and deleting material, over several years.

Close Encounters refers to or comments on all the landmark "first contact" movies, like *The Day the Earth Stood Still* (1951); in fact, it updates them for a new, media-savvy and skeptical generation still recovering from the Vietnam War and Watergate. Spielberg may have been optimistic about aliens, but he depicted government authorities as potentially paranoid and duplicitous conspirators. Driving the story was the widely believed myth that the government was covering up evidence of UFOs.

Separating Spielberg from earlier sci-fi film-makers was his unparalleled access to funding. He could afford to hire whatever experts he needed, to shoot in locations of his choice, and to spend almost as long as he wanted to film his story. He may have concerned himself too much with the technical aspects of the film. François Truffaut, the French director hired to add a bit of prestige to the project, said later, "I never had the impression of playing a role, only of lending my carnal envelope." He also referred to the film as "a grand cartoon strip."

Although unhappy with his performance, Richard Dreyfuss thought, "This movie would be potentially the most important film ever made." Early audiences agreed. Viewers in New York's Ziegfeld Theater burst into spontaneous applause at the first image of the film, a blinding light accompanied by a John Williams crescendo on the soundtrack. *Close Encounters* went on to gross some

$270 million. Spielberg received his first Oscar nomination for the film, and he would return to the subject with *E.T. The Extra-Terrestrial* (1982). During a lull in shooting *E.T.*, he and George Lucas initiated a joint project, *Raiders of the Lost Ark* (1981).

While filming *1941* in 1979, Spielberg spent nineteen weekends shooting additional material for *Close Encounters*. He released a new version of the film, *The Special Edition of Close Encounters of the Third Kind*, in 1980. Spielberg cut almost sixteen minutes from the original film, replacing it with seven minutes of outtakes and six minutes of new footage, including Richard Dreyfuss's Ray Neary entering the mother ship. (A 1998 "Director's Cut" eliminated the mother ship scenes.) For years, home-video versions were based in part on the *Special Edition*; only a 1990 Criterion laserdisc included the original cut. A 2007 DVD includes the original theatrical release.

National Lampoon's Animal House

Universal, 1978. Sound, color, 1.85. 109 minutes. Rated R.

Cast: John Belushi (John [Bluto] Blutarsky), Tim Matheson (Eric [Otter] Stratton), John Vernon (Dean Vernon Wormer), Verna Bloom (Marion Wormer), Thomas Hulce (Larry Kroger), Cesare Danova (Mayor Carmine DePasto), Peter Riegert (Donald "Boone" Schoenstein), Mary Louise Weller (Mandy Pepperidge), Stephen Furst (Kent Dorfman), James Daughton (Greg Marmalard), Bruce McGill (Daniel Simpson [D-Day] Day), Mark Metcalf (Doug Neidermeyer), DeWayne Jessie (Otis Day), Karen Allen (Katy), James Widdoes (Robert Hoover), Martha Smith (Babs Jansen), Sarah Holcomb (Clorette DePasto), Lisa Baur (Shelly), Kevin Bacon (Chip Diller), Donald Sutherland (Dave Jennings), Douglas Kenney (Stork), Christian Miller (Hardbar), Bruce Bonnheim (B.B.), Joshua Daniel (Mothball), Junior (Trooper), Sunny Johnson (Otter's Co-Ed), Stacy Grooman (Sissy), Stephen Bishop (Charming guy with guitar), Eliza Garrett (Brunella), Aseneth Jurgenson (Beth), Katherine Denning (Noreen), Raymone Robinson (Mean dude), Robert Elliott (Meaner dude), Reginald H. Farmer (Meanest dude), Jebidiah R. Dumas (Gigantic dude), Priscilla Lauris (Dean's secretary), Rick Eby (Omega), John Freeman (Man on street), Sean McCartin (Lucky boy), Helen Vick (Sorority girl), Rick Greenough (Mongol).

Credits: Directed by John Landis. Written by Harold Ramis, Douglas Kenney & Chris Miller. Produced by Matty Simmons & Ivan Reitman. Director of photography: Charles Correll. Art Director: John J. Lloyd. Edited by George Folsey, Jr. Music: Elmer Bernstein. Casting by Michael Chinich. Costumes by Deborah Nadoolman. Unit production manager: Peter MacGregor-Scott. First assistant director: Cliff Coleman. Script supervisor: Katherine Wooten. Sound: William B. Kaplan. Special effects: Henry Millar. Make-up: Lynn Brooks, Gerald Soucie. Hair stylist: Marilyn Phillips. Stunt coordinator: Gary R. McLarty. Titles & optical effects: Universal Title. "Animal House" and "Dream Girl" composed and performed by Stephen Bishop. "Money" performed by John Belushi. Color by Technicolor. A Matty Simmons/Ivan Reitman production.

Additional Cast: John Landis, Judith Belushi, Robert Cray (Bandmember, Otis Day and the Knights).

Additional Credits: Production dates: October 24 to November 30, 1977. Premiered in New York City on July 27, 1978.

Other Versions: Basis for the television series *Delta House* (1979).

Available: Universal Home Video DVD (2003). ISBN: 0-7832-6356-2. UPC: 0-25192-15502-4.

A film that divided critics on its release, *National Lampoon's Animal House* became one of the more influential comedies of the 1970s. Embraced by younger viewers, it has been used as a blueprint by a succeeding generation of comedy filmmakers. Those connected with the project now like to say that when it was being filmed, it was considered a throwaway product. But *Animal House*, as it is usually referred to, was actually a canny, carefully thought out attempt to exploit two different franchises, *National Lampoon* and *Saturday Night Live*. Created and produced by Lorne Michaels, the latter had made celebrities of its comedian performers, many of them drafted from the Second City troupe.

National Lampoon magazine was a spin-off from the venerable *Harvard Lampoon*, founded in 1876 as a sort of American version of *Punch*. Formed by Doug Kenney, Henry Beard, and Robert Hoffman in 1970, *National Lampoon* reached its height of popularity in the mid-1970s, when the franchise name was backing a radio show, records, several parody books, and even an off-Broadway play, *The National Lampoon Show*. The play was produced by *Lampoon* publisher Matty Simmons, the Brooklyn-born former editor of *Diners' Club Magazine*, and Ivan Reitman.

Born in Czechoslovakia, Reitman grew up in Toronto, where he pursued a musical career before becoming a key figure in the rise of Canadian exploitation films at the end of the 1960s. Reitman had always hoped to make a *Lampoon* movie, and after the success of the play Simmons was enthusiastic as well. The first treatment was written by Doug Kenney, Chris Miller (who wrote a number of college-themed stories for the magazine), and Harold Ramis.

A veteran of Chicago's Second City comedy group, Ramis became, along with Miller, the prime creative force behind the screenplay. In Ramis's account, they submitted an admittedly over-the-top story filled with rape and vomit that shocked executives at Universal, where Reitman and Simmons had a development deal. Nine drafts later, Universal agreed to a budget a little under $3 million, provided John Belushi was in the cast. Ramis knew Belushi through Second City, and wrote the part of Bluto Blutarsky specifically for the actor. Universal wanted other *Saturday Night Live* actors in the film as well (the part of D-Day was written with Dan Aykroyd in mind), but only Belushi would agree to appear.

In an interview Reitman gave immediately before the film's release, he said that he approached Richard Lester, Bob Rafelson, and others about directing the project. When John Landis was mentioned, Reitman remembered his *Schlock* (1971) as "a pretty mediocre movie," but thought better of *Kentucky Fried Movie* (1977), a pastiche of Z-budget movies seen through the filter of late-night television. It was a critic-proof approach to tastelessness: complaining about bad writing, acting, set design, and the like was beside the point. Landis wanted his work to look ugly, the jokes to bomb, the seams to show.

A high-school dropout, Landis clashed with the *Lampoon* personnel, especially when he decided to cast Peter Riegert in a part Ramis had written for himself. But Landis also mollified Universal by getting Donald Sutherland, the highest-paid cast member, to appear as a stoned English professor. The rest of the cast were largely drawn from the struggling ranks. *Animal House* became a sort of incubator of talent, with Karen Allen, Kevin Bacon, and Tom Hulce going on to significant careers.

Each generation claims comedy for its own, and each likes to believe it has pushed the bounds of propriety for risky, edgy laughs that parents wouldn't appreciate. At the time, right-wing writers howled about how *Animal House* was contributing to the vulgarization of American culture. (Liberal critics, on the other hand, endorsed the film, perhaps because its villains were drawn—anachronistically—as wealthy, pro-war, anti-evolution, bedrock conservatives.) Today, the *Animal House*'s casual, even unconscious racism seems more appalling.

Landis had a fan's appreciation of film history, with little sense of proportion or discrimination between good and bad. He loved threadbare horror movies and rock-bottom musicals as much as cinema masterpieces. He had seen enough silent slapstick, Three Stooges shorts, and Warner Brothers cartoons to use them as a source of gags, confident that his audience wouldn't know any better. (Two unacknowledged sources for the film were the "beach blanket" teen party pics of the 1960s and 1973's *American Graffiti*.)

Fashioning a coherent story line proved more difficult. Landis could use rougher words and show more skin, but he couldn't develop a romance between Riegert and Allen any more convincing than that between Frankie Avalon and Annette Funicello in *Beach Blanket Bingo* (1965). He turned Belushi into a modern-day Harpo Marx, then left the actor with nothing else to do but flex his eyebrows. Landis did hit some high points, like the swirling chaos of a parade of floats and marching bands that uses jokes from Buster Keaton's *Cops* (1922), or Belushi's anguished wail, "Seven years of college down the drain." But, like the magazine, the director couldn't resist cheap, ugly jokes. "What are you studying?" Tom Hulce asks a date. "Primitive cultures," she replies, and Landis immediately cuts to a shot of shrieking, sweaty black musicians. The threat of interracial rape serves as a punch line to the sequence.

Preview screenings went so well that Universal wound up spending more on publicity than what the film itself cost. *Animal House* grossed almost $150 million, an unheard-of amount for a comedy. Although *Variety* called it a "soft-pedalled, punches-pulled parody," it unleashed the floodgates for other randy, teen-oriented comedies. Reitman directed *Meatballs* (1979), a sort of *Animal House* at summer camp, and has veered ever since between high- and lowbrow projects.

Landis directed Belushi again in *The Blues Brothers* (1980), but the comedian could not establish a stable film career before his death in 1982. "National Lampoon" became an umbrella title for several comedies, such as *National Lampoon's Vacation* (1983). Harold Ramis took a significant role in *Ghostbusters* (1984), a comedy franchise that also featured Bill Murray (and Reitman as director). Ramis's most accomplished film may be *Groundhog Day* (1993), which is also on the Registry.

Days of Heaven

Paramount, 1978. Sound, color, 1.78. 94 minutes. Rated PG.

Cast: Richard Gere (Bill), Brooke Adams (Abby), Sam Shepard (The Farmer), Linda Manz (Linda), Robert Wilke (The farm foreman), Jackie Shultis (Linda's friend), Stuart Margolin (Mill foreman), Tim Scott (Harvest hand), Gene Bell (Dancer), Doug Kershaw (Fiddler), Richard Libertini (Vaudeville leader), Frenchie Lemond (Vaudeville wrestler), Sahbra Markus (Vaudeville dancer), Bob Wilson (Accountant), Muriel Jolliffe (Headmistress), John Wilkinson (Preacher), King Cole (Farm worker).

Credits: Written and directed by Terrence Malick. Produced by Bert and Harold Schneider. Executive producer: Jacob Brackman. Director of photography: Nestor Almendros. Art director: Jack Fisk. Edited by Billy Weber. Music composed and conducted by Ennio Morricone. Costumes designed by Patricia Norris. Additional photography: Haskell Wexler. Additional music: Leo Kottke. Color consultant: Bob McMillan. Re-recording mixer: John Wilkinson. First assistant director: Skip Cosper. Technical advisor: Clenton Owensby. Casting: Dianne Crittenden. Second unit director: Jacob Brackman. Title design: Dan Perri. Additional editors: Caroline Ferriol, Marion Segal, Susan Martin. Special sound effects: James Cox. Set decorator: Robert Gould. Script supervisor: Wally Bennett. Production manager: Les Kimber. Sound effects by Neiman-Tillar Associates. Special effects: John Thomas, Mel Merrells. Men's wardrobe: Jered Green. Camera operators: John Bailey, Rod Parkhurst. Sound mixers: George Ronconi, Barry Thomas. Hair stylist: Bertine Taylor. Makeup: Jamie Brown. Time lapse photography: Ken Middleham. Prints in Metrocolor. Lenses and Panaflex Camera by Panavision. Re-recording by Glen Glenn Sound. Dolby System. An O.P. production.

Additional credits: Filming began October 1976. Opened September 13, 1978.

Awards: Oscar for Best Cinematography.

Available: Criterion Collection DVD (2007). UPC: 715515026321.

Director Terrence Malick first met Bert Schneider while he was trying to find a distributor for *Badlands* (1973, a Registry title). Malick had established a reputation as a writer on the basis of scripts for two commercial failures and work on Jack Nicholson's *Drive, He Said* (1971). At the time Schneider was one of the most influential producers in Hollywood; his films included the Registry titles *Easy Rider* (1969), *Five Easy Pieces* (1970), and *The Last Picture Show* (1971). Schneider had won a documentary Oscar for *Hearts and Minds* (1974, directed by Peter Davis), but now had trouble duplicating those successes.

Malick's next script, *Days of Heaven*, followed three migrants who flee Chicago to work in the wheat fields of the Texas panhandle just as World War I was starting. A romantic triangle involving a ranch owner leads to violence. Malick had been unable to find funding, in part because he didn't have any stars. During a trip to Cuba, Schneider agreed to produce the film with his brother Herbert.

Schneider worked up a deal with Barry Diller at Paramount, getting Malick final cut in return for personally guaranteeing the budget. The cast now included Richard Gere, a former television actor who would grab attention as a potential serial killer in *Looking for Mr. Goodbar* (1977); Brooke Adams, whose striking features suited the period settings; and Sam Shepard, a musician and stage actor who became for many the pre-eminent playwright of his generation.

Just as important as the casting was the hiring of Nestor Almendros as cinematographer. Born in Spain in 1930, Almendros moved to Cuba until he was forced to leave after participating in student protests in 1955. He returned to Cuba to form a film collective in 1959, but fled to France for political reasons. Almendros found work with French New Wave directors like Eric Rohmer and François Truffaut, developing a cinematic style that eschewed filters, fill lighting, and other "glossy" techniques.

Almendros' contribution to *Days of Heaven* cannot be overestimated. Once the cast and crew began shooting in Alberta, Canada, Malick realized that his script wasn't working. He essentially discarded it, working with Almendros to improvise a visual story instead. As camera operator John Bailey put it, Malick's "dramatic scenes themselves do not necessarily follow conventional structure of revealing dramatic dialogue. It's more fragmented and impressionistic." To Shepard, Malick's films were "like poems. You can analyze them to death, but it's still not going to get to what this poem is doing to you."

Animal House may not be directly responsible for the Porky's and American Pie series, or the other titles in the growing genre of gross-out comedy. But it is still evoked today whenever filmmakers want their work to be perceived as "outrageous." MGM pushed *College* (2008), for example, as following "in the classic footsteps of *Animal House*, *American Pie*, and *Old School*."

Almendros faced resistance from some crew members, upset by his tendency to reject what were considered tried-and-true techniques. They didn't want to use the small, light dolly Almendros preferred, and insisted on the older tripod gear heads from an earlier era. The cinematographer praised the work by art director Jack Fisk, who constructed a mansion in the middle of rolling fields of wheat. As Bailey pointed out, Fisk not only strove for period authenticity, he built the interiors for shooting, so the camera could wend in and out of rooms and corridors.

Malick's methods were extremely time-consuming, perhaps because he was still searching for a story. He would rehearse the cast and crew in the middle of the day, when the sunlight was flat, and shoot just before sundown—the "golden hour," as cinematographers call it. As Almendros later admitted in his autobiography, this approach would play havoc with editing, and also led to some of the rumors surrounding the production. That there was no artificial lighting used, for example, or that all the shots were handheld. Almendros and Malick quickly realized that many shots would have to be taken from a tripod. "Very few decisions as I remember were made strictly because of the light," Haskell Wexler said later. According to Bailey, all of the interior scenes required lighting of some sort.

Schneider was sensitive to the rumors about *Days of Heaven*; he was also losing his own money, not Paramount's. As the production dragged on, Almendros had to leave after fifty-nine working days to meet a prior commitment to shoot Truffaut's *The Man Who Loved Women* (1977). He was replaced by Wexler, who photographed the last nineteen days of the production.

Notoriously indecisive, Malick needed some two years to fashion his footage into final shape. Ten editors are listed in the credits (two more if you include sound editors), and they spent much of their time whittling away the original story.

The director felt he needed to eliminate what he considered dramatically dishonest or implausible. (Editing took so long that Gere's *Looking for Mr. Goodbar* was filmed and released before *Days of Heaven* came out.)

Malick was able to realize his visual ambitions to an extent undreamed of by an earlier generation of filmmakers. Where Frank Capra or John Ford would have had to rely on soundstages for interior scenes, Malick had an actual house on location. He could show a real train crossing a landscape, and stay with it as actors clambered off or on—not switch to stock footage or process shots. He could forgo model shots, matte paintings, cornstarch posing as snow, things filmmakers from the 1930s had only dreamed about.

Unfortunately, he could not imagine a world beyond the tired romantic conventions of the past. Furthermore, Malick removed so much material from the original script that he had to insert a voice-over by newcomer Linda Manz to make sense of the story. *Days of Heaven* resembles *Badlands* set in an earlier time, only without that film's narrative focus and drive. Critics were divided, generally applauding Almendros and complaining about the plot. Not everyone appreciated the film's visual splendor. After one classroom screening, director Arthur Penn became incensed about a shot of a wine glass sitting on a river bottom. "How did we get to the bottom of a river?" he asked. "Why are we watching a movie from the point of view of a wine glass?"

Few moviegoers of the time bothered to find out. *Days of Heaven* performed so poorly at the box office that Schneider, who was forced to refinance his deal with Barry Diller at Paramount to cover Malick's overages, essentially retired from filmmaking. So did Malick, who spent part of the next fifteen years teaching philosophy in France. It took him until 1998 to direct another feature, *The Thin Red Line*.

Halloween

Compass International Pictures, 1978. Sound, color, 2.35. 91 minutes. Rated R.

Cast: Donald Pleasance (Loomis), Jamie Lee Curtis (Laurie), Nancy Loomis (Annie), P.J. Soles (Lynda), Charles Cyphers (Brackett), Kyle Richards (Lindsey), Brian Andrews (Tommy), John Michael Graham (Bob), Nancy Stephens (Marion), Arthur Malet (Graveyard keeper), Mickey Yablans (Richie), Brent Le Page (Lonnie), Adam Hollander (Keith), Robert Phalen (Dr. Wynn), Tony Moran (Michael, age 23), Will Sandin (Michael, age 6), Sandy Johnson (Judith Myers), David Kyle (Boyfriend), Peter Griffith (Laurie's father), Nick Castle (The shape [Michael Myers]), Jim Windburn (Stunt).

Credits: Directed by John Carpenter. Screenplay by John Carpenter and Debra Hill. Produced by Debra Hill. Executive producer: Irwin Yablans. Director of photography: Dean Cundey. Film editors: Tommy Wallace, Charles Bornstein. Music by John Carpenter. Associate producer: Kool Lusby. Production manager: Don Behrns. Production designer: Tommy

Wallace. Camera operator: Ray Stella. Set decorator/property master: Craig Stearns. Assistant director: Rick Wallace. Sound mixer: Tommy Causey. Makeup: Erica Ulland. Wardrobe: Beth Rodgers. Panaglide: Ray Stella. Supervising sound editor: William Stevenson. Orchestration: Dan Wyman. Music coordinator: Bob Walters. Music performed by The Bowling Green Philharmonic Orchestra [John Carpenter]. Filmed in Panavision and Metrocolor. Titles and opticals: MGM. A Moustapha Akkad presentation of a Debra Hill production.

Additional Credits: Title on screen: *John Carpenter's Halloween*. Released October 25, 1978.

Other Versions: *Halloween II* (1981), *Halloween III* (1982), *Halloween 4: The Return of Michael Myers* (1988), *Halloween 5* (1989), *Halloween: The Curse of Michael Myers* (1995), *Halloween H20: 20 Years Later* (1998), *Halloween: Resurrection* (2002), *Halloween* (2007, a remake directed by Rob Zombie), *Halloween II* (2009).

Available: Anchor Bay Entertainment DVD (2007). UPC: 0-1313-12284-9-6.

Generations of filmmakers have used the horror genre as a way of breaking into the industry. Few directors have been as commercially successful in the genre as John Carpenter. Born in 1948, he grew up in Kentucky, where his father taught music theory at Western Kentucky University. Carpenter received a grounding in music, but was more interested in movies. By the age of eight he was making stop-motion animation films on an 8mm camera. He dropped out of college in 1968 to attend film school at the University of Southern California, where he worked on the Oscar-winning short *The Resurrection of Bronco Billy* (1970). Starting with $1,000, he expanded a student film he wrote with his roommate Dan O'Bannon into *Dark Star* (1974), a spoof of science fiction films.

Carpenter borrowed the idea for his next feature, the contemporary cop thriller *Assault on Precinct 13* (1976), from the Howard Hawks Western *Rio Bravo* (1959). The film received respectful reviews (and was remade in 2005). Producer Irwin Yablans, who distributed it in the United States, asked Carpenter to prepare a low-budget film about a killer who targets babysitters. Carpenter wrote *The Babysitter Murders* with his girlfriend at the time, Debra Hill. Born in Haddonfield, New Jersey, in 1950, Hill had worked on educational films and as a script supervisor. She was "certainly the most influential woman in my professional life," Carpenter said later.

It was Yablans who thought of setting the film on October 31 and calling it *Halloween*. While peddling *Assault on Precinct 13* in Europe, the producer met financier Moustapha Akkad, who had been financing films with Middle Eastern themes. The two formed Compass International in order to market and distribute *Halloween*, using $300,000 that Akkad had left over from *Lion of the Desert* (1981).

The script for *Halloween* showed how attuned Hill and Carpenter were to the demands of their audience and the realities of low-budget filmmaking. The plot stripped away almost everything that writers used to justify previous horror films, reducing the story to killer and victim, outside and inside, evil and good. The writers set the story in a generic Midwest suburb, limited most of the characters to teens and children, and staged stalkings and murders in dens, bedrooms, and laundry rooms. Carpenter and Hill took authority away from the figures who gave a semblance of sanity to earlier horror films. The scientists, doctors, and police in *Halloween* were singularly ineffective.

As Hill said later, "We didn't want it to be gory. The idea was that you couldn't kill evil." A distributor who knew his audience, Yablans still wanted a shock to scare viewers every ten minutes during the film. Out of necessity, Carpenter made most of these false ones, jolts that usually turned out to be nothing more than musical stings. The small budget precluded extensive special effects and location shooting. Southern California locations fill in for the Midwest suburb of Haddonfield, and all Carpenter has to depict a mental institution is a sign on a chain-link fence.

What set *Halloween* apart from other horror films was Carpenter's extensive use of subjective camera, which in turn was made possible by Steadicam technology. Subjective camera, where the audience sees the same as what one of the characters in the film is seeing, goes back to the nineteenth century. Hawks employed it in *Rio Bravo*, as did Alfred Hitchcock in *The Birds* (1963). (Robert Montgomery's 1946 version of *Lady in the Lake* is told entirely in the "first person," from the viewpoint of detective Philip Marlowe.) For low-budget filmmakers, the problem with subjective camera had been the expensive rails and cranes necessary for smooth cinematography. The Steadicam, invented by Garrett Brown, eliminated the jerkiness associated with handheld cameras. Referred to as a Panaglide in the credits, the device enabled operator Ray Stella to mimic the killer's viewpoint and movements in a graceful, visually seductive fashion.

The subjective camera implicated viewers in the violence occurring on the screen; coupled with the script's insistence that there was no rational explanation for the killer's behavior, it prevented moviegoers from distancing themselves from the sex and murders they were watching. (Although

Carpenter denied it later, *Halloween* made a direct connection between sex and death; to be fair, it's hard to find a horror movie that doesn't.)

This was the motion picture debut for Jamie Lee Curtis, the daughter of movie stars Tony Curtis and Janet Leigh. It took her several years to break out of "scream queen" typecasting, although she returned to the franchise after a long absence with *Halloween H20* (1998). Donald Pleasance was the third choice for the role of Loomis; he only agreed to the film because his daughter had liked *Assault on Precinct 13*. Like most of the crew, the other actors were struggling to find a toehold in the industry. "Everyone had something to prove with *Halloween*," cinematographer Dean Cundey said. "It was a very hard time to break into mainstream Hollywood."

Halloween broke another mold by succeeding through word of mouth rather than through reviews. The film opened in Kansas City, Missouri,

spreading out gradually to the rest of the country. It eventually made over $50 million theatrically, none of which went to the cast. (Pleasance, at $20,000, was the highest-paid actor; Curtis made $8,000.) However, the film's success at the box office helped legitimize the slasher genre, and turned the movie into a franchise. Copycat films appeared almost at once, a few of which became franchises of their own.

Carpenter went on to remake Howard Hawks' *The Thing* (kids in *Halloween* watch its opening credits on television, and later tune in to *Forbidden Planet*). He also worked as a writer, director, composer, and/or producer on several commercially successful films: *Escape from New York* (1980), *Starman* (1984), etc. Debra Hill continued to work with Carpenter, then formed a production company with her friend Lynda Obst. She succumbed to cancer in 2005, the same year Akkad died in a terrorist bombing in Syria.

The Deer Hunter

Universal, 1978. Sound, color, 2.35. 183 minutes. Rated R.

Cast: Robert De Niro (Michael), John Cazale (Stan), John Savage (Steven), Meryl Streep (Linda), Christopher Walken (Nick), George Dzundza (John), Shirley Stoler (Steven's mother), Chuck Aspegren (Axel), Rutanya Alda (Angela), Pierre Segui (Julien), Mady Kaplan (Axel's girl), Amy Wright (Bridesmaid), Mary Ann Haenel (Stan's girl), Richard Kuss (Linda's father), Joe Grifasi (Bandleader), Christopher Colombi, Jr. (Wedding man), Victoria Karnafel (Sad looking girl), Jack Scardino (Cold old man), Joe Strnad (Bingo caller), Helen Tomko (Helen), Paul D'Amato (Sergeant), Dennis Watlington (Cab driver), Charlene Darrow (Red head), Jane-Colette Disko (Girl checker), Michael Wollet (Stock boy), Robert Beard, Joe Dzizmba (World war veterans), Father Stephen Kopestonsky (Priest), John F. Buchmelter, III (Bar patron), Frank Devore (Barman), Tom Becker (Doctor), Lynn Kongkham (Nurse), Nong-nuj Timruang (Bar girl), Po Pao Pee (Chinese referee), Dale Burroughs (Embassy guard), Parris Hicks (Sergeant), Samui Muang-Intata (Chinese bodyguard), Sapox Colisium (Chinese man), Vitoon Winiwtoon (NVA officer), Somsak Sengvilai (V.C. referee), Charan Nusvanon (Chinese boss), Jiam Gongtongsmoot (Chinese man at door); Chai Peyawan, Mana Hansa, Sombot Jumpanoi (South Vietnamese prisoners); Phip Manee (Woman in village); Ding Santos, Krieng Chaiyapuk, Ot Palapoo, Chok Chai Mahasoke (V.C. guards).

Credits: Directed by Michael Cimino. Screenplay by Deric Washburn. Story by Michael Cimino & Deric Washburn and Louis Garfinkle & Quinn K. Redeker. Produced by Barry Spikings, Michael Deeley, Michael Cimino, John Peverall. Executive in charge of production: Elliot Schick. Associate producers: Marion Rosenberg, Joann Carelli. Production consultant: Joann Carelli. Director of photography: Vilmos Zsigmond. Editor: Peter Zinner. Music by Stanley Myers. Art directors: Ron Hobbs and Kim Swados. Casting by Cis Corman. Main title theme performed by John Williams. Set decorator, USA: Dick Goddard. Set decorator, Thailand: Alan Hicks. Hair stylist: Mary Keats. Supervising sound effects editor: James J. Klinger. Assistant editors: Flo Williamson, Thomas K. Avildsen, Penelope Shaw. Assistant director: Charles Okun. Military technical advisor: Richard Dioguardi. Stunt coordinator, USA: Carey Loftin. Stunt coordinator, Thailand: Buddy van Horn. Filmed in Panavision. Color by Technicolor. Dolby consultant: Steve Katz. An EMI presentation.

Additional Credits: Released December 8, 1978.

Awards: Oscars for Best Picture, Director, Actor in a Supporting Role (Walken), Film Editing, Sound.
Available: Universal Home Video DVD (2005). ISBN: 1-4170-5444-1. UPC: 0-25192-79762-0.

Director Michael Cimino had directed a single feature before *The Deer Hunter*, *Thunderbolt and Lightfoot* (1974), an offbeat action film starring Clint Eastwood and Jeff Bridges. He did well enough for Eastwood to offer him a three-picture deal with his production company, but Cimino had bigger goals in mind.

Born in New York City (sources range from 1939 to 1943), Cimino enjoyed a privileged childhood and earned an MFA at Yale. For six months as a medic in the Army Reserves, he was a attached to a Green Beret unit, the initial inspiration for *The Deer Hunter*. Back in New York, Cimino studied acting and ballet while training as an apprentice editor for documentary producers. For several years he directed commercials (including Kool cigarettes and L'eggs hosiery), then received his first screen credit as coauthor, with Deric Washburn, of *Silent Running*, a 1972 sci-fi adventure. He then cowrote, with John Milius, a sequel to *Dirty Harry*, *Magnum Force* (1973). *Thunderbolt and Lightfoot* followed.

Cimino saw *The Deer Hunter* as an opportunity to remove the Vietnam War from a debate between liberals and conservatives, in effect to refight it on his own terms. The story would try to make hippies and rednecks irrelevant, to de-emphasize the government's motives and tactics in favor of the patriotism and heroism of the soldiers involved. Cimino built his story around six friends in a Pennsylvania steel town; three go to war, but all must face consequences. Or, in the director's metaphor, all must play Russian roulette in one form or another.

He pitched *The Deer Hunter* to a number of studios, but only EMI Films, a subsidiary of the music company, was interested. The budget was set at around $7 million, and Cimino faced such strict time limitations that he was forced to dress sets for winter in the midst of heat waves. He wrote a script while scouting locations, ultimately settling on eight locations in Ohio, Pennsylvania, and West Virginia to stand in for the steel town of Clairton. Cimino sent his material to several writers for advice, then worked with Deric Washburn on the final draft. (In a 2002 interview with Nancy Griffin, Cimino said that EMI approached him with a story about a U.S. soldier who remains in Saigon to play Russian roulette; Louis Garfinkle and Quinn K. Redeker wrote a screenplay with some similar plot elements, and received screen credit after arbitration.)

Roy Scheider had been considered for the lead role, but once Robert De Niro agreed to the part, the rest of the cast fell into place quickly. De Niro was instrumental in obtaining Meryl Streep, who had appeared in *Julia* (1977), but who was primarily known as a stage actress. This was John Cazale's fifth and last film. He was suffering from bone cancer and would die before the film's release. Many of the other cast members were nonactors: steelworkers, an actual priest, etc. Both John Savage and Christopher Walken had been around for a while—Walken had been a child actor, and once danced in a nightclub act with Mamie Van Doren—but their appearances here helped define their future careers.

Shooting started on June 27, 1977, with a wedding sequence that ended up occupying over an hour of screen time. That summer production moved to the Cascade Mountains in Washington for a month, where Cimino shot hunting sequences that were supposed to be occurring outside Pittsburgh. The next stage took place in Thailand, where some six thousand extras were used to stage the fall of Saigon. The crew shot the film's prisoner of war torture sequences in the Katchanaburi district near the River Kwai. Cimino instructed his actors to slap each other for real when the script required it in order to get more realistic performances. As Walken said later, "When somebody belts you fifty times, you don't have to fake a reaction. You don't have trouble shaking." A helicopter accident almost killed cinematographer Vilmos Zsigmond, and forced De Niro and Savage to jump some thirty feet into a river.

By this time EMI had agreed to share costs with Universal, who would distribute the film in most areas. (The final budget was estimated at $15 million, more than twice the original cost.) Cimino's first cut was close to four hours, alarming studio executives. He came back with a three-hour cut; Universal wanted a two-hour version. But after two previews, audiences responded better to the longer *Deer Hunter*.

On its release in December 1978, *The Deer Hunter* was a qualified success. It grossed about twice its budget, and did well overseas. Many critics praised it, but a significant number reviewed it harshly. It received nine Oscar nominations, winning five awards. However, protestors picketed the film outside the Oscar ceremonies. De Niro would later call this his most physically challenging film, and cited a reunion scene with Savage as some of his best work. But Streep was quoted as calling her role "a man's view of a woman."

Working with Zsigmond, among the most talented cinematographers of his time, Cimino achieved a layered visual style dense with information. His frames are as crammed with people and props as a Sternberg movie. Cimino the writer thinks in operatic terms, inflating the mundane to high emotion, turning pop ephemera into spiritual epiphanies. When he is on, the effect is uncanny. A mentally disturbed Nicky (Walken) lurches into a Saigon strip joint, with Gladys Knight and the Pips' "Midnight Train to Georgia" barely discernible on the soundtrack. The lyrics match not only Nicky's mood, but his place in the narrative.

Cimino strips away what doesn't interest him, focusing—at length—on moments of intense emotion. He is also masterful with sweeping gestures—a parade of refugees on a dirt road, body bags and coffins lined up in a hospital courtyard, the flood of humanity on a Saigon street at night. As well as anyone in his period, he knew how to operate the machinery of filmmaking.

So how could someone so astute about craft make such regrettable choices? There are mountains in western Pennsylvania, for example; Cimino didn't have to go to Washington to film patently false landscapes. But he was always willing to sacrifice reality for image, as in the film's insistence that Russian roulette was the central pursuit of Vietcong captors and whacked-out, off-duty soldiers. *The Deer Hunter* seems to be saying that life is like a game of Russian roulette, but what does that actually mean? How useful is it in explaining how people live? Is Cimino exploiting a taboo subject for gratuitous purposes? Is he responsible for the rash of copycat suicides that followed the film's release?

By the time *The Deer Hunter* had opened, Cimino was hard at work on his next project. Originally called *The Johnson County War*, it would be released as *Heaven's Gate* in 1980.

Powers of Ten

Frame enlargement from *Powers of Ten. Courtesy of Eames Demetrios*

Pyramid Films, 1977. Sound, color, 1.37. 9 Minutes.
Featuring: Paul Bruhwiler, Etsu Garfias.
Credits: Made by the office of Charles and Ray Eames for IBM. Music composed and performed by Elmer Bernstein. Narrated by Philip Morrison. For the Eames Office: Alex Funke, Michael Wiener, Ron Rosselle and Dennis Carmichael, Wendy Vanguard, Cy Didjurgis, Don Amundson, Michael Russell, Sam Passalaqua. Consultation: John Fessler, Owen Gingerich, Kenneth Johnson, John Paul Revel and Philip Morrison. With thanks to: Chicago Aerial Survey, Graphic Films, Modern Film Effects, NASA, Norman Hodgkin. With much gratitude to Kees Boeke.
Additional Credits: Directed by Charles and Ray Eames. Production supervisors: Alex Funke, Michael Wiener.
Available: Image Entertainment DVD *The Films of Charles & Ray Eames Volume 1* (2000). UPC: 0-14381-9210-2. Also on order from the Eames Office (*www.eamesgallery.com*).

As an educational film that's both informative and fun to watch, *Powers of Ten* is a rare exception to what can be a dreary genre. Conceived by the architectural and design team of Charles and Ray Eames, the film deals with the concept of scale, and how the size of an object changes relative to how and where it is viewed. Disarmingly direct in concept and execution, the film conveys a striking amount of information with a minimum of fuss. It's one of the few educational films that is tied so closely to the medium's capabilities that it simply would not work as well in any other format.

Influential painters and architects, Charles and Ray Eames are perhaps most famous for their furniture designs, especially their chairs. Starting with *Blacktop* in 1952, they also made over 125 films, smart, compact shorts that display considerable technical dexterity as well as ingratiating humor. For one film, the Eames Office staff invented an optical slide printer and animation stand; for another, one of the first computer-controlled movie cameras. Charles shot montages for his friend Billy Wilder's *The Spirit of St. Louis* (1957), and was a consultant with Ray on Robert Wise's *Executive Suite* (1954). But the bulk of their work was in the instructional field, often commissioned by IBM.

The 1977 version of *Powers of Ten* is actually the third filmed by the Eames team, and the last completed before Charles' death in 1978. In 1963 they shot a two-minute prototype, *Truck*

Test, to experiment with the idea of an accelerating camera. The second draft, called *Rough Sketch* (the complete title is *Rough Sketch for a Proposed Film on the Relative Size of Things in the Universe*), is very similar to the final film. In fact, the same actor appears in both.

The third version centers on a man at a picnic in Chicago. It shows what would happen if the camera moved ten times (a power of ten) farther away from the man every ten seconds. Within a minute the camera has pulled back to outer space, then out of the Earth's orbit, through the solar system, and eventually out of the Milky Way. It's a journey that's dizzying and exhilarating at the same time, and one that illustrates a wide variety of scientific principles and theories. When the camera reaches the limits of the known universe, it begins to reverse, speeding back down to Chicago until it reaches the hand of the picnicker. Then it begins a journey to subatomic space, ending on the threshold of quarks.

Powers of Ten took about eighteen months to shoot, at a cost of less than $100,000. It was filmed at 901 Washington Boulevard in Venice, for years the headquarters of the Eames Office. Paul Bruhwiler, a Swiss designer, and Eames staffer Etsu Garfias played the picnickers. The film was narrated by Philip Morrison, a longtime friend of the Eames and an astrophysicist who taught at MIT. Elmer Bernstein composed the score for this and many other Eames films. The production supervisors were Alex Funke and Michael Wiener. (Funke would later win an Oscar for his special effects work in *Total Recall*, 1990, and shot miniatures for *The Lord of the Rings*, 2001.) While Charles Eames shot the opening of the film, there is no director of photography credit. Charles and Ray are the directors of the film, and were in charge of the creative aspects of the movie. Other traditional credits don't really work for *Powers of Ten*, as it was a collaborative effort.

Distributed through Pyramid Films, *Powers of Ten* became one of the most popular educational films of all time, selling prints to tiny public school systems as well as to Harvard University. Prints can still be purchased, in both 16 and 35mm. The film is also available on video and DVD; more than fifty other Eames films are available on video. The original elements are preserved at the Library of Congress, along with some 750,000 slides, photographs, and prints from the Eames Office.

Ray Eames collaborated with Philip and Phylis Morrison on *Powers of Ten*, the first volume in the Scientific American Library (New York: W.H. Freeman, 1982). The definitive book on the Eames Office is *Eames Design* by Ray Eames and John and Marilyn Neuhart (New York: Harry N. Abrams, 1989). An excellent introduction to the work of Charles and Ray Eames is *An Eames Primer* by Eames Demetrios (New York: Universe, 2001); Demetrios also wrote *Powers of Ten Interactive*, a CD-ROM available from the Eames Office.

Manhattan

United Artists, 1979. Sound, B&W, 2.35. 96 minutes. Rated R.

Cast: Woody Allen (Isaac Davis), Diane Keaton (Mary Wilke), Michael Murphy (Yale), Mariel Hemingway (Tracy), Meryl Streep (Jill), Anne Byrne (Emily), Karen Ludwig (Connie), Michael O'Donoghue (Dennis), Tisa Farrow (Party guest), Damion Sheller (Ike's son), Wallace Shawn (Jeremiah), Helen Hanft (Party guest), Bella Abzug (Guest of honor), Victor Truro (Party guest), Gary Weis (Television director), Kenny Vance (Television producer), Charles Levin (Television actor #1), Karen Allen (Television actor #2), David Rasche (Television actor #3), Mary Linn Baker [Mark Linn-Baker] (Shakespearean actor), Frances Conroy (Shakespearean actress), Bill Anthony (Porsche owner #1), John Doumanian (Porsche owner #2), Ray Serra (Pizzeria waiter).

Credits: Directed by Woody Allen. Written by Woody Allen and Marshall Brickman. Produced by Charles H. Joffe. Executive producer: Robert Greenhut. Director of photography: Gordon Willis. Production designer: Mel Bourne. Costume designer: Albert Wolsky. Film editor: Susan E. Morse. Casting: Juliet Taylor. Music by George Gershwin. "Rhapsody in Blue" performed by The New York Philharmonic, conducted by Zubin Mehta. Music adapted and arranged by Tom Pierson. Production manager: Martin Danzig. Assistant director: Fredric B. Blankfein. Unit supervisor: Michael Peyser. Script supervisor: Kay Chapin. Camera operator: Fred Schuler. Gaffer: Dusty Wallace. Key grip: Robert Ward. Set decorator: Robert Drumheller. Costumer: Clifford Capone. Wardrobe supervisor: C.J. Donnelly. Hair stylist: Romaine Greene. Makeup artist: Fern Buchner. Sound mixer: James Sabat. Re-recording mixer: Jack Higgins. Sound editor: Dan Sable. Prints by Technicolor. A Jack Rollins–Charles H. Joffe production.

Additional Credits: Released April 25, 1979.

Available: MGM Home Entertainment DVD (2000). ISBN: 0-7928-4610-9. UPC: 0-27616-85115-4.

The success of *Annie Hall*, both critically and at the box office, seemed a vindication of Woody Allen's personal, introspective approach to filmmaking. For his next project, *Interiors*, he abandoned comedy completely, instead writing and directing a family melodrama in the style of Ingmar Bergman. Allen didn't even appear in *Interiors*, feeling that he had enough viewer support to break with his past work. But *Interiors*, for which Allen adopted an icy style to tell an overwrought story, got a mixed reception from critics and performed poorly in theaters.

Manhattan in one sense was a retreat on Allen's part, back to the same settings and essentially the same characters that audiences had loved in *Annie Hall*. But there were crucial differences. Allen's style of filmmaking was now more elaborate and ambitious. He used black-and-white, a format that had basically disappeared from mainstream movies. The lack of color gave *Manhattan* the aura of a "serious" film, the type that played in art-house theaters. (It was a tactic other directors would employ as well: Martin Scorsese with *Raging Bull*, Steven Spielberg with *Schindler's List*.) Allen also used the 2.35 widescreen format for the first time, and later insisted that the format be retained for the film's television broadcasts and video releases.

Upping the ante was a soundtrack built around melodies by George Gershwin. Allen claimed in interviews that the inspiration for *Manhattan* came from hearing an album of Gershwin's overtures, and the film opens with a crescendo from "Rhapsody in Blue," joined in short order by Allen's voice-over narration. When they were wedded to landscape shots of the broad city skyline, Allen was placing himself on the same level with the iconic architecture and music of the city.

The lush cinematography and score backed up a series of vignettes about wealthy, self-involved overachievers whose neuroses masked an astonishing lack of morals. People lose themselves, Allen said, "because they don't deal with their sense of spiritual emptiness." He intended the film to be "a metaphor for everything wrong with our culture," with, as John L. Sullivan's producers might have said, a little sex. But placing these characters within such opulent and carefully selected settings had the paradoxical effect of making it seem as if Allen approved of them. For the audience, *Manhattan* was entry into a world of privilege that was usually closed off. Viewers didn't want to criticize Allen's characters, they wanted to share in their good luck.

The plot of *Annie Hall* dealt with the shifting balance of power in a relationship by imagining first one and then the other partner betraying their affair. *Manhattan* offered instead two romantic triangles, each operating on

deception and self-loathing. But on a more fundamental level, *Annie Hall* was really about finding a character and actress for Allen to play off of. Diane Keaton's presence made his self-deprecating quips and paranoid reactions funnier, or at least easier to swallow. *Manhattan* lacks that central antagonist, unless Allen was playing against the city itself. It's one thing to give your film a seal of approval from an ex-girlfriend playing a ditzy but lovable free spirit. It's a different matter entirely to suggest, as Allen does, that Manhattan itself is beaming affectionately on him as he turns his preoccupations into one-liners.

Annie Hall featured a number of cameos and up-and-coming actors; *Manhattan* had a cast with narrower appeal. This was the sixth Woody Allen film Diane Keaton had acted in, and after starring in *Interiors* she seemed to have exhausted her potential for the director. She would not have another leading role for Allen until she filled in for Mia Farrow in *Manhattan Murder Mystery* (1993). Michael Murphy had honed his persona as a smoothly glib scoundrel in several Robert Altman films. Meryl Streep was on the verge of breaking through as a major star, and is about as limited here as she was in *Kramer vs. Kramer* that same year. Mariel Hemingway, still a teenager during filming, had previously appeared with her sister Margaux in *Lipstick* (1976), a sordid, preposterous rape thriller. Playing seventeen to Allen's character's forty-two may have seemed like a step up from her debut in an exploitation flick.

Critics of the time stepped gingerly around the age issue in *Manhattan*. "Relationships aren't really the point of the movie," argued Roger Ebert, who also wrote that Hemingway's "certain grave intelligence" ruled out any sense of "an unhealthy interest on Woody's part in innocent young girls." The subsequent events in Allen's life cast a pall over *Manhattan*. When Allen left his longtime partner Mia Farrow for her adopted daughter Soon-Yi Previn (twenty-four years his junior), one-liners couldn't assuage the emotional pain the incident caused. That may be one reason why Allen told an interviewer in 2001 that he was embarrassed by *Manhattan*. "I looked at it and begged them not to release the movie," he recalled. "I said I'd do a free one to make it up."

Alien

Twentieth Century-Fox, 1979. Sound, color, 2.35. 117 minutes. Rated R.
Cast: Tom Skerritt (Dallas), Sigourney Weaver (Ripley), Veronica Cartwright (Lambert), Harry Dean Stanton (Brett), John Hurt (Kane), Ian Holm (Ash), Yaphet Kotto (Parker).
Credits: Directed by Ridley Scott. Screenplay by Dan O'Bannon. Story by Dan O'Bannon and Ronald Shusett. Produced by Gordon Carroll, David Giler and Walter Hill. Executive producer: Ronald Shusett. Associate producer: Ivor Powell. Music by Jerry Goldsmith. Conducted by Lionel Newman. Film editor: Terry Rawlings. Director of photography: Derek Vanlint. Production designer: Michael Seymour. Art directors: Les Dilley, Roger Christian. "Alien" design: H.R. Giger. "Alien" head effects created by Carlo Rambaldi. Special effects supervisors: Brian Johnson, Nick Allder. Title design: Steven Frankfurt Communications, R. Greenberg Associates, Tony Silver Films. Visual design consultant: Dan O'Bannon. Concept artist: Ron Cobb. Production manager: Garth Thomas. Editor: Peter Weatherley. Sound editor: Jim Shields. Production sound mixer: Derrick Leather. 1st assistant director: Paul Ibbetson. Costume design: John Mollo. Make-up supervisor: Tommy Manderson. Make-up: Pat Hay. Hairdresser: Sarah Monzani. Set decorator: Ian Whittaker. Stunt co-ordinator: Ray Scammell. Stunt work: Eddie Powell. Recorded in Dolby Stereo. Filmed in Panavision. Prints by DeLuxe. A Brandywine–Ronald Shusett production.
Additional Cast: Baloji Badejo ("Alien"), Helen Horton (Voice of "Mother").
Additional Credits: Production dates: July 5, 1978 to December 1978. Released May 25, 1979.
Awards: Oscar for Best Effects–Visual Effects (H.R. Giger, Carlo Rambaldi, Brian Johnson, Nick Allder).
Other Versions: *Aliens* (1986), directed by James Cameron. *Alien 3* (1992), directed by David Fincher. *Alien Resurrection* (1997), directed by Jean-Pierre Jeunet. *AVP: Alien vs. Predator* (2004), directed by Paul W.S. Anderson. *AVP: Alien vs. Predator—Requiem* (2007), directed by Colin and Greg Strause.
Available: Twentieth Century Fox Home Entertainment DVD (2004). UPC: 024543098508.

At the time of its release, some critics saw *Alien* as a corrective to essentially upbeat science fiction films like *Close Encounters of the Third Kind* and *Star Wars* (both 1977). For screenwriter Dan O'Bannon, it was a chance to make *Dark Star* the right way. After an unhappy childhood in St. Louis, O'Bannon studied film at USC, where he met aspiring director John Carpenter. The two collaborated on *Dark Star*, a zero-budget comedy set aboard a spaceship. Originally a student film, it received a theatrical release in 1974. Undeniably clever, *Dark Star* was undone by its limited financing, resulting in a monster O'Bannon compared to a beach ball.

Producer Ron Shusett, a fan of *Dark Star*, approached O'Bannon for help with a script that eventually became *Total Recall* (1990). Shusett read the opening pages of O'Bannon's *Alien* script, added some crucial suggestions, and began pitching it to studios. They were about to sign a deal with Roger Corman when Mark Haggerty, another producer, brought the script to Brandywine, a new production company formed by writer and director Walter Hill and producers David Giler and Gordon Carroll. Accounts differ over how much the Brandywine people changed the script. Giler credits Brandywine with providing a blue-collar atmosphere to the story, turning it into the equivalent of "truckers in space." The selling pitch for the project now was "*Jaws* in space."

Twentieth Century-Fox, flush with funds from *Star Wars*, turned *Alien* into a big-budget project, partly on the understanding that Hill would direct it. But Hill decided that he didn't have the temperament to work with special effects, leading to the hiring of Ridley Scott. The English-born director had only completed one feature, *The Duellists* (1977), a period melodrama based on a Joseph Conrad story. But he had an extensive background in directing for television and in advertising. (Ridley Scott Associates has been responsible for over three thousand commercials for clients ranging from Chanel to Apple.) Scott believes that it was his detailed storyboards for the script that won him the job.

Scott trained for years as a graphic designer, and the ultimate "look" of *Alien* was arguably as responsible as other elements for its success. Scott won the admiration of O'Bannon by agreeing that the monster would be based on paintings by the Swiss surrealist H.R. Giger, whom O'Bannon had met during a European film project that eventually fell apart. Brought into the mainstream by *Alien*, Giger's sleek, overtly sexual, and brutally vicious monsters had a profound impact on popular culture. Other visual aspects of the film, notably the spaceship designs, were the result of work by artists like Ron Cobb.

The Fox studio exerted some influence over the production, by suggesting that the lead role be changed to a woman, for example. Ripley, originally intended for Veronica Cartwright but then cast with Sigourney Weaver, was one of the crucial creations in science fiction, a heroine who did away with the musty misogyny of authors like Arthur Clarke and Ray Bradbury. Powerful, independent women would soon dominate the genre, and spread into other areas of pop culture as well. *Alien* wasn't the first film to do this—there's Jane Fonda as *Barbarella* back in 1968, for example. But Scott managed to present a potentially divisive character in a matter-of-fact way that appealed to a broad audience, even if she had to strip to her underwear at the climax.

The production took place in England, with the cast increasingly dispirited by the gloomy spaceship set. The resulting film was new primarily in Scott's use of technology, not in any narrative sense. As a story, *Alien* is little more than *The Thing* (1951) set on a spaceship instead of in an Arctic lab. In the same Hawksian manner as that film, characters—some officers, some scientists, some just working slobs—sit around talking until disaster strikes. Then they must cohere to solve problems, picked off one by one in the meantime. O'Bannon freely admitted to stealing from a variety of other sources, while Scott has cited everything from *The Old Dark House* (1932) to *The Texas Chainsaw Massacre* (1974) as influences. (The makers of 1958's *It! The Terror from Beyond Space* filed a lawsuit against Fox that was settled quietly.)

But narrative issues are secondary to what made *Alien* such a popular phenomenon. The sci-fi aspects of the film seemed limited, almost perfunctory, not that far removed from what was available to the public in 1979. Secondhand, broken-down, unreliable equipment; shoddy working conditions; tired, hostile employees arguing over job definitions, pay raises, bonuses—day-to-day life in the future didn't look all that different from the night shift in a chemical plant.

The film's set pieces would become well known through word of mouth almost as soon as the picture opened. Like the attacks in *Jaws* (1975), they became something viewers anticipated, even looked forward to. For better or worse, *Alien* brought the extremes of "body horror" from films like *The Texas Chainsaw Massacre* into the mainstream. The puncturings, dismemberments, even the autopsies were filmed in vivid detail. When Scott added Jerry Goldsmith's tense score to an effects track that alternated between throbbing heartbeats and wheezing gasps, then piled on flashing strobe lights to imagery made more confusing by clouds of steam, he showed a subsequent generation of filmmakers the state-of-the-art way to scare an audience.

Many critics were dismissive of *Alien* when it was released. *Variety* referred to it as "an old-fashioned scary movie set in a highly realistic sci-fi future, made all the more believable by expert technical craftsmanship." It also complained, "The price paid for the excitement, and it's a small one, is very little involvement with the characters themselves. But it really doesn't matter when the screaming starts." The film initiated one of the Fox studio's most successful franchises, resulting in three direct sequels and two spinoffs as of 2008.

Apocalypse Now

Paramount, 1979. Sound, color, 2.35. 153 minutes. Rated R.

Cast: Marlon Brando (Colonel Kurtz), Robert Duvall (Lt. Colonel Kilgore), Martin Sheen (Captain Willard), Frederic Forrest (Chief), Albert Hall (Chief), Sam Bottoms (Lance), Larry Fishburne (Clean), Dennis Hopper (Photo journalist), G.D. Spradlin (General), Harrison Ford (Colonel), Jerry Ziesmer (Civilian), Scott Glenn (Colby), Bo Byers (Sergeant MP #1), James Keane (Kilgore's gunner), Kerry Rossall (Mike from San Diego), Ron McQueen (Injured soldier), Tom Mason (Supply sergeant), Cynthia Wood (Playmate of the Year); Colleen Camp, Linda Carpenter (Playmates); Jack Thibeau (Soldier in trench), Glenn Walken (Lieutenant Carlsen), George Cantero (Soldier with suitcase), Damien Leake (Machine gunner), Herb Rice (Roach), William Upton (Spotter), Larry Carney (Sergeant MP #2), Marc Coppola (AFRS announcer), Daniel Kiewit (Major from New Jersey), Father Elias (Catholic priest), Bill Graham (Agent), Hattie James (Voice of Clean's mother), Jerry Ross (Johnny from Malibu), Dick White (Helicopter pilot).

Credits: Directed and produced by Francis Coppola. Written by John Milius and Francis Coppola. Narration by Michael Herr. Co-produced by Fred Roos, Gray Frederickson, Tom Sternberg. Photography by Vittorio Storaro. Production designer: Dean Tavoularis. Supervising editor: Richard Marks. Editors: Walter Murch, Gerald B. Greenberg, Lisa Fruchtman. Associate producer: Mona Skager. Creative consultant: Dennis Jakob. Music by Carmine Coppola and Francis Coppola. Sound montage and design by Walter Murch. Special assistant to the producers: Doug Claybourne. Executive assistants: Melissa Mathison, Jack Fritz. Music produced by David Rubinson. Art director: Angelo Graham. Set decorator: George R. Nelson. Production managers: Leon Chooluck, Barrie Osborne. Assistant director: Jerry Ziesmer.

Production sound recording: Nathan Boxer. Supervising sound editor: Richard Cirincione. Sound re-recording mixers: Mark Berger, Richard Beggs. Special effects coordinators: Joseph Lombardi, A.D. Flowers. Casting: Terry Liebling, Vic Ramos. Stunt coordinator: Terry J. Leonard. Filmed in Technovision. Titles: Wayne Fitzgerald. Color by Technicolor. Recorded in Dolby Stereo. A Francis Ford Coppola presentation of an Omni Zoetrope release.

Additional Cast: Francis Ford Coppola (Director of TV crew), Vittorio Storaro (TV photographer).

Additional Credits: Music by Mickey Hart. Production dates: March 1976 to August 1977. Released August 15, 1979.

Awards: Oscars for Best Cinematography, Sound.

Other Versions: Coppola oversaw a new edit of the material, *Apocalypse Now Redux* (2001). Directed by Fax Bahr and George Hickenlooper, *Hearts of Darkness: A Filmmaker's Apocalypse* (1991) is a feature-length documentary about the making of *Apocalypse Now.*

Available: Paramount Home Entertainment DVD (2006). ISBN: 1-4157-2093-2. UPC: 0-9736-07068-4-0.

The idea for *Apocalypse Now* was originally developed by screenwriter John Milius and director George Lucas as part of a financing deal between Warner Brothers and American Zoetrope, a production company formed by Lucas and Francis Ford Coppola. When Warners canceled the deal, Lucas went on to make *American Graffiti* (1973) and *Star Wars* (1977). Coppola, meanwhile, immersed himself in two *Godfather* movies (1972 and 1974) and *The Conversation* (1974). (All five of these films are on the Registry.)

Coppola, who thought *Apocalypse Now* should be released for the nation's bicentennial, began to think about directing it himself. Based loosely on Joseph Conrad's *Heart of Darkness*, the story was set in Vietnam at the height of the war. In it, Willard, a psychologically damaged assassin, is sent upriver to terminate Kurtz, an AWOL officer who has attracted a cult of followers. Lucas and his producer Gary Kurtz had envisioned shooting the project on 16mm for under $3 million, but Coppola decided to make the film without the support of studios, using largely his own money.

The director was surprised when stars like Steve McQueen, Jack Nicholson, and Al Pacino turned down his requests to appear in the film. In desperation, he cast Marlon Brando as Kurtz, agreeing to the actor's demands: $11 million for three weeks of work. Harvey Keitel agreed to play Willard, and Coppola filled the rest of the cast with actors from previous films, such as Robert Duvall, Frederic Forrest, and Harrison Ford. When he left for the Philippines in March 1976, Coppola had $17 million for what was planned as a fourteen-week shoot. He also had a release date: April 7, 1977.

A month later, Coppola replaced Keitel with Martin Sheen, whose career had been somewhat static since *Badlands* (1972). Editor and sound designer Walter Murch later said about Keitel, "You tend to watch *him* rather than watch things *through* him." Sheen's open face helped make him more appropriate for a role as an observer, but he was also much easier to manipulate than Keitel. Coppola exploited Sheen's trouble with alcoholism in a notorious hotel room scene, filming the actor with multiple cameras as if for a rehearsal, egging him on when he suffered a heart attack, and then using the material in the final film.

Typhoons that May destroyed sets and forced the production to close. Coppola returned to San Francisco with only eight minutes of film, already $3 million over budget. Back in the Philippines that September, he was spending $150,000 a day on the production. And that was before Brando arrived.

The actor was embarrassed about his weight, over 300 pounds. Despite his previous assurances, he had yet to read Conrad's novel. Brando spent a week arguing with Coppola over the script. When he finally did read *Heart of Darkness* (some accounts say Coppola read it out loud to him), he shaved his head and adopted the name "Kurtz." Since he had insisted on using the name "Colonel Leighley" previously, dialogue for scenes that had been filmed earlier had to be re-recorded.

Coppola now had only two weeks to film with his star. The centerpiece of Brando's performance was a forty-five-minute improvisation which editors pared down to two minutes in the release print. Biographer Patricia Bosworth calculates that between 1975 and 1979, Brando earned $10 million for what amounted to one hour of performing in three films and a television miniseries.

The disasters and dalliances that marked the production of *Apocalypse Now* have been the subject of several articles, a book by Coppola's wife Eleanor, and even a feature-length documentary, *Hearts of Darkness: A Filmmaker's Apocalypse* (1991). Production stopped for a month in December 1976. Sheen suffered his heart attack that March, followed by Coppola's own temporary breakdown. Filming finally ended that May.

When he returned to San Francisco for postproduction, Coppola was almost $20 million over budget. He mortgaged all of his assets for the $10 million needed for editing. Four teams worked on the film. Walter Murch cut from the start to the sampan massacre. Jerry Greenberg did the famous helicopter attack. Lisa Fruchtman put together the Playboy Bunnies concert. Supervising editor Richie Marks was responsible for the rest.

Murch told interviewer Michael Ondaatje that the script originally had a voice-over narration that was dropped in August 1977. But the editor kept reinserting a voice-over so the story would make sense. That narration had been written by Milius and Coppola, but in the spring of 1978, Michael Herr joined the production. His book *Dispatches* had been the definitive account of what the war was like from a personal, ground-level perspective. Herr contributed a total of seven narrations, each dutifully recorded by Sheen. Murch described a "year of evolution" during which a new narration would affect the structure of the entire movie. "The film would change as a result, and then maybe six weeks later we'd go through the whole process again."

The multiple edits indicated that Coppola was unwilling to let go of the project, and was perhaps unsure of what he really had. Some people close to the director thought he was suffering from manic depression, and for years he took prescription lithium. By the time Coppola was ready to release *Apocalypse Now*, *The Deer Hunter* had already amassed five Oscars.

Apocalypse Now contains some of the most memorable scenes and imagery of the 1970s, including a spectacular turn by Robert Duvall that distills everything right and wrong about the nation's involvement in the war into a few crystalline moments. "I love the smell of napalm in the morning" became one of the defining lines of the era. Murch's complex sound design, Vittorio Storaro's precise cinematography, the canny use of music (like Wagner's "Ride of the Valkyries"), the intermingling of real and staged characters and incidents, and Coppola's grandiose vision inspire filmmakers to this day. Despite the personal turmoil around the production, the first half of *Apocalypse Now* is a burst of sustained brilliance that few directors—Coppola included—will ever match again.

In 2001, Coppola released *Apocalypse Now Redux*, a version with approximately forty-nine minutes of deleted footage re-inserted into the original film, as well as a newly engineered soundtrack. The new version adds as many problems as it solves.

The Black Stallion

United Artists, 1979. Sound, color, 1.85. 117 minutes. Rated G.

Cast: Kelly Reno (Alec Ramsey), Mickey Rooney (Henry Dailey), Teri Garr (Alec's mother), Clarence Muse (Snoe), Hoyt Axton (Alec's father), Michael Higgins (Neville), Ed McNamara (Jake), Dogmi Larbi (Arab), John Burton (Jockey #1), John Buchanan (Jockey #2), Kristen Vigard (Becky), Fausto Tozzi (Rescue captain), John Karlson (Archeologist), Leopoldo Trieste (Priest), Frank Cousins (African chieftain), Don Hudson (Taurog), Marne Maitland (*Drake* captain), Tom Dahlgren (Veterinarian).

Credits: Directed by Carroll Ballard. Screenplay by Melissa Mathison & Jeanne Rosenberg and William D. Wittliff. From the novel *The Black Stallion* by Walter Farley. Produced by Fred Roos and Tom Sternberg. Executive producer: Francis Coppola. Director of photography: Caleb Deschanel. Editor: Robert Dalva. Art directors: Aurelio Crugnola, Earl Preston. Music by Carmine Coppola. Production managers: Alessandro von Normann, Ted Holliday. Horse trainer: Corky Randall. Stunt coordinator: Glenn (J.R.) Randall. Supervising sound editor: Alan Splet. Second unit photographed by Stephen H. Burum. Additional photography: Robert Dalva. Assistant director: Doug Claybourne. Optical effects: Modern Film Effects. Titles by Colossal Pictures. Color by Technicolor. Recorded in Dolby Stereo. A Francis Ford Coppola presentation from Omni Zoetrope Studios.

Additional Credits: The Black Stallion is portrayed by Cass-Olé. Additional horses: Junior, Star, Fae-Jur, Olympic, Rex. Shown at the New York Film Festival, September 1979. Commercial release October 13, 1979.

Other Versions: Sequel, *The Black Stallion Returns* (1983), directed by Robert Dalva. Prequel: *The Young Black Stallion* (2003), directed by Simon Wincer.

Available: MGM Home Entertainment DVD (1007). UPC: 027616626998.

Walter Farley's nineteen "Black Stallion" novels have sold over seventy-three million copies since the series originated in 1941. *The Black Stallion* was the first book written by Farley, who grew up in Syracuse, New York, and whose uncle was a professional horseman. He began writing the story in high school, revising it through college and while working as an advertising copywriter. By the time the book became a hit, Farley was in the Army, where he wrote the first of many sequels, *The Black Stallion Returns*.

The books had long been favorites of Francis Ford Coppola, and with some of the profits from *The Godfather* he purchased the movie rights to the entire series. Coppola was attempting to expand his filmmaking capabilities in several directions, establishing Zoetrope, his own production company; pondering the purchases of distributor Cinema 5 and the entire United Artists studio; and announcing a series of children's films, of which *The Black Stallion* would be the first. He assigned Walter Murch and Carroll Ballard to write a screenplay. Murch, the extraordinary sound editor on films like *The Conversation* (1974), had also been a writer on *THX 1138* (1971), George Lucas's first feature. Like Coppola, Ballard had been a film student at UCLA. Since graduating, he had produced *Harvest* (1967), a documentary, and worked on television projects.

Neither Murch nor Ballard, nor Gill Dennis, who helped on the initial draft, liked the book. "I thought it was kind of a *Leave It to Beaver* story," Ballard told Coppola biographer Michael Schumacher. While the opening was unusual, with hero Alec Ramsey shipwrecked on a desert island, "when he gets back home, it's like a million movies, with the horse winning the big race and everything."

Although he was involved with *Apocalypse Now* (1979), Coppola persisted in developing the *Stallion* script. Eventually three writers got screen credit: Jeanne Rosenberg, who had been a script supervisor on a low-budget horror film; William D. Wittliff, who had one television writing credit;

and Melissa Mathison, Coppola's former babysitter. Coppola had already given up future profits on *The Black Stallion* to finance *Apocalypse Now*, and as the start of filming approached, he threatened to cancel the entire production due to arguments with Ballard over the script.

Although "we were in a terrible mess," as Ballard put it, shooting started in the summer of 1977. Instead of using a professional child actor, Ballard chose Kelly Reno, a thirteen-year-old who grew up on a ranch in Colorado. An excellent rider, Reno did all of his stunts in the movie, except riding on the racetrack. There, "I was too small to hold him back," Reno explained, the "him" being prize Arabian show horse Cass-Olé.

The first sequences shot were in and around Toronto, with Reno and costars Teri Garr and Mickey Rooney. Rooney, who had played jockeys in two films and a horse trainer in *National Velvet* (1944), received an Academy Award nomination for his performance as a retired horseman. Bad weather caused extensive delays before Ballard opened the second half of production on Sardinia. Additional scenes were shot at Rome's Cinecittà Studios.

The scope of *The Black Stallion* slowed filmmaking to a crawl. Ballard was not only working with a lead actor who was an amateur actor, but with unpredictable animals on demanding locations. Although Cass-Olé was being handled by Corky Randall, whose credits included *Ben-Hur* (1959) and Roy Rogers movies, the horse was required to perform especially difficult stunts, such as swimming out to a rescue boat. According to *Arabian-Horse-World* magazine, this last scene required stunt doubles for Cass-Olé.

Despite the delays, Coppola was adamant in his support of the film. According to Schumacher, United Artists executives hated the finished product, and considered shelving it. After a screening at the New York Film Festival, *The Black Stallion* had a limited opening. Word-of-mouth helped make it one of the top-performing films of the year.

What endeared the film to audiences was its child's point of view. Ballard, in conjunction with the screenwriters and editor Robert Dalva, constructed a world filled with visual details strong enough to advance the story without dialogue. Stunningly photographed by former USC film school student Caleb Deschanel, the images have the clarity and immensity of those seen by children. They exist on the border of fantasy, and needed lighting so specific that it's no wonder the film endured delays.

Crucial to the success of *The Black Stallion* was its pacing. The film proceeds in fits and starts, expanding and contracting time as a child would perceive it. Dalva received an Oscar nomination in part for the film's climactic match race, built up from camera angles and sound, the gasping of a horse used as a rhythmic device and then merged slowly with the score, crowd sounds swelling and diminishing before, startlingly, a flashback to the desert island. Just as impressive is the minute of film before the race starts, where Dalva cuts among two dozen angles and close-ups to build tension. For sheer terror, few sequences of the time match the opening shipwreck, a dazzling display of cinematography and editing. (A total of twenty-three associate, assistant, sound, dialogue, and additional editors received credit.)

At a time when children's films were often tawdry and uninspired, *The Black Stallion* took its audience seriously, giving youngsters a story and filmmaking that matched the best films geared toward adults. Reno appeared in the sequel, but was injured in an automobile accident and has subsequently left the industry. With the success of *The Black Stallion*, Ballard suffered the equivalent of typecasting. He has directed few films, the majority of them animal related. *Never Cry Wolf* (1983), *Fly Away Home* (1996), and *Duma* (2005) all show the same rich visuals and languid pacing. Coppola oversaw one more children's project, 1983's *The Secret Garden*, but has been too overextended to see through his original plans for younger viewers.

All That Jazz

Twentieth Century-Fox, Columbia Pictures, 1979. Sound, color, 1.85. 123 minutes. Rated R.

Cast: Roy Scheider (Joe Gideon), Jessica Lange (Angelique), Ann Reinking (Kate Jagger), Leland Palmer (Audrey Paris), Cliff Gorman (Davis Newman), Ben Vereen (O'Connor Flood), Erzsebet Foldi (Michelle), Michael Tolan (Dr. Ballinger), Max Wright (Joshua Penn), William LeMassena (Jonesy Hecht), Chris Chase (Leslie Perry), Deborah Geffner (Victoria), Kathryn Doby (Kathryn), Anthony Holland (Paul Dann), Robert Hitt (Ted Christopher), David Margulies (Larry Goldie), Sue Paul (Stacy), Keith Gordon (Young Joe), Frankie Man (Comic), Alan Heim (Eddie), John Lithgow (Lucas Sergeant), Robert Levine (Dr. Hyman), Phil Friedman (Murray Nathan), Stephen Strimpell (Alvin

Rackmil), Leonard Drum (Insurance man), Eugene Troobnick (Insurance doctor), Jules Fisher (Himself), Ben Masters (Dr. Garry), Catherine Shirriff (Nurse Briggs), Joanna Merlin (Nurse Pierce), Leah Ayres (Nurse Capobianco), Nancy Beth Bird (Nurse Bates), Harry Agress (Resident MD), C.C.H. Pounder (Nurse Blake), Tito Goya (Attendant), Tiger Haynes (Porter), Lotta Palfi-Andor (Old woman); K.C. Townsend, Melanie Hunter, Rita Bennett (Strippers); Gary Bayer (Intern), Wallace Shawn (Assistant insurance man). Principal dancers: Sandhal Bergman, Eileen Casey, Bruce Davis, Gary Flannery, Jennifer Nairn-Smith, Danny Ruvolo, Leland Schwantes, John Sowkinski, Candace Tovar, Rima Vetter. Fan dancers: Trudy Carson, Mary Sue Finnerty, Lesley Kingley, P.J. Mann, Cathy Rice, Sonja Stuart, Terri Treas.

Credits: Directed by Bob Fosse. Written by Robert Alan Aurthur and Bob Fosse. Produced by Robert Alan Aurthur. Executive producer: Daniel Melnick. Associate producers: Kenneth Utt, Wolfgang Glattes. Director of photography: Giuseppe Rotunno. Editor: Alan Heim. Production designer: Philip Rosenberg. Fantasy designer: Tony Walton. Costume designer: Albert Wolsky. Music arranged and conducted by Ralph Burns. Choreography by Bob Fosse. Production manager: Kenneth Utt. First assistant director: Wolfgang Glattes. Casting by Howard Feuer, Jeremy Ritzer. Musical coordinator: Stanley Lebowsky. Supervising sound editor: Maurice Schell. Sound mixers: Chris Newman, Peter Ilardi. Make-up: Fern Buchner. Color by Technicolor. Prints by De Luxe.

Additional Credits: Released December 20, 1979.

Awards: Oscars for Best Film Editing, Music—Best Original Song Score and Its Adaptation or Best Adaptation Score, Costume Design, Art Direction–Set Decoration.

Available: Twentieth Century Fox Home Video DVD (2007). UPC: 024543434795.

Winning a Tony for directing *Pippin* and an Oscar for directing *Cabaret* made Bob Fosse feel "terrific for six days. Then, after seven, I thought, it's all false. They made me feel I fooled everybody." The choreographer and director was rehearsing *Chicago* when he fell ill and eventually underwent bypass surgery. After recuperating, he proceeded with work on *Chicago*, which opened the same season as Michael Bennett's *A Chorus Line*.

Fosse then pursued a project at Paramount called *Ending*, written by his friend Bob Aurthur. It would star Keith Carradine and deal with "intimate and universal emotions in dying," according to biographer Martin Gottfried. Fosse reconsidered the project, saying, "I didn't know if I could live with that kind of pain for a year and a half . . . I wanted music and dancing in it." Instead, he and Aurthur interviewed family, friends, and collaborators ranging from screenwriter Paddy Chayefsky to composers John Kander and Fred Ebb, Dr. Edwin Ettinger (who performed his heart surgery), and dancer Gwen Verdon. Armed with the transcripts, Fosse and Aurthur wrote a screenplay over the summer of 1977.

The premise now concerned a compulsive Broadway choreographer who was editing a movie about an abrasive comedian while directing a musical starring his estranged wife, a famous dancer. In other words, Fosse himself. The story would show how "Joe Gideon" dealt with his impending death after driving himself to a heart attack. Fosse got executive producer Daniel Melnick, the former head of MGM, to back the project at his new studio, Columbia, with a budget set at $6 million.

After interrupting work on the film to open the Broadway show *Dancin'*, a sort of career retrospective of his choreography, Fosse began casting. He hired Richard Dreyfuss, not yet the star he would become after *Close Encounters of the Third Kind* (1977), to play the Gideon role. But after eight weeks of rehearsal, Dreyfuss quit, not confident that he could handle his dance scenes. Fosse considered playing the role himself, but agent Sam Cohn suggested Roy Scheider. Melnick, who had wanted Paul Newman, had to be convinced that Scheider would fit.

Fosse was particular about his crew, hiring Tony Walton as set designer and Giuseppe Rotunno as director of photography. Walton had won a Tony for the scenic design for *Pippin*, while Rotunno shot several Federico Fellini features. Filming an opening audition sequence at the Palace Theatre, Fosse complained about Aurthur's persistent coughing. Aurthur, who learned that he was suffering from terminal lung cancer, tried to continue his producing duties from a hospital bed. He ended his relationship with Fosse, and died in November 1978.

Gottfried finds traces of *Sweet Charity*, *Cabaret*, and even *Lenny* in the dance numbers and fantasy sequences that make up the majority of *All That Jazz*. The opening audition number, set to "On Broadway," encapsulates much of Fosse's approach to dance, even while it borrows heavily from the concept behind *A Chorus Line*. On the other hand, the director was reaching for realism, going so far as to film actual open heart surgery, performed by Dr. John Hutchinson. (The address on Gideon's prescription bottle was Fosse's own.) As he did with his earlier films, Fosse went catastrophically behind on his schedule. He was $4 million over his budget when Columbia decided to pull the plug.

Melnick and his colleague Sherry Lansing brought a rough cut of the film to Twentieth Century-Fox, which agreed to add enough to the budget for the director to shoot the four musical numbers he wanted for the death sequence. In return, Fox would split the distribution of *All That Jazz* with Columbia. The final four songs sum up both Fosse's career and his perception of himself. For example, Gottfried compares "They'll Be Some Changes Made" to "Steam Heat," a tune Fosse choreographed in *The Pajama Game*.

Critical reception to *All That Jazz* was mixed. Vincent Canby at the *New York Times* concluded, "Not even Fellini, Ingmar Bergman, or Woody Allen—all of whom are similarly guilt-ridden—has ever celebrated himself quite so cruelly." Few critics found fault with the film's musical numbers, even though some of them veered into vulgarity and parody, hallmarks of Fosse's previous work. The objections were about his approach to the story, which was characteristically maudlin and unfair. Like Chayefsky, Fosse believed that if he criticized himself first, he was free to attack anyone else, friend or stranger. In Fosse's eyes, his alter ego Joe Gideon may be a substance-abusing, womanizing cheat, but at least he isn't as bad as the people he has to deal with: starstruck actress, sycophantic producer, talentless lyricist, duplicitous rival director. In a similar tactic, Fosse tries to defuse critics by including a bad review of his work in the film. Its harsh remarks give Gideon a heart attack. If legitimate critics wanted to point out how pompous, garish, and self-serving the closing number is, would they be putting Fosse at risk?

While *All That Jazz* won four Oscars, none of them went to Fosse. He would direct only one more film, *Star 80* (1983), before his death in 1987 of a massive heart attack.

Ann Reinking performing in *All That Jazz*.

Free Radicals

Direct Film Company, 1958. Sound, B&W, 1.37. 5 minutes.
Credits: A film by Len Lye. Music by the Bagirmi Tribe of Africa.
Additional Credits: Produced by Ann Zeiss.
Notes: Lye re-edited *Free Radicals* in 1979, removing approximately one minute of footage. Assistants on revised version: Paul Barnes, Steven Jones. This version was sponsored by the New Zealand Film Commission.
Available: 16mm prints from Canyon Cinema (*www.canyoncinema.com*). Re:Voir VHS *Rhythms* (2001). ISBN: 3-493551-000242.

Over the course of fifty years, Len Lye created some of the most daring and influential films in the history of the medium. A noted sculptor, painter, and poet as well as filmmaker, Lye was born in New Zealand in 1901. He discovered Maori and Aboriginal art at an early age, and later studied Polynesian dance. They would remain significant influences throughout his career.

Motion became the dominant theme in Lye's art. While still an adolescent, he read about how artists like Constable and the Dadaists grappled with movement in painting. As he wrote later, "All of a sudden it hit me—if there was such a thing as composing music, there could be such a thing as composing motion. After all, there are melodic figures, why can't there be figures of motion?" Lye moved to Australia to study animation, where he began some uncompleted experimental work. By 1929 he was living in London, where he showed his first film, *Tusalava*, an abstract animation with Maori and Samoan overtones that was projected to live music by Jack Ellit.

Lye's breakthrough film was *A Colour Box* (1935), in which he painted directly onto clear celluloid; final prints were released in the Dufaycolor process. Relying solely on lines, dots, patterns, and colors, Lye was able to "animate" "La Belle Créole," a jaunty, percussion-heavy pop tune. He may have been inspired in part by the wave patterns formed by sound on optical soundtracks. In an idea that would be copied by everyone from Walt Disney to Harry Smith, he assigned visual motifs to individual instruments: a strong vertical line for violins, a profusion of dots for pianos. John Grierson, a filmmaker and critic who at the time was the head of a film unit in the public relations office of Britain's General Post Office (GPO), was so taken with a test reel Lye prepared that he commissioned a full version of *A Colour Box*. With the addition of a "cheaper parcel post" tag line, the film could be released as advertising.

Lye developed his style through a succession of commercials for the GPO, Imperial Airways, and Shell Oil. His figures became more complex, and he began incorporating live footage, altered through masking, stenciling, double exposures, overprinting, and a variety of other techniques, notably jump cuts. Lye continued to rely on Latin-influenced big band music, which not only gave his movies a percussive base for editing, but also helped turn them into the some of the most exuberant and joyful artwork of the period. Above all, Lye became a master at not just bringing a kinetic energy to inanimate shapes and objects, but through music and editing finding ways to choreograph them. In his hands they could hop, glide, spin—in short, dance.

With the outbreak of World War II, Lye began making more straightforward documentaries, accepting assignments from the Ministry of Information and from *The March of Time* in the United States. Lye moved to New York in 1944, where he worked full-time for *The March of Time* until the series ended in 1951. He also created kinetic sculpture, fashioning pieces that spun and vibrated to their own metallic soundtracks.

In 1952 Lye released his first "rayogram" or "shadowcast" film, *Color Cry*. He placed string, cloth, and strips of metal on raw stock, covered them with sheets of colored gelatin, and exposed the film with brief bursts of light. It was edited to a rendition of "Fox Chase" by blues musician Sonny Terry, a song that reminded Lye of an escaped slave fleeing a lynch mob.

Lye began a film project he called *Anions* around this time. "I messed around in a form of film doodling trying to find a kinetic image, scratching one on the black emulsion of 16mm film for 4 or 5 months trying to make a 'jump' image that matched up with an ephemeral image-feeling I felt in the back of my skull," he wrote later. But funding was a constant problem. In the meantime, he applied for a grant for a project on "Music Programming on T-V," and completed *Rhythm* (1957) as a sample automobile commercial for Chrysler.

To make *Rhythm*, Lye took stock footage supplied by advertising agency McCann Erickson, ninety minutes of an automobile factory scenes reminiscent of *Master Hands* (1936), and distilled it down to one minute synchronized to African drumming. An audacious exercise in jump cutting, *Rhythm* pulses and throbs while still telling a story, one filled with in-jokes and blithe asides. It took first prize in an art directors' festival until it was disqualified because Chrysler refused to broadcast it.

Lye returned to *Anions*, solving his creative problems with the film in order to meet a deadline to compete in the 1958 International Experimental Film Festival in Brussels. (In a 1963 article called "Is Film Art?" Lye wrote that NBC, CBS, Dupont, Kodak, "and many other institutions" refused to help finance the work.) For the film, now titled *Free Radicals*, Lye scratched shapes onto black 16mm film, timing it to percussive music performed by the Bagirmi Tribe.

Free Radicals strips away most of the effects Lye used earlier in his career: color, recognizable shapes, even melody. He "drew" with instruments ranging from needles to arrowheads to saw teeth, suggesting landscapes, stars, tribesmen, all of which he made "dance" with a grace and vigor that remain startling today. What seems effortless in viewing took a staggering amount of forethought and concentration. Lye wrote later about his wife Ann finding him "standing crouched over a piece of film with my etching needle stuck in it. If I couldn't complete the etched line by forcing the needle to complete the design on the film, then the continuity of a dozen or so designs which preceded it would be lost. So, I wriggled my whole body to get a compressed feeling into my shoulders—trying to get a pent-up feeling of inexorable precision into the fingers of both hands which grasped the needle and, with a sudden jump, pulled the needle through the celluloid and completed the design."

The film won a prize in the Brussels competition, and Lye used similar materials in films like *Prime Time* (1958), *Particles in Space* (revised in 1979), and *Tal Farlow* (completed posthumously in 1980), but for financial reasons he was forced to give up serious filmmaking until shortly before his death. A leading kinetic sculptor in the 1960s, he returned to film in 1978, releasing a revised version of *Free Radicals* the following year. By that time his methods had been adopted in some form or another by almost every experimental filmmaker, and by a large number of commercial artists as well. Lye died in 1980, after halting chemotherapy treatments for leukemia.

Garlic Is As Good As Ten Mothers

Flower Films, 1980. Color, sound, 1.37. 51 minutes.
Featuring: Anzonini del Puerto (Flamenco singer, sausage maker), Kathleen Bendel (Garlic queen), Harrod Blank (Youth saved from dysentery), Mary T. Brown (Cook who uses garlic salt), Robert Charles (La Veielle [Vieille] Maison, Truckee, CA), Henry Chung (Hunan Restaurant, San Francisco), Rose "Pistolias" Evangelisti (Cook, garlic lover), Val Filice (Garlic grower, squid chef), George Flintroy (Flint's Barbeque, Oakland), Lloyd John Harris (Publisher *Garlic Times*), Michael Goodwin (Interviewer, recordist, writer, garlic peeler), Maura Hagerty (Irish garlic eater), Werner Herzog (Film director, *Nosferatu*), Charles Perry (Antivampire writer), Ruth Reichl (Food writer, *New West Magazine*), Lina Stevens (Belly dancer), Alice Waters (Chez Panisse Restaurant, Berkeley), Warren Weber (Organic farmer with Ph.D in Shakespeare), Deborah Wright (Singer, "Garlic Is the Spice of Life"). Chris Pray (Narration).
The Musicians: Flamenco songs: Anzonini del Puerto, with guitar by Kenneth Parker and clapping by Roberto Zamora. Cajun music: The Balfa Brothers with Danny Poullard and Tracy Schwartz; the Louisiana Playboys. French provincial music: Le Camembert. Swiss-Italian music: Irene Herrmann and Paul Hostetter; Ricard Tunzi and Matteo Gasserlind. "Bar be que Bess" sung by Bessie Jackson (1930). Mexican string music: The Marin String Band. Vera Cruz harp group: Bones Jarochos (Courtesy Arhoolie Records). Moroccan music: Feenjon Group (Courtesy Monitor Records). "The Garlic Waltz," composed and sung by Ruthie Gordon.
Credits: Produced, directed and photographed by Les Blank. Editing and sound recording by Maureen Gosling. Researcher: Marina Hersch. Apprentice editors: Maura Hagerty, Frances Politeo. Extra sound and camera: Wim Wenders, John Lumsdraine, James Schnell, Gabriela Schultz, Chris Strachwitz, Michael Goodwin, Charles Plusnick. Interview in Spanish: Merle Linda Wolin. Translator: Paul Shalmy. Sound mix: Marcus Berger at the Saul Zaentz Company. Titles: Licita Fernandez. Mouthwash commercial Courtesy of Lever Bros. Lab: Monaco Labs in San Francisco.
Available: Flower Films VHS and DVD (*www.lesblank.com*).

By 1977, Les Blank had been making films for some twenty years, from commercial and educational films to his own independent projects. His work documented several strands of ethnic music and culture. Yet he found it impossible to find funding for his latest project, a documentary about garlic. The National Endowment for the Arts turned down his grant proposal, calling it "silly," according to Blank. But the director had enough raw stock to start filming Alice Waters at the Chez Panisse restaurant in Berkeley. "I would use any excuse just to hang out in her kitchen."

Blank may have been technically unemployed, but his Flower Films was still distributing his earlier titles to universities, film societies, and other markets. The filmmaker had built up a network of supporters over the years, and he turned to them for help with his newest project. In February 1979, he sent out a request for financial help to those on his mailing list. "I have been making this film over a 3-year period with my own money," he added. That August, he told reporter Ed Halter that he hoped to film garlic material in Korea and France.

He also screened segments of the unfinished film wherever he could. When allowed, Blank would bring AromaRound with him. This was the improved version of his earlier SmellaRound, which he used when screening *Always For Pleasure* (1978), his documentary look at New Orleans culture. SmellaRound consisted of a pot of rice and beans that Blank would simmer in the back of a theater; for AromaRound, he simmered garlic butter or baked whole heads of garlic in a toaster oven.

In later interviews, Blank spoke about the dangers of basing a film on passion instead of a budget. "The garlic film had nothing but resistance from funding sources. I did it anyway, because I like Alice Waters and her principles . . . in the end, German television paid for it."

Time eventually caught up to Blank and his obsessions. Although still a cult figure in 1979, Alice Waters has since become a renowned chef and author. She is currently director of the Chez Panisse Foundation, a board member of local farmers' markets, and an international spokesperson for the "slow food" movement. Blank's film also helped popularize the Gilroy, California, Garlic Festival, which began in 1978 and now draws over 100,000 visitors annually.

As film critic Carrie Rickey has noted, "The shape of a Blank movie is unstructure." *Garlic Is As Good As Ten Mothers* proceeds on a sort of free-association basis, with Blank cutting among dozens of interviews and locations to develop themes and arguments. Archival songs mix with live musical performances, Spanish cuisine with Chinese, garlic lovers with garlic haters. In the process, the director leaves in material that most other filmmakers would take out. Blank shows the stitches and seams holding his film together, revealing to viewers the methods behind his creative process.

Along the way you either accept Blank's theses or watch in exasperation as zealots and missionaries make outlandish statements. Garlic is "one of the foods and medicines that has been at the very foundations of civilization," says Marion Cunningham, author of the Fannie Farmer cookbooks. A self-professed vampire refuses to look at the camera; Blank then cuts to German film director Werner Herzog, who muses in the backseat of a car about why he didn't include garlic in his 1979 version of *Nosferatu*.

In the midst of filming *Garlic*, Blank released *Werner Herzog Eats His Shoe* (1979), a twenty-two minute short in which Herzog does just that, to fulfill a vow he made to filmmaker Errol Morris, at the time working on his first film, *Gates of Heaven* (1978). Blank's relationship with Herzog led to his most fascinating film, *Burden of Dreams* (1982), a documentary about the making of Herzog's *Fitzcarraldo*. A pitiless yet at the same time sympathetic account of a jungle epic gone disastrously wrong, it is one of the best documentaries ever made about the mania that drives filmmaking. Blank is currently working on projects involving calypso music, radical environmentalism, Alabama outsider artist Butch Anthony, durians, sustainable agriculture, and documentarian Ricky Leacock.

Return of the Secaucus Seven

Libra/Specialty Films, 1980. Color, sound, 1.33. 104 minutes. Rated R.
Cast: Bruce MacDonald (Mike), Maggie Renzi (Katie [Sipriani]), Adam Lefevre (J.T.), Maggie Cousineau (Frances), Gordon Clapp (Chip [Hollister]), Jean Passanante (Irene), Karen Trott (Maura [Tolliver]), Mark Arnott (Jeff), David Strathairn (Ron [Desjardins]), John Sayles (Howie), Marisa Smith (Carol), Amy Schewel (Lacey [Summers]), Carolyn Brooks (Meg), Eric Forsythe (Captain), Nancy Mette (Lee), Betsy Julia Robinson (Amy), Cora Bennett (Singer), John Mendillo (Bartender), Steven Zaitz (Singer), Brian Johnston (Norman), Ernie Bashaw (Officer), Jack LaValle (Booking officer), Jessica MacDonald (Stacey), Benjamin Zaitz (Benjamin), Jeffrey Nelson (The Man).
Credits: Written, directed and edited by John Sayles. Produced by William Aydelott, Jeffrey Nelson. Director of photography: Austin De Besche. Score directed and produced by Mason Daring. Written and performed by Guy Van Duser, Bill Staines, Timothy Jackson, Mason Daring. Camera: William Aydelott. Assistant camera: Frank Coleman. Sound: Wayne Wadhams. Gaffer/Key grip: David Arndt. Assistant sound: Fred Burnham. Technical assistant: Michael Rubin. Script supervisor: Elizabeth Shafer. Credit and location stills: Fred Burnham. Assistant to director: Donald McLane. Production assistants: Logan Goodman, Wendell Lees, Carolyn Brooks. Caterer: Ita Roberts. Costume consultant: Deborah Shaw. Assistant editor/Locations: Steven Zaitz. Assistant editor/Unit manager: Maggie Renzi. Post production services: Aydelott Associates. Sound transfer: Bill Gitt. Mix: Magno Sound. Negative cutting: Tri Film Services. Titles: EFX Unlimited. Printing: Du Art Film Labs. Filmed in North Conway, New Hampshire. A Libra/Specialty Films release of a Salsipuedes Productions production.
Additional Credits: Screened at the New Directors/New Films series, New York City, on April 11, 1980.
Available: Metro Goldwyn Mayer Home Entertainment DVD (2003). ISBN: 0-7928-5812-3. UPC: 0-27616-88648-4.

The debut feature for writer, director, and editor John Sayles, *Return of the Secaucus Seven* is an early example of what would become known as "indie films." Born in Schenectady, New York, in 1950, Sayles, the son of educators, received a liberal education in a largely blue-collar society. That dichotomy may be the most distinctive characteristic of his work.

After studying psychology in college, Sayles worked in a variety of menial and laboring jobs to support his writing. He also developed a circle of creative friends in summer theater. His 1977 novel *Union Dues* helped him obtain screenwriting work with producer Roger Corman. Sayles used the money from scripts for films like *Piranha* (1978) to put together his own feature project. "We were just making a movie out of the blue," he said later. "We really didn't know anything about the business."

Sayles based much of the movie on his experiences as an actor in summer theater, drawing on colleagues he had worked with before, like David Strathairn, an approach that made rehearsals easier. "With a very low budget, five-week shoot, you have little time for actors." He took Corman's strategy of disciplined budgeting to new extremes, setting his story in a handful of existing locations that required few props and almost no set dressing. Sayles later boasted that the crew could walk to some of the locations.

Sayles had very deliberate ideas about the script, and did not allow improvisation except for underlying asides in a few group scenes. In part this was to save film, as he did not have the financing for more than two or three takes of any one shot. The director had equally deliberate ideas about shooting, eschewing almost all camera movement because of the time required to light and stage such shots. Sayles made the decision to film in 16mm instead of 35mm partly for financial reasons, but also because he envisioned selling the finished film to public television. That's why the film wasn't made in a widescreen format.

Most of the seven-man crew came from the Boston area. One camera operator had worked on ski documentaries for Warren Miller. The musicians in the film were all under contract to one of the film's producers, an agent in real life.

How seven friends who met as twenty-something anti-war demonstrators coped with life in their thirties became the focus of the film's plot. As one critic put it, *Return of the Secaucus Seven* was about the intersection between culture and politics. In Sayles's words, the male characters chose a "downwardly mobile" path, while the women were adjusting to new possibilities opening up as result of the feminist movement. The subjects and themes of the film echo a Swiss movie directed by Alain Tanner in 1976, *Jonah Who Will Be 25 in the Year 2000*, only condensed and pared.

In a way Sayles was simply taking the narrative apparatus of a film like *Piranha*, which threw a group of disparate characters together, and stripping away the monsters. He was arguing that his characters, with their hopes and problems, their tangled relationships and damaging choices, were as worthy of attention as the larger-than-life, inherently artificial characters played by Hollywood stars in Hollywood movies.

The gamble was whether or not Sayles's taste—his observations, likes and dislikes—could win over moviegoers. The writer in Sayles made a brilliant choice with the title of the project, which allied the film's characters with a movement of the preceding decade that remained popular with his target audience. Suddenly the people in the film weren't aimless, self-centered poseurs, they were martyrs to a cause. Some of the film's topics, like biological clocks and locals priced out of the towns they grew up in, are startlingly prescient for the time.

But Sayles could make poor writing decisions as well. He could betray his vision of the common man by having a desk clerk cite centaurs during a monologue about career goals. At one point the women bond by reciting dialogue from *Salt of the Earth* (1954), a film that was absurdly obscure at the time. One scene features an extended debate about the Boston Police Strike of 1919.

He was also feeling his way as a director. In later interviews he referred continually to the lack of money, which prevented him from being able to correct what he now perceives as mistakes. As his longtime companion Maggie Renzi noted, "We had no costume designer, no makeup or hair." Many of the cast members tend to act with their heads, lifting their chins when making a point, and they often have trouble making eye contact. There is a stiffness, even wariness, to some of the performances. And not many directors would pose nude in their debut film.

In editing the film, Sayles was forced to use the material on hand, even if it included flash frames or a shaky camera. He was also locked into his original script, which consisted of long conversations broken up by brief bits of horseplay. Influenced by the films of director Robert Altman, Sayles hit upon an important strategy. By cutting among two or three separate conversations, he could imply movement and progress within scenes that were actually static. He could also highlight secondary characters, like the auto mechanic played by Strathairn.

Sayles seems apologetic about some of his decisions today. Transitions in the film's montages feel too short, for example. Working in 16mm, he could fashion dissolves only on multiples of eight. An eight-frame dissolve would last about a third of a second, for example. "I just had to make that guess and the optical was done and that was that," he said. The director might also harbor some bitterness about *The Big Chill*, a 1983 film by Lawrence Kasdan that took the premise of this film and turned it into a glossy, superficial, star-driven, and entertaining comic blockbuster. "Very different people," was how Sayles characterized Kasdan's story.

Sayles has followed his stubbornly independent path in over a dozen features, while also building a reputation as a premiere script doctor. He continues to work with Maggie Renzi, who has produced most of his subsequent films. In retrospect, *Return of the Secaucus Seven* helped put into place a new paradigm for filmmaking, one that would be exploited by a generation of indie filmmakers in the coming decade.

Atlantic City

Paramount, 1980. Sound, color, 1.85. 104 minutes. Rated R.
Cast: Burt Lancaster (Lou [Pascal]), Susan Sarandon (Sally [Matthews]), Kate Reid (Grace), Michel Piccoli (Joseph), Hollis McLaren (Chrissie), Robert Joy (Dave [Matthews]), Al Waxman (Alfie), Robert Goulet (Singer), Moses Znaimer (Felix), Angus MacInnes (Vinnie), Sean Sullivan (Buddy), Wally Shawn (Waiter), Harvey Atkin (Bus driver), Norma Dell'Agnese (Jeanne), Louis Del Grande (Mr. Shapiro), John McCurry (Fred), Eleanor Beecroft (Mrs. Reese), Cec Linder (President of hospitalHospital), Sean McCaan (Detective), Vincent Glorioso (Young doctorDoctor), Adele Chatfield-Taylor (Florist), Tony Angelo (Poker playerPlayer), Sis Clark (Toll booth Booth operatorOperator), Gennaro Consalvo (Casino guard-Guard), Lawrence McGuire (Pit Boss), Ann Burns, Marie Burns, Jean Burns (Singers in casinoCasino), Connie Collins (Connie Bishop), John Allmond (Police Commissioner), John Burns (Anchorman).
Credits: Directed by Louis Malle. Written by John Guare. Produced by Denis Heroux. Executive producers: Joseph Beaubien, Gabriel Boustany

[Boustiani]. Associate producers: Justine Heroux, Larry Nesis. Production coordinator: Vincent Malle. Production designer: Ann Pritchard. Editor: Suzanne Baron. Sound: Jean-Claude Laureux. Director of photography: Richard Ciupka, C.S.C. Music composed and conducted by Michel Legrand. Costume designer: Francois Barbeau. Lenses and Panaflex Camera by Panavision. An International Cinema Corporation and Selta Films presentation of a John Kemeny, Denis Heroux production. A Cine-Neighbor Inc. (Montréal) and Selta Films–Elie Kfouri (Paris) co-production, produced with the participation of Famous Players Limited and the Canadian Film Development Corporation.

Additional Credits: Set designer: Gretchen Rau. Production dates: October 31, 1979 to January 1980. Shown at the Venice Film Festival, August 1980. Opened April 3, 1981.

Available: Paramount Home Video DVD (2002). ISBN 0-7921-7914-5. UPC: 0-97360-14604-2.

Although he was grouped with the French New Wave early in his career, director Louis Malle extended his range further than most of his contemporaries. Born into a wealthy family in 1932, Malle received a strict Catholic education before studying political science at the Sorbonne. Switching to film, he was chosen by oceanographer Jacques-Yves Costeau to codirect *The Silent World* (1956). The first of several documentaries in his résumé, *The Silent World* also showed Malle's growing interest in the world's more exotic locations. His first feature film, generally referred to in the United States as *Elevator to the Gallows* (1958), was characteristic of the director's delight with genre pictures and movie stars, in this case Jeanne Moreau. Malle worked several times with Moreau and with Brigitte Bardot, filming them with a respect, even reverence, they did not always receive from other directors.

The Lovers (1958) revealed a preoccupation with sex that would grow stronger throughout Malle's career. Despite the clichés about their country, most New Wave directors were curiously indifferent to sex in their films. Malle not only centered many of his films around sex, he used its shock value as a selling point for his films. *Murmur of the Heart* (1971) treated incest in a lighthearted manner; *Pretty Baby* (1978) presented model Brooke Shields as a twelve-year-old prostitute.

Atlantic City, the follow-up to *Pretty Baby*, came together quickly. Malle had the promise of French and Canadian financing if he could shoot a film within a narrow time frame. Sarandon, who had appeared in *Pretty Baby*, wanted to work with Malle again, and suggested playwright John Guare when the director could not wrestle the script he was working on into shooting shape.

In plays like *The House of Blue Leaves*, Guare addressed success, materialism, celebrity, and other aspects of American culture through absurdity and black humor. These elements all appear in *Atlantic City*, but tempered, first of all by Malle's sympathy for the characters he dissects, but also because the film's rundown locations have their own unassailable poignancy, and because Burt Lancaster agreed to play the lead, an aging petty crook who is forced to confront his delusions.

Lancaster had spent the previous decade alternating between European art films and Hollywood escapism (Bernardo Bertolucci's *1900* in 1976, *Twilight's Last Gleaming* the following year). He brought a relaxed serenity, a sense that he was through fighting useless fights, to his role as Lou Pascal, a numbers runner holed up in a faded apartment building. It was an approach that melded perfectly with Malle's calm, nonjudgmental depiction of emotional and physical violence.

Atlantic City at the time was undergoing a transformation from tired seaside resort to a collection of gambling casinos, and Malle seized upon the demolition of once-grand hotels as an all-purpose metaphor: for the characters in his story, for the decline of American culture, for almost anything. As a result, *Atlantic City* can feel facile, mean-spirited, too willing to stoop to obvious points. (What else can explain the graceless cameo by Robert Goulet, playing a lounge singer performing at the dedication of a new hospital wing?) Its moments of beauty arise almost by accident, like the sunset sky that frames the murder of a drug dealer, or the intersecting planes revealed by a high-angle shot of the boardwalk. Or, in a typically provocative Malle moment, Sarandon rubbing lemon juice over her arms and breasts while Lancaster watches from an adjoining apartment.

Guare's plot revolves around Lancaster's response to an unexpected windfall: stolen cocaine left behind by Sarandon's murdered brother. Like the characters in the Ealing Studios comedy *Tight Little Island* (1949), Lancaster goes on a mild spree, buying a spiffy suit, tipping a rest room attendant, taking Sarandon to expensive restaurants. The cocaine becomes a liberating force for people trapped by debt in lives they don't want, echoing the themes from an earlier spate of counterculture films extolling drugs. *Atlantic City* is a throwback to the cycle of downbeat character studies like *Midnight Cowboy* and *Scarecrow*. It was also Malle's attempt to deal with the multiple characters and story lines used by Robert Altman. But thanks to Lancaster, the film is more resonant as a tribute or farewell—to a classical style of filmmaking as well as to the city's lost splendor.

Critics at the time were enthralled by Lancaster's performance; most also remarked on how "European" the film felt. Lancaster would appear in several more movies, notably *Local Hero* (1983) and *Field of Dreams* (1989), before dying in 1994. For the next decade, Sarandon moved toward commercial projects, like the vampire thriller *The Hunger* (1983), while also becoming more open about her political views. Malle, on the other hand, followed *Atlantic City* with what may have been his most unusual film, *My Dinner with Andre* (1981). Its costar Wallace Shawn can be seen here briefly as a waiter. The Oscar-nominated *Au revoir les enfants* (1987) and *Vanya on 42nd Street* (1994) are highlights of Malle's later career. He died of cancer in 1995.

The Life and Times of Rosie the Riveter

First Run Features, 1980. Sound, color, 1.37. 65 minutes.
Featuring: Lola Weixel, Margaret Wright, Lyn Childs, Gladys Belcher, Wanita Allen.
Credits: Written, produced and directed by Connie Field. Associate producers: Ellen Geiger, Lorraine Kahn, Jane Scantlebury, Bonnie Bellow. Photography: Cathy Zheutlin, Bonnie Friedman, Robert Handley, Emiko Omori. Additional photography: Gordon Quinn, Frances Reid, Dan Drasin, Este Gardner, Debbie Hoffman, Judy Hoffman. Edited by Lucy Massie Phenix, Connie Field. Contributing editor: Peter Adair. Assistant editor: Robert Epstein. Sound recording: Marilyn Lulford, Chat Gunter, Clyde Stringer. Additional sound recording: Este Gardner, Terry Kelley, Lorna Rasmussen, Liz Stevens. Sound editor: Alice Erber. A Clarity Films production.
Additional Credits: Premiered at the New York Film Festival on September 27, 1980.
Available: Clarity Films DVD (*www.clarityfilms.org*).

During World War II, the United States government made a concerted effort to increase the number of women in the civilian workforce. One of the outgrowths of this campaign was "Rosie the Riveter," a fictional defense worker who was the home-front equivalent to "G.I. Joe." The Four Vagabonds recorded "Rosie the Riveter," a song written by Redd Evans and John Jacob Loeb, in 1943. It became popular enough to be used in *Follow the Band* (1943), where it was sung by The King Sisters, and the following year in *Rosie the Riveter*, sung by Kirby Grant.

Follow the Band was released in April 1943. The following month, the May 29 issue of *The Saturday Evening Post* featured a Norman Rockwell cover of a female welder whose lunchbox had "Rosie" written on it. Within a month, real-life Rosies were popping up in newspapers, such as Rose Bonavita, who worked in a defense plant in Tarrytown, New York. Rose Will Monroe was "discovered" by actor Walter Pidgeon in an aircraft factory in Michigan. (Pidgeon was on a tour to raise defense funds.) Monroe later appeared in posters and a government-sponsored short film.

During the war some six million women entered the workforce for the first time. After peace was declared, the number of working women dropped, but not to pre-war levels. Although women continued to be presented in traditional roles in culture, the war brought about a permanent change in society. But by the 1970s, "Rosie

World War II posters like this one by Cyrus Hungerford helped draw women into the workforce, as documented in *The Life and Times of Rosie the Riveter*. *Prints & Photographs Division, Library of Congress, LC-USZC4-5601*

the Riveter" was a largely forgotten artifact of an earlier time. Documentarian Connie Field set out to to explore the truth behind the image.

Field was following two trends by documentarians: to re-examine World War II, as in *The World at War* (1975), and to show the history of the labor movement from a feminist perspective, as in *Union Maids* (1977) and *With Babies and Banners* (1978). Field employed a familiar approach to documentary filmmaking, combining archival footage, photographs, and music with newly filmed oral histories. Where Field is distinct from other documentarians is in her patience and selectivity. She interviewed over seven hundred people in preparing and filming *The Life and Times of Rosie the Riveter*, but distilled the onscreen interviews down to five women. By following their stories in depth, she could provide a sense of the dramatic changes the women underwent, while still making her own points.

The Life and Times follows a chronological pattern, allowing the five participants to explain their backgrounds, their first days on the job, the problems they faced, and then the aftermath to the declaration of peace. Field's subjects include vivid details, like how much money a factory worker made in the 1930s, the subtle and overt discrimination women and minorities faced, what it was like to plow a field, and the limited jobs open to women. The structure of the film—cross-cutting among the women, contrasting them with archival material—allows its facts to emerge gradually, without belaboring political points.

In retrospect at least, Field's five witnesses seem keenly aware of the steps they were taking. Describing the reaction of men when she first started working in a factory, Lola Weixel says, "When a woman walked in, a man went to war," an evenhanded acknowledgment that hostile reactions had a variety of causes. The women generally seem proud of their accomplishments, but the racism they encountered is still galling. Field can be more pointed in these sections, cutting from a newsreel extolling hygiene in plants to a witness describing

how black women weren't allowed to use "whites only" showers.

After the armistice, with up to 70,000 soldiers discharged every month, the women interviewed predictably lost their jobs. Meanwhile, newsreel clips try to re-establish pre-war roles for women. The film also relies heavily on printed documentation: photographs, newspaper clippings, posters, and other ephemera. Field uses zoom lenses and slow pans to give a sense of movement to this static material, a technique that is often credited today to Ken Burns.

Field showed *The Life and Times* at the New York Film Festival in 1980. It was picked up by First Run Features, founded in 1979 to help distribute independent film, and received a brief theatrical release in 1981. It was later broadcast as part of the PBS series, *The American Experience*.

Field has continued making documentaries with Clarity Films. Perhaps as a result of her discoveries in *The Life and Times of Rosie the Riveter*, she has focused on racial issues. *Freedom on My Mind* (1994) examined the history of the civil rights movement in Mississippi. Her current project is *Have You Heard from Johannesburg?*, a series of films on apartheid in South Africa, *Apartheid and the Club of the West* has been screening in film festivals since November 2006.

Raging Bull

United Artists, 1980. Sound, B&W and color, 1.85. 129 minutes.

Cast: Robert De Niro (Jake La Motta), Joe Pesci (Joey), Cathy Moriarty (Vickie La Motta), Frank Vincent (Salvy), Nicholas Colasanto (Tommy Como), Mario Gallo (Mario), Bernie Allen (Comedian), Joseph Bono (Guido), Lori Anne Flax (Irma), Theresa Saldana (Lenore), Frank Adonis (Patsy), Bill Hanrahan (Eddie Eagan), Don Dunphy (Radio announcer, Dauthuille fight), Frank Topham (Toppy), Charles Scorsese (Charlie—man with Como), Rita Bennett (Emma—Miss 48's), James V. Christy (Dr. Pinto). Fighters: Floyd Anderson (Jimmy Reeves), Johnny Barnes (Sugar Ray Robinson), Eddie Mustafa Muhammad (Billy Fox), Kevin Mahon (Tony Janiro), Louis Raftis (Marcel Cerdan), Johnny Turner (Laurent Dauthuille).

Credits: Director: Martin Scorsese. Screenplay by Paul Schrader and Mardik Martin. Based on the book by Jake La Motta with Joseph Carter and Peter Savage. Consultant: Jake La Motta. Producers: Irwin Winkler and Robert Chartoff. Produced in association with Peter Savage. Associate producer: Hal W. Polaire. Director of photography: Michael Chapman. Editor: Thelma Schoonmaker. Production designer in New York: Gene Rudolf. Art directors in Los Angeles: Alan Manser, Kirk Axtell. Visual consultant in Los Angeles: Gene Rudolf. Casting: Cis Corman. Music: Pietro Mascagni (*Cavalleria Rusticana*: Intermezzo; *Guglielmo Ratcliff*: Intermezzo; *Silvano*: Barcarolle). Orchestra of Bologna Munic-op Thetra; Arturo Basile, Conductor. Production manager: James D. Brubaker. First assistant directors: Jerry Grandey, Allan Wertheim. Sound effects supervising editor: Frank Warner. Stunt coordinator: Jim Nickerson. Makeup created by Michael Westmore. Costume designer: Richard Bruno. Sound mixers: Les Lazarowitz, Michael Evje. Script supervisor: Hannah Scheel. Art director in New York: Sheldon Haber. Set decorators: Fred Weiler, Phil Abramson. Boxing technical advisor: Al Silvani. Title design by Dan Perri. Recorded in Dolby Stereo.

Additional Cast: Mardik Martin (Copa waiter), Peter Savage (Jackie Curtie), Martin Scorsese (Barbizon stagehand). Voice of Ted Husing announcing the actual La Motta-Robinson fight (February 14, 1951).

Additional Credits: Production dates April to October 1979. Released in New York City on November 14, 1980.

Awards: Oscars for Best Actor, Film Editing.

Available: MGM Home Entertainment DVD (2005). ISBN: 0-7928-6332-1. UPC: 0-27716-91512-2.

Robert De Niro read Jake La Motta's autobiography while he was working on *The Godfather Part II* (1974), for which he won his first Oscar. La Motta, a one-time middleweight champion, was an Italian from New York City, a reason why De Niro felt that Martin Scorsese would be the ideal director for the project. But Scorsese professed to dislike sports movies, and found little of interest about La Motta. It wasn't until September 1978, a particularly low point in Scorsese's life, that the director began to understand the significance of the project.

Seen as a cautionary tale, La Motta's rise and fall could be applied to Scorsese as well. He had come off several critical hits to make *New York New*

Using cinematography and editing for visceral impact in *Raging Bull*.

York (1977), an expensive faux musical that failed with both reviewers and moviegoers. Like La Motta, Scorsese had gone through a divorce, was in poor health, and prone to substance abuse. De Niro, drawn to the project because it was an acting showcase with intensely physical and emotional scenes, was also using *Raging Bull* as a way to pull Scorsese out of a potentially devastating slide. As Scorsese put it, "I kind of woke up and said, 'This is the picture that has to be made, and I'll make it that way. These are the reasons why it has to be made.' I understood then what Jake was, but only after having gone through a similar experience myself."

When he optioned the book, De Niro hired Mardik Martin, one of the writers of *Mean Streets* (1973), to adopt it into a screenplay. Both Scorsese and De Niro were disappointed with what Martin submitted. Scorsese asked Paul Schrader, the writer of *Taxi Driver* (1976), to help. Schrader restructured what had been a chronological story line, altered the part of La Motta's friend Peter Savage (a pseudonym for Pete Petrella) into his brother Joey, and added what he once considered his finest piece of writing: a three-page soliloquy in which La Motta, in jail on a morals charge, masturbates over memories of the women in his life, only to smash his hand against the cell wall when remorse renders him impotent.

United Artists executives blanched when they read Schrader's take. Producers Robert Chartoff and Irwin Winkler had been looking for a corrective to their previous boxing movie, *Rocky* (1976), but *Raging Bull* in this form was too strong. De Niro took Scorsese to the Caribbean island of St. Martin for three weeks to rewrite the script.

"I always thought there was something very decent about him somewhere," De Niro said about La Motta, who received a consultant credit on the finished film. But finding that spark of humanity

became secondary to depicting the fighter's primal appetites, the driving narrative force to both the script and the film. For De Niro the project became a series of moments in the fighter's life, moments of complete emotional and physical exposure. The actor was more concerned with the truthfulness of his work, how real and honest it was, than with judging La Motta's real and perceived flaws. Part of this truthfulness extended to De Niro's regimen of training, not just getting into fighting shape, but gaining weight to show the fighter's dissolute decline.

Scorsese saw the dozen or so fights included in the film as a series of puzzles to be solved, as well as a violent correlative to what the La Motta character was experiencing in day-to-day life. In the first fight against Jimmy Reeves, the editing is almost subliminal, the action reduced to a blur, editor Thelma Schoonmaker slamming together half-second shots that elide the beginnings and ends of punches. Cinematographer Michael Chapman shot in a style reminiscent of newsreels, but was free to move his camera in any direction in the ring, following Scorsese's meticulous pre-planning. (Both photographer and director realized that the film would be too grotesquely bloody in color after shooting some 8mm test footage.)

By the fourth and fifth fight, Scorsese is covering entire bouts in two or three still photographs, saving the most brutal imagery for a fight in which La Motta takes a dive, and his last rematch with Sugar Ray Robinson. It's a measure of the creative expertise in *Raging Bull* that the fights ultimately become secondary to the human drama.

De Niro suggested Joe Pesci to Scorsese as La Motta's brother Joey. Pesci, a former child actor, had been a member of Joey Dee and the Starliters, the house band at New York City's Peppermint Lounge in the 1960s. When De Niro approached him, Pesci was ready to leave show business entirely. He recommended seventeen-year-old Cathy Moriarty to casting director Cis Corman as La Motta's wife Vickie. After rehearsing with De Niro and Scorsese for three months, Moriarty was hired in February 1979.

Shooting began in April 1979, with a schedule of five weeks of fight scenes, ten weeks of dramatic scenes, two months off for De Niro to gain sixty pounds, and then three weeks of "fat" scenes. (Scorsese also took time off to marry Isabella Rossellini.) Scorsese became obsessed with the editing of the film, particularly the sound, and threatened to take his name off the project when Irwin Winkler insisted on sending the print to the lab to be duplicated before the director felt it was finished. By that time the real Joey La Motta was suing Joe Pesci for $2.5 million, and movie star Marcello Mastroianni was belittling De Niro's acting methods.

Consistently voted onto top ten lists for the year, the decade, and sports movies in general, *Raging Bull* found both Scorsese and De Niro deeply committed to filmmaking as a process, a way to test their skills, and as a chance for them to reinterpret the 1950s and '60s. What they had to say about La Motta—that he really was a raging bull with elemental appetites, that he might have been a better person had he not been forced to compromise by the mob, that he was a masochist who lashed out at those around him in order to earn his punishments—was ultimately not as interesting as how they said it. They were targeting an audience that largely didn't know anything about La Motta or boxing, and many viewers may have subsequently mistaken technique for insight. Scorsese, De Niro, and Pesci would work together again on *GoodFellas* (1990), another Registry title.

Raiders of the Lost Ark

Harrison Ford as Indiana Jones in *Raiders of the Lost Ark*.

Paramount, 1981. Sound, color, 2.35. 115 minutes. Rated PG.
Cast: Harrison Ford (Indy [Indiana Jones]), Karen Allen (Marion [Ravenwood]), Paul Freeman (Belloq), Ronald Lacey (Toht), John Rhys-Davies (Sallah), Alfred Molina (Satipo), Wolf Kahler (Dietrich), Anthony Higgins (Gobler), Denholm Elliott (Brody), Vic Tablian (Barranca), Don Fellows (Col. Musgrove), William Hootkins (Major Eaton), Bill Reimbold (Bureaucrat), Fred Sorenson (Jock), Patrick Durkin (Australian climber), Matthew Scurfield (2nd Nazi), Malcolm Weaver (Ratty Nepalese), Sonny Caldinez (Mean Mongolian), Anthony Chinn (Mohan), Pat Roach (Giant Sherpa), Christopher Frederick (Otto), Tutte Lemkow (Imam), Ishaq Bux (Omar), Kiran Shah (Abu), Souad Messaoudi (Fayah), Vic Tablian (Monkey man), Terry Richards (Arab swordsman), Pat Roach (1st mechanic), Steve Hanson (German agent), Frank Marshall (Pilot), Martin Kreidt (Young soldier), George Harris (Katanga), Eddie Tagoe (Messenger pirate), John Rees (Sergeant), Tony Vogel (Tall captain), Ted Grossman (Peruvian porter).
Credits: Directed by Steven Spielberg. Screenplay by Lawrence Kasdan. Story by George Lucas and Philip Kaufman. Produced by Frank Marshall. Executive producers: George Lucas, Howard Kazanjian. Production designer: Norman Reynolds. Director of photography: Douglas Slocombe. Associate producer: Robert Watts. Editor: Michael Kahn. Music: John Williams. Casting: Mike

Fenton & Jane Feinberg, Mary Selway. Second unit director: Michael Moore. Stunt co-ordinator: Glenn Randall. Costume design: Deborah Nadoolman. Visual effects supervisor: Richard Edlund. Mechanical effects supervisor: Kit West. Additional photography: Paul Beeson. Art director: Leslie Dilley. Set decorator: Michael Ford. Chief make-up artist: Tom Smith. Make-up artist: Dickie Mills. Chief hairdresser: Patricia McDermott. Hairdresser: Mike Lockey. Stunt arranger: Peter Diamond. Sound design: Ben Burtt. Supervising sound effects editor: Richard L. Anderson. Production sound: Roy Charman. Special visual effects production at Industrial Light and Magic. A Paramount Pictures presentation of a Lucasfilm Ltd. production.
Additional Credits: Photographed in France, Tunisia, Hawaii, EMI Elstree Studios, Borehamwood, England. Released June 12, 1981.
Awards: Oscars for Art Direction–Set Decoration, Effects–Visual Effects, Editing, Sound.
Other Versions: Sequels include *Indiana Jones and the Temple of Doom* (1984), *Indiana Jones and the Last Crusade* (1989), *Indiana Jones and the Kingdom of the Crystal Skull* (2008), all directed by Steven Spielberg. The television series *The Young Indiana Jones Chronicles* ran in 1992.
Available: Paramount VHS (1999). ISBN: 0-7921-5784-2. UPC: 0-9736-01376-1-3. Paramount DVD (2003). UPC: 097360612547.

Now a franchise of four features, *Raiders of the Lost Ark* was hatched on a beach on Maui, as George Lucas, recuperating from *Star Wars*, and Steven Spielberg, almost ready to release *Close Encounters of the Third Kind*, were discussing their next projects. Spielberg wanted to do a James Bond picture, but Lucas said he had a better idea: an old-fashioned adventure about an archeologist searching the world for treasure. Lucas agreed that Spielberg would direct it.

First came Spielberg's *1941* (1979), a World War II comedy that remains his most problematic film. Since its budget ballooned out of control, he approached *Raiders* as a director-for-hire, out to prove he could film frugally and responsibly. Lucas and Spielberg demanded from studios an unprecedented share of profits, requiring a year of negotiations between the filmmakers and Michael D. Eisner, at the time the head of Paramount. The deal would ultimately give Lucasfilm the negative, but also required the production company to supply Paramount with four sequels.

Although he was deeply involved in *The Empire Strikes Back*, the first *Star Wars* sequel, Lucas exerted considerable control over the *Raiders* script. Its hero, Indiana Jones, was a wish fulfillment fantasy for Lucas: a hero, a brain, a playboy, and a practical joker who was quick with a quip. Indy's style and humor was more frat boy than man of the world, however. Lucas claimed that the inspiration for the story came from the serials and series films of the 1930s and '40s—*Flash Gordon*, *Batman*, Zorro, Lash La Rue, etc.—but the sensibility driving *Raiders* was more attuned to television of the 1950s and adolescence in the 1960s. In the first Indiana Jones film, at least, girls are still kind of icky, villains sport monocles and bad accents, and nothing says manliness more than knocking back shots from an unlabeled bottle of liquor.

Neither Lucas nor Spielberg had actually seen the serials they were updating, and both were dismayed after screening fifteen chapters of *Don Winslow of the Navy*. "I was so depressed that I walked out of the theater thinking, 'How can I get out of this?'" Spielberg said later.

Writer and director Philip Kaufman added a crucial element to the story, the search for the Ark of the Covenant. It was an angle that appealed to Spielberg's religious interests, both his perception of himself as a Jewish outsider and his desire to portray Judaism in a heroic light.

Spielberg hired screenwriter Lawrence Kasdan on the basis of his script for *Continental Divide* (1981), a romance that was eventually filmed with John Belushi and Blair Brown. Kasdan thinks his affinity for Howard Hawks—for snappy patter and strong woman characters—may have gotten him the job. Kasdan met with Spielberg and Lucas for five days of intense meetings, then used taped transcripts of their discussions to fashion a script over the next six months. The two directors offered a slew of ideas that wound up in the film: a giant boulder that menaces Indy, a monkey that uses the Nazi salute, for example, as well as some that ended up in the first sequel.

Spielberg had planned to cast Amy Irving as Marion Ravenwood, Indy's love interest, but broke up with her before filming started. Karen Allen got the part instead, according to Spielberg because of her spunkiness in *National Lampoon's Animal House* (1978). Allen later faulted aspects of her character. "I couldn't understand why Marion would wear a dress in the desert. Was she going to seduce Belloq?" She tried improvising scenes with Paul Freeman, who played Belloq, but Spielberg wasn't interested in veering from the script.

Lucas and Spielberg cast Tom Selleck in the lead role, but a few weeks before shooting was to start they learned he was committed to a CBS television series, *Magnum P.I.* Harrison Ford, Han Solo in *Star Wars*, was an obvious choice for a replacement.

Filming took place over sixteen weeks, with Lucas present for five of them (and responsible for some second unit footage). Some *Star Wars* locations in Tunisia were used, as well as several *Star Wars* crew members. This was Spielberg's first collaboration with producer Frank Marshall; they would continue to work together throughout the 1980s (along with Marshall's future wife Kathleen Kennedy). With their help, and that of Lucas's collaborator Howard Kazanjian, *Raiders* became the first film Spielberg finished on budget.

It may be difficult to judge today how purely escapist *Raiders* was on its release. Adventure films of the time were not only B-movies, they were almost uniformly conservative, even redneck, movies about car chases, shoot-outs, and fistfights. Spielberg was working on a more highbrow level, evoking *Only Angels Have Wings* (1939) and *Citizen Kane* (1941) more than *Smokey and the Bandit* (1977). At the same time he was reaching for the *Star Wars/Close Encounters* audience:

juvenile, uninterested in irony and complexity, most likely completely unaware of the targets of the film's satire. How old movies used backlots and process footage to pass for foreign locales, for example. Here Hawaii passed for South America, and Tunisia did double duty as Egypt and a mysterious volcanic island.

It's not clear how aware Spielberg was at the time of some of the film's narrative overtones. Most viewers can appreciate how the end of the movie refers to Passover, a connection emphasized by several shots reminiscent of Paramount's earlier blockbuster, *The Ten Commandments* (1956). But did Spielberg really want to suggest that the only way to be saved was to not watch the end of his film? And is it coincidence that his death-dealing wraiths resemble silent movie actresses of the 1920s?

Where *Raiders* succeeds best is in its stunt-work, in its intricately constructed set pieces, and in Michael Kahn's marvelously quick and clean editing. The film's punches, kicks, crashes, swordfights, whippings, topplings, and collisions stand up to anything from Hollywood's Golden Age. Combined with Ford's macho insouciance, they were an enormous influence on filmmakers, both in the United States and abroad. Jackie Chan, for example, has used both the general plotline and specific stunts from *Raiders* in several of his movies.

Few imitators were able to duplicate Spielberg's technique, his ability to depict the cause-and-effect clockwork of action scenes, his grasp of details large and small. As Allen noted, "It's all bits and pieces—it could take weeks to move from one part of the frame to another." Spielberg's hold on those pieces is what gave *Raiders* its life, what made it exciting. The film earned over $360 million, and was Paramount's box-office champion until *Forrest Gump* in 1994.

Chan Is Missing

New Yorker Films, 1982. Sound, B&W, 1.37. 76 minutes.

Cast: Wood Moy (Jo), Marc Hayashi (Steve), Laureen Chew (Amy), Peter Wang (Henry), Presco Tabios (Presco), Frankie Alarcon (Frankie), Judy Nihei (Lawyer), Ellen Yeung (Mrs. Chan), George Woo (George), Emily Yamasaki (Jenny), Virginia R. Cerenio (Jenny's Friend), Roy Chan (Mr. Lee), Leong Pui Chee (Mr. Fong).

Credits: Produced and directed by Wayne Wang. Script: Terrel Seltzer, Wayne Wang. Narration: Isaac Cronin, Wayne Wang. Cinematography: Michael Chin. Additional cinematography: Kathleen Beeler. Sound recording: Curtis Choy. Additional sound recording: Sara Chin. Edited by Wayne Wang. Editorial consulting: Rick Schmidt. Music: Robert Kikuchi-Yngojo. Chinese pop music: Sam Hui, courtesy Polygram Records, Ltd. Suspense music courtesy Steve Shapiro/Sound Service. Production management: Sara Chin. Production assistance: Julian Low, Don Wong, Bob Yano. Continuity: Piera Kwan. Production grant from The American Film Institute in association with The National Endowment for the Arts. Copyright 1981 Wayne Wang Productions.

Additional Credits: Opened theatrically June 4, 1982.

Available: Koch Lorber Films DVD (2006). ISBN: 1-4172-0096-0. UPC: 7-41952-30809-6.

Despite the presence of some Asian-American stars in the early days of Hollywood, the film industry usually relied on Caucasians in disguise when depicting Asians. Just as many whites appeared in blackface, actors like Paul Muni, Louise Rainer, and Katharine Hepburn taped their eyes and wore makeup for films like *The Good Earth* (1937) and *Dragon Seed* (1944).

By the 1980s, the same San Francisco Chinatown extolled by Rodgers and Hammerstein in *Flower Drum Song* as an exotic spot for tourists had grown into a mature, self-assured community eager to deal with the mainstream. The benefits of the civil rights movement extended to Asian-Americans as well as African-Americans, leading to a willingness among younger members to both assert their independence and stake their claim to ethnic legitimacy. This wary, tentative pride is one of the distinguishing characteristics of *Chan Is Missing*, one of a handful of Asian-American features since the silent era.

Street theater became a popular method of expressing the changing mood in San Francisco's Chinatown. The Asian-American Theatre Company came from this movement. It coincided with a growing prominence of Chinese culture in general, from the international success of Bruce Lee to the burgeoning film industry in Hong Kong. When Wayne Wang arrived in San Francisco committed to making a film about Chinese Americans there, he found a full complement of professionals—actors and creative technicians—ready to help him.

Born in Hong Kong in 1949, days after his family fled Communist China, Wang went to college in California, earning a masters in film and television. He moved to Hong Kong, where he directed segments of films and TV episodes, but soon returned to San Francisco. There he codirected *A Man, a Woman and a Killer* (1975) before becoming involved in community activism. He had originally intended his next project to be an experimental film. *Fire over Water* would be a combination of city symphony à la *Menschen am Sontag* and ethnic documentary. Wang started work with a $10,000 grant from the American Film Institute.

Most of his crew had day jobs, limiting the time Wang could shoot to ten consecutive weekends. They tended to work for free or for deferred salaries, proud to be contributing to a legitimately Asian-American project. For an actor like Wood Moy, the struggle for acceptance had been a lifelong one. A New York native, Wood became interested in acting while attending St. John's University in Shanghai. When he returned to the United States, he formed his own theater group, balancing the need for an income with the desire to portray Chinese characters with honesty and dignity. It was a time when Asian-Americans were limited in what they were allowed to do—essentially working in restaurants, laundries, and printing. Wood was in fact working in a printing plant when he decided to return to acting in his fifties. His most notable film role prior to *Chan Is Missing* was as a launderer in the 1978 version of *Invasion of the Body Snatchers*.

Wood was one of the first actors cast in *Chan*, and he participated in the auditions to find his screen partner. Marc Hayashi was a veteran of street theater, someone attuned to pop culture, able to mix traditional with contemporary. Mutt to Wood's Jeff, he was also adept at improvising, sometimes throwing his more conservative elder.

Wang started with an experimental framework, but the film was shifting into a more feature-oriented mode. With a premise tied to the search for an elusive Chan Hung, *Chan* became a snapshot of Chinatown, a cross-section that ranged from community service organizations to businesses to homes and tourist sites like the Golden Gate Bridge. Along the way Michael Chin's camera captured souvenir parlors, martial arts movie theaters, classrooms, government offices, and the cramped alleys and apartments of Chinatown.

As sound recordist Curtis Choy put it, this was collective filmmaking, with contributions from everyone involved. While Wang wanted, in Choy's words, "to invert film conventions," the cast and crew guided him through the many layers and complications of Chinatown life. An

outsider himself, Wang could provide a fresh angle on overly familiar locations and situations. His documentary impulses, his love of faces, particularly of the elderly, shine through in many sequences. Manilatown Senior Center provides the backdrop for some of the film's most moving footage: portraits of members dancing, sitting, staring with stoic expressions into the camera. Almost all of the scene was shot on the spur of the moment.

Chan Is Missing is a film attuned to the fortuitous, the accidental, the stumbled-across. Like the opening shot, filmed through the windshield of Wood's cab as he drives down a street, the reflections of the buildings marking a perfect line between light and dark, between blindness and sight, between insight and confusion. The only real plot: Jo (Wood's role) and his nephew Steve (Hayashi) need to talk to Chan Hung about $4,000 they want to invest in subleasing a taxi license. Their search will take them through all that Chinatown offers.

But what does the search mean? Can Chan, a sort of Chinese Everyman, ever be "found"? As Jo and Steve circle around their target, different aspects of his character emerge: immigrant, husband, father, adulterer, worker, anti-Communist, dropout, even potential criminal. But the true core of the film is a remarkable handheld shot filmed in one take on a pier near the Golden Gate Bridge. In the shot, which lasts almost three minutes, Jo confronts Steve about Chan, in the process exposing the central conflicts between their generations. "That scene is my proudest moment as an actor," Hayashi said later.

Wang throws in halfhearted references to the conventions of mainstream film—there's a noirish search of an apartment, a chase of sorts down city sidewalks—but the thrust of the film is exploratory, experimental. So experimental that the cast and crew alike complained loudly when Wang screened a rough cut. Aided with a $12,500 grant from the National Endowment for the Arts, the director returned to the film with screenwriter Isaac Cronin, writing a narration that made many of the implied themes more explicit, removing much of the film's ambiguity.

The revised version of the film received its public premiere during the 1982 Asian American Film Festival in San Francisco. Stephen Gong, now a film archivist, described an enraptured audience fully tuned in to a movie that depicted their lives, their destinies. Vincent Canby at *The New York Times* called the film "a matchless delight." Critical reaction like that was strong enough to merit a theatrical release for the film, albeit one limited to art-house theaters in larger cities. The repercussions for Wang were significant. He embarked on a directing career that included art-house titles like *Smoke* and *Blue in the Face* (both 1995) as well as commercial films like *The Joy Luck Club* (1993) and *Last Holiday* (2006).

E.T. The Extra-Terrestrial

Universal, 1982. Sound, color, 1.85. 115 minutes. Rated PG.
Cast: Dee Wallace (Mary), Peter Coyote ([Keys]), Robert Macnaughton (Michael), Drew Barrymore (Gertie), Henry Thomas (Elliott), K.C. Martel (Greg), Sean Frye (Steve), Tom Howell [C. Thomas Howell] (Tyler), Erika Eleniak (Elliott's girlfriend), David O'Dell (Schoolboy), Richard Swingler (Science teacher), Frank Toth (Policeman), Robert Barton (Ultra sound man), Michael Darrell (Van man); David Berkson, David Carlberg, Milt Kogan, Alexander Lampone, Rhoda Makoff, Robert Murphy, Richard Pesavento, Tom Sherry, Susan Cameron, Will Fowler, Jr., Barbara Hartnett, Di Ann Lampone, Mary Stein, Mitchell Suskin (Medical unit).
Credits: Directed by Steven Spielberg. Written by Melissa Mathison. Produced by Steven Spielberg & Kathleen Kennedy. Director of photography: Allen Daviau. Production designer: James D. Bissell. Edited by Carol Littleton. Music by John Williams. Production supervisor: Frank Marshall. Associate producer: Melissa Mathison. Production associates: Michael Burmeister, Lance Young. Assistant directors: Katy M. Emde, Daniel Attias. Animation supervisor: Samuel Comstock. "E.T." creator: Carlo Rambaldi. Visual effects supervisor: Dennis Muren. Makeup: Robert Sidell. Hairstyles: Lola McNally. Costumes: Deborah Scott. Supervising sound editor: Charles L. Campbell. Sound recording: Gene S. Cantamessa, Robert Knudson, Robert W. Glass, Jr., Don Digirolamo. Casting director: Marci Liroff. Stunts: Glenn Randall. An Amblin Entertainment production.
Additional Credits: Production dates: September 8, 1981 to December 1981. Reshoots: January, February 1982. Released June 11, 1982. Extended version runs 120 minutes.
Awards: Oscars for Best Music—Original Score, Sound, Effects—Visual Effects, Effects—Sound Effects Editing.
Available: Universal Studios Home Entertainment DVD (2005). UPC: 025192866425.

One of the highest-grossing films of all time, *E.T. the Extra-Terrestrial* is to date Steven Spielberg's most autobiographical feature. Set in a suburbia resembling his childhood homes in Phoenix, Arizona, and Los Gatos, California, the film features incidents taken directly from the director's life. It was "a very personal story," he said. "*E.T.* is a film that was inside me for many years and could only come out after a lot of suburban psychodrama." Specifically, it was an attempt to address his parents' divorce, and his estimation of himself as an outsider. On another occasion he said, "I always felt *E.T.* was a minority story."

While the germ of the story was contained in Spielberg's psyche, the project started with *Night Skies*, a script he commissioned from John Sayles (*Return of the Secaucus Seven*, 1980). The Sayles story was the flip side of *Close Encounters of the Third Kind* (1977), one in which the aliens were hostile instead of welcoming. Spielberg was set to produce *Night Skies* at Columbia, but while preparing *Raiders of the Lost Ark* (1981), he began having misgivings about the project. Actor Harrison Ford's future wife Melissa Mathison was on the London set of *Raiders*, and Spielberg began "pouring my heart out" to her. Under his direction, she began writing a very different screenplay, one in which a benevolent space creature stranded from his crew befriends a ten-year-old boy.

Spielberg's idea essentially updated elements of *Peter Pan* to contemporary suburbia, complete with flying sequences, and with the alien as a sort of Tinkerbell. Like J.M. Barrie, Spielberg gave himself over completely to a child's imagination, zeroing in on the fears and desires of a ten-year-old, "where I've sort of been for thirty-four years anyway."

E.T. is the director's most lyrical film, the closest he has come to "pure" cinema. Long passages of the film are without dialogue, and many of the lines in the film are irrelevant, background conversations. Instead of following a strict plot, Spielberg offers images and sounds that feel deeply personal: a quarter moon, sliced by clouds, in an autumnal sky; pine trees swaying in the wind; the monotonous symmetry of suburban streets; a Halloween that verges on anarchy. Home is a sanctuary, but also a retreat constantly under threat. Adults are either Mom or unfathomable, capricious, cruel, and anonymous figures.

The key to the success of *E.T.* was Spielberg's ability to ground the story in a suburban reality that his audience could recognize. Equally important was finding a way to make his characters more appealing than typical suburban residents. Again, the script wasn't as important as finding the proper actors and giving them the right direction. A San Antonio native, Henry Thomas had appeared only in a local musical when he was cast in *Raggedy Man* (1981), a Sissy Spacek vehicle. "I felt the best way to work with Henry in *E.T.* was not to be his director but his buddy," Spielberg explained. They played Pac-Man together during lunch. Robert

Macnaughton (also spelled MacNaughton) had worked in television. Six years old at the time, Drew Barrymore had also appeared in a handful of small roles. None of them had previously revealed the personality or depth that Spielberg elicited.

Unlike his previous blockbusters, Spielberg was working with a relatively small budget, $10.5 million, and a short shooting schedule of sixty-five days. (More than a million went to E.T. himself, basically an animatronic puppet designed by Carlo Rambaldi.) For the first time in his career, Spielberg did without storyboards, a move that was risky but also liberating. He limited his use of special effects, going back to simple tricks that could be filmed easily. The Halloween sequence is a good example of how effective the newly relaxed shooting methods could be.

E.T. grossed $11.8 million during its opening weekend, and by 2008 had made $980 million (adjusted for inflation). Universal ultimately licensed more than two hundred tie-ins to the movie, everything from ice cream to bedsheets.

Sales of Reese's Pieces, the candy Elliott uses to lure E.T. out of hiding, went up 65 percent. A $40 million E.T. ride opened at the Universal Studios theme park in 1991.

The film became a cultural phenomenon, dissected by pundits who interpreted it in dozens of ways (you can find it described as everything from a religious parable to a dog story). It spoke to a broad spectrum of the population, proof of the power of Spielberg's vision and his ability to connect to the masses. Not everyone fell under its spell. Some complained about the occasionally intrusive score by John Williams, others about the maudlin, drawn-out ending.

Spielberg waited until 1988 to release the film to the home market, and has resisted efforts to make a sequel (although he and Mathison did write an E.T. II treatment in July 1982). The director has since employed digital technology to alter the original version, erasing guns from some shots, for example. His next project at the time, *Poltergeist*, used a similar setting to tell a much darker story.

Blade Runner

Warner Bros., 1982. Sound, color, 2.35. 117 minutes. Rated R.

Cast: Harrison Ford ([Rick] Deckard), Rutger Hauer (Roy Batty), Sean Young (Rachael), Edward James Olmos (Gaff), M. Emmet Walsh (Bryant), Daryl Hannah (Pris), William Sanderson (J.F. Sebastian), Brion James (Leon), Joe Turkel (Dr. Tyrell), Joanna Cassidy (Zhora), James Hong (Chew), Morgan Paull (Holden), Kevin Thompson (Bear), John Edward Allen (Kaiser), Hy Pike (Taffey Lewis), Kimiro Hiroshige (Cambodian lady), Robert Okazaki (Sushi master), Carolyn DeMirjian (Saleslady).

Credits: Directed by Ridley Scott. Screenplay by Hampton Fancher and David Peoples. Based on the novel *Do Androids Dream of Electric Sheep?* by Philip K. Dick. Produced by Michael Deeley. Executive producers: Brian Kelly, Hampton Fancher. Associate producer: Ivor Powell. Supervising editor: Terry Rawlings. Music composed, arranged, performed and produced by Vangelis. Production designed by Lawrence G. Paull. Director of photography: Jordan Cronenweth. Special photographic effects supervisors: Douglas Trumbull, Richard Yuricich, David Dryer. Visual futurist: Syd Mead. Executive in charge of production: C.O. Erickson. Production executive: Katherine Haber. Unit production manager: John W. Rogers. First assistant directors: Newton Arnold, Peter Cornberg. Costumes designed by Charles Knode and Michael Kaplan. Art director: David Snyder. Additional photography: Steven Poster, Brian Tufano. Casting by Mike Fenton and Jane Feinberg. Sound Mixer: Bud Alper. Make up artist: Marvin G. Westmore. Hair stylist: Shirley L. Padgett. Editor: Marsha Nakashima. Color by Technicolor. Filmed in Panavision. Dolby Stereo. The Ladd Company in association with Sir Run Run Shaw through Warner Bros. A Jerry Perenchio and Bud Yorkin presentation of a Michael Deeley–Ridley Scott production.

Additional Cast: Charles Knapp, Leo Gorcey, Jr. (Bartenders); Kelly Hine (Show girl); Sharon Hesky, Rose Mascari (Barflies); Suan Rhee, Horilo Kimuri (Geishas); Kai Wong, Kit Wong (Chinese); Hiro Okazaki, Steve Pope, Robert Reiter (Policemen).

Additional Credits: Narration written by Darryl Ponicsan (version discarded), Roland Kibbee. Production dates: March 9 to June 1981. Released June 25, 1982. The 70mm release has a 2.20 aspect ratio.

Available: Warner Home Entertainment DVD, *Blade Runner Five-Disc Ultimate Collector's Edition* (2007). UPC: 085391144847.

One of the most imitated science fiction films of the past forty years, *Blade Runner* helped legitimize the genre, paradoxically by ignoring many of its signature elements. It also introduced the work of Philip K. Dick to a broader audience. The author's novels have since become the source material for more than a half-dozen feature films, and the unacknowledged inspiration for several others.

Born in Chicago in 1929, Dick was a sickly child who immersed himself in fantasy books and opera. He began writing science fiction in his early twenties, selling his first novel in 1953 and writing short stories at an astonishing pace. He had some ambivalence about the genre, also writing several "realist" works that were lost or published posthumously. Despite a tumultuous private life and an increasing dependence on drugs, Dick managed to write three novels and a children's story in 1966. The novel *Do Androids Dream of Electric Sheep?* was published two years later, and became the first of Dick's work to be optioned to the movies. While Dick was earning the growing admiration of the sci-fi community, he was also committed to a psychiatric clinic, and made his first suicide attempt in 1972. The following year, United Artists extended its option on *Do Androids Dream of Electric Sheep?*, and in 1974 two separate screenwriters consulted with Dick about how to adapt it.

Hampton Fancher, an actor who worked primarily in episodic television, wrote an adaptation in 1977 that caught the attention of Michael Deeley, a veteran producer who started out as a film editor in the 1950s. He approached Ridley Scott, whose reputation had skyrocketed after directing *Alien* (1979). "It was called *Dangerous Days*," Scott remembered later, "and Deeley had come to see me when I was actually mixing *Alien*." But Scott preferred to work on *Dune* (eventually directed by David Lynch and released in 1984), a big-budget version of Frank Herbert's best-selling novel, until progress on that film came to a standstill. Scott remembered the *Dangerous Days* script, and told Deeley, "You know, if you guys had to expand this into something more spectacular, we can push this right outside and onto the street and create this universe of futuristic urban future."

By now the project was called *Blade Runner*, the title coming from a William S. Burroughs screen treatment of a novel by Alan E. Nourse. Deeley and Scott hired screenwriter David Webb Peoples, a former editor who had cowritten a documentary about nuclear scientists. Scott also consulted architects and industrial designers like Syd Mead about how a futuristic world would look. "Serious futurists, great speculators, great imagination, looking to the future, where the big test is saying, 'Draw me a car in 30 years' time without it looking like bad science fiction.'"

Scott now viewed *Aliens* as a C-movie elevated to an A level by its look and its monster. For *Blade Runner*, "My special effect, behind it all, would be the world." Dick's story remained relatively intact, but was embellished with Scott's visual flourishes. The film looked real, a place where characters lived rather than a collection of sets to act in. Many of the ideas in *Blade Runner* were prescient: the pervasive commercials, genetic engineering, and reliance on video, for example. (The filmmakers made miscalculations as well, like cathode ray tubes instead of flat panel screens.)

Some of the stylistic choices—the frequent rain, scenes set at night—were to help disguise the wires and cables needed for special effects, but they also connected the story to film noir. As actor M. Emmet Walsh recalled, "Ridley said, 'Smoke! We need smoke. Do you smoke?' I said, 'I'm not a smoker.' He said, 'We'll give him a cigar.' He wanted just, you know, atmosphere. Everything's atmosphere."

Scott's methods led to clashes with Walsh and with Harrison Ford, cast as hero Rick Deckard, a retired cop forced back to work to find a half-dozen killers. (Scott and Ford play down their differences today.) But the most notable aspect of *Blade Runner* was its sense of morality. Like Dick's novel, the film raised questions about free will and individuality that are still difficult to answer. Dick's original title asked whether machines created by man could develop feelings and emotions, an issue both "replicants" and humans confront in the film. Many viewers have chosen to reduce this question to whether or not Deckard is a replicant, or android.

In Scott's original version, the answer was spelled out clearly. "This character always in my mind was a replicant," he said. But producers found his cut too confusing, and edited it to include a voice-over. Gone were some scenes, such as Deckard's daydream about a unicorn, that helped settle the cop's status. Added was aerial footage left over from Stanley Kubrick's *The Shining* (1980) to provide a more upbeat ending. Scott struggled with the film's narrative structure for years, deleting the voice-over, fiddling with edits, improving special effects. By 2008, seven different versions were available.

The basic look and themes of the film remain just as influential as when it was originally released. Several directors, whether directly or indirectly, have commented on Scott's vision of the future. In *Brazil* (1985), Terry Gilliam's take is markedly more cynical. Steven Spielberg's *A.I.* (2001) offers a modicum of hope, while Tim Burton's *Batman* (1989) toys with the sadism and despair lurking underneath Scott's film. *Blade Runner* was a box-office failure in 1982, perhaps because it was competing with more accessible sci-fi films like *E.T. The Extra-Terrestrial* and *Star Trek II: The Wrath of Khan*. But the film helped establish Ford and Scott as two of the more significant figures in the film industry over the past three decades.

Fast Times at Ridgemont High

Universal, 1982. Sound, color, 1.85. 89 minutes. Rated R.

Cast: Sean Penn (Jeff Spicoli), Jennifer Jason Leigh (Stacy Hamilton), Judge Reinhold (Brad Hamilton), Phoebe Cates (Linda Barrett), Brian Backer (Mark "Rat" Ratner), Robert Romanus (Mike Damone), Ray Walston (Mr. Hand), Scott Thomson (Arnold), Vincent Schiavelli (Mr. Vargas), Amanda Wyss (Lisa), D.W. Brown (Ron Johnson), Forest Whitaker (Charles Jefferson), Kelli Maroney (Cindy), Tom Nolan (Dennis Taylor), Blair Ashleigh (Pat Bernardo), Eric Stoltz (Stoner Bud), Stanley Davis, Jr. (Jefferson's brother), James Russo (Robber) James Bershad [Bolt] (Greg), Nicolas Coppola [Cage] (Brad's Bud), Reginald H. Farmer (Vice principal), Anthony Edwards (Stoner Bud), Pamela Springsteen (Dina Phillips), Stuart Cornfeld (Pirate King), Sonny Davis (Businessman), Michael Wyle (Brad's Bud), David E. Price (Desmond), Patrick Brennan (Curtis Spicoli); Julie Guilmette, Shelly O'Neill (Perry's Pizza waitresses); Stu Nahan (Himself), Duane Tucker (Dr. Brandt), Martin Brest (Dr. Miller); Douglas Brian Martin, Steven M. Martin (Angry twins); Nancy Wilson (Beautiful girl in car); David Resnik, Eric Leroy (Pee Wee) Burdette, David Doolittle, Tom B. Bralley, Reeves Nevo (Reeves Nevo & The Cinch); Virginia Peters (Restaurant waitress), Laurie Hendricks (Nurse), Lois Brandt (Mrs. O'Rourke), Ellen Fenwick (Stacey's Mom), Cherie Effron (Girl #1), Suzanne Marie Fava (Girl #2), Lana Clarkson (Mrs. Vargas), Roy Holmer [Homer] Wallack (Santa Claus); Ava Lazar, Lorie Sutton (Playmates).

Credits: Directed by Amy Heckerling. Produced by Art Linson, Irving Azoff. Screenplay by Cameron Crowe, based on his book. Executive producer: C.O. Erickson. Director of photography: Matthew F. Leonetti. Additional photography by James Glennon. Art director: Dan Lomino. Edited by Eric Jenkins. Costumes by Marilyn Vance. Casting by Don Phillips. Unit production manager: C.O. Erickson. First assistant director: Albert Shapiro. Sound: Tom Overton. Music editor: Jim Weidman. Music coordinator: Bob Destocki. Additional scoring by Joe Walsh. Make-up: Frank Griffin. Hair stylist: Jan Brandow. Color by Technicolor. Ultracam 35 equipment: Leonetti Cine Rentals.

Additional Credits: Production dates: November 10 to December 28, 1981. Released August 13, 1982.

Other Versions: *The Wild Life* (1984, directed by Art Linson and written by Cameron Crowe), is often regarded as a semi sequel. Amy Heckerling directed a television series, *Fast Times*, in 1986.

Available: Universal DVD (2004). ISBN: 1-4170-1100-9. UPC: 0-25192-5442-1.

Cameron Crowe was writing for *Rolling Stone* while still a teenager, having graduated from high school three years early. He sold the idea for a book about life in high school with the premise that he would go undercover as a student himself, covering a typical year (1978–79) in Redondo Beach, California. The resulting *Fast Times at Ridgemont High: A True Story* was published in 1981. Crowe sold the film rights to the book before it was published, and adapted the book into a screenplay himself.

The producers were Irving Azoff, a noted manager of rock groups, primarily in California, and Art Linson, a Chicago native and UCLA law graduate. Linson was the producer and one of the writers on *American Hot Wax* (1978), a sanitized biopic about early rock promoter Alan Freed. (Crowe had a bit part in the film.) Together, Azoff and Linson brought a degree of rock credibility to the project, resulting in a best-selling soundtrack that featured a number of Azoff's clients.

Director Amy Heckerling, born in New York City in 1954, cites *Mad* magazine as an early influence. *Mean Streets* (1973) convinced her to study film at the American Film Institute, where her short movies won her a brief contract at MGM. Heckerling signed on to *Fast Times* realizing it would be an extremely difficult shoot. She was not only working with a largely untested cast, but had limited time to film in the Sherman Oaks Galleria, a critical location in the story.

The plot to *Fast Times* followed the structure of Crowe's book, but the emphases changed considerably as a result of the performers cast and Heckerling's interests. Crowe was surprised at how conservative his classmates were, calling them "Reagan children" and "scary." Ironically, he himself took a conservative approach to the subject and his writing. His subsequent career has been marked by old-fashioned, crowd-pleasing comic dramas that rely on glib catch phrases and time-specific cultural references.

Heckerling's career has also been marked by ups and downs, including hits like *National Lampoon's European Vacation* (1985) and *Clueless* (1999) as well as commercial disappointments like *Johnny Dangerously* (1984). Her work has been compromised by her quest for commercial justification, by her efforts to recapture the same broad audience that took to this film.

So what were young filmgoers responding to when they embraced *Fast Times* on its release? The music, including songs from Danny Elfman, Jackson Browne, The Go-Go's, most of the members of The Eagles, and Atlantic Records mainstays like The Cars and Led Zeppelin, certainly helped. *Fast Times* was also safely within the template established by *National Lampoon's Animal House* (1978) and popularized in 1981 by *Porky's*.

The film not only helped define stereotypes in the form of Sean Penn's stoned surfer and Phoebe Cates's naive flirt, but also reduced adult characters to teen size, much as Steven Spielberg reduced Warner Brothers cartoon characters into *Tiny Toons*. Robert Romanus's sleazy ticket scalper is a pint-sized variant on the Rat Pack of the 1950s, while Brian Backer's fumbling lover could be seen as a teen-aged Woody Allen.

But, crucial to its success with moviegers, *Fast Times* broke away from genre expectations.

Like *American Graffiti* (1973), there are only a handful of adult characters in the film. Parents are almost completely absent. The film depicts its characters' homes with surprising honesty. Where most teen movies imagined a world of relative wealth, here the characters live in dreary apartment houses or suburban developments with dried-up lawns. Work equals dead-end jobs in fast-food restaurants. Drugs and drink are dangerous; sex, cold, mechanical, and unsatisfying.

This last topic is perhaps *Fast Times'* area of greatest success. In showing the increasingly desperate attempts by Stacy Hamilton to cope with her pregnancy, Jennifer Jason Leigh gave a performance of startling depth and maturity. She has displayed the same high standards throughout her career, whether throwing out an impersonation

of a fast-talking 1930s heroine in *The Hudsucker Proxy* (1994) or co-directing an incisive account of upper-class angst in *The Anniversary Party* (2001).

Despite its generally poor reviews (Roger Ebert famously called it a "scuz-pit" of a movie), *Fast Times* has been an enduring hit with its target audience. It also served as an incubator for up-and-coming performers, notably Sean Penn. Actor Nick Nolte described Penn in real life living much like his Jeff Spicoli character; he has rarely been as open and light-hearted in his other films. Other future Oscar winners in the cast include Forest Whitaker and Nicolas Cage, appearing here under the surname Coppola. Cameron Crowe's script for *The Wild Life* (1984), a loose sequel to *Fast Times*, was a critical and box-office failure, but he would win an Academy Award for the screenplay for 2000's *Almost Famous*.

Koyaanisqatsi

Island Alive, 1982. Sound, color, 1.85. 86 minutes.

Credits: Produced and directed by Godfrey Reggio. Concept: Godfrey Reggio. Scenario: Ron Fricke, Godfrey Reggio, Michael Hoenig, Alton Walpole. Creative Consultant: Bradford Smith. Associate producers: Lawrence S. Taub, T. Michael Powers, Alton Walpole, Roger McNew, Mel Lawrence. Director of photography: Ron Fricke. Music: Philip Glass. Philip Glass music produced and recorded by Kurt Munkacsi. Conducted by Michael Riesman. Music Director & Additional Music: Michael Hoenig. Editors: Alton Walpole, Ron Fricke. Dramaturge: Walter Bachauer. Audio & Electronic Engineering: Michael Stocker. Music & Effects Editor: David Rivas. Re-recording Mixer: Steve Maslow. Camera assistants: Robert Hill, David Brownlow, Roger McNew, Neil Bockman. Associate editor: Anne Miller. Assistant editors: Robert Hill, Tove Johnson, Susan Marcinkus. Distribution research: Ronald P. Gold. Distribution & promotion: Mel Lawrence. Consultants to the director: Jeffrey Lew, T.A. Price, Belle Carpenter, Langdon Winner, Cybele Carpenter, Barbara Pecarich. Additional cinematography: Hilary Harris, Louis Schwartzberg. Associate cinematographer: Christine Gibson. Micro Chip still photography: Phillip Harrington. Rock Painting still photography: Karl Kernberger. Still photography animation: Wayne V. McGee. Special camera modification: Reinhard Lichter. Pilots for aerial cinematography: Bruce Adams, Elizabeth Emerson, Dan Williams. Explosive engineer: Russ Deal. Title design: Paul Pascarella. Dolby Stereo. Stock footage: Energy Productions (Cinematography by Louis Schwartzberg), National Film Archives (NASA—Larry Heflin), Consolidated Demolition, Inc., MacGillivray-Freeman, Screen Presentation, Norton Air Force Base, Sherman Grinberg Library, U.S. Geological Survey. A Francis Ford Coppola presentation of an IRE production.

Additional Credits: Screened at the New York Film Festival on October 4, 1982.

Other Versions: Sequels: *Powaqqatsi* (1988), *Naqoyqatsi* (2002).

Available: MGM Home Entertainment DVD (2002). ISBN: 0-7928-5333-4. UPC: 0-27616-87893-9.

Seven years in the making, *Koyaanisqatsi* is the first in a trilogy of documentaries dealing with the impact of technology on human society. Almost entirely wordless, the film consists of carefully composed images married to the first film score by minimalist composer Philip Glass. With the imprimatur

of Francis Ford Coppola, and strategic screenings at film festivals, it enjoyed a surprising run at the box office.

It was the first feature for Godfrey Reggio, once a member of a religious order and later a political activist. Born in New Orleans in 1940, Reggio spent fourteen years with the Christian Brothers, living, as he put it, "in the Middle Ages." Upon leaving the order, he was a founder of the Institute for Regional Education (IRE) in Santa Fe, New Mexico. In 1974, Reggio began working on a mass media campaign about technology and the use of surveillance to control human behavior. Funded in part by the American Civil Liberties Union, the campaign included a graphic book inserted as a supplement to a Sunday newspaper and over a half-dozen public service announcements that he said later "worked beautifully in a non-narrative form."

In 1975 Reggio began collaborating with cinematographer Ron Fricke, expanding on the visual ideas he developed in his "Privacy Campaign" spots. In his biographical references Reggio sometimes presents himself as an inventor of a new visual style, but he was actually working from the same principles that Charles Sheeler and Paul Strand used when filming *Manhatta* in 1921. *Koyaanisqatsi* can be seen as an updating of the "city symphony" genre that also includes *The Twenty-Four-Dollar Island* (1927), *A Bronx Morning*

(1931), and many others. Reggio was working with more sophisticated equipment, but his canvas was essentially the same.

One element missing from the early city documentaries was sound, and Reggio had the good fortune to obtain the services of Philip Glass. Actually, both described a more drawn-out process, as Glass had never composed for a film before agreeing to meet with Reggio. He watched some forty minutes of material, including footage of clouds near the Grand Canyon and the Four Corners. Reggio screened it first with a nondescript electronic score, then backed by Glass's own compositions. "It's better with your music," he told Glass, who agreed.

Glass divided Reggio's finished cut into a dozen or so sections, composing individual themes for them. Reggio promptly recut his film to the music, foiling Glass's original intentions but also inspiring the composer to revise much of his material. Reggio and Fricke revised their film as well, reshooting footage as their concept of the film's "narrative" changed.

"What he did was take the ambiance of the music, not the structure of the music," Glass said approvingly. "We spent about three years, a very leisurely pace. That was a tremendous advantage because we had time to look at things, to rewrite things, to recut things. We got into the habit of working interactively . . . every one of the sections of *Koyaanisqatsi* went through that process several times."

In interviews, Reggio insists that *Koyaanisqatsi* has no message. "These films are meant to provoke, they are meant to offer an experience rather than an idea or information or a story," he has said. However, he will make some admissions: "The basic idea for the film is the transiting from old nature into a technological milieu. It's not that we use technology, we live technology. We are no longer conscious of its presence." But Reggio, who thanked veteran editor Roger Spottiswoode in his closing credits, is smart enough to realize that placing any two film images together forces viewers to give a larger meaning to them. So even without a narration, Reggio's editing scheme and Glass's score produce a "narrative" for viewers to follow.

So what does *Koyaanisqatsi* "say"? Like many of the city symphonies, the film's structure suggests the passage of a day, from dawn to night, beginning with largely rural images and then progressing to urban ones. Or it could be a creation myth,

starting from fire, progressing to deserts, then water and cultivation, to technology. Gradually, inevitably, the film turns into a condemnation of our technological society.

Many of the images, filled with rich hues, sped up or in slow motion, have a hypnotic beauty emphasized by Glass's circular musical themes. "What I decided to do in making this film was rip out all of the foreground of a traditional film, the foreground being the actors, the characterization, the story, and move the background into the foreground, make that the subject," Reggio said.

It's a strategy used by experimental filmmakers before Reggio, notably James Benning, whose *8½ x 11* (1974) includes a number of similarly staged shots. In fact, similar visual and editing strategies can be found in several titles in the National Film Registry: *Westinghouse Works* (note Reggio's overhead crane shot in the Oscar Meyer factory), *Star Theater*, *H₂O*, *Master Hands*, *Powers of Ten*. (Reggio also cited Luis Buñuel's *Los Olvidados* as an inspiration.) The director may have intended to "slip the grip with some freak show," but he was actually following a well-worn path.

Which may be why several critics objected to the film when it was released. Vincent Canby in *The New York Times* referred to it as a coffee-table film, while *Variety* complained that it was "an overblown non-narrative image piece." Canby was onto something. *Koyaanisqatsi* is a collection of achingly beautiful images that by themselves might mean little. The film's subtitle—"Life out of Balance"—imposes an artificial viewpoint. For much of the time, the only thing "out of balance" is how fast or slow Reggio manipulates the footage.

What may have also galled many viewers was Reggio's tendency to make flip editorial comments. Comparing commuters to hot dogs on an assembly line, for example, or tilting up from clogged traffic to a billboard for a resort casino. Reggio holds onto shots until they practically shout "metaphor": bees in a hive, ants on a hill, arterial freeways with cars as corpuscles.

For some viewers, *Koyaanisqatsi* functioned as a "head trip," just as *2001: A Space Odyssey* was an excuse to get high. It was successful enough for Reggio to complete the trilogy, receiving financial help in the second part from George Lucas and in the third from Steven Soderbergh. Each subsequent film offered a larger canvas, a more expansive soundtrack, more experimentation with film stocks, special effects, and more pointed commentary.

It's notable how smoothly Reggio's style slipped into the mainstream. MTV may have been the first, appropriating as Reggio did NASA stock footage for interstitial programming simply for the pure beauty of its imagery.

But *The Blue Planet* and in fact vast swatches of the Discovery Channel use the same style of nature photography. Fricke has gone on to direct *Chronos* (1985) and *Baraka* (1992), similarly non-verbal documentaries.

Tootsie

Columbia, 1982. Sound, color, 2.35. 116 minutes. Rated PG.

Cast: Dustin Hoffman (Michael Dorsey/Dorothy Michaels), Jessica Lange (Julie), Teri Garr (Sandy), Dabney Coleman (Ron), George Gaynes (John Van Horn), Geena Davis (April), Doris Belack (Rita), Charles Durning (Les), Bill Murray (Jeff), Sydney Pollack (George Fields), Ellen Foley (Jacqui), Peter Gatto (Rick), Lynne Thigpen (Jo), Ronald L. Schwary (Phil Weintraub), Debra Lincoln (Mrs. Mallory), Amy Lawrence (Amy), Kenny Sinclair (Boy), Susan Merson (Page), Michael Ryan (Middle-Aged Man), Robert D. Wilson (Stage Hand), James Carruthers (Middle-Aged Man), Estelle Getty (Middle-Aged Woman), Christine Ebersole (Linda), Bernie Pollack (Actor #1), Sam Stoneburner (Actor #2), Marjorie Lovett (Salesgirl), Willy Switkes (Man at Cab), Gregory Camillucci (Maitre d'), Barbara Spiegel (Billie), Tony Craig (Joel Spector), Walter Cline (Bartender), Suzanne von Schaack (Party Girl), Anne Shropshire (Mrs. Crawley), Pamela Lincoln (Secretary), Mary Donnet (Receptionist), Bernie Passeltiner (Mac), Mallory Jones (Girl #1), Patti Cohane (Girl #2), Murray Schisgal (Party Guest), Greg Gorman (Photographer), Anne Prager (Acting Student), John Carpenter (First Actor), Rob Levine (Second Actor), Richard Whiting (Priest), Jim Jansen (Stage Manager #2), Susan Egbert (Diane), Kay Self (Acting Student), Tom Mardirosian (Stage Manager), Richard Wirth (Mel—Technical Director), Gavin Reed (Director).

Credits: Directed by Sydney Pollack. Screenplay by Larry Gelbart and Murray Schisgal. Story by Don McGuire and Larry Gelbart. Produced by Sydney Pollack and Dick Richards. Executive producer: Charles Evans. Director of photography: Owen Roizman. Production designed by Peter Larkin. Edited by Fredric Steinkamp, William Steinkamp. Music by Dave Grusin. Original Songs: Lyrics by Alan & Marilyn Bergman. Music by Dave Grusin. "Tootsie," "It Might Be You" sung by Stephen Bishop. Costumes designed by Ruth Morley. Casting by Lynn Stalmaster, Toni Howard & Associates. Assistant director: David McGiffert. Mr. Hoffman's Make-Up Created and Designed by Dorothy Pearl, George Masters. Mr. Hoffman's Make-Up: Allen Weisinger. Make-Up Artist: C. Romania Ford. Costume supervisor: Bernie Pollack. Set decorator: Tom Tonery. Sound mixer: Les Lazarowitz. Titles & Opticals by Pacific Title. Lenses and Panaflex Camera by Panavision. Color by Technicolor. From Columbia—Delphi Productions. A Columbia Pictures presentation of a Mirage/Punch production.

Additional Credits: Premiered in Los Angeles on December 1, 1982.

Awards: Oscar for Best Supporting Actress (Lange).

Available: Columbia Pictures DVD (2001). ISBN: 0-7678-3402-X. UPC: 0-43396-03747-2. Sony Pictures DVD (2008). UPC: 043396191716.

Acknowledged as one of the finest actors of his generation, Dustin Hoffman is also, famously, one of the most indecisive. Early in his career he took on difficult roles; in the late 1970s he sought more commercial, mainstream projects. It was three years between his turn as a divorced father in the extremely popular *Kramer vs. Kramer* (1979) and the release of *Tootsie*, a movie that underwent several revisions and personnel changes.

Hoffman and playwright Murray Schisgal (*Luv*) worked on a script about a man in drag right around the time of *Kramer vs. Kramer*. One of the actor's early collaborators, Schisgal receives a screenplay credit, although by most accounts he contributed primarily to the first draft. Don McGuire, an actor, producer, director, and novelist as well as screenwriter, was working on a drag comedy called either *Paging Donna Darling* or *Would I Lie to You?* in the 1970s. Plans for it were fairly advanced, with a director and lead actors cast (and even other writers assigned for revisions). McGuire died in 1979, but in subsequent arbitration he received a story credit for *Tootsie*.

The other credited writer on *Tootsie* was Larry Gelbart, who started writing comedy professionally while still a teenager. Having worked in radio and television (where he was on Sid Caesar's staff), Gelbart was one of the writers of the Tony-winning Broadway musical *A Funny Thing Happened on the Way to the Forum*. In the 1970s he returned to television, most famously as one of the creative forces behind the television series *M*A*S*H*. In later interviews, Gelbart described working with Hoffman for a year on the script.

By that time original director Hal Ashby had been replaced by Sydney Pollack, a former actor who worked with Robert Redford on a half-dozen films. This was the first comedy Pollack directed, and he not only took a producing credit, he allowed Hoffman to persuade him to return to acting. As agent George Fields, he is effortlessly commanding and quite funny. Pollack continued acting intermittently, taking an important part in *Michael Clayton* (2007). He would direct seven more features before his death in 2008.

Pollack and Hoffman at some point soured on Gelbart's writing. (In Gelbart's words, Hoffman thought he had "a subtext of contempt for his ideas.") Several uncredited writers were brought onto the project, most notably Elaine May, who received $450,000 for three weeks' work. She is generally regarded as supplying many of the farcical complications to the plot. Whoever was responsible must have been inspired by *Some Like*

It Hot (1959), not in terms of plot but in terms of how the characters play out their roles.

Drag comedies, and drag dramas for that matter, have a long tradition in American culture. Drag was a crucial component of early two-reel slapstick comedies, and a favored device for melodramatic actors like Lon Chaney and Lionel Barrymore. Imported from London, where Shakespeare helped make drag an enduring theatrical gimmick, *Charley's Aunt* was filmed several times, in 1930 with Charles Ruggles, in 1941 with Jack Benny, and, as the musical *Where's Charley?* with Ray Bolger in 1952. Maybe each generation gets the drag comedy it deserves: from fast-paced but harmless in the 1920s to the violent and suicidal *Some Like It Hot* in the 1950s to the defiantly perverse and hallucinogenic *The Rocky Horror Picture Show* in the 1970s.

In *Tootsie*, Hoffman's Michael Dorsey/Dorothy Michaels combines the Tony Curtis and Jack Lemmon roles in *Some Like It Hot* into one character. Like Curtis, Hoffman falls in love with a woman while disguised as a woman; like Lemmon, Hoffman becomes an object of desire as a woman. Charles Durning, a veteran of stage and television whose film career took off after *The Sting* (1973), functions as the Joe E. Brown character in *Tootsie*: good-hearted, clueless, but relentless. Pollack cast Jessica Lange, still regarded a bit skeptically for making her feature debut in the 1976 remake of *King Kong*, while Hoffman is reported to have brought Bill Murray into the project. A *Saturday Night Live* alumnus, Murray helped turned broad comedies like *Caddyshack* (1980) and *Stripes* (1981) into blockbuster hits. He appeared unbilled in advertising because he didn't want his fans to mistake *Tootsie* for one of his typical outings.

The three affairs at the core of *Tootsie* give Hoffman the opportunity to express his visions of sexual relationships. With Charles Durning he is amusingly guarded; with Jessica Lange, he is so smitten he can't think straight; and with Teri Garr, he is callous, insensitive, and deceitful. Garr's performance is in some ways the most moving in the film, or at least the one that seems to be based on a believable personal history.

"We never, ever laughed on that set," Pollack said in a documentary about the film. "It's not laugh comedy—it is for the audience, but not for us—it's Chekhov." As film critic Joe Morgenstern noted, "He kept 'looking for the meat' in *Tootsie*—for the truth of what the characters want, of what they feel they're doing and why they're doing it." Speaking about another movie, Pollack said, "The first rule of any love story is you can't make one character attractive at the expense of the other." This evenhanded approach, a combination of respect and tolerance, helped *Tootsie* win over moviegoers who might have been dubious about a cross-dressing comedy.

Apart from relationships, the rest of *Tootsie* consists of brisk but affectionate satires of television soap operas, in particular *General Hospital*, and enough personal details to ground the story in a truth filmgoers could recognize. Hoffman was notoriously difficult to work with, for example, giving his character's obsessive self-editing and narcissism in the film a funny edge. Dorothy Michaels' willingness to appear on a patently ridiculous soap opera mirrors Hoffman's own peculiar career choices, from sci-fi adventures like *Outbreak* (1995) and *Sphere* (1998) to outsized supporting roles in *The Messenger: The Story of Joan of Arc* (1999) and *Perfume: The Story of a Murderer* (2006).

El Norte

Cinecom International Films/Island Alive, 1983. Sound, color, 1.78. 141 minutes. Rated R.
Cast: Zaide Silvia Gutierrez (Rosa Xuncax), David Villalpando (Enrique Xuncax), Ernesto Gomez Cruz (Arturo Xuncax), Alicia del Lago (Lupe Xuncax), Stella Quan (Josefita), Eraclio Zepeda (Pedro), Rodrigo Puebla (El Puma), Rodolfo Alejandre (Don Ramon), Emilio del Haro (Truck driver), Mike Gomez (Jaime), John Martin (Border guard), Ron Joseph (Border guard), Abel Franco (Raimundo), Trinidad Silva (Monty), Lupe Ontiveros (Nacha), Tony Plana (Carlos [busboy]), Enrique Castillo (Jorge [dishwasher]), Momo Yashima (English teacher), Jo Marie Ward (Helen Rogers), Diane Civita (Alice Harper), George O'Hanlan, Jr. (Doctor Murphy), Jorge Moreno (Man in bus).
Credits: Directed by Gregory Nava. Screenplay by Gregory Nava and Anna Thomas. Original story: Gregory Nava. Produced by Anna

Thomas. Cinematography: James Glennon. Film editor: Betsy Blankett. Production sound: Robert Yerington. Sound design: Michael C. Moore. Color by Du Art Film Laboratories. Guatemalan dialogue translations: Arturo Arias. Mexican dialogue translations: Eraclio Zepeda. Traditional and original music composed and performed by Los Folkloristas. Traditional and original harp music composed and performed by Melecio Martinez. Marimba and atmospheric music composed and performed by Emil Richards. Mariachi music arranged and performed by Mariachi Nuevo Uclatlan. An Independent Productions presentation, in association with American Playhouse. Produced in association with American Playhouse with funds from Public Television Stations and the Corporation for Public Broadcasting. Additional production funding provided by Channel Four Television, Great Britain.

Additional Credits: Premiered in Telluride, Colorado, during September 1983. Released theatrically January 1984.

Available: Criterion DVD (2009). ISBN: 978-1-60465-109-6. UPC: 7-15515-03472-2.

Written, produced, and directed by the husband-and-wife team of Gregory Nava and Anna Thomas, *El Norte* shows the immigration process through the eyes of participants. Epic in scope, the film is broken into three parts. The first starts in Guatemala, where political oppression threatens a native Indian village. Brother and sister Enrique and Rosa Xuncax (played by David Villalpando and Zaide Silvia Gutierrez) flee first to Mexico, then to the United States. Although specific in detail, their journey mirrors the general migration from Central America north in search of money and security.

Nava has said in interviews that his family has lived in southern California since the 1880s. "I came from a border family. I have lots of aunts and uncles who were born and raised in Tijuana," he explained. "I've been raised in that border world, with that tremendous clash between the cultures." Nava and his future wife Thomas both attended film school at UCLA. Their first feature collaboration, *The Confessions of Amans* (1976), was a historical romance shot in Spain. "All of the work that I do, I try to have a strong mythic underpinning to it," Nava said.

In the *El Norte* screenplay, Nava and Thomas zero in on a particular family, but add mythic qualities to the journey Enrique and Rosa take. The screenplay was based on years of research, but as Thomas told an interviewer, "Nobody goes to the movies to hear a lecture. We didn't want *El Norte* to look like a docu-drama, or have any stylistic elements that would remind people of journalism or 'rough-around-the-edges' documentary. The style we aimed for is the dream realism that comes from Mayan culture." Like the characters in Elia Kazan's *America America* (1963), the Amerindians here believe in spirits and spells, in folk cures and curses.

The pair's insistence on shooting in Spanish with Hispanic actors made financing the film difficult. They spent two years submitting their script to studios, but it wasn't until Lindsay Law, an executive producer at the PBS *American Playhouse* series, read it that the project got off the ground. Law advanced half the budget; Nava and Thomas got additional funding by selling broadcast rights to England's Channel 4.

It was impossible to shoot in Guatemala, so Nava opted for Chiapas, a Mexican state on the Guatemalan border. They faced obstacles there, but scenes shot in Morelos in central Mexico proved more dangerous. Cameraman James Glennon was chased by gunmen when he tried to return to Los Angeles, where his wife was giving birth. They took his exposed negative; Nava and Thomas eventually had to pay a ransom in Mexico City to get it back. (In other accounts, Nava said that he was threatened at gunpoint, and that Mexican police kidnapped the film's accountant.) As a result, they rebuilt a Guatemalan village in California to shoot most of *El Norte*'s opening.

Nava elicits affecting performances from his cast, many of them nonactors, and succeeds in building a dreamlike atmosphere in the opening sequences. As a stylist, however, he is prone to overemphasis, to the use of close-up inserts to repeat points, and to forcing metaphorical meanings on material that may not need it. A viewer may be entranced by the appearance of butterflies during a departure scene, or distracted by trying to figure out how the shot was accomplished, or worried about whether or not the scene is symbolic. The dozens of lit candles featured in several interior shots can be seen as a romantic gesture, an idealized vision of beauty, or a fire hazard. As a director, Nava can be variable. A fight with a "coyote" who had promised to bring Rosa and Enrique across the border is shot and edited with precision and flair; the subsequent scene, involving U.S. Border Patrol agents, is garishly lit and flatly acted.

The destinies Rosa and Enrique face are closely intertwined but also too schematic to be entirely credible. The culture they encounter in San Diego is seductive but corrupt, beset by literal rats in Rosa's case and metaphorical ones in Enrique's. Nava and Thomas suggest that their Amerindian society in Guatemala is superior, but can offer only folk songs and colorful costumes as proof.

The film premiered at the Telluride Film Festival over Labor Day weekend in 1983. It received a theatrical release through Cinecom International Films and Island Alive (which also handled a soundtrack album). It was also broadcast on PBS in 1985 and again in 1987. Nava reissued a "director's cut" thorough Artisan Entertainment in 2000. Not one of those three distributors exists in the same form today. A VHS version was released by CBS Fox Home Video, another company no longer in business. Until Criterion released a DVD in 2009, *El Norte* was a difficult film to see.

After *El Norte*, Nava and Thomas chose to work within the Hollywood film industry rather than outside it. Films like *A Time of Destiny* (1988),

My Family (1995), *Selena* (1997, a biopic of the murdered Mexican pop singer), and *Bordertown* (2007) received mixed critical reactions. Nava also produced, wrote, and directed *American Family*

(2002), a television series broadcast on CBS and PBS. Zaide Silvia Gutierrez and David Villalpando have both gone on to extensive careers in film and television, primarily in Mexico.

Zaide Silvia Gutierrez and David Villalpando play siblings in *El Norte*. Photo courtesy of The Criterion Collection

This Is Spinal Tap

Embassy Pictures, 1984. Sound, color, 1.85. 83 minutes. Rated R.

Cast: Christopher Guest (Nigel Tufnel), Michael McKean (David St. Hubbins), Harry Shearer (Derek Smalls), Rob Reiner (Marty DiBergi), June Chadwick (Jeanine Pettibone), Tony Hendra (Ian Faith), Bruno Kirby (Tommy Pischedda). Special appearances by Ed Begley, Jr. (John "Stumpy" Pepys), Paul Benedict (Tucker "Smitty" Brown), Zane Buzby (*Rolling Stone* reporter), Billy Crystal (Morty the Mime), Howard Hesseman (Terry Ladd), Patrick MacNee [Macnee] (Sir Denis Eton-Hogg), Paul Shaffer (Artie Fufkin), Fred Willard (Lt. Hookstratten). Also starring: R. J. Parnell (Mick Shrimpton), David Kaff (Viv Savage), Fran Drescher (Bobbi Flekman), Joyce Hyser (Belinda), Vicki Blue (Cindy), Angelica [Anjelica] Huston (Polly Deutsch); Kimberly Stringer, Chazz Dominguez, Shari Hall (Heavy metal fans); Jean Cromie (Ethereal fan), Patrick Maher (New York M.C.), Danny Kortchmar (Ronnie Pudding), Memo Vera (Bartender), Julie Payne (Mime Waitress), Dana Carvey (Mime Waiter), Sandy Helberg (Angelo DiMentibello), Robin Mencken [Menken] (Angelo's Associate), Jennifer Child (Limo groupie), J.J. Barry (Rack jobber), George McDaniel (Southern rock promoter), Anne Churchill (Reba), Paul Shortino (Duke Fame); Cherie Darr, Lara Cody (Fame groupies); Andrew J. Lederer (Student promoter), Russ Kunkel (Eric "Stumpy Joe" Childs); Diana Duncan, Gina Marie Pitrello ("Jamboree Bop" Dancers); Gloria Gifford (Airport security officer), Archie Hahn (Room service guy), Charles Levin (Disc 'n' Dat manager), Wonderful Smith (Janitor); Chris Romano, Daniel Rodgers (Little Druids); Fred Asparagus (Joe "Mama" Besser), Rodney Kemerer (L.A. party guest), Robert Bauer (Moke).

Credits: Directed by Rob Reiner. Written by Christopher Guest, Michael McKean, Harry Shearer, Rob Reiner. Produced by Karen Murphy. Director of photography: Peter Smokler. Supervising film editor: Robert Leighton. Casting by Eve Brandstein. Film editors: Kent Beyda, Kim Secrist. Executive in charge of production: Lindsay Doran. Unit production manager: Cary Glieberman. Production designer: Bryan Jones. Costume stylist: Renée Johnston. Sound mixer: Bob Eber. Hair & Make-up supervisor: Michele Payne. Supervising sound editor: John Brasher. Music editor: Kenneth Karman. The real Ian Faith: Derek Sutton. Titles, opticals & color by CFI. Dolby stereo. Music & lyrics by Christopher Guest, Michael McKean, Harry Shearer, Rob Reiner. Music performed by Christopher Guest, Michael McKean, Harry Shearer, R.J. Parnell, David Kaff.

Additional Credits: Released March 2, 1984.

Available: MGM Home Entertainment DVD (2000). ISBN:0-7928-4658-3. UPC: 0-27616-85280-9.

Originally conceived as a joke for *The T.V. Show*, the rock group Spinal Tap became the subject of *This Is Spinal Tap* on the basis of a twenty-minute demonstration reel put together by its four principal writers and comedians, Rob Reiner, Christopher Guest, Michael McKean, and Harry Shearer. All had extensive experience in comedy before meeting on *The T.V. Show*, an ABC special. Reiner was the son of Carl Reiner, a writer, director, and actor whose work on television included *The Dick Van Dyke Show*. Born in 1947 in the Bronx, Rob Reiner grew up surrounded by comedians. He studied acting in college before forming "The Session," a comedy troupe that also featured Richard Dreyfuss. Reiner occasionally appeared in another troupe, "The Committee," then started getting parts playing hippies on television shows like *The Beverly Hillbillies*. Along with Steve Martin, he was a staff writer on *The Smothers Brothers Show*, but his big break was a recurring role as "Meathead" on Norman Lear's *All in the Family*. A contract to develop television shows at ABC didn't pan out; nor did his marriage to Penny Marshall, the Laverne in the hit series *Laverne & Shirley*.

One of the supporting stars of *Laverne & Shirley* was Michael McKean, a New York native who ten years earlier had paired with Christopher Guest to write rock songs. McKean moved to Los Angeles in 1970, where he joined Harry Shearer in "The Credibility Gap," another comedy troupe. Shearer, born in 1943, had been a fairly successful child actor, with credits on *The Jack Benny Show* and the pilot of *Leave It to Beaver*. After the Gap disbanded in 1976, Shearer wrote for a variety of television shows, and had two stints in the cast of *Saturday Night Live*.

Christopher Guest was born in New York City in 1948, the son of Peter Haden-Guest, a British diplomat at the United Nations. A fan of folk and country music, he learned guitar and mandolin and played in bluegrass bands before turning to rock and roll. Guest performed on *National Lampoon* radio shows, and played guitar on an album McKean made as his "Lenny" character from *Laverne & Shirley*.

After Spinal Tap appeared on *The T.V. Show* in 1979, it took Reiner almost four years to secure financing for *This Is Spinal Tap*. One crucial backer was Norman Lear, who had purchased Embassy Pictures in 1982. Embassy would end up releasing the film.

The film was structured and photographed like a documentary, with *The Last Waltz* (1978), Martin Scorsese's concert film about The Band, a clear model. (Reiner appears on camera as Marty DiBergi, a Scorsese lookalike who conducts inane interviews.) But *This Is Spinal Tap* also embraced the entire history of televised rock and roll, from phony British kinescopes of a Spinal Tap forerunner performing "Gimme Some Money" to the manufactured psychedelia of "(Listen to the) Flower People," shot on a set that could have come from *The Smothers Brothers Show*.

Christopher Guest spoke about some of the filming methods in a 2007 interview. Guest and the others worked from an outline that was between twenty-five and thirty pages long. Through improvisations and personal experiences, the actors figured out everything they could about the backgrounds for their characters. "But there was no dialogue written down in any form and we didn't really rehearse. We tried to get everything while it was spontaneous. I would guess that we never went past three takes."

What distinguished *This Is Spinal Tap* from other rock parodies was the fact that the leads were all musicians themselves. "We tried to make the music enjoyable up to a point," Guest said, arguing that in order to parody something you have to get it right first. Songs like "(Tonight I'm Gonna) Rock Ya Tonite" and "Stonehenge" sound as if any heavy metal band might have played them. "But the lyrics are insane," Guest adds. What's more, the actors didn't have to guess about the bland hotel rooms, cheap fast food restaurants, and rundown concert halls looked like: they had experienced them firsthand, just as they had dealt with the clueless promoters, oblivious record executives, and pushy publicists who litter the film.

Another distinguishing characteristic of *This Is Spinal Tap* is the affection and sympathy the actors hold for their characters. McKean, Guest, and Shearer want viewers to appreciate the conviction and hard work the Spinal Tap members put into their music. They made be deluded, but they are not evil. It is their petty jealousies and miscommunications that drive the plot, which ultimately boils down to a story of love and friendship. (Chipped away from the original four-hour cut were several scenes involving Bruno Kirby, the acts that opened for Spinal Tap, and other subplots.)

Starting with 1996's *Waiting for Guffman*, Guest would develop this theme of art substituting for thwarted love in a series of "mockumentaries," including *Best in Show* (2000), *A Mighty Wind* (2003), and *For Your Consideration* (2006). McKean has gone on to an extensive career on film and in television, and recently has been appearing on the Broadway stage. Harry Shearer has recorded albums of his own music and worked with his wife, singer Judith Owen. He also periodically uses satellite feeds to deconstruct television newscasts. His greatest fame today is as one of the most important voice actors on *The Simpsons*. For a time Reiner was one of the most commercially successful directors in Hollywood, responsible for hits like *When Harry Met Sally . . .* (1989), *Misery* (1990), and *A Few Good Men* (1992). Spinal Tap, on the other hand, has had trouble matching its earlier hits. The group disbanded in the face of public indifference, but surviving members reunited for a concert tour in 1992 and have occasionally performed together since then.

Stranger Than Paradise

Left to right: Richard Edson, Eszter Balint, John Lurie in *Stranger Than Paradise. Courtesy of The Criterion Collection*

Samuel Goldwyn Company, 1984. Sound, B&W, 1.85. 89 minutes. Rated R.

Cast: John Lurie (Willie), Eszter Balint (Eva), Richard Edson (Eddie), Cecillia Stark (Aunt Lotte), Danny Rosen (Billy), Rammellzee (Man with money), Tom DiCillo (Airline agent), Richard Boes (Factory worker); Rockets Redglare, Harvey Perr, Brian J. Burchill (Poker players); Sara Driver (Girl with hat), Paul Sloane (Motel owner).

Credits: Written and directed by Jim Jarmusch. Part One (The New World) from an idea by Jim Jarmusch and John Lurie. Produced by Sara Driver. Executive producer: Otto Grokenberger. Director of photography: Tom DiCillo. Production manager: Sara Driver. Music by John Lurie. Edited by Jim Jarmusch and Melody London. Sound: Greg Curry (Part one), Drew Kunin (Parts two and three). Assistant camera: Paul Gibson (Part one), James Hayman (Parts two and three), Li Shin Yu (Part three). Gaffer/grip: Frank Prinzi. Production: Stephen Torton, Guido Chiesa, Louis Tancredi, Matt Buchwald, Una McClure, Tom Jarmusch, Sam Edwards. Sound editing: Melody London, John Auerbach. Mix: Jack Cooley at Magno Sound. Titles: Suzanne Fletcher. Titles shot by Cynosure films. A Grokenberger Film Produktion, Munich, and Cinesthesia Productions, Inc., production. Co-produced by ZDF. With special help from Paul Bartel. Music performed by The Paradise Quartet. Viola: Jill B. Jaffe. Violin: Mary L. Rowell. Violin: Kay Stern. Cello: Eugene Moye. "I Put a Spell on You" written and performed by Screamin' Jay Hawkins.

Additional Credits: Received a limited release on October 1, 1984.

Available: MGM Home Entertainment DVD (2000). ISB: 0-7928-4683-4. UPC: 0-27616-85287-8. Criterion Collection DVD (2007). UPC: 7-15515-02402-0.

In the 1970s, the film studies program at New York University positioned itself as an alternative to more mainstream films schools at UCLA and USC. Headed at the time by Laslo Benedek, the NYU Graduate School was located in the heart of the Lower East Side. Students wanted to be Martin Scorsese or Arthur Penn, independent directors who thrived outside Hollywood; they included Joel Coen, Spike Lee, and, for a time, Jim Jarmusch.

Jarmusch was born in 1953 in Akron, Ohio, the son of a Goodyear Tire and Rubber executive and a reporter for the local newspaper. He studied literature at Columbia University before entering NYU. Nicholas Ray, at the time suffering from terminal brain cancer, taught a third-year directing course, and Jarmusch became his student assistant. Jarmusch also plunged into the post-punk East Village scene, performing in a rock band and befriending John Lurie, a musician with the Lounge Lizards. Lurie appeared in Jarmusch's student film *Permanent Vacation* (1980). Because Jarmusch worked on *Lightning Over Water* (1980), a Wim Wenders documentary about Nicholas Ray, Wenders gave him about forty minutes' worth of film ends from *The State of Things*, enough footage to start making *Stranger Than Paradise*.

Jarmusch collaborated with Lurie on the script for the original version of the film, which later became the basis of "The New World" section of the final release. This first part, about a half-hour long, involved a hipster (played by Lurie), his desolate apartment, and a cousin (Eszter Balint) who arrives from Budapest. They eat, watch television, go to movies, read newspapers, play solitaire, shoplift, and listen to a cassette of "I Put a Spell on You." Occasionally Eddie (Richard Edson) drops by.

Additional financing from German producer Otto Grokenberger allowed Jarmusch and his crew to shoot two more segments, one in Cleveland ("One Year Later") and one in Florida ("Paradise"). These include more card games, movies, and television, as well as a few new characters and some driving sequences.

Jarmusch used an inheritance and industry connections to complete the film and enter it at the Cannes Film Festival, where it won the Palme d'Or in 1984. It opened theatrically after screening at the New York Film Festival, and was embraced by counterculture media. Jarmusch joined the Coen brothers and Spike Lee as an example of successful New York independent filmmakers. The Coens made their mark in *Blood Simple* (1984) by adopting polished, stylized cinematography and editing; Lee broke through by emphasizing race in *She's Gotta Have It* (1986).

Jarmusch, on the other hand, took a minimalist stance on filmmaking. He claimed influences like Andy Warhol, Robert Bresson, William Burroughs, and Jack Kerouac. "I am interested in the non-dramatic moments in life," he said in an interview. "I'm not at all attracted to making films that are about drama." It's a typically ambiguous remark from a filmmaker who carefully controls every element of his movies. In *Stranger Than Paradise*, as in all of Jarmusch's work, the look of the film—what is cool and what isn't, who is in and who is out—*is* the drama.

For Jarmusch and his colleagues, cool became the defining element of their work. And in the East Village in the early 1980s, the detritus of 1950s pop culture was the epitome of cool. The fedoras and beer cans and drab furniture in tenement apartments that fill out

Stranger Than Paradise could have come straight from *Pull My Daisy* (1959). Left unspoken was the influence of drugs, although the episodic nature of the script, and the use of black leader between shots, mimic the gaps and blackouts that can result from indulging.

Once *Stranger Than Paradise* leaves New York City, Jarmusch's vision reverts to Robert Frank landscapes, to French New Wave ennui, and to the druggy listlessness of beatniks. In the Cleveland section of the film, Jarmusch finds the same sort of grimy factories that Michael Cimino used in *The Deer Hunter*. But Jarmusch strips them of their context and narrative meaning, presenting them as pure imagery. Expecting more wouldn't be cool: you either get it or you don't. By dismissing the standards of mainstream film, Jarmusch doesn't have to answer for nonexistent plotting, poor acting, repetitive music, tawdry locations. They are all part of the point he is making.

Stranger Than Paradise made over $2 million in its initial release, an excellent return on its budget, but small change for mainstream Hollywood. Jarmusch continued his wayward, obscure style in films like *Down by Law* (1986) and *Mystery Train* (1989) with diminishing results. When the lethargic Western *Dead Man* (1995) failed at the box office despite a cast that included Johnny Depp and Robert Mitchum, Jarmusch blamed Harvey Weinstein, his distributor. His most recent films, *Broken Flowers* (2005) and *The Limits of Control* (2009), were financial disappointments.

The Terminator

Orion, 1984. Sound, color, 1.85. 107 minutes. Rated R.

Cast: Arnold Schwarzenengger (Terminator), Michael Biehn (Kyle Reese), Linda Hamilton (Sarah Connor), Lance Henriksen (Vukovich), Paul Winfield (Lt. Traxler), Rick Rossovich (Matt), Bess Motta (Ginger), Earl Boen (Silverman), Dick Miller (Pawn shop clerk), Shawn Schepps (Nancy), Bruce M. Kerner (Desk sergeant), Franco Columbu (Future Terminator), Bill Paxton (Punk leader); Brad Rearden, Brian Thompson (Punks); William Wisher, Jr., Ken Fritz, Tom Oberhaus (Policemen).

Credits: Directed by James Cameron. Written by James Cameron with Gale Anne Hurd. Additional dialogue: William Wisher. Acknowledgement to the works of Harlan Ellison. Produced by Gale Anne Hurd. Executive producers: John Daly and Derek Gibson. Director of photography: Adam Greenberg. Edited by Mark Goldblatt. Music by Brad Fiedel. Casting by Stanzi Stokes. Executive in charge of production: Bruce M. Kerner. Special Terminator effects created by Stan Winston. Special visual effects by Fantasy II. Production manager and post production supervisor: Donna Smith. First assistant director: Betsy Magruder. Art director: George Costello. Set decorator: Maria Rebman Caso. Supervising sound editor: David Campling. Sound effects: Mayflower Films, Inc. Synthesizer sound effects: Robert Garrett. Music editor: Emilie Robertson. Music consultant: Budd Carr. Production sound mixer: Richard

Lightstone. Stunt coordinator: Ken Fritz. Script supervisor: Brenda Weisman. Costume designer: Hilary Wright. Hair stylist: Peter Tothpal. Makeup artist: Jefferson Dawn. Special effects: Roger George, Frank DeMarco. Special effects coordinator: Ernest D. Farino. GMF Robots supplied and operated by Ellison Machinery Co. Motoman robots supplied and operated by Yaskawa Electric America. Sound recorded at Glen Glenn Sound. Prints by DeLuxe. A Euro Film Funding Limited feature. A Hemdale presentation of a Pacific Western Production. Copyright Cinema '84, a Greenberg Brothers partnership.

Additional Credits: Production dates: February to June 1984. Released October 26, 1984.

Other Versions: Sequels: *Terminator 2: Judgment Day* (1991), *Terminator 3: Rise of the Machines* (2003), *Terminator Salvation* (2009).

Available: MGM DVD (2001). UPC: 027616854735.

A surprise box-office hit, *The Terminator* gave new impetus to a flagging science fiction genre; more important, it boosted the careers of star Arnold Schwarzenegger, producer Gale Anne Hurd, and director James Cameron. It also initiated a successful movie franchise that has lasted three decades.

Born in Canada in 1954, Cameron became a movie fan after seeing Stanley Kubrick's *2001: A Space Odyssey* (1968) and George Lucas's *Star Wars* (1977). Cameron studied to be a marine biologist, then turned to physics at California State University. By his early twenties he had dropped out of school, marrying a waitress and becoming a truck driver. He also wrote and studied film on his own, finishing a test reel that got him a job with Roger Corman. With Corman he progressed from special effects and set design to directing a negligible horror sequel, *Piranha II: The Spawning* (1981).

Hurd enjoyed a privileged upbringing in Palm Springs, California. An academic overachiever, she majored in economics and communications at Stanford, pursuing a film career with Corman after she graduated in 1977. As his assistant, Hurd learned everything from budgeting to publicity. She met Cameron while she was supervising reshoots for *Humanoids from the Deep* (1980); he was doing model work and special effects on *Battle Beyond the Stars* (1980).

After the *Piranha* debacle, Cameron decided to work on his own project, turning to an idea about an android from the future sent to the past to murder the mother of a potential world leader. With Hurd's help, he finished a draft in May 1982. Cameron's longtime friend William Wisher also contributed scenes and dialogue. To insure that he would direct the script, Cameron sold his rights to Hurd for one dollar. The two set up a production deal with John Daly at Hemdale Pictures.

Cameron initially envisioned either Lance Henriksen or Michael Biehn in the role of the deadly Terminator, but Orion executive Michael Medavoy, who would be distributing the movie, argued for Arnold Schwarzenegger. A fitness and bodybuilding celebrity with a thick Austrian accent, Schwarzenegger had pursued an acting career with admirable doggedness but little luck, appearing in everything from television to documentaries without establishing himself as much more than a muscle-bound extra. *Conan the Barbarian* (1982), a pulp fantasy for which he played the title role, found enough of an audience to merit a sequel, postponing his participation in *The Terminator* for almost two years.

The delay gave Cameron the opportunity to fine-tune his script, as well as to prepare storyboards for the production. As a result, *The Terminator* is one of the most tightly plotted and cleverly shot films of its time. Presented first as a whodunit, it evolves into a dystopian sci-fi adventure with religious overtones. Without knowing the full implications of the plot, viewers can still follow Cameron's story line, which places complex moral questions in a truly life-or-death setting. Cameron's bold visual style and relentless pacing set *Terminator* apart from exploitation films, but it was his careful attention to the audience, to making sure shots and scenes conveyed the right information, that helped make the movie so popular.

Remarkably, during preproduction Cameron was also writing sequels to two major successes, *Alien* (1979) and *First Blood* (1982). He used essentially the same premise for what became *Aliens* (1986) and *Rambo: First Blood, Part 2* (1985), sending the main characters from the originals back to their worst nightmares, and then doubling the size of the villains they faced.

By the time *Terminator* filming began on March 19, 1984, Cameron knew exactly what he wanted from his actors, his stunt people, his crew, and even the notoriously independent Stan Winston, hired as the special effects coordinator. The ten-week shoot started smoothly, but the last eight weeks were predominately at night, and included scenes that used thousands of rounds of explosive squibs. Schwarzenegger was dumbfounded by Cameron's recklessness in demonstrating stunts, while Linda Hamilton, cast as heroine Sarah Connor, complained about his personality. "He didn't make a lot of room in this movie to satisfy his actors," she told a reporter later. "He had a reputation for not treating people very well and that's exactly what happened with me on that film." (Hamilton would later marry Cameron, after he divorced both his first wife and Gale Anne Hurd.)

After principal photography was completed in June, Cameron continued writing *Aliens* while overseeing editing of *The Terminator*. He later claimed that he came to blows with Hemdale's Daly, who wanted him to discard the film's final ten minutes. He was also dismayed at the publicity campaign devised by Orion, whose executives predicted that the movie would disappear after three weeks. But *The Terminator* not only received excellent reviews, it outperformed expensive and high-profile titles like *Dune* and *2010: The Year We Make Contact*.

Critics offered many reasons for *The Terminator*'s success: the Sarah Connor character, who evolves from a waitress into a credible action heroine; Schwarzenegger's cannily robotic turn as an unstoppable android; a strong supporting cast consisting of Cameron cronies like Henriksen and Bill Paxton as well as Roger Corman stalwarts like Dick Miller; Winston's imaginative effects; outstanding stunts, cinematography and editing; and the carefully modulated story line.

But the foremost factor in the film was Cameron himself. He wasn't afraid to make large gestures, bathing the screen in blood-red light, distorting sound while slowing down action to expand time and build up suspense, injecting moments of black humor, and carefully preparing viewers for his big set pieces.

He introduces a police office that will shortly be destroyed in a complicated shot almost forty seconds long. Two cops—Henriksen's Vukovich and Paul Winfield's Traxler—stride past cubicles trading exposition about two inexplicable murders, the camera preceding them. Briskly professional, technically dexterous, it is a throwaway moment handled with unusual, even obsessive attention to detail and pacing.

Cameron was subsequently involved with some of the most ambitious and successful films of the past twenty years, notably *Titanic* (1997), the first $200 million production. Despite massive overruns, it earned over a billion dollars and won eleven Oscars. For the next decade Cameron concentrated on television and on documentaries while promoting the use of 3-D technology for features. He wrote and directed *Terminator 2: Judgment Day* (1991), but did not take part in the third or fourth sequels.

Some have noticed plot similarities between the first two *Terminator* movies and *Cyborg 2087*, a low-budget sci-fi film released in 1966. Cameron has been reticent about two lawsuits initiated by science fiction author Harlan Ellison, who cited resemblances between *The Terminator* and two episodes he wrote for TV's *The Outer Limits*: "Soldier" and "Demon with a Glass Hand." Ellison won both cases.

Back to the Future

Universal, 1985. Sound, color, 1.85. 116 minutes. Rated PG.

Cast: Michael J. Fox (Marty McFly), Christopher Lloyd (Dr. Emmett Brown), Lea Thompson (Lorraine Baines), Crispin Glover (George McFly), Thomas F. Wilson (Biff Tannen), Claudia Wells (Jennifer Parker), Marc McClure (Dave McFly), Wendie Jo Sperber (Linda McFly), George DiCenzo (Sam Baines), James Tolkan (Mr. Strickland), Jeffrey Jay Cohen (Skinhead), Casey Siemaszko (3-D), Billy Zane (Match), Harry Waters, Jr. (Marvin Berry), Donald Fullilove (Goldie Wilson), Lisa Freeman (Babs), Cristen Kauffman (Betty), Elsa Raven (Clocktower lady), Will Hare (Pa Peabody), Ivy Bethune (Ma Peabody), Frances Lee McCain (Stella Baines), Jason Marin (Sherman Peabody), Katherine Britton (Peabody daughter), Jason Hervey (Milton Baines), Maia Brewton (Sally Baines), Courtney Gains (Dixon), Richard L. Duran (Terrorist), Jeff O'Haco (Terrorist van driver), Johnny Green (Scooter kid #1), Jamie Abbott (Scooter kid #2), Norman Alden (Lou), Read Morgan (Cop), Sachi Parker (Bystander #1), Robert Krantz (Bystander #2), Gary Riley (Guy #1), Karen Petrasek (Girl #1), Buck Flower (Bum); Tommy Thomas, Granville "Danny" Young, David Harold Brown, Lloyd L. Tolbert (Starlighters); Paul Hanson, Lee Brownfield, Robert DeLapp (Pinheads).

Credits: Directed by Robert Zemeckis. Written by Robert Zemeckis & Bob Gale. Produced by Bob Gale and Neil Canton. Executive producers: Steven Spielberg, Frank Marshall, Kathleen Kennedy. Director of photography: Dean Cundey. Production designed by Lawrence G. Paull. Edited by Arthur Schmidt, Harry Keramidas. Music by Alan Silvestri. "The Power of Love" performed by Huey Lewis and the News. Written by Huey Lewis and Chris Hayes. Casting by Mike Fenton, Jane Feinberg, Judy Taylor. Unit production managers: Dennis E. Jones, Jack Grossberg. First assistant director: David McGiffert. Visual effects produced at Industrial Light & Magic. Make-up created by Ken Chase. Art director: Todd Hallowell. Set decorator: Hal Gausman. Script continuity: Nancy B. Hansen. Production sound mixer: William B. Kaplan. Costume designer: Deborah L. Scott. Hair stylist: Dorothy Byrne. Special effects supervisor: Kevin Pike. Music supervisor: Bones Howe. Supervising sound editors: Charles L. Campbell, Robert Rutledge. Opticals by Movie Magic. Title design: Nina Saxon. Stunt coordinator: Walter Scott. Panavision. Technicolor. Dolby Stereo.

Additional Credits: Production dates: November 26, 1984 to April 1985. Released July 3, 1985.

Other Versions: Sequels *Back to the Future II* (1989), *Back to the Future III* (1990).
Available: Universal Studios DVD (2002). ISBN: 0-7832-6993-5. UPC: 0-25192-21212-3.

One of the cleverest of the 1980s blockbusters, *Back to the Future* proved popular enough to support a trilogy that extended to 1990. The script was the work of Robert Zemeckis and Robert Gale, long-term collaborators who were also protégés of director Steven Spielberg. Gale was born in St. Louis in 1951, the son of an attorney and a violinist. He switched from Tulane to the University of Southern California, where he met Zemeckis.

A year younger than his partner, Zemeckis was born in Chicago, where he made 8mm shorts as a way to learn the process of filmmaking. "I was fascinated by the illusion of movies before anything else," he told one interviewer. "Always trying to figure out how they did something, how they did a visual effect or an action sequence." He cited *Bonnie and Clyde* (1967) as the movie that showed him the potential of the medium. With Gale at USC, he embarked on what he called "guerrilla filmmaking," exploring how to photograph chases and action. Their final USC film, *Field of Honor*, won a student academy award.

Gale and Zemeckis wrote a series of "spec" scripts to television shows, but turned down a long-term writing contract to concentrate on feature films. Director John Milius offered to let them expand an idea he was developing; *1941*, the resulting World War II comedy, was directed by Steven Spielberg.

Spielberg also produced *I Wanna Hold Your Hand* (1978) and *Used Cars* (1980), two witty, fast-paced comedies directed by Zemeckis. Both did poorly at the box office. "You go into a complete crash when the movie opens and no one wants to see it," Zemeckis remembered. "Just because movies work with audiences doesn't mean anybody wants to go see them."

By this time, Zemeckis and Gale had completed the script for *Back to the Future*, but could not get financing from any studio. "I have a stack of rejection letters from every studio in town except Steven," Zemeckis said. Worried about his reputation in the industry, he hoped to work outside Spielberg's umbrella. It took three years before Michael Douglas offered him *Romancing the Stone* (released in 1984). When it became the top-grossing film of 1985, *Back to the Future* was suddenly a hot prospect.

"Steven's name had become synonymous with a certain kind of film," Zemeckis said. "It had become a brand name, and to have him associated with *Back to the Future* was a perfect fit." The director had hoped to cast Michael J. Fox in the lead, but chose Eric Stoltz because Fox was tied to a TV show. But as Zemeckis remembered later, "You can't make creative decisions for corporate reasons." After shooting for four weeks, he realized that Stoltz was not working in the part. Spielberg helped convince Universal executives to scrap $4 million worth of footage and start over again.

The plot to *Back to the Future* sends a suburban Los Angeles teenager from the 1980s to the 1950s, where he is enmeshed in a welter of Oedipal conflicts while trying to return to the present. Part of the pleasure in watching the film is recognizing how many genres and plot lines have been ransacked by Zemeckis and Gale. Gang fights, mad scientists, teen lust, rock'n'roll, and class warfare are all tied to a story line whose built-in deadlines converge in an expertly timed climax. As Zemeckis points out, "Because of the story it's considered to be this giant special effects movie." But only some thirty shots required special effects, and most of those were for lightning. The 1950s settings, while charming, never dominated the story; they were a backdrop to an involving human drama.

Zemeckis brought an exuberance to *Back to the Future* that is reflected in its nimble pacing and gee-whiz tone. While enamored of technology, the director is also fixated on his audience, determined to win its approval. More so than many of his contemporaries, his best films are tied to their times. *Back to the Future* is forever anchored to 1985 by its pop songs, brand names, hairstyles, and plot twists.

Back to the Future was a box-office sensation, in part for its humor and adventure, but also because of Zemeckis's warm portrayal of its characters. He shot its two sequels back to back, extending the story to a dystopian future and back to the Wild West frontier.

With Spielberg as executive producer, Zemeckis helmed *Who Framed Roger Rabbit* (1988), a groundbreaking combination of animation and live action. Like Spielberg, he branched into producing, forming Dark Castle Entertainment with Joel Silver and Gilbert Adler. As a director, Zemeckis continued to extend the use of special effects, helping pioneer 3-D performance capture technology in films like *The Polar Express* (2004) and *Beowulf* (2007). He won a directing Oscar for the effects-laden *Forrest Gump* (1994), which also won Best Picture. In the relatively small-scale *Cast Away* (2000), he made perhaps his most emotionally complicated picture.

Sherman's March

First Run Features, 1986. Sound, color, 1.37. 157 minutes.

Featuring: Pat Rendleman, Charleen Swansea, Joyous Perrin.

Credits: Camera, sound, editing: Ross McElwee. Assistant editors: Kate Davis, Alyson Denny, Meredith Woods. Narration: Ross McElwee. Reading of historical narration: Richard Leacock. New York statue camerawork: Michel Negroponte. Sound mix: Richard Bock. Negative conformer: Dick Cohen. Map: Stephen Nichols. Thanks to: Alexandra Anthony, Adam Bartos, Ted Bogosian, Michael Callahan, David Fanning, Tom Gunning, Alfred Guzzetti, Jeanne Jordon, Richard Leacock, Julie Levinson, Michel Negroponte, Dede McElwee Nichols, Edward Pincus, Dick Rogers, Irwin Young. With special gratitude to: Steven Ascher, Marilyn Levine, Peter McGhee, Robb Moss, Dr. & Mrs. Ross McElwee. Partially funded by: Boston Film/Video Foundation, New England Regional Fellowship Program, John Simon Guggenheim Memorial Foundation, Massachusetts Artists Foundation, Inc., Massachusetts Council on the Arts and Humanities, Pinewood Foundation, WGBH Educational Foundation.

Additional Credits: Directed by Ross McElwee. Full title: *Sherman's March: A Meditation on the Possibility of Romantic Love in the South During an*

Era of Nuclear Weapons Proliferation. Premiered in New York City on September 5, 1986.

Available: First Run Features DVD (2004). UPC: 7-20229-91097-2.

In *Sherman's March*, filmmaker Ross McElwee journeys through the contemporary South, using a diary format to document the culture and people of a region he views with a cautious, even reluctant, sympathy. Born in Charlotte, North Carolina, in 1947, McElwee attended college in Boston, studying film at the Massachusetts Institute of Technology under Richard Leacock and Ed Pincus. After working as a studio cameraman for a local TV station in Charlotte, North Carolina, he freelanced as a cinematographer and editor on independent documentaries. He also started making his own films in 1976.

As he explains in an opening monologue, McElwee received a $9,000 Guggenheim grant to make a documentary about William Tecumseh Sherman, the Union general who enacted his theory of "total war" in a swath of destruction across the South at the tail end of the Civil War. Just before filming started, McElwee broke up with a girlfriend. While he dutifully documents biographical details about Sherman, McElwee switches the focus of the film to his personal problems, using them as a springboard to investigate the South in general.

To make his observations more palatable to a filmgoing audience accustomed to treating documentaries as medicine, McElwee adopted the personality of a naïf, a Pangloss who wanders through a landscape that has become alien. It was a convenient but not especially accurate role to play. After all, he was a world traveler who had shot anthropological footage in Africa for John Marshall (*The Hunters*, 1957) and who had been making his own films for over a decade. By posing as an innocent, he could present uncomfortable material without ostensibly commenting on it. And by focusing the film's narrative on himself, he could add political and social situations that an audience might not otherwise want to see.

"I only knew I wanted to make some sort of film about my homeland," he wrote about *Sherman's March*. "I never intended for it to be an historical documentary. I assumed that racial relations in the so-called 'New South' would be a major theme . . . but other themes became more dominant." McElwee traveled through the South for four months (his journey amusingly traced on the same sort of maps used in educational films), "and shot, or was ready to shoot, nearly every day."

He ended up with close to twenty-five hours of footage. The first cut of the film was eight hours, a four to one ratio that is unheard of in documentaries. It's an indication of how carefully McElwee husbanded his film stock, and how attuned he was to the overall shape of his project, that there was very little footage to discard. Still, it took the filmmaker two and a half years to edit the project down to its current running time.

Viewed as an anthropological documentary, *Sherman's March* offers a fascinating portrait of a South of survivalists, religious zealots, struggling artists, and noveau riche. McElwee films some of his subjects as if they were as exotic or unknowable as African bushmen, at times seemingly flabbergasted at what he was recording. What *Sherman's March* doesn't provide is an explanation of how the social systems he observes got that way, or how they operate. Instead, McElwee offers oblique and occasionally very funny comments about situations in his narration. "Some of us hope that by raising some issues, other people will find the answers," he said about his voice-over.

McElwee filmed himself delivering monologues to the camera while he was preparing his other material. They separated McElwee's work from mainstream documentaries, and at first he had not intended to use them. But, as he said later, "there was a sense that something was missing." At the time McElwee's presence in his film stirred some controversy with conservative critics. McElwee made himself part of the interviews he filmed, sometimes even allowing himself to be glimpsed in windows and mirrors, holding his camera and a microphone. "In the conventions of documentary filmmaking, those are the parts that you would cut out," he said, "but to me it seemed extremely important to allow those references to stay in."

He chose not to address another criticism of the film, the fact that he was directing his interviews rather than "documenting" them. The illusion offered by cinema verité filmmakers was that they were just observing reality, but McElwee made no pretense at objectivity. The fact that his film ended up concentrating on his thwarted relationships with a series of women renders objectivity irrelevant. McElwee has acknowledged that his film can be criticized for being too solipsistic, but objects to accusations that he exploited relationships or invaded anyone's privacy. "To some degree, they're playing along with the game, too," he said about the people he filmed.

In reviews, critics compared McElwee to everyone from Woody Allen to Mark Twain. Twain and McElwee do share a willingness to revel in social absurdities, but McElwee seems modest where Twain could be bitter and savage. A closer comparison might be to the comic writer Dave Barry, whose view of the South ranges from fond to exasperated. McElwee has always cited *Diaries* (1982) by his teacher Ed Pincus as an important personal influence on his filmmaking.

McElwee's personality was engaging enough for his film to merit a theatrical release, despite its extreme length. *Sherman's March* received generally positive reviews and made enough of a profit to enable McElwee to continue his autobiographical musings in features like *Bright Leaves* (2003). Many see McElwee's influence in a cycle of first-person documentaries like *Roger & Me* (1999) by Michael Moore. McElwee continues to teach filmmaking at Harvard University.

Charleen Swansea and Ross McElwee, two of the figures in *Sherman's March*. *This photograph was taken in 1994; courtesy of Ross McElwee*

Hoosiers

Orion, 1986. Sound, color, 1.86. 116 minutes. Rated PG.

Cast: Gene Hackman (Coach Norman Dale), Barbara Hershey (Myra Fleener), Dennis Hopper (Shooter), Sheb Wooley (Cletus), Fern Persons (Opal Fleener), Chelcie Ross (George), Robert Swan (Rollin), Michael O'Guinne (Rooster), Wil Dewitt (Reverend Doty), John Robert Thompson (Sheriff Finley), Michael Sassone (Preacher Purl), Gloria Dorson (Millie), Mike Dalzell (Mayor Carl), Calvert L. Welker (Junior), Eric Gilliom (J. June); Robert Boyle, Jerry D. Petro (Referees, Oolitic); Sam Smiley (Referee, Cedar Knob), Tom McConnell (Coach, Cedar Knob), Dennis Farkas ("Gorilla" player, Cedar Knob), Tim Fogarty (Referee, Verdi), Don Stratigos (Referee, Logootee), Ken Strunk (Referee, Dugger); Jerry D. Larrison, Thomas W. Marshall (Referees, Terhune); Gary Long, C.W. Mundy (Coaches, Jasper), Jeff Moster (Player, Jasper), Ralph H. Shively (Doc Buggins); Rich Komenich, Scott Miley, Robert Sutton (Reporters); Ray Crowe (Coach, State), Ray Craft (Official, finals), Tom Carnegie (P.A. announcer, finals), Hilliard Gates (Radio announcer, finals); Geoff Brewer, Dean Ferrandini, Gary Jensen (Stunts); Laura Robling, Nancy Harris, Libbey Schenck (Hickory cheerleaders); The Hickory Huskers: Brad Boyle (Whit), Steve Hollar (Rade), Brad Long (Buddy), David Neidorf (Everett), Kent Poole (Merle), Wade Schenck (Ollie), Scott Summers (Strap), Maris Valainis (Jimmy [Chitwood]).

Credits: Directed by David Anspaugh. Written by Angelo Pizzo. Produced by Carter De Haven and Angelo Pizzo. Executive producers: John Daly, Derek Gibson. Director of photography: Fred Murphy. Production designer: David Nichols. Film editor: C. Timothy O'Meara. Music by Jerry Goldsmith. Associate producer: Graham Henderson. Unit production manager: Graham Henderson. First assistant director: Herb Adelman. Casting: Ken Carlson of Carlson-Dowd, Inc. Costume designer: Jane Anderson. Script supervisor: Marilyn Bailey. Supervising sound editor: Bill Phillips. Music supervisor: Budd Carr. Orchestrations by Arthur Morton. Production sound mixer: David Brownlow. Makeup artist: Ronnie Spector. Hair dresser: Daniel Marc. Steadicam operator: Randy Nolen. Basketball coordinator: Spyridon "Strats" Stratigos. Technical advisors: Tom McConnell, Tom Abernathy. Title design: Phill Norman. Titles and opticals: Pacific Title. Dolby Stereo. Filmed entirely in the state of Indiana. A Hemdale Film Corporation presentation of a Carter De Haven production.

Additional Credits: Production dates: October 21 to December 1985. Released November 14, 1986.

Available: MGM Home Entertainment DVD (2005). ISBN: 0-7928-4359-2. UPC: 0-27616-8018-2-1. Two disc version (2005). UPC: 027616902412.

Loosely based on the Milan Indians, a small-town basketball team that won the Indiana State Championships in 1954, *Hoosiers* began as a collaboration between two Indiana natives and college roommates. During a Christmas break from USC film school, writer Angelo Pizzo attended a high school game in Bloomington, Indiana. It inspired him to pursue a film project with David Anspaugh, who was working his way up from associate producer on television series to producing and directing individual episodes and pilots.

The Milan Indians story gave Pizzo a framework for what became *Hoosiers*, but not much more. "The essence of all drama is conflict," he told reporter Bill Kauffman in 2006. The Indians didn't face any real problems, got along with each other, and took the championship without much trouble. Pizzo used versions of his own childhood friends in their place. The Indians coach at the time, Marvin Wood, was twenty-six. "I wrote it that way and the movie didn't work. If he had failed, he still had the rest of his life," Pizzo revealed. Instead, the writer based fictional coach Norman Dale on Robert Duvall's role as Mac Sledge, an alcoholic, over-the-hill country singer who redeems himself in *Tender Mercies* (1983). Dale's coaching technique, and his violence, came from college coaching legend Bobby Knight.

Hoosiers also owes an unacknowledged debt to *Rocky* (1976), whose plot it parallels in several key aspects: flawed hero seeking a second chance, alcoholic assistant, spinster love interest, for example. *Hoosiers* appeared after several other sports-related hits, like the Oscar-winning *Chariots of Fire* (1981), whose synthesized score Jerry Goldsmith seems to be aping here. Pizzo drew from so many other popular films that his script at times seems like code, a shorthand account of the formula for sports movies. All he had to do is set up a scene, and viewers could tell what would happen. But *Breaking Away* (1979), set in his native Bloomington, was not one of Pizzo's favorite films. "I saw my hometown being depicted and I didn't recognize any of the people in it. Those people didn't belong in Bloomington," he told Kauffman. That's why he felt "in a movie called *Hoosiers*, you'd better get Indiana right."

Financing came from Hemdale Film Corporation, a British company that also backed *The Terminator* (1984) and *Platoon* (1986). Pizzo attributes Hemdale's participation to the fact that one of its founders had an alcoholic father similar to "Shooter" in the script.

Holding the film together is Gene Hackman, giving an effortless performance as a complicated, difficult, even ornery coach. Hackman doesn't ask for sympathy; if anything, he plays up Dale's sense of wronged isolation. As the love interest, Barbara Hershey struggles in an underwritten part, while Dennis Hopper, badly in need of redemption in real life, hams it up as the town drunk. It was a showy enough job to win an Oscar nomination.

Still, what makes the picture seem authentic for many viewers are its Indiana locations. Much of *Hoosiers* was shot in and around New Richmond, a town that still proclaims its connection to the movie. (Anspaugh noted that it rained almost every day of the shoot, adding an unexpectedly melancholy note to the film.) Furthermore, as Pizzo said, "We determined not only to shoot in Indiana but to hire only real Indiana basketball players. We had open casting calls and reduced them not by reading but by basketball playing." Apart from Maris Valainis, who starred as Jimmy Chitwood, few of the players pursued acting subsequently. (Valainis is now a golf pro in Southern California.)

Carefully middlebrow, *Hoosiers* opened to generally positive reviews (*Variety* called it "both rousing and too conventional") and surprisingly strong ticket sales. Anspaugh and Pizzo exploited their sports niche with *Rudy* (1993), an underdog football story set at Notre Dame University, and *The Game of Their Lives* (2005), about an underdog soccer team from the United States that defeats England during the 1950 World Cup.

Hollywood Reporter journalist Brooks Boliek attributed the film's selection to the National Film Registry to a letter-writing campaign started by Bonnie Britton, at the time a film critic for the *Indianapolis Star*. "I mentioned it in one of my columns," she admitted, and Library of Congress staffers were subsequently inundated with requests from Indiana citizens. "It shows how the public process can work," said Gregory Lukow, the assistant chief of the library's Motion Picture, Broadcasting and Recorded Sound Division.

Tin Toy

Pixar, 1988. Sound, color, 1.78. 5 minutes.

Cast: Tinny (as the Tin Toy), Billy (as himself), Gumbo, Les, Flip 'n Beth, Ace, Clocky, Spot, Zoo Train, Chrome Dome, Eben's Car, Rallye Guy, Fire Hydrant, Helicopter Sheep, Toypot, Frodo, Bouncy, RenderMan.

Credits: Direction, animation and story: John Lasseter. Technical directors: William Reeves, Eben Ostby. Additional animation: William Reeves, Eben Ostby, Craig Good. Modeling: William Reeves, Eben Ostby, John Lasseter, Craig Good. Sound: Gary Rydstrom, Sprocket Systems. Production coordination: Ralph Guggenheim, Susan Anderson, Deirdre Warin. Best Boy: Tony Apodaca.

Awards: Oscar for Best Short Film—Animated.

Available: Buena Vista Home Entertainment DVD *Pixar Short Films* (2007). ISBN: 0-7888-7402-0. UPC: 786936723489.

The fourth short film from Pixar, *Tin Toy* was the first to fully explore the themes that would make the studio a leading force in animation. Pixar can be traced back to a 1979 division of Lucasfilm that largely focused on developing RenderMan, a computer animation software program. When he left Apple Computer in 1985, Steve Jobs purchased the division from George Lucas and renamed it Pixar. His main product was the Pixar Image Computer, a powerful graphics unit aimed at government agencies and hospitals. To show off the computer's capabilities, Jobs hired John Lasseter to make a cartoon short.

Born in Hollywood in 1957, Lasseter grew up with an affection for classic Disney and Warner Brothers cartoons. Encouraged by his mother, a high school art teacher, he pursued animation as a career, taking part in the first animation class taught at the California Institute for the Arts in 1975. (CalArts was formed in 1961 by Walt Disney and his brother Roy.) After winning two Student Academy Awards in 1979 and 1980, he took a job as animator at the Walt Disney Company, contributing to films like *The Fox and the Hound* (1981). Lasseter left Disney for Lucasfilm in 1983, where he met Ed Catmull, one of the principal architects of RenderMan.

Lasseter later called Catmull "one of the most amazing people I've ever known in my life," and it was Catmull who opened his eyes to the potential for computer animation. The process had previously been used to create backgrounds or the occasional character. No one, Lasseter included, believed that computer animation could support a film by itself, without any drawing by hand. But Catmull wasn't worried about the technology—he was looking for someone who understood story and characters.

Lasseter first worked on what would become *The Adventures of André and Wally B.* (1984), an amusing but primitive one-gag short that helped persuade Lucas to get out of computer animation. Steve Jobs had more faith in the company, pouring in millions in financing. But his primary goal was to sell the Pixar Image Computer, a $125,000 image processor. The animation department was left on its own, giving Lasseter the freedom to design and write *Luxo Jr.* (1986). Another breakthrough, the film showed Lasseter's facility at imbuing inanimate objects with personalities. His characters and story became more important than the film's animating techniques. (The Luxo lamp would later become a mascot for the studio.) *Red's Dream* (1987) introduced far more complex art design, including rainy weather and a bike shop location that featured tens of thousands of polygon shapes.

Tin Toy was another advance, the first time Pixar attempted to animate a human being, the first to employ complicated camera movements, and the first to exploit pop culture of the 1950s and '60s. (The baby came out so poorly that Pixar for years resisted using human characters.) The animation is significantly smoother and more polished than *The Adventures of André and Wally B.* four years earlier; it is also far busier, with up to a dozen characters moving at once, and incorporating several reflective surfaces.

But again, story and characters were more important than animation techniques. Lasseter tapped into a plot line and time period that appealed to two generations at once. Older viewers, especially parents, could appreciate references to TV shows like *The Price Is Right* and Lasseter's loving variations on period toys. Younger viewers who didn't know anything about the 1950s could delight in the film's tension and slapstick. And everyone could respond to the emotional pull of the story, the decision of "Tinny" to remain true to his destiny despite potential personal loss. The cartoon even gave a subtle demonstration of how toys help babies develop motor skills. (As the camera crosses over a sofa, you can see a copy of the July 1987 issue of *Sunset* magazine, complete with mailing label. It's a detail that not only pins the making of the cartoon to a specific time; it also helps define Billy's parents.)

A tour de force on several levels, *Tin Toy* showed a commitment to production values, to intelligent scripting, and to uplifting sentiments that was largely missing from animation of the time. The film pointed the way to *Toy Story* (1995), the studio's first feature, also a Registry title. When *Tin Toy* won an animation Oscar, it validated both Catmull's dream of computer animation and Lasseter's approach to narrative. Pixar began to attract the most talented personnel in the industry.

The Thin Blue Line

Third Floor Productions/American Playhouse/Miramax, 1988. Sound, color, 1.85. 101 minutes.

Featuring: Interviews (in order of appearance): Randall Adams, David Harris; Gus Rose, Jackie Johnson, Marshall Touchton (Homicide detectives in Dallas); Dale Holt (Internal Affairs investigator in Dallas), Sam Kittrell (Police detective in Vidor); Hootie Nelson, Dennis Johnson, Floyd Jackson (Friends of David Harris in Vidor); Edith James, Dennis White (Defense attorneys); Don Metcalfe (Judge); Emily Miller, R.L. Miller (Surprise eyewitnesses); Elba Carr (Employee at Fas-Gas), Michael Randell (Third surprise eyewitness), Melvyn Carson Bruder (Appellate attorney). Re-enactments (of the crime scene, interrogation and drive-in movie): Adam Goldfine (Randall Adams), Derek Horton (David Harris), Ron Thornhill (Robert Wood), Marianne Leone (Teresa Turko), Amanda Caprio (Popcorn lady), Michael Nicoll (Interrogation officer), Michael Cirilla (2nd interrogation officer), Phyllis Rodgers (Stenographer).

Credits: Directed by Errol Morris. Produced by Mark Lipson. Executive producer: Lindsay Law. Directors of photography: Stefan Czapsky, Robert Chappell. Associate producer: Brad Fuller. Production designer: Ted Bafaloukos. Editor: Paul Barnes. Original music composed by Philip Glass. Music produced by Kurt Mankasci. Music conducted by Michael Riesman. Production manager: Shelley Houis. Sound: Brad Fuller. Assistant producer: David Hohmann. Additional photography: Philip Carr-Foster, Ned Burgess, Peter Sova, Tom Sigel. Art director: Lester Cohen. Courtroom drawings: Christine Cornell. Re-recording mixers: Jack Leahy, Samuel Lehmer. Color by Du Art Laboratories, Inc. Dolby stereo. An American Playhouse presentation of an Errol Morris Film. Produced in association with American Playhouse with funds from Public Television Stations, The Corporation for Public Broadcasting, The National Endowment for the Arts, The Chubb Group of Insurance Companies, Channel 4 (U.K.), The Program Development Company. Clips from *Swinging Cheerleaders* (1974), *The Student Body* (1975), *Boston Blackie* (1952), *Dillinger* (1945). Special thanks: Julia Sheehan, The Criminal Justice Center, Sam Houston State University, Dr. George Beto and Dr. Peter Phillips, Volker Schlondorff.

Additional Credits: Released August 25, 1988.

Available: MGM Home Entertainment DVD (2005). ISBN: 0-7928-6470-0. UPC: 0-27616-90232-0.

"Truth is not subjective," Errol Morris told an interviewer in 2000, two years after the release of *The Thin Blue Line*. Born in Hewlett on Long Island, New York, in 1948, Morris studied the cello, then history, and finally philosophy at the University of California at Berkeley. He became interested in filmmaking at the Pacific Film Archives, and with backing from family and a classmate started making documentaries. *Gates of Heaven* (1978, about pet cemeteries) was quirky; *Vernon, Florida* (1981, a postmodern travelogue made when another project fell through) lacked relevance for mainstream viewers. Unable to finance additional projects, Morris worked for two years as a private detective.

In the later 1980s, Morris was in Dallas hoping to make a film about Dr. James Grigson, a forensic psychologist known as "Dr. Death" for his testimony in capital murder cases. Through Grigson, Morris learned about Randall Dale Adams, a convicted cop killer who had been sentenced to death. During a routine traffic stop on a night in November 1976, Dallas policeman Robert Wood was shot and killed. In the car that Wood had pulled to the side of the road were Adams, at the time a drifter and day laborer living in a motel with his brother, and David Ray Harris, a sixteen-year-old runaway.

The Thin Blue Line is built around the legwork a good detective would be expected to do when investigating a crime. Morris interviewed everyone involved, marshaled all the available facts, and constructed timelines. He compared evidence from other crimes, got witnesses to recant testimony, and essentially proved that Harris had committed the murder, not Adams. Morris had the makings of a textbook documentary, one that could have featured charts and diagrams, talking heads, and a narrator making an impassioned plea for Adams' release.

But was it possible to show the truth rather than proclaim it? Wouldn't evidence seem more irrefutable if viewers drew their own conclusions about it? Couldn't Adams' case be presented in a way that allowed only one logical conclusion? Morris took a daring step by deciding not just to reconstruct the crime for viewers, but to present a half-dozen versions of it, like *Rashomon* (1950) emphasizing a different element each time. By the cumulative weight of details, and by penetrating interviews, he hoped to steer viewers to the truth.

In traditional documentaries, style was something to be avoided. A director might allow cinematographers the occasional visual flourish, but the primary focus of filmmakers was to record facts. Morris approached this project like a feature film, hiring production designer Ted Bafaloukos to give *The Thin Blue Line* a distinctive look, and composer Philip Glass to give it just as distinctive a sound.

He also cast actors to play the people involved and staged them as a feature director might. Although scenes are listed as "re-enactments" in the credits, Morris has since pulled back from that usage. In an interview in 2000, he said,

> When I hear the term re-enactment, what I think is the intention to tell people, "This is what it looked like." There is none of that in my filmmaking. There were no re-enactments per se in *The Thin Blue Line*. Re-enactment to me suggests that you are showing people what really happened, that you're

showing them some picture of the world. I have done something very different. I have shown people pictures of belief, untruth, falsehood, confusion. I have taken people back into what they thought they might have seen, thought might have been out there, but it's clear they were wrong or delusional.

Is it "wrong" for a documentarian to increase the tension of a scene by adding sinister music and atmospheric lighting? What about staging scenes that never took place? Who is the ultimate guide for the viewer? According to *Washington Post* reporter Hal Hinson, "The same characteristics of Morris' style that make it an engrossing story of tragic coincidence and justice gone wrong disqualify it as a factual document . . . you can't help but feel uncomfortable with the way he has hyped his material." Or do the ends justify the means? Is it permissible to "smudge the distinction between fact and fiction" to right an injustice? Shouldn't Morris just come out and say what he thinks is true?

By tailoring his message for moviegoers, Morris perhaps felt he was presenting the best possible version of the incident. For the most part *The Thin Blue Line* received enthusiastic reviews, although Morris has become defensive about the subsequent plague of police-oriented reality shows on television. It would be unfair to those who haven't seen *The Thin Blue Line* to discuss its outcome; the lawsuits that arose after the documentary do not detract from its accomplishments as a movie. Morris has gone on to a distinguished career as a director of documentaries, helping establish an interviewing style that has become pervasive in the field. (He named his filming apparatus the "Interrotron.") He has also directed commercials for Apple Computer, American Express, Miller High Life beer, Volkswagen, and other clients.

Uksuum Cauyai: The Drums of Winter

Uksuum Cauyai: Missionary sisters dressed in Eskimo kuspiks (cloth over parkas) and wearing ceremonial masks, taken circa 1920. *Photo credit: Oregon Province Jesuit Archives.*

Sarah Elder and Leonard Kamerling, 1988. Sound, color, 1.37. 90 minutes. **Credits:** Produced, directed and written by Sarah Elder and Leonard Kamerling. Edited by Sarah Elder. Photographed by Leonard Kamerling. Sound recorded by Sarah Elder. Yup'ik Language and Culture Consultant: Walkie Charles. Yup'ik Language Translators: David Chanar, Walkie Charles, Lucy Coolidge, Oscar Kawagley. Sound editor: Ray Karpicki. Editing consultant: Vincent Stenerson. Assistant film editors: Meri Weingarten, Valerie Kantakos. Dance Myth Voice: Walkie Charles. Elder Voice: William Tyson. Trecca Voice: Serge Lecomte. Zagoskin voice: Rudy Krejci. Drebert Voice: Russell Stratton. Keyes Voice: Lee Salisbury. Negative conforming: J.G. Films. Sound re-recording: Mel Zelniker. Titles: The Optical House, N.Y. Archival material courtesy of: Moravian Church Archives, Newark Museum, Oregon Province Archives of the Society of Jesus, People of Emmonak, Sophie Lee. Potlatch footage (1970) filmed by Ed Eisenson. Courtesy of The Village of Emmonak and Community Enterprise Development Corp. Myth on the Origin of Dancing from Cyril Chanar. Excerpts from *Alaska Missionary* by Rev. Ferdinand Drebert; *Lt. Zagoskin's Travels in Russian America*, edited by H.N. Michael; Fr. Joseph Trecca's letters. Presented by the Alaska Native Heritage Film Project and The Emmonak Dancers. Major Funding Provided by: National Endowment for the Arts Folk Arts Program; Alaska State Council on the Arts; Institute of Alaska Native Arts, Inc.; Rock Foundation. Additional funding and support provided by: Fairbanks North Star Borough School District, Kellogg Foundation, University of Alaska Foundation, University of Alaska Museum.

Available: Documentary Educational Resources DVD (2005; *www.der.org*).

Suspicions about bias in documentaries became more pronounced after the development of cinema verité in the 1960s. Ethnographic filmmakers shifted away from the style of a Robert Flaherty or Margaret Mead, who presented idealized versions of native life that were outdated even as they were filming them. While some complained that these early documentaries were not factual, others objected to how the films presented an often false narrative for the cultures they were depicting.

With *The Hunters* (1957) and his other Kalahari films, John Marshall tried to do away with recreating aspects of native life. As he acknowledged, this proved more difficult than he expected. For Sarah Elder, who was studying anthropology at Sarah Lawrence College in the 1960s, *The Hunters* and Robert Gardner's *Dead Birds* (1965) were startling experiences. "My God, there's nobody in these films who are representing themselves or speaking for themselves," she told reporter Cynthia Miller. "The whole thing is this kind of fantastical imaginary, carved out by the filmmakers." After watching documentaries made by the North Vietnamese, Elder decided to become a filmmaker herself, focusing on "people who had no empowerment in their lives."

After working with Marshall and Tim Asch at Documentary Educational Resources, Elder traveled to Alaska in 1972. There she became both principal and the entire teaching staff at the newly formed high school in the village of Emmonak. In Alaska she met Leonard Kamerling. As he told Miller, "In the mid-'60s, I took a year off from college and joined VISTA, and I ended up in a small Yup'ik village in Southwest Alaska, where I had my worldview turned around rather dramatically." Back in school, Kamerling was influenced by a ten-hour series of films about the Netsilik Eskimos made by Dr. Asen Balicki. Kamerling called the series "the most radical thing I had ever seen. It did away with the narrator and any mediation for the viewer."

Kamerling used the same approach for the first film he made with Elder. *Tununeremiut: The People of Tununuk* (1972) examined a small Yup'ik village off the Bering Sea coast. They subsequently collaborated on other documentaries that covered different aspects of Yup'ik life: *At the Time of Whaling* (1974), *On the Spring Ice* (1975), etc. Elder's interest in Eskimo Dance, brought about by a chance conversation with Pentecostal missionaries, led to *Uksuum Cauyai*.

Elder and Kamerling began filming *Uksuum Cauyai* in 1977, with Kamerling operating the camera. They arranged lighting and camera angles with the cooperation of Yup'ik leaders, intent on presenting what the natives wanted rather than interpreting it themselves. In addition to the dances, they interviewed several Yup'ik parents and students about the history of Eskimo Dance and its practices and meanings.

The footage was edited at the University of Alaska. It took a year to translate the Yup'ik dialogue into English, a crucial step for structuring the material. According to Kamerling, "Funds were a constant problem in completing this film and we had to stop the editing process several times as a result." They finished two documentaries, *Everyday Choices* and *Overture on Ice*, before obtaining the financing to complete *Uksuum Cauyai*.

The delay was "serendipitous," wrote Kamerling, adding, "We were more mature as filmmakers and could see deeper into the complex story of Yup'ik dance and reciprocal gift giving, and we also obtained additional interviews and rare archival materials that gave the film an important historical context." In the late 1980s, Elder and Kamerling also interviewed young villagers about their dance experiences, as well as other figures. The filmmakers found and incorporated footage that had been shot by Ed Eisenson in 1970 and left unedited in a fish storage shed.

Uksuum Cauyai is filmed in the straightforward, unadorned style of a news program, with a camera that rarely moves and focus kept intently on the dances and their participants. Background information emerges slowly. As interviewees refer obliquely to the past, when the government prohibited both dances and the use of native languages, the filmmakers cut to archival footage and letters. Gradually the film tackles the potlatch tradition, the greatest sticking point to an understanding between native and missionary beliefs. Elder's editing allows both sides to express their opinions, a difficult balancing act.

The dozen or so dances are the highlights of the film. They have a hypnotic power that Kamerling and Elder capture in extended takes and judicious cutting. As René Astruc, a Jesuit priest stationed in Alaska since 1956, says, the dances erase a sense of time, an effect that can be either alarming or liberating. Apart from its value as an ethnographic document, *Uksuum Cauyai* offers a poignant look at a vanishing culture. Not only are most of the dancers elderly, but around the fringes of society you can see the arrival of modern life: cartons of cigarettes, bottles of Pine-Sol, an elder singing Doc Watson's 1975 version of Lucille Leatherman's "Curly Headed Baby."

Elder and Kamerling continued working together on a number of Alaska-based films. Elder was a cofounder of the Alaska Native Heritage Film Center at the University of Alaska Museum in Fairbanks. Recently, she has served as professor of documentary film in the Department of Media Study at the University of Buffalo, State University of New York. Kamerling is presently curator at the Alaska Center for Documentary Film at the University of Alaska Museum of the North. He is researching contemporary Ainu culture in Japan, and has begun production on *They Came to Teach—A History of Bush Teachers in Alaska.*

sex, lies, and videotape

Miramax, 1989. Sound, color, 1.85. 100 minutes. Rated R.

Cast: James Spader (Graham), Andie MacDowell (Ann), Peter Gallagher (John), Laura San Giacomo (Cynthia), Ron Vawter (Therapist), Steven Brill (Barfly), Alexandra Root (Girl on tape), Earl T. Taylor (Landlord), David Foil (John's colleague).

Credits: Written and directed by Steven Soderbergh. Produced by Robert Newmyer, John Hardy. Executive producers: Nancy Tenenbaum, Nick Wechsler, Morgan Mason. Photographed by Walt Lloyd. Music by Cliff Martinez. Casting by Deborah Aquila. Unit production manager: John Hardy. First assistant director: Michael Dempsey. Script supervisor: Elizabeth Lambert. Second assistant director: Alexandra Root. Production executive: John Kao. Art director: Joanne Schmidt. Set decorator: Victoria Spader. Production sound mixer: Paul Ledford. Boom operator: Stephen Tyler. Key grip: J.D. Streett. Gaffer: Phil Beard. Make-up and costuming: James Ryder. Hair stylists: Sabrina Lopez, Amanda Schuler. Wardrobe: Amanda Moore. Sound editing, re-recording, music recording: Larry Blake. Picture editing: Steven Soderbergh. Film stock: Agfa XT320. Negative processing: Allied + WBS Labs, Dallas. Prints: CFI. Dolby Stereo. Filmed on location in Baton Rouge, Louisiana. An Outlaw production.

Additional Credits: Production dates: August 1 to September 1988. Screened at the Sundance Film Festival on January 20, 1989.

Available: Columbia TriStar Home Video DVD (1998). ISBN: 0-7678-1215-8. UPC: 0-43396-90489-7.

Born in 1963, Steven Soderbergh became interested in movies at thirteen, when he decided that he didn't have the skills to play baseball. His father, a dean at Louisiana State University, helped him take college animation courses while he was still a teenager. After completing high school, Soderbergh left home for Hollywood to break into the motion picture industry. He found work as an editor on a television series, but eventually returned chastened to Baton Rouge. Working in a video production house, he directed a Grammy-nominated concert film for the rock group Yes. He also wrote screenplays which didn't sell, leading to what he described as a self-destructive depression fueled by alcohol. "I was involved with a relationship with a woman in which I was deceptive and mentally manipulative," he said later. "I got involved with a number of other women simultaneously." When therapy didn't work, Soderbergh translated his experiences into the short film *Winston* (1987). This became the germ of *sex, lies, and videotape.*

Soderbergh used his director's reel as an entry to pitch a script for a feature built around an impotent man who videotapes women talking about sex. Nancy Tenenbaum, a producer with the independent production company Skouras Pictures, was an early supporter of the project. But most of the money for *sex, lies, and videotape* came from producers Bobby Newmyer, Nick Wechsler, and Larry Estes at RCA/Columbia Home Video. They expected a soft-core straight-to-video piece with plenty of nudity to justify an R rating. This was at odds with Soderbergh's original concept of a sober, black-and-white film along the lines of French New Wave cinema. This tension between art and commerce became part of the creative process behind the film.

With a budget of around a million dollars, Soderbergh now had the opportunity to upgrade his cast. Andie MacDowell was a fairly well-known model anxious to establish a career in film. She had appeared in glamorous parts in several movies that would not have appealed to Soderbergh, yet he still cast her as a prim, repressed housewife. MacDowell's Southern background may have helped during her audition, but it was more likely a series of Calvin Klein television ads in which she spoke about the South that got her the part. For James Spader, whose good looks and prep school background had trapped him in a "Brat Pack" niche of ingénue roles, *sex, lies, and videotape* was a chance to prove that he could act. He persuaded Soderbergh to cast Peter Gallagher as the villain in the story, but at the time Spader was not at all sure that the film wouldn't fail.

It was a feeling shared by the movie's producers, who when viewing the dailies kept pressuring Soderbergh for more skin. "I'm not seeing any flesh," Estes said. "Why is that?" But for the director, the film had evolved into a critique of yuppie culture, which he viewed with something like self-loathing. *sex, lies, and videotape* exposed the shallowness of its characters' lives and the emptiness of a society oriented toward consumption, but in a manner that didn't threaten its target audience, who were yuppies themselves. By choosing attractive settings and performers, and by making sex a vague metaphor for larger problems, Soderbergh could let viewers fantasize about an unattainable lifestyle while still concluding that it was not for them.

Soderbergh started shooting on August 1, 1988, and finished five weeks later. He entered the movie in the Sundance Film Festival, which began in late January 1989, forcing him into a grueling editing schedule. He carried the first finished print to Park City himself, still unsure if his work would ever receive theatrical exhibition. The screenings went well enough for Soderbergh to win an audience prize at the end of the festival, but he returned to Los Angeles without a distributor.

Todd McCarthy's rave review in *Variety* stirred up interest in both Soderbergh and his film. While he juggled offers for his next project, Estes and Newmyer reviewed distribution deals from New Line, Samuel Goldwyn Pictures, and Miramax, a company run by Harvey and Bob Weinstein. Formerly concert promoters, they initially forged a position in the industry by distributing soft-core porn and concert films. Acquisitions like *Pelle the Conqueror, The Thin Blue Line* (both 1988), and *My Left Foot* (1989) helped legitimize the company; more important, through relentless publicity and advertising, the Weinsteins actually got audiences to see their films. They offered Estes $2 million for the theatrical rights to *sex, lies, and videotape*, far more than other distributors.

In May 1989, the Weinsteins brought the film to Cannes, where it won the Palme d'Or. Back in the United States, they prepared television ads to promote it, unheard of for an independent project with such a small budget (and with no hope of Miramax receiving any home video income). Soderbergh objected to the emphasis on sex in the Miramax campaign, and questioned the wisdom of screening the film in five or six hundred theaters instead of sticking to the standard art-house circuit. But when *sex, lies, and videotape* grossed almost $25 million in the domestic market (and another $30 million in other territories), the Weinsteins felt vindicated.

Soderbergh had mixed feelings. "When I look at it now, it looks like something made by someone who wants to think he's deep but really isn't," he said later. In his subsequent films, Soderbergh alternated between dark, difficult works like *Kafka* (1991) that failed to find viewers, and more mainstream projects like *King of the Hill* (1993) that likewise performed poorly. It wasn't until 1998's *Out of Sight* that he regained his commercial touch. That film also introduced him to one of his most consistent creative collaborators, George Clooney. Together they have established a franchise with the *Ocean's Eleven* movies, while exploring more challenging projects like *Solaris* (2002), a remake of a Russian science fiction film. Soderbergh is one of the few directors working today who backs up his commercial clout with morally aware choices. He has also been a quiet but significant contributor to film preservation projects. Clooney has spoken about Soderbergh's "fear of success," but few of the directors' peers are as astute about the marketplace and as adventurous about the art and technology of filmmaking.

Do the Right Thing

Universal, 1989. Sound, color, 1.85. 120 minutes. Rated R.

Cast: Danny Aiello (Sal), Ossie Davis (Da Mayor), Ruby Dee (Mother Sister), Richard Edson (Vito), Giancarlo Esposito (Buggin' Out), Spike Lee (Mookie), Bill Nunn (Radio Raheem), John Turturro (Pino), Paul Benjamin (ML), Frankie Faison (Coconut Sid), Robin Harris (Sweet Dick Willie), Joie Lee (Jade), Miguel Sandoval (Officer Ponte), Rick Aiello (Officer Long), John Savage (Clifton), Sam Jackson (Mister Señor Love Daddy), Rosie Perez (Tina), Roger Guenveur Smith (Smiley), Steve White (Ahmad), Martin Lawrence (Cee), Leonard Thomas (Punchy), Christa Rivers (Ella), Frank Vincent (Charlie), Luis Ramos (Stevie), Richard Habersham (Eddie), Gwen McGee (Louise), Steve Park (Sonny), Ginny Yang (Kim), Sherwin Park (Korean child), Shawn Elliott (Puerto Rican Icee Man), Diva Osorio (Carmen), Chris Delaney, Angel Ramirez, Sixto Ramos, Nelson Vasquez (Stevie's friends), Travell Lee Toulson (Hector), Joel Nagle (Sergeant), David E. Weinberg (Plainclothes detective), Yattee Brown, Mecca Brunson, Shawn Stainback, Soquana Wallace (Double Dutch girls); Danny Aiello, III (Stunt double—Sal), Mharaka Washington (Stunt driver); Gary Frith, Andy Duppin, Rashon Khan, Erik Koniger, Malcolm Livingston, David S. Lomax, Dominic Marcus, Eric A. Payne, Roy Thomas, Tom Wright (Stunt players).

Credits: Produced, written and directed by Spike Lee. Coproducer: Monty Ross. Line producer: Jon Kilik. Photographed by Ernest Dickerson. Editor: Barry Alexander Brown. Original music score: Bill Lee. Production design: Wynn Thomas. Casting: Robi Reed. Costumes: Ruth Carter. Sound design: Skip Lievsay. Stunt coordinator: Eddie Smith. Color by Du Art Laboratories. Prints by Deluxe. Dolby Stereo. A Forty Acres and a Mule Filmworks production.

Additional Credits: Released June 30, 1989.

Available: Criterion DVD (2001). ISBN: 1-55940-910-X. UPC: 7-15515-01122-8.

Set in a predominantly African-American block in the Bedford-Stuyvesant section of Brooklyn, *Do the Right Thing* sets out to explore various forms of racism and possible responses to them. It was the third feature written and directed by Spike Lee. The son of jazz musician Bill Lee, he was born in 1957, grew up in New York City, and attended Morehouse College in Atlanta and the film school at New York University. His student film *Joe's Bed-Stuy Barbershop: We Cut Heads* (1980), an affectionate, fast-paced short, led to a trying half-decade in which Lee had trouble financing feature projects. He financed *She's Gotta Have It* (1986) essentially on credit cards; it was successful enough at the box office for Lee to receive backing from Columbia for his next feature, *School Daze* (1988).

According to a "making of" book Lee wrote with Lisa Jones, the inspiration behind *Do the Right Thing* came from an incident in Howard Beach, a neighborhood in Queens, New York. On December 20, 1986, three blacks were assaulted by local white teenagers; one, Michael Griffith, was struck and killed by a car as he tried to escape. Lee began writing his script in December 1988, deciding to limit the story to one block in a Brooklyn neighborhood on the hottest day of the summer. It was a strategy that would allow his characters to operate at the height of passion, to let what he perceived as long-simmering tensions erupt. (As *Variety* pointed out, Elmer Rice used a strikingly similar approach in his Pulitzer Prize–winning play *Street Scene*, filmed in 1931. For that matter, so did Sidney Kingsley in his play *Dead End*, filmed in 1937.)

Unhappy with Dawn Steele at Columbia, Lee hoped to receive financing through Jeffrey Katzenberg at Touchstone or Ned Tannen at Paramount instead. While writing, he consulted with cinematographer Ernest Dickerson over the visual scheme he wanted. Lee later cited the "Chinese angles" in *The Third Man* (1949) and the cinematography in Godfrey Reggio's *Powaqqatsi* (1988) as influences. He also borrowed a crucial scene from *The Night of the Hunter* (1955).

Lee sent drafts to a number of actors, including Robert De Niro, Matt Dillon, and Laurence Fishburne. But when Paramount turned down Lee's script at the end of April, the entire project was in jeopardy. Sam Kitt at Universal offered Lee $6.5 million, a million less than the figure the director was discussing with Paramount. That forced Lee to cut a week from his production schedule.

With a ninety-three-page script, he would have to shoot over two pages a day. However, he would be allowed to keep the inflammatory ending that worried Paramount executives.

By this time much of the cast had been settled. The husband-and-wife team of Ossie Davis and Ruby Dee took important parts, but the film was also an opportunity for several untested performers. Bill Nunn, Rosie Perez, Frankie Faison, and Martin Lawrence all had their careers boosted by the film. Danny Aiello took a lead role as the owner of a neighborhood pizzeria. A former bus dispatcher, union politician, nightclub bouncer, and petty crook, Aiello had entered acting when he was forty. Big, streetwise, and unmistakably Italian, he had appeared in two Woody Allen comedies and had made a strong impression in *Moonstruck* (1987). Appearing as his son was John Turturro, another Italian-American and another actor fearless in his approach to the material. Lee cast both himself and his sister Joie Lee in big parts.

Do the Right Thing was shown at the Cannes Film Festival in May 1989, and opened in the United States at the end of June. The film elicited a firestorm of protest from critics and commentators. Entire episodes of *The Oprah Winfrey Show* and ABC's *Nightline* were devoted to the movie. In his book about the film, Ed Guerrero cites five *New York Times* articles about it, and notes that Lee made the cover of three magazines. The controversy undoubtedly helped the film's box-office performance.

Thanks to the polarizing nature of his script, and Lee's strident directing style, *Do the Right Thing* became a litmus test for attitudes about race. But it's easier today to separate the film from its political surroundings, just as it's easier to question some of Lee's choices. Had a different actor incited the riot that makes up the film's climax, Lee could have better defended his position on violence. "Am I advocating violence?" he wrote. "No, but the days of twenty-five million Blacks being silent while our fellow brothers and sisters are exploited, oppressed, and murdered, have to come to an end."

Judging from the film itself, the causes for the riot are difficult to explain and impossible to justify, as are several other moments in the piece. Perez complained later that Lee exploited her in the film's nude scenes, and it's clear in the opening credits that the director is fetishizing her in exactly the same way "white" media would. Lee implicitly endorses Tawana Brawley, whose allegations of being a victim of kidnapping and rape were judged hoaxes; by using "Fight the Power" as a theme song, he appears to agree with Public Enemy's own form of racism. In a sports argument with Turturro's character, Lee insists against all evidence that New York Mets pitcher Dwight Gooden is the victim of a racist white press. But the most troubling aspect of *Do the Right Thing* may be its anti-intellectualism. The volume of the mob repeatedly drowns out reason.

Lee is, of course, entitled to his opinions; by playing a fictional role, he can also express these opinions while still claiming not to hold to them himself. Viewers can decide for themselves how well his choices have played out. Is Lee simply documenting racism or espousing it, presenting violence or promoting it? Film critic Scott MacDonald astutely pointed out that while the social structure Lee dramatizes leads to discrimination and violence, *Do the Right Thing* as a film

production was an example of exactly the opposite: blacks and whites united successfully in a common cause.

The film received two Academy Award nominations, for Aiello and for Lee's script, and earned close to $30 million. But the director complained that bad reviews hurt the film's take by making whites afraid to go to movie theaters. In Lee's logic, if you don't like *Do the Right Thing*, you are racist. He has blamed racism for the poor performance of his other films as well. As Guerrero wrote, "Lee is viewed by Hollywood's executive offices as a marginal small to mid-budget maker of 'niche market' films. This is because Lee never had the full backing and benefit of the industry's vast promotional publicity machine, which is reserved for mainstream movies." But one could just as easily argue that Lee never earned the right to use this machine, not with this film and not with many of his subsequent "mainstream" productions.

Water and Power

Lookout Mountain Films, 1989. Sound, color, 1.37. 55 minutes.
Cast: Joel Lorimen, Beth Block, George Lockwood, Megan Williams, Ric Stafford, Chris Casady, Amy Halperin, Mike Pestel, Tom Leeser, Adam Dubov, Carlos Durazo, Bill Stobaugh, Beverly Bernacke, Byron Werner, Jon Lee, James Valentine, Jan Nordstrom.
Credits: A film by Pat O'Neill. Audio design and production: George Lockwood. Electronic design, motion control software: Mark Madel. Mechanical design and construction: Joe Louis. Optical printer, finder of lost negatives: Beth Block. Animators: Diana Krumins, Megan Williams, Diana Wilson. Musicians: John Bergamo, percussion; Greg Johnson, percussion; Robert Lloyd, piano; Kurt Festinger, flute, saxophone; Vivian Miller, alto. Special thanks to: Jay Cassidy, Scott Greiger, David Pann, Harry Frazer, Jacky De Haviland, Dan Kohne, Bill Robinson, David Berry, Jim Shaw, Patty Podesta, James Sullivan, David Wilson, Carmen Vigil. Partially funded by The National Endowment for the Arts.
Additional Credits: Written, photographed, edited, and directed by Pat O'Neill. Screened at the New York Film Festival on October 1, 1989.
Available: Canyon Cinema, *www.canyoncinema.com.*

Before the development of optical printers, special effects for films were created in camera, or painted by hand onto exposed celluloid. Dissolving from one scene to another meant rewinding exposed film for the required number of frames while estimating the speed and duration of fading in and out. Double exposures and matte shots required similar calculations. Optical printers, which essentially rephotographed two filmstrips onto a third, gave cinematographers the ability to experiment more freely with dissolves, fades, wipes, and other editing strategies.

Speaking about optical printers, Pat O'Neill told reporter David Pagel, "I wanted the equipment.

I wanted to have a way of rephotographing film." For O'Neill, a printer gave him the means to compare and contrast elements in static shots—"to make films that either have no cuts, or that have pauses between shots," as he said to interviewer David E. James. "Finding the point at which content is both unstable and balanced led me to the use of multiple images laid over one another." These two techniques, using printers to alter and shape exposed footage, and combining several layers of imagery, became the hallmarks of O'Neill's work.

A sculptor and painter as well as a filmmaker, O'Neill began making abstract movies in the 1960s. Some of his inspiration may have come from the "city symphony" films of the 1920s (the Registry includes titles like *Manhatta*, 1921). Author Scott MacDonald finds a connection between O'Neill's use of time-lapse photography and double or multiple exposures and artists like Marie Mencken and Godfrey Reggio (whose *Koyaanisqatsi*, 1982, is also a Registry title). But several factors set O'Neill's films apart.

O'Neill's patience, example. *Water and Power* was filmed over a period of ten years, using footage he shot in the Owens Valley and other areas in and around Los Angeles. In a talk he gave in 1974, he said, "One thing I've always liked to do is just sit and look at the sky when it's perfectly blue and flat . . . and then watch the things in your own nervous system. You start seeing little white things, and you see flaws in your eyeball surface and so on, and very often, also, if there's a screen like that and you've been looking at something, then you turn to a flat surface, and you get after-images that are complementary in color and value to what you've just been looking at." His landscapes are concrete and mysterious at the same time, with surfaces that support more than one interpretation, or which are used for more than one image.

Another distinctive factor was O'Neill's commercial work. In 1974 he formed Lookout Mountain Films. Two years later he purchased two optical printers and began work on special effects for feature films and advertising. "Sometimes whole years would go by when we did nothing but work," he said later. His SFX house contributed the lightning bolt effects from Darth Vader's fingers in the second *Star Wars* feature (*The Empire Strikes Back*, 1980), for example. The commercial work served as training for O'Neill's more personal films. It also positioned O'Neill apart from the avant-garde tradition. O'Neill admitted that the Owens Valley locations in *Water and Power* were influenced more by Roman Polanski's *Chinatown* (1974) than by the work of experimental filmmakers. *Water and Power* makes use of features like *The Ten Commandments* (1923), *The Last Command* (1928), and *Detour* (1945), repurposing both the sound and imagery invented by Hollywood.

One more crucial element in *Water and Power* was the development of motion control technology, computer software that enables cinematographers to match or repeat pans, tracks, and other camera movements in separate times and locations. Combined with O'Neill's mastery of optical printing, motion control software enabled him to devise remarkably complex shots that flowed seamlessly from real to abstract. About six minutes into *Water and Power*, O'Neill shows a high angle of a Los Angeles traffic intersection. As time-lapse photography takes us through a day, the camera begins to pan to the right, up the street. As twilight descends, O'Neill begins introducing artificial elements—streaks of light, a building outlined in artificial neon, a volcano appearing on the horizon.

One critic wrote about a "metallic sheen" to O'Neill's films, a result of his lustrous exposures and stately pans. Equally characteristic is how O'Neill manipulates time and commingles locations. The time-lapse photography adds unexpected grace notes: how a gas station sign revolves in time to the soundtrack, as do marchers in a parade.

O'Neill paid as much attention to editing sound as he did to visuals. Tough-guy patter and soundtrack scores blend with jazz and classical music. At times imagery seems to fail him, the screen falling black while music and dialogue suggest narratives. "*Water and Power* was a landscape film that gradually became animated by the beginnings of human stories," he told Pagel. "That was how I solved in my own head the question of the way we could look at some of these places—by putting action in them." His goal was to depict "geographic time . . . like evidence. It's just physical."

Narrative is a factor in but not a solution to *Water and Power*. The stories in the film do not resolve any more than the landscapes or occasional graphics do. O'Neill's script for the film, published in *Millennium Film Journal* (Summer 1991), include several handwritten pages filled with notes about f-stops, dissolve durations, filters, and ordinal points, but also typewritten notes about troubling dreams. "I wanted things that seemed completely chaotic but that would occasionally organize themselves in some way, then go right on to something else," he explained in a lecture.

That's not much help for average viewers, who not only may not recognize O'Neill's cinematic allusions, but who are also likely to be baffled by intertitles like "Osmotic Pressure." No matter how much energy they spend trying to decipher *Water and Power*, the film remains deliberately, defiantly, obscure. O'Neill has complained that art critics don't cover films very well, or "seem to be interested only in the narrative. I have chosen to use the language of one tradition while working in another, at my own peril. What I do has not really been on the plate of the people who write about avant-garde film."

O'Neill tried working within a more traditional narrative framework with *The Decay of Fiction* (2002), which used the Ambassador Hotel in Los Angeles as the backdrop for characters enacting a variety of story lines. It was "a huge bust financially," he said. "But I did get what I wanted out of it." *Another Kind of Record*, a collection of his artwork, was published in 2008.

GoodFellas

Warner Bros., 1990. Sound, color, 2.35. 145 minutes. Rated R.

Cast: Robert De Niro (James Conway), Ray Liotta (Henry Hill), Joe Pesci (Tommy DeVito), Lorraine Bracco (Karen Hill), Paul Sorvino (Paul Cicero), Frank Sivero (Frankie Carbone), Tony Darrow (Sonny Bunz), Mike Starr (Frenchy), Frank Vincent (Billy Batts), Chuck Low (Morris Kessler), Frank DiLeo (Tuddy Cicero), Henny Youngman (Himself), Gina Mastrogiacomo (Janice Rossi), Catherine Scorsese (Tommy's mother), Charles Scorsese (Vinnie), Suzanne Shepherd (Karen's mother), Debi Mazar (Sandy), Margo Winkler (Belle Kessler), Welker White (Lois Byrd), Jerry Vale (Himself), Julie Garfield (Mickey Conway), Christopher Serrone (Young Henry), Elaine Kagan (Henry's mother), Beau Starr (Henry's father), Kevin Corrigan (Michael Hill), Michael Imperioli (Spider), Robbie Vinton (Bobby Vinton), John Williams (Johnny Roastbeef), Daniel P. Conte (Dr. Dan), Tony Conforti (Tony), Frank Pellegrino (Johnny Dio), Ronald Maccone (Ronnie), Tony Sirico (Tony Stacks), Joseph D'Onofrio (Young Tommy), Steve Forleo (City Detective #1), Richard Dioguardi (City Detective #2), Frank Adonis (Anthony Stabile), John Manca (Nickey Eyes), Joseph Bono (Mikey Frazese), Katherine Wallach (Diane), Mark Evan Jacobs (Bruce), Angela Pietropinto (Cicero's wife), Marianne Leone (Tuddy's wife), Marie Michaels (Mrs. Carbone), Lo Nardo (Frenchy's wife), Melissa Prophet (Angie), Illeana Douglas (Rosie), Susan Varon (Susan), Elizabeth Whitcraft (Tommy's girlfriend @ Copa), Clem Caserta (Joe Buddha), Samuel L. Jackson (Stacks Edwards), Fran McGee (Johnny Roastbeef's wife), Paul Herman (Dealer), Edward McDonald (Himself), Edward Hayes (Defense attorney).

Credits: Directed by Martin Scorsese. Screenplay by Nicholas Pileggi & Martin Scorsese. Based on the book *Wiseguy* by Nicholas Pileggi. Produced by Irwin Winkler. Executive producer: Barbara De Fina. Director of photography: Michael Ballhaus. Production designer: Kristi Zea. Film editor: Thelma Schoonmaker. Casting: Ellen Lewis. Associate producer: Bruce Pustin. Unit production manager: Bruce Pustin. Costume designer: Richard Bruno. Titles: Elaine & Saul Bass. Second unit director: Joseph Reidy. Art director: Maher Ahmad. Set decorator: Les Bloom. Supervising sound editor: Skip Lievsay. Production sound mixer: James Sabat. Sound recordist: Frank Graziadei. Make-up artists: Allen Weisinger, Carl Fullerton. Hair stylists: Bill Farley, Alan D'Angerio. Stunt coordinator: Michael Russo. Camera and lenses by Arriflex. Color by Technicolor. Dolby Stereo SR. A Warner Bros. presentation of an Irwin Winkler production.

Additional Credits: Production dates: May 3 to August 9, 1989. Premiered in New York City on September 18, 1990.

Awards: Oscar for Best Actor in a Supporting Role (Pesci).

Available: Warner Home Video DVD (2004). ISBN: 0-7907-5834-2. UPC: 0-85391-91222-4.

Nicholas Pileggi worked for twelve years as a reporter for the Associated Press, based in New York City and focusing on crime. After becoming a contributing editor to *New York* magazine, he published his first book, a nonfiction look at a private detective, in 1976. It took almost ten years for his next book, *Wiseguy: Life in a Mafia Family*, to be printed. Based on interviews with Henry Hill, it expanded on an article that first appeared in *New York*.

Born in Brooklyn in 1941, Hill served in the Army, then began working for Paul Vario, an underboss in the Lucchese crime family. Vario's group was among the most violent in the city, responsible for everything from hijackings, arson, and drug dealing to murder. Hill served time for extortion, then played parts in a point-shaving scandal involving the Boston College basketball team and in a multimillion-dollar robbery from a Lufthansa terminal at Kennedy Airport. Worried for his life, Hill testified against Vario and other gangsters, then entered the Federal Witness Protection Program. That's where Pileggi found him, the only witness in the program willing to talk to a reporter.

Martin Scorsese was working on *The Color of Money* (1986), a sequel to *The Hustler* (1961), when he saw Pileggi's article. Producer Irwin Winkler was in Paris making *'Round Midnight* (1986) when he made an offer for Pileggi's book. Fortunately, Winkler wanted to work with Scorsese, whom he compared to a jazz musician: "He doesn't know all the notes he's going to hit, but he knows the melody he's going to stick to."

Scorsese saw the project as a return to material he felt he understood best: "*GoodFellas* is going back to the same period as *Mean Streets*, the early sixties, to the world I grew up in and knew from an angle slightly different from that in *Mean Streets*." Since *Raging Bull* (1980), Scorsese had made two comedies and a sequel; before he would start on *GoodFellas*, he directed an adaptation of the Nikos Kazantzakis novel *The Last Temptation of Christ* (1988) and the "Life Lessons" segment in the omnibus movie *New York Stories* (1989). Before it would finance the project, Warner Brothers insisted on casting a major star, so *GoodFellas* would be an opportunity for Scorsese to work with Robert De Niro for the first time in seven years.

First the director needed a script. For the first time since *Mean Streets* (1973), Scorsese would be taking a feature writing credit. He and Pileggi went through a dozen versions of the screenplay, an exhaustive series of revisions of scenes from the book. "Visual style had to be completely redone in our writing sessions," he said. "Every one of those twelve drafts was fun," Pileggi remembered later, even the nuts-and-bolts business of changing names. For example, Paul Vario became Paul Cicero (played by Paul Sorvino), while Tommy DeSimone became Tommy DeVito (Joe Pesci). De Niro took the role of Jimmy Conway (based on Jimmy "The Gent" Burke), essentially a supporting part, and recommended Ray Liotta to Scorsese after seeing him appear as a psychotic crook in *Something Wild* (1986).

In translating the script's visual style to film, Scorsese's longtime cinematographer Michael Ballhaus devised a challenging shooting scheme that tried to do away with middle-focus lenses. The 32mm lens is one of the cameraman's real bulwarks, used for the medium shots that predominate in feature films. "We're using a lot of long lenses, so there's nothing in between, no 32s—it's like 24 or 28 or 18, and then it's 50 and 85," Ballhaus explained. Scorsese wanted a film "that's *almost* in the style of a documentary," so Ballhaus also went with a harsh, direct light look, "not soft and not bounced."

The ersatz documentary style gave Scorsese the freedom to take the plot in any direction he wanted, shifting to different points of view, time frames, even different versions of the same scene. "The plot may be extremely confusing," he admitted later. "But it doesn't matter. It's the exploration of a lifestyle." The director repeated the extended, sinuous shots he used in *Mean Streets* and *Raging Bull*, notably in a three-minute, one-take tour de force that glided from 60th Street down a flight of stairs, through corridors and then a restaurant kitchen, and onto the crowded floor of the Copacabana nightclub. But he also sped up the pace of his cutting. "I guess the main thing that's happened in the past ten years is that the scenes have to be quicker and shorter. *GoodFellas* is sort of my version of MTV . . . but even that's old-fashioned."

GoodFellas also upped the ante for violence, made all the more abrasive by Pesci's no-holds-barred, Oscar-winning performance as a murderous thug. Both Pesci and Sorvino used the analogy of soldiers who kill for the government to justify the film's brutality. Scorsese saw the film as explaining how gangsters worked, showing a process or business to viewers. "The main purpose of the gangster, especially in *GoodFellas*, is to make money," he said. "*GoodFellas* is an indictment. I had to do it in such a way as to make people angry about the state of things, about organized crime and how and why it works."

Not everyone agreed. *Variety*'s Joseph McBride found the film "dramatically unsatisfying," "simultaneously fascinating and repellent," for example. On the other hand, filmmakers as varied as Jon Favreau and Richard Linklater cite the influence of *GoodFellas* on their own work, and the links between Scorsese's film and television's *The Sopranos* are obvious. De Niro and Scorsese teamed again immediately for a remake of *Cape Fear* (1991). The two also worked with Pileggi and Pesci in *Casino* (1995), the third film in Scorsese's informal gangster trilogy.

Dances with Wolves

Orion Pictures, 1990. Sound, color, 2.35. 181 minutes. Rated PG-13.

Cast: Kevin Costner (Lt. John J. Dunbar), Mary McDonnell (Stands With a Fist), Graham Greene (Kicking Bird), Rodney A. Grant (Wind in His Hair), Floyd Red Crow Westerman (Ten Bears), Tantoo Cardinal (Black Shawl), Jimmy Herman (Stone Calf), Charles Rocket (Lieutenant Elgin), Robert Pastorelli (Timmons), Larry Joshua (Sergeant Bauer), Tony Pierce (Spivey), Tom Everett (Sergeant Pepper), Maury Chaykin (Major Fambrough), Nathan Lee Chasing His Horse (Smiles a Lot), Michael Spears (Otter), Jason R. Lone Hill (Worm), Doris Leader Charge (Pretty Shield), Kirk Baltz (Edwards), Wayne Grace (Major), Donald Hotton (General Tide), Annie Costner (Christine), Conor Duffy (Willie), Elisa Daniel (Christine's Mother), Percy White Plume (Big Warrior), John Tail (Escort Warrior), Steve Reevis (Sioux #1/Warrior #1), Sheldon Wolfchild (Sioux #2/Warrior #2), Wes Studi (Toughest Pawnee), Buffalo Child (Pawnee #1), Clayton Big Eagle (Pawnee #2), Richard Leader Charge (Pawnee #3); Redwing Ted Nez, Marvin Holy (Sioux Warriors); Raymond Newholy (Sioux Courier); David J. Fuller (Kicking Bird's Son), Ryan White Bull (Kicking Bird's Eldest Son), Otakuye Conroy (Kicking Bird's Daughter), Maretta Big Crow (Village Mother), Steve Chambers (Guard), William H. Burton (General's Aide), Bill W. Curry (Confederate Cavalryman); Nick Thompson, Carter Hanner (Confederate Soldiers); Kent Hays (Wagon Driver), Robert Goldman (Union Soldier), Frank P. Costanza (Tucker), James A. Mitchell (Ray), R. L. Curtin (Ambush Wagon Driver), Justin (Cisco), Teddy & Buck (Two Socks).

Credits: Directed by Kevin Costner. Screenplay by Michael Blake, based on his novel. Produced by Jim Wilson, Kevin Costner. Executive producer: Jake Eberts. Edited by Neil Travis. Director of photography: Dean Semler. Music composed and conducted by John Barry. Costume designer: Elsa Zamparelli. Production designer: Jeffrey Beecroft. Casting by Elisabeth Leustig. Associate producer: Bonnie Arnold. First assistant director: Douglas C. Metzger. Art director: William Ladd Skinner. Set decorator: Lisa Dean. Editors: William Hoy, Stephen Potter, Chip Masamitsu. Script supervisor: Jan Evans. Production sound mixers: Russell Williams, Mary Jo Devenney. Sound design: Robert Fitzgerald. Supervising sound editors: Hari Ryatt, Robert Fitzgerald. Chief makeup: Frank Karrisosa. Chief hairstylist: Elle Elliott. Stunt coordinator: Norman L. Howell. Title design: David L. Aaron, Jay Johnson. Color by DeLuxe. Panavision. Dolby Stereo. A Tig Productions presentation.

Additional Credits: Kevin Reynolds assisted in directing the buffalo hunt. Limited opening: November 9, 1990.

Awards: Oscars for Best Picture, Director, Writing—Screenplay Based on Material from Another Medium, Cinematography, Editing, Music—Original Score, Sound.

Available: MGM Home Entertainment DVD (2003). UPC: 027616880598. MGM Home Entertainment DVD (2004). ISBN: 0-7928-6042-X. UPC: 0-27616-90573-4.

When Kevin Costner set out to make *Dances with Wolves*, the Western genre had almost disappeared. The last Western epic, *Heaven's Gate* (1980), had ruined United Artists, and even well-regarded genre pieces like *Silverado* (1985) performed poorly at the box office. Costner had accepted a role in the latter film just for a chance to be in a Western, and it was largely due to his box-office appeal that *Dances with Wolves* got made at all.

Born in Compton, California, in 1955, Costner had a normal suburban upbringing, despite moving frequently. He majored in marketing at California State University at Fullerton, but gave up a career as a salesman to act with the South Coast Actor's Co-Op. His early film roles were in exploitation films like *Sizzle Beach, U.S.A.* (released 1986). When he did win legitimate parts, his work was often edited out in final cuts. He ended up delivering one line in *Frances* (1982), and was a corpse in *The Big Chill* (1983). *The Untouchables* (1987), where he played federal agent Eliot Ness, changed his fortunes, and he ended the 1980s with a string of successes culminating in *Field of Dreams* (1989).

By that time Costner had formed his own company, Tig Productions, with Jim Wilson, the director of one of Costner's early films, *Stacy's Knights* (1983). The film was written by Michael Blake, who was trying to pitch an idea for a movie about a post–Civil War veteran who learns to embrace a Native American lifestyle. Costner convinced Blake to write the story as a novel first, then purchased the movie rights. Thirty-six at the time, he also decided to make the project his debut as a director. Costner, Wilson, and Blake collaborated closely on the shooting script for *Dances with Wolves*; their first goal was to make sure everything was as accurate as possible. From locating a buffalo herd of 3,500 head in South Dakota to hiring 250 Sioux actors and advisors, the filmmakers faced huge logistical problems made more difficult by the fact that expertise in shooting a Western was in short supply. Wilson still seemed stunned, and proud, by the film's scope at the end of the production. He added up the requirements for a buffalo hunt that is the centerpiece of the picture: "a helicopter, 10 pickup trucks, 24 bareback Indian riders, 150 extras, 20 wranglers to hand a herd of 3,500 real buffalo, 25 recreated buffalo, and 7 cameras."

The film opens in Tennessee during the Civil War. In a scene reminiscent of Ambrose Bierce, Lt. John J. Dunbar rides recklessly across a field, instigating a battle that leads to a Union victory. Sickened by war, Dunbar heads to the frontier, where he is slowly drawn into Sioux culture. Cinematographer Dean Semler shot the "Tennessee" footage in South Dakota with 250 Civil War re-enactors. Production designer Jeffrey Beecroft used 10,000 gallons of paint to dress the landscape for "autumn." Fortunately, Semler was able to shoot most of the rest of the film in sequence, following the seasons from summer to winter.

Descriptions of *Dances with Wolves* tend to bog down in numbers, statistics, the enormous size of the production. Fittingly, much of the movie is about process: how to burn carcasses, how to move a load of skins up a hill, how to build a teepee. Riding a horse becomes an expression of personality, as does starting a fire or drawing a bow. At the time of filming, news reports referred to a production out of control, a *"Kevin's Gate."* Reviewers greeted the final film with sighs of relief (although director Sam Fuller complained that Blake's script borrowed from his *Run of the Arrow*, 1957). Far from an idiosyncratic epic, *Dances with Wolves* was defiantly mainstream, a movie with no hidden messages and no discernible subtext, no sharp angles or uncomfortable surprises. It was the perfect Western for people who didn't like Westerns, or who didn't know what Westerns could achieve.

Blake wrote that the project made him "immeasurably sad," adding "Among all the Indian groups, there was a spirituality that was transcendent and a way of life that was marvelous. *Dances with Wolves* is about my devastation to think that way of life is gone and we had no chance to learn from it." Blake and his fellow filmmakers tried to capture Native American spirituality by depicting white characters as villainous bigots, apart from the sensitive, saintly Dunbar. They also included grand flourishes that were unintentionally funny—such as how Dunbar and the Sioux form a circle around an enemy, then open fire on him. But no one could question Costner's commitment to the material, his love for the South Dakota landscape, and his determination to make a worthwhile film.

Finished for around $19 million, *Dances with Wolves* grossed over ten times that amount, making it the most successful modern-day Western. Costner later prepared a director's cut that added an hour of additional footage. Although he has continued to direct and produce as well as star in movies, *Dances with Wolves* marked the commercial highpoint of his career. (2003's *Open Range*, which Costner directed and starred in along with Robert Duvall, is a far more accomplished Western.) Michael Blake wrote a sequel called *The Holy Road* that he hopes to adapt to film. Published in 2001, it takes place ten years after *Dances with Wolves*.

Daughters of the Dust

Geechee Girls Productions, American Playhouse Theatrical Films, Kino International, 1991. Sound, color, 1.85. 112 minutes.

Cast: Adisa Anderson (Eli Peazant), Barbara-O (Yellow Mary Peazant), Cheryl Lynn Bruce (Viola Peazant), Cora Lee Day (Nana Peazant), Geraldine Dunston (Viola's mother), Vertamae Grosvenor (Hairbraider), Tommy Hicks (Mr. Snead), Trula Hoosier (Trula), Kaycee Moore (Haagar Peazant), Eartha D. Robinson (Myown Peazant), Alva Rodgers [Rogers] (Eula Peazant), Cornell Royal (Daddy Mac), Catherine Tarver (Woman with baby), Bahni Turpin (Iona Peazant), Kai-Lynne Warren (The Unborn Child), Umar Abdurrahman (Bilal Muhammed); Marcus Humphrey, Bernard Wilson (Boatmen); Jabario Cuthbert (Ninnyjugs); Yolanda Simmons, Ebony Hills (Teenage girls); Sherry Jackson (Older cousin), Malik Farrakhan (Newlywed man), Althea Lang (Newlywed woman); Jasmine Lee, Dalisia Robinson (Peazant babies); Willie Faulkner, Joe Taylor, Frank Brown, Rueben Fripp (Peazant men); Derrick Coaxum, Neil Howard (Peazant boys); Jared Warren, Zenovia Green, Taira Miller, Tiffanye Hills (Peazant children); Jamar Freeman (Pete), Detrell Freeman (Re-Pete); Vivian Dawson, Inez Griffin (Rice Huskers); M. Cochise Anderson (St. Julien Lastchild).

Credits: Produced, written, and directed by Julie Dash. Executive producer: Lindsay Law. Associate producers: J. Bernard Nicolas, Pamm R. Jackson, Floyd Webb, Arthur J. Fielder [Arthur Jafa]. Director of photography: A. Jaffa Fielder [Arthur Jafa]. Editors: Amy Carey, Joseph Burton. Production designer: Kerry Marshall. Music composed by John Barnes. Costume designer: Arline Burks. Casting director: Len Hunt. First assistant directors: C.C. Barnes, Nandi Bowe. Gullah language consultant: Ronald Daise. Historical consultant: Margaret Washington-Creel. Makeup supervisor: Rose Chatterton. Hairstyles created by Pamela Ferrel. Sound mixer: Veda Campbell. Supervising sound editor: Michael Payne. An American Playhouse Theatrical Films presentation, in association with WMG Films, of a Geechee Girls Production.

Additional Credits: Screened at the Sundance Film Festival during January 1991.

Available: Kino Video DVD (1999). UPC: 7-38329-01332-5.

Born in 1952, Julie Dash grew up in the Queensbridge housing projects in Long Island City, New York. When she was a teenager, she accompanied a friend to a cinema workshop at the Studio Museum in Harlem. Two years later, Dash completed her first short, but was not considering a career in filmmaking. Majoring in psychology at the City College of New York, she also wrote and produced a short documentary for the New York Urban Coalition.

Moving to California, Dash received a fellowship to the American Film Institute, then worked for the Motion Picture Association of America. She earned four grants from the National Endowment for the Arts and one from the Guggenheim Foundation, enabling her to work on screenplays and short films. In 1986, she moved to Atlanta, where she directed educational films for the National Black Women's Health Project.

As early as 1975, Dash was working on a project about the migration of African-American women to the North in the early twentieth century. The story evolved into *Daughters of the Dust*, one day in the life of a Gullah community on the Sea Islands off the coast of Georgia and South Carolina. Also known as Geechee, the Gullah culture grew from the descendants of slaves brought by ship from Africa. Isolated in space and time, they developed their own dialect and rituals. Dash set her story during a family reunion in 1902 that also marked the departure of many siblings for the mainland and eventually the North.

To assemble financing for the film, Dash spent two weeks shooting scenes on St. Helena Island with cameraman Arthur Jafa, preparing a combination of trailer and demonstration reel for investors. She screened her footage at a PBS workshop at Sundance, where Lynn Holst, a vice-president of development for *American Playhouse*, became involved. She persuaded *American Playhouse* executive producer Lindsay Law to invest in the project; his participation ensured additional funding from the Corporation for Public Broadcasting. The eventual budget was $800,000.

Even in the film's early stages, Dash's artistic strategies were evident. In articles and interviews, she spoke about the need to adopt a different method of storytelling, one suited for her target audience. "Most characters in American narrative film are grounded in parameters dictated by the archetypal Greek god and goddesses of classical western literature," she wrote in her notes on the film. "The crucial underlying references for the Peazant family in *Daughters of the Dust* are the dei ties of classical West African cosmologies." Nana (played by Cora Lee Day), the great-grandmother and matriarch of the Peazant family, represented Obatala, a Yoruba god of the sky. Eula Peazant (Alva Rogers) was Oya Yansa, the winds of change; her husband Eli (Adisa Anderson) was Ogun, similar to Pluto.

Daughters of the Dust was not the first film to assign metaphorical meanings to its characters, but it was the first independent film of the 1990s to lean so heavily on symbolism while still relating a functional narrative. Dash broke the story line into impressionistic vignettes, some proceeding in chronological order, others not. Crucial to this approach was a means of tying individual scenes together. Dash's solution was to utilize a steadily moving camera that glided over the landscape and the characters' faces, emphasizing their unity. To this she added a spare, atmospheric score by John

Barnes that placed all of the events on the same temporal plane. (Dash called both *The Blood of Jesus*, directed in 1941 by Spencer Williams, and *Ganga & Hess*, directed in 1973 by Bill Gunn, visual influences.)

Academics had no trouble deciphering Dash's intentions and strategies. *Daughters of the Dust* was popular at film festivals and on campuses, where it received thoughtful reviews. Mainstream filmgoers expecting a story along the lines of *Sounder* (1972) or *The Color Purple* (1985), cited by Dash as films her investors preferred, had a harder time appreciating the director's intentions. In response, Dash wrote, "When a work is so densely seeded within black culture, a lot of people who are not from the culture will say they find the film inaccessible or they will say they find it not engaging. What they are saying is that they do not feel privileged by the film, so they choose not to engage or allow themselves to become engaged."

Or, as a character intones on the soundtrack, "I am the first and the last. I am the honored one and the scorned one. I am the whore and the holy one. I am the wife and the virgin. I am the silence that you can not understand." Evoking a mysticism that extended beyond conventional spirituality, Dash set for herself the goal to "focus on and depict experiences that have never been shown on the screen before." Dash later wrote a novel, also called *Daughters of the Dust*, that elaborated on the lives of the characters in her film. She has also directed several music videos and television films.

Boyz n the Hood

Columbia Pictures, 1991. Sound, color, 2.35. 112 minutes. Rated R.

Cast: Larry [Laurence] Fishburne (Furious Styles), Ice Cube (Doughboy), Cuba Gooding, Jr. (Tre Styles), Nia Long (Brandi), Morris Chestnut (Ricky Baker), Tyra Ferrell (Mrs. Baker), Angela Bassett (Reva Styles), Meta King (Brandi's Mom), Whitman May (The Old Man), Hudhail Al-Amir (S.A.T. Man), Lloyd Avery, II (Knucklehead #2), Mia Bell (Female Club Member), Lexie Bigham (Mad Dog), Kenneth A. Brown (Little Chris), Nicole Brown (Brandi, Age 10), Ceal (Sheryl), Darneicea Corley (Keisha), John Cothran, Jr. (Lewis Crump), Na' Blonka Durden (Trina), Ousaun Elam (Utility Stunt #1), Susan Falcon (Mrs. Olaf), Jesse Ferguson (Officer Coffey), Dedrick D. Gobert (Dooky), Redge Green (Chris), Kareem J. Grimes (Ice Cream Truck Kid), Tammy Hanson (Rosa), Valentino Harrison (Bobby, Age 10), Desi Arnez Hines, II (Tre, Age 10), Baha Jackson (Doughboy, Age 10), Dee Dee Jacobs (Renee), Kirk Kinder (Officer Graham), Regina King (Shalika), Leanear Lane (Gangster #2), Whitman Mayo (The Old Man), Donovan McCrary (Ricky, Age 10), Don Nelson (Gangster #1), Jimmy Lee Newman (Kid), Malcolm Norrington (Knucklehead #1), Alysia M. Rogers (Shanice), Esther Scott (Tisha's Grandmother), Leonette Scott (Tisha), Vonté Sweet (Ric Rock), Baldwin C. Sykes (Monster), Raymond D. Turner (Ferris), Yolanda Whittaker (Yo-Yo), Gerard Williams (Utility Stunt #2).

Credits: Written and directed by John Singleton. Produced by Steve Nicolaides. Director of photography: Charles Mills. Art director: Bruce Bellamy. Edited by Bruce Cannon. Original music score by Stanley Clarke. Casting: Jaki Brown. Unit production manager: Steve Nicolaides. 1st Assistant director: Don Wilderons. 2nd Assistant director: Eric Jones. Music supervisor: Raoul Roach. Color by DeLuxe. Dolby Stereo.

Additional Cast: John Singleton (Mailman).

Additional Credits: Production dates: October 1 to November 28, 1990. Premiered in Los Angeles on July 2, 1991.

Available: Columbia TriStar Home Entertainment 2-disc Anniversary Edition DVD (2003). ISBN: 0-7678-7651-2. UPC: 0-43396-07319-7.

By the end of the 1980s, the first wave of blaxploitation films had died out, in part because blacks had assimilated into the film industry, in part due to the habitual caution of film executives to finance African-American movies. By coincidence, two black projects began shooting around the same time. *New Jack City*, written and directed by Mario Van Peebles, the son of iconoclastic independent filmmaker Melvin Van Peebles, took place in an Eastern urban setting. *Boyz n the Hood*, by first-time director John Singleton, was embedded deep within South Central Los Angeles.

Born in 1968, Singleton grew up in a split home, spending weekends with his father. Enrolling in film school at USC, he won several writing awards, a stepping-stone to earning representation at the Creative Artists Agency. Stephanie Allain, an executive at Columbia, read his script for *Boyz n the Hood*, and pushed for the studio to buy it. Singleton agreed to sell it only if he was allowed to direct.

Working through casting director Jaki Brown, Singleton selected largely untried actors. Cuba Gooding, Jr., who has the key role of Tre Styles, had appeared in two previous films, but this was the turning point in his career. This was the film debut for Morris Chestnut, who plays Ricky, one of Tre's friends. Playing Ricky's brother Doughboy was Ice Cube (born O'Shea Jackson), a former member of the hip-hop group NWA who had just released his first solo album. Anchoring the film was veteran actor Laurence Fishburne as Tre's father Furious Styles. Playing the conscience of the film as well as its voice of reason, Fishburne was also instrumental in the casting of Angela Bassett and Tyra Ferrell as mothers. The film was shot entirely on location in South Central. Singleton and producer Steve Nicolaides later claimed that they tried to refrain from associating with gangs, but productions notes credited the director with hiring three local gang members as consultants.

Singleton sets out his intentions in an opening title: "One out of every twenty-one Black American males will be murdered in their lifetime." His story proceeds to depict the troubled lives of three friends growing up in South Central from 1984 to 1991. Like that opening title, Singleton's script is earnest, if a bit tongue-tied. It sometimes settles for easy dramatic answers, pat solutions to problems that deserve more analysis. Especially with Fishburne's character, Singleton can seem didactic, preaching, even self-righteous.

On the other hand, Singleton had just entered his twenties, and his film is marked by a burning enthusiasm. His grasp of life in South Central is key to the film's realistic atmosphere: the trash-strewn alleyways, fast-food restaurants, liquor stores, front porches and stoops seem just as authentic today as they were fifteen years ago. Some of this authenticity may be due to the fact that many of the actors were Singleton's age, and almost all of his crew was African-American.

The first half-hour of the episodic script, set in 1984, introduces the main characters. The bulk of the film plays out their destinies in the present. In interviews and in subsequent films like *Baby Boy* (2001), Singleton revealed his real interest to be the lack of fathers, and father figures, in the black community: "My main message is that African-American men have to take more responsibility for raising their children, especially their boys. Fathers have to teach their boys to be men." That is the essential message of *Boyz n the Hood*, delivered cryptically at one point by Furious Styles: "Best way you can destroy a people, you take away their ability to reproduce themselves."

But many filmgoers fastened on its depiction of violence instead, delivered in terms recognizable from *Rebel Without a Cause*. A minor offense triggers a feud that leaves four dead, and that forces Tre to choose between his friends and his future.

Made for around six million dollars, *Boyz n the Hood* grossed close to ten times that, making it one of the most profitable films of 1991. (Like *New Jack City*, *Boyz N the Hood* was the occasion for violence during its opening run.) Singleton earned both screenwriting and directing nominations at the Academy Awards, the youngest directing nominee to date. His subsequent career, including diversions into blaxploitation with a 2000 remake of *Shaft*, had its disappointments. But in 2005 Singleton produced *Hustle & Flow* and directed *Four Brothers*, two assured films more concerned with entertaining than preaching.

One surprise has been the subsequent careers of the actors in this film—a reflection of how seriously both the industry and filmgoers have taken Singleton's picture. Some, like Fishburne, who had a significant role in the *Matrix* trilogy but also in B-movies like *Biker Boyz*, have become increasingly irrelevant. Others, like Nia Long and Morris Chestnut, never truly fulfilled their potential. Gooding won a Best Supporting Oscar for a stunt role in *Jerry Maguire*, a film that has lost a lot of its original luster. Of all the actors, Ice Cube has been on some levels the most successful. He gave a strong performance in *Three Kings*, but he has also written, produced, directed, and starred in films like the *Friday* and *Barbershop* series.

Beauty and the Beast

Walt Disney Pictures, 1991. Sound, color, 1.85. 84 minutes. Rated G.
Voice Cast: Robby Benson (Beast), Jesse Corti (Le Fou), Rex Everhart (Maurice), Angela Lansbury (Mrs. Potts), Paige O'Hara (Belle), Jerry Orbach (Lumiere), Bradley Michael Pierce (Chip), David Ogden Stiers (Cogsworth/Narrator), Richard White (Gaston), Jo Anne Worley (Wardrobe), Mary Kay Bergman (Babette), Brian Cummins (Stove), Alvin Epstein (Bookseller), Tony Jay (Monsieur D'Arque), Alec Murphy (Baker), Kimmy Robertson (Featherduster), Hal Smith (Philippe), Kath Soucie (Bimbette), Frank Welker (Footstool/featured special vocal effects).
Credits: Directed by Gary Trousdale and Kirk Wise. Animation screenplay by Linda Woolverton. Produced by Don Hahn. Executive producer: Howard Ashman. Songs by Howard Ashman and Alan Menken. Original score by Alan Menken. Associate producer: Sarah McArthur. Art director: Brian McEntee. Edited by John Carnochan. Artistic supervisors: Story: Robert Allers. Layout: Ed Ghertner. Background: Lisa Keene. Cleanup: Vera Lanpher. Visual effects: Randy Fullmer. Computer graphic images: Jim Hillin. Story: Brenda Chapman, Burney Mattinson,

Brian Pimental, Joe Ranft, Kelly Asbury, Christopher Sanders, Kevin Harkey, Bruce Woodside, Tom Ellery, Robert Lence. Supervising animators: James Baxter (Belle), Glen Keane (Beast), Andreas Deja (Gaston), Nik Ranieri (Lumiere), Will Finn (Cogsworth), David Pruiksma (Mrs. Potts and Chip), Rueben A. Aquino (Maurice), Chris Wahl (Le Fou), Russ Edmonds (Philippe), Larry White (Wolves), Tony Anselmo (Wardrobe). Casting by Albert Tavares. Prints by Technicolor. Produced and distributed on Eastman Film. Dolby Stereo. A Walt Disney Pictures production, in association with Silver Screen Partners IV.
Additional Credits: Sound editors: Julia Evershade, Michael Benavente, Jessica Gallavan, J. H. Arrufat, Ron Bartlett. Opened in New York City on November 13, 1991.
Awards: Oscars for Best Original Score, Original Song ("Beauty and the Beast").
Other Versions: Disney released an expanded IMAX edition in 2002.
Available: Walt Disney Studios Home Entertainment DVD (2002). ISBN: 0-7888-3369-3. UPC: 786936171631.

By the time of Walt Disney's death in 1966, his film empire was almost moribund. The remarkable string of feature cartoons from the 1940s and '50s had been replaced by frankly dull entries like *The Rescuers* (1977) and *The Great Mouse Detective* (1986). In 1979, Don Bluth, complaining about the lack of energy and invention in the company's products, led an exodus of animators from the studio. Disney's long-running television anthology series *The Wonderful World of Disney* was canceled in 1983. Despite its steady supply of live-action PG-rated films, the Disney brand was synonymous with the sort of family entertainment that no one liked anymore.

Born in 1942, Michael Eisner started out in the entertainment industry as a page at NBC, and later held programming jobs at all three major networks. Hired by Barry Diller at ABC, Eisner followed him to Paramount in 1976, where he became CEO of the studio. He oversaw several blockbuster films, but left Paramount when he was not named chairman after Diller's departure. Instead, Eisner became the chairman and CEO of the Walt Disney Company in 1984.

Eisner brought with him Jeffrey Katzenberg, a one-time agent and former assistant to Diller who had helped develop some of Paramount's biggest franchises. As the new chair of film production, Katzenberg set out to revitalize the animation department. One of his first projects was *The Little Mermaid* (1989), which transformed the Hans Christian Andersen fairy tale into the equivalent of an animated Broadway musical. It was enormously popular in part because of its score, but also because it followed in the tradition of the great Disney cartoon features of the past.

Beauty and the Beast used *Little Mermaid*'s songwriters, Howard Ashman and Alan Menken. Ashman had been a book editor in New York City when he started writing plays and song lyrics. Menken studied piano and violin in high school, and after graduating from NYU gave up pre-med to focus on music. He met Ashman at the Lehman Engle Musical Theater Workshop at EMI. Their Broadway musical version of *Little Shop of Horrors* brought them to the attention of Disney, where they first worked on songs for *Oliver & Company* (1988).

The screenplay for *Beauty and the Beast* passed through several drafts and writers until Linda Woolverton's version was accepted. (Walt Disney himself had tried to develop the project in the 1930s and again in the 1950s.) Previously a children's television writer, Woolverton stayed relatively true to the outlines of the original French story, which can be traced back to the eighteenth century. The new version still featured a beast cast under a spell, an enchanted castle, an imprisoned father ransomed by his daughter Belle, and a curse that could only be undone by true love. Edited away were Belle's sisters; added was a modern sensibility that gave Belle feminist longings and an amusingly blockheaded suitor named Gaston.

Like their work in *The Little Mermaid*, Ashman and Menken's songs, in particular "Be My Guest," brought an ingenious form of razzle-dazzle that had been missing for many years from Disney films. The furiously paced lyrics, dense with insults and one-liners, were handled as just another melodic element by Menken. Merged with animation, they became show-stopping delights—in part because directors Gary Trousdale and Kirk Wise insisted on including jokes, either essential or peripheral, in as many shots as possible. A village boy chases a pig through the middle of "Belle," the opening song, for example. (Its lyrics are shared, à la *Love Me Tonight*, 1932, by all the villagers.) In a gag Disney would have loved, the song ends with Gaston shooting down a goose flying overhead.

The quality of the film's animation is variable; how the characters walk is especially problematic. However, the tour de force moments—again, "Be My Guest" but also some frightening interludes in a forest filled with snarling wolves—are as lively and imaginative as the best Disney features. The studio made extensive use of previews, even showing a "work in progress" at the 1991 New York Film Festival that persuaded animators to expand "Be My Guest."

Beauty and the Beast was an instant sensation with both audiences and critics when it was released. Older viewers responded to the film's connection to the Disney movies they saw as children, as well as its many allusions to everything from *The Bride of Frankenstein* (1935) to *Citizen Kane* (1941). Youngsters were entranced by a story with real depth, emotions, and mystery, one that didn't talk down to them and that didn't pretend that the world was free from pain. The spiritual element of the plot—its retribution and resurrection, for example—received less attention than its depiction of Belle as a modern-day corrective to Snow White. Did children understand that during their courtship, Belle was asking the Beast to destroy the very parts of his personality that made her love him?

The film is dedicated to Ashman, who died of AIDS before the film opened. *Beauty and the Beast* became an important revenue stream for Disney, which produced a live version at Walt Disney World, another for *Disney on Ice*, and a Broadway version that ran for over five thousand performances. The studio was equally successful with the animated features *Aladdin* (1992) and *The Lion King* (1994), but in recent years the animation department has again suffered from a loss of direction. Currently it is under the direction of John Lasseter, the head of Pixar.

Unforgiven

Unforgiven's Bill Munny (Clint Eastwood), no longer able to deny his destiny as a killer to the Schofield Kid (Jaimz Woolvett).

Warner Bros., 1992. Sound, color, 2.35. 130 minutes. Rated R.

Cast: Clint Eastwood (Bill Munny), Gene Hackman (Little Bill Daggett), Morgan Freeman (Ned Logan), Richard Harris (English Bob), Jaimz Woolvett (The "Schofield Kid"), Saul Rubinek (W. W. Beauchamp), Frances Fisher (Strawberry Alice), Anna Thomson (Delilah Fitzgerald), David Mucci (Quick Mike), Rob Campbell (Davey Bunting), Anthony James (Skinny Dubois), Tara Dawn Frederick (Little Sue), Beverley Elliott (Silky), Liisa Repo-Martell (Faith), Josie Smith (Crow Creek Kate), Shane Meier (Will Munny), Aline Levasseur (Penny Munny), Cherrilene Cardinal (Sally Two Trees), Robert Koons (Crocker), Ron White (Clyde Ledbetter), Mina E. Mina (Muddy Chandler), Henry Kope (German Joe Schultz), Jeremy Ratchford (Deputy Andy Russell), John Pyper-Ferguson (Charley Hecker), Jefferson Mappin (Fatty Rossiter), Walter Marsh (Barber), Garner Butler (Eggs Anderson), Larry Reese (Tom Luckinbill), Blair Haynes (Paddy McGee), Frank C. Turner (Fuzzy), Sam Karas (Thirsty Thurston), Lochlyn Munro (Texas Slim), Ben Cardinal (Johnny Foley), Philip Hayes (Lippy MacGregor), Michael Charrois (Wiggens), Bill Davidson (Buck Barthol), Paul McLean (Train person #1), James Herman (Train person #2), Michael Maurer (Train person #3), Larry Joshua (Bucky), George Orrison ("The Shadow"), Gregory Goossen (Fighter).

Credits: Directed and produced by Clint Eastwood. Written by David Webb Peoples. Executive producer: David Valdes. Director of photography: Jack N. Green. Production designed by Henry Bumstead. Edited by Joel Cox. Music score by Lennie Niehaus. Associate producer: Julian Ludwig. Production manager: Bob Gray. First assistant director: Scott Maitland. Casting by Phyllis Huffman. Art directors: Rick Roberts, Adrian Gorton. Set designer: James J. Murakami. Script supervisor: Lloyd Nelson. Supervising sound editors: Alan Robert Murray, Walter Newman. Sound mixer: Rob Young. Technical consultant: Buddy Van Horn. Wardrobe Department Head: Glenn Wright. Head Make-up artist: Mike Hancock. Head hair stylist: Iloe Flewelling. Special effects coordinator: John Frazier. Titles and optics by Pacific Title. Color by Technicolor. Filmed in Panavision. Dolby Stereo. "Dedicated to Sergio and Don." A Warner Bros. presentation of a Malpaso production.

Additional Credits: Musical themes by Clint Eastwood. Production dates: August 21 to November 12, 1991. Premiered in Los Angeles on August 3, 1992.

Awards: Oscars for Best Picture, Directing, Supporting Actor (Hackman), Film Editing.

Available: Warner Home Video DVD (2002). ISBN: 0-7907-7269-8. UPC: 085392345724.

After *The Outlaw Josey Wales* (1976, a Registry title), Clint Eastwood's career veered between lowbrow, often violent movies and films in which he explored less predictable aspects of his screen persona. Quiet, low-key comedies like *Bronco Billy* 1980) and period dramas like *Honkytonk Man* (1982) showed a relaxed, amiable Eastwood. *Tightrope* (1984) and *Pale Rider* (1985) presented his earlier characters in a more skeptical light, acknowledging shortcomings and contradictions. The actor and director still showed a propensity for brainless action films like *Pink Cadillac* (1989) and *The Rookie* (1990), but even these were made with a craftsmanship and attention to detail that separated him from other filmmakers.

Still, by working within the system, by amassing credits in disreputable genres, and by expressing conservative attitudes in an industry that valued liberal outlooks, he failed to earn the respect awarded to many younger filmmakers. In the beginning of the 1990s, Eastwood also had to cope with a series of personal crises often recounted in gossip columns. After the poor box-office performance of *The Rookie*, he turned to a screenplay he had optioned years earlier. It was written on spec (i.e., without a contract) by David Webb Peoples, a former film editor who gained attention by revising a script for *Blade Runner* (1982). Francis Ford Coppola had optioned what would eventually become *Unforgiven*, but allowed his rights to lapse. Eastwood got a copy of the script as a writing sample, and optioned it in 1984.

Taking place largely in Big Whiskey, Wyoming, in 1880, *Unforgiven* addressed the central themes in Westerns, in particular how violence defined the frontier. When Eastwood decided to film the project in 1990, he gave it a broader canvas than many of his previous movies. His vision encompassed an entire society on the verge of turmoil, from a sheriff imposing law through force of will to a saloonkeeper trading in flesh, from working farmers and ranchers to killers and outcasts.

Erected in a remote section of Alberta, the town of Big Whiskey, designed by Hollywood veteran Henry Bumstead, had real buildings, not false-front sets. For the cast, Eastwood gathered respected actors like Gene Hackman and Morgan Freeman, and then gave them the freedom to develop fully rounded characters. Cinematographer Jack N. Green captured extraordinary landscapes, one of the prerequisites of the genre, but also used deep focus, low lighting, and subjective camera movements to draw viewers into an intricately realized world.

At this stage in his career, Eastwood was uniquely qualified to comment on the genre. He was the last movie star to establish a career in Westerns, through his *Rawhide* television show and his "Man with No Name" trilogy directed by Sergio Leone. Throughout the 1970s and '80s, he almost single-handedly upheld the Western tradition even as he questioned its values.

As with many other movie stars, much of Eastwood's career was based on violence. He examined it in detail in the first *Dirty Harry* (1971) and in *Tightrope*, offering nuanced and troubling takes on its corrupting influence. On the other hand, he was willing to exploit violence for commercial favor. In *Unforgiven* he would tackle the subject head on, showing its corrosive effects on both killer and victim, in the process summing up both

his beliefs and his career, and displaying a maturity and understanding sometimes missing from his earlier movies.

Written in the style of revisionist anti-Westerns of the 1970s, Peoples' script depicted a world in which almost everyone was both villain and victim. In adapting the story, Eastwood showed a remarkable empathy with all sides of conflicts. No one is absolutely wrong in the film; as director Jean Renoir once put it, "Everyone has his reasons." An initial burst of violence erupts from a character's psychological inadequacies. Hackman's sheriff, Little Bill Daggett, may resort to grotesque beatings, but he is trying to maintain a fragile stability in his town. Using quirky humor to sketch in their personalities, Eastwood made his characters real enough so that their actions could startle and dismay.

Eastwood's Bill Munny, a reformed killer and pig farmer, is the most complex figure in *Unforgiven*. With his friend Ned Logan (played by Freeman), he spends much of the film determined to deny his personality. Identified in the opening credits as "a man of notoriously vicious and intemperate disposition," he keeps insisting, "I ain't like that anymore." It's been eleven years since he's fired a gun, he's given up liquor, and he even has trouble staying on his horse. When he decides to collect a bounty by killing two outlaw cowboys, it's apparently because he wants to save his pig farm and help his young children.

But good motives aren't enough. Munny's efforts to kill for the "right" reasons unleash a monster he has spent years repressing, one whose violence is even more ghastly than the slashings, whippings, and outhouse shootings that precede him. This is the heart of darkness in the American dream, the truth behind the gunslingers and gangsters who fill our movies, the real consequence to conquering the frontier. The beatings and shootings in *Unforgiven* occur at the same narrative points they would in other Western plots, but here they provide no catharsis, no reassurance. Instead they are grisly, even appalling.

For someone with Eastwood's background and reputation, *Unforgiven* was a daring statement. The film ran counter to almost everything the genre promised, and did so with an authority and conviction that was impossible to argue with. Eastwood's lean, sinewy filmmaking style, his appreciation for acting, and his respect for a Western tradition embodied by John Ford, Budd Boetticher, and other masters added to the stature of *Unforgiven*. (Eastwood dedicated the film to Sergio Leone and Don Siegel.)

For some critics, *Unforgiven* marked an amazing resurgence for a one-time action star. For others, it was the culmination of a career of dedication and hard work. *Unforgiven* has influenced every subsequent Western, and its moral standing and filmmaking expertise place Eastwood among the best directors working in the industry. His subsequent career has been marked by equally challenging movies like *Mystic River* (2003) and *Flags of Our Fathers* (2006), award-winning efforts that on the level of pure craftsmanship are among the best-made titles of our time.

Groundhog Day

Columbia, 1993. Sound, color, 1.85. 101 minutes. Rated PG.

Cast: Bill Murray (Phil [Connors]), Andie MacDowell (Rita), Chris Elliott (Larry), Stephen Tobolowsky (Ned [Ryerson]), Brian Doyle-Murray (Buster), Marita Geraghty (Nancy), Angela Paton (Mrs. Lancaster), Ric Ducommun (Gus), Rick Overton (Ralph), Robin Duke (Doris the waitress), Carol Bivins (Anchorwoman), Willie Garson (Phil's assistant Kenny), Ken Hudson Campbell (Man in hallway), Les Podewell (Old man), Rod Sell (Groundhog official), Tom Milanovich (State trooper), John Watson, Sr. (Bartender), Peggy Roeder (Piano teacher), Harold Ramis (Neurologist), David Pasquesi (Psychiatrist), Lee R. Sellars (Cop), Chet Dubowski (Bank guard Felix), Don Erickson (Bank guard Herman), Sandy Maschmeyer (Phil's movie date), Leighanne O'Neil (Fan on street); Evangeline Binkley, Samuel Mages, Ben Zwick (*Jeopardy!* viewers); Hynden Walsh (Debbie), Michael Shannon (Fred), Timothy Hendrickson (Waiter Bill), Martha Webster (Waitress Alice), Angela Gollan (Piano student), Shaun Chaiyabhat (Boy in tree), Dianne B. Shaw (E.R. nurse); Barbara Ann Grimes, Ann Heekin, Lucina Paquet (Flat tire ladies); Brenda Pickleman (Buster's wife), Amy Murdoch (Buster's daughter), Eric Saiet (Buster's son), Lindsay Reinsch (Woman with cigarette), Roger Adler (Guitar player), Ben A. Fish (Bass player), Don Rio McNichols (Drum player), Brian Willig (Saxophone player); Richard Henzel, Rob Riley (D.J. voices).

Credits: Directed by Harold Ramis. Screenplay by Danny Rubin and Harold Ramis. Story by Danny Rubin. Produced by Trevor Albert and Harold Ramis. Executive producer: C. O. Erickson. Director of photography: John Bailey. Production designer: David Nichols. Edited by Pembroke J. Herring. Costume designer: Jennifer Butler. Music by George Fenton. Casting by Howard Feuer. Unit production manager: C. O. Erickson. 1st assistant director: Michael Haley. Associate producer: Whitney White. Art director: Peter Lansdown Smith. Script supervisor: Judi Townsend. Costume supervisor: Mike Butler. Key makeup: Dorothy Pearl. Makeup: Deborah K. Dee. Key hair stylist: Emanuel "Manny" Millar. Hair stylist: Gunnar Swanson. Stunt coordinator: Rick LeFevour. Special effects: Tom Ryba. Supervising sound editor: George H. Anderson. Production mixer: Les Lazarowitz. Opticals by Cinema Research Corporation. Title design: Pittard/Sullivan/Fitzgerald. Filmed in Panavision. Prints by Technicolor. Dolby Stereo. A Columbia Pictures presentation of a Trevor Albert production.

Additional Credits: Production dates: March 16 to June 10, 1992. Released February 12, 1993.

Available: Sony Pictures DVD (2008). UPC: 043396226456.

As a follow-up to *National Lampoon's Animal House* (1978, a Registry title), screenwriter Harold Ramis cowrote *Meatballs* (1979). The film was a showcase for Bill Murray, like Ramis a veteran of Chicago's Second City comedy troupe. The success of *Meatballs* won Ramis the chance to direct a feature, *Caddyshack* (1980), which also featured Murray, along with comedians like Rodney Dangerfield. Next up was *Stripes* (1981), in which Ramis acted with Murray as well as contributing to the screenplay. While the settings—summer camp, country club, military maneuvers—might change, the essential narrative engine behind all these films remained the same: anarchic comedy among male cronies, interrupted at times by sentimental passages.

With *Ghostbusters* (1984), Ramis found a way to expand his formula by tying it to a special-effects adventure plot; the result was the most financially successful film comedy of its time. It also cemented Murray's status as movie star. Born in Evanston, Illinois, in 1950, he received a Jesuit education before dropping out of college to follow his older brother, Brian Doyle-Murray, into Second City. After working in Chicago, he moved to New York for the *National Lampoon Radio Hour*. Murray replaced a departing Chevy Chase on *Saturday Night Live*; there he developed several memorable characters. Murray also honed his personality as a performer, becoming the sort of jaded, cynical wisecracker whose inner pain was impossible to miss.

Ghostbusters was so successful that it enabled Murray to develop his own projects. He starred in a remake of *The Razor's Edge* (1984) and was the principal creative force behind *Scrooged* (1988), a retelling of Charles Dickens' *A Christmas Carol*. Murray codirected the underrated *Quick Change* (1990), a story with thematic resemblances to *Groundhog Day* and another effort on his part to make something more ambitious than the slapstick of *Ghostbusters II* (1989).

Trevor Albert, an associate producer on the Ramis-scripted *Club Paradise* (1986), was intrigued enough by Danny Rubin's script for *Groundhog Day* to want it as his first producing credit. Rubin, who had a background in theater and in writing industrial films, saw the story as a way to broach existential issues in an entertainment medium. His plot concerned a self-absorbed television weatherman who finds himself in a time warp in which he repeats the same February 2nd over and over again.

Albert sent the screenplay to Ramis, who agreed to direct and produce as long as he could rewrite it. For one thing, Rubin's script started in the middle of the story, with no explanation for what was happening. Ramis used a more conventional narrative approach to introduce the characters: Phil Connors, the weatherman; Rita, his producer (played by Andie MacDowell); and Larry, his cameraman (Chris Elliott). They are on assignment in Punxsutawney, Pennsylvania, covering the annual Groundhog Day celebration, when bad weather forces them to stay over for the night. But as each day dawns, Connors finds himself in the same situations, meeting the same people, making the same mistakes.

Connors' disdain for Punxsutawney, its people, his job, his coworkers, and life in general fuels the opening of the film, but his increasing desperation as he relives the same day over and over lifts *Groundhog Day* into an entirely new world of comedy. "What would you do if you were stuck in one place and everyday was exactly the same and nothing that you did mattered?" Connors asks at once point, and it is a question that Rubin and Ramis want viewers to answer as well.

How we make choices, what we decide is important, how we live our lives are issues that few films, let alone comedies, tackle. Ramis has cited Frank Capra's *It's a Wonderful Life* (1946) as an influence, but what distinguishes *Groundhog Day* is its consistent inventiveness, its willingness to stretch logic to the limit. Ramis's upbeat tone, a corrective to Murray's dyspeptic persona, softens the story's cruel moments. As a result, Connors comes off like Wile E. Coyote in the Road Runner cartoons, his increasingly elaborate schemes still doomed to failure. According to Albert, Ramis's lack of cynicism was crucial to the film. "It would have been very easy in the hands of another director to turn it much darker," he said.

Because it can function as a sort of spiritual primer, *Groundhog Day* has been described by fans as "Buddhist" or "Jesuit" or leaning toward several other denominations. It is equally rewarding as a working out of various schools of philosophical thought. Rubin explained the point of the film as "doing what you can do in the moment to make things better instead of making things worse," while Ramis spoke about "living a life in service to others."

What may be most satisfying about *Groundhog Day* is its refusal to judge. Connors, who at first sees the people of Punxsutawney as hicks and morons, learns to view them as humans. Moviegoers who applaud Connors' cynical quips and put-downs gradually see the emptiness of his life. When Connors "embraces where he is and what he can do," as Ramis put it, he finds a form of salvation. If that upbeat message ignores the reality of the tramps and hoboes in the film, it still speaks to the hopes of a wide audience.

Ramis continues to work as a writer, actor, producer, and director, both in mainstream projects like *Analyze This* (1999) and in darker works like *The Ice Harvest* (2005). Murray has also alternated between middlebrow movies like *Garfield* and esoteric films like *The Life Aquatic with Steve Zissou* (both 2004).

Schindler's List

Universal, 1993. Sound, color, 1.85. 195 minutes. Rated R.

Cast: Liam Neeson (Oskar Schindler), Ben Kingsley (Itzhak Stern), Ralph Fiennes (Amon Goeth), Caroline Goodall (Emilie Schindler), Jonathan Sagalle (Poldek Pfefferberg), Embeth Davidtz (Helen Hirsch), Malgoscha Gebel (Victoria Klonowska), Shmulik [Shmuel] Levy (Wilek Chilowicz), Mark Ivanir (Marcel Goldberg), Béatrice Macola (Ingrid), Andrzej Seweryn (Julian Scherner), Friedrich von Thun (Rolf Czurda), Krzysztof Luft (Herman Toffel), Harry Nehring (Leo John), Norbert Weisser (Albert Hujar), Adi Nitzan (Mila Pfefferberg).

Credits: Directed by Steven Spielberg. Screenplay by Steven Zaillian. Based on the novel by Thomas Keneally. Produced by Steven Spielberg, Gerald R. Molen, Branko Lustig. Executive producer: Kathleen Kennedy. Director of photography: Janusz Kaminski. Film edited by Michael Kahn. Production designer: Allan Starski. Music by John Williams. Co-producer: Lew Rywin. Violin solos by Itzhak Perlman. Costume designer: Anna Biedrzycka-Sheppard. Casting: Lucky Englander and Fritz Fleischhacker, Magdalena Szwarcbart, Tova Cypin and Liat Meiron, Juliet Taylor. Unit production manager: Branko Lustig. First assistant director: Sergio Mimica-Gezzan. Consultant: Leopold Page. Associate producers: Irving Glovin, Robert Raymond. Art directors: Maciej Walczak, Ewa Tarnowska, Ryszard Melliwa, Grzegorz Piatowski. Visual effects supervisor: Steve Price. Special effects coordinator: Bruce Minkus. Makeup supervisor: Christina Smith. Hair supervisor: Judith A. Cory. Supervising sound editors: Charles L. Campbell, Louis L. Edemann. Production sound mixers: Ronald Judkins, Robert C. Jackson. Prints by DeLuxe. A Universal Pictures presentation of an Amblin Entertainment production.

Additional Credits: Production dates: March 1 to May 23, 1983. Premiered in Washington, D.C., on November 30, 1993.

Awards: Oscars for Best Picture, Director, Writing—Screenplay Based on Material from Another Medium, Cinematography, Editing, Music—Original Score, Art Direction–Set Decoration.

Available: Universal Studios DVD (2004). ISBN: 0-7832-9728-9. UPC: 0-25192-38662-6.

Although he was responsible for some of the most popular, and profitable, films of his time, Steven Spielberg in the 1980s still struggled to be accepted as a "serious" director. *The Color Purple* (1985) and *Empire of the Sun* (1987) marked tentative steps in that direction; the latter, an adaptation of a J.G.

Ballard novel about a young boy's experiences in Shanghai during the Japanese occupation, also fit in with the director's interest in World War II. Before those two projects, he asked Universal to purchase the film rights to Thomas Keneally's 1982 "non-fiction novel" *Schindler's List*. Keneally started his extensive research after an encounter with Poldek Pfefferberg, who owned a Beverly Hills luggage store. Pfefferberg had two filing cabinets filled with documents about Oskar Schindler, a Nazi factory owner who saved the lives of some 1,200 Jews during the Holocaust. He not only persuaded Keneally to tackle the project, he accompanied the author on trips through the United States, Europe, and Israel, providing introductions, translations, and other help. In his memoir *Searching for Schindler*, Keneally makes it clear how important Pfefferberg was to the success of the original novel.

Spielberg had never dealt directly in film with his Jewish background, although he would tell interviewers that his empathy for aliens and outsiders was a result of his own feelings of ostracism growing up as a Jew. He also credits a classroom screening of *The Twisted Cross* (1956), an anti-Nazi documentary, with making the Holocaust a real event, rather than a school topic, for him. Apart from his amateur work, Spielberg directed three features about World War II (furthermore, the *Indiana Jones* series roughly coincided with the rise of Nazism). But, he shied away from *Schindler's List*, even after meeting Pfefferberg, one of the *Schindlerjuden*, in 1983.

At the time, the Holocaust had almost never been covered directly in movies, apart from documentaries like Alain Resnais' *Night and Fog* (1955). There were several obstacles: questions of taste and decency, or of exploiting the victims and glamorizing the Nazis, for example. In 1983, Spielberg believed he wasn't emotionally or intellectually ready to tackle the subject. He was also worried about alienating his audience. Through his years of success, he had formed an unspoken pact with moviegoers, the sense that he would not cheat them or let them down. As he said to a *Wall Street Journal* reporter in 1987, "I think some people would like me to make a movie that explores the dark side and provides no easy answer to make the audience feel better when they return to their cars. If those critics want more pain in my films, they can give me $2 million—that's all it would take to make a film about pain—and I'll make that movie."

But *Schindler's List* gave Spielberg the opportunity to make a Holocaust film that, while

serious and accurate, would not dwell relentlessly on misery. He faced some criticism for choosing a story that would, in the words of Rabbi Eli Hecht, "glorify a latter-day Robin Hood who profited at the expense of Polish Jewry." But he also found a means, as Keneally did, to focus on a society and culture that allowed the Holocaust to occur, and not just to depict how its victims suffered.

Keneally wrote a screenplay draft, as did Kurt Luedtke, but Spielberg didn't proceed until he read a version by Steve Zaillian. (Martin Scorsese, who hired Zaillian, had considered adapting the book in 1988.) Spielberg received the go-ahead from Universal executive Sidney Sheinberg on rather stringent terms, including a short seventy-six-day shooting schedule and a tight budget of $22 million. Spielberg also had to shoot *Jurassic Park* first. He continued working on *Jurassic Park* after flying to Poland to start *Schindler's List*. He wound up finishing principal photography on *Schindler's List* four days under schedule.

Spielberg told cinematographer Janusz Kaminski that he didn't just want a documentary look. "We want people to see this film in fifteen years and not have a sense when it was made," Kaminski said. He added that Spielberg "got rid of the crane, got rid of the Steadicam, got rid of the zoom lenses, got rid of everything that for me might be considered a safety net." Almost half of the film was shot with handheld cameras. Using black-and-white required altering the production design and returning to an older style of lighting. The result was a film that immersed viewers in the reality of the Holocaust experience to an extent never achieved in mainstream features before.

Press notes listed extraordinary statistics: 126 speaking parts, 30,000 extras, 148 sets, 210 crew members. What participants noted was Spielberg's commitment to accuracy and truth. Emotionally, it was a devastating production. "My kids saw me cry for the first time," he said. "I would come home and weep, not because I was feeling sorry for anybody—I would weep because it was so bloody painful."

The film opened to unusually strong reviews and extraordinary ticket sales. Against all expectations, *Schindler's List* was a box-office phenomenon across the world, attracting attention from political and religious leaders. It became the most honored of all Spielberg's works, but its greatest legacy may be the Shoah Visual History Foundation, formed in 1994 to collect and catalog the testimonies of Holocaust survivors. In 2006, the foundation became the University of Southern California Shoah Foundation Institute. Spielberg also helps fund the Steven Spielberg Jewish Film Archive at the Hebrew University of Jerusalem and the United States Holocaust Museum's Steven Spielberg Film and Video Archive.

Hoop Dreams

Basketball as a way of life. Arthur Agee in *Hoop Dreams*.
Courtesy of The Criterion Collection

Fine Line Features, 1994. Sound, color, 1.33. 171 minutes.

Featuring: William Gates, Arthur Agee, Emma Gates, Curtis Gates, Sheila Agee, Arthur "Bo" Agee, Earl Smith, Gene Pingatore, Isiah Thomas, Sister Marilyn Hopewell, Bill Gleason, Patricia Weir, Marjorie Heard, Luther Bedford, Aretha Mitchell, Shannon Johnson, Tomika Agee, Joe "Sweetie" Agee, Jazz Agee, Catherine Mines, Alicia Mines, Alvin Bibbs, Willie Gates, James Kelly, Michael O'Brie, Dick Vitale, Kevin O'Neill, Bobby Knight, Joey Meyer, Frank Du Bois, Spike Lee, Bo Ellis, Bob Gibbons, Dennis Doyle, Clarence Webb, Stan Wilson, Derrick Zinneman, Tim Gray, Myron Gordon.

Credits: Directed by Steve James. Produced by Frederick Marx, Steve James, Peter Gilbert. Director of photography: Peter Gilbert. Edited by Frederick Marx, Steve James, Bill Haugse. Creative consultant, co-producer: Gordon Quinn. Sound: Adam Singer, Tom Yore. Music producer: Ben Sidran. Executive producers: Gordon Quinn, Catherine Allan. Post-production supervisor: Susanne Suffredin. Executive in charge for KTCA: Gerry Richman. KTCA production manager: Emily Stevens. Additional music: Tom Yore. Additional photography: Gordon Quinn, Ed Scott, Sid Lubitsch, Kevin McCarey, Mirko Popadic, Jim Morrissette, Jim Fetterley. Additional sound: Ed Scott, Mirko Popadic, Bill Jenkins. Narrator: Steven James. Technical consultant: Jim Morrissette. Kartemquin On-line: Frederick Marx, Melissa Sterne. Colorists: Craig Leffel, Robert Jung, Oscar Oboza, Jr. Post-production supervisor: Fenell Doremus. Audio mix: Ric Coken, Chuck Rapp, Corey Coken, Bryen Hensley, Margaret M.S. Marvin, Zenith Audio Services. Title design: George Eastman. Program support: The John D. and Catherine T. MacArthur Foundation, The Corporation for Public Broadcasting, Public Broadcasting Service, Dan and Lucia Woods-Lindley, Illinois Arts Council, NEA Regional Grants—Midwest, Pru and Frank Beidler. Originally produced for the Public Broadcast Service. A Kartemquin Films and KTCA TV (Public Television, Saint Paul, Minneapolis) production.

Additional Credits: Screened at the Sundance Film Festival during January 1994 and at the New York Film Festival on October 9, 1994. Opened theatrically October 14, 1994.

Available: Criterion DVD (2005). ISBN: 1-55940-958-4. UPC: 7-15515-01602-5.

The genesis of *Hoop Dreams* was a half-hour documentary about how Chicago area high schools recruited grade-school students. Of the three principal filmmakers involved, producer Frederick Marx had been a teacher and film critic before producing and directing "personal essay" films like *Dreams from China* (1989). Cinematographer Peter Gilbert had worked with documentarians Barbara Kopple and Michael Apted and had also shot music videos. Director Steve James had made *Grassroots Chicago* (1991), an activist documentary, for Kartemquin Films.

Founded by Gordon Quinn and Jerry Blumenthal, Kartemquin Films has been an influential documentary production house in Chicago since 1967. Quinn encouraged the filmmakers to take on a project that ultimately would entail filming over a period of five years. Originally their goal had been to focus on the impact basketball had on black culture. Gene Pingatore, a coach at St. Joseph High School, introduced them to insurance agent and unofficial talent scout Earl Smith, who in turn brought them to fourteen-year-old Arthur Agee. Agee and his family agreed to participate in the film; the producers approached three other players and their families as well, deciding to cover William Gates, another teenager, in case Agee's story did not work out.

At that point the only financing the filmmakers received was a $2500 NEA grant. Money was one reason why Gilbert decided to shoot the project on Betacam video (using borrowed and donated equipment), but he also acknowledged that video allowed him to shoot with fewer lighting requirements. Both Agee and Gates were accepted into St. Joseph's, a private school in Westchester that counted basketball star Isiah Thomas among its graduates. The filmmakers not only documented the experiences of the boys at school, but covered their families and homes as well. "We were struck by how little the cameras affected their lives," James said later. "We built up a level of trust and understanding with the families so that eventually, the cameras became routine."

The producers could not anticipate the reversals the boys would encounter over the next three years; as they admitted later, the first lesson they had to learn was to "get the footage while it was there." In the final cut, the freshman and sophomore years at St. Joseph's cover about a half-hour of screen time, edited down from a total of twenty-two shooting days. "We were still trying to raise money," Gilbert confessed. The filmmakers also had to decide how big a role they wanted to play in the lives of their subjects. "Our interest in them went beyond filmmaking," James said. "We were the only people in William's life who had no vested interest in his success."

In following Agee and Gates so closely, the filmmakers could incidentally capture a world mainstream filmgoers had never seen before. *Hoop Dreams* documents a culture in which goals have been twisted out of shape, one in which sports can be a viable escape from poverty, but also a route to dissipation and loss. The filmmakers present crucial decisions—to either fund a student or not, to demand an adolescent to play through injuries, to ignore the outside factors affecting performance—without judgment, without pointing out heroes or villains, and, remarkably, without exploiting their subjects. And when one student is forced to leave St. Joseph's for an inner-city public school, the film can effectively double its viewpoint and provide a detailed comparison between the rich and the poor. "Do you all wonder sometimes how am I living?" Arthur's mother asks when her public aid is cut to $268 a month.

After amassing some 250 hours of material, Marx, James, and Bill Haugse reduced it to a first cut of roughly eight hours. The final cut, about half that length, was still considered excessively long, especially in a market that had seen only three commercially successful documentaries in the previous decade. But Gilbert sent VHS copies to Kopple and Apted, who became strong supporters of the project. After winning an award at the 1994 Sundance Film Festival, *Hoop Dreams* received a slot at the New York Film Festival that fall and a distribution deal with New Line Cinema.

Reviews were overwhelmingly positive, with Chicago film critics Gene Siskel and Roger Ebert campaigning heavily for the film. Nevertheless, *Hoop Dreams* was not nominated for a documentary Oscar. The resulting scandal forced a change in the Academy of Motion Picture Arts and Sciences' nominating procedures for documentaries. Meanwhile, the film earned some $8 million in movie theaters. The filmmakers split their profits with the Gates and Agee families, who received close to $200,000 each.

All three producers have continued to work in film. Steve James, for example, recently directed *Reel Paradise* (2005), about independent producer John Pierson's efforts to run a movie theater on a South Seas island, and worked with Gilbert on *At the Death House Door* (2008). Gates is now a pastor in his old neighborhood, while Agee has a sports radio show and leads the Arthur Agee Role Model Foundation. Like the filmmakers, they found success by accepting the changes in their plans and goals. "When we were filming this," James said, "it was one surprise after another. We didn't start out to make the film we ended up making. William and Arthur gave us something far grander and more insightful."

Toy Story

Buena Vista Pictures, 1995. Sound, color, 1.85. 80 minutes. Rated G.
Voice Cast: Tom Hanks (Woody), Tim Allen (Buzz Lightyear), Don Rickles (Mr. Potato Head), Jim Varney (Slinky Dog), Wallace Shawn (Rex), John Ratzenberger (Hamm), Annie Potts (Bo Peep), John Morris (Andy), Erik Von Detten (Sid), Laurie Metcalf (Mrs. Davis), R. Lee Ermey (Sergeant), Sarah Freeman (Hannah), Penn Jillette (TV announcer).
Credits: Directed by John Lasseter. Screenplay by Joss Whedon, Andrew Stanton, Joel Cohen and Alec Sokolow. Original story by John Lasseter, Pete Docter, Andrew Stanton, Joe Ranft. Produced by Ralph Guggenheim, Bonnie Arnold. Executive producers: Edwin Catmull, Steve Jobs. Supervising technical director: William Reeves. Music by Randy Newman. Songs written & performed by Randy Newman. Art director: Ralph Eggleston. Film editors: Robert Gordon, Lee Unkrich. Supervising animator: Pete Docter. Sound design: Gary Rydstrom. Production supervisor: Karen Robert Jackson. Story supervisors: Joe Ranft, Robert Lence. Story coordinator: Susan E. Levin. Directing animators: Rich Quade, Ash Brannon. Animation managers: Triva Von Klark, B.Z. Petroff. Associate technical director: Eben Fiske Ostby. Technical department manager: Allison Smith Murphy.

Camera manager: Julie M. McDonald. Computer systems manager: David H. Ching. Post production supervisor: Patsy Bougé. Rerecording mixers: Gary Summers, Gary Rydstrom. Supervising sound editor: Tim Holland. Title design: Susan Bradley. Titles by Buena Vista Imaging. Rendered by RenderMan. Processing by Monaco Labs. Prints by Technicolor. Produced and distributed on Eastman Film. Dolby Digital Stereo. A Walt Disney Pictures presentation of a Pixar production.
Additional Credits: Premiered in Los Angeles on November 19, 1995.
Other Versions: Sequels *Toy Story 2* (1999), directed by John Lasseter and Ash Brannon; *Toy Story 3* (2010), directed by Lee Unkrich.
Available: Buena Vista Home Entertainment DVD (2005). ISBN: 0-7888-6117-4. UPC: 786936294507.

Before *Tin Toy* (1988, a Registry title) won an Oscar, Pixar head Steve Jobs had seriously considered shutting down the animation unit led by John Lasseter. Instead, Lasseter was allowed to develop *Knick Knack* (1989), a short comedy that takes place largely inside a snow globe. He thought about doing commercials and television shows, and pursued talks with Walt Disney Pictures to develop *Tin Toy* into a feature. With the hardware division shuttered, the company also focused on rendering software.

By 1990, Pixar was losing more than $8 million a year, money that Jobs was personally guaranteeing. A year later, Jobs fired almost half of the Pixar animators. Fortunately, executives Alvy Ray Smith and Ed Catmull learned that Disney was still interested in a feature film. Even better was the fact that Jeffrey Katzenberg, named head of Disney's animation division when Michael Eisner took over the company, was willing to let Pixar work on its own. Rather than be subject to creative decisions by Disney animators, Pixar would be allowed to develop and animate its own script.

Negotiations took months, but in March 1991, Lasseter gave Katzenberg a treatment for a story called *Toy Story*. Written by Lasseter, Andrew Stanton, and Pete Docter, it sent Tinny from *Tin Toy* on a journey through garbage dumps and yard sales to a kindergarten playground. This led to a contract with Disney, signed in July, that gave Katzenberg total creative control over the final product, and an option for two more films. His first advice: turn *Toy Story* into a buddy comedy along the lines of *48 Hrs.* (1982).

A second treatment developed the themes that would eventually be used in the movie. Toys were sentient beings whose goal was to please children. Their biggest fear was being replaced or left behind by their owners. These two ideas drove everything that happened in the story. Ironically, Lasseter gradually realized that he had to abandon Tinny because he was "too antiquated" for narrative purposes. (In 2005, Tinny's relatives became the focus of the short *One Man Band*.)

Instead, Pixar writers set up a conflict between a cowboy and a spaceman, a collision of cultures between the Wild West and the Space Age that fixed *Toy Story* in a period roughly around 1960. This was an astute commercial ploy as well as a nod to Lasseter's own childhood. *Toy Story* would be directed not only at children, but at their parents when they themselves were young.

The film evolved in much the same way features had during Disney's heyday, with short tests leading to refinements in characters and gags. Woody, a "talking" puppet, gained his drawstring after June 1992, well along in the process, for example. Lasseter and Docter attended one of Robert McKee's screenwriting seminars for help in mastering the feature film format. Lasseter also studied features like *Midnight Run* (1988) and *The French Connection* (1971) to learn how they handled character interactions and chases. As director Peter Jackson would note later, *Toy Story* and other Pixar films succeed in part because they employ the techniques of live-action films.

Disney assigned the team of Joel Cohen and Alec Sokolow to work on the script. They delivered seven drafts before being superseded by Joss Whedon, who spent four months rewriting. Whedon wanted to the Barbie doll to be an action heroine, using an approach similar to one he would take in *Buffy the Vampire Slayer* (1992), but Mattel refused to license the character. Disney also wanted the film to have songs, like its animation hit *Beauty and the Beast* (1991). Lasseter didn't want his characters to sing, but he did agree to use music to comment on the plot.

Lasseter began casting the voice actors for *Toy Story* in January 1993, after a shooting script was approved. He wanted Tom Hanks for Woody because, "Even when he's yelling at somebody, he's likable." When comedian Billy Crystal turned down the part of Buzz Lightyear, Lasseter cast Tim Allen, the star of *Home Improvement*, a television sitcom produced by Disney.

After viewing footage in November 1993, Peter Schneider, president of Walt Disney Feature Animation, ordered Pixar to stop work on *Toy Story*. It took four months of rewriting (including brightening Woody's character, making him less surly and argumentative) before Disney allowed production to start again. Pixar went on a hiring spree to meet production deadlines. At one point twenty-seven animators and sixty-one artists and engineers were working on *Toy Story*. The script was still being revised, with a sequence between

Buzz Lightyear and cult aliens arriving late in the production. (Chris Sanders, who had worked on *Beauty and the Beast*, designed the aliens.)

Schneider, now a firm backer of the film, announced that it would open in time for Thanksgiving 1995. Test screenings were held that July, with additional material and edits made on the advice of Michael Eisner and others. Some $145 million was committed to publicity, almost all of it from firms like Burger King and Nestlé who had commercial tie-ins. (The actual budget for the film was well under $30 million.)

The film not only received glowing reviews, it was a commercial blockbuster of unexpected proportions. It was also one of the finest features of any sort, live action or animation, to be released that year. As Tom Hanks put it later, "I wasn't prepared

for how seamless it was; I wasn't prepared for how deep it was." It's not just that Lasseter and his staff built a convincing world and believable characters; they found a story with humor, excitement, and, in the best Disney tradition, sheer terror. It was a narrative that embraced diversity, that helped overcome fears, that brought uplift without preaching.

According to George Lucas, "*Toy Story* became the standard in the industry because it set a whole new precedent for quality." Under Lasseter, and such key contributors as Andrew Stanton and Joe Ranft, Pixar went on a creative spree unmatched by anyone since Walt Disney himself. In films like *Finding Nemo* (2003) and *WALL-E* (2008), Pixar has done more than define the best in contemporary animation, it has provided some of the finest and most influential movies of the decade.

Fargo

Gramercy Pictures, 1996. Dolby Stereo, color, 1.85. 98 minutes. Rated R.
Cast: Frances McDormand (Marge Gunderson), William H. Macy (Jerry Lundegaard), Steve Buscemi (Carl Showalter), Harve Presnell (Wade Gustafson), Peter Stormare (Gaear Grimsrud), Kristin Rudrüd (Jean Lundegaard), Tony Denman (Scotty Lundegaard), Gary Houston (Irate customer), Sally Wingert (Irate customer's wife), Kurt Schweickhardt (Car salesman), Larissa Kokernot (Hooker #1), Melissa Peterman (Hooker #2), Steven Reevis (Shep Proudfoot), Warren Keith (Reilly Diefenbach), Steve Edelman (Morning show host), Sharon Anderson (Morning show hostess), Larry Brandenburg (Stan Grossman), James Gaulke (State trooper), J. Todd Anderson (Victim in field), Michelle Suzanne LeDoux (Victim in car), John Carroll Lynch (Norm Gunderson), Bruce Bohne (Lou), Petra Boden (Cashier), Steve Park (Mike Yanagita), Wayne Evenson (Customer), Cliff Rakerd (Officer Olson), Jessica Shepherd (Hotel clerk), Peter Schmitz (Airport lot attendant), Steve Schaefer (Mechanic), Michelle Hutchinson (Escort), David Lomax (Man in hallway), José Feliciano (Himself), Don William Skahill (Night parking attendant), Bain Boehlke (Mr. Mohra), Rose Stockton (Valerie), Robert Ozasky (Bismarck cop #1), John Bandemer (Bismarck cop #2), Don Wescott (Bark beetle narrator), Jery Hewitt (Stunt coordinator); Jery Hewitt, Jennifer Lamb, Danny Downey (Stunt players).
Credits: Directed by Joel Coen. Written by Ethan Coen, Joel Coen. Produced by Ethan Coen. Executive producers: Tim Bevan, Eric Fellner. Line producer: John Cameron. Director of photography: Roger Deakins. Production designer: Rick Heinrichs. Costume designer: Mary Zophres. Music by Carter Burwell. Film editor: Roderick Jaynes [Joel and Ethan Coen]. Associate editor: Tricia Cooke. Supervising sound editor: Skip Lievsay. Sound mixer: Allan Byer. Casting by John Lyons. Key makeup artist: John Blake. Key hairstylist: Daniel Curet. Costume supervisor: Sister Daniels. Dialect coach: Elizabeth Himmelstein. Dolby Stereo Digital Spectral Recording. Color by Du Art.
Additional Credits: Production dates: January 23 to April 21, 1995. Released March 8, 1996.
Awards: Oscars for Best Actress (McDormand), Writing—Screenplay Written Directly for the Screen.
Available: MGM Home Entertainment DVD (2003). ISBN: 0-7928-5805-0. UPC: 0-27616-88415-2.

Of the independent filmmakers who broke into the marketplace during the 1980s, the Coen brothers, Joel and Ethan, had the most extensive training. Joel, born 1954, and Ethan, born 1957, grew up in a suburb of Minneapolis and went to college in

Massachusetts. Joel attended film school at New York University while Ethan received an undergraduate degree in philosophy from Princeton. But from an early age the two were interested in film, reshooting movies they saw on TV on a Super-8 millimeter camera.

After film school, Joel found work as a production assistant on industrial films and music videos. He was hired as an assistant editor on *The Evil Dead* (1981) by director Sam Raimi, and it was through Raimi that the brothers received an extensive course in low-budget filmmaking. They learned how to use simple tricks to achieve the look and polish of Hollywood movies. Having crew members carry a camera mounted on a two-by-four, for example, instead of laying rails down for a tracking shot. Raimi also showed them that tastes were shifting: violence and gore once thought unacceptable were now considered fine for mainstream audiences.

Perhaps the most important lesson the brothers learned was how to keep control over their own projects. "We come from low budget filmmaking and are still practitioners of it," Joel said after *Fargo* opened. "In order to be precise, in shepherding your resources in order to get the most bang for your buck, we had to thoroughly think out how we were going to shoot each scene."

"The Coens have always been extremely smart about what size movies they make for the audience they're after," producer Jim Jacks said. The brothers' first film, *Blood Simple* (1984), earned over two million dollars on a budget of approximately $750,000. The story, a mingling of film noir and slasher genres, won over critics and viewers by playing with narrative formulas in a way that kept everyone in on the joke. Their subsequent films continued to toy with film stereotypes. *Raising Arizona* (1987) was a comedy that wed Chuck Jones slapstick and landscapes with the deliberately moronic humor of The Three Stooges. *The Hudsucker Proxy* (1994) grafted *His Girl Friday* onto *It's a Wonderful Life*; 2000's *O Brother, Where Are Thou?* (the novel director John Sullivan wants to adapt in *Sullivan's Travels*) was a rural musical and chain-gang comedy.

The brothers wrote their screenplays together and operated on the set together as well. Although Joel took the directing credit, Ethan had as much say during shooting. The brothers also edited their films under the pseudonym Roderick Jaynes. They tended to work with the same people when possible. Barry Sonnenfeld shot their first three features before departing to direct his own movies; since then the brothers have worked with cinematographer Roger Deakins. *Blood Simple* was the film debut for Frances McDormand; she subsequently married Joel.

The brothers' early films, released through Twentieth Century-Fox, generally eked out small profits, except for *Miller's Crossing* (1990), an unacknowledged adaptation of Dashiell Hammett's *The Glass Key*. *The Hudsucker Proxy*, produced by Scott Rudin and released through Warner Brothers, was an impressive failure, earning less than $4 million on a budget of $25 million. By this point the brothers' limitations were becoming obvious. The Coens kept such a tight control over their work that it could seem airless on the screen. They were smarter than the characters they wrote about, and dismissive of mainstream culture. Viewers came to their movies to snicker at rubes and deadbeats, and to congratulate themselves on being better than the losers they were watching.

Fargo was a return to the Coens' roots, an examination of the culture they experienced while growing up as well as of the Minnesota landscape in all its winter glory (or "Siberia with family restaurants," as Joel described it). The film was also a return to the thriller format they used in *Blood Simple*, but with a crucial twist: this time they added a subplot told from the point of view of a small-town sheriff who was smart, incorruptible,

and seven months' pregnant. Including Marge Gunderson (played by Frances McDormand) and a host of supporting characters who were unfailingly polite in typical Minnesotan fashion allowed the Coens to put the screws to their villains, who were involved in a kidnapping scheme that goes awry.

In interviews, the Coens described car salesman Jerry Lundegaard (played by William H. Macy) as a "schmuck" and "numbnuts." A veteran of stage, screen, and television, Macy read for the part three times, even flying to New York for an audition. Before *Fargo*, Steve Buscemi had become typecast as a bug-eyed killer in a string of independent films; for his role as inept thug Carl Showalter, the Coens allowed him to take his shtick to extremes. The Coens had seen Peter Stormare on stage, and wrote a part for him in *Miller's Crossing*, but the actor was tied to previous commitments. Gaear Grimsrud, a monosyllabic killer, was written specifically for him. "We often write for a particular actor," Joel said in one interview. "The rhythm of the speech and the way people talk, that's frequently a way that we get into imagining characters."

Fargo opens with the title "This is a true story," and even after the film opened the brothers were insisting that the crimes in the film actually took place. When the *New York Post* revealed that the script was entirely fictional, the Coens shrugged off the ensuing flurry of publicity. They were equally noncommittal after a Japanese woman killed herself after failing to find a treasure mentioned in the film. McDormand explained the "true story" ruse as an experiment: "If an audience thinks it is true, will they go with it longer?"

Money from *Fargo* came in part from Eric Fellner, a producer at Working Title. Joel Cohen met Fellner during the making of *Hidden Agenda*, which starred McDormand. The film was released through Gramercy Pictures, a specialty division of PolyGram. (PolyGram was later purchased by Universal.) *Fargo* earned about $25 million domestically on its release, and twice that worldwide. More than the profits, the two Oscars the film won (along with five other nominations) established the Coens as commercial—and not just artistic—moviemakers. While they continue to make their own pitiless, "aggressively idiosyncratic" films, they have also branched out, producing documentaries, for example, as well as Terry Zwigoff's *Bad Santa* (2003). Their adaptation of the Cormac McCarthy novel *No Country for Old Men* (2007) won a Best Picture Oscar.